Table of Atomic Masses*

Element	Symbol	Atomic Number	Atomic Mass	Element	Symbol	Atomic Number	Atomic Mass	Element	Symbol	Atomic Number	Atomic Mass
Actinium	Ac	89	[227]§	Gold	Au	79	197.0	Praseodymium	Pr	59	140.9
Aluminum	Al	13	26.98	Hafnium	Hf	72	178.5	Promethium	Pm	61	[145]
Americium	Am	95	[243]	Hassium	Hs	108	[265]	Protactinium	Pa	91	[231]
Antimony	Sb	51	121.8	Helium	He	2	4.003	Radium	Ra	88	226
Argon	Ar	18	39.95	Holmium	Ho	67	164.9	Radon	Rn	86	[222]
Arsenic	As	33	74.92	Hydrogen	H	1	1.008	Rhenium	Re	75	186.2
Astatine	At	85	[210]	Indium	In	49	114.8	Rhodium	Rh	45	102.9
Barium	Ba	56	137.3	Iodine	I	53	126.9	Roentgenium	Rg	111	[272]
Berkelium	Bk	97	[247]	Iridium	Ir	77	192.2	Rubidium	Rb	37	85.47
Beryllium	Be	4	9.012	Iron	Fe	26	55.85	Ruthenium	Ru	44	101.1
Bismuth	Bi	83	209.0	Krypton	Kr	36	83.80	Rutherfordium	Rf	104	[261]
Bohrium	Bh	107	[264]	Lanthanum	La	57	138.9	Samarium	Sm	62	150.4
Boron	B	5	10.81	Lawrencium	Lr	103	[260]	Scandium	Sc	21	44.96
Bromine	Br	35	79.90	Lead	Pb	82	207.2	Seaborgium	Sg	106	[263]
Cadmium	Cd	48	112.4	Lithium	Li	3	6.9419	Selenium	Se	34	78.96
Calcium	Ca	20	40.08	Lutetium	Lu	71	175.0	Silicon	Si	14	28.09
Californium	Cf	98	[251]	Magnesium	Mg	12	24.31	Silver	Ag	47	107.9
Carbon	C	6	12.01	Manganese	Mn	25	54.94	Sodium	Na	11	22.99
Cerium	Ce	58	140.1	Meitnerium	Mt	109	[268]	Strontium	Sr	38	87.62
Cesium	Cs	55	132.90	Mendelevium	Md	101	[258]	Sulfur	S	16	32.07
Chlorine	Cl	17	35.45	Mercury	Hg	80	200.6	Tantalum	Ta	73	180.9
Chromium	Cr	24	52.00	Molybdenum	Mo	42	95.94	Technetium	Tc	43	[98]
Cobalt	Co	27	58.93	Neodymium	Nd	60	144.2	Tellurium	Te	52	127.6
Copper	Cu	29	63.55	Neon	Ne	10	20.18	Terbium	Tb	65	158.9
Curium	Cm	96	[247]	Neptunium	Np	93	[237]	Thallium	Tl	81	204.4
Darmstadtium	Ds	110	[271]	Nickel	Ni	28	58.69	Thorium	Th	90	232.0
Dubnium	Db	105	[262]	Niobium	Nb	41	92.91	Thulium	Tm	69	168.9
Dysprosium	Dy	66	162.5	Nitrogen	N	7	14.01	Tin	Sn	50	118.7
Einsteinium	Es	99	[252]	Nobelium	No	102	[259]	Titanium	Ti	22	47.88
Erbium	Er	68	167.3	Osmium	Os	76	190.2	Tungsten	W	74	183.9
Europium	Eu	63	152.0	Oxygen	O	8	16.00	Uranium	U	92	238.0
Fermium	Fm	100	[257]	Palladium	Pd	46	106.4	Vanadium	V	23	50.94
Fluorine	F	9	19.00	Phosphorus	P	15	30.97	Xenon	Xe	54	131.3
Francium	Fr	87	[223]	Platinum	Pt	78	195.1	Ytterbium	Yb	70	173.0
Gadolinium	Gd	64	157.3	Plutonium	Pu	94	[244]	Yttrium	Y	39	88.91
Gallium	Ga	31	69.72	Polonium	Po	84	[209]	Zinc	Zn	30	65.38
Germanium	Ge	32	72.59	Potassium	K	19	39.10	Zirconium	Zr	40	91.22

*The values given here are to four significant figures where possible. §A value given in parentheses denotes the mass of the longest-lived isotope.

Study Card to Accompany Zumdahl's *Introductory Chemistry* Series

Measurements and Calculations

Table 2.2 The Commonly Used Prefixes in the Metric System p. 19

Prefix	Symbol	Meaning	Power of 10 for Scientific Notation
mega	M	1,000,000.000000001	10^6
kilo	k	1000	10^3
deci	d	0.1	10^{-1}
centi	c	0.01	10^{-2}
milli	m	0.001	10^{-3}
micro	μ	0.000001	10^{-6}
nano	n	0.000000001	10^{-9}

Table 2.6 Some Examples of Commonly Used Units p. 22

length	A dime is 1 mm thick. A quarter is 2.5 cm in diameter. The average height of an adult man is 1.8 m.
mass	A nickel has a mass of about 5 g. A 120-lb woman has a mass of about 55 kg.
volume	A 12-oz can of soda has a volume of about 360 mL. A half gallon of milk is equal to about 2 L of milk.

$1\ cm^3 = 1\ mL$
density of $H_2O(l) = 1.0$ g/mL
density = mass/volume
Avogadro's number = 6.022×10^{23}

Energy

Heat Required = Q = specific heat capacity × mass × ΔT
Specific heat capacity of $H_2O(l) = 4.184$ J/g °C
Kinetic energy = $mv^2/2$
Exothermic reactions produce heat
Endothermic reactions absorb heat

Kinds of Chemical Reactions

p. 191

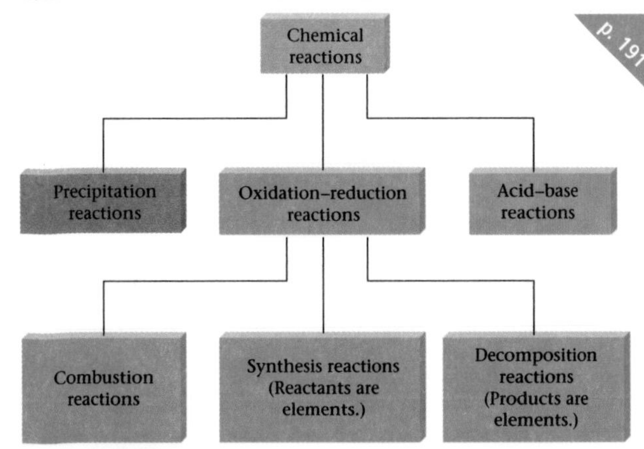

Figure 7.12 Summary of classes of reactions.

Atomic Structure

$^{23}_{11}\text{Na}$
Mass number (A) (number of protons and neutrons)
Element symbol
Atomic number (Z) (number of protons)

$A - Z = \#n^0$ $\quad\quad$ $\#p^+ - \#e^- =$ charge

Gases

STP: 0 °C, 1 atm
Volume of 1 mole of ideal gas at STP = 22.4 L
$PV = nRT$ (Ideal Gas Law)
$R = 0.08206$ L atm/K mol
Process at constant n and T: $P_1V_1 = P_2V_2$ (Boyle's law)
Process at constant n and P: $V_1/T_1 = V_2/T_2$ (Charles's law)
Process at constant T and P: $V_1/n_1 = V_2/n_2$ (Avogadro's law)

Types of Crystalline Solids

p. 459

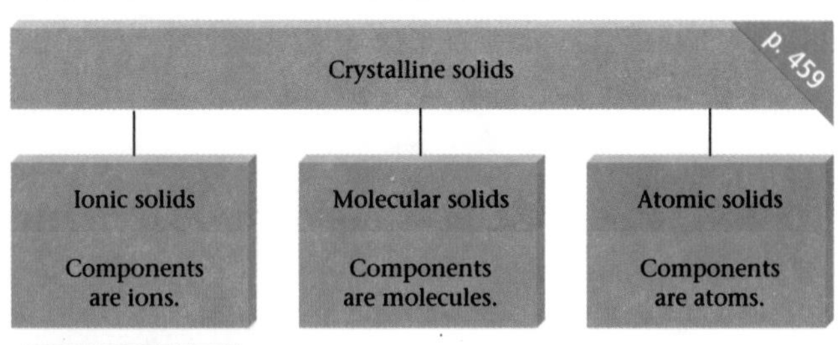

Figure 14.13 The classes of crystalline solids.

Solutions

$$\text{Mass percent} = \frac{\text{mass of solute}}{\text{mass of solution}} \times 100\%$$ (p. 481)

$$M = \text{molarity} = \frac{\text{moles of solute}}{\text{liters of solution}} = \frac{\text{mol}}{\text{L}}$$ (p. 483)

Mass of solute = (molar mass of solute) × (L of solution) (Molarity)

$$\text{Normality} = N = \frac{\text{number of equivalents}}{\text{1 liter of solution}} = \frac{\text{equivalents}}{\text{liter}} = \frac{\text{equiv}}{\text{L}}$$ (p. 499)

Acids and Bases

Common Strong Acids: HCl, HNO_3, H_2SO_4, $HClO_4$, HI
Common Weak Acids: HSO_4^-, CH_3COOH (often written $HC_2H_3O_2$), HF
Common Strong Bases: NaOH, KOH
Common Weak Bases: NH_3

$K_w = 10^{-14} = [H^+][OH^-]$ (ion-product constant for water) (p. 523)

$pH = -\log[H^+]$ (p. 526)

$pOH = -\log[OH^-]$ (p. 527)

$pH + pOH = 14.00$ (p. 529)

Equilibrium Constants

$aA + bB \rightleftharpoons cC + dD$, $K = [C]^c[D]^d/[A]^a[B]^b$ (p. 553)
$A_2B_3\ (s) \rightleftharpoons 2A^{3+}(aq) + 3B^{2-}(aq)$, $K_{sp} = [A^{3+}]^2[B^{2-}]^3$
[X] = Molarity of X

Study Card to Accompany Zumdahl's *Introductory Chemistry* Series

Chemical Bonding

Table 12.4 Arrangements of Electron Pairs and the Resulting Molecular Structures for Two, Three, and Four Electron Pairs p. 388

Number of Electron Pairs	Bonds	Electron Pair Arrangement	Ball-and-Stick Model	Molecular Structure	Partial Lewis Structure	Ball-and-Stick Model
2	2	Linear	 180°	Linear	A—B—A	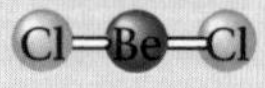 Cl—Be—Cl
3	3	Trigonal planar (triangular)	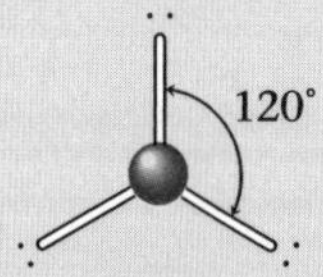 120°	Trigonal planar (triangular)	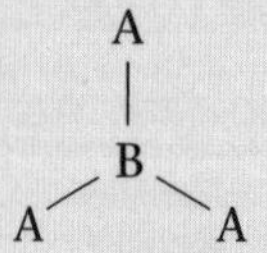 A, B, A, A	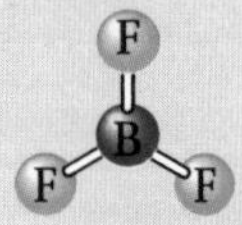 F, B, F, F
4	4	Tetrahedral	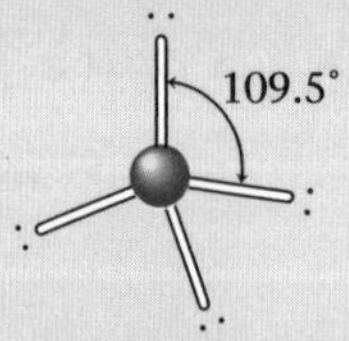 109.5°	Tetrahedral	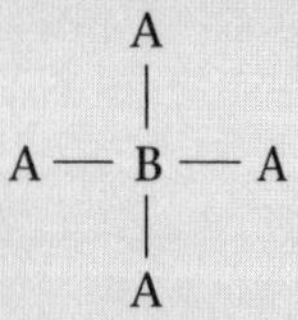 A, A—B—A, A	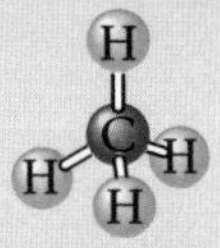 H, C, H, H, H
4	3	Tetrahedral	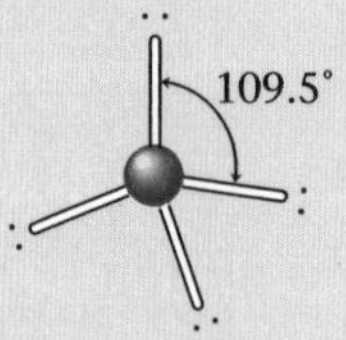 109.5°	Trigonal pyramid	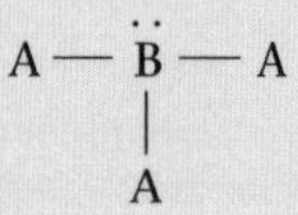 A—B̈—A, A	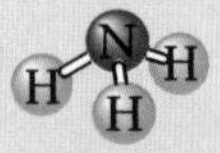 N, H, H, H
4	2	Tetrahedral	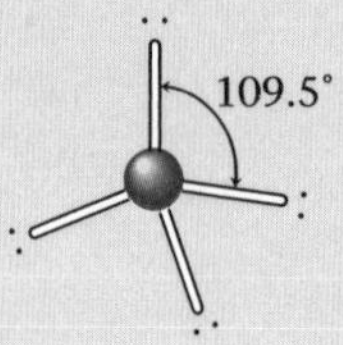 109.5°	Bent or V-shaped	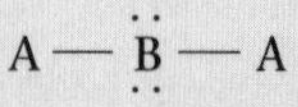 A—B—A (with two lone pairs on B)	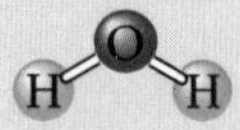 O, H, H

Common Lewis Dot Fragments

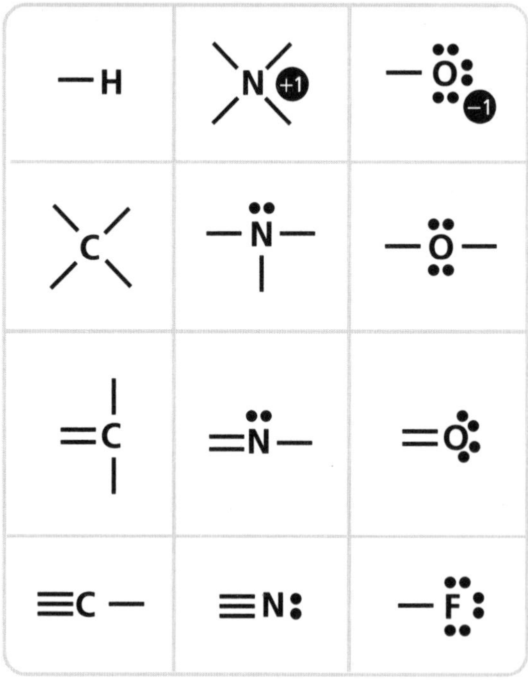

—H	N (+1)	—O: (−1)
C	—N̈—	—O—
=C	=N̈—	=O:
≡C —	≡N:	—F:

Oxidation–Reduction Reactions

Oxidation is loss of electrons (OIL)
Reduction is gain of electrons (RIG)

Rules for Assigning Oxidation States

p. 586

1. The oxidation state of an atom in an uncombined element is 0.
2. The oxidation state of a monatomic ion is the same as its charge.
3. Oxygen is assigned an oxidation state of −2 in most of its covalent compounds. Important exception: peroxides (compounds containing the O_2^{2-} group), in which each oxygen is assigned an oxidation state of −1.
4. In its covalent compounds with nonmetals, hydrogen is assigned an oxidation state of +1.
5. In binary compounds, the element with the greater electronegativity is assigned a negative oxidation state equal to its charge as an anion in its ionic compounds.
6. For an electrically neutral compound, the sum of the oxidation states must be zero.
7. For an ionic species, the sum of the oxidation states must equal the overall charge.

TAKE A LOOK AT WHAT'S NEW IN *INTRODUCTORY CHEMISTRY, 7E*

▸ An expanded focus on problem solving

- The importance of becoming a good independent problem solver is emphasized in a new Section 8.4.
- **New questions** contained within the examples model for students the questions they should be asking themselves while solving problems.

▸ A revised art program

The book's full-color art program has been redrawn to make figures more pedagogically useful. In particular, the authors have added numeric formulas within the molecular representations to help students visualize this important connection.

▸ Revised end-of-chapter questions with more than 170 new Active Learning Problems

- To add interest and variety, the authors have significantly revised each chapter's end-of-chapter questions.

▸ Revised *Chemistry in Focus* boxes

New topics include using bees to detect drugs and bombs at airports and analyzing isotopes in human hair to identify disaster victims' country of origin. **More than *40 end-of-chapter questions*** corresponding to the ***Chemistry in Focus*** boxes have been added.

▸ A robust technology support program that gives you a choice between two leading online learning systems

Online Web Learning

UMassAmherst

(See back page for details.)

Photo Credit: PhotoDisc/Getty Images

POWERFUL PEDAGOGY

The book's **full-color art program** has been redrawn to make figures more pedagogically useful. Specifically, the authors have added numeric formulas within the molecular representations to help students visualize this important connection.

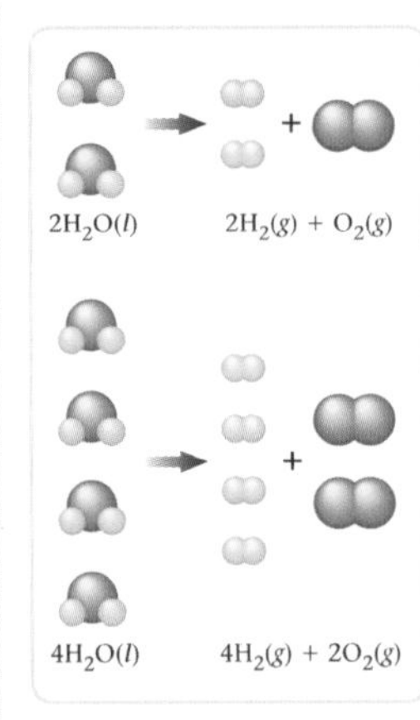

One way to answer this question is to mu
2 (which will give us 4 mol of H_2O).

$$2[2H_2O(l) \rightarrow 2H_2(g) + C$$
$$4H_2O(l) \rightarrow 4H_2(g) + 2$$

Now we can state that

4 mol of H_2O yields 4 mol of H_2 p

which answers the question of how many mol
mol of H_2O.

Next, suppose we decompose 5.8 mol of w
of products are formed in this process? We co
rebalancing the chemical equation as follows: I
of the balanced equation

$$2H_2O(l) \rightarrow 2H_2(g) + C$$

by 2, to give

$$H_2O(l) \rightarrow H_2(g) + \tfrac{1}{2}O$$

Now, because we have 5.8 mol of H_2O, we m

$$5.8[H_2O(l) \rightarrow H_2(g) + \tfrac{1}{2}($$

CHAPTER 9 REV

Key Terms

mole ratio (9.2)
stoichiometry (9.3)
limiting reactant (limiting reagent) (9.4
theoretical yield (9.6)
percent yield (9.6)

Summary

1. A balanced equation relates the numbers of m cules of reactants and products. It can also be pressed in terms of the numbers of moles of r tants and products.
2. The process of using a chemical equation to ca late the relative amounts of reactants and prod involved in the reaction is called doing stoichion ric calculations. To convert between moles of r tants and moles of products, we use mole ratios rived from the balanced equation.
3. Often reactants are not mixed in stoichiome quantities (they do not "run out" at the same tir In that case, we must use the limiting reactant to culate the amounts of products formed.
4. The actual yield of a reaction is usually less thar theoretical yield. The actual yield is often expres as a percentage of the theoretical yield, which called the percent yield.

Active Learning Questions

These questions are designed to be considered by gro of students in class. Often these questions work well introducing a particular topic in class.

1. Relate Active Learning Question 2 from Chapter the concepts of chemical stoichiometry.
2. You are making cookies and are missing a key in dient—eggs. You have plenty of the other ingr

Questions and Problems

■ dentoes problems assignable in OWL
directs you to the *Chemistry in Focus* feature in the chap indicates visual problems
VP Even-numbered exercises have answers in the back of this book and solutions in the Solutions Guide.

All even-numbered exercises have answers in the bac this book and solutions in the *Solutions Guide.*

9.1 Information Given by Chemical Equations

QUESTIONS

1. What do the coefficients of a balanced chem equation tell us about the proportions in wh atoms and molecules react on an individual (mic scopic) basis?
2. What do the coefficients of a balanced chem equation tell us about the proportions in which s stances react on a macroscopic (mole) basis?
3. Although *mass* is a property of matter we can c veniently measure in the laboratory, the coefficie of a balanced chemical equation are *not* directly terpreted on the basis of mass. Explain why.
4. For the balanced chemical equation $H_2 + Br_2 \rightarrow 2H$ explain why we do *not* expect to produce 2 g of if 1 g of H_2 is reacted with 1 g of Br_2.

PROBLEMS

5. For each of the following reactions, give the balan equation for the reaction and state the meaning the equation in terms of the numbers of *indivi molecules* and in terms of *moles of molecules.*
   a. $PCl_3(l) + H_2O(l) \rightarrow H_3PO_3(aq) + HCl(g)$
   b. $XeF_2(g) + H_2O(l) \rightarrow Xe(g) + HF(g) + O_2(g)$
   c. $S(s) + HNO_3(aq) \rightarrow H_2SO_4(aq) + H_2O(l) + NO$
   d. $NaHSO_3(s) \rightarrow Na_2SO_3(s) + SO_2(g) + H_2O(l)$
6. For each of the following reactions, balance chemical equation and state the stoichiometric *me ing* of the equation in terms of the numbers of *i vidual molecules* reacting and in terms of *moles of m ecules* reacting.

Questions and Problems are keyed to chapter sections and arranged in matched pairs. Answers to the even-numbered problems appear at the back of the book. **Additional Problems** incorporate materials from multiple sections to provide a level of challenge.

Summaries reinforce key chapter concepts.

Active Learning Questions promote collaborative learning.

Cumulative Reviews follow every two to three chapters, combining questions and problems from the chapters just covered.

CUMULATIVE REVIEW for CHAPTERS 8 - 9

QUESTIONS

1. What does the average *atomic mass* of an element represent? What unit is used for average atomic mass? Express the atomic mass unit in grams. Why is the average atomic mass for an element typically *not* a whole number?
2. Perhaps the most important concept in introductory chemistry concerns what a *mole* of a substance represents. The mole concept will come up again and again in later chapters in this book. What does one mole of a substance represent on a microscopic, atomic basis? What does one mole of a substance represent on a macroscopic, mass basis? Why have chemists defined the mole in this manner?
3. How do we know that 16.00 g of oxygen contains the same number of atoms as does 12.01 g of carbon, and that 22.99 g of sodium contains the same number of atoms as each of these? How do we know that 106.0 g of Na_2CO_3 contains the same number

masses. For example, the compound CH_4 co 74.87% carbon by mass. Rather than giving stu the data in this form, a teacher might instea "When 1.000 g of a compound was analyzed, found to contain 0.7487 g of carbon, with t mainder consisting of hydrogen." Using the pound you chose for Question 7, and the p composition data you calculated, reword you as suggested in this problem in terms of actua perimental" masses. Then from these masses, late the empirical formula of your compound.

9. Balanced chemical equations give us informati terms of individual molecules reacting in the portions indicated by the coefficients, and a terms of macroscopic amounts (that is, moles). a balanced chemical equation of your choice, a terpret in words the meaning of the equation c molecular and macroscopic levels.
10. Consider the *unbalanced* equation for the co

AN ENHANCED PROBLEM-SOLVING FOCUS

Learning to Solve Problems

Imagine today is the first day of your new job. The problem is that you don't know how to get there. However, as luck would have it, a friend does know the way and offers to drive you. What should you do while you sit in the passenger seat? If your goal is simply to get to work today, you might not pay attention to how to get there. However, you will need to get there on your own tomorrow, so you should pay attention to distances, signs, and turns. The difference between these two approaches is the difference between taking a passive role (going along for the ride) and an active role (learning how to do it yourself). In this section, we will emphasize that you should take an active role in reading the text, especially the solutions to the practice problems.

One of the great rewards of studying chemistry is that you become a good problem solver. Being able to solve problems is a talent that will serve you well in all walks of life. It is our purpose in this text to help you learn to solve problems in a flexible, creative way based on understanding the fundamental ideas of chemistry. We call this approach **conceptual problem**

▶ A new Section 8.4 shows students how becoming independent problem solvers will benefit them in college and beyond.

The mass percents of all the elements in a compound add up to 100%, although rounding-off effects may produce a small deviation. Adding up the percentages is a good way to check the calculations. In this case, the sum of the mass percents is 52.14% + 13.13% + 34.73% = 100.00%.

EXAMPLE 8.9 Calculating Mass Percent

Carvone is a substance that occurs in two forms, both of which have the same molecular formula ($C_{10}H_{14}O$) and molar mass. One type of carvone gives caraway seeds their characteristic smell; the other is responsible for the smell of spearmint oil. Compute the mass percent of each element in carvone.

SOLUTION

Where Are We Going?

We want to determine the mass percent of each element in carvone.

What Do We Know?

- The formula for carvone is $C_{10}H_{14}O$.
- We know the atomic masses of carbon (12.01 g/mol), hydrogen (1.008 g/mol), and oxygen (16.00 g/mol).
- The mass of isopentyl acetate is 1×10^{-6} g.
- There are 6.022×10^{23} molecules in 1 mole.

What Do We Need To Know?

- The mass of each element (we'll use 1 mol carvone)
- Molar mass of carvone

How Do We Get There?

Because the formula for carvone is $C_{10}H_{14}O$, the masses of the various elements in 1 mole of carvone are

$$\text{Mass of C in 1 mol} = 10\ \cancel{\text{mol}} \times 12.01\ \frac{\text{g}}{\cancel{\text{mol}}} = 120.1\ \text{g}$$

$$\text{Mass of H in 1 mol} = 14\ \cancel{\text{mol}} \times 1.008\ \frac{\text{g}}{\cancel{\text{mol}}} = 14.11\ \text{g}$$

$$\text{Mass of O in 1 mol} = 1\ \cancel{\text{mol}} \times 16.00\ \frac{\text{g}}{\cancel{\text{mol}}} = 16.00\ \text{g}$$

$$\text{Mass of 1 mol } C_{10}H_{14}O = 150.21\ \text{g}$$

$$\text{Molar mass} = 150.2\ \text{g}$$

(rounding to the correct number of significant figures)

MATH SKILL BUILDER
The 120.1 limits the sum to one decimal place.

Next we find the fraction of the total mass contributed by each element and convert it to a percentage.

$$\text{Mass percent of C} = \frac{120.1\ \text{g C}}{150.2\ \text{g } C_{10}H_{14}O} \times 100\% = 79.96\%$$

$$\text{Mass percent of H} = \frac{14.11\ \text{g H}}{150.2\ \text{g } C_{10}H_{14}O} \times 100\% = 9.394\%$$

$$\text{Mass percent of O} = \frac{16.00\ \text{g O}}{150.2\ \text{g } C_{10}H_{14}O} \times 100\% = 10.65\%$$

▶ **Examples** model a thoughtful, step-by-step approach to problem solving.

New questions contained within the examples model for students the questions they should be asking themselves while solving problems.

Math Skill Builder tips emphasize math skills critical for success in chemistry.

Self-Check Exercises allow students to practice the skills they just learned. Solutions appear in the back of the book.

ROBUST TECHNOLOGY RESOURCES

OWL Online Web Learning (available with an e-book)

Providing end-of-chapter questions drawn directly from Zumdahl/DeCoste's Seventh Edition, **OWL** offers you more assignable, gradable content than any other online learning system, a modern intuitive interface with most tasks just a click away, and a three-step assignment wizard with assignments that are ready to use "out of the box." **OWL** makes homework management a breeze and has already helped hundreds of thousands of students master chemistry through tutorials, interactive simulations, and algorithmically generated homework questions that provide instant, answer-specific feedback.

For more information or to see a demo, please contact your Cengage Learning representative or visit us on the web at **www.cengage.com/owl**

Enhanced WebAssign (available with an e-book)

This proven homework system—which includes text-specific problems pulled directly from Zumdahl/DeCoste's Seventh Edition—allows you to easily assign, collect, grade, and record homework assignments via the web. Learning activities include "Practice It" visual exercises, "Watch It" lecture videos from Thinkwell®, "Chat About It" online help, and "Read It" links to the PDF of the e-book.

For more information or to see a demo, please contact your Cengage Learning representative. Visit www.webassign.net to learn more.

ChemWork®

Both ***OWL*** and ***Enhanced WebAssign*** now include ***ChemWork,*** a set of unique assignments developed by Steven and Susan Zumdahl. ***ChemWork*** assignments focus on coaching students through the process of becoming independent problem solvers, just as you would coach them during office hours. ***ChemWork*** helps students develop true problem-solving ability.

For details on the complete teaching and learning package that accompanies ***Introductory Chemistry: A Foundation, Seventh Edition,*** please turn to the authors' preface.

Annotated Instructor's Edition

This **Annotated Instructor's Edition** includes the student text for *Introductory Chemistry: A Foundation* along with a extensive program of annotations, printed in the wrap-around margins, which has been developed by Donald DeCoste of the University of Illinois. Based on many years of teaching experience in this course, the annotations furnish instructors and teaching assistants with practical solutions to problems frequently encountered by students in this course. The annotations also offer helpful tips for teaching the material in the chapter and guidelines for setting up chemistry demonstrations in class. In addition, the annotations program provides information on incorporating electronic support materials, lab experiments, and test bank questions into the course presentation. We hope you find the annotations useful.

Brief Contents

This **Annotated Instructor's Edition** is intended to serve as your guide to any of the three student versions you may choose to use:

✔ *Introductory Chemistry: A Foundation*, Seventh Edition

✔ *Introductory Chemistry*, Seventh Edition

✔ *Basic Chemistry*, Seventh Edition

ANNOTATED INSTRUCTOR'S EDITION

SEVENTH EDITION

Introductory Chemistry

A FOUNDATION

Steven S. Zumdahl
University of Illinois

Donald J. DeCoste
University of Illinois

BROOKS/COLE
CENGAGE Learning

Australia • Brazil • Japan • Korea • Mexico • Singapore • Spain • United Kingdom • United States

***Introductory Chemistry: A Foundation*, Seventh Edition, Annotated Instructor's Edition**
Steven S. Zumdahl and Donald J. DeCoste

Publisher: Charles Hartford

Development Editor: Alyssa White

Senior Content Project Manager: Cathy Brooks

Art Directors: Jill Haber, Cate Barr

Senior Marketing Manager: Nicole Hamm

Senior Technology Project Manager: Rebecca Berardy-Schwartz

Assistant Editor: Stephanie VanCamp

Editorial Assistant: Jon Olafsson

Photo Researcher: Sharon Donahue

Senior Marketing Communications Manager: Linda Yip

Print Buyer: Judy Inouye

Permissions Editor: Roberta Broyer

Text Designer: Janet Theurer

Production Service: Graphic World Inc.

Production Project Manager, Graphic World: Megan Greiner

Copyeditor: Graphic World Inc.

Illustrators: Jessica Broekman, Rossi Art, and Graphic World Inc.

Cover Designer: Brian Salisbury

Cover Image: Radius Images/Photo Library

OWL Producers: Stephen Battisti, Cindy Stein, David Hart (Center for Educational Software Development; University of Massachusetts, Amherst)

Compositor: Graphic World Inc.

Library of Congress Control Number: 2009934046

ISBN-13: 978-0-538-73635-0

ISBN-10: 0-538-73635-6

Brooks/Cole
20 Davis Drive
Belmont, CA 94002-3098
USA

Printed in the United States of America
1 2 3 4 5 6 7 13 12 11 10 09

BRIEF CONTENTS

CONTENTS

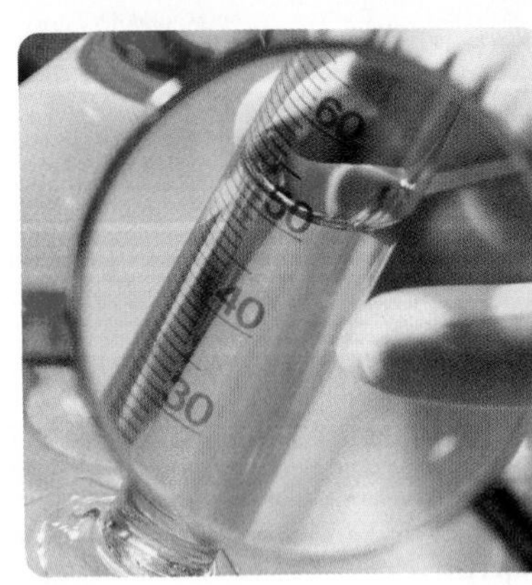

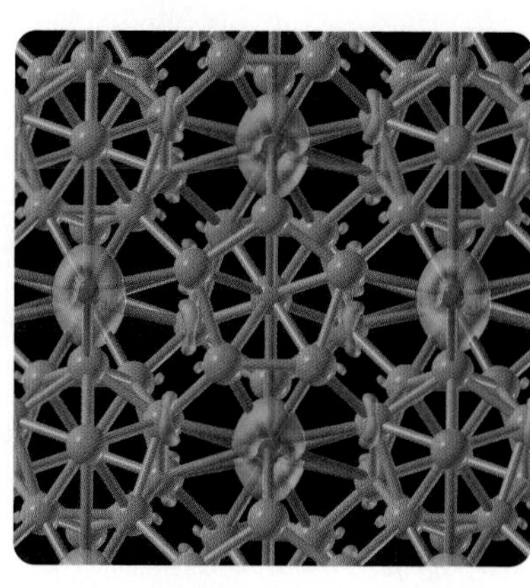

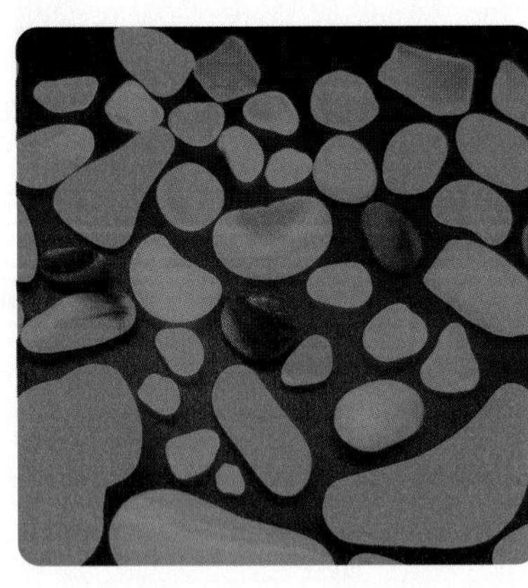

PREFACE

The seventh edition of *Introductory Chemistry* continues toward the goals we have pursued for the first six editions: to make chemistry interesting, accessible, and understandable to the beginning student. For this edition, we have included additional support for instructors and students to help achieve these goals.

Learning chemistry can be very rewarding. And even the novice, we believe, can relate the macroscopic world of chemistry—the observation of color changes and precipitate formation—to the microscopic world of ions and molecules. To achieve that goal, instructors are making a sincere attempt to provide more interesting and more effective ways to learn chemistry, and we hope that *Introductory Chemistry* will be perceived as a part of that effort. In this text we have presented concepts in a clear and sensible manner using language and analogies that students can relate to. We have also written the book in a way that supports active learning. In particular, the Active Learning Questions, found at the end of each chapter, provide excellent material for collaborative work by students. In addition, we have connected chemistry to real-life experience at every opportunity, from chapter opening discussions of chemical applications to "Chemistry in Focus" features throughout the book. We are convinced that this approach will foster enthusiasm and real understanding as the student uses this text. Highlights of the *Introductory Chemistry* program are described below.

New to This Edition

Building on the success of previous editions of *Introductory Chemistry,* the following changes have been made to further enhance the text:

Updates to the Student Text and Instructor's Annotated Edition

Changes to the student text and the accompanying Instructor's Annotated Edition are outlined below:

Instructor's Annotated Edition The marginal annotations have been revised and expanded to include point-of-use references to print and new media.

Section 8.4: Learning to Solve Problems We have added a new section that emphasizes the importance of conceptual problem solving in which students are shown how to think their way through a problem. The students will learn that this "big picture approach" produces more long-term, meaningful learning rather than simply memorizing specific steps that are soon forgotten.

Problem-Solving Approach in *Examples* Using the general conceptual problem-solving approach outlined in the new Section 8.4, we have introduced a series of questions into the in-chapter *Examples.* This more active approach helps students think their way through the solution to the problem. We use this approach for most of the quantitative *Examples* beginning in Section 8.4.

Section 9.4: The Concept of Limiting Reactants We have added a new section that helps students better understand the concept of a limiting reactant. Familiar examples such as making sandwiches and lemonade are used, as well as molecular-level illustrations of chemistry reactions. Students will learn how to think about limiting reactants before being asked to make mass–mass calculations to determine which reactant is limiting for a given reaction.

New Active Learning Questions We have written new Active Learning Questions for each chapter (over 170 new problems in all). In addition, many of the new problems include visual components such as graphs or molecular-level illustrations.

New End-of-Chapter Questions Using the "Chemistry in Focus" boxes We have written new end-of-chapter questions that specifically address topics covered in the "Chemistry in Focus" boxes (over 40 new questions in all).

Art Program We have revised almost every figure in the textbook to better serve visual learners. Most of the glassware, orbitals, graphs, and flowcharts have been redrawn.

"Chemistry in Focus" boxes Approximately 20% of the "Chemistry in Focus" boxes in the seventh edition are new, and many more have been revised, with up-to-date topics such as hybrid cars, artificial sweeteners, and positron emission tomography (PET).

End-of-Chapter Exercises We have replaced 20% of the end-of-chapter questions and problems and cumulative review exercises. As before, the margin of the Annotated Instructor's Edition includes answers to all of the Self-Check end-of-chapter exercises, along with additional examples for all Example problems. In the student edition, answers to Self-Check Exercises and to even-numbered exercises are provided at the back of the book.

NEW!

Enhanced Teaching Resources for the Instructor

OWL

OWL: Online Web-based Learning by Roberta Day and Beatrice Botch of the University of Massachusetts, Amherst, and William Vining of the State University of New York at Oneonta (ISBN-10: 0-538-73740-9; ISBN-13: 978-0-538-73740-1). Developed at the University of Massachusetts, Amherst, and class-tested by tens of thousands of chemistry students, OWL is a fully customizable and flexible web-based learning system. OWL supports mastery learning and offers numerical, chemical, and contextual parameterization to produce thousands of problems correlated to this text. The OWL system also features a database of simulations, tutorials, and exercises, as well as end-of-chapter problems from the text. In addition, OWL now includes *ChemWork* assignments, which help students learn key chemical concepts while guiding them in the process to become problem solvers. (See description below.) With OWL, you get the most widely used online learning system available for chemistry with unsurpassed reliability and dedicated training and support. Also new in OWL is *Go Chemistry*™—27 mini-video lectures covering key chemistry concepts that students can view onscreen or download to their portable video player to study on the go! The optional **eBook**

in OWL includes the complete electronic version of the text, fully integrated and linked to OWL homework problems. Most e-Books in OWL are interactive and offer highlighting, notetaking, and bookmarking features that can all be saved. In addition, the eBook includes links to Thinkwell® mini-video lectures. To view an OWL demo and for more information, visit **www.cengage.com/owl** or contact your Cengage Learning, Brooks/Cole representative.

ChemWork Offered in both OWL and *Enhanced WebAssign*®, *ChemWork* assignments offer students another opportunity to practice. These problems are designed for students to use in one of two ways: to *learn* the problem-solving process (while doing actual homework problems) or as a *capstone* assignment to determine whether they understand how to solve problems (perhaps in final preparation for an exam). *ChemWork* assignments test students' understanding of core concepts from each chapter. Students who solve a particular problem with no assistance can proceed directly to the answer and receive congratulations. However, students who need help can get assistance through a series of hints. The procedure for assisting students is modeled after the way a teacher would help with a homework problem in his or her office. The hints are usually in the form of interactive questions that guide students through the problem-solving process. Students cannot receive the right answer from the system; rather it encourages them to continue working on the problem through this system of multiple hints. *ChemWork* is chemically and numerically parameterized so that each student in the course receives a unique set of problems.

Enhanced WebAssign® *Enhanced WebAssign,* a robust, easy-to-use online learning system, includes algorithmic textbook problems with rich media learning resources, such as *ChemWork* assignments and Thinkwell® mini-video lectures. Instructors can create assignments from a ready-to-use database of textbook questions or write and customize their own exercises.

PowerLecture with ExamView® and JoinIn™ Instructor's DVD (ISBN-10: 0-538-73643-7; ISBN-13: 978-0-538-73643-5): PowerLecture is a one-stop digital library and presentation tool that includes:

- **Prepared Microsoft® PowerPoint® Lecture Slides** that cover all key points from the text in a convenient format that you can enhance with your own materials or with additional interactive video and animations from the CD-ROM for personalized, media-enhanced lectures.
- **Image Libraries** in PowerPoint® and JPEG formats that contain electronic files for all text art, most photographs, and all numbered tables in the text. These files can be used to print transparencies or to enhance PowerPoint® lectures.
- **JoinIn™ "Clicker" Slides** include questions that are written specifically for the use of *Introductory Chemistry* with the classroom response system of your choice, and allows you to seamlessly display student answers.
- **ExamView®** testing software, with all the test items from the Online Test Bank in electronic format. The electronic test bank by Steven S. Zumdahl and Donald J. DeCoste provides over 1600 multiple-choice, true-false, short-answer, matching, and completion questions. Approximately 200 questions from the previous edition

have been made into algorithms, which enable you to create even more customized tests.

NEW! Enhanced Learning Resources for the Student

Student Companion Website Accessible from **www.cengage.com/chemistry/zumdahl,** this site provides online study tools, including practice tests and flashcards.

***GoChemistry*™ for General Chemistry** (27-Module Set) (ISBN-10: 0-495-38228-0; ISBN-13: 978-0-495-38228-7) *GoChemistry*™ is a set of easy-to-use essential videos that can be downloaded to your video iPod or portable video player—ideal for the student on the go! Developed by award-winning chemists, these new electronic tools are designed to help students quickly review essential chemistry topics. Mini-video lectures include animations and problems for a quick summary of key concepts. Selected *GoChemistry* modules have e-flashcards to briefly introduce a key concept and then test student understanding of the basics with a series of questions. *GoChemistry* also plays on QuickTime, iTunes, and iPhones. Modules are also available separately. To purchase, enter ISBN 0-495-38228-0 at **www.ichapters.com.**

OWL **OWL for General Chemistry** by Roberta Day and Beatrice Botch of the University of Massachusetts, Amherst, and William Vining of the State University of New York at Oneonta [OWL Instant Access (4 Semesters) ISBN-10: 0-495-05099-7; ISBN-13: 978-0-495-05099-5]. See the previous description in the Instructor Support Materials.

Emphasis on Reaction Chemistry

We continue to emphasize chemical reactions early in the book, leaving the more abstract material on orbitals for later chapters. In a course in which many students encounter chemistry for the first time, it seems especially important that we present the chemical nature of matter before we discuss the theoretical intricacies of atoms and orbitals. Reactions are inherently interesting to students and can help us draw them to chemistry. In particular, reactions can form the basis for fascinating classroom demonstrations and laboratory experiments.

We have therefore chosen to emphasize reactions before going on to the details of atomic structure. Relying only on very simple ideas about the atom, Chapters 6 and 7 represent a thorough treatment of chemical reactions, including how to recognize a chemical change and what a chemical equation means. The properties of aqueous solutions are discussed in detail, and careful attention is given to precipitation and acid–base reactions. In addition, a simple treatment of oxidation–reduction reactions is given. These chapters should provide a solid foundation, relatively early in the course, for reaction-based laboratory experiments.

For instructors who feel that it is desirable to introduce orbitals early in the course, prior to chemical reactions, the chapters on atomic theory and bonding (Chapters 11 and 12) can be covered directly after Chapter 4. Chapter 5 deals solely with nomenclature and can be used wherever it is needed in a particular course.

Development of Problem-Solving Skills

Problem solving is a high priority in chemical education. We all want our students to acquire problem-solving skills. Fostering the development of such skills has been a central focus of the earlier editions of this text and we have maintained this approach in this edition.

In the first chapters we spend considerable time guiding students to an understanding of the importance of learning chemistry. At the same time, we explain that the complexities that can make chemistry frustrating at times can also provide the opportunity to develop the problem-solving skills that are beneficial in any profession. Learning to think like a chemist is useful to everyone. To emphasize this idea, we apply scientific thinking to some real-life problems in Chapter 1.

One reason chemistry can be challenging for beginning students is that they often do not possess the required mathematical skills. Thus we have paid careful attention to such fundamental mathematical skills as using scientific notation, rounding off to the correct number of significant figures, and rearranging equations to solve for a particular quantity. And we have meticulously followed the rules we have set down, so as not to confuse students.

Attitude plays a crucial role in achieving success in problem solving. Students must learn that a systematic, thoughtful approach to problems is better than brute force memorization. We foster this attitude early in the book, using temperature conversions as a vehicle in Chapter 2. Throughout the book we encourage an approach that starts with trying to represent the essence of the problem using symbols and/or diagrams, and ends with thinking about whether the answer makes sense. We approach new concepts by carefully working through the material before we give mathematical formulas or overall strategies. We encourage a thoughtful step-by-step approach rather than the premature use of algorithms. Once we have provided the necessary foundation, we highlight important rules and processes in skill development boxes so that students can locate them easily.

We have written a new section (Section 8.4: Learning to Solve Problems) so that students will better understand how to think their way through a problem. We discuss how to solve problems in a flexible, creative way based on understanding the fundamental ideas of chemistry and asking and answering key questions. We model this approach in the in-text *Examples* throughout the text.

Many of the worked examples are followed by Self-Check Exercises, which provide additional practice. The Self-Check Exercises are keyed to end-of-chapter exercises to offer another opportunity for students to practice a particular problem-solving skill or understand a particular concept.

We have expanded the number of end-of-chapter exercises. As in the first six editions, the end-of-chapter exercises are arranged in "matched pairs," meaning that both problems in the pair explore similar topics. An Additional Problems section includes further practice in chapter concepts as well as more challenging problems. Cumulative reviews, which appear after every few chapters, test concepts from the preceding chapter block. Answers for all even-numbered exercises appear in a special section at the end of the student edition.

Handling the Language of Chemistry and Applications

We have gone to great lengths to make this book "student friendly" and have received enthusiastic feedback from students who have used it.

As in the earlier editions, we present a systematic and thorough treatment of chemical nomenclature. Once this framework is established, students can progress through the book comfortably.

Along with chemical reactions, applications form an important part of descriptive chemistry. Because students are interested in chemistry's impact on their lives, we have included many new "Chemistry in Focus" boxes, which describe current applications of chemistry. These special interest boxes cover such topics as new technology to replace the incandescent lightbulb, using bees to detect drugs and bombs at airports, and analyzing isotopes in human hair to identify disaster victims' country of origin.

Visual Impact of Chemistry

In response to instructors' requests to include graphic illustrations of chemical reactions, phenomena, and processes, we use a full-color design that enables color to be used functionally, thoughtfully, and consistently to help students understand chemistry and to make the subject more inviting to them. We have included only those photos that illustrate a chemical reaction or phenomenon or that make a connection between chemistry and the real world. Many new photos enhance the seventh edition.

Choices of Coverage

For the convenience of instructors, four versions of the seventh edition are available: two paperback versions and two hardbound versions. *Basic Chemistry,* Seventh Edition, a paperback text, provides basic coverage of chemical concepts and applications through acid–base chemistry and has 16 chapters. *Introductory Chemistry,* Seventh Edition, available in hardcover and paperback, expands the coverage to 19 chapters with the addition of equilibrium, oxidation–reduction reactions and electrochemistry, radioactivity, and nuclear energy. Finally, *Introductory Chemistry: A Foundation,* Seventh Edition, a hardbound text, has 21 chapters, with the final two chapters providing a brief introduction to organic and biological chemistry.

Supplements for the Text

A main focus of this revision is to provide instructors and students with an unparalleled level of support. In addition to the media components described previously, we offer the following materials.

For the Student

Student Companion Website Accessible from **www.cengage.com/chemistry/zumdahl,** this site provides online study tools, including practice tests and flashcards.

Study Guide by Donald J. DeCoste of the University of Illinois contains Chapter Discussions and Learning Review (practice chapter tests) (ISBN-10: 0-538-73640-2; ISBN-13: 978-0-538-73640-4).

Solutions Guide by James F. Hall, University of Massachusetts, Lowell, contains detailed solutions for the even-numbered end-of-chapter questions and exercises and cumulative review exercises (ISBN-10: 0-538-73641-0; ISBN-13: 978-0-538-73641-1).

Introductory Chemistry in the Laboratory by James F. Hall contains experiments organized according to the topical presentation in the text. Annotations in the Annotated Instructor's Edition indicate where the experiments from this manual are relevant to chapter content. The lab manual has been updated and revised for this edition (ISBN-10: 0-538-73642-9; ISBN-13: 978-0-538-73642-8).

For the Instructor

Annotated Instructor's Edition The Annotated Instructor's Edition gathers a wealth of teaching support in one convenient package. The AIE contains all 21 chapters (the full contents of *Introductory Chemistry: A Foundation,* Seventh Edition). Annotations in the wrap-around margins of the AIE include:

- Answers to Self-Check Exercises, at point-of-use.
- Answers to all end-of-chapter questions and exercises, at point-of-use.
- Additional Examples with answers to supplemental worked-out Examples in the text.
- Technology Information about incorporating animations and video clips from the electronic support materials in lecture.
- Teaching Support Suggestions for specific lecture/instruction methods, activities, and in-class demonstrations to help convey concepts.
- An Overview of the chapter's learning objectives.
- Teaching Tips: Guidelines for highlighting critical information in the chapter.
- Misconceptions: Tips on where students may have trouble or be confused with a topic.
- Demonstrations: Detailed instructions for in-class demonstrations and activities. (These are similar to material in Teaching Support, and may be referenced in Teaching Support annotations.)
- Laboratory Experiments: Information on which labs in the Laboratory Manual are relevant to chapter content.
- Background Information: Explanations of conventions used in the text.
- Icons mark material correlations between the main text and the electronic support materials, the Test Bank, and the Laboratory Manual.
- Historical Notes: Biographical or other historical information about science and scientists.

PowerLecture with ExamView® and JoinIn™ Instructor's DVD (ISBN-10: 0-538-73643-7; ISBN-13: 978-0-538-73643-5): PowerLecture is a one-stop digital library and presentation tool that includes:

- **Prepared Microsoft® PowerPoint® Lecture Slides** that cover all key points from the text in a convenient format that you can enhance with your own materials or with additional interactive video and animations from the CD-ROM for personalized, media-enhanced lectures.

- **Image Libraries** in PowerPoint® and JPEG formats that contain electronic files for all text art, most photographs, and all numbered tables in the text. These files can be used to print transparencies or to enhance PowerPoint® lectures.
- **JoinIn™ "Clicker" Slides** include questions that are written specifically for the use of *Introductory Chemistry* with the classroom response system of your choice, and allows you to seamlessly display student answers.
- ***Complete Solutions Manual*** (James F. Hall, University of Massachusetts, Lowell) The *Complete Solutions Manual* contains detailed solutions to all of the end-of chapter problems, problems, and cumulative review exercises.
- **Answers to Active Learning Questions** from the end-of-chapter questions, written by Donald J. DeCoste.
- ***Instructor's Guide for Introductory Chemistry in the Laboratory*** by James F. Hall includes general notes about each experiment, estimated completion time, materials required, and answers to both pre- and post-laboratory questions. Annotations in the AIE indicate where experiments from this manual are relevant to chapter content. The lab manual has been updated and revised for this edition.
- **Sample Chapters** from the *Student Solutions Manual* and *Study Guide.*
- **ExamView®** testing software, with all the test items from the Online Test Bank in electronic format. The electronic test bank by Steven S. Zumdahl and Donald J. DeCoste provides over 1600 multiple-choice, true-false, short-answer, matching, and completion questions. Approximately 200 questions from the previous edition have been made into algorithms, which enable you to create even more customized tests.

Acknowledgments

This book represents the collaborative efforts of many talented and dedicated people to whom we are greatly indebted. Charles Hartford, Publisher, was extremely supportive of the revision. Charlie asked good questions and provided helpful and creative ideas. We also wish to thank Cathy Brooks, Content Project Manager, who has an eye for detail and an uncanny ability to do everything at once and all of it well. We appreciate the efforts of Alyssa White, Development Editor, who, along with her other tasks, was instrumental in making sure the art was appealing and correct. We are grateful to have worked with Sharon Donahue, Photo Researcher, who once again displayed her remarkable ability for finding outstanding photos.

Jim Hall of the University of Massachusetts, Lowell, contributed in many different ways to the success of this project. He has been a tremendous help with the end-of-chapter questions and problems and the cumulative review exercises, along with writing the *Solutions Guides, Introductory Chemistry in the Laboratory,* and the *Instructor's Guide for Introductory Chemistry in the Laboratory.*

We especially appreciate the efforts of Gretchen Adams of the University of Illinois for her work on revising the PowerPoint® media component,

Richard Triplett of Des Moines Area Community College for reviewing the ancillaries, and Linda Bush for revising the test bank.

Thanks to others who provided valuable assistance on this revision: Stephanie VanCamp, Assistant Editor for the ancillaries; Rebecca Berardy-Schwartz, Technology Project Manager; Jon Olaffson, Editorial Assistant; Nicole Hamm, Marketing Manager; Megan Greiner, Project Manager (Graphic World); Jill Haber and Cate Barr, Art Directors; Betty Litt, Copyeditor; and David Shinn, who checked the textbook and solutions for accuracy.

Our sincerest appreciation goes to all of the reviewers whose feedback and suggestions contributed to the success of this project.

Angela Bickford
Northwest Missouri State University

Simon Bott
University of Houston

Jabe Breland
St. Petersburg College

Frank Calvagna
Rock Valley College

Jing-Yi Chin
Suffolk County Community College

Carl David
University of Connecticut

Cory DiCarlo
Grand Valley State University

Cathie Keenan
Chaffey College

Pamela Kimbrough
Crafton Hills College

Wendy Lewis
Stark State College of Technology

Guillermo Muhlmann
Capital Community College

Lydia Martinez Rivera
University of Texas at San Antonio

Sharadha Sambasivan
Suffolk County Community College

Perminder Sandhu
Bellevue Community College

Lois Schadewald
Normandale Community College

Marie Villarba
Seattle Central Community College

About the Annotated Instructor's Edition

Testing

This icon marks where test items available in the *Test Bank* correlate to chapter material.

Laboratory Experiments

This icon marks where laboratory experiments in *Introductory Chemistry in the Laboratory* by James Hall are relevant to chapter content. The lab manual has been updated and revised for this edition.

Lecture Demonstrations

The margin notes contain detailed instructions for selected demonstrations. In addition, brief **Lecture Demonstration** annotations reference the supplement *Lecture Demonstrations Resource Guide,* by Frederick H. Juergens. The guide contains more than 750 references for lecture demonstrations taken from nine prominent sources. The numbers in the Lecture Demonstration annotations are keyed to the numbered demonstrations in the guide and are placed as appropriate throughout the AIE.

Electronic Support Material

PowerLecture: This 2-DVD package includes the Chemistry Multimedia Library, which contains animations, simulations, and movies for all chemistry subjects, organized by topic for lecture presentations. Annotations for the PowerLecture are referenced in the margins throughout the Annotated Instructor's Edition.

ChemWork: Refined over ten years of use by thousands of students, ChemWork builds and enhances students' problem-solving skills. Online assignments function as a "personal instructor" to help students learn how to solve challenging problems and learn how to think like chemists. Annotations for ChemWork assignments are included at the beginning of the end-of-chapter Review.

Chapter 1

Objectives

In this chapter, our objectives are for the students to:

SECTION 1.1

- Understand the importance of learning chemistry.

SECTION 1.2

- Define chemistry.

SECTION 1.3

- Understand scientific thinking.

SECTION 1.4

- Describe the method scientists use to study nature.

SECTION 1.5

- Develop successful strategies for learning chemistry.

1 Chemistry: An Introduction

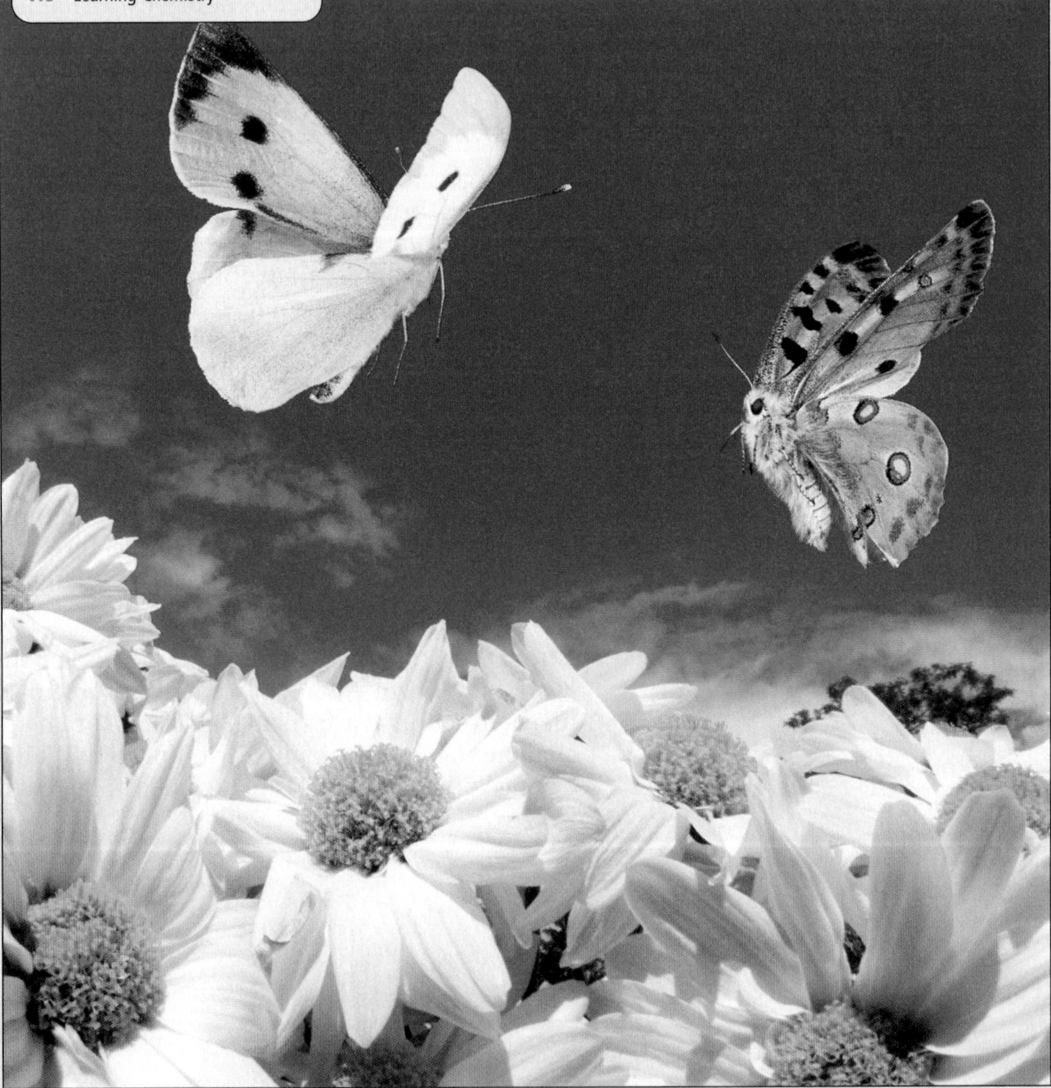

Chemistry deals with the natural world. *(Dr. John Brackenbury/Science Photo Library/Photo Researchers, Inc.)*

ChemWork Refined over ten years of use by thousands of students, **ChemWork** builds and enhances students' problems-solving skills. Online assignments function as a "personal instructor" to help students learn how to solve challenging problems and learn how to think like chemists. Annotations for **ChemWork** assignments are included at the beginning of the end-of-chapter review.

PowerLecture This 2-DVD package includes the Chemistry Multimedia Library, which contains animations, simulations, and movies for all chemistry subjects, organized by topic for lecture presentations. Annotations for **PowerLecture** are referenced in the margins throughout the Annotated Instructor's Edition.

OWL Sign in to OWL at **www.cengage.com/owl** to view tutorials and simulations, develop problem-solving skills, and complete online homework assigned by your professor.

Did you ever see a fireworks display on July Fourth and wonder how it's possible to produce those beautiful, intricate designs in the air? Have you read about dinosaurs—how they ruled the earth for millions of years and then suddenly disappeared? Although the extinction happened 65 million years ago and may seem unimportant, could the same thing happen to us? Have you ever wondered why an ice cube (pure water) floats in a glass of water (also pure water)? Did you know that the "lead" in your pencil is made of the same substance (carbon) as the diamond in an engagement ring? Did you ever wonder how a corn plant or a palm tree grows seemingly by magic, or why leaves turn beautiful colors in autumn? Do you know how the battery works to start your car or run your calculator? Surely some of these things and many others in the world around you have intrigued you. The fact is that we can explain all of these things in convincing ways using the models of chemistry and the related physical and life sciences.

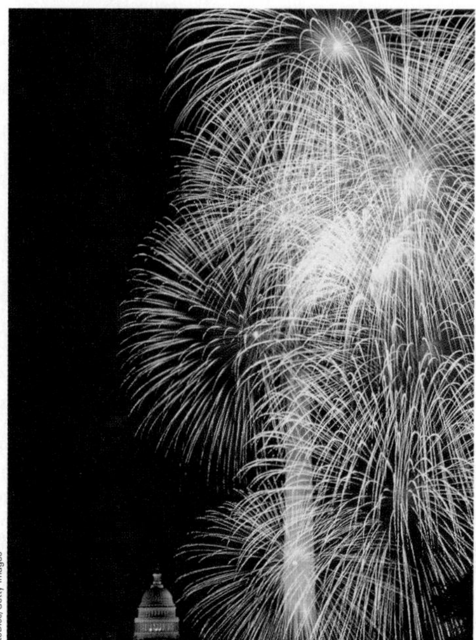
PhotoDisc/Getty Images

Fireworks are a beautiful illustration of chemistry in action.

1.1 Chemistry: An Introduction

OBJECTIVE: To understand the importance of learning chemistry.

Although chemistry might seem to have little to do with dinosaurs, knowledge of chemistry was the tool that enabled paleontologist Luis W. Alvarez and his coworkers from the University of California at Berkeley to "crack the case" of the disappearing dinosaurs. The key was the relatively high level of iridium found in the sediment that represents the boundary between the earth's Cretaceous (K) and Tertiary (T) periods—the time when the dinosaurs disappeared virtually overnight (on the geological scale). The Berkeley researchers knew that meteorites also have unusually high iridium content (relative to the earth's composition), which led them to suggest that a large meteorite impacted the earth 65 million years ago, causing the climatic changes that wiped out the dinosaurs.

Section 1.1

Project

Begin focusing on an Element of the Week. Feature a bulletin board with a celebrity element each week. Highlight its properties, uses, and characteristics. Assign an element to each student. Have the students research their element, including its name, symbol, properties, uses, and characteristics.

PowerLecture Videos:
Interview: Jacqueline Barton
Interview: James Cusumano
Interview: Jeanette Grasselli Brown

A knowledge of chemistry is useful to almost everyone—chemistry occurs all around us all of the time, and an understanding of chemistry is useful to doctors, lawyers, mechanics, business people, firefighters, and poets among others. Chemistry is important—there is no doubt about that. It lies at the heart of our efforts to produce new materials that make our lives safer and easier, to produce new sources of energy that are abundant and nonpolluting, and to understand and control the many diseases that threaten us and our food supplies. Even if your future career does not require the daily use of chemical principles, your life will be greatly influenced by chemistry.

A strong case can be made that the use of chemistry has greatly enriched all of our lives. However, it is important to understand that the principles of chemistry are inherently neither good nor bad—it's what we do with this knowledge that really matters. Although humans are clever, resourceful, and concerned about others, they also can be greedy, selfish, and ignorant. In addition, we tend to be shortsighted; we concentrate too much on the present and do not think enough about the long-range implications of our actions. This type of thinking has already caused us a great deal of trouble—severe environmental damage has occurred on many fronts. We cannot place all the responsibility on the chemical companies, because everyone has contributed to these problems. However, it is less important to lay blame than to figure out how to solve these problems. An important part of the answer must rely on chemistry.

One of the "hottest" fields in the chemical sciences is environmental chemistry—an area that involves studying our environmental ills and finding creative ways to address them. For example, meet Bart Eklund, who works in the atmospheric chemistry field for Radian Corporation in Austin, Texas. Bart's interest in a career in environmental science was fostered by two environmental chemistry courses and two ecology courses he took as an undergraduate. His original plan to gain several years of industrial experience and then to return to school for a graduate degree changed when he discovered that professional advancement with a B.S. degree was possible in the environmental research field. The multidisciplinary nature of environmental problems has allowed Bart to pursue his interest in several fields at the same time. You might say that he specializes in being a generalist.

Courtesy, Bart Eklund

Bart Eklund checking air quality at a hazardous waste site.

The environmental consulting field appeals to Bart for a number of reasons: the chance to define and solve a number of research problems; the simultaneous work on a number of diverse projects; the mix of desk, field, and laboratory work; the travel; and the opportunity to perform rewarding work that has a positive effect on people's lives.

Among his career highlights are the following:

- Spending a winter month doing air sampling in the Grand Tetons, where he also met his wife and learned to ski;
- Driving sampling pipes by hand into the rocky ground of Death Valley Monument in California;
- Working regularly with experts in their fields and with people who enjoy what they do;
- Doing vigorous work in 100 °F weather while wearing a rubberized suit, double gloves, and a respirator; and
- Getting to work in and see Alaska, Yosemite Park, Niagara Falls, Hong Kong, the People's Republic of China, Mesa Verde, New York City, and dozens of other interesting places.

Bart Eklund's career demonstrates how chemists are helping to solve our environmental problems. It is how we use our chemical knowledge that makes all the difference.

An example that shows how technical knowledge can be a "double-edged sword" is the case of chlorofluorocarbons (CFCs). When the compound CCl_2F_2 (originally called Freon-12) was first synthesized, it was hailed as a near-miracle substance. Because of its noncorrosive nature and its unusual ability to resist decomposition, Freon-12 was rapidly applied in refrigeration and air-conditioning systems, cleaning applications, the blowing of foams used for insulation and packing materials, and many other ways. For years everything seemed fine—the CFCs actually replaced more dangerous materials, such as the ammonia formerly used in refrigeration systems. The CFCs were definitely viewed as "good guys." But then a problem was discovered—the ozone in the upper atmosphere that protects us from the high-energy radiation of the sun began to decline. What was happening to cause the destruction of the vital ozone?

Much to everyone's amazement, the culprits turned out to be the seemingly beneficial CFCs. Inevitably, large quantities of CFCs had leaked into the atmosphere but nobody was very worried about this development because these compounds seemed totally benign. In fact, the great stability of the CFCs (a tremendous advantage for their various applications) was in the end a great disadvantage when they were released into the environment. Professor F. S. Rowland and his colleagues at the University of California at Irvine demonstrated that the CFCs eventually drifted to high altitudes in the atmosphere, where the energy of the sun stripped off chlorine atoms. These chlorine atoms in turn promoted the decomposition of the ozone in the upper atmosphere. (We will discuss this in more detail in Chapter 13.) Thus a substance that possessed many advantages in earth-bound applications turned against us in the atmosphere. Who could have guessed it would turn out this way?

The good news is that the U.S. chemical industry is leading the way to find environmentally safe alternatives to CFCs, and the levels of CFCs in the atmosphere are already dropping.

The saga of the CFCs demonstrates that we can respond relatively quickly to a serious environmental problem if we decide to do so. Also, it is important to understand that chemical manufacturers have a new attitude about the environment—they are now among the leaders in finding ways to address our environmental ills. The industries that apply the chemical sciences are now determined to be part of the solution rather than part of the problem.

A chemist in the laboratory.

As you can see, learning chemistry is both interesting and important. A chemistry course can do more than simply help you learn the principles of chemistry, however. A major by-product of your study of chemistry is that you will become a better problem solver. One reason chemistry has the reputation of being "tough" is that it often deals with rather complicated systems that require some effort to figure out. Although this might at first seem like a disadvantage, you can turn it to your advantage if you have the right attitude. Recruiters for companies of all types maintain that one of the first things they look for in a prospective employee is the ability to solve problems. We will spend a good deal of time solving various types of problems in this book by using a systematic, logical approach that will serve you well in solving any kind of problem in any field. Keep this broader goal in mind as you learn to solve the specific problems connected with chemistry.

PowerLecture Animation: Underwater Diver Exploring the Sea

Although learning chemistry is often not easy, it's never impossible. In fact, anyone who is interested, patient, and willing to work can learn

1.1 Chemistry: An Introduction 3

Section 1.2

Test Bank: 1

PowerLecture Animation: Ocean Waves

DEMONSTRATION

Carbon Tower

Materials

250-mL beaker

Paper towels

Concentrated sulfuric acid

Sucrose

Stirring rod

Procedure Place 50 g of sucrose in the beaker. Place the beaker on a mat of paper towels in a fume hood. Add 50 mL concentrated sulfuric acid to the sugar and step back to observe.

Teaching Notes Have students note the color changes as the reaction proceeds (white, yellow, brown, black). Ask students which element found in sugar could account for this color change.

Note the steam emitted from the black carbon residue that rises out of the beaker. Ask students to propose an explanation of the source of the steam.

Safety and Disposal The reaction releases SO_2 gas, which is irritating to some students. The smell of the reaction is that of burned sugar. Be sure not to handle the tower unless you wash it with sodium bicarbonate solution. You can dispose of the washed tower in a trashcan. You can clean the beaker with soap and water.

Alternative If you do not have a fume hood, this demonstration is found on the Chemistry in Motion videotape or videodisk with the title "Sulfuric Acid and Sugar."

CHEMISTRY *IN* FOCUS

Dr. Ruth—Cotton Hero

AP Photo/Ric Risberg

Ruth Benerito, the inventor of easy-care cotton.

Dr. Ruth Rogan Benerito may have saved the cotton industry in the United States. In the 1960s, synthetic fibers posed a serious competitive threat to cotton, primarily because of wrinkling. Synthetic fibers such as polyester can be formulated to be highly resistant to wrinkles both in the laundering process and in wearing. On the other hand, 1960s' cotton fabrics wrinkled easily—white cotton shirts had to be ironed to look good. This requirement put cotton at a serious disadvantage and endangered an industry very important to the economic health of the South.

During the 1960s Ruth Benerito worked as a scientist for the Department of Agriculture, where she was instrumental in developing the chemical treatment of cotton to make it wrinkle resistant. In so doing she enabled cotton to remain a preeminent fiber in the market—a place it continues to hold today. She was honored with the Lemelson–MIT Lifetime Achievement Award for Inventions in 2002 when she was 86 years old.

Dr. Benerito, who holds 55 patents, including the one for wrinkle-free cotton awarded in 1969, began her career when women were not expected to enter scientific fields. However, her mother, who was an artist, adamantly encouraged her to be anything she wanted to be.

Dr. Benerito graduated from high school at 14 and attended Newcomb College, the women's college associated with Tulane University. She majored in chemistry with minors in physics and math. At that time she was one of only two women allowed to take the physical chemistry course at Tulane. She earned her B.S. degree in 1935 at age 19 and subsequently earned a master's degree at Tulane and a Ph.D. at the University of Chicago.

In 1953 Dr. Benerito began working in the Agriculture Department's Southern Regional Research Center in New Orleans, where she mainly worked on cotton and cotton-related products. She also invented a special method for intravenous feeding in long-term medical patients.

Since her retirement in 1986, she has continued to tutor science students to keep busy. Everyone who knows Dr. Benerito describes her as a class act.

the fundamentals of chemistry. In this book we will try very hard to help you understand what chemistry is and how it works and to point out how chemistry applies to the things going on in your life.

Our sincere hope is that this text will motivate you to learn chemistry, make its concepts understandable to you, and demonstrate how interesting and vital the study of chemistry is.

1.2 What Is Chemistry?

OBJECTIVE: To define chemistry.

Chemical and physical changes will be discussed in Chapter 3.

Chemistry can be defined as *the science that deals with the materials of the universe and the changes that these materials undergo.* Chemists are involved in activities as diverse as examining the fundamental particles of matter,

TEACHING TIPS

- Connecting the real world to the atomic/molecular world is difficult for many students. Encourage students to visualize the atomic/molecular world by drawing pictures. For example, a Bunsen burner works by reacting methane and oxygen to form carbon dioxide and water vapor. A representation of this is given in Figure 6.4 and can be shown to your students, along with a working Bunsen burner.
- Discuss student ideas of what everyday objects look like on an atomic/molecular level. Include in your discussion examples such as air, water, salt, and sugar. Don't worry about the details (subatomic particles) here. The idea is to get the students thinking and ready to continue with Chapter 3. Further details will be developed there. The students' responses will give you an idea of their entering perceptions.

The launch of the space shuttle gives clear indications that chemical reactions are occurring.

looking for molecules in space, synthesizing and formulating new materials of all types, using bacteria to produce such chemicals as insulin, and inventing new diagnostic methods for early detection of disease.

Chemistry is often called the central science—and with good reason. Most of the phenomena that occur in the world around us involve chemical changes, changes where one or more substances become different substances. Here are some examples of chemical changes:

Wood burns in air, forming water, carbon dioxide, and other substances.

A plant grows by assembling simple substances into more complex substances.

The steel in a car rusts.

Eggs, flour, sugar, and baking powder are mixed and baked to yield a cake.

The definition of the term *chemistry* is learned and stored in the brain.

Emissions from a power plant lead to the formation of acid rain.

As we proceed, you will see how the concepts of chemistry allow us to understand the nature of these and other changes and thus help us manipulate natural materials to our benefit.

1.3 Solving Problems Using a Scientific Approach

 **Test Bank: 3**

Section 1.3

TEACHING TIP

Students should understand that much of "scientific thinking" is logical or analytical thinking.

OBJECTIVE: To understand scientific thinking.

One of the most important things we do in everyday life is solve problems. In fact, most of the decisions you make each day can be described as solving problems.

It's 8:30 A.M. on Friday. Which is the best way to drive to school to avoid traffic congestion?

You have two tests on Monday. Should you divide your study time equally or allot more time to one than to the other?

Your car stalls at a busy intersection and your little brother is with you. What should you do next?

These are everyday problems of the type we all face. What process do we use to solve them? You may not have thought about it before, but there are several steps that almost everyone uses to solve problems:

1. Recognize the problem and state it clearly. Some information becomes known, or something happens that requires action. In science we call this step *making an observation.*
2. Propose *possible* solutions to the problem or *possible* explanations for the observation. In scientific language, suggesting such a possibility is called *formulating a hypothesis.*

PowerLecture Video: Richard Feynman Speaks about Space Shuttle

CHEMISTRY IN FOCUS

A Mystifying Problem

To illustrate how science helps us solve problems, consider a true story about two people, David and Susan (not their real names). Several years ago David and Susan were healthy 40-year-olds living in California, where David was serving in the Air Force. Gradually Susan became quite ill, showing flu-like symptoms including nausea and severe muscle pains. Even her personality changed: she became uncharacteristically grumpy. She seemed like a totally different person from the healthy, happy woman of a few months earlier. Following her doctor's orders, she rested and drank a lot of fluids, including large quantities of coffee and orange juice from her favorite mug, part of a 200-piece set of pottery dishes recently purchased in Italy. However, she just got sicker, developing extreme abdominal cramps and severe anemia.

During this time David also became ill and exhibited symptoms much like Susan's: weight loss, excruciating pain in his back and arms, and uncharacteristic fits of temper. The disease became so debilitating that he retired early from the Air Force and the couple moved to Seattle. For a short time their health improved, but after they unpacked all their belongings (including those pottery dishes), their health began to deteriorate again. Susan's body became so sensitive that she could not tolerate the weight of a blanket. She was near death. What was wrong? The doctors didn't know, but one suggested she might have porphyria, a rare blood disease.

Desperate, David began to search the medical literature himself. One day while he was reading about porphyria, a phrase jumped off the page: "Lead poisoning can sometimes be confused with porphyria." Could the problem be lead poisoning?

We have described a very serious problem with life-or-death implications. What should David do next? Overlooking for a moment the obvious response of calling the couple's doctor immediately to discuss the possibility of lead poisoning, could David solve the problem via scientific thinking? Let's use the three steps described in Section 1.3 to attack the problem one part at a time. This is important: usually we solve complex problems by breaking them down into manageable parts. We can then assemble the solution to the overall problem from the answers we have found "piecemeal."

In this case there are many parts to the overall problem:

What is the disease?

Where is it coming from?

Can it be cured?

Let's attack "What is the disease?" first.

Observation: David and Susan are ill with the symptoms described. Is the disease lead poisoning?

Hypothesis: The disease is lead poisoning.

Experiment: If the disease is lead poisoning, the symptoms must match those known to characterize lead poisoning. Look up the symptoms of lead poisoning. David did this and found that they matched the couple's symptoms almost exactly.

This discovery points to lead poisoning as the source of their problem, but David needed more evidence.

Observation: Lead poisoning results from high levels of lead in the bloodstream.

Hypothesis: The couple have high levels of lead in their blood.

Experiment: Perform a blood analysis. Susan arranged for such an analysis, and the results showed high lead levels for both David and Susan.

3. Decide which of the solutions is the best or decide whether the explanation proposed is reasonable. To do this we search our memory for any pertinent information or we seek new information. In science we call searching for new information *performing an experiment.*

Italian pottery.

This confirms that lead poisoning is probably the cause of the trouble, but the overall problem is still not solved. David and Susan are likely to die unless they find out where the lead is coming from.

Observation: There is lead in the couple's blood.

Hypothesis: The lead is in their food or drink when they buy it.

Experiment: Find out whether anyone else who shopped at the same store was getting sick (no one was). Also note that moving to a new area did not solve the problem.

Observation: The food they buy is free of lead.

Hypothesis: The dishes they use are the source of the lead poisoning.

Experiment: Find out whether their dishes contain lead. David and Susan learned that lead compounds are often used to put a shiny finish on pottery objects. And laboratory analysis of their Italian pottery dishes showed that lead was present in the glaze.

Observation: Lead is present in their dishes, so the dishes are a possible source of their lead poisoning.

Hypothesis: The lead is leaching into their food.

Experiment: Place a beverage, such as orange juice, in one of the cups and then analyze the beverage for lead. The results showed high levels of lead in drinks that had been in contact with the pottery cups.

After many applications of the scientific method, the problem is solved. We can summarize the answer to the problem (David and Susan's illness) as follows: the Italian pottery they used for everyday dishes contained a lead glaze that contaminated their food and drink with lead. This lead accumulated in their bodies to the point where it interfered seriously with normal functions and produced severe symptoms. This overall explanation, which summarizes the hypotheses that agree with the experimental results, is called a *theory* in science. This explanation accounts for the results of all the experiments performed.*

We could continue to use the scientific method to study other aspects of this problem, such as

What types of food or drink leach the most lead from the dishes?

Do all pottery dishes with lead glazes produce lead poisoning?

As we answer questions using the scientific method, other questions naturally arise. By repeating the three steps over and over, we can come to understand a given phenomenon thoroughly.

*"David" and "Susan" recovered from their lead poisoning and are now publicizing the dangers of using lead-glazed pottery. This happy outcome is the answer to the third part of their overall problem, "Can the disease be cured?" They simply stopped eating from that pottery!

As we will discover in the next section, scientists use these same procedures to study what happens in the world around us. The important point here is that scientific thinking can help you in all parts of your life. It's worthwhile to learn how to think scientifically—whether you want to be a scientist, an auto mechanic, a doctor, a politician, or a poet!

Section 1.4

MISCONCEPTION

Some students believe that theories become laws once a theory has been accepted. Theories never become laws. They are different things. Laws tell us what happens; theories are our attempts to explain why.

 Test Bank: 2, 4

1.4 The Scientific Method

OBJECTIVE: To describe the method scientists use to study nature.

In the last section we began to see how the methods of science are used to solve problems. In this section we will further examine this approach.

Science is a framework for gaining and organizing knowledge. Science is not simply a set of facts but also a plan of action—a *procedure* for processing and understanding certain types of information. Although scientific thinking is useful in all aspects of life, in this text we will use it to understand how the natural world operates. The process that lies at the center of scientific inquiry is called the **scientific method.** As we saw in the previous section, it consists of the following steps:

Steps in the Scientific Method

1. *State the problem and collect data (make observations).* Observations may be *qualitative* (the sky is blue; water is a liquid) or *quantitative* (water boils at 100 °C; a certain chemistry book weighs 4.5 pounds). A qualitative observation does not involve a number. A quantitative observation is called a **measurement** and does involve a number (and a unit, such as pounds or inches). We will discuss measurements in detail in Chapter 2.
2. *Formulate hypotheses.* A hypothesis is a *possible* explanation for the observation.
3. *Perform experiments.* An experiment is something we do to test the hypothesis. We gather new information that allows us to decide whether the hypothesis is supported by the new information we have learned from the experiment. Experiments always produce new observations, and this brings us back to the beginning of the process again.

Quantitative observations involve a number. Qualitative ones do not.

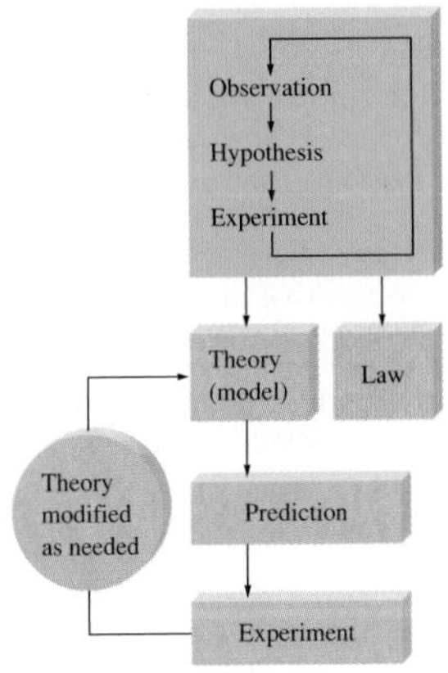

To explain the behavior of a given part of nature, we repeat these steps many times. Gradually we accumulate the knowledge necessary to understand what is going on.

Once we have a set of hypotheses that agrees with our various observations, we assemble them into a theory that is often called a *model.* A **theory** (model) is a set of tested hypotheses that gives an overall explanation of some part of nature (see Figure 1.1).

It is important to distinguish between observations and theories. An observation is something that is witnessed and can be recorded. A theory is an *interpretation*—a possible explanation of *why* nature behaves in a particular way. Theories inevitably change as more information becomes available. For example, the motions of the sun and stars have remained virtually the same over the thousands of years during which humans have been observing them, but our explanations—our theories—have changed greatly since ancient times.

The point is that we don't stop asking questions just because we have devised a theory that seems to account satisfactorily for some aspect of natural behavior. We continue doing experiments to refine our theories. We generally do this by using the theory to make a prediction and then doing an experiment (making a new observation) to see whether the results bear out this prediction.

Observation
Hypothesis
Experiment
Theory (model)
Law
Theory modified as needed
Prediction
Experiment

Figure 1.1
The various parts of the scientific method.

TEACHING SUPPORT

ACTIVITY

Name Game

This whole-class activity is meant to help students learn about the scientific method.

Start by thinking of a category for a name such as "a female name with five letters." Don't tell the students the category, but tell them you are thinking of a name, and ask someone to guess it. If the students guess a name outside the category, tell them the guess is incorrect. If they guess a name in your chosen category, say, "That could be right." You might write the answers in columns on the board labeled correct and incorrect. After several correct answers, ask them to determine the category.

What can the students learn from this activity? First, scientists make observations and try to look for patterns. They develop hypotheses to explain these patterns. Some of these hypotheses sound good initially but later turn out to be incorrect. These mistakes can usually be discovered by making more observations. Although we can never be sure that the hypothesis is correct, we can become more confident as we make more observations that fit. After many different names have been presented, the "female five-letter name" theory will become apparent. Discuss how this relates to the scientific method (students made observations, looked for patterns, and developed a hypothesis; they then used new observations to refine the theory).

TEACHING SUPPORT

ACTIVITY

Models

As part of your discussion of theories (models) in science, bring some models (toys) to class and place them on the front desk. Examples include a car, truck, horse, boat, and molecule (ball-and-stick methane is a simple one). Tell the class you

Law: A summary of observed behavior.

Theory: An explanation of behavior.

Always remember that theories (models) are human inventions. They represent our attempts to explain observed natural behavior in terms of our human experiences. We must continue to do experiments and refine our theories to be consistent with new knowledge if we hope to approach a more nearly complete understanding of nature.

As we observe nature, we often see that the same observation applies to many different systems. For example, studies of innumerable chemical changes have shown that the total mass of the materials involved is the same before and after the change. We often formulate such generally observed behavior into a statement called a **natural law.** The observation that the total mass of materials is not affected by a chemical change in those materials is called the law of conservation of mass.

You must recognize the difference between a law and a theory. A law is a summary of observed (measurable) behavior, whereas a theory is an explanation of behavior. *A law tells what happens; a theory (model) is our attempt to explain why it happens.*

In this section, we have described the scientific method (which is summarized in Figure 1.1) as it might ideally be applied. However, it is important to remember that science does not always progress smoothly and efficiently. Scientists are human. They have prejudices; they misinterpret data; they can become emotionally attached to their theories and thus lose objectivity; and they play politics. Science is affected by profit motives, budgets, fads, wars, and religious beliefs. Galileo, for example, was forced to recant his astronomical observations in the face of strong religious resistance. Lavoisier, the father of modern chemistry, was beheaded because of his political affiliations. And great progress in the chemistry of nitrogen fertilizers resulted from the desire to produce explosives to fight wars. The progress of science is often slowed more by the frailties of humans and their institutions than by the limitations of scientific measuring devices. The scientific method is only as effective as the humans using it. It does not automatically lead to progress.

PowerLecture Animation: Rubber O-Ring
PowerLecture Video: Big Bang

1.5 Learning Chemistry

OBJECTIVE: To develop successful strategies for learning chemistry.

Chemistry courses have a universal reputation for being difficult. There are some good reasons for this. For one thing, the language of chemistry is unfamiliar in the beginning; many terms and definitions need to be memorized. As with any language, *you must know the vocabulary* before you can communicate effectively. We will try to help you by pointing out those things that need to be memorized.

But memorization is only the beginning. Don't stop there or your experience with chemistry will be frustrating. Be willing to do some thinking, and learn to trust yourself to figure things out. To solve a typical chemistry problem, you must sort through the given information and decide what is really crucial.

It is important to realize that chemical systems tend to be complicated—there are typically many components—and we must make approximations in describing them. Therefore, trial and error play a major role in solving chemical problems. In tackling a complicated system, a practicing chemist really does not expect to be right the first time he or she analyzes the problem. The usual practice is to make several simplifying assumptions and then give it a try. If the answer obtained doesn't make sense, the chemist adjusts the assumptions, using feedback from the first attempt, and tries

Section 1.5

MISCONCEPTION

Students often come to a chemistry course believing that the subject of chemistry consists of many disparate facts to be memorized. While there is certainly a "language of chemistry," students should also understand that the topics and ideas are related. What they learn should have consistency and should make sense to them. While this sounds obvious to us, students often think of science as counterintuitive.

will point to one, and they should shout out its name. Expect to be greeted with shouts of "car," "truck," and so on. Write these names on the board, thank the students for being so responsive, but inform them that they are wrong. Ask them to reconsider. You will probably be greeted with more specifics such as "blue car." Again, thank them, but tell them they are wrong. Ask the students to talk with each other. Eventually someone may say "model car," "toy horse," or something similar. Congratulate them on their thinking skills. (If they do not come to this conclusion, help them by saying things such as "What makes a car a car? Can I drive this car?") Discuss the nature and purpose of models in science. In particular, make sure the students understand the difference between a scientific model and "reality."

TEACHING SUPPORT

ACTIVITY

Can a Tape Recorder Learn?

Bring a tape recorder with a blank tape to class. Tell the students you are going to teach it the names of some of your students. Walk over to a student and say, "The name of this student is [push Record] (name)." Continue this for a few students. Then, rewind the tape, go back to the first student, and ask, "What is this student's name?" Press Play. Continue this for the next few students. Ask the class, "Did I teach the tape recorder? Did the tape recorder learn?" Discuss learning and teaching with your students.

Most students will state that the tape recorder is not learning. They will respond that the tape recorder is recording what you say and then "saying" it back. Push the students a little further and say, "But didn't the tape recorder get all of the answers right? Wouldn't it deserve an 'A'?" Most students will tell you "no"; use this reply to your advantage.

While most students believe that it is obvious that the tape recorder is not learning, these same students might act like tape recorders in class. Students often genuinely believe that their role is to simply remember what you say and what is in the text without assimilating it.

CHEMISTRY *IN* FOCUS

Chemistry: An Important Component of Your Education

What is the purpose of education? Because you are spending considerable time, energy, and money to pursue an education, this is an important question.

Some people seem to equate education with the storage of facts in the brain. These people apparently believe that education simply means memorizing the answers to all of life's present and future problems. Although this is clearly unreasonable, many students seem to behave as though this were their guiding principle. These students want to memorize lists of facts and to reproduce them on tests. They regard as unfair any exam questions that require some original thought or some processing of information. Indeed, it might be tempting to reduce education to a simple filling up with facts, because that approach can produce short-term satisfaction for both student and teacher. And of course, storing facts in the brain *is* important. You cannot function without knowing that red means stop, electricity is hazardous, ice is slippery, and so on.

However, mere recall of abstract information, without the ability to process it, makes you little better than a talking encyclopedia. Former students always seem to bring the same message when they return to campus. The characteristics that are most important to their success are a knowledge of the fundamentals of their fields, the ability to recognize and solve problems, and the ability to communicate effectively. They also emphasize the importance of a high level of motivation.

How does studying chemistry help you achieve these characteristics? The fact that chemical systems are complicated is really a blessing, though one that is well disguised. Studying chemistry will not by itself make you a good problem solver, but it can help you develop a positive, aggressive attitude toward problem solving and can help boost your confidence. Learning to "think like a chemist" can be valuable to anyone in any field. In fact, the chemical industry is heavily populated at all levels and in all areas by chemists and chemical engineers. People who were trained as chemical professionals often excel not only in chemical research and production but also in the areas of personnel, marketing, sales, development, finance, and management. The point is that much of what you learn in this course can be applied to any field of endeavor. So be careful not to take too narrow a view of this course. Try to look beyond short-term frustration to long-term benefits. It may not be easy to learn to be a good problem solver, but it's well worth the effort.

Students pondering the structure of a molecule.

again. The point is this: in dealing with chemical systems, do not expect to understand immediately everything that is going on. In fact, it is typical (even for an experienced chemist) *not* to understand at first. Make an attempt to solve the problem and then analyze the feedback. *It is no disaster to make a mistake as long as you learn from it.*

The only way to develop your confidence as a problem solver is to practice solving problems. To help you, this book contains examples worked out in detail. Follow these through carefully, making sure you understand each step. These examples are usually followed by a similar exercise (called a self-check exercise) that you should try on your own (detailed solutions of the self-check exercises are given at the end of each chapter). Use the self-check exercises to test whether you are understanding the material as you go along.

To complete the point, go to the students in a different order to show that the tape recorder is no longer correct. Ask a question such as "Why is the sky blue?" When the tape recorder answers "Bob," discuss that the tape recorder does not even know what is being asked. Tell the students that a major goal this year is to learn to think scientifically and they cannot do so if they are merely tape recorders.

Many students have the wrong goals about learning chemistry. Most understand and accept that they will have to commit some material to memory (the language of chemistry). However, students generally do not recognize what it means to "understand." For many students, simply knowing (that is, memorizing) constitutes understanding.

There are questions and problems at the end of each chapter. The questions review the basic concepts of the chapter and give you an opportunity to check whether you properly understand the vocabulary introduced. Some of the problems are really just exercises that are very similar to examples done in the chapter. If you understand the material in the chapter, you should be able to do these exercises in a straightforward way. Other problems require more creativity. These contain a knowledge gap—some unfamiliar territory that you must cross—and call for thought and patience on your part. For this course to be really useful to you, it is important to go beyond the questions and exercises. Life offers us many exercises, routine events that we deal with rather automatically, but the real challenges in life are true problems. This course can help you become a more creative problem solver.

As you do homework, be sure to use the problems correctly. If you cannot do a particular problem, do not immediately look at the solution. Review the relevant material in the text and then try the problem again. Don't be afraid to struggle with a problem. Looking at the solution as soon as you get stuck short-circuits the learning process.

Learning chemistry takes time. Use all the resources available to you and study on a regular basis. Don't expect too much of yourself too soon. You may not understand everything at first, and you may not be able to do many of the problems the first time you try them. This is normal. It doesn't mean you can't learn chemistry. Just remember to keep working and to keep learning from your mistakes, and you will make steady progress.

CHAPTER 1 REVIEW

Key Terms

chemistry (1.2)
scientific method (1.4)
theory (1.4)
natural law (1.4)

F directs you to the *Chemistry in Focus* feature in the chapter
VP indicates visual problems
OWL interactive versions of these problems are assignable in OWL

Active Learning Questions

These questions are designed to be considered by groups of students in class. Often these questions work well for introducing a particular topic in class.

1. Discuss how a hypothesis can become a theory. Can a theory become a law? Explain.
2. Make five qualitative and five quantitative observations about the room in which you now sit.
3. List as many chemical reactions you can think of that are part of your everyday life. Explain.
4. Differentiate between a "theory" and a "scientific theory."
5. Describe three situations when you used the scientific method (outside of school) in the past month.
6. Scientific models do not describe reality. They are simplifications and therefore incorrect at some level. So why are models useful?
7. Theories should inspire questions. Discuss a scientific theory you know and the questions it brings up.
8. Describe how you would set up an experiment to test the relationship between completion of assigned homework and the final grade you receive in the course.
9. If all scientists use the scientific method to try to arrive at a better understanding of the world, why do so many debates arise among scientists?
10. As stated in the text, there is no one scientific method. However, making observations, formulating hypotheses, and performing experiments are generally

TEACHING SUPPORT

ANALOGIES FOR TEACHING AND LEARNING

You will need the following materials:

Water
0.10 *M* NaOH
Universal indicator
1-L Erienmeyer flask
0.10 *M* HCl
Vegetable oil
250-mL Erienmeyer flasks (4)

Empty Pitcher

Show the students a large flask filled with water and an empty 250-mL flask. Explain that in this analogy the teacher is the large flask, the small flask is the student, and the water is knowledge. In this analogy, the student starts out empty (knowing nothing). The teacher pours knowledge into the student. Discuss the problems with this analogy. First, students do come into class with ideas about the subject material, even if some are erroneous. Second, the knowledge the students attain is not the same as the knowledge the teacher has; knowledge is not simply transferred. Finally, learning is not a passive activity.

Oil and Water

In this activity a flask of water represents the teacher. Another flask with some vegetable oil represents the student. This shows the students come with knowledge and that this knowledge differs from the teacher's knowledge. The knowledge (water) flows from the teacher to the student, and it takes a lot of work to get it to mix with the student's initial knowledge. This is demonstrated by capping the flask that represents the student and mixing it vigorously. Show the students the product of this work and let them watch as the water and oil slowly separate. "This is a lot of work for nothing. If learning is truly like this—that is, 'cram as much as you can in your head for a test, and then let it out afterward'—then we are all wasting our time." In this analogy the teacher does all of the work.

Active Learning

In this activity, the teacher's knowledge is represented by an aqueous acidic solution. The student is represented by a basic solution containing several drops of universal indicator. When the acidic solution (knowledge) flows, the students' knowledge changes (shown by a change in color). Like the oil and

components of "doing science." Read the following passage, and list any observations, hypotheses, and experiments. Support your answer.

Joyce and Frank are eating raisins and drinking ginger ale. Frank accidentally drops a raisin into his ginger ale. They both notice that the raisin falls to the bottom of the glass. Soon, the raisin rises to the surface of the ginger ale, and then sinks. Within a couple of minutes, it rises and sinks again. Joyce asks, "I wonder why that happened?" Frank says, "I don't know, but let's see if it works in water." Joyce fills a glass with water and drops the raisin into the glass. After a few minutes, Frank says, "No, it doesn't go up and down in the water." Joyce closely observes the raisins in the two glasses and states, "Look, there are bubbles on the raisins in the ginger ale but not on the raisins in the water." Frank says, "It must be the bubbles that make the raisin rise." Joyce asks, "OK, but then why do they sink again?"

11. In Section 1.3 the statement is made that it is worthwhile for scientists, auto mechanics, doctors, politicians, and poets to take a scientific approach to their professions. Discuss how each of these people could use a scientific approach in his or her profession.

VP 12. As part of a science project, you study traffic patterns in your city at an intersection in the middle of downtown. You set up a device that counts the cars passing through this intersection for a 24-hour period during a weekday. The graph of hourly traffic looks like this.

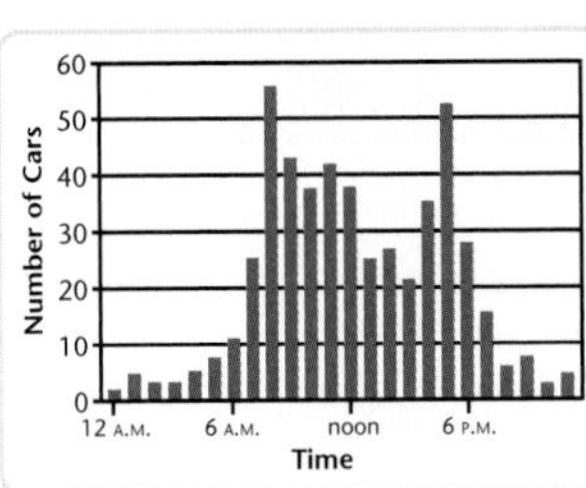

a. At what time(s) does the highest number of cars pass through the intersection?
b. At what time(s) does the lowest number of cars pass through the intersection?
c. Briefly describe the trend in numbers of cars over the course of the day.
d. Provide a hypothesis explaining the trend in numbers of cars over the course of the day.
e. Provide a possible experiment that could test your hypothesis.

VP 13. Confronted with the box shown in the diagram, you wish to discover something about its internal workings. You have no tools and cannot open the box. You pull on rope B, and it moves rather freely. When you pull on rope A, rope C appears to be pulled slightly into the box. When you pull on rope C, rope A almost disappears into the box.*

*From Yoder, Suydam, and Snavely, *Chemistry* (New York: Harcourt Brace Jovanovich, 1975), pp. 9–11.

a. Based on these observations, construct a model for the interior mechanism of the box.
b. What further experiments could you do to refine your model?

Questions and Problems

1.1 Chemistry: An Introduction

QUESTIONS

1. Chemistry is an intimidating academic subject for many students. You are not alone if you are afraid of not doing well in this course! Why do you suppose the study of chemistry is so intimidating for many students? What about having to take a chemistry course bothers you? Make a list of your concerns and bring them to class for discussion with your fellow students and your instructor.
2. The first paragraphs in this chapter ask you if you have ever wondered how and why various things in our everyday lives happen the way they do. For your next class meeting, make a list of five similar chemistry-related things for discussion with your instructor and the other students in your class.
3. This section presents several ways our day-to-day lives have been enriched by chemistry. List three materials or processes involving chemistry that you feel have contributed to such an enrichment and explain your choices.
4. The "Chemistry in Focus" segment titled *Dr. Ruth—Cotton Hero* discusses the enormous contribution of Dr. Ruth Rogan Benerito to the survival of the cotton fabric industry in the United States. In the discussion, it was mentioned that Dr. Benerito became a chemist when women were not expected to be interested in, or good at, scientific subjects. Has this attitude changed? Among your own friends, approximately how many of your female friends are studying a science? How many plan to pursue a career in science? Discuss.

All even-numbered Questions and Problems have answers in the back of this book and solutions in the Solutions Guide.

ChemWork

Using Metric System Definitions
Identifying Significant Figures
Rounding Numbers
Using Significant Figures in Calculations
Length Conversions
Metric Mileage
Speed Conversions
Unit Conversions
Changing Temperature Scales
Temperature Conversions
Density for Osmium
Density of Atoms
Finding the Density of a Liquid
Classifying Matter
Identifying Chemical Properties
Identifying Chemical Changes

water analogy, the student begins with some knowledge (different from the teacher). The students do not just take the knowledge; that new knowledge interacts with what the students already know. The new knowledge changes their understanding, and they don't end up just like the teacher. The interaction is achieved by the students taking an active role in understanding the material.

Answers to End-of-Chapter Exercises

1. The answer depends on the student's experiences.

2. The answer depends on the student's experiences.

3. Answer depends on student responses/examples.

4. Answers will depend on the student's responses.

5. The answer depends on the student's experiences.

6. Answers will depend on the student's choices.

7. David and Susan first recognized the problem (unexplained medical problems). A possible explanation was then proposed (the glaze on their pottery dishes might be causing lead poisoning). The explanation was tested by experiment (it was determined that the glaze did contain lead). A full discussion of this scenario is given in the text.

8. Recognize the problem and state it clearly; propose possible solutions or explanations; decide which solution/explanation is best through experiments.

9. A hypothesis is a tentative explanation for an observed event. So before proposing a hypothesis, repeated observations are necessary to make sure that the phenomenon repeats itself. A theory collects together hypotheses about all aspects of an event in an attempt to explain the event.

1.2 What Is Chemistry?

QUESTIONS

5. This textbook provides a specific definition of chemistry: the study of the materials of which the universe is made and the transformations that these materials undergo. Obviously, such a general definition has to be very broad and nonspecific. From your point of view at this time, how would *you* define chemistry? In your mind, what are "chemicals"? What do "chemists" do?

6. We use chemical reactions in our everyday lives, too, not just in the science laboratory. Give at least five examples of chemical transformations that you use in your daily activities. Indicate what the "chemical" is in each of your examples and how you recognize that a chemical change has taken place.

1.3 Solving Problems Using a Scientific Approach

QUESTIONS

7. Read the "Chemistry in Focus" segment *A Mystifying Problem* and discuss how David and Susan analyzed the situation, arriving at the theory that the lead glaze on the pottery was responsible for their symptoms.

8. Being a scientist is very much like being a detective. Detectives such as Sherlock Holmes or Miss Marple perform a very systematic analysis of a crime to solve it, much like a scientist does when addressing a scientific investigation. What are the steps that scientists (or detectives) use to solve problems?

1.4 The Scientific Method

QUESTIONS

9. Why does a scientist make repeated *observations* of phenomena? Is an observation the same as a *theory?* Why (or why not)? Is a *hypothesis* the same as a *theory?* When does a set of hypotheses *become* a theory?

10. Observations may be either qualitative or quantitative. Quantitative observations are usually referred to as *measurements.* List five examples of *qualitative observations* you might make around your home or school. List five examples of *measurements* you might make in everyday life.

11. Several words are used in this section that students sometimes may find hard to distinguish. Write your *own* definitions of the following terms, and bring them to class for discussion with your instructor and fellow students: *theory, experiment, natural law, hypothesis.*

12. Although, in general, science has advanced our standard of living tremendously, there is sometimes a "dark side" to science. Give an example of the misuse of science and explain how this has had an adverse effect on our lives.

13. Although science *should* lead to solutions to problems that are completely independent of outside forces, very often in history scientific investigations have been influenced by prejudice, profit motives, fads, wars, religious beliefs, and other forces. Your textbook mentions the case of Galileo having to change his theories about astronomy based on intervention by religious authorities. Can you give three additional examples of how scientific investigations have been similarly influenced by nonscientific forces?

1.5 Learning Chemistry

QUESTIONS

14. Although reviewing your lecture notes and reading your textbook are important, why does the study of chemistry depend so much on problem solving? Can you learn to solve problems yourself just by looking at the solved examples in your textbook or study guide? Discuss.

15. Why is the ability to solve problems important in the study of chemistry? Why is it that the *method* used to attack a problem is as important as the answer to the problem itself?

16. Students approaching the study of chemistry must learn certain basic facts (such as the names and symbols of the most common elements), but it is much more important that they learn to think critically and to go beyond the specific examples discussed in class or in the textbook. Explain how learning to do this might be helpful in any career, even one far removed from chemistry.

17. The "Chemistry in Focus" segment *Chemistry: An Important Component of Your Education* discusses how studying chemistry can be beneficial not only in your chemistry courses but in your studies in general. What are some characteristics of a good student, and how does studying chemistry help achieve these characteristics?

All even-numbered Questions and Problems have answers in the back of this book and solutions in the Solutions Guide.

10. Answers will depend on student responses. A quantitative observation must include a number, such as "There are three windows in this room." A qualitative observation could include something like "The chair is blue."

11. A theory is a set of tested hypotheses that gives an overall explanation of an observed phenomenon. A hypothesis is a possible explanation for an observation. An experiment is some measurement or gathering of information we do to test a hypothesis. A natural law is a statement of some generally observed behavior, sometimes mathematical in format, which we then try to explain with our theory.

12. The answer depends on the student's responses/examples.

13. The answer depends on the student's experiences.

14. Chemistry is not just a set of facts that have to be memorized. To be successful in chemistry, you have to be able to apply what you have learned to new situations, new phenomena, new experiments. Rather than just learning a list of facts or studying someone else's solution to a problem, your instructor hopes you will learn *how* to solve problems *yourself,* so that you will be able to apply what you have learned in future circumstances.

15. Chemistry is the study of very real interactions among different samples of matter. When we first begin to study chemistry, we try to be as general and nonspecific as possible, trying to learn the basic principles for application to many situations in the future. At the beginning of study, the solution to a problem is not as important as learning how to recognize and interpret the problem, and how to propose reasonable, testable hypotheses.

16. In real-life situations, the problems and applications likely to be encountered are not simple textbook examples. You must be able to observe an event, hypothesize a cause, and then test this hypothesis. You must be able to carry what has been learned in class forward to new, different situations.

17. A good student will learn the background and fundamentals of the subject from the classes and textbook; will develop the ability to recognize and solve problems and to extend what was learned in the classroom to "real" situations; will learn to make careful observations; and will be able to communicate effectively. Whereas some academic subjects may emphasize use of one or more of these skills, chemistry makes extensive use of all of them.

Chapter 2

Objectives

In this chapter, our objectives are for the students to:

SECTION 2.1

- Show how very large or very small numbers can be expressed as the product of a number between 1 and 10 and a power of 10.

SECTION 2.2

- Learn the English, metric, and SI systems of measurement.

SECTION 2.3

- Use the metric system for measuring length, volume, and mass.

SECTION 2.4

- Understand how uncertainty in a measurement arises.
- Learn to indicate a measurement's uncertainty by using significant figures.

SECTION 2.5

- Learn to determine the number of significant figures in a calculated result.

SECTION 2.6

- Learn how dimensional analysis can be used to solve various types of problems.

SECTION 2.7

- Learn the three temperature scales.
- Learn to convert from one scale to another.
- Continue to develop problem-solving skills.

SECTION 2.8

- Define density and its units.

2 Measurements and Calculations

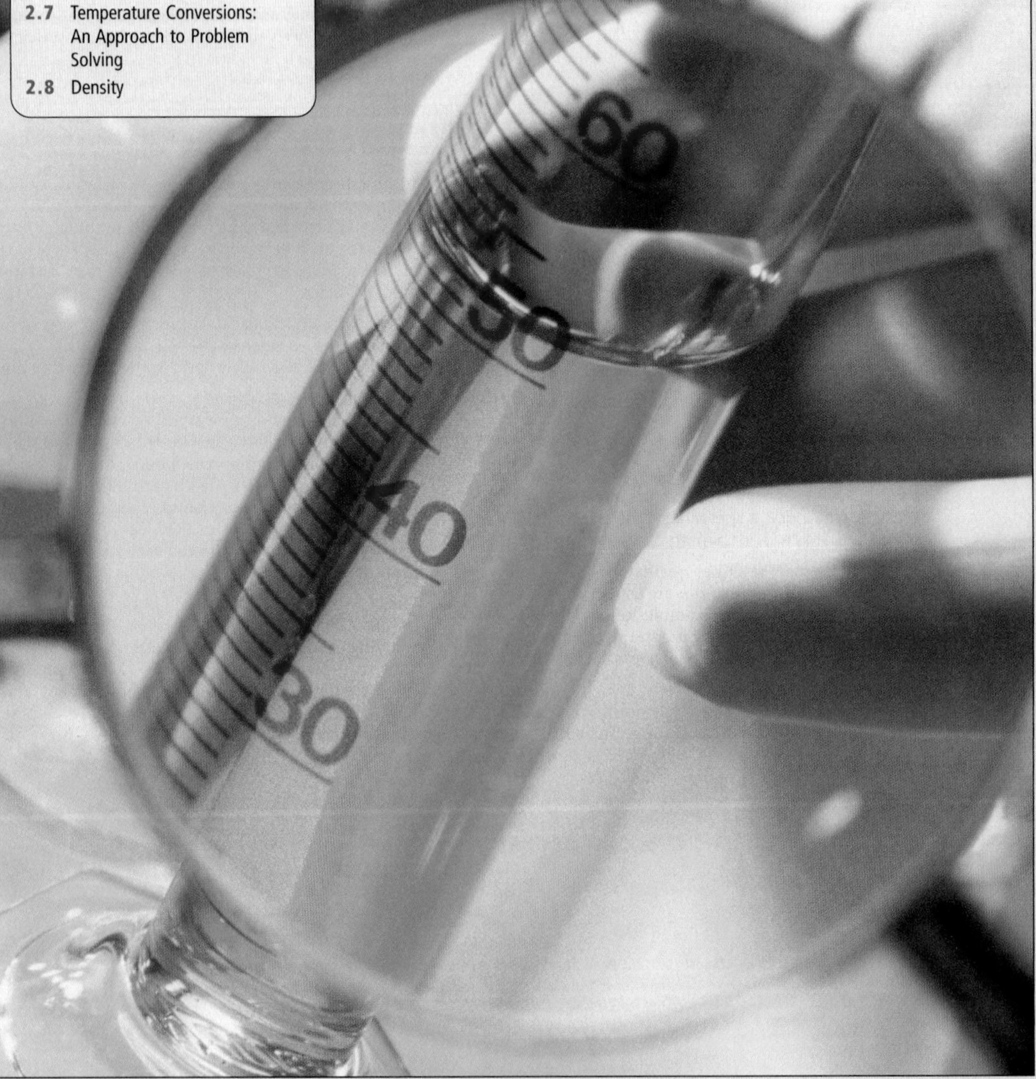

An enlarged view of a graduated cylinder *(Masterfile)*

ChemWork Refined over ten years of use by thousands of students, **ChemWork** builds and enhances students' problems-solving skills. Online assignments function as a "personal instructor" to help students learn how to solve challenging problems and learn how to think like chemists. Annotations for **ChemWork** assignments are included at the beginning of the end-of-chapter review.

PowerLecture This 2-DVD package includes the Chemistry Multimedia Library, which contains animations, simulations, and movies for all chemistry subjects, organized by topic for lecture presentations. Annotations for **PowerLecture** are referenced in the margins throughout the Annotated Instructor's Edition.

Test Bank: 1–10, 61, 62

Section 2.1

OWL Sign in to OWL at **www.cengage.com/owl** to view tutoritals and simulations, develop problem-solving skills, and complete online homework assigned by your professor.

As we pointed out in Chapter 1, making observations is a key part of the scientific process. Sometimes observations are *qualitative* ("the substance is a yellow solid") and sometimes they are *quantitative* ("the substance weighs 4.3 grams"). A quantitative observation is called a **measurement.** Measurements are very important in our daily lives. For example, we pay for gasoline by the gallon, so the gas pump must accurately measure the gas delivered to our fuel tank. The efficiency of the modern automobile engine depends on various measurements, including the amount of oxygen in the exhaust gases, the temperature of the coolant, and the pressure of the lubricating oil. In addition, cars with traction control systems have devices to measure and compare the rates of rotation of all four wheels. As we will see in the "Chemistry in Focus" discussion in this chapter, measuring devices have become very sophisticated in dealing with our fast-moving and complicated society.

As we will discuss in this chapter, a measurement always consists of two parts: a number and a unit. Both parts are necessary to make the measurement meaningful. For example, suppose a friend tells you that she saw a bug 5 long. This statement is meaningless as it stands. Five what? If it's 5 millimeters, the bug is quite small. If it's 5 centimeters, the bug is quite large. If it's 5 meters, run for cover!

The point is that for a measurement to be meaningful, it must consist of both a number and a unit that tells us the scale being used.

In this chapter we will consider the characteristics of measurements and the calculations that involve measurements.

A gas pump measures the amount of gasoline delivered.

MATH MISCONCEPTION

Scientific Notation

Students often confuse negative and positive exponents. For example, to change 93,000,000 to scientific notation we move the decimal point to the left, so many students will claim that it is equal to 9.3×10^{-7}. This makes sense to these students because if we convert 9.3×10^{-7} to normal notation, we move the decimal point to the left. Listen to the students as they solve these problems and deal with students on an individual basis.

The chemistry course may be the first time a student is asked to report and manipulate numbers using scientific notation. While students may be familiar with exponents, they are generally not comfortable using them. For example, many students will say that 1×10^{-7} is larger than 1×10^{-3} because "7" is larger than "3." Other students are likely to disregard the exponent entirely—for example, 2.3×10^3 is said to be larger than 1.8×10^6 because "2.3" is larger than "1.8."

2.1 Scientific Notation

OBJECTIVE: To show how very large or very small numbers can be expressed as the product of a number between 1 and 10 and a power of 10.

A measurement must always consist of a number *and* a unit.

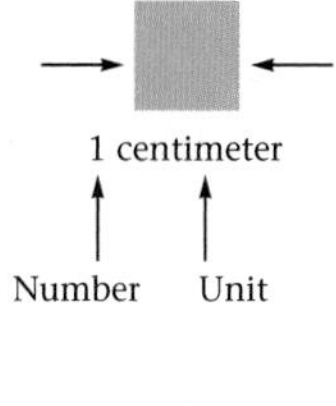

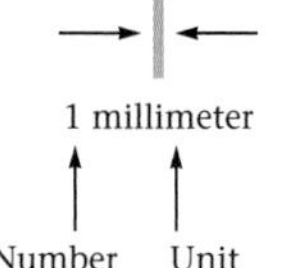

The numbers associated with scientific measurements are often very large or very small. For example, the distance from the earth to the sun is approximately 93,000,000 (93 million) miles. Written out, this number is rather bulky. Scientific notation is a method for making very large or very small numbers more compact and easier to write.

To see how this is done, consider the number 125, which can be written as the product

$$125 = 1.25 \times 100$$

Because $100 = 10 \times 10 = 10^2$, we can write

$$125 = 1.25 \times 100 = 1.25 \times 10^2$$

Similarly, the number 1700 can be written

$$1700 = 1.7 \times 1000$$

and because $1000 = 10 \times 10 \times 10 = 10^3$, we can write

$$1700 = 1.7 \times 1000 = 1.7 \times 10^3$$

TEACHING TIPS

- You will find that the students have used scientific notation to some extent in math classes. Point out that numbers in science are often very large or very small, so using scientific notation is very helpful. It makes an excellent shorthand way of writing numbers.
- Work plenty of examples in class for each type of situation. This practice will give the students more confidence in doing problems on their own.

MATH MISCONCEPTION

Scientific Notation and Calculators

A common mistake for students is to use the calculator incorrectly so that they multiply by 10 twice. For example, when entering the number 2.1×10^7 into the calculator, a student may enter "2.1" "×" "10" "EE" "7," even though the "EE" button represents "×10." The student has effectively entered 2.1×10^8 and the answer will be incorrect by a factor of 10.

TEACHING TIPS

- When introducing scientific notation, use familiar numbers such as 1000 and 5000. Students will easily see that $1000 = 10 \times 10 \times 10 = 1 \times 10^3$, and $5000 = 5 \times 10 \times 10 \times 10 = 5 \times 10^3$.
- If students need extra help with scientific notation, direct them to the Appendix.

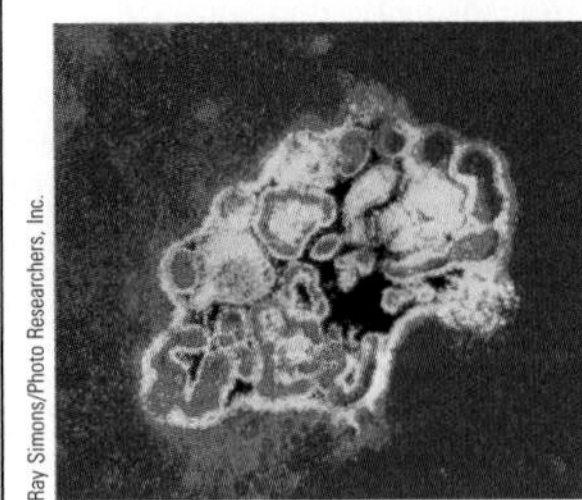

When describing very small distances, such as the diameter of a swine flu virus (shown here magnified 16,537 times), it is convenient to use scientific notation.

Scientific notation simply expresses a number as *a product of a number between 1 and 10 and the appropriate power of 10.* For example, the number 93,000,000 can be expressed as

$$93{,}000{,}000 = 9.3 \times 10{,}000{,}000 = \underset{\text{Number between 1 and 10}}{9.3} \times \underset{\text{Appropriate power of 10 } (10{,}000{,}000 = 10^7)}{10^7}$$

The easiest way to determine the appropriate power of 10 for scientific notation is to start with the number being represented and count the number of places the decimal point must be moved to obtain a number between 1 and 10. For example, for the number

9 3 0 0 0 0 0 0
7 6 5 4 3 2 1

MATH SKILL BUILDER
Keep one digit to the left of the decimal point.

we must move the decimal point seven places to the left to get 9.3 (a number between 1 and 10). To compensate for every move of the decimal point to the left, we must multiply by 10. That is, each time we move the decimal point to the left, we make the number smaller by one power of 10. So for each move of the decimal point to the left, we must multiply by 10 to restore the number to its original magnitude. Thus moving the decimal point seven places to the left means we must multiply 9.3 by 10 seven times, which equals 10^7:

$$93{,}000{,}000 = 9.3 \times 10^7$$

We moved the decimal point seven places to the left, so we need 10^7 to compensate.

MATH SKILL BUILDER
Moving the decimal point to the left requires a positive exponent.

Remember: whenever the decimal point is moved to the *left,* the exponent of 10 is *positive.*

We can represent numbers smaller than 1 by using the same convention, but in this case the power of 10 is negative. For example, for the number 0.010 we must move the decimal point two places to the right to obtain a number between 1 and 10:

0.0 1 0
1 2

MATH SKILL BUILDER
Moving the decimal point to the right requires a negative exponent.

This requires an exponent of −2, so $0.010 = 1.0 \times 10^{-2}$. Remember: whenever the decimal point is moved to the *right,* the exponent of 10 is *negative.*

Next consider the number 0.000167. In this case we must move the decimal point four places to the right to obtain 1.67 (a number between 1 and 10):

0.0 0 0 1 6 7
1 2 3 4

MATH SKILL BUILDER
Read the Appendix if you need a further discussion of exponents and scientific notation.

Moving the decimal point four places to the right requires an exponent of −4. Therefore,

$$0.000167 = 1.67 \times 10^{-4}$$

We moved the decimal point four places to the right.

We summarize these procedures below.

Using Scientific Notation

- Any number can be represented as the product of a number between 1 and 10 and a power of 10 (either positive or negative).
- The power of 10 depends on the number of places the decimal point is moved and in which direction. The *number of places* the decimal point is moved determines the *power of 10.* The *direction* of the move determines whether the power of 10 is *positive* or *negative.* If the decimal point is moved to the left, the power of 10 is positive; if the decimal point is moved to the right, the power of 10 is negative.

MATH SKILL BUILDER
$100 = 1.0 \times 10^2$
$0.010 = 1.0 \times 10^{-2}$

MATH SKILL BUILDER
Left Is Positive; remember LIP.

EXAMPLE 2.1 Scientific Notation: Powers of 10 (Positive)

MATH SKILL BUILDER
A number that is greater than 1 will always have a positive exponent when written in scientific notation.

Represent the following numbers in scientific notation.

a. 238,000

b. 1,500,000

SOLUTION

a. First we move the decimal point until we have a number between 1 and 10, in this case 2.38.

2 3 8 0 0 0
5 4 3 2 1 The decimal point was moved five places to the left.

Because we moved the decimal point five places to the left, the power of 10 is positive 5. Thus $238{,}000 = 2.38 \times 10^5$.

b. 1 5 0 0 0 0 0
6 5 4 3 2 1 The decimal point was moved six places to the left, so the power of 10 is 6.

Thus $1{,}500{,}000 = 1.5 \times 10^6$. ■

EXAMPLE 2.2 Scientific Notation: Powers of 10 (Negative)

MATH SKILL BUILDER
A number that is less than 1 will always have a negative exponent when written in scientific notation.

Represent the following numbers in scientific notation.

a. 0.00043

b. 0.089

SOLUTION

a. First we move the decimal point until we have a number between 1 and 10, in this case 4.3.

0 . 0 0 0 4 3
1 2 3 4 The decimal point was moved four places to the right.

Because we moved the decimal point four places to the right, the power of 10 is negative 4. Thus $0.00043 = 4.3 \times 10^{-4}$.

Additional Examples

Example 2.1

Express each number in scientific notation.

1. 12,500 — 1.25×10^4
2. 247 — 2.47×10^2
3. 10 — 1×10^1
4. 3,500,000 — 3.5×10^6
5. 1430 — 1.43×10^3

Example 2.2

Express each number in scientific notation.

1. 0.135 — 1.35×10^{-1}
2. 0.0024 — 2.4×10^{-3}
3. 0.104 — 1.04×10^{-1}
4. 0.0306 — 3.06×10^{-2}
5. 0.00000072 — 7.2×10^{-7}

Self Check

Answers to Self-Check Exercise 2.1

$357 = 3.57 \times 10^2$

$0.0055 = 5.5 \times 10^{-3}$

Test Bank: 11–24

Section 2.2

TEACHING TIPS

- Challenge your students to go an entire day without ever using a unit. Students often complain about our emphasis on keeping track of units. However, the same students often do not realize that they use units all of the time. For example, challenge them to go into their favorite fast-food restaurant and order "two" and see if they get what they want.
- Have students focus on learning only one conversion between English and metric for each parameter (e.g., length, volume, mass). This will permit them to switch between systems. They usually can convert successfully within a given system.
- When introducing the metric system, ask the students to give examples of the use of the metric system in their lives. This discussion should introduce the idea of a liter and a meter in a more natural way. Most students are not familiar with the large and small prefixes needed in the metric system. Use the PowerPoint slide or transparency of Table 2.2 to introduce them.

b. 0.0 8 9
   1 2   The power of 10 is negative 2 because the decimal point was moved two places to the right.

Thus $0.089 = 8.9 \times 10^{-2}$.

Self-Check EXERCISE 2.1 Write the numbers 357 and 0.0055 in scientific notation. If you are having difficulty with scientific notation at this point, reread the Appendix.

See Problems 2.5 through 2.14. ■

2.2 Units

OBJECTIVE: To learn the English, metric, and SI systems of measurement.

The **units** part of a measurement tells us what *scale* or *standard* is being used to represent the results of the measurement. From the earliest days of civilization, trade has required common units. For example, if a farmer from one region wanted to trade some of his grain for the gold of a miner who lived in another region, the two people had to have common standards (units) for measuring the amount of the grain and the weight of the gold.

The need for common units also applies to scientists, who measure quantities such as mass, length, time, and temperature. If every scientist had her or his own personal set of units, complete chaos would result. Unfortunately, although standard systems of units did arise, different systems were adopted in different parts of the world. The two most widely used systems are the **English system** used in the United States and the **metric system** used in most of the rest of the industrialized world.

The metric system has long been preferred for most scientific work. In 1960 an international agreement set up a comprehensive system of units called the **International System** (*le Système Internationale* in French), or **SI.** The SI units are based on the metric system and units derived from the metric system. The most important fundamental SI units are listed in Table 2.1. Later in this chapter we will discuss how to manipulate some of these units.

Because the fundamental units are not always a convenient size, the SI system uses prefixes to change the size of the unit. The most commonly used prefixes are listed in Table 2.2. Although the fundamental unit for length is the meter (m), we can also use the decimeter (dm), which represents one-tenth (0.1) of a meter; the centimeter (cm), which represents one one-hundredth (0.01) of a meter; the millimeter (mm), which represents one one-thousandth (0.001) of a meter; and so on. For example, it's much more convenient to specify the diameter of a certain contact lens as 1.0 cm than as 1.0×10^{-2} m.

Table 2.1 Some Fundamental SI Units

Physical Quantity	Name of Unit	Abbreviation
mass	kilogram	kg
length	meter	m
time	second	s
temperature	kelvin	K

CHEMISTRY IN FOCUS

Critical Units!

How important are conversions from one unit to another? If you ask the National Aeronautics and Space Administration (NASA), very important! In 1999 NASA lost a $125 million Mars Climate Orbiter because of a failure to convert from English to metric units.

The problem arose because two teams working on the Mars mission were using different sets of units. NASA's scientists at the Jet Propulsion Laboratory in Pasadena, California, assumed that the thrust data for the rockets on the Orbiter they received from Lockheed Martin Astronautics in Denver, which built the spacecraft, were in metric units. In reality, the units were English. As a result the Orbiter dipped 100 kilometers lower into the Mars atmosphere than planned and the friction from the atmosphere caused the craft to burn up.

NASA's mistake refueled the controversy over whether Congress should require the United States to switch to the metric system. About 95% of the world now uses the metric system, and the United States is slowly switching from English to metric. For example, the automobile industry has adopted metric fasteners and we buy our soda in two-liter bottles.

Units can be very important. In fact, they can mean the difference between life and death on some occasions. In 1983, for example, a Canadian jetliner almost ran out of fuel when someone pumped 22,300 pounds of fuel into the aircraft instead of 22,300 kilograms. Remember to watch your units!

NASA

Artist's conception of the lost Mars Climate Orbiter.

Table 2.2 The Commonly Used Prefixes in the Metric System

Prefix	Symbol	Meaning	Power of 10 for Scientific Notation
mega	M	1,000,000	10^{6}
kilo	k	1000	10^{3}
deci	d	0.1	10^{-1}
centi	c	0.01	10^{-2}
milli	m	0.001	10^{-3}
micro	μ	0.000001	10^{-6}
nano	n	0.000000001	10^{-9}

Measurements consist of both a number and a unit, and both are crucial. Just as you would not report a measurement without a numerical value, you would not report a measurement without a unit. You already use units in your daily life, whether you tell somebody, "Let's meet in one hour" (hour is the unit), or you and your friends order two pizzas for dinner (pizza is the unit).

Section 2.3

DEMONSTRATION

Length Bring a regular yardstick and a meter stick to class. Point out how they are similar and how they are different. Discuss which is easier to use, as the meter stick is based on 10 and the yardstick is based on 12 (inches to a foot) and 3 (feet to a yard).

Volume Bring several interesting shapes of glassware to class. For example, use a graduated cylinder, a volumetric flask, an Erlenmeyer flask, a pipet, a buret, and a 1-liter soda bottle. You can use these containers to discuss the fact that liquids take the shape of their container and to indicate that different measuring devices are used for different purposes.

Mass Bring a kilogram mass and a playing card (mass about 1 g).

Test Bank: 25–28

TEACHING TIP

Some metric units are already meaningful to the students. Bring in a 1-L water bottle (and show how it is equal to 1.05 qt). Also, most packaged foods (such as cereals) give "weights" in both grams and ounces. It is helpful if the students have a feel for the size of a liter, a gram, and a meter.

2.3 Measurements of Length, Volume, and Mass

OBJECTIVE: To understand the metric system for measuring length, volume, and mass.

The fundamental SI unit of length is the **meter,** which is a little longer than a yard (1 meter = 39.37 inches). In the metric system fractions of a meter or multiples of a meter can be expressed by powers of 10, as summarized in Table 2.3.

The English and metric systems are compared on the ruler shown in Figure 2.1. Note that

$$1 \text{ inch} = 2.54 \text{ centimeters}$$

Other English–metric equivalences are given in Section 2.6.

Volume is the amount of three-dimensional space occupied by a substance. The fundamental unit of volume in the SI system is based on the volume of a cube that measures 1 meter in each of the three directions. That is, each edge of the cube is 1 meter in length. The volume of this cube is

$$1 \text{ m} \times 1 \text{ m} \times 1 \text{ m} = (1 \text{ m})^3 = 1 \text{ m}^3$$

or, in words, one cubic meter.

In Figure 2.2 this cube is divided into 1000 smaller cubes. Each of these small cubes represents a volume of 1 dm^3, which is commonly called the **liter** (rhymes with "meter" and is slightly larger than a quart) and abbreviated L.

The meter was originally defined, in the eighteenth century, as one ten-millionth of the distance from the equator to the North Pole and then, in the late nineteenth century, as the distance between two parallel marks on a special metal bar stored in a vault in Paris. More recently, for accuracy and convenience, a definition expressed in terms of light waves has been adopted.

Table 2.3 The Metric System for Measuring Length

Unit	Symbol	Meter Equivalent
kilometer	km	1000 m or 10^3 m
meter	m	1 m
decimeter	dm	0.1 m or 10^{-1} m
centimeter	cm	0.01 m or 10^{-2} m
millimeter	mm	0.001 m or 10^{-3} m
micrometer	μm	0.000001 m or 10^{-6} m
nanometer	nm	0.000000001 m or 10^{-9} m

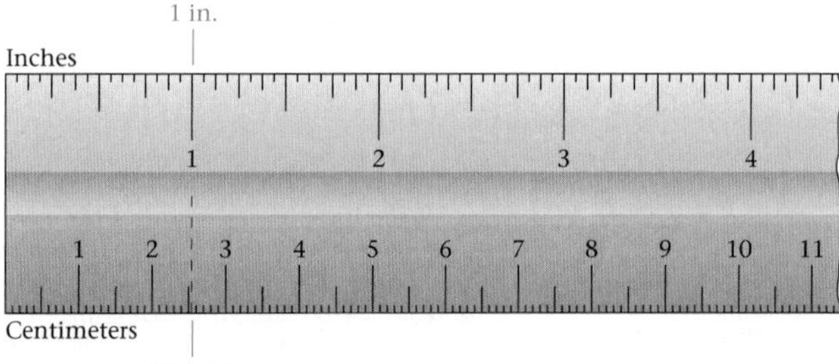

Figure 2.1
Comparison of English and metric units for length on a ruler.

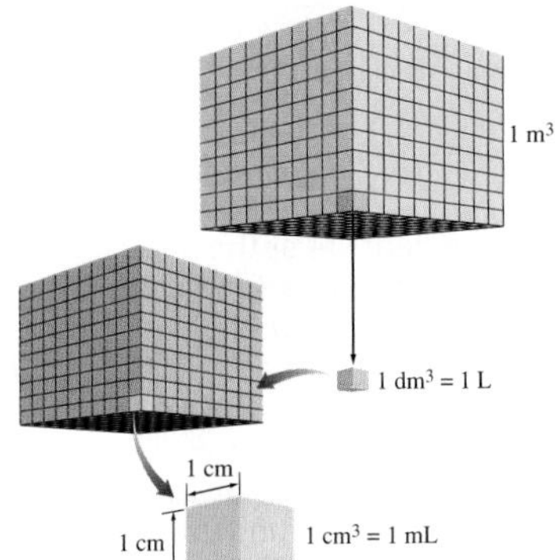

Figure 2.2
The largest drawing represents a cube that has sides 1 m in length and a volume of 1 m^3. The middle-size cube has sides 1 dm in length and a volume of 1 dm^3, or 1 L. The smallest cube has sides 1 cm in length and a volume of 1 cm^3, or 1 mL.

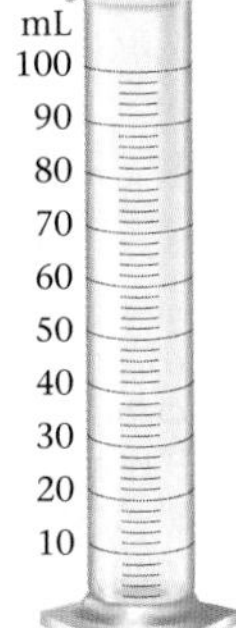

Figure 2.3
A 100-mL graduated cylinder.

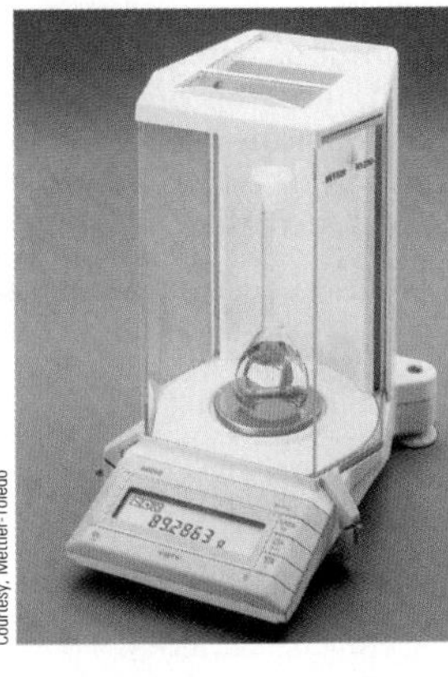
Courtesy, Mettler-Toledo

Figure 2.4
An electronic analytical balance used in chemistry labs.

The cube with a volume of 1 dm^3 (1 liter) can in turn be broken into 1000 smaller cubes, each representing a volume of 1 cm^3. This means that each liter contains 1000 cm^3. One cubic centimeter is called a **milliliter** (abbreviated mL), a unit of volume used very commonly in chemistry. This relationship is summarized in Table 2.4.

The *graduated cylinder* (see Figure 2.3), commonly used in chemical laboratories for measuring the volumes of liquids, is marked off in convenient units of volume (usually milliliters). The graduated cylinder is filled to the desired volume with the liquid, which then can be poured out.

Another important measurable quantity is **mass,** which can be defined as the quantity of matter present in an object. The fundamental SI unit of mass is the **kilogram.** Because the metric system, which existed before the SI system, used the gram as the fundamental unit, the prefixes for the various mass units are based on the **gram,** as shown in Table 2.5.

In the laboratory we determine the mass of an object by using a balance. A balance compares the mass of the object to a set of standard masses ("weights"). For example, the mass of an object can be determined by using a single-pan balance (Figure 2.4).

To help you get a feeling for the common units of length, volume, and mass, some familiar objects are described in Table 2.6.

Table 2.4 The Relationship of the Liter and Milliliter

Unit	Symbol	Equivalence
liter	L	1 L = 1000 mL
milliliter	mL	$\frac{1}{1000}$ L = 10^{-3} L = 1 mL

Table 2.5 The Most Commonly Used Metric Units for Mass

Unit	Symbol	Gram Equivalent
kilogram	kg	1000 g = 10^3 g = 1 kg
gram	g	1 g
milligram	mg	0.001 g = 10^{-3} g = 1 mg

2.3 Measurements of Length, Volume, and Mass 21

CHEMISTRY *IN* FOCUS

Measurement: Past, Present, and Future

Measurement lies at the heart of doing science. We obtain the data for formulating laws and testing theories by doing measurements. Measurements also have very practical importance; they tell us if our drinking water is safe, whether we are anemic, and the exact amount of gasoline we put in our cars at the filling station.

Although the fundamental measuring devices we consider in this chapter are still widely used, new measuring techniques are being developed every day to meet the challenges of our increasingly sophisticated world. For example, engines in modern automobiles have oxygen sensors that analyze the oxygen content in the exhaust gases. This information is sent to the computer that controls the engine functions so that instantaneous adjustments can be made in spark timing and air–fuel mixtures to provide efficient power with minimum air pollution.

As another example, consider airline safety: How do we rapidly, conveniently, and accurately determine whether a given piece of baggage contains an explosive device? A thorough hand-search of each piece of luggage is out of the question. Scientists are now developing a screening procedure that bombards the luggage with high-energy particles that cause any substance present to emit radiation characteristic of that substance. This radiation is monitored to identify luggage with unusually large quantities of nitrogen, because most chemical explosives are based on compounds containing nitrogen.

Ben Osborne/Stone/Getty Images

A pollution control officer measuring the oxygen content of river water.

Scientists are also examining the natural world to find supersensitive detectors because many organisms are sensitive to tiny amounts of chemicals in their environments—recall, for example, the sensitive noses of bloodhounds. One of these natural measuring devices uses the sensory hairs from Hawaiian red swimming crabs, which are connected to electrical analyzers and used to detect hormones down to levels of 10^{-8} g/L. Likewise, tissues from pineapple cores can be used to detect tiny amounts of hydrogen peroxide.

These types of advances in measuring devices have led to an unexpected problem: detecting all kinds of substances in our food and drinking water scares us. Although these substances were always there, we didn't worry so much when we couldn't detect them. Now that we know they are present what should we do about them? How can we assess whether these trace substances are harmful or benign? Risk assessment has become much more complicated as our sophistication in taking measurements has increased.

Table 2.6 Some Examples of Commonly Used Units

length	A dime is 1 mm thick. A quarter is 2.5 cm in diameter. The average height of an adult man is 1.8 m.
mass	A nickel has a mass of about 5 g. A 120-lb woman has a mass of about 55 kg.
volume	A 12-oz can of soda has a volume of about 360 mL. A half gallon of milk is equal to about 2 L of milk.

TEACHING TIPS

- Now is an excellent time to discuss the difference between mass and weight. In daily life we often use these terms interchangeably. They have very different meanings to a chemist, however. Because our language does not have a verb for mass, we use the term *weigh* in chemistry to mean finding the mass of the substance on a balance.
- Ask students to compare the relationship between a liter and a quart, a gram and a pound, and a kilometer and a mile. Try to get them to relate these ideas to the familiar objects in everyday life without actually converting the units.

2.4 Uncertainty in Measurement

OBJECTIVES: To understand how uncertainty in a measurement arises. • To learn to indicate a measurement's uncertainty by using significant figures.

When you measure the amount of something by counting, the measurement is exact. For example, if you asked your friend to buy four apples from the store and she came back with three or five apples, you would be surprised. However, measurements are not always exact. For example, whenever a measurement is made with a device such as a ruler or a graduated cylinder, an estimate is required. We can illustrate this by measuring the pin shown in Figure 2.5a. We can see from the ruler that the pin is a little longer than 2.8 cm and a little shorter than 2.9 cm. Because there are no graduations on the ruler between 2.8 and 2.9, we must estimate the pin's length between 2.8 and 2.9 cm. We do this by *imagining* that the distance between 2.8 and 2.9 is broken into 10 equal divisions (Figure 2.5b) and estimating to which division the end of the pin reaches. The end of the pin appears to come about halfway between 2.8 and 2.9, which corresponds to 5 of our 10 imaginary divisions. So we estimate the pin's length as 2.85 cm. The result of our measurement is that the pin is approximately 2.85 cm in length, but we had to rely on a visual estimate, so it might actually be 2.84 or 2.86 cm.

Andrew Lambert/Leslie Garland Picture Library/Alamy Images

A student performing a titration in the laboratory.

Because the last number is based on a visual estimate, it may be different when another person makes the same measurement. For example, if five different people measured the pin, the results might be

Person	Result of Measurement
1	2.85 cm
2	2.84 cm
3	2.86 cm
4	2.85 cm
5	2.86 cm

Note that the first two digits in each measurement are the same regardless of who made the measurement; these are called the *certain* numbers of the measurement. However, the third digit is estimated and can vary; it is called an *uncertain* number. When one is making a measurement, the custom is to record all of the certain numbers plus the *first* uncertain number. It would not make any sense to try to measure the pin to the third decimal place (thousandths of a centimeter), because this ruler requires an estimate of even the second decimal place (hundredths of a centimeter).

Every measurement has some degree of uncertainty.

It is very important to realize that *a measurement always has some degree of uncertainty.* The uncertainty of a measurement depends on the

Section 2.4

TEACHING TIP

To illustrate uncertainty in measurements, bring to class several pieces of glassware used to measure volume. Show students the glassware. Draw the shape of a representative piece of the glassware on the board, marking the drawing to show the meniscus of a liquid between two of the lines. Because the volume falls between the lines, there is uncertainty involved in the reading. Have students write down the result of the measurement. Then compare results. The number recorded for this measurement will vary from student to student only in the last digit. Thus only one uncertain digit is present.

PowerLecture Animation: Chemistry Apparatus (no sound)

Section 2.5

TEACHING TIPS

- Students have the most trouble determining whether zeros are significant. Be sure to do examples with zeros in various locations within the number. Also, make students explain *why* a zero is or is not a significant figure. The explanation should go beyond a mere citation of a rule. Let students know that for the sake of measurement, 2.40 means something different from 2.4 (although according to their calculators both are equivalent).
- Students often have trouble determining which numbers qualify as "exact numbers." Be sure to discuss numbers that are exact as you encounter them in examples. Help the students recognize numbers from definitions and from counting objects as being exact.
- The easiest way to determine the number of significant figures in a number is to write the number in scientific notation. In this notation there are no leading zeros, all zeros in the middle of the number are significant, and trailing zeros are recorded only if they are significant.

Test Bank: 29–62
Lecture Demonstration: 1.4

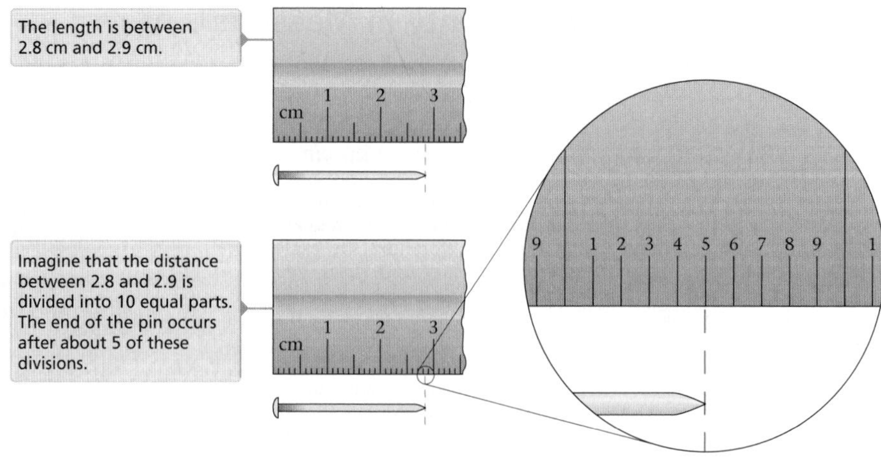
The length is between 2.8 cm and 2.9 cm.
Imagine that the distance between 2.8 and 2.9 is divided into 10 equal parts. The end of the pin occurs after about 5 of these divisions.
cm
1
2
3
9 1 2 3 4 5 6 7 8 9 1

Figure 2.5
Measuring a pin.

measuring device. For example, if the ruler in Figure 2.5 had marks indicating hundredths of a centimeter, the uncertainty in the measurement of the pin would occur in the thousandths place rather than the hundredths place, but some uncertainty would still exist.

The numbers recorded in a measurement (all the certain numbers plus the first uncertain number) are called **significant figures.** The number of significant figures for a given measurement is determined by the inherent uncertainty of the measuring device. For example, the ruler used to measure the pin can give results only to hundredths of a centimeter. Thus, when we record the significant figures for a measurement, we automatically give information about the uncertainty in a measurement. The uncertainty in the last number (the estimated number) is usually assumed to be ± 1 unless otherwise indicated. For example, the measurement 1.86 kilograms can be interpreted as 1.86 ± 0.01 kilograms, where the symbol $\pm$ means plus or minus. That is, it could be 1.86 kg − 0.01 kg = 1.85 kg or 1.86 kg + 0.01 kg = 1.87 kg.

2.5 Significant Figures

OBJECTIVE: To learn to determine the number of significant figures in a calculated result.

We have seen that any measurement involves an estimate and thus is uncertain to some extent. We signify the degree of certainty for a particular measurement by the number of significant figures we record.

Because doing chemistry requires many types of calculations, we must consider what happens when we do arithmetic with numbers that contain uncertainties. It is important that we know the degree of uncertainty in the final result. Although we will not discuss the process here, mathematicians have studied how uncertainty accumulates and have designed a set of rules

TEACHING SUPPORT

ACTIVITY

Bring in yardsticks, meter sticks, and rulers (English and metric). Have students measure the length of the room in yards and centimeters. Have them convert the yards to centimeters, and the centimeters to yards, and compare the results. This leads to a good discussion of uncertainty and to a meaningful look at significant figures.

to determine how many significant figures the result of a calculation should have. You should follow these rules whenever you carry out a calculation. The first thing we need to do is learn how to count the significant figures in a given number. To do this we use the following rules:

Rules for Counting Significant Figures

1. *Nonzero integers.* Nonzero integers *always* count as significant figures. For example, the number 1457 has four nonzero integers, all of which count as significant figures.
2. *Zeros.* There are three classes of zeros:
   a. *Leading zeros* are zeros that *precede* all of the nonzero digits. They *never* count as significant figures. For example, in the number 0.0025, the three zeros simply indicate the position of the decimal point. The number has only two significant figures, the 2 and the 5.
   b. *Captive zeros* are zeros that fall *between* nonzero digits. They *always* count as significant figures. For example, the number 1.008 has four significant figures.
   c. *Trailing zeros* are zeros at the *right end* of the number. They are significant only if the number is written with a decimal point. The number one hundred written as 100 has only one significant figure, but written as 100., it has three significant figures.
3. *Exact numbers.* Often calculations involve numbers that were not obtained using measuring devices but were determined by counting: 10 experiments, 3 apples, 8 molecules. Such numbers are called *exact numbers.* They can be assumed to have an unlimited number of significant figures. Exact numbers can also arise from definitions. For example, 1 inch is defined as *exactly* 2.54 centimeters. Thus in the statement 1 in. = 2.54 cm, neither 2.54 nor 1 limits the number of significant figures when it is used in a calculation.

MATH SKILL BUILDER
Leading zeros are never significant figures.

MATH SKILL BUILDER
Captive zeros are always significant figures.

MATH SKILL BUILDER
Trailing zeros are sometimes significant figures.

MATH SKILL BUILDER
Exact numbers never limit the number of significant figures in a calculation.

Rules for counting significant figures also apply to numbers written in scientific notation. For example, the number 100. can also be written as 1.00×10^2, and both versions have three significant figures. Scientific notation offers two major advantages: the number of significant figures can be indicated easily, and fewer zeros are needed to write a very large or a very small number. For example, the number 0.000060 is much more conveniently represented as 6.0×10^{-5}, and the number has two significant figures, written in either form.

MATH SKILL BUILDER
Significant figures are easily indicated by scientific notation.

EXAMPLE 2.3 Counting Significant Figures

Give the number of significant figures for each of the following measurements.

a. A sample of orange juice contains 0.0108 g of vitamin C.

b. A forensic chemist in a crime lab weighs a single hair and records its mass as 0.0050060 g.

c. The distance between two points was found to be 5.030×10^3 ft.

d. In yesterday's bicycle race, 110 riders started but only 60 finished.

LABORATORY EXPERIMENT

Relevant laboratory experiments for this section are Experiment 1, The Laboratory Balance: Mass Determinations, and Experiment 2, The Use of Volumetric Glassware, from *Introductory Chemistry in the Laboratory* by James Hall.

Additional Examples

Example 2.3

Give the number of significant figures for each measurement.

1. The mass of a single eyelash is 0.000304 g. (3)
2. The length of a skid mark is 1.270×10^2 m. (4)
3. A 125-g sample of chocolate chip cookies contains 10 g of chocolate. (3,1)
4. The volume of soda remaining in a can after a spill is 0.09020 L. (4)
5. A dose of antibiotic is 4.0×10^{-1} cm³. (2)

SOLUTION

a. The number contains three significant figures. The zeros to the left of the 1 are leading zeros and are not significant, but the remaining zero (a captive zero) is significant.

b. The number contains five significant figures. The leading zeros (to the left of the 5) are not significant. The captive zeros between the 5 and the 6 are significant, and the trailing zero to the right of the 6 is significant because the number contains a decimal point.

c. This number has four significant figures. Both zeros in 5.030 are significant.

d. Both numbers are exact (they were obtained by counting the riders). Thus these numbers have an unlimited number of significant figures.

Self-Check **EXERCISE 2.2** Give the number of significant figures for each of the following measurements.

a. 0.00100 m

b. 2.0800×10^2 L

c. 480 Corvettes

See Problems 2.33 and 2.34. ■

Rounding Off Numbers

When you perform a calculation on your calculator, the number of digits displayed is usually greater than the number of significant figures that the result should possess. So you must "round off" the number (reduce it to fewer digits). The rules for **rounding off** follow.

These rules reflect the way calculators round off.

Rules for Rounding Off

1. If the digit to be removed
   a. is less than 5, the preceding digit stays the same. For example, 1.33 rounds to 1.3.
   b. is equal to or greater than 5, the preceding digit is increased by 1. For example, 1.36 rounds to 1.4, and 3.15 rounds to 3.2.
2. In a series of calculations, carry the extra digits through to the final result and *then* round off.* This means that you should carry all of the digits that show on your calculator until you arrive at the final number (the answer) and then round off, using the procedures in Rule 1.

We need to make one more point about rounding off to the correct number of significant figures. Suppose the number 4.348 needs to be

*This practice will not be followed in the worked-out examples in this text, because we want to show the correct number of significant figures in each step of the example.

Self Check

Answers to Self-Check Exercise 2.2

a. Three significant figures. The leading zeros (to the left of the 1) do not count, but the trailing zeros do.

b. Five significant figures. The one captive zero and the two trailing zeros all count.

c. This is an exact number obtained by counting the cars. It has an unlimited number of significant figures.

TEACHING TIP

Students have had practice rounding off numbers in math class. Often, however, they do not know when to round off during a problem. Be sure to emphasize Rule 2, as the students use calculators. In general, students should carry all calculator digits until the end of the problem and then round off to the correct number of significant figures.

Background Information

- When developing worksheet problems and exams, it is important to follow the steps used in "Rules for Rounding Off" when constructing the answers and choices for answers. Otherwise, the students' correct answer and your correct answer may differ, leading students to believe they have done the calculations incorrectly.
- Students should also pay attention to significant figures throughout the school year (not just in this chapter). This text gives answers rounded to correct significant figures throughout. Having students be aware of the number of significant figures in their answers reminds them that in science measurements have limitations. All atomic masses in the text have been rounded to four significant figures, so this consideration will not limit the number of significant figures in the answer for a calculation.

Lecture Demonstration: 1.6

rounded to two significant figures. In doing this, we look *only* at the *first number* to the right of the 3:

4.348
↑
Look at this number to round off to two significant figures.

MATH SKILL BUILDER
Do not round off sequentially. The number 6.8347 rounded to three significant figures is 6.83, not 6.84.

The number is rounded to 4.3 because 4 is less than 5. It is incorrect to round sequentially. For example, do *not* round the 4 to 5 to give 4.35 and then round the 3 to 4 to give 4.4.

When rounding off, *use only the first number to the right of the last significant figure.*

Determining Significant Figures in Calculations

Next we will learn how to determine the correct number of significant figures in the result of a calculation. To do this we will use the following rules.

Rules for Using Significant Figures in Calculations

1. For *multiplication* or *division,* the number of significant figures in the result is the same as that in the measurement with the *smallest number* of significant figures. We say this measurement is *limiting,* because it limits the number of significant figures in the result. For example, consider this calculation:

$$4.56 \times 1.4 = 6.384 \xrightarrow{\text{Round off}} 6.4$$

4.56: Three significant figures; 1.4: Limiting (two significant figures); 6.4: Two significant figures

Because 1.4 has only two significant figures, it limits the result to two significant figures. Thus the product is correctly written as 6.4, which has two significant figures. Consider another example. In the division $\frac{8.315}{298}$, how many significant figures should appear in the answer? Because 8.315 has four significant figures, the number 298 (with three significant figures) limits the result. The calculation is correctly represented as

$$\frac{8.315}{298} = 0.0279027 \xrightarrow{\text{Round off}} 2.79 \times 10^{-2}$$

8.315: Four significant figures; 298: Limiting (three significant figures); 0.0279027: Result shown on calculator; 2.79×10^{-2}: Three significant figures

(continued)

TEACHING TIP

You can discuss using significant figures with addition and subtraction by reminding your students that we assume the estimated number to be ± unless otherwise indicated. The answer 31.1 mL, therefore, indicates a range of 31.0 mL to 31.2 mL. To show this, have your students recalculate the answer twice, once by assuming the upper limits and once by assuming the lowers limits. In this case the students should calculate the following:

$12.12 + 18.1 + 1.014 = 31.234 \rightarrow 31.2$

$12.10 + 17.9 + 1.012 = 31.012 \rightarrow 31.0$

So we can say the answer is 31.1, which implies 31.1 ± 0.1.

Additional Examples

Example 2.4

Without calculating, determine the correct number of significant figures in each answer.

1. 17.1 + 0.77 + 241 (3)
2. 47.2 − 9 (2)
3. 1.27 × 3.1416 (3)
4. $\frac{0.072}{4.36}$ (2)
5. the cost of 2 tickets to a concert at $27.50 per ticket (4)

MATH SKILL BUILDER
If you need help in using your calculator, see the Appendix.

2. For *addition* or *subtraction,* the limiting term is the one with the smallest number of decimal places. For example, consider the following sum:

```
 12.11
 18.0     Limiting term (has one decimal place)
  1.013
 31.123  Round off > 31.1
                      ↑
                One decimal place
```

Why is the answer limited by the term with the smallest number of decimal places? Recall that the last digit reported in a measurement is actually an uncertain number. Although 18, 18.0, and 18.00 are treated as the same quantities by your calculator, they are different to a scientist. The problem above can be thought of as follows:

```
 12.11? mL
 18.0?? mL
  1.013 mL
 31.1?? mL
```

Because the term 18.0 is reported only to the tenths place, our answer must be reported this way as well.

The correct result is 31.1 (it is limited to one decimal place because 18.0 has only one decimal place). Consider another example:

```
  0.6875
 −0.1      Limiting term (one decimal place)
  0.5875
          Round off > 0.6
```

Note that *for multiplication and division, significant figures are counted. For addition and subtraction, the decimal places are counted.*

Now we will put together the things you have learned about significant figures by considering some mathematical operations in the following examples.

EXAMPLE 2.4 Counting Significant Figures in Calculations

Without performing the calculations, tell how many significant figures each answer should contain.

a. 5.19
   1.9
   +0.842

b. 1081 − 7.25

c. 2.3 × 3.14

d. the total cost of 3 boxes of candy at $2.50 a box

SOLUTION

a. The answer will have one digit after the decimal place. The limiting number is 1.9, which has one decimal place, so the answer has two significant figures.

b. The answer will have no digits after the decimal point. The number 1081 has no digits to the right of the decimal point and limits the result, so the answer has four significant figures.

c. The answer will have two significant figures because the number 2.3 has only two significant figures (3.14 has three).

d. The answer will have three significant figures. The limiting factor is 2.50 because 3 (boxes of candy) is an exact number. ■

EXAMPLE 2.5 Calculations Using Significant Figures

Carry out the following mathematical operations and give each result to the correct number of significant figures.

a. 5.18×0.0208

b. $(3.60 \times 10^{-3}) \times (8.123) \div 4.3$

c. $21 + 13.8 + 130.36$

d. $116.8 - 0.33$

e. $(1.33 \times 2.8) + 8.41$

SOLUTION

Limiting terms — Round to this digit.

a. $5.18 \times 0.0208 = 0.107744 \Rightarrow 0.108$

The answer should contain three significant figures because each number being multiplied has three significant figures (Rule 1). The 7 is rounded to 8 because the following digit is greater than 5.

Round to this digit.

b. $\frac{(3.60 \times 10^{-3})(8.123)}{4.3} = 6.8006 \times 10^{-3} \Rightarrow 6.8 \times 10^{-3}$

Limiting term

Because 4.3 has the least number of significant figures (two), the result should have two significant figures (Rule 1).

c. $21 + 13.8 + 130.36 = 165.16 \Rightarrow 165$

In this case 21 is limiting (there are no digits after the decimal point). Thus the answer must have no digits after the decimal point, in accordance with the rule for addition (Rule 2).

d. $116.8 - 0.33 = 116.47 \Rightarrow 116.5$

Because 116.8 has only one decimal place, the answer must have only one decimal place (Rule 2). The 4 is rounded up to 5 because the digit to the right (7) is greater than 5.

e. $1.33 \times 2.8 = 3.724 \Rightarrow 3.7$

3.7 ← Limiting term

$3.7 + 8.41 = 12.11 \Rightarrow 12.1$

Note that in this case we multiplied and then rounded the result to the correct number of significant figures before we performed the addition so that we would know the correct number of decimal places.

MATH SKILL BUILDER
When we multiply and divide in a problem, perform all calculations before rounding the answer to the correct number of significant figures.

MATH SKILL BUILDER
When we multiply (or divide) and then add (or subtract) in a problem, round the first answer from the first operation (in this case, multiplication) before performing the next operation (in this case, addition). We need to know the correct number of decimal places.

Self-Check **EXERCISE 2.3** Give the answer for each calculation to the correct number of significant figures.

a. 12.6×0.53

b. $(12.6 \times 0.53) - 4.59$

c. $(25.36 - 4.15) \div 2.317$

See Problems 2.47 through 2.52. ■

Self Check

Answers to Self-Check Exercise 2.3

a. 6.7

b. 2.1

c. 9.154

Additional Examples

Example 2.5

Give the correct power of 10 for each answer.

1. $(1.71 \times 10^3)(2.0 \times 10^2) =$ $3.4 \times$ ______ (10^5)

2. $\frac{1.64 \times 10^{-2}}{1.2 \times 10^{-2}} =$ $1.4 \times$ ______ (10^0)

3. Solve the following, giving the answer in scientific notation with the correct significant figures.

a. $(1.83 \times 10^{-4})(7.55 \times 10^7) =$ 1.38×10^4

b. $3.3 \times 5280 =$ 1.7×10^4

c. $\frac{(5.0 \times 10^{-4})(8.51 \times 10^{-2})}{2.92 \times 10^4} =$ 1.5×10^{-9}

d. $1.842 + 45.2 + 87.55 =$ 1.346×10^2

e. $714.3 - 18.56 =$ 6.957×10^2

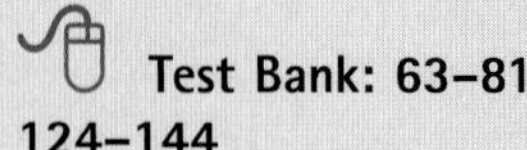

Test Bank: 63–81, 124–144

Section 2.6

MISCONCEPTION

Students often confuse achieving a correct answer with possessing a conceptual understanding of a system, and dimensional analysis aids this misconception. Dimensional analysis is a double-edged sword—it is both extremely useful and quite dangerous. It is useful because it allows students to solve problems by considering only the units. It is dangerous for the same reason; that is, it can allow students to solve problems they do not understand.

MISCONCEPTION

It is important to differentiate between achieving the correct answer and understanding the underlying concepts of the problem. As an example, you may wish to give the students this problem:

There are 2 igals in 1 odonku, and 6 odonkus in 4 falgers. If you have 3 igals, how many falgers is this?

Most students eventually get the answer "1 falger." Once they have solved the problem, ask them questions such as "What is an igal? an odonku? a falger?" While we expect the students to be able to do the mathematical mechanics illustrated by this problem, students should also strive to understand the problems they are solving.

2.6 Problem Solving and Dimensional Analysis

OBJECTIVE: To learn how dimensional analysis can be used to solve various types of problems.

Suppose that the boss at the store where you work on weekends asks you to pick up 2 dozen doughnuts on the way to work. However, you find that the doughnut shop sells by the doughnut. How many doughnuts do you need?

This "problem" is an example of something you encounter all the time: converting from one unit of measurement to another. Examples of this occur in cooking (The recipe calls for 3 cups of cream, which is sold in pints. How many pints do I buy?); traveling (The purse costs 250 pesos. How much is that in dollars?); sports (A recent Tour de France bicycle race was 3215 kilometers long. How many miles is that?); and many other areas.

How do we convert from one unit of measurement to another? Let's explore this process by using the doughnut problem.

$$2 \text{ dozen doughnuts} = ? \text{ individual doughnuts}$$

where ? represents a number you don't know yet. The essential information you must have is the definition of a dozen:

$$1 \text{ dozen} = 12$$

You can use this information to make the needed conversion as follows:

$$2 \text{ dozen doughnuts} \times \frac{12}{1 \text{ dozen}} = 24 \text{ doughnuts}$$

MATH SKILL BUILDER
Since 1 dozen = 12, when we multiply by $\frac{12}{1 \text{ dozen}}$, we are multiplying by 1. The unit "dozen" cancels.

You need to buy 24 doughnuts.

Note two important things about this process.

1. The factor $\frac{12}{1 \text{ dozen}}$ is a conversion factor based on the definition of the term *dozen*. This conversion factor is a ratio of the two parts of the definition of a dozen given above.
2. The unit "dozen" itself cancels.

Now let's generalize a bit. To change from one unit to another we will use a conversion factor.

$$\text{Unit}_1 \times \text{conversion factor} = \text{Unit}_2$$

The **conversion factor** is a ratio of the two parts of the statement that relates the two units. We will see this in more detail on the following pages.

Earlier in this chapter we considered a pin that measured 2.85 cm in length. What is the length of the pin in inches? We can represent this problem as

$$2.85 \text{ cm} \rightarrow ? \text{ in.}$$

Table 2.7 English–Metric and English–English Equivalents

Length	1 m = 1.094 yd
	2.54 cm = 1 in.
	1 mi = 5280. ft
	1 mi = 1760. yd
Mass	1 kg = 2.205 lb
	453.6 g = 1 lb
Volume	1 L = 1.06 qt
	1 ft^3 = 28.32 L

The question mark stands for the number we want to find. To solve this problem, we must know the relationship between inches and centimeters. In Table 2.7, which gives several equivalents between the English and metric systems, we find the relationship

$$2.54 \text{ cm} = 1 \text{ in.}$$

MATH MISCONCEPTION

Equivalence Statements

Even students who can correctly use equivalence statements may not realize that when you multiply a given value by an equivalence statement, you are effectively multiplying that value by "1," because the values in the numerator and the denominator are equivalent. This point should be emphasized.

This is called an **equivalence statement.** In other words, 2.54 cm and 1 in. stand for *exactly the same distance*. (See Figure 2.1.) The respective numbers are different because they refer to different *scales* (*units*) of distance.

The equivalence statement 2.54 cm = 1 in. can lead to either of two conversion factors:

$$\frac{2.54 \text{ cm}}{1 \text{ in.}} \quad \text{or} \quad \frac{1 \text{ in.}}{2.54 \text{ cm}}$$

Note that these *conversion factors* are *ratios of the two parts of the equivalence statement* that relates the two units. Which of the two possible conversion factors do we need? Recall our problem:

$$2.85 \text{ cm} = ? \text{ in.}$$

That is, we want to convert from units of centimeters to inches:

$$2.85 \text{ cm} \times \text{conversion factor} = ? \text{ in.}$$

We choose a conversion factor that cancels the units we want to discard and leaves the units we want in the result. Thus we do the conversion as follows:

MATH SKILL BUILDER
Units cancel just as numbers do.

$$2.85 \text{ cm} \times \frac{1 \text{ in.}}{2.54 \text{ cm}} = \frac{2.85 \text{ in.}}{2.54} = 1.12 \text{ in.}$$

Note two important facts about this conversion:

1. The centimeter units cancel to give inches for the result. This is exactly what we had wanted to accomplish. Using the other conversion factor $\left(2.85 \text{ cm} \times \frac{2.54 \text{ cm}}{1 \text{ in.}}\right)$ would not work because the units would not cancel to give inches in the result.
2. As the units changed from centimeters to inches, the number changed from 2.85 to 1.12. Thus 2.85 cm has exactly the same value (is the same length) as 1.12 in. Notice that in this conversion, the number decreased from 2.85 to 1.12. This makes sense because the inch is a larger unit of length than the centimeter is. That is, it takes fewer inches to make the same length in centimeters.

MATH SKILL BUILDER
When you finish a calculation, always check to make sure that the answer makes sense.

The result in the foregoing conversion has three significant figures as required. Caution: Noting that the term 1 appears in the conversion, you might think that because this number appears to have only one significant figure, the result should have only one significant figure. That is, the answer should be given as 1 in. rather than 1.12 in. However, in the equivalence statement 1 in. = 2.54 cm, the 1 is an exact number (by definition). In other words, exactly 1 in. equals 2.54 cm. Therefore, the 1 does not limit the number of significant digits in the result.

MATH SKILL BUILDER
When exact numbers are used in a calculation, they never limit the number of significant digits.

We have seen how to convert from centimeters to inches. What about the reverse conversion? For example, if a pencil is 7.00 in. long, what is its length in centimeters? In this case, the conversion we want to make is

$$7.00 \text{ in.} \rightarrow ? \text{ cm}$$

What conversion factor do we need to make this conversion?

Remember that two conversion factors can be derived from each equivalence statement. In this case, the equivalence statement 2.54 cm = 1 in. gives

$$\frac{2.54 \text{ cm}}{1 \text{ in.}} \quad \text{or} \quad \frac{1 \text{ in.}}{2.54 \text{ cm}}$$

TEACHING TIPS

- Be sure to help the students understand how to use equivalence statements. An equivalence statement relates the same quantity in two different units. The statement can be used to generate two different conversion factors. Students must learn to use the correct conversion factor in setting up problems. Their choice should indicate the unit they need or want on the top of the factor and the unit they are trying to eliminate on the bottom of the conversion factor.
- When doing examples in class, give both of the possible conversion factors. Ask students to choose the one that will produce the correct result. This practice reinforces the ideas that all conversion factors can be written in two ways and that the student must choose the appropriate one based on the desired units.
- Students often think they already know how to convert units. Frequently, they do not use units on their conversion factors. As the problems become more complex, this omission becomes an increasing difficulty. Encourage all students to place proper units on the conversion factors. Ask them to set up problems and show how the units work out for the final result without actually doing the calculation.
- Asking students to consider whether their answer makes sense is a good way to check on the magnitude and the sign of the answer. Students are often reluctant to do so, which leads to many careless mistakes in calculations.

MATH MISCONCEPTION

Equivalence Statements

Students frequently interpret equivalence statements incorrectly. For example, consider the equivalence statement 1 L = 1.0567 qt. While a student may be able to correctly use this statement to convert a given number of liters to the correct number of quarts, this same student may claim that a quart is larger than a liter (because 1.0567 is larger than 1). It is useful to bring in two empty 1-L bottles and add 1 L of water to one bottle and 1 quart of water to the other bottle to show the difference.

TEACHING TIP

Discuss with the students which conversions come from definitions (such as 1 inch = 2.54 centimeters) and which are the result of measurements. Knowing the difference helps students to decide which conversion limits the number of significant figures.

Additional Examples

Example 2.6

1. A new baby weighs 7.8 lb. What is its mass in kilograms? **3.5 kg**
2. A piece of lumber is 88.4 cm long. What is its length in millimeters? **884 mm** in inches? **34.8 in.**
3. A bottle of soda contains 2.0 L. What is its volume in quarts? **2.12 qt**

Again, we choose which factor to use by looking at the *direction* of the required change. For us to change from inches to centimeters, the inches must cancel. Thus the factor

$$\frac{2.54\text{ cm}}{1\text{ in.}}$$

is used, and the conversion is done as follows:

$$7.00\text{ in.} \times \frac{2.54\text{ cm}}{1\text{ in.}} = (7.00)(2.54)\text{ cm} = 17.8\text{ cm}$$

Here the inch units cancel, leaving centimeters as required.

Note that in this conversion, the number increased (from 7.00 to 17.8). This makes sense because the centimeter is a smaller unit of length than the inch. That is, it takes more centimeters to make the same length in inches. *Always take a moment to think about whether your answer makes sense.* This will help you avoid errors.

Consider the direction of the required change in order to select the correct conversion factor.

Changing from one unit to another via conversion factors (based on the equivalence statements between the units) is often called **dimensional analysis.** We will use this method throughout our study of chemistry.

We can now state some general steps for doing conversions by dimensional analysis.

Converting from One Unit to Another

Step 1 To convert from one unit to another, use the equivalence statement that relates the two units. The conversion factor needed is a ratio of the two parts of the equivalence statement.

Step 2 Choose the appropriate conversion factor by looking at the direction of the required change (make sure the unwanted units cancel).

Step 3 Multiply the quantity to be converted by the conversion factor to give the quantity with the desired units.

Step 4 Check that you have the correct number of significant figures.

Step 5 Ask whether your answer makes sense.

We will now illustrate this procedure in Example 2.6.

EXAMPLE 2.6 Conversion Factors: One-Step Problems

An Italian bicycle has its frame size given as 62 cm. What is the frame size in inches?

SOLUTION

We can represent the problem as

$$62\text{ cm} = ?\text{ in.}$$

In this problem we want to convert from centimeters to inches.

$$62\text{ cm} \times \text{conversion factor} = ?\text{ in.}$$

Step 1 To convert from centimeters to inches, we need the equivalence statement 1 in. = 2.54 cm. This leads to two conversion factors:

$$\frac{1\text{ in.}}{2.54\text{ cm}} \quad \text{and} \quad \frac{2.54\text{ cm}}{1\text{ in.}}$$

Step 2 In this case, the direction we want is

Centimeters → inches

so we need the conversion factor $\frac{1 \text{ in.}}{2.54 \text{ cm}}$. We know this is the one we want because using it will make the units of centimeters cancel, leaving units of inches.

Step 3 The conversion is carried out as follows:

$$62 \text{ cm} \times \frac{1 \text{ in.}}{2.54 \text{ cm}} = 24 \text{ in.}$$

Step 4 The result is limited to two significant figures by the number 62. The centimeters cancel, leaving inches as required.

Step 5 Note that the number decreased in this conversion. This makes sense; the inch is a larger unit of length than the centimeter.

Self-Check **EXERCISE 2.4** Wine is often bottled in 0.750-L containers. Using the appropriate equivalence statement from Table 2.7, calculate the volume of such a wine bottle in quarts.

See Problems 2.59 and 2.60. ■

Next we will consider a conversion that requires several steps.

EXAMPLE 2.7 Conversion Factors: Multiple-Step Problems

The length of the marathon race is approximately 26.2 mi. What is this distance in kilometers?

SOLUTION

The problem before us can be represented as follows:

$$26.2 \text{ mi} = ? \text{ km}$$

We could accomplish this conversion in several different ways, but because Table 2.7 gives the equivalence statements 1 mi = 1760 yd and 1 m = 1.094 yd, we will proceed as follows:

Miles → yards → meters → kilometers

This process will be carried out one conversion at a time to make sure everything is clear.

MILES → YARDS: We convert from miles to yards using the conversion factor $\frac{1760 \text{ yd}}{1 \text{ mi}}$.

$$26.2 \cancel{\text{mi}} \times \frac{1760 \text{ yd}}{1 \cancel{\text{mi}}} = 46{,}112 \text{ yd}$$

Result shown on calculator

46,112 yd → Round off → 46,100 yd = 4.61×10^4 yd

Self Check

Answer to Self-Check Exercise 2.4

$$0.750 \text{ L} \times \frac{1.06 \text{ qt}}{1 \text{ L}} = 0.795 \text{ qt}$$

Additional Examples

Example 2.7

1. In the Olympics one swimming event has a distance of 100. m. How long is the race in feet? **328 ft**
2. How many seconds are in one day? **86,400 s**
3. Your car has a 5.00-L engine. What is the size of this engine in cubic inches? **305 in.^{3}**

YARDS → METERS: The conversion factor used to convert yards to meters is $\frac{1\text{ m}}{1.094\text{ yd}}$.

$$4.61 \times 10^4 \cancel{\text{yd}} \times \frac{1\text{ m}}{1.094 \cancel{\text{yd}}} = 4.213894 \times 10^4\text{ m}$$

Result shown on calculator

$$4.213894 \times 10^4\text{ m} \xrightarrow{\text{Round off}} 4.21 \times 10^4\text{ m}$$

METERS → KILOMETERS: Because 1000 m = 1 km, or 10^3 m = 1 km, we convert from meters to kilometers as follows:

$$4.21 \times 10^4 \cancel{\text{m}} \times \frac{1\text{ km}}{10^3 \cancel{\text{m}}} = 4.21 \times 10^1\text{ km} = 42.1\text{ km}$$

Thus the marathon (26.2 mi) is 42.1 km.

Once you feel comfortable with the conversion process, you can combine the steps. For the above conversion, the combined expression is

miles → yards → meters → kilometers

$$26.2 \cancel{\text{mi}} \times \frac{1760 \cancel{\text{yd}}}{1 \cancel{\text{mi}}} \times \frac{1 \cancel{\text{m}}}{1.094 \cancel{\text{yd}}} \times \frac{1\text{ km}}{10^3 \cancel{\text{m}}} = 42.1\text{ km}$$

Note that the units cancel to give the required kilometers and that the result has three significant figures.

MATH SKILL BUILDER
Remember that we are rounding off at the end of each step to show the correct number of significant figures. However, in doing a multistep calculation, *you* should retain the extra numbers that show on your calculator and round off only at the end of the calculation.

Self Check

Answer to Self-Check Exercise 2.5

$$225 \frac{\text{mi}}{\text{h}} \times \frac{1760\text{ yd}}{1\text{ mi}} \times \frac{1\text{ m}}{1.094\text{ yd}} \times \frac{1\text{ km}}{1000\text{ m}} = 362 \frac{\text{km}}{\text{h}}$$

Test Bank: 82–99

Self-Check EXERCISE 2.5 Racing cars at the Indianapolis Motor Speedway now routinely travel around the track at an average speed of 225 mi/h. What is this speed in kilometers per hour?

See Problems 2.65 and 2.66. ■

Units provide a very valuable check on the validity of your solution. Always use them.

Recap: Whenever you work problems, remember the following points:

1. Always include the units (a measurement always has two parts: a number *and* a unit).
2. Cancel units as you carry out the calculations.
3. Check that your final answer has the correct units. If it doesn't, you have done something wrong.
4. Check that your final answer has the correct number of significant figures.
5. Think about whether your answer makes sense.

Section 2.7

TEACHING TIPS

- This section provides an excellent opportunity to emphasize relationships instead of simply memorizing formulas. The relationships among the temperature scales can be related to graphing a straight line. See Teaching Support. This activity relates to the students' math backgrounds. It offers a good opportunity for cross-curricular teaching with the math department.
- One way to assess how well students understand temperature scales is to invent a new scale and ask the students to make conversions between this new scale and the others.

2.7 Temperature Conversions: An Approach to Problem Solving

OBJECTIVES: To learn the three temperature scales. • To learn to convert from one scale to another. • To continue to develop problem-solving skills.

TEACHING SUPPORT

GRAPHING TEMPERATURE SCALES

To relate the temperature scales by graphing, you can do the following:

Kelvin/Celsius Graph the freezing and boiling points of water on a graph with the *x*-axis as Celsius and the *y*-axis as Kelvin. Draw a line through the points and write the equation for the line in the form $y = mx + b$. Have students determine the slope and *y*-intercept. Show them that this is the equation for converting between the scales. Also point out that the size of the degrees is the same (the slope is 1) and that the nonzero *y*-intercept indicates that the zero points of the two scales differ by 273.

Fahrenheit/Celsius Make a new graph relating Celsius (*x*-axis) and Fahrenheit (*y*-axis) degrees

When the doctor tells you your temperature is 102 degrees and the weatherperson on TV says it will be 75 degrees tomorrow, they are using the **Fahrenheit scale.** Water boils at 212 °F and freezes at 32 °F, and normal body temperature is 98.6 °F (where °F signifies "Fahrenheit degrees"). This temperature scale is widely used in the United States and Great Britain, and it is the scale employed in most of the engineering sciences. Another temperature scale, used in Canada and Europe and in the physical and life sciences in most countries, is the **Celsius scale.** In keeping with the metric system, which is based on powers of 10, the freezing and boiling points of water on the Celsius scale are assigned as 0 °C and 100 °C, respectively. On both the Fahrenheit and the Celsius scales, the unit of temperature is called a degree, and the symbol for it is followed by the capital letter representing the scale on which the units are measured: °C or °F.

Although 373 K is often stated as 373 degrees Kelvin, it is more correct to say 373 kelvins.

Still another temperature scale used in the sciences is the **absolute** or **Kelvin scale.** On this scale water freezes at 273 K and boils at 373 K. On the Kelvin scale, the unit of temperature is called a kelvin and is symbolized by K. Thus, on the three scales, the boiling point of water is stated as 212 Fahrenheit degrees (212 °F), 100 Celsius degrees (100 °C), and 373 kelvins (373 K).

The three temperature scales are compared in Figures 2.6 and 2.7. There are several important facts you should note.

1. The size of each temperature unit (each degree) is the same for the Celsius and Kelvin scales. This follows from the fact that the *difference* between the boiling and freezing points of water is 100 units on both of these scales.
2. The Fahrenheit degree is smaller than the Celsius and Kelvin units. Note that on the Fahrenheit scale there are 180 Fahrenheit degrees between the boiling and freezing points of water, as compared with 100 units on the other two scales.
3. The zero points are different on all three scales.

LABORATORY EXPERIMENT

A relevant laboratory experiment for this section is Experiment 3, The Measurement of Temperature: Boiling Point Determination, from *Introductory Chemistry in the Laboratory* by James Hall.

TEACHING TIP

The main advantage of the Kelvin scale is that it is an absolute scale. That is, a doubling of temperature implies a double of average kinetic energy. This is because on the Kelvin scale, the lowest possible value is zero (known as absolute zero). This also means that there are no negative temperatures on the Kelvin scale.

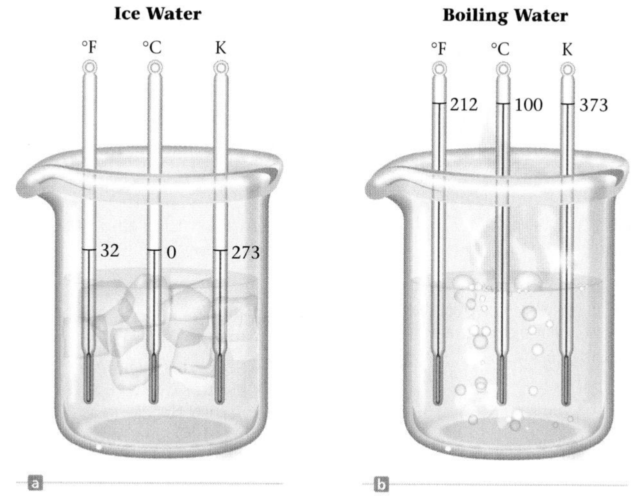

Ice Water
°F °C K
32 0 273

Boiling Water
°F °C K
212 100 373

a b

Figure 2.6
Thermometers based on the three temperature scales in a ice water and b boiling water.

for the boiling and freezing points of water. Once again draw a line through the points and have students write the $y = mx + b$ form for the equation of the line. Point out that the slope of the line is the relationship between the sizes of the degrees (how many on each scale between boiling and freezing) and that the zero points on the scales differ by 32. The equation for converting between Celsius and Fahrenheit is shown from the graph.

Now invent a temperature scale and ask students to write an equation for converting from Celsius to your imaginary scale. The number of degrees between the boiling and freezing points of water should be different from any of the common scales. The difference in the zero points should also be different from 273 and 32. If students understand the relationship between the imaginary scale and the Celsius scale, they should be able to write an equation for converting between the two.

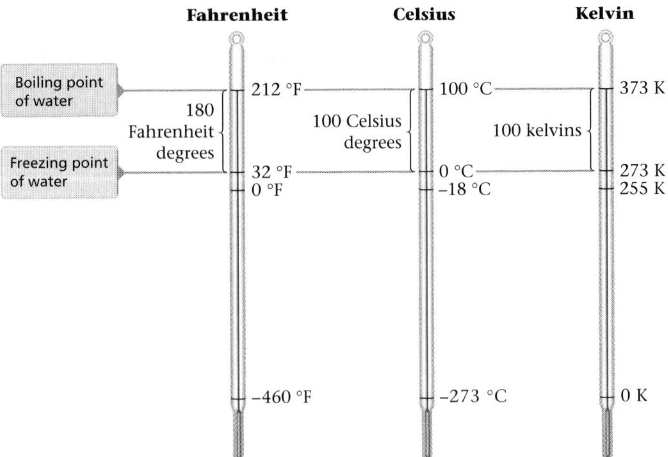

Figure 2.7
The three major temperature scales.

In your study of chemistry, you will sometimes need to convert from one temperature scale to another. We will consider in some detail how this is done. In addition to learning how to change temperature scales, you should also use this section as an opportunity to further develop your skills in problem solving.

Converting Between the Kelvin and Celsius Scales

It is relatively simple to convert between the Celsius and Kelvin scales because the temperature unit is the same size; only the zero points are different. Because 0 °C corresponds to 273 K, converting from Celsius to Kelvin requires that we add 273 to the Celsius temperature. We will illustrate this procedure in Example 2.8.

Additional Examples

Example 2.8

1. The temperature is a balmy 28.5 °C. Convert it to the Kelvin scale. 301.5 K
2. The freezing point of nitrogen is −210 °C. What is this temperature on the Kelvin scale? 63 K

EXAMPLE 2.8 Temperature Conversion: Celsius to Kelvin

Boiling points will be discussed further in Chapter 14.

The boiling point of water at the top of Mt. Everest is 70. °C. Convert this temperature to the Kelvin scale. (The decimal point after the temperature reading indicates that the trailing zero is significant.)

SOLUTION

In solving problems, it is often helpful to draw a diagram that depicts what the words are telling you.

This problem asks us to find 70. °C in units of kelvins. We can represent this problem simply as

$$70.\ °C = ?\ K$$

In doing problems, it is often helpful to draw a diagram in which we try to represent the words in the problem with a picture. This problem can be diagramed as shown in Figure 2.8a.

In this picture we have shown what we want to find: "What temperature (in kelvins) is the same as 70. °C?" We also know from Figure 2.7 that 0 °C represents the same temperature as 273 K. How many degrees above 0 °C is 70. °C? The answer, of course, is 70. Thus we must add 70. to 0 °C to reach 70. °C. Because degrees are the *same size* on both the Celsius scale

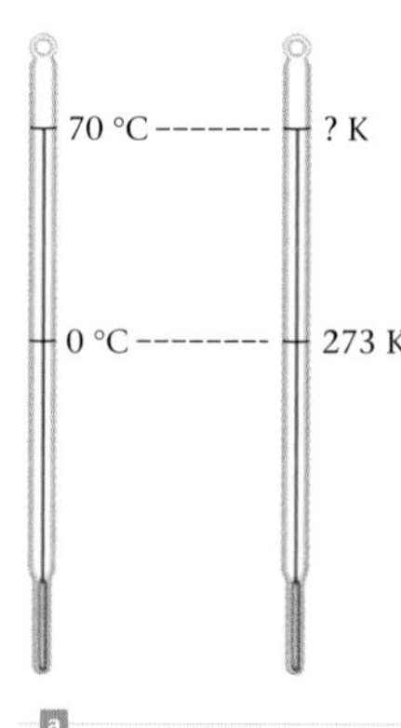

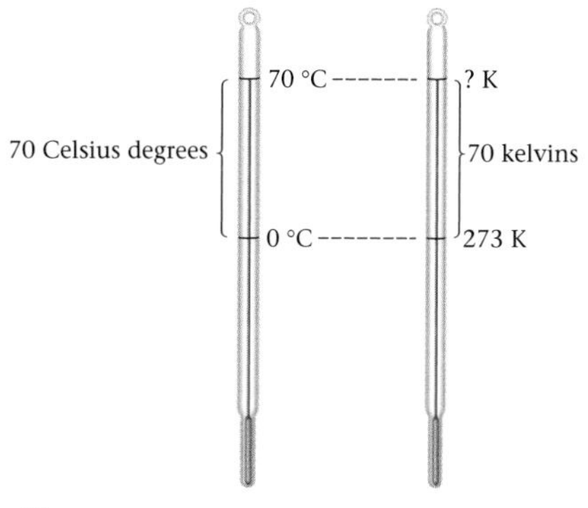

Figure 2.8 Converting 70. °C to units measured on the Kelvin scale.

a *We know 0 °C = 273 K. We want to know 70. °C = ? K.*

b *There are 70 degrees on the Celsius scale between 0 °C and 70. °C. Because units on these scales are the same size, there are also 70 kelvins in this same distance on the Kelvin scale.*

and the Kelvin scale (see Figure 2.8b), we must also add 70. to 273 K (same temperature as 0 °C) to reach ? K. That is,

$$? \text{ K} = 273 + 70. = 343 \text{ K}$$

Thus 70. °C corresponds to 343 K.

Note that to convert from the Celsius to the Kelvin scale, we simply add the temperature in °C to 273. That is,

$$T_{°C} + 273 = T_K$$

Temperature in Celsius degrees — Temperature in kelvins

Using this formula to solve the present problem gives

$$70. + 273 = 343$$

(with units of kelvins, K), which is the correct answer. ■

We can summarize what we learned in Example 2.8 as follows: to convert from the Celsius to the Kelvin scale, we can use the formula

$$T_{°C} + 273 = T_K$$

Temperature in Celsius degrees — Temperature in kelvins

EXAMPLE 2.9 Temperature Conversion: Kelvin to Celsius

Liquid nitrogen boils at 77 K. What is the boiling point of nitrogen on the Celsius scale?

SOLUTION

The problem to be solved here is 77 K = ? °C. Let's explore this question by examining the picture on the following page representing the two

Additional Examples

Example 2.9

1. If your body temperature is 312 K, what is it on the Celsius scale?

   39 °C

2. If your outdoor thermometer reads 300. K, should you wear a jacket?

   No

   What is it on the Celsius scale?

   27.0 °C

CHEMISTRY *IN* **FOCUS**

Tiny Thermometers

Can you imagine a thermometer that has a diameter equal to one one-hundredth of a human hair? Such a device has actually been produced by scientists Yihica Gao and Yoshio Bando of the National Institute for Materials Science in Tsukuba, Japan. The thermometer they constructed is so tiny that it must be read using a powerful electron microscope.

It turns out that the tiny thermometers were produced by accident. The Japanese scientists were actually trying to make tiny (nanoscale) gallium nitride wires. However, when they examined the results of their experiment, they discovered tiny tubes of carbon atoms that were filled with elemental gallium. Because gallium is a liquid over an unusually large temperature range, it makes a perfect working liquid for a thermometer. Just as in mercury thermometers, which have mostly been phased out because of the toxicity of mercury, the gallium expands as the temperature increases. Therefore, gallium moves up the tube as the temperature increases.

These minuscule thermometers are not useful in the normal macroscopic world—they can't even be seen with the naked eye. However, they should be valuable for monitoring temperatures from 50 °C to 500 °C in materials in the nanoscale world.

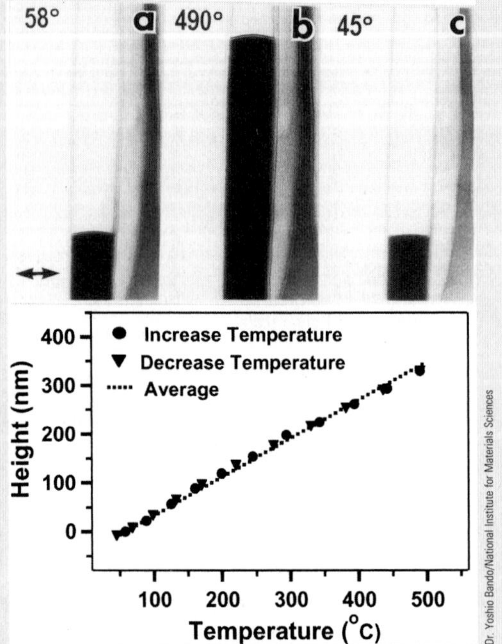

Dr. Yoshio Bando/National Institute for Materials Sciences

Liquid gallium expands within a carbon nanotube as the temperature increases (left to right).

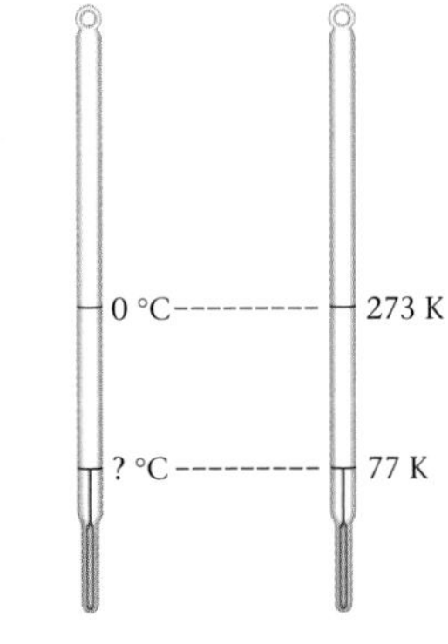

temperature scales. One key point is to recognize that 0 °C = 273 K. Also note that the difference between 273 K and 77 K is 196 kelvins (273 − 77 = 196). That is, 77 K is 196 kelvins below 273 K. The degree size is the same on these two temperature scales, so 77 K must correspond to 196 Celsius degrees below zero or −196 °C. Thus 77 K = ? °C = −196 °C.

We can also solve this problem by using the formula

$$T_{°C} + 273 = T_K$$

However, in this case we want to solve for the Celsius temperature, $T_{°C}$. That is, we want to isolate$T_{°C}$ on one side of the equals sign. To do this we use an important general principle: doing *the same thing on both sides of the equals sign* preserves the equality. In other words, it's always okay to perform the same operation on both sides of the equals sign.

38

To isolate $T_{°C}$ we need to subtract 273 from both sides:

$$T_{°C} + \underbrace{273 - 273}_{\text{Sum is zero}} = T_K - 273$$

to give

$$T_{°C} = T_K - 273$$

Using this equation to solve the problem, we have

$$T_{°C} = T_K - 273 = 77 - 273 = -196$$

So, as before, we have shown that

$$77 \text{ K} = -196 \text{ °C}$$

Self-Check **EXERCISE 2.6** Which temperature is colder, 172 K or −75 °C?

See Problems 2.73 and 2.74. ■

Self Check

Answer to Self-Check Exercise 2.6

172 K = −101 °C, which is a lower temperature than −75 °C. 172 K is colder than −75 °C.

In summary, because the Kelvin and Celsius scales have the same size unit, to switch from one scale to the other we must simply account for the different zero points. We must add 273 to the Celsius temperature to obtain the temperature on the Kelvin scale:

$$T_K = T_{°C} + 273$$

To convert from the Kelvin scale to the Celsius scale, we must subtract 273 from the Kelvin temperature:

$$T_{°C} = T_K - 273$$

Converting Between the Fahrenheit and Celsius Scales

The conversion between the Fahrenheit and Celsius temperature scales requires two adjustments:

1. For the different size units
2. For the different zero points

To see how to adjust for the different unit sizes, consider the diagram in Figure 2.9. Note that because 212 °F = 100 °C and 32 °F = 0 °C,

$$212 - 32 = 180 \text{ Fahrenheit degrees} = 100 - 0 = 100 \text{ Celsius degrees}$$

Thus

$$180. \text{ Fahrenheit degrees} = 100. \text{ Celsius degrees}$$

MATH SKILL BUILDER
Remember, it's okay to do the same thing to both sides of the equation.

Dividing both sides of this equation by 100. gives

$$\frac{180.}{100.} \text{ Fahrenheit degrees} = \frac{\cancel{100.}}{\cancel{100.}} \text{ Celsius degrees}$$

or

$$1.80 \text{ Fahrenheit degrees} = 1.00 \text{ Celsius degree}$$

The factor 1.80 is used to convert from one degree size to the other.

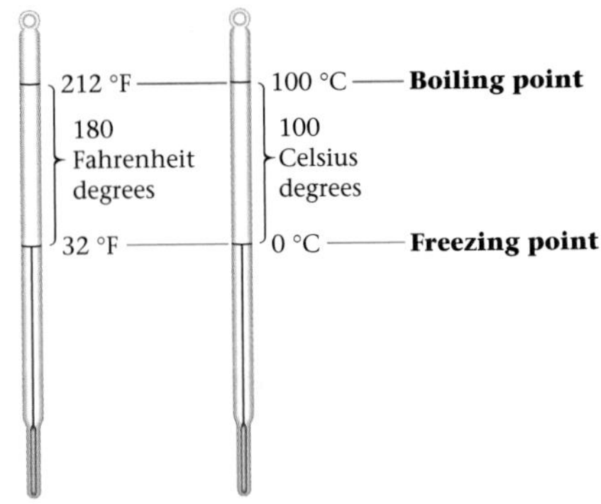

Figure 2.9
Comparison of the Celsius and Fahrenheit scales.

Next we have to account for the fact that 0 °C is *not* the same as 0 °F. In fact, 32 °F = 0 °C. Although we will not show how to derive it, the equation to convert a temperature in Celsius degrees to the Fahrenheit scale is

$$T_{°F} = 1.80(T_{°C}) + 32$$

Temperature in °F   Temperature in °C

In this equation the term $1.80(T_{°C})$ adjusts for the difference in degree size between the two scales. The 32 in the equation accounts for the different zero points. We will now show how to use this equation.

Additional Examples

Example 2.10 and Example 2.11

1. You're traveling in a metric country and get sick. Your temperature is 39 °C. What is it on the Fahrenheit scale? **102 °F**
2. Convert 32 °C to Fahrenheit. **89.6 °F**
3. The boiling point of nitrogen is −196 °C. What is this temperature on the Fahrenheit scale? **−321 °F**

EXAMPLE 2.10

Temperature Conversion: Celsius to Fahrenheit

On a summer day the temperature in the laboratory, as measured on a lab thermometer, is 28 °C. Express this temperature on the Fahrenheit scale.

SOLUTION

This problem can be represented as 28 °C = ? °F. We will solve it using the formula

$$T_{°F} = 1.80\,(T_{°C}) + 32$$

In this case,

$$T_{°F} = ?\,°F = 1.80(28) + 32 = 50.4 + 32$$

($T_{°C}$ ↓ points to 28; 50.4 Rounds off to 50)

$$= 50. + 32 = 82$$

Thus 28 °C = 82 °F. ■

Note that 28 °C is approximately equal to 82 °F. Because the numbers are just reversed, this is an easy reference point to remember for the two scales.

EXAMPLE 2.11

Temperature Conversion: Celsius to Fahrenheit

Express the temperature −40. °C on the Fahrenheit scale.

SOLUTION

We can express this problem as −40. °C = ? °F. To solve it we will use the formula

$$T_{°F} = 1.80\,(T_{°C}) + 32$$

In this case,

$$T_{°F} = ?\,°F = 1.80(\underset{T_{°C}}{-40.}) + 32 = -72 + 32 = -40$$

So −40 °C = −40 °F. This is a very interesting result and is another useful reference point.

Self-Check **EXERCISE 2.7** Hot tubs are often maintained at 41 °C. What is this temperature in Fahrenheit degrees?

See Problems 2.75 through 2.78. ■

Self Check

Answer to Self-Check Exercise 2.7

41 °C = 106 °F

To convert from Celsius to Fahrenheit, we have used the equation

$$T_{°F} = 1.80\,(T_{°C}) + 32$$

To convert a Fahrenheit temperature to Celsius, we need to rearrange this equation to isolate Celsius degrees ($T_{°C}$). Remember, we can always do the same operation to both sides of the equation. First subtract 32 from each side:

$$T_{°F} - 32 = 1.80\,(T_{°C}) + \underbrace{32 - 32}_{\text{Sum is zero}}$$

to give

$$T_{°F} - 32 = 1.80(T_{°C})$$

Next divide both sides by 1.80

$$\frac{T_{°F} - 32}{1.80} = \frac{\cancel{1.80}(T_{°C})}{\cancel{1.80}}$$

to give

$$\frac{T_{°F} - 32}{1.80} = T_{°C}$$

or

Temperature in °F

$$T_{°C} = \frac{T_{°F} - 32}{1.80}$$

Temperature in °C

$$T_{°C} = \frac{T_{°F} - 32}{1.80}$$

EXAMPLE 2.12 Temperature Conversion: Fahrenheit to Celsius

One of the body's responses to an infection or injury is to elevate its temperature. A certain flu victim has a body temperature of 101 °F. What is this temperature on the Celsius scale?

SOLUTION

The problem is 101 °F = ? °C. Using the formula

$$T_{°C} = \frac{T_{°F} - 32}{1.80}$$

yields

$$T_{°C} = ?\ °C = \frac{\overset{T_{°F}}{101} - 32}{1.80} = \frac{69}{1.80} = 38$$

That is, 101 °F = 38 °C.

Self-Check EXERCISE 2.8 An antifreeze solution in a car's radiator boils at 239 °F. What is this temperature on the Celsius scale?

See Problems 2.75 through 2.78. ■

In doing temperature conversions, you will need the following formulas.

Temperature Conversion Formulas

- Celsius to Kelvin $T_K = T_{°C} + 273$
- Kelvin to Celsius $T_{°C} = T_K - 273$
- Celsius to Fahrenheit $T_{°F} = 1.80(T_{°C}) + 32$
- Fahrenheit to Celsius $T_{°C} = \frac{T_{°F} - 32}{1.80}$

2.8 Density

OBJECTIVE: To define density and its units.

Lead has a greater density than feathers.

When you were in elementary school, you may have been embarrassed by your answer to the question "Which is heavier, a pound of lead or a pound of feathers?" If you said lead, you were undoubtedly thinking about density, not mass. **Density** can be defined as the amount of matter present *in a given volume* of substance. That is, density is mass per unit volume, the ratio of the mass of an object to its volume:

$$\text{Density} = \frac{\text{mass}}{\text{volume}}$$

It takes a much bigger volume to make a pound of feathers than to make a pound of lead. This is because lead has a much greater mass per unit volume—a greater density.

Additional Examples

Example 2.12

1. Ray Bradbury wrote a book titled *Fahrenheit 451.* What is this temperature on the Celsius scale? 253 °C
2. Pork is considered to be well done when its internal temperature reaches 160 °F. What is this temperature on the Celsius scale? 71 °C

Self Check

Answer to Self-Check Exercise 2.8

239 °F = 115 °C

Lecture Demonstration: 1.7, 1.8

 **Test Bank: 100–123**

Section 2.8

DEMONSTRATION

Use a 1-L soda bottle to prepare a demonstration of density. Add 500 mL of vegetable oil and 500 mL of water (colored with food coloring). Tighten the top and shake. Allow the liquids to settle. Ask the students which liquid is more dense. You can extend your discussion to include an introduction to the immiscibility of oil and water. You can then ask students if a density column could be made from different concentrations of the same substance. See Teaching Support for the construction of such a column.

TEACHING SUPPORT

DEMONSTRATION

Rainbow Density Column

Materials

300 g sucrose	Separatory funnel
Food coloring	Rubber tubing
6 beakers or cups	Large cylinder (1000-mL graduated)

Procedure The night before the demonstration prepare six solutions of sugar water as described in the table.

Color	Dye	Sugar Concentration	Sugar Mass
Red	Red	0%	0 g
Orange	Red: yellow (1:1)	10%	14 g
Yellow	Yellow	20%	28 g
Green	Green	30%	42 g
Blue	Blue	40%	56 g
Violet	Blue: red (1:1)	60%	84 g

The density of a liquid can be determined easily by weighing a known volume of the substance as illustrated in Example 2.13.

EXAMPLE 2.13

Calculating Density

Suppose a student finds that 23.50 mL of a certain liquid weighs 35.062 g. What is the density of this liquid?

SOLUTION

We can calculate the density of this liquid simply by applying the definition

$$\text{Density} = \frac{\text{mass}}{\text{volume}} = \frac{35.062 \text{ g}}{23.50 \text{ mL}} = 1.492 \text{ g/mL}$$

This result could also be expressed as 1.492 g/cm^3 because 1 mL = 1 cm^3. ■

The volume of a solid object is often determined indirectly by submerging it in water and measuring the volume of water displaced. In fact, this is the most accurate method for measuring a person's percent body fat. The person is submerged momentarily in a tank of water, and the increase in volume is measured (see Figure 2.10). It is possible to calculate the body density by using the person's weight (mass) and the volume of the person's body determined by submersion. Fat, muscle, and bone have different densities (fat is less dense than muscle tissue, for example), so the fraction of the person's body that is fat can be calculated. The more muscle and the less fat a person has, the higher his or her body density. For example, a muscular person weighing 150 lb has a smaller body volume (and thus a higher density) than a fat person weighing 150 lb.

EXAMPLE 2.14

Determining Density

The most common units for density are g/mL = g/cm^3.

At a local pawn shop a student finds a medallion that the shop owner insists is pure platinum. However, the student suspects that the medallion may actually be silver and thus much less valuable. The student buys the medallion only after the shop owner agrees to refund the price if the medallion is

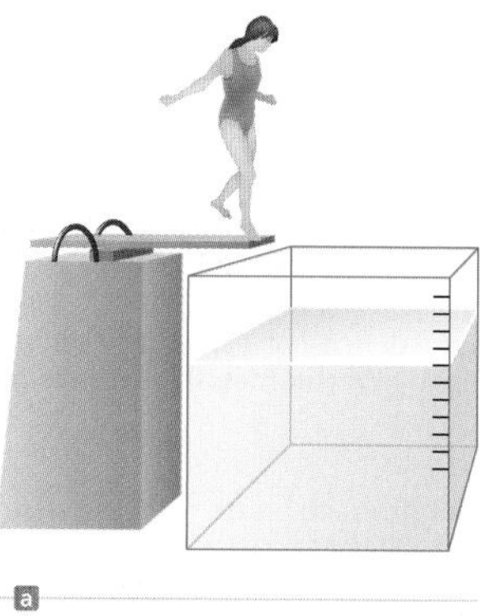

a Tank of water

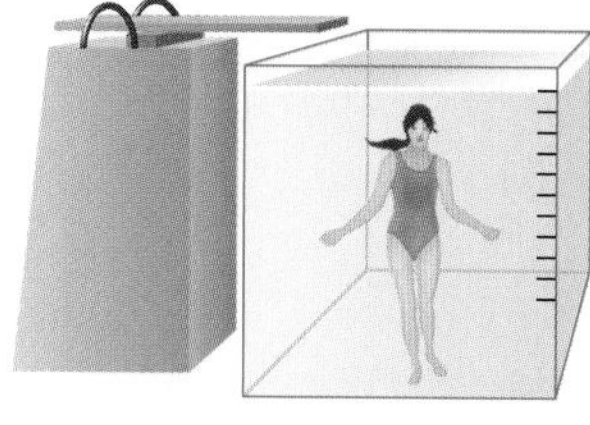

b Person submerged in the tank, raising the level of the water

Figure 2.10

LABORATORY EXPERIMENT

A relevant laboratory experiment for this section is Experiment 4, Recrystallization and Melting Point Determination, from *Introductory Chemistry in the Laboratory* by James Hall.

Additional Example

Example 2.13

1. A block has a volume of 25.3 cm^3. Its mass is 21.7 g. Calculate the density of the block.

0.858 g/cm^3

MATH MISCONCEPTION

Density

The concept of density may be the first time a student has dealt with a ratio of measurements. Students often confuse mass and density—that is, students often believe that a substance with a larger mass is also the more dense substance.

MINI-DEMO

You can use a large graduated cylinder filled with colored water to measure the density of an object. Use an object with a known density first (such as a cylinder of a pure metal) to show that the method works. Then use an irregularly shaped object such as a stone.

Lecture Demonstration: 1.9–1.14

Make the colored water for each solution (140 mL) first, adjusting the colors to the desired shade for a clear distinction between them before adding the sugar. Then dissolve the sugar in the water. You can use a microwave to warm the water to dissolve the sugar. The liquids can be transported to school in foam cups with lids.

Place the tall cylinder on a ring stand. Connect the hose to the bottom of the separatory funnel. Suspend the separatory funnel in an iron ring above the tall cylinder so that the hose reaches very near the bottom of the cylinder. Fill the separatory funnel with red solution (be sure the stopcock is closed). Add the red solution to the cylinder, being careful to fill the tube completely with the solution. Close the stopcock just before all of the red solution drains out. Add the orange solution and slowly open the stopcock to add it to the column. Again, close the stopcock before all of the solution has quite drained out of the separatory funnel. Add the remaining solutions in the same manner in order of increasing concentration. You

Additional Example

Example 2.14

1. A student fills a graduated cylinder to 25.0 mL with liquid. She then immerses a solid in the liquid. The volume of the liquid rises to 33.9 mL. The mass of the solid is 63.5 g. What is its density?

   7.1 g/mL

returned within two days. The student, a chemistry major, then takes the medallion to her lab and measures its density as follows. She first weighs the medallion and finds its mass to be 55.64 g. She then places some water in a graduated cylinder and reads the volume as 75.2 mL. Next she drops the medallion into the cylinder and reads the new volume as 77.8 mL. Is the medallion platinum (density = 21.4 g/cm^3) or silver (density = 10.5 g/cm^3)?

SOLUTION

The densities of platinum and silver differ so much that the measured density of the medallion will show which metal is present. Because by definition

$$\text{Density} = \frac{\text{mass}}{\text{volume}}$$

to calculate the density of the medallion, we need its mass and its volume. The mass of the medallion is 55.64 g. The volume of the medallion can be obtained by taking the difference between the volume readings of the water in the graduated cylinder before and after the medallion was added.

$$\text{Volume of medallion} = 77.8 \text{ mL} - 75.2 \text{ mL} = 2.6 \text{ mL}$$

The volume appeared to increase by 2.6 mL when the medallion was added, so 2.6 mL represents the volume of the medallion. Now we can use the measured mass and volume of the medallion to determine its density:

$$\text{Density of medallion} = \frac{\text{mass}}{\text{volume}} = \frac{55.64 \text{ g}}{2.6 \text{ mL}} = 21 \text{ g/mL}$$

or

$$= 21 \text{ g/cm}^3$$

The medallion is really platinum.

Self Check

Answer to Self-Check Exercise 2.9

The density = 0.785 g/mL. This density identifies the liquid as isopropyl alcohol.

Self-Check EXERCISE 2.9 A student wants to identify the main component in a commercial liquid cleaner. He finds that 35.8 mL of the cleaner weighs 28.1 g. Of the following possibilities, which is the main component of the cleaner?

Substance	Density, g/cm^3
chloroform	1.483
diethyl ether	0.714
isopropyl alcohol	0.785
toluene	0.867

See Problems 2.89 and 2.90. ■

Additional Examples

Example 2.15

1. Isopropyl alcohol has a density of 0.785 g/mL. What volume should be measured to obtain 20.0 g of the liquid? 31.8 mL

2. A student needs 150 cm^3 of salt for an experiment. The density of salt is 2.16 g/cm^3. How many 1-lb boxes of salt should he buy at the grocery store? 324 g needs one 1-lb box

3. A beaker contains 725 mL of water. The density of water is 1.00 g/mL. Calculate the volume of water in liters. 0.725 L Find the mass of the water. 0.725 g

EXAMPLE 2.15 Using Density in Calculations

Mercury has a density of 13.6 g/mL. What volume of mercury must be taken to obtain 225 g of the metal?

SOLUTION

To solve this problem, start with the definition of density,

$$\text{Density} = \frac{\text{mass}}{\text{volume}}$$

and then rearrange this equation to isolate the required quantity. In this case we want to find the volume. Remember that we maintain an equality

should end up with a rainbow column. The layers will be visible for at least 24 hours if the column remains undisturbed. You can also stir the column at the end of the demonstration, which mixes the colors and shows the students that the density was based on concentration, not miscibility.

Variation Students can construct their own columns by using 10-mL graduated cylinders and Beral pipets for the addition of the colors. They must add the solutions from most to least dense.

TEACHING SUPPORT

ACTIVITY

The Density of Clay

Give each student/group a piece of clay and have water, balances, graduated cylinders, and rulers available for students to use. Have each student/group determine the density of the clay. They should investigate questions such as "Does the amount of clay affect the density?"; "Does

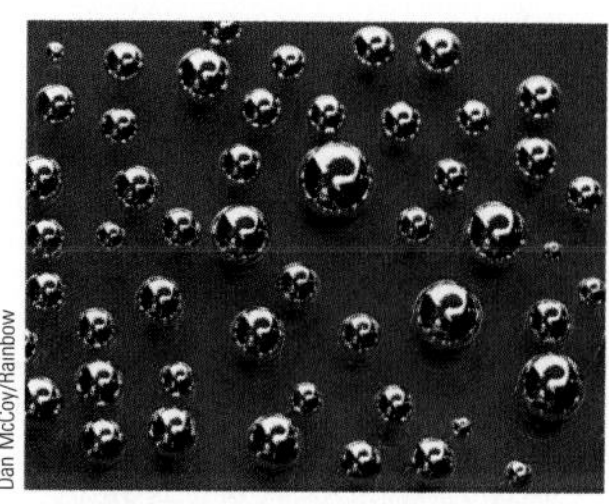
Dan McCoy/Rainbow

Spherical droplets of mercury, a very dense liquid.

when we do the same thing to both sides. For example, if we multiply *both sides* of the density definition by volume,

$$\text{Volume} \times \text{density} = \frac{\text{mass}}{\cancel{\text{volume}}} \times \cancel{\text{volume}}$$

volume cancels on the right, leaving

$$\text{Volume} \times \text{density} = \text{mass}$$

We want the volume, so we now divide both sides by density,

$$\frac{\text{Volume} \times \cancel{\text{density}}}{\cancel{\text{density}}} = \frac{\text{mass}}{\text{density}}$$

to give

$$\text{Volume} = \frac{\text{mass}}{\text{density}}$$

Now we can solve the problem by substituting the given numbers:

$$\text{Volume} = \frac{225 \text{ g}}{13.6 \text{ g/mL}} = 16.5 \text{ mL}$$

We must take 16.5 mL of mercury to obtain an amount that has a mass of 225 g. ■

The densities of various common substances are given in Table 2.8.

Besides being a tool for the identification of substances, density has many other uses. For example, the liquid in your car's lead storage battery (a solution of sulfuric acid) changes density because the sulfuric acid is consumed as the battery discharges. In a fully charged battery, the density of the solution is about 1.30 g/cm^3. When the density falls below 1.20 g/cm^3, the battery has to be recharged. Density measurement is also used to determine the amount of antifreeze, and thus the level of protection against freezing, in the cooling system of a car. Water and antifreeze have different densities, so the measured density of the mixture tells us how much of each is present. The device used to test the density of the solution—a hydrometer—is shown in Figure 2.11.

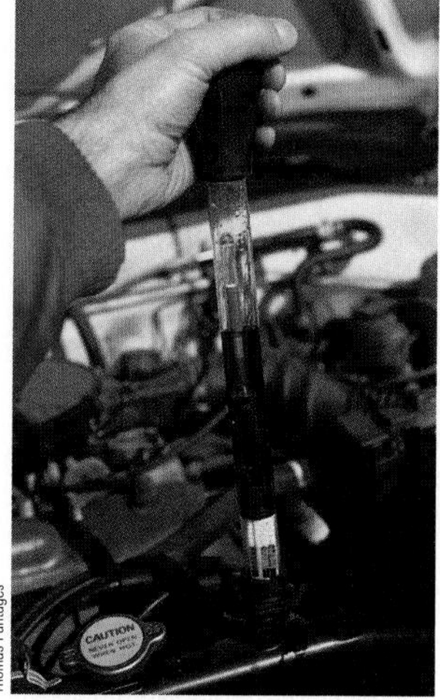
Thomas Pantages

Figure 2.11 A hydrometer being used to determine the density of the antifreeze solution in a car's radiator.

Table 2.8 Densities of Various Common Substances at 20 °C

Substance	Physical State	Density (g/cm^3)
oxygen	gas	0.00133*
hydrogen	gas	0.000084*
ethanol	liquid	0.785
benzene	liquid	0.880
water	liquid	1.000
magnesium	solid	1.74
salt (sodium chloride)	solid	2.16
aluminum	solid	2.70
iron	solid	7.87
copper	solid	8.96
silver	solid	10.5
lead	solid	11.34
mercury	liquid	13.6
gold	solid	19.32

*At 1 atmosphere pressure

the shape of the clay affect the density?"; and "How does the density of a hollow ball of clay compare to your previous answers?"

There are two common ways for students to determine the density of the clay. In both cases the student needs to determine the mass of the clay by using a balance. To determine the volume, a student may use water displacement, which means he or she must understand that the clay will displace its volume of water. In this method, place some water in a graduated cylinder and note the volume reading. Then put the piece of clay into the cylinder, and determine the volume of water displaced. This volume is the volume of the clay. Another way to determine the volume would be to mold the clay into an easily measured geometric shape, such as a cube. Then the student can use a ruler, make the proper measurements, and calculate the volume. The density of the clay is the ratio of the mass to the volume.

TEACHING TIP

Specific gravity is used in measuring the density of solutions such as the sulfuric acid in a car battery to determine its state of charge, and to test whether an alcoholic beverage has completed its fermentation process. A hydrometer is the instrument used to find the specific gravity of a solution.

In certain situations, the term *specific gravity* is used to describe the density of a liquid. **Specific gravity** is defined as the ratio of the density of a given liquid to the density of water at 4 °C. Because it is a ratio of densities, specific gravity has no units.

CHAPTER 2 REVIEW

Key Terms

measurement (p. 15)
scientific notation (2.1)
units (2.2)
English system (2.2)
metric system (2.2)
SI units (2.2)
volume (2.3)
mass (2.3)
significant figures (2.4)
rounding off (2.5)
conversion factor (2.6)
equivalence statement (2.6)
dimensional analysis (2.6)
Fahrenheit scale (2.7)
Celsius scale (2.7)
Kelvin (absolute) scale (2.7)
density (2.8)
specific gravity (2.8)

Summary

1. A quantitative observation is called a measurement and always consists of a number and a unit.
2. We can conveniently express very large or very small numbers using scientific notation, which represents the number as a number between 1 and 10 multiplied by 10 raised to a power.
3. Units give a scale on which to represent the results of a measurement. The three systems discussed are the English, metric, and SI systems. The metric and SI systems use prefixes (Table 2.2) to change the size of the units.
4. The mass of an object represents the quantity of matter in that object.
5. All measurements have a degree of uncertainty, which is reflected in the number of significant figures used to express them. Various rules are used to round off to the correct number of significant figures in a calculated result.
6. We can convert from one system of units to another by a method called dimensional analysis, in which conversion factors are used.
7. Temperature can be measured on three different scales: Fahrenheit, Celsius, and Kelvin. We can readily convert among these scales.
8. Density is the amount of matter present in a given volume (mass per unit volume). That is,

$$\text{Density} = \frac{\text{mass}}{\text{volume}}$$

F directs you to the *Chemistry in Focus* feature in the chapter
VP indicates visual problems
OWL interactive versions of these problems are assignable in OWL.

Active Learning Questions

These questions are designed to be considered by groups of students in class. Often these questions work well for introducing a particular topic in class.

1. a. There are 365 days/year, 24 hours/day, 12 months/year, and 60 minutes/hour. How many minutes are there in one month?
   b. There are 24 hours/day, 60 minutes/hour, 7 days/week, and 4 weeks/month. How many minutes are there in one month?
   c. Why are these answers different? Which (if either) is more correct and why?
2. You go to a convenience store to buy candy and find the owner to be rather odd. He allows you to buy pieces only in multiples of four, and to buy four, you need \$0.23. He allows you only to use 3 pennies and 2 dimes. You have a bunch of pennies and dimes, and instead of counting them, you decide to weigh them. You have 636.3 g of pennies, and each penny weighs an average of 3.03 g. Each dime weighs an average of 2.29 g. Each piece of candy weighs an average of 10.23 g.
   a. How many pennies do you have?
   b. How many dimes do you need to buy as much candy as possible?
   c. How much would all of your dimes weigh?
   d. How many pieces of candy could you buy (based on the number of dimes from part b)?
   e. How much would this candy weigh?
   f. How many pieces of candy could you buy with twice as many dimes?
3. When a marble is dropped into a beaker of water, it sinks to the bottom. Which of the following is the best explanation?
   a. The surface area of the marble is not large enough for the marble to be held up by the surface tension of the water.
   b. The mass of the marble is greater than that of the water.

ChemWork

Atomic Who Am I
Nuclear Particles
Components of the Atom
Elementary Atomic Structure
Naming Elements
Symbols for Elements
Beginning to Name Compounds
Beginning to Write Formulas for Compounds
Naming Acids
Naming Compounds
Predicting Ions
Properties of Elements

For this activity, use modeling clay that does not readily absorb water. Clay is a useful material for this kind of activity because it allows for experimentation with density. For example, students should see that neither the shape of the object nor its size affects the density of the clay, as long as the object is not hollow. Many students confuse density with mass, and it is good for them to see that a large sample of clay has the same density as a small piece. When a piece of clay is formed with a cavity in its center, it has a much greater volume and essentially the same mass (although the mass of air adds a little to the total), and thus is less dense than a solid sample of clay.

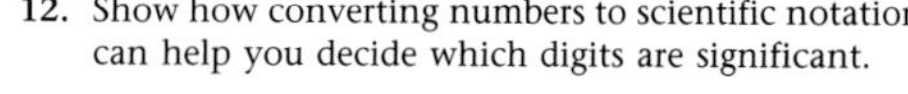

c. The marble weighs more than an equivalent volume of the water.
d. The force from dropping the marble breaks the surface tension of the water.
e. The marble has greater mass and volume than the water.

Explain each choice. That is, for choices you did not pick, explain why you feel they are wrong, and justify the choice you did pick.

4. Consider water in each graduated cylinder as shown:

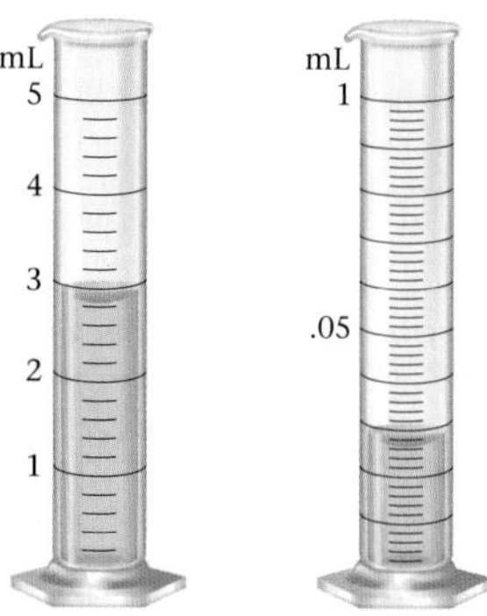

You add both samples of water to a beaker. How would you write the number describing the total volume? What limits the precision of this number?

5. What is the numerical value of a conversion factor? Why must this be true?

6. For each of the following numbers, indicate which zeros are significant and explain. Do not merely cite the rule that applies, but explain the rule.

a. 10.020 b. 0.002050 c. 190 d. 270

7. Consider the addition of "15.4" to "28." What would a mathematician say the answer is? What would a scientist say? Justify the scientist's answer, not merely citing the rule, but explaining it.

8. Consider multiplying "26.2" by "16.43." What would a mathematician say the answer is? What would a scientist say? Justify the scientist's answer, not merely citing the rule, but explaining it.

9. In lab you report a measured volume of 128.7 mL of water. Using significant figures as a measure of the error, what range of answers does your reported volume imply? Explain.

10. Sketch two pieces of glassware: one that can measure volume to the thousandths place, and one that can measure volume only to the ones place.

11. Oil floats on water but is "thicker" than water. Why do you think this fact is true?

12. Show how converting numbers to scientific notation can help you decide which digits are significant.

13. You are driving 65 mph and take your eyes off the road "just for a second." How many feet do you travel in this time?

14. You have a 1.0-cm^3 sample of lead and a 1.0-cm^3 sample of glass. You drop each in a separate beaker of water. How do the volumes of water that are displaced by the samples compare? Explain.

VP 15. The beakers shown below have different precisions.

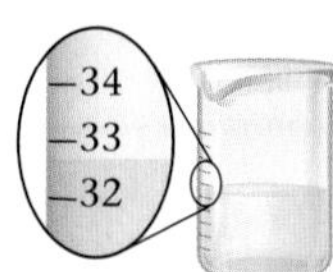

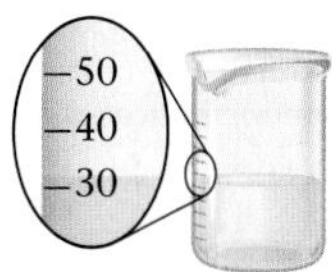

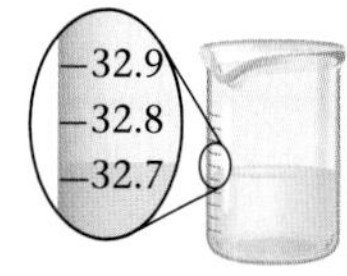

a. Label the amount of water in each of the three beakers to the correct number of significant figures.
b. Is it possible for each of the three beakers to contain the exact same amount of water? If no, why not? If yes, did you report the volumes as the same in part a? Explain.
c. Suppose you pour the water from these three beakers into one container. What should be the volume in the container reported to the correct number of significant figures?

16. True or False? For any mathematical operation performed on two measurements, the number of significant figures in the answer is the same as the least number of significant figures in either of the measurements. Explain your answer.

17. Complete the following and explain each in your own words: leading zeros are (never/sometimes/always) significant; captive zeros are (never/sometimes/always) significant; and trailing zeros are (never/sometimes/always) significant.

For any statement with an answer of "sometimes," give examples of when the zero is significant and when it is not, and explain.

VP 18. For each of the following figures, a through d, decide which block is more dense: the orange block, the blue block, or it cannot be determined. Explain your answers.

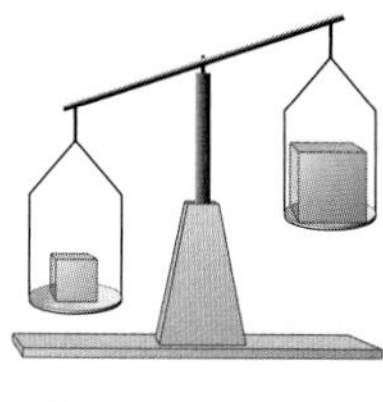

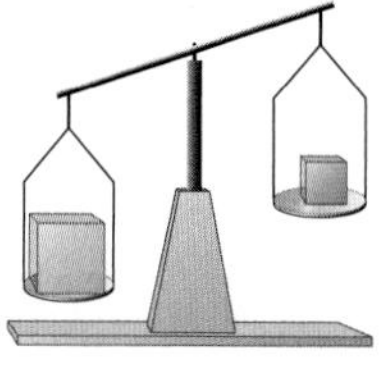

Chapter Review 47

Answers to End-of-Chapter Exercises

1. measurement

2. "Scientific notation" means we have to put the decimal point after the first significant figure, and then express the order of magnitude of the number as a power of 10. So we want to put the decimal point after the first 2:

$2421 \rightarrow 2.421 \times 10^{\text{to some power}}$

To be able to move the decimal point three places to the left in going from 2421 to 2.421 means you will need a power of 10^3 after the number, where the exponent 3 shows that you moved the decimal point three places to the left:

$2421 \rightarrow 2.421 \times 10^{\text{to some power}} = 2.421 \times 10^3$

3. (a) 9.651; (b) 3.521; (c) 9.3241; (d) 1.002

4. (a) 10^4; (b) 10^{-3}; (c) 10^2; (d) 10^{-30}

5. (a) positive; (b) positive; (c) negative; (d) negative

6. (a) negative; (b) zero; (c) positive; (d) negative

7. (a) 5.012×10^{-1}; (b) 5.012×10^6; (c) 5.012×10^{-6}; (d) 5.012×10^0; (e) 5.012×10^3; (f) 5.012×10^{-3}

8. (a) 2789; (b) 0.002789; (c) 93,000,000; (d) 42.89; (e) 99,990; (f) 0.00009999

9. (a) six places to the right; (b) five places to the left; (c) one place to the right; (d) the decimal point does not have to be moved; (e) 18 places to the right; (f) 16 places to the left

10. (a) three places to the left; (b) one place to the left; (c) five places to the right; (d) one place to the left; (e) two places to the right; (f) two places to the left

11. (a) 9.782×10^4 (b) 4.214×10^4; (c) 8.214×10^{-5}; (d) 3.914×10^{-4}; (e) 9.271×10^2; (f) 4.781×10^{-1}

12. (a) 6244; (b) 0.09117; (c) 82.99; (d) 0.0001771; (e) 545.1; (f) 0.00002934

13. (a) 9.681×10^{-4}; (b) 1×10^{-5}; (c) 1×10^7; (d) 5×10^3; (e) 3.233×10^{-7}; (f) 1×10^4; (g) 1×10^{-9}; (h) 6.7×10^4

14. (a) 3.1×10^3; (b) 1×10^6; (c) 1 or 1×10^0; (d) 1.8×10^{-5}; (e) 1×10^7; (f) 1.00×10^6; (g) 1.00×10^{-7} (h) 1×10^1

15. mass, kilogram; length, meter; temperature, Kelvin

16. Answer depends on student's examples.

17. 25 m^2 is approximately 30 yd^2.

18. about ¼ pound

19. about 12 gal

20. about an inch

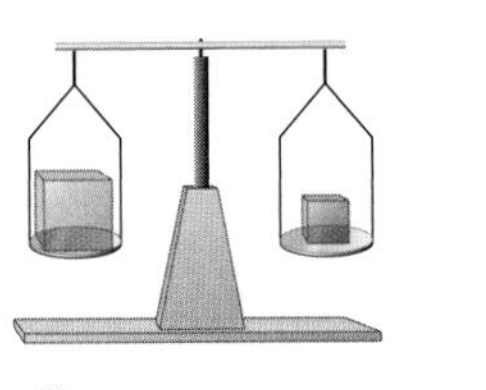

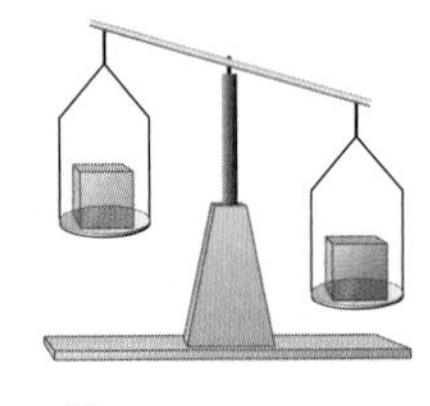

VP 19. For the pin shown below, why is the third digit determined for the length of the pin uncertain? Considering that the third digit is uncertain, explain why the length of the pin is indicated as 2.85 cm rather than, for example, 2.83 or 2.87 cm.

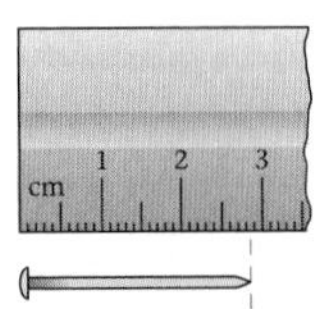

VP 20. Why can the length of the pin shown below not be recorded as 2.850 cm?

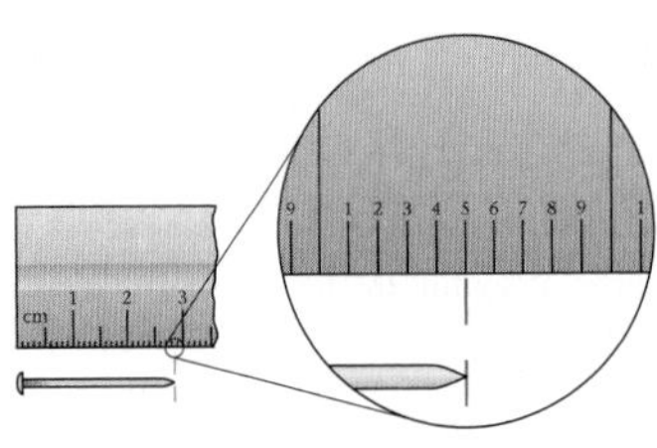

VP 21. Use the figure below to answer the following questions.

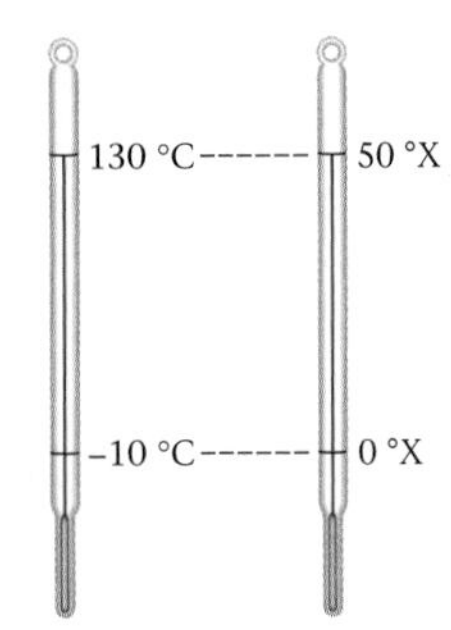

a. Derive the relationship between °C and °X.
b. If the temperature outside is 22.0 °C, what is the temperature in units of °X?
c. Convert 58.0 °X to units of °C, K, and °F.

Questions and Problems

2.1 Scientific Notation

QUESTIONS

1. A ______ represents a quantitative observation.
2. Although your textbook lists the rules for converting an ordinary number to scientific notation, oftentimes students remember such rules better if they put them into their own words. Pretend you are helping your 12-year-old niece with her math homework, and write a paragraph explaining to her how to convert the ordinary number 2421 to scientific notation.
3. When a large or small number is written in standard scientific notation, the number is expressed as the product of a *number* between 1 and 10, multiplied by the appropriate *power* of 10. For each of the following numbers, indicate what number between 1 and 10 would be appropriate when expressing the numbers in standard scientific notation.

   a. 9651 c. 93,241
   b. 0.003521 d. 0.000001002
4. When a large or small number is written in standard scientific notation, the number is expressed as the product of a *number* between 1 and 10, multiplied by the appropriate *power* of 10. For each of the following numbers, indicate what power of 10 would be appropriate when expressing the numbers in standard scientific notation.

   a. 82,350
   b. 0.009375
   c. 251
   d. 0.000000000000000000000000000009109

PROBLEMS

5. Will the power of 10 have a *positive* or a *negative* exponent when each of the following numbers is rewritten in standard scientific notation?

   a. 42,751 c. 0.002045
   b. 1253 d. 0.1089
6. Will the power of 10 have a *positive, negative,* or *zero* exponent when each of the following numbers is rewritten in standard scientific notation?

   a. 0.9091 c. 9091
   b. 9.091 d. 0.00000009091
7. Express each of the following numbers in *standard* scientific notation.

   a. 0.5012
   b. 5,012,000
   c. 0.000005012
   d. 5.012
   e. 5012
   f. 0.005012

All even-numbered Questions and Problems have answers in the back of this book and solutions in the Solutions Guide.

8. Rewrite each of the following as an "ordinary" decimal number.

a. 2.789×10^3
b. 2.789×10^{-3}
c. 9.3×10^7
d. 4.289×10^1
e. 9.999×10^4
f. 9.999×10^{-5}

9. By how many places must the decimal point be moved, and in which direction, to convert each of the following to "ordinary" decimal numbers?

a. 4.311×10^6
b. 7.895×10^{-5}
c. 8.712×10^1
d. 4.995×10^0
e. 2.331×10^{18}
f. 1.997×10^{-16}

10. By how many places must the decimal point be moved, and in which direction, to convert each of the following to standard scientific notation?

a. 5993
b. −72.14
c. 0.00008291
d. 62.357
e. 0.01014
f. 324.9

11. Write each of the following numbers in *standard* scientific notation.

a. 97,820
b. 42.14×10^3
c. 0.08214×10^{-3}
d. 0.0003914
e. 927.1
f. $4.781 \times 10^2 \times 10^{-3}$

12. Write each of the following numbers as "ordinary" decimal numbers.

a. 6.244×10^3
b. 9.117×10^{-2}
c. 8.299×10^1
d. 1.771×10^{-4}
e. 5.451×10^2
f. 2.934×10^{-5}

13. Write each of the following numbers in *standard* scientific notation.

a. 1/1033
b. $1/10^5$
c. $1/10^{-7}$
d. 1/0.0002
e. 1/3,093,000
f. $1/10^{-4}$
g. $1/10^9$
h. 1/0.000015

14. Write each of the following numbers in *standard* scientific notation.

a. 1/0.00032
b. $10^3/10^{-3}$
c. $10^3/10^3$
d. 1/55,000
e. $(10^5)(10^4)(10^{-4})/(10^{-2})$
f. $43.2/(4.32 \times 10^{-5})$
g. $(4.32 \times 10^{-5})/432$
h. $1/(10^5)(10^{-6})$

2.2 Units

QUESTIONS

15. What are the fundamental units of mass, length, and temperature in the metric system?

16. Give several examples of how *prefixes* are used in the metric system to indicate quantities that are multiples or divisions of the fundamental units of the metric system.

2.3 Measurements of Length, Volume, and Mass

QUESTIONS

Students often have trouble relating measurements in the metric system to the English system they have grown up with. Give the approximate English system equivalents for each of the following metric system descriptions in Exercises 17–20.

17. My new kitchen floor will require 25 square meters of linoleum.

18. My recipe for chili requires a 125-g can of tomato paste.

19. The gas tank in my new car holds 48 liters.

20. I need some 2.5-cm-long nails to hang up this picture.

21. The road sign I just passed says "New York City 100 km," which is about ______ mi.

22. Which contains more soda, a 2-liter bottle or a 2-quart bottle?

23. The tablecloth on my dining room table is 2 m long, which is ______ cm or about ______ in.

24. Who is taller, a man who is 1.62 m tall or a woman who is 5 ft 6 in. tall?

25. The fundamental SI unit of length is the meter. However, we often deal with larger or smaller lengths or distances for which multiples or fractions of the fundamental unit are more useful. For each of the following situations, suggest what fraction or multiple of the meter might be the most appropriate measurement.

a. the distance between Chicago and Saint Louis
b. the size of your bedroom
c. the dimensions of this textbook
d. the thickness of a hair

26. Which metric unit of length or distance is most comparable in scale to each of the following English system units for making measurements?

a. an inch
b. a yard
c. a mile

27. The unit of volume in the metric system is the liter, which consists of 1000 milliliters. How many liters or milliliters is each of the following common English system measurements approximately equivalent to?

a. a gallon of gasoline
b. a pint of milk
c. a cup of water

28. Which metric system unit is most appropriate for measuring the distance between two cities?

a. meters
b. millimeters
c. centimeters
d. kilometers

All even-numbered Questions and Problems have answers in the back of this book and solutions in the Solutions Guide.

21. 62

22. 2-liter bottle

23. 200 cm; 79 in. (80 in. to one significant figure)

24. the woman

25. (a) kilometers; (b) meters; (c) centimeters; (d) millimeters or micrometers

26. (a) centimeter; (b) meter; (c) kilometer

27. (a) about 4 liters; (b) about ½ liter; (c) about ¼ liter

28. d

29. When we use a measuring instrument to the limits of its precision, we *estimate* between the smallest scale divisions on the instrument for the last significant digit. As this last digit is estimated, it is uncertain.

30. Typically we read the scale on measuring devices to 0.1 unit of the smallest scale division on the device. We estimate this final significant figure, which makes the final significant figure in the measurement uncertain.

31. The third digit is uncertain because the scale of the ruler is marked only to the nearest tenth.

32. The scale of the ruler is marked to the nearest tenth of a centimeter. Writing 2.850 would imply that the scale was marked to the nearest hundredth of a centimeter (and that the zero in the thousandths place had been estimated).

33. (a) three; (b) two; (c) two; (d) four

34. (a) three: the relationship is exact; (b) two; (c) five; (d) probably two

35. increase the preceding digit by 1

36. It is better to round off only the final answer and to carry through extra digits in intermediate calculations. If there are enough steps to the calculation, rounding off in each step may lead to a cumulative error in the final answer.

37. (a) 2.55×10^5; (b) 2.56×10^{-4}; (c) 4.79×10^4; (d) 8.21×10^3

38. (a) 4.18×10^{-6}; (b) 3.87×10^4; (c) 9.11×10^{-30}; (d) 5.46×10^6

39. (a) 4.34×10^5; (b) 9.34×10^4; (c) 9.916×10^1; (d) 9.327×10^0

40. (a) 8.8×10^{-4}; (b) 9.375×10^4; (c) 8.97×10^{-1}; (d) 1.00×10^3

41. Because the only operations in the calculation are multiplication and division, the number of significant figures is limited by the factor of 0.15, which has only two significant figures.

2.4 Uncertainty in Measurement

QUESTIONS

29. If you were to measure the width of this page using a ruler, and you used the ruler to the limits of precision permitted by the scale on the ruler, the last digit you would write down for the measurement would be *uncertain* no matter how careful you were. Explain.

30. What does it mean to say that every measurement we make with a measuring device contains some measure of *uncertainty?*

31. For the pin shown in Figure 2.5, why is the third figure determined for the length of the pin uncertain? Considering that the third figure is uncertain, explain why the length of the pin is indicated as 2.85 cm rather than, for example, 2.83 or 2.87 cm.

32. Why can the length of the pin shown in Figure 2.5 not be recorded as 2.850 cm?

2.5 Significant Figures

QUESTIONS

33. Indicate the number of significant figures in each of the following:

a. 250. b. 250 c. 2.5×10^2 d. 250.0

34. Indicate the number of significant figures implied in each of the following statements:

a. One inch is equivalent to 2.54 cm.
b. My chemistry instructor gave us 24 homework problems to solve this week!
c. My monthly car payment is $249.75.
d. It's about 2500 mi from California to Hawaii.

Rounding Off Numbers

QUESTIONS

35. When we round off a number, if the number to the right of the digit to be rounded is greater than 5, then we should ______.

36. In a multiple-step calculation, is it better to round off the numbers to the correct number of significant figures in each step of the calculation or to round off only the final answer? Explain.

37. Round off each of the following numbers to three significant digits, and express the result in standard scientific notation.

a. 254,931 c. 47.85×10^3
b. 0.00025615 d. 0.08214×10^5

38. Round off each of the following numbers to three significant digits, and express the result in standard scientific notation.

a. 0.004175×10^{-3}
b. 38,652
c. 0.0000000000000000000000000000009109
d. 5.455×10^6

39. Round off each of the following numbers to the indicated number of significant digits and write the answer in standard scientific notation.

a. 4341×10^2 to three significant digits
b. 93.441×10^3 to three significant digits
c. 0.99155×10^2 to four significant digits
d. 9.3265 to four significant digits

40. Round off each of the following numbers to the indicated number of significant digits and write the answer in standard scientific notation.

a. 0.0008751 to two significant digits
b. 93,745 to four significant digits
c. 0.89724 to three significant digits
d. 9.995×10^2 to three significant digits

Determining Significant Figures in Calculations

QUESTIONS

41. Consider the calculation indicated below:

$$\frac{2.21 \times 0.072333 \times 0.15}{4.995}$$

Explain why the answer to this calculation should be reported to only two significant digits.

42. Suppose a group of objects were to be weighed separately on a scale and then the individual masses *added together* to determine the total mass of the group of objects. What would determine how many significant digits should appear in the reported total mass? Give an example of such a calculation.

43. When the calculation $(2.31)(4.9795 \times 10^3)/(1.9971 \times 10^4)$ is performed, how many significant digits should be reported for the answer? You should *not* need to perform the calculation.

44. Try this with your calculator: Enter 2 ÷ 3 and press the = sign. What does your calculator say is the answer? What would be wrong with that answer if the 2 and 3 were experimentally determined numbers?

45. When the sum 4.9965 + 2.11 + 3.887 is calculated, to how many decimal places should the answer be reported? You should *not* need to perform the calculation.

46. How many digits after the decimal point should be reported when the calculation (10,434 − 9.3344) is performed?

PROBLEMS

Note: See the Appendix for help in doing mathematical operations with numbers that contain exponents.

47. Evaluate each of the following mathematical expressions, and express the answer to the correct number of significant digits.

a. 44.2124 + 0.81 + 7.335
b. 9.7789 + 3.3315 − 2.21
c. 0.8891 + 0.225 + 4.14
d. (7.223 + 9.14 + 3.7795)/3.1

All even-numbered Questions and Problems have answers in the back of this book and solutions in the Solutions Guide.

42. The total mass would be determined by the number of decimal places available on the readout of the scale/balance. For example, if a balance whose readout is to the nearest 0.01 g were used, the total mass would be reported to the second decimal place. For example, 42.05 g + 29.15 g + 31.09 g would be reported as 102.29 to the second decimal place. Even though there are only four significant figures in each of the measurements, there are five significant figures in the answer because we look at the decimal place when adding (or subtracting) numbers.

43. three (based on 2.31)

44. Most calculators would say 0.66666666. If the 2 and 3 were experimentally determined numbers, this quotient would imply far too many significant figures.

45. two decimal places (based on 2.11)

46. none

47. (a) 52.36; (b) 10.90; (c) 5.25; (d) 6.5

48. (a) 2.3; (b) 9.1×10^2; (c) 1.323×10^3; (d) 6.63×10^{-13}

49. (a) two; (b) two; (c) two; (d) three (assuming the sum in the numerator is considered to the second decimal place)

50. (a) one; (b) four; (c) two; (d) three

51. (a) two; (b) two; (c) four; (d) three

52. (a) 2.045; (b) 3.8×10^3; (c) 5.19×10^{-5}; (d) 3.8418×10^{-7}

53. conversion factor

54. an infinite number, a definition

55. $\frac{1\text{ mi}}{1760\text{ yd}}$; $\frac{1760\text{ yd}}{1\text{ mi}}$

56. $\frac{2.54\text{ cm}}{1\text{ in.}}$; $\frac{1\text{ in.}}{2.54\text{ cm}}$

57. $0.79/1 lb

58. 1 lb/$0.79

59. (a) 31.8 cm; (b) 4.92 in.; (c) 0.4759 mi; (d) 1.38 m; (e) 391 sec; (f) 0.523 m; (g) 4.60 yd; (h) 0.501 lb

60. (a) 50.5 in.; (b) 3.11 ft; (c) 452 mm; (d) 76.12 cm; (e) 1.32 qt; (f) 8.42 pt; (g) 13.7 lb; (h) 28.0 oz

61. (a) 2.82 km; (b) 10.5 qt; (c) 19.56 J; (d) 0.9950 atm; (e) 6.03×10^{-26} kg; (f) 117 cm; (g) 88.0 fl oz; (h) 3.21 m

62. (a) 1.03598 atm; (b) 3.13 qt; (c) 0.510 kg; (d) 1.007 cal; (e) 8617 ft; (f) 9.04 qt; (g) 262 g; (h) 1.76 qt

63. 377 g

64. 4117 km

65. Boston–New York trains are faster.

66. 1×10^{-8} cm; 4×10^{-9} in.; 0.1 nm

67. Celsius

48. Evaluate each of the following mathematical expressions, and express the answer to the correct number of significant digits.

a. $(4.771 + 2.3)/3.1$
b. $5.02 \times 10^2 + 4.1 \times 10^2$
c. $1.091 \times 10^3 + 2.21 \times 10^2 + 1.14 \times 10^1$
d. $(2.7991 \times 10^{-6})/(4.22 \times 10^6)$

49. *Without actually performing the calculations indicated,* tell to how many significant digits the answer to the calculation should be expressed.

a. $(0.196)(0.08215)(295)/(1.1)$
b. $(4.215 + 3.991 + 2.442)/(0.22)$
c. $(7.881)(4.224)(0.00033)/(2.997)$
d. $(6.219 + 2.03)/(3.1159)$

50. *Without actually performing the calculations indicated,* tell to how many significant digits the answer to the calculation should be expressed.

a. $\dfrac{(9.7871)(2)}{(0.00182)(43.21)}$
b. $(67.41 + 0.32 + 1.98)/(18.225)$
c. $(2.001 \times 10^{-3})(4.7 \times 10^{-6})(68.224 \times 10^{-2})$
d. $(72.15)(63.9)[1.98 + 4.8981]$

51. How many significant digits should be used to report the answer to each of the following calculations? Do not perform the calculations.

a. $(2.7518 + 9.01 + 3.3349)/(2.1)$
b. $(2.7751 \times 1.95)/(.98)$
c. $12.0078/3.014$
d. $(0.997 + 4.011 + 3.876)/(1.86 \times 10^{-3})$

52. Evaluate each of the following and write the answer to the appropriate number of significant figures.

a. $(2.0944 + 0.0003233 + 12.22)/(7.001)$
b. $(1.42 \times 10^2 + 1.021 \times 10^3)/(3.1 \times 10^{-1})$
c. $(9.762 \times 10^{-3})/(1.43 \times 10^2 + 4.51 \times 10^1)$
d. $(6.1982 \times 10^{-4})^2$

2.6 Problem Solving and Dimensional Analysis

QUESTIONS

53. A ______ represents a ratio based on an equivalence statement between two measurements.

54. How many significant figures are understood for the numbers in the following definition: 1 mi = 5280 ft?

55. Given that 1 mi = 1760 yd, determine what conversion factor is appropriate to convert 1849 yd to miles; to convert 2.781 mi to yards.

56. Given that 1 in. = 2.54 cm exactly, indicate what conversion factor is appropriate to convert 12.3 in. to centimeters; to convert 63.52 cm to inches.

For Exercises 57 and 58, apples cost \$0.79 per pound.

57. What conversion factor is appropriate to express the cost of 5.3 lb of apples?

58. What conversion factor could be used to determine how many pounds of apples could be bought for \$2.00?

PROBLEMS

Note: Appropriate equivalence statements for various units are found inside the back cover of this book.

59. Perform each of the following conversions, being sure to set up the appropriate conversion factor in each case.

a. 12.5 in. to centimeters
b. 12.5 cm to inches
c. 2513 ft to miles
d. 4.53 ft to meters
e. 6.52 min to seconds
f. 52.3 cm to meters
g. 4.21 m to yards
h. 8.02 oz to pounds

60. Perform each of the following conversions, being sure to set up the appropriate conversion factor in each case.

a. 4.21 ft to inches
b. 37.3 in. to feet
c. 45.2 cm to millimeters
d. 761.2 mm to centimeters
e. 1.25 L to quarts
f. 4.21 qt to pints
g. 6.21 kg to pounds
h. 1.75 lb to ounces

61. Perform each of the following conversions, being sure to set up the appropriate conversion factor in each case.

a. 1.75 mi to kilometers
b. 2.63 gal to quarts
c. 4.675 calories to joules
d. 756.2 mm Hg to atmospheres
e. 36.3 atomic mass units to kilograms
f. 46.2 in. to centimeters
g. 2.75 qt to fluid ounces
h. 3.51 yd to meters

62. Perform each of the following conversions, being sure to set up the appropriate conversion factor in each case.

a. 104.971 kilopascals to atmospheres
b. 6.25 pt to quarts
c. 18.0 oz to kilograms
d. 4.213 joules to calories
e. 1.632 mi to feet
f. 4.52 qt to pints
g. 9.25 oz to grams
h. 56.2 fluid ounces to quarts

63. 12.01 g of carbon contains 6.02×10^{23} carbon atoms. What is the mass in grams of 1.89×10^{25} carbon atoms?

64. Los Angeles and Honolulu are 2558 mi apart. What is this distance in kilometers?

65. The United States has high-speed trains running between Boston and New York capable of speeds up to 160 mi/h. Are these trains faster or slower than the fastest trains in the United Kingdom, which reach speeds of 225 km/h?

66. The radius of an atom is on the order of 10^{-10} m. What is this radius in centimeters? in inches? in nanometers?

All even-numbered Questions and Problems have answers in the back of this book and solutions in the Solutions Guide.

68. freezing/melting

69. 212 °F, 100 °C

70. 273

71. 100

72. Fahrenheit (F)

73. (a) 317 K; (b) 618 °C; (c) 253 K; (d) 0 °C

74. (a) 195 K; (b) 502 °C; (c) 216 °C; (d) 297 K

75. (a) 7.2 °C; (b) 46 °C; (c) −23 °C; (d) 5500 °C (assuming two sig. figs.)

76. (a) 173 °F; (b) 104 °F; (c) −459 °F; (d) 90. °F

77. (a) gallium is in the liquid state over the temperature range of this thermometer; (b) 122 °F to 932 °F

78. (a) 2 °C; (b) 28 °C; (c) −5.8 °F (−6 °F); (d) −40 °C (−40 is where both temperature scales have the same value)

79. Density represents the mass per unit volume of a substance.

80. g/cm^3 (g/mL)

81. lead

82. 100 $in.^3$

83. Gases are mostly empty space, so there is less mass in a given volume than for solids and liquids, and therefore gases have *lower* densities.

84. Density is a characteristic property of a pure substance.

85. Gold is most dense; hydrogen is least dense; 1 g of hydrogen would occupy the larger volume.

86. copper

87. (a) 1.55 g/cm^3; (b) 0.51 g/cm^3; (c) 1.01 g/cm^3; (d) 0.0896 g/cm^3

88. (a) 22 g/cm^3; (b) 0.034 g/cm^3; (c) 0.962 g/cm^3; (d) 2.1×10^{-5} g/cm^3

89. 390. g; 27.2 mL

90. 2.94×10^3 g; 159 mL

91. 0.929 g/mL

92. float

93. 81.7 mL

94. 11.7 mL

95. (a) 23.1 cm^3; (b) 3.68 cm^3; (c) 56.8 cm^3; (d) 4.76 cm^3

96. (a) 966 g; (b) 394 g; (c) 567 g; (d) 135 g

97. (a) three; (b) three; (c) three

98. (a) 301,100,000,000, 000,000,000,000; (b) 5,091,000,000; (c) 720; (d) 123,400; (e) 0.000432002; (f) 0.03001; (g) 0.00000029901; (h) 0.42

99. (a) 4.25×10^2; (b) 7.81×10^{-4}; (c) 2.68×10^4; (d) 6.54×10^{-4}; (e) 7.26×10^1

100. (a) cm; (b) m; (c) km; (d) cm; (e) mm

101. (a) 0.104 ft, 3.18 cm; (b) 0.530 gal, 2.01 L; (c) 0.500 mi., 0.805 km; (d) 110.6 cm^3; (e) 196 g; (f) 57 mL, 0.78 kg

102. (a) 5.07×10^4 kryll; (b) 0.12 blim; (c) 3.70×10^{-5} $blim^2$

103. 1.1 h

104. 20. in.

105. highway, 19 km/L; city, 16 km/L

106. $1.33

107. 24 capsules

108. °X = 1.26 °C + 14

109. 3.8 g/cm^3; the ball will sink

110. 3.50 g/L (3.50×10^{-3} g/cm^3)

111. (a) 2.98×10^5 cm^3; (b) 1.84 cm^3; (c) 2.20 cm^3; (d) 25.0 cm^3

112. 959 g

113. three

114. (a) negative; (b) negative; (c) positive; (d) zero; (e) negative

115. (a) positive; (b) negative; (c) negative; (d) zero

116. (a) 2, positive; (b) 11, negative; (c) 3, positive; (d) 5, negative; (e) 5, positive; (f) 0, zero; (g) 1, negative; (h) 7, negative

117. (a) 4, positive; (b) 6, negative; (c) 0, zero; (d) 5, positive; (e) 2, negative

118. (a) 1, positive; (b) 3, negative; (c) 0, zero; (d) 3, positive; (e) 9, negative

119. (a) 5.29×10^2; (b) 2.4×10^8; (c) 3.01×10^{17}; (d) 7.8444×10^4; (e) 3.442×10^{-4}; (f) 9.02×10^{-10}; (g) 4.3×10^{-2}; (h) 8.21×10^{-2}

120. (a) 0.0000298; (b) 4,358,000,000; (c) 0.0000019928; (d) 602,000,000,000,000, 000,000,000; (e) 0.101; (f) 0.00787; (g) 98,700,000; (h) 378.99; (i) 0.1093; (j) 2.9004; (k) 0.00039; (l) 0.00000001904

2.7 Temperature Conversions

QUESTIONS

67. The temperature scale used in everyday life in most of the world except the United States is the ______ scale.

68. The ______ point of water is at 32° on the Fahrenheit temperature scale.

69. The normal boiling point of water is ______ °F, or ______ °C.

70. The freezing point of water is ______ K.

71. On both the Celsius and Kelvin temperature scales, there are ______ degrees between the normal freezing and boiling points of water.

72. On which temperature scale (°F, °C, or K) does 1 degree represent the smallest change in temperature?

PROBLEMS

73. Make the following temperature conversions:

    a. 44.2 °C to kelvins
    b. 891 K to °C
    c. −20 °C to kelvins
    d. 273.1 K to °C

74. Make the following temperature conversions:

    a. −78.1 °C to kelvins
    b. 775 K to °C
    c. 489 K to °C
    d. 24.3 °C to kelvins

75. Convert the following Fahrenheit temperatures to Celsius degrees.

    a. a chilly morning in early autumn, 45 °F
    b. a hot, dry day in the Arizona desert, 115 °F
    c. the temperature in winter when my car won't start, −10 °F
    d. the surface of a star, 10,000 °F

76. Convert the following Celsius temperatures to Fahrenheit degrees.

    a. the boiling temperature of ethyl alcohol, 78.1 °C
    b. a hot day at the beach on a Greek isle, 40. °C
    c. the lowest possible temperature, −273 °C
    d. the body temperature of a person with hypothermia, 32 °C

77. The "Chemistry in Focus" segment *Tiny Thermometers* states that the temperature range for the carbon nanotube gallium thermometers is 50 °C to 500 °C.

    a. What properties of gallium make it useful in a thermometer?
    b. Determine the useful temperature range for the gallium thermometer in Fahrenheit units.

78. Perform the indicated temperature conversions.

    a. 275 K to °C
    b. 82 °F to °C
    c. −21 °C to °F
    d. −40 °F to °C (Notice anything unusual about your answer?)

2.8 Density

QUESTIONS

79. What does the *density* of a substance represent?

80. The most common units for density are ______ .

81. A kilogram of lead occupies a much smaller volume than a kilogram of water, because ______ has a much higher density.

82. If a solid block of glass, with a volume of exactly 100 $in.^3$, is placed in a basin of water that is full to the brim, then ______ of water will overflow from the basin.

83. Is the density of a gaseous substance likely to be larger or smaller than the density of a liquid or solid substance at the same temperature? Why?

84. What property of density makes it useful as an aid in identifying substances?

85. Referring to Table 2.8, which substance listed is most dense? Which substance is least dense? For the two substances you have identified, for which one would a 1.00-g sample occupy the larger volume?

86. Referring to Table 2.8, determine whether copper, silver, lead, or mercury is the least dense.

PROBLEMS

87. For the masses and volumes indicated, calculate the density in grams per cubic centimeter.

    a. mass = 452.1 g; volume = 292 cm^3
    b. mass = 0.14 lb; volume = 125 mL
    c. mass = 1.01 kg; volume = 1000 cm^3
    d. mass = 225 mg; volume = 2.51 mL

88. For the masses and volumes indicated, calculate the density in grams per cubic centimeter.

    a. mass = 122.4 g; volume = 5.5 cm^3
    b. mass = 19,302 g; volume = 0.57 m^3
    c. mass = 0.0175 kg; volume = 18.2 mL
    d. mass = 2.49 g; volume = 0.12 m^3

89. The element bromine at room temperature is a liquid with a density of 3.12 g/mL. Calculate the mass of 125 mL of bromine. What volume does 85.0 g of bromine occupy?

90. Isopropyl alcohol (rubbing alcohol) has a density of 0.785 g/mL. What is the mass of 3.75 L of isopropyl alcohol? What volume would 125 g of isopropyl alcohol occupy?

91. If 1000. mL of linseed oil has a mass of 929 g, calculate the density of linseed oil.

92. A material will float on the surface of a liquid if the material has a density less than that of the liquid. Given that the density of water is approximately 1.0 g/mL under many conditions, will a block of material having a volume of 1.2×10^4 $in.^3$ and weighing 3.5 lb float or sink when placed in a reservoir of water?

All even-numbered Questions and Problems have answers in the back of this book and solutions in the Solutions Guide.

121. (a) 1.023×10^{-3}; (b) 3.203×10^{-2}; (c) 5.9933×10^6; (d) 5.9933×10^6; (e) 5.9933×10^6; (f) 2.054×10^2; (g) 3.2×10^1; (h) 5.9933×10^6

122. (a) 1×10^{-2}; (b) 1×10^2; (c) 5.5×10^{-2}; (d) 3.1×10^9; (e) 1×10^3; (f) 1×10^8; (g) 2.9×10^2; (h) 3.453×10^4

123. meter

124. kelvin, K

125. 100 km

126. centimeter

93. Iron has a density of 7.87 g/cm^3. If 52.4 g of iron is added to 75.0 mL of water in a graduated cylinder, to what volume reading will the water level in the cylinder rise?

94. The density of pure silver is 10.5 g/cm^3 at 20 °C. If 5.25 g of pure silver pellets is added to a graduated cylinder containing 11.2 mL of water, to what volume level will the water in the cylinder rise?

95. Use the information in Table 2.8 to calculate the volume of 50.0 g of each of the following substances.

a. sodium chloride
b. mercury
c. benzene
d. silver

96. Use the information in Table 2.8 to calculate the mass of 50.0 cm^3 of each of the following substances.

a. gold
b. iron
c. lead
d. aluminum

Additional Problems

97. Indicate the number of significant digits in the answer when each of the following expressions is evaluated (you do *not* have to evaluate the expression).

a. (6.25)/(74.1143)
b. (1.45)(0.08431)(6.022×10^{23})
c. (4.75512)(9.74441)/(3.14)

98. Express each of the following as an "ordinary" decimal number.

a. 3.011×10^{23}
b. 5.091×10^{9}
c. 7.2×10^{2}
d. 1.234×10^{5}
e. 4.32002×10^{-4}
f. 3.001×10^{-2}
g. 2.9901×10^{-7}
h. 4.2×10^{-1}

99. Write each of the following numbers in standard scientific notation, rounding off the numbers to three significant digits.

a. 424.6174
b. 0.00078145
c. 26,755
d. 0.0006535
e. 72.5654

100. Which unit of length in the metric system would be most appropriate in size for measuring each of the following items?

a. the dimensions of this page
b. the size of the room in which you are sitting
c. the distance from New York to London
d. the diameter of a baseball
e. the diameter of a common pin

101. Make the following conversions.

a. 1.25 in. to feet and to centimeters
b. 2.12 qt to gallons and to liters
c. 2640 ft to miles and to kilometers
d. 1.254 kg lead to its volume in cubic centimeters
e. 250. mL ethanol to its mass in grams
f. 3.5 in.^{3} of mercury to its volume in milliliters and its mass in kilograms

102. On the planet Xgnu, the most common units of length are the blim (for long distances) and the kryll (for shorter distances). Because the Xgnuese have 14 fingers, perhaps it is not surprising that 1400 kryll = 1 blim.

a. Two cities on Xgnu are 36.2 blim apart. What is this distance in kryll?
b. The average Xgnuese is 170 kryll tall. What is this height in blims?
c. This book is presently being used at Xgnu University. The area of the cover of this book is 72.5 square krylls. What is its area in square blims?

103. You pass a road sign saying "New York 110 km." If you drive at a constant speed of 100. km/h, how long should it take you to reach New York?

104. At the mall, you decide to try on a pair of French jeans. Naturally, the waist size of the jeans is given in centimeters. What does a waist measurement of 52 cm correspond to in inches?

105. Suppose your car is rated at 45 mi/gal for highway use and 38 mi/gal for city driving. If you wanted to write your friend in Spain about your car's mileage, what ratings in kilometers per liter would you report?

106. You are in Paris, and you want to buy some peaches for lunch. The sign in the fruit stand indicates that peaches cost 2.45 euros per kilogram. Given that 1 euro is equivalent to approximately \$1.20, calculate what a pound of peaches will cost in dollars.

107. For a pharmacist dispensing pills or capsules, it is often easier to weigh the medication to be dispensed rather than to count the individual pills. If a single antibiotic capsule weighs 0.65 g, and a pharmacist weighs out 15.6 g of capsules, how many capsules have been dispensed?

108. On the planet Xgnu, the natives have 14 fingers. On the official Xgnuese temperature scale (°X), the boiling point of water (under an atmospheric pressure similar to earth's) is 140 °X, whereas water freezes at 14 °X. Derive the relationship between °X and °C.

109. For a material to float on the surface of water, the material must have a density less than that of water (1.0 g/mL) and must not react with the water or dissolve in it. A spherical ball has a radius of 0.50 cm and weighs 2.0 g. Will this ball float or sink when placed in water? (*Note:* Volume of a sphere = $\frac{4}{3}\pi r^3$.)

110. A gas cylinder having a volume of 10.5 L contains 36.8 g of gas. What is the density of the gas?

111. Using Table 2.8, calculate the volume of 25.0 g of each of the following:

a. hydrogen gas (at 1 atmosphere pressure)
b. mercury
c. lead
d. water

112. Ethanol and benzene dissolve in each other. When 100. mL of ethanol is dissolved in 1.00 L of benzene, what is the mass of the mixture? (See Table 2.8.)

113. When 2891 is written in scientific notation, the exponent indicating the power of 10 is ______.

All even-numbered Questions and Problems have answers in the back of this book and solutions in the Solutions Guide.

127. 250. mL

128. 0.105 m

129. 62.1 mi/h; not a violation

130. 1 kg

131. 4.25 g

132. 10

133. significant figures (digits)

134. 2.8 (the hundredths place is estimated)

135. (a) one; (b) one; (c) four; (d) two; (e) infinite (definition); (f) one

136. (a) 0.000426; (b) 4.02×10^{-5}; (c) 5.99×10^{6}; (d) 400.; (e) 0.00600

137. (a) 0.7556; (b) 293; (c) 17.01; (d) 432.97

138. (a) 2149.6; (b) 5.37×10^{3}; (c) 3.83×10^{-2}; (d) -8.64×10^{5}

139. (a) 5.57×10^{7}; (b) 2.38×10^{-1}; (c) 4.72; (d) 8.08×10^{8}

140. (a) 7.6166×10^{6}; (b) 7.24×10^{3}; (c) 1.92×10^{-5}; (d) 2.4482×10^{-3}

141. 1 L/1000 cm^3; 1000 cm^3/1 L

142. 1 yr/12 mo; 12 mo/1 yr

143. (a) 84.3 mm; (b) 2.41 m; (c) 2.945×10^{-5} cm; (d) 0.4045 km; (e) 14.45 km; (f) 4.22 cm; (g) 2.353×10^{5} mm; (h) 0.9033 μm

144. (a) 25.7 kg; (b) 3.38 gal; (c) 0.132 qt; (d) 1.09×10^{4} mL; (e) 2.03×10^{3} g; (f) 0.58 qt

145. 1.5×10^{8} km; 1.5×10^{13} cm

146. for exactly 6 gross, 864 pencils

147. (a) 273 K; (b) 298 K; (c) 310. K; (d) 373 K; (e) 98 K; (f) 485 K

148. (a) 352 K; (b) −18 °C; (c) −43 °C; (d) 257 °F

149. (a) 110 g/cm^3; (b) 1.1×10^{-3} g/cm^3; (c) 9.1×10^{-3} g/cm^3; (d) 9.4×10^{-2} g/cm^3

150. 78.2 g

151. 38.2 g

152. 0.59 g/cm^3

153. 3.8 g/mL

154. (a) 23 °F; (b) 32 °F; (c) −321 °F; (d) −459 °F; (e) 187 °F; (f) −459 °F

155. (a) 10^{3}; (b) 10^{9}; (c) 10^{-2}; (d) 10^{-3}

156. (a) 100 km, 62 mi; (b) 2.69×10^{4} lb

157. (a) The text mentions oxygen sensors in automobile exhaust systems, detection of nitrogen-containing compounds in airline baggage, use of sensory hair from crabs to detect low levels of hormones, and use of pineapple extracts to detect hydrogen peroxide; (b) We can now detect the presence of impurities or contaminants to much lower levels than was possible in the past. Although that may seem helpful, we now have to determine whether these contaminants were always present and are not harmful or if they are something new that we should be concerned about.

158. 8×10^{-11} lb/gal

114. For each of the following numbers, if the number is rewritten in scientific notation, will the exponent of the power of 10 be positive, negative, or zero?

a. $1/10^3$
b. 0.00045
c. 52,550
d. 7.21
e. 1/3

115. For each of the following numbers, if the number is rewritten in scientific notation, will the exponent of the power of 10 be positive, negative, or zero?

a. 4,915,442
b. 1/1000
c. 0.001
d. 3.75

116. For each of the following numbers, by how many places does the decimal point have to be moved to express the number in standard scientific notation? In each case, is the exponent positive or negative?

a. 102
b. 0.00000000003489
c. 2500
d. 0.00003489
e. 398,000
f. 1
g. 0.3489
h. 0.0000003489

117. For each of the following numbers, by how many places must the decimal point be moved to express the number in standard scientific notation? In each case, will the exponent be positive, negative, or zero?

a. 55,651
b. 0.000008991
c. 2.04
d. 883,541
e. 0.09814

118. For each of the following numbers, by how many places must the decimal point be moved to express the number in standard scientific notation? In each case, will the exponent be positive, negative, or zero?

a. 72.471
b. 0.008941
c. 9.9914
d. 6519
e. 0.000000008715

119. Express each of the following numbers in scientific (exponential) notation.

a. 529
b. 240,000,000
c. 301,000,000,000,000,000
d. 78,444
e. 0.0003442
f. 0.000000000902
g. 0.043
h. 0.0821

120. Express each of the following as an "ordinary" decimal number.

a. 2.98×10^{-5}
b. 4.358×10^{9}
c. 1.9928×10^{-6}
d. 6.02×10^{23}
e. 1.01×10^{-1}
f. 7.87×10^{-3}
g. 9.87×10^{7}
h. 3.7899×10^{2}
i. 1.093×10^{-1}
j. 2.9004×10^{0}
k. 3.9×10^{-4}
l. 1.904×10^{-8}

121. Write each of the following numbers in *standard* scientific notation.

a. 102.3×10^{-5}
b. 32.03×10^{-3}
c. 59933×10^{2}
d. 599.33×10^{4}
e. 5993.3×10^{3}
f. 2054×10^{-1}
g. $32{,}000{,}000 \times 10^{-6}$
h. 59.933×10^{5}

122. Write each of the following numbers in *standard* scientific notation. See the Appendix if you need help multiplying or dividing numbers with exponents.

a. $1/10^2$
b. $1/10^{-2}$
c. $55/10^3$
d. $(3.1 \times 10^6)/10^{-3}$
e. $(10^6)^{1/2}$
f. $(10^6)(10^4)/(10^2)$
g. 1/0.0034
h. $3.453/10^{-4}$

123. The fundamental unit of length or distance in the metric system is the ______ .

124. The SI unit of temperature is the ______ .

125. Which distance is farther, 100 km or 50 mi?

126. The unit of volume corresponding to 1/1000 of a liter is referred to as 1 milliliter, or 1 cubic ______ .

127. The volume 0.250 L could also be expressed as ______ mL.

128. The distance 10.5 cm could also be expressed as ______ m.

129. Would an automobile moving at a constant speed of 100 km/h violate a 65-mph speed limit?

130. Which weighs more, 100 g of water or 1 kg of water?

131. Which weighs more, 4.25 g of gold or 425 mg of gold?

132. The length 100 mm can also be expressed as ______ cm.

133. When a measurement is made, the certain numbers plus the first uncertain number are called the ______ of the measurement.

134. In the measurement of the length of the pin indicated in Figure 2.5, what are the *certain* numbers in the measurement shown?

135. Indicate the number of significant figures in each of the following:

a. This book contains over 500 pages.
b. A mile is just over 5000 ft.
c. A liter is equivalent to 1.059 qt.
d. The population of the United States is approaching 250 million.
e. A kilogram is 1000 g.
f. The Boeing 747 cruises at around 600 mph.

136. Round off each of the following numbers to three significant digits.

a. 0.00042557
b. 4.0235×10^{-5}
c. 5,991,556
d. 399.85
e. 0.0059998

137. Round off each of the following numbers to the indicated number of significant digits.

a. 0.75555 to four digits
b. 292.5 to three digits
c. 17.005 to four digits
d. 432.965 to five digits

138. Evaluate each of the following, and write the answer to the appropriate number of significant figures.

a. $149.2 + 0.034 + 2000.34$
b. $1.0322 \times 10^3 + 4.34 \times 10^3$

All even-numbered Questions and Problems have answers in the back of this book and solutions in the Solutions Guide.

c. $4.03 \times 10^{-2} - 2.044 \times 10^{-3}$
d. $2.094 \times 10^{5} - 1.073 \times 10^{6}$

139. Evaluate each of the following, and write the answer to the appropriate number of significant figures.

a. $(0.0432)(2.909)(4.43 \times 10^{8})$
b. $(0.8922)/[(0.00932)(4.03 \times 10^{2})]$
c. $(3.923 \times 10^{2})(2.94)(4.093 \times 10^{-3})$
d. $(4.9211)(0.04434)/[(0.000934)(2.892 \times 10^{-7})]$

140. Evaluate each of the following, and write the answer to the appropriate number of significant figures.

a. $(2.9932 \times 10^{4})[2.4443 \times 10^{2} + 1.0032 \times 10^{1}]$
b. $[2.34 \times 10^{2} + 2.443 \times 10^{-1}]/(0.0323)$
c. $(4.38 \times 10^{-3})^{2}$
d. $(5.9938 \times 10^{-6})^{1/2}$

141. Given that 1 L = 1000 cm^3, determine what conversion factor is appropriate to convert 350 cm^3 to liters; to convert 0.200 L to cubic centimeters.

142. Given that 12 months = 1 year, determine what conversion factor is appropriate to convert 72 months to years; to convert 3.5 years to months.

143. Perform each of the following conversions, being sure to set up clearly the appropriate conversion factor in each case.

a. 8.43 cm to millimeters
b. 2.41×10^{2} cm to meters
c. 294.5 nm to centimeters
d. 404.5 m to kilometers
e. 1.445×10^{4} m to kilometers
f. 42.2 mm to centimeters
g. 235.3 m to millimeters
h. 903.3 nm to micrometers

144. Perform each of the following conversions, being sure to set up clearly the appropriate conversion factor(s) in each case.

a. 908 oz to kilograms
b. 12.8 L to gallons
c. 125 mL to quarts
d. 2.89 gal to milliliters
e. 4.48 lb to grams
f. 550 mL to quarts

145. The mean distance from the earth to the sun is 9.3×10^{7} mi. What is this distance in kilometers? in centimeters?

146. Given that one gross = 144 items, how many pencils are contained in 6 gross?

147. Convert the following temperatures to kelvins.

a. 0 °C
b. 25 °C
c. 37 °C
d. 100 °C
e. −175 °C
f. 212 °C

148. Carry out the indicated temperature conversions.

a. 175 °F to kelvins
b. 255 K to Celsius degrees
c. −45 °F to Celsius degrees
d. 125 °C to Fahrenheit degrees

149. For the masses and volumes indicated, calculate the density in grams per cubic centimeter.

a. mass = 234 g; volume = 2.2 cm^3
b. mass = 2.34 kg; volume = 2.2 m^3
c. mass = 1.2 lb; volume = 2.1 ft^3
d. mass = 4.3 ton; volume = 54.2 yd^3

150. A sample of a liquid solvent has a density of 0.915 g/mL. What is the mass of 85.5 mL of the liquid?

151. An organic solvent has a density of 1.31 g/mL. What volume is occupied by 50.0 g of the liquid?

152. A solid metal sphere has a volume of 4.2 ft^3. The mass of the sphere is 155 lb. Find the density of the metal sphere in grams per cubic centimeter.

153. A sample containing 33.42 g of metal pellets is poured into a graduated cylinder initially containing 12.7 mL of water, causing the water level in the cylinder to rise to 21.6 mL. Calculate the density of the metal.

154. Convert the following temperatures to Fahrenheit degrees.

a. −5 °C
b. 273 K
c. −196 °C
d. 0 K
e. 86 °C
f. −273 °C

155. For each of the following descriptions, identify the power of 10 being indicated by the *prefix* in the measurement.

a. The sign on the interstate highway says to tune my AM radio to 540 *kilo*hertz for traffic information.
b. My new digital camera has a two-*giga*byte flash memory card.
c. The shirt I bought for my dad on my European vacation shows the sleeve length in *centi*meters.
d. My brother's camcorder records on 8-*milli*meter tape cassettes.

156. The "Chemistry in Focus" segment *Critical Units!* discusses the importance of unit conversions. Read the segment and make the proper unit conversions to answer the following questions.

a. The Mars Climate Orbiter burned up because it dipped lower in the Mars atmosphere than planned. How many miles lower than planned did it dip?
b. A Canadian jetliner almost ran out of fuel because someone pumped less fuel into the aircraft than was thought. How many more pounds of fuel should have been pumped into the aircraft?

157. Read the "Chemistry in Focus" segment *Measurement: Past, Present, and Future* and answer the following questions.

a. Give three examples of how developing sophisticated measuring devices is useful in our society.
b. Explain how advances in measurement abilities can be a problem.

158. The "Chemistry in Focus" segment *Measurement: Past, Present, and Future* states that hormones can be detected to a level of 10^{-8} g/L. Convert this level to units of pounds per gallon.

All even-numbered Questions and Problems have answers in the back of this book and solutions in the Solutions Guide.

Chapter Review 55

Chapter 3

Objectives

In this chapter, our objectives are for the students to:

SECTION 3.1

- Learn about matter and its three states.

SECTION 3.2

- Learn to distinguish between physical and chemical properties.
- Learn to distinguish between physical and chemical changes.

SECTION 3.3

- Understand the definitions of elements and compounds.

SECTION 3.4

- Learn to distinguish between mixtures and pure substances.

SECTION 3.5

- Learn two methods of separating mixtures.

3 Matter

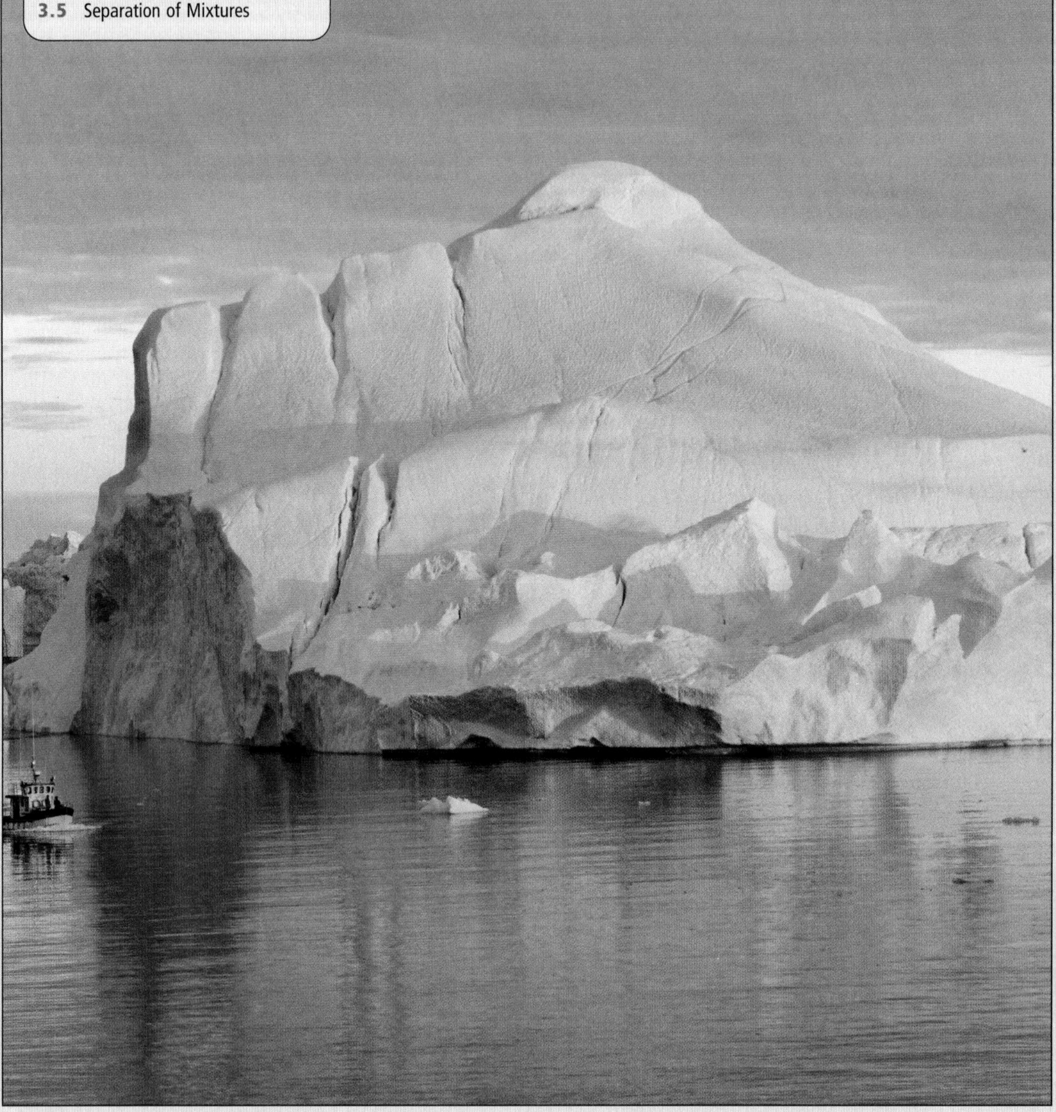

An iceberg in Greenland. *(Frank Krahmer/Masterfile)*

ChemWork Refined over ten years of use by thousands of students, **ChemWork** builds and enhances students' problems-solving skills. Online assignments function as a "personal instructor" to help students learn how to solve challenging problems and learn how to think like chemists. Annotations for **ChemWork** assignments are included at the beginning of the end-of-chapter review.

PowerLecture This 2-DVD package includes the Chemistry Multimedia Library, which contains animations, simulations, and movies for all chemistry subjects, organized by topic for lecture presentations. Annotations for **PowerLecture** are referenced in the margins throughout the Annotated Instructor's Edition.

OWL Sign in to OWL at **www.cengage.com/owl** to view tutoritals and simulations, develop problem-solving skills, and complete online homework assigned by your professor.

Why does soda fizz when you open the bottle?

As you look around you, you must wonder about the properties of matter. How do plants grow and why are they green? Why is the sun hot? Why does a hot dog get hot in a microwave oven? Why does wood burn whereas rocks do not? What is a flame? How does soap work? Why does soda fizz when you open the bottle? When iron rusts, what's happening? And why doesn't aluminum rust? How does a cold pack for an athletic injury, which is stored for weeks or months at room temperature, suddenly get cold when you need it? How does a hair permanent work?

The answers to these and endless other questions lie in the domain of chemistry. In this chapter we begin to explore the nature of matter: how it is organized and how and why it changes.

Test Bank: 1–4, 44–46

3.1 Matter

OBJECTIVE: To learn about matter and its three states.

Section 3.1

TEACHING TIP

It is important to emphasize an atomic/molecular view of chemistry from the beginning. One reason why students find the subject so difficult is that they do not relate the microscopic to the macroscopic. By thinking only in macroscopic terms, ideas such as compound, mixture, and chemical change are often memorized rather than understood. This is why we start immediately with an atomic/molecular perspective (note Figure 3.2, for example).

Matter, the "stuff" of which the universe is composed, has two characteristics: it has mass and it occupies space. Matter comes in a great variety of forms: the stars, the air that you are breathing, the gasoline that you put in your car, the chair on which you are sitting, the turkey in the sandwich you may have had for lunch, the tissues in your brain that enable you to read and comprehend this sentence, and so on.

To try to understand the nature of matter, we classify it in various ways. For example, wood, bone, and steel share certain characteristics. These things are all rigid; they have definite shapes that are difficult to change. On the other hand, water and gasoline, for example, take the shape of any container into which they are poured (see Figure 3.1). Even so, 1 L of water has a volume of 1 L whether it is in a pail or a beaker. In contrast, air takes the shape of its container and fills any container uniformly.

The substances we have just described illustrate the three **states of matter: solid, liquid,** and **gas.** These are defined and illustrated in Table 3.1. The state of a given sample of matter depends on the strength of the forces among the particles contained in the matter; the stronger these forces, the more rigid the matter. We will discuss this in more detail in the next section.

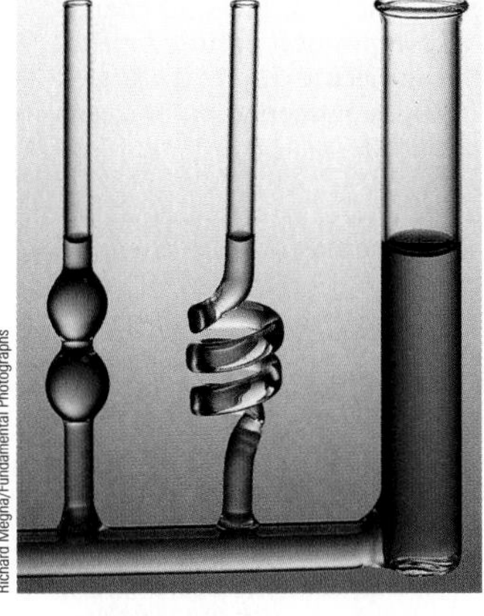

Figure 3.1 Liquid water takes the shape of its container.

Table 3.1 The Three States of Matter

State	Definition	Examples
solid	rigid; has a fixed shape and volume	ice cube, diamond, iron bar
liquid	has a definite volume but takes the shape of its container	gasoline, water, alcohol, blood
gas	has no fixed volume or shape; takes the shape and volume of its container	air, helium, oxygen

3.2 Physical and Chemical Properties and Changes

OBJECTIVES: To learn to distinguish between physical and chemical properties. • To learn to distinguish between physical and chemical changes.

How does this lush vegetation grow in a tropical rain forest, and why is it green?

Brian Parker/Tom Stack & Associates

When you see a friend, you immediately respond and call him or her by name. We can recognize a friend because each person has unique characteristics or properties. The person may be thin and tall, may have blonde hair and blue eyes, and so on. The characteristics just mentioned are examples of **physical properties.** Substances also have physical properties. Typical physical properties of a substance include odor, color, volume, state (gas, liquid, or solid), density, melting point, and boiling point. We can also describe a pure substance in terms of its **chemical properties,** which refer to its ability to form new substances. An example of a chemical change is wood burning in a fireplace, giving off heat and gases and leaving a residue of ashes. In this process, the wood is changed to several new substances. Other examples of chemical changes include the rusting of the steel in our cars, the digestion of food in our stomachs, and the growth of grass in our yards. In a chemical change a given substance changes to a fundamentally different substance or substances.

EXAMPLE 3.1 Identifying Physical and Chemical Properties

Classify each of the following as a physical or a chemical property.

a. The boiling point of a certain alcohol is 78 °C.

b. Diamond is very hard.

c. Sugar ferments to form alcohol.

d. A metal wire conducts an electric current.

SOLUTION

Items (a), (b), and (d) are physical properties; they describe inherent characteristics of each substance, and no change in composition occurs. A metal wire has the same composition before and after an electric current has passed through it. Item (c) is a chemical property of sugar. Fermentation of sugars involves the formation of a new substance (alcohol).

Self-Check EXERCISE 3.1 Which of the following are physical properties and which are chemical properties?

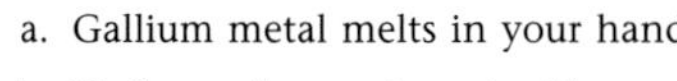

a. Gallium metal melts in your hand.

b. Platinum does not react with oxygen at room temperature.

c. This page is white.

d. The copper sheets that form the "skin" of the Statue of Liberty have acquired a greenish coating over the years.

See Problems 3.11 through 3.14. ■

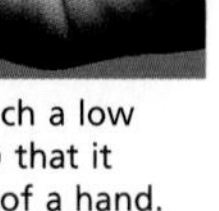

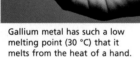

Gallium metal has such a low melting point (30 °C) that it melts from the heat of a hand.

© Cengage Learning

Matter can undergo changes in both its physical and its chemical properties. To illustrate the fundamental differences between physical and chemical changes, we will consider water. As we will see in much more detail in later chapters, a sample of water contains a very large number of individual

DEMONSTRATION

These demonstrations allow the students to take an atomic/molecular perspective. The second demonstration specifically addresses states of matter.

1. Demonstrate the movement of the molecules in water by placing a drop of food coloring in a beaker of water and allowing it to mix without stirring.
2. Use small (marble-sized) Styrofoam balls to demonstrate the differences among solids, liquids, and gases at the atomic/molecular level. Glue a number of balls together in an orderly fashion to represent a solid. Place a handful of loose balls in a beaker to represent a liquid. The balls can be poured and flow over one another; the liquid will take the shape of its container. Place just a few balls in a quart jar with a lid and shake the jar to illustrate a gas. If you leave the top off the jar and shake, the gas will escape from the container.

Test Bank: 5–19, 39, 47–53

Self Check

Answers to Self-Check Exercise 3.1

Items (a) and (c) are physical properties. When solid gallium melts, it forms liquid gallium. Items (b) and (d) reflect the ability to change composition and are thus chemical properties. Statement (b) means that platinum does not react with oxygen to form some new substance. Statement (d) means that copper reacts with air to form a new substance, which is green.

Section 3.2

Additional Examples

Example 3.1

Classify each of the following as a physical or chemical property:

1. Ice melts at 0 °C. — Physical property
2. Propane burns in the air. — Chemical property
3. Lead is a very dense metal. — Physical property
4. Leaves turn colors in the fall. — Chemical property

The letters indicate atoms and the lines indicate attachments (bonds) between atoms.

units (called molecules), each made up of two atoms of hydrogen and one atom of oxygen—the familiar H_2O. This molecule can be represented as

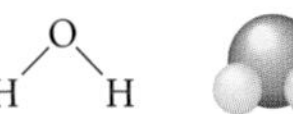

The purpose here is to give an overview. Don't worry about the precise definitions of *atom* and *molecule* now. We will explore these concepts more fully in Chapter 4.

where the letters stand for atoms and the lines show attachments (called bonds) between atoms, and the molecular model (on the right) represents water in a more three-dimensional fashion.

What is really occurring when water undergoes the following changes?

Solid (ice)  Liquid (water)  Gas (steam)

Melting Boiling

Chip Clark

An iron pyrite crystal (gold color) on a white quartz crystal.

We will describe these changes of state precisely in Chapter 14, but you already know something about these processes because you have observed them many times.

When ice melts, the rigid solid becomes a mobile liquid that takes the shape of its container. Continued heating brings the liquid to a boil, and the water becomes a gas or vapor that seems to disappear into "thin air." The changes that occur as the substance goes from solid to liquid to gas are represented in Figure 3.2. In ice the water molecules are locked into fixed positions (although they are vibrating). In the liquid the molecules are still very close together, but some motion is occurring; the positions of the molecules are no longer fixed as they are in ice. In the gaseous state the molecules are much farther apart and move randomly, hitting each other and the walls of the container.

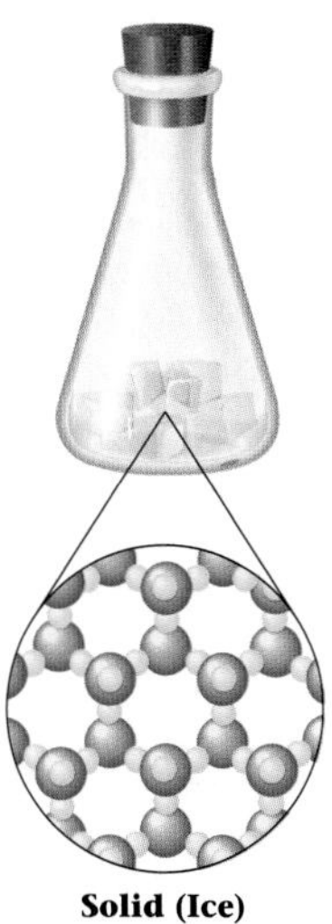
Solid (Ice)

a Solid: the water molecules are locked into rigid positions and are close together.

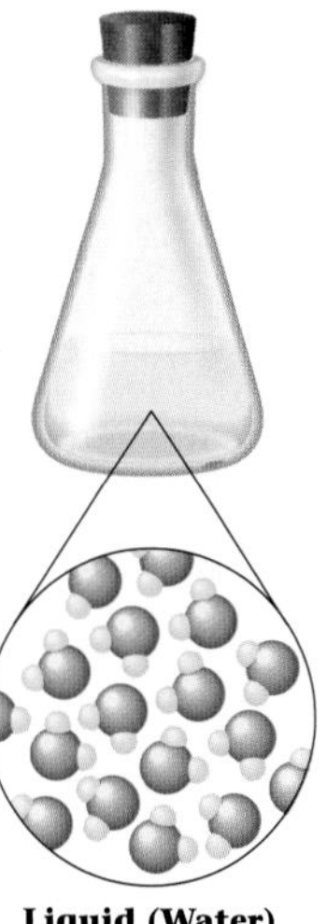
Liquid (Water)

b Liquid: the water molecules are still close together but can move around to some extent.

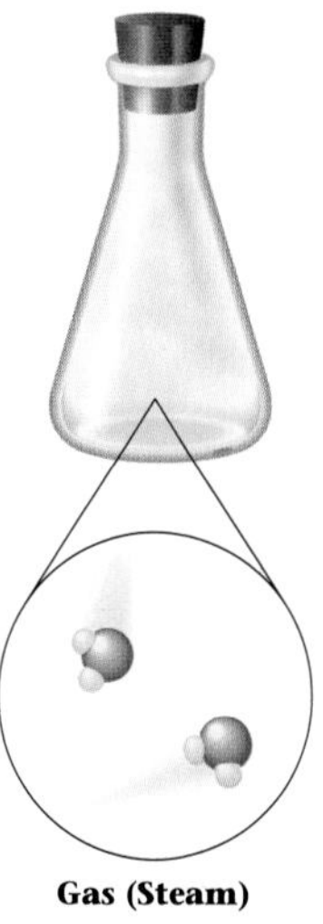
Gas (Steam)

c Gas: the water molecules are far apart and move randomly.

Figure 3.2
The three states of water (where red spheres represent oxygen atoms and blue spheres represent hydrogen atoms).

TEACHING TIP

To illustrate the difference between a physical change and a chemical change, compare representations (b) and (c) from Figure 3.2 (a physical change from liquid water to gaseous water) to the chemical change when liquid water is electrolyzed to produce the gases H_2 and O_2. Use the equation in the text to represent the electrolysis of water chemical change.

DEMONSTRATION

Genie in the Bottle—A Chemical Change

Materials

- 5000-mL Florence flask or Erlenmeyer flask
- 100-mL beaker
- 30% hydrogen peroxide
- Aluminum foil
- Manganese dioxide
- Tea bag
- Rubber stopper

Procedure Cover the flask with aluminum foil. Before class cut open a tea bag and remove the tea. Refill the bag with about two spatulas of manganese dioxide and staple the bag closed. Be sure the string is attached. Just before class, measure out about 50 mL of 30% hydrogen peroxide using the 100-mL beaker and pour it into the flask. Carefully suspend the tea bag containing the manganese dioxide above the hydrogen peroxide and hold it in place with a rubber stopper.

Tell the students a story about a genie in the bottle. When you are ready to release the genie, remove the stopper and step back. A large puff of steam will be released. The flask will be very hot!

Safety and Cleanup
The 30% hydrogen peroxide is corrosive and should be stored under refrigeration. This demonstration can also be done with 10% hydrogen peroxide, with less dramatic results. The flask remains hot for some time. Dispose of the chemicals using correct procedures for your area.

DEMONSTRATION

Chemical versus Physical Change

Before class prepare a mixture of iron filings and sulfur. Show students that a mixture can be separated by physical means—in this case, by using a magnet to separate the iron filings from the sulfur. Place a small amount of the mixture in a test tube. Heat the tube in the flame of a Bunsen burner until it changes to a reddish brown color. Now show the students that the new compound, iron sulfide, cannot be separated into iron filings and sulfur by using a magnet.

PowerLecture Animation: Sea Life
PowerLecture Video: Separating Iron from Cereal Flakes

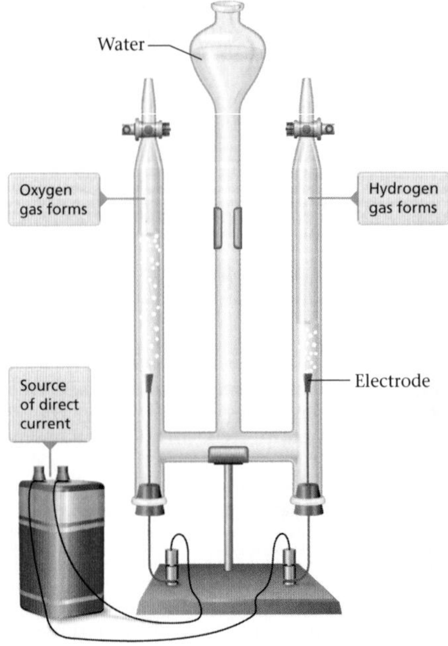

Figure 3.3
Electrolysis, the decomposition of water by an electric current, is a chemical process.

The most important thing about all these changes is that the water molecules are still intact. The motions of individual molecules and the distances between them change, but *H_2O molecules are still present.* These changes of state are **physical changes** because they do not affect the composition of the substance. In each state we still have water (H_2O), not some other substance.

Now suppose we run an electric current through water as illustrated in Figure 3.3. Something very different happens. The water disappears and is replaced by two new gaseous substances, hydrogen and oxygen. An electric current actually causes the water molecules to come apart—the water *decomposes* to hydrogen and oxygen. We can represent this process as follows:

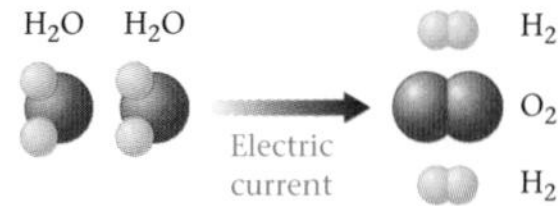

This is a **chemical change** because water (consisting of H_2O molecules) has changed into different substances: hydrogen (containing H_2 molecules) and oxygen (containing O_2 molecules). Thus in this process, the H_2O molecules have been replaced by O_2 and H_2 molecules. Let us summarize:

Physical and Chemical Changes

1. A *physical change* involves a change in one or more physical properties, but no change in the fundamental components that make up the substance. The most common physical changes are changes of state: solid ⇔ liquid ⇔ gas.
2. A *chemical change* involves a change in the fundamental components of the substance; a given substance changes into a different substance or substances. Chemical changes are called **reactions:** silver tarnishes by reacting with substances in the air; a plant forms a leaf by combining various substances from the air and soil; and so on.

EXAMPLE 3.2 Identifying Physical and Chemical Changes

Classify each of the following as a physical or a chemical change.

a. Iron metal is melted.

b. Iron combines with oxygen to form rust.

c. Wood burns in air.

d. A rock is broken into small pieces.

Jim Pickerell/Stock Connection

Oxygen combines with the chemicals in wood to produce flames. Is a physical or chemical change taking place?

SOLUTION

a. Melted iron is just liquid iron and could cool again to the solid state. This is a physical change.

b. When iron combines with oxygen, it forms a different substance (rust) that contains iron and oxygen. This is a chemical change because a different substance forms.

c. Wood burns to form different substances (as we will see later, they include carbon dioxide and water). After the fire, the wood is no longer in its original form. This is a chemical change.

d. When the rock is broken up, all the smaller pieces have the same composition as the whole rock. Each new piece differs from the original only in size and shape. This is a physical change.

Self-Check EXERCISE 3.2 Classify each of the following as a chemical change, a physical change, or a combination of the two.

a. Milk turns sour.

b. Wax is melted over a flame and then catches fire and burns.

See Problems 3.17 and 3.18. ■

3.3 Elements and Compounds

OBJECTIVE: To understand the definitions of elements and compounds.

Element: a substance that cannot be broken down into other substances by chemical methods.

As we examine the chemical changes of matter, we encounter a series of fundamental substances called **elements.** Elements cannot be broken down into other substances by chemical means. Examples of elements are iron,

Additional Examples

Example 3.2

Classify each of the following as a physical or chemical change.

1. You make scrambled eggs. — Chemical change
2. You step on and crush a piece of chalk. — Physical change
3. You light a candle. — Chemical change
4. Steam from your shower condenses on the mirror. — Physical change

Self Check

Answers to Self-Check Exercise 3.2

a. Milk turns sour because new substances are formed. This is a chemical change.

b. Melting wax is a physical change (a change of state). When wax burns, new substances are formed. This is a chemical change.

 **Test Bank: 20–25, 40, 55**

Section 3.3

TEACHING TIP

Students should be able to draw atomic/molecular representations differentiating between the concepts of "element" and "compound." These representations should show that elements can be made of atoms or molecules, but compounds must consist of molecules (although table salt, for example, consists of NaCl "units," not molecules).

aluminum, oxygen, and hydrogen. All of the matter in the world around us contains elements. The elements sometimes are found in an isolated state, but more often they are combined with other elements. Most substances contain several elements combined together.

Compound: a substance composed of a given combination of elements that can be broken down into those elements by chemical methods.

The atoms of certain elements have special affinities for each other. They bind together in special ways to form **compounds,** substances that have the same composition no matter where we find them. Because compounds are made of elements, they can be broken down into elements through chemical changes:

Compounds ⇨ Elements
Chemical changes

Water is an example of a compound. Pure water always has the same composition (the same relative amounts of hydrogen and oxygen) because it consists of H_2O molecules. Water can be broken down into the elements hydrogen and oxygen by chemical means, such as by the use of an electric current (see Figure 3.3).

PowerLecture Animation: Water Droplet/Molecules

As we will discuss in more detail in Chapter 4, each element is made up of a particular kind of atom: a pure sample of the element aluminum contains only aluminum atoms, elemental copper contains only copper atoms, and so on. Thus an element contains only one kind of atom; a sample of iron contains many atoms, but they are all iron atoms. Samples of certain pure elements do contain molecules; for example, hydrogen gas contains H—H (usually written H_2) molecules, and oxygen gas contains O—O (O_2) molecules. However, any pure sample of an element contains only atoms of that element, *never* any atoms of any other element.

A compound *always* contains atoms of *different* elements. For example, water contains hydrogen atoms and oxygen atoms, and there are always exactly twice as many hydrogen atoms as oxygen atoms because water consists of H—O—H molecules. A different compound, carbon dioxide, consists of CO_2 molecules and so contains carbon atoms and oxygen atoms (always in the ratio 1:2).

Test Bank: 26–36, 41–43, 54

A compound, although it contains more than one type of atom, *always has the same composition*—that is, the same combination of atoms. The properties of a compound are typically very different from those of the elements it contains. For example, the properties of water are quite different from the properties of pure hydrogen and pure oxygen.

Section 3.4

3.4 Mixtures and Pure Substances

OBJECTIVE: To learn to distinguish between mixtures and pure substances.

TEACHING TIPS

- Students should be able to draw atomic/molecular representations differentiating between the concepts of "mixture" and "pure substance." These representations should show the difference between a "homogeneous mixture" and a "heterogeneous mixture." Students can often cite the definitions, but do not have a clear picture of what such mixtures look like at an atomic level.
- Packaged food items provide familiar examples of mixtures (such as dry cake mixtures). Bring in a few examples. You can use the labels on these items when studying nomenclature in Chapter 5.

Virtually all of the matter around us consists of mixtures of substances. For example, if you closely observe a sample of soil, you will see that it has many types of components, including tiny grains of sand and remnants of plants. The air we breathe is a complex mixture of such gases as oxygen, nitrogen, carbon dioxide, and water vapor. Even the sparkling water from a drinking fountain contains many substances besides water.

A **mixture** can be defined as something that has variable composition. For example, wood is a mixture (its composition varies greatly depending on the tree from which it originates); wine is a mixture (it can be red or pale yellow, sweet or dry); coffee is a mixture (it can be strong, weak, or bitter); and, although it looks very pure, water pumped from deep in the earth is a mixture (it contains dissolved minerals and gases).

PowerLecture Video: Comparison of a Compound and a Mixture

CHEMISTRY IN FOCUS

Concrete—An Ancient Material Made New

Concrete, which was invented more than 2000 years ago by the ancient Romans, is being transformed into a high-tech building material through the use of our knowledge of chemistry. There is little doubt that concrete is the world's most important material. It is used to construct highways, bridges, buildings, floors, countertops, and countless other objects. In its simplest form concrete consists of about 70% sand and gravel, 15% water, and 15% cement (a mixture prepared by heating and grinding limestone, clay, shale, and gypsum). Because concrete forms the skeleton of much of our society, improvements to make it last longer and perform better are crucial.

One new type of concrete is Ductal, which was developed by the French company Lafarge. Unlike traditional concrete, which is brittle and can rupture suddenly under a heavy load, Ductal can bend. Even better, Ductal is five times stronger than traditional concrete. The secret behind Ductal's near-magical properties lies in the addition of small steel or polymeric fibers, which are dispersed throughout the structure. The fibers eliminate the need for steel reinforcing bars (rebar) for structures such as bridges. Bridges built of Ductal are lighter, thinner, and much more corrosion resistant than bridges built with traditional concrete containing rebar.

In another innovation, the Hungarian company Litracon has developed a translucent concrete material by incorporating optical fibers of various diameters into the concrete. With this light-transmitting concrete, architects can design buildings with translucent concrete walls and concrete floors that can be lighted from below.

Another type of concrete being developed by the Italian company Italcementi Group has a self-cleaning surface. This new material is made by mixing titanium oxide particles into the concrete. Titanium oxide can absorb ultraviolet light and promote the decomposition of pollutants that would otherwise darken the surface of the building. This material has already been used for several buildings in Italy. One additional bonus of using this material for buildings and roads in cities is that it may actually act to reduce air pollution very significantly.

Concrete is an ancient material, but one that is showing the flexibility to be a high-tech material. Its adaptability will ensure that it finds valuable uses far into the future.

An object made of translucent concrete.

A **pure substance,** on the other hand, will always have the same composition. Pure substances are either elements or compounds. For example, pure water is a compound containing individual H_2O molecules. However, as we find it in nature, liquid water always contains other substances in addition to pure water—it is a mixture. This is obvious from the different tastes, smells, and colors of water samples obtained from various locations. However, if we take great pains to purify samples of water from various sources (such as oceans, lakes, rivers, and the earth's interior), we always end up with the same pure substance—water, which is made up only of H_2O molecules. Pure water always has the same physical and chemical properties

MISCONCEPTION

Students often confuse mixtures and compounds. It is important to emphasize a molecular-level view. Instead of having students memorizing definitions of "mixture" and "compound," have them show you the difference at a molecular level.

Although we say we can separate mixtures into pure substances, it is virtually impossible to separate mixtures into totally pure substances. No matter how hard we try, some impurities (components of the original mixture) remain in each of the "pure substances."

and is always made of molecules containing hydrogen and oxygen in exactly the same proportions, regardless of the original source of the water. The properties of a pure substance make it possible to identify that substance conclusively.

Mixtures can be separated into pure substances: elements and/or compounds.

Mixtures  Two or more pure substances

For example, the mixture known as air can be separated into oxygen (element), nitrogen (element), water (compound), carbon dioxide (compound), argon (element), and other pure substances.

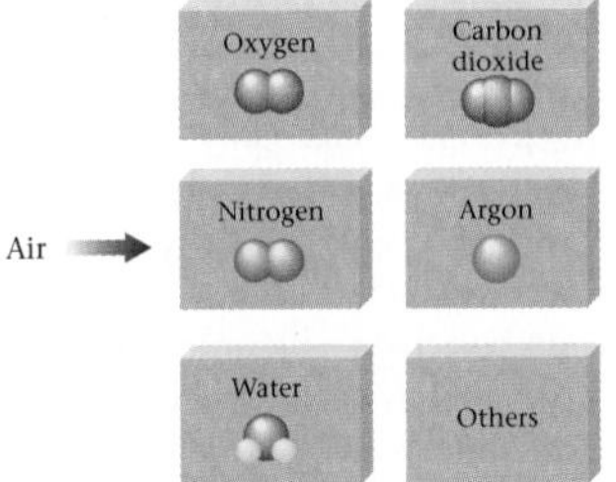

PowerLecture Video: Homogeneous Mixtures: Air and Brass

A solution is a homogeneous mixture.

Mixtures can be classified as either homogeneous or heterogeneous. A **homogeneous mixture** is *the same throughout*. For example, when we dissolve some salt in water and stir well, all regions of the resulting mixture have the same properties. A homogeneous mixture is also called a **solution.** Of course, different amounts of salt and water can be mixed to form various solutions, but a homogeneous mixture (a solution) does not vary in composition from one region to another (see Figure 3.4).

TEACHING TIP

Discuss the difference between mixtures and compounds by using a cooking analogy. Just as a mixture of hydrogen (H_2) and oxygen (O_2) is not the same as water (H_2O), so a mixture of eggs, flour, sugar, and milk is not a cake. Only when the ingredients react do we get a cake.

Richard Megna/Fundamental Photographs

Figure 3.4
When table salt is stirred into water *(left)*, a homogeneous mixture called a solution forms *(right)*.

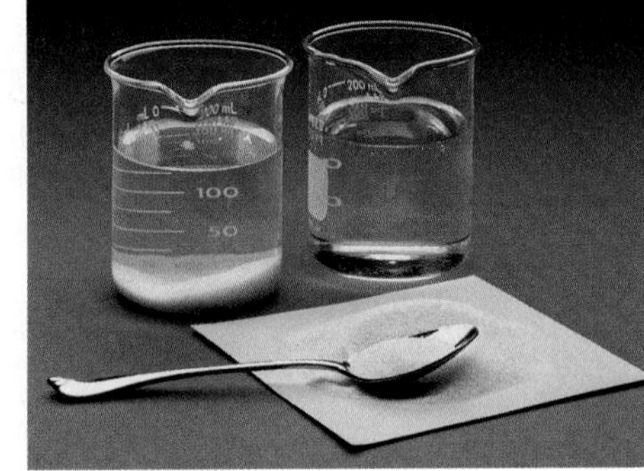

Figure 3.5
Sand and water do not mix to form a uniform mixture. After the mixture is stirred, the sand settles back to the bottom.

Coffee is a solution that has variable composition. It can be strong or weak.

The air around you is a solution—it is a homogeneous mixture of gases. Solid solutions also exist. Brass is a homogeneous mixture of the metals copper and zinc.

A **heterogeneous mixture** contains regions that have different properties from those of other regions. For example, when we pour sand into water, the resulting mixture has one region containing water and another, very different region containing mostly sand (see Figure 3.5).

EXAMPLE 3.3 Distinguishing Between Mixtures and Pure Substances

Identify each of the following as a pure substance, a homogeneous mixture, or a heterogeneous mixture.

a. gasoline
b. a stream with gravel at the bottom
c. air
d. brass
e. copper metal

SOLUTION

a. Gasoline is a homogeneous mixture containing many compounds.
b. A stream with gravel on the bottom is a heterogeneous mixture.
c. Air is a homogeneous mixture of elements and compounds.
d. Brass is a homogeneous mixture containing the elements copper and zinc. Brass is not a pure substance because the relative amounts of copper and zinc are different in different brass samples.
e. Copper metal is a pure substance (an element).

Self-Check **EXERCISE 3.3** Classify each of the following as a pure substance, a homogeneous mixture, or a heterogeneous mixture.

a. maple syrup
b. the oxygen and helium in a scuba tank
c. oil and vinegar salad dressing
d. common salt (sodium chloride)

See Problems 3.29 through 3.31. ■

3.5 Separation of Mixtures

OBJECTIVE: To learn two methods of separating mixtures.

We have seen that the matter found in nature is typically a mixture of pure substances. For example, seawater is water containing dissolved minerals. We can separate the water from the minerals by boiling, which changes the water to steam (gaseous water) and leaves the minerals behind as solids. If we collect and cool the steam, it condenses to pure water. This separation process, called **distillation,** is shown in Figure 3.6.

When we carry out the distillation of salt water, water is changed from the liquid state to the gaseous state and then back to the liquid state. These

The separation of a mixture sometimes occurs in the natural environment and can be to our benefit (see photo on p. 66).

Self Check

Answers to Self-Check Exercise 3.3

a. Maple syrup is a homogeneous mixture of sugar and other substances dispersed uniformly in water.

b. Helium and oxygen form a homogeneous mixture.

c. Oil and vinegar salad dressing is a heterogeneous mixture.

d. Common salt (sodium chloride) is a pure substance, so it always has the same composition. (Commercial iodized salt has iodine added to it and so would be a homogeneous mixture.)

Section 3.5

LABORATORY EXPERIMENT

Relevant laboratory experiments for this section are Experiment 4, Recrystallization and Melting Point Determination; Experiment 6, Simple Distillation; Experiment 7, Properties of Some Representative Elements; and Experiment 8, Thin-Layer Chromatography; from *Introductory Chemistry in the Laboratory* by James Hall. Experiment 7 could also be used during study of Section 4.8.

Additional Examples

Example 3.3

Identify each of the following as a pure substance, a homogeneous mixture, or a heterogeneous mixture.

1. "pure" apple juice — Homogeneous mixture
2. table salt — Pure substance
3. chocolate chip cookies — Heterogeneous mixture

Test Bank: 37, 38

Lecture Demonstration: 1.17

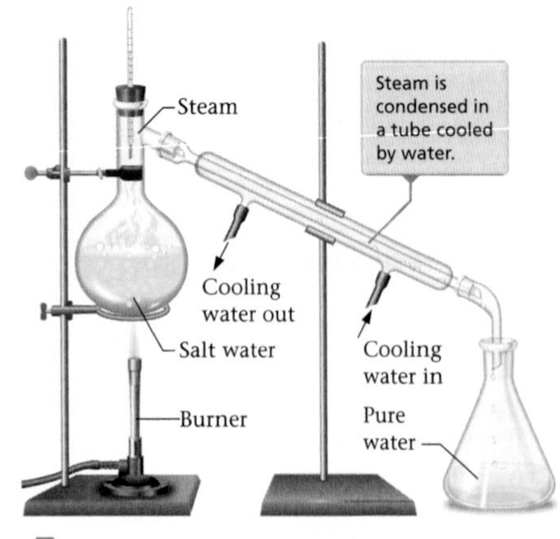

a

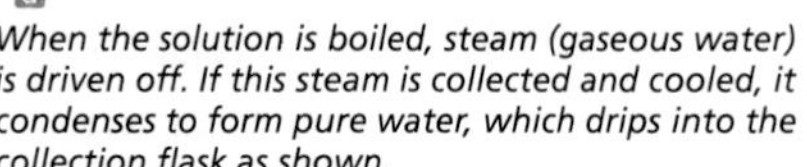
When the solution is boiled, steam (gaseous water) is driven off. If this steam is collected and cooled, it condenses to form pure water, which drips into the collection flask as shown.

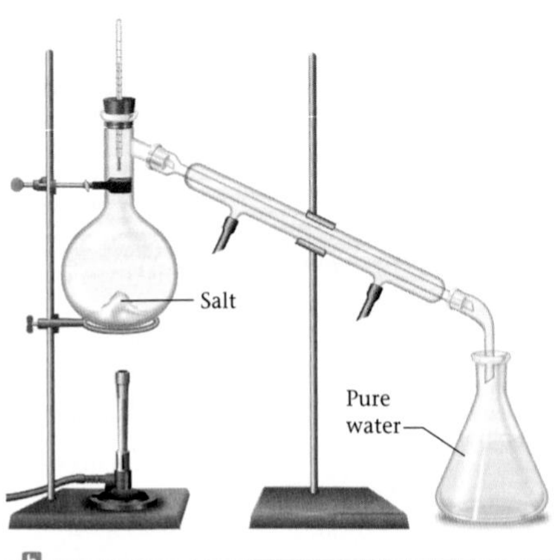

b

After all of the water has been boiled off, the salt remains in the original flask and the water is in the collection flask.

Figure 3.6
Distillation of a solution consisting of salt dissolved in water.

changes of state are examples of physical changes. We are separating a mixture of substances, but we are not changing the composition of the individual substances. We can represent this as shown in Figure 3.7.

Suppose we scooped up some sand with our sample of seawater. This sample is a heterogeneous mixture, because it contains an undissolved solid as well as the saltwater solution. We can separate out the sand by simple **filtration.** We pour the mixture onto a mesh, such as a filter paper, which allows the liquid to pass through and leaves the solid behind (see Figure 3.8). The salt can then be separated from the water by distillation. The total separation process is represented in Figure 3.9. All the changes involved are physical changes.

We can summarize the description of matter given in this chapter with the diagram shown in Figure 3.10. Note that a given sample of matter can be a pure substance (either an element or a compound) or, more commonly, a mixture (homogeneous or heterogeneous). We have seen that all matter exists as elements or can be broken down into elements, the most fundamental substances we have encountered up to this point. We will have more to say about the nature of elements in the next chapter.

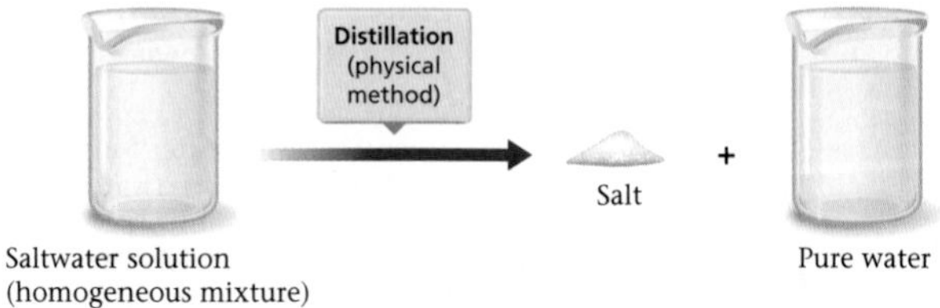

Figure 3.7
No chemical change occurs when salt water is distilled.

TEACHING SUPPORT

DEMONSTRATION

Simple Distillation

Materials

Distillation setup (Figure 3.6)

50 mL 0.1 M $CuSO_4$ solution

Procedure Place the copper sulfate solution in the flask over the burner. Begin heating the system. Be sure the condenser has water running through it. After some time elapses and the copper sulfate solution is boiling gently, point out that the liquid collecting in the receiver flask is colorless. The blue color remains in the original flask. The water in the solution is turning to steam and then condensing and collecting in the receiving flask. If all of the water is boiled off (do not do this—it takes too long and you may crack the flask), only crystals of copper sulfate will remain.

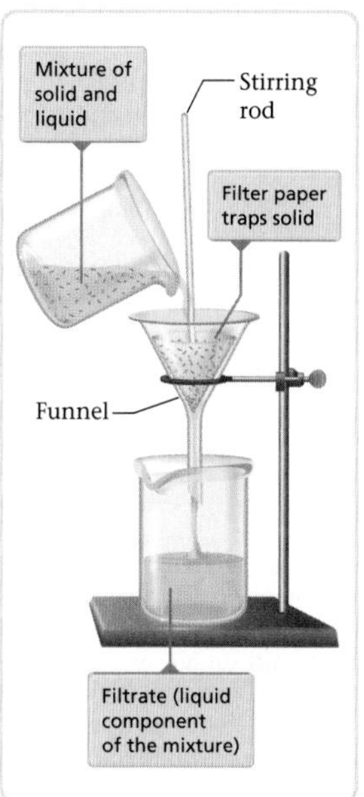

Figure 3.8
Filtration separates a liquid from a solid. The liquid passes through the filter paper, but the solid particles are trapped.

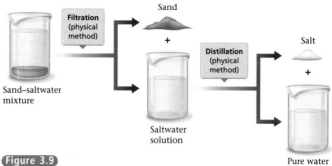

Figure 3.9
Separation of a sand–saltwater mixture.

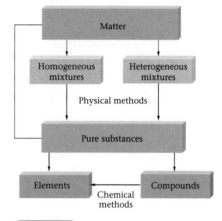

Figure 3.10
The organization of matter.

TEACHING TIP

Although we can separate mixtures into pure substances, it is virtually impossible to separate mixtures into *totally* pure substances. No matter how hard we try, some impurities remain in each of the "pure substances."

PowerLecture Video: Separation of Water, Sand, and Copper Sulfate

PowerLecture Video: Paper Chromatography of Ink

CHAPTER 3 REVIEW

Key Terms

matter (3.1)
states of matter (3.1)
solid (3.1)
liquid (3.1)
gas (3.1)
physical properties (3.2)
chemical properties (3.2)
physical change (3.2)
chemical change (3.2)
reaction (3.2)
element (3.3)
compound (3.3)
mixture (3.4)
pure substance (3.4)
homogeneous mixture (3.4)
solution (3.4)
heterogeneous mixture (3.4)
distillation (3.5)
filtration (3.5)

ChemWork

Identifying Isotopes
Comparing Number of Hydrogen Atoms
Determining Moles of a Compound
Molar Mass
Molecular Stoichiometry
Moles of a Compound
Stoichiometry Conversions
Calculating Percent Composition
Comparing Atoms of Different Elements
Percent Composition
Percent Composition for Polyatomic Salts
Burning Glucose
Empirical and Molecular Formulas
Balancing Chemical Equations
Characteristics of Chemical Equations
Burning Pentane
Finding the Amount of Compound in an Impure Sample
Finding the Mass of Lithium Carbonate
Thermite Stoichiometry
Finding Maximum Moles of Product
Formation of Sodium Amide
Formation of Sodium Sulfite
Making Acrylonitrile
Nylon Stoichiometry

F directs you to the *Chemistry in Focus* feature in the chapter
VP indicates visual problems
OWL interactive versions of these problems are assignable in OWL.

Summary

1. Matter can exist in three states—solid, liquid, and gas—and can be described in terms of its physical and chemical properties. Chemical properties describe a substance's ability to undergo a change to a different substance. Physical properties are the characteristics a substance exhibits as long as no chemical change occurs.
2. A physical change involves a change in one or more physical properties, but no change in composition. A chemical change transforms a substance into a new substance or substances.
3. A mixture has variable composition. A homogeneous mixture has the same properties throughout; a heterogeneous mixture does not. A pure substance always has the same composition. We can physically separate mixtures of pure substances by distillation and filtration.
4. Pure substances are of two types: elements, which cannot be broken down chemically into simpler substances, and compounds, which can be broken down chemically into elements.

Active Learning Questions

These questions are designed to be considered by groups of students in class. Often these questions work well for introducing a particular topic in class.

1. When water boils, you can see bubbles rising to the surface of the water. Of what are these bubbles made?
   a. air
   b. hydrogen and oxygen gas
   c. oxygen gas
   d. water vapor
   e. carbon dioxide gas
2. If you place a glass rod over a burning candle, the glass turns black. What is happening to each of the following (physical change, chemical change, both, or neither) as the candle burns? Explain.
   a. the wax
   b. the wick
   c. the glass rod
3. The boiling of water is a
   a. physical change because the water disappears.
   b. physical change because the gaseous water is chemically the same as the liquid.
   c. chemical change because heat is needed for the process to occur.
   d. chemical change because hydrogen and oxygen gases are formed from water.
   e. chemical and physical change.

   Explain your answer.
4. Is there a difference between a homogeneous mixture of hydrogen and oxygen in a 2:1 ratio and a sample of water vapor? Explain.
5. Sketch a magnified view (showing atoms and/or molecules) of each of the following and explain why the specified type of mixture is
   a. a heterogeneous mixture of two different compounds
   b. a homogeneous mixture of an element and a compound
6. Are all physical changes accompanied by chemical changes? Are all chemical changes accompanied by physical changes? Explain.
7. Why would a chemist find fault with the phrase "pure orange juice"?
8. Are separations of mixtures physical or chemical changes? Explain.
9. Explain the terms *element, atom,* and *compound.* Provide an example and microscopic drawing of each.
10. Mixtures can be classified as either homogeneous or heterogeneous. Compounds cannot be classified in this way. Why not? In your answer, explain what is meant by heterogeneous and homogeneous.
11. Provide microscopic drawings down to the atoms for Figure 3.10 in your text.
12. Look at Table 2.8 in your text. How do the densities of gases, liquids, and solids compare to each other? Use microscopic pictures to explain why this is true.

VP 13. Label each of the following as an atomic element, a molecular element, or a compound.

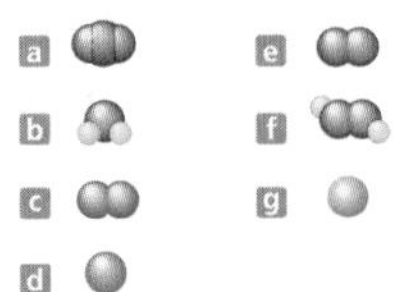

VP 14. Match each description below with the following microscopic pictures. More than one picture may fit each description. A picture may be used more than once or not used at all.

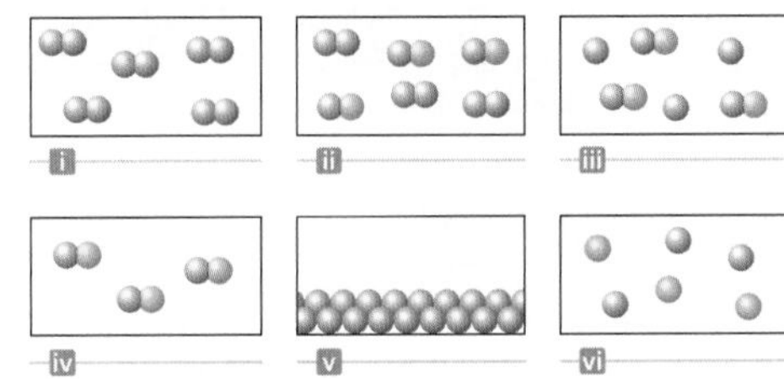

a. a gaseous compound
b. a mixture of two gaseous elements
c. a solid element
d. a mixture of gaseous element and a gaseous compound

Questions and Problems

3.1 Matter

QUESTIONS

1. What are the two characteristic properties of *matter?*
2. What is the chief factor that determines the *physical state* of a sample of matter?
3. Of the three states of matter, ______ and ______ are not very compressible.
4. Gases and ______ take on the shape of the container in which they are located.
5. Compare and contrast the ease with which molecules are able to move relative to each other in the three states of matter.
6. Matter in the ______ state has no shape and fills completely whatever container holds it.
7. What similarities are there between the liquid and gaseous states of matter? What differences are there between these two states?
8. A sample of matter that is "rigid" has (stronger/weaker) forces among the particles in the sample than does a sample that is not rigid.
9. Consider three 10-g samples of water: one as ice, one as liquid, and one as vapor. How do the volumes of these three samples compare with one another? How is this difference in volume related to the physical state involved?
10. In a sample of a gaseous substance, more than 99% of the overall volume of the sample is empty space. How is this fact reflected in the properties of a gaseous substance, compared with the properties of a liquid or solid substance?

3.2 Physical and Chemical Properties and Changes

QUESTIONS

11. Elemental bromine is a dense, dark-red, pungent-smelling liquid. Are these characteristics of elemental bromine physical or chemical properties?
12. Elemental bromine reacts vigorously with elemental sodium metal to form a white solid. Does this characteristic of elemental bromine represent a physical or a chemical property?

(For Exercises 13–14) Magnesium metal is very malleable, and is able to be pounded and stretched into long, thin, narrow "ribbons" that are often used in the introductory chemistry lab as a source of the metal. If a strip of magnesium ribbon is ignited in a Bunsen burner flame, the magnesium burns brightly and produces a quantity of white magnesium oxide powder.

13. From the information given above, indicate one *chemical* property of magnesium metal.
14. From the information given above, indicate one *physical* property of magnesium metal.
15. Choose a chemical substance with which you are familiar, and give an example of a *chemical change* that might take place to the substance.
16. Which of the following does *not* represent a physical property/change?
    a. Elemental sulfur boils at 445 °C.
    b. Elemental sulfur is yellow in its most common form.
    c. Elemental sulfur burns with a dark blue flame in the air to form a gaseous material.
    d. Elemental sulfur is rigid and hard.
17. Classify each of the following as a *physical* or *chemical* change or property.
    a. Oven cleaners contain sodium hydroxide, which converts the grease/oil spatters inside the oven to water-soluble materials, which can be washed away.
    b. A rubber band stretches when you pull on it.
    c. A cast-iron frying pan will rust if it is not dried after washing.
    d. Concentrated hydrochloric acid has a choking, pungent odor.
    e. Concentrated hydrochloric acid will burn a hole in cotton jeans because the acid breaks down the cellulose fibers in cotton.
    f. Copper compounds often form beautiful blue crystals when a solution of a given copper compound is evaporated slowly.
    g. Copper metal combines with substances in the air to form a green "patina" that protects the copper from further reaction.
    h. Bread turns brown when you heat it in a toaster.
    i. When you use the perfume your boyfriend gave you for your birthday, the liquid of the perfume evaporates quickly from your skin.
    j. If you leave your steak on the gas grill too long, the steak will turn black and char.
    k. Hydrogen peroxide fizzes when it is applied to a cut or scrape.
18. Classify each of the following as a *physical* or *chemical* change or property.
    a. A fireplace poker glows red when you heat it in the fire.
    b. A marshmallow turns black when toasted too long in a campfire.
    c. Hydrogen peroxide dental strips will make your teeth whiter.
    d. If you wash your jeans with chlorine bleach, they will fade.
    e. If you spill some nail polish remover on your skin, it will evaporate quickly.
    f. When making ice cream at home, salt is added to lower the temperature of the ice being used to freeze the mixture.
    g. A hair clog in your bathroom sink drain can be cleared with drain cleaner.

All even-numbered Questions and Problems have answers in the back of this book and solutions in the Solutions Guide.

Answers to End-of-Chapter Exercises

1. has mass; occupies space

2. forces among the particles in the matter

3. liquids; solids

4. liquids

5. In solids, molecular motion is very restricted; in gases, molecular motion is very free and random; in liquids, the motion is greater than that in solids but less than that in gases.

6. gaseous

7. Liquids and gases both have no rigid shape and take on the shape of the container. Liquids are essentially incompressible; gases are readily compressible.

8. stronger

9. The gaseous sample has a much larger volume than either the solid or the liquid. Although all three samples contain the same number of molecules, there is a great deal of empty space in the gaseous sample.

10. Because gases are mostly empty space, they can be *compressed* easily to smaller volumes. In solids and liquids, most of the sample's bulk volume is filled with the molecules, leaving little empty space.

11. physical

12. chemical

13. magnesium burns

14. malleable, ductile

15. The answer depends on the student's selection of a substance.

16. c

17. (a) chemical; (b) physical; (c) chemical; (d) physical; (e) chemical; (f) physical; (g) chemical; (h) chemical; (i) physical; (j) chemical; (k) chemical

18. (a) physical; (b) chemical; (c) chemical; (d) chemical; (e) physical; (f) physical; (g) chemical; (h) physical; (i) physical; (j) physical; (k) chemical

19. compounds

20. Compounds consist of two or more elements combined together chemically in a fixed composition, no matter what their source may be. For example, water on earth consists of molecules containing one oxygen atom and two hydrogen atoms. Water on Mars (or any other planet) has the same composition.

21. compounds

22. compounds

23. the same/identical/constant

24. In general, the properties of a compound are very different from the properties of its constituent elements. For example, the properties of water are altogether different from the properties of the elements (hydrogen gas and oxygen gas) that make it up.

25. mixture

26. no; heating causes a reaction to form iron(II) sulfide, a pure substance

27. *Homogeneous* means there are no variations in composition in different areas of the mixture.

28. Heterogeneous mixtures: salad dressing, jelly beans, the change in my pocket; solutions: window cleaner, shampoo, rubbing alcohol

29. (a) mixture; (b) mixture; (c) relatively pure substance; (d) mixture

30. (a) primarily a pure compound, but fillers and anti-caking agents may have been added; (b) mixture; (c) mixture; (d) pure substance

31. (a) heterogeneous; (b) more or less homogeneous; (c) heterogeneous; (d) heterogeneous; (e) heterogeneous

32. Concrete is a mixture. It consists of sand, gravel, water, and cement (which consists of limestone, clay, shale, and gypsum). The composition of concrete can vary.

h. The perfume your boyfriend gave you for your birthday smells like flowers.
i. Mothballs pass directly into the gaseous state in your closet without first melting.
j. A log of wood is chopped up with an axe into smaller pieces of wood.
k. A log of wood is burned in a fireplace.

3.3 Elements and Compounds

QUESTIONS

19. Although some elements are found in an isolated state, most elements are found combined as ______ with other elements.

20. What is a *compound?* What are compounds composed of? What is true about the composition of a compound, no matter where we happen to find the compound?

21. Certain elements have special affinities for other elements. This causes them to bind together in special ways to form ______ .

22. ______ can be broken down into the component elements by chemical changes.

23. The composition of a given pure compound is always ______ no matter what the source of the compound.

24. How do the properties of a compound, in general, compare to the properties of the elements that constitute it? Give an example of a common compound and the elements of which it is composed to illustrate your answer.

3.4 Mixtures and Pure Substances

QUESTIONS

25. If iron filings are placed with excess powdered sulfur in a beaker, the iron filings are still attracted by a magnet and could be separated from the sulfur with the magnet. Would this combination of iron and sulfur represent a *mixture* or a *pure substance?*

26. If the combination of iron filings and sulfur in Question 25 is heated strongly, the iron reacts with the sulfur to form a solid that is no longer attracted by the magnet. Would this still represent a "mixture?" Why or why not?

27. What does it mean to say that a solution is a *homogeneous mixture?*

28. Give three examples of heterogeneous *mixtures* and three examples of *solutions* that you might use in everyday life.

29. Classify the following as *mixtures* or *pure substances.*
a. the vegetable soup you had for lunch
b. the fertilizer your dad spreads on the front lawn in the spring
c. the salt you sprinkle on your French fries
d. the hydrogen peroxide you cleaned a cut finger with

30. Classify the following as *mixtures* or *pure substances.*
a. the sugar you just put into your coffee while studying
b. the perfume you dab on before you go on a date
c. the black pepper you grind onto your salad at dinner
d. the distilled water you use in your iron so it won't get clogged

31. Classify the following mixtures as *heterogeneous* or *homogeneous.*
a. soil
b. mayonnaise
c. Italian salad dressing
d. the wood from which the desk you are studying on is made
e. sand at the beach

F 32. Read the "Chemistry in Focus" segment *Concrete—An Ancient Material Made New* and classify concrete as an element, a mixture, or a compound. Defend your answer.

3.5 Separation of Mixtures

QUESTIONS

33. Describe how the process of *distillation* could be used to separate a solution into its component substances. Give an example.

34. Describe how the process of *filtration* could be used to separate a mixture into its components. Give an example.

35. In a common laboratory experiment in general chemistry, students are asked to determine the relative amounts of benzoic acid and charcoal in a solid mixture. Benzoic acid is relatively soluble in hot water, but charcoal is not. Devise a method for separating the two components of this mixture.

36. During a filtration or distillation experiment, we separate a mixture into its individual components. Do the chemical identities of the components of the mixture change during such a process? Explain.

Additional Problems

37. If powdered elemental zinc and powdered elemental sulfur are poured into a metal beaker and then heated strongly, a very vigorous chemical reaction takes place, and the ______ zinc sulfide is formed.

38. Pure substance X is melted, and the liquid is placed in an electrolysis apparatus such as that shown in Figure 3.3. When an electric current is passed through the liquid, a brown solid forms in one chamber and a white solid forms in the other chamber. Is substance X a compound or an element?

All even-numbered Questions and Problems have answers in the back of this book and solutions in the Solutions Guide.

33. Consider a solution of salt in water. Because water boils at a much lower temperature than sodium chloride does, the water can be boiled off, and the steam can be collected and condensed. This procedure separates the two substances.

34. Consider a mixture of salt (sodium chloride) and sand. Salt is soluble in water; sand is not. The mixture is added to water and stirred to dissolve the salt, and is then filtered. The salt solution passes through the filter; the sand remains on the filter. The water can then be evaporated from the salt.

35. Add water to the sample and heat to boiling; this should dissolve the benzoic acid but not the charcoal. Filter to remove the charcoal, and then cool the filtrate to crystallize the benzoic acid.

36. Each component of the mixture retains its own identity during the separation.

37. compound

38. compound

39. compound; loses mass when heated; change in physical properties

39. If a piece of hard white blackboard chalk is heated strongly in a flame, the mass of the piece of chalk will decrease, and eventually the chalk will crumble into a fine white dust. Does this change suggest that the chalk is composed of an element or a compound?

40. During a very cold winter, the temperature may remain below freezing for extended periods. However, fallen snow can still disappear, even though it cannot melt. This is possible because a solid can vaporize directly, without passing through the liquid state. Is this process (sublimation) a physical or a chemical change?

41. Discuss the similarities and differences between a liquid and a gas.

42. In gaseous substances, the individual molecules are relatively (close/far apart) and are moving freely, rapidly, and randomly.

43. The fact that solutions of potassium chromate are bright yellow is an example of a ______ property.

44. The fact that the substance copper(II) sulfate pentahydrate combines with ammonia in solution to form a new compound is an example of a ______ property.

(For Exercises 45–46) Solutions containing nickel(II) ion are usually bright green in color. When potassium hydroxide is added to such a nickel(II) solution, a pale-green fluffy solid forms and settles out of the solution.

45. The fact that a reaction takes place when potassium hydroxide is added to a solution of nickel(II) ions is an example of a ______ property.

46. The fact that a solution of nickel(II) ion is bright green is an example of a ______ property.

47. The processes of melting and evaporation involve changes in the ______ of a substance.

48. ______ is the process of making a chemical reaction take place by passage of an electric current through a substance or solution.

49. Classify each of the following as a *physical* or *chemical* change or property.

a. Milk curdles if a few drops of lemon juice are added to it.
b. Butter turns rancid if it is left exposed at room temperature.
c. Salad dressing separates into layers after standing.
d. Milk of magnesia neutralizes stomach acid.
e. The steel in a car has rust spots.
f. A person is asphyxiated by breathing carbon monoxide.
g. Sulfuric acid spilled on a laboratory notebook page causes the paper to char and disintegrate.
h. Sweat cools the body as the sweat evaporates from the skin.
i. Aspirin reduces fever.
j. Oil feels slippery.
k. Alcohol burns, forming carbon dioxide and water.

50. Classify the following mixtures as *homogeneous* or *heterogeneous*.

a. the freshman class at your school
b. salsa
c. mashed potatoes
d. cream of tomato soup
e. cream of mushroom soup

51. Classify the following mixtures as *homogeneous* or *heterogeneous*.

a. potting soil
b. white wine
c. your sock drawer
d. window glass
e. granite

52. Mixtures can be heterogeneous or homogeneous. Give two examples of each type. Explain why you classified each example as you did.

53. Give three examples each of *heterogeneous* mixtures and *homogeneous* mixtures.

54. The fact that water freezes at 0 °C is an example of a ______ property, whereas the fact that water can be broken down by electricity into hydrogen gas and oxygen gas is a ______ property.

55. Choose an element or compound with which you are familiar in everyday life. Give two *physical* properties and two *chemical* properties of your choice of element or compound.

56. Oxygen forms molecules in which there are two oxygen atoms, O_2. Phosphorus forms molecules in which there are four phosphorus atoms, P_4. Does this mean that O_2 and P_4 are "compounds" because they contain multiple atoms? O_2 and P_4 react with each other to form diphosphorus pentoxide, P_2O_5. Is P_2O_5 a "compound"? Why (or why not)?

57. Give an example of each of the following:

a. a heterogeneous mixture
b. a homogeneous mixture
c. an element
d. a compound
e. a physical property or change
f. a chemical property or change
g. a solution

58. Distillation and filtration are important methods for separating the components of mixtures. Suppose we had a mixture of sand, salt, and water. Describe how filtration and distillation could be used sequentially to separate this mixture into the three separate components.

59. Sketch the apparatus commonly used for simple distillation in the laboratory and identify each component.

60. The properties of a compound are often very different from the properties of the elements making up the compound. Water is an excellent example of this idea. Discuss.

All even-numbered Questions and Problems have answers in the back of this book and solutions in the Solutions Guide.

50. (a) heterogeneous; (b) heterogeneous; (c) homogeneous (if no lumps!); (d) heterogeneous (although it may appear homogeneous); (e) heterogeneous

51. (a) heterogeneous; (b) homogeneous; (c) heterogeneous; (d) homogeneous; (e) heterogeneous

52. Answers depend on student responses.

53. Answer depends on student choices/examples.

54. physical, chemical

55. Answer depends on student choice/example.

56. O_2 and P_4 are both still elements, even though the ordinary forms of these elements consist of molecules containing more than one atom (but all atoms in each respective molecule are the same). P_2O_5 is a compound, because it is made up of two or more different elements (not all the atoms in the P_2O_5 molecule are the same).

57. Answers will depend on student responses.

58. Assuming there is enough water present in the mixture to have dissolved all the salt, filter the mixture to separate out the sand from the mixture. Then distill the filtrate (consisting of salt and water), which will boil off the water, leaving the salt.

59. See Figure 3.6.

60. The most obvious difference is the physical states: water is a liquid under room conditions, hydrogen and oxygen are both gases. Hydrogen is flammable. Oxygen supports combustion. Water does neither.

40. physical

41. Liquids and gases both flow freely and take on the shapes of their containers. The molecules in liquids are relatively close together and interact, whereas the molecules in gases are far apart from each other and do not interact.

42. far apart

43. physical

44. chemical

45. chemical

46. physical

47. state

48. electrolysis

49. (a) physical; (b) chemical; (c) physical; (d) chemical; (e) chemical; (f) chemical; (g) chemical; (h) physical; (i) chemical; (j) physical; (k) chemical

Answers to Cumulative Review Exercises

Chapters 1–3

1. Obviously, this answer depends on your own experiences in studying and learning about chemistry. We hope that by now you have at least gotten over any "fear" of chemistry that you had initially. Perhaps you have begun to appreciate why one leading chemical manufacturer has as its corporate slogan "better living through chemistry."

2. After having covered three chapters in this book, you should have adopted an "active" approach to your study of chemistry. You can't just sit and take notes in class, or just review the solved examples in the textbook. You must learn to *interpret* problems and reduce them to simple mathematical relationships.

3. The steps of the scientific method are as follows: (1) make observations of the system and state the problem clearly; (2) formulate an explanation or hypothesis to try to explain your observations; and (3) perform one or more experiments to test the validity of your hypothesis. For the case of the liquid material, we first have to state the problem: we have a sample of clear liquid that may be either a pure compound or a mixture, and we want to determine which it is. The liquid is completely homogeneous, so we can't tell anything just by looking at it.

CUMULATIVE REVIEW for CHAPTERS 1-3

QUESTIONS

1. In the exercises for Chapter 1 of this text, you were asked to give your *own* definition of what chemistry represents. After having completed a few more chapters in this book, has your definition changed? Do you have a better appreciation for what chemists do? Explain.
2. Early on in this text, some aspects of the best way to go about learning chemistry were presented. In *beginning* your study of chemistry, you may initially have approached studying chemistry as you would any of your other academic subjects (taking notes in class, reading the text, memorizing facts, and so on). Discuss why the ability to sort through and analyze facts and the ability to propose and solve problems are so much more important in learning chemistry.
3. You have learned the basic way in which scientists analyze problems, propose models to explain the systems under consideration, and then experiment to test their models. Suppose you have a sample of a liquid material. You are not sure whether the liquid is a pure *compound* (for example, water or alcohol) or a *solution*. How could you apply the scientific method to study the liquid and to determine which type of material the liquid is?
4. Many college students would not choose to take a chemistry course if it were not required for their major. Do you have a better appreciation of *why* chemistry is a required course for your own particular major or career choice? Discuss.
5. In Chapter 2 of this text, you were introduced to the International System (SI) of measurements. What are the basic units of this system for mass, distance, time, and temperature? What are some of the prefixes used to indicate common multiples and subdivisions of these basic units? Give three examples of the *use* of such prefixes, and explain why the prefix is appropriate to the quantity or measurement being indicated.
6. Most people think of science as being a specific, exact discipline, with a "correct" answer for every problem. Yet you were introduced to the concept of *uncertainty* in scientific measurements. What is meant by "uncertainty"? How does uncertainty creep into measurements? How is uncertainty *indicated* in scientific measurements? Can uncertainty ever be completely eliminated in experiments? Explain.
7. After studying a few chapters of this text, and perhaps having done a few lab experiments and taken a few quizzes in chemistry, you are probably sick of hearing the term *significant figures*. Most chemistry teachers make a big deal about significant figures. Why is reporting the correct number of significant figures so important in science? Summarize the rules for deciding whether a figure in a calculation is "significant." Summarize the rules for rounding off numbers. Summarize the rules for doing arithmetic with the correct number of significant figures.
8. This chemistry course may have been the first time you have encountered the method of *dimensional analysis* in problem solving. Explain what are meant by a *conversion factor* and an *equivalence statement*. Give an everyday example of how you might use dimensional analysis to solve a simple problem.
9. You have learned about several temperature scales so far in this text. Describe the Fahrenheit, Celsius, and Kelvin temperature scales. How are these scales defined? Why were they defined this way? Which of these temperature scales is the most fundamental? Why?
10. What is *matter?* What is matter composed of? What are some of the different types of matter? How do these types of matter differ and how are they the same?
11. It is important to be able to distinguish between the *physical* and the *chemical* properties of chemical substances. Choose a chemical substance you are familiar with, then use the Internet or a handbook of chemical information to list three physical properties and three chemical properties of the substance.
12. What is an *element* and what is a *compound?* Give examples of each. What does it mean to say that a compound has a *constant composition?* Would samples of a particular compound here and in another part of the world have the same composition and properties?
13. What is a mixture? What is a solution? How do mixtures differ from pure substances? What are some of the techniques by which mixtures can be resolved into their components?

PROBLEMS

14. For each of the following, make the indicated conversion.
    a. 0.0008917 to standard scientific notation
    b. 2.795×10^{-4} to ordinary decimal notation
    c. 4.913×10^{3} to ordinary decimal notation
    d. 85,100,000 to standard scientific notation
    e. $5.751 \times 10^{5} \times 2.119 \times 10^{-4}$ to standard scientific notation.
    f. $\dfrac{2.791 \times 10^{-5}}{8.219 \times 10^{3}}$
15. For each of the following, make the indicated conversion, showing explicitly the conversion factor(s) you used.
    a. 493.2 g to kilograms
    b. 493.2 g to pounds
    c. 9.312 mi to kilometers
    d. 9.312 mi to feet

72

If the unknown liquid is a mixture, we should be able to separate the components of the mixture by distillation (see Chapter 3). If the liquid is a mixture of two pure liquids, the liquids should boil at their characteristic temperatures during distillation. If the liquid is a solution of a solid material, then the liquid portion should boil off, leaving a solid residue behind. If the unknown liquid is a pure substance, rather than a mixture, it should boil away at a constant, uniform temperature. Let's hypothesize that the liquid is a mixture.

Now we perform the experiment: we begin heating the liquid in a distillation apparatus, monitoring the temperature with a thermometer. At 65 °C, the liquid begins to boil, and a clear, sweet-smelling liquid begins to collect in the receiving container. The temperature remains at 65 °C until approximately half the liquid has distilled, whereupon it rises suddenly to 100 °C. At this point, we change receiving flasks. The temperature remains at 100 °C until the remainder of the liquid boils. We notice that this second fraction of liquid collected has no odor.

e. 4.219 m to feet
f. 4.219 m to centimeters
g. 429.2 mL to liters
h. 2.934 L to quarts

16. Without performing the actual calculations, determine to how many significant figures the results of the following calculations should be reported.

a. $\frac{(2.991)(4.3785)(1.97)}{(2.1)}$
b. $\frac{(5.2)}{(1.9311 + 0.4297)}$
c. 1.782 + 0.00035 + 2.11
d. (6.521)(5.338 + 2.11)
e. 9 − 0.000017
f. (4.2005 + 2.7)(7.99118)
g. $(5.12941 \times 10^4)(4.91 \times 10^{-3})(0.15)$
h. 97.215 + 42.1 − 56.3498

17. Chapter 2 introduced the Kelvin and Celsius temperature scales and related them to the Fahrenheit temperature scale commonly used in the United States.

a. How is the size of the temperature unit (degree) related between the Kelvin and Celsius scale?
b. How does the size of the temperature unit (degree) on the Fahrenheit scale compare to the temperature unit on the Celsius scale?
c. What is the normal freezing point of water on each of the three temperature scales?
d. Convert 27.5 °C to kelvins and to Fahrenheit degrees.
e. Convert 298.1 K to Celsius degrees and to Fahrenheit degrees.
f. Convert 98.6 °F to kelvins and to Celsius degrees.

18. a. Given that 100. mL of ethyl alcohol weighs 78.5 g, calculate the density of ethyl alcohol.
b. What volume would 1.59 kg of ethyl alcohol occupy?
c. What is the mass of 1.35 L of ethyl alcohol?
d. Pure aluminum metal has a density of 2.70 g/cm^3. Calculate the volume of 25.2 g of pure aluminum.
e What will a rectangular block of pure aluminum having dimensions of 12.0 cm × 2.5 cm × 2.5 cm weigh?

19. Which of the following represent physical properties or changes, and which represent chemical properties or changes?

a. You curl your hair with a curling iron.
b. You curl your hair by getting a "permanent wave" at the hair salon.
c. Ice on your sidewalk melts when you put salt on it.
d. A glass of water evaporates overnight when it is left on the bedside table.
e. Your steak chars if the skillet is too hot.
f. Alcohol feels cool when it is spilled on the skin.
g. Alcohol ignites when a flame is brought near it.
h. Baking powder causes biscuits to rise.

Based on the observations that two separate fractions that had different boiling points were collected, and that only one of the fractions had a noticeable odor, we can conclude that our hypothesis that the unknown liquid was a mixture is correct.

4. Some courses, particularly those in your major field, have obvious and immediate utility. Other courses—chemistry included—provide general background knowledge that will prove useful in understanding your own major, or other subjects related to your major.

5. The basic units are mass, kilogram; distance, meter; time, second; temperature, Kelvin. Common prefixes used to indicate multiples of the basic units are milli-, 10^{-3}; centi-, 10^{-2}; deci-, 10^{-1}; kilo, 10^3; mega, 10^6; giga, 10^9. Examples depend on student choices.

6. Whenever a scientific measurement is made, we always employ the instrument or measuring device to the limits of its precision. This usually means that we *estimate* the last significant figure of the measurement. An example of the uncertainty in the last significant figure is given for measuring the length of a pin in the text in Figure 2.5. Scientists appreciate the limits of experimental techniques and instruments and always *assume* that the last digit in a number representing a measurement has been estimated. Because instruments or measuring devices always have a limit to their precision, uncertainty cannot be completely excluded from measurements.

(Please refer to p. A32 for answers to Exercises 7–19.)

4 Chemical Foundations: Elements, Atoms, and Ions

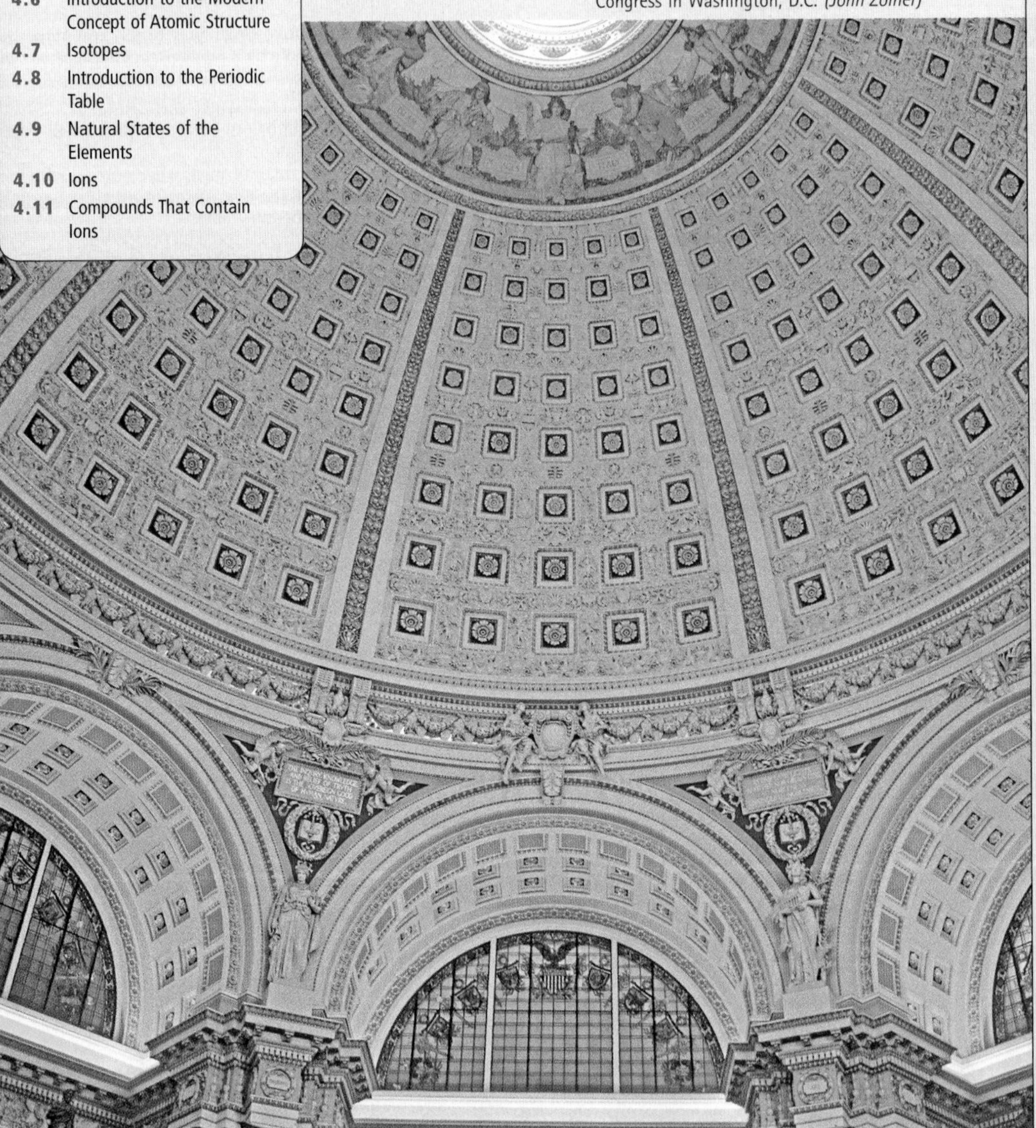

Gold leafing on the ceiling of the Library of Congress in Washington, D.C. *(John Zoiner)*

Chapter 4

Objectives

In this chapter, our objectives are for the students to:

SECTION 4.1

- Learn about the relative abundances of the elements.
- Learn the names of some elements.

SECTION 4.2

- Learn the symbols of some elements.

SECTION 4.3

- Learn about Dalton's theory of atoms.
- Understand and illustrate the law of constant composition.

SECTION 4.4

- Learn how a formula describes a compound's composition.

SECTION 4.5

- Learn about the internal parts of an atom.
- Understand Rutherford's experiment to characterize the atom's structure.

SECTION 4.6

- Understand some important features of subatomic particles.

SECTION 4.7

- Learn about the terms *isotope, atomic number, and mass number.*
- Understand the use of the symbol $^{A}_{Z}X$ to describe a given atom.

SECTION 4.8

- Learn about various features of the periodic table.
- Learn some of the properties of metals, nonmetals, and metalloids.

SECTION 4.9

- Learn the natures of the common elements.

SECTION 4.10

- Understand the formation of ions from their parent atoms, and learn to name them.
- Learn how the periodic table can help predict which ion a given element forms.

SECTION 4.11

- Learn how ions combine to form neutral compounds.

OWL Sign in to OWL at **www.cengage.com/owl** to view tutorials and simulations, develop problem-solving skills, and complete online homework assigned by your professor.

go Chemistry Download mini-lecture videos for key concept review and exam prep from OWL or purchase them from **www.ichapters.com**

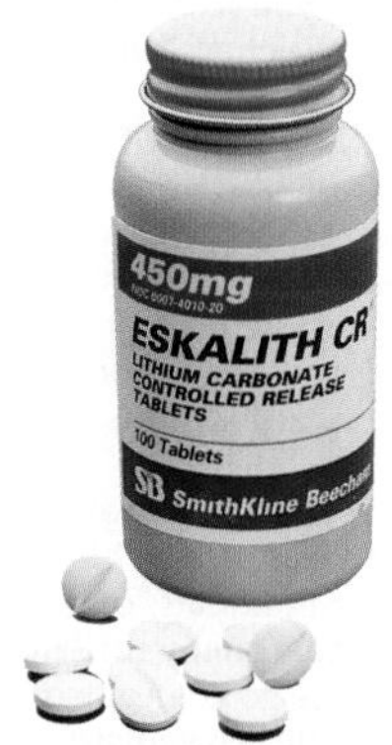

© Cengage Learning

Lithium is administered in the form of lithium carbonate pills.

The Granger Collection, New York

Robert Boyle at 62 years of age.

The chemical elements are very important to each of us in our daily lives. Although certain elements are present in our bodies in tiny amounts, they can have a profound impact on our health and behavior. As we will see in this chapter, lithium can be a miracle treatment for someone with bipolar disorder, and our cobalt levels can have a remarkable impact on whether we behave violently.

Since ancient times, humans have used chemical changes to their advantage. The processing of ores to produce metals for ornaments and tools and the use of embalming fluids are two applications of chemistry that were used before 1000 B.C.

The Greeks were the first to try to explain why chemical changes occur. By about 400 B.C. they had proposed that all matter was composed of four fundamental substances: fire, earth, water, and air.

The next 2000 years of chemical history were dominated by alchemy. Some alchemists were mystics and fakes who were obsessed with the idea of turning cheap metals into gold. However, many alchemists were sincere scientists, and this period saw important events: the elements mercury, sulfur, and antimony were discovered, and alchemists learned how to prepare acids.

The first scientist to recognize the importance of careful measurements was the Irishman Robert Boyle (1627–1691). Boyle is best known for his pioneering work on the properties of gases, but his most important contribution to science was probably his insistence that science should be firmly grounded in experiments. For example, Boyle held no preconceived notions about how many elements there might be. His definition of the term *element* was based on experiments: a substance was an element unless it could be broken down into two or more simpler substances. For example, air could not be an element as the Greeks believed, because it could be broken down into many pure substances.

As Boyle's experimental definition of an element became generally accepted, the list of known elements grew, and the Greek system of four elements died. But although Boyle was an excellent scientist, he was not always right. For some reason he ignored his own definition of an element and clung to the alchemists' views that metals were not true elements and that a way would be found eventually to change one metal into another.

4.1 The Elements

OBJECTIVES: To learn about the relative abundances of the elements. • To learn the names of some elements.

In studying the materials of the earth (and other parts of the universe), scientists have found that all matter can be broken down chemically into about 100 different elements. At first it might seem amazing that the millions of known substances are composed of so few fundamental elements. Fortunately for those trying to understand and systematize it, nature often uses a relatively small number of fundamental units to assemble even extremely

Test Bank: 1, 2

Section 4.1

TEACHING TIPS

- Remind students of the similarity between the letters in the alphabet and the atoms of the various elements. In the same way we can make many words from 26 letters, millions of compounds can be made using only the 100 or so elements. Putting the same elements together in different ways results in different compounds with very different properties. For example, the words *ADD* and *DAD* both consist of the same letters, but the order of the letters gives them different meanings. This discussion will help later (for example, in Chapter 6 you can use this analogy to help students understand why we do not change subscripts in a chemical formula).
- Use Tables 4.1 and 4.2 when you cover Chapter 8. You can have the students rank the elements according to mole percent and compare their answers.

Lecture Demonstration: 2.1

ChemWork Refined over ten years of use by thousands of students, **ChemWork** builds and enhances students' problems-solving skills. Online assignments function as a "personal instructor" to help students learn how to solve challenging problems and learn how to think like chemists. Annotations for **ChemWork** assignments are included at the beginning of the end-of-chapter review.

PowerLecture This 2-DVD package includes the Chemistry Multimedia Library, which contains animations, simulations, and movies for all chemistry subjects, organized by topic for lecture presentations. Annotations for **PowerLecture** are referenced in the margins throughout the Annotated Instructor's Edition.

complex materials. For example, proteins, a group of substances that serve the human body in almost uncountable ways, are all made by linking together a few fundamental units to form huge molecules. A nonchemical example is the English language, where hundreds of thousands of words are constructed from only 26 letters. If you take apart the thousands of words in an English dictionary, you will find only these 26 fundamental components. In much the same way, when we take apart all of the substances in the world around us, we find only about 100 fundamental building blocks—the elements. Compounds are made by combining atoms of the various elements, just as words are constructed from the 26 letters of the alphabet. And just as you had to learn the letters of the alphabet before you learned to read and write, you need to learn the names and symbols of the chemical elements before you can read and write chemistry.

Presently about 116 different elements are known,* 88 of which occur naturally. (The rest have been made in laboratories.) The elements vary tremendously in abundance. In fact, only 9 elements account for most of the compounds found in the earth's crust. In Table 4.1, the elements are listed in order of their abundance (mass percent) in the earth's crust, oceans, and atmosphere. Note that nearly half of the mass is accounted for by oxygen alone. Also note that the 9 most abundant elements account for over 98% of the total mass.

Jeremy Woodhouse/PhotoDisc/Getty Images

Footprints in the sand of the Namib Desert in Namibia.

Oxygen, in addition to accounting for about 20% of the earth's atmosphere (where it occurs as O_2 molecules), is found in virtually all the rocks, sand, and soil on the earth's crust. In these latter materials, oxygen is not present as O_2 molecules but exists in compounds that usually contain silicon and aluminum atoms. The familiar substances of the geological world, such as rocks and sand, contain large groups of silicon and oxygen atoms bound together to form huge clusters.

The list of elements found in living matter is very different from the list of elements found in the earth's crust. Table 4.2 shows the distribution of elements in the human body. Oxygen, carbon, hydrogen, and nitrogen form the basis for all biologically important molecules. Some elements found in the body (called trace elements) are crucial for life, even though they are present in relatively small amounts. For example, chromium helps the body use sugars to provide energy.

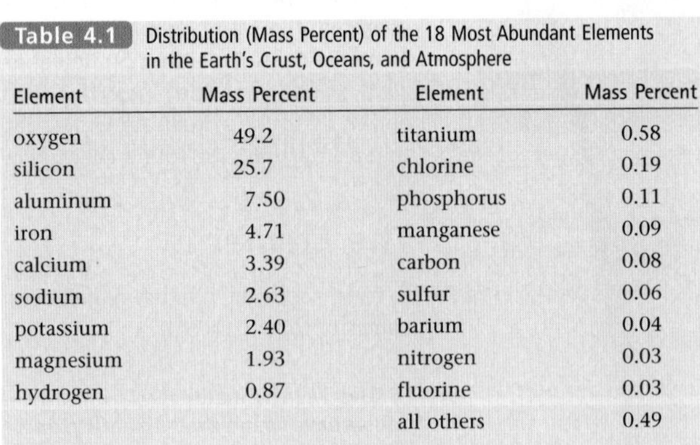
Table 4.1 Distribution (Mass Percent) of the 18 Most Abundant Elements in the Earth's Crust, Oceans, and Atmosphere

Element	Mass Percent	Element	Mass Percent
oxygen	49.2	titanium	0.58
silicon	25.7	chlorine	0.19
aluminum	7.50	phosphorus	0.11
iron	4.71	manganese	0.09
calcium	3.39	carbon	0.08
sodium	2.63	sulfur	0.06
potassium	2.40	barium	0.04
magnesium	1.93	nitrogen	0.03
hydrogen	0.87	fluorine	0.03
		all others	0.49

*This number changes as new elements are made in particle accelerators.

DEMONSTRATION

Bring samples of a variety of elements to class. Have students identify them and tell a use for each (if they know one). You can also bring in rocks and minerals and discuss the fact that elements in rocks are combined with other elements and are not pure. Very few elements are mined as pure substances.

Table 4-2 Abundance of Elements in the Human Body

Major Elements	Mass Percent	Trace Elements (in alphabetical order)
oxygen	65.0	arsenic
carbon	18.0	chromium
hydrogen	10.0	cobalt
nitrogen	3.0	copper
calcium	1.4	fluorine
phosphorus	1.0	iodine
magnesium	0.50	manganese
potassium	0.34	molybdenum
sulfur	0.26	nickel
sodium	0.14	selenium
chlorine	0.14	silicon
iron	0.004	vanadium
zinc	0.003	

One more general comment is important at this point. As we have seen, elements are fundamental to understanding chemistry. However, students are often confused by the many different ways that chemists use the term *element.* Sometimes when we say *element,* we mean a single atom of that element. We might call this the microscopic form of an element. Other times when we use the term *element,* we mean a sample of the element large enough to weigh on a balance. Such a sample contains many, many atoms of the element, and we might call this the macroscopic form of the element. There is yet a further complication. As we will see in more detail in Section 4.9 the macroscopic forms of several elements contain molecules rather than individual atoms as the fundamental components. For example, chemists know that oxygen gas consists of molecules with two oxygen atoms connected together (represented as O—O or more commonly as O_2). Thus when we refer to the element oxygen we might mean a single atom of oxygen, a single O_2 molecule, or a macroscopic sample containing many O_2 molecules. Finally, we often use the term *element* in a generic fashion. When we say the human body contains the element sodium or lithium, we do not mean that free elemental sodium or lithium is present. Rather, we mean that atoms of these elements are present in some form. In this text we will try to make clear what we mean when we use the term *element* in a particular case.

MISCONCEPTION

Students often have difficulty understanding what is meant by chemical terms such as *element.* It is important to emphasize the various ways we use the term *element* in chemistry. We might mean a single atom, a molecule such as N or O, or a large sample such as a bar of aluminum or the graphite ("lead") in a pencil. Be sure to help students realize that chemists use terms in many ways. They need to look at the context of the word to be sure that they understand what is intended. Chemists are accustomed to thinking about things at the macroscopic and microscopic levels simultaneously. Encourage students to think while they read and to consider how the terms are used.

4.2 Symbols for the Elements

OBJECTIVE: To learn the symbols of some elements.

The names of the chemical elements have come from many sources. Often an element's name is derived from a Greek, Latin, or German word that describes some property of the element. For example, gold was originally called *aurum,* a Latin word meaning "shining dawn," and lead was known as *plumbum,* which means "heavy." The names for chlorine and iodine come

Section 4.2

TEACHING TIPS

- Water pipes were once made of lead. This is the origin of the word *plumber.*
- The only way to learn the symbols of the elements is to memorize them. It is beneficial if the students learn not to confuse some symbol pairs such as Na/S, K/P, and Mg/Mn.

DEMONSTRATION

Check Out This Cereal!

Materials

Box of cereal (use one with 100% iron or "reduced iron" on the label; Total or Special K works well)

Bar magnet or magnetic stirrer magnet

Large Ziploc bag

Large beaker

Magnetic stir plate (optional)

Procedure Place about a cup of the cereal into the Ziploc bag. Have a student crush the cereal into small pieces. Pour the crushed cereal into the beaker and cover it with water. Stir until the cereal becomes soggy. Place the magnetic stirrer into the beaker and place the setup on the stir plate. Start stirring and continue for 15–20 minutes. If you are not using a stir plate, attach the stirrer to a pencil or paint stick and stir the mixture for about 10 minutes. Remove the magnet from the mixture and show the students the dark-colored iron filings on the magnet. You can then remove the filings to a piece of white paper and show the students they are attracted to a magnet held under the paper.

Test Bank: 3–31

CHEMISTRY IN FOCUS

Trace Elements: Small but Crucial

We all know that certain chemical elements, such as calcium, carbon, nitrogen, phosphorus, and iron, are essential for humans to live. However, many other elements that are present in tiny amounts in the human body are also essential to life. Examples are chromium, cobalt, iodine, manganese, and copper. Chromium assists in the metabolism of sugars, cobalt is present in vitamin B_{12}, iodine is necessary for the proper functioning of the thyroid gland, manganese appears to play a role in maintaining the proper calcium levels in bones, and copper is involved in the production of red blood cells.

It is becoming clear that certain trace elements are very important in determining human behavior. For example, lithium (administered as lithium carbonate) has been a miracle drug for some people afflicted with bipolar disorder, a disease that produces oscillatory behavior between inappropriate "highs" and the blackest of depressions. Although its exact function remains unknown, lithium seems to moderate the levels of neurotransmitters (compounds that are essential to nerve function), thus relieving some of the extreme emotions in sufferers of bipolar disorder.

In addition, a chemist named William Walsh has done some very interesting studies on the inmates of Stateville Prison in Illinois. By analyzing the trace elements in the hair of prisoners, he has found intriguing relationships between the behavior of the inmates and their trace element profile. For example, Walsh found an inverse relationship between the level of cobalt in the prisoner's body and the degree of violence in his behavior.

Besides the levels of trace elements in our bodies, the various substances in the water, the food we consume, and the air we breathe also are of great importance to our health. For example, many scientists are concerned about our exposure to aluminum, through aluminum compounds used in water purification, baked goods and cheese (sodium aluminum phosphate acts as a leavening agent and also is added to cheese to make it softer and easier to melt), and the aluminum that dissolves from our cookware and utensils. The effects of exposure to low levels of aluminum on humans are not presently clear, but there are some indications that we should limit our intake of this element.

Another example of low-level exposure to an element is the fluoride placed in many water supplies and toothpastes to control tooth decay by making tooth enamel more resistant to dissolving. However, the exposure of large numbers of people to fluoride is quite controversial—many people think it is harmful.

The chemistry of trace elements is fascinating and important. Keep your eye on the news for further developments.

from Greek words describing their colors, and the name for bromine comes from a Greek word meaning "stench." In addition, it is very common for an element to be named for the place where it was discovered. You can guess where the elements francium, germanium, californium,* and americium* were first found. Some of the heaviest elements are named after famous scientists—for example, einsteinium* and nobelium.*

We often use abbreviations to simplify the written word. For example, it is much easier to put MA on an envelope than to write out Massachusetts, and we often write USA instead of United States of America. Likewise, chemists have invented a set of abbreviations or **element symbols** for the chemical elements. These symbols usually consist of the first letter or the

*These elements are made artificially. They do not occur naturally.

first two letters of the element names. The first letter is always capitalized, and the second is not. Examples include

fluorine	F	neon	Ne
oxygen	O	silicon	Si
carbon	C		

In the symbol for an element, only the first letter is capitalized.

Sometimes, however, the two letters used are not the first two letters in the name. For example,

zinc	Zn	cadmium	Cd
chlorine	Cl	platinum	Pt

Walter Urie/West Light/Corbis

Various forms of the element gold.

The symbols for some other elements are based on the original Latin or Greek name.

Current Name	Original Name	Symbol
gold	aurum	Au
lead	plumbum	Pb
sodium	natrium	Na
iron	ferrum	Fe

A list of the most common elements and their symbols is given in Table 4.3. You can also see the elements represented on a table in the inside front cover of this text. We will explain the form of this table (which is called the periodic table) in later chapters.

Table 4.3 The Names and Symbols of the Most Common Elements

Element	Symbol	Element	Symbol
aluminum	Al	lithium	Li
antimony (stibium)*	Sb	magnesium	Mg
argon	Ar	manganese	Mn
arsenic	As	mercury (hydrargyrum)	Hg
barium	Ba	neon	Ne
bismuth	Bi	nickel	Ni
boron	B	nitrogen	N
bromine	Br	oxygen	O
cadmium	Cd	phosphorus	P
calcium	Ca	platinum	Pt
carbon	C	potassium (kalium)	K
chlorine	Cl	radium	Ra
chromium	Cr	silicon	Si
cobalt	Co	silver (argentium)	Ag
copper (cuprum)	Cu	sodium (natrium)	Na
fluorine	F	strontium	Sr
gold (aurum)	Au	sulfur	S
helium	He	tin (stannum)	Sn
hydrogen	H	titanium	Ti
iodine	I	tungsten (wolfram)	W
iron (ferrum)	Fe	uranium	U
lead (plumbum)	Pb	zinc	Zn

*Where appropriate, the original name is shown in parentheses so that you can see where some of the symbols came from.

TEACHING TIP

Consider having the students rewrite Table 4.3 using alternative grouping. For example, create a group of elements that have symbols dissimilar to their names, a group of elements that begin with the letter "C," a group of elements that have double letters for symbols, and so on.

Test Bank: 32–34, 49, 50

Section 4.3

TEACHING TIP

This section provides another opportunity to discuss the difference between laws and theories. Dalton's atomic theory is relatively simple in scope, as it should be. Dalton was trying to explain laws such as the law of constant composition. His success makes the model successful, but not absolutely correct (a model is always a simplification). For example, Dalton's theory does not explain questions such as "Why and how do atoms stick together to form molecules?" and "Why and how do molecules stick together to form liquids and solids?" Of course, no model answers all questions.

Lecture Demonstration: 2.3

PowerLecture Video: Mg Metal Burning

4.3 Dalton's Atomic Theory

OBJECTIVES: To learn about Dalton's theory of atoms. • To understand and illustrate the law of constant composition.

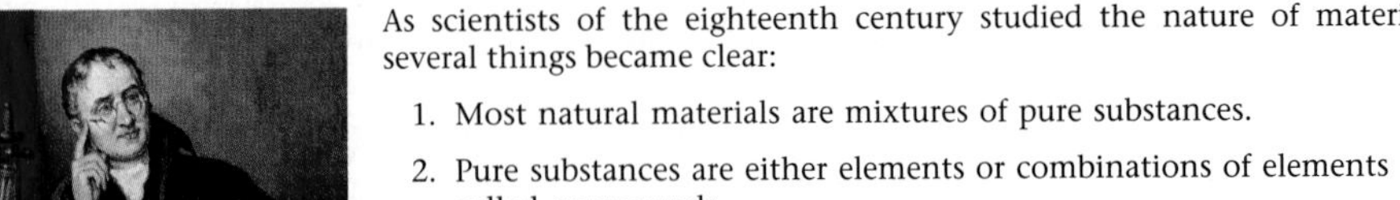

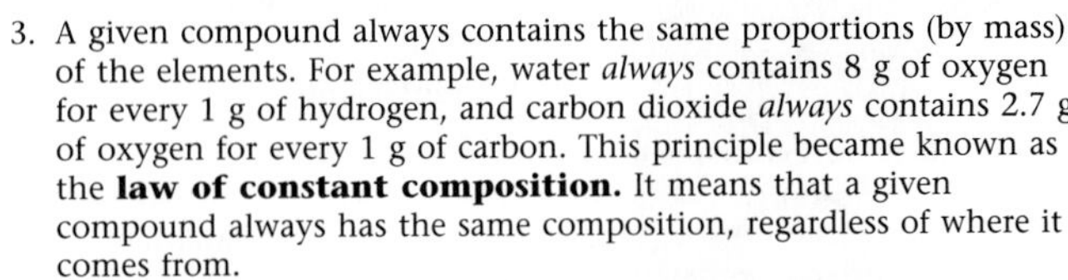

Figure 4.1

John Dalton (1766–1844) was an English scientist who made his living as a teacher in Manchester. Although Dalton is best known for his atomic theory, he made contributions in many other areas, including meteorology (he recorded daily weather conditions for 46 years, producing a total of 200,000 data entries). A rather shy man, Dalton was colorblind to red (a special handicap for a chemist) and suffered from lead poisoning contracted from drinking stout (strong beer or ale) that had been drawn through lead pipes.

As scientists of the eighteenth century studied the nature of materials, several things became clear:

1. Most natural materials are mixtures of pure substances.
2. Pure substances are either elements or combinations of elements called compounds.
3. A given compound always contains the same proportions (by mass) of the elements. For example, water *always* contains 8 g of oxygen for every 1 g of hydrogen, and carbon dioxide *always* contains 2.7 g of oxygen for every 1 g of carbon. This principle became known as the **law of constant composition.** It means that a given compound always has the same composition, regardless of where it comes from.

John Dalton (Figure 4.1), an English scientist and teacher, was aware of these observations, and in about 1808 he offered an explanation for them that became known as **Dalton's atomic theory.** The main ideas of this theory (model) can be stated as follows:

Dalton's Atomic Theory

1. Elements are made of tiny particles called **atoms.**
2. All atoms of a given element are identical.
3. The atoms of a given element are different from those of any other element.
4. Atoms of one element can combine with atoms of other elements to form compounds. A given compound always has the same relative numbers and types of atoms.
5. Atoms are indivisible in chemical processes. That is, atoms are not created or destroyed in chemical reactions. A chemical reaction simply changes the way the atoms are grouped together.

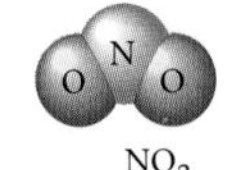

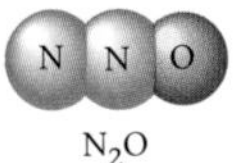

Figure 4.2

Dalton pictured compounds as collections of atoms. Here NO, NO_2, and N_2O are represented. Note that the number of atoms of each type in a molecule is given by a subscript, except that the number 1 is always assumed and never written.

Dalton's model successfully explained important observations such as the law of constant composition. This law makes sense because if a compound always contains the same relative numbers of atoms, it will always contain the same proportions by mass of the various elements.

Like most new ideas, Dalton's model was not accepted immediately. However, Dalton was convinced he was right and *used his model to predict* how a given pair of elements might combine to form more than one compound. For example, nitrogen and oxygen might form a compound containing one atom of nitrogen and one atom of oxygen (written NO), a compound containing two atoms of nitrogen and one atom of oxygen (written N_2O), a compound containing one atom of nitrogen and two atoms of oxygen (written NO_2), and so on (Figure 4.2). When the existence of these substances was verified, it was a triumph for Dalton's model. Because Dalton was able to predict correctly the formation of multiple compounds between two elements, his atomic theory became widely accepted.

TEACHING SUPPORT

HISTORICAL NOTE

John Dalton, the son of a poor English weaver, showed an unusual talent for mathematical science at an early age. In fact, he started a school in his village when he was 12 years old. Dalton's consuming interest as a boy was the study of the atmosphere, and he kept meticulous records of the weather for most of his life. Dalton never married and his only form of relaxation was bowling, which he did every Thursday afternoon. Dalton was a tall, gaunt, rather unattractive fellow who was not an effective public speaker. He was very unsuccessful as a lecturer and made his living mainly as a private tutor.

CHEMISTRY IN FOCUS

No Laughing Matter

Sometimes solving one problem leads to another. One such example involves the catalytic converters now required on all automobiles sold around much of the world. The purpose of these converters is to remove harmful pollutants such as CO and NO_2 from automobile exhausts. The good news is that these devices are quite effective and have led to much cleaner air in congested areas. The bad news is that these devices produce significant amounts of nitrous oxide, N_2O, commonly known as laughing gas because when inhaled it produces relaxation and mild inebriation. It was long used by dentists to make their patients more tolerant of some painful dental procedures.

The problem with N_2O is not that it is an air pollutant but that it is a "greenhouse gas." Certain molecules, such as CO_2, CH_4, N_2O, and others, strongly absorb infrared light ("heat radiation"), which causes the earth's atmosphere to retain more of its heat energy. Human activities have significantly increased the concentrations of these gases in the atmosphere. Mounting evidence suggests that the earth is warming as a result, leading to possible dramatic climatic changes.

A recent study by the Environmental Protection Agency (EPA) indicates that N_2O now accounts for over 7% of the greenhouse gases in the atmosphere and that automobiles equipped with catalytic converters produce nearly half of this N_2O. Ironically, N_2O is not regulated, because the Clean Air Act of 1970 was written to control smog—not greenhouse gases. The United States and other industrialized nations are now negotiating to find ways to control global warming, but no agreement is in place.

The N_2O situation illustrates just how complex environmental issues are. Clean may not necessarily be "green."

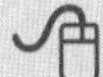 **Test Bank: 36–48**

Section 4.4

4.4 Formulas of Compounds

OBJECTIVE: To learn how a formula describes a compound's composition.

A **compound** is a distinct substance that is composed of the atoms of two or more elements and always contains exactly the same relative masses of those elements. In light of Dalton's atomic theory, this simply means that a compound always contains the same relative *numbers* of atoms of each element. For example, water always contains two hydrogen atoms for each oxygen atom.

Here, *relative* refers to ratios.

The types of atoms and the number of each type in each unit (molecule) of a given compound are conveniently expressed by a **chemical formula.** In a chemical formula the atoms are indicated by the element symbols, and the number of each type of atom is indicated by a subscript, a number that appears to the right of and below the symbol for the element. The formula for water is written H_2O, indicating that each molecule of water contains two atoms of hydrogen and one atom of oxygen (the subscript 1 is always understood and not written). Following are some general rules for writing formulas:

Rules for Writing Formulas

1. Each atom present is represented by its element symbol.
2. The number of each type of atom is indicated by a subscript written to the right of the element symbol.
3. When only one atom of a given type is present, the subscript 1 is not written.

TEACHING TIPS

- Relate the formulas of simple compounds to drawings of the molecules. Place a formula on the board and have students draw a representation of it. Focus on the number and kind of atoms in the molecule; don't worry about shape at this time. Ideas for some interactive examples are H_2O, NH_3, CO_2, CH_4, and CO.
- You may also wish to include the idea of a coefficient at this time. For example, have students draw a representation of 2CO or $4H_2O$. This exercise can lead to a good discussion of the difference between a coefficient and a subscript, which will help when balancing equations in Chapter 6.

Additional Examples

Example 4.1

Write the formula for each of the following compounds, listing the elements in the order given.

1. a molecule containing six carbon atoms and six hydrogen atoms C_6H_6
2. a compound containing half as many calcium atoms as chlorine atoms $CaCl_2$
3. a compound containing equal numbers of sodium and nitrogen atoms, but three times as many oxygen atoms as nitrogen atoms $NaNO_3$

Self Check

Answers to Self-Check Exercise 4.1

a. P_4O_{10}

b. UF_6

c. $AlCl_3$

Section 4.5

EXAMPLE 4.1 Writing Formulas of Compounds

Write the formula for each of the following compounds, listing the elements in the order given.

a. Each molecule of a compound that has been implicated in the formation of acid rain contains one atom of sulfur and three atoms of oxygen.

b. Each molecule of a certain compound contains two atoms of nitrogen and five atoms of oxygen.

c. Each molecule of glucose, a type of sugar, contains six atoms of carbon, twelve atoms of hydrogen, and six atoms of oxygen.

SOLUTION

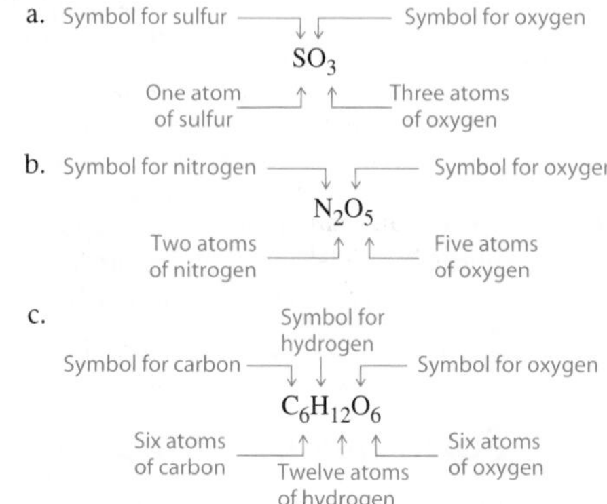

Self-Check EXERCISE 4.1 Write the formula for each of the following compounds, listing the elements in the order given.

a. A molecule contains four phosphorus atoms and ten oxygen atoms.

b. A molecule contains one uranium atom and six fluorine atoms.

c. A molecule contains one aluminum atom and three chlorine atoms.

See Problems 4.19 and 4.20. ■

4.5 The Structure of the Atom

OBJECTIVES: To learn about the internal parts of an atom. • To understand Rutherford's experiment to characterize the atom's structure.

Dalton's atomic theory, proposed in about 1808, provided such a convincing explanation for the composition of compounds that it became generally accepted. Scientists came to believe that *elements consist of atoms* and that *compounds are a specific collection of atoms* bound together in some way. But what is an atom like? It might be a tiny ball of matter that is the same throughout with no internal structure—like a ball bearing. Or the atom

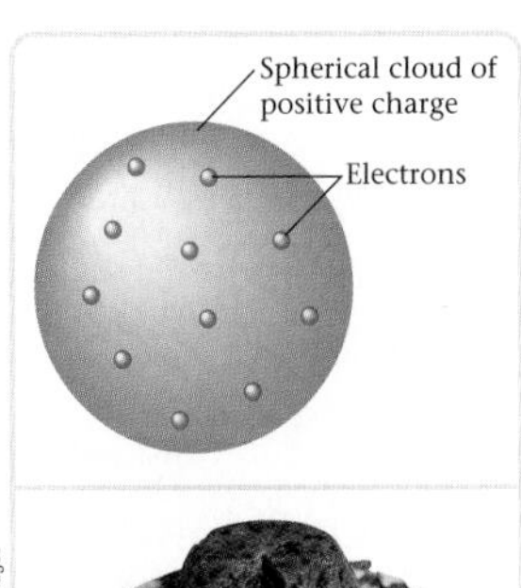

StockFood/Getty Images

Figure 4.3
One of the early models of the atom was the plum pudding model, in which the electrons were pictured as embedded in a positively charged spherical cloud, much as raisins are distributed in an old-fashioned plum pudding.

Some historians credit J. J. Thomson for the plum pudding model.

might be composed of parts—it might be made up of a number of subatomic particles. But if the atom contains parts, there should be some way to break up the atom into its components.

Many scientists pondered the nature of the atom during the 1800s, but it was not until almost 1900 that convincing evidence became available that the atom has a number of different parts.

A physicist in England named J. J. Thomson showed in the late 1890s that the atoms of any element can be made to emit tiny negative particles. (He knew the particles had a negative charge because he could show that they were repelled by the negative part of an electric field.) Thus he concluded that all types of atoms must contain these negative particles, which are now called **electrons.**

On the basis of his results, Thomson wondered what an atom must be like. Although he knew that atoms contain these tiny negative particles, he also knew that whole atoms are not negatively *or* positively charged. Thus he concluded that the atom must also contain positive particles that balance exactly the negative charge carried by the electrons, giving the atom a zero overall charge.

Another scientist pondering the structure of the atom was William Thomson (better known as Lord Kelvin and no relation to J. J. Thomson). Lord Kelvin got the idea (which might have occurred to him during dinner) that the atom might be something like plum pudding (a pudding with raisins randomly distributed throughout). Kelvin reasoned that the atom might be thought of as a uniform "pudding" of positive charge with enough negative electrons scattered within to counterbalance that positive charge (see Figure 4.3). Thus the plum pudding model of the atom came into being.

If you had taken this course in 1910, the plum pudding model would have been the only picture of the atom described. However, our ideas about the atom were changed dramatically in 1911 by a physicist named Ernest Rutherford (Figure 4.4), who learned physics in J. J. Thomson's laboratory in the late 1890s. By 1911 Rutherford had become a distinguished scientist with many important discoveries to his credit. One of his main areas of interest involved alpha particles (α particles), positively charged particles with a mass approximately 7500 times that of an electron. In studying the flight of these particles through air, Rutherford found that some of the α particles were deflected by something in the air. Puzzled by this, he designed an experiment that involved directing α particles toward a thin metal foil. Surrounding the foil was a detector coated with a substance that produced tiny

MISCONCEPTION

Most of your students will not relate to the idea of a plum pudding model for the atom. You might make a similar analogy using chocolate chip cookie dough, with the dough being the uniform positive charge and the scattered chips representing the electrons to counterbalance the positive charge.

Corbis-Bettmann

Figure 4.4
Ernest Rutherford (1871–1937) was born on a farm in New Zealand. In 1895 he placed second in a scholarship competition to attend Cambridge University but was awarded the scholarship when the winner decided to stay home and get married. Rutherford was an intense, hard-driving person who became a master at designing just the right experiment to test a given idea. He was awarded the Nobel Prize in chemistry in 1908.

TEACHING SUPPORT

HISTORICAL NOTES

John Joseph (J. J.) Thomson was chosen to head the Cavendish Laboratory in Cambridge, England, in 1884, when he was only 28 years old. Thomson was known for his gift in designing experiments, but he was not mechanically inclined and needed help to build the apparatus needed to perform the experiments. In the 1890s, one of the most common ways to study electricity was to build a glass tube with metal electrodes in each end, one of which was coated with zinc sulfide. When the air was pumped out of the tube, called a cathode ray tube, and a battery was hooked to wires connected to the electrodes, a bright,

TEACHING TIPS

- Ernest Marsden, Rutherford's undergraduate student, is often credited with discovering the evidence that led Rutherford to decide that particles were reflected from the nucleus of the gold atoms. This story provides an excellent opportunity to talk with students about the possibility that they might also be involved in research even as undergraduates, and that not all discoveries are made by people who have completed their formal education.
- Organize Rutherford's observations and conclusions into a table to help students appreciate the importance of the experiment.

Lecture Demonstration: 2.5, 2.6

PowerLecture Animations: Rutherford Experiment Alpha Particles Deflected by Nucleus

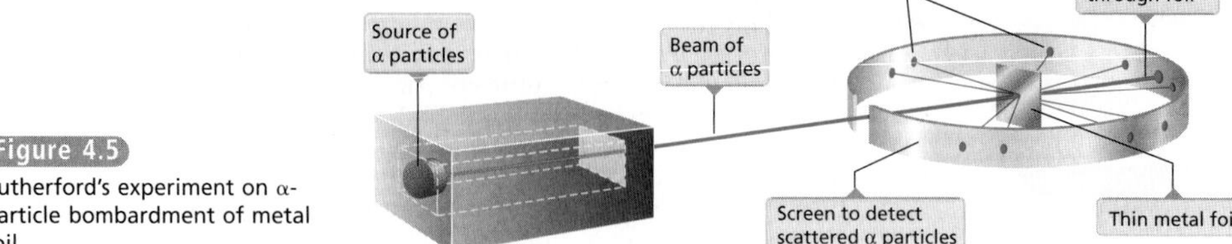

Figure 4.5 Rutherford's experiment on α-particle bombardment of metal foil.

flashes wherever it was hit by an α particle (Figure 4.5). The results of the experiment were very different from those Rutherford anticipated. Although most of the α particles passed straight through the foil, some of the particles were deflected at large angles, as shown in Figure 4.5, and some were reflected backward.

This outcome was a great surprise to Rutherford. (He described this result as comparable to shooting a gun at a piece of paper and having the bullet bounce back.) Rutherford knew that if the plum pudding model of the atom was correct, the massive α particles would crash through the thin foil like cannonballs through paper (as shown in Figure 4.6a). So he expected the α particles to travel through the foil experiencing, at most, very minor deflections of their paths.

Rutherford concluded from these results that the plum pudding model for the atom could not be correct. The large deflections of the α particles could be caused only by a center of concentrated positive charge that would repel the positively charged α particles, as illustrated in Figure 4.6b. Most of the α particles passed directly through the foil because the atom is mostly open space. The deflected α particles were those that had a "close encounter" with the positive center of the atom, and the few reflected α particles were those that scored a "direct hit" on the positive center. In Rutherford's mind these results could be explained only in terms of a **nuclear atom**—an atom with a dense center of positive charge (the **nucleus**) around which tiny electrons moved in a space that was otherwise empty.

One of Rutherford's coworkers in this experiment was an undergraduate named Ernest Marsden who, like Rutherford, was from New Zealand.

He concluded that the nucleus must have a positive charge to balance the negative charge of the electrons and that it must be small and dense.

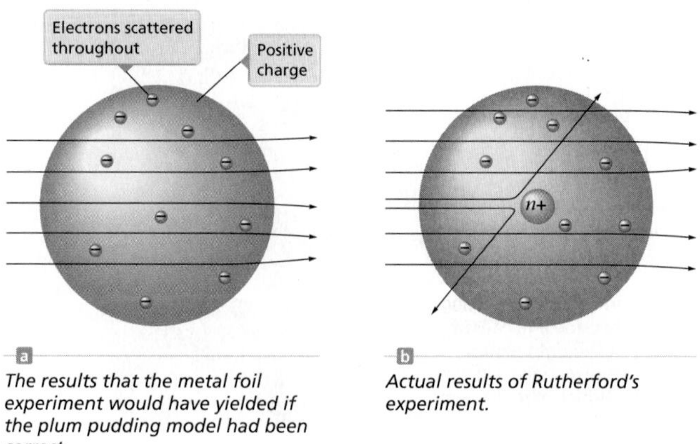

Figure 4.6

a *The results that the metal foil experiment would have yielded if the plum pudding model had been correct.*

b *Actual results of Rutherford's experiment.*

glowing spot was observed in the zinc sulfide. After ten years of trying to figure out what caused the glow, Thomson finally concluded it must be due to a stream of negative particles that he called corpuscles of electricity—we now call them electrons.

By the time of Thomson's discovery in 1897, the Cavendish had become the most distinguished laboratory in England (and had acknowledged the growing women's rights movement by allowing women to enter the laboratory). However, despite the prominence of Thomson and his laboratory, the suggestion that these particles came from inside atoms (that is, were subatomic particles) was not received with enthusiasm by the scientific community. In fact, in the 1890s many physicists did not even believe in the existence of atoms.

If the atom were expanded to the size of a huge stadium, the nucleus would be only about as big as a fly at the center.

What was it made of? By 1919 Rutherford concluded that the nucleus of an atom contained what he called protons. A **proton** has the same magnitude (size) of charge as the electron, but its charge is *positive*. We say that the proton has a charge of 1+ and the electron a charge of 1−.

Rutherford reasoned that the hydrogen atom has a single proton at its center and one electron moving through space at a relatively large distance from the proton (the hydrogen nucleus). He also reasoned that other atoms must have nuclei (the plural of *nucleus*) composed of many protons bound together somehow. In addition, Rutherford and a coworker, James Chadwick, were able to show in 1932 that most nuclei also contain a neutral particle that they named the **neutron.** A neutron is slightly more massive than a proton but has no charge.

4.6 Introduction to the Modern Concept of Atomic Structure

OBJECTIVE: To understand some important features of subatomic particles.

In this model the atom is called a nuclear atom because the positive charge is localized in a small, compact structure (the nucleus) and not spread out uniformly, as in the plum pudding view.

The *chemistry* of an atom arises from its electrons.

In the years since Thomson and Rutherford, a great deal has been learned about atomic structure. The simplest view of the atom is that it consists of a tiny nucleus (about 10^{-13} cm in diameter) and electrons that move about the nucleus at an average distance of about 10^{-8} cm from it (Figure 4.7). To visualize how small the nucleus is compared with the size of the atom, consider that if the nucleus were the size of a grape, the electrons would be about one *mile* away on average. The nucleus contains protons, which have a positive charge equal in magnitude to the electron's negative charge, and neutrons, which have almost the same mass as a proton but no charge. The neutrons' function in the nucleus is not obvious. They may help hold the protons (which repel each other) together to form the nucleus, but we will not be concerned with that here. The relative masses and charges of the electron, proton, and neutron are shown in Table 4.4.

An important question arises at this point: *"If all atoms are composed of these same components, why do different atoms have different chemical properties?"* The answer lies in the number and arrangement of the electrons. The space in which the electrons move accounts for most of the atomic volume. The electrons are the parts of atoms that "intermingle" when atoms combine to form molecules. Therefore, the number of electrons a given atom possesses greatly affects the way it can interact with other atoms. As a result, atoms of different elements, which have different numbers of electrons, show different chemical behavior. Although the atoms of different elements also differ in their numbers of protons, it is the number of electrons that really determines chemical behavior. We will discuss how this happens in later chapters.

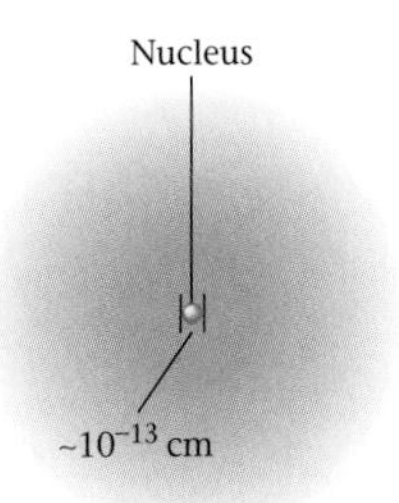

Figure 4.7 A nuclear atom viewed in cross section. (The symbol ~ means approximately.) This drawing does not show the actual scale. The nucleus is actually *much* smaller compared with the size of an atom.

Table 4.4 The Mass and Charge of the Electron, Proton, and Neutron

Particle	Relative Mass*	Relative Charge
electron	1	1−
proton	1836	1+
neutron	1839	none

*The electron is arbitrarily assigned a mass of 1 for comparison.

Section 4.6

TEACHING TIPS

- It is worthwhile to emphasize the tiny size of the nucleus compared to the atom. One example is given in the text: If the nucleus were the size of a grape, the radius of the atom would be about one mile.
- Emphasize here that questioning theories is what science is all about. Theories are always questioned so as to refine and improve them or to refute them.

 **Test Bank: 51–53**

TEACHING SUPPORT

HISTORICAL NOTES

Radioactivity was discovered accidentally by Antoine-Henri Becquerel in 1896, when he stored a piece of potassium uranyl sulfate in a drawer with some photographic plates and found that the rock emitted radiation that exposed the plates. Although Becquerel was later awarded a Nobel Prize for his discovery (in 1903), he didn't understand the composition of the radiation in 1896. The first clue to the nature of radioactivity came in 1897, when J. J. Thomson discovered the corpuscles of electricity now called electrons.

The first person to study radioactivity in a systematic way was Ernest Rutherford. In his studies at the Cavendish Lab, he learned that radioactive materials spewed out huge numbers of particles that traveled at speeds of thousands of

Test Bank: 35, 56, 57, 60, 61, 63

Section 4.7

TEACHING TIPS

- Students learned in Section 4.5 that the overall charge on an atom is zero. At this point you need to emphasize that the charge is zero because the number of negatively charged electrons equals the number of positively charged protons.
- The discovery of the proton offers an excellent example of how and why models change. Dalton's model of the atom did not account for isotopes because he assumed that all atoms of an element are exactly alike. As knowledge expands, models change to accommodate the new information.
- The mass number represents the sum of the *numbers* of protons and neutrons. Students often confuse this idea, believing that the mass number should be the sum of the *masses* of the protons and neutrons. Be careful to make sure they are clear on this point.

Lecture Demonstration: 2.7

4.7 Isotopes

OBJECTIVES: To learn about the terms isotope, atomic number, and mass number. • To understand the use of the symbol $^{A}_{Z}X$ to describe a given atom.

We have seen that an atom has a nucleus with a positive charge due to its protons and has electrons in the space surrounding the nucleus at relatively large distances from it.

All atoms of the same element have the same number of protons (the element's atomic number) and the same number of electrons.

As an example, consider a sodium atom, which has 11 protons in its nucleus. Because an atom has no overall charge, the number of electrons must equal the number of protons. Therefore, a sodium atom has 11 electrons in the space around its nucleus. It is *always* true that a sodium atom has 11 protons and 11 electrons. However, each sodium atom also has neutrons in its nucleus, and different types of sodium atoms exist that have different numbers of neutrons.

In a free atom, the positive and negative charges always balance to yield a net zero charge.

When Dalton stated his atomic theory in the early 1800s, he assumed all of the atoms of a given element were identical. This idea persisted for over a hundred years, until James Chadwick discovered that the nuclei of most atoms contain neutrons as well as protons. (This is a good example of how a theory changes as new observations are made.) After the discovery of the neutron, Dalton's statement that all atoms of a given element are identical had to be changed to "All atoms of the same element contain the same number of protons and electrons, but atoms of a given element may have different numbers of neutrons."

To illustrate this idea, consider the sodium atoms represented in Figure 4.8. These atoms are **isotopes,** or *atoms with the same number of protons but different numbers of neutrons.* The number of protons in a nucleus is called the atom's **atomic number.** The *sum* of the number of neutrons and the number of protons in a given nucleus is called the atom's **mass number.** To specify which of the isotopes of an element we are talking about, we use the symbol

Atomic number: the number of protons. Mass number: the sum of protons and neutrons.

$$^{A}_{Z}X$$

where

X = the symbol of the element
A = the mass number (number of protons and neutrons)
Z = the atomic number (number of protons)

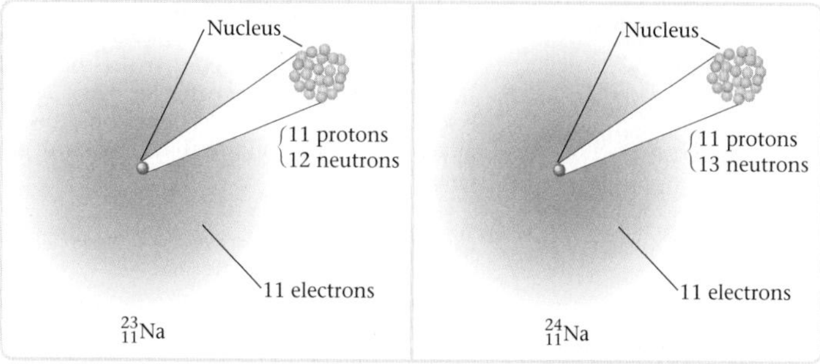

Figure 4.8
Two isotopes of sodium. Both have 11 protons and 11 electrons, but they differ in the number of neutrons in their nuclei.

miles per second. Rutherford found two distinct types of particles, which he named *alpha* and *beta* rays (now called particles). He found that while alpha particles were stopped by a sheet of paper, the beta particles were highly penetrating. (In 1900 Becquerel showed that beta particles were actually high-speed electrons.)

In 1898 Rutherford moved to McGill University in Canada, where he continued his life's work—the study of alpha particles. After four years of work Rutherford concluded that alpha particles are helium nuclei. One of the curious things Rutherford learned about alpha particles is that they don't travel in a straight line through air, because they are deflected by oxygen and nitrogen molecules. After moving to the University of Manchester in 1907 and winning the Nobel Prize in 1908, Rutherford was determined

CHEMISTRY *IN* FOCUS

"Whair" Do You Live?

Picture a person who has been the victim of a crime in a large city in the eastern United States. The person has been hit in the head and, as a result, has total amnesia. The person's ID has been stolen, but the authorities suspect he may not be from the local area. Is there any way to find out where the person might be from? The answer is yes. Recent research indicates that the relative amounts of the isotopes of hydrogen and oxygen in a person's hair indicate in which part of the United States a person lives.

Support for this idea has come from a recent study by James Ehleringer, a chemist at the University of Utah in Salt Lake City. Noting that the concentrations of hydrogen-2 (deuterium) and oxygen-18 in drinking water vary significantly from region to region in the United States (see accompanying illustration), Ehleringer and his colleagues collected hair samples from barbershops in 65 cities and 18 states. Their analyses showed that 86% of the variations in the hydrogen and oxygen isotopes in the hair samples result from the isotopic composition of the local water. Based on their results, the group was able to develop estimates of the isotopic signature of peoples' hair from various regions of the country. Although this method cannot be used to pinpoint a person's place of residence, it can give a general region. This method might be helpful for the amnesia victim described above by showing where to look for his family. His picture could be shown on TV in the region indicated by analysis of his hair. Another possible use of this technique is identifying the country of origin of victims of a natural disaster in a tourist region with visitors from all over the world. In fact, a similar technique was used to specify the countries of origin of the victims of the tsunami that devastated southern Asia in December 2004.

An interesting verification of this technique occurred when the researchers examined a strand of hair from a person who had recently moved from Beijing, China, to Salt Lake City. Analysis of various parts of the hair showed a distinct change in isotopic distribution corresponding to his change of residence. Thus the isotopes of elements can provide useful information in unexpected ways.

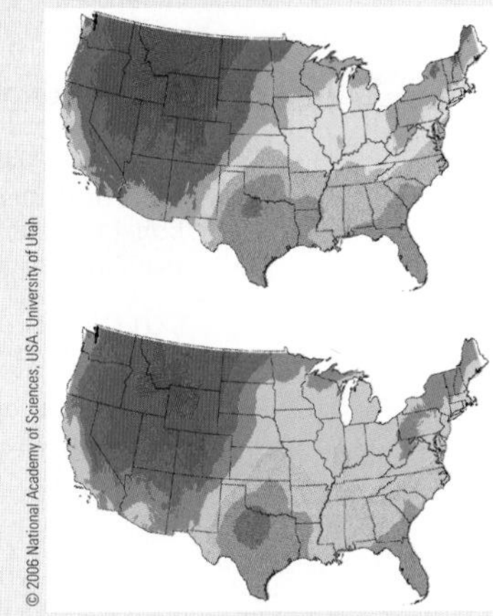

Maps of predicted concentrations of hydrogen-2 (top) and oxygen-18 (bottom). Red represents the highest concentration, and blue represents the lowest concentration of each isotope.

For example, the symbol for one particular type of sodium atom is written

$$^{23}_{11}\text{Na}$$

Mass number (number of protons and neutrons)
Element symbol
Atomic number (number of protons)

The particular atom represented here is called sodium-23, because it has a mass number of 23. Let's specify the number of each type of subatomic particle. From the atomic number 11 we know that the nucleus contains

to find out how alpha particles were deflected by matter. With the help of his assistant, Hans Geiger, and an undergraduate, Ernest Marsden, he set up an experiment in which alpha particles were directed at a thin metal foil, backed by a metal screen that gave flashes of light when struck by an alpha particle. To see the tiny flashes the scientists had to sit in the absolute dark for more than an hour before the experiment. In 1909 Marsden was able to demonstrate that one in 8000 of the alpha particles rebounded from the foil—and the age of the nuclear atom was born.

Additional Examples

Example 4.2

Determine the number of each of the three types of subatomic particles for each of the following.

1. $^{60}_{27}Co$ # protons = # electrons = 27; # neutrons = 33 (60 − 27)
2. $^{37}_{17}Cl$ # protons = # electrons = 17; # neutrons = 20 (37 − 17)
3. $^{238}_{92}U$ # protons = # electrons = 92; # neutrons = 146 (238 − 92)

11 protons. And because the number of electrons is equal to the number of protons, we know that this atom contains 11 electrons. How many neutrons are present? We can calculate the number of neutrons from the definition of the mass number

$$\text{Mass number} = \text{number of protons} + \text{number of neutrons}$$

or, in symbols,

$$A = Z + \text{number of neutrons}$$

We can isolate (solve for) the number of neutrons by subtracting Z from both sides of the equation

$$A - Z = Z - Z + \text{number of neutrons}$$
$$A - Z = \text{number of neutrons}$$

This is a general result. You can always determine the number of neutrons present in a given atom by subtracting the atomic number from the mass number. In this case ($^{23}_{11}Na$), we know that $A = 23$ and $Z = 11$. Thus

$$A - Z = 23 - 11 = 12 = \text{number of neutrons}$$

In summary, sodium-23 has 11 electrons, 11 protons, and 12 neutrons.

EXAMPLE 4.2 Interpreting Symbols for Isotopes

In nature, elements are usually found as a mixture of isotopes. Three isotopes of elemental carbon are $^{12}_{6}C$ (carbon-12), $^{13}_{6}C$ (carbon-13), and $^{14}_{6}C$ (carbon-14). Determine the number of each of the three types of subatomic particles in each of these carbon atoms.

SOLUTION

The number of protons and electrons is the same in each of the isotopes and is given by the atomic number of carbon, 6. The number of neutrons can be determined by subtracting the atomic number (Z) from the mass number (A):

$$A - Z = \text{number of neutrons}$$

The numbers of neutrons in the three isotopes of carbon are

$$^{12}_{6}C\text{: number of neutrons} = A - Z = 12 - 6 = 6$$
$$^{13}_{6}C\text{: number of neutrons} = 13 - 6 = 7$$
$$^{14}_{6}C\text{: number of neutrons} = 14 - 6 = 8$$

In summary,

Symbol	Number of Protons	Number of Electrons	Number of Neutrons
$^{12}_{6}C$	6	6	6
$^{13}_{6}C$	6	6	7
$^{14}_{6}C$	6	6	8

Self Check

Answers to Self-Check Exercise 4.2

protons = # electrons = 38; # neutrons = 52 (90 − 38)

Self-Check EXERCISE 4.2 Give the number of protons, neutrons, and electrons in the atom symbolized by $^{90}_{38}Sr$. Strontium-90 occurs in fallout from nuclear testing. It can accumulate in bone marrow and may cause leukemia and bone cancer.

See Problems 4.39 and 4.42. ■

C H E M I S T R Y *IN* **FOCUS**

Isotope Tales

The atoms of a given element typically consist of several isotopes—atoms with the same number of protons but different numbers of neutrons. It turns out that the ratio of isotopes found in nature can be very useful in natural detective work. One reason is that the ratio of isotopes of elements found in living animals and humans reflects their diets. For example, African elephants that feed on grasses have a different $^{13}C/^{12}C$ ratio in their tissues than elephants that primarily eat tree leaves. This difference arises because grasses have a different growth pattern than leaves do, resulting in different amounts of ^{13}C and ^{12}C being incorporated from the CO_2 in the air. Because leaf-eating and grass-eating elephants live in different areas of Africa, the observed differences in the $^{13}C/^{12}C$ isotope ratios in elephant ivory samples have enabled authorities to identify the sources of illegal samples of ivory.

Another case of isotope detective work involves the tomb of King Midas, who ruled the kingdom Phyrgia in the eighth century B.C. Analysis of nitrogen isotopes in the king's decayed casket has revealed details about the king's diet. Scientists have learned that the $^{15}N/^{14}N$ ratios of carnivores are higher than those of herbivores, which in turn are higher than those of plants. It turns out that the organism responsible for decay of the king's wooden casket has an unusually large requirement for nitrogen. The source of this nitrogen was the body of the dead king. Because the decayed wood under his now-decomposed body showed a high $^{15}N/^{14}N$ ratio, researchers feel sure that the king's diet was rich in meat.

A third case of historical isotope detective work concerns the Pueblo ancestor people (commonly called the Anasazi), who lived in what is now northwestern New Mexico between A.D. 900 and 1150. The center of their civilization, Chaco Canyon, was a thriving cultural center boasting dwellings made of hand-hewn sandstone and more than 200,000 logs. The sources of the logs have always been controversial. Many theories have been advanced concerning the distances over which the logs were hauled. Recent research by Nathan B. English, a geochemist at the University of Arizona in Tucson, has used the distribution of strontium isotopes in the wood to identify the probable sources of the logs. This effort has enabled scientists to understand more clearly the Anasazi building practices.

These stories illustrate how isotopes can serve as valuable sources of biologic and historical information.

Paul Chesley/National Geographic/Getty Images

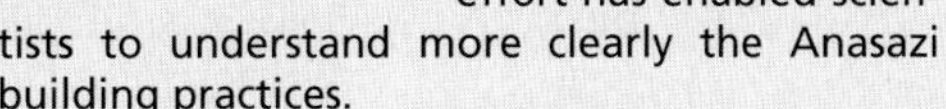

Ancient Anasazi Indian cliff dwellings.

Self-Check **EXERCISE 4.3** Give the number of protons, neutrons, and electrons in the atom symbolized by $^{201}_{80}Hg$.

See Problems 4.39 and 4.42. ■

EXAMPLE 4.3 Writing Symbols for Isotopes

Write the symbol for the magnesium atom (atomic number 12) with a mass number of 24. How many electrons and how many neutrons does this atom have?

Self Check

Answers to Self-Check Exercise 4.3

protons = # electrons = 80; # neutrons = 121 (201 − 80)

Additional Examples

Example 4.3

Write the symbol for each of the following atoms, and list the number of protons, neutrons, and electrons for each.

1. the cesium atom with a mass number of 132

   $^{132}_{55}Cs$; # protons = # electrons = 55; # neutrons = 77 (132 − 55)

2. the iron atom with a mass number of 56

   $^{56}_{26}Fe$; # protons = # electrons = 26; # neutrons = 30 (56 − 26)

Example 4.4

Write the symbol for each of the following.

1. the krypton atom that has 48 neutrons $^{84}_{36}Kr$
2. the nitrogen atom that has 6 neutrons $^{13}_{7}N$

Self Check

Answers to Self-Check Exercise 4.4

$^{32}_{15}P$

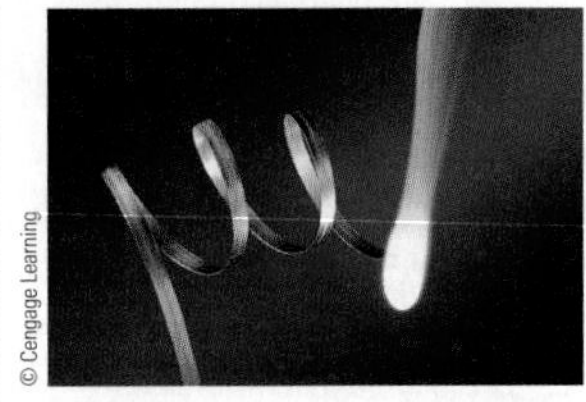

Magnesium burns in air to give a bright white flame.

SOLUTION

The atomic number 12 means the atom has 12 protons. The element magnesium is symbolized by Mg. The atom is represented as

$$^{24}_{12}Mg$$

and is called magnesium-24. Because the atom has 12 protons, it must also have 12 electrons. The mass number gives the total number of protons and neutrons, which means that this atom has 12 neutrons (24 − 12 = 12). ■

EXAMPLE 4.4 Calculating Mass Number

Write the symbol for the silver atom ($Z = 47$) that has 61 neutrons.

SOLUTION

The element symbol is $^{A}_{Z}Ag$, where we know that $Z = 47$. We can find A from its definition, $A = Z +$ number of neutrons. In this case,

$$A = 47 + 61 = 108$$

The complete symbol for this atom is $^{108}_{47}Ag$.

Self-Check EXERCISE 4.4 Give the symbol for the phosphorus atom ($Z = 15$) that contains 17 neutrons.

See Problem 4.42. ■

Section 4.8

TEACHING TIPS

- Use the PowerPoint slide or transparency of Figure 4.11 to illustrate the important features of the periodic table. Be sure to include the groups and their names, as well as the metals, nonmetals, and metalloids. Show students how many more metals there are than nonmetals. List the metalloids for students as they may not know that aluminum is a metal and boron is a nonmetal. The other elements along both sides of the heavy stair-step line are metalloids. Discuss the location of hydrogen and the size of the table if the actinides and lanthanides were included in their proper places.
  Talk about the newly discovered element 118. Explain the three-letter symbol. This symbol is simply the number of the element using Latin. For example, 118 (Uuo) is called *ununoctium.* Once the Union of Pure and Applied Chemists has agreed on a name for these elements, the number names will be changed. Students might be interested to know that these elements do not have official names yet because they are so new.
- Students should learn the names of the common groups on the periodic table. This will simplify your discussion later in the course.
- Ask students to think of common metal items that illustrate the properties of metals. Examples include copper wire, aluminum foil, silver spoons, and hammered copper utensils.
- The reasons underlying the structure of the periodic table and the trends it shows are not introduced until Chapter 11. Focus students' attention on the locations of groups of elements and the separation between metals and nonmetals.

4.8 Introduction to the Periodic Table

OBJECTIVES: To learn about various features of the periodic table. • To learn some of the properties of metals, nonmetals, and metalloids.

In any room where chemistry is taught or practiced, you are almost certain to find a chart called the **periodic table** hanging on the wall. This chart shows all of the known elements and gives a good deal of information about each. As our study of chemistry progresses, the usefulness of the periodic table will become more obvious. This section will simply introduce it.

A simple version of the periodic table is shown in Figure 4.9. Note that each box of this table contains a number written over one, two, or three letters. The letters are the symbols for the elements. The number shown above each symbol is the atomic number (the number of protons and also the number of electrons) for that element. For example, carbon (C) has atomic number 6:

6
C

1 1A Alkali metals	2 2A Alkaline earth metals	3	4	5	6	7	8	9	10	11	12	13 3A	14 4A	15 5A	16 6A	17 7A Halogens	18 8A Noble gases
		Transition metals															
1 H																	2 He
3 Li	4 Be											5 B	6 C	7 N	8 O	9 F	10 Ne
11 Na	12 Mg											13 Al	14 Si	15 P	16 S	17 Cl	18 Ar
19 K	20 Ca	21 Sc	22 Ti	23 V	24 Cr	25 Mn	26 Fe	27 Co	28 Ni	29 Cu	30 Zn	31 Ga	32 Ge	33 As	34 Se	35 Br	36 Kr
37 Rb	38 Sr	39 Y	40 Zr	41 Nb	42 Mo	43 Tc	44 Ru	45 Rh	46 Pd	47 Ag	48 Cd	49 In	50 Sn	51 Sb	52 Te	53 I	54 Xe
55 Cs	56 Ba	57 La*	72 Hf	73 Ta	74 W	75 Re	76 Os	77 Ir	78 Pt	79 Au	80 Hg	81 Tl	82 Pb	83 Bi	84 Po	85 At	86 Rn
87 Fr	88 Ra	89 Ac†	104 Rf	105 Db	106 Sg	107 Bh	108 Hs	109 Mt	110 Ds	111 Rg	112 Uub	113 Uut	114 Uuq	115 Uup			118 Uuo

*Lanthanides	58 Ce	59 Pr	60 Nd	61 Pm	62 Sm	63 Eu	64 Gd	65 Tb	66 Dy	67 Ho	68 Er	69 Tm	70 Yb	71 Lu
†Actinides	90 Th	91 Pa	92 U	93 Np	94 Pu	95 Am	96 Cm	97 Bk	98 Cf	99 Es	100 Fm	101 Md	102 No	103 Lr

Figure 4.9
The periodic table.

Lead (Pb) has atomic number 82:

82
Pb

Notice that elements 112 through 115 and 118 have unusual three-letter designations beginning with U. These are abbreviations for the systematic names of the atomic numbers of these elements. "Regular" names for these elements will be chosen eventually by the scientific community.

Note that the elements are listed on the periodic table in order of increasing atomic number. They are also arranged in specific horizontal rows and vertical columns. The elements were first arranged in this way in 1869 by Dmitri Mendeleev, a Russian scientist. Mendeleev arranged the elements in this way because of similarities in the chemical properties of various "families" of elements. For example, fluorine and chlorine are reactive gases that form similar compounds. It was also known that sodium and potassium behave very similarly. Thus the name *periodic table* refers to the fact that as we increase the atomic numbers, every so often an element occurs with

Mendeleev actually arranged the elements in order of increasing atomic mass rather than atomic number.

LABORATORY EXPERIMENT

A relevant laboratory experiment for this section is Experiment 7, Properties of Some Representative Elements, from *Introductory Chemistry in the Laboratory* by James Hall (this lab can also be used during a study of Section 3.5).

PowerLecture Simulation: Periodic Table

DEMONSTRATION

Bring samples of metals, metalloids, and nonmetals to class. Probably the simplest metalloid to bring to class is a piece of silicon. It looks very much like a metal but is brittle. Use these samples to illustrate the properties of each group. You can have the students classify each item, and justify their classifications through the properties.

properties similar to those of an earlier (lower-atomic-number) element. For example, the elements

9 F
17 Cl
35 Br
53 I
85 At

Throughout the text, we will highlight the location of various elements by presenting a small version of the periodic table.

all show similar chemical behavior and so are listed vertically, as a "family" of elements.

These families of elements with similar chemical properties that lie in the same vertical column on the periodic table are called **groups.** Groups are often referred to by the number over the column (see Figure 4.9). Note that the group numbers are accompanied by the letter A on the periodic table in Figure 4.9 and the one inside the front cover of the text. For simplicity we will delete the A's when we refer to groups in the text. Many of the groups have special names. For example, the first column of elements (Group 1) has the name **alkali metals.** The Group 2 elements are called the **alkaline earth metals,** the Group 7 elements are the **halogens,** and the elements in Group 8 are called the **noble gases.** A large collection of elements that spans many vertical columns consists of the **transition metals.**

There's another convention recommended by the International Union of Pure and Applied Chemistry for group designations that uses numbers 1 through 18 and includes the transition metals (see Fig. 4.9). Do not confuse that system with the one used in this text, where only the representative elements have group numbers (1 through 8).

Most of the elements are **metals.** Metals have the following characteristic physical properties:

Physical Properties of Metals

1. Efficient conduction of heat and electricity
2. Malleability (they can be hammered into thin sheets)
3. Ductility (they can be pulled into wires)
4. A lustrous (shiny) appearance

Nonmetals sometimes have one or more metallic properties. For example, solid iodine is lustrous, and graphite (a form of pure carbon) conducts electricity.

For example, copper is a typical metal. It is lustrous (although it tarnishes readily); it is an excellent conductor of electricity (it is widely used in electrical wires); and it is readily formed into various shapes, such as pipes for water systems. Copper is one of the transition metals—the metals shown in the center of the periodic table. Iron, aluminum, and gold are other familiar elements that have metallic properties. All of the elements shown to the left of and below the heavy "stair-step" black line in Figure 4.9 are classified as metals, except for hydrogen (Figure 4.10).

The relatively small number of elements that appear in the upper-right corner of the periodic table (to the right of the heavy line in Figures 4.9 and 4.10) are called **nonmetals.** Nonmetals generally lack those properties that characterize metals and show much more variation in their properties than metals do. Whereas almost all metals are solids at normal temperatures,

92 Chapter 4 Chemical Foundations: Elements, Atoms, and Ions

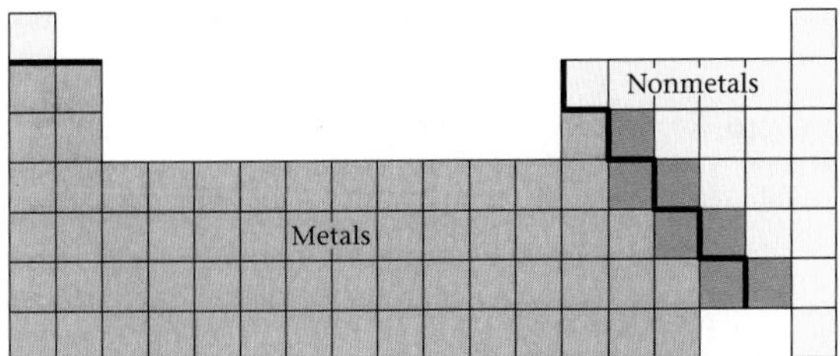

Figure 4.10
The elements classified as metals and as nonmetals.

many nonmetals (such as nitrogen, oxygen, chlorine, and neon) are gaseous and one (bromine) is a liquid. Several nonmetals (such as carbon, phosphorus, and sulfur) are also solids.

The elements that lie close to the "stair-step" line as shown in blue in Figure 4.10 often show a mixture of metallic and nonmetallic properties. These elements, which are called **metalloids** or **semimetals,** include silicon, germanium, arsenic, antimony, and tellurium.

As we continue our study of chemistry, we will see that the periodic table is a valuable tool for organizing accumulated knowledge and that it helps us predict the properties we expect a given element to exhibit. We will also develop a model for atomic structure that will explain why there are groups of elements with similar chemical properties.

EXAMPLE 4.5 Interpreting the Periodic Table

API/Explorer/Photo Researchers, Inc.

Indonesian men carrying chunks of elemental sulfur in baskets.

For each of the following elements, use the periodic table in the front of the book to give the symbol and atomic number and to specify whether the element is a metal or a nonmetal. Also give the named family to which the element belongs (if any).

a. iodine b. magnesium c. gold d. lithium

SOLUTION

a. Iodine (symbol I) is element 53 (its atomic number is 53). Iodine lies to the right of the stair-step line in Figure 4.10 and thus is a nonmetal. Iodine is a member of Group 7, the family of halogens.

b. Magnesium (symbol Mg) is element 12 (atomic number 12). Magnesium is a metal and is a member of the alkaline earth metal family (Group 2).

c. Gold (symbol Au) is element 79 (atomic number 79). Gold is a metal and is not a member of a named vertical family. It is classed as a transition metal.

d. Lithium (symbol Li) is element 3 (atomic number 3). Lithium is a metal in the alkali metal family (Group 1).

Self-Check **EXERCISE 4.5** Give the symbol and atomic number for each of the following elements. Also indicate whether each element is a metal or a nonmetal and whether it is a member of a named family.

a. argon b. chlorine c. barium d. cesium

See Problems 4.53 and 4.54. ■

Additional Examples

Example 4.5

For each of the following elements, use the periodic table to give the symbol and atomic number and specify whether the element is a metal or nonmetal. Also, give the family to which the element belongs (if any).

1. strontium

   Sr, atomic number = 38. Strontium is a metal and a member of the alkaline earth family (Group 2).

2. silicon

   Si, atomic number = 14. Silicon is a metalloid and a member of Group 4.

3. xenon

   Xe, atomic number = 54. Xenon is a nonmetal and a member of the noble gas family (Group 8).

Self Check

Answers to Self-Check Exercise 4.5

Element	*Symbol*	*Atomic Number*	*Metal or Nonmetal?*	*Family*
argon	Ar	18	nonmetal	noble gases
chlorine	Cl	17	nonmetal	halogen
barium	Ba	56	metal	alkaline earth metals
cesium	Cs	55	metal	alkali metals

CHEMISTRY IN FOCUS

Putting the Brakes on Arsenic

The toxicity of arsenic is well known. Indeed, arsenic has often been the poison of choice in classic plays and films—rent *Arsenic and Old Lace* sometime. Contrary to its treatment in the aforementioned movie, arsenic poisoning is a serious, contemporary problem. For example, the World Health Organization estimates that 77 million people in Bangladesh are at risk from drinking water that contains large amounts of naturally occurring arsenic. Recently, the Environmental Protection Agency announced more stringent standards for arsenic in U.S. public drinking water supplies. Studies show that prolonged exposure to arsenic can lead to a higher risk of bladder, lung, and skin cancers as well as other ailments, although the levels of arsenic that induce these symptoms remain in dispute in the scientific community.

Cleaning up arsenic-contaminated soil and water poses a significant problem. One approach is to find plants that will leach arsenic from the soil. Such a plant, the brake fern, recently has been shown to have a voracious appetite for arsenic. Research led by Lenna Ma, a chemist at the University of Florida in Gainesville, has shown that the brake fern accumulates arsenic at a rate 200 times that of the average plant. The arsenic, which becomes concentrated in fronds that grow up to 5 feet long, can be easily harvested and hauled away. Researchers are now investigating the best way to dispose of the plants so the arsenic can be isolated. The fern (*Pteris vittata*) looks promising for putting the brakes on arsenic pollution.

Tara Piasio/IFAS/University of Florida

Lenna Ma and Pteris vittata*—called the brake fern.*

Section 4.9

TEACHING TIPS

- Although students will generally have access to a periodic table during most exams and quizzes, it is a good idea that they become familiar with the locations of elements on the periodic table, some physical properties, and the names and symbols of at least the common elements.
- Use Figure 4.13 to introduce the idea of a balanced chemical equation to the students (which they will consider in more detail in Chapter 6). You can relate the formulas of the reactants and products to the representations of the molecules.

4.9 Natural States of the Elements

OBJECTIVE: To learn the natures of the common elements.

As we have noted, the matter around us consists mainly of mixtures. Most often these mixtures contain compounds, in which atoms from different elements are bound together. Most elements are quite reactive: their atoms tend to combine with those of other elements to form compounds. Thus we do not often find elements in nature in pure form—uncombined with other elements. However, there are notable exceptions. The gold nuggets found at Sutter's Mill in California that launched the Gold Rush in 1849 are virtually pure elemental gold. And platinum and silver are often found in nearly pure form.

A gold nugget weighing 13 lb, 7 oz, which came to be called Tom's Baby, was found by Tom Grove near Breckenridge, Colorado, on July 23, 1887.

Gold, silver, and platinum are members of a class of metals called *noble metals* because they are relatively unreactive. (The term *noble* implies a class set apart.)

Other elements that appear in nature in the uncombined state are the elements in Group 8: helium, neon, argon, krypton, xenon, and radon. Because the atoms of these elements do not combine readily with those of other elements, we call them the *noble gases*. For example, helium gas is found in uncombined form in underground deposits with natural gas.

Recall that a molecule is a collection of atoms that behaves as a unit. Molecules are always electrically neutral (zero charge).

When we take a sample of air (the mixture of gases that constitute the earth's atmosphere) and separate it into its components, we find several pure elements present. One of these is argon. Argon gas consists of a collection of separate argon atoms, as shown in Figure 4.11.

Air also contains nitrogen gas and oxygen gas. When we examine these two gases, however, we find that they do not contain single atoms, as argon does, but instead contain **diatomic molecules:** molecules made up of *two atoms,* as represented in Figure 4.12. In fact, any sample of elemental oxygen gas at normal temperatures contains O_2 molecules. Likewise, nitrogen gas contains N_2 molecules.

Hydrogen is another element that forms diatomic molecules. Though virtually all of the hydrogen found on earth is present in compounds with other elements (such as with oxygen in water), when hydrogen is prepared as a free element it contains diatomic H_2 molecules. For example, an electric current can be used to decompose water (see Figure 4.13 and Figure 3.3 on p. 60) into elemental hydrogen and oxygen containing H_2 and O_2 molecules, respectively.

MISCONCEPTION

Some students believe that because oxygen is a diatomic molecule, the subscript for oxygen must be a "2" in all compounds.

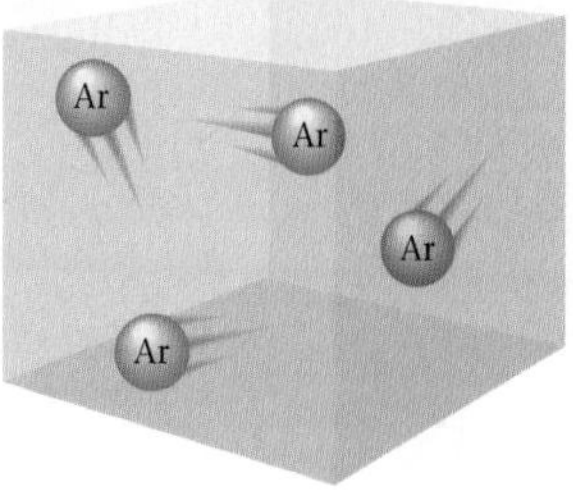

Figure 4.11
Argon gas consists of a collection of separate argon atoms.

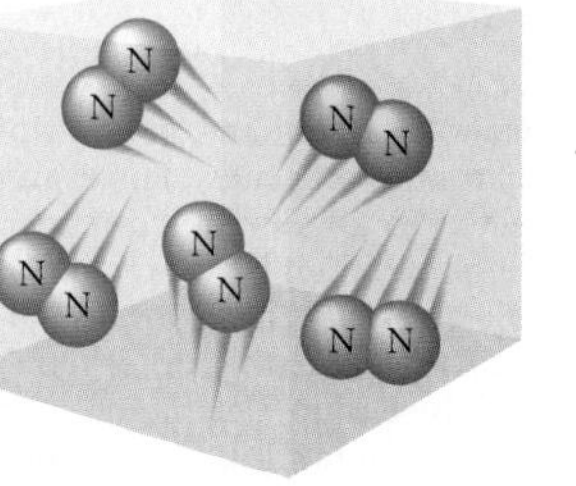

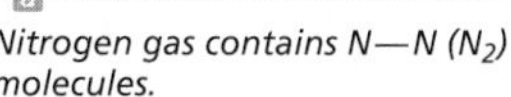

a Nitrogen gas contains N—N (N_2) molecules.

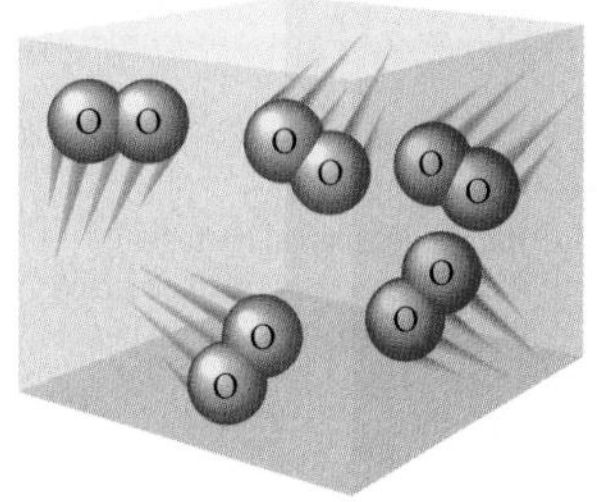

b Oxygen gas contains O—O (O_2) molecules.

Figure 4.12
Gaseous nitrogen and oxygen contain diatomic (two-atom) molecules.

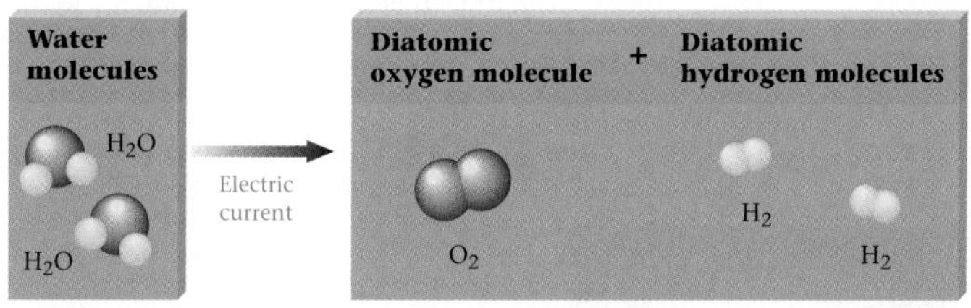

Figure 4.13
The decomposition of two water molecules (H_2O) to form two hydrogen molecules (H_2) and one oxygen molecule (O_2). Note that only the grouping of the atoms changes in this process; no atoms are created or destroyed. There must be the same number of H atoms and O atoms before and after the process. Thus the decomposition of two H_2O molecules (containing four H atoms and two O atoms) yields one O_2 molecule (containing two O atoms) and two H_2 molecules (containing a total of four H atoms).

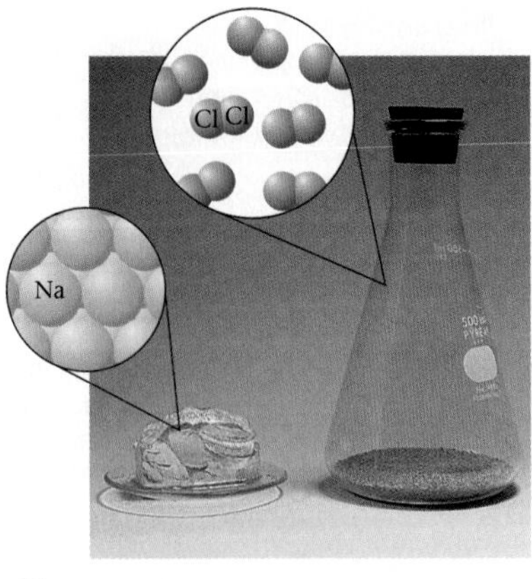

Figure 4.14

a Sodium chloride (common table salt) can be decomposed to its elements.

b Sodium metal (on the left) and chlorine gas.

The only elemental hydrogen found naturally on earth occurs in the exhaust gases of volcanoes.

Several other elements, in addition to hydrogen, nitrogen, and oxygen, exist as diatomic molecules. For example, when sodium chloride is melted and subjected to an electric current, chlorine gas is produced (along with sodium metal). This chemical change is represented in Figure 4.14. Chlorine gas is a pale green gas that contains Cl_2 molecules.

Chlorine is a member of Group 7, the halogen family. All the elemental forms of the Group 7 elements contain diatomic molecules. Fluorine is a pale yellow gas containing F_2 molecules. Bromine is a brown liquid made up of Br_2 molecules. Iodine is a lustrous, purple solid that contains I_2 molecules.

Table 4.5 lists the elements that contain diatomic molecules in their pure, elemental forms.

So far we have seen that several elements are gaseous in their elemental forms at normal temperatures (~25 °C). The noble gases (the Group 8 elements) contain individual atoms, whereas several other gaseous elements contain diatomic molecules (H_2, N_2, O_2, F_2, and Cl_2).

Only two elements are liquids in their elemental forms at 25 °C: the nonmetal bromine (containing Br_2 molecules) and the metal mercury. The metals gallium and cesium almost qualify in this category; they are solids at 25 °C, but both melt at ~30 °C.

~ means "approximately."

Platinum is a noble metal used in jewelry and in many industrial processes.

Table 4.5 Elements That Exist as Diatomic Molecules in Their Elemental Forms

Element Present	Elemental State at 25 °C	Molecule
hydrogen	colorless gas	H_2
nitrogen	colorless gas	N_2
oxygen	pale blue gas	O_2
fluorine	pale yellow gas	F_2
chlorine	pale green gas	Cl_2
bromine	reddish brown liquid	Br_2
iodine	lustrous, dark purple solid	I_2

96 Chapter 4 Chemical Foundations: Elements, Atoms, and Ions

Liquid bromine in a flask with bromine vapor.

Figure 4.15

In solid metals, the spherical atoms are packed closely together.

The other elements are solids in their elemental forms at 25 °C. For metals these solids contain large numbers of atoms packed together much like marbles in a jar (see Figure 4.15).

The structures of solid nonmetallic elements are more varied than those of metals. In fact, different forms of the same element often occur. For example, solid carbon occurs in three forms. Different forms of a given element are called *allotropes*. The three allotropes of carbon are the familiar diamond and graphite forms plus a form that has only recently been discovered called *buckminsterfullerene*. These elemental forms have very different properties because of their different structures (see Figure 4.16). Diamond is the hardest natural substance known and is often used for industrial cutting tools. Diamonds are also valued as gemstones. Graphite, by contrast, is a rather soft material useful for writing (pencil "lead" is really graphite) and (in the form of a powder) for lubricating locks. The rather odd name given to buckminsterfullerene comes from the structure of the C_{60} molecules that form this allotrope. The soccer-ball-like structure contains five- and six-member rings reminiscent of the structure of geodesic domes suggested by the late industrial designer Buckminster Fuller. Other "fullerenes" containing molecules with more than 60 carbon atoms have also been discovered, leading to a new area of chemistry.

Cut diamond, held over coal.

DEMONSTRATION

The allotropes of carbon can be illustrated using simple models. Diamond can be represented by a toothpick and gumdrop (or clay) model. Graphite can be shown by using pieces of chicken wire. Buckminsterfullerene can be illustrated by a soccer ball.

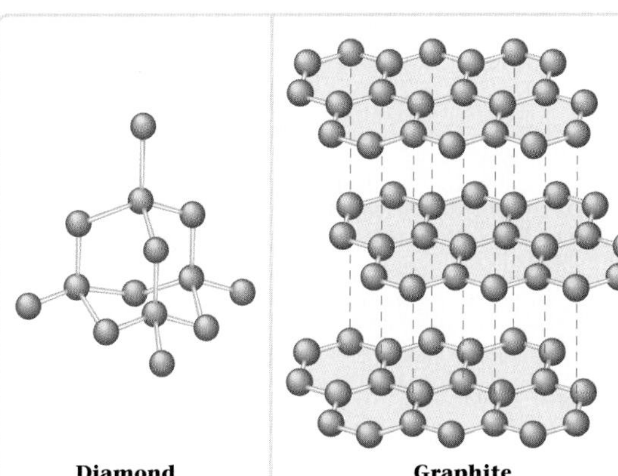

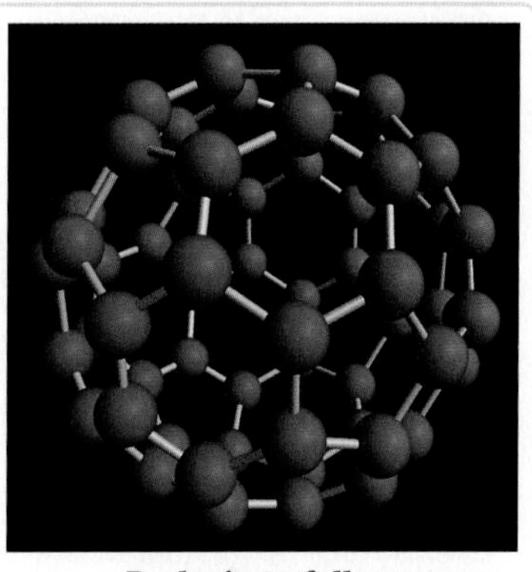

Figure 4.16

The three solid elemental forms of carbon (allotropes): diamond, graphite, and buckminsterfullerene. The representations of diamond and graphite are fragments of much larger structures that extend in all directions from the parts shown here. Buckminsterfullerene contains C_{60} molecules, one of which is shown.

Section 4.10

TEACHING TIPS

- Make sure that the students realize the atoms of an element are neutral. Charge is shown only for ions. Emphasize that ions are formed by the gain and loss of electrons. This concept is difficult for students because they tend to think about gain and loss using positive numbers. It is very important that they understand from the beginning that a positive ion is formed by losing electrons and a negative ion is formed by gaining electrons. In chemistry the positive number (protons) remains the same.
- Now is an excellent time to teach the notation for writing basic equations. $Na \rightarrow Na^+ + e^-$ shows how a neutral atom can lose an electron to have a positive charge. Students sometimes have difficulty in putting the electrons on the correct side when writing these equations.
- When naming ions, be sure to emphasize the difference in the suffix of the name. Students tend to slide over the ending and miss the *-ide* that distinguishes the ion from an atom.
- Students need to learn the charges for the ions formed from the elements in Groups 1, 2, 3, 6, and 7 of the periodic table. This will help them name compounds correctly later on.
- While the students are naming ions and writing their charges, ask them to look for any patterns. They should be able to discover that the nonmetals form ions with negative charges and the metals form ions with positive charges that match their group numbers. They may also notice that transition metals have a variety of charges.

4.10 Ions

OBJECTIVES: To understand the formation of ions from their parent atoms, and learn to name them. • To learn how the periodic table can help predict which ion a given element forms.

go Chemistry **Module 2: Predicting Ion Charges** covers concepts in this section.

We have seen that an atom has a certain number of protons in its nucleus and an equal number of electrons in the space around the nucleus. This results in an exact balance of positive and negative charges. We say that an atom is a neutral entity—it has *zero net charge.*

We can produce a charged entity, called an **ion,** by taking a neutral atom and adding or removing one or more electrons. For example, a sodium atom ($Z = 11$) has eleven protons in its nucleus and eleven electrons outside its nucleus.

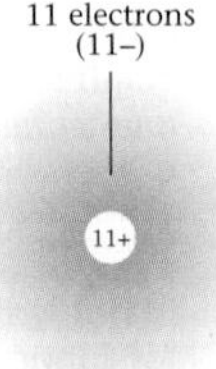

An ion has a net positive or negative charge.

If one of the electrons is lost, there will be eleven positive charges but only ten negative charges. This gives an ion with a net positive one (1+) charge: $(11+) + (10-) = 1+$. We can represent this process as follows:

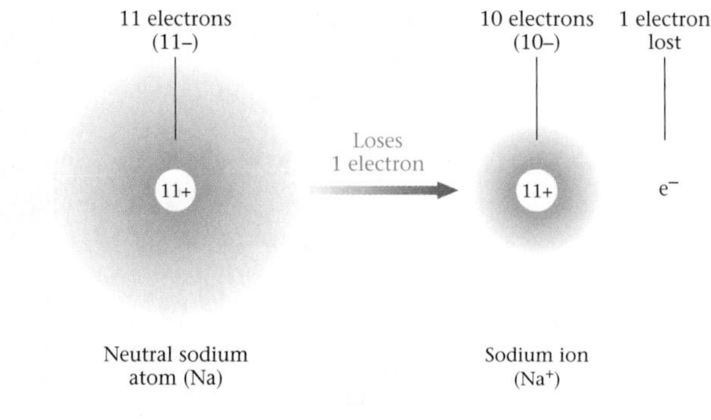

or, in shorthand form, as

$$Na \rightarrow Na^+ + e^-$$

where Na represents the neutral sodium atom, Na^+ represents the 1+ ion formed, and e^- represents an electron.

Test Bank: 133–161

A positive ion, called a **cation** (pronounced *cat' eye on*), is produced when one or more electrons are *lost* from a neutral atom. We have seen that sodium loses one electron to become a 1+ cation. Some atoms lose more than one electron. For example, a magnesium atom typically loses two electrons to form a 2+ cation:

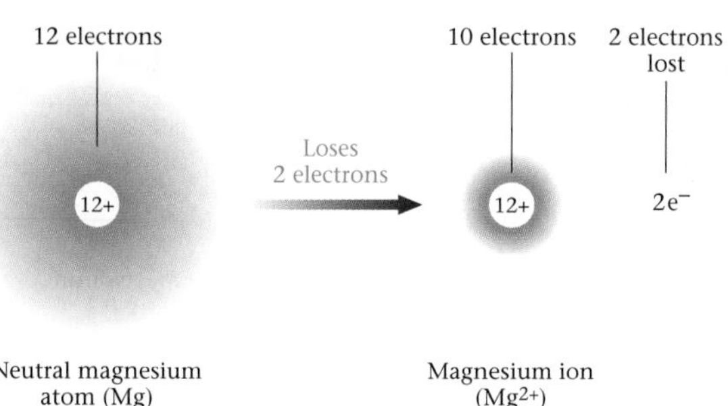

We usually represent this process as follows:

$$Mg \rightarrow Mg^{2+} + 2e^-$$

Aluminum forms a 3+ cation by losing three electrons:

13 electrons

10 electrons

3 electrons lost

Loses 3 electrons

13+

13+

$3e^-$

Neutral aluminum atom (Al)

Aluminum ion (Al^{3+})

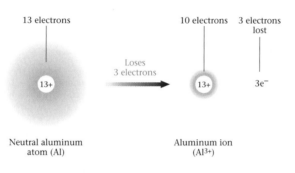

Note the size decreases dramatically when an atom loses one or more electrons to form a positive ion.

or

$$Al \rightarrow Al^{3+} + 3e^-$$

A cation is named using the name of the parent atom. Thus Na^+ is called the sodium ion (or sodium cation), Mg^{2+} is called the magnesium ion (or magnesium cation), and Al^{3+} is called the aluminum ion (or aluminum cation).

When electrons are *gained* by a neutral atom, an ion with a negative charge is formed. A negatively charged ion is called an **anion** (pronounced *an' ion*). An atom that gains one extra electron forms an anion with a

4.10 Ions 99

1− charge. An example of an atom that forms a 1− anion is the chlorine atom, which has seventeen protons and seventeen electrons:

Note the size increases dramatically when an atom gains one or more electrons to form a negative ion.

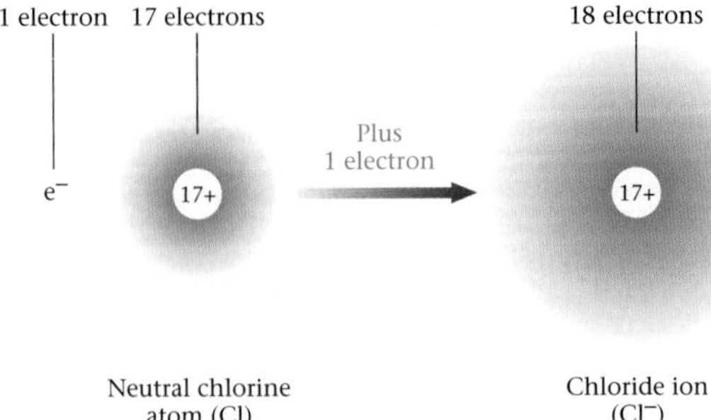

or

$$Cl + e^- \rightarrow Cl^-$$

Note that the anion formed by chlorine has eighteen electrons but only seventeen protons, so the net charge is (18−) + (17+) = 1−. Unlike a cation, which is named for the parent atom, an anion is named by taking the root name of the atom and changing the ending. For example, the Cl^- anion produced from the Cl (chlorine) atom is called the *chloride* ion (or chloride anion). Notice that the word *chloride* is obtained from the root of the atom name (*chlor-*) plus the suffix *-ide*. Other atoms that add one electron to form 1− ions include

The name of an anion is obtained by adding *-ide* to the root of the atom name.

fluorine	$F + e^- \rightarrow F^-$	(*fluor*ide ion)
bromine	$Br + e^- \rightarrow Br^-$	(*brom*ide ion)
iodine	$I + e^- \rightarrow I^-$	(*iod*ide ion)

Note that the name of each of these anions is obtained by adding *-ide* to the root of the atom name.

Some atoms can add two electrons to form 2− anions. Examples include

oxygen	$O + 2e^- \rightarrow O^{2-}$	(*ox*ide ion)
sulfur	$S + 2e^- \rightarrow S^{2-}$	(*sulf*ide ion)

Note that the names for these anions are derived in the same way as those for the 1− anions.

It is important to recognize that ions are always formed by removing electrons from an atom (to form cations) or adding electrons to an atom (to form anions). *Ions are never formed by changing the number of protons* in an atom's nucleus.

It is essential to understand that isolated atoms do not form ions on their own. Most commonly, ions are formed when metallic elements combine with nonmetallic elements. As we will discuss in detail in Chapter 7, when metals and nonmetals react, the metal atoms tend to lose one or more electrons, which are in turn gained by the atoms of the nonmetal. Thus reactions between metals and nonmetals tend to form compounds that contain metal cations and nonmetal anions. We will have more to say about these compounds in Section 4.11.

100 Chapter 4 Chemical Foundations: Elements, Atoms, and Ions

1	2										3	4	5	6	7	8
Li^+	Be^{2+}													O^{2-}	F^-	
Na^+	Mg^{2+}										Al^{3+}			S^{2-}	Cl^-	
K^+	Ca^{2+}										Ga^{3+}			Se^{2-}	Br^-	
Rb^+	Sr^{2+}	Transition metals form cations with various charges.									In^{3+}			Te^{2-}	I^-	
Cs^+	Ba^{2+}															

Figure 4.17
The ions formed by selected members of Groups 1, 2, 3, 6, and 7.

Ion Charges and the Periodic Table

For Groups 1, 2, and 3, the charges of the cations equal the group numbers.

We find the periodic table very useful when we want to know what type of ion is formed by a given atom. Figure 4.17 shows the types of ions formed by atoms in several of the groups on the periodic table. Note that the Group 1 metals all form 1+ ions (M^+), the Group 2 metals all form 2+ ions (M^{2+}), and the Group 3 metals form 3+ ions (M^{3+}). Thus for Groups 1 through 3 the charges of the cations formed are identical to the group numbers.

In contrast to the Group 1, 2, and 3 metals, most of the many *transition metals* form cations with various positive charges. For these elements there is no easy way to predict the charge of the cation that will be formed.

Note that metals always form positive ions. This tendency to lose electrons is a fundamental characteristic of metals. Nonmetals, on the other hand, form negative ions by gaining electrons. Note that the Group 7 atoms all gain one electron to form 1− ions and that all the nonmetals in Group 6 gain two electrons to form 2− ions.

At this point you should memorize the relationships between the group number and the type of ion formed, as shown in Figure 4.17. You will understand why these relationships exist after we further discuss the theory of the atom in Chapter 11.

4.11 Compounds That Contain Ions

OBJECTIVE: To learn how ions combine to form neutral compounds.

Melting means that the solid, where the ions are locked into place, is changed to a liquid, where the ions can move.

Chemists have good reasons to believe that many chemical compounds contain ions. For instance, consider some of the properties of common table salt, sodium chloride (NaCl). It must be heated to about 800 °C to melt and to almost 1500 °C to boil (compare to water, which boils at 100 °C). As a solid, salt will not conduct an electric current, but when melted it is a very good conductor. Pure water does not conduct electricity (does not allow an electric current to flow), but when salt is dissolved in water, the resulting solution readily conducts electricity (see Figure 4.18).

Chemists have come to realize that we can best explain these properties of sodium chloride (NaCl) by picturing it as containing Na^+ ions and Cl^- ions packed together as shown in Figure 4.19. Because the positive and negative charges attract each other very strongly, it must be heated to a very high temperature (800 °C) before it melts.

To explore further the significance of the electrical conductivity results, we need to discuss briefly the nature of electric currents. An electric current

Section 4.11

DEMONSTRATION

Conductivity

Materials

Conductivity apparatus
6 beakers
Sugar
Distilled water
1 *M* HCl
1 *M* acetic acid
NaCl
Wash bottle/distilled water

Procedure Place the distilled water in a beaker. Ask for a prediction of conductivity. Test the water with the conductivity apparatus. Place tap water in a beaker. Test its conductivity. Ask students how tap water differs from distilled water.

Note Be sure to rinse the conductivity apparatus after each test.

Add a spoonful of sugar to a beaker containing distilled water and test its conductivity. Add a spoonful of salt to a beaker containing distilled water and test its conductivity. In a similar manner, test solutions of HCl and acetic acid. Summarize the results of the test in a table.

Teaching Notes Ask students why distilled water does not conduct electricity but tap water does. What must be present for conductivity to occur? Have students draw molecular-level pictures of the sugar and sodium chloride solutions. Based on these results, have students predict what the HCl solution might look like at the molecular level. Finally, ask students to propose a hypothesis for how the acetic acid solution might differ from the HCl solution.

TEACHING TIPS

- Students need to think about ionic compounds on the molecular (ionic) level. Be sure to have them draw pictures when they begin writing formulas for these compounds. The idea that the compound is composed of both cations and anions lays a strong foundation for the more advanced concepts introduced later in the course. Once students can see the ions in a compound, making the total charge be a net of zero is more understandable. Students can then see how many of each ion are needed to attain a zero charge.
- Be sure to point out that atoms do not spontaneously gain or lose electrons. The gain and loss of electrons are always paired. One atom loses electrons while another atom gains electrons simultaneously.

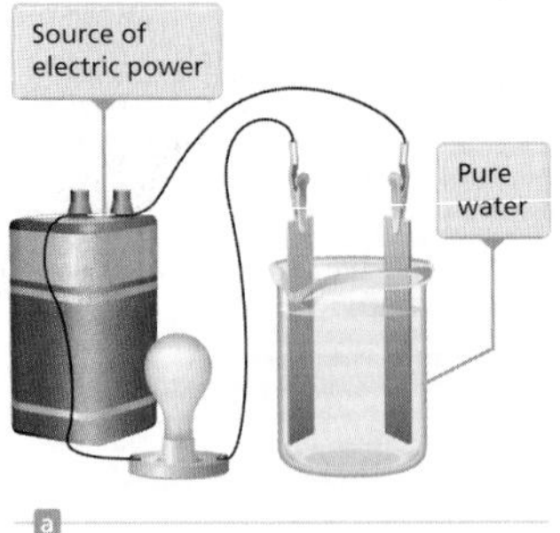

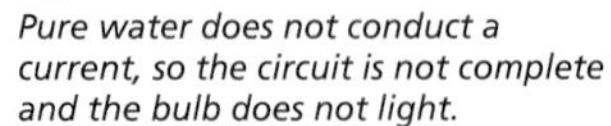

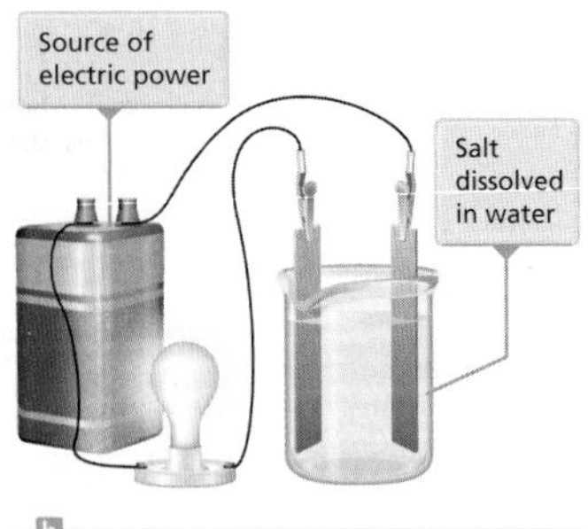

Figure 4.18

a Pure water does not conduct a current, so the circuit is not complete and the bulb does not light.

b Water containing dissolved salt conducts electricity and the bulb lights.

A substance containing ions that can move can conduct an electric current.

Dissolving NaCl causes the ions to be randomly dispersed in the water, allowing them to move freely. Dissolving is not the same as melting, but both processes free the ions to move.

An ionic compound cannot contain only anions or only cations, because the net charge of a compound must be zero.

can travel along a metal wire because *electrons are free to move* through the wire; the moving electrons carry the current. In ionic substances the ions carry the current. Thus substances that contain ions can conduct an electric current *only if the ions can move*—the current travels by the movement of the charged ions. In solid NaCl the ions are tightly held and cannot move, but when the solid is melted and changed to a liquid, the structure is disrupted and the ions can move. As a result, an electric current can travel through the melted salt.

The same reasoning applies to NaCl dissolved in water. When the solid dissolves, the ions are dispersed throughout the water and can move around in the water, allowing it to conduct a current.

Thus, we recognize substances that contain ions by their characteristic properties. They often have very high melting points, and they conduct an electric current when melted or when dissolved in water.

Many substances contain ions. In fact, whenever a compound forms between a metal and a nonmetal, it can be expected to contain ions. We call these substances **ionic compounds.**

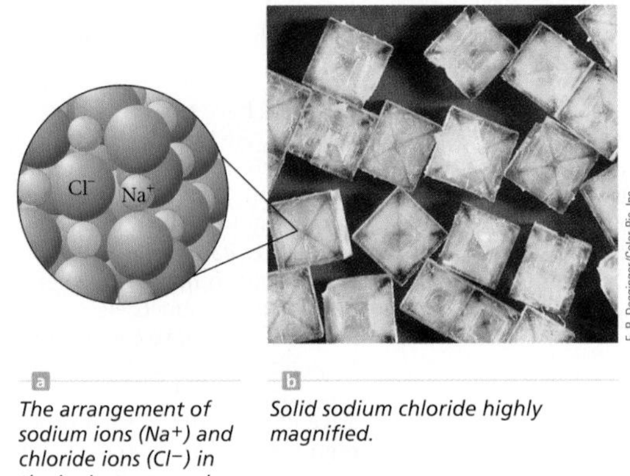

Figure 4.19

a The arrangement of sodium ions (Na^+) and chloride ions (Cl^-) in the ionic compound sodium chloride.

b Solid sodium chloride highly magnified.

One fact very important to remember is that *a chemical compound must have a net charge of zero*. This means that if a compound contains ions, then

The net charge of a compound (zero) is the sum of the positive and negative charges.

1. Both positive ions (cations) and negative ions (anions) must be present.
2. The numbers of cations and anions must be such that the net charge is zero.

For example, note that the formula for sodium chloride is written NaCl, indicating one of each type of these elements. This makes sense because sodium chloride contains Na^+ ions and Cl^- ions. Each sodium ion has a 1+ charge and each chloride ion has a 1− charge, so they must occur in equal numbers to give a net charge of zero.

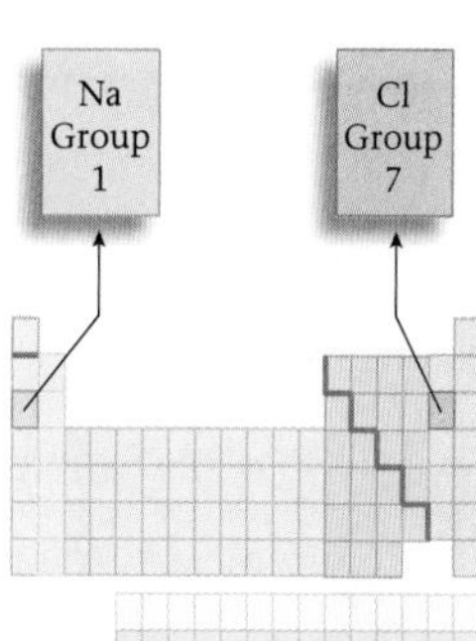

And for *any* ionic compound,

$$\text{Total charge of cations} + \text{Total charge of anions} = \text{Zero net charge}$$

Consider an ionic compound that contains the ions Mg^{2+} and Cl^-. What combination of these ions will give a net charge of zero? To balance the 2+ charge on Mg^{2+}, we will need two Cl^- ions to give a net charge of zero.

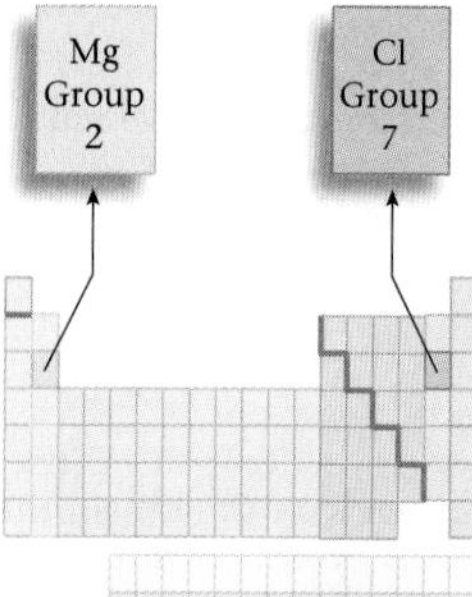

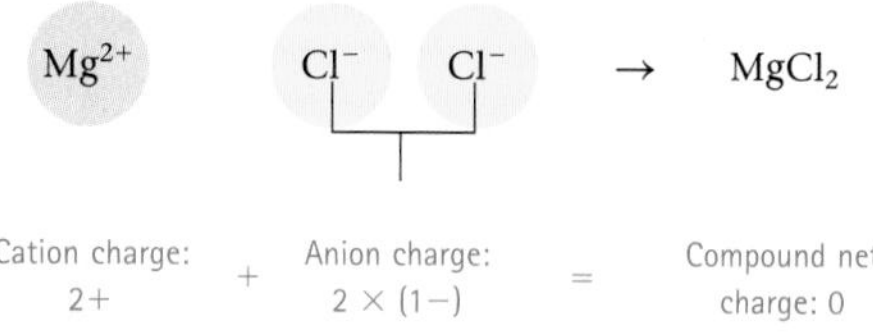

This means that the formula of the compound must be $MgCl_2$. Remember that subscripts are used to give the relative numbers of atoms (or ions).

Now consider an ionic compound that contains the ions Ba^{2+} and O^{2-}. What is the correct formula? These ions have charges of the same size (but opposite sign), so they must occur in equal numbers to give a net charge of zero. The formula of the compound is BaO, because $(2+) + (2-) = 0$.

Similarly, the formula of a compound that contains the ions Li^+ and N^{3-} is Li_3N, because three Li^+ cations are needed to balance the charge of the N^{3-} anion.

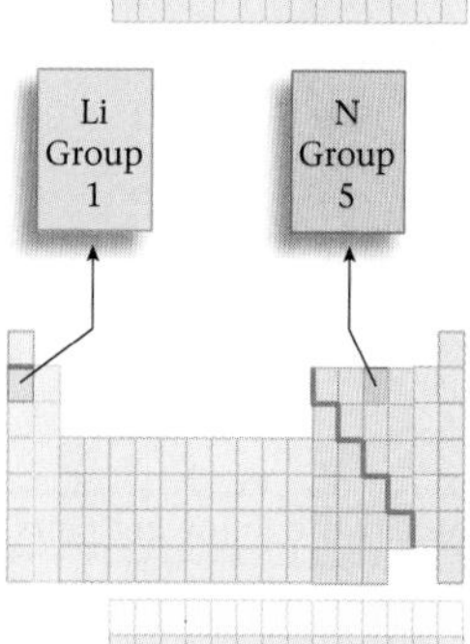

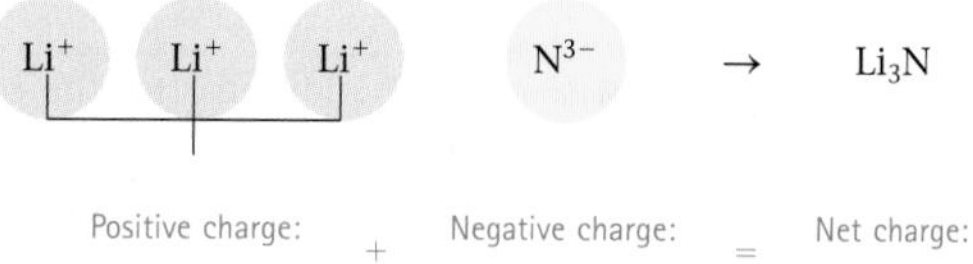

4.11 Compounds That Contain Ions 103

Additional Examples

Example 4.6

Use the pairs of ions below to give the formula for the compound containing these ions.

1. Ba^{2+} and O^{2-} — BaO
2. Al^{3+} and S^{2-} — Al_2S_3
3. K^+ and P^{3-} — K_3P

EXAMPLE 4.6 Writing Formulas for Ionic Compounds

The pairs of ions contained in several ionic compounds are listed below. Give the formula for each compound.

a. Ca^{2+} and Cl^- b. Na^+ and S^{2-} c. Ca^{2+} and P^{3-}

The subscript 1 in a formula is not written.

SOLUTION

a. Ca^{2+} has a 2+ charge, so two Cl^- ions (each with the charge 1−) will be needed.

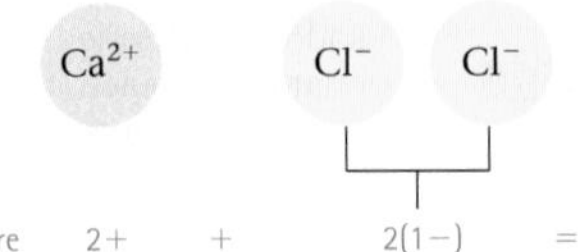

The formula is $CaCl_2$.

b. In this case S^{2-}, with its 2− charge, requires two Na^+ ions to produce a zero net charge.

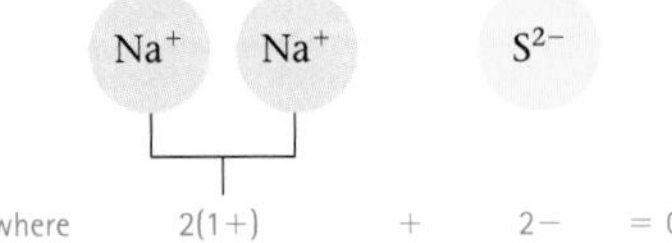

The formula is Na_2S.

c. We have the ions Ca^{2+} (charge 2+) and P^{3-} (charge 3−). We must figure out how many of each are needed to balance exactly the positive and negative charges. Let's try two Ca^{2+} and one P^{3-}.

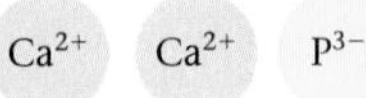

The resulting net charge is 2(2+) + (3−) = (4+) + (3−) = 1−. This doesn't work because the net charge is not zero. We can obtain the same total positive and total negative charges by having three Ca^{2+} ions and two P^{3-} ions.

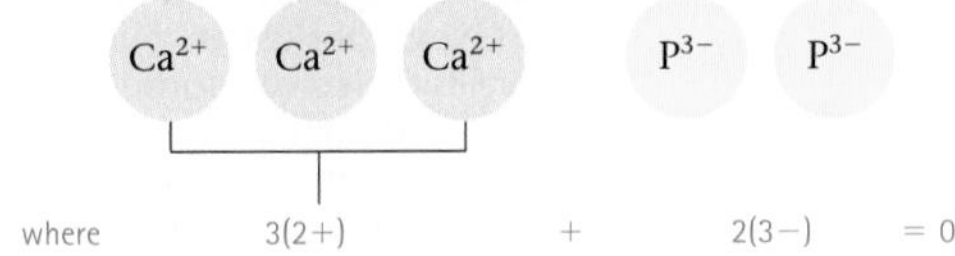

Thus the formula must be Ca_3P_2.

Self-Check EXERCISE 4.6 Give the formulas for the compounds that contain the following pairs of ions.

a. K^+ and I^- b. Mg^{2+} and N^{3-} c. Al^{3+} and O^{2-}

See Problems 4.83 and 4.84. ■

Self Check

Answers to Self-Check Exercise 4.6

a. KI

b. Mg_3N_2

c. Al_2O_3

CHAPTER 4 REVIEW

Key Terms

element symbols (4.2)
law of constant composition (4.3)
Dalton's atomic theory (4.3)
atom (4.3)
compound (4.4)
chemical formula (4.4)
electron (4.5)
nuclear atom (4.5)
nucleus (4.5)
proton (4.5)
neutron (4.5)
isotopes (4.7)
atomic number, *Z* (4.7)
mass number, *A* (4.7)
periodic table (4.8)
groups (4.8)
alkali metals (4.8)
alkaline earth metals (4.8)
halogens (4.8)
noble gases (4.8)
transition metals (4.8)
metals (4.8)
nonmetals (4.8)
metalloids (semimetals) (4.8)
diatomic molecule (4.9)
ion (4.10)
cation (4.10)
anion (4.10)
ionic compound (4.11)

Summary

1. Of the more than 100 different elements now known, only 9 account for about 98% of the total mass of the earth's crust, oceans, and atmosphere. In the human body, oxygen, carbon, hydrogen, and nitrogen are the most abundant elements.
2. Elements are represented by symbols that usually consist of the first one or two letters of the element's name. Sometimes, however, the symbol is taken from the element's original Latin or Greek name.
3. The law of constant composition states that a given compound always contains the same proportions by mass of the elements of which it is composed.
4. Dalton accounted for this law with his atomic theory. He postulated that all elements are composed of atoms; that all atoms of a given element are identical, but that atoms of different elements are different; that chemical compounds are formed when atoms combine; and that atoms are not created or destroyed in chemical reactions.
5. A compound can be represented by a chemical formula that uses the symbol for each type of atom and gives the number of each type of atom that appears in a molecule of the compound.
6. Atoms consist of a nucleus containing protons and neutrons, surrounded by electrons that occupy a large volume relative to the size of the nucleus. Electrons have a relatively small mass (1/1836 of the proton mass) and a negative charge. Protons have a positive charge equal in magnitude (but opposite in sign) to that of the electron. A neutron has a slightly greater mass than the proton but no charge.
7. Isotopes are atoms with the same number of protons but different numbers of neutrons.
8. The periodic table displays the elements in rows and columns in order of increasing atomic number. Elements that have similar chemical properties fall into vertical columns called groups. Most of the elements are metals. These occur on the left-hand side of the periodic table; the nonmetals appear on the right-hand side.
9. Each chemical element is composed of a given type of atom. These elements may exist as individual atoms or as groups of like atoms. For example, the noble gases contain single, separated atoms. However, elements such as oxygen, nitrogen, and chlorine exist as diatomic (two-atom) molecules.
10. When an atom loses one or more electrons, it forms a positive ion called a cation. This behavior is characteristic of metals. When an atom gains one or more electrons, it becomes a negatively charged ion called an anion. This behavior is characteristic of nonmetals. Oppositely charged ions form ionic compounds. A compound is always neutral overall—it has zero net charge.
11. The elements in Groups 1 and 2 on the periodic table form 1+ and 2+ cations, respectively. Group 7 atoms can gain one electron to form 1− ions. Group 6 atoms form 2− ions.

F directs you to the *Chemistry in Focus* feature in the chapter
VP indicates visual problems
OWL interactive versions of these problems are assignable in OWL

Active Learning Questions

These questions are designed to be considered by groups of students in class. Often these questions work well for introducing a particular topic in class.

1. Knowing the number of protons in the atom of a neutral element enables you to determine which of the following?
   a. the number of neutrons in the atom of the neutral element
   b. the number of electrons in the atom of the neutral element
   c. the name of the element
   d. two of the above
   e. none of the above

   Explain.

ChemWork

Concentration of Chloride Ions
Concentration of Ions
Diluting a Solution
Dilution of Solutions
Dilution Volume
Making Solutions
Molarity of Solutions
Predicting Precipitates
What Is the Precipitate?
Concentration of Ions After Precipitation of Silver Chloride
Determining Mass Percent
Finding the Mass of a Product
Precipitation of Barium Phosphate
Precipitation of Silver Chloride
Solution Stoichiometry
Concentration of a Base
Neutralization Reaction
The Percent of Sulfur in Coal
Assigning Oxidation States

Answers to End-of-Chapter Exercises

1. fire, earth, water, air

2. Robert Boyle

3. Boyle insisted that science be founded solidly on experiment and that no preconceptions should prejudice the experiments.

4. About 116 elements are known. Of these, 88 occur naturally, with the remainder being manmade. Table 4.1 lists the most common elements on the earth.

5. oxygen, silicon, aluminum, iron, calcium

6. (a) trace elements are those elements that, while present in the body only in small quantities, are essential to life; (b) depends on student choice/example

7. *C:* Cadmium, Cd; calcium, Ca; californium, Cf; carbon, C; cerium, Ce; cesium, Cs; chlorine, Cl; chromium, Cr; cobalt, Co; copper, Cu; curium, Cm

S: samarium, Sm; scandium, Sc; seaborgium, Sg; selenium, Se; silicon, Si; silver, Ag; sodium, Na; strontium, Sr; sulfur, S

T: tantalum, Ta; technetium, Tc; tellurium, Te; terbium, Tb; thallium, Tl; thorium, Th; thulium, Tm; tin, Sn; titanium, Ti; tungsten, W

8. Answer depends on student choices/examples.

9. (a) 4; (b) 11; (c) 12; (d) 3; (e) 8; (f) 9; (g) 13; (h) 7; (i) 6; (j) 5

10. (a) 9; (b) 6; (c) 8; (d) 12; (e) 11; (f) 13; (g) 3; (h) 5; (i) 4; (j) 2

11. cobalt; Rb; radon; Ra; uranium

12. zirconium; Cs; selenium; Au; cerium

13. (a) potassium; (b) germanium; (c) phosphorus; (d) carbon; (e) nitrogen; (f) sodium; (g) neon; (h) iodine

14. *B:* barium, Ba; berkelium, Bk; beryllium, Be; bismuth, Bi; bohrium, Bh; boron, B; bromine, Br

N: neodymium, Nd; neon, Ne; neptunium, Np; nickel, Ni; niobium, Nb; nitrogen, N; nobelium, No

P: palladium, Pd; phosphorus, P; platinum, Pt; plutonium, Pu; polonium, Po; potassium, K; praseodymium, Pr; promethium, Pm; protactinium, Pa

S: samarium, Sm; scandium, Sc; seaborgium, Sg; selenium, Se; silicon, Si; silver, Ag; sodium, Na; strontium, Sr; sulfur, S

15. Catalytic converters are designed to prevent NO_2, a pollutant, from entering the atmosphere from automobile exhaust systems. Such converters, however, produce N_2O, which, though not considered a pollutant, is nonetheless a "greenhouse" gas.

---

2. The average mass of a carbon atom is 12.011. Assuming you could pick up one carbon atom, what is the chance that you would randomly get one with a mass of 12.011?

   a. 0%
   b. 0.011%
   c. about 12%
   d. 12.011%
   e. greater than 50%
   f. none of the above

   Explain.

3. How is an ion formed?

   a. by either adding or subtracting protons from the atom
   b. by either adding or subtracting neutrons from the atom
   c. by either adding or subtracting electrons from the atom
   d. all of the above
   e. two of the above

   Explain.

4. The formula of water, H_2O, suggests which of the following?

   a. There is twice as much mass of hydrogen as oxygen in each molecule.
   b. There are two hydrogen atoms and one oxygen atom per water molecule.
   c. There is twice as much mass of oxygen as hydrogen in each molecule.
   d. There are two oxygen atoms and one hydrogen atom per water molecule.
   e. Two of the above.

   Explain.

5. The vitamin niacin (nicotinic acid, $C_6H_5NO_2$) can be isolated from a variety of natural sources, such as liver, yeast, milk, and whole grain. It also can be synthesized from commercially available materials. Which source of nicotinic acid, from a nutritional view, is best for use in a multivitamin tablet? Why?

6. One of the best indications of a useful theory is that it raises more questions for further experimentation than it originally answered. How does this apply to Dalton's atomic theory? Give examples.

7. Dalton assumed that all atoms of the same element are identical in all their properties. Explain why this assumption is not valid.

8. How does Dalton's atomic theory account for the law of constant composition?

9. Which of the following is true about the state of an individual atom?

   a. An individual atom should be considered to be a solid.
   b. An individual atom should be considered to be a liquid.
   c. An individual atom should be considered to be a gas.
   d. The state of the atom depends on which element it is.
   e. An individual atom cannot be considered to be a solid, liquid, or gas.

   For choices you did not pick, explain what you feel is wrong with them, and justify the choice you did pick.

10. These questions concern the work of J. J. Thomson:

    a. From Thomson's work, which particles do you think he would feel are most important in the formation of compounds (chemical changes) and why?
    b. Of the remaining two subatomic particles, which do you place second in importance for forming compounds and why?
    c. Come up with three models that explain Thomson's findings and evaluate them. To be complete you should include Thomson's findings.

11. Heat is applied to an ice cube until only steam is present. Draw a sketch of this process, assuming you can see it at an extremely high level of magnification. What happens to the size of the molecules? What happens to the total mass of the sample?

12. What makes a carbon atom different from a nitrogen atom? How are they alike?

13. Hundreds of years ago, alchemists tried to turn lead into gold. Is this possible? If not, why not? If yes, how would you do it?

14. Chlorine has two prominent isotopes, ^{37}Cl and ^{35}Cl. Which is more abundant? How do you know?

15. Differentiate between an atomic element and a molecular element. Provide an example and microscopic drawing of each.

16. Science often develops by using the known theories and expanding, refining, and perhaps changing these theories. As discussed in Section 4.5, Rutherford used Thompson's ideas when thinking about his model of the atom. What if Rutherford had not known about Thompson's work? How might Rutherford's model of the atom have been different?

17. Rutherford was surprised when some of the α-particles bounced back. He was surprised because he was thinking of Thompson's model of the atom. What if Rutherford believed atoms were as Dalton envisioned them? What do you suppose Rutherford would have expected, and what would have surprised him?

18. It is good practice to actively read the textbook and to try to verify claims that are made when you can. The following claim is made in your textbook: "... if the nucleus were the size of a grape, the electrons would be about one mile away on average."

    Provide mathematical support for this statement.

19. Why is the term "sodium chloride molecule" incorrect but the term "carbon dioxide molecule" is correct?

20. Both atomic elements and molecular elements exist. Are there such entities as atomic compounds and molecular compounds? If so, provide an example and microscopic drawing. If not, explain why not.

21. Now that you have gone through Chapter 4, go back to Section 4.3 and review Dalton's Atomic Theory. Which of the premises are no longer accepted? Explain your answer.

VP 22. Write the formula for each of the following substances, listing the elements in the order given.

a. 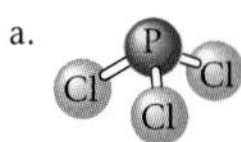

List the phosphorus atom first.

b. a molecule containing two boron atoms and six hydrogen atoms

c. a compound containing one calcium atom for every two chlorine atoms

d. 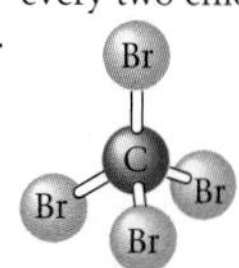

List the carbon atom first.

e. a compound containing two iron atoms for every three oxygen atoms

f. a molecule containing three hydrogen atoms, one phosphorus atom, and four oxygen atoms

VP 23. Use the following figures to identify the element or ion. Write the symbol for each, using the $^A_Z X$ format.

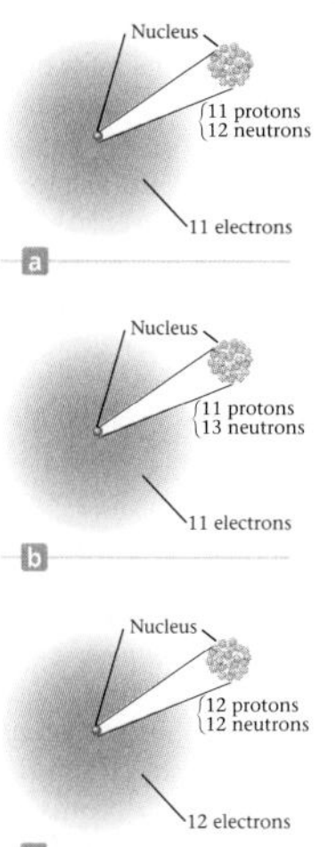

Questions and Problems

4.1 The Elements

QUESTIONS

1. What were the four fundamental substances postulated by the Greeks?

2. Who was the first scientist generally accredited with putting the study of chemistry on a firm experimental basis?

3. In addition to his important work on the properties of gases, what other valuable contributions did Robert Boyle make to the development of the study of chemistry?

4. How many elements are presently known? How many of these elements occur naturally, and how many are synthesized artificially? What are the most common elements present on the earth?

5. What are the five most abundant elements (by mass) in the earth's crust, oceans, and atmosphere?

F 6. Read the "Chemistry in Focus" segment *Trace Elements: Small but Crucial,* and answer the following questions.

a. What is meant by the term *trace element?*

b. Name two essential trace elements in the body and list their function(s).

4.2 Symbols for the Elements

Note: Refer to the tables on the inside front cover when appropriate.

QUESTIONS

7. The letters *C*, *S*, and *T* have been very popular when naming the elements, and there are ten or more elements whose names begin with each of these letters. Without looking in your textbook, see if you can list the symbol and name of five elements for each letter.

8. The symbols for most elements are based on the first few letters of the respective element's common English name. In some cases, however, the symbol seems to have nothing to do with the element's common name. Give three examples of elements whose symbols are not directly derived from the element's common English name.

9. Find the symbol in Column 2 for each name in Column 1.

Column 1	Column 2
a. helium	1. Si
b. sodium	2. So
c. silver	3. S
d. sulfur	4. He
e. bromine	5. C
f. potassium	6. Co
g. neon	7. Ba
h. barium	8. Br
i. cobalt	9. K
j. carbon	10. Po
	11. Na
	12. Ag
	13. Ne
	14. Ca

All even-numbered Questions and Problems have answers in the back of this book and solutions in the Solutions Guide.

16. (a) Elements are made of tiny particles called atoms.
(b) All atoms of a given element are identical.
(c) The atoms of a given element are different from those of any other element.
(d) A given compound always has the same numbers and types of atoms.
(e) Atoms are neither created nor destroyed in chemical processes. A chemical reaction simply changes the way the atoms are grouped together.

17. A compound is a distinct substance that is composed of two or more elements and always contains exactly the same relative masses of those elements.

18. According to Dalton, all atoms of the same element are *identical;* in particular, every atom of a given element has the same *mass* as every other atom of that element. If a given compound always contains the *same relative numbers* of atoms of each kind, and those atoms always have the same *masses,* then the compound made from those elements always contains the same relative masses of its elements.

19. (a) C_6H_6; (b) $AlCl_3$; (c) Na_2S; (d) N_2O_4; (e) $NaHCO_3$; (f) KI

20. (a) CO_2; (b) CO; (c) $CaCO_3$; (d) H_2SO_4; (e) $BaCl_2$; (f) Al_2S_3

21. (a) electron; He postulated that because he had detected negative particles in the atom, there must also be positive particles to counterbalance the charge. (b) He saw the atom as a uniform "pudding" of positive charge, with electrons scattered through like the raisins in a pudding to balance the charge.

22. (a) False; Rutherford's bombardment experiments with metal foil suggested that the α particles were being deflected by coming near a *dense, positively charged* atomic nucleus. (b) False; the proton and the electron have opposite charges, but the mass of the electron is *much smaller* than the mass of the proton. (c) True

23. Neutrons are found in the nucleus and have no charge.

24. The protons and neutrons are found in the nucleus. The protons are positively charged; the neutrons have no charge. The protons and neutrons each weigh approximately the same.

25. The proton and neutron have similar (but not identical) masses. Either of these particles has a mass about 2000 times greater than that of the electron. The protons and neutrons make up most of the mass of the atom, but the electrons make the greatest contribution to the atom's chemical properties.

26. neutron; electron

27. 10^{-13} cm; 10^{-15} m

28. The electrons; outside the nucleus

29. Although all atoms of a given element contain the same number of protons in the nucleus, different atoms may have different numbers of neutrons. Isotopes are atoms of the same element with different mass numbers.

30. The atomic number represents the number of protons in the nucleus of the atom, and makes the atom a particular element. The mass number represents the total number of protons and neutrons in the nucleus of an atom, and distinguishes one isotope of an element from another.

31. An isolated atom has no charge; therefore, the number of negatively charged electrons must equal the number of positively charged protons.

32. Neutrons are uncharged and contribute only to the mass.

33. Dalton's original assumption was reasonable for his time, but as mass determination techniques improved, it was discovered that a given element may be composed of several isotopes. Isotopes have the same number of protons and electrons, and so are chemically identical, but they differ in the number of neutrons, which causes some physical differences.

34. Atoms of the same element (atoms with the same number of protons in the nucleus) may have different numbers of neutrons, and so will have different masses.

37. (a) $^{13}_{6}C$; (b) $^{12}_{6}C$; (c) $^{14}_{6}C$; (d) $^{11}_{5}B$; (e) $^{10}_{5}B$; (f) $^{10}_{5}B$

38. (a) $^{54}_{26}Fe$; (b) $^{56}_{26}Fe$; (c) $^{57}_{26}Fe$; (d) $^{14}_{7}N$; (e) $^{15}_{7}N$; (f) $^{15}_{7}N$

39. (a) 56 protons, 74 neutrons, 56 electrons; (b) 56 protons, 80 neutrons, 56 electrons; (c) 22 protons, 24 neutrons, 22 electrons; (d) 22 protons, 26 neutrons, 22 electrons; (e) 3 protons, 3 neutrons, 3 electrons; (f) 3 protons, 4 neutrons, 3 electrons

10. Find the name in Column 2 that corresponds to each symbol in Column 1.

Column 1	Column 2
a. Si	1. sulfur
b. O	2. copper
c. Fe	3. molybdenum
d. W	4. strontium
e. Ni	5. platinum
f. Zn	6. oxygen
g. Mo	7. protactinium
h. Pt	8. iron
i. Sr	9. silicon
j. Cu	10. nitrogen
	11. nickel
	12. tungsten
	13. zinc
	14. gold

11. Use the periodic table inside the front cover of this book to find the symbol or name for each of the following elements.

Symbol	Name
Co	______
______	rubidium
Rn	______
______	radium
U	______

12. Use the periodic table inside the front cover of this book to find the symbol or name for each of the following elements.

Symbol	Name
Zr	______
______	cesium
Se	______
______	gold
Ce	______

13. For each of the following chemical symbols, give the name of the corresponding element.

a. K	e. N
b. Ge	g. Ne
c. P	f. Na
d. C	h. I

14. Several chemical elements have English names beginning with the letters B, N, P, or S. For each letter, list the English *names* for two elements whose names begin with that letter, and give the symbols for the elements you choose (the symbols do not necessarily need to begin with the same letters).

4.3 Dalton's Atomic Theory

QUESTIONS

15. The "Chemistry in Focus" segment *No Laughing Matter* ends with the statement "Clean may not necessarily be 'green.'" Read this segment and explain the statement.

16. Correct each of the following misstatements from Dalton's atomic theory.
    a. Elements are made of tiny particles called molecules.
    b. All atoms of a given element are very similar.
    c. The atoms of a given element may be the same as those of another element.
    d. A given compound may vary in the relative number and types of atoms depending on the source of the compound.
    e. A chemical reaction may involve the gain or loss of atoms as it takes place.

4.4 Formulas of Compounds

QUESTIONS

17. What is a compound?

18. A given compound always contains the same relative masses of its constituent elements. How is this related to the relative numbers of each kind of atom present?

19. Based on the following word descriptions, write the formula for each of the indicated substances.
    a. a compound whose molecules each contain six carbon atoms and six hydrogen atoms
    b. an aluminum compound in which there are three chlorine atoms for each aluminum atom
    c. a compound in which there are two sodium atoms for every sulfur atom
    d. a compound whose molecules each contain two nitrogen atoms and four oxygen atoms
    e. a compound in which there is an equal number of sodium, hydrogen, and carbon atoms but there are three times as many oxygen atoms as atoms of the other three elements
    f. a compound that has equal numbers of potassium and iodide atoms

20. Based on the following word descriptions, write the formula for each of the indicated substances.
    a. a compound whose molecules contain twice as many oxygen atoms as carbon atoms
    b. a compound whose molecules contain an equal number of carbon and oxygen atoms
    c. a compound in which there is an equal number of calcium and carbon atoms but there are three times as many atoms of oxygen as of the other two elements
    d. a compound whose molecules contain twice as many hydrogen atoms as sulfur atoms and four times as many oxygen atoms as sulfur atoms
    e. a compound in which there are twice as many chlorine atoms as barium atoms
    f. a compound in which there are three sulfur atoms for every two aluminum atoms

All even-numbered Questions and Problems have answers in the back of this book and solutions in the Solutions Guide.

35.

Atomic Number	*Symbol*	*Name*
8	O	oxygen
29	Cu	copper
78	Pt	platinum
15	P	phosphorus
17	Cl	chlorine
50	Sn	tin
30	Zn	zinc

36.

Z	*Symbol*	*Name*
14	Si	silicon
54	Xe	xenon
79	Au	gold
56	Ba	barium
53	I	iodine
50	Sn	tin
48	Cd	cadmium

4.5 The Structure of the Atom

QUESTIONS

21. Scientists J. J. Thomson and William Thomson (Lord Kelvin) made numerous contributions to our understanding of the atom's structure.
    a. Which subatomic particle did J. J. Thomson discover, and what did this lead him to postulate about the nature of the atom?
    b. William Thomson postulated what became known as the "plum pudding" model of the atom's structure. What did this model suggest?

22. Indicate whether each of the following statements is true or false. If false, correct the statement so that it becomes true.
    a. Rutherford's bombardment experiments with metal foil suggested that the alpha particles were being deflected by coming near a large, negatively charged atomic nucleus.
    b. The proton and the electron have similar masses but opposite electrical charges.
    c. Most atoms also contain neutrons, which are slightly heavier than protons but carry no charge.

4.6 Introduction to the Modern Concept of Atomic Structure

QUESTIONS

23. Where are neutrons found in an atom? Are neutrons positively charged, negatively charged, or electrically uncharged?

24. What two common types of particles are found in the nucleus of the atom? What are the relative charges of these particles? What are the relative masses of these particles?

25. Do the proton and the neutron have exactly the same mass? How do the masses of the proton and the neutron compare to the mass of the electron? Which particles make the greatest contribution to the mass of an atom? Which particles make the greatest contribution to the chemical properties of an atom?

26. The proton and the (electron/neutron) have almost equal masses. The proton and the (electron/neutron) have charges that are equal in magnitude but opposite in nature.

27. An average atomic nucleus has a diameter of about ________ m.

28. Which particles in an atom are most responsible for the chemical properties of the atom? Where are these particles located in the atom?

4.7 Isotopes

QUESTIONS

29. Explain what we mean when we say that a particular element consists of several *isotopes*.

30. Imagine you are talking to a friend who has never taken any science courses. Explain to your friend what are meant by the *atomic number* and *mass number* of a nucleus.

31. For an isolated atom, why do we expect the number of electrons present in the atom to be the *same* as the number of protons in the nucleus of the atom?

32. Why do we not necessarily expect the number of neutrons in the nucleus of an atom to be the same as the number of protons?

33. Dalton's original atomic theory proposed that all atoms of a given element are *identical*. Did this turn out to be true after further experimentation was carried out? Explain.

34. Are all atoms of the same element identical? If not, how can they differ?

35. For each of the following elements, use the periodic table on the inside cover of this book to write the element's atomic number, symbol, or name.

Atomic Number	Symbol	Name
8	______	______
______	Cu	______
78	______	______
______	______	phosphorus
17	______	______
______	Sn	______
______	______	zinc

36. For each of the following elements, use the periodic table on the inside cover of this book to write the element's atomic number, symbol, or name.

Atomic Number	Symbol	Name
14	Si	______
______	Xe	xenon
79	______	gold
56	______	barium
______	I	iodine
______	Sn	tin
48	______	cadmium

37. Write the atomic symbol ($^{A}_{Z}X$) for each of the isotopes described below.
    a. the isotope of carbon with 7 neutrons
    b. the isotope of carbon with 6 neutrons
    c. $Z = 6$, number of neutrons = 8
    d. atomic number 5, mass number 11
    e. number of protons = 5, number of neutrons = 5
    f. the isotope of boron with mass number 10

38. Write the atomic symbol ($^{A}_{Z}X$) for each of the isotopes described below.
    a. $Z = 26$, $A = 54$
    b. the isotope of iron with 30 neutrons
    c. number of protons-26, number of neutrons-31
    d. the isotope of nitrogen with 7 neutrons
    e. $Z = 7$, $A = 15$
    f. atomic number 7, number of neutrons-8

All even-numbered Questions and Problems have answers in the back of this book and solutions in the Solutions Guide.

40. The relative amounts of ^{2}H and ^{18}O in a person's hair, compared to other isotopes of these elements, vary significantly from region to region in the United States and is related to the isotopic abundances in the drinking water in a region.

41. Isotopes are atoms that contain the same number of protons but a different number of neutrons. The text gives an example in which ivory from African elephants was identified as coming from a specific region based on the ratio of ^{13}C to ^{12}C in the ivory.

42.

Name	*Symbol*	*Atomic Number*	*Mass Number*	*Number of Neutrons*
oxygen	$^{17}_{8}O$	8	17	9
oxygen	$^{17}_{8}O$	8	17	9
Neon	$^{20}_{10}Ne$	10	20	10
iron	$^{56}_{26}Fe$	26	56	30
plutonium	$^{244}_{94}Pu$	94	244	150
mercury	$^{202}_{80}Hg$	80	202	122
cobalt	$^{59}_{27}Co$	27	59	32
nickel	$^{56}_{28}Ni$	28	56	28
fluorine	$^{19}_{9}F$	9	19	10
chromium	$^{50}_{24}Cr$	24	50	26

43. False; they are arranged in order of increasing atomic number (nuclear charge).

44. vertical, groups

45. Metals are excellent conductors of heat and electricity; they are malleable, ductile, and generally lustrous (when a fresh surface is exposed).

46. Metallic elements are found toward the *left* and *bottom* of the periodic table; there are far more metallic elements than nonmetals.

47. Mercury is a liquid at room temperature.

48. nonmetallic gaseous elements: oxygen, nitrogen, fluorine, chlorine, hydrogen, and the noble gases; no metallic gaseous elements at room conditions

49. metal, mercury; nonmetal, bromine (normal room conditions)

50. A metalloid is an element that has some properties common to both metallic and nonmetallic elements. The metalloids are found in the "stair-step" region marked on most periodic tables.

51. (a) Group 1, alkali metals; (b) Group 2, alkaline earth elements; (c) Group 8, noble gases; (d) Group 7, halogens; (e) Group 2, alkaline earth elements; (f) Group 8, noble gases; (g) Group 1, alkali metals

52. (a) fluorine, chlorine, bromine, iodine, astatine; (b) lithium, sodium, potassium, rubidium, cesium, francium; (c) beryllium, magnesium, calcium, strontium, barium, radium; (d) helium, neon, argon, krypton, xenon, radon

53. (a) Sr, $Z = 38$, Group 2, metal; (b) I, $Z = 53$, Group 7, nonmetal; (c) Si, $Z = 14$, Group 4, metalloid; (d) Cs, $Z = 55$, Group 1, metal; (e) S, $Z = 16$, Group 6, nonmetal

54. Arsenic, atomic number 33, is located on the dividing line between the metallic elements and the non-metallic elements, and is therefore classified as a metalloid. Arsenic is in Group 5 of the periodic table, whose other principal members are N, P, Sb, and Bi.

55. compounds (and mixtures of compounds)

56. Most elements are too reactive to be found in the uncombined form in nature and are found only in compounds.

57. argon

58. These elements are found uncombined in nature and do not readily react with other elements. Although these elements were once thought to form no compounds, this now has been shown to be untrue.

59. diatomic

60. diatomic gases: H_2, N_2, O_2, F_2, Cl_2; monatomic gases: He, Ne, Kr, Xe, Rn, Ar

61. electricity

62. chlorine

63. liquids: bromine, mercury (gallium); gases: hydrogen, nitrogen, oxygen, fluorine, chlorine, helium, neon, argon, krypton, xenon, radon

64. diamond

65. zero

66. electrons

67. loses three

68. 3+

69. cations, anions

70. *-ide*

71. The answer depends on the student's selection.

72. nonmetallic

73. (a) 54; (b) 18; (c) 23; (d) 10; (e) 54; (f) 80

74. (a) 36; (b) 36; (c) 21; (d) 36; (e) 80; (f) 27

75. (a) Ca: 20 protons, 20 electrons; Ca^{2+}: 20 protons, 18 electrons; (b) P: 15 protons, 15 electrons; P^{3-}: 15 protons, 18 electrons; (c) Br: 35 protons, 35 electrons; Br^-: 35 protons, 36 electrons; (d) Fe: 26 protons, 26 electrons; Fe^{3+}: 26 protons, 23 electrons; (e) Al: 13 protons, 13 electrons; Al^{3+}: 13 protons, 10 electrons; (f) N: 7 protons, 7 electrons; N^{3-}: 7 protons, 10 electrons

76. (a) two electrons gained; (b) three electrons gained; (c) three electrons lost; (d) two electrons lost; (e) one electron lost; (f) two electrons lost

77. (a) I^-; (b) Sr^{2+}; (c) Cs^+; (d) Ra^{2+}; (e) F^-; (f) Al^{3+}

78. (a) P^{3-}; (b) Ra^{2+}; (c) At^-; (d) no ion; (e) Cs^+; (f) Se^{2-}

79. high melting point; conducts current when dissolved

80. Sodium chloride is an *ionic* compound, consisting of Na^+ and Cl^- *ions*. When NaCl is dissolved in water, these ions are *set free* and can move independently to conduct the electric current. Sugar crystals, although they may *appear* similar visually, contain *no* ions. When sugar is

39. How many protons and neutrons are contained in the nucleus of each of the following atoms? Assuming each atom is uncharged, how many electrons are present?

a. $^{130}_{56}Ba$ c. $^{46}_{22}Ti$ e. $^{6}_{3}Li$
b. $^{136}_{56}Ba$ d. $^{48}_{22}Ti$ f. $^{7}_{3}Li$

F 40. Read the "Chemistry in Focus" segment *"Whair" Do You Live?* How can isotopes be used to identify the general region of a person's place of residence?

F 41. Read the "Chemistry in Focus" segment *Isotope Tales.* Define the term *isotope,* and explain how isotopes can be used to answer scientific and historical questions.

42. Complete the following table.

Name	Symbol	Atomic Number	Mass Number	Number of Neutrons
____	$^{17}_{8}O$	____	____	____
____	____	8	____	9
____	____	10	20	____
iron	____	____	56	____
____	$^{244}_{94}Pu$	____	____	____
____	$^{202}_{80}Hg$	____	____	____
cobalt	____	____	59	____
____	____	28	56	____
____	$^{19}_{9}F$	____	____	____
chromium	____	____	____	26

4.8 Introduction to the Periodic Table

QUESTIONS

43. True or false? The elements are arranged in the periodic table in order of increasing mass.

44. In which direction on the periodic table, horizontal or vertical, are elements with similar chemical properties aligned? What are families of elements with similar chemical properties called?

45. List the characteristic physical properties that distinguish the metallic elements from the nonmetallic elements.

46. Where are the metallic elements found on the periodic table? Are there more metallic elements or nonmetallic elements?

47. Most, but not all, metallic elements are solids under ordinary laboratory conditions. Which metallic elements are *not* solids?

48. List five nonmetallic elements that exist as gaseous substances under ordinary conditions. Do any metallic elements ordinarily occur as gases?

49. Under ordinary conditions, only a few pure elements occur as liquids. Give an example of a metallic and a nonmetallic element that ordinarily occur as liquids.

50. What is a *metalloid?* Where are the metalloids found on the periodic table?

51. Write the number and name (if any) of the group (family) to which each of the following elements belongs.

a. cesium e. strontium
b. Ra f. Xe
c. Rn g. Rb
d. chlorine

52. Without looking at your textbook or the periodic table, name three elements in each of the following groups (families).

a. halogens
b. alkali metals
c. alkaline earth metals
d. noble/inert gases

53. For each of the following elements, use the tables on the inside cover of this book to give the chemical symbol, atomic number, and group number of each element, and to specify whether each element is a metal, nonmetal, or metalloid.

a. strontium c. silicon e. sulfur
b. iodine d. cesium

F 54. The "Chemistry in Focus" segment *Putting the Brakes on Arsenic* discusses the dangers of arsenic and a possible help against arsenic pollution. Is arsenic a metal, a nonmetal, or a metalloid? What other elements are in the same group on the periodic table as arsenic?

4.9 Natural States of the Elements

QUESTIONS

55. Most substances are composed of ____ rather than elemental substances.

56. Are most of the chemical elements found in nature in the elemental form or combined in compounds? Why?

57. The noble gas present in relatively large concentrations in the atmosphere is ____.

58. Why are the elements of Group 8 referred to as the noble or inert gas elements?

59. Molecules of nitrogen gas and oxygen gas are said to be ____, which means they consist of pairs of atoms.

60. Give three examples of gaseous elements that exist as diatomic molecules. Give three examples of gaseous elements that exist as monatomic species.

61. A simple way to generate elemental hydrogen gas is to pass ____ through water.

62. If sodium chloride (table salt) is melted and then subjected to an electric current, elemental ____ gas is produced, along with sodium metal.

All even-numbered Questions and Problems have answers in the back of this book and solutions in the Solutions Guide.

63. Most of the elements are solids at room temperature. Give three examples of elements that are *liquids* at room temperature, and three examples of elements that are *gases* at room temperature.

64. The two most common elemental forms of carbon are graphite and ______.

4.10 Ions

QUESTIONS

65. An isolated atom has a net charge of ______.

66. Ions are produced when an atom gains or loses ______.

67. A simple ion with a 3+ charge (for example, Al^{3+}) results when an atom (gains/loses) ______ electrons.

68. An ion that has three more protons in the nucleus than there are electrons outside the nucleus will have a charge of ______.

69. Positive ions are called ______, whereas negative ions are called ______.

70. Simple negative ions formed from single atoms are given names that end in ______.

71. Based on their location in the periodic table, give the symbols for three elements that would be expected to form positive ions in their reactions.

72. The tendency to *gain* electrons is a fundamental property of the ______ elements.

73. How many electrons are present in each of the following ions?

a. Ba^{2+} c. Mn^{2+} e. Cs^{+}
b. P^{3-} d. Mg^{2+} f. Pb^{2+}

74. How many electrons are present in each of the following ions?

a. Se^{2-} c. Cr^{3+} e. Bi^{3+}
b. Br^{-} d. Rb^{+} f. Cu^{2+}

75. For the following processes that show the formation of ions, use the periodic table to indicate the number of electrons and protons present in both the *ion* and the *neutral atom* from which the ion is made.

a. $Ca \rightarrow Ca^{2+} + 2e^{-}$
b. $P + 3e^{-} \rightarrow P^{3-}$
c. $Br + e^{-} \rightarrow Br^{-}$
d. $Fe \rightarrow Fe^{3+} + 3e^{-}$
e. $Al \rightarrow Al^{3+} + 3e^{-}$
f. $N + 3e^{-} \rightarrow N^{3-}$

76. For the following ions, indicate whether electrons must be *gained* or *lost* from the parent neutral atom, and *how many* electrons must be gained or lost.

a. O^{2-} c. Cr^{3+} e. Rb^{+}
b. P^{3-} d. Sn^{2+} f. Pb^{2+}

77. For each of the following atomic numbers, use the periodic table to write the formula (including the charge) for the simple *ion* that the element is most likely to form.

a. 53 c. 55 e. 9
b. 38 d. 88 f. 13

78. On the basis of the element's location in the periodic table, indicate what simple ion each of the following elements is most likely to form.

a. P c. At e. Cs
b. Ra d. Rn f. Se

4.11 Compounds That Contain Ions

QUESTIONS

79. List some properties of a substance that would lead you to believe it consists of ions. How do these properties differ from those of nonionic compounds?

80. Why does a solution of sodium chloride in water conduct an electric current, whereas a solution of sugar in water does not?

81. Why does an ionic compound conduct an electric current when the compound is melted but not when it is in the solid state?

82. Why must the total number of positive charges in an ionic compound equal the total number of negative charges?

83. For each of the following positive ions, use the concept that a chemical compound must have a net charge of zero to predict the formula of the simple compounds that the positive ions would form with the Cl^{-}, S^{2-}, and N^{3-} ions.

a. K^{+} c. Al^{3+} e. Li^{+}
b. Mg^{2+} d. Ca^{2+}

84. For each of the following negative ions, use the concept that a chemical compound must have a net charge of zero to predict the formula of the simple compounds that the negative ions would form with the Cs^{+}, Ba^{2+}, and Al^{3+} ions.

a. I^{-} c. P^{3-} e. H^{-}
b. O^{2-} d. Se^{2-}

Additional Problems

85. For each of the following elements, give the chemical symbol and atomic number.

a. astatine e. lead
b. xenon f. selenium
c. radium g. argon
d. strontium h. cesium

86. Give the group number (if any) in the periodic table for the elements listed in problem 85. If the group has a family name, give that name.

All even-numbered Questions and Problems have answers in the back of this book and solutions in the Solutions Guide.

dissolved in water, it dissolves as uncharged *molecules.* No electrically charged species are present in a sugar solution to carry the electric current.

81. In the solid state, ions are rigidly held in fixed positions and cannot move. In the liquid state, ions are free to move and can conduct an electric current.

82. The total number of positive charges must equal the total number of negative charges so that the crystals of an ionic compound have *no net charge.* A macroscopic sample of compound ordinarily has no net charge.

83. (a) KCl, K_2S, K_3N; (b) $MgCl_2$, MgS, Mg_3N_2; (c) $AlCl_3$, Al_2S_3, AlN; (d) $CaCl_2$, CaS, Ca_3N_2; (e) LiCl, Li_2S, Li_3N

84. (a) CsI, BaI_2, AlI_3; (b) Cs_2O, BaO, Al_2O_3; (c) Cs_3P, Ba_3P_2, AlP; (d) Cs_2Se, BaSe, Al_2Se_3; (e) CsH, BaH_2, AlH_3

85. (a) At, $Z = 85$; (b) Xe, $Z = 54$; (c) Ra, $Z = 88$; (d) Sr, $Z = 38$; (e) Pb, $Z = 82$; (f) Se, $Z = 34$; (g) Ar, $Z = 18$; (h) Cs, $Z = 55$

86. (a) 7, halogens; (b) 8, noble gases; (c) 2, alkaline earth elements; (d) 2, alkaline earth elements; (e) 4; (f) 6; (g) 8, noble gases; (h) 1, alkali metals

87. See bottom of page.

88. Group 3: boron, B, 5; aluminum, Al, 13; gallium, Ga, 31; indium, In, 49; Group 5: nitrogen, N, 7; phosphorus, P, 15; arsenic, As, 33; antimony, Sb, 51; Group 8: helium, He, 2; neon, Ne, 10; argon, Ar, 18; krypton, Kr, 36

89. The atomic number represents the number of protons in the nucleus; the mass number represents the total number of protons and neutrons. No two elements have the same atomic number, but two elements *may* have the same mass number.

87.

	Element	*Symbol*	*Atomic Number*
Group 1	hydrogen	H	1
	lithium	Li	3
	sodium	Na	11
	potassium	K	19
Group 2	beryllium	Be	4
	magnesium	Mg	12
	calcium	Ca	20
	strontium	Sr	38

87. (*cont.*)

	Element	*Symbol*	*Atomic Number*
Group 6	oxygen	O	8
	sulfur	S	16
	selenium	Se	34
	tellurium	Te	52
Group 7	fluorine	F	9
	chlorine	Cl	17
	bromine	Br	35
	iodine	I	53

87. List the names, symbols, and atomic numbers of the top four elements in Groups 1, 2, 6, and 7.

88. List the names, symbols, and atomic numbers of the top four elements in Groups 3, 5, and 8.

89. What is the difference between the atomic number and the mass number of an element? Can atoms of two different elements have the same atomic number? Could they have the same mass number? Why or why not?

90. Which subatomic particles contribute most to the atom's mass? Which subatomic particles determine the atom's chemical properties?

91. Is it possible for the same two elements to form more than one compound? Is this consistent with Dalton's atomic theory? Give an example.

92. Carbohydrates, a class of compounds containing the elements carbon, hydrogen, and oxygen, were originally thought to contain one water molecule (H_2O) for each carbon atom present. The carbohydrate glucose contains six carbon atoms. Write a general formula showing the relative numbers of each type of atom present in glucose.

93. When iron rusts in moist air, the product is typically a mixture of two iron–oxygen compounds. In one compound, there is an equal number of iron and oxygen atoms. In the other compound, there are three oxygen atoms for every two iron atoms. Write the formulas for the two iron oxides.

94. How many protons and neutrons are contained in the nucleus of each of the following atoms? For an atom of the element, how many electrons are present?

a. $^{63}_{29}Cu$ b. $^{80}_{35}Br$ c. $^{24}_{12}Mg$

95. Though the common isotope of aluminum has a mass number of 27, isotopes of aluminum have been isolated (or prepared in nuclear reactors) with mass numbers of 24, 25, 26, 28, 29, and 30. How many neutrons are present in each of these isotopes? Why are they all considered aluminum atoms, even though they differ greatly in mass? Write the atomic symbol for each isotope.

96. The principal goal of alchemists was to convert cheaper, more common metals into gold. Considering that gold had no particular practical uses (for example, it was too soft to be used for weapons), why do you think early civilizations placed such emphasis on the value of gold?

97. How did Robert Boyle define an element?

98. Give the chemical symbol for each of the following elements.

a. iodine
b. silicon
c. tungsten
d. iron
e. copper
f. cobalt

99. Give the chemical symbol for each of the following elements.

a. barium
b. potassium
c. cesium
d. lead
e. platinum
f. gold

100. Give the chemical symbol for each of the following elements.

a. bromine
b. bismuth
c. mercury
d. vanadium
e. fluorine
f. calcium

101. Give the chemical symbol for each of the following elements.

a. silver
b. aluminum
c. cadmium
d. antimony
e. tin
f. arsenic

102. For each of the following chemical symbols, give the name of the corresponding element.

a. Os
b. Zr
c. Rb
d. Rn
e. U
f. Mn
g. Ni
h. Br

103. For each of the following chemical symbols, give the name of the corresponding element.

a. Te
b. Pd
c. Zn
d. Si
e. Cs
f. Bi
g. F
h. Ti

104. Write the simplest formula for each of the following substances, listing the elements in the order given.

a. a molecule containing one carbon atom and two oxygen atoms
b. a compound containing one aluminum atom for every three chlorine atoms
c. perchloric acid, which contains one hydrogen atom, one chlorine atom, and four oxygen atoms
d. a molecule containing one sulfur atom and six chlorine atoms

105. For each of the following atomic numbers, write the name and chemical symbol of the corresponding element. (Refer to Figure 4.11.)

a. 7
b. 10
c. 11
d. 28
e. 22
f. 18
g. 36
h. 54

106. Write the atomic symbol (^A_ZX) for each of the isotopes described below.

a. $Z = 6$, number of neutrons = 7
b. the isotope of carbon with a mass number of 13
c. $Z = 6$, $A = 13$
d. $Z = 19$, $A = 44$
e. the isotope of calcium with a mass number of 41
f. the isotope with 19 protons and 16 neutrons

All even-numbered Questions and Problems have answers in the back of this book and solutions in the Solutions Guide.

90. Most of an atom's mass is concentrated in the nucleus: the *protons* and *neutrons* that constitute the nucleus have similar masses and are each nearly 2000 times more massive than electrons. The chemical properties of an atom depend on the number and location of the *electrons* it possesses. Electrons are found in the outer regions of the atom and are involved in interactions between atoms.

91. yes; law of multiple proportions

92. $C_6H_{12}O_6$

93. FeO and Fe_2O_3

94. (a) 29 electrons, 34 neutrons, 29 electrons; (b) 35 protons, 45 neutrons, 35 electrons; (c) 12 protons, 12 neutrons, 12 electrons

95. See bottom of page.

96. The chief use of gold in ancient times was as *ornamentation,* whether in statuary or in jewelry. Gold possesses an especially beautiful luster; since it is relatively soft and malleable, it can be worked finely by artisans. Among the metals, gold is inert to attack by most substances in the environment.

97. Boyle defined an element as a substance that could not be broken down into simpler substances.

98. (a) I; (b) Si; (c) W; (d) Fe; (e) Cu; (f) Co

99. (a) Ba; (b) K; (c) Cs; (d) Pb; (e) Pt; (f) Au

100. (a) Br; (b) Bi; (c) Hg; (d) V; (e) F; (f) Ca

101. (a) Ag; (b) Al; (c) Cd; (d) Sb; (e) Sn; (f) As

102. (a) osmium; (b) zirconium; (c) rubidium; (d) radon; (e) uranium; (f) manganese; (g) nickel; (h) bromine

103. (a) tellurium; (b) palladium; (c) zinc; (d) silicon; (e) cesium; (f) bismuth; (g) fluorine; (h) titanium

95.

Mass Number	*Symbol*	*Number of Neutrons*
24	$^{24}_{13}Al$	11
25	$^{25}_{13}Al$	12
26	$^{26}_{13}Al$	13
28	$^{28}_{13}Al$	15
29	$^{29}_{13}Al$	16
30	$^{30}_{13}Al$	17

107. How many protons and neutrons are contained in the nucleus of each of the following atoms? In an atom of each element, how many electrons are present?

a. $^{41}_{22}Ti$ d. $^{86}_{36}Kr$
b. $^{64}_{30}Zn$ e. $^{75}_{33}As$
c. $^{76}_{32}Ge$ f. $^{41}_{19}K$

108. Complete the following table.

Symbol	Protons	Neutrons	Mass Number
$^{41}_{20}Ca$	______	______	______
______	25	30	______
______	47	______	109
$^{45}_{21}Sc$	______	______	______

109. For each of the following elements, use the table on the inside front cover of the book to give the chemical symbol and atomic number and to specify whether the element is a metal or a nonmetal. Also give the named family to which the element belongs (if any).

a. carbon
b. selenium
c. radon
d. beryllium

All even-numbered Questions and Problems have answers in the back of this book and solutions in the Solutions Guide.

104. (a) CO_2; (b) $AlCl_3$; (c) $HClO_4$; (d) SCl_6

105. (a) nitrogen, N; (b) neon, Ne; (c) sodium, Na; (d) nickel, Ni; (e) titanium, Ti; (f) argon, Ar; (g) krypton, Kr; (h) xenon, Xe

106. (a) $^{13}_{6}C$; (b) $^{13}_{6}C$; (c) $^{13}_{6}C$; (d) $^{44}_{19}K$; (e) $^{41}_{20}Ca$; (f) $^{35}_{19}K$

107. (a) 22 protons, 19 neutrons, 22 electrons; (b) 30 protons, 34 neutrons, 30 electrons; (c) 32 protons, 44 neutrons, 32 electrons; (d) 36 protons, 50 neutrons, 36 electrons; (e) 33 protons, 42 neutrons, 33 electrons; (f) 19 protons, 22 neutrons, 19 electrons

108. $^{41}_{20}Ca$, 20, 21, 41; $^{55}_{25}Mn$, 25, 30, 55; $^{109}_{47}Ag$, 47, 62, 109; $^{45}_{21}Sc$, 21, 24, 45

109. (a) C, $Z = 6$, nonmetal; (b) Se, $Z = 34$, nonmetal; (c) Rn, $Z = 86$, nonmetal, noble gas; (d) Be, $Z = 4$, metal, alkaline earth element

Chapter 5

Objectives

In this chapter, our objectives are for the students to:

SECTION 5.1

- Understand why it is necessary to have a system for naming compounds.

SECTION 5.2

- Learn to name binary compounds of a metal and a nonmetal.

SECTION 5.3

- Learn to name binary compounds containing only nonmetals.

SECTION 5.4

- Review the naming of Type I, Type II, and Type III binary compounds.

SECTION 5.5

- Learn the names of common polyatomic ions and how to use them in naming compounds.

SECTION 5.6

- Learn how the anion composition determines the acid's name.
- Learn names for common acids.

SECTION 5.7

- Learn to write the formula of a compound, given its name.

5 Nomenclature

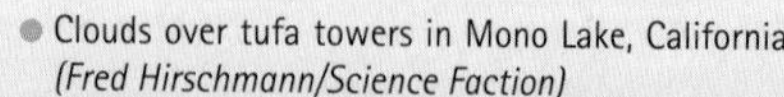

Clouds over tufa towers in Mono Lake, California. *(Fred Hirschmann/Science Faction)*

ChemWork Refined over ten years of use by thousands of students, **ChemWork** builds and enhances students' problems-solving skills. Online assignments function as a "personal instructor" to help students learn how to solve challenging problems and learn how to think like chemists. Annotations for **ChemWork** assignments are included at the beginning of the end-of-chapter review.

PowerLecture This 2-DVD package includes the Chemistry Multimedia Library, which contains animations, simulations, and movies for all chemistry subjects, organized by topic for lecture presentations. Annotations for **PowerLecture** are referenced in the margins throughout the Annotated Instructor's Edition.

OWL Sign in to OWL at **www.cengage.com/owl** to view tutorials and simulations, develop problem-solving skills, and complete online homework assigned by your professor.

go Chemistry Download mini-lecture videos for key concept review and exam prep from OWL or purchase them from **www.ichapters.com**

When chemistry was an infant science, there was no system for naming compounds. Names such as sugar of lead, blue vitriol, quicklime, Epsom salts, milk of magnesia, gypsum, and laughing gas were coined by early chemists. Such names are called *common names.* As our knowledge of chemistry grew, it became clear that using common names for compounds was not practical. More than four million chemical compounds are currently known. Memorizing common names for all these compounds would be impossible.

The solution, of course, is a *system* for naming compounds in which the name tells something about the composition of the compound. After learning the system, you should be able to name a compound when you are given its formula. And, conversely, you should be able to construct a compound's formula, given its name. In the next few sections we will specify the most important rules for naming compounds other than organic compounds (those based on chains of carbon atoms).

An artist using plaster of Paris, a gypsum plaster.

Bob Daemmrich/The Image Works

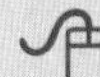

Test Bank: (5a) 2

Section 5.1

TEACHING TIPS

- Stress that learning the language of chemistry, by naming compounds and writing their formulas, is fundamental to being successful in chemistry. Tell students that they will use this skill for the remainder of the course.
- Stress that learning to name compounds does not involve memorizing a seemingly endless list of chemicals. Systematic rules for naming compounds exist and, by knowing only a few rules, students can name almost any compound they will encounter in this course.
- Students should also understand that we keep the rules as simple as possible (much the same way as we keep our scientific models as simple as possible). We add complications (such as prefixes and Roman numerals) only when they are required for clarity. For example, the name sodium(I) chloride is not necessarily wrong, merely redundant. Therefore, the name sodium chloride suffices.
- Bring in a variety of food labels while the students are studying nomenclature. Have them write the formulas for as many of the ingredients as they can. It is encouraging to be able to identify more ingredients the more they learn about naming compounds.

5.1 Naming Compounds

OBJECTIVE: To understand why it is necessary to have a system for naming compounds.

We will begin by discussing the system for naming **binary compounds**—compounds composed of two elements. We can divide binary compounds into two broad classes:

1. Compounds that contain a metal and a nonmetal
2. Compounds that contain two nonmetals

We will describe how to name compounds in each of these classes in the next several sections. Then, in succeeding sections, we will describe the systems used for naming more complex compounds.

Sugar of Lead

In ancient Roman society it was common to boil wine in a lead-lined vessel, driving off much of the water to produce a very sweet, viscous syrup called *sapa.* This syrup was commonly used as a sweetener for many types of food and drink.

We now realize that a major component of this syrup was lead acetate, $Pb(C_2H_3O_2)_2$. This compound has a very sweet taste—hence its original name, sugar of lead.

Many historians believe that the fall of the Roman Empire was due at least in part to lead poisoning, which causes lethargy and mental malfunctions. One major source of this lead was the sapa syrup. In addition, the Romans' highly advanced plumbing system employed lead water pipes, which allowed lead to be leached into their drinking water.

Sadly, this story is more relevant to today's society than you might think. Lead-based solder was widely used for many years to connect the copper pipes in water systems in homes and commercial buildings. There is evidence that dangerous amounts of lead can be leached from these soldered joints into drinking water. In fact, large quantities of lead have been found in the water that some drinking fountains and water coolers dispense. In response to these problems, the U.S. Congress has passed a law banning lead from the solder used in plumbing systems for drinking water.

Art Resource, NY

An ancient painting showing Romans drinking wine.

Test Bank: (5a) 1, 3–13, 15, 21, 53, 67, 68, 72, 82, 83, 85

Section 5.2

TEACHING TIPS

- Students can determine the charges of the ions in Table 5.1 from their positions in the periodic table, with the exception of Ag^+. Students should appreciate that the periodic table contains a great deal of information—it is a valuable resource.
- Type I ionic compounds are named simply by "naming the ions." You may wish to ask students a question such as, "How do we know that the formula for sodium chloride cannot be $NaCl_2$?" In this way you set the stage for Roman numerals and prefixes.
- Type I compounds are relatively easy for students because they have only one set of naming rules at this point. Be sure to review the rules for each type of compound as you progress through the chapter. This repetition will help students to build on their prior knowledge.

5.2 Naming Binary Compounds That Contain a Metal and a Nonmetal (Types I and II)

OBJECTIVE: To learn to name binary compounds of a metal and a nonmetal.

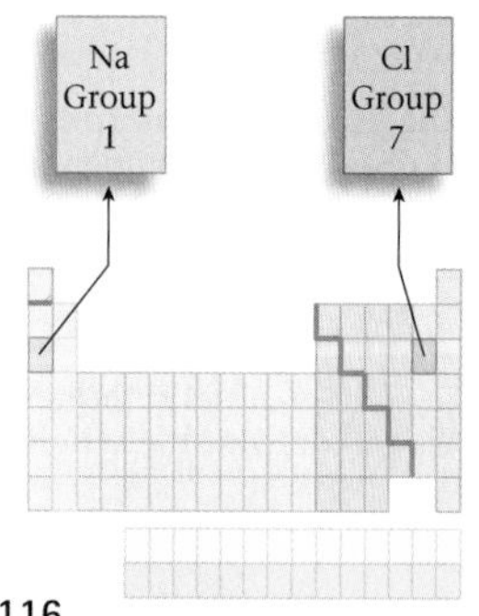

As we saw in Section 4.11, when a metal such as sodium combines with a nonmetal such as chlorine, the resulting compound contains ions. The metal loses one or more electrons to become a cation, and the nonmetal gains one or more electrons to form an anion. The resulting substance is called a **binary ionic compound.** Binary ionic compounds contain a positive ion (cation), which is always written first in the formula, and a negative ion (anion). *To name these compounds we simply name the ions.*

In this section we will consider binary ionic compounds of two types based on the cations they contain. Certain metal atoms form only one cation. For example, the Na atom always forms Na^+, *never* Na^{2+} or Na^{3+}. Likewise, Cs always forms Cs^+, Ca always forms Ca^{2+}, and Al always forms Al^{3+}. We will call compounds that contain this type of metal atom Type I binary compounds and the cations they contain Type I cations. Examples of Type I cations are Na^+, Ca^{2+}, Cs^+, and Al^{3+}.

go Chemistry **Module 3: Names to Formulas of Ionic Compounds** covers concepts in this section.

go Chemistry **Module 4: The Mole** covers concepts in this section.

go Chemistry **Module 5: Predicting the Water Solubility of Common Ionic Compounds** covers concepts in this section.

go Chemistry **Module 6: Writing Net Ionic Equations** covers concepts in this section.

Table 5.1 Common Simple Cations and Anions

Cation	Name	Anion	Name*
H^+	hydrogen	H^-	hydride
Li^+	lithium	F^-	fluoride
Na^+	sodium	Cl^-	chloride
K^+	potassium	Br^-	bromide
Cs^+	cesium	I^-	iodide
Be^{2+}	beryllium	O^{2-}	oxide
Mg^{2+}	magnesium	S^{2-}	sulfide
Ca^{2+}	calcium		
Ba^{2+}	barium		
Al^{3+}	aluminum		
Ag^+	silver		
Zn^{2+}	zinc		

*The root is given in color.

Other metal atoms can form two or more cations. For example, Cr can form Cr^{2+} and Cr^{3+} and Cu can form Cu^+ and Cu^{2+}. We will call such ions Type II cations and their compounds Type II binary compounds.

In summary:

Type I compounds: The metal present forms only one type of cation.

Type II compounds: The metal present can form two (or more) cations that have different charges.

Some common cations and anions and their names are listed in Table 5.1. You should memorize these. They are an essential part of your chemical vocabulary.

Type I Binary Ionic Compounds

The following rules apply for Type I ionic compounds:

A simple cation has the same name as its parent element.

Rules for Naming Type I Ionic Compounds

1. The cation is always named first and the anion second.
2. A simple cation (obtained from a single atom) takes its name from the name of the element. For example, Na^+ is called sodium in the names of compounds containing this ion.
3. A simple anion (obtained from a single atom) is named by taking the first part of the element name (the root) and adding *-ide*. Thus the Cl^- ion is called chloride.

We will illustrate these rules by naming a few compounds. For example, the compound NaI is called sodium iodide. It contains Na^+ (the sodium cation, named for the parent metal) and I^- (iodide: the root of *iodine* plus *-ide*). Similarly, the compound CaO is called calcium oxide because it contains Ca^{2+} (the calcium cation) and O^{2-} (the oxide anion).

5.2 Naming Binary Compounds That Contain a Metal and a Nonmetal (Types I and II) 117

The rules for naming binary compounds are also illustrated by the following examples:

Compound	Ions Present	Name
NaCl	Na^+, Cl^-	sodium chloride
KI	K^+, I^-	potassium iodide
CaS	Ca^{2+}, S^{2-}	calcium sulfide
CsBr	Cs^+, Br^-	cesium bromide
MgO	Mg^{2+}, O^{2-}	magnesium oxide

It is important to note that in the *formulas* of ionic compounds, simple ions are represented by the element symbol: Cl means Cl^-, Na means Na^+, and so on. However, when *individual ions* are shown, the charge is always included. Thus the formula of potassium bromide is written KBr, but when the potassium and bromide ions are shown individually, they are written K^+ and Br^-.

Additional Examples

Example 5.1

Name each binary compound.

1. KCl

   potassium chloride

2. ZnS

   zinc sulfide

3. $CaBr_2$

   calcium bromide

4. BaH_2

   barium hydride

5. Al_2S_3

   aluminum sulfide

EXAMPLE 5.1 Naming Type I Binary Compounds

Name each binary compound.

a. CsF b. $AlCl_3$ c. MgI_2

SOLUTION

We will name these compounds by systematically following the rules given above.

a. CsF

Step 1 Identify the cation and anion. Cs is in Group 1, so we know it will form the 1+ ion Cs^+. Because F is in Group 7, it forms the 1− ion F^-.

Step 2 Name the cation. Cs^+ is simply called cesium, the same as the element name.

Step 3 Name the anion. F^- is called fluoride: we use the root name of the element plus *-ide*.

Step 4 Name the compound by combining the names of the individual ions. The name for CsF is cesium fluoride. (Remember that the name of the cation is always given first.)

b.

Compound	Ions Present	Ion Names	Comments
$AlCl_3$ (Cation)	Al^{3+}	aluminum	Al (Group 3) always forms Al^{3+}.
$AlCl_3$ (Anion)	Cl^-	chloride	Cl (Group 7) always forms Cl^-.

The name of $AlCl_3$ is aluminum chloride.

c.

Compound	Ions Present	Ion Names	Comments
MgI_2 (Cation)	Mg^{2+}	magnesium	Mg (Group 2) always forms Mg^{2+}.
MgI_2 (Anion)	I^-	iodide	I (Group 7) gains one electron to form I^-.

The name of MgI_2 is magnesium iodide.

Self-Check **EXERCISE 5.1** Name the following compounds.

a. Rb_2O b. SrI_2 c. K_2S

See Problems 5.9 and 5.10. ■

Self Check

Answers to Self-Check Exercise 5.1

a. rubidium oxide

b. strontium iodide

c. potassium sulfide

Example 5.1 reminds us of three things:

1. Compounds formed from metals and nonmetals are ionic.
2. In an ionic compound the cation is always named first.
3. The *net* charge on an ionic compound is always zero. Thus, in CsF, one of each type of ion (Cs^+ and F^-) is required: (1+) + (1−) = 0 charge. In $AlCl_3$, however, three Cl^- ions are needed to balance the charge of Al^{3+}: (3+) + 3 (1−) = 0 charge. In MgI_2, two I^- ions are needed for each Mg^{2+} ion: (2+) + 2 (1−) = 0 charge.

Type II Binary Ionic Compounds

TEACHING TIP

Make a clear distinction between Type I and Type II cations. This effort reinforces the reasons for the Roman numerals in the names of the compounds. Ask students, for example, "How is 'iron oxide' different from 'magnesium oxide'?"

So far we have considered binary ionic compounds (Type I) containing metals that always give the same cation. For example, sodium always forms the Na^+ ion, calcium always forms the Ca^{2+} ion, and aluminum always forms the Al^{3+} ion. As we said in the previous section, we can predict with certainty that each Group 1 metal will give a 1+ cation and each Group 2 metal will give a 2+ cation. Aluminum always forms Al^{3+}.

Type II binary ionic compounds contain a metal that can form more than one type of cation.

However, there are many metals that can form more than one type of cation. For example, lead (Pb) can form Pb^{2+} or Pb^{4+} in ionic compounds. Also, iron (Fe) can produce Fe^{2+} or Fe^{3+}, chromium (Cr) can produce Cr^{2+} or Cr^{3+}, gold (Au) can produce Au^+ or Au^{3+}, and so on. This means that if we saw the name gold chloride, we wouldn't know whether it referred to the compound AuCl (containing Au^+ and Cl^-) or the compound $AuCl_3$ (containing Au^{3+} and three Cl^- ions). Therefore, we need a way of specifying which cation is present in compounds containing metals that can form more than one type of cation.

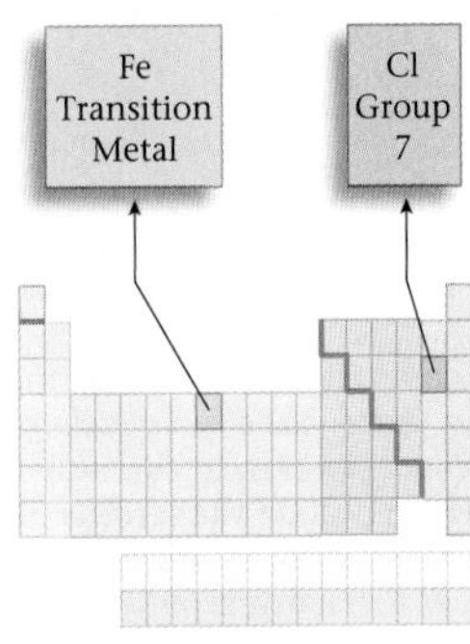

Chemists have decided to deal with this situation by using a Roman numeral to specify the charge on the cation. To see how this works, consider the compound $FeCl_2$. Iron can form Fe^{2+} or Fe^{3+}, so we must first decide which of these cations is present. We can determine the charge on the iron cation, because we know it must just balance the charge on the two 1− anions (the chloride ions). Thus if we represent the charges as

$$(?+) + 2\,(1-) = 0$$

(?+)	+ 2 (1−)	= 0
↑ Charge on iron cation	↑ Charge on Cl^-	↑ Net charge

we know that ? must represent 2 because

$$(2+) + 2(1-) = 0$$

FeCl$_3$ must contain Fe^{3+} to balance the charge of three Cl^- ions.

The compound $FeCl_2$, then, contains one Fe^{2+} ion and two Cl^- ions. We call this compound iron(II) chloride, where the II tells the charge of the iron cation. That is, Fe^{2+} is called iron(II). Likewise, Fe^{3+} is called iron(III). And $FeCl_3$, which contains one Fe^{3+} ion and three Cl^- ions, is called iron(III) chloride. Remember that the Roman numeral tells the *charge* on the ion, not the number of ions present in the compound.

TEACHING TIPS

- If a cation is not listed in Table 5.2, its charge can be obtained from the number and type of anions present in a given compound. However, this information does not tell the student whether a Roman numeral is required in the name of the compound.
- Students should use the periodic table when they cannot remember whether a cation has more than one possible charge. Cations from Groups 1, 2, or 3 have only one possible charge and that charge is the same as the group number. Cations formed from transition metals may have more than one charge.

MISCONCEPTION

Students often make the mistake of assuming that the Roman numeral tells us the number of ions present in the compound, because in many cases the Roman numeral is the same as one of the subscripts. Use an example such as iron(II) oxide with the formula FeO to show that the Roman numeral relates only to the charge.

© Cengage Learning

Copper(II) sulfate crystals.

Table 5.2 Common Type II Cations

Ion	Systematic Name	Older Name
Fe^{3+}	iron(III)	ferric
Fe^{2+}	iron(II)	ferrous
Cu^{2+}	copper(II)	cupric
Cu^{+}	copper(I)	cuprous
Co^{3+}	cobalt(III)	cobaltic
Co^{2+}	cobalt(II)	cobaltous
Sn^{4+}	tin(IV)	stannic
Sn^{2+}	tin(II)	stannous
Pb^{4+}	lead(IV)	plumbic
Pb^{2+}	lead(II)	plumbous
Hg^{2+}	mercury(II)	mercuric
Hg_2^{2+}*	mercury(I)	mercurous

*Mercury(I) ions always occur bound together in pairs to form Hg_2^{2+}.

Note that in the preceding examples the Roman numeral for the cation turned out to be the same as the subscript needed for the anion (to balance the charge). This is often not the case. For example, consider the compound PbO_2. Since the oxide ion is O^{2-}, for PbO_2 we have

$$(?+) + 2(2-) = 0$$

Charge on lead ion; (4−) Charge on two O^{2-} ions; Net charge

Thus the charge on the lead ion must be 4+ to balance the 4− charge of the two oxide ions. The name of PbO_2 is therefore lead(IV) oxide, where the IV indicates the presence of the Pb^{4+} cation.

There is another system for naming ionic compounds containing metals that form two cations. *The ion with the higher charge has a name ending in* -ic, *and the one with the lower charge has a name ending in* -ous. In this system, for example, Fe^{3+} is called the ferric ion, and Fe^{2+} is called the ferrous ion. The names for $FeCl_3$ and $FeCl_2$, in this system, are ferric chloride and ferrous chloride, respectively. Table 5.2 gives both names for many Type II cations. We will use the system of Roman numerals exclusively in this text; the other system is falling into disuse.

To help distinguish between Type I and Type II cations, remember that Group 1 and 2 metals are always Type I. On the other hand, transition metals are almost always Type II.

Rules for Naming Type II Ionic Compounds

1. The cation is always named first and the anion second.
2. Because the cation can assume more than one charge, the charge is specified by a Roman numeral in parentheses.

EXAMPLE 5.2 Naming Type II Binary Compounds

Give the systematic name of each of the following compounds.

a. CuCl b. HgO c. Fe_2O_3 d. MnO_2 e. $PbCl_4$

SOLUTION

All these compounds include a metal that can form more than one type of cation; thus we must first determine the charge on each cation. We do this by recognizing that a compound must be electrically neutral; that is, the positive and negative charges must balance exactly. We will use the known charge on the anion to determine the charge of the cation.

a. In CuCl we recognize the anion as Cl^-. To determine the charge on the copper cation, we invoke the principle of charge balance.

$$(?+) + (1-) = 0$$

↑ Charge on copper ion ↑ Charge on Cl^- ↑ Net charge (must be zero)

In this case, ?+ must be 1+ because $(1+) + (1-) = 0$. Thus the copper cation must be Cu^+. Now we can name the compound by using the regular steps.

Compound		Ions Present	Ion Names	Comments
CuCl	Cation →	Cu^+	copper(I)	Copper forms other cations (it is a transition metal), so we must include the I to specify its charge.
	Anion →	Cl^-	chloride	

The name of CuCl is copper(I) chloride.

b. In HgO we recognize the O^{2-} anion. To yield zero net charge, the cation must be Hg^{2+}.

Compound		Ions Present	Ion Names	Comments
HgO	Cation →	Hg^{2+}	mercury(II)	The II is necessary to specify the charge.
	Anion →	O^{2-}	oxide	

The name of HgO is mercury(II) oxide.

c. Because Fe_2O_3 contains three O^{2-} anions, the charge on the iron cation must be 3+.

$$2(3+) + 3(2-) = 0$$

↑ Fe^{3+} ↑ O^{2-} ↑ Net charge

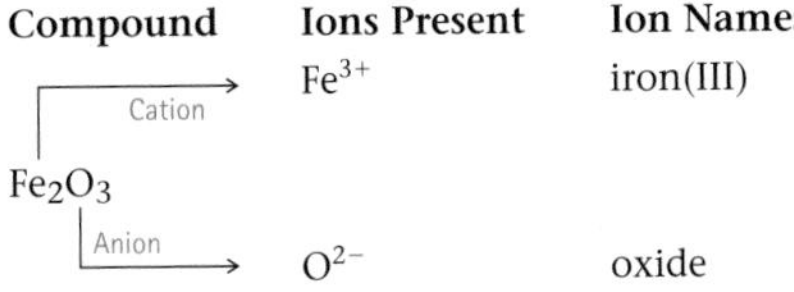

Compound		Ions Present	Ion Names	Comments
Fe_2O_3	Cation →	Fe^{3+}	iron(III)	Iron is a transition metal and requires a III to specify the charge on the cation.
	Anion →	O^{2-}	oxide	

The name of Fe_2O_3 is iron(III) oxide.

Additional Examples

Example 5.2

Name each binary compound.

1. $CoCl_3$

   cobalt(III) chloride

2. CuI

   copper(I) iodide

3. $SnBr_4$

   tin(IV) bromide

4. $HgCl_2$

   mercury(II) chloride

5. PbS

   lead(II) sulfide

DEMONSTRATION

Bring samples of copper(I) chloride and copper(II) chloride to class. Show students the difference in the colors of the compounds, indicating differences in the copper ions present. Another compound that shows similar differences in color with different ion charges is cobalt(II) chloride and cobalt(III) chloride.

d. MnO_2 contains two O^{2-} anions, so the charge on the manganese cation is 4+.

$$\underset{Mn^{4+}}{(4+)} + \underset{O^{2-}}{2(2-)} = \underset{\text{Net charge}}{0}$$

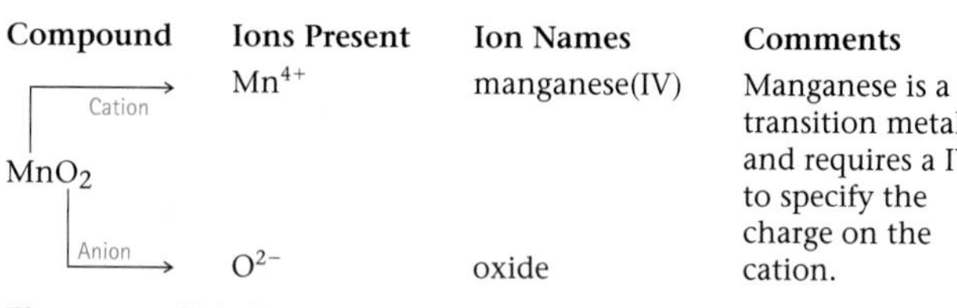

The name of MnO_2 is manganese(IV) oxide.

e. Because $PbCl_4$ contains four Cl^- anions, the charge on the lead cation is 4+.

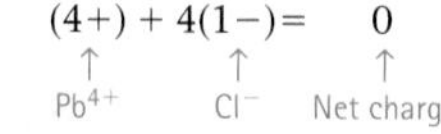

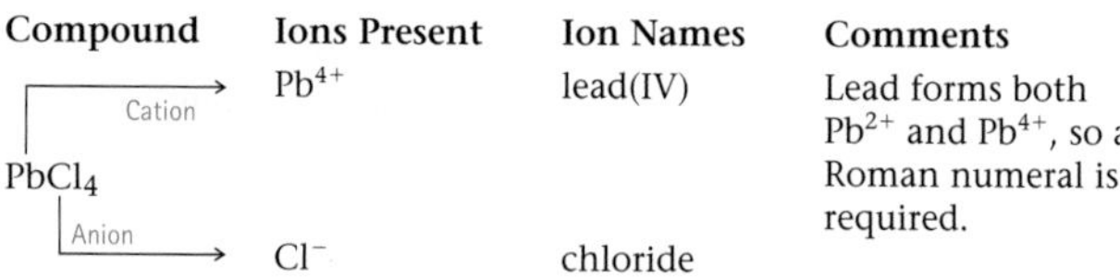

Compound
Ions Present
Ion Names
Comments
Cation
Pb^{4+}
lead(IV)
Lead forms both Pb^{2+} and Pb^{4+}, so a Roman numeral is required.
$PbCl_4$
Anion
Cl^-
chloride

The name for $PbCl_4$ is lead(IV) chloride. ■

Sometimes transition metals form only one ion, such as silver, which forms Ag^+; zinc, which forms Zn^{2+}; and cadmium, which forms Cd^{2+}. In these cases, chemists do not use a Roman numeral, although it is not "wrong" to do so.

The use of a Roman numeral in a systematic name for a compound is required only in cases where more than one ionic compound forms between a given pair of elements. This occurs most often for compounds that contain transition metals, which frequently form more than one cation. *Metals that form only one cation do not need to be identified by a Roman numeral.* Common metals that do not require Roman numerals are the Group 1 elements, which form only 1+ ions; the Group 2 elements, which form only 2+ ions; and such Group 3 metals as aluminum and gallium, which form only 3+ ions.

As shown in Example 5.2, when a metal ion that forms more than one type of cation is present, the charge on the metal ion must be determined by balancing the positive and negative charges of the compound. To do this, you must be able to recognize the common anions and you must know their charges (see Table 5.1).

EXAMPLE 5.3 Naming Binary Ionic Compounds: Summary

Give the systematic name of each of the following compounds.

a. $CoBr_2$

b. $CaCl_2$

c. Al_2O_3

d. $CrCl_3$

Additional Examples

Example 5.3

Name each binary compound.

1. SnI_4

   tin(IV) iodide
2. K_3N

   potassium nitride
3. HgO

   mercury(II) oxide
4. RbF

   rubidium fluoride
5. NaH

   sodium hydride
6. CrF_2

   chromium(II) fluoride
7. $MgBr_2$

   magnesium bromide
8. MnI_2

   manganese(II) iodide
9. Li_2O

   lithium oxide

SOLUTION

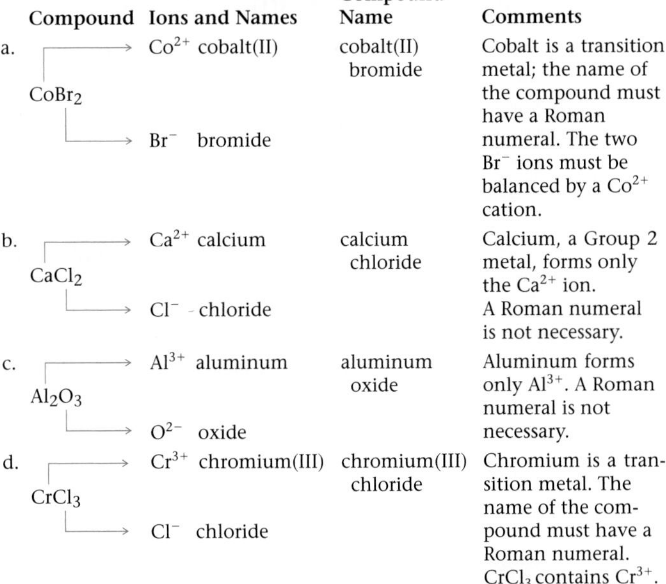

	Compound	Ions and Names	Compound Name	Comments
a.	$CoBr_2$	Co^{2+} cobalt(II) Br^- bromide	cobalt(II) bromide	Cobalt is a transition metal; the name of the compound must have a Roman numeral. The two Br^- ions must be balanced by a Co^{2+} cation.
b.	$CaCl_2$	Ca^{2+} calcium Cl^- chloride	calcium chloride	Calcium, a Group 2 metal, forms only the Ca^{2+} ion. A Roman numeral is not necessary.
c.	Al_2O_3	Al^{3+} aluminum O^{2-} oxide	aluminum oxide	Aluminum forms only Al^{3+}. A Roman numeral is not necessary.
d.	$CrCl_3$	Cr^{3+} chromium(III) Cl^- chloride	chromium(III) chloride	Chromium is a transition metal. The name of the compound must have a Roman numeral. $CrCl_3$ contains Cr^{3+}.

Self-Check **EXERCISE 5.2** Give the names of the following compounds.

a. $PbBr_2$ and $PbBr_4$ b. FeS and Fe_2S_3 c. $AlBr_3$ d. Na_2S e. $CoCl_3$

See Problems 5.9, 5.10, and 5.13 through 5.16. ■

The following flow chart is useful when you are naming binary ionic compounds:

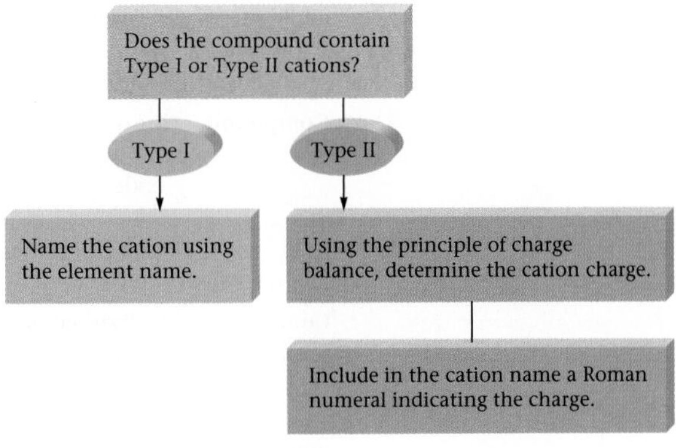

Self Check

Answers to Self-Check Exercise 5.2

a. lead(II) bromide; lead(IV) bromide

b. iron(II) sulfide; iron(III) sulfide

c. aluminum bromide

d. sodium sulfide

e. cobalt(III) chloride

5.2 Naming Binary Compounds That Contain a Metal and a Nonmetal (Types I and II) 123

Test Bank: (5a) 14, 16–19, 86

Section 5.3

TEACHING TIPS

- Consider starting with examples such as NO and NO_2. Ask students to name these compounds. This exercise will lead naturally to a discussion of prefixes. Like Roman numerals, prefixes are used only for clarity. For example, two "carbon oxides" are possible, and we must use prefixes to differentiate between them (carbon monoxide and carbon dioxide). We make the rules more complicated only when it is required.
- Students need to learn the prefixes given in Table 5.3. This makes naming compounds and writing formulas much easier.
- In naming Type III compounds, two vowels sometimes appear together (one from the prefix and one from the root name). We eliminate the vowel on the end of the prefix to make the pronunciation of the name easier. For example, tetraoxide becomes tetroxide and monooxide becomes monoxide.

5.3 Naming Binary Compounds That Contain Only Nonmetals (Type III)

OBJECTIVE: To learn how to name binary compounds containing only nonmetals.

Table 5.3 Prefixes Used to Indicate Numbers in Chemical Names

Prefix	Number Indicated
mono-	1
di-	2
tri-	3
tetra-	4
penta-	5
hexa-	6
hepta-	7
octa-	8

Binary compounds that contain only nonmetals are named in accordance with a system similar in some ways to the rules for naming binary ionic compounds, but there are important differences. *Type III binary compounds contain only nonmetals.* The following rules cover the naming of these compounds.

Rules for Naming Type III Binary Compounds

1. The first element in the formula is named first, and the full element name is used.
2. The second element is named as though it were an anion.
3. Prefixes are used to denote the numbers of atoms present. These prefixes are given in Table 5.3.
4. The prefix *mono-* is never used for naming the first element. For example, CO is called carbon monoxide, *not* monocarbon monoxide.

We will illustrate the application of these rules in Example 5.4.

EXAMPLE 5.4 Naming Type III Binary Compounds

Name the following binary compounds, which contain two nonmetals (Type III).

a. BF_3 b. NO c. N_2O_5

SOLUTION

a. BF_3

Rule 1 Name the first element, using the full element name: boron.

Rule 2 Name the second element as though it were an anion: fluoride.

Rules 3 and 4 Use prefixes to denote numbers of atoms. One boron atom: do not use *mono-* in first position. Three fluorine atoms: use the prefix *tri-*.

The name of BF_3 is boron trifluoride.

b.

Compound	Individual Names	Prefixes	Comments
NO	nitrogen	none	*Mono-* is not used
	oxide	*mono-*	for the first element.

The name for NO is nitrogen monoxide. Note that the second *o* in *mono-* has been dropped for easier pronunciation. The *common* name for NO, which is often used by chemists, is nitric oxide.

c.

Compound	Individual Names	Prefixes	Comments
N_2O_5	nitrogen	*di-*	two N atoms
	oxide	*penta-*	five O atoms

The name for N_2O_5 is dinitrogen pentoxide. The *a* in *penta-* has been dropped for easier pronunciation.

Additional Examples

Example 5.4

Name the following Type III compounds.

1. I_2O_7

   diiodine heptoxide
2. CO_2

   carbon dioxide
3. CF_4

   carbon tetrafluoride
4. NH_3

   ammonia
5. PCl_3

   phosphorus trichloride

A piece of copper metal about to be placed in nitric acid (*left*). Copper reacts with nitric acid to produce colorless NO, which immediately reacts with the oxygen in the air to form reddish-brown NO_2 gas and Cu^{2+} ions in solution (which produce the green color) (*right*).

Self-Check **EXERCISE 5.3** Name the following compounds.

a. CCl_4 b. NO_2 c. IF_5

See Problems 5.17 and 5.18. ■

The previous examples illustrate that, to avoid awkward pronunciation, we often drop the final *o* or *a* of the prefix when the second element is oxygen. For example, N_2O_4 is called dinitrogen tetroxide, *not* dinitrogen tetr*a*oxide, and CO is called carbon monoxide, *not* carbon mon*o*oxide.

Water and ammonia are always referred to by their common names.

Some compounds are always referred to by their common names. The two best examples are water and ammonia. The systematic names for H_2O and NH_3 are never used.

To make sure you understand the procedures for naming binary nonmetallic compounds (Type III), study Example 5.5 and then do Self-Check Exercise 5.4.

EXAMPLE 5.5 Naming Type III Binary Compounds: Summary

Name each of the following compounds.

a. PCl_5 c. SF_6 d. SO_2
b. P_4O_6 d. SO_3 f. N_2O_3

SOLUTION

Compound	Name
a. PCl_5	phosphorus pentachloride
b. P_4O_6	tetraphosphorus hexoxide
c. SF_6	sulfur hexafluoride
d. SO_3	sulfur trioxide
e. SO_2	sulfur dioxide
f. N_2O_3	dinitrogen trioxide

Self Check

Answers to Self-Check Exercise 5.3

a. carbon tetrachloride

b. nitrogen dioxide

c. iodine pentafluoride

Additional Examples

Example 5.5

Name the following Type III compounds.

1. CO

   carbon monoxide

2. NO_2

   nitrogen dioxide

3. SeF_6

   selenium hexafluoride

4. N_2O

   dinitrogen monoxide

5. H_2O

   water

Self-Check EXERCISE 5.4 Name the following compounds.

a. SiO_2 b. O_2F_2 c. XeF_6

See Problems 5.17 and 5.18.

Self Check

Answers to Self-Check Exercise 5.4

a. silicon dioxide

b. dioxygen difluoride

c. xenon hexafluoride

5.4 Naming Binary Compounds: A Review

OBJECTIVE: To review the naming of Type I, Type II, and Type III binary compounds.

Section 5.4

TEACHING TIPS

- Most students can name compounds if they are identified by type. This section provides an opportunity to review the types and have students practice on a variety of compounds rather than just those of a particular type.
- Figure 5.1 is a convenient flow chart to help students systematically name compounds. They need to be encouraged to use this type of device to help them think through a difficult problem. The chart is also found in the PowerPoint and transparency package.

Because different rules apply for naming various types of binary compounds, we will now consider an overall strategy to use for these compounds. We have considered three types of binary compounds, and naming each of them requires different procedures.

Type I: Ionic compounds with metals that always form a cation with the same charge

Type II: Ionic compounds with metals (usually transition metals) that form cations with various charges

Type III: Compounds that contain only nonmetals

In trying to determine which type of compound you are naming, use the periodic table to help identify metals and nonmetals and to determine which elements are transition metals.

The flow chart given in Figure 5.1 should help you as you name binary compounds of the various types.

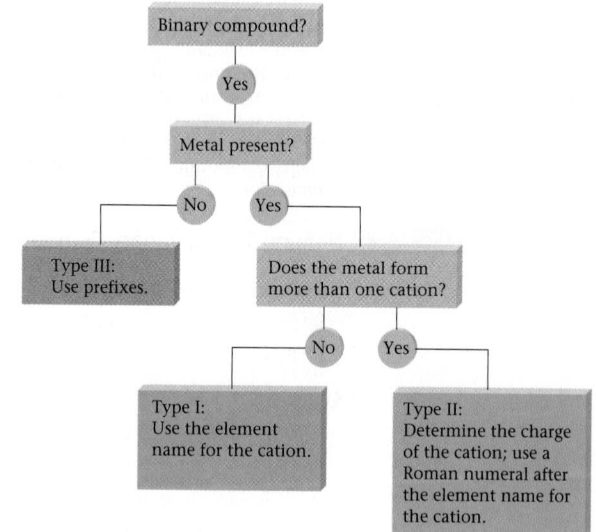

Figure 5.1
A flow chart for naming binary compounds.

CHEMISTRY *IN* FOCUS

Chemophilately

Philately is the study of postage stamps. Chemophilately, a term coined by the Israeli chemist Zvi Rappoport, refers to the study of stamps that have some sort of chemical connection. Collectors estimate that more than 2000 chemical-related stamps have been printed throughout the world. Relatively few of these stamps have been produced in the United States. One example is a 29¢ stamp honoring minerals that shows a copper nugget.

Courtesy, Daniel Rabinovich

Chemists also have been honored on U.S. postage stamps. One example is a 29¢ stamp printed in 1993 honoring Percy L. Julian, an African-American chemist who was the grandson of slaves. Julian is noted for his synthesis of steroids used to treat glaucoma and rheumatoid arthritis. As a holder of more than 100 patents, he was inducted into the National Inventors Hall of Fame in 1990.

Courtesy, Daniel Rabinovich

In 1983 the United States issued a stamp honoring Joseph Priestley, whose experiments led to the discovery of oxygen.

Courtesy, Whitman Publishing LLC

A stamp from 2005 pictures J. Willard Gibbs, a Yale professor who was instrumental in developing thermodynamics—the study of energy and its transformations.

In 2008, a 41¢ stamp was issued that honors Linus C. Pauling, who pioneered the concept of the chemical bond. Pauling received two Nobel Prizes: one for his work on chemical bonds and the other for his work championing world peace. His stamp includes drawings of red blood cells to commemorate his work on the study of hemoglobin, which led to the classification of sickle cell anemia as a molecular disease.

Courtesy, Daniel Rabinovich

Postal chemistry also shows up in postmarks from places in the United States with chemical names. Examples include Radium, KS, Neon, KY, Boron, CA, Bromide, OK, and Telluride, CO.

Courtesy, Daniel Rabinovich

Chemophilately—further proof that chemistry is everywhere!

127

Additional Examples

Example 5.6

Name each of the following compounds.

1. AsF_3

   arsenic trifluoride

2. Al_2S_3

   aluminum sulfide

3. $SnBr_4$

   tin(IV) bromide

4. CS_2

   carbon disulfide

5. CdS

   cadmium sulfide

6. AgCl

   silver chloride

7. KI

   potassium iodide

8. NO

   nitrogen monoxide

9. P_2O_5

   diphosphorus pentoxide

10. $FeCl_3$

    iron(III) chloride

EXAMPLE 5.6 Naming Binary Compounds: Summary

Name the following binary compounds.

a. CuO c. B_2O_3 e. K_2S g. NH_3

b. SrO d. $TiCl_4$ f. OF_2

SOLUTION

a.

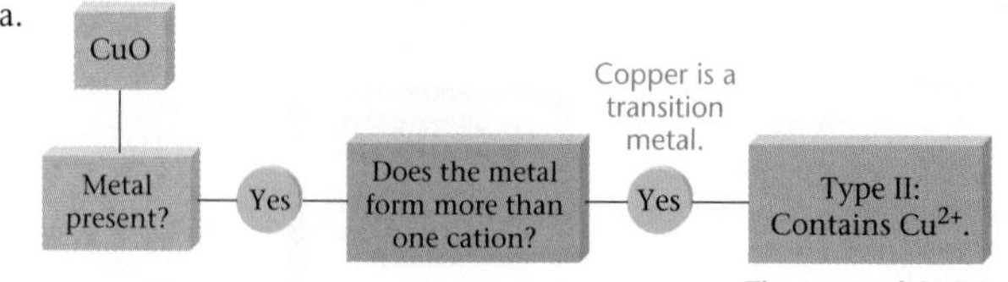

b.

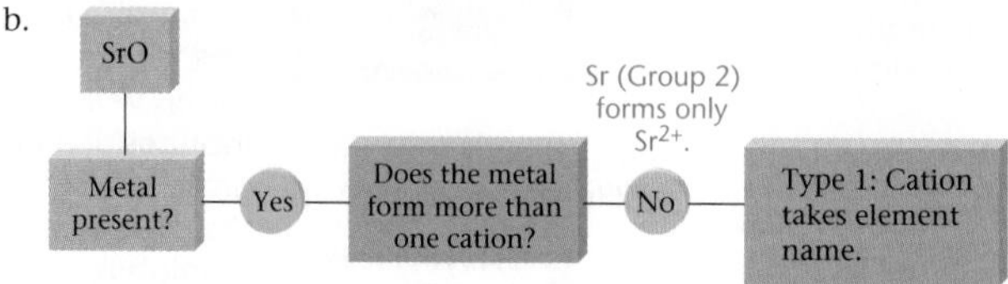

c.

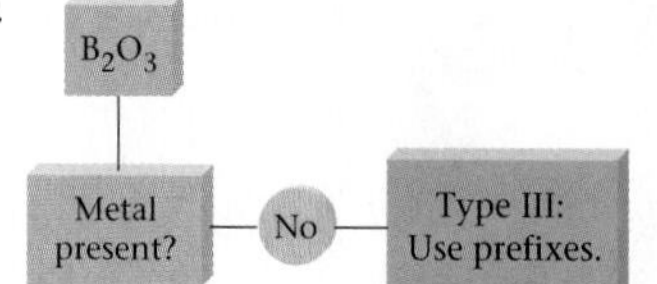

d.

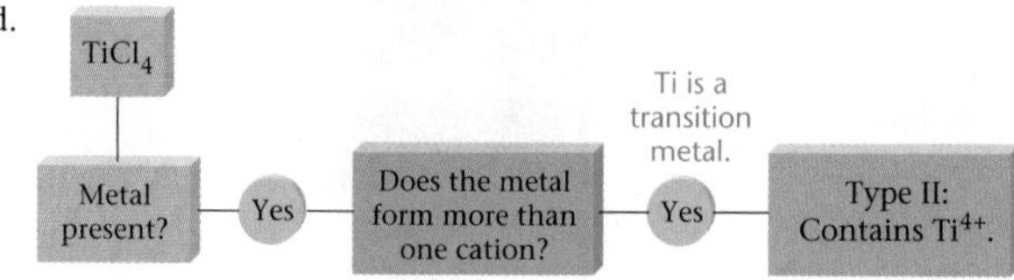

e.

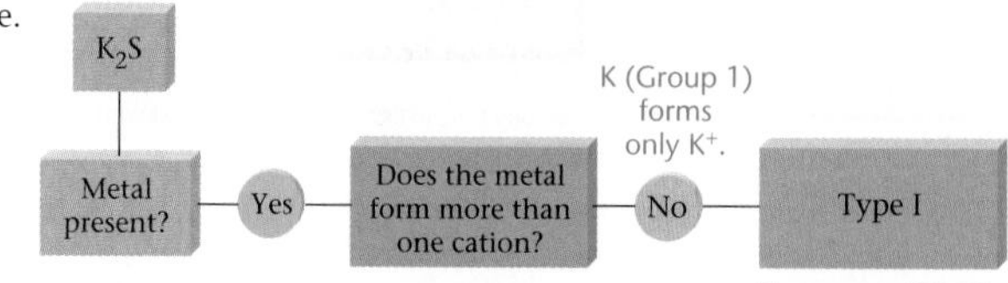

f.

OF_2 → Metal present? → No → Type III

The name of OF_2 is oxygen difluoride.

g.

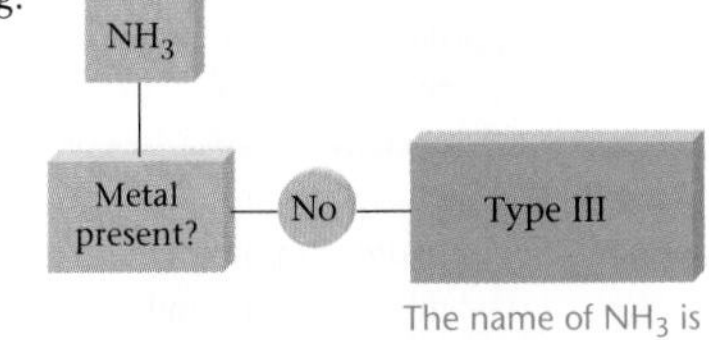

The name of NH_3 is ammonia. The systematic name is never used.

Self-Check **EXERCISE 5.5** Name the following binary compounds.

a. ClF_3 d. MnO_2

b. VF_5 e. MgO

c. CuCl f. H_2O

See Problems 5.19 through 5.22. ■

Self Check

Answers to Self-Check Exercise 5.5

a. chlorine trifluoride

b. vanadium(V) fluoride

c. copper(I) chloride

d. manganese(IV) oxide

e. magnesium oxide

f. water

Test Bank: (5a) 20, 22–30, 32–52, 87–90

5.5 Naming Compounds That Contain Polyatomic Ions

OBJECTIVE: To learn the names of common polyatomic ions and how to use them in naming compounds.

Section 5.5

Ionic compounds containing polyatomic ions are not binary compounds, because they contain more than two elements.

The names and charges of polyatomic ions must be memorized. They are an important part of the vocabulary of chemistry.

A type of ionic compound that we have not yet considered is exemplified by ammonium nitrate, NH_4NO_3, which contains the **polyatomic ions** NH_4^+ and NO_3^-. As their name suggests, polyatomic ions are charged entities composed of several atoms bound together. Polyatomic ions are assigned special names that you *must memorize* to name the compounds containing them. The most important polyatomic ions and their names are listed in Table 5.4.

Note in Table 5.4 that several series of polyatomic anions exist that contain an atom of a given element and different numbers of oxygen atoms. These anions are called **oxyanions.** When there are two members in such a series, the name of the one with the smaller number of oxygen atoms ends in *-ite,* and the name of the one with the larger number ends in *-ate.* For example, SO_3^{2-} is sulfite and SO_4^{2-} is sulfate. When more than two oxyanions make up a series, *hypo-* (less than) and *per-* (more than) are used as prefixes to name the members of the series with the fewest and the most oxygen

MISCONCEPTION

Students should think of polyatomic ions as a "unit." Many students know that if NaCl is dissolved in water, Na^+ ions and Cl^- ions are present. However, they are often confused about the ions present when $NaNO_3$ dissolves. Instead of the NO_3^- ion, students often think individual nitrogen and oxygen ions are present.

5.5 Naming Compounds That Contain Polyatomic Ions 129

TEACHING TIPS

- In the long run, it is helpful for students to know the common polyatomic ions. Use Table 5.4 to help in learning their names. There are groups of ions that are related as part of a series, which makes remembering the names and charges easier. For example, nitrate and nitrite differ by only an oxygen atom, as do sulfate and sulfite. Show students that the charge is the same but the number of oxygens changes. Also, point out that when hydrogen is added to a polyatomic ion (as in hydrogen sulfate or hydrogen carbonate), the charge on the polyatomic ion changes by one.
- Chlorine is used to illustrate the series of ions formed between the halogens and oxygen. You can also show how other halogens (bromine, for example) form a series of anions with oxygen.
- If students learn the names and formulas for the *-ate* polyatomic ions and understand the concepts in the oxygen and hydrogen anion series, they will be able to write formulas for almost all of the common polyatomic ions.

Table 5.4 Names of Common Polyatomic Ions

Ion	Name	Ion	Name
NH_4^+	ammonium	CO_3^{2-}	carbonate
NO_2^-	nitrite	HCO_3^-	hydrogen carbonate (bicarbonate is a widely used common name)
NO_3^-	nitrate		
SO_3^{2-}	sulfite		
SO_4^{2-}	sulfate	ClO^-	hypochlorite
HSO_4^-	hydrogen sulfate (bisulfate is a widely used common name)	ClO_2^-	chlorite
		ClO_3^-	chlorate
		ClO_4^-	perchlorate
OH^-	hydroxide	$C_2H_3O_2^-$	acetate
CN^-	cyanide	MnO_4^-	permanganate
PO_4^{3-}	phosphate	$Cr_2O_7^{2-}$	dichromate
HPO_4^{2-}	hydrogen phosphate	CrO_4^{2-}	chromate
$H_2PO_4^-$	dihydrogen phosphate	O_2^{2-}	peroxide

atoms, respectively. The best example involves the oxyanions containing chlorine:

ClO^- *hypo*chlorite
ClO_2^- chlor*ite*
ClO_3^- chlor*ate*
ClO_4^- *per*chlor*ate*

Naming ionic compounds that contain polyatomic ions is very similar to naming binary ionic compounds. For example, the compound NaOH is called sodium hydroxide, because it contains the Na^+ (sodium) cation and the OH^- (hydroxide) anion. To name these compounds, *you must learn to recognize the common polyatomic ions.* That is, you must learn the *composition* and *charge* of each of the ions in Table 5.4. Then when you see the formula $NH_4C_2H_3O_2$, you should immediately recognize its two "parts":

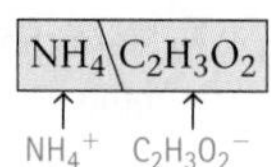

The correct name is ammonium acetate.

Remember that when a metal is present that forms more than one cation, a Roman numeral is required to specify the cation charge, just as in naming Type II binary ionic compounds. For example, the compound $FeSO_4$ is called iron(II) sulfate, because it contains Fe^{2+} (to balance the 2− charge on SO_4^{2-}). Note that to determine the charge on the iron cation, you must know that sulfate has a 2− charge.

EXAMPLE 5.7 Naming Compounds That Contain Polyatomic Ions

Give the systematic name of each of the following compounds.

a. Na_2SO_4 c. $Fe(NO_3)_3$ e. Na_2SO_3
b. KH_2PO_4 d. $Mn(OH)_2$ f. NH_4ClO_3

Additional Examples

Example 5.7

Name each of these compounds.

1. $Cu(NO_3)_2$

   copper(II) nitrate
2. $PbCO_3$

   lead(II) carbonate
3. $KHSO_4$

   potassium hydrogen sulfate
4. NH_4I

   ammonium iodide
5. NaCN

   sodium cyanide

SOLUTION

	Compound	Ions Present	Ion Names	Compound Name
a.	Na_2SO_4	two Na^+ SO_4^{2-}	sodium sulfate	sodium sulfate
b.	KH_2PO_4	K^+ $H_2PO_4^-$	potassium dihydrogen phosphate	potassium dihydrogen phosphate
c.	$Fe(NO_3)_3$	Fe^{3+} three NO_3^-	iron(III) nitrate	iron(III) nitrate
d.	$Mn(OH)_2$	Mn^{2+} two OH^-	manganese(II) hydroxide	manganese(II) hydroxide
e.	Na_2SO_3	two Na^+ SO_3^{2-}	sodium sulfite	sodium sulfite
f.	NH_4ClO_3	NH_4^+ ClO_3^-	ammonium chlorate	ammonium chlorate

Self-Check **EXERCISE 5.6** Name each of the following compounds.

a. $Ca(OH)_2$
b. Na_3PO_4
c. $KMnO_4$
d. $(NH_4)_2Cr_2O_7$
e. $Co(ClO_4)_2$
f. $KClO_3$
g. $Cu(NO_2)_2$

See Problems 5.35 and 5.36. ■

Self Check

Answers to Self-Check Exercise 5.6

a. calcium hydroxide
b. sodium phosphate
c. potassium permanganate
d. ammonium dichromate
e. cobalt(II) perchlorate
f. potassium chlorate
g. copper(II) nitrite

Example 5.7 illustrates that when more than one polyatomic ion appears in a chemical formula, parentheses are used to enclose the ion and a subscript is written after the closing parenthesis. Other examples are $(NH_4)_2SO_4$ and $Fe_3(PO_4)_2$.

In naming chemical compounds, use the strategy summarized in Figure 5.2. If the compound being considered is binary, use the procedure summarized in Figure 5.1. If the compound has more than two elements, ask yourself whether it has any polyatomic ions. Use Table 5.4 to help you recognize these ions until you have committed them to memory. If a polyatomic ion is present, name the compound using procedures very similar to those for naming binary ionic compounds.

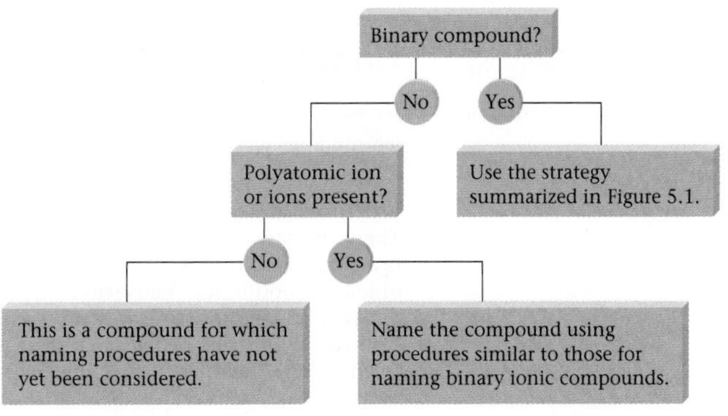

Figure 5.2
Overall strategy for naming chemical compounds.

Additional Examples

Example 5.8

Name the following compounds.

1. $Ca(HCO_3)_2$

   calcium hydrogen carbonate, calcium bicarbonate

2. MgI_2

   magnesium iodide

3. $KMnO_4$

   potassium permanganate

4. Sb_2O_3

   antimony(III) oxide

5. $Fe(OH)_2$

   iron(II) hydroxide

Self Check

Answers to Self-Check Exercise 5.7

a. sodium hydrogen carbonate (often called sodium bicarbonate)

b. barium sulfate

c. cesium perchlorate

d. bromine pentafluoride

e. sodium bromide

f. potassium hypochlorite

g. zinc(II) phosphate

Section 5.6

TEACHING TIP

Students are briefly introduced to acids in this chapter. Acids are reactants in many reactions in upcoming chapters and are used in early experiments, so this brief introduction is important.

Test Bank: (5a) 31, 53–123

EXAMPLE 5.8 Summary of Naming Binary Compounds and Compounds That Contain Polyatomic Ions

Name the following compounds.

a. Na_2CO_3
b. $FeBr_3$
c. $CsClO_4$
d. PCl_3
e. $CuSO_4$

SOLUTION

	Compound	Name	Comments
a.	Na_2CO_3	sodium carbonate	Contains $2Na^+$ and CO_3^{2-}.
b.	$FeBr_3$	iron(III) bromide	Contains Fe^{3+} and $3Br^-$.
c.	$CsClO_4$	cesium perchlorate	Contains Cs^+ and ClO_4^-.
d.	PCl_3	phosphorus trichloride	Type III binary compound (both P and Cl are nonmetals).
e.	$CuSO_4$	copper(II) sulfate	Contains Cu^{2+} and SO_4^{2-}.

Self-Check **EXERCISE 5.7** Name the following compounds.

a. $NaHCO_3$
b. $BaSO_4$
c. $CsClO_4$
d. BrF_5
e. NaBr
f. KOCl
g. $Zn_3(PO_4)_2$

See Problems 5.29 through 5.36. ■

Although we have emphasized that a Roman numeral is required in the name of a compound that contains a transition metal ion, certain transition metals form only one ion. Common examples are zinc (forms only Zn^{2+}) and silver (forms only Ag^+). For these cases the Roman numeral is omitted from the name.

5.6 Naming Acids

OBJECTIVES: To learn how the anion composition determines the acid's name. • To learn names for common acids.

When dissolved in water, certain molecules produce H^+ ions (protons). These substances, which are called **acids,** were first recognized by the sour taste of their solutions. For example, citric acid is responsible for the tartness of lemons and limes. Acids will be discussed in detail later. Here we simply present the rules for naming acids.

An acid can be viewed as a molecule with one or more H^+ ions attached to an anion. The rules for naming acids depend on whether the anion contains oxygen.

Rules for Naming Acids

1. If the *anion does not contain oxygen,* the acid is named with the prefix *hydro-* and the suffix *-ic* attached to the root name for the element. For example, when gaseous HCl (hydrogen chloride) is dissolved in water, it forms hydrochloric acid. Similarly, hydrogen cyanide (HCN) and dihydrogen sulfide (H_2S) dissolved in water are called hydrocyanic acid and hydrosulfuric acid, respectively.
2. When the *anion contains oxygen,* the acid name is formed from the root name of the central element of the anion or the anion name, with a suffix of *-ic* or *-ous.* When the anion name ends in *-ate,* the suffix *-ic* is used. For example,

Acid	Anion	Name
H_2SO_4	SO_4^{2-} (sulfate)	sulfuric acid
H_3PO_4	PO_4^{3-} (phosphate)	phosphoric acid
$HC_2H_3O_2$	$C_2H_3O_2^-$ (acetate)	acetic acid

When the anion name ends in *-ite,* the suffix *-ous* is used in the acid name. For example,

Acid	Anion	Name
H_2SO_3	SO_3^{2-} (sulfite)	sulfurous acid
HNO_2	NO_2^- (nitrite)	nitrous acid

Table 5.5 Names of Acids That Do Not Contain Oxygen

Acid	Name
HF	hydrofluoric acid
HCl	hydrochloric acid
HBr	hydrobromic acid
HI	hydroiodic acid
HCN	hydrocyanic acid
H_2S	hydrosulfuric acid

The application of Rule 2 can be seen in the names of the acids of the oxyanions of chlorine below.

Acid	Anion	Name
$HClO_4$	perchlor*ate*	perchlor*ic* acid
$HClO_3$	chlor*ate*	chlor*ic* acid
$HClO_2$	chlor*ite*	chlor*ous* acid
HClO	hypochlor*ite*	hypochlor*ous* acid

The rules for naming acids are given in schematic form in Figure 5.3. The names of the most important acids are given in Table 5.5 and Table 5.6. These should be memorized.

Table 5.6 Names of Some Oxygen-Containing Acids

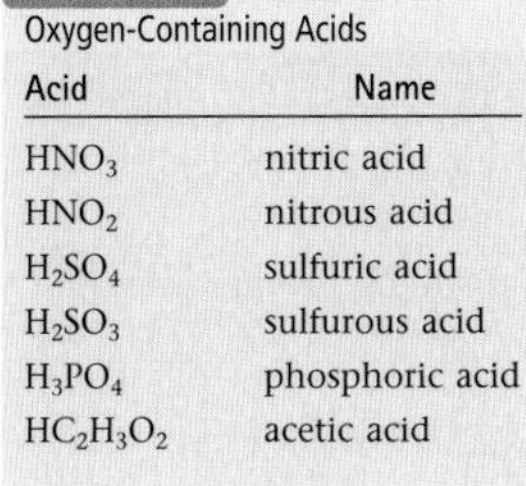

Acid	Name
HNO_3	nitric acid
HNO_2	nitrous acid
H_2SO_4	sulfuric acid
H_2SO_3	sulfurous acid
H_3PO_4	phosphoric acid
$HC_2H_3O_2$	acetic acid

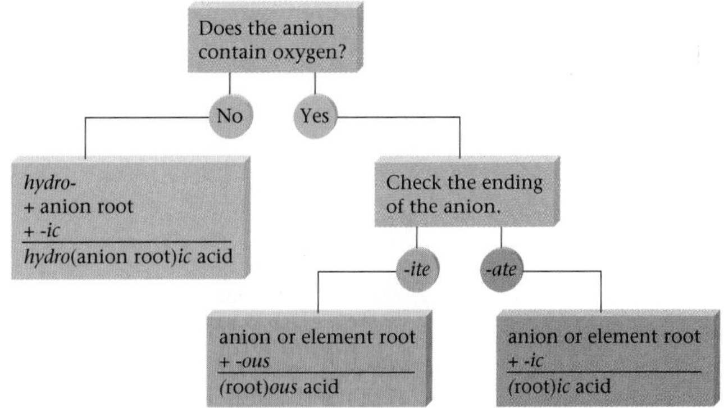

Figure 5.3 A flow chart for naming acids. The acid is considered as one or more H^+ ions attached to an anion.

TEACHING TIP

Ask students to name the oxyacids containing bromine as well as those containing chlorine. This exercise provides an opportunity to review the naming system for the polyatomic ions and extend it to acids.

Additional Examples

Name the following acids.

1. HF

   hydrofluoric acid

2. H_3PO_3

   phosphorus acid

3. HNO_3

   nitric acid

4. $HBrO_4$

   bromic acid

5. H_2S

   hydrosulfuric acid

 **Test Bank: (5b) 1–99**

Section 5.7

TEACHING TIPS

- Writing formulas from names is usually easier for students than naming formulas because Type I and Type II cations are identified by name. Students must know the polyatomic ions and their charges to write formulas correctly.
- Students often forget parentheses when writing formulas, especially when a polyatomic ion requires a subscript. For example, $Ca(OH)_2$ is frequently written by beginning students as $CaOH_2$. You may want to relate this point to math and the grouping of algebraic symbols with parentheses.

PowerLecture Video: Formation of Ionic Compounds

Additional Examples

Example 5.9

Write the correct formula for each compound.

1. sodium nitrate

   $NaNO_3$

2. ammonium dichromate

   $NH_4Cr_2O_7$

3. mercury(II) iodide

   HgI_2

4. barium carbonate

   $BaCO_3$

5. magnesium bromide

   $MgBr_2$

6. hydrochloric acid

   $HCl(aq)$

7. carbon disulfide

   CS_2

8. nickel(II) perchlorate

   $Ni(ClO_4)_2$

9. cesium fluoride

   CsF

10. hypobromous acid

    HBrO

5.7 Writing Formulas from Names

OBJECTIVE: To learn to write the formula of a compound, given its name.

So far we have started with the chemical formula of a compound and decided on its systematic name. Being able to reverse the process is also important. Often a laboratory procedure describes a compound by name, but the label on the bottle in the lab shows only the formula of the chemical it contains. It is essential that you are able to get the formula of a compound from its name. In fact, you already know enough about compounds to do this. For example, given the name calcium hydroxide, you can write the formula as $Ca(OH)_2$ because you know that calcium forms only Ca^{2+} ions and that, since hydroxide is OH^-, two of these anions are required to give a neutral compound. Similarly, the name iron(II) oxide implies the formula FeO, because the Roman numeral II indicates the presence of the cation Fe^{2+} and the oxide ion is O^{2-}.

We emphasize at this point that it is essential to learn the name, composition, and charge of each of the common polyatomic anions (and the NH_4^+ cation). If you do not recognize these ions by formula and by name, you will not be able to write the compound's name given its formula or the compound's formula given its name. You must also learn the names of the common acids.

EXAMPLE 5.9 Writing Formulas from Names

Give the formula for each of the following compounds.

a. potassium hydroxide
b. sodium carbonate
c. nitric acid
d. cobalt(III) nitrate
e. calcium chloride
f. lead(IV) oxide
g. dinitrogen pentoxide
h. ammonium perchlorate

SOLUTION

Name	Formula	Comments
a. potassium hydroxide	KOH	Contains K^+ and OH^-.
b. sodium carbonate	Na_2CO_3	We need two Na^+ to balance CO_3^{2-}.
c. nitric acid	HNO_3	Common strong acid; memorize.
d. cobalt(III) nitrate	$Co(NO_3)_3$	Cobalt(III) means Co^{3+}; we need three NO_3^- to balance Co^{3+}.
e. calcium chloride	$CaCl_2$	We need two Cl^- to balance Ca^{2+}; Ca (Group 2) always forms Ca^{2+}.
f. lead(IV) oxide	PbO_2	Lead(IV) means Pb^{4+}; we need two O^{2-} to balance Pb^{4+}.
g. dinitrogen pentoxide	N_2O_5	*Di-* means two; *pent(a)-* means five.
h. ammonium perchlorate	NH_4ClO_4	Contains NH_4^+ and ClO_4^-.

Self-Check **EXERCISE 5.8** Write the formula for each of the following compounds.

a. ammonium sulfate
b. vanadium(V) fluoride
c. disulfur dichloride
d. rubidium peroxide
e. aluminum oxide

See Problems 5.41 through 5.46. ■

CHAPTER 5 REVIEW

Key Terms

binary compound (5.1)
binary ionic compound (5.2)
polyatomic ion (5.5)
oxyanion (5.5)
acid (5.6)

F directs you to the *Chemistry in Focus* feature in the chapter
VP indicates visual problems
WL interactive versions of these problems are assignable in OWL

Summary

1. Binary compounds can be named systematically by following a set of relatively simple rules. For compounds containing both a metal and a nonmetal, the metal is always named first, followed by a name derived from the root name for the nonmetal. For compounds containing a metal that can form more than one cation (Type II), we use a Roman numeral to specify the cation's charge. In binary compounds containing only nonmetals (Type III), prefixes are used to specify the numbers of atoms.
2. Polyatomic ions are charged entities composed of several atoms bound together. These have special names that must be memorized. Naming ionic compounds that contain polyatomic ions is very similar to naming binary ionic compounds.
3. The names of acids (molecules with one or more H^+ ions attached to an anion) depend on whether the anion contains oxygen.

Active Learning Questions

These questions are designed to be considered by groups of students in class. Often these questions work well for introducing a particular topic in class.

1. In some cases the Roman numeral in a name is the same as a subscript in the formula, and in some cases it is not. Provide an example (formula and name) for each of these cases. Explain why the Roman numeral is not necessarily the same as the subscript.
2. The formulas $CaCl_2$ and $CoCl_2$ look very similar. What is the name for each compound? Why do we name them differently?
3. The formulas MgO and CO look very similar. What is the name for each compound? Why do we name them differently?
4. Explain how to use the periodic table to determine that there are two chloride ions for every magnesium ion in magnesium chloride and one chloride ion for every sodium ion in sodium chloride. Then write the formulas for calcium oxide and potassium oxide and explain how you got them.
5. What is the general formula for an ionic compound formed by elements in the following groups? Explain your reasoning and provide an example for each (name and formula).
   a. Group 1 with group 7
   b. Group 2 with group 7
   c. Group 1 with group 6
   d. Group 2 with group 6
6. An element forms an ionic compound with chlorine, leading to a compound having the formula XCl_2. The ion of element X has mass number 89 and 36 electrons. Identify the element X, tell how many neutrons it has, and name the compound.
7. VP Name each of the following compounds.

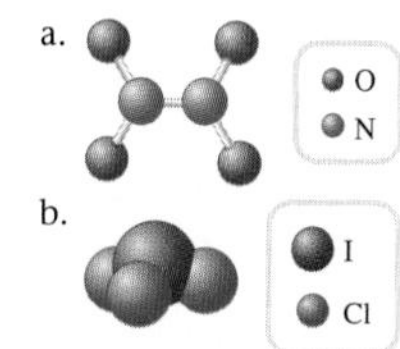

c. SO_3
d. P_2S_5

Self Check

Answers to Self-Check Exercise 5.8

a. $(NH_4)_2SO_4$
b. VF_5
c. S_2Cl_2
d. Rb_2O_2
e. Al_2O_3

ChemWork

Using a Manometer to Find Pressure
Predicting Gas Behavior
Gas Law Variables
Finding Moles of a Gas
Finding the Volume of a Gas
Mass of a Gas
Volume of a Balloon
Converting Ethene to Ethane
Density of a Gas
Gas Stoichiometry
Molar Mass of a Gas
Production of Oxygen Gas
Reacting a Gas with Calcium Silicate
Collecting a Gas over Water
Characteristics of Gases
Kinetic Molecular Theory

Answers to End-of-Chapter Exercises

1. (a) It was very sweet-tasting; (b) lead(II) acetate, plumbous acetate; (c) There are millions of known chemical compounds, and a system of nomenclature is essential for communication among scientists.

2. A binary chemical compound contains only two elements; the major types are ionic (compounds of a metal and a nonmetal) and nonionic or molecular (compounds between two nonmetals). Answers depend on student responses.

3. positive; negative

4. cation (positive ion)

5. cation

6. Some substances do not contain molecules; the formula we write reflects only the relative number of each type of atom present.

7. *-ous, -ic*

8. Roman numeral

9. (a) sodium bromide; (b) magnesium chloride; (c) aluminum phosphide; (d) strontium bromide; (e) silver iodide; (f) potassium sulfide

10. (a) lithium chloride; (b) barium fluoride; (c) calcium oxide; (d) aluminum iodide; (e) magnesium sulfide; (f) rubidium oxide

11. (a) correct; (b) incorrect; lead(II) chloride; (c) correct; (d) incorrect; sodium sulfide; (e) correct

12. (a) correct; (b) incorrect; copper(I) oxide; (c) incorrect; potassium oxide; (d) correct; (e) incorrect; rubidium sulfide

13. (a) tin(IV) chloride; (b) iron(III) sulfide; (c) lead(IV) oxide; (d) chromium(III) sulfide; (e) copper(II) oxide; (f) copper(I) oxide

14. (a) copper(II) chloride; (b) chromium(III) oxide; (c) mercury(II) chloride; (d) mercury(I) oxide; (e) gold(III) bromide; (f) manganese(IV) oxide

15. (a) cuprous chloride; (b) ferric oxide; (c) mercurous chloride; (d) manganous chloride; (e) titanic oxide; (f) plumbous oxide

16. (a) cobaltic chloride; (b) ferrous bromide; (c) plumbic oxide; (d) stannic chloride; (e) mercuric iodide; (f) ferrous sulfide

17. (a) krypton diflouride; (b) diselenium hexasulfide; (c) arsenic trihydride; (d) xenon tetroxide; (e) bromine trifluoride; (f) diphosphorus pentasulfide

18. (a) chlorine pentafluoride; (b) xenon dichloride; (c) selenium dioxide; (d) dinitrogen trioxide; (e) diiodine hexachloride; (f) carbon disulfide

8. Why do we call $Ba(NO_3)_2$ barium nitrate but call $Fe(NO_3)_2$ iron(II) nitrate?

9. What is the difference between sulfuric acid and hydrosulfuric acid?

Questions and Problems

5.1 Naming Compounds

QUESTIONS

1. The "Chemistry in Focus" segment *Sugar of Lead* discusses $Pb(C_2H_3O_2)_2$, which originally was known as sugar of lead.
   a. Why was it called sugar of lead?
   b. What is the systematic name for $Pb(C_2H_3O_2)_2$?
   c. Why is it necessary to have a *system* for the naming of chemical compounds?

2. What is a *binary* chemical compound? What are the two major *types* of binary chemical compounds? Give three examples of each type of binary compound.

5.2 Naming Binary Compounds That Contain a Metal and a Nonmetal (Types I and II)

QUESTIONS

3. Cations are ______ ions, and anions are ______ ions.

4. In naming ionic compounds, we always name the ______ first.

5. In a simple binary ionic compound, which ion (cation/anion) has the same name as its parent element?

6. When we write the formula for an ionic compound, we are merely indicating the relative numbers of each type of ion in the compound, *not* the presence of "molecules" in the compound with that formula. Explain.

7. For a metallic element that forms two stable cations, the ending ______ is used to indicate the cation of lower charge and the ending ______ is used to indicate the cation of higher charge.

8. We indicate the charge of a metallic element that forms more than one cation by adding a ______ after the name of the cation.

9. Give the name of each of the following simple binary ionic compounds.
   a. NaBr d. $SrBr_2$
   b. $MgCl_2$ e. AgI
   c. AlP f. K_2S

10. Give the name of each of the following simple binary ionic compounds.
   a. LiCl d. AlI_3
   b. BaF_2 e. MgS
   c. CaO f. Rb_2O

11. In each of the following, identify which names are incorrect for the given formulas, and give the correct name.
   a. CaH_2, calcium hydride
   b. $PbCl_2$, lead(IV) chloride
   c. CrI_3, chromium(III) iodide
   d. Na_2S, disodium sulfide
   e. $CuBr_2$, cupric bromide

12. In each of the following, identify which names are incorrect for the given formulas, and give the correct name.
   a. $MnCl_2$, manganese(II) chloride
   b. Cu_2O, copper(II) oxide
   c. K_2O, potassium(I) oxide
   d. ZnS, zinc sulfide
   e. Rb_2S, rubidium(II) sulfide

13. Write the name of each of the following ionic substances, using the system that includes a Roman numeral to specify the charge of the cation.
   a. $SnCl_4$ d. Cr_2S_3
   b. Fe_2S_3 e. CuO
   c. PbO_2 f. Cu_2O

14. Write the name of each of the following ionic substances, using the system that includes a Roman numeral to specify the charge of the cation.
   a. $CuCl_2$ d. Hg_2O
   b. Cr_2O_3 e. $AuBr_3$
   c. $HgCl_2$ f. MnO_2

15. Write the name of each of the following ionic substances, using *–ous* or *–ic* endings to indicate the charge of the cation.
   a. CuCl d. $MnCl_2$
   b. Fe_2O_3 e. TiO_2
   c. Hg_2Cl_2 f. PbO

16. Write the name of each of the following ionic substances, using *–ous* or *–ic* endings to indicate the charge of the cation.
   a. $CoCl_3$ d. $SnCl_4$
   b. $FeBr_2$ e. HgI_2
   c. PbO_2 f. FeS

5.3 Naming Binary Compounds That Contain Only Nonmetals (Type III)

QUESTIONS

17. Write the name of each of the following binary compounds of nonmetallic elements.
   a. KrF_2
   b. Se_2S_6
   c. AsH_3
   d. XeO_4
   e. BrF_3
   f. P_2S_5

All even-numbered Questions and Problems have answers in the back of this book and solutions in the Solutions Guide.

19. (a) iron(II) phosphide, ferrous phosphide; (b) calcium bromide; (c) dinitrogen pentoxide; (d) lead(IV) chloride, plumbic chloride; (e) disulfur decafluoride; (f) copper(I) oxide, cuprous oxide

20. (a) lead(IV) sulfide, plumbic sulfide; (b) lead(II) sulfide, plumbous sulfide; (c) silicon dioxide; (d) tin(IV) fluoride, stannic fluoride; (e) dichlorine heptoxide; (f) cobalt(III) sulfide, cobaltic sulfide

21. (a) magnesium sulfide, ionic; (b) aluminum chloride, ionic; (c) phosphorus trihydride (common name: phosphine), nonionic; (d) chlorine monobromide, nonionic; (e) lithium oxide, ionic; (f) tetraphosphorus decoxide, nonionic

22. (a) barium fluoride; (b) radium oxide; (c) dinitrogen oxide; (d) rubidium oxide; (e) diarsenic pent(a)oxide; (f) calcium nitride

18. Write the name of each of the following binary compounds of nonmetallic elements.

a. ClF_5 d. N_2O_3
b. $XeCl_2$ e. I_2Cl_6
c. SeO_2 f. CS_2

5.4 Naming Binary Compounds: A Review

QUESTIONS

19. Name each of the following binary compounds, using the periodic table to determine whether the compound is likely to be ionic (containing a metal and a nonmetal) or nonionic (containing only nonmetals).

a. Fe_3P_2 d. $PbCl_4$
b. $CaBr_2$ e. S_2F_{10}
c. N_2O_5 f. Cu_2O

20. Name each of the following binary compounds, using the periodic table to determine whether the compound is likely to be ionic (containing a metal and a nonmetal) or nonionic (containing only nonmetals).

a. PbS_2 d. SnF_4
b. PbS e. Cl_2O_7
c. SiO_2 f. Co_2S_3

21. Name each of the following binary compounds, using the periodic table to determine whether the compound is likely to be ionic (containing a metal and a nonmetal) or nonionic (containing only nonmetals).

a. MgS d. ClBr
b. $AlCl_3$ e. Li_2O
c. PH_3 f. P_4O_{10}

22. Name each of the following binary compounds, using the periodic table to determine whether the compound is likely to be ionic (containing a metal and a nonmetal) or nonionic (containing only nonmetals).

a. BaF_2 d. Rb_2O
b. RaO e. As_2O_5
c. N_2O f. Ca_3N_2

5.5 Naming Compounds That Contain Polyatomic Ions

QUESTIONS

23. What is a *polyatomic* ion? Give examples of five common polyatomic ions.

24. What is an *oxyanion?* List the series of oxyanions that chlorine and bromine form and give their names.

25. For the oxyanions of sulfur, the ending *-ite* is used for SO_3^{2-} to indicate that it contains ______ than does SO_4^{2-}.

26. In naming oxyanions, when there are more than two members in the series for a given element, what prefixes are used to indicate the oxyanions in the series with the *fewest* and the *most* oxygen atoms?

27. Complete the following list by filling in the missing names or formulas of the oxyanions of chlorine.

ClO_4^- ______
______ hypochlorite
ClO_3^- ______
______ chlorite

28. A series of oxyanions of iodine, comparable to the series for chlorine discussed in the text, also exists. Write the formulas and names for the oxyanions of iodine.

29. Write the formula for each of the following phosphorus-containing ions, including the overall charge of the ion.

a. phosphide
b. phosphate
c. phosphite
d. hydrogen phosphate

30. Write the formula for each of the following nitrogen-containing polyatomic ions, including the overall charge of the ion.

a. nitrate
b. nitrite
c. ammonium
d. cyanide

31. Chlorine occurs in several common polyatomic anions. List the formulas of as many such anions as you can, along with the names of the anions.

32. Carbon occurs in several common polyatomic anions. List the formulas of as many such anions as you can, along with the names of the anions.

33. Give the name of each of the following polyatomic ions.

a. HCO_3^- d. OH^-
b. $C_2H_3O_2^-$ e. NO_2^-
c. CN^- f. HPO_4^{2-}

34. Give the name of each of the following polyatomic ions.

a. NH_4^+ d. HSO_3^-
b. $H_2PO_4^-$ e. ClO_4^-
c. SO_4^{2-} f. IO_3^-

35. Name each of the following compounds, which contain polyatomic ions.

a. NH_4NO_3 d. Na_2HPO_4
b. $Ca(HCO_3)_2$ e. $KClO_4$
c. $MgSO_4$ f. $Ba(C_2H_3O_2)_2$

36. Name each of the following compounds, which contain polyatomic ions.

a. $NaMnO_4$ d. $Ca(ClO)_2$
b. $AlPO_4$ e. $BaCO_3$
c. $CrCO_3$ f. $CaCrO_4$

All even-numbered Questions and Problems have answers in the back of this book and solutions in the Solutions Guide.

27. ClO_4^-, perchlorate; ClO^-, hypochlorite; ClO_3^-, chlorate; ClO_2^-, chlorite

28. IO^-, hypoiodite; IO_2^-, iodite; IO_3^-, iodate; IO_4^-, periodate

29. (a) P^{3-}; (b) PO_4^{3-}; (c) PO_3^{3-}; (d) HPO_4^{2-}

30. (a) NO_3^-; (b) NO_2^-; (c) NH_4^+; (d) CN^-

31. Cl^-, chloride; ClO^-, hypochlorite; ClO_2^-, chlorite; ClO_3^-, chlorate; ClO_4^-, perchlorate

32. CN^-, cyanide; CO_3^{2-}, carbonate; HCO_3^-, hydrogen carbonate; $C_2H_3O_2^-$, acetate

33. (a) hydrogen carbonate, bicarbonate; (b) acetate; (c) cyanide; (d) hydroxide; (e) nitrite; (f) hydrogen phosphate

34. (a) ammonium ion; (b) dihydrogen phosphate ion; (c) sulfate ion; (d) hydrogen sulfite ion (bisulfite ion); (e) perchlorate ion; (f) iodate ion

35. (a) ammonium nitrate; (b) calcium hydrogen carbonate, calcium bicarbonate; (c) magnesium sulfate; (d) sodium hydrogen phosphate; (e) potassium perchlorate; (f) barium acetate

36. (a) sodium permanganate; (b) aluminum phosphate; (c) chromium(II) carbonate, chromous carbonate; (d) calcium hypochlorite; (e) barium carbonate; (f) calcium chromate

23. A polyatomic ion is a group of atoms bound together that, as a unit, carries an electrical charge. Answers depend on student responses.

24. An oxyanion is a polyatomic ion containing a given element and one or more oxygen atoms. The oxyanions of chlorine and bromine are given here:

Oxyanion	*Name*	*Oxyanion*	*Name*
ClO^-	hypochlorite	BrO^-	hypobromite
ClO_2^-	chlorite	BrO_2^-	bromite
ClO_3^-	chlorate	BrO_3^-	bromate
ClO_4^-	perchlorate	BrO_4^-	perbromate

25. one fewer oxygen atom

26. *hypo-* (fewest); *per-* (most)

37. An acid produces H^+ ions when dissolved in water.

38. oxygen

39. (a) hydrochloric acid; (b) sulfuric acid; (c) nitric acid; (d) hydroiodic acid; (e) nitrous acid; (f) chloric acid; (g) hydrobromic acid; (h) hydrofluoric acid; (i) acetic acid

40. (a) hypochlorous acid; (b) sulfurous acid; (c) bromic acid; (d) hypoiodous acid; (e) perbromic acid; (f) hydrosulfuric acid; (g) hydroselenic acid; (h) phosphorous acid

41. (a) $CoCl_2$; (b) $CoCl_3$; (c) Na_3P; (d) FeO; (e) CaH_2; (f) MnO_2; (g) MgI_2; (h) Cu_2S

42. (a) MgF_2; (b) FeI_3; (c) HgS; (d) Ba_3N_2; (e) $PbCl_2$; (f) SnF_4; (g) Ag_2O; (h) K_2Se

43. (a) CS_2; (b) H_2O; (c) N_2O_3; (d) Cl_2O_7; (e) CO_2; (f) NH_3; (g) XeF_4

44. (a) N_2O; (b) NO_2; (c) N_2O_4; (d) SF_6; (e) PBr_3; (f) Cl_4; (g) OCl_2

45. (a) NH_4NO_3; (b) $Mg(C_2H_3O_2)_2$; (c) CaO_2; (d) $KHSO_4$; (e) $FeSO_4$; (f) $KHCO_3$; (g) $CoSO_4$; (h) $LiClO_4$

46. (a) $NH_4C_2H_3O_2$; (b) $Fe(OH)_2$; (c) $Co_2(CO_3)_3$; (d) $BaCr_2O_7$; (e) $PbSO_4$; (f) KH_2PO_4; (g) Li_2O_2; (h) $Zn(ClO_3)_2$

47. (a) H_2S; (b) $HBrO_4$; (c) $HC_2H_3O_2$; (d) HBr; (e) $HClO_2$; (f) H_2Se; (g) H_2SO_3; (h) $HClO_4$

48. (a) HCN; (b) HNO_3; (c) H_2SO_4; (d) H_3PO_4; (e) HClO or HOCl; (f) HBr; (g) $HBrO_2$; (h) HF

49. (a) Na_2O_2; (b) $Ca(ClO_3)_2$; (c) RbOH; (d) $Zn(NO_3)_2$; (e) $(NH_4)_2Cr_2O_7$; (f) $H_2S(aq)$; (g) $CaBr_2$; (h) $HOCl(aq)$; (i) K_2SO_4; (j) $HNO_3(aq)$; (k) $Ba(C_2H_3O_2)_2$; (l) Li_2SO_3

5.6 Naming Acids

QUESTIONS

37. Give a simple definition of an *acid.*

38. Many acids contain the element ________ in addition to hydrogen.

39. Name each of the following acids.

a. HCl
b. H_2SO_4
c. HNO_3
d. HI
e. HNO_2
f. $HClO_3$
g. HBr
h. HF
i. $HC_2H_3O_2$

40. Name each of the following acids.

a. HOCl
b. H_2SO_3
c. $HBrO_3$
d. HOI
e. $HBrO_4$
f. H_2S
g. H_2Se
h. H_3PO_3

5.7 Writing Formulas from Names

PROBLEMS

41. Write the formula for each of the following simple binary ionic compounds.

a. cobalt(II) chloride
b. cobaltic chloride
c. sodium phosphide
d. iron(II) oxide
e. calcium hydride
f. manganese(IV) oxide
g. magnesium iodide
h. copper(I) sulfide

42. Write the formula for each of the following simple binary ionic compounds.

a. magnesium fluoride
b. ferric iodide
c. mercuric sulfide
d. barium nitride
e. plumbous chloride
f. stannic fluoride
g. silver oxide
h. potassium selenide

43. Write the formula for each of the following binary compounds of nonmetallic elements.

a. carbon disulfide
b. water
c. dinitrogen trioxide
d. dichlorine heptoxide
e. carbon dioxide
f. ammonia
g. xenon tetrafluoride

44. Write the formula for each of the following binary compounds of nonmetallic elements.

a. dinitrogen oxide
b. nitrogen dioxide
c. dinitrogen tetraoxide (tetroxide)
d. sulfur hexafluoride
e. phosphorus tribromide
f. carbon tetraiodide
g. oxygen dichloride

45. Write the formula for each of the following compounds that contain polyatomic ions. Be sure to enclose the polyatomic ion in parentheses if more than one such ion is needed to balance the oppositely charged ion(s).

a. ammonium nitrate
b. magnesium acetate
c. calcium peroxide
d. potassium hydrogen sulfate
e. iron(II) sulfate
f. potassium hydrogen carbonate
g. cobalt(II) sulfate
h. lithium perchlorate

46. Write the formula for each of the following compounds that contain polyatomic ions. Be sure to enclose the polyatomic ion in parentheses if more than one such ion is needed to balance the oppositely charged ions.

a. ammonium acetate
b. ferrous hydroxide
c. cobalt(III) carbonate
d. barium dichromate
e. lead(II) sulfate
f. potassium dihydrogen phosphate
g. lithium peroxide
h. zinc chlorate

47. Write the formula for each of the following acids.

a. hydrosulfuric acid
b. perbromic acid
d. acetic acid
d. hydrobromic acid
e. chlorous acid
f. hydroselenic acid
g. sulfurous acid
h. perchloric acid

48. Write the formula for each of the following acids.

a. hydrocyanic acid
b. nitric acid
c. sulfuric acid
d. phosphoric acid
e. hypochlorous acid
f. hydrobromic acid
g. bromous acid
h. hydrofluoric acid

49. Write the formula for each of the following substances.

a. sodium peroxide
b. calcium chlorate
c. rubidium hydroxide
d. zinc nitrate
e. ammonium dichromate
f. hydrosulfuric acid
g. calcium bromide
h. hypochlorous acid
i. potassium sulfate
j. nitric acid
k. barium acetate
l. lithium sulfite

All even-numbered Questions and Problems have answers in the back of this book and solutions in the Solutions Guide.

50. (a) $Ca(HSO_4)_2$; (b) $Zn_3(PO_4)_2$; (c) $Fe(ClO_4)_3$; (d) $Co(OH)_3$; (e) K_2CrO_4; (f) $Al(H_2PO_4)_3$; (g) $LiHCO_3$; (h) $Mn(C_2H_3O_2)_2$; (i) $MgHPO_4$; (j) Cs_2ClO_2; (k) BaO_2; (l) $NiCO_3$

51.

Formula	*Roman Numeral Name*	*-ous/-ic Name*
FeO	iron(II) oxide	ferrous oxide
Fe_2O_3	iron(III) oxide	ferric oxide
FeS	iron(II) sulfide	ferrous sulfide
Fe_2S_3	iron(III) sulfide	ferric sulfide
$FeCl_2$	iron(II) chloride	ferrous chloride
$FeCl_3$	iron(III) chloride	ferric chloride

50. Write the formula for each of the following substances.

a. calcium hydrogen sulfate
b. zinc phosphate
c. iron(III) perchlorate
d. cobaltic hydroxide
e. potassium chromate
f. aluminum dihydrogen phosphate
g. lithium bicarbonate
h. manganese(II) acetate
i. magnesium hydrogen phosphate
j. cesium chlorite
k. barium peroxide
l. nickelous carbonate

Additional Problems

51. Iron forms both 2+ and 3+ cations. Write formulas for the oxide, sulfide, and chloride compound of each iron cation, and give the name of each compound in both the nomenclature method that uses Roman numerals to specify the charge of the cation and the *-ous*/*-ic* notation.

52. Before an electrocardiogram (ECG) is recorded for a cardiac patient, the ECG leads are usually coated with a moist paste containing sodium chloride. What property of an ionic substance such as NaCl is being made use of here?

53. Nitrogen and oxygen form numerous binary compounds, including NO, NO_2, N_2O_4, N_2O_5, and N_2O. Give the name of each of these oxides of nitrogen.

54. On some periodic tables, hydrogen is listed both as a member of Group 1 and as a member of Group 7. Write an equation showing the formation of H^+ ion and an equation showing the formation of H^- ion.

55. List the names and formulas of five common oxyacids.

56. Complete the following list by filling in the missing oxyanion or oxyacid for each pair.

ClO_4^-	______
______	HIO_3
ClO^-	______
BrO_2^-	______
______	$HClO_2$

57. Name the following compounds.

a. $Ca(C_2H_3O_2)_2$
b. PCl_3
c. $Cu(MnO_4)_2$
d. $Fe_2(CO_3)_3$
e. $LiHCO_3$
f. Cr_2S_3
g. $Ca(CN)_2$

58. Name the following compounds.

a. $AuBr_3$
b. $Co(CN)_3$
c. $MgHPO_4$
d. B_2H_6
e. NH_3
f. Ag_2SO_4
g. $Be(OH)_2$

59. Name the following compounds.

a. $HClO_3$
b. $CoCl_3$
c. B_2O_3
d. H_2O
e. $HC_2H_3O_2$
f. $Fe(NO_3)_3$
g. $CuSO_4$

60. Name the following compounds.

a. $(NH_4)_2CO_3$
b. NH_4HCO_3
c. $Ca_3(PO_4)_2$
d. H_2SO_3
e. MnO_2
f. HIO_3
g. KH

61. Most metallic elements form *oxides*, and often the oxide is the most common compound of the element that is found in the earth's crust. Write the formulas for the oxides of the following metallic elements.

a. potassium
b. magnesium
c. iron(II)
d. iron(III)
e. zinc(II)
f. lead(II)
g. aluminum

62. Consider a hypothetical simple ion M^{4+}. Determine the formula of the compound this ion would form with each of the following anions.

a. acetate
b. permanganate
c. oxide
d. hydrogen phosphate
e. hydroxide
f. nitrite

63. Consider a hypothetical element M, which is capable of forming stable simple cations that have charges of 1+, 2+, and 3+, respectively. Write the formulas of the compounds formed by the various M cations with each of the following anions.

a. chromate
b. dichromate
c. sulfide
d. bromide
e. bicarbonate
f. hydrogen phosphate

64. Consider the hypothetical metallic element M, which is capable of forming stable simple cations that have charges of 1+, 2+, and 3+, respectively. Consider also the nonmetallic elements D, E, and F, which form anions that have charges of 1−, 2−, and 3−, respectively. Write the formulas of all possible compounds between metal M and nonmetals D, E, and F.

65. Complete Table 5.A (on page 140) by writing the names and formulas for the ionic compounds formed when the cations listed across the top combine with the anions shown in the left-hand column.

66. Complete Table 5.B (on page 140) by writing the formulas for the ionic compounds formed when the anions listed across the top combine with the cations shown in the left-hand column.

67. The noble metals gold, silver, and platinum are often used in fashioning jewelry because they are relatively ______.

68. The noble gas ______ is frequently found in underground deposits of natural gas.

69. The elements of Group 7 (fluorine, chlorine, bromine, and iodine) consist of molecules containing ______ atom(s).

All even-numbered Questions and Problems have answers in the back of this book and solutions in the Solutions Guide.

52. A moist paste of NaCl would contain Na^+ and Cl^- ions in solution and would serve as a *conductor* of electrical impulses.

53. NO, nitrogen monoxide; NO_2, nitrogen dioxide; N_2O_4, dinitrogen tetr(a)oxide; N_2O_5, dinitrogen pent(a)oxide; N_2O, dinitrogen monoxide

54. $H \rightarrow H^+$ (hydrogen ion) + e^-; $H + e^- \rightarrow H^-$ (hydride ion)

55. Answers will depend on student choices.

56. ClO_4^-, $HClO_4$; IO_3^-, HIO_3; ClO^-, $HClO$; BrO_2^-, $HBrO_2$; ClO_2^-, $HClO_2$

57. (a) calcium acetate; (b) phosphorus trichloride; (c) copper(II) permanganate; (d) iron(III) carbonate; (e) lithium hydrogen carbonate; (f) chromium(III) sulfide; (g) calcium cyanide

58. (a) gold(III) bromide (auric bromide); (b) cobalt(III) cyanide (cobaltic cyanide); (c) magnesium hydrogen phosphate; (d) diboron hexahydride (common name diborane); (e) ammonia; (f) silver(I) sulfate (usually called silver sulfate); (g) beryllium hydroxide

59. (a) chloric acid; (b) cobalt(III) chloride; (c) diboron trioxide; (d) water; (e) acetic acid; (f) iron(III) nitrate; (g) copper(II) sulfate

60. (a) ammonium carbonate; (b) ammonium hydrogen carbonate, ammonium bicarbonate; (c) calcium phosphate; (d) sulfurous acid; (e) manganese(IV) oxide; (f) iodic acid; (g) potassium hydride

61. (a) K_2O; (b) MgO; (c) FeO; (d) Fe_2O_3; (e) ZnO; (f) PbO; (g) Al_2O_3

62. (a) $M(C_2H_3O_2)_4$; (b) $M(MnO_4)_4$; (c) MO_2; (d) $M(HPO_4)_2$; (e) $M(OH)_4$; (f) $M(NO_2)_4$

63. (a) M_2CrO_4, $MCrO_4$, $M_2(CrO_4)_3$; (b) $M_2Cr_2O_7$, MCr_2O_7, $M_2(Cr_2O_7)_3$; (c) M_2S, MS, M_2S_3; (d) MBr, MBr_2, MBr_3; (e) $MHCO_3$, $M(HCO_3)_2$, $M(HCO_3)_3$; (f) M_2HPO_4, $MHPO_4$, $M_2(HPO_4)_3$

64. M^+ compounds: MD, M_2E, M_3F; M^{2+} compounds: MD_2, ME, M_3F_2; M^{3+} compounds: MD_3, M_2E_3, MF

65. Fe^{2+}: $FeCO_3$, iron(II) carbonate; $Fe(BrO_3)_2$, iron(II) bromate; $Fe(C_2H_3O_2)_2$, iron(II) acetate; $Fe(OH)_2$, iron(II) hydroxide; $Fe(HCO_3)_2$, iron(II) hydrogen carbonate; $Fe_3(PO_4)_2$, iron(II) phosphate; $FeSO_3$, iron(II) sulfite; $Fe(ClO_4)_2$, iron(II) perchlorate; $FeSO_4$, iron(II) sulfate; FeO, iron(II) oxide; $FeCl_2$, iron(II) chloride

Table 5.A

Ions	Fe^{2+}	Al^{3+}	Na^+	Ca^{2+}	NH_4^+	Fe^{3+}	Ni^{2+}	Hg_2^{2+}	Hg^{2+}
CO_3^{2-}									
BrO_3^-									
$C_2H_3O_2^-$									
OH^-									
HCO_3^-									
PO_4^{3-}									
SO_3^{2-}									
ClO_4^-									
SO_4^{2-}									
O^{2-}									
Cl^-									

Table 5.B

Ions	nitrate	sulfate	hydrogen sulfate	dihydrogen phosphate	oxide	chloride
calcium						
strontium						
ammonium						
aluminum						
iron(III)						
nickel(II)						
silver(I)						
gold(III)						
potassium						
mercury(II)						
barium						

70. Under what physical state at room temperature do each of the halogen elements exist?

71. When an atom gains two electrons, the ion formed has a charge of ______.

72. An ion with one more electron than it has protons has a ______ charge.

73. An atom that has lost three electrons will have a charge of ______.

74. An atom that has gained one electron has a charge of ______.

75. For each of the negative ions listed in column 1, use the periodic table to find in column 2 the total number of electrons the ion contains. A given answer may be used more than once.

Column 1	Column 2
[1] Se^{2-}	[a] 18
[2] S^{2-}	[b] 35
[3] P^{3-}	[c] 52
[4] O^{2-}	[d] 34
[5] N^{3-}	[e] 36
[6] I^-	[f] 54
[7] F^-	[g] 10
[8] Cl^-	[h] 9
[9] Br^-	[i] 53
[10] At^-	[j] 86

76. For each of the following processes that show the formation of ions, complete the process by indicating the number of electrons that must be gained or lost to form the ion. Indicate the total number of electrons in the ion, and in the atom from which it was made.

a. $Al \rightarrow Al^{3+}$
b. $S \rightarrow S^{2-}$
c. $Cu \rightarrow Cu^+$
d. $F \rightarrow F^-$
e. $Zn \rightarrow Zn^{2+}$
f. $P \rightarrow P^{3-}$

77. For each of the following atomic numbers, use the periodic table to write the formula (including the charge) for the simple *ion* that the element is most likely to form.

a. 36 d. 81
b. 31 e. 35
c. 52 f. 87

78. For the following pairs of ions, use the principle of electrical neutrality to predict the formula of the binary compound that the ions are most likely to form.

a. Na^+ and S^{2-} e. Cu^{2+} and Br^-
b. K^+ and Cl^- f. Al^{3+} and I^-
c. Ba^{2+} and O^{2-} g. Al^{3+} and O^{2-}
d. Mg^{2+} and Se^{2-} h. Ca^{2+} and N^{3-}

All even-numbered Questions and Problems have answers in the back of this book and solutions in the Solutions Guide.

Al^{3+}: $Al_2(CO_3)_3$, aluminum carbonate; $Al(BrO_3)_3$, aluminum bromate; $Al(C_2H_3O_2)_3$, aluminum acetate; $Al(OH)_3$, aluminum hydroxide; $Al(HCO_3)_3$, aluminum hydrogen carbonate; $AlPO_4$, aluminum phosphate; $Al_2(SO_4)_3$, aluminum sulfite; $Al(ClO_4)_3$, aluminum perchlorate; $Al_2(SO_4)_3$, aluminum sulfate; Al_2O_3, aluminum oxide; $AlCl_3$, aluminum chloride

Na^+: Na_2CO_3, sodium carbonate; $NaBrO_3$, sodium bromate; $NaC_2H_3O_2$, sodium acetate; $NaOH$, sodium hydroxide; $NaHCO_3$, sodium hydrogen carbonate; Na_3PO_4, sodium phosphate; Na_2SO_3, sodium sulfite; $NaClO_4$, sodium perchlorate; Na_2SO_4, sodium sulfate; Na_2O, sodium oxide; $NaCl$, sodium chloride

Ca^{2+}: $CaCO_3$, calcium carbonate; $Ca(BrO_3)_2$, calcium bromate; $Ca(C_2H_3O_2)_2$, calcium acetate; $Ca(OH)_2$, calcium hydroxide; $Ca(HCO_3)_2$, calcium hydrogen carbonate; $Ca_3(PO_4)_2$, calcium phosphate; $CaSO_3$, calcium sulfite; $Ca(ClO_4)_2$, calcium perchlorate; $CaSO_4$, calcium sulfate; CaO, calcium oxide; $CaCl_2$, calcium chloride

NH_4^+: $(NH_4)_2CO_3$, ammonium carbonate; NH_4BrO_3, ammonium bromate; $NH_4C_2H_3O_2$, ammonium actetate; NH_4HCO_3, ammonium hydrogen carbonate; $(NH_4)_3PO_4$, ammonium phosphate; $(NH_4)_2SO_3$, ammonium sulfite; NH_4ClO_4, ammonium perchlorate; $(NH_4)_2SO_4$, ammonium sulfate; $(NH_4)_2O$, ammonium oxide; NH_4Cl, ammonium chloride

Fe^{3+}: $Fe_2(CO_3)_3$, iron(III) carbonate; $Fe(BrO_3)_3$, iron(III) bromate; $Fe(C_2H_3O_2)_3$, iron(III) acetate; $Fe(OH)_3$, iron(III) hydroxide; $FePO_4$, iron(III) phosphate; $Fe_2(SO_3)_3$, iron(III) sulfite; $Fe(ClO_4)_3$, iron(III) perchlorate; $Fe_2(SO_4)_3$, iron(III) sulfate; Fe_2O_3, iron(III) oxide; $FeCl_3$, iron(III) chloride

Ni^{2+}: $NiCO_3$, nickel(II) carbonate; $Ni(BrO_3)_2$, nickel(II) bromate; $Ni(C_2H_3O_2)_2$, nickel(II) acetate; $Ni(OH)_2$, nickel(II) hydroxide; $Ni(HCO_3)_2$, nickel(II) hydrogen, nirbonate; $Ni_3(PO_4)_2$, nickel(II) phosphate; $NiSO_3$, nickel(II) sulfite; $Ni(ClO_4)_2$, nickel(II) perchlorate; $NiSO_4$, nickel(II) sulfate; NiO, nickel(II) oxide; $NiCl_2$, nickel(II) chloride

Hg_2^{2+}: Hg_2CO_3, mercury(I) carbonate; $Hg_2(BrO_3)_2$, mercury(I) bromate; $Hg_2(C_2H_3O_2)_2$, mercury(I) acetate; $Hg_2(OH)_2$, mercury(I) hydroxide; $Hg_2(HCO_3)_2$, mercury(I) hydrogen carbonate; $(Hg_2)_3(PO_4)_2$, mercury(I) phosphate; Hg_2SO_3, mercury(I) sulfite; $Hg_2(ClO_4)_2$, mercury(I) perchlorate; Hg_2SO_4, mercury(I) sulfate; Hg_2O, mercury(I) oxide; Hg_2Cl_2, mercury(I) chloride

Hg^{2+}: $HgCO_3$, mercury(II) carbonate; $Hg(BrO_3)_2$, mercury(II) bromate; $Hg(C_2H_3O_2)_2$, mercury(II) acetate; $Hg(OH)_2$, mercury(II) hydroxide;

79. Give the name of each of the following simple binary ionic compounds.

a. BeO
b. MgI_2
c. Na_2S
d. Al_2O_3
e. HCl
f. LiF
g. Ag_2S
h. CaH_2

80. In which of the following pairs is the name incorrect? Give the correct name for the formulas indicated.

a. Ag_2O, disilver monoxide
b. N_2O, dinitrogen monoxide
c. Fe_2O_3, iron(II) oxide
d. PbO_2, plumbous oxide
e. $Cr_2(SO_4)_3$, chromium(III) sulfate

81. Write the name of each of the following ionic substances, using the system that includes a Roman numeral to specify the charge of the cation.

a. $FeBr_2$
b. CoS
c. Co_2S_3
d. SnO_2
e. Hg_2Cl_2
f. $HgCl_2$

82. Write the name of each of the following ionic substances, using *-ous* or *-ic* endings to indicate the charge of the cation.

a. $SnCl_2$
b. FeO
c. SnO_2
d. PbS
e. Co_2S_3
f. $CrCl_2$

83. Name each of the following binary compounds.

a. XeF_6
b. OF_2
c. AsI_3
d. N_2O_4
e. Cl_2O
f. SF_6

84. Name each of the following compounds.

a. $Fe(C_2H_3O_2)_3$
b. BrF
c. K_2O_2
d. $SiBr_4$
e. $Cu(MnO_4)_2$
f. $CaCrO_4$

85. Which oxyanion of nitrogen contains a larger number of oxygen atoms, the nitr*ate* ion or the nitr*ite* ion?

86. Write the formula for each of the following carbon-containing polyatomic ions, including the overall charge of the ion.

a. carbonate
b. hydrogen carbonate
c. acetate
d. cyanide

87. Write the formula for each of the following chromium-containing ions, including the overall charge of the ion.

a. chromous
b. chromate
c. chromic
d. dichromate

88. Give the name of each of the following polyatomic anions.

a. CO_3^{2-}
b. ClO_3^-
c. SO_4^{2-}
d. PO_4^{3-}
e. ClO_4^-
f. MnO_4^-

89. Name each of the following compounds, which contain polyatomic ions.

a. LiH_2PO_4
b. $Cu(CN)_2$
c. $Pb(NO_3)_2$
d. Na_2HPO_4
e. $NaClO_2$
f. $Co_2(SO_4)_3$

90. Choose any five simple cations and any five polyatomic anions, and write the formulas for all possible compounds between the cations and the anions. Give the name of each compound.

91. Write the formula for each of the following binary compounds of nonmetallic elements.

a. sulfur dioxide
b. dinitrogen monoxide
c. xenon tetrafluoride
d. tetraphosphorus decoxide
e. phosphorus pentachloride
f. sulfur hexafluoride
g. nitrogen dioxide

92. Write the formula of each of the following ionic substances.

a. sodium dihydrogen phosphate
b. lithium perchlorate
c. copper(II) hydrogen carbonate
d. potassium acetate
e. barium peroxide
f. cesium sulfite

93. Write the formula for each of the following compounds, which contain polyatomic ions. Be sure to enclose the polyatomic ion in parentheses if more than one such ion is needed to balance the oppositely charged ion(s).

a. silver(I) perchlorate (usually called silver perchlorate)
b. cobalt(III) hydroxide
c. sodium hypochlorite
d. potassium dichromate
e. ammonium nitrite
f. ferric hydroxide
g. ammonium hydrogen carbonate
h. potassium perbromate

All even-numbered Questions and Problems have answers in the back of this book and solutions in the Solutions Guide.

$Hg(HCO_3)_2$, mercury(II) hydrogen carbonate; $Hg_3(PO_4)_2$, mercury(II) phosphate; $HgSO_3$, mercury(II) sulfite; $Hg(ClO_4)_2$, mercury(II) perchlorate; $HgSO_4$, mercury(II) sulfate; HgO, mercury(II) oxide; $HgCl_2$, mercury(II) chloride

66. See table below.

67. unreactive

68. helium

69. two

70. F_2, Cl_2 (gas); Br_2 (liquid); I_2, At_2 (solid)

71. 2−

72. 1−

73. 3+

74. 1−

75. (1) e; (2) a; (3) a; (4) g; (5) g; (6) f; (7) g; (8) a; (9) e; (10) j

76. (a) Al(13e) → Al^{3+}(10e) + $3e^-$; (b) S(16e) + $2e^-$ → S^{2-}(18e); (c) Cu(29e) → Cu^+(28e) + e^-; (d) F(9e) + e^- → F^-(10e); (e) Zn(30e) → Zn^{2+}(28e) + $2e^-$; (f) P(15e) + $3e^-$ → P^{3-}(18e)

77. (a) none likely (noble gas); (b) Ga^{3+}; (c) Te^{2-}; (d) Tl^{3+}; (e) Br^-; (f) Fr^+

78. (a) Na_2S; (b) KCl; (c) BaO; (d) MgSe; (e) $CuBr_2$; (f) AlI_3; (g) Al_2O_3; (h) Ca_3N_2

79. (a) beryllium oxide; (b) magnesium iodide; (c) sodium sulfide; (d) aluminum oxide; (e) hydrogen chloride, hydrochloric acid; (f) lithium fluoride; (g) silver sulfide; (h) calcium hydride

80. (a) silver(I) oxide or just silver oxide; (b) correct; (c) iron(III) oxide; (d) plumbic oxide; (e) correct

81. (a) iron(II) bromide; (b) cobalt(II) sulfide; (c) cobalt(III) sulfide; (d) tin(IV) oxide; (e) mercury(I) chloride; (f) mercury(II) chloride

82. (a) stannous chloride; (b) ferrous oxide; (c) stannic oxide; (d) plumbous sulfide;

66.

Nitrate	*Sulfate*	*Hydrogen sulfate*	*Dihydrogen phosphate*	*Oxide*	*Chloride*
$Ca(NO_3)_2$	$CaSO_4$	$Ca(HSO_4)_2$	$Ca(H_2PO_4)_2$	CaO	$CaCl_2$
$Sr(NO_3)_2$	$SrSO_4$	$Sr(HSO_4)_2$	$Sr(H_2PO_4)_2$	SrO	$SrCl_2$
NH_4NO_3	$(NH_4)_2SO_4$	NH_4HSO_4	$NH_4H_2PO_4$	$(NH_4)_2O$	NH_4Cl
$Al(NO_3)_3$	$Al_2(SO_4)_3$	$Al(HSO_4)_3$	$Al(H_2PO_4)_3$	Al_2O_3	$AlCl_3$
$Fe(NO_3)_3$	$Fe_2(SO_4)_3$	$Fe(HSO_4)_3$	$Fe(H_2PO_4)_3$	Fe_2O_3	$FeCl_3$
$Ni(NO_3)_2$	$NiSO_4$	$Ni(HSO_4)_2$	$Ni(H_2PO_4)_2$	NiO	$NiCl_2$
$AgNO_3$	Ag_2SO_4	$AgHSO_4$	AgH_2PO_4	Ag_2O	AgCl
$Au(NO_3)_3$	$Au_2(SO_4)_3$	$Au(HSO_4)_3$	$Au(H_2PO_4)_3$	Au_2O_3	$AuCl_3$
KNO_3	K_2SO_4	$KHSO_4$	KH_2PO_4	K_2O	KCl
$Hg(NO_3)_2$	$HgSO_4$	$Hg(HSO_4)_2$	$Hg(H_2PO_4)_2$	HgO	$HgCl_2$
$Ba(NO_3)_2$	$BaSO_4$	$Ba(HSO_4)_2$	$Ba(H_2PO_4)_2$	BaO	$BaCl_2$

(e) cobaltic sulfide; (f) chromous chloride

83. (a) xenon hexafluoride; (b) oxygen difluoride; (c) arsenic triiodide; (d) dinitrogen tetraoxide (tetroxide); (e) dichlorine monoxide; (f) sulfur hexafluoride

84. (a) iron(III) acetate; (b) bromine monofluoride; (c) potassium peroxide; (d) silicon tetrabromide; (e) copper(II) permanganate; (f) calcium chromate

85. nitrate

86. (a) CO_3^{2-}; (b) HCO_3^-; (c) $C_2H_3O_2^-$; (d) CN^-

87. (a) Cr^{2+}; (b) CrO_4^-; (c) Cr^{3+}; (d) $Cr_2O_7^{2-}$

88. (a) carbonate; (b) chlorate; (c) sulfate; (d) phosphate; (e) perchlorate; (f) permanganate

89. (a) lithium dihydrogen phosphate; (b) copper(II) cyanide; (c) lead(II) nitrate; (d) sodium hydrogen phosphate; (e) sodium chlorite; (f) cobalt(III) sulfate

90. Answers will depend on student choices.

91. (a) SO_2; (b) N_2O; (c) XeF_4; (d) P_4O_{10}; (e) PCl_5; (f) SF_6; (g) NO_2

92. (a) NaH_2PO_4; (b) $LiClO_4$; (c) $Cu(HCO_3)_2$; (d) $KC_2H_3O_2$; (e) BaO_2; (f) Cs_2SO_3

93. (a) $AgClO_4$; (b) $Co(OH)_3$; (c) $NaClO$; (d) $K_2Cr_2O_7$; (e) NH_4NO_2; (f) $Fe(OH)_3$; (g) NH_4HCO_3; (h) $KBrO_4$

CUMULATIVE REVIEW for CHAPTERS 4-5

QUESTIONS

1. What is an element? Which elements are most abundant on the earth? Which elements are most abundant in the human body?

2. Without consulting any reference, write the name and symbol for as many elements as you can. How many could you name? How many symbols did you write correctly?

3. The symbols for the elements silver (Ag), gold (Au), and tungsten (W) seem to bear no relation to their English names. Explain and give three additional examples.

4. Without consulting your textbook or notes, state as many points as you can of Dalton's atomic theory. Explain in your own words each point of the theory.

5. What is a compound? What is meant by the *law of constant composition* for compounds and why is this law so important to our study of chemistry?

6. What is meant by a *nuclear atom?* Describe the points of Rutherford's model for the nuclear atom and how he tested this model. Based on his experiments, how did Rutherford envision the structure of the atom? How did Rutherford's model of the atom's structure differ from Kelvin's "plum pudding" model?

7. Consider the neutron, the proton, and the electron.
   a. Which is(are) found in the nucleus?
   b. Which has the largest relative mass?
   c. Which has the smallest relative mass?
   d. Which is negatively charged?
   e. Which is electrically neutral?

8. What are *isotopes?* To what do the *atomic number* and the *mass number* of an isotope refer? How are specific isotopes indicated symbolically (give an example and explain)? Do the isotopes of a given element have the same chemical and physical properties? Explain.

9. Complete the following table by giving the symbol, name, atomic number, and/or group(family) number as required.

Symbol	Name	Atomic Number	Group Number
Ca	______	______	______
I	______	______	______
______	cesium	______	______
______	______	16	______
______	arsenic	______	______
Sr	______	______	______
______	______	14	______
Rn	______	______	______
______	radium	______	______
Se	______	______	______

10. Are most elements found in nature in the elemental or the combined form? Why? Name several elements that are usually found in the elemental form.

11. What are *ions?* How are ions formed from atoms? Do isolated atoms form ions spontaneously? To what do the terms *cation* and *anion* refer? In terms of subatomic particles, how is an ion related to the atom from which it is formed? Does the nucleus of an atom change when the atom is converted into an ion? How can the periodic table be used to predict what ion an element's atoms will form?

12. What are some general physical properties of ionic compounds such as sodium chloride? How do we know that substances such as sodium chloride consist of positively and negatively charged particles? Since ionic compounds are made up of electrically charged particles, why doesn't such a compound have an overall electric charge? Can an ionic compound consist only of cations or anions (but not both)? Why not?

13. What principle do we use in writing the formula of an ionic compound such as NaCl or MgI_2? How do we know that *two* iodide ions are needed for each magnesium ion, whereas only one chloride ion is needed per sodium ion?

14. When writing the name of an ionic compound, which is named first, the anion or the cation? Give an example. What ending is added to the root name of an element to show that it is a simple anion in a Type I ionic compound? Give an example. What *two* systems are used to show the charge of the cation in a Type II ionic compound? Give examples of each system for the same compound. What general type of element is involved in Type II compounds?

15. Describe the system used to name Type III binary compounds (compounds of nonmetallic elements). Give several examples illustrating the method. How does this system differ from that used for ionic compounds? How is the system for Type III compounds similar to those for ionic compounds?

16. What is a *polyatomic* ion? Without consulting a reference, list the formulas and names of at least ten polyatomic ions. When writing the overall formula of an ionic compound involving polyatomic ions, why are parentheses used around the formula of a polyatomic ion when more than one such ion is present? Give an example.

17. What is an *oxyanion?* What special system is used in a series of related oxyanions that indicates the relative number of oxygen atoms in each ion? Give examples.

18. What is an *acid?* How are acids that do *not* contain oxygen named? Give several examples. Describe the naming system for the oxyacids. Give examples of a series of oxyacids illustrating this system.

142

Answers to Cumulative Review Exercises

Chapters 4–5

1. An element is a substance that cannot be broken down into simpler substances by ordinary chemical means. Only the elements of atomic number 92 and lower occur naturally; elements past atomic number 92 have been created in the laboratory. The five most abundant elements on the earth by mass are oxygen, silicon, aluminum, iron, and calcium.

2. Although you don't have to memorize all the elements, you should at least be able to give the symbol or name for the most common elements (listed in Table 4.3).

3. These symbols are derived from the name of the element in another language (Ag, argentum; Au, aurum; W, wolfram). Examples depend on student choices.

4. The main postulates of Dalton's theory are: (1) elements are made up of tiny particles called atoms; (2) all atoms of a given element are identical; (3) although all atoms of a given element are identical, these atoms are different from the atoms of all other elements; (4) atoms of one element can combine with atoms of another element to form a compound that will always have the same relative numbers and types of atoms for its composition; and (5) atoms are merely rearranged into new groupings during an ordinary chemical reaction,

PROBLEMS

19. Complete the following table by giving the symbol, name, atomic number, and/or group (family) number as required.

Symbol	Name	Atomic Number	Group Number
Al	______	______	______
______	radon	______	______
______	sulfur	______	______
______	______	38	______
Br	______	______	______
______	carbon	______	______
Ba	______	______	______
______	______	88	______
______	______	11	______
K	______	______	______
______	germanium	______	______
______	______	17	______

20. Your text indicates that the Group 1, Group 2, Group 7, and Group 8 elements all have "family" names (alkali metals, alkaline earth metals, halogens, and noble gases, respectively). Without looking at your textbook, name as many elements in each family as you can. What similarities are there among the members of a family? Why?

21. Using the periodic table on the inside cover of this book, for each of the following symbols, write the name of the element and its atomic number.

a. Mg
b. Ga
c. Sn
d. Sb
e. Sr
f. Si
g. Cs
h. Ca
i. Cr
j. Co
k. Cu
l. Ag
m. U
n. As
o. At
p. Ar
q. Zn
r. Mn
s. Se
t. W
u. Ra
v. Rn
w. Ce
x. Zr
y. Al
z. Pd

22. How many electrons, protons, and neutrons are found in isolated atoms having the following atomic symbols?

a. $^{17}_{8}O$
b. $^{235}_{92}U$
c. $^{37}_{17}Cl$
d. $^{3}_{1}H$
e. $^{4}_{2}He$
f. $^{119}_{50}Sn$
g. $^{124}_{54}Xe$
h. $^{64}_{30}Zn$

23. What simple ion does each of the following elements most commonly form?

a. Mg
b. F
c. Ag
d. Al
e. O
f. Ba
g. Na
h. Br
i. K
j. Ca
k. S
l. Li
m. Cl

24. For each of the following simple ions, indicate the number of protons and electrons the ion contains.

a. Mg^{2+}
b. Fe^{2+}
c. Fe^{3+}
d. F^-
e. Ni^{2+}
f. Zn^{2+}
g. Co^{3+}
h. N^{3-}
i. S^{2-}
j. Rb^+
k. Se^{2-}
l. K^+

25. Using the ions indicated in Problem 24, write the formulas and give the names for all possible simple ionic compounds involving these ions.

26. Write the formula for each of the following binary ionic compounds.

a. copper(I) iodide
b. cobaltous chloride
c. silver sulfide
d. mercurous bromide
e. mercuric oxide
f. chromium(III) sulfide
g. plumbic oxide
h. potassium nitride
i. stannous fluoride
j. ferric oxide

27. Which of the following formula–name pairs are incorrect? Explain why for each case.

a. $Ag(NO_3)_2$ silver nitrate
b. Fe_2Cl ferrous chloride
c. NaH_2PO_4 sodium hydrogen phosphate
d. NH_4S ammonium sulfide
e. $KC_2H_3O_2$ potassium acetate
f. $Ca(ClO_4)_2$ calcium perchlorate
g. $K_2Cr_2O_7$ potassium dichromate
h. BaOH barium hydroxide
i. Na_2O_2 sodium peroxide
j. $Ca(CO_3)_2$ calcium carbonate

28. Give the name of each of the following polyatomic ions.

a. NH_4^+
b. SO_3^{2-}
c. NO_3^-
d. SO_4^{2-}
e. NO_2^-
f. CN^-
g. OH^-
h. ClO_4^-
i. ClO^-
j. PO_4^{3-}

29. Using the negative polyatomic ions listed in Table 5.4, write formulas for each of their sodium and calcium compounds.

30. Give the name of each of the following compounds.

a. XeO_2
b. ICl_5
c. PCl_3
d. CO
e. OF_2
f. P_2O_5
g. AsI_3
h. SO_3

31. Write formulas for each of the following compounds.

a. mercuric chloride
b. iron(III) oxide
c. sulfurous acid
d. calcium hydride
e. potassium nitrate
f. aluminum fluoride
g. dinitrogen monoxide
h. sulfuric acid
i. potassium nitride
j. nitrogen dioxide
k. silver acetate
l. acetic acid
m. platinum(IV) chloride
n. ammonium sulfide
o. cobalt(III) bromide
p. hydrofluoric acid

and no atom is ever destroyed and no new atom is ever created during such a reaction.

5. A compound is a distinct, pure substance that is composed of two or more elements held together by chemical bonds. In addition, a given compound always contains exactly the same relative masses of its constituent elements. This latter statement is termed the law of constant composition. The law of constant composition results from the fact that a given compound is made up of molecules containing a particular type and number of each constituent atom. For example, water's composition by mass (88.8% oxygen, 11.2% hydrogen) results from the fact that each and every water molecule contains one oxygen atom (relative mass 16.0) and two hydrogen atoms (relative mass 1.008 each). The law of constant composition is important to our study of chemistry because it means that we can always assume that any sample of a given pure substance, from whatever source, will be identical to any other sample.

6. The expression "nuclear atom" indicates that the atom has a dense center of positive charge (nucleus) around which the electrons move through primarily empty space. Rutherford's experiment involved shooting a beam of α particles at a thin sheet of metal foil. According to the "plum pudding" model of the atom, these positively charged α particles should have passed through the foil. Rutherford detected that a small number of α particles bounced backward to the source of α particles or were deflected from the foil at large angles. Rutherford realized that his observations could be explained if the atoms of the metal foil had a small, dense, positively charged nucleus, with a significant amount of empty space between nuclei. The empty space between nuclei would allow most of the α particles to pass through the foil. If an α particle were to hit a nucleus head-on, it would be deflected backward. If a positively charged α particle passed *near* a positively charged nucleus, then the α particle would be deflected by the repulsive forces. Rutherford's experiment disproved the "plum pudding" model, which envisioned the atom as a uniform sphere of positive charge, with enough negatively charged electrons scattered throughout to balance out the positive charge.

7. (a) protons and neutrons; (b) neutron; (c) electron; (d) electron; (e) neutron

(Please refer to page A32 in this book for answers to Exercises 8–31.)

Chapter 6

Objectives

In this chapter our objectives are for the students to:

SECTION 6.1

- Learn the signals that show a chemical reaction has occurred.

SECTION 6.2

- Learn to identify the characteristics of a chemical reaction and the information given by a chemical equation.

SECTION 6.3

- Learn how to write a balanced equation for a chemical reaction.

6 Chemical Reactions: An Introduction

Lightning over Seattle, Washington. *(Chuck Pefley/Tips Images)*

ChemWork Refined over ten years of use by thousands of students, **ChemWork** builds and enhances students' problems-solving skills. Online assignments function as a "personal instructor" to help students learn how to solve challenging problems and learn how to think like chemists. Annotations for **ChemWork** assignments are included at the beginning of the end-of-chapter review.

PowerLecture This 2-DVD package includes the Chemistry Multimedia Library, which contains animations, simulations, and movies for all chemistry subjects, organized by topic for lecture presentations. Annotations for **PowerLecture** are referenced in the margins throughout the Annotated Instructor's Edition.

OWL Sign in to OWL at **www.cengage.com/owl** to view tutorials and simulations, develop problem-solving skills, and complete online homework assigned by your professor.

go Chemistry Download mini-lecture videos for key concept review and exam prep from OWL or purchase them from **www.ichapters.com**

Chemistry is about change. Grass grows. Steel rusts. Hair is bleached, dyed, "permed," or straightened. Natural gas burns to heat houses. Nylon is produced for jackets, swimsuits, and pantyhose. Water is decomposed to hydrogen and oxygen gas by an electric current. Grape juice ferments in the production of wine. The bombardier beetle concocts a toxic spray to shoot at its enemies (see "Chemistry in Focus," p. 153).

These are just a few examples of chemical changes that affect each of us. Chemical reactions are the heart and soul of chemistry, and in this chapter we will discuss the fundamental ideas about chemical reactions.

Nylon is a strong material that makes sturdy parasails.

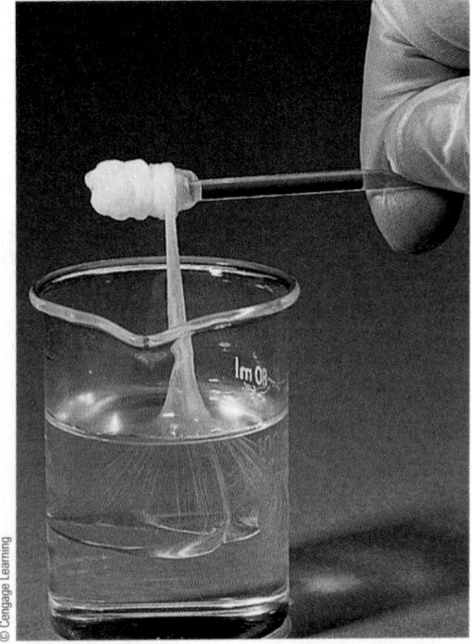

Production of plastic film for use in containers such as soft drink bottles *(left)*. Nylon being drawn from the boundary between two solutions containing different reactants *(right)*.

Test Bank: 1

Section 6.1

6.1 Evidence for a Chemical Reaction

OBJECTIVE: To learn the signals that show a chemical reaction has occurred.

Energy and chemical reactions will be discussed in more detail in Chapter 7.

How do we know when a chemical reaction has occurred? That is, what are the clues that a chemical change has taken place? A glance back at the processes in the introduction suggests that *chemical reactions often give a*

TEACHING TIP

Students should understand that the clues suggesting that a chemical reaction has occurred (Table 6.1) are not absolute. Now can be a good time to review the difference between chemical and physical changes. For example, a color change is evident (clue #1) when food coloring is added to water; a solid forms (clue #2) when water freezes or melted wax cools; and bubbles form and heat is absorbed (clues #3 and #4, respectively) when water is heated to boiling. However, all of these are physical changes. These clues are all *macroscopic* clues. We also need to consider what occurs *microscopically* to best differentiate between chemical and physical changes.

Lecture Demonstration:
4.2, 4.18, 4.19

DEMONSTRATION

Traffic Light Chemistry

Materials 6 g dextrose, 10 g NaOH, indigo carmine indicator solution (1%), 1-L soda bottle (clear, colorless)

Preparation Make the traffic light solution by adding 6 g dextrose and 10 g NaOH to 500 mL of water. Make 100 mL of indigo carmine indicator solution (1%).

Presentation Place the traffic light solution in the soda bottle. Add 75 mL of indigo carmine indicator solution to the soda bottle and tighten the cap. At the beginning of the demonstration, the solution should be yellow. Gently swirl the bottle to produce a red solution. Shake the bottle to make the solution green.

Teaching Notes If the red solution does not return, adjust the amount of indicator solution. In this oxidation–reduction reaction, oxygen is the oxidizing agent. Opening the top reinvigorates the reaction.

PowerLecture Video:
Hydrogen Balloon Ignited

Table 6.1 Some Clues That a Chemical Reaction Has Occurred

1. The color changes.
2. A solid forms.
3. Bubbles form.
4. Heat and/or a flame is produced, or heat is absorbed.

visual signal. Steel changes from a smooth, shiny material to a reddish-brown, flaky substance when it rusts. Hair changes color when it is bleached. Solid nylon is formed when two particular liquid solutions are brought into contact. A blue flame appears when natural gas reacts with oxygen. Chemical reactions, then, often give *visual* clues: a color changes, a solid forms, bubbles are produced (see Figure 6.1), a flame occurs, and so on. However, reactions are not always visible. Sometimes the only signal that a reaction is occurring is a change in temperature as heat is produced or absorbed (see Figure 6.2).

Table 6.1 summarizes common clues to the occurrence of a chemical reaction, and Figure 6.3 gives some examples of reactions that show these clues.

Figure 6.1 Bubbles of hydrogen and oxygen gas form when an electric current is used to decompose water.

© Cengage Learning

Figure 6.2

a An injured girl wearing a cold pack to help prevent swelling. The pack is activated by breaking an ampule; this initiates a chemical reaction that absorbs heat rapidly, lowering the temperature of the area to which the pack is applied.

b A hot pack used to warm hands and feet in winter. When the package is opened, oxygen from the air penetrates a bag containing solid chemicals. The resulting reaction produces heat for several hours.

a When colorless hydrochloric acid is added to a red solution of cobalt(II) nitrate, the solution turns blue, a sign that a chemical reaction has taken place.

b A solid forms when a solution of sodium dichromate is added to a solution of lead nitrate.

c Bubbles of hydrogen gas form when calcium metal reacts with water.

d Methane gas reacts with oxygen to produce a flame in a Bunsen burner.

Figure 6.3

6.2 Chemical Equations

OBJECTIVE: To learn to identify the characteristics of a chemical reaction and the information given by a chemical equation.

Chemists have learned that a chemical change always involves a rearrangement of the ways in which the atoms are grouped. For example, when the methane, CH_4, in natural gas combines with oxygen, O_2, in the air and burns, carbon dioxide, CO_2, and water, H_2O, are formed. A chemical change such as this is called a **chemical reaction.** We represent a chemical reaction by writing a **chemical equation** in which the chemicals present before the reaction (the **reactants**) are shown to the left of an arrow and the chemicals formed by the reaction (the **products**) are shown to the right of an arrow. The arrow indicates the direction of the change and is read as "yields" or "produces":

$$\text{Reactants} \rightarrow \text{Products}$$

For the reaction of methane with oxygen, we have

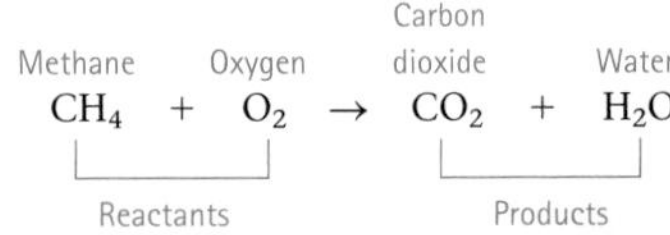

Note from this equation that the products contain the same atoms as the reactants but that the atoms are associated in different ways. That is, a *chemical reaction involves changing the ways the atoms are grouped.*

It is important to recognize that **in a chemical reaction, atoms are neither created nor destroyed.** *All atoms present in the reactants must be accounted for among the products.* In other words, there must be the same number of each type of atom on the product side as on the reactant side of the arrow. Making sure that the equation for a reaction obeys this rule is called **balancing the chemical equation** for a reaction.

DEMONSTRATION

Handwarming Chemistry

Before class, measure 25 g of iron powder (100 mesh works well) into a small Ziploc bag. Add 1 g sodium chloride. Close the bag and mix well. Add about 1 tablespoon of vermiculite (small pieces from a plant store) and mix again. When you are ready to perform the demonstration in class, open the bag, add 5 mL water, and reseal the bag. Squeeze and shake the bag by having students pass it around the class. After approximately 2 minutes, significant heat will be produced. *Note:* The bag can be regenerated by opening it to let in air before resealing it. Oxygen is the limiting reactant.

Section 6.2

TEACHING TIP

In this section students learn that a chemical reaction involves rearrangement of elements. It is very helpful to use simple models of the reactants that you can take apart and rearrange to show students that atoms are conserved in a chemical reaction (toothpicks and gumdrops or clay work well if you do not have ball-and-stick models). Use Figure 6.4 to help in this discussion.

Test Bank: 2, 3

PowerLecture Videos:
Conservation of Matter: Hydrolic Acid and Sodium Carbonate
Conservation of Matter: Lead Iodide Precipitation

DEMONSTRATION

Fire on Demand

Materials Potassium chlorate (*s*), sugar (*s*), evaporating dish or fire-resistant pad, concentrated sulfuric acid, dropper

Procedure Place equal amounts of potassium chlorate and sugar in a beaker. Mix well, but do not grind! For an evaporating dish you will need about a teaspoon of each solid. Place the mixture in the center of the evaporating dish or in the center of the fire-resistant pad. Carefully add one drop of concentrated sulfuric acid to the pile of solid and **step back.**

Safety Notes This reaction produces sparks, so clear the area around the reaction. It also produces smoke, so perform it in a well-ventilated area. Potassium chlorate is a dangerous chemical, and you should never grind it (it may explode). Do not make more of the mixture than you will need in a day.

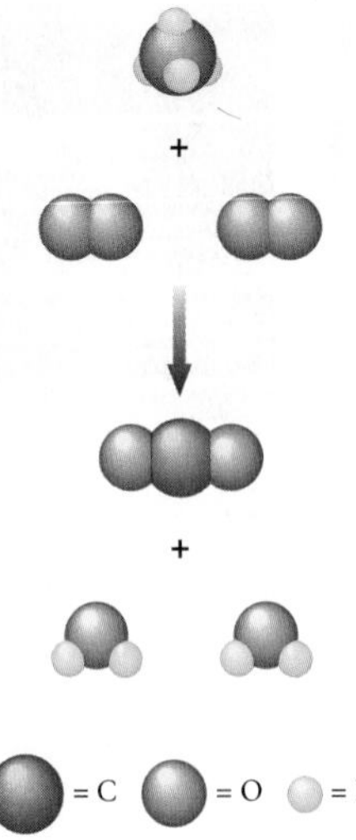

Figure 6.4
The reaction between methane and oxygen to give water and carbon dioxide. Note that there are four oxygen atoms in the products *and* in the reactants; none has been gained or lost in the reaction. Similarly, there are four hydrogen atoms and one carbon atom in the reactants *and* in the products. The reaction simply changes the way the atoms are grouped.

The equation that we have shown for the reaction between CH_4 and O_2 is not balanced. We can see that it is not balanced by taking the reactants and products apart.

$$CH_4 + O_2 \longrightarrow CO_2 + H_2O$$

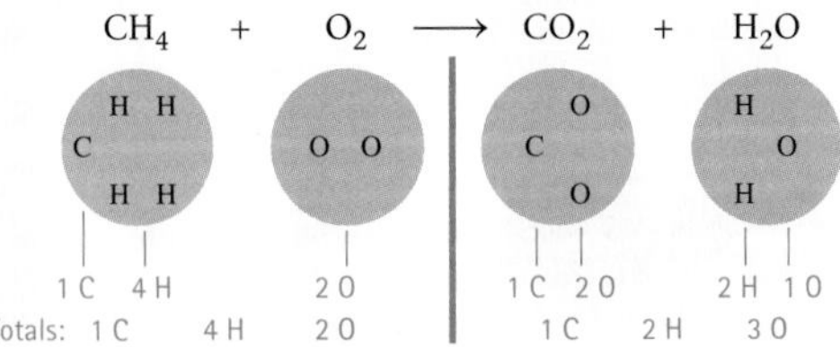

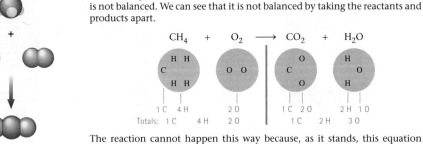

The reaction cannot happen this way because, as it stands, this equation states that one oxygen atom is created and two hydrogen atoms are destroyed. A reaction is only rearrangement of the way the atoms are grouped; atoms are not created or destroyed. The total number of each type of atom must be the same on both sides of the arrow. We can fix the imbalance in this equation by involving one more O_2 molecule on the left and by showing the production of one more H_2O molecule on the right.

$$CH_4 + O_2 + O_2 \longrightarrow CO_2 + H_2O + H_2O$$

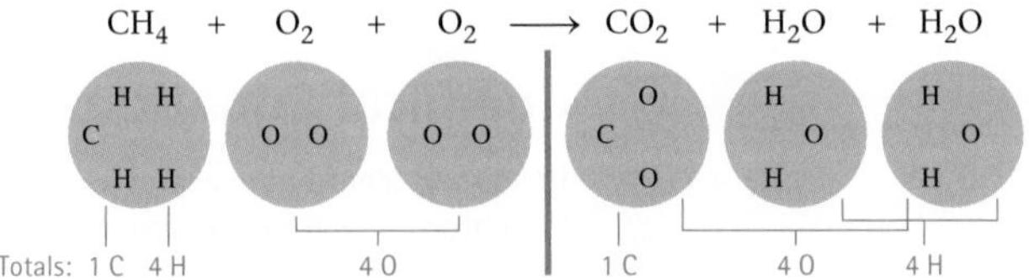

This *balanced chemical equation* shows the actual numbers of molecules involved in this reaction (see Figure 6.4).

When we write the balanced equation for a reaction, we group like molecules together. Thus

$$CH_4 + O_2 + O_2 \longrightarrow CO_2 + H_2O + H_2O$$

is written

$$CH_4 + 2O_2 \longrightarrow CO_2 + 2H_2O$$

The chemical equation for a reaction provides us with two important types of information:

1. The identities of the reactants and products
2. The relative numbers of each

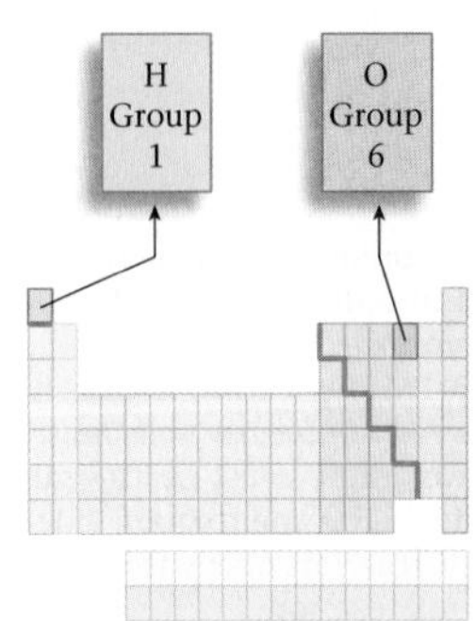

Physical States

Besides specifying the compounds involved in the reaction, we often indicate in the equation the *physical states* of the reactants and products by using the following symbols:

Symbol	State
(*s*)	solid
(*l*)	liquid
(*g*)	gas
(*aq*)	dissolved in water (in aqueous solution)

Richard Megna/Fundamental Photographs

The reactant potassium metal (stored in mineral oil to prevent oxidation).

b *The reactant water.*

c *The reaction of potassium with water. The flame occurs because hydrogen gas, $H_2(g)$, produced by the reaction burns in air [reacts with $O_2(g)$] at the high temperatures caused by the reaction.*

Figure 6.5

For example, when solid potassium reacts with liquid water, the products are hydrogen gas and potassium hydroxide; the latter remains dissolved in the water. From this information about the reactants and products, we can write the equation for the reaction. Solid potassium is represented by K(*s*); liquid water is written as $H_2O(l)$; hydrogen gas contains diatomic molecules and is represented as $H_2(g)$; potassium hydroxide dissolved in water is written as KOH(*aq*). So the *unbalanced* equation for the reaction is

Solid potassium		Water		Hydrogen gas		Potassium hydroxide dissolved in water
$K(s)$	$+$	$H_2O(l)$	$\rightarrow$	$H_2(g)$	$+$	$KOH(aq)$

This reaction is shown in Figure 6.5.

The hydrogen gas produced in this reaction then reacts with the oxygen gas in the air, producing gaseous water and a flame. The *unbalanced* equation for this second reaction is

$$H_2(g) + O_2(g) \rightarrow H_2O(g)$$

Both of these reactions produce a great deal of heat. In Example 6.1 we will practice writing the unbalanced equations for reactions. Then, in the next section, we will discuss systematic procedures for balancing equations.

EXAMPLE 6.1 Chemical Equations: Recognizing Reactants and Products

Write the *unbalanced* chemical equation for each of the following reactions.

a. Solid mercury(II) oxide decomposes to produce liquid mercury metal and gaseous oxygen.

b. Solid carbon reacts with gaseous oxygen to form gaseous carbon dioxide.

c. Solid zinc is added to an aqueous solution containing dissolved hydrogen chloride to produce gaseous hydrogen that bubbles out of the solution and zinc chloride that remains dissolved in the water.

Additional Examples

Example 6.1

Write the *unbalanced* chemical equation for each of the following reactions.

1. Gaseous ammonia reacts with gaseous hydrogen chloride to form solid ammonium chloride.

   $NH_3(g) + HCl(g) \rightarrow NH_4Cl(s)$

2. Iron metal reacts with oxygen gas in the air to form solid iron(II) oxide.

   $Fe(s) + O_2(g) \rightarrow FeO(s)$

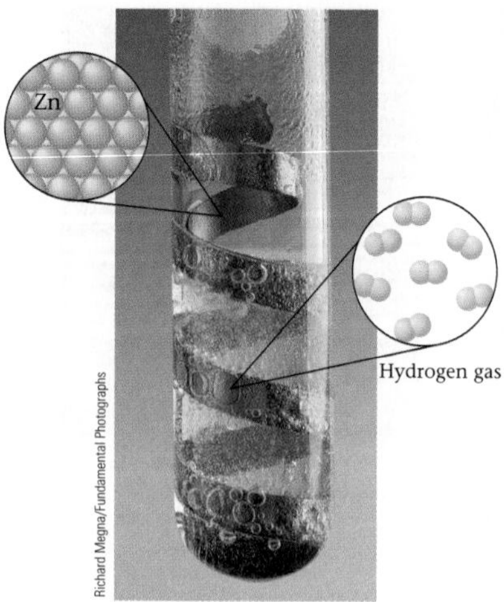

Zinc metal reacts with hydrochloric acid to produce bubbles of hydrogen gas.

SOLUTION

a. In this case we have only one reactant, mercury(II) oxide. The name mercury(II) oxide means that the Hg^{2+} cation is present, so one O^{2-} ion is required for a zero net charge. Thus the formula is HgO, which is written HgO(*s*) in this case because it is given as a solid. The products are liquid mercury, written Hg(*l*), and gaseous oxygen, written $O_2(g)$. (Remember that oxygen exists as a diatomic molecule under normal conditions.) The unbalanced equation is

$$\underset{\text{Reactant}}{HgO(s)} \rightarrow \underbrace{Hg(l) + O_2(g)}_{\text{Products}}$$

b. In this case, solid carbon, written C(*s*), reacts with oxygen gas, $O_2(g)$, to form gaseous carbon dioxide, which is written $CO_2(g)$. The equation (which happens to be balanced) is

$$\underbrace{C(s) + O_2(g)}_{\text{Reactants}} \rightarrow \underset{\text{Product}}{CO_2(g)}$$

c. In this reaction solid zinc, Zn(*s*), is added to an aqueous solution of hydrogen chloride, which is written HCl(*aq*) and called hydrochloric acid. These are the reactants. The products of the reaction are gaseous hydrogen, $H_2(g)$, and aqueous zinc chloride. The name zinc chloride means that the Zn^{2+} ion is present, so two Cl^- ions are needed to achieve a zero net charge. Thus zinc chloride dissolved in water is written $ZnCl_2(aq)$. The unbalanced equation for the reaction is

Because Zn forms only the Zn^{2+} ion, a Roman numeral is usually not used. Thus $ZnCl_2$ is commonly called zinc chloride.

$$\underbrace{Zn(s) + HCl(aq)}_{\text{Reactants}} \rightarrow \underbrace{H_2(g) + ZnCl_2(aq)}_{\text{Products}}$$

150 Chapter 6 Chemical Reactions: An Introduction

Self-Check

EXERCISE 6.1 Identify the reactants and products and write the *unbalanced* equation (including symbols for states) for each of the following chemical reactions.

a. Solid magnesium metal reacts with liquid water to form solid magnesium hydroxide and hydrogen gas.

b. Solid ammonium dichromate (review Table 5.4 if this compound is unfamiliar) decomposes to solid chromium(III) oxide, gaseous nitrogen, and gaseous water.

c. Gaseous ammonia reacts with gaseous oxygen to form gaseous nitrogen monoxide and gaseous water.

See Problems 6.13 through 6.34. ■

Self Check

Answers to Self-Check Exercise 6.1

a. $Mg(s) + H_2O(l) \rightarrow Mg(OH)_2(s) + H_2(g)$

b. $(NH_4)_2Cr_2O_7(s) \rightarrow Cr_2O_3(s) + N_2(g) + H_2O(g)$

c. $NH_3(g) + O_2(g) \rightarrow NO(g) + H_2O(g)$

Test Bank: 4–76

6.3 Balancing Chemical Equations

OBJECTIVE: To learn how to write a balanced equation for a chemical reaction.

Trial and error is often useful for solving problems. It's okay to make a few wrong turns before you get to the right answer.

As we saw in the previous section, an unbalanced chemical equation is not an accurate representation of the reaction that occurs. Whenever you see an equation for a reaction, you should ask yourself whether it is balanced. The principle that lies at the heart of the balancing process is that **atoms are conserved in a chemical reaction.** That is, atoms are neither created nor destroyed. They are just grouped differently. The same number of each type of atom is found among the reactants and among the products.

Chemists determine the identity of the reactants and products of a reaction by experimental observation. For example, when methane (natural gas) is burned in the presence of sufficient oxygen gas, the products are always carbon dioxide and water. **The identities (formulas) of the compounds must never be changed in balancing a chemical equation.** In other words, the subscripts in a formula cannot be changed, nor can atoms be added to or subtracted from a formula.

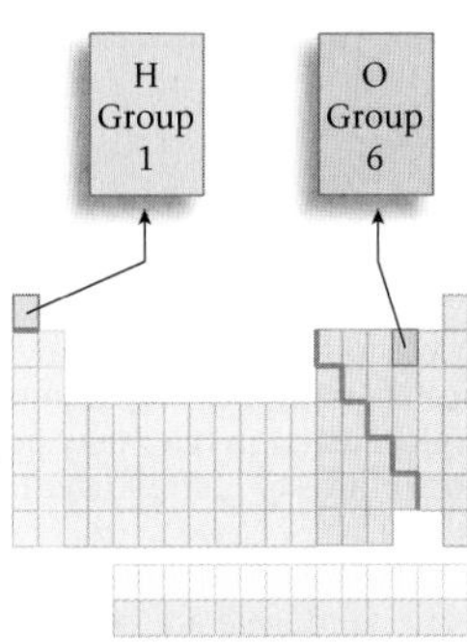

Most chemical equations can be balanced by trial and error—that is, by inspection. Keep trying until you find the numbers of reactants and products that give the same number of each type of atom on both sides of the arrow. For example, consider the reaction of hydrogen gas and oxygen gas to form liquid water. First, we write the unbalanced equation from the description of the reaction.

$$H_2(g) + O_2(g) \rightarrow H_2O(l)$$

We can see that this equation is unbalanced by counting the atoms on both sides of the arrow.

$$H_2(g) + O_2(g) \longrightarrow H_2O(l)$$

H H | O O | H O H

2 H | 2 O | 2 H, 1 O

Reactants	Products
2 H	2 H
2 O	1 O

We have one more oxygen atom in the reactants than in the product. Because we cannot create or destroy atoms and because we *cannot change the formulas* of the reactants or products, we must balance the equation by adding more molecules of reactants and/or products. In this case we need

Section 6.3

TEACHING TIPS

- Remind students they need to know the diatomic elements to write correct equations.
- Students often want to change the subscripts on the reactants or products to balance the equation. Remind them that this action changes the substances in the reaction. Once they have decided on the reactants and products, they can change only the coefficients to balance the equation. Consider using models to show how changing the subscripts changes the nature of the compound.

one more oxygen atom on the right, so we add another water molecule (which contains one O atom). Then we count all of the atoms again.

Reactants	Products
2 H	4 H
2 O	2 O

$$H_2(g) + O_2(g) \longrightarrow H_2O(l) + H_2O(l)$$

Totals: 2 H 2 O | 4 H 2 O

We have balanced the oxygen atoms, but now the hydrogen atoms have become unbalanced. There are more hydrogen atoms on the right than on the left. We can solve this problem by adding another hydrogen molecule (H_2) to the reactant side.

Reactants	Products
4 H	4 H
2 O	2 O

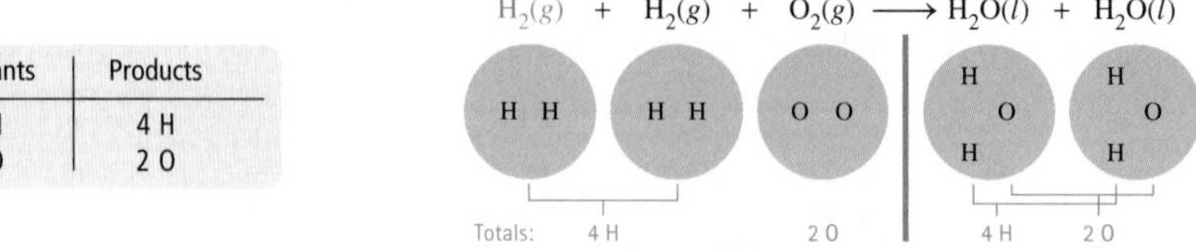

The equation is now balanced. We have the same numbers of hydrogen and oxygen atoms represented on both sides of the arrow. Collecting like molecules, we write the balanced equation as

$$2H_2(g) + O_2(g) \rightarrow 2H_2O(l)$$

Consider next what happens if we multiply every part of this balanced equation by 2:

$$2 \times [2H_2(g) + O_2(g) \rightarrow 2H_2O(l)]$$

to give

$$4H_2(g) + 2O_2(g) \rightarrow 4H_2O(l)$$

This equation is balanced (count the atoms to verify this). In fact, we can multiply or divide *all parts* of the original balanced equation by any number to give a new balanced equation. Thus each chemical reaction has many possible balanced equations. Is one of the many possibilities preferred over the others? Yes.

The accepted convention is that the "best" balanced equation is the one with the *smallest integers (whole numbers)*. These integers are called the **coefficients** for the balanced equation. Therefore, for the reaction of hydrogen and oxygen to form water, the "correct" balanced equation is

$$2H_2(g) + O_2(g) \rightarrow 2H_2O(l)$$

The coefficients 2, 1 (never written), and 2, respectively, are the smallest *integers* that give a balanced equation for this reaction.

Next we will balance the equation for the reaction of liquid ethanol, C_2H_5OH, with oxygen gas to form gaseous carbon dioxide and water. This reaction, among many others, occurs in engines that burn a gasoline–ethanol mixture called gasohol.

The first step in obtaining the balanced equation for a reaction is always to identify the reactants and products from the description given for the reaction. In this case we are told that liquid ethanol, $C_2H_5OH(l)$, reacts

TEACHING TIP

A good example involves the reaction of hydrogen and oxygen to form water. We can take the equation

$$H_2(g) + O_2(g) \rightarrow H_2O(l)$$

and "balance" it in the following way:

$$H_2(g) + O_2(g) \rightarrow H_2O_2(l)$$

Water and hydrogen peroxide are very different chemicals. Use the Elephant's Toothpaste demonstration to show students how hydrogen peroxide differs from water.

DEMONSTRATION

Elephant's Toothpaste

Materials 1-L cylinder, 50 mL liquid detergent (Dawn works best), 50 mL 30% hydrogen peroxide, 50 mL 6.0 *M* KI solution, plastic dishwashing tub or tray

Preparation Make the KI solution by placing 8.3 g KI in 50 mL water. Premeasure all of the solutions for the demonstration.

Performance Place the cylinder in the plastic tub or tray (to catch the foam). Add the hydrogen peroxide to the cylinder. Add the liquid detergent to the cylinder and swirl to mix. Add the KI and step back. Large amounts of foam will bubble out of the top of the cylinder, forming the elephant's toothpaste.

Teaching Notes Discuss the evidence for the chemical reaction observed here (the bubbles and the heat, seen as steam). There is also a color change to observe.

CHEMISTRY IN FOCUS

The Beetle That Shoots Straight

If someone said to you, "Name something that protects itself by spraying its enemies," your answer would almost certainly be "a skunk." Of course, you would be correct, but there is another correct answer—the bombardier beetle. When threatened, this beetle shoots a boiling stream of toxic chemicals at its enemy. How does this clever beetle accomplish this? Obviously, the boiling mixture cannot be stored inside the beetle's body all the time. Instead, when endangered, the beetle mixes chemicals that produce the hot spray. The chemicals involved are stored in two compartments. One compartment contains the chemicals hydrogen peroxide (H_2O_2) and methylhydroquinone ($C_7H_8O_2$). The key reaction is the decomposition of hydrogen peroxide to form oxygen gas and water:

$$2H_2O_2(aq) \rightarrow 2H_2O(l) + O_2(g)$$

Hydrogen peroxide also reacts with the hydroquinones to produce other compounds that become part of the toxic spray.

However, none of these reactions occurs very fast unless certain enzymes are present. (Enzymes are natural substances that speed up biologic reactions by means we will not discuss here.) When the beetle mixes the hydrogen peroxide and hydroquinones with the enzyme, the decomposition of H_2O_2 occurs rapidly, producing a hot mixture pressurized by the formation of oxygen gas. When the gas pressure becomes high enough, the hot spray is ejected in one long stream or in short bursts. The beetle has a highly accurate aim and can shoot several attackers with one batch of spray.

Thomas Eisner

A bombardier beetle defending itself.

with gaseous oxygen, $O_2(g)$, to produce gaseous carbon dioxide, $CO_2(g)$, and gaseous water, $H_2O(g)$. Therefore, the unbalanced equation is

$$\underset{\text{Liquid ethanol}}{C_2H_5OH(l)} + \underset{\text{Gaseous oxygen}}{O_2(g)} \rightarrow \underset{\text{Gaseous carbon dioxide}}{CO_2(g)} + \underset{\text{Gaseous water}}{H_2O(g)}$$

In balancing equations, start by looking at the most complicated molecule.

When one molecule in an equation is more complicated (contains more elements) than the others, it is best to start with that molecule. The most complicated molecule here is C_2H_5OH, so we begin by considering the products that contain the atoms in C_2H_5OH. We start with carbon. The only product that contains carbon is CO_2. Because C_2H_5OH contains two carbon atoms, we place a 2 before the CO_2 to balance the carbon atoms.

C_2H_5OH

2 C, 6 H, 1 O

$$\underbrace{C_2H_5OH(l)}_{\text{2 C atoms}} + O_2(g) \longrightarrow \underbrace{2CO_2(g)}_{\text{2 C atoms}} + H_2O(g)$$

Remember, we cannot change the formula of any reactant or product when we balance an equation. We can only place coefficients in front of the formulas.

153

Eventually we get the right answer (so trial and error is a reasonable method). However, it would have been better not to have balanced the oxygen as the second step. This is why step 3 tells students to start with the most complicated molecule. Encourage them to leave the elements and diatomic molecules until last when balancing equations. This choice simplifies the trial-and-error process.

- Using recipes as analogies for chemical equations is a good idea. Recipes in which we are given only the ingredients (and product) involved are analogous to unbalanced equations. They are useful up to a point, but we eventually need the amounts if we are to do anything with the equation (or the recipe). Also, the amounts in a recipe can be changed, but all amounts must then be changed by the same amount, just as we can multiply all coefficients by 2, for example. (Of course, we can change a recipe by adding just a touch more salt, but this does not increase the amount of product.)
- Emphasize that the equation represents the ratio of the amounts of chemicals that react or are produced. An individual coefficient is as meaningless as a recipe that gives the required amount of only one ingredient.
- Students should indicate the states of the reactants and products in an equation so that this habit becomes part of the process for writing and balancing the equation.

TEACHING TIPS

- For the reaction

$$C_2H_5OH(g) + O_2(g) \rightarrow CO_2(g) + H_2O(l)$$

consider balancing the equation in the following way:

$$C_2H_5OH(g) + O_2(g) \rightarrow 2CO_2(g) + H_2O(l)$$

(carbon is balanced)

$$C_2H_5OH(g) + 2O_2(g) \rightarrow 2CO_2(g) + H_2O(l)$$

(oxygen is balanced)

$$C_2H_5OH(g) + 2O_2(g) \rightarrow 2CO_2(g) + 3H_2O(l)$$

(hydrogen is balanced; oxygen is now unbalanced)

$$C_2H_5OH(g) + 3O_2(g) \rightarrow 2CO_2(g) + 3H_2O(l)$$

(the equation is balanced)

TEACHING TIP

When students are first learning to balance equations, encourage them to write the number of each kind of atom as they work. This practice will reduce the number of simple errors.

Next we consider hydrogen. The only product containing hydrogen is H_2O. C_2H_5OH contains six hydrogen atoms, so we need six hydrogen atoms on the right. Because each H_2O contains two hydrogen atoms, we need three H_2O molecules to yield six hydrogen atoms. So we place a 3 before the H_2O.

	H—O—H
O—C—O	H—O—H
O—C—O	H—O—H
4 O atoms	3 O atoms

$$C_2H_5OH(l) + O_2(g) \longrightarrow 2CO_2(g) + 3H_2O(g)$$

(5 + 1) H → 6 H (left); (3 × 2) H → 6 H (right)

Finally, we count the oxygen atoms. On the left we have three oxygen atoms (one in C_2H_5OH and two in O_2), and on the right we have seven oxygen atoms (four in $2CO_2$ and three in $3H_2O$). We can correct this imbalance if we have three O_2 molecules on the left. That is, we place a coefficient of 3 before the O_2 to produce the balanced equation.

$$C_2H_5OH(l) + 3O_2(g) \longrightarrow 2CO_2(g) + 3H_2O(g)$$

1 O + (3 × 2) O = 7 O (left); (2 × 2) O + 3 O = 7 O (right)

At this point you may have a question: why did we choose O_2 on the left when we balanced the oxygen atoms? Why not use C_2H_5OH, which has an oxygen atom? The answer is that if we had changed the coefficient in front of C_2H_5OH, we would have unbalanced the hydrogen and carbon atoms. Now we count all of the atoms as a check to make sure the equation is balanced.

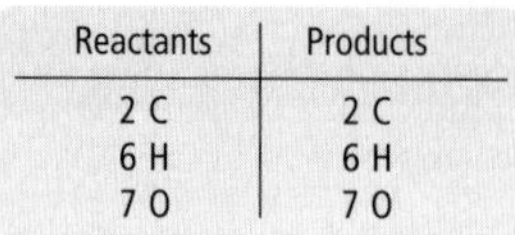

Reactants	Products
2 C	2 C
6 H	6 H
7 O	7 O

$$C_2H_5OH(l) + 3O_2(g) \longrightarrow 2CO_2(g) + 3H_2O(g)$$

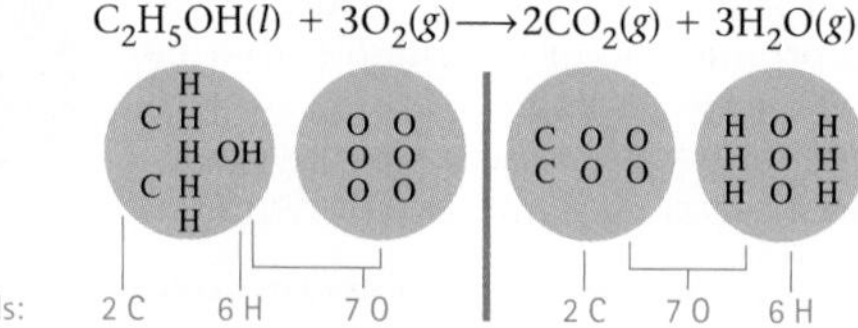

The equation is now balanced. We have the same numbers of all types of atoms on both sides of the arrow. Notice that these coefficients are the smallest integers that give a balanced equation.

The process of writing and balancing the equation for a chemical reaction consists of several steps:

How to Write and Balance Equations

Step 1 Read the description of the chemical reaction. What are the reactants, the products, and their states? Write the appropriate formulas.

Step 2 Write the *unbalanced* equation that summarizes the information from step 1.

Step 3 Balance the equation by inspection, starting with the most complicated molecule. Proceed element by element to determine what coefficients are necessary so that the same number of each type of atom appears on both the reactant side and the product side. Do not change the identities (formulas) of any of the reactants or products.

(continued)

Step 4 Check to see that the coefficients used give the same number of each type of atom on both sides of the arrow. (Note that an "atom" may be present in an element, a compound, or an ion.) Also check to see that the coefficients used are the smallest integers that give the balanced equation. This can be done by determining whether all coefficients can be divided by the same integer to give a set of smaller *integer* coefficients.

Additional Examples

Example 6.2

Write the *balanced* chemical equation for each of the following reactions.

1. Nitrogen monoxide gas reacts with hydrogen gas to form nitrogen gas and water.

   $2NO(g) + 2H_2(g) \rightarrow N_2(g) + 2H_2O(l)$

2. Lithium metal reacts with chlorine gas to form solid lithium chloride.

   $2Li(s) + Cl_2(aq) \rightarrow 2LiCl(s)$

EXAMPLE 6.2 Balancing Chemical Equations I

For the following reaction, write the unbalanced equation and then balance the equation: solid potassium reacts with liquid water to form gaseous hydrogen and potassium hydroxide that dissolves in the water.

SOLUTION

Step 1 From the description given for the reaction, we know that the reactants are solid potassium, $K(s)$, and liquid water, $H_2O(l)$. The products are gaseous hydrogen, $H_2(g)$, and dissolved potassium hydroxide, $KOH(aq)$.

Step 2 The unbalanced equation for the reaction is

$$K(s) + H_2O(l) \rightarrow H_2(g) + KOH(aq)$$

Step 3 Although none of the reactants or products is very complicated, we will start with KOH because it contains the most elements (three). We will arbitrarily consider hydrogen first. Note that on the reactant side of the equation in step 2, there are two hydrogen atoms but on the product side there are three. If we place a coefficient of 2 in front of both H_2O and KOH, we now have four H atoms on each side.

$$K(s) + 2H_2O(l) \rightarrow H_2(g) + 2KOH(aq)$$

4 H atoms | 2 H atoms | 2 H atoms

Also note that the oxygen atoms balance.

$$K(s) + 2H_2O(l) \rightarrow H_2(g) + 2KOH(aq)$$

2 O atoms | 2 O atoms

However, the K atoms do not balance; we have one on the left and two on the right. We can fix this easily by placing a coefficient of 2 in front of $K(s)$ to give the balanced equation:

$$2K(s) + 2H_2O(l) \rightarrow H_2(g) + 2KOH(aq)$$

Step 4

CHECK: There are 2 K, 4 H, and 2 O on both sides of the arrow, and the coefficients are the smallest integers that give a balanced equation. We know this because we cannot divide through by a given integer to give a set of smaller *integer* (whole-number) coefficients. For example, if we divide all of the coefficients by 2, we get

Reactants	Products
2 K	2 K
4 H	4 H
2 O	2 O

$$K(s) + H_2O(l) \rightarrow \tfrac{1}{2}H_2(g) + KOH(aq)$$

This is not acceptable because the coefficient for H_2 is not an integer. ■

Additional Examples

Example 6.3

Write the *balanced* chemical equation for each of the following reactions.

1. Iron metal reacts with oxygen gas in the air to form iron(III) oxide.

   $4Fe(s) + 3O_2(g) \rightarrow 2Fe_2O_3(s)$

2. Diboron trioxide reacts with water to form boric acid, $B(OH)_3$.

   $B_2O_3(s) + 3H_2O(l) \rightarrow 2B(OH)_3(aq)$

Self Check

Answer to Self-Check Exercise 6.2

$C_3H_8(g) + 5O_2(g) \rightarrow 3CO_2(g) + 4H_2O(g)$

EXAMPLE 6.3 Balancing Chemical Equations II

Under appropriate conditions at 1000 °C, ammonia gas reacts with oxygen gas to produce gaseous nitrogen monoxide (common name, nitric oxide) and gaseous water. Write the unbalanced and balanced equations for this reaction.

SOLUTION

Step 1 The reactants are gaseous ammonia, $NH_3(g)$, and gaseous oxygen, $O_2(g)$. The products are gaseous nitrogen monoxide, $NO(g)$, and gaseous water, $H_2O(g)$.

Step 2 The unbalanced equation for the reaction is

Reactants	Products
1 N	1 N
3 H	2 H
2 O	2 O

$$NH_3(g) + O_2(g) \rightarrow NO(g) + H_2O(g)$$

Step 3 In this equation there is no molecule that is obviously the most complicated. Three molecules contain two elements, so we arbitrarily start with NH_3. We arbitrarily begin by looking at hydrogen. A coefficient of 2 for NH_3 and a coefficient of 3 for H_2O give six atoms of hydrogen on both sides.

$$\underbrace{2NH_3(g)}_{6\ H} + O_2(g) \rightarrow NO(g) + \underbrace{3H_2O(g)}_{6\ H}$$

We can balance the nitrogen by giving NO a coefficient of 2.

$$\underbrace{2NH_3(g)}_{2\ N} + O_2(g) \rightarrow \underbrace{2NO(g)}_{2\ N} + 3H_2O(g)$$

$\frac{5}{2} = 2\frac{1}{2}$
O—O
O—O
O+O

$2\frac{1}{2}\ O_2$ contains 5 O atoms

Finally, we note that there are two atoms of oxygen on the left and five on the right. The oxygen can be balanced with a coefficient of $\frac{5}{2}$ for O_2, because $\frac{5}{2} \times O_2$ gives five oxygen atoms.

$$2NH_3(g) + \underbrace{\tfrac{5}{2}O_2(g)}_{5\ O} \rightarrow \underbrace{2NO(g)}_{2\ O} + \underbrace{3H_2O(g)}_{3\ O}$$

However, the convention is to have integer (whole-number) coefficients, so we multiply the entire equation by 2.

$$2 \times [2NH_3(g) + \tfrac{5}{2}O_2(g) \rightarrow 2NO(g) + 3H_2O(g)]$$

or

$$2 \times 2NH_3(g) + 2 \times \tfrac{5}{2}O_2(g) \rightarrow 2 \times 2NO(g) + 2 \times 3H_2O(g)$$
$$4NH_3(g) + 5O_2(g) \rightarrow 4NO(g) + 6H_2O(g)$$

Step 4

Reactants	Products
4 N	4 N
12 H	12 H
10 O	10 O

CHECK: There are 4 N, 12 H, and 10 O atoms on both sides, so the equation is balanced. These coefficients are the smallest integers that give a balanced equation. That is, we cannot divide all coefficients by the same integer and obtain a smaller set of *integers*.

Self-Check EXERCISE 6.2 Propane, C_3H_8, a liquid at 25 °C under high pressure, is often used for gas grills and as a fuel in rural areas where there is no natural gas pipeline. When liquid propane is released from its storage tank, it changes to propane gas that reacts with oxygen gas (it "burns") to give gaseous carbon dioxide and gaseous water. Write and balance the equation for this reaction.

HINT: This description of a chemical process contains many words, some of which are crucial to solving the problem and some of which are not. First sort out the important information and use symbols to represent it.

See Problems 6.37 through 6.44. ■

EXAMPLE 6.4 Balancing Chemical Equations III

Richard Megna/Fundamental Photographs

Decorations on glass are produced by etching with hydrofluoric acid.

Glass is sometimes decorated by etching patterns on its surface. Etching occurs when hydrofluoric acid (an aqueous solution of HF) reacts with the silicon dioxide in the glass to form gaseous silicon tetrafluoride and liquid water. Write and balance the equation for this reaction.

SOLUTION

Step 1 From the description of the reaction we can identify the reactants:

hydrofluoric acid	$HF(aq)$
solid silicon dioxide	$SiO_2(s)$

and the products:

gaseous silicon tetrafluoride	$SiF_4(g)$
liquid water	$H_2O(l)$

Step 2 The unbalanced equation is

$$SiO_2(s) + HF(aq) \rightarrow SiF_4(g) + H_2O(l)$$

Reactants	Products
1 Si	1 Si
1 H	2 H
1 F	4 F
2 O	1 O

Step 3 There is no clear choice here for the most complicated molecule. We arbitrarily start with the elements in SiF_4. The silicon is balanced (one atom on each side), but the fluorine is not. To balance the fluorine, we need a coefficient of 4 before the HF.

$$SiO_2(s) + 4HF(aq) \rightarrow SiF_4(g) + H_2O(l)$$

Reactants	Products
1 Si	1 Si
4 H	2 H
4 F	4 F
2 O	1 O

Hydrogen and oxygen are not balanced. Because we have four hydrogen atoms on the left and two on the right, we place a 2 before the H_2O:

$$SiO_2(s) + 4HF(aq) \rightarrow SiF_4(g) + 2H_2O(l)$$

This balances the hydrogen *and* the oxygen (two atoms on each side).

Reactants	Products
1 Si	1 Si
4 H	4 H
4 F	4 F
2 O	2 O

Step 4

CHECK: $SiO_2(s) + 4HF(aq) \rightarrow SiF_4(g) + 2H_2O(l)$

Totals: 1 Si, 2 O, 4 H, 4 F → 1 Si, 4 F, 4 H, 2 O

All atoms check, so the equation is balanced.

Self-Check EXERCISE 6.3

Give the balanced equation for each of the following reactions.

a. When solid ammonium nitrite is heated, it produces nitrogen gas and water vapor.

b. Gaseous nitrogen monoxide (common name, nitric oxide) decomposes to produce dinitrogen monoxide gas (common name, nitrous oxide) and nitrogen dioxide gas.

c. Liquid nitric acid decomposes to reddish-brown nitrogen dioxide gas, liquid water, and oxygen gas. (This is why bottles of nitric acid become yellow upon standing.)

If you are having trouble writing formulas from names, review the appropriate sections of Chapter 5. It is very important that you are able to do this.

See Problems 6.37 through 6.44. ■

Additional Examples

Example 6.4

Write the *balanced* chemical equation for each of the following reactions.

1. Solid iron(III) oxide reacts with aqueous nitric acid to form aqueous iron(III) nitrate and water.

$Fe_2O_3(s) + 6HNO_3(aq) \rightarrow 2Fe(NO_3)_3(aq) + 3H_2O(l)$

2. Hydrogen sulfide gas reacts with aqueous lead(II) nitrate to form solid lead(II) sulfide and aqueous nitric acid.

$H_2S(g) + Pb(NO_3)_2(aq) \rightarrow PbS(s) + 2HNO_3(aq)$

Self Check

Answers to Self-Check Exercise 6.3

a. $NH_4NO_2(s) \rightarrow N_2(g) + 2H_2O(g)$ (balanced)

b. $3NO(g) \rightarrow N_2O(g) + NO_2(g)$ (balanced)

c. $4HNO_3(l) \rightarrow 4NO_2(g) + 2H_2O(l) + O_2(g)$ (balanced)

ChemWork

Big Balloon

Doing Work

Exothermic or Endothermic

Kinetic and Potential Energy

Acid–Base Calorimetry

Carbon Energy Changes

Releasing Heat During Combustion

Swimming and Calorimetry

Calculating Enthalpy

Using Hess's Law

Enthalpy of Formation

CHAPTER 6 REVIEW

F directs you to the *Chemistry in Focus* feature in the chapter

VP indicates visual problems

OWL interactive versions of these problems are assignable in OWL

Key Terms

chemical reaction (6.2)
chemical equation (6.2)
reactant (6.2)
product (6.2)
balancing a chemical equation (6.2)
coefficient (6.3)

Summary

1. Chemical reactions usually give some kind of visual signal—a color changes, a solid forms, bubbles form, heat and/or flame is produced.
2. A chemical equation represents a chemical reaction. Reactants are shown on the left side of an arrow and products on the right. In a chemical reaction, atoms are neither created nor destroyed; they are merely rearranged. A balanced chemical equation gives the relative numbers of reactant and product molecules.
3. A chemical equation for a reaction can be balanced by using a systematic approach. First identify the reactants and products and write the formulas. Next write the unbalanced equation. Then balance by trial and error, starting with the most complicated molecule(s). Finally, check to be sure the equation is balanced.

Active Learning Questions

These questions are designed to be considered by groups of students in class. Often these questions work well for introducing a particular topic in class.

1. The following are actual student responses to the question: Why is it necessary to balance chemical equations?
   a. The chemicals will not react until you have added the correct ratios.
   b. The correct products will not form unless the right amounts of reactants have been added.
   c. A certain number of products cannot form without a certain number of reactants.
   d. The balanced equation tells you how much reactant you need, and allows you to predict how much product you will make.
   e. A ratio must be established for the reaction to occur as written.

   Justify the best choice, and, for choices you did not pick, explain what is wrong with them.
2. What information do we get from a formula? From an equation?
3. Given the equation for the reaction: $N_2 + H_2 \rightarrow NH_3$, draw a molecular diagram that represents the reaction (make sure it is balanced).
4. What do the subscripts in a chemical formula represent? What do the coefficients in a balanced chemical equation represent?
5. Can the subscripts in a chemical formula be fractions? Explain.
6. Can the coefficients in a balanced chemical equation be fractions? Explain.
7. Changing the subscripts of chemicals can mathematically balance the equations. Why is this unacceptable?
8. Table 6.1 lists some clues that a chemical reaction has occurred. However, these events do not necessarily prove the existence of a chemical change. Give an example for each of the clues that is not a chemical reaction but a physical change.
9. Use molecular-level drawings to show the difference between physical and chemical changes.
10. It is stated in Section 6.3 of the text that to balance equations by inspection you start "with the most complicated molecule." What does this mean? Why is it best to do this?
11. Which of the following statements concerning balanced chemical equations are true? There may be more than one true statement.
    a. Atoms are neither created nor destroyed.
    b. The coefficients indicate the mass ratios of the substances used.
    c. The sum of the coefficients on the reactant side always equals the sum of the coefficients on the product side.
12. Consider the generic chemical equation $aA + bB \rightarrow cC + dD$ (where a, b, c, and d represent coefficients for the chemicals A, B, C, and D, respectively).
    a. How many possible values are there for "c"? Explain your answer.
    b. How many possible values are there for "c/d"? Explain your answer.

158 Chapter 6 Chemical Reactions: An Introduction

13. How is the balancing of chemical equations related to the law of conservation of mass?

14. Which of the following correctly describes the balanced chemical equation given below? There may be more than one true statement. If a statement is incorrect, explain why it is incorrect.

$$4Al + 3O_2 \rightarrow 2Al_2O_3$$

a. For every 4 atoms of aluminum that react with 6 atoms of oxygen, 2 molecules of aluminum oxide are produced.

b. For every 4 moles of aluminum that reacts with 3 moles of oxygen, 2 moles of aluminum (III) oxide is produced.

c. For every 4 grams of aluminum that reacts with 3 grams of oxygen, 2 grams of aluminum oxide is produced.

15. Which of the following correctly balances the chemical equation given below? There may be more than one correct balanced equation. If a balanced equation is incorrect, explain why it is incorrect.

$$CaO + C \rightarrow CaC_2 + CO_2$$

a. $CaO_2 + 3C \rightarrow CaC_2 + CO_2$

b. $2CaO + 5C \rightarrow 2CaC_2 + CO_2$

c. $CaO + 2\frac{1}{2}C \rightarrow CaC_2 + \frac{1}{2}CO_2$

d. $4CaO + 10C \rightarrow 4CaC_2 + 2CO_2$

VP 16. The reaction of an element X (△) with element Y (○) is represented in the following diagram. Which of the elements best describes this reaction?

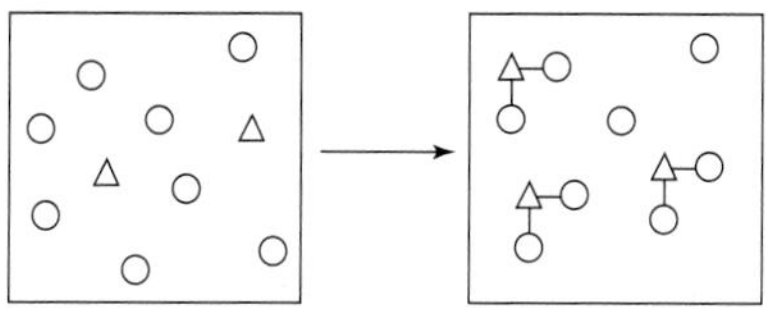

a. $3X + 8Y \rightarrow X_3Y_8$

b. $3X + 6Y \rightarrow X_3Y_6$

c. $X + 2Y \rightarrow XY_2$

d. $3X + 8Y \rightarrow 3XY_2 + 2Y$

Questions and Problems

6.1 Evidence for a Chemical Reaction

QUESTIONS

1. How do we *know* when a chemical reaction is taking place? Can you think of an example of how each of the five senses (sight, hearing, taste, touch, smell) might be used in detecting when a chemical reaction has taken place?

2. These days many products are available to whiten teeth at home. Many of these products contain a peroxide that bleaches stains from the teeth. What evidence is there that the bleaching process is a chemical reaction?

3. Although these days many people have "self-cleaning" ovens, if your oven gets *really* dirty you may have to resort to one of the spray-on oven cleaner preparations sold in supermarkets. What evidence is there that such oven cleaners work by a chemical reaction?

4. Small cuts and abrasions on the skin are frequently cleaned using hydrogen peroxide solution. What evidence is there that treating a wound with hydrogen peroxide causes a chemical reaction to take place?

5. You have probably had the unpleasant experience of discovering that a flashlight battery has gotten old and begun to leak. Is there evidence that this change is due to a chemical reaction?

6. If you've ever left bread in a toaster too long, you know that the bread eventually burns and turns black. What evidence is there that this represents a chemical process?

6.2 Chemical Equations

QUESTIONS

7. What are the substances to the *left* of the arrow in a chemical equation called? To the *right* of the arrow? What does the arrow itself mean?

8. In an ordinary chemical reaction, ______ are neither created nor destroyed.

9. In a chemical reaction, the total number of atoms present after the reaction is complete is (larger than/smaller than/the same as) the total number of atoms present before the reaction began.

10. What does "balancing" an equation accomplish?

11. Why are the *physical states* of the reactants and products often indicated when writing a chemical equation?

12. When indicating the physical state of a reactant or product in a chemical equation, how do we indicate that a reactant is a solid? A liquid? A gaseous substance?

PROBLEMS

Note: In some of the following problems you will need to write a chemical formula from the name of the compound. Review Chapter 5 if you are having trouble.

13. A common experiment to determine the relative reactivity of metallic elements is to place a pure sample of one metal into an aqueous solution of a

All even-numbered Questions and Problems have answers in the back of this book and solutions in the Solutions Guide.

Answers to End-of-Chapter Exercises

1. precipitate forms, gas evolves, color changes, heat evolves, etc.

2. Most of these products contain a peroxide, which decomposes and releases oxygen gas.

3. The oven cleaner is a relatively clear liquid when applied, but it turns into a thick, opaque, soapy layer after it reacts with oils and greases on the oven walls.

4. Bubbling takes place as the hydrogen peroxide chemically decomposes into water and oxygen gas.

5. The battery container is typically one of the electrodes in the battery; the leak develops because the metal has dissolved.

6. The appearance of the black color actually signals the breakdown of starches and sugars in the bread to elemental carbon. You may also see steam coming from the bread (water produced by the breakdown of the carbohydrates).

7. reactants; products; the arrow signifies a chemical reaction

8. atoms

9. the same as

10. Balancing an equation ensures that no atoms are created or destroyed during the reaction. The total mass after the reaction must be the same as the total mass before the reaction.

11. In many reactions, the physical state of the reactants or products may influence whether or not the reaction takes place. For example, some metallic elements do not react with cold water but will react vigorously with steam.

12. Solid, (*s*); liquid, (*l*); gas, (*g*)

13. $Zn(s) + CuSO_4(aq) \rightarrow ZnSO_4(aq) + Cu(s)$

14. $H_2O_2(aq) \rightarrow H_2O(l) + O_2(g)$

15. $H_2(g) + O_2(g) \rightarrow H_2O(g)$

16. $N_2H_4(l) \rightarrow N_2(g) + H_2(g)$

17. $KI(aq) + H_2O(l) \rightarrow KOH(aq) + I_2(s) + H_2(g)$

18. $C_3H_8(g) + O_2(g) \rightarrow CO_2(g) + H_2O(g)$; $C_3H_8(g) + O_2(g) \rightarrow CO(g) + H_2O(g)$

19. $B_2O_3(s) + Mg(s) \rightarrow B(g) + MgO(s)$

20. $CaCO_3(s) + HCl(aq) \rightarrow CaCl_2(aq) + H_2O(l) + CO_2(g)$

21. $P_4(s) + Cl_2(g) \rightarrow PCl_3(s)$

22. $SiO_2(s) + C(s) \rightarrow Si(s) + CO(g)$

23. $NH_4NO_3(s) \rightarrow N_2O(g) + H_2O(g)$

24. $Fe(s) + H_2O(g) \rightarrow FeO(s) + H_2(g)$

25. $C_2H_2(g) + O_2(g) \rightarrow CO_2(g) + H_2O(g)$

26. $SO_2(g) + H_2O(l) \rightarrow H_2SO_3(aq)$; $SO_3(g) + H_2O(l) \rightarrow H_2SO_4(aq)$

27. $BaO(s) + Al(s) \rightarrow Ba(s) + Al_2O_3(s)$; $CaO(s) + Al(s) \rightarrow Ca(s) + Al_2O_3(s)$; $SrO(s) + Al(s) \rightarrow Sr(s) + Al_2O_3(s)$

28. $NO(g) + O_3(g) \rightarrow NO_2(g) + O_2(g)$

29. $CH_4(g) + Cl_2(g) \rightarrow CCl_4(l) + HCl(g)$

30. $P_4(s) + O_2(g) \rightarrow P_2O_5(s)$

31. $CaO(s) + H_2O(g) \rightarrow Ca(OH)_2(s)$

32. $Xe(g) + F_2(g) \rightarrow XeF_4(s)$

33. $SnO_2(s) + C(s) \rightarrow Sn(l) + CO(g)$

compound of another metallic element. If the pure metal you are adding is more reactive than the metallic element in the compound, then the pure metal will *replace* the metallic element in the compound. For example, if you place a piece of pure zinc metal into a solution of copper(II) sulfate, the zinc will slowly dissolve to produce zinc sulfate solution, and the copper(II) ion of the copper(II) sulfate will be converted to metallic copper. Write the unbalanced equation for this process.

14. Hydrogen peroxide, H_2O_2, is often used to cleanse wounds. Hydrogen peroxide is ordinarily stable in dilute solution at room temperature, but its decomposition into water and oxygen gas is catalyzed by many enzymes and metal ions (the iron contained in blood, for example). Hydrogen peroxide is useful in the treatment of wounds because the oxygen gas produced both helps to clean the wound and suppresses the growth of anaerobic bacteria. Write the unbalanced equation for the decomposition of aqueous hydrogen peroxide into water and oxygen gas.

15. If a sample of pure hydrogen gas is ignited very carefully, the hydrogen burns gently, combining with the oxygen gas of the air to form water vapor. Write the unbalanced chemical equation for this reaction.

16. Liquid hydrazine, N_2H_4, has been used as a fuel for rockets. When the rocket is to be launched, a catalyst causes the liquid hydrazine to decompose quickly into elemental nitrogen and hydrogen gases. The rapid expansion of the product gases and the heat released by the reaction provide the thrust for the rocket. Write the unbalanced equation for the reaction of hydrazine to produce nitrogen and hydrogen gases.

17. If electricity of sufficient voltage is passed into a solution of potassium iodide in water, a reaction takes place in which elemental hydrogen gas and elemental iodine are produced, leaving a solution of potassium hydroxide. Write the unbalanced equation for this process.

18. Your family may have a "gas grill" for outdoor cooking. Gas grills typically use bottled propane gas (C_3H_8), which burns in air (oxygen) to produce carbon dioxide gas and water vapor. Write the unbalanced chemical equation for this process. Gas grills should never be used indoors, however, because if the supply of oxygen is restricted, the products of the reaction tend to be water vapor and toxic carbon monoxide, instead of nontoxic carbon dioxide. Write the unbalanced chemical equation for this process.

19. Elemental boron is produced in one industrial process by heating diboron trioxide with magnesium metal, also producing magnesium oxide as a by-product. Write the unbalanced chemical equation for this process.

20. Many over-the-counter antacid tablets are now formulated using calcium carbonate as the active ingredient, which enables such tablets to also be used as dietary calcium supplements. As an antacid for gastric hyperacidity, calcium carbonate reacts by combining with hydrochloric acid found in the stomach, producing a solution of calcium chloride, converting the stomach acid to water, and releasing carbon dioxide gas (which the person suffering from stomach problems may feel as a "burp"). Write the unbalanced chemical equation for this process.

21. Phosphorus trichloride is used in the manufacture of certain pesticides, and may be synthesized by direct combination of its constituent elements. Write the unbalanced chemical equation for this process.

22. Pure silicon, which is needed in the manufacturing of electronic components, may be prepared by heating silicon dioxide (sand) with carbon at high temperatures, releasing carbon monoxide gas. Write the unbalanced chemical equation for this process.

23. Nitrous oxide gas (systematic name: dinitrogen monoxide) is used by some dental practitioners as an anesthetic. Nitrous oxide (and water vapor as by-product) can be produced in small quantities in the laboratory by careful heating of ammonium nitrate. Write the unbalanced chemical equation for this reaction.

24. Although there are many processes by which pure metallic substances corrode, one simple process is the reaction of the metal with moisture (water) to produce the oxide of the metal and hydrogen gas. Write an unbalanced chemical equation showing the reaction of iron metal with water to produce solid iron(II) oxide and hydrogen gas.

25. Acetylene gas (C_2H_2) is often used by plumbers, welders, and glass blowers because it burns in oxygen with an intensely hot flame. The products of the combustion of acetylene are carbon dioxide and water vapor. Write the unbalanced chemical equation for this process.

26. The burning of high-sulfur fuels has been shown to cause the phenomenon of "acid rain." When a high-sulfur fuel is burned, the sulfur is converted to sulfur dioxide (SO_2) and sulfur trioxide (SO_3). When sulfur dioxide and sulfur trioxide gas dissolve in water in the atmosphere, sulfurous acid and sulfuric acid are produced, respectively. Write the unbalanced chemical equations for the reactions of sulfur dioxide and sulfur trioxide with water.

27. The Group 2 metals (Ba, Ca, Sr) can be produced in the elemental state by the reaction of their oxides with aluminum metal at high temperatures, also producing solid aluminum oxide as a by-product. Write the unbalanced chemical equations for the reactions of barium oxide, calcium oxide, and strontium oxide with aluminum.

28. There are fears that the protective ozone layer around the earth is being depleted. Ozone, O_3, is produced by the interaction of ordinary oxygen gas in the atmosphere with ultraviolet light and lightning discharges.

All even-numbered Questions and Problems have answers in the back of this book and solutions in the Solutions Guide.

160 Chapter 6 Chemical Reactions: An Introduction

The oxides of nitrogen (which are common in automobile exhaust gases), in particular, are known to decompose ozone. For example, gaseous nitric oxide (NO) reacts with ozone gas to produce nitrogen dioxide gas and oxygen gas. Write the unbalanced chemical equation for this process.

29. Carbon tetrachloride was widely used for many years as a solvent until its harmful properties became well established. Carbon tetrachloride may be prepared by the reaction of natural gas (methane, CH_4) and elemental chlorine gas in the presence of ultraviolet light. Write the unbalanced chemical equation for this process.

30. When elemental phosphorus, P_4, burns in oxygen gas, it produces an intensely bright light, a great deal of heat, and massive clouds of white solid phosphorus(V) oxide (P_2O_5) product. Given these properties, it is not surprising that phosphorus has been used to manufacture incendiary bombs for warfare. Write the unbalanced equation for the reaction of phosphorus with oxygen gas to produce phosphorus(V) oxide.

31. Calcium oxide is sometimes very challenging to store in the chemistry laboratory. This compound reacts with moisture in the air and is converted to calcium hydroxide. If a bottle of calcium oxide is left on the shelf too long, it gradually absorbs moisture from the humidity in the laboratory. Eventually the bottle cracks and spills the calcium hydroxide that has been produced. Write the unbalanced chemical equation for this process.

32. Although they were formerly called the inert gases, the heavier elements of Group 8 do form relatively stable compounds. For example, at high temperatures in the presence of an appropriate catalyst, xenon gas will combine directly with fluorine gas to produce solid xenon tetrafluoride. Write the unbalanced chemical equation for this process.

33. The element tin often occurs in nature as the oxide, SnO_2. To produce pure tin metal from this sort of tin ore, the ore usually is heated with coal (carbon). This produces pure molten tin, with the carbon being removed from the reaction system as the gaseous byproduct carbon monoxide. Write the unbalanced equation for this process.

34. Nitric acid, HNO_3, can be produced by reacting high-pressure ammonia gas with oxygen gas at around 750 °C in the presence of a platinum catalyst. Water is a by-product of the reaction. Write the unbalanced chemical equation for this process.

6.3 Balancing Chemical Equations

QUESTIONS

35. When balancing chemical equations, beginning students are often tempted to change the numbers *within* a formula (the subscripts) to balance the equation. Why is this never permitted? What effect does changing a subscript have?

F 36. The "Chemistry in Focus" segment *The Beetle That Shoots Straight* discusses the bombardier beetle and the chemical reaction of the decomposition of hydrogen peroxide.

$$H_2O_2(aq) \rightarrow H_2O(l) + O_2(g)$$

The balanced equation given in the segment is

$$2H_2O_2(aq) \rightarrow 2H_2O(l) + O_2(g)$$

Why can't we balance the equation in the following way?

$$H_2O_2(aq) \rightarrow H_2(g) + O_2(g)$$

Use molecular level pictures like those in Section 6.3 to support your answer.

PROBLEMS

37. Balance each of the following chemical equations.
   a. $FeCl_3(aq) + KOH(aq) \rightarrow Fe(OH)_3(s) + KCl(aq)$
   b. $Pb(C_2H_3O_2)_2(aq) + KI(aq) \rightarrow PbI_2(s) + KC_2H_3O_2(aq)$
   c. $P_4O_{10}(s) + H_2O(l) \rightarrow H_3PO_4(aq)$
   d. $Li_2O(s) + H_2O(l) \rightarrow LiOH(aq)$
   e. $MnO_2(s) + C(s) \rightarrow Mn(s) + CO_2(g)$
   f. $Sb(s) + Cl_2(g) \rightarrow SbCl_3(s)$
   g. $CH_4(g) + H_2O(g) \rightarrow CO(g) + H_2(g)$
   h. $FeS(s) + HCl(aq) \rightarrow FeCl_2(aq) + H_2S(g)$

38. Balance each of the following chemical equations.
   a. $Zn(s) + CuO(s) \rightarrow ZnO(s) + Cu(l)$
   b. $P_4(s) + F_2(g) \rightarrow PF_3(g)$
   c. $Xe(g) + F_2(g) \rightarrow XeF_4(s)$
   d. $NH_4Cl(g) + Mg(OH)_2(s) \rightarrow NH_3(g) + H_2O(g) + MgCl_2(s)$
   e. $SiO(s) + Cl_2(g) \rightarrow SiCl_4(l) + O_2(g)$
   f. $Cs_2O(s) + H_2O(l) \rightarrow CsOH(aq)$
   g. $N_2O_3(g) + H_2O(l) \rightarrow HNO_2(aq)$
   h. $Fe_2O_3(s) + H_2SO_4(l) \rightarrow Fe_2(SO_4)_3(s) + H_2O(g)$

39. Balance each of the following chemical equations.
   a. $K_2SO_4(aq) + BaCl_2(aq) \rightarrow BaSO_4(s) + KCl(aq)$
   b. $Fe(s) + H_2O(g) \rightarrow FeO(s) + H_2(g)$
   c. $NaOH(aq) + HClO_4(aq) \rightarrow NaClO_4(aq) + H_2O(l)$
   d. $Mg(s) + Mn_2O_3(s) \rightarrow MgO(s) + Mn(s)$
   e. $KOH(s) + KH_2PO_4(aq) \rightarrow K_3PO_4(aq) + H_2O(l)$
   f. $NO_2(g) + H_2O(l) + O_2(g) \rightarrow HNO_3(aq)$
   g. $BaO_2(s) + H_2O(l) \rightarrow Ba(OH)_2(aq) + O_2(g)$
   h. $NH_3(g) + O_2(g) \rightarrow NO(g) + H_2O(l)$

40. Balance each of the following chemical equations.
   a. $Na_2SO_4(aq) + CaCl_2(aq) \rightarrow CaSO_4(s) + NaCl(aq)$
   b. $Fe(s) + H_2O(g) \rightarrow Fe_3O_4(s) + H_2(g)$
   c. $Ca(OH)_2(aq) + HCl(aq) \rightarrow CaCl_2(aq) + H_2O(l)$
   d. $Br_2(g) + H_2O(l) + SO_2(g) \rightarrow HBr(aq) + H_2SO_4(aq)$
   e. $NaOH(s) + H_3PO_4(aq) \rightarrow Na_3PO_4(aq) + H_2O(l)$
   f. $NaNO_3(s) \rightarrow NaNO_2(s) + O_2(g)$
   g. $Na_2O_2(s) + H_2O(l) \rightarrow NaOH(aq) + O_2(g)$
   h. $Si(s) + S_8(s) \rightarrow Si_2S_4(s)$

All even-numbered Questions and Problems have answers in the back of this book and solutions in the Solutions Guide.

34. $NH_3(g) + O_2(g) \rightarrow HNO_3(aq) + H_2O(l)$

35. The subscripts in a formula really define what compound is present, because the subscripts represent the proportions in which the elements combine to form the compound. Changing the subscripts would change the identity of the compound.

36. We cannot change the identities or formulas of the reactants or products in a chemical equation when balancing the equation. The proposed equation has changed one of the products from water to hydrogen gas.

37. (a) $FeCl_3(aq) + 3KOH(aq) \rightarrow Fe(OH)_3(s) + 3KCl(aq)$; (b) $Pb(C_2H_3O_2)_2(aq) + 2KI(aq) \rightarrow PbI_2(s) + 2KC_2H_3O_2(aq)$; (c) $P_4O_{10}(s) + 6H_2O(l) \rightarrow 4H_3PO_4(aq)$; (d) $Li_2O(s) + H_2O(l) \rightarrow 2LiOH(aq)$; (e) already balanced; (f) $2Sb(s) + 3Cl_2(g) \rightarrow 2SbCl_3(s)$; (g) $CH_4(g) + H_2O(g) \rightarrow CO(g) + 3H_2(g)$; (h) $FeS(s) + 2HCl(aq) \rightarrow FeCl_2(aq) + H_2S(g)$

38. (a) $Zn(s) + CuO(s) \rightarrow ZnO(s) + Cu(l)$; (b) $P_4(s) + 6F_2(g) \rightarrow 4PF_3(g)$; (c) $Xe(g) + 2F_2(g) \rightarrow XeF_4(s)$; (d) $2NH_4Cl(g) + Mg(OH)_2(s) \rightarrow 2NH_3(g) + 2H_2O(g) + MgCl_2(s)$; (e) $2SiO(s) + 4Cl_2(g) \rightarrow 2SiCl_4(l) + O_2(g)$; (f) $Cs_2O(s) + H_2O(l) \rightarrow 2CsOH(aq)$; (g) $N_2O_3(g) + H_2O(l) \rightarrow 2HNO_2(aq)$; (h) $Fe_2O_3(s) + 3H_2SO_4(l) \rightarrow Fe_2(SO_4)_3(s) + 3H_2O(g)$

39. (a) $K_2SO_4(aq) + BaCl_2(aq) \rightarrow BaSO_4(s) + 2KCl(aq)$; (b) $Fe(s) + H_2O(g) \rightarrow FeO(s) + H_2(g)$; (c) $NaOH(aq) + HClO_4(aq) \rightarrow NaClO_4(aq) + H_2O(l)$; (d) $3Mg(s) + Mn_2O_3(s) \rightarrow 3MgO(s) + 2Mn(s)$; (e) $2KOH(s) + KH_2PO_4(aq) \rightarrow K_3PO_4(aq) + 2H_2O(l)$; (f) $4NO_2(g) + 2H_2O(l) + O_2(g) \rightarrow 4HNO_3(aq)$; (g) $2BaO_2(s) + 2H_2O(l) \rightarrow 2Ba(OH)_2(aq) + O_2(g)$; (h) $4NH_3(g) + 5O_2(g) \rightarrow 4NO(g) + 6H_2O(l)$

40. (a) $Na_2SO_4(aq) + CaCl_2(aq) \rightarrow CaSO_4(s) + 2NaCl(aq)$; (b) $3Fe(s) + 4H_2O(g) \rightarrow Fe_3O_4(s) + 4H_2(g)$; (c) $Ca(OH)_2(aq) + 2HCl(aq) \rightarrow CaCl_2(aq) + 2H_2O(l)$; (d) $Br_2(g) + 2H_2O(l) + SO_2(g) \rightarrow 2HBr(aq) + H_2SO_4(aq)$; (e) $3NaOH(s) + H_3PO_4(aq) \rightarrow Na_3PO_4(aq) + 3H_2O(l)$; (f) $2NaNO_3(s) \rightarrow 2NaNO_2(s) + O_2(g)$; (g) $2Na_2O_2(s) + 2H_2O(l) \rightarrow 4NaOH(aq) + O_2(g)$; (h) $4Si(s) + S_8(s) \rightarrow 2Si_2S_4(s)$

41. Balance each of the following chemical equations.

a. $Fe_3O_4(s) + H_2(g) \rightarrow Fe(l) + H_2O(g)$
b. $K_2SO_4(aq) + BaCl_2(aq) \rightarrow BaSO_4(s) + KCl(aq)$
c. $HCl(aq) + FeS(s) \rightarrow FeCl_2(aq) + H_2S(g)$
d. $Br_2(g) + H_2O(l) + SO_2(g) \rightarrow HBr(aq) + H_2SO_4(aq)$
e. $CS_2(l) + Cl_2(g) \rightarrow CCl_4(l) + S_2Cl_2(g)$
f. $Cl_2O_7(g) + Ca(OH)_2(aq) \rightarrow Ca(ClO_4)_2(aq) + H_2O(l)$
g. $PBr_3(l) + H_2O(l) \rightarrow H_3PO_3(aq) + HBr(g)$
h. $Ba(ClO_3)_2(s) \rightarrow BaCl_2(s) + O_2(s)$

42. Balance each of the following chemical equations.

a. $NaCl(s) + SO_2(g) + H_2O(g) + O_2(g) \rightarrow Na_2SO_4(s) + HCl(g)$
b. $Br_2(l) + I_2(s) \rightarrow IBr_3(s)$
c. $Ca_3N_2(s) + H_2O(l) \rightarrow Ca(OH)_2(aq) + PH_3(g)$
d. $BF_3(g) + H_2O(g) \rightarrow B_2O_3(s) + HF(g)$
e. $SO_2(g) + Cl_2(g) \rightarrow SOCl_2(l) + Cl_2O(g)$
f. $Li_2O(s) + H_2O(l) \rightarrow LiOH(aq)$
g. $Mg(s) + CuO(s) \rightarrow MgO(s) + Cu(l)$
h. $Fe_3O_4(s) + H_2(g) \rightarrow Fe(l) + H_2O(g)$

43. Balance each of the following chemical equations.

a. $KO_2(s) + H_2O(l) \rightarrow KOH(aq) + O_2(g) + H_2O_2(aq)$
b. $Fe_2O_3(s) + HNO_3(aq) \rightarrow Fe(NO_3)_3(aq) + H_2O(l)$
c. $NH_3(g) + O_2(g) \rightarrow NO(g) + H_2O(g)$
d. $PCl_5(l) + H_2O(l) \rightarrow H_3PO_4(aq) + HCl(g)$
e. $C_2H_5OH(l) + O_2(g) \rightarrow CO_2(g) + H_2O(l)$
f. $CaO(s) + C(s) \rightarrow CaC_2(s) + CO_2(g)$
g. $MoS_2(s) + O_2(g) \rightarrow MoO_3(s) + SO_2(g)$
h. $FeCO_3(s) + H_2CO_3(aq) \rightarrow Fe(HCO_3)_2(aq)$

44. Balance each of the following chemical equations.

a. $Ba(NO_3)_2(aq) + Na_2CrO_4(aq) \rightarrow BaCrO_4(s) + NaNO_3(aq)$
b. $PbCl_2(aq) + K_2SO_4(aq) \rightarrow PbSO_4(s) + KCl(aq)$
c. $C_2H_5OH(l) + O_2(g) \rightarrow CO_2(g) + H_2O(l)$
d. $CaC_2(s) + H_2O(l) \rightarrow Ca(OH)_2(s) + C_2H_2(g)$
e. $Sr(s) + HNO_3(aq) \rightarrow Sr(NO_3)_2(aq) + H_2(g)$
f. $BaO_2(s) + H_2SO_4(aq) \rightarrow BaSO_4(s) + H_2O_2(aq)$
g. $AsI_3(s) \rightarrow As(s) + I_2(s)$
h. $CuSO_4(aq) + KI(s) \rightarrow CuI(s) + I_2(s) + K_2SO_4(aq)$

Additional Problems

45. Acetylene gas, C_2H_2, is used in welding because it generates an extremely hot flame when it is combusted with oxygen. The heat generated is sufficient to melt the metals being welded together. Carbon dioxide gas and water vapor are the chemical products of this reaction. Write the unbalanced chemical equation for the reaction of acetylene with oxygen.

46. Sodium commonly forms the peroxide, Na_2O_2, when reacted with pure oxygen, rather than the simple oxide, Na_2O, as we might expect. Sodium peroxide is fairly reactive. If sodium peroxide is added to water, oxygen gas is evolved, leaving a solution of sodium hydroxide. Write unbalanced chemical equations for the reaction of sodium with oxygen to form sodium peroxide and for the reaction of sodium peroxide with water.

47. Crude gunpowders often contain a mixture of potassium nitrate and charcoal (carbon). When such a mixture is heated until reaction occurs, a solid residue of potassium carbonate is produced. The explosive force of the gunpowder comes from the fact that two gases are also produced (carbon monoxide and nitrogen), which increase in volume with great force and speed. Write the unbalanced chemical equation for the process.

48. The sugar sucrose, which is present in many fruits and vegetables, reacts in the presence of certain yeast enzymes to produce ethyl alcohol (ethanol) and carbon dioxide gas. Balance the following equation for this reaction of sucrose.

$$C_{12}H_{22}O_{11}(aq) + H_2O(l) \rightarrow C_2H_5OH(aq) + CO_2(g)$$

49. Methanol (methyl alcohol), CH_3OH, is a very important industrial chemical. Formerly, methanol was prepared by heating wood to high temperatures in the absence of air. The complex compounds present in wood are degraded by this process into a charcoal residue and a volatile portion that is rich in methanol. Today, methanol is instead synthesized from carbon monoxide and elemental hydrogen. Write the balanced chemical equation for this latter process.

50. The Hall process is an important method by which pure aluminum is prepared from its oxide (alumina, Al_2O_3) by indirect reaction with graphite (carbon). Balance the following equation, which is a simplified representation of this process.

$$Al_2O_3(s) + C(s) \rightarrow Al(s) + CO_2(g)$$

51. Iron oxide ores, commonly a mixture of FeO and Fe_2O_3, are given the general formula Fe_3O_4. They yield elemental iron when heated to a very high temperature with either carbon monoxide or elemental hydrogen. Balance the following equations for these processes.

$$Fe_3O_4(s) + H_2(g) \rightarrow Fe(s) + H_2O(g)$$
$$Fe_3O_4(s) + CO(g) \rightarrow Fe(s) + CO_2(g)$$

52. The elements of Group 1 all react with sulfur to form the metal sulfides. Write balanced chemical equations for the reactions of the Group 1 elements with sulfur.

53. When steel wool (iron) is heated in pure oxygen gas, the steel wool bursts into flame and a fine powder consisting of a mixture of iron oxides (FeO and Fe_2O_3) forms. Write *separate* unbalanced equations for the reaction of iron with oxygen to give each of these products.

54. One method of producing hydrogen peroxide is to add barium peroxide to water. A precipitate of barium oxide forms, which may then be filtered off to leave a solution of hydrogen peroxide. Write the balanced chemical equation for this process.

55. When elemental boron, B, is burned in oxygen gas, the product is diboron trioxide. If the diboron

All even-numbered Questions and Problems have answers in the back of this book and solutions in the Solutions Guide.

41. (a) $Fe_3O_4(s) + 4H_2(g) \rightarrow 3Fe(l) + 4H_2O(g)$; (b) $K_2SO_4(aq) + BaCl_2(aq) \rightarrow BaSO_4(s) + 2KCl(aq)$; (c) $2HCl(aq) + FeS(s) \rightarrow FeCl_2(aq) + H_2S(g)$; (d) $Br_2(g) + 2H_2O(l) + SO_2(g) \rightarrow 2HBr(aq) + H_2SO_4(aq)$; (e) $CS_2(l) + 3Cl_2(g) \rightarrow CCl_4(l) + S_2Cl_2(g)$; (f) $Cl_2O_7(g) + Ca(OH)_2(aq) \rightarrow Ca(ClO_4)_2(aq) + H_2O(l)$; (g) $PBr_3(l) + 3H_2O(l) \rightarrow H_3PO_3(aq) + 3HBr(g)$; (h) $Ba(ClO_3)_2(s) \rightarrow BaCl_2(s) + 3O_2(s)$

42. (a) $4NaCl(s) + 2SO_2(g) + 2H_2O(g) + O_2(g) \rightarrow 2Na_2SO_4(s) + 4HCl(g)$; (b) $3Br_2(l) + I_2(s) \rightarrow 2IBr_3(s)$; (c) $Ca(s) + 2H_2O(g) \rightarrow Ca(OH)_2(aq) + H_2(g)$; (d) $2BF_3(g) + 3H_2O(g) \rightarrow B_2O_3(s) + 6HF(g)$; (e) $SO_2(g) + 2Cl_2(g) \rightarrow SOCl_2(l) + Cl_2O(g)$; (f) $Li_2O(s) + H_2O(l) \rightarrow 2LiOH(aq)$; (g) $Mg(s) + CuO(s) \rightarrow MgO(s) + Cu(l)$; (h) $Fe_3O_4(s) + 4H_2(g) \rightarrow 3Fe(l) + 4H_2O(g)$

43. (a) $4KO_2(s) + 6H_2O(l) \rightarrow 4KOH(aq) + O_2(g) + 4H_2O_2(aq)$; (b) $Fe_2O_3(s) + 6HNO_3(aq) \rightarrow 2Fe(NO_3)_3(aq) + 3H_2O(l)$; (c) $4NH_3(g) + 5O_2(g) \rightarrow 4NO(g) + 6H_2O(g)$; (d) $PCl_5(l) + 4H_2O(l) \rightarrow H_3PO_4(aq) + 5HCl(g)$; (e) $C_2H_5OH(l) + 3O_2(g) \rightarrow 2CO_2(g) + 3H_2O(l)$; (f) $2CaO(s) + 5C(s) \rightarrow 2CaC_2(s) + CO_2(g)$; (g) $2MoS_2(s) + 7O_2(g) \rightarrow 2MoO_3(s) + 4SO_2(g)$; (h) $FeCO_3(s) + H_2CO_3(aq) \rightarrow Fe(HCO_3)_2(aq)$

44. (a) $Ba(NO_3)_2(aq) + Na_2CrO_4(aq) \rightarrow BaCrO_4(s) + 2NaNO_3(aq)$; (b) $PbCl_2(aq) + K_2SO_4(aq) \rightarrow PbSO_4(s) + 2KCl(aq)$; (c) $C_2H_5OH(l) + 3O_2(g) \rightarrow 2CO_2(g) + 3H_2O(l)$; (d) $CaC_2(s) + 2H_2O(l) \rightarrow Ca(OH)_2(s) + C_2H_2(g)$; (e) $Sr(s) + 2HNO_3(aq) \rightarrow Sr(NO_3)_2(aq) + H_2(g)$; (f) $BaO_2(s) + H_2SO_4(aq) \rightarrow BaSO_4(s) + H_2O_2(aq)$; (g) $2AsI_3(s) \rightarrow 2As(s) + 3I_2(s)$; (h) $2CuSO_4(aq) + 4KI(s) \rightarrow 2CuI(s) + I_2(s) + 2K_2SO_4(aq)$

45. $C_2H_2(g) + O_2(g) \rightarrow CO_2(g) + H_2O(g)$

46. $Na(s) + O_2(g) \rightarrow Na_2O_2(s)$; $Na_2O_2(s) + H_2O(l) \rightarrow NaOH(aq) + O_2(g)$

47. $KNO_3(s) + C(s) \rightarrow K_2CO_3(s) + CO(g) + N_2(g)$

48. $C_{12}H_{22}O_{11}(aq) + H_2O(l) \rightarrow 4C_2H_5OH(aq) + 4CO_2(g)$

49. $2H_2(g) + CO(g) \rightarrow CH_3OH(l)$

50. $2Al_2O_3(s) + 3C(s) \rightarrow 4Al(s) + 3CO_2(g)$

51. $Fe_3O_4(s) + 4H_2(g) \rightarrow 3Fe(s) + 4H_2O(g)$; $Fe_3O_4(s) + 4CO(g) \rightarrow 3Fe(s) + 4CO_2(g)$

52. $2Li(s) + S(s) \rightarrow Li_2S(s)$; $2Na(s) + S(s) \rightarrow Na_2S(s)$; $2K(s) + S(s) \rightarrow K_2S(s)$; $2Rb(s) + S(s) \rightarrow Rb_2S(s)$; $2Cs(s) + S(s) \rightarrow Cs_2S(s)$; $2Fr(s) + S(s) \rightarrow Fr_2S(s)$

trioxide is then reacted with a measured quantity of water, it reacts with the water to form what is commonly known as boric acid, $B(OH)_3$. Write a balanced chemical equation for each of these processes.

56. A common experiment in introductory chemistry courses involves heating a weighed mixture of potassium chlorate, $KClO_3$, and potassium chloride. Potassium chlorate decomposes when heated, producing potassium chloride and evolving oxygen gas. By measuring the volume of oxygen gas produced in this experiment, students can calculate the relative percentage of $KClO_3$ and KCl in the original mixture. Write the balanced chemical equation for this process.

57. A common demonstration in chemistry courses involves adding a tiny speck of manganese(IV) oxide to a concentrated hydrogen peroxide, H_2O_2, solution. Hydrogen peroxide is unstable, and it decomposes quite spectacularly under these conditions to produce oxygen gas and steam (water vapor). Manganese(IV) oxide is a catalyst for the decomposition of hydrogen peroxide and is not consumed in the reaction. Write the balanced equation for the decomposition reaction of hydrogen peroxide.

58. The benches in many undergraduate chemistry laboratories are often covered by a film of white dust. This may be due to poor housekeeping, but the dust is usually ammonium chloride, produced by the gaseous reaction in the laboratory of hydrogen chloride and ammonia; most labs have aqueous solutions of these common reagents. Write the balanced chemical equation for the reaction of gaseous ammonia and hydrogen chloride to form solid ammonium chloride.

59. Glass is a mixture of several compounds, but a major constituent of most glass is calcium silicate, $CaSiO_3$. Glass can be etched by treatment with hydrogen fluoride: HF attacks the calcium silicate of the glass, producing gaseous and water-soluble products (which can be removed by washing the glass). For example, the volumetric glassware in chemistry laboratories is often graduated by using this process. Balance the following equation for the reaction of hydrogen fluoride with calcium silicate.

$$CaSiO_3(s) + HF(g) \rightarrow CaF_2(aq) + SiF_4(g) + H_2O(l)$$

60. Fish has a "fishy" taste and odor because of the presence of nitrogen compounds called amines in the protein of the fish. Amines such as methyl amine, CH_3NH_2, can be thought of as close relatives of ammonia, NH_3, in which a hydrogen atom of ammonia is replaced by a carbon-containing group. When fish is served, it is often accompanied by lemon (or vinegar in some countries), which reduces the fishy odor and taste. Is there evidence that the action of the lemon juice or vinegar represents a chemical reaction?

61. If you had a "sour stomach," you might try an over-the-counter antacid tablet to relieve the problem. Can you think of evidence that the action of such an antacid is a chemical reaction?

62. When iron wire is heated in the presence of sulfur, the iron soon begins to glow, and a chunky, blue-black mass of iron(II) sulfide is formed. Write the unbalanced chemical equation for this reaction.

63. When finely divided solid sodium is dropped into a flask containing chlorine gas, an explosion occurs and a fine powder of sodium chloride is deposited on the walls of the flask. Write the unbalanced chemical equation for this process.

64. If aqueous solutions of potassium chromate and barium chloride are mixed, a bright yellow solid (barium chromate) forms and settles out of the mixture, leaving potassium chloride in solution. Write a balanced chemical equation for this process.

65. When hydrogen sulfide, H_2S, gas is bubbled through a solution of lead(II) nitrate, $Pb(NO_3)_2$, a black precipitate of lead(II) sulfide, PbS, forms, and nitric acid, HNO_3, is produced. Write the unbalanced chemical equation for this reaction.

66. If an electric current is passed through aqueous solutions of sodium chloride, sodium bromide, and sodium iodide, the elemental halogens are produced at one electrode in each case, with hydrogen gas being evolved at the other electrode. If the liquid is then evaporated from the mixture, a residue of sodium hydroxide remains. Write balanced chemical equations for these electrolysis reactions.

67. When a strip of magnesium metal is heated in oxygen, it bursts into an intensely white flame and produces a finely powdered dust of magnesium oxide. Write the unbalanced chemical equation for this process.

68. When small amounts of acetylene gas are needed, a common process is to react calcium carbide with water. Acetylene gas is evolved rapidly from this combination even at room temperature, leaving a residue of calcium hydroxide. Write the balanced chemical equation for this process.

69. When solid red phosphorus, P_4, is burned in air, the phosphorus combines with oxygen, producing a choking cloud of tetraphosphorus decoxide. Write the unbalanced chemical equation for this reaction.

70. When copper(II) oxide is boiled in an aqueous solution of sulfuric acid, a strikingly blue solution of copper(II) sulfate forms along with additional water. Write the unbalanced chemical equation for this reaction.

71. When lead(II) sulfide is heated to high temperatures in a stream of pure oxygen gas, solid lead(II) oxide forms with the release of gaseous sulfur dioxide. Write the unbalanced chemical equation for this reaction.

72. When sodium sulfite is boiled with sulfur, the sulfite ions, SO_3^{2-}, are converted to thiosulfate ions, $S_2O_3^{2-}$, resulting in a solution of sodium thiosulfate, $Na_2S_2O_3$. Write the unbalanced chemical equation for this reaction.

All even-numbered Questions and Problems have answers in the back of this book and solutions in the Solutions Guide.

60. The senses we call "odor" and "taste" are really chemical reactions of the receptors in our body with molecules in the food we are eating. The fact that the receptors no longer detect the "fishy" odor or taste suggests that adding the lemon juice or vinegar has changed the nature of the amines in the fish.

61. Many antacids contain HCO_3^- or CO_3^{2-} ion, which both react with H^+ to evolve $CO_2(g)$.

62. $Fe(s) + S(s) \rightarrow FeS(s)$

63. $Na(s) + Cl_2(g) \rightarrow NaCl(s)$

64. $K_2CrO_4(aq) + BaCl_2(aq) \rightarrow BaCrO_4(s) + 2KCl(aq)$

65. $H_2S(g) + Pb(NO_3)_2(aq) \rightarrow PbS(s) + HNO_3(aq)$

66. $2NaCl(aq) + 2H_2O(l) \rightarrow Cl_2(g) + H_2(g) + 2NaOH(aq, s)$
$2NaBr(aq) + 2H_2O(l) \rightarrow Br_2(l) + H_2(g) + 2NaOH(aq, s)$
$2NaI(aq) + 2H_2O(l) \rightarrow I_2(s) + H_2(g) + 2NaOH(aq, s)$

67. $Mg(s) + O_2(g) \rightarrow MgO(s)$

68. $CaC_2(s) + 2H_2O(l) \rightarrow Ca(OH)_2(s) + C_2H_2(g)$

69. $P_4(s) + O_2(g) \rightarrow P_4O_{10}(g)$

70. $CuO(s) + H_2SO_4(aq) \rightarrow CuSO_4(aq) + H_2O(l)$

71. $PbS(s) + O_2(g) \rightarrow PbO(s) + SO_2(g)$

72. $Na_2SO_3(aq) + S(s) \rightarrow Na_2S_2O_3(aq)$

53. $Fe(s) + O_2(g) \rightarrow FeO(s)$; $Fe(s) + O_2(g) \rightarrow Fe_2O_3(s)$

54. $BaO_2(s) + H_2O(l) \rightarrow BaO(s) + H_2O_2(aq)$

55. $4B(s) + 3O_2(g) \rightarrow 2B_2O_3(s)$; $B_2O_3(s) + 3H_2O(l) \rightarrow 2B(OH)_3(s)$

56. $2KClO_3(s) \rightarrow 2KCl(s) + 3O_2(g)$

57. $2H_2O_2(aq) \rightarrow 2H_2O(g) + O_2(g)$

58. $NH_3(g) + HCl(g) \rightarrow NH_4Cl(s)$

59. $CaSiO_3(s) + 6HF(g) \rightarrow CaF_2(aq) + SiF_4(g) + 3H_2O(l)$

73. Balance each of the following chemical equations.

a. $Cl_2(g) + KBr(aq) \rightarrow Br_2(l) + KCl(aq)$
b. $Cr(s) + O_2(g) \rightarrow Cr_2O_3(s)$
c. $P_4(s) + H_2(g) \rightarrow PH_3(g)$
d. $Al(s) + H_2SO_4(aq) \rightarrow Al_2(SO_4)_3(aq) + H_2(g)$
e. $PCl_3(l) + H_2O(l) \rightarrow H_3PO_3(aq) + HCl(aq)$
f. $SO_2(g) + O_2(g) \rightarrow SO_3(g)$
g. $C_7H_{16}(l) + O_2(g) \rightarrow CO_2(g) + H_2O(g)$
h. $C_2H_6(g) + O_2(g) \rightarrow CO_2(g) + H_2O(g)$

74. Balance each of the following chemical equations.

a. $Cl_2(g) + KI(aq) \rightarrow KCl(aq) + I_2(s)$
b. $CaC_2(s) + H_2O(l) \rightarrow Ca(OH)_2(s) + C_2H_2(g)$
c. $NaCl(s) + H_2SO_4(l) \rightarrow Na_2SO_4(s) + HCl(g)$
d. $CaF_2(s) + H_2SO_4(l) \rightarrow CaSO_4(s) + HF(g)$
e. $K_2CO_3(s) \rightarrow K_2O(s) + CO_2(g)$
f. $BaO(s) + Al(s) \rightarrow Al_2O_3(s) + Ba(s)$
g. $Al(s) + F_2(g) \rightarrow AlF_3(s)$
h. $CS_2(g) + Cl_2(g) \rightarrow CCl_4(l) + S_2Cl_2(g)$

75. Balance each of the following chemical equations.

a. $SiCl_4(l) + Mg(s) \rightarrow Si(s) + MgCl_2(s)$
b. $NO(g) + Cl_2(g) \rightarrow NOCl(g)$
c. $MnO_2(s) + Al(s) \rightarrow Mn(s) + Al_2O_3(s)$
d. $Cr(s) + S_8(s) \rightarrow Cr_2S_3(s)$
e. $NH_3(g) + F_2(g) \rightarrow NH_4F(s) + NF_3(g)$
f. $Ag_2S(s) + H_2(g) \rightarrow Ag(s) + H_2S(g)$
g. $O_2(g) \rightarrow O_3(g)$
h. $Na_2SO_3(aq) + S_8(s) \rightarrow Na_2S_2O_3(aq)$

76. Balance each of the following chemical equations.

a. $Pb(NO_3)_2(aq) + K_2CrO_4(aq) \rightarrow PbCrO_4(s) + KNO_3(aq)$
b. $BaCl_2(aq) + Na_2SO_4(aq) \rightarrow BaSO_4(s) + NaCl(aq)$
c. $CH_3OH(l) + O_2(g) \rightarrow CO_2(g) + H_2O(g)$
d. $Na_2CO_3(aq) + S(s) + SO_2(g) \rightarrow CO_2(g) + Na_2S_2O_3(aq)$
e. $Cu(s) + H_2SO_4(aq) \rightarrow CuSO_4(aq) + SO_2(g) + H_2O(l)$
f. $MnO_2(s) + HCl(aq) \rightarrow MnCl_2(aq) + Cl_2(g) + H_2O(l)$
g. $As_2O_3(s) + KI(aq) + HCl(aq) \rightarrow AsI_3(s) + KCl(aq) + H_2O(l)$
h. $Na_2S_2O_3(aq) + I_2(aq) \rightarrow Na_2S_4O_6(aq) + NaI(aq)$

All even-numbered Questions and Problems have answers in the back of this book and solutions in the Solutions Guide.

73. (a) $Cl_2(g) + 2KBr(aq) \rightarrow Br_2(l) + 2KCl(aq)$; (b) $2Cr(s) + 3O_2(g) \rightarrow 2Cr_2O_3(s)$; (c) $P_4(s) + 6H_2(g) \rightarrow 4PH_3(g)$; (d) $2Al(s) + 3H_2SO_4(aq) \rightarrow Al_2(SO_4)_3(aq) + 3H_2(g)$; (e) $PCl_3(l) + 3H_2O(l) \rightarrow H_3PO_3(aq) + 3HCl(aq)$; (f) $2SO_2(g) + O_2(g) \rightarrow 2SO_3(g)$; (g) $C_7H_{16}(l) + 11O_2(g) \rightarrow 7CO_2(g) + 8H_2O(g)$; (h) $2C_2H_6(g) + 7O_2(g) \rightarrow 4CO_2(g) + 6H_2O(g)$

74. (a) $Cl_2(g) + 2KI(aq) \rightarrow 2KCl(aq) + I_2(s)$; (b) $CaC_2(s) + 2H_2O(l) \rightarrow Ca(OH)_2(s) + C_2H_2(g)$; (c) $2NaCl(s) + H_2SO_4(l) \rightarrow Na_2SO_4(s) + 2HCl(g)$; (d) $CaF_2(s) + H_2SO_4(l) \rightarrow CaSO_4(s) + 2HF(g)$; (e) $K_2CO_3(s) \rightarrow K_2O(s) + CO_2(g)$; (f) $3BaO(s) + 2Al(s) \rightarrow Al_2O_3(s) + 3Ba(s)$; (g) $2Al(s) + 3F_2(g) \rightarrow 2AlF_3(s)$; (h) $CS_2(g) + 3Cl_2(g) \rightarrow CCl_4(l) + S_2Cl_2(g)$

75. (a) $SiCl_4(l) + 2Mg(s) \rightarrow Si(s) + 2MgCl_2(s)$; (b) $2NO(g) + Cl_2(g) \rightarrow 2NOCl(g)$; (c) $3MnO_2(s) + 4Al(s) \rightarrow 3Mn(s) + 2Al_2O_3(s)$; (d) $16Cr(s) + 3S_8(s) \rightarrow 8Cr_2S_3(s)$; (e) $4NH_3(g) + 3F_2(g) \rightarrow 3NH_4F(s) + NF_3(g)$; (f) $Ag_2S(aq) + H_2(g) \rightarrow 2Ag(s) + H_2S(g)$; (g) $3O_2(g) \rightarrow 2O_3(g)$; (h) $8Na_2SO_3(aq) + S_8(s) \rightarrow 8Na_2S_2O_3(aq)$

76. (a) $Pb(NO_3)_2(aq) + K_2CrO_4(aq) \rightarrow PbCrO_4(s) + 2KNO_3(aq)$; (b) $BaCl_2(aq) + Na_2SO_4(aq) \rightarrow BaSO_4(s) + 2NaCl(aq)$; (c) $2CH_3OH(l) + 3O_2(g) \rightarrow 2CO_2(g) + 4H_2O(g)$; (d) $Na_2CO_3(aq) + S(s) + SO_2(g) \rightarrow CO_2(g) + Na_2S_2O_3(aq)$; (e) $Cu(s) + 2H_2SO_4(aq) \rightarrow CuSO_4(aq) + SO_2(g) + 2H_2O(l)$; (f) $MnO_2(s) + 4HCl(aq) \rightarrow MnCl_2(aq) + Cl_2(g) + 2H_2O(l)$; (g) $As_2O_3(s) + 6KI(aq) + 6HCl(aq) \rightarrow 2AsI_3(s) + 6KCl(aq) + 3H_2O(l)$; (h) $2Na_2S_2O_3(aq) + I_2(aq) \rightarrow Na_2S_4O_6(aq) + 2NaI(aq)$

Chapter 7

Objectives

In this chapter, our objectives are for the students to:

SECTION 7.1

- Learn about some of the factors that cause reactions to occur.

SECTION 7.2

- Learn to identify the solid that forms in a precipitation reaction.

SECTION 7.3

- Learn to describe reactions in solutions by writing molecular, complete ionic, and net ionic equations.

SECTION 7.4

- Learn the key characteristics of the reactions between strong acids and strong bases.

SECTION 7.5

- Learn the general characteristics of a reaction between a metal and a nonmetal.
- Understand electron transfer as a driving force for a chemical reaction.

SECTION 7.6

- Learn various classification schemes for reactions.

SECTION 7.7

- Consider additional classes of chemical reactions.

7 Reactions in Aqueous Solutions

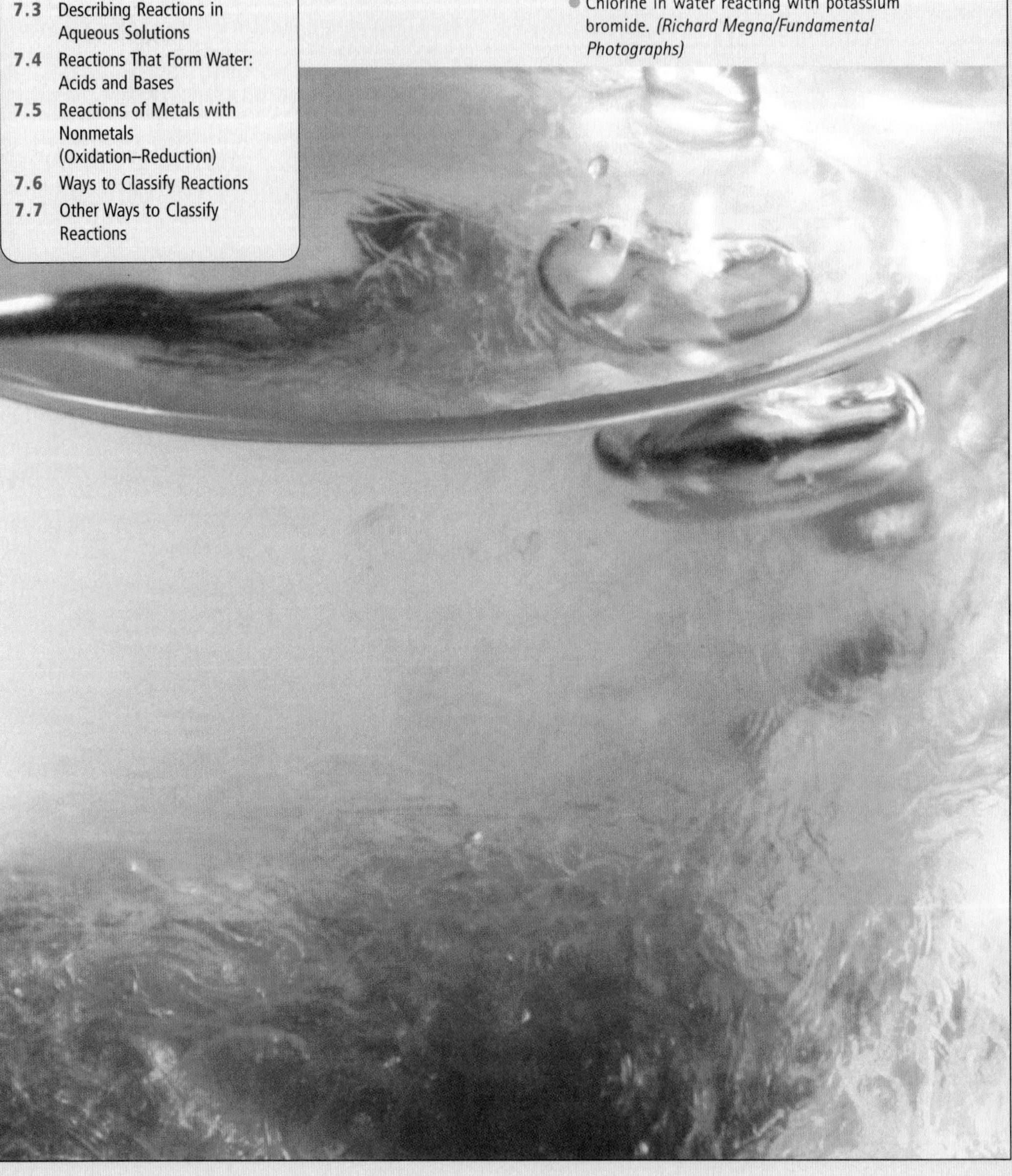

Chlorine in water reacting with potassium bromide. *(Richard Megna/Fundamental Photographs)*

ChemWork Refined over ten years of use by thousands of students, **ChemWork** builds and enhances students' problems-solving skills. Online assignments function as a "personal instructor" to help students learn how to solve challenging problems and learn how to think like chemists. Annotations for **ChemWork** assignments are included at the beginning of the end-of-chapter review.

PowerLecture This 2-DVD package includes the Chemistry Multimedia Library, which contains animations, simulations, and movies for all chemistry subjects, organized by topic for lecture presentations. Annotations for **PowerLecture** are referenced in the margins throughout the Annotated Instructor's Edition.

OWL Sign in to OWL at **www.cengage.com/owl** to view tutorials and simulations, develop problem-solving skills, and complete online homework assigned by your professor.

go Chemistry Download mini-lecture videos for key concept review and exam prep from OWL or purchase them from **www.ichapters.com**

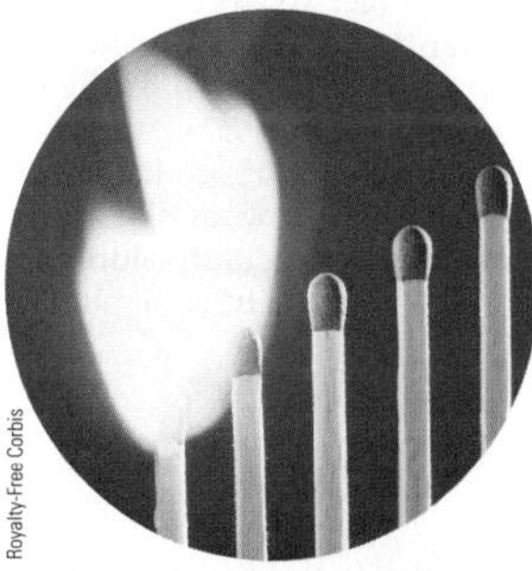

Royalty-Free Corbis

A burning match involves several chemical reactions.

The chemical reactions that are most important to us occur in water—in aqueous solutions. Virtually all of the chemical reactions that keep each of us alive and well take place in the aqueous medium present in our bodies. For example, the oxygen you breathe dissolves in your blood, where it associates with the hemoglobin in the red blood cells. While attached to the hemoglobin it is transported to your cells, where it reacts with fuel (from the food you eat) to provide energy for living. However, the reaction between oxygen and fuel is not direct—the cells are not tiny furnaces. Instead, electrons are transferred from the fuel to a series of molecules that pass them along (this is called the respiratory chain) until they eventually reach oxygen. Many other reactions are also crucial to our health and well-being. You will see numerous examples of these as you continue your study of chemistry.

In this chapter we will study some common types of reactions that take place in water, and we will become familiar with some of the driving forces that make these reactions occur. We will also learn how to predict the products for these reactions and how to write various equations to describe them.

 **Test Bank: 1**

Section 7.1

7.1 Predicting Whether a Reaction Will Occur

OBJECTIVE: To learn about some of the factors that cause reactions to occur.

In this text we have already seen many chemical reactions. Now let's consider an important question: Why does a chemical reaction occur? What causes reactants to "want" to form products? As chemists have studied reactions, they have recognized several "tendencies" in reactants that drive them to form products. That is, there are several "driving forces" that pull reactants toward products—changes that tend to make reactions go in the direction of the arrow. The most common of these driving forces are

1. Formation of a solid
2. Formation of water
3. Transfer of electrons
4. Formation of a gas

When two or more chemicals are brought together, if any of these things can occur, a chemical change (a reaction) is likely to take place. Accordingly, when we are confronted with a set of reactants and want to predict whether a reaction will occur and what products might form, we will consider these driving forces. They will help us organize our thoughts as we encounter new reactions.

TEACHING TIPS

- Explain that chemists make predictions based on the driving forces in a reaction and their own databases (mostly in their memories) of chemical reactions. The more experience someone has, the easier it becomes to predict the correct products for a reaction.
- Now is an excellent time to review polyatomic ions. Students will need them to write chemical equations in this chapter.

PowerLecture Video: Reaction: $CaCO_3$ + HCl

7.2 Reactions in Which a Solid Forms

OBJECTIVE: To learn to identify the solid that forms in a precipitation reaction.

One driving force for a chemical reaction is the formation of a solid, a process called **precipitation.** The solid that forms is called a **precipitate,** and the reaction is known as a **precipitation reaction.** For example,

Test Bank: 2–14, 22, 23, 29

Section 7.2

TEACHING TIP

Many teachers identify precipitation reactions by the term *double-displacement reactions,* but we use only the term *precipitation* to emphasize the driving force in this type of reaction. The term *double-displacement* is discussed as an alternative way to classify chemical reactions in Section 7.7.

TEACHING SUPPORT

BACKGROUND INFORMATION

This chapter introduces the concept of a *driving force.* Driving forces for natural processes are complex, and we would not expect students to understand at this point the "why" of driving forces. At this time students need to become aware that important driving forces exist and what some of them are. The "why" of these forces is usually explained in terms of achieving the lowest possible randomness (entropy), but these ideas would not make sense to students at this point in their study of chemistry. For now, it is enough that students understand that predictable driving forces exist.

LABORATORY EXPERIMENT

A relevant laboratory experiment for this section is Experiment 10, Precipitation Reactions, from *Introductory Chemistry in the Laboratory* by James Hall.

Lecture Demonstration: 4.3, 4.4, 4.5

PowerLecture Video: Reaction: Lead Iodide Precipitation

DEMONSTRATION

0.1 *M* K_2CrO_4 and 0.1 *M* $Ba(NO_3)_2$ can be used to illustrate the example shown in Figure 7.1. Place the yellow potassium chromate solution in a beaker and the barium nitrate solution in a graduated cylinder. Slowly pour the barium nitrate into the potassium chromate solution.

Note You can also use many other combinations for this illustration. For example, another yellow precipitate forms from the reaction of KI and $Pb(NO_3)_2$.

Lecture Demonstration: 4.1

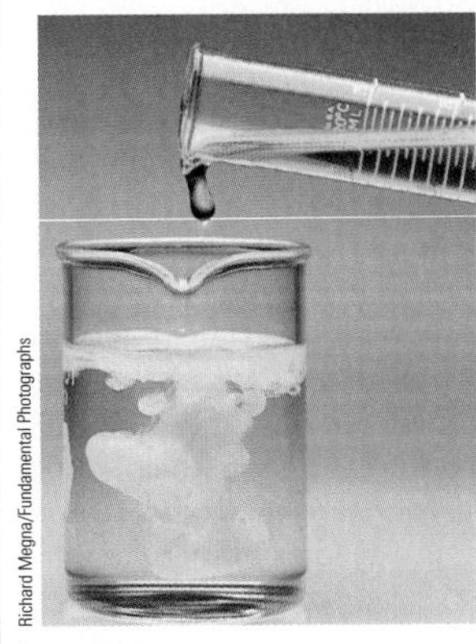

Richard Megna/Fundamental Photographs

Figure 7.1
The precipitation reaction that occurs when yellow potassium chromate, $K_2CrO_4(aq)$, is mixed with a colorless barium nitrate solution, $Ba(NO_3)_2(aq)$.

when an aqueous (water) solution of potassium chromate, $K_2CrO_4(aq)$, which is yellow, is added to a colorless aqueous solution containing barium nitrate, $Ba(NO_3)_2(aq)$, a yellow solid forms (see Figure 7.1). The fact that a solid forms tells us that a reaction—a chemical change—has occurred. That is, we have a situation where

$$\text{Reactants} \rightarrow \text{Products}$$

What is the equation that describes this chemical change? To write the equation, we must decipher the identities of the reactants and products. The reactants have already been described: $K_2CrO_4(aq)$ and $Ba(NO_3)_2(aq)$. Is there some way in which we can predict the identities of the products? What is the yellow solid? The best way to predict the identity of this solid is to first *consider what products are possible.* To do this we need to know what chemical species are present in the solution that results when the reactant solutions are mixed. First, let's think about the nature of each reactant in an aqueous solution.

What Happens When an Ionic Compound Dissolves in Water?

The designation $Ba(NO_3)_2(aq)$ means that barium nitrate (a white solid) has been dissolved in water. Note from its formula that barium nitrate contains the Ba^{2+} and NO_3^- ions. *In virtually every case when a solid containing ions dissolves in water, the ions separate* and move around independently. That is, $Ba(NO_3)_2(aq)$ does not contain $Ba(NO_3)_2$ units. Rather, it contains separated Ba^{2+} and NO_3^- ions. In the solution there are two NO_3^- ions for every Ba^{2+} ion. Chemists know that separated ions are present in this solution because it is an excellent conductor of electricity (see Figure 7.2). Pure water does not conduct an electric current. Ions must be present in water for a current to flow.

When each unit of a substance that dissolves in water produces separated ions, the substance is called a **strong electrolyte.** Barium nitrate is a strong electrolyte in water, because each $Ba(NO_3)_2$ unit produces the separated ions (Ba^{2+}, NO_3^-, NO_3^-).

Similarly, aqueous K_2CrO_4 also behaves as a strong electrolyte. Potassium chromate contains the K^+ and CrO_4^{2-} ions, so an aqueous solution of

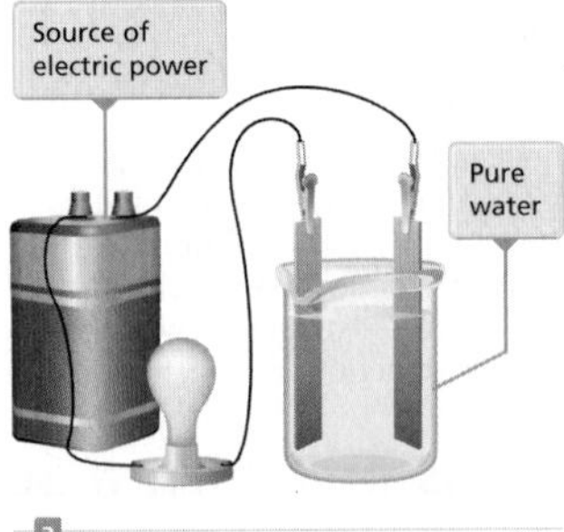

a Pure water does not conduct an electric current. The lamp does not light.

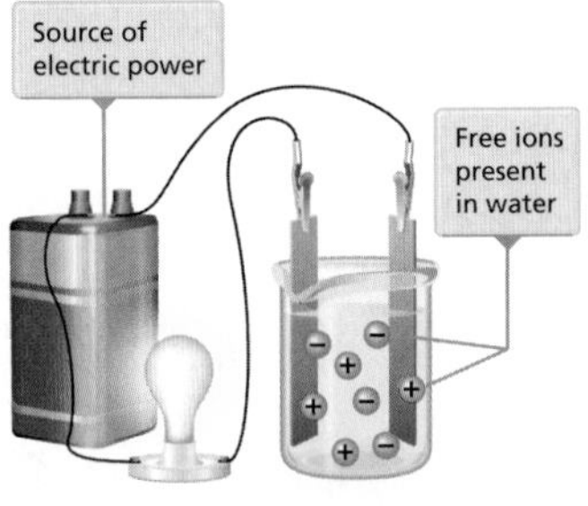

b When an ionic compound is dissolved in water, current flows and the lamp lights. The result of this experiment is strong evidence that ionic compounds dissolved in water exist in the form of separated ions.

Figure 7.2
Electrical conductivity of aqueous solutions.

TEACHING SUPPORT

BACKGROUND INFORMATION

One of the most valuable properties of water is its ability to dissolve many different substances. For example, salt "disappears" when you sprinkle it into the water used to cook vegetables, as does sugar when you add it to your iced tea. In each case the "disappearing" substance is obviously still present—you can taste it. What happens when a solid dissolves? To understand this process, we need to consider the nature of water. Liquid water consists of a collection of H_2O molecules. An individual H_2O molecule is "bent" or V-shaped, with an H—O—H angle of approximately 105 degrees.

potassium chromate (which is prepared by dissolving solid K_2CrO_4 in water) contains these separated ions. That is, $K_2CrO_4(aq)$ does not contain K_2CrO_4 units but instead contains K^+ cations and CrO_4^{2-} anions, which move around independently. (There are two K^+ ions for each CrO_4^{2-} ion.)

The idea introduced here is very important: when ionic compounds dissolve, the *resulting solution contains the separated ions*. Therefore, we can represent the mixing of $K_2CrO_4(aq)$ and $Ba(NO_3)_2(aq)$ in two ways. We usually write these reactants as

$$K_2CrO_4(aq) + Ba(NO_3)_2(aq) \rightarrow \text{Products}$$

However, a more accurate representation of the situation is

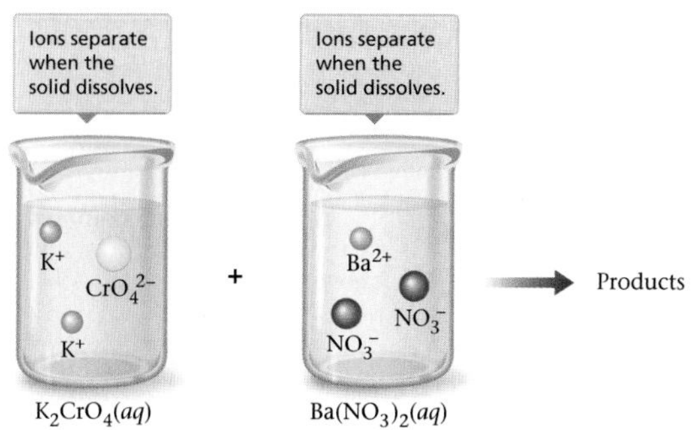

We can express this information in equation form as follows:

$$\underbrace{2K^+(aq) + CrO_4^{2-}(aq)}_{\text{The ions in } K_2CrO_4(aq)} + \underbrace{Ba^{2+}(aq) + 2NO_3^-(aq)}_{\text{The ions in } Ba(NO_3)_2(aq)} \rightarrow \text{Products}$$

Thus the *mixed solution* contains four types of ions: K^+, CrO_4^{2-}, Ba^{2+}, and NO_3^-. Now that we know what the reactants are, we can make some educated guesses about the possible products.

How to Decide What Products Form

Which of these ions combine to form the yellow solid observed when the original solutions are mixed? This is not an easy question to answer. Even an experienced chemist is not sure what will happen in a new reaction. The chemist tries to think of the various possibilities, considers the likelihood of each possibility, and then makes a prediction (an educated guess). Only after identifying each product experimentally can the chemist be sure what reaction actually has taken place. However, an educated guess is very useful because it indicates what kinds of products are most likely. It gives us a place to start. So the best way to proceed is first to think of the various possibilities and then to decide which of them is most likely.

What are the possible products of the reaction between $K_2CrO_4(aq)$ and $Ba(NO_3)_2(aq)$ or, more accurately, what reaction can occur among the ions K^+, CrO_4^{2-}, Ba^{2+}, and NO_3^-? We already know some things that will help us

The O—H bonds in the water molecule are covalent bonds formed by electron sharing between the oxygen and hydrogen atoms. However, the electrons of the bond are not shared equally between these atoms. For reasons we will discuss in later chapters, oxygen has a greater attraction for electrons than does hydrogen. If the electrons were shared equally between the two atoms, both would be electrically neutral because, on average, the number of electrons around each would equal the number of protons in that nucleus. Because the oxygen atom has a greater attraction for electrons, the shared electrons tend to spend more time close to the oxygen than to either of the hydrogens. Thus the oxygen atom gains a slight excess of negative charge, and the hydrogen atoms become slightly positive. Because of this unequal charge distribution, water is said to be a polar molecule. This polarity gives water its great ability to dissolve compounds.

DEMONSTRATION

Lights Out!

Materials Saturated $Ba(OH)_2$, 3 *M* H_2SO_4, beaker, stirring plate and stir bar or student volunteer stirrer, conductivity tester

Preparation Make saturated barium hydroxide by dissolving the maximum amount possible in distilled water. Decant the solution from the solid for use.

Presentation Place 25 mL distilled water and one drop of 3 *M* sulfuric acid into the beaker. Add the stirring bar and place the beaker on the stir plate. Place the conductivity tester in the beaker, out of the way of the spinning stir bar. Add the barium hydroxide solution dropwise, observing the light. Continue adding barium hydroxide until the light goes out. Stop and discuss this result with the students. End the demonstration by asking for a prediction of what will happen if more barium hydroxide is added to the solution. Add more barium hydroxide and discuss the results with the students.

Teaching Notes This demonstration provides a practical connection between the macroscopic and microscopic worlds. Draw the solutions before the reaction on a molecular level. Discuss how conductivity tells us that ions are present in the solution. Proceed with the demonstration until the light goes out. Now discuss on a molecular level what is present in the beaker (water and solid $BaSO_4$) and explain how this composition differs from what was present before the reaction. Finally, after the student predictions, explain that the light comes on again as a result of the addition of more barium and hydroxide ions that do not form a precipitate, as all of the sulfate has been consumed.

TEACHING TIPS

- Review how ionic compounds are formed. Remind students that both positive and negative ions are needed to form a compound, and that compounds must be electrically neutral.
- To help students decide which products can form, list all possible combinations and then begin eliminating the unlikely ones.
- Students sometimes have trouble remembering to eliminate the starting reactants as possible products. Use molecular-level drawings to show why these substances cannot be products in the reaction.
- It is obvious that you should focus on the precipitate when discussing precipitation reactions. However, it is just as important to spend an equal amount of time discussing what are in the two solutions before they are mixed together. Students must understand the nature of the solutions to be able to appreciate the reaction.

decide. We know that a *solid compound must have a zero net charge.* This means that the product of our reaction must contain *both anions and cations* (negative and positive ions). For example, K^+ and Ba^{2+} could not combine to form the solid because such a solid would have a positive charge. Similarly, CrO_4^{2-} and NO_3^- could not combine to form a solid because that solid would have a negative charge.

Something else that will help us is an observation that chemists have made by examining many compounds: *most ionic materials contain only two types of ions*—one type of cation and one type of anion. This idea is illustrated by the following compounds (among many others):

Compound	Cation	Anion
$NaCl$	Na^+	Cl^-
KOH	K^+	OH^-
Na_2SO_4	Na^+	SO_4^{2-}
NH_4Cl	NH_4^+	Cl^-
Na_2CO_3	Na^+	CO_3^{2-}

All the possible combinations of a cation and an anion to form uncharged compounds from among the ions K^+, CrO_4^{2-}, Ba^{2+}, and NO_3^- are shown below:

	NO_3^-	CrO_4^{2-}
K^+	KNO_3	K_2CrO_4
Ba^{2+}	$Ba(NO_3)_2$	$BaCrO_4$

So the compounds that *might* make up the solid are

K_2CrO_4 $BaCrO_4$
KNO_3 $Ba(NO_3)_2$

Which of these possibilities is most likely to represent the yellow solid? We know it's not K_2CrO_4 or $Ba(NO_3)_2$; these are the reactants. They were present (dissolved) in the separate solutions that were mixed initially. The only real possibilities are KNO_3 and $BaCrO_4$. To decide which of these is more likely to represent the yellow solid, we need more facts. An experienced chemist, for example, knows that KNO_3 is a white solid. On the other hand, the CrO_4^{2-} ion is yellow. Therefore, the yellow solid most likely is $BaCrO_4$.

We have determined that one product of the reaction between $K_2CrO_4(aq)$ and $Ba(NO_3)_2(aq)$ is $BaCrO_4(s)$, but what happened to the K^+ and NO_3^- ions? The answer is that these ions are left dissolved in the solution. That is, KNO_3 does not form a solid when the K^+ and NO_3^- ions are present in water. In other words, if we took the white solid $KNO_3(s)$ and put it in water, it would totally dissolve (the white solid would "disappear," yielding a colorless solution). So when we mix $K_2CrO_4(aq)$ and $Ba(NO_3)_2(aq)$, $BaCrO_4(s)$ forms but KNO_3 is left behind in solution [we write it as $KNO_3(aq)$]. (If we poured the mixture through a filter to remove the solid $BaCrO_4$ and then evaporated all of the water, we would obtain the white solid KNO_3.)

After all this thinking, we can finally write the unbalanced equation for the precipitation reaction:

$$K_2CrO_4(aq) + Ba(NO_3)_2(aq) \rightarrow BaCrO_4(s) + KNO_3(aq)$$

We can represent this reaction in pictures as follows:

PowerLecture Video: Reaction: Lead Chromate Precipitation

Note that the K^+ and NO_3^- ions are not involved in the chemical change. They remain dispersed in the water before and after the reaction.

Using Solubility Rules

In the example considered above we were finally able to identify the products of the reaction by using two types of chemical knowledge:

1. Knowledge of facts
2. Knowledge of concepts

For example, knowing the colors of the various compounds proved very helpful. This represents factual knowledge. Awareness of the concept that solids always have a net charge of zero was also essential. These two kinds of knowledge allowed us to make a good guess about the identity of the solid that formed. As you continue to study chemistry, you will see that a balance of factual and conceptual knowledge is always required. You must both *memorize* important facts and *understand* crucial concepts to succeed.

Solids must contain both anions and cations in the relative numbers necessary to produce zero net charge.

In the present case we are dealing with a reaction in which an ionic solid forms—that is, a process in which ions that are dissolved in water combine to give a solid. We know that for a solid to form, both positive and negative ions must be present in relative numbers that give zero net charge. However, oppositely charged ions in water do not always react to form a solid, as we have seen for K^+ and NO_3^-. In addition, Na^+ and Cl^- can coexist in water in very large numbers with no formation of solid NaCl. In other words, when solid NaCl (common salt) is placed in water, it dissolves—the white solid "disappears" as the Na^+ and Cl^- ions are dispersed throughout the water. (You probably have observed this phenomenon in preparing salt water to cook food.) The following two statements, then, are really saying the same thing.

1. Solid NaCl is very soluble in water.
2. Solid NaCl does not form when one solution containing Na^+ is mixed with another solution containing Cl^-.

To predict whether a given pair of dissolved ions will form a solid when mixed, we must know some facts about the solubilities of various types of ionic compounds. In this text we will use the term **soluble solid** to mean a solid that readily dissolves in water; the solid "disappears" as the ions are dispersed in the water. The terms **insoluble solid** and **slightly soluble solid** are taken to mean the same thing: a solid where such a tiny amount dissolves in water that it is undetectable with the naked eye. The solubility information about common solids that is summarized in Table 7.1 is based on observations of the behavior of many compounds. This is factual knowledge that you will need to predict what will happen in chemical reactions where a solid might form. This information is summarized in Figure 7.3.

Table 7.1 General Rules for Solubility of Ionic Compounds (Salts) in Water at 25 °C

1. Most nitrate (NO_3^-) salts are soluble.
2. Most salts of Na^+, K^+, and NH_4^+ are soluble.
3. Most chloride salts are soluble. Notable exceptions are $AgCl$, $PbCl_2$, and Hg_2Cl_2.
4. Most sulfate salts are soluble. Notable exceptions are $BaSO_4$, $PbSO_4$, and $CaSO_4$.
5. Most hydroxide compounds are only slightly soluble.* The important exceptions are $NaOH$ and KOH. $Ba(OH)_2$ and $Ca(OH)_2$ are only moderately soluble.
6. Most sulfide (S^{2-}), carbonate (CO_3^{2-}), and phosphate (PO_4^{3-}) salts are only slightly soluble.*

*The terms *insoluble* and *slightly soluble* really mean the same thing: such a tiny amount dissolves that it is not possible to detect it with the naked eye.

go Chemistry **Module 5: Predicting the Water Solubility of Common Ionic Compounds** covers concepts in this section.

Notice that in Table 7.1 and Figure 7.3 the term *salt* is used to mean *ionic compound*. Many chemists use the terms *salt* and *ionic compound* interchangeably. In Example 7.1, we will illustrate how to use the solubility rules to predict the products of reactions among ions.

EXAMPLE 7.1

Identifying Precipitates in Reactions Where a Solid Forms

$AgNO_3$ is usually called silver nitrate rather than silver(I) nitrate because silver forms only Ag^+.

When an aqueous solution of silver nitrate is added to an aqueous solution of potassium chloride, a white solid forms. Identify the white solid and write the balanced equation for the reaction that occurs.

SOLUTION

First let's use the description of the reaction to represent what we know:

$$AgNO_3(aq) + KCl(aq) \rightarrow \text{White solid}$$

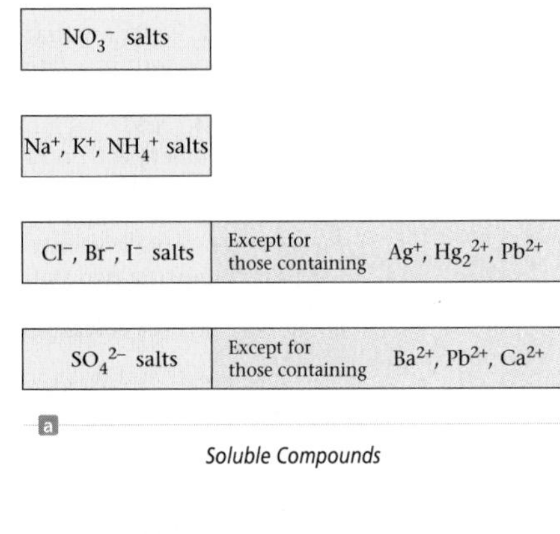

Figure 7.3 Solubilities of common compounds.

PowerLecture Video: Reaction: Iron(III) + NaOH

TEACHING TIPS

- Use the PowerPoint and transparency for Figure 7.3 to help the students decide the identities of precipitates.
- Compounds we call *slightly soluble* are virtually insoluble in water and most of the compound remains a solid in water.
- Use at least one example in class in which two solutions are mixed and no solid forms (for example, Na_2SO_4 and KCl). Students should not think that a solid *always* forms whenever two solutions of ionic compounds are mixed.

PowerLecture Video: Reaction: $AgNO_3$ + NaCl

MISCONCEPTION

Students often conserve subscripts in precipitation reactions. Emphasizing what the solutions look like at a molecular level, and that the products must be electrically neutral, helps students understand why subscripts need not be conserved.

Additional Examples

Example 7.1

1. When an aqueous solution of barium nitrate is added to an aqueous solution of sodium sulfate, a white solid forms. Identify the white solid and write the balanced equation for the reaction that occurs.

   $Ba(NO_3)_2(aq) + Na_2SO_4(aq) \rightarrow BaSO_4(s) + 2NaNO_3(aq)$. Students deduce the identity of the solid by knowing that a solid forms (this is given in the problem) and that sodium nitrate is not the solid (from the solubility rules).

2. When an aqueous solution of lead(II) nitrate is added to an aqueous solution of potassium iodide, a yellow solid forms. Identify the yellow solid and write the balanced equation for the reaction that occurs.

   $Pb(NO_3)_2(aq) + 2KI(aq) \rightarrow PbI_2(s) + 2KNO_3(aq)$. Students deduce the identity of the solid by knowing that a solid forms (this is given in the problem) and that potassium nitrate is not the solid (from the solubility rules).

PowerLecture Simulation: Solubility of Ionic Compounds

Remember, try to determine the essential facts from the words and represent these facts by symbols or diagrams. To answer the main question (What is the white solid?), we must establish what ions are present in the mixed solution. That is, we must know what the reactants are really like. Remember that *when ionic substances dissolve in water, the ions separate.* So we can write the equation

$$\underbrace{Ag^+(aq) + NO_3^-(aq)}_{\text{Ions in } AgNO_3(aq)} + \underbrace{K^+(aq) + Cl^-(aq)}_{\text{Ions in } KCl(aq)} \rightarrow \text{Products}$$

or using pictures

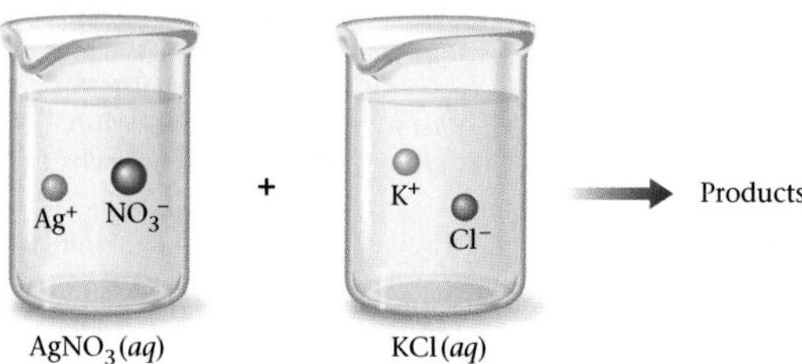

to represent the ions present in the mixed solution before any reaction occurs. In summary:

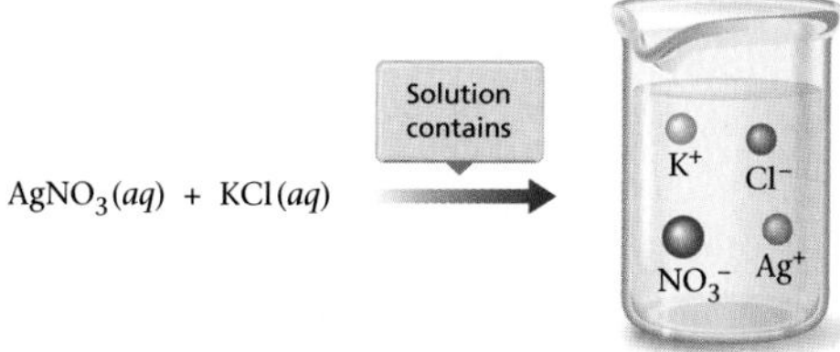

	NO_3^-	Cl^-
Ag^+	$AgNO_3$	$AgCl$
K^+	KNO_3	KCl

Now we will consider what solid *might* form from this collection of ions. Because the solid must contain both positive and negative ions, the possible compounds that can be assembled from this collection of ions are

$AgNO_3$	$AgCl$
KNO_3	KCl

$AgNO_3$ and KCl are the substances already dissolved in the reactant solutions, so we know that they do not represent the white solid product. We are left with two possibilities:

AgCl
KNO_3

7.2 Reactions in Which a Solid Forms 173

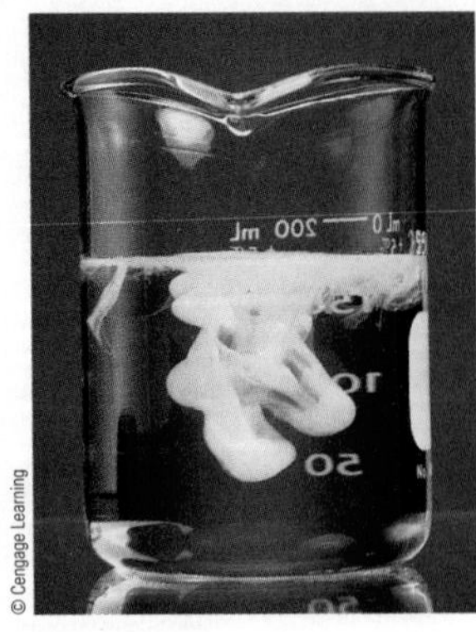

Figure 7.4
Precipitation of silver chloride occurs when solutions of silver nitrate and potassium chloride are mixed. The K^+ and NO_3^- ions remain in solution.

Another way to obtain these two possibilities is by *ion interchange*. This means that in the reaction of $AgNO_3(aq)$ and $KCl(aq)$, we take the cation from one reactant and combine it with the anion of the other reactant.

$$Ag^+ + NO_3^- + K^+ + Cl^- \rightarrow \text{Products}$$

Possible solid products

Ion interchange also leads to the following possible solids:

AgCl or KNO_3

To decide whether AgCl or KNO_3 is the white solid, we need the solubility rules (Table 7.1). Rule 2 states that most salts containing K^+ are soluble in water. Rule 1 says that most nitrate salts (those containing NO_3^-) are soluble. So the salt KNO_3 is water-soluble. That is, when K^+ and NO_3^- are mixed in water, a solid (KNO_3) does *not* form.

On the other hand, Rule 3 states that although most chloride salts (salts that contain Cl^-) are soluble, AgCl is an exception. That is, AgCl(*s*) is insoluble in water. Thus the white solid must be AgCl. Now we can write

$$AgNO_3(aq) + KCl(aq) \rightarrow AgCl(s) + ?$$

What is the other product?

To form AgCl(*s*), we have used the Ag^+ and Cl^- ions:

$$Ag^+(aq) + NO_3^-(aq) + K^+(aq) + Cl^-(aq) \rightarrow AgCl(s)$$

This leaves the K^+ and NO_3^- ions. What do they do? Nothing. Because KNO_3 is very soluble in water (Rules 1 and 2), the K^+ and NO_3^- ions remain separate in the water; the KNO_3 remains dissolved and we represent it as $KNO_3(aq)$. We can now write the full equation:

$$AgNO_3(aq) + KCl(aq) \rightarrow AgCl(s) + KNO_3(aq)$$

Figure 7.4 shows the precipitation of AgCl(*s*) that occurs when this reaction takes place. In graphic form, the reaction is

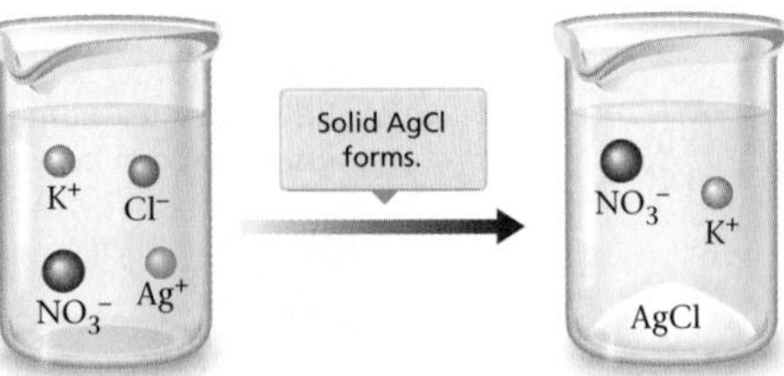

■

PowerLecture Video: Precipitation Reactions

The following strategy is useful for predicting what will occur when two solutions containing dissolved salts are mixed.

How to Predict Precipitates When Solutions of Two Ionic Compounds Are Mixed

Step 1 Write the reactants as they actually exist before any reaction occurs. Remember that when a salt dissolves, its ions separate.

Step 2 Consider the various solids that could form. To do this, simply *exchange the anions* of the added salts.

Step 3 Use the solubility rules (Table 7.1) to decide whether a solid forms and, if so, to predict the identity of the solid.

EXAMPLE 7.2 Using Solubility Rules to Predict the Products of Reactions

Using the solubility rules in Table 7.1, predict what will happen when the following solutions are mixed. Write the balanced equation for any reaction that occurs.

a. $KNO_3(aq)$ and $BaCl_2(aq)$

b. $Na_2SO_4(aq)$ and $Pb(NO_3)_2(aq)$

c. $KOH(aq)$ and $Fe(NO_3)_3(aq)$

SOLUTION (a)

Step 1 $KNO_3(aq)$ represents an aqueous solution obtained by dissolving solid KNO_3 in water to give the ions $K^+(aq)$ and $NO_3^-(aq)$. Likewise, $BaCl_2(aq)$ is a solution formed by dissolving solid $BaCl_2$ in water to produce $Ba^{2+}(aq)$ and $Cl^-(aq)$. When these two solutions are mixed, the following ions will be present:

$$\underbrace{K^+,\quad NO_3^-,}_{\text{From } KNO_3(aq)}\quad \underbrace{Ba^{2+},\quad Cl^-}_{\text{From } BaCl_2(aq)}$$

Step 2 To get the possible products, we exchange the anions.

$$K^+ \quad NO_3^- \quad Ba^{2+} \quad Cl^-$$

This yields the possibilities KCl and $Ba(NO_3)_2$. These are the solids that *might* form. Notice that two NO_3^- ions are needed to balance the 2+ charge on Ba^{2+}.

Step 3 The rules listed in Table 7.1 indicate that both KCl and $Ba(NO_3)_2$ are soluble in water. So no precipitate forms when $KNO_3(aq)$ and $BaCl_2(aq)$ are mixed. All of the ions remain dissolved in the solution. This means that no reaction takes place. That is, no chemical change occurs.

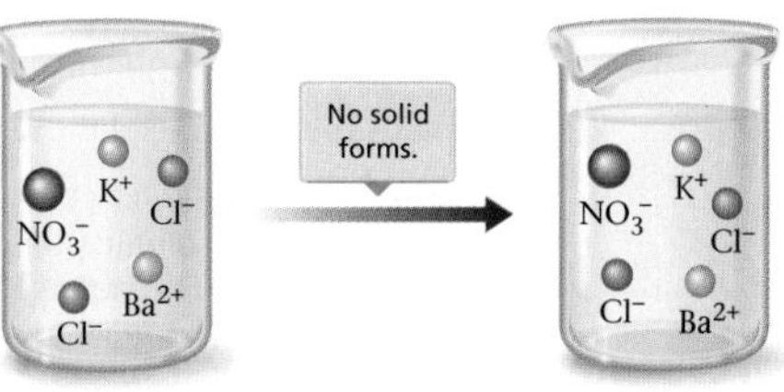

Additional Examples

Example 7.2

Using the solubility rules in Table 7.1, predict what will happen when the following solutions are mixed. Write the balanced equation for any reaction that occurs.

1. $Ba(NO_3)_2(aq) + K_3PO_4(aq)$

   $3Ba(NO_3)_2(aq) + 2K_3PO_4(aq) \rightarrow Ba_3(PO_4)_2(s) + 6KNO_3(aq)$

2. $Na_2SO_4(aq) + KCl(aq)$

   no reaction

SOLUTION (b)

Step 1 The following ions are present in the mixed solution before any reaction occurs:

$$Na^+, \quad SO_4^{2-}, \quad Pb^{2+}, \quad NO_3^-$$

From $Na_2SO_4(aq)$ — From $Pb(NO_3)_2(aq)$

Step 2 Exchanging anions

$$Na^+ \quad SO_4^{2-} \quad Pb^{2+} \quad NO_3^-$$

yields the *possible* solid products $PbSO_4$ and $NaNO_3$.

Step 3 Using Table 7.1, we see that $NaNO_3$ is soluble in water (Rules 1 and 2) but that $PbSO_4$ is only slightly soluble (Rule 4). Thus, when these solutions are mixed, solid $PbSO_4$ forms. The balanced reaction is

$$Na_2SO_4(aq) + Pb(NO_3)_2(aq) \rightarrow PbSO_4(s) + 2NaNO_3(aq)$$

Remains dissolved

which can be represented as

SOLUTION (c)

Step 1 The ions present in the mixed solution before any reaction occurs are

$$K^+, \quad OH^-, \quad Fe^{3+}, \quad NO_3^-$$

From $KOH(aq)$ — From $Fe(NO_3)_3(aq)$

Step 2 Exchanging anions

$$K^+ \quad OH^- \quad Fe^{3+} \quad NO_3^-$$

yields the possible solid products KNO_3 and $Fe(OH)_3$.

Step 3 Rules 1 and 2 (Table 7.1) state that KNO_3 is soluble, whereas $Fe(OH)_3$ is only slightly soluble (Rule 5). Thus, when these solutions are mixed, solid $Fe(OH)_3$ forms. The balanced equation for the reaction is

$$3KOH(aq) + Fe(NO_3)_3(aq) \rightarrow Fe(OH)_3(s) + 3KNO_3(aq)$$

176 Chapter 7 Reactions in Aqueous Solutions

which can be represented as

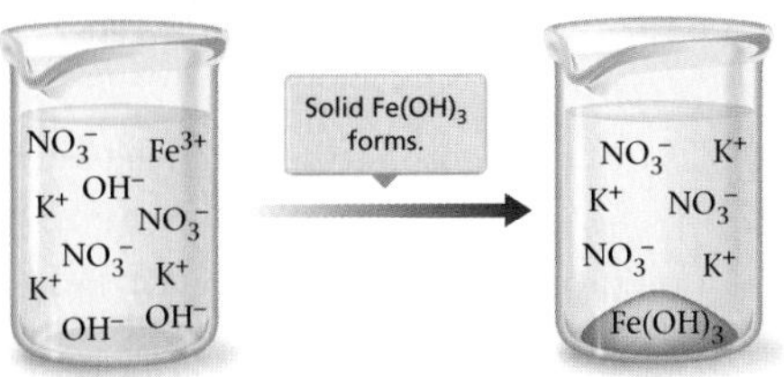

Self-Check **EXERCISE 7.1** Predict whether a solid will form when the following pairs of solutions are mixed. If so, identify the solid and write the balanced equation for the reaction.

a. $Ba(NO_3)_2(aq)$ and $NaCl(aq)$

b. $Na_2S(aq)$ and $Cu(NO_3)_2(aq)$

c. $NH_4Cl(aq)$ and $Pb(NO_3)_2(aq)$

See Problems 7.17 and 7.18. ■

7.3 Describing Reactions in Aqueous Solutions

OBJECTIVE: To learn to describe reactions in solutions by writing molecular, complete ionic, and net ionic equations.

Much important chemistry, including virtually all of the reactions that make life possible, occurs in aqueous solutions. We will now consider the types of equations used to represent reactions that occur in water. For example, as we saw earlier, when we mix aqueous potassium chromate with aqueous barium nitrate, a reaction occurs to form solid barium chromate and dissolved potassium nitrate. One way to represent this reaction is by the equation

$$K_2CrO_4(aq) + Ba(NO_3)_2(aq) \rightarrow BaCrO_4(s) + 2KNO_3(aq)$$

This is called the **molecular equation** for the reaction; it shows the complete formulas of all reactants and products. However, although this equation shows the reactants and products of the reaction, it does not give a very clear picture of what actually occurs in solution. As we have seen, aqueous solutions of potassium chromate, barium nitrate, and potassium nitrate contain the individual ions, not molecules as is implied by the molecular equation. Thus the **complete ionic equation,**

$$\underbrace{2K^+(aq) + CrO_4^{2-}(aq)}_{\text{Ions from } K_2CrO_4} + \underbrace{Ba^{2+}(aq) + 2NO_3^-(aq)}_{\text{Ions from } Ba(NO_3)_2} \rightarrow BaCrO_4(s) + 2K^+(aq) + 2NO_3^-(aq)$$

A strong electrolyte is a substance that completely breaks apart into ions when dissolved in water. The resulting solution readily conducts an electric current.

better represents the actual forms of the reactants and products in solution. *In a complete ionic equation, all substances that are strong electrolytes are represented as ions.* Notice that $BaCrO_4$ is not written as the separate ions, because it is present as a solid; it is not dissolved.

Self Check

Answers to Self-Check Exercise 7.1

a. Exchanging the anions gives the possible solid products $BaCl_2$ and $NaNO_3$. Using Table 7.1, we see that both substances are very soluble (Rules 1, 2, and 3). Thus no solid forms.

b. $Na_2S(aq) + Cu(NO_3)_2(aq) \rightarrow CuS(s) + 2NaNO_3(aq)$

c. $2NH_4Cl(aq) + Pb(NO_3)_2(aq) \rightarrow PbCl_2(s) + 2NH_4NO_3(aq)$

Section 7.3

TEACHING TIPS

- Drawing molecular-level pictures when first discussing reactions in aqueous solutions is helpful for students.
- Molecular equations contain the complete formulas for all reactants and products. Complete ionic equations provide a window into the microscopic world. These equations show substances as they are in solution or at the molecular level.
- Remind students that a new product is often a solid and must not be written as ions if it is insoluble.
- Remind students that charges must be balanced in both ionic and net ionic equations.

Test Bank: 15–17, 20–21, 24–26, 30–32

TEACHING SUPPORT

ACTIVITY

Materials Each student/group will need water samples and access to a solution of silver nitrate (~0.1 *M*). Empty film canisters work well for bringing in water samples (and drugstores will often give these to you in bulk).

Purpose The purpose is to help students see that most water samples contain chloride ions. In addition, students will see an example of a precipitation reaction and write a net ionic equation.

Discussion Most likely all of the water samples students bring in will contain chloride ions to some extent (even bottled drinking water, which may surprise the students). The distilled water from the school should be free of chloride ions. Before adding the silver nitrate, have students predict which samples will be high in chloride ions and which will be low. Then have them compare their predictions to the actual results.

The net ionic equation in all cases is $Ag^+(aq) + Cl^-(aq) \rightarrow AgCl(s)$.

go Chemistry Module 6: Writing Net Ionic Equations covers concepts in this section.

The complete ionic equation reveals that only some of the ions participate in the reaction. Notice that the K^+ and NO_3^- ions are present in solution both before and after the reaction. Ions such as these, which do not participate directly in a reaction in solution, are called **spectator ions.** The ions that participate in this reaction are the Ba^{2+} and CrO_4^{2-} ions, which combine to form solid $BaCrO_4$:

$$Ba^{2+}(aq) + CrO_4^{2-}(aq) \rightarrow BaCrO_4(s)$$

The net ionic equation includes only those components that undergo a change in the reaction.

This equation, called the **net ionic equation,** includes only those components that are directly involved in the reaction. Chemists usually write the net ionic equation for a reaction in solution, because it gives the actual forms of the reactants and products and includes only the species that undergo a change.

Types of Equations for Reactions in Aqueous Solutions

Three types of equations are used to describe reactions in solutions.

1. The *molecular equation* shows the overall reaction but not necessarily the actual forms of the reactants and products in solution.
2. The *complete ionic equation* represents all reactants and products that are strong electrolytes as ions. All reactants and products are included.
3. The *net ionic equation* includes only those components that undergo a change. Spectator ions are not included.

To make sure these ideas are clear, we will do another example. In Example 7.2 we considered the reaction between aqueous solutions of lead nitrate and sodium sulfate. The molecular equation for this reaction is

$$Pb(NO_3)_2(aq) + Na_2SO_4(aq) \rightarrow PbSO_4(s) + 2NaNO_3(aq)$$

Because any ionic compound that is dissolved in water is present as the separated ions, we can write the complete ionic equation as follows:

$$Pb^{2+}(aq) + 2NO_3^-(aq) + 2Na^+(aq) + SO_4^{2-}(aq) \rightarrow PbSO_4(s) + 2Na^+(aq) + 2NO_3^-(aq)$$

The $PbSO_4$ is not written as separate ions because it is present as a solid. The ions that take part in the chemical change are the Pb^{2+} and the SO_4^{2-} ions, which combine to form solid $PbSO_4$. Thus the net ionic equation is

$$Pb^{2+}(aq) + SO_4^{2-}(aq) \rightarrow PbSO_4(s)$$

The Na^+ and NO_3^- ions do not undergo any chemical change; they are spectator ions.

EXAMPLE 7.3 Writing Equations for Reactions

For each of the following reactions, write the molecular equation, the complete ionic equation, and the net ionic equation.

a. Aqueous sodium chloride is added to aqueous silver nitrate to form solid silver chloride plus aqueous sodium nitrate.

b. Aqueous potassium hydroxide is mixed with aqueous iron(III) nitrate to form solid iron(III) hydroxide and aqueous potassium nitrate.

Because silver is present as Ag^+ in all of its common ionic compounds, we usually delete the (I) when naming silver compounds.

Additional Examples

Example 7.3

For each of the following reactions, write the balanced molecular equation, the balanced complete ionic equation, and the balanced net ionic equation.

1. Aqueous silver nitrate is added to aqueous sodium chromate to form solid silver chromate and aqueous sodium nitrate.

   molecular: $2AgNO_3(aq) + Na_2CrO_4(aq) \rightarrow Ag_2CrO_4(s) + 2NaNO_3(aq)$;

   complete ionic: $2Ag^+(aq) + 2NO_3^-(aq) + 2Na^+(aq) + CrO_4^{2-}(aq) \rightarrow Ag_2CrO_4(s) + 2Na^+(aq) + 2NO_3^-(aq)$;

   net ionic: $2Ag^+(aq) + CrO_4^{2-}(aq) \rightarrow Ag_2CrO_4(s)$

2. Aqueous nickel(II) nitrate is added to aqueous potassium carbonate to form solid nickel(II) carbonate and aqueous potassium nitrate.

   molecular: $Ni(NO_3)_2(aq) + K_2CO_3(aq) \rightarrow NiCO_3(s) + 2KNO_3(aq)$;

   complete ionic: $Ni^{2+}(aq) + 2NO_3^-(aq) + 2K^+(aq) + CO_3^{2-}(aq) \rightarrow NiCO_3(s) + 2K^+(aq) + 2NO_3^-(aq)$;

   net ionic: $Ni^{2+}(aq) + CO_3^{2-}(aq) \rightarrow NiCO_3(s)$

TEACHING SUPPORT

DEMONSTRATION

Colorful Precipitates

Materials 12 test tubes (18 × 150 mm), test tube rack, nickel(II) chloride, potassium iodide, sodium sulfate, sodium nitrate, sodium carbonate, lead(II) nitrate, barium chloride, copper(II) chloride, potassium chloride, silver nitrate, ammonium thiocyanate.

Preparation Prepare dilute solutions of each of the listed compounds by adding 1 teaspoon of each to 500 mL of distilled water. Label the test tubes as follows:

1. $AgNO_3$
2. NH_4SCN
3. $NiCl_2$
4. Na_2CO_3
5. $Pb(NO_3)_2$
6. KI
7. $NaNO_3$
8. KCl
9. $BaCl_2$
10. Na_2SO_4
11. $CuCl_2$
12. Na_2CO_3

SOLUTION

a. *Molecular equation:*

$$NaCl(aq) + AgNO_3(aq) \rightarrow AgCl(s) + NaNO_3(aq)$$

Complete ionic equation:

$$Na^+(aq) + Cl^-(aq) + Ag^+(aq) + NO_3^-(aq) \rightarrow AgCl(s) + Na^+(aq) + NO_3^-(aq)$$

Net ionic equation:

$$Cl^-(aq) + Ag^+(aq) \rightarrow AgCl(s)$$

b. *Molecular equation:*

$$3KOH(aq) + Fe(NO_3)_3(aq) \rightarrow Fe(OH)_3(s) + 3KNO_3(aq)$$

Complete ionic equation:

$$3K^+(aq) + 3OH^-(aq) + Fe^{3+}(aq) + 3NO_3^-(aq) \rightarrow Fe(OH)_3(s) + 3K^+(aq) + 3NO_3^-(aq)$$

Net ionic equation:

$$3OH^-(aq) + Fe^{3+}(aq) \rightarrow Fe(OH)_3(s)$$

Self-Check **EXERCISE 7.2** For each of the following reactions, write the molecular equation, the complete ionic equation, and the net ionic equation.

a. Aqueous sodium sulfide is mixed with aqueous copper(II) nitrate to produce solid copper(II) sulfide and aqueous sodium nitrate.

b. Aqueous ammonium chloride and aqueous lead(II) nitrate react to form solid lead(II) chloride and aqueous ammonium nitrate.

See Problems 7.25 through 7.30. ■

7.4 Reactions That Form Water: Acids and Bases

OBJECTIVE: To learn the key characteristics of the reactions between strong acids and strong bases.

Don't taste chemicals!

In this section we encounter two very important classes of compounds: acids and bases. Acids were first associated with the sour taste of citrus fruits. In fact, the word *acid* comes from the Latin word *acidus,* which means "sour." Vinegar tastes sour because it is a dilute solution of acetic acid; citric acid is responsible for the sour taste of a lemon. Bases, sometimes called *alkalis,* are characterized by their bitter taste and slippery feel, like wet soap. Most commercial preparations for unclogging drains are highly basic.

Acids have been known for hundreds of years. For example, the *mineral acids* sulfuric acid, H_2SO_4, and nitric acid, HNO_3, so named because they were originally obtained by the treatment of minerals, were discovered around 1300. However, it was not until the late 1800s that the essential nature of acids was discovered by Svante Arrhenius, then a Swedish graduate student in physics.

Fill each test tube one-third full of solution.

Presentation Pour the contents of test tube 1 into test tube 2. Ask students to make observations, write an ionic equation for the reaction, and name the precipitate. Repeat for the remaining test tubes, pairing 3 and 4, 5 and 6, 7 and 8, 9 and 10, and 11 and 12.

Teaching Notes Students can write the molecular, complete ionic, and net ionic equations for each reaction as you perform the demonstration.

Silver nitrate and ammonium thiocyanate produce a brown precipitate, silver thiocyanate (all ions are aqueous):

$$Ag^+ + NO_3^- + NH_4^+ + SCN^- \rightarrow AgSCN(s) + NH_4^+ + NO_3^-$$

(Ions such as K^+ and NO_3^- that do not enter the reaction are called spectator ions.)

Self Check

Answers to Self-Check Exercise 7.2

a. *Molecular equation:*

$Na_2S(aq) + Cu(NO_3)_2(aq) \rightarrow CuS(s) + 2NaNO_3(aq)$

Complete ionic equation:

$2Na^+(aq) + S^{2-}(aq) + Cu^{2+}(aq) + 2NO_3^-(aq) \rightarrow CuS(s) + 2Na^+(aq) + 2NO_3^-(aq)$

Net ionic equation:

$S^{2-}(aq) + Cu^{2+}(aq) \rightarrow CuS(s)$

b. *Molecular equation:*

$2NH_4Cl(aq) + Pb(NO_3)_2(aq) \rightarrow PbCl_2(s) + 2NH_4NO_3(aq)$

Complete ionic equation:

$2NH_4^+(aq) + 2Cl^-(aq) + Pb^{2+}(aq) + 2NO_3^-(aq) \rightarrow PbCl_2(s) + 2NH_4^+(aq) + 2NO_3^-(aq)$

Net ionic equation:

$2Cl^-(aq) + Pb^{2+}(aq) \rightarrow PbCl_2(s)$

Test Bank: 18, 27–28, 33

Section 7.4

LABORATORY EXPERIMENT

A relevant laboratory experiment for this section is Experiment 11, Properties and Reactions of Acids and Bases, from *Introductory Chemistry in the Laboratory* by James Hall.

DEMONSTRATION

Use the conductivity apparatus to show that acids and bases in solution conduct electricity. You may also want to show students litmus paper and use it to test each solution. Be sure to test distilled water to show its lack of conductivity.

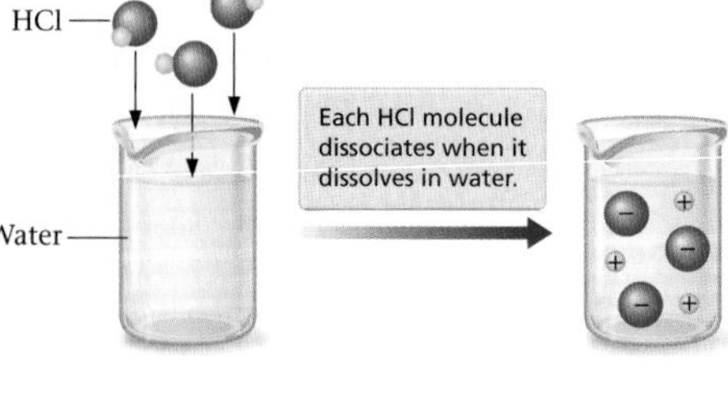
HCl
Water
Each HCl molecule dissociates when it dissolves in water.

Figure 7.5 When gaseous HCl is dissolved in water, each molecule dissociates to produce H^+ and Cl^- ions. That is, HCl behaves as a strong electrolyte.

The Nobel Prize in chemistry was awarded to Arrhenius in 1903 for his studies of solution conductivity.

Arrhenius, who was trying to discover why only certain solutions could conduct an electric current, found that conductivity arose from the presence of ions. In his studies of solutions, Arrhenius observed that when the substances HCl, HNO_3, and H_2SO_4 were dissolved in water, they behaved as strong electrolytes. He suggested that this was the result of ionization reactions in water.

$$HCl \xrightarrow{H_2O} H^+(aq) + Cl^-(aq)$$
$$HNO_3 \xrightarrow{H_2O} H^+(aq) + NO_3^-(aq)$$
$$H_2SO_4 \xrightarrow{H_2O} H^+(aq) + HSO_4^-(aq)$$

Arrhenius proposed that an **acid** *is a substance that produces H^+ ions (protons) when it is dissolved in water.*

Studies show that when HCl, HNO_3, and H_2SO_4 are placed in water, *virtually every molecule* dissociates to give ions. This means that when 100 molecules of HCl are dissolved in water, 100 H^+ ions and 100 Cl^- ions are produced. Virtually no HCl molecules exist in aqueous solution (see Figure 7.5). Because these substances are strong electrolytes that produce H^+ ions, they are called **strong acids.**

The Arrhenius definition of an acid: a substance that produces H^+ ions in aqueous solution.

Arrhenius also found that *aqueous solutions that exhibit basic behavior* always contain hydroxide ions. He defined a **base** as a *substance that produces hydroxide ions (OH^-) in water.* The base most commonly used in the chemical laboratory is sodium hydroxide, NaOH, which contains Na^+ and OH^- ions and is very soluble in water. Sodium hydroxide, like all ionic substances, produces separated cations and anions when it is dissolved in water.

$$NaOH(s) \xrightarrow{H_2O} Na^+(aq) + OH^-(aq)$$

Stephen P. Parker/Photo Researchers, Inc.

The marsh marigold is a beautiful but poisonous plant. Its toxicity results partly from the presence of erucic acid.

Although dissolved sodium hydroxide is usually represented as NaOH(*aq*), you should remember that the solution really contains separated Na^+ and OH^- ions. In fact, for every 100 units of NaOH dissolved in water, 100 Na^+ and 100 OH^- ions are produced.

Potassium hydroxide (KOH) has properties markedly similar to those of sodium hydroxide. It is very soluble in water and produces separated ions.

Lecture Demonstration: 4.7

$$KOH(s) \xrightarrow{H_2O} K^+(aq) + OH^-(aq)$$

Because these hydroxide compounds are strong electrolytes that contain OH^- ions, they are called **strong bases.**

When strong acids and strong bases (hydroxides) are mixed, the fundamental chemical change that always occurs is that *H^+ ions react with OH^- ions to form water.*

$$H^+(aq) + OH^-(aq) \rightarrow H_2O(l)$$

Water is a very stable compound, as evidenced by the abundance of it on the earth's surface. Therefore, when substances that can form water are

Nickel chloride and sodium carbonate produce a pale blue precipitate, nickel carbonate:

$$Ni^{2+} + 2Cl^- + 2Na^+ + CO_3^{2-} \rightarrow NiCO_3(s) + 2Cl^- + 2Na^+$$

Lead nitrate and potassium iodide produce a yellow precipitate, lead iodide:

$$Pb^{2+} + 2NO_3^- + 2K^+ + 2I^- \rightarrow PbI_2(s) + 2NO_3^- + 2K^+$$

Sodium nitrate and potassium chloride produce no reaction:

$$Na^+ + NO_3^- + K^+ + Cl^- \rightarrow \text{no reaction}$$

Barium chloride and sodium sulfate produce a white precipitate, barium sulfate:

$$Ba^{2+} + 2Cl^- + 2Na^+ + SO_4^{2-} \rightarrow BaSO_4(s) + 2Cl^- + 2Na^+$$

Copper(II) chloride and sodium carbonate produce a pale blue precipitate, copper(II) carbonate:

$$Cu^{2+} + 2Cl^- + 2Na^+ + CO_3^{2-} \rightarrow CuCO_3(s) + 2Cl^- + 2Na^+$$

mixed, there is a strong tendency for the reaction to occur. In particular, the hydroxide ion OH^- has a high affinity for H^+ ions, because water is produced in the reaction between these ions.

Hydrochloric acid is an aqueous solution that contains dissolved hydrogen chloride. It is a strong electrolyte.

The tendency to form water is the second of the driving forces for reactions that we mentioned in Section 7.1. Any compound that produces OH^- ions in water reacts vigorously with any compound that can furnish H^+ ions to form H_2O. For example, the reaction between hydrochloric acid and aqueous sodium hydroxide is represented by the following molecular equation:

$$HCl(aq) + NaOH(aq) \rightarrow H_2O(l) + NaCl(aq)$$

Because HCl, NaOH, and NaCl exist as completely separated ions in water, the complete ionic equation for this reaction is

$$H^+(aq) + Cl^-(aq) + Na^+(aq) + OH^-(aq) \rightarrow H_2O(l) + Na^+(aq) + Cl^-(aq)$$

Notice that the Cl^- and Na^+ are spectator ions (they undergo no changes), so the net ionic equation is

$$H^+(aq) + OH^-(aq) \rightarrow H_2O(l)$$

Thus the only chemical change that occurs when these solutions are mixed is that water is formed from H^+ and OH^- ions.

EXAMPLE 7.4 Writing Equations for Acid–Base Reactions

Nitric acid is a strong acid. Write the molecular, complete ionic, and net ionic equations for the reaction of aqueous nitric acid and aqueous potassium hydroxide.

SOLUTION

Molecular equation:

$$HNO_3(aq) + KOH(aq) \rightarrow H_2O(l) + KNO_3(aq)$$

Complete ionic equation:

$$H^+(aq) + NO_3^-(aq) + K^+(aq) + OH^-(aq) \rightarrow H_2O(l) + K^+(aq) + NO_3^-(aq)$$

Net ionic equation:

$$H^+(aq) + OH^-(aq) \rightarrow H_2O(l)$$

Note that K^+ and NO_3^- are spectator ions and that the formation of water is the driving force for this reaction. ■

There are two important things to note as we examine the reaction of hydrochloric acid with aqueous sodium hydroxide and the reaction of nitric acid with aqueous potassium hydroxide.

1. The net ionic equation is the same in both cases; water is formed.

$$H^+(aq) + OH^-(aq) \rightarrow H_2O(l)$$

2. Besides water, which is *always a product* of the reaction of an acid with OH^-, the second product is an ionic compound, which might precipitate or remain dissolved, depending on its solubility.

$$HCl(aq) + NaOH(aq) \rightarrow H_2O(l) + NaCl(aq)$$
$$HNO_3(aq) + KOH(aq) \rightarrow H_2O(l) + KNO_3(aq)$$
Dissolved ionic compounds

This ionic compound is called a **salt.** In the first case the salt is sodium chloride, and in the second case the salt is potassium nitrate. We can obtain these soluble salts in solid form (both are white solids) by evaporating the water.

Additional Examples

Example 7.4

1. Hydrobromic acid is a strong acid. Write the balanced molecular, balanced complete ionic, and balanced net ionic equations for the reaction of aqueous hydrobromic acid and aqueous sodium hydroxide.

   molecular: $HBr(aq) + NaOH(aq) \rightarrow H_2O(l) + NaBr(aq)$;

   complete ionic: $H^+(aq) + Br^-(aq) + Na^+(aq) + OH^-(aq) \rightarrow H_2O(l) + Na^+(aq) + Br^-(aq)$;

   net ionic: $H^+(aq) + OH^-(aq) \rightarrow H_2O(l)$

2. Sulfuric acid is a strong acid. Write the balanced molecular, balanced complete ionic, and balanced net ionic equations for the reaction of aqueous sulfuric acid and aqueous potassium hydroxide.

   molecular: $H_2SO_4(aq) + 2KOH(aq) \rightarrow 2H_2O(l) + K_2SO_4(aq)$;

   complete ionic: $2H^+(aq) + SO_4^{2-}(aq) + 2K^+(aq) + 2OH^-(aq) \rightarrow 2H_2O(l) + 2K^+(aq) + SO_4^{2-}(aq)$;

   net ionic: $H^+(aq) + OH^-(aq) \rightarrow H_2O(l)$

TEACHING SUPPORT

BACKGROUND INFORMATION

Svante Arrhenius

The basis for the conductivity properties of solutions was first correctly identified by Svante Arrhenius (1859–1927), then a Swedish graduate student in physics, who carried out research on the nature of solutions at the University of Uppsala in the early 1880s. Arrhenius came to believe that the conductivity of solutions arose from the presence of ions, an idea that was at first scorned by the majority of the scientific establishment. However, in the late 1890s when atoms were found to contain charged particles, the ionic theory suddenly made sense and became widely accepted. As Arrhenius postulated, the extent to which a solution can conduct an

Test Bank: 38–48

Section 7.5

LABORATORY EXPERIMENT

A relevant laboratory experiment for this section is Experiment 12, Oxidation–Reduction Reactions, from *Introductory Chemistry in the Laboratory* by James Hall.

PowerLecture Video: Reaction: Zinc and Sulfur

DEMONSTRATION

Making Salt

Materials 1-L cylinder one-third filled with dry sand, salt shaker filled with salt and with a wire attached long enough to reach out the top of the cylinder, deflagrating spoon, stopper to fit the cylinder, Na metal, knife, Cl_2 gas (lecture bottle), tweezers, wash bottle/water.

Preparation Bury the salt shaker completely in the sand in the cylinder with the wire extending up and out the top of the cylinder. In the hood, fill the cylinder with Cl_2 gas and stopper it firmly, catching the wire between the stopper and the glass.

Presentation Cut a small piece of sodium to fit in the deflagrating spoon. Use a paper towel to dry off the oil. Place the sodium in the deflagrating spoon. Squirt the sodium with a small amount of water to ignite it. Immediately remove the stopper from the cylinder and lower the deflagrating spoon into the cylinder. Once the sodium has gone out and white smoke is evident, remove the spoon. Ask students what the product is. As they respond, pull the salt shaker out of the cylinder.

PowerLecture Video: Production of Sodium Chloride

Both strong acids and strong bases are strong electrolytes.

Drano contains a strong base.

Summary of Strong Acids and Strong Bases

The following points about strong acids and strong bases are particularly important.

1. The common strong acids are aqueous solutions of HCl, HNO_3, and H_2SO_4.
2. A strong acid is a substance that completely dissociates (ionizes) in water. (Each molecule breaks up into an H^+ ion plus an anion.)
3. A strong base is a metal hydroxide compound that is very soluble in water. The most common strong bases are NaOH and KOH, which completely break up into separated ions (Na^+ and OH^- or K^+ and OH^-) when they are dissolved in water.
4. The net ionic equation for the reaction of a strong acid and a strong base (contains OH^-) is always the same: it shows the production of water.

$$H^+(aq) + OH^-(aq) \rightarrow H_2O(l)$$

5. In the reaction of a strong acid and a strong base, one product is always water and the other is always an ionic compound called a salt, which remains dissolved in the water. This salt can be obtained as a solid by evaporating the water.
6. The reaction of H^+ and OH^- is often called an acid–base reaction, where H^+ is the acidic ion and OH^- is the basic ion.

7.5 Reactions of Metals with Nonmetals (Oxidation–Reduction)

OBJECTIVES: To learn the general characteristics of a reaction between a metal and a nonmetal. • To understand electron transfer as a driving force for a chemical reaction.

In Chapter 4 we spent considerable time discussing ionic compounds—compounds formed in the reaction of a metal and a nonmetal. A typical example is sodium chloride, formed by the reaction of sodium metal and chlorine gas:

$$2Na(s) + Cl_2(g) \rightarrow 2NaCl(s)$$

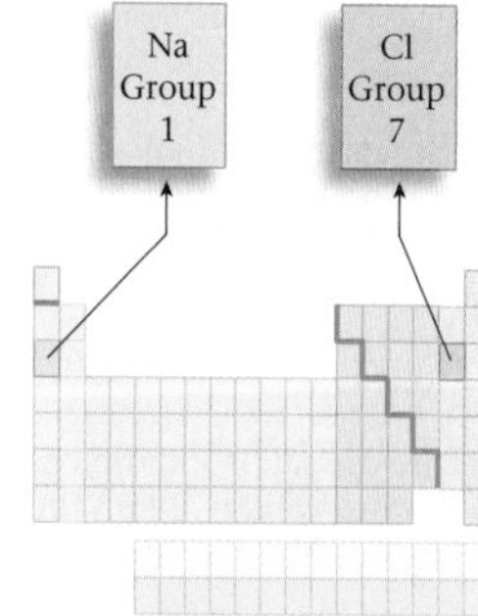

Let's examine what happens in this reaction. Sodium metal is composed of sodium atoms, each of which has a net charge of zero. (The positive charges of the eleven protons in its nucleus are exactly balanced by the negative charges on the eleven electrons.) Similarly, the chlorine molecule consists of two uncharged chlorine atoms (each has seventeen protons and seventeen electrons). However, in the product (sodium chloride), the sodium is present as Na^+ and the chlorine as Cl^-. By what process do the neutral atoms become ions? The answer is that one electron is transferred from each sodium atom to each chlorine atom.

$$Na + Cl \rightarrow Na^+ + Cl^-$$
(e^- transferred from Na to Cl)

After the electron transfer, each sodium has ten electrons and eleven protons (a net charge of 1+), and each chlorine has eighteen electrons and seventeen protons (a net charge of 1−).

electric current depends directly on the number of ions present. Some materials, such as sodium chloride, readily produce ions in aqueous solution and thus are strong electrolytes. Other substances, such as acetic acid, produce relatively few ions when dissolved in water and are weak electrolytes. A third class consists of materials, such as sugar, that form virtually no ions when dissolved in water and are nonelectrolytes.

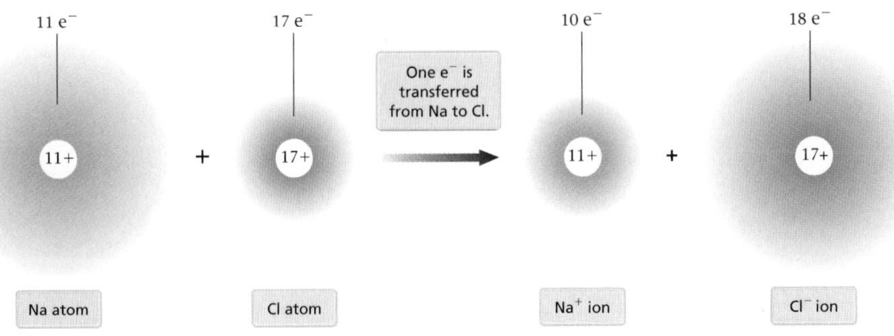

Figure 7.6
The thermite reaction gives off so much heat that the iron formed is molten.

Thus the reaction of a metal with a nonmetal to form an ionic compound involves the transfer of one or more electrons from the metal (which forms a cation) to the nonmetal (which forms an anion). This tendency to transfer electrons from metals to nonmetals is the third driving force for reactions that we listed in Section 7.1. A reaction that *involves a transfer of electrons* is called an **oxidation–reduction reaction.**

There are many examples of oxidation–reduction reactions in which a metal reacts with a nonmetal to form an ionic compound. Consider the reaction of magnesium metal with oxygen,

$$2Mg(s) + O_2(g) \rightarrow 2MgO(s)$$

which produces a bright, white light useful in camera flash units. Note that the reactants contain uncharged atoms, but the product contains ions:

$$MgO$$
Contains Mg^{2+}, O^{2-}

Therefore, in this reaction, each magnesium atom loses two electrons ($Mg \rightarrow Mg^{2+} + 2e^-$) and each oxygen atom gains two electrons ($O + 2e^- \rightarrow O^{2-}$). We might represent this reaction as follows:

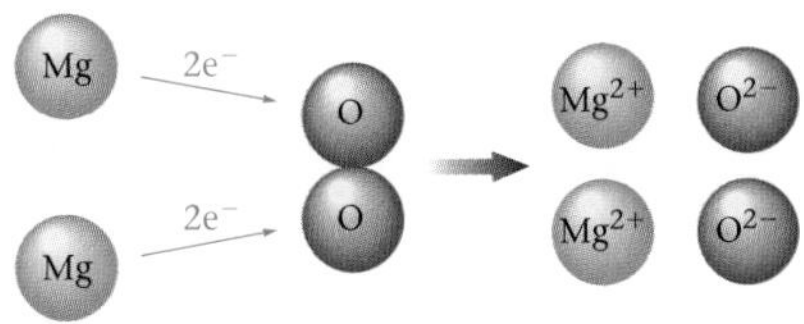

Another example is

$$2Al(s) + Fe_2O_3(s) \rightarrow 2Fe(s) + Al_2O_3(s)$$

which is a reaction (called the thermite reaction) that produces so much energy (heat) that the iron is initially formed as a liquid (see Figure 7.6). In this case the aluminum is originally present as the elemental metal (which contains uncharged Al atoms) and ends up in Al_2O_3, where it is present as Al^{3+} cations (the $2Al^{3+}$ ions just balance the charge of the $3O^{2-}$ ions). Therefore, in the reaction each aluminum atom loses three electrons.

$$Al \rightarrow Al^{3+} + 3e^-$$

This equation is read, "An aluminum atom yields an aluminum ion with a 3+ charge and three electrons."

The opposite process occurs with the iron, which is initially present as Fe^{3+} ions in Fe_2O_3 and ends up as uncharged atoms in the elemental iron. Thus each iron cation gains three electrons to form an uncharged atom:

$$Fe^{3+} + 3e^- \rightarrow Fe$$

TEACHING TIPS

- Discuss the importance of oxidation–reduction reactions in daily life. Batteries, corrosion, and combustion are all oxidation–reduction reactions.
- Point out that the loss or gain of electrons can take place only if another element is present to accept or donate electrons. If you do the Making Salt demonstration, point out that chlorine gas doesn't react alone; neither does sodium metal. Yet if you ignite the sodium and place it in the chlorine gas, the two elements react to form ions.
- It is easier for students to begin with oxidation–reduction reactions between two elements. Once they understand this type of reaction, you can move on to more complicated reactions such as $2NaBr + Cl_2 \rightarrow 2NaCl + Br_2$. Reactions of this type are sometimes classified as single-displacement reactions. Once again, students may be confused by this term because they do not understand what it means to be single-displacement when two elements are changing places. We choose to classify all oxidation–reduction reactions as reactions in which electrons are transferred between atoms. This approach focuses students' attention on the driving force for the reaction. The term *single-displacement* is discussed in Section 7.7 as an alternative way to classify reactions.

Teaching Notes Chlorine gas is toxic and choking. Be careful when removing the stopper. The reaction produces intense heat and light.

The reaction is $2Na(s) + Cl_2(g) \rightarrow 2NaCl(s)$.

Lecture Demonstration: 4.8, 4.9

PowerLecture Video: Thermite Reaction

PowerLecture Video: Zinc and Iodine

We can represent this reaction in schematic form as follows:

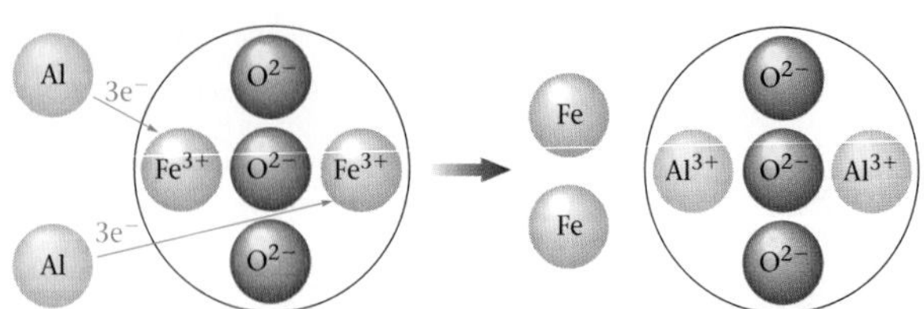

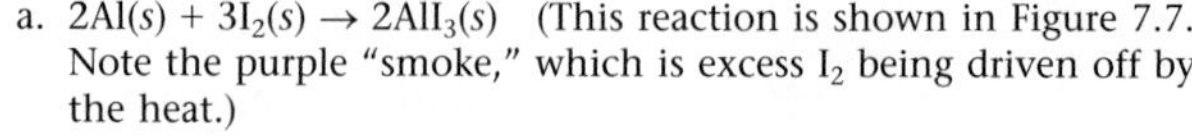

EXAMPLE 7.5 Identifying Electron Transfer in Oxidation–Reduction Reactions

For each of the following reactions, show how electrons are gained and lost.

a. $2Al(s) + 3I_2(s) \rightarrow 2AlI_3(s)$ (This reaction is shown in Figure 7.7. Note the purple "smoke," which is excess I_2 being driven off by the heat.)

b. $2Cs(s) + F_2(g) \rightarrow 2CsF(s)$

Figure 7.7 When powdered aluminum and iodine (shown in the foreground) are mixed (and a little water added), they react vigorously.

SOLUTION

a. In AlI_3 the ions are Al^{3+} and I^- (aluminum always forms Al^{3+}, and iodine always forms I^-). In $Al(s)$ the aluminum is present as uncharged atoms. Thus aluminum goes from Al to Al^{3+} by losing three electrons ($Al \rightarrow Al^{3+} + 3e^-$). In I_2 each iodine atom is uncharged. Thus each iodine atom goes from I to I^- by gaining one electron ($I + e^- \rightarrow I^-$). A schematic for this reaction is

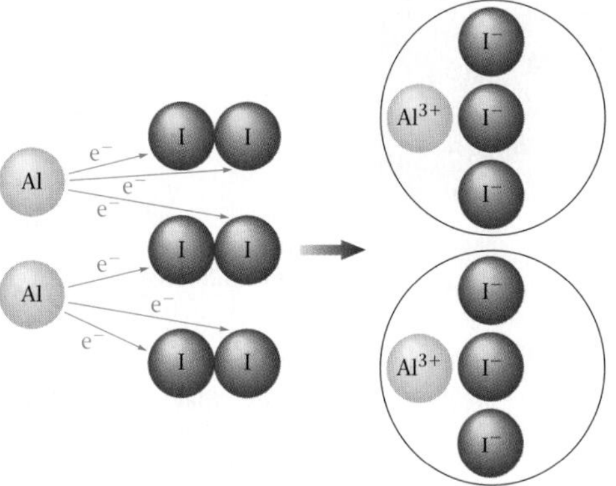

b. In CsF the ions present are Cs^+ and F^-. Cesium metal, $Cs(s)$, contains uncharged cesium atoms, and fluorine gas, $F_2(g)$, contains uncharged fluorine atoms. Thus in the reaction each cesium atom loses one electron ($Cs \rightarrow Cs^+ + e^-$) and each fluorine atom gains one electron ($F + e^- \rightarrow F^-$). The schematic for this reaction is

Additional Examples

Example 7.5

For each of the following reactions, show how electrons are gained and lost.

1. $4Al(s) + 3O_2(g) \rightarrow 2Al_2O_3(s)$

   Each Al atom loses 3 electrons (for a total of 12 electrons). Each oxygen atom gains 2 electrons (for a total of 12 electrons).

2. $4Na(s) + O_2(g) \rightarrow 2Na_2O(s)$

   Each Na atom loses 1 electron (for a total of 4 electrons). Each oxygen atom gains 2 electrons (for a total of 4 electrons).

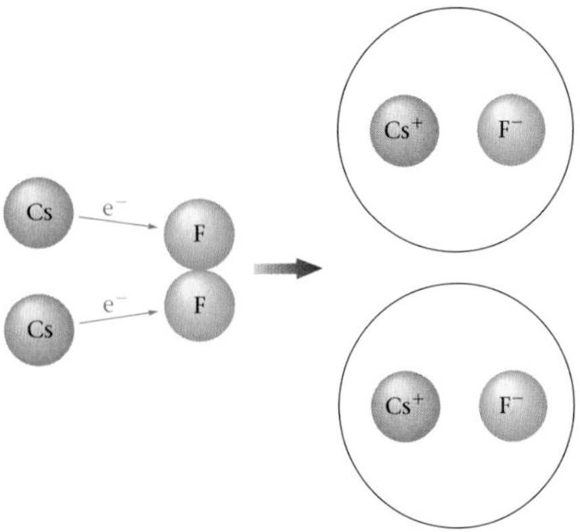

Self-Check **EXERCISE 7.3** For each reaction, show how electrons are gained and lost.

a. $2Na(s) + Br_2(l) \rightarrow 2NaBr(s)$

b. $2Ca(s) + O_2(g) \rightarrow 2CaO(s)$

See Problems 7.47 and 7.48. ■

So far we have emphasized electron transfer (oxidation–reduction) reactions that involve a metal and a nonmetal. Electron transfer reactions can also take place between two nonmetals. We will not discuss these reactions in detail here. All we will say at this point is that one sure sign of an oxidation–reduction reaction between nonmetals is the presence of oxygen, $O_2(g)$, as a reactant or product. In fact, oxidation got its name from oxygen. Thus the reactions

$$CH_4(g) + 2O_2(g) \rightarrow CO_2(g) + 2H_2O(g)$$

and

$$2SO_2(g) + O_2(g) \rightarrow 2SO_3(g)$$

are electron transfer reactions, even though it is not obvious at this point.

We can summarize what we have learned about oxidation–reduction reactions as follows:

Characteristics of Oxidation–Reduction Reactions

1. When a metal reacts with a nonmetal, an ionic compound is formed. The ions are formed when the metal transfers one or more electrons to the nonmetal, the metal atom becoming a cation and the nonmetal atom becoming an anion. *Therefore, a metal–nonmetal reaction can always be assumed to be an oxidation–reduction reaction, which involves electron transfer.*
2. Two nonmetals can also undergo an oxidation–reduction reaction. At this point we can recognize these cases only by looking for O_2 as a reactant or product. When two nonmetals react, the compound formed is not ionic.

Self Check

Answers to Self-Check Exercise 7.3

a. The compound NaBr contains Na^+ and Br^- ions. Thus each sodium atom loses one electron ($Na \rightarrow Na^+ + e^-$), and each bromine atom gains one electron ($Br + e^- \rightarrow Br^-$).

b. The compound CaO contains Ca^{2+} and O^{2-} ions. Thus each calcium atom loses two electrons ($Ca \rightarrow Ca^{2+} + 2e^-$), and each oxygen atom gains two electrons ($O + 2e^- \rightarrow O^{2-}$).

PowerLecture Video: Reaction: Mg Oxidation

Test Bank: 34–37, 49–60

Section 7.6

TEACHING TIPS

- Have students design lists of clues to identify different types of reactions. For example, the clues to recognizing a precipitation reaction are that a solid forms and that the reactants and products are ionic.
- Students can also make flow charts or concept maps to assist in the classification of reactions. Make sure they take the time to identify the types of reactions by all names. For example, precipitation reactions are also called double-displacement reactions and some oxidation–reduction reactions are called single-displacement, combination, or combustion reactions.
- Remind students that once they have written the correct formulas for a chemical reaction, they still need to balance the chemical equation.
- Once students have been introduced to these three ways of classifying reactions, it is a good idea to have them practice as a class. Have them classify a series of reactions and then engage in a class discussion in which students explain how they identified a given type of reaction.

Lecture Demonstration: 4.6

7.6 Ways to Classify Reactions

OBJECTIVE: To learn various classification schemes for reactions.

So far in our study of chemistry we have seen many, many chemical reactions—and this is just Chapter 7. In the world around us and in our bodies, literally millions of chemical reactions are taking place. Obviously, we need a system for putting reactions into meaningful classes that will make them easier to remember and easier to understand.

In Chapter 7 we have so far considered the following "driving forces" for chemical reactions:

- Formation of a solid
- Formation of water
- Transfer of electrons

We will now discuss how to classify reactions involving these processes. For example, in the reaction

$$K_2CrO_4(aq) + Ba(NO_3)_2(aq) \rightarrow BaCrO_4(s) + 2KNO_3(aq)$$

Solution Solution Solid formed Solution

solid $BaCrO_4$ (a precipitate) is formed. Because the *formation of a solid when two solutions are mixed* is called *precipitation,* we call this a **precipitation reaction.**

Notice in this reaction that two anions (NO_3^- and CrO_4^{2-}) are simply exchanged. Note that CrO_4^{2-} was originally associated with K^+ in K_2CrO_4 and that NO_3^- was associated with Ba^{2+} in $Ba(NO_3)_2$. In the products these associations are reversed. Because of this double exchange, we sometimes call this reaction a double-exchange reaction or **double-displacement reaction.** We might represent such a reaction as

$$AB + CD \rightarrow AD + CB$$

So we can classify a reaction such as this one as a precipitation reaction or as a double-displacement reaction. Either name is correct, but the former is more commonly used by chemists.

In this chapter we have also considered reactions in which water is formed when a strong acid is mixed with a strong base. All of these reactions had the same net ionic equation:

$$H^+(aq) + OH^-(aq) \rightarrow H_2O(l)$$

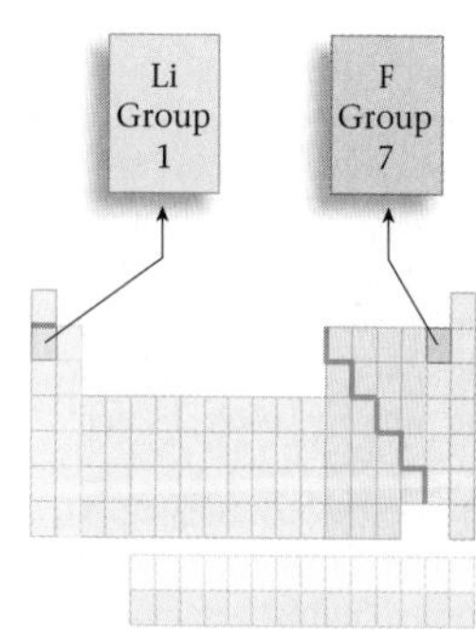

The H^+ ion comes from a strong acid, such as $HCl(aq)$ or $HNO_3(aq)$, and the origin of the OH^- ion is a strong base, such as $NaOH(aq)$ or $KOH(aq)$. An example is

$$HCl(aq) + KOH(aq) \rightarrow H_2O(l) + KCl(aq)$$

We classify these reactions as **acid–base reactions.** You can recognize this as an acid–base reaction because it *involves an H^+ ion that ends up in the product water.*

The third driving force is electron transfer. We see evidence of this driving force particularly in the "desire" of a metal to donate electrons to nonmetals. An example is

$$2Li(s) + F_2(g) \rightarrow 2LiF(s)$$

Lecture Demonstration: 4.8, 4.9

where each lithium atom loses one electron to form Li^+, and each fluorine atom gains one electron to form the F^- ion. The process of electron transfer is also called oxidation–reduction. Thus we classify the preceding reaction as an **oxidation–reduction reaction.**

An additional driving force for chemical reactions that we have not yet discussed is *formation of a gas*. A reaction in aqueous solution that forms a gas (which escapes as bubbles) is pulled toward the products by this event. An example is the reaction

$$2HCl(aq) + Na_2CO_3(aq) \rightarrow CO_2(g) + H_2O(l) + NaCl(aq)$$

for which the net ionic equation is

$$2H^+(aq) + CO_3^{2-}(aq) \rightarrow CO_2(g) + H_2O(l)$$

Note that this reaction forms carbon dioxide gas as well as water, so it illustrates two of the driving forces that we have considered. Because this reaction involves H^+ that ends up in the product water, we classify it as an acid–base reaction.

Consider another reaction that forms a gas:

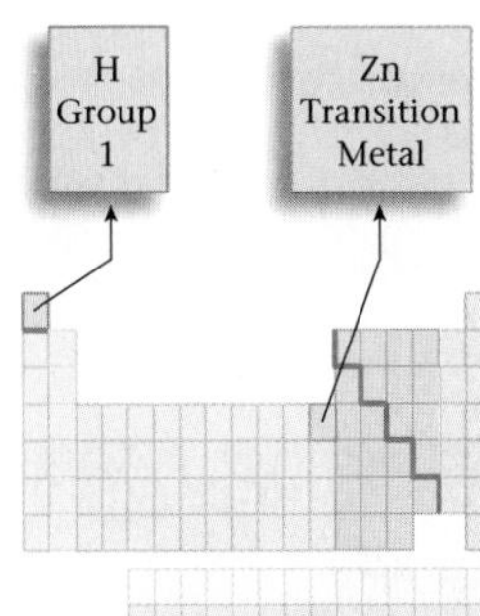

$$Zn(s) + 2HCl(aq) \rightarrow H_2(g) + ZnCl_2(aq)$$

How might we classify this reaction? A careful look at the reactants and products shows the following:

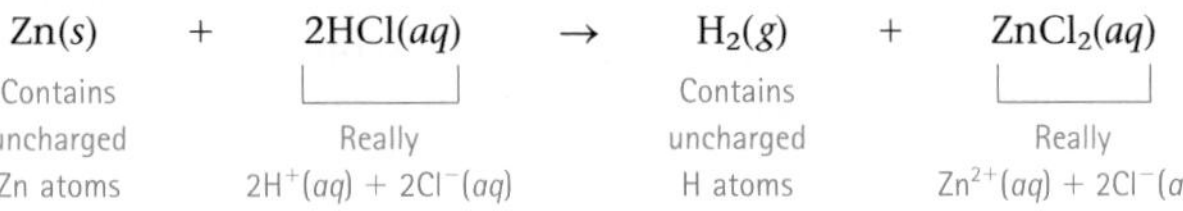

Note that in the reactant zinc metal, Zn exists as uncharged atoms, whereas in the product it exists as Zn^{2+}. Thus each Zn atom loses two electrons. Where have these electrons gone? They have been transferred to two H^+ ions to form H_2. The schematic for this reaction is

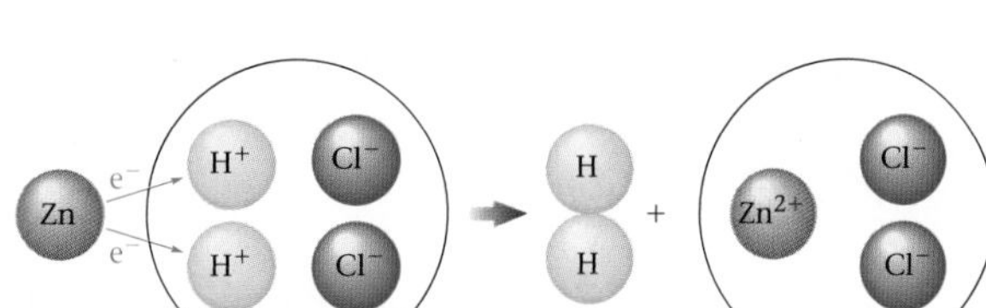

Zn metal Solution of HCl H_2 molecule Solution of $ZnCl_2$

This is an electron transfer process, so the reaction can be classified as an oxidation–reduction reaction.

Another way this reaction is sometimes classified is based on the fact that a *single* type of anion (Cl^-) has been exchanged between H^+ and Zn^{2+}. That is, Cl^- is originally associated with H^+ in HCl and ends up associated with Zn^{2+} in the product $ZnCl_2$. We can call this a *single-replacement reaction* in contrast to double-displacement reactions, in which two types of anions are exchanged. We can represent a single replacement as

$$A + BC \rightarrow B + AC$$

7.6 Ways to Classify Reactions 187

CHEMISTRY *IN* FOCUS

Oxidation–Reduction Reactions Launch the Space Shuttle

Launching into space a vehicle that weighs millions of pounds requires unimaginable quantities of energy—all furnished by oxidation–reduction reactions.

Notice from Figure 7.8 that three cylindrical objects are attached to the shuttle orbiter. In the center is a tank about 28 feet in diameter and 154 feet long that contains liquid oxygen and liquid hydrogen (in separate compartments). These fuels are fed to the orbiter's rocket engines, where they react to form water and release a huge quantity of energy.

$$2H_2 + O_2 \rightarrow 2H_2O + \text{energy}$$

Note that we can recognize this reaction as an oxidation–reduction reaction because O_2 is a reactant.

Two solid-fuel rockets 12 feet in diameter and 150 feet long are also attached to the orbiter. Each rocket contains 1.1 million pounds of fuel: ammonium perchlorate (NH_4ClO_4) and powdered aluminum mixed with a binder ("glue"). Because the rockets are so large, they are built in segments and assembled at the launch site as shown in Figure 7.9. Each segment is filled with the syrupy propellant (Figure 7.10), which then solidifies to a consistency much like that of a hard rubber eraser.

The oxidation–reduction reaction between the ammonium perchlorate and the aluminum is represented as follows:

$$3NH_4ClO_4(s) + 3Al(s) \rightarrow Al_2O_3(s) + AlCl_3(s) + 3NO(g) + 6H_2O(g) + \text{energy}$$

It produces temperatures of about 5700 °F and 3.3 million pounds of thrust in each rocket.

Thus we can see that oxidation–reduction reactions furnish the energy to launch the space shuttle.

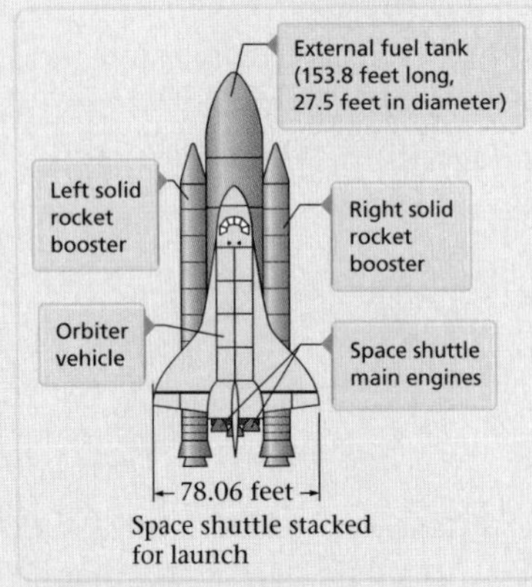

Figure 7.8 For launch, the space shuttle orbiter is attached to two solid-fuel rockets (left and right) and a fuel tank (center) that supplies hydrogen and oxygen to the orbiter's engines. *(Reprinted with permission from* Chemical and Engineering News, *September 19, 1988. Copyright © 1988 American Chemical Society.)*

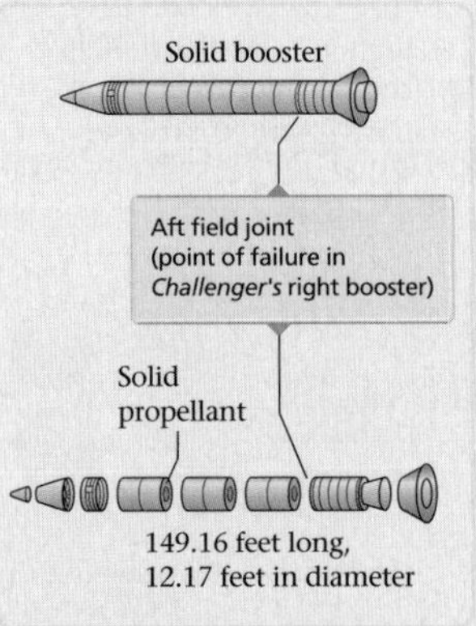

Figure 7.9 The solid-fuel rockets are assembled from segments to make loading the fuel more convenient. *(Reprinted with permission from* Chemical and Engineering News, *September 19, 1988. Copyright © 1988 American Chemical Society.)*

Figure 7.10 A rocket segment being filled with the propellant mixture.

188

7.7 Other Ways to Classify Reactions

OBJECTIVE: To consider additional classes of chemical reactions.

So far in this chapter we have classified chemical reactions in several ways. The most commonly used of these classifications are

- Precipitation reactions
- Acid–base reactions
- Oxidation–reduction reactions

However, there are still other ways to classify reactions that you may encounter in your future studies of chemistry. We will consider several of these in this section.

Combustion Reactions

Many chemical reactions that involve oxygen produce energy (heat) so rapidly that a flame results. Such reactions are called **combustion reactions.** We have considered some of these reactions previously. For example, the methane in natural gas reacts with oxygen according to the following balanced equation:

$$CH_4(g) + 2O_2(g) \rightarrow CO_2(g) + 2H_2O(g)$$

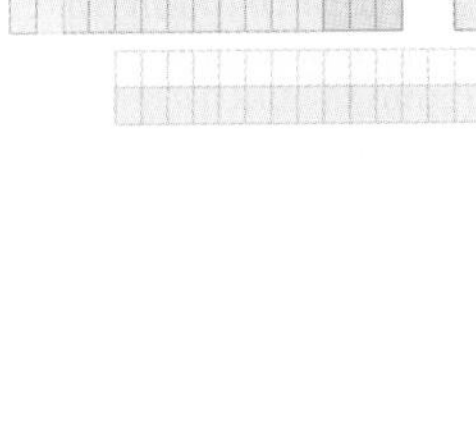

This reaction produces the flame of the common laboratory burner and is used to heat most homes in the United States. Recall that we originally classified this reaction as an oxidation–reduction reaction in Section 7.5. Thus we can say that the reaction of methane with oxygen is both an oxidation–reduction reaction and a combustion reaction. Combustion reactions, in fact, are a special class of oxidation–reduction reactions (see Figure 7.11).

There are many combustion reactions, most of which are used to provide heat or electricity for homes or businesses or energy for transportation. Some examples are:

- Combustion of propane (used to heat some rural homes)

$$C_3H_8(g) + 5O_2(g) \rightarrow 3CO_2(g) + 4H_2O(g)$$

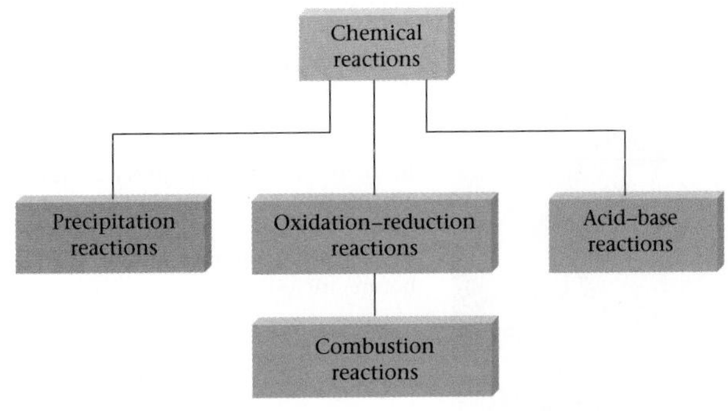

Figure 7.11
Classes of reactions. Combustion reactions are a special type of oxidation–reduction reaction.

Test Bank: 61–73

Section 7.7

TEACHING TIPS

- A useful clue to help students identify combustion reactions is to look for molecular oxygen and a carbon-containing molecule as reactants. The products of many combustion reactions are carbon dioxide and water. A good example to use is

$$CH_3CH_2OH + 3O_2 \rightarrow 2CO_2 + 3H_2O$$
Ethyl alcohol

- Most students can write products for double-displacement and single-displacement reactions, but not for synthesis and decomposition reactions.

Lecture Demonstration: 3.6

- Combustion of gasoline* (used to power cars and trucks)

$$2C_8H_{18}(l) + 25O_2(g) \rightarrow 16CO_2(g) + 18H_2O(g)$$

- Combustion of coal* (used to generate electricity)

$$C(s) + O_2(g) \rightarrow CO_2(g)$$

Synthesis (Combination) Reactions

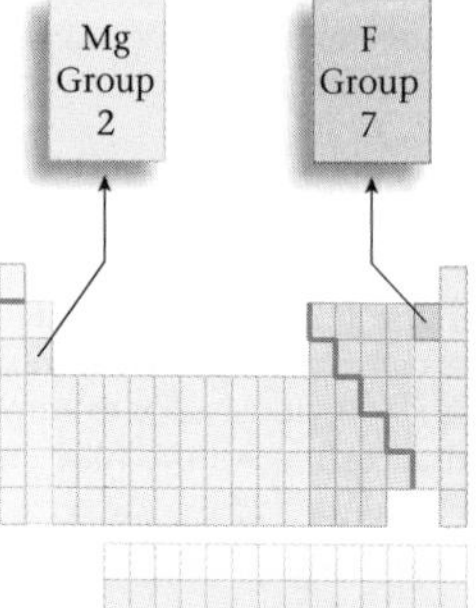

One of the most important activities in chemistry is the synthesis of new compounds. Each of our lives has been greatly affected by synthetic compounds such as plastic, polyester, and aspirin. When a given compound is formed from simpler materials, we call this a **synthesis** (or **combination**) **reaction.**

In many cases synthesis reactions start with elements, as shown by the following examples:

- Synthesis of water $2H_2(g) + O_2(g) \rightarrow 2H_2O(l)$
- Synthesis of carbon dioxide $C(s) + O_2(g) \rightarrow CO_2(g)$
- Synthesis of nitrogen monoxide $N_2(g) + O_2(g) \rightarrow 2NO(g)$

Notice that each of these reactions involves oxygen, so each can be classified as an oxidation–reduction reaction. The first two reactions are also commonly called combustion reactions because they produce flames. The reaction of hydrogen with oxygen to produce water, then, can be classified three ways: as an oxidation–reduction reaction, as a combustion reaction, and as a synthesis reaction.

There are also many synthesis reactions that do not involve oxygen:

Lecture Demonstration: 4.11

- Synthesis of sodium chloride $2Na(s) + Cl_2(g) \rightarrow 2NaCl(s)$
- Synthesis of magnesium fluoride $Mg(s) + F_2(g) \rightarrow MgF_2(s)$

We have discussed the formation of sodium chloride before and have noted that it is an oxidation–reduction reaction; uncharged sodium atoms lose electrons to form Na^+ ions, and uncharged chlorine atoms gain electrons to form Cl^- ions. The synthesis of magnesium fluoride is also an oxidation–reduction reaction because Mg^{2+} and F^- ions are produced from the uncharged atoms.

We have seen that synthesis reactions in which the reactants are elements are oxidation–reduction reactions as well. In fact, we can think of these synthesis reactions as another subclass of the oxidation–reduction class of reactions.

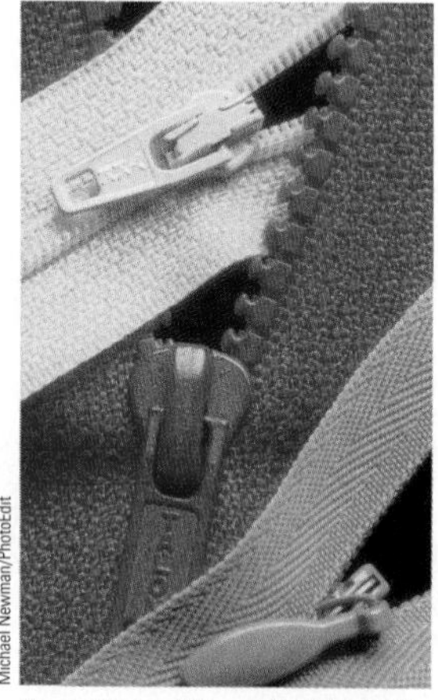

Michael Newman/PhotoEdit

Formation of the colorful plastics used in these zippers is an example of a synthetic reaction.

Decomposition Reactions

In many cases a compound can be broken down into simpler compounds or all the way to the component elements. This is usually accomplished by heating or by the application of an electric current. Such reactions are called **decomposition reactions.** We have discussed decomposition reactions before, including

- Decomposition of water

$$2H_2O(l) \xrightarrow[\text{current}]{\text{Electric}} 2H_2(g) + O_2(g)$$

*This substance is really a complex mixture of compounds, but the reaction shown is representative of what takes place.

Chemical reactions

Precipitation reactions | Oxidation–reduction reactions | Acid–base reactions

Combustion reactions | Synthesis reactions (Reactants are elements.) | Decomposition reactions (Products are elements.)

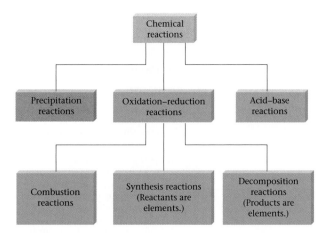

Figure 7.12
Summary of classes of reactions.

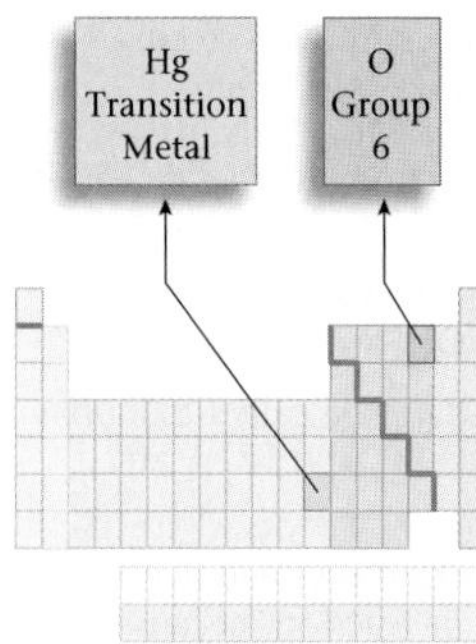

- Decomposition of mercury(II) oxide

$$2HgO(s) \xrightarrow[\text{Heat}]{} 2Hg(l) + O_2(g)$$

Because O_2 is involved in the first reaction, we recognize it as an oxidation–reduction reaction. In the second reaction, HgO, which contains Hg^{2+} and O^{2-} ions, is decomposed to the elements, which contain uncharged atoms. In this process each Hg^{2+} gains two electrons and each O^{2-} loses two electrons, so this is both a decomposition reaction and an oxidation–reduction reaction.

A decomposition reaction, in which a compound is broken down into its elements, is just the opposite of the synthesis (combination) reaction, in which elements combine to form the compound. For example, we have just discussed the synthesis of sodium chloride from its elements. Sodium chloride can be decomposed into its elements by melting it and passing an electric current through it:

$$2NaCl(l) \xrightarrow[\text{Electric current}]{} 2Na(l) + Cl_2(g)$$

There are other schemes for classifying reactions that we have not considered. However, we have covered many of the classifications that are commonly used by chemists as they pursue their science in laboratories and industrial plants.

It should be apparent that many important reactions can be classified as oxidation–reduction reactions. As shown in Figure 7.12, various types of reactions can be viewed as subclasses of the overall oxidation–reduction category.

EXAMPLE 7.6 Classifying Reactions

Classify each of the following reactions in as many ways as possible.

a. $2K(s) + Cl_2(g) \rightarrow 2KCl(s)$

b. $Fe_2O_3(s) + 2Al(s) \rightarrow Al_2O_3(s) + 2Fe(s)$

PowerLecture Animations:
Mercury II Oxide Decomposition
Combustion of Propane
PCl_3 Formation

Additional Examples

Example 7.6

Classify each of the following reactions in as many ways as possible.

1. $2C_2H_2(s) + 5O_2(g) \rightarrow 4CO_2(g) + 2H_2O(s)$

   combustion, oxidation–reduction

2. $2Ni(s) + 4O_2(g) \rightarrow 2NiO(g)$

   synthesis, oxidation–reduction

c. $2Mg(s) + O_2(g) \rightarrow 2MgO(s)$

d. $HNO_3(aq) + NaOH(aq) \rightarrow H_2O(l) + NaNO_3(aq)$

e. $KBr(aq) + AgNO_3(aq) \rightarrow AgBr(s) + KNO_3(aq)$

f. $PbO_2(s) \rightarrow Pb(s) + O_2(g)$

SOLUTION

a. This is both a synthesis reaction (elements combine to form a compound) and an oxidation–reduction reaction (uncharged potassium and chlorine atoms are changed to K^+ and Cl^- ions in KCl).

b. This is an oxidation–reduction reaction. Iron is present in $Fe_2O_3(s)$ as Fe^{3+} ions and in elemental iron, Fe(*s*), as uncharged atoms. So each Fe^{3+} must gain three electrons to form Fe. The reverse happens to aluminum, which is present initially as uncharged aluminum atoms, each of which loses three electrons to give Al^{3+} ions in Al_2O_3. Note that this reaction might also be called a single-replacement reaction because O is switched from Fe to Al.

c. This is both a synthesis reaction (elements combine to form a compound) and an oxidation–reduction reaction (each magnesium atom loses two electrons to give Mg^{2+} ions in MgO, and each oxygen atom gains two electrons to give O^{2-} in MgO).

d. This is an acid–base reaction. It might also be called a double-displacement reaction because NO_3^- and OH^- "switch partners."

e. This is a precipitation reaction that might also be called a double-displacement reaction in which the anions Br^- and NO_3^- are exchanged.

f. This is a decomposition reaction (a compound breaks down into elements). It also is an oxidation–reduction reaction, because the ions in PbO_2 (Pb^{4+} and O^{2-}) are changed to uncharged atoms in the elements Pb(*s*) and $O_2(g)$. That is, electrons are transferred from O^{2-} to Pb^{4+} in the reaction.

Self-Check EXERCISE 7.4

Classify each of the following reactions in as many ways as possible.

a. $4NH_3(g) + 5O_2(g) \rightarrow 4NO(g) + 6H_2O(g)$

b. $S_8(s) + 8O_2(g) \rightarrow 8SO_2(g)$

c. $2Al(s) + 3Cl_2(g) \rightarrow 2AlCl_3(s)$

d. $2AlN(s) \rightarrow 2Al(s) + N_2(g)$

e. $BaCl_2(aq) + Na_2SO_4(aq) \rightarrow BaSO_4(s) + 2NaCl(aq)$

f. $2Cs(s) + Br_2(l) \rightarrow 2CsBr(s)$

g. $KOH(aq) + HCl(aq) \rightarrow H_2O(l) + KCl(aq)$

h. $2C_2H_2(g) + 5O_2(g) \rightarrow 4CO_2(g) + 2H_2O(l)$

See Problems 7.53 and 7.54. ■

Self Check

Answers to Self-Check Exercise 7.4

a. oxidation–reduction reaction; combustion reaction

b. synthesis reaction; oxidation–reduction reaction; combustion reaction

c. synthesis reaction; oxidation–reduction reaction

d. decomposition reaction; oxidation–reduction reaction

e. precipitation reaction (and double-displacement)

f. synthesis reaction; oxidation–reduction reaction

g. acid–base reaction (and double-displacement)

h. combustion reaction; oxidation–reduction reaction

CHAPTER 7 REVIEW

Key Terms

precipitation (7.2)
precipitate (7.2)
precipitation reaction (7.2, 7.6)
strong electrolyte (7.2)
soluble solid (7.2)
insoluble (slightly soluble) solid (7.2)
molecular equation (7.3)
complete ionic equation (7.3)
spectator ions (7.3)
net ionic equation (7.3)
acid (7.4)
strong acid (7.4)
base (7.4)
strong base (7.4)
salt (7.4)
oxidation–reduction reaction (7.5, 7.6)
precipation reaction (7.6)
double-displacement reaction (7.6)
acid–base reaction (7.6)
combustion reaction (7.7)
synthesis (combination) reaction (7.7)
decomposition reaction (7.7)

Summary

1. Four driving forces that favor chemical change (chemical reaction) are formation of a solid, formation of water, transfer of electrons, and formation of a gas.
2. A reaction where a solid forms is called a precipitation reaction. General rules on solubility help predict whether a solid—and what solid—will form when two solutions are mixed.
3. Three types of equations are used to describe reactions in solution: (1) the molecular equation, which shows the complete formulas of all reactants and products; (2) the complete ionic equation, in which all reactants and products that are strong electrolytes are shown as ions; and (3) the net ionic equation, which includes only those components of the solution that undergo a change. Spectator ions (those ions that remain unchanged in a reaction) are not included in a net ionic equation.
4. A strong acid is a compound in which virtually every molecule dissociates in water to give an H^+ ion and an anion. Similarly, a strong base is a metal hydroxide compound that is soluble in water, giving OH^- ions and cations. The products of the reaction of a strong acid and a strong base are water and a salt.
5. Reactions of metals and nonmetals involve a transfer of electrons and are called oxidation–reduction reactions. A reaction between a nonmetal and oxygen is also an oxidation–reduction reaction. Combustion reactions involve oxygen and are a subgroup of oxidation–reduction reactions.
6. When a given compound is formed from simpler materials, such as elements, the reaction is called a synthesis or combination reaction. The reverse process, which occurs when a compound is broken down into its component elements, is called a decomposition reaction. These reactions are also subgroups of oxidation–reduction reactions.

F directs you to the *Chemistry in Focus* feature in the chapter
VP indicates visual problems
OWL interactive versions of these problems are assignable in OWL.

Active Learning Questions

These questions are designed to be considered by groups of students in class. Often these questions work well for introducing a particular topic in class.

1. Consider the mixing of aqueous solutions of lead(II) nitrate and sodium iodide to form a solid.
   a. Name the possible products, and determine the formulas of these possible products.
   b. What is the precipitate? How do you know?
   c. Must the subscript for an ion in a reactant stay the same as the subscript of that ion in a product? Explain your answer.
2. Assume a highly magnified view of a solution of HCl that allows you to "see" the HCl. Draw this magnified view. If you dropped in a piece of magnesium, the magnesium would disappear and hydrogen gas would be released. Represent this change using symbols for the elements, and write the balanced equation.
3. Why is the formation of a solid evidence of a chemical reaction? Use a molecular-level drawing in your explanation.
4. Sketch molecular-level drawings to differentiate between two soluble compounds: one that is a strong electrolyte, and one that is not an electrolyte.
5. Mixing an aqueous solution of potassium nitrate with an aqueous solution of sodium chloride does not result in a chemical reaction. Why?
6. Why is the formation of water evidence of a chemical reaction? Use a molecular-level drawing in your explanation.
7. Use the Arrhenius definition of acids and bases to write the net ionic equation for the reaction of an acid with a base.

ChemWork

How Many Lines for H?
Electron Transitions in H
Hydrogen Wavelengths
Electron Designations
Quantum Numbers
Quantum Numbers 2
Electron Configurations
Identifying Elements by Configurations
Modern Atomic Theory and Electron Configurations
Writing Electron Configurations
Atomic Properties
Atomic Size
Comparing Atomic Properties
Comparing Atomic Radii
Comparing Ionization Energies
Identifying Elements by Atomic Properties
Ionization Energies of Atoms
Periodic Trends for First Ionization Energies
Periodic Trends in Atomic Radii

8. Why is the transfer of electrons evidence of a chemical reaction? Use a molecular-level drawing in your explanation.

9. Why is the formation of a gas evidence of a chemical reaction? Use a molecular-level drawing in your explanation.

10. Label each of the following statements as true or false. Explain your answers, and provide an example for each that supports your answer.
   a. All nonelectrolytes are insoluble.
   b. All insoluble substances are nonelectrolytes.
   c. All strong electrolytes are soluble.
   d. All soluble substances are strong electrolytes.

11. Look at Figure 7.2 in the text. It is possible for a weak electrolyte solution to cause the bulb to glow brighter than a strong electrolyte. Explain how this is possible.

12. What is the purpose of spectator ions? If they are not present as part of the reaction, why are they present at all?

13. Which of the following **must** be an oxidation–reduction reaction? Explain your answer, and include an example oxidation–reduction reaction for all that apply.
   a. A metal reacts with a nonmetal.
   b. A precipitation reaction.
   c. An acid–base reaction.

14. If an element is a reactant or product in a chemical reaction, the reaction must be an oxidation–reduction reaction. Why is this true?

VP 15. Match each name below with the following microscopic pictures of that compound in aqueous solution.

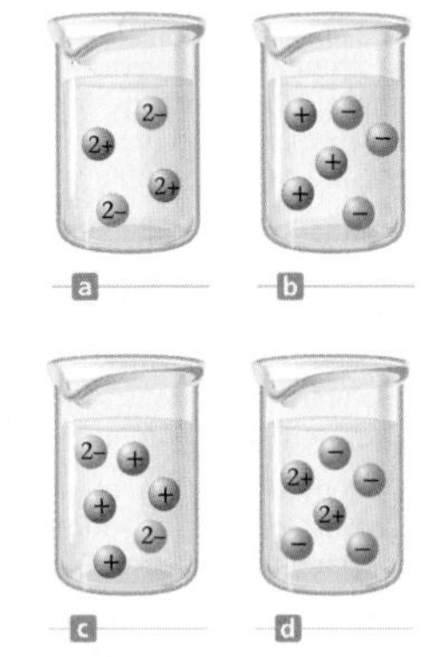

a. barium nitrate
b. sodium chloride
c. potassium carbonate
d. magnesium sulfate

Which picture best represents $HNO_3(aq)$? Why aren't any of the pictures a good representation of $HC_2H_3O_2(aq)$?

VP 16. On the basis of the general solubility rules given in Table 7.1, predict the identity of the precipitate that forms when aqueous solutions of the following substances are mixed. If no precipitate is likely, indicate which rules apply.

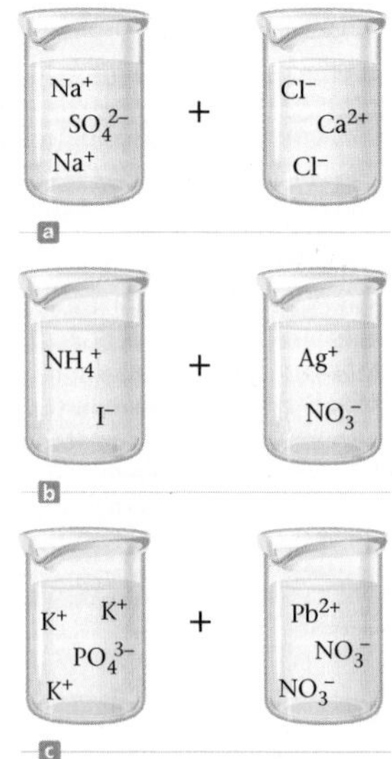

VP 17. Write the balanced formula and net ionic equation for the reaction that occurs when the contents of the two beakers are added together. What colors represent the spectator ions in each reaction?

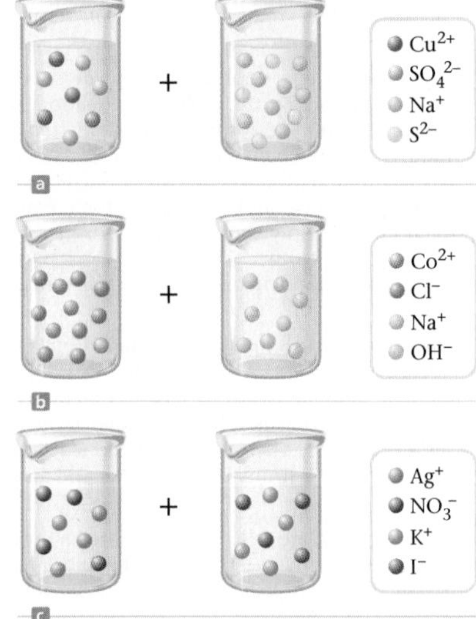

Answers to End-of-Chapter Exercises

1. Water is the most universal of all liquids; water has high heat capacity; water is very polar.

2. Driving forces are types of *changes* in a system that pull a reaction in the *direction of product formation;* driving forces include formation of a *solid,* formation of *water,* formation of a *gas,* and transfer of electrons.

3. precipitation

4. a reactant in aqueous solution is indicated with (*aq*); formation of a solid is indicated with (*s*)

5. The ions separate, become hydrated, and behave independently.

6. There are twice as many chloride ions as magnesium ions.

7. A substance is a strong electrolyte if the substance completely dissociates into individual ions when dissolved.

8. The simplest evidence is that solutions of ionic substances conduct electricity.

9. Answer depends on student examples.

10. Answer depends on student choices.

11. (a) insoluble; Rule 6; (b) insoluble; Rule 5; (c) soluble; Rules 2 and 4; (d) soluble; Rule 2; (e) insoluble; Rule 6; (f) insoluble; Rule 6; (g) insoluble; Rule 3; (h) insoluble, Rule 4

12. (a) soluble; Rule 3; (b) soluble; Rule 2; (c) soluble; Rule 2; (d) insoluble; Rule 5; (e) soluble; Rule 2; (f) soluble; Rule 1; (g) soluble; Rule 4; (h) insoluble; Rule 6

13. (a) Rule 2; (b) Rule 1; (c) Rule 2; (d) Rule 4; (e) Rule 3

14. (a) Rule 6; (b) Rule 6; (c) Rule 6; (d) Rule 3; (e) Rule 4

15. (a) CuS; (b) $Ba_3(PO_4)_2$; (c) AgCl; (d) $CoCO_3$; (e) $CaSO_4$; (f) Hg_2Cl_2

16. (a) $MnCO_3$, Rule 6; (b) $CaSO_4$, Rule 4; (c) Hg_2Cl_2, Rule 3; (d) no precipitate, most sodium and nitrate salts are soluble; (e) $Ni(OH)_2$, Rule 5; (f) $BaSO_4$, Rule 4

17. (a) $NH_4Cl(aq) + H_2SO_4(aq) \rightarrow$ no precipitate; (b) $2K_2CO_3(aq) + SnCl_4(aq) \rightarrow \underline{Sn(CO_3)_2(s)} +$ $4KCl(aq)$; (c) $2NH_4Cl(aq) + Pb(NO_3)_2(aq) \rightarrow$ $\underline{PbCl_2(s)} + 2NH_4NO_3(aq)$; (d) $CuSO_4(aq) +$ $2KOH(aq) \rightarrow \underline{Cu(OH)_2(s)} + K_2SO_4(aq)$; (e) $Na_3PO_4(aq) + CrCl_3(aq) \rightarrow \underline{CrPO_4(s)} +$ $3NaCl(s)$; (f) $3(NH_4)_2S(aq) + 2FeCl_3(aq) \rightarrow$ $\underline{Fe_2S_3(s)} + 6NH_4Cl(aq)$

18. (a) $Na_2CO_3(aq) + CuSO_4(aq) \rightarrow Na_2SO_4(aq) +$ $\underline{CuCO_3(s)}$; (b) $HCl(aq) + AgC_2H_3O_2(aq) \rightarrow$ $HC_2H_3O_2(aq) + \underline{AgCl(s)}$; (c) no precipitate; (d) $3(NH_4)_2S(aq) + 2FeCl_3(aq) \rightarrow 6NH_4Cl(aq) +$ $\underline{Fe_2S_3(s)}$; (e) $H_2SO_4(aq) + Pb(NO_3)_2(aq) \rightarrow$ $2HNO_3(aq) + \underline{PbSO_4(s)}$; (f) $2K_3PO_4(aq) +$ $3CaCl_2(aq) \rightarrow 6KCl(aq) + \underline{Ca_3(PO_4)_2(s)}$

Questions and Problems

7.1 Predicting Whether a Reaction Will Occur

QUESTIONS

1. Why is water an important solvent? Although you have not yet studied water in detail, can you think of some properties of water that make it so important?

2. What is a "driving force"? What are some of the driving forces discussed in this section that tend to make reactions likely to occur? Can you think of any other possible driving forces?

7.2 Reactions in Which a Solid Forms

QUESTIONS

3. A reaction in aqueous solution that results in the formation of a *solid* is called a ______ reaction.

4. When writing the chemical equation for a reaction, how do you indicate that a given reactant is dissolved in water? How do you indicate that a precipitate has formed as a result of the reaction?

5. Describe briefly what happens when an ionic substance is dissolved in water.

6. When the ionic solute $MgCl_2$ is dissolved in water, what can you say about the number of chloride ions present in the solution compared to the number of magnesium ions in the solution?

7. What is meant by a *strong electrolyte?* Give two examples of substances that behave in solution as strong electrolytes.

8. How do chemists know that the ions behave independently of one another when an ionic solid is dissolved in water?

9. Suppose you are trying to help your friend understand the general solubility rules for ionic substances in water. Explain in general terms to your friend what the solubility rules mean, and give an example of how the rules could be applied in determining the identity of the precipitate in a reaction between solutions of two ionic compounds.

10. Using the general solubility rules given in Table 7.1, write the formulas and names of five ionic substances that would not be expected to be appreciably soluble in water. Indicate *why* each of the substances would not be expected to be soluble.

11. On the basis of the general solubility rules given in Table 7.1, predict which of the following substances are *not* likely to be soluble in water. Indicate which specific rule(s) led to your conclusion.

    a. PbS
    b. $Mg(OH)_2$
    c. Na_2SO_4
    d. $(NH_4)_2S$
    e. $BaCO_3$
    f. $AlPO_4$
    g. $PbCl_2$
    h. $CaSO_4$

12. On the basis of the general solubility rules given in Table 7.1, predict which of the following substances are likely to be appreciably soluble in water. Indicate which specific rule(s) led to your conclusion.

    a. $BaCl_2$
    b. $NH_4C_2H_3O_2$
    c. Na_2S
    d. $Fe(OH)_3$
    e. K_2CO_3
    f. $Au(NO_3)_3$
    g. $ZnSO_4$
    h. Fe_2S_3

13. On the basis of the general solubility rules given in Table 7.1, for each of the following compounds, explain why the compound would be expected to be appreciably soluble in water. Indicate which of the solubility rules covers each substance's particular situation.

    a. potassium sulfide
    b. cobalt(III) nitrate
    c. ammonium phosphate
    d. cesium sulfate
    e. strontium chloride

14. On the basis of the general solubility rules given in Table 7.1, for each of the following compounds, explain why the compound would *not* be expected to be appreciably soluble in water. Indicate which of the solubility rules covers each substance's particular situation.

    a. copper(II) sulfide
    b. iron(III) carbonate
    c. zinc phosphate
    d. lead(II) chloride
    e. barium sulfate

15. On the basis of the general solubility rules given in Table 7.1, predict the identity of the precipitate that forms when aqueous solutions of the following substances are mixed. If no precipitate is likely, indicate which rules apply.

    a. copper(II) chloride, $CuCl_2$, and ammonium sulfide, $(NH_4)_2S$
    b. barium nitrate, $Ba(NO_3)_2$, and potassium phosphate, K_3PO_4
    c. silver acetate, $AgC_2H_3O_2$, and calcium chloride, $CaCl_2$
    d. potassium carbonate, K_2CO_3, and cobalt(II) chloride, $CoCl_2$
    e. sulfuric acid, H_2SO_4, and calcium nitrate, $Ca(NO_3)_2$
    f. mercurous acetate, $Hg_2(C_2H_3O_2)_2$, and hydrochloric acid, HCl

16. On the basis of the general solubility rules given in Table 7.1, predict the identity of the precipitate that forms when aqueous solutions of the following substances are mixed. If no precipitate is likely, indicate which rules apply.

    a. sodium carbonate, Na_2CO_3, and manganese(II) chloride, $MnCl_2$
    b. potassium sulfate, K_2SO_4, and calcium acetate, $Ca(C_2H_3O_2)_2$
    c. hydrochloric acid, HCl, and mercurous acetate, $Hg_2(C_2H_3O_2)_2$
    d. sodium nitrate, $NaNO_3$, and lithium sulfate, Li_2SO_4
    e. potassium hydroxide, KOH, and nickel(II) chloride, $NiCl_2$
    f. sulfuric acid, H_2SO_4, and barium chloride, $BaCl_2$

All even-numbered Questions and Problems have answers in the back of this book and solutions in the Solutions Guide.

19. (a) $Na_2SO_4(aq) + CaCl_2(aq) \rightarrow CaSO_4(s) + 2NaCl(aq)$; (b) $Co(C_2H_3O_2)_2(aq) + Na_2S(aq) \rightarrow CoS(s) + 2NaC_2H_3O_2(aq)$; (c) $2KOH(aq) + NiCl_2(aq) \rightarrow Ni(OH)_2(s) + 2KCl(aq)$

20. (a) $CaCl_2(aq) + 2AgNO_3(aq) \rightarrow Ca(NO_3)_2(aq) + 2AgCl(s)$; (b) $2AgNO_3(aq) + K_2CrO_4(aq) \rightarrow Ag_2CrO_4(s) + 2KNO_3(aq)$; (c) $BaCl_2(aq) + K_2SO_4(aq) \rightarrow BaSO_4(s) + 2KCl(aq)$

21. (a) $(NH_4)_2SO_4(aq) + Ba(NO_3)_2(aq) \rightarrow 2NH_4NO_3(aq) + \underline{BaSO_4(s)}$; (b) $H_2S(aq) + NiSO_4(aq) \rightarrow H_2SO_4(aq) + \underline{NiS(s)}$; (c) $FeCl_3(aq) + 3NaOH(aq) \rightarrow 3NaCl(aq) + \underline{Fe(OH)_3(s)}$

22. (a) $Na_2CO_3(aq) + K_2SO_4(aq) \rightarrow$ no precipitate; all combinations are soluble; (b) $CuCl_2(aq) + (NH_4)_2CO_3(aq) \rightarrow 2NH_4Cl(aq) + \underline{CuCO_3(s)}$; (c) $K_3PO_4(aq) + AlCl_3(aq) \rightarrow 3KCl(aq) + \underline{AlPO_4(s)}$

23. The net ionic equation indicates only those ions that are involved in forming the precipitate.

24. Spectator ions are ions that *remain in solution* during a precipitation/double-displacement reaction. For example, in the reaction $BaCl_2(aq) + K_2SO_4(aq) \rightarrow BaSO_4(s) + 2KCl(aq)$, the K^+ and Cl^- ions are spectator ions.

25. Answer depends on student choice of examples.

26. (a) $Ca^{2+}(aq) + SO_4^{2-}(aq) \rightarrow CaSO_4(s)$; (b) $Ni^{2+}(aq) + 2OH^-(aq) \rightarrow Ni(OH)_2(s)$; (c) $2Fe^{3+}(aq) + 3S^{2-}(aq) \rightarrow Fe_2S_3(s)$

27. $Cu^{2+}(aq) + CrO_4^{2-}(aq) \rightarrow CuCrO_4(s)$; $Co^{3+}(aq) + CrO_4^{2-}(aq) \rightarrow Co_2(CrO_4)_3(s)$; $Ba^{2+}(aq) + CrO_4^{2-}(aq) \rightarrow BaCrO_4(s)$; $Fe^{3+}(aq) + CrO_4^{2-}(aq) \rightarrow Fe_2(CrO_4)_3(s)$

28. $Ag^+(aq) + Cl^-(aq) \rightarrow AgCl(s)$; $Pb^{2+}(aq) + 2Cl^-(aq) \rightarrow PbCl_2(s)$; $Hg_2^{2+}(aq) + 2Cl^-(aq) \rightarrow Hg_2Cl_2(s)$

29. $Ca^{2+}(aq) + C_2O_4^{2-}(aq) \rightarrow CaC_2O_4(s)$

30. $Co^{2+}(aq) + S^{2-}(aq) \rightarrow CoS(s)$; $2Co^{3+}(aq) + 3S^{2-}(aq) \rightarrow Co_2S_3(s)$; $Fe^{2+}(aq) + S^{2-}(aq) \rightarrow FeS(s)$; $2Fe^{3+}(aq) + 3S^{2-}(aq) \rightarrow Fe_2S_3(s)$

31. Strong acids ionize completely in water; they are also strong electrolytes.

32. The strong bases are those hydroxide compounds that dissociate fully when dissolved in water. The strong bases that are highly soluble in water (NaOH, KOH) are also strong electrolytes.

33. $H^+(aq) + OH^-(aq) \rightarrow H_2O(l)$

34. acids: HCl (hydrochloric), HNO_3 (nitric), H_2SO_4 (sulfuric); bases: hydroxides of Group 1A elements: NaOH, KOH, RbOH, CsOH

35. 1000; 1000

36. A salt is the ionic product remaining in solution when an acid neutralizes a base. For example, in the reaction $HCl(aq) + NaOH(aq) \rightarrow NaCl(aq) + H_2O(l)$, sodium chloride is the salt produced by the neutralization reaction.

37. $HCl(aq) \rightarrow H^+(aq) + Cl^-(aq)$; $HNO_3(aq) \rightarrow H^+(aq) + NO_3^-(aq)$; $H_2SO_4(aq) \rightarrow H^+(aq) + HSO_4^-(aq)$;

PROBLEMS

17. On the basis of the general solubility rules given in Table 7.1, write a balanced molecular equation for the precipitation reactions that take place when the following aqueous solutions are mixed. Underline the formula of the precipitate (solid) that forms. If no precipitation reaction is likely for the reactants given, explain why.
    a. ammonium chloride, NH_4Cl, and sulfuric acid, H_2SO_4
    b. potassium carbonate, K_2CO_3, and tin(IV) chloride, $SnCl_4$
    c. ammonium chloride, NH_4Cl, and lead(II) nitrate, $Pb(NO_3)_2$
    d. copper(II) sulfate, $CuSO_4$, and potassium hydroxide, KOH
    e. sodium phosphate, Na_3PO_4, and chromium(III) chloride, $CrCl_3$
    f. ammonium sulfide, $(NH_4)_2S$, and iron(III) chloride, $FeCl_3$

18. On the basis of the general solubility rules given in Table 7.1, write a balanced molecular equation for the precipitation reactions that take place when the following aqueous solutions are mixed. Underline the formula of the precipitate (solid) that forms. If no precipitation reaction is likely for the solutes given, so indicate.
    a. sodium carbonate, Na_2CO_3, and copper(II) sulfate, $CuSO_4$
    b. hydrochloric acid, HCl, and silver acetate, $AgC_2H_3O_2$
    c. barium chloride, $BaCl_2$, and calcium nitrate, $Ca(NO_3)_2$
    d. ammonium sulfide, $(NH_4)_2S$, and iron(III) chloride, $FeCl_3$
    e. sulfuric acid, H_2SO_4, and lead(II) nitrate, $Pb(NO_3)_2$
    f. potassium phosphate, K_3PO_4, and calcium chloride, $CaCl_2$

19. Balance each of the following equations that describe precipitation reactions.
    a. $Na_2SO_4(aq) + CaCl_2(aq) \rightarrow CaSO_4(s) + NaCl(aq)$
    b. $Co(C_2H_3O_2)_2(aq) + Na_2S(aq) \rightarrow CoS(s) + NaC_2H_3O_2(aq)$
    c. $KOH(aq) + NiCl_2(aq) \rightarrow Ni(OH)_2(s) + KCl(aq)$

20. Balance each of the following equations that describe precipitation reactions.
    a. $CaCl_2(aq) + AgNO_3(aq) \rightarrow Ca(NO_3)_2(aq) + AgCl(s)$
    b. $AgNO_3(aq) + K_2CrO_4(aq) \rightarrow Ag_2CrO_4(s) + KNO_3(aq)$
    c. $BaCl_2(aq) + K_2SO_4(aq) \rightarrow BaSO_4(s) + KCl(aq)$

21. For each of the following precipitation reactions, complete and balance the equation, indicating clearly which product is the precipitate. If no reaction would be expected, so indicate.
    a. $(NH_4)_2SO_4(aq) + Ba(NO_3)_2(aq) \rightarrow$
    b. $H_2S(aq) + NiSO_4(aq) \rightarrow$
    c. $FeCl_3(aq) + NaOH(aq) \rightarrow$

22. For each of the following precipitation reactions, complete and balance the equation, indicating clearly which product is the precipitate. If no reaction would be expected, so indicate.
    a. $Na_2CO_3(aq) + K_2SO_4(aq) \rightarrow$
    b. $CuCl_2(aq) + (NH_4)_2CO_3(aq) \rightarrow$
    c. $K_3PO_4(aq) + AlCl_3(aq) \rightarrow$

7.3 Describing Reactions in Aqueous Solutions

QUESTIONS

23. What is a net ionic equation? What species are shown in such an equation, and which species are not shown?

24. What are *spectator ions?* Write an example of an equation in which spectator ions are present and identify them.

PROBLEMS

25. Based on the general solubility rules given in Table 7.1, propose five combinations of aqueous ionic reagents that likely would form a precipitate when they are mixed. Write the balanced full molecular equation and the balanced net ionic equation for each of your choices.

26. Write balanced net ionic equations for the reactions that occur when the following aqueous solutions are mixed. If no reaction is likely to occur, so indicate.
    a. calcium nitrate and sulfuric acid
    b. nickel(II) nitrate and sodium hydroxide
    c. ammonium sulfide and iron(III) chloride

27. Many chromate (CrO_4^{2-}) salts are insoluble, and most have brilliant colors that have led to their being used as pigments. Write balanced net ionic equations for the reactions of Cu^{2+}, Co^{3+}, Ba^{2+}, and Fe^{3+} with chromate ion.

28. The procedures and principles of qualitative analysis are covered in many introductory chemistry laboratory courses. In qualitative analysis, students learn to analyze mixtures of the common positive and negative ions, separating and confirming the presence of the particular ions in the mixture. One of the first steps in such an analysis is to treat the mixture with hydrochloric acid, which precipitates and removes silver ion, lead(II) ion, and mercury(I) ion from the aqueous mixture as the insoluble chloride salts. Write balanced net ionic equations for the precipitation reactions of these three cations with chloride ion.

29. Many plants are poisonous because their stems and leaves contain oxalic acid, $H_2C_2O_4$, or sodium oxalate, $Na_2C_2O_4$; when ingested, these substances cause swelling of the respiratory tract and suffocation. A standard analysis for determining the amount of oxalate ion, $C_2O_4^{2-}$, in a sample is to precipitate this species as calcium oxalate, which is insoluble in water. Write the net ionic equation for the reaction between sodium oxalate and calcium chloride, $CaCl_2$, in aqueous solution.

All even-numbered Questions and Problems have answers in the back of this book and solutions in the Solutions Guide.

$HClO_4(aq) \rightarrow H^+(aq) + ClO_4^-(aq)$

38. $RbOH(s) \rightarrow Rb^+(aq) + OH^-(aq)$; $CsOH(s) \rightarrow Cs^+(aq) + OH^-(aq)$

39. (a) KCl; (b) $RbNO_3$; (c) $NaClO_4$; (d) CsBr(*aq*)

40. (a) $H_2SO_4(aq) + 2KOH(aq) \rightarrow K_2SO_4(aq) + 2H_2O(l)$; (b) $HNO_3(aq) + NaOH(aq) \rightarrow NaNO_3(aq) + H_2O(l)$; (c) $2HCl(aq) + Ca(OH)_2(aq) \rightarrow CaCl_2(aq) + 2H_2O(l)$; (d) $2HClO_4(aq) + Ba(OH)_2(aq) \rightarrow Ba(ClO_4)_2(aq) + 2H_2O(l)$

41. One species loses electrons (oxidation); another species gains electrons (reduction).

42. Answer depends on student choice of example: $2Na(s) + Cl_2(g) \rightarrow 2NaCl(s)$ is an example.

43. an event that helps to convert reactants to products; some elements tend to lose electrons, others tend to gain them; a transfer of electrons would be favorable

44. The metal loses electrons; the nonmetal gains electrons.

45. Each calcium atom would lose two electrons. Each fluorine atom would gain one electron (so the F_2 molecule would gain two electrons). One calcium atom would be required to react with one fluorine, F_2, molecule. Calcium ions are charged 2+; fluoride ions are charged 1−.

46. Each magnesium atom would lose two electrons. Each oxygen atom would gain two electrons (so the O_2 molecule would gain four electrons). Two magnesium atoms would be required to react with each O_2 molecule. Magnesium ions are charged 2+; oxide ions are charged 2−.

47. Each Mg loses two electrons to become Mg^{2+}; each Cl gains one electron to become Cl^-; one Mg atom would provide the electrons for two Cl atoms.

48. Each potassium atom loses one electron. The sulfur atom gains two electrons. So two potassium atoms are required to react with one sulfur atom.

$$2 \times (K \rightarrow K^+ + e^-)$$
$$S + 2e^- \rightarrow S^{2-}$$

49. (a) $2Co(s) + 3Br_2(l) \rightarrow 2CoBr_3(s)$; cobalt is oxidized, bromine is reduced; (b) $2Al(s) + 3H_2SO_4(aq) \rightarrow Al_2(SO_4)_3(aq) + 3H_2(g)$; aluminum is oxidized, hydrogen is reduced; (c) $2Na(s) + 2H_2O(l) \rightarrow 2NaOH(aq) + H_2(g)$; sodium is oxidized; hydrogen is reduced; (d) $4Cu(s) + O_2(g) \rightarrow 2Cu_2O(s)$; copper is oxidized, oxygen is reduced

50. (a) $P_4(s) + 5O_2(g) \rightarrow P_4O_{10}(s)$; (b) $MgO(s) + C(s) \rightarrow Mg(s) + CO(g)$; (c) $Sr(s) + 2H_2O(l) \rightarrow Sr(OH)_2(aq) + H_2(g)$; (d) $Co(s) + 2HCl(aq) \rightarrow CoCl_2(aq) + H_2(g)$

51. (a) and (b): Answer depends on student choice of examples.

30. Another step in the qualitative analysis of cations (see Exercise 28) involves precipitating some of the metal ions as the insoluble sulfides (followed by subsequent treatment of the mixed sulfide precipitate to separate the individual ions). Write balanced net ionic equations for the reactions of Co(II), Co(III), Fe(II), and Fe(III) ions with sulfide ion, S^{2-}.

7.4 Reactions That Form Water: Acids and Bases

QUESTIONS

31. What is meant by a *strong acid?* Are the strong acids also strong *electrolytes?* Explain.

32. What is meant by a *strong base?* Are the strong bases also strong *electrolytes?* Explain.

33. The same net ionic process takes place when any strong acid reacts with any strong base. Write the equation for that process.

34. Write the formulas and names of three common strong acids and strong bases.

35. If 1000 NaOH units were dissolved in a sample of water, the NaOH would produce ______ Na^+ ions and ______ OH^- ions.

36. What is a *salt?* Give two balanced chemical equations showing how a salt is formed when an acid reacts with a base.

PROBLEMS

37. Write balanced equations showing how three of the common strong acids ionize to produce hydrogen ion.

38. In addition to the strong bases NaOH and KOH discussed in this chapter, the hydroxide compounds of other Group 1 elements behave as strong bases when dissolved in water. Write equations for RbOH and CsOH that show which ions form when they dissolve in water.

39. What salt would form when each of the following strong acid/strong base reactions takes place?
   a. $HCl(aq) + KOH(aq) \rightarrow$
   b. $RbOH(aq) + HNO_3(aq) \rightarrow$
   c. $HClO_4(aq) + NaOH(aq) \rightarrow$
   d. $HBr(aq) + CsOH(aq) \rightarrow$

40. Complete the following acid–base reactions by indicating the acid and base that must have reacted in each case to produce the indicated salt.
   a. ______ + ______ $\rightarrow K_2SO_4(aq) + 2H_2O(l)$
   b. ______ + ______ $\rightarrow NaNO_3(aq) + H_2O(l)$
   c. ______ + ______ $\rightarrow CaCl_2(aq) + 2H_2O(l)$
   d. ______ + ______ $\rightarrow Ba(ClO_4)_2(aq) + 2H_2O(l)$

7.5 Reactions of Metals with Nonmetals (Oxidation–Reduction)

QUESTIONS

41. What is an oxidation–reduction reaction? What is transferred during such a reaction?

42. Give an example of a simple chemical reaction that involves the *transfer of electrons* from a metallic element to a nonmetallic element.

43. What do we mean when we say that the transfer of electrons can be the "driving force" for a reaction? Give an example of a reaction where this happens.

44. If atoms of a metallic element (such as sodium) react with atoms of a nonmetallic element (such as sulfur), which element loses electrons and which element gains them?

45. If atoms of the metal calcium were to react with molecules of the nonmetal fluorine, F_2, how many electrons would each calcium atom lose? How many electrons would each fluorine atom gain? How many calcium atoms would be needed to react with one fluorine molecule? What charges would the resulting calcium and fluoride ions have?

46. If oxygen molecules, O_2, were to react with magnesium atoms, how many electrons would each magnesium atom lose? How many electrons would each oxygen atom gain? How many magnesium atoms would be needed to react with each oxygen molecule? What charges would the resulting magnesium and oxide ions have?

PROBLEMS

47. For the reaction $Mg(s) + Cl_2(g) \rightarrow MgCl_2(s)$, illustrate how electrons are gained and lost during the reaction.

48. For the reaction $2K(s) + S(g) \rightarrow K_2S(s)$, show how electrons are gained and lost by the atoms.

49. Balance each of the following oxidation–reduction reactions. For each, indicate which substance is being oxidized and which is being reduced.
   a. $Co(s) + Br_2(l) \rightarrow CoBr_3(s)$
   b. $Al(s) + H_2SO_4(aq) \rightarrow Al_2(SO_4)_3(aq) + H_2(g)$
   c. $Na(s) + H_2O(l) \rightarrow NaOH(aq) + H_2(g)$
   d. $Cu(s) + O_2(g) \rightarrow Cu_2O(s)$

50. Balance each of the following oxidation–reduction chemical reactions.
   a. $P_4(s) + O_2(g) \rightarrow P_4O_{10}(s)$
   b. $MgO(s) + C(s) \rightarrow Mg(s) + CO(g)$
   c. $Sr(s) + H_2O(l) \rightarrow Sr(OH)_2(aq) + H_2(g)$
   d. $Co(s) + HCl(aq) \rightarrow CoCl_2(aq) + H_2(g)$

7.6 Ways to Classify Reactions

QUESTIONS

51. a. Give two examples each of a single-displacement reaction and of a double-replacement reaction. How are the two reaction types similar, and how are they different?
   b. Give two examples each of a reaction in which formation of water is the driving force and in which formation of a gas is the driving force.

All even-numbered Questions and Problems have answers in the back of this book and solutions in the Solutions Guide.

52. The reaction includes aluminum metal as a reactant and products that contain aluminum ions. For this reaction, electrons must be transferred. That is, to make an aluminum cation, electrons must be removed from the metal. An oxidation reduction is one that involves transfers of electrons.

53. (a) precipitation; (b) oxidation–reduction; (c) precipitation; (d) acid–base; (e) oxidation–reduction; (f) acid–base; (g) precipitation; (h) oxidation–reduction; (i) precipitation

54. (a) oxidation–reduction; (b) oxidation–reduction; (c) acid–base; (d) acid–base, precipitation; (e) precipitation; (f) precipitation; (g) oxidation–reduction; (h) oxidation–reduction; (i) acid–base

55. A combustion reaction is typically a reaction in which an element or compound reacts with oxygen so quickly and with so much energy released that a flame results. In addition to the carbon dioxide and water chemical products, combustion reactions are a major source of heat energy.

56. oxidation–reduction

57. production of a compound from simpler substances (elements or simpler compounds)

58. A decomposition reaction is one in which a given compound is broken down into simpler compounds or constituent elements. The reactions $CaCO_3(s) \rightarrow CaO(s) + CO_2(g)$ and $2HgO(s) \rightarrow 2Hg(l) + O_2(g)$ represent decomposition reactions. Such reactions often may be classified in other ways. For example, the reaction of $HgO(s)$ is also an oxidation–reduction reaction.

59. (a) $2C_6H_6(l) + 15O_2(g) \rightarrow 12CO_2(g) + 6H_2O(g)$; (b) $C_5H_{12}(l) + 8O_2(g) \rightarrow 5CO_2(g) + 6H_2O(g)$; (c) $C_2H_6O(l) + 3O_2(g) \rightarrow 2CO_2(g) + 3H_2O(g)$

60. (a) $C_3H_8(g) + 5O_2(g) \rightarrow 3CO_2(g) + 4H_2O(g)$; (b) $C_2H_4(g) + 3O_2(g) \rightarrow 2CO_2(g) + 2H_2O(g)$; (c) $2C_8H_{18}(l) + 25O_2(g) \rightarrow 16CO_2(g) + 18H_2O(g)$

61. Answer depends on student selection of examples.

62. Answer depends on student selection.

63. (a) $CaO(s) + H_2O(l) \rightarrow Ca(OH)_2(s)$; (b) $4Fe(s) + 3O_2(g) \rightarrow 2Fe_2O_3(s)$; (c) $P_2O_5(s) + 3H_2O(l) \rightarrow 2H_3PO_4(aq)$

64. (a) $8Fe(s) + S_8(s) \rightarrow 8FeS(s)$; (b) $4Co(s) + 3O_2(g) \rightarrow 2Co_2O_3(s)$; (c) $Cl_2O_7(g) + H_2O(l) \rightarrow 2HClO_4(aq)$

65. (a) $CaSO_4(s) \rightarrow CaO(s) + SO_3(g)$; (b) $Li_2CO_3(s) \rightarrow Li_2O(s) + CO_2(g)$; (c) $2LiHCO_3(s) \rightarrow Li_2CO_3(s) + H_2O(g) + CO_2(g)$; (d) $C_6H_6(l) \rightarrow 6C(s) + 3H_2(g)$; (e) $4PBr_3(l) \rightarrow P_4(s) + 6Br_2(l)$

66. (a) $2Al(s) + 3Br_2(g) \rightarrow 2AlBr_3(s)$; (b) $Zn(s) + 2HClO_4(aq) \rightarrow Zn(ClO_4)_2(aq) + H_2(g)$; (c) $3Na(s) + P(s) \rightarrow Na_3P(s)$; (d) $CH_4(g) + 4Cl_2(g) \rightarrow CCl_4(l) + 4HCl(g)$; (e) $Cu(s) + 2AgNO_3(aq) \rightarrow Cu(NO_3)_2(aq) + 2Ag(s)$

52. The reaction between ammonium perchlorate and aluminum is discussed in the Chemistry in Focus segment *Oxidation–Reduction Reactions Launch the Space Shuttle*. The reaction is labeled as an oxidation–reduction reaction. Explain why this is an oxidation–reduction reaction and defend your answer.

53. Identify each of the following unbalanced reaction equations as belonging to one or more of the following categories: precipitation, acid–base, or oxidation–reduction.

a. $K_2SO_4(aq) + Ba(NO_3)_2(aq) \rightarrow BaSO_4(s) + KNO_3(aq)$
b. $HCl(aq) + Zn(s) \rightarrow H_2(g) + ZnCl_2(aq)$
c. $HCl(aq) + AgNO_3(aq) \rightarrow HNO_3(aq) + AgCl(s)$
d. $HCl(aq) + KOH(aq) \rightarrow H_2O(l) + KCl(aq)$
e. $Zn(s) + CuSO_4(aq) \rightarrow ZnSO_4(aq) + Cu(s)$
f. $NaH_2PO_4(aq) + NaOH(aq) \rightarrow Na_3PO_4(aq) + H_2O(l)$
g. $Ca(OH)_2(aq) + H_2SO_4(aq) \rightarrow CaSO_4(s) + H_2O(l)$
h. $ZnCl_2(aq) + Mg(s) \rightarrow Zn(s) + MgCl_2(aq)$
i. $BaCl_2(aq) + H_2SO_4(aq) \rightarrow BaSO_4(s) + HCl(aq)$

54. Identify each of the following unbalanced reaction equations as belonging to one or more of the following categories: precipitation, acid–base, or oxidation–reduction.

a. $H_2O_2(aq) \rightarrow H_2O(l) + O_2(g)$
b. $H_2SO_4(aq) + Zn(s) \rightarrow ZnSO_4(aq) + H_2(g)$
c. $H_2SO_4(aq) + NaOH(aq) \rightarrow Na_2SO_4(aq) + H_2O(l)$
d. $H_2SO_4(aq) + Ba(OH)_2(aq) \rightarrow BaSO_4(s) + H_2O(l)$
e. $AgNO_3(aq) + CuCl_2(aq) \rightarrow Cu(NO_3)_2(aq) + AgCl(s)$
f. $KOH(aq) + CuSO_4(aq) \rightarrow Cu(OH)_2(s) + K_2SO_4(aq)$
g. $Cl_2(g) + F_2(g) \rightarrow ClF(g)$
h. $NO(g) + O_2(g) \rightarrow NO_2(g)$
i. $Ca(OH)_2(s) + HNO_3(aq) \rightarrow Ca(NO_3)_2(aq) + H_2O(l)$

7.7 Other Ways to Classify Reactions

QUESTIONS

55. How do we define a *combustion* reaction? In addition to the chemical products, what other products do combustion reactions produce? Give two examples of balanced chemical equations for combustion reactions.

56. Reactions involving the combustion of fuel substances make up a subclass of ______ reactions.

57. What is a *synthesis* or *combination* reaction? Give an example. Can such reactions also be classified in other ways? Give an example of a synthesis reaction that is also a *combustion* reaction. Give an example of a synthesis reaction that is also an *oxidation–reduction* reaction, but that does not involve combustion.

58. What is a *decomposition* reaction? Give an example. Can such reactions also be classified in other ways?

PROBLEMS

59. Complete and balance each of the following combustion reactions.

a. $C_6H_6(l) + O_2(g) \rightarrow$
b. $C_5H_{12}(l) + O_2(g) \rightarrow$
c. $C_2H_6O(l) + O_2(g) \rightarrow$

60. Complete and balance each of the following combustion reactions.

a. $C_3H_8(g) + O_2(g) \rightarrow$
b. $C_2H_4(g) + O_2(g) \rightarrow$
c. $C_8H_{18}(l) + O_2(g) + H_2O(g) \rightarrow$

61. By now, you are familiar with enough chemical compounds to begin to write your own chemical reaction equations. Write two examples of what we mean by a *combustion* reaction.

62. By now, you are familiar with enough chemical compounds to begin to write your own chemical reaction equations. Write two examples each of what we mean by a *synthesis* reaction and by a *decomposition* reaction.

63. Balance each of the following equations that describe synthesis reactions.

a. $CaO(s) + H_2O(l) \rightarrow Ca(OH)_2(s)$
b. $Fe(s) + O_2(g) \rightarrow Fe_2O_3(s)$
c. $P_2O_5(s) + H_2O(l) \rightarrow H_3PO_4(aq)$

64. Balance each of the following equations that describe synthesis reactions.

a. $Fe(s) + S_8(s) \rightarrow FeS(s)$
b. $Co(s) + O_2(g) \rightarrow Co_2O_3(s)$
c. $Cl_2O_7(g) + H_2O(l) \rightarrow HClO_4(aq)$

65. Balance each of the following equations that describe decomposition reactions.

a. $CaSO_4(s) \rightarrow CaO(s) + SO_3(g)$
b. $Li_2CO_3(s) \rightarrow Li_2O(s) + CO_2(g)$
c. $LiHCO_3(s) \rightarrow Li_2CO_3(s) + H_2O(g) + CO_2(g)$
d. $C_6H_6(l) \rightarrow C(s) + H_2(g)$
e. $PBr_3(l) \rightarrow P_4(s) + Br_2(l)$

66. Balance each of the following equations that describe oxidation–reduction reactions.

a. $Al(s) + Br_2(l) \rightarrow AlBr_3(s)$
b. $Zn(s) + HClO_4(aq) \rightarrow Zn(ClO_4)_2(aq) + H_2(g)$
c. $Na(s) + P(s) \rightarrow Na_3P(s)$
d. $CH_4(g) + Cl_2(g) \rightarrow CCl_4(l) + HCl(g)$
e. $Cu(s) + AgNO_3(aq) \rightarrow Cu(NO_3)_2(aq) + Ag(s)$

Additional Problems

67. Distinguish between the *molecular* equation, the *complete ionic* equation, and the *net ionic* equation for a reaction in solution. Which type of equation most clearly shows the species that actually react with one another?

68. Using the general solubility rules given in Table 7.1, name three reactants that would form precipitates with each of the following ions in aqueous solution. Write the net ionic equation for each of your suggestions.

a. chloride ion
b. calcium ion
c. iron(III) ion
d. sulfate ion
e. mercury(I) ion, Hg_2^{2+}
f. silver ion

All even-numbered Questions and Problems have answers in the back of this book and solutions in the Solutions Guide.

67. molecular equation (normal, uncharged formulas); complete ionic (shows compounds broken up into the ions they contain; all ions shown); net ionic (shows *only* the ions that form the precipitate)

68. (a) silver ion: $Ag^+(aq) + Cl^-(aq) \rightarrow AgCl(s)$; lead(II) ion: $Pb^{2+}(aq) + 2Cl^-(aq) \rightarrow PbCl_2(s)$; mercury(I) ion: $Hg_2^{2+}(aq) + 2Cl^-(aq) \rightarrow Hg_2Cl_2(s)$; (b) sulfate ion: $Ca^{2+}(aq) + SO_4^{2-}(aq) \rightarrow CaSO_4(s)$; carbonate ion: $Ca^{2+}(aq) + CO_3^{2-}(aq) \rightarrow CaCO_3(s)$; phosphate ion: $3Ca^{2+}(aq) + 2PO_4^{3-}(aq) \rightarrow Ca_3(PO_4)_2(s)$; (c) hydroxide ion: $Fe^{3+}(aq) + 3OH^-(aq) \rightarrow Fe(OH)_3(s)$; sulfide ion: $2Fe^{3+}(aq) + 3S^{2-}(aq) \rightarrow Fe_2S_3(s)$; phosphate ion: $Fe^{3+}(aq) + PO_4^{3-}(aq) \rightarrow FePO_4(s)$; (d) barium ion: $Ba^{2+}(aq) + SO_4^{2-}(aq) \rightarrow BaSO_4(s)$; calcium ion: $Ca^{2+}(aq) + SO_4^{2-}(aq) \rightarrow CaSO_4(s)$; lead(II) ion: $Pb^{2+}(aq) + SO_4^{2-}(aq) \rightarrow PbSO_4(s)$; (e) chloride ion: $Hg_2^{2+}(aq) + 2Cl^-(aq) \rightarrow Hg_2Cl_2(s)$; sulfide ion: $Hg_2^{2+}(aq) + S^{2-}(aq) \rightarrow Hg_2S(s)$; carbonate ion: $Hg_2^{2+}(aq) + CO_3^{2-}(aq) \rightarrow Hg_2CO_3(s)$; (f) chloride ion: $Ag^+(aq) + Cl^-(aq) \rightarrow AgCl(s)$; hydroxide ion: $Ag^+(aq) + OH^-(aq) \rightarrow AgOH(s)$; carbonate ion: $2Ag^+(aq) + CO_3^{2-}(aq) \rightarrow Ag_2CO_3(s)$

69. (a) $2Fe^{3+}(aq) + 3CO_3^{2-}(aq) \rightarrow Fe_2(CO_3)_3(s)$; (b) $Hg_2^{2+}(aq) + 2Cl^-(aq) \rightarrow Hg_2Cl_2(s)$; (c) no precipitate; (d) $Cu^{2+}(aq) + S^{2-}(aq) \rightarrow CuS(s)$; (e) $Pb^{2+}(aq) + 2Cl^-(aq) \rightarrow PbCl_2(s)$; (f) $Ca^{2+}(aq) + CO_3^{2-}(aq) \rightarrow CaCO_3(s)$; (g) $Au^{3+}(aq) + 3OH^-(aq) \rightarrow Au(OH)_3(s)$

70. (a) $HNO_3(aq) + KOH(aq) \rightarrow H_2O(l) + \underline{KNO_3(aq)}$; (b) $H_2SO_4(aq) + Ba(OH)_2(aq) \rightarrow \underline{BaSO_4(s)} + 2H_2O(l)$; (c) $HClO_4(aq) + NaOH(aq) \rightarrow H_2O(l) + \underline{NaClO_4(aq)}$; (d) $2HCl(aq) + Ca(OH)_2(aq) \rightarrow \underline{CaCl_2(aq)} + H_2O(l)$

71. Ag^+: AgCl, Ag_2CO_3, AgOH, Ag_3PO_4, Ag_2S, Ag_2SO_4; Ba^{2+}: $BaCO_3$, $Ba(OH)_2$, $Ba_3(PO_4)_2$, BaS, $BaSO_4$; Ca^{2+}: $CaCO_3$, $Ca(OH)_2$, $Ca_3(PO_4)_2$, CaS, $CaSO_4$; Fe^{3+}: $Fe_2(CO_3)_3$, $Fe(OH)_3$, $FePO_4$, Fe_2S_3; Hg_2^{2+}: Hg_2Cl_2, Hg_2CO_3, $Hg_2(OH)_2$, $(Hg_2)_3(PO_4)_2$, Hg_2S; Na^+: all common salts are soluble; Ni^{2+}: $NiCO_3$, $Ni(OH)_2$, $Ni_3(PO_4)_2$, NiS; Pb^{2+}: $PbCl_2$, $PbCO_3$, $Pb(OH)_2$, $Pb_3(PO_4)_2$, PbS, $PbSO_4$

72. (a) soluble (Rule 2: most potassium salts are soluble); (b) soluble (Rule 2: most ammonium salts are soluble); (c) insoluble (Rule 6: most carbonate salts are only slightly soluble); (d) insoluble (Rule 6: most phosphate salts are only slightly soluble); (e) soluble (Rule 2: most sodium salts are soluble); (f) insoluble (Rule 6: most carbonate salts are only slightly soluble); (g) soluble (Rule 3: most chloride salts are soluble)

69. Without first writing a full molecular or ionic equation, write the net ionic equations for any precipitation reactions that occur when aqueous solutions of the following compounds are mixed. If no reaction occurs, so indicate.

a. iron(III) nitrate and sodium carbonate
b. mercurous nitrate and sodium chloride
c. sodium nitrate and ruthenium nitrate
d. copper(II) sulfate and sodium sulfide
e. lithium chloride and lead(II) nitrate
f. calcium nitrate and lithium carbonate
g. gold(III) chloride and sodium hydroxide

70. Complete and balance each of the following molecular equations for strong acid/strong base reactions. Underline the formula of the *salt* produced in each reaction.

a. $HNO_3(aq) + KOH(aq) \rightarrow$
b. $H_2SO_4(aq) + Ba(OH)_2(aq) \rightarrow$
c. $HClO_4(aq) + NaOH(aq) \rightarrow$
d. $HCl(aq) + Ca(OH)_2(aq) \rightarrow$

71. For the cations listed in the left-hand column, give the formulas of the precipitates that would form with each of the anions in the right-hand column. If no precipitate is expected for a particular combination, so indicate.

Cations	Anions
Ag^+	$C_2H_3O_2^-$
Ba^{2+}	Cl^-
Ca^{2+}	CO_3^{2-}
Fe^{3+}	NO_3^-
Hg_2^{2+}	OH^-
Na^+	PO_4^{3-}
Ni^{2+}	S^{2-}
Pb^{2+}	SO_4^{2-}

72. On the basis of the general solubility rules given in Table 7.1, predict which of the following substances are likely to be soluble in water.

a. potassium hexacyanoferrate(III), $K_3Fe(CN)_6$
b. ammonium molybdate, $(NH_4)_2MoO_4$
c. osmium(II) carbonate, $OsCO_3$
d. gold(III) phosphate, $AuPO_4$
e. sodium hexanitrocobaltate(III), $Na_3Co(NO_2)_6$
f. barium carbonate, $BaCO_3$
g. iron(III) chloride, $FeCl_3$

73. On the basis of the general solubility rules given in Table 7.1, predict the identity of the precipitate that forms when aqueous solutions of the following substances are mixed. If no precipitate is likely, indicate why (which rules apply).

a. iron(III) chloride and sodium hydroxide
b. nickel(II) nitrate and ammonium sulfide
c. silver nitrate and potassium chloride
d. sodium carbonate and barium nitrate
e. potassium chloride and mercury(I) nitrate
f. barium nitrate and sulfuric acid

74. On the basis of the general solubility rules given in Table 7.1, write a balanced molecular equation for the precipitation reactions that take place when the following aqueous solutions are mixed. Underline the formula of the precipitate (solid) that forms. If no precipitation reaction is likely for the reactants given, so indicate.

a. silver nitrate and hydrochloric acid
b. copper(II) sulfate and ammonium carbonate
c. iron(II) sulfate and potassium carbonate
d. silver nitrate and potassium nitrate
e. lead(II) nitrate and lithium carbonate
f. tin(IV) chloride and sodium hydroxide

75. For each of the following *un*balanced molecular equations, write the corresponding *balanced net ionic equation* for the reaction.

a. $HCl(aq) + AgNO_3(aq) \rightarrow AgCl(s) + HNO_3(aq)$
b. $CaCl_2(aq) + Na_3PO_4(aq) \rightarrow Ca_3(PO_4)_2(s) + NaCl(aq)$
c. $Pb(NO_3)_2(aq) + BaCl_2(aq) \rightarrow PbCl_2(s) + Ba(NO_3)_2(aq)$
d. $FeCl_3(aq) + NaOH(aq) \rightarrow Fe(OH)_3(s) + NaCl(aq)$

76. Most sulfide compounds of the transition metals are insoluble in water. Many of these metal sulfides have striking and characteristic colors by which we can identify them. Therefore, in the analysis of mixtures of metal ions, it is very common to precipitate the metal ions by using dihydrogen sulfide (commonly called hydrogen sulfide), H_2S. Suppose you had a mixture of Fe^{2+}, Cr^{3+}, and Ni^{2+}. Write net ionic equations for the precipitation of these metal ions by the use of H_2S.

77. What strong acid and what strong base would react in aqueous solution to produce the following salts?

a. potassium perchlorate, $KClO_4$
b. cesium nitrate, $CsNO_3$
c. potassium chloride, KCl
d. sodium sulfate, Na_2SO_4

78. Using the general solubility rules given in Table 7.1, name three reactants that would form precipitates with each of the following ions in aqueous solutions. Write the balanced molecular equation for each of your suggested reactants.

a. sulfide ion
b. carbonate ion
c. hydroxide ion
d. phosphate ion

79. For the reaction $16Fe(s) + 3S_8(s) \rightarrow 8Fe_2S_3(s)$, show how electrons are gained and lost by the atoms.

80. Balance the equation for each of the following oxidation–reduction chemical reactions.

a. $Na(s) + O_2(g) \rightarrow Na_2O_2(s)$
b. $Fe(s) + H_2SO_4(aq) \rightarrow FeSO_4(aq) + H_2(g)$
c. $Al_2O_3(s) \rightarrow Al(s) + O_2(g)$
d. $Fe(s) + Br_2(l) \rightarrow FeBr_3(s)$
e. $Zn(s) + HNO_3(aq) \rightarrow Zn(NO_3)_2(aq) + H_2(g)$

81. Identify each of the following unbalanced reaction equations as belonging to one or more of the following categories: precipitation, acid–base, or oxidation–reduction.

a. $Fe(s) + H_2SO_4(aq) \rightarrow Fe_2(SO_4)_3(aq) + H_2(g)$

All even-numbered Questions and Problems have answers in the back of this book and solutions in the Solutions Guide.

73. (a) $Fe(OH)_3$, Rule 5; (b) NiS, Rule 6; (c) AgCl, Rule 3; (d) $BaCO_3$, Rule 6; (e) Hg_2Cl_2, Rule 3; (f) $BaSO_4$, Rule 4

74. (a) $AgNO_3(aq) + HCl(aq) \rightarrow \underline{AgCl}(s) + HNO_3(aq)$; (b) $CuSO_4(aq) + (NH_4)_2CO_3(aq) \rightarrow \underline{CuCO_3}(s) + (NH_4)_2SO_4(aq)$; (c) $FeSO_4(aq) + K_2CO_3(aq) \rightarrow \underline{FeCO_3}(s) + K_2SO_4(aq)$; (d) no reaction; (e) $Pb(NO_3)_2(aq) + Li_2CO_3(aq) \rightarrow \underline{PbCO_3}(s) + 2LiNO_3(aq)$; (f) $SnCl_4(aq) + 4NaOH(aq) \rightarrow \underline{Sn(OH)_4}(s) + 4NaCl(aq)$

75. (a) Rule 3, $Ag^+(aq) + Cl^-(aq) \rightarrow AgCl(s)$; (b) Rule 6, $3Ca^{2+}(aq) + 2PO_4^{3-}(aq) \rightarrow Ca_3(PO_4)_2(s)$; (c) Rule 3, $Pb^{2+}(aq) + 2Cl^-(aq) \rightarrow PbCl_2(s)$; (d) Rule 6, $Fe^{3+}(aq) + 3OH^-(aq) \rightarrow Fe(OH)_3(s)$

76. $Fe^{2+}(aq) + S^{2-}(aq) \rightarrow FeS(s)$; $2Cr^{3+}(aq) + 3S^{2-}(aq) \rightarrow Cr_2S_3(s)$; $Ni^{2+}(aq) + S^{2-}(aq) \rightarrow NiS(s)$

77. (a) potassium hydroxide and perchloric acid; (b) cesium hydroxide and nitric acid; (c) potassium hydroxide and hydrochloric acid; (d) sodium hydroxide and sulfuric acid

78. These anions tend to form insoluble precipitates with many metal ions. The following are illustrative for cobalt(II) chloride, tin(II) chloride, and copper(II) nitrate reacting with sodium salts of the given anions.

(a) $CoCl_2(aq) + Na_2S(aq) \rightarrow CoS(s) + 2NaCl(aq)$; $SnCl_2(aq) + Na_2S(aq) \rightarrow SnS(s) + 2NaCl(aq)$; $Cu(NO_3)_2(aq) + Na_2S(aq) \rightarrow CuS(s) + 2NaNO_3(aq)$; (b) $CoCl_2(aq) + Na_2CO_3(aq) \rightarrow CoCO_3(s) + 2NaCl(aq)$; $SnCl_2(aq) + Na_2CO_3(aq) \rightarrow SnCO_3(s) + 2NaCl(aq)$; $Cu(NO_3)_2(aq) + Na_2CO_3(aq) \rightarrow CuCO_3(s) + 2NaNO_3(aq)$; (c) $CoCl_2(aq) + 2NaOH(aq) \rightarrow Co(OH)_2(s) + 2NaCl(aq)$; $SnCl_2(aq) + 2NaOH(aq) \rightarrow Sn(OH)_2(s) + 2NaCl(aq)$; $Cu(NO_3)_2(aq) + 2NaOH(aq) \rightarrow Cu(OH)_2(s) + 2NaNO_3(aq)$; (d) $3CoCl_2(aq) + 2Na_3PO_4(aq) \rightarrow Co_3(PO_4)_2(s) + 6NaCl(aq)$; $3SnCl_2(aq) + 2Na_3PO_4(aq) \rightarrow Sn_3(PO_4)_2(s) + 6NaCl(aq)$; $3Cu(NO_3)_2(aq) + 2Na_3PO_4(aq) \rightarrow Cu_3(PO_4)_2(s) + 6NaNO_3(aq)$

79. Iron atoms lose three electrons to become Fe^{3+} ions; sulfur atoms gain two electrons to become S^{2-} ions.

80. (a) $2Na(s) + O_2(g) \rightarrow Na_2O_2(s)$; (b) $Fe(s) + H_2SO_4(aq) \rightarrow FeSO_4(aq) + H_2(g)$; (c) $2Al_2O_3(s) \rightarrow 4Al(s) + 3O_2(g)$; (d) $2Fe(s) + 3Br_2(l) \rightarrow 2FeBr_3(s)$; (e) $Zn(s) + 2HNO_3(aq) \rightarrow Zn(NO_3)_2(aq) + H_2(g)$

81. (a) oxidation–reduction; (b) acid–base; (c) oxidation–reduction; (d) acid–base; (e) precipitation; (f) precipitation; (g) acid–base; (h) precipitation; (i) oxidation–reduction

82. (a) $2C_4H_{10}(l) + 13O_2(g) \rightarrow 8CO_2(g) + 10H_2O(g)$; (b) $C_4H_{10}O(l) + 6O_2(g) \rightarrow 4CO_2(g) + 5H_2O(g)$; (c) $2C_4H_{10}O_2(l) + 11O_2(g) \rightarrow 8CO_2(g) + 10H_2O(g)$

b. $HClO_4(aq) + RbOH(aq) \rightarrow RbClO_4(aq) + H_2O(l)$
c. $Ca(s) + O_2(g) \rightarrow CaO(s)$
d. $H_2SO_4(aq) + NaOH(aq) \rightarrow Na_2SO_4(aq) + H_2O(l)$
e. $Pb(NO_3)_2(aq) + Na_2CO_3(aq) \rightarrow PbCO_3(s) + NaNO_3(aq)$
f. $K_2SO_4(aq) + CaCl_2(aq) \rightarrow KCl(aq) + CaSO_4(s)$
g. $HNO_3(aq) + KOH(aq) \rightarrow KNO_3(aq) + H_2O(l)$
h. $Ni(C_2H_3O_2)_2(aq) + Na_2S(aq) \rightarrow NiS(s) + NaC_2H_3O_2(aq)$
i. $Ni(s) + Cl_2(g) \rightarrow NiCl_2(s)$

82. Complete and balance each of the following equations that describe combustion reactions.

a. $C_4H_{10}(l) + O_2(g) \rightarrow$
b. $C_4H_{10}O(l) + O_2(g) \rightarrow$
c. $C_4H_{10}O_2(l) + O_2(g) \rightarrow$

83. Balance each of the following equations that describe synthesis reactions.

a. $FeO(s) + O_2(g) \rightarrow Fe_2O_3(s)$
b. $CO(g) + O_2(g) \rightarrow CO_2(g)$
c. $H_2(g) + Cl_2(g) \rightarrow HCl(g)$
d. $K(s) + S_8(s) \rightarrow K_2S(s)$
e. $Na(s) + N_2(g) \rightarrow Na_3N(s)$

84. Balance each of the following equations that describe decomposition reactions.

a. $NaHCO_3(s) \rightarrow Na_2CO_3(s) + H_2O(g) + CO_2(g)$
b. $NaClO_3(s) \rightarrow NaCl(s) + O_2(g)$
c. $HgO(s) \rightarrow Hg(l) + O_2(g)$
d. $C_{12}H_{22}O_{11}(s) \rightarrow C(s) + H_2O(g)$
e. $H_2O_2(l) \rightarrow H_2O(l) + O_2(g)$

85. Write a balanced oxidation–reduction equation for the reaction of each of the metals in the left-hand column with each of the nonmetals in the right-hand column.

Ba	O_2
K	S
Mg	Cl_2
Rb	N_2
Ca	Br_2
Li	

86. Sulfuric acid, H_2SO_4, oxidizes many metallic elements. One of the effects of acid rain is that it produces sulfuric acid in the atmosphere, which then reacts with metals used in construction. Write balanced oxidation–reduction equations for the reaction of sulfuric acid with Fe, Zn, Mg, Co, and Ni.

87. Although the metals of Group 2 of the periodic table are not nearly as reactive as those of Group 1, many of the Group 2 metals will combine with common nonmetals, especially at elevated temperatures. Write balanced chemical equations for the reactions of Mg, Ca, Sr, and Ba with Cl_2, Br_2, and O_2.

88. For each of the following metals, how many electrons will the metal atoms lose when the metal reacts with a nonmetal?

a. sodium
b. potassium
c. magnesium
d. barium
e. aluminum

89. For each of the following nonmetals, how many electrons will each atom of the nonmetal gain in reacting with a metal?

a. oxygen
b. fluorine
c. nitrogen
d. chlorine
e. sulfur

90. There is much overlapping of the classification schemes for reactions discussed in this chapter. Give an example of a reaction that is, at the same time, an oxidation–reduction reaction, a combustion reaction, and a synthesis reaction.

91. Classify the reactions represented by the following unbalanced equations by as many methods as possible. Balance the equations.

a. $I_4O_9(s) \rightarrow I_2O_6(s) + I_2(s) + O_2(g)$
b. $Mg(s) + AgNO_3(aq) \rightarrow Mg(NO_3)_2(aq) + Ag(s)$
c. $SiCl_4(l) + Mg(s) \rightarrow MgCl_2(s) + Si(s)$
d. $CuCl_2(aq) + AgNO_3(aq) \rightarrow Cu(NO_3)_2(aq) + AgCl(s)$
e. $Al(s) + Br_2(l) \rightarrow AlBr_3(s)$

92. Classify the reactions represented by the following unbalanced equations by as many methods as possible. Balance the equations.

a. $C_3H_8O(l) + O_2(g) \rightarrow CO_2(g) + H_2O(g)$
b. $HCl(aq) + AgC_2H_3O_2(aq) \rightarrow AgCl(s) + HC_2H_3O_2(aq)$
c. $HCl(aq) + Al(OH)_3(s) \rightarrow AlCl_3(aq) + H_2O(l)$
d. $H_2O_2(aq) \rightarrow H_2O(l) + O_2(g)$
e. $N_2H_4(l) + O_2(g) \rightarrow N_2(g) + H_2O(g)$

93. Corrosion of metals costs us billions of dollars annually, slowly destroying cars, bridges, and buildings. Corrosion of a metal involves the oxidation of the metal by the oxygen in the air, typically in the presence of moisture. Write a balanced equation for the reaction of each of the following metals with O_2: Zn, Al, Fe, Cr, and Ni.

94. Elemental chlorine, Cl_2, is very reactive, combining with most metallic substances. Write a balanced equation for the reaction of each of the following metals with Cl_2: Na, Al, Zn, Ca, and Fe.

95. Give a balanced molecular chemical equation to illustrate each of the following types of reactions.

a. a synthesis (combination) reaction
b. a precipitation reaction
c. a double-displacement reaction
d. an acid–base reaction
e. an oxidation–reduction reaction
f. a combustion reaction

All even-numbered Questions and Problems have answers in the back of this book and solutions in the Solutions Guide.

83. (a) $4FeO(s) + O_2(g) \rightarrow 2Fe_2O_3(s)$; (b) $2CO(g) + O_2(g) \rightarrow 2CO_2(g)$; (c) $H_2(g) + Cl_2(g) \rightarrow 2HCl(g)$; (d) $16K(s) + S_8(s) \rightarrow 8K_2S(s)$; (e) $6Na(s) + N_2(g) \rightarrow 2Na_3N(s)$

84. (a) $2NaHCO_3(s) \rightarrow Na_2CO_3(s) + H_2O(g) + CO_2(g)$; (b) $2NaClO_3(s) \rightarrow 2NaCl(s) + 3O_2(g)$; (c) $2HgO(s) \rightarrow 2Hg(l) + O_2(g)$; (d) $C_{12}H_{22}O_{11}(s) \rightarrow 12C(s) + 11H_2O(g)$; (e) $2H_2O_2(l) \rightarrow 2H_2O(l) + O_2(g)$

85. $2Ba + O_2 \rightarrow 2BaO$, $Ba + S \rightarrow BaS$, $Ba + Cl_2 \rightarrow BaCl_2$, $3Ba + N_2 \rightarrow Ba_3N_2$, $Ba + Br_2 \rightarrow BaBr_2$; $4K + O_2 \rightarrow 2K_2O$, $2K + S \rightarrow K_2S$, $2K + Cl_2 \rightarrow 2KCl$, $6K + N_2 \rightarrow 2K_3N$, $2K + Br_2 \rightarrow 2KBr$; $2Mg + O_2 \rightarrow 2MgO$, $Mg + S \rightarrow MgS$, $Mg + Cl_2 \rightarrow MgCl_2$, $3Mg + N_2 \rightarrow Mg_3N_2$, $Mg + Br_2 \rightarrow MgBr_2$; $4Rb + O_2 \rightarrow 2Rb_2O$, $2Rb + S \rightarrow Rb_2S$, $2Rb + Cl_2 \rightarrow 2RbCl$, $6Rb + N_2 \rightarrow 2Rb_3N$, $2Rb + Br_2 \rightarrow 2RbBr$; $2Ca + O_2 \rightarrow 2CaO$, $Ca + S \rightarrow CaS$, $Ca + Cl_2 \rightarrow CaCl_2$, $3Ca + N_2 \rightarrow Ca_3N_2$, $Ca + Br_2 \rightarrow CaBr_2$; $4Li + O_2 \rightarrow 2Li_2O$, $2Li + S \rightarrow Li_2S$, $2Li + Cl_2 \rightarrow 2LiCl$, $6Li + N_2 \rightarrow 2Li_3N$, $2Li + Br_2 \rightarrow 2LiBr$

86. $Fe(s) + H_2SO_4(aq) \rightarrow FeSO_4(aq) + H_2(g)$; $Zn(s) + H_2SO_4(aq) \rightarrow ZnSO_4(aq) + H_2(g)$; $Mg(s) + H_2SO_4(aq) \rightarrow MgSO_4(aq) + H_2(g)$; $Co(s) + H_2SO_4(aq) \rightarrow CoSO_4(aq) + H_2(g)$; $Ni(s) + H_2SO_4(aq) \rightarrow NiSO_4(aq) + H_2(g)$

87. $Mg + Cl_2 \rightarrow MgCl_2$, $Ca + Cl_2 \rightarrow CaCl_2$, $Sr + Cl_2 \rightarrow SrCl_2$, $Ba + Cl_2 \rightarrow BaCl_2$; $Mg + Br_2 \rightarrow MgBr_2$; $Ca + Br_2 \rightarrow CaBr_2$, $Sr + Br_2 \rightarrow SrBr_2$, $Ba + Br_2 \rightarrow BaBr_2$; $2Mg + O_2 \rightarrow 2MgO$, $2Ca + O_2 \rightarrow 2CaO$, $2Sr + O_2 \rightarrow 2SrO$, $2Ba + O_2 \rightarrow 2BaO$

88. (a) one; (b) one; (c) two; (d) two; (e) three

89. (a) two, $O + 2e^- \rightarrow O^{2-}$; (b) one, $F + e^- \rightarrow F^-$; (c) three, $N + 3e^- \rightarrow N^{3-}$; (d) one, $Cl + e^- \rightarrow Cl^-$; (e) two, $S + 2e^- \rightarrow S^{2-}$

90. The reaction $C(s) + O_2(g) \rightarrow CO_2(g)$ is such an example.

91. (a) $2I_4O_9(s) \rightarrow 2I_2O_6(s) + 2I_2(s) + 3O_2(g)$, oxidation–reduction, decomposition; (b) $Mg(s) + 2AgNO_3(aq) \rightarrow Mg(NO_3)_2(aq) + 2Ag(s)$, oxidation–reduction, single-displacement; (c) $SiCl_4(l) + 2Mg(s) \rightarrow 2MgCl_2(s) + Si(s)$, oxidation–reduction, single-displacement; (d) $CuCl_2(aq) + 2AgNO_3(aq) \rightarrow 2AgCl(s) + Cu(NO_3)_2(aq)$, precipitation, double-displacement; (e) $2Al(s) + 3Br_2(l) \rightarrow 2AlBr_3(s)$, oxidation–reduction, synthesis

92. (a) $2C_3H_8O(l) + 9O_2(g) \rightarrow 6CO_2(g) + 8H_2O(g)$, oxidation–reduction, combustion; (b) $HCl(aq) + AgC_2H_3O_2(aq) \rightarrow AgCl(s) + HC_2H_3O_2(aq)$, precipitation, double-displacement; (c) $3HCl(aq) + Al(OH)_3(s) \rightarrow AlCl_3(aq) + 3H_2O(l)$, acid–base, double-displacement; (d) $2H_2O_2(aq) \rightarrow 2H_2O(l) + O_2(g)$, oxidation–reduction, decomposition; (e) $N_2H_4(l) + O_2(g) \rightarrow N_2(g) + 2H_2O(g)$, oxidation–reduction, combustion

CUMULATIVE REVIEW for CHAPTERS 6-7

QUESTIONS

1. What kind of *visual* evidence indicates that a chemical reaction has occurred? Give an example of each type of evidence you have mentioned. Do *all* reactions produce visual evidence that they have taken place?
2. What, in general terms, does a chemical equation indicate? What are the substances indicated to the left of the arrow called in a chemical equation? To the right of the arrow?
3. What does it mean to "balance" an equation? Why is it so important that equations be balanced? What does it mean to say that atoms must be *conserved* in a balanced chemical equation? How are the physical states of reactants and products indicated when writing chemical equations?
4. When balancing a chemical equation, why is it *not* permissible to adjust the subscripts in the formulas of the reactants and products? What would changing the subscripts within a formula do? What do the *coefficients* in a balanced chemical equation represent? Why is it acceptable to adjust a substance's coefficient but not permissible to adjust the subscripts within the substance's formula?
5. What is meant by the *driving force* for a reaction? Give some examples of driving forces that make reactants tend to form products. Write a balanced chemical equation illustrating each type of driving force you have named.
6. Explain to your friend what chemists mean by a *precipitation* reaction. What is the driving force in a precipitation reaction? Using the information provided about solubility in these chapters, write balanced molecular and net ionic equations for five examples of precipitation reactions.
7. Define the term *strong electrolyte*. What types of substances tend to be strong electrolytes? What does a solution of a strong electrolyte contain? Give a way to determine if a substance is a strong electrolyte.
8. Summarize the simple solubility rules for ionic compounds. How do we use these rules in determining the identity of the solid formed in a precipitation reaction? Give examples including balanced complete and net ionic equations.
9. In general terms, what are the *spectator ions* in a precipitation reaction? Why are the spectator ions not included in writing the net ionic equation for a precipitation reaction? Does this mean that the spectator ions do not have to be present in the solution?
10. Describe some physical and chemical properties of *acids* and *bases*. What is meant by a *strong* acid or base? Are strong acids and bases also strong electrolytes? Give several examples of strong acids and strong bases.
11. What is a *salt?* How are salts formed by acid–base reactions? Write chemical equations showing the formation of three different salts. What other product is formed when an aqueous acid reacts with an aqueous base? Write the net ionic equation for the formation of this substance.
12. What do we call reactions in which electrons are transferred between atoms or ions? What do we call a *loss* of electrons by an atom or ion? What is it called when an atom or ion *gains* electrons? Can we have a process in which electrons are lost by one species without there also being a process in which the electrons are gained by another species? Why? Give three examples of equations in which there is a transfer of electrons between a metallic element and a nonmetallic element. In your examples, identify which species loses electrons and which species gains electrons.
13. What is a *combustion* reaction? Are combustion reactions a unique type of reaction, or are they a special case of a more general type of reaction? Write an equation that illustrates a combustion reaction.
14. Give an example of a *synthesis* reaction and of a *decomposition* reaction. Are synthesis and decomposition reactions always also oxidation–reduction reactions? Explain.
15. List and define all the ways of classifying chemical reactions that have been discussed in the text. Give a balanced chemical equation as an example of each type of reaction, and show clearly how your example fits the definition you have given.

PROBLEMS

16. The element carbon undergoes many inorganic reactions, as well as being the basis for the field of organic chemistry. Write balanced chemical equations for the reactions of carbon described below.
    a. Carbon burns in an excess of oxygen (for example, in the air) to produce carbon dioxide.
    b. If the supply of oxygen is limited, carbon will still burn, but will produce carbon monoxide rather than carbon dioxide.
    c. If molten lithium metal is treated with carbon, lithium carbide, Li_2C_2, is produced.
    d. Iron(II) oxide reacts with carbon above temperatures of about 700 °C to produce carbon monoxide gas and molten elemental iron.
    e. Carbon reacts with fluorine gas at high temperatures to make carbon tetrafluoride.
17. Balance each of the following chemical equations.
    a. $Na_2SO_4(aq) + BaCl_2(aq) \rightarrow BaSO_4(s) + NaCl(aq)$
    b. $Zn(s) + H_2O(g) \rightarrow ZnO(s) + H_2(g)$
    c. $NaOH(aq) + H_3PO_4(aq) \rightarrow Na_3PO_4(aq) + H_2O(l)$
    d. $Al(s) + Mn_2O_3(s) \rightarrow Al_2O_3(s) + Mn(s)$
    e. $C_7H_6O_2(s) + O_2(g) \rightarrow CO_2(g) + H_2O(g)$

201

93. $2Zn(s) + O_2(g) \rightarrow 2ZnO(s)$; $4Al(s) + 3O_2(g) \rightarrow 2Al_2O_3(s)$; $2Fe(s) + O_2(g) \rightarrow 2FeO(s)$; $4Fe(s) + 3O_2(g) \rightarrow 2Fe_2O_3(s)$; $2Cr(s) + O_2(g) \rightarrow 2CrO(s)$; $4Cr(s) + 3O_2(g) \rightarrow 2Cr_2O_3(s)$; $2Ni(s) + O_2(g) \rightarrow 2NiO(s)$

94. $2Na(s) + Cl_2(g) \rightarrow 2NaCl(s)$; $2Al(s) + 3Cl_2(g) \rightarrow 2AlCl_3(s)$; $Zn(s) + Cl_2(g) \rightarrow ZnCl_2(s)$; $Ca(s) + Cl_2(g) \rightarrow CaCl_2(s)$; $2Fe(s) + 3Cl_2(g) \rightarrow 2FeCl_3(s)$

95. Answers depend on student choice of examples.

Answers to Cumulative Review Exercises

Chapters 6–7

1. There are numerous ways we can recognize that a chemical reaction has taken place. In some reactions there may be a color change. In many reactions of ionic solutes a solid precipitate may form when the ions are combined. In some reactions bubbles of a gaseous product may form. In some reactions (particularly in the combustion of organic chemical substances with oxygen gas) heat, light, and a flame may be produced. All chemical reactions do produce some evidence that the reaction has occurred, but sometimes this evidence may not be visual and may not be very obvious.

2. A chemical equation indicates the substances necessary for a given chemical reaction, and the substances produced by that chemical reaction. The substances to the left of the arrow are called the *reactants*; those to the right of the arrow are called the *products*. A *balanced* equation indicates the relative numbers of molecules in the reaction.

3. When we "balance" a chemical equation, we adjust the coefficients of the reactants and products in the equation so that the same total numbers of atoms of each element are present both before and after the reaction has taken place. Balancing chemical equations is so important because a balanced chemical equation shows us not only the identities of the reactants and products but also the relative numbers of each involved in the process; this information is necessary if we are to do any sort of calculation involving the amounts of reactants required for a process or are to calculate the yield expected

f. $C_6H_{14}(l) + O_2(g) \rightarrow CO_2(g) + H_2O(g)$
g. $C_3H_8O(l) + O_2(g) \rightarrow CO_2(g) + H_2O(g)$
h. $Mg(s) + HClO_4(aq) \rightarrow Mg(ClO_4)_2(aq) + H_2(g)$

18. The reagent shelf in a general chemistry lab contains aqueous solutions of the following substances: silver nitrate, sodium chloride, acetic acid, nitric acid, sulfuric acid, potassium chromate, barium nitrate, phosphoric acid, hydrochloric acid, lead nitrate, sodium hydroxide, and sodium carbonate. Suggest how you might prepare the following pure substances using these reagents and any normal laboratory equipment. If it is *not* possible to prepare a substance using these reagents, indicate why.

a. $BaCrO_4(s)$
b. $NaC_2H_3O_2(s)$
c. $AgCl(s)$
d. $PbSO_4(s)$
e. $Na_2SO_4(s)$
f. $BaCO_3(s)$

19. The common strong acids are HCl, HNO_3, and H_2SO_4, whereas NaOH and KOH are the common strong bases. Write the neutralization reaction equations for each of these strong acids with each of these strong bases in aqueous solution.

20. Classify each of the following chemical equations in as *many* ways as possible based on what you have learned. Balance each equation.

a. $FeO(s) + HNO_3(aq) \rightarrow Fe(NO_3)_2(aq) + H_2O(l)$
b. $Mg(s) + CO_2(g) + O_2(g) \rightarrow MgCO_3(s)$
c. $NaOH(s) + CuSO_4(aq) \rightarrow Cu(OH)_2(s) + Na_2SO_4(aq)$
d. $HI(aq) + KOH(aq) \rightarrow KI(aq) + H_2O(l)$
e. $C_3H_8(g) + O_2(g) \rightarrow CO_2(g) + H_2O(g)$
f. $Co(NH_3)_6Cl_2(s) \rightarrow CoCl_2(s) + NH_3(g)$
g. $HCl(aq) + Pb(C_2H_3O_2)_2(aq) \rightarrow HC_2H_3O_2(aq) + PbCl_2(s)$
h. $C_{12}H_{22}O_{11}(s) \rightarrow C(s) + H_2O(g)$
i. $Al(s) + HNO_3(aq) \rightarrow Al(NO_3)_3(aq) + H_2(g)$
j. $B(s) + O_2(g) \rightarrow B_2O_3(s)$

21. In Column 1 are listed some reactive metals; in Column 2 are listed some nonmetals. Write a balanced chemical equation for the combination/synthesis reaction of each element in Column 1 with each element in Column 2.

Column 1	Column 2
sodium, Na	fluorine gas, F_2
calcium, Ca	oxygen gas, O_2
aluminum, Al	sulfur, S
magnesium, Mg	chlorine gas, Cl_2

22. Give balanced equations for two examples of each of the following types of reactions.

a. precipitation
b. single-displacement
c. combustion
d. synthesis
e. oxidation–reduction
f. decomposition
g. acid–base neutralization

23. Using the general solubility rules discussed in Chapter 7, give the formulas of five substances that would be expected to be readily soluble in water and five substances that would be expected to *not* be very soluble in water. For each of the substances you choose, indicate the specific solubility rule you applied to make your prediction.

24. Write the balanced net ionic equation for the reaction that takes place when aqueous solutions of the following solutes are mixed. If no reaction is likely, explain why no reaction would be expected for that combination of solutes.

a. potassium nitrate and sodium chloride
b. calcium nitrate and sulfuric acid
c. ammonium sulfide and lead(II) nitrate
d. sodium carbonate and iron(III) chloride
e. mercurous nitrate and calcium chloride
f. silver acetate and potassium chloride
g. phosphoric acid (H_3PO_4) and calcium nitrate
h. sulfuric acid and nickel(II) sulfate

25. Complete and balance the following equations.

a. $Pb(NO_3)_2(aq) + Na_2S(aq) \rightarrow$
b. $AgNO_3(aq) + HCl(aq) \rightarrow$
c. $Mg(s) + O_2(g) \rightarrow$
d. $H_2SO_4(aq) + KOH(aq) \rightarrow$
e. $BaCl_2(aq) + H_2SO_4(aq) \rightarrow$
f. $Mg(s) + H_2SO_4(aq) \rightarrow$
g. $Na_3PO_3(aq) + CaCl_2(aq) \rightarrow$
h. $C_4H_{10}(l) + O_2(g) \rightarrow$

from a process. When we say that atoms must be conserved when writing a balanced chemical equation, we mean that the number of atoms of each element must be the same after the reaction is complete as before the reaction was attempted. No atoms are created or destroyed during a chemical reaction; they are just arranged into new combinations. We often indicate the physical states of the reactants and products for a chemical reaction because sometimes the physical state is important for the reaction to be successful. The physical states are indicated by using letters in parentheses after the formula: (*s*), (*l*), (*g*), or (*aq*).

4. Never change the *subscripts* of a *formula:* changing the subscripts changes the *identity* of a substance and makes the equation invalid. When balancing a chemical equation, we adjust only the *coefficients* in front of a formula: changing a coefficient changes the *number* of molecules being used in the reaction, *without* changing the *identity* of the substance.

5. The concept of a "driving force" for chemical reactions, at this point, is a rather nebulous idea. Clearly, there must be some reason why certain substances react when combined and why other substances can be combined without anything happening. If you go on with further studies in chemistry, you will learn that there is a mathematical thermodynamic function that can be used to predict exactly what will happen when a given set of reactants is combined. Even at this point, however, we can use some generalizations about what sorts of events tend to make a reaction take place. A reaction is likely to occur if any of the following things occur as a result of the reaction: formation of a solid, formation of water (or another nonionized molecule), formation of a gas, or the transfer of electrons from one species to another.

6. A precipitation reaction is one in which a solid is produced when two aqueous solutions are combined. The driving force in such a reaction is the formation of the solid thus removing ions from the solution. Examples depend on student input.

7. A strong electrolyte is one that completely dissociates into ions when dissolved in water; that is, each unit of the substance that dissolves in water produces separated, free ions. Ionic compounds, since they already consist of ions in the solid state, are strong electrolytes if they are soluble in water. Certain acids and bases also behave as strong electrolytes. A solution of a strong electrolyte actually consists of free, separated ions moving through the solvent independently of one another (there are no molecules or clusters of combined positive and negative ions). An apparatus for experimentally determining whether a substance is an electrolyte is shown in Figure 7.2 in the text.

8. Nearly all compounds containing the nitrate, sodium, potassium, and ammonium ions are soluble in water. Most salts containing the chloride and sulfate ions are soluble in water, with specific exceptions (see Table 7.1). Most compounds containing the hydroxide, sulfide, carbonate, and phosphate ions are *not* soluble in water (unless the compound also contains Na^+, K^+, or NH_4^+). For example, suppose we combine barium chloride and sulfuric acid solutions:

$BaCl_2(aq) + H_2SO_4(aq) \rightarrow BaSO_4(s) + 2HCl(aq)$

$Ba^{2+}(aq) + SO_4^{2-}(aq) \rightarrow BaSO_4(s)$ [net ionic reaction]

Because barium sulfate is not soluble in water, a precipitate of $BaSO_4(s)$ forms.

(*Please refer to page A32 in this book for answers to Exercises 9–25.*)

Chapter 8

Objectives

In this chapter our objectives are for the students to:

SECTION 8.1

- Understand the concept of average mass and explore how counting can be done by weighing.

SECTION 8.2

- Understand atomic mass and its experimental determination.

SECTION 8.3

- Understand the mole concept and Avogadro's number.
- Learn to convert among moles, mass, and number of atoms in a given sample.

SECTION 8.4

- Understand how to solve problems by asking and answering a series of questions.

SECTION 8.5

- Understand the definition of molar mass.
- Learn to convert between moles and mass of a given sample of a chemical compound.

SECTION 8.6

- Learn to find the mass percent of an element in a given compound.

SECTION 8.7

- Understand the meaning of empirical formulas of compounds.

SECTION 8.8

- Learn to calculate empirical formulas.

SECTION 8.9

- Learn to calculate the molecular formula of a compound, given its empirical formula and molar mass.

8 Chemical Composition

These glass bottles contain silicon dioxide. *(James L. Amos/Peter Arnold)*

ChemWork Refined over ten years of use by thousands of students, **ChemWork** builds and enhances students' problems-solving skills. Online assignments function as a "personal instructor" to help students learn how to solve challenging problems and learn how to think like chemists. Annotations for **ChemWork** assignments are included at the beginning of the end-of-chapter review.

PowerLecture This 2-DVD package includes the Chemistry Multimedia Library, which contains animations, simulations, and movies for all chemistry subjects, organized by topic for lecture presentations. Annotations for **PowerLecture** are referenced in the margins throughout the Annotated Instructor's Edition.

OWL Sign in to OWL at **www.cengage.com/owl** to view tutorials and simulations, develop problem-solving skills, and complete online homework assigned by your professor.

One very important chemical activity is the synthesis of new substances. Nylon, the artificial sweetener aspartame (Nutra-Sweet®), Kevlar used in bulletproof vests and the body parts of exotic cars, polyvinyl chloride (PVC) for plastic water pipes, Teflon, Nitinol (the alloy that remembers its shape even after being severely distorted), and so many other materials that make our lives easier—all originated in some chemist's laboratory. Some of the new materials have truly amazing properties such as the plastic that listens and talks, described in the "Chemistry in Focus" on page 206. When a chemist makes a new substance, the first order of business is to identify it. What is its composition? What is its chemical formula?

In this chapter we will learn to determine a compound's formula. Before we can do that, however, we need to think about counting atoms. How do we determine the number of each type of atom in a substance so that we can write its formula? Of course, atoms are too small to count individually. As we will see in this chapter, we typically count atoms by weighing them. So let us first consider the general principle of counting by weighing.

AP Photo/Remy de la Mauviniere

The Enzo Ferrari has a body made of carbon fiber composite materials.

8.1 Counting by Weighing

OBJECTIVE: To understand the concept of average mass and explore how counting can be done by weighing.

Suppose you work in a candy store that sells gourmet jelly beans by the bean. People come in and ask for 50 beans, 100 beans, 1000 beans, and so on, and you have to count them out—a tedious process at best. As a good problem solver, you try to come up with a better system. It occurs to you that it might be far more efficient to buy a scale and count the jelly beans by weighing them. How can you count jelly beans by weighing them? What information about the individual beans do you need to know?

Assume that all of the jelly beans are identical and that each has a mass of 5 g. If a customer asks for 1000 jelly beans, what mass of jelly beans would be required? Each bean has a mass of 5 g, so you would need 1000 beans × 5 g/bean, or 5000 g (5 kg). It takes just a few seconds to weigh out 5 kg of jelly beans. It would take much longer to count out 1000 of them.

In reality, jelly beans are not identical. For example, let's assume that you weigh 10 beans individually and get the following results:

Bean	Mass
1	5.1 g
2	5.2 g
3	5.0 g
4	4.8 g
5	4.9 g
6	5.0 g
7	5.0 g
8	5.1 g
9	4.9 g
10	5.0 g

Section 8.1

TEACHING TIPS

- Using analogies to cooking and daily life is helpful for beginning students.
- Students often spend so much time on the mechanics of solving these problems that they lose the "big picture" of what they are trying to learn. Keep talking to them about the idea that we are determining chemical quantities to decide how much we will have or how much we may need of a particular substance.

LABORATORY EXPERIMENT

A relevant laboratory experiment for this section is Experiment 13, Counting by Weighing, from *Introductory Chemistry in the Laboratory* by James Hall.

CHEMISTRY IN FOCUS

Plastic That Talks and Listens!

Imagine a plastic so "smart" that it can be used to sense a baby's breath, measure the force of a karate punch, sense the presence of a person 100 ft away, or make a balloon that sings. There is a plastic film capable of doing all these things. It's called **polyvinylidene difluoride (PVDF),** which has the structure

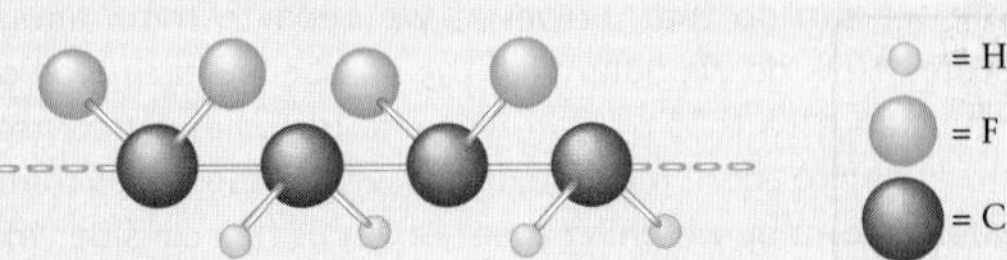

When this polymer is processed in a particular way, it becomes piezoelectric and pyroelectric. A *piezoelectric* substance produces an electric current when it is physically deformed or, alternatively, undergoes a deformation when a current is applied. A *pyroelectric* material is one that develops an electrical potential in response to a change in its temperature.

Because PVDF is piezoelectric, it can be used to construct a paper-thin microphone; it responds to sound by producing a current proportional to the deformation caused by the sound waves. A ribbon of PVDF plastic one-quarter of an inch wide could be strung along a hallway and used to listen to all the conversations going on as people walk through. On the other hand, electric pulses can be applied to the PVDF film to produce a speaker. A strip of PVDF film glued to the inside of a balloon can play any song stored on a microchip attached to the film—hence a balloon that can sing happy birthday at a party. The PVDF film also can be used to construct a sleep apnea monitor, which, when placed beside the mouth of a sleeping infant, will set off an alarm if the breathing stops, thus helping to prevent sudden infant death syndrome (SIDS). The same type of film is used by the U.S. Olympic karate team to measure the force of kicks and punches as the team trains. Also, gluing two strips of film together gives a material that curls in response to a current, creating an artificial muscle. In addition, because the PVDF film is pyroelectric, it responds to the infrared (heat) radiation emitted by a human as far away as 100 ft, making it useful for burglar alarm systems. Making the PVDF polymer piezoelectric and pyroelectric requires some very special processing, which makes it costly ($10 per square foot), but this seems a small price to pay for its near-magical properties.

Can we count these nonidentical beans by weighing? Yes. The key piece of information we need is the *average mass* of the jelly beans. Let's compute the average mass for our 10-bean sample.

$$\text{Average mass} = \frac{\text{total mass of beans}}{\text{number of beans}}$$

$$= \frac{5.1\text{ g} + 5.2\text{ g} + 5.0\text{ g} + 4.8\text{ g} + 4.9\text{ g} + 5.0\text{ g} + 5.0\text{ g} + 5.1\text{ g} + 4.9\text{ g} + 5.0\text{ g}}{10}$$

$$= \frac{50.0}{10} = 5.0\text{ g}$$

The average mass of a jelly bean is 5.0 g. Thus, to count out 1000 beans, we need to weigh out 5000 g of beans. This sample of beans, in which the beans have an average mass of 5.0 g, can be treated exactly like a sample where all of the beans are identical. Objects do not need to have identical masses to be counted by weighing. We simply need to know the average mass of the objects. For purposes of counting, the objects *behave as though they were all identical,* as though they each actually had the average mass.

Suppose a customer comes into the store and says, "I want to buy a bag of candy for each of my kids. One of them likes jelly beans and the other one

206

TEACHING TIP

The concept of counting atoms from the mass of a sample is difficult for students to understand. Develop the idea slowly. Many students learn to work the problems without really understanding this section. This leads to trouble later when they try to solve more complex problems. Return to the candy analogy to assist in developing this concept. You can also use a hardware store analogy of buying nails by weight, or a banking analogy of counting rolled coins by weighing them.

TEACHING SUPPORT

ACTIVITY

You can demonstrate the jelly bean concept of counting by weighing by using a balance and small candy packages (such as M&Ms). Place the candies from one package on the balance. Have the students determine the mass per candy. Now give the students (individually or in teams) a package and have them use the mass per candy to predict the number of candies in their package from the mass of the package. Assemble the results on the board. Have the students open the package, and count the candies. Record the actual counts next to the predicted counts. Compare and discuss the differences.

likes mints. Please put a scoopful of jelly beans in a bag and a scoopful of mints in another bag." Then the customer recognizes a problem. "Wait! My kids will fight unless I bring home exactly the same number of candies for each one. Both bags must have the same number of pieces because they'll definitely count them and compare. But I'm really in a hurry, so we don't have time to count them here. Is there a simple way you can be sure the bags will contain the same number of candies?"

You need to solve this problem quickly. Suppose you know the average masses of the two kinds of candy:

Jelly beans: average mass = 5 g
Mints: average mass = 15 g

You fill the scoop with jelly beans and dump them onto the scale, which reads 500 g. Now the key question: What mass of mints do you need to give the same number of mints as there are jelly beans in 500 g of jelly beans? Comparing the average masses of the jelly beans (5 g) and mints (15 g), you realize that each mint has three times the mass of each jelly bean:

$$\frac{15\text{ g}}{5\text{ g}} = 3$$

This means that you must weigh out an amount of mints that is three times the mass of the jelly beans:

$$3 \times 500\text{ g} = 1500\text{ g}$$

You weigh out 1500 g of mints and put them in a bag. The customer leaves with your assurance that both the bag containing 500 g of jelly beans and the bag containing 1500 g of mints contain the same number of candies.

In solving this problem, you have discovered a principle that is very important in chemistry: two samples containing different types of components, A and B, both *contain the same number of components if the ratio of the sample masses is the same as the ratio of the masses of the individual components* of A and B.

Let's illustrate this rather intimidating statement by using the example we just discussed. The individual components have the masses 5 g (jelly beans) and 15 g (mints). Consider several cases.

- Each sample contains 1 component:

Mass of mint = 15 g
Mass of jelly bean = 5 g

- Each sample contains 10 components:

$$10\ \cancel{\text{mints}} \times \frac{15\text{ g}}{\cancel{\text{mint}}} = 150\text{ g of mints}$$

$$10\ \cancel{\text{jelly beans}} \times \frac{5\text{ g}}{\cancel{\text{jelly bean}}} = 50\text{ g of jelly beans}$$

- Each sample contains 100 components:

$$100\ \cancel{\text{mints}} \times \frac{15\text{ g}}{\cancel{\text{mint}}} = 1500\text{ g of mints}$$

$$100\ \cancel{\text{jelly beans}} \times \frac{5\text{ g}}{\cancel{\text{jelly bean}}} = 500\text{ g of jelly beans}$$

Note in each case that the ratio of the masses is always 3 to 1:

$$\frac{1500}{500} = \frac{150}{50} = \frac{15}{5} = \frac{3}{1}$$

TEACHING SUPPORT

BACKGROUND

The Chemistry of Jelly Beans

Jelly beans, used here as an example of counting by weighing, are actually quite interesting from a chemical point of view. It takes up to 7 days to make a jelly bean with a soft center and, surprisingly, before now candy makers have not known why. Gregory Ziegler, Associate Professor of Food Science at Penn State University, decided to solve the mystery of how a jelly bean can have a soft center and a hard outer shell.

A jelly bean is made from the inside out, starting with its center. A mixture of corn syrup, sugar, and appropriate flavorings is cooked in a big kettle and then poured into a molding tray. Overnight the centers become hard and tough—not good to eat. The next step involves "engrossing," in which a sugar shell is added to surround the center. Candy makers must then wait 2 to 4 days for the center to soften.

TEACHING TIPS

- The idea that different samples with identical mass ratios contain the same number of objects is a difficult one for many students. Consider using the following example.

  Suppose we have two blocks: a red block and a yellow block. The red block weighs 1.0 ounce, and the yellow block weighs 4.0 ounces. Now suppose we have 16 of each color block. What is the mass of each sample? The sample of red blocks weighs 16.0 ounces and the sample of yellow blocks weighs 64.0 ounces. But note that 16.0 ounces is also 1.0 pound, so 64.0 ounces is 4.0 pounds. The relative masses of the blocks are:

	1 Block	16 Blocks
Red	1.0 ounce	1.0 pound
Yellow	4.0 ounces	4.0 pounds

  The relative masses stay the same (1:4), but the units change.

  You can make an analogy between ounces and pounds in this case and amu's and grams in the case of the periodic table. In the blocks example, the number 16 is analogous to Avogadro's number.

- The relative values of coins can be used as an analogy to relative masses. A penny has a relative value of 1, a nickel a relative value of 5, a dime a relative value of 10, and a quarter a relative value of 25. Inflation, however, keeps these values from being absolute (once upon a time, for example, you could actually buy something for a penny!). Suppose (as has been suggested) the U.S. government phases out pennies in circulation. Then we could think of the nickel as having a relative value of 1, a dime as having a relative value of 2, and a quarter as having a relative value of 5.

This is the ratio of the masses of the individual components:

$$\frac{\text{Mass of mint}}{\text{Mass of jelly bean}} = \frac{15}{5} = \frac{3}{1}$$

Any two samples, one of mints and one of jelly beans, that have a *mass ratio* of 15/5 = 3/1 will contain the same number of components. And these same ideas apply also to atoms, as we will see in the next section.

Test Bank: 2, 12

Section 8.2

8.2 Atomic Masses: Counting Atoms by Weighing

OBJECTIVE: To understand atomic mass and its experimental determination.

TEACHING TIPS

- Even though students may understand counting candy by weighing, they may find it hard to transfer the idea to counting atoms or molecules by mass. This concept seems much more abstract and confusing for them.
- We first introduce counting atoms by weighing using atomic mass units. These are not units with which students are familiar. It helps to reassure students that we will soon work with more familiar units (grams).
- Refer back to the candy analogy or activity from Section 8.1. The average mass of a candy does not represent the mass of a particular candy. Similarly, the average mass of an atom does not represent the mass of an individual atom. This reasoning allows you to introduce the idea that atoms are slightly different in mass without the necessity of developing the idea of isotopes at the same time.

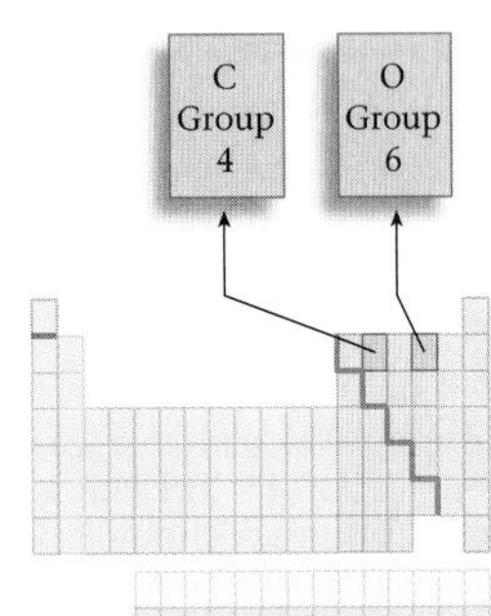

In Chapter 6 we considered the balanced equation for the reaction of solid carbon and gaseous oxygen to form gaseous carbon dioxide:

$$C(s) + O_2(g) \rightarrow CO_2(g)$$

Now suppose you have a small pile of solid carbon and want to know how many oxygen molecules are required to convert all of this carbon into carbon dioxide. The balanced equation tells us that one oxygen molecule is required for each carbon atom.

$$C(s) \quad + \quad O_2(g) \quad \rightarrow \quad CO_2(g)$$

1 atom reacts with 1 molecule to yield 1 molecule

To determine the number of oxygen molecules required, we must know how many carbon atoms are present in the pile of carbon. But individual atoms are far too small to see. We must learn to count atoms by weighing samples containing large numbers of them.

In the last section we saw that we can easily count things like jelly beans and mints by weighing. Exactly the same principles can be applied to counting atoms.

Because atoms are so tiny, the normal units of mass—the gram and the kilogram—are much too large to be convenient. For example, the mass of a single carbon atom is 1.99×10^{-23} g. To avoid using terms like 10^{-23} when describing the mass of an atom, scientists have defined a much smaller unit of mass called the **atomic mass unit,** which is abbreviated **amu.** In terms of grams,

$$1 \text{ amu} = 1.66 \times 10^{-24} \text{ g}$$

Now let's return to our problem of counting carbon atoms. To count carbon atoms by weighing, we need to know the mass of individual atoms, just as we needed to know the mass of the individual jelly beans. Recall from Chapter 4 that the atoms of a given element exist as isotopes. The isotopes of carbon are ${}^{12}_{6}C$, ${}^{13}_{6}C$, and ${}^{14}_{6}C$. Any sample of carbon contains a mixture of these isotopes, always in the same proportions. Each of these isotopes has a slightly different mass. Therefore, just as with the nonidentical jelly beans, we need to use an average mass for the carbon atoms. The **average atomic mass** for carbon atoms is 12.01 amu. This means that any sample of carbon from nature *can be treated as though it were composed of identical carbon atoms,* each with a mass of 12.01 amu. Now that we know the average mass of the carbon atom, we can count carbon atoms by weighing samples of natural carbon. For example, what mass of natural carbon

Ziegler and his colleagues actually used magnetic resonance imaging (MRI) to study the softening process. They found that the moisture from the outer shell is drawn into the center, which softens the center and hardens the shell. The driving force for this movement of water to the center is osmosis. The water flows toward the center, which is a more concentrated "solution" than the shell, trying to equalize the two concentrations. (Osmosis also explains how pickles are made. When cucumbers are placed in a brine [NaCl*(aq)*] solution, water flows out of the cucumber into the brine, shrinking the cucumber into a pickle. Again, in this case, water flows from the more dilute to the more concentrated solution.)

must we take to have 1000 carbon atoms present? Because 12.01 amu is the average mass,

MATH SKILL BUILDER
Remember that 1000 is an exact number here.

$$\text{Mass of 1000 natural carbon atoms} = (1000\ \cancel{\text{atoms}})\left(12.01\ \frac{\text{amu}}{\cancel{\text{atom}}}\right)$$
$$= 12{,}010\ \text{amu} = 12.01 \times 10^3\ \text{amu}$$

Now let's assume that when we weigh the pile of natural carbon mentioned earlier, the result is 3.00×10^{20} amu. How many carbon atoms are present in this sample? We know that an average carbon atom has the mass 12.01 amu, so we can compute the number of carbon atoms by using the equivalence statement

$$1\ \text{carbon atom} = 12.01\ \text{amu}$$

to construct the appropriate conversion factor,

$$\frac{1\ \text{carbon atom}}{12.01\ \text{amu}}$$

The calculation is carried out as follows:

$$3.00 \times 10^{20}\ \cancel{\text{amu}} \times \frac{1\ \text{carbon atom}}{12.01\ \cancel{\text{amu}}} = 2.50 \times 10^{19}\ \text{carbon atoms}$$

The principles we have just discussed for carbon apply to all the other elements as well. All the elements as found in nature typically consist of a mixture of various isotopes. So to count the atoms in a sample of a given element by weighing, we must know the mass of the sample and the average mass for that element. Some average masses for common elements are listed in Table 8.1.

Table 8.1 Average Atomic Mass Values for Some Common Elements

Element	Average Atomic Mass (amu)
Hydrogen	1.008
Carbon	12.01
Nitrogen	14.01
Oxygen	16.00
Sodium	22.99
Aluminum	26.98

EXAMPLE 8.1 Calculating Mass Using Atomic Mass Units (amu)

Calculate the mass, in amu, of a sample of aluminum that contains 75 atoms.

SOLUTION

To solve this problem we use the average mass for an aluminum atom: 26.98 amu. We set up the equivalence statement:

$$1\ \text{Al atom} = 26.98\ \text{amu}$$

It gives the conversion factor we need:

MATH SKILL BUILDER
The 75 in this problem is an exact number—the number of atoms.

$$75\ \cancel{\text{Al atoms}} \times \frac{26.98\ \text{amu}}{1\ \cancel{\text{Al atom}}} = 2024\ \text{amu}$$

Self-Check **EXERCISE 8.1** Calculate the mass of a sample that contains 23 nitrogen atoms.

See Problems 8.5 and 8.8. ■

The opposite calculation can also be carried out. That is, if we know the mass of a sample, we can determine the number of atoms present. This procedure is illustrated in Example 8.2.

TEACHING TIP

Point out that someone has already measured the masses of atoms and we have a table of average atomic masses as a result of that work (the periodic table).

Additional Examples

Example 8.1

1. Calculate the mass (in amu) of a sample of carbon that contains 62 atoms.

   744.6 amu

2. Calculate the mass (in amu) of a sample of iron that contains 15 atoms.

   837.8 amu

Self Check

Answer to Self-Check Exercise 8.1

322.2 amu

Now that the curing process is understood, candy makers hope to find a way to speed up the jelly bean manufacturing process so that they do not have to store the jelly beans for several days but can instead ship them quickly to market.

Additional Examples

Example 8.2

1. Calculate the number of copper atoms present in a sample that has a mass of 1779.4 amu.

   28.00 atoms

2. Calculate the number of argon atoms present in a sample that has a mass of 3755.3 amu.

   94.00 atoms

Self Check

Answer to Self-Check Exercise 8.2

18.0 O atoms

Test Bank: 1, 4–13, 15–33, 44, 50, 51, 54, 138, 140

EXAMPLE 8.2 Calculating the Number of Atoms from the Mass

Calculate the number of sodium atoms present in a sample that has a mass of 1172.49 amu.

SOLUTION

We can solve this problem by using the average atomic mass for sodium (see Table 8.1) of 22.99 amu. The appropriate equivalence statement is

$$1 \text{ Na atom} = 22.99 \text{ amu}$$

which gives the conversion factor we need:

$$1172.49 \cancel{\text{amu}} \times \frac{1 \text{ Na atom}}{22.99 \cancel{\text{amu}}} = 51.00 \text{ Na atoms}$$

Self-Check EXERCISE 8.2 Calculate the number of oxygen atoms in a sample that has a mass of 288 amu.

See Problems 8.6 and 8.7. ■

To summarize, we have seen that we can count atoms by weighing if we know the average atomic mass for that type of atom. This is one of the fundamental operations in chemistry, as we will see in the next section.

The average atomic mass for each element is listed in tables found inside the front cover of this book. Chemists often call these values the *atomic weights* for the elements, although this terminology is passing out of use.

8.3 The Mole

OBJECTIVES: To understand the mole concept and Avogadro's number. • To learn to convert among moles, mass, and number of atoms in a given sample.

In the previous section we used atomic mass units for mass, but these are extremely small units. In the laboratory a much larger unit, the gram, is the convenient unit for mass. In this section we will learn to count atoms in samples with masses given in grams.

Let's assume we have a sample of aluminum that has a mass of 26.98 g. What mass of copper contains exactly the same number of atoms as this sample of aluminum?

26.98 g aluminum	⟵ Contains the same number of atoms ⟶	? grams copper

To answer this question, we need to know the average atomic masses for aluminum (26.98 amu) and copper (63.55 amu). Which atom has the greater atomic mass, aluminum or copper? The answer is copper. If we have 26.98 g of aluminum, do we need more or less than 26.98 g of copper to have the same number of copper atoms as aluminum atoms? We need more than 26.98 g of copper because each copper atom has a greater mass than each aluminum atom. Therefore, a given number of copper atoms will weigh more than an equal number of aluminum atoms. How much copper do we need? Because the average masses of aluminum and copper atoms are 26.98 amu and 63.55 amu, respectively, 26.98 g of aluminum and 63.55 g of copper

Section 8.3

TEACHING TIPS

- This section provides the bridge between amu units and grams. The reasoning used to explain the relative atomic masses on the periodic table is the concept of mass ratios introduced in Section 8.1. Students can memorize the definitions but to get a real understanding of the ideas presented here, you will need to proceed slowly and use many examples.
- Students need to realize that a mole really describes the number of objects present, just as "a dozen" means 12. This connection between a mole as a number and the mass of a sample is essential because we count atoms by weighing samples containing large numbers of them.
- The mole is a crucial concept in this chapter. An understanding of this concept is important for many later topics in the course.

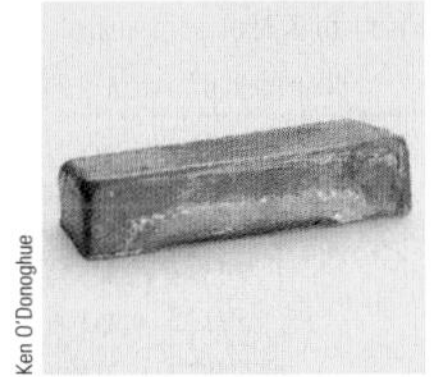
Lead bar
207.2 g

Silver bars
107.9 g

Pile of copper
63.55 g

Figure 8.1
All these samples of pure elements contain the *same number* (a mole) of atoms: 6.022×10^{23} atoms.

Ken O'Donoghue

contain exactly the same number of atoms. So we need 63.55 g of copper. As we saw in the first section when we were discussing candy, *samples in which the ratio of the masses is the same as the ratio of the masses of the individual atoms always contain the same number of atoms.* In the case just considered, the ratios are

$$\frac{26.98\text{ g}}{63.55\text{ g}} = \frac{26.98\text{ amu}}{63.55\text{ amu}}$$

Ratio of sample masses — Ratio of atomic masses

Therefore, 26.98 g of aluminum contains the same number of aluminum atoms as 63.55 g of copper contains copper atoms.

Now compare carbon (average atomic mass, 12.01 amu) and helium (average atomic mass, 4.003 amu). A sample of 12.01 g of carbon contains the same number of atoms as 4.003 g of helium. In fact, if we weigh out samples of all the elements such that each sample has a mass equal to that element's average atomic mass in grams, these samples all contain the same number of atoms (Figure 8.1). This number (the number of atoms present in all of these samples) assumes special importance in chemistry. It is called the mole, the unit all chemists use in describing numbers of atoms. The **mole** (abbreviated mol) can be defined as *the number equal to the number of carbon atoms in 12.01 grams of carbon*. Techniques for counting atoms very precisely have been used to determine this number to be 6.022×10^{23}. This number is called **Avogadro's number.** *One mole of something consists of 6.022×10^{23} units of that substance.* Just as a dozen eggs is 12 eggs, a mole of eggs is 6.022×10^{23} eggs. And a mole of water contains 6.022×10^{23} H_2O molecules.

Ken O'Donoghue

Figure 8.2
One-mole samples of iron (nails), iodine crystals, liquid mercury, and powdered sulfur.

This definition of the mole is slightly different from the SI definition but is used because it is easier to understand at this point.

Avogadro's number (to four significant figures) is 6.022×10^{23}. One mole of *anything* is 6.022×10^{23} units of that substance.

The magnitude of the number 6.022×10^{23} is very difficult to imagine. To give you some idea, 1 mole of seconds represents a span of time 4 million times as long as the earth has already existed! One mole of marbles is enough to cover the entire earth to a depth of 50 miles! However, because atoms are so tiny, a mole of atoms or molecules is a perfectly manageable quantity to use in a reaction (Figure 8.2).

How do we use the mole in chemical calculations? Recall that Avogadro's number is defined such that a 12.01-g sample of carbon contains 6.022×10^{23} atoms. By the same token, because the average atomic mass of hydrogen is 1.008 amu (Table 8.1), 1.008 g of hydrogen contains 6.022×10^{23} hydrogen atoms. Similarly, 26.98 g of aluminum contains 6.022×10^{23} aluminum atoms. The point is that a sample of *any* element that weighs a number of grams equal to the average atomic mass of that element contains 6.022×10^{23} atoms (1 mol) of that element.

Table 8.2 shows the masses of several elements that contain 1 mole of atoms.

DEMONSTRATION

Bring a dozen eggs, a gross of pencils, and a ream of paper to class. Show the students the eggs and ask them to determine how many eggs are in 5 dozen. Have a student explain how he or she got the answer. Do a similar thing with the pencils and the paper. Once the students are familiar with calculating the number of objects of a given type, write the number of objects in a mole on the board. Ask the students to determine how many atoms of aluminum are in a mole of aluminum. Repeat this idea with several different elements and amounts. Be sure that students can relate that the process used is the same regardless of the unit.

DEMONSTRATION

Moles and Molecules

Materials Four 500-mL beakers, sugar, sulfur, water

Procedure Place the following in separate, labeled beakers: 18 mL water (labeled *1 mol water*), 342 g sugar (labeled *1 mol sugar*), 256 g sulfur (labeled *1 mol sulfur*), 342 mL water (labeled *342 g water*)

Show the students the beakers each containing one mole. Note the differences in mass and volume. Note that the number of molecules (6.022×10^{23}) is the same in each case.

Now use the beaker containing sugar and the one containing 342 g water. Emphasize that they have the same mass. Ask the students how the number of molecules in the beakers compares. The sugar contains 6.022×10^{23} molecules while the water contains $19(6.022 \times 10^{23}) = 1.14 \times 10^{25}$ molecules of water.

Extending the Idea Ask students to determine the ratio of the molecules in the sugar beaker to the molecules in the water beaker. How does this compare to the ratio of moles from sugar to water?

TEACHING TIPS

- Some students memorize the equivalence statement 1 mol = 6.022×10^{-23}. Presumably this is because we have dealt with many small numbers (e.g., diameter of an atom, mass of a proton). Because we generally use Avogadro's number to mean the number of atoms or molecules in a sample, the students should understand that a mole must be larger than 1. This is a good time to review scientific notation.
- Notice that we define the mole differently from the SI definition: "the mole is the amount of substance that contains as many entities as there are in exactly 0.012 kg of carbon 12." Our definition is "the mole is the number equal to the number of carbon atoms in 12.01 g of carbon." We believe our definition is easier for students to understand at this point. It more strongly emphasizes both that the mole is fundamentally a number and that the periodic table contains average atomic masses.
- Make sure that students understand that *mol* means mole and not molecule.
- Students do not need to memorize the average atomic masses for elements. These masses are given on the periodic table.

Table 8.2 Comparison of 1-Mol Samples of Various Elements

Element	Number of Atoms Present	Mass of Sample (g)
Aluminum	6.022×10^{23}	26.98
Gold	6.022×10^{23}	196.97
Iron	6.022×10^{23}	55.85
Sulfur	6.022×10^{23}	32.07
Boron	6.022×10^{23}	10.81
Xenon	6.022×10^{23}	131.3

The mass of 1 mole of an element is equal to its average atomic mass in grams.

In summary, *a sample of an element with a mass equal to that element's average atomic mass expressed in grams contains 1 mole of atoms.*

To do chemical calculations, you *must* understand what the mole means and how to determine the number of moles in a given mass of a substance. However, before we do any calculations, let's be sure that the process of counting by weighing is clear. Consider the following "bag" of H atoms (symbolized by dots), which contains 1 mole (6.022×10^{23}) of H atoms and has a mass of 1.008 g. Assume the bag itself has no mass.

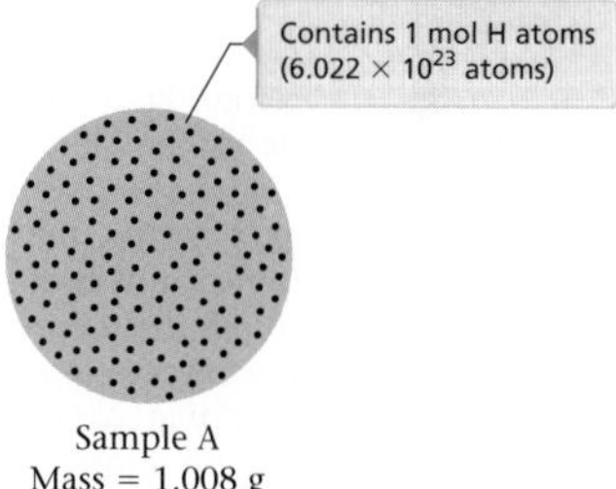

Now consider another "bag" of hydrogen atoms in which the number of hydrogen atoms is unknown.

A 1-mol sample of graphite (a form of carbon) weighs 12.01 g

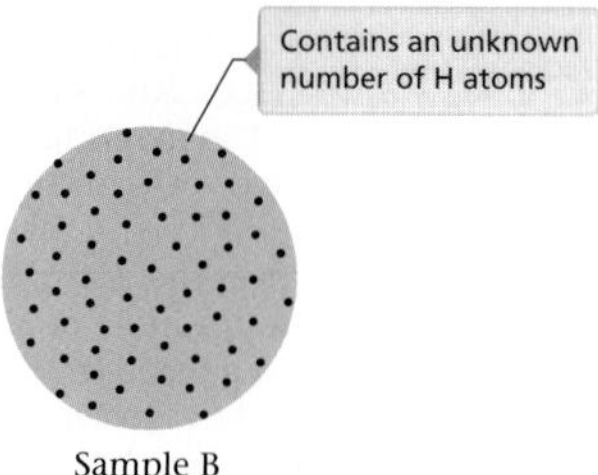

We want to find out how many H atoms are present in sample ("bag") B. How can we do that? We can do it by weighing the sample. We find the mass of sample B to be 0.500 g.

How does this measured mass help us determine the number of atoms in sample B? We know that 1 mole of H atoms has a mass of 1.008 g. Sample B has a mass of 0.500 g, which is approximately half the mass of a mole of H atoms.

TEACHING SUPPORT

HISTORICAL NOTE

Naming the number 6.022×10^{23} as Avogadro's number honors Amadeo Avogadro (1776–1856), the Italian chemist who first realized that equal volumes of gases at the same pressure contain equal numbers of particles (atoms or molecules). This idea, known as Avogadro's hypothesis, was advanced by Avogadro in 1811 but went unnoticed for about half a century. It was not until 1860, after Avogadro's death, that another Italian chemist, Stanislao Cannizzaro, used Avogadro's hypothesis to determine the molar masses of several compounds. In so doing, he proved the correctness of Avogadro's idea.

Have your students investigate the lives and careers of Avogadro and Cannizzaro to understand more fully their monumental contributions to chemistry.

Sample A Mass = 1.008 g		Sample B Mass = 0.500 g
Contains 1 mol H atoms	→ Because the mass of B is about half the mass of A	Must contain about 1/2 mol H atoms

We carry out the actual calculation by using the equivalence statement

$$1 \text{ mol H atoms} = 1.008 \text{ g H}$$

to construct the conversion factor we need:

$$0.500 \text{ g H} \times \frac{1 \text{ mol H}}{1.008 \text{ g H}} = 0.496 \text{ mol H in sample B}$$

MATH SKILL BUILDER
In demonstrating how to solve problems requiring more than one step, we will often break the problem into smaller steps and report the answer to each step in the correct number of significant figures. While it may not always affect the final answer, it is a better idea to wait until the final step to round your answer to the correct number of significant figures.

Let's summarize. We know the mass of 1 mole of H atoms, so we can determine the number of moles of H atoms in any other sample of pure hydrogen by weighing the sample and *comparing* its mass to 1.008 g (the mass of 1 mole of H atoms). We can follow this same process for any element, because we know the mass of 1 mol for each of the elements.

Also, because we know that 1 mol is 6.022×10^{23} units, once we know the *moles* of atoms present, we can easily determine the *number* of atoms present. In the case considered above, we have approximately 0.5 mole of H atoms in sample B. This means that about 1/2 of 6×10^{23}, or 3×10^{23}, H atoms is present. We carry out the actual calculation by using the equivalence statement

$$1 \text{ mol} = 6.022 \times 10^{23}$$

to determine the conversion factor we need:

$$0.496 \text{ mol H atoms} \times \frac{6.022 \times 10^{23} \text{ H atoms}}{1 \text{ mol H atoms}} = 2.99 \times 10^{23} \text{ H atoms in sample B}$$

These procedures are illustrated in Example 8.3.

EXAMPLE 8.3 Calculating Moles and Number of Atoms

Aluminum (Al), a metal with a high strength-to-weight ratio and a high resistance to corrosion, is often used for structures such as high-quality bicycle frames. Compute both the number of moles of atoms and the number of atoms in a 10.0-g sample of aluminum.

© Cengage Learning

A bicycle with an aluminum frame.

SOLUTION

In this case we want to change from mass to moles of atoms:

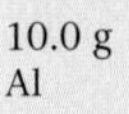
10.0 g Al

? moles of Al atoms

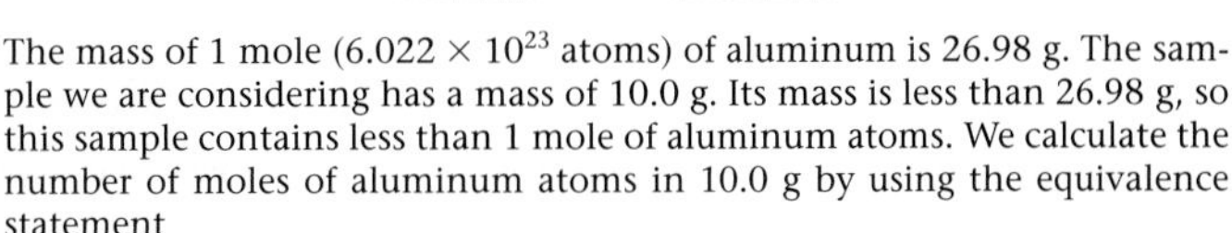

The mass of 1 mole (6.022×10^{23} atoms) of aluminum is 26.98 g. The sample we are considering has a mass of 10.0 g. Its mass is less than 26.98 g, so this sample contains less than 1 mole of aluminum atoms. We calculate the number of moles of aluminum atoms in 10.0 g by using the equivalence statement

$$1 \text{ mol Al} = 26.98 \text{ g Al}$$

Additional Examples

Example 8.3

1. Calculate the number of moles of atoms and the number of atoms in a 25.0-g sample of calcium.

   0.624 mol Ca; 3.76×10^{23} Ca atoms

2. Calculate the number of moles of atoms and the number of atoms in a 57.7-g sample of sulfur.

   1.80 mol S; 1.08×10^{24} S atoms

TEACHING TIPS

- You may wish to go back to Tables 4.1 and 4.2 and have students rank the elements according to abundance by mole percent.
- Either Avogadro's number or atomic masses can limit the number of significant figures in a result. Be sure that the students recognize that these numbers are not exact.

TEACHING SUPPORT

ACTIVITY

Bring samples of several elements to class along with a balance. Weigh a sample of an element. Have students determine the number of moles and the number of atoms or molecules in the sample.

Remind students to express their answers in scientific notation with correct significant figures. This helps them remember that these considerations are important for every problem in chemistry.

to construct the appropriate conversion factor:

$$10.0 \text{ g Al} \times \frac{1 \text{ mol Al}}{26.98 \text{ g Al}} = 0.371 \text{ mol Al}$$

Next we convert from moles of atoms to the number of atoms, using the equivalence statement

$$6.022 \times 10^{23} \text{ Al atoms} = 1 \text{ mol Al atoms}$$

We have

$$0.371 \text{ mol Al} \times \frac{6.022 \times 10^{23} \text{ Al atoms}}{1 \text{ mol Al}} = 2.23 \times 10^{23} \text{ Al atoms}$$

We can summarize this calculation as follows:

$$10.0 \text{ g Al} \times \frac{1 \text{ mol}}{26.98 \text{ g}} \Rightarrow 0.371 \text{ mol Al}$$

$$0.371 \text{ mol Al atoms} \times \frac{6.022 \times 10^{23} \text{ Al atoms}}{\text{mol}} \Rightarrow 2.23 \times 10^{23} \text{ Al atoms}$$

■

Additional Examples

Example 8.4

1. Calculate the number of atoms in a 23.6-mg sample of zinc.

   2.17×10^{20} Zn atoms

2. Calculate the number of atoms in a 128.3-mg sample of silver.

   7.16×10^{20} Ag atoms

EXAMPLE 8.4 Calculating the Number of Atoms

A silicon chip used in an integrated circuit of a microcomputer has a mass of 5.68 mg. How many silicon (Si) atoms are present in this chip? The average atomic mass for silicon is 28.09 amu.

PhotoDisc/Getty Images

A silicon chip of the type used in electronic equipment.

SOLUTION

Our strategy for doing this problem is to convert from milligrams of silicon to grams of silicon, then to moles of silicon, and finally to atoms of silicon:

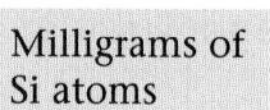

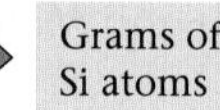

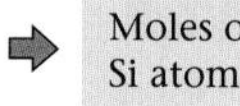

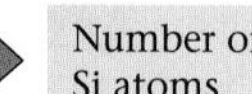

where each arrow in the schematic represents a conversion factor. Because 1 g = 1000 mg, we have

$$5.68 \text{ mg Si} \times \frac{1 \text{ g Si}}{1000 \text{ mg Si}} = 5.68 \times 10^{-3} \text{ g Si}$$

Next, because the average mass of silicon is 28.09 amu, we know that 1 mole of Si atoms weighs 28.09 g. This leads to the equivalence statement

$$1 \text{ mol Si atoms} = 28.09 \text{ g Si}$$

Thus,

$$5.68 \times 10^{-3} \text{ g Si} \times \frac{1 \text{ mol Si}}{28.09 \text{ g Si}} = 2.02 \times 10^{-4} \text{ mol Si}$$

Using the definition of a mole ($1 \text{ mol} = 6.022 \times 10^{23}$), we have

$$2.02 \times 10^{-4} \text{ mol Si} \times \frac{6.022 \times 10^{23} \text{ atoms}}{1 \text{ mol Si}} = 1.22 \times 10^{20} \text{ Si atoms}$$

We can summarize this calculation as follows:

$$5.68 \text{ mg Si} \times \frac{1 \text{ g}}{1000 \text{ mg}} \Rightarrow 5.68 \times 10^{-3} \text{ g Si}$$

$$5.68 \times 10^{-3} \text{ g Si} \times \frac{1 \text{ mol}}{28.09 \text{ g}} \Rightarrow 2.02 \times 10^{-4} \text{ mol Si}$$

$$2.02 \times 10^{-4} \text{ mol Si} \times \frac{6.022 \times 10^{23} \text{ Si atoms}}{\text{mol}} \Rightarrow 1.22 \times 10^{20} \text{ Si atoms}$$

PROBLEM SOLVING: DOES THE ANSWER MAKE SENSE?

When you finish a problem, always think about the "reasonableness" of your answers. In Example 8.4, 5.68 mg of silicon is clearly much less than 1 mole of silicon (which has a mass of 28.09 g), so the final answer of 1.22×10^{20} atoms (compared to 6.022×10^{23} atoms in a mole) at least lies in the right direction. That is, 1.22×10^{20} atoms is a smaller number than 6.022×10^{23}. Also, always include the units as you perform calculations and make sure the correct units are obtained at the end. Paying careful attention to units and making this type of general check can help you detect errors such as an inverted conversion factor or a number that was incorrectly entered into your calculator.

As you can see, the problems are getting more complicated to solve. In the next section we will discuss strategies that will help you become a better problem solver.

Self Check

Answers to Self-Check Exercise 8.3

8.30×10^{-4} mol Cr
4.32×10^{-2} g Cr

Self-Check EXERCISE 8.3 Chromium (Cr) is a metal that is added to steel to improve its resistance to corrosion (for example, to make stainless steel). Calculate both the number of moles in a sample of chromium containing 5.00×10^{20} atoms and the mass of the sample.

The values for the average masses of the atoms of the elements are listed inside the front cover of this book.

See Problems 8.19 through 8.24. ■

8.4 Learning to Solve Problems

Section 8.4

OBJECTIVE: To understand how to solve problems by asking and answering a series of questions.

TEACHING TIP

When encountering new problems, students often try to memorize a specific solution and then apply it to a new problem. This approach often leads to wrong answers and can be frustrating. In this section, we offer a general approach to problem solving in which the students think through a problem and ask questions (much like we would ask the students in a one-on-one help session). The eventual goal is to get the students to ask and answer these questions on their own.

Imagine today is the first day of your new job. The problem is that you don't know how to get there. However, as luck would have it, a friend does know the way and offers to drive you. What should you do while you sit in the passenger seat? If your goal is simply to get to work today, you might not pay attention to how to get there. However, you will need to get there on your own tomorrow, so you should pay attention to distances, signs, and turns. The difference between these two approaches is the difference between taking a passive role (going along for the ride) and an active role (learning how to do it yourself). In this section, we will emphasize that you should take an active role in reading the text, especially the solutions to the practice problems.

One of the great rewards of studying chemistry is that you become a good problem solver. Being able to solve complex problems is a talent that will serve you well in all walks of life. It is our purpose in this text to help you learn to solve problems in a flexible, creative way based on understanding the fundamental ideas of chemistry. We call this approach **conceptual problem**

solving. The ultimate goal is to be able to solve new problems (that is, problems you have not seen before) on your own. In this text, we will provide problems, but instead of giving solutions for you to memorize, we will explain how to think about the solutions to the problems. Although the answers to these problems are important, it is even more important that you understand the process—the thinking necessary to get to the answer. At first we will be solving the problem for you (we will be "driving"). However, it is important that you do not take a passive role. While studying the solution, it is crucial that you interact—think through the problem with us, that is, take an active role so that eventually you can "drive" by yourself. Do not skip the discussion and jump to the answer. Usually, the solution involves asking a series of questions. Make sure that you understand each step in the process.

Although actively studying our solutions to the problems is helpful, at some point you will need to know how to think about these problems on your own. If we help you too much as you solve the problems, you won't really learn effectively. If we always "drive," you won't interact as meaningfully with the material. Eventually you need to learn to drive by yourself. Because of this, we will provide more help on the earlier problems and less as we proceed in later chapters. The goal is for you to learn how to solve a problem because you understand the main concepts and ideas in the problem.

Consider, for example, that you now know how to get from home to work. Does this mean that you can drive from work to home? Not necessarily, as you probably know from experience. If you have only memorized the directions from home to work and do not understand fundamental principles such as "I traveled north to get to the workplace, so my house is south of the workplace," you may find yourself stranded. Part of conceptual problem solving is understanding these fundamental principles.

Of course, there are many more places to go than from home to work and back. In a more complicated example, suppose you know how to get from your house to work (and back) and from your house to the library (and back). Can you get from work to the library without having to go back home? Probably not, if you have only memorized directions and you do not have a "big picture" of where your house, your workplace, and the library are relative to one another. Getting this big picture—a real understanding of the situation—is the other part of conceptual problem solving.

In conceptual problem solving, we let the problem guide us as we solve it. We ask a series of questions as we proceed and use our knowledge of fundamental principles to answer these questions. Learning this approach requires some patience, but the reward is that you become an effective solver of any new problem that confronts you in daily life or in your work in any field.

To help us as we proceed to solve a problem, the following organizing principles will be useful to us.

1. First, we need to read the problem and decide on the final goal. Then we sort through the facts given, focusing on keywords and often drawing a diagram of the problem. In this part of the analysis, we need to state the problem as simply and as visually as possible. We can summarize this process as **"Where Are We Going?"**
2. We need to work backward from the final goal in order to decide where to start. For example, in a stoichiometry problem we always start with the chemical reaction. Then as we proceed, we ask a series of questions, such as "What are the reactants and products?," "What is the balanced equation?," and "What are the amounts of the reactants?" Our understanding of the fundamental principles of chemistry will enable us to answer each of these simple questions

TEACHING TIP

We have written solutions throughout the remainder of the text to the quantitative Example Problems in this format. Encourage the students to read through these solutions and to try to answer the questions ("Where Are We Going?," etc.) on their own as they progress through the text.

and eventually will lead us to the final solution. We can summarize this process as "**How Do We Get There?**"

3. Once we get the solution of the problem, then we ask ourselves: "Does it make sense?" That is, does our answer seem reasonable? We call this the **Reality Check.** It always pays to check your answer.

Using a conceptual approach to problem solving will enable you to develop real confidence as a problem solver. You will no longer panic when you see a problem that is different in some ways from those you have solved in the past. Although you might be frustrated at times as you learn this method, we guarantee that it will pay dividends later and should make your experience with chemistry a positive one that will prepare you for any career you choose.

To summarize, a creative problem solver has an understanding of fundamental principles and a big picture of the situation. One of our major goals in this text is to help you become a creative problem solver. We will do this first by giving you lots of guidance on how to solve problems. We will "drive," but we hope you will be paying attention instead of just "going along for the ride." As we move forward, we will gradually shift more of the responsibility to you. As you gain confidence in letting the problem guide you, you will be amazed at how effective you can be at solving some really complex problems, just like the ones you will confront in real life.

An Example of Conceptual Problem Solving

Let's look at how conceptual problem solving works in practice. Because we used a driving analogy before, let's consider a problem about driving.

> Estimate the amount of money you would spend on gasoline to drive from New York, New York, to Los Angeles, California.

Where Are We Going?

The first thing we need to do is state the problem in words or as a diagram so that we understand the problem.

In this case, we are trying to estimate how much money we will spend on gasoline. How are we going to do this? We need to understand what factors cause us to spend more or less money. This requires us to ask, "**What Information Do We Need?**," and "**What Do We Know?**"

Consider two people traveling in separate cars. Why might one person spend more money on gasoline than does the other person? In other words, if you were told that the two people spent different amounts of money on gasoline for a trip, what are some reasons you could give? Consider this, and write down some ideas before you continue reading.

Three factors that are important in this case are

- The price of a gallon of gasoline
- The distance of the trip between New York and Los Angeles
- The average gas mileage of the car we are driving

What do we know, or what are we given in the problem? In this problem, we are not given any of these values but are asked to estimate the cost of gasoline. So we need to estimate the required information. For example, the distance between New York and Los Angeles is about 3000 miles. The cost of gasoline varies over time and location, but a reasonable estimate is \$2.00 a gallon. Gas mileage also varies, but we will assume it is about 30 miles per gallon.

Now that we have the necessary information, we will solve the problem.

TEACHING TIP

The example of conceptual problem solving used in the text is different from many of the problems the students will encounter because, in this example, they have to determine some of the information (they estimate, for example, the average gas mileage of the car and the price of a gallon of gas). Assure the students that they will often be given this type of information although there may be cases in which they will be asked to determine some of it.

If you have time in class, consider having the students work together on a different example problem to make sure they understand the approach. Choosing a non-chemistry example is a good idea so the students can focus more on the approach than the chemistry. For example, you could tell them that banks often count coins by weighing them and you could ask "How much is 2 pounds of nickels worth?" Ask the students to use the conceptual problem solving approach to answer this question and have the students work in groups to decide what they would need to know to solve this problem and then develop a solution. For example, they would need to know the average mass of a nickel and how many nickels there are in a dollar. If you decide to give them the average mass of a nickel in grams (~5.0 g per nickel) they would also have to know the conversion between grams and pounds (453.59 g = 1 lb.). The solution is

$$2 \text{ pounds} \times \frac{453.59 \text{ grams}}{1 \text{ pound}} \times \frac{1 \text{ nickel}}{5.0 \text{ grams}} \times \frac{\$1}{20 \text{ nickels}} = \$9$$

This answer has 1 significant figure as dictated by what is given (2 pounds). When you first introduce chemistry problems with this approach, it will be a good idea to go back to this example and the one in the text for reassurance.

How Do We Get There?

To set up the solution, we need to understand how the information affects our answer. Let's consider the relationship between the three factors we identified and our final answer.

- Price of gasoline: directly related. The more a gallon of gasoline costs, the more we will spend in total.
- Distance: directly related. The farther we travel, the more we will spend on gasoline.
- Gas mileage: inversely related. The better our gas mileage (the higher the number), the less we will spend on gasoline.

It should make sense, then, that we multiply the distance and price (because they are directly related) and then divide by the gas mileage (because it is inversely related). We will use dimensional analysis as discussed in Chapter 2. First let's determine how much gasoline we will need for our trip.

$$3000 \cancel{\text{miles}} \times \frac{1 \text{ gal}}{30 \cancel{\text{miles}}} = 100 \text{ gallons of gasoline}$$

Notice how the distance is in the numerator and the gas mileage is in the denominator, just as we determined they each should be. So, we will need about 100 gallons of gasoline. How much will this much gasoline cost?

$$100 \cancel{\text{gallons}} \times \frac{\$2.00}{1 \cancel{\text{gallon}}} = \$200$$

Notice that the price of a gallon of gas is in the numerator, just as predicted. So, given our information, we estimate the total cost of gasoline to be $200. The final step is to consider if this answer is reasonable.

REALITY CHECK Does our answer make sense? This is always a good question to consider, and our answer will depend on our familiarity with the situation. Sometimes we may not have a good feel for what the answer should be, especially when we are learning a new concept. Other times we may have only a rough idea and may be able to claim that the answer seems reasonable, although we cannot say it is exactly right. This will usually be the case, and it is the case here if you are familiar with how much you spend on gasoline. For example, the price to fill up the tank for an average car (at $2.00 per gallon) is around $20 to $40. So, if our answer is under $100, we should be suspicious. An answer in the thousands of dollars is way too high. So, an answer in the hundreds of dollars seems reasonable.

8.5 Molar Mass

OBJECTIVES: To understand the definition of molar mass. • To learn to convert between moles and mass of a given sample of a chemical compound.

A chemical compound is, fundamentally, a collection of atoms. For example, methane (the major component of natural gas) consists of molecules each containing one carbon atom and four hydrogen atoms (CH_4). How can we calculate the mass of 1 mole of methane? That is, what is the mass of 6.022×10^{23} CH_4 molecules? Because each CH_4 molecule contains one carbon atom and four hydrogen atoms, 1 mole of CH_4 molecules consists of

Note that when we say 1 mole of methane, we mean 1 mole of methane *molecules*.

Section 8.5

MISCONCEPTION

Some students, when asked to give the number of hydrogen atoms in 10.0 g (or any given mass) of water, will quickly respond "2." Now is a good time to review what a subscript means.

Test Bank: 14, 34–43, 45–49, 52, 53, 55–93, 95, 135–137, 139, 141, 142

MATH MISCONCEPTION

Molar Mass

Molar mass, like density, is a ratio of two numbers. Students often confuse the mass of a sample with the molar mass of a compound. You can help the students by giving them problems such as the following:

If 0.400 mole of a compound has a mass of 17.6 g, what is the molar mass of the compound?

By dividing 17.6 g by 0.400 mol, we see that the compound has a molar mass of 44.0 g/mol.

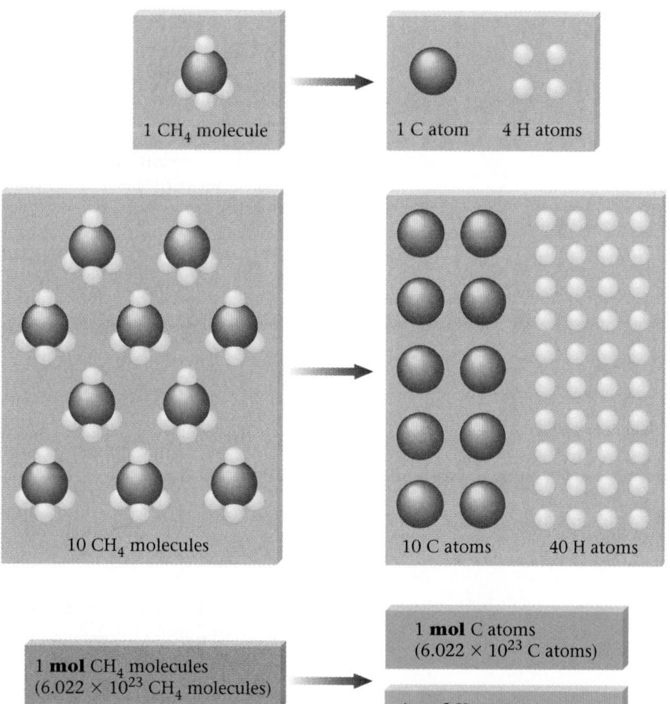

Figure 8.3
Various numbers of methane molecules showing their constituent atoms.

MATH SKILL BUILDER
Remember that the least number of decimal places limits the number of significant figures in addition.

1 mole of carbon atoms and 4 moles of hydrogen atoms (Figure 8.3). The mass of 1 mole of methane can be found by summing the masses of carbon and hydrogen present:

$$\begin{aligned} \text{Mass of 1 mol C} &= 1 \times 12.01 \text{ g} = 12.01 \text{ g} \\ \text{Mass of 4 mol H} &= 4 \times 1.008 \text{ g} = \underline{4.032 \text{ g}} \\ \text{Mass of 1 mol } CH_4 &= 16.04 \text{ g} \end{aligned}$$

A substance's molar mass (in grams) is the mass of 1 mole of that substance.

The quantity 16.04 g is called the molar mass for methane: the mass of 1 mole of CH_4 molecules. The **molar mass*** of any substance is the *mass (in grams) of 1 mole of the substance.* The molar mass is obtained by summing the masses of the component atoms.

EXAMPLE 8.5 Calculating Molar Mass

Calculate the molar mass of sulfur dioxide, a gas produced when sulfur-containing fuels are burned. Unless "scrubbed" from the exhaust, sulfur dioxide can react with moisture in the atmosphere to produce acid rain.

*The term *molecular weight* was traditionally used instead of *molar mass*. The terms *molecular weight* and *molar mass* mean exactly the same thing. Because the term *molar mass* more accurately describes the concept, it will be used in this text.

TEACHING TIPS

- The term *molar mass* has replaced *molecular weight* because molar mass more accurately describes the concept.
- It is difficult for students to translate a formula into moles at this point. For example, 1 mole of methane molecules contains 4 moles of hydrogen atoms. Be sure to have students practice this translation and have them justify their answers.
- Emphasize that molar mass is the mass *per one mole* of substance. For example, one mole of diatomic oxygen gas has a mass of 32.00 g. A sample containing two moles of oxygen gas has a mass of 64.00 g.

Additional Examples

Example 8.5

Here are some additional examples to use for molar mass calculations. Each answer has been rounded to four significant figures.

1. Water

   H_2O; 18.02 g/mol

2. Ammonia

   NH_3; 17.03 g/mol

3. C_3H_8

   propane; 44.09 g/mol

4. $C_6H_{12}O_6$

   glucose; 180.2 g/mol

Here are some additional examples to use for molar mass calculations for ionic compounds. These can also be used to review naming ionic compounds. Each answer has been rounded to four significant figures.

1. Calcium sulfate

   $CaSO_4$; 136.2 g/mol

2. Sodium carbonate

   Na_2CO_3; 106.0 g/mol

3. Barium hydroxide

   $Ba(OH)_2$; 171.3 g/mol

SOLUTION

Where Are We Going?

We want to determine the molar mass of sulfur dioxide in units of g/mol.

What Do We Know?

- The formula for sulfur dioxide is SO_2, which means that 1 mole of SO_2 molecules contains 1 mole of sulfur atoms and 2 moles of oxygen atoms.

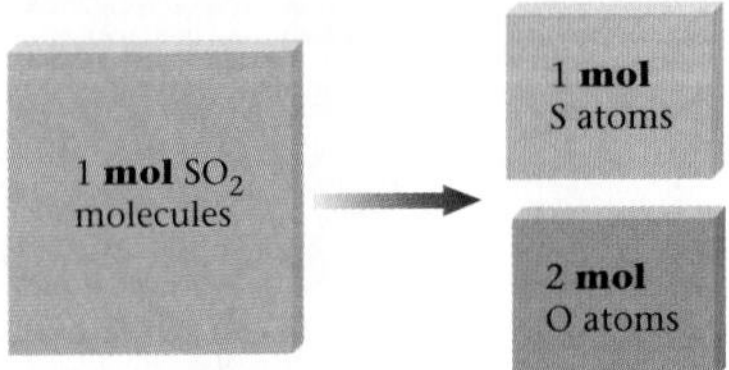

- We know the atomic masses of sulfur (32.07 g/mol) and oxygen (16.00 g/mol).

How Do We Get There?

We need to find the mass of 1 mole of SO_2 molecules, which is the molar mass of SO_2.

$$\begin{aligned} &\text{Mass of 1 mol S} = 1 \times 32.07 &&= 32.07\text{ g} \\ &\text{Mass of 2 mol O} = 2 \times 16.00 &&= \underline{32.00\text{ g}} \\ &\text{Mass of 1 mol SO}_2 &&= 64.07\text{ g} = \text{molar mass} \end{aligned}$$

The molar mass of SO_2 is 64.07 g. It represents the mass of 1 mole of SO_2 molecules.

REALITY CHECK The answer is greater than the atomic masses of sulfur and oxygen. The units (g/mol) are correct, and the answer is reported to the correct number of significant figures (to two decimal places).

Self-Check **EXERCISE 8.4** Polyvinyl chloride (called PVC), which is widely used for floor coverings ("vinyl") and for plastic pipes in plumbing systems, is made from a molecule with the formula C_2H_3Cl. Calculate the molar mass of this substance.

See Problems 8.27 through 8.30. ■

Self Check

Answer to Self-Check Exercise 8.4

The molar mass of C_2H_3Cl is 62.49 g (rounding to the correct number of significant figures).

Some substances exist as a collection of ions rather than as separate molecules. For example, ordinary table salt, sodium chloride (NaCl), is composed of an array of Na^+ and Cl^- ions. There are no NaCl molecules present. In some books the term **formula weight** is used instead of molar mass for ionic compounds. However, in this book we will apply the term *molar mass* to both ionic and molecular substances.

To calculate the molar mass for sodium chloride, we must realize that 1 mole of NaCl contains 1 mole of Na^+ ions and 1 mole of Cl^- ions.

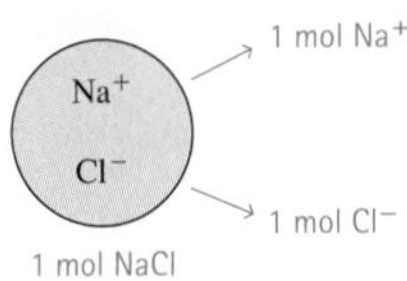

The mass of the electron is so small that Na^+ and Na have the same mass for our purposes, even though Na^+ has one electron fewer than Na. Also the mass of Cl virtually equals the mass of Cl^- even though it has one more electron than Cl.

Therefore, the molar mass (in grams) for sodium chloride represents the sum of the mass of 1 mole of sodium ions and the mass of 1 mole of chloride ions.

$$\begin{aligned} \text{Mass of 1 mol } Na^+ &= 22.99 \text{ g} \\ \text{Mass of 1 mol } Cl^- &= \underline{35.45 \text{ g}} \\ \text{Mass of 1 mol NaCl} &= 58.44 \text{ g} = \text{molar mass} \end{aligned}$$

The molar mass of NaCl is 58.44 g. It represents the mass of 1 mole of sodium chloride.

EXAMPLE 8.6

Calculating Mass from Moles

Calcium carbonate, $CaCO_3$ (also called calcite), is the principal mineral found in limestone, marble, chalk, pearls, and the shells of marine animals such as clams.

a. Calculate the molar mass of calcium carbonate.

b. A certain sample of calcium carbonate contains 4.86 mol. What is the mass in grams of this sample?

SOLUTION

a. Where Are We Going?

We want to determine the molar mass of calcium carbonate in units of g/mol.

What Do We Know?

- The formula for calcium carbonate is $CaCO_3$. One mole of $CaCO_3$ contains 1 mole of Ca, 1 mole of C, and 3 moles of O.
- We know the atomic masses of calcium (40.08 g/mol), carbon (12.01 g/mol), and oxygen 16.00 g/mol).

How Do We Get There?

Calcium carbonate is an ionic compound composed of Ca^{2+} and CO_3^{2-} ions. One mole of calcium carbonate contains 1 mole of Ca^{2+} and 1 mole of CO_3^{2-} ions. We calculate the molar mass by summing the masses of the components.

$$\begin{aligned} &\text{Mass of 1 mol } Ca^{2+} = 1 \times 40.08 \text{ g} = 40.08 \text{ g} \\ &\text{Mass of 1 mol } CO_3^{2-} \text{ (contains 1 mol C and 3 mol O):} \\ &\quad \text{1 mol C} \quad = 1 \times 12.01 \text{ g} = 12.01 \text{ g} \\ &\quad \text{3 mol O} \quad = 3 \times 16.00 \text{ g} = \underline{48.00 \text{ g}} \\ &\qquad \text{Mass of 1 mol } CaCO_3 = 100.09 \text{ g} = \text{molar mass} \end{aligned}$$

REALITY CHECK The answer is greater than the atomic masses of calcium, carbon, and oxygen. The units (g/mol) are correct, and the answer is reported to the correct number of significant figures (to two decimal places).

b. Where Are We Going?

We want to determine the mass of 4.86 moles of $CaCO_3$.

What Do We Know?

- From part a, we know that the molar mass of $CaCO_3$ is 100.09 g/mol.
- We have 4.86 mol $CaCO_3$.

Additional Examples

Example 8.6

1. Calculate the mass of 1.48 moles of potassium oxide, (K_2O).

   139 g

2. Calculate the mass of 4.85 moles of acetic acid, $HC_2H_3O_2$. Vinegar is a dilute solution of acetic acid.

   291 g

TEACHING TIP

Students should not round off the atomic masses when calculating molar masses—for example, using 1 for hydrogen and 12 for carbon. If the students develop this habit now, they will have trouble obtaining the correct answer to stoichiometry problems later in the course.

Self Check

Answer to Self-Check Exercise 8.5

142.05 g/mol; 2.112 mol Na_2SO_4

How Do We Get There?

We determine the mass of 4.86 moles of $CaCO_3$ by using the molar mass.

$$4.86 \text{ mol } CaCO_3 \times \frac{100.09 \text{ g } CaCO_3}{1 \text{ mol } CaCO_3} = 486 \text{ g } CaCO_3$$

This can be diagrammed as follows:

$$4.86 \text{ mol } CaCO_3 \times \frac{100.09 \text{ g}}{\text{mol}} \Rightarrow 486 \text{ g } CaCO_3$$

REALITY CHECK We have a bit less than 5 moles of $CaCO_3$, which has a molar mass of about 100 g/mol. We should expect an answer a bit less than 500 g, so our answer makes sense. The number of significant figures in our answer (486 g) is three, as required by the initial number of moles (4.86 mol).

Self-Check EXERCISE 8.5 Calculate the molar mass for sodium sulfate, Na_2SO_4. A sample of sodium sulfate with a mass of 300.0 g represents what number of moles of sodium sulfate?

For average atomic masses, look inside the front cover of this book.

See Problems 8.35 through 8.38. ■

In summary, the molar mass of a substance can be obtained by summing the masses of the component atoms. The molar mass (in grams) represents the mass of 1 mole of the substance. Once we know the molar mass of a compound, we can compute the number of moles present in a sample of known mass. The reverse, of course, is also true as illustrated in Example 8.7.

Additional Examples

Example 8.7

1. Formaldehyde, which in the past was used to preserve biologic samples, has the formula H_2CO. How many moles of formaldehyde does a 7.55-g sample represent?

   0.251 mol formaldehyde

2. How many moles of tetraphosphorus decoxide does a 250.0-g sample represent?

   0.8805 mol

EXAMPLE 8.7 Calculating Moles from Mass

Juglone, a dye known for centuries, is produced from the husks of black walnuts. It is also a natural herbicide (weed killer) that kills off competitive plants around the black walnut tree but does not affect grass and other noncompetitive plants. The formula for juglone is $C_{10}H_6O_3$.

a. Calculate the molar mass of juglone.

b. A sample of 1.56 g of pure juglone was extracted from black walnut husks. How many moles of juglone does this sample represent?

Lyntha Scott Eiler/Library of Ethnographic Field Collection/Library of Congress

Black walnuts with and without their green hulls.

SOLUTION

a. Where Are We Going?

We want to determine the molar mass of juglone in units of g/mol.

What Do We Know?

- The formula for juglone is $C_{10}H_6O_3$. One mole of juglone contains 10 moles of C, 6 moles of H, and 3 moles of O.
- We know the atomic masses of carbon (12.01 g/mol), hydrogen (1.008 g/mol), and oxygen (16.00 g/mol).

How Do We Get There?

The molar mass is obtained by summing the masses of the component atoms. In 1 mole of juglone there are 10 moles of carbon atoms, 6 moles of hydrogen atoms, and 3 moles of oxygen atoms.

MATH SKILL BUILDER
The 120.1 limits the sum to one decimal place.

$$\begin{aligned} \text{Mass of 10 mol C} &= 10 \times 12.01 \text{ g} = 120.1 \text{ g} \\ \text{Mass of 6 mol H} &= 6 \times 1.008 \text{ g} = 6.048 \text{ g} \\ \text{Mass of 3 mol O} &= 3 \times 16.00 \text{ g} = \underline{48.00 \text{ g}} \\ \text{Mass of 1 mol } C_{10}H_6O_3 &= 174.1 \text{ g} = \text{molar mass} \end{aligned}$$

REALITY CHECK Ten moles of carbon would have a mass of about 120 g, and our answer is higher than this. The units (g/mol) are correct, and the answer is reported to the correct number of significant figures (to two decimal places).

b. Where Are We Going?

We want to determine the number of moles of juglone in a sample with mass of 1.56 g.

What Do We Know?

- From part a, we know that the molar mass of juglone is 174.1 g/mol.
- We have 1.56 g of juglone.

How Do We Get There?

The mass of 1 mole of this compound is 174.1 g, so 1.56 g is much less than a mole. We can determine the exact fraction of a mole by using the equivalence statement

$$1 \text{ mol} = 174.1 \text{ g juglone}$$

to derive the appropriate conversion factor:

$$1.56 \text{ g juglone} \times \frac{1 \text{ mol juglone}}{174.1 \text{ g juglone}} = 0.00896 \text{ mol juglone}$$
$$= 8.96 \times 10^{-3} \text{ mol juglone}$$

$$1.56 \text{ g juglone} \times \frac{1 \text{ mol}}{174.1 \text{ g}} \Rightarrow 8.96 \times 10^{-3} \text{ mol juglone}$$

REALITY CHECK The mass of 1 mole of juglone is 174.1 g, so 1.56 g is much less than 1 mole. Our answer has units of mol, and the number of significant figures in our answer is three, as required by the initial mass of 1.56 g. ■

EXAMPLE 8.8 Calculating Number of Molecules

Isopentyl acetate, $C_7H_{14}O_2$, the compound responsible for the scent of bananas, can be produced commercially. Interestingly, bees release about 1 μg (1×10^{-6} g) of this compound when they sting. This attracts other bees, which then join the attack. How many moles and how many molecules of isopentyl acetate are released in a typical bee sting?

Additional Examples

Example 8.8

1. How many water molecules are in a 10.0-g sample of water?

   3.34×10^{23} water molecules

2. Sucrose, or table sugar, has the formula $C_{12}H_{22}O_{11}$. How many molecules of sugar are in a 5.00-lb bag of sugar?

   3.99×10^{24} sugar molecules

SOLUTION

Where Are We Going?

We want to determine the number of moles and the number of molecules of isopentyl acetate in a sample with mass of 1×10^{-6} g.

What Do We Know?

- The formula for isopentyl acetate is $C_7H_{14}O_2$.
- We know the atomic masses of carbon (12.01 g/mol), hydrogen (1.008 g/mol), and oxygen (16.00 g/mol).
- The mass of isopentyl acetate is 1×10^{-6} g.
- There are 6.022×10^{23} molecules in 1 mol.

How Do We Get There?

We are given a mass of isopentyl acetate and want the number of molecules, so we must first compute the molar mass.

$$7 \cancel{\text{mol C}} \times 12.01 \frac{\text{g}}{\cancel{\text{mol}}} = 84.07 \text{ g C}$$

$$14 \cancel{\text{mol H}} \times 1.008 \frac{\text{g}}{\cancel{\text{mol}}} = 14.11 \text{ g H}$$

$$2 \cancel{\text{mol O}} \times 16.00 \frac{\text{g}}{\cancel{\text{mol}}} = 32.00 \text{ g O}$$

$$\text{Molar mass} = 130.18 \text{ g}$$

This means that 1 mole of isopentyl acetate (6.022×10^{23} molecules) has a mass of 130.18 g.

Next we determine the number of moles of isopentyl acetate in 1 μg, which is 1×10^{-6} g. To do this, we use the equivalence statement

1 mol isopentyl acetate = 130.18 g isopentyl acetate

which yields the conversion factor we need:

$$1 \times 10^{-6} \cancel{\text{g } C_7H_{14}O_2} \times \frac{1 \text{ mol } C_7H_{14}O_2}{130.18 \cancel{\text{g } C_7H_{14}O_2}} = 8 \times 10^{-9} \text{ mol } C_7H_{14}O_2$$

Using the equivalence statement 1 mol = 6.022×10^{23} units, we can determine the number of molecules:

$$8 \times 10^{-9} \cancel{\text{mol } C_7H_{14}O_2} \times \frac{6.022 \times 10^{23} \text{ molecules}}{1 \cancel{\text{mol } C_7H_{14}O_2}} = 5 \times 10^{15} \text{ molecules}$$

This very large number of molecules is released in each bee sting.

REALITY CHECK The mass of isopentyl acetate released in each sting (1×10^{-6} g) is much less than the mass of 1 mole of $C_7H_{14}O_2$, so the number of moles should be less than 1 mol, and it is (8×10^{-9} mol). The number of molecules should be much less than 6.022×10^{23}, and it is (5×10^{15} molecules).

Our answers have the proper units, and the number of significant figures in our answer is one, as required by the initial mass.

Self-Check **EXERCISE 8.6** The substance Teflon, the slippery coating on many frying pans, is made from the C_2F_4 molecule. Calculate the number of C_2F_4 units present in 135 g of Teflon.

See Problems 8.39 and 8.40. ■

Self Check

Answer to Self-Check Exercise 8.6

8.13×10^{23} C_2F_4 units

Test Bank: 94, 96–109, 111

8.6 Percent Composition of Compounds

OBJECTIVE: To learn to find the mass percent of an element in a given compound.

So far we have discussed the composition of compounds in terms of the numbers of constituent atoms. It is often useful to know a compound's composition in terms of the *masses* of its elements. We can obtain this information from the formula of the compound by comparing the mass of each element present in 1 mole of the compound to the total mass of 1 mole of the compound. The mass fraction for each element is calculated as follows:

MATH SKILL BUILDER
$\text{Percent} = \frac{\text{Part}}{\text{Whole}} \times 100\%$

$$\text{Mass fraction for a given element} = \frac{\text{mass of the element present in 1 mole of compound}}{\text{mass of 1 mole of compound}}$$

The mass fraction is converted to *mass percent* by multiplying by 100%.

We will illustrate this concept using the compound ethanol, an alcohol obtained by fermenting the sugar in grapes, corn, and other fruits and grains. Ethanol is often added to gasoline as an octane enhancer to form a fuel called gasohol. The added ethanol has the effect of increasing the octane of the gasoline and also lowering the carbon monoxide in automobile exhaust.

The formula for ethanol is written C_2H_5OH, although you might expect it to be written simply as C_2H_6O.

Note from its formula that each molecule of ethanol contains two carbon atoms, six hydrogen atoms, and one oxygen atom. This means that each mole of ethanol contains 2 moles of carbon atoms, 6 moles of hydrogen atoms, and 1 mole of oxygen atoms. We calculate the mass of each element present and the molar mass for ethanol as follows:

$$\text{Mass of C} = 2\ \cancel{\text{mol}} \times 12.01\ \frac{\text{g}}{\cancel{\text{mol}}} = 24.02\ \text{g}$$

$$\text{Mass of H} = 6\ \cancel{\text{mol}} \times 1.008\ \frac{\text{g}}{\cancel{\text{mol}}} = 6.048\ \text{g}$$

$$\text{Mass of O} = 1\ \cancel{\text{mol}} \times 16.00\ \frac{\text{g}}{\cancel{\text{mol}}} = 16.00\ \text{g}$$

$$\text{Mass of 1 mol } C_2H_5OH = 46.07\ \text{g} = \text{molar mass}$$

The **mass percent** (sometimes called the weight percent) of carbon in ethanol can be computed by comparing the mass of carbon in 1 mole of ethanol with the total mass of 1 mole of ethanol and multiplying the result by 100%.

$$\text{Mass percent of C} = \frac{\text{mass of C in 1 mol } C_2H_5OH}{\text{mass of 1 mol } C_2H_5OH} \times 100\% = \frac{24.02\ \text{g}}{46.07\ \text{g}} \times 100\% = 52.14\%$$

That is, ethanol contains 52.14% by mass of carbon. The mass percents of hydrogen and oxygen in ethanol are obtained in a similar manner.

$$\text{Mass percent of H} = \frac{\text{mass of H in 1 mol } C_2H_5OH}{\text{mass of 1 mol } C_2H_5OH} \times 100\% = \frac{6.048\ \text{g}}{46.07\ \text{g}} \times 100\% = 13.13\%$$

$$\text{Mass percent of O} = \frac{\text{mass of O in 1 mol } C_2H_5OH}{\text{mass of 1 mol } C_2H_5OH} \times 100\% = \frac{16.00\ \text{g}}{46.07\ \text{g}} \times 100\% = 34.73\%$$

MATH SKILL BUILDER
Sometimes, because of rounding-off effects, the sum of the mass percents in a compound is not exactly 100%.

Section 8.6

TEACHING TIPS

- Use two simple ball-and-stick models of the same molecule (water is a good example) to make your discussion of percent composition more concrete. Show the students one model and ask them how to determine the percent by mass of each of the different colored balls in the model. The model can be taken apart to illustrate that the first step is to determine the mass of all of the balls of the same color. After a discussion of percentages, display both models and ask students to determine the percent by mass in a sample consisting of two models. Give them time to calculate this answer if they do not recognize that the percent composition must be the same for a sample containing one model as it is for the sample containing two models. Use this discussion to explain that the sample size does not influence the percent composition.
- Let students know that we can use percent composition data to determine the formulas for compounds. While we reserve the details until Section 8.8, it is good for students to know where we are going.
- Bring a sample of a compound to class to use in discussing percent composition. Good examples include copper(II) nitrate, hydrogen peroxide, and potassium permanganate. Put the formula for the compound on the board and use it to illustrate the mass percent calculations.

PowerLecture Simulation: Compounds, Molecules, and Moles

TEACHING TIPS

- Remind students that a percentage is just a fraction multiplied by 100—it represents a part of the whole. You may need to spend some time in class working with students on the concept of percentages.

Additional Examples

Example 8.9

1. Determine the mass percent of each element in sulfuric acid, (H_2SO_4).

   2.055% hydrogen by mass, 32.70% sulfur by mass, 65.25% oxygen by mass

2. Rubbing alcohol is an aqueous solution of isopropyl alcohol. Isopropyl alcohol has the formula C_3H_7OH. Determine the mass percent of each element in isopropyl alcohol.

   59.96% carbon by mass, 13.42% hydrogen by mass, 26.62% oxygen by mass

The mass percents of all the elements in a compound add up to 100%, although rounding-off effects may produce a small deviation. Adding up the percentages is a good way to check the calculations. In this case, the sum of the mass percents is 52.14% + 13.13% + 34.73% = 100.00%.

EXAMPLE 8.9 Calculating Mass Percent

Carvone is a substance that occurs in two forms, both of which have the same molecular formula ($C_{10}H_{14}O$) and molar mass. One type of carvone gives caraway seeds their characteristic smell; the other is responsible for the smell of spearmint oil. Compute the mass percent of each element in carvone.

SOLUTION

Where Are We Going?

We want to determine the mass percent of each element in carvone.

What Do We Know?

- The formula for carvone is $C_{10}H_{14}O$.
- We know the atomic masses of carbon (12.01 g/mol), hydrogen (1.008 g/mol), and oxygen (16.00 g/mol).
- The mass of isopentyl acetate is 1×10^{-6} g.
- There are 6.022×10^{23} molecules in 1 mole.

What Do We Need To Know?

- The mass of each element (we'll use 1 mol carvone)
- Molar mass of carvone

How Do We Get There?

Because the formula for carvone is $C_{10}H_{14}O$, the masses of the various elements in 1 mole of carvone are

$$\text{Mass of C in 1 mol} = 10\ \cancel{\text{mol}} \times 12.01\ \frac{\text{g}}{\cancel{\text{mol}}} = 120.1\ \text{g}$$

$$\text{Mass of H in 1 mol} = 14\ \cancel{\text{mol}} \times 1.008\ \frac{\text{g}}{\cancel{\text{mol}}} = 14.11\ \text{g}$$

$$\text{Mass of O in 1 mol} = 1\ \cancel{\text{mol}} \times 16.00\ \frac{\text{g}}{\cancel{\text{mol}}} = 16.00\ \text{g}$$

$$\text{Mass of 1 mol } C_{10}H_{14}O = 150.21\ \text{g}$$

$$\text{Molar mass} = 150.2\ \text{g}$$

(rounding to the correct number of significant figures)

MATH SKILL BUILDER
The 120.1 limits the sum to one decimal place.

Next we find the fraction of the total mass contributed by each element and convert it to a percentage.

$$\text{Mass percent of C} = \frac{120.1\ \text{g C}}{150.2\ \text{g } C_{10}H_{14}O} \times 100\% = 79.96\%$$

$$\text{Mass percent of H} = \frac{14.11\ \text{g H}}{150.2\ \text{g } C_{10}H_{14}O} \times 100\% = 9.394\%$$

$$\text{Mass percent of O} = \frac{16.00\ \text{g O}}{150.2\ \text{g } C_{10}H_{14}O} \times 100\% = 10.65\%$$

TEACHING SUPPORT

ACTIVITY

The nutrition labels on snack foods list the mass of sodium per serving. Have students choose a snack food or drink and record the mass of sodium per serving and the number of servings in the container and bring it to class. In class, have students determine the number of moles and of atoms of sodium per serving and for the whole container. Assemble the data for all of the snacks on the board. Which snacks contain the most sodium per serving? Which contain the least sodium?

REALITY CHECK Add the individual mass percent values—they should total 100% within a small range due to rounding off. In this case, the percentages add up to 100.00%.

Self-Check **EXERCISE 8.7** Penicillin, an important antibiotic (antibacterial agent), was discovered accidentally by the Scottish bacteriologist Alexander Fleming in 1928, although he was never able to isolate it as a pure compound. This and similar antibiotics have saved millions of lives that would otherwise have been lost to infections. Penicillin, like many of the molecules produced by living systems, is a large molecule containing many atoms. One type of penicillin, penicillin F, has the formula $C_{14}H_{20}N_2SO_4$. Compute the mass percent of each element in this compound.

See Problems 8.45 through 8.50. ■

Self Check

Answer to Self-Check Exercise 8.7

53.81% C, 6.453% H, 8.969% N, 10.27% S, 20.49% O

 **Test Bank: 113, 114**

8.7 Formulas of Compounds

OBJECTIVE: To understand the meaning of empirical formulas of compounds.

Section 8.7

Assume that you have mixed two solutions, and a solid product (a precipitate) forms. How can you find out what the solid is? What is its formula? There are several possible approaches you can take to answering these questions. For example, we saw in Chapter 7 that we can usually predict the identity of a precipitate formed when two solutions are mixed in a reaction of this type if we know some facts about the solubilities of ionic compounds.

However, although an experienced chemist can often predict the product expected in a chemical reaction, the only sure way to identify the product is to perform experiments. Usually we compare the physical properties of the product to the properties of known compounds.

Sometimes a chemical reaction gives a product that has never been obtained before. In such a case, a chemist determines what compound has been formed by determining which elements are present and how much of each. These data can be used to obtain the formula of the compound. In Section 8.6 we used the formula of the compound to determine the mass of each element present in a mole of the compound. To obtain the formula of an unknown compound, we do the opposite. That is, we use the measured masses of the elements present to determine the formula.

Recall that the formula of a compound represents the relative numbers of the various types of atoms present. For example, the molecular formula CO_2 tells us that for each carbon atom there are two oxygen atoms in each molecule of carbon dioxide. So to determine the formula of a substance we need to count the atoms. As we have seen in this chapter, we can do this by weighing. Suppose we know that a compound contains only the elements carbon, hydrogen, and oxygen, and we weigh out a 0.2015-g sample for analysis. Using methods we will not discuss here, we find that this 0.2015-g sample of compound contains 0.0806 g of carbon, 0.01353 g of hydrogen, and 0.1074 g of oxygen. We have just learned how to convert these masses to numbers of atoms by using the atomic mass of each element. We begin by converting to moles.

Carbon

$$(0.0806 \cancel{\text{g C}}) \times \frac{1 \text{ mol C atoms}}{12.01 \cancel{\text{g C}}} = 0.00671 \text{ mol C atoms}$$

DEMONSTRATION

Bring samples of compounds with the same empirical formula but different molecular formulas to class. You could use formaldehyde, acetic acid, and glucose, all of which have the empirical formula CH_2O. Show students the compounds and the empirical formula. Then show the molecular formula for each compound. You might then discuss or demonstrate some of the properties of each compound.

Hydrogen

$$(0.01353 \cancel{\text{g H}}) \times \frac{1 \text{ mol H atoms}}{1.008 \cancel{\text{g H}}} = 0.01342 \text{ mol H atoms}$$

Oxygen

$$(0.1074 \cancel{\text{g O}}) \times \frac{1 \text{ mol O atoms}}{16.00 \cancel{\text{g O}}} = 0.006713 \text{ mol O atoms}$$

Let's review what we have established. We now know that 0.2015 g of the compound contains 0.00671 mole of C atoms, 0.01342 mole of H atoms, and 0.006713 mole of O atoms. Because 1 mol is 6.022×10^{23}, these quantities can be converted to actual numbers of atoms.

Carbon

$$(0.00671 \cancel{\text{mol C atoms}}) \frac{(6.022 \times 10^{23} \text{ C atoms})}{1 \cancel{\text{mol C atoms}}} = 4.04 \times 10^{21} \text{ C atoms}$$

Hydrogen

$$(0.01342 \cancel{\text{mol H atoms}}) \frac{(6.022 \times 10^{23} \text{ H atoms})}{1 \cancel{\text{mol H atoms}}} = 8.08 \times 10^{21} \text{ H atoms}$$

Oxygen

$$(0.006713 \cancel{\text{mol O atoms}}) \frac{(6.022 \times 10^{23} \text{ O atoms})}{1 \cancel{\text{mol O atoms}}} = 4.043 \times 10^{21} \text{ O atoms}$$

These are the numbers of the various types of atoms *in 0.2015 g of compound.* What do these numbers tell us about the formula of the compound? Note the following:

1. The compound contains the same number of C and O atoms.
2. There are twice as many H atoms as C atoms or O atoms.

We can represent this information by the formula CH_2O, which expresses the *relative* numbers of C, H, and O atoms present. Is this the true formula for the compound? In other words, is the compound made up of CH_2O molecules? It may be. However, it might also be made up of $C_2H_4O_2$ molecules, $C_3H_6O_3$ molecules, $C_4H_8O_4$ molecules, $C_5H_{10}O_5$ molecules, $C_6H_{12}O_6$ molecules, and so on. Note that each of these molecules has the required 1:2:1 ratio of carbon to hydrogen to oxygen atoms (the ratio shown by experiment to be present in the compound).

When we break a compound down into its separate elements and "count" the atoms present, we learn only the ratio of atoms—we get only the *relative* numbers of atoms. The formula of a compound that expresses the smallest whole-number ratio of the atoms present is called the **empirical formula** or *simplest formula*. A compound that contains the molecules $C_4H_8O_4$ has the same empirical formula as a compound that contains $C_6H_{12}O_6$ molecules. The empirical formula for both is CH_2O. The actual formula of a compound—the one that gives the composition of the molecules that are present—is called the **molecular formula.** The sugar called glucose is made of molecules with the molecular formula $C_6H_{12}O_6$ (Figure 8.4). Note from the molecular formula for glucose that the empirical formula is CH_2O. We can represent the molecular formula as a multiple (by 6) of the empirical formula:

$$C_6H_{12}O_6 = (CH_2O)_6$$

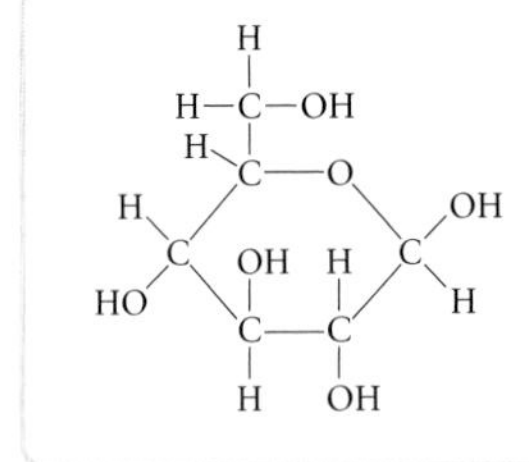

Figure 8.4

The glucose molecule. The molecular formula is $C_6H_{12}O_6$, as can be verified by counting the atoms. The empirical formula for glucose is CH_2O.

In the next section, we will explore in more detail how to calculate the empirical formula for a compound from the relative masses of the elements present. As we will see in Sections 8.8 and 8.9, we must know the molar mass of a compound to determine its molecular formula.

228 Chapter 8 Chemical Composition

EXAMPLE 8.10 Determining Empirical Formulas

In each case below, the molecular formula for a compound is given. Determine the empirical formula for each compound.

a. C_6H_6. This is the molecular formula for benzene, a liquid commonly used in industry as a starting material for many important products.

b. $C_{12}H_4Cl_4O_2$. This is the molecular formula for a substance commonly called dioxin, a powerful poison that sometimes occurs as a by-product in the production of other chemicals.

c. $C_6H_{16}N_2$. This is the molecular formula for one of the reactants used to produce nylon.

SOLUTION

a. $C_6H_6 = (CH)_6$; CH is the empirical formula. Each subscript in the empirical formula is multiplied by 6 to obtain the molecular formula.

b. $C_{12}H_4Cl_4O_2$; $C_{12}H_4Cl_4O_2 = (C_6H_2Cl_2O)_2$; $C_6H_2Cl_2O$ is the empirical formula. Each subscript in the empirical formula is multiplied by 2 to obtain the molecular formula.

c. $C_6H_{16}N_2 = (C_3H_8N)_2$; C_3H_8N is the empirical formula. Each subscript in the empirical formula is multiplied by 2 to obtain the molecular formula. ■

8.8 Calculation of Empirical Formulas

OBJECTIVE: To learn to calculate empirical formulas.

As we said in the previous section, one of the most important things we can learn about a new compound is its chemical formula. To calculate the empirical formula of a compound, we first determine the relative masses of the various elements that are present.

One way to do this is to measure the masses of elements that react to form the compound. For example, suppose we weigh out 0.2636 g of pure nickel metal into a crucible and heat this metal in the air so that the nickel can react with oxygen to form a nickel oxide compound. After the sample has cooled, we weigh it again and find its mass to be 0.3354 g. The gain in mass is due to the oxygen that reacts with the nickel to form the oxide. Therefore, the mass of oxygen present in the compound is the total mass of the product minus the mass of the nickel:

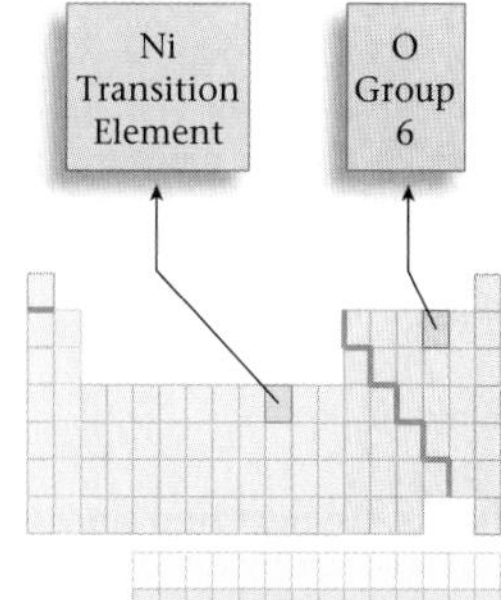

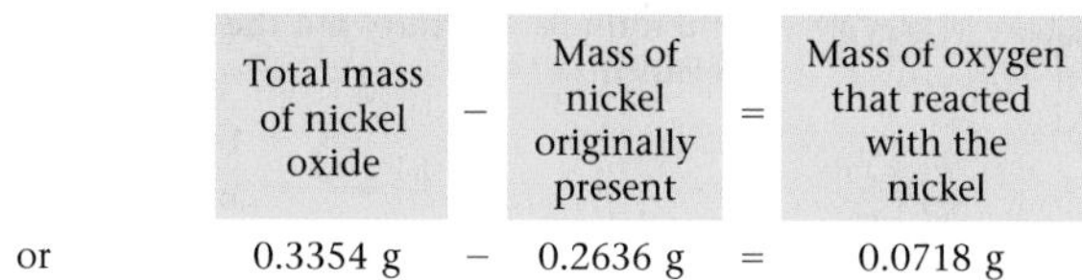

or 0.3354 g − 0.2636 g = 0.0718 g

Note that the mass of nickel present in the compound is the nickel metal originally weighed out. So we know that the nickel oxide contains 0.2636 g of nickel and 0.0718 g of oxygen. What is the empirical formula of this compound?

Additional Examples

Example 8.10

Determine the empirical formula from each of the following molecular formulas.

1. H_2O_2. This is hydrogen peroxide, a substance commonly diluted with water and used as a disinfectant.

   HO

2. C_4H_{10}. This is butane, commonly used in lighters.

   C_2H_5

3. CCl_4. This is carbon tetrachloride, an organic solvent.

   CCl_4

TEACHING TIP

Remind students that subscripts outside the parentheses have an effect on the number of each atom inside the parentheses. You can relate this point to the distributive property for multiplication over addition. This review will remind students to multiply the subscripts to obtain the number of atoms.

Section 8.8

TEACHING TIP

The key concept in this section is that the mass of each element in a compound is an indicator of the number of atoms of the element in the compound, but only if the mass is converted to moles.

Test Bank: 3, 96, 110, 116–123

To answer this question we must convert the masses to numbers of atoms, using atomic masses:

Four significant figures allowed.

$$0.2636\ \cancel{\text{g Ni}} \times \frac{1\ \text{mol Ni atoms}}{58.69\ \cancel{\text{g Ni}}} = 0.004491\ \text{mol Ni atoms}$$

Three significant figures allowed.

$$0.0718\ \cancel{\text{g O}} \times \frac{1\ \text{mol O atoms}}{16.00\ \cancel{\text{g O}}} = 0.00449\ \text{mol O atoms}$$

These mole quantities represent numbers of atoms (remember that a mole of atoms is 6.022×10^{23} atoms). It is clear from the moles of atoms that the compound contains an equal number of Ni and O atoms, so the formula is NiO. This is the *empirical formula;* it expresses the smallest whole-number (integer) ratio of atoms:

$$\frac{0.004491\ \text{mol Ni atoms}}{0.00449\ \text{mol O atoms}} = \frac{1\ \text{Ni}}{1\ \text{O}}$$

That is, this compound contains equal numbers of nickel atoms and oxygen atoms. We say the ratio of nickel atoms to oxygen atoms is 1:1 (1 to 1).

EXAMPLE 8.11 Calculating Empirical Formulas

An oxide of aluminum is formed by the reaction of 4.151 g of aluminum with 3.692 g of oxygen. Calculate the empirical formula for this compound.

SOLUTION

Where Are We Going?

We want to determine the empirical formula for the aluminum oxide, Al_xO_y. That is, we want to solve for x and y.

What Do We Know?

- The compound contains 4.151 g of aluminum and 3.692 g of oxygen.
- We know the atomic masses of aluminum (26.98 g/mol), and oxygen (16.00 g/mol).

What Do We Need To Know?

- x and y represent moles of atoms in 1 mole of the compound, so we need to determine the relative number of moles of Al and O.

How Do We Get There?

Al Group 3

O Group 6

We need to know the relative numbers of each type of atom to write the formula, so we must convert these masses to moles of atoms to get the empirical formula. We carry out the conversion by using the atomic masses of the elements.

$$4.151\ \cancel{\text{g Al}} \times \frac{1\ \text{mol Al}}{26.98\ \cancel{\text{g Al}}} = 0.1539\ \text{mol Al atoms}$$

$$3.692\ \cancel{\text{g O}} \times \frac{1\ \text{mol O}}{16.00\ \cancel{\text{g O}}} = 0.2308\ \text{mol O atoms}$$

Because chemical formulas use only whole numbers, we next find the integer (whole-number) ratio of the atoms. To do this we start by dividing both numbers by the smallest of the two. This converts the smallest number to 1.

Additional Examples

Example 8.11

1. A 1.500-g sample of a compound containing only carbon and hydrogen is found to contain 1.198 g of carbon. Determine the empirical formula for this compound.

   CH_3

2. A 3.450-g sample of nitrogen reacts with 1.970 g of oxygen. Determine the empirical formula for this compound.

   N_2O

TEACHING TIP

In these problems students worry when the ratio of moles of atoms is not an integer, thinking that the calculation may be incorrect. Warn them to be careful of calculation errors, but also to remember that a noninteger result is a fraction in decimal form. Some easily recognized fractions in decimal form are

1/2 = 0.500

1/3 = 0.333

1/4 = 0.25

2/3 = 0.667

3/4 = 0.75

In cases in which a noninteger is obtained, students should look for one of these fractions and multiply each of the atom ratios by the denominator of the fraction to obtain a whole number.

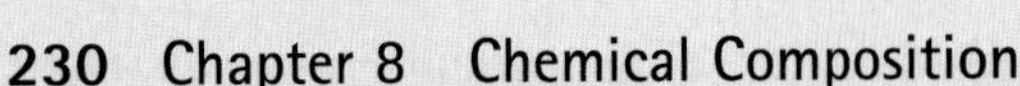

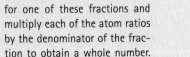

$$\frac{0.1539 \text{ mol Al}}{0.1539} = 1.000 \text{ mol Al atoms}$$

$$\frac{0.2308 \text{ mol O}}{0.1539} = 1.500 \text{ mol O atoms}$$

Note that dividing both numbers of moles of atoms by the *same* number does not change the *relative* numbers of oxygen and aluminum atoms. That is,

$$\frac{0.2308 \text{ mol O}}{0.1539 \text{ mol Al}} = \frac{1.500 \text{ mol O}}{1.000 \text{ mol Al}}$$

Thus we know that the compound contains 1.500 moles of O atoms for every 1.000 mole of Al atoms, or, in terms of individual atoms, we could say that the compound contains 1.500 O atoms for every 1.000 Al atom. However, because only *whole* atoms combine to form compounds, we must find a set of *whole numbers* to express the empirical formula. When we multiply both 1.000 and 1.500 by 2, we get the integers we need.

We might express these data as:

$Al_{1.000 \text{ mol}}O_{1.500 \text{ mol}}$

or

$Al_{2.000 \text{ mol}}O_{3.000 \text{ mol}}$

or

Al_2O_3

$$1.500 \text{ O} \times 2 = 3.000 = 3 \text{ O atoms}$$

$$1.000 \text{ Al} \times 2 = 2.000 = 2 \text{ Al atoms}$$

Therefore, this compound contains two Al atoms for every three O atoms, and the empirical formula is Al_2O_3. Note that the *ratio* of atoms in this compound is given by each of the following fractions:

$$\frac{0.2308 \text{ O}}{0.1539 \text{ Al}} = \frac{1.500 \text{ O}}{1.000 \text{ Al}} = \frac{\frac{3}{2}\text{O}}{1 \text{ Al}} = \frac{3 \text{ O}}{2 \text{ Al}}$$

The smallest whole-number ratio corresponds to the subscripts of the empirical formula, Al_2O_3.

REALITY CHECK The values for x and y are whole numbers. ■

Sometimes the relative numbers of moles you get when you calculate an empirical formula will turn out to be nonintegers, as was the case in Example 8.11. When this happens, you must convert to the appropriate whole numbers. This is done by multiplying all the numbers by the same small integer, which can be found by trial and error. The multiplier needed is almost always between 1 and 6. We will now summarize what we have learned about calculating empirical formulas.

Steps for Determining the Empirical Formula of a Compound

Step 1 Obtain the mass of each element present (in grams).

Step 2 Determine the number of moles of each type of atom present.

Step 3 Divide the number of moles of each element by the smallest number of moles to convert the smallest number to 1. If all of the numbers so obtained are integers (whole numbers), these are the subscripts in the empirical formula. If one or more of these numbers are not integers, go on to step 4.

Step 4 Multiply the numbers you derived in step 3 by the smallest integer that will convert all of them to whole numbers. This set of whole numbers represents the subscripts in the empirical formula.

MISCONCEPTION

Students will often divide the mass of oxygen or mass percent of oxygen by 32.00 instead of 16.00. Let students know that we are determining the ratio of oxygen *atoms* in the compound.

Additional Examples

Example 8.12

1. When a 2.000-g sample of iron metal is heated in air, it reacts with oxygen to achieve a final mass of 2.573 g. Determine the empirical formula for this iron oxide.

   FeO [iron(II) oxide]

2. A 4.550-g sample of cobalt reacts with 5.475 g chlorine to form a binary compound. Determine the empirical formula for this compound.

   $CoCl_2$ [cobalt(II) chloride]

EXAMPLE 8.12 Calculating Empirical Formulas for Binary Compounds

When a 0.3546-g sample of vanadium metal is heated in air, it reacts with oxygen to achieve a final mass of 0.6330 g. Calculate the empirical formula of this vanadium oxide.

SOLUTION

Where Are We Going?

We want to determine the empirical formula for the vanadium oxide, V_xO_y. That is, we want to solve for x and y.

What Do We Know?

- The compound contains 0.3546 g of vanadium and has a total mass of 0.6330 g.
- We know the atomic masses of vanadium (50.94 g/mol) and oxygen (16.00 g/mol).

What Do We Need To Know?

- We need to know the mass of oxygen in the sample.
- x and y represent moles of atoms in 1 mole of the compound, so we need to determine the relative number of moles of V and O.

How Do We Get There?

Step 1 All the vanadium that was originally present will be found in the final compound, so we can calculate the mass of oxygen that reacted by taking the following difference:

Total mass of compound	−	Mass of vanadium in compound	=	Mass of oxygen in compound
0.6330 g	−	0.3546 g	=	0.2784 g

Step 2 Using the atomic masses (50.94 for V and 16.00 for O), we obtain

$$0.3546 \cancel{\text{g V}} \times \frac{1 \text{ mol V atoms}}{50.94 \cancel{\text{g V}}} = 0.006961 \text{ mol V atoms}$$

$$0.2784 \cancel{\text{g O}} \times \frac{1 \text{ mol O atoms}}{16.00 \cancel{\text{g O}}} = 0.01740 \text{ mol O atoms}$$

Step 3 Then we divide both numbers of moles by the smaller, 0.006961.

$$\frac{0.006961 \text{ mol V atoms}}{0.006961} = 1.000 \text{ mol V atoms}$$

$$\frac{0.01740 \text{ mol O atoms}}{0.006961} = 2.500 \text{ mol O atoms}$$

Because one of these numbers (2.500) is not an integer, we go on to step 4.

MATH SKILL BUILDER
$V_{1.000}O_{2.500}$ becomes V_2O_5.

Step 4 We note that $2 \times 2.500 = 5.000$ and $2 \times 1.000 = 2.000$, so we multiply both numbers by 2 to get integers.

$$2 \times 1.000 \text{ V} = 2.000 \text{ V} = 2 \text{ V}$$
$$2 \times 2.500 \text{ O} = 5.000 \text{ O} = 5 \text{ O}$$

This compound contains 2 V atoms for every 5 O atoms, and the empirical formula is V_2O_5.

REALITY CHECK The values for x and y are whole numbers.

Self-Check **EXERCISE 8.8** In a lab experiment it was observed that 0.6884 g of lead combines with 0.2356 g of chlorine to form a binary compound. Calculate the empirical formula of this compound.

See Problems 8.61, 8.63, 8.65, and 8.66. ■

The same procedures we have used for binary compounds also apply to compounds containing three or more elements, as Example 8.13 illustrates.

EXAMPLE 8.13

Calculating Empirical Formulas for Compounds Containing Three or More Elements

A sample of lead arsenate, an insecticide used against the potato beetle, contains 1.3813 g of lead, 0.00672 g of hydrogen, 0.4995 g of arsenic, and 0.4267 g of oxygen. Calculate the empirical formula for lead arsenate.

SOLUTION

Where Are We Going?

We want to determine the empirical formula for lead arsenate, $Pb_aH_bAs_cO_d$. That is, we want to solve for a, b, c, and d.

What Do We Know?

- The compound contains 1.3813 g of Pb, 0.00672 g of H, 0.4995 g of As, and 0.4267 g of O.
- We know the atomic masses of lead (207.2 g/mol), hydrogen (1.008 g/mol), arsenic (74.92 g/mol), and oxygen (16.00 g/mol).

What Do We Need To Know?

- a, b, c, and d represent moles of atoms in 1 mole of the compound, so we need to determine the relative number of moles of Pb, H, As, and O.

How Do We Get There?

Step 1 The compound contains 1.3813 g Pb, 0.00672 g H, 0.4995 g As, and 0.4267 g O.

Step 2 We use the atomic masses of the elements present to calculate the moles of each.

$$1.3813 \text{ g Pb} \times \frac{1 \text{ mol Pb}}{207.2 \text{ g Pb}} = 0.006667 \text{ mol Pb}$$

$$0.00672 \text{ g H} \times \frac{1 \text{ mol H}}{1.008 \text{ g H}} = 0.00667 \text{ mol H}$$

$$0.4995 \text{ g As} \times \frac{1 \text{ mol As}}{74.92 \text{ g As}} = 0.006667 \text{ mol As}$$

$$0.4267 \text{ g O} \times \frac{1 \text{ mol O}}{16.00 \text{ g O}} = 0.02667 \text{ mol O}$$

Self Check

Answer to Self-Check Exercise 8.8

$PbCl_2$

Additional Examples

Example 8.13

1. Phosphoric acid is found in some soft drinks. A sample of phosphoric acid contains 0.3086 g of hydrogen, 3.161 g of phosphorus, and 6.531 g of oxygen. Determine the empirical formula for phosphoric acid.

   H_3PO_4

2. *Para*-dichlorobenzene is often used in chemistry labs when studying melting points. A sample of *para*-dichlorobenzene contains 5.657 g of carbon, 0.3165 g of hydrogen, and 5.566 g of chlorine. Determine the empirical formula for this compound.

   C_3H_2Cl

Step 3 Now we divide by the smallest number of moles.

$$\frac{0.006667 \text{ mol Pb}}{0.006667} = 1.000 \text{ mol Pb}$$

$$\frac{0.00667 \text{ mol H}}{0.006667} = 1.00 \text{ mol H}$$

$$\frac{0.006667 \text{ mol As}}{0.006667} = 1.000 \text{ mol As}$$

$$\frac{0.02667 \text{ mol O}}{0.006667} = 4.000 \text{ mol O}$$

The numbers of moles are all whole numbers, so the empirical formula is $PbHAsO_4$.

REALITY CHECK The values for *a, b, c,* and *d* are whole numbers.

Self Check

Answer to Self-Check Exercise 8.9

CNH_3O_2

Self-Check **EXERCISE 8.9** Sevin, the commercial name for an insecticide used to protect crops such as cotton, vegetables, and fruit, is made from carbamic acid. A chemist analyzing a sample of carbamic acid finds 0.8007 g of carbon, 0.9333 g of nitrogen, 0.2016 g of hydrogen, and 2.133 g of oxygen. Determine the empirical formula for carbamic acid.

See Problems 8.57 and 8.59. ■

TEACHING TIP

Point out that percent composition can be used to determine the empirical formula for a compound by using the percentages to determine the mass of each element present. Remind students that a percentage can be converted to grams if the size of the sample is known. If no sample size is given in the problem, students can assume a 100-g sample (for ease in doing the math) and find the mass of each element from its percentage. Then they can use the masses to find the formula as before. However, many students end up knowing that they should assume 100.0 g but do not understand why. Consider doing an example twice, once assuming 100.0 g and once assuming 50.00 g, to show students that it doesn't matter what sample size we assume.

When a compound is analyzed to determine the relative amounts of the elements present, the results are usually given in terms of percentages by masses of the various elements. In Section 8.6 we learned to calculate the percent composition of a compound from its formula. Now we will do the opposite. Given the percent composition, we will calculate the empirical formula.

MATH SKILL BUILDER
Percent by mass for a given element means the grams of that element in 100 g of the compound.

To understand this procedure, you must understand the meaning of *percent*. Remember that percent means parts of a given component per 100 parts of the total mixture. For example, if a given compound is 15% carbon (by mass), the compound contains 15 g of carbon per 100 g of compound.

Calculation of the empirical formula of a compound when one is given its percent composition is illustrated in Example 8.14.

EXAMPLE 8.14 **Calculating Empirical Formulas from Percent Composition**

Cisplatin, the common name for a platinum compound that is used to treat cancerous tumors, has the composition (mass percent) 65.02% platinum, 9.34% nitrogen, 2.02% hydrogen, and 23.63% chlorine. Calculate the empirical formula for cisplatin.

SOLUTION

Where Are We Going?

We want to determine the empirical formula for cisplatin, $Pt_aN_bH_cCl_d$. That is, we want to solve for *a, b, c,* and *d.*

What Do We Know?

- The compound has the composition (mass percent) 65.02% Pt, 9.34% N, 2.02% H, and 23.63% Cl.
- We know the atomic masses of platinum (195.1 g/mol), nitrogen (14.01 g/mol), hydrogen (1.008 g/mol), and chlorine (35.45 g/mol).

Additional Examples

Example 8.14

1. The simplest amino acid, glycine, has the following mass percents: 32.00% carbon, 6.714% hydrogen, 42.63% oxygen, and 18.66% nitrogen. Determine the empirical formula for glycine.

   $C_2H_5O_2N$

What Do We Need To Know?

- a, b, c, and d represent moles of atoms in 1 mole of the compound, so we need to determine the relative number of moles of Pt, N, H, and Cl.
- We have mass percent data, and to get to the number of moles we need to know the mass of each element (g) in the sample.

How Do We Get There?

Step 1 Determine how many grams of each element are present in 100 g of compound. Cisplatin is 65.02% platinum (by mass), which means there is 65.02 g of platinum (Pt) per 100.00 g of compound. Similarly, a 100.00-g sample of cisplatin contains 9.34 g of nitrogen (N), 2.02 g of hydrogen (H), and 26.63 g of chlorine (Cl).

If we have a 100.00-g sample of cisplatin, we have 65.02 g Pt, 9.34 g N, 2.02 g H, and 23.63 g Cl.

Step 2 Determine the number of moles of each type of atom. We use the atomic masses to calculate moles.

$$65.02\ \cancel{\text{g Pt}} \times \frac{1\ \text{mol Pt}}{195.1\ \cancel{\text{g Pt}}} = 0.3333\ \text{mol Pt}$$

$$9.34\ \cancel{\text{g N}} \times \frac{1\ \text{mol N}}{14.01\ \cancel{\text{g N}}} = 0.667\ \text{mol N}$$

$$2.02\ \cancel{\text{g H}} \times \frac{1\ \text{mol H}}{1.008\ \cancel{\text{g H}}} = 2.00\ \text{mol H}$$

$$23.63\ \cancel{\text{g Cl}} \times \frac{1\ \text{mol Cl}}{35.45\ \cancel{\text{g Cl}}} = 0.6666\ \text{mol Cl}$$

Step 3 Divide through by the smallest number of moles.

$$\frac{0.3333\ \text{mol Pt}}{0.3333} = 1.000\ \text{mol Pt}$$

$$\frac{0.667\ \text{mol N}}{0.3333} = 2.00\ \text{mol N}$$

$$\frac{2.00\ \text{mol H}}{0.3333} = 6.01\ \text{mol H}$$

$$\frac{0.6666\ \text{mol Cl}}{0.3333} = 2.000\ \text{mol Cl}$$

The empirical formula for cisplatin is $PtN_2H_6Cl_2$. Note that the number for hydrogen is slightly greater than 6 because of rounding-off effects.

REALITY CHECK The values for a, b, c, and d are whole numbers.

2. A compound has been analyzed and found to have the following mass percent composition: 66.75% copper, 10.84% phosphorus, and 22.41% oxygen. Determine the empirical formula for this compound.

Cu_3PO_4

Self-Check EXERCISE 8.10 The most common form of nylon (Nylon-6) is 63.68% carbon, 12.38% nitrogen, 9.80% hydrogen, and 14.14% oxygen. Calculate the empirical formula for Nylon-6.

See Problems 8.67 through 8.74. ■

Self Check

Answer to Self-Check Exercise 8.10

$C_6NH_{11}O$

Note from Example 8.14 that once the percentages are converted to masses, this example is the same as earlier examples in which the masses were given directly.

Test Bank: 97, 112, 115, 124–134

Section 8.9

TEACHING TIPS

- Students should understand that unless they are given the molar mass for a compound, they can calculate only the empirical formula for the compound.
- Tell students that they must first calculate the empirical formula before they can determine the molecular formula for a compound. This point leads to a discussion of how we can use the molar mass of an empirical formula.

Additional Examples

Example 8.15

1. A compound containing carbon, hydrogen, and oxygen is found to be 40.00% carbon and 6.700% hydrogen by mass. The molar mass of this compound is between 115 g/mol and 125 g/mol. Determine the molecular formula for this compound.

   $C_4H_8O_4$

2. Caffeine is a compound containing carbon, hydrogen, nitrogen, and oxygen. The mass percent composition of caffeine is 49.47% carbon, 5.191% hydrogen, 28.86% nitrogen, and 16.48% oxygen. The molar mass of caffeine is approximately 194 g/mol. Determine the molecular formula for caffeine.

   $C_8H_{10}N_4O_2$

8.9 Calculation of Molecular Formulas

OBJECTIVE: To learn to calculate the molecular formula of a compound, given its empirical formula and molar mass.

If we know the composition of a compound in terms of the masses (or mass percentages) of the elements present, we can calculate the empirical formula but not the molecular formula. For reasons that will become clear as we consider Example 8.15, to obtain the molecular formula we must know the molar mass. In this section we will consider compounds where both the percent composition and the molar mass are known.

EXAMPLE 8.15 Calculating Molecular Formulas

A white powder is analyzed and found to have an empirical formula of P_2O_5. The compound has a molar mass of 283.88 g. What is the compound's molecular formula?

SOLUTION

Where Are We Going?

We want to determine the molecular formula (P_xO_y) for a compound. That is, we want to solve for *x* and *y*.

What Do We Know?

- The empirical formula of the compound is P_2O_5.
- The molar mass of the compound is 283.88 g/mol.
- We know the atomic masses of phosphorus (30.97 g/mol) and oxygen (16.00 g/mol).
- The molecular formula contains a whole number of empirical formula units. So, the molecular formula will be $P_{2x}O_{5y}$.

What Do We Need To Know?

- We need to know the empirical formula mass.

How Do We Get There?

To obtain the molecular formula, we must compare the empirical formula mass to the molar mass. The empirical formula mass for P_2O_5 is the mass of 1 mole of P_2O_5 units.

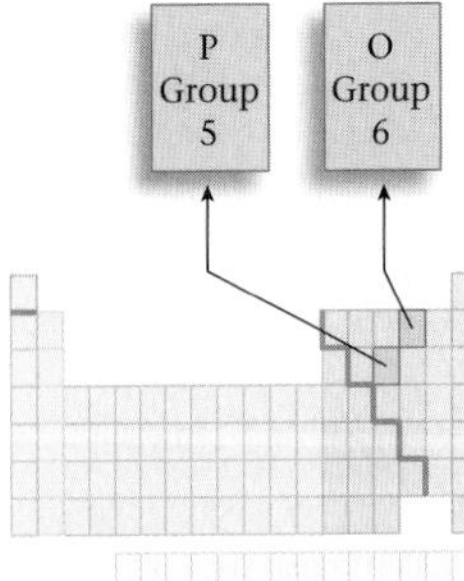

Atomic mass of P

$$\text{2 mol P: } 2 \times 30.97\text{ g} = 61.94\text{ g}$$
$$\text{5 mol O: } 5 \times 16.00\text{ g} = 80.00\text{ g}$$
$$141.94\text{ g} \quad \text{Mass of 1 mole of } P_2O_5 \text{ units}$$

Atomic mass of O

Recall that the molecular formula contains a whole number of empirical formula units. That is,

$$\text{Molecular formula} = (\text{empirical formula})_n$$

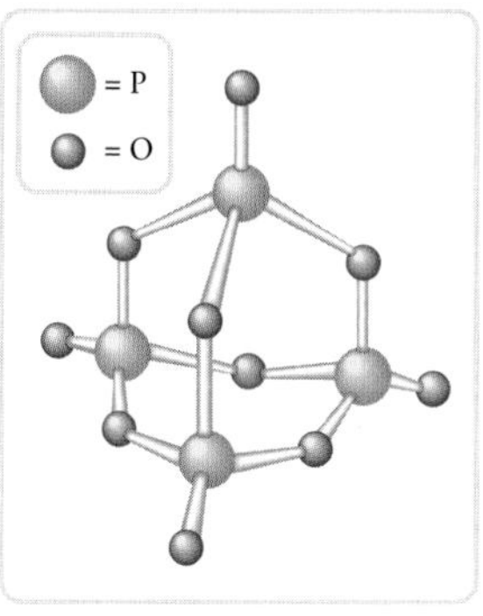

Figure 8.5
The structure of P_4O_{10} as a "ball-and-stick" model. This compound has a great affinity for water and is often used as a desiccant, or drying agent.

where n is a small whole number. Now, because

$$\text{Molecular formula} = n \times \text{empirical formula}$$

then

$$\text{Molar mass} = n \times \text{empirical formula mass}$$

Solving for n gives

$$n = \frac{\text{molar mass}}{\text{empirical formula mass}}$$

Thus, to determine the molecular formula, we first divide the molar mass by the empirical formula mass. This tells us how many empirical formula masses there are in one molar mass.

$$\frac{\text{Molar mass}}{\text{Empirical formula mass}} = \frac{283.88 \text{ g}}{141.94 \text{ g}} = 2$$

This result means that $n = 2$ for this compound, so the molecular formula consists of two empirical formula units, and the molecular formula is $(P_2O_5)_2$, or P_4O_{10}. The structure of this interesting compound is shown in Figure 8.5.

REALITY CHECK The values for x and y are whole numbers. Also, the ratio of P:O in the molecular formula (4:10) is 2:5.

Self-Check EXERCISE 8.11 A compound used as an additive for gasoline to help prevent engine knock shows the following percent composition:

71.65% Cl 24.27% C 4.07% H

The molar mass is known to be 98.96 g. Determine the empirical formula and the molecular formula for this compound.

See Problems 8.81 and 8.82. ■

Self Check

Answer to Self-Check Exercise 8.11

$Cl_2C_2H_4$

It is important to realize that the molecular formula is always an integer multiple of the empirical formula. For example, the sugar glucose (see Figure 8.4) has the empirical formula CH_2O and the molecular formula $C_6H_{12}O_6$. In this case there are six empirical formula units in each glucose molecule:

$$(CH_2O)_6 = C_6H_{12}O_6$$

In general, we can represent the molecular formula in terms of the empirical formula as follows:

$$(\text{Empirical formula})_n = \text{molecular formula}$$

where n is an integer. If $n = 1$, the molecular formula is the same as the empirical formula. For example, for carbon dioxide the empirical formula (CO_2) and the molecular formula (CO_2) are the same, so $n = 1$. On the other hand, for tetraphosphorus decoxide the empirical formula is P_2O_5 and the molecular formula is $P_4O_{10} = (P_2O_5)_2$. In this case $n = 2$.

TEACHING SUPPORT

CHALLENGE YOUR STUDENTS

You might want to challenge your best students to determine the molecular formula for a compound when the molar mass for the compound is not given. Give the students the mass of a sample of the compound and the number of moles of the compound contained in the sample. They can then put information on determining molar mass of a compound together with the information they have learned in this section to find the molecular formula for the compound.

ChemWork

Bond Types between Atoms
Bond Types in Compounds
Classifying Bonds in Molecules
Comparing Bond Polarity
Comparing Bonds
Comparing Electronegatives
Predicting Bonds Between Atoms
Atomic and Ionic Size
Electron Configurations for Ions
Electron Configurations of Ions
Noble Gas Configurations and Ions
Calculating ΔH for Ionization Reactions
Calculating Heat of Formation
Estimating ΔH
Lewis Structures
Relative Bond Lengths
Resonance
Shapes of Molecules
Structure and Polarity

CHAPTER 8 REVIEW

Key Terms

atomic mass unit (amu) (8.2)
average atomic mass (8.2)
mole (8.3)
Avogadro's number (8.3)
conceptual problem solving (8.4)
molar mass (8.5)
mass percent (8.6)
empirical formula (8.7)
molecular formula (8.7)

F directs you to the *Chemistry in Focus* feature in the chapter
VP indicates visual problems
OWL interactive versions of these problems are assignable in OWL

Summary

1. We can count individual units by weighing if we know the average mass of the units. Thus, when we know the average mass of the atoms of an element as that element occurs in nature, we can calculate the number of atoms in any given sample of that element by weighing the sample.
2. A mole is a unit of measure equal to 6.022×10^{23}, which is called Avogadro's number. One mole of any substance contains 6.022×10^{23} units.
3. One mole of an element has a mass equal to the element's atomic mass expressed in grams. The molar mass of any compound is the mass (in grams) of 1 mole of the compound and is the sum of the masses of the component atoms.
4. Percent composition consists of the mass percent of each element in a compound:

$$\text{Mass percent} = \frac{\text{mass of a given element in 1 mole of compound}}{\text{mass of 1 mole of compound}} \times 100\%$$

5. The empirical formula of a compound is the simplest whole-number ratio of the atoms present in the compound; it can be derived from the percent composition of the compound. The molecular formula is the exact formula of the molecules present; it is always an integer multiple of the empirical formula. The diagram in the left column summarizes these different ways of expressing the same information.

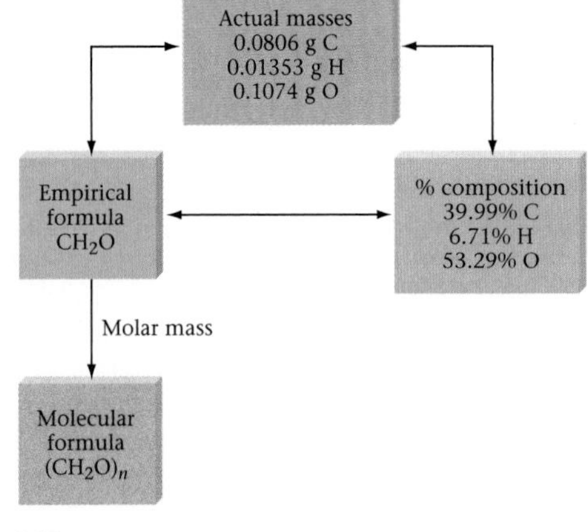

Active Learning Questions

These questions are designed to be considered by groups of students in class. Often these questions work well for introducing a particular topic in class.

1. In chemistry, what is meant by the term *mole?* What is the importance of the mole concept?
2. What is the difference between the empirical and molecular formulas of a compound? Can they ever be the same? Explain.
3. A substance A_2B is 60% A by mass. Calculate the percent B (by mass) for AB_2.
4. Give the formula for calcium phosphate and then answer the following questions:
   a. Calculate the percent composition of each of the elements in this compound.
   b. If you knew that there was 50.0 g of phosphorus in your sample, how many grams of calcium phosphate would you have? How many moles of calcium phosphate would this be? How many formula units of calcium phosphate?
5. How would you find the number of "chalk molecules" it takes to write your name on the board? Explain what you would need to do, and provide a sample calculation.
6. A 0.821-mol sample of a substance composed of diatomic molecules has a mass of 131.3 g. Identify this molecule.
7. How many molecules of water are there in a 10.0-g sample of water? How many hydrogen atoms are there in this sample?
8. What is the mass (in grams) of one molecule of ammonia?
9. Consider separate 100.0-g samples of each of the following: NH_3, N_2O, N_2H_4, HCN, HNO_3. Arrange these samples from largest mass of nitrogen to smallest mass of nitrogen and prove/explain your order.
10. A molecule has a mass of 4.65×10^{-23} g. Provide two possible chemical formulas for such a molecule.
11. Differentiate between the terms *atomic mass* and *molar mass*.

12. Consider Figure 4.19 in the text. Why is it that the formulas for ionic compound are always empirical formulas?

13. Why do we need to count atoms by weighing them?

14. The following claim is made in your text: 1 mole of marbles is enough to cover the entire earth to a depth of 50 miles.

    Provide mathematical support for this claim. Is it reasonably accurate?

15. Estimate the length of time it would take you to count to Avogadro's number. Provide mathematical support.

16. Suppose Avogadro's number was 1000 instead of 6.022×10^{23}. How, if at all, would this affect the relative masses on the periodic table? How, if at all, would this affect the absolute masses of the elements?

17. Estimate the number of atoms in your body and provide mathematical support. Because it is an estimate, it need not be exact, although you should choose your number wisely.

18. Consider separate equal mass samples of magnesium, zinc, and silver. Rank them from greatest to least number of atoms and support your answer.

19. You have a 20.0-g sample of silver metal. You are given 10.0 g of another metal and told that this sample contains twice the number of atoms as the sample of silver metal. Identify this metal.

20. How would you find the number of "ink molecules" it takes to write your name on a piece of paper with your pen? Explain what you would need to do, and provide a sample calculation.

21. True or false. The atom with the largest subscript in a formula is the atom with the largest percent by mass in the compound.

    If true, explain why with an example. If false, explain why and provide a counterexample. In either case, provide mathematical support.

VP 22. Which of the following compounds have the same empirical formulas?

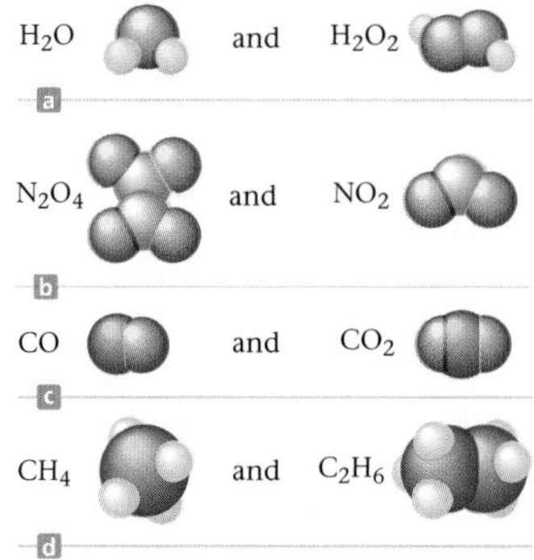

VP 23. The percent by mass of nitrogen is 46.7% for a species containing only nitrogen and oxygen. Which of the following could be this species?

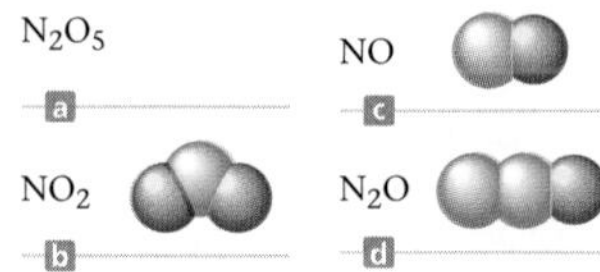

VP 24. Calculate the molar mass of the following substances.

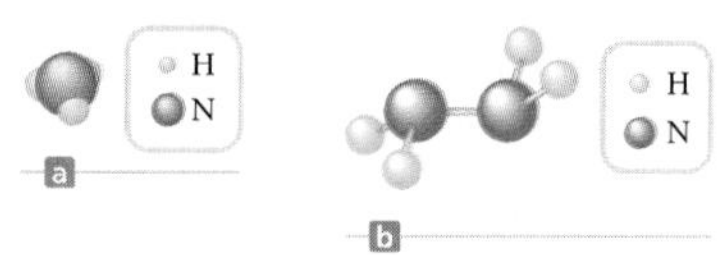

VP 25. Give the empirical formula for each of the compounds represented below.

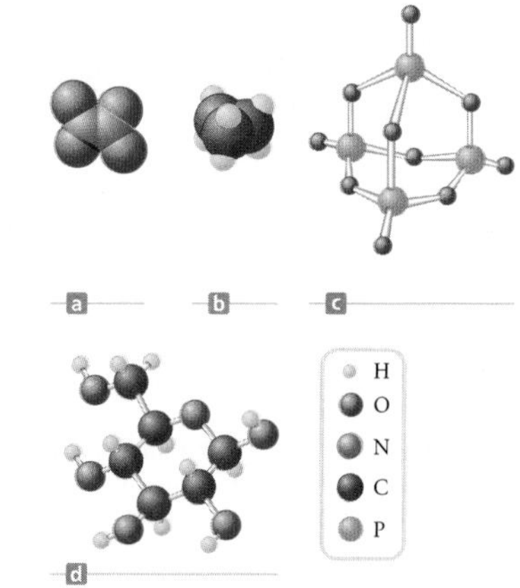

Questions and Problems*

8.1 Counting by Weighing

PROBLEMS

1. Merchants usually sell small nuts, washers, and bolts by weight (like jelly beans!) rather than by individually counting the items. Suppose a particular type of washer weighs 0.110 g on the average. What would 100 such washers weigh? How many washers would there be in 100. g of washers?

2. The Chemistry in Focus segment *Plastic That Talks and Listens!* discusses polyvinylidene difluoride (PVDF). What is the empirical formula of PVDF? Note: An empirical formula is the simplest whole-number ratio of atoms in a compound. This is discussed more fully in Sections 8.7 and 8.8 of your text.

*The element symbols and formulas are given in some problems but not in others to help you learn this necessary "vocabulary."

All even-numbered Questions and Problems have answers in the back of this book and solutions in the Solutions Guide.

Answers to End-of-Chapter Exercises

1. 11.0 g, 909 washers

2. The empirical formula is the lowest whole-number ratio of atoms in the compound. The graphic of PVDF shows four of each type of atom (carbon, hydrogen, and fluorine). So, the empirical formula is CHF.

Chapter Review 239

3. unit of mass defined to more simply describe relative masses on an atomic scale; 1.66×10^{-24} g

4. The average atomic mass takes into account the various isotopes of an element and the relative abundances in which those isotopes are found.

5. (a) 1.50×10^{3} amu; (b) 1.955×10^{8} amu; (c) 7.22×10^{22} amu; (d) 24.31 amu; (e) 3.821×10^{25} amu

6. (a) one; (b) five; (c) ten; (d) 50; (e) ten

7. 55.85 amu; 1.67×10^{4} amu; 99

8. A sample containing 35 tin atoms would weigh 4155 amu; 2967.5 amu of tin would represent 25 tin atoms.

9. 6.022×10^{23}

10. 26.98

11. 3.012×10^{23} (0.5002 mol); 19.56 g K

12. 3.011×10^{23} atoms Ne; 2.002 g He

13. 0.504 g H

14. 177 g

15. 4.04×10^{-23} g

16. 1.99×10^{-23} g

17. 1 mole of He atoms = 4.003 g; 4 moles of H atoms = 4.032 g; 4 moles of H atoms has mass slightly larger than 1 mole of He atoms

18. 0.50 mol Ne atoms

19. (a) 0.245 mol; (b) 1.24 mol; (c) 1.07×10^{-3} mol; (d) 2.61×10^{-8} mol; (e) 1.06 mol

20. (a) 3.500 moles of F atoms; (b) 2.000 mmol Hg; (c) 3.000 mol Si; (d) 0.2500 mol Pt; (e) 100.0 mol Mg; (f) 0.5000 mol Mo

21. (a) 1.74 g Li; (b) 40.7 g Al; (c) 18.1 g Pb; (d) 6.50×10^{3} g Cr; (e) 2.37×10^{5} g Fe; (f) 2.55×10^{-3} g Mg

8.2 Atomic Masses: Counting Atoms by Weighing

QUESTIONS

3. Define the *amu*. What is one amu equivalent to in grams?
4. What do we mean by the *average* atomic mass of an element? What is "averaged" to arrive at this number?

PROBLEMS

5. Using the average atomic masses for each of the following elements (see the table inside the cover of this book), calculate the mass (in amu) of each of the following samples.
   a. 125 carbon atoms
   b. 5 million potassium atoms
   c. 1.04×10^{22} lithium atoms
   d. 1 atom of magnesium
   e. 3.011×10^{23} iodine atoms
6. Using the average atomic masses for each of the following elements (see the table inside the front cover of this book), calculate the number of atoms present in each of the following samples.
   a. 40.08 amu of calcium
   b. 919.5 amu of tungsten
   c. 549.4 amu of manganese
   d. 6345 amu of iodine
   e. 2072 amu of lead
7. What is the average atomic mass (in amu) of iron atoms? What would 299 iron atoms weigh? How many iron atoms are present in a sample of iron that has a mass of 5529.2 amu?
8. The atomic mass of tin is 118.7 amu. What would be the mass of 35 tin atoms? How many tin atoms are contained in a sample of tin that has a mass of 2967.5 amu?

8.3 The Mole

QUESTIONS

9. There are ______ iron atoms present in 55.85 g of iron.
10. There are 6.022×10^{23} aluminum atoms present in ______ g of aluminum.

PROBLEMS

11. Suppose you have a sample of sodium weighing 11.50 g. How many atoms of sodium are present in the sample? What mass of potassium would you need to have the same number of potassium atoms as there are sodium atoms in the sample of sodium?
12. Consider a sample of neon gas weighing 10.09 g. How many atoms of neon are present in the sample? What mass of helium gas would you need for the helium sample to contain the same number of atoms as the neon sample?
13. What mass of hydrogen contains the same number of atoms as 7.00 g of nitrogen?
14. What mass of cobalt contains the same number of atoms as 57.0 g of fluorine?
15. If an average sodium atom has a mass of 3.82×10^{-23} g, what is the mass of a magnesium atom in grams?
16. If an average aluminum atom has a mass of 4.48×10^{-23} g, what is the average mass of a carbon atom in grams?
17. Which has the smaller mass, 1 mole of He atoms or 4 moles of H atoms?
18. Which weighs less, 0.50 mole of neon atoms or 1.0 mole of boron atoms?
19. Use the average atomic masses given inside the front cover of this book to calculate the number of *moles* of the element present in each of the following samples.
    a. 4.95 g of neon
    b. 72.5 g of nickel
    c. 115 mg of silver
    d. 6.22 μg of uranium (μ is a standard abbreviation meaning "micro")
    e. 135 g of iodine
20. Use the average atomic masses given inside the front cover of this book to calculate the number of *moles* of the element present in each of the following samples.
    a. 66.50 g of fluorine atoms
    b. 401.2 mg of mercury
    c. 84.27 g of silicon
    d. 48.78 g of platinum
    e. 2431 g of magnesium
    f. 47.97 g of molybdenum
21. Use the average atomic masses given inside the front cover of this book to calculate the mass in grams of each of the following samples.
    a. 0.251 mole of lithium
    b. 1.51 moles of aluminum
    c. 8.75×10^{-2} moles of lead
    d. 125 moles of chromium
    e. 4.25×10^{3} moles of iron
    f. 0.000105 mole of magnesium
22. Use the average atomic masses given inside the front cover of this book to calculate the mass in grams of each of the following samples.
    a. 0.00552 mole of calcium
    b. 6.25 mmol of boron (1 mmol = 1/1000 mole)
    c. 135 moles of aluminum
    d. 1.34×10^{-7} moles of barium
    e. 2.79 moles of phosphorus
    f. 0.0000997 mole of arsenic
23. Using the average atomic masses given inside the front cover of this book, calculate the number of *atoms* present in each of the following samples.

All even-numbered Questions and Problems have answers in the back of this book and solutions in the Solutions Guide.

22. (a) 0.221 g; (b) 0.0676 g; (c) 3.64×10^{3} g; (d) 1.84×10^{-5} g; (e) 86.4 g (f) 7.47×10^{-3} g

23. (a) 8.37×10^{21} atoms; (b) 9.0×10^{20} atoms; (c) 1.4×10^{19} atoms; (d) 4.95×10^{25} atoms; (e) 9.97×10^{23} atoms; (f) 3.52×10^{22} atoms; (g) 1.41×10^{24} atoms

a. 1.50 g of silver, Ag
b. 0.0015 mole of copper, Cu
c. 0.0015 g of copper, Cu
d. 2.00 kg of magnesium, Mg
e. 2.34 oz of calcium, Ca
f. 2.34 g of calcium, Ca
g. 2.34 moles of calcium, Ca

24. Using the average atomic masses given inside the front cover of this book, calculate the indicated quantities.

a. the mass in grams of 125 iron atoms
b. the mass in amu of 125 iron atoms
c. the number of moles of iron atoms in 125 g of iron
d. the mass in grams of 125 moles of iron
e. the number of iron atoms in 125 g of iron
f. the number of iron atoms in 125 moles of iron

8.5 Molar Mass

QUESTIONS

25. The ______ of a substance is the mass (in grams) of 1 mole of the substance.

26. Describe in your own words how the *molar mass* of a compound may be calculated.

PROBLEMS

27. Give the name and calculate the molar mass for each of the following substances.

a. H_3PO_4
b. Fe_2O_3
c. $NaClO_4$
d. $PbCl_2$
e. HBr
f. $Al(OH)_3$

28. Give the name and calculate the molar mass for each of the following substances.

a. $KHCO_3$
b. Hg_2Cl_2
c. H_2O_2
d. $BeCl_2$
e. $Al_2(SO_4)_3$
f. $KClO_3$

29. Write the formula and calculate the molar mass for each of the following substances.

a. barium chloride
b. aluminum nitrate
c. iron(II) chloride
d. sulfur dioxide
e. calcium acetate

30. Write the formula and calculate the molar mass for each of the following substances.

a. lithium perchlorate
b. sodium hydrogen sulfate
c. magnesium carbonate
d. aluminum bromide
e. chromium(III) sulfide

31. Calculate the number of *moles* of the indicated substance present in each of the following samples.

a. 21.4 mg of nitrogen dioxide
b. 1.56 g of copper(II) nitrate
c. 2.47 g of carbon disulfide
d. 5.04 g of aluminum sulfate
e. 2.99 g of lead(II) chloride
f. 62.4 g of calcium carbonate

32. Calculate the number of *moles* of the indicated substance present in each of the following samples.

a. 47.2 g of aluminum oxide
b. 1.34 kg of potassium bromide
c. 521 mg of germanium
d. 56.2 μg of uranium
e. 29.7 g of sodium acetate
f. 1.03 g of sulfur trioxide

33. Calculate the number of *moles* of the indicated substance in each of the following samples.

a. 41.5 g of $MgCl_2$
b. 135 mg of Li_2O
c. 1.21 kg of Cr
d. 62.5 g of H_2SO_4
e. 42.7 g of C_6H_6
f. 135 g of H_2O_2

34. Calculate the number of moles of the indicated substance present in each of the following samples.

a. 1.95×10^{-3} g of lithium carbonate
b. 4.23 kg of calcium chloride
c. 1.23 mg of strontium chloride
d. 4.75 g of calcium sulfate
e. 96.2 mg of nitrogen(IV) oxide
f. 12.7 g of mercury(I) chloride

35. Calculate the mass in grams of each of the following samples.

a. 1.25 moles of aluminum chloride
b. 3.35 moles of sodium hydrogen carbonate
c. 4.25 millimol of hydrogen bromide (1 millimol = 1/1000 mole)
d. 1.31×10^{-3} moles of uranium
e. 0.00104 mole of carbon dioxide
f. 1.49×10^2 moles of iron

36. Calculate the mass in grams of each of the following samples.

a. 1.21 moles of hydrogen sulfide
b. 4.22×10^{-3} moles of lithium sulfide
c. 224 moles of ferric chloride
d. 7.29 mmol of sodium carbonate (1 mmol = 1/1000 mole)
e. 8.14×10^3 moles of sodium acetate
f. 0.00793 mole of phosphine, PH_3

37. Calculate the mass in grams of each of the following samples.

a. 0.251 mole of ethyl alcohol, C_2H_6O
b. 1.26 moles of carbon dioxide
c. 9.31×10^{-4} moles of gold(III) chloride

All even-numbered Questions and Problems have answers in the back of this book and solutions in the Solutions Guide.

29. (a) $BaCl_2$, 208.2 g; (b) $Al(NO_3)_3$, 213.0 g; (c) $FeCl_2$, 126.75 g; (d) SO_2, 64.07 g; (e) $Ca(C_2H_3O_2)_2$, 158.17 g

30. (a) $LiClO_4$; 106.39 g; (b) $NaHSO_4$; 120.07 g; (c) $MgCO_3$; 84.32 g; (d) $AlBr_3$; 266.7 g; (e) Cr_2S_3; 200.2 g

31. (a) 4.65×10^{-4} mol; (b) 8.32×10^{-3} mol; (c) 0.0324 mol; (d) 0.0147 mol; (e) 0.0108 mol; (f) 0.623 mol

32. (a) 0.463 mol; (b) 11.3 mol; (c) 7.18×10^{-3} mol; (d) 2.36×10^{-7} mol; (e) 0.362 mol; (f) 0.0129 mol

33. (a) 0.436 mol; (b) 4.52×10^{-3} mol/ 4.52 mmol; (c) 23.3 mol; (d) 0.637 mol; (e) 0.547 mol; (f) 3.97 mol

34. (a) 2.64×10^{-5} mol; (b) 38.1 mol; (c) 7.76×10^{-6} mol; (d) 3.49×10^{-2} mol; (e) 2.09×10^{-3} mol; (f) 2.69×10^{-2} mol

35. (a) 167 g; (b) 281 g; (c) 0.344 g; (d) 0.312 g; (e) 0.0458 g; (f) 8.32×10^3 g

36. (a) 41.2 g; (b) 0.194 g; (c) 3.63×10^4 g; (d) 0.773 g; (e) 6.68×10^5 g; (f) 0.270 g

37. (a) 11.6 g; (b) 55.5 g; (c) 0.282 g; (d) 658 g; (e) 0.0199 g

24. (a) 1.16×10^{-20} g; (b) 6.98×10^3 amu; (c) 2.24 mol; (d) 6.98×10^3 g; (e) 1.35×10^{24} atoms; (f) 7.53×10^{25} atoms

25. molar mass

26. The molar mass is calculated by summing the individual atomic masses of the atoms in the formula.

27. (a) phosphoric acid; 97.99 g; (b) iron(III) oxide, ferric oxide; 159.70 g; (c) sodium perchlorate; 122.44 g; (d) lead(II) chloride, plumbous chloride; 278.1 g; (e) hydrogen bromide; 80.91 g; (f) aluminum hydroxide; 78.00 g

28. (a) potassium hydrogen carbonate; 100.12 g; (b) mercury(I) chloride, mercurous chloride; 472.1 g; (c) hydrogen peroxide; 34.02 g; (d) beryllium chloride; 79.91 g; (e) aluminum sulfate; 342.2 g; (f) potassium chlorate; 122.55 g

d. 7.74 moles of sodium nitrate
e. 0.000357 mole of iron

38. Calculate the mass in grams of each of the following samples.

a. 0.994 mole of benzene, C_6H_6
b. 4.21 moles of calcium hydride
c. 1.79×10^{-4} moles of hydrogen peroxide, H_2O_2
d. 1.22 mmol of glucose, $C_6H_{12}O_6$ (1 mmol = 1/1000 mole).
e. 10.6 moles of tin
f. 0.000301 mole of strontium fluoride

39. Calculate the number of *molecules* present in each of the following samples.

a. 4.75 mmol of phosphine, PH_3
b. 4.75 g of phosphine, PH_3
c. 1.25×10^{-2} g of lead(II) acetate, $Pb(CH_3CO_2)_2$
d. 1.25×10^{-2} moles of lead(II) acetate, $Pb(CH_3CO_2)_2$
e. a sample of benzene, C_6H_6, which contains a total of 5.40 moles of carbon

40. Calculate the number of *molecules* present in each of the following samples.

a. 6.37 moles of carbon monoxide
b. 6.37 g of carbon monoxide
c. 2.62×10^{-6} g of water
d. 2.62×10^{-6} moles of water
e. 5.23 g of benzene, C_6H_6

41. Calculate the number of *moles* of carbon atoms present in each of the following samples.

a. 1.271 g of ethanol, C_2H_5OH
b. 3.982 g of 1,4-dichlorobenzene, $C_6H_4Cl_2$
c. 0.4438 g of carbon suboxide, C_3O_2
d. 2.910 g of methylene chloride, CH_2Cl_2

42. Calculate the number of *moles* of sulfur atoms present in each of the following samples.

a. 2.01 g of sodium sulfate
b. 2.01 g of sodium sulfite
c. 2.01 g of sodium sulfide
d. 2.01 g of sodium thiosulfate, $Na_2S_2O_3$

8.6 Percent Composition of Compounds

QUESTIONS

43. The mass fraction of an element present in a compound can be obtained by comparing the mass of the particular element present in 1 mole of the compound to the ______ mass of the compound.

44. The mass percentage of a given element in a compound must always be (greater/less) than 100%.

PROBLEMS

45. Calculate the percent by mass of each element in the following compounds.

a. $HClO_3$
b. UF_4
c. CaH_2
d. Ag_2S
e. $NaHSO_3$
f. MnO_2

46. Calculate the percent by mass of each element in the following compounds.

a. ZnO
b. Na_2S
c. $Mg(OH)_2$
d. H_2O_2
e. CaH_2
f. K_2O

47. Calculate the percent by mass of the element listed *first* in the formulas for each of the following compounds.

a. methane, CH_4
b. sodium nitrate, $NaNO_3$
c. carbon monoxide, CO
d. nitrogen dioxide, NO_2
e. 1-octanol, $C_8H_{18}O$
f. calcium phosphate, $Ca_3(PO_4)_2$
g. 3-phenylphenol, $C_{12}H_{10}O$
h. aluminum acetate, $Al(C_2H_3O_2)_3$

48. Calculate the percent by mass of the element listed *first* in each of the following compounds.

a. barium peroxide, BaO_2
b. barium oxide, BaO
c. cobalt(II) bromide, $CoBr_2$
d. cobalt(III) bromide, $CoBr_3$
e. tin(II) chloride, $SnCl_2$
f. tin(IV) chloride, $SnCl_4$
g. lithium hydride, LiH
h. aluminum hydride, AlH_3

49. Calculate the percent by mass of the element listed *first* in the formulas for each of the following compounds.

a. adipic acid, $C_6H_{10}O_4$
b. ammonium nitrate, NH_4NO_3
c. caffeine, $C_8H_{10}N_4O_2$
d. chlorine dioxide, ClO_2
e. cyclohexanol, $C_6H_{11}OH$
f. dextrose, $C_6H_{12}O_6$
g. eicosane, $C_{20}H_{42}$
h. ethanol, C_2H_5OH

50. Calculate the percent by mass of the element listed *first* in each of the following compounds.

a. iodine monochloride, ICl
b. nitrogen(I) oxide, N_2O
c. nitrogen(II) oxide, NO
d. mercuric chloride, $HgCl_2$
e. mercurous chloride, Hg_2Cl_2
f. sulfur hexafluoride, SF_6
g. xenon difluoride, XeF_2
h. manganese(IV) oxide, MnO_2

51. For each of the following samples of ionic substances, calculate the number of moles and mass of the positive ions present in each sample.

a. 4.25 g of ammonium iodide, NH_4I
b. 6.31 moles of ammonium sulfide, $(NH_4)_2S$
c. 9.71 g of barium phosphide, Ba_3P_2
d. 7.63 moles of calcium phosphate, $Ca_3(PO_4)_2$

All even-numbered Questions and Problems have answers in the back of this book and solutions in the Solutions Guide.

38. (a) 77.6 g; (b) 177 g; (c) 6.09×10^{-3} g; (d) 0.220 g; (e) 1.26×10^3 g; (f) 3.78×10^{-2} g

39. (a) 2.86×10^{21} molecules; (b) 8.42×10^{22} molecules; (c) 2.31×10^{19} formula units; (d) 7.53×10^{21} formula units; (e) 5.42×10^{23} molecules

40. (a) 3.84×10^{24} molecules; (b) 1.37×10^{23} molecules; (c) 8.76×10^{16} molecules; (d) 1.58×10^{18} molecules; (e) 4.03×10^{22} molecules

41. (a) 0.05518 mol C; (b) 0.1625 mol C; (c) 0.01957 mol C; (d) 0.03426 mol C

42. (a) 0.0141 mol S; (b) 0.0159 mol S; (c) 0.0258 mol S; (d) 0.0127 mol S

43. molar

44. less

45. (a) 1.193% H, 41.97% Cl, 56.83% O; (b) 75.80% U, 24.20% F; (c) 95.21% Ca, 4.789% H; (d) 87.06% Ag, 12.94% S; (e) 22.09% Na, 0.9686% H, 30.82% S, 46.12% O; (f) 63.19% Mn, 36.81% O

46. (a) 80.34% Zn; 19.66% O; (b) 58.91% Na; 41.09% S; (c) 41.68% Mg; 54.86% O; 3.456% H; (d) 5.926% H; 94.06% O; (e) 95.20% Ca; 4.789% H; (f) 83.01% K; 16.99% O

47. (a) 74.88% C; (b) 27.05% Na; (c) 42.88% C; (d) 30.45% N; (e) 73.79% C; (f) 38.76% Ca; (g) 84.67% C; (h) 13.22% Al

48. (a) 81.10% Ba; (b) 89.56% Ba; (c) 26.94% Co; (d) 19.73% Co; (e) 62.61% Sn; (f) 45.57% Sn; (g) 87.32% Li; (h) 89.92% Al

49. (a) 49.32% C; (b) 35.00% N; (c) 49.47% C; (d) 52.56% Cl; (e) 71.92% C; (f) 39.99% C; (g) 85.03% C; (h) 52.14% C

50. (a) 78.16% I; (b) 63.65% N; (c) 46.68% N; (d) 73.89% Hg; (e) 84.98% Hg; (f) 21.96% S; (g) 77.55% Xe; (h) 63.19% Mn

51. (a) 0.529 g NH_4^+; (b) 227 g NH_4^+; (c) 8.44 g Ba^{2+}; (d) 918 g Ca^{2+}

52. For each of the following ionic substances, calculate the percentage of the overall molar mass of the compound that is represented by the *negative* ions in the substance.

a. ammonium sulfide
b. calcium chloride
c. barium oxide
d. nickel(II) sulfate

8.7 Formulas of Compounds

QUESTIONS

53. What experimental evidence about a new compound must be known before its formula can be determined?

54. Explain to a friend who has not yet taken a chemistry course what is meant by the *empirical formula* of a compound.

55. Give the empirical formula that corresponds to each of the following molecular formulas.

a. sodium peroxide, Na_2O_2
b. terephthalic acid, $C_8H_6O_4$
c. phenobarbital, $C_{12}H_{12}N_2O_3$
d. 1,4-dichloro-2-butene, $C_4H_6Cl_2$

56. Which of the following pairs of compounds have the same *empirical* formula?

a. acetylene, C_2H_2, and benzene, C_6H_6
b. ethane, C_2H_6, and butane, C_4H_{10}
c. nitrogen dioxide, NO_2, and dinitrogen tetroxide, N_2O_4
d. diphenyl ether, $C_{12}H_{10}O$, and phenol, C_6H_5OH

8.8 Calculation of Empirical Formulas

PROBLEMS

57. A compound was analyzed and was found to contain the following percentages of the elements by mass: barium, 89.56%; oxygen, 10.44%. Determine the empirical formula of the compound.

58. A compound was analyzed and was found to contain the following percentages of the elements by mass: nitrogen, 11.64%; chlorine, 88.36%. Determine the empirical formula of the compound.

59. A 0.5998-g sample of a new compound has been analyzed and found to contain the following masses of elements: carbon, 0.2322 g; hydrogen, 0.05848 g; oxygen, 0.3091 g. Calculate the empirical formula of the compound.

60. A compound was analyzed and was found to contain the following percentages of the elements by mass: boron, 78.14%; hydrogen, 21.86%. Determine the empirical formula of the compound.

61. If a 1.271-g sample of aluminum metal is heated in a chlorine gas atmosphere, the mass of aluminum chloride produced is 6.280 g. Calculate the empirical formula of aluminum chloride.

62. A compound was analyzed and was found to contain the following percentages of the elements by mass: tin, 45.56%; chlorine, 54.43%. Determine the empirical formula of the compound.

63. When 3.269 g of zinc is heated in pure oxygen, the sample gains 0.800 g of oxygen in forming the oxide. Calculate the empirical formula of zinc oxide.

64. If cobalt metal is mixed with excess sulfur and heated strongly, a sulfide is produced that contains 55.06% cobalt by mass. Calculate the empirical formula of the sulfide.

65. If 1.25 g of aluminum metal is heated in an atmosphere of fluorine gas, 3.89 g of aluminum fluoride results. Determine the empirical formula of aluminum fluoride.

66. If 2.50 g of aluminum metal is heated in a stream of fluorine gas, it is found that 5.28 g of fluorine will combine with the aluminum. Determine the empirical formula of the compound that results.

67. A compound used in the nuclear industry has the following composition: uranium, 67.61%; fluorine, 32.39%. Determine the empirical formula of the compound.

68. A compound was analyzed and was found to contain the following percentages of the elements by mass: lithium, 46.46%; oxygen, 53.54%. Determine the empirical formula of the compound.

69. A compound has the following percentage composition by mass: copper, 33.88%; nitrogen, 14.94%; oxygen, 51.18%. Determine the empirical formula of the compound.

70. When lithium metal is heated strongly in an atmosphere of pure nitrogen, the product contains 59.78% Li and 40.22% N on a mass basis. Determine the empirical formula of the compound.

71. A compound has been analyzed and has been found to have the following composition: copper, 66.75%; phosphorus, 10.84%; oxygen, 22.41%. Determine the empirical formula of the compound.

72. A compound was analyzed and was found to contain the following percentages of the elements by mass: cobalt, 71.06%; oxygen, 28.94%. Determine the empirical formula of the compound.

73. When 1.00 mg of lithium metal is reacted with fluorine gas (F_2), the resulting fluoride salt has a mass of 3.73 mg. Calculate the empirical formula of lithium fluoride.

74. Phosphorus and chlorine form two binary compounds, in which the percentages of phosphorus are 22.55% and 14.87%, respectively. Calculate the empirical formulas of the two binary phosphorus–chlorine compounds.

All even-numbered Questions and Problems have answers in the back of this book and solutions in the Solutions Guide.

55. (a) NaO; (b) $C_4H_3O_2$; (c) $C_{12}H_{12}N_2O_3$; (d) C_2H_3Cl

56. a, c

57. Li_2O

58. NCl_3

59. CH_3O

60. BH_3

61. $AlCl_3$

62. $SnCl_4$

63. ZnO

64. Co_2S_3

65. AlF_3

66. AlF_3

67. UF_6

68. Li_2O

69. CuN_2O_6 [$Cu(NO_3)_2$]

70. Li_3N

71. Cu_3PO_4

72. Co_2O_3

73. LiF

74. PCl_3, PCl_5

52. (a) 47.06% S^{2-}; (b) 63.89% Cl^-; (c) 10.44% O^{2-}; (d) 62.08% SO_4^{2-}

53. empirical formula: composition by mass must be known; molecular formula: composition by mass *and* molar mass must be known

54. The empirical formula indicates the smallest whole-number ratio of the number and type of atoms present in a molecule. For example, both NO_2 and N_2O_4 have two oxygen atoms for every nitrogen atom and therefore have the same empirical formula.

8.9 Calculation of Molecular Formulas

QUESTIONS

75. How does the *molecular* formula of a compound differ from the *empirical* formula? Can a compound's empirical and molecular formulas be the same? Explain.

76. What information do we need to determine the molecular formula of a compound if we know only the empirical formula?

PROBLEMS

77. A binary compound of boron and hydrogen has the following percentage composition: 78.14% boron, 21.86% hydrogen. If the molar mass of the compound is determined by experiment to be between 27 and 28 g, what are the empirical and molecular formulas of the compound?

78. A compound with empirical formula CH was found by experiment to have a molar mass of approximately 78 g. What is the molecular formula of the compound?

79. A compound with the empirical formula CH_2 was found to have a molar mass of approximately 84 g. What is the molecular formula of the compound?

80. A compound with empirical formula C_2H_5O was found in a separate experiment to have a molar mass of approximately 90 g. What is the molecular formula of the compound?

81. A compound having an approximate molar mass of 165–170 g has the following percentage composition by mass: carbon, 42.87%; hydrogen, 3.598%; oxygen, 28.55%; nitrogen, 25.00%. Determine the empirical and molecular formulas of the compound.

82. NO_2 (nitrogen dioxide) and N_2O_4 (dinitrogen tetroxide) have the same empirical formula, NO_2. Confirm this by calculating the percent by mass of each element present in the two compounds.

Additional Problems

83. Use the periodic table inside the front cover of this text to determine the atomic mass (per mole) or molar mass of each of the substances in column 1, and find that mass in column 2.

Column 1	Column 2
(1) molybdenum	(a) 33.99 g
(2) lanthanum	(b) 79.9 g
(3) carbon tetrabromide	(c) 95.94 g
(4) mercury(II) oxide	(d) 125.84 g
(5) titanium(IV) oxide	(e) 138.9 g
(6) manganese(II) chloride	(f) 143.1 g
(7) phosphine, PH_3	(g) 156.7 g
(8) tin(II) fluoride	(h) 216.6 g
(9) lead(II) sulfide	(i) 239.3 g
(10) copper(I) oxide	(j) 331.6 g

84. Complete the following table.

Mass of Sample	Moles of Sample	Atoms in Sample
5.00 g Al	______	______
______	0.00250 mol Fe	______
______	______	2.6×10^{24} atoms Cu
0.00250 g Mg	______	______
______	2.7×10^{-3} mol Na	______
______	______	1.00×10^4 atoms U

85. Complete the following table.

Mass of Sample	Moles of Sample	Molecules in Sample	Atoms in Sample
4.24 g C_6H_6	______	______	______
______	0.224 mol H_2O	______	______
______	______	2.71×10^{22} molecules CO_2	______
______	1.26 mol HCl	______	______
______	______	4.21×10^{24} molecules H_2O	______
0.297 g CH_3OH	______	______	______

86. Consider a hypothetical compound composed of elements X, Y, and Z with the empirical formula X_2YZ_3. Given that the atomic masses of X, Y, and Z are 41.2, 57.7, and 63.9, respectively, calculate the percentage composition by mass of the compound. If the molecular formula of the compound is found by molar mass determination to be actually $X_4Y_2Z_6$, what is the percentage of each element present? Explain your results.

87. A binary compound of magnesium and nitrogen is analyzed, and 1.2791 g of the compound is found to contain 0.9240 g of magnesium. When a second sample of this compound is treated with water and heated, the nitrogen is driven off as ammonia, leaving a compound that contains 60.31% magnesium and 39.69% oxygen by mass. Calculate the empirical formulas of the two magnesium compounds.

88. When a 2.118-g sample of copper is heated in an atmosphere in which the amount of oxygen present is restricted, the sample gains 0.2666 g of oxygen in forming a reddish-brown oxide. However, when 2.118 g of copper is heated in a stream of pure oxygen, the sample gains 0.5332 g of oxygen. Calculate the empirical formulas of the two oxides of copper.

89. Hydrogen gas reacts with each of the halogen elements to form the hydrogen halides (HF, HCl, HBr, HI). Calculate the percent by mass of hydrogen in each of these compounds.

90. Calculate the number of atoms of each element present in each of the following samples.

a. 4.21 g of water
b. 6.81 g of carbon dioxide
c. 0.000221 g of benzene, C_6H_6
d. 2.26 moles of $C_{12}H_{22}O_{11}$

All even-numbered Questions and Problems have answers in the back of this book and solutions in the Solutions Guide.

75. empirical formula: smallest whole-number ratio of atoms present; molecular formula: actual number of atoms in a molecule

76. molar mass

77. empirical formula = BH_3; molecular formula = B_2H_6

78. C_6H_6

79. C_6H_{12}

80. $C_4H_{10}O_2$

81. molecular formula $C_6H_6O_3N_3$

82. Both are 30.45% N, 69.55% O

83. [1] c; [2] e; [3] j; [4] h; [5] b; [6] d; [7] a; [8] g; [9] i; [10] f

84. 5.00 g Al, 0.185 mol, 1.12×10^{23} atoms; 0.140 g Fe, 0.00250 mol, 1.51×10^{21} atoms; 2.7×10^2 g Cu, 4.3 mol, 2.6×10^{24} atoms; 0.00250 g Mg, 1.03×10^{-4} mol, 6.19×10^{19} atoms; 0.062 g Na, 2.7×10^{-3} mol, 1.6×10^{21} atoms; 3.95×10^{-18} g U, 1.66×10^{-20} mol, 1.00×10^4 atoms

85. 4.24 g, 0.0543 mol, 3.27×10^{22} molecules, 3.92×10^{23} atoms; 4.04 g, 0.224 mol, 1.35×10^{23} molecules, 4.05×10^{23} atoms; 1.98 g, 0.0450 mol, 2.71×10^{22} molecules, 8.13×10^{22} atoms; 45.9 g, 1.26 mol, 7.59×10^{23} molecules, 1.52×10^{24} atoms; 126 g, 6.99 mol, 4.21×10^{24} molecules, 1.26×10^{25} atoms; 0.297 g, 0.00927 mol, 5.58×10^{21} molecules, 3.35×10^{22} atoms

86. 24.8% X, 17.4% Y, 57.8% Z. If the molecular formula were actually $X_4Y_2Z_6$, the percent composition would be the same: the *relative* mass of each element present would not change. The molecular formula is always a whole-number multiple of the empirical formula.

87. Mg_3N_2, MgO

88. Cu_2O, CuO

89. HF, 20.01 g, 5.037% H; HCl, 36.46 g, 2.765% H; HBr, 80.91 g, 1.246% H; HI, 127.9 g, 0.7881% H

91. Calculate the mass in grams of each of the following samples.

a. 10,000,000,000 nitrogen molecules
b. 2.49×10^{20} carbon dioxide molecules
c. 7.0983 moles of sodium chloride
d. 9.012×10^{-6} moles of 1,2-dichloroethane, $C_2H_4Cl_2$

92. Calculate the mass of carbon in grams, the percent carbon by mass, and the number of individual carbon atoms present in each of the following samples.

a. 7.819 g of carbon suboxide, C_3O_2
b. 1.53×10^{21} molecules of carbon monoxide
c. 0.200 mole of phenol, C_6H_6O

93. Find the item in column 2 that best explains or completes the statement or question in column 1.

Column 1

(1) 1 amu
(2) 1008 amu
(3) mass of the "average" atom of an element
(4) number of carbon atoms in 12.01 g of carbon
(5) 6.022×10^{23} molecules
(6) total mass of all atoms in 1 mole of a compound
(7) smallest whole-number ratio of atoms present in a molecule
(8) formula showing actual number of atoms present in a molecule
(9) product formed when any carbon-containing compound is burned in O_2
(10) have the same empirical formulas, but different molecular formulas

Column 2

(a) 6.022×10^{23}
(b) atomic mass
(c) mass of 1000 hydrogen atoms
(d) benzene, C_6H_6, and acetylene, C_2H_2
(e) carbon dioxide
(f) empirical formula
(g) 1.66×10^{-24} g
(h) molecular formula
(i) molar mass
(j) 1 mole

94. Calculate the number of grams of iron that contain the same number of atoms as 2.24 g of cobalt.

95. Calculate the number of grams of cobalt that contain the same number of atoms as 2.24 g of iron.

96. Calculate the number of grams of mercury that contain the same number of atoms as 5.00 g of tellurium.

97. Calculate the number of grams of lithium that contain the same number of atoms as 1.00 kg of zirconium.

98. Given that the molar mass of carbon tetrachloride, CCl_4, is 153.8 g, calculate the mass in grams of 1 molecule of CCl_4.

99. Calculate the mass in grams of hydrogen present in 2.500 g of each of the following compounds.

a. benzene, C_6H_6
b. calcium hydride, CaH_2
c. ethyl alcohol, C_2H_5OH
d. serine, $C_3H_7O_3N$

100. Calculate the mass in grams of nitrogen present in 5.000 g of each of the following compounds.

a. glycine, $C_2H_5O_2N$
b. magnesium nitride, Mg_3N_2
c. calcium nitrate
d. dinitrogen tetroxide

101. A strikingly beautiful copper compound with the common name "blue vitriol" has the following elemental composition: 25.45% Cu, 12.84% S, 4.036% H, 57.67% O. Determine the empirical formula of the compound.

102. A magnesium salt has the following elemental composition: 16.39% Mg, 18.89% N, 64.72% O. Determine the empirical formula of the salt.

103. The mass 1.66×10^{-24} g is equivalent to 1 ______.

104. Although exact isotopic masses are known with great precision for most elements, we use the *average* mass of an element's atoms in most chemical calculations. Explain.

105. Using the average atomic masses given in Table 8.1, calculate the number of atoms present in each of the following samples.

a. 160,000 amu of oxygen
b. 8139.81 amu of nitrogen
c. 13,490 amu of aluminum
d. 5040 amu of hydrogen
e. 367,495.15 amu of sodium

106. If an average sodium atom weighs 22.99 amu, how many sodium atoms are contained in 1.98×10^{13} amu of sodium? What will 3.01×10^{23} sodium atoms weigh?

107. Using the average atomic masses given inside the front cover of this text, calculate how many *moles* of each element the following *masses* represent.

a. 1.5 mg of chromium
b. 2.0×10^{-3} g of strontium
c. 4.84×10^4 g of boron
d. 3.6×10^{-6} μg of californium
e. 1.0 ton (2000 lb) of iron
f. 20.4 g of barium
g. 62.8 g of cobalt

108. Using the average atomic masses given inside the front cover of this text, calculate the *mass in grams* of each of the following samples.

a. 5.0 moles of potassium
b. 0.000305 mole of mercury
c. 2.31×10^{-5} moles of manganese
d. 10.5 moles of phosphorus
e. 4.9×10^4 moles of iron
f. 125 moles of lithium
g. 0.01205 mole of fluorine

All even-numbered Questions and Problems have answers in the back of this book and solutions in the Solutions Guide.

97. 76.1 g Li

98. 2.554×10^{-22} g

99. (a) 0.1936 g H; (b) 0.1197 g H; (c) 0.3282 g H; (d) 0.1678 g H

100. (a) 0.9331 g N; (b) 1.388 g N; (c) 0.8537 g N; (d) 1.522 g N

101. $CuSH_{10}O_9$ [$CuSO_4 \cdot 5H_2O$]

102. MgN_2O_6 [$Mg(NO_3)_2$]

103. atomic mass unit

104. The average mass takes into account not only the exact masses of the isotopes of an element, but also the relative abundance of the isotopes in nature.

105. (a) 1.0×10^4 O atoms; (b) 581 N atoms; (c) 500 Al atoms; (d) 5.00×10^3 H atoms; (e) 1.599×10^4 Na atoms

106. 8.61×10^{11} sodium atoms; 6.92×10^{24} amu

107. (a) 2.9×10^{-5} mol Cr; (b) 2.3×10^{-5} mol Sr; (c) 4.48×10^3 mol B; (d) 1.4×10^{-14} mol Cf; (e) 1.6×10^4 mol Fe; (f) 0.149 mol Ba; (g) 1.07 mol Co

90. (a) 2.82×10^{23} H atoms, 1.41×10^{23} O atoms; (b) 9.32×10^{22} C atoms, 1.86×10^{23} O atoms; (c) 1.02×10^{19} C atoms and H atoms; (d) 1.63×10^{25} C atoms, 2.99×10^{25} H atoms, 1.50×10^{25} O atoms

91. (a) 4.7×10^{-13} g N_2; (b) 0.0182 g CO_2; (c) 414.8 g NaCl; (d) 8.918×10^{-4} g $C_2H_4Cl_2$

92. (a) 4.141 g C, 52.96% C, 2.076×10^{23} atoms C; (b) 0.0305 g C, 42.88% C, 1.53×10^{21} atoms C; (c) 14.4 g C, 76.6% C, 7.23×10^{23} atoms C

93. [1] g; [2] c; [3] b; [4] a; [5] j; [6] i; [7] f; [8] h; [9] e; [10] d

94. 2.12 g Fe

95. 2.36 g Co

96. 7.86 g Hg

109. Using the average atomic masses given inside the front cover of this text, calculate the number of *atoms* present in each of the following samples.

a. 2.89 g of gold
b. 0.000259 mole of platinum
c. 0.000259 g of platinum
d. 2.0 lb of magnesium
e. 1.90 mL of liquid mercury (density = 13.6 g/mL)
f. 4.30 moles of tungsten
g. 4.30 g of tungsten

110. Calculate the molar mass for each of the following substances.

a. ferrous sulfate
b. mercuric iodide
c. stannic oxide
d. cobaltous chloride
e. cupric nitrate

111. Calculate the molar mass for each of the following substances.

a. adipic acid, $C_6H_{10}O_4$
b. caffeine, $C_8H_{10}N_4O_2$
c. eicosane, $C_{20}H_{42}$
d. cyclohexanol, $C_6H_{11}OH$
e. vinyl acetate, $C_4H_6O_2$
f. dextrose, $C_6H_{12}O_6$

112. Calculate the number of *moles* of the indicated substance present in each of the following samples.

a. 21.2 g of ammonium sulfide
b. 44.3 g of calcium nitrate
c. 4.35 g of dichlorine monoxide
d. 1.0 lb of ferric chloride
e. 1.0 kg of ferric chloride

113. Calculate the number of *moles* of the indicated substance present in each of the following samples.

a. 1.28 g of iron(II) sulfate
b. 5.14 mg of mercury(II) iodide
c. 9.21 μg of tin(IV) oxide
d. 1.26 lb of cobalt(II) chloride
e. 4.25 g of copper(II) nitrate

114. Calculate the mass in grams of each of the following samples.

a. 2.6×10^{-2} moles of copper(II) sulfate, $CuSO_4$
b. 3.05×10^3 moles of tetrafluoroethylene, C_2F_4
c. 7.83 mmol (1 mmol = 0.001 mol) of 1,4-pentadiene, C_5H_8
d. 6.30 moles of bismuth trichloride, $BiCl_3$
e. 12.2 moles of sucrose, $C_{12}H_{22}O_{11}$

115. Calculate the mass in grams of each of the following samples.

a. 3.09 moles of ammonium carbonate
b. 4.01×10^{-6} moles of sodium hydrogen carbonate
c. 88.02 moles of carbon dioxide
d. 1.29 mmol of silver nitrate
e. 0.0024 mole of chromium(III) chloride

116. Calculate the number of *molecules* present in each of the following samples.

a. 3.45 g of $C_6H_{12}O_6$
b. 3.45 moles of $C_6H_{12}O_6$
c. 25.0 g of ICl_5
d. 1.00 g of B_2H_6
e. 1.05 mmol of $Al(NO_3)_3$

117. Calculate the number of moles of hydrogen atoms present in each of the following samples.

a. 2.71 g of ammonia
b. 0.824 mole of water
c. 6.25 mg of sulfuric acid
d. 451 g of ammonium carbonate

118. Calculate the percent by mass of each element in the following compounds.

a. calcium phosphate
b. cadmium sulfate
c. iron(III) sulfate
d. manganese(II) chloride
e. ammonium carbonate
f. sodium hydrogen carbonate
g. carbon dioxide
h. silver(I) nitrate

119. Calculate the percent by mass of the element mentioned *first* in the formulas for each of the following compounds.

a. sodium azide, NaN_3
b. copper(II) sulfate, $CuSO_4$
c. gold(III) chloride, $AuCl_3$
d. silver nitrate, $AgNO_3$
e. rubidium sulfate, Rb_2SO_4
f. sodium chlorate, $NaClO_3$
g. nitrogen triiodide, NI_3
h. cesium bromide, CsBr

120. Calculate the percent by mass of the element mentioned *first* in the formulas for each of the following compounds.

a. iron(II) sulfate
b. silver(I) oxide
c. strontium chloride
d. vinyl acetate, $C_4H_6O_2$
e. methanol, CH_3OH
f. aluminum oxide
g. potassium chlorite
h. potassium chloride

121. A 1.2569-g sample of a new compound has been analyzed and found to contain the following masses of elements: carbon, 0.7238 g; hydrogen, 0.07088 g; nitrogen, 0.1407 g; oxygen, 0.3214 g. Calculate the empirical formula of the compound.

122. A 0.7221-g sample of a new compound has been analyzed and found to contain the following masses of elements: carbon, 0.2990 g; hydrogen, 0.05849 g; nitrogen, 0.2318 g; oxygen, 0.1328 g. Calculate the empirical formula of the compound.

All even-numbered Questions and Problems have answers in the back of this book and solutions in the Solutions Guide.

108. (a) 2.0×10^2 g K; (b) 0.0612 g Hg; (c) 1.27×10^{-3} g Mn; (d) 325 g P; (e) 2.7×10^6 g Fe; (f) 868 g Li; (g) 0.2290 g F

109. (a) 8.83×10^{21} Au atoms; (b) 1.56×10^{20} Pt atoms; (c) 7.99×10^{17} Pt atoms; (d) 2.2×10^{25} Mg atoms; (e) 7.75×10^{22} Hg atoms; (f) 2.59×10^{24} W atoms; (g) 1.41×10^{22} W atoms

110. (a) 151.9 g; (b) 454.4 g; (c) 150.7 g; (d) 129.8 g; (e) 187.6 g

111. (a) 146.14 g; (b) 194.20 g; (c) 282.5 g; (d) 100.16 g; (e) 86.09 g; (f) 180.16 g

112. (a) 0.311 mol; (b) 0.270 mol; (c) 0.0501 mol; (d) 2.8 mol; (e) 6.2 mol

113. (a) 8.43×10^{-3} mol; (b) 1.13×10^{-5} mol; (c) 6.11×10^{-8} mol; (d) 4.41 mol; (e) 2.27×10^{-2} mol

114. (a) 4.2 g; (b) 3.05×10^5 g; (c) 0.533 g; (d) 1.99×10^3 g; (e) 4.18×10^3 g

115. (a) 297 g; (b) 3.37×10^{-4} g; (c) 3874 g; (d) 0.219 g; (e) 0.38 g

116. (a) 1.15×10^{22} molecules; (b) 2.08×10^{24} molecules; (c) 4.95×10^{22} molecules; (d) 2.18×10^{22} molecules; (e) 6.32×10^{20} formula units (substance is ionic)

117. (a) 0.477 mol; (b) 1.65 mol; (c) 1.27×10^{-4} mol; (d) 37.5 mol

118. (a) 38.76% Ca, 19.97% P, 41.27% O; (b) 53.91% Cd, 15.38% S, 30.70% O; (c) 27.93% Fe, 24.06% S, 48.01% O; (d) 43.66% Mn, 56.34% Cl; (e) 29.16% N, 8.392% H, 12.50% C, 49.95% O; (f) 27.37% Na, 1.200% H, 14.30% C, 57.14% O; (g) 27.29% C, 72.71% O; (h) 63.51% Ag, 8.246% N, 28.25% O

119. (a) 35.36% Na; (b) 39.81% Cu; (c) 64.93% Au; (d) 63.51% Ag; (e) 64.01% Rb; (f) 21.60% Na; (g) 3.550% N; (h) 62.45% Cs

120. (a) 36.76% Fe; (b) 93.10% Ag; (c) 55.28% Sr; (d) 55.80% C; (e) 37.48% C; (f) 52.92% Al; (g) 36.70% K; (h) 52.45% K

246 Chapter 8 Chemical Composition

123. When 2.004 g of calcium is heated in pure nitrogen gas, the sample gains 0.4670 g of nitrogen. Calculate the empirical formula of the calcium nitride formed.

124. When 4.01 g of mercury is strongly heated in air, the resulting oxide weighs 4.33 g. Calculate the empirical formula of the oxide.

125. When 1.00 g of metallic chromium is heated with elemental chlorine gas, 3.045 g of a chromium chloride salt results. Calculate the empirical formula of the compound.

126. When barium metal is heated in chlorine gas, a binary compound forms that consists of 65.95% Ba and 34.05% Cl by mass. Calculate the empirical formula of the compound.

All even-numbered Questions and Problems have answers in the back of this book and solutions in the Solutions Guide.

121. $C_6H_7NO_2$

122. $C_3H_7N_2O$

123. Ca_3N_2

124. HgO

125. $CrCl_3$

126. $BaCl_2$

Chapter 9

Objectives

In this chapter our objectives are for the students to:

SECTION 9.1

- Understand the molecular and mass information given in a balanced equation.

SECTION 9.2

- Learn to use a balanced equation to determine the relationships between moles of reactants and moles of products.

SECTION 9.3

- Learn to relate masses of reactants and products in a chemical reaction.

SECTION 9.4

- Understand what is meant by the term *limiting reactant.*

SECTION 9.5

- Learn to recognize the limiting reactant in a reaction.
- Learn to use the limiting reactant to do stoichiometric calculations.

SECTION 9.6

- Learn to calculate actual yield as a percentage of theoretical yield.

9 Chemical Quantities

Doctors administering the polio vaccine in Niger. *(Jean-Marc Giboux/Getty Images)*

ChemWork Refined over ten years of use by thousands of students, **ChemWork** builds and enhances students' problems-solving skills. Online assignments function as a "personal instructor" to help students learn how to solve challenging problems and learn how to think like chemists. Annotations for **ChemWork** assignments are included at the beginning of the end-of-chapter review.

PowerLecture This 2-DVD package includes the Chemistry Multimedia Library, which contains animations, simulations, and movies for all chemistry subjects, organized by topic for lecture presentations. Annotations for **PowerLecture** are referenced in the margins throughout the Annotated Instructor's Edition.

OWL Sign in to OWL at **www.cengage.com/owl** to view tutorials and simulations, develop problem-solving skills, and complete online homework assigned by your professor.

go Chemistry Download mini-lecture videos for key concept review and exam prep from OWL or purchase them from **www.ichapters.com**

Suppose you work for a consumer advocate organization and you want to test a company's advertising claims about the effectiveness of its antacid. The company claims that its product neutralizes 10 times as much stomach acid per tablet as its nearest competitor. How would you test the validity of this claim?

Or suppose that after graduation you go to work for a chemical company that makes methanol (methyl alcohol), a substance used as a starting material for the manufacture of products such as antifreeze and aviation fuels. You are working with an experienced chemist who is trying to improve the company's process for making methanol from the reaction of gaseous hydrogen with carbon monoxide gas. The first day on the job, you are instructed to order enough hydrogen and carbon monoxide to produce 6.0 kg of methanol in a test run. How would you determine how much carbon monoxide and hydrogen you should order?

Methanol is a starting material for some jet fuels.

Royalty-Free Corbis

More than 10 *billion* pounds of methanol is produced annually.

After you study this chapter, you will be able to answer these questions.

9.1 Information Given by Chemical Equations

OBJECTIVE: To understand the molecular and mass information given in a balanced equation.

Reactions are what chemistry is really all about. Recall from Chapter 6 that chemical changes are actually rearrangements of atom groupings that can be described by chemical equations. These chemical equations tell us the identities (formulas) of the reactants and products and also show how much of each reactant and product participates in the reaction. The numbers (coefficients) in the balanced chemical equation enable us to determine just how much product we can get from a given quantity of reactants. It is important to recognize that the coefficients in a balanced equation give us the *relative* numbers of molecules. That is, we are interested in the *ratio* of the coefficients, not individual coefficients.

To illustrate this idea, consider a nonchemical analogy. Suppose you are in charge of making deli sandwiches at a fast-food restaurant. A particular type of sandwich requires 2 slices of bread, 3 slices of meat, and 1 slice of cheese. We can represent making the sandwich with the following equation:

$$2 \text{ slices bread} + 3 \text{ slices meat} + 1 \text{ slice cheese} \rightarrow 1 \text{ sandwich}$$

 **Test Bank: 1–4**

Section 9.1

TEACHING TIPS

- Remind students that chemistry problems often require a balanced chemical equation. Be sure they remember to write the equation first, and then balance it before working the problem.
- Recipe analogies can help students relate to chemical equations and quantities. Explain that in a recipe (for chocolate chip cookies, for example) one needs to know the ingredients just as in a chemistry equation we need to know the reactants and products. An unbalanced chemical equation is like a recipe that lists the ingredients but not the amounts of each needed. A balanced chemical equation is like a recipe that includes both the amounts and the ingredients. It can be increased or decreased by multiplying by the appropriate factor. For a cookie recipe you can double or halve the recipe, just as you can multiply a chemical equation by 2 or by 1/2.
- Consider using Active Learning Questions 1–3 as an introduction to this chapter (have students work together on these problems before you present the material). You can then tell students that all of the concepts in the chapter are included in these questions. You can also return to these problems if students have difficulty later in the chapter.

TEACHING TIPS

- Emphasize that the coefficients in a balanced equation represent the mole *ratios*. An individual coefficient is meaningless (just as an amount of a single ingredient in a recipe is meaningless without the other amounts).

Your boss sends you to the store to get enough ingredients to make 50 sandwiches. How do you figure out how much of each ingredient to buy? Because you need enough to make 50 sandwiches, you multiply the preceding equation by 50.

$$50(2 \text{ slices bread}) + 50(3 \text{ slices meat}) + 50(1 \text{ slice cheese}) \rightarrow 50(1 \text{ sandwich})$$

That is

$$100 \text{ slices bread} + 150 \text{ slices meat} + 50 \text{ slices cheese} \rightarrow 50 \text{ sandwiches}$$

Notice that the numbers 100:150:50 correspond to the ratio 2:3:1, which represents the coefficients in the "balanced equation" of making a sandwich. If you were asked to make any number of sandwiches, it would be easy to use the original sandwich equation to determine how much of each ingredient you need.

The equation for a chemical reaction gives you the same type of information. It indicates the relative numbers of reactant and product molecules involved in the reaction. Using the equation permits us to determine the amounts of reactants needed to give a certain amount of product or to predict how much product we can make from a given quantity of reactants.

go Chemistry **Module 7: Simple Stoichiometry** covers concepts in this section.

To illustrate how this idea works with a chemistry example, consider the reaction between gaseous carbon monoxide and hydrogen to produce liquid methanol, $CH_3OH(l)$. The reactants and products are

$$\text{Unbalanced: } \underbrace{CO(g) + H_2(g)}_{\text{Reactants}} \rightarrow \underbrace{CH_3OH(l)}_{\text{Product}}$$

Because atoms are just rearranged (not created or destroyed) in a chemical reaction, we must always balance a chemical equation. That is, we must choose coefficients that give the same number of each type of atom on both sides. Using the smallest set of integers that satisfies this condition gives the balanced equation

$$\text{Balanced: } CO(g) + 2H_2(g) \rightarrow CH_3OH(l)$$

CHECK: Reactants: 1 C, 1 O, 4 H; Products: 1 C, 1 O, 4 H

Again, the coefficients in a balanced equation give the *relative* numbers of molecules. That is, we could multiply this balanced equation by any number and still have a balanced equation. For example, we could multiply by 12:

$$12[CO(g) + 2H_2(g) \rightarrow CH_3OH(l)]$$

to obtain

$$12CO(g) + 24H_2(g) \rightarrow 12CH_3OH(l)$$

This is still a balanced equation (check to be sure). Because 12 represents a dozen, we could even describe the reaction in terms of dozens:

$$1 \text{ dozen } CO(g) + 2 \text{ dozen } H_2(g) \rightarrow 1 \text{ dozen } CH_3OH(l)$$

We could also multiply the original equation by a very large number, such as 6.022×10^{23}:

$$6.022 \times 10^{23}[CO(g) + 2H_2(g) \rightarrow CH_3OH(l)]$$

which leads to the equation

$$6.022 \times 10^{23}\ CO(g) + 2(6.022 \times 10^{23})\ H_2(g) \rightarrow 6.022 \times 10^{23}\ CH_3OH(l)$$

One mole is 6.022×10^{23} units.

Just as 12 is called a dozen, chemists call 6.022×10^{23} a *mole* (abbreviated mol). Our equation, then, can be written in terms of moles:

$$1 \text{ mol } CO(g) + 2 \text{ mol } H_2(g) \rightarrow 1 \text{ mol } CH_3OH(l)$$

Table 9.1 Information Conveyed by the Balanced Equation for the Production of Methanol

$CO(g)$	+	$2H_2(g)$	→	$CH_3OH(l)$
1 molecule CO	+	2 molecules H_2	→	1 molecule CH_3OH
1 dozen CO molecules	+	2 dozen H_2 molecules	→	1 dozen CH_3OH molecules
6.022×10^{23} CO molecules	+	$2(6.022 \times 10^{23})$ H_2 molecules	→	6.022×10^{23} CH_3OH molecules
1 mol CO molecules	+	2 mol H_2 molecules	→	1 mol CH_3OH molecules

Various ways of interpreting this balanced chemical equation are given in Table 9.1.

EXAMPLE 9.1 Relating Moles to Molecules in Chemical Equations

Propane is often used as a fuel for outdoor grills.

Propane, C_3H_8, is a fuel commonly used for cooking on gas grills and for heating in rural areas where natural gas is unavailable. Propane reacts with oxygen gas to produce heat and the products carbon dioxide and water. This combustion reaction is represented by the unbalanced equation

$$C_3H_8(g) + O_2(g) \rightarrow CO_2(g) + H_2O(g)$$

Give the balanced equation for this reaction, and state the meaning of the equation in terms of numbers of molecules and moles of molecules.

SOLUTION

Using the techniques explained in Chapter 6, we can balance the equation.

$$C_3H_8(g) + 5O_2(g) \rightarrow 3CO_2(g) + 4H_2O(g)$$

CHECK: 3 C, 8 H, 10 O → 3 C, 8 H, 10 O

This equation can be interpreted in terms of molecules as follows:

1 molecule of C_3H_8 reacts with 5 molecules of O_2 to give 3 molecules of CO_2 plus 4 molecules of H_2O

or as follows in terms of moles (of molecules):

1 mol C_3H_8 reacts with 5 mol O_2 to give 3 mol CO_2 plus 4 mol H_2O ■

9.2 Mole–Mole Relationships

OBJECTIVE: To learn to use a balanced equation to determine relationships between moles of reactants and moles of products.

Now that we have discussed the meaning of a balanced chemical equation in terms of moles of reactants and products, we can use an equation to predict the moles of products that a given number of moles of reactants will yield. For example, consider the decomposition of water to give hydrogen and oxygen, which is represented by the following balanced equation:

$$2H_2O(l) \rightarrow 2H_2(g) + O_2(g)$$

This equation tells us that 2 mol H_2O yields 2 mol H_2 and 1 mol O_2.

Now suppose that we have 4 mol water. If we decompose 4 mol water, how many moles of products do we get?

Additional Examples

Example 9.1

Give the balanced equation for each of the following, and state the meaning of the equation in terms of numbers of molecules and moles of molecules.

1. $NO(g) + H_2(g) \rightarrow N_2(g) + H_2O(l)$

   $2NO(g) + 2H_2(g) \rightarrow N_2(g) + 2H_2O(l)$; 2 molecules (or 2 moles) of NO react with 2 molecules (or 2 moles) of hydrogen gas to give 1 molecule (or 1 mole) of nitrogen gas and 2 molecules (or 2 moles) of water.

2. $SiH_4(g) + NH_3(g) \rightarrow Si_3N_4(s) + H_2(g)$

   $3SiH_4(g) + 4NH_3(g) \rightarrow Si_3N_4(s) + 12H_2(g)$; 3 molecules (or 3 moles) of SiH_4 react with 4 molecules (or 4 moles) of ammonia to give 1 molecule (or 1 mole) of Si_3N_4 and 12 molecules (or 12 moles) of hydrogen gas.

Test Bank: 5–14, 78, 82, 83, 88

Section 9.2

TEACHING TIPS

Students often have difficulty understanding what a mole ratio represents. Spend some time explaining that a mole ratio relates the moles of one substance in the chemical equation to the moles of another substance through an equivalence statement. The confusion arises when students assume that equivalence means equality. The moles on either side of an equivalence statement are not equal; they are equivalent amounts.

For example, in Example 9.2 the equivalence statement between H_2O and O_2 is 2 mol H_2O = 1 mol O_2. This means that if you begin with 2 mol water, you will produce 1 mol oxygen. The two amounts are not equal to each other but they are equivalent for this equation.

MISCONCEPTION

Students often think of the coefficients as the amounts of reactants and products involved in the reaction. For example, for

$$2H_2 + O_2 \rightarrow 2H_2O$$

many students who are asked, "Given 1.0 mole (or any number) of H_2, how many moles of O_2 are required and how much water is produced?" will answer "1.0 mol O_2 and 2.0 mol H_2O," because these are the coefficients in the balanced equation. Emphasize that the coefficients are only important as ratios and each individual coefficient is meaningless.

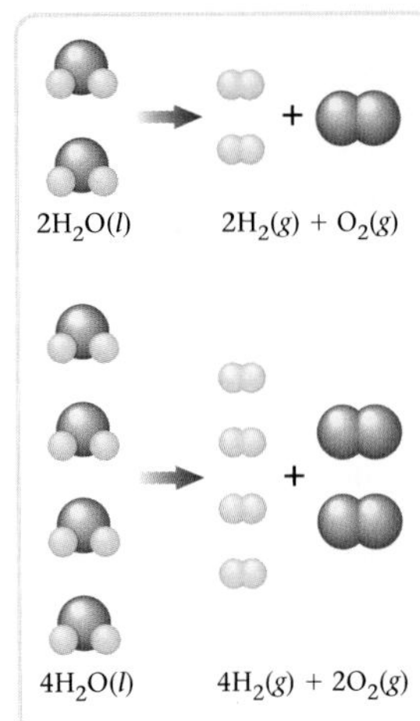

One way to answer this question is to multiply the entire equation by 2 (which will give us 4 mol H_2O).

$$2[2H_2O(l) \rightarrow 2H_2(g) + O_2(g)]$$
$$4H_2O(l) \rightarrow 4H_2(g) + 2O_2(g)$$

Now we can state that

4 mol H_2O yields 4 mol H_2 plus 2 mol O_2

which answers the question of how many moles of products we get with 4 mol H_2O.

Next, suppose we decompose 5.8 mol water. What numbers of moles of products are formed in this process? We could answer this question by rebalancing the chemical equation as follows: First, we divide *all coefficients* of the balanced equation

$$2H_2O(l) \rightarrow 2H_2(g) + O_2(g)$$

by 2, to give

$$H_2O(l) \rightarrow H_2(g) + \tfrac{1}{2}O_2(g)$$

Now, because we have 5.8 mol H_2O, we multiply this equation by 5.8.

$$5.8[H_2O(l) \rightarrow H_2(g) + \tfrac{1}{2}O_2(g)]$$

This gives

$$5.8H_2O(l) \rightarrow 5.8H_2(g) + 5.8(\tfrac{1}{2})O_2(g)$$
$$5.8H_2O(l) \rightarrow 5.8H_2(g) + 2.9O_2(g)$$

This equation with noninteger coefficients makes sense only if the equation means moles (of molecules) of the various reactants and products.

(Verify that this is a balanced equation.) Now we can state that

5.8 mol H_2O yields 5.8 mol H_2 plus 2.9 mol O_2

This procedure of rebalancing the equation to obtain the number of moles involved in a particular situation always works, but it can be cumbersome. In Example 9.2 we will develop a more convenient procedure, which uses conversion factors, or **mole ratios,** based on the balanced chemical equation.

EXAMPLE 9.2 Determining Mole Ratios

What number of moles of O_2 will be produced by the decomposition of 5.8 moles of water?

SOLUTION

Where Are We Going?

We want to determine the number of moles of O_2 produced by the decomposition of 5.8 moles of H_2O.

What Do We Know?

- The balanced equation for the decomposition of water is

$$2H_2O \rightarrow 2H_2 + O_2$$

- We start with 5.8 mol H_2O.

How Do We Get There?

Our problem can be diagrammed as follows:

5.8 mol H_2O → yields → ? mol O_2

Additional Examples

Example 9.2

Methane burns in oxygen to form carbon dioxide and water according to the balanced equation

$$CH_4(g) + 2O_2(g) \rightarrow CO_2(g) + 2H_2O(g)$$

1. What number of moles of oxygen gas is required to react with 7.4 moles of methane?

   14.8 mol $O_2(g)$

2. How many moles of carbon dioxide gas will be produced by reacting 2.6 moles of oxygen with excess methane?

   1.3 mol $CO_2(g)$

To answer this question, we need to know the relationship between moles of H_2O and moles of O_2 in the balanced equation (conventional form):

$$2H_2O(l) \rightarrow 2H_2(g) + O_2(g)$$

From this equation we can state that

2 mol H_2O —yields→ 1 mol O_2

which can be represented by the following equivalence statement:

$$2 \text{ mol } H_2O = 1 \text{ mol } O_2$$

We now want to use this equivalence statement to obtain the conversion factor (mole ratio) that we need. Because we want to go from moles of H_2O to moles of O_2, we need the mole ratio

$$\frac{1 \text{ mol } O_2}{2 \text{ mol } H_2O}$$

so that mol H_2O will cancel in the conversion from moles of H_2O to moles of O_2.

$$5.8 \cancel{\text{mol } H_2O} \times \frac{1 \text{ mol } O_2}{2 \cancel{\text{mol } H_2O}} = 2.9 \text{ mol } O_2$$

So if we decompose 5.8 mol H_2O, we will get 2.9 mol O_2.

REALITY CHECK Note that this is the same answer we obtained earlier when we rebalanced the equation to give

$$5.8H_2O(l) \rightarrow 5.8H_2(g) + 2.9O_2(g) \;\blacksquare$$

The statement 2 mol H_2O = 1 mol O_2 is obviously not true in a literal sense, but it correctly expresses the chemical equivalence between H_2O and O_2.

MATH SKILL BUILDER
For a review of equivalence statements and dimensional analysis, see Section 2.6.

We saw in Example 9.2 that to determine the moles of a product that can be formed from a specified number of moles of a reactant, we can use the balanced equation to obtain the appropriate mole ratio. We will now extend these ideas in Example 9.3.

EXAMPLE 9.3 Using Mole Ratios in Calculations

Calculate the number of moles of oxygen required to react exactly with 4.30 moles of propane, C_3H_8, in the reaction described by the following balanced equation:

$$C_3H_8(g) + 5O_2(g) \rightarrow 3CO_2(g) + 4H_2O(g)$$

SOLUTION

Where Are We Going?

We want to determine the number of moles of O_2 required to react with 4.30 mol C_3H_8.

What Do We Know?

- The balanced equation for the reaction is

$$C_3H_8 + 5O_2 \rightarrow 3CO_2 + 4H_2O$$

- We start with 4.30 mol C_3H_8.

How Do We Get There?

In this case the problem can be stated as follows:

4.30 mol C_3H_8 —requires→ ? mol O_2

Additional Examples

Example 9.3

Hydrogen sulfide gas reacts with oxygen to produce sulfur dioxide gas and water according to the balanced equation

$$2H_4S(g) + 3O_2(g) \rightarrow 2SO_2(g) + 2H_2O(l)$$

1. How many moles of oxygen gas are required to react with 5.6 moles of hydrogen sulfide?

   8.4 mol $O_2(g)$

2. How many moles of sulfur dioxide gas will be produced by reacting 7.3 moles of hydrogen sulfide with excess oxygen?

   7.3 mol $SO_2(g)$

3. How many moles of sulfur dioxide gas will be produced by reacting 7.3 moles of oxygen with excess hydrogen sulfide?

   4.9 mol $SO_2(g)$

To solve this problem, we need to consider the relationship between the reactants C_3H_8 and O_2. Using the balanced equation, we find that

$$1 \text{ mol } C_3H_8 \text{ requires } 5 \text{ mol } O_2$$

which can be represented by the equivalence statement

$$1 \text{ mol } C_3H_8 = 5 \text{ mol } O_2$$

This leads to the required mole ratio

$$\frac{5 \text{ mol } O_2}{1 \text{ mol } C_3H_8}$$

for converting from moles of C_3H_8 to moles of O_2. We construct the conversion ratio this way so that mol C_3H_8 cancels:

$$4.30 \cancel{\text{mol } C_3H_8} \times \frac{5 \text{ mol } O_2}{1 \cancel{\text{mol } C_3H_8}} = 21.5 \text{ mol } O_2$$

We can now answer the original question:

$$4.30 \text{ mol } C_3H_8 \text{ requires } 21.5 \text{ mol } O_2$$

REALITY CHECK According to the balanced equation, more O_2 is required (by mol) than C_3H_8 by a factor of 5. With about 4 mol C_3H_8, we would expect about 20 mol of O_2, which is close to our answer.

Self Check

Answer to Self-Check Exercise 9.1

12.9 mol CO_2

Test Bank: 15–48, 76, 77, 79, 84

Self-Check **EXERCISE 9.1** Calculate the moles of CO_2 formed when 4.30 moles of C_3H_8 reacts with the required 21.5 moles of O_2.

HINT: Use the moles of C_3H_8, and obtain the mole ratio between C_3H_8 and CO_2 from the balanced equation.

See Problems 9.15 and 9.16. ■

Section 9.3

TEACHING TIPS

- Remind students that conversion factors such as 44.01 g C_3H_8 = 1 mol C_3H_8 and 32.00 g O_2 = 1 mol O_2 come from the molar masses on the periodic table. We use the coefficients in the balanced equation when relating two different substances.
- Use diagrams and flow charts to help students think through these problems. Try to be consistent in your approach. Begin with the balanced equation each time and write in what is known and what is being sought.

9.3 Mass Calculations

OBJECTIVE: To learn to relate masses of reactants and products in a chemical reaction.

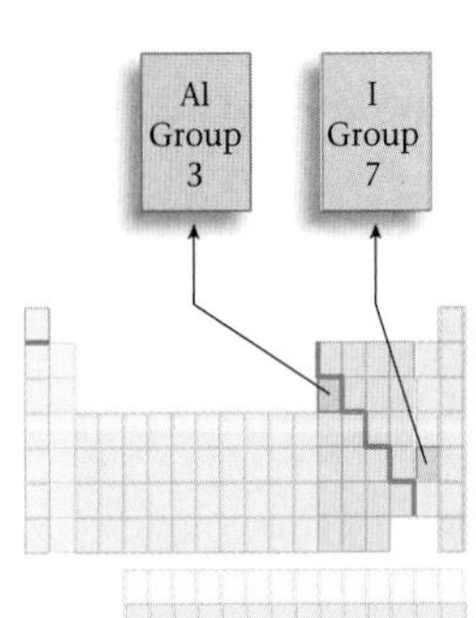

In the last section we saw how to use the balanced equation for a reaction to calculate the numbers of moles of reactants and products for a particular case. However, moles represent numbers of molecules, and we cannot count molecules directly. In chemistry we count by weighing. Therefore, in this section we will review the procedures for converting between moles and masses and will see how these procedures are applied to chemical calculations.

To develop these procedures we will consider the reaction between powdered aluminum metal and finely ground iodine to produce aluminum iodide. The balanced equation for this vigorous chemical reaction is

$$2Al(s) + 3I_2(s) \rightarrow 2AlI_3(s)$$

Suppose we have 35.0 g of aluminum. What mass of I_2 should we weigh out to react exactly with this amount of aluminum?

To answer this question, let's use the problem-solving strategy discussed in Chapter 8.

Aluminum (*left*) and iodine (*right*), shown at the top, react vigorously to form aluminum iodide. The purple cloud results from excess iodine vaporized by the heat of the reaction.

Where Are We Going?

We want to find the mass of iodine (I_2) that will react with 35.0 g of aluminum (Al). We know from the balanced equation that

$$2 \text{ mol Al requires } 3 \text{ mol } I_2$$

This can be written as the mole ratio

$$\frac{3 \text{ mol } I_2}{2 \text{ mol Al}}$$

We can use this ratio to calculate moles of I_2 needed from the moles of Al present. However, this leads us to two questions:

1. How many moles of Al are present?
2. How do we convert moles of I_2 to mass of I_2 as required by the problem?

We need to be able to convert from grams to moles and from moles to grams.

How Do We Get There?

The problem states that we have 35.0 g of aluminum, so we must convert from grams to moles of aluminum. This is something we already know how to do. Using the table of average atomic masses inside the front cover of this book, we find the atomic mass of aluminum to be 26.98. This means that 1 mole of aluminum has a mass of 26.98 g. We can use the equivalence statement

$$1 \text{ mol Al} = 26.98 \text{ g}$$

to find the moles of Al in 35.0 g.

$$35.0 \cancel{\text{g Al}} \times \frac{1 \text{ mol Al}}{26.98 \cancel{\text{g Al}}} = 1.30 \text{ mol Al}$$

Now that we have moles of Al, we can find the moles of I_2 required.

$$1.30 \cancel{\text{mol Al}} \times \frac{3 \text{ mol } I_2}{2 \cancel{\text{mol Al}}} = 1.95 \text{ mol } I_2$$

We now know the *moles* of I_2 required to react with the 1.30 moles of Al (35.0 g). The next step is to convert 1.95 moles of I_2 to grams so we will know how much to weigh out. We do this by using the molar mass of I_2. The atomic mass of iodine is 126.9 g (for 1 mole of I atoms), so the molar mass of I_2 is

$$2 \times 126.9 \text{ g/mol} = 253.8 \text{ g/mol} = \text{mass of 1 mol } I_2$$

Now we convert the 1.95 moles of I_2 to grams of I_2.

$$1.95 \cancel{\text{mol } I_2} \times \frac{253.8 \text{ g } I_2}{\cancel{\text{mol } I_2}} = 495 \text{ g } I_2$$

We have solved the problem. We need to weigh out 495 g of iodine (contains I_2 molecules) to react exactly with the 35.0 g of aluminum. We will further develop procedures for dealing with masses of reactants and products in Example 9.4.

REALITY CHECK We have determined that 495 g of I_2 is required to react with 35.0 g Al. Does this answer make sense? We know from the

LABORATORY EXPERIMENT

A relevant laboratory experiment for this section is Experiment 16, Stoichiometry of Magnesium Oxide, from *Introductory Chemistry in the Laboratory* by James Hall.

9.3 Mass Calculations 255

molar masses of Al and I_2 (26.98 g/mol and 253.8 g/mol) that the mass of 1 mol I_2 is almost 10 times as great as that of 1 mol Al. We also know that we need a greater number of moles of I_2 compared with Al (by a 3:2 ratio). So, we should expect to get a mass of I_2 that is well over 10 times as great as 35.0 g, and we did.

Additional Examples

Example 9.4

Solutions of sodium hydroxide absorb carbon dioxide from the air, forming sodium carbonate according to the balanced equation

$$2NaOH(aq) + CO_2(g) \rightarrow Na_2CO_3(g) + H_2O(l)$$

1. Calculate the mass of carbon dioxide gas that is required to react with a solution containing 10.0 g of sodium hydroxide.

   5.50 g $CO_2(g)$

2. Calculate the mass of sodium carbonate that is produced when 10.0 g of sodium hydroxide reacts with an excess of carbon dioxide.

   13.2 g $Na_2CO_3(g)$

EXAMPLE 9.4 Using Mass–Mole Conversions with Mole Ratios

Propane, C_3H_8, when used as a fuel, reacts with oxygen to produce carbon dioxide and water according to the following unbalanced equation:

$$C_3H_8(g) + O_2(g) \rightarrow CO_2(g) + H_2O(g)$$

What mass of oxygen will be required to react exactly with 96.1 g of propane?

SOLUTION

Where Are We Going?

We want to determine the mass of O_2 required to react exactly with 96.1 g C_3H_8.

What Do We Know?

- The unbalanced equation for the reaction is

$$C_3H_8 + O_2 \rightarrow CO_2 + H_2O.$$

- We start with 96.1 g mol C_3H_8.
- We know the atomic masses of carbon, hydrogen, and oxygen from the periodic table.

What Do We Need To Know?

- We need to know the balanced equation.
- We need the molar masses of O_2 and C_3H_8.

How Do We Get There?

Always balance the equation for the reaction first.

To deal with the amounts of reactants and products, we first need the balanced equation for this reaction:

$$C_3H_8(g) + 5O_2(g) \rightarrow 3CO_2(g) + 4H_2O(g)$$

Our problem, in schematic form, is

96.1 g propane	requires	? grams O_2

MATH SKILL BUILDER
Remember that to show the correct significant figures in each step, we are rounding off after each calculation. In doing problems, you should carry extra numbers, rounding off only at the end.

Using the ideas we developed when we discussed the aluminum–iodine reaction, we will proceed as follows:

1. We are given the number of grams of propane, so we must convert to moles of propane (C_3H_8).
2. Then we can use the coefficients in the balanced equation to determine the moles of oxygen (O_2) required.
3. Finally, we will use the molar mass of O_2 to calculate grams of oxygen.

We can sketch this strategy as follows:

$$C_3H_8(g) \quad + \quad 5O_2(g) \quad \rightarrow \quad 3CO_2(g) \quad + \quad 4H_2O(g)$$

96.1 g C_3H_8 → (1) → ? moles C_3H_8 → (2) → ? moles O_2 → (3) → ? grams O_2

Thus the first question we must answer is, *How many moles of propane are present in 96.1 g of propane?* The molar mass of propane is 44.09 g ($3 \times 12.01 + 8 \times 1.008$). The moles of propane present can be calculated as follows:

$$96.1\ \cancel{g\ C_3H_8} \times \frac{1\ \text{mol}\ C_3H_8}{44.09\ \cancel{g\ C_3H_8}} = 2.18\ \text{mol}\ C_3H_8$$

Next we recognize that each mole of propane reacts with 5 mol of oxygen. This gives us the equivalence statement

$$1\ \text{mol}\ C_3H_8 = 5\ \text{mol}\ O_2$$

from which we construct the mole ratio

$$\frac{5\ \text{mol}\ O_2}{1\ \text{mol}\ C_3H_8}$$

that we need to convert from moles of propane molecules to moles of oxygen molecules.

$$2.18\ \cancel{\text{mol}\ C_3H_8} \times \frac{5\ \text{mol}\ O_2}{1\ \cancel{\text{mol}\ C_3H_8}} = 10.9\ \text{mol}\ O_2$$

Notice that the mole ratio is set up so that the moles of C_3H_8 cancel and the resulting units are moles of O_2.

Because the original question asked for the *mass* of oxygen needed to react with 96.1 g of propane, we must convert the 10.9 mol O_2 to grams, using the molar mass of O_2 ($32.00 = 2 \times 16.00$).

$$10.9\ \cancel{\text{mol}\ O_2} \times \frac{32.0\ g\ O_2}{1\ \cancel{\text{mol}\ O_2}} = 349\ g\ O_2$$

Therefore, 349 g of oxygen is required to burn 96.1 g of propane. We can summarize this problem by writing out a "conversion string" that shows how the problem was done.

$$96.1\ \cancel{g\ C_3H_8} \overset{1}{\times} \frac{1\ \cancel{\text{mol}\ C_3H_8}}{44.09\ \cancel{g\ C_3H_8}} \overset{2}{\times} \frac{5\ \cancel{\text{mol}\ O_2}}{1\ \cancel{\text{mol}\ C_3H_8}} \overset{3}{\times} \frac{32.0\ g\ O_2}{1\ \cancel{\text{mol}\ O_2}} = 349\ g\ O_2$$

MATH SKILL BUILDER
Use units as a check to see that you have used the correct conversion factors (mole ratios).

This is a convenient way to make sure the final units are correct. The procedure we have followed is summarized below.

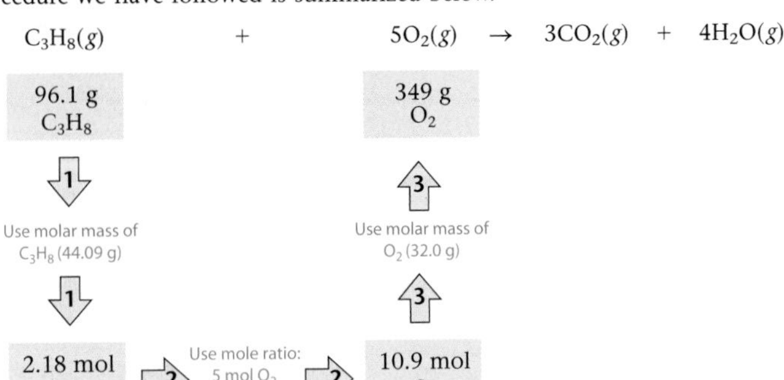

REALITY CHECK According to the balanced equation, more O_2 is required (by moles) than C_3H_8 by a factor of 5. Because the molar mass of C_3H_8 is not much greater than that of O_2, we should expect that a greater mass of oxygen is required, and our answer confirms this.

Self Check

Answer to Self-Check Exercise 9.2

132 g CO_2

Self-Check **EXERCISE 9.2** What mass of carbon dioxide is produced when 96.1 g of propane reacts with sufficient oxygen?

See Problems 9.23 through 9.26. ■

Self Check

Answer to Self-Check Exercise 9.3

72.1 g H_2O

Self-Check **EXERCISE 9.3** Calculate the mass of water formed by the complete reaction of 96.1 g of propane with oxygen.

See Problems 9.23 through 9.26. ■

So far in this chapter, we have spent considerable time "thinking through" the procedures for calculating the masses of reactants and products in chemical reactions. We can summarize these procedures in the following steps:

Steps for Calculating the Masses of Reactants and Products in Chemical Reactions

Step 1 Balance the equation for the reaction.

Step 2 Convert the masses of reactants or products to moles.

Step 3 Use the balanced equation to set up the appropriate mole ratio(s).

Step 4 Use the mole ratio(s) to calculate the number of moles of the desired reactant or product.

Step 5 Convert from moles back to masses.

The process of using a chemical equation to calculate the relative masses of reactants and products involved in a reaction is called **stoichiometry** (pronounced stoi´ kē-ŏm´ i-trē). Chemists say that the balanced equation for a chemical reaction describes the stoichiometry of the reaction.

We will now consider a few more examples that involve chemical stoichiometry. Because real-world examples often involve very large or very small masses of chemicals that are most conveniently expressed by using scientific notation, we will deal with such a case in Example 9.5.

EXAMPLE 9.5 Stoichiometric Calculations: Using Scientific Notation

For a review of writing formulas of ionic compounds, see Chapter 5.

Solid lithium hydroxide has been used in space vehicles to remove exhaled carbon dioxide from the living environment. The products are solid lithium carbonate and liquid water. What mass of gaseous carbon dioxide can 1.00×10^3 g of lithium hydroxide absorb?

SOLUTION

Where Are We Going?

We want to determine the mass of carbon dioxide absorbed by 1.00×10^3 g of lithium hydroxide.

What Do We Know?

- The names of the reactants and products.
- We start with 1.00×10^3 g of lithium hydroxide.
- We can obtain the atomic masses from the periodic table.

What Do We Need To Know?

- We need to know the balanced equation for the reaction, but we first have to write the formulas for the reactants and products.
- We need the molar masses of lithium hydroxide and carbon dioxide.

Astronaut Sidney M. Gutierrez changes the lithium hydroxide canisters on space shuttle *Columbia*.

NASA

How Do We Get There?

Step 1 Using the description of the reaction, we can write the unbalanced equation

$$LiOH(s) + CO_2(g) \rightarrow Li_2CO_3(s) + H_2O(l)$$

The balanced equation is

$$2LiOH(s) + CO_2(g) \rightarrow Li_2CO_3(s) + H_2O(l)$$

Check this for yourself.

Step 2 We convert the given mass of LiOH to moles, using the molar mass of LiOH, which is 6.941 g + 16.00 g + 1.008 g = 23.95 g.

$$1.00 \times 10^3 \text{ g LiOH} \times \frac{1 \text{ mol LiOH}}{23.95 \text{ g LiOH}} = 41.8 \text{ mol LiOH}$$

Step 3 The appropriate mole ratio is

$$\frac{1 \text{ mol } CO_2}{2 \text{ mol LiOH}}$$

Additional Examples

Example 9.5

Thionyl chloride, which is used as a drying agent in many synthetic chemistry experiments, reacts with water to form sulfur dioxide gas and hydrogen chloride gas:

$$SOCl_2(l) + H_2O(l) \rightarrow SO_2(g) + 2HCl(g)$$

1. Calculate the mass of water consumed by the complete reaction of 3.50×10^2 g of thionyl chloride.

   53.0 g $H_2O(l)$

2. Calculate the mass of hydrogen chloride produced by the complete reaction of 3.50×10^2 g of thionyl chloride.

   2.14×10^2 g $HCl(g)$

DEMONSTRATION

The reaction between baking soda and an acid is a quick, fun demonstration to illustrate a neutralization reaction. Use a 2-L soda bottle with a stopper to fit. Wrap a teaspoon of baking soda in a tissue in a cigar shape with the ends twisted closed. Make the "cigar" thin enough to fit through the opening in the soda bottle. Place 100 mL of vinegar in the soda bottle before the demonstration. When you are ready to do the demo, stuff the "cigar" into the bottle and stopper it. Shake gently to mix and don't aim at any people. The stopper should shoot across the room. You might then discuss the resulting reaction:

$$NaHCO_3(s) + HC_2H_3O_2(aq) \rightarrow NaC_2H_3O_2(aq) + H_2O(l) + CO_2(g)$$

You can also discuss what might happen to the carbon dioxide gas if this were to occur in the stomach.

Step 4 Using this mole ratio, we calculate the moles of CO_2 needed to react with the given mass of LiOH.

$$41.8 \text{ mol LiOH} \times \frac{1 \text{ mol } CO_2}{2 \text{ mol LiOH}} = 20.9 \text{ mol } CO_2$$

Step 5 We calculate the mass of CO_2 by using its molar mass (44.01 g).

$$20.9 \text{ mol } CO_2 \times \frac{44.01 \text{ g } CO_2}{1 \text{ mol } CO_2} = 920. \text{ g } CO_2 = 9.20 \times 10^2 \text{ g } CO_2$$

Thus 1.00×10^3 g of LiOH(s) can absorb 920. g of $CO_2(g)$.

We can summarize this problem as follows:

$$2LiOH(s) \quad + \quad CO_2(g) \rightarrow Li_2CO_3(s) + H_2O(l)$$

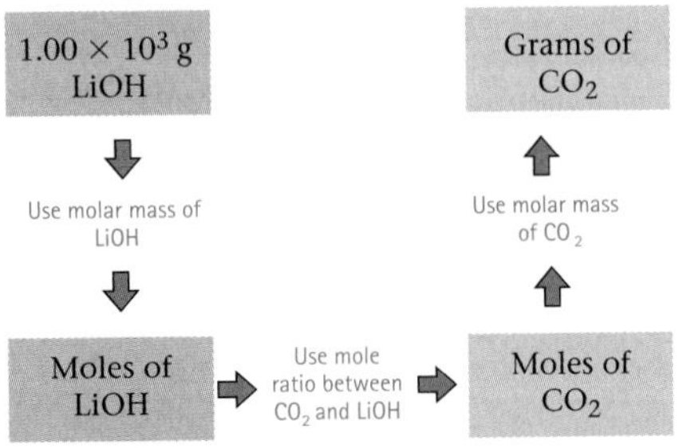

1.00×10^3 g LiOH → (Use molar mass of LiOH) → Moles of LiOH → (Use mole ratio between CO_2 and LiOH) → Moles of CO_2 → (Use molar mass of CO_2) → Grams of CO_2

The conversion string is

$$1.00 \times 10^3 \text{ g LiOH} \times \frac{1 \text{ mol LiOH}}{23.95 \text{ g LiOH}} \times \frac{1 \text{ mol } CO_2}{2 \text{ mol LiOH}} \times \frac{44.01 \text{ g } CO_2}{1 \text{ mol } CO_2} = 9.19 \times 10^2 \text{ g } CO_2$$

MATH SKILL BUILDER
Carrying extra significant figures and rounding off only at the end gives an answer of 919 g CO_2.

REALITY CHECK According to the balanced equation, there is a 2:1 mole ratio of LiOH to CO_2. There is about a 1:2 molar mass ratio of LiOH:CO_2 (23.95:44.01). We should expect about the same mass of CO_2 as LiOH, and our answer confirms this (1000 g compared to 920 g).

Self Check

Answers to Self-Check Exercise 9.4

a. 7.56 g HF

b. 3.41 g H_2O

Self-Check **EXERCISE 9.4** Hydrofluoric acid, an aqueous solution containing dissolved hydrogen fluoride, is used to etch glass by reacting with the silica, SiO_2, in the glass to produce gaseous silicon tetrafluoride and liquid water. The unbalanced equation is

$$HF(aq) + SiO_2(s) \rightarrow SiF_4(g) + H_2O(l)$$

a. Calculate the mass of hydrogen fluoride needed to react with 5.68 g of silica. *Hint:* Think carefully about this problem. What is the balanced equation for the reaction? What is given? What do you need to calculate? Sketch a map of the problem before you do the calculations.

b. Calculate the mass of water produced in the reaction described in part a.

See Problems 9.23 through 9.26. ■

EXAMPLE 9.6 Stoichiometric Calculations: Comparing Two Reactions

Baking soda, $NaHCO_3$, is often used as an antacid. It neutralizes excess hydrochloric acid secreted by the stomach. The balanced equation for the reaction is

$$NaHCO_3(s) + HCl(aq) \rightarrow NaCl(aq) + H_2O(l) + CO_2(g)$$

Milk of magnesia, which is an aqueous suspension of magnesium hydroxide, $Mg(OH)_2$, is also used as an antacid. The balanced equation for the reaction is

$$Mg(OH)_2(s) + 2HCl(aq) \rightarrow 2H_2O(l) + MgCl_2(aq)$$

Which antacid can consume the most stomach acid, 1.00 g of $NaHCO_3$ or 1.00 g of $Mg(OH)_2$?

SOLUTION

Where Are We Going?

We want to compare the neutralizing power of two antacids, $NaHCO_3$ and $Mg(OH)_2$. In other words, how many moles of HCl will react with 1.00 g of each antacid?

What Do We Know?

- The balanced equations for the reactions.
- We start with 1.00 g each of $NaHCO_3$ and $Mg(OH)_2$.
- We can obtain atomic masses from the periodic table.

What Do We Need to Know?

- We need the molar masses of $NaHCO_3$ and $Mg(OH)_2$.

How Do We Get There?

The antacid that reacts with the larger number of moles of HCl is more effective because it will neutralize more moles of acid. A schematic for this procedure is

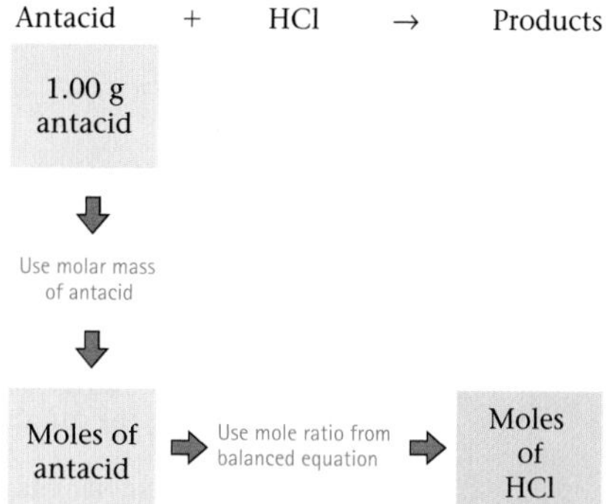

Notice that in this case we do not need to calculate how many grams of HCl react; we can answer the question with moles of HCl. We will now solve this problem for each antacid. Both of the equations are balanced, so we can proceed with the calculations.

Using the molar mass of $NaHCO_3$, which is 22.99 g + 1.008 g + 12.01 g + 3(16.00 g) = 84.01 g, we determine the moles of $NaHCO_3$ in 1.00 g of $NaHCO_3$.

Additional Examples

Example 9.6

Which of the following results in a greater mass of product?

1.00 g of hydrogen gas reacting with an excess of oxygen gas to produce water

or

1.00 g of hydrogen gas reacting with an excess of nitrogen gas to produce ammonia (NH_3)

8.94 g of water is produced, compared with 5.63 g of ammonia.

PowerLecture Video: Reaction: Antacid Tablet in Water

CHEMISTRY *IN* FOCUS

Cars of the Future

There is a great deal of concern about how we are going to sustain our personal transportation system in the face of looming petroleum shortages (and the resultant high costs) and the challenges of global warming. The era of large gasoline-powered cars as the primary means of transportation in the United States seems to be drawing to a close. The fact that discoveries of petroleum are not keeping up with the rapidly increasing global demand for oil has caused skyrocketing prices. In addition, the combustion of gasoline produces carbon dioxide (about 1 lb of CO_2 per mile for many cars), which has been implicated in global warming.

So what will the car of the future in the United States be like? It seems that we are moving rapidly toward cars that have an electrical component as part of the power train. Hybrid cars, which use a small gasoline motor in conjunction with a powerful battery, have been quite successful. By supplementing the small gasoline engine, which would be inadequate by itself, with power from the battery, the typical hybrid gets 40 to 50 miles per gallon of gasoline. In this type of hybrid car, both the battery and the engine are used to power the wheels of the car as needed.

Another type of system that involves both a gasoline engine and a battery is the so-called "plug-in hybrid." In this car, the battery is the sole source of power to the car's wheels. The gasoline engine is only used to charge the battery as needed. One example of this type of car is the Chevrolet Volt, which is slated for production in 2010. The Volt is being designed to run about 40 miles on each battery charge. The car would be plugged into a normal household electric outlet overnight to recharge the battery. For trips longer than 40 miles, the gasoline engine would turn on to charge the battery.

Another type of "electrical car" being tested is one powered by a hydrogen–oxygen fuel cell. An example of such a car is the Honda FCX Clarity. The Clarity stores hydrogen in a tank that holds 4.1 kg of H_2 at a pressure of 5000 lb per square inch. The H_2 is sent to a fuel cell, where it reacts with oxygen from the air supplied by an air compressor. About 200 of these cars are going to be tested in Southern Califor-

$$1.00\ \text{g NaHCO}_3 \times \frac{1\ \text{mol NaHCO}_3}{84.01\ \text{g NaHCO}_3} = 0.0119\ \text{mol NaHCO}_3$$

$$= 1.19 \times 10^{-2}\ \text{mol NaHCO}_3$$

Next we determine the moles of HCl, using the mole ratio $\frac{1\ \text{mol HCl}}{1\ \text{mol NaHCO}_3}$.

$$1.19 \times 10^{-2}\ \text{mol NaHCO}_3 \times \frac{1\ \text{mol HCl}}{1\ \text{mol NaHCO}_3} = 1.19 \times 10^{-2}\ \text{mol HCl}$$

Thus 1.00 g of $NaHCO_3$ neutralizes 1.19×10^{-2} mol HCl. We need to compare this to the number of moles of HCl that 1.00 g of $Mg(OH)_2$ neutralizes.

Using the molar mass of $Mg(OH)_2$, which is 24.31 g + 2(16.00 g) + 2(1.008 g) = 58.33 g, we determine the moles of $Mg(OH)_2$ in 1.00 g of $Mg(OH)_2$.

$$1.00\ \text{g Mg(OH)}_2 \times \frac{1\ \text{mol Mg(OH)}_2}{58.33\ \text{g Mg(OH)}_2} = 0.0171\ \text{mol Mg(OH)}_2$$

$$= 1.71 \times 10^{-2}\ \text{mol Mg(OH)}_2$$

262

nia in the next 3 years, leased to people who live near one of the three 24-hour public hydrogen stations. The Clarity gets about 72 miles per kilogram of hydrogen. One obvious advantage of a car powered by an H_2/O_2 fuel cell is that the combustion product is only H_2O. However, there is a catch (it seems there is always a catch). Currently, 95% of hydrogen produced is obtained by natural gas (CH_4), and CO_2 is a by-product of this process. Intense research is now being conducted to find economically feasible ways to produce H_2 from water.

It appears that our cars of the future will have an electrical drive component. Whether it will involve a conventional battery or a fuel cell will depend on technological developments and costs.

Horizon Fuel Cell Technologies Pte. Ltd.

Even model cars are becoming "green." The H-racer from Horizon Fuel Cell Technologies uses a hydrogen–oxygen fuel cell.

Courtesy Honda Motors USA

The Honda FCX Clarity is powered by a hydrogen–oxygen fuel cell.

To determine the moles of HCl that react with this amount of $Mg(OH)_2$, we use the mole ratio $\frac{2 \text{ mol HCl}}{1 \text{ mol Mg(OH)}_2}$.

$$1.71 \times 10^{-2} \cancel{\text{mol Mg(OH)}_2} \times \frac{2 \text{ mol HCl}}{1 \cancel{\text{mol Mg(OH)}_2}} = 3.42 \times 10^{-2} \text{ mol HCl}$$

Therefore, 1.00 g of $Mg(OH)_2$ neutralizes 3.42×10^{-2} mol HCl. We have already calculated that 1.00 g of $NaHCO_3$ neutralizes only 1.19×10^{-2} mol HCl. Therefore, $Mg(OH)_2$ is a more effective antacid than $NaHCO_3$ on a mass basis.

Self-Check **EXERCISE 9.5** In Example 9.6 we answered one of the questions we posed in the introduction to this chapter. Now let's see if you can answer the other question posed there. Determine what mass of carbon monoxide and what mass of hydrogen are required to form 6.0 kg of methanol by the reaction

$$CO(g) + 2H_2(g) \rightarrow CH_3OH(l)$$

See Problem 9.39. ■

Self Check

Answers to Self-Check Exercise 9.5

5.3×10^3 g CO
7.7×10^2 g H_2

Section 9.4

TEACHING TIPS

- It is useful to use a real-life example when introducing limiting reactants. Students seem to relate easily to kitchen experiences yet have difficulty applying the same concepts to chemical equations. By working with real-life experiences first and addressing the concepts in this context, students have an opportunity to become comfortable with the concept before applying it to an unfamiliar setting.
- Using a concrete analogy helps students better understand calculations, especially with problems involving a limiting reactant. Problems in which a reactant is limiting are conceptually the same as the cases in which no reactant is limiting. However, students seem to have much more difficulty dealing with limiting reactants. For example, some will calculate the amount of product that could be made from each reactant and then add them. Or, they may add the moles of each given reactant for the total. They almost never make these types of mistakes in the analogies, though, so it is helpful to be very explicit about these points.
- Use molecular diagrams like those shown in the text to make counting molecules more concrete (and similar to real-life experience).

9.4 The Concept of Limiting Reactants

OBJECTIVE: To understand what is meant by the term "limiting reactant."

Earlier in this chapter, we discussed making sandwiches. Recall that the sandwich-making process could be described as follows:

$$2 \text{ pieces bread} + 3 \text{ slices meat} + 1 \text{ slice cheese} \rightarrow 1 \text{ sandwich}$$

In our earlier discussion, we always purchased the ingredients in the correct ratios so that we used all the components, with nothing left over.

Now assume that you came to work one day and found the following quantities of ingredients:

20 slices of bread
24 slices of meat
12 slices of cheese

How many sandwiches can you make? What will be left over?

To solve this problem, let's see how many sandwiches we can make with each component.

Bread: $$20 \text{ slices bread} \times \frac{1 \text{ sandwich}}{2 \text{ slices of bread}} = 10 \text{ sandwiches}$$

Meat: $$24 \text{ slices meat} \times \frac{1 \text{ sandwich}}{3 \text{ slices of meat}} = 8 \text{ sandwiches}$$

Cheese: $$12 \text{ slices cheese} \times \frac{1 \text{ sandwich}}{1 \text{ slice of cheese}} = 12 \text{ sandwiches}$$

How many sandwiches can you make? The answer is 8. When you run out of meat, you must stop making sandwiches. The meat is the limiting ingredient.

What do you have left over? Making 8 sandwiches requires 16 pieces of bread. You started with 20 pieces, so you have 4 pieces of bread left. You also used 8 pieces of cheese for the 8 sandwiches, so you have $12 - 8 = 4$ pieces of cheese left.

In this example, the ingredient present in the largest number (the meat) was actually the component that limited the number of sandwiches you could make. This situation arose because each sandwich required 3 slices of meat—more than the quantity required of any other ingredient.

You probably have been dealing with limiting-reactant problems for most of your life. For example, suppose a lemonade recipe calls for 1 cup of sugar for every 6 lemons. You have 12 lemons and 3 cups of sugar. Which ingredient is limiting, the lemons or the sugar?*

A Closer Look

go Chemistry **Module 8a: Stoichiometry and Limiting Reactants (Pt. 1)** covers concepts in this section.

When molecules react with each other to form products, considerations very similar to those involved in making sandwiches arise. We can illustrate these ideas with the reaction of $N_2(g)$ and $H_2(g)$ to form $NH_3(g)$:

$$N_2(g) + 3H_2(g) \rightarrow 2NH_3(g)$$

*The ratio of lemons to sugar that the recipe calls for is 6 lemons to 1 cup of sugar. We can calculate the number of lemons required to "react with" the 3 cups of sugar as follows:

$$3 \text{ cups sugar} \times \frac{6 \text{ lemons}}{1 \text{ cup sugar}} = 18 \text{ lemons}$$

Thus 18 lemons would be required to use up 3 cups of sugar. However, we have only 12 lemons, so the lemons are limiting.

PowerLecture Video: Reaction: Burning of Methanol

PowerLecture Videos: Reaction: Limiting Reagent Demonstration with Zn + HCl Limiting Reactant

Consider the following container of $N_2(g)$ and $H_2(g)$:

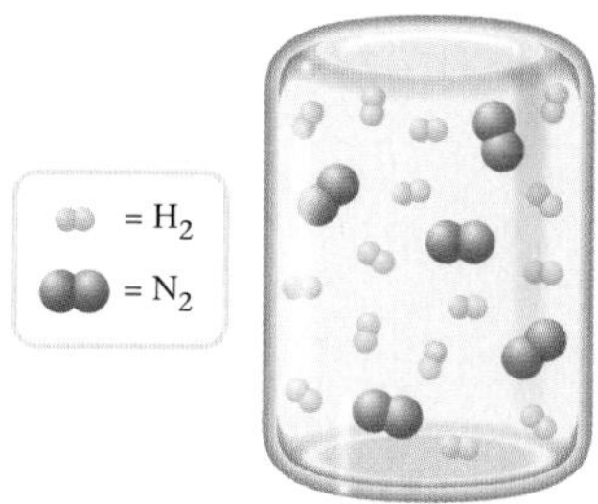

What will this container look like if the reaction between N_2 and H_2 proceeds to completion? To answer this question, you need to remember that each N_2 requires 3 H_2 molecules to form 2 NH_3. To make things more clear, we will circle groups of reactants:

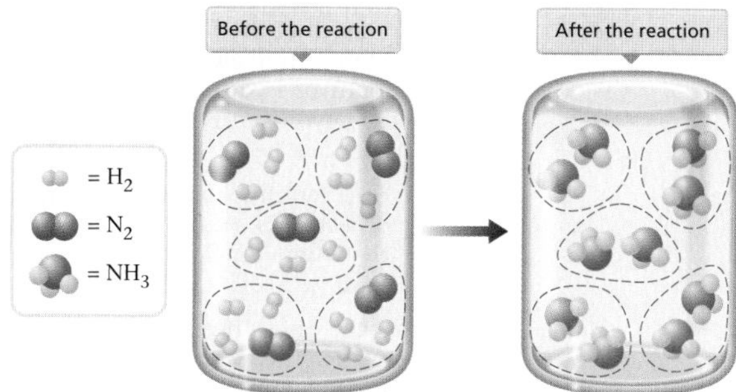

In this case, the mixture of N_2 and H_2 contained just the number of molecules needed to form NH_3 with nothing left over. That is, the ratio of the number of H_2 molecules to N_2 molecules was

$$\frac{15\ H_2}{5\ N_2} = \frac{3\ H_2}{1\ N_2}$$

This ratio exactly matches the numbers in the balanced equation

$$3H_2(g) + N_2(g) \rightarrow 2NH_3(g).$$

This type of mixture is called a *stoichiometric mixture*—one that contains the relative amounts of reactants that matches the numbers in the balanced equation. In this case, all reactants will be consumed to form products.

Now consider another container of $N_2(g)$ and $H_2(g)$:

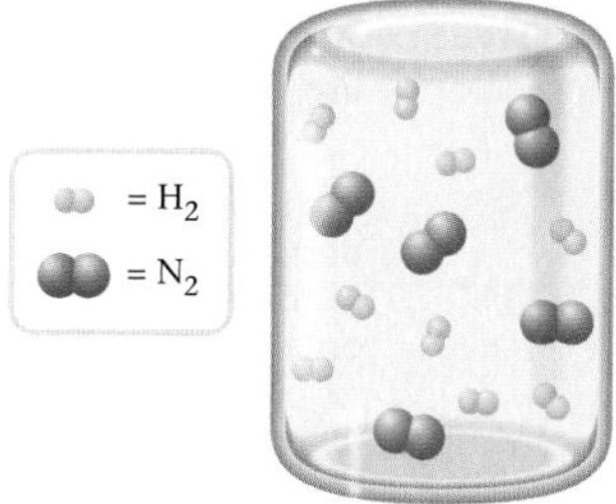

9.4 The Concept of Limiting Reactants 265

What will the container look like if the reaction between $N_2(g)$ and $H_2(g)$ proceeds to completion? Remember that each N_2 requires 3 H_2. Circling groups of reactants, we have

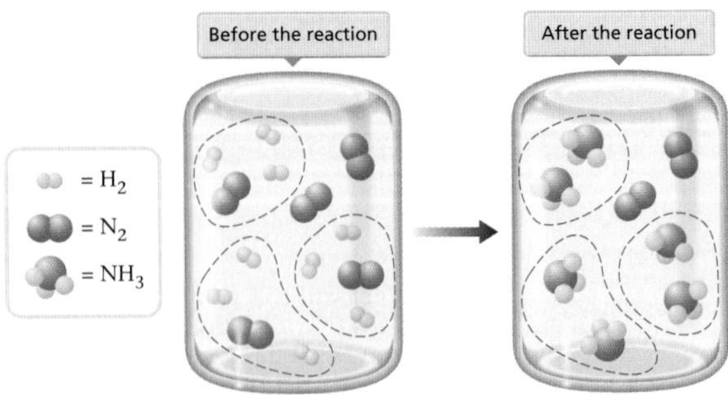

In this case, the hydrogen (H_2) is limiting. That is, the H_2 molecules are used up before all of the N_2 molecules are consumed. In this situation, the amount of hydrogen limits the amount of product (ammonia) that can form—hydrogen is the limiting reactant. Some N_2 molecules are left over in this case because the reaction runs out of H_2 molecules first.

To determine how much product can be formed from a given mixture of reactants, we have to look for the reactant that is limiting—the one that runs out first and thus limits the amount of product that can form.

In some cases, the mixture of reactants might be stoichiometric—that is, all reactants run out at the same time. In general, however, you cannot assume that a given mixture of reactants is a stoichiometric mixture, so you must determine whether one of the reactants is limiting.

Test Bank: 15, 49–69, 71, 80, 81, 85–93

The reactant that runs out first and thus limits the amounts of products that can form is called the **limiting reactant (limiting reagent).**

Lecture Demonstration: 3.4, 3.6

To this point, we have considered examples where the numbers of reactant molecules could be counted. In "real life" you can't count the molecules directly—you can't see them, and, even if you could, there would be far too many to count. Instead, you must count by weighing. We must therefore explore how to find the limiting reactant, given the masses of the reactants.

Section 9.5

PowerLecture Simulation: Limiting Reactants

9.5 Calculations Involving a Limiting Reactant

OBJECTIVES: To learn to recognize the limiting reactant in a reaction. • To learn to use the limiting reactant to do stoichiometric calculations.

LABORATORY EXPERIMENT

A relevant laboratory experiment for this section is Experiment 15, Stoichiometry and the Limiting Reactant, from *Introductory Chemistry in the Laboratory* by James Hall.

Manufacturers of cars, bicycles, and appliances order parts in the same proportion as they are used in their products. For example, auto manufacturers order four times as many wheels as engines and bicycle manufacturers order twice as many pedals as seats. Likewise, when chemicals are mixed together so that they can undergo a reaction, they are often mixed in stoichiometric quantities—that is, in exactly the correct amounts so that all

AP photo/Kevin Rivoli

Farmer Rodney Donala looks out over his corn fields in front of his 30,000-gallon tank (at right) of anhydrous ammonia, a liquid fertilizer.

reactants "run out" (are used up) at the same time. To clarify this concept, we will consider the production of hydrogen for use in the manufacture of ammonia. Ammonia, a very important fertilizer itself and a starting material for other fertilizers, is made by combining nitrogen from the air with hydrogen. The hydrogen for this process is produced by the reaction of methane with water according to the balanced equation

$$CH_4(g) + H_2O(g) \rightarrow 3H_2(g) + CO(g)$$

Let's consider the question, *What mass of water is required to react exactly with 249 g of methane?* That is, how much water will just use up all of the 249 g of methane, leaving no methane or water remaining?

This problem requires the same strategies we developed in the previous section. Again, drawing a map of the problem is helpful.

$$CH_4(g) + H_2O(g) \rightarrow 3H_2(g) + CO(g)$$

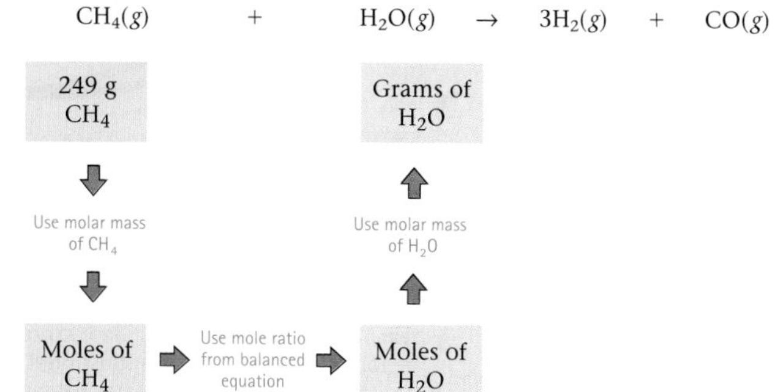

Module 8b: Stoichiometry and Limiting Reactants (Pt. 2) covers concepts in this section.

We first convert the mass of CH_4 to moles, using the molar mass of CH_4 (16.04 g/mol).

$$249 \text{ g } \cancel{CH_4} \times \frac{1 \text{ mol } CH_4}{16.04 \text{ g } \cancel{CH_4}} = 15.5 \text{ mol } CH_4$$

Because in the balanced equation 1 mol CH_4 reacts with 1 mol H_2O, we have

$$15.5 \cancel{\text{mol } CH_4} \times \frac{1 \text{ mol } H_2O}{1 \cancel{\text{mol } CH_4}} = 15.5 \text{ mol } H_2O$$

Therefore, 15.5 mol H_2O will react exactly with the given mass of CH_4. Converting 15.5 mol H_2O to grams of H_2O (molar mass = 18.02 g/mol) gives

$$15.5 \cancel{\text{mol } H_2O} \times \frac{18.02 \text{ g } H_2O}{1 \cancel{\text{mol } H_2O}} = 279 \text{ g } H_2O$$

This result means that if 249 g of methane is mixed with 279 g of water, both reactants will "run out" at the same time. The reactants have been mixed in stoichiometric quantities.

If, on the other hand, 249 g of methane is mixed with 300 g of water, the methane will be consumed before the water runs out. The water will be in *excess*. In this case, the quantity of products formed will be determined by the quantity of methane present. Once the methane is consumed, no more products can be formed, even though some water still remains. In this situation, the amount of methane *limits* the amount of products that can be formed. Recall from Section 9.4 that we call such a reactant the limiting reactant or the limiting reagent. In any stoichiometry problem where reactants

The reactant that is consumed first limits the amounts of products that can form.

TEACHING TIP

Consider beginning your discussion of this section by using several examples that include simple equations and starting with moles, not masses. A good example for beginning the discussion is

$$2Na + Cl_2 \rightarrow 2NaCl$$

Have students consider what occurs if we add 2 mol Na to 1 mol Cl_2. The result is 0 mol Na, 0 mol Cl_2, and 2 mol NaCl. Next ask what will result from mixing 0.5 mol Cl_2 and 2 mol Na. Students must now consider the limit that the 0.5 mol Cl_2 places on the system. They should find that the result would now be 1 mol NaCl, 0 mol Cl_2, and 1 mol Na. Once this idea is clear, move on to solving problems with more complex equations or beginning with masses.

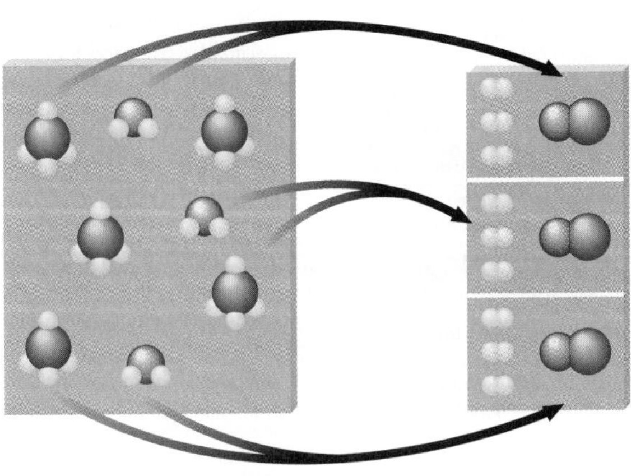

Figure 9.1

A mixture of $5CH_4$ and $3H_2O$ molecules undergoes the reaction $CH_4(g) + H_2O(g) \rightarrow 3H_2(g) + CO(g)$. Note that the H_2O molecules are used up first, leaving two CH_4 molecules unreacted.

are not mixed in stoichiometric quantities, it is essential to determine which reactant is limiting to calculate correctly the amounts of products that will be formed. This concept is illustrated in Figure 9.1. Note from this figure that because there are fewer water molecules than CH_4 molecules, the water is consumed first. After the water molecules are gone, no more products can form. So in this case water is the limiting reactant.

EXAMPLE 9.7 Stoichiometric Calculations: Identifying the Limiting Reactant

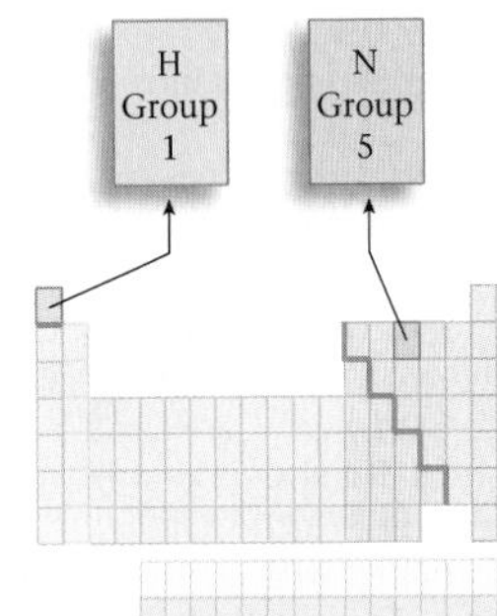

Suppose 25.0 kg (2.50×10^4 g) of nitrogen gas and 5.00 kg (5.00×10^3 g) of hydrogen gas are mixed and reacted to form ammonia. Calculate the mass of ammonia produced when this reaction is run to completion.

SOLUTION

Where Are We Going?

We want to determine the mass of ammonia produced given the masses of both reactants.

What Do We Know?

- The names of the reactants and products.
- We start with 2.50×10^4 g of nitrogen gas and 5.00×10^3 g of hydrogen gas.
- We can obtain the atomic masses from the periodic table.

What Do We Need To Know?

- We need to know the balanced equation for the reaction, but we first have to write the formulas for the reactants and products.
- We need the molar masses of nitrogen gas, hydrogen gas, and ammonia.
- We need to determine the limiting reactant.

PROBLEM-SOLVING TIP

Another way of presenting a limiting reactant problem is shown here.

Sulfur and oxygen react to form sulfur trioxide: $2S + 3O_2 \rightarrow 2SO_3$. Calculate the number of moles of SO_3 formed when 6.0 moles of each reactant is present initially and the reaction goes to completion.

Set up a table that includes all of the known information.

	$2S$	$+\ 3O_2$	$\rightarrow 2SO_3$
Initial	6	6	0
Change	−?	−?	+?
End	?	?	?

Six moles of each reactant (and no product) is shown in the "initial" row. The "change" row shows the change in moles for each chemical. The "end" row shows the final reaction mixture.

Since the reaction is complete, one (or possibly both) of the end values for sulfur or oxygen must be zero. But which one? We can decide by realizing a crucial point: *the ratio of the numbers in the "change" row must be the same as the ratio of the coefficients in the balanced equation.* Consider the two possibilities:

	$2S$	$+\ 3O_2$	$\rightarrow 2SO_3$
Initial	6	6	0
Change	−6	−9	+6
End	0	−3	6

	$2S$	$+\ 3O_2$	$\rightarrow 2SO_3$
Initial	6	6	0
Change	−4	−6	+4
End	2	0	4

In the first table, we assume all of the sulfur reacts. In the second table, we assume all of the oxygen is consumed. We can see why sulfur is not limiting by looking at the first table—we need 3 more moles of oxygen than we have. These tables give us all the needed information: which reactant is limiting, how much of the excess reactant is left over, and how much product is formed.

DEMONSTRATION

Limiting Reactants

Materials Five test tubes (18 × 159 mm), test tube rack, distilled water, two 10-mL graduated cylinders, 0.20 *M* NaI, 0.10 *M* $Pb(NO_3)_2$

Preparation Add 10.0 mL of 0.10 *M* $Pb(NO_3)_2$ to each of the test tubes.

Presentation Add the following amounts of water to the respective test tubes: 8.0 mL, 6.0 mL, 4.0 mL, 2.0 mL, 0 mL. Add the following amounts of 0.20 *M* NaI to the respective test tubes: 2.0 mL, 4.0 mL, 6.0 mL, 8.0 mL, 10.0 mL. Note that the volume in each test tube is now the same. Let the test tubes stand for several minutes and notice the amount of precipitate in each. There will be an increase in product from tubes 1 through 3, but this amount levels off for tubes 4 and 5.

Disposal Decant the excess solution and dispose of it as required. Dry the precipitates and dispose of them as required.

How Do We Get There?

The unbalanced equation for this reaction is

$$N_2(g) + H_2(g) \rightarrow NH_3(g)$$

which leads to the balanced equation

$$N_2(g) + 3H_2(g) \rightarrow 2NH_3(g)$$

This problem is different from the others we have done so far in that we are mixing *specified amounts of two reactants* together. To know how much product forms, we must determine which reactant is consumed first. That is, we must determine which is the limiting reactant in this experiment. To do so we must add a step to our normal procedure. We can map this process as follows:

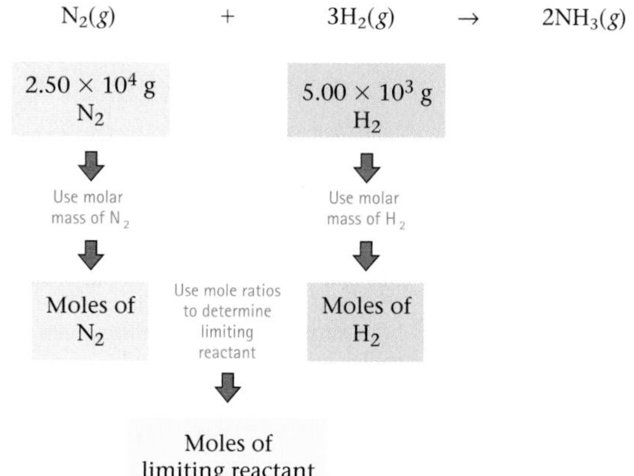

We will use the moles of the limiting reactant to calculate the moles and then the grams of the product.

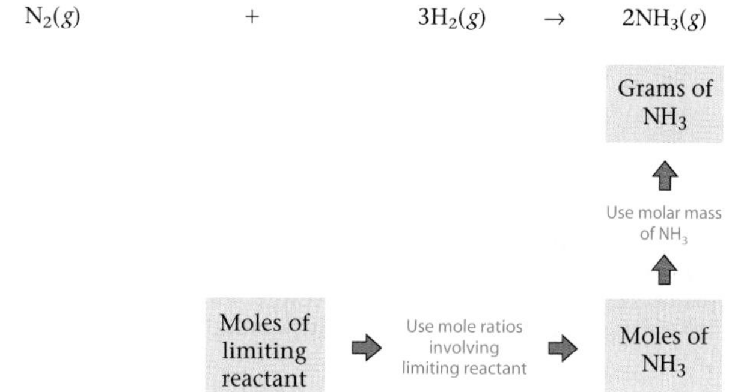

We first calculate the moles of the two reactants present:

$$2.50 \times 10^4 \text{ g N}_2 \times \frac{1 \text{ mol N}_2}{28.02 \text{ g N}_2} = 8.92 \times 10^2 \text{ mol N}_2$$

$$5.00 \times 10^3 \text{ g H}_2 \times \frac{1 \text{ mol H}_2}{2.016 \text{ g H}_2} = 2.48 \times 10^3 \text{ mol H}_2$$

MISCONCEPTION

Students often think that the reactant for which we have fewer moles or less mass must be the limiting reactant. Provide examples in which this is not the case.

Lecture Demonstration: 3.7

Additional Examples

Example 9.7

Aluminum reacts with chlorine gas to form aluminum chloride according to the balanced equation

$$2Al(s) + 3Cl_2(g) \rightarrow AlCl_3(s)$$

In a certain experiment, 10.0 g of aluminum is reacted with 35.0 g of chlorine gas.

1. What mass of aluminum chloride will be produced, assuming a complete reaction?

   21.9 g $AlCl_3(s)$

2. What mass of which reactant is left after the reaction?

   1.1 g $Al(s)$

Teaching Notes Have students predict what will happen before you add the NaI. It is important to explain that the water is added to the test tubes to keep the volumes of the solutions constant. Ask the students what changes in the test tubes. Which reactant is the limiting reactant? How could the students tell for sure? Since we have not yet discussed molarity, students cannot calculate the amounts of products unless you tell them the mass of each reactant in each test tube.

Now we must determine which reactant is limiting (will be consumed first). We have 8.92×10^2 moles of N_2. Let's determine *how many moles of H_2 are required to react with this much N_2*. Because 1 mole of N_2 reacts with 3 moles of H_2, the number of moles of H_2 we need to react completely with 8.92×10^2 moles of N_2 is determined as follows:

8.92×10^2 mol N_2

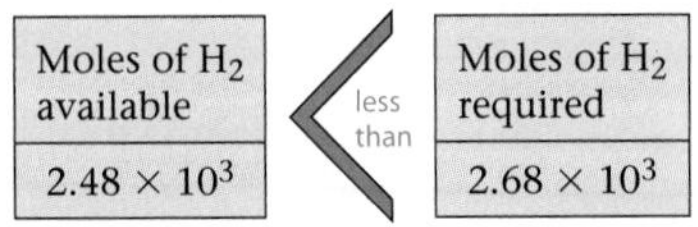

$$8.92 \times 10^2 \cancel{\text{mol } N_2} \times \frac{3 \text{ mol } H_2}{1 \cancel{\text{mol } N_2}} = 2.68 \times 10^3 \text{ mol } H_2$$

Is N_2 or H_2 the limiting reactant? The answer comes from the comparison

Moles of H_2 available		Moles of H_2 required
2.48×10^3	less than	2.68×10^3

We see that 8.92×10^2 mol N_2 requires 2.68×10^3 mol H_2 to react completely. However, only 2.48×10^3 mol H_2 is present. This means that the hydrogen will be consumed before the nitrogen runs out, so hydrogen is the *limiting reactant* in this particular situation.

Note that in our effort to determine the limiting reactant, we could have started instead with the given amount of hydrogen and calculated the moles of nitrogen required.

2.48×10^3 mol H_2

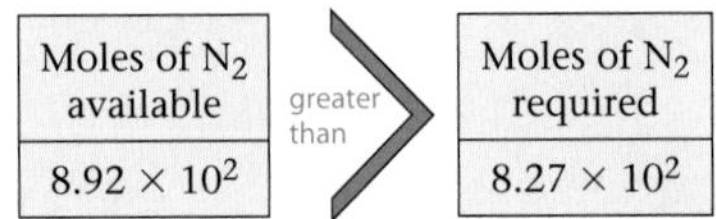

$$2.48 \times 10^3 \cancel{\text{mol } H_2} \times \frac{1 \text{ mol } N_2}{3 \cancel{\text{mol } H_2}} = 8.27 \times 10^2 \text{ mol } N_2$$

Thus 2.48×10^3 mol H_2 requires 8.27×10^2 mol N_2. Because 8.92×10^2 mol N_2 is actually present, the nitrogen is in excess.

Moles of N_2 available		Moles of N_2 required
8.92×10^2	greater than	8.27×10^2

Always check to see which, if any, reactant is limiting when you are given the amounts of two or more reactants.

If nitrogen is in excess, hydrogen will "run out" first; again we find that hydrogen limits the amount of ammonia formed.

Because the moles of H_2 present are limiting, we must use this quantity to determine the moles of NH_3 that can form.

$$2.48 \times 10^3 \cancel{\text{mol } H_2} \times \frac{2 \text{ mol } NH_3}{3 \cancel{\text{mol } H_2}} = 1.65 \times 10^3 \text{ mol } NH_3$$

Next we convert moles of NH_3 to mass of NH_3.

$$1.65 \times 10^3 \cancel{\text{mol } NH_3} \times \frac{17.03 \text{ g } NH_3}{1 \cancel{\text{mol } NH_3}} = 2.81 \times 10^4 \text{ g } NH_3 = 28.1 \text{ kg } NH_3$$

Therefore, 25.0 kg of N_2 and 5.00 kg of H_2 can form 28.1 kg of NH_3.

270 Chapter 9 Chemical Quantities

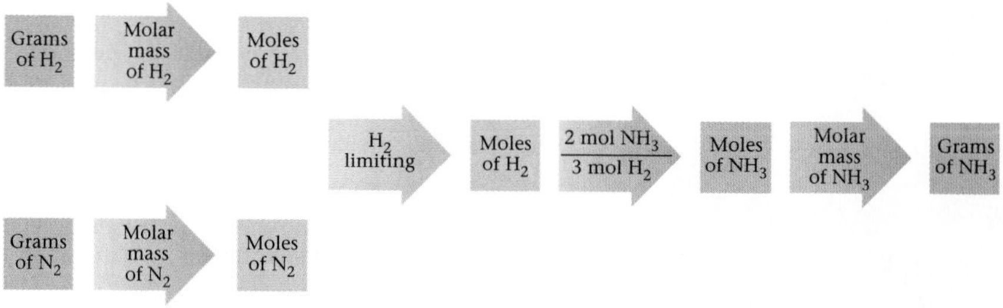

Lecture Demonstration: 3.8

Figure 9.2

A map of the procedure used in Example 9.7.

REALITY CHECK If neither reactant were limiting, we would expect an answer of 30.0 kg of NH_3 because mass is conserved (25.0 kg + 5.0 kg = 30.0 kg). Because one of the reactants (H_2 in this case) is limiting, the answer should be less than 30.0 kg, which it is. ■

The strategy used in Example 9.7 is summarized in Figure 9.2.

The following list summarizes the steps to take in solving stoichiometry problems in which the amounts of two (or more) reactants are given.

Steps for Solving Stoichiometry Problems Involving Limiting Reactants

Step 1 Write and balance the equation for the reaction.

Step 2 Convert known masses of reactants to moles.

Step 3 Using the numbers of moles of reactants and the appropriate mole ratios, determine which reactant is limiting.

Step 4 Using the amount of the limiting reactant and the appropriate mole ratios, compute the number of moles of the desired product.

Step 5 Convert from moles of product to grams of product, using the molar mass (if this is required by the problem).

Additional Examples

Example 9.8

Iron(III) oxide reacts with carbon monoxide to form iron metal and carbon dioxide gas:

$$Fe_2O_3(s) + 3CO(g) \rightarrow 2Fe(s) + 3CO_2(g)$$

In a certain experiment, 5.0 g of iron(III) oxide is reacted with 5.0 g of carbon monoxide gas.

1. What mass of iron will be produced, assuming a complete reaction?

   3.5 g Fe(*s*)

2. What mass of carbon dioxide will be produced, assuming a complete reaction?

   4.1 g $CO_2(g)$

EXAMPLE 9.8 Stoichiometric Calculations: Reactions Involving the Masses of Two Reactants

Nitrogen gas can be prepared by passing gaseous ammonia over solid copper(II) oxide at high temperatures. The other products of the reaction are solid copper and water vapor. How many grams of N_2 are formed when 18.1 g of NH_3 is reacted with 90.4 g of CuO?

SOLUTION

Where Are We Going?

We want to determine the mass of nitrogen produced given the masses of both reactants.

Copper(II) oxide reacting with ammonia in a heated tube.

What Do We Know?

- The names or formulas of the reactants and products.
- We start with 18.1 g of NH_3 and 90.4 g of CuO.
- We can obtain the atomic masses from the periodic table.

What Do We Need To Know?

- We need to know the balanced equation for the reaction, but we first have to write the formulas for the reactants and products.
- We need the molar masses of NH_3, CuO, and N_2.
- We need to determine the limiting reactant.

How Do We Get There?

Step 1 From the description of the problem, we obtain the following balanced equation:

$$2NH_3(g) + 3CuO(s) \rightarrow N_2(g) + 3Cu(s) + 3H_2O(g)$$

Step 2 Next, from the masses of reactants available we must compute the moles of NH_3 (molar mass = 17.03 g) and of CuO (molar mass = 79.55 g).

$$18.1 \text{ g } \cancel{NH_3} \times \frac{1 \text{ mol } NH_3}{17.03 \text{ g } \cancel{NH_3}} = 1.06 \text{ mol } NH_3$$

$$90.4 \text{ g } \cancel{CuO} \times \frac{1 \text{ mol CuO}}{79.55 \text{ g } \cancel{CuO}} = 1.14 \text{ mol CuO}$$

Step 3 To determine which reactant is limiting, we use the mole ratio between CuO and NH_3.

$$1.06 \cancel{\text{mol } NH_3} \times \frac{3 \text{ mol CuO}}{2 \cancel{\text{mol } NH_3}} = 1.59 \text{ mol CuO}$$

Then we compare how much CuO we have with how much of it we need.

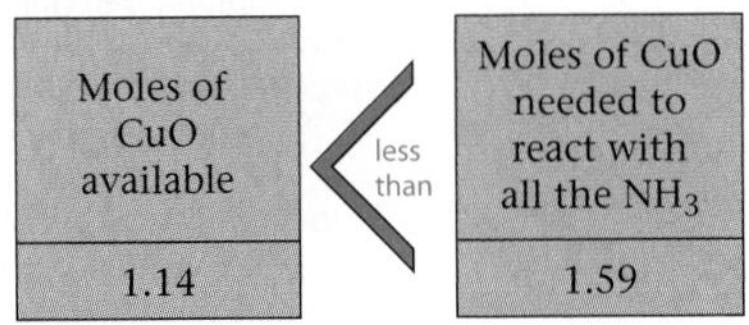

Therefore, 1.59 mol CuO is required to react with 1.06 mol NH_3, but only 1.14 mol CuO is actually present. So the amount of CuO is limiting; CuO will run out before NH_3 does.

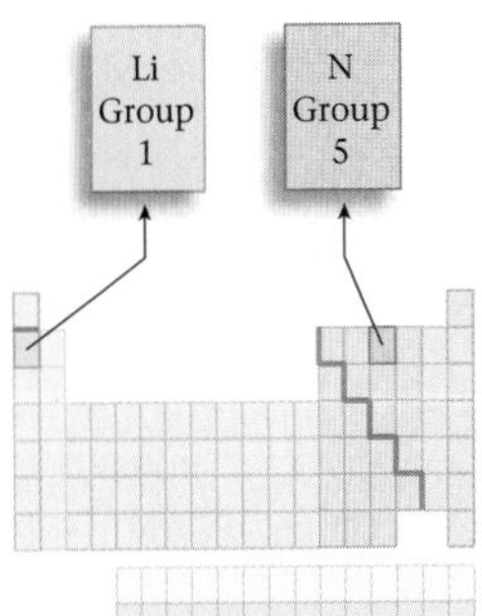

Step 4 CuO is the limiting reactant, so we must use the amount of CuO in calculating the amount of N_2 formed. Using the mole ratio between CuO and N_2 from the balanced equation, we have

$$1.14 \cancel{\text{mol CuO}} \times \frac{1 \text{ mol } N_2}{3 \cancel{\text{mol CuO}}} = 0.380 \text{ mol } N_2$$

Step 5 Using the molar mass of N_2 (28.02), we can now calculate the mass of N_2 produced.

$$0.380 \cancel{\text{mol } N_2} \times \frac{28.02 \text{ g } N_2}{1 \cancel{\text{mol } N_2}} = 10.6 \text{ g } N_2$$

Self-Check **EXERCISE 9.6** Lithium nitride, an ionic compound containing the Li^+ and N^{3-} ions, is prepared by the reaction of lithium metal and nitrogen gas. Calculate the mass of lithium nitride formed from 56.0 g of nitrogen gas and 56.0 g of lithium in the unbalanced reaction

$$Li(s) + N_2(g) \rightarrow Li_3N(s)$$

See Problems 9.51 through 9.54. ■

9.6 Percent Yield

OBJECTIVE: To learn to calculate actual yield as a percentage of theoretical yield.

In the previous section we learned how to calculate the amount of products formed when specified amounts of reactants are mixed together. In doing these calculations, we used the fact that the amount of product is controlled by the limiting reactant. Products stop forming when one reactant runs out.

The amount of product calculated in this way is called the **theoretical yield** of that product. It is the amount of product predicted from the amounts of reactants used. For instance, in Example 9.8, 10.6 g of nitrogen represents the theoretical yield. This is the *maximum amount* of nitrogen that can be produced from the quantities of reactants used. Actually, however, the amount of product predicted (the theoretical yield) is seldom obtained. One reason for this is the presence of side reactions (other reactions that consume one or more of the reactants or products).

Percent yield is important as an indicator of the efficiency of a particular reaction.

The *actual yield* of product, which is the amount of product *actually obtained,* is often compared to the theoretical yield. This comparison, usually expressed as a percentage, is called the **percent yield.**

$$\frac{\text{Actual yield}}{\text{Theoretical yield}} \times 100\% = \text{percent yield}$$

For example, *if* the reaction considered in Example 9.8 *actually* gave 6.63 g of nitrogen instead of the *predicted* 10.6 g, the percent yield of nitrogen would be

$$\frac{6.63\ \cancel{g\ N_2}}{10.6\ \cancel{g\ N_2}} \times 100\% = 62.5\%$$

EXAMPLE 9.9 Stoichiometric Calculations: Determining Percent Yield

In Section 9.1, we saw that methanol can be produced by the reaction between carbon monoxide and hydrogen. Let's consider this process again. Suppose 68.5 kg (6.85×10^4 g) of $CO(g)$ is reacted with 8.60 kg (8.60×10^3 g) of $H_2(g)$.

a. Calculate the theoretical yield of methanol.

b. If 3.57×10^4 g of CH_3OH is actually produced, what is the percent yield of methanol?

SOLUTION (a)

Where Are We Going?

We want to determine the theoretical yield of methanol and the percent yield given an actual yield.

Lecture Demonstration: 3.3, 3.5

Self Check

Answer to Self-Check Exercise 9.6

93.7 g Li_3N

Section 9.6

TEACHING TIPS

- Students may find it difficult to understand that the answers to stoichiometry problems are actually theoretical yields. It is useful to make a clear distinction between theoretical yield and actual yield. Point out that an actual yield must be determined by someone in the laboratory, while a theoretical yield can be determined by solving limiting reactant problems.
- Now is an excellent time to review the concept of percentages. You may want to have students review percent composition problems from Chapter 8 as part of this effort.

 **Test Bank: 72–75**

Additional Examples

Example 9.9

1. In a certain experiment, the expected yield is 1.352 g. The actual yield was 1.279 g. Determine the percent yield.

   94.60%

2. Urea is formed by the reaction of ammonia and carbon dioxide:

   $$2NH_3(g) + CO_2(g) \rightarrow CN_2H_4O(s) + 2H_2O(l)$$

   In a certain experiment 100.0 g of ammonia is reacted with 100.0 g of carbon dioxide and 120.0 g of urea is produced. Determine the percent yield for this reaction.

   88.23%

What Do We Know?

- From Section 9.1 we know the balanced equation is

$$2H_2 + CO \rightarrow CH_3OH$$

- We start with 6.85×10^4 g of CO and 8.60×10^3 g of H_2.
- We can obtain the atomic masses from the periodic table.

What Do We Need To Know?

- We need the molar masses of H_2, CO, and CH_3OH.
- We need to determine the limiting reactant.

How Do We Get There?

Step 1 The balanced equation is

$$2H_2(g) + CO(g) \rightarrow CH_3OH(l)$$

Step 2 Next we calculate the moles of reactants.

$$6.85 \times 10^4 \text{ g CO} \times \frac{1 \text{ mol CO}}{28.01 \text{ g CO}} = 2.45 \times 10^3 \text{ mol CO}$$

$$8.60 \times 10^3 \text{ g } H_2 \times \frac{1 \text{ mol } H_2}{2.016 \text{ g } H_2} = 4.27 \times 10^3 \text{ mol } H_2$$

Step 3 Now we determine which reactant is limiting. Using the mole ratio between CO and H_2 from the balanced equation, we have

$$2.45 \times 10^3 \text{ mol CO} \times \frac{2 \text{ mol } H_2}{1 \text{ mol CO}} = 4.90 \times 10^3 \text{ mol } H_2$$

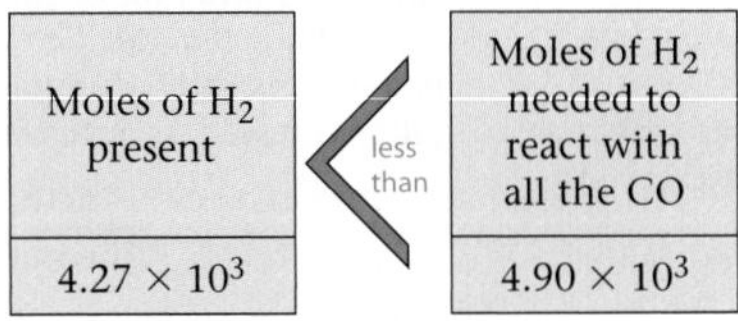

We see that 2.45×10^3 mol CO requires 4.90×10^3 mol H_2. Because only 4.27×10^3 mol H_2 is actually present, *H_2 is limiting.*

Step 4 We must therefore use the amount of H_2 and the mole ratio between H_2 and CH_3OH to determine the maximum amount of methanol that can be produced in the reaction.

$$4.27 \times 10^3 \text{ mol } H_2 \times \frac{1 \text{ mol } CH_3OH}{2 \text{ mol } H_2} = 2.14 \times 10^3 \text{ mol } CH_3OH$$

This represents the theoretical yield in moles.

Step 5 Using the molar mass of CH_3OH (32.04 g), we can calculate the theoretical yield in grams.

$$2.14 \times 10^3 \text{ mol } CH_3OH \times \frac{32.04 \text{ g } CH_3OH}{1 \text{ mol } CH_3OH} = 6.86 \times 10^4 \text{ g } CH_3OH$$

So, from the amounts of reactants given, the maximum amount of CH_3OH that can be formed is 6.86×10^4 g. This is the *theoretical yield.*

SOLUTION (b)

The percent yield is

$$\frac{\text{Actual yield (grams)}}{\text{Theoretical yield (grams)}} \times 100\% = \frac{3.57 \times 10^4 \text{ g } CH_3OH}{6.86 \times 10^4 \text{ g } CH_3OH} \times 100\% = 52.0\%$$

Self-Check **EXERCISE 9.7** Titanium(IV) oxide is a white compound used as a coloring pigment. In fact, the page you are now reading is white because of the presence of this compound in the paper. Solid titanium(IV) oxide can be prepared by reacting gaseous titanium(IV) chloride with oxygen gas. A second product of this reaction is chlorine gas.

$$TiCl_4(g) + O_2(g) \rightarrow TiO_2(s) + Cl_2(g)$$

a. Suppose 6.71×10^3 g of titanium(IV) chloride is reacted with 2.45×10^3 g of oxygen. Calculate the maximum mass of titanium(IV) oxide that can form.

b. If the percent yield of TiO_2 is 75%, what mass is actually formed?

See Problems 9.63 and 9.64. ■

CHAPTER 9 REVIEW

Key Terms

mole ratio (9.2)
stoichiometry (9.3)
limiting reactant (limiting reagent) (9.4)
theoretical yield (9.6)
percent yield (9.6)

 directs you to the *Chemistry in Focus* feature in the chapter

 indicates visual problems

 interactive versions of these problems are assignable in OWL.

Summary

1. A balanced equation relates the numbers of molecules of reactants and products. It can also be expressed in terms of the numbers of moles of reactants and products.
2. The process of using a chemical equation to calculate the relative amounts of reactants and products involved in the reaction is called doing stoichiometric calculations. To convert between moles of reactants and moles of products, we use mole ratios derived from the balanced equation.
3. Often reactants are not mixed in stoichiometric quantities (they do not "run out" at the same time). In that case, we must use the limiting reactant to calculate the amounts of products formed.
4. The actual yield of a reaction is usually less than its theoretical yield. The actual yield is often expressed as a percentage of the theoretical yield, which is called the percent yield.

Active Learning Questions

These questions are designed to be considered by groups of students in class. Often these questions work well for introducing a particular topic in class.

1. Relate Active Learning Question 2 from Chapter 2 to the concepts of chemical stoichiometry.
2. You are making cookies and are missing a key ingredient—eggs. You have plenty of the other ingredients, except that you have only 1.33 cups of butter and no eggs. You note that the recipe calls for 2 cups of butter and 3 eggs (plus the other ingredients) to make 6 dozen cookies. You telephone a friend and have him bring you some eggs.

   a. How many eggs do you need?
   b. If you use all the butter (and get enough eggs), how many cookies can you make?

   Unfortunately, your friend hangs up before you tell him how many eggs you need. When he arrives, he has a surprise for you—to save time he has broken the eggs in a bowl for you. You ask him how many he brought, and he replies, "All of them, but I spilled some on the way over." You weigh the eggs and find that they weigh 62.1 g. Assuming that an average egg weighs 34.21 g:

   c. How much butter is needed to react with all the eggs?
   d. How many cookies can you make?
   e. Which will you have left over, eggs or butter?
   f. How much is left over?
   g. Relate this question to the concepts of chemical stoichiometry.

Self Check

Answers to Self-Check Exercise 9.7

2.83×10^3 g TiO_2

2.12×10^3 g TiO_2

ChemWork

Bonding Characteristics 1
Bonding Characteristics 2
Bonding Characteristics 3
Bonding Characteristics 4
Chlorine Oxide Fluorides
Colorful Molecules
Hybridization
Hybridization in an Organic Molecule
Molecular Structures
Polyatomic Ion Structure
Molecular Orbitals in Homonuclear Ions
Molecular Orbital Predictions
Molecular Orbitals in Heteronuclear Ions

VP 3. Nitrogen (N_2) and hydrogen (H_2) react to form ammonia (NH_3). Consider the mixture of N_2 (●●) and H_2 (○○) in a closed container as illustrated below:

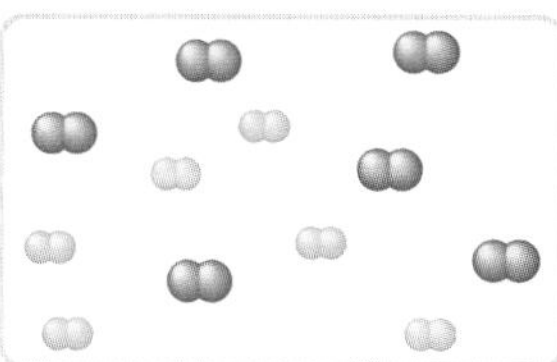

Assuming the reaction goes to completion, draw a representation of the product mixture. Explain how you arrived at this representation.

4. Which of the following equations best represents the reaction for Question 3?

a. $6N_2 + 6H_2 \rightarrow 4NH_3 + 4N_2$
b. $N_2 + H_2 \rightarrow NH_3$
c. $N + 3H \rightarrow NH_3$
d. $N_2 + 3H_2 \rightarrow 2NH_3$
e. $2N_2 + 6H_2 \rightarrow 4NH_3$

For choices you did not pick, explain what you feel is wrong with them, and justify the choice you did pick.

5. You know that chemical A reacts with chemical B. You react 10.0 g A with 10.0 g B. What information do you need to know to determine the amount of product that will be produced? Explain.

6. If 10.0 g of hydrogen gas is reacted with 10.0 g of oxygen gas according to the equation

$$2H_2 + O_2 \rightarrow 2H_2O$$

we should not expect to form 20.0 g of water. Why not? What mass of water can be produced with a complete reaction?

7. The limiting reactant in a reaction:

a. has the lowest coefficient in a balanced equation.
b. is the reactant for which you have the fewest number of moles.
c. has the lowest ratio: moles available/coefficient in the balanced equation.
d. has the lowest ratio: coefficient in the balanced equation/moles available.
d. None of the above.

For choices you did not pick, explain what you feel is wrong with them, and justify the choice you did pick.

8. Given the equation $3A + B \rightarrow C + D$, if 4 moles of A is reacted with 2 moles of B, which of the following is true?

a. The limiting reactant is the one with the higher molar mass.
b. A is the limiting reactant because you need 6 moles of A and have 4 moles.
c. B is the limiting reactant because you have fewer moles of B than moles of A.
d. B is the limiting reactant because three A molecules react with every one B molecule.
e. Neither reactant is limiting.

For choices you did not pick, explain what you feel is wrong with them, and justify the choice you did pick.

9. What happens to the weight of an iron bar when it rusts?

a. There is no change because mass is always conserved.
b. The weight increases.
c. The weight increases, but if the rust is scraped off, the bar has the original weight.
d. The weight decreases.

Justify your choice and, for choices you did not pick, explain what is wrong with them. Explain what it means for something to rust.

10. Consider the equation $2A + B \rightarrow A_2B$. If you mix 1.0 mole of A and 1.0 mole of B, how many moles of A_2B can be produced?

11. What is meant by the term *mole ratio*? Give an example of a mole ratio, and explain how it is used in solving a stoichiometry problem.

12. Which would produce a greater number of moles of product: a given amount of hydrogen gas reacting with an excess of oxygen gas to produce water, or the same amount of hydrogen gas reacting with an excess of nitrogen gas to make ammonia? Support your answer.

13. Consider a reaction represented by the following balanced equation

$$2A + 3B \rightarrow C + 4D$$

You find that it requires equal masses of A and B so that there are no reactants left over. Which of the following is true? Justify your choice.

a. The molar mass of A must be greater than the molar mass of B.
b. The molar mass of A must be less than the molar mass of B.
c. The molar mass of A must be the same as the molar mass of B.

14. Consider a chemical equation with two reactants forming one product. If you know the mass of each reactant, what else do you need to know to determine the mass of the product? Why isn't the mass necessarily the sum of the mass of the reactants? Provide a real example of such a reaction, and support your answer mathematically.

15. Consider the balanced chemical equation

$$A + 5B \rightarrow 3C + 4D$$

When equal masses of A and B are reacted, which is limiting, A or B? Justify your choice.

a. If the molar mass of A is greater than the molar mass of B, then A must be limiting.

b. If the molar mass of A is less than the molar mass of B, then A must be limiting.
c. If the molar mass of A is greater than the molar mass of B, then B must be limiting.
d. If the molar mass of A is less than the molar mass of B, then B must be limiting.

16. Which of the following reaction mixtures would produce the greatest amount of product, assuming all went to completion? Justify your choice.

Each involves the reaction symbolized by the equation

$$2H_2 + O_2 \rightarrow 2H_2O$$

a. 2 moles of H_2 and 2 moles of O_2.
b. 2 moles of H_2 and 3 moles of O_2.
c. 2 moles of H_2 and 1 mole of O_2.
d. 3 moles of H_2 and 1 mole of O_2.
e. Each would produce the same amount of product.

17. Baking powder is a mixture of cream of tartar ($KHC_4H_4O_6$) and baking soda ($NaHCO_3$). When it is placed in an oven at typical baking temperatures (as part of a cake, for example), it undergoes the following reaction (CO_2 makes the cake rise):

$$KHC_4H_4O_6(s) + NaHCO_3(s) \rightarrow KNaC_4H_4O_6(s) + H_2O(g) + CO_2(g)$$

You decide to make a cake one day, and the recipe calls for baking powder. Unfortunately, you have no baking powder. You do have cream of tartar and baking soda, so you use stoichiometry to figure out how much of each to mix.

Of the following choices, which is the best way to make baking powder? The amounts given in the choices are in teaspoons (that is, you will use a teaspoon to measure the baking soda and cream of tartar). Justify your choice.

Assume a teaspoon of cream of tartar has the same mass as a teaspoon of baking soda.

a. Add equal amounts of baking soda and cream of tartar.
b. Add a bit more than twice as much cream of tartar as baking soda.
c. Add a bit more than twice as much baking soda as cream of tartar.
d. Add more cream of tartar than baking soda, but not quite twice as much.
e. Add more baking soda than cream of tartar, but not quite twice as much.

VP 18. You have seven closed containers each with equal masses of chlorine gas (Cl_2). You add 10.0 g of sodium to the first sample, 20.0 g of sodium to the second sample, and so on (adding 70.0 g of sodium to the seventh sample). Sodium and chloride react to form sodium chloride according to the equation

$$2Na(s) + Cl_2(g) \rightarrow 2NaCl(s)$$

After each reaction is complete, you collect and measure the amount of sodium chloride formed. A graph of your results is shown below.

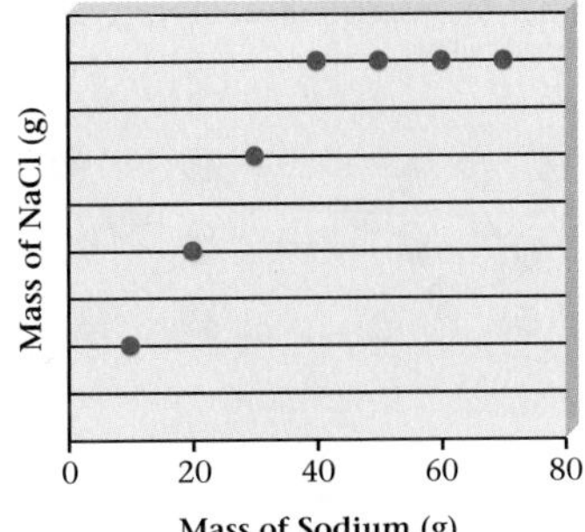

Answer the following questions:

a. Explain the shape of the graph.
b. Calculate the mass of NaCl formed when 20.0 g of sodium is used.
c. Calculate the mass of Cl_2 in each container.
d. Calculate the mass of NaCl formed when 50.0 g of sodium is used.
e. Identify the leftover reactant and determine its mass for parts b and d above.

VP 19. You have a chemical in a sealed glass container filled with air. The setup is sitting on a balance as shown below. The chemical is ignited by means of a magnifying glass focusing sunlight on the reactant. After the chemical has completely burned, which of the following is true? Explain your answer.

a. The balance will read less than 250.0 g.
b. The balance will read 250.0 g.
c. The balance will read greater than 250.0 g.
d. Cannot be determined without knowing the identity of the chemical.

VP 20. Consider an iron bar on a balance as shown.

As the iron bar rusts, which of the following is true? Explain your answer.

a. The balance will read less than 75.0 g.
b. The balance will read 75.0 g.
c. The balance will read greater than 75.0 g.
d. The balance will read greater than 75.0 g, but if the bar is removed, the rust scraped off, and the bar replaced, the balance will read 75.0 g.

Answers to End-of-Chapter Exercises

1. relative numbers of molecules of reactants and products

2. The coefficients of the balanced chemical equation indicate the *relative numbers of molecules* (or moles) of each reactant that combine, as well as the number of molecules (or moles) of each product formed.

3. The units of mass are a human invention; atoms/molecules react on an individual particle basis.

4. Balanced chemical equations tell us in what molar ratios substances combine to form products, not in what mass proportions they combine.

5. (a) $PCl_3(l) + 3H_2O(l) \rightarrow H_3PO_3(aq) + 3HCl(g)$, 1 molecule/mol of liquid PCl_3 reacts with 3 molecules/mol of liquid water to produce 1 molecule/mol of phosphorous acid and 3 molecules/mol of gaseous hydrogen chloride; (b) $2XeF_2(g) + 2H_2O(l) \rightarrow 2Xe(g) + 4HF(g) + O_2(g)$, 2 molecules/mol of gaseous xenon difluoride reacts with 2 molecules/mol of liquid water to produce 2 atoms/mol of gaseous xenon, 4 molecules/mol of gaseous hydrogen fluoride, and 1 molecule/mol of oxygen gas; (c) $S(s) + 6HNO_3(aq) \rightarrow H_2SO_4(aq) + 2H_2O(l) + 6NO_2(g)$, 1 atom/mol of solid sulfur reacts with 6 molecules/mol nitric acid to produce 1 molecule/mol of sulfuric acid, 2 molecules/mol of liquid water, and 6 molecules/mol of gaseous nitrogen dioxide; (d) $2NaHSO_3(s) \rightarrow Na_2SO_3(s) + SO_2(g) + H_2O(l)$, 2 formula units/mol of solid sodium hydrogen sulfite reacts to produce 1 formula unit/mol of sodium sulfite, 1 molecule/mol of sulfur dioxide gas, and 1 molecule/mol of liquid water.

VP 21. Consider the reaction between $NO(g)$ and $O_2(g)$ represented below.

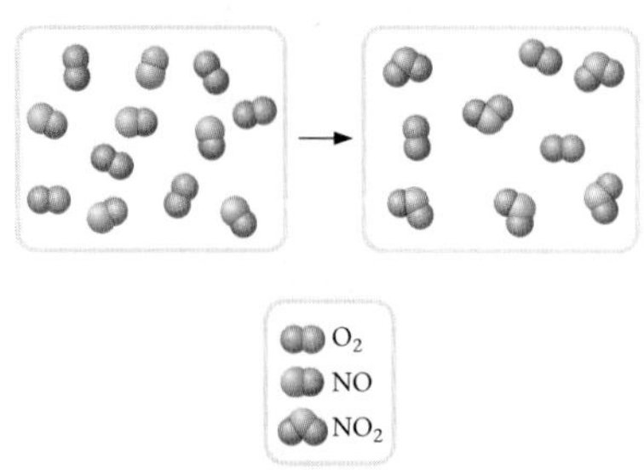

What is the balanced equation for this reaction, and what is the limiting reactant?

Questions and Problems

9.1 Information Given by Chemical Equations

QUESTIONS

1. What do the coefficients of a balanced chemical equation tell us about the proportions in which atoms and molecules react on an individual (microscopic) basis?
2. What do the coefficients of a balanced chemical equation tell us about the proportions in which substances react on a macroscopic (mole) basis?
3. Although *mass* is a property of matter we can conveniently measure in the laboratory, the coefficients of a balanced chemical equation are *not* directly interpreted on the basis of mass. Explain why.
4. For the balanced chemical equation $H_2 + Br_2 \rightarrow 2HBr$, explain why we do *not* expect to produce 2 g of HBr if 1 g of H_2 is reacted with 1 g of Br_2.

PROBLEMS

5. For each of the following reactions, give the balanced equation for the reaction and state the meaning of the equation in terms of the numbers of *individual molecules* and in terms of *moles of molecules*.
   a. $PCl_3(l) + H_2O(l) \rightarrow H_3PO_3(aq) + HCl(g)$
   b. $XeF_2(g) + H_2O(l) \rightarrow Xe(g) + HF(g) + O_2(g)$
   c. $S(s) + HNO_3(aq) \rightarrow H_2SO_4(aq) + H_2O(l) + NO_2(g)$
   d. $NaHSO_3(s) \rightarrow Na_2SO_3(s) + SO_2(g) + H_2O(l)$
6. For each of the following reactions, balance the chemical equation and state the stoichiometric *meaning* of the equation in terms of the numbers of *individual molecules* reacting and in terms of *moles of molecules* reacting.
   a. $(NH_4)_2CO_3(s) \rightarrow NH_3(g) + CO_2(g) + H_2O(g)$
   b. $Mg(s) + P_4(s) \rightarrow Mg_3P_2(s)$
   c. $Si(s) + S_8(s) \rightarrow Si_2S_4(l)$
   d. $C_2H_5OH(l) + O_2(g) \rightarrow CO_2(g) + H_2O(g)$

9.2 Mole–Mole Relationships

QUESTIONS

7. Consider the reaction represented by the chemical equation
   $$KOH(s) + SO_2(g) \rightarrow KHSO_3(s)$$
   Since the coefficients of the balanced chemical equation are all equal to 1, we know that exactly 1 g of KOH will react with exactly 1 g of SO_2. True or false? Explain.
8. For the balanced chemical equation for the decomposition of hydrogen peroxide
   $$2H_2O_2(aq) \rightarrow 2H_2O(l) + O_2(g)$$
   explain why we know that decomposition of 2 g of hydrogen peroxide will *not* result in the production of 2 g of water and 1 g of oxygen gas.
9. Consider the balanced chemical equation
   $$4Al(s) + 3O_2(g) \rightarrow 2Al_2O_3(s).$$
   What mole ratio would you use to calculate how many moles of oxygen gas would be needed to react completely with a given number of moles of aluminum metal? What mole ratio would you use to calculate the number of moles of product that would be expected if a given number of moles of aluminum metal reacts completely?
10. Consider the balanced chemical equation
   $$Fe_2O_3(s) + 3H_2SO_4(aq) \rightarrow Fe_2(SO_4)_3(s) + 3H_2O(l).$$
   What mole ratio would you use to calculate the number of moles of sulfuric acid needed to react completely with a given number of moles of iron(III) oxide? What mole ratios would you use to calculate the number of moles of each product that would be produced if a given number of moles of $Fe_2O_3(s)$ reacts completely?

PROBLEMS

11. For each of the following balanced chemical equations, calculate how many *moles* of product(s) would be produced if 0.500 mole of the first reactant were to react completely.
   a. $CO_2(g) + 4H_2(g) \rightarrow CH_4(g) + 2H_2O(l)$
   b. $BaCl_2(aq) + 2AgNO_3(aq) \rightarrow 2AgCl(s) + Ba(NO_3)_2(aq)$
   c. $C_3H_8(g) + 5O_2(g) \rightarrow 4H_2O(l) + 3CO_2(g)$
   d. $3H_2SO_4(aq) + 2Fe(s) \rightarrow Fe_2(SO_4)_3(aq) + 3H_2(g)$
12. For each of the following balanced chemical equations, calculate how many *moles* of product(s) would be produced if 0.250 mole of the first reactant were to react completely.
   a. $4Bi(s) + 3O_2(g) \rightarrow 2Bi_2O_3(s)$
   b. $SnO_2(s) + 2H_2(g) \rightarrow Sn(s) + 2H_2O(g)$
   c. $SiCl_4(l) + 2H_2O(l) \rightarrow SiO_2(s) + 4HCl(g)$
   d. $2N_2(g) + 5O_2(g) + 2H_2O(l) \rightarrow 4HNO_3(aq)$
13. For each of the following balanced chemical equations, calculate how many *grams* of the product(s)

All even-numbered Questions and Problems have answers in the back of this book and solutions in the Solutions Guide.

6. (a) $(NH_4)_2CO_3(s) \rightarrow 2NH_3(g) + CO_2(g) + H_2O(g)$. One formula unit of solid ammonium carbonate decomposes to produce two molecules of ammonia gas, one molecule of carbon dioxide gas, and one molecule of water vapor. One mole of solid ammonium carbonate decomposes into two moles of gaseous ammonia, one mole of carbon dioxide gas, and one mole of water vapor.

(b) $6Mg(s) + P_4(s) \rightarrow 2Mg_3P_2(s)$.
Six atoms of magnesium metal react with one molecule of solid phosphorus (P_4) to make two formula units of solid magnesium phosphide. Six moles of magnesium metal react with one mole of phosphorus solid (P_4) to produce two moles of solid magnesium phosphide.

(c) $4Si(s) + S_8(s) \rightarrow 2Si_2S_4(l)$.
Four atoms of solid silicon react with one molecule of solid sulfur (S_8) to form two molecules of liquid disilicon tetrasulfide. Four moles of solid silicon react with one mole of solid sulfur (S_8) to form two moles of liquid disilicon tetrasulfide.

(d) $C_2H_5OH(l) + 3O_2(g) \rightarrow 2CO_2(g) + 3H_2O(g)$.

would be produced by complete reaction of 0.125 mole of the first reactant.

a. $AgNO_3(aq) + LiOH(aq) \rightarrow AgOH(s) + LiNO_3(aq)$
b. $Al_2(SO_4)_3(aq) + 3CaCl_2(aq) \rightarrow 2AlCl_3(aq) + 3CaSO_4(s)$
c. $CaCO_3(s) + 2HCl(aq) \rightarrow CaCl_2(aq) + CO_2(g) + H_2O(l)$
d. $2C_4H_{10}(g) + 13O_2(g) \rightarrow 8CO_2(g) + 10H_2O(g)$

14. For each of the following balanced chemical equations, calculate how many *grams* of the product(s) would be produced by complete reaction of 0.750 mole of the first (or only) reactant.

a. $C_5H_{12}(l) + 8O_2(g) \rightarrow 5CO_2(g) + 6H_2O(l)$
b. $2CH_3OH(l) + 3O_2(g) \rightarrow 4H_2O(l) + 2CO_2(g)$
c. $Ba(OH)_2(aq) + H_3PO_4(aq) \rightarrow BaHPO_4(s) + 2H_2O(l)$
d. $C_6H_{12}O_6(aq) \rightarrow 2C_2H_5OH(aq) + 2CO_2(g)$

15. For each of the following *unbalanced* equations, indicate how many *moles* of the *second reactant* would be required to react exactly with *0.275 mol* of the *first reactant.* State clearly the mole ratio used for the conversion.

a. $Cl_2(g) + KI(aq) \rightarrow I_2(s) + KCl(aq)$
b. $Co(s) + P_4(s) \rightarrow Co_3P_2(s)$
c. $Zn(s) + HNO_3(aq) \rightarrow ZnNO_3(aq) + H_2(g)$
d. $C_5H_{12}(l) + O_2(g) \rightarrow CO_2(g) + H_2O(g)$

16. For each of the following *unbalanced* equations, indicate how many *moles* of the *first product* are produced if *0.625 mole* of the *second product* forms. State clearly the mole ratio used for each conversion.

a. $KO_2(s) + H_2O(l) \rightarrow O_2(g) + KOH(s)$
b. $SeO_2(g) + H_2Se(g) \rightarrow Se(s) + H_2O(g)$
c. $CH_3CH_2OH(l) + O_2(g) \rightarrow CH_3CHO(aq) + H_2O(l)$
d. $Fe_2O_3(s) + Al(s) \rightarrow Fe(l) + Al_2O_3(s)$

9.3 Mass Calculations

QUESTIONS

17. What quantity serves as the conversion factor between the mass of a sample and how many moles the sample contains?

18. What does it mean to say that the balanced chemical equation for a reaction describes the *stoichiometry* of the reaction?

PROBLEMS

19. Using the average atomic masses given inside the front cover of this book, calculate how many *moles* of each substance the following masses represent.

a. 4.15 g of silicon, Si
b. 2.72 mg of gold(III) chloride, $AuCl_3$
c. 1.05 kg of sulfur, S
d. 0.000901 g of iron(III) chloride, $FeCl_3$
e. 5.62×10^3 g of magnesium oxide, MgO

20. Using the average atomic masses given inside the front cover of this book, calculate how many *moles* of each substance the following masses represent.

a. 72.4 mg of argon, Ar
b. 52.7 g of carbon disulfide, CS_2
c. 784 kg of iron, Fe
d. 0.00104 g of calcium chloride, $CaCl_2$
e. 1.26×10^3 g of nickel(II) sulfide, NiS

21. Using the average atomic masses given inside the front cover of this book, calculate the *mass in grams* of each of the following samples.

a. 2.17 moles of germanium, Ge
b. 4.24 mmol of lead(II) chloride (1 mmol = 1/1000 mol)
c. 0.0971 mole of ammonia, NH_3
d. 4.26×10^3 moles of hexane, C_6H_{14}
e. 1.71 moles of iodine monochloride, ICl

22. Using the average atomic masses given inside the front cover of this book, calculate the *mass in grams* of each of the following samples.

a. 2.23 moles of propane, C_3H_8
b. 9.03 mmol of argon, Ar (1 mmol = 1/1000 mol)
c. 5.91×10^6 moles of silicon dioxide, SiO_2
d. 0.000104 mole of copper(II) chloride, $CuCl_2$
e. 0.000104 mole of copper(I) chloride, CuCl

23. For each of the following *unbalanced* equations, calculate how many *moles* of the second reactant would be required to react completely with 0.413 *moles* of the first reactant.

a. $Co(s) + F_2(g) \rightarrow CoF_3(s)$
b. $Al(s) + H_2SO_4(aq) \rightarrow Al_2(SO_4)_3(aq) + H_2(g)$
c. $K(s) + H_2O(l) \rightarrow KOH(aq) + H_2(g)$
d. $Cu(s) + O_2(g) \rightarrow Cu_2O(s)$

24. For each of the following *unbalanced* equations, calculate how many *moles* of the second reactant would be required to react completely with 0.557 *grams* of the first reactant.

a. $Al(s) + Br_2(l) \rightarrow AlBr_3(s)$
b. $Hg(s) + HClO_4(aq) \rightarrow Hg(ClO_4)_2(aq) + H_2(g)$
c. $K(s) + P(s) \rightarrow K_3P(s)$
d. $CH_4(g) + Cl_2(g) \rightarrow CCl_4(l) + HCl(g)$

25. For each of the following *unbalanced* equations, calculate how many *grams of each product* would be produced by complete reaction of 12.5 g of the reactant indicated in boldface. Indicate clearly the mole ratio used for the conversion.

a. $TiBr_4(g) + \mathbf{H_2}(g) \rightarrow Ti(s) + HBr(g)$
b. $\mathbf{SiH_4}(g) + NH_3(g) \rightarrow Si_3N_4(s) + H_2(g)$
c. $NO(g) + \mathbf{H_2}(g) \rightarrow N_2(g) + 2H_2O(l)$
d. $\mathbf{Cu_2S}(s) \rightarrow Cu(s) + S(g)$

26. For each of the following *balanced* equations, calculate how many *grams of each product* would be produced by complete reaction of 15.0 g of the reactant indicated in boldface.

a. $\mathbf{2BCl_3}(s) + 3H_2(g) \rightarrow 2B(s) + 6HCl(g)$
b. $\mathbf{2Cu_2S}(s) + 3O_2(g) \rightarrow 2Cu_2O(s) + 2SO_2(g)$
c. $2Cu_2O(s) + \mathbf{Cu_2S}(s) \rightarrow 6Cu(s) + SO_2(g)$
d. $CaCO_3(s) + \mathbf{SiO_2}(s) \rightarrow CaSiO_3(s) + CO_2(g)$

All even-numbered Questions and Problems have answers in the back of this book and solutions in the Solutions Guide.

One molecule of liquid ethanol burns with three molecules of oxygen gas to produce two molecules of carbon dioxide gas and three molecules of water vapor. One mole of liquid ethanol burns with three moles of oxygen gas to produce two moles of gaseous carbon dioxide and three moles of water vapor.

7. False. Balanced chemical equations are in molecule/mole ratios, not mass ratios.

8. Balanced chemical equations tell us in what molar ratios substances combine to form products, not in what mass proportions they combine. How could 2 g of reactant produce a total of 3 g of products?

9. $\frac{3 \text{ mol } O_2}{4 \text{ mol Al}}; \frac{2 \text{ mol } Al_2O_3}{4 \text{ mol Al}}$

10. $\frac{3 \text{ mol } H_2SO_4}{1 \text{ mol } Fe_2O_3}; \frac{1 \text{ mol } Fe_2(SO_4)_3}{1 \text{ mol } Fe_2O_3}; \frac{3 \text{ mol } H_2O}{1 \text{ mol } Fe_2O_3}$

11. (a) 0.500 mol CH_4; 1.00 mol H_2O; (b) 1.00 mol AgCl; 0.500 mol $Ba(NO_3)_2$; (c) 2.00 mol H_2O; 1.50 mol CO_2; (d) 0.167 mol $Fe_2(SO_4)_3$; 0.500 mol H_2

12. (a) 0.125 mol Bi_2O_3; (b) 0.250 mol Sn; 0.500 mol H_2O; (c) 0.250 mol SiO_2; 1.00 mol HCl; (d) 0.500 mol HNO_3

13. (a) 15.6 g AgOH; 8.62 g $LiNO_3$; (b) 33.3 g $AlCl_3$; 51.1 g $CaSO_4$; (c) 13.9 g $CaCl_2$; 5.50 g CO_2; 2.25 g H_2O; (d) 22.0 g CO_2; 11.3 g H_2

14. (a) 165 g CO_2; 81.1 g H_2O; (b) 27.0 g H_2O; 33.0 g CO_2; (c) 175 g $BaHPO_4$; 27.0 g H_2O; (d) 69.1 g C_2H_5OH; 66.0 g CO_2

15. (a) 0.550 mol; (b) 0.0458 mol; (c) 0.550 mol; (d) 2.20 mol

16. (a) 0.469 mol O_2; (b) 0.938 mol Se; (c) 0.625 mol CH_3CHO; (d) 1.25 mol Fe

17. the molar mass of the substance

18. Stoichiometry is the process of using a chemical equation to calculate the relative masses of reactants and products involved in a reaction.

19. (a) 0.148 mol; (b) 8.97×10^{-6} mol; (c) 32.7 mol; (d) 5.55×10^{-6} mol; (e) 139 mol

20. (a) 1.81×10^{-3} mol; (b) 0.692 mol; (c) 1.40×10^4 mol; (d) 9.37×10^{-6} mol; (e) 13.9 mol

21. (a) 158 g; (b) 1.18 g; (c) 1.65 g; (d) 3.67×10^5 g; (e) 278 g

22. (a) 98.3 g; (b) 0.361 g; (c) 3.55×10^8 g; (d) 0.0140 g; (e) 0.0103 g

23. (a) 0.620 mol; (b) 0.620 mol; (c) 0.413 mol; (d) 0.103 mol

24. (a) 0.0310 mol; (b) 0.00555 mol; (c) 0.00475 mol; (d) 0.139 mol

25. (a) 148 g Ti, 1.00 × 10^3 g HBr; (b) 18.2 g Si_3N_4, 3.14 g H_2; (c) 86.9 g N_2, 112 g H_2O; (d) 9.98 g Cu, 2.52 g S

26. (a) 1.38 g B, 14.0 g HCl; (b) 13.5 g Cu_2O, 6.04 g SO_2; (c) 35.9 g Cu, 6.04 g SO_2; (d) 29.0 g $CaSiO_3$, 11.0 g CO_2

27. 0.443 g NH_3

28. 1.52 g C_2H_2

29. 18.3 g CO_2, 11.7 g CO

30. 0.959 g Na_2CO_3

31. 45.0 mg

32. 2.68 g ethyl alcohol

33. 3.32 g SO_2

34. 0.443 g NH_3

35. 6.39 g O_2

36. 8.62 kg Hg

37. 0.437 g N_2, 0.250 g O_2, 0.562 g H_2O

38. 0.501 g C

27. "Smelling salts," which are used to revive someone who has fainted, typically contain ammonium carbonate, $(NH_4)_2CO_3$. Ammonium carbonate decomposes readily to form ammonia, carbon dioxide, and water. The strong odor of the ammonia usually restores consciousness in the person who has fainted. The unbalanced equation is

$$(NH_4)_2CO_3(s) \rightarrow NH_3(g) + CO_2(g) + H_2O(g)$$

Calculate the mass of ammonia gas that is produced if 1.25 g of ammonium carbonate decomposes completely.

28. Calcium carbide, CaC_2, can be produced in an electric furnace by strongly heating calcium oxide (lime) with carbon. The unbalanced equation is

$$CaO(s) + C(s) \rightarrow CaC_2(s) + CO(g)$$

Calcium carbide is useful because it reacts readily with water to form the flammable gas acetylene, C_2H_2, which is used extensively in the welding industry. The unbalanced equation is

$$CaC_2(s) + H_2O(l) \rightarrow C_2H_2(g) + Ca(OH)_2(s)$$

What mass of acetylene gas, C_2H_2, would be produced by complete reaction of 3.75 g of calcium carbide?

29. When elemental carbon is burned in the open atmosphere, with plenty of oxygen gas present, the product is carbon dioxide.

$$C(s) + O_2(g) \rightarrow CO_2(g)$$

However, when the amount of oxygen present during the burning of the carbon is restricted, carbon monoxide is more likely to result.

$$2C(s) + O_2(g) \rightarrow 2CO(g)$$

What mass of each product is expected when a 5.00-g sample of pure carbon is burned under each of these conditions?

30. If baking soda (sodium hydrogen carbonate) is heated strongly, the following reaction occurs:

$$2NaHCO_3(s) \rightarrow Na_2CO_3(s) + H_2O(g) + CO_2(g)$$

Calculate the mass of sodium carbonate that will remain if a 1.52-g sample of sodium hydrogen carbonate is heated.

31. Although we usually think of substances as "burning" only in oxygen gas, the process of rapid oxidation to produce a flame may also take place in other strongly oxidizing gases. For example, when iron is heated and placed in pure chlorine gas, the iron "burns" according to the following (unbalanced) reaction:

$$Fe(s) + Cl_2(g) \rightarrow FeCl_3(s)$$

How many milligrams of iron(III) chloride result when 15.5 mg of iron is reacted with an excess of chlorine gas?

32. When yeast is added to a solution of glucose or fructose, the sugars are said to undergo *fermentation* and ethyl alcohol is produced.

$$C_6H_{12}O_6(aq) \rightarrow 2C_2H_5OH(aq) + 2CO_2(g)$$

This is the reaction by which wines are produced from grape juice. Calculate the mass of ethyl alcohol, C_2H_5OH, produced when 5.25 g of glucose, $C_6H_{12}O_6$, undergoes this reaction.

33. Sulfurous acid is unstable in aqueous solution and gradually decomposes to water and sulfur dioxide gas (which explains the choking odor associated with sulfurous acid solutions).

$$H_2SO_3(aq) \rightarrow H_2O(l) + SO_2(g)$$

If 4.25 g of sulfurous acid undergoes this reaction, what mass of sulfur dioxide is released?

34. Small quantities of ammonia gas can be generated in the laboratory by heating an ammonium salt with a strong base. For example, ammonium chloride reacts with sodium hydroxide according to the following balanced equation:

$$NH_4Cl(s) + NaOH(s) \rightarrow NH_3(g) + NaCl(s) + H_2O(g)$$

What mass of ammonia gas is produced if 1.39 g of ammonium chloride reacts completely?

35. Elemental phosphorus burns in oxygen with an intensely hot flame, producing a brilliant light and clouds of the oxide product. These properties of the combustion of phosphorus have led to its being used in bombs and incendiary devices for warfare.

$$P_4(s) + 5O_2(g) \rightarrow 2P_2O_5(s)$$

If 4.95 g of phosphorus is burned, what mass of oxygen does it combine with?

36. Although we tend to make less use of mercury these days because of the environmental problems created by its improper disposal, mercury is still an important metal because of its unusual property of existing as a liquid at room temperature. One process by which mercury is produced industrially is through the heating of its common ore cinnabar (mercuric sulfide, HgS) with lime (calcium oxide, CaO).

$$4HgS(s) + 4CaO(s) \rightarrow 4Hg(l) + 3CaS(s) + CaSO_4(s)$$

What mass of mercury would be produced by complete reaction of 10.0 kg of HgS?

37. Ammonium nitrate has been used as a high explosive because it is unstable and decomposes into several gaseous substances. The rapid expansion of the gaseous substances produces the explosive force.

$$NH_4NO_3(s) \rightarrow N_2(g) + O_2(g) + H_2O(g)$$

Calculate the mass of each product gas if 1.25 g of ammonium nitrate reacts.

38. If common sugars are heated too strongly, they char as they decompose into carbon and water vapor. For example, if sucrose (table sugar) is heated, the reaction is

$$C_{12}H_{22}O_{11}(s) \rightarrow 12C(s) + 11H_2O(g)$$

What mass of carbon is produced if 1.19 g of sucrose decomposes completely?

All even-numbered Questions and Problems have answers in the back of this book and solutions in the Solutions Guide.

39. Thionyl chloride, $SOCl_2$, is used as a very powerful drying agent in many synthetic chemistry experiments in which the presence of even small amounts of water would be detrimental. The unbalanced chemical equation is

$$SOCl_2(l) + H_2O(l) \rightarrow SO_2(g) + HCl(g)$$

Calculate the mass of water consumed by complete reaction of 35.0 g of $SOCl_2$.

40. In the "Chemistry in Focus" segment *Cars of the Future,* the claim is made that the combustion of gasoline for some cars causes about 1 lb of CO_2 to be produced for each mile traveled.

Estimate the gas mileage of a car that produces about 1 lb of CO_2 per mile traveled. Assume gasoline has a density of 0.75 g/mL and is 100% octane (C_8H_{18}). While this last part is not true, it is close enough for an estimation. The reaction can be represented by the following *un*balanced chemical equation:

$$C_8H_{18} + O_2 \rightarrow CO_2 + H_2O$$

9.5 Calculations Involving a Limiting Reactant

QUESTIONS

41. Imagine you are chatting with a friend who has not yet taken a chemistry course. How would you explain the concept of *limiting reactant* to her? Your textbook uses the analogy of an automobile manufacturer ordering four wheels for each engine ordered as an example. Can you think of another analogy that might help your friend to understand the concept?

42. Explain how one determines which reactant in a process is the limiting reactant. Does this depend only on the masses of the reactant present? Is the mole ratio in which the reactants combine involved?

43. What is the *theoretical yield* for a reaction, and how does this quantity depend on the limiting reactant?

44. What does it mean to say a reactant is present "in excess" in a process? Can the *limiting reactant* be present in excess? Does the presence of an excess of a reactant affect the mass of products expected for a reaction?

PROBLEMS

45. For each of the following *unbalanced* reactions, suppose exactly 5.00 g of *each reactant* is taken. Determine which reactant is limiting, and also determine what mass of the excess reagent will remain after the limiting reactant is consumed.

a. $Na_2B_4O_7(s) + H_2SO_4(aq) + H_2O(l) \rightarrow H_3BO_3(s) + Na_2SO_4(aq)$
b. $CaC_2(s) + H_2O(l) \rightarrow Ca(OH)_2(s) + C_2H_2(g)$
c. $NaCl(s) + H_2SO_4(l) \rightarrow HCl(g) + Na_2SO_4(s)$
d. $SiO_2(s) + C(s) \rightarrow Si(l) + CO(g)$

46. For each of the following *unbalanced* chemical equations, suppose that exactly 5.00 g of *each* reactant is taken. Determine which reactant is limiting, and calculate what mass of each product is expected (assuming that the limiting reactant is completely consumed).

a. $S(s) + H_2SO_4(aq) \rightarrow SO_2(g) + H_2O(l)$
b. $MnO_2(s) + H_2SO_4(l) \rightarrow Mn(SO_4)_2(s) + H_2O(l)$
c. $H_2S(g) + O_2(g) \rightarrow SO_2(g) + H_2O(l)$
d. $AgNO_3(aq) + Al(s) \rightarrow Ag(s) + Al(NO_3)_3(aq)$

47. For each of the following *unbalanced* chemical equations, suppose 10.0 g of *each* reactant is taken. Show by calculation which reactant is the limiting reagent. Calculate the mass of each product that is expected.

a. $C_3H_8(g) + O_2(g) \rightarrow CO_2(g) + H_2O(g)$
b. $Al(s) + Cl_2(g) \rightarrow AlCl_3(s)$
c. $NaOH(s) + CO_2(g) \rightarrow Na_2CO_3(s) + H_2O(l)$
d. $NaHCO_3(s) + HCl(aq) \rightarrow NaCl(aq) + H_2O(l) + CO_2(g)$

48. For each of the following *unbalanced* chemical equations, suppose that exactly 1.00 g of *each* reactant is taken. Determine which reactant is limiting, and calculate what mass of the product in boldface is expected (assuming that the limiting reactant is completely consumed).

a. $CS_2(l) + O_2(g) \rightarrow \mathbf{CO_2}(g) + SO_2(g)$
b. $NH_3(g) + CO_2(g) \rightarrow CN_2H_4O(s) + \mathbf{H_2O}(g)$
c. $H_2(g) + MnO_2(s) \rightarrow MnO(s) + \mathbf{H_2O}(g)$
d. $I_2(l) + Cl_2(g) \rightarrow \mathbf{ICl}(g)$

49. For each of the following *unbalanced* chemical equations, suppose 1.00 g of *each* reactant is taken. Show by calculation which reactant is limiting. Calculate the mass of each product that is expected.

a. $UO_2(s) + HF(aq) \rightarrow UF_4(aq) + H_2O(l)$
b. $NaNO_3(aq) + H_2SO_4(aq) \rightarrow Na_2SO_4(aq) + HNO_3(aq)$
c. $Zn(s) + HCl(aq) \rightarrow ZnCl_2(aq) + H_2(g)$
d. $B(OH)_3(s) + CH_3OH(l) \rightarrow B(OCH_3)_3(s) + H_2O(l)$

50. For each of the following *unbalanced* chemical equations, suppose 10.0 mg of *each* reactant is taken. Show by calculation which reactant is limiting. Calculate the mass of each product that is expected.

a. $CO(g) + H_2(g) \rightarrow CH_3OH(l)$
b. $Al(s) + I_2(s) \rightarrow AlI_3(s)$
c. $Ca(OH)_2(aq) + HBr(aq) \rightarrow CaBr_2(aq) + H_2O(l)$
d. $Cr(s) + H_3PO_4(aq) \rightarrow CrPO_4(s) + H_2(g)$

51. Lead(II) carbonate, also called "white lead," was formerly used as a pigment in white paints. However, because of its toxicity, lead can no longer be used in paints intended for residential homes. Lead(II) carbonate is prepared industrially by reaction of aqueous lead(II) acetate with carbon dioxide gas. The unbalanced equation is

$$Pb(C_2H_3O_2)_2(aq) + H_2O(l) + CO_2(g) \rightarrow PbCO_3(s) + HC_2H_3O_2(aq)$$

Suppose an aqueous solution containing 1.25 g of lead(II) acetate is treated with 5.95 g of carbon dioxide. Calculate the theoretical yield of lead carbonate.

All even-numbered Questions and Problems have answers in the back of this book and solutions in the Solutions Guide.

39. 5.30 g

40. Gas mileage is about 19 miles per gallon.

Balanced equation: $2C_8H_{18} + 25O_2 \rightarrow 16CO_2 + 18H_2O$

$$1 \text{ gallon of gasoline} \times \frac{3.7854 \text{ L}}{1 \text{ gallon}} \times \frac{1000 \text{ mL}}{1 \text{ L}} \times \frac{0.75 \text{ g } C_8H_{18}}{1 \text{ mL}} \times \frac{1 \text{ mol } C_8H_{18}}{114.224 \text{ g } C_8H_{18}} \times \frac{16 \text{ mol } CO_2}{2 \text{ mol } C_8H_{18}} \times \frac{44.01 \text{ g } CO_2}{1 \text{ mol } CO_2} \times \frac{1 \text{ lb } CO_2}{453.59 \text{ g } CO_2} \times \frac{1 \text{ mile}}{1 \text{ lb } CO_2} =$$

19.29 miles traveled

41. Answer depends on student explanation.

42. To determine the limiting reactant, first calculate the number of moles of each reactant present. Then determine how these numbers of moles correspond to the stoichiometric ratio indicated by the balanced chemical equation for the reaction. For each reactant, use the stoichiometric ratios from the balanced chemical equation to calculate how much of the *other* reactants would be required to react completely.

43. The theoretical yield is the stoichiometric amount of product that should form if the limiting reactant is completely consumed.

44. A reactant is present in excess if there is more of that reactant present than is required to react with the limiting reactant. The limiting reactant, by definition, cannot be present in excess. No.

45. (a) $Na_2B_4O_7$ is limiting, 2.56 g H_2SO_4 remaining, 2.76 g H_2O remaining; (b) CaC_2 is limiting, 2.18 g water remaining; (c) NaCl is limiting, 0.80 g H_2SO_4 remaining; (d) SiO_2 is limiting, 3.00 g C remaining

46. (a) H_2SO_4 is limiting, 4.90 g SO_2, 0.918 g H_2O; (b) H_2SO_4 is limiting, 6.30 g $Mn(SO_4)_2$, 0.918 g H_2O; (c) O_2 is limiting, 6.67 g SO_2, 1.88 g H_2O; (d) $AgNO_3$ is limiting, 3.18 g Ag, 2.09 g $Al(NO_3)_3$

47. (a) O_2 is limiting, 8.25 g CO_2, 4.51 g H_2O; (b) Cl_2 is limiting, 12.5 g $AlCl_3$; (c) NaOH is limiting, 13.3 g Na_2CO_3, 2.25 g H_2O; (d) $NaHCO_3$ is limiting, 6.95 g NaCl, 2.14 g H_2O, 5.24 g CO_2

48. (a) O_2 is limiting, 0.458 g CO_2; (b) CO_2 is limiting, 0.409 g H_2O; (c) MnO_2 is limiting, 0.207 g H_2O; (d) I_2 is limiting, 1.28 g ICl

49. (a) UO_2 is the limiting reactant, 1.16 g UF_4, 0.133 g H_2O; (b) $NaNO_3$ is the limiting reactant, 0.836 g Na_2SO_4, 0.741 g HNO_3; (c) HCl is the limiting reactant, 1.87 g $ZnCl_2$, 0.0276 g H_2; (d) CH_3OH is the limiting reactant, 1.08 g $B(OCH_3)_3$, 0.562 g H_2O

50. (a) CO is limiting reactant, 11.4 mg CH_3OH; (b) I_2 is limiting reactant, 10.7 mg AlI_3; (c) HBr is limiting reactant, 12.4 mg $CaBr_2$, 2.23 mg H_2O; (d) H_3PO_4 is limiting reactant, 15.0 mg $CrPO_4$, 0.309 mg H_2

51. 1.03 g $PbCO_3$

52. CuO

53. 46.4 kg Pb

54. 1.79 g Fe_2O_3

55. No

56. Sodium sulfate is the limiting reactant; calcium chloride is present in excess.

57. BaO_2 is limiting, 0.301 g H_2O_2

58. 0.67 kg SiC

59. The *theoretical yield* represents the yield we calculate from the stoichiometry of the reaction and the masses of reactants taken for the experiment. The *actual yield* is what is actually obtained in an experiment. The *percent yield* is the ratio of what is actually obtained to the theoretical amount that could be obtained, converted to a percentage.

60. If the reaction occurs in a solvent, the product may have a substantial solubility in the solvent; the reaction may come to equilibrium before the full yield of product is achieved (see Chapter 17); loss of product may occur through operator error.

61. 85.4%

62. 1.86 g in theory; 81.3% yield

63. theoretical yield, 25.2 g; percent yield, 20.9%

52. Copper(II) sulfate has been used extensively as a fungicide (kills fungus) and herbicide (kills plants). Copper(II) sulfate can be prepared in the laboratory by reaction of copper(II) oxide with sulfuric acid. The unbalanced equation is

$$CuO(s) + H_2SO_4(aq) \rightarrow CuSO_4(aq) + H_2O(l)$$

If 2.49 g of copper(II) oxide is treated with 5.05 g of pure sulfuric acid, which reactant would limit the quantity of copper(II) sulfate that could be produced?

53. Lead(II) oxide from an ore can be reduced to elemental lead by heating in a furnace with carbon.

$$PbO(s) + C(s) \rightarrow Pb(l) + CO(g)$$

Calculate the expected yield of lead if 50.0 kg of lead oxide is heated with 50.0 kg of carbon.

54. If steel wool (iron) is heated until it glows and is placed in a bottle containing pure oxygen, the iron reacts spectacularly to produce iron(III) oxide.

$$Fe(s) + O_2(g) \rightarrow Fe_2O_3(s)$$

If 1.25 g of iron is heated and placed in a bottle containing 0.0204 mole of oxygen gas, what mass of iron(III) oxide is produced?

55. A common method for determining how much chloride ion is present in a sample is to precipitate the chloride from an aqueous solution of the sample with silver nitrate solution and then to weigh the silver chloride that results. The balanced net ionic reaction is

$$Ag^+(aq) + Cl^-(aq) \rightarrow AgCl(s)$$

Suppose a 5.45-g sample of pure sodium chloride is dissolved in water and is then treated with a solution containing 1.15 g of silver nitrate. Will this quantity of silver nitrate be capable of precipitating *all* the chloride ion from the sodium chloride sample?

56. Although many sulfate salts are soluble in water, calcium sulfate is not (Table 7.1). Therefore, a solution of calcium chloride will react with sodium sulfate solution to produce a precipitate of calcium sulfate. The balanced equation is

$$CaCl_2(aq) + Na_2SO_4(aq) \rightarrow CaSO_4(s) + 2NaCl(aq)$$

If a solution containing 5.21 g of calcium chloride is combined with a solution containing 4.95 g of sodium sulfate, which is the limiting reactant? Which reactant is present in excess?

57. Hydrogen peroxide is used as a cleaning agent in the treatment of cuts and abrasions for several reasons. It is an oxidizing agent that can directly kill many microorganisms; it decomposes upon contact with blood, releasing elemental oxygen gas (which inhibits the growth of anaerobic microorganisms); and it foams upon contact with blood, which provides a cleansing action. In the laboratory, small quantities of hydrogen peroxide can be prepared by the action of an acid on an alkaline earth metal peroxide, such as barium peroxide.

$$BaO_2(s) + 2HCl(aq) \rightarrow H_2O_2(aq) + BaCl_2(aq)$$

What amount of hydrogen peroxide should result when 1.50 g of barium peroxide is treated with 25.0 mL of hydrochloric acid solution containing 0.0272 g of HCl per mL?

58. Silicon carbide, SiC, is one of the hardest materials known. Surpassed in hardness only by diamond, it is sometimes known commercially as carborundum. Silicon carbide is used primarily as an abrasive for sandpaper and is manufactured by heating common sand (silicon dioxide, SiO_2) with carbon in a furnace.

$$SiO_2(s) + C(s) \rightarrow CO(g) + SiC(s)$$

What mass of silicon carbide should result when 1.0 kg of pure sand is heated with an excess of carbon?

9.6 Percent Yield

QUESTIONS

59. Your text talks about several sorts of "yield" when experiments are performed in the laboratory. Students often confuse these terms. Define, compare, and contrast what are meant by *theoretical* yield, *actual* yield, and *percent* yield.

60. The text explains that one reason why the actual yield for a reaction may be less than the theoretical yield is side reactions. Suggest some other reasons why the percent yield for a reaction might not be 100%.

61. According to his prelaboratory theoretical yield calculations, a student's experiment should have produced 1.44 g of magnesium oxide. When he weighed his product after reaction, only 1.23 g of magnesium oxide was present. What is the student's percent yield?

62. Small quantities of oxygen gas can be generated in the laboratory by heating potassium chlorate.

$$2KClO_3(s) \rightarrow 2KCl(s) + 3O_2(g)$$

If 4.74 g of potassium chlorate is heated, what theoretical mass of oxygen gas should be produced? If only 1.51 g of oxygen is actually obtained, what is the percent yield?

PROBLEMS

63. The compound sodium thiosulfate pentahydrate, $Na_2S_2O_3{\cdot}5H_2O$, is important commercially to the photography business as "hypo," because it has the ability to dissolve unreacted silver salts from photographic film during development. Sodium thiosulfate pentahydrate can be produced by boiling elemental sulfur in an aqueous solution of sodium sulfite.

$$S_8(s) + Na_2SO_3(aq) + H_2O(l) \rightarrow Na_2S_2O_3{\cdot}5H_2O(s) \quad \text{(unbalanced)}$$

All even-numbered Questions and Problems have answers in the back of this book and solutions in the Solutions Guide.

What is the theoretical yield of sodium thiosulfate pentahydrate when 3.25 g of sulfur is boiled with 13.1 g of sodium sulfite? Sodium thiosulfate pentahydrate is very soluble in water. What is the percent yield of the synthesis if a student doing this experiment is able to isolate (collect) only 5.26 g of the product?

64. Alkali metal hydroxides are sometimes used to "scrub" excess carbon dioxide from the air in closed spaces (such as submarines and spacecraft). For example, lithium hydroxide reacts with carbon dioxide according to the unbalanced chemical equation

$$LiOH(s) + CO_2(g) \rightarrow Li_2CO_3(s) + H_2O(g)$$

Suppose a lithium hydroxide canister contains 155 g of LiOH(*s*). What mass of $CO_2(g)$ will the canister be able to absorb? If it is found that after 24 hours of use the canister has absorbed 102 g of carbon dioxide, what percentage of its capacity has been reached?

65. Although they were formerly called the inert gases, at least the heavier elements of Group 8 do form relatively stable compounds. For example, xenon combines directly with elemental fluorine at elevated temperatures in the presence of a nickel catalyst.

$$Xe(g) + 2F_2(g) \rightarrow XeF_4(s)$$

What is the theoretical mass of xenon tetrafluoride that should form when 130. g of xenon is reacted with 100. g of F_2? What is the percent yield if only 145 g of XeF_4 is actually isolated?

66. A common undergraduate laboratory analysis for the amount of sulfate ion in an unknown sample is to precipitate and weigh the sulfate ion as barium sulfate.

$$Ba^{2+}(aq) + SO_4^{2-}(aq) \rightarrow BaSO_4(s)$$

The precipitate produced, however, is very finely divided, and frequently some is lost during filtration before weighing. If a sample containing 1.12 g of sulfate ion is treated with 5.02 g of barium chloride, what is the theoretical yield of barium sulfate to be expected? If only 2.02 g of barium sulfate is actually collected, what is the percent yield?

Additional Problems

67. Natural waters often contain relatively high levels of calcium ion, Ca^{2+}, and hydrogen carbonate ion (bicarbonate), HCO_3^-, from the leaching of minerals into the water. When such water is used commercially or in the home, heating of the water leads to the formation of solid calcium carbonate, $CaCO_3$, which forms a deposit ("scale") on the interior of boilers, pipes, and other plumbing fixtures.

$$Ca(HCO_3)_2(aq) \rightarrow CaCO_3(s) + CO_2(g) + H_2O(l)$$

If a sample of well water contains 2.0×10^{-3} mg of $Ca(HCO_3)_2$ per milliliter, what mass of $CaCO_3$ scale would 1.0 mL of this water be capable of depositing?

68. One process for the commercial production of baking soda (sodium hydrogen carbonate) involves the following reaction, in which the carbon dioxide is used in its solid form ("dry ice") both to serve as a source of reactant and to cool the reaction system to a temperature low enough for the sodium hydrogen carbonate to precipitate:

$$NaCl(aq) + NH_3(aq) + H_2O(l) + CO_2(s) \rightarrow NH_4Cl(aq) + NaHCO_3(s)$$

Because they are relatively cheap, sodium chloride and water are typically present in excess. What is the expected yield of $NaHCO_3$ when one performs such a synthesis using 10.0 g of ammonia and 15.0 g of dry ice, with an excess of NaCl and water?

69. A favorite demonstration among chemistry instructors, to show that the properties of a compound differ from those of its constituent elements, involves iron filings and powdered sulfur. If the instructor takes samples of iron and sulfur and just mixes them together, the two elements can be separated from one another with a magnet (iron is attracted to a magnet, sulfur is not). If the instructor then combines and *heats* the mixture of iron and sulfur, a reaction takes place and the elements combine to form iron(II) sulfide (which is not attracted by a magnet).

$$Fe(s) + S(s) \rightarrow FeS(s)$$

Suppose 5.25 g of iron filings is combined with 12.7 g of sulfur. What is the theoretical yield of iron(II) sulfide?

70. When the sugar glucose, $C_6H_{12}O_6$, is burned in air, carbon dioxide and water vapor are produced. Write the balanced chemical equation for this process, and calculate the theoretical yield of carbon dioxide when 1.00 g of glucose is burned completely.

71. When elemental copper is strongly heated with sulfur, a mixture of CuS and Cu_2S is produced, with CuS predominating.

$$Cu(s) + S(s) \rightarrow CuS(s)$$
$$2Cu(s) + S(s) \rightarrow Cu_2S(s)$$

What is the theoretical yield of CuS when 31.8 g of Cu(*s*) is heated with 50.0 g of S? (Assume only CuS is produced in the reaction.) What is the percent yield of CuS if only 40.0 g of CuS can be isolated from the mixture?

72. Barium chloride solutions are used in chemical analysis for the quantitative precipitation of sulfate ion from solution.

$$Ba^{2+}(aq) + SO_4^{2-}(aq) \rightarrow BaSO_4(s)$$

Suppose a solution is known to contain on the order of 150 mg of sulfate ion. What mass of barium chloride should be added to guarantee precipitation of all the sulfate ion?

73. The traditional method of analysis for the amount of chloride ion present in a sample is to dissolve the

All even-numbered Questions and Problems have answers in the back of this book and solutions in the Solutions Guide.

64. $2LiOH(s) + CO_2(g) \rightarrow Li_2CO_3(s) + H_2O(g)$. 142 g of CO_2 can be ultimately absorbed; 102 g is 71.8% of the canister's capacity.

65. theoretical yield, 205 g; percent yield, 70.7%

66. theoretical, 2.72 g $BaSO_4$; percent, 74.3%

67. 1.2×10^{-6} g

68. 28.6 g $NaHCO_3$

69. Fe is limiting, 8.26 g FeS

70. $C_6H_{12}O_6 + 6O_2 \rightarrow 6CO_2 + 6H_2O$; 1.47 g CO_2

71. Cu is limiting, 47.8 g CuS, 83.7%

72. at least 325 mg

73. 0.520 g $AgNO_3$, 0.439 g AgCl

sample in water and then slowly to add a solution of silver nitrate. Silver chloride is very insoluble in water, and by adding a slight excess of silver nitrate, it is possible effectively to remove all chloride ion from the sample.

$$Ag^+(aq) + Cl^+(aq) \rightarrow AgCl(s)$$

Suppose a 1.054-g sample is known to contain 10.3% chloride ion by mass. What mass of silver nitrate must be used to completely precipitate the chloride ion from the sample? What mass of silver chloride will be obtained?

74. For each of the following reactions, give the balanced equation for the reaction and state the meaning of the equation in terms of numbers of *individual molecules* and in terms of *moles* of molecules.

a. $UO_2(s) + HF(aq) \rightarrow UF_4(aq) + H_2O(l)$
b. $NaC_2H_3O_2(aq) + H_2SO_4(aq) \rightarrow Na_2SO_4(aq) + HC_2H_3O_2(aq)$
c. $Mg(s) + HCl(aq) \rightarrow MgCl_2(aq) + H_2(g)$
d. $B_2O_3(s) + H_2O(l) \rightarrow B(OH)_3(aq)$

75. True or false? For the reaction represented by the balanced chemical equation

$$Mg(OH)_2(aq) + 2HCl(aq) \rightarrow 2H_2O(l) + MgCl_2(aq)$$

for 0.40 mole of $Mg(OH)_2$, 0.20 mol of HCl will be needed.

76. Consider the balanced equation

$$C_3H_8(g) + 5O_2(g) \rightarrow 3CO_2(g) + 4H_2O(g)$$

What mole ratio enables you to calculate the number of moles of oxygen needed to react exactly with a given number of moles of $C_3H_8(g)$? What mole ratios enable you to calculate how many moles of each product form from a given number of moles of C_3H_8?

77. For each of the following balanced reactions, calculate how many *moles of each product* would be produced by complete conversion of *0.50 mole* of the reactant indicated in boldface. Indicate clearly the mole ratio used for the conversion.

a. $\mathbf{2H_2O_2}(l) \rightarrow 2H_2O(l) + O_2(g)$
b. $\mathbf{2KClO_3}(s) \rightarrow 2KCl(s) + 3O_2(g)$
c. $\mathbf{2Al}(s) + 6HCl(aq) \rightarrow 2AlCl_3(aq) + 3H_2(g)$
d. $\mathbf{C_3H_8}(g) + 5O_2(g) \rightarrow 3CO_2(g) + 4H_2O(g)$

78. For each of the following balanced equations, indicate how many *moles of the product* could be produced by complete reaction of *1.00 g* of the reactant indicated in boldface. Indicate clearly the mole ratio used for the conversion.

a. $\mathbf{NH_3}(g) + HCl(g) \rightarrow NH_4Cl(s)$
b. $\mathbf{CaO}(s) + CO_2(g) \rightarrow CaCO_3(s)$
c. $\mathbf{4Na}(s) + O_2(g) \rightarrow 2Na_2O(s)$
d. $\mathbf{2P}(s) + 3Cl_2(g) \rightarrow 2PCl_3(l)$

79. Using the average atomic masses given inside the front cover of the text, calculate how many *moles* of each substance the following masses represent.

a. 4.21 g of copper(II) sulfate
b. 7.94 g of barium nitrate
c. 1.24 mg of water
d. 9.79 g of tungsten
e. 1.45 lb of sulfur
f. 4.65 g of ethyl alcohol, C_2H_5OH
g. 12.01 g of carbon

80. Using the average atomic masses given inside the front cover of the text, calculate the *mass in grams* of each of the following samples.

a. 5.0 moles of nitric acid
b. 0.000305 mole of mercury
c. 2.31×10^{-5} mole of potassium chromate
d. 10.5 moles of aluminum chloride
e. 4.9×10^4 moles of sulfur hexafluoride
f. 125 moles of ammonia
g. 0.01205 mole of sodium peroxide

81. For each of the following *incomplete* and *unbalanced* equations, indicate how many *moles* of the *second reactant* would be required to react completely with *0.145 mol* of the *first reactant.*

a. $BaCl_2(aq) + H_2SO_4 \rightarrow$
b. $AgNO_3(aq) + NaCl(aq) \rightarrow$
c. $Pb(NO_3)_2(aq) + Na_2CO_3(aq) \rightarrow$
d. $C_3H_8(g) + O_2(g) \rightarrow$

82. One step in the commercial production of sulfuric acid, H_2SO_4, involves the conversion of sulfur dioxide, SO_2, into sulfur trioxide, SO_3.

$$2SO_2(g) + O_2(g) \rightarrow 2SO_3(g)$$

If 150 kg of SO_2 reacts completely, what mass of SO_3 should result?

83. Many metals occur naturally as sulfide compounds; examples include ZnS and CoS. Air pollution often accompanies the processing of these ores, because toxic sulfur dioxide is released as the ore is converted from the sulfide to the oxide by roasting (smelting). For example, consider the unbalanced equation for the roasting reaction for zinc:

$$ZnS(s) + O_2(g) \rightarrow ZnO(s) + SO_2(g)$$

How many kilograms of sulfur dioxide are produced when 1.0×10^2 kg of ZnS is roasted in excess oxygen by this process?

84. If sodium peroxide is added to water, elemental oxygen gas is generated:

$$Na_2O_2(s) + H_2O(l) \rightarrow NaOH(aq) + O_2(g)$$

Suppose 3.25 g of sodium peroxide is added to a large excess of water. What mass of oxygen gas will be produced?

All even-numbered Questions and Problems have answers in the back of this book and solutions in the Solutions Guide.

74. (a) $UO_2(s) + 4HF(aq) \rightarrow UF_4(aq) + 2H_2O(l)$. One formula unit of uranium(IV) oxide combines with four molecules of hydrofluoric acid, producing one uranium(IV) fluoride molecule and two water molecules. One mole of uranium(IV) oxide combines with four moles of hydrofluoric acid to produce one mole of uranium(IV) fluoride and two moles of water. (b) $2NaC_2H_3O_2(aq) + H_2SO_4(aq) \rightarrow Na_2SO_4(aq) + 2HC_2H_3O_2(aq)$. Two molecules (formula units) of sodium acetate react exactly with one molecule of sulfuric acid, producing one molecule (formula unit) of sodium acetate and two molecules of acetic acid. Two moles of sodium acetate combine with one mole of sulfuric acid, producing one mole of sodium sulfate and two moles of acetic acid. (c) $Mg(s) + 2HCl(aq) \rightarrow MgCl_2(aq) + H_2(g)$. One magnesium atom reacts with two hydrochloric acid molecules (formula units) to produce one molecule (formula unit) of magnesium chloride and one molecule of hydrogen gas. One mole of magnesium combines with two moles of hydrochloric acid, producing one mole of magnesium chloride and one mole of gaseous hydrogen. (d) $B_2O_3(s) + 3H_2O(l) \rightarrow 2B(OH)_3(s)$. One molecule (formula unit) of diboron trioxide reacts exactly with three molecules of water, producing two molecules of boron trihydroxide (boric acid). One mole of diboron trioxide combines with three moles of water to produce two moles of boron trihydroxide (boric acid).

75. False

76. for O_2, 5 mol O_2/1 mol C_3H_8; for CO_2, 3 mol CO_2/1 mol C_3H_8; for H_2O, 4 mol H_2O/1 mol C_3H_8

77. (a) 0.50 mol H_2O, 0.25 mol O_2; (b) 0.50 mol KCl, 0.75 mol O_2; (c) 0.50 mol $AlCl_3$, 0.75 mol H_2; (d) 1.5 mol CO_2, 2.0 mol H_2O

78. (a) 0.0588 mol NH_4Cl; (b) 0.0178 mol $CaCO_3$; (c) 0.0217 mol Na_2O; (d) 0.0323 mol PCl_3

79. (a) 0.0264 mol; (b) 0.0304 mol; (c) 6.88×10^{-5} mol; (d) 5.32×10^{-2} mol; (e) 20.5 mol; (f) 0.101 mol; (g) 1.00 mol

80. (a) 3.2×10^2 g HNO_3; (b) 0.0612 g Hg; (c) 4.49×10^{-3} g K_2CrO_4; (d) 1.40×10^3 g $AlCl_3$; (e) 7.2×10^6 g SF_6; (f) 2.13×10^3 g NH_3; (g) 0.9397 g Na_2O_2

81. (a) 0.145 mol; (b) 0.145 mol; (c) 0.145 mol; (d) 0.725 mol

82. 1.9×10^2 kg SO_3

83. 66 kg

84. 0.667 g O_2

85. When elemental copper is placed in a solution of silver nitrate, the following oxidation–reduction reaction takes place, forming elemental silver:

$$Cu(s) + 2AgNO_3(aq) \rightarrow Cu(NO_3)_2(aq) + 2Ag(s)$$

What mass of copper is required to remove all the silver from a silver nitrate solution containing 1.95 mg of silver nitrate?

86. When small quantities of elemental hydrogen gas are needed for laboratory work, the hydrogen is often generated by chemical reaction of a metal with acid. For example, zinc reacts with hydrochloric acid, releasing gaseous elemental hydrogen:

$$Zn(s) + 2HCl(aq) \rightarrow ZnCl_2(aq) + H_2(g)$$

What mass of hydrogen gas is produced when 2.50 g of zinc is reacted with excess aqueous hydrochloric acid?

87. The gaseous hydrocarbon acetylene, C_2H_2, is used in welders' torches because of the large amount of heat released when acetylene burns with oxygen.

$$2C_2H_2(g) + 5O_2(g) \rightarrow 4CO_2(g) + 2H_2O(g)$$

How many grams of oxygen gas are needed for the complete combustion of 150 g of acetylene?

88. For each of the following *unbalanced* chemical equations, suppose exactly 5.0 g of each reactant is taken. Determine which reactant is limiting, and calculate what mass of each product is expected, assuming that the limiting reactant is completely consumed.

a. $Na(s) + Br_2(l) \rightarrow NaBr(s)$
b. $Zn(s) + CuSO_4(aq) \rightarrow ZnSO_4(aq) + Cu(s)$
c. $NH_4Cl(aq) + NaOH(aq) \rightarrow NH_3(g) + H_2O(l) + NaCl(aq)$
d. $Fe_2O_3(s) + CO(g) \rightarrow Fe(s) + CO_2(g)$

89. For each of the following *unbalanced* chemical equations, suppose 25.0 g of each reactant is taken. Show by calculation which reactant is limiting. Calculate the theoretical yield in grams of the product in boldface.

a. $C_2H_5OH(l) + O_2(g) \rightarrow \mathbf{CO_2}(g) + H_2O(l)$
b. $N_2(g) + O_2(g) \rightarrow \mathbf{NO}(g)$
c. $NaClO_2(aq) + Cl_2(g) \rightarrow ClO_2(g) + \mathbf{NaCl}(aq)$
d. $H_2(g) + N_2(g) \rightarrow \mathbf{NH_3}(g)$

90. Hydrazine, N_2H_4, emits a large quantity of energy when it reacts with oxygen, which has led to hydrazine's use as a fuel for rockets:

$$N_2H_4(l) + O_2(g) \rightarrow N_2(g) + 2H_2O(g)$$

How many moles of each of the gaseous products are produced when 20.0 g of pure hydrazine is ignited in the presence of 20.0 g of pure oxygen? How many grams of each product are produced?

91. Although elemental chlorine, Cl_2, is added to drinking water supplies primarily to kill microorganisms, another beneficial reaction that also takes place removes sulfides (which would impart unpleasant odors or tastes to the water). For example, the noxious-smelling gas hydrogen sulfide (its odor resembles that of rotten eggs) is removed from water by chlorine by the following reaction:

$$H_2S(aq) + Cl_2(aq) \rightarrow HCl(aq) + S_8(s) \quad \text{(unbalanced)}$$

What mass of sulfur is removed from the water when 50. L of water containing 1.5×10^{-5} g of H_2S per liter is treated with 1.0 g of $Cl_2(g)$?

92. Before going to lab, a student read in his lab manual that the percent yield for a difficult reaction to be studied was likely to be only 40.% of the theoretical yield. The student's prelab stoichiometric calculations predict that the theoretical yield should be 12.5 g. What is the student's actual yield likely to be?

All even-numbered Questions and Problems have answers in the back of this book and solutions in the Solutions Guide.

85. 0.365 mg

86. 0.0771 g H_2

87. 4.6×10^2 g

88. (a) Br_2 is limiting reactant, 6.4 g NaBr; (b) $CuSO_4$ is limiting reactant, 5.1 g $ZnSO_4$, 2.0 g Cu; (c) NH_4Cl is limiting reactant, 1.6 g NH_3, 1.7 g H_2O, 5.5 g NaCl; (d) Fe_2O_3 is limiting reactant, 3.5 g Fe, 4.1 g CO_2

89. (a) O_2 is limiting, 22.9 g CO_2; (b) O_2 is limiting, 46.9 g NO; (c) $NaClO_2$ is limiting, 16.2 g NaCl; (d) N_2 is limiting, 30.4 g NH_3

90. 0.624 mol N_2, 17.5 g N_2; 1.25 mol H_2O, 22.5 g H_2O

91. 7.1×10^{-4} g S_8 removed

92. 5.0 g

Answers to Cumulative Review Exercises

Chapters 8–9

1. The average atomic mass of an element represents the weighted average mass, on the relative atomic scale, of all the isotopes of an element. Average atomic masses usually are given in terms of atomic mass units (1 amu = 1.66×10^{24} g). For example, the average atomic mass of sodium is 22.99 amu, which represents the average mass of all the sodium atoms in the world (including all the various isotopes and their relative abundances). So that we will be able to use the mass of a sample of sodium to count the number of atoms of sodium present in the sample, we consider that every sodium atom in a sample has exactly the same mass (the average atomic mass). The average atomic mass of an element is typically not a whole number of amu's because of the presence of the different isotopes of the element, each with its own relative abundance. Since the relative abundance of an element can be any random number, when the weighted-average atomic mass of the element is calculated, the average is unlikely to be a whole number.

2. On a microscopic basis, one mole of a substance represents Avogadro's number (6.022×10^{23}) of individual units (atoms or molecules) of the substance. On a macroscopic basis, one mole of a substance represents the amount of substance present when the molar mass of the substance in grams is taken. Chemists have chosen these definitions so that a simple relationship will exist between measurable amounts of substances (grams) and the actual number of atoms or molecules present, and so that the number of particles present in samples of *different* substances can easily be compared.

3. It's all relative. The mass of each substance mentioned in this question happens to be the molar mass of that substance. Each of the three samples of elemental substances mentioned (O, C, and Na) contains Avogadro's number (6.022×10^{23}) of atoms of its respective element. For the compound Na_2CO_3 given, since each unit of Na_2CO_3 contains two sodium atoms, one carbon atom, and three oxygen atoms, it's not surprising that a sample having a mass equal to the molar mass of Na_2CO_3 should contain one molar mass of carbon, two molar masses of sodium, and three molar masses of oxygen: 12.01 g + 2(22.99 g) + 3(16.00 g) = 106.0 g.

4. The molar mass of a compound is the mass in grams of one mole of the compound and is calculated by summing the average atomic masses of all the atoms present in a molecule of the compound. For example, for H_3PO_4: molar mass H_3PO_4 = 3(1.008 g) + 1(30.97 g) + 4(16.00 g) = 97.99 g.

CUMULATIVE REVIEW for CHAPTERS 8 - 9

QUESTIONS

1. What does the average *atomic mass* of an element represent? What unit is used for average atomic mass? Express the atomic mass unit in grams. Why is the average atomic mass for an element typically *not* a whole number?

2. Perhaps the most important concept in introductory chemistry concerns what a *mole* of a substance represents. The mole concept will come up again and again in later chapters in this book. What does one mole of a substance represent on a microscopic, atomic basis? What does one mole of a substance represent on a macroscopic, mass basis? Why have chemists defined the mole in this manner?

3. How do we know that 16.00 g of oxygen contains the same number of atoms as does 12.01 g of carbon, and that 22.99 g of sodium contains the same number of atoms as each of these? How do we know that 106.0 g of Na_2CO_3 contains the same number of carbon atoms as does 12.01 g of carbon, but three times as many oxygen atoms as in 16.00 g of oxygen, and twice as many sodium atoms as in 22.99 g of sodium?

4. Define *molar mass*. Using H_3PO_4 as an example, calculate the molar mass from the atomic masses of the elements.

5. What is meant by the *percent composition* by mass for a compound? Describe in general terms how this information is obtained by experiment for new compounds. How can this information be calculated for known compounds?

6. Define, compare, and contrast what are meant by the *empirical* and *molecular* formulas for a substance. What does each of these formulas tell us about a compound? What information must be known for a compound before the molecular formula can be determined? Why is the molecular formula an *integer multiple* of the empirical formula?

7. When chemistry teachers prepare an exam question on determining the empirical formula of a compound, they usually take a known compound and calculate the percent composition of the compound from the formula. They then give students this percent composition data and have the students calculate the original formula. Using a compound of *your* choice, first use the molecular formula of the compound to calculate the percent composition of the compound. Then use this percent composition data to calculate the empirical formula of the compound.

8. Rather than giving students straight percent composition data for determining the empirical formula of a compound (see Question 7), sometimes chemistry teachers will try to emphasize the experimental nature of formula determination by converting the percent composition data into actual experimental masses. For example, the compound CH_4 contains 74.87% carbon by mass. Rather than giving students the data in this form, a teacher might say instead, "When 1.000 g of a compound was analyzed, it was found to contain 0.7487 g of carbon, with the remainder consisting of hydrogen." Using the compound you chose for Question 7, and the percent composition data you calculated, reword your data as suggested in this problem in terms of actual "experimental" masses. Then from these masses, calculate the empirical formula of your compound.

9. Balanced chemical equations give us information in terms of individual molecules reacting in the proportions indicated by the coefficients, and also in terms of macroscopic amounts (that is, moles). Write a balanced chemical equation of your choice, and interpret in words the meaning of the equation on the molecular and macroscopic levels.

10. Consider the *unbalanced* equation for the combustion of propane:

$$C_3H_8(g) + O_2(g) \rightarrow CO_2(g) + H_2O(g)$$

First, balance the equation. Then, for a given amount of propane, write the mole ratios that would enable you to calculate the number of moles of each product as well as the number of moles of O_2 that would be involved in a complete reaction. Finally, show how these mole ratios would be applied if 0.55 mole of propane is combusted.

11. In the practice of chemistry one of the most important calculations concerns the masses of products expected when particular masses of reactants are used in an experiment. For example, chemists judge the practicality and efficiency of a reaction by seeing how close the amount of product actually obtained is to the expected amount. Using a balanced chemical equation and an amount of starting material of your choice, summarize and illustrate the various steps needed in such a calculation for the expected amount of product.

12. What is meant by a *limiting reactant* in a particular reaction? In what way is the reaction "limited"? What does it mean to say that one or more of the reactants are present *in excess?* What happens to a reaction when the limiting reactant is used up?

13. For a balanced chemical equation of your choice, and using 25.0 g of each of the reactants in your equation, illustrate and explain how you would determine which reactant is the limiting reactant. Indicate *clearly* in your discussion how the choice of limiting reactant follows from your calculations.

14. What do we mean by the *theoretical yield* for a reaction? What is meant by the *actual yield?* Why might the actual yield for an experiment be *less* than the theoretical yield? Can the actual yield be *more* than the theoretical yield?

286

PROBLEMS

15. Consider 2.45-g samples of each of the following elements or compounds. Calculate the number of moles of the element or compound present in each sample.

a. $Fe_2O_3(s)$
b. $P_4(s)$
c. $Cl_2(g)$
d. $Hg_2O(s)$
e. $HgO(s)$
f. $Ca(NO_3)_2(s)$
g. $C_3H_8(g)$
h. $Al_2(SO_4)_3(s)$

16. Calculate the percent by mass of the element whose symbol occurs *first* in the following compounds' formulas.

a. $C_6H_6(l)$
b. $Na_2SO_4(s)$
c. $CS_2(l)$
d. $AlCl_3(s)$
e. $Cu_2O(s)$
f. $CuO(s)$
g. $Co_2O_3(s)$
h. $C_6H_{12}O_6(s)$

17. A compound was analyzed and was found to have the following percent composition by mass: sodium, 43.38%; carbon, 11.33%; oxygen, 45.29%. Determine the empirical formula of the compound.

18. For each of the following balanced equations, calculate how many grams of each product would form if 12.5 g of the reactant listed *first* in the equation reacts completely (there is an excess of the second reactant).

a. $SiC(s) + 2Cl_2(g) \rightarrow SiCl_4(l) + C(s)$
b. $Li_2O(s) + H_2O(l) \rightarrow 2LiOH(aq)$
c. $2Na_2O_2(s) + 2H_2O(l) \rightarrow 4NaOH(aq) + O_2(g)$
d. $SnO_2(s) + 2H_2(g) \rightarrow Sn(s) + 2H_2O(l)$

19. For the reactions in Question 18, suppose that instead of an *excess* of the second reactant, only 5.00 g of the second reactant is available. Indicate which substance is the limiting reactant in each reaction.

20. Depending on the concentration of oxygen gas present when carbon is burned, either of two oxides may result.

$2C(s) + O_2(g) \rightarrow 2CO(g)$
(restricted amount of oxygen)

$C(s) + O_2(g) \rightarrow CO_2(g)$
(unrestricted amount of oxygen)

Suppose that experiments are performed in which duplicate 5.00-g samples of carbon are burned under both conditions. Calculate the theoretical yield of product for each experiment.

21. A traditional analysis for samples containing calcium ion was to precipitate the calcium ion with sodium oxalate ($Na_2C_2O_4$) solution and then to collect and weigh either the calcium oxalate itself or the calcium oxide produced by heating the oxalate precipitate:

$$Ca^{2+}(aq) + C_2O_4^{2-}(aq) \rightarrow CaC_2O_4(s)$$

Suppose a sample contained 0.1014 g of calcium ion. What theoretical yield of calcium oxalate would be expected? If only 0.2995 g of calcium oxalate is collected, what percentage of the theoretical yield does that represent?

5. The percent composition (by mass) of a compound shows the relative amount of each element present in the compound on a mass basis. For compounds whose formulas are known (and whose molar masses are therefore known), the percentage of a given element present in the compound is given by

$$\frac{\text{mass of the element present}}{\text{molar mass of the compound}} \times 100$$

When a new compound is prepared whose formula is not known, the percent composition must be determined on an experimental basis. An elemental analysis must be done of a sample of the new compound to see what mass of each element is present in the sample.

6. The *empirical* formula of a compound represents the *relative* number of atoms of each type present in a molecule of the compound, whereas the *molecular* formula represents the *actual* number of atoms of each type present in a real molecule. For example, both acetylene (molecular formula C_2H_2) and benzene (molecular formula C_6H_6) have the same relative number of carbon and hydrogen atoms, and thus have the same empirical formula (CH). The molar mass of the compound must be determined before calculating the actual molecular formula. Since real molecules cannot contain fractional *parts* of atoms, the molecular formula is always a *whole-number multiple* of the empirical formula.

7. Answer depends on student choice of example.

8. Answer depends on student examples chosen for Exercise 7.

9. Answer depends on student choice of example.

(Please refer to page A32 in this book for answers to Exercises 10–21.)

Chapter 10

Objectives

In this chapter our objectives are for the students to:

SECTION 10.1

- Understand the general properties of energy.

SECTION 10.2

- Understand the concepts of temperature and heat.

SECTION 10.3

- Consider the direction of energy flow as heat.

SECTION 10.4

- Understand how energy flow affects internal energy.

SECTION 10.5

- Understand how heat is measured.

SECTION 10.6

- Consider the heat (enthalpy) of chemical reactions.

SECTION 10.7

- Understand Hess's law.

SECTION 10.8

- See how the quality of energy changes as it is used.

SECTION 10.9

- Consider the energy resources of our world.

SECTION 10.10

- Understand energy as a driving force for natural processes.

10 Energy

A hummingbird exerts a great deal of energy in order to hover. *(Image by © Raven Regan/Design Pics/Corbis)*

ChemWork Refined over ten years of use by thousands of students, **ChemWork** builds and enhances students' problems-solving skills. Online assignments function as a "personal instructor" to help students learn how to solve challenging problems and learn how to think like chemists. Annotations for **ChemWork** assignments are included at the beginning of the end-of-chapter review.

PowerLecture This 2-DVD package includes the Chemistry Multimedia Library, which contains animations, simulations, and movies for all chemistry subjects, organized by topic for lecture presentations. Annotations for **PowerLecture** are referenced in the margins throughout the Annotated Instructor's Edition.

OWL Sign in to OWL at **www.cengage.com/owl** to view tutorials and simulations, develop problem-solving skills, and complete online homework assigned by your professor.

Energy is at the center of our very existence as individuals and as a society. The food that we eat furnishes the energy to live, work, and play, just as the coal and oil consumed by manufacturing and transportation systems power our modern industrialized civilization.

Huge quantities of carbon-based fossil fuels have been available for the taking. This abundance of fuels has led to a world society with a huge appetite for energy, consuming millions of barrels of petroleum every day. We are now dangerously dependent on the dwindling supplies of oil, and this dependence is an important source of tension among nations in today's world. In an incredibly short time we have moved from a period of ample and cheap supplies of petroleum to one of high prices and uncertain supplies. If our present standard of living is to be maintained, we must find alternatives to petroleum. To do this, we need to know the relationship between chemistry and energy, which we explore in this chapter.

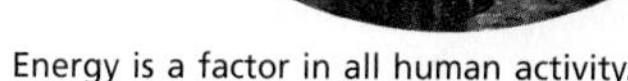

Energy is a factor in all human activity.

Chad Ehler/Stock Connection

10.1 The Nature of Energy

OBJECTIVE: To understand the general properties of energy.

Although energy is a familiar concept, it is difficult to define precisely. For our purposes we will define **energy** as *the ability to do work or produce heat.* We will define these terms below.

Energy can be classified as either potential or kinetic energy. **Potential energy** is energy due to position or composition. For example, water behind a dam has potential energy that can be converted to work when the water flows down through turbines, thereby creating electricity. Attractive and repulsive forces also lead to potential energy. The energy released when gasoline is burned results from differences in attractive forces between the nuclei and electrons in the reactants and products. The **kinetic energy** of an object is energy due to the motion of the object and depends on the mass of the object m and its velocity v: $KE = \frac{1}{2}mv^2$.

One of the most important characteristics of energy is that it is conserved. The **law of conservation of energy** states *that energy can be converted from one form to another but can be neither created nor destroyed.* That is, the energy of the universe is constant.

Although the energy of the universe is constant, it can be readily converted from one form to another. Consider the two balls in Figure 10.1a. Ball A, because of its initially higher position, has more potential energy than ball B. When ball A is released, it moves down the hill and strikes ball B. Eventually, the arrangement shown in Figure 10.1b is achieved. What has happened in going from the initial to the final arrangement? The potential

TEACHING SUPPORT

DEMONSTRATION

Chemiluminescence: Seeing the Light!

Materials

Several lightsticks of any color
Knife
3 clear plastic cups
Funnel
Several feet of clear plastic tubing (purchase from a hardware store)
3% hydrogen peroxide solution (drugstores carry it)

Preparation Attach the tubing to the funnel and decide how you want to arrange it for the demonstration. Possibilities include a random curve, a spiral, a zigzag pattern, or an artistic arrangement of your own design. Use clamps and a ringstand to achieve the desired effect.

Section 10.1

TEACHING TIP

It is helpful to use practical examples when introducing the concept of energy. Students can relate to examples from everyday life. Once these ideas have been discussed in this way, move to a discussion that incorporates more scientific terminology.

Test Bank: 39–42

MINI-DEMO

Begin with a textbook sitting on the edge of the desk. Ask the students whether it has energy and what type it has. Knock the book to the floor. Discuss the changes in energy that occurred as a result of the drop. Ask again whether the book has energy and what type it has. Pick up the book. Have you given the book energy? Continue to use this example to discuss the ideas of kinetic energy, potential energy, and conservation of energy.

As an example to differentiate between kinetic energy and potential energy, use some object (such as an eraser). Hold the object over your head in front of you and ask, "What will happen when I let go?" The students know it will fall to the ground. Release the object and use it to discuss potential energy (which the object has as you are holding it and as it falls to the ground) and kinetic energy (which it has as it falls). As the object gets closer to the ground, the potential energy decreases and the kinetic energy increases. The object transfers this energy to the ground.

PowerLecture Video:
Vaporizing of CO_2 Inside a Plastic Bag, Lifting a Book

PowerLecture Animations:
Man Climbing Ladder (no sound)
Man Diving off Board (no sound)

TEACHING TIP

Another example of a state function is displacement. For example, if two students go from the chemistry room to the school cafeteria, they are both the same distance away from you. They may have taken different routes—one student may have traveled a greater distance—but they end up with the same displacement from you.

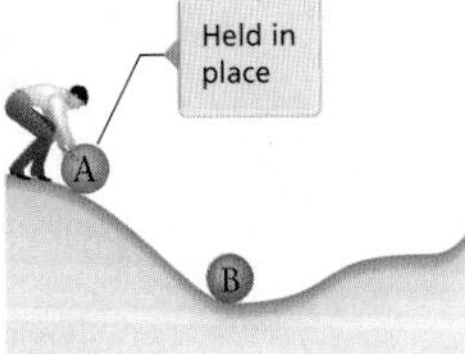

Initial

a In the initial positions, ball A has a higher potential energy than ball B.

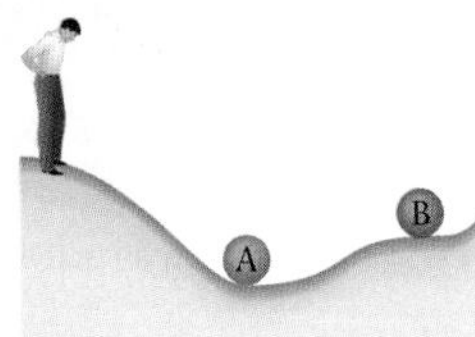

Final

b After A has rolled down the hill, the potential energy lost by A has been converted to random motions of the components of the hill (fractional heating) and to an increase in the potential energy of B.

Figure 10.1

energy of A has decreased because its position was lowered. However, this energy cannot disappear. Where is the energy lost by A?

Initially, the potential energy of A is changed to kinetic energy as the ball rolls down the hill. Part of this energy is transferred to B, causing it to be raised to a higher final position. Thus the potential energy of B has been increased, which means that **work** (force acting over a distance) has been performed on B. Because the final position of B is lower than the original position of A, however, some of the energy is still unaccounted for. Both balls in their final positions are at rest, so the missing energy cannot be attributed to their motions.

What has happened to the remaining energy? The answer lies in the interaction between the hill's surface and the ball. As ball A rolls down the hill, some of its kinetic energy is transferred to the surface of the hill as heat. This transfer of energy is called *frictional heating*. The temperature of the hill increases very slightly as the ball rolls down. Thus the energy stored in A in its original position (potential energy) is distributed to B through work and to the surface of the hill by heat.

Imagine that we perform this same experiment several times, varying the surface of the hill from very smooth to very rough. In rolling to the bottom of the hill (see Figure 10.1), A always loses the same amount of energy because its position always changes by exactly the same amount. The way that this energy transfer is divided between work and heat, however, depends on the specific conditions—the *pathway*. For example, the surface of the hill might be so rough that the energy of A is expended completely through frictional heating: A is moving so slowly when it hits B that it cannot move B to the next level. In this case, no work is done. Regardless of the condition of the hill's surface, the *total energy* transferred will be constant, although the amounts of heat and work will differ. Energy change is independent of the pathway, whereas work and heat are both dependent on the pathway.

This brings us to a very important idea, the state function. A **state function** is a property of the system that changes independently of its pathway. Let's consider a nonchemical example. Suppose you are traveling from Chicago to Denver. Which of the following are state functions?

- Distance traveled
- Change in elevation

Because the distance traveled depends on the route taken (that is, the *pathway* between Chicago and Denver), it is *not* a state function. On the other hand, the change in elevation depends only on the difference between Denver's elevation (5280 ft) and Chicago's elevation (580 ft). The change in elevation is always 5280 ft − 580 ft = 4700 ft; it does not depend on the route taken between the two cities.

We can also learn about state functions from the example illustrated in Figure 10.1. Because ball A always goes from its initial position on the hill to the bottom of the hill, its energy change is always the same, regardless of whether the hill is smooth or bumpy. This energy is a state function—a given change in energy is independent of the pathway of the process. In contrast, work and heat are *not* state functions. For a given change in the position of A, a smooth hill produces more work and less heat than a rough hill does. That is, for a given change in the position of A, the change in energy is always the same (state function) but the way the resulting energy is distributed as heat or work depends on the nature of the hill's surface (heat and work are not state functions).

Use the knife to slice through one end of a lightstick. Pour the contents of the lightstick into one of the plastic cups. The main liquid is thick and colored. A small glass vial is found inside the lightstick as well. Separate the small glass vial (containing hydrogen peroxide) from the rest of the contents and discard it. Place about 5 mL of hydrogen peroxide into a small container (a film cannister works well). You can use additional lightsticks in the same manner to make a longer demonstration.

Presentation Discuss different forms of energy with the students. We most often "see" energy changes in chemical reactions as heat. Light is another form of energy that is observed in some chemical reactions. Show an unactivated lightstick, noting the noise that the small vial of hydrogen peroxide makes when the vial is shaken gently. Bend the lightstick to break the vial of hydrogen peroxide and observe the production of light from the chemical reaction. Pass the lighted stick around the class to have the

10.2 Temperature and Heat

OBJECTIVE: To understand the concepts of temperature and heat.

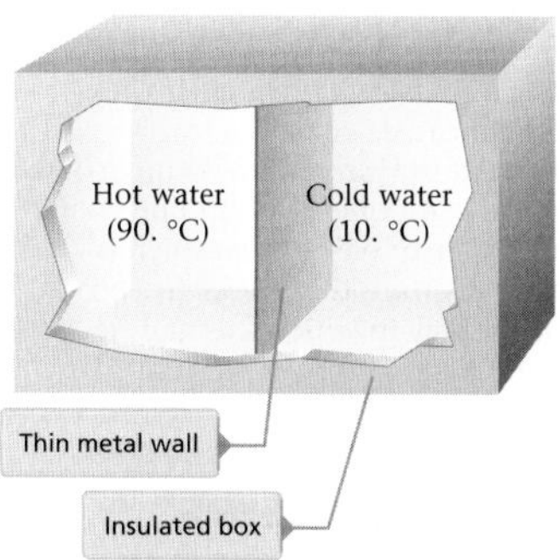

Figure 10.2
Equal masses of hot water and cold water separated by a thin metal wall in an insulated box.

What does the temperature of a substance tell us about that substance? Put another way, how is warm water different from cold water? The answer lies in the motions of the water molecules. **Temperature** is a *measure of the random motions of the components of a substance.* That is, the H_2O molecules in warm water are moving around more rapidly than the H_2O molecules in cold water.

Consider an experiment in which we place 1.00 kg of hot water (90. °C) next to 1.00 kg of cold water (10. °C) in an insulated box. The water samples are separated from each other by a thin metal plate (see Figure 10.2). You already know what will happen: the hot water will cool down and the cold water will warm up.

Assuming that no energy is lost to the air, can we determine the final temperature of the two samples of water? Let's consider how to think about this problem.

First picture what is happening. Remember that the H_2O molecules in the hot water are moving faster than those in the cold water (see Figure 10.3). As a result, energy will be transferred through the metal wall from the hot water to the cold water. This energy transfer will cause the H_2O molecules in the hot water to slow down and the H_2O molecules in the cold water to speed up.

Thus we have a transfer of energy from the hot water to the cold water. This flow of energy is called heat. **Heat** can be defined as a *flow of energy due to a temperature difference.* What will eventually happen? The two water samples will reach the same temperature (see Figure 10.4). At this point, how does the energy lost by the hot water compare to the energy gained by the cold water? They must be the same (remember that energy is conserved).

We conclude that the final temperature is the average of the original temperatures:

$$T_{\text{final}} = \frac{T_{\substack{\text{hot}\\\text{initial}}} + T_{\substack{\text{cold}\\\text{initial}}}}{2} = \frac{90.\ ^\circ\text{C} + 10.\ ^\circ\text{C}}{2} = 50.\ ^\circ\text{C}$$

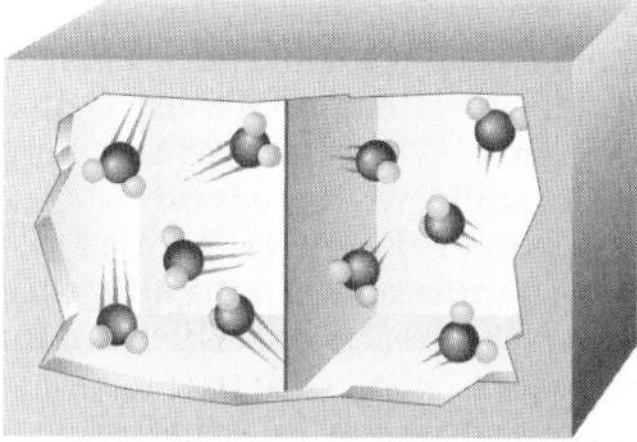

Figure 10.3
The H_2O molecules in hot water have much greater random motions than the H_2O molecules in cold water.

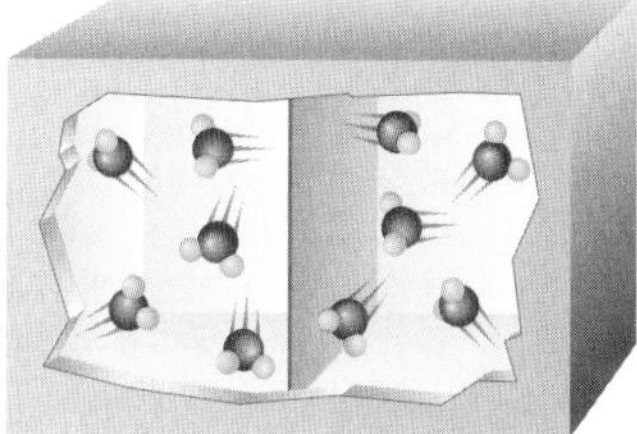

Figure 10.4
The water samples now have the same temperature (50. °C) and have the same random motions.

students observe whether heat is also a product of the reaction. Dim the lights and pour the contents of the previously dissected lightstick into the funnel and follow it with the hydrogen peroxide solution from the film cannister. The solution should begin to glow as it passes through the tubing.

Teaching Notes More discussion of chemiluminescence can be accomplished after the students have an understanding of the role that electrons play in atoms. This demonstration can be done again in Chapter 11 with a more detailed explanation of the source of the energy. The reaction between the hydrogen peroxide and the phenyl oxalate ester in the lightstick causes a transfer of energy to the dye molecules, which in turn excites the electrons in the dye. The electrons release this energy in the form of light.

Section 10.2

Test Bank: 43, 44

PowerLecture Video: Transfer of Thermal Energy from Heated Bar to Cool Water

TEACHING TIPS

- Some students have difficulty distinguishing between temperature and heat. It is important to talk about heat as a flow of energy and temperature as a measure of the "vigor" of the random motions of the components of a substance. Thermal energy is the energy that a substance contains due to the random motions of its components. Heat is the way that thermal energy is transferred from one object to another. Use Figures 10.2 through 10.4 to illustrate this point. Have students focus on the motion of the molecules in the compartments. Note that the molecules never mix, yet energy is transferred from one compartment to the other. The temperature in one compartment goes down and the temperature in the other compartment goes up. The energy flows from the higher-temperature compartment to the lower-temperature compartment.
- We take a molecular perspective to discuss temperature and heat. This approach allows students to have a better understanding of the difference between these concepts.

PowerLecture Animation: Kinetic-Molecular Theory-Heat Transfer

PowerLecture Video: Transfer of Thermal Energy to Water by Drilling

Test Bank: 36–38

Section 10.3

TEACHING TIP

To check the understanding of your students, ask them to label the following as endothermic or exothermic.

1. Your hand gets cold when you touch ice. (exothermic)
2. The ice melts when you touch it. (endothermic)
3. Ice cream melts. (endothermic)
4. Propane is burning in a propane torch. (exothermic)
5. Water drops on your skin after swimming evaporate. (endothermic)
6. Two chemicals mixing in a beaker give off heat. (exothermic)

PowerLecture Video: Reaction of Sodium and Chlorine

PowerLecture Video: NASA Space Shuttle Liftoff

PowerLecture Video: Reaction: Gummi Bear and $KClO_3$

For the hot water, the temperature change is

$$\text{Change in temperature (hot)} = \Delta T_{\text{hot}} = 90.\ ^\circ\text{C} - 50.\ ^\circ\text{C} = 40.\ ^\circ\text{C}$$

The temperature change for the cold water is

$$\text{Change in temperature (cold)} = \Delta T_{\text{cold}} = 50.\ ^\circ\text{C} - 10.\ ^\circ\text{C} = 40.\ ^\circ\text{C}$$

In this example, the masses of hot water and cold water are equal. If they were unequal, this problem would be more complicated.

Let's summarize the ideas we have introduced in this section. Temperature is a measure of the random motions of the components of an object. Heat is a *flow* of energy due to a temperature difference. We say that the random motions of the components of an object constitute the *thermal energy* of that object. The flow of energy called heat is the way in which thermal energy is transferred from a hot object to a colder object.

10.3 Exothermic and Endothermic Processes

OBJECTIVE: To consider the direction of energy flow as heat.

In this section we will consider the energy changes that accompany chemical reactions. To explore this idea, let's consider the striking and burning of a match. Energy is clearly released through heat as the match burns. To discuss this reaction, we divide the universe into two parts: the system and the surroundings. The **system** is the part of the universe on which we wish to focus attention; the **surroundings** include everything else in the universe. In this case we define the system as the reactants and products of the reaction. The surroundings consist of the air in the room and anything else other than the reactants and products.

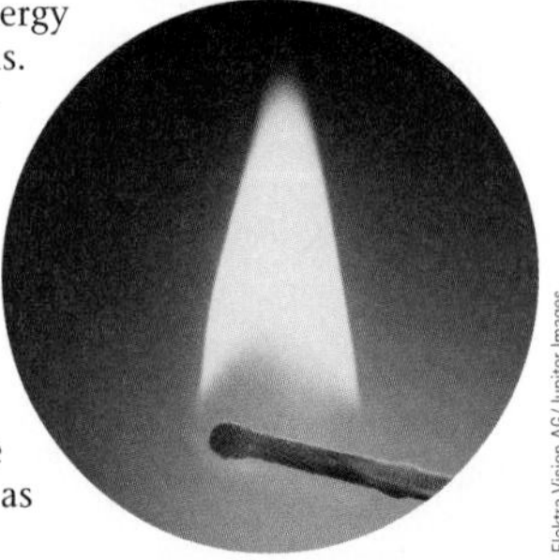

A burning match releases energy.

Elektra Vision AG/Jupiter Images

When a process results in the evolution of heat, it is said to be **exothermic** (*exo-* is a prefix meaning "out of"); that is, energy flows *out of the system*. For example, in the combustion of a match, energy flows out of the system as heat. Processes that absorb energy from the surroundings are said to be **endothermic.** When the heat flow moves *into a system,* the process is endothermic. Boiling water to form steam is a common endothermic process.

Where does the energy, released as heat, come from in an exothermic reaction? The answer lies in the difference in potential energies between the products and the reactants. Which has lower potential energy, the reactants or the products? We know that total energy is conserved and that energy flows from the system into the surroundings in an exothermic reaction. Thus *the energy gained by the surroundings must be equal to the energy lost by the system.* In the combustion of a match, the burned match has lost potential energy (in this case potential energy stored in the bonds of the reactants), which was transferred through heat to the surroundings (see Figure 10.5). The heat flow into the surroundings results from a lowering of the potential energy of the reaction system. *In any exothermic reaction, some of the potential energy stored in the chemical bonds is converted to thermal energy (random kinetic energy) via heat.*

TEACHING SUPPORT

DEMONSTRATION

An Endothermic Reaction

Materials

250-mL beaker
Second smaller beaker
Wooden splint or tongue depressor
Wooden board
Wash bottle and water
Barium hydroxide hydrate
Ammonium thiocyanate

Preparation Measure about 20 g of $Ba(OH)_2 \cdot 8H_2O$ crystals into the 250-mL beaker. Place about 10 g of ammonium thiocyanate in the smaller beaker.

Presentation Place a small pool of water on the board. Place the 250-mL beaker on the board. Add the ammonium thiocyanate to the barium hydroxide hydrate in the 250-mL beaker.

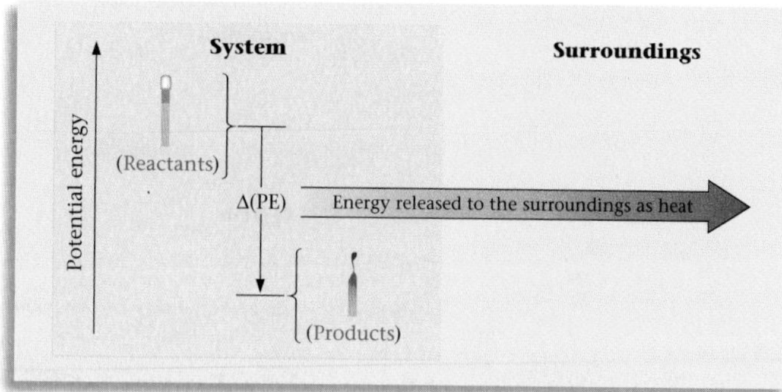

Figure 10.5

The energy changes accompanying the burning of a match.

10.4 Thermodynamics

OBJECTIVE: To understand how energy flow affects internal energy.

The study of energy is called **thermodynamics.** The law of conservation of energy is often called the **first law of thermodynamics** and is stated as follows:

The energy of the universe is constant.

The **internal energy,** E, of a system can be defined most precisely as the sum of the kinetic and potential energies of all "particles" in the system. The internal energy of a system can be changed by a flow of work, heat, or both. That is,

$$\Delta E = q + w$$

where

Δ ("delta") means a change in the function that follows

q represents heat

w represents work

Thermodynamic quantities always consist of two parts: a *number,* giving the magnitude of the change, and a *sign,* indicating the direction of the flow. *The sign reflects the system's point of view.* For example, when a quantity of energy flows *into* the system via heat (an endothermic process), q is equal to $+x$, where the *positive* sign indicates that the *system's energy is increasing.* On the other hand, when energy flows *out of* the system via heat (an exothermic process), q is equal to $-x$, where the *negative* sign indicates that the *system's energy is decreasing.*

In this text the same conventions apply to the flow of work. If the system does work on the surroundings (energy flows out of the system), w is negative. If the surroundings do work on the system (energy flows into the system), w is positive. We define work from the system's point of view to be consistent for all thermodynamic quantities. That is, in this convention the signs of both q and w reflect what happens to the system; thus we use $\Delta E = q + w$.

Test Bank: 16–19, 45–47, 50, 52

Section 10.4

TEACHING TIPS

- It is important that students think of energy from the system's point of view. Now is an excellent time to reinforce the idea that numbers representing thermodynamic quantities have two parts: the magnitude and the sign. It will be a new idea for many students to think about sign as a representation of direction. This idea is the key concept on which to focus attention.
- Emphasize that the sign convention is arbitrary. That is, because chemists chose to take the system's point of view, all signs are determined relative to the system.

PowerLecture Animation: Work vs. Energy Flow

Stir the two solids together with the wooden splint. After 2–3 minutes the substances will be liquid and the beaker will be frozen to the board. You can lift the beaker and the board will stick to the bottom of it quite tightly.

Teaching Notes Ammonium chloride (7 g) or ammonium nitrate (10 g) can be substituted for the ammonium thiocyanate. The smell of ammonia is evident during the reaction. The reaction is unusual because two solids actually react without being dissolved in a solvent.

If you do not have access to these chemicals, you can use the following chemicals to create a demonstration of endothermic and exothermic reactions. For an endothermic process, dissolve about 15 g of ammonium nitrate in about 100 mL of water (many ammonium compounds dissolve endothermically). For an exothermic process, dissolve calcium chloride or sodium hydroxide. Allow the students to touch the beaker before and after dissolution.

Test Bank: 1–15, 20–27, 32–35, 48, 49

Section 10.5

TEACHING TIPS

- In this section students learn the difference between calories in real life and calories for the chemist. It offers an opportunity to talk about the differences in the way scientists use language and the way we use language in our daily lives.
- This section also provides an excellent opportunity to review the process of unit conversion and to remind students that units should always be part of the calculations and the answers in chemistry.
- Point out the relationship between the calorie used in chemistry and the more familiar food Calorie, which really is a kilocalorie. This difference can be seen by the students in the Calorie Value of Nuts experiment in the laboratory manual.

Additional Examples

Example 10.1

1. Express 34.8 cal of energy in units of joules.

   146 J

2. Express 47.3 J of energy in units of calories.

   11.3 cal

Self Check

Answer to Self-Check Exercise 10.1

The conversion factor needed is $\frac{1 \text{ cal}}{4.184 \text{ J}}$, and the conversion is $28.4 \cancel{\text{J}} \times \frac{1 \text{ cal}}{4.184 \text{ J}} = 6.79 \text{ cal}$

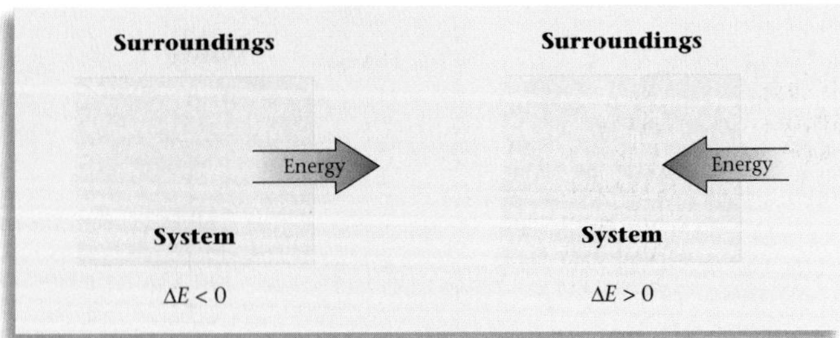

10.5 Measuring Energy Changes

OBJECTIVE: To understand how heat is measured.

Diet drinks are now labeled as "low joule" instead of "low calorie" in European countries.

Earlier in this chapter we saw that when we heat a substance to a higher temperature, we increase the motions of the components of the substance—that is, we increase the thermal energy of the substance. Different materials respond differently to being heated. To explore this idea we need to introduce the common units of energy: the *calorie* and the *joule* (pronounced "jewel").

In the metric system the **calorie** is defined as the amount of energy (heat) required to raise the temperature of one gram of water by one Celsius degree. The "calorie" with which you are probably familiar is used to measure the energy content of food and is actually a kilocalorie (1000 calories), written with a capital *C* (Calorie) to distinguish it from the calorie used in chemistry. The **joule** (an SI unit) can be most conveniently defined in terms of the calorie:

$$1 \text{ calorie} = 4.184 \text{ joules}$$

or using the normal abbreviations

$$1 \text{ cal} = 4.184 \text{ J}$$

You need to be able to convert between calories and joules. We will consider that conversion process in Example 10.1.

EXAMPLE 10.1 Converting Calories to Joules

Express 60.1 cal of energy in units of joules.

SOLUTION

By definition 1 cal = 4.184 J, so the conversion factor needed is $\frac{4.184 \text{ J}}{1 \text{ cal}}$, and the result is

$$60.1 \cancel{\text{cal}} \times \frac{4.184 \text{ J}}{1 \cancel{\text{cal}}} = 251 \text{ J}$$

Note that the 1 in the denominator is an exact number by definition and so does not limit the number of significant figures.

Self-Check EXERCISE 10.1 How many calories of energy correspond to 28.4 J?

See Problems 10.25 through 10.30. ■

TEACHING SUPPORT

DEMONSTRATION

Spontaneous Combustion

Materials

Potassium permanganate
Fireproof pad or evaporating dish
Glycerine
Spatula

Presentation Pile 5.0 g of potassium permanganate on the fireproof pad or in the evaporating dish. With a spatula form a depression in the center of the pile. Add about 1 mL of glycerine to the pile and step back. After a few seconds a white puff of smoke is produced, followed by a purplish flame.

CHEMISTRY IN FOCUS

Coffee: Hot and Quick(lime)

Convenience and speed are the watchwords of our modern society. One new product that fits these requirements is a container of coffee that heats itself with no batteries needed. Consumers can now buy a 10-ounce container of Wolfgang Puck gourmet latte that heats itself to 145 °F in 6 minutes and stays hot for 30 minutes. What kind of chemical magic makes this happen? Pushing a button on the bottom of the container. This action allows water to mix with calcium oxide, or quicklime (see accompanying figure). The resulting reaction

$$CaO(s) + H_2O(l) \rightarrow Ca(OH)_2(s)$$

releases enough energy as heat to bring the coffee to a pleasant drinking temperature.

Other companies are experimenting with similar technology to heat liquids such as tea, hot chocolate, and soup.

A different reaction is now being used to heat MREs (meals ready-to-eat) for soldiers on the battlefield. In this case the energy to heat the meals is furnished by mixing magnesium iron oxide with water to produce an exothermic reaction.

Clearly, chemistry is "hot stuff."

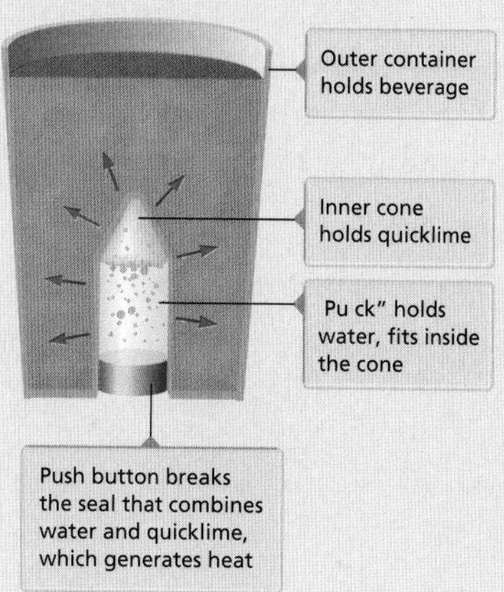
Outer container holds beverage
Inner cone holds quicklime
Pu ck" holds water, fits inside the cone
Push button breaks the seal that combines water and quicklime, which generates heat

TEACHING TIP

Using a molecular perspective enables us to explain why the amount of energy required to raise the temperature of water by 1 °C is directly related to the amount of water.

Now think about heating a substance from one temperature to another. How does the amount of substance heated affect the energy required? In 2 g of water there are twice as many molecules as in 1 g of water. It takes twice as much energy to change the temperature of 2 g of water by 1 °C, because we must change the motions of twice as many molecules in a 2-g sample as in a 1-g sample. Also, as we would expect, it takes twice as much energy to raise the temperature of a given sample of water by 2 degrees as it does to raise the temperature by 1 degree.

EXAMPLE 10.2 Calculating Energy Requirements

Determine the amount of energy (heat) in joules required to raise the temperature of 7.40 g water from 29.0 °C to 46.0 °C.

SOLUTION

Where Are We Going?

We want to determine the amount of energy (heat in joules) needed to increase the temperature of 7.40 g water from 29.0 °C to 46.0 °C.

What Do We Know?

- The mass of water is 7.40 g, and the temperature is increased from 29.0 °C to 46.0 °C.

Additional Examples

Example 10.2

1. Determine the amount of energy as heat that is required to raise the temperature of 1.0 L of water from 25.0 °C to boiling (100.0 °C). Answer in joules and calories. (1.0 L of water has a mass of 1.0 kg.)

   314,000 J (314 kJ); 7.50×10^4 cal (75.0 kcal)

2. If 455 J of heat is transferred to 25.0 g of water at 45.0 °C, what is the final temperature of the water?

   49.3 °C

What Information Do We Need?

- The amount of heat needed to raise 1.00 g water by 1.00 °C. From the text we see that 4.184 J of energy is required.

How Do We Get There?

In solving any kind of problem, it is often useful to draw a diagram that represents the situation. In this case, we have 7.40 g of water that is to be heated from 29.0 °C to 46.0 °C.

7.40 g water, T = 29.0 °C ⇨ (? energy) 7.40 g water, T = 46.0 °C

Our task is to determine how much energy is required to accomplish this task.

From the discussion in the text, we know that 4.184 J of energy is required to raise the temperature of *one* gram of water by *one* Celsius degree.

1.00 g water, T = 29.0 °C ⇨ (4.184 J) 1.00 g water, T = 30.0 °C

Because in our case we have 7.40 g of water instead of 1.00 g, it will take 7.40 × 4.184 J to raise the temperature by one degree.

7.40 g water, T = 29.0 °C ⇨ (7.40 × 4.184 J) 7.40 g water, T = 30.0 °C

However, we want to raise the temperature of our sample of water by more than 1 °C. In fact, the temperature change required is from 29.0 °C to 46.0 °C. This is a change of 17.0 °C (46.0 °C − 29.0 °C = 17.0 °C). Thus we will have to supply 17.0 times the energy necessary to raise the temperature of 7.40 g of water by 1 °C.

7.40 g water, T = 29.0 °C ⇨ (17.0 × 7.40 × 4.184 J) 7.40 g water, T = 46.0 °C

This calculation is summarized as follows:

$$4.184\frac{\text{J}}{\text{g °C}} \times 7.40\text{ g} \times 17.0\text{ °C} = 526\text{ J}$$

Energy per gram of water per degree of temperature × Actual grams of water × Actual temperature change = Energy required

MATH SKILL BUILDER
The result you will get on your calculator is 4.184 × 7.40 × 17.0 = 526.3472, which rounds off to 526.

We have shown that 526 J of energy (as heat) is required to raise the temperature of 7.40 g of water from 29.0 °C to 46.0 °C. Note that because 4.184 J of energy is required to heat 1 g of water by 1 °C, the units are J/g °C (joules per gram per Celsius degree).

REALITY CHECK The units (J) are correct, and the answer is reported to the correct number of significant figures (three).

Self-Check EXERCISE 10.2 Calculate the joules of energy required to heat 454 g of water from 5.4 °C to 98.6 °C.

See Problems 10.31 through 10.36. ■

Self Check

Answer to Self-Check Exercise 10.2

We know that it takes 4.184 J of energy to change the temperature of each gram of water by 1 °C, so we must multiply 4.184 by the mass of water (454 g) and the temperature change (98.6 °C − 5.4 °C = 93.2 °C).

$$4.184\frac{\text{J}}{\text{g °C}} \times 454\text{ g} \times 93.2\text{ °C} = 1.77 \times 10^5\text{ J}$$

TEACHING SUPPORT

DEMONSTRATION

Heat Up or Chill Out?

Materials

Ammonium chloride (50 g)
Calcium chloride, anhydrous (30 g)
2 small Ziploc storage bags
Graduated cylinder
Water

Preparation Measure 30 g calcium chloride and place it in a small Ziploc bag, label it "hot," and seal it. Measure 50 g ammonium chloride and place it into a second Ziploc bag, label it "cold," and seal it.

Presentation Introduce the idea that dissolving a solid can be an exothermic or endothermic process. Explain that common hot or cold packs used to relieve sore muscles are often based on this idea. Measure about 25 mL of wa-

Nature Has Hot Plants

The voodoo lily (Titan Arum) is a beautiful and seductive plant. The exotic-looking lily features an elaborate reproductive mechanism—a purple spike that can reach nearly 3 feet in length and is cloaked by a hoodlike leaf. But approach to the plant reveals bad news—it smells terrible!

Despite its antisocial odor, this putrid plant has fascinated biologists for many years because of its ability to generate heat. At the peak of its metabolic activity, the plant's blossom can be as much as 15 °C above its surrounding temperature. To generate this much heat, the metabolic rate of the plant must be close to that of a flying hummingbird!

What's the purpose of this intense heat production? For a plant faced with limited food supplies in the very competitive tropical climate where it grows, heat production seems like a great waste of energy. The answer to this mystery is that the voodoo lily is pollinated mainly by carrion-loving insects. Thus the lily prepares a malodorous mixture of chemicals characteristic of rotting meat, which it then "cooks" off into the surrounding air to attract flesh-feeding beetles and flies. Then, once the insects enter the pollination chamber, the high temperatures there (as high as 110 °F) cause the insects to remain very active to better carry out their pollination duties.

The voodoo lily is only one of many thermogenic (heat-producing) plants. These plants are of special interest to biologists because they provide opportunities to study metabolic reactions that are quite subtle in "normal" plants.

Titan Arum is reputedly the largest flower in the world.

Table 10.1 The Specific Heat Capacities of Some Common Substances

Substance	Specific Heat Capacity (J/g °C)
water (*l*)* (liquid)	4.184
water (*s*) (ice)	2.03
water (*g*) (steam)	2.0
aluminum (*s*)	0.89
iron (*s*)	0.45
mercury (*l*)	0.14
carbon (*s*)	0.71
silver (*s*)	0.24
gold (*s*)	0.13

*The symbols (*s*), (*l*), and (*g*) indicate the solid, liquid, and gaseous states, respectively.

So far we have seen that the energy (heat) required to change the temperature of a substance depends on

1. The amount of substance being heated (number of grams)
2. The temperature change (number of degrees)

There is, however, another important factor: the identity of the substance.

Different substances respond differently to being heated. We have seen that 4.184 J of energy raises the temperature of 1 g of water by 1 °C. In contrast, this same amount of energy applied to 1 g of gold raises its temperature by approximately 32 °C! The point is that some substances require relatively large amounts of energy to change their temperatures, whereas others require relatively little. Chemists describe this difference by saying that substances have different heat capacities. *The amount of energy required to change the temperature of one gram of a substance by one Celsius degree* is called its **specific heat capacity** or, more commonly, its *specific heat.* The specific heat capacities for several substances are listed in Table 10.1. You can see from the table that the specific heat capacity for water is very high compared to those of the other substances listed. This is why lakes and seas are much slower to respond to cooling or heating than are the surrounding land masses.

TEACHING TIP

Students often do many problems involving water. Be sure to include some examples in which the specific heat capacities for other substances are needed.

MINI-DEMO

Use a heat conductivity apparatus (the apparatus looks like a star with a central circle of metal and spokes emanating from it) to demonstrate the specific heat capacities for various metals. Different metal spheres (shot) are attached to the ends of the spokes with paraffin. The apparatus is then heated at the center with a Bunsen burner. The heat travels out the spokes and the paraffin melts, causing the metal spheres to drop off at different times according to their specific heat capacities.

PowerLecture Simulation: Heat Transfer between Substances

PowerLecture Simulation: Specific Heat Capacity

ter into the graduated cylinder. Open one of the plastic bags and pour in the water. Rezip the bag closed and shake it to mix the contents well. Repeat the process with the other plastic bag. Pass both bags around the class so that students can directly observe the temperature change associated with dissolving the solids.

Teaching Notes The heats of dissolution for the packs are

$$NH_4Cl(s) \rightarrow NH_4^+(aq) + Cl^-(aq) \qquad \Delta H = 15.2\ \text{kJ}$$

$$CaCl_2(s) \rightarrow Ca^{2+}(aq) + 2Cl^-(aq) \qquad \Delta H = -82.8\ \text{kJ}$$

Be sure that students don't hold the hot pack too long—it generates enough heat to produce discomfort. Dispose of the contents according to regulations. You may also want to bring in commercial hot and cold packs to demonstrate their use.

Additional Examples

Example 10.3

1. Determine the amount of energy as heat that is required to raise the temperature of a 10.0-g sample of aluminum from 25 °C to 58 °C. Answer in joules and calories.

   294 J; 70. cal

2. If 294 J of heat is transferred to a 10.0-g sample of silver at 25 °C, what is the final temperature of the silver?

   148 °C

EXAMPLE 10.3 Calculations Involving Specific Heat Capacity

a. What quantity of energy (in joules) is required to heat a piece of iron weighing 1.3 g from 25 °C to 46 °C?

b. What is the answer in calories?

SOLUTION

Where Are We Going?

We want to determine the amount of energy (units of joules and calories) to increase the temperature of 1.3 g, of iron from 25° C to 46° C.

What Do We Know?

- The mass of iron is 1.3 g, and the temperature is increased from 25° C to 46° C.

What Information Do We Need?

- We need the specific heat capacity of iron and the conversion factor between joules and calories.

How Do We Get There?

a. It is helpful to draw the following diagram to represent the problem.

1.3 g iron T = 25 °C	⇨ ? joules	1.3 g iron T = 46 °C

From Table 10.1 we see that the specific heat capacity of iron is 0.45 J/g °C. That is, it takes 0.45 J to raise the temperature of a 1-g piece of iron by 1 °C.

1.0 g iron T = 25 °C	⇨ 0.45 J	1.0 g iron T = 26 °C

In this case our sample is 1.3 g, so 1.3 × 0.45 J is required for *each* degree of temperature increase.

1.3 g iron T = 25 °C	⇨ 1.3 × 0.45 J	1.3 g iron T = 26 °C

Because the temperature increase is 21 °C (46 °C − 25 °C = 21 °C), the total amount of energy required is

$$0.45 \frac{\text{J}}{\text{g °C}} \times 1.3 \text{ g} \times 21 \text{ °C} = 12 \text{ J}$$

MATH SKILL BUILDER
The result you will get on your calculator is 0.45 × 1.3 × 21 = 12.285, which rounds off to 12.

1.3 g iron T = 25 °C	⇨ 21 × 1.3 × 0.45 J	1.3 g iron T = 46 °C

Note that the final units are joules, as they should be.

b. To calculate this energy in calories, we can use the definition 1 cal = 4.184 J to construct the appropriate conversion factor. We want to change from joules to calories, so cal must be in the numerator and J in the denominator, where it cancels:

$$12 \cancel{\text{J}} \times \frac{1 \text{ cal}}{4.184 \cancel{\text{J}}} = 2.9 \text{ cal}$$

Remember that 1 in this case is an exact number by definition and therefore does not limit the number of significant figures (the number 12 is limiting here).

REALITY CHECK The units (joules and calories) are correct, and the answer is reported to the correct number of significant figures (two).

Self-Check EXERCISE 10.3 A 5.63-g sample of solid gold is heated from 21 °C to 32 °C. How much energy (in joules and calories) is required?

See Problems 10.31 through 10.36. ■

Note that in Example 10.3, to calculate the energy (heat) required, we took the product of the specific heat capacity, the sample size in grams, and the change in temperature in Celsius degrees.

Energy (heat) required (Q)	=	Specific heat capacity (s)	×	Mass (m) in grams of sample	×	Change in temperature (ΔT) in °C

We can represent this by the following equation:

MATH SKILL BUILDER
The symbol Δ (the Greek letter delta) is shorthand for "change in."

$$Q = s \times m \times \Delta T$$

where

Q = energy (heat) required

s = specific heat capacity

m = mass of the sample in grams

ΔT = change in temperature in Celsius degrees

This equation always applies when a substance is being heated (or cooled) and no change of state occurs. Before you begin to use this equation, however, make sure you understand what it means.

EXAMPLE 10.4 Specific Heat Capacity Calculations: Using the Equation

A 1.6-g sample of a metal that has the appearance of gold requires 5.8 J of energy to change its temperature from 23 °C to 41 °C. Is the metal pure gold?

SOLUTION

Where Are We Going?

We want to determine if a metal is gold.

What Do We Know?

- The mass of metal is 1.6 g, and 5.8 J of energy is required to increase the temperature from 23° C to 41° C.

What Information Do We Need?

- We need the specific heat capacity of gold.

Self Check

Answer to Self-Check Exercise 10.3

From Table 10.1, the specific heat capacity for solid gold is 0.13 J/g °C. Because it takes 0.13 J to change the temperature of *one* gram of gold by *one* Celsius degree, we must multiply 0.13 by the sample size (5.63 g) and the change in temperature (32 °C − 21 °C = 11 °C).

$$0.13 \frac{J}{g\ °C} \times 5.63\ g \times 11\ °C = 8.1\ J$$

We can change this energy to units of calories as follows:

$$8.1\ J \times \frac{1\ cal}{4.184\ J} = 1.9\ cal$$

Additional Examples

Example 10.4

1. A 2.6-g sample of a metal requires 15.6 J of energy to change its temperature from 21 °C to 34 °C. Use the information in Table 10.1 to identify this metal.

   iron (Fe)

2. A sample of gold requires 3.1 J of energy to change its temperature from 19 °C to 27 °C. What is the mass of this sample of gold?

   3.0 g

CHEMISTRY IN FOCUS

Firewalking: Magic or Science?

For millennia people have been amazed at the ability of Eastern mystics to walk across beds of glowing coals without any apparent discomfort. Even in the United States, thousands of people have performed feats of firewalking as part of motivational seminars. How can this be possible? Do firewalkers have supernatural powers?

Actually, there are good scientific explanations of why firewalking is possible. First, human tissue is mainly composed of water, which has a relatively large specific heat capacity. This means that a large amount of energy must be transferred from the coals to change significantly the temperature of the feet. During the brief contact between feet and coals involved in firewalking, there is relatively little time for energy flow, so the feet do not reach a high enough temperature to cause damage.

Also, although the surface of the coals has a very high temperature, the red-hot layer is very thin. Therefore, the quantity of energy available to heat the feet is smaller than might be expected.

Thus, although firewalking is impressive, there are several scientific reasons why anyone with the proper training should be able to do it on a properly prepared bed of coals. (Don't try this on your own!)

AP Photo/Itsuo Inouye

A group of firewalkers in Japan.

How Do We Get There?

We can represent the data given in this problem by the following diagram:

1.6 g metal $T = 23$ °C	⇨ 5.8 J	1.6 g metal $T = 41$ °C

$$\Delta T = 41\text{ °C} - 23\text{ °C} = 18\text{ °C}$$

Using the data given, we can calculate the value of the specific heat capacity for the metal and compare this value to the one for gold given in Table 10.1. We know that

$$Q = s \times m \times \Delta T$$

or, pictorially,

1.6 g metal $T = 23$ °C	⇨ $5.8\text{ J} = ? \times 1.6 \times 18$	1.6 g metal $T = 41$ °C

When we divide both sides of the equation

$$Q = s \times m \times \Delta T$$

300

TEACHING SUPPORT

DEMONSTRATION

The Fireproof Balloon

Materials

Black balloons (9-in. diameter)
Candle
Medium-size beaker or plastic cup

Preparation Place approximately 25 mL of water into one balloon. Place it along with several additional balloons into the cup or beaker, making sure that the water balloon is easy to remove.

Presentation Place a lighted candle on a flat, level surface. Ask for a volunteer. Have the volunteer take a balloon, blow it up, and tie it off with a knot. Demonstrate the process yourself by picking up the water balloon and

by $m \times \Delta T$, we get

$$\frac{Q}{m \times \Delta T} = s$$

Thus, using the data given, we can calculate the value of s. In this case,

Q = energy (heat) required = 5.8 J

m = mass of the sample = 1.6 g

ΔT = change in temperature = 18 °C (41 °C − 23 °C = 18 °C)

MATH SKILL BUILDER
The result you will get on your calculator is 5.8/(1.6 × 18) = 0.2013889, which rounds off to 0.20.

Thus

$$s = \frac{Q}{m \times \Delta T} = \frac{5.8\text{ J}}{(1.6\text{ g})(18\text{ °C})} = 0.20\text{ J/g °C}$$

From Table 10.1, the specific heat capacity for gold is 0.13 J/g °C. Thus the metal must not be pure gold.

Self-Check EXERCISE 10.4 A 2.8-g sample of pure metal requires 10.1 J of energy to change its temperature from 21 °C to 36 °C. What is this metal? (Use Table 10.1.)

See Problems 10.31 through 10.36. ■

10.6 Thermochemistry (Enthalpy)

OBJECTIVE: To consider the heat (enthalpy) of chemical reactions.

We have seen that some reactions are exothermic (produce heat energy) and other reactions are endothermic (absorb heat energy). Chemists also like to know exactly how much energy is produced or absorbed by a given reaction. To make that process more convenient, we have invented a special energy function called **enthalpy,** which is designated by H. For a reaction occurring under conditions of constant pressure, the change in enthalpy (ΔH) is equal to the energy that flows as heat. That is,

$$\Delta H_p = \text{heat}$$

where the subscript "p" indicates that the process has occurred under conditions of constant pressure and Δ means "a change in." Thus the enthalpy change for a reaction (that occurs at constant pressure) is the same as the heat for that reaction.

EXAMPLE 10.5 Enthalpy

When 1 mole of methane (CH_4) is burned at constant pressure, 890 kJ of energy is released as heat. Calculate ΔH for a process in which a 5.8-g sample of methane is burned at constant pressure.

SOLUTION

Where Are We Going?

We want to determine ΔH for the reaction of 5.8 g of methane (CH_4) with oxygen at constant pressure.

Self Check

Answer to Self-Check Exercise 10.4

Table 10.1 lists the specific heat capacities of several metals. We want to calculate the specific heat capacity (s) for this metal and then use Table 10.1 to identify the metal. Using the equation

$$Q = s \times m \times \Delta T$$

we can solve for s by dividing both sides by m (the mass of the sample) and by ΔT:

$$\frac{Q}{m \times \Delta T} = s$$

In this case,

Q = energy (heat) required = 10.1 J

m = 2.8 g

ΔT = temperature change = 36 °C − 21 °C = 15 °C

so

$$s = \frac{Q}{m \times \Delta T} = \frac{10.1\text{ J}}{(2.8\text{ g})(15\text{ °C})} = 0.24\text{ J/g °C}$$

Table 10.1 shows that silver has a specific heat capacity of 0.24 J/g °C. The metal is silver.

Section 10.6

Test Bank: 28–31, 51, 53–56

blowing it up. (*Note:* As you do so, be careful to keep your hand in front of the balloon to conceal the mass of water in the balloon.) Now hold your balloon over the flame (making sure that the flame is over the bottom of the balloon where the water is). Ask the volunteer to repeat the experiment with his or her balloon. At the end of the demonstration, heat the balloon containing the water on its side while holding it over a trashcan.

Teaching Notes The water in the balloon will absorb the heat from the candle flame and prevent the balloon from breaking. Be sure not to set the water balloon down or it will be evident that it contains water.

Additional Examples

Example 10.5

1. When 1 mole of sulfur dioxide reacts with excess oxygen to form sulfur trioxide at constant pressure, 198.2 kJ of energy is released as heat. Calculate ΔH for a process in which a 12.8-g sample of sulfur dioxide reacts with excess oxygen at constant pressure.

   39.6 kJ

2. When 1 mole of hydrogen gas reacts with excess oxygen to form water at constant pressure, 241.8 kJ of energy is released as heat. Calculate ΔH for a process in which a 15.0-g sample of hydrogen gas reacts with excess oxygen at constant pressure.

   1.80×10^3 kJ

Self Check

Answer to Self-Check Exercise 10.5

We are told that 1652 kJ of energy is *released* when 4 moles of Fe reacts. We first need to determine what number of moles the 1.00 g of Fe represents.

$$1.00 \text{ g Fe} \times \frac{1 \text{ mol}}{55.85 \text{ g}} = 1.79 \times 10^{-2} \text{ mol Fe}$$

$$1.79 \times 10^{-2} \text{ mol Fe} \times \frac{1652 \text{ kJ}}{4 \text{ mol Fe}} = 7.39 \text{ kJ}$$

Thus 7.39 kJ of energy (as heat) is released when 1.00 g of iron reacts.

What Do We Know?

- When 1 mol CH_4 is burned, 890 kJ of energy is released.
- We have 5.8 g of CH_4.

What Information Do We Need?

- Molar mass of methane, which we can get from the atomic masses of carbon (12.01 g/mol) and hydrogen (1.008 g/mol). The molar mass is 16.0 g/mol.

How Do We Get There?

At constant pressure, 890 kJ of energy per mole of CH_4 is produced as heat:

$$q_p = \Delta H = -890 \text{ kJ/mol } CH_4$$

Note that the minus sign indicates an exothermic process. In this case, a 5.8-g sample of CH_4 (molar mass = 16.0 g/mol) is burned. Since this amount is smaller than 1 mol, less than 890 kJ will be released as heat. The actual value can be calculated as follows:

$$5.8 \text{ g } \cancel{CH_4} \times \frac{1 \text{ mol } CH_4}{16.0 \text{ g } \cancel{CH_4}} = 0.36 \text{ mol } CH_4$$

and

$$0.36 \text{ } \cancel{\text{mol } CH_4} \times \frac{-890 \text{ kJ}}{\cancel{\text{mol } CH_4}} = -320 \text{ kJ}$$

Thus, when a 5.8-g sample of CH_4 is burned at constant pressure,

$$\Delta H = \text{heat flow} = -320 \text{ kJ}$$

REALITY CHECK The mass of methane burned is less than 1 mol, so less than 890 kJ will be released as heat. The answer has two significant figures as required by the given quantities.

Self-Check EXERCISE 10.5 The reaction that occurs in the heat packs used to treat sports injuries is

$$4Fe(s) + 3O_2(g) \rightarrow 2Fe_2O_3(s) \qquad \Delta H = -1652 \text{ kJ}$$

How much heat is released when 1.00 g of Fe(*s*) is reacted with excess $O_2(g)$?

See Problems 10.40 and 10.41. ■

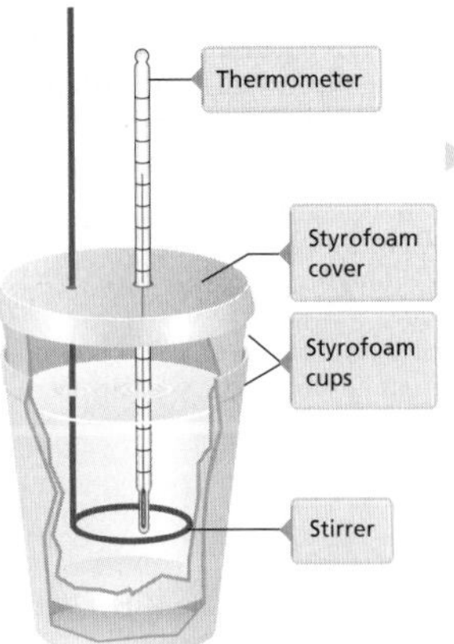

Figure 10.6
A coffee-cup calorimeter made of two Styrofoam cups.

Calorimetry

A **calorimeter** (see Figure 10.6) is a device used to determine the heat associated with a chemical reaction. The reaction is run in the calorimeter and the temperature change of the calorimeter is observed. Knowing the temperature change that occurs in the calorimeter and the heat capacity of the calorimeter enables us to calculate the heat energy released or absorbed by the reaction. Thus we can determine ΔH for the reaction.

Once we have measured the ΔH values for various reactions, we can use these data to *calculate* the ΔH values of other reactions. We will see how to carry out these calculations in the next section.

CHEMISTRY IN FOCUS

Methane: An Important Energy Source

Methane is the main component of natural gas, a valuable fossil fuel. It is such a good fuel because the combustion of methane with oxygen

$$CH_4(g) + 2O_2(g) \rightarrow CO_2(g) + 2H_2O(g)$$

produces 55 kJ of energy per gram of methane. Natural gas, which is associated with petroleum deposits and contains as much as 97% methane, originated from the decomposition of plants in ancient forests that became buried in natural geological processes.

Although the methane in natural gas represents a tremendous source of energy for our civilization, an even more abundant source of methane lies in the depths of the ocean. The U.S. Geological Survey estimates that 320,000 trillion cubic feet of methane is trapped in the deep ocean near the United States. This amount is 200 times the amount of methane contained in the natural gas deposits in the United States. In the ocean, the methane is trapped in cavities formed by water molecules that are arranged very much like the water molecules in ice. These structures are called methane hydrates.

Although extraction of methane from the ocean floor offers tremendous potential benefits, it also carries risks. Methane is a "greenhouse gas"—its presence in the atmosphere helps to trap the heat from the sun. As a result, any accidental release of the methane from the ocean could produce serious warming of the earth's climate. As usual, environmental trade-offs accompany human activities.

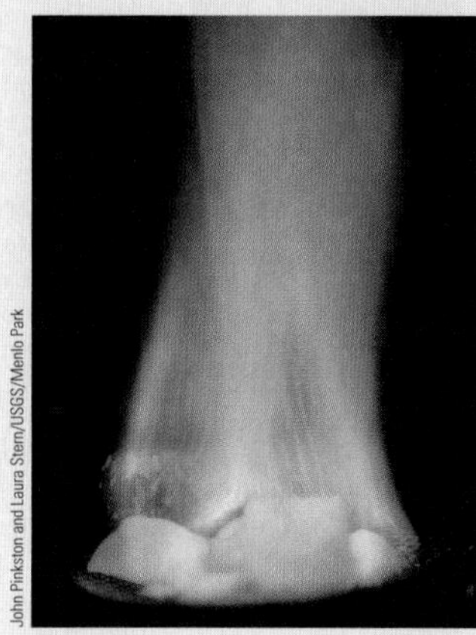
John Pinkston and Laura Stern/USGS/Menlo Park

Flaming pieces of methane hydrate.

MINI-DEMO

Lighting a Cheeto or a nut can bring the concept of calorimetry into the real world. Discuss the fact that to obtain the nutrition information on food someone has to determine the calorie value for the food. Using a calorimeter is one way to do so.

10.7 Hess's Law

OBJECTIVE: To understand Hess's law.

Section 10.7

 **Test Bank: 57**

PowerLecture Animation: Hess's Law

One of the most important characteristics of enthalpy is that it is a state function. That is, the change in enthalpy for a given process is independent of the pathway for the process. Consequently, *in going from a particular set of reactants to a particular set of products, the change in enthalpy is the same whether the reaction takes place in one step or in a series of steps.* This principle, which is known as **Hess's law,** can be illustrated by examining the oxidation of nitrogen to produce nitrogen dioxide. The overall reaction can be written in one step, where the enthalpy change is represented by ΔH_1.

$$N_2(g) + 2O_2(g) \rightarrow 2NO_2(g) \qquad \Delta H_1 = 68 \text{ kJ}$$

This reaction can also be carried out in two distinct steps, with the enthalpy changes being designated as ΔH_2 and ΔH_3:

$$N_2(g) + O_2(g) \rightarrow 2NO(g) \qquad \Delta H_2 = 180 \text{ kJ}$$
$$2NO(g) + O_2(g) \rightarrow 2NO_2(g) \qquad \Delta H_3 = -112 \text{ kJ}$$
$$\text{Net reaction: } N_2(g) + 2O_2(g) \rightarrow 2NO_2(g) \qquad \Delta H_2 + \Delta H_3 = 68 \text{ kJ}$$

303

TEACHING TIPS

- Once students understand that energy changes can be measured in a calorimeter, the next logical question is, How can anyone measure all of the energy changes in the world? What if the reaction is unpleasant, or is an explosion, or is very complex—how can we measure the energy change then? To answer this question, Hess's law is useful. It provides an excellent example of how a chemist can extend knowledge by applying information gathered from simple systems to more complex systems.
- Hess's law problems relate well to the mathematics of equations. As students are already familiar with manipulating algebraic equations, this section is a good place to show the overlap of math and science. The two characteristics of enthalpy changes are easily related to algebraic concepts.
- An analogy you can use with Hess's law is paying for something at a store. If the net result is to pay the store \$8, this goal can be achieved in many ways. For example, you can give the store one \$5 bill and three \$1 bills, or you can pay with a \$10 bill and get \$2 in change. No matter how many steps are involved in the process, the payment is the same.

Note that the sum of the two steps gives the net, or overall, reaction and that

$$\Delta H_1 = \Delta H_2 + \Delta H_3 = 68 \text{ kJ}$$

The importance of Hess's law is that it allows us to *calculate* heats of reaction that might be difficult or inconvenient to measure directly in a calorimeter.

Characteristics of Enthalpy Changes

To use Hess's law to compute enthalpy changes for reactions, it is important to understand two characteristics of ΔH for a reaction:

1. If a reaction is reversed, the sign of ΔH is also reversed.
2. The magnitude of ΔH is directly proportional to the quantities of reactants and products in a reaction. If the coefficients in a balanced reaction are multiplied by an integer, the value of ΔH is multiplied by the same integer.

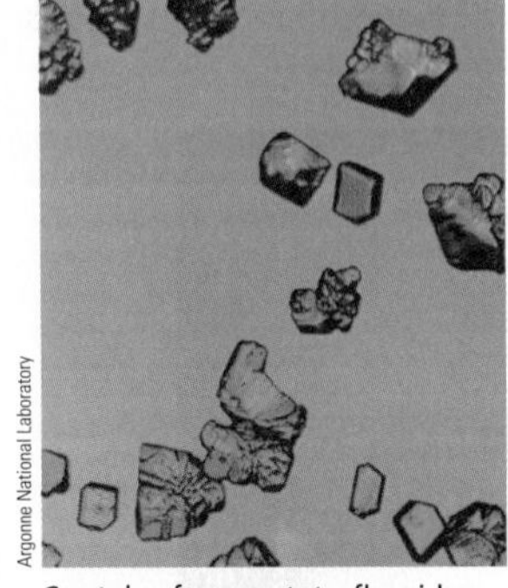

Argonne National Laboratory

Crystals of xenon tetrafluoride, the first reported binary compound containing a noble gas element.

Both these rules follow in a straightforward way from the properties of enthalpy changes. The first rule can be explained by recalling that the *sign* of ΔH indicates the *direction* of the heat flow at constant pressure. If the direction of the reaction is reversed, the direction of the heat flow also will be reversed. To see this, consider the preparation of xenon tetrafluoride, which was the first binary compound made from a noble gas:

$$Xe(g) + 2F_2(g) \rightarrow XeF_4(s) \qquad \Delta H = -251 \text{ kJ}$$

This reaction is exothermic, and 251 kJ of energy flows into the surroundings as heat. On the other hand, if the colorless XeF_4 crystals are decomposed into the elements, according to the equation

$$XeF_4(s) \rightarrow Xe(g) + 2F_2(g)$$

the opposite energy flow occurs because 251 kJ of energy must be added to the system to produce this endothermic reaction. Thus, for this reaction, $\Delta H = +251$ kJ.

The second rule comes from the fact that ΔH is an extensive property, depending on the amount of substances reacting. For example, since 251 kJ of energy is evolved for the reaction

$$Xe(g) + 2F_2(g) \rightarrow XeF_4(s)$$

then for a preparation involving twice the quantities of reactants and products, or

$$2Xe(g) + 4F_2(g) \rightarrow 2XeF_4(s)$$

twice as much heat would be evolved:

$$\Delta H = 2(-251 \text{ kJ}) = -502 \text{ kJ}$$

PowerLecture Simulation: Hess's Law

EXAMPLE 10.6 Hess's Law

Two forms of carbon are graphite, the soft, black, slippery material used in "lead" pencils and as a lubricant for locks, and diamond, the brilliant, hard gemstone. Using the enthalpies of combustion for graphite (−394 kJ/mol) and diamond (−396 kJ/mol), calculate ΔH for the conversion of graphite to diamond:

$$C_{graphite}(s) \rightarrow C_{diamond}(s)$$

Additional Example

Example 10.6

Given the following data,

$4CuO(s) \rightarrow 2Cu_2O(s) + O_2(g)$
$\Delta H = 288$ kJ

$Cu_2O(s) \rightarrow Cu(s) + CuO(s)$
$\Delta H = 11$ kJ

calculate ΔH for the following reaction:

$2Cu(s) + O_2(g) \rightarrow 2CuO(s)$
−310. kJ

TEACHING SUPPORT

BACKGROUND INFORMATION

The bombadier beetle (see the Chemistry in Focus, "The Beetle That Shoots Straight," in Chapter 6) is an amazing insect "knowledgeable" about thermochemistry and Hess's law. The beetle protects itself from predators by mixing chemicals within its abdomen and spraying its enemy with the resulting concoction. The chemicals are hydroquinone [$C_6H_4(OH)_2(aq)$] and hydrogen peroxide (H_2O_2). As these chemicals are mixed with a catalyst (enzyme), a fast exothermic reaction takes place that produces quinone ($C_6H_4O_2$) and water. The heat of reaction for this process is −204 kJ. This heat raises the entire solution to its boiling point and the resulting vapor is shot out in spurts (up to 30) as a hot mist with appropriate sound effects!

SOLUTION

Where Are We Going?

We want to determine ΔH for the conversion of graphite to diamond.

What Do We Know?

The combustion reactions are

$$C_{graphite}(s) + O_2(g) \rightarrow CO_2(g) \quad \Delta H = -394 \text{ kJ}$$
$$C_{diamond}(s) + O_2(g) \rightarrow CO_2(g) \quad \Delta H = -396 \text{ kJ}$$

How Do We Get There?

Note that if we reverse the second reaction (which means we must change the sign of ΔH) and sum the two reactions, we obtain the desired reaction:

$$C_{graphite}(s) + O_2(g) \rightarrow CO_2(g) \quad \Delta H = -394 \text{ kJ}$$
$$CO_2(g) \rightarrow C_{diamond}(s) + O_2(g) \quad \Delta H = -(-396 \text{ kJ})$$
$$\overline{C_{graphite}(s) \rightarrow C_{diamond}(s) \quad \Delta H = 2 \text{ kJ}}$$

Thus 2 kJ of energy is required to change 1 mole of graphite to diamond. This process is endothermic.

Self-Check **EXERCISE 10.6** From the following information

$$S(s) + \tfrac{3}{2}O_2 \rightarrow SO_3(g) \quad \Delta H = -395.2 \text{ kJ}$$
$$2SO_2(g) + O_2(g) \rightarrow 2SO_3(g) \quad \Delta H = -198.2 \text{ kJ}$$

calculate ΔH for the reaction

$$S(s) + O_2(g) \rightarrow SO_2(g)$$

See Problems 10.45 through 10.48. ■

10.8 Quality Versus Quantity of Energy

OBJECTIVE: To see how the quality of energy changes as it is used.

One of the most important characteristics of energy is that it is conserved. Thus the total energy content of the universe will always be what it is now. If that is the case, why are we concerned about energy? For example, why should we worry about conserving our petroleum supply? Surprisingly, the "energy crisis" is not about the *quantity* of energy, but rather about the *quality* of energy. To understand this idea, consider an automobile trip from Chicago to Denver. Along the way you would put gasoline into the car to get to Denver. What happens to that energy? The energy stored in the bonds of the gasoline and of the oxygen that reacts with it is changed to thermal energy, which is spread along the highway to Denver. The total quantity of energy remains the same as before the trip but the energy concentrated in the gasoline becomes widely distributed in the environment:

$$\text{gasoline}(l) + O_2(g) \rightarrow CO_2(g) + H_2O(l) + \text{energy}$$

↑ C_8H_{18} and other similar compounds

↓ Spread along the highway, heating the road and the air

The appropriate steps for illustrating Hess's law follow.

$$C_6H_4(OH)_2(aq) \rightarrow C_6H_4O_2(aq) + H_2(g) \quad \Delta H = 177 \text{ kJ}$$
$$H_2O_2(aq) \rightarrow H_2O(l) + \tfrac{1}{2}O_2(g) \quad \Delta H = -95 \text{ kJ}$$
$$H_2(g) + \tfrac{1}{2}O_2(g) \rightarrow H_2O(l) \quad \Delta H = -286 \text{ kJ}$$
$$\overline{C_6H_4(OH)_2(aq) + H_2O_2(aq) \rightarrow C_6H_4O_2(aq) + 2H_2O(l) \quad \Delta H = -204 \text{ kJ}}$$

Self Check

Answer to Self-Check Exercise 10.6

Noting the reactants and products in the desired reaction

$$S(s) + O_2(g) \rightarrow SO_2(g)$$

we need to reverse the second equation and multiply it by $\tfrac{1}{2}$. This action reverses the sign and cuts the amount of energy by a factor of 2:

$$\tfrac{1}{2}[2SO_3(g) \rightarrow 2SO_2(g) + O_2(g)] \quad \Delta H = \frac{198.2 \text{ kJ}}{2}$$

or

$$SO_3(g) \rightarrow SO_2(g) + \tfrac{1}{2}O_2(g) \quad \Delta H = 99.1 \text{ kJ}$$

Now we add this reaction to the first reaction:

$$S(s) + \tfrac{3}{2}O_2(g) \rightarrow SO_3(g) \quad \Delta H = -395.2 \text{ kJ}$$
$$+ \; SO_3(g) \rightarrow SO_2(g) + \tfrac{1}{2}O_2(g) \quad \Delta H = 99.1 \text{ kJ}$$
$$\overline{S(s) + O_2(g) \rightarrow SO_2(g) \quad \Delta H = -296.1 \text{ kJ}}$$

Section 10.8

TEACHING TIP

This section introduces the concept that energy naturally changes from useful forms to less useful forms. Each energy transformation results in the same amount of energy but in a less useful form. The focus on the quality of energy, rather than the quantity of energy, is the key idea to present here.

Which energy is easier to use to do work: the concentrated energy in the gasoline or the thermal energy spread from Chicago to Denver? Of course, the energy concentrated in the gasoline is more convenient to use.

This example illustrates a very important general principle: when we utilize energy to do work, we degrade its usefulness. In other words, when we use energy the *quality* of that energy (its ease of use) is lowered.

In summary,

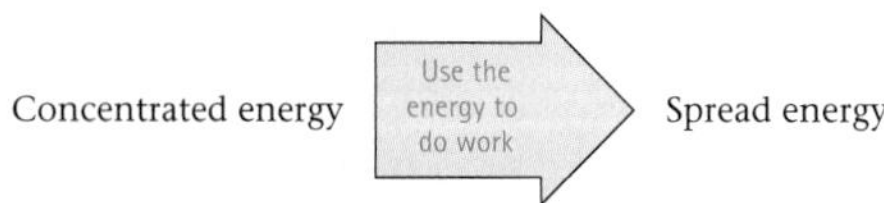

You may have heard someone mention the "heat death" of the universe. Eventually (many eons from now), all energy will be spread evenly throughout the universe and everything will be at the same temperature. At this point it will no longer be possible to do any work. The universe will be "dead."

We don't have to worry about the heat death of the universe anytime soon, of course, but we do need to think about conserving "quality" energy supplies. The energy stored in petroleum molecules got there over millions of years through plants and simple animals absorbing energy from the sun and using this energy to construct molecules. As these organisms died and became buried, natural processes changed them into the petroleum deposits we now access for our supplies of gasoline and natural gas.

Petroleum is highly valuable because it furnishes a convenient, concentrated source of energy. Unfortunately, we are using this fuel at a much faster rate than natural processes can replace it, so we are looking for new sources of energy. The most logical energy source is the sun. *Solar energy* refers to using the sun's energy directly to do productive work in our society. We will discuss energy supplies in the next section.

Section 10.9

Test Bank: 58, 59

TEACHING TIP

This section offers an excellent opportunity for students to work on a cross-curricular project with the social science department. Have them research energy resources in the news and on the Web. They can make classroom presentations on alternative resources, have a debate about the advantages and disadvantages of different fuels, or discuss the implications of our energy use for the future.

10.9 Energy and Our World

OBJECTIVE: To consider the energy resources of our world.

Woody plants, coal, petroleum, and natural gas provide a vast resource of energy that originally came from the sun. By the process of photosynthesis, plants store energy that can be claimed by burning the plants themselves or the decay products that have been converted over millions of years to **fossil fuels.** Although the United States currently depends heavily on petroleum for energy, this dependency is a relatively recent phenomenon, as shown in Figure 10.7. In this section we discuss some sources of energy and their effects on the environment.

Petroleum and Natural Gas

Although how they were produced is not completely understood, petroleum and natural gas were most likely formed from the remains of marine organisms that lived approximately 500 million years ago. **Petroleum** is a thick, dark liquid composed mostly of compounds called *hydrocarbons* that contain carbon and hydrogen. (Carbon is unique among elements in the extent to which it can bond to itself to form chains of various lengths.) Table 10.2 gives the formulas and names for several common hydrocarbons. **Natural**

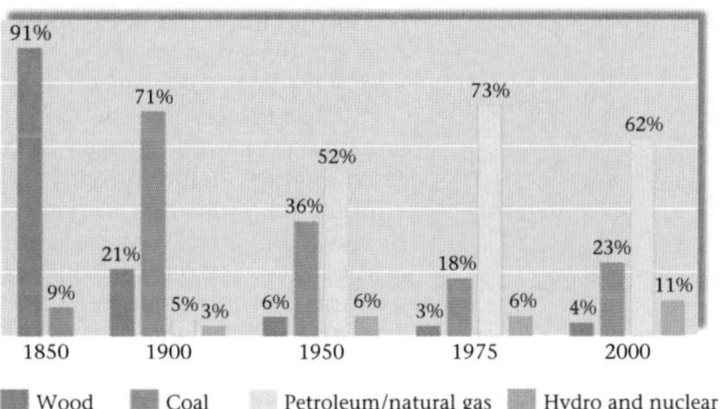

Figure 10.7
Energy sources used in the United States.

gas, usually associated with petroleum deposits, consists mostly of methane, but it also contains significant amounts of ethane, propane, and butane.

The composition of petroleum varies somewhat, but it includes mostly hydrocarbons having chains that contain from 5 to more than 25 carbons. To be used efficiently, the petroleum must be separated into fractions by boiling. The lighter molecules (having the lowest boiling points) can be boiled off, leaving the heavier ones behind. The commercial uses of various petroleum fractions are shown in Table 10.3.

The petroleum era began when the demand for lamp oil during the Industrial Revolution outstripped the traditional sources: animal fats and whale oil. In response to this increased demand, Edwin Drake drilled the first oil well in 1859 at Titusville, Pennsylvania. The petroleum from this well was refined to produce *kerosene* (fraction C_{10}–C_{18}), which served as an excellent lamp oil. *Gasoline* (fraction C_5–C_{10}) had limited use and was often discarded. This situation soon changed. The development of the electric light decreased the need for kerosene, and the advent of the "horseless carriage" with its gasoline-powered engine signaled the birth of the gasoline age.

As gasoline became more important, new ways were sought to increase the yield of gasoline obtained from each barrel of petroleum. William Burton invented a process at Standard Oil of Indiana called *pyrolytic (high-temperature) cracking*. In this process, the heavier molecules of the kerosene fraction are heated to about 700 °C, causing them to break (crack) into the smaller molecules of hydrocarbons in the gasoline fraction. As cars became larger, more efficient internal combustion engines were designed. Because of the uneven burning of the gasoline then available, these engines "knocked,"

Table 10.2 Names and Formulas for Some Common Hydrocarbons

Formula	Name
CH_4	Methane
C_2H_6	Ethane
C_3H_8	Propane
C_4H_{10}	Butane
C_5H_{12}	Pentane
C_6H_{14}	Hexane
C_7H_{16}	Heptane
C_8H_{18}	Octane

Table 10.3 Uses of the Various Petroleum Fractions

Petroleum Fraction in Terms of Numbers of Carbon Atoms	Major Uses
C_5–C_{10}	Gasoline
C_{10}–C_{18}	Kerosene
	Jet fuel
C_{15}–C_{25}	Diesel fuel
	Heating oil
	Lubricating oil
$>C_{25}$	Asphalt

Additional Activity

Have students determine energy use inking with fuel and electric bills. Estimate an average yearly consumption of

Electricity in kilowatt hours (1 kWh = 3595 J)
Natural gas in therms or BTUs (1 therm = 1054 kJ)
Oil in gallons

Once this exercise is complete, find the annual class average. Then determine the annual city average, state average, and country average.

A similar exercise can be done using gasoline. Determine the weekly consumption of gasoline by an individual. Next determine the average consumption of gasoline in your school. Finally determine the cost of this fuel.

producing unwanted noise and even engine damage. Intensive research to find additives that would promote smoother burning produced tetraethyl lead, $(C_2H_5)_4Pb$, a very effective "antiknock" agent.

The addition of tetraethyl lead to gasoline became a common practice, and by 1960, gasoline contained as much as 3g of lead per gallon. As we have discovered so often in recent years, technological advances can produce environmental problems. To prevent air pollution from automobile exhaust, catalytic converters have been added to car exhaust systems. The effectiveness of these converters, however, is destroyed by lead. The use of leaded gasoline also greatly increased the amount of lead in the environment, where it can be ingested by animals and humans. For these reasons, the use of lead in gasoline has been phased out, requiring extensive (and expensive) modifications of engines and of the gasoline refining process.

Coal

Coal was formed from the remains of plants that were buried and subjected to high pressure and heat over long periods of time. Plant materials have a high content of cellulose, a complex molecule whose empirical formula is CH_2O but whose molar mass is approximately 500,000 g/mol. After the plants and trees that grew on the earth at various times and places died and were buried, chemical changes gradually lowered the oxygen and hydrogen content of the cellulose molecules. Coal "matures" through four stages: lignite, subbituminous, bituminous, and anthracite. Each stage has a higher carbon-to-oxygen and carbon-to-hydrogen ratio; that is, the relative carbon content gradually increases. Typical elemental compositions of the various coals are given in Table 10.4. The energy available from the combustion of a given mass of coal increases as the carbon content increases. Anthracite is the most valuable coal, and lignite is the least valuable.

Roland Weinrauch/dpa/Corbis

Coal is an important and plentiful fuel in the United States, currently furnishing approximately 20% of our energy. As the supply of petroleum decreases, the share of the energy supply from coal could eventually increase to as high as 30%. However, coal is expensive and dangerous to mine underground, and the strip mining of fertile farmland in the Midwest or of scenic land in the West causes obvious problems. In addition, the burning of coal, especially high-sulfur coal, yields air pollutants such as sulfur dioxide, which, in turn, can lead to acid rain. However, even if coal were pure carbon, the carbon dioxide produced when it was burned would still have significant effects on the earth's climate.

Table 10.4 Element Composition of Various Types of Coal

	Mass Percent of Each Element				
Type of Coal	C	H	O	N	S
Lignite	71	4	23	1	1
Subbituminous	77	5	16	1	1
Bituminous	80	6	8	1	5
Anthracite	92	3	3	1	1

Effects of Carbon Dioxide on Climate

The earth receives a tremendous quantity of radiant energy from the sun, about 30% of which is reflected back into space by the earth's atmosphere. The remaining energy passes through the atmosphere to the earth's surface. Some of this energy is absorbed by plants for photosynthesis and some by the oceans to evaporate water, but most of it is absorbed by soil, rocks, and water, increasing the temperature of the earth's surface. This energy is, in turn, radiated from the heated surface mainly as *infrared radiation,* often called *heat radiation.*

The atmosphere, like window glass, is transparent to visible light but does not allow all the infrared radiation to pass back into space. Molecules in the atmosphere, principally H_2O and CO_2, strongly absorb infrared radiation and radiate it back toward the earth, as shown in Figure 10.8. A net amount of thermal energy is retained by the earth's atmosphere, causing the earth to be much warmer than it would be without its atmosphere. In a way, the atmosphere acts like the glass of a greenhouse, which is transparent to visible light but absorbs infrared radiation, thus raising the temperature inside the building. This **greenhouse effect** is seen even more spectacularly on Venus, where the dense atmosphere is thought to be responsible for the high surface temperature of that planet.

Thus the temperature of the earth's surface is controlled to a significant extent by the carbon dioxide and water content of the atmosphere. The effect of atmospheric moisture (humidity) is readily apparent in the Midwest, for example. In summer, when the humidity is high, the heat of the sun is retained well into the night, giving very high nighttime temperatures. In winter, the coldest temperatures always occur on clear nights, when the low humidity allows efficient radiation of energy back into space.

The atmosphere's water content is controlled by the water cycle (evaporation and precipitation), and the average has remained constant over the years. However, as fossil fuels have been used more extensively, the carbon dioxide concentration has increased—up about 20% from 1880 to the present. Projections indicate that the carbon dioxide content of the atmosphere

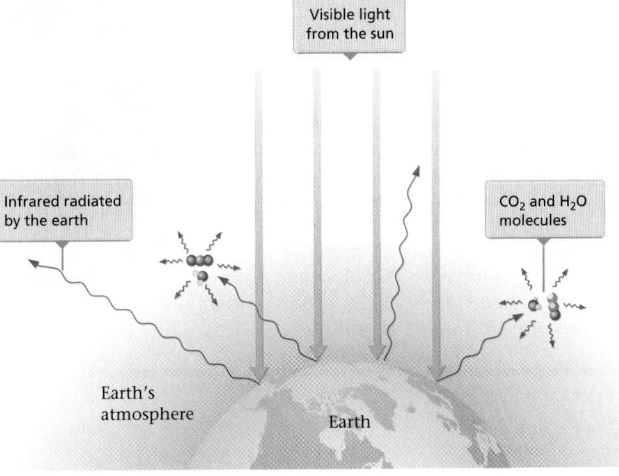

Figure 10.8
The earth's atmosphere is transparent to visible light from the sun. This visible light strikes the earth, and part of it is changed to infrared radiation. The infrared radiation from the earth's surface is strongly absorbed by CO_2, H_2O, and other molecules present in smaller amounts (for example, CH_4 and N_2O) in the atmosphere. In effect, the atmosphere traps some of the energy, acting like the glass in a greenhouse and keeping the earth warmer than it would otherwise be.

CHEMISTRY *IN* FOCUS

Seeing the Light

We are about to have a revolution in lighting. The incandescent light bulb developed by Thomas Edison in the late nineteenth century still dominates our lighting systems. However, this is about to change because Edison's light bulb is so inefficient: about 95% of the energy goes to heat instead of light. In the United States, 22% of total electricity production goes for lighting, for a cost of about $58 million. Globally, illumination consumes about 19% of electricity, and demand for lighting is expected to grow by 60% in the next 25 years. Given energy prices and the problems associated with global warming, we must find more efficient lighting devices.

In the short term, the answer appears to be compact fluorescent lights (CFLs). These bulbs, which have a screw-type base, draw only about 20% as much energy as incandescent bulbs for a comparable amount of light production. Although they cost four times as much, CFLs last ten times as long as incandescent bulbs. CFLs produce light from a type of compound called a phosphor that coats the inner walls of the bulb. The phosphor is mixed with a small amount of mercury (about 5 mg per bulb). When the bulb is turned on, a beam of electrons is produced. The electrons are absorbed by mercury atoms, which are caused to emit ultraviolet (UV) light. This UV light is absorbed by phosphor, which then emits visible light (a process called fluorescence). It is estimated that replacing all of the incandescent bulbs in our homes with CFLs would reduce our electrical demand in the United States by the equivalent of the power produced by 20 new 1000-MW nuclear power plants. This is a very significant savings.

Although the amount of mercury in each bulb is small (breaking a single CFL would not endanger a normal adult), recycling large numbers of CFLs does present potential pollution hazards. Research is now underway to find ways to alleviate this danger. For example, Professor Robert Hurt and his colleagues at Brown University have found that selenium prepared as tiny particles has a very high affinity for mercury and can be used in recycling operations to prevent dangerous occupational exposure to mercury.

Another type of lighting device that looks to be very valuable in the near future is the light-emitting diode (LED). An LED is a solid-state semiconductor designed to emit visible light when its electrons fall to lower energy levels. The tiny glowing light that indicates an audio system or television is on is an LED. In recent years, LEDs have been used in traffic lights, turn signals on cars, flashlights, and street lights. The use of LEDs for holiday lighting is rapidly increasing. It is estimated that LEDs eventually will reduce energy consumption for holiday lighting by 90%. The light production of LEDs per amount of energy consumed has increased dramatically in recent months, and the costs are decreasing steadily. Currently, LED lights are ten times more expensive than CFLs but last more than 15 years. Thus dramatic changes are occurring in the methods for lighting, and we all need to do our part to make our lives more energy efficient.

A compact fluorescent light bulb (CFL).

310

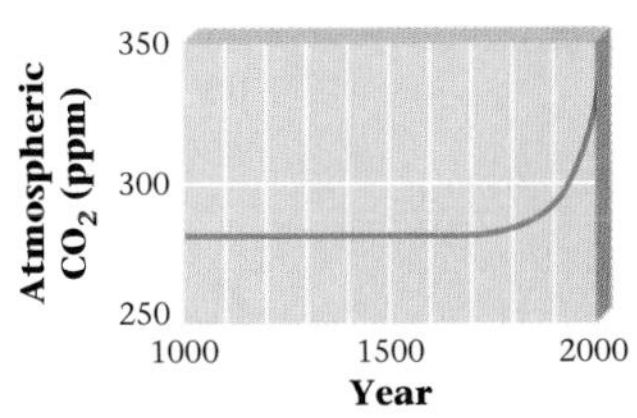

Figure 10.9

The atmospheric CO_2 concentration over the past 1000 years, based on ice core data and direct readings (since 1958). Note the dramatic increase in the past 100 years.

may be double in the twenty-first century what it was in 1880. This trend *could* increase the earth's average temperature by as much as 10 °C, causing dramatic changes in climate and greatly affecting the growth of food crops.

How well can we predict the long-term effects of carbon dioxide? Because weather has been studied for a period of time that is minuscule compared with the age of the earth, the factors that control the earth's climate in the long range are not clearly understood. For example, we do not understand what causes the earth's periodic ice ages. So it is difficult to estimate the effects of the increasing carbon dioxide levels.

In fact, the variation in the earth's average temperature over the past century is somewhat confusing. In the northern latitudes during the past century, the average temperature rose by 0.8 °C over a period of 60 years, then cooled by 0.5 °C during the next 25 years, and finally warmed by 0.2 °C in the succeeding 15 years. Such fluctuations do not match the steady increase in carbon dioxide. However, in southern latitudes and near the equator during the past century, the average temperature showed a steady rise totaling 0.4 °C. This figure is in reasonable agreement with the predicted effect of the increasing carbon dioxide concentration over that period. Another significant fact is that the last 10 years of the twentieth century have been the warmest decade on record.

Although the exact relationship between the carbon dioxide concentration in the atmosphere and the earth's temperature is not known at present, one thing is clear: The increase in the atmospheric concentration of carbon dioxide is quite dramatic (see Figure 10.9). We must consider the implications of this increase as we consider our future energy needs.

New Energy Sources

As we search for the energy sources of the future, we need to consider economic, climatic, and supply factors. There are several potential energy sources: the sun (solar), nuclear processes (fission and fusion), biomass (plants), and synthetic fuels. Direct use of the sun's radiant energy to heat our homes and run our factories and transportation systems seems a sensible long-term goal. But what do we do now? Conservation of fossil fuels is one obvious step, but substitutes for fossil fuels also must be found. There is much research going on now to solve this problem.

Section 10.10

Test Bank: 60

TEACHING TIP

In this section we discuss the "why" of energy. As in previous chapters, we emphasize that scientists want to know not only the "what" about a particular topic but also the "why." Energy is a driving force in chemical reactions. In this section we discuss why this driving force arises and use the "why" as a basis for introducing the concept of entropy on a qualitative level.

10.10 Energy as a Driving Force

OBJECTIVE: To understand energy as a driving force for natural processes.

A major goal of science is to understand why things happen as they do. In particular, we are interested in the driving forces of nature. Why do things occur in a particular direction? For example, consider a log that has burned in a fireplace, producing ashes and heat energy. If you are sitting in front of the fireplace, you would be very surprised to see the ashes begin to absorb heat from the air and reconstruct themselves into the log. It just doesn't happen. That is, the process that always occurs is

$$\text{log} + O_2(g) \rightarrow CO_2(g) + H_2O(g) + \text{ashes} + \text{energy}$$

The reverse of this process

$$CO_2(g) + H_2O(g) + \text{ashes} + \text{energy} \rightarrow \text{log} + O_2(g)$$

never happens.

Consider another example. A gas is trapped in one end of a vessel as shown below.

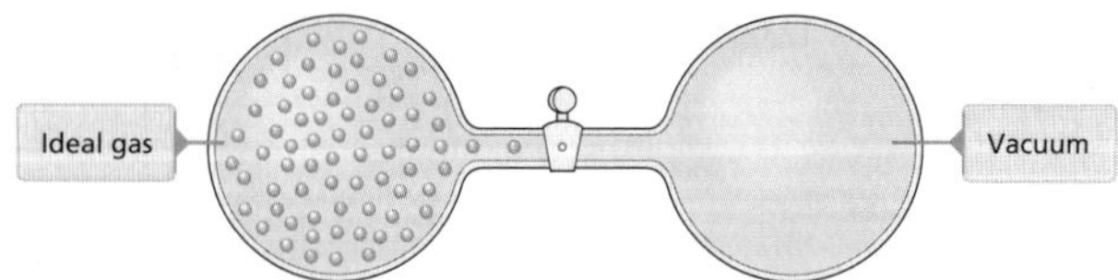

When the valve is opened, what always happens? The gas spreads evenly throughout the entire container.

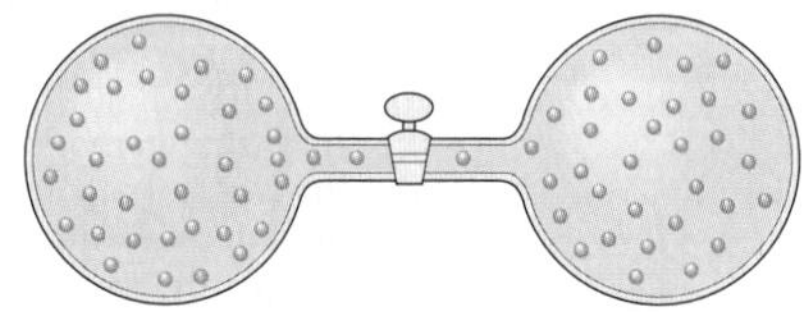

You would be very surprised to see the following process occur spontaneously:

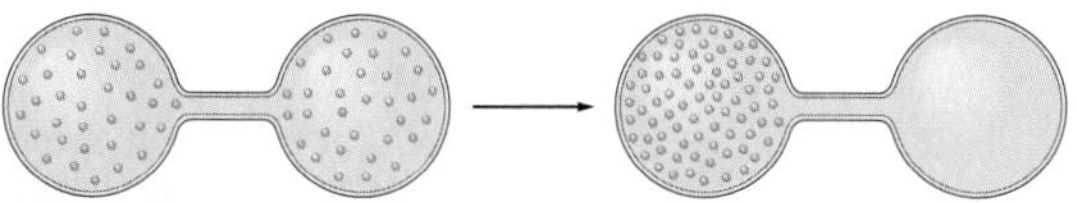

So, why does this process

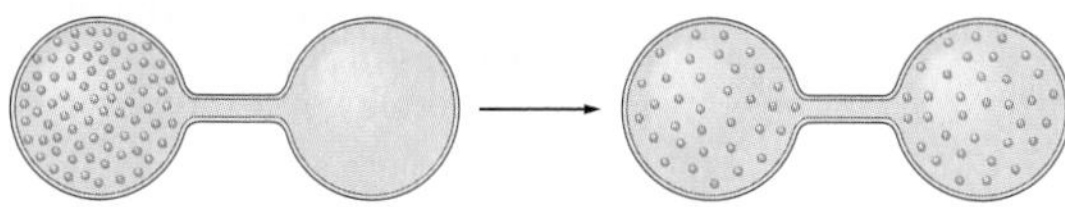

PowerLecture Animation: Dispersion of Energy from an Exothermic Reaction

occur spontaneously but the reverse process

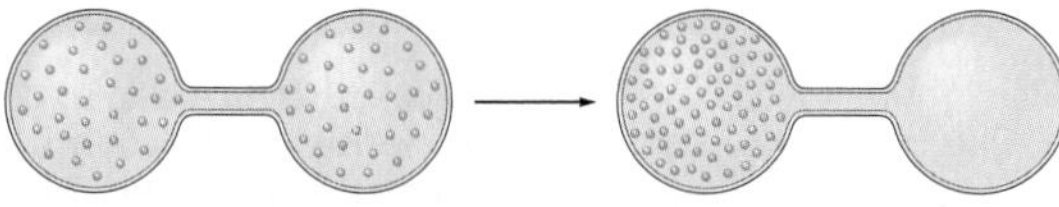

never occurs?

In many years of analyzing these and many other processes, scientists have discovered two very important driving forces:

- Energy spread
- Matter spread

Energy spread means that in a given process, concentrated energy is dispersed widely. This distribution happens every time an exothermic process occurs. For example, when a Bunsen burner burns, the energy stored in the fuel (natural gas—mostly methane) is dispersed into the surrounding air:

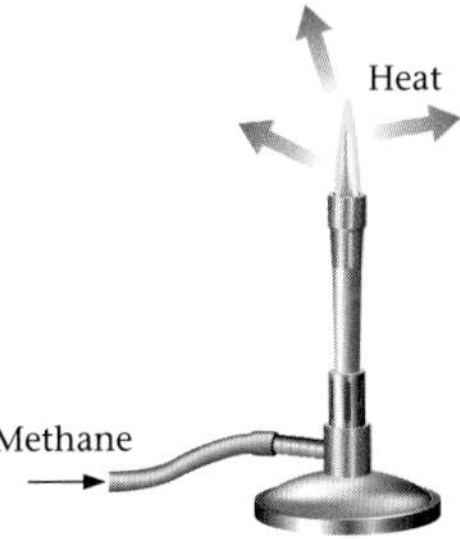

The energy that flows into the surroundings through heat increases the thermal motions of the molecules in the surroundings. In other words, this process increases the random motions of the molecules in the surroundings. *This always happens in every exothermic process.*

Matter spread means exactly what it says: the molecules of a substance are spread out and occupy a larger volume.

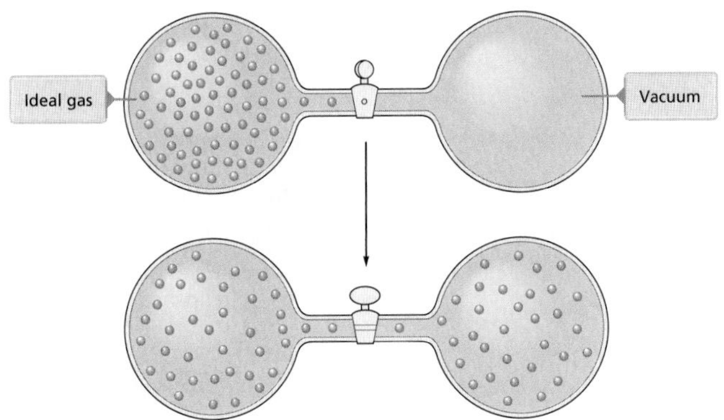

After looking at thousands of processes, scientists have concluded that these two factors are the important driving forces that cause events to occur. That is, processes are favored if they involve energy spread and matter spread.

Do these driving forces ever occur in opposition? Yes, they do—in many, many processes.

For example, consider ordinary table salt dissolving in water.

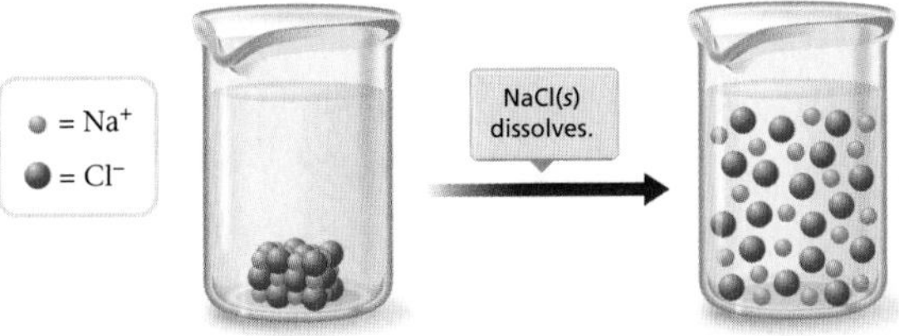

TEACHING TIP

The first law of thermodynamics tells us that energy is conserved. The second law gives us some indication of the natural direction of energy flows (the second law is often described as "time's arrow"). For example, the first law cannot explain why we could not "uncook" an egg by putting a cooked egg in the refrigerator, or why a ball that has just rolled down a hill (and has transferred energy to the hill) could not roll up the hill by spontaneously gathering the newly transferred energy from the hill. The second law informs us that these phenomena are impossible.

PowerLecture Animation: Entropy and Dissolution of $KMnO_4$

This process occurs spontaneously. You observe it every time you add salt to water to cook potatoes or pasta. Surprisingly, dissolving salt in water is *endothermic.* This process seems to go in the wrong direction—it involves energy concentration, not energy spread. Why does the salt dissolve? Because of matter spread. The Na^+ and Cl^- that are closely packed in the solid NaCl become spread around randomly in a much larger volume in the resulting solution. Salt dissolves in water because the favorable matter spread overcomes an unfavorable energy change.

Entropy

Entropy is a function we have invented to keep track of the natural tendency for the components of the universe to become disordered—entropy (designated by the letter *S*) is a measure of disorder or randomness. As randomness increases, *S* increases. Which has lower entropy, solid water (ice) or gaseous water (steam)? Remember that ice contains closely packed, ordered H_2O molecules, and steam has widely dispersed, randomly moving H_2O molecules (see Figure 10.10). Thus ice has more order and a lower value of *S*.

What do you suppose happens to the disorder of the universe as energy spread and matter spread occur during a process?

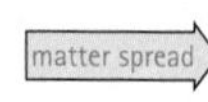

Faster random motions of the molecules in surroundings

matter spread → Components of matter are dispersed—they occupy a larger volume

PowerLecture Video: Sand not Reacting

It seems clear that both energy spread and matter spread lead to greater entropy (greater disorder) in the universe. This idea leads to a very important conclusion that is summarized in the **second law of thermodynamics:**

The entropy of the universe is always increasing.

A **spontaneous process** is one that occurs in nature without outside intervention—it happens "on its own." The second law of thermodynamics

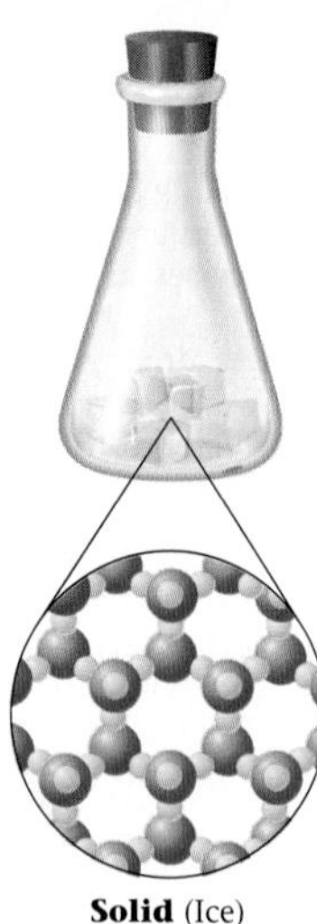
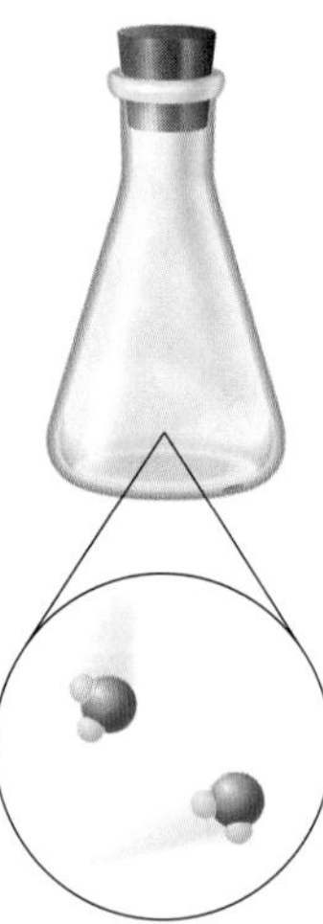

Solid (Ice) **Gas** (Steam)

Figure 10.10
Comparing the entropies of ice and steam.

PowerLecture Animation: H_2O Molecules Evaporating and Dispersing helps us to understand why certain processes are spontaneous and others are not. It also helps us to understand the conditions necessary for a process to be spontaneous. For example, at 1 atm (1 atmosphere of pressure), ice will spontaneously melt above a temperature of 0 °C but not below this temperature. A process is spontaneous only if the entropy of the universe increases as a result of the process. That is, all processes that occur in the universe lead to a net increase in the disorder of the universe. As the universe "runs," it is always heading toward more disorder. We are plunging slowly but inevitably toward total randomness—the heat death of the universe. But don't despair; it will not happen soon.

CHAPTER 10 REVIEW

Key Terms

energy (10.1)
potential energy (10.1)
kinetic energy (10.1)
law of conservation of energy (10.1)
work (10.1)
state function (10.1)
temperature (10.2)
heat (10.2)
system (10.3)
surroundings (10.3)
exothermic (10.3)
endothermic (10.3)
thermodynamics (10.4)
first law of thermodynamics (10.4)
internal energy (10.4)
calorie (10.5)
joule (10.5)
specific heat capacity (10.5)
enthalpy (10.6)
calorimeter (10.6)
Hess's law (10.7)
fossil fuels (10.9)
petroleum (10.9)
natural gas (10.9)
coal (10.9)
greenhouse effect (10.9)
energy spread (10.10)
matter spread (10.10)
entropy (10.10)
second law of thermodynamics (10.10)
spontaneous process (10.10)

Summary

1. One of the fundamental characteristics of energy is that it is conserved. Energy is changed in form but it is not produced or consumed in a process. Thermodynamics is the study of energy and its changes.
2. In a process some functions—called state functions—depend only on the beginning and final states of the system, not on the specific pathway followed. Energy is a state function. Other functions, such as heat and work, depend on the specific pathway followed and are not state functions.
3. The temperature of a substance indicates the vigor of the random motions of the components of that substance. The thermal energy of an object is the energy content of the object as produced by its random motions.

F directs you to the *Chemistry in Focus* feature in the chapter
VP indicates visual problems
OWL interactive versions of these problems are assignable in OWL

4. Heat is a flow of energy between two objects due to a temperature difference in the two objects. In an exothermic reaction, energy as heat flows out of the system into its surroundings. In an endothermic process, energy as heat flows from the surroundings into the system.
5. The internal energy of an object is the sum of the kinetic (due to motion) and potential (due to position) energies of the object. Internal energy can be changed by two types of energy flows, work (w) and heat (q): $\Delta E = q + w$.
6. A calorimeter is used to measure the heats of chemical reactions. The common units for heat are joules and calories.
7. The specific heat capacity of a substance (the energy required to change the temperature of one gram of the substance by one Celsius degree) is used to calculate temperature changes when a substance is heated.
8. The change in enthalpy for a process is equal to the heat for that process run at constant pressure.
9. Hess's law allows the calculation of the heat of a given reaction from known heats of related reactions.
10. Although energy is conserved in every process, the quality (usefulness) of the energy decreases with each use.
11. Our world has many sources of energy. The use of these sources affects the environment in various ways.
12. Natural processes occur in the direction that leads to an increase in the disorder (entropy) of the universe. The principal driving forces for processes are energy spread and matter spread.

ChemWork

Comparing Boiling Points
Identifying Intermolecular Forces
Intermolecular Forces
Properties and Intermolecular Forces
Ranking Boiling Points
Ranking Intermolecular Forces
Ranking Melting Points
Ranking Vapor Pressures
Unit Cells
X-ray Diffraction
Calculating Density of a Metal
Determining Types of Solids
Forces in Solids
Tetrahedral Holes
Calculating the Temperature of a Mixture
Heating Ice Cubes
Predicting Properties
Pressure Cooker
Vapor Pressure of Acetone
Phase Diagrams
Sulfur Phase Diagrams

Answers to End-of-Chapter Exercises

1. energy

2. Potential energy is energy due to position or composition. A stone at the top of a hill possesses potential energy because the stone may eventually roll down the hill. A gallon of gasoline possesses potential energy because heat will be released when the gasoline is burned.

3. $KE = \frac{1}{2}mv^2$

4. The total energy of the universe is constant. Energy cannot be created or destroyed, but can only be converted from one form to another.

5. A state function is a property of a system that changes independently of the pathway taken to make the change in the system.

6. Ball A initially possesses potential energy by virtue of its position at the top of the hill. As ball A rolls down the hill, its potential energy is converted to kinetic energy and frictional (heat) energy. When ball A reaches the bottom of the hill and hits ball B, it transfers its kinetic energy to ball B. Ball A then has only the potential energy corresponding to its new position.

7. *Temperature* is a measure of the random motions of the particles in a substance; that is, temperature is a measure of the average kinetic energies of the particles. *Heat* is the energy that flows because of a temperature difference.

8. The hot tea is at a higher temperature, which means the particles in the hot tea have higher average kinetic energies. When the tea spills on the skin, energy flows from the hot tea to the skin, until the tea and skin are at the same temperature. This sudden inflow of energy causes the burn.

Active Learning Questions

These questions are designed to be considered by groups of students in class. Often these questions work well for introducing a particular topic in class.

1. Look at Figure 10.1 in your text. Ball A has stopped moving. However, energy must be conserved. So what happened to the energy of ball A?

2. A friend of yours reads that the process of water freezing is exothermic. This friend tells you that this can't be true because exothermic implies "hot," and ice is cold. Is the process of water freezing exothermic? If so, explain this process so your friend can understand it. If not, explain why not.

3. You place hot metal into a beaker of cold water.
   a. Eventually what is true about the temperature of the metal compared to that of the water? Explain why this is true.
   b. Label this process as endothermic or exothermic if we consider the system to be
      i. the metal. Explain.
      ii. the water. Explain.

4. What does it mean when the heat for a process is reported with a negative sign?

5. You place 100.0 g of a hot metal in 100.0 g of cold water. Which substance (metal or water) undergoes a larger temperature change? Why is this?

6. Explain why aluminum cans make good storage containers for soft drinks. Styrofoam cups can be used to keep coffee hot and cola cold. How can this be?

7. In Section 10.7, two characteristics of enthalpy changes for reactions are listed. What are these characteristics? Explain why these characteristics are true.

8. What is the difference between *quality* and *quantity* of energy? Are both conserved? Is either conserved?

9. What is meant by the term *driving forces?* Why are *matter spread* and *energy spread* considered to be driving forces?

10. Give an example of a process in which *matter spread* is a driving force and an example of a process in which *energy spread* is a driving force, and explain each. These examples should be different from the ones given in the text.

11. Explain in your own words what is meant by the term *entropy*. Explain how both *matter spread* and *energy spread* are related to the concept of entropy.

12. Consider the processes

$$H_2O(g) \rightarrow H_2O(l)$$
$$H_2O(l) \rightarrow H_2O(g)$$

   a. Which process is favored by energy spread? Explain.
   b. Which process is favored by matter spread? Explain.
   c. How does temperature affect which process is favored? Explain.

13. What if energy was not conserved? How would this affect our lives?

14. The internal energy of a system is said to be the sum of the kinetic and potential energies of all the particles in the system. Section 10.1 discusses *potential energy* and *kinetic energy* in terms of a ball on a hill. Explain *potential energy* and *kinetic energy* for a chemical reaction.

15. Hydrogen gas and oxygen gas react violently to form water.
   a. Which is lower in energy: a mixture of hydrogen gases, or water? Explain.
   b. Sketch an energy-level diagram (like Figure 10.5) for this reaction and explain it.

16. Consider four 100.0-g samples of water, each in a separate beaker at 25.0 °C. Into each beaker you drop 10.0 g of a different metal that has been heated to 95.0 °C. Assuming no heat loss to the surroundings, which water sample will have the highest final temperature? Explain your answer.
   a. The water to which you have added aluminum (c = 0.89 J/g °C).
   b. The water to which you have added iron (c = 0.45 J/g °C).
   c. The water to which you have added copper (c = 0.20 J/g °C).
   d. The water to which you have added lead (c = 0.14 J/g °C).
   e. Because the masses of the metals are the same, the final temperatures would be the same.

17. For each of the following situations a–c, use the following choices i–iii to complete the statement "The final temperature of the water should be"
      i. Between 50 °C and 90 °C
      ii. 50 °C
      iii. Between 10 °C and 50 °C
   a. A 100.0-g sample of water at 90 °C is added to a 100.0-g sample of water at 10 °C.
   b. A 100.0-g sample of water at 90 °C is added to a 500.0-g sample of water at 10 °C.
   c. You have a Styrofoam cup with 50.0 g of water at 10 °C. You add a 50.0-g iron ball at 90 °C to the water.

18. How is Hess's law a restatement of the first law of thermodynamics?

19. Does the entropy of the system increase or decrease for each of the following? Explain.
   a. the evaporation of alcohol
   b. the freezing of water
   c. dissolving NaCl in water

9. The thermal energy of an object represents the random motions of the particles of matter that constitute the object.

10. Temperature is the concept by which we express the thermal energy contained in a sample. We cannot measure the motions of the particles/kinetic energy in a sample of matter directly. We know, however, that if two objects are at different temperatures, the one with the higher temperature has molecules that have higher average kinetic energies than the molecules of the object at the lower temperature.

11. The *system* is the part of the universe upon which we wish to focus attention (for example, the actual molecules that are reacting). The *surroundings* include everything else in the universe.

12. When the chemical system evolves energy, the energy evolved from the reacting chemicals is transferred to the surroundings.

VP 20. Predict the sign of ΔS° for each of the following changes.

a.

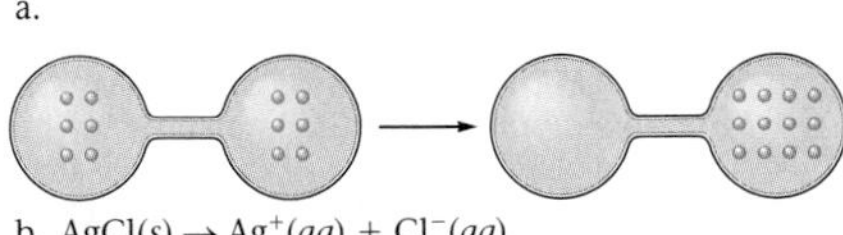

b. $AgCl(s) \rightarrow Ag^+(aq) + Cl^-(aq)$
c. $2H_2(g) + O_2 \rightarrow 2H_2O(l)$
d. $H_2O(l) \rightarrow H_2O(g)$

Questions and Problems

10.1 The Nature of Energy

QUESTIONS

1. ______ represents the ability to do work or to produce heat.
2. What is meant by *potential* energy? Give an example of an object or material that possesses potential energy.
3. What is the kinetic energy of a particle of mass m moving through space with velocity v?
4. Explain what we mean by the *law of conservation of energy*.
5. What is meant by a *state* function? Give an example.
6. In Figure 10.1, what kind of energy does ball A possess initially when at rest at the top of the hill? What kind of energies are involved as ball A moves down the hill? What kind of energy does ball A possess when it reaches the bottom of the hill and *stops* moving after hitting ball B? Where did the energy gained by ball B, allowing it to move up the hill, come from?

10.2 Temperature and Heat

QUESTIONS

7. Students often confuse what is meant by *heat* and *temperature*. Define each. How are the two concepts related?
8. If you spilled a cup of freshly brewed *hot* tea on yourself, you would be burned. If you spilled the same quantity of *iced* tea on yourself, you would not be burned. Explain.
9. What does the *thermal energy* of an object represent?
10. How are the *temperature* of an object and the *thermal energy* of an object related?

10.3 Exothermic and Endothermic Processes

QUESTIONS

11. In studying heat flows for chemical processes, what do we mean by the terms *system* and *surroundings*?
12. When a chemical system evolves energy, where does the energy go?
13. The combustion of methane, CH_4, is an exothermic process. Therefore, the products of this reaction must possess (higher/lower) total potential energy than do the reactants.
14. In any process, the energy gained by the surroundings must be ______ to the energy lost by the system.

10.4 Thermodynamics

QUESTIONS

15. What do we mean by *thermodynamics?* What is the *first law of thermodynamics?*
16. The ______ energy, E, of a system represents the sum of the kinetic and potential energies of all particles within the system.
17. Explain the meaning of each of the terms in the equation $\Delta E = q + w$.
18. If q for a process is a negative number, then the system is (gaining/losing) energy.
19. For an endothermic process, q will have a (positive/negative) sign.
20. If w for a process is a positive number, then the system must be (gaining/losing) energy from the surroundings.

10.5 Measuring Energy Changes

QUESTIONS

21. How is the *calorie* defined? How does a *Calorie* differ from a *calorie?* How is the *joule* related to the calorie?
22. Write the conversion factors that would be necessary to perform each of the following conversions:
    a. an energy given in calories to its equivalent in joules
    b. an energy given in joules to its equivalent in calories
    c. an energy given in calories to its equivalent in kilocalories
    d. an energy given in kilojoules to its equivalent in joules

PROBLEMS

23. If 8.40 kJ of heat is needed to raise the temperature of a sample of metal from 15 °C to 20 °C, how many kilojoules of heat will be required to raise the temperature of the same sample of metal from 25 °C to 40 °C?
24. If it takes 654 J of energy to warm a 5.51-g sample of water, how much energy would be required to warm 55.1 g of water by the same amount?

All even-numbered Questions and Problems have answers in the back of this book and solutions in the Solutions Guide.

13. lower

14. exactly equal to

15. Thermodynamics is the study of energy and energy transfers. The first law of thermodynamics is the same as the law of conservation of energy, which is usually stated as "the energy of the universe is constant."

16. internal

17. ΔE represents the change in internal energy of the system (the internal energy represents the total of the kinetic and potential energies of all the particles in the system); q represents the heat energy that flows during a process; w represents the work done by, or upon, a system during a process.

18. losing

19. positive

20. gaining

21. The calorie represents the amount of energy required to warm one gram of water by one Celsius degree. The "Calorie" or "nutritional" calorie represents 1000 calories (one kilocalorie). The joule is the SI unit of energy and 1 calorie is equivalent to 4.184 joules. The joule has a specific SI definition as the energy required to exert a force of 1 newton over a distance of 1 meter, but we tend to use the experimental definition above in terms of heating water.

22. (a) $\frac{1\text{ J}}{4.184\text{ cal}}$; (b) $\frac{4.184\text{ cal}}{1\text{ J}}$; (c) $\frac{1\text{ kcal}}{1000\text{ cal}}$; (d) $\frac{1000\text{ J}}{1\text{ kJ}}$

23. 25.2 kJ

24. 6540 J = 6.54 kJ

25. (a) 315 kJ, 3.15×10^3 J; (b) 0.315 kJ, 315 J; (c) 5.90 kJ, 5.90×10^3 J; (d) 5.90 kJ, 5.90×10^3 J

26. (a) 8.254 kcal; (b) 0.0415 kcal; (c) 8.231 kcal; (d) 752.9 kcal

27. (a) 155.9 kcal; (b) 0.239 kcal; (c) 1.000 kcal; (d) 1040. kcal

28. (a) 243 kJ to 3 significant figures; (b) 0.004184 kJ; (c) 0.000251 kJ; (d) 0.4503 kJ

29. (a) 2.616 kJ; (b) 8.241×10^4 J; (c) 2.201×10^5 J; (d) 29.68 kcal

30. (a) 9.174×10^4 cal; (b) 425.7 cal; (c) 1.032 kcal; (d) 383.8 kJ

31. 6.02 J/g °C

32. 5.8×10^2 J (two significant figures)

33. 18 °C (two significant figures)

34. 28.6 °C/29 °C

35. 1.8×10^2 J

36. exothermic

37. Approximately 63 kJ (~60 kJ to one significant figure)

25. Convert the following numbers of calories or kilocalories into joules and kilojoules (Remember: *Kilo* means 1000.)

a. 75.2 kcal
b. 75.2 cal
c. 1.41×10^3 cal
d. 1.41 kcal

26. Convert the following numbers of calories into kilocalories. (Remember: *kilo* means 1000.)

a. 8254 cal
b. 41.5 cal
c. 8.231×10^3 cal
d. 752,900 cal

27. Convert the following numbers of kilojoules into kilocalories. (Remember: *kilo* means 1000.)

a. 652.1 kJ
b. 1.00 kJ
c. 4.184 kJ
d. 4.351×10^3 kJ

28. Convert the following numbers of joules into kilojoules. (Remember: *kilo* means 1000.)

a. 243,000 J
b. 4.184 J
c. 0.251 J
d. 450.3 J

29. Perform the indicated conversions.

a. 625.2 cal into kilojoules
b. 82.41 kJ into joules
c. 52.61 kcal into joules
d. 124.2 kJ into kilocalories

30. Perform the indicated conversions.

a. 91.74 kcal into calories
b. 1.781 kJ into calories
c. 4.318×10^3 J into kilocalories
d. 9.173×10^4 cal into kilojoules

31. If 69.5 kJ of heat is applied to a 1012-g block of metal, the temperature of the metal increases by 11.4 °C. Calculate the specific heat capacity of the metal in J/g °C.

32. What quantity of heat energy must have been applied to a block of aluminum weighing 42.7 g if the temperature of the block of aluminum increased by 15.2 °C? (See Table 10.1.)

33. If 125 J of heat energy is applied to a block of silver weighing 29.3 g, by how many degrees will the temperature of the silver increase? (See Table 10.1.)

34. If 100. J of heat energy is applied to a 25-g sample of mercury, by how many degrees will the temperature of the sample of mercury increase? (See Table 10.1.)

35. What quantity of heat is required to raise the temperature of 55.5 g of gold from 20 °C to 45 °C? (See Table 10.1.)

36. The "Chemistry in Focus" segment *Coffee: Hot and Quick(lime)* discusses self-heating cups of coffee using the chemical reaction between quicklime, CaO(*s*), and water. Is this reaction endothermic or exothermic?

37. The "Chemistry in Focus" segment *Nature Has Hot Plants* discusses thermogenic, or heat-producing, plants. For some plants, enough heat is generated to increase the temperature of the blossom by 15 °C. About how much heat is required to increase the temperature of 1 L of water by 15 °C?

38. In the "Chemistry in Focus" segment *Firewalking: Magic or Science?*, it is claimed that one reason people can walk on hot coals is that human tissue is mainly composed of water. Because of this, a large amount of heat must be transferred from the coals to change significantly the temperature of the feet. How much heat must be transferred to 100.0 g of water to change its temperature by 35 °C?

10.6 Thermochemistry (Enthalpy)

QUESTIONS

39. What do we mean by the *enthalpy change* for a reaction that occurs at constant pressure?

40. What is a *calorimeter?*

PROBLEMS

41. The enthalpy change for the reaction of hydrogen gas with fluorine gas to produce hydrogen fluoride is −542 kJ for the equation *as written*:

$$H_2(g) + F_2(g) \rightarrow 2HF(g) \quad \Delta H = -542 \text{ kJ}$$

a. What is the enthalpy change *per mole* of hydrogen fluoride produced?
b. Is the reaction exothermic or endothermic as written?
c. What would be the enthalpy change for the *reverse* of the given equation (that is, for the decomposition of HF into its constituent elements)?

42. For the reaction $S(s) + O_2(g) \rightarrow SO_2(g)$, $\Delta H = -296$ kJ per mole of SO_2 formed.

a. Calculate the quantity of heat released when 1.00 g of sulfur is burned in oxygen.
b. Calculate the quantity of heat released when 0.501 mole of sulfur is burned in air.
c. What quantity of energy is required to break up 1 mole of $SO_2(g)$ into its constituent elements?

10.7 Hess's Law

QUESTIONS

43. The "Chemistry in Focus" segment *Methane: An Important Energy Source* discusses methane as a fuel. Determine ΔH for methane in terms of kJ/mol.

44. When ethanol (grain alcohol, C_2H_5OH) is burned in oxygen, approximately 1360 kJ of heat energy is released per mole of ethanol.

$$C_2H_5OH(l) + 3O_2(g) \rightarrow 2CO_2(g) + 3H_2O(g)$$

a. What quantity of heat is released for each *gram* of ethanol burned?
b. What is ΔH for the reaction *as written*?
c. How much heat is released when sufficient ethanol is burned so as to produce 1 mole of water vapor?

All even-numbered Questions and Problems have answers in the back of this book and solutions in the Solutions Guide.

38. 14.6 kJ (~15 kJ to one significant figure)

39. The enthalpy change is the heat that flows on a molar basis for a reaction at constant pressure.

40. A calorimeter is an insulated device in which reactions are performed and temperature changes measured, enabling the calculation of heat flows. See Figure 10.6.

41. (a) −271 kJ/mol HF; (b) exothermic; (c) +542 kJ for the reverse of the reaction as written

42. (a) −9.23 kJ; (b) −148 kJ; (c) +296 kJ/mol

43. 8.8×10^2 kJ/mol

44. (a) −29.5 kJ (b) $\Delta H = -1360$ kJ; (c) 453 kJ/mol H_2O

45. a + [−b] kJ or (a − b) kJ

46. −220 kJ

47. −296.1 kJ

48. −233 kJ

49. The energy is converted to the energy of motion of the car, and to friction as the car's tires interact with the road. Once the potential energy has been dispersed, it cannot be reused.

50. Once everything in the universe is at the same temperature, no further thermodynamic work can be done. Even though the total energy of the universe will be the same, the energy will have been dispersed evenly, making it effectively useless.

51. Petroleum is especially useful because it is a concentrated, easy-to-transport, easy-to-use source of energy.

52. Concentrated sources of energy, such as petroleum, are being used so as to disperse the energy they contain, making that energy unavailable for human use.

53. These sources of energy originally came from living plants and animals, which used their metabolic processes to store energy.

54. Petroleum consists mainly of hydrocarbons, which are molecules containing chains of carbon atoms with hydrogen atoms attached to the chains. The fractions are based on the number of carbon atoms in the chains: for example, gasoline is a mixture of hydrocarbons with 5–10 carbon atoms in the chains, whereas asphalt is a mixture of hydrocarbons with 25 or more carbon atoms in the chains. Different fractions have different physical properties and uses, but all can be combusted to produce energy. See Table 10.3.

55. Natural gas consists primarily of methane, with small amounts of ethane, propane, and butane. It is generally found in association with petroleum deposits.

56. Tetraethyl lead was used as an additive for gasoline to promote smoother running of engines. It is no longer widely used because of concerns about the lead being released into the environment as the leaded gasoline burns.

PROBLEMS

45. Given the following hypothetical data:

$$X(g) + Y(g) \rightarrow XY(g) \text{ for which } \Delta H = a \text{ kJ}$$
$$X(g) + Z(g) \rightarrow XZ(g) \text{ for which } \Delta H = b \text{ kJ}$$

Calculate ΔH for the reaction

$$Y(g) + XZ(g) \rightarrow XY(g) + Z(g)$$

46. Given the following data:

$$C(s) + O_2(g) \rightarrow CO_2(g) \qquad \Delta H = -393 \text{ kJ}$$
$$2CO(g) + O_2(g) \rightarrow 2CO_2(g) \qquad \Delta H = -566 \text{ kJ}$$

Calculate ΔH for the reaction $2C(s) + O_2(g) \rightarrow CO(g)$.

47. Given the following data:

$$S(s) + \tfrac{3}{2}O_2(g) \rightarrow SO_3(g) \qquad \Delta H = -395.2 \text{ kJ}$$
$$2SO_2(g) + O_2(g) \rightarrow 2SO_3(g) \qquad \Delta H = -198.2 \text{ kJ}$$

Calculate ΔH for the reaction $S(s) + O_2(g) \rightarrow SO_2(g)$.

48. Given the following data:

$$2O_3(g) \rightarrow 3O_2(g) \qquad \Delta H = -427 \text{ kJ}$$
$$O_2(g) \rightarrow 2O(g) \qquad \Delta H = +495 \text{ kJ}$$
$$NO(g) + O_3(g) \rightarrow NO_2(g) + O_2(g) \qquad \Delta H = -199 \text{ kJ}$$

Calculate ΔH for the reaction

$$NO(g) + O_2(g) \rightarrow NO_2(g)$$

10.8 Quality Versus Quantity of Energy

QUESTIONS

49. Consider gasoline in your car's gas tank. What happens to the energy stored in the gasoline when you drive your car? Although the total energy in the universe remains constant, can the energy stored in the gasoline be reused once it is dispersed to the environment?

50. Although the total energy of the universe will remain constant, why will energy no longer be useful once everything in the universe is at the same temperature?

51. Why are petroleum products especially useful as sources of energy?

52. Why is the "quality" of energy decreasing in the universe?

10.9 Energy and Our World

QUESTIONS

53. Where did the energy stored in wood, coal, petroleum, and natural gas originally come from?

54. What does petroleum consist of? What are some "fractions" into which petroleum is refined? How are these fractions related to the sizes of the molecules involved?

55. What does natural gas consist of? Where is natural gas commonly found?

56. What was tetraethyl lead used for in the petroleum industry? Why is it no longer commonly used?

57. What are the four "stages" of coal formation? How do the four types of coal differ?

58. What is the "greenhouse effect"? Why is a certain level of greenhouse gases beneficial, but too high a level dangerous to life on earth? What is the most common greenhouse gas?

10.10 Energy as a Driving Force

QUESTIONS

59. What do chemists mean by a "driving force"?

60. What does it mean to say that "energy spread" and "matter spread" are driving forces in chemical reactions?

61. If a reaction occurs readily but has an endothermic heat of reaction, what must be the driving force for the reaction?

62. Does a double-displacement reaction such as

$$NaCl(aq) + AgNO_3(aq) \rightarrow AgCl(s) + NaNO_3(aq)$$

result in a matter spread or in a concentration of matter?

63. What do we mean by *entropy?* Why does the entropy of the universe increase during a spontaneous process?

64. A chunk of ice at room temperature melts, even though the process is endothermic. Why?

Additional Problems

65. Consider a sample of *steam* (water in the gaseous state) at 150 °C. Describe what happens to the molecules in the sample as the sample is slowly cooled until it liquefies and then solidifies.

66. Convert the following numbers of kilojoules into kilocalories. (Remember: *kilo* means 1000.)

a. 462.4 kJ
b. 18.28 kJ
c. 1.014 kJ
d. 190.5 kJ

67. Perform the indicated conversions.

a. 85.21 cal into joules
b. 672.1 J into calories
c. 8.921 kJ into joules
d. 556.3 cal into kilojoules

68. Calculate the amount of energy required (in calories) to heat 145 g of water from 22.3 °C to 75.0 °C.

69. It takes 1.25 kJ of energy to heat a certain sample of pure silver from 12.0 °C to 15.2 °C. Calculate the mass of the sample of silver.

70. What quantity of heat energy would have to be applied to a 25.1-g block of iron in order to raise the temperature of the iron sample by 17.5 °C? (See Table 10.1.)

71. The specific heat capacity of gold is 0.13 J/g °C. Calculate the specific heat capacity of gold in cal/g °C.

All even-numbered Questions and Problems have answers in the back of this book and solutions in the Solutions Guide.

57. Coal matures through four stages: lignite, subbituminous, bituminous, and anthracite. The four types of coal differ in the ratio of carbon to the other elements. Anthracite has the highest fraction of carbon in it; when burned, it releases a larger amount of heat for a given mass.

58. The greenhouse effect is a warming effect due to the presence of gases in the atmosphere that absorb infrared radiation that has reached the earth from the sun; the gases do not allow the energy to pass back into space. A limited greenhouse effect is desirable because it moderates the temperature changes in the atmosphere that would otherwise be more drastic between daytime when the sun is shining and nighttime. Having too high a concentration of greenhouse gases, however, will elevate the temperature of the earth too much, affecting climate, crops, the polar ice caps, the temperatures of the oceans, and so on. Carbon dioxide produced by combustion reactions is our greatest concern as a greenhouse gas.

59. A driving force is some factor that tends to make a process occur.

60. If a proposed reaction involves either or both of those phenomena, the reaction will tend to be favorable.

61. an increase in entropy

62. Formation of a solid precipitate represents a concentration of matter.

63. Entropy is a measure of the randomness or disorder in a system. The entropy of the universe increases because the natural tendency is for things to become more disordered.

64. The molecules in liquid water are moving around freely and are therefore more "disordered" than when the molecules are held rigidly in a solid lattice in ice. The entropy increases during melting.

65. As the steam is cooled from 150 °C to 100 °C, the molecules of vapor gradually slow down as they lose kinetic energy. At 100 °C, the steam condenses into liquid water, and the temperature remains at 100 °C until all the steam has condensed. As the liquid water cools, the molecules in the liquid move more and more slowly as they lose kinetic energy. At 0 °C, the liquid water freezes.

66. (a) 110.5 kcal; (b) 4.369 kcal; (c) 0.2424 kcal; (d) 45.53 kcal

67. (a) 356.5 J; (b) 160.6 cal; (c) 8921 J; (d) 2.328 kJ

68. 7.65 kcal

69. 1627 g = 1.6×10^3 g

70. 2.0×10^2 J (two significant figures)

71. 0.31 cal/g °C

72. 3.8×10^5 J

73. For a given mass of substance, the substance with the *smallest* specific heat capacity (gold, 0.13 J/g °C) will undergo the *largest* increase in temperature. Conversely, the substance with the largest specific heat capacity (water, 4.184 J/g °C) will undergo the smallest increase in temperature.

74. 62.5 °C = 63 °C

75. 22.3 °C = 22 °C

76. 9.0

77. For any substance, $Q = s \times m \times \Delta T$. The basic calculation for each of the substances is the same: Heat required = 150. g × (specific heat capacity) × 11.2 °C. (See table at bottom of page.)

78. See table at bottom of page.

79. (a) 41 kJ; (b) 129 kJ; (c) 47 kJ (d) When the surroundings deliver work to the system, $w > 0$. This is the case for (a) and (b).

80. (a) exothermic; (b) exothermic; (c) endothermic; (d) endothermic

81. (a) −1652 kJ; (b) −826 kJ; (c) −7.39 kJ; (d) O_2 is the limiting reactant, −34.4 kJ heat released.

82. $\frac{1}{2}C + F \rightarrow A + B + D$ $\Delta H = 47.0$ kJ

83. 4900 mL or 4.9 L

84. Approximately 9 hr

72. Calculate the amount of energy required (in joules) to heat 2.5 kg of water from 18.5 °C to 55.0 °C.

73. If 10. J of heat is applied to 5.0-g samples of each of the substances listed in Table 10.1, which substance's temperature will increase the most? Which substance's temperature will increase the least?

74. A 50.0-g sample of water at 100. °C is poured into a 50.0-g sample of water at 25 °C. What will be the final temperature of the water?

75. A 25.0-g sample of pure iron at 85 °C is dropped into 75 g of water at 20. °C. What is the final temperature of the water–iron mixture?

76. If it takes 4.5 J of energy to warm 5.0 g of aluminum from 25 °C to a certain higher temperature, then it will take ______ J to warm 10. g of aluminum over the same temperature interval.

77. For each of the substances listed in Table 10.1, calculate the quantity of heat required to heat 150. g of the substance by 11.2 °C.

78. Suppose you had 10.0-g samples of each of the substances listed in Table 10.1 and that 1.00 kJ of heat is applied to each of these samples. By what amount would the temperature of each sample be raised?

79. Calculate ΔE for each of the following.

a. $q = -47$ kJ, $w = +88$ kJ
b. $q = +82$ kJ, $w = +47$ kJ
c. $q = +47$ kJ, $w = 0$
d. In which of these cases do the surroundings do work on the system?

80. Are the following processes exothermic or endothermic?

a. the combustion of gasoline in a car engine
b. water condensing on a cold pipe
c. $CO_2(s) \rightarrow CO_2(g)$
d. $F_2(g) \rightarrow 2F(g)$

81. The overall reaction in commercial heat packs can be represented as

$$4Fe(s) + 3O_2(g) \rightarrow 2Fe_2O_3(s) \qquad \Delta H = -1652 \text{ kJ}$$

a. How much heat is released when 4.00 mol iron is reacted with excess O_2?
b. How much heat is released when 1.00 mol Fe_2O_3 is produced?
c. How much heat is released when 1.00 g iron is reacted with excess O_2?
d. How much heat is released when 10.0 g Fe and 2.00 g O_2 are reacted?

82. Consider the following equations:

$$3A + 6B \rightarrow 3D \qquad \Delta H = -403 \text{ kJ/mol}$$
$$E + 2F \rightarrow A \qquad \Delta H = -105.2 \text{ kJ/mol}$$
$$C \rightarrow E + 3D \qquad \Delta H = +64.8 \text{ kJ/mol}$$

Suppose the first equation is reversed and multiplied by $\frac{1}{6}$, the second and third equations are divided by 2, and the three adjusted equations are added. What is the net reaction and what is the overall heat of this reaction?

83. It has been determined that the body can generate 5500 kJ of energy during one hour of strenuous exercise. Perspiration is the body's mechanism for eliminating this heat. How many grams and how many liters of water would have to be evaporated through perspiration to rid the body of the heat generated during two hours of exercise? (The heat of vaporization of water is 40.6 kJ/mol.)

84. One way to lose weight is to exercise! Walking briskly at 4.0 miles per hour for an hour consumes about 400 kcal of energy. How many hours would you have to walk at 4.0 miles per hour to lose one pound of body fat? One gram of body fat is equivalent to 7.7 kcal of energy. There are 454 g in 1 lb.

All even-numbered Questions and Problems have answers in the back of this book and solutions in the Solutions Guide.

77.

Substance	*Specific Heat Capacity*	*Heat Required*
water (*l*)	4.184 J/g °C	7.03×10^3 J
water (*s*)	2.03 J/g °C	3.41×10^3 J
water (*g*)	2.0 J/g °C	3.4×10^3 J
aluminum	0.89 J/g °C	1.5×10^3 J
iron	0.45 J/g °C	7.6×10^2 J
mercury	0.14 J/g °C	2.4×10^2 J
carbon	0.71 J/g °C	1.2×10^3 J
silver	0.24 J/g °C	4.0×10^2 J
gold	0.13 J/g °C	2.2×10^2 J

78.

Substance	*Specific Heat Capacity*	*Temperature Change*
water (*l*)	4.184 J/g °C	23.9 °C
water (*s*)	2.03 J/g °C	49.3 °C
water (*g*)	2.0 J/g °C	50. °C
aluminum	0.89 J/g °C	1.1×10^2 °C
iron	0.45 J/g °C	2.2×10^2 °C
mercury	0.14 J/g °C	7.1×10^2 °C
carbon	0.71 J/g °C	1.4×10^2 °C
silver	0.24 J/g °C	4.2×10^2 °C
gold	0.13 J/g °C	7.7×10^2 °C

Chapter 11

Objectives

In this chapter, our objectives are for the students to:

SECTION 11.1

- Describe Rutherford's model of the atom.

SECTION 11.2

- Explore the nature of electromagnetic radiation.

SECTION 11.3

- See how atoms emit light.

SECTION 11.4

- Understand how the emission spectrum of hydrogen demonstrates the quantized nature of energy.

SECTION 11.5

- Learn about Bohr's model of the hydrogen atom.

SECTION 11.6

- Understand how the electron's position is represented in the wave mechanical model.

SECTION 11.7

- Learn about the shapes of orbitals designated by *s*, *p*, and *d*.

SECTION 11.8

- Review the energy levels and orbitals of the wave mechanical model of the atom.
- Learn about electron spin.

SECTION 11.9

- Understand how the principal energy levels fill with electrons in atoms beyond hydrogen.
- Learn about valence electrons and core electrons.

SECTION 11.10

- Learn about the electron configurations of atoms with *Z* greater than 18.

SECTION 11.11

- Understand the general trends in atomic properties in the periodic table.

11 Modern Atomic Theory

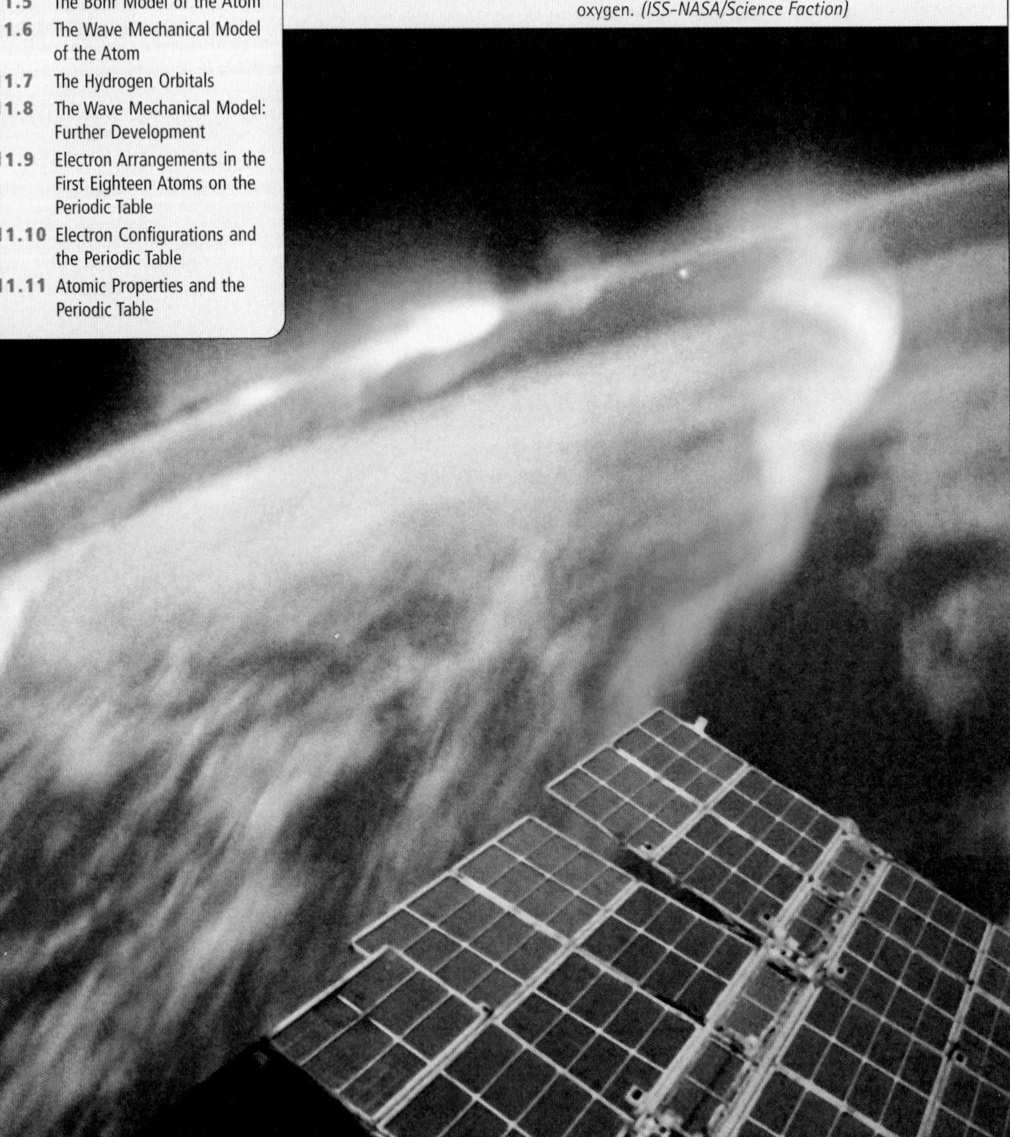

The Aurora Australis from space. The colors are due to spectral emissions of nitrogen and oxygen. *(ISS-NASA/Science Faction)*

OWL Sign in to OWL at **www.cengage.com/owl** to view tutorials and simulations, develop problem-solving skills, and complete online homework assigned by your professor.

go Chemistry Download mini-lecture videos for key concept review and exam prep from OWL or purchase them from **www.ichapters.com**

The concept of atoms is a very useful one. It explains many important observations, such as why compounds always have the same composition (a specific compound always contains the same types and numbers of atoms) and how chemical reactions occur (they involve a rearrangement of atoms).

Once chemists came to "believe" in atoms, a logical question followed: What are atoms like? What is the structure of an atom? In Chapter 4 we learned to picture the atom with a positively charged nucleus composed of protons and neutrons at its center and electrons moving around the nucleus in a space very large compared to the size of the nucleus.

In this chapter we will look at atomic structure in more detail. In particular, we will develop a picture of the electron arrangements in atoms—a picture that allows us to account for the chemistry of the various elements. Recall from our discussion of the periodic table in Chapter 4 that, although atoms exhibit a great variety of characteristics, certain elements can be grouped together because they behave similarly. For example, fluorine, chlorine, bromine, and iodine (the halogens) show great chemical similarities. Likewise, lithium, sodium, potassium, rubidium, and cesium (the alkali metals) exhibit many similar properties, and the noble gases (helium, neon, argon, krypton, xenon, and radon) are all very nonreactive. Although the members of each of these groups of elements show great similarity *within* the group, the differences in behavior *between* groups are striking. In this chapter we will see that it is the way the electrons are arranged in various atoms that accounts for these facts.

Alkali metals Halogens Noble gases

Owaki-Kulla/Corbis

A neon sign celebrating Route 66.

11.1 Rutherford's Atom

OBJECTIVE: To describe Rutherford's model of the atom.

go Chemistry **Module 11: Periodic Trends** covers concepts in this section.

Remember that in Chapter 4 we discussed the idea that an atom has a small positive core (called the nucleus) with negatively charged electrons moving around the nucleus in some way (Figure 11.1). This concept of a *nuclear atom* resulted from Ernest Rutherford's experiments in which he bombarded metal foil with α particles (see Section 4.5). Rutherford and his coworkers were able to show that the nucleus of the atom is composed of positively charged particles called *protons* and neutral particles called *neutrons*. Rutherford also found that the nucleus is apparently very small compared to the size of the entire atom. The electrons account for the rest of the atom.

Section 11.1

TEACHING TIP

This section reviews the basic components of the atom. It offers an opportunity to revisit these components and to emphasize models and how they change over time.

ChemWork Refined over ten years of use by thousands of students, **ChemWork** builds and enhances students' problems-solving skills. Online assignments function as a "personal instructor" to help students learn how to solve challenging problems and learn how to think like chemists. Annotations for **ChemWork** assignments are included at the beginning of the end-of-chapter review.

PowerLecture This 2-DVD package includes the Chemistry Multimedia Library, which contains animations, simulations, and movies for all chemistry subjects, organized by topic for lecture presentations. Annotations for **PowerLecture** are referenced in the margins throughout the Annotated Instructor's Edition.

Test Bank: 1–5

Section 11.2

TEACHING TIP

Students often consider the forms of electromagnetic radiation outside the visible range (radio, X rays, infrared, microwaves) to be entirely different from light. Use the PowerPoint and transparency of the electromagnetic spectrum (Figure 11.4) to show the range of frequencies for each type of radiation.

PowerLecture Animation: Electromagnetic Waves from Lightbulb (no sound)

LABORATORY EXPERIMENT

A relevant laboratory experiment for this section is Experiment 17, Line Spectra: Evidence for Atomic Structure, from *Introductory Chemistry in the Laboratory* by James Hall.

DEMONSTRATION

A long Slinky can be used to demonstrate the properties of waves. Have a student volunteer to hold one end of the Slinky. You can hold the other end and move it back and forth to make a wave. You can then discuss wavelength, frequency, and amplitude. You can tie a ribbon to one point on the Slinky and show that it does not traverse along the length of the Slinky. The ribbon simply moves back and forth in the same place. The energy actually seems to move through the point, rather than carrying it along the wave.

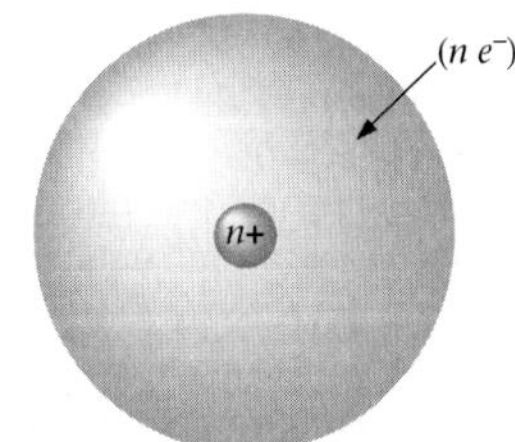

Figure 11.1
Rutherford's atom. The nuclear charge ($n+$) is balanced by the presence of n electrons moving in some way around the nucleus.

A major question left unanswered by Rutherford's work was, What are the electrons doing? That is, how are the electrons arranged and how do they move? Rutherford suggested that electrons might revolve around the nucleus like the planets revolve around the sun in our solar system. He couldn't explain, however, why the negative electrons aren't attracted into the positive nucleus, causing the atom to collapse.

At this point it became clear that more observations of the properties of atoms were needed to understand the structure of the atom more fully. To help us understand these observations, we need to discuss the nature of light and how it transmits energy.

11.2 Electromagnetic Radiation

OBJECTIVE: To explore the nature of electromagnetic radiation.

If you hold your hand a few inches from a brightly glowing light bulb, what do you feel? Your hand gets warm. The "light" from the bulb somehow transmits energy to your hand. The same thing happens if you move close to the glowing embers of wood in a fireplace—you receive energy that makes you feel warm. The energy you feel from the sun is a similar example.

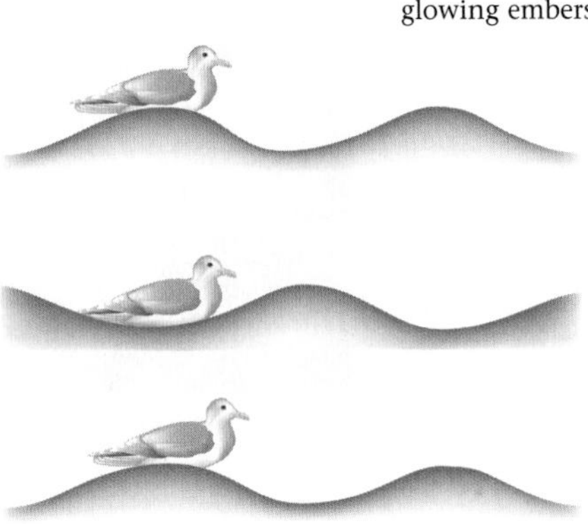

Figure 11.2
A seagull floating on the ocean moves up and down as waves pass.

In all three of these instances, energy is being transmitted from one place to another by light—more properly called **electromagnetic radiation.** Many kinds of electromagnetic radiation exist, including the X rays used to make images of bones, the "white" light from a light bulb, the microwaves used to cook hot dogs and other food, and the radio waves that transmit voices and music. How do these various types of electromagnetic radiation differ from one another? To answer this question we need to talk about waves. To explore the characteristics of waves, let's think about ocean waves. In Figure 11.2 a seagull is shown floating on the ocean and being raised and lowered by the motion of the water surface as waves pass by. Notice that the gull just moves up and down as the waves pass—it is not moved forward. A particular wave is characterized by three properties: *wavelength, frequency,* and *speed.*

The **wavelength** (symbolized by the Greek letter lambda, λ) is the distance between two consecutive wave peaks (see Figure 11.3). The **frequency** of the wave (symbolized by the Greek letter nu, ν) indicates how many wave peaks pass a certain point per given time period. This idea can best be understood by thinking about how many times the seagull in Figure 11.2 goes up and down per minute. The *speed* of a wave indicates how fast a given peak travels through the water.

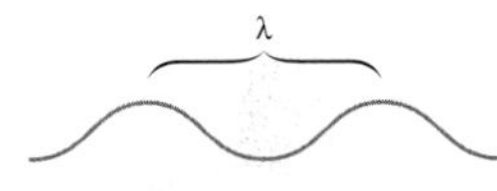

Figure 11.3
The wavelength of a wave is the distance between peaks.

Although it is more difficult to picture than water waves, light (electromagnetic radiation) also travels as waves. The various types of electromagnetic radiation (X rays, microwaves, and so on) differ in their wavelengths. The classes of electromagnetic radiation are shown in Figure 11.4. Notice that X rays have very short wavelengths, whereas radiowaves have very long wavelengths.

CHEMISTRY *IN* FOCUS

Light as a Sex Attractant

Parrots, which are renowned for their vibrant colors, apparently have a secret weapon that enhances their colorful appearance—a phenomenon called fluorescence. Fluorescence occurs when a substance absorbs ultraviolet (UV) light, which is invisible to the human eye, and converts it to visible light. This phenomenon is widely used in interior lighting in which long tubes are coated with a fluorescent substance. The fluorescent coating absorbs UV light (produced in the interior of the tube) and emits intense white light, which consists of all wavelengths of visible light.

Interestingly, scientists have shown that parrots have fluorescent feathers that are used to attract the opposite sex. Note in the accompanying photos that a budgerigar parrot has certai feathers that produce fluorescence. Kathryn E. Arnold of the University of Glasgow in Scotland examined the skins of 700 Australian parrots from museum collections and found that the feathers that showed fluorescence were always display feathers—ones that were fluffed or waggled during courtship. To test her theory that fluorescence is a significant aspect of parrot romance, Arnold studied the behavior of a parrot toward birds of the opposite sex. In some cases, the potential mate had a UV-blocking substance applied to its feathers, blocking its fluorescence. Arnold's study revealed that parrots always preferred partners that showed fluorescence over those in which the fluorescence was blocked. Perhaps on your next date you might consider wearing a shirt with some fluorescent decoration!

The back and front of a budgerigar parrot. In the photo at the right, the same parrot is seen under ultraviolet light.

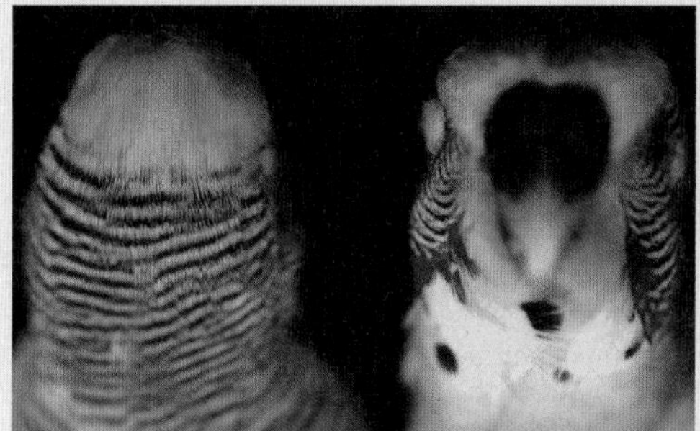

Andrey K. Geim/High Field Magnet Laboratory/University of Nijmegen

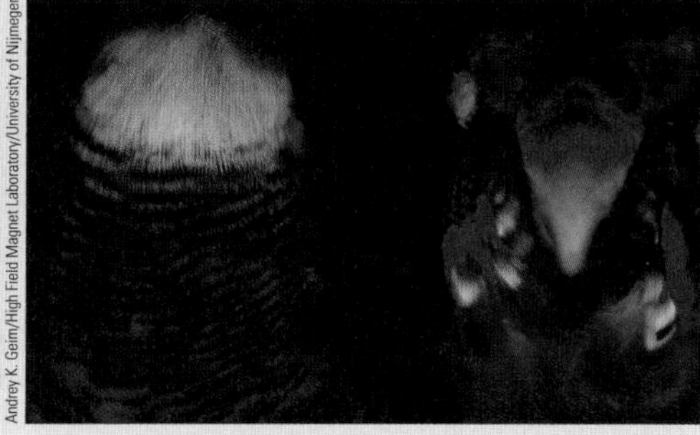

PowerLecture Animation: Refraction of White Light

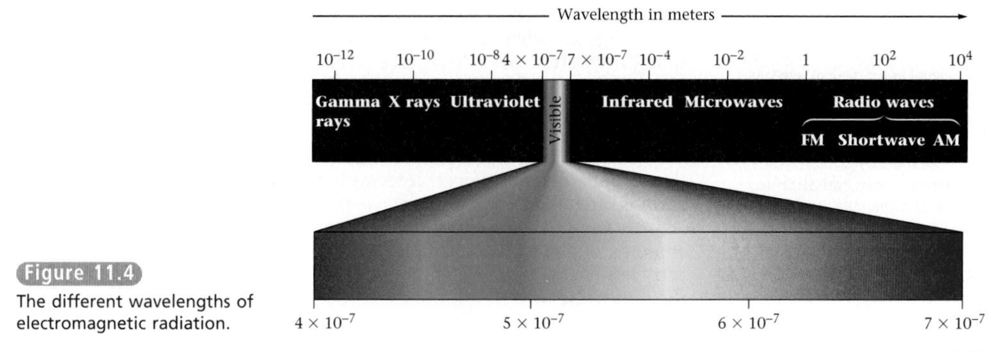

Figure 11.4
The different wavelengths of electromagnetic radiation.

325

CHEMISTRY *IN* FOCUS

Atmospheric Effects

The gaseous atmosphere of the earth is crucial to life in many different ways. One of the most important characteristics of the atmosphere is the way its molecules absorb radiation from the sun.

If it weren't for the protective nature of the atmosphere, the sun would "fry" us with its high-energy radiation. We are protected by the atmospheric ozone, a form of oxygen consisting of O_3 molecules, which absorbs high-energy radiation and thus prevents it from reaching the earth. This explains why we are so concerned that chemicals released into the atmosphere are destroying this high-altitude ozone.

The atmosphere also plays a central role in controlling the earth's temperature, a phenomenon called the *greenhouse effect.* The atmospheric gases CO_2, H_2O, CH_4, N_2O, and others do not absorb light in the visible region. Therefore, the visible light from the sun passes through the atmosphere to warm the earth. In turn, the earth radiates this energy back toward space as infrared radiation. (For example, think of the heat radiated from black asphalt on a hot summer day.) But the gases listed earlier are strong *absorbers* of *infrared* waves, and they reradiate some of this energy back toward the earth as shown in Figure 11.7. Thus these gases act as an insulating blanket keeping the earth much warmer than it would be without them. (If these gases were not present, all of the heat the earth radiates would be lost into space.)

However, there is a problem. When we burn fossil fuels (coal, petroleum, and natural gas), one of the products is CO_2. Because we use such huge quantities of fossil fuels, the CO_2 content in the atmosphere is increasing gradually but significantly. This should cause the earth to get warmer, eventually changing the weather patterns on the earth's surface and melting the polar ice caps, which would flood many low-lying areas.

Because the natural forces that control the earth's temperature are not very well understood at this point, it is difficult to decide whether the greenhouse warming has already started. But many scientists think it has. For example, the 1980s and 1990s were among the warmest years the earth has experienced since people started keeping records. Also, studies at the Scripps Institution of Oceanography indicate that the average temperatures of surface waters in the world's major oceans have risen since the 1960s in close

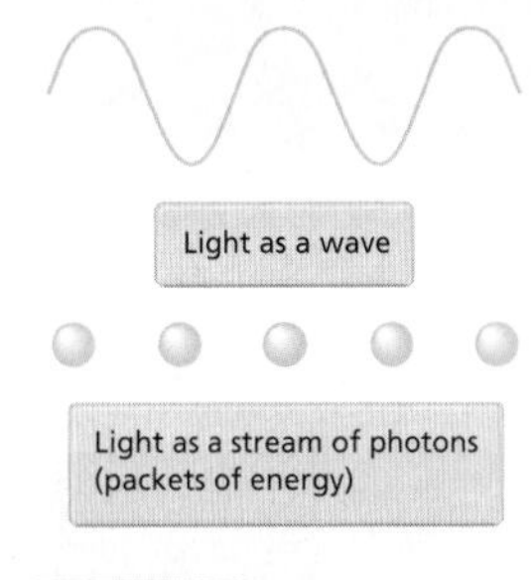

Figure 11.5
Electromagnetic radiation (a beam of light) can be pictured in two ways: as a wave and as a stream of individual packets of energy called photons.

Radiation provides an important means of energy transfer. For example, the energy from the sun reaches the earth mainly in the forms of visible and ultraviolet radiation. The glowing coals of a fireplace transmit heat energy by infrared radiation. In a microwave oven, the water molecules in food absorb microwave radiation, which increases their motions; this energy is then transferred to other types of molecules by collisions, increasing the food's temperature.

Thus we visualize electromagnetic radiation ("light") as a wave that carries energy through space. Sometimes, however, light doesn't behave as though it were a wave. That is, electromagnetic radiation can sometimes have properties that are characteristic of particles. (You will learn more about this idea in later courses.) Another way to think of a beam of light traveling through space, then, is as a stream of tiny packets of energy called **photons.**

What is the exact nature of light? Does it consist of waves or is it a stream of particles of energy? It seems to be both (see Figure 11.5). This situation is often referred to as the wave–particle nature of light.

Different wavelengths of electromagnetic radiation carry different amounts of energy. For example, the photons that correspond to red light carry less energy than the photons that correspond to blue light. In general, the longer the wavelength of light, the lower the energy of its photons (see Figure 11.6).

agreement with the predictions of models based on the increase in CO_2 concentrations. Studies also show that Arctic sea ice, the Greenland Ice Sheet, and various glaciers are melting much faster in recent years. These changes indicate that global warming is occurring.

The greenhouse effect is something we must watch closely. Controlling it may mean lowering our dependence on fossil fuels and increasing our reliance on nuclear, solar, or other power sources. In recent years, the trend has been in the opposite direction.

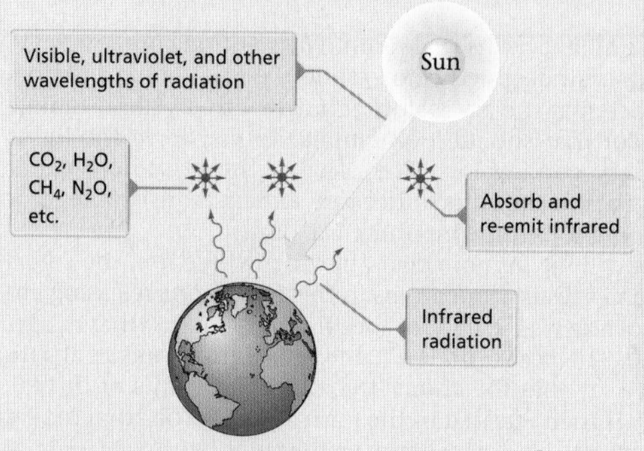

Figure 11.7

Certain gases in the earth's atmosphere absorb and re-emit some of the infrared (heat) radiation produced by the earth. This keeps the earth warmer than it would be otherwise.

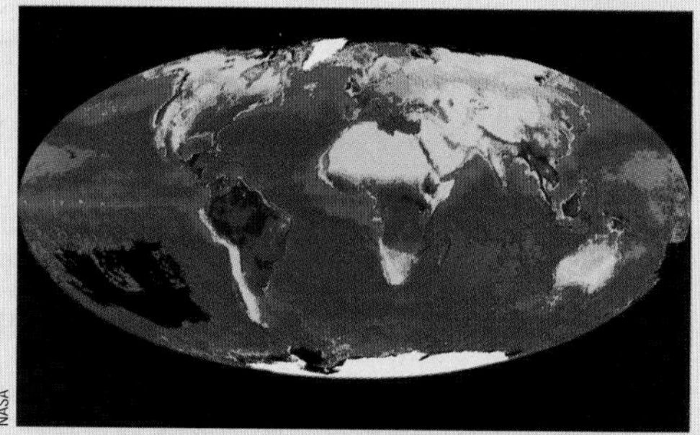

A composite satellite image of the earth's biomass constructed from the radiation given off by living matter over a multiyear period.

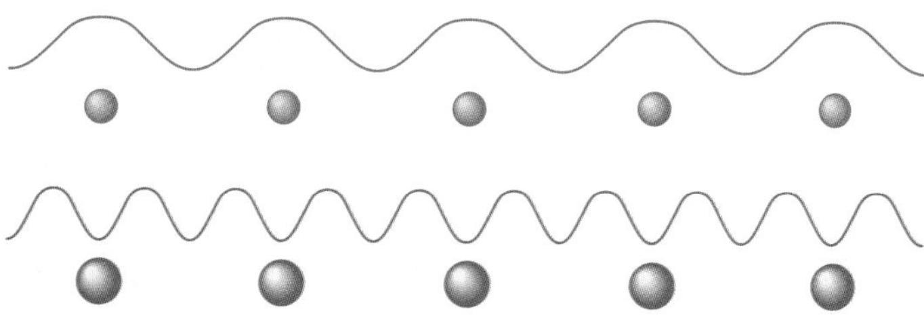

Figure 11.6

A photon of red light (relatively long wavelength) carries less energy than does a photon of blue light (relatively short wavelength).

11.3 Emission of Energy by Atoms

OBJECTIVE: To see how atoms emit light.

Consider the results of the experiment shown on page 328. This experiment is run by dissolving compounds containing the Li^+ ion, the Cu^{2+} ion, and the Na^+ ion in separate dishes containing methyl alcohol (with a little water added to help dissolve the compounds). The solutions are then set on fire.

327

PowerLecture Simulation: The Electromagnetic Spectrum and Planck's Equation

Section 11.3

DEMONSTRATION

Burning Rainbows

Materials Several evaporating dishes, nitrate salts of various metals (Li, Sr, Cu, Ba, K, Na), stirring rods, methanol in a labeled wash bottle, water in a wash bottle, matches

Presentation Place a pea-sized amount of each salt in a separate evaporating dish. Add a small amount of water to just begin dissolution. Add about 10 mL of methanol using the wash bottle. Stir each mixture with a separate stirring rod. Light each dish with a match and dim the lights.

Teaching Notes The amount of methanol added will determine how long each dish burns. Be careful to plan for this outcome. Initially the methanol will burn as blue to colorless. Stirring may be necessary to produce color. **Keep the methanol bottle away** from this demonstration or a flash fire may occur.

Variation Build a trough ½″ × ½″ × 10″ from aluminum foil. Make sure the narrow ends are folded up and are leakproof. Add about 1.0 g of the metal salts in the following order: Sr, Li, Na, Ba, Cu, K. Add a drop of water to each salt pile to aid in dissolution. Add enough methanol to cover the salts. Light the trough with a match.

PowerLecture Animation: Electron Cloud; Neutron; Proton; Nucleus (no sound)

Test Bank: 8–14

Section 11.4

PowerLecture Video: Flame Tests

TEACHING TIPS

- This discussion is very significant. Discuss the ramifications of seeing only certain colors. Also consider discussing white light.
- A commonly used analogy for the energy levels within an atom is a staircase. A person can move from one step to another or even move up two or three steps and down a similar number. It is not possible, however, to move up or down by only part of a step. Within atoms, electron energies are quantized—the energy levels are like stairsteps. Electrons can change only between established energy levels, not in between those levels. Compare this idea to using a ramp, which is like continuous energies.
- Distinguish between an emission spectrum for an atom and light emitted by an atom. To see an emission spectrum, the light must be separated into its component parts. This task is accomplished by using a prism or a diffraction grating.

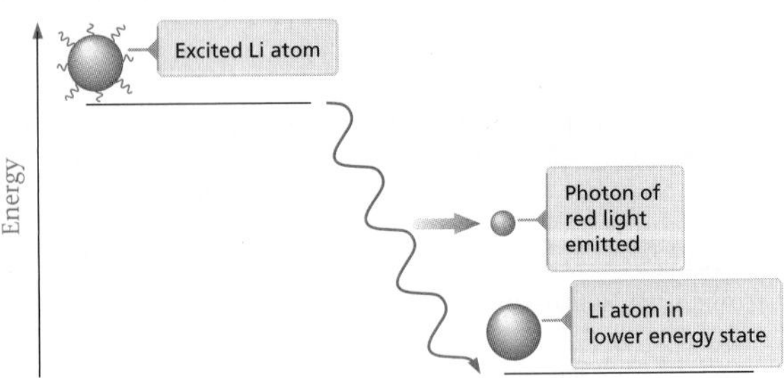

Figure 11.8

An excited lithium atom emitting a photon of red light to drop to a lower energy state.

© Cengage Learning

When salts containing Li^+, Cu^{2+}, and Na^+ dissolved in methyl alcohol are set on fire, brilliant colors result: Li^+, red; Cu^{2+}, green; and Na^+, yellow.

Notice the brilliant colors that result. The solution containing Li^+ gives a beautiful, deep-red color, while the Cu^{2+} solution burns green. Notice that the Na^+ solution burns with a yellow–orange color, a color that should look familiar to you from the lights used in many parking lots. The color of these "sodium vapor lights" arises from the same source (the sodium atom) as the color of the burning solution containing Na^+ ions.

As we will see in more detail in the next section, the colors of these flames result from atoms in these solutions releasing energy by emitting visible light of specific wavelengths (that is, specific colors). The heat from the flame causes the atoms to absorb energy—we say that the atoms become *excited*. Some of this excess energy is then released in the form of light. The atom moves to a lower energy state as it emits a photon of light.

Lithium emits red light because its energy change corresponds to photons of red light (see Figure 11.8). Copper emits green light because it undergoes a different energy change than lithium; the energy change for copper corresponds to the energy of a photon of green light. Likewise, the energy change for sodium corresponds to a photon with a yellow–orange color.

To summarize, we have the following situation. When atoms receive energy from some source—they become excited—they can release this energy by emitting light. The emitted energy is carried away by a photon. Thus the energy of the photon corresponds exactly to the energy change experienced by the emitting atom. High-energy photons correspond to short-wavelength light and low-energy photons correspond to long-wavelength light. The photons of red light therefore carry less energy than the photons of blue light because red light has a longer wavelength than blue light does.

11.4 The Energy Levels of Hydrogen

OBJECTIVE: To understand how the emission spectrum of hydrogen demonstrates the quantized nature of energy.

An atom can lose energy by *emitting* a photon.

As we learned in the last section, an atom with excess energy is said to be in an *excited state*. An excited atom can release some or all of its excess energy by emitting a photon (a "particle" of electromagnetic radiation) and thus move to a lower energy state. The lowest possible energy state of an atom is called its *ground state*.

We can learn a great deal about the energy states of hydrogen atoms by observing the photons they emit. To understand the significance of this, you need to remember that the *different wavelengths of light carry different amounts*

Lecture Demonstration: 7.1, 7.4

DEMONSTRATION

Atomic Spectra

Materials Several gas discharge tubes of various elements and an apparatus to power them, or samples of metal salts and evaporating dishes as used in the Burning Rainbows Demonstration in Section 11.3, diffraction spectroscopes or small pieces of diffraction grating (one per student)

Preparation You can make simple spectroscopes from a piece of diffraction grating and small black film canisters. Use a one-hole punch to punch a hole in the center of the gray top of the film canister. Then use a craft knife to cut a slit in the bottom of the film canister. Cut the diffraction grating into pieces slightly bigger than the hole punched in the top of the film canister. Using a small amount of superglue, affix the diffraction grating to the inside of the top of the film canister, covering the hole. Snap the top back on the bottom and test the spectroscope.

Presentation Distribute a spectroscope or diffractio[n] grating to each student. Have students use the spectro[scopes] to look at an incandescent light and find the rain[bow] to either side of the slit in the tube. (*Note:* Stu[dents] often look through the wrong end of th[e] spectroscope. They should look through the end con

Each photon of blue light carries a larger quantity of energy than a photon of red light.

A particular color (wavelength) of light carries a particular amount of energy per photon.

of energy per photon. Recall that a beam of red light has lower-energy photons than a beam of blue light.

When a hydrogen atom absorbs energy from some outside source, it uses this energy to enter an excited state. It can release this excess energy (go back to a lower state) by emitting a photon of light (Figure 11.9). We can picture this process in terms of the energy-level diagram shown in Figure 11.10. The important point here is that *the energy contained in the photon corresponds to the change in energy that the atom experiences* in going from the excited state to the lower state.

Consider the following experiment. Suppose we take a sample of H atoms and put a lot of energy into the system (as represented in Figure 11.9). When we study the photons of visible light emitted, we see only certain colors (Figure 11.11). That is, *only certain types of photons* are produced. We don't see all colors, which would add up to give "white light"; we see only selected colors. This is a very significant result. Let's discuss carefully what it means.

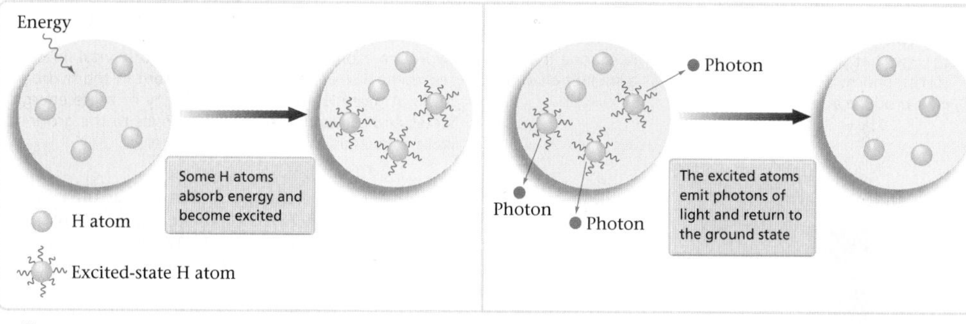

A sample of H atoms receives energy from an external source, which causes some of the atoms to become excited (to possess excess energy).

The excited H atoms can release the excess energy by emitting photons. The energy of each emitted photon corresponds exactly to the energy lost by each excited atom.

Figure 11.9

Figure 11.10 When an excited H atom returns to a lower energy level, it emits a photon that contains the energy released by the atom. Thus the energy of the photon corresponds to the difference in energy between the two states.

410 nm 434 nm 486 nm 656 nm

Figure 11.11 When excited hydrogen atoms return to lower energy states, they emit photons of certain energies, and thus certain colors. Shown here are the colors and wavelengths (in nanometers) of the photons in the visible region that are emitted by excited hydrogen atoms.

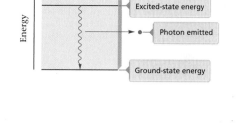

TEACHING TIPS

- Discuss how hydrogen can have multiple lines even though it has only one electron. Students often forget that they are observing many thousands of atoms simultaneously when observing a line emission spectrum.
- Point out that the quantized nature of atoms is a surprise and nonintuitive. It is comforting to students to realize that this topic is complicated even to people who have been studying it for a while.
- Now is an excellent time to discuss the colors of streetlights. Mercury vapor lights have a blue cast, whereas sodium lights are yellow and neon lights are more orange. You may also want to discuss the difference between an incandescent light and a vapor light. Many students think that all lights are the same. They do not realize that an incandescent lamp produces a continuous spectrum since the tiny filament is radiating all wavelengths of visible light, while vapor lamps (like many streetlights) are more like gas discharge tubes in their operation.

PowerLecture Simulation: Atomic Absorption and Emission

PowerLecture Animations: Electron Cloud; Neutron; Proton; Nucleus (no sound)
The Line Spectrum of Hydrogen

taining the diffraction grating, not the slit end.) You can also have students observe fluorescent lights with the spectroscopes. Once the students are proficient at using the spectroscopes, set up the gas discharge tube. Darken the room and have students observe the spectrum from the tube. They should see a line emission spectrum. Then change the gas discharge tube to a different element and repeat the process. (*Note:* The gas discharge apparatus uses high voltage; be sure to unplug it before changing the tube.) Have students compare the emission spectra from different elements.

Variation If you do not have access to a gas discharge apparatus and tubes, you can use the solutions from the Burning Rainbows Demonstration to do the same thing. Use only one evaporating dish at a time and use a little extra salt to obtain good color.

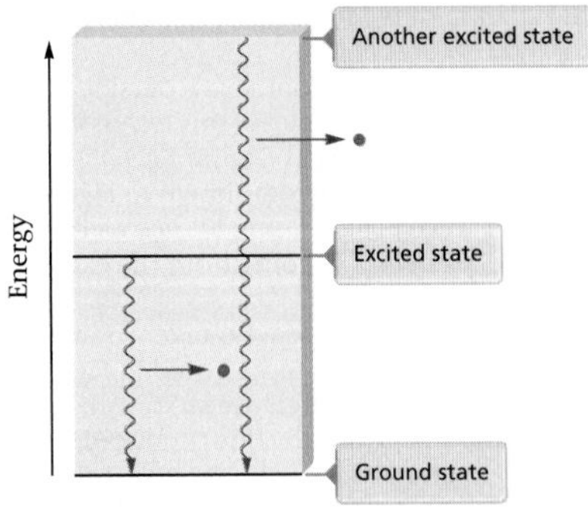

Figure 11.12
Hydrogen atoms have several excited-state energy levels. The color of the photon emitted depends on the energy change that produces it. A larger energy change may correspond to a blue photon, whereas a smaller change may produce a red photon.

Figure 11.13
Each photon emitted by an excited hydrogen atom corresponds to a particular energy change in the hydrogen atom. In this diagram the horizontal lines represent discrete energy levels present in the hydrogen atom. A given H atom can exist in any of these energy states and can undergo energy changes to the ground state as well as to other excited states.

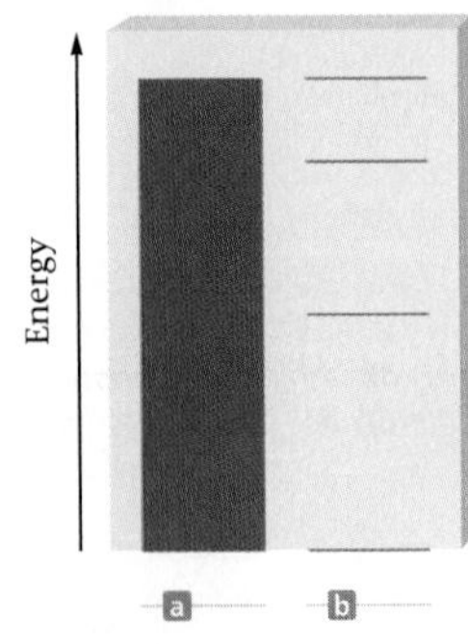

Figure 11.14
a Continuous energy levels. Any energy value is allowed.
b Discrete (quantized) energy levels. Only certain energy states are allowed.

Because only certain photons are emitted, we know that only certain energy changes are occurring (Figure 11.12). This means that the hydrogen atom must have *certain discrete energy levels* (Figure 11.13). Excited hydrogen atoms *always* emit photons with the same discrete colors (wavelengths)—those shown in Figure 11.11. They *never* emit photons with energies (colors) in between those shown. So we can conclude that all hydrogen atoms have the same set of discrete energy levels. We say the energy levels of hydrogen are **quantized.** That is, only *certain values are allowed.* Scientists have found that the energy levels of *all* atoms are quantized.

The quantized nature of the energy levels in atoms was a surprise when scientists discovered it. It had been assumed previously that an atom could exist at any energy level. That is, everyone had assumed that atoms could have a continuous set of energy levels rather than only certain discrete values (Figure 11.14). A useful analogy here is the contrast between the elevations allowed by a ramp, which vary continuously, and those allowed by a set of steps, which are discrete (Figure 11.15). The discovery of the quantized nature of energy has radically changed our view of the atom, as we will see in the next few sections.

a *A ramp varies continously in elevation.*

b *A flight of stairs allows only certain elevations; the elevations are quantized.*

Figure 11.15
The difference between continuous and quantized energy levels can be illustrated by comparing a flight of stairs with a ramp.

11.5 The Bohr Model of the Atom

OBJECTIVE: To learn about Bohr's model of the hydrogen atom.

In 1911 at the age of twenty-five, Niels Bohr (Figure 11.16) received his Ph.D. in physics. He was convinced that the atom could be pictured as a small positive nucleus with electrons orbiting around it.

Over the next two years, Bohr constructed a model of the hydrogen atom with quantized energy levels that agreed with the hydrogen emission results we have just discussed. Bohr pictured the electron moving in circular orbits corresponding to the various allowed energy levels. He suggested that the electron could jump to a different orbit by absorbing or emitting a photon of light with exactly the correct energy content. Thus, in the Bohr atom, the energy levels in the hydrogen atom represented certain allowed circular orbits (Figure 11.17).

At first Bohr's model appeared very promising. It fit the hydrogen atom very well. However, when this model was applied to atoms other than hydrogen, it did not work. In fact, further experiments showed that the Bohr model is fundamentally incorrect. Although the Bohr model paved the way for later theories, it is important to realize that the current theory of atomic structure is not the same as the Bohr model. Electrons do *not* move around the nucleus in circular orbits like planets orbiting the sun. Surprisingly, as we shall see later in this chapter, we do not know exactly how the electrons move in an atom.

Figure 11.16
Niels Hendrik David Bohr (1885–1962) as a boy lived in the shadow of his younger brother Harald, who played on the 1908 Danish Olympic Soccer Team and later became a distinguished mathematician. In school, Bohr received his poorest marks in composition and struggled with writing during his entire life. In fact, he wrote so poorly that he was forced to dictate his Ph.D. thesis to his mother. He is one of the very few people who felt the need to write rough drafts of postcards. Nevertheless, Bohr was a brilliant physicist. After receiving his Ph.D. in Denmark, he constructed a quantum model for the hydrogen atom by the time he was 27. Even though his model later proved to be incorrect, Bohr remained a central figure in the drive to understand the atom. He was awarded the Nobel Prize in physics in 1922.

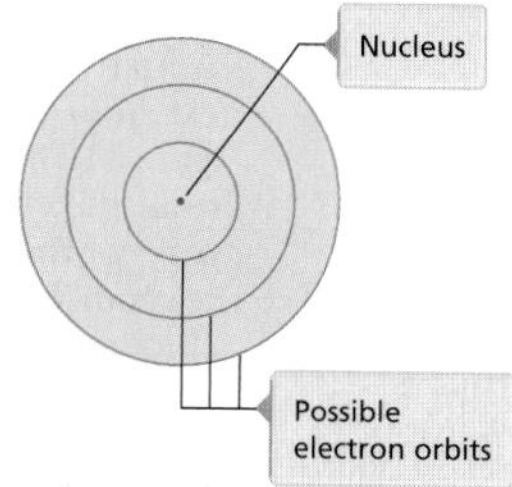

Figure 11.17
The Bohr model of the hydrogen atom represented the electron as restricted to certain circular orbits around the nucleus.

11.6 The Wave Mechanical Model of the Atom

OBJECTIVE: To understand how the electron's position is represented in the wave mechanical model.

By the mid-1920s it had become apparent that the Bohr model was incorrect. Scientists needed to pursue a totally new approach. Two young physicists, Louis Victor de Broglie from France and Erwin Schrödinger from Austria, suggested that because light seems to have both wave and particle characteristics (it behaves simultaneously as a wave and as a stream of particles), the electron might also exhibit both of these characteristics. Although everyone

Test Bank: 15

Section 11.5

TEACHING TIPS

- Emphasize that although the Bohr model of the atoms is important historically, it does not represent an accurate model for the atom.
- Point out that Bohr's model is no longer accepted because it is considered fundamentally incorrect (which explains why the section is so short). A discussion of this model is useful in discussing the nature of science. The Bohr model is a relatively simple model whose sole intent was to explain the results of the hydrogen emission spectrum. It succeeded in doing so, which is why it was considered powerful. However, this model does not fit polyelectronic atoms and electrons do not move in fixed orbits.

PowerLecture Animations: Electron Cloud; Neutron; Proton; Nucleus (no sound)
Electromagnetic Waves from Lightbulb (no sound)
Electronic Transitions in Hydrogen Atoms
Models of the Atom; Current, Ancient, and Bohr (no sound)

Test Bank: 16

Section 11.6

TEACHING TIPS

- This section introduces the idea of probability as a model for understanding nature. This concept will be new to all students and most will find it confusing. It is a fundamental change from determinism in looking at the world and it is under-

TEACHING TIPS

standable that students will have difficulty with it. For example, students tend to think of orbitals as physical structures and will find it difficult to think of them as probability distributions. Section 11.7 describes the orbital as a *potential space* for an electron. This concept is a good way for the students to think about it initially.

- The firefly example offers a way for students to understand the difference between an orbit and an orbital. Many students confuse orbitals and orbits. An *orbit* describes a particular path that an object follows as it travels around another. For example, the moon has an orbit about the earth. Electrons do not follow a particular path around the nucleus. An *orbital* describes the volume around the nucleus where an electron is likely to be found. The exact path of an electron in this area is not known, in the same way that the exact path of the firefly is not known.

PowerLecture Animation: Electrons Orbiting Nucleus vs. Electron Cloud

The Granger Collection/New York

Louis Victor de Broglie

had assumed that the electron was a tiny particle, these scientists said it might be useful to find out whether it could be described as a wave.

When Schrödinger carried out a mathematical analysis based on this idea, he found that it led to a new model for the hydrogen atom that seemed to apply equally well to other atoms—something Bohr's model failed to do. We will now explore a general picture of this model, which is called the **wave mechanical model** of the atom.

In the Bohr model, the electron was assumed to move in circular orbits. In the wave mechanical model, on the other hand, the electron states are described by orbitals. *Orbitals are nothing like orbits.* To approximate the idea of an orbital, picture a single male firefly in a room in the center of which an open vial of female sex-attractant hormones is suspended. The room is extremely dark and there is a camera in one corner with its shutter open. Every time the firefly "flashes," the camera records a pinpoint of light and thus the firefly's position in the room at that moment. The firefly senses the sex attractant, and as you can imagine, it spends a lot of time at or close to it. However, now and then the insect flies randomly around the room.

When the film is taken out of the camera and developed, the picture will probably look like Figure 11.18. Because a picture is brightest where the film has been exposed to the most light, the color intensity at any given point tells us how often the firefly visited a given point in the room. Notice that, as we might expect, the firefly spent the most time near the room's center.

Figure 11.18
A representation of the photo of the firefly experiment. Remember that a picture is brightest where the film has been exposed to the most light. Thus the intensity of the color reflects how often the firefly visited a given point in the room. Notice that the brightest area is in the center of the room near the source of the sex attractant.

Now suppose you are watching the firefly in the dark room. You see it flash at a given point far from the center of the room. Where do you expect to see it next? There is really no way to be sure. The firefly's flight path is not precisely predictable. However, if you had seen the time-exposure picture of the firefly's activities (Figure 11.18), you would have some idea where to look next. Your best chance would be to look more toward the center of the room. Figure 11.18 suggests there is the highest probability (the highest odds, the greatest likelihood) of finding the firefly at any particular moment near the center of the room. You *can't be sure* the firefly will fly toward the center of the room, but it *probably* will. So the time-exposure picture is a kind of "probability map" of the firefly's flight pattern.

According to the wave mechanical model, the electron in the hydrogen atom can be pictured as being something like this firefly. Schrödinger found that he could not precisely describe the electron's path. His mathematics enabled him only to predict the probabilities of finding the electron at given points in space around the nucleus. In its ground state the hydrogen electron has a probability map like that shown in Figure 11.19. The more intense the color at a particular point, the more probable that the electron will be found at that point at a given instant. The model gives *no information about when* the electron occupies a certain point in space or *how it moves.* In fact, we have good reasons to believe that we can *never know* the details of electron motion, no matter how sophisticated our models may become. But one thing we feel confident about is that the electron *does not* orbit the nucleus in circles as Bohr suggested.

Figure 11.19
The probability map, or orbital, that describes the hydrogen electron in its lowest possible energy state. The more intense the color of a given dot, the more likely it is that the electron will be found at that point. We have no information about when the electron will be at a particular point or about how it moves. Note that the probability of the electron's presence is highest closest to the positive nucleus (located at the center of this diagram), as might be expected.

Test Bank: 17–19, 64–66

11.7 The Hydrogen Orbitals

OBJECTIVE: To learn about the shapes of orbitals designated by *s*, *p*, and *d*.

Figure 11.20
a The hydrogen 1*s* orbital.
b The size of the orbital is defined by a sphere that contains 90% of the total electron probability. That is, the electron can be found *inside* this sphere 90% of the time. The 1*s* orbital is often represented simply as a sphere. However, the most accurate picture of the orbital is the probability map represented in a.

The probability map for the hydrogen electron shown in Figure 11.19 is called an **orbital.** Although the probability of finding the electron decreases at greater distances from the nucleus, the probability of finding it even at great distances from the nucleus never becomes exactly zero. A useful analogy might be the lack of a sharp boundary between the earth's atmosphere and "outer space." The atmosphere fades away gradually, but there are always a few molecules present. Because the edge of an orbital is "fuzzy," an orbital does not have an exactly defined size. So chemists arbitrarily define its size as the sphere that contains 90% of the total electron probability (Figure 11.20b). This means that the electron spends 90% of the time inside this surface and 10% somewhere outside this surface. (Note that we are *not* saying the electron travels only on the *surface* of the sphere.) The orbital represented in Figure 11.20 is named the **1*s* orbital,** and it describes the hydrogen electron's lowest energy state (the ground state).

In Section 11.4 we saw that the hydrogen atom can absorb energy to transfer the electron to a higher energy state (an excited state). In terms of the obsolete Bohr model, this meant the electron was transferred to an orbit with a larger radius. In the wave mechanical model, these higher energy states correspond to different kinds of orbitals with different shapes.

At this point we need to stop and consider how the hydrogen atom is organized. Remember, we showed earlier that the hydrogen atom has discrete energy levels. We call these levels **principal energy levels** and label them with integers (Figure 11.21). Next we find that each of these levels is subdivided into **sublevels.** The following analogy should help you understand this. Picture an inverted triangle (Figure 11.22). We divide the principal levels into various numbers of sublevels. Principal level 1 consists of one sublevel, principal level 2 has two sublevels, principal level 3 has three sublevels, and principal level 4 has four sublevels.

Like our triangle, the principal energy levels in the hydrogen atom contain sublevels. As we will see presently, these sublevels contain spaces for the electron that we call orbitals. Principal energy level 1 consists of just one sublevel, or one type of orbital. The spherical shape of this orbital is shown in Figure 11.20. We label this orbital 1*s*. The number 1 is for the principal energy level, and *s* is a shorthand way to label a particular sublevel (type of orbital).

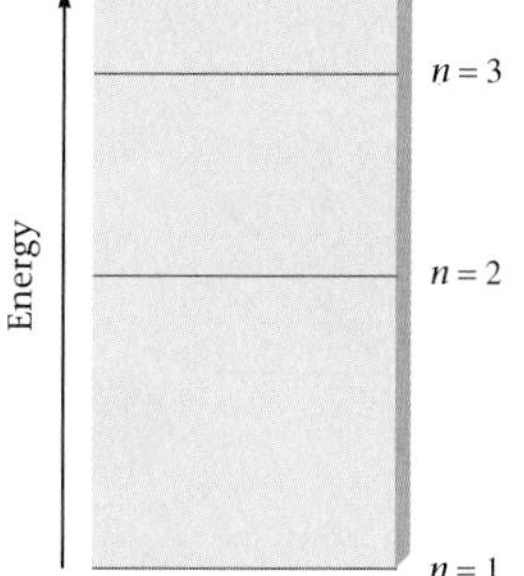

Figure 11.21
The first four principal energy levels in the hydrogen atom. Each level is assigned an integer, *n*.

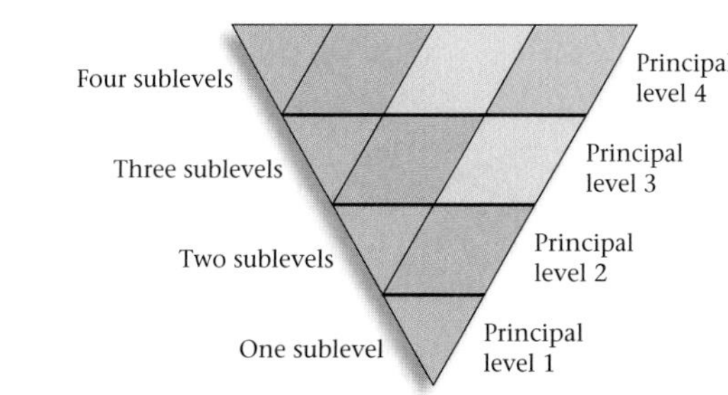

Figure 11.22
An illustration of how principal levels can be divided into sublevels.

Section 11.7

TEACHING TIPS

- The shapes of orbitals are mathematically determined, a point that is outside the scope of an introductory chemistry course. Students should understand that the shapes of these orbitals are not intuitive.
- Solid models can be used to demonstrate the shapes of the *s*, *p*, and *d* orbitals. Remind students that the electron probability is high within the shape but there is no set path for the electron.

Lecture Demonstration: 7.7

PowerLecture Animations: Atom Showng Electron Cloud (no sound)
1*s* Orbital

PowerLecture Animations:
3*s* Orbital Shape (no sound)
$3d_{z^2}$ Orbital Shape (no sound)
$3d_{yz}$ Orbital Shape (no sound)
$3d_{xy}$ Orbital Shape (no sound)
$3d_{x^2-y^2}$ Orbital Shape (no sound)

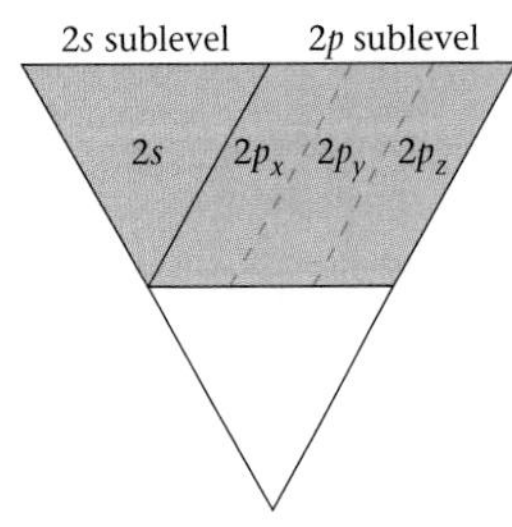

Figure 11.23
Principal level 2 shown divided into the 2*s* and 2*p* sublevels.

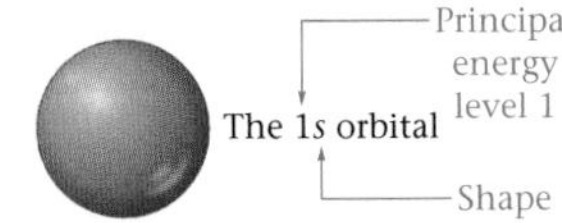

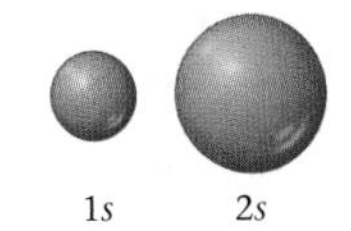

Figure 11.24
The relative sizes of the 1*s* and 2*s* orbitals of hydrogen.

Principal energy level 2 has two sublevels. (Note the correspondence between the principal energy level number and the number of sublevels.) These sublevels are labeled 2*s* and 2*p*. The 2*s* sublevel consists of one orbital (called the 2*s*), and the 2*p* sublevel consists of three orbitals (called $2p_x$, $2p_y$, and $2p_z$). Let's return to the inverted triangle to illustrate this. Figure 11.23 shows principal level 2 divided into the sublevels 2*s* and 2*p* (which is subdivided into $2p_x$, $2p_y$, and $2p_z$). The orbitals have the shapes shown in Figures 11.24 and 11.25. The 2*s* orbital is spherical like the 1*s* orbital but larger in size (see Figure 11.24). The three 2*p* orbitals are not spherical but have two "lobes." These orbitals are shown in Figure 11.25 both as electron probability maps and as surfaces that contain 90% of the total electron probability. Notice that the label *x*, *y*, or *z* on a given 2*p* orbital tells along which axis the lobes of that orbital are directed.

What we have learned so far about the hydrogen atom is summarized in Figure 11.26. Principal energy level 1 has one sublevel, which contains the 1*s* orbital. Principal energy level 2 contains two sublevels, one of which contains the 2*s* orbital and one of which contains the 2*p* orbitals (three of them). Note that each orbital is designated by a symbol or label. We summarize the information given by this label in the following box.

TEACHING TIP

Students can become confused about the meanings of the following terms: *principal energy level*, *sublevel*, and *orbital*. Point out that the principal energy level gives the region of energy for the electrons. It also turns out that a given principal quantum number indicates the number of sublevels available on that energy level. The sublevels are lettered *s*, *p*, *d*, and *f* based on the shapes of the orbitals within them. An orbital represents a specific region of probability that can contain at most two electrons.

Orbital Labels

1. The number tells the principal energy level.
2. The letter tells the shape. The letter *s* means a spherical orbital; the letter *p* means a two-lobed orbital. The *x*, *y*, or *z* subscript on a *p* orbital label tells along which of the coordinate axes the two lobes lie.

One important characteristic of orbitals is that as the level number increases, the average distance of the electron in that orbital from the nucleus also increases. That is, when the hydrogen electron is in the 1*s* orbital (the ground state), it spends most of its time much closer to the nucleus than when it occupies the 2*s* orbital (an excited state).

PowerLecture Animation: Electrons Orbiting Nucleus vs. Electron Cloud

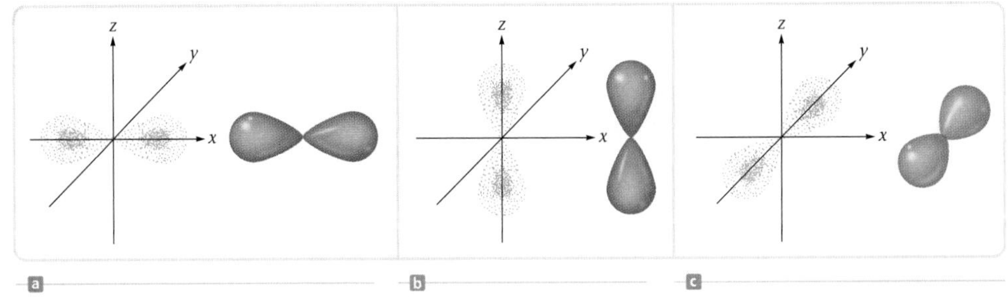

Figure 11.25
The three 2*p* orbitals: a $2p_x$, b $2p_z$, c $2p_y$. The *x*, *y*, or *z* label indicates along which axis the two lobes are directed. Each orbital is shown both as a probability map and as a surface that encloses 90% of the electron probability.

PowerLecture Animations:
1*s* Orbital Shape (no sound)
2*s* Orbital Shape (no sound)
$2p_x$ Orbital Shape (no sound)
$2p_y$ Orbital Shape (no sound)
$2p_z$ Orbital Shape (no sound)

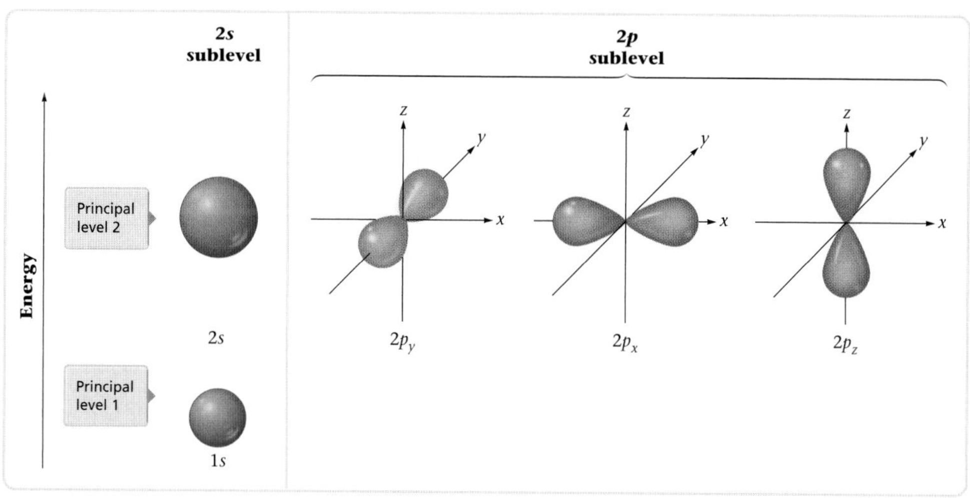

Figure 11.26
A diagram of principal energy levels 1 and 2 showing the shapes of orbitals that compose the sublevels.

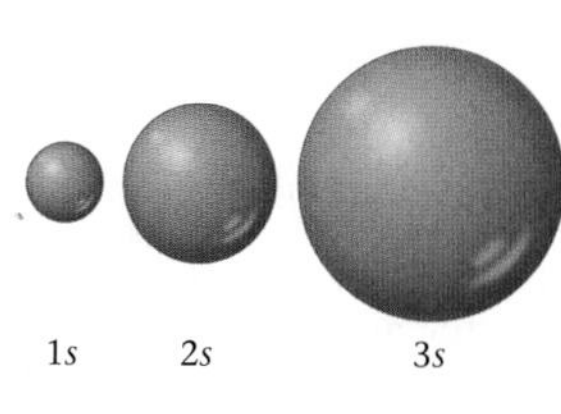

Figure 11.27
The relative sizes of the spherical 1s, 2s, and 3s orbitals of hydrogen.

You may be wondering at this point why hydrogen, which has only one electron, has more than one orbital. It is best to think of an orbital as a *potential space* for an electron. The hydrogen electron can occupy only a single orbital at a time, but the other orbitals are still available should the electron be transferred into one of them. For example, when a hydrogen atom is in its ground state (lowest possible energy state), the electron is in the 1*s* orbital. By adding the correct amount of energy (for example, a specific photon of light), we can excite the electron to the 2*s* orbital or to one of the 2*p* orbitals.

So far we have discussed only two of hydrogen's energy levels. There are many others. For example, level 3 has three sublevels (see Figure 11.22), which we label 3*s*, 3*p*, and 3*d*. The 3*s* sublevel contains a single 3*s* orbital, a spherical orbital larger than 1*s* and 2*s* (Figure 11.27). Sublevel 3*p* contains three orbitals: $3p_x$, $3p_y$, and $3p_z$, which are shaped like the 2*p* orbitals except that they are larger. The 3*d* sublevel contains five 3*d* orbitals with the shapes and labels shown in Figure 11.28. (You do not need to memorize the 3*d* orbital shapes and labels. They are shown for completeness.)

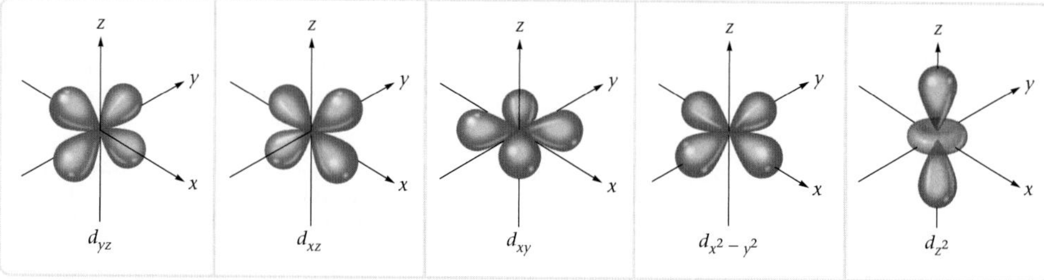

Figure 11.28
The shapes and labels of the five 3*d* orbitals.

PowerLecture Animation: Orbital Image Collage (no sound)

TEACHING SUPPORT

BACKGROUND INFORMATION

Polyelectronic Atoms

The quantum mechanical model gives a description of the hydrogen atom that agrees very well with experimental data. However, the model would not be very useful if it did not account for the properties of the other atoms as well.

To see how the model applies to polyelectronic atoms—that is, atoms with more than one electron—let's consider helium, which has two protons in its nucleus and two electrons. Three energy contributions must be considered in the description of the helium atom: (1) the kinetic energy of the electrons as they move around the nucleus, (2) the potential energy of attraction between the nucleus and the electrons, and (3) the potential energy of repulsion between the two electrons.

PowerLecture Animations:
$3d_{x^2-y^2}$ Orbital
$3d_{xy}$ Orbital
$3d_{xz}$ Orbital
$3d_{yz}$ Orbital
$3d_{z^2}$ Orbital

Notice as you compare levels 1, 2, and 3 that a new type of orbital (sublevel) is added in each principal energy level. (Recall that the *p* orbitals are added in level 2 and the *d* orbitals in level 3.) This makes sense because in going farther out from the nucleus, there is more space available and thus room for more orbitals.

It might help you to understand that the number of orbitals increases with the principal energy level if you think of a theater in the round. Picture a round stage with circular rows of seats surrounding it. The farther from the stage a row of seats is, the more seats it contains because the circle is larger. Orbitals divide up the space around a nucleus somewhat like the seats in this circular theater. The greater the distance from the nucleus, the more space there is and the more orbitals we find.

The pattern of increasing numbers of orbitals continues with level 4. Level 4 has four sublevels labeled 4*s*, 4*p*, 4*d*, and 4*f*. The 4*s* sublevel has a single 4*s* orbital. The 4*p* sublevel contains three orbitals ($4p_x$, $4p_y$, and $4p_z$). The 4*d* sublevel has five 4*d* orbitals. The 4*f* sublevel has seven 4*f* orbitals.

The 4*s*, 4*p*, and 4*d* orbitals have the same shapes as the earlier *s*, *p*, and *d* orbitals, respectively, but are larger. We will not be concerned here with the shapes of the *f* orbitals.

Test Bank: 20–31

Section 11.8

TEACHING TIP

The idea of electron spin is abstract and difficult for many students. Focus your discussion on the important point that for two electrons to occupy the same orbital, their spins must be opposite. An analogy to a magnet is often useful.

11.8 The Wave Mechanical Model: Further Development

OBJECTIVES: To review the energy levels and orbitals of the wave mechanical model of the atom. • To learn about electron spin.

A model for the atom is of little use if it does not apply to all atoms. The Bohr model was discarded because it could be applied only to hydrogen. The wave mechanical model can be applied to all atoms in basically the same form as the one we have just used for hydrogen. In fact, the major triumph of this model is its ability to explain the periodic table of the elements. Recall that the elements on the periodic table are arranged in vertical groups, which contain elements that typically show similar chemical properties. The wave mechanical model of the atom allows us to explain, based on electron arrangements, why these similarities occur. We will see in due time how this is done.

Remember that an atom has as many electrons as it has protons to give it a zero overall charge. Therefore, all atoms beyond hydrogen have more than one electron. Before we can consider the atoms beyond hydrogen, we must describe one more property of electrons that determines how they can be arranged in an atom's orbitals. This property is spin. Each electron appears to be spinning as a top spins on its axis. Like the top, an electron can spin only in one of two directions. We often represent spin with an arrow: either ↑ or ↓. One arrow represents the electron spinning in the one direction, and the other represents the electron spinning in the opposite direction. For our purposes, what is most important about electron spin is that two electrons must have *opposite* spins to occupy the same orbital. That is, two electrons that have the same spin cannot occupy the same orbital. This leads to the **Pauli exclusion principle:** an atomic orbital can hold a maximum of two electrons, and those two electrons must have opposite spins.

Before we apply the wave mechanical model to atoms beyond hydrogen, we will summarize the model for convenient reference.

DEMONSTRATION

Use two bar magnets or cow magnets (available from Educational Innovations or local farm supply resources) to illustrate electron spin. Suspend both magnets on separate pieces of fishing line wrapped around their middles. Bring the magnets together and illustrate how they twist apart when the same poles are close to each other. Explain that in a similar manner electrons with the same spin repel each other, so electrons in the same orbital have opposite spins.

Although the helium atom can be readily described in terms of the quantum mechanical model, the Schrödinger equation that results cannot be solved exactly. The difficulty arises in dealing with the repulsions between the electrons. Since the electron pathways are unknown, the electron repulsions cannot be calculated exactly. This issue is called the *electron correlation problem*.

The electron correlation problem occurs with all polyelectronic atoms. To treat these systems using the quantum mechanical model, we must make approximations. Most commonly, the approximation used is to treat each electron as if it were moving in a *field of charge that is the net result of the nuclear attraction and the average repulsions of all the other electrons.*

Now let's single out the outermost electron of the sodium atom and consider the forces that this electron feels. The electron is clearly attracted to the highly charged nucleus. However, it also feels the repulsions caused by the other

Principal Components of the Wave Mechanical Model of the Atom

1. Atoms have a series of energy levels called **principal energy levels,** which are designated by whole numbers symbolized by *n; n* can equal 1, 2, 3, 4, . . . Level 1 corresponds to $n = 1$, level 2 corresponds to $n = 2$, and so on.
2. The energy of the level increases as the value of *n* increases.
3. Each principal energy level contains one or more *types* of orbitals, called **sublevels.**
4. The number of sublevels present in a given principal energy level equals *n*. For example, level 1 contains one sublevel (1*s*); level 2 contains two sublevels (two types of orbitals), the 2*s* orbital and the three 2*p* orbitals; and so on. These are summarized in the following table. The number of each type of orbital is shown in parentheses.

n	Sublevels (Types of Orbitals) Present
1	1*s*(1)
2	2*s*(1) 2*p*(3)
3	3*s*(1) 3*p*(3) 3*d*(5)
4	4*s*(1) 4*p*(3) 4*d*(5) 4*f*(7)

5. The *n* value is always used to label the orbitals of a given principal level and is followed by a letter that indicates the type (shape) of the orbital. For example, the designation 3*p* means an orbital in level 3 that has two lobes (a *p* orbital always has two lobes).
6. An orbital can be empty or it can contain one or two electrons, but never more than two. If two electrons occupy the same orbital, they must have opposite spins.
7. The shape of an orbital does not indicate the details of electron movement. It indicates the probability distribution for an electron residing in that orbital.

EXAMPLE 11.1 Understanding the Wave Mechanical Model of the Atom

Indicate whether each of the following statements about atomic structure is true or false.

a. An *s* orbital is always spherical in shape.

b. The 2*s* orbital is the same size as the 3*s* orbital.

c. The number of lobes on a *p* orbital increases as *n* increases. That is, a 3*p* orbital has more lobes than a 2*p* orbital.

d. Level 1 has one *s* orbital, level 2 has two *s* orbitals, level 3 has three *s* orbitals, and so on.

e. The electron path is indicated by the surface of the orbital.

SOLUTION

a. True. The size of the sphere increases as *n* increases, but the shape is always spherical.

PowerLecture Animation: Electron Spin (no sound)

TEACHING TIP

The summary box highlights aspects of the wave mechanical model of the atom. These points are not intuitive to students nor can they be predicted. They are the "what" but not the "why" of the model. Students should appreciate the difference.

Additional Examples

Example 11.1

Indicate whether each of the following statements about atomic structure is true or false.

1. The shape of a given type of orbital changes as *n* increases.

   False. The shape of a given orbital stays the same while the size increases.

2. The number of types of orbitals in a given energy level is the same as the value of *n*.

   True. For example, in $n = 2$ there are two types of orbitals (*s* and *p*).

3. The hydrogen atom has a 3*s* orbital.

   True. There are no electrons in the 3*s* orbital for a hydrogen atom in its lowest energy state, but the orbital is a potential space, not a physical structure.

10 electrons. The net effect is that the electron is not bound nearly as tightly to the nucleus as it would be if the other electrons were not present. We say that the electron is *screened* or *shielded* from the nuclear charge by the repulsions of the other electrons.

This picture of polyelectronic atoms leads to *hydrogenlike orbitals* for these atoms. They have the same general shapes as the orbitals for hydrogen, but their sizes and energies are different. The differences occur because of the interplay between nuclear attraction and electron repulsions.

One especially important difference between polyelectronic atoms and the hydrogen atom is that for hydrogen all the orbitals in a given principal quantum level have the same energy (they are said to be *degenerate*). This is not the case for polyelectronic atoms, where for a given principal level the orbitals vary in energy as follows:

$$E_{ns} < E_{np} < E_{nd} < E_{nf}$$

PowerLecture Animation: Orbital Energies

b. False. The 3*s* orbital is larger (the electron is farther from the nucleus on average) than the 2*s* orbital.

c. False. A *p* orbital always has two lobes.

d. False. Each principal energy level has only one *s* orbital.

e. False. The electron is *somewhere inside* the orbital surface 90% of the time. The electron does not move around *on* this surface.

Self-Check EXERCISE 11.1 Define the following terms.

a. Bohr orbits

b. orbitals

c. orbital size

d. sublevel

See Problems 11.37 through 11.44. ■

Self Check

Answers to Self-Check Exercise 11.1

a. Circular pathways for electrons in the Bohr model

b. Three-dimensional probability maps that represent the likelihood that the electron will occupy a given point in space

c. The surface that contains 90% of the total electron probability

d. A set of orbitals of a given type of orbital within a principal energy level; for example, there are three sublevels in principal energy level 3 (*s*, *p*, *d*)

Test Bank: 32–37

Section 11.9

PowerLecture Animation: Electron Configurations and Periodic Blocks (no sound)

PowerLecture Simulation: Atomic Orbital Energies

11.9 Electron Arrangements in the First Eighteen Atoms on the Periodic Table

OBJECTIVES: To understand how the principal energy levels fill with electrons in atoms beyond hydrogen. • To learn about valence electrons and core electrons.

We will now describe the electron arrangements in atoms with $Z = 1$ to $Z = 18$ by placing electrons in the various orbitals in the principal energy levels, starting with $n = 1$, and then continuing with $n = 2$, $n = 3$, and so on. For the first eighteen elements, the individual sublevels fill in the following order: 1*s*, then 2*s*, then 2*p*, then 3*s*, then 3*p*.

The most attractive orbital to an electron in an atom is always the 1*s*, because in this orbital the negatively charged electron is closer to the positively charged nucleus than in any other orbital. That is, the 1*s* orbital involves the space around the nucleus that is closest to the nucleus. As *n* increases, the orbital becomes larger—the electron, on average, occupies space farther from the nucleus.

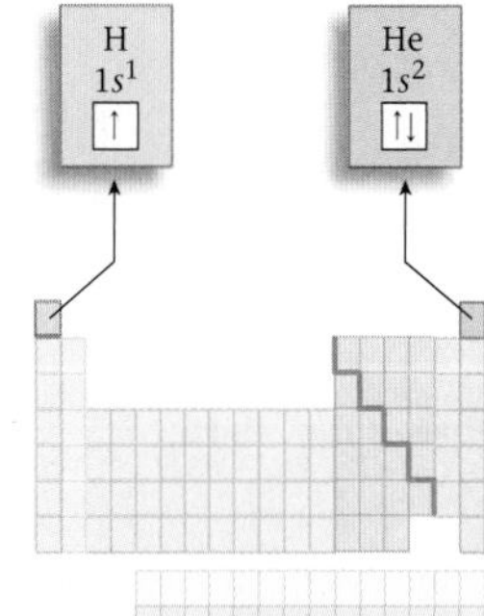

So in its ground state hydrogen has its lone electron in the 1*s* orbital. This is commonly represented in two ways. First, we say that hydrogen has the electron arrangement, or **electron configuration,** $1s^1$. This just means there is one electron in the 1*s* orbital. We can also represent this configuration by using an **orbital diagram,** also called a **box diagram,** in which orbitals are represented by boxes grouped by sublevel with small arrows indicating the electrons. For *hydrogen,* the electron configuration and box diagram are

The arrow represents an electron spinning in a particular direction. The next element is *helium,* $Z = 2$. It has two protons in its nucleus and so has two electrons. Because the 1*s* orbital is the most desirable, both electrons go there

TEACHING TIPS

- For polyelectronic atoms, the third electron goes to the 2*s* orbital. In the hydrogen atom, the 2*s* and 2*p* orbitals have the same energy. However, multiple electrons change this. With multiple electrons, in a given energy level the *s* orbitals are lower in energy (and thus filled first) than the *p* orbitals, which in turn are lower in energy than the *d* orbitals.
- When explaining the filling of the *p* orbitals, it may be helpful to use the analogy of a restaurant with three

In other words, when electrons are placed in a particular quantum level, they "prefer" the orbitals in the order *s, p, d,* and *f.* Why does this happen? Although an electron in the 2*s* orbital spends most of its time a little farther from the nucleus than does an electron in the 2*p* orbital, it spends a small but very significant amount of time very near the nucleus. We say that the 2*s* electron *penetrates* to the nucleus more than for the 2*p* orbital. This *penetration effect* causes an electron in a 2*s* orbital to be attracted to the nucleus more strongly than an electron in a 2*p* orbital. That is, the 2*s* orbital is lower in energy than the 2*p* orbitals in a polyelectronic atom. The same thing happens in the other principal quantum levels.

but with opposite spins. For helium, the electron configuration and box diagram are

Two electrons in 1*s* orbital

He: $1s^2$ 1*s* [↑↓]

The opposite electron spins are shown by the opposing arrows in the box.

Lithium ($Z = 3$) has three electrons, two of which go into the 1*s* orbital. That is, two electrons fill that orbital. The 1*s* orbital is the only orbital for $n = 1$, so the third electron must occupy an orbital with $n = 2$—in this case the 2*s* orbital. This gives a $1s^22s^1$ configuration. The electron configuration and box diagram are

Li
$1s^2\ 2s^1$
[↑↓] [↑]

Be
$1s^2\ 2s^2$
[↑↓] [↑↓]

Li: $1s^22s^1$ 1*s* [↑↓] 2*s* [↑]

The next element, *beryllium,* has four electrons, which occupy the 1*s* and 2*s* orbitals with opposite spins.

Be: $1s^22s^2$ 1*s* [↑↓] 2*s* [↑↓]

Boron has five electrons, four of which occupy the 1*s* and 2*s* orbitals. The fifth electron goes into the second type of orbital with $n = 2$, one of the 2*p* orbitals.

B: $1s^22s^22p^1$ 1*s* [↑↓] 2*s* [↑↓] 2*p* [↑][ ][ ]

B Group 3 | C Group 4 | N Group 5

Because all the 2*p* orbitals have the same energy, it does not matter which 2*p* orbital the electron occupies.

Carbon, the next element, has six electrons: two electrons occupy the 1*s* orbital, two occupy the 2*s* orbital, and two occupy 2*p* orbitals. There are three 2*p* orbitals, so each of the mutually repulsive electrons occupies a different 2*p* orbital. For reasons we will not consider, in the separate 2*p* orbitals the electrons have the same spin.

The configuration for carbon could be written $1s^22s^22p^12p^1$ to indicate that the electrons occupy separate 2*p* orbitals. However, the configuration is usually given as $1s^22s^22p^2$, and it is understood that the electrons are in different 2*p* orbitals.

C: $1s^22s^22p^2$ 1*s* [↑↓] 2*s* [↑↓] 2*p* [↑][↑][ ]

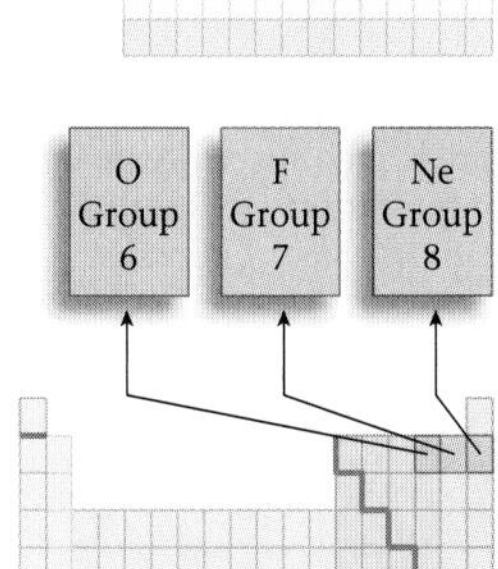

Note the like spins for the unpaired electrons in the 2*p* orbitals.

The configuration for *nitrogen,* which has seven electrons, is $1s^22s^22p^3$. The three electrons in 2*p* orbitals occupy separate orbitals and have like spins.

N: $1s^22s^22p^3$ 1*s* [↑↓] 2*s* [↑↓] 2*p* [↑][↑][↑]

The configuration for *oxygen,* which has eight electrons, is $1s^22s^22p^4$. One of the 2*p* orbitals is now occupied by a pair of electrons with opposite spins, as required by the Pauli exclusion principle.

O: $1s^22s^22p^4$ 1*s* [↑↓] 2*s* [↑↓] 2*p* [↑↓][↑][↑]

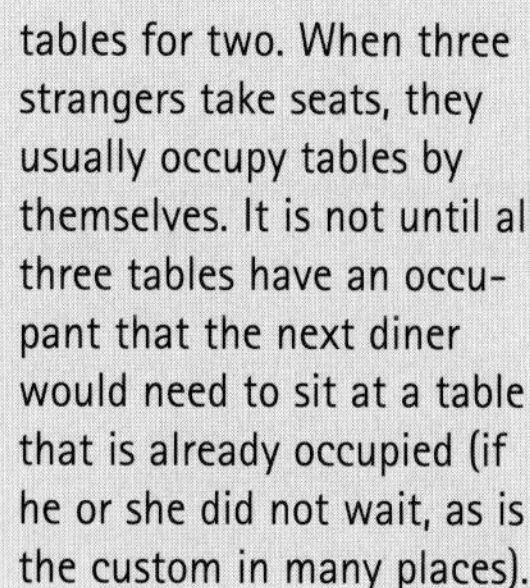

tables for two. When three strangers take seats, they usually occupy tables by themselves. It is not until all three tables have an occupant that the next diner would need to sit at a table that is already occupied (if he or she did not wait, as is the custom in many places).

- Encourage students to use the periodic table to assist them in figuring out electron configurations. Once they see that they can just move across the rows, filling electrons into the *s* and *p* orbitals, electron configurations become much easier to write. This should be used to emphasize the periodicity of the periodic table (even though the table was invented before the discovery of electrons).

Lecture Demonstration: 7.10

PowerLecture Animation: Hund's Rule (no sound)

Lecture Demonstration: 7.11

TEACHING SUPPORT

HISTORICAL BACKGROUND

Dmitri Ivanovich Mendeleev (1834–1907), born in Siberia as the youngest of 17 children, taught chemistry at the University of St. Petersburg. In 1860, Mendeleev heard the Italian chemist Cannizzaro lecture on a reliable method for determining the correct atomic masses of the elements. This important development paved the way for Mendeleev's own brilliant contribution to chemistry—the periodic table. In 1861, Mendeleev returned to St. Petersburg, where he wrote a book on organic chemistry. Later, he also wrote a book on inorganic chemistry, and he was struck by the fact that the systematic approach characterizing organic chemistry was lacking in inorganic chemistry. In attempting to systematize inorganic chemistry, he eventually arranged the elements in the form of the periodic table.

TEACHING TIPS

- Students often become confused about using the core notation for writing electron configurations. It may be easier to have them use only the long form for electron configurations until Chapter 12 when an explanation of bonding makes the core notation a useful form for writing the configurations. The biggest advantage of the core notation is the emphasis it places on the outer electrons that are used in bonding. Be sure students understand that in the core notation the last noble gas is used and the outer electrons are written after it.
- Point out that the periodic table (developed by considering chemical properties of the elements) was created before the discovery of electrons. The wave mechanical model is consistent with the positions on the periodic table, which offers strong support for the model.

Additional Examples

Example 11.2

1. Write the orbital diagram for sodium.

1s	2s	2p	3s
↑↓	↑↓	↑↓ ↑↓ ↑↓	↑

2. Write the orbital diagram for silicon.

1s	2s	2p	3s	3p
↑↓	↑↓	↑↓ ↑↓ ↑↓	↑↓	↑ ↑

H $1s^1$							He $1s^2$
Li $2s^1$	Be $2s^2$	B $2p^1$	C $2p^2$	N $2p^3$	O $2p^4$	F $2p^5$	Ne $2p^6$
Na $3s^1$	Mg $3s^2$	Al $3p^1$	Si $3p^2$	P $3p^3$	S $3p^4$	Cl $3p^5$	Ar $3p^6$

Figure 11.29 The electron configurations in the sublevel last occupied for the first eighteen elements.

The electron configurations and orbital diagrams for *fluorine* (nine electrons) and *neon* (ten electrons) are

		1s	2s	2p
F:	$1s^22s^22p^5$	↑↓	↑↓	↑↓ ↑↓ ↑
Ne:	$1s^22s^22p^6$	↑↓	↑↓	↑↓ ↑↓ ↑↓

With neon, the orbitals with $n = 1$ and $n = 2$ are completely filled.

For *sodium,* which has eleven electrons, the first ten electrons occupy the 1*s*, 2*s*, and 2*p* orbitals, and the eleventh electron must occupy the first orbital with $n = 3$, the 3*s* orbital. The electron configuration for sodium is $1s^22s^22p^63s^1$. To avoid writing the inner-level electrons, we often abbreviate the configuration $1s^22s^22p^63s^1$ as $[Ne]3s^1$, where [Ne] represents the electron configuration of neon, $1s^22s^22p^6$.

The orbital diagram for sodium is

1s	2s	2p	3s
↑↓	↑↓	↑↓ ↑↓ ↑↓	↑

The next element, *magnesium,* $Z = 12$, has the electron configuration $1s^22s^22p^63s^2$, or $[Ne]3s^2$.

The next six elements, *aluminum* through *argon,* have electron configurations obtained by filling the 3*p* orbitals one electron at a time. Figure 11.29 summarizes the electron configurations of the first eighteen elements by giving the number of electrons in the type of orbital (sublevel) occupied last.

EXAMPLE 11.2 Writing Orbital Diagrams

Write the orbital diagram for magnesium.

SOLUTION

Magnesium ($Z = 12$) has twelve electrons that are placed successively in the 1*s*, 2*s*, 2*p*, and 3*s* orbitals to give the electron configuration $1s^22s^22p^63s^2$. The orbital diagram is

1s	2s	2p	3s
↑↓	↑↓	↑↓ ↑↓ ↑↓	↑↓

Only occupied orbitals are shown here.

Self-Check EXERCISE 11.2 Write the complete electron configuration and the orbital diagram for each of the elements aluminum through argon.

See Problems 11.49 through 11.54. ■

Mendeleev was a versatile genius who was interested in many fields of science. He worked on many problems associated with Russia's natural resources, such as coal, salt, and various metals. Being particularly interested in the petroleum industry, he visited the United States in 1876 to study the Pennsylvania oil fields. His interests also included meteorology and hot-air balloons. In 1887, he made an ascent in a balloon to study a total eclipse of the sun.

CHEMISTRY IN FOCUS

A Magnetic Moment

An anesthetized frog lies in the hollow core of an electromagnet. As the current in the coils of the magnet is increased, the frog magically rises and floats in midair (see photo). How can this happen? Is the electromagnet an antigravity machine? In fact, there is no magic going on here. This phenomenon demonstrates the magnetic properties of all matter. We know that iron magnets attract and repel each other depending on their relative orientations. Is a frog magnetic like a piece of iron? If a frog lands on a steel manhole cover, will it be trapped there by magnetic attractions? Of course not. The magnetism of the frog, as with most objects, shows up only in the presence of a strong inducing magnetic field. In other words, the powerful electromagnet surrounding the frog in the experiment described above *induces* a magnetic field in the frog that opposes the inducing field. The opposing magnetic field in the frog repels the inducing field, and the frog lifts up until the magnetic force is balanced by the gravitational pull on its body. The frog then "floats" in air.

How can a frog be magnetic if it is not made of iron? It's the electrons. Frogs are composed of cells containing many kinds of molecules. Of course, these molecules are made of atoms—carbon atoms, nitrogen atoms, oxygen atoms, and other types. Each of these atoms contains electrons that are moving around the atomic nuclei. When these electrons sense a strong magnetic field, they respond by moving in a fashion that produces magnetic fields aligned to oppose the inducing field. This phenomenon is called *diamagnetism.*

All substances, animate and inanimate, because they are made of atoms, exhibit diamagnetism. Andre Geim and his colleagues at the University of Nijmegan, the Netherlands, have levitated frogs, grasshoppers, plants, and water droplets, among other objects. Geim says that, given a large enough electromagnet, even humans can be levitated. He notes, however, that constructing a magnet strong enough to float a human would be very expensive, and he sees no point in it. Geim does point out that inducing weightlessness with magnetic fields may be a good way to pretest experiments on weightlessness intended as research for future space flights—to see if the ideas fly as well as the objects.

A live frog levitated in a magnetic field.

At this point it is useful to introduce the concept of **valence electrons**—that is, *the electrons in the outermost (highest) principal energy level of an atom.* For example, nitrogen, which has the electron configuration $1s^22s^22p^3$, has electrons in principal levels 1 and 2. Therefore, level 2 (which has 2*s* and 2*p* sublevels) is the valence level of nitrogen, and the 2*s* and 2*p* electrons are the valence electrons. For the sodium atom (electron configuration $1s^22s^22p^63s^1$, or $[Ne]3s^1$), the valence electron is the electron in the 3*s* orbital, because in this case principal energy level 3 is the outermost level that contains an electron. The valence electrons are the most important electrons to chemists because, being the outermost electrons, they are the ones involved when atoms attach to each other (form bonds), as we will see in the next chapter. The inner electrons, which are known as **core electrons,** are not involved in bonding atoms to each other.

Self Check

Answers to Self-Check Exercise 11.2

Element	*Electron Configuration*	*Orbital Diagram* 1*s*	2*s*	2*p*	3*s*	3*p*
Al	$1s^22s^22p^63s^23p^1$ $[Ne]3s^23p^1$	↑↓	↑↓	↑↓ ↑↓ ↑↓	↑↓	↑ ☐ ☐
Si	$[Ne]3s^23p^2$	↑↓	↑↓	↑↓ ↑↓ ↑↓	↑↓	↑ ↑ ☐
P	$[Ne]3s^23p^3$	↑↓	↑↓	↑↓ ↑↓ ↑↓	↑↓	↑ ↑ ↑
S	$[Ne]3s^23p^4$	↑↓	↑↓	↑↓ ↑↓ ↑↓	↑↓	↑↓ ↑ ↑
Cl	$[Ne]3s^23p^5$	↑↓	↑↓	↑↓ ↑↓ ↑↓	↑↓	↑↓ ↑↓ ↑
Ar	$[Ne]3s^23p^6$	↑↓	↑↓	↑↓ ↑↓ ↑↓	↑↓	↑↓ ↑↓ ↑↓

Test Bank: 37–63, 67–81

Note in Figure 11.29 that a very important pattern is developing: except for helium, *the atoms of elements in the same group (vertical column of the periodic table) have the same number of electrons in a given type of orbital* (sublevel), except that the orbitals are in different principal energy levels. Remember that the elements were originally organized into groups on the periodic table on the basis of similarities in chemical properties. Now we understand the reason behind these groupings. Elements with the same valence electron arrangement show very similar chemical behavior.

Section 11.10

11.10 Electron Configurations and the Periodic Table

OBJECTIVE: To learn about the electron configurations of atoms with Z greater than 18.

In the previous section we saw that we can describe the atoms beyond hydrogen by simply filling the atomic orbitals starting with level $n = 1$ and working outward in order. This works fine until we reach the element *potassium* ($Z = 19$), which is the next element after argon. Because the $3p$ orbitals are fully occupied in argon, we might expect the next electron to go into a $3d$ orbital (recall that for $n = 3$ the sublevels are $3s$, $3p$, and $3d$). However, experiments show that the chemical properties of potassium are very similar to those of lithium and sodium. Because we have learned to associate similar chemical properties with similar valence-electron arrangements, we predict that the valence-electron configuration for potassium is $4s^1$, resembling sodium ($3s^1$) and lithium ($2s^1$). That is, we expect the last electron in potassium to occupy the $4s$ orbital instead of one of the $3d$ orbitals. This means that principal energy level 4 begins to fill before level 3 has been completed. This conclusion is confirmed by many types of experiments. So the electron configuration of potassium is

$$\text{K: } 1s^2 2s^2 2p^6 3s^2 3p^6 4s^1, \text{ or } [\text{Ar}]4s^1$$

The next element is *calcium*, with an additional electron that also occupies the $4s$ orbital.

$$\text{Ca: } 1s^2 2s^2 2p^6 3s^2 3p^6 4s^2, \text{ or } [\text{Ar}]4s^2$$

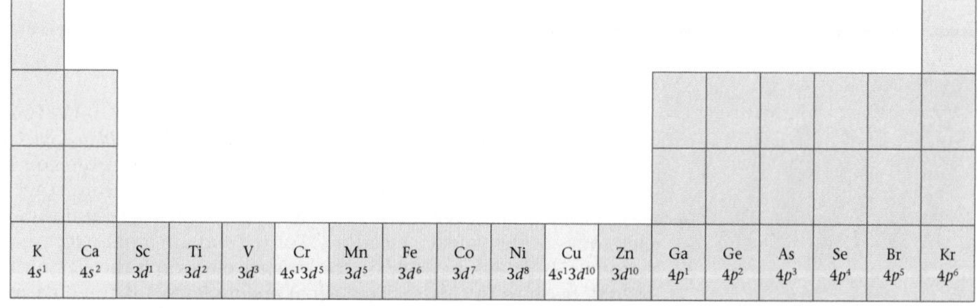

Figure 11.30

Partial electron configurations for the elements potassium through krypton. The transition metals shown in green (scandium through zinc) have the general configuration $[\text{Ar}]4s^2 3d^n$, except for chromium and copper.

TEACHING TIP

Encourage students to use the periodic table as a guide in writing electron configurations. Here understanding the structure of the table can be much more useful than memorizing an order of filling. Each row guides students through an energy level. Each block guides them through a sublevel. Use the PowerPoint and transparency for Figure 11.31 to discuss this process.

DEMONSTRATION

On an overhead projector place two Petri dishes. Cover the bottom of each dish to a depth of 1 cm with water. Cut *small* samples of Na and K metals. Dry each with a paper towel. Add the Na to one dish and the K to the other. Observe the results and compare the reactions. Both metals skate around on the surface of the water, and they may burst into flames or smoke.

TEACHING TIPS

- Point out that Cu and Cr are notable exceptions to the expected electron configurations. The reasons for these exceptions are quite complicated.
- It is very important that students realize that with an understanding of how the periodic table is put together, they can figure out the expected electron configuration of any element. They need not memorize these configurations.

PowerLecture Simulations:
Atomic Electron Configurations
Electron Configurations, Tutorial Style

CHEMISTRY IN FOCUS

The Chemistry of Bohrium

One of the best uses of the periodic table is to predict the properties of newly discovered elements. For example, the artificially synthesized element bohrium ($Z = 107$) is found in the same family as manganese, technetium, and rhenium and is expected to show chemistry similar to these elements. The problem, of course, is that only a few atoms of bohrium (Bh) can be made at a time and the atoms exist for only a very short time (about 17 seconds). It's a real challenge to study the chemistry of an element under these conditions. However, a team of nuclear chemists led by Heinz W. Gaggeler of the University of Bern in Switzerland isolated six atoms of ^{267}Bh and prepared the compound BhO_3Cl. Analysis of the decay products of this compound helped define the thermochemical properties of BhO_3Cl and showed that bohrium seems to behave as might be predicted from its position in the periodic table.

The 4*s* orbital is now full.

After calcium the next electrons go into the 3*d* orbitals to complete principal energy level 3. The elements that correspond to filling the 3*d* orbitals are called transition metals. Then the 4*p* orbitals fill. Figure 11.30 gives partial electron configurations for the elements potassium through krypton.

Note from Figure 11.30 that all of the transition metals have the general configuration $[Ar]4s^2 3d^n$ except chromium ($4s^1 3d^5$) and copper ($4s^1 3d^{10}$). The reasons for these exceptions are complex and will not be discussed here.

Instead of continuing to consider the elements individually, we will now look at the overall relationship between the periodic table and orbital filling. Figure 11.31 shows which type of orbital is filling in each area of the periodic table. Note the points in the box below.

Orbital Filling

1. In a principal energy level that has *d* orbitals, the *s* orbital from the *next* level fills before the *d* orbitals in the current level. That is, the $(n + 1)s$ orbitals always fill before the *nd* orbitals. For example, the 5*s* orbitals fill for rubidium and strontium before the 4*d* orbitals fill for the second row of transition metals (yttrium through cadmium).
2. After lanthanum, which has the electron configuration $[Xe]6s^2 5d^1$, a group of fourteen elements called the **lanthanide series,** or the lanthanides, occurs. This series of elements corresponds to the filling of the seven 4*f* orbitals.
3. After actinium, which has the configuration $[Rn]7s^2 6d^1$, a group of fourteen elements called the **actinide series,** or the actinides, occurs. This series corresponds to the filling of the seven 5*f* orbitals.
4. Except for helium, the group numbers indicate the sum of electrons in the *ns* and *np* orbitals in the highest principal energy level that contains electrons (where *n* is the number that indicates a particular principal energy level). These electrons are the valence electrons, the electrons in the outermost principal energy level of a given atom.

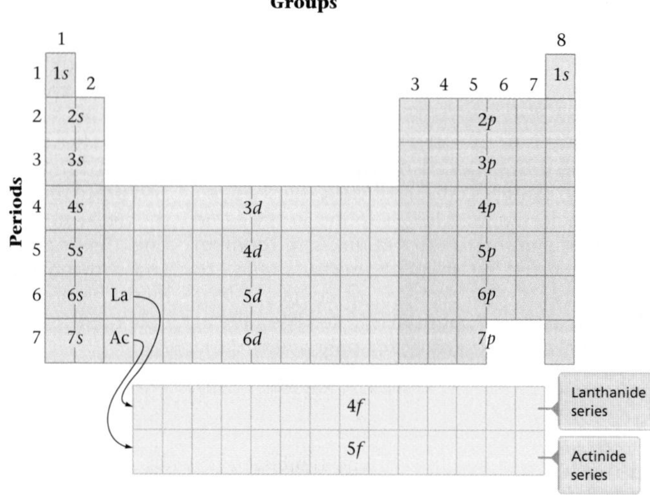

Figure 11.31
The orbitals being filled for elements in various parts of the periodic table. Note that in going along a horizontal row (a period), the $(n + 1)s$ orbital fills before the nd orbital. The group label indicates the number of valence electrons (the number of s plus the number of p electrons in the highest occupied principal energy level) for the elements in each group.

*After the 6*s* orbital is full, one electron goes into a 5*d* orbital. This corresponds to the element lanthanum ($[Xe]6s^2 5d^1$). After lanthanum, the 4*f* orbitals fill with electrons.

**After the 7*s* orbital is full, one electron goes into 6*d*. This is actinium ($[Rn]7s^2 6d^1$). The 5*f* orbitals then fill.

To help you further understand the connection between orbital filling and the periodic table, Figure 11.32 shows the orbitals in the order in which they fill.

A periodic table is almost always available to you. If you understand the relationship between the electron configuration of an element and its position on the periodic table, you can figure out the expected electron configuration of any atom.

EXAMPLE 11.3 Determining Electron Configurations

Using the periodic table inside the front cover of the text, give the electron configurations for sulfur (S), gallium (Ga), hafnium (Hf), and radium (Ra).

SOLUTION

Sulfur is element 16 and resides in Period 3, where the 3*p* orbitals are being filled (see Figure 11.33). Because sulfur is the fourth among the "3*p* elements," it must have four 3*p* electrons. Sulfur's electron configuration is

$$S: 1s^2 2s^2 2p^6 3s^2 3p^4, \text{ or } [Ne]3s^2 3p^4$$

Gallium is element 31 in Period 4 just after the transition metals (see Figure 11.33). It is the first element in the "4*p* series" and has a $4p^1$ arrangement. Gallium's electron configuration is

$$Ga: 1s^2 2s^2 2p^6 3s^2 3p^6 4s^2 3d^{10} 4p^1, \text{ or } [Ar]4s^2 3d^{10} 4p^1$$

Hafnium is element 72 and is found in Period 6, as shown in Figure 11.33. Note that it occurs just after the lanthanide series (see Figure 11.31).

Additional Examples

Example 11.3

Give the electron configuration for the following elements:

1. Bromine (Br)

   $1s^2 2s^2 2p^6 3s^2 3p^6 4s^2 3d^{10} 4p^5$ or $[Ar]4s^2 3d^{10} 4p^5$

2. Tin (Sn)

   $1s^2 2s^2 2p^6 3s^2 3p^6 4s^2 3d^{10} 4p^6 5s^2 4d^{10} 5p^2$ or $[Kr]5s^2 4d^{10} 5p^2$

3. Polonium (Po)

   $1s^2 2s^2 2p^6 3s^2 3p^6 4s^2 3d^{10} 4p^6 5s^2 4d^{10} 5p^6 6s^2 4f^{14} 5d^{10} 6p^4$ or $[Xe]6s^2 4f^{14} 5d^{10} 6p^4$

Order of filling of orbitals

6d
5f**
7s
6p
5d
4f*
6s
5p
4d
5s
4p
3d
4s
3p
3s
2p
2s
1s

Figure 11.32
A box diagram showing the order in which orbitals fill to produce the atoms in the periodic table. Each box can hold two electrons.

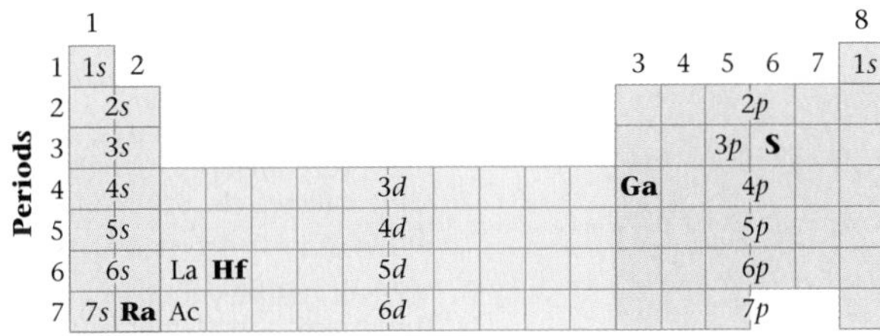

Figure 11.33
The positions of the elements considered in Example 11.3.

Thus the $4f$ orbitals are already filled. Hafnium is the second member of the $5d$ transition series and has two $5d$ electrons. Its electron configuration is

$$\text{Hf: } 1s^2 2s^2 2p^6 3s^2 3p^6 4s^2 3d^{10} 4p^6 5s^2 4d^{10} 5p^6 6s^2 4f^{14} 5d^2, \text{ or } [\text{Xe}] 6s^2 4f^{14} 5d^2$$

Radium is element 88 and is in Period 7 (and Group 2), as shown in Figure 11.33. Thus radium has two electrons in the $7s$ orbital, and its electron configuration is

$$\text{Ra: } 1s^2 2s^2 2p^6 3s^2 3p^6 4s^2 3d^{10} 4p^6 5s^2 4d^{10} 5p^6 6s^2 4f^{14} 5d^{10} 6p^6 7s^2, \text{ or } [\text{Rn}] 7s^2$$

Self-Check EXERCISE 11.3 Using the periodic table inside the front cover of the text, predict the electron configurations for fluorine, silicon, cesium, lead, and iodine. If you have trouble, use Figure 11.31.

See Problems 11.59 through 11.68. ■

Self Check

Answers to Self-Check Exercise 11.3

F: $1s^2 2s^2 2p^5$ or $[\text{He}] 2s^2 2p^5$

Si: $1s^2 2s^2 2p^6 3s^2 3p^2$ or $[\text{Ne}] 3s^2 3p^2$

Cs: $1s^2 2s^2 2p^6 3s^2 3p^6 4s^2 3d^{10} 4p^6 5s^2 4d^{10} 5p^6 6s^1$ or $[\text{Xe}] 6s^1$

Pb: $1s^2 2s^2 2p^6 3s^2 3p^6 4s^2 3d^{10} 4p^6 5s^2 4d^{10} 5p^6 6s^2 4f^{14} 5d^{10} 6p^2$ or $[\text{Xe}] 6s^2 4f^{14} 5d^{10} 6p^2$

I: $1s^2 2s^2 2p^6 3s^2 3p^6 4s^2 3d^{10} 4p^6 5s^2 4d^{10} 5p^5$ or $[\text{Kr}] 5s^2 4d^{10} 5p^5$

Summary of the Wave Mechanical Model and Valence-Electron Configurations

The concepts we have discussed in this chapter are very important. They allow us to make sense of a good deal of chemistry. When it was first observed that elements with similar properties occur periodically as the atomic number increases, chemists wondered why. Now we have an explanation. The wave mechanical model pictures the electrons in an atom as arranged in orbitals, with each orbital capable of holding two electrons. As we build up the atoms, the same types of orbitals recur in going from one principal energy level to another. This means that particular valence-electron configurations recur periodically. For reasons we will explore in the next chapter, elements with a particular type of valence configuration all show very similar chemical behavior. Thus groups of elements, such as the alkali metals, show similar chemistry because all the elements in that group have the same type of valence-electron arrangement. This concept, which explains so much chemistry, is the greatest contribution of the wave mechanical model to modern chemistry.

For reference, the valence-electron configurations for all the elements are shown on the periodic table in Figure 11.34. Note the following points:

1. The group labels for Groups 1, 2, 3, 4, 5, 6, 7, and 8 indicate the *total number* of valence electrons for the atoms in these groups. For

11.10 Electron Configurations and the Periodic Table 345

example, all the elements in Group 5 have the configuration ns^2np^3. (Any d electrons present are always in the next lower principal energy level than the valence electrons and so are not counted as valence electrons.)

2. The elements in Groups 1, 2, 3, 4, 5, 6, 7, and 8 are often called the **main-group elements,** or **representative elements.** Remember that every member of a given group (except for helium) has the same valence-electron configuration, except that the electrons are in different principal energy levels.

3. We will not be concerned in this text with the configurations for the *f*-transition elements (lanthanides and actinides), although they are included in Figure 11.34.

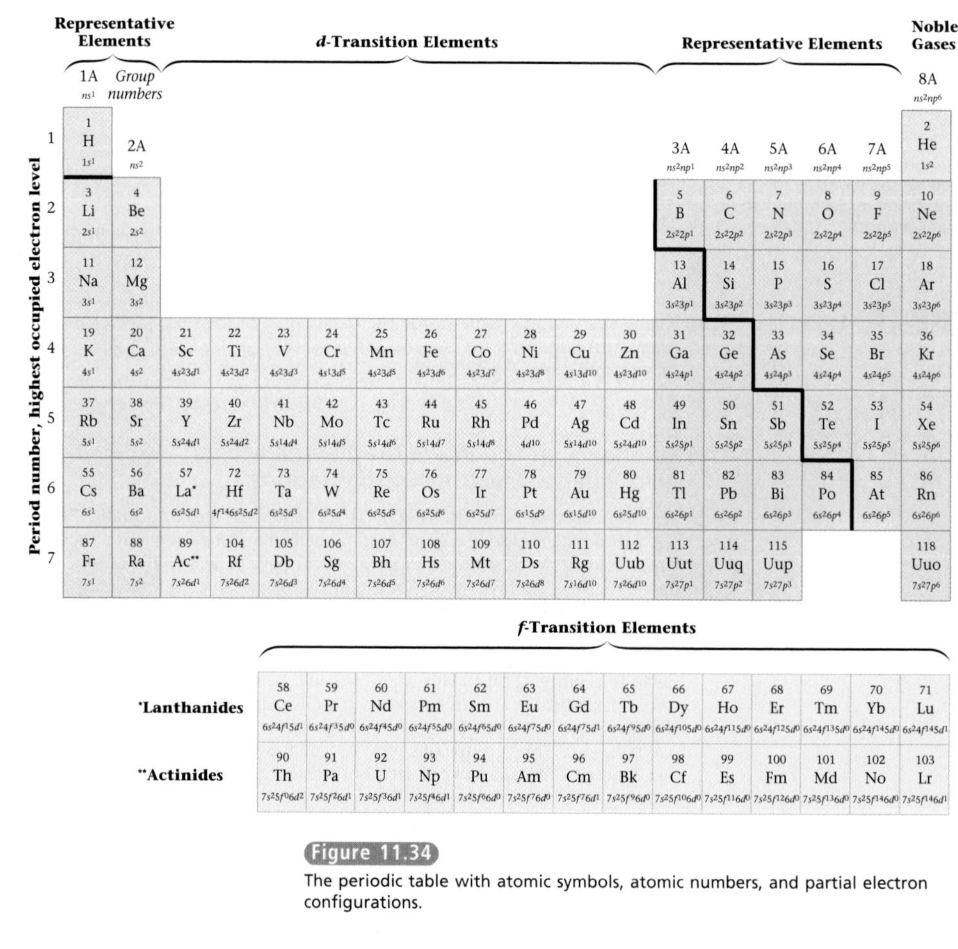

Figure 11.34
The periodic table with atomic symbols, atomic numbers, and partial electron configurations.

11.11 Atomic Properties and the Periodic Table

OBJECTIVE: To understand the general trends in atomic properties in the periodic table.

With all of this talk about electron probability and orbitals, we must not lose sight of the fact that chemistry is still fundamentally a science based on the observed properties of substances. We know that wood burns, steel rusts, plants grow, sugar tastes sweet, and so on because we *observe* these phenomena. The atomic theory is an attempt to help us understand why these things occur. If we understand why, we can hope to better control the chemical events that are so crucial in our daily lives.

In the next chapter we will see how our ideas about atomic structure help us understand how and why atoms combine to form compounds. As we explore this, and as we use theories to explain other types of chemical behavior later in the text, it is important that we distinguish the observation (steel rusts) from the attempts to explain why the observed event occurs (theories). The observations remain the same over the decades, but the theories (our explanations) change as we gain a clearer understanding of how nature operates. A good example of this is the replacement of the Bohr model for atoms by the wave mechanical model.

Because the observed behavior of matter lies at the heart of chemistry, you need to understand thoroughly the characteristic properties of the various elements and the trends (systematic variations) that occur in those properties. To that end, we will now consider some especially important properties of atoms and see how they vary, horizontally and vertically, on the periodic table.

Metals and Nonmetals

The most fundamental classification of the chemical elements is into metals and nonmetals. **Metals** typically have the following physical properties: a lustrous appearance, the ability to change shape without breaking (they can be pulled into a wire or pounded into a thin sheet), and excellent conductivity of heat and electricity. **Nonmetals** typically do not have these physical properties, although there are some exceptions. (For example, solid iodine is lustrous; the graphite form of carbon is an excellent conductor of electricity; and the diamond form of carbon is an excellent conductor of heat.) However, it is the *chemical* differences between metals and nonmetals that interest us the most: *metals tend to lose electrons to form positive ions, and nonmetals tend to gain electrons to form negative ions.* When a metal and a nonmetal react, a transfer of one or more electrons from the metal to the nonmetal often occurs.

Most of the elements are classified as metals, as is shown in Figure 11.35. Note that the metals are found on the left side and at the center of the periodic table. The relatively few nonmetals are in the upper-right corner of the table. A few elements exhibit both metallic and nonmetallic behavior; they are classified as **metalloids** or semimetals.

It is important to understand that simply being classified as a metal does not mean that an element behaves exactly like all other metals. For example, some metals can lose one or more electrons much more easily than others. In particular, cesium can give up its outermost electron (a 6*s* electron)

Gold leaf being applied to the dome of the courthouse in Huntington, West Virginia.

TEACHING SUPPORT

BACKGROUND INFORMATION

History of the Periodic Table

The periodic table was originally constructed to represent the patterns observed in the chemical properties of the elements. As chemistry progressed during the eighteenth and nineteenth centuries, it became evident that the earth is composed of a great many elements with very different properties. Things are much more complicated than the simple model of earth, air, fire, and water suggested by the ancients. At first, the array of elements and properties was bewildering. Gradually, however, patterns were noticed.

The first chemist to recognize such patterns was Johann Dobereiner (1780–1849), who found several groups of three elements that have similar properties—for example, chlorine, bromine, and iodine. However, as Dobereiner attempted

Section 11.11

TEACHING TIP

Transparency and PowerPoint Figure 11.34 can help tie together the information presented in this chapter. It leads naturally to a discussion of periodic trends.

Test Bank: 82–100

Lecture Demonstration: 7.8

PowerLecture Animation: Periodic Table Trends

DEMONSTRATION

Roman Candle

Materials Test tube (200 × 24 mm), 600-mL beaker, sand, dropper, copper(II) chloride, potassium chlorate, granulated sugar, powdered iron, strontium nitrate, sulfuric acid (concentrated)

Preparation Measure 35.0 g potassium chlorate and 10.00 g granulated sugar separately and then mix them uniformly. (*Caution:* Do not grind this mixture together. An explosion may result.) Prepare this mixture fresh for each demonstration; do not store it. Starting with the bottom, prepare four zones of chemicals in the test tube as follows: (1) mixture of 3.0 g strontium nitrate and 9.0 g potassium chlorate/sugar (red color); (2) mixture of 2.0 g copper(II) chloride and 10.0 g potassium chlorate/sugar (blue color); (3) mixture of 3.0 g powdered iron and 9.0 g potassium chlorate/sugar (yellow sparks); (4) 12.0 g potassium chlorate/sugar (white color). Embed the test tube upright in the beaker containing the sand.

Performance (*Note:* This demonstration produces lots of smoke. Perform it in a well-ventilated area or outside. Use a safety shield to protect the audience.) When ready, add one or two drops of concentrated sulfuric acid to the test tube and *step back.* The test tube sometimes begins to melt in this demonstration. Be careful to wait for it to cool after the demonstration. The test tube can be discarded.

Teaching Notes You can use this demonstration as a review of the colors produced in the flame test. Ask students what chemical produces each color.

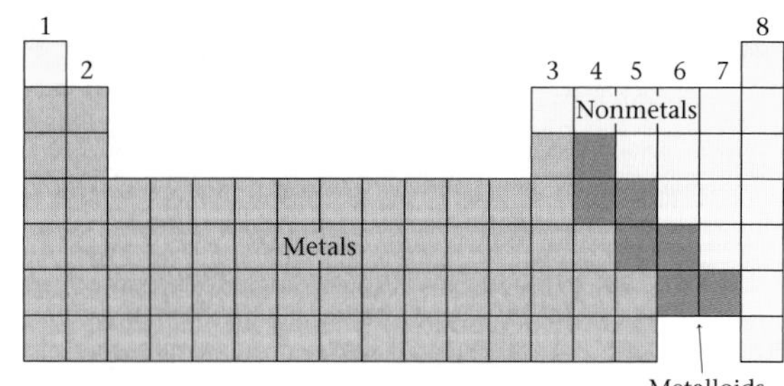

Figure 11.35
The classification of elements as metals, nonmetals, and metalloids.

more easily than can lithium (a 2*s* electron). In fact, for the alkali metals (Group 1) the ease of giving up an electron varies as follows:

$$\text{Cs} > \text{Rb} > \text{K} > \text{Na} > \text{Li}$$

Loses an electron most easily

Note that as we go down the group, the metals become more likely to lose an electron. This makes sense because as we go down the group, the electron being removed resides, on average, farther and farther from the nucleus. That is, the 6*s* electron lost from Cs is much farther from the attractive positive nucleus—and so is easier to remove—than the 2*s* electron that must be removed from a lithium atom.

The same trend is also seen in the Group 2 metals (alkaline earth metals): the farther down in the group the metal resides, the more likely it is to lose an electron.

Just as metals vary somewhat in their properties, so do nonmetals. In general, the elements that can most effectively pull electrons from metals occur in the upper-right corner of the periodic table.

As a general rule, we can say that the most chemically active metals appear in the lower-left region of the periodic table, whereas the most chemically active nonmetals appear in the upper-right region. The properties of the semimetals, or metalloids, lie between the metals and the nonmetals, as might be expected.

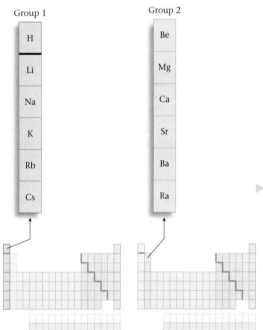

Group 1: H, Li, Na, K, Rb, Cs

Group 2: Be, Mg, Ca, Sr, Ba, Ra

PowerLecture Videos:
Reaction: Lithium and Water
Reaction: Potassium and Water

Ionization Energies

The **ionization energy** of an atom is the energy required to remove an electron from an individual atom in the gas phase:

$$\text{M}(g) \xrightarrow{\text{Ionization energy}} \text{M}^{+}(g) + e^{-}$$

As we have noted, the most characteristic chemical property of a metal atom is losing electrons to nonmetals. Another way of saying this is to say that *metals have relatively low ionization*

to expand this model of *triads* (as he called them) to the rest of the known elements, it became clear that this idea was severely limited.

The next notable attempt was made by the English chemist John Newlands, who in 1864 suggested that elements should be arranged in *octaves,* based on the idea that certain properties seemed to repeat for every eighth tone. Even though this model managed to group several elements with similar properties, it was not generally successful.

The present form of the periodic table was conceived independently by two chemists: Julius Lothar Meyer (1830–1895), a German, and Dmitri Ivanovich Mendeleev (1834–1907), a Russian. Usually, Mendeleev is given most of the credit, because he emphasized how useful the table could be in predicting the existence and properties of still unknown elements. For example, in 1872 when Mendeleev first published his table, the elements gallium, scandium, and germanium were unknown. Mendeleev correctly

CHEMISTRY *IN* FOCUS

Fireworks

These brightly colored fireworks are the result of complex mixtures of chemicals.

Eyewire/Alamy Images

The art of using mixtures of chemicals to produce explosives is an ancient one. Black powder—a mixture of potassium nitrate, charcoal, and sulfur—was being used in China well before A.D. 1000, and it has been used through the centuries in military explosives, in construction blasting, and for fireworks.

Before the nineteenth century, fireworks were confined mainly to rockets and loud bangs. Orange and yellow colors came from the presence of charcoal and iron filings. However, with the great advances in chemistry in the nineteenth century, new compounds found their way into fireworks. Salts of copper, strontium, and barium added brilliant colors. Magnesium and aluminum metals gave a dazzling white light.

How do fireworks produce their brilliant colors and loud bangs? Actually, only a handful of different chemicals are responsible for most of the spectacular effects. To produce the noise and flashes, an oxidizer (something with a strong affinity for electrons) is reacted with a metal such as magnesium or aluminum mixed with sulfur. The resulting reaction produces a brilliant flash, which is due to the aluminum or magnesium burning, and a loud report is produced by the rapidly expanding gases. For a color effect, an element with a colored flame is included.

Yellow colors in fireworks are due to sodium. Strontium salts give the red color familiar from highway safety flares. Barium salts give a green color.

Although you might think that the chemistry of fireworks is simple, achieving the vivid white flashes and the brilliant colors requires complex combinations of chemicals. For example, because the white flashes produce high flame temperatures, the colors tend to wash out. Another problem arises from the use of sodium salts. Because sodium produces an extremely bright yellow color, sodium salts cannot be used when other colors are desired. In short, the manufacture of fireworks that produce the desired effects and are also safe to handle requires very careful selection of chemicals.*

*The chemical mixtures in fireworks are very dangerous. *Do not* experiment with chemicals on your own.

energies—a relatively small amount of energy is needed to remove an electron from a typical metal.

Recall that metals at the bottom of a group lose electrons more easily than those at the top. In other words, ionization energies tend to decrease in going from the top to the bottom of a group.

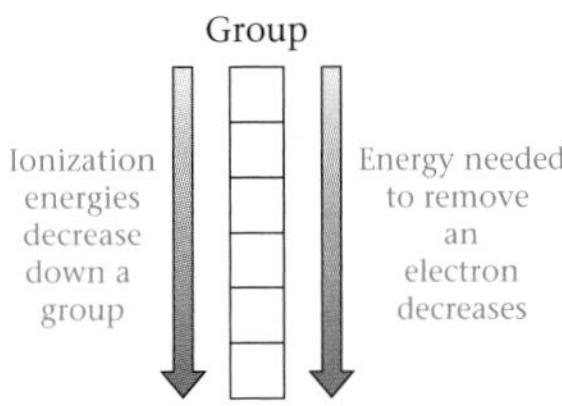
Group
Ionization energies decrease down a group
Energy needed to remove an electron decreases

349

predicted the existence and properties of these elements from gaps in his periodic table.

Using his table, Mendeleev also was able to correct several values for atomic masses. For example, the original atomic mass of 76 of indium was based on the assumption that indium oxide had the formula InO. This atomic mass placed indium, which has metallic properties, among the nonmetals. Mendeleev assumed that the atomic mass was probably incorrect and proposed that the formula of indium oxide was really In_2O_3. Based on this correct formula, indium has an atomic mass of approximately 113, placing the element among the metals. Mendeleev also corrected the atomic masses of beryllium and uranium. Because of its obvious usefulness, Mendeleev's periodic table was almost universally adopted, and it remains one of the most valuable tools at the chemist's disposal.

TEACHING TIPS

- Students should understand the reasons for the periodic trends. It is important to focus on why each trend occurs and not simply on what the trend is.
- Students can easily understand why atomic size increases as we move down the periodic table. It is much harder for them to understand why it decreases as we move from left to right. Focus the students' attention on adding electrons at approximately the same distance from the nucleus while at the same time increasing the nuclear charge.
- Make sure students understand the trends related to atomic size across rows and down groups in the periodic table. If they understand these trends, the trends for ionization energy are much easier to grasp. Students should be able to see that the trends for atomic size and ionization energy are consistent with one another.

PowerLecture Animation: Fireworks

MISCONCEPTION

Many students believe that alkali metals "want" to lose an electron—that is, the potassium atom, for example, will release energy to become an ion. Or they believe that less energy is required to remove the second electron from calcium, for example, than the first because calcium "wants" to lose two electrons. Energy is always required to remove an electron, and successive electrons can be removed only with an increasing amount of energy.

PowerLecture Animation: Electronic Transitions in Fireworks

PowerLecture Animations:
Atoms of Hydrogen and Oxygen (no sound)
Five Atoms with Electron Clouds (no sound)

In contrast to metals, nonmetals have relatively large ionization energies. Nonmetals tend to gain, not lose, electrons. Recall that metals appear on the left side of the periodic table and nonmetals appear on the right. Thus it is not surprising that ionization energies tend to increase from left to right across a given period on the periodic table.

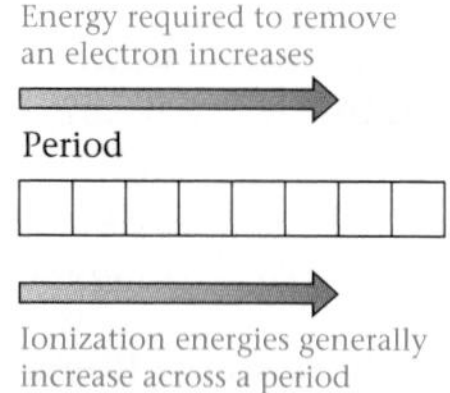

In general, the elements that appear in the lower-left region of the periodic table have the lowest ionization energies (and are therefore the most chemically active metals). On the other hand, the elements with the highest ionization energies (the most chemically active nonmetals) occur in the upper-right region of the periodic table.

Atomic Size

The sizes of atoms vary as shown in Figure 11.36. Notice that atoms get larger as we go down a group on the periodic table and that they get smaller as we go from left to right across a period.

We can understand the increase in size that we observe as we go down a group by remembering that as the principal energy level increases, the average distance of the electrons from the nucleus also increases. So atoms get bigger as electrons are added to larger principal energy levels.

Figure 11.36 Relative atomic sizes for selected atoms. Note that atomic size increases down a group and decreases across a period.

TEACHING TIP

Some students do not understand that a high ionization energy means that it is difficult to remove an electron from an atom. Discuss the attraction of the electron for the nucleus and point out that this attraction must be overcome (requiring energy) to remove the electron.

TEACHING SUPPORT

BACKGROUND INFORMATION

Atomic Radius

Just as the size of an orbital cannot be specified exactly, neither can the size of an atom. We must make some arbitrary choices to obtain values for atomic radii. These values can be obtained by measuring the distances between atoms in chemical compounds. For example, in the bromine molecule, the distance between the two nuclei is known to be 229 pm. The bromine atomic radius is assumed to be half this distance, or 114 pm. These radii are often called *covalent atomic radii* because of the way they are determined (from the distances between atoms in covalent bonds).

For nonmetallic atoms that do not form diatomic molecules, the atomic radii are estimated from their various covalent compounds. The radii for

Explaining the decrease in **atomic size** across a period requires a little thought about the atoms in a given row (period) of the periodic table. Recall that the atoms in a particular period all have their outermost electrons in a given principal energy level. That is, the atoms in Period 1 have their outer electrons in the 1*s* orbital (principal energy level 1), the atoms in Period 2 have their outermost electrons in principal energy level 2 (2*s* and 2*p* orbitals), and so on (see Figure 11.31). Because all the orbitals in a given principal energy level are expected to be the same size, we might expect the atoms in a given period to be the same size. However, remember that the number of protons in the nucleus increases as we move from atom to atom in the period. The resulting increase in positive charge on the nucleus tends to pull the electrons closer to the nucleus. So instead of remaining the same size across a period as electrons are added in a given principal energy level, the atoms get smaller as the electron "cloud" is drawn in by the increasing nuclear charge.

CHAPTER 11 REVIEW

Key Terms

electromagnetic radiation (11.2)
wavelength (11.2)
frequency (11.2)
photon (11.2)
quantized energy levels (11.4)
wave mechanical model (11.6)
orbital (11.7)
principal energy levels (11.7)
sublevels (11.7)
Pauli exclusion principle (11.8)
electron configuration (11.9)
orbital (box) diagram (11.9)
valence electrons (11.9)
core electrons (11.9)
lanthanide series (11.10)
actinide series (11.10)
main-group (representative) elements (11.10)
metals (11.11)
nonmetals (11.11)
metalloids (11.11)
ionization energy (11.11)
atomic size (11.11)

F directs you to the *Chemistry in Focus* feature in the chapter
VP indicates visual problems
OWL interactive versions of these problems are assignable in OWL

Summary

1. Energy travels through space by electromagnetic radiation ("light"), which can be characterized by the wavelength and frequency of the waves. Light can also be thought of as packets of energy called photons. Atoms can gain energy by absorbing a photon and can lose energy by emitting a photon.
2. The emissions of energy from hydrogen atoms produce only certain energies as hydrogen changes from a higher to a lower energy. This shows that the energy levels of hydrogen are quantized.
3. The Bohr model of the hydrogen atom postulated that the electron moved in circular orbits corresponding to the various allowed energy levels. Though it worked well for hydrogen, the Bohr model did not work for other atoms.
4. The wave mechanical model explains atoms by postulating that the electron has both wave and particle characteristics. Electron states are described by orbitals, which are probability maps indicating how likely it is to find the electron at a given point in space. The orbital size can be thought of as a surface containing 90% of the total electron probability.
5. According to the Pauli exclusion principle, an atomic orbital can hold a maximum of two electrons, and those electrons must have opposite spins.
6. Atoms have a series of energy levels, called principal energy levels (n), which contain one or more sublevels (types of orbitals). The number of sublevels increases with increasing n.
7. Valence electrons are the *s* and *p* electrons in the outermost principal energy level of an atom. Core electrons are the inner electrons of an atom.
8. Metals are found at the left and center of the periodic table. The most chemically active metals are found in the lower-left corner of the periodic table. The most chemically active nonmetals are located in the upper-right corner.

metal atoms (*metallic radii*) are obtained from half the distances between metal atoms in solid metal crystals.

The values of atomic radii are significantly smaller than might be expected from the 90% electron density volumes of isolated atoms, because when atoms form bonds, their electron "clouds" interpenetrate. However, these values form a self-consistent data set that can be used to discuss the trends in atomic radii.

Also note that atomic radii decrease in going from left to right across a period. This decrease can be explained in terms of the increasing effective nuclear charge (decreasing shielding) in going from left to right. This means that the valence electrons are drawn closer to the nucleus, decreasing the size of the atom.

Atomic radius increases down a group, because of the increases in the orbital sizes in successive principal quantum levels.

ChemWork

Types of Concentration
Lattice Energy and Enthalpy
Solubility and Solvents
Comparing Solubility
Solubility of a Gas
Composition of Vapor
Raoult's Law
Vapor Pressure
Boiling Point Determination
Osmotic Pressure
Mixture Composition and Freezing Point

Answers to End-of-Chapter Exercises

1. positively; negatively

2. Rutherford's experiments determined that the atom had a nucleus containing positively charged particles called protons. He established that the nucleus was very small compared to the overall size of the atom. He was not able to determine where the electrons were in the atom or what they were doing.

3. Electromagnetic radiation is energy propagated through space as waves; at the "speed of light" in a vacuum.

4. The different forms of electromagnetic radiation all exhibit the same wavelike behavior and are propagated through space at the same speed (the "speed of light"). The types of electromagnetic radiation differ in their frequency (and wavelength) and in the resulting amount of energy carried per photon.

5. The wavelength represents the distance between corresponding points on two successive waves. The energy of a photon is inversely proportional to the wavelength ($E = hc/\lambda$).

6. The frequency of electromagnetic radiation represents how many waves pass a given location per second. The speed of electromagnetic

9. Ionization energy, the energy required to remove an electron from a gaseous atom, decreases going down a group and increases going from left to right across a period.

10. For the representative elements, atomic size increases going down a group but decreases going from left to right across a period.

Active Learning Questions

These questions are designed to be considered by groups of students in class. Often these questions work well for introducing a particular topic in class.

1. How does probability fit into the description of the atom?
2. What is meant by an *orbital?*
3. Account for the fact that the line that separates the metals from the nonmetals on the periodic table is diagonal downward to the right instead of horizontal or vertical.
4. Consider the following statements: "The ionization energy for the potassium atom is negative because when K loses an electron to become K^+, it achieves a noble gas electron configuration." Indicate everything that is correct in this statement. Indicate everything that is incorrect. Correct the mistaken information and explain the error.
5. In going across a row of the periodic table, protons and electrons are added and ionization energy generally increases. In going down a column of the periodic table, protons and electrons are also being added but ionization energy generally decreases. Explain.
6. Which is larger, the H 1*s* orbital or the Li 1*s* orbital? Why? Which has the larger radius, the H atom or the Li atom? Why?
7. True or false? The hydrogen atom has a 3*s* orbital. Explain.
8. Differentiate among the terms *energy level, sublevel,* and *orbital.*
9. Make sense of the fact that metals tend to lose electrons and nonmetals tend to gain electrons. Use the periodic table to support your answer.
10. Show how using the periodic table helps you find the expected electron configuration of any element.

For Questions 11–13, you will need to consider ionizations beyond the first ionization energy. For example, the second ionization energy is the energy to remove a second electron from an element.

11. Compare the first ionization energy of helium to its second ionization energy, remembering that both electrons come from the 1*s* orbital.
12. Which would you expect to have a larger second ionization energy, lithium or beryllium? Why?
13. The first four ionization energies for elements X and Y are shown below. The units are not kJ/mol.

	X	Y
first	170	200
second	350	400
third	1800	3500
fourth	2500	5000

Identify the elements X and Y. There may be more than one answer, so explain completely.

14. Explain what is meant by the term "excited state" as it applies to an electron. Is an electron in an excited state higher or lower in energy than an electron in the ground state? Is an electron in an excited state more or less stable than an electron in the ground state?
15. What does it mean when we say energy levels are *quantized?*
16. What evidence do we have that energy levels in an atom are quantized? State and explain the evidence.
17. Explain the hydrogen emission spectrum. Why is it significant that the color emitted is not white? How does the emission spectrum support the idea of quantized energy levels?
18. There are an infinite number of allowed transitions in the hydrogen atom. Why don't we see more lines in the emission spectrum for hydrogen?
19. You have learned that each orbital is allowed two electrons, and this pattern is evident on the periodic table. What if each orbital was allowed three electrons? How would this change the appearance of the periodic table? For example, what would be the atomic numbers of the noble gases?
20. Atom A has valence electrons that are lower in energy than the valence electrons of Atom B. Which atom has the higher ionization energy? Explain.

VP 21. Consider the following waves representing electromagnetic radiation:

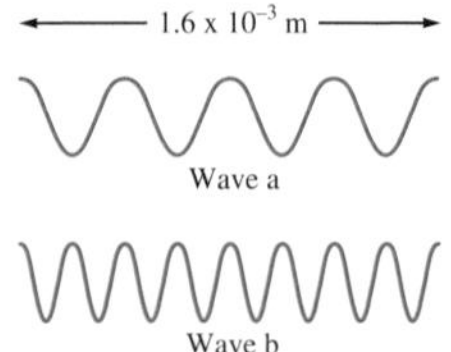

Questions and Problems

11.1 Rutherford's Atom

QUESTIONS

1. An atom has a small ______ charged core called the nucleus, with ______ charged electrons moving in the space around the nucleus.

All even-numbered Questions and Problems have answers in the back of this book and solutions in the Solutions Guide.

radiation represents how fast the waves propagate through space. The frequency and the speed are not the same.

7. higher

8. The greenhouse gases do not absorb light in the visible wavelengths. Therefore, this light passes through the atmosphere and warms the earth, keeping the earth much warmer than it would be without these gases. As more we are increasing our use of fossil fuels, the level of CO_2 in the atmosphere is increasing gradually but significantly. An increase in the level of CO_2 will warm the earth further, eventually changing the weather patterns on the earth's surface and melting the polar ice caps.

9. The atoms in salts emit light of characteristic wavelengths because of how their internal electron structures interact with the applied energy. Each element's atoms have a different electron structure, so each atom emits light differently from all other atoms.

10. exactly equal to

11. The ground state represents the lowest-energy state of the atom.

12. It is emitted as a photon.

13. $E = hc/\lambda$; short-wavelength light carries more energy

14. absorbs

15. The emission of light by excited atoms has been the key interconnection between the macroscopic world we can observe and measure and what is happening on a microscopic basis inside an atom.

16. When excited hydrogen atoms emit their excess energy, the photons of radiation emitted always have exactly the same wavelength and energy. This means that the hydrogen atom possesses only certain allowed energy states, and that the photons emitted correspond to the electron changing from one

TEACHING SUPPORT

BACKGROUND INFORMATION

Ionization Energy

In general, as we go *across a period from left to right, the first ionization energy increases.* This trend is consistent with the idea that electrons added in the same principal quantum level do not completely shield the increasing nuclear charge caused by the added protons. Thus electrons in the same principal quantum level are generally more strongly bound as we move to the right on the periodic table, and ionization energy values generally increase as electrons are added to a given principal quantum level.

By contrast, *first ionization energy decreases in going down a group.* This pattern can be seen most clearly by focusing on the Group 1A elements (the alkali metals) and the Group 8A elements (the noble gases). The decrease in

2. What major conclusions did Rutherford draw about the atom based on his gold foil bombardment experiments? What questions were left unanswered by Rutherford's experiments?

11.2 Electromagnetic Radiation

QUESTIONS

3. What is *electromagnetic radiation?* At what speed does electromagnetic radiation travel?
4. How are the different types of electromagnetic radiation similar? How do they differ?
5. What does the *wavelength* of electromagnetic radiation represent? How is the wavelength of radiation related to the *energy* of the photons of the radiation?
6. What do we mean by the *frequency* of electromagnetic radiation? Is the frequency the same as the *speed* of the electromagnetic radiation?
7. The "Chemistry in Focus" segment *Light as a Sex Attractant* discusses fluorescence. In fluorescence, ultraviolet radiation is absorbed and intense white visible light is emitted. Is ultraviolet radiation a higher or a lower energy radiation than visible light?
8. The "Chemistry in Focus" segment *Atmospheric Effects* discusses the greenhouse effect. How do the greenhouse gases CO_2, H_2O, and CH_4 have an effect on the temperature of the atmosphere?

11.3 Emission of Energy by Atoms

QUESTIONS

9. When lithium salts are heated in a flame, they emit red light. When copper salts are heated in a flame in the same manner, they emit green light. Why do we know that lithium salts will never emit green light, and copper salts will never emit red light?
10. The energy of a photon of visible light emitted by an excited atom is _______ the energy change that takes place within the atom itself.

11.4 The Energy Levels of Hydrogen

QUESTIONS

11. What does the *ground state* of an atom represent?
12. When an atom in an excited state returns to its ground state, what happens to the excess energy of the atom?
13. How is the energy carried per photon of light related to the wavelength of the light? Does short-wavelength light carry more energy or less energy than long-wavelength light?
14. When an atom _______ energy from outside, the atom goes from a lower energy state to a higher energy state.
15. Describe briefly why the study of electromagnetic radiation has been important to our understanding of the arrangement of electrons in atoms.
16. What does it mean to say that the hydrogen atom has *discrete energy levels?* How is this fact reflected in the radiation that excited hydrogen atoms emit?
17. Because a given element's atoms emit only certain photons of light, only certain _______ are occurring in those particular atoms.
18. How does the energy possessed by an emitted photon compare to the difference in energy levels that gave rise to the emission of the photon?
19. The energy levels of hydrogen (and other atoms) are said to be _______, which means that only certain energy values are allowed.
20. When a tube containing hydrogen atoms is energized by passing several thousand volts of electricity into the tube, the hydrogen emits light that, when passed through a prism, resolves into the "bright line" spectrum shown in Figure 11.11. Why do hydrogen atoms emit bright lines of specific wavelengths rather than a continuous spectrum?

11.5 The Bohr Model of the Atom

QUESTIONS

21. What are the essential points of Bohr's theory of the structure of the hydrogen atom?
22. According to Bohr, what happens to the electron when a hydrogen atom absorbs a photon of light of sufficient energy?
23. How does the Bohr theory account for the observed phenomenon of the emission of discrete wavelengths of light by excited atoms?
24. Why was Bohr's theory for the hydrogen atom initially accepted, and why was it ultimately discarded?

11.6 The Wave Mechanical Model of the Atom

QUESTIONS

25. What major assumption (that was analogous to what had already been demonstrated for electromagnetic radiation) did de Broglie and Schrödinger make about the motion of tiny particles?
26. Discuss briefly the difference between an orbit (as described by Bohr for hydrogen) and an orbital (as described by the more modern, wave mechanical picture of the atom).
27. Why was Schrödinger not able to describe exactly the pathway an electron takes as it moves through the space of an atom?
28. Section 11.6 uses a "firefly" analogy to illustrate how the wave mechanical model for the atom differs from Bohr's model. Explain this analogy.

All even-numbered Questions and Problems have answers in the back of this book and solutions in the Solutions Guide.

ionization energy in going down a group occurs largely because the electrons being removed are, on average, farther from the nucleus. As *n* increases, the size of the orbital increases, and the electron is easier to remove.

Some discontinuities in ionization energy occur in going across a period. For example, for Period 2, boron has a lower ionization energy than beryllium, and oxygen has a lower value than nitrogen. These exceptions to the normal trend can be explained in terms of electron repulsions. The decrease in ionization energy in going from beryllium to boron reflects the fact that the electrons in the filled 2*s* orbital provide some shielding for electrons in the 2*p* orbital from the nuclear charge. The decrease in ionization energy in going from nitrogen to oxygen reflects the extra electron repulsions in the doubly occupied oxygen 2*p* orbital.

of these allowed energy states to another allowed energy state. The energy of the photon emitted corresponds to the energy difference between the allowed states. If the hydrogen atom did *not* possess discrete energy levels, then the photons emitted would have random wavelengths and energies.

17. transitions of electrons

18. They are identical.

19. quantized

20. Energy is emitted at wavelengths corresponding to specific transitions for the electron among the energy levels of hydrogen.

21. Bohr pictured electrons as moving in circular orbits corresponding to the various allowed energy states. He suggested that an electron could jump to a different orbit by absorbing or emitting a photon with energy content corresponding to the difference in energy between the orbits.

22. The electron moves to an orbit farther from the nucleus of the atom.

23. Bohr suggested that an electron could jump to a different orbit by absorbing or emitting a photon of light with exactly the correct energy content (corresponding to the difference in energy between the orbits). Since the energy levels of a given atom are fixed and definite, then the atom should always emit energy at the same discrete wavelengths.

24. Bohr's theory explained the experimentally observed line spectrum of hydrogen exactly. The theory was discarded because the calculated properties did not correspond closely to experimental measurements for atoms other than hydrogen.

25. Schrödinger and de Broglie reasoned that, since light seems to have both wave and particle characteristics, then perhaps the electron might also exhibit both characteristics. That is, al-

11.7 The Hydrogen Orbitals

QUESTIONS

29. Your text describes the probability map for an *s* orbital using an analogy to the earth's atmosphere. Explain this analogy.

30. When students first see a drawing of the *p* orbitals, they often question how the electron is able to jump through the nucleus to get from one lobe of the *p* orbital to the other. How would you explain this?

31. What are the differences between the 2*s* orbital and the 1*s* orbital of hydrogen? How are they similar?

32. What overall shape do the 2*p* and 3*p* orbitals have? How do the 2*p* orbitals differ from the 3*p* orbitals? How are they similar?

33. The higher the principal energy level, *n*, the (closer to/farther from) the nucleus is the electron.

34. When the electron in hydrogen is in the $n =$ ______ principal energy level, the atom is in its ground state.

35. Although a hydrogen atom has only one electron, the hydrogen atom possesses a complete set of available orbitals. What purpose do these additional orbitals serve?

36. Complete the following table.

Value of *n*	Possible Sublevels
1	______
2	______
3	______
4	______

11.8 The Wave Mechanical Model: Further Development

QUESTIONS

37. When describing the electrons in an orbital, we use arrows pointing upward and downward (↑ and ↓) to indicate what property?

38. Why can only two electrons occupy a particular orbital? What is this idea called?

39. How does the *energy* of a principal energy level depend on the value of *n*? Does a higher value of *n* mean a higher or lower energy?

40. The number of sublevels in a principal energy level (increases/decreases) as *n* increases.

41. According to the Pauli exclusion principle, a given orbital can contain only ______ electrons.

42. According to the Pauli exclusion principle, the electrons within a given orbital must have ______ spins.

43. Which of the following orbital designations is(are) possible?

a. 1*s* c. 2*d*
b. 2*p* d. 4*f*

44. Which of the following orbital designations is(are) *not* possible?

a. 3*f* c. 2*d*
b. 4*d* d. 1*p*

11.9 Electron Arrangements in the First Eighteen Atoms on the Periodic Table

QUESTIONS

45. Which orbital is the *first* to be filled in any atom? Why?

46. When a hydrogen atom is in its ground state, in which orbital is its electron found? Why?

47. Where are the *valence electrons* found in an atom, and why are these particular electrons most important to the chemical properties of the atom?

48. How are the electron arrangements in a given group (vertical column) of the periodic table related? How is this relationship manifested in the properties of the elements in the given group?

PROBLEMS

49. Write the full electron configuration ($1s^22s^2$, etc.) for each of the following elements.

a. magnesium, $Z = 12$
b. lithium, $Z = 3$
c. oxygen, $Z = 8$
d. sulfur, $Z = 16$

50. To which element does each of the following electron configurations correspond?

a. $1s^22s^22p^63s^23p^2$ c. $1s^22s^22p^6$
b. $1s^22s^2$ d. $1s^22s^22p^63s^23p^6$

51. Write the full electron configuration ($1s^22s^2$, etc.) for each of the following elements.

a. phosphorus, $Z = 15$
b. calcium, $Z = 20$
c. potassium, $Z = 19$
d. boron, $Z = 5$

52. To which element does each of the following electron configurations correspond?

a. $1s^22s^22p^63s^23p^64s^23d^{10}4p^4$
b. $1s^22s^22p^63s^23p^64s^23d^1$
c. $1s^22s^22p^63s^23p^4$
d. $1s^22s^22p^63s^23p^64s^23d^{10}4p^65s^24d^{10}5p^5$

53. Write the complete orbital diagram for each of the following elements, using boxes to represent orbitals and arrows to represent electrons.

a. helium, $Z = 2$ c. krypton, $Z = 36$
b. neon, $Z = 10$ d. xenon, $Z = 54$

All even-numbered Questions and Problems have answers in the back of this book and solutions in the Solutions Guide.

though the electron behaves as a discrete particle, perhaps the properties of the electron in the atom could be treated as if they were wavelike.

26. An orbit refers to a definite, exact circular pathway around the nucleus, in which Bohr postulated that an electron would be found. An orbital represents a region of space in which there is a high probability of finding the electron.

27. Schrödinger's mathematical treatment could only describe the movement of the electron through the atom in terms of the *probability* of finding the electron in a given region of space within the atom, but not at a particular point within the atom at a particular time. Any experimental attempt to determine the exact position of the electron within an atom would, in fact, disturb the electron from wherever it had been.

28. The firefly analogy is intended to demonstrate the concept of a probability map for electron density. In the wave mechanical model of the atom, we cannot say specifically where the electron is in the atom; we can say only where there is a high probability of finding the electron. The analogy is to imagine a time-exposure photograph of a firefly in a closed room. Most of the time, the firefly will be found near the center of the room.

29. Although the probability of finding the electron decreases at greater distances from the nucleus, the probability of finding it even at great distances from the nucleus never becomes exactly zero. The probability becomes increasingly less as you move away from the nucleus, similar to the way the atmosphere becomes increasingly thinner as you move away from the surface of the earth.

30. The drawing is a contour map, indicating a 90% probability that the electron is within the region of space bounded by that region. The electron may be anywhere within this region.

31. The 2*s* orbital is similar in shape to the 1*s* orbital, but is larger.

32. two-lobed ("dumbbell"-shaped); lower in energy and closer to the nucleus; similar shape

33. farther from

34. 1

35. The other orbitals serve as the excited states for hydrogen.

36.

Value of n	*Possible Subshells*
1	1*s*
2	2*s*, 2*p*
3	3*s*, 3*p*, 3*d*
4	4*s*, 4*p*, 4*d*, 4*f*

54. Write the complete orbital diagram for each of the following elements, using boxes to represent orbitals and arrows to represent electrons.

a. magnesium, $Z = 12$
b. argon, $Z = 18$
c. lithium, $Z = 3$
d. arsenic, $Z = 33$

55. The "Chemistry in Focus" segment *A Magnetic Moment* discusses the ability to levitate a frog in a magnetic field because electrons, when sensing a strong magnetic field, respond by opposing it. This is called *diamagnetism*. Atoms that are diamagnetic have all paired electrons. Which columns among the representative elements in the periodic table consist of diamagnetic atoms? Consider orbital diagrams when answering this question.

56. For each of the following, give an atom and its complete electron configuration that would be expected to have the indicated number of valence electrons.

a. one
b. three
c. five
d. seven

11.10 Electron Configurations and the Periodic Table

QUESTIONS

57. Why do we believe that the valence electrons of calcium and potassium reside in the 4*s* orbital rather than in the 3*d* orbital?

58. Would you expect the valence electrons of rubidium and strontium to reside in the 5*s* or the 4*d* orbitals? Why?

PROBLEMS

59. Using the symbol of the previous noble gas to indicate the core electrons, write the electron configuration for each of the following elements.

a. arsenic, $Z = 33$
b. titanium, $Z = 22$
c. strontium, $Z = 38$
d. chlorine, $Z = 17$

60. To which element does each of the following abbreviated electron configurations refer?

a. $[Ne]3s^2 3p^1$
b. $[Ar]4s^1$
c. $[Ar]4s^2 3d^{10} 4p^5$
d. $[Kr]5s^2 4d^{10} 5p^2$

61. Using the symbol of the previous noble gas to indicate the core electrons, write the electron configuration for each of the following elements.

a. scandium, $Z = 21$
b. yttrium, $Z = 39$
c. lanthanum, $Z = 57$
d. actinium, $Z = 89$

62. Using the symbol of the previous noble gas to indicate the core electrons, write the valence shell electron configuration for each of the following elements.

a. phosphorus, $Z = 15$
b. chlorine, $Z = 17$
c. magnesium, $Z = 12$
d. zinc, $Z = 30$

63. How many 3*d* electrons are found in each of the following elements?

a. nickel, $Z = 28$
b. vanadium, $Z = 23$
c. manganese, $Z = 25$
d. iron, $Z = 26$

64. How many 4*d* electrons are found in each of the following elements?

a. yttrium, $Z = 39$
b. zirconium, $Z = 40$
c. strontium, $Z = 38$
d. cadmium, $Z = 48$

65. For each of the following elements, indicate which set of orbitals is filled last.

a. radium, $Z = 88$
b. iodine, $Z = 53$
c. gold, $Z = 79$
d. lead, $Z = 82$

66. For each of the following elements, indicate which set of orbitals is being filled last.

a. plutonium, $Z = 94$
b. nobelium, $Z = 102$
c. praseodymium, $Z = 59$
d. radon, $Z = 86$

67. Write the valence shell electron configuration of each of the following elements, basing your answer on the element's location on the periodic table.

a. rubidium, $Z = 37$
b. barium, $Z = 56$
c. titanium, $Z = 22$
d. germanium, $Z = 32$

68. The "Chemistry in Focus" segment *The Chemistry of Bohrium* discusses element 107, bohrium (Bh). What is the expected electron configuration of Bh?

11.11 Atomic Properties and the Periodic Table

QUESTIONS

69. What are some of the physical properties that distinguish the metallic elements from the nonmetals? Are these properties absolute, or do some nonmetallic elements exhibit some metallic properties (and vice versa)?

70. What types of ions do the metals and the nonmetallic elements form? Do the metals lose or gain electrons in doing this? Do the nonmetallic elements gain or lose electrons in doing this?

71. Give some similarities that exist among the elements of Group 1.

72. Give some similarities that exist among the elements of Group 7.

73. Which of the following elements most easily gives up electrons during reactions: Li, K, or Cs? Explain your choice.

74. Which elements in a given period (horizontal row) of the periodic table lose electrons most easily? Why?

75. Where are the most nonmetallic elements located on the periodic table? Why do these elements pull electrons from metallic elements so effectively during a reaction?

All even-numbered Questions and Problems have answers in the back of this book and solutions in the Solutions Guide.

37. electron spin

38. Electrons have an intrinsic spin (they spin on their own axes). Geometrically, there are only two senses possible for spin (clockwise or counterclockwise). This means only two electrons can occupy an orbital, with the opposite sense or direction of spin. This idea is called the Pauli exclusion principle.

39. The higher the value of *n*, the higher the energy.

40. increases

41. two

42. paired (opposite spin)

43. (a) possible; (b) possible; (c) not possible; (d) possible

44. (a) not possible; (b) possible; (c) possible; (d) not possible

45. 1*s*; closest to nucleus and lowest in energy

46. For a hydrogen atom in its ground state, the electron is in the 1*s* orbital. The 1*s* orbital has the lowest energy of all hydrogen orbitals.

47. The valence electrons are those in the outermost energy shell; these electrons come "in contact with" other atoms for reaction.

48. similar type of orbitals being filled in the same way; chemical properties of the members of the group are similar

49. (a) $1s^2\,2s^2\,2p^6\,3s^2$; (b) $1s^2\,2s^1$; (c) $1s^2\,2s^2\,2p^4$; (d) $1s^2\,2s^2\,2p^6\,3s^2\,3p^4$

50. (a) silicon; (b) beryllium; (c) neon; (d) argon

51. (a) $1s^2\,2s^2\,2p^6\,3s^2\,3p^3$; (b) $1s^2\,2s^2\,2p^6\,3s^2\,3p^6\,4s^2$; (c) $1s^2\,2s^2\,2p^6\,3s^2\,3p^6\,4s^1$; (d) $1s^2\,2s^2\,2p^1$

52. (a) selenium; (b) scandium; (c) sulfur; (d) iodine

53. See bottom of page.

54. See bottom of page.

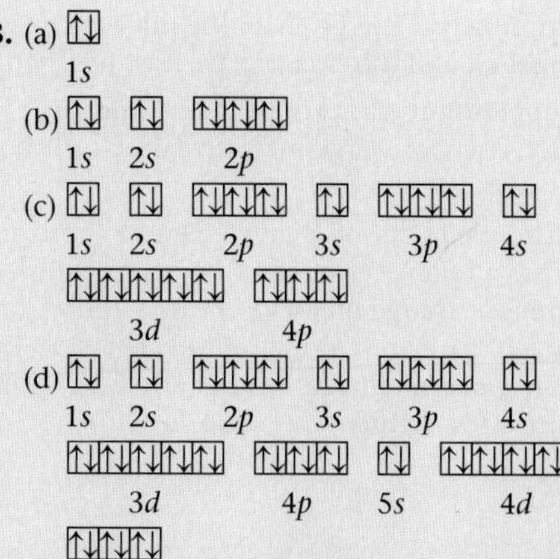

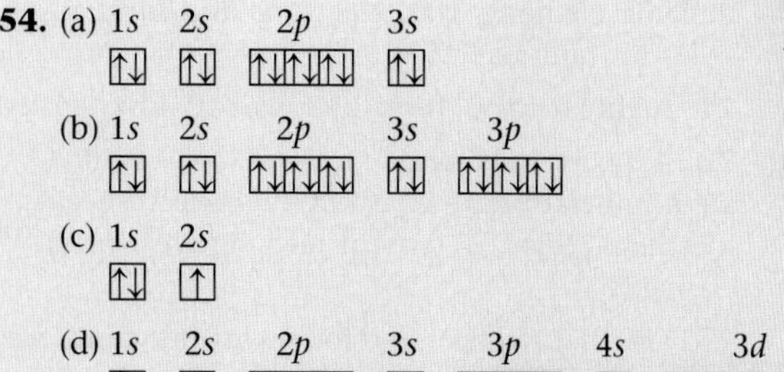

76. Why do the metallic elements of a given period (horizontal row) typically have much lower ionization energies than do the nonmetallic elements of the same period?

77. What are the *metalloids?* Where are the metalloids found on the periodic table?

F 78. The "Chemistry in Focus" segment *Fireworks* discusses some of the chemicals that give rise to the colors of fireworks. How do these colors support the existence of quantized energy levels in atoms?

PROBLEMS

79. In each of the following groups, which element is least reactive?

a. Group 1
b. Group 7
c. Group 2
d. Group 6

80. In each of the following sets of elements, which element would be expected to have the highest ionization energy?

a. Cs, K, Li
b. Ba, Sr, Ca
c. I, Br, Cl
d. Mg, Si, S

81. Arrange the following sets of elements in order of increasing atomic size.

a. Sn, Xe, Rb, Sr
b. Rn, He, Xe, Kr
c. Pb, Ba, Cs, At

82. In each of the following sets of elements, indicate which element has the smallest atomic size.

a. Na, K, Rb
b. Na, Si, S
c. N, P, As
d. N, O, F

Additional Problems

83. Consider the bright line spectrum of hydrogen shown in Figure 11.11. Which line in the spectrum represents photons with the highest energy? With the lowest energy?

84. The speed at which electromagnetic radiation moves through a vacuum is called the ______.

85. The portion of the electromagnetic spectrum between wavelengths of approximately 400 and 700 nanometers is called the ______ region.

86. A beam of light can be thought of as consisting of a stream of light particles called ______.

87. The lowest possible energy state of an atom is called the ______ state.

88. The energy levels of hydrogen (and other atoms) are ______, which means that only certain values of energy are allowed.

89. According to Bohr, the electron in the hydrogen atom moved around the nucleus in circular paths called ______.

90. In the modern theory of the atom, a(n) ______ represents a region of space in which there is a high probability of finding an electron.

91. Electrons found in the outermost principal energy level of an atom are referred to as ______ electrons.

92. An element with partially filled *d* orbitals is called a(n) ______.

93. The ______ of electromagnetic radiation represents the number of waves passing a given point in space each second.

94. Only two electrons can occupy a given orbital in an atom, and to be in the same orbital, they must have opposite ______.

95. One bit of evidence that the present theory of atomic structure is "correct" lies in the magnetic properties of matter. Atoms with *unpaired* electrons are attracted by magnetic fields and thus are said to exhibit *paramagnetism*. The degree to which this effect is observed is directly related to the *number* of unpaired electrons present in the atom. On the basis of the electron orbital diagrams for the following elements, indicate which atoms would be expected to be paramagnetic, and tell how many unpaired electrons each atom contains.

a. phosphorus, $Z = 15$
b. iodine, $Z = 53$
c. germanium, $Z = 32$

96. Without referring to your textbook or a periodic table, write the full electron configuration, the orbital box diagram, and the noble gas shorthand configuration for the elements with the following atomic numbers.

a. $Z = 19$
b. $Z = 22$
c. $Z = 14$
d. $Z = 26$
e. $Z = 30$

97. Without referring to your textbook or a periodic table, write the full electron configuration, the orbital box diagram, and the noble gas shorthand configuration for the elements with the following atomic numbers.

a. $Z = 21$
b. $Z = 15$
c. $Z = 36$
d. $Z = 38$
e. $Z = 30$

98. Write the general valence configuration (for example, ns^1 for Group 1) for the group in which each of the following elements is found.

a. barium, $Z = 56$
b. bromine, $Z = 35$
c. tellurium, $Z = 52$
d. potassium, $Z = 19$
e. sulfur, $Z = 16$

99. How many valence electrons does each of the following atoms have?

a. titanium, $Z = 22$
b. iodine, $Z = 53$
c. radium, $Z = 88$
d. manganese, $Z = 25$

All even-numbered Questions and Problems have answers in the back of this book and solutions in the Solutions Guide.

55. Group 2 (ns^2) and Group 8 ($ns^2\ np^6$) are the only groups where all electrons are paired.

56. Specific answers depend on student choice of elements. Any Group 1 element would have one valence electron. Any Group 3 element would have three valence electrons. Any Group 5 element would have five valence electrons. Any Group 7 element would have seven valence electrons.

57. based on the experimental properties of K and Ca; K's properties are similar to those of the other members of Group 1; Ca's properties are similar to those of the other members of Group 2

58. The properties of Rb and Sr suggest that they are members of Groups 1 and 2, respectively, and so must be filling the 5*s* orbital. The 5*s* orbital is lower in energy than (and fills before) the 4*d* orbitals.

59. (a) [Ar] $4s^23d^{10}4p^3$; (b) [Ar] $4s^2\ 3d^2$; (c) [Kr]$5s^2$; (d) [Ne] $3s^23p^5$

60. (a) aluminum; (b) potassium; (c) bromine; (d) tin

61. (a) [Ar]$4s^23d^1$; (b) [Kr]$5s^24d^1$; (c) [Xe]$6s^25d^1$; (d) [Rn]$7s^26d^1$

62. (a) [Ne]$3s^23p^3$; (b) [Ne]$3s^23p^5$; (c) [Ne]$3s^2$; (d) [Ar]$4s^23d^{10}$

63. (a) eight; (b) three; (c) five; (d) six

64. (a) 1; (b) 2; (c) 0; (d) 10

65. (a) 7*s*; (b) 5*p*; (c) 5*d*; (d) 6*p*

66. (a) 5*f*; (b) 5*f*; (c) 4*f*; (d) 6*p*

67. (a) [Kr] $5s^1$ (b) [Xe] $6s^2$ (c) [Ar] $4s^2\ 3d^2$ (d) [Ar] $4s^2\ 3d^{10}4p^2$

68. [Rn] $7s^25f^{14}6d^5$

69. metals: lustrous, malleable, ductile, conductors of heat and electricity; nonmetals: nonlustrous, brittle, nonconductors

70. The metallic elements lose electrons and form positive ions (cations); the nonmetallic elements gain electrons and form negative ions (anions).

71. highly reactive, form 1+ ions, soft, low density

72. All exist as diatomic molecules (F_2, Cl_2, Br_2, I_2); are nonmetals; have relatively high electronegativities; and form 1− ions in reacting with metallic elements.

73. Cs: the valence electron is farther from the nucleus in Cs than in Li or K.

74. Elements at the left of a period (horizontal row) lose electrons most readily; at the left of a period (given principal energy level) the nuclear charge is the smallest and the electrons are least tightly held.

75. upper-right corner of periodic table; high ionization energies, larger effective nuclear charge pulling on the subshell

76. The elements of a given period (horizontal row) have valence electrons in the same subshells, but nuclear charge increases across a period going from left to right. Atoms at the left side have smaller nuclear charges and bind their valence electrons less tightly.

100. In the text (Section 11.6) it was mentioned that current theories of atomic structure suggest that all matter and all energy demonstrate both particle-like and wave-like properties under the appropriate conditions, although the wave-like nature of matter becomes apparent only in very small and very fast-moving particles. The relationship between wavelength (λ) observed for a particle and the mass and velocity of that particle is called the de Broglie relationship. It is

$$\lambda = h/mv$$

in which h is Planck's constant (6.63×10^{-34} J · s),* m represents the mass of the particle in kilograms, and v represents the velocity of the particle in meters per second. Calculate the "de Broglie wavelength" for each of the following, and use your numerical answers to explain why macroscopic (large) objects are not ordinarily discussed in terms of their "wave-like" properties.

a. an electron moving at 0.90 times the speed of light
b. a 150-g ball moving at a speed of 10. m/s
c. a 75-kg person walking at a speed of 2 km/h

101. Light waves move through space at a speed of ______ meters per second.

102. How do we know that the energy levels of the hydrogen atom are not *continuous,* as physicists originally assumed?

103. How does the attractive force that the nucleus exerts on an electron change with the principal energy level of the electron?

104. Into how many sublevels is the third principal energy level of hydrogen divided? What are the names of the orbitals that constitute these sublevels? What are the general shapes of these orbitals?

105. A student writes the electron configuration of carbon ($Z = 6$) as $1s^32s^3$. Explain to him what is *wrong* with this configuration.

106. Write three orbital designations that would be *incorrect* and explain *why* each is incorrect. For example, 1*p* would be an incorrect orbital designation because there is no *p* subshell in the first orbit.

107. Why do we believe that the three electrons in the 2*p* sublevel of nitrogen occupy different orbitals?

108. Write the full electron configuration ($1s^22s^2$, etc.) for each of the following elements.

a. bromine, $Z = 35$
b. xenon, $Z = 54$
c. barium, $Z = 56$
d. selenium, $Z = 34$

*Note that s is the abbreviation for "seconds."

109. Write the complete orbital diagram for each of the following elements, using boxes to represent orbitals and arrows to represent electrons.

a. scandium, $Z = 21$
b. sulfur, $Z = 16$
c. potassium, $Z = 19$
d. nitrogen, $Z = 7$

110. How many valence electrons does each of the following atoms have?

a. nitrogen, $Z = 7$
b. chlorine, $Z = 17$
c. sodium, $Z = 11$
d. aluminum, $Z = 13$

111. What name is given to the series of ten elements in which the electrons are filling the 3*d* sublevel?

112. Using the symbol of the previous noble gas to indicate the core electrons, write the valence shell electron configuration for each of the following elements.

a. zirconium, $Z = 40$
b. iodine, $Z = 53$
c. germanium, $Z = 32$
d. cesium, $Z = 55$

113. Using the symbol of the previous noble gas to indicate core electrons, write the valence shell electron configuration for each of the following elements.

a. titanium, $Z = 22$
b. selenium, $Z = 34$
c. antimony, $Z = 51$
d. strontium, $Z = 38$

114. Identify the element corresponding to each of the following electron configurations.

a. $1s^22s^22p^63s^23p^64s^23d^{10}4p^4$
b. $[Ar]4s^23d^{10}4p^4$
c. $1s^22s^22p^63s^23p^64s^23d^{10}4p^65s^1$
d. $1s^22s^22p^63s^23p^64s^23d^3$

115. Write the shorthand valence shell electron configuration of each of the following elements, basing your answer on the element's location on the periodic table.

a. nickel, $Z = 28$
b. niobium, $Z = 41$
c. hafnium, $Z = 72$
d. astatine, $Z = 85$

116. Metals have relatively (low/high) ionization energies, whereas nonmetals have relatively (high/low) ionization energies.

117. In each of the following sets of elements, indicate which element shows the most active chemical behavior.

a. B, Al, In b. Na, Al, S c. B, C, F

118. In each of the following sets of elements, indicate which element has the smallest atomic size.

a. Ba, Ca, Ra b. P, Si, Al c. Rb, Cs, K

All even-numbered Questions and Problems have answers in the back of this book and solutions in the Solutions Guide.

77. Metalloids are elements that have both metallic and nonmetallic properties. They are located along either side of the "stair-step" toward the right side of the periodic table.

78. When substances absorb energy, the electrons become excited (move to higher energy levels). Upon returning to the ground state, energy is released, some of which is in the visible spectrum. Because we see colors, this tells us only certain wavelengths of light are released, which means that only certain transitions are allowed. This is what is meant by quantized energy levels. If all wavelengths of light were emitted, we would see white light.

79. (a) Li; (b) At; (c) Be; (d) Po

80. (a) Li; (b) Ca; (c) Cl; (d) S

81. (a) Xe < Sn < Sr < Rb; (b) He < Kr < Xe < Rn; (c) At < Pb < Ba < Cs

82. (a) Na; (b) S; (c) N; (d) F

83. The highest-energy photons are responsible for the line at 410 nm; the lowest-energy photons give rise to the line at 656 nm.

84. speed of light

85. visible

86. photons

87. ground

88. quantized

89. orbits

90. orbital

91. valence

92. transition metal

93. frequency

94. spins

95. (a) paramagnetic, three unpaired electrons; (b) paramagnetic, one unpaired electron; (c) paramagnetic, two unpaired electrons

96. See bottom of page

96. (a) $1s^22s^22p^63s^23p^64s^1$; $[Ar]4s^1$;

↑↓	↑↓	↑↓ ↑↓ ↑↓	↑↓	↑↓ ↑↓ ↑↓	↑
1*s*	2*s*	2*p*	3*s*	3*p*	4*s*

(b) $1s^22s^22p^63s^23p^64s^23d^2$; $[Ar]4s^23d^2$;

↑↓	↑↓	↑↓ ↑↓ ↑↓	↑↓	↑↓ ↑↓ ↑↓	↑↓
1*s*	2*s*	2*p*	3*s*	3*p*	4*s*

↑	↑			

3*d*

(c) $1s^22s^22p^63s^23p^2$; $[Ne]3s^23p^2$;

↑↓	↑↓	↑↓ ↑↓ ↑↓	↑↓	↑ ↑
1*s*	2*s*	2*p*	3*s*	3*p*

(d) $1s^22s^22p^63s^23p^64s^23d^6$; $[Ar]4s^23d^6$;

↑↓	↑↓	↑↓ ↑↓ ↑↓	↑↓	↑↓ ↑↓ ↑↓	↑↓
1*s*	2*s*	2*p*	3*s*	3*p*	4*s*

↑↓	↑	↑	↑	↑

3*d*

(e) $1s^22s^22p^63s^23p^64s^23d^{10}$; $[Ar]4s^23d^{10}$;

↑↓	↑↓	↑↓ ↑↓ ↑↓	↑↓	↑↓ ↑↓ ↑↓	↑↓
1*s*	2*s*	2*p*	3*s*	3*p*	4*s*

↑↓	↑↓	↑↓	↑↓	↑↓

3*d*

(Please refer to page A27 in this book for answers to Exercises 97–118.)

Chapter 12

Objectives

In this chapter, our objectives are for the students to:

SECTION 12.1

- Learn about ionic and covalent bonds and explain how they are formed.
- Learn about the polar covalent bond.

SECTION 12.2

- Understand the nature of bonds and their relationship to electronegativity.

SECTION 12.3

- Understand bond polarity and how it is related to molecular polarity.

SECTION 12.4

- Learn about stable electron configurations.
- Learn to predict the formulas of ionic compounds.

SECTION 12.5

- Learn about ionic structures.
- Understand factors governing ionic size.

SECTION 12.6

- Learn to write Lewis structures.

SECTION 12.7

- Learn to write Lewis structures for molecules with multiple bonds.

SECTION 12.8

- Understand molecular structure and bond angles.

SECTION 12.9

- Learn to predict molecular geometry from the number of electron pairs.

SECTION 12.10

- Learn to apply the VSEPR model to molecules with double bonds.

12 Chemical Bonding

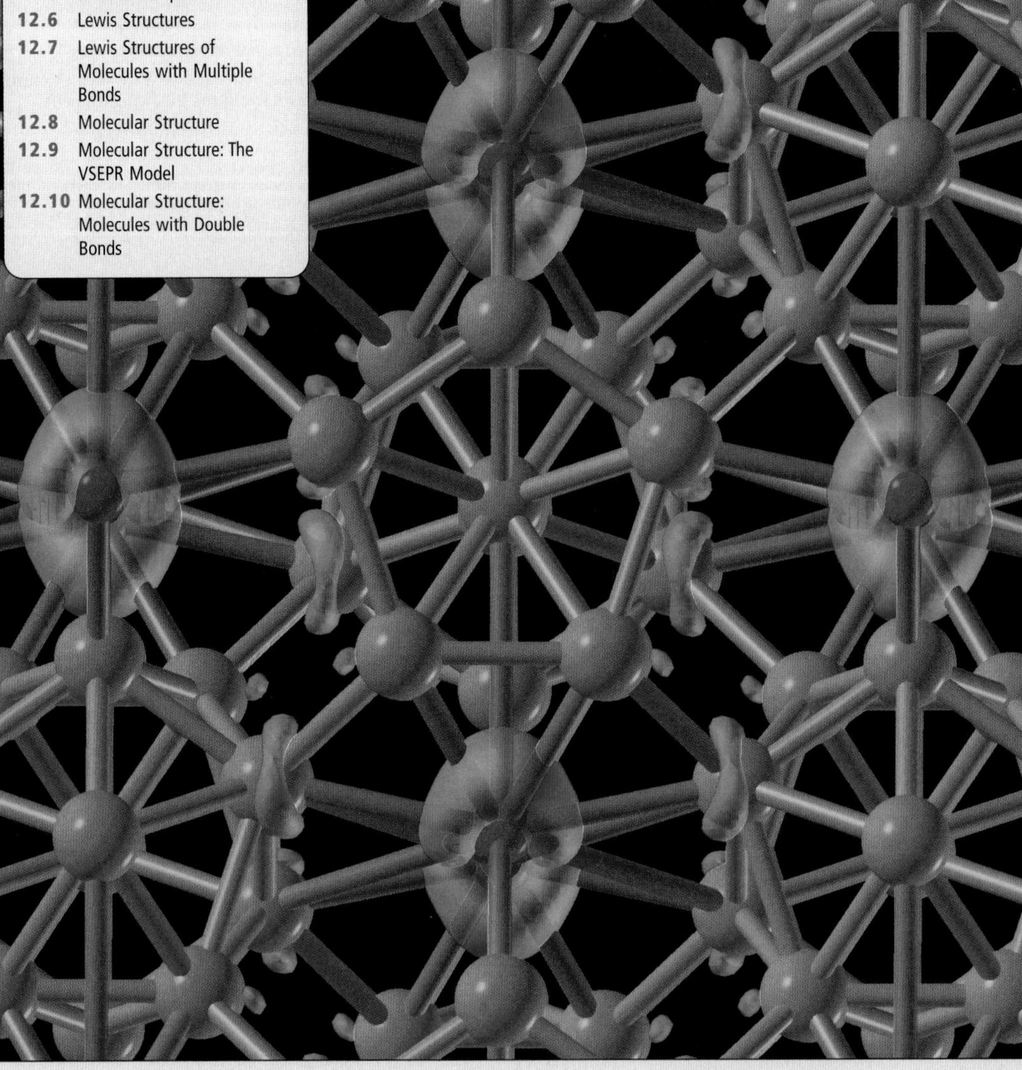

The ionic structure of boron. *(Artem Oganov/Stony Brook University, New York)*

ChemWork Refined over ten years of use by thousands of students, **ChemWork** builds and enhances students' problems-solving skills. Online assignments function as a "personal instructor" to help students learn how to solve challenging problems and learn how to think like chemists. Annotations for **ChemWork** assignments are included at the beginning of the end-of-chapter review.

PowerLecture This 2-DVD package includes the Chemistry Multimedia Library, which contains animations, simulations, and movies for all chemistry subjects, organized by topic for lecture presentations. Annotations for **PowerLecture** are referenced in the margins throughout the Annotated Instructor's Edition.

OWL Sign in to OWL at **www.cengage.com/owl** to view tutorials and simulations, develop problem-solving skills, and complete online homework assigned by your professor.

go Chemistry Download mini-lecture videos for key concept review and exam prep from OWL or purchase them from **www.ichapters.com**

The world around us is composed almost entirely of compounds and mixtures of compounds. Rocks, coal, soil, petroleum, trees, and human beings are all complex mixtures of chemical compounds in which different kinds of atoms are bound together. Most of the pure elements found in the earth's crust also contain many atoms bound together. In a gold nugget each gold atom is bound to many other gold atoms, and in a diamond many carbon atoms are bonded very strongly to each other. Substances composed of unbound atoms do exist in nature, but they are very rare. (Examples include the argon atoms in the atmosphere and the helium atoms found in natural gas reserves.)

Tino Hammid

Diamond, composed of carbon atoms bonded together to produce one of the hardest materials known, makes a beautiful gemstone.

The manner in which atoms are bound together has a profound effect on the chemical and physical properties of substances. For example, both graphite and diamond are composed solely of carbon atoms. However, graphite is a soft, slippery material used as a lubricant in locks, and diamond is one of the hardest materials known, valuable both as a gemstone and in industrial cutting tools. Why do these materials, both composed solely of carbon atoms, have such different properties? The answer lies in the different ways in which the carbon atoms are bound to each other in these substances.

Molecular bonding and structure play the central role in determining the course of chemical reactions, many of which are vital to our survival. Most reactions in biological systems are very sensitive to the structures of the participating molecules; in fact, very subtle differences in shape sometimes serve to channel the chemical reaction one way rather than another. Molecules that act as drugs must have exactly the right structure to perform their functions correctly. Structure also plays a central role in our senses of smell and taste. Substances have a particular odor because they fit into the specially shaped receptors in our nasal passages. Taste is also dependent on molecular shape, as we discuss in the "Chemistry in Focus" on page 383.

To understand the behavior of natural materials, we must understand the nature of chemical bonding and the factors that control the structures of compounds. In this chapter, we will present various classes of compounds that illustrate the different types of bonds. We will then develop models to describe the structure and bonding that characterize the materials found in nature.

Test Bank: 1–4, 12, 45

12.1 Types of Chemical Bonds

Section 12.1

OBJECTIVES: To learn about ionic and covalent bonds and explain how they are formed. • To learn about the polar covalent bond.

A water molecule.

What is a chemical bond? Although there are several possible ways to answer this question, we will define a **bond** as a force that holds groups of two or more atoms together and makes them function as a unit. For example, in water the fundamental unit is the H—O—H molecule, which we describe as

TEACHING TIPS

- Ionic and covalent bonding are the two extremes of bonding. Students should understand that attractive forces between molecules lie along a continuum.
- Focus students' attention on where the electrons "spend more time." Are they shared equally between two atoms or do they spend more time closer to one atom in the bond? This focus will help students understand the concept of bond polarity.

TEACHING SUPPORT

BACKGROUND INFORMATION

Models originate from our observations of the properties of nature. For example, the concept of bonds arose from observations that most chemical processes involve collections of atoms and that chemical reactions involve rearrangements of the ways the atoms are grouped. Therefore, to understand reactions, we must understand the forces that bind atoms together.

Natural processes are characterized by a tendency toward lower energy. Collections of atoms occur because the aggregated state has lower energy than the separated atoms. Why? As we saw earlier, the best explanations for the energy change involve atoms sharing electrons or atoms transferring electrons to become ions. In the case of electron sharing, we find it convenient to assume that individual bonds occur between pairs of atoms.

TEACHING TIP

While the electrons are simultaneously attracted to both nuclei, the nuclei of the hydrogen atoms repel each other.

PowerLecture Video: Comparison of a Molecular Compound and an Ionic Compound

Lecture Demonstration: 2.9, 2.10

Lecture Demonstration: 2.11, 2.12

PowerLecture Animation: Interatomic Electrostatic Interactions

PowerLecture Animation: Covalent Bonding

being held together by the two O—H bonds. We can obtain information about the strength of a bond by measuring the energy required to break the bond, the **bond energy.**

Atoms can interact with one another in several ways to form aggregates. We will consider specific examples to illustrate the various types of chemical bonds.

In Chapter 7 we saw that when solid sodium chloride is dissolved in water, the resulting solution conducts electricity, a fact that convinces chemists that sodium chloride is composed of Na^+ and Cl^- ions. Thus, when sodium and chlorine react to form sodium chloride, electrons are transferred from the sodium atoms to the chlorine atoms to form Na^+ and Cl^- ions, which then aggregate to form solid sodium chloride. The resulting solid sodium chloride is a very sturdy material; it has a melting point of approximately 800 °C. The strong bonding forces present in sodium chloride result from the attractions among the closely packed, oppositely charged ions. This is an example of **ionic bonding.** Ionic substances are formed when an atom that loses electrons relatively easily reacts with an atom that has a high affinity for electrons. In other words, an **ionic compound** results when a metal reacts with a nonmetal.

Metal
Nonmetal
Ionic compound
M + X
e⁻
M⁺ X⁻

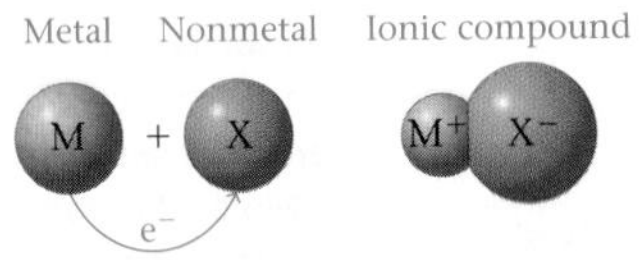

We have seen that a bonding force develops when two very different types of atoms react to form oppositely charged ions. But how does a bonding force develop between two identical atoms? Let's explore this situation by considering what happens when two hydrogen atoms are brought close together, as shown in Figure 12.1. When hydrogen atoms are close together, the two electrons are simultaneously attracted to both nuclei. Note in Figure 12.1b how the electron probability increases between the two nuclei indicating that the electrons are shared by the two nuclei.

The type of bonding we encounter in the hydrogen molecule and in many other molecules where *electrons are shared by nuclei* is called **covalent bonding.** Note that in the H_2 molecule the electrons reside primarily in the space between the two nuclei, where they are attracted simultaneously by both protons. Although we will not go into detail about it here, the increased attractive forces in this area lead to the formation of the H_2 molecule from

Two separate hydrogen atoms.
Hydrogen atoms sufficiently far apart to have no interaction
H atom
H atom
a
When two hydrogen atoms come close together, the two electrons are attracted simultaneously by both nuclei. This produces the bond. Note the relatively large electron probability between the nuclei indicating sharing of the electrons.
H_2 molecule
b

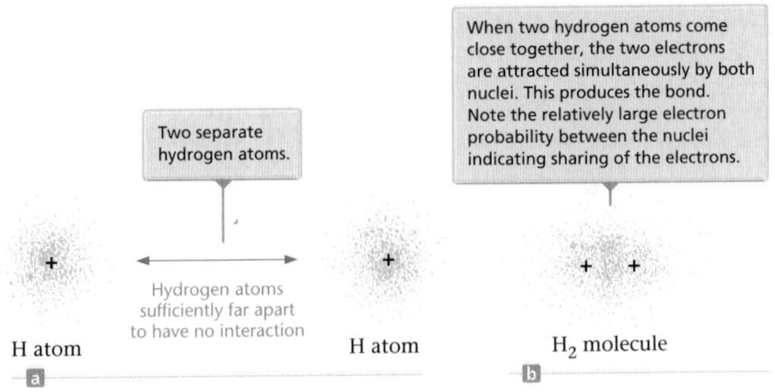

Figure 12.1 The formation of a bond between two hydrogen atoms.

The bonding model provides a framework to systematize chemical behavior by enabling us to think of molecules as a collection of common fundamental components. A typical biomolecule, such as a protein, contains hundreds of atoms and might seem discouragingly complex. However, if we think of a protein as being constructed of individual bonds, C—C, C—H, C—N, C—O, N—H, and so on, it helps tremendously in predicting and understanding the protein's behavior. The essential idea is that we expect a given bond to behave about the same way in any molecular environment. Used in this way, the model of the chemical bond has helped chemists to systematize the reactions of the millions of existing compounds.

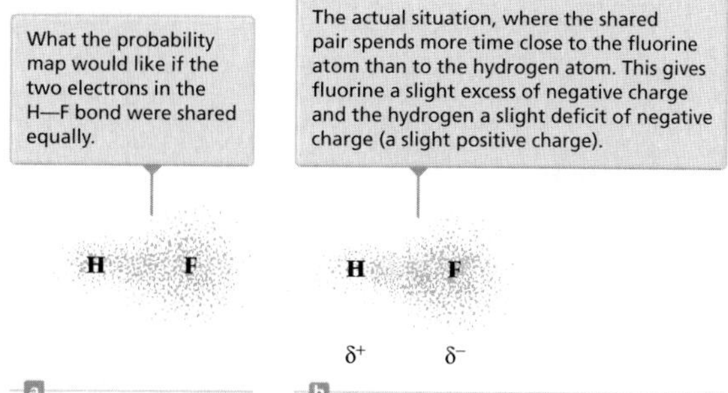
What the probability map would like if the two electrons in the H—F bond were shared equally.
The actual situation, where the shared pair spends more time close to the fluorine atom than to the hydrogen atom. This gives fluorine a slight excess of negative charge and the hydrogen a slight deficit of negative charge (a slight positive charge).
H
F
H
F
δ+
δ−
a
b

Figure 12.2
Probability representations of the electron sharing in HF.

the two separated hydrogen atoms. When we say that a bond is formed between the hydrogen atoms, we mean that the H_2 molecule is more stable than two separated hydrogen atoms by a certain quantity of energy (the bond energy).

Ionic and covalent bonds are the extreme bond types.

So far we have considered two extreme types of bonding. In ionic bonding, the participating atoms are so different that one or more electrons are transferred to form oppositely charged ions. The bonding results from the attractions among these ions. In covalent bonding, two identical atoms share electrons equally. The bonding results from the mutual attraction of the two nuclei for the shared electrons. Between these extremes are intermediate cases in which the atoms are not so different that electrons are completely transferred but are different enough so that unequal sharing of electrons results, forming what is called a **polar covalent bond.** The hydrogen fluoride (HF) molecule contains this type of bond, which produces the following charge distribution,

$$\underset{\delta^+}{H}-\underset{\delta^-}{F}$$

where δ (delta) is used to indicate a partial or fractional charge.

The most logical explanation for the development of *bond polarity* (the partial positive and negative charges on the atoms in such molecules as HF) is that the electrons in the bonds are not shared equally. For example, we can account for the polarity of the HF molecule by assuming that the fluorine atom has a stronger attraction than the hydrogen atom for the shared electrons (Figure 12.2). Because bond polarity has important chemical implications, we find it useful to assign a number that indicates an atom's ability to attract shared electrons. In the next section we show how this is done.

12.2 Electronegativity

OBJECTIVE: To understand the nature of bonds and their relationship to electronegativity.

We saw in the previous section that when a metal and a nonmetal react, one or more electrons are transferred from the metal to the nonmetal to give ionic bonding. On the other hand, two identical atoms react to form a covalent bond in which electrons are shared equally. When *different* nonmetals react, a bond forms in which electrons are shared *unequally,* giving a polar

Test Bank: 5, 6, 8–11, 13–25, 29–44, 46

Section 12.2

TEACHING TIPS

- This section develops the concept of electronegativity and its trends on the periodic table. It is important to focus students' attention on how electronegativity relates to ionization energy.
- Students can memorize electronegativity trends, but it is important that they understand the reasons behind these trends (just as they should understand trends for atomic radius and ionization energy).
- Students should be able to compare the electronegativity values of two elements in the same group or same period. They should not memorize the actual electronegativity numbers but rather be able to predict which is greater.

TEACHING TIPS

- The relationship between the difference in electronegativity and bond type is rather arbitrary and serves as only a rough guide. The transition between polar covalent and ionic bonding, for example, is not a sharp one and the students should recognize this fact.
- Remind students that the electronegativity values of the lightest noble gases are zero. When we say that the elements in the upper-right corner of the periodic table are the most electronegative, we do not include the noble gases. Have students explain why.

Increasing electronegativity

Decreasing electronegativity

H 2.1

Li 1.0, Be 1.5, B 2.0, C 2.5, N 3.0, O 3.5, F 4.0

Na 0.9, Mg 1.2, Al 1.5, Si 1.8, P 2.1, S 2.5, Cl 3.0

K 0.8, Ca 1.0, Sc 1.3, Ti 1.5, V 1.6, Cr 1.6, Mn 1.5, Fe 1.8, Co 1.9, Ni 1.9, Cu 1.9, Zn 1.6, Ga 1.6, Ge 1.8, As 2.0, Se 2.4, Br 2.8

Rb 0.8, Sr 1.0, Y 1.2, Zr 1.4, Nb 1.6, Mo 1.8, Tc 1.9, Ru 2.2, Rh 2.2, Pd 2.2, Ag 1.9, Cd 1.7, In 1.7, Sn 1.8, Sb 1.9, Te 2.1, I 2.5

Cs 0.7, Ba 0.9, La–Lu 1.0–1.2, Hf 1.3, Ta 1.5, W 1.7, Re 1.9, Os 2.2, Ir 2.2, Pt 2.2, Au 2.4, Hg 1.9, Tl 1.8, Pb 1.9, Bi 1.9, Po 2.0, At 2.2

Fr 0.7, Ra 0.9, Ac 1.1, Th 1.3, Pa 1.4, U 1.4, Np–No 1.4–1.3

< 1.5

1.5–1.9

2.0–2.9

3.0–4.0

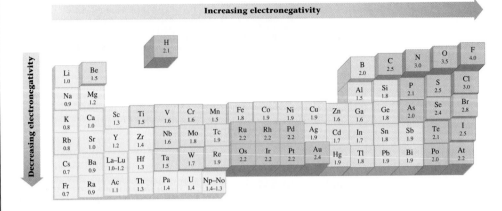

Figure 12.3 Electronegativity values for selected elements. Note that electronegativity generally increases across a period and decreases down a group. Note also that metals have relatively low electronegativity values and that nonmetals have relatively high values.

covalent bond. The unequal sharing of electrons between two atoms is described by a property called **electronegativity:** *the relative ability of an atom in a molecule to attract shared electrons to itself.*

Chemists determine electronegativity values for the elements (Figure 12.3) by measuring the polarities of the bonds between various atoms. Note that electronegativity generally increases going from left to right across a period and decreases going down a group for the representative elements. The range of electronegativity values is from 4.0 for fluorine to 0.7 for cesium and francium. Remember, the higher the atom's electronegativity value, the closer the shared electrons tend to be to that atom when it forms a bond.

The polarity of a bond depends on the *difference* between the electronegativity values of the atoms forming the bond. If the atoms have very similar electronegativities, the electrons are shared almost equally and the bond shows little polarity. If the atoms have very different electronegativity values, a very polar bond is formed. In extreme cases one or more electrons are actually transferred, forming ions and an ionic bond. For example, when an element from Group 1 (electronegativity values of about 0.8) reacts with an element from Group 7 (electronegativity values of about 3), ions are formed and an ionic substance results.

The relationship between electronegativity and bond type is shown in Table 12.1. The various types of bonds are summarized in Figure 12.4.

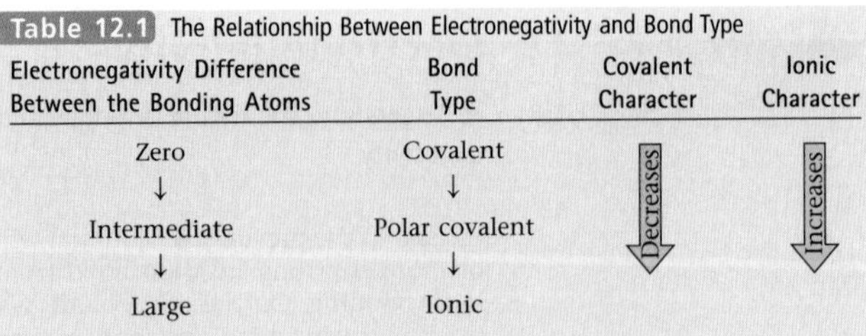

Table 12.1 The Relationship Between Electronegativity and Bond Type

Electronegativity Difference Between the Bonding Atoms	Bond Type	Covalent Character	Ionic Character
Zero	Covalent	Decreases ↓	Increases ↓
↓	↓		
Intermediate	Polar covalent		
↓	↓		
Large	Ionic		

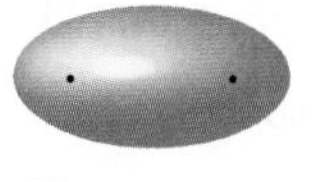

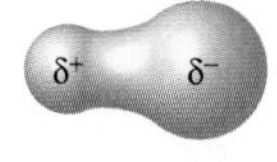

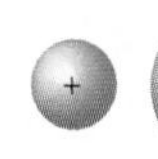

a A covalent bond formed between identical atoms.

b A polar covalent bond, with both ionic and covalent components.

c An ionic bond, with no electron sharing.

Figure 12.4
The three possible types of bonds.

EXAMPLE 12.1

Using Electronegativity to Determine Bond Polarity

Using the electronegativity values given in Figure 12.3, arrange the following bonds in order of increasing polarity: H—H, O—H, Cl—H, S—H, and F—H.

SOLUTION

The polarity of the bond increases as the difference in electronegativity increases. From the electronegativity values in Figure 12.3, the following variation in bond polarity is expected (the electronegativity value appears below each element).

Bond	Electronegativity Values	Difference in Electronegativity Values	Bond Type	Polarity
H—H	(2.1)(2.1)	$2.1 - 2.1 = 0$	Covalent	Increasing ↓
S—H	(2.5)(2.1)	$2.5 - 2.1 = 0.4$	Polar covalent	
Cl—H	(3.0)(2.1)	$3.0 - 2.1 = 0.9$	Polar covalent	
O—H	(3.5)(2.1)	$3.5 - 2.1 = 1.4$	Polar covalent	
F—H	(4.0)(2.1)	$4.0 - 2.1 = 1.9$	Polar covalent	

Therefore, in order of increasing polarity, we have

H—H S—H Cl—H O—H F—H

Least polar → Most polar

Self-Check EXERCISE 12.1 For each of the following pairs of bonds, choose the bond that will be more polar.

a. H—P, H—C

b. O—F, O—I

c. N—O, S—O

d. N—H, Si—H

See Problems 12.17 through 12.20. ■

Additional Examples

Example 12.1

On the basis of the electronegativity values given in Figure 12.3, indicate which is the more polar bond in each of the following pairs.

1. H—S or H—F

   H—F

2. O—S or O—F

   O—F

3. N—S or N—Cl

   N—Cl

4. C—S or C—Cl

   C—Cl

Self Check

Answers to Self-Check Exercise 12.1

a. H—C

b. O—I

c. S—O

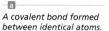

d. N—H

Test Bank: 47–49

Section 12.3

MISCONCEPTION

Students will often confuse dipole moments in a molecule with the overall polarity of a molecule. Molecules with polar bonds may be nonpolar molecules (CCl_4 is an example). The three-dimensional shape affects the overall polarity of a molecule (a concept discussed in more detail in Sections 12.8–12.10).

12.3 Bond Polarity and Dipole Moments

OBJECTIVE: To understand bond polarity and how it is related to molecular polarity.

We saw in Section 12.1 that hydrogen fluoride has a positive end and a negative end. A molecule such as HF that has a center of positive charge and a center of negative charge is said to have a **dipole moment.** The dipolar character of a molecule is often represented by an arrow. This arrow points toward the negative charge center, and its tail indicates the positive center of charge:

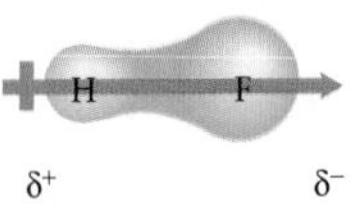

Any diatomic (two-atom) molecule that has a polar bond has a dipole moment. Some polyatomic (more than two atoms) molecules also have dipole moments. For example, because the oxygen atom in the water molecule has a greater electronegativity than the hydrogen atoms, the electrons are not shared equally. This results in a charge distribution (Figure 12.5) that causes the molecule to behave as though it had two centers of charge—one positive and one negative. So the water molecule has a dipole moment.

The fact that the water molecule is polar (has a dipole moment) has a profound impact on its properties. In fact, it is not overly dramatic to state that the polarity of the water molecule is crucial to life as we know it on earth. Because water molecules are polar, they can surround and attract both positive and negative ions (Figure 12.6). These attractions allow ionic materials to dissolve in water. Also, the polarity of water molecules causes them to attract each other strongly (Figure 12.7). This means that much energy is required to change water from a liquid to a gas (the molecules must be separated from each other to undergo this change of state). Therefore, it is the polarity of the water molecule that causes water to remain a liquid at the temperatures on the earth's surface. If it were nonpolar, water would be a gas and the oceans would be empty.

δ+ H, O 2δ−, H δ+

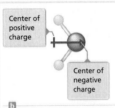

a The charge distribution in the water molecule. The oxygen has a charge of 2δ− because it pulls δ− of charge from each hydrogen atom (δ− + δ− = 2δ−).

Center of positive charge

Center of negative charge

b The water molecule behaves as if it had a positive end and a negative end, as indicated by the arrow.

Figure 12.5

PowerLecture Animation: Polar Molecules

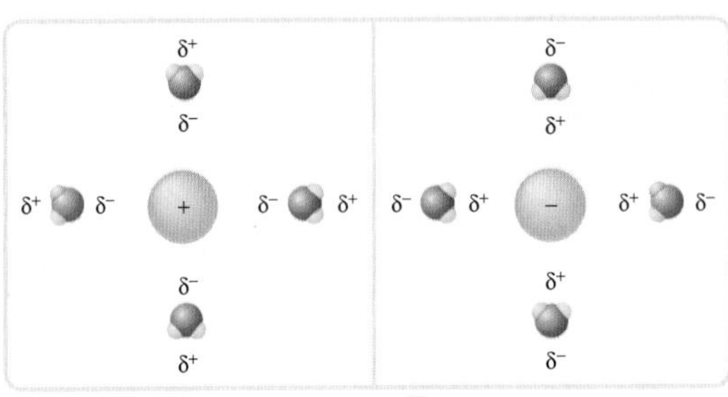

a *Polar water molecules are strongly attracted to positive ions by their negative ends.*

b *They are also strongly attracted to negative ions by their positive ends.*

Figure 12.6

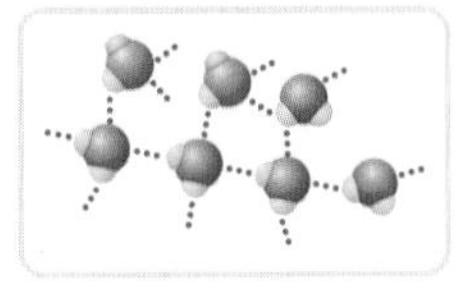

Figure 12.7
Polar water molecules are strongly attracted to each other.

Lecture Demonstration: 8.1

TEACHING TIPS

- Remember to keep your examples to simple molecules in this section. We have not yet discussed molecular shape, which plays a role in determining the polarity of more complex molecules.
- The polarity of a molecule has a profound impact on its chemical and physical properties. For example, water is a liquid and methane (CH_4) is a gas at room temperature, even though both have similar molar masses. Relating molecular shape to polarity to properties provides a "big picture" so students can recognize where we are going with this information.
- Students are often confused about why we use minus and plus signs to show charges on ions and instead use δ^- and δ^+ to show the charges on polar atoms in a molecule. The difficulty comes from not understanding that full and partial charges differ.
- Now is an excellent time to discuss the importance of polarity in molecules by using the properties of water. Discuss the ability of water to dissolve polar and ionic substances (Figure 12.6) and the strong attraction that water molecules have for each other (Figure 12.7), which results in a high boiling point for water.

Test Bank: 50–77

Section 12.4

12.4 Stable Electron Configurations and Charges on Ions

OBJECTIVES: To learn about stable electron configurations. • To learn to predict the formulas of ionic compounds.

We have seen many times that when a metal and a nonmetal react to form an ionic compound, the metal atom loses one or more electrons to the nonmetal. In Chapter 5, where binary ionic compounds were introduced, we saw that in these reactions, Group 1 metals always form 1+ cations, Group 2 metals always form 2+ cations, and aluminum in Group 3 always forms a 3+ cation. For the nonmetals, the Group 7 elements always form 1− anions, and the Group 6 elements always form 2− anions. This is further illustrated in Table 12.2.

Notice something very interesting about the ions in Table 12.2: they all have the electron configuration of neon, a noble gas. That is, sodium loses its one valence electron (the 3*s*) to form Na^+, which has an [Ne] electron configuration. Likewise, Mg loses its two valence electrons to form Mg^{2+}, which also has an [Ne] electron configuration. On the other hand, the nonmetal atoms gain just the number of electrons needed for them to achieve the noble gas electron configuration. The O atom gains two electrons and the F atom gains one electron to give O^{2-} and F^-, respectively, both of which have the [Ne] electron configuration. We can summarize these observations as follows:

Electron Configurations of Ions

1. Representative (main-group) metals form ions by losing enough electrons to achieve the configuration of the previous noble gas (that is, the noble gas that occurs before the metal in question on the periodic table). For example, note from the periodic table inside the front cover of the text that neon is the noble gas previous to sodium and magnesium. Similarly, helium is the noble gas previous to lithium and beryllium.
2. Nonmetals form ions by gaining enough electrons to achieve the configuration of the next noble gas (that is, the noble gas that follows the element in question on the periodic table). For example, note that neon is the noble gas that follows oxygen and fluorine, and argon is the noble gas that follows sulfur and chlorine.

Table 12.2 The Formation of Ions by Metals and Nonmetals

Group	Ion Formation	Electron Configuration: Atom		Ion
1	$Na \rightarrow Na^+ + e^-$	$[Ne]3s^1$	$\xrightarrow{e^- \text{ lost}}$	[Ne]
2	$Mg \rightarrow Mg^{2+} + 2e^-$	$[Ne]3s^2$	$\xrightarrow{2e^- \text{ lost}}$	[Ne]
3	$Al \rightarrow Al^{3+} + 3e^-$	$[Ne]3s^23p^1$	$\xrightarrow{3e^- \text{ lost}}$	[Ne]
6	$O + 2e^- \rightarrow O^{2-}$	$[He]2s^22p^4 + 2e^-$	$\rightarrow [He]2s^22p^6 =$	[Ne]
7	$F + e^- \rightarrow F^-$	$[He]2s^22p^5 + e^-$	$\rightarrow [He]2s^22p^6 =$	[Ne]

TEACHING TIPS

- This is an excellent time to review the electron configurations for atoms and write electron configurations for ions. Emphasize that we can predict the ion that forms from a particular atom by achieving a noble gas electron configuration. The concept that there is a strong tendency for atoms to adopt a noble gas configuration is central to understanding the electronic structure of ions and the Lewis structures of molecules. This concept is emphasized in this chapter and should be stressed in class discussions. However, it does not explain why the atom achieves this configuration. Science is about observing patterns (laws) and developing explanations (theories or models). The fact that the atoms in a compound have a tendency to achieve a noble gas electron configuration is an observation, not an explanation. Knowing this tendency helps us to make predictions, but it does not answer the "why?" question. From this observation, students should be able to predict, for example, that a sodium atom will lose only one electron when becoming an ion, and that a calcium atom will lose two electrons. However, the reason is not because the atoms "want" to have a noble gas electron configuration. This is a subtle but important distinction. See the Background Information on Ionic Compounds in Section 12.5 for a discussion of this.

PowerLecture Animations:
Mg^{2+} Cation Formation
F^- Anion Formation

PowerLecture Simulation:
Electron Configurations of Ions

TEACHING TIPS

- You may want to begin your discussion of bonding by using a simple example of ionic bonding and another of covalent bonding to illustrate how atoms attain the electron configurations of noble gases. One possibility is NaCl, in which Na loses an electron to Cl so that the sodium ion has the same electron configuration as Ne and the chloride ion has the same electron configuration as Ar. In the case of H_2, each hydrogen atom shares an electron with the other, so that both have the same electron configuration as He.
- Students already know how to predict the charge on an ion from the group number on the periodic table. Now is a good time to review this point and to indicate that students now can also predict the charge on an ion by looking at the valence-electron configuration.
- Now is a good time to review predicting the products in chemical reactions between elements. Students can now predict the correct product by using the valence-electron configurations for each atom. Once they have determined the number of electrons that are lost or gained to achieve the core electron configuration of a noble gas, they will be able to determine the charge on the ion and from there the formula for the product in the reaction.

Atoms in stable compounds almost always have a noble gas electron configuration.

This brings us to an important general principle. In observing millions of stable compounds, chemists have learned that **in almost all stable chemical compounds of the representative elements, all of the atoms have achieved a noble gas electron configuration.** The importance of this observation cannot be overstated. It forms the basis for all of our fundamental ideas about why and how atoms bond to each other.

We have already seen this principle operating in the formation of ions (see Table 12.2). We can summarize this behavior as follows: when representative metals and nonmetals react, they transfer electrons in such a way that both the cation and the anion have noble gas electron configurations.

On the other hand, when nonmetals react with each other, they share electrons in ways that lead to a noble gas electron configuration for each atom in the resulting molecule. For example, oxygen ([He]$2s^22p^4$), which needs two more electrons to achieve an [Ne] configuration, can get these electrons by combining with two H atoms (each of which has one electron),

		2s	2p
O:	[He]	↑↓	↑↓ ↑· ↑·
			H H

to form water, H_2O. This fills the valence orbitals of oxygen.

In addition, each H shares two electrons with the oxygen atom,

O
H H

which fills the H 1s orbital, giving it a $1s^2$ or [He] electron configuration. We will have much more to say about covalent bonding in Section 12.6.

At this point let's summarize the ideas we have introduced so far.

Electron Configurations and Bonding

1. When a *nonmetal and a Group 1, 2, or 3 metal* react to form a binary ionic compound, the ions form in such a way that the valence-electron configuration of the *nonmetal* is *completed* to achieve the configuration of the *next* noble gas, and the valence orbitals of the *metal* are *emptied* to achieve the configuration of the *previous* noble gas. In this way both ions achieve noble gas electron configurations.
2. When *two nonmetals* react to form a covalent bond, they share electrons in a way that completes the valence-electron configurations of both atoms. That is, both nonmetals attain noble gas electron configurations by sharing electrons.

Predicting Formulas of Ionic Compounds

Now that we know something about the electron configurations of atoms, we can explain *why* these various ions are formed.

To show how to predict what ions form when a metal reacts with a nonmetal, we will consider the formation of an ionic compound from calcium and oxygen. We can predict what compound will form by considering the valence electron configurations of the following two atoms:

Ca: [Ar]$4s^2$
O: [He]$2s^22p^4$

From Figure 12.3 we see that the electronegativity of oxygen (3.5) is much greater than that of calcium (1.0), giving a difference of 2.5. Because of this large difference, electrons are transferred from calcium to oxygen to form an oxygen anion and a calcium cation. How many electrons are transferred? We can base our prediction on the observation that noble gas configurations are the most stable. Note that oxygen needs two electrons to fill its valence orbitals (2*s* and 2*p*) and achieve the configuration of neon ($1s^2 2s^2 2p^6$), which is the next noble gas.

$$O + 2e^- \rightarrow O^{2-}$$
$$[He]2s^2 2p^4 + 2e^- \rightarrow [He]2s^2 2p^6, \text{ or } [Ne]$$

And by losing two electrons, calcium can achieve the configuration of argon (the previous noble gas).

$$Ca \rightarrow Ca^{2+} + 2e^-$$
$$[Ar]4s^2 \rightarrow [Ar] + 2e^-$$

Two electrons are therefore transferred as follows:

$$Ca + O \rightarrow Ca^{2+} + O^{2-}$$

2e⁻

To predict the formula of the ionic compound, we use the fact that chemical compounds are always electrically neutral—they have the same total quantities of positive and negative charges. In this case we must have equal numbers of Ca^{2+} and O^{2-} ions, and the empirical formula of the compound is CaO.

The same principles can be applied to many other cases. For example, consider the compound formed from aluminum and oxygen. Aluminum has the electron configuration $[Ne]3s^2 3p^1$. To achieve the neon configuration, aluminum must lose three electrons, forming the Al^{3+} ion.

$$Al \rightarrow Al^{3+} + 3e^-$$
$$[Ne]3s^2 3p^1 \rightarrow [Ne] + 3e^-$$

$3 \times (2-)$ balances $2 \times (3+)$.

Therefore, the ions will be Al^{3+} and O^{2-}. Because the compound must be electrically neutral, there will be three O^{2-} ions for every two Al^{3+} ions, and the compound has the empirical formula Al_2O_3.

Table 12.3 shows common elements that form ions with noble gas electron configurations in ionic compounds.

Notice that our discussion in this section refers to metals in Groups 1, 2, and 3 (the representative metals). The transition metals exhibit more complicated behavior (they form a variety of ions), which we will not be concerned with in this text.

Table 12.3 Common Ions with Noble Gas Configurations in Ionic Compounds

Group 1	Group 2	Group 3	Group 6	Group 7	Electron Configuration
Li^+	Be^{2+}				[He]
Na^+	Mg^{2+}	Al^{3+}	O^{2-}	F^-	[Ne]
K^+	Ca^{2+}		S^{2-}	Cl^-	[Ar]
Rb^+	Sr^{2+}		Se^{2-}	Br^-	[Kr]
Cs^+	Ba^{2+}		Te^{2-}	I^-	[Xe]

12.4 Stable Electron Configurations and Charges on Ions 367

Section 12.5

TEACHING TIP

Styrofoam balls of different sizes and colors can be used as good models of the packing of ionic solids.

12.5 Ionic Bonding and Structures of Ionic Compounds

OBJECTIVES: To learn about ionic structures. • To understand factors governing ionic size.

When metals and nonmetals react, the resulting ionic compounds are very stable; large amounts of energy are required to "take them apart." For example, the melting point of sodium chloride is approximately 800 °C. The strong bonding in these ionic compounds results from the attractions among the oppositely charged cations and anions.

We write the formula of an ionic compound such as lithium fluoride simply as LiF, but this is really the empirical, or simplest, formula. The actual solid contains huge and equal numbers of Li^+ and F^- ions packed together in a way that maximizes the attractions of the oppositely charged ions. A representative part of the lithium fluoride structure is shown in Figure 12.8a. In this structure the larger F^- ions are packed together like hard spheres, and the much smaller Li^+ ions are interspersed regularly among the F^- ions. The structure shown in Figure 12.8b represents only a tiny part of the actual structure, which continues in all three dimensions with the same pattern as that shown.

When spheres are packed together, they do not fill up all of the space. The spaces (holes) that are left can be occupied by smaller spheres.

The structures of virtually all binary ionic compounds can be explained by a model that involves packing the ions as though they were hard spheres. The larger spheres (usually the anions) are packed together, and the small ions occupy the interstices (spaces or holes) among them.

To understand the packing of ions it helps to realize that *a cation is always smaller than the parent atom, and an anion is always larger than the parent atom.* This makes sense because when a metal loses all of its valence electrons to form a cation, it gets much smaller. On the other hand, in forming an anion, a nonmetal gains enough electrons to achieve the next noble gas electron configuration and so becomes much larger. The relative sizes of the Group 1 and Group 7 atoms and their ions are shown in Figure 12.9.

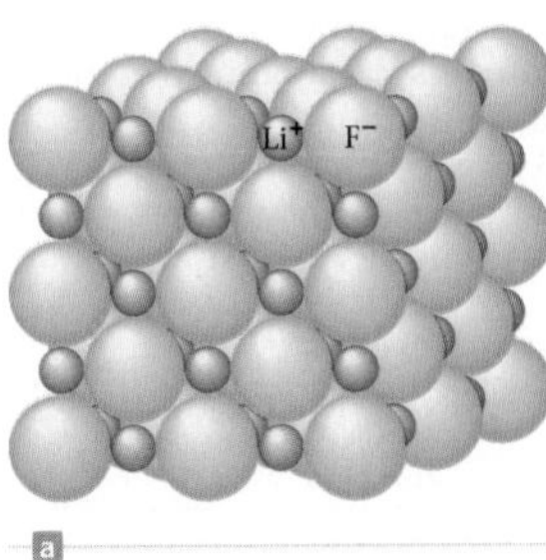

a *This structure represents the ions as packed spheres.*

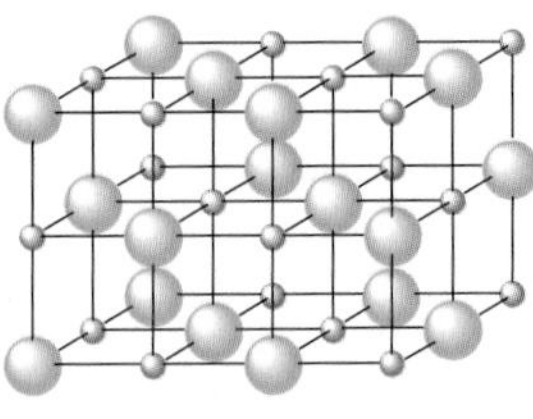

b *This structure shows the positions (centers) of the ions. The spherical ions are packed in the way that maximizes the ionic attractions.*

Figure 12.8
The structure of lithium fluoride.

TEACHING SUPPORT

BACKGROUND INFORMATION

Ionic Compounds

At the beginning of this discussion, emphasize that when chemists use the term *ionic compound,* they are usually referring to the solid state of that compound. In the solid state, the ions are close together. That is, solid ionic compounds contain a large collection of positive and negative ions packed together in a way that minimizes the −..− and +..+ repulsions and maximizes the +..− attractions. This situation stands in contrast to the gas phase of an ionic substance, in which the ions are quite far apart on average. In the gas phase, a pair of ions may get close enough to interact, but large collections of ions do not exist. Thus, when we speak of the stability of an ionic compound, we are referring to the solid state, where the large attractive forces present among oppositely charge ions tend to stabilize (favor the formation of) the ions. For example, the O^{2-} ion is not stable as an isolated, gas-phase species but, of course, is very stable in many solid ionic com-

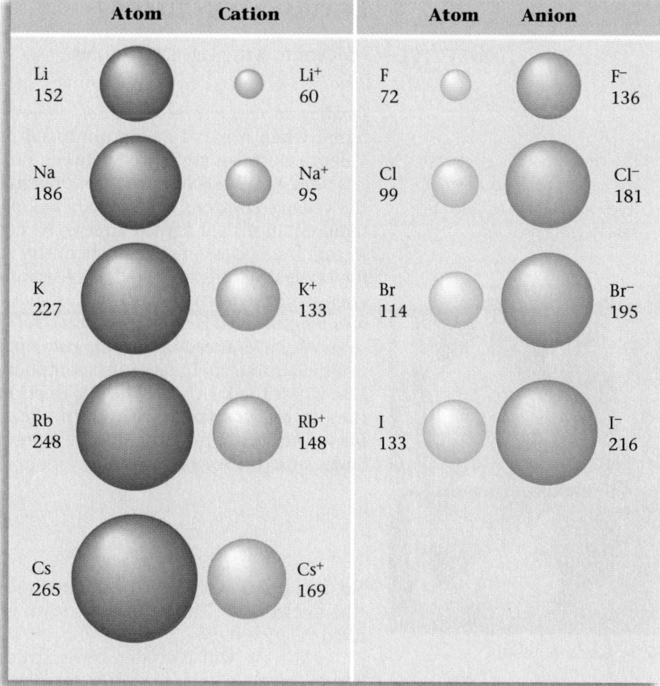

Figure 12.9

Relative sizes of some ions and their parent atoms. Note that cations are smaller and anions are larger than their parent atoms. The sizes (radii) are given in units of picometers (1 pm $= 10^{-12}$ m).

Ionic Compounds Containing Polyatomic Ions

So far in this chapter we have discussed only binary ionic compounds, which contain ions derived from single atoms. However, many compounds contain polyatomic ions: charged species composed of several atoms. For example, ammonium nitrate contains the NH_4^+ and NO_3^- ions. These ions with their opposite charges attract each other in the same way as do the simple ions in binary ionic compounds. However, the *individual* polyatomic ions are held together by covalent bonds, with all of the atoms behaving as a unit. For example, in the ammonium ion, NH_4^+, there are four N—H covalent bonds. Likewise the nitrate ion, NO_3^-, contains three covalent N—O bonds. Thus, although ammonium nitrate is an ionic compound because it contains the NH_4^+ and NO_3^- ions, it also contains covalent bonds in the individual polyatomic ions. When ammonium nitrate is dissolved in water, it behaves as a strong electrolyte like the binary ionic compounds sodium chloride and potassium bromide. As we saw in Chapter 7, this occurs because when an ionic solid dissolves, the ions are freed to move independently and can conduct an electric current.

The common polyatomic ions, which are listed in Table 5.4, are all held together by covalent bonds.

TEACHING TIP

Students have difficulty understanding polyatomic ions. It is difficult for them to see that these atoms are bonded together covalently and will not break up into atoms or simple ions. For example, when sodium sulfate dissolves in water, sodium and sulfate ions are formed, but the sulfate ion cannot break into sulfur and oxygen ions because the sulfur and oxygen are covalently bonded together.

PowerLecture Animation: Ionic Radii of Main Group Elements

PowerLecture Simulation: Sizes of Atoms and Ions

pounds. That is, MgO(*s*), which contains Mg^{2+} and O^{2-} ions, is very stable, but the isolated, gas-phase ion pair Mg^{2+}.. O^{2-} is not energetically favorable in comparison with the separate, neutral gaseous atoms. Keep in mind that in this section, and in most other cases where we are describing the nature of ionic compounds, the discussion usually refers to the solid state, where many ions are interacting simultaneously.

When *two nonmetals* react to form a covalent bond, they share electrons in a way that completes the valence-electron configurations of both atoms. That is, both nonmetals attain noble gas electron configurations.

When *a nonmetal and a representative (main-group) metal* react to form a binary ionic compound, the ions form so that the valence-electron configuration of the nonmetal achieves the electron configuration of the next noble gas atom and the valence orbitals of the metal are emptied. In this way, both ions achieve noble gas electron configurations.

Test Bank: 7, 78–83

Section 12.6

TEACHING TIPS

- Drawing Lewis structures provides a way for students to use their knowledge about electron configurations to predict bonding in covalent molecules.
- You can effectively show why noble gases do not generally form compounds by drawing the Lewis structures for several noble gases. However, it is a good idea to deemphasize the drawing of Lewis structures for atoms. It is shown here to introduce simple Lewis structures (diatomic molecules in particular). But students are later confused when confronted with a molecule such as carbon monoxide (CO), for which we cannot draw the Lewis structure of the molecule directly from the Lewis structures of the atoms.

12.6 Lewis Structures

OBJECTIVE: To learn to write Lewis structures.

Remember that the electrons in the highest principal energy level of an atom are called the valence electrons.

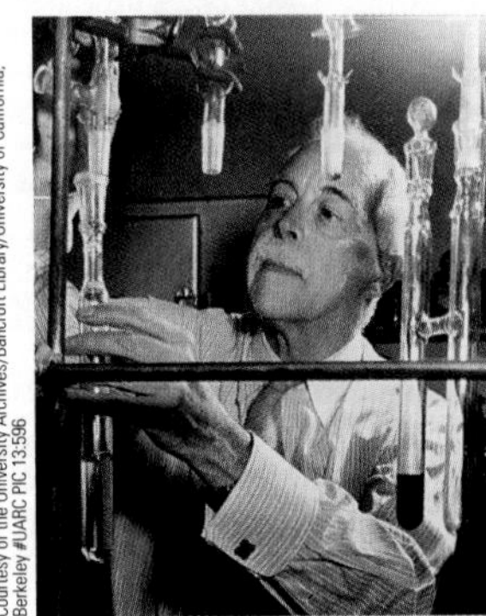

G. N. Lewis in his lab.

go Chemistry **Module 12: Drawing Lewis Electron Dot Structures** covers concepts in this section.

Bonding involves just the valence electrons of atoms. Valence electrons are transferred when a metal and a nonmetal react to form an ionic compound. Valence electrons are shared between nonmetals in covalent bonds.

The **Lewis structure** is a representation of a molecule that shows how the valence electrons are arranged among the atoms in the molecule. These representations are named after G. N. Lewis, who conceived the idea while lecturing to a class of general chemistry students in 1902. The rules for writing Lewis structures are based on observations of many molecules from which chemists have learned that the *most important requirement for the formation of a stable compound is that the atoms achieve noble gas electron configurations.*

We have already seen this rule operate in the reaction of metals and nonmetals to form binary ionic compounds. An example is the formation of KBr, where the K^+ ion has the [Ar] electron configuration and the Br^- ion has the [Kr] electron configuration. In writing Lewis structures, *we include only the valence electrons.* Using dots to represent valence electrons, we write the Lewis structure for KBr as follows:

K^+	$[:\ddot{\underset{..}{Br}}:]^-$
Noble gas configuration [Ar]	Noble gas configuration [Kr]

No dots are shown on the K^+ ion because it has lost its only valence electron (the 4*s* electron). The Br^- ion is shown with eight electrons because it has a filled valence shell.

Next we will consider Lewis structures for molecules with covalent bonds, involving nonmetals in the first and second periods. The principle of achieving a noble gas electron configuration applies to these elements as follows:

1. Hydrogen forms stable molecules where it shares two electrons. That is, it follows a **duet rule.** For example, when two hydrogen atoms, each with one electron, combine to form the H_2 molecule, we have

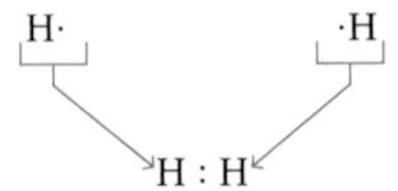

By sharing electrons, each hydrogen in H_2 has, in effect, two electrons; that is, each hydrogen has a filled valence shell.

H [↑] 1*s* + H [↓] 1*s* → H_2 [↑↓] [He] configuration

2. Helium does not form bonds because its valence orbital is already filled; it is a noble gas. Helium has the electron configuration $1s^2$ and can be represented by the Lewis structure

He:
[He] configuration

TEACHING SUPPORT

BACKGROUND INFORMATION

Lewis Structures: Comments About the Octet Rule

- The second-row elements C, N, O, and F should always be assumed to obey the octet rule.
- The second-row elements B and Be often have fewer than eight electrons around them in their compounds. These electron-deficient compounds are very reactive.
- The second-row elements never exceed the octet rule, since their valence orbitals (2*s* and 2*p*) can accommodate only eight electrons.

Carbon, nitrogen, oxygen, and fluorine almost always obey the octet rule in stable molecules.

3. The second-row nonmetals carbon through fluorine form stable molecules when they are surrounded by enough electrons to fill the valence orbitals—that is, the one $2s$ and the three $2p$ orbitals. Eight electrons are required to fill these orbitals, so these elements typically obey the **octet rule;** they are surrounded by eight electrons. An example is the F_2 molecule, which has the following Lewis structure:

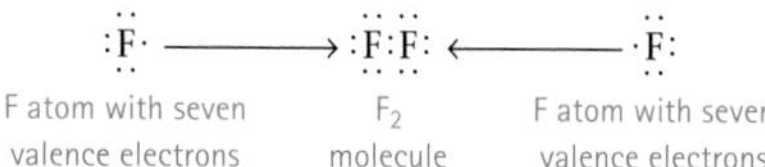

Note that each fluorine atom in F_2 is, in effect, surrounded by eight valence electrons, two of which are shared with the other atom. This is a **bonding pair** of electrons, as we discussed earlier. Each fluorine atom also has three pairs of electrons that are not involved in bonding. These are called **lone pairs** or **unshared pairs.**

4. Neon does not form bonds because it already has an octet of valence electrons (it is a noble gas). The Lewis structure is

Note that only the valence electrons ($2s^22p^6$) of the neon atom are represented by the Lewis structure. The $1s^2$ electrons are core electrons and are not shown.

Lewis structures show only valence electrons.

Next we want to develop some general procedures for writing Lewis structures for molecules. Remember that Lewis structures involve only the valence electrons of atoms, so before we proceed, we will review the relationship of an element's position on the periodic table to the number of valence electrons it has. Recall that the group number gives the total number of valence electrons. For example, all Group 6 elements have six valence electrons (valence configuration ns^2np^4).

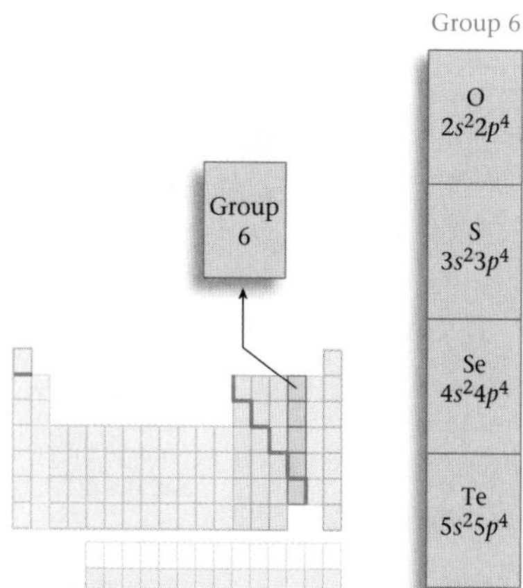

- Third-row and heavier elements often satisfy the octet rule but can exceed the octet rule, presumably by using their empty valence d orbitals.
- When writing the Lewis structure for a molecule, satisfy the octet rule for the atoms first. If electrons remain after the octet rule has been satisfied, then place them on the elements having available d orbitals (elements in Period 3 or beyond).

TEACHING TIPS

- The rules for writing Lewis structures help students consistently write correct Lewis structures. Many students who do not follow these rules will be less successful in drawing correct Lewis structures, especially for more complex molecules.
- Emphasize that to write correct structures for molecules it is necessary to sum all the valence electrons from all the atoms. Make sure that students do not attach valence electrons to individual atoms and then try to write a Lewis structure. This method can sometimes produce a correct structure but often fails for molecules containing multiple bonds and for complex molecules.

PowerLecture Simulation: Drawing Lewis Structures (1)

Similarly, all Group 7 elements have seven valence electrons (valence configuration ns^2np^5).

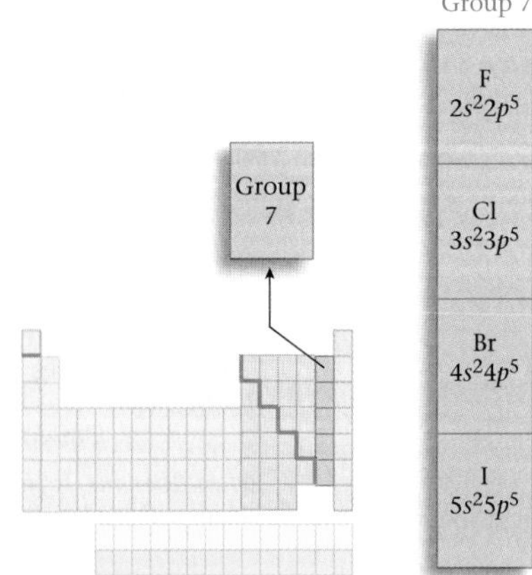

In writing the Lewis structure for a molecule, we need to keep the following things in mind:

1. We must include all the valence electrons from all atoms. The total number of electrons available is the sum of all the valence electrons from all the atoms in the molecule.
2. Atoms that are bonded to each other share one or more pairs of electrons.
3. The electrons are arranged so that each atom is surrounded by enough electrons to fill the valence orbitals of that atom. This means two electrons for hydrogen and eight electrons for second-row nonmetals.

The best way to make sure we arrive at the correct Lewis structure for a molecule is to use a systematic approach. We will use the approach summarized by the following rules.

Steps for Writing Lewis Structures

Step 1 Obtain the sum of the valence electrons from all of the atoms. Do not worry about keeping track of which electrons come from which atoms. It is the *total* number of valence electrons that is important.

Step 2 Use one pair of electrons to form a bond between each pair of bound atoms. For convenience, a line (instead of a pair of dots) is often used to indicate each pair of bonding electrons.

Step 3 Arrange the remaining electrons to satisfy the duet rule for hydrogen and the octet rule for each second-row element.

To see how these rules are applied, we will write the Lewis structures of several molecules.

CHEMISTRY *IN* FOCUS

To Bee or Not to Bee

One of the problems we face in modern society is how to detect illicit substances, such as drugs and explosives, in a convenient, accurate manner. Trained dogs are often used for this purpose because of their acute sense of smell. Now several researches are trying to determine whether insects, such as honeybees and wasps, can be even more effective chemical detectors. In fact, studies have shown that bees can be trained in just a few minutes to detect the smell of almost any chemical.

Scientists at Los Alamos National Laboratory in New Mexico are designing a portable device using bees that possibly could be used to sniff out drugs and bombs at airports, border crossings, and schools. They call their study the Stealthy Insect Sensor Project. The Los Alamos project is based on the idea that bees can be trained to associate the smell of a particular chemical with a sugary treat. Bees stick out their "tongues" when they detect a food source. By pairing a drop of sugar water with the scent of TNT (trinitrotoluene) or C-4 (composition 4) plastic explosive about six times, the bees can be trained to extend their proboscis at a whiff of the chemical alone. The bee bomb detector is about half the size of a shoe box and weighs 4 lb. Inside the box, bees are lined up in a row and strapped into straw-like tubes, then exposed to puffs of air as a camera monitors their reactions. The signals from the video camera are sent to a computer, which analyzes the bees' behavior and signals when the bees respond to the particular scent they have been trained to detect.

A project at the University of Georgia uses tiny parasitic wasps as a chemical detector. Wasps do not extend their tongues when they detect a scent. Instead, they communicate the discovery of a scent by body movements that the scientists call "dances." The device, called the Wasp Hound, contains a team of wasps in a hand-held ventilated cartridge that has a fan at one end to draw in air from outside. If the scent is one the wasps do not recognize, they continue flying randomly. However, if the scent is one the wasps have been conditioned to recognize, they cluster around the opening. A video camera paired with a computer analyzes their behavior and signals when a scent is detected.

The insect sensors are now undergoing field trials, which typically compare the effectiveness of insects to that of trained dogs. Initial results appear promising, but the effectiveness of these devices remains to be proved.

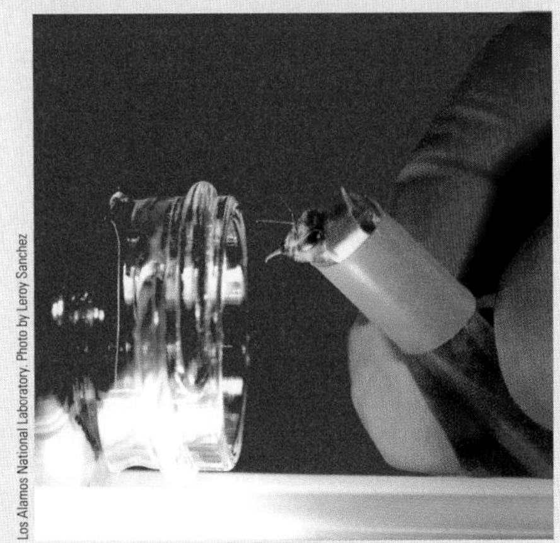

Los Alamos National Laboratory. Photo by Leroy Sanchez

A honeybee receives a fragrant reminder of its target scent each morning and responds by sticking out its proboscis.

EXAMPLE 12.2 Writing Lewis Structures: Simple Molecules

Write the Lewis structure of the water molecule.

SOLUTION

We will follow the steps listed on page 372.

373

Additional Examples

Example 12.2

Write Lewis structures for each of the following molecules.

1. CCl_4

```
       ..
      :Cl:
   ..  |  ..
  :Cl—C—Cl:
   ''  |  ''
      :Cl:
       ''
```

2. PH_3

```
     ..
  H—P—H
     |
     H
```

Step 1 Find the sum of the *valence* electrons for H_2O.

$$\underset{\substack{\text{H} \\ \text{(Group 1)}}}{\overset{\uparrow}{1}} + \underset{\substack{\text{H} \\ \text{(Group 1)}}}{\overset{\uparrow}{1}} + \underset{\substack{\text{O} \\ \text{(Group 6)}}}{\overset{\uparrow}{6}} = 8 \text{ valence electrons}$$

Step 2 Using a pair of electrons per bond, we draw in the two O—H bonds, using a line to indicate each pair of bonding electrons.

H—O—H

Note that

H—O—H represents H : O : H

Step 3 We arrange the remaining electrons around the atoms to achieve a noble gas electron configuration for each atom. Four electrons have been used in forming the two bonds, so four electrons (8 − 4) remain to be distributed. Each hydrogen is satisfied with two electrons (duet rule), but oxygen needs eight electrons to have a noble gas electron configuration. So the remaining four electrons are added to oxygen as two lone pairs. Dots are used to represent the lone pairs.

H—Ö—H Lone pairs

This is the correct Lewis structure for the water molecule. Each hydrogen shares two electrons, and the oxygen has four electrons and shares four to give a total of eight.

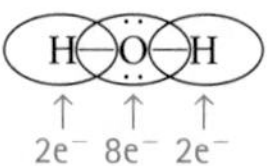

Note that a line is used to represent a shared pair of electrons (bonding electrons) and dots are used to represent unshared pairs.

H—Ö—H might also be drawn as H:Ö:H

Self-Check EXERCISE 12.2 Write the Lewis structure for HCl.

See Problems 12.59 through 12.62. ■

12.7 Lewis Structures of Molecules with Multiple Bonds

OBJECTIVE: To learn how to write Lewis structures for molecules with multiple bonds.

Now let's write the Lewis structure for carbon dioxide.

Step 1 Summing the valence electrons gives

$$\underset{\substack{\text{C} \\ \text{(Group 4)}}}{\overset{\uparrow}{4}} + \underset{\substack{\text{O} \\ \text{(Group 6)}}}{\overset{\uparrow}{6}} + \underset{\substack{\text{O} \\ \text{(Group 6)}}}{\overset{\uparrow}{6}} = 16$$

Self Check

Self-Check Exercise 12.2

H—C̈l:

Test Bank: 84–98, 101, 102

Section 12.7

TEACHING TIPS

- Writing Lewis structures for more complex molecules or ions can be difficult for students. A student encountering Lewis structures for the first time has no way of knowing if the carbon dioxide molecule is in the order O—C—O or C—O—O. It is helpful to tell students that atoms are usually symmetrically arranged in molecules.
- Tell students to arrange the electrons to make single bonds between the atoms first and then add double or triple bonds to complete the octets and use all the available electrons.
- The concept of resonance offers an opportunity to discuss the limitations of the bonding model we have developed.
- Students have more trouble writing Lewis structures for ions than for molecules. They are not sure what to do with the charge and how many electrons are available for the Lewis structure.

PowerLecture Simulation: Drawing Lewis Structures (2)

CHEMISTRY *IN* FOCUS

Hiding Carbon Dioxide

As we discussed in Chapter 11 (see "Chemistry in Focus: Atmospheric Effects," page 326), global warming seems to be a reality. At the heart of this issue is the carbon dioxide produced by society's widespread use of fossil fuels. For example, in the United States, CO_2 makes up 81% of greenhouse gas emissions. Thirty percent of this CO_2 comes from coal-fired power plants used to produce electricity. One way to solve this problem would be to phase out coal-fired power plants. However, this outcome is not likely because the United States possesses so much coal (at least a 250-year supply) and coal is so cheap (about $0.03 per pound). Recognizing this fact, the U.S. government has instituted a research program to see if the CO_2 produced at power plants can be captured and sequestered (stored) underground in deep geological formations. The factors that need to be explored to determine whether sequestration is feasible are the capacities of underground storage sites and the chances that the sites will leak.

The injection of CO_2 into the earth's crust is already being undertaken by various oil companies. Since 1996, the Norwegian oil company Statoil has separated more than 1 million tons of CO_2 annually from natural gas and pumped it into a saltwater aquifer beneath the floor of the North Sea. In western Canada a group of oil companies has injected CO_2 from a North Dakota synthetic fuels plant into oil fields in an effort to increase oil recovery. The oil companies expect to store 22 million tons of CO_2 there and to produce 130 million barrels of oil over the next 20 years.

Sequestration of CO_2 has great potential as one method for decreasing the rate of global warming. Only time will tell whether it will work.

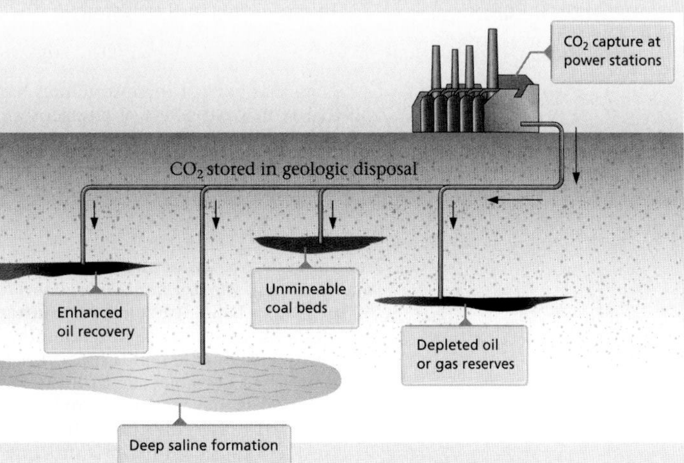

MISCONCEPTION

Students often look at a species that has a negative charge and think that an electron has been removed (since negative usually connotes something has been removed). Likewise, students often think an electron has been added to a positively charged ion.

O—C—O

represents

O:C:O

$:\ddot{O}—C—\ddot{O}:$

represents

$:\ddot{O}:C:\ddot{O}:$

Step 2 Form a bond between the carbon and each oxygen:

$$O—C—O$$

Step 3 Next, distribute the remaining electrons to achieve noble gas electron configurations on each atom. In this case twelve electrons (16 − 4) remain after the bonds are drawn. The distribution of these electrons is determined by a trial-and-error process. We have six pairs of electrons to distribute. Suppose we try three pairs on each oxygen to give

$$:\ddot{O}—C—\ddot{O}:$$

Is this correct? To answer this question we need to check two things:

1. The total number of electrons. There are sixteen valence electrons in this structure, which is the correct number.
2. The octet rule for each atom. Each oxygen has eight electrons around it, but the carbon has only four. This cannot be the correct Lewis structure.

How can we arrange the sixteen available electrons to achieve an octet for each atom? Suppose we place two shared pairs between the carbon and each oxygen:

PowerLecture Simulation: Resonance Structures

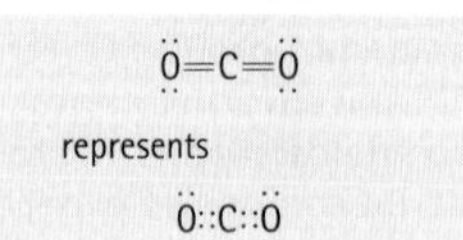

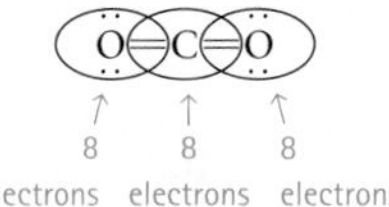

Now each atom is surrounded by eight electrons, and the total number of electrons is sixteen, as required. This is the correct Lewis structure for carbon dioxide, which has two *double* bonds. A **single bond** involves two atoms sharing one electron pair. A **double bond** involves two atoms sharing two pairs of electrons.

:O≡C—Ö: represents :O:::C:Ö:

In considering the Lewis structure for CO_2, you may have come up with

:O≡C—Ö: or :Ö—C≡O:

Note that both of these structures have the required sixteen electrons and that both have octets of electrons around each atom (verify this for yourself). Both of these structures have a **triple bond** in which three electron pairs are shared. Are these valid Lewis structures for CO_2? Yes. So there really are three Lewis structures for CO_2:

:Ö—C≡O: Ö=C=Ö :O≡C—Ö:

This brings us to a new term, **resonance.** A molecule shows resonance when *more than one Lewis structure can be drawn for the molecule.* In such a case we call the various Lewis structures **resonance structures.**

Of the three resonance structures for CO_2 shown above, the one in the center with two double bonds most closely fits our experimental information about the CO_2 molecule. In this text we will not be concerned about how to choose which resonance structure for a molecule gives the "best" description of that molecule's properties.

Next let's consider the Lewis structure of the CN^- (cyanide) ion.

Step 1 Summing the valence electrons, we have

CN^-

4 + 5 + 1 = 10

Note that the negative charge means an extra electron must be added.

Step 2 Draw a single bond (C—N).

Step 3 Next, we distribute the remaining electrons to achieve a noble gas configuration for each atom. Eight electrons remain to be distributed. We can try various possibilities, such as

C̈—N̈ or :C̈—N: or :C—N̈:

These structures are incorrect. To show why none is a valid Lewis structure, count the electrons around the C and N atoms. In the left structure, neither

CHEMISTRY IN FOCUS

Broccoli—Miracle Food?

Eating the right foods is critical to our health. In particular, certain vegetables, although they do not enjoy a very jazzy image, seem especially important. A case in point is broccoli, a vegetable with a humble reputation that packs a powerful chemistry wallop.

Broccoli contains a chemical called sulforaphane, which has the following Lewis structure:

$$CH_3—\underset{\underset{:\ddot{O}:}{\|}}{S}—(CH_2)_4—\ddot{N}=C=\ddot{S}:$$

Experiments indicate that sulforaphane furnishes protection against certain cancers by increasing the production of enzymes (called phase 2 enzymes) that "mop up" reactive molecules that can harm DNA. Sulforaphane also seems to combat bacteria. For example, among the most common harmful bacteria in humans is *Helicobacter pylori (H. pylori),* which has been implicated in the development of several diseases of the stomach, including inflammation, cancer, and ulcers. Antibiotics are clearly the best treatment for *H. pylori* infections. However, especially in developing countries, where *H. pylori* is rampant, antibiotics are often too expensive to be available to the general population. In addition, the bacteria sometimes evade antibiotics by "hiding" in cells on the stomach walls and then reemerging after treatment ends.

Studies at Johns Hopkins in Baltimore and Vandoeuvre-les Nancy in France have shown that sulforaphane kills *H. pylori* (even when it has taken refuge in stomach-wall cells) at concentrations that are achievable by eating broccoli. The scientists at Johns Hopkins also found that sulforaphane seems to inhibit stomach cancer in mice. Although there are no guarantees that broccoli will keep you healthy, it might not hurt to add it to your diet.

atom satisfies the octet rule. In the center structure, C has eight electrons but N has only four. In the right structure, the opposite is true. Remember that both atoms must simultaneously satisfy the octet rule. Therefore, the correct arrangement is

:C≡N:

represents

:C:::N:

$$:C{\equiv}N:$$

(Satisfy yourself that both carbon and nitrogen have eight electrons.) In this case we have a triple bond between C and N, in which three electron pairs are shared. Because this is an anion, we indicate the charge outside of square brackets around the Lewis structure.

$$[:C{\equiv}N:]^-$$

In summary, sometimes we need double or triple bonds to satisfy the octet rule. Writing Lewis structures is a trial-and-error process. Start with single bonds between the bonded atoms and add multiple bonds as needed.

We will write the Lewis structure for NO_2^- in Example 12.3 to make sure the procedures for writing Lewis structures are clear.

Additional Examples

Example 12.3

Write Lewis structures for each of these molecules.

1. SO_2

$$\ddot{O}=\ddot{S}—\ddot{O}: \leftrightarrow :\ddot{O}—\ddot{S}=\ddot{O}$$

2. CO_3^{2-}

$$\left[\begin{array}{c} \ddot{O} \\ \| \\ C \\ :\ddot{O}{/}\quad{\backslash}\ddot{O}: \end{array} \leftrightarrow \begin{array}{c} :\ddot{O}: \\ | \\ C \\ :\ddot{O}{/}\quad{\backslash\backslash}\ddot{O} \end{array} \leftrightarrow \begin{array}{c} :\ddot{O}: \\ | \\ C \\ \ddot{O}{//}\quad{\backslash}\ddot{O}: \end{array} \right]^{2-}$$

Self Check

Answer to Self-Check Exercise 12.3

$\dot{\ddot{O}}=\ddot{O}-\ddot{O}: \leftrightarrow :\ddot{O}-\ddot{O}=\dot{\ddot{O}}$

Additional Examples

Example 12.4

Write Lewis structures for each of the following molecules.

1. NI_3

:Ï—N̈—Ï:, with :Ï: bonded below N

2. PO_4^{3-}

[P bonded to four :Ö: atoms]$^{3-}$

3. SCN^- (C is the central atom)

$[:\ddot{S}-C\equiv N: \leftrightarrow \dot{\ddot{S}}=C=\ddot{N}]^-$

EXAMPLE 12.3 Writing Lewis Structures: Resonance Structures

Write the Lewis structure for the NO_2^- anion.

SOLUTION

Step 1 Sum the valence electrons for NO_2^-.

Valence electrons: 6 (O) + 5 (N) + 6 (O) + 1 (−1 charge) = 18 electrons

Step 2 Put in single bonds.

O—N—O

Step 3 Satisfy the octet rule. In placing the electrons, we find there are two Lewis structures that satisfy the octet rule:

$[\ddot{O}=\ddot{N}-\ddot{O}:]^-$ and $[:\ddot{O}-\ddot{N}=\ddot{O}]^-$

Verify that each atom in these structures is surrounded by an octet of electrons. Try some other arrangements to see whether other structures exist in which the eighteen electrons can be used to satisfy the octet rule. It turns out that these are the only two that work. Note that this is another case where resonance occurs; there are two valid Lewis structures.

Self-Check EXERCISE 12.3 Ozone is a very important constituent of the atmosphere. At upper levels it protects us by absorbing high-energy radiation from the sun. Near the earth's surface it produces harmful air pollution. Write the Lewis structure for ozone, O_3.

See Problems 12.63 through 12.68. ■

Now let's consider a few more cases in Example 12.4.

EXAMPLE 12.4 Writing Lewis Structures: Summary

Give the Lewis structure for each of the following:

a. HF e. CF_4
b. N_2 f. NO^+
c. NH_3 g. NO_3^-
d. CH_4

You may wonder how to decide which atom is the central atom in molecules of binary compounds. In cases where there is one atom of a given element and several atoms of a second element, the single atom is almost always the central atom of the molecule.

SOLUTION

In each case we apply the three steps for writing Lewis structures. Recall that lines are used to indicate shared electron pairs and that dots are used to indicate nonbonding pairs (lone pairs). The table on page 379 summarizes our results.

Self-Check EXERCISE 12.4 Write the Lewis structures for the following molecules:

a. NF_3 d. PH_3 g. NH_4^+
b. O_2 e. H_2S h. ClO_3^-
c. CO f. SO_4^{2-} i. SO_2

See Problems 12.55 through 12.68. ■

Self Check

Answers to Self-Check Exercise 12.4

a. :F̈—N̈—F̈:, with :F̈: bonded below N

b. $\dot{\ddot{O}}=\dot{\ddot{O}}$ c. $:C\equiv O:$

d. H—P̈—H, with H bonded below P

e. H—S̈—H

f. [S bonded to four :Ö: atoms]$^{2-}$

g. [N bonded to four H atoms]$^+$

h. [:Ö—C̈l—Ö:, with :Ö: bonded below Cl]$^-$

i. $\dot{\ddot{O}}=\ddot{S}-\ddot{O}: \leftrightarrow :\ddot{O}-\ddot{S}=\dot{\ddot{O}}$

Molecule or Ion	Total Valence Electrons	Draw Single Bonds	Calculate Number of Electrons Remaining	Use Remaining Electrons to Achieve Noble Gas Configurations	*Check* Atom	*Check* Electrons
a. HF	1 + 7 = 8	H—F	8 − 2 = 6	H—F̤̈:	H F	2 8
b. N_2	5 + 5 = 10	N—N	10 − 2 = 8	:N≡N:	N	8
c. NH_3	5 + 3(1) = 8	H—N—H, with H below N	8 − 6 = 2	H—N̈—H, with H below N	H N	2 8
d. CH_4	4 + 4(1) = 8	H—C—H, with H above and below C	8 − 8 = 0	H—C—H, with H above and below C	H C	2 8
e. CF_4	4 + 4(7) = 32	F—C—F, with F above and below C	32 − 8 = 24	:F̤̈—C—F̤̈:, with :F̤̈: above and below C	F C	8 8
f. NO^+	5 + 6−1 = 10	N—O	10 − 2 = 8	[:N≡O:]$^+$	N O	8 8
g. NO_3^-	5 + 3(6)+1 = 24	[O—N(—O)—O], O above N, two O below	24 − 6 = 18	[:Ö: above N (single bond); N=O lower left; N—O lower right]$^-$	N O	8 8
			NO_3^- shows resonance	[:Ö: above N (single bond); N—O lower left; N=O lower right]$^-$	N O	8 8
				[:O: above N (double bond); N—O lower left; N—O lower right]$^-$	N O	8 8

Remember, when writing Lewis structures, you don't have to worry about which electrons come from which atoms in a molecule. It is best to think of a molecule as a new entity that uses all the available valence electrons from the various atoms to achieve the strongest possible bonds. Think of the valence electrons as belonging to the molecule, rather than to the individual atoms. Simply distribute all the valence electrons so that noble gas electron configurations are obtained for each atom, without regard to the origin of each particular electron.

Some Exceptions to the Octet Rule

The idea that covalent bonding can be predicted by achieving noble gas electron configurations for all atoms is a simple and very successful idea. The rules we have used for Lewis structures describe correctly the bonding in

TEACHING TIP

Remind students that many elements usually obey the octet rule. If an atom that can exceed the octet rule is bonded to atoms that obey the octet rule, the available electrons should be distributed to form octets on all the atoms. Then any remaining electrons can be placed on atoms that can exceed the octet rule.

PowerLecture Animation: Reaction of NH_3 + BF_3

PowerLecture Video: O_2 and N_2 Poured on Magnets

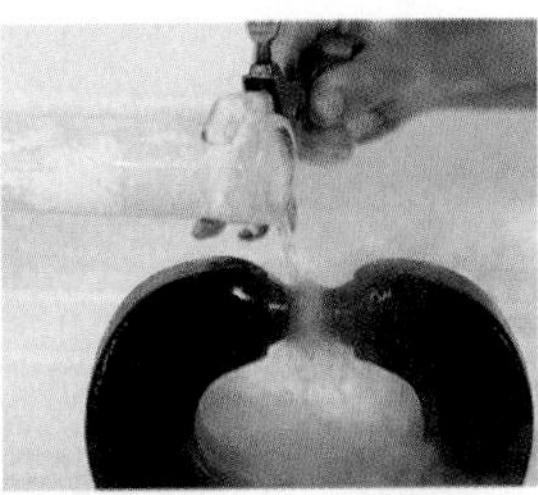

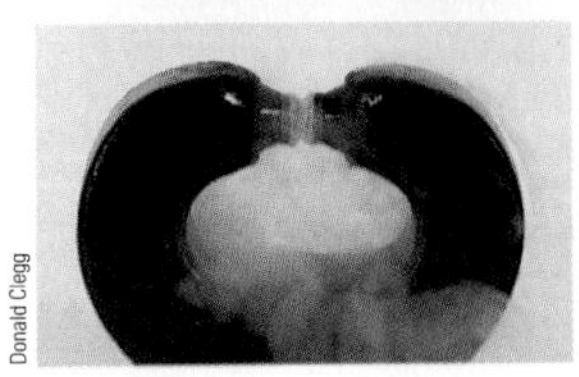

Donald Clegg

Figure 12.10 When liquid oxygen is poured between the poles of a magnet, it "sticks" until it boils away. This shows that the O_2 molecule has unpaired electrons (is paramagnetic).

most molecules. However, with such a simple model, some exceptions are inevitable. Boron, for example, tends to form compounds in which the boron atom has fewer than eight electrons around it—that is, it does not have a complete octet. Boron trifluoride, BF_3, a gas at normal temperatures and pressures, reacts very energetically with molecules such as water and ammonia that have unshared electron pairs (lone pairs).

$$\text{H}_2\ddot{\text{O}}\text{:} \longleftarrow \text{Lone pairs} \longrightarrow \text{:NH}_3$$

The violent reactivity of BF_3 with electron-rich molecules arises because the boron atom is electron-deficient. The Lewis structure that seems most consistent with the properties of BF_3 (twenty-four valence electrons) is

$$\text{:}\ddot{\text{F}}\text{:} - \text{B}(-\text{:}\ddot{\text{F}}\text{:})_2$$

Note that in this structure the boron atom has only six electrons around it. The octet rule for boron could be satisfied by drawing a structure with a double bond between the boron and one of the fluorines. However, experiments indicate that each B—F bond is a single bond in accordance with the above Lewis structure. This structure is also consistent with the reactivity of BF_3 with electron-rich molecules. For example, BF_3 reacts vigorously with NH_3 to form H_3NBF_3.

$$\text{H}_3\text{N:} + \text{BF}_3 \rightarrow \text{H}_3\text{N}-\text{BF}_3$$

Note that in the product H_3NBF_3, which is very stable, boron has an octet of electrons.

It is also characteristic of beryllium to form molecules where the beryllium atom is electron-deficient.

The compounds containing the elements carbon, nitrogen, oxygen, and fluorine are accurately described by Lewis structures in the vast majority of cases. However, there are a few exceptions. One important example is the oxygen molecule, O_2. The following Lewis structure that satisfies the octet rule can be drawn for O_2 (see Self-Check Exercise 12.4).

$$\ddot{\text{O}}=\ddot{\text{O}}$$

Paramagnetic substances have unpaired electrons and are drawn toward the space between a magnet's poles.

However, this structure does not agree with the *observed behavior* of oxygen. For example, the photos in Figure 12.10 show that when liquid oxygen is poured between the poles of a strong magnet, it "sticks" there until it boils away. This provides clear evidence that oxygen is paramagnetic—that is, it contains unpaired electrons. However, the above Lewis structure shows only pairs of electrons. That is, no unpaired electrons are shown. There is no simple Lewis structure that satisfactorily explains the paramagnetism of the O_2 molecule.

Any molecule that contains an odd number of electrons does not conform to our rules for Lewis structures. For example, NO and NO_2 have eleven and seventeen valence electrons, respectively, and conventional Lewis structures cannot be drawn for these cases.

Even though there are exceptions, most molecules can be described by Lewis structures in which all the atoms have noble gas electron configurations, and this is a very useful model for chemists.

TEACHING SUPPORT

BACKGROUND INFORMATION

Fundamental Properties of Models

- Models are human inventions, always based on an incomplete understanding of how nature works. *A model does not equal reality.*
- Models are often wrong. This property derives from the first property. Models are based on speculation and are always oversimplifications.
- Models tend to become more complicated as they age. As flaws are discovered in our models, we "patch" them and thus add more detail.
- It is very important to understand the assumptions inherent in a particular model before you use it to interpret observations or to make predictions. Simple models usually involve very restrictive assumptions and can be expected to yield only qualitative information. Asking for a sophisticated explanation from a simple model is like expecting to get an

12.8 Molecular Structure

OBJECTIVE: To understand molecular structure and bond angles.

So far in this chapter we have considered the Lewis structures of molecules. These structures represent the arrangement of the *valence electrons* in a molecule. We use the word *structure* in another way when we talk about the **molecular structure** or **geometric structure** of a molecule. These terms refer to the three-dimensional arrangement of the *atoms* in a molecule. For example, the water molecule is known to have the molecular structure

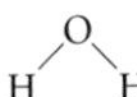

which is often called "bent" or "V-shaped." To describe the structure more precisely, we often specify the **bond angle.** For the H_2O molecule the bond angle is about 105°.

O
H H
~105°

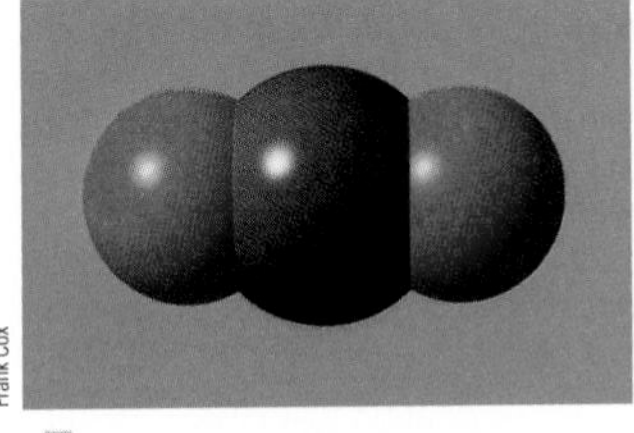

a Computer graphic of a linear molecule containing three atoms

b Computer graphic of a trigonal planar molecule

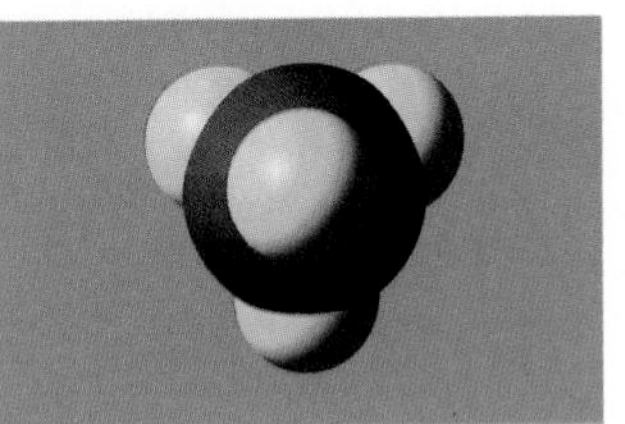

c Computer graphic of a tetrahedral molecule

Frank Cox

On the other hand, some molecules exhibit a **linear structure** (all atoms in a line). An example is the CO_2 molecule.

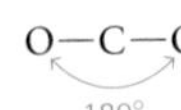

Note that a linear molecule has a 180° bond angle.

A third type of molecular structure is illustrated by BF_3, which is planar or flat (all four atoms in the same plane) with 120° bond angles.

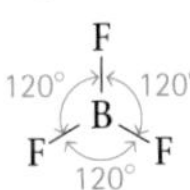

The name usually given to this structure is **trigonal planar structure,** although triangular might seem to make more sense.

Another type of molecular structure is illustrated by methane, CH_4. This molecule has the molecular structure shown in Figure 12.11, which is called a **tetrahedral structure** or a **tetrahedron.** The dashed lines shown connecting the H atoms define the four identical triangular faces of the tetrahedron.

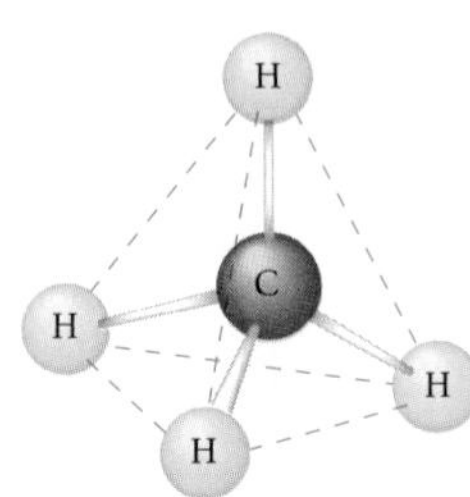

Figure 12.11
The tetrahedral molecular structure of methane. This representation is called a ball-and-stick model; the atoms are represented by balls and the bonds by sticks. The dashed lines show the outline of the tetrahedron.

Section 12.8

Test Bank: 103

TEACHING TIP

Use models in class to demonstrate each of the shapes in this section. It is difficult for students to visualize the shapes of molecules without models. Students can make models at home to help them with problems by using toothpicks and gumdrops or marshmallows.

LABORATORY EXPERIMENT

A relevant laboratory experiment for this section and Section 12.9 is Experiment 14, Length of a Mole, from *Introductory Chemistry in the Laboratory* by James Hall.

accurate mass for a diamond using a bathroom scale.

- To use a model effectively, we must understand its strengths and weaknesses and ask only appropriate questions. An illustration of this point is the simple aufbau principle used to account for the electron configurations of the elements. Although this model correctly predicts the configuration for most atoms, chromium and copper, for example, do not agree with its predictions. Detailed studies show that the configurations of chromium and copper result from complex electron interactions that are not taken into account in the simple model. This discrepancy does not mean that we should discard the simple model that is so useful for most atoms. Instead, we must apply it with caution and not expect it to be correct in every case.
- When a model is wrong, we often learn much more than when it is right. If a model makes a wrong prediction, it usually means we do not understand some fundamental characteristics of nature. We often learn by making mistakes.

Test Bank: 26–28, 99, 100, 104–114

Section 12.9

TEACHING TIP

When teaching the VSEPR model, stress the difference between the arrangement of the electron pairs and the molecular structure. For example, point out the differences between $BeCl_2$ and water. This exercise will help students see the difference between electron pair structure and molecular shape. Many students do not understand why water should have a bent shape and $BeCl_2$ is linear.

Lecture Demonstration: 8.2

PowerLecture Animations: VSEPR Electron-Pair Geometry: 2-Electron Pairs VSEPR

In the next section we will discuss these various molecular structures in more detail. In that section we will learn how to predict the molecular structure of a molecule by looking at the molecule's Lewis structure.

12.9 Molecular Structure: The VSEPR Model

OBJECTIVE: To learn to predict molecular geometry from the number of electron pairs.

The structures of molecules play a very important role in determining their properties. For example, as we see in the "Chemistry in Focus" on page 383, taste is directly related to molecular structure. Structure is particularly important for biological molecules; a slight change in the structure of a large biomolecule can completely destroy its usefulness to a cell and may even change the cell from a normal one to a cancerous one.

Many experimental methods now exist for determining the molecular structure of a molecule—that is, the three-dimensional arrangement of the atoms. These methods must be used when accurate information about the structure is required. However, it is often useful to be able to predict the *approximate* molecular structure of a molecule. In this section we consider a simple model that allows us to do this. This model, called the **valence shell electron pair repulsion (VSEPR) model,** is useful for predicting the molecular structures of molecules formed from nonmetals. The main idea of this model is that *the structure around a given atom is determined by minimizing repulsions between electron pairs.* This means that the bonding and nonbonding electron pairs (lone pairs) around a given atom are positioned *as far apart as possible.* To see how this model works, we will first consider the molecule $BeCl_2$, which has the following Lewis structure (it is an exception to the octet rule):

:C̈l—Be—C̈l:

Note that there are two pairs of electrons around the beryllium atom. What arrangement of these electron pairs allows them to be as far apart as possible to minimize the repulsions? The best arrangement places the pairs on opposite sides of the beryllium atom at 180° from each other.

—Be—
180°

This is the maximum possible separation for two electron pairs. Now that we have determined the optimal arrangement of the electron pairs around the central atom, we can specify the molecular structure of $BeCl_2$—that is, the positions of the atoms. Because each electron pair on beryllium is shared with a chlorine atom, the molecule has a **linear structure** with a 180° bond angle.

:C̈l—Be—C̈l:
180°

Whenever two pairs of electrons are present around an atom, they should always be placed at an angle of 180° to each other to give a linear arrangement.

Next let's consider BF_3, which has the following Lewis structure (it is another exception to the octet rule):

```
    :F̈:
     |
:F̈—B—F̈:
```

TEACHING SUPPORT

ACTIVITY

Materials Each student/group will need nine uninflated balloons. You can decrease the number of balloons used by not having each group make each geometry.

Directions Have the students blow up the balloons to the same size. Have them make three geometries: tie two balloons together, tie three balloons together, and tie four balloons together.

Discussion This activity is especially good for understanding tetrahedral geometry because it is now seen to be "natural." While model kits are good, the angles are predetermined; in this case, the students see that the geometries discussed in the book occur simply because the balloons cannot occupy the same space. This is analogous to saying that electrons repel each other and electron pairs try to get as far apart from one another as possible. The knot represents the center atom, and each balloon represents an electron pair.

CHEMISTRY *IN* FOCUS

Taste—It's the Structure That Counts

Why do certain substances taste sweet, sour, bitter, or salty? Of course, it has to do with the taste buds on our tongues. But how do these taste buds work? For example, why does sugar taste sweet to us? The answer to this question remains elusive, but it does seem clear that sweet taste depends on how certain molecules fit the "sweet receptors" in our taste buds.

One of the mysteries of the sweet taste sensation is the wide variety of molecules that taste sweet. For example, the many types of sugars include glucose and sucrose (table sugar). The first artificial sweetener was probably the Romans' sapa (see "Chemistry in Focus: Sugar of Lead" in Chapter 5), made by boiling wine in lead vessels to produce a syrup that contained lead acetate, $Pb(C_2H_3O_2)_2$, called sugar of lead because of its sweet taste. Other widely used modern artificial sweeteners include saccharin, aspartame, sucralose, and steviol, whose structures are shown in the accompanying figure. The structure of steviol is shown in simplified form. Each vertex represents a carbon atom, and not all of the hydrogen atoms are shown. Note the great disparity of structures for these sweet-tasting molecules. It's certainly not obvious which structural features trigger a sweet sensation when these molecules interact with the taste buds.

The pioneers in relating structure to sweet taste were two chemists, Robert S. Shallenberger and Terry E. Acree of Cornell University, who almost thirty years ago suggested that all sweet-tasting substances must contain a common feature they called a glycophore. They postulated that a glycophore always contains an atom or group of atoms that have available electrons located near a hydrogen atom attached to a relatively electronegative atom. Murray Goodman, a chemist at the University of California at San Diego, expanded the definition of a glycophore to include a hydrophobic ("water-hating") region. Goodman finds that a "sweet molecule" tends to be L-shaped with positively and negatively charged regions on the upright of the L and a hydrophobic region on the base of the L. For a molecule to be sweet, the L must be planar. If the L is twisted in one direction, the molecule has a bitter taste. If the molecule is twisted in the other direction, the molecule is tasteless.

The latest model for the sweet-taste receptor, proposed by Piero Temussi of the University of Naples, postulates that there are four binding sites on the receptor that can be occupied independently. Small sweet-tasting molecules might bind to one of the sites, while a large molecule would bind to more than one site simultaneously.

So the search goes on for a better artificial sweetener. One thing's for sure; it all has to do with molecular structure.

Saccharin

Sucralose

Aspartame (Nutra-Sweet™)

Steviol

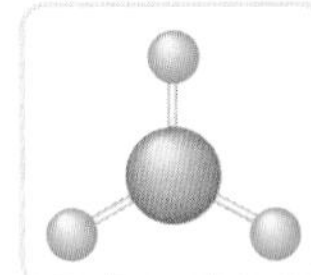

Here the boron atom is surrounded by three pairs of electrons. What arrangement minimizes the repulsions among three pairs of electrons? Here the greatest distance between electron pairs is achieved by angles of 120°.

Lecture Demonstration: 8.3

PowerLecture Animations:
VSEPR Electron-Pair Geometry: 3-Electron Pairs
Rotating Molecular Structure of BF_3

In the case of three balloons, if one is a lone pair, the shape is bent or V-shaped (like SO_2); if there are two lone pairs, it is linear (like CO_2). With four balloons, if there is one lone pair, the shape is trigonal pyramid (like NH_3); with two lone pairs, the shape is bent or V-shaped (like H_2O); with three lone pairs, the shape is linear (like HCl).

Many students initially believe that a central atom with four other atoms around it will naturally form a square planar geometry. This activity can be used to confront this misconception. Once the tetrahedral geometry is naturally formed, you can show that it requires an input of energy to make a square planar geometry. This indicates that the square planar geometry is higher in energy and, therefore, less stable. In addition, if you drop the square planar geometry on the floor, it naturally converts back to the tetrahedral geometry.

If you wish, you could have the students do five balloons (trigonal bipyramid, like PCl_5) and/or six balloons (octahedral, like SF_6). These geometries are not in the text.

PowerLecture Animation: VSEPR Electron-Pair Geometry: 4-Electron Pairs

Because each of the electron pairs is shared with a fluorine atom, the molecular structure is

F (top), B (center), F (bottom left), F (bottom right), angles 120°, 120°, 120° or F, B, F- - - -F

This is a planar (flat) molecule with a triangular arrangement of F atoms, commonly described as a trigonal planar structure. *Whenever three pairs of electrons are present around an atom, they should always be placed at the corners of a triangle (in a plane at angles of 120° to each other).*

Next let's consider the methane molecule, which has the Lewis structure

```
    H                H
    |                ..
H—C—H     or     H:C:H
    |                ..
    H                H
```

There are four pairs of electrons around the central carbon atom. What arrangement of these electron pairs best minimizes the repulsions? First we try a square planar arrangement:

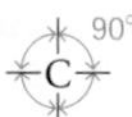

The carbon atom and the electron pairs are all in a plane represented by the surface of the paper, and the angles between the pairs are all 90°.

Is there another arrangement with angles greater than 90° that would put the electron pairs even farther away from each other? The answer is yes. We can get larger angles than 90° by using the following three-dimensional structure, which has angles of approximately 109.5°.

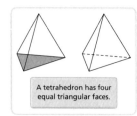

A tetrahedron has four equal triangular faces.

In this drawing the wedge indicates a position above the surface of the paper and the dashed lines indicate positions behind that surface. The solid line indicates a position on the surface of the page. The figure formed by connecting the lines is called a tetrahedron, so we call this arrangement of electron pairs the **tetrahedral arrangement.**

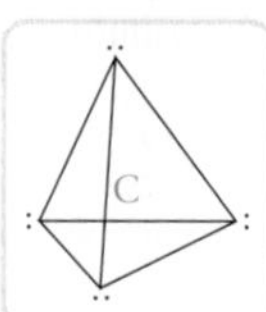

This is the maximum possible separation of four pairs around a given atom. *Whenever four pairs of electrons are present around an atom, they should always be placed at the corners of a tetrahedron (the tetrahedral arrangement).*

Now that we have the arrangement of electron pairs that gives the least repulsion, we can determine the positions of the atoms and thus the molecular structure of CH_4. In methane each of the four electron pairs is shared

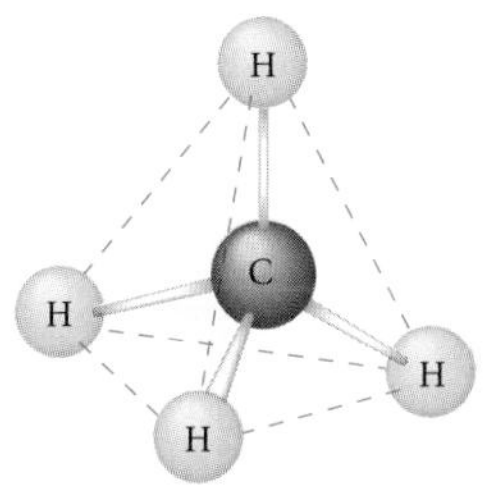

Figure 12.12
The molecular structure of methane. The tetrahedral arrangement of electron pairs produces a tetrahedral arrangement of hydrogen atoms.

between the carbon atom and a hydrogen atom. Thus the hydrogen atoms are placed as shown in Figure 12.12, and the molecule has a tetrahedral structure with the carbon atom at the center.

Recall that the main idea of the VSEPR model is to find the arrangement of electron pairs around the central atom that minimizes the repulsions. Then we can determine the *molecular structure* by knowing how the electron pairs are shared with the peripheral atoms. A systematic procedure for using the VSEPR model to predict the structure of a molecule is outlined below.

Steps for Predicting Molecular Structure Using the VSEPR Model

Step 1 Draw the Lewis structure for the molecule.

Step 2 Count the electron pairs and arrange them in the way that minimizes repulsion (that is, put the pairs as far apart as possible).

Step 3 Determine the positions of the atoms from the way the electron pairs are shared.

Step 4 Determine the name of the molecular structure from the positions of the atoms.

EXAMPLE 12.5 Predicting Molecular Structure Using the VSEPR Model, I

Ammonia, NH_3, is used as a fertilizer (injected into the soil) and as a household cleaner (in aqueous solution). Predict the structure of ammonia using the VSEPR model.

SOLUTION

Step 1 Draw the Lewis structure.

$$\mathrm{H-\ddot{N}-H}$$
$$\mathrm{|}$$
$$\mathrm{H}$$

Step 2 Count the pairs of electrons and arrange them to minimize repulsions. The NH_3 molecule has four pairs of electrons around the N atom: three bonding pairs and one nonbonding pair. From the discussion of the methane molecule, we know that the best arrangement of four electron pairs is the tetrahedral structure shown in Figure 12.13a.

Step 3 Determine the positions of the atoms. The three H atoms share electron pairs as shown in Figure 12.13b.

Step 4 Name the molecular structure. It is very important to recognize that the name of the molecular structure is always based on the *positions of the atoms. The placement of the electron pairs determines the structure, but the name is based on the positions of the atoms.* Thus it is incorrect to say that the NH_3 molecule is tetrahedral. It has a tetrahedral arrangement of electron pairs but *not* a tetrahedral arrangement of atoms. The molecular structure of ammonia is a **trigonal pyramid** (one side is different from the other three) rather than a tetrahedron. ■

Additional Examples

Example 12.5

Describe the molecular structure (shape) of the following molecules using the VSEPR model.

1. Cl_2O

   bent (V shape)

2. N_2O (N is the central atom)

   linear

PowerLecture Simulations:
Determining Electron-Pair Geometry (1)
Determining Electron-Pair Geometry (2)

PowerLecture Simulation:
Determining Molecular Geometry (1)

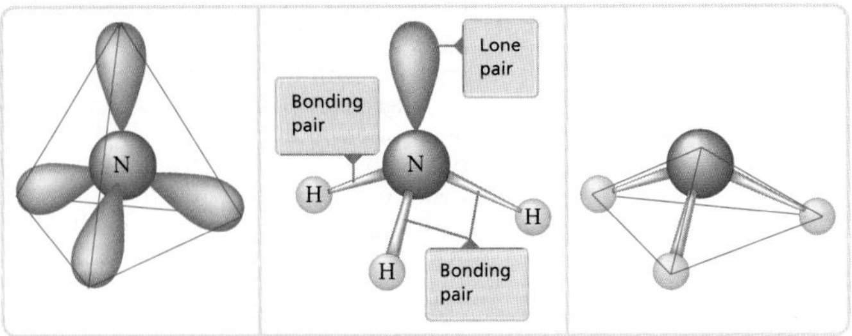

Figure 12.13

a — *The tetrahedral arrangement of electron pairs around the nitrogen atom in the ammonia molecule.*

b — *Three of the electron pairs around nitrogen are shared with hydrogen atoms as shown, and one is a lone pair. Although the arrangement of electron pairs is tetrahedral, as in the methane molecule, the hydrogen atoms in the ammonia molecule occupy only three corners of the tetrahedron. A lone pair occupies the fourth corner.*

c — *The NH_3 molecule has the trigonal pyramid structure (a pyramid with a triangle as a base).*

Additional Examples

Example 12.6

Describe the molecular structure (shape) of the following molecules using the VSEPR model.

1. H_2Se

   bent (V shape)

2. ClO_4^-

   tetrahedral

EXAMPLE 12.6 Predicting Molecular Structure Using the VSEPR Model, II

Describe the molecular structure of the water molecule.

SOLUTION

Step 1 The Lewis structure for water is

H—Ö—H (two lone pairs on O)

Step 2 There are four pairs of electrons: two bonding pairs and two nonbonding pairs. To minimize repulsions, these are best arranged in a tetrahedral structure as shown in Figure 12.14a.

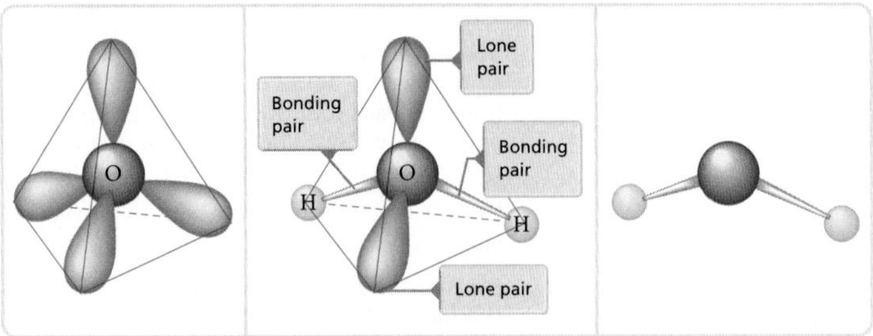

Figure 12.14

a — *The tetrahedral arrangement of the four electron pairs around oxygen in the water molecule.*

b — *Two of the electron pairs are shared between oxygen and the hydrogen atoms, and two are lone pairs.*

c — *The V-shaped molecular structure of the water molecule.*

PowerLecture Animation: Rotating Molecular Structure of NH_3

Self Check

Answers to Self-Check Exercise 12.5

a. 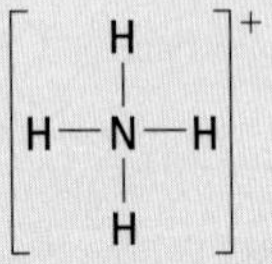 tetrahedral arrangement of electrons; tetrahedral molecular structure

b. 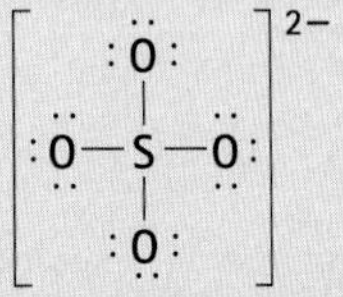 tetrahedral arrangement of electrons; tetrahedral molecular structure

c. 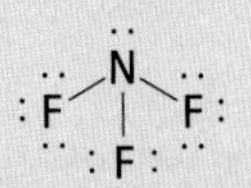 tetrahedral arrangement of electrons; trigonal pyramid molecular structure

d. H—S̈—H (two lone pairs on S) tetrahedral arrangement of electrons; bent or V-shaped molecular structure

e. 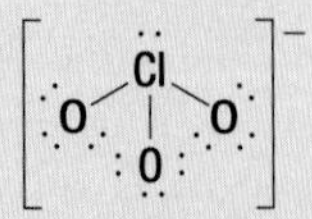 tetrahedral arrangement of electrons; trigonal pyramid molecular structure

f. :F̈—Be—F̈: linear arrangement of electrons; linear molecular structure

Step 3 Although H_2O has a tetrahedral arrangement of *electron pairs,* it is *not a tetrahedral molecule*. The *atoms* in the H_2O molecule form a V shape, as shown in Figure 12.14b and c.

Step 4 The molecular structure is called V-shaped or bent.

MISCONCEPTION

It is crucial that students write the Lewis structure first. Many students believe they can predict the shape from the formula. However, it is easy to show counterexamples. For example, CO_2 is linear, while OF_2 is bent; BF_3 is trigonal planar, while NH_3 is trigonal pyramid.

Self-Check EXERCISE 12.5 Predict the arrangement of electron pairs around the central atom. Then sketch and name the molecular structure for each of the following molecules or ions.

a. NH_4^+ d. H_2S

b. SO_4^{2-} e. ClO_3^-

c. NF_3 f. BeF_2

See Problems 12.81 through 12.84. ■

The various molecules we have considered are summarized in Table 12.4 on the following page. Note the following general rules.

Rules for Predicting Molecular Structure Using the VSEPR Model

1. Two pairs of electrons on a central atom in a molecule are always placed 180° apart. This is a linear arrangement of pairs.
2. Three pairs of electrons on a central atom in a molecule are always placed 120° apart in the same plane as the central atom. This is a trigonal planar (triangular) arrangement of pairs.
3. Four pairs of electrons on a central atom in a molecule are always placed 109.5° apart. This is a tetrahedral arrangement of electron pairs.
4. When *every pair* of electrons on the central atom is *shared* with another atom, the molecular structure has the same name as the arrangement of electron pairs.

Number of Pairs	Name of Arrangement
2	linear
3	trigonal planar
4	tetrahedral

5. When one or more of the electron pairs around a central atom are unshared (lone pairs), the name for the molecular structure is *different* from that for the arrangement of electron pairs (see rows 4 and 5 in Table 12.4).

12.10 Molecular Structure: Molecules with Double Bonds

OBJECTIVE: To learn to apply the VSEPR model to molecules with double bonds.

Up to this point we have applied the VSEPR model only to molecules (and ions) that contain single bonds. In this section we will show that this model applies equally well to species with one or more double bonds. We will develop the procedures for dealing with molecules with double bonds by considering examples whose structures are known.

Section 12.10

LABORATORY EXPERIMENT

A relevant laboratory experiment for this section is Experiment 18, Lewis Structures and Molecular Shapes, from *Introductory Chemistry in the Laboratory* by James Hall.

Table 12.4 Arrangements of Electron Pairs and the Resulting Molecular Structures for Two, Three, and Four Electron Pairs

Number of Electron Pairs	Bonds	Electron Pair Arrangement	Ball-and-Stick Model	Molecular Structure	Partial Lewis Structure	Ball-and-Stick Model
2	2	Linear	180°	Linear	A—B—A	Cl—Be—Cl
3	3	Trigonal planar (triangular)	120°	Trigonal planar (triangular)	A, B, A, A	F, B, F, F
4	4	Tetrahedral	109.5°	Tetrahedral	A, A—B—A, A	H, C, H, H, H
4	3	Tetrahedral	109.5°	Trigonal pyramid	A—B̈—A, A	N, H, H, H
4	2	Tetrahedral	109.5°	Bent or V-shaped	A—B̈—A	O, H, H

First we will examine the structure of carbon dioxide, a substance that may be contributing to the warming of the earth. The carbon dioxide molecule has the Lewis structure

$$\ddot{\underset{\cdot\cdot}{O}}=C=\ddot{\underset{\cdot\cdot}{O}}$$

as discussed in Section 12.7. Carbon dioxide is known by experiment to be a linear molecule. That is, it has a 180° bond angle.

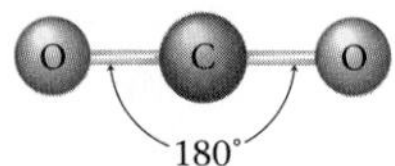

Recall from Section 12.9 that two electron pairs around a central atom can minimize their mutual repulsions by taking positions on opposite sides of the atom (at 180° from each other). This causes a molecule like $BeCl_2$, which has the Lewis structure

$$:\ddot{\underset{\cdot\cdot}{Cl}}—Be—\ddot{\underset{\cdot\cdot}{Cl}}:$$

to have a linear structure. Now recall that CO_2 has two double bonds and is known to be linear, so the double bonds must be at 180° from each other. Therefore, we conclude that each double bond in this molecule acts *effectively* as one repulsive unit. This conclusion makes sense if we think of a bond in terms of an electron density "cloud" between two atoms. For example, we can picture the single bonds in $BeCl_2$ as follows:

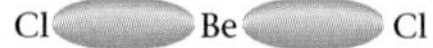

CHEMISTRY IN FOCUS

Minimotor Molecule

Our modern society is characterized by a continual quest for miniaturization. Our computers, cell phones, portable music players, calculators, and many other devices have been greatly downsized over the last several years. The ultimate in miniaturization—machines made of single molecules. Although this idea sounds like an impossible dream, recent advances place us on the doorstep of such devices. For example, Hermann E. Gaub and his coworkers at the Center for Nanoscience at Ludwig-Maximilians University in Munich have just reported a single molecule that can do simple work.

Gaub and his associates constructed a polymer about 75 nm long by hooking together many light-sensitive molecules called azobenzenes:

```
   H     H           H     H
    \   /             \   /
     C—C               C—C
    //  \\    ..  ..  //  \\
H—C      C—N=N—C      C—H
    \   /             \   /
     C=C               C=C
    /   \             /   \
   H     H           H     H
```

Azobenzene is ideal for this application because its bonds are sensitive to specific wavelengths of light. When azobenzene absorbs light of 420 nm, it becomes extended; light at 365 nm causes the molecule to contract.

To make their tiny machine, the German scientists attached one end of the azobenzene polymer to a tiny, bendable lever similar to the tip of an atomic-force microscope. The other end of the polymer was attached to a glass surface. Flashes of 365-nm light caused the molecule to contract, bending the lever down and storing mechanical energy. Pulses of 420-nm radiation then extended the molecule, causing the lever to rise and releasing the stored energy. Eventually, one can imagine having the lever operate some part of a nanoscale machine. It seems we are getting close to the ultimate in miniature machines.

The minimum repulsion between these two electron density clouds occurs when they are on opposite sides of the Be atom (180° angle between them).

Each double bond in CO_2 involves the sharing of four electrons between the carbon atom and an oxygen atom. Thus we might expect the bonding cloud to be "fatter" than for a single bond:

However, the repulsive effects of these two clouds produce the same result as for single bonds; the bonding clouds have minimum repulsions when they are positioned on opposite sides of the carbon. The bond angle is 180°, and so the molecule is linear:

In summary, examination of CO_2 leads us to the conclusion that in using the VSEPR model for molecules with double bonds, each double bond should be treated the same as a single bond. In other words, although a double bond involves four electrons, these electrons are restricted to the space between a given pair of atoms. Therefore, these four electrons do not function as two independent pairs but are "tied together" to form one effective repulsive unit.

We reach this same conclusion by considering the known structures of other molecules that contain double bonds. For example, consider the ozone molecule, which has eighteen valence electrons and exhibits two resonance structures:

$$:\ddot{\underset{..}{O}}-\ddot{O}=\ddot{O}: \longleftrightarrow :\ddot{O}=\ddot{O}-\ddot{\underset{..}{O}}:$$

The ozone molecule is known to have a bond angle close to 120°. Recall that 120° angles represent the minimum repulsion for three pairs of electrons.

PowerLecture Simulation: Determining Molecular Geometry (2)

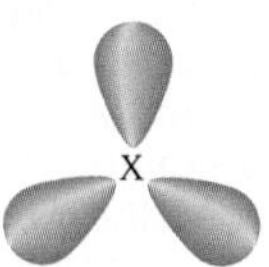

This indicates that the double bond in the ozone molecule is behaving as one effective repulsive unit:

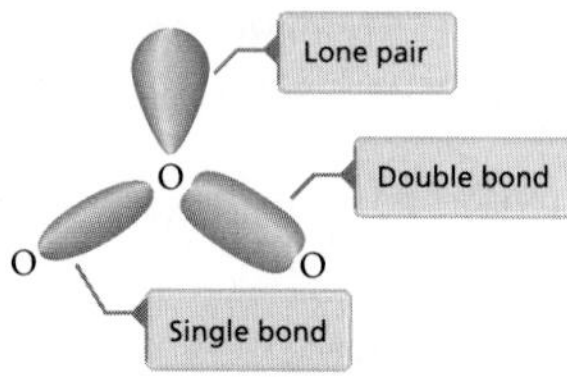

These and other examples lead us to the following rule: *When using the VSEPR model to predict the molecular geometry of a molecule, a double bond is counted the same as a single electron pair.*

Thus CO_2 has two "effective pairs" that lead to its linear structure, whereas O_3 has three "effective pairs" that lead to its bent structure with a 120° bond angle. Therefore, to use the VSEPR model for molecules (or ions) that have double bonds, we use the same steps as those given in Section 12.9, but we count any double bond the same as a single electron pair. Although we have not shown it here, triple bonds also count as one repulsive unit in applying the VSEPR model.

Additional Examples

Example 12.7

Describe the molecular structure (shape) of the following molecules using the VSEPR model.

1. C_2H_2

   linear

2. CO_3^{2-}

   trigonal planar

EXAMPLE 12.7 Predicting Molecular Structure Using the VSEPR Model, III

Predict the structure of the nitrate ion.

SOLUTION

Step 1 The Lewis structures for NO_3^- are

$$\left[\begin{array}{c} :\ddot{O}: \\ \| \\ N \\ :\ddot{\underset{..}{O}}\diagup \quad \diagdown \ddot{\underset{..}{O}}: \end{array}\right]^- \leftrightarrow \left[\begin{array}{c} :\ddot{O}: \\ | \\ N \\ \ddot{O}\diagup\!\!\diagup \quad \diagdown \ddot{\underset{..}{O}}: \end{array}\right]^- \leftrightarrow \left[\begin{array}{c} :\ddot{O}: \\ | \\ N \\ :\ddot{\underset{..}{O}}\diagup \quad \diagdown\!\!\diagdown \ddot{O} \end{array}\right]^-$$

Step 2 In each resonance structure there are effectively three pairs of electrons: the two single bonds and the double bond (which counts as one pair).

These three "effective pairs" will require a trigonal planar arrangement (120° angles).

Step 3 The atoms are all in a plane, with the nitrogen at the center and the three oxygens at the corners of a triangle (trigonal planar arrangement).

Step 4 The NO_3^- ion has a trigonal planar structure. ■

CHAPTER 12 REVIEW

F directs you to the *Chemistry in Focus* feature in the chapter
VP indicates visual problems
OWL interactive versions of these problems are assignable in OWL

Key Terms

bond (12.1)
bond energy (12.1)
ionic bonding (12.1)
ionic compound (12.1)
covalent bonding (12.1)
polar covalent bond (12.1)
electronegativity (12.2)
dipole moment (12.3)
Lewis structure (12.6)
duet rule (12.6)
octet rule (12.6)
bonding pair (12.6)
lone (unshared) pair (12.6)
single bond (12.7)
double bond (12.7)
triple bond (12.7)
resonance (12.7)
resonance structure (12.7)
molecular (geometric) structure (12.8)
bond angle (12.8)
linear structure (12.8)
trigonal planar structure (12.8)
tetrahedral structure (12.8)
valence shell electron pair repulsion (VSEPR) model (12.9)
tetrahedral arrangement (12.9)
trigonal pyramid (12.9)

Summary

1. Chemical bonds hold groups of atoms together. They can be classified into several types. An ionic bond is formed when a transfer of electrons occurs to form ions; in a purely covalent bond, electrons are shared equally between identical atoms. Between these extremes lies the polar covalent bond, in which electrons are shared unequally between atoms with different electronegativities.
2. Electronegativity is defined as the relative ability of an atom in a molecule to attract the electrons shared in a bond. The difference in electronegativity values between the atoms involved in a bond determines the polarity of that bond.
3. In stable chemical compounds, the atoms tend to achieve a noble gas electron configuration. In the formation of a binary ionic compound involving representative elements, the valence-electron configuration of the nonmetal is completed: it achieves the configuration of the next noble gas. The valence orbitals of the metal are emptied to give the electron configuration of the previous noble gas. Two nonmetals share the valence electrons so that both atoms have completed valence-electron configurations (noble gas configurations).
4. Lewis structures are drawn to represent the arrangement of the valence electrons in a molecule. The rules for drawing Lewis structures are based on the observation that nonmetal atoms tend to achieve noble gas electron configurations by sharing electrons. This leads to a duet rule for hydrogen and to an octet rule for many other atoms.
5. Some molecules have more than one valid Lewis structure, a property called resonance. Although Lewis structures in which the atoms have noble gas electron configurations correctly describe most molecules, there are some notable exceptions, including O_2, NO, NO_2, and the molecules that contain Be and B.
6. The molecular structure of a molecule describes how the atoms are arranged in space.
7. The molecular structure of a molecule can be predicted by using the valence shell electron pair repulsion (VSEPR) model. This model bases its prediction on minimizing the repulsions among the electron pairs around an atom, which means arranging the electron pairs as far apart as possible.

Active Learning Questions

These questions are designed to be considered by groups of students in class. Often these questions work well for introducing a particular topic in class.

1. Using only the periodic table, predict the most stable ion for Na, Mg, Al, S, Cl, K, Ca, and Ga. Arrange these elements from largest to smallest radius and explain why the radius varies as it does.

ChemWork

Reaction Rates
Initial Rates
Competing Rates
First-Order Rate Law
Integrated Rate Laws
Percent Completion 1
Percent Completion 2
Percent Completion 3
Time and First-Order Kinetics
Time and Second-Order Kinetics
Time and Zero-Order Kinetics
Activation Energy
The Chirping Cricket
Rate Law Concepts

Answers to End-of-Chapter Exercises

1. A *chemical bond* is a force that holds groups of two or more atoms together and makes them function as a unit.

2. The *bond energy* represents the energy required to break a chemical bond.

3. An ionic bond is created when a metallic element reacts with a nonmetallic element.

4. A covalent bond represents the *sharing* of electrons by nuclei.

5. In Cl_2, the bonding is pure covalent with the electron pair shared equally between the two atoms. In HCl, although there is a shared pair, it is drawn more closely to the Cl atom and the bond is polar covalent.

6. In H_2 and HF, the bonding is covalent in nature, with an electron pair being shared between the atoms. In H_2, the two atoms are identical and so the sharing is equal; in HF, the two atoms are different and so the bonding is polar covalent. Both of these are in marked contrast to the situation in NaF: NaF is an ionic compound, and an electron is completely transferred from sodium to fluorine, thereby producing the separate ions.

7. electronegativity

8. A bond is polar if the centers of positive and negative charge do not coincide at the same point. The bond has a negative end and a positive end. Any molecule in which the atoms in the bonds are not identical will have polar bonds (although the molecule as a whole may not be polar). Two simple examples are HCl and HF.

9. large

10. the difference in electronegativity between the atoms in the bond

11. (a) H is most electronegative; K is least electronegative; (b) F is most electronegative; Na is least electronegative; (c) F is most electronegative; B is least electronegative

12. (a) I is most electronegative, Rb is least electronegative; (b) Mg is most electronegative, Ca and Sr have similar electronegativities; (c) Br is most electronegative, K is least electronegative

13. (a) covalent; (b) ionic; (c) polar covalent

14. (a) ionic; (b) polar covalent; (c) covalent

15. a and b

16. c and d

17. (a) H—F; (b) H—Cl; (c) H—Cl; (d) H—Br

18. (a) O—Br; (b) N—F; (c) P—O; (d) H—O

19. (a) Na—F; (b) Ca—O; (c) Cs—Cl; (d) Mg—N

20. (a) Ca—Cl; (b) Ba—Cl; (c) Fe—I; (d) Be—F

21. an electrical effect that occurs in molecules with separate centers of positive and negative charge

22. The presence of strong bond dipoles and a large overall dipole moment makes water a very polar substance. Properties of water that are dependent on its dipole moment involve its freezing point, melting point, vapor pressure, and ability to dissolve many substances.

23. (a) chlorine; (b) oxygen; (c) fluorine

24. (a) H; (b) Cl; (c) I

25. (a) $^{\delta+}C \rightarrow F^{\delta-}$
(b) $^{\delta+}Si \rightarrow C^{\delta-}$
(c) $^{\delta+}C \rightarrow O^{\delta-}$
(d) $^{\delta+}B \rightarrow C^{\delta-}$

26. (a) $^{\delta+}S \rightarrow O\ \delta-$;
(b) $^{\delta+}S \rightarrow N\ \delta-$;
(c) $^{\delta+}S \rightarrow F\ \delta-$;
(d) $^{\delta+}S \rightarrow Cl\ \delta-$

27. (a) $^{\delta+}Si \rightarrow H^{\delta-}$; (b) P—H (the atoms have nearly the same electronegativity); (c) $^{\delta+}H \rightarrow S^{\delta-}$; (d) $^{\delta+}H \rightarrow Cl^{\delta-}$

2. Write the proper charges so that an alkali metal, a noble gas, and a halogen have the same electron configurations. What is the number of protons in each? The number of electrons in each? Arrange them from smallest to largest radii and explain your ordering rationale.
3. What is meant by a *chemical bond?*
4. Why do atoms form bonds with one another? What can make a molecule favored compared with the lone atoms?
5. How does a bond between Na and Cl differ from a bond between C and O? What about a bond between N and N?
6. In your own words, what is meant by the term *electronegativity?* What are the trends across and down the periodic table for electronegativity? Explain them, and describe how they are consistent with trends of ionization energy and atomic radii.
7. Explain the difference between ionic bonding and covalent bonding. How can we use the periodic table to help us determine the type of bonding between atoms?
8. True or false? In general, a larger atom has a smaller electronegativity. Explain.
9. Why is there an octet rule (and what does *octet* mean) in writing Lewis structures?
10. Does a Lewis structure tell which electrons came from which atoms? Explain.
11. If lithium and fluorine react, which has more attraction for an electron? Why?
12. In a bond between fluorine and iodine, which has more attraction for an electron? Why?
13. We use differences in electronegativity to account for certain properties of bond.
What if all atoms had the same electronegativity values? How would bonding between atoms be affected? What are some differences we would notice?
14. Explain how you can use the periodic table to predict the formula of compounds.
15. Why do we only consider the valence electrons in drawing Lewis structures?
16. How do we determine the total number of valence electrons for an ion? Provide an example of an anion and a cation, and explain your answer.
17. What is the main idea in the valence shell electron pair repulsion (VSEPR) theory?
18. The molecules NH_3 and BF_3 have the same general formula (AB_3) but different shapes.
   a. Find the shape of each of the above molecules.
   b. Provide more examples of real molecules that have the same general formulas but different shapes.
19. How do we deal with multiple bonds in VSEPR theory?
20. In Section 12.10 of your text, the term "effective pairs" is used. What does this mean?
21. VP Consider the ions Sc^{3+}, Cl^-, K^+, Ca^{2+}, and S^{2-}. Match these ions to the following pictures that represent the relative sizes of the ions.

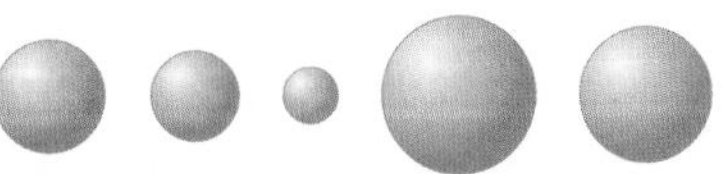

22. VP Write the name of each of the following shapes of molecules.

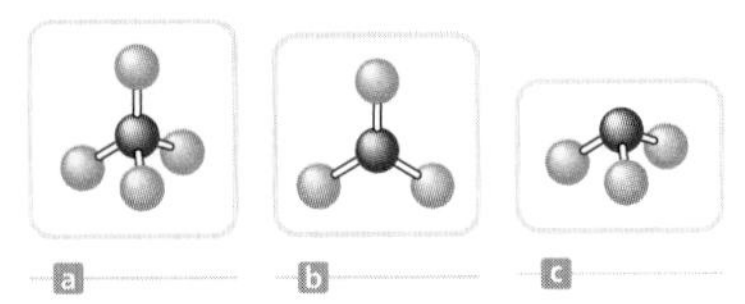

Questions and Problems

12.1 Types of Chemical Bonds

QUESTIONS

1. In general terms, what is a chemical *bond?*
2. What does the *bond energy* of a chemical bond represent?
3. A What sorts of elements react to form *ionic* compounds?
4. In general terms, what is a *covalent* bond?
5. Describe the type of bonding that exists in the $Cl_2(g)$ molecule. How does this type of bonding differ from that found in the $HCl(g)$ molecule? How is it similar?
6. Compare and contrast the bonding found in the $H_2(g)$ and $HF(g)$ molecules with that found in $NaF(s)$.

12.2 Electronegativity

QUESTIONS

7. The relative ability of an atom in a molecule to attract electrons to itself is called the atom's ______.
8. What does it mean to say that a bond is *polar?* Give two examples of molecules with *polar* bonds. Indicate in your examples the direction of the polarity.
9. A bond between atoms having a (small/large) difference in electronegativity will be ionic.
10. What factor determines the relative level of polarity of a polar covalent bond?

All even-numbered Questions and Problems have answers in the back of this book and solutions in the Solutions Guide.

28. (a) $^{\delta+}H \rightarrow C^{\delta-}$; (b) $^{\delta+}N \rightarrow O^{\delta-}$; (c) $^{\delta+}S \rightarrow N^{\delta-}$; (d) $^{\delta+}C \rightarrow N^{\delta-}$

29. When forming ionic bonds, the element forming the positive ion loses enough electrons to have the same configuration as the previous noble gas. The element forming the negative ion gains enough electrons to have the same configuration as the next noble gas. When forming covalent compounds, electrons are shared in such a way that as many atoms as possible in the molecu have a configuration analogous to a noble gas.

30. preceding

31. gaining

32. Atoms in covalent molecules gain a configu ration like that of a noble gas by sharing one c more pairs of electrons between atoms: suc shared pairs of electrons "belong" to each of th bonding atoms at the same time. In ionic bon

PROBLEMS

11. In each of the following groups, which element is the most electronegative? Which is the least electronegative?
    a. K, Na, H
    b. F, Br, Na
    c. B, N, F
12. In each of the following groups, which element is the most electronegative? Which is the least electronegative?
    a. Rb, Sr, I
    b. Ca, Mg, Sr
    c. Br, Ca, K
13. On the basis of the electronegativity values given in Figure 12.3, indicate whether each of the following bonds would be expected to be ionic, covalent, or polar covalent.
    a. O—O
    b. Al—O
    c. B—O
14. On the basis of the electronegativity values given in Figure 12.3, indicate whether each of the following bonds would be expected to be covalent, polar covalent, or ionic.
    a. K—Cl
    b. Br—Cl
    c. Cl—Cl
15. Which of the following molecules contain polar covalent bonds?
    a. water, H_2O
    b. carbon monoxide, CO
    c. fluorine, F_2
    d. nitrogen, N_2
16. Which of the following molecules contain polar covalent bonds?
    a. sulfur, S_8
    b. fluorine, F_2
    c. iodine monochloride, ICl
    d. hydrogen bromide, HBr
17. On the basis of the electronegativity values given in Figure 12.3, indicate which is the more polar bond in each of the following pairs.
    a. H—F or H—Cl
    b. H—Cl or H—I
    c. H—Br or H—Cl
    d. H—I or H—Br
18. On the basis of the electronegativity values given in Figure 12.3, indicate which is the more polar bond in each of the following pairs.
    a. O—Cl or O—Br
    b. N—O or N—F
    c. P—S or P—O
    d. H—O or H—N
19. Which bond in each of the following pairs has the greater ionic character?
    a. Na—F or Na—I
    b. Ca—S or Ca—O
    c. Li—Cl or Cs—Cl
    d. Mg—N or Mg—P
20. Which bond in each of the following pairs has less ionic character?
    a. Na—Cl or Ca—Cl
    b. Cs—Cl or Ba—Cl
    c. Fe—I or Fe—F
    d. Be—F or Ba—F

12.3 Bond Polarity and Dipole Moments

QUESTIONS

21. What is a *dipole moment?* Give four examples of molecules that possess dipole moments, and draw the direction of the dipole as shown in Section 12.3.
22. Why is the presence of a dipole moment in the water molecule so important? What are some properties of water that are determined by its polarity?

PROBLEMS

23. In each of the following diatomic molecules, which end of the molecule is negative relative to the other end?
    a. hydrogen chloride, HCl
    b. carbon monoxide, CO
    c. bromine monofluoride, BrF
24. In each of the following diatomic molecules, which end of the molecule is positive relative to the other end?
    a. hydrogen fluoride, HF
    b. chlorine monofluoride, ClF
    c. iodine monochloride, ICl
25. For each of the following bonds, draw a figure indicating the direction of the bond dipole, including which end of the bond is positive and which is negative.
    a. C—F
    b. Si—C
    c. C—O
    d. B—C
26. For each of the following bonds, draw a figure indicating the direction of the bond dipole, including which end of the bond is positive and which is negative.
    a. S—O
    b. S—N
    c. S—F
    d. S—Cl
27. For each of the following bonds, draw a figure indicating the direction of the bond dipole, including which end of the bond is positive and which is negative.
    a. Si—H
    b. P—H
    c. S—H
    d. Cl—H
28. For each of the following bonds, draw a figure indicating the direction of the bond dipole, including which end of the bond is positive and which is negative.
    a. H—C
    b. N—O
    c. N—S
    d. N—C

All even-numbered Questions and Problems have answers in the back of this book and solutions in the Solutions Guide.

g, one atom completely donates one or more ectrons to another atom, and then the resulting ns behave independently of one another (they e not "attached" to one another, although they e mutually attracted).

3. (a) Cl^-; Ar; (b) Sr^{2+}; Kr; (c) O^{2-}; Ne;) Rb^+; Kr

4. (a) Br^-, Kr; (b) Cs^+, Xe; (c) P^{3-}, Ar; (d) S^{2-}, Ar

35. (a) Na^+, Mg^{2+}, Al^{3+}; $1s^22s^22p^6$; (b) Li^+, Be^{2+}; $1s^2$; (c) K^+, Ca^{2+} from the A group elements; $1s^22s^22p^63s^23p^6$; (d) Rb^+, Sr^{2+} from the A group elements; $1s^22s^22p^63s^23p^64s^23d^{10}4p^6$

36. (a) F^-, O^{2-}, N^{3-}; (b) Cl^-, S^{2-}, P^{3-}; (c) F^-, O^{2-}, N^{3-}; (d) Br^-, Se^{2-}, As^{3-}

37. (a) Al_2S_3; (b) RaO; (c) CaF_2; (d) Cs_3N; (e) Rb_3P

38. (a) $AlBr_3$; (b) Al_2O_3; (c) AlP; (d) AlH_3

39. (a) Ba^{2+}[Xe], S^{2-}[Ar]; (b) Sr^{2+}[Kr], F^-[Ne]; (c) Mg^{2+}[Ne], O^{2-}[Ne]; (d) Al^{3+}[Ne], S^{2-}[Ar]

40. Answers depend on student choice of examples.

41. The formula represents only the smallest whole-number ratio (empirical formula).

42. An ionic solid such as NaCl consists of an array of alternating positively and negatively charged ions: that is, each positive ion has as its nearest neighbors a group of negative ions, and each negative ion has a group of positive ions surrounding it. In most ionic solids, the ions are packed as tightly as possible.

43. Positive ions are smaller because the valence shell has been lost.

44. In forming an anion, an atom gains additional electrons in its outermost (valence) shell. Having additional electrons in the valence shell increases the repulsive forces between electrons, and the outermost shell becomes larger to accommodate this.

45. (a) H; (b) N; (c) Al^{3+}; (d) F

46. (a) F^- is larger than Li^+. The F^- ion has a filled $n = 2$ shell. A lithium atom has *lost* the electron from its $n = 2$ shell, leaving the $n = 1$ shell as its outermost. (b) Cl^- is larger than Na^+, since its valence electrons are in the $n = 3$ shell (Na^+ has lost its 3*s* electron). (c) Ca is larger than Ca^{2+}. Positive ions are always smaller than the atoms from which they are formed. (d) I^- is larger. Both Cs^+ and I^- have the same electron configuration (isoelectronic with Xe) and have their valence electrons in the same shell. However, Cs^+ has two more positive charges in its nucleus than does I^-; this charge causes the $n = 5$ shell of Cs^+ to be smaller than that of I^- (the electrons are pulled in closer to the nucleus by the positive charge).

12.4 Stable Electron Configurations and Charges on Ions

QUESTIONS

29. What does it mean when we say that in forming bonds, atoms try to achieve an electron configuration analogous to a noble gas?

30. The metallic elements lose electrons when reacting, and the resulting positive ions have an electron configuration analogous to the ______ noble gas element.

31. Nonmetals form negative ions by (losing/gaining) enough electrons to achieve the electron configuration of the next noble gas.

32. Explain how the atoms in *covalent* molecules achieve electron configurations similar to those of the noble gases. How does this differ from the situation in ionic compounds?

PROBLEMS

33. Which simple ion would each of the following elements be expected to form? What noble gas has an analogous electron configuration to each of the ions?
   a. chlorine, $Z = 17$
   b. strontium, $Z = 38$
   c. oxygen, $Z = 8$
   d. rubidium, $Z = 37$

34. Which simple ion would each of the following elements be expected to form? Which noble gas has an analogous electron configuration to each of the ions?
   a. bromine, $Z = 35$
   b. cesium, $Z = 55$
   c. phosphorus, $Z = 15$
   d. sulfur, $Z = 16$

35. For each of the following numbers of electrons, give the formula of a *positive ion* that would have that number of electrons, and write the complete electron configuration for each ion.
   a. 10 electrons
   b. 2 electrons
   c. 18 electrons
   d. 36 electrons

36. Give the formula of a *negative* ion that would have the same number of electrons as each of the following *positive* ions.
   a. Na^+
   b. Ca^{2+}
   c. Al^{3+}
   d. Rb^+

37. On the basis of their electron configurations, predict the formula of the simple binary ionic compounds likely to form when the following pairs of elements react with each other.
   a. aluminum, Al, and sulfur, S
   b. radium, Ra, and oxygen, O
   c. calcium, Ca, and fluorine, F
   d. cesium, Cs, and nitrogen, N
   e. rubidium, Rb, and phosphorus, P

38. On the basis of their electron configurations, predict the formula of the simple binary ionic compound likely to form when the following pairs of elements react with each other.
   a. aluminum and bromine
   b. aluminum and oxygen
   c. aluminum and phosphorus
   d. aluminum and hydrogen

39. Name the noble gas atom that has the same electron configuration as each of the ions in the following compounds.
   a. barium sulfide, BaS
   b. strontium fluoride, SrF_2
   c. magnesium oxide, MgO
   d. aluminum sulfide, Al_2S_3

40. Atoms form ions so as to achieve electron configurations similar to those of the noble gases. For the following pairs of noble gas configurations, give the formulas of two simple ionic compounds that would have comparable electron configurations.
   a. [He] and [Ne]
   b. [Ne] and [Ne]
   c. [He] and [Ar]
   d. [Ne] and [Ar]

12.5 Ionic Bonding and Structures of Ionic Compounds

QUESTIONS

41. Is the formula we write for an ionic compound the *molecular* formula or the *empirical* formula? Why?

42. Describe in general terms the structure of ionic solids such as NaCl. How are the ions packed in the crystal?

43. Why are cations always smaller than the atoms from which they are formed?

44. Why are anions always larger than the atoms from which they are formed?

PROBLEMS

45. For each of the following pairs, indicate which species is smaller. Explain your reasoning in terms of the electron structure of each species.
   a. H or H^-
   b. N or N^{3-}
   c. Al or Al^{3+}
   d. F or Cl

46. For each of the following pairs, indicate which species is larger. Explain your reasoning in terms of the electron structure of each species.
   a. Li^+ or F^-
   b. Na^+ or Cl^-
   c. Ca^{2+} or Ca
   d. Cs^+ or I^-

47. For each of the following pairs, indicate which is smaller.
   a. Fe or Fe^{3+} b. Cl or Cl^- c. Al^{3+} or Na^+

48. For each of the following pairs, indicate which is larger.
   a. I or F b. F or F^- c. Na^+ or F^-

All even-numbered Questions and Problems have answers in the back of this book and solutions in the Solutions Guide.

47. (a) Fe^{3+}; (b) Cl; (c) Al^{3+}

48. (a) I; (b) F^-; (c) F^-

49. The valence electrons are found in the outermost principal energy level; they are most affected because they are at the "outside edge" of the atom.

50. When atoms form covalent bonds, they try to attain a valence-electron configuration similar to that of the following noble gas element. When the elements in the first few horizontal rows of the periodic table form covalent bonds, they attempt to achieve the configurations of the noble gases helium (two valence electrons, duet rule) and neon and argon (eight valence electrons, octet rule).

51. noble gas electron configuration

52. These elements attain a total of eight valence electrons, giving the valence-electron configurations of the noble gases Ne and Ar.

53. 4 electrons (2 pairs)

54. Two atoms in a molecule are connected by a triple bond if the atoms share three pairs of electrons (six electrons) to complete their outermost shells. A simple molecule containing a triple bond is acetylene, C_2H_2 (H:C:::C:H).

55. (a) :I· (b) Al· (c) :Xe: (d) Sr:

56. (a) Mg:; (b) :Br·; (c) :S·; (d) :Si

57. (a) 16; (b) 12; (c) 20; (d) 26

58. (a) 24; (b) 16; (c) 20; (d) 14

59. (a) :Br—N—Br: with :Br: bonded below N

(b) H—F:

(c) C bonded to four :Br: atoms

(d) H—C—C—H

60. (a) H—H (b) H—Cl:

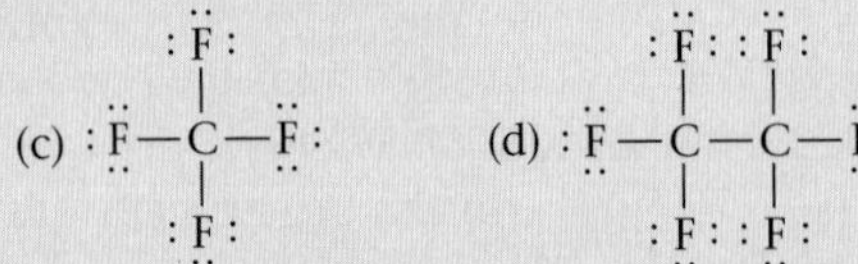

(c) C bonded to four :F: atoms (d) two C atoms bonded to each other, each bonded to three :F: atoms

(c) H—C—C—C—C—H, each C bonded to two H

(d) Si bonded to four :Cl: atoms

61. (a) H—C—C—H, each C bonded to two H (b) F—N—F with F bonded below N

12.6 and 12.7 Lewis Structures

QUESTIONS

49. Why are the *valence* electrons of an atom the only electrons likely to be involved in bonding to other atoms?

50. Explain what the "duet" and "octet" rules are and how they are used to describe the arrangement of electrons in a molecule.

51. What type of structure must each atom in a compound usually exhibit for the compound to be stable?

52. When elements in the second and third periods occur in compounds, what number of electrons in the valence shell represents the most stable electron arrangement? Why?

PROBLEMS

53. How many electrons are involved when two atoms in a molecule are connected by a "double bond"? Write the Lewis structure of a molecule containing a double bond.

54. What does it mean when two atoms in a molecule are connected by a "triple bond"? Write the Lewis structure of a molecule containing a triple bond.

55. Write the simple Lewis structure for each of the following atoms.

a. I ($Z = 53$) c. Xe ($Z = 54$)
b. Al ($Z = 13$) d. Sr ($Z = 38$)

56. Write the simple Lewis structure for each of the following atoms.

a. Mg ($Z = 12$) c. S ($Z = 16$)
b. Br ($Z = 35$) d. Si ($Z = 14$)

57. Give the *total* number of valence electrons in each of the following molecules.

a. N_2O c. C_3H_8
b. B_2H_6 d. NCl_3

58. Give the *total* number of valence electrons in each of the following molecules.

a. B_2O_3 c. C_2H_6O
b. CO_2 d. NO_2

59. Write a Lewis structure for each of the following simple molecules. Show all bonding valence electron pairs as lines and all nonbonding valence electron pairs as dots.

a. NBr_3 c. CBr_4
b. HF d. C_2H_2

60. Write a Lewis structure for each of the following simple molecules. Show all bonding valence electron pairs as lines and all nonbonding valence electron pairs as dots.

a. H_2 c. CF_4
b. Hcl d. C_2F_6

61. Write a Lewis structure for each of the following simple molecules. Show all bonding valence electron pairs as lines and all nonbonding valence electron pairs as dots.

a. C_2H_6 c. C_4H_{10}
b. NF_3 d. $SiCl_4$

62. Write a Lewis structure for each of the following molecules. Show all bonding valence electron pairs as lines and all nonbonding valence electron pairs as dots.

a. PCl_3 c. $C_2H_4Cl_2$
b. $CHCl_3$ d. N_2H_4

F 63. The "Chemistry in Focus" segment *Broccoli–Miracle Food?* discusses the health benefits of eating broccoli and gives a Lewis structure for sulforaphane, a chemical in broccoli. Draw possible resonance structures for sulforaphane.

F 64. The "Chemistry in Focus" segment *Hiding Carbon Dioxide* discusses attempts at sequestering (storing) underground CO_2 produced at power plants so as to diminish the greenhouse effect. Draw all resonance structures of the CO_2 molecule.

65. Write a Lewis structure for each of the following polyatomic ions. Show all bonding valence electron pairs as lines and all nonbonding valence electron pairs as dots. For those ions that exhibit resonance, draw the various possible resonance forms.

a. sulfate ion, SO_4^{2-}
b. phosphate ion, PO_4^{3-}
c. sulfite ion, SO_3^{2-}

66. Write a Lewis structure for each of the following polyatomic ions. Show all bonding valence electron pairs as lines and all nonbonding valence electron pairs as dots. For those ions that exhibit resonance, draw the various possible resonance forms.

a. chlorate ion, ClO_3^-
b. peroxide ion, O_2^{2-}
c. acetate ion, $C_2H_3O_2^-$

67. Write a Lewis structure for each of the following polyatomic ions. Show all bonding valence electron pairs as lines and all nonbonding valence electron pairs as dots. For those ions that exhibit resonance, draw the various possible resonance forms.

a. chlorite ion, ClO_2^-
b. perbromate ion, BrO_4^-
c. cyanide ion, CN^-

68. Write a Lewis structure for each of the following polyatomic ions. Show all bonding valence electron pairs as lines and all nonbonding valence electron pairs as dots. For those ions that exhibit resonance, draw the various possible resonance forms.

a. carbonate ion, CO_3^{2-}
b. ammonium ion, NH_4^+
c. hypochlorite ion, ClO^-

All even-numbered Questions and Problems have answers in the back of this book and solutions in the Solutions Guide.

62. (a)

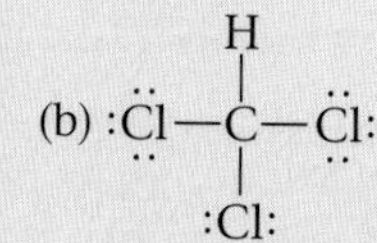

(b) :Cl—C(H)(Cl:)—Cl:

(c) :Cl—C(H)(H)—C(H)(H)—Cl:

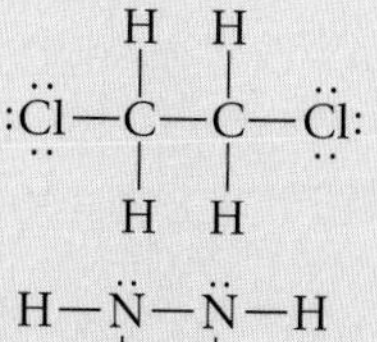

(d) 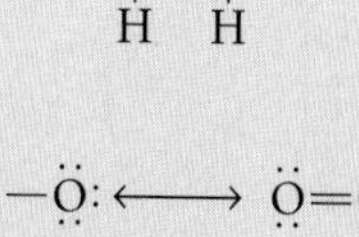 H—N(H)—N(H)—H

64.

:O≡C—O: ⟷ O=C=O ⟷ :O—C≡O:

63.

CH_3—S(=O:)—$(CH_2)_4$—N=C=S

CH_3—S(=O:)—$(CH_2)_4$—N≡C—S:

CH_3—S(=O:)—$(CH_2)_4$—N—C≡S:

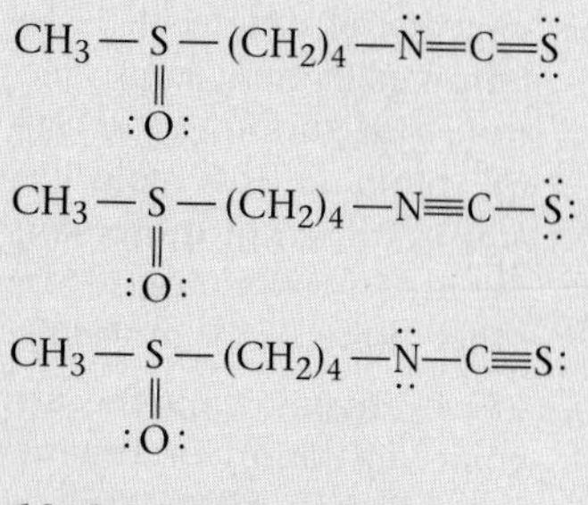

64. See bottom of page

65. (a) 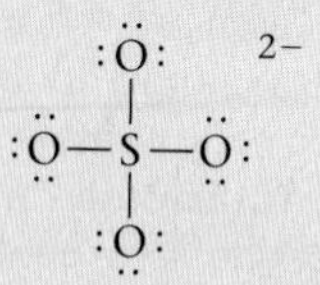 [:O—S(:O:)(:O:)—O:] 2−

(b) 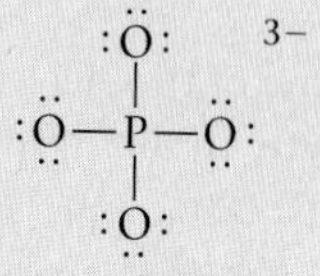 [:O—P(:O:)(:O:)—O:] 3−

(c) 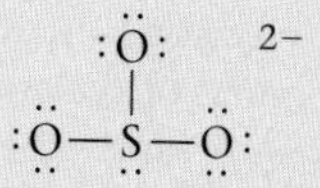 [:O—S(:O:)—O:] 2−

66. See bottom of next page

67. (a) 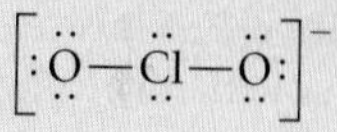 [:O—Cl—O:]⁻

(b) 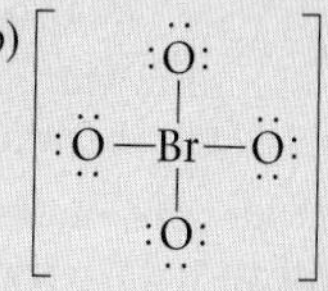 [:O—Br(:O:)(:O:)—O:]⁻

(c) 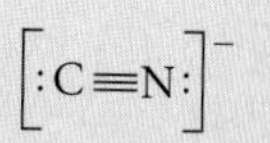 [:C≡N:]⁻

68. See bottom of next page

69. bent (V-shaped); four pairs; bond angle ~106°

70. The geometric structure of NH_3 is that of a trigonal pyramid. The nitrogen atom of NH_3 is surrounded by four electron pairs (three are bonding, one is a lone pair). The H N H bond angle is somewhat less than 109.5° (because of the presence of the lone pair).

71. trigonal planar; three pairs; bond angle 120°

72. SiF_4 has a tetrahedral geometric structure; eight pairs of electrons on Si; ~109.5°

73. The shape plays a very big role in the reactivity of the molecule, especially in biological molecules, where a slight change in shape can render a molecule useless to a cell.

74. The general molecular structure of a molecule is determined by how many electron pairs surround the central atom in the molecule, and by which of those pairs are used for bonding to the other atoms of the molecule.

75. by maximizing the angular separation of the valence electron pairs

76. Geometry shows that only two points in space are needed to indicate a straight line. A diatomic molecule represents two points in space.

77. One of the electron pairs is a lone (nonbonding) pair.

78. In NF_3, the nitrogen atom has *four* pairs of valence electrons; in BF_3, only *three* pairs of valence electrons surround the boron atom. The nonbonding pair on nitrogen in NF_3 pushes the three F atoms out of the plane of the N atom.

79. (a) 4 pairs, tetrahedral; (b) 4 pairs, tetrahedral; (c) 4 pairs, tetrahedral

80. (a) four pairs of electrons in a (distorted) tetrahedral arrangement; (b) four pairs of electrons in a (slightly distorted) tetrahedral arrangement; (c) four pairs of electrons in a tetrahedral arrangement

81. (a) trigonal pyramidal; (b) nonlinear/V-shaped; (c) tetrahedral

82. (a) trigonal pyramidal; (b) trigonal pyramidal; (c) non-linear (bent, V-shaped)

83. (a) tetrahedral; (b) tetrahedral; (c) tetrahedral

12.8 Molecular Structure

QUESTIONS

69. What is the geometric structure of the water molecule? How many pairs of valence electrons are there on the oxygen atom in the water molecule? What is the approximate H—O—H bond angle in water?

70. What is the geometric structure of the ammonia molecule? How many pairs of electrons surround the nitrogen atom in NH_3? What is the approximate H—N—H bond angle in ammonia?

71. What is the geometric structure of the boron trifluoride molecule, BF_3? How many pairs of valence electrons are present on the boron atom in BF_3? What are the approximate F—B—F bond angles in BF_3?

72. What is the geometric structure of the SiF_4 molecule? How many pairs of valence electrons are present on the silicon atom of SiF_4? What are the approximate F—Si—F bond angles in SiF_4?

12.9 Molecular Structure: The VSEPR Model

QUESTIONS

73. Why is the geometric structure of a molecule important, especially for biological molecules?

74. What general principles determine the molecular structure (shape) of a molecule?

75. How is the structure around a given atom related to repulsion between valence electron pairs on the atom?

76. Why are all diatomic molecules *linear,* regardless of the number of valence electron pairs on the atoms involved?

77. Although the valence electron pairs in ammonia have a tetrahedral arrangement, the overall geometric structure of the ammonia molecule is *not* described as being tetrahedral. Explain.

78. Although both the BF_3 and NF_3 molecules contain the same number of atoms, the BF_3 molecule is flat, whereas the NF_3 molecule is trigonal pyramidal. Explain.

PROBLEMS

79. For the indicated atom in each of the following molecules or ions, give the number and arrangement of the electron pairs around that atom.
   a. As in AsO_4^{3-}
   b. Se in SeO_4^{2-}
   c. S in H_2S

80. For the indicated atom in each of the following molecules or ions, give the number and arrangement of the electron pairs around that atom.
   a. S in SO_3^{2-}
   b. S in HSO_3^-
   c. S in HS^-

81. Using the VSEPR theory, predict the molecular structure of each of the following molecules.
   a. NCl_3 b. H_2Se c. $SiCl_4$

82. Using the VSEPR theory, predict the molecular structure of each of the following molecules.
   a. NI_3 b. AsH_3 c. OF_2

83. Using the VSEPR theory, predict the molecular structure of each of the following polyatomic ions.
   a. sulfate ion, SO_4^{2-}
   b. phosphate ion, PO_4^{3-}
   c. ammonium ion, NH_4^+

84. Using the VSEPR theory, predict the molecular structure of each of the following polyatomic ions.
   a. dihydrogen phosphate ion, $H_2PO_4^-$
   b. perchlorate ion, ClO_4^-
   c. sulfite ion, SO_3^{2-}

85. For each of the following molecules or ions, indicate the bond angle expected between the central atom and any two adjacent hydrogen atoms.
   a. H_2O b. NH_3 c. NH_4^+ d. CH_4

86. For each of the following molecules or ions, indicate the bond angle expected between the central atom and any two adjacent chlorine atoms.
   a. Cl_2O b. NCl_3 c. CCl_4 d. C_2Cl_4

F 87. The "Chemistry in Focus" segment *Taste–It's the Structure That Counts* discusses artificial sweeteners. What are the expected bond angles around the nitrogen atom in aspartame?

F 88. The "Chemistry in Focus" segment *Minimotor Molecule* discusses a tiny polymer (75 nm long) made of azobenzenes that can do work. Consider the Lewis structure shown in this segment. What are the expected bond angles around the carbon atoms in the structure? What about the C—N—N bond angle?

Additional Problems

89. What is *resonance?* Give three examples of molecules or ions that exhibit resonance, and draw Lewis structures for each of the possible resonance forms.

90. When two atoms share two pairs of electrons, a(n) ________ bond is said to exist between them.

91. The geometric arrangement of electron pairs around a given atom is determined principally by the tendency to minimize ________ between the electron pairs.

92. In each case, which of the following pairs of bonded elements forms the more polar bond?
   a. S—F or S—Cl
   b. N—O or P—O
   c. C—H or Si—H

All even-numbered Questions and Problems have answers in the back of this book and solutions in the Solutions Guide.

66. (a) ClO_3^- (:Ö—C̈l—Ö: with :Ö: bonded below Cl)$^-$

(b) O_2^{2-} (:Ö—Ö:)$^{2-}$

(c) $C_2H_3O_2^-$ (H—C(H)(H)—C(=O:)—Ö:)$^-$ ↔ (H—C(H)(H)—C(—Ö:)=O)$^-$

68. (a) [:O:=C(—Ö:)(—Ö:) ↔ :Ö:—C(=O)(—Ö:) ↔ :Ö:—C(—Ö:)(=O)]$^{2-}$

(b) [H—N(H)(H)—H]$^+$

(c) [:C̈l—Ö:]$^-$

93. In each case, which of the following pairs of bonded elements forms the more polar bond?

a. Br—Cl or Br—F
b. As—S or As—O
c. Pb—C or Pb—Si

94. What do we mean by the *bond energy* of a chemical bond?

95. A(n) ______ chemical bond represents the equal sharing of a pair of electrons between two nuclei.

96. For each of the following pairs of elements, identify which element would be expected to be more electronegative. It should not be necessary to look at a table of actual electronegativity values.

a. Be or Ba
b. N or P
c. F or Cl

97. On the basis of the electronegativity values given in Figure 12.3, indicate whether each of the following bonds would be expected to be ionic, covalent, or polar covalent.

a. H—O c. H—H
b. O—O d. H—Cl

98. Which of the following molecules contain polar covalent bonds?

a. carbon monoxide, CO
b. chlorine, Cl_2
c. iodine monochloride, ICl
d. phosphorus, P_4

99. On the basis of the electronegativity values given in Figure 12.3, indicate which is the more polar bond in each of the following pairs.

a. N—P or N—O c. N—S or N—C
b. N—C or N—O d. N—F or N—S

100. In each of the following molecules, which end of the molecule is negative relative to the other end?

a. carbon monoxide, CO
b. iodine monobromide, IBr
c. hydrogen iodide, HI

101. For each of the following bonds, draw a figure indicating the direction of the bond dipole, including which end of the bond is positive and which is negative.

a. N—Cl c. N—S
b. N—P d. N—C

102. Write the electron configuration for each of the following atoms and for the simple ion that the element most commonly forms. In each case, indicate which noble gas has the same electron configuration as the ion.

a. aluminum, $Z = 13$
b. bromine, $Z = 35$
c. calcium, $Z = 20$
d. lithium, $Z = 3$
e. fluorine, $Z = 9$

103. What simple ion does each of the following elements most commonly form?

a. sodium e. sulfur
b. iodine f. magnesium
c. potassium g. aluminum
d. calcium h. nitrogen

104. On the basis of their electron configurations, predict the formula of the simple binary ionic compound likely to form when the following pairs of elements react with each other.

a. sodium, Na, and selenium, Se
b. rubidium, Rb, and fluorine, F
c. potassium, K, and tellurium, Te
d. barium, Ba, and selenium, Se
e. potassium, K, and astatine, At
f. francium, Fr, and chlorine, Cl

105. Which noble gas has the same electron configuration as each of the ions in the following compounds?

a. calcium bromide, $CaBr_2$
b. aluminum selenide, Al_2Se_3
c. strontium oxide, SrO
d. potassium sulfide, K_2S

106. For each of the following pairs, indicate which is smaller.

a. Rb^+ or Na^+ c. F^- or I^-
b. Mg^{2+} or Al^{3+} d. Na^+ or K^+

107. Write the Lewis structure for each of the following atoms.

a. He ($Z = 2$)
b. Br ($Z = 35$)
c. Sr ($Z = 38$)
d. Ne ($Z = 10$)
e. I ($Z = 53$)
f. Ra ($Z = 88$)

108. What is the *total* number of *valence* electrons in each of the following molecules?

a. HNO_3 c. H_3PO_4
b. H_2SO_4 d. $HClO_4$

109. Write a Lewis structure for each of the following simple molecules. Show all bonding valence electron pairs as lines and all nonbonding valence electron pairs as dots.

a. GeH_4 c. NI_3
b. Icl d. PF_3

110. Write a Lewis structure for each of the following simple molecules. Show all bonding valence electron pairs as lines and all nonbonding valence electron pairs as dots.

a. N_2H_4 c. NCl_3
b. C_2H_6 d. $SiCl_4$

111. Write a Lewis structure for each of the following simple molecules. Show all bonding valence electron pairs as lines and all nonbonding valence electron pairs as dots. For those molecules that exhibit

All even-numbered Questions and Problems have answers in the back of this book and solutions in the Solutions Guide.

84. (a) basically tetrahedral arrangement of the oxygens around the phosphorus; (b) tetrahedral; (c) trigonal pyramid

85. (a) <109.5°; (b) <109.5°; (c) 109.5°; (d) 109.5°

86. (a) approximately tetrahedral (a little less than 109.5°); (b) approximately tetrahedral (a little less than 109.5°); (c) tetrahedral (109.5°); (d) trigonal planar (120°) because of the double bond

87. The bond angles would be expected to be slightly less than the 109.5° angle expected for four electron pairs due to one of the electron pairs being nonbonding.

88. 120° around the carbon atoms in the rings; 120° also for the C—N—N and N—N—C bond angles. The double bonds influence the bond angles greatly, with each atom having only three "effective pairs" of electrons around the atom.

89. Resonance exists when more than one valid Lewis structure can be drawn for a molecule. The actual bonding/structure is thought to be somewhere "in between" the various possible Lewis structures.

90. double

91. repulsion

92. (a) S—F; (b) P—O; (c) C—H

93. (a) Br—F; (b) As—O; (c) Pb—C

94. The bond energy is the energy required to break the bond.

95. covalent

96. (a) Be; (b) N; (c) F

97. (a) polar covalent; (b) covalent; (c) covalent; (d) polar covalent

98. a, c

99. (a) N—P is more polar; (b) the bonds are of the same polarity; (c) the bonds are of the same polarity; (d) N—F is more polar

100. (a) O; (b) Br; (c) I

101. (a) N—Cl atoms of same electronegativity; (b) $^{\delta+}P \rightarrow N^{\delta-}$; (c) $^{\delta+}S \rightarrow N^{\delta-}$; (d) $^{\delta+}C \rightarrow N^{\delta-}$

102. (a) Al: $1s^22s^22p^63s^23p^1$; Al^{3+}: $1s^22s^22p^6$; Ne has the same configuration as Al^{3+}; (b) Br: $1s^22s^22p^63s^23p^64s^2 3d^{10}4p^5$; Br^-: $1s^22s^22p^63s^2 3p^64s^2 3d^{10}4p^6$; Kr has the same configuration as Br^-; (c) Ca: $1s^22s^22p^63s^23p^64s^2$; Ca^{2+}: $1s^22s^22p^63s^23p^6$; Ar has the same configuration as Ca^{2+}; (d) Li: $1s^22s^1$; Li^+: $1s^2$; He has the same configuration as Li^+; (e) F: $1s^22s^22p^5$; F^-: $1s^22s^22p^6$; Ne has the same configuration as F^-

103. (a) Na^+; (b) I^-; (c) K^+; (d) Ca^{2+}; (e) S^{2-}; (f) Mg^{2+}; (g) Al^{3+}; (h) N^{3-}

104. (a) Na_2Se; (b) RbF; (c) K_2Te; (d) BaSe; (e) KAt; (f) FrCl

105. (a) Ca^{2+}[Ar], Br^-[Kr]; (b) Al^{3+}[Ne], Se^{2-}[Kr]; (c) Sr^{2+}[Kr], O^{2-}[Ne]; (d) K^+[Ar], S^{2-}[Ar]

106. (a) Na^+; (b) Al^{3+}; (c) F^-; (d) Na^+

107. The number of dots is indicated: (a) 2; (b) 7; (c) 2; (d) 8; (e) 7; (f) 2

108. (a) 24; (b) 32; (c) 32; (d) 32

109. (a) H—Ge—H (with H bonded above and below Ge)

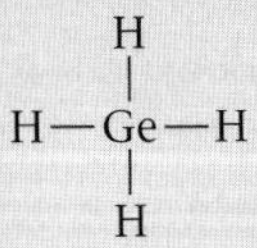

(b) :I—Cl:

(c) :I—N—I: (with :I: bonded below N)

(d) :F—P—F: (with :F: bonded below P)

110.

(a) N_2H_4 H—N—N—H (each N bonded to one H below)

(b) C_2H_6 H—C—C—H (each C bonded to H above and H below)

(c) NCl_3 :Cl—N—Cl: (with :Cl: bonded below N)

(d) $SiCl_4$:Cl—Si—Cl: (with :Cl: bonded above and below Si)

111. (a)

O=S—O: ↔ :O—S=O

(b) :N≡N—O:

(c)

O=O—O: ↔ :O—O=O

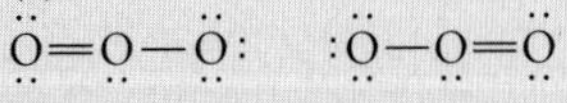

112. See bottom of page

113. In BeF_2, there are only two valence electron pairs in Be; in H_2O, there are four valence electron pairs on O.

114. (a) four pairs arranged tetrahedrally; (b) four pairs arranged tetrahedrally; (c) three pairs arranged trigonally (planar)

115. (a) nonlinear/V-shaped; (b) nonlinear/V-shaped; (c) tetrahedral

116. (a) trigonal pyramid; (b) nonlinear (V-shaped); (c) tetrahedral

117. (a) <109.5°; (b) 109.5°; (c) 180°; (d) 120°

resonance, draw the various possible resonance forms.

a. SO_2
b. N_2O (N in center)
c. O_3

112. Write a Lewis structure for each of the following polyatomic ions. Show all bonding valence electron pairs as lines and all nonbonding valence electron pairs as dots. For those ions that exhibit resonance, draw the various possible resonance forms.

a. nitrate ion
b. carbonate ion
c. ammonium ion

113. Why is the molecular structure of H_2O nonlinear, whereas that of BeF_2 is linear, even though both molecules consist of three atoms?

114. For the indicated atom in each of the following molecules, give the number and the arrangement of the electron pairs around that atom.

a. C in CCl_4
b. Ge in GeH_4
c. B in BF_3

115. Using the VSEPR theory, predict the molecular structure of each of the following molecules.

a. Cl_2O
b. OF_2
c. $SiCl_4$

116. Using the VSEPR theory, predict the molecular structure of each of the following polyatomic ions.

a. chlorate ion
b. chlorite ion
c. perchlorate ion

117. For each of the following molecules, indicate the bond angle expected between the central atom and any two adjacent chlorine atoms.

a. Cl_2O
b. CCl_4
c. $BeCl_2$
d. BCl_3

118. Using the VSEPR theory, predict the molecular structure of each of the following molecules or ions containing multiple bonds.

a. SO_2
b. SO_3
c. HCO_3^- (hydrogen is bonded to oxygen)
d. HCN

119. Using the VSEPR theory, predict the molecular structure of each of the following molecules or ions containing multiple bonds.

a. CO_3^{2-}
b. HNO_3 (hydrogen is bonded to oxygen)
c. NO_2^-
d. C_2H_2

120. Explain briefly how substances with ionic bonding differ in properties from substances with covalent bonding.

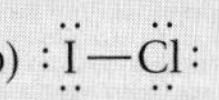

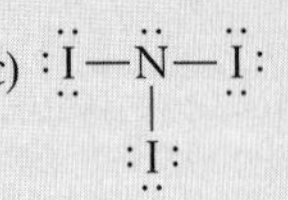

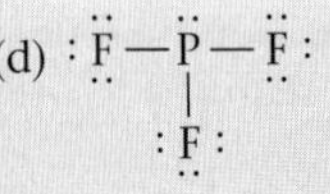

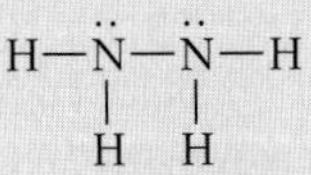

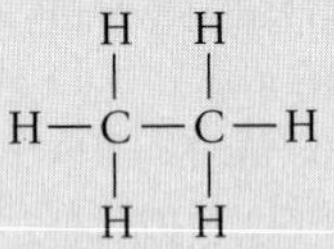

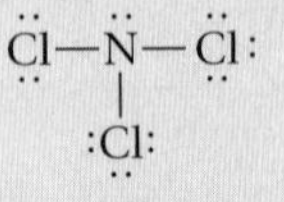

121. Explain the difference between a covalent bond formed between two atoms of the same element and a covalent bond formed between atoms of two different elements.

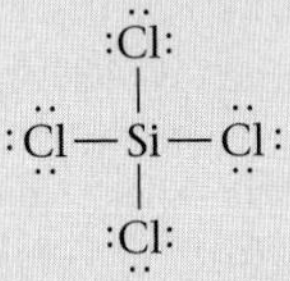

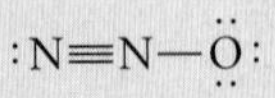

All even-numbered Questions and Problems have answers in the back of this book and solutions in the Solutions Guide.

112.

(a) NO_3^- $[O=N—O:]^-$ (with :O: bonded below N) ↔ $[:O—N—O:]^-$ (with O double-bonded below N) ↔ $[:O—N=O]^-$ (with :O: bonded below N)

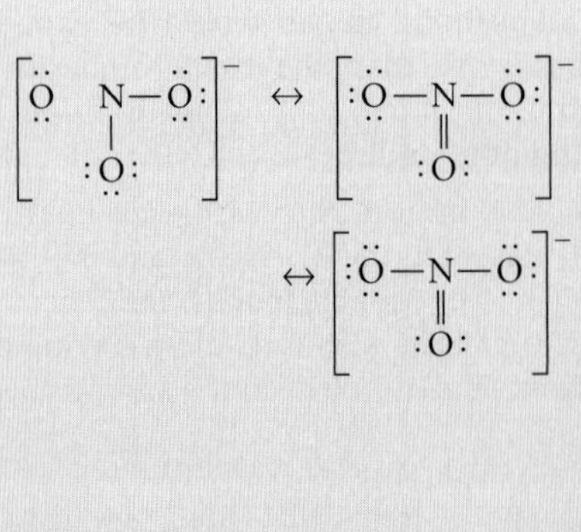

(b) CO_3^{2-} $[O=C—O:]^{2-}$ (with :O: bonded below C) ↔ $[:O—C=O]^{2-}$ (with :O: bonded below C) ↔ $[:O—C—O:]^{2-}$ (with O double-bonded below C)

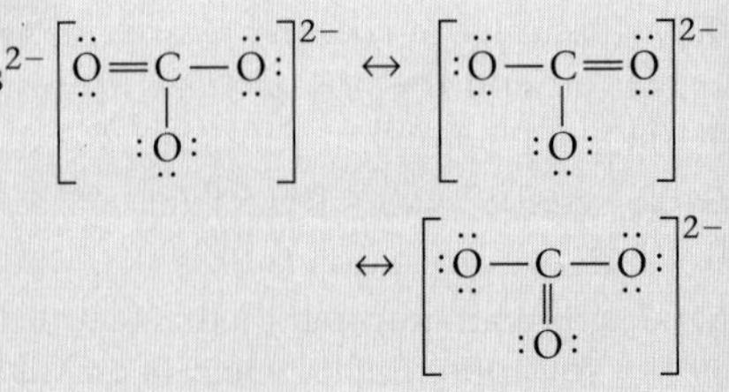

(c) NH_4^+ $[H—N—H]^+$ (with H bonded above and below N)

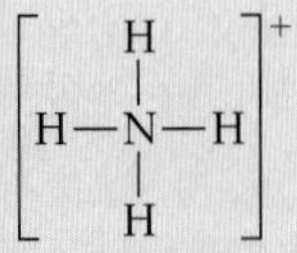

QUESTIONS

1. What is *potential* energy? What is *kinetic* energy? What do we mean by the *law of conservation of energy?* What do scientists mean by *work?* Explain what scientists mean by a *state function* and give an example of one.

2. What does *temperature* measure? Are the molecules in a beaker of warm water moving at the same speed as the molecules in a beaker of cold water? Explain. What is *heat?* Is *heat* the same as *temperature?*

3. When describing a reaction, a chemist might refer to the *system* and the *surroundings*. Explain each of these terms. If a reaction is *endothermic,* does heat travel from the surroundings into the system, or from the system into the surroundings? Suppose a reaction between ionic solutes is performed in aqueous solution, and the temperature of the solution increases. Is the reaction exothermic or endothermic? Explain.

4. What is the study of energy and energy changes called? What is the "first law" of thermodynamics and what does it mean? What do scientists mean by the *internal energy* of a system? Is the *internal energy* the same as *heat?*

5. How is the *calorie* defined? Is the *thermodynamic calorie* the same as the *Calorie* we are careful of when planning our diets? Although the calorie is our "working unit" of energy (based on its experimental definition), the SI unit of energy is the *joule*. How are joules and calories related? What does the *specific heat capacity* of a substance represent? What common substance has a relatively high specific heat capacity, which makes it useful for cooling purposes?

6. What is the *enthalpy* change for a process? Is enthalpy a state function? In what experimental apparatus are enthalpy changes measured?

7. Hess's law is often confusing to students. Imagine you are talking to a friend who has not taken any science courses. Using the reactions

$$P_4(s) + 6Cl_2(g) \rightarrow 4PCl_3(g) \qquad \Delta H = -2.44 \times 10^3 \text{ kJ}$$
$$4PCl_5(g) \rightarrow P_4(s) + 10Cl_2(g) \qquad \Delta H = 3.43 \times 10^3 \text{ kJ}$$

Explain to your friend how Hess's law can be used to calculate the enthalpy change for the reaction

$$PCl_5(g) \rightarrow PCl_3(g) + Cl_2(g)$$

8. The first law of thermodynamics indicates that the total energy content of the universe is constant. If this is true, why do we worry about "energy conservation"? What do we mean by the *quality* of energy, rather than the *quantity?* Give an example. Although the quantity of energy in the universe may be constant, is the *quality* of that energy changing?

9. What do *petroleum* and *natural gas* consist of? Indicate some petroleum "fractions" and explain what they are used for. What does it mean to "crack" petroleum and why is this done? What was tetraethyl lead used for, and why has its use been drastically reduced? What is the *greenhouse effect,* and why are scientists concerned about it?

10. What is a *driving force?* Name two common and important driving forces, and give an example of each. What is *entropy?* Although the total *energy* of the universe is constant, is the *entropy* of the universe constant? What is a spontaneous process?

11. Suppose we have separate 25-g samples of iron, silver, and gold. If 125 J of heat energy is applied separately to each of the three samples, show by calculation which sample will end up at the highest temperature.

12. Methane, CH_4, is the major component of natural gas. Methane burns in air, releasing approximately 890 kJ of heat energy per mole.

$$CH_4(g) + 2O_2(g) \rightarrow CO_2(g) + 2H_2O(g)$$

a. What quantity of heat is released if 0.521 mole of methane is burned?
b. What quantity of heat is released if 1.25 g of methane is burned?
c. What quantity of methane must have reacted if 1250 kJ of heat energy was released?

13. What is *electromagnetic radiation?* Give some examples of such radiation. Explain what the *wavelength* (λ) and *frequency* (ν) of electromagnetic radiation represent. Sketch a representation of a wave and indicate on your drawing one wavelength of the wave. At what speed does electromagnetic radiation move through space? How is this speed related to λ and ν?

14. Explain what it means for an atom to be in an *excited state* and what it means for an atom to be in its *ground state*. How does an excited atom *return* to its ground state? What is a *photon?* How is the wavelength (color) of light related to the energy of the photons being emitted by an atom? How is the energy of the photons being *emitted* by an atom related to the energy changes taking place *within* the atom?

15. Do atoms in excited states emit radiation randomly, at any wavelength? Why? What does it mean to say that the hydrogen atom has only certain *discrete energy levels* available? How do we know this? Why was the quantization of energy levels surprising to scientists when it was first discovered?

16. Describe Bohr's model of the hydrogen atom. How did Bohr envision the relationship between the electron and the nucleus of the hydrogen atom? How did Bohr's model explain the emission of only discrete wavelengths of light by excited hydrogen atoms? Why did Bohr's model not stand up as more experiments were performed using elements other than hydrogen?

118. (a) nonlinear (V-shaped); (b) trigonal planar; (c) basically trigonal planar around C, distorted somewhat by H; (d) linear

119. (a) trigonal planar; (b) basically trigonal planar; (c) nonlinear/V-shaped; (d) linear

120. Ionic compounds tend to be hard, crystalline substances with relatively high melting and boiling points. Covalently bonded substances tend to be gases, liquids, or relatively soft solids, with much lower melting and boiling points.

121. same element, equally shared; different elements, shared unequally

Answers to Cumulative Review Exercises

Chapters 10–12

1. Potential energy is energy due to the position of an object or its composition. Kinetic energy is the energy an object possesses due to its mass and its velocity. The law of conservation of energy states that energy cannot be created or destroyed, but can only be converted from one form to another. Work represents a force acting over a distance. A state function is a property of a system that changes independently of the pathway used to produce the change.

2. Temperature is a measure of the random motions of the components of a substance: in other words, temperature is a measure of the average kinetic energy of the particles in a sample. The molecules in warm water must be moving faster than the molecules in cold water (the molecules have the same mass, so if the temperature is higher, the average velocity of the particles must be higher in the warm water). Heat is the energy that flows because of a difference in temperature.

3. The system represents what we want to focus upon. Typically, this means the chemicals in the reaction. The surroundings represent everything else in the universe, such as the water in which the chemicals of interest are dissolved. An endothermic reaction is one in which energy flows into the system from the surroundings. If the temperature of the surroundings increases (the water), then the chemicals reacting must have transferred energy to the surroundings: the reaction would therefore be exothermic.

4. Thermodynamics is the study of energy and energy changes. The first law of thermodynamics is the law of conservation of energy: the energy of the universe is constant. Energy cannot be created or destroyed, only

17. Schrödinger and de Broglie suggested a "wave–particle duality" for small particles—that is, if electromagnetic radiation showed some particle-like properties, then perhaps small particles might exhibit some wave-like properties. Explain. How does the wave mechanical picture of the atom fundamentally differ from the Bohr model? How do wave mechanical *orbitals* differ from Bohr's *orbits?* What does it mean to say that an orbital represents a probability map for an electron?

18. Describe the general characteristics of the first (lowest-energy) hydrogen atomic orbital. How is this orbital designated symbolically? Does this orbital have a sharp "edge"? Does the orbital represent a surface upon which the electron travels at all times?

19. Use the wave mechanical picture of the hydrogen atom to describe what happens when the atom absorbs energy and moves to an "excited" state. What do the *principal energy levels* and their sublevels represent for a hydrogen atom? How do we designate specific principal energy levels and sublevels in hydrogen?

20. Describe the sublevels and orbitals that constitute the third and fourth principal energy levels of hydrogen. How is each of the orbitals designated and what are the general shapes of their probability maps?

21. Describe *electron spin*. How does electron spin affect the total number of electrons that can be accommodated in a given orbital? What does the *Pauli exclusion principle* tell us about electrons and their spins?

22. Summarize the postulates of the wave mechanical model of the atom.

23. List the *order* in which the orbitals are filled as the atoms beyond hydrogen are built up. How many electrons overall can be accommodated in the first and second principal energy levels? How many electrons can be placed in a given *s* subshell? In a given *p* subshell? In a specific *p* orbital? Why do we assign unpaired electrons in the 2*p* orbitals of carbon, nitrogen, and oxygen?

24. Which are the *valence* electrons in an atom? Choose three elements and write their electron configurations, circling the valence electrons in the configurations. Why are the valence electrons more important to an atom's chemical properties than are the core electrons or the nucleus?

25. Sketch the overall shape of the periodic table and indicate the general regions of the table that represent the various *s, p, d,* and *f* orbitals being filled. How is an element's position in the periodic table related to its chemical properties?

26. Using the general periodic table you developed in Question 25, show how the valence-electron configuration of most of the elements can be written just by knowing the relative *location* of the element on the table. Give specific examples.

27. What are the *representative elements?* In what region(s) of the periodic table are these elements found? In what general area of the periodic table are the *metallic* elements found? In what general area of the table are the *nonmetals* found? Where in the table are the *metalloids* located?

28. You have learned how the properties of the elements vary *systematically,* corresponding to the electron structures of the elements being considered. Discuss how the *ionization energies* and *atomic sizes* of elements vary, both within a vertical group (family) of the periodic table and within a horizontal row (period).

29. In general, what do we mean by a *chemical bond?* What does the *bond energy* tell us about the strength of a chemical bond? Name the principal types of chemical bonds.

30. What do we mean by *ionic* bonding? Give an example of a substance whose particles are held together by ionic bonding. What experimental evidence do we have for the existence of ionic bonding? In general, what types of substances react to produce compounds having ionic bonding?

31. What do we mean by *covalent* bonding and *polar covalent* bonding? How are these two bonding types similar and how do they differ? What circumstance must exist for a bond to be purely covalent? How does a polar covalent bond differ from an ionic bond?

32. What is meant by *electronegativity*? How is the difference in electronegativity between two bonded atoms related to the polarity of the bond? Using Figure 12.3, give an example of a bond that would be nonpolar and of a bond that would be highly polar.

33. What does it mean to say that a molecule has a dipole moment? What is the *difference* between a polar bond and a polar molecule (one that has a dipole moment)? Give an example of a molecule that has polar bonds and that has a dipole moment. Give an example of a molecule that has polar bonds, but that does *not* have a dipole moment. What are some implications of the fact that water has a dipole moment?

34. How is the attainment of a noble gas electron configuration important to our ideas of how atoms bond to each other? When atoms of a metal react with atoms of a nonmetal, what type of electron configurations do the resulting ions attain? Explain how the atoms in a covalently bonded compound can attain noble gas electron configurations.

35. Give evidence that ionic bonds are very strong. Does an ionic substance contain discrete molecules? With what general type of structure do ionic compounds occur? Sketch a representation of a general structure for an ionic compound. Why is a cation always smaller and an anion always larger than the respective parent atom? Describe the bonding in an ionic compound containing polyatomic ions.

transferred from one place to another or from one form to another. The internal energy of a system, *E*, represents the total of the kinetic and potential energies of all particles in a system. A flow of heat may be produced when there is a change in internal energy in the system, but it is not correct to say that the system "contains" the heat: part of the internal energy is *converted* to heat energy during the process (under other conditions, the change in internal energy might be expressed as work rather than a heat flow).

5. The calorie is defined as the quantity of heat required to warm one gram of water by one Celsius degree. The nutritional Calorie (uppercase C) represents 1000 calories. Although the joule is the "official" SI unit of energy, we tend to relate the joule to the calorie since the definition of the calorie is experimental and easy to comprehend: 1 calorie = 4.184 joules. The specific heat capacity of a substance represents the quantity of heat required to warm one gram of the substance by one Celsius degree (which means that the specific heat capacity of water must be 1.00 calorie/J °C as that is also our definition of the calorie). Water's specific heat capacity is higher than that of most other substances, and given its other properties, water is often used for cooling purposes.

6. The enthalpy change represents the heat energy that flows (at constant pressure) on a molar basis when a reaction occurs. The enthalpy change is a state function (which we make great use of in Hess's law calculations). Enthalpy changes are typically measured in insulated reaction vessels called calorimeters (a simple calorimeter is shown in Figure 10.6).

7. If it is possible to combine algebraically two or more chemical equations in such a way as to generate a desired chemical equation, then the heat of the desired chemical equation can be obtained from the heats of the given equations by combining their heats in the same algebraic way the chemical equations were combined. In this example, the desired chemical equation can be obtained by adding together the two given equations, combining terms, then dividing by four. Therefore the heat for the desired equation can be calculated by adding the heats of reaction for the two given equations and then dividing the sum by four.

8. Consider petroleum. A gallon of gasoline contains concentrated, stored energy. We can use that energy to make our car move, but when we do, the energy stored in the gasoline is dispersed throughout the environment. Although the energy is still there (it is conserved), it is no longer in a concentrated, useful form. Thus, although the energy content of the universe remains constant, the energy that is now stored in concentrated forms in oil, coal, wood, and other sources is gradually being dispersed to the universe, where it can do no work.

9. Petroleum and natural gas both consist primarily of hydrocarbons: chains of carbon atoms with hydrogen atoms attached to the chains. Natural gas

36. Why does a Lewis structure for a molecule show only the valence electrons? What is the most important factor for the formation of a stable compound? How do we use this requirement when writing Lewis structures?

37. In writing Lewis structures for molecules, what is meant by the *duet rule?* To which element does the duet rule apply? What do we mean by the *octet rule?* Why is attaining an octet of electrons important for an atom when it forms bonds to other atoms? What is a bonding *pair* of electrons? What is a nonbonding (or *lone*) pair of electrons?

38. For three simple molecules of your own choice, *apply* the rules for writing Lewis structures. Write your discussion as if you are explaining the method to someone who is *not* familiar with Lewis structures.

39. What does a *double* bond between two atoms represent in terms of the number of electrons shared? What does a *triple* bond represent? When writing a Lewis structure, explain how we recognize when a molecule must contain double or triple bonds. What are *resonance structures?*

40. Although many simple molecules fulfill the octet rule, some common molecules are exceptions to this rule. Give three examples of molecules whose Lewis structures are exceptions to the octet rule.

41. What do we mean by the *geometric structure* of a molecule? Draw the geometric structures of at least four simple molecules of your choosing and indicate the bond angles in the structures. Explain the main ideas of the *valence shell electron pair repulsion (VSEPR) theory.* Using several examples, explain how you would *apply* the VSEPR theory to predict their geometric structures.

42. What bond angle results when there are only two valence electron pairs around an atom? What bond angle results when there are three valence pairs? What bond angle results when there are four pairs of valence electrons around the central atom in a molecule? Give examples of molecules containing these bond angles.

43. How do we predict the geometric structure of a molecule whose Lewis structure indicates that the molecule contains a double or triple bond? Give an example of such a molecule, write its Lewis structure, and show how the geometric shape is derived.

44. Write the electron configuration for the following atoms, using the appropriate noble gas to abbreviate the configuration of the core electrons.

a. Sr, $Z = 38$	d. K, $Z = 19$
b. Al, $Z = 13$	e. S, $Z = 16$
c. Cl, $Z = 17$	f. As, $Z = 33$

45. Based on the electron configuration of the simple ions that the pairs of elements given below would be expected to form, predict the formula of the simple binary compound that would be formed by each pair.

a. Al and F	d. Mg and P
b. Li and N	e. Al and O
c. Ca and S	f. K and S

46. Draw the Lewis structure for each of the following molecules or ions. Indicate the number and spatial orientation of the electron pairs around the boldface atom in each formula. Predict the simple geometric structure of each molecule or ion, and indicate the approximate bond angles around the boldface atom.

a. $H_2\mathbf{O}$	d. $\mathbf{Cl}O_4^-$
b. $\mathbf{P}H_3$	e. $\mathbf{B}F_3$
c. $\mathbf{C}Br_4$	f. $\mathbf{Be}F_2$

typically consists of molecules with four or fewer carbon atoms, with petroleum representing larger chains of carbon atoms. The various fractions into which petroleum is separated are based on the approximate number of carbon atoms in the chains. Gasoline, for example, consists of small chains of 5–10 carbon atoms (which makes it a volatile liquid); home heating oil consists of the fraction with 15–25 carbon atoms in the chains (which makes the oil thicker and less volatile); asphalt consists of the fraction with the longest chains, which makes it a nonvolatile semi-solid useful for paving roads. "Cracking" was a process invented to produce a larger fraction of gasoline from crude petroleum: longer chains of carbon atoms are broken down during cracking to give more of the shorter chains characteristic of gasoline. Tetraethyl lead was used as an additive for gasoline to prevent engines from knocking; as engine technology has improved, the need for tetraethyl lead has decreased dramatically. The greenhouse effect considers that some gases prevent heat energy absorbed by the earth from the sun from being radiated back into space. The presence of water vapor in the atmosphere moderates the temperature of the earth, preventing heat from being radiated back into space at night. But as combustion of fossil fuels increases, the concentration of carbon dioxide in the atmosphere is increasing. Carbon dioxide also prevents heat from being radiated back to space, so if there is too much carbon dioxide in the atmosphere, the earth's average temperature will increase. It is feared that an increase in the earth's average temperature may eventually produce severe climatological changes (such as changes in ocean currents and melting of the polar icecaps).

10. A "driving force" is an effect that tends to make a process occur. Two important driving forces are dispersion of energy during a process or dispersion of matter during a process ("energy spread" and "matter spread"). For example, a log burns in a fireplace because the energy contained in the log is dispersed to the universe when it burns. If we put a teaspoon of sugar into a glass of water, the dissolving of the sugar is a favorable process because the matter of the sugar is dispersed when it dissolves. Entropy is a measure of the randomness or disorder in a system. The entropy of the universe is constantly increasing because of "matter spread" and "energy spread." A spontaneous process is one that occurs without outside intervention: the spontaneity of a reaction depends on the energy spread and matter spread if the reaction takes place. A reaction that disperses energy and also disperses matter will always be spontaneous. Reactions that require an input of energy may still be spontaneous if the matter spread is large enough.

(Please refer to p. A32 in this book for answers to Exercises 11–46.)

Chapter 13

Objectives

In this chapter, our objectives are for the students to:

SECTION 13.1

- Learn about atmospheric pressure and how barometers work.
- Learn the various units of pressure.

SECTION 13.2

- Understand the law that relates the pressure and volume of a gas.
- Do calculations involving this law.

SECTION 13.3

- Learn about absolute zero.
- Learn about the law relating the volume and temperature of a sample of gas at constant moles and pressure, and do calculations involving this law.

SECTION 13.4

- Understand the law relating the volume and number of moles of a sample of gas at constant temperature and pressure, and do calculations involving this law.

SECTION 13.5

- Understand the ideal gas law and use it in calculations.

SECTION 13.6

- Understand the relationship between the partial and total pressures of a gas mixture, and use this relationship in calculations.

SECTION 13.7

- Understand the relationship between laws and models (theories).

SECTION 13.8

- Understand the basic postulates of the kinetic molecular theory.

SECTION 13.9

- Understand the term *temperature*.
- Learn how the kinetic molecular theory explains the gas laws.

SECTION 13.10

- Understand the molar volume of an ideal gas.
- Learn the definition of STP.
- Use these concepts and the ideal gas equation.

13 Gases

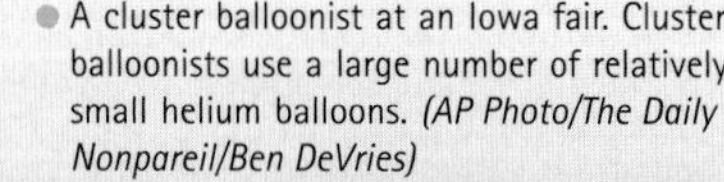

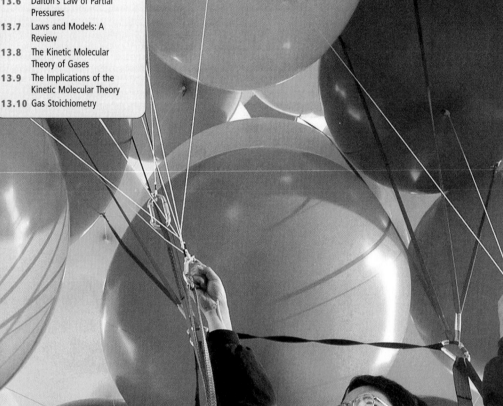

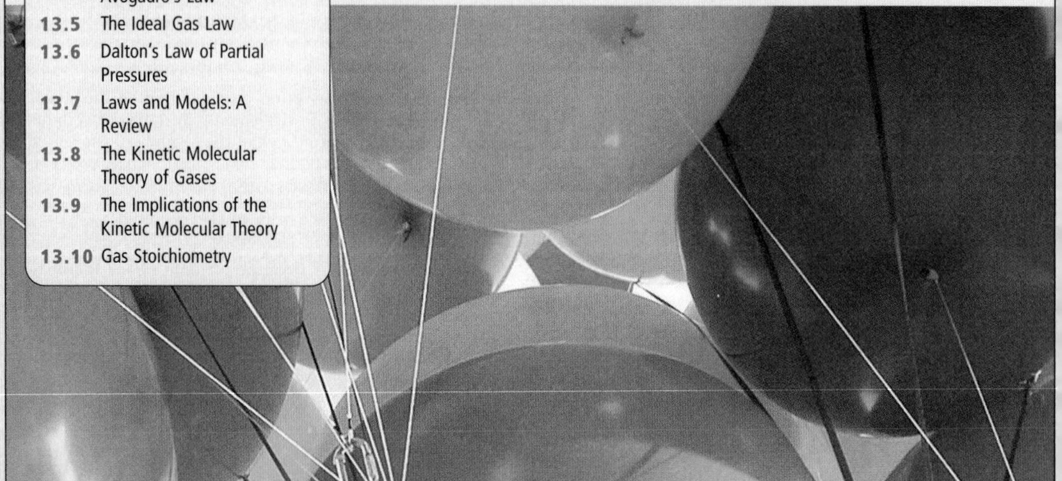

A cluster balloonist at an Iowa fair. Cluster balloonists use a large number of relatively small helium balloons. *(AP Photo/The Daily Nonpareil/Ben DeVries)*

OWL Sign in to OWL at **www.cengage.com/owl** to view tutorials and simulations, develop problem-solving skills, and complete online homework assigned by your professor.

go Chemistry Download mini-lecture videos for key concept review and exam prep from OWL or purchase them from **www.ichapters.com**

We live immersed in a gaseous solution. The earth's atmosphere is a mixture of gases that consists mainly of elemental nitrogen, N_2, and oxygen, O_2. The atmosphere both supports life and acts as a waste receptacle for the exhaust gases that accompany many industrial processes. The chemical reactions of these waste gases in the atmosphere lead to various types of pollution, including smog and acid rain. The two main sources of pollution are transportation and the production of electricity. The combustion of fuel in vehicles produces CO, CO_2, NO, and NO_2, along with unburned fragments of the petroleum used as fuel. The combustion of coal and petroleum in power plants produces NO_2 and SO_2 in the exhaust gases. These mixtures of chemicals can be activated by absorbing light to produce the photochemical smog that afflicts most large cities. The SO_2 in the air reacts with oxygen to produce SO_3 gas, which combines with water in the air to produce droplets of sulfuric acid (H_2SO_4), a major component of acid rain.

The gases in the atmosphere also shield us from harmful radiation from the sun and keep the earth warm by reflecting heat radiation back toward the earth. In fact, there is now great concern that an increase in atmospheric carbon dioxide, a product of the combustion of fossil fuels, is causing a dangerous warming of the earth. (See "Chemistry in Focus: Atmospheric Effects," in Chapter 11.)

In this chapter we will look carefully at the properties of gases. First, we will see how measurements of gas properties lead to various types of laws—statements that show how the properties are related to each other. Then we will construct a model to explain why gases behave as they do. This model will show how the behavior of the individual particles of a gas leads to the observed properties of the gas itself (a collection of many, many particles).

The study of gases provides an excellent example of the scientific method in action. It illustrates how observations lead to natural laws, which in turn can be accounted for by models.

AP Photo/Steve Holland

Steve Fossett flies his balloon *Solo Spirit,* over the east coast of Australia during his attempt to make the first solo balloon flight around the world.

 **Test Bank: 1–9**

Section 13.1

TEACHING TIPS

- Use real-world examples to introduce the concept of pressure. Some good examples are automobile tires, basketballs, balloons, and soda bottles.
- This chapter emphasizes the scientific method in action. Focus on how observations lead to natural laws, and how we try to explain these laws with theories or models.

  Students should understand that while laws are based on observations, the laws do not explain *why* the observation occurs. Laws can help us make predictions, but they are not explanations. Knowing the law of gravity, for example, allows us to predict that if we drop a pen it will fall to the ground. It does not explain why the pen fell, what gravity is, or how gravity "works." To explain the observations, we must develop models or theories. We want each model to be as simple as possible as long as it answers the questions we wish to answer.
- We have taken an atomic/molecular-level perspective throughout the text, so our model for understanding the behavior of gases is based on looking at a gas as a collection of individual particles.

13.1 Pressure

OBJECTIVES: To learn about atmospheric pressure and how barometers work. • To learn the various units of pressure.

A gas uniformly fills any container, is easily compressed, and mixes completely with any other gas (see Section 3.1). One of the most obvious properties of a gas is that it exerts pressure on its surroundings. For example, when you blow up a balloon, the air inside pushes against the elastic sides of the balloon and keeps it firm.

ChemWork Refined over ten years of use by thousands of students, **ChemWork** builds and enhances students' problems-solving skills. Online assignments function as a "personal instructor" to help students learn how to solve challenging problems and learn how to think like chemists. Annotations for **ChemWork** assignments are included at the beginning of the end-of-chapter review.

PowerLecture This 2-DVD package includes the Chemistry Multimedia Library, which contains animations, simulations, and movies for all chemistry subjects, organized by topic for lecture presentations. Annotations for **PowerLecture** are referenced in the margins throughout the Annotated Instructor's Edition.

Lecture Demonstration: 5.1, 5.2

Dry air (air from which the water vapor has been removed) is 78.1% N_2 molecules, 20.9% O_2 molecules, 0.9% Ar atoms, and 0.03% CO_2 molecules, along with smaller amounts of Ne, He, CH_4, Kr, and other trace components.

As a gas, water occupies 1200 times as much space as it does as a liquid at 25 °C and atmospheric pressure.

Soon after Torricelli died, a German physicist named Otto von Guericke invented an air pump. In a famous demonstration for the King of Prussia in 1683, Guericke placed two hemispheres together, pumped the air out of the resulting sphere through a valve, and showed that teams of horses could not pull the hemispheres apart. Then, after secretly opening the air valve, Guericke easily separated the hemispheres by hand. The King of Prussia was so impressed that he awarded Guericke a lifetime pension!

a The pressure exerted by the gases in the atmosphere can be demonstrated by boiling water in a can and then turning off the heat and sealing the can.

b As the can cools, the water vapor condenses, lowering the gas pressure inside the can. This causes the can to crumple.

Figure 13.1

The gases most familiar to us form the earth's atmosphere. The pressure exerted by this gaseous mixture that we call air can be dramatically demonstrated by the experiment shown in Figure 13.1. A small volume of water is placed in a metal can and the water is boiled, which fills the can with steam. The can is then sealed and allowed to cool. Why does the can collapse as it cools? It is the atmospheric pressure that crumples the can. When the can is cooled after being sealed so that no air can flow in, the water vapor (steam) inside the can condenses to a very small volume of liquid water. As a gas, the water vapor filled the can, but when it is condensed to a liquid, the liquid does not come close to filling the can. The H_2O molecules formerly present as a gas are now collected in a much smaller volume of liquid, and there are very few molecules of gas left to exert pressure outward and counteract the air pressure. As a result, the pressure exerted by the gas molecules in the atmosphere smashes the can.

A device that measures atmospheric pressure, the **barometer,** was invented in 1643 by an Italian scientist named Evangelista Torricelli (1608–1647), who had been a student of the famous astronomer Galileo. Torricelli's barometer is constructed by filling a glass tube with liquid mercury and inverting it in a dish of mercury, as shown in Figure 13.2. Notice that a large quantity of mercury stays in the tube. In fact, at sea level the height of this column of mercury averages 760 mm. Why does this mercury stay in the tube, seemingly in defiance of gravity? Figure 13.2 illustrates how the pressure exerted by the atmospheric gases on the surface of mercury in the dish keeps the mercury in the tube.

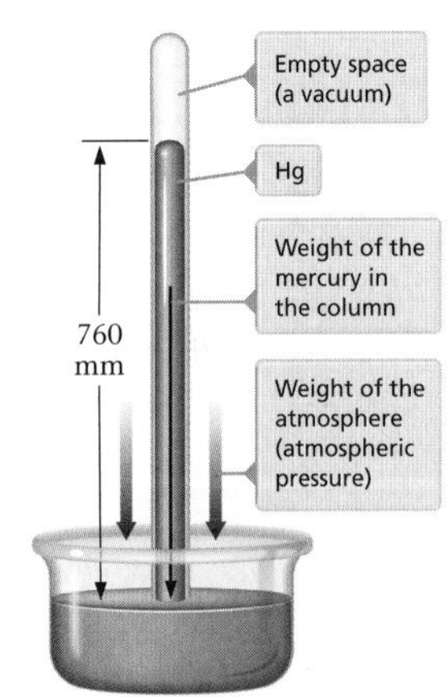

Figure 13.2

When a glass tube is filled with mercury and inverted in a dish of mercury at sea level, the mercury flows out of the tube until a column approximately 760 mm high remains (the height varies with atmospheric conditions). Note that the pressure of the atmosphere balances the weight of the column of mercury in the tube.

DEMONSTRATION

Collapsing Can

Materials Heating unit (hot plate or ring stand, ring and burner), aluminum fluid can (a washed-out gallon ditto fluid can or paint thinner can works well), rubber stopper to fit the opening in the can, hot pad

Preparation Thoroughly wash out the can to remove any remains of flammable solvents. Place about 50 mL of water into the clean can.

Presentation Place the rubber stopper in the opening of the can so that it fits securely but not tightly. Heat the water to boiling and the stopper pops out of the can. Ask students why the stopper popped out of the can. When ready to proceed, remove the can from the heat source and seal the opening firmly with the stopper or a screw cap. Allow the can to stand on the demonstration table. Within about one minute, the can will collapse with very visible results!

Teaching Notes Ask students what the pressure was inside the can before it was heated. Ask what the pressure is when the stopper pops and steam is escaping from the unsealed container. Ask what the pressure is when the can is sealed. In all these cases, have students compare the pressure inside the can to the atmospheric pressure. The can collapses because as it cools the steam condenses back to water, leaving a lower pressure inside the can than atmospheric pressure. The atmosphere crushes the can.

Variation If you cannot find gallon cans for this demonstration, you can use an aluminum soda can. Place about 10 mL of water in the can, heat the water to boiling, and invert the can into a tub of cold water using tongs. The can will collapse immediately with a loud bang.

Lecture Demonstration: 5.3

PowerLecture Video: Collapsing Can

Atmospheric pressure results from the mass of the air being pulled toward the center of the earth by gravity—in other words, it results from the weight of the air. Changing weather conditions cause the atmospheric pressure to vary, so the height of the column of Hg supported by the atmosphere at sea level varies; it is not always 760 mm. The meteorologist who says a "low" is approaching means that the atmospheric pressure is going to decrease. This condition often occurs in conjunction with a storm.

Atmospheric pressure also varies with altitude. For example, when Torricelli's experiment is done in Breckenridge, Colorado (elevation 9600 feet), the atmosphere supports a column of mercury only about 520 mm high because the air is "thinner." That is, there is less air pushing down on the earth's surface at Breckenridge than at sea level.

Units of Pressure

Mercury is used to measure pressure because of its high density. By way of comparison, the column of water required to measure a given pressure would be 13.6 times as high as a mercury column used for the same purpose.

Because instruments used for measuring pressure (see Figure 13.3) often contain mercury, the most commonly used units for pressure are based on the height of the mercury column (in millimeters) that the gas pressure can support. The unit **mm Hg** (millimeters of mercury) is often called the **torr** in honor of Torricelli. The terms *torr* and *mm Hg* are used interchangeably by chemists. A related unit for pressure is the **standard atmosphere** (abbreviated atm).

$$1 \text{ standard atmosphere} = 1.000 \text{ atm} = 760.0 \text{ mm Hg} = 760.0 \text{ torr}$$

The SI unit for pressure is the **pascal** (abbreviated Pa).

$$1 \text{ standard atmosphere} = 101{,}325 \text{ Pa}$$

Thus 1 atmosphere is about 100,000 or 10^5 pascals. Because the pascal is so small we will use it sparingly in this book. A unit of pressure that is employed

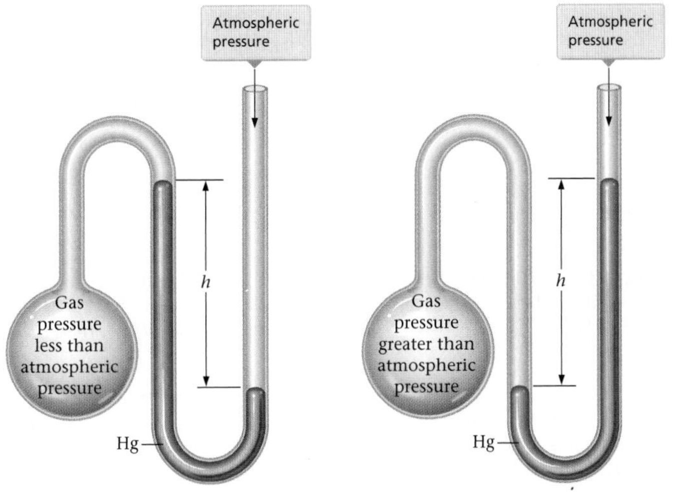

Figure 13.3 A device (called a manometer) for measuring the pressure of a gas in a container. The pressure of the gas is equal to *h* (the difference in mercury levels) in units of torr (equivalent to mm Hg).

TEACHING TIPS

- You might want to discuss how barometers work. If you are fortunate enough to have a classroom barometer, you can discuss it while you show students how it operates.
- Pressure conversion problems provide a means to have students review unit conversions and begin thinking about gases. These problems prepare students for the conversions they will need later in the chapter.

DEMONSTRATION

Make a water barometer using a large test tube and a dish of water. Fill the test tube with water, cover the end with your fingers, invert the test tube in the dish of water, and remove your hand. The water will stay in the test tube because the weight of the atmosphere pressing down on the water is greater than the weight of the water in the tube. The atmosphere can hold water to a height of about 34 feet. We calculate this height by knowing that the atmosphere can hold up about 760 mm Hg (assuming a pressure of about 1.0 atm) and that mercury is 13.6 times as dense as water. Thus the atmosphere can hold up a column of roughly 760 × 13.6 mm, or about 34 feet. This demonstration provides an excellent way to explain why mercury barometers are preferable to water barometers.

Additional Examples

Example 13.1

1. The height of mercury in a mercury barometer is measured to be 732 mm. Represent this pressure in atm, torr, and pascals.

   0.963 atm; 732 torr; 9.76×10^4 Pa

2. The pressure of a gas is measured to be 2.79×10^5 Pa. Represent this pressure in atm, torr, and psi.

   2.75 atm; 2.10×10^3 torr; 40.4 psi

1.000 atm
760.0 mm Hg
760.0 torr
14.69 psi
101,325 Pa

in the engineering sciences and that we use for measuring tire pressure is pounds per square inch, abbreviated psi.

$$1.000 \text{ atm} = 14.69 \text{ psi}$$

Sometimes we need to convert from one unit of pressure to another. We do this by using conversion factors. The process is illustrated in Example 13.1.

EXAMPLE 13.1 Pressure Unit Conversions

Ken O'Donoghue

Checking the air pressure in a tire.

The pressure of the air in a tire is measured to be 28 psi. Represent this pressure in atmospheres, torr, and pascals.

SOLUTION

Where Are We Going?

We want to convert from units of pounds per square inch to units of atmospheres, torr, and pascals.

What Do We Know?

- 28 psi

What Information Do We Need?

- We need the equivalence statements for the units.

How Do We Get There?

To convert from pounds per square inch to atmospheres, we need the equivalence statement

$$1.000 \text{ atm} = 14.69 \text{ psi}$$

which leads to the conversion factor

$$\frac{1.000 \text{ atm}}{14.69 \text{ psi}}$$

$$28 \cancel{\text{psi}} \times \frac{1.000 \text{ atm}}{14.69 \cancel{\text{psi}}} = 1.9 \text{ atm}$$

To convert from atmospheres to torr, we use the equivalence statement

$$1.000 \text{ atm} = 760.0 \text{ torr}$$

which leads to the conversion factor

$$\frac{760.0 \text{ torr}}{1.000 \text{ atm}}$$

$$1.9 \cancel{\text{atm}} \times \frac{760.0 \text{ torr}}{1.000 \cancel{\text{atm}}} = 1.4 \times 10^3 \text{ torr}$$

MATH SKILL BUILDER
$1.9 \times 760.0 = 1444$
1444 ➡ $1400 = 1.4 \times 10^3$
Round off

To change from torr to pascals, we need the equivalence statement

$$1.000 \text{ atm} = 101{,}325 \text{ Pa}$$

which leads to the conversion factor

$$\frac{101{,}325 \text{ Pa}}{1.000 \text{ atm}}$$

$$1.9 \cancel{\text{atm}} \times \frac{101{,}325 \text{ Pa}}{1.000 \cancel{\text{atm}}} = 1.9 \times 10^5 \text{ Pa}$$

MATH SKILL BUILDER
$1.9 \times 101{,}325 = 192{,}517.5$
192,517.5 ➡ $190{,}000 = 1.9 \times 10^5$
Round off

REALITY CHECK The units on the answers are the units required.

TEACHING SUPPORT

HISTORICAL BACKGROUND

Robert Boyle

Robert Boyle, the fourteenth child of the Earl of Cork, was born at Lismore Castle, Ireland, on January 25, 1627. Boyle was a true child prodigy who began studies at Eton at age eight (he was already speaking Greek and Latin) and traveled through Europe with a tutor at age eleven. On his travels he observed demonstrations by the German Otto von Guericke, who had developed an air pump. Guericke's favorite "trick" was to seal two hemispheres together and then remove the air from inside. The difference in pressure between the atmosphere and the inside of the sphere was so great that teams of horses pulling in opposite directions could not separate them.

Self-Check **EXERCISE 13.1** On a summer day in Breckenridge, Colorado, the atmospheric pressure is 525 mm Hg. What is this air pressure in atmospheres?

See Problems 13.7 through 13.12. ■

Self Check

Answer to Self-Check Exercise 13.1

0.691 atm

13.2 Pressure and Volume: Boyle's Law

Section 13.2

Test Bank: 10–14, 16–17

OBJECTIVES: To understand the law that relates the pressure and volume of a gas. • To do calculations involving this law.

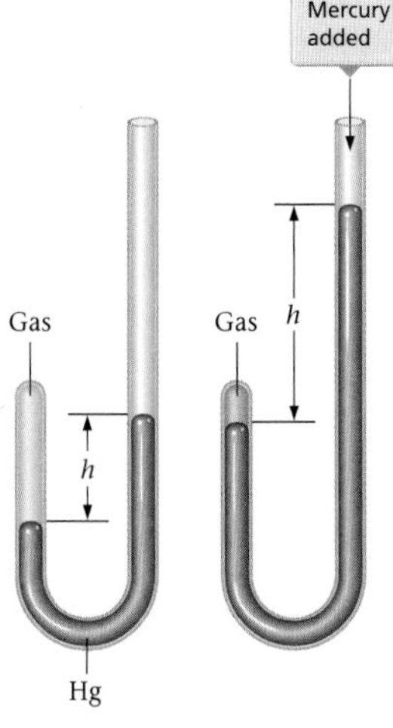

Figure 13.4
A J-tube similar to the one used by Boyle. The pressure on the trapped gas can be changed by adding or withdrawing mercury.

For Boyle's law to hold, the amount of gas (moles) must not be changed. The temperature must also be constant.

The fact that the constant is sometimes 1.40×10^3 instead of 1.41×10^3 is due to experimental error (uncertainties in measuring the values of P and V).

The first careful experiments on gases were performed by the Irish scientist Robert Boyle (1627–1691). Using a J-shaped tube closed at one end (Figure 13.4), which he reportedly set up in the multi-story entryway of his house, Boyle studied the relationship between the pressure of the trapped gas and its volume. Representative values from Boyle's experiments are given in Table 13.1. The units given for the volume (cubic inches) and pressure (inches of mercury) are the ones Boyle used. Keep in mind that the metric system was not in use at this time.

First let's examine Boyle's observations (Table 13.1) for general trends. Note that as the pressure increases, the volume of the trapped gas decreases. In fact, if you compare the data from experiments 1 and 4, you can see that as the pressure is doubled (from 29.1 to 58.2), the volume of the gas is halved (from 48.0 to 24.0). The same relationship can be seen in experiments 2 and 5 and in experiments 3 and 6 (approximately).

We can see the relationship between the volume of a gas and its pressure more clearly by looking at the product of the values of these two properties ($P \times V$) using Boyle's observations. This product is shown in the last column of Table 13.1. Note that for all the experiments,

$$P \times V = 1.4 \times 10^3 \text{ (in Hg)} \times \text{in.}^3$$

with only a slight variation due to experimental error. Other similar measurements on gases show the same behavior. This means that the relationship of the pressure and volume of a gas can be expressed in words as

pressure times volume equals a constant

Table 13.1 A Sample of Boyle's Observations (moles of gas and temperature both constant)

			Pressure × Volume (in Hg) × (in.³)	
Experiment	Pressure (in Hg)	Volume (in.³)	Actual	Rounded*
1	29.1	48.0	1396.8	1.40×10^3
2	35.3	40.0	1412.0	1.41×10^3
3	44.2	32.0	1414.4	1.41×10^3
4	58.2	24.0	1396.8	1.40×10^3
5	70.7	20.0	1414.0	1.41×10^3
6	87.2	16.0	1395.2	1.40×10^3
7	117.5	12.0	1410.0	1.41×10^3

*Three significant figures are allowed in the product because both of the numbers that are multiplied together have three significant figures.

TEACHING TIPS

- Boyle's law is an excellent example of an inverse relationship and provides an opportunity to use graphing to illustrate the application of a math concept.
- Have the students plot the data from Table 13.1 and observe the shape of the graph. The resulting shape (half a hyperbola) is indicative of an inverse relationship, and students should learn to recognize that the equation for an inverse relationship should be $xy = k$ or, in this case, $PV = k$. Table 13.1 shows the constant for the data that students graphed.
- You cannot overemphasize that for Boyle's law to hold true, the temperature and amount of gas must be held constant. Certain activities, such as filling a tire or a basketball with air, seem on the surface to be at odds with Boyle's law. Students often reason this way: "If I add more gas to a container such as a basketball, the volume and pressure both increase. Thus, as pressure increases, so does volume." As a consequence, students may believe that pressure and volume are directly related.

Guericke would then discreetly let the air back in and separate the hemispheres himself. Boyle was intrigued by this demonstration and proceeded to develop an even better air pump. Using this pump he evacuated a chamber and demonstrated that a feather and a lump of coal both fall at the same rate. He also showed that sound could not travel in a vacuum. Boyle later carried out his famous experiments in which he discovered the inverse relationship between gas volume and pressure.

In 1661 Boyle published *The Sceptical Chymist*, in which he abandoned the ancient view of the four elements and took the position that an element must be defined by experiment.

Boyle died in London on December 30, 1691.

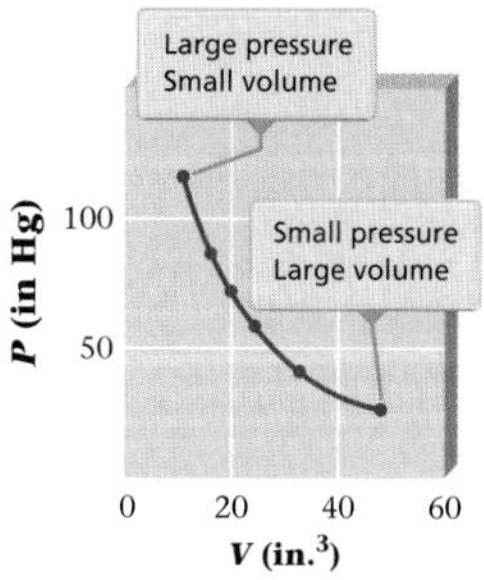

Large pressure
Small volume

Small pressure
Large volume

P (in Hg): 100, 50

V (in.³): 0, 20, 40, 60

Figure 13.5
A plot of P versus V from Boyle's data in Table 13.1.

or in terms of an equation as

$$PV = k$$

which is called **Boyle's law,** where k is a constant at a specific temperature for a given amount of gas. For the data we used from Boyle's experiment, $k = 1.41 \times 10^3$ (in Hg) $\times$ in.^{3}.

It is often easier to visualize the relationships between two properties if we make a graph. Figure 13.5 uses the data given in Table 13.1 to show how pressure is related to volume. This relationship, called a plot or a graph, shows that V decreases as P increases. When this type of relationship exists, we say that volume and pressure are inversely related or *inversely proportional;* when one increases, the other decreases. Boyle's law is illustrated by the gas samples in Figure 13.6.

Boyle's law means that if we know the volume of a gas at a given pressure, we can predict the new volume if the pressure is changed, *provided that neither the temperature nor the amount of gas is changed.* For example, if we represent the original pressure and volume as P_1 and V_1 and the final values as P_2 and V_2, using Boyle's law we can write

$$P_1V_1 = k$$

and

$$P_2V_2 = k$$

We can also say

$$P_1V_1 = k = P_2V_2$$

or simply

$$P_1V_1 = P_2V_2$$

This is really another way to write Boyle's law. We can solve for the final volume (V_2) by dividing both sides of the equation by P_2.

$$\frac{P_1V_1}{P_2} = \frac{P_2V_2}{P_2}$$

Canceling the P_2 terms on the right gives

$$\frac{P_1}{P_2} \times V_1 = V_2$$

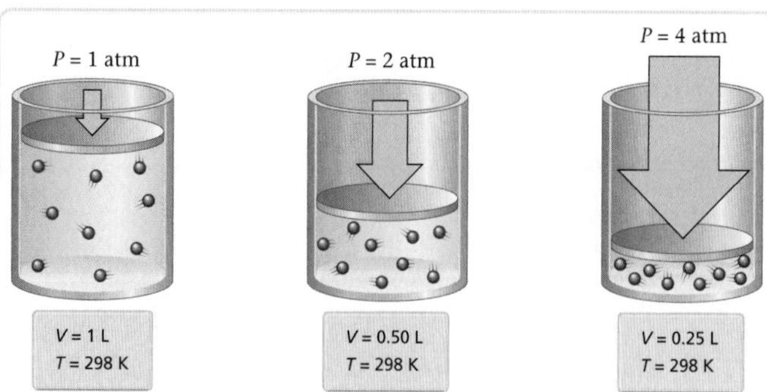

Figure 13.6
Illustration of Boyle's law. These three containers contain the same number of molecules. At 298 K, $P \times V = 1$ L atm in all three containers.

DEMONSTRATION

One qualitative demonstration of pressure–volume relationships involves the use of a syringe that is mounted between two blocks of wood (4″ × 4″ × ½″). The top of the syringe's plunger is attached to one block, and the base of the syringe (with a plastic cap glued to the needle opening to prevent the escape of air) is attached to the other. The apparatus should stand unsupported with air trapped in the syringe. Attach the apparatus to a ring stand for stability during the demonstration. To present the demonstration, show students the apparatus and ask what will happen when a chemistry text is added to the top of the apparatus. Add one. Repeat the process, pointing out that the volume of gas decreases with increasing "book" pressure.

Lecture Demonstration: 5.4, 5.5, 5.7, 5.8, 5.9, 5.10, 5.11

TEACHING TIPS

- Emphasize that in Boyle's law both the temperature and the amount of gas are constant. This point is important in working through the initial gas laws toward the ideal gas equation.
- Students sometimes confuse the idea of an inverse relationship with that of a line having a negative slope. A linear graph with a negative slope is a direct relationship between the variables. To make this distinction clear, focus on the idea that *inverse* means the relationship varies as the reciprocal ($1/x$). Have students focus on the shape of the graph in Figure 13.5. Ask them to tell you what will happen to the pressure as the volume becomes extremely large (the pressure approaches zero, but will never reach zero). As the volume gets smaller, the pressure increases (as the volume goes to zero, the pressure goes to infinity). Thus the graph must not touch the axes—it is a hyperbola, not a straight line.

PowerLecture Animation: Boyle's Law: A Molecular-Level View

or

$$V_2 = V_1 \times \frac{P_1}{P_2}$$

This equation tells us that we can calculate the new gas volume (V_2) by multiplying the original volume (V_1) by the ratio of the original pressure to the final pressure (P_1/P_2), as illustrated in Example 13.2.

EXAMPLE 13.2 Calculating Volume Using Boyle's Law

Freon-12 (the common name for the compound CCl_2F_2) was widely used in refrigeration systems, but has now been replaced by other compounds that do not lead to the breakdown of the protective ozone in the upper atmosphere. Consider a 1.5-L sample of gaseous CCl_2F_2 at a pressure of 56 torr. If pressure is changed to 150 torr at a constant temperature,

a. Will the volume of the gas increase or decrease?

b. What will be the new volume of the gas?

SOLUTION

Where Are We Going?

We want to determine if the volume will increase or decrease when the pressure is changed, and we want to calculate the new volume.

What Do We Know?

- We know the initial and final pressures and the initial volume.
- The amount of gas and temperature are held constant.
- Boyle's law: $P_1V_1 = P_2V_2$

How Do We Get There?

a. As the first step in a gas law problem, always write down the information given, in the form of a table showing the initial and final conditions.

Initial Conditions	Final Conditions
$P_1 = 56$ torr	$P_2 = 150$ torr
$V_1 = 1.5$ L	$V_2 = ?$

Drawing a picture also is often helpful. Notice that the pressure is increased from 56 torr to 150 torr, so the volume must decrease:

$P_1V_1 \rightarrow P_2V_2$

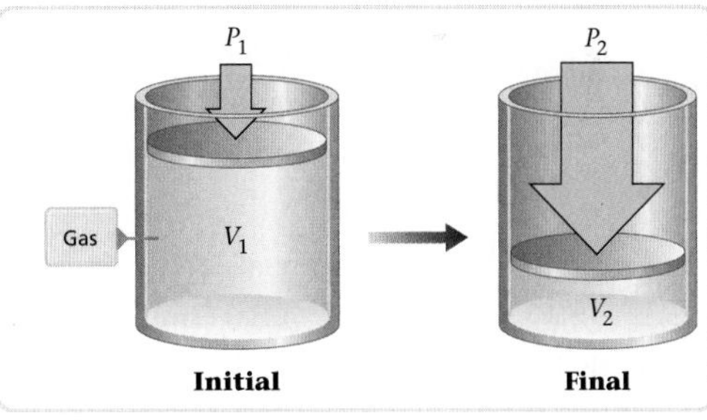

Additional Examples

Example 13.2

1. A sample of helium gas has a pressure of 3.54 atm in a container with a volume of 23.1 L. This sample is transferred to a new container and the pressure is measured to be 1.87 atm. What is the volume of the new container? Assume constant temperature.

   43.7 L

2. A steel tank of argon gas has a pressure of 34.6 atm. If all of the argon is transferred to a new tank with a volume of 456 L, the pressure is measured to be 2.94 atm. What is the volume of the original container? Assume constant temperature.

   38.7 L

TEACHING TIP

Remind students that they should check their answers to confirm that they "make sense." Go through an example and show students how to predict in advance whether volume and pressure should increase or decrease. Then show them that this prediction allows them to see whether their answer makes sense.

We can verify this by using Boyle's law in the form

$$V_2 = V_1 \times \frac{P_1}{P_2}$$

Note that V_2 is obtained by "correcting" V_1 using the ratio P_1/P_2. Because P_1 is less than P_2, the ratio P_1/P_2 is a fraction that is less than 1. Thus V_2 must be a fraction of (smaller than) V_1; the volume decreases.

The fact that the volume decreases in Example 13.2 makes sense because the pressure was increased. *To help catch errors, make it a habit to check whether an answer to a problem makes physical sense.*

b. We calculate V_2 as follows:

$$V_2 = V_1 \times \frac{P_1}{P_2} = \underset{V_1}{1.5\text{ L}} \times \frac{\overset{P_1}{56\text{ torr}}}{\underset{P_2}{150\text{ torr}}} = 0.56\text{ L}$$

REALITY CHECK Because the pressure increases, we expect the volume to decrease. The pressure increased by almost a factor of three, and the volume decreased by about a factor of three.

Self Check

Answer to Self-Check Exercise 13.2

1.22 L

Self-Check EXERCISE 13.2 A sample of neon to be used in a neon sign has a volume of 1.51 L at a pressure of 635 torr. Calculate the volume of the gas after it is pumped into the glass tubes of the sign, where it shows a pressure of 785 torr.

See Problems 13.21 and 13.22. ■

Additional Examples

Example 13.3

1. A sample of neon gas has a pressure of 7.43 atm in a container with a volume of 45.1 L. This sample is transferred to a container with a volume of 18.4 L. What is the new pressure of the neon gas? Assume constant temperature.

   18.2 atm

2. A steel tank of oxygen gas has a volume of 2.00 L. If all of the oxygen is transferred to a new tank with a volume of 5.50 L, the pressure is measured to be 6.75 atm. What was the original pressure of the oxygen gas? Assume constant temperature.

   18.6 atm

EXAMPLE 13.3 Calculating Pressure Using Boyle's Law

In an automobile engine the gaseous fuel–air mixture enters the cylinder and is compressed by a moving piston before it is ignited. In a certain engine the initial cylinder volume is 0.725 L. After the piston moves up, the volume is 0.075 L. The fuel–air mixture initially has a pressure of 1.00 atm. Calculate the pressure of the compressed fuel–air mixture, assuming that both the temperature and the amount of gas remain constant.

SOLUTION

Where Are We Going?

We want to determine the new pressure of a fuel–air mixture that has undergone a volume change.

What Do We Know?

- We know the initial and final volumes and the initial pressure.
- The amount of gas and temperature are held constant.
- Boyle's law: $P_1V_1 = P_2V_2$

MATH SKILL BUILDER

$$P_1V_1 = P_2V_2$$
$$\frac{P_1V_1}{V_2} = \frac{P_2\cancel{V_2}}{\cancel{V_2}}$$
$$P_1 \times \frac{V_1}{V_2} = P_2$$
$$\frac{0.725}{0.075} = 9.666\ldots$$
$$9.666 \Rightarrow 9.7$$
Round off

How Do We Get There?

We summarize the given information in the following table:

Initial Conditions	Final Conditions
$P_1 = 1.00$ atm	$P_2 = ?$
$V_1 = 0.725$ L	$V_2 = 0.075$ L

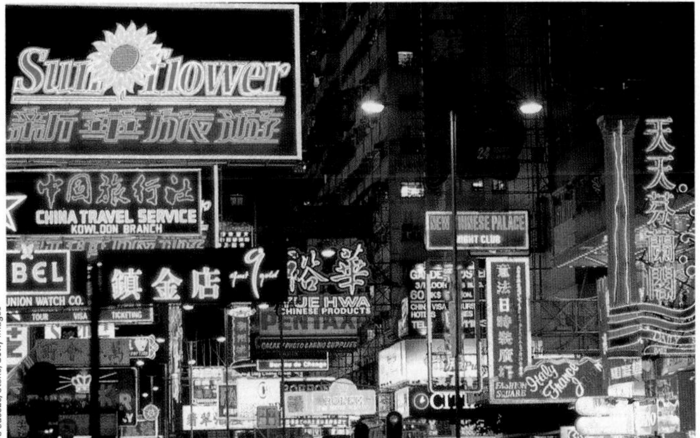

Dave Jacobs/Stone/Getty Images

Neon signs in Hong Kong.

Then we solve Boyle's law in the form $P_1V_1 = P_2V_2$ for P_2 by dividing both sides by V_2 to give the equation

$$P_2 = P_1 \times \frac{V_1}{V_2} = 1.00 \text{ atm} \times \frac{0.725 \not{L}}{0.075 \not{L}} = 9.7 \text{ atm}$$

REALITY CHECK Because the volume decreases, we expect the pressure to increase. The volume decreased by about a factor of 10, and the pressure increased by about a factor of 10. ■

13.3 Volume and Temperature: Charles's Law

OBJECTIVES: To learn about absolute zero. • To learn about the law relating the volume and temperature of a sample of gas at constant moles and pressure, and to do calculations involving that law.

John A. Rizzo/PhotoDisc/Getty Images

In the century following Boyle's findings, scientists continued to study the properties of gases. The French physicist Jacques Charles (1746–1823), who was the first person to fill a balloon with hydrogen gas and who made the first solo balloon flight, showed that the volume of a given amount of gas (at constant pressure) increases with the temperature of the gas. That is, the volume increases when the temperature increases. A plot of the volume of a given sample of gas (at constant pressure) versus its temperature (in Celsius degrees) gives a straight line. This type of relationship is called *linear,* and this behavior is shown for several gases in Figure 13.7.

The solid lines in Figure 13.7 are based on actual measurements of temperature and volume for the gases listed. As we cool the gases they eventually liquefy, so we cannot determine any experimental points below this

The air in a balloon expands when it is heated. This means that some of the air escapes from the balloon, lowering the air density inside and thus making the balloon buoyant.

Presentation Show the balloon and basket to the students, discussing the fact that it just hovers. Ask for suggestions about how to get the balloon to rise. Place the silver side of the balloon over a hot plate (be careful not to get the balloon too close). Observe the balloon expanding. When it appears close to capacity, remove it from the heat and release it. The balloon will rise. As it cools, the balloon will descend.

Teaching Notes Make sure the balloon is not fully inflated before you heat it. You may also use a heat gun or hair blow dryer to warm the balloon. It is effective to repeat this demonstration. The second time you heat the balloon, ask students what is happening to the mass of the balloon. This exercise can be used to lead into a discussion of the balloon's density. Extend this discussion to explain how the balloon rises as a result of its change in density (mass is constant, volume increases).

Lecture Demonstration: 5.12, 5.13, 5.14, 5.15, 5.16, 5.17, 5.18

PowerLecture Animation: Charles's Law: A Molecular-Level View

Test Bank: 18, 20, 21, 23–25, 75

Section 13.3

LABORATORY EXPERIMENTS

A relevant laboratory experiment for this section is Experiment 20, Charles's Law: Volume and Temperature, from *Introductory Chemistry in the Laboratory* by James Hall.

DEMONSTRATION

Helium Hot-Air Balloon

Materials Commercial Mylar helium balloon (filled), twist tie, hot plate, small paper cup and string (optional)

Preparation Remove about 5% of the helium from a Mylar balloon. Reseal the balloon with a twist tie. Attach a paper cup to the balloon to form its basket if desired. Adjust the helium and weight of the basket until the balloon just hovers.

TEACHING TIPS

- One of the most common mistakes for beginning students is to forget that they must convert temperatures to the Kelvin scale to work gas problems correctly. Discuss this point with students as you do examples. Remind them that this conversion is important because a negative temperature will result in a negative volume, which does not make sense.
- In Chapter 10 we saw that temperature measures the average kinetic energy of a sample. Does a gas sample at 40 °C have an average kinetic energy twice that of a gas sample at 20 °C? No. Although 40 = 2 × 20, 0 °C is not the lowest possible temperature. To compare relative average kinetic energies by comparing temperatures, we need to have a temperature scale in which zero is the lowest possible temperature (the absolute scale).
- Point out that volume is directly related to temperature only if a graph of V versus T hits the origin (0,0), as seen in Figures 13.7 and 13.8. That is, in Figure 13.7, a doubling of the temperature does not give rise to a doubling of the volume. This is the case in Figure 13.8, however.

PowerLecture Video: Liquid Nitrogen and Balloons

PowerLecture Animation: Charles's Law: A Graphical View

Temperatures such as 0.00000002 K have been obtained in the laboratory, but 0 K has never been reached.

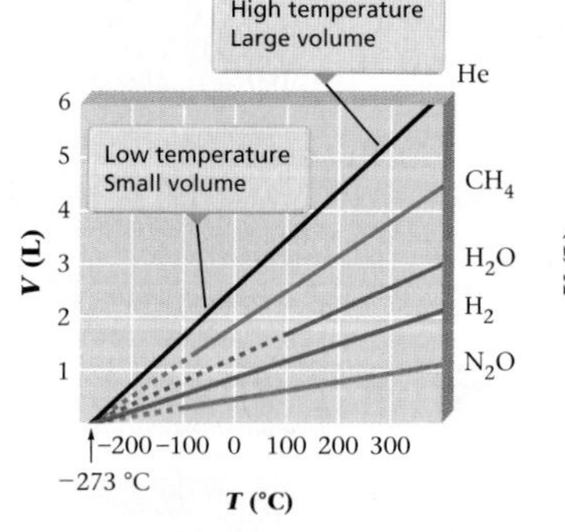

Figure 13.7 Plots of V (L) versus T (°C) for several gases. Note that each sample of gas contains a different number of moles to spread out the plots.

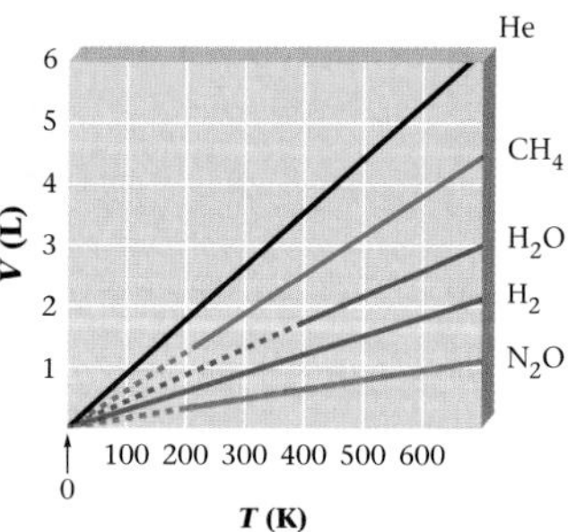

Figure 13.8 Plots of V versus T as in Figure 13.7, except that here the Kelvin scale is used for temperature.

temperature. However, when we extend each straight line (which is called *extrapolation* and is shown here by a dashed line), something very interesting happens. *All* of the lines extrapolate to zero volume at the same temperature: −273 °C. This suggests that −273 °C is the lowest possible temperature, because a negative volume is physically impossible. In fact, experiments have shown that matter cannot be cooled to temperatures lower than −273 °C. Therefore, this temperature is defined as **absolute zero** on the Kelvin scale.

When the volumes of the gases shown in Figure 13.7 are plotted against temperature on the Kelvin scale rather than the Celsius scale, the plots shown in Figure 13.8 result. These plots show that the volume of each gas is *directly proportional to the temperature* (in kelvins) and extrapolates to zero when the temperature is 0 K. Let's illustrate this statement with an example. Suppose we have 1 L of gas at 300 K. When we double the temperature of this gas to 600 K (without changing its pressure), the volume also doubles, to 2 L. Verify this type of behavior by looking carefully at the lines for various gases shown in Figure 13.8.

The direct proportionality between volume and temperature (in kelvins) is represented by the equation known as **Charles's law:**

$$V = bT$$

where T is in kelvins and b is the proportionality constant. Charles's law holds for a given sample of gas at constant pressure. It tells us that (for a given amount of gas at a given pressure) the volume of the gas is directly proportional to the temperature on the Kelvin scale:

$$V = bT \quad \text{or} \quad \frac{V}{T} = b = \text{constant}$$

From Figure 13.8 for Helium

V (L)	T (K)	b
0.7	100	0.01
1.7	200	0.01
2.7	300	0.01
3.7	400	0.01
5.7	600	0.01

Notice that in the second form, this equation states that the *ratio* of V to T (in kelvins) must be constant. (This is shown for helium in the margin.) Thus, when we triple the temperature (in kelvins) of a sample of gas, the volume of the gas triples as well.

$$\frac{V}{T} = \frac{3 \times V}{3 \times T} = b = \text{constant}$$

We can also write Charles's law in terms of V_1 and T_1 (the initial conditions) and V_2 and T_2 (the final conditions).

$$\frac{V_1}{T_1} = b \quad \text{and} \quad \frac{V_2}{T_2} = b$$

Charles's law in the form $V_1/T_1 = V_2/T_2$ applies only when both the amount of gas (moles) and the pressure are constant.

Thus

$$\frac{V_1}{T_1} = \frac{V_2}{T_2}$$

We will illustrate the use of this equation in Examples 13.4 and 13.5.

Additional Examples

Example 13.4

1. A 2.45-L sample of nitrogen gas is collected at 273 K and heated to 325 K. Calculate the volume of the nitrogen gas at 325 K. Assume constant pressure.

   2.92 L

2. A sample of methane gas is collected at 285 K and cooled to 245 K. At 245 K the volume of the gas is 75.0 L. Calculate the volume of the methane gas at 285 K. Assume constant pressure.

   87.2 L

EXAMPLE 13.4 Calculating Volume Using Charles's Law, I

A 2.0-L sample of air is collected at 298 K and then cooled to 278 K. The pressure is held constant at 1.0 atm.

a. Does the volume increase or decrease?

b. Calculate the volume of the air at 278 K.

SOLUTION

Where Are We Going?

We want to determine if the volume will increase or decrease when the temperature is changed, and we want to calculate the new volume.

What Do We Know?

- We know the initial and final temperatures and the initial volume.
- The amount of gas and pressure are held constant.
- Charles's law: $\frac{V_1}{T_1} = \frac{V_2}{T_2}$.

How Do We Get There?

a. Because the gas is cooled, the volume of the gas must decrease:

$$\frac{V}{T} = \text{constant}$$

T is decreased, so *V* must decrease to maintain a constant ratio.

b. To calculate the new volume, V_2, we will use Charles's law in the form

$$\frac{V_1}{T_1} = \frac{V_2}{T_2}$$

$\frac{V_1}{T_1} \Rightarrow \frac{V_2}{T_2}$

Temperature smaller, volume smaller

We are given the following information:

Initial Conditions	Final Conditions
$T_1 = 298$ K	$T_2 = 278$ K
$V_1 = 2.0$ L	$V_2 = ?$

We want to solve the equation

$$\frac{V_1}{T_1} = \frac{V_2}{T_2}$$

for V_2. We can do this by multiplying both sides by T_2 and canceling.

$$T_2 \times \frac{V_1}{T_1} = \frac{V_2}{\cancel{T_2}} \times \cancel{T_2} = V_2$$

Thus

$$V_2 = T_2 \times \frac{V_1}{T_1} = 278 \cancel{K} \times \frac{2.0 \text{ L}}{298 \cancel{K}} = 1.9 \text{ L}$$

REALITY CHECK Because the temperature decreases, we expect the volume to decrease. The temperature decreased slightly, so we would expect the volume to decrease slightly. ■

Additional Examples

Example 13.5

1. A sample of oxygen gas has a volume of 4.55 L at 25 °C. Calculate the volume of the oxygen gas when the temperature is raised to 45 °C. Assume constant pressure.

   4.86 L

2. A sample of hydrogen gas is collected at 34 °C and heated to 68 °C. At 68 °C the volume of hydrogen is 26.0 L. Calculate the volume of the hydrogen sample at 34 °C. Assume constant pressure.

   23.4 L

EXAMPLE 13.5 Calculating Volume Using Charles's Law, II

A sample of gas at 15 °C (at 1 atm) has a volume of 2.58 L. The temperature is then raised to 38 °C (at 1 atm).

a. Does the volume of the gas increase or decrease?

b. Calculate the new volume.

SOLUTION

Where Are We Going?

We want to determine if the volume will increase or decrease when the temperature is changed, and we want to calculate the new volume.

What Do We Know?

- We know the initial and final temperatures and the initial volume.
- The amount of gas and pressure are held constant.
- Charles's law: $\frac{V_1}{T_1} = \frac{V_2}{T_2}$.

How Do We Get There?

a. In this case we have a given sample (constant amount) of gas that is heated from 15 °C to 38 °C *while the pressure is held constant.* We know from Charles's law that the volume of a given sample of gas is directly proportional to the temperature (at constant pressure). So the increase in temperature will *increase* the volume; the new volume will be greater than 2.58 L.

b. To calculate the new volume, we use Charles's law in the form

$$\frac{V_1}{T_1} = \frac{V_2}{T_2}$$

We are given the following information:

Initial Conditions	**Final Conditions**
$T_1 = 15$ °C	$T_2 = 38$ °C
$V_1 = 2.58$ L	$V_2 = ?$

As is often the case, the temperatures are given in Celsius degrees. However, for us to use Charles's law, the temperature *must be in kelvins.* Thus we must convert by adding 273 to each temperature.

USGA photo by T. Casadevall

Researchers take samples from a steaming volcanic vent at Mount Baker in Washington.

Initial Conditions	**Final Conditions**
$T_1 = 15\ ^\circ C = 15 + 273$	$T_2 = 38\ ^\circ C = 38 + 273$
$= 288\ K$	$= 311\ K$
$V_1 = 2.58\ L$	$V_2 = ?$

Solving for V_2 gives

$$V_2 = V_1 \times \frac{T_2}{T_1} = 2.58\ L\left(\frac{311\ \cancel{K}}{288\ \cancel{K}}\right) = 2.79\ L$$

REALITY CHECK Because the temperature increases, we expect the volume to increase.

Self-Check EXERCISE 13.3 A child blows a bubble that contains air at 28 °C and has a volume of 23 cm^3 at 1 atm. As the bubble rises, it encounters a pocket of cold air (temperature 18 °C). If there is no change in pressure, will the bubble get larger or smaller as the air inside cools to 18 °C? Calculate the new volume of the bubble.

See Problems 13.29 and 13.30. ■

Notice from Example 13.5 that we adjust the volume of a gas for a temperature change by multiplying the original volume by the ratio of the Kelvin temperatures—final (T_2) over initial (T_1). Remember to check whether your answer makes sense. When the temperature increases (at constant pressure), the volume must increase, and vice versa.

EXAMPLE 13.6 Calculating Temperature Using Charles's Law

In former times, gas volume was used as a way to measure temperature using devices called gas thermometers. Consider a gas that has a volume of 0.675 L at 35 °C and 1 atm pressure. What is the temperature (in units of °C) of a room where this gas has a volume of 0.535 L at 1 atm pressure?

Self Check

Answer to Self-Check Exercise 13.3

smaller, 22 cm^3

Additional Examples

Example 13.6

1. Consider a gas with a volume of 5.65 L at 27 °C and 1 atm pressure. At what temperature will this gas have a volume of 6.69 L and 1 atm pressure?

   82 °C (355 K)

2. Consider a gas with a volume of 9.25 L at 47 °C and 1 atm pressure. At what temperature does this gas have a volume of 3.50 L and 1 atm pressure?

   −152 °C (121 K)

SOLUTION

Where Are We Going?

We want to determine the new temperature of a gas given that the volume has decreased at constant pressure.

What Do We Know?

- We know the initial and final volumes and the initial temperature.
- The amount of gas and pressure are held constant.
- Charles's law: $\frac{V_1}{T_1} = \frac{V_2}{T_2}$.

How Do We Get There?

The information given in the problem is

Initial Conditions	**Final Conditions**
$T_1 = 35\ °C = 35 + 273 = 308\ K$	$T_2 = ?$
$V_1 = 0.675\ L$	$V_2 = 0.535\ L$
$P_1 = 1\ atm$	$P_2 = 1\ atm$

The pressure remains constant, so we can use Charles's law in the form

$$\frac{V_1}{T_1} = \frac{V_2}{T_2}$$

and solve for T_2. First we multiply both sides by T_2.

$$T_2 \times \frac{V_1}{T_1} = \frac{V_2}{\cancel{T_2}} \times \cancel{T_2} = V_2$$

Next we multiply both sides by T_1.

$$\cancel{T_1} \times T_2 \times \frac{V_1}{\cancel{T_1}} = T_1 \times V_2$$

This gives

$$T_2 \times V_1 = T_1 \times V_2$$

Now we divide both sides by V_1 (multiply by $1/V_1$),

$$\frac{1}{\cancel{V_1}} \times T_2 \times \cancel{V_1} = \frac{1}{V_1} \times T_1 \times V_2$$

and obtain

$$T_2 = T_1 \times \frac{V_2}{V_1}$$

We have now isolated T_2 on one side of the equation, and we can do the calculation.

$$T_2 = T_1 \times \frac{V_2}{V_1} = (308\ K) \times \frac{0.535\ \cancel{L}}{0.675\ \cancel{L}} = 244\ K$$

To convert from units of K to units of °C, we subtract 273 from the Kelvin temperature.

$$T_{°C} = T_K - 273 = 244 - 273 = -29\ °C$$

The room is very cold; the new temperature is -29 °C.

REALITY CHECK Because the volume is smaller, we expect the temperature to be lower. ■

13.4 Volume and Moles: Avogadro's Law

OBJECTIVE: To understand the law relating the volume and the number of moles of a sample of gas at constant temperature and pressure, and to do calculations involving this law.

What is the relationship between the volume of a gas and the number of molecules present in the gas sample? Experiments show that when the number of moles of gas is doubled (at constant temperature and pressure), the volume doubles. In other words, the volume of a gas is directly proportional to the number of moles if temperature and pressure remain constant. Figure 13.9 illustrates this relationship, which can also be represented by the equation

$$V = an \quad \text{or} \quad \frac{V}{n} = a$$

where V is the volume of the gas, n is the number of moles, and a is the proportionality constant. Note that this equation means that the ratio of V to n is constant as long as the temperature and pressure remain constant. Thus, when the number of moles of gas is increased by a factor of 5, the volume also increases by a factor of 5,

$$\frac{V}{n} = \frac{\cancel{5} \times V}{\cancel{5} \times n} = a = \text{constant}$$

and so on. In words, this equation means that *for a gas at constant temperature and pressure, the volume is directly proportional to the number of moles of gas.* This relationship is called **Avogadro's law** after the Italian scientist Amadeo Avogadro, who first postulated it in 1811.

For cases where the number of moles of gas is changed from an initial amount to another amount (at constant T and P), we can represent Avogadro's law as

$$\underset{\text{Initial amount}}{\frac{V_1}{n_1}} = a = \underset{\text{Final amount}}{\frac{V_2}{n_2}}$$

or

$$\frac{V_1}{n_1} = \frac{V_2}{n_2}$$

We will illustrate the use of this equation in Example 13.7.

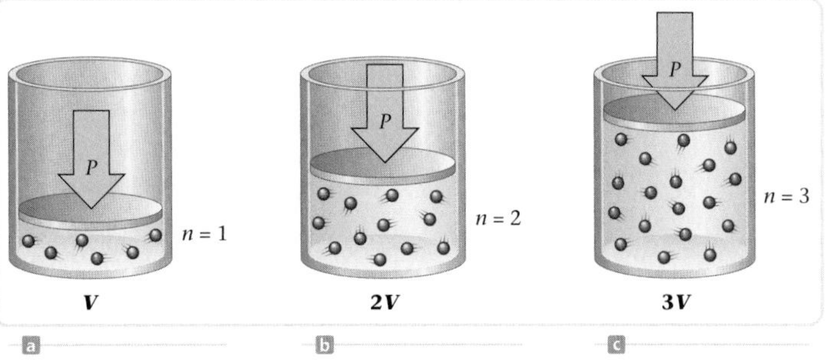

Figure 13.9 The relationship between volume V and number of moles n. As the number of moles is increased from 1 to 2 (a) to (b), the volume doubles. When the number of moles is tripled (c), the volume is also tripled. The temperature and pressure remain the same in these cases.

Test Bank: 22, 26–28, 76, 78, 83

Section 13.4

TEACHING TIP

At this point all four variables (P, V, T, and n) have been used in gas law problems. Now is an excellent time to focus on problem-solving skills. Be sure students write down what they know from the problem, what they are looking for, and what they need to know to find the answer.

DEMONSTRATION

To show a qualitative demonstration of Avogadro's law, you can blow up a balloon. Plan on some discussion about why this is a constant-pressure situation (since the balloon is very flexible, the pressure inside the balloon is essentially always equal to the atmospheric pressure). You can also place a small piece of dry ice in an inflated balloon and tie it. As the dry ice sublimes (and the moles of gas increase), the volume of the balloon will increase.

DEMONSTRATION

The Candle and the Tumbler

Materials A candle, a glass, a test tube that fits over the candle, clay, and matches

Preparation Light the candle and let some wax drip onto the bottom of the glass. Blow out the candle and fix the candle to the glass before the wax solidifies. Add water to the glass until the candle is half-submerged (do not get the wick of the candle wet).

Presentation Light the candle. Quickly place the test tube over the candle, submerging the opening of the test tube. Ask the students to write their observations and to develop an explanation.

Discussion This is a complex system. As the test tube is placed over the flame, the air inside the test tube is heated, causing the air to expand and some to escape the test tube (sometimes evidenced by the bubbling of air through the water if the test tube is placed over the candle and into the water with the correct speed). The reaction consumes oxygen (and generates carbon dioxide and water), and eventually the flame goes out. Once the flame is out, the air cools while the amount of gas inside the test tube remains constant. A decrease in temperature gives rise to a lower pressure. Atmospheric pressure pushes water into the test tube until the pressure inside the tube and the weight of the water equal atmospheric pressure. Of course, oxygen is consumed in the reaction, but carbon dioxide (and water) is generated. While the reaction gives rise to a net decrease in moles of gas, this decrease is not enough to account for the amount of water that enters the test tube.

Many students will initially claim that the fire uses up oxygen, so the amount of gas inside the tube is less after the reaction than before it. According to this explanation, the pressure is decreased and atmospheric pressure will push the water into the tube.

Although this explanation is incorrect, it involves good thinking on the students' part. First, they know that oxygen is used up in the process of burning. Second, they understand that a decrease in the amount of gas will cause a decrease in pressure. Third, they know that atmospheric pressure will force water into the tube. In fact, this idea is so attractive that many texts (usually at the middle-school level) use this activity to demonstrate that air is about 20% oxygen by volume; having the volume change by about 15%–25% is common.

In reality, the idea that oxygen being used up is the sole cause of the rise in water level fails for several reasons. Most importantly, it disregards the fact that another gas (carbon dioxide) is a product of the reaction. It also neglects any effect resulting from a temperature difference. In addition, careful observation will reveal that the water level doesn't start rising significantly until the flame goes out. If oxygen being "used up" was the sole cause, the water level should increase smoothly over the course of the reaction. The fact that the water level rises dramatically only after the flame is very low or out suggests that the heat has a great deal to do with this phenomenon.

EXAMPLE 13.7 Using Avogadro's Law in Calculations

Suppose we have a 12.2-L sample containing 0.50 mol oxygen gas, O_2, at a pressure of 1 atm and a temperature of 25 °C. If all of this O_2 is converted to ozone, O_3, at the same temperature and pressure, what will be the volume of the ozone formed?

SOLUTION

Where Are We Going?

We want to determine the volume of ozone (O_3) formed from 0.50 mol O_2 given the volume of oxygen.

What Do We Know?

- We know the initial number of moles of oxygen and the volume of oxygen.
- The temperature and pressure are held constant.
- Avogadro's law: $\frac{V_1}{T_1} = \frac{V_2}{T_2}$.

What Information Do We Need?

- We need the balanced equation for the reaction to determine the number of moles of ozone formed.

How Do We Get There?

To do this problem we need to compare the moles of gas originally present to the moles of gas present after the reaction. We know that 0.50 mol O_2 is present initially. To find out how many moles of O_3 will be present after the reaction, we need to use the balanced equation for the reaction.

$$3O_2(g) \rightarrow 2O_3(g)$$

We calculate the moles of O_3 produced by using the appropriate mole ratio from the balanced equation.

$$0.50 \cancel{\text{mol } O_2} \times \frac{2 \text{ mol } O_3}{3 \cancel{\text{mol } O_2}} = 0.33 \text{ mol } O_3$$

Avogadro's law states that

$$\frac{V_1}{n_1} = \frac{V_2}{n_2}$$

where V_1 is the volume of n_1 moles of O_2 gas and V_2 is the volume of n_2 moles of O_3 gas. In this case we have

Initial Conditions	Final Conditions
$n_1 = 0.50$ mol	$n_2 = 0.33$ mol
$V_1 = 12.2$ L	$V_2 = ?$

Solving Avogadro's law for V_2 gives

$$V_2 = V_1 \times \frac{n_2}{n_1} = 12.2 \text{ L} \left(\frac{0.33 \cancel{\text{mol}}}{0.50 \cancel{\text{mol}}}\right) = 8.1 \text{ L}$$

MATH SKILL BUILDER

$$\frac{V_1}{n_1} = \frac{V_2}{n_2}$$

$$n_2 \times \frac{V_1}{n_1} = \frac{V_2}{\cancel{n_2}} \times \cancel{n_2}$$

$$V_1 \times \frac{n_2}{n_1} = V_2$$

REALITY CHECK Note that the volume decreases, as it should, because fewer molecules are present in the gas after O_2 is converted to O_3.

PowerLecture Animation: Relationship Between Gas Quantity and Volume

Additional Examples

Example 13.7

1. If 2.55 moles of helium gas occupies a volume of 59.5 L at a particular temperature and pressure, what volume does 7.83 moles of helium occupy under the same conditions?

   183 L

2. If 4.35 g of neon gas occupies a volume of 15.0 L at a particular temperature and pressure, what volume does 2.00 g of neon gas occupy under the same conditions?

   6.90 L

Lecture Demonstration: 5.20, 5.21, 5.22

Self-Check **EXERCISE 13.4** Consider two samples of nitrogen gas (composed of N_2 molecules). Sample 1 contains 1.5 mol N_2 and has a volume of 36.7 L at 25 °C and 1 atm. Sample 2 has a volume of 16.5 L at 25 °C and 1 atm. Calculate the number of moles of N_2 in Sample 2.

See Problems 13.41 through 13.44. ■

13.5 The Ideal Gas Law

OBJECTIVE: To understand the ideal gas law and use it in calculations.

We have considered three laws that describe the behavior of gases as it is revealed by experimental observations.

Constant n means a constant number of moles of gas.

Boyle's law: $PV = k$ or $V = \frac{k}{P}$ (at constant T and n)

Charles's law: $V = bT$ (at constant P and n)

Avogadro's law: $V = an$ (at constant T and P)

These relationships, which show how the volume of a gas depends on pressure, temperature, and number of moles of gas present, can be combined as follows:

$$V = R\left(\frac{Tn}{P}\right)$$

where R is the combined proportionality constant and is called the **universal gas constant.** When the pressure is expressed in atmospheres and the volume is in liters, R always has the value 0.08206 L atm/K mol. We can rearrange the above equation by multiplying both sides by P,

$R = 0.08206 \frac{\text{L atm}}{\text{K mol}}$

$$P \times V = \cancel{P} \times R\left(\frac{Tn}{\cancel{P}}\right)$$

to obtain the **ideal gas law** written in its usual form,

$$PV = nRT$$

The ideal gas law involves all the important characteristics of a gas: its pressure (P), volume (V), number of moles (n), and temperature (T). Knowledge of any three of these properties is enough to define completely the condition of the gas, because the fourth property can be determined from the ideal gas law.

It is important to recognize that the ideal gas law is based on experimental measurements of the properties of gases. A gas that obeys this equation is said to behave *ideally.* That is, this equation defines the behavior of an **ideal gas.** Most gases obey this equation closely at pressures of approximately 1 atm or lower, when the temperature is approximately 0 °C or higher. You should assume ideal gas behavior when working problems involving gases in this text.

The ideal gas law can be used to solve a variety of problems. Example 13.8 demonstrates one type, where you are asked to find one property characterizing the condition of a gas given the other three properties.

EXAMPLE 13.8 Using the Ideal Gas Law in Calculations

A sample of hydrogen gas, H_2, has a volume of 8.56 L at a temperature of 0 °C and a pressure of 1.5 atm. Calculate the number of moles of H_2 present in this gas sample. (Assume that the gas behaves ideally.)

Self Check

Answer to Self-Check Exercise 13.4

0.67 mol

Lecture Demonstration: 5.23

PowerLecture Video: The Ideal Gas Law *PV-nRT*

Test Bank: 12, 19, 29–39, 41–56, 74, 77, 79–81

Section 13.5

TEACHING TIPS

- Remind students that when they solve problems using the ideal gas law, they must ensure that all units for variables are the same as those in the gas constant *R*. Show that all of the units of *R* (except those for the variable) cancel with units on numbers given in the problem.
- Now is another opportunity to help students improve their problem-solving skills. Remind them to write down the information from the problem, decide what they are solving for, decide what they need to solve for that variable, and finally solve the problem. Remind students to consider the answer and check whether it makes sense with what they predicted should happen.
- Emphasize how the ideal gas law can be used to derive all of the other gas laws.

DEMONSTRATION

Marshmallow Man

Materials Bag of large marshmallows, toothpicks, vacuum pump, vacuum chamber

Preparation Assemble a marshmallow man from marshmallows and toothpicks. Use a pen to give him a face. Seat him on the platform of the vacuum chamber (you may need to prop him up with a small beaker).

Presentation Place the vacuum chamber over the marshmallow man. Attach the vacuum pump. Turn on the pump. Observe the marshmallow man getting larger as the pressure decreases. When the pressure is released, marshmallow man deflates, never to inflate the same way again.

Teaching Notes A marshmallow has a large amount of air trapped in the tiny cells in its structure. As the surrounding pressure decreases, the cells swell. If the pump is very strong, the marshmallow man may suddenly deflate (the cells burst).

Variation If you do not have access to a vacuum pump, you can place a single large marshmallow in an Erlenmeyer flask and stopper it tightly. Insert the needle of a large plastic syringe through the stopper and remove air from the flask with one quick pull of the plunger. (Veterinary supply houses carry large syringes.)

SOLUTION

Where Are We Going?

We want to determine the number of moles of hydrogen gas (H_2) present given conditions of temperature, pressure, and volume.

What Do We Know?

- We know the temperature, pressure, and volume of hydrogen gas.
- Ideal gas law: $PV = nRT$.

What Information Do We Need?

- $R = 0.08206$ L atm/mol K.

How Do We Get There?

In this problem we are given the pressure, volume, and temperature of the gas: $P = 1.5$ atm, $V = 8.56$ L, and $T = 0$ °C. Remember that the temperature must be changed to the Kelvin scale.

$$T = 0\ °C = 0 + 273 = 273\ K$$

We can calculate the number of moles of gas present by using the ideal gas law, $PV = nRT$. We solve for n by dividing both sides by RT:

$$\frac{PV}{RT} = n\frac{\cancel{RT}}{\cancel{RT}}$$

to give

$$\frac{PV}{RT} = n$$

Thus

$$n = \frac{PV}{RT} = \frac{(1.5\ \cancel{atm})(8.56\ \cancel{L})}{\left(0.08206\ \frac{\cancel{L}\ \cancel{atm}}{\cancel{K}\ mol}\right)(273\ \cancel{K})} = 0.57\ mol$$

Self-Check EXERCISE 13.5 A weather balloon contains 1.10×10^5 mol He and has a volume of 2.70×10^6 L at 1.00 atm pressure. Calculate the temperature of the helium in the balloon in kelvins and in Celsius degrees.

See Problems 13.53 through 13.60. ■

EXAMPLE 13.9 Ideal Gas Law Calculations Involving Conversion of Units

What volume is occupied by 0.250 mol carbon dioxide gas at 25 °C and 371 torr?

SOLUTION

Where Are We Going?

We want to determine the volume of carbon dioxide gas (CO_2) given the number of moles, pressure, and temperature.

What Do We Know?

- We know the number of moles, pressure, and temperature of the carbon dioxide.
- Ideal gas law: $PV = nRT$.

LABORATORY EXPERIMENT

A relevant laboratory experiment for this section is Experiment 21, Molar Mass of a Volatile Liquid, from *Introductory Chemistry in the Laboratory* by James Hall.

Additional Examples

Example 13.8

1. A 2.50-mol sample of nitrogen gas has a volume of 5.50 L at a temperature of 27 °C. Calculate the pressure of the nitrogen gas.

   11.2 atm

2. A 5.00-mol sample of oxygen gas has a pressure of 1.25 atm at 22 °C. What volume does this gas occupy?

   96.8 L

Self Check

Answer to Self-Check Exercise 13.5

299 K = 26 °C

Additional Examples

Example 13.9

1. A sample of neon gas has a volume of 3.45 L at 25 °C and a pressure of 565 torr. Calculate the number of moles of neon present in this gas sample.

   0.105 mol

2. A 0.250-mol sample of argon gas has a volume of 9.00 L at a pressure of 875 mm Hg. What is the temperature (in °C) of the gas?

   232 °C

What Information Do We Need?

- $R = 0.08206$ L atm/mol K.

How Do We Get There?

We can use the ideal gas law to calculate the volume, but we must first convert pressure to atmospheres and temperature to the Kelvin scale.

MATH SKILL BUILDER

$$PV = nRT$$
$$\frac{\not{P}V}{\not{P}} = \frac{nRT}{P}$$
$$V = \frac{nRT}{P}$$

$$P = 371 \text{ torr} = 371 \not{\text{torr}} \times \frac{1.000 \text{ atm}}{760.0 \not{\text{torr}}} = 0.488 \text{ atm}$$
$$T = 25\ °\text{C} = 25 + 273 = 298 \text{ K}$$

We solve for V by dividing both sides of the ideal gas law ($PV = nRT$) by P.

$$V = \frac{nRT}{P} = \frac{(0.250 \not{\text{mol}})\left(0.08206 \frac{\text{L} \not{\text{atm}}}{\not{\text{K}} \not{\text{mol}}}\right)(298 \not{\text{K}})}{0.488 \not{\text{atm}}} = 12.5 \text{ L}$$

The volume of the sample of CO_2 is 12.5 L.

Self-Check EXERCISE 13.6 Radon, a radioactive gas formed naturally in the soil, can cause lung cancer. It can pose a hazard to humans by seeping into houses, and there is concern about this problem in many areas. A 1.5-mol sample of radon gas has a volume of 21.0 L at 33 °C. What is the pressure of the gas?

See Problems 13.53 through 13.60. ■

Note that R has units of L atm/K mol. Accordingly, whenever we use the ideal gas law, we must express the volume in units of liters, the temperature in kelvins, and the pressure in atmospheres. When we are given data in other units, we must first convert to the appropriate units.

The ideal gas law can also be used to calculate the changes that will occur when the conditions of the gas are changed as illustrated in Example 13.10.

EXAMPLE 13.10 Using the Ideal Gas Law Under Changing Conditions

Suppose we have a 0.240-mol sample of ammonia gas at 25 °C with a volume of 3.5 L at a pressure of 1.68 atm. The gas is compressed to a volume of 1.35 L at 25 °C. Use the ideal gas law to calculate the final pressure.

SOLUTION

Where Are We Going?

We want to use the ideal gas law equation to determine the pressure of ammonia gas given a change in volume.

What Do We Know?

- We know the initial number of moles, pressure, volume, and temperature of the ammonia.
- We know the new volume.
- Ideal gas law: $PV = nRT$.

Self Check

Answer to Self-Check Exercise 13.6

1.8 atm

Additional Examples

Example 13.10

1. Consider a sample of helium gas at 23 °C with a volume of 5.60 L at a pressure of 2.45 atm. The pressure is changed to 8.75 atm and the gas is cooled to 15 °C. Calculate the new volume of the gas using the ideal gas law equation.

   1.53 L

2. Consider a sample of helium gas at 28 °C with a volume of 3.80 L at a pressure of 3.15 atm. The gas expands to a volume of 9.50 L and the gas is heated to 43 °C. Calculate the new pressure of the gas using the ideal gas law equation.

   1.32 atm

TEACHING TIPS

- Encourage students to use the ideal gas law to solve most gas law problems, even when some conditions do not change. All the other gas laws can be derived from the ideal gas law. If students understand how to do this, they need not memorize the other gas laws. Encourage the use of finesse and understanding to replace the brute-force method of memorizing formulas and plugging numbers into them.
- An almost infinite number of kinds of gas law problems exist. Expose your students to many different types. Ask them to find mass instead of moles, or density or molar mass for a gas. These types of problems bring together information that students have learned earlier in the course and provide a more challenging environment for them. By asking different types of questions you also encourage students to work toward understanding the concepts instead of memorizing formulas and equations.

Self Check

Answer to Self-Check Exercise 13.7

4.9 L

How Do We Get There?

In this case we have a sample of ammonia gas in which the conditions are changed. We are given the following information:

Initial Conditions	Final Conditions
$V_1 = 3.5$ L	$V_2 = 1.35$ L
$P_1 = 1.68$ atm	$P_2 = ?$
$T_1 = 25\text{ °C} = 25 + 273 = 298$ K	$T_2 = 25\text{ °C} = 25 + 273 = 298$ K
$n_1 = 0.240$ mol	$n_2 = 0.240$ mol

Note that both n and T remain constant—only P and V change. Thus we could simply use Boyle's law ($P_1V_1 = P_2V_2$) to solve for P_2. However, we will use the ideal gas law to solve this problem in order to introduce the idea that one equation—the ideal gas equation—can be used to do almost any gas problem. The key idea here is that in using the ideal gas law to describe a change in conditions for a gas, we always *solve the ideal gas equation in such a way that the variables that change are on one side of the equals sign and the constant terms are on the other side.* That is, we start with the ideal gas equation in the conventional form ($PV = nRT$) and rearrange it so that all the terms that change are moved to one side and all the terms that do not change are moved to the other side. In this case the pressure and volume change, and the temperature and number of moles remain constant (as does R, by definition). So we write the ideal gas law as

$$\underset{\text{Change}}{PV} = \underset{\text{Remain constant}}{nRT}$$

Because n, R, and T remain the same in this case, we can write $P_1V_1 = nRT$ and $P_2V_2 = nRT$. Combining these gives

$$P_1V_1 = nRT = P_2V_2 \quad \text{or} \quad P_1V_1 = P_2V_2$$

and

$$P_2 = P_1 \times \frac{V_1}{V_2} = (1.68\text{ atm})\left(\frac{3.5\text{ }\cancel{L}}{1.35\text{ }\cancel{L}}\right) = 4.4\text{ atm}$$

REALITY CHECK Does this answer make sense? The volume was decreased (at constant temperature and constant number of moles), which means that the pressure should increase, as the calculation indicates.

Self-Check EXERCISE 13.7 A sample of methane gas that has a volume of 3.8 L at 5 °C is heated to 86 °C at constant pressure. Calculate its new volume.

See Problems 13.61 and 13.62. ■

Note that in solving Example 13.10, we actually obtained Boyle's law ($P_1V_1 = P_2V_2$) from the ideal gas equation. You might well ask, "Why go to all this trouble?" The idea is to learn to use the ideal gas equation to solve all types of gas law problems. This way you will never have to ask yourself, "Is this a Boyle's law problem or a Charles's law problem?"

We continue to practice using the ideal gas law in Example 13.11. Remember, the key idea is to rearrange the equation so that the quantities that change are moved to one side of the equation and those that remain constant are moved to the other.

EXAMPLE 13.11 Calculating Volume Changes Using the Ideal Gas Law

A sample of diborane gas, B_2H_6, a substance that bursts into flames when exposed to air, has a pressure of 0.454 atm at a temperature of −15 °C and a volume of 3.48 L. If conditions are changed so that the temperature is 36 °C and the pressure is 0.616 atm, what will be the new volume of the sample?

SOLUTION

Where Are We Going?

We want to use the ideal gas law equation to determine the volume of diborane gas.

What Do We Know?

- We know the initial pressure, volume, and temperature of the diborane gas.
- We know the new temperature and pressure.
- Ideal gas law: $PV = nRT$.

How Do We Get There?

We are given the following information:

Initial Conditions	Final Conditions
$P_1 = 0.454$ atm	$P_2 = 0.616$ atm
$V_1 = 3.48$ L	$V_2 = ?$
$T_1 = -15\ °C = 273 - 15 = 258$ K	$T_2 = 36\ °C = 273 + 36 = 309$ K

MATH SKILL BUILDER

$$PV = nRT$$

$$\frac{PV}{T} = \frac{nR\not{T}}{\not{T}}$$

$$\frac{PV}{T} = nR$$

Note that the value of n is not given. However, we know that n is constant (that is, $n_1 = n_2$) because no diborane gas is added or taken away. Thus, in this experiment, n is constant and P, V, and T change. Therefore, we rearrange the ideal gas equation ($PV = nRT$) by dividing both sides by T,

$$\underset{\text{Change}}{\frac{PV}{T}} = \underset{\text{Constant}}{nR}$$

which leads to the equation

$$\frac{P_1V_1}{T_1} = nR = \frac{P_2V_2}{T_2}$$

or

$$\frac{P_1V_1}{T_1} = \frac{P_2V_2}{T_2}$$

We can now solve for V_2 by dividing both sides by P_2 and multiplying both sides by T_2.

$$\frac{1}{P_2} \times \frac{P_1V_1}{T_1} = \frac{\not{P_2}V_2}{T_2} \times \frac{1}{\not{P_2}} = \frac{V_2}{T_2}$$

$$T_2 \times \frac{P_1V_1}{P_2T_1} = \frac{V_2}{\not{T_2}} \times \not{T_2} = V_2$$

That is,

$$\frac{T_2P_1V_1}{P_2T_1} = V_2$$

Additional Examples

Example 13.11

1. Consider a sample of hydrogen gas at 63 °C with a volume of 3.65 L at a pressure of 4.55 atm. The pressure is changed to 2.75 atm and the gas is cooled to −35 °C. Calculate the new volume of the gas.

   4.28 L

2. Consider a sample of oxygen gas at 27 °C with a volume of 9.55 L at a pressure of 2.97 atm. The pressure is changed to 8.25 atm and the gas is heated to 125 °C. Calculate the new volume of the gas using the ideal gas law equation.

   4.56 L

CHEMISTRY IN FOCUS

Snacks Need Chemistry, Too!

Have you ever wondered what makes popcorn pop? The popping is linked with the properties of gases. What happens when a gas is heated? Charles's law tells us that if the pressure is held constant, the volume of the gas must increase as the temperature is increased. But what happens if the gas being heated is trapped at a constant volume? We can see what happens by rearranging the ideal gas law ($PV = nRT$) as follows:

$$P = \left(\frac{nR}{V}\right)T$$

When n, R, and V are held constant, the pressure of a gas is directly proportional to the temperature. Thus, as the temperature of the trapped gas increases, its pressure also increases. This is exactly what happens inside a kernel of popcorn as it is heated. The moisture inside the kernel vaporized by the heat produces increasing pressure. The pressure finally becomes so great that the kernel breaks open, allowing the starch inside to expand to about 40 times its original size.

What's special about popcorn? Why does it pop while "regular" corn doesn't? William da Silva, a biologist at the University of Campinas in Brazil, has traced the "popability" of popcorn to its outer casing, called the pericarp. The molecules in the pericarp of popcorn, which are packed in a much more orderly way than in regular corn, transfer heat unusually quickly, producing a very fast pressure jump that pops the kernel. In addition, because the pericarp of popcorn is much thicker and stronger than that of regular corn, it can withstand more pressure, leading to a more explosive pop when the moment finally comes.

Popcorn popping.

It is sometimes convenient to think in terms of the ratios of the initial temperature and pressure and the final temperature and pressure. That is,

$$V_2 = \frac{T_2P_1V_1}{T_1P_2} = V_1 \times \frac{T_2}{T_1} \times \frac{P_1}{P_2}$$

Always convert the temperature to the Kelvin scale and the pressure to atmospheres when applying the ideal gas law.

Substituting the information given yields

$$V_2 = \frac{309 \cancel{K}}{258 \cancel{K}} \times \frac{0.454 \cancel{atm}}{0.616 \cancel{atm}} \times 3.48 \text{ L} = 3.07 \text{ L}$$

Self-Check EXERCISE 13.8 A sample of argon gas with a volume of 11.0 L at a temperature of 13 °C and a pressure of 0.747 atm is heated to 56 °C and a pressure of 1.18 atm. Calculate the final volume.

See Problems 13.61 and 13.62. ■

Self Check

Answer to Self-Check Exercise 13.8

8.01 L

The equation obtained in Example 13.11,

$$\frac{P_1V_1}{T_1} = \frac{P_2V_2}{T_2}$$

is often called the **combined gas law** equation. It holds when the amount of gas (moles) is held constant. While it may be convenient to remember this equation, it is not necessary because you can always use the ideal gas equation.

13.6 Dalton's Law of Partial Pressures

OBJECTIVE: To understand the relationship between the partial and total pressures of a gas mixture, and to use this relationship in calculations.

Many important gases contain a mixture of components. One notable example is air. Scuba divers who are going deeper than 150 feet use another important mixture, helium and oxygen. Normal air is not used because the nitrogen present dissolves in the blood in large quantities as a result of the high pressures experienced by the diver under several hundred feet of water. When the diver returns too quickly to the surface, the nitrogen bubbles out of the blood just as soda fizzes when it's opened, and the diver gets "the bends"—a very painful and potentially fatal condition. Because helium gas is only sparingly soluble in blood, it does not cause this problem.

Studies of gaseous mixtures show that each component behaves independently of the others. In other words, a given amount of oxygen exerts the same pressure in a 1.0-L vessel whether it is alone or in the presence of nitrogen (as in the air) or helium.

Among the first scientists to study mixtures of gases was John Dalton. In 1803, Dalton summarized his observations in this statement: *For a mixture of gases in a container, the total pressure exerted is the sum of the partial pressures of the gases present. The* **partial pressure** *of a gas is the pressure that the gas would exert if it were alone in the container.* This statement, known as **Dalton's law of partial pressures,** can be expressed as follows for a mixture containing three gases:

$$P_{\text{total}} = P_1 + P_2 + P_3$$

where the subscripts refer to the individual gases (gas 1, gas 2, and gas 3). The pressures P_1, P_2, and P_3 are the partial pressures; that is, each gas is responsible for only part of the total pressure (Figure 13.10).

MATH SKILL BUILDER

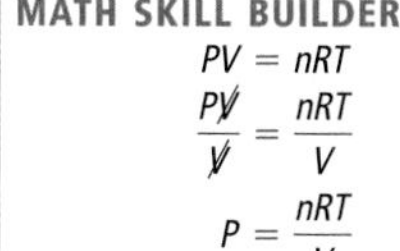

$$PV = nRT$$

$$\frac{PV}{V} = \frac{nRT}{V}$$

$$P = \frac{nRT}{V}$$

Assuming that each gas behaves ideally, we can calculate the partial pressure of each gas from the ideal gas law:

$$P_1 = \frac{n_1RT}{V},\ P_2 = \frac{n_2RT}{V},\ P_3 = \frac{n_3RT}{V}$$

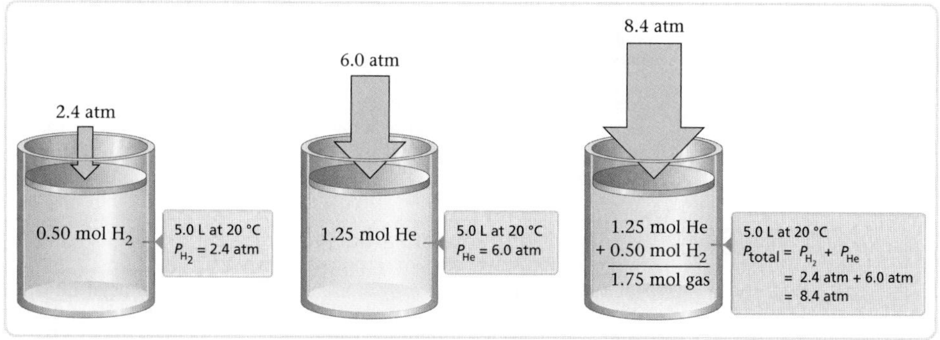

Figure 13.10
When two gases are present, the total pressure is the sum of the partial pressures of the gases.

Section 13.6

TEACHING TIPS

- When introducing Dalton's law of partial pressures, encourage students to think about the mixtures of gases at the molecular level. The presence of additional gases does not affect the number of times that a particular gas molecule hits the side of the container (since it is mostly empty space anyway). This discussion will help students understand why the pressures are additive.
- The observations summarized by Dalton's law of partial pressures are extremely important when developing a theory to explain the gas laws.
- We will develop a theory of gases that is dependent on these two statements.

Test Bank: 57–60

LABORATORY EXPERIMENT

A relevant laboratory experiment for this section is Experiment 19, Preparation and Properties of Oxygen Gas, from *Introductory Chemistry in the Laboratory* by James Hall.

DEMONSTRATION

Egg in a Bottle

Materials Flask with an opening slightly smaller than the egg you intend to use, peeled hard-boiled egg, water, hot plate

Preparation Hard-boil the egg the evening before the demonstration and allow it to cool.

Presentation Peel the hard-boiled egg and show the students that it will not fit through the opening into the bottle. Explain to them that knowledge of gas laws will help put the egg in the bottle. Place about one-half inch of water in the flask. Heat the water to boiling using the hot plate. Remove the flask from the hot plate and place the egg over the opening to the bottle. The egg will be pushed into the bottle with considerable force and noise. Now ask the students how we can remove the egg from the bottle. After discussing some options, pour out the water from the flask. Tip the bottle upside down and show the students the egg will not fall out. With the egg in the neck of the flask, blow hard into the flask. The egg will pop out into your mouth!

Teaching Notes You can use a small coffee stirrer to open the egg valve slightly and make removing the egg by blowing slightly easier. You can also use a quart milk bottle or any other quart bottle with an opening the correct size. Remember that these bottles are not Pyrex and must be heated slowly. Fill the bottle with hot water and empty it. Then fill the bottle with almost boiling water, let it sit 5–10 seconds, and empty it, immediately placing the egg on the opening. Place the small end of the egg on the opening or the egg may split as it enters the bottle.

Lecture Demonstration: 5.29, 5.30, 5.31

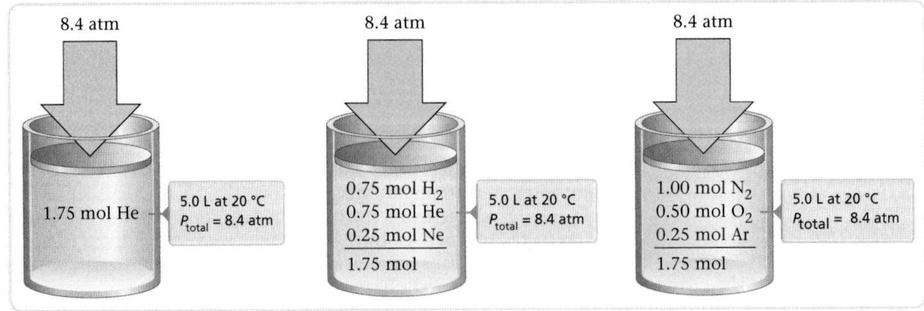

Figure 13.11 The total pressure of a mixture of gases depends on the number of moles of gas particles (atoms or molecules) present, not on the identities of the particles. Note that these three samples show the same total pressure because each contains 1.75 mol gas. The detailed nature of the mixture is unimportant.

The total pressure of the mixture, P_{total}, can be represented as

$$\begin{aligned} P_{total} &= P_1 + P_2 + P_3 = \frac{n_1RT}{V} + \frac{n_2RT}{V} + \frac{n_3RT}{V} \\ &= n_1\left(\frac{RT}{V}\right) + n_2\left(\frac{RT}{V}\right) + n_3\left(\frac{RT}{V}\right) \\ &= (n_1 + n_2 + n_3)\left(\frac{RT}{V}\right) \\ &= n_{total}\left(\frac{RT}{V}\right) \end{aligned}$$

where n_{total} is the sum of the numbers of moles of the gases in the mixture. Thus, for a mixture of ideal gases, it is the *total number of moles of particles* that is important, not the *identity* of the individual gas particles. This idea is illustrated in Figure 13.11.

The fact that the pressure exerted by an ideal gas is affected by the *number* of gas particles and is independent of the *nature* of the gas particles tells us two important things about ideal gases:

1. The volume of the individual gas particle (atom or molecule) must not be very important.
2. The forces among the particles must not be very important.

If these factors were important, the pressure of the gas would depend on the nature of the individual particles. For example, an argon atom is much larger than a helium atom. Yet 1.75 mol argon gas in a 5.0-L container at 20 °C exerts the same pressure as 1.75 mol helium gas in a 5.0-L container at 20 °C.

The same idea applies to the forces among the particles. Although the forces among gas particles depend on the nature of the particles, this seems to have little influence on the behavior of an ideal gas. We will see that these observations strongly influence the model that we will construct to explain ideal gas behavior.

EXAMPLE 13.12 **Using Dalton's Law of Partial Pressures, I**

Mixtures of helium and oxygen are used in the "air" tanks of underwater divers for deep dives. For a particular dive, 12 L of O_2 at 25 °C and 1.0 atm and 46 L of He at 25 °C and 1.0 atm were both pumped into a 5.0-L tank. Calculate the partial pressure of each gas and the total pressure in the tank at 25 °C.

SOLUTION

Where Are We Going?

We want to determine the partial pressure of helium and oxygen and the total pressure in the tank.

What Do We Know?

- We know the initial volume, pressure, and temperature of both gases.
- We know the final volume of the tank.
- The temperature remains constant.
- Ideal gas law: $PV = nRT$.
- Dalton's law of partial pressures: $P_{total} = P_1 + P_2 + \ldots$

What Information Do We Need?

- $R = 0.08206$ L atm/mol K.

How Do We Get There?

MATH SKILL BUILDER

$$PV = nRT$$
$$\frac{PV}{RT} = \frac{n\cancel{RT}}{\cancel{RT}}$$
$$\frac{PV}{RT} = n$$

Because the partial pressure of each gas depends on the moles of that gas present, we must first calculate the number of moles of each gas by using the ideal gas law in the form

$$n = \frac{PV}{RT}$$

From the above description we know that $P = 1.0$ atm, $V = 12$ L for O_2 and 46 L for He, and $T = 25 + 273 = 298$ K. Also, $R = 0.08206$ L atm/K mol (as always).

$$\text{Moles of } O_2 = n_{O_2} = \frac{(1.0\ \cancel{\text{atm}})(12\ \cancel{\text{L}})}{(0.08206\ \cancel{\text{L}}\ \cancel{\text{atm}}/\cancel{\text{K}}\ \text{mol})(298\ \cancel{\text{K}})} = 0.49\ \text{mol}$$

$$\text{Moles of He} = n_{He} = \frac{(1.0\ \cancel{\text{atm}})(46\ \cancel{\text{L}})}{(0.08206\ \cancel{\text{L}}\ \cancel{\text{atm}}/\cancel{\text{K}}\ \text{mol})(298\ \cancel{\text{K}})} = 1.9\ \text{mol}$$

The tank containing the mixture has a volume of 5.0 L, and the temperature is 25 °C (298 K). We can use these data and the ideal gas law to calculate the partial pressure of each gas.

$$P = \frac{nRT}{V}$$

$$P_{O_2} = \frac{(0.49\ \cancel{\text{mol}})(0.08206\ \cancel{\text{L}}\ \text{atm}/\cancel{\text{K}}\ \cancel{\text{mol}})(298\ \cancel{\text{K}})}{5.0\ \cancel{\text{L}}} = 2.4\ \text{atm}$$

$$P_{He} = \frac{(1.9\ \cancel{\text{mol}})(0.08206\ \cancel{\text{L}}\ \text{atm}/\cancel{\text{K}}\ \cancel{\text{mol}})(298\ \cancel{\text{K}})}{5.0\ \cancel{\text{L}}} = 9.3\ \text{atm}$$

The total pressure is the sum of the partial pressures.

$$P_{total} = P_{O_2} + P_{He} = 2.4\ \text{atm} + 9.3\ \text{atm} = 11.7\ \text{atm}$$

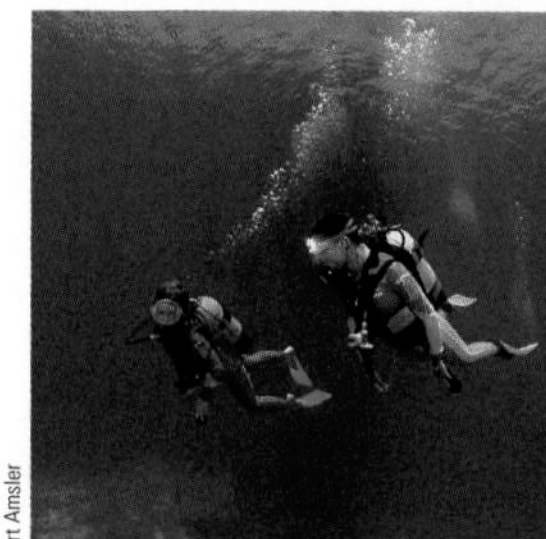

Kurt Amsler

Divers use a mixture of oxygen and helium in their breathing tanks when diving to depths greater than 150 feet.

REALITY CHECK The volume of each gas decreased, and the pressure of each gas increased. The partial pressure of helium is greater than that of oxygen, which makes sense because the initial temperatures and pressures of helium and oxygen were the same, but the initial volume of helium was much greater than that of oxygen.

Additional Examples

Example 13.12

1. A 5.00-g sample of helium gas is added to a 5.00-g sample of neon gas in a 2.50-L container at 27 °C. Calculate the partial pressure of each gas and the total pressure.

   12.3 atm He; 2.44 atm Ne; 14.7 atm total

2. Equal masses of oxygen and nitrogen gas are present in a container. Which gas exerts the larger partial pressure? By what factor?

   N_2 exerts a partial pressure that is 1.14 times as great as the partial pressure of O_2.

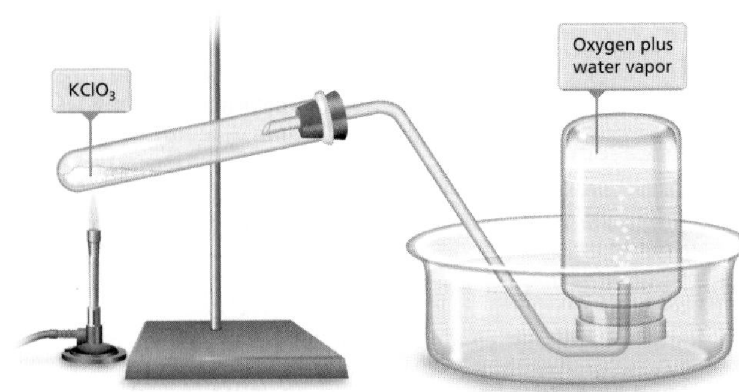

Figure 13.12
The production of oxygen by thermal decomposition of $KClO_3$.

Self-Check EXERCISE 13.9 A 2.0-L flask contains a mixture of nitrogen gas and oxygen gas at 25 °C. The total pressure of the gaseous mixture is 0.91 atm, and the mixture is known to contain 0.050 mol N_2. Calculate the partial pressure of oxygen and the moles of oxygen present.

See Problems 13.67 through 13.70. ■

Table 13.2 The Vapor Pressure of Water as a Function of Temperature

T (°C)	P (torr)
0.0	4.579
10.0	9.209
20.0	17.535
25.0	23.756
30.0	31.824
40.0	55.324
60.0	149.4
70.0	233.7
90.0	525.8

A mixture of gases occurs whenever a gas is collected by displacement of water. For example, Figure 13.12 shows the collection of the oxygen gas that is produced by the decomposition of solid potassium chlorate. The gas is collected by bubbling it into a bottle that is initially filled with water. Thus the gas in the bottle is really a mixture of water vapor and oxygen. (Water vapor is present because molecules of water escape from the surface of the liquid and collect as a gas in the space above the liquid.) Therefore, the total pressure exerted by this mixture is the sum of the partial pressure of the gas being collected and the partial pressure of the water vapor. The partial pressure of the water vapor is called the vapor pressure of water. Because water molecules are more likely to escape from hot water than from cold water, the *vapor pressure* of water increases with temperature. This is shown by the values of vapor pressure at various temperatures in Table 13.2.

EXAMPLE 13.13 Using Dalton's Law of Partial Pressures, II

A sample of solid potassium chlorate, $KClO_3$, was heated in a test tube (see Figure 13.12) and decomposed according to the reaction

$$2KClO_3(s) \rightarrow 2KCl(s) + 3O_2(g)$$

The oxygen produced was collected by displacement of water at 22 °C. The resulting mixture of O_2 and H_2O vapor had a total pressure of 754 torr and a volume of 0.650 L. Calculate the partial pressure of O_2 in the gas collected and the number of moles of O_2 present. The vapor pressure of water at 22 °C is 21 torr.

SOLUTION

Where Are We Going?

We want to determine the partial pressure of oxygen collected by water displacement and the number of moles of O_2 present.

What Do We Know?

- We know the temperature, total pressure, and volume of gas collected by water displacement.

Self Check

Answers to Self-Check Exercise 13.9

0.024 mol, 0.29 atm

Additional Examples

Example 13.13

1. A sample of oxygen gas is saturated with water vapor at 30.0 °C. The total pressure is 753 torr, and the vapor pressure of water at 30.0 °C is 31.824 torr. What is the partial pressure of the oxygen gas in atm?

   0.949 atm

2. A sample of oxygen gas is saturated with water vapor at 27 °C. The total pressure is 785.0 torr, and the partial pressure of oxygen is 758.3 torr. What is the vapor pressure of water at 27 °C?

   26.7 torr

- We know the vapor pressure of water at this temperature.
- Ideal gas law: $PV = nRT$.
- Dalton's law of partial pressures: $P_{total} = P_1 + P_2 + \ldots$

What Information Do We Need?

- $R = 0.08206$ L atm/mol K.

How Do We Get There?

We know the total pressure (754 torr) and the partial pressure of water (vapor pressure = 21 torr). We can find the partial pressure of O_2 from Dalton's law of partial pressures:

$$P_{total} = P_{O_2} + P_{H_2O} = P_{O_2} + 21 \text{ torr} = 754 \text{ torr}$$

or

$$P_{O_2} + 21 \text{ torr} = 754 \text{ torr}$$

We can solve for P_{O_2} by subtracting 21 torr from both sides of the equation.

$$P_{O_2} = 754 \text{ torr} - 21 \text{ torr} = 733 \text{ torr}$$

Next we solve the ideal gas law for the number of moles of O_2.

$$n_{O_2} = \frac{P_{O_2}V}{RT}$$

In this case, $P_{O_2} = 733$ torr. We change the pressure to atmospheres as follows:

$$\frac{733 \cancel{\text{torr}}}{760 \cancel{\text{torr}}/\text{atm}} = 0.964 \text{ atm}$$

MATH SKILL BUILDER

$$PV = nRT$$
$$\frac{PV}{RT} = \frac{n\cancel{RT}}{\cancel{RT}}$$
$$\frac{PV}{RT} = n$$

Then,

$$V = 0.650 \text{ L}$$
$$T = 22 \text{ °C} = 22 + 273 = 295 \text{ K}$$
$$R = 0.08206 \text{ L atm/K mol}$$

so

$$n_{O_2} = \frac{(0.964 \cancel{\text{atm}})(0.650 \cancel{\text{L}})}{(0.08206 \cancel{\text{L}} \cancel{\text{atm}}/\cancel{\text{K}} \text{ mol})(295 \cancel{\text{K}})} = 2.59 \times 10^{-2} \text{ mol}$$

Self-Check EXERCISE 13.10 Consider a sample of hydrogen gas collected over water at 25 °C where the vapor pressure of water is 24 torr. The volume occupied by the gaseous mixture is 0.500 L, and the total pressure is 0.950 atm. Calculate the partial pressure of H_2 and the number of moles of H_2 present.

See Problems 13.71 through 13.74. ■

Self Check

Answers to Self-Check Exercise 13.10

1.88×10^{-2} mol, $P = 0.918$ atm

13.7 Laws and Models: A Review

OBJECTIVE: To understand the relationship between laws and models (theories).

Section 13.7

In this chapter we have considered several properties of gases and have seen how the relationships among these properties can be expressed by various laws written in the form of mathematical equations. The most useful of these is the ideal gas equation, which relates all the important gas properties. However, under certain conditions gases do not obey the ideal gas equation. For

TEACHING TIP

Now is a good time to review the difference between laws and models. The gas laws allow students to predict the behavior of gases, while the kinetic molecular theory explains why gases behave in the manner they do.

DEMONSTRATION

Before class, make the following apparatus. Use an Erlenmeyer flask or round-bottom flask with a small, narrow mouth. Place about 5 mL of water in the flask and heat the water to boiling. Continue heating until only about 1 mL of water remains. Now for the tricky part. Remove the flask from the heat and, while holding it with a towel so you don't burn your fingers, cover the opening with a balloon (partially inflated or containing a little soapy solution works best). A partner can be of great assistance in getting the balloon on the flask. As the flask cools, the balloon will be drawn into the flask. The hardest part is getting the balloon over the mouth of the warm flask without splitting or puncturing it. Be patient and practice.

In class, show the flask to the students and challenge them for explanations.

PowerLecture Animations:
Motion of High and Low Temperature Gas Molecules
Relationship Between Gas Quantity and Pressure
Relationship Between Gas Temperature and Pressure Structure of a Gas
Visualizing Molecular Motion: Many Molecules

example, at high pressures and/or low temperatures, the properties of gases deviate significantly from the predictions of the ideal gas equation. On the other hand, as the pressure is lowered and/or the temperature is increased, almost all gases show close agreement with the ideal gas equation. This means that an ideal gas is really a hypothetical substance. At low pressures and/or high temperatures, real gases *approach* the behavior expected for an ideal gas.

At this point we want to build a model (a theory) to explain *why* a gas behaves as it does. We want to answer the question, *What are the characteristics of the individual gas particles that cause a gas to behave as it does?* However, before we do this let's briefly review the scientific method. Recall that a law is a generalization about behavior that has been observed in many experiments. Laws are very useful; they allow us to predict the behavior of similar systems. For example, a chemist who prepares a new gaseous compound can assume that that substance will obey the ideal gas equation (at least at low P and/or high T).

However, laws do not tell us *why* nature behaves the way it does. Scientists try to answer this question by constructing theories (building models). The models in chemistry are speculations about how individual atoms or molecules (microscopic particles) cause the behavior of macroscopic systems (collections of atoms and molecules in large enough numbers so that we can observe them).

A model is considered successful if it explains known behavior and predicts correctly the results of future experiments. But a model can never be proved absolutely true. In fact, by its very nature *any model is an approximation* and is destined to be modified, at least in part. Models range from the simple (to predict approximate behavior) to the extraordinarily complex (to account precisely for observed behavior). In this text, we use relatively simple models that fit most experimental results.

Section 13.8

TEACHING TIPS

- The postulates for the kinetic molecular theory form the basis for understanding the behavior of gases. Encourage students to develop a mental movie of an ideal gas on a molecular level that can form the basis for understanding the theory.
- Point out that we previously encountered four of these postulates, and are now bringing them all together. Postulate 1 comes from Dalton's atomic theory (discussed in Chapter 4). Postulates 2 and 4 come from Dalton's law of partial pressures. Postulate 5 was discussed in Chapter 10.
- Stress that we are talking about *ideal* gases. For example, we know postulate 4 to be false as evidenced by steam condensing on a cool mirror during a hot shower. It is important for students to understand that although our model for gases assumes ideal behavior and gases are not ideal, we can still use the model to predict behavior and understand gases. The difficulties with real gases surface in small volumes and at large pressures. Under most everyday conditions, the ideal gas law does allow us to predict the behavior of gases.

13.8 The Kinetic Molecular Theory of Gases

OBJECTIVE: To understand the basic postulates of the kinetic molecular theory.

go Chemistry **Module 16: Gas Law and the Kinetic Molecular Theory** covers concepts in this section.

A relatively simple model that attempts to explain the behavior of an ideal gas is the **kinetic molecular theory.** This model is based on speculations about the behavior of the individual particles (atoms or molecules) in a gas. The assumptions (postulates) of the kinetic molecular theory can be stated as follows:

Postulates of the Kinetic Molecular Theory of Gases

1. Gases consist of tiny particles (atoms or molecules).
2. These particles are so small, compared with the distances between them, that the volume (size) of the individual particles can be assumed to be negligible (zero).
3. The particles are in constant random motion, colliding with the walls of the container. These collisions with the walls cause the pressure exerted by the gas.
4. The particles are assumed not to attract or to repel each other.
5. The average kinetic energy of the gas particles is directly proportional to the Kelvin temperature of the gas.

Test Bank: 61–65

Lecture Demonstration: 5.32, 5.33

PowerLecture Simulation: The Kinetic Molecular Theory

The kinetic energy referred to in postulate 5 is the energy associated with the motion of a particle. Kinetic energy (*KE*) is given by the equation $KE = \frac{1}{2}mv^2$, where m is the mass of the particle and v is the velocity (speed) of the particle. The greater the mass or velocity of a particle, the greater its kinetic energy. Postulate 5 means that if a gas is heated to higher temperatures, the average speed of the particles increases; therefore, their kinetic energy increases.

Although real gases do not conform exactly to the five assumptions listed here, we will see in the next section that these postulates do indeed explain *ideal* gas behavior—behavior shown by real gases at high temperatures and/or low pressures.

13.9 The Implications of the Kinetic Molecular Theory

OBJECTIVES: To understand the term *temperature*. • To learn how the kinetic molecular theory explains the gas laws.

In this section we will discuss the *qualitative* relationships between the kinetic molecular (KM) theory and the properties of gases. That is, without going into the mathematical details, we will show how the kinetic molecular theory explains some of the observed properties of gases.

The Meaning of Temperature

In Chapter 2 we introduced temperature very practically as something we measure with a thermometer. We know that as the temperature of an object increases, the object feels "hotter" to the touch. But what does temperature really mean? How does matter change when it gets "hotter"? In Chapter 10 we introduced the idea that temperature is an index of molecular motion. The kinetic molecular theory allows us to further develop this concept. As postulate 5 of the KM theory states, the temperature of a gas reflects how rapidly, on average, its individual gas particles are moving. At high temperatures the particles move very fast and hit the walls of the container frequently, whereas at low temperatures the particles' motions are more sluggish and they collide with the walls of the container much less often. Therefore, temperature really is a measure of the motions of the gas particles. In fact, the Kelvin temperature of a gas is directly proportional to the average kinetic energy of the gas particles.

The Relationship Between Pressure and Temperature

To see how the meaning of temperature given above helps to explain gas behavior, picture a gas in a rigid container. As the gas is heated to a higher temperature, the particles move faster, hitting the walls more often. And, of course, the impacts become more forceful as the particles move faster. If the pressure is due to collisions with the walls, the gas pressure should increase as temperature is increased.

Is this what we observe when we measure the pressure of a gas as it is heated? Yes. A given sample of gas in a rigid container (if the volume is not changed) shows an increase in pressure as its temperature is increased.

Section 13.9

TEACHING TIPS

- Begin the section with a review of temperature and what it means. Apply this concept to the mental movie of the molecular level of gases to help students understand how things change at that level as the temperature changes (see "Technology"). Encourage them to think about the model for gases at the molecular level.
- Once students see the molecular-level action of gases with changing temperature, proceed to investigate and develop models for the molecular level to illustrate the *P*, *T* and *V*, *T* relationships. Now is an opportune time for students to begin to think as chemists. Observing gases at the macroscopic level allows us to predict behavior, while developing a model at the microscopic level allows us to understand why gases behave as they do.

Lecture Demonstration: 5.34

DEMONSTRATION

Add 100 mL of water (and a couple of drops of food coloring if desired) to a 250-mL beaker and place a 50-mL beaker upside down in the water. Set this apparatus on a hot plate and then heat the water to boiling (the smaller beaker will "bounce" in the larger beaker). Allow the water to boil for a few minutes and then remove it from the heat. Water will rise in the 50-mL beaker. As the water boils, steam enters the 50-mL beaker and pushes the air out (which is why the beaker "bounces"). After a few minutes, the small beaker is filled with steam (with very little air). As this system cools, the steam condenses, which lowers the pressure in the 50-mL beaker. Atmospheric pressure then pushes the water up into the 50-mL beaker.

DEMONSTRATION

Place about 50 small balls (or beads) in a one-quart closed jar to simulate a sample of gas. Shake the jar and ask students to tell you how pressure, volume, moles, and temperature are represented (*pressure* can be "heard" as the collisions with the container; *volume* is the volume of the jar; *moles* is a function of the number of particles; *temperature* is related to how fast the jar is shaken). Ask students to tell you how to increase the pressure of the gas sample and demonstrate their suggestions (shake the jar faster, add more balls, transfer all of the balls to a smaller container and shake at the same rate).

Use this opportunity to demonstrate which factors must be held constant and why. For example, if students tell you to increase the temperature, remove most of the balls and shake a little faster. They will "hear" that the pressure has been decreased. Spend time discussing several possibilities.

PowerLecture Video: Air Bags in Car Collisions

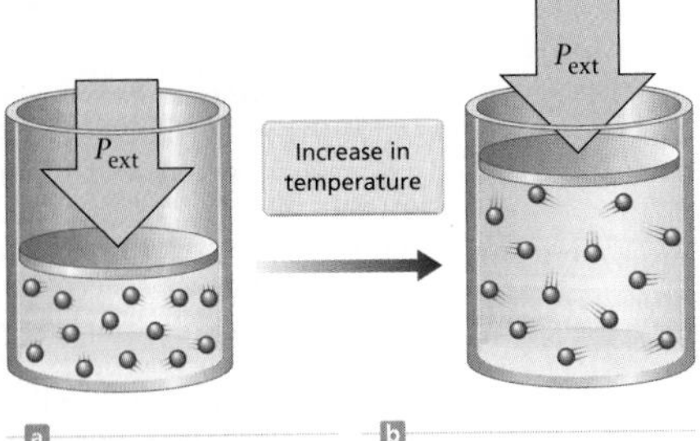

Figure 13.13

a A gas confined in a cylinder with a movable piston. The gas pressure P_{gas} is just balanced by the external pressure P_{ext}. That is, $P_{gas} = P_{ext}$.

b The temperature of the gas is increased at constant pressure P_{ext}. The increased particle motions at the higher temperature push back the piston, increasing the volume of the gas.

The Relationship Between Volume and Temperature

Now picture the gas in a container with a movable piston. As shown in Figure 13.13a, the gas pressure P_{gas} is just balanced by an external pressure P_{ext}. What happens when we heat the gas to a higher temperature? As the temperature increases, the particles move faster, causing the gas pressure to increase. As soon as the gas pressure P_{gas} becomes greater than P_{ext} (the pressure holding the piston), the piston moves up until $P_{gas} = P_{ext}$. Therefore, the KM model predicts that the volume of the gas will increase as we raise its temperature at a constant pressure (Figure 13.13b). This agrees with experimental observations (as summarized by Charles's law).

Additional Examples

Example 13.14

1. Use the kinetic molecular theory to predict what will happen to the pressure of a gas when the number of moles is increased at constant volume and temperature.
2. Use the kinetic molecular theory to predict what will happen to the volume of a gas when the number of moles is increased at constant pressure and temperature.

(See answers on opposite page.)

Test Bank: 66–73, 84, 85

EXAMPLE 13.14 Using the Kinetic Molecular Theory to Explain Gas Law Observations

Use the KM theory to predict what will happen to the pressure of a gas when its volume is decreased (n and T constant). Does this prediction agree with the experimental observations?

SOLUTION

When we decrease the gas's volume (make the container smaller), the particles hit the walls more often because they do not have to travel so far between the walls. This would suggest an increase in pressure. This prediction on the basis of the model is in agreement with experimental observations of gas behavior (as summarized by Boyle's law). ■

In this section we have seen that the predictions of the kinetic molecular theory generally fit the behavior observed for gases. This makes it a useful and successful model.

Section 13.10

13.10 Gas Stoichiometry

OBJECTIVES: To understand the molar volume of an ideal gas. • To learn the definition of STP. • To use these concepts and the ideal gas equation.

We have seen repeatedly in this chapter just how useful the ideal gas equation is. For example, if we know the pressure, volume, and temperature for a given sample of gas, we can calculate the number of moles present:

TEACHING TIPS

- Discussing the relationship between volume and temperature at constant pressure is complex because for the pressure to remain constant, the volume must change. When the temperature increases, the volume changes due to an instantaneous increase in pressure (the volume increase then brings the pressure back to its original value).
- Consider discussing a semi-quantitative relationship between pressure and volume for mathematically inclined students. Imagine a sample of gas in a cubic container with sides of length 1 ft. If we transfer this sample to a cube with sides of length 2 ft, the gas particles will have to travel (on average) twice as far from one wall to the next, and half as many collisions will occur (decreasing the pressure by a factor of 2). In addition, the area of each wall will be four times as large (4 ft^2 versus 1 ft^2). Because pressure is a measure of force per area, this will cause the pressure to decrease by a factor of 4. Thus the pressure should be reduced overall by a factor of 8 (2 × 4). This result is consistent with Boyle's law, since the second container has a volume 8 times larger than that of the first container.

$n = PV/RT$. This fact makes it possible to do stoichiometric calculations for reactions involving gases. We will illustrate this process in Example 13.15.

EXAMPLE 13.15

Gas Stoichiometry: Calculating Volume

Calculate the volume of oxygen gas produced at 1.00 atm and 25 °C by the complete decomposition of 10.5 g of potassium chlorate. The balanced equation for the reaction is

$$2KClO_3(s) \rightarrow 2KCl(s) + 3O_2(g)$$

SOLUTION

Where Are We Going?

We want to determine the volume of oxygen gas collected by the decomposition of $KClO_3$.

What Do We Know?

- We know the temperature and pressure of oxygen gas.
- We know the mass of $KClO_3$.
- The balanced equation: $2KClO_3(s) \rightarrow 2KCl(s) = 3O_2(g)$.
- Ideal gas law: $PV = nRT$.

What Information Do We Need?

- $R = 0.08206$ L atm/mol K.
- We need the number of moles of oxygen gas.
- Molar mass of $KClO_3$.

How Do We Get There?

This is a stoichiometry problem very much like the type we considered in Chapter 9. The only difference is that in this case, we want to calculate the volume of a gaseous product rather than the number of grams. To do so, we can use the relationship between moles and volume given by the ideal gas law.

We'll summarize the steps required to do this problem in the following schematic:

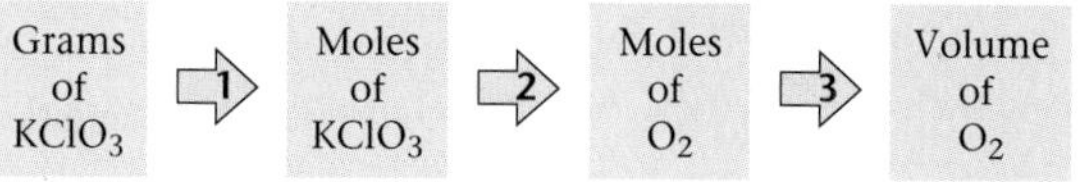

MATH SKILL BUILDER
$\frac{10.5}{122.6} = 0.085644$
0.085644 ➡ 0.0856
Round off
$0.0856 = 8.56 \times 10^{-2}$

Step 1 To find the moles of $KClO_3$ in 10.5 g, we use the molar mass of $KClO_3$ (122.6 g).

$$10.5 \text{ g } \cancel{KClO_3} \times \frac{1 \text{ mol } KClO_3}{122.6 \text{ g } \cancel{KClO_3}} = 8.56 \times 10^{-2} \text{ mol } KClO_3$$

Step 2 To find the moles of O_2 produced, we use the mole ratio of O_2 to $KClO_3$ derived from the balanced equation.

$$8.56 \times 10^{-2} \text{ } \cancel{\text{mol } KClO_3} \times \frac{3 \text{ mol } O_2}{2 \text{ } \cancel{\text{mol } KClO_3}} = 1.28 \times 10^{-1} \text{ mol } O_2$$

TEACHING TIP

Review the basics of stoichiometry before beginning to work gas stoichiometry problems. Now is a good time to review the mole and mole ratio and to revisit unit conversions. Also assure students that there is no conceptual difference between "gas stoichiometry" and the stoichiometry they have already learned. We always need to determine quantities in moles. In Chapter 9 we converted mass to moles by using the molar mass of the substance. Here we convert conditions of a gas (pressure, temperature, and volume) to moles by using the ideal gas law equation.

Example 13.15

1. Consider the reaction represented by the equation $P_4(s) + 6H_2(g) \longrightarrow 4PH_3(g)$. What volume of hydrogen gas at 27 °C and 1.25 atm is required to react with 5.65 g of phosphorus?

   5.39 L

2. When calcium carbonate is heated strongly, carbon dioxide is evolved as shown by the following equation: $CaCO_3(s) \longrightarrow CaO(s) + CO_2(g)$. If 6.25 g of calcium carbonate is heated, what volume of carbon dioxide would be produced when collected at 22 °C and 1.05 atm?

   1.44 L

Answers

1. When we increase the number of moles of gas at constant volume and temperature, the gas particles are moving at the same average speed. With more gas particles, more collisions with the walls of the container will occur. Since pressure is due to collisions with the walls, the gas pressure should increase as the number of moles of gas increases.

2. Picture the gas in a container with a movable piston as shown in Figure 13.13. When we increase the number of moles of gas at constant pressure and temperature, the gas particles are moving at the same average speed. With more gas particles, more collisions with the walls of the container will occur. Since pressure is due to collisions with the walls, the gas pressure should increase as the number of moles of gas increases. As soon as the pressure of the gas inside the container is greater than the external pressure, the piston moves up until the internal and external pressures are equal. We predict that the volume of the gas increases with an increasing number of moles of gas (which is verified by Avogadro's law).

Step 3 To find the volume of oxygen produced, we use the ideal gas law $PV = nRT$, where

$P = 1.00$ atm
$V = ?$
$n = 1.28 \times 10^{-1}$ mol, the moles of O_2 we calculated
$R = 0.08206$ L atm/K mol
$T = 25$ °C $= 25 + 273 = 298$ K

Solving the ideal gas law for V gives

$$V = \frac{nRT}{P} = \frac{(1.28 \times 10^{-1} \cancel{\text{mol}})\left(0.08206 \frac{\text{L} \cancel{\text{atm}}}{\cancel{\text{K}} \cancel{\text{mol}}}\right)(298 \cancel{\text{K}})}{1.00 \cancel{\text{atm}}} = 3.13 \text{ L}$$

Thus 3.13 L of O_2 will be produced.

Self Check

Answer to Self-Check Exercise 13.11

6.47 L

Self-Check EXERCISE 13.11 Calculate the volume of hydrogen produced at 1.50 atm and 19 °C by the reaction of 26.5 g of zinc with excess hydrochloric acid according to the balanced equation

$$Zn(s) + 2HCl(aq) \rightarrow ZnCl_2(aq) + H_2(g)$$

See Problems 13.85 through 13.92. ■

In dealing with the stoichiometry of reactions involving gases, it is useful to define the volume occupied by 1 mole of a gas under certain specified conditions. For 1 mole of an ideal gas at 0 °C (273 K) and 1 atm, the volume of the gas given by the ideal gas law is

$$V = \frac{nRT}{P} = \frac{(1.00 \cancel{\text{mol}})(0.08206 \text{ L } \cancel{\text{atm}}/\cancel{\text{K}} \cancel{\text{mol}})(273 \cancel{\text{K}})}{1.00 \cancel{\text{atm}}} = 22.4 \text{ L}$$

This volume of 22.4 L is called the **molar volume** of an ideal gas.

STP: 0 °C and 1 atm

The conditions 0 °C and 1 atm are called **standard temperature and pressure** (abbreviated **STP**). Properties of gases are often given under these conditions. Remember, the molar volume of an ideal gas is 22.4 L *at STP.* That is, 22.4 L contains 1 mole of an ideal gas at STP.

Additional Examples

Example 13.16

1. A sample of argon gas has a volume of 3.45 L at STP. What is the mass of the argon?

   6.15 g

2. A sample of hydrogen gas occupies a volume of 15.0 L at STP. What volume will this sample occupy at 22 °C and 2.50 atm?

   6.48 L

EXAMPLE 13.16 Gas Stoichiometry: Calculations Involving Gases at STP

A sample of nitrogen gas has a volume of 1.75 L at STP. How many moles of N_2 are present?

SOLUTION

Where Are We Going?

We want to determine the number of moles of nitrogen gas.

What Do We Know?

- The nitrogen gas has a volume of 1.75 L at STP.

What Information Do We Need?

- STP = 1.00 atm, 0 °C.
- At STP, 1 mole of an ideal gas occupies a volume of 22.4 L.

How Do We Get There?

We could solve this problem by using the ideal gas equation, but we can take a shortcut by using the molar volume of an ideal gas at STP. Because 1 mole

DEMONSTRATION

Molar Volume of a Gas

Materials One quart-sized Ziploc plastic bag, dry ice (100 – 125 g), balance, graduated cylinder (1 L if possible)

Presentation Find the mass of the dry ice and plastic bag. Place the dry ice in the plastic bag, press out the air in the bag, and seal it closed. Observe the bag as it inflates with carbon dioxide. Open the bag, press out the gas in it, and find the mass again. Remove the dry ice and fill the bag with water. Measure the volume of the bag by pouring the water into the graduated cylinder. Determine the mass of CO_2 that filled the bag and convert this amount to moles. Find the molar volume of CO_2 by dividing the volume of the bag by the moles of CO_2 generated.

Teaching Notes The volume you obtain will be larger than 22.4 L, because the conditions are not at STP. You can have students correct their molar volume to STP for a closer comparison (since CO_2 is not an ideal gas, the answer will not be exact).

of an ideal gas at STP has a volume of 22.4 L, a 1.75-L sample of N_2 at STP contains considerably less than 1 mol. We can find how many moles by using the equivalence statement

$$1.000 \text{ mol} = 22.4 \text{ L (STP)}$$

which leads to the conversion factor we need:

$$1.75 \cancel{\text{L N}_2} \times \frac{1.000 \text{ mol N}_2}{22.4 \cancel{\text{L N}_2}} = 7.81 \times 10^{-2} \text{ mol N}_2$$

Self-Check EXERCISE 13.12 Ammonia is commonly used as a fertilizer to provide a source of nitrogen for plants. A sample of $NH_3(g)$ occupies a volume of 5.00 L at 25 °C and 15.0 atm. What volume will this sample occupy at STP?

See Problems 13.95 through 13.98. ■

Standard conditions (STP) and molar volume are also useful in carrying out stoichiometric calculations on reactions involving gases, as shown in Example 13.17.

EXAMPLE 13.17 Gas Stoichiometry: Reactions Involving Gases at STP

Quicklime, CaO, is produced by heating calcium carbonate, $CaCO_3$. Calculate the volume of CO_2 produced at STP from the decomposition of 152 g of $CaCO_3$ according to the reaction

$$CaCO_3(s) \rightarrow CaO(s) + CO_2(g)$$

SOLUTION

Where Are We Going?

We want to determine the volume of carbon dioxide produced from 152 g of $CaCO_3$.

What Do We Know?

- We know the temperature and pressure of carbon dioxide gas (STP).
- We know the mass of $CaCO_3$.
- The balanced equation: $CaCO_3(s) \rightarrow CaO(s) = CO_2(g)$.

What Information Do We Need?

- STP = 1.00 atm, 0 °C.
- At STP, 1 mole of an ideal gas occupies a volume of 22.4 L.
- We need the number of moles of carbon dioxide gas.
- Molar mass of $CaCO_3$.

How Do We Get There?

The strategy for solving this problem is summarized by the following schematic:

Self Check

Answer to Self-Check Exercise 13.12

68.8 L

DEMONSTRATION

Density of Gases

Materials Balloons filled with a variety of gases (helium, methane, carbon dioxide, air), ribbons or string

Preparation Fill the balloons all to about equal volume. It is helpful to use a different color for each type of gas. You can generate CO_2 by using dry ice. If you have lecture bottles of any gases, they may provide a resource for filling the balloons. Tie a ribbon or string to each balloon. Be sure the string is at least a meter long. Gather the balloons together and be sure to hold them together at the necks so the students cannot observe the densities before the demonstration.

Presentation Find a volunteer for each balloon. Give the volunteer the balloon, and have the student hold the neck of the balloon with one hand and the end of the string with the other hand. Have all the volunteers hold the balloons about 6 feet from the floor. Ask the volunteers to drop the balloons at the same time. Observe the order in which the balloons fall (or rise). You will need to repeat the demonstration to actually have the students observe the order—the first time they just see what happens. (It is important to have the strings so that the volunteers do not lose the balloons.)

Teaching Notes You can write the gases on the board and have students match each balloon color with the gas and explain how they arrived at their conclusion. You can also use this exercise to review many concepts by asking students to order the balloons from largest to smallest based on pressure, volume, temperature, number of particles, mass of gas, density, average kinetic energy, and average speed of particles.

Additional Examples

Example 13.17

1. When magnesium reacts with hydrochloric acid, hydrogen gas is produced: $Mg(s) + 2HCl(aq) \rightarrow MgCl_2(aq) + H_2(g)$. Calculate the volume of hydrogen gas produced at STP by reacting 5.00 g Mg and an excess of $HCl(aq)$.

   4.61 L

2. When subjected to an electric current, water decomposes to hydrogen and oxygen gas: $2H_2O(l) \rightarrow 2H_2(g) + O_2(g)$. If 25.0 g of water is decomposed, what volume of oxygen gas is produced at STP?

   15.5 L

Lecture Demonstration: 5.24, 5.25, 5.26

ChemWork

- Calculating an Equilibrium Constant from Concentration
- Calculating K from Equilibrium Concentrations
- Finding K from Concentration
- Calculating Equilibrium Pressures
- Calculating K_p in a Homogeneous System
- Converting between K and K_p
- Calculating K_p in a Heterogeneous System
- Heterogeneous Equilibrium
- Calculating Equilibrium Concentrations from Initial Concentrations
- Calculating K_p from Equilibrium Pressures
- Determining an Equilibrium Concentration
- Equilibrium Concentrations for NOCl
- Equilibrium Concentrations for Phosphorus Pentachloride
- Equilibrium in an Ammonia System
- Finding Equilibrium Pressures from K and Initial Pressures
- Le Châtelier's Principle
- Predicting Equilibrium Composition Changes
- Predicting the Effect of Changes on K

Step 1 Using the molar mass of $CaCO_3$ (100.1 g), we calculate the number of moles of $CaCO_3$.

$$152 \text{ g } \cancel{CaCO_3} \times \frac{1 \text{ mol } CaCO_3}{100.1 \text{ g } \cancel{CaCO_3}} = 1.52 \text{ mol } CaCO_3$$

Step 2 Each mole of $CaCO_3$ produces 1 mole of CO_2, so 1.52 moles of CO_2 will be formed.

Step 3 We can convert the moles of CO_2 to volume by using the molar volume of an ideal gas, because the conditions are STP.

$$1.52 \text{ } \cancel{\text{mol } CO_2} \times \frac{22.4 \text{ L } CO_2}{1 \text{ } \cancel{\text{mol } CO_2}} = 34.1 \text{ L } CO_2$$

Thus the decomposition of 152 g of $CaCO_3$ produces 34.1 L of CO_2 atSTP. ■

Remember that the molar volume of an ideal gas is 22.4 L at STP.

Note that the final step in Example 13.17 involves calculating the volume of gas from the number of moles. Because the conditions were specified as STP, we were able to use the molar volume of a gas at STP. If the conditions of a problem are different from STP, we must use the ideal gas law to compute the volume, as we did in Section 13.5.

CHAPTER 13 REVIEW

F directs you to the *Chemistry in Focus* feature in the chapter
VP indicates visual problems
OWL interactive versions of these problems are assignable in OWL

Key Terms

barometer (13.1)
mm Hg (13.1)
torr (13.1)
standard atmosphere (13.1)
pascal (13.1)
Boyle's law (13.2)
absolute zero (13.3)
Charles's law (13.3)
Avogadro's law (13.4)
universal gas constant (13.5)
ideal gas law (13.5)
ideal gas (13.5)
combined gas law (13.5)
partial pressure (13.6)
Dalton's law of partial pressures (13.6)
kinetic molecular theory (13.8)
molar volume (13.10)
standard temperature and pressure (STP) (13.10)

Summary

1. Atmospheric pressure is measured with a barometer. The most commonly used units of pressure are mm Hg (torr), atmospheres, and pascals (the SI unit).
2. Boyle's law states that the volume of a given amount of gas is inversely proportional to its pressure (at constant temperature): $PV = k$ or $P = k/V$. That is, as pressure increases, volume decreases.
3. Charles's law states that, for a given amount of gas at constant pressure, the volume is directly proportional to the temperature (in kelvins): $V = bT$. At −273 °C (0 K), the volume of a gas extrapolates to zero, and this temperature is called absolute zero.
4. Avogadro's law states that for a gas at constant temperature and pressure, the volume is directly proportional to the number of moles of gas: $V = an$.
5. These three laws can be combined into the ideal gas law, $PV = nRT$, where R is called the universal gas constant. This equation makes it possible to calculate any one of the properties—volume, pressure, temperature, or moles of gas present—given the other three. A gas that obeys this equation is said to behave ideally.
6. From the ideal gas equation we can derive the combined gas law,

$$\frac{P_1V_1}{T_1} = \frac{P_2V_2}{T_2}$$

which holds when the amount of gas (moles) remains constant.
7. The pressure of a gas mixture is described by Dalton's law of partial pressures, which states that the total pressure of the mixture of gases in a container is the sum of the partial pressures of the gases that make up the mixture.

8. The kinetic molecular theory of gases is a model that accounts for ideal gas behavior. This model assumes that a gas consists of tiny particles with negligible volumes, that there are no interactions among particles, and that the particles are in constant motion, colliding with the container walls to produce pressure.

Active Learning Questions

These questions are designed to be considered by groups of students in class. Often these questions work well for introducing a particular topic in class.

1. As you increase the temperature of a gas in a sealed, rigid container, what happens to the density of the gas? Would the results be the same if you did the same experiment in a container with a movable piston at a constant external pressure? Explain.

VP 2. A diagram in a chemistry book shows a magnified view of a flask of air.

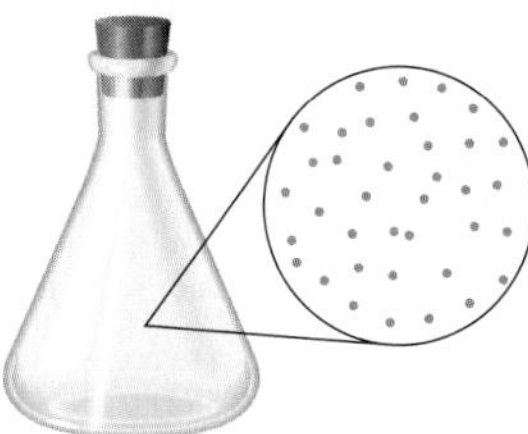

What do you suppose is between the dots (which represent air molecules)?

a. air
b. dust
c. pollutants
d. oxygen
e. nothing

3. If you put a drinking straw in water, place your finger over the opening, and lift the straw out of the water, some water stays in the straw. Explain.

4. A chemistry student relates the following story: I noticed my tires were a bit low and went to the gas station. As I was filling the tires I thought about the kinetic molecular (KM) theory. I noticed the tires because the volume was low, and I realized that I was increasing both the pressure and volume of the tires. "Hmmm," I thought, "that goes against what I learned in chemistry, where I was told pressure and volume are inversely proportional." What is the fault of the logic of the chemistry student in this situation? Explain under what conditions pressure and volume are inversely related (draw pictures and use the KM theory).

5. Chemicals X and Y (both gases) react to form the gas XY, but it takes some time for the reaction to occur. Both X and Y are placed in a container with a piston (free to move), and you note the volume. As the reaction occurs, what happens to the volume of the container? Explain your answer.

6. Which statement best explains why a hot-air balloon rises when the air in the balloon is heated?

a. According to Charles's law, the temperature of a gas is directly related to its volume. Thus the volume of the balloon increases, decreasing the density.
b. Hot air rises inside the balloon, which lifts the balloon.
c. The temperature of a gas is directly related to its pressure. The pressure therefore increases, which lifts the balloon.
d. Some of the gas escapes from the bottom of the balloon, thus decreasing the mass of gas in the balloon. This decreases the density of the gas in the balloon, which lifts the balloon.
e. Temperature is related to the velocity of the gas molecules. Thus the molecules are moving faster, hitting the balloon more, and lifting the balloon.

For choices you did not pick, explain what you feel is wrong with them, and justify the choice you did pick.

7. If you release a helium balloon, it soars upward and eventually pops. Explain this behavior.

8. If you have any two gases in different containers that are the same size at the same pressure and same temperature, what is true about the moles of each gas? Why is this true?

9. Using postulates of the kinetic molecular theory, give a molecular interpretation of Boyle's law, Charles's law, and Dalton's law of partial pressures.

10. Rationalize the following observations.

a. Aerosol cans will explode if heated.
b. You can drink through a soda straw.
c. A thin-walled can will collapse when the air inside is removed by a vacuum pump.
d. Manufacturers produce different types of tennis balls for high and low altitudes.

11. Show how Boyle's law and Charles's law are special cases of the ideal gas law.

12. Look at the demonstration discussed in Figure 13.1. How would this demonstration change if water was not added to the can? Explain.

13. How does Dalton's law of partial pressures help us with our model of ideal gases? That is, which postulates of the kinetic molecular theory does it support?

14. Draw molecular-level views that show the differences among solids, liquids, and gases.

15. Explain how increasing the number of moles of gas affects the pressure (assuming constant volume and temperature).

16. Explain how increasing the number of moles of gas affects the volume (assuming constant pressure and temperature).

17. Gases are said to exert pressure. Provide a molecular-level explanation for this.

Chapter Review 437

18. Why is it incorrect to say that a sample of helium at 50 °C is twice as hot as a sample of helium at 25 °C?

19. We can use different units for pressure or volume, but we must use units of Kelvin for temperature. Why must we use the Kelvin temperature scale?

20. Estimate the mass of air at normal conditions that takes up the volume of your head. Provide support for your answer.

21. You are holding two balloons of the same volume. One balloon contains 1.0 g of helium. The other balloon contains neon. Calculate the mass of neon in the balloon.

VP 22. You have helium gas in a two-bulbed container connected by a valve as shown below. Initially the valve is closed.

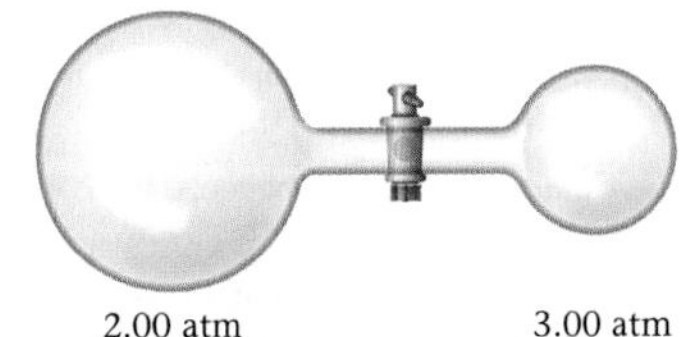

2.00 atm 3.00 atm

a. When the valve is opened, will the total pressure in the apparatus be less than 5.00 atm, equal to 5.00 atm, or greater than 5.00 atm? Explain your answer.
b. The left bulb has a volume of 9.00 L, and the right bulb has a volume of 3.00 L. Calculate the final pressure after the valve is opened.

VP 23. Use the graphs below to answer the following questions.

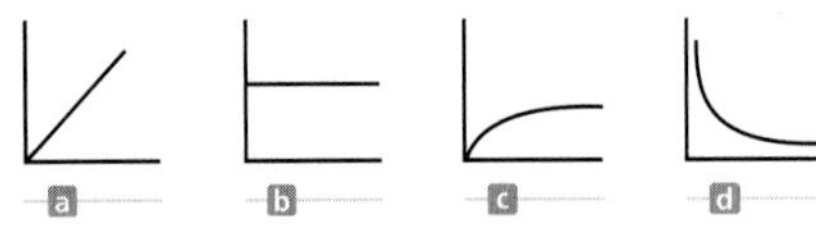

a. Which of the above graphs best represents the relationship between the pressure and temperature (measured in kelvins) of 1 mole of an ideal gas?
b. Which of the above graphs best represents the relationship between the pressure and volume of 1 mole of an ideal gas?
c. Which of the above graphs best represents the relationship between the volume and temperature (measured in kelvins) of 1 mole of an ideal gas.

Questions and Problems

13.1 Pressure

QUESTIONS

1. The introduction to this chapter says that "we live immersed in a gaseous solution." What does that mean?

2. How are the three states of matter similar, and how do they differ?

3. Figure 13.1 shows an experiment that can be used effectively to demonstrate the pressure exerted by the atmosphere. Write an explanation of this experiment to a friend who has not yet taken any science courses to help him understand the concept of atmospheric pressure.

4. Describe a simple mercury barometer. How is such a barometer used to measure the pressure of the atmosphere?

5. If two gases that do not react with each other are placed in the same container, they will ______ completely with each other.

6. What are the common units used to measure pressure? Which unit is an experimental unit derived from the device used to measure atmospheric pressure?

PROBLEMS

7. Make the indicated pressure conversions.
   a. 45.2 kPa to atmospheres
   b. 755 mm Hg to atmospheres
   c. 802 torr to kilopascals
   d. 1.04 atm to millimeters of mercury

8. Make the indicated pressure conversions.
   a. 14.9 psi to atmospheres
   b. 795 torr to atmospheres
   c. 743 mm Hg to kilopascals
   d. 99,436 Pa to kilopascals

9. Make the indicated pressure conversions.
   a. 699 mm Hg to atmospheres
   b. 18.2 psi to mm Hg
   c. 862 mm Hg to torr
   d. 795 mm Hg to psi

10. Make the indicated pressure conversions.
   a. 17.3 psi to kilopascals
   b. 1.15 atm to psi
   c. 4.25 atm to mm Hg
   d. 224 psi to atmospheres

11. Make the indicated pressure conversions.
   a. 1.54×10^5 Pa to atmospheres
   b. 1.21 atm to pascals
   c. 97,345 Pa to mm Hg
   d. 1.32 kPa to pascals

12. Make the indicated pressure conversions.
   a. 6.42 atm to kilopascals
   b. 4.21 atm to torr
   c. 794 mm Hg to atmospheres
   d. 27.2 psi to atmospheres

All even-numbered Questions and Problems have answers in the back of this book and solutions in the Solutions Guide.

Answers to End-of-Chapter Exercises

1. The atmosphere is a homogeneous mixture of gases.

2. Solids are rigid and incompressible and have definite shapes and volumes. Liquids are less rigid than solids; although they have definite volumes, liquids take the shape of their containers. Gases have no fixed volume or shape; they take the volume and shape of their container and are affected more by changes in their pressure and temperature than are solids or liquids.

3. A small amount of water is added to a metal can. The can is heated so as to boil the water and fill the can with steam (gaseous water). The heat is then removed and the can is sealed off. As the steam in the can cools, it condenses back to a liquid. Because the gas in the can has condensed, the pressure of the atmosphere is much larger than the pressure of gas in the can, and the atmospheric pressure causes the can to collapse.

4. A mercury barometer consists of a tube filled with mercury that is then inverted over a reservoir of mercury, the surface of which is open to the atmosphere. The pressure of the atmosphere is reflected in the height to which the column of mercury in the tube is supported.

5. mix

6. Pressure units include mm Hg, torr, pascals, and psi. The unit "mm Hg" is derived from the barometer, because in a traditional mercury barometer, we measure the height of the mercury column (in millimeters) above the reservoir of mercury.

7. (a) 0.446 atm; (b) 0.993 atm; (c) 107 kPa; (d) 790 mm Hg

8. (a) 1.01 atm; (b) 1.05 atm; (c) 99.1 kPa; (d) 99.436 kPa

9. (a) 0.920 atm; (b) 941 mm Hg; (c) 862 torr; (d) 15.4 psi

10. (a) 119 kPa; (b) 16.9 psi; (c) 3.23×10^3 mm Hg; (d) 15.2 atm

11. (a) 1.52 atm; (b) 1.23×10^5 Pa; (c) 730.14 mm Hg; (d) 1.32×10^3 Pa

12. (a) 651 kPa; (b) 3.20×10^3 torr; (c) 1.04 atm; (d) 1.85 atm

13.2 Pressure and Volume: Boyle's Law

QUESTIONS

13. Pretend that you're talking to a friend who has not yet taken any science courses, and describe how you would explain Boyle's law to her.

14. In Figure 13.4, when additional mercury is added to the right-hand arm of the J-shaped tube, the volume of the gas trapped above the mercury in the left-hand arm of the J-tube decreases. Explain.

15. The volume of a sample of ideal gas is inversely proportional to the ______ on the gas at constant temperature.

16. A mathematical expression that summarizes Boyle's law is ______.

PROBLEMS

17. For each of the following sets of pressure/volume data, calculate the new volume of the gas sample after the pressure change is made. Assume that the temperature and the amount of gas remain the same.

a. V = 125 mL at 755 mm Hg; V = ? mL at 780 mm Hg
b. V = 223 mL at 1.08 atm; V = ? mL at 0.951 atm
c. V = 3.02 L at 103 kPa; V = ? L at 121 kPa

18. For each of the following sets of pressure/volume data, calculate the new volume of the gas sample after the pressure change is made. Assume that the temperature and the amount of gas remain the same.

a. V = 375 mL at 1.15 atm; V = ? mL at 775 mm Hg
b. V = 195 mL at 1.08 atm; V = ? mL at 135 kPa
c. V = 6.75 L at 131 kPa; V = ? L at 765 mm Hg

19. For each of the following sets of pressure/volume data, calculate the missing quantity. Assume that the temperature and the amount of gas remain constant.

a. V = 19.3 L at 102.1 kPa; V = 10.0 L at ? kPa
b. V = 25.7 mL at 755 torr; V = ? at 761 mm Hg
c. V = 51.2 L at 1.05 atm; V = ? at 112.2 kPa

20. For each of the following sets of pressure/volume data, calculate the missing quantity after the change is made. Assume that the temperature and the amount of gas remain the same.

a. V = 125 mL at 755 mm Hg; V = 137 mL at ? mm Hg
b. V = 331 mL at 1.08 atm; V = 299 mL at ? atm
c. V = 3.02 L at 789 mm Hg; V = ? L at 135 kPa

21. What volume of gas would result if 225 mL of neon gas is compressed from 1.02 atm to 2.99 atm at constant temperature?

22. If the pressure on a 1.04-L sample of gas is doubled at constant temperature, what will be the new volume of the gas?

23. A sample of helium gas with a volume of 29.2 mL at 785 mm Hg is compressed at constant temperature until its volume is 15.1 mL. What will be the new pressure in the sample?

24. What pressure would have to be applied to a 27.2-mL sample of gas at 25 °C and 1.00 atm to compress its volume to 1.00 mL without a change in temperature?

13.3 Volume and Temperature: Charles's Law

QUESTIONS

25. Pretend that you're talking to a friend who has not yet taken any science courses, and describe how you would explain the concept of absolute zero to him.

26. Figures 13.7 and 13.8 show volume/temperature data for several samples of gases. Why do all the lines seem to extrapolate to the same point at −273 °C? Explain.

27. The volume of a sample of ideal gas is ______ proportional to its temperature (K) at constant pressure.

28. A mathematical expression that summarizes Charles's law is ______.

PROBLEMS

29. A favorite demonstration in introductory chemistry is to illustrate how the volume of a gas is affected by temperature by blowing up a balloon at room temperature and then placing the balloon into a container of dry ice or liquid nitrogen (both of which are *very* cold). Suppose a balloon containing 1.15 L of air at 25.2 °C is placed into a flask containing liquid nitrogen at −78.5 °C. What will the volume of the sample become (at constant pressure)?

30. Suppose a 375-mL sample of neon gas at 78 °C is cooled to 22 °C at constant pressure. What will be the new volume of the neon sample?

31. For each of the following sets of volume/temperature data, calculate the missing quantity after the change is made. Assume that the pressure and the amount of gas remain the same.

a. V = 2.03 L at 24 °C; V = 3.01 L at ? °C
b. V = 127 mL at 273 K; V = ? mL at 373 K
c. V = 49.7 mL at 34 °C; V = ? at 350 K

32. For each of the following sets of volume/temperature data, calculate the missing quantity. Assume that the pressure and the mass of gas remain constant.

a. V = 73.5 mL at 0 °C; V = ? at 25 °C
b. V = 15.2 L at 298 K; V = 10.0 L at ? °C
c. V = 1.75 mL at 2.3 K; V = ? at 0 °C

33. For each of the following sets of volume/temperature data, calculate the missing quantity after the change is made. Assume that the pressure and the amount of gas remain the same.

a. V = 9.14 L at 24 °C; V = ? at 48 °C
b. V = 24.9 mL at −12 °C; V = 49.9 mL at ? °C
c. V = 925 mL at 25 K; V = ? at 273 K

All even-numbered Questions and Problems have answers in the back of this book and solutions in the Solutions Guide.

26. Charles's law indicates that an ideal gas decreases by 1/273 of its volume for every Celsius degree its temperature is lowered. This means an ideal gas would approach a volume of zero at −273 °C.

27. directly

28. $V = bT$; $V_1/T_1 = V_2/T_2$

29. 0.750 L

30. 315 mL

31. (a) 440 K, 167 °C; (b) 174 mL; (c) 56.7 mL

32. (a) 80.2 mL; (b) −77 °C (196 K); (c) 208 mL (2.1×10^2 mL)

33. (a) 9.88 L; (b) 523 K, 250 °C; (c) 1.01×10^4 mL

13. student explanation

14. Additional mercury increases the pressure on the gas sample, causing the volume of the gas upon which the pressure is exerted to decrease (Boyle's law).

15. pressure

16. $PV = k$; $P_1V_1 = P_2V_2$

17. (a) 121 mL; (b) 253 mL; (c) 2.57 L

18. (a) 423 mL; (b) 158 mL; (c) 8.67 L

19. (a) 197 kPa; (b) 25.5 mL; (c) 48.6 L

20. (a) 689 mm Hg; (b) 1.20 atm; (c) 2.35 L

21. 76.8 mL

22. 0.520 L

23. 1.52×10^3 mm Hg

24. 27.2 atm

25. student explanation

34. For each of the following sets of volume/temperature data, calculate the missing quantity. Assume that the pressure and the mass of gas remain constant.

a. $V = 2.01 \times 10^2$ L at 1150 °C; $V = 5.00$ L at ? °C
b. $V = 44.2$ mL at 298 K; $V = ?$ at 0 K
c. $V = 44.2$ mL at 298 K; $V = ?$ at 0 °C

35. Suppose 1.25 L of argon is cooled from 291 K to 78 K. What will be the new volume of the argon sample?

36. Suppose a 125-mL sample of argon is cooled from 450 K to 250 K at constant pressure. What will be the volume of the sample at the lower temperature?

37. If a 375-mL sample of neon gas is heated from 24 °C to 72 °C at constant pressure, what will be the volume of the sample at the higher temperature?

38. A sample of gas has a volume of 127 mL in a boiling water bath at 100 °C. Calculate the volume of the sample of gas at 10 °C intervals after the heat source is turned off and the gas sample begins to cool down to the temperature of the laboratory, 20 °C.

13.4 Volume and Moles: Avogadro's Law

QUESTIONS

39. At conditions of constant temperature and pressure, the volume of a sample of ideal gas is ______ proportional to the number of moles of gas present.

40. A mathematical expression that summarizes Avogadro's law is ______.

PROBLEMS

41. If 0.00901 mol neon gas at a particular temperature and pressure occupies a volume of 242 mL, what volume would 0.00703 mol neon occupy under the same conditions?

42. If 1.04 g of chlorine gas occupies a volume of 872 mL at a particular temperature and pressure, what volume will 2.08 g of chlorine gas occupy under the same conditions?

43. If 3.25 mol argon gas occupies a volume of 100. L at a particular temperature and pressure, what volume does 14.15 mol argon occupy under the same conditions?

44. If 2.71 g of argon gas occupies a volume of 4.21 L, what volume will 1.29 mol argon occupy under the same conditions?

13.5 The Ideal Gas Law

QUESTIONS

45. What do we mean by an *ideal* gas?

46. Under what conditions do *real* gases behave most ideally?

47. Show how Boyle's gas law can be derived from the ideal gas law.

48. Show how Charles's gas law can be derived from the ideal gas law.

PROBLEMS

49. Given the following sets of values for three of the gas variables, calculate the unknown quantity.

a. $P = 782.4$ mm Hg; $V = ?$; $n = 0.1021$ mol; $T = 26.2$ °C
b. $P = ?$ mm Hg; $V = 27.5$ mL; $n = 0.007812$ mol; $T = 16.6$ °C
c. $P = 1.045$ atm; $V = 45.2$ mL; $n = 0.002241$ mol; $T = ?$ °C

50. Given each of the following sets of values for an ideal gas, calculate the unknown quantity.

a. $P = 782$ mm Hg; $V = ?$; $n = 0.210$ mol; $T = 27$ °C
b. $P = ?$ mm Hg; $V = 644$ mL; $n = 0.0921$ mol; $T = 303$ K
c. $P = 745$ mm Hg; $V = 11.2$ L; $n = 0.401$ mol; $T = ?$ K

51. What mass of neon gas is required to fill a 5.00-L container to a pressure of 1.02 atm at 25 °C?

52. What pressure will exist in a 10.0-L flask containing 12.2 g of argon gas at 25 °C?

53. What volume will 2.04 g of helium gas occupy at 100. °C and 785 mm Hg pressure?

54. At what temperature will 40.0 g of argon gas have a pressure of 1.00 atm when confined in a 25.0-L tank?

55. What mass of helium gas is needed to pressurize a 100.0-L tank to 255 atm at 25 °C? What mass of oxygen gas would be needed to pressurize a similar tank to the same specifications?

56. Suppose that a 1.25-g sample of neon gas is confined in a 10.1-L container at 25 °C. What will be the pressure in the container? Suppose the temperature is then raised to 50 °C. What will the new pressure be after the temperature is increased?

57. At what temperature will a 1.0-g sample of neon gas exert a pressure of 500. torr in a 5.0-L container?

58. At what temperature would 4.25 g of oxygen gas, O_2, exert a pressure of 784 mm Hg in a 2.51-L container?

59. What pressure exists in a 200-L tank containing 5.0 kg of neon gas at 300. K?

60. Which flask will have the higher pressure: a 5.00-L flask containing 4.15 g of helium at 298 K, or a 10.0-L flask containing 56.2 g of argon at 303 K?

61. Suppose a 24.3-mL sample of helium gas at 25 °C and 1.01 atm is heated to 50. °C and compressed to a volume of 15.2 mL. What will be the pressure of the sample?

62. Suppose that 1.29 g of argon gas is confined to a volume of 2.41 L at 29 °C. What would be the pressure in the container? What would the pressure become if the temperature were raised to 42 °C without a change in volume?

All even-numbered Questions and Problems have answers in the back of this book and solutions in the Solutions Guide.

34. (a) 35.4 K = −238 °C; (b) 0 mL (absolute zero; a real gas would condense to a solid or liquid); (c) 40.5 mL

35. 0.335 L/0.34 L

36. 69.4 mL (69 mL to two significant figures)

37. 436 mL

38. 90 °C, 124 mL; 80 °C, 121 mL; 70 °C, 117 mL; 60 °C, 113 mL; 50 °C, 110 mL; 40 °C, 107 mL; 30 °C, 103 mL; 20 °C, 99.8. mL

39. directly

40. $V = an$; $V_1/n_1 = V_2/n_2$

41. 189 mL

42. 1744 mL (1.74×10^3 mL)

43. 435 L

44. 80.1 L

45. An ideal gas is one that obeys the ideal gas law exactly.

46. Real gases behave most ideally at relatively high temperatures and relatively low pressures. We usually assume that a real gas's behavior approaches ideal behavior if the temperature is over 0 °C (273 K) and the pressure is 1 atm or lower.

47. student explanation

48. For an ideal gas, $PV = nRT$ is true under any conditions. Consider a particular sample of gas (n remains constant) at a particular fixed pressure (P remains constant). Suppose that at temperature T_1 the volume of the gas sample is V_1. For this set of conditions, the ideal gas equation would be given by $PV_1 = nRT_1$. If the temperature of the gas sample changes to a new temperature, T_2, then the volume of the gas sample changes to a new volume, V_2. For this new set of conditions, the ideal gas equation would be given by $PV_2 = nRT_2$. If we make a *ratio* of these two expressions for the ideal gas equation for this gas sample, and cancel out terms that are constant for this situation (P, n, and R), we get

$$\frac{PV_1}{PV_2} = \frac{nRT_1}{nRT_2}, \text{ or } \frac{V_1}{V_2} = \frac{T_1}{T_2},$$

which can be rearranged to the familiar form of Charles's law,

$$\frac{V_1}{T_1} = \frac{V_2}{T_2}.$$

49. (a) 2.44 L; (b) 6.76 atm (5.14×10^3 mm Hg); (c) 257 K/−16 °C

50. (a) 5.02 L; (b) 3.56 atm = 2.70×10^3 mm Hg; (c) 334 K

51. 4.21 g

52. 0.747 atm

53. 15.1 L

54. 304 K, 31 °C

55. 4.16×10^3 g He, 3.33×10^4 g O_2

56. 0.150 atm; 0.163 atm

57. 81.0 K

58. 238 K/−35 °C

59. 31 atm (2 significant figures)

60. The helium (5.07 atm) is at a higher pressure than the argon (3.50 atm).

63. What will the volume of the sample become if 459 mL of an ideal gas at 27 °C and 1.05 atm is cooled to 15 °C and 0.997 atm?

F 64. The "Chemistry in Focus" segment *Snacks Need Chemistry, Too!* discusses why popcorn "pops." You can estimate the pressure inside a kernel of popcorn at the time of popping by using the ideal gas law. Basically, you determine the mass of water released when the popcorn pops by measuring the mass of the popcorn both before and after popping. Assume that the difference in mass is the mass of water vapor lost on popping. Assume that the popcorn pops at the temperature of the cooking oil (225 °C) and that the volume of the "container" is the volume of the unpopped kernel. Although we are making several assumptions, we can at least get some idea of the magnitude of the pressure inside the kernel.

Assuming a total volume of 2.0 mL for 20 kernels and a mass of 0.250 g of water lost from them on popping, calculate the pressure inside the kernels just before they "pop."

13.6 Dalton's Law of Partial Pressures

QUESTIONS

65. Explain why the measured properties of a mixture of gases depend only on the total number of moles of particles, not on the identity of the individual gas particles. How is this observation summarized as a law?

66. We often collect small samples of gases in the laboratory by bubbling the gas into a bottle or flask containing water. Explain why the gas becomes saturated with water vapor and how we must take the presence of water vapor into account when calculating the properties of the gas sample.

PROBLEMS

67. If a gaseous mixture is made of 2.41 g of He and 2.79 g of Ne in an evacuated 1.04-L container at 25 °C, what will be the partial pressure of each gas and the total pressure in the container?

68. Suppose that 1.28 g of neon gas and 2.49 g of argon gas are confined in a 9.87-L container at 27 °C. What would be the pressure in the container?

69. A tank contains a mixture of 52.5 g of oxygen gas and 65.1 g of carbon dioxide gas at 27 °C. The total pressure in the tank is 9.21 atm. Calculate the partial pressure (in atm) of each gas in the mixture.

70. What mass of neon gas would be required to fill a 3.00-L flask to a pressure of 925 mm Hg at 26 °C? What mass of argon gas would be required to fill a similar flask to the same pressure at the same temperature?

71. A sample of oxygen gas is saturated with water vapor at 27 °C. The total pressure of the mixture is 772 torr, and the vapor pressure of water is 26.7 torr at 27 °C. What is the partial pressure of the oxygen gas?

72. Suppose a gaseous mixture of 1.15 g helium and 2.91 g argon is placed in a 5.25-L container at 273 °C. What pressure would exist in the container?

73. A 500.-mL sample of O_2 gas at 24 °C was prepared by decomposing a 3% aqueous solution of hydrogen peroxide, H_2O_2, in the presence of a small amount of manganese catalyst by the reaction

$$2H_2O_2(aq) \rightarrow 2H_2O(g) + O_2(g)$$

The oxygen thus prepared was collected by displacement of water. The total pressure of gas collected was 755 mm Hg. What is the partial pressure of O_2 in the mixture? How many moles of O_2 are in the mixture? (The vapor pressure of water at 24 °C is 23 mm Hg.)

74. Small quantities of hydrogen gas can be prepared in the laboratory by the addition of aqueous hydrochloric acid to metallic zinc.

$$Zn(s) + 2HCl(aq) \rightarrow ZnCl_2(aq) + H_2(g)$$

Typically, the hydrogen gas is bubbled through water for collection and becomes saturated with water vapor. Suppose 240. mL of hydrogen gas is collected at 30. °C and has a total pressure of 1.032 atm by this process. What is the partial pressure of hydrogen gas in the sample? How many moles of hydrogen gas are present in the sample? How many grams of zinc must have reacted to produce this quantity of hydrogen? (The vapor pressure of water is 32 torr at 30 °C.)

13.7 Laws and Models: A Review

QUESTIONS

75. What is a scientific *law?* What is a *theory?* How do these concepts differ? Does a law explain a theory, or does a theory attempt to explain a law?

76. When is a scientific theory considered to be successful? Are all theories successful? Will a theory that has been successful in the past necessarily be successful in the future?

13.8 The Kinetic Molecular Theory of Gases

QUESTIONS

77. What do we assume about the volume of the actual molecules themselves in a sample of gas, compared to the bulk volume of the gas overall? Why?

78. Collisions of the molecules in a sample of gas with the walls of the container are responsible for the gas's observed ______.

79. Temperature is a measure of the average ______ of the molecules in a sample of gas.

80. The kinetic molecular theory of gases suggests that gas particles exert ______ attractive or repulsive forces on each other.

All even-numbered Questions and Problems have answers in the back of this book and solutions in the Solutions Guide.

67. P_{total} = 17.5 atm; P_{He} = 14.2 atm; P_{Ne} = 3.25 atm

68. 0.314 atm

69. 4.84 atm O_2; 4.37 atm CO_2

70. 3.00 g Ne; 5.94 g Ar

71. 745 torr

72. 3.07 atm

73. 1.98×10^{-2} mol O_2

74. $P_{hydrogen}$ = 0.990 atm; 9.55×10^{-3} mol H_2; 0.625 g Zn

75. A law is a statement that expresses generally observed behavior. A theory consists of a set of hypotheses that attempts to explain the observed behavior.

76. A theory is successful if it explains known experimental observations. Theories that have been successful in the past may not be successful in the future (for example, as technology evolves, more sophisticated experiments may be possible in the future).

77. volume of molecules negligible compared to bulk volume of gas; explains compressibility of gases

78. pressure

79. kinetic energy

80. no

61. 1.75 atm

62. 0.332 atm; 0.346 atm

63. 464 mL

64. ~283 (2.8×10^2 atm) atm

65. We assume that the molecules themselves occupy no volume, and that they do not interact with each other, so that the overall properties of the mixture depend only on the total quantity of gas present.

66. As a gas is bubbled through water, the bubbles of gas become saturated with water vapor, thus forming a gaseous mixture. The total pressure for a sample of gas that has been collected by bubbling through water is made up of two components: the pressure of the sample gas and the pressure of water vapor. The partial pressure of the gas equals the total pressure of the sample minus the vapor pressure of water.

13.9 The Implications of the Kinetic Molecular Theory

QUESTIONS

81. How is the phenomenon of temperature explained on the basis of the kinetic molecular theory? What microscopic property of gas molecules is reflected in the temperature measured?

82. Explain, in terms of the kinetic molecular theory, how an increase in the temperature of a gas confined to a rigid container causes an increase in the pressure of the gas.

13.10 Gas Stoichiometry

QUESTIONS

83. What is the *molar volume* of a gas? Do all gases that behave ideally have the same molar volume?

84. What conditions are considered "standard temperature and pressure" (STP) for gases? Suggest a reason why these particular conditions might have been chosen for STP.

PROBLEMS

85. Calcium oxide can be used to "scrub" carbon dioxide from air.

$$CaO(s) + CO_2(g) \rightarrow CaCO_3(s)$$

What mass of CO_2 could be absorbed by 1.25 g of CaO? What volume would this CO_2 occupy at STP?

86. Consider the following reaction:

$$C(s) + O_2(g) \rightarrow CO_2(g)$$

What volume of oxygen gas at 25 °C and 1.02 atm would be required to react completely with 1.25 g of carbon?

87. Consider the following reaction for the combustion of octane, C_8H_{18}:

$$2C_8H_{18}(l) + 25O_2(g) \rightarrow 16CO_2(g) + 18H_2O(l)$$

What volume of oxygen gas at STP would be needed for the complete combustion of 10.0 g of octane?

88. Although we generally think of combustion reactions as involving oxygen gas, other rapid oxidation reactions are also referred to as combustions. For example, if magnesium metal is placed into chlorine gas, a rapid oxidation takes place, and magnesium chloride is produced.

$$Mg(s) + Cl_2(g) \rightarrow MgCl_2(s)$$

What volume of chlorine gas, measured at STP, is required to react completely with 1.02 g of magnesium?

89. Ammonia and gaseous hydrogen chloride combine to form ammonium chloride.

$$NH_3(g) + HCl(g) \rightarrow NH_4Cl(s)$$

If 4.21 L of $NH_3(g)$ at 27 °C and 1.02 atm is combined with 5.35 L of $HCl(g)$ at 26 °C and 0.998 atm, what mass of $NH_4Cl(s)$ will be produced? Which gas is the limiting reactant? Which gas is present in excess?

90. Calcium carbide, CaC_2, reacts with water to produce acetylene gas, C_2H_2.

$$CaC_2(s) + 2H_2O(l) \rightarrow C_2H_2(g) + Ca(OH)_2(s)$$

What volume of acetylene at 25 °C and 1.01 atm is generated by the complete reaction of 2.49 g of calcium carbide? What volume would this quantity of acetylene occupy at STP?

91. Many transition metal salts are hydrates: they contain a fixed number of water molecules bound per formula unit of the salt. For example, copper(II) sulfate most commonly exists as the pentahydrate, $CuSO_4 \cdot 5H_2O$. If 5.00 g of $CuSO_4 \cdot 5H_2O$ is heated strongly so as to drive off all of the waters of hydration as water vapor, what volume will this water vapor occupy at 350. °C and a pressure of 1.04 atm?

92. If water is added to magnesium nitride, ammonia gas is produced when the mixture is heated.

$$Mg_3N_2(s) + 3H_2O(l) \rightarrow 3MgO(s) + 2NH_3(g)$$

If 10.3 g of magnesium nitride is treated with water, what volume of ammonia gas would be collected at 24 °C and 752 mm Hg?

93. What volume does a mixture of 14.2 g of He and 21.6 g of H_2 occupy at 28 °C and 0.985 atm?

94. What volume does a mixture of 26.2 g of O_2 and 35.1 g of N_2 occupy at 35 °C and 755 mm Hg?

95. A sample of helium gas occupies a volume of 25.2 mL at 95 °C and a pressure of 892 mm Hg. Calculate the volume of the gas at STP.

96. What volume does 5.02 g of helium occupy at STP? What volume would 42.1 g of argon occupy under the same conditions?

97. A mixture contains 5.00 g *each* of O_2, N_2, CO_2, and Ne gas. Calculate the volume of this mixture at STP. Calculate the partial pressure of each gas in the mixture at STP.

98. A gaseous mixture contains 6.25 g of He and 4.97 g of Ne. What volume does the mixture occupy at STP? Calculate the partial pressure of each gas in the mixture at STP.

99. Consider the following *unbalanced* chemical equation for the combination reaction of sodium metal and chlorine gas:

$$Na(s) + Cl_2(g) \rightarrow NaCl(s)$$

What volume of chlorine gas, measured at STP, is necessary for the complete reaction of 4.81 g of sodium metal?

All even-numbered Questions and Problems have answers in the back of this book and solutions in the Solutions Guide.

81. Temperature reflects the speed/kinetic energy of the molecules (on average): molecules move faster at higher temperatures.

82. If the temperature of a sample of gas is increased, the average kinetic energy of the particles of gas increases. This means that the speeds of the particles increase. If the particles have a higher speed, they hit the walls of the container more frequently and with greater force, thereby increasing the pressure.

83. volume occupied by one mole of ideal gas at STP; yes

84. STP = 0 °C, 1 atm pressure. These conditions were chosen because they are easy to attain and reproduce *experimentally*. The barometric pressure within a laboratory will usually be near 1 atm, and 0 °C can be attained with a simple ice bath.

85. 0.981 g CO_2; 0.499 L

86. 2.50 L O_2

87. 24.5 L O_2

88. 0.940 L

89. 9.31 g NH_4Cl; NH_3 is the limiting reactant

90. 0.941 L; 0.870 L

91. 4.92 L $H_2O(g)$

92. 5.03 L (dry volume)

93. 357 L

94. 52.7 L

95. 21.9 mL

96. 28.1 L He; 23.6 L Ar

97. 15.6 L at STP; P_{oxygen} = 0.225 atm; $P_{nitrogen}$ = 0.256 atm; $P_{carbon\ dioxide}$ = 0.163 atm; P_{neon} = 0.356 atm

98. 40.5 L; P_{He} = 0.864 atm; P_{Ne} = 0.136 atm

99. 2.34 L Cl_2

100. Welders commonly use an apparatus that contains a tank of acetylene (C_2H_2) gas and a tank of oxygen gas. When burned in pure oxygen, acetylene generates a large amount of heat.

$$2C_2H_2(g) + 5O_2(g) \rightarrow 2H_2O(g) + 4CO_2(g)$$

What volume of carbon dioxide gas at STP is produced if 1.00 g of acetylene is combusted completely?

101. During the making of steel, iron(II) oxide is reduced to metallic iron by treatment with carbon monoxide gas.

$$FeO(s) + CO(g) \rightarrow Fe(s) + CO_2(g)$$

Suppose 1.45 kg of Fe reacts. What volume of $CO(g)$ is required, and what volume of $CO_2(g)$ is produced, each measured at STP?

102. Consider the following reaction:

$$Zn(s) + 2HCl(aq) \rightarrow ZnCl_2(aq) + H_2(g)$$

What mass of zinc metal should be taken so as to produce 125 mL of H_2 measured at STP when reacted with excess hydrochloric acid?

Additional Problems

103. When doing any calculation involving gas samples, we must express the temperature in terms of the ______ temperature scale.

104. Two moles of ideal gas occupy a volume that is ______ the volume of 1 mole of ideal gas under the same temperature and pressure conditions.

105. Summarize the postulates of the kinetic molecular theory for gases. How does the kinetic molecular theory account for the observed properties of temperature and pressure?

106. Give a formula or equation that represents each of the following gas laws.

a. Boyle's law
b. Charles's law
c. Avogadro's law
d. the ideal gas law
e. the combined gas law

107. For a mixture of gases in the same container, the total pressure exerted by the mixture of gases is the ______ of the pressures that those gases would exert if they were alone in the container under the same conditions.

108. A helium tank contains 25.2 L of helium at 8.40 atm pressure. Determine how many 1.50-L balloons at 755 mm Hg can be inflated with the gas in the tank, assuming that the tank will also have to contain He at 755 mm Hg after the balloons are filled (that is, it is not possible to empty the tank completely). The temperature is 25 °C in all cases.

109. As weather balloons rise from the earth's surface, the pressure of the atmosphere becomes less, tending to cause the volume of the balloons to expand. However, the temperature is much lower in the upper atmosphere than at sea level. Would this temperature effect tend to make such a balloon expand or contract? Weather balloons do, in fact, expand as they rise. What does this tell you?

110. When ammonium carbonate is heated, three gases are produced by its decomposition.

$$(NH_4)_2CO_3(s) \rightarrow 2NH_3(g) + CO_2(g) + H_2O(g)$$

What total volume of gas is produced, measured at 453 °C and 1.04 atm, if 52.0 g of ammonium carbonate is heated?

111. Carbon dioxide gas, in the dry state, may be produced by heating calcium carbonate.

$$CaCO_3(s) \rightarrow CaO(s) + CO_2(g)$$

What volume of CO_2, collected dry at 55 °C and a pressure of 774 torr, is produced by complete thermal decomposition of 10.0 g of $CaCO_3$?

112. Carbon dioxide gas, saturated with water vapor, can be produced by the addition of aqueous acid to calcium carbonate.

$$CaCO_3(s) + 2H^+(aq) \rightarrow Ca^{2+}(aq) + H_2O(l) + CO_2(g)$$

How many moles of $CO_2(g)$, collected at 60. °C and 774 torr total pressure, are produced by the complete reaction of 10.0 g of $CaCO_3$ with acid? What volume does this wet CO_2 occupy? What volume would the CO_2 occupy at 774 torr if a desiccant (a chemical drying agent) were added to remove the water? (The vapor pressure of water at 60. °C is 149.4 mm Hg.)

113. Sulfur trioxide, SO_3, is produced in enormous quantities each year for use in the synthesis of sulfuric acid.

$$S(s) + O_2(g) \rightarrow SO_2(g)$$
$$2SO_2(g) + O_2(g) \rightarrow 2SO_3(g)$$

What volume of $O_2(g)$ at 350. °C and a pressure of 5.25 atm is needed to completely convert 5.00 g of sulfur to sulfur trioxide?

114. Calculate the volume of $O_2(g)$ produced at 25 °C and 630. torr when 50.0 g of $KClO_3(s)$ is heated in the presence of a small amount of MnO_2 catalyst.

115. If 10.0 g of liquid helium at 1.7 K is completely vaporized, what volume does the helium occupy at STP?

116. Perform the indicated pressure conversions.

a. 752 mm Hg into pascals
b. 458 kPa into atmospheres
c. 1.43 atm into mm Hg
d. 842 torr into mm Hg

117. Convert the following pressures into mm Hg.

a. 0.903 atm
b. 2.1240×10^6 Pa
c. 445 kPa
d. 342 torr

All even-numbered Questions and Problems have answers in the back of this book and solutions in the Solutions Guide.

100. 1.72 L

101. 4.52×10^4 L CO is required; 4.52×10^4 L CO_2 is produced

102. 0.365 g

103. Kelvin (absolute)

104. twice

105. Gases consist of tiny particles, which are so small that the fraction of the bulk volume of the gas occupied by the particles is negligible. The particles of a gas are in constant random motion and collide with the walls of the container (giving rise to the pressure of the gas). The particles of a gas do not attract or repel each other. The average kinetic energy of the particles in the gas is reflected in the temperature of the gas.

106. (a) $PV = k$; $P_1V_1 = P_2V_2$; (b) $V = bT$; $V_1/T_1 = V_2/T_2$; (c) $V = an$; $V_1/n_1 = V_2/n_2$; (d) $PV = nRT$; (e) $P_1V_1/T_1 = P_2V_2/T_2$

107. sum

108. 125 balloons

109. Although a decrease in temperature would tend to decrease the volume of a gas sample, the change in pressure for a weather balloon is more dramatic and has a larger influence on the volume of the balloon.

110. 124 L

111. 2.64 L CO_2

112. 0.0999 mol CO_2; 3.32 L wet; 2.68 L dry

113. 2.28 L O_2

114. 18.1 L O_2

115. 56.0 L He

116. (a) 1.00×10^5 Pa; (b) 4.52 atm; (c) 1087 (1.09×10^3) mm Hg; (d) 842 mm Hg

117. (a) 686 mm Hg; (b) 1.5931×10^4 mm Hg; (c) 3.34×10^3 mm Hg; (d) 342 mm Hg

118. (a) 8.60×10^4 Pa;
(b) 2.21×10^5 Pa;
(c) 8.88×10^4 Pa;
(d) 4.3×10^3 Pa

119. (a) 426 L;
(b) 0.127 atm;
(c) 2.87×10^4 L

120. (a) 128 mL;
(b) 1.3×10^{-2} L; (c) 9.8 L

121. yes (calculated volume 3 L)

122. 2.55×10^3 mm Hg

123. 922 mL

124. (a) 57.3 mL;
(b) 448 K = 175 °C;
(c) zero (absolute zero; a real gas would condense to a solid or liquid)

125. (a) 541 K (268 °C);
(b) 0.30 mL;
(c) 7.21×10^3 K (6940 °C)

126. 123 mL

127. 30.3 L

128. 2.59 g

129. (a) 84.9 K;
(b) 2.25 atm;
(c) 15.8 L (1.58×10^4 mL)

130. (a) 61.8 K;
(b) 0.993 atm;
(c) 1.66×10^4 L

131. 1.24 atm

132. 487 mol gas needed; 7.79 kg CH_4; 13.6 kg N_2; 21.4 kg CO_2

133. 273 K (0 °C)

134. 0.42 atm

135. 2.8 L

136. 2.51×10^3 K

137. 13 atm

138. 32.4 L

139. 0.967 atm

140. 3.43 L N_2; 10.3 L H_2

141. 4.221 L of each product

118. Convert the following pressures into pascals.
   a. 645 mm Hg
   b. 221 kPa
   c. 0.876 atm
   d. 32 torr

119. For each of the following sets of pressure/volume data, calculate the missing quantity. Assume that the temperature and the amount of gas remain constant.
   a. $V = 123$ L at 4.56 atm; $V = ?$ at 1002 mm Hg
   b. $V = 634$ mL at 25.2 mm Hg; $V = 166$ mL at ? atm
   c. $V = 443$ L at 511 torr; $V = ?$ at 1.05 kPa

120. For each of the following sets of pressure/volume data, calculate the missing quantity. Assume that the temperature and the amount of gas remain constant.
   a. $V = 255$ mL at 1.00 mm Hg; $V = ?$ at 2.00 torr
   b. $V = 1.3$ L at 1.0 kPa; $V = ?$ at 1.0 atm
   c. $V = 1.3$ L at 1.0 kPa; $V = ?$ at 1.0 mm Hg

121. A particular balloon is designed by its manufacturer to be inflated to a volume of no more than 2.5 L. If the balloon is filled with 2.0 L of helium at sea level, is released, and rises to an altitude at which the atmospheric pressure is only 500. mm Hg, will the balloon burst?

122. What pressure is needed to compress 1.52 L of air at 755 mm Hg to a volume of 450 mL (at constant temperature)?

123. An expandable vessel contains 729 mL of gas at 22 °C. What volume will the gas sample in the vessel have if it is placed in a boiling water bath (100. °C)?

124. For each of the following sets of volume/temperature data, calculate the missing quantity. Assume that the pressure and the amount of gas remain constant.
   a. $V = 100.$ mL at 74 °C; $V = ?$ at −74 °C
   b. $V = 500.$ mL at 100 °C; $V = 600.$ mL at ? °C
   c. $V = 10{,}000$ L at 25 °C; $V = ?$ at 0 K

125. For each of the following sets of volume/temperature data, calculate the missing quantity. Assume that the pressure and the amount of gas remain constant.
   a. $V = 22.4$ L at 0 °C; $V = 44.4$ L at ? K
   b. $V = 1.0 \times 10^{-3}$ mL at −272 °C; $V = ?$ at 25 °C
   c. $V = 32.3$ L at −40 °C; $V = 1000.$ L at ? °C

126. A 75.2-mL sample of helium at 12 °C is heated to 192 °C. What is the new volume of the helium (assuming constant pressure)?

127. If 5.12 g of oxygen gas occupies a volume of 6.21 L at a certain temperature and pressure, what volume will 25.0 g of oxygen gas occupy under the same conditions?

128. If 23.2 g of a given gas occupies a volume of 93.2 L at a particular temperature and pressure, what mass of the gas occupies a volume of 10.4 L under the same conditions?

129. Given each of the following sets of values for three of the gas variables, calculate the unknown quantity.
   a. $P = 21.2$ atm; $V = 142$ mL; $n = 0.432$ mol; $T = ?$ K
   b. $P = ?$ atm; $V = 1.23$ mL; $n = 0.000115$ mol; $T =$ 293 K
   c. $P = 755$ mm Hg; $V = ?$ mL; $n = 0.473$ mol; $T =$ 131 °C

130. Given each of the following sets of values for three of the gas variables, calculate the unknown quantity.
   a. $P = 1.034$ atm; $V = 21.2$ mL; $n = 0.00432$ mol; $T = ?$ K
   b. $P = ?$ atm; $V = 1.73$ mL; $n = 0.000115$ mol; $T =$ 182 K
   c. $P = 1.23$ mm Hg; $V = ?$ L; $n = 0.773$ mol; $T =$ 152 °C

131. What is the pressure inside a 10.0-L flask containing 14.2 g of N_2 at 26 °C?

132. Suppose three 100.-L tanks are to be filled separately with the gases CH_4, N_2, and CO_2, respectively. What mass of each gas is needed to produce a pressure of 120. atm in its tank at 27 °C?

133. At what temperature does 4.00 g of helium gas have a pressure of 1.00 atm in a 22.4-L vessel?

134. What is the pressure in a 100.-mL flask containing 55 mg of oxygen gas at 26 °C?

135. A weather balloon is filled with 1.0 L of helium at 23 °C and 1.0 atm. What volume does the balloon have when it has risen to a point in the atmosphere where the pressure is 220 torr and the temperature is −31 °C?

136. At what temperature does 100. mL of N_2 at 300. K and 1.13 atm occupy a volume of 500. mL at a pressure of 1.89 atm?

137. If 1.0 mol $N_2(g)$ is injected into a 5.0-L tank already containing 50. g of O_2 at 25 °C, what will be the total pressure in the tank?

138. A gaseous mixture contains 12.1 g of N_2 and 4.05 g of He. What is the volume of this mixture at STP?

139. A flask of hydrogen gas is collected at 1.023 atm and 35 °C by displacement of water from the flask. The vapor pressure of water at 35 °C is 42.2 mm Hg. What is the partial pressure of hydrogen gas in the flask?

140. Consider the following chemical equation:

$$N_2(g) + 3H_2(g) \rightarrow 2NH_3(g)$$

What volumes of nitrogen gas and hydrogen gas, each measured at 11 °C and 0.998 atm, are needed to produce 5.00 g of ammonia?

141. Consider the following *unbalanced* chemical equation:

$$C_6H_{12}O_6(s) + O_2(g) \rightarrow CO_2(g) + H_2O(g)$$

What volume of oxygen gas, measured at 28 °C and 0.976 atm, is needed to react with 5.00 g of $C_6H_{12}O_6$? What volume of each product is produced under the same conditions?

All even-numbered Questions and Problems have answers in the back of this book and solutions in the Solutions Guide.

142. Consider the following *unbalanced* chemical equation:

$$Cu_2S(s) + O_2(g) \rightarrow Cu_2O(s) + SO_2(g)$$

What volume of oxygen gas, measured at 27.5 °C and 0.998 atm, is required to react with 25 g of copper(I) sulfide? What volume of sulfur dioxide gas is produced under the same conditions?

143. When sodium bicarbonate, $NaHCO_3(s)$, is heated, sodium carbonate is produced, with the evolution of water vapor and carbon dioxide gas.

$$2NaHCO_3(s) \rightarrow Na_2CO_3(s) + H_2O(g) + CO_2(g)$$

What total volume of gas, measured at 29 °C and 769 torr, is produced when 1.00 g of $NaHCO_3(s)$ is completely converted to $Na_2CO_3(s)$?

144. What volume does 35 moles of N_2 occupy at STP?

145. A sample of oxygen gas has a volume of 125 L at 25 °C and a pressure of 0.987 atm. Calculate the volume of this oxygen sample at STP.

146. A mixture contains 5.0 g of He, 1.0 g of Ar, and 3.5 g of Ne. Calculate the volume of this mixture at STP. Calculate the partial pressure of each gas in the mixture at STP.

147. What volume of CO_2 measured at STP is produced when 27.5 g of $CaCO_3$ is decomposed?

$$CaCO_3(s) \rightarrow CaO(s) + CO_2(g)$$

148. Concentrated hydrogen peroxide solutions are explosively decomposed by traces of transition metal ions (such as Mn or Fe):

$$2H_2O_2(aq) \rightarrow 2H_2O(l) + O_2(g)$$

What volume of pure $O_2(g)$, collected at 27 °C and 764 torr, would be generated by decomposition of 125 g of a 50.0% by mass hydrogen peroxide solution?

All even-numbered Questions and Problems have answers in the back of this book and solutions in the Solutions Guide.

142. 5.8 L O_2; 3.9 L SO_2

143. 0.291 L

144. 7.8×10^2 L

145. 113 L

146. 32 L; $P_{He} = 0.86$ atm; $P_{Ar} = 0.017$ atm; $P_{Ne} = 0.12$ atm

147. 6.16 L

148. 22.4 L O_2

Chapter 14

Objectives

In this chapter, our objectives are for the students to:

SECTION 14.1

- Learn some of the important features of water.

SECTION 14.2

- Learn about interactions among water molecules.
- Understand and use heat of fusion and heat of vaporization.

SECTION 14.3

- Learn about dipole–dipole attraction, hydrogen bonding, and London dispersion forces.
- Understand the effect of these forces on the properties of liquids.

SECTION 14.4

- Understand the relationship among vaporization, condensation, and vapor pressure.

SECTION 14.5

- Learn about the various types of crystalline solids.

SECTION 14.6

- Understand the interparticle forces in crystalline solids.
- Learn about how the bonding in metals determines metallic properties.

14 Liquids and Solids

Ice, the solid form of water, provides recreation for this ice climber. *(Vandystadt/Tips Images)*

ChemWork Refined over ten years of use by thousands of students, **ChemWork** builds and enhances students' problems-solving skills. Online assignments function as a "personal instructor" to help students learn how to solve challenging problems and learn how to think like chemists. Annotations for **ChemWork** assignments are included at the beginning of the end-of-chapter review.

PowerLecture This 2-DVD package includes the Chemistry Multimedia Library, which contains animations, simulations, and movies for all chemistry subjects, organized by topic for lecture presentations. Annotations for **PowerLecture** are referenced in the margins throughout the Annotated Instructor's Edition.

OWL Sign in to OWL at **www.cengage.com/owl** to view tutorials and simulations, develop problem-solving skills, and complete online homework assigned by your professor.

go Chemistry Download mini-lecture videos for key concept review and exam prep from OWL or purchase them from **www.ichapters.com**

You have only to think about water to appreciate how different the three states of matter are. Flying, swimming, and ice skating are all done in contact with water in its various states. We swim in liquid water and skate on water in its solid form (ice). Airplanes fly in an atmosphere containing water in the gaseous state (water vapor). To allow these various activities, the arrangements of the water molecules must be significantly different in their gas, liquid, and solid forms.

In Chapter 13 we saw that the particles of a gas are far apart, are in rapid random motion, and have little effect on each other. Solids are obviously very different from gases. Gases have low densities, have high compressibilities, and completely fill a container. Solids have much greater densities than gases, are compressible only to a very slight extent, and are rigid; a solid maintains its shape regardless of its container. These properties indicate that the components of a solid are close together and exert large attractive forces on each other.

The properties of liquids lie somewhere between those of solids and of gases—but not midway between, as can be seen from some of the properties of the three states of water. For example, it takes about seven times more energy to change liquid water to steam (a gas) at 100 °C than to melt ice to form liquid water at 0 °C.

$$H_2O(s) \rightarrow H_2O(l) \qquad \text{energy required} \cong 6 \text{ kJ/mol}$$
$$H_2O(l) \rightarrow H_2O(g) \qquad \text{energy required} \cong 41 \text{ kJ/mol}$$

Robert Y. Ono/Corbis

Wind surfers use liquid water for recreation.

These values indicate that going from the liquid to the gaseous state involves a much greater change than going from the solid to the liquid. Therefore, we can conclude that the solid and liquid states are more similar than the liquid and gaseous states. This is also demonstrated by the densities of the three states of water (Table 14.1). Note that water in its gaseous state is about 2000 times less dense than in the solid and liquid states and that the latter two states have very similar densities.

We find in general that the liquid and solid states show many similarities and are strikingly different from the gaseous state (see Figure 14.1). The best way to picture the solid state is in terms of closely packed, highly ordered particles in contrast to the widely spaced, randomly arranged particles of a gas. The liquid state lies in between, but its properties indicate that it much more closely resembles the solid than the gaseous state. It is useful to picture a liquid in terms of particles that are generally quite close together, but with a more disordered arrangement than for the solid state and with some empty spaces. For most substances, the solid state has a higher density than the liquid, as Figure 14.1 suggests. However, water is an exception to this rule.

Liquids and Solids 447

PowerLecture Video: Structure of a Liquid

PowerLecture Animation: Structure of a Solid

Test Bank: 1–3, 6

Table 14.1 Densities of the Three States of Water

State	Density (g/cm³)
solid (0 °C, 1 atm)	0.9168
liquid (25 °C, 1 atm)	0.9971
gas (100 °C, 1 atm)	5.88×10^{-4}

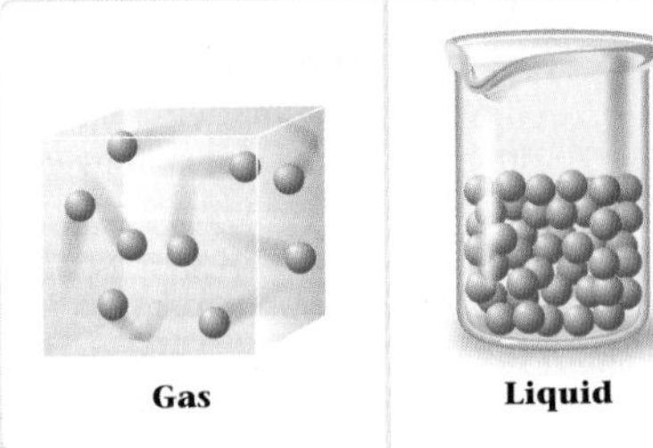

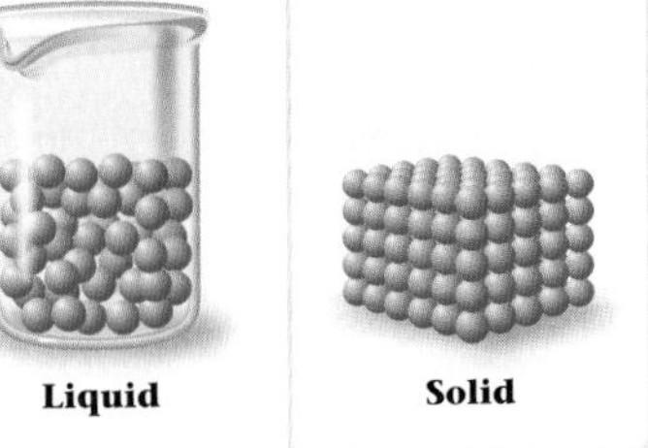

Figure 14.1
Representations of the gas, liquid, and solid states.

Ice has an unusual amount of empty space and so is less dense than liquid water, as indicated in Table 14.1.

In this chapter we will explore the important properties of liquids and solids. We will illustrate many of these properties by considering one of the earth's most important substances: water.

Section 14.1

TEACHING TIPS

- This section provides an opportunity to review the specific heat capacity for water.
- As water is such a common molecule, you have a choice of many interesting phenomena to discuss in class. This section offers an opportunity to discuss the density of ice (and why it floats), why pipes burst when they freeze (and why human tissue does not behave the same way after freezing), why potholes form in road surfaces in the winter, and how water can crack large rocks and cause them to fall. If students are familiar with pressure cookers, now is an excellent time to explain why foods cook faster in them.

14.1 Water and Its Phase Changes

OBJECTIVE: To learn some of the important features of water.

In the world around us we see many solids (soil, rocks, trees, concrete, and so on), and we are immersed in the gases of the atmosphere. But the liquid we most commonly see is water; it is virtually everywhere, covering about 70% of the earth's surface. Approximately 97% of the earth's water is found in the oceans, which are actually mixtures of water and huge quantities of dissolved salts.

Water is one of the most important substances on earth. It is crucial for sustaining the reactions within our bodies that keep us alive, but it also affects our lives in many indirect ways. The oceans help moderate the earth's temperature. Water cools automobile engines and nuclear power plants. Water provides a means of transportation on the earth's surface and acts as a medium for the growth of the myriad creatures we use as food, and much more.

The water we drink often has a taste because of the substances dissolved in it. It is not pure water.

Pure water is a colorless, tasteless substance that at 1 atm pressure freezes to form a solid at 0 °C and vaporizes completely to form a gas at 100 °C. This means that (at 1 atm pressure) the liquid range of water occurs between the temperatures 0 °C and 100 °C.

What happens when we heat liquid water? First the temperature of the water rises. Just as with gas molecules, the motions of the water molecules increase as it is heated. Eventually the temperature of the water reaches 100 °C; now bubbles develop in the interior of the liquid, float to the surface, and burst—the boiling point has been reached. An interesting thing happens at the boiling point: even though heating continues, the temperature stays at 100 °C until all the water has changed to vapor. Only when all of the water has changed to the gaseous state does the temperature begin to rise

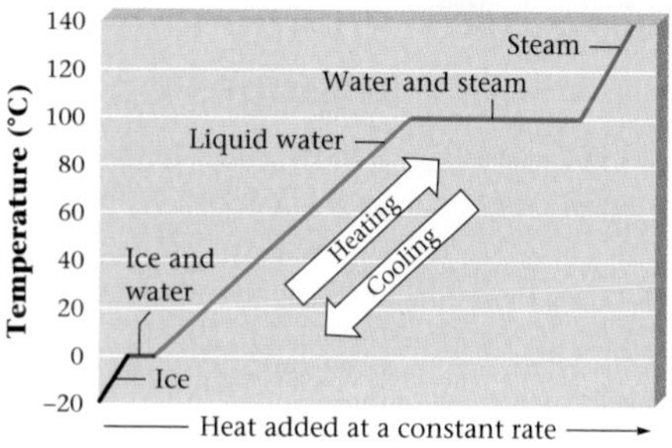

Figure 14.2 The heating/cooling curve for water heated or cooled at a constant rate. The plateau at the boiling point is longer than the plateau at the melting point, because it takes almost seven times as much energy (and thus seven times the heating time) to vaporize liquid water as to melt ice. Note that to make the diagram clear, the blue line is not drawn to scale. It actually takes more energy to melt ice and boil water than to heat water from 0 °C to 100 °C.

Lecture Demonstration: 10.22

again. (We are now heating the vapor.) At 1 atm pressure, liquid water always changes to gaseous water at 100 °C, the **normal boiling point** for water.

PowerLecture Video: Changes of State

The experiment just described is represented in Figure 14.2, which is called the **heating/cooling curve** for water. Going from left to right on this graph means energy is being added (heating). Going from right to left on the graph means that energy is being removed (cooling).

When liquid water is cooled, the temperature decreases until it reaches 0 °C, where the liquid begins to freeze (see Figure 14.2). The temperature remains at 0 °C until all the liquid water has changed to ice and then begins to drop again as cooling continues. At 1 atm pressure, water freezes (or, in the opposite process, ice melts) at 0 °C. This is called the **normal freezing point** of water. Liquid and solid water can coexist indefinitely if the temperature is held at 0 °C. However, at temperatures below 0 °C liquid water freezes, while at temperatures above 0 °C ice melts.

Interestingly, water expands when it freezes. That is, one gram of ice at 0 °C has a greater volume than one gram of liquid water at 0 °C. This has very important practical implications. For instance, water in a confined space can break its container when it freezes and expands. This accounts for the bursting of water pipes and engine blocks that are left unprotected in freezing weather.

The expansion of water when it freezes also explains why ice cubes float. Recall that density is defined as mass/volume. When one gram of liquid water freezes, its volume becomes greater (it expands). Therefore, the *density* of one gram of ice is less than the density of one gram of water, because in the case of ice we divide by a slightly larger volume. For example, at 0 °C the density of liquid water is

Test Bank: 5, 7–16

$$\frac{1.00 \text{ g}}{1.00 \text{ mL}} = 1.00 \text{ g/mL}$$

and the density of ice is

PowerLecture Animation: Structure of a Diamond

$$\frac{1.00 \text{ g}}{1.09 \text{ mL}} = 0.917 \text{ g/mL}$$

The lower density of ice also means that ice floats on the surface of lakes as they freeze, providing a layer of insulation that helps to prevent lakes and rivers from freezing solid in the winter. This means that aquatic life continues to have liquid water available through the winter.

Section 14.2

TEACHING TIPS

- Intermolecular forces are introduced now to help explain differences in energy requirements for melting and for vaporization. The detailed discussion of intermolecular forces occurs in Section 14.3.
- Students will need to be reminded that energy is required to change phase even though the temperature does not change during that time. The energy applied to the system is used to overcome the intermolecular forces. This demonstrates clearly that heat is not the same as temperature.
- Remind students that a phase change takes place when no temperature change occurs and that no change of phase occurs when the temperature is changing.

14.2 Energy Requirements for the Changes of State

OBJECTIVES: To learn about interactions among water molecules. • To understand and use heat of fusion and heat of vaporization.

It is important to recognize that changes of state from solid to liquid and from liquid to gas are *physical* changes. No *chemical* bonds are broken in these processes. Ice, water, and steam all contain H_2O molecules. When water is boiled to form steam, water molecules are separated from each other (see Figure 14.3) but the individual molecules remain intact.

The bonding forces that hold the atoms of a molecule together are called **intramolecular** (within the molecule) **forces.** The forces that occur among molecules that cause them to aggregate to form a solid or a liquid are called **intermolecular** (between the molecules) **forces.** These two types of forces are illustrated in Figure 14.4.

Remember that temperature is a measure of the random motions (average kinetic energy) of the particles in a substance.

It takes energy to melt ice and to vaporize water, because intermolecular forces between water molecules must be overcome. In ice the molecules are virtually locked in place, although they can vibrate about their positions. When energy is added, the vibrational motions increase, and the molecules eventually achieve the greater movement and disorder characteristic of liquid water. The ice has melted. As still more energy is added, the gaseous state is eventually reached, in which the individual molecules are far apart and interact relatively little. However, the gas still consists of water molecules. It would take *much* more energy to overcome the covalent bonds and decompose the water molecules into their component atoms.

The energy required to melt 1 mole of a substance is called the **molar heat of fusion.** For ice, the molar heat of fusion is 6.02 kJ/mol. The energy required to change 1 mole of liquid to its vapor is called the **molar heat of vaporization.** For water, the molar heat of vaporization is 40.6 kJ/mol at 100 °C. Notice in Figure 14.2 that the plateau that corresponds to the vaporization of water is much longer than that for the melting of ice. This occurs because it takes much more energy (almost seven times as much) to vaporize a mole of water than to melt a mole of ice. This is consistent with our models of solids, liquids, and gases (see Figure 14.1). In liquids, the particles (molecules) are relatively close together, so most of the intermolecular forces are still present. However, when the molecules go from the liquid to the gaseous state, they must be moved far apart. To separate the molecules enough to form a gas, virtually all of the intermolecular forces must be overcome, and this requires large quantities of energy.

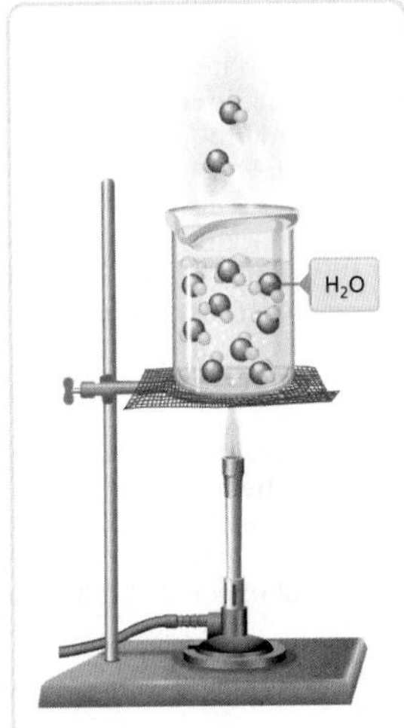

Figure 14.3
Both liquid water and gaseous water contain H_2O molecules. In liquid water the H_2O molecules are close together, whereas in the gaseous state the molecules are widely separated. The bubbles contain gaseous water.

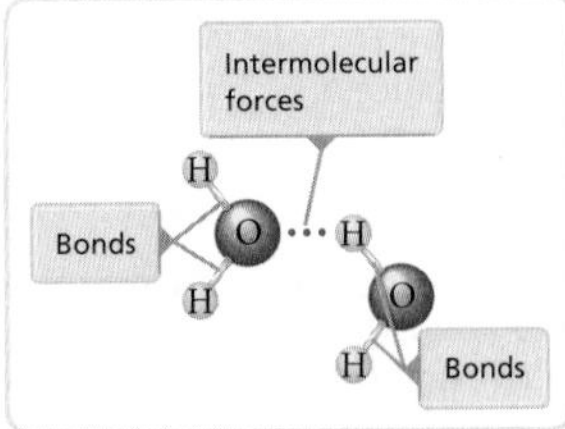

Figure 14.4
Intramolecular (bonding) forces exist between the atoms in a molecule and hold the molecule together. Intermolecular forces exist between molecules. These are the forces that cause water to condense to a liquid or form a solid at low enough temperatures. Intermolecular forces are typically much weaker than intramolecular forces.

CHEMISTRY *IN* FOCUS

Whales Need Changes of State

Sperm whales are prodigious divers. They commonly dive a mile or more into the ocean, hovering at that depth in search of schools of squid or fish. To remain motionless at a given depth, the whale must have the same density as the surrounding water. Because the density of seawater increases with depth, the sperm whale has a system that automatically increases its density as it dives. This system involves the spermaceti organ found in the whale's head. Spermaceti is a waxy substance with the formula

$$CH_3-(CH_2)_{15}-O-\underset{\displaystyle O}{\underset{\|}{C}}-(CH_2)_{14}-CH_3$$

which is a liquid above 30 °C. At the ocean surface the spermaceti in the whale's head is a liquid, warmed by the flow of blood through the spermaceti organ. When the whale dives, this blood flow decreases and the colder water causes the spermaceti to begin freezing. Because solid spermaceti is more dense than the liquid state, the sperm whale's density increases as it dives, matching the increase in the water's density.* When the whale wants to resurface, blood flow through the spermaceti organ increases, remelting the spermaceti and making the whale more buoyant. So the sperm whale's sophisticated density-regulating mechanism is based on a simple change of state.

Flip Nicklin/Minden Pictures

A sperm whale.

*For most substances, the solid state is more dense than the liquid state. Water is an important exception.

EXAMPLE 14.1 Calculating Energy Changes: Solid to Liquid

Calculate the energy required to melt 8.5 g of ice at 0 °C. The molar heat of fusion for ice is 6.02 kJ/mol.

SOLUTION

Where Are We Going?

We want to determine the energy (in kJ) required to melt 8.5 g of ice at 0 °C.

What Do We Know?

- We have 8.5 g of ice (H_2O) at 0 °C.
- The molar heat of fusion of ice is 6.02 kJ/mol.

What Information Do We Need?

- We need to know the number of moles of ice in 8.5 g.

How Do We Get There?

The molar heat of fusion is the energy required to melt *1 mole* of ice. In this problem we have 8.5 g of solid water. We must find out how many moles of

451

Additional Examples

Example 14.1

1. Calculate the energy released when 15.5 g of ice freezes at 0 °C. The molar heat of fusion of ice is 6.02 kJ/mol.

   5.18 kJ

2. Calculate the energy required to melt 12.5 g of ice at 0 °C and change it to water at 25 °C. The specific heat capacity of liquid water is 4.18 J/g °C and the molar heat of fusion of ice is 6.02 kJ/mol.

   5.48 kJ

ice this mass represents. Because the molar mass of water is 16 + 2(1) = 18, we know that 1 mole of water has a mass of 18 g, so we can convert 8.5 g of H_2O to moles of H_2O.

$$8.5 \text{ g } \cancel{H_2O} \times \frac{1 \text{ mol } H_2O}{18 \text{ g } \cancel{H_2O}} = 0.47 \text{ mol } H_2O$$

Because 6.02 kJ of energy is required to melt a mole of solid water, our sample will take about half this amount (we have approximately half a mole of ice). To calculate the exact amount of energy required, we will use the equivalence statement

6.02 kJ required for 1 mol H_2O

which leads to the conversion factor we need:

$$0.47 \cancel{\text{mol } H_2O} \times \frac{6.02 \text{ kJ}}{\cancel{\text{mol } H_2O}} = 2.8 \text{ kJ}$$

This can be represented symbolically as

0.47 mol ice → ($\frac{6.02 \text{ kJ}}{\text{mol}}$) → 2.8 kJ required

REALITY CHECK Because we have just under half of 1 mole of ice, our answer should be about half the molar heat of fusion of ice. The answer of 2.8 kJ is just under half of 6.02 kJ, so this answer makes sense. ■

Additional Examples

Example 14.2

1. Calculate the energy required to vaporize 35.0 g of water at 100 °C. The molar heat of vaporization of water is 40.6 kJ/mol.

   78.9 kJ

2. Calculate the energy required to heat 22.5 g of water at 0 °C and change it to steam at 100 °C. The specific heat capacity of liquid water is 4.18 J/g °C and the molar heat of vaporization of water is 40.6 kJ/mol.

   60.1 kJ

TEACHING TIP

When working multistep problems, associate each step with its location on the heating curve.

EXAMPLE 14.2 Calculating Energy Changes: Liquid to Gas

Specific heat capacity was discussed in Section 10.5.

Calculate the energy (in kJ) required to heat 25 g of liquid water from 25 °C to 100. °C and change it to steam at 100. °C. The specific heat capacity of liquid water is 4.18 J/g °C, and the molar heat of vaporization of water is 40.6 kJ/mol.

SOLUTION

Where Are We Going?

We want to determine the energy (in kJ) required to heat and vaporize a given quantity of water.

What Do We Know?

- We have 25 g of H_2O at 25 °C. The water will be heated to 100. °C and then vaporized at 100. °C
- The specific heat capacity of liquid water is 4.18 J/g °C.
- The molar vaporization of water is 40.6 kJ/mol.
- $Q = s \times m \times \Delta T$.

What Information Do We Need?

- We need to know the number of moles of water in 25 g.

How Do We Get There?

This problem can be split into two parts: (1) heating the water to its boiling point and (2) converting the liquid water to vapor at the boiling point.

Step 1: Heating to Boiling We must first supply energy to heat the liquid water from 25 °C to 100. °C. Because 4.18 J is required to heat *one* gram of water by *one* Celsius degree, we must multiply by both the mass of water (25 g) and the temperature change (100. °C − 25 °C = 75 °C),

Energy required (Q)	=	Specific heat capacity (s)	×	Mass of water (m)	×	Temperature change (ΔT)

which we can represent by the equation

$$Q = s \times m \times \Delta T$$

Thus

$$Q = 4.18\frac{\text{J}}{\text{g}\,^\circ\text{C}} \times 25\ \text{g} \times 75\ ^\circ\text{C} = 7.8 \times 10^3\ \text{J}$$

Energy required to heat 25 g of water from 25 °C to 100. °C; Specific heat capacity; Mass of water; Temperature change

$$= 7.8 \times 10^3\ \text{J} \times \frac{1\ \text{kJ}}{1000\ \text{J}} = 7.8\ \text{kJ}$$

Step 2: Vaporization Now we must use the molar heat of vaporization to calculate the energy required to vaporize the 25 g of water at 100. °C. The heat of vaporization is given *per mole* rather than per gram, so we must first convert the 25 g of water to moles.

$$25\ \text{g H}_2\text{O} \times \frac{1\ \text{mol H}_2\text{O}}{18\ \text{g H}_2\text{O}} = 1.4\ \text{mol H}_2\text{O}$$

We can now calculate the energy required to vaporize the water.

$$\frac{40.6\ \text{kJ}}{\text{mol H}_2\text{O}} \times 1.4\ \text{mol H}_2\text{O} = 57\ \text{kJ}$$

Molar heat of vaporization; Moles of water

The total energy is the sum of the two steps.

$$7.8\ \text{kJ} + 57\ \text{kJ} = 65\ \text{kJ}$$

Heat from 25 °C to 100. °C; Change to vapor

Self-Check **EXERCISE 14.1** Calculate the total energy required to melt 15 g of ice at 0 °C, heat the water to 100. °C, and vaporize it to steam at 100. °C.

HINT: Break the process into three steps and then take the sum.

See Problems 14.15 through 14.18. ■

Self Check

Answer to Self-Check Exercise 14.1

45 kJ (5.0 + 6.3 + 34)

Lecture Demonstration: 10.1

Test Bank: 17–31

Section 14.3

TEACHING TIPS

- Be sure to help students draw a clear distinction between *intra*molecular forces (covalent and ionic bonds) and *inter*molecular forces.
- This section offers an excellent opportunity to review the main concepts from bonding and prepare students to look at the forces that exist between molecules. It is especially helpful to review the concept of a dipole and consider what it means before moving into intermolecular forces. Now is the time to tie in electronegativity and arrangement of atoms to polarity of molecules.
- Some students think that dipole–dipole interactions and hydrogen bonds are completely unrelated. Stress that all of these interactions result from polarity.
- Students are often confused by the term *hydrogen bond.* They have the misconception that the hydrogen bond is the O—H, N—H, or F—H bond and not the attractive force between the dipoles. We have used dashed lines to represent hydrogen bonds to help students see this idea more clearly. Stress that a hydrogen bond is an attractive force between molecules.
- Students have trouble deciding when molecules should have hydrogen bonds between them. Use examples such as NH_3, CH_3OH, and HF to show that in each case the hydrogen is bonded directly to the N, O, or F. Molecules such as $(CH_3)_3N$ do not form hydrogen bonds even though they contain both N and H, because no hydrogen is bonded to the N to produce the dipole needed for a hydrogen bond.

14.3 Intermolecular Forces

OBJECTIVES: To learn about dipole–dipole attraction, hydrogen bonding, and London dispersion forces. • To understand the effect of these forces on the properties of liquids.

go Chemistry **Module 17: Intermolecular Forces** covers concepts in this section.

We have seen that covalent bonding forces within molecules arise from the sharing of electrons, but how do intermolecular forces arise? Actually several types of intermolecular forces exist. To illustrate one type, we will consider the forces that exist among water molecules.

The polarity of a molecule was discussed in Section 12.3.

As we saw in Chapter 12, water is a polar molecule—it has a dipole moment. When molecules with dipole moments are put together, they orient themselves to take advantage of their charge distributions. Molecules with dipole moments can attract each other by lining up so that the positive and negative ends are close to each other, as shown in Figure 14.5a. This is called a **dipole–dipole attraction.** In the liquid, the dipoles find the best compromise between attraction and repulsion, as shown in Figure 14.5b.

Dipole–dipole forces are typically only about 1% as strong as covalent or ionic bonds, and they become weaker as the distance between the dipoles increases. In the gas phase, where the molecules are usually very far apart, these forces are relatively unimportant.

See Section 12.2 for a discussion of electronegativity.

Particularly strong dipole-dipole forces occur between molecules in which hydrogen is bound to a highly electronegative atom, such as nitrogen, oxygen, or fluorine. Two factors account for the strengths of these interactions: the great polarity of the bond and the close approach of the dipoles, which is made possible by the very small size of the hydrogen atom. Because dipole–dipole attractions of this type are so unusually strong, they are given a special name—**hydrogen bonding.** Figure 14.6 illustrates hydrogen bonding among water molecules.

Hydrogen bonding has a very important effect on various physical properties. For example, the boiling points for the covalent compounds of hydrogen with the elements in Group 6 are given in Figure 14.7. Note that the boiling point of water is much higher than would be expected from the trend shown by the other members of the series. Why? Because the especially large electronegativity value of the oxygen atom compared with that of the other group members causes the O—H bonds to be much more polar

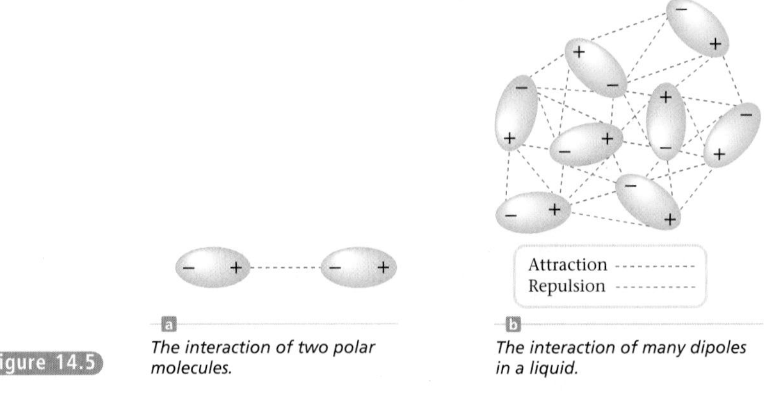

Figure 14.5

a The interaction of two polar molecules.

b The interaction of many dipoles in a liquid.

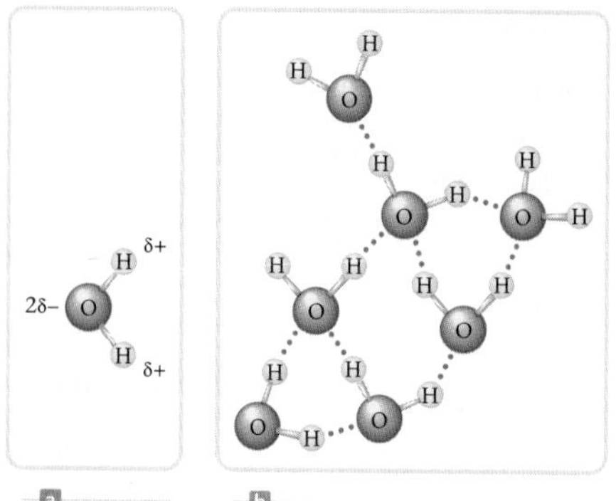

Figure 14.6

a The polar water molecule. b Hydrogen bonding among water molecules. The small size of the hydrogen atoms allows the molecules to get very close and thus to produce strong interactions.

PowerLecture Animations: HCl Molecules Cooling from Gas to Liquid
Intermolecular Forces: Hydrogen Bonding Forces

PowerLecture Animation: Induced Dipoles in Neighboring I_2 Molecules

PowerLecture Animation: Graph of Boiling Points of Compounds with Hydrogen

PowerLecture Animation: Intermolecular Forces: London Dispersion Forces

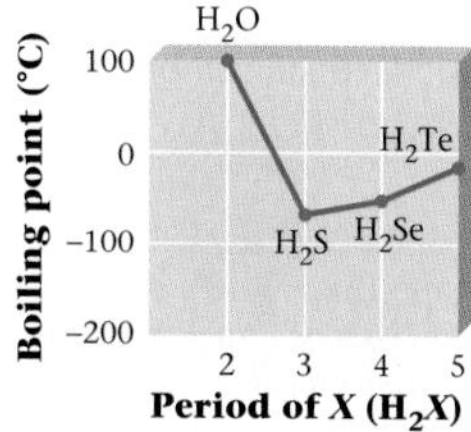

Figure 14.7

The boiling points of the covalent hydrides of elements in Group 6.

than the S—H, Se—H, or Te—H bonds. This leads to very strong hydrogen-bonding forces among the water molecules. An unusually large quantity of energy is required to overcome these interactions and separate the molecules to produce the gaseous state. That is, water molecules tend to remain together in the liquid state even at relatively high temperatures—hence the very high boiling point of water.

However, even molecules without dipole moments must exert forces on each other. We know this because all substances—even the noble gases—exist in the liquid and solid states at very low temperatures. There must be forces to hold the atoms or molecules as close together as they are in these condensed states. The forces that exist among noble gas atoms and nonpolar molecules are called **London dispersion forces.** To understand the origin of these forces, consider a pair of noble gas atoms. Although we usually assume that the electrons of an atom are uniformly distributed about the nucleus (see Figure 14.8a), this is apparently not true at every instant. Atoms

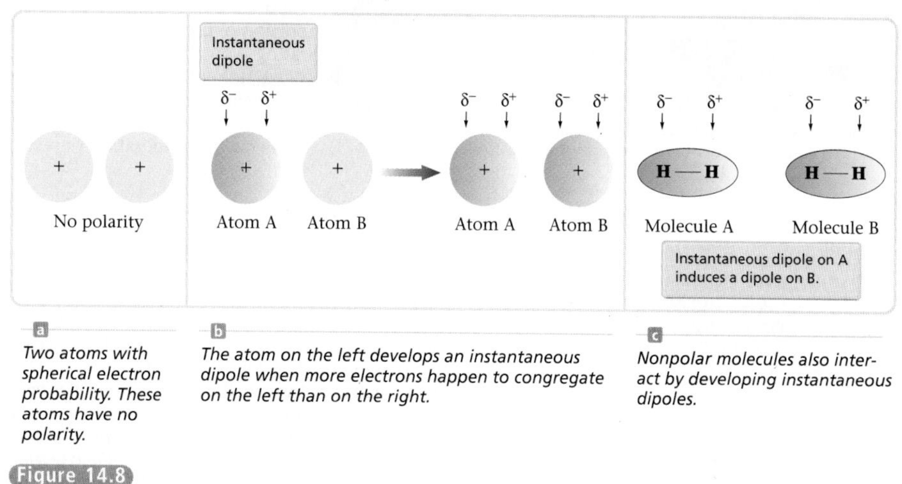

a *Two atoms with spherical electron probability. These atoms have no polarity.*

b *The atom on the left develops an instantaneous dipole when more electrons happen to congregate on the left than on the right.*

c *Nonpolar molecules also interact by developing instantaneous dipoles.*

Figure 14.8

Students find it difficult to visualize what happens within a molecule to produce London dispersion forces. This concept is challenging to represent with a picture. It is easiest to begin talking about these forces by using small, nonpolar molecules.

- London dispersion forces exist not only among noble gas atoms and nonpolar molecules, but also between all molecules. They are generally important only among noble gas atoms and nonpolar molecules because they are relatively weak.

PowerLecture Animation: Vaporization of High-Energy Molecules of a Liquid

Test Bank: 32–34

Table 14.2 The Freezing Points of the Group 8 Elements

Element	Freezing Point (°C)
helium*	−272.0 (25 atm)
neon	−248.6
argon	−189.4
krypton	−157.3
xenon	−111.9

*Helium will not freeze unless the pressure is increased above 1 atm.

can develop a temporary dipolar arrangement of charge as the electrons move around the nucleus (see Figure 14.8b). This *instantaneous dipole* can then *induce* a similar dipole in a neighboring atom, as shown in Figure 14.8b. The interatomic attraction thus formed is both weak and short-lived, but it can be very significant for large atoms and large molecules, as we will see.

The motions of the atoms must be greatly slowed down before the weak London dispersion forces can lock the atoms into place to produce a solid. This explains, for instance, why the noble gas elements have such low freezing points (see Table 14.2).

Nonpolar molecules such as H_2, N_2, and I_2, none of which has a permanent dipole moment, also attract each other by London dispersion forces (see Figure 14.8c). London forces become more significant as the sizes of atoms or molecules increase. Larger size means there are more electrons available to form the dipoles.

Section 14.4

14.4 Evaporation and Vapor Pressure

OBJECTIVE: To understand the relationship among vaporization, condensation, and vapor pressure.

TEACHING TIPS

- The idea that evaporation is an endothermic process is difficult for many students to grasp. Take time to explain that the temperature of the liquid drops because the higher-kinetic-energy molecules are going to the gas phase. Energy flows in if the container is not insulated; the temperature of the liquid will then remain constant.
- The familiar scents of fingernail polish remover and rubbing alcohol tell us that these liquids evaporate relatively easily.

We all know that a liquid can evaporate from an open container. This is clear evidence that the molecules of a liquid can escape the liquid's surface and form a gas. This process, which is called **vaporization** or **evaporation,** requires energy to overcome the relatively strong intermolecular forces in the liquid.

The fact that vaporization requires energy has great practical significance; in fact, one of the most important roles that water plays in our world is to act as a coolant. Because of the strong hydrogen bonding among its molecules in the liquid state, water has an unusually large heat of vaporization (41 kJ/mol). A significant portion of the sun's energy is spent evaporating water from the oceans, lakes, and rivers rather than warming the earth. The vaporization of water is also crucial to our body's temperature-control system, which relies on the evaporation of perspiration.

Photolink/PhotoDisc/Getty Images

Water is used to absorb heat from nuclear reactors. The water is then cooled in cooling towers before it is returned to the environment.

Vapor Pressure

Vapor, not *gas,* is the term we customarily use for the gaseous state of a substance that exists naturally as a solid or liquid at 25 °C and 1 atm.

A system at equilibrium is dynamic on the molecular level, but shows no visible changes.

When we place a given amount of liquid in a container and then close it, we observe that the amount of liquid at first decreases slightly but eventually becomes constant. The decrease occurs because there is a transfer of molecules from the liquid to the vapor phase (Figure 14.9). However, as the number of vapor molecules increases, it becomes more and more likely that some of them will return to the liquid. The process by which vapor molecules form a liquid is called **condensation.** Eventually, the same number of molecules are leaving the liquid as are returning to it: the rate of condensation equals the rate of evaporation. *At this point no further change occurs in the amounts of liquid or vapor, because the two opposite processes exactly balance each other;* the system is at *equilibrium*. Note that this system is highly *dynamic* on the mo-

PowerLecture Animations: Phase Change: Liquid to Gas
Phase Change: Gas to Liquid

Lecture Demonstration: 10.14, 10.16, 10.17

DEMONSTRATION

You will need a beaker of room-temperature water, a thermometer, and an electric fan. Have a student come to the front of the room and read the thermometer. Then ask students to tell you what will happen when you place the thermometer in front of the running fan. Many will believe the thermometer will read a cooler temperature. It does not (the fan does not cool the air, although some students believe that it does). Then put the tip of the thermometer in the water and have a student read the temperature. Place the wet thermometer in front of the fan; the temperature will decrease significantly. Use this demonstration to explain the cooling effect of evaporation. We feel cooler in front of a fan because of the sweat that evaporates from our skin. *Note:* You can also perform this demonstration without the fan to show that it is just the evaporation of water that lowers the temperature. The fan merely serves to remove the warmer air more quickly from around the bulb of the thermometer.

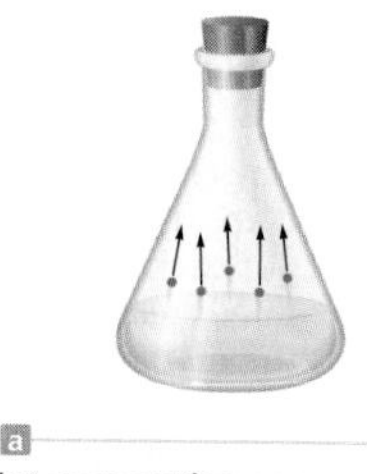

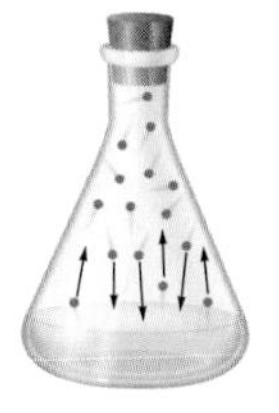

a Net evaporation occurs at first, so the amount of liquid decreases slightly.

a As the number of vapor molecules increases, the rate of condensation increases. Finally the rate of condensation equals the rate of evaporation. The system is at equilibrium.

Figure 14.9 Behavior of a liquid in a closed container.

lecular level—molecules are constantly escaping from and entering the liquid. However, there is no *net* change because the two opposite processes just *balance* each other. As an analogy, consider two island cities connected by a bridge. Suppose the traffic flow on the bridge is the same in both directions. There is motion—we can see the cars traveling across the bridge—but the number of cars in each city is not changing because an equal number enter and leave each one. The result is no *net* change in the number of autos in each city: an equilibrium exists.

The pressure of the vapor present at equilibrium with its liquid is called the *equilibrium vapor pressure* or, more commonly, the **vapor pressure** of the liquid. A simple barometer can be used to measure the vapor pressure of a liquid, as shown in Figure 14.10. Because mercury is so dense, any common liq-

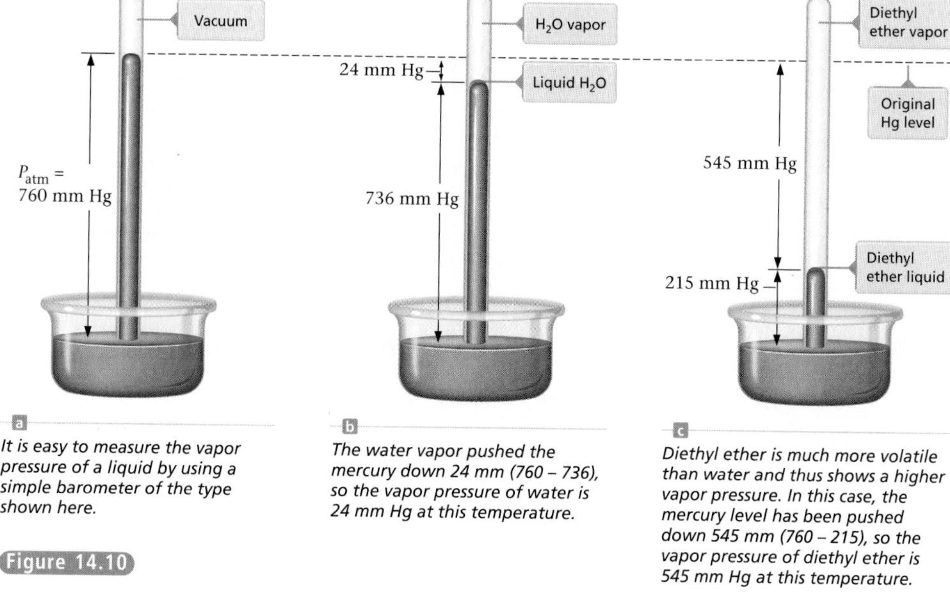

a *It is easy to measure the vapor pressure of a liquid by using a simple barometer of the type shown here.*

b *The water vapor pushed the mercury down 24 mm (760 – 736), so the vapor pressure of water is 24 mm Hg at this temperature.*

c *Diethyl ether is much more volatile than water and thus shows a higher vapor pressure. In this case, the mercury level has been pushed down 545 mm (760 – 215), so the vapor pressure of diethyl ether is 545 mm Hg at this temperature.*

Figure 14.10

PowerLecture Video: Vapor Pressure Lowering: Liquid/Vapor Equilibrium

TEACHING TIP

Vapor pressure is really the beginning of introducing the concept of equilibrium to students. The idea that molecules are changing between the gas and liquid phases at constant, equal rates is new for students. Focus their attention on Figure 14.9 to help them understand what is taking place at the molecular level.

PowerLecture Animation: Dynamic Liquid/Gas Equilibrium

DEMONSTRATION

Cooling by Evaporation

Materials Four thermometers, 4 circles of filter paper, fine copper wire or small rubber bands, small containers of water, methanol, ethanol, acetone

Preparation Wrap the bulb of each thermometer with a half-circle of filter paper and secure it with fine copper wire or a small rubber band.

Presentation Note the temperature of the room on the board. You will need four student volunteers to assist in this demonstration. Ask each volunteer to obtain one of the containers of liquid and a thermometer. Have the students dip the thermometer into the liquid, wetting the filter paper. Remove the thermometers from the liquids and observe what happens to the temperature. Continue observations for each thermometer until the lowest temperature is reached. Note that the student volunteers must hold the thermometers still, and not wave them in the air to speed the process. Record the lowest temperature for each liquid on a table on the board. While students are waiting to find the lowest temperature for each substance, use reference materials to have other students find the boiling point of each substance and record these data on the board as well.

Teaching Notes Ask students to explain why the temperature drops when the thermometers covered with wet filter paper are exposed to the air. On the basis of the observations of the behavior of the four liquids, what is the relationship between the normal boiling point and the effectiveness of each liquid in cooling by evaporation? You can relate this discussion to the technique used to relieve high fevers by giving the person a sponge bath or a rubdown with alcohol.

Lecture Demonstration: 10.18

LABORATORY EXPERIMENT

A relevant laboratory experiment for this section is Experiment 21, Molar Mass of a Volatile Liquid, from *Introductory Chemistry in the Laboratory* by James Hall.

Additional Examples

Example 14.3

Predict which substance in each of the following pairs will show the largest vapor pressure at a given temperature.

1. $H_2O(l)$, $HF(l)$

   HF. Hydrogen bonding occurs in both samples, but H_2O has two O—H bonds, which are capable of hydrogen bonding with other water molecules.

2. $CH_3OCH_3(l)$, $CH_3CH_2OH(l)$

   CH_3OCH_3. No hydrogen bonding can exist in CH_3OCH_3 because the hydrogen atoms are attached to carbon atoms, not the oxygen. Hydrogen bonding does occur in CH_3CH_2OH.

uid injected at the bottom of the column of mercury floats to the top, where it produces a vapor, and the pressure of this vapor pushes some mercury out of the tube. When the system reaches equilibrium, the vapor pressure can be determined from the change in the height of the mercury column.

In effect, we are using the space above the mercury in the tube as a closed container for each liquid. However, in this case as the liquid vaporizes, the vapor formed creates a pressure that pushes some mercury out of the tube and lowers the mercury level. The mercury level stops changing when the excess liquid floating on the mercury comes to equilibrium with the vapor. The change in the mercury level (in millimeters) from its initial position (before the liquid was injected) to its final position is equal to the vapor pressure of the liquid.

The vapor pressures of liquids vary widely (see Figure 14.10). Liquids with high vapor pressures are said to be *volatile*—they evaporate rapidly.

The vapor pressure of a liquid at a given temperature is determined by the *intermolecular forces* that act among the molecules. Liquids in which the intermolecular forces are large have relatively low vapor pressures, because such molecules need high energies to escape to the vapor phase. For example, although water is a much smaller molecule than diethyl ether, $C_2H_5—O—C_2H_5$, the strong hydrogen-bonding forces in water cause its vapor pressure to be much lower than that of ether (see Figure 14.10).

EXAMPLE 14.3 Using Knowledge of Intermolecular Forces to Predict Vapor Pressure

Predict which substance in each of the following pairs will show the largest vapor pressure at a given temperature.

a. $H_2O(l)$, $CH_3OH(l)$

b. $CH_3OH(l)$, $CH_3CH_2CH_2CH_2OH(l)$

SOLUTION

a. Water contains two polar O—H bonds; methanol (CH_3OH) has only one. Therefore, the hydrogen bonding among H_2O molecules is expected to be much stronger than that among CH_3OH molecules. This gives water a lower vapor pressure than methanol.

b. Each of these molecules has one polar O—H bond. However, because $CH_3CH_2CH_2CH_2OH$ is a much larger molecule than CH_3OH, it has much greater London forces and thus is less likely to escape from its liquid. Thus $CH_3CH_2CH_2CH_2OH(l)$ has a lower vapor pressure than $CH_3OH(l)$. ■

14.5 The Solid State: Types of Solids

OBJECTIVE: To learn about the various types of crystalline solids.

Solids play a very important role in our lives. The concrete we drive on, the trees that shade us, the windows we look through, the paper that holds this print, the diamond in an engagement ring, and the plastic lenses in eyeglasses are all important solids. Most solids, such as wood, paper, and glass, contain mixtures of various components. However, some natural solids, such as diamonds and table salt, are nearly pure substances.

Section 14.5

TEACHING TIP

Relate chemistry to earth science by bringing some samples of crystalline solids to class. Quartz and calcite are favorites, and a graphite rod or copper wire is a good example of an atomic solid.

Test Bank: 35

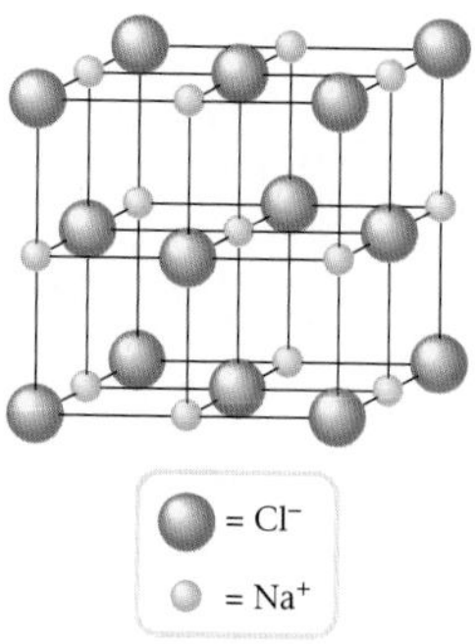

Figure 14.11
The regular arrangement of sodium and chloride ions in sodium chloride, a crystalline solid.

a Quartz, SiO_2

b Rock salt, NaCl

c Iron pyrite, FeS_2

Figure 14.12
Several crystalline solids.

Many substances form **crystalline solids**—those with a regular arrangement of their components. This is illustrated by the partial structure of sodium chloride shown in Figure 14.11. The highly ordered arrangement of the components in a crystalline solid produces beautiful, regularly shaped crystals such as those shown in Figure 14.12.

There are many different types of crystalline solids. For example, both sugar and salt have beautiful crystals that we can easily see. However, although both dissolve readily in water, the properties of the resulting solutions are quite different. The salt solution readily conducts an electric current; the sugar solution does not. This behavior arises from the different natures of the components in these two solids. Common salt, NaCl, is an ionic solid that contains Na^+ and Cl^- ions. When solid sodium chloride dissolves in water, sodium ions and chloride ions are distributed throughout the resulting solution. These ions are free to move through the solution to conduct an electric current. Table sugar (sucrose), on the other hand, is composed of neutral molecules that are dispersed throughout the water when the solid dissolves. No ions are present, and the resulting solution does not conduct electricity. These examples illustrate two important types of crystalline solids: **ionic solids,** represented by sodium chloride; and **molecular solids,** represented by sucrose.

A third type of crystalline solid is represented by elements such as graphite and diamond (both pure carbon), boron, silicon, and all metals. These substances, which contain atoms of only one element covalently bonded to each other, are called **atomic solids.**

We have seen that crystalline solids can be grouped conveniently into three classes as shown in Figure 14.13. Notice that the names of the three classes come from the components of the solid. An ionic solid contains ions,

Lecture Demonstration: 10.6, 10.7

Crystalline solids		
Ionic solids	Molecular solids	Atomic solids
Components are ions.	Components are molecules.	Components are atoms.

Figure 14.13
The classes of crystalline solids.

PowerLecture Animations:
Boiling Water
NaCl Formation Reaction

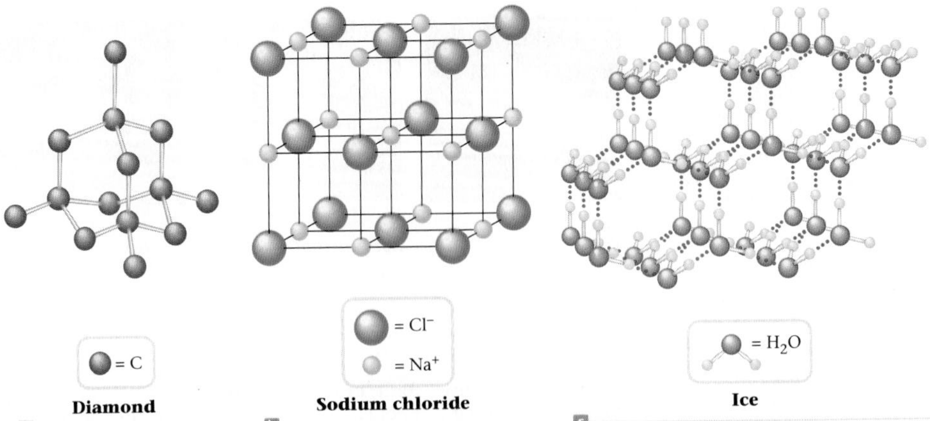

Diamond

a An atomic solid. Each sphere represents a carbon atom in diamond.

Sodium chloride

b An ionic solid. The spheres represent alternating Na^+ and Cl^- ions in solid sodium chloride.

Ice

c A molecular solid. Each unit of three spheres represents an H_2O molecule in ice. The dashed lines show the hydrogen bonding among the polar water molecules.

Figure 14.14
Examples of three types of crystalline solids. Only part of the structure is shown in each case. The structures continue in three dimensions with the same patterns.

Test Bank: 36–41

a molecular solid contains molecules, and an atomic solid contains atoms. Examples of the three types of solids are shown in Figure 14.14.

The internal forces in a solid determine many of the properties of the solid.

The properties of a solid are determined primarily by the nature of the forces that hold the solid together. For example, although argon, copper, and diamond are all atomic solids (their components are atoms), they have strikingly different properties. Argon has a very low melting point (−189 °C), whereas diamond and copper melt at high temperatures (about 3500 °C and 1083 °C, respectively). Copper is an excellent conductor of electricity (it is widely used for electrical wires), whereas both argon and diamond are insulators. The shape of copper can easily be changed; it is both malleable (will form thin sheets) and ductile (can be pulled into a wire). Diamond, on the other hand, is the hardest natural substance known. The marked differences in properties among these three atomic solids are due to differences in bonding. We will explore the bonding in solids in the next section.

Section 14.6

TEACHING TIPS

- Models of different crystal structures can be very effectively used to discuss the different types of solids.
- Remind students that the formulas for ionic solids are empirical formulas, not molecular formulas.
- Styrofoam balls of two different sizes can be glued together to show how the smaller cations fit in the empty spaces between larger anions.

14.6 Bonding in Solids

OBJECTIVES: To understand the interparticle forces in crystalline solids. • To learn about how the bonding in metals determines metallic properties.

Ionic solids were also discussed in Section 12.5.

We have seen that crystalline solids can be divided into three classes, depending on the fundamental particle or unit of the solid. Ionic solids consist of oppositely charged ions packed together, molecular solids contain molecules, and atomic solids have atoms as their fundamental particles. Examples of the various types of solids are given in Table 14.3.

PowerLecture Animations:
Molecular Solids
Structure of Diamond

Table 14.3 Examples of the Various Types of Solids

Type of Solid	Examples	Fundamental Unit(s)
ionic	sodium chloride, NaCl(*s*)	Na^+, Cl^- ions
ionic	ammonium nitrate, $NH_4NO_3(s)$	NH_4^+, NO_3^- ions
molecular	dry ice, $CO_2(s)$	CO_2 molecules
molecular	ice, $H_2O(s)$	H_2O molecules
atomic	diamond, C(*s*)	C atoms
atomic	iron, Fe(*s*)	Fe atoms
atomic	argon, Ar(*s*)	Ar atoms

Ionic Solids

Ionic solids are stable substances with high melting points that are held together by the strong forces that exist between oppositely charged ions. The structures of ionic solids can be visualized best by thinking of the ions as spheres packed together as efficiently as possible. For example, in NaCl the larger Cl^- ions are packed together much like one would pack balls in a box. The smaller Na^+ ions occupy the small spaces ("holes") left among the spherical Cl^- ions, as represented in Figure 14.15.

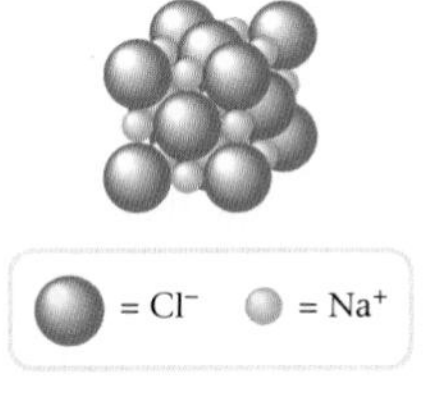

Figure 14.15 The packing of Cl^- and Na^+ ions in solid sodium chloride.

PowerLecture Video: KBr Crystal Shape

PowerLecture Animation: Formation of Ionic Solids

Molecular Solids

In a molecular solid the fundamental particle is a molecule. Examples of molecular solids include ice (contains H_2O molecules), dry ice (contains CO_2 molecules), sulfur (contains S_8 molecules), and white phosphorus (contains P_4 molecules). The latter two substances are shown in Figure 14.16.

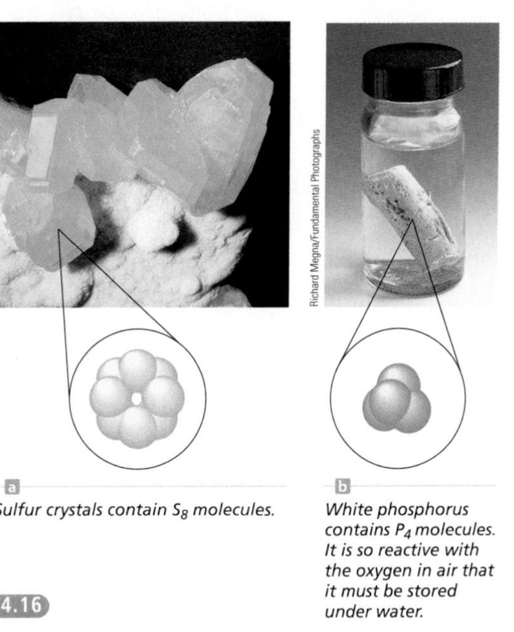

a *Sulfur crystals contain S_8 molecules.*

b *White phosphorus contains P_4 molecules. It is so reactive with the oxygen in air that it must be stored under water.*

Figure 14.16

14.6 Bonding in Solids 461

Molecular solids tend to melt at relatively low temperatures because the intermolecular forces that exist among the molecules are relatively weak. If the molecule has a dipole moment, dipole–dipole forces hold the solid together. In solids with nonpolar molecules, London dispersion forces hold the solid together.

Part of the structure of solid phosphorus is represented in Figure 14.17. Note that the distances between P atoms in a given molecule are much shorter than the distances between the P_4 molecules. This is because the covalent bonds *between atoms* in the molecule are so much stronger than the London dispersion forces *between molecules*.

Atomic Solids

The properties of atomic solids vary greatly because of the different ways in which the fundamental particles, the atoms, can interact with each other. For example, the solids of the Group 8 elements have very low melting points (see Table 14.2), because these atoms, having filled valence orbitals, cannot form covalent bonds with each other. So the forces in these solids are the relatively weak London dispersion forces.

On the other hand, diamond, a form of solid carbon, is one of the hardest substances known and has an extremely high melting point (about 3500 °C). The incredible hardness of diamond arises from the very strong covalent carbon–carbon bonds in the crystal, which lead to a giant

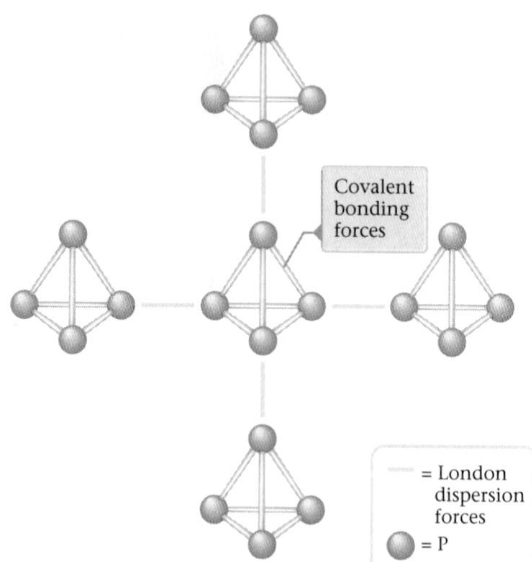

Figure 14.17
A representation of part of the structure of solid phosphorus, a molecular solid that contains P_4 molecules.

molecule. In fact, the entire crystal can be viewed as one huge molecule. A small part of the diamond structure is represented in Figure 14.14a. In diamond each carbon atom is bound covalently to four other carbon atoms to produce a very stable solid. Several other elements also form solids whereby the atoms join together covalently to form giant molecules. Silicon and boron are examples.

At this point you might be asking yourself, "Why aren't solids such as a crystal of diamond, which is a 'giant molecule,' classified as molecular solids?" The answer is that, by convention, a solid is classified as a molecular solid only if (like ice, dry ice, sulfur, and phosphorus) it contains small molecules. Substances like diamond that contain giant molecules are called network solids.

Lecture Demonstration: 10.9

Bonding in Metals

Metals represent another type of atomic solid. Metals have familiar physical properties: they can be pulled into wires, can be hammered into sheets, and are efficient conductors of heat and electricity. However, although the shapes of most pure metals can be changed relatively easily, metals are also durable and have high melting points. These facts indicate that it is difficult to separate metal atoms but relatively easy to slide them past each other. In other words, the bonding in most metals is *strong* but *nondirectional*.

Lecture Demonstration: 10.10, 10.11

The simplest picture that explains these observations is the **electron sea model,** which pictures a regular array of metal atoms in a "sea" of valence electrons that are shared among the atoms in a nondirectional way and that are quite mobile in the metal crystal. The mobile electrons can conduct heat and electricity, and the atoms can be moved rather easily, as, for example, when the metal is hammered into a sheet or pulled into a wire.

Because of the nature of the metallic crystal, other elements can be introduced relatively easily to produce substances called alloys. An **alloy** is best defined as *a substance that contains a mixture of elements and has metallic properties.* There are two common types of alloys.

PowerLecture Animation: Electron Sea Model

In a **substitutional alloy** some of the host metal atoms are *replaced* by other metal atoms of similar sizes. For example, in brass approximately one-third of the atoms in the host copper metal have been replaced by zinc atoms, as shown in Figure 14.18a. Sterling silver (93% silver and 7% copper) and pewter (85% tin, 7% copper, 6% bismuth, and 2% antimony) are other examples of substitutional alloys.

An **interstitial alloy** is formed when some of the interstices (holes) among the closely packed metal atoms are occupied by atoms much smaller than the host atoms, as shown in Figure 14.18b. Steel, the

T.J. Florian/Rainbow

A steel sculpture in Chicago.

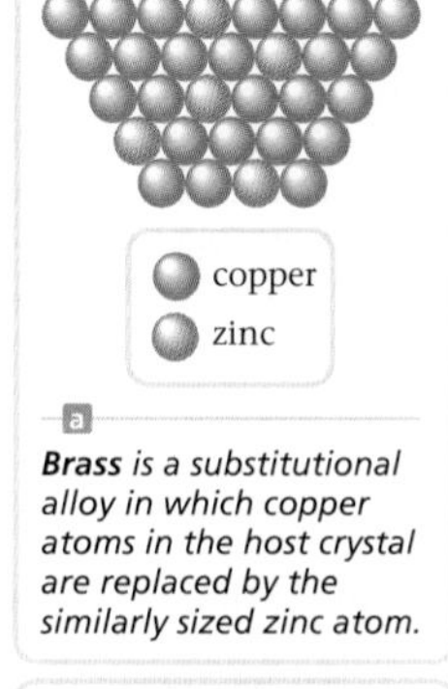

a

Brass is a substitutional alloy in which copper atoms in the host crystal are replaced by the similarly sized zinc atom.

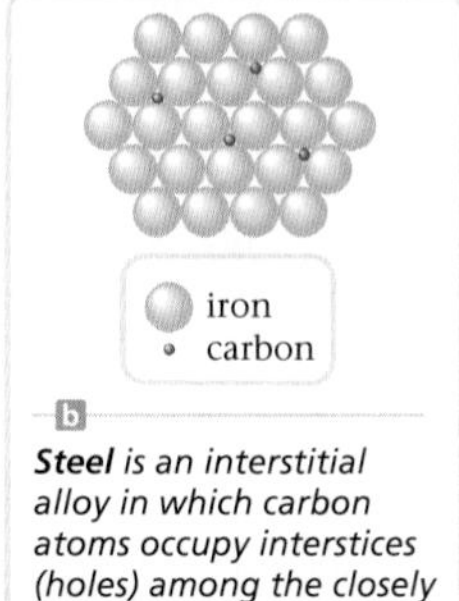

b

Steel is an interstitial alloy in which carbon atoms occupy interstices (holes) among the closely packed iron atoms.

Figure 14.18
Two types of alloys.

CHEMISTRY IN FOCUS

Metal with a Memory

A distraught mother walks into the optical shop carrying her mangled pair of $400 eyeglasses. Her child had gotten into her purse, found her glasses, and twisted them into a pretzel. She hands them to the optometrist with little hope that they can be salvaged. The optometrist says not to worry and drops the glasses into a dish of warm water where the glasses magically spring back to their original shape. The optometrist hands the restored glasses to the woman and says there is no charge for repairing them.

How can the frames "remember" their original shape when placed in warm water? The answer is a nickel–titanium alloy called Nitinol that was developed in the late 1950s and early 1960s at the Naval Ordnance Laboratory in White Oak, Maryland, by William J. Buehler. (The name Nitinol comes from *Ni*ckel *Ti*tanium *N*aval *O*rdnance *L*aboratory.)

Nitinol has the amazing ability to remember a shape originally impressed in it. For example, note the accompanying photos. What causes Nitinol to behave this way? Although the details are too complicated to describe here, this phenomenon results from two different forms of solid Nitinol. When Nitinol is heated to a sufficiently high temperature, the Ni and Ti atoms arrange themselves in a way that leads to the most compact and regular pattern of the atoms—a form called austenite (A). When the alloy is cooled, its atoms rearrange slightly to a form called martensite (M). The shape desired (for example, the word *ICE*) is set into the alloy at a high temperature (A form), then the metal is cooled, causing it to assume the M form. In this process no visible change is noted. Then, if the image is deformed, it will magically return if the alloy is heated (hot water works fine) to a temperature that changes it back to the A form.

Nitinol has many medical applications, including hooks used by orthopedic surgeons to attach ligaments and tendons to bone and "baskets" to catch blood clots. In the latter case a length of Nitinol wire is shaped into a tiny basket and this shape is set at a high temperature. The

best-known interstitial alloy, contains carbon atoms in the "holes" of an iron crystal. The presence of interstitial atoms changes the properties of the host metal. Pure iron is relatively soft, ductile, and malleable because of the absence of strong directional bonding. The spherical metal atoms can be moved rather easily with respect to each other. However, when carbon, which forms strong directional bonds, is introduced into an iron crystal, the presence of the directional carbon–iron bonds makes the resulting alloy harder, stronger, and less ductile than pure iron. The amount of carbon directly affects the properties of steel. *Mild steels* (containing less than 0.2% carbon) are still ductile and malleable and are used for nails, cables, and chains. *Medium steels* (containing 0.2–0.6% carbon) are harder than mild steels and are used in rails and structural steel beams. *High-carbon steels* (containing 0.6–1.5% carbon) are tough and hard and are used for springs, tools, and cutlery.

Many types of steel contain other elements in addition to iron and carbon. Such steels are often called *alloy steels* and can be viewed as being mixed interstitial (carbon) and substitutional (other metals) alloys. An example is stainless steel, which has chromium and nickel atoms substituted for some of the iron atoms. The addition of these metals greatly increases the steel's resistance to corrosion.

464

wires forming the basket are then straightened so they can be inserted as a small bundle through a catheter. When the wires warm up in the blood, the basket shape springs back and acts as a filter to stop blood clots from moving to the heart.

One of the most promising consumer uses of Nitinol is for eyeglass frames. Nitinol is also now being used for braces to straighten crooked teeth.

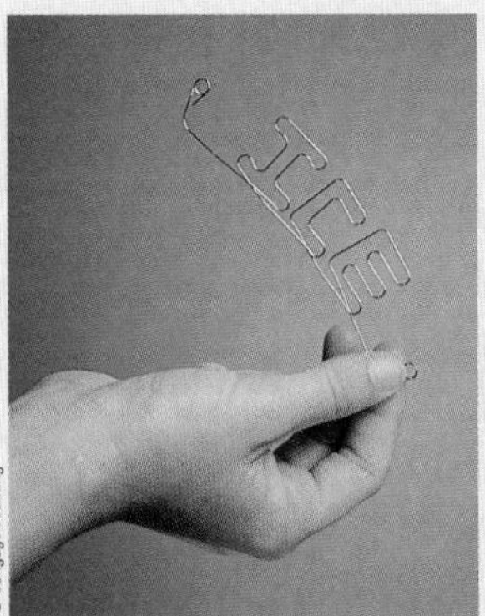

The word ICE is formed from Nitinol wire.

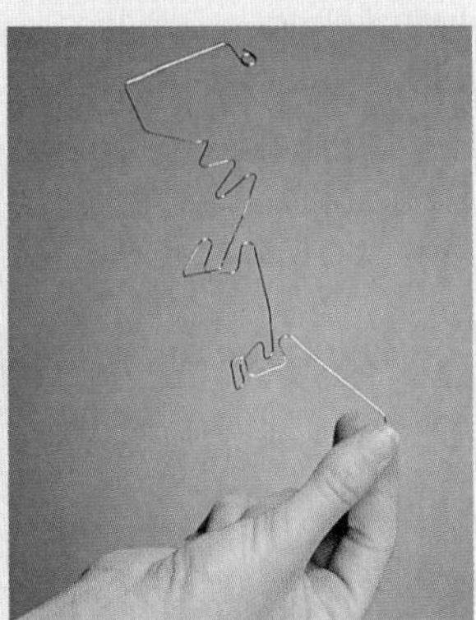
The wire is stretched to obliterate the word ICE.

The wire pops back to ICE when immersed in warm water.

EXAMPLE 14.4 Identifying Types of Crystalline Solids

Name the type of crystalline solid formed by each of the following substances:

a. ammonia
b. iron
c. cesium fluoride
d. argon
e. sulfur

SOLUTION

a. Solid ammonia contains NH_3 molecules, so it is a molecular solid.
b. Solid iron contains iron atoms as the fundamental particles. It is an atomic solid.
c. Solid cesium fluoride contains the Cs^+ and F^- ions. It is an ionic solid.

465

Additional Examples

Example 14.4

Name the type of crystalline solid formed by each of the following substances.

1. water

   molecular solid

2. calcium oxide

   ionic solid

3. krypton

   atomic solid

d. Solid argon contains argon atoms, which cannot form covalent bonds to each other. It is an atomic solid.

e. Sulfur contains S_8 molecules, so it is a molecular solid.

Self-Check EXERCISE 14.2 Name the type of crystalline solid formed by each of the following substances:

a. sulfur trioxide

b. barium oxide

c. gold

See Problems 14.41 and 14.42. ■

CHAPTER 14 REVIEW

Ⓕ directs you to the *Chemistry in Focus* feature in the chapter

VP indicates visual problems

OWL interactive versions of these problems are assignable in OWL

Key Terms

normal boiling point (14.1)
heating/cooling curve (14.1)
normal freezing point (14.1)
intramolecular forces (14.2)
intermolecular forces (14.2)
molar heat of fusion (14.2)
molar heat of vaporization (14.2)
dipole–dipole attraction (14.3)
hydrogen bonding (14.3)
London dispersion forces (14.3)
vaporization (evaporation) (14.4)
condensation (14.4)
vapor pressure (14.4)
crystalline solid (14.5)
ionic solid (14.5)
molecular solid (14.5)
atomic solid (14.5)
electron sea model (14.6)
alloy (14.6)
substitutional alloy (14.6)
interstitial alloy (14.6)

Summary

1. Liquids and solids exhibit some similarities and are very different from the gaseous state.

2. The temperature at which a liquid changes its state to a gas (at 1 atm pressure) is called the normal boiling point of that liquid. Similarly, the temperature at which a liquid freezes (at 1 atm pressure) is the normal freezing point. Changes of state are physical changes, not chemical changes.

3. To convert a substance from the solid to the liquid and then to the gaseous state requires the addition of energy. Forces among the molecules in a solid or a liquid must be overcome by the input of energy. The energy required to melt 1 mole of a substance is called the molar heat of fusion, and the energy required to change 1 mole of liquid to the gaseous state is called the molar heat of vaporization.

4. There are several types of intermolecular forces. Dipole–dipole interactions occur when molecules with dipole moments attract each other. A particularly strong dipole–dipole interaction called hydrogen bonding occurs in molecules that contain hydrogen bonded to a very electronegative element such as N, O, or F. London dispersion forces occur when instantaneous dipoles in atoms or nonpolar molecules lead to relatively weak attractions.

5. The change of a liquid to its vapor is called vaporization or evaporation. The process whereby vapor molecules form a liquid is called condensation. In a closed container, the pressure of the vapor over its liquid reaches a constant value called the vapor pressure of the liquid.

6. Many solids are crystalline (contain highly regular arrangements of their components). The three types

Self Check

Answers to Self-Check Exercise 14.2

a. molecular solid

b. ionic solid

c. atomic solid

ChemWork

Conjugate Acids and Bases
Ranking Acids by Strength
Calculating pH
Properties of Acids
Calculating pH of a Weak Acid
Working with Weak Acids
Calculating pH for a Weak Base
pH for Strong Acids and Bases
Ranking Solutions by pH
Using ICE to Determine pH
Classifying Salt Solutions
Comparing the pH of Salt Solutions
Determining pH of a Salt Solution 1
Determining pH of a Salt Solution 2
Determining pH of a Salt Solution 3

Answers to End-of-Chapter Exercises

1. lower

2. less

3. Ice floats on liquid water. Water expands in volume when it freezes.

4. Because it requires so much more energy to vaporize water than to melt ice, this suggests that the gaseous state is significantly different from the liquid state, but that the liquid and solid states are relatively similar.

5. From –5 °C to 0 °C, molecules within the solid vibrate faster and faster as the temperature increases; at 0 °C, the solid melts as the heat being applied is used to break apart the forces between molecules; above 0 °C, the molecules within the liquid move increasingly faster as additional heat is applied.

6. See Figure 14.2.

7. Physical; no chemical bonds are broken within molecules.

8. When a solid is heated, the molecules begin to vibrate/move more quickly. When enough energy has been added to overcome the intermolecular forces that hold the molecules in a crystal lattice, the solid melts. As the liquid is heated, the molecules begin to move more quickly and more randomly. When enough energy has been added, molecules having sufficient kinetic energy will begin to escape from the surface of the liquid. Once the pressure of the vapor coming from the liquid is equal to the pressure above the liquid, the liquid boils. Only intermolecular forces need to be overcome in this process: no chemical bonds are broken.

9. *Intra*molecular forces are forces within a given molecule (i.e., the bonds between the atoms); *inter*molecular forces are forces between or among different molecules.

of crystalline solids are ionic, molecular, and atomic solids. In ionic solids, the ions are packed together in a way that maximizes the attractions of oppositely charged ions and minimizes the repulsions among identically charged ions. Molecular solids are held together by dipole–dipole attractions if the molecules are polar and by London dispersion forces if the molecules are nonpolar. Atomic solids are held together by covalent bonding forces or London dispersion forces, depending on the atoms present.

Active Learning Questions

These questions are designed to be considered by groups of students in class. Often these questions work well for introducing a particular topic in class.

1. You seal a container half-filled with water. Which best describes what occurs in the container?
   a. Water evaporates until the air becomes saturated with water vapor; at this point, no more water evaporates.
   b. Water evaporates until the air becomes overly saturated (supersaturated) with water, and most of this water recondenses; this cycle continues until a certain amount of water vapor is present, and then the cycle ceases.
   c. The water does not evaporate because the container is sealed.
   d. Water evaporates, and then water evaporates and recondenses simultaneously and continuously.
   e. The water evaporates until it is eventually all in vapor form.

   Justify your choice and for choices you did not pick, explain what is wrong with them.
2. Explain the following: You add 100 mL of water to a 500-mL round-bottomed flask and heat the water until it is boiling. You remove the heat and stopper the flask, and the boiling stops. You then run cool water over the neck of the flask, and the boiling begins again. It seems as though you are boiling water by cooling it.
3. Is it possible for the dispersion forces in a particular substance to be stronger than hydrogen-bonding forces in another substance? Explain your answer.
4. Does the nature of intermolecular forces change when a substance goes from a solid to a liquid, or from a liquid to a gas? What causes a substance to undergo a phase change?
5. How does vapor pressure change with changing temperature? Explain.
6. What occurs when the vapor pressure of a liquid is equal to atmospheric pressure? Explain.
7. What is the vapor pressure of water at 100 °C? How do you know?
8. How do the following physical properties depend on the strength of intermolecular forces? Explain.
   a. melting point
   b. boiling point
   c. vapor pressure
9. Look at Figure 14.2. Why doesn't temperature increase continuously over time? That is, why does the temperature stay constant for periods of time?
10. Which are stronger, intermolecular or intramolecular forces for a given molecule? What observation(s) have you made that supports this position? Explain.
11. Why does water evaporate at all?
12. Sketch a microscopic picture of water and distinguish between *intramolecular bonds* and *intermolecular forces*. Which correspond to the bonds we draw in Lewis structures?
13. Which has the stronger intermolecular forces: N_2 or H_2O? Explain.
14. Which gas would behave more ideally at the same conditions of pressure and temperature: CO or N_2? Why?
15. You have seen that the water molecule has a bent shape and therefore is a polar molecule. This accounts for many of water's interesting properties. What if the water molecule were linear? How would this affect the properties of water? How would life be different?
16. True or false? Methane (CH_4) is more likely to form stronger hydrogen bonding than is water because each methane molecule has twice as many hydrogen atoms. Provide a concise explanation of hydrogen bonding to go with your answer.
17. Why should it make sense that N_2 exists as a gas? Given your answer, how is it possible to make liquid nitrogen? Explain why lowering the temperature works.
18. White phosphorus and sulfur both are called molecular solids even though each is made of only phosphorus and sulfur, respectively. How can they be considered molecular solids? If this is true, why isn't diamond (which is made up only of carbon) a molecular solid?
19. Why is it incorrect to use the term "molecule of NaCl" but correct to use the term "molecule of H_2O"? Is the term "molecule of diamond" correct? Explain.
20. Which would you predict should be larger for a given substance: ΔH_{vap} or ΔH_{fus}? Explain why.

10. intramolecular; intermolecular

11. In ice, water molecules are in regular, fixed positions in the ice crystal; strong hydrogen-bonding forces exist. In liquid water, enough energy has been applied that the molecules are no longer fixed in position, but strong hydrogen bonding still exists, maintaining the bulk nature. In water vapor, enough energy has been applied to overcome the intermolecular forces, and the molecules move independently and exert no forces on each other.

12. The quantity of energy that must be applied to melt one mole of the substance.

13.

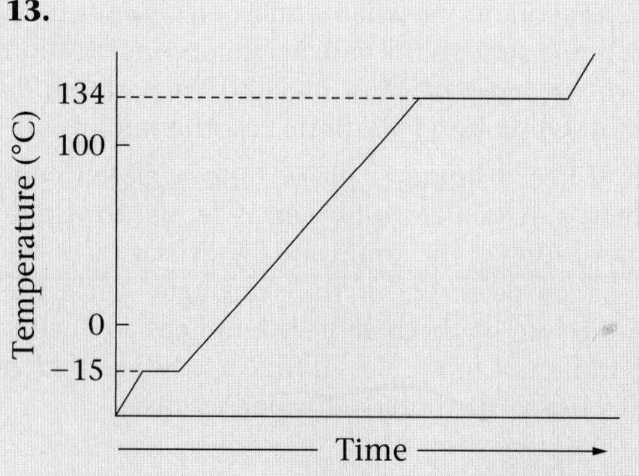

14. (a) In going from a liquid to a gas, a considerably larger amount of the heat being applied has to be converted to the kinetic energy of the atoms escaping from the liquid; (b) 10.9 kJ; (c) −2.00 kJ (heat is evolved); (d) 1.13 kJ

15. 0.106 mol benzene; melting: 1.05 kJ; boiling: 3.24 kJ; more energy is required to overcome the forces holding the molecules in the liquid state to vaporize ($l \rightarrow g$) than to just allow the molecules to begin moving ($s \rightarrow l$)

16. 2.44 kJ; −10.6 kJ (heat is evolved)

17. 33.1 kJ

18. 2.60 kJ/mol

19. The molecules would orient with the iodine (δ+) on one molecule aimed toward the chlorine (δ−) on an adjacent molecule: $^{\delta+}I—Cl^{\delta-}\cdots\cdots{}^{\delta+}I—Cl^{\delta-}$

20. weaker

21. Hydrogen bonding is possible when hydrogen atoms are bonded to highly electronegative atoms such as oxygen, nitrogen, or fluorine. The small size of the hydrogen atom allows the dipoles to approach each other more closely than with other atoms.

22. The hydrogen bonding that can exist when H is bonded to O (or N or F) is an additional intermolecular force, which means additional energy must be added to separate the molecules during boiling.

23. Dipole–dipole forces are very distance-dependent; in the gaseous state, the molecules are too far apart.

24. London dispersion forces are instantaneous dipole forces that arise when the electron cloud of an atom is momentarily distorted by a nearby dipole, temporarily separating the centers of positive and negative charge in the atom.

25. (a) London dispersion forces; (b) dipole–dipole forces (polar molecules); London dispersion forces; (c) hydrogen bonding (H bonded to O); London dispersion forces; (d) London dispersion forces

26. (a) London dispersion forces; (b) hydrogen bonding (H bonded to N); London dispersion forces; (c) London dispersion forces; (d) dipole–dipole forces (polar molecules); London dispersion forces

27. The boiling points increase with an increase in molar mass. As the noble gas atoms increase in size, London dispersion forces become stronger.

28. An increase in the heat of fusion is observed for an increase in the size of the halogen atom (the electron cloud of a larger atom is more easily polarized by a neighboring dipole, thus giving larger London dispersion forces).

29. Both water and ammonia molecules are capable of hydrogen bonding. As ammonia is first bubbled into water, the ammonia molecules begin to hydrogen-bond to the water molecules and to draw the water molecules closer together.

30. For a homogeneous mixture to form, the forces between molecules of the two substances being mixed must be at least *comparable in magnitude* to the intermolecular forces within each separate substance. In the case of a water–ethanol mixture, the forces that exist when water and ethanol are mixed are stronger than water–water or ethanol–ethanol forces in the separate substances. Ethanol and water molecules can approach one another more closely in the mixture than either substance's molecules could approach a like molecule in the separate substances. Strong hydrogen bonding occurs in both ethanol and water.

VP 21. In the diagram below, which lines represent the hydrogen bonds?

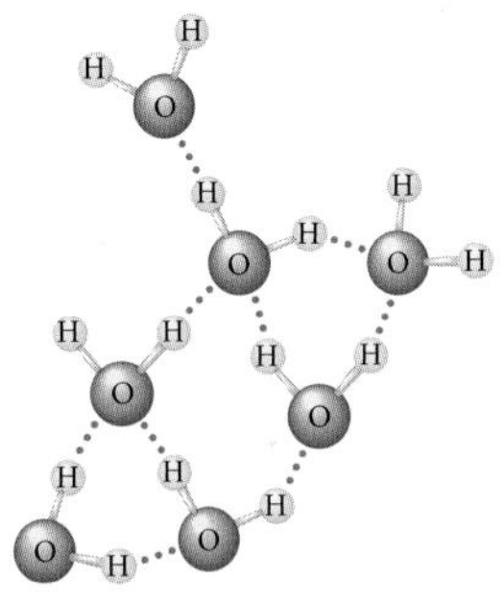

a. The dotted lines between the hydrogen atoms of one water molecule and the oxygen atoms of a different water molecule.
b. The solid lines between a hydrogen atom and oxygen atom in the same water molecule.
c. Both the solid lines and dotted lines represent the hydrogen bonds.
d. There are no hydrogen bonds represented in the diagram.

VP 22. Use the heating/cooling curve below to answer the following questions.

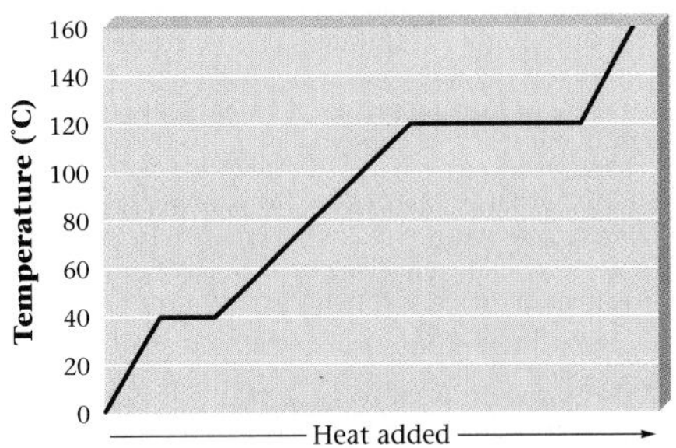

a. What is the freezing point of the liquid?
b. What is the boiling point of the liquid?
c. Which is greater: the heat of fusion or the heat of vaporization? Explain.

VP 23. Assume the two-dimensional structure of an ionic compound, M_xA_y, is

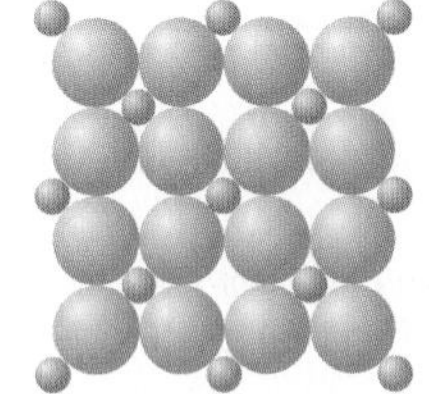

What is the empirical formula of this ionic compound?

Questions and Problems

14.1 Water and Its Phase Changes

QUESTIONS

1. Gases have (higher/lower) densities than liquids or solids.
2. Liquids and solids are (more/less) compressible than are gases.
3. What evidence do we have that the solid form of water is less dense than the liquid form of water at its freezing/melting point?
4. The enthalpy (ΔH) of *vaporization* of water is about seven times larger than water's enthalpy of *fusion* (41 kJ/mol versus 6 kJ/mol). What does this tell us about the relative similarities among the solid, liquid, and gaseous states of water?
5. Consider a sample of ice being heated from −5 °C to +5 °C. Describe on both a macroscopic and a microscopic basis what happens to the ice as the temperature reaches 0 °C.
6. Sketch a heating/cooling curve for water, starting out at −20 °C and going up to 120 °C, applying heat to the sample at a constant rate. Mark on your sketch the portions of the curve that represent the melting of the solid and the boiling of the liquid.

14.2 Energy Requirements for the Changes of State

QUESTIONS

7. Are changes in state *physical* or *chemical* changes for molecular solids? Why?
8. Describe in detail the microscopic processes that take place when a solid melts and when a liquid boils. What kind of forces must be overcome? Are any chemical bonds broken during these processes?
9. Explain the difference between *intra*molecular and *inter*molecular forces.
10. The forces that connect two hydrogen atoms to an oxygen atom in a water molecule are (intermolecular/intramolecular), but the forces that hold water molecules close together in an ice cube are (intermolecular/intramolecular).
11. Discuss the similarities and differences between the arrangements of molecules and the forces between molecules in liquid water versus steam, and in liquid water versus ice.
12. What does the *molar heat of fusion* of a substance represent?

All even-numbered Questions and Problems have answers in the back of this book and solutions in the Solutions Guide.

31. Evaporation is when a substance passes from the liquid state to the gaseous state; condensation is the reverse of this process. Evaporation is endothermic; condensation is exothermic.

32. When a liquid is placed into a closed container, a dynamic equilibrium is set up, in which vaporization of the liquid and condensation of the vapor are occurring at the same rate. Once the equilibrium has been achieved, there is a net concentration of molecules in the vapor state, which gives rise to the observed vapor pressure.

33. A dynamic equilibrium occurs when two opposite processes take place at the same speed in a container, so that there is no net change in the system over time. In a closed vessel containing a liquid, evaporation and condensation occur at the same speed, so that there is a fixed quantity of material in the vapor state at any given time (which represents the vapor pressure).

PROBLEMS

13. The following data have been collected for substance X. Construct a heating curve for substance X. (The drawing does not need to be absolutely to scale, but it should clearly show relative differences.)

normal melting point	−15 °C
molar heat of fusion	2.5 kJ/mol
normal boiling point	134 °C
molar heat of vaporization	55.3 kJ/mol

14. The molar heat of fusion of aluminum metal is 10.79 kJ/mol, whereas its heat of vaporization is 293.4 kJ/mol.
    a. Why is the heat of fusion of aluminum so much smaller than the heat of vaporization?
    b. What quantity of heat would be required to vaporize 1.00 g of aluminum at its normal boiling point?
    c. What quantity of heat would be evolved if 5.00 g of liquid aluminum freezes at its normal freezing point?
    d. What quantity of heat would be required to melt 0.105 mole of aluminum at its normal melting point?

15. The molar heat of fusion of benzene is 9.92 kJ/mol. Its molar heat of vaporization is 30.7 kJ/mol. Calculate the heat required to melt 8.25 g of benzene at its normal melting point. Calculate the heat required to vaporize 8.25 g of benzene at its normal boiling point. Why is the heat of vaporization more than three times the heat of fusion?

16. The molar heats of fusion and vaporization for silver are 11.3 kJ/mol and 250. kJ/mol, respectively. Silver's normal melting point is 962 °C, and its normal boiling point is 2212 °C. What quantity of heat is required to melt 12.5 g of silver at 962 °C? What quantity of heat is liberated when 4.59 g of silver vapor condenses at 2212 °C?

17. Given that the specific heat capacities of ice and steam are 2.06 J/g °C and 2.03 J/g °C, respectively, and considering the information about water given in Exercise 16, calculate the total quantity of heat evolved when 10.0 g of steam at 200. °C is condensed, cooled, and frozen to ice at −50. °C.

18. It requires 113 J to melt 1.00 g of sodium metal at its normal melting point of 98 °C. Calculate the *molar heat of fusion* of sodium.

14.3 Intermolecular Forces

QUESTIONS

19. Consider the iodine monochloride molecule, ICl. Because chlorine is more electronegative than iodine, this molecule is a dipole. How would you expect iodine monochloride molecules in the gaseous state to orient themselves with respect to each other as the sample is cooled and the molecules begin to aggregate? Sketch the orientation you would expect.

20. Dipole–dipole forces become ________ as the distance between the dipoles increases.

21. The text implies that hydrogen bonding is a special case of very strong dipole–dipole interactions possible among only certain atoms. What atoms in addition to hydrogen are necessary for hydrogen bonding? How does the small size of the hydrogen atom contribute to the unusual strength of the dipole–dipole forces involved in hydrogen bonding?

22. The normal boiling point of water is unusually high, compared to the boiling points of H_2S, H_2Se, and H_2Te. Explain this observation in terms of the *hydrogen bonding* that exists in water, but that does not exist in the other compounds.

23. Why are the dipole–dipole interactions between polar molecules *not* important in the vapor phase?

24. What are London dispersion forces, and how do they arise?

PROBLEMS

25. What type of intermolecular forces is active in the liquid state of each of the following substances?
    a. Ne
    b. CO
    c. CH_3OH
    d. Cl_2

26. Discuss the types of intermolecular forces acting in the liquid state of each of the following substances.
    a. Xe
    b. NH_3
    c. F_2
    d. ICl

27. The boiling points of the noble gas elements are listed below. Comment on the trend in the boiling points. Why do the boiling points vary in this manner?

He	−272 °C	Kr	−152.3 °C
Ne	−245.9 °C	Xe	−107.1 °C
Ar	−185.7 °C	Rn	−61.8 °C

28. The heats of fusion of three substances are listed below. Explain the trend this list reflects.

HI	2.87 kJ/mol
HBr	2.41 kJ/mol
HCl	1.99 kJ/mol

29. When dry ammonia gas (NH_3) is bubbled into a 125-mL sample of water, the volume of the sample (initially, at least) *decreases* slightly. Suggest a reason for this.

All even-numbered Questions and Problems have answers in the back of this book and solutions in the Solutions Guide.

34. A liquid is injected at the bottom of the column of mercury and rises to the surface of the mercury, where the liquid evaporates into the vacuum above the mercury column. As the liquid evaporates, the pressure of the vapor increases in the space above the mercury and presses down on the mercury. The level of mercury therefore drops, and the amount by which the mercury level drops (in mm Hg) is equivalent to the vapor pressure of the liquid.

35. (a) CH_3OH: Both substances are capable of hydrogen bonding, but CH_3OH has a much smaller molar mass; (b) CH_3CH_3: The CH_3CH_2OH molecule is capable of hydrogen bonding, which raises the boiling point; (c) CH_4: Hydrogen bonding is possible in H_2O but not in CH_4.

36. (a) HF: Although both substances are capable of hydrogen bonding, water has two O–H bonds that can be involved in hydrogen bonding versus only one F–H bond in HF. (b) CH_3OCH_3: Because no H is attached to the O atom, no hydrogen bonding can exist. Thus, the molecule should be relatively more volatile than CH_3CH_2OH even though it contains the same number of atoms of each element. (c) CH_3SH: Hydrogen bonding is not as important for an S–H bond (because S has a lower electronegativity than O). Since there is relatively little hydrogen bonding, CH_3SH is more volatile than CH_3OH.

37. Oxygen is considerably more electronegative than nitrogen, so that although hydrogen bonding does exist in both liquids, it is much stronger in H_2O than in NH_3.

38. Both substances have the same molar mass. Ethyl alcohol contains a hydrogen atom directly bonded to an oxygen atom, however. Therefore, hydrogen bonding can exist in ethyl alcohol, whereas only weak dipole–dipole forces exist in dimethyl ether. Dimethyl ether is more volatile; ethyl alcohol has a higher boiling point.

39. A crystalline solid is a solid with a regular, repeating microscopic arrangement of its components in a lattice; the highly ordered arrangement on a microscopic basis is frequently reflected macroscopically in regularly shaped crystals.

40. *Ionic* solids have positive and negative ions as their fundamental particles; a simple example is sodium chloride, in which Na^+ and Cl^- ions are held together by strong electrostatic forces. *Molecular* solids have molecules as their fundamental particles, with the molecules being held together in the crystal by dipole–dipole forces, hydrogen-bonding forces, or London dispersion forces (depending on the identity of the substance); simple examples of molecular solids include ice (H_2O) and ordinary table sugar (sucrose). *Atomic* solids have simple atoms as their fundamental particles, with the atoms being held to-

30. When 50 mL of liquid water at 25 °C is added to 50 mL of ethanol (ethyl alcohol), also at 25 °C, the combined volume of the mixture is considerably *less* than 100 mL. Give a possible explanation.

14.4 Evaporation and Vapor Pressure

QUESTIONS

31. What is *evaporation*? What is *condensation*? Which of these processes is endothermic and which is exothermic?

32. If you've ever opened a bottle of rubbing alcohol or other solvent on a warm day, you may have heard a little "whoosh" as the vapor that had built up above the liquid escapes. Describe on a microscopic basis how a vapor pressure builds up in a closed container above a liquid. What processes in the container give rise to this phenomenon?

33. What do we mean by a *dynamic equilibrium?* Describe how the development of a vapor pressure above a liquid represents such an equilibrium.

34. Consider Figure 14.10. Imagine you are talking to a friend who has not taken any science courses, and explain how the figure demonstrates the concept of vapor pressure and enables it to be measured.

PROBLEMS

35. Which substance in each pair would be expected to have a lower boiling point? Explain your reasoning.

a. CH_3OH or $CH_3CH_2CH_2OH$
b. CH_3CH_3 or CH_3CH_2OH
c. H_2O or CH_4

36. Which substance in each pair would be expected to show the largest vapor pressure at a given temperature? Explain your reasoning.

a. $H_2O(l)$ or $HF(l)$
b. $CH_3OCH_3(l)$ or $CH_3CH_2OH(l)$
c. $CH_3OH(l)$ or $CH_3SH(l)$

37. Although water and ammonia differ in molar mass by only one unit, the boiling point of water is over 100 °C higher than that of ammonia. What forces in liquid water that do *not* exist in liquid ammonia could account for this observation?

38. Two molecules that contain the same number of each kind of atom but that have different molecular structures are said to be *isomers* of each other. For example, both ethyl alcohol and dimethyl ether (shown below) have the formula C_2H_6O and are isomers. Based on considerations of intermolecular forces, which substance would you expect to be more volatile? Which would you expect to have the higher boiling point? Explain.

dimethyl ether	ethyl alcohol
$CH_3—O—CH_3$	$CH_3—CH_2—OH$

14.5 The Solid State: Types of Solids

QUESTIONS

39. What are crystalline solids? What kind of microscopic structure do such solids have? How is this microscopic structure reflected in the macroscopic appearance of such solids?

40. On the basis of the smaller units that make up the crystals, cite three types of crystalline solids. For each type of crystalline solid, give an example of a substance that forms that type of solid.

14.6 Bonding in Solids

QUESTIONS

41. How do *ionic* solids differ in structure from *molecular* solids? What are the fundamental particles in each? Give two examples of each type of solid and indicate the individual particles that make up the solids in each of your examples.

42. A common prank on college campuses is to switch the salt and sugar on dining hall tables, which is usually easy because the substances look so much alike. Yet, despite the similarity in their appearance, these two substances differ greatly in their properties, since one is a molecular solid and the other is an ionic solid. How do the properties differ and why?

43. Ionic solids are generally considerably harder than most molecular solids. Explain.

44. Although crystals of table salt (sodium chloride) and table sugar (sucrose) look very similar to the naked eye, the melting point of sucrose (186 °C) is several hundred degrees less than the melting point of sodium chloride (801 °C). Explain.

45. The forces holding together a molecular solid are much (stronger/weaker) than the forces between particles in an ionic solid.

46. Explain the overall trend in melting points given below in terms of the forces among particles in the solids indicated.

Hydrogen, H_2	−259 °C
Ethyl alcohol, C_2H_5OH	−114 °C
Water, H_2O	0 °C
Sucrose, $C_{12}H_{22}O_{11}$	186 °C
Calcium chloride, $CaCl_2$	772 °C

47. What is a *network* solid? Give an example of a network solid and describe the bonding in such a solid. How does a network solid differ from a molecular solid?

48. Ionic solids do not conduct electricity in the solid state, but are strong conductors in the liquid state and when dissolved in water. Explain.

All even-numbered Questions and Problems have answers in the back of this book and solutions in the Solutions Guide.

gether in the crystal by either covalent bonding (as in graphite or diamond) or metallic bonding (as in copper or other metals).

41. The fundamental particles in ionic solids are positively and negatively charged ions in an alternating array in which each type of ion is surrounded by several oppositely charged ions. In a molecular solid, the fundamental particles are molecules; although the *intra*molecular forces holding individual molecules together are strong, the *inter*molecular forces between adjacent molecules are not as strong as in an ionic solid.

42. sugar: molecular solid, relatively "soft," melts at a relatively low temperature, dissolves as molecules, does not conduct electricity when dissolved or melted; salt: ionic solid, relatively "hard," melts at a high temperature, dissolves as positively and negatively charged ions, conducts electricity when dissolved or melted

43. The very strong electrostatic forces between the ions in an ionic solid make it very difficult to move or displace ions relative to each other. In a molecular solid, the intermolecular forces are considerably less strong in magnitude.

44. Sodium chloride is an ionic substance in which a crystal lattice of alternating positive and negative ions holds the substance together with very strong forces that are difficult to overcome. Sucrose is a molecular substance in which the molecules are held together in the solid by dipole–dipole (and H-bonding) forces, which are weaker than the ionic forces.

45. weaker

46. In liquid hydrogen, the only intermolecular forces are weak London dispersion forces. In ethyl alcohol and water we have hydrogen bonding possible, but the hydrogen bonding forces are weaker in ethyl alcohol because of the influence of the remainder of the molecule. In sucrose, we also have hydrogen bonding possible, but now at several places in the molecule, leading to stronger forces. In calcium chloride, we have an ionic crystal lattice with even stronger forces between the particles.

47. A network solid has strong covalent bonding between all the atoms, which results in the solid effectively being one large molecule (diamond is the best example). In a molecular solid, individual molecules are held together by covalent bonds, but the forces *between* the molecules are typically only dipole–dipole or London dispersion forces.

48. Although ions exist in both the solid and liquid states, in the solid state the ions are rigidly held in place in the crystal lattice and cannot move so as to conduct an electric current.

49. What is an *alloy?* Explain the differences in structure between substitutional and interstitial alloys. Give an example of each type.

50. The "Chemistry in Focus" segment *Metal with a Memory* discusses Nitinol, an alloy that "remembers" a shape originally impressed in it. Which elements compose Nitinol, and why is it classified as an alloy?

Additional Problems

MATCHING

For Exercises 51–60 choose one of the following terms to match the definition or description given.

a. alloy
b. specific heat
c. crystalline solid
d. dipole–dipole attraction
e. equilibrium vapor pressure
f. intermolecular
g. intramolecular
h. ionic solids
i. London dispersion forces
j. molar heat of fusion
k. molar heat of vaporization
l. molecular solids
m. normal boiling point
n. semiconductor

51. boiling point at pressure of 1 atm

52. energy required to melt 1 mole of a substance

53. forces between atoms in a molecule

54. forces between molecules in a solid

55. instantaneous dipole forces for nonpolar molecules

56. lining up of opposite charges on adjacent polar molecules

57. maximum pressure of vapor that builds up in a closed container

58. mixture of elements having metallic properties overall

59. repeating arrangement of component species in a solid

60. solids that melt at relatively low temperatures

61. Given the densities and conditions of ice, liquid water, and steam listed in Table 14.1, calculate the volume of 1.0 g of water under each of these circumstances.

62. In carbon compounds a given group of atoms can often be arranged in more than one way. This means that more than one structure may be possible for the same atoms. For example, both the molecules diethyl ether and 1-butanol have the same number of each type of atom, but they have different structures and are said to be *isomers* of one another.

diethyl ether	$CH_3—CH_2—O—CH_2—CH_3$
1-butanol	$CH_3—CH_2—CH_2—CH_2—OH$

Which substance would you expect to have the larger vapor pressure? Why?

63. Which of the substances in each of the following sets would be expected to have the highest boiling point? Explain why.

a. Ga, KBr, O_2
b. Hg, NaCl, He
c. H_2, O_2, H_2O

64. Which of the substances in each of the following sets would be expected to have the lowest melting point? Explain why.

a. H_2, N_2, O_2
b. Xe, NaCl, C (diamond)
c. Cl_2, Br_2, I_2

65. When a person has a severe fever, one therapy to reduce the fever is an "alcohol rub." Explain how the evaporation of alcohol from the person's skin removes heat energy from the body.

66. What is steel?

67. Some properties of potassium metal are summarized in the following table:

Normal melting point	63.5 °C
Normal boiling point	765.7 °C
Molar heat of fusion	2.334 kJ/mol
Molar heat of vaporization	79.87 kJ/mol
Specific heat of the solid	0.75 J/g °C

a. Calculate the quantity of heat required to heat 5.00 g of potassium from 25.3 °C to 45.2 °C.
b. Calculate the quantity of heat required to melt 1.35 moles of potassium at its normal melting point.
c. Calculate the quantity of heat required to vaporize 2.25 g of potassium at its normal boiling point.

68. What are some important uses of water, both in nature and in industry? What is the liquid range for water?

69. Describe, on both a microscopic and a macroscopic basis, what happens to a sample of water as it is cooled from room temperature to 50 °C below its normal freezing point.

70. Cake mixes and other packaged foods that require cooking often contain special directions for use at high elevations. Typically these directions indicate that the food should be cooked longer above 5000 ft. Explain why it takes longer to cook something at higher elevations.

71. Why is there no change in *intra*molecular forces when a solid is melted? Are intramolecular forces stronger or weaker than intermolecular forces?

72. What do we call the energies required, respectively, to melt and to vaporize 1 mole of a substance? Which of these energies is always larger for a given substance? Why?

All even-numbered Questions and Problems have answers in the back of this book and solutions in the Solutions Guide.

49. An alloy is a mixture of elements that as a whole shows metallic properties. In a substitutional alloy, some of the host metal atoms are *replaced* by other metal atoms. In an interstitial alloy, small atoms occupy the spaces *between* the host metal atoms.

50. Nitinol is an alloy of nickel and titanium. When nickel and titanium are heated to a sufficiently high temperature during the production of Nitinol, the atoms arrange themselves in a compact and regular pattern of the atoms.

51. m **52.** j
53. g **54.** f
55. i **56.** d
57. e **58.** a
59. c **60.** l

61. ice, 1.1 cm^3; liquid, 1.0 cm^3; vapor, 3.1×10^3 cm^3

62. Dimethyl ether has the larger vapor pressure. No hydrogen bonding is possible because the O atom does not have a hydrogen atom attached. Hydrogen bonding can occur *only* when a hydrogen atom is *directly* attached to a strongly electronegative atom (such as N, O, or F). Hydrogen bonding is possible in ethanol (ethanol contains an −OH group).

63. (a) KBr; (b) NaCl; (c) H_2O

64. (a) H_2. London dispersion forces are the only intermolecular forces present in these nonpolar molecules; typically these forces become larger with increasing atomic size (as the atoms become bigger, the edge of the electron cloud lies farther from the nucleus and becomes more easily distorted). (b) Xe. Only the relatively weak London forces exist in a crystal of Xe atoms, whereas in NaCl strong ionic forces exist, and in diamond strong covalent bonding exists between carbon atoms. (c) Cl_2. Only London forces exist among such nonpolar molecules.

65. To evaporate, a liquid must absorb the heat of vaporization. When alcohol is applied to a feverish person, this heat is taken from the skin.

66. *Steel* is a general term applied to alloys consisting primarily of iron, but with small amounts of other substances added. Whereas pure iron itself is relatively soft, malleable, and ductile, steels are typically much stronger and harder and much less subject to damage.

67. (a) 75 J; (b) 3.15 kJ; (c) 4.60 kJ

68. Water is the solvent in which cellular processes take place in living creatures. Water in the oceans moderates the earth's temperature. Water is used in industry as a

73. The molar heat of vaporization of carbon disulfide, CS_2, is 28.4 kJ/mol at its normal boiling point of 46 °C. How much energy (heat) is required to vaporize 1.0 g of CS_2 at 46 °C? How much heat is evolved when 50. g of CS_2 is condensed from the vapor to the liquid form at 46 °C?

74. Which is stronger, a dipole–dipole attraction between two molecules or a covalent bond between two atoms within the same molecule? Explain.

75. For a liquid to boil, the intermolecular forces in the liquid must be overcome. Based on the types of intermolecular forces present, arrange the expected boiling points of the liquid states of the following substances in order from lowest to highest: NaCl(*l*), He(*l*), CO(*l*), H_2O(*l*).

76. What are *London dispersion forces* and how do they arise in a nonpolar molecule? Are London forces typically stronger or weaker than dipole–dipole attractions between polar molecules? Are London forces stronger or weaker than covalent bonds? Explain.

77. Discuss the types of intermolecular forces acting in the liquid state of each of the following substances.

a. N_2
b. NH_3
c. He
d. CO_2 (linear, nonpolar)

78. Explain how the evaporation of water acts as a coolant for the earth.

79. What do we mean when we say a liquid is *volatile?* Do volatile liquids have large or small vapor pressures? What types of intermolecular forces occur in highly volatile liquids?

80. Although methane, CH_4, and ammonia, NH_3, differ in molar mass by only one unit, the boiling point of ammonia is over 100 °C higher than that of methane (a nonpolar molecule). Explain.

81. Which type of solid is likely to have the highest melting point—an ionic solid, a molecular solid, or an atomic solid? Explain.

82. What types of intermolecular forces exist in a crystal of ice? How do these forces differ from the types of intermolecular forces that exist in a crystal of solid oxygen?

83. Discuss the *electron sea model* for metals. How does this model account for the fact that metals are very good conductors of electricity?

84. Water is unusual in that its solid form (ice) is less dense than its liquid form. Discuss some implications of this fact.

85. Describe in detail the microscopic processes that take place when a liquid boils. What kind of forces must be overcome? Are any chemical bonds broken during these processes?

86. Water at 100 °C (its normal boiling point) could certainly give you a bad burn if it were spilled on the skin, but steam at 100 °C could give you a much *worse* burn. Explain.

87. What is a *dipole–dipole attraction?* Give three examples of liquid substances in which you would expect dipole–dipole attractions to be large.

88. What is meant by *hydrogen bonding?* Give three examples of substances that would be expected to exhibit hydrogen bonding in the liquid state.

89. Although the noble gas elements are monatomic and could not give rise to dipole–dipole forces or hydrogen bonding, these elements still can be liquefied and solidified. Explain.

90. Describe, on a microscopic basis, the processes of *evaporation* and *condensation.* Which process requires an input of energy? Why?

All even-numbered Questions and Problems have answers in the back of this book and solutions in the Solutions Guide.

cooling agent, and it serves as a means of transportation. The liquid range is 0 °C to 100 °C at 1 atm pressure.

69. From room temperature to 0 °C, the average kinetic energy of the molecules decreases, and the molecules slow down. At 0 °C, the liquid freezes, with the molecules forming a crystal lattice characterized by much greater order than in the liquid state; molecules no longer move freely but can only vibrate somewhat. As the temperature is lowered further, molecular vibrations decrease in intensity.

70. At higher altitudes, the boiling points of liquids are lower because there is a lower atmospheric pressure above the liquid. The temperature at which food cooks is determined by the temperature to which the water in the food can be heated before it escapes as steam. Thus, food cooks at a lower temperature at high elevations where the boiling point of water is lowered.

71. *Intra*molecular forces are the forces between atoms that hold a group of atoms together as a molecule. When the solid is melted, it is the *inter*molecular forces *between* molecules that are overcome. Intramolecular forces are typically stronger.

72. Heat of fusion (melt); heat of vaporization (boil). The heat of vaporization is always larger, because virtually all of the intermolecular forces must be overcome to form a gas. In a liquid, considerable intermolecular forces remain. Going from a solid to a liquid requires less energy than going from a liquid to a gas.

73. 0.37 kJ; −19 kJ

74. Dipole–dipole interactions are typically 1% as strong as a covalent bond. Dipole–dipole interactions represent electrostatic attractions between portions of molecules that carry only a *partial* positive or negative charge, and such forces require the molecules that are interacting to come *near* each other.

Please refer to p. A27 in this book for answers to Exercises 75–90.

Chapter 15

Objectives

In this chapter, our objectives are for the students to:

SECTION 15.1

- Understand the process of dissolving.
- Learn why certain components dissolve in water.

SECTION 15.2

- Learn qualitative terms associated with the concentration of a solution.

SECTION 15.3

- Understand the concentration term *mass percent* and learn how to calculate it.

SECTION 15.4

- Understand molarity.
- Learn to use molarity to calculate the number of moles of solute present.

SECTION 15.5

- Learn to calculate the concentration of a solution made by diluting a stock solution.

SECTION 15.6

- Understand the strategy for solving stoichiometric problems for solution reactions.

SECTION 15.7

- Learn how to do calculations involved in acid–base reactions.

SECTION 15.8

- Learn about normality and equivalent weight.
- Learn to use these concepts in stoichiometric calculations.

15 Solutions

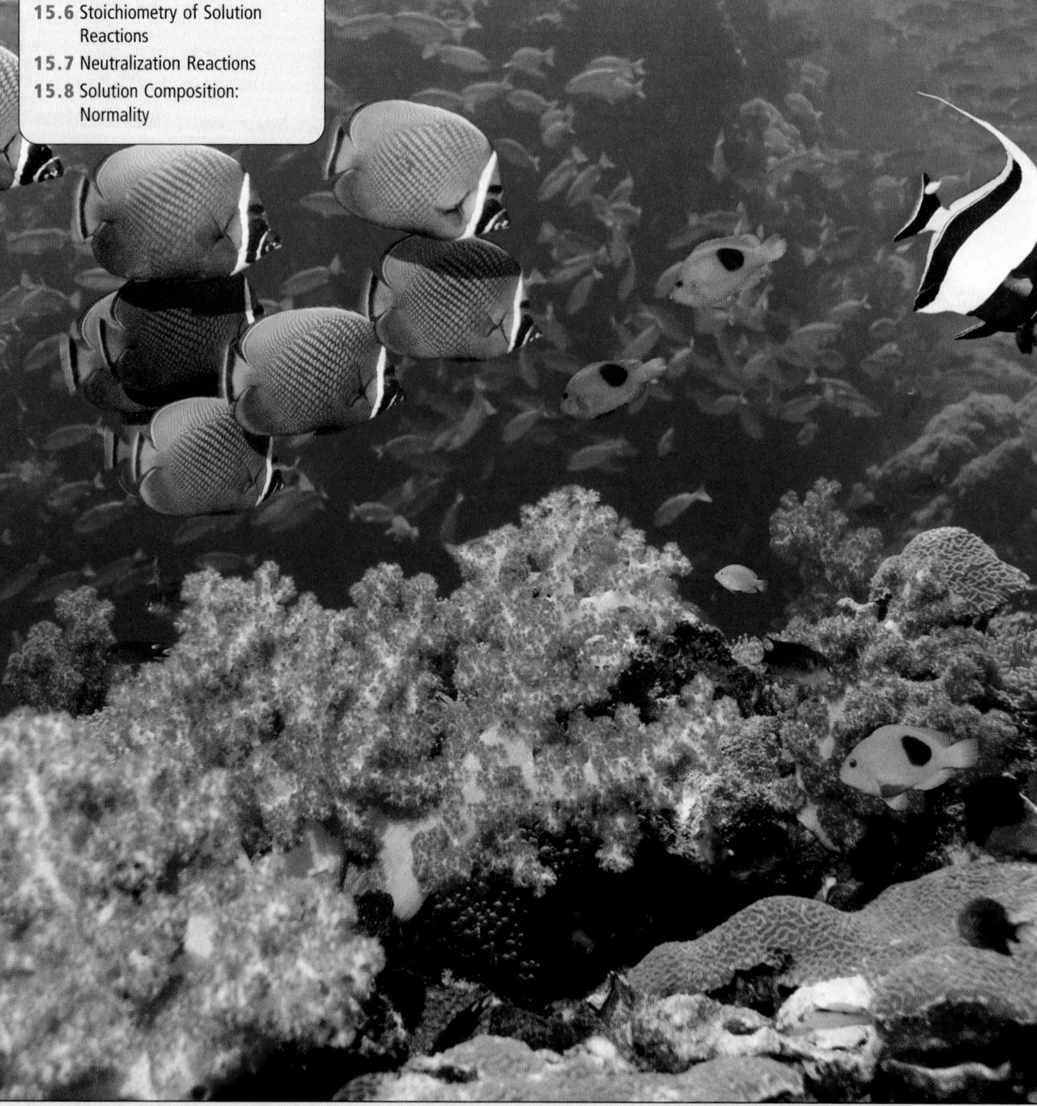

Seawater is an aqueous solution. *(Georgette Douwma/Getty Images)*

ChemWork Refined over ten years of use by thousands of students, **ChemWork** builds and enhances students' problems-solving skills. Online assignments function as a "personal instructor" to help students learn how to solve challenging problems and learn how to think like chemists. Annotations for **ChemWork** assignments are included at the beginning of the end-of-chapter review.

PowerLecture This 2-DVD package includes the Chemistry Multimedia Library, which contains animations, simulations, and movies for all chemistry subjects, organized by topic for lecture presentations. Annotations for **PowerLecture** are referenced in the margins throughout the Annotated Instructor's Edition.

OWL Sign in to OWL at **www.cengage.com/owl** to view tutorials and simulations, develop problem-solving skills, and complete online homework assigned by your professor.

Most of the important chemistry that keeps plants, animals, and humans functioning occurs in aqueous solutions. Even the water that comes out of a tap is not pure water but a solution of various materials in water. For example, tap water may contain dissolved chlorine to disinfect it, dissolved minerals that make it "hard," and traces of many other substances that result from natural and human-initiated pollution. We encounter many other chemical solutions in our daily lives: air, shampoo, orange soda, coffee, gasoline, cough syrup, and many others.

A **solution** is a homogeneous mixture, a mixture in which the components are uniformly intermingled. This means that a sample from one part is the same as a sample from any other part. For example, the first sip of coffee is the same as the last sip.

The atmosphere that surrounds us is a gaseous solution containing $O_2(g)$, $N_2(g)$, and other gases randomly dispersed. Solutions can also be solids. For example, brass is a homogeneous mixture—a solution—of copper and zinc.

These examples illustrate that a solution can be a gas, a liquid, or a solid (see Table 15.1). The substance present in the largest amount is called the **solvent,** and the other substance or substances are called **solutes.** For example, when we dissolve a teaspoon of sugar in a glass of water, the sugar is the solute and the water is the solvent.

Aqueous solutions are solutions with water as the solvent. Because they are so important, in this chapter we will concentrate on the properties of aqueous solutions.

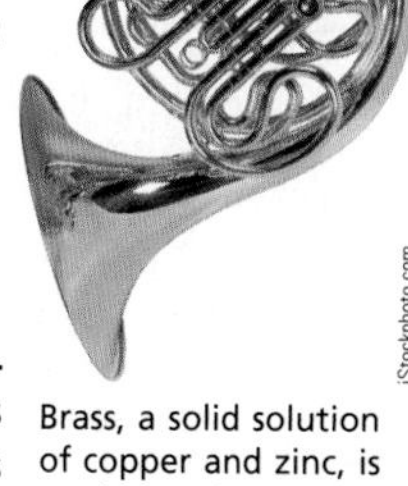

iStockphoto.com

Brass, a solid solution of copper and zinc, is used to make musical instruments and many other objects.

Test Bank: 1–4

Section 15.1

15.1 Solubility

OBJECTIVES: To understand the process of dissolving. • To learn why certain components dissolve in water.

What happens when you put a teaspoon of sugar in your iced tea and stir it, or when you add salt to water for cooking vegetables? Why do the sugar and salt "disappear" into the water? What does it mean when something dissolves—that is, when a solution forms?

Table 15.1 Various Types of Solutions

Example	State of Solution	Original State of Solute	State of Solvent
air, natural gas	gas	gas	gas
vodka in water, antifreeze in water	liquid	liquid	liquid
brass	solid	solid	solid
carbonated water (soda)	liquid	gas	liquid
seawater, sugar solution	liquid	solid	liquid

TEACHING TIPS

- Introduce the topic of solubility by using examples from daily life. Then move to the molecular level to help students understand how a substance dissolves.
- Entropy is also a driving force for dissolving.
- This is an excellent opportunity to repeat the conductivity demonstration used in earlier chapters. It will remind students that we can tell whether a solution contains ions by assessing its conductivity.

LABORATORY EXPERIMENT

A relevant laboratory experiment for this section is Experiment 23, Properties of Solutions, from *Introductory Chemistry in the Laboratory* by James Hall.

PowerLecture Video: Comparison of a Solution and a Mixture

Lecture Demonstration: 11.1, 11.3

DEMONSTRATION

You can show the immiscibility of oil and water by dissolving a little food coloring in 50 mL of water in a 25-mL flask and adding 50 mL of vegetable oil to the water. Stopper the flask and shake it. Allow the flask to stand. Two layers will result.

Lecture Demonstration: 11.8

DEMONSTRATION

Sum of the Parts

Materials Beaker, marbles (to fill the beaker), about 1/4 cup sand, about 1/2 cup sugar, 2-cup measuring cup, two 100-mL graduated cylinders, food coloring, about 75 mL of alcohol (isopropanol or ethanol, 70%–100%)

Preparation Mark the 100-mL line on the graduated cylinder with a grease pencil so it can be seen clearly by the class.

Presentation Begin with the beaker full of marbles. Ask students whether the beaker is full. Ask for predictions about what will happen if the sand is poured into the beaker of marbles, then do it. Discuss whether the beaker is now full. (If you don't mind the mess generated by wet sand, you can pour water into the sand/marble mixture until it is about to overflow.)

Next, turn to a new system. Place 1 cup of water into the 2-cup measuring cup. Ask the class what the final volume will be when 1/2 cup sugar is added to the measuring cup. Add the sugar and stir to dissolve all the sugar. Note the final volume. Discuss why the volume is not 2.5 cups but is more than 2 cups.

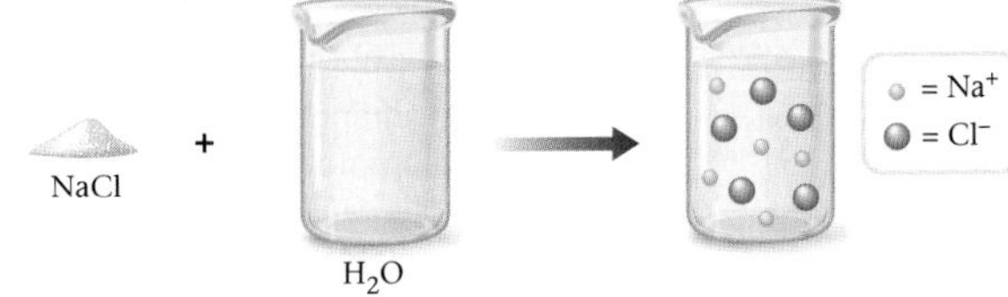

Figure 15.1 When solid sodium chloride dissolves, the ions are dispersed randomly throughout the solution.

We saw in Chapter 7 that when sodium chloride dissolves in water, the resulting solution conducts an electric current. This convinces us that the solution contains *ions* that can move (this is how the electric current is conducted). The dissolving of solid sodium chloride in water is represented in Figure 15.1. Notice that in the solid state the ions are packed closely together. However, when the solid dissolves, the ions are separated and dispersed throughout the solution. The strong ionic forces that hold the sodium chloride crystal together are overcome by the strong attractions between the ions and the polar water molecules. This process is represented in Figure 15.2. Notice that each polar water molecule orients itself in a way to maximize its attraction with a Cl^- or Na^+ ion. The negative end of a water molecule is attracted to a Na^+ ion, while the positive end is attracted to a Cl^- ion. The strong forces holding the positive and negative ions in the solid are replaced by strong water–ion interactions, and the solid dissolves (the ions disperse).

Cations are positive ions.
Anions are negative ions.

It is important to remember that when an ionic substance (such as a salt) dissolves in water, it breaks up into *individual* cations and anions, which are dispersed in the water. For instance, when ammonium nitrate, NH_4NO_3, dissolves in water, the resulting solution contains NH_4^+ and NO_3^- ions, which move around independently. This process can be represented as

$$NH_4NO_3(s) \xrightarrow{H_2O(l)} NH_4^+(aq) + NO_3^-(aq)$$

where (aq) indicates that the ions are surrounded by water molecules.

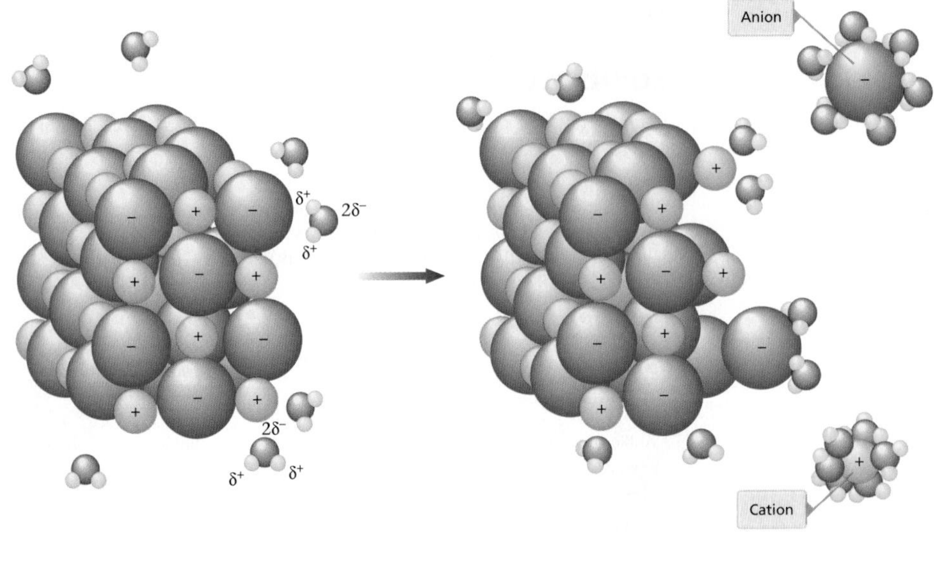

Figure 15.2 Polar water molecules interact with the positive and negative ions of a salt. These interactions replace the strong ionic forces holding the ions together in the undissolved solid, thus assisting in the dissolving process.

PowerLecture Animations:
Dissolution of a Salt (A)
Dissolution of a Salt (B)

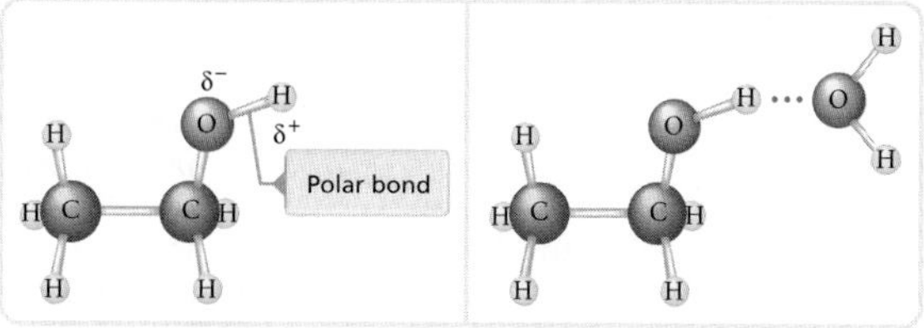

a
The ethanol molecule contains a polar O—H bond similar to those in the water molecule.

b
The polar water molecule interacts strongly with the polar O—H bond in ethanol.

Figure 15.3

A satellite photo of an oil spill in Tokyo Bay.

AP Photo/Science & Technology Ministry

Water also dissolves many nonionic substances. Sugar is one example of a nonionic solute that is very soluble in water. Another example is ethanol, C_2H_5OH. Wine, beer, and mixed drinks are aqueous solutions of ethanol (and other substances). Why is ethanol so soluble in water? The answer lies in the structure of the ethanol molecule (Figure 15.3a). The molecule contains a polar O—H bond like those in water, which makes it very compatible with water. Just as hydrogen bonds form among water molecules in pure water (see Figure 14.6), ethanol molecules can form hydrogen bonds with water molecules in a solution of the two. This is shown in Figure 15.3b.

The sugar molecule (common table sugar has the chemical name sucrose) is shown in Figure 15.4. Notice that this molecule has many polar O—H groups, each of which can hydrogen-bond to a water molecule. Because of the attractions between sucrose and water molecules, solid sucrose is quite soluble in water.

Many substances do not dissolve in water. For example, when petroleum leaks from a damaged tanker, it does not disperse uniformly in the water (does not dissolve) but rather floats on the surface because its density is less than that of water. Petroleum is a mixture of molecules like the one shown in Figure 15.5. Since carbon and hydrogen have very similar electronegativities, the bonding electrons are shared almost equally and the

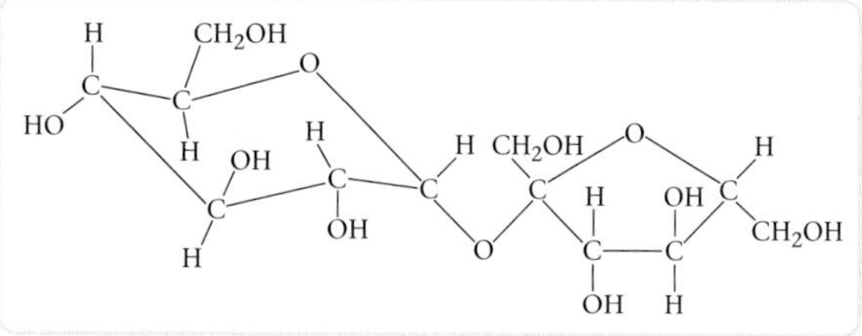

Figure 15.4
The structure of common table sugar (called sucrose). The large number of polar O—H groups in the molecule causes sucrose to be very soluble in water.

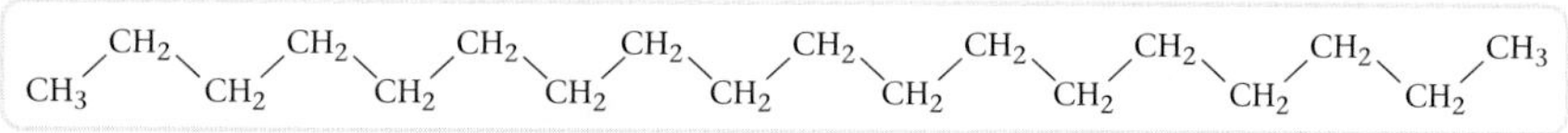

Figure 15.5
A molecule typical of those found in petroleum. The bonds are not polar.

Finally, ask what happens when liquids are mixed. Begin by measuring 50 mL of water into the 100-mL graduated cylinder. In a second graduated cylinder, measure 50 mL of water. Color one water sample blue with food coloring and the other yellow. Ask students to predict the final volume when the two water samples are mixed. Mix the two samples in one graduated cylinder. Record the volume. Discuss the color change. (Did a reaction occur? If not, why did the colors change? Did the volumes add?) Now repeat the experiment, this time using 50 mL of water and 50 mL of alcohol. Mix the two samples and note the volume. Discuss why the volume is less than the sum of the individual volumes.

Teaching Notes Addition of sugar or alcohol interferes with the attractions between water molecules. The molecules assume a more compact arrangement that reduces the volume to less than the sum of the independent volumes.

DEMONSTRATION

Dissolving Peanuts

Packing materials (known as "peanuts") are now made from both polystyrene and starch. The old polystyrene peanuts do not dissolve in water. You can, however, dissolve them in acetone by filling a large beaker full of peanuts and adding a little acetone to it. The peanuts will shrink down to a small gooey mass in the acetone. These peanuts are not particularly friendly to the environment, since most are discarded if they are not reused. Bring in a sample of "biodegradable" peanuts as well. They are made of starch and will dissolve in water. You can put some of these into a Ziploc bag, add water, and then seal. Shake the bag and watch the peanuts disappear into solution. Discuss how this result is helpful in cleaning up landfills.

TEACHING TIPS

- Students can remember "like dissolves like" but often have trouble figuring out which substances are alike and which are not. Use the structures of molecules such as CH_3OH and water to highlight similarities.
- Explaining why two nonpolar substances mix is difficult without bringing in the concept of entropy.

PowerLecture Video: Oil and Water Not Mixing

CHEMISTRY *IN* FOCUS

Water, Water, Everywhere, But . . .

Although more than two thirds of the earth is covered by water, the earth is facing increasing water shortages as the global population grows. Why is that? The problem is that most of the earth's water is ocean water, which contains such high concentrations of dissolved minerals that the ocean water can't be consumed by humans and it kills crops. Humans need "fresh water" to sustain their lives. This fresh water is ultimately derived from rain, which supplies water to our lakes, rivers, and underground aquifers. However, as our populations are expanding, our supply of useable water is running short.

Because the earth has so much "salt water," the obvious answer to the water problem would seem to be removing minerals from ocean water, a process called "desalination." We know how to desalinate seawater. By forcing seawater through special membranes that trap the dissolved ions but allow water molecules to pass through, we can produce useable water. This is the most common method for producing drinking water in the Middle East and other arid regions. Worldwide more than 13,000 desalination plants produce more than 12 billion gallons of useable water every day.

Given the widespread use of desalination in the world, why is the process not used very much in the United States? The answer is simple: cost. Because the desalination process requires high-pressure pumps to force seawater through the special membranes, a great deal of electricity is needed. Also, the special membranes are very expensive. Thus, desalination costs currently are 30% higher than the costs of traditional sources of water. However, as water supplies are becoming tighter, major users of water are more willing to bear the higher costs of desalination. Water-challenged California is a good example. Poseidon Resources Corporation recently signed a contract to build a $300 million desalination plant in Carlsbad, California, a city just north of San Diego. This facility will be the largest in the Western Hemisphere, producing enough water for 100,000 homes (50 million gallons per day). A schematic diagram of this plant is shown on the next page.

Poseidon is planning a second plant in Huntington Beach, California, and as many as 20 other similar projects are in the planning stages. This technology could go a long way toward satisfying our thirst in the future.

bonds are essentially nonpolar. The resulting molecule with its nonpolar bonds cannot form attractions to the polar water molecules and this prevents it from being soluble in water. This situation is represented in Figure 15.6.

Notice in Figure 15.6 that the water molecules in liquid water are associated with each other by hydrogen-bonding interactions. For a solute to dissolve in water, a "hole" must be made in the water structure for each solute

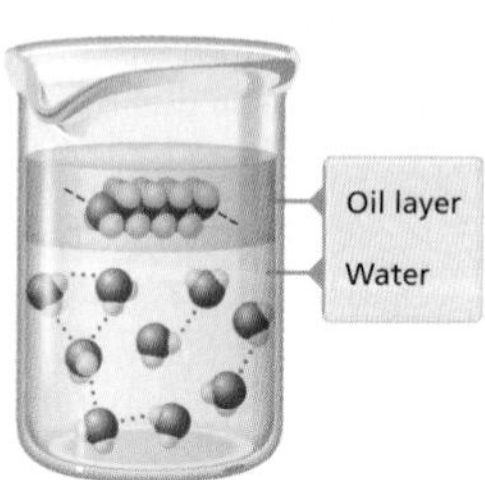

Figure 15.6 An oil layer floating on water. For a substance to dissolve, the water–water hydrogen bonds must be broken to make a "hole" for each solute particle. However, the water–water interactions will break only if they are replaced by similar strong interactions with the solute.

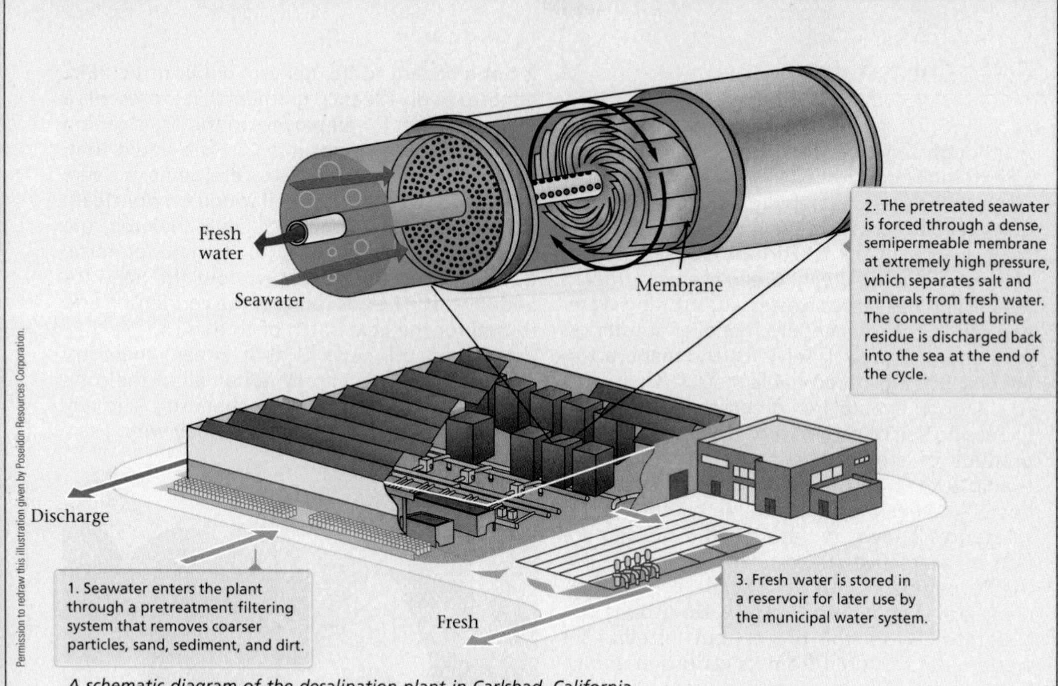
Fresh water
Seawater
Membrane
2. The pretreated seawater is forced through a dense, semipermeable membrane at extremely high pressure, which separates salt and minerals from fresh water. The concentrated brine residue is discharged back into the sea at the end of the cycle.
Discharge
1. Seawater enters the plant through a pretreatment filtering system that removes coarser particles, sand, sediment, and dirt.
Fresh
3. Fresh water is stored in a reservoir for later use by the municipal water system.
Permission to redraw this illustration given by Poseidon Resources Corporation.

A schematic diagram of the desalination plant in Carlsbad, California.

particle. This will occur only if the lost water–water interactions are replaced by similar water–solute interactions. In the case of sodium chloride, strong interactions occur between the polar water molecules and the Na^+ and Cl^- ions. This allows the sodium chloride to dissolve. In the case of ethanol or sucrose, hydrogen-bonding interactions can occur between the O—H groups on these molecules and water molecules, making these substances soluble as well. But oil molecules are not soluble in water, because the many water–water interactions that would have to be broken to make "holes" for these large molecules are not replaced by favorable water–solute interactions.

These considerations account for the observed behavior that "*like dissolves like.*" In other words, we observe that a given solvent usually dissolves solutes that have polarities similar to its own. For example, water dissolves most polar solutes, because the solute–solvent interactions formed in the solution are similar to the water–water interactions present in the pure solvent. Likewise, nonpolar solvents dissolve nonpolar solutes. For example, dry-cleaning solvents used for removing grease stains from clothes are nonpolar liquids. "Grease" is composed of nonpolar molecules, so a nonpolar solvent is needed to remove a grease stain.

Section 15.2

DEMONSTRATION

Saturating a Solution

You can illustrate the terms *unsaturated, saturated,* and *supersaturated* by making a supersaturated solution of $Na_2S_2O_3$ before class. To do so, place 300 mL of water in a 600-mL beaker and add $Na_2S_2O_3$ until crystals remain after stirring. Heat the solution to boiling and allow it to cool slowly, undisturbed. In class begin by adding about 1 g $Na_2S_2O_3$ to 300 mL of water in a 600-mL beaker. Tell students that this is an unsaturated solution. Next place 300 mL of water in another 600-mL beaker and add $Na_2S_2O_3$ until no more will dissolve. Tell students that this is a saturated solution. They can identify it easily since there are crystals on the bottom. Finally bring out your previously prepared beaker of supersaturated $Na_2S_2O_3$. Explain how you made the solution and then add a single crystal of $Na_2S_2O_3$ to the supersaturated solution. Observe the crystallization and then discuss the resulting solution with the class. Ask students whether the solution is now saturated. How can they tell?

 **Test Bank: 5, 6**

DEMONSTRATION

Concentrating on Concentration

Prepare a relatively concentrated solution of a colorful substance such as $CuSO_4$ or $Ni(NO_3)_2$. You can even use food coloring in water. In class make several dilutions of the solution in different beakers. Discuss the concentrations of the solutions relative to each other, showing students that a given solute can be concentrated with respect to one solution but dilute with respect to another solution. Use this idea to show that qualitative terms for concentration are useful, but that we need to have a way of determining the exact amount of solute in a solution.

CHEMISTRY *IN* FOCUS

Green Chemistry

Although some chemical industries have been culprits in the past for fouling the earth's environment, that situation is rapidly changing. In fact, a quiet revolution is sweeping through chemistry from academic labs to *Fortune* 500 companies. Chemistry is going green. *Green chemistry* means minimizing hazardous wastes, substituting water and other environmentally friendlier substances for traditional organic solvents, and manufacturing products out of recyclable materials.

A good example of green chemistry is the increasing use of carbon dioxide, one of the by-products of the combustion of fossil fuels. For example, the Dow Chemical Company is now using CO_2 rather than chlorofluorocarbons (CFCs; substances known to catalyze the decomposition of protective stratospheric ozone) to put the "sponginess" into polystyrene egg cartons, meat trays, and burger boxes. Dow does not generate CO_2 for this process but instead uses waste gases captured from its various manufacturing processes.

Another very promising use of carbon dioxide is as a replacement for the solvent perchloroethylene (PERC; $\mathrm{Cl_2C{=}CCl_2}$), now used by about 80% of dry cleaners in the United States. Chronic exposure to PERC has been linked to kidney and liver damage and cancer. Although PERC is not a hazard to the general public (little PERC adheres to dry-cleaned garments), it represents a major concern for employees in the dry-cleaning industry. At high pressures CO_2 is a liquid that, when used with appropriate detergents, is a very effective solvent for the soil found on dry-clean-only fabrics. When the pressure is lowered, the CO_2 immediately changes to its gaseous form, quickly drying the clothes without the need for added heat. The gas can then be condensed and reused for the next batch of clothes.

The good news is that green chemistry makes sense economically. When all of the costs are taken into account, green chemistry is usually cheaper chemistry as well. Everybody wins.

Michael Newman/PhotoEdit

The dry-cleaning agent PERC is a health concern for workers in the dry-cleaning industry.

15.2 Solution Composition: An Introduction

OBJECTIVE: To learn qualitative terms associated with the concentration of a solution.

Even for very soluble substances, there is a limit to how much solute can be dissolved in a given amount of solvent. For example, when you add sugar to a glass of water, the sugar rapidly disappears at first. However, as you continue to add more sugar, at some point the solid no longer dissolves but collects at the bottom of the glass. When a solution contains as much solute as will dissolve at that temperature, we say it is **saturated.** If a solid solute is

---

DEMONSTRATION

Supersaturation

Materials Heating unit, 500-mL Erlenmeyer flask, 100-mL beaker, sodium acetate trihydrate, baking dish (8″ × 8″ glass pan or smaller)

Preparation Measure 175 g of sodium acetate trihydrate. Place it in a 500-mL flask containing 50 mL of water. Heat the flask slowly on a heating unit (a water bath makes it easier to heat), swirling the flask occasionally until a clear, homogeneous solution is obtained. Remove the flask from the heat and invert a 100-mL beaker over the mouth of the flask. Allow the solution to cool undisturbed until it reaches room temperature (1–3 hours). *Note:* Be careful not to jar the solution or it will crystallize out. Cover the solution with parafilm until needed. Place 1 or 2 crystals of sodium acetate trihydrate in the baking dish.

Presentation Slowly pour the solution of supersaturated sodium trihydrate on the crystals in the baking

added to a solution already saturated with that solute, the added solid does not dissolve. A solution that has *not* reached the limit of solute that will dissolve in it is said to be **unsaturated.** When more solute is added to an unsaturated solution, it dissolves.

Although a chemical compound always has the same composition, a solution is a mixture and the amounts of the substances present can vary in different solutions. For example, coffee can be strong or weak. Strong coffee has more coffee dissolved in a given amount of water than weak coffee. To describe a solution completely, we must specify the amounts of solvent and solute. We sometimes use the qualitative terms *concentrated* and *dilute* to describe a solution. A relatively large amount of solute is dissolved in a **concentrated** solution (strong coffee is concentrated). A relatively small amount of solute is dissolved in a **dilute** solution (weak coffee is dilute).

Although these qualitative terms serve a useful purpose, we often need to know the exact amount of solute present in a given amount of solution. In the next several sections, we will consider various ways to describe the composition of a solution.

15.3 Solution Composition: Mass Percent

OBJECTIVE: To understand the concentration term *mass percent* and learn how to calculate it.

Describing the composition of a solution means specifying the amount of solute present in a given quantity of the solution. We typically give the amount of solute in terms of mass (number of grams) or in terms of moles. The quantity of solution is defined in terms of mass or volume.

One common way of describing a solution's composition is **mass percent** (sometimes called *weight percent*), which expresses the mass of solute present in a given mass of solution. The definition of mass percent is

The mass of the solution is the sum of the masses of the solute and the solvent.

$$\text{Mass percent} = \frac{\text{mass of solute}}{\text{mass of solution}} \times 100\%$$
$$= \frac{\text{grams of solute}}{\text{grams of solute} + \text{grams of solvent}} \times 100\%$$

For example, suppose a solution is prepared by dissolving 1.0 g of sodium chloride in 48 g of water. The solution has a mass of 49 g (48 g of H_2O plus 1.0 g of NaCl), and there is 1.0 g of solute (NaCl) present. The mass percent of solute, then, is

$$\frac{1.0 \text{ g solute}}{49 \text{ g solution}} \times 100\% = 0.020 \times 100\% = 2.0\% \text{ NaCl}$$

EXAMPLE 15.1 **Solution Composition: Calculating Mass Percent**

A solution is prepared by mixing 1.00 g of ethanol, C_2H_5OH, with 100.0 g of water. Calculate the mass percent of ethanol in this solution.

SOLUTION

Where Are We Going?

We want to determine the mass percent of a given ethanol solution.

dish. Crystallization occurs immediately, forming a tower of solid sodium acetate.

Teaching Notes After the demonstration is complete, the solid can be cut up with a spatula and returned to the flask. The supersaturated solution is restored by heating as in the preparation. The mixture can be used repeatedly if not contaminated. Small amounts of water may need to be added to compensate for evaporation losses.

PowerLecture Videos:
Precipitation of Lead Iodide: Saturated Solution
Dissolution of Nickel Chloride: Unsaturated Solution

Section 15.3

TEACHING TIPS

- Now is a good time to review the math concept of percent. Students often forget to calculate the mass of the entire solution, instead using the mass of the solvent and leaving out the mass of the solute. Be sure that they understand that a percent is the amount as a portion of the total (in this case the sum of the masses of the solvent and solute).
- A common example of a solution with a concentration expressed in mass percent is vinegar. You may want to bring a bottle to class to show a label giving a mass percent.

 **Test Bank: 7–11**

LABORATORY EXPERIMENT

A relevant laboratory experiment for this section is Experiment 26, Acid–Base Titrations, from *Introductory Chemistry in the Laboratory* by James Hall.

Additional Examples

Example 15.1

1. A solution is prepared by mixing 2.50 g of calcium chloride with 50.0 g of water. Calculate the mass percent of calcium chloride in this solution.

   4.76% $CaCl_2$

2. A 75.0-g sample of a solution is known to contain 23.8 g of glucose. Calculate the mass percent of glucose in this solution.

   31.7% glucose

What Do We Know?

- We have 1.00 g ethanol (C_2H_5OH) in 100.0 g water (H_2O).
- Mass percent = $\frac{\text{mass of solute}}{\text{mass of solution}} \times 100\%$.

How Do We Get There?

In this case we have 1.00 g of solute (ethanol) and 100.0 g of solvent (water). We now apply the definition of mass percent.

$$\begin{aligned}\text{Mass percent } C_2H_5OH &= \left(\frac{\text{grams of } C_2H_5OH}{\text{grams of solution}}\right) \times 100\% \\ &= \left(\frac{1.00 \text{ g } C_2H_5OH}{100.0 \text{ g } H_2O + 1.00 \text{ g } C_2H_5OH}\right) \times 100\% \\ &= \frac{1.00 \text{ g}}{101.0 \text{ g}} \times 100\% \\ &= 0.990\% \ C_2H_5OH\end{aligned}$$

REALITY CHECK The percent mass is just under 1%, which makes sense because we have 1.00 g of ethanol in a bit more than 100.0 g of solution.

Self Check

Answer to Self-Check Exercise 15.1

3.50%

Self-Check EXERCISE 15.1 A 135-g sample of seawater is evaporated to dryness, leaving 4.73 g of solid residue (the salts formerly dissolved in the seawater). Calculate the mass percent of solute present in the original seawater.

See Problems 15.15 and 15.16. ■

Additional Examples

Example 15.2

1. Vinegar is a solution of acetic acid in water and typically contains 5.00% acetic acid by mass. Calculate the mass of acetic acid in a 250.0-g sample of vinegar.

   12.5 g

2. Concentrated hydrochloric acid solution contains 37.2% by mass HCl. What mass of HCl is contained in 35.5 g of concentrated HCl?

   13.2 g

EXAMPLE 15.2 Solution Composition: Determining Mass of Solute

Although milk is not a true solution (it is really a suspension of tiny globules of fat, protein, and other substrates in water), it does contain a dissolved sugar called lactose. Cow's milk typically contains 4.5% by mass of lactose, $C_{12}H_{22}O_{11}$. Calculate the mass of lactose present in 175 g of milk.

SOLUTION

Where Are We Going?

We want to determine the mass of lactose present in 175 g of milk.

What Do We Know?

- We have 175 g of milk.
- Milk contains 4.5% by mass of lactose, $C_{12}H_{22}O_{11}$.
- Mass percent = $\frac{\text{mass of solute}}{\text{mass of solution}} \times 100\%$.

How Do We Get There?

Using the definition of mass percent, we have

$$\text{Mass percent} = \frac{\text{grams of solute}}{\text{grams of solution}} \times 100\%$$

We now substitute the quantities we know:

$$\text{Mass percent} = \frac{\overset{\text{Mass of lactose}}{\text{grams of solute}}}{\underset{\text{Mass of milk}}{175\text{ g}}} \times 100\% = \overset{\text{Mass percent}}{4.5\%}$$

We now solve for grams of solute by multiplying both sides by 175 g,

$$\cancel{175\text{ g}} \times \frac{\text{grams of solute}}{\cancel{175\text{ g}}} \times 100\% = 4.5\% \times 175\text{ g}$$

and then dividing both sides by 100%,

$$\text{Grams of solute} \times \frac{\cancel{100\%}}{\cancel{100\%}} = \frac{4.5\cancel{\%}}{100\cancel{\%}} \times 175\text{ g}$$

to give

$$\text{Grams of solute} = 0.045 \times 175\text{ g} = 7.9\text{ g lactose}$$

Self-Check EXERCISE 15.2 What mass of water must be added to 425 g of formaldehyde to prepare a 40.0% (by mass) solution of formaldehyde? This solution, called formalin, is used to preserve biological specimens.

HINT: Substitute the known quantities into the definition for mass percent, and then solve for the unknown quantity (mass of solvent).

See Problems 15.17 and 15.18. ■

Self Check

Answer to Self-Check Exercise 15.2

638 g water

Test Bank: 12–39, 50, 64, 65, 69–72, 74

15.4 Solution Composition: Molarity

OBJECTIVES: To understand molarity. • To learn to use molarity to calculate the number of moles of solute present.

When a solution is described in terms of mass percent, the amount of solution is given in terms of its mass. However, it is often more convenient to measure the volume of a solution than to measure its mass. Because of this, chemists often describe a solution in terms of concentration. We define the *concentration* of a solution as the amount of solute in a *given volume* of solution. The most commonly used expression of concentration is **molarity (*M*).** Molarity describes the amount of solute in moles and the volume of the solution in liters. Molarity is *the number of moles of solute per volume of solution in liters*. That is

$$M = \text{molarity} = \frac{\text{moles of solute}}{\text{liters of solution}} = \frac{\text{mol}}{\text{L}}$$

A solution that is 1.0 molar (written as 1.0 M) contains 1.0 mole of solute per liter of solution.

Section 15.4

TEACHING TIPS

- Students need to understand the importance of calculations involving molarity. This concept will be used in solution stoichiometry, titration, and acid–base calculations.
- Emphasize that molarity is an important term because we are often interested in moles of reactants or products. Let students know that they will be performing stoichiometric calculations with solutions and remind them that they need to work in units of moles.
- Stress that the definition for molarity involves two amounts: the number of moles of solute and the volume of solution. Students need to understand that molarity is a ratio.

MATH MISCONCEPTION

Molarity

Molarity, like density (and molar mass), is a ratio of two numbers. Students often believe that if, for example, solution A has a greater concentration than solution B, then solution A must have a greater number of moles of solute than solution B. This is not necessarily the case. For example, present the following situation:

Solution A: dissolve 5 moles of sugar in 10 L of solution: concentration = 0.5 M

Solution B: dissolve 1 mole of sugar in 1 L of solution: concentration = 1.0 M

Solution B has fewer moles of sugar, but a greater concentration than solution A.

Additional Examples

Example 15.3

1. Calculate the molarity of a solution prepared by dissolving 15.6 g of solid KBr in enough water to make 1.25 L of solution.

   0.105 *M*

2. Calculate the molarity of a solution prepared by dissolving 250.0 g of solid $Ca(NO_3)_2$ in enough water to make 2.50 L of solution.

   0.609 *M*

Additional Examples

Example 15.4

1. Calculate the molarity of a solution prepared by dissolving 2.80 g of solid NaCl in enough water to make 135 mL of solution.

   0.355 *M*

2. Calculate the molarity of a solution prepared by dissolving 8.55 g of $MgCl_2$ in enough water to make 65.0 L of solution.

   1.38 *M*

EXAMPLE 15.3 Solution Composition: Calculating Molarity, I

Calculate the molarity of a solution prepared by dissolving 11.5 g of solid NaOH in enough water to make 1.50 L of solution.

SOLUTION

Where Are We Going?

We want to determine the concentration (*M*) of a solution of NaOH.

What Do We Know?

- 11.5 g of NaOH is dissolved in 1.50 L of solution.
- $M = \frac{\text{moles of solute}}{\text{liters of solution}}$.

What Information Do We Need?

- We need to know the number of moles of NaOH in 11.5 g NaOH.

How Do We Get There?

We have the mass (in grams) of solute, so we need to convert the mass of solute to moles (using the molar mass of NaOH). Then we can divide the number of moles by the volume in liters.

Mass of solute → (Use molar mass) → Moles of solute → (Moles / Liters) → Molarity

We compute the number of moles of solute, using the molar mass of NaOH (40.0 g).

$$11.5 \text{ g NaOH} \times \frac{1 \text{ mol NaOH}}{40.0 \text{ g NaOH}} = 0.288 \text{ mol NaOH}$$

Then we divide by the volume of the solution in liters.

$$\text{Molarity} = \frac{\text{moles of solute}}{\text{liters of solution}} = \frac{0.288 \text{ mol NaOH}}{1.50 \text{ L solution}} = 0.192\ M \text{ NaOH}$$ ■

EXAMPLE 15.4 Solution Composition: Calculating Molarity, II

Calculate the molarity of a solution prepared by dissolving 1.56 g of gaseous HCl into enough water to make 26.8 mL of solution.

SOLUTION

Where Are We Going?

We want to determine the concentration (*M*) of a solution of HCl.

What Do We Know?

- 1.56 g of HCl is dissolved in 26.8 mL of solution.
- $M = \frac{\text{moles of solute}}{\text{liters of solution}}$.

What Information Do We Need?

- We need to know the number of moles of HCl in 1.56 g.
- We need to know the volume of the solution in liters.

How Do We Get There?

We must change 1.56 g of HCl to moles of HCl, and then we must change 26.8 mL to liters (because molarity is defined in terms of liters). First we calculate the number of moles of HCl (molar mass = 36.5 g).

$$1.56 \text{ g HCl} \times \frac{1 \text{ mol HCl}}{36.5 \text{ g HCl}} = 0.0427 \text{ mol HCl}$$

$$= 4.27 \times 10^{-2} \text{ mol HCl}$$

Next we change the volume of the solution from milliliters to liters, using the equivalence statement 1 L = 1000 mL, which gives the appropriate conversion factor.

$$26.8 \text{ mL} \times \frac{1 \text{ L}}{1000 \text{ mL}} = 0.0268 \text{ L}$$

$$= 2.68 \times 10^{-2} \text{ L}$$

Finally, we divide the moles of solute by the liters of solution.

$$\text{Molarity} = \frac{4.27 \times 10^{-2} \text{ mol HCl}}{2.68 \times 10^{-2} \text{ L solution}} = 1.59\ M \text{ HCl}$$

Self-Check EXERCISE 15.3 Calculate the molarity of a solution prepared by dissolving 1.00 g of ethanol, C_2H_5OH, in enough water to give a final volume of 101 mL.

See Problems 15.37 through 15.42. ■

It is important to realize that the description of a solution's composition may not accurately reflect the true chemical nature of the solute as it is present in the dissolved state. Solute concentration is always written in terms of the form of the solute *before* it dissolves. For example, describing a solution as 1.0 *M* NaCl means that the solution was prepared by dissolving 1.0 mole of solid NaCl in enough water to make 1.0 L of solution; it does not mean that the solution contains 1.0 mole of NaCl units. Actually the solution contains 1.0 mole of Na^+ ions and 1.0 mole of Cl^- ions. That is, it contains 1.0 *M* Na^+ and 1.0 *M* Cl^-.

EXAMPLE 15.5 Solution Composition: Calculating Ion Concentration from Molarity

Remember, ionic compounds separate into the component ions when they dissolve in water.

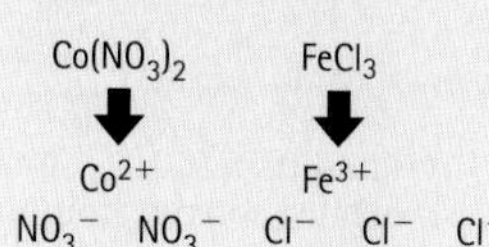

Give the concentrations of all the ions in each of the following solutions:

a. 0.50 *M* $Co(NO_3)_2$

b. 1 *M* $FeCl_3$

SOLUTION

a. When solid $Co(NO_3)_2$ dissolves, it produces ions as follows:

$$Co(NO_3)_2(s) \xrightarrow{H_2O(l)} Co^{2+}(aq) + 2NO_3^-(aq)$$

TEACHING TIP

Beginning students often struggle when asked to determine the concentration of ions in a solution. Emphasize that students should write an equation for the dissociation of the ions in solution and use the mole ratios in the balanced equation to determine the concentrations of the ions. For example, a 1 *M* solution of $CaCl_2$ contains Ca^{2+} ions in a concentration of 1 *M* and a Cl^- ion concentration of 2 *M* since two moles of chloride ion are found in the solution for each mole of calcium ion.

Self Check

Answer to Self-Check Exercise 15.3

0.215 *M*

Additional Examples

Example 15.5

Give the concentrations of all ions in each of the following solutions:

1. 1.20 *M* Na_2SO_4

   2.40 *M* Na^+,
   1.20 *M* SO_4^{2-}

2. 0.750 *M* K_2CrO_4

   1.50 *M* K^+,
   0.750 *M* CrO_4^{2-}

TEACHING TIPS

- When students are calculating ion concentrations from molarity, have them draw microscopic pictures of the solutions to emphasize the relative numbers of each ion.
- Some students may have difficulty rearranging the definition of molarity (M = moles of solute/volume solution) to solve for the appropriate variable. You may want to show how this is done by working some examples with the students.

Self Check

Answers to Self-Check Exercise 15.4

a. 0.20 M Na^+, 0.10 M CO_3^{2-}

b. 0.20 M Al^{3+}, 0.30 M SO_4^{2-}

Additional Examples

Example 15.6

1. How many moles of Na^+ ions are present in 42.0 mL of a 0.350 M NaCl solution?

   1.47×10^{-2} mol Na^+

2. How many moles of Na^+ ions are present in 42.0 mL of a 0.350 M Na_3PO_4 solution?

   4.41×10^{-2} mol Na^+

which we can represent as

$$1 \text{ mol } Co(NO_3)_2(s) \xrightarrow{H_2O(l)} 1 \text{ mol } Co^{2+}(aq) + 2 \text{ mol } NO_3^-(aq)$$

Therefore, a solution that is 0.50 M $Co(NO_3)_2$ contains 0.50 M Co^{2+} and (2×0.50) M NO_3^-, or 1.0 M NO_3^-.

b. When solid $FeCl_3$ dissolves, it produces ions as follows:

$$FeCl_3(s) \xrightarrow{H_2O(l)} Fe^{3+}(aq) + 3Cl^-(aq)$$

or

$$1 \text{ mol } FeCl_3(s) \xrightarrow{H_2O(l)} 1 \text{ mol } Fe^{3+}(aq) + 3 \text{ mol } Cl^-(aq)$$

A solution that is 1 M $FeCl_3$ contains 1 M Fe^{3+} ions and 3 M Cl^- ions.

Self-Check EXERCISE 15.4 Give the concentrations of the ions in each of the following solutions:

a. 0.10 M Na_2CO_3

b. 0.010 M $Al_2(SO_4)_3$

See Problems 15.49 and 15.50. ■

MATH SKILL BUILDER

$M = \frac{\text{moles of solute}}{\text{liters of solution}}$

Liters × M ➡ Moles of solute

Often we need to determine the number of moles of solute present in a given volume of a solution of known molarity. To do this, we use the definition of molarity. When we multiply the molarity of a solution by the volume (in liters), we get the moles of solute present in that sample:

$$\text{Liters of solution} \times \text{molarity} = \cancel{\text{liters of solution}} \times \frac{\text{moles of solute}}{\cancel{\text{liters of solution}}} = \text{moles of solute}$$

EXAMPLE 15.6

Solution Composition: Calculating Number of Moles from Molarity

Tom Pantages

A solution of cobalt(II) nitrate.

How many moles of Ag^+ ions are present in 25 mL of a 0.75 M $AgNO_3$ solution?

SOLUTION

Where Are We Going?

We want to determine the number of moles of Ag^+ in a solution.

What Do We Know?

- We have 25 mL of 0.75 M $AgNO_3$.
- $M = \frac{\text{moles of solute}}{\text{liters of solution}}$.

How Do We Get There?

A 0.75 M $AgNO_3$ solution contains 0.75 M Ag^+ ions and 0.75 M NO_3^- ions. Next we must express the volume in liters. That is, we must convert from mL to L.

$$25 \text{ mL} \times \frac{1 \text{ L}}{1000 \text{ mL}} = 0.025 \text{ L} = 2.5 \times 10^{-2} \text{ L}$$

Now we multiply the volume times the molarity.

$$2.5 \times 10^{-2} \text{ L solution} \times \frac{0.75 \text{ mol Ag}^+}{\text{L solution}} = 1.9 \times 10^{-2} \text{ mol Ag}^+$$

Self-Check EXERCISE 15.5 Calculate the number of moles of Cl^- ions in 1.75 L of 1.0×10^{-3} M $AlCl_3$.

See Problems 15.49 and 15.50. ■

A **standard solution** is a solution whose *concentration is accurately known*. When the appropriate solute is available in pure form, a standard solution can be prepared by weighing out a sample of solute, transferring it completely to a *volumetric flask* (a flask of accurately known volume), and adding enough solvent to bring the volume up to the mark on the neck of the flask. This procedure is illustrated in Figure 15.7.

EXAMPLE 15.7 Solution Composition: Calculating Mass from Molarity

To analyze the alcohol content of a certain wine, a chemist needs 1.00 L of an aqueous 0.200 M $K_2Cr_2O_7$ (potassium dichromate) solution. How much solid $K_2Cr_2O_7$ (molar mass = 294.2 g) must be weighed out to make this solution?

SOLUTION

Where Are We Going?

We want to determine the mass of $K_2Cr_2O_7$ needed to make a given solution.

What Do We Know?

- We want 1.00 L of 0.200 M $K_2Cr_2O_7$.

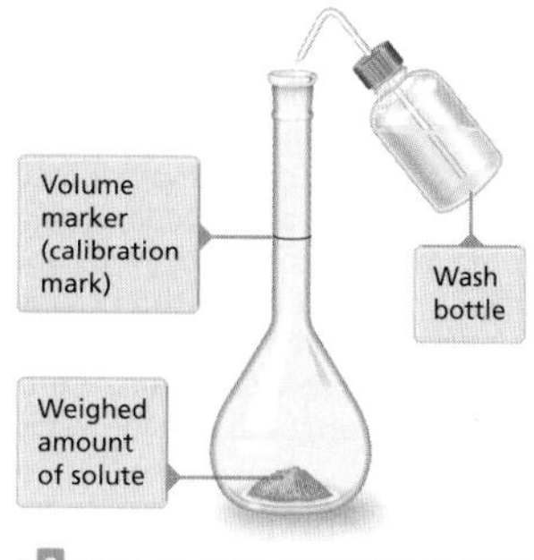

a *Put a weighed amount of a substance (the solute) into the volumetric flask, and add a small quantity of water.*

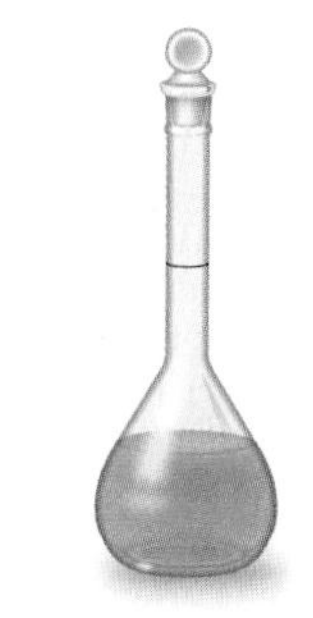

b *Dissolve the solid in the water by gently swirling the flask (with the stopper in place).*

c *Add more water (with gentle swirling) until the level of the solution just reaches the mark etched on the neck of the flask. Then mix the solution thoroughly by inverting the flask several times.*

Figure 15.7
Steps involved in the preparation of a standard aqueous solution.

DEMONSTRATION

Prepare a standard solution of a colorful compound in class to illustrate the proper method for making solutions. Good examples are potassium permanganate, copper sulfate, and copper nitrate. Use a volumetric flask, balance, and distilled water. This standard solution can then be used to illustrate making dilutions in Section 15.5.

Self Check

Answer to Self-Check Exercise 15.5

5.3×10^{-3} mol Cl^-

Additional Examples

Example 15.7

1. What mass of $NaNO_3$ is required to make 2.50 L of a 0.150 M solution of $NaNO_3$?

   31.9 g

2. What mass of $(NH_4)_2SO_4$ is required to make 1.25 L of a 0.250 M solution of $(NH_4)_2SO_4$?

   41.3 g

PowerLecture Video: Preparation of an Aqueous Solution by Direct Addition

- The molar mass of $K_2Cr_2O_7$ is 294.2 g/mol.
- $M = \frac{\text{moles of solute}}{\text{liters of solution}}$.

How Do We Get There?

We need to calculate the number of grams of solute ($K_2Cr_2O_7$) present (and thus the mass needed to make the solution). First we determine the number of moles of $K_2Cr_2O_7$ present by multiplying the volume (in liters) by the molarity.

Liters × *M* ➡ Moles of solute

$$1.00 \text{ L solution} \times \frac{0.200 \text{ mol } K_2Cr_2O_7}{\text{L solution}} = 0.200 \text{ mol } K_2Cr_2O_7$$

Then we convert the moles of $K_2Cr_2O_7$ to grams, using the molar mass of $K_2Cr_2O_7$ (294.2 g).

$$0.200 \text{ mol } K_2Cr_2O_7 \times \frac{294.2 \text{ g } K_2Cr_2O_7}{\text{mol } K_2Cr_2O_7} = 58.8 \text{ g } K_2Cr_2O_7$$

Therefore, to make 1.00 L of 0.200 *M* $K_2Cr_2O_7$, the chemist must weigh out 58.8 g of $K_2Cr_2O_7$ and dissolve it in enough water to make 1.00 L of solution. This is most easily done by using a 1.00-L volumetric flask (see Figure 15.7).

Self Check

Answer to Self-Check Exercise 15.6

930 g formaldehyde

Self-Check EXERCISE 15.6 Formalin is an aqueous solution of formaldehyde, HCHO, used as a preservative for biologic specimens. How many grams of formaldehyde must be used to prepare 2.5 L of 12.3 *M* formalin?

See Problems 15.51 and 15.52. ■

Test Bank: 40–45, 53, 62, 73

15.5 Dilution

Section 15.5

OBJECTIVE: To learn to calculate the concentration of a solution made by diluting a stock solution.

TEACHING TIP

The key concept in this section is the idea that the concentrated solution contains the same number of moles of solute as the dilute solution. Students are confused about this idea because they think of *dilute* as containing less solute than *concentrated.* In this case the solution has increased in volume but the number of moles of solute has remained the same. Stress that concentration is the amount of solute per volume available.

To save time and space in the laboratory, solutions that are routinely used are often purchased or prepared in concentrated form (called *stock solutions*). Water (or another solvent) is then added to achieve the molarity desired for a particular solution. The process of adding more solvent to a solution is called **dilution.** For example, the common laboratory acids are purchased as concentrated solutions and diluted with water as they are needed. A typical dilution calculation involves determining how much water must be added to an amount of stock solution to achieve a solution of the desired concentration. The key to doing these calculations is to remember that *only water is added in the dilution.* The amount of solute in the final, more dilute solution is the *same* as the amount of solute in the original, concentrated stock solution. That is,

The molarities of stock solutions of the common concentrated acids are:

Sulfuric (H_2SO_4)	18 *M*
Nitric (HNO_3)	16 *M*
Hydrochloric (HCl)	12 *M*

Moles of solute after dilution = moles of solute before dilution

Dilution with water doesn't alter the number of moles of solute present.

The number of moles of solute stays the same but more water is added, increasing the volume, so the molarity decreases.

$$M = \frac{\text{moles of solute}}{\text{volume (L)}}$$

Remains constant (moles of solute)
Decreases (*M*)
Increases (water added) (volume)

PowerLecture Video: Dilution

For example, suppose we want to prepare 500. mL of 1.00 *M* acetic acid, $HC_2H_3O_2$, from a 17.5 *M* stock solution of acetic acid. What volume of the stock solution is required?

The first step is to determine the number of moles of acetic acid needed in the final solution. We do this by multiplying the volume of the solution by its molarity.

$$\text{Volume of dilute solution (liters)} \times \text{molarity of dilute solution} = \text{moles of solute present}$$

The number of moles of solute present in the more dilute solution equals the number of moles of solute that must be present in the more concentrated (stock) solution, because this is the only source of acetic acid.

Because molarity is defined in terms of liters, we must first change 500. mL to liters and then multiply the volume (in liters) by the molarity.

MATH SKILL BUILDER
Liters × *M* ➡ Moles of solute

$$\underset{V_{\text{dilute solution}}\ (\text{in mL})}{500.\ \cancel{\text{mL solution}}} \times \underset{\text{Convert mL to L}}{\frac{1\ \text{L solution}}{1000\ \cancel{\text{mL solution}}}} = 0.500\ \text{L solution}$$

$$0.500\ \cancel{\text{L solution}} \times \underset{M_{\text{dilute solution}}}{\frac{1.00\ \text{mol}\ HC_2H_3O_2}{\cancel{\text{L solution}}}} = 0.500\ \text{mol}\ HC_2H_3O_2$$

Now we need to find the volume of 17.5 *M* acetic acid that contains 0.500 mole of $HC_2H_3O_2$. We will call this unknown volume *V*. Because volume × molarity = moles, we have

$$V\ (\text{in liters}) \times \frac{17.5\ \text{mol}\ HC_2H_3O_2}{\text{L solution}} = 0.500\ \text{mol}\ HC_2H_3O_2$$

Solving for V $\left(\text{by dividing both sides by } \frac{17.5\ \text{mol}}{\text{L solution}}\right)$ gives

$$V = \frac{0.500\ \cancel{\text{mol}\ HC_2H_3O_2}}{\frac{17.5\ \cancel{\text{mol}\ HC_2H_3O_2}}{\text{L solution}}} = 0.0286\ \text{L, or 28.6 mL, of solution}$$

Therefore, to make 500. mL of a 1.00 *M* acetic acid solution, we take 28.6 mL of 17.5 *M* acetic acid and dilute it to a total volume of 500. mL. This process is illustrated in Figure 15.8. Because the moles of solute remain the same before and after dilution, we can write

$$\underset{\text{Initial Conditions}}{\underset{\text{Molarity before dilution}}{M_1} \times \underset{\text{Volume before dilution}}{V_1}} = \text{moles of solute} = \underset{\text{Final Conditions}}{\underset{\text{Molarity after dilution}}{M_2} \times \underset{\text{Volume after dilution}}{V_2}}$$

We can check our calculations on acetic acid by showing that $M_1 \times V_1 = M_2 \times V_2$. In the above example, $M_1 = 17.5\ M$, $V_1 = 0.0286$ L, $V_2 = 0.500$ L, and $M_2 = 1.00\ M$, so

$$M_1 \times V_1 = 17.5\ \frac{\text{mol}}{\text{L}} \times 0.0286\ \text{L} = 0.500\ \text{mol}$$

$$M_2 \times V_2 = 1.00\ \frac{\text{mol}}{\text{L}} \times 0.500\ \text{L} = 0.500\ \text{mol}$$

and therefore

$$M_1 \times V_1 = M_2 \times V_2$$

This shows that the volume (V_2) we calculated is correct.

DEMONSTRATION

If you did the demonstration in Section 15.4, use the standard solution you prepared. If you did not, then make a colored solution before class by putting food coloring in water. Arbitrarily choose a concentration for the food-coloring solution at the beginning of the demonstration. Begin with the concentration of your standard or food-coloring solution. Use a pipet to transfer 1 mL of the standard solution to a small container. Add 9 mL water to the solution and have students calculate the concentration of the new solution. Repeat the process, using the new solution to create a more dilute solution for successive dilutions. *Note:* You can do this demonstration on the overhead projector by using a well tray and drops of solution (measured with a Beral pipet). Even when the color is no longer evident, the solution contains solute in a concentration that can be calculated.

TEACHING TIP

The formula $M_1V_1 = M_2V_2$ works well but some students memorize it without understanding why it works. Emphasize what each variable means, and point out that the formula works only because the number of moles of solute is the same both before and after dilution. Consider asking a question in which students are asked to solve for the volume of water that must be added to achieve a dilution (see, for example, the second problem in the Additional Examples for Example 15.8). Students will need to think about what they are solving for instead of just plugging numbers into an equation.

PowerLecture Video: Creating a Solution: Dilution Method

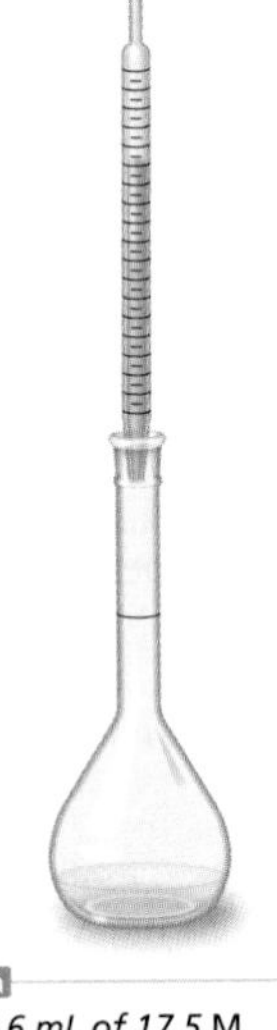

a 28.6 mL of 17.5 M acetic acid solution is transferred to a volumetric flask that already contains some water.

b Water is added to the flask (with swirling) to bring the volume to the calibration mark, and the solution is mixed by inverting the flask several times.

c The resulting solution is 1.00 M acetic acid.

Figure 15.8

Additional Examples

Example 15.8

1. What volume of 19 M NaOH must be used to prepare 1.0 L of a 0.15 M NaOH solution?

   7.9 mL

2. What volume of water is needed to prepare 500.0 mL of a 0.250 M $Ca(NO_3)_2$ solution from a 5.00 M $Ca(NO_3)_2$ solution?

   475 mL

EXAMPLE 15.8 Calculating Concentrations of Diluted Solutions

What volume of 16 M sulfuric acid must be used to prepare 1.5 L of a 0.10 M H_2SO_4 solution?

Tom Pantages

Approximate dilutions can be carried out using a calibrated beaker. Here, concentrated sulfuric acid is being added to water to make a dilute solution.

SOLUTION

Where Are We Going?

We want to determine the volume of sulfuric acid needed to prepare a given volume of a more dilute solution.

What Do We Know?

Initial Conditions (concentrated)	Final Conditions (dilute)
$M_1 = 16\ \frac{\text{mol}}{\text{L}}$	$M_2 = 0.10\ \frac{\text{mol}}{\text{L}}$
$V_1 = ?$	$V_2 = 1.5\ \text{L}$

$$\text{Moles of solute} = M_1 \times V_1 = M_2 \times V_2$$

How Do We Get There?

We can solve the equation

$$M_1 \times V_1 = M_2 \times V_2$$

for V_1 by dividing both sides by M_1,

$$\frac{\cancel{M_1} \times V_1}{\cancel{M_1}} = \frac{M_2 \times V_2}{M_1}$$

to give

$$V_1 = \frac{M_2 \times V_2}{M_1}$$

Now we substitute the known values of M_2, V_2, and M_1.

$$V_1 = \frac{\left(0.10 \frac{\cancel{mol}}{\cancel{L}}\right)(1.5\ L)}{16 \frac{\cancel{mol}}{\cancel{L}}} = 9.4 \times 10^{-3}\ L$$

$$9.4 \times 10^{-3}\ \cancel{L} \times \frac{1000\ mL}{1\ \cancel{L}} = 9.4\ mL$$

It is always best to add concentrated acid to water, not water to the acid. That way, if any splashing occurs accidentally, it is dilute acid that splashes.

Therefore, $V_1 = 9.4 \times 10^{-3}$ L, or 9.4 mL. To make 1.5 L of 0.10 M H_2SO_4 using 16 M H_2SO_4, we must take 9.4 mL of the concentrated acid and dilute it with water to a final volume of 1.5 L. The correct way to do this is to add the 9.4 mL of acid to about 1 L of water and then dilute to 1.5 L by adding more water.

Self-Check EXERCISE 15.7 What volume of 12 M HCl must be taken to prepare 0.75 L of 0.25 M HCl?

See Problems 15.57 and 15.58. ■

15.6 Stoichiometry of Solution Reactions

OBJECTIVE: To understand the strategy for solving stoichiometric problems for solution reactions.

Because so many important reactions occur in solution, it is important to be able to do stoichiometric calculations for solution reactions. The principles needed to perform these calculations are very similar to those developed in Chapter 9. It is helpful to think in terms of the following steps:

Steps for Solving Stoichiometric Problems Involving Solutions

Step 1 Write the balanced equation for the reaction. For reactions involving ions, it is best to write the net ionic equation.

Step 2 Calculate the moles of reactants.

Step 3 Determine which reactant is limiting.

Step 4 Calculate the moles of other reactants or products, as required.

Step 5 Convert to grams or other units, if required.

See Section 7.3 for a discussion of net ionic equations.

Self Check

Answer to Self-Check Exercise 15.7

16 mL

Test Bank: 46–49, 51, 52, 54, 63, 66–68

Section 15.6

TEACHING TIPS

- Begin this section with a review of basic stoichiometry. The steps outlined in the text form the basis for a review of the principles involved in solving stoichiometry problems.
- Assure students that the concepts involved in "solution stoichiometry" problems are the same as those for other stoichiometry problems they have done in the past. In all cases we use the mole ratios in the balanced chemical equation to convert from moles of one substance to moles of another. In Chapter 9 we converted from mass to moles using the molar mass. In Chapter 13 we used the ideal gas law equation to convert conditions of a gas (P, V, T) to moles. Here we convert from volume of solution to moles by using the concentration of the solution.
- Remind students to balance all chemical equations before beginning a problem.
- Now is a good time to review writing net ionic equations. Using a net ionic equation simplifies the work done in solving these solution problems. It also focuses students' attention on the species reacting and, therefore, on what is being asked.

LABORATORY EXPERIMENT

A relevant laboratory experiment for this section is Experiment 24, Determination of Calcium in Calcium Supplements, from *Introductory Chemistry in the Laboratory* by James Hall.

Additional Examples

Example 15.9

1. Calculate the mass of solid sodium sulfate that must be added to 250.0 mL of a 0.200 *M* solution of barium nitrate to precipitate all of the barium ions in the form of barium sulfate. Also calculate the mass of barium sulfate formed.

   7.10 g Na_2SO_4 required; 11.7 g $BaSO_4$ produced

2. Calculate the mass of NaI that must be added to 425.0 mL of a 0.100 *M* $Pb(NO_3)_2$ solution to precipitate all of the Pb^{2+} ions as PbI_2. Also calculate the mass of PbI_2 formed.

   12.7 g NaI required; 19.6 g PbI_2 produced

DEMONSTRATION

When working problems in solution stoichiometry, students find it more interesting if you can show them the reaction in class. Before class, make dilute solutions of the reactants for the examples you plan to present. For each example, after you write the reactants on the board, stop and mix the chemicals together. Have students name the products and complete the equation. Balance the equation and proceed with the solution stoichiometry problem. This provides an excellent opportunity for students to be involved actively in a review of earlier topics while solving a new problem.

EXAMPLE 15.9 Solution Stoichiometry: Calculating Mass of Reactants and Products

Calculate the mass of solid NaCl that must be added to 1.50 L of a 0.100 *M* $AgNO_3$ solution to precipitate all of the Ag^+ ions in the form of AgCl. Calculate the mass of AgCl formed.

SOLUTION

Where Are We Going?

We want to determine the mass of NaCl.

What Do We Know?

- We have 1.50 L of a 0.100 *M* $AgNO_3$ solution.

What Information Do We Need?

- We need the balanced equation between $AgNO_3$ and NaCl.
- We need the molar mass of NaCl.

How Do We Get There?

Step 1 *Write the balanced equation for the reaction.*
When added to the $AgNO_3$ solution (which contains Ag^+ and NO_3^- ions), the solid NaCl dissolves to yield Na^+ and Cl^- ions. Solid AgCl forms according to the following balanced net ionic reaction:

$$Ag^+(aq) + Cl^-(aq) \rightarrow AgCl(s)$$

This reaction was discussed in Section 7.2.

Step 2 *Calculate the moles of reactants.*
In this case we must add enough Cl^- ions to just react with all the Ag^+ ions present, so we must calculate the moles of Ag^+ ions present in 1.50 L of a 0.100 *M* $AgNO_3$ solution. (Remember that a 0.100 *M* $AgNO_3$ solution contains 0.100 *M* Ag^+ ions and 0.100 *M* NO_3^- ions.)

MATH SKILL BUILDER
Liters × *M* ➡ Moles of solute

$$1.50\ \cancel{L} \times \frac{0.100 \text{ mol } Ag^+}{\cancel{L}} = 0.150 \text{ mol } Ag^+$$

Moles of Ag^+ present in 1.50 L of 0.100 *M* $AgNO_3$

Richard Megna/Fundamental Photographs

When aqueous sodium chloride is added to a solution of silver nitrate, a white silver chloride precipitate forms.

Step 3 *Determine which reactant is limiting.*
In this situation we want to add just enough Cl^- to react with the Ag^+ present. That is, we want to precipitate *all* the Ag^+ in the solution. Thus the Ag^+ present determines the amount of Cl^- needed.

Step 4 *Calculate the moles of Cl^- required.*
We have 0.150 mole of Ag^+ ions and, because one Ag^+ ion reacts with one Cl^- ion, we need 0.150 mole of Cl^-,

$$0.150\ \cancel{\text{mol } Ag^+} \times \frac{1 \text{ mol } Cl^-}{1\ \cancel{\text{mol } Ag^+}} = 0.150 \text{ mol } Cl^-$$

so 0.150 mole of AgCl will be formed.

$$0.150 \text{ mol } Ag^+ + 0.150 \text{ mol } Cl^- \rightarrow 0.150 \text{ mol AgCl}$$

Step 5 *Convert to grams of NaCl required.*
To produce 0.150 mol Cl^-, we need 0.150 mol NaCl. We calculate the mass of NaCl required as follows:

$$0.150 \text{ ~~mol NaCl~~} \times \frac{58.4 \text{ g NaCl}}{\text{~~mol NaCl~~}} = 8.76 \text{ g NaCl}$$

Moles → Mass
times molar mass

The mass of AgCl formed is

$$0.150 \text{ ~~mol AgCl~~} \times \frac{143.3 \text{ g AgCl}}{\text{~~mol AgCl~~}} = 21.5 \text{ g AgCl} ■$$

EXAMPLE 15.10

Solution Stoichiometry: Determining Limiting Reactants and Calculating Mass of Products

See Section 7.2 for a discussion of this reaction.

When $Ba(NO_3)_2$ and K_2CrO_4 react in aqueous solution, the yellow solid $BaCrO_4$ is formed. Calculate the mass of $BaCrO_4$ that forms when 3.50×10^{-3} mole of solid $Ba(NO_3)_2$ is dissolved in 265 mL of 0.0100 *M* K_2CrO_4 solution.

SOLUTION

Where Are We Going?

We want to determine the mass of $BaCrO_4$ that forms in a reaction of known amounts of solutions.

What Do We Know?

- We react 3.50×10^{-3} mol $BaNO_3$ with 265 mL of 0.0100 *M* K_2CrO_4.

What Information Do We Need?

- We will need the balanced equation between $BaNO_3$ and K_2CrO_4.
- We will need the molar mass of $BaCrO_4$.

Barium chromate precipitating.

Richard Megna/Fundamental Photographs

How Do We Get There?

Step 1 The original K_2CrO_4 solution contains the ions K^+ and CrO_4^{2-}. When the $Ba(NO_3)_2$ is dissolved in this solution, Ba^{2+} and NO_3^- ions are added. The Ba^{2+} and CrO_4^{2-} ions react to form solid $BaCrO_4$. The balanced net ionic equation is

$$Ba^{2+}(aq) + CrO_4^{2-}(aq) \rightarrow BaCrO_4(s)$$

Step 2 Next we determine the moles of reactants. We are told that 3.50×10^{-3} mole of $Ba(NO_3)_2$ is added to the K_2CrO_4 solution. Each formula unit of $Ba(NO_3)_2$ contains one Ba^{2+} ion, so 3.50×10^{-3} mole of $Ba(NO_3)_2$ gives 3.50×10^{-3} mole of Ba^{2+} ions in solution.

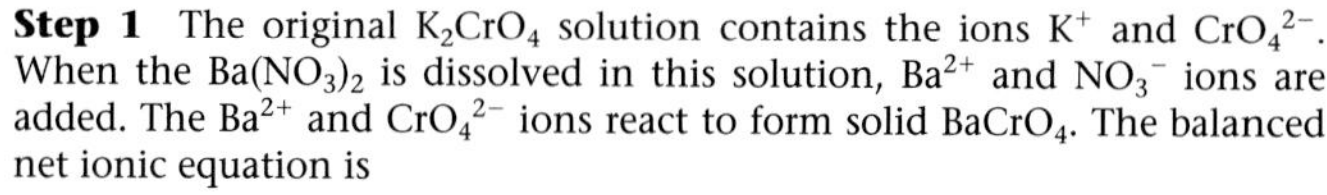

3.50×10^{-3} mol $Ba(NO_3)_2$ → 3.50×10^{-3} mol Ba^{2+}
dissolves to give

Because $V \times M$ = moles of solute, we can compute the moles of K_2CrO_4 in the solution from the volume and molarity of the original solution. First we must convert the volume of the solution (265 mL) to liters.

$$265 \text{ ~~mL~~} \times \frac{1 \text{ L}}{1000 \text{ ~~mL~~}} = 0.265 \text{ L}$$

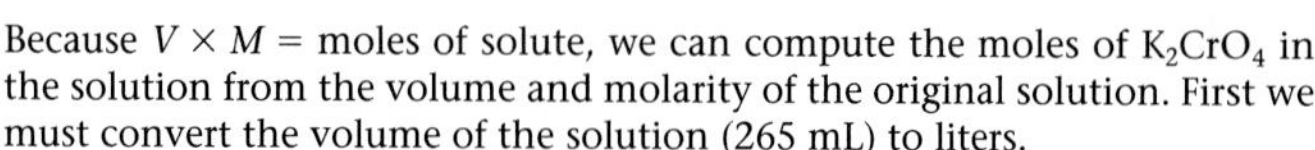

Additional Examples

Example 15.10

1. Calculate the mass of the white solid $CaCO_3$ that forms when 25.0 mL of a 0.100 *M* $Ca(NO_3)_2$ solution is mixed with 20.0 mL of a 0.150 *M* Na_2CO_3 solution.

   0.250 g $CaCO_3$

2. Calculate the mass of the blood-red solid Ag_2CrO_4 that forms when 50.0 mL of a 0.250 *M* $AgNO_3$ solution is mixed with 30.0 mL of a 0.250 *M* K_2CrO_4 solution.

   2.07 g Ag_2CrO_4

TEACHING TIP

Include some examples in class in which a salt dissolves to produce multiple moles of ion per mole of compound. Such examples illustrate the need for writing net ionic equations when solving solution stoichiometry problems.

PowerLecture Video: Neutralization of a Strong Acid by a Strong Base

Next we determine the number of moles of K_2CrO_4, using the molarity of the K_2CrO_4 solution (0.0100 *M*).

$$0.265\ \cancel{L} \times \frac{0.0100\ \text{mol}\ K_2CrO_4}{\cancel{L}} = 2.65 \times 10^{-3}\ \text{mol}\ K_2CrO_4$$

We know that

2.65×10^{-3} mol K_2CrO_4 → (dissolves to give) 2.65×10^{-3} mol CrO_4^{2-}

so the solution contains 2.65×10^{-3} mole of CrO_4^{2-} ions.

Step 3 The balanced equation tells us that one Ba^{2+} ion reacts with one CrO_4^{2-} ion. Because the number of moles of CrO_4^{2-} ions (2.65×10^{-3}) is smaller than the number of moles of Ba^{2+} ions (3.50×10^{-3}), the CrO_4^{2-} will run out first.

$$Ba^{2+}(aq) + CrO_4^{2-}(aq) \rightarrow BaCrO_4(s)$$

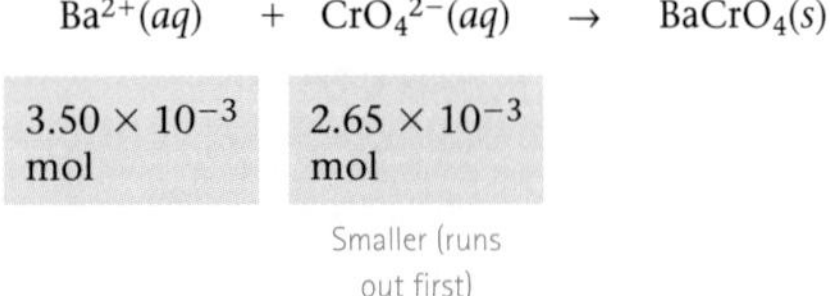

Therefore, the CrO_4^{2-} is limiting.

Step 4 The 2.65×10^{-3} mole of CrO_4^{2-} ions will react with 2.65×10^{-3} mole of Ba^{2+} ions to form 2.65×10^{-3} mole of $BaCrO_4$.

2.65×10^{-3} mol Ba^{2+} + 2.65×10^{-3} mol CrO_4^{2-} → 2.65×10^{-3} mol $BaCrO_4(s)$

Step 5 The mass of $BaCrO_4$ formed is obtained from its molar mass (253.3 g) as follows:

$$2.65 \times 10^{-3}\ \cancel{\text{mol}\ BaCrO_4} \times \frac{253.3\ \text{g}\ BaCrO_4}{\cancel{\text{mol}\ BaCrO_4}} = 0.671\ \text{g}\ BaCrO_4$$

Self-Check EXERCISE 15.8 When aqueous solutions of Na_2SO_4 and $Pb(NO_3)_2$ are mixed, $PbSO_4$ precipitates. Calculate the mass of $PbSO_4$ formed when 1.25 L of 0.0500 *M* $Pb(NO_3)_2$ and 2.00 L of 0.0250 *M* Na_2SO_4 are mixed.

HINT: Calculate the moles of Pb^{2+} and SO_4^{2-} in the mixed solution, decide which ion is limiting, and calculate the moles of $PbSO_4$ formed.

See Problems 15.65 through 15.68. ■

Self Check

Answer to Self-Check Exercise 15.8

15.2 g $PbSO_4$

Test Bank: 55–59

15.7 Neutralization Reactions

OBJECTIVE: To learn how to do calculations involved in acid–base reactions.

So far we have considered the stoichiometry of reactions in solution that result in the formation of a precipitate. Another common type of solution reaction occurs between an acid and a base. We introduced these reactions in Section 7.4. Recall from that discussion that an acid is a substance that furnishes H^+ ions. A strong acid, such as hydrochloric acid, HCl, dissociates (ionizes) completely in water.

$$HCl(aq) \rightarrow H^+(aq) + Cl^-(aq)$$

Strong bases are water-soluble metal hydroxides, which are completely dissociated in water. An example is NaOH, which dissolves in water to give Na^+ and OH^- ions.

$$NaOH(s) \xrightarrow{H_2O(l)} Na^+(aq) + OH^-(aq)$$

When a strong acid and a strong base react, the net ionic reaction is

$$H^+(aq) + OH^-(aq) \rightarrow H_2O(l)$$

An acid–base reaction is often called a **neutralization reaction.** When just enough strong base is added to react exactly with the strong acid in a solution, we say the acid has been *neutralized*. One product of this reaction is always water. The steps in dealing with the stoichiometry of any neutralization reaction are the same as those we followed in the previous section.

EXAMPLE 15.11 Solution Stoichiometry: Calculating Volume in Neutralization Reactions

What volume of a 0.100 *M* HCl solution is needed to neutralize 25.0 mL of a 0.350 *M* NaOH solution?

SOLUTION

Where Are We Going?

We want to determine the volume of a given solution of HCl required to react with a known amount of NaOH.

What Do We Know?

- We have 25.0 mL of 0.350 *M* NaOH.
- The concentration of the HCl solution is 0.100 *M*.

What Information Do We Need?

- We need the balanced equation between HCl and NaOH.

How Do We Get There?

Step 1 *Write the balanced equation for the reaction.*
Hydrochloric acid is a strong acid, so all the HCl molecules dissociate to produce H^+ and Cl^- ions. Also, when the strong base NaOH dissolves, the solution contains Na^+ and OH^- ions. When these two solutions are mixed, the H^+ ions from the hydrochloric acid react with the OH^- ions from the sodium

Section 15.7

TEACHING TIP

This section presents an opportunity to help students learn to solve problems by thinking through the problem. These problems are applications of material that students have seen previously. Work with them to think through each problem. Focus students' attention on the basic requirements for solving problems in chemistry: writing down what is known, writing a balanced equation, determining what is being asked for, deciding what needs to be found to obtain what is asked for, and finally solving the problem.

Additional Examples

Example 15.11

1. What volume of 0.150 *M* HNO_3 solution is needed to neutralize 45.0 mL of a 0.550 *M* KOH solution?

   165 mL

2. What volume of 1.00×10^{-2} *M* HCl solution is needed to neutralize 35.0 mL of a 5.00×10^{-3} *M* $Ba(OH)_2$ solution?

   35.0 mL

PowerLecture Animation: Proton Transfer

hydroxide solution to form water. The balanced net ionic equation for the reaction is

$$H^+(aq) + OH^-(aq) \rightarrow H_2O(l)$$

Step 2 *Calculate the moles of reactants.*
In this problem we are given a volume (25.0 mL) of 0.350 *M* NaOH, and we want to add just enough 0.100 *M* HCl to provide just enough H^+ ions to react with all the OH^-. Therefore, we must calculate the number of moles of OH^- ions in the 25.0-mL sample of 0.350 *M* NaOH. To do this, we first change the volume to liters and multiply by the molarity.

$$25.0 \text{ mL NaOH} \times \frac{1 \text{ L}}{1000 \text{ mL}} \times \frac{0.350 \text{ mol OH}^-}{\text{L NaOH}} = 8.75 \times 10^{-3} \text{ mol OH}^-$$

Moles of OH^- present in 25.0 mL of 0.350 *M* NaOH

Step 3 *Determine which reactant is limiting.*
This problem requires the addition of just enough H^+ ions to react exactly with the OH^- ions present, so the number of moles of OH^- ions present determines the number of moles of H^+ that must be added. The OH^- ions are limiting.

Step 4 *Calculate the moles of H^+ required.*
The balanced equation tells us that the H^+ and OH^- ions react in a 1:1 ratio, so 8.75×10^{-3} mole of H^+ ions is required to neutralize (exactly react with) the 8.75×10^{-3} mole of OH^- ions present.

Step 5 Calculate the volume of 0.100 M *HCl required.*
Next we must find the volume (*V*) of 0.100 *M* HCl required to furnish this amount of H^+ ions. Because the volume (in liters) times the molarity gives the number of moles, we have

$$V \times \frac{0.100 \text{ mol H}^+}{\text{L}} = 8.75 \times 10^{-3} \text{ mol H}^+$$

Unknown volume (in liters) — Moles of H^+ needed

Now we must solve for *V* by dividing both sides of the equation by 0.100.

$$V \times \frac{0.100 \text{ mol H}^+}{0.100 \text{ L}} = \frac{8.75 \times 10^{-3} \text{ mol H}^+}{0.100}$$

$$V = 8.75 \times 10^{-2} \text{ L}$$

Changing liters to milliliters, we have

$$V = 8.75 \times 10^{-2} \text{ L} \times \frac{1000 \text{ mL}}{\text{L}} = 87.5 \text{ mL}$$

Therefore, 87.5 mL of 0.100 *M* HCl is required to neutralize 25.0 mL of 0.350 *M* NaOH.

Self-Check EXERCISE 15.9 Calculate the volume of 0.10 *M* HNO_3 needed to neutralize 125 mL of 0.050 *M* KOH.

See Problems 15.69 through 15.74. ■

Self Check

Answer to Self-Check Exercise 15.9

63 mL

Test Bank: 60–61

15.8 Solution Composition: Normality

OBJECTIVES: To learn about normality and equivalent weight. • To learn to use these concepts in stoichiometric calculations.

Normality is another unit of concentration that is sometimes used, especially when dealing with acids and bases. The use of normality focuses mainly on the H^+ and OH^- available in an acid–base reaction. Before we discuss normality, however, we need to define some terms. One **equivalent of an acid** is the *amount of that acid that can furnish 1 mole of H^+ ions*. Similarly, one **equivalent of a base** is defined as the *amount of that base that can furnish 1 mole of OH^- ions*. The **equivalent weight** of an acid or a base is the mass in grams of 1 equivalent (equiv) of that acid or base.

The common strong acids are HCl, HNO_3, and H_2SO_4. For HCl and HNO_3 each molecule of acid furnishes one H^+ ion, so 1 mole of HCl can furnish 1 mole of H^+ ions. This means that

1 mol HCl $\xrightarrow{\text{produces}}$ 1 mol H^+

1 mol HCl = 1 equiv HCl

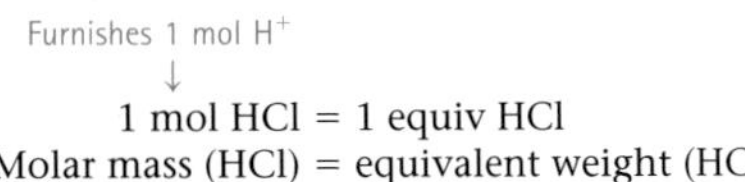

$$1 \text{ mol HCl} = 1 \text{ equiv HCl}$$
$$\text{Molar mass (HCl)} = \text{equivalent weight (HCl)}$$

Likewise, for HNO_3,

$$1 \text{ mol } HNO_3 = 1 \text{ equiv } HNO_3$$
$$\text{Molar mass } (HNO_3) = \text{equivalent weight } (HNO_3)$$

However, H_2SO_4 can furnish *two* H^+ ions per molecule, so 1 mole of H_2SO_4 can furnish *two* moles of H^+. This means that

1 mol H_2SO_4 $\xrightarrow{\text{furnishes}}$ 2 mol H^+

$\frac{1}{2}$ mol H_2SO_4 $\xrightarrow{\text{furnishes}}$ 1 mol H^+

$\frac{1}{2}$ mol H_2SO_4 = 1 equiv H_2SO_4 ⇨ 1 mol H^+

Because each mole of H_2SO_4 can furnish 2 moles of H^+, we need only to take $\frac{1}{2}$ mole of H_2SO_4 to get 1 equiv of H_2SO_4. Therefore,

$$\tfrac{1}{2} \text{ mol } H_2SO_4 = 1 \text{ equiv } H_2SO_4$$

and

$$\text{Equivalent weight } (H_2SO_4) = \tfrac{1}{2} \text{ molar mass } (H_2SO_4)$$
$$= \tfrac{1}{2}(98 \text{ g}) = 49 \text{ g}$$

The equivalent weight of H_2SO_4 is 49 g.

The common strong bases are NaOH and KOH. For NaOH and KOH, each formula unit furnishes one OH^- ion, so we can say

$$1 \text{ mol NaOH} = 1 \text{ equiv NaOH}$$
$$\text{Molar mass (NaOH)} = \text{equivalent weight (NaOH)}$$
$$1 \text{ mol KOH} = 1 \text{ equiv KOH}$$
$$\text{Molar mass (KOH)} = \text{equivalent weight (KOH)}$$

These ideas are summarized in Table 15.2.

Section 15.8

TEACHING TIPS

- It may help to introduce the idea of equivalents from the standpoint of equivalence statements. Since Chapter 2 on measurement, students have been using equivalence statements to convert from one system to another. In this section an equivalence exists between moles of hydrogen (or hydroxide) ion and an equivalent. If students can view it as a conversion, this perspective will simplify their thinking about normality.
- Be sure that students begin these problems by writing an equation for the dissociation of one mole of the acid or base. This step will help them see the number of hydrogen ions or hydroxide ions produced.

Table 15.2 The Molar Masses and Equivalent Weights of the Common Strong Acids and Bases

	Molar Mass (g)	Equivalent Weight (g)
Acid		
HCl	36.5	36.5
HNO_3	63.0	63.0
H_2SO_4	98.0	$49.0 = \frac{98.0}{2}$
Base		
NaOH	40.0	40.0
KOH	56.1	56.1

Additional Examples

Example 15.12

1. Arsenic acid, H_3AsO_4, can furnish three H^+ ions per molecule. Calculate the equivalent weight of H_3AsO_4.

   47.31 g

2. Calculate the equivalent weight of HBr.

   80.91 g

EXAMPLE 15.12 Solution Stoichiometry: Calculating Equivalent Weight

Phosphoric acid, H_3PO_4, can furnish three H^+ ions per molecule. Calculate the equivalent weight of H_3PO_4.

SOLUTION

Where Are We Going?

We want to determine the equivalent weight of phosphoric acid.

What Do We Know?

- The formula for phosphoric acid is H_3PO_4.
- The equivalent weight of an acid is the amount of acid that can furnish 1 mole of H^+ ions.

What Information Do We Need?

- We need to know the molar mass of H_3PO_4.

How Do We Get There?

The key point here involves how many protons (H^+ ions) each molecule of H_3PO_4 can furnish.

H_3PO_4 ⇨ (furnishes) ? H^+

Because each H_3PO_4 can furnish three H^+ ions, 1 mole of H_3PO_4 can furnish 3 moles of H^+ ions:

1 mol H_3PO_4 ⇨ (furnishes) 3 mol H^+

So 1 equiv of H_3PO_4 (the amount that can furnish 1 mole of H^+) is one-third of a mole.

$\frac{1}{3}$ mol H_3PO_4 ⇨ (furnishes) 1 mol H^+

This means the equivalent weight of H_3PO_4 is one-third its molar mass.

$$\text{Equivalent weight} = \frac{\text{Molar mass}}{3}$$

$$\text{Equivalent weight } (H_3PO_4) = \frac{\text{molar mass } (H_3PO_4)}{3}$$
$$= \frac{98.0\text{ g}}{3} = 32.7\text{ g} ■$$

Normality (***N***) is defined as the number of equivalents of solute per liter of solution.

$$\text{Normality} = N = \frac{\text{number of equivalents}}{\text{1 liter of solution}} = \frac{\text{equivalents}}{\text{liter}} = \frac{\text{equiv}}{\text{L}}$$

This means that a 1 N solution contains 1 equivalent of solute per liter of solution. Notice that when we multiply the volume of a solution in liters by the normality, we get the number of equivalents.

MATH SKILL BUILDER
Liters × Normality ➡ Equiv

$$N \times V = \frac{\text{equiv}}{\cancel{L}} \times \cancel{L} = \text{equiv}$$

EXAMPLE 15.13 Solution Stoichiometry: Calculating Normality

A solution of sulfuric acid contains 86 g of H_2SO_4 per liter of solution. Calculate the normality of this solution.

Whenever you need to calculate the concentration of a solution, first write the appropriate definition. Then decide how to calculate the quantities shown in the definition.

SOLUTION

Where Are We Going?

We want to determine the normality of a given solution of H_2SO_4.

What Do We Know?

- We have 86 g of H_2SO_4 per liter of solution.
- $N = \frac{\text{equivalents}}{\text{L}}$.

What Information Do We Need?

- We need to know the molar mass of H_2SO_4.

How Do We Get There?

To find the number of equivalents present, we must calculate the number of equivalents represented by 86 g of H_2SO_4. To do this calculation, we focus on the definition of the equivalent: it is the amount of acid that furnishes 1 mole of H^+. Because H_2SO_4 can furnish two H^+ ions per molecule, 1 equiv of H_2SO_4 is $\frac{1}{2}$ mole of H_2SO_4, so

$$\text{Equivalent weight } (H_2SO_4) = \frac{\text{molar mass } (H_2SO_4)}{2}$$
$$= \frac{98.0\text{ g}}{2} = 49.0\text{ g}$$

TEACHING TIP

The key idea in understanding normality is to determine equivalents. This step is analogous to determining moles in other solution problems.

Additional Examples

Example 15.13

1. A solution of phosphoric acid contains 50.0 g of H_3PO_4 per liter of solution. Calculate the normality of this solution.

   1.53 N

2. A solution of hydrochloric acid contains 25.0 g of HCl per liter of solution. Calculate the normality of this solution.

   0.686 N

We have 86 g of H_2SO_4.

$$86 \text{ g } \cancel{H_2SO_4} \times \frac{1 \text{ equiv } H_2SO_4}{49.0 \text{ g } \cancel{H_2SO_4}} = 1.8 \text{ equiv } H_2SO_4$$

$$N = \frac{\text{equiv}}{\text{L}} = \frac{1.8 \text{ equiv } H_2SO_4}{1.0 \text{ L}} = 1.8\ N\ H_2SO_4$$

REALITY CHECK We know that 86 g is more than 1 equiv of H_2SO_4 (49 g), so this answer makes sense.

Self Check

Answer to Self-Check Exercise 15.10

0.558 *N*

Self-Check EXERCISE 15.10 Calculate the normality of a solution containing 23.6 g of KOH in 755 mL of solution.

See Problems 15.79 and 15.80. ■

The main advantage of using equivalents is that 1 equiv of acid contains the same number of available H^+ ions as the number of OH^- ions present in 1 equiv of base. That is,

0.75 equiv (base) will react exactly with 0.75 equiv (acid).

0.23 equiv (base) will react exactly with 0.23 equiv (acid).

And so on.

In each of these cases, the *number of* H^+ ions furnished by the sample of acid is the same as the *number of* OH^- ions furnished by the sample of base. The point is that *n equivalents of any acid will exactly neutralize n equivalents of any base.*

n equiv acid ← reacts exactly with → *n* equiv base

Because we know that equal equivalents of acid and base are required for neutralization, we can say that

$$\text{equiv (acid)} = \text{equiv (base)}$$

That is,

$$N_{acid} \times V_{acid} = \text{equiv (acid)} = \text{equiv (base)} = N_{base} \times V_{base}$$

Therefore, for any neutralization reaction, the following relationship holds:

$$N_{acid} \times V_{acid} = N_{base} \times V_{base}$$

Additional Examples

Example 15.14

1. What volume of 0.500 *N* NaOH is required to react exactly with 125 mL of 0.500 *N* H_2SO_4?

   125 mL

2. What volume of 1.00 *N* H_3PO_4 is required to react exactly with 25.0 mL of 0.500 *N* NaOH?

   12.5 mL

EXAMPLE 15.14 **Solution Stoichiometry: Using Normality in Calculations**

What volume of a 0.075 *N* KOH solution is required to react exactly with 0.135 L of 0.45 *N* H_3PO_4?

SOLUTION

Where Are We Going?

We want to determine the volume of a given solution of KOH required to react with a known solution of H_3PO_4.

What Do We Know?

- We have 0.135 L of 0.45 *N* H_3PO_4.
- The concentration of the KOH solution is 0.075 *N*.
- We know $\text{equivalents}_{acid} = \text{equivalents}_{base}$.
- $N_{acid} \times V_{acid} = N_{base} \times V_{base}$

How Do We Get There?

We know that for neutralization, equiv (acid) = equiv (base), or

$$N_{acid} \times V_{acid} = N_{base} \times V_{base}$$

We want to calculate the volume of base, V_{base}, so we solve for V_{base} by dividing both sides by N_{base}.

$$\frac{N_{acid} \times V_{acid}}{N_{base}} = \frac{\cancel{N_{base}} \times V_{base}}{\cancel{N_{base}}} = V_{base}$$

Now we can substitute the given values $N_{acid} = 0.45\ N$, $V_{acid} = 0.135$ L, and $N_{base} = 0.075\ N$ into the equation.

$$V_{base} = \frac{N_{acid} \times V_{acid}}{N_{base}} = \frac{\left(0.45\ \frac{\cancel{\text{equiv}}}{\cancel{\text{L}}}\right)(0.135\ \text{L})}{0.075\ \frac{\cancel{\text{equiv}}}{\cancel{\text{L}}}} = 0.81\ \text{L}$$

This gives $V_{base} = 0.81$ L, so 0.81 L of 0.075 *N* KOH is required to react exactly with 0.135 L of 0.45 *N* H_3PO_4.

Self-Check EXERCISE 15.11 What volume of 0.50 *N* H_2SO_4 is required to react exactly with 0.250 L of 0.80 *N* KOH?

See Problems 15.85 and 15.86. ■

Self Check

Answer to Self-Check Exercise 15.11

0.40 L

CHAPTER 15 REVIEW

Key Terms

solution (p. 475)
solvent (p. 475)
solute (p. 475)
aqueous solution (p. 475)
saturated (15.2)
unsaturated (15.2)
concentrated (15.2)
dilute (15.2)
mass percent (15.3)
molarity (*M*) (15.4)
standard solution (15.4)
dilution (15.5)
neutralization reaction (15.7)
equivalent of an acid (15.8)
equivalent of a base (15.8)
equivalent weight (15.8)
normality (*N*) (15.8)

F directs you to the *Chemistry in Focus* feature in the chapter
VP indicates visual problems
OWL interactive versions of these problems are assignable in OWL

Summary

1. A solution is a homogeneous mixture. The solubility of a solute in a given solvent depends on the interactions between the solvent and solute particles. Water dissolves many ionic compounds and compounds with polar molecules, because strong forces occur between the solute and the polar water molecules.

ChemWork

Calculating K_{sp} from Solubility

Calculation of Solubility with Common Anions

Calculation of Solubility with Common Cations

Calculating Solubility from K_{sp}

Comparing Solubilities

Determining K_{sp} from Solubility with a Common Ion

Precipitation Stoichiometry and Equilibrium

HgI Concentration

Nonpolar solvents tend to dissolve nonpolar solutes. "Like dissolves like."

2. Solution composition can be described in many ways. Two of the most important are in terms of mass percent of solute:

$$\text{Mass percent} = \frac{\text{mass of solute}}{\text{mass of solution}} \times 100\%$$

and molarity:

$$\text{Molarity} = \frac{\text{moles of solute}}{\text{liters of solution}}$$

3. A standard solution is one whose concentration is accurately known. Solutions are often made from a stock solution by dilution. When a solution is diluted, only solvent is added, which means that

Moles of solute after dilution = moles of solute before dilution

4. Normality is defined as the number of equivalents per liter of solution. One equivalent of acid is the amount of acid that furnishes 1 mole of H^+ ions. One equivalent of base is the amount of base that furnishes 1 mole of OH^- ions.

Active Learning Questions

These questions are designed to be considered by groups of students in class. Often these questions work well for introducing a particular topic in class.

1. You have a solution of table salt in water. What happens to the salt concentration (increases, decreases, or stays the same) as the solution boils? Draw pictures to explain your answer.

2. Consider a sugar solution (solution A) with concentration x. You pour one-third of this solution into a beaker, and add an equivalent volume of water (solution B).
   a. What is the ratio of sugar in solutions A and B?
   b. Compare the volumes of solutions A and B.
   c. What is the ratio of the concentrations of sugar in solutions A and B?

3. You need to make 150.0 mL of a 0.10 M NaCl solution. You have solid NaCl, and your lab partner has a 2.5 M NaCl solution. Explain how you each independently make the solution you need.

4. You have two solutions containing solute A. To determine which solution has the highest concentration of A in molarity, which of the following must you know? (There may be more than one answer.)
   a. the mass in grams of A in each solution
   b. the molar mass of A
   c. the volume of water added to each solution
   d. the total volume of the solution

   Explain your answer.

5. Which of the following do you need to know to calculate the molarity of a salt solution? (There may be more than one answer.)
   a. the mass of salt added
   b. the molar mass of the salt
   c. the volume of water added
   d. the total volume of the solution

   Explain your answer.

6. Consider separate aqueous solutions of HCl and H_2SO_4 with the same concentrations in terms of molarity. You wish to neutralize an aqueous solution of NaOH. For which acid solution would you need to add more volume (in mL) to neutralize the base?
   a. The HCl solution.
   b. The H_2SO_4 solution.
   c. You need to know the acid concentrations to answer this question.
   d. You need to know the volume and concentration of the NaOH solution to answer this question.
   e. c and d

   Explain your answer.

7. Draw molecular-level pictures to differentiate between concentrated and dilute solutions.

8. Can one solution have a greater concentration than another in terms of weight percent, but a lower concentration in terms of molarity? Explain.

9. Explain why the formula $M_1V_1 = M_2V_2$ works when solving dilution problems.

10. You have equal masses of different solutes dissolved in equal volumes of solution. Which of the solutes listed below would make the solution with the highest concentration measured in molarity? Defend your answer.

    NaCl, $MgSO_4$, LiF, KNO_3

11. Which of the following solutions contains the greatest number of particles? Support your answer.
    a. 400.0 mL of 0.10 M sodium chloride
    b. 300.0 mL of 0.10 M calcium chloride
    c. 200.0 mL of 0.10 M iron(III) chloride
    d. 200.0 mL of 0.10 M potassium bromide
    e. 800.0 mL of 0.10 M sucrose (table sugar)

12. As with all quantitative problems in chemistry, make sure not to get "lost in the math." In particular, work on visualizing solutions at a molecular level. For example, consider the following.

    You have two separate beakers with aqueous solutions, one with 4 "units" of potassium sulfate and one with 3 "units" of barium nitrate.
    a. Draw molecular-level diagrams of both solutions.
    b. Draw a molecular-level diagram of the mixture of the two solutions before a reaction has taken place.
    c. Draw a molecular-level diagram of the product and solution formed after the reaction has taken place.

Answers to End-of-Chapter Exercises

1. Specific answers depend on student choices.

2. A *non*homogeneous mixture may differ in composition in various places in the mixture, whereas a solution (a homogeneous mixture) has the same composition throughout. Examples of nonhomogeneous mixtures include spaghetti sauce, a jar of jelly beans, and a mixture of salt and sugar.

VP 13. The figures below are molecular-level representations of four aqueous solutions of the same solute. Arrange the solutions from most to least concentrated.

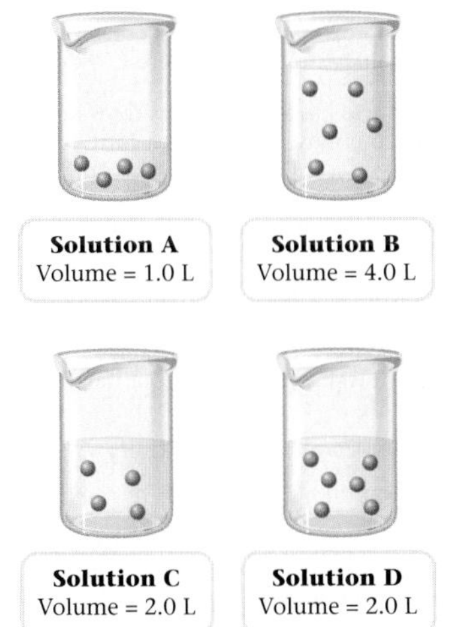

VP 14. The drawings below represent aqueous solutions. Solution A is 2.00 L of a 2.00 *M* aqueous solution of copper(II) nitrate. Solution B is 2.00 L of a 3.00 *M* aqueous solution of potassium hydroxide.

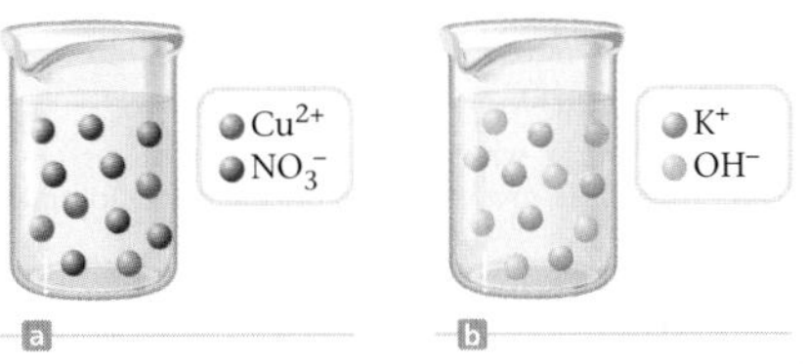

a. Draw a picture of the solution made by mixing solutions A and B together after the precipitation reaction takes place. Make sure this picture shows the correct relative volume compared to solutions A and B and the correct relative number of ions, along with the correct relative amount of solid formed.

b. Determine the concentrations (in *M*) of all ions left in solution (from part a) and the mass of solid formed.

Questions and Problems

15.1 Solubility

QUESTIONS

1. A solution is a *homogeneous mixture.* Can you give an example of a gaseous homogeneous mixture? A liquid homogeneous mixture? A solid homogeneous mixture?

2. How do the properties of a *non*homogeneous (heterogeneous) mixture differ from those of a solution? Give two examples of *non*homogeneous mixtures.

3. Suppose you dissolved a teaspoon of sugar in a glass of water. Which substance is the *solvent?* Which substance is the *solute?*

4. A metallic alloy, such as brass, is an example of a ________ solution.

5. In Chapter 14, you learned that the bonding forces in ionic solids such as NaCl are very strong, yet many ionic solids dissolve readily in water. Explain.

6. An oil spill spreads out on the *surface* of water, rather than *dissolving* in the water. Explain why.

F 7. The "Chemistry in Focus" segment *Water, Water Everywhere, But . . .* discusses the desalinization of ocean water. Explain why many salts are soluble in water. Include molecular-level diagrams in your answer.

F 8. The "Chemistry in Focus" segment *Green Chemistry* discusses the use of gaseous carbon dioxide in place of CFCs and of liquid carbon dioxide in place of the dry-cleaning chemical PERC. Would you expect carbon dioxide to be very soluble in water? Explain your answer.

15.2 Solution Composition: An Introduction

QUESTIONS

9. What does it mean to say that a solution is *saturated* with a solute?

10. If additional solute is added to a(n) ________ solution, it will dissolve.

11. A solution is a homogeneous mixture and, unlike a compound, has ________ composition.

12. The label "concentrated H_2SO_4" on a bottle means that there is a relatively ________ amount of H_2SO_4 present in the solution.

15.3 Solution Composition: Mass Percent

QUESTIONS

13. How do we define the *mass percent* composition of a solution? Give an example of a solution, and explain the relative amounts of solute and solvent present in the solution in terms of the mass percent composition.

14. A solution that is 9% by mass glucose contains 9 g of glucose in every ________ g of solution.

PROBLEMS

15. Calculate the percent by mass of solute in each of the following solutions.

a. 2.14 g of potassium chloride dissolved in 12.5 g of water

All even-numbered Questions and Problems have answers in the back of this book and solutions in the Solutions Guide.

3. Water is the solvent, sugar the solute.

4. solid

5. When an ionic solute dissolves in water, a given ion is pulled into solution by the attractive ion–dipole forces exerted by several water molecules. Since the action is by *several* water molecules, it is possible that the cumulative forces between the water molecules and the ion might be stronger than the forces between the ion and its oppositely charged neighbors.

6. "Like dissolves like." The hydrocarbons in oil have intermolecular forces that are very different from those in water, so the oil spreads out rather than dissolving in the water.

7. Salts are composed of positive and negative ions packed closely together in a crystal lattice. The crystal is held together by the ionic forces among oppositely charged particles in the solid. When a crystal of a salt is placed in water, the polar water molecules arrange their dipoles around the ions of the crystal in such a way as to attract the ions. For example, a positive ion at a corner of the crystal will be surrounded by a group of water molecules aiming the negative end of their dipoles at the positive ion. If the forces of attraction of the water molecules for the positive ion are larger than the ionic forces holding the ion in the crystal, then the ion will leave the crystal and enter solution (see Figure 15.2).

8. Carbon dioxide is somewhat soluble in water, especially if pressurized (otherwise, the soda you may be drinking while studying chemistry would be "flat"). Carbon dioxide's solubility in water is approximately 1.5 g/L at 25 °C under a pressure of approximately 1 atm. Although the carbon dioxide molecule overall is nonpolar, that is because the two individual C–O bond dipoles cancel each other due to the linearity of the molecule. However these bond dipoles are able to interact with water, making CO_2 more soluble in water than nonpolar molecules such as O_2 or N_2 that do not possess individual bond dipoles.

9. A saturated solution is one that contains the maximum amount of solute possible at a particular temperature. A saturated solution is one that is in equilibrium with undissolved solute.

10. unsaturated

11. variable

12. large

13. The mass percent of a component in a solution is the mass of that component, divided by the total mass of the solution, multiplied by 100%.

14. 100.

15. (a) 14.6%; (b) 7.89%; (c) 5.40%; (d) 4.10%

16. (a) 0.116%; (b) 0.0116%; (c) 10.4%; (d) 10.4%

b. 2.14 g of potassium chloride dissolved in 25.0 g of water
c. 2.14 g of potassium chloride dissolved in 37.5 g of water
d. 2.14 g of potassium chloride dissolved in 50.0 g of water

16. Calculate the percent by mass of solute in each of the following solutions.

a. 6.11 mg of calcium chloride dissolved in 5.25 g of water
b. 6.11 mg of calcium chloride dissolved in 52.5 g of water
c. 6.11 g of calcium chloride dissolved in 52.5 g of water
d. 6.11 kg of calcium chloride dissolved in 52.5 kg of water

17. Calculate the mass, in grams, of solute present in each of the following solutions.

a. 375 g of 1.51% ammonium chloride solution
b. 125 g of 2.91% sodium chloride solution
c. 1.31 kg of 4.92% potassium nitrate solution
d. 478 mg of 12.5% ammonium nitrate solution

18. Calculate how many grams of solute and solvent are needed to prepare the following solutions.

a. 525 g of 3.91% iron(III) chloride solution
b. 225 g of 11.9% sucrose solution
c. 1.45 kg of 12.5% sodium chloride solution
d. 635 g of 15.1% potassium nitrate solution

19. A sample of an iron alloy contains 92.1 g Fe, 2.59 g C, and 1.59 g Cr. Calculate the percent by mass of each component present in the alloy sample.

20. Consider the iron alloy described in Question 19. Suppose it is desired to prepare 1.00 kg of this alloy. What mass of each component would be necessary?

21. An aqueous solution is to be prepared that will be 7.51% by mass ammonium nitrate. What mass of NH_4NO_3 and what mass of water will be needed to prepare 1.25 kg of the solution?

22. If 67.1 g of $CaCl_2$ is added to 275 g of water, calculate the mass percent of $CaCl_2$ in the solution.

23. A solution is to be prepared that will be 4.50% by mass calcium chloride. To prepare 175 g of the solution, what mass of calcium chloride will be needed?

24. How many grams of KBr are contained in 125 g of a 6.25% (by mass) KBr solution?

25. What mass of each solute is present in 285 g of a solution that contains 5.00% by mass NaCl and 7.50% by mass Na_2CO_3?

26. Hydrogen peroxide solutions sold in drugstores as an antiseptic typically contain 3.0% of the active ingredient, H_2O_2. Hydrogen peroxide decomposes into water and oxygen gas when applied to a wound according to the balanced chemical equation

$$2H_2O_2(aq) \rightarrow 2H_2O(l) + O_2(g)$$

What approximate mass of hydrogen peroxide solution would be needed to produce 1.00 g of oxygen gas?

27. Sulfuric acid has a great affinity for water, and for this reason, the most concentrated form of sulfuric acid available is actually a 98.3% solution. The density of concentrated sulfuric acid is 1.84 g/mL. What mass of sulfuric acid is present in 1.00 L of the concentrated solution?

28. A solvent sold for use in the laboratory contains 0.95% of a stabilizing agent that prevents the solvent from reacting with the air. What mass of the stabilizing agent is present in 1.00 kg of the solvent?

15.4 Solution Composition: Molarity

QUESTIONS

29. A solution you used in last week's lab experiment was labeled "3 *M* HCl." Describe in words the composition of this solution.

30. A solution labeled "0.110 *M* $CaCl_2$" would contain ______ mol Ca^{2+} and ______ mol Cl^- in each liter of the solution.

31. What is a *standard* solution? Describe the steps involved in preparing a standard solution.

32. To prepare 500. mL of 1.02 *M* sugar solution, which of the following would you need?

a. 500. mL of water and 1.02 mole of sugar
b. 1.02 mole of sugar and enough water to make the total volume 500. mL
c. 500. g of water and 1.02 mole of sugar
d. 0.51 mole of sugar and enough water to make the total volume 500. mL

PROBLEMS

33. For each of the following solutions, the number of moles of solute is given, followed by the total volume of the solution prepared. Calculate the molarity of each solution.

a. 0.521 mol NaCl; 125 mL
b. 0.521 mol NaCl; 250. mL
c. 0.521 mol NaCl; 500. mL
d. 0.521 mol NaCl; 1.00 L

34. For each of the following solutions, the number of moles of solute is given, followed by the total volume of the solution prepared. Calculate the molarity of each solution.

a. 0.754 mol KNO_3; 225 mL
b. 0.0105 mol $CaCl_2$; 10.2 mL
c. 3.15 mol NaCl; 5.00 L
d. 0.499 mol NaBr; 100. mL

All even-numbered Questions and Problems have answers in the back of this book and solutions in the Solutions Guide.

17. (a) 5.66 g; (b) 3.64 g; (c) 64.5 g; (d) 0.0598 g

18. (a) 20.5 g $FeCl_3$; 504.5 g (505 g) water; (b) 26.8 g sucrose; 198.2 g (198 g) water; (c) 181.3 g (181 g) NaCl; 1268.7 (1269 g) water; (d) 95.9 g KNO_3; 539.1 (539) g water

19. 95.7% Fe; 2.69% C; 1.65% Cr

20. 921 g Fe; 26.9 g C; 16.5 g Cr

21. 93.9 g NH_4NO_3; 1156.1 g water (1160 g)

22. 19.6% $CaCl_2$

23. 7.88 g $CaCl_2$

24. 7.81 g KBr

25. 14.3 g NaCl; 21.4 g Na_2CO_3

26. approximately 71 g

27. 1809 g (1.81×10^3 g)

28. 9.5 g

29. Each liter of the solution contained 3 moles of hydrogen chloride.

30. 0.110 mol; 0.220 mol

31. A standard solution is one whose concentration is known very accurately and with high precision. For stable, stoichiometric solutes, a standard solution is typically prepared by weighing out a precise amount of solute, and then dissolving the solute in a precise amount of solvent or to a precise final volume (using a volumetric flask).

32. b

33. (a) 4.17 *M*; (b) 2.08 *M*; (c) 1.04 *M*; (d) 0.521 *M*

34. (a) 3.35 *M*; (b) 1.03 *M*; (c) 0.630 *M*; (d) 4.99 *M*

35. (a) 2.40 *M*; (b) 1.20 *M*; (c) 0.801 *M*; (d) 0.601 *M*

36. (a) 0.403 *M*; (b) 0.169 *M*; (c) 0.629 *M*; (d) 0.829 *M*

35. For each of the following solutions, the mass of solute is given, followed by the total volume of the solution prepared. Calculate the molarity of each solution.

a. 3.51 g NaCl; 25 mL
b. 3.51 g NaCl; 50. mL
c. 3.51 g NaCl; 75 mL
d. 3.51 g NaCl; 1.00 L

36. For each of the following solutions, the mass of solute is given, followed by the total volume of the solution prepared. Calculate the molarity of each solution.

a. 5.59 g $CaCl_2$; 125 mL
b. 2.34 g $CaCl_2$; 125 mL
c. 8.73 g $CaCl_2$; 125 mL
d. 11.5 g $CaCl_2$; 125 mL

37. A laboratory assistant needs to prepare 225 mL of 0.150 *M* $CaCl_2$ solution. How many grams of calcium chloride will she need?

38. What mass of potassium bromide is contained in 135 mL of 0.251 *M* KBr solution?

39. Standard solutions of calcium ion used to test for water hardness are prepared by dissolving pure calcium carbonate, $CaCO_3$, in dilute hydrochloric acid. A 1.745-g sample of $CaCO_3$ is placed in a 250.0-mL volumetric flask and dissolved in HCl. Then the solution is diluted to the calibration mark of the volumetric flask. Calculate the resulting molarity of calcium ion.

40. An alcoholic iodine solution ("tincture" of iodine) is prepared by dissolving 5.15 g of iodine crystals in enough alcohol to make a volume of 225 mL. Calculate the molarity of iodine in the solution.

41. If 42.5 g of NaOH is dissolved in water and diluted to a final volume of 225 mL, calculate the molarity of the solution.

42. It is desired to prepare a standard solution of potassium nitrate. If 1.21 g of KNO_3 is placed in a 25.0-mL volumetric flask, and the solute is then dissolved and diluted to the calibration mark on the flask, what will be the molarity of the solution?

43. How many *moles* of the indicated solute does each of the following solutions contain?

a. 4.25 mL of 0.105 *M* $CaCl_2$ solution
b. 11.3 mL of 0.405 *M* NaOH solution
c. 1.25 L of 12.1 *M* HCl solution
d. 27.5 mL of 1.98 *M* NaCl solution

44. How many *moles* of the indicated solute does each of the following solutions contain?

a. 12.5 mL of 0.104 *M* HCl
b. 27.3 mL of 0.223 *M* NaOH
c. 36.8 mL of 0.501 *M* HNO_3
d. 47.5 mL of 0.749 *M* KOH

45. What *mass* of the indicated solute does each of the following solutions contain?

a. 2.50 L of 13.1 *M* HCl solution
b. 15.6 mL of 0.155 *M* NaOH solution
c. 135 mL of 2.01 *M* HNO_3 solution
d. 4.21 L of 0.515 *M* $CaCl_2$ solution

46. What *mass* of the indicated solute does each of the following solutions contain?

a. 17.8 mL of 0.119 *M* $CaCl_2$
b. 27.6 mL of 0.288 *M* KCl
c. 35.4 mL of 0.399 *M* $FeCl_3$
d. 46.1 mL of 0.559 *M* KNO_3

47. What mass of NaOH pellets is required to prepare 3.5 L of 0.50 *M* NaOH solution?

48. What mass of solute is present in 225 mL of 0.355 *M* KBr solution?

49. Calculate the number of moles of the indicated ion present in each of the following solutions.

a. Na^+ ion in 1.00 L of 0.251 *M* Na_2SO_4 solution
b. Cl^- ion in 5.50 L of 0.10 *M* $FeCl_3$ solution
c. NO_3^- ion in 100. mL of 0.55 *M* $Ba(NO_3)_2$ solution
d. NH_4^+ ion in 250. mL of 0.350 *M* $(NH_4)_2SO_4$ solution

50. Calculate the number of moles of *each* ion present in each of the following solutions.

a. 10.2 mL of 0.451 *M* $AlCl_3$ solution
b. 5.51 L of 0.103 *M* Na_3PO_4 solution
c. 1.75 mL of 1.25 *M* $CuCl_2$ solution
d. 25.2 mL of 0.00157 *M* $Ca(OH)_2$ solution

51. An experiment calls for 125 mL of 0.105 *M* NaCl solution. What mass of NaCl is required? What mass of NaCl would be required for 1.00 L of the same solution?

52. Strong acid solutions may have their concentration determined by reaction with measured quantities of standard sodium carbonate solution. What mass of Na_2CO_3 is needed to prepare 250. mL of 0.0500 *M* Na_2CO_3 solution?

15.5 Dilution

QUESTIONS

53. When a concentrated stock solution is diluted to prepare a less concentrated reagent, the number of ________ is the same both before and after the dilution.

54. When the volume of a given solution is doubled (by adding water), the new concentration of solute is ________ the original concentration.

PROBLEMS

55. Calculate the new molarity if each of the following dilutions is made. Assume the volumes are additive.

a. 55.0 mL of water is added to 25.0 mL of 0.119 *M* NaCl solution
b. 125 mL of water is added to 45.3 mL of 0.701 *M* NaOH solution
c. 550. mL of water is added to 125 mL of 3.01 *M* KOH solution
d. 335 mL of water is added to 75.3 mL of 2.07 *M* $CaCl_2$ solution

All even-numbered Questions and Problems have answers in the back of this book and solutions in the Solutions Guide.

50. (a) 4.60×10^{-3} mol Al^{3+}, 1.38×10^{-2} mol Cl^-; (b) 1.70 mol Na^+, 0.568 mol PO_4^{3-}; (c) 2.19×10^{-3} mol Cu^{2+}, 4.38×10^{-3} mol Cl^-; (d) 3.96×10^{-5} mol Ca^{2+}, 7.91×10^{-5} mol OH^-

51. 0.767 g NaCl, 6.14 g NaCl

52. 1.33 g

53. moles of solute

54. half

55. (a) 0.0372 *M*; (b) 0.186 *M*; (c) 0.557 *M*; (d) 0.380 *M*

56. (a) 0.0717 *M*; (b) 1.69 *M*; (c) 0.0426 *M*; (d) 0.625 *M*

37. 3.75 g $CaCl_2$

38. 4.03 g KBr

39. 0.06973 *M*

40. 0.0902 *M*

41. 4.72 *M*

42. 0.479 *M*

43. (a) 4.46×10^{-4} mol; (b) 4.58×10^{-3} mol; (c) 15.1 mol; (d) 0.0545 mol

44. (a) 0.00130 mol; (b) 0.00609 mol; (c) 0.0184 mol; (d) 0.0356 mol

45. (a) 1.19×10^3 g HCl; (b) 9.67×10^{-2} g NaOH; (c) 17.1 g HNO_3; (d) 241 g $CaCl_2$

46. (a) 0.235 g; (b) 0.593 g; (c) 2.29 g; (d) 2.61 g

47. 70. g

48. 9.51 g

49. (a) 0.502 mol Na^+; (b) 1.7 mol Cl^-; (c) 0.11 mol NO_3^-; (d) 0.175 mol NH_4^+

57. HCl, 56 mL; HNO_3, 42 mL; H_2SO_4, 38 mL; $HC_2H_3O_2$, 39 mL; H_3PO_4, 45 mL

58. 0.541 L (541 mL)

59. Dilute 48.1 mL of the 2.00 *M* solution to a final volume of 275 mL.

60. Dilute 48.3 mL of the 1.01 *M* solution to a final volume of 325 mL.

61. 167 mL water

62. 10.3 mL

63. 7.33 mL

64. 31.2 mL

65. 31.7 mL

66. 0.523 g

67. 0.976 g $PbCrO_4$

68. 0.300 g

69. 26.6 mL

70. 378 mL

71. 0.02559 *M*

72. 1.8×10^{-4} *M*

73. (a) 3.85 mL; (b) 3.57 mL; (c) 4.29 mL; (d) 15.4 mL

56. Calculate the new molarity if each of the following dilutions is made. Assume the volumes are additive.

a. 25.0 mL of water is added to 10.0 mL of 0.251 *M* $CaCl_2$ solution
b. 97.5 mL of water is added to 125 mL of 3.00 *M* HCl solution
c. 25.0 mL of 0.851 *M* NH_3 solution is transferred by pipet to a 500.-mL volumetric flask and water is added to the 500.-mL mark
d. 25.0 mL of 1.25 *M* NaCl solution is diluted with an equal volume of water

57. Many laboratories keep bottles of 3.0 *M* solutions of the common acids on hand. Given the following molarities of the concentrated acids, determine how many milliliters of each concentrated acid would be required to prepare 225 mL of a 3.0 *M* solution of the acid.

Acid	Molarity of Concentrated Reagent
HCl	12.1 *M*
HNO_3	15.9 *M*
H_2SO_4	18.0 *M*
$HC_2H_3O_2$	17.5 *M*
H_3PO_4	14.9 *M*

58. For convenience, one form of sodium hydroxide that is sold commercially is the saturated solution. This solution is 19.4 *M*, which is approximately 50% by mass sodium hydroxide. What volume of this solution would be needed to prepare 3.50 L of 3.00 *M* NaOH solution?

59. How would you prepare 275 mL of 0.350 *M* NaCl solution using an available 2.00 *M* solution?

60. Suppose 325 mL of 0.150 *M* NaOH is needed for your experiment. How would you prepare this if all that is available is a 1.01 *M* NaOH solution?

61. How much *water* must be added to 500. mL of 0.200 *M* HCl to produce a 0.150 *M* solution? (Assume that the volumes are additive.)

62. An experiment calls for 100. mL of 1.25 *M* HCl. All that is available in the lab is a bottle of concentrated HCl, whose label indicates that it is 12.1 *M*. How much of the concentrated HCl would be needed to prepare the desired solution?

15.6 Stoichiometry of Solution Reactions

PROBLEMS

63. The amount of nickel(II) present in an aqueous solution can be determined by precipitating the nickel with the organic chemical reagent dimethylglyoxime [$CH_3C(NOH)C(NOH)CH_3$, commonly abbreviated as "DMG"].

$$Ni^{2+}(aq) + 2DMG(aq) \rightarrow Ni(DMG)_2(s)$$

How many milliliters of 0.0703 *M* DMG solution is required to precipitate all the nickel(II) present in 10.0 mL of 0.103 *M* nickel(II) sulfate solution?

64. Generally only the carbonates of the Group 1 elements and the ammonium ion are soluble in water; most other carbonates are *insoluble*. How many milliliters of 0.125 *M* sodium carbonate solution would be needed to precipitate the calcium ion from 37.2 mL of 0.105 *M* $CaCl_2$ solution?

$$Na_2CO_3(aq) + CaCl_2(aq) \rightarrow CaCO_3(s) + 2NaCl(s)$$

65. Many metal ions are precipitated from solution by the sulfide ion. As an example, consider treating a solution of copper(II) sulfate with sodium sulfide solution:

$$CuSO_4(aq) + Na_2S(aq) \rightarrow CuS(s) + Na_2SO_4(aq)$$

What volume of 0.105 *M* Na_2S solution would be required to precipitate all of the copper(II) ion from 27.5 mL of 0.121 *M* $CuSO_4$ solution?

66. Calcium oxalate, CaC_2O_4, is very insoluble in water. What mass of sodium oxalate, $Na_2C_2O_4$, is required to precipitate the calcium ion from 37.5 mL of 0.104 *M* $CaCl_2$ solution?

67. When aqueous solutions of lead(II) ion are treated with potassium chromate solution, a bright yellow precipitate of lead(II) chromate, $PbCrO_4$, forms. How many grams of lead chromate form when a 1.00-g sample of $Pb(NO_3)_2$ is added to 25.0 mL of 1.00 *M* K_2CrO_4 solution?

68. Aluminum ion may be precipitated from aqueous solution by addition of hydroxide ion, forming $Al(OH)_3$. A large excess of hydroxide ion must not be added, however, because the precipitate of $Al(OH)_3$ will redissolve as a soluble compound containing aluminum ions and hydroxide ions begins to form. How many grams of solid NaOH should be added to 10.0 mL of 0.250 *M* $AlCl_3$ to just precipitate all the aluminum?

15.7 Neutralization Reactions

PROBLEMS

69. What volume of 0.502 *M* NaOH solution would be required to neutralize 27.2 mL of 0.491 *M* HNO_3 solution?

70. What volume of 0.995 *M* HCl solution could be neutralized by 125 mL of 3.01 *M* NaOH solution?

71. A sample of sodium hydrogen carbonate solid weighing 0.1015 g requires 47.21 mL of a hydrochloric acid solution to react completely.

$$HCl(aq) + NaHCO_3(s) \rightarrow NaCl(aq) + H_2O(l) + CO_2(g)$$

Calculate the molarity of the hydrochloric acid solution.

72. The total acidity in water samples can be determined by neutralization with standard sodium hydroxide solution. What is the total concentration of hydrogen ion, H^+, present in a water sample if 100. mL of the sample requires 7.2 mL of 2.5×10^{-3} *M* NaOH to be neutralized?

All even-numbered Questions and Problems have answers in the back of this book and solutions in the Solutions Guide.

73. What volume of 1.00 *M* NaOH is required to neutralize each of the following solutions?

a. 25.0 mL of 0.154 *M* acetic acid, $HC_2H_3O_2$
b. 35.0 mL of 0.102 *M* hydrofluoric acid, HF
c. 10.0 mL of 0.143 *M* phosphoric acid, H_3PO_4
d. 35.0 mL of 0.220 *M* sulfuric acid, H_2SO_4

74. What volume of 0.101 *M* HNO_3 is required to neutralize each of the following solutions?

a. 12.7 mL of 0.501 *M* NaOH
b. 24.9 mL of 0.00491 *M* $Ba(OH)_2$
c. 49.1 mL of 0.103 *M* NH_3
d. 1.21 L of 0.102 *M* KOH

15.8 Solution Composition: Normality

QUESTIONS

75. One equivalent of an acid is the amount of the acid required to provide ______.

76. A solution that contains 1 equivalent of acid or base per liter is said to be a ______ solution.

77. Explain why the equivalent weight of H_2SO_4 is half the molar mass of this substance. How many hydrogen ions does each H_2SO_4 molecule produce when reacting with an excess of OH^- ions?

78. How many equivalents of hydroxide ion are needed to react with 1.53 equivalents of hydrogen ion? How did you know this when no balanced chemical equation was provided for the reaction?

PROBLEMS

79. For each of the following solutions, calculate the normality.

a. 25.2 mL of 0.105 *M* HCl diluted with water to a total volume of 75.3 mL
b. 0.253 *M* H_3PO_4
c. 0.00103 *M* $Ca(OH)_2$

80. For each of the following solutions, the mass of solute taken is indicated, along with the total volume of solution prepared. Calculate the normality of each solution.

a. 0.113 g NaOH; 10.2 mL
b. 12.5 mg $Ca(OH)_2$; 100. mL
c. 12.4 g H_2SO_4; 155 mL

81. Calculate the normality of each of the following solutions.

a. 0.250 *M* HCl
b. 0.105 *M* H_2SO_4
c. 5.3×10^{-2} *M* H_3PO_4

82. Calculate the normality of each of the following solutions.

a. 0.134 *M* NaOH
b. 0.00521 *M* $Ca(OH)_2$
c. 4.42 *M* H_3PO_4

83. A solution of phosphoric acid, H_3PO_4, is found to contain 35.2 g of H_3PO_4 per liter of solution. Calculate the molarity and normality of the solution.

84. A solution of the sparingly soluble base $Ca(OH)_2$ is prepared in a volumetric flask by dissolving 5.21 mg of $Ca(OH)_2$ to a total volume of 1000. mL. Calculate the molarity and normality of the solution.

85. How many milliliters of 0.50 *N* NaOH are required to neutralize exactly 15.0 mL of 0.35 *N* H_2SO_4?

86. What volume of 0.104 *N* H_2SO_4 is required to neutralize 15.2 mL of 0.152 *N* NaOH? What volume of 0.104 *M* H_2SO_4 is required to neutralize 15.2 mL of 0.152 *M* NaOH?

$$H_2SO_4(aq) + 2NaOH(aq) \rightarrow Na_2SO_4(aq) + 2H_2O(l)$$

87. What volume of 0.151 *N* NaOH is required to neutralize 24.2 mL of 0.125 *N* H_2SO_4? What volume of 0.151 *N* NaOH is required to neutralize 24.1 mL of 0.125 *M* H_2SO_4?

88. Suppose that 27.34 mL of standard 0.1021 *M* NaOH is required to neutralize 25.00 mL of an unknown H_2SO_4 solution. Calculate the molarity and the normality of the unknown solution.

Additional Problems

89. A mixture is prepared by mixing 50.0 g of ethanol, 50.0 g of water, and 5.0 g of sugar. What is the mass percent of each component in the mixture? How many grams of the mixture should one take in order to have 1.5 g of sugar? How many grams of the mixture should one take to have 10.0 g of ethanol?

90. Explain the difference in meaning between the following two solutions: "50. g of NaCl dissolved in 1.0 L of water" and "50. g of NaCl dissolved in enough water to make 1.0 L of solution." For which solution can the molarity be calculated directly (using the molar mass of NaCl)?

91. Suppose 50.0 mL of 0.250 *M* $CoCl_2$ solution is added to 25.0 mL of 0.350 *M* $NiCl_2$ solution. Calculate the concentration, in moles per liter, of each of the ions present after mixing. Assume that the volumes are additive.

92. If 500. g of water is added to 75 g of 25% NaCl solution, what is the percent by mass of NaCl in the diluted solution?

93. Calculate the mass of AgCl formed, and the concentration of silver ion remaining in solution, when 10.0 g of solid $AgNO_3$ is added to 50. mL of 1.0×10^{-2} *M* NaCl solution. Assume there is no volume change upon addition of the solid.

94. Baking soda (sodium hydrogen carbonate, $NaHCO_3$) is often used to neutralize spills of acids on the benchtop in the laboratory. What mass of $NaHCO_3$ would be needed to neutralize a spill consisting of 25.2 mL of 6.01 *M* hydrochloric acid solution?

All even-numbered Questions and Problems have answers in the back of this book and solutions in the Solutions Guide.

85. 11 mL

86. 22.2 mL; 11.1 mL

87. 20.0 mL; 39.9 mL

88. 0.05583 *M;* 0.1117 *N*

89. 47.6% ethanol, 47.6% water, 4.8% sugar; 31 g solution; 21.0 g solution

90. Molarity is defined as the number of moles of solute contained in 1 liter of *total* solution volume (solute plus solvent after mixing). In the first example, the total volume after mixing is *not* known and the molarity cannot be calculated. In the second example, the final volume after mixing is known and the molarity can be calculated simply.

91. 0.167 *M* Co^{2+}; 0.117 *M* Ni^{2+}; 0.567 *M* Cl^-

92. 3.3%

93. 0.072 g AgCl form; 1.2 *M* remaining silver ion concentration

94. 12.7 g

95. 11 mL H_2S

74. (a) 63.0 mL; (b) 2.42 mL; (c) 50.1 mL; (d) 1.22 L

75. 1 mole of hydrogen ions (protons)

76. 1 *N*

77. Each H_2SO_4 molecule provides two H^+ ions when it ionizes completely. To obtain one mole of H^+ ions, therefore, only one-half mole of H_2SO_4 is needed.

78. 1.53 equivalents OH^- ion. By definition, one equivalent of OH^- ion exactly neutralizes one equivalent of H^+ ion.

79. (a) 0.0351 *N;* (b) 0.759 *N;* (c) 0.00206 *N*

80. (a) 0.277 *N;* (b) 3.37×10^{-3} *N;* (c) 1.63 *N*

81. (a) 0.250 *N;* (b) 0.210 *N;* (c) 0.16 *N*

82. (a) 0.134 *N;* (b) 0.0104 *N;* (c) 13.3 *N*

83. 0.359 *M;* 1.08 *N*

84. 7.03×10^{-5} *M;* 1.41×10^{-4} *N*

95. Many metal ions form insoluble sulfide compounds when a solution of the metal ion is treated with hydrogen sulfide gas. For example, nickel(II) precipitates nearly quantitatively as NiS when H_2S gas is bubbled through a nickel ion solution. How many milliliters of gaseous H_2S at STP are needed to precipitate all the nickel ion present in 10. mL of 0.050 *M* $NiCl_2$ solution?

96. Strictly speaking, the solvent is the component of a solution that is present in the largest amount on a *mole* basis. For solutions involving water, water is almost always the solvent because there tend to be many more water molecules present than molecules of any conceivable solute. To see why this is so, calculate the number of moles of water present in 1.0 L of water. Recall that the density of water is very nearly 1.0 g/mL under most conditions.

97. Aqueous ammonia is typically sold by chemical supply houses as the saturated solution, which has a concentration of 14.5 mol/L. What volume of NH_3 at STP is required to prepare 100. mL of concentrated ammonia solution?

98. What volume of hydrogen chloride gas at STP is required to prepare 500. mL of 0.100 *M* HCl solution?

99. What do we mean when we say that "like dissolves like"? Do two molecules have to be identical to be able to form a solution in one another?

100. The concentration of a solution of HCl is 33.1% by mass, and its density was measured to be 1.147 g/mL. How many milliliters of the HCl solution are required to obtain 10.0 g of HCl?

101. An experiment calls for 1.00 g of silver nitrate, but all that is available in the laboratory is a 0.50% solution of $AgNO_3$. Assuming the density of the silver nitrate solution to be very nearly that of water because it is so dilute, determine how many milliliters of the solution should be used.

102. If 14.2 g of $CaCl_2$ is added to a 50.0-mL volumetric flask, and after dissolving the salt, water is added to the calibration mark of the flask, calculate the molarity of the solution.

103. A solution is 0.1% by mass calcium chloride. Therefore, 100. g of the solution contains ________ g of calcium chloride.

104. Calculate the mass percent of KNO_3 in each of the following solutions.

a. 5.0 g of KNO_3 in 75 g of water
b. 2.5 mg of KNO_3 in 1.0 g of water
c. 11 g of KNO_3 in 89 g of water
d. 11 g of KNO_3 in 49 g of water

105. A 15.0% (by mass) NaCl solution is available. Determine what mass of the solution should be taken to obtain the following quantities of NaCl.

a. 10.0 g
b. 25.0 g
c. 100.0 g
d. 1.00 lb

106. A certain grade of steel is made by dissolving 5.0 g of carbon and 1.5 g of nickel per 100. g of molten iron. What is the mass percent of each component in the finished steel?

107. A sugar solution is prepared in such a way that it contains 10.% dextrose by mass. What quantity of this solution do we need to obtain 25 g of dextrose?

108. How many grams of Na_2CO_3 are contained in 500. g of a 5.5% by mass Na_2CO_3 solution?

109. What mass of KNO_3 is required to prepare 125 g of 1.5% KNO_3 solution?

110. A solution contains 7.5% by mass NaCl and 2.5% by mass KBr. What mass of *each* solute is contained in 125 g of the solution?

111. How many moles of each ion are present in 11.7 mL of 0.102 *M* Na_3PO_4 solution?

112. For each of the following solutions, the number of moles of solute is given, followed by the total volume of solution prepared. Calculate the molarity.

a. 0.10 mole of $CaCl_2$; 25 mL
b. 2.5 moles of KBr; 2.5 L
c. 0.55 mole of $NaNO_3$; 755 mL
d. 4.5 moles of Na_2SO_4; 1.25 L

113. For each of the following solutions, the mass of the solute is given, followed by the total volume of solution prepared. Calculate the molarity.

a. 5.0 g of $BaCl_2$; 2.5 L
b. 3.5 g of KBr; 75 mL
c. 21.5 g of Na_2CO_3; 175 mL
d. 55 g of $CaCl_2$; 1.2 L

114. If 125 g of sucrose, $C_{12}H_{22}O_{11}$, is dissolved in enough water to make 450. mL of solution, calculate the molarity.

115. Concentrated hydrochloric acid is made by pumping hydrogen chloride gas into distilled water. If concentrated HCl contains 439 g of HCl per liter, what is the molarity?

116. If 1.5 g of NaCl is dissolved in enough water to make 1.0 L of solution, what is the molarity of NaCl in the solution?

117. How many *moles* of the indicated solute does each of the following solutions contain?

a. 1.5 L of 3.0 *M* H_2SO_4 solution
b. 35 mL of 5.4 *M* NaCl solution
c. 5.2 L of 18 *M* H_2SO_4 solution
d. 0.050 L of 1.1×10^{-3} *M* NaF solution

118. How many *moles* and how many *grams* of the indicated solute does each of the following solutions contain?

a. 4.25 L of 0.105 *M* KCl solution
b. 15.1 mL of 0.225 *M* $NaNO_3$ solution
c. 25 mL of 3.0 *M* HCl
d. 100. mL of 0.505 *M* H_2SO_4

119. If 10. g of $AgNO_3$ is available, what volume of 0.25 *M* $AgNO_3$ solution can be prepared?

All even-numbered Questions and Problems have answers in the back of this book and solutions in the Solutions Guide.

96. 56 mol

97. 32.5 L NH_3

98. 1.12 L HCl at STP

99. Two substances will be miscible if they have similar intermolecular forces; molecules do not have to be identical, but a similarity in structure will help solubility.

100. 26.3 mL

101. 200 g solution (2.0×10^2 g solution)

102. 2.56 *M*

103. 0.1 g $CaCl_2$

104. (a) 6.3% KNO_3; (b) 0.25% KNO_3; (c) 11% KNO_3; (d) 18% KNO_3

105. (a) 66.7 g solution; (b) 167 g solution; (c) 667 g solution; (d) 3.02×10^3 g solution

106. 4.7% C; 1.4% Ni; 93.9% Fe

107. 250 g solution

108. 28 g Na_2CO_3

109. 1.9 g KNO_3

110. 9.4 g NaCl; 3.1 g KBr

111. 1.19×10^{-4} mol PO_4^{3-}; 3.58×10^{-4} mol Na^+

112. (a) 4.0 *M*; (b) 1.0 *M*; (c) 0.73 *M*; (d) 3.6 *M*

113. (a) 9.6×10^{-3} *M*; (b) 0.39 *M*; (c) 1.16 *M*; (d) 0.41 *M*

114. 0.812 *M*

115. 12.0 *M*

116. 0.026 *M*

117. (a) 4.5 mol H_2SO_4; (b) 0.19 mol NaCl; (c) 94 mol H_2SO_4; (d) 5.5×10^{-5} mol NaF

118. (a) 0.446 mol, 33.3 g; (b) 0.00340 mol, 0.289 g; (c) 0.075 mol, 2.7 g; (d) 0.0505 mol, 4.95 g

119. 0.24 L

120. (a) 0.938 mol Na^+, 0.313 mol PO_4^{3-}; (b) 0.042 mol H^+, 0.021 mol SO_4^{2-}; (c) 0.0038 mol Al^{3+}, 0.011 mol Cl^-; (d) 1.88 mol Ba^{2+}, 3.75 mol Cl^-

120. Calculate the number of moles of *each* ion present in each of the following solutions.

a. 1.25 L of 0.250 *M* Na_3PO_4 solution
b. 3.5 mL of 6.0 *M* H_2SO_4 solution
c. 25 mL of 0.15 *M* $AlCl_3$ solution
d. 1.50 L of 1.25 *M* $BaCl_2$ solution

121. Calcium carbonate, $CaCO_3$, can be obtained in a very pure state. Standard solutions of calcium ion are usually prepared by dissolving calcium carbonate in acid. What mass of $CaCO_3$ should be taken to prepare 500. mL of 0.0200 *M* calcium ion solution?

122. Calculate the new molarity when 150. mL of water is added to each of the following solutions.

a. 125 mL of 0.200 *M* HBr
b. 155 mL of 0.250 *M* $Ca(C_2H_3O_2)_2$
c. 0.500 L of 0.250 *M* H_3PO_4
d. 15 mL of 18.0 *M* H_2SO_4

123. How many milliliters of 18.0 *M* H_2SO_4 are required to prepare 35.0 mL of 0.250 *M* solution?

124. When 50. mL of 5.4 *M* NaCl is diluted to a final volume of 300. mL, what is the concentration of NaCl in the diluted solution?

125. When 10. L of water is added to 3.0 L of 6.0 *M* H_2SO_4, what is the molarity of the resulting solution? Assume the volumes are additive.

126. How many milliliters of 0.10 *M* Na_2S solution are required to precipitate all the nickel, as NiS, from 25.0 mL of 0.20 *M* $NiCl_2$ solution?

$$NiCl_2(aq) + Na_2S(aq) \rightarrow NiS(s) + 2NaCl(aq)$$

127. How many grams of $Ba(NO_3)_2$ are required to precipitate all the sulfate ion present in 15.3 mL of 0.139 *M* H_2SO_4 solution?

$$Ba(NO_3)_2(aq) + H_2SO_4(aq) \rightarrow BaSO_4(s) + 2HNO_3(aq)$$

128. What volume of 0.150 *M* HNO_3 solution is needed to exactly neutralize 35.0 mL of 0.150 *M* NaOH solution?

129. What volume of 0.250 *M* HCl is required to neutralize each of the following solutions?

a. 25.0 mL of 0.103 *M* sodium hydroxide, NaOH
b. 50.0 mL of 0.00501 *M* calcium hydroxide, $Ca(OH)_2$
c. 20.0 mL of 0.226 *M* ammonia, NH_3
d. 15.0 mL of 0.0991 *M* potassium hydroxide, KOH

130. For each of the following solutions, the mass of solute taken is indicated, as well as the total volume of solution prepared. Calculate the normality of each solution.

a. 15.0 g of HCl; 500. mL
b. 49.0 g of H_2SO_4; 250. mL
c. 10.0 g of H_3PO_4; 100. mL

131. Calculate the normality of each of the following solutions.

a. 0.50 *M* acetic acid, $HC_2H_3O_2$
b. 0.00250 *M* sulfuric acid, H_2SO_4
c. 0.10 *M* potassium hydroxide, KOH

132. A sodium dihydrogen phosphate solution was prepared by dissolving 5.0 g of NaH_2PO_4 in enough water to make 500. mL of solution. What are the molarity and normality of the resulting solution?

133. How many milliliters of 0.105 *M* NaOH are required to neutralize exactly 14.2 mL of 0.141 *M* H_3PO_4?

134. If 27.5 mL of 3.5×10^{-2} *N* $Ca(OH)_2$ solution is needed to neutralize 10.0 mL of nitric acid solution of unknown concentration, what is the normality of the nitric acid?

All even-numbered Questions and Problems have answers in the back of this book and solutions in the Solutions Guide.

121. 1.00 g $CaCO_3$

122. (a) 0.0909 *M;* (b) 0.127 *M;* (c) 0.192 *M;* (d) 1.6 *M*

123. 0.486 mL

124. 0.90 *M*

125. 1.4 *M*

126. 50. mL

127. 0.556 g $Ba(NO_3)_2$

128. 35.0 mL

129. (a) 10.3 mL; (b) 2.00 mL; (c) 18.1 mL; (d) 5.95 mL

130. (a) 0.822 *N* HCl; (b) 4.00 *N* H_2SO_4; (c) 3.06 *N* H_3PO_4

131. (a) 0.50 *N* $HC_2H_3O_2$; (b) 0.00500 *N* H_2SO_4; (c) 0.10 *N* KOH

132. 0.083 *M* NaH_2PO_4; 0.17 *N* NaH_2PO_4

133. 57.2 mL

134. 9.6×10^{-2} *N* HNO_3

Answers to Cumulative Review Exercises

Chapters 13–15

1. Gases have no fixed volume or shape, but rather take on the shape and volume of the container in which they are confined. In contrast, a sample of solid has its own intrinsic volume and shape, and is very incompressible; a sample of liquid has an intrinsic volume, but does take on the shape of its container.

2. The pressure of the atmosphere represents the mass of the gases in the atmosphere pressing down on the surface of the earth. The device most commonly used to measure the pressure of the atmosphere is the mercury barometer shown in Figure 13.2. A simple experiment to demonstrate the pressure of the atmosphere is shown in Figure 13.1.

3. The SI unit of pressure is the *pascal,* but this unit is rarely used in everyday situations because it is too small to be practical. Rather, we tend to use units of pressure that are based on the simple instruments used to measure pressures, the mercury barometer and the manometer (see Figures 13.2 and 13.3).

The *mercury barometer,* used for measuring the pressure of the atmosphere, consists of a column of mercury that is held in a vertical glass tube by the atmosphere. The pressure of the atmosphere is indicated in terms of the height of the surface of the mercury in the long tube (relative to the surface of the mercury in the reservoir). As the atmospheric pressure changes, the height of the mercury column changes. The height of the mercury column is given in radio and TV weather reports in *inches of mercury,* but most scientific applications would quote the height in *millimeters of mercury* (mm Hg, torr). Pressures are also quoted in *standard atmospheres,* where 1 atm is equivalent to a pressure of 760 mm Hg.

The *mercury manometer* is used to measure the pressure of samples of gas in the laboratory. A manometer consists basically of a U-shaped tube filled with mercury, with one arm of the U open to the atmosphere and the other arm of the U connected to the gas sample to be measured. If the pressure of the gas sample is the same as the pressure of the atmosphere, then the mercury levels will be the same in both sides of the U. If the pressure of the gas is not the same as the atmospheric pressure, then the difference in height of the mercury levels can be used to determine by how many mm Hg the pressure of the gas sample differs from atmospheric pressure.

4. Boyle's law says that the volume of a gas sample will decrease if you squeeze it harder (at constant temperature, for a fixed amount of gas). Two mathematical statements of Boyle's law are

$$P \times V = \text{constant}$$
$$P_1 \times V_1 = P_2 \times V_2$$

These two mathematical formulas say the same thing: if the pressure on a sample of gas is increased, the volume of the sample will decrease. A graph of Boyle's law data is given as Figure 13.5: this type of graph ($xy = k$) is known to mathematicians as a *hyperbola*.

5. The qualification is necessary because the volume of a gas sample is dependent on all its properties. The properties of a gas are all interrelated (as shown by the ideal gas law, $PV = nRT$). If we want to use one of the derivative gas laws (Boyle's, Charles's, or Avogadro's gas law), which isolate how the volume of a gas sample varies with just one of its properties, then we must keep all the other properties constant while studying that one property.

6. Charles's law says that if you heat a sample of gas, the volume of the sample will increase (assuming the pressure and amount of gas remain the same). When the temperature is given in kelvins, Charles's law expresses a *direct* proportionality (if you *increase* T, then V *increases*), whereas Boyle's law expresses an *inverse* proportionality (if you *increase* P, then V *decreases*). Two mathematical statements of Charles's law are $V = bT$ and $(V_1/T_1) = (V_2/T_2)$. With this second formulation, we can determine volume–temperature information for a given gas sample under two sets of conditions. Charles's law holds true only if the amount of gas remains the same (the volume of a gas sample would increase if more gas were present) and also if the pressure remains the same (a change in pressure also changes the volume of a gas sample). A graph of volume versus temperature (at constant pressure) for an ideal gas is a straight line with an intercept at −273 °C (see Figure 13.7).

CUMULATIVE REVIEW for CHAPTERS 13-15

QUESTIONS

1. What are some of the general properties of gases that distinguish them from liquids and solids?
2. How does the pressure of the atmosphere arise? Sketch a representation of the device commonly used to measure the pressure of the atmosphere. Your textbook described a simple experiment to demonstrate the pressure of the atmosphere. Explain this experiment.
3. What is the SI unit of pressure? What units of pressure are commonly used in the United States? Why are these common units more convenient to use than the SI unit? Describe a *manometer* and explain how such a device can be used to measure the pressure of gas samples.
4. Your textbook gives several definitions and formulas for Boyle's law for gases. Write, in your *own* words, what this law really tells us about gases. Now write two mathematical expressions that describe Boyle's law. Do these two expressions tell us different things, or are they different representations of the same phenomena? Sketch the general shape of a graph of pressure versus volume for an ideal gas.
5. When using Boyle's law in solving problems in the textbook, you may have noticed that questions were often qualified by stating that "the temperature and amount of gas remain the same." Why was this qualification necessary?
6. What does Charles's law tell us about how the volume of a gas sample varies as the temperature of the sample is changed? How does this volume–temperature relationship *differ* from the volume–pressure relationship of Boyle's law? Give two mathematical expressions that describe Charles's law. For Charles's law to hold true, why must the pressure and amount of gas remain the same? Sketch the general shape of a graph of volume versus temperature (at constant pressure) for an ideal gas.
7. Explain how the concept of absolute zero came about through Charles's studies of gases. *Hint:* What would happen to the volume of a gas sample at absolute zero (if the gas did not liquefy first)? What temperature scale is defined with its lowest point as the absolute zero of temperature? What is absolute zero in Celsius degrees?
8. What does Avogadro's law tell us about the relationship between the volume of a sample of gas and the number of molecules the gas contains? Why must the temperature and pressure be held constant for valid comparisons using Avogadro's law? Does Avogadro's law describe a direct or an inverse relationship between the volume and the number of moles of gas?
9. What do we mean specifically by an *ideal* gas? Explain why the *ideal gas law* ($PV = nRT$) is actually a combination of Boyle's, Charles's, and Avogadro's gas laws. What is the numerical value and what are the specific units of the universal gas constant, *R*? Why is close attention to *units* especially important when doing ideal gas law calculations?
10. Dalton's law of partial pressures concerns the properties of mixtures of gases. What is meant by the *partial pressure* of an individual gas in a mixture? How does the *total pressure* of a gaseous mixture depend on the partial pressures of the individual gases in the mixture? How does Dalton's law help us realize that in an ideal gas sample, the volume of the individual molecules is insignificant compared with the bulk volume of the sample?
11. What happens to a gas sample when it is collected by displacement of, or by bubbling through, water? How is this taken into account when calculating the pressure of the gas?
12. Without consulting your textbook, list and explain the main postulates of the kinetic molecular theory for gases. How do these postulates help us account for the following bulk properties of a gas: the pressure of the gas and why the pressure of the gas increases with increased temperature; the fact that a gas fills its entire container; and the fact that the volume of a given sample of gas increases as its temperature is increased.
13. What does "STP" stand for? What conditions correspond to STP? What is the volume occupied by one mole of an ideal gas at STP?
14. In general, how do we envision the structures of solids and liquids? Explain how the densities and compressibilities of solids and liquids contrast with those properties of gaseous substances. How do we know that the structures of the solid and liquid states of a substance are more comparable to each other than to the properties of the substance in the gaseous state?
15. Describe some of the physical properties of water. Why is water one of the most important substances on earth?
16. Define the *normal* boiling point of water. Why does a sample of boiling water remain at the same temperature until all the water has been boiled? Define the normal freezing point of water. Sketch a representation of a heating/cooling curve for water, marking clearly the normal freezing and boiling points.
17. Are changes in state physical or chemical changes? Explain. What type of forces must be overcome to melt or vaporize a substance (are these forces *intra*molecular or *inter*molecular)? Define the *molar heat of fusion* and *molar heat of vaporization.* Why is the molar heat of vaporization of water so much larger than its molar heat of fusion? Why does the boiling point of a liquid vary with altitude?

18. What is a *dipole–dipole attraction?* How do the strengths of dipole–dipole forces compare with the strengths of typical covalent bonds? What is *hydrogen bonding?* What conditions are necessary for hydrogen bonding to exist in a substance or mixture? What experimental evidence do we have for hydrogen bonding?

19. Define *London dispersion forces.* Draw a picture showing how London forces arise. Are London forces relatively strong or relatively weak? Explain. Although London forces exist among all molecules, for what type of molecule are they the *only* major intermolecular force?

20. Why does the process of *vaporization* require an input of energy? Why is it so important that water has a large heat of vaporization? What is *condensation?* Explain how the processes of vaporization and condensation represent an *equilibrium* in a closed container. Define the *equilibrium vapor pressure* of a liquid. Describe how this pressure arises in a closed container. Describe an experiment that demonstrates vapor pressure and enables us to measure the magnitude of that pressure. How is the magnitude of a liquid's vapor pressure related to the intermolecular forces in the liquid?

21. Define a *crystalline solid.* Describe in detail some important types of crystalline solids and name a substance that is an example of each type of solid. Explain how the particles are held together in each type of solid (the interparticle forces that exist). How do the interparticle forces in a solid influence the bulk physical properties of the solid?

22. Define the bonding that exists in metals and how this model explains some of the unique physical properties of metals. What are metal *alloys?* Identify the two main types of alloys, and describe how their structures differ. Give several examples of each type of alloy.

23. Define a *solution.* Describe how an ionic solute such as NaCl dissolves in water to form a solution. How are the strong bonding forces in a crystal of ionic solute overcome? Why do the ions in a solution not attract each other so strongly as to reconstitute the ionic solute? How does a molecular solid such as sugar dissolve in water? What forces between water molecules and the molecules of a molecular solid may help the solute dissolve? Why do some substances *not* dissolve in water at all?

24. Define a *saturated* solution. Does saturated mean the same thing as saying the solution is *concentrated?* Explain. Why does a solute dissolve only to a particular extent in water? How does formation of a saturated solution represent an equilibrium?

25. The concentration of a solution may be expressed in various ways. Suppose 5.00 g of NaCl were dissolved in 15.0 g of water, which resulted in 16.1 mL of solution after mixing. Explain how you would calculate the *mass percent* of NaCl and the *molarity* of NaCl.

26. When a solution is diluted by adding additional solvent, the *concentration* of solute changes but the *amount* of solute present does not change. Explain. Suppose 250. mL of water is added to 125 mL of 0.551 *M* NaCl solution. Explain *how* you would calculate the concentration of the solution after dilution.

27. What is one *equivalent* of an acid? What does an equivalent of a base represent? How is the equivalent weight of an acid or a base related to the substance's molar mass? Give an example of an acid and a base that have equivalent weights *equal* to their molar masses. Give an example of an acid and a base that have equivalent weights that are *not equal* to their molar masses. What is a *normal* solution of an acid or a base? How is the *normality* of an acid or a base solution related to its *molarity?* Give an example of a solution whose normality is equal to its molarity, and an example of a solution whose normality is *not* the same as its molarity.

PROBLEMS

28. a. If the pressure on a 125-mL sample of gas is increased from 755 mm Hg to 899 mm Hg at constant temperature, what will the volume of the sample become?
    b. If a sample of gas is compressed from an initial volume of 455 mL at 755 mm Hg to a final volume of 327 mL at constant temperature, what will be the new pressure in the gas sample?

29. a. If the temperature of a 255-mL sample of gas is increased from 35 °C to 55 °C at constant pressure, what will be the new volume of the gas sample?
    b. If a 325-mL sample of gas at 25 °C is immersed in liquid nitrogen at −196 °C, what will be the new volume of the gas sample?

30. Calculate the indicated quantity for each gas sample.
    a. The volume occupied by 1.15 g of helium gas at 25 °C and 1.01 atm pressure.
    b. The partial pressure of each gas if 2.27 g of H_2 and 1.03 g of He are confined to a 5.00-L container at 0 °C.
    c. The pressure existing in a 9.97-L tank containing 42.5 g of argon gas at 27 °C.

31. Chlorine gas, Cl_2, can be generated in small quantities by addition of concentrated hydrochloric acid to manganese(IV) oxide.

$$MnO_2(s) + 4HCl(aq) \rightarrow MnCl_2(aq) + 2H_2O(l) + Cl_2(g)$$

The chlorine gas is bubbled through water to dissolve any traces of HCl remaining and then is dried by bubbling through concentrated sulfuric acid.

After drying, what volume of Cl_2 gas at STP would be expected if 4.05 g of MnO_2 is treated with excess concentrated HCl?

32. When calcium carbonate is heated strongly, it evolves carbon dioxide gas.

$$CaCO_3(s) \rightarrow CaO(s) + CO_2(g)$$

7. The volume of a gas sample changes by the same factor (i.e., linearly) for each degree by which its temperature is changed (for a fixed amount of gas at a constant pressure). Charles realized that, if a gas were cooled, the volume of a gas sample would decrease by a constant factor for each degree by which the temperature was lowered. When Charles plotted his experimental data and extrapolated the linear data to very low temperatures that he could not measure experimentally, he realized that there would be an ultimate temperature where the volume of a gas sample would shrink to zero if the temperature were lowered any further. The same ultimate temperature was calculated no matter which gas sample was used for the experiment. This temperature—where the volume of an ideal gas sample would approach zero as a limit—is called the absolute zero of temperature. Unlike the Fahrenheit and Celsius temperature scales, which were defined by humans with experimentally convenient reference points, the absolute zero of temperature is a fundamental, natural reference point for the measurement of temperatures. The Kelvin (or absolute) temperature scale is defined with absolute zero as its lowest temperature, with all temperatures positive relative to this point. The size of the Kelvin degree was chosen to be the same size as the Celsius degree. Absolute zero (0 K) corresponds to −273 °C.

8. Avogadro's law says that the volume of a sample of gas is directly proportional to the number of moles (or molecules) of gas present (at constant temperature and pressure). Avogadro's law holds true only for gas samples compared under the same conditions of temperature and pressure. Avogadro's law expresses a direct proportionality: the more gas in a sample, the larger the sample's volume.

9. An *ideal gas* is defined to be a gas that obeys the *ideal gas law* (recognizing that the ideal gas law is based on the experimental measurement of the properties of gases). *Boyle's law* tells us that the volume of a gas is inversely proportional to its pressure (at constant temperature for a fixed amount of gas):

$$V = (\text{constant})/P$$

Charles's law indicates that the volume of a gas sample is related to its temperature (at constant pressure for a fixed amount of gas):

$$V = (\text{constant}) \times T$$

Avogadro's law shows that the volume of a gas sample is proportional to the number of moles of gas (at constant pressure and temperature):

$$V = (\textit{constant}) \times n$$

If we combine these relationships (and constants) to show how the volume of a gas is proportional to all its properties simultaneously, we obtain

$$V = (\text{constant}) \times \frac{T \times n}{P}$$

which can be arranged to the familiar form of the ideal gas law:

$$P \times V \times n \times R \times T$$

or just

$$PV = nRT$$

where R is the universal gas constant, which has the value 0.08206 L atm/mol K.

Although it is always important to pay attention to the units when solving a problem, this consideration is especially crucial when solving gas problems involving the universal gas constant, R. The numerical value of 0.08206 for R applies only when the properties of the gas sample are given in the units specified for the constant: volume in liters (not mL), pressure in atmospheres (not mm Hg, torr, or Pa), amount of gas in moles (not g), and temperature in kelvins (not °F or °C).

10. The "partial" pressure of an individual gas in a mixture of gases represents the pressure the gas would exert in the same container at the same temperature if it were the *only* gas present. The *total* pressure in a mixture of gases is the sum of the individual partial pressures of the gases present in the mixture. The fact that the partial pressures of the gases in a mixture are additive suggests that the total pressure in a container is a function of the *number* of molecules present, and not of the identity of the molecules or of any other property (such as the molecules' inherent atomic size).

11. When a gas is bubbled through water or is collected by displacing water, the gas becomes saturated with water vapor. A correction must be applied to the pressure of the gas to take into account the vapor pressure of water.

(Please refer to p. A32 in this book for answers to Exercises 12–38.)

If 1.25 g of $CaCO_3$ is heated, what mass of CO_2 would be produced? What volume would this quantity of CO_2 occupy at STP?

33. If an electric current is passed through molten sodium chloride, elemental chlorine gas is generated (see Chapter 18) as the sodium chloride is decomposed.

$$2NaCl(l) \rightarrow 2Na(s) + Cl_2(g)$$

What volume of chlorine gas measured at 767 mm Hg at 25 °C would be generated by complete decomposition of 1.25 g of NaCl?

34. Calculate the indicated quantity for each solution.
a. The percent by mass of solute when 2.05 g of NaCl is dissolved in 19.2 g of water.
b. The mass of solute contained in 26.2 g of 10.5% $CaCl_2$ solution.
c. The mass of NaCl required to prepare 225 g of 5.05% NaCl solution.

35. Calculate the indicated quantity for each solution.
a. The mass of solute present in 235 mL of 0.251 *M* NaOH solution.
b. The molarity of the solution when 0.293 mole of KNO_3 is dissolved in water to a final volume of 125 mL.
c. The number of moles of HCl present in 5.05 L of 6.01 *M* solution.

36. Calculate the molarities of the solutions resulting when the indicated dilutions are made. Assume that the volumes are additive.
a. 25 mL of water is added to 12.5 mL of 1.515 *M* NaOH solution.
b. 75.0 mL of 0.252 *M* HCl is diluted to a volume of 225 mL.
c. 52.1 mL fo 0.751 *M* HNO_3 is added to 250. mL of water.

37. Calculate the volume (in milliliters) of each of the following acid solutions that would be required to neutralize 36.2 mL of 0.259 *M* NaOH solution.
a. 0.271 *M* HCl
b. 0.119 *M* H_2SO_4
c. 0.171 *M* H_3PO_4

38. If 125 mL of concentrated sulfuric acid solution (density 1.84 g/mL, 98.3% H_2SO_4 by mass) is diluted to a final volume of 3.01 L, calculate the following information.
a. the mass of pure H_2SO_4 in the 125-mL sample.
b. the molarity of the *concentrated* acid solution
c. the molarity of the *dilute* acid solution
d. the normality of the dilute acid solution
e. the quantity of the dilute acid solution needed to neutralize 45.3 mL of 0.532 *M* NaOH solution

Chapter 16

Objectives

In this chapter, our objectives are for the students to:

SECTION 16.1

- Learn about two models of acids and bases and the relationship of conjugate acid–base pairs.

SECTION 16.2

- Understand what acid strength means.
- Understand the relationship between acid strength and the strength of the conjugate base.

SECTION 16.3

- Learn about the ionization of water.

SECTION 16.4

- Understand pH and pOH.
- Learn to find pOH and pH for various solutions.
- Learn to use a calculator in these calculations.

SECTION 16.5

- Learn to calculate the pH of solutions of strong acids.

SECTION 16.6

- Understand the general characteristics of buffered solutions.

16 Acids and Bases

Gargoyles on the Notre Dame cathedral in Paris in need of restoration from decades of acid rain. *(Witold Skrypczak/SuperStock)*

ChemWork Refined over ten years of use by thousands of students, **ChemWork** builds and enhances students' problems-solving skills. Online assignments function as a "personal instructor" to help students learn how to solve challenging problems and learn how to think like chemists. Annotations for **ChemWork** assignments are included at the beginning of the end-of-chapter review.

PowerLecture This 2-DVD package includes the Chemistry Multimedia Library, which contains animations, simulations, and movies for all chemistry subjects, organized by topic for lecture presentations. Annotations for **PowerLecture** are referenced in the margins throughout the Annotated Instructor's Edition.

OWL Sign in to OWL at **www.cengage.com/owl** to view tutorials and simulations, develop problem-solving skills, and complete online homework assigned by your professor.

go Chemistry Download mini-lecture videos for key concept review and exam prep from OWL or purchase them from **www.ichapters.com**

Acids are very important substances. They cause lemons to be sour, digest food in the stomach (and sometimes cause heartburn), dissolve rock to make fertilizer, dissolve your tooth enamel to form cavities, and clean the deposits out of your coffee maker. Acids are essential industrial chemicals. In fact, the chemical in first place in terms of the amount manufactured in the United States is sulfuric acid, H_2SO_4. Eighty *billion* pounds of this material are used every year in the manufacture of fertilizers, detergents, plastics, pharmaceuticals, storage batteries, and metals. The acid–base properties of substances also can be used to make interesting novelties such as the foaming chewing gum described on page 517.

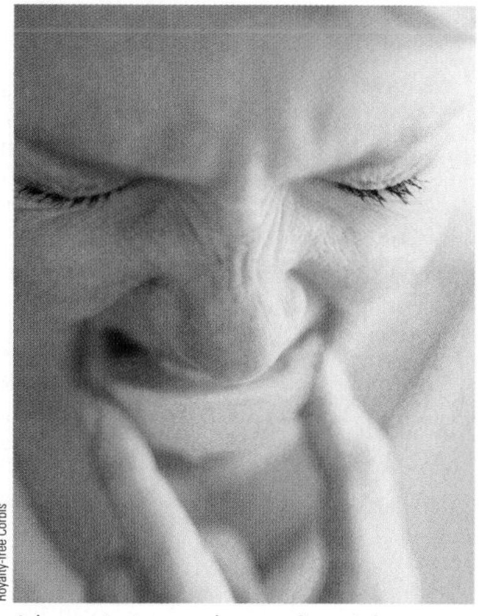

Royalty-free Corbis

A lemon tastes sour because it contains citric acid.

In this chapter we will consider the most important properties of acids and of their opposites, the bases.

Test Bank: 1–6

Section 16.1

16.1 Acids and Bases

OBJECTIVE: To learn about two models of acids and bases and the relationship of conjugate acid–base pairs.

Don't taste chemical reagents!

© Cengage Learning

The label on a bottle of concentrated hydrochloric acid.

Acids were first recognized as substances that taste sour. Vinegar tastes sour because it is a dilute solution of acetic acid; citric acid is responsible for the sour taste of a lemon. Bases, sometimes called *alkalis,* are characterized by their bitter taste and slippery feel. Most hand soaps and commercial preparations for unclogging drains are highly basic.

The first person to recognize the essential nature of acids and bases was Svante Arrhenius. On the basis of his experiments with electrolytes, Arrhenius postulated that **acids** *produce hydrogen ions in aqueous solution,* whereas **bases** *produce hydroxide ions* (review Section 7.4).

For example, when hydrogen chloride gas is dissolved in water, each molecule produces ions as follows:

$$HCl(g) \xrightarrow{H_2O} H^+(aq) + Cl^-(aq)$$

This solution is the strong acid known as hydrochloric acid. On the other hand, when solid sodium hydroxide is dissolved in water, its ions separate producing a solution containing Na^+ and OH^- ions.

TEACHING TIPS

- Spend some time developing the model for acid–base pairs in this section. Students need to be able to look at a chemical equation and identify the acid–base pairs.
- The Brønsted–Lowry definition of acids and bases is preferable because it emphasizes that for one reactant to act like an acid, the other reactant must act like a base.
- It is important that students recognize how these substances work together. A proton donor must have a substance to accept the proton. The idea that water can act as both an acid and a base can be developed here.
- This occasion is the first time students have seen the hydronium ion. Be sure that they understand how it forms from the donation of a proton to water.

Lecture Demonstration: 14.1

Lecture Demonstration: 14.2, 14.3

PowerLecture Animation: Brønsted-Lowry Reaction

PowerLecture Animations:
Strong Base: NaOH
Reaction: Nitric Acid and Water
Reaction: Ammonia and Water
Reaction: Hydrogen Carbonate Ion and Water
Reaction: NH_3 and HF

$$NaOH(s) \xrightarrow{H_2O} Na^+(aq) + OH^-(aq)$$

This solution is called a strong base.

Although the **Arrhenius concept of acids and bases** was a major step forward in understanding acid–base chemistry, this concept is limited because it allows for only one kind of base—the hydroxide ion. A more general definition of acids and bases was suggested by the Danish chemist Johannes Brønsted and the English chemist Thomas Lowry. In the **Brønsted–Lowry model,** *an acid is a proton (H^+) donor, and a base is a proton acceptor.* According to the Brønsted–Lowry model, the general reaction that occurs when an acid is dissolved in water can best be represented as an acid (HA) donating a proton to a water molecule to form a new acid (the **conjugate acid**) and a new base (the **conjugate base**).

Recall that (*aq*) means the substance is hydrated—it has water molecules clustered around it.

$$\underset{\text{Acid}}{HA(aq)} + \underset{\text{Base}}{H_2O(l)} \rightarrow \underset{\text{Conjugate acid}}{H_3O^+(aq)} + \underset{\text{Conjugate base}}{A^-(aq)}$$

This model emphasizes the significant role of the polar water molecule in pulling the proton from the acid. Note that the conjugate base is everything that remains of the acid molecule after a proton is lost. The conjugate acid is formed when the proton is transferred to the base. A **conjugate acid–base pair** consists of two substances related to each other by the donating and accepting of a *single proton.* In the above equation there are two conjugate acid–base pairs: HA (acid) and A^- (base), and H_2O (base) and H_3O^+ (acid). For example, when hydrogen chloride is dissolved in water it behaves as an acid.

Acid–conjugate base pair

$$HCl(aq) + H_2O(l) \rightarrow H_3O^+(aq) + Cl^-(aq)$$

Base–conjugate acid pair

In this case HCl is the acid that loses an H^+ ion to form Cl^-, its conjugate base. On the other hand, H_2O (behaving as a base) gains an H^+ ion to form H_3O^+ (the conjugate acid).

How can water act as a base? Remember that the oxygen of the water molecule has two unshared electron pairs, either of which can form a covalent bond with an H^+ ion. When gaseous HCl dissolves in water, the following reaction occurs:

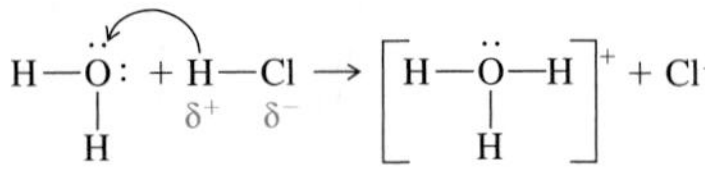

$$H-\ddot{\underset{|}{\overset{}{O}}}:_{H} + \overset{\delta^+}{H}-\overset{\delta^-}{Cl} \rightarrow \left[H-\ddot{\underset{|}{O}}_{H}-H\right]^+ + Cl^-$$

Note that an H^+ ion is transferred from the HCl molecule to the water molecule to form H_3O^+, which is called the **hydronium ion.**

EXAMPLE 16.1 Identifying Conjugate Acid–Base Pairs

Which of the following represent conjugate acid–base pairs?

a. HF, F^-

b. NH_4^+, NH_3

c. HCl, H_2O

Additional Examples

Example 16.1

Which of the following represent conjugate acid–base pairs?

1. $HClO_4$, ClO_4^-
2. HCl, ClO^-
3. $H_2PO_4^-$, HPO_4^{2-}
4. HNO_3, NO_3^-

1, 3, and 4

CHEMISTRY IN FOCUS

Gum That Foams

Mad Dawg chewing gum is a practical joker's dream come true. It is noticeably sour when someone first starts to chew it, but the big surprise comes about ten chews later when brightly colored foam oozes from the person's mouth. Although the effect is dramatic, the cause is simple acid–base chemistry.

The foam consists of sugar and saliva churned into a bubbling mess by carbon dioxide released from the gum. The carbon dioxide is formed when sodium bicarbonate ($NaHCO_3$) present in the gum is mixed with citric acid and malic acid (also present in the gum) in the moist environment of the mouth. As $NaHCO_3$ dissolves in the water of the saliva, it separates into its ions:

$$NaHCO_3(s) \xrightarrow{H_2O} Na^+(aq) + HCO_3^-(aq)$$

The bicarbonate ion, when exposed to H^+ ions from acids, decomposes to carbon dioxide and water:*

$$H^+(aq) + HCO_3^-(aq) \rightarrow H_2O(l) + CO_2(g)$$

The acids present in the gum also cause it to be sour, stimulating extra salivation and thus extra foam.

Although the chemistry behind Mad Dawg is well understood, the development of the gum into a safe, but fun, product was not so easy. In fact, early versions of the gum exploded because the acids and the sodium bicarbonate mixed prematurely. As solids, citric and malic acids and sodium bicarbonate do not react with each other. However, the presence of water frees the ions to move and react. In the manufacture of the gum, colorings and flavorings are applied as aqueous solutions. The water caused the gum to explode in early attempts to manufacture it. The makers of Mad Dawg obviously solved the problem. Buy some Mad Dawg and cut it open to see how they did it.

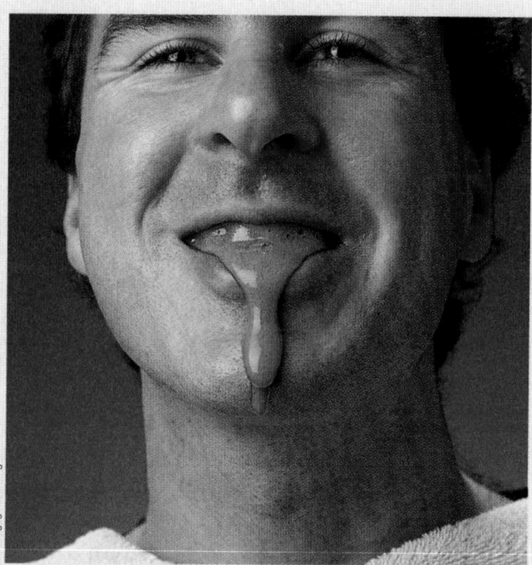

Chewing Mad Dawg gum.

*This reaction is often used to power "bottle rockets" by adding vinegar (dilute acetic acid) to baking soda (sodium bicarbonate).

SOLUTION

a. and b. HF, F^- and NH_4^+, NH_3 are conjugate acid–base pairs because the two species differ by one H^+.

$$HF \rightarrow H^+ + F^-$$
$$NH_4^+ \rightarrow H^+ + NH_3$$

c. HCl and H_2O are not a conjugate acid–base pair because they are not related by the removal or addition of one H^+. The conjugate base of HCl is Cl^-. The conjugate acid of H_2O is H_3O^+. ■

Additional Examples

Example 16.2

Write the conjugate base for each of the following.

1. H_2S

   HS^-

2. HS^-

   S^{2-}

3. NH_3

   NH_2^-

4. H_2SO_3

   HSO_3^-

Self Check

Answers to Self-Check Exercise 16.1

a, d

Section 16.2

TEACHING TIP

Have students draw molecular-level pictures to illustrate the difference between strong acids and weak acids. This idea is important to the understanding of how acids behave.

Test Bank: 7, 8, 10, 11

EXAMPLE 16.2 Writing Conjugate Bases

Write the conjugate base for each of the following:

a. $HClO_4$ b. H_3PO_4 c. $CH_3NH_3^+$

SOLUTION

To get the conjugate base for an acid, we must remove an H^+ ion.

a. $\underset{\text{Acid}}{HClO_4} \rightarrow H^+ + \underset{\text{Conjugate base}}{ClO_4^-}$

b. $\underset{\text{Acid}}{H_3PO_4} \rightarrow H^+ + \underset{\text{Conjugate base}}{H_2PO_4^-}$

c. $\underset{\text{Acid}}{CH_3NH_3^+} \rightarrow H^+ + \underset{\text{Conjugate base}}{CH_3NH_2}$

Self-Check EXERCISE 16.1 Which of the following represent conjugate acid–base pairs?

a. H_2O, H_3O^+

b. OH^-, HNO_3

c. H_2SO_4, SO_4^{2-}

d. $HC_2H_3O_2$, $C_2H_3O_2^-$

See Problems 16.7 through 16.14. ■

16.2 Acid Strength

OBJECTIVES: To understand what acid strength means. • To understand the relationship between acid strength and the strength of the conjugate base.

We have seen that when an acid dissolves in water, a proton is transferred from the acid to water:

$$HA(aq) + H_2O(l) \rightarrow H_3O^+(aq) + A^-(aq)$$

In this reaction a new acid, H_3O^+ (called the conjugate acid), and a new base, A^- (the conjugate base), are formed. The conjugate acid and base can react with one another,

$$H_3O^+(aq) + A^-(aq) \rightarrow HA(aq) + H_2O(l)$$

to re-form the parent acid and a water molecule. Therefore, this reaction can occur "in both directions." The forward reaction is

$$HA(aq) + H_2O(l) \rightarrow H_3O^+(aq) + A^-(aq)$$

and the reverse reaction is

$$H_3O^+(aq) + A^-(aq) \rightarrow HA(aq) + H_2O(l)$$

Note that the products in the forward reaction are the reactants in the reverse reaction. We usually represent the situation in which the reaction can occur in both directions by double arrows:

$$HA(aq) + H_2O(l) \rightleftharpoons H_3O^+(aq) + A^-(aq)$$

This situation represents a competition for the H^+ ion between H_2O (in the forward reaction) and A^- (in the reverse reaction). If H_2O "wins" this competition—that is, if H_2O has a very high attraction for H^+ compared to A^-—then the solution will contain mostly H_3O^+ and A^-. We describe this situation by saying that the H_2O molecule is a much stronger base (more attraction for H^+) than A^-. In this case the forward reaction predominates:

$$HA(aq) + H_2O(l) \Rightarrow H_3O^+(aq) + A^-(aq)$$

We say that the acid HA is **completely ionized** or **completely dissociated.** This situation represents a **strong acid.**

The opposite situation can also occur. Sometimes A^- "wins" the competition for the H^+ ion. In this case A^- is a much stronger base than H_2O and the reverse reaction predominates:

$$HA(aq) + H_2O(l) \Leftarrow H_3O^+(aq) + A^-(aq)$$

Here, A^- has a much larger attraction for H^+ than does H_2O, and most of the HA molecules remain intact. This situation represents a **weak acid.**

We can determine what is actually going on in a solution by measuring its ability to conduct an electric current. Recall from Chapter 7 that a solution can conduct a current in proportion to the number of ions that are present (see Figure 7.2). When 1 mole of solid sodium chloride is dissolved in 1 L of water, the resulting solution is an excellent conductor of an electric current because the Na^+ and Cl^- ions separate completely. We call NaCl a strong electrolyte. Similarly, when 1 mole of hydrogen chloride is dissolved in 1 L of water, the resulting solution is an excellent conductor. Therefore, hydrogen chloride is also a strong electrolyte, which means that each HCl molecule must produce H^+ and Cl^- ions. This tells us that the forward reaction predominates:

A hydrochloric acid solution readily conducts electric current, as shown by the brightness of the bulb.

$$HCl(aq) + H_2O(l) \rightleftharpoons H_3O^+(aq) + Cl^-(aq)$$

(Accordingly, the arrow pointing right is longer than the arrow pointing left.) In solution there are virtually no HCl molecules, only H^+ and Cl^- ions. This shows that Cl^- is a very poor base compared to the H_2O molecule; it has virtually no ability to attract H^+ ions in water. This aqueous solution of hydrogen chloride (called *hydrochloric acid*) is a strong acid.

In general, the strength of an acid is defined by the position of its ionization (dissociation) reaction:

$$HA(aq) + H_2O(l) \rightleftharpoons H_3O^+(aq) + A^-(aq)$$

A strong acid is one for which *the forward reaction predominates*. This means that almost all the original HA is dissociated (ionized) (see Figure 16.1a). There is an important connection between the strength of an acid and that of its conjugate base. *A strong acid contains a relatively weak conjugate base*—one that has a low attraction for protons. A strong acid can be described as an acid whose conjugate base is a much weaker base than water (Figure 16.2). In this case the water molecules win the competition for the H^+ ions.

A strong acid is completely dissociated in water. No HA molecules remain. Only H_3O^+ and A^- are present.

In contrast to hydrochloric acid, when acetic acid, $HC_2H_3O_2$, is dissolved in water, the resulting solution conducts an electric current only weakly. That is, acetic acid is a weak electrolyte, which means that only a few ions are present. In other words, for the reaction

$$HC_2H_3O_2(aq) + H_2O(l) \rightleftharpoons H_3O^+(aq) + C_2H_3O_2^-(aq)$$

DEMONSTRATION

Glowing Acids

Use the conductivity apparatus to show students various solutions of strong and weak acids. The brightness of the light is evident for strong acids, and the weakly lit bulb is apparent for weak acids. You can use this demonstration to discuss the difference in the number of ions produced in strong and weak acids.

Lecture Demonstration: 14.5

PowerLecture Animations:
Weak Acid: HF
Strong Acid: NaOH

TEACHING TIP

We use the terms *ionized* and *dissociated* interchangeably when discussing acids.

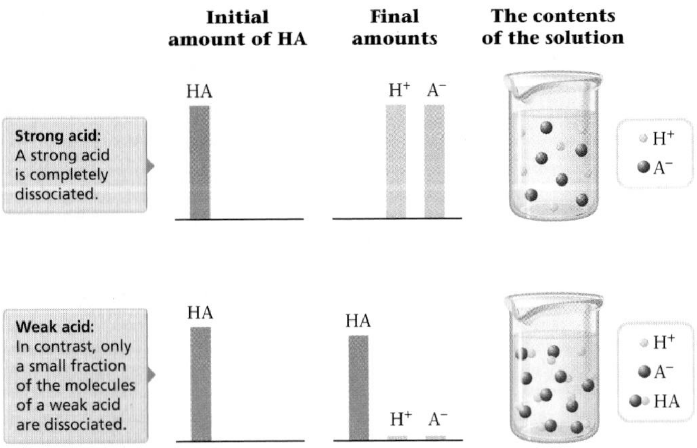

	Initial amount of HA	Final amounts	The contents of the solution
Strong acid: A strong acid is completely dissociated.	HA	H^+ A^-	H^+, A^-
Weak acid: In contrast, only a small fraction of the molecules of a weak acid are dissociated.	HA	HA, H^+ A^-	H^+, A^-, HA

Figure 16.1
Graphical representation of the behavior of acids of different strengths in aqueous solution.

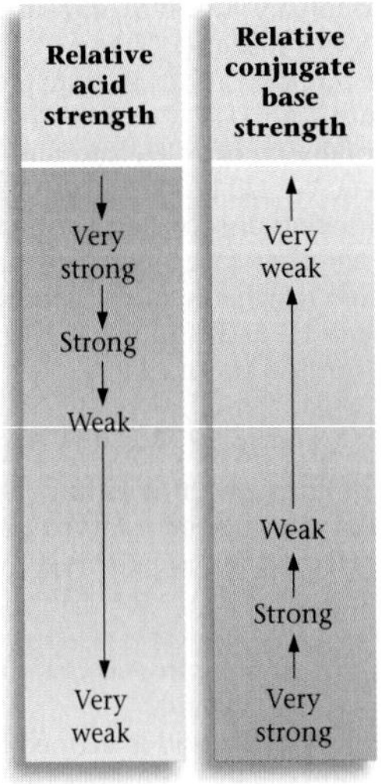

Relative acid strength	Relative conjugate base strength
Very strong	Very weak
Strong	
Weak	Weak
	Strong
Very weak	Very strong

Figure 16.2
The relationship of acid strength and conjugate base strength for the dissociation reaction

$$\underset{\text{Acid}}{HA(aq)} + H_2O(l) \rightleftharpoons H_3O^+(aq) + \underset{\text{Conjugate base}}{A^-(aq)}$$

PowerLecture Simulation: Acid Ionization

the reverse reaction predominates (thus the arrow pointing left is longer). In fact, measurements show that only about one in one hundred (1%) of the $HC_2H_3O_2$ molecules is dissociated (ionized) in a 0.1 *M* solution of acetic acid. Thus acetic acid is a weak acid. When acetic acid molecules are placed in water, almost all of the molecules remain undissociated. This tells us that the acetate ion, $C_2H_3O_2^-$, is an effective base—it very successfully attracts H^+ ions in water. This means that acetic acid remains largely in the form of $HC_2H_3O_2$ molecules in solution. A weak acid is one for which the *reverse reaction predominates.*

$$HA(aq) + H_2O(l) \Leftarrow H_3O^+(aq) + A^-(aq)$$

Most of the acid originally placed in the solution is still present as HA at equilibrium. That is, a weak acid dissociates (ionizes) only to a very small extent in aqueous solution (see Figure 16.1b). In contrast to a strong acid, a weak acid has a conjugate base that is a much stronger base than water. In this case a water molecule is not very successful in pulling an H^+ ion away from the conjugate base. *A weak acid contains a relatively strong conjugate base* (Figure 16.2).

The various ways of describing the strength of an acid are summarized in Table 16.1.

Table 16.1 Ways to Describe Acid Strength

Property	Strong Acid	Weak Acid
the acid ionization (dissociation) reaction	forward reaction predominates	reverse reaction predominates
strength of the conjugate base compared with that of water	A^- is a much weaker base than H_2O	A^- is a much stronger base than H_2O

520 Chapter 16 Acids and Bases

CHEMISTRY *IN* FOCUS

Carbonation—A Cool Trick

The sensations of taste and smell greatly affect our daily experience. For example, memories are often triggered by an odor that matches one that occurred when an event was originally stored in our memory banks. Likewise, the sense of taste has a powerful effect on our lives. For example, many people crave the intense sensation produced by the compounds found in chili peppers.

One sensation that is quite refreshing for most people is the effect of a chilled, carbonated beverage in the mouth. The sharp, tingling sensation experienced is not directly due to the bubbling of the dissolved carbon dioxide in the beverage. Rather, it arises because protons are produced as the CO_2 interacts with the water in the tissues of the mouth:

$$CO_2 + H_2O \rightleftharpoons H^+ + HCO_3^-$$

This reaction is speeded up by a biologic catalyst—an enzyme—called carbonic anhydrase. The acidification of the fluids in the nerve endings in the mouth leads to the sharp sensation produced by carbonated drinks.

Carbon dioxide also stimulates nerve sites that detect "coolness" in the mouth. In fact, researchers have identified a mutual enhancement between cooling and the presence of CO_2. Studies show that at a given concentration of CO_2, a colder drink feels more "pungent" than a warmer one. When tests were conducted on drinks in which the carbon dioxide concentration was varied, the results showed that a drink felt colder as the CO_2 concentration was increased, even though the drinks were all actually at the same temperature.

Thus a beverage can seem colder if it has a higher concentration of carbon dioxide. At the same time, cooling a carbonated beverage can intensify the tingling sensation caused by the acidity induced by the CO_2. This is truly a happy synergy.

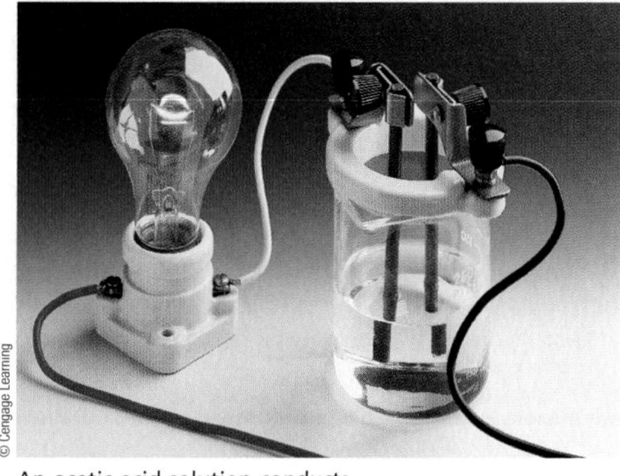

An acetic acid solution conducts only a small amount of current as shown by the dimly lit bulb.

The common strong acids are sulfuric acid, $H_2SO_4(aq)$; hydrochloric acid, $HCl(aq)$; nitric acid, $HNO_3(aq)$; and perchloric acid, $HClO_4(aq)$. Sulfuric acid is actually a **diprotic acid,** an acid that can furnish two protons. The acid H_2SO_4 is a strong acid that is virtually 100% dissociated in water:

$$H_2SO_4(aq) \rightarrow H^+(aq) + HSO_4^-(aq)$$

The HSO_4^- ion is also an acid but it is a weak acid:

$$HSO_4^-(aq) \rightleftharpoons H^+(aq) + SO_4^{2-}(aq)$$

Most of the HSO_4^- ions remain undissociated.

Most acids are **oxyacids,** in which the acidic hydrogen is attached to an oxygen atom (several oxyacids are shown at the bottom of the following page). The strong acids we have mentioned, except hydrochloric acid, are typical examples. **Organic acids,** those with a carbon-atom backbone, commonly contain the **carboxyl group:**

```
     O
    //
 —C
    \
     O—H
```

Acids of this type are usually weak. An example is acetic acid, CH_3COOH, which is often written as $HC_2H_3O_2$.

TEACHING TIPS

- This occasion is the first time students have been introduced to chemical equilibrium. It will be discussed in more detail in Chapter 17. For now, emphasize the competition for a proton between a conjugate base and water in determining which reaction (forward or reverse) dominates.
- After discussing forward and reverse reactions, students should understand that $C_2H_3O_2^-$ is a stronger base than H_2O, and that H_2O is a stronger base than Cl^-.
- In discussing the phrase "A weak acid contains a relatively strong conjugate base," emphasize the term *relatively*. The conjugate base of a weak acid is not a strong base in the same way that NaOH is a strong base: for the reaction of the conjugate base in water, the reverse reaction dominates. However, if we compare two unequally weak acids, the conjugate base of the weaker of the two acids is a stronger base, although both bases are considered weak (compared to OH^-).

CHEMISTRY *IN* FOCUS

Plants Fight Back

Plants sometimes do not seem to get much respect. We often think of them as rather dull life forms. We are used to animals communicating with each other, but we think of plants as mute. However, this perception is now changing. It is now becoming clear that plants communicate with other plants and also with insects. Ilya Roskin and his colleagues at Rutgers University, for example, have found that tobacco plants under attack by disease signal distress using the chemical salicylic acid, a precursor of aspirin. When a tobacco plant is infected with tobacco mosaic virus (TMV), which forms dark blisters on leaves and causes them to pucker and yellow, the sick plant produces large amounts of salicylic acid to alert its immune system to fight the virus. In addition, some of the salicylic acid is converted to methyl salicylate, a volatile compound that evaporates from the sick plant. Neighboring plants absorb this chemical and turn it back to salicylic acid, thus triggering their immune systems to protect them against the impending attack by TMV. Thus, as a tobacco plant gears up to fight an attack by TMV, it also warns its neighbors to be ready for this virus.

In another example of plant communication, a tobacco leaf under attack by a caterpillar emits a chemical signal that attracts a parasitic wasp that stings and kills the insect. Even more impressive is the ability of the plant to customize the emitted signal so that the wasp attracted will be the one that specializes in killing the particular caterpillar involved in the attack. The plant does this by changing the proportions of two chemicals emitted when a caterpillar chews on a leaf. Studies have shown that other plants, such as corn and cotton, also emit wasp-attracting chemicals when they face attack by caterpillars.

This research shows that plants can "speak up" to protect themselves. Scientists hope to learn to help them do this even more effectively.

Salicylic acid

Methyl salicylate

Agricultural Research Service/USDA

A wasp lays its eggs on a gypsy moth caterpillar on the leaf of a corn plant.

Phosphoric acid

Acetic acid

Nitrous acid

Hypochlorous acid

522

There are some important acids in which the acidic proton is attached to an atom other than oxygen. The most significant of these are the hydrohalic acids HX, where X represents a halogen atom. Examples are $HCl(aq)$, a strong acid, and $HF(aq)$, a weak acid.

16.3 Water as an Acid and a Base

OBJECTIVE: To learn about the ionization of water.

A substance is said to be *amphoteric* if it can behave either as an acid or as a base. Water is the most common **amphoteric substance.** We can see this clearly in the **ionization of water,** which involves the transfer of a proton from one water molecule to another to produce a hydroxide ion and a hydronium ion.

$$H_2O(l) + H_2O(l) \rightleftharpoons H_3O^+(aq) + OH^-(aq)$$

In this reaction one water molecule acts as an acid by furnishing a proton, and the other acts as a base by accepting the proton. The forward reaction for this process does not occur to a very great extent. That is, in pure water only a tiny amount of H_3O^+ and OH^- exist. At 25 °C the actual concentrations are

$$[H_3O^+] = [OH^-] = 1.0 \times 10^{-7}\ M$$

Notice that in pure water the concentrations of $[H_3O^+]$ and $[OH^-]$ are equal because they are produced in equal numbers in the ionization reaction.

One of the most interesting and important things about water is that the mathematical *product* of the H_3O^+ and OH^- concentrations is always constant. We can find this constant by multiplying the concentrations of H_3O^+ and OH^- at 25 °C:

$$[H_3O^+][OH^-] = (1.0 \times 10^{-7})(1.0 \times 10^{-7}) = 1.0 \times 10^{-14}$$

We call this constant K_w. Thus at 25 °C

$$[H_3O^+][OH^-] = 1.0 \times 10^{-14} = K_w$$

To simplify the notation we often write H_3O^+ as just H^+. Thus we would write the K_w expression as follows:

$$[H^+][OH^-] = 1.0 \times 10^{-14} = K_w$$

$\mathbf{K_w}$ is called the **ion-product constant** for water. The units are customarily omitted when the value of the constant is given and used.

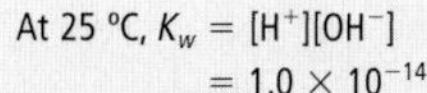
At 25 °C, $K_w = [H^+][OH^-] = 1.0 \times 10^{-14}$

It is important to recognize the meaning of K_w. In any aqueous solution at 25 °C, *no matter what it contains,* the product of $[H^+]$ and $[OH^-]$ must always equal 1.0×10^{-14}. This means that if the $[H^+]$ goes up, the $[OH^-]$ must go down so that the product of the two is still 1.0×10^{-14}. For example, if HCl gas is dissolved in water, increasing the $[H^+]$, the $[OH^-]$ must decrease.

There are three possible situations we might encounter in an aqueous solution. If we add an acid (an H^+ donor) to water, we get an *acidic solution.* In this case, because we have added a source of H^+, the $[H^+]$ will be greater than the $[OH^-]$. On the other hand, if we add a base (a source of OH^-) to water, the $[OH^-]$ will be greater than the $[H^+]$. This is a *basic solution.* Finally, we might have a situation in which $[H^+] = [OH^-]$. This is called a *neutral solution.* Pure water is automatically neutral but we can also obtain a neutral

PowerLecture Animation: Self-Ionization of Water

Test Bank: 12–19

Section 16.3

TEACHING TIP

Use an equation with two water molecules on the reactant side to show students that water acts as an acid and as a base. In this way, students can see that a proton is donated from one water molecule and accepted by the other water molecule. This knowledge allows them to correctly identify acid–base pairs.

DEMONSTRATION

You can use a conductivity tester to demonstrate that pure water does not conduct a current. Thus, in the autoionization of water, the reverse reaction must dominate—there are very few ions present.

TEACHING TIPS

- Students have no experience with the concept of an equilibrium constant. When you discuss the idea that K_w is a constant, be prepared for students who reason as follows: "Pure water contains $1.0 \times 10^{-7}\ M\ H^+$ and $1.0 \times 10^{-7}\ M\ OH^-$. If we add 1.0 mole of HCl to 1 L of water, the concentration of H^+ is about 1.0 *M*. So isn't $K_w = [H^+][OH^-] = [1.0\ M][1.0 \times 10^{-7}\ M] = 1.0 \times 10^{-7}$?" These students do not understand that the added H^+ will react with OH^-, lowering the concentration of OH^-. If 1.0 mole of H^+ is added to 1 L of water, the OH^- concentration will be 1.0×10^{-14} *M*. This will not be obvious to students at this point.

- Emphasize the definitions of acidic, basic, and neutral solutions. Note, however, that the focus should be on the relationship of the concentrations of the ions, not on the pH of the solution.

Additional Examples

Example 16.3

Calculate $[H^+]$ or $[OH^-]$ as required for each of the following at 25 °C and state whether the solution is neutral, acidic, or basic.

1. $[H^+] = 3.4 \times 10^{-4}$ *M*

   $[OH^-] = 2.9 \times 10^{-11}$ *M*; acidic

2. $[H^+] = 2.6 \times 10^{-8}$ *M*

   $[OH^-] = 3.9 \times 10^{-7}$ *M*; basic

3. $[OH^-] = 6.2 \times 10^{-9}$ *M*

   $[H^+] = 1.6 \times 10^{-6}$ *M*; acidic

4. $[OH^-] = 8.1 \times 10^{-3}$ *M*

   $[H^+] = 1.2 \times 10^{-12}$ *M*; basic

solution by adding equal amounts of H^+ and OH^-. It is very important that you understand the definitions of neutral, acidic, and basic solutions. In summary:

Remember that H^+ represents H_3O^+.

1. In a **neutral solution,** $[H^+] = [OH^-]$
2. In an **acidic solution,** $[H^+] > [OH^-]$
3. In a **basic solution,** $[OH^-] > [H^+]$

In each case, however, $K_w = [H^+][OH^-] = 1.0 \times 10^{-14}$.

EXAMPLE 16.3 Calculating Ion Concentrations in Water

Calculate $[H^+]$ or $[OH^-]$ as required for each of the following solutions at 25 °C, and state whether the solution is neutral, acidic, or basic.

a. 1.0×10^{-5} *M* OH^- b. 1.0×10^{-7} *M* OH^- c. 10.0 *M* H^+

SOLUTION

a. **Where Are We Going?**

We want to determine $[H^+]$ in a solution of given $[OH^-]$ at 25 °C.

What Do We Know?

- At 25 °C, $K_w = [H^+][OH^-] = 1.0 \times 10^{-14}$
- $[OH^-] = 1.0 \times 10^{-5}$ *M*

How Do We Get There?

MATH SKILL BUILDER

$K_w = [H^+][OH^-]$

$\frac{K_w}{[OH^-]} = [H^+]$

We know that $K_w = [H^+][OH^-] = 1.0 \times 10^{-14}$. We need to calculate the $[H^+]$. However, the $[OH^-]$ is given—it is 1.0×10^{-5} *M*—so we will solve for $[H^+]$ by dividing both sides by $[OH^-]$.

$$[H^+] = \frac{1.0 \times 10^{-14}}{[OH^-]} = \frac{1.0 \times 10^{-14}}{1.0 \times 10^{-5}} = 1.0 \times 10^{-9}\ M$$

Because $[OH^-] = 1.0 \times 10^{-5}$ *M* is greater than $[H^+] = 1.0 \times 10^{-9}$ *M*, the solution is basic. (Remember: The more negative the exponent, the smaller the number.)

b. **Where Are We Going?**

We want to determine $[H^+]$ in a solution of given $[OH^-]$ at 25 °C.

What Do We Know?

- At 25 °C, $K_w = [H^+][OH^-] = 1.0 \times 10^{-14}$
- $[OH^-] = 1.0 \times 10^{-7}$ *M*

How Do We Get There?

Again the $[OH^-]$ is given, so we solve the K_w expression for $[H^+]$.

$$[H^+] = \frac{1.0 \times 10^{-14}}{[OH^-]} = \frac{1.0 \times 10^{-14}}{1.0 \times 10^{-7}} = 1.0 \times 10^{-7}\ M$$

Here $[H^+] = [OH^-] = 1.0 \times 10^{-7}$ *M*, so the solution is neutral.

c. **Where Are We Going?**

We want to determine $[OH^-]$ in a solution of given $[H^+]$ at 25 °C.

What Do We Know?

- At 25 °C, $K_w = [H^+][OH^-] = 1.0 \times 10^{-14}$
- $[H^+] = 10.0\ M$

How Do We Get There?

MATH SKILL BUILDER
$K_w = [H^+][OH^-]$
$\frac{K_w}{[H^+]} = [OH^-]$

In this case the $[H^+]$ is given, so we solve for $[OH^-]$.

$$[OH^-] = \frac{1.0 \times 10^{-14}}{[H^+]} = \frac{1.0 \times 10^{-14}}{10.0} = 1.0 \times 10^{-15}\ M$$

Now we compare $[H^+] = 10.0\ M$ with $[OH^-] = 1.0 \times 10^{-15}\ M$. Because $[H^+]$ is greater than $[OH^-]$, the solution is acidic.

Self-Check EXERCISE 16.2 Calculate $[H^+]$ in a solution in which $[OH^-] = 2.0 \times 10^{-2}\ M$. Is this solution acidic, neutral, or basic?

See Problems 16.31 through 16.34. ■

EXAMPLE 16.4 Using the Ion-Product Constant in Calculations

Is it possible for an aqueous solution at 25 °C to have $[H^+] = 0.010\ M$ and $[OH^-] = 0.010\ M$?

SOLUTION

The concentration 0.010 *M* can also be expressed as $1.0 \times 10^{-2}\ M$. Thus, if $[H^+] = [OH^-] = 1.0 \times 10^{-2}\ M$, the product

$$[H^+][OH^-] = (1.0 \times 10^{-2})(1.0 \times 10^{-2}) = 1.0 \times 10^{-4}$$

This is not possible. The product of $[H^+]$ and $[OH^-]$ must always be 1.0×10^{-14} in water at 25 °C, so a solution could not have $[H^+] = [OH^-] = 0.010\ M$. If H^+ and OH^- are added to water in these amounts, they will react with each other to form H_2O,

$$H^+ + OH^- \rightarrow H_2O$$

until the product $[H^+][OH^-] = 1.0 \times 10^{-14}$.

This is a general result. When H^+ and OH^- are added to water in amounts such that the product of their concentrations is greater than 1.0×10^{-14}, they will react to form water until enough H^+ and OH^- are consumed so that $[H^+][OH^-] = 1.0 \times 10^{-14}$. ■

16.4 The pH Scale

OBJECTIVE: To understand pH and pOH. • To learn to find pOH and pH for various solutions. • To learn to use a calculator in these calculations.

To express small numbers conveniently, chemists often use the "p scale," which is based on common logarithms (base 10 logs). In this system, if *N* represents some number, then

$$pN = -\log N = (-1) \times \log N$$

Self Check

Answer to Self-Check Exercise 16.2

$[H^+] = 5.0 \times 10^{-13}\ M$, basic

Additional Examples

Example 16.4

1. Which is greater, $[OH^-]$ or $[H^+]$, if $[H^+] = 2.8 \times 10^{-5}\ M$ in an aqueous solution at 25 °C?

   $[H^+]$ is greater than $[OH^-]$

2. How many times greater is $[OH^-]$ than $[H^+]$ if $[H^+] = 1.0 \times 10^{-9}\ M$ in an aqueous solution at 25 °C?

   1.0×10^5 times greater

Test Bank: 9, 20–26, 28–34

Section 16.4

TEACHING TIPS

- Explain to students that logs are a shorthand way of writing exponents. Now is an excellent time to make sure that students understand how to use their particular calculator for determining logs.
- Students with programmable calculators must type in the expression exactly as it is shown to be evaluated. Many students using these calculators forget to type the parentheses in a mathematical expression. For example, if the parentheses are left out of the expression $-\log(1.0 \times 10^{-7})$, the answer will be 0.
- Significant figures in logs are especially difficult for students. Because logs are taught on calculators instead of using log tables, students often do not understand the concepts of the characteristic and the mantissa. The easiest way to teach them to use proper significant figures in logs is to explain that the number of significant figures in the original number is equal to the number of places to the right of the decimal in the log of the number.

CHEMISTRY *IN* FOCUS

Airplane Rash

Because airplanes remain in service for many years, it is important to spot corrosion that might weaken the structure at an early stage. In the past, looking for minute signs of corrosion has been very tedious and labor-intensive, especially for large planes. This situation has changed, however, thanks to the paint system developed by Gerald S. Frankel and Jian Zhang of Ohio State University. The paint they created turns pink in areas that are beginning to corrode, making these areas easy to spot.

The secret to the paint's magic is phenolphthalein, the common acid–base indicator that turns pink in a basic solution. The corrosion of the aluminum skin of the airplane involves a reaction that forms OH^- ions, producing a basic area at the site of the corrosion that turns the phenolphthalein pink. Because this system is highly sensitive, corrosion can be corrected before it damages the plane.

Next time you fly, if the plane has pink spots you might want to wait for a later flight!

Lecture Demonstration: 14.6

PowerLecture Animation: H_3O^+, OH^-, and pH

go Chemistry **Module 9a: pH (Pt. 1)** covers concepts in this section.

That is, the p means to take the log of the number that follows and multiply the result by −1. For example, to express the number 1.0×10^{-7} on the p scale, we need to take the negative log of 1.0×10^{-7}.

$$p(1.0 \times 10^{-7}) = -\log(1.0 \times 10^{-7}) = 7.00$$

The pH scale provides a compact way to represent solution acidity.

Because the $[H^+]$ in an aqueous solution is typically quite small, using the p scale in the form of the **pH scale** provides a convenient way to represent solution acidity. The pH is defined as

$$pH = -\log[H^+]$$

go Chemistry **Module 9b: pH (Pt. 2)** covers concepts in this section.

To obtain the pH value of a solution, we must compute the negative log of the $[H^+]$.

In the case where $[H^+] = 1.0 \times 10^{-5}\ M$, the solution has a pH value of 5.00.

To represent pH to the appropriate number of significant figures, you need to know the following rule for logarithms: *the number of decimal places for a log must be equal to the number of significant figures in the original number.* Thus

2 significant figures

$$[H^+] = 1.0 \times 10^{-5}\ M$$

and

$$pH = 5.00$$

2 decimal places

526

EXAMPLE 16.5 Calculating pH

Calculate the pH value for each of the following solutions at 25 °C.

a. A solution in which $[H^+] = 1.0 \times 10^{-9}$ *M*

b. A solution in which $[OH^-] = 1.0 \times 10^{-6}$ *M*

SOLUTION

a. For this solution $[H^+] = 1.0 \times 10^{-9}$.

$$-\log 1.0 \times 10^{-9} = 9.00$$
$$\text{pH} = 9.00$$

b. In this case we are given the $[OH^-]$. Thus we must first calculate $[H^+]$ from the K_w expression. We solve

$$K_w = [H^+][OH^-] = 1.0 \times 10^{-14}$$

for $[H^+]$ by dividing both sides by $[OH^-]$.

$$[H^+] = \frac{1.0 \times 10^{-14}}{[OH^-]} = \frac{1.0 \times 10^{-14}}{1.0 \times 10^{-6}} = 1.0 \times 10^{-8}$$

Now that we know the $[H^+]$, we can calculate the pH because $\text{pH} = -\log[H^+] = -\log[1.0 \times 10^{-8}] = 8.00$.

Self-Check EXERCISE 16.3 Calculate the pH value for each of the following solutions at 25 °C.

a. A solution in which $[H^+] = 1.0 \times 10^{-3}$ *M*

b. A solution in which $[OH^-] = 5.0 \times 10^{-5}$ *M*

See Problems 16.41 through 16.44. ■

Table 16.2 The Relationship of the H^+ Concentration of a Solution to Its pH

$[H^+]$	pH
1.0×10^{-1}	1.00
1.0×10^{-2}	2.00
1.0×10^{-3}	3.00
1.0×10^{-4}	4.00
1.0×10^{-5}	5.00
1.0×10^{-6}	6.00
1.0×10^{-7}	7.00

Because the pH scale is a log scale based on 10, *the pH changes by 1 for every power-of-10 change in the $[H^+]$.* For example, a solution of pH 3 has an H^+ concentration of 10^{-3} *M,* which is 10 times that of a solution of pH 4 ($[H^+] = 10^{-4}$ *M*) and 100 times that of a solution of pH 5. This is illustrated in Table 16.2. Also note from Table 16.2 that *the pH decreases as the $[H^+]$ increases.* That is, a lower pH means a more acidic solution. The pH scale and the pH values for several common substances are shown in Figure 16.3.

The pH decreases as $[H^+]$ increases, and vice versa.

We often measure the pH of a solution by using a pH meter, an electronic device with a probe that can be inserted into a solution of unknown pH. A pH meter is shown in Figure 16.4. Colored indicator paper is also commonly used to measure the pH of a solution when less accuracy is needed. A drop of the solution to be tested is placed on this special paper, which promptly turns to a color characteristic of a given pH (see Figure 16.5).

Log scales similar to the pH scale are used for representing other quantities. For example,

$$\text{pOH} = -\log[OH^-]$$

The symbol p means −log.

Therefore, in a solution in which

$$[OH^-] = 1.0 \times 10^{-12} \text{ } M$$

the pOH is

$$-\log[OH^-] = -\log(1.0 \times 10^{-12}) = 12.00$$

PowerLecture Simulation: The pH Scale

Products with a pH in the 6–8 range include bottled water (which is usually slightly basic due to bicarbonates) and milk (which is slightly acidic).

Additional Examples

Example 16.5

Calculate the pH value for each of the following aqueous solutions at 25 °C.

1. A solution in which $[H^+] = 2.1 \times 10^{-5}$ *M*

   pH = 4.68

2. A solution in which $[OH^-] = 5.9 \times 10^{-8}$ *M*

   pH = 6.77

Self Check

Answers to Self-Check Exercise 16.3

a. pH = 3.00

b. pH = 9.70

TEACHING TIP

Point out that a change of 1 in pH represents a change of a factor of 10 in hydrogen ion concentration.

DEMONSTRATION

Use pH paper or a pH meter (if one is available) to show the pH of various solutions. Some possible solutions are vinegar, HCl, NaOH, liquid drain cleaner, salt water, lemon juice, other fruit juices, and soap solutions. You may want to bring in some samples of household items for pH testing. As you find the pH of each item, have students classify it as acidic, basic, or neutral.

Students may be surprised to learn that most of the products they buy have a pH outside the 6–8 range. Fruits, fruit juices, and soft drinks all have pH values lower than 6. In fact, many food products are acidic. Also, many household cleaners (such as ammonia) are basic, as are antacid tablets.

PowerLecture Simulation: The pH Scale

PoweLecture Animation: pH Meter

	$[H^+]$	pH	
Basic	10^{-14}	14	1 *M* NaOH
	10^{-13}	13	
	10^{-12}	12	Ammonia (household cleaner)
	10^{-11}	11	
	10^{-10}	10	
	10^{-9}	9	
Neutral	10^{-8}	8	Blood
	10^{-7}	7	Pure water
	10^{-6}	6	Milk
	10^{-5}	5	
Acidic	10^{-4}	4	
	10^{-3}	3	Vinegar, Lemon juice
	10^{-2}	2	Stomach acid
	10^{-1}	1	
	10^{0}	0	1 *M* HCl

Figure 16.3 The pH scale and pH values of some common substances.

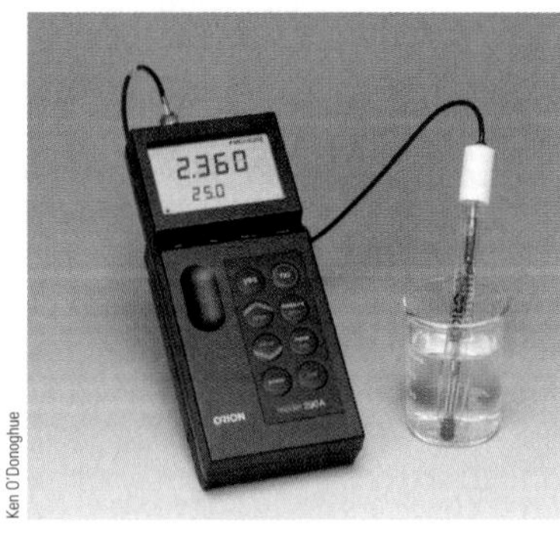

Ken O'Donoghue

Figure 16.4 A pH meter. The electrodes on the right are placed in the solution with unknown pH. The difference between the $[H^+]$ in the solution sealed into one of the electrodes and the $[H^+]$ in the solution being analyzed is translated into an electrical potential and registered on the meter as a pH reading.

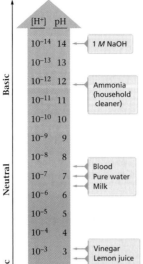

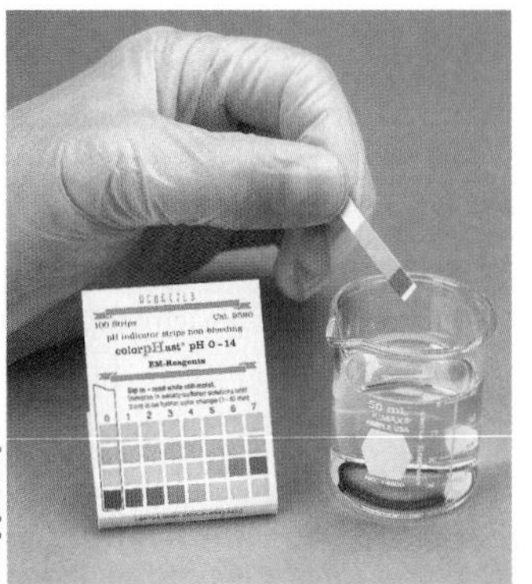

Figure 16.5 Indicator paper being used to measure the pH of a solution. The pH is determined by comparing the color that the solution turns the paper to the color chart.

Additional Examples

Example 16.6

Calculate the pH and pOH values for each of the following aqueous solutions at 25 °C.

1. A solution in which $[H^+] = 3.6 \times 10^{-9}$ *M*

   pH = 8.44; pOH = 5.56

2. A solution in which $[OH^-] = 9.2 \times 10^{-2}$ *M*

   pOH = 1.04; pH = 12.96

EXAMPLE 16.6 Calculating pH and pOH

Calculate the pH and pOH for each of the following solutions at 25 °C.

a. 1.0×10^{-3} *M* OH^-

b. 1.0 *M* H^+

SOLUTION

a. We are given the $[OH^-]$, so we can calculate the pOH value by taking $-\log[OH^-]$.

$$\text{pOH} = -\log[OH^-] = -\log(1.0 \times 10^{-3}) = 3.00$$

To calculate the pH, we must first solve the K_w expression for $[H^+]$.

$$[H^+] = \frac{K_w}{[OH^-]} = \frac{1.0 \times 10^{-14}}{1.0 \times 10^{-3}} = 1.0 \times 10^{-11}\ M$$

Now we compute the pH.

$$pH = -\log[H^+] = -\log(1.0 \times 10^{-11}) = 11.00$$

b. In this case we are given the $[H^+]$ and we can compute the pH.

$$pH = -\log[H^+] = -\log(1.0) = 0$$

We next solve the K_w expression for $[OH^-]$.

$$[OH^-] = \frac{K_w}{[H^+]} = \frac{1.0 \times 10^{-14}}{1.0} = 1.0 \times 10^{-14}\ M$$

Now we compute the pOH.

$$pOH = -\log[OH^-] = -\log(1.0 \times 10^{-14}) = 14.00$$ ■

We can obtain a convenient relationship between pH and pOH by starting with the K_w expression $[H^+][OH^-] = 1.0 \times 10^{-14}$ and taking the negative log of both sides.

$$-\log([H^+][OH^-]) = -\log(1.0 \times 10^{-14})$$

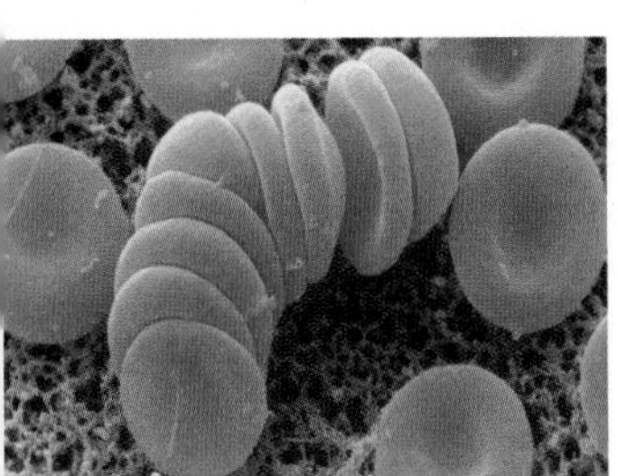

Red blood cells can exist only over a narrow range of pH.

Because the log of a product equals the sum of the logs of the terms—that is, $\log(A \times B) = \log A + \log B$—we have

$$\underbrace{-\log[H^+]}_{pH} \underbrace{-\log[OH^-]}_{pOH} = -\log(1.0 \times 10^{-14}) = 14.00$$

which gives the equation

$$pH + pOH = 14.00$$

This means that once we know either the pH or the pOH for a solution, we can calculate the other. For example, if a solution has a pH of 6.00, the pOH is calculated as follows:

$$\begin{aligned} pH + pOH &= 14.00 \\ pOH &= 14.00 - pH \\ pOH &= 14.00 - 6.00 = 8.00 \end{aligned}$$

EXAMPLE 16.7 **Calculating pOH from pH**

The pH of blood is about 7.4. What is the pOH of blood?

SOLUTION

$$\begin{aligned} pH + pOH &= 14.00 \\ pOH &= 14.00 - pH \\ &= 14.00 - 7.4 \\ &= 6.6 \end{aligned}$$

The pOH of blood is 6.6.

Self-Check EXERCISE 16.4 A sample of rain in an area with severe air pollution has a pH of 3.5. What is the pOH of this rainwater?

See Problems 16.45 and 16.46. ■

Additional Examples

Example 16.7

1. The pH of a solution is 5.67. What is the pOH of the solution?

   pOH = 8.33

2. The pH of a solution is 9.23. What is the pOH of the solution?

   pOH = 4.77

Self Check

Answer to Self-Check Exercise 16.4

pOH = 10.5

TEACHING TIPS

- Some calculators have an inverse log key, while others use 10^x for the inverse log function. This variation can cause difficulties for students. Be sure they understand how to use their calculators to find inverse logs.
- This occasion offers another opportunity to review significant figures. Once again, students may become confused about how many significant figures to put in the inverse log concentration. Remind students that the correct number of significant figures will be the same as the number of digits to the right of the decimal in the log number.

It is also possible to find the $[H^+]$ or $[OH^-]$ from the pH or pOH. To find the $[H^+]$ from the pH, we must go back to the definition of pH:

$$pH = -\log[H^+]$$

or

$$-pH = \log[H^+]$$

To arrive at $[H^+]$ on the right-hand side of this equation we must "undo" the log operation. This is called taking the *antilog* or the *inverse* log.

$$\text{Inverse log}\,(-pH) = \text{inverse log}\,(\log[H^+])$$
$$\text{Inverse log}\,(-pH) = [H^+]$$

MATH SKILL BUILDER
This operation may involve a 10^x key on some calculators.

There are different methods for carrying out the inverse log operation on various calculators. One common method is the two-key (inv) (log) sequence. (Consult the user's manual for your calculator to find out how to do the antilog or inverse log operation.) The steps in going from pH to $[H^+]$ are as follows:

Steps for Calculating $[H^+]$ from pH

Step 1 Take the inverse log (antilog) of $-pH$ to give $[H^+]$ by using the (inv) (log) keys in that order. (Your calculator may require different keys for this operation.)

Step 2 Press the minus [−] key.

Step 3 Enter the pH.

For practice, we will convert pH = 7.0 to $[H^+]$.

$$pH = 7.0$$
$$-pH = -7.0$$

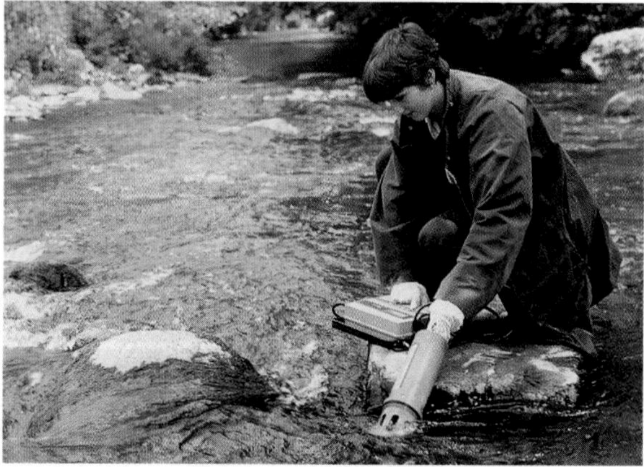

David Woodfall/Stone/Getty Images

Measuring the pH of the water in a river.

The inverse log of -7.0 gives 1×10^{-7}.

$$[H^+] = 1 \times 10^{-7}\,M$$

This process is illustrated further in Example 16.8.

EXAMPLE 16.8 Calculating $[H^+]$ from pH

The pH of a human blood sample was measured to be 7.41. What is the $[H^+]$ in this blood?

SOLUTION

$$\begin{aligned} pH &= 7.41 \\ -pH &= -7.41 \\ [H^+] &= \text{inverse log of } -7.41 = 3.9 \times 10^{-8} \\ [H^+] &= 3.9 \times 10^{-8}\,M \end{aligned}$$

Notice that because the pH has two decimal places, we need two significant figures for $[H^+]$.

Self-Check **EXERCISE 16.5** The pH of rainwater in a polluted area was found to be 3.50. What is the $[H^+]$ for this rainwater?

See Problems 16.49 and 16.50. ■

A similar procedure is used to change from pOH to $[OH^-]$, as shown in Example 16.9.

EXAMPLE 16.9 Calculating $[OH^-]$ from pOH

The pOH of the water in a fish tank is found to be 6.59. What is the $[OH^-]$ for this water?

SOLUTION

We use the same steps as for converting pH to $[H^+]$, except that we use the pOH to calculate the $[OH^-]$.

$$\begin{aligned} pOH &= 6.59 \\ -pOH &= -6.59 \\ [OH^-] &= \text{inverse log of } -6.59 = 2.6 \times 10^{-7} \\ [OH^-] &= 2.6 \times 10^{-7}\,M \end{aligned}$$

Note that two significant figures are required.

Self-Check **EXERCISE 16.6** The pOH of a liquid drain cleaner was found to be 10.50. What is the $[OH^-]$ for this cleaner?

See Problems 16.51 and 16.52. ■

Additional Examples

Example 16.8

1. The pH of a solution is 3.14. What is the $[H^+]$ of the solution?

   $[H^+] = 7.2 \times 10^{-4}\,M$

2. The pH of a solution is 8.53. What is the $[H^+]$ of the solution?

   $[H^+] = 3.0 \times 10^{-9}\,M$

Self Check

Answer to Self-Check Exercise 16.5

$[H^+] = 3.2 \times 10^{-4}\,M$

Additional Examples

Example 16.9

1. The pOH of a solution is 5.67. What is the $[OH^-]$ of the solution?

   $[OH^-] = 2.1 \times 10^{-6}\,M$

2. The pOH of a solution is 11.28. What is the $[OH^-]$ of the solution?

   $[OH^-] = 5.2 \times 10^{-12}\,M$

Self Check

Answer to Self-Check Exercise 16.6

$[OH^-] = 3.2 \times 10^{-11}\,M$

CHEMISTRY IN FOCUS

Garden-Variety Acid–Base Indicators

What can flowers tell us about acids and bases? Actually, some flowers can tell us whether the soil they are growing in is acidic or basic. For example, in acidic soil, bigleaf hydrangea blossoms will be blue; in basic (alkaline) soil, the flowers will be red. What is the secret? The pigment in the flower is an acid–base indicator.

Generally, acid–base indicators are dyes that are weak acids. Because indicators are usually complex molecules, we often symbolize them as HIn. The reaction of the indicator with water can be written as

$$HIn(aq) + H_2O(l) \rightleftharpoons H_3O^+(aq) + In^-(aq)$$

To work as an acid–base indicator, the conjugate acid–base forms of these dyes must have different colors. The acidity level of the solution will determine whether the indicator is present mainly in its acidic form (HIn) or its basic form (In^-).

When placed in an acidic solution, most of the basic form of the indicator is converted to the acidic form by the reaction

$$In^-(aq) + H^+(aq) \rightarrow HIn(aq)$$

When placed in a basic solution, most of the acidic form of the indicator is converted to the basic form by the reaction

$$HIn(aq) + OH^-(aq) \rightarrow In^-(aq) + H_2O(l)$$

It turns out that many fruits, vegetables, and flowers can act as acid–base indicators. Red, blue, and purple plants often contain a class of chemicals called anthocyanins, which change color based on the acidity level of the surroundings. Perhaps the most famous of these plants is red cabbage. Red cabbage contains a mixture of anthocyanins and other pigments that allow it to be used as a "universal indicator." Red cabbage juice appears deep red at a pH of 1–2, purple at a pH of 4, blue at a pH of 8, and green at a pH of 11.

Test Bank: 27, 35–45

Section 16.5

16.5 Calculating the pH of Strong Acid Solutions

OBJECTIVE: To learn to calculate the pH of solutions of strong acids.

TEACHING TIP

Focus students' attention on the molecular view of a strong acid. Once they understand that the acid ionizes completely in solution, they are ready to find the hydrogen ion concentration and the pH.

In this section we will learn to calculate the pH for a solution containing a strong acid of known concentration. For example, if we know a solution contains 1.0 *M* HCl, how can we find the pH of the solution? To answer this question we must know that when HCl dissolves in water, each molecule dissociates (ionizes) into H^+ and Cl^- ions. That is, we must know that HCl is a strong acid. Thus, although the label on the bottle says 1.0 *M* HCl, the solution contains virtually no HCl molecules. A 1.0 *M* HCl solution contains H^+ and Cl^- ions rather than HCl molecules. Typically, container labels indicate the substance(s) used to make up the solution but do not necessarily describe the solution components after dissolution. In this case,

$$1.0\ M\ HCl \rightarrow 1.0\ M\ H^+ \text{ and } 1.0\ M\ Cl^-$$

Therefore, the $[H^+]$ in the solution is 1.0 *M*. The pH is then

$$pH = -\log[H^+] = -\log(1.0) = 0$$

LABORATORY EXPERIMENT

A relevant laboratory experiment for this section is Experiment 26, Acid-Base Titrations, from *Introductory Chemistry in the Laboratory* by James Hall.

532

TEACHING SUPPORT

CHALLENGE YOUR STUDENTS

If you have excellent mathematics students looking for additional challenges, ask them to calculate the pH of 1.0 L of water after 1.0×10^{-7} mole of HCl is added. The answer 7.00 is not correct because H^+ is coming from both the water and HCl; thus the pH is lower than 7.00. The students might decide to add the H^+ from the HCl (1.0×10^{-7} *M*) to that in pure water (1.0×10^{-7} *M*) to give 2.0×10^{-7} *M*, which leads to a pH of 6.70 [from taking $-\log(2.0 \times 10^{-7})$]. However, the added H^+ from the HCl shifts the equilibrium to the left, using up some H^+. Thus, the pH must be higher than 6.70 but lower than 7.00. The pH of the solution is actually 6.79.

Other natural indicators include the skins of beets (which change from red to purple in very basic solutions), blueberries (which change from blue to red in acidic solutions), and a wide variety of flower petals, including delphiniums, geraniums, morning glories, and, of course, hydrangeas.

Royalty-free Corbis

Neil Holmes/Homes Garden Photos/Alamy

EXAMPLE 16.10 Calculating the pH of Strong Acid Solutions

Calculate the pH of 0.10 *M* HNO_3.

SOLUTION

HNO_3 is a strong acid, so the ions in solution are H^+ and NO_3^-. In this case,

$$0.10\ M\ HNO_3 \rightarrow 0.10\ M\ H^+ \text{ and } 0.10\ M\ NO_3^-$$

Thus

$$[H^+] = 0.10\ M \qquad \text{and} \qquad pH = -\log(0.10) = 1.00$$

Self-Check EXERCISE 16.7 Calculate the pH of a solution of 5.0×10^{-3} *M* HCl.

See Problems 16.57 and 16.58. ■

533

Additional Examples

Example 16.10

1. Calculate the pH of 0.025 *M* $HClO_4$.

   pH = 1.60

2. Calculate the pH of 1.2×10^{-5} *M* HBr.

   pH = 4.92

Self Check

Answer to Self-Check Exercise 16.7

pH = 2.30

Section 16.6

TEACHING TIP

The concept of a buffer is quite complex. It is important to go slowly when you explain how a buffer works. Students need to see each of the possibilities and what happens.

LABORATORY EXPERIMENT

A relevant laboratory experiment for this section is Experiment 27, Buffered Solutions, from *Introductory Chemistry in the Laboratory* by James Hall.

Test Bank: 15, 46–49

DEMONSTRATION

Show the effects of a buffer by making an acetic acid/sodium acetate buffer solution (0.1 *M* for each) in one flask. In another flask, place the same amount of distilled water. Measure the pH of each (using paper or a pH meter). Then add a drop of H^+ or hydroxide to each flask and recheck the pH. Repeat the process several times.

PowerLecture Animations:
pH Change for HCl Addition to Phosphate Buffer
pH Change for HCl Addition to H_2O
Adding an Acid to a Buffer

16.6 Buffered Solutions

OBJECTIVE: To understand the general characteristics of buffered solutions.

Water: pH = 7
0.01 *M* HCl: pH = 2

A **buffered solution** is one that resists a change in its pH even when a strong acid or base is added to it. For example, when 0.01 mole of HCl is added to 1 L of pure water, the pH changes from its initial value of 7 to 2, a change of 5 pH units. However, when 0.01 mole of HCl is added to a solution containing both 0.1 *M* acetic acid ($HC_2H_3O_2$) and 0.1 *M* sodium acetate ($NaC_2H_3O_2$), the pH changes from an initial value of 4.74 to 4.66, a change of only 0.08 pH unit. The latter solution is buffered—it undergoes only a very slight change in pH when a strong acid or base is added to it.

Buffered solutions are vitally important to living organisms whose cells can survive only in a very narrow pH range. Many goldfish have died because their owners did not realize the importance of buffering the aquarium water at an appropriate pH. For humans to survive, the pH of the blood must be maintained between 7.35 and 7.45. This narrow range is maintained by several different buffering systems.

For goldfish to survive, the pH of the water must be carefully controlled.

A solution is **buffered** by the *presence of a weak acid and its conjugate base*. An example of a buffered solution is an aqueous solution that contains acetic acid and sodium acetate. The sodium acetate is a salt that furnishes acetate ions (the conjugate base of acetic acid) when it dissolves. To see how this system acts as a buffer, we must recognize that the species present in this solution are

$$HC_2H_3O_2, \quad Na^+, \quad C_2H_3O_2^-$$

When $NaC_2H_3O_2$ is dissolved, it produces the separated ions

What happens in this solution when a strong acid such as HCl is added? In pure water, the H^+ ions from the HCl would accumulate, thus lowering the pH.

$$HCl \xrightarrow{100\%} H^+ + Cl^-$$

However, this buffered solution contains $C_2H_3O_2^-$ ions, which are basic. That is, $C_2H_3O_2^-$ has a strong affinity for H^+, as evidenced by the fact that $HC_2H_3O_2$ is a weak acid. This means that the $C_2H_3O_2^-$ and H^+ ions do not exist together in large numbers. Because the $C_2H_3O_2^-$ ion has a high affinity for H^+, these two combine to form $HC_2H_3O_2$ molecules. Thus the H^+ from the added HCl does not accumulate in solution but reacts with the $C_2H_3O_2^-$ as follows:

$$H^+(aq) + C_2H_3O_2^-(aq) \rightarrow HC_2H_3O_2(aq)$$

Next consider what happens when a strong base such as sodium hydroxide is added to the buffered solution. If this base were added to pure water, the OH^- ions from the solid would accumulate and greatly change (raise) the pH.

$$NaOH \xrightarrow{100\%} Na^+ + OH^-$$

However, in the buffered solution the OH^- ion, which has a *very strong* affinity for H^+, reacts with $HC_2H_3O_2$ molecules as follows:

$$HC_2H_3O_2(aq) + OH^-(aq) \rightarrow H_2O(l) + C_2H_3O_2^-(aq)$$

PowerLecture Simulation: Buffer Solutions

Table 16.3 The Characteristics of a Buffer

1. The solution contains a weak acid HA and its conjugate base A^-.
2. The buffer resists changes in pH by reacting with any added H^+ or OH^- so that these ions do not accumulate.
3. Any added H^+ reacts with the base A^-.
   $H^+(aq) + A^-(aq) \rightarrow HA(aq)$
4. Any added OH^- reacts with the weak acid HA.
   $OH^-(aq) + HA(aq) \rightarrow H_2O(l) + A^-(aq)$

This happens because, although $C_2H_3O_2^-$ has a strong affinity for H^+, OH^- has a much stronger affinity for H^+ and thus can remove H^+ ions from acetic acid molecules.

Note that the buffering materials dissolved in the solution prevent added H^+ or OH^- from building up in the solution. Any added H^+ is trapped by $C_2H_3O_2^-$ to form $HC_2H_3O_2$. Any added OH^- reacts with $HC_2H_3O_2$ to form H_2O and $C_2H_3O_2^-$.

The general properties of a buffered solution are summarized in Table 16.3.

CHAPTER 16 REVIEW

F directs you to the *Chemistry in Focus* feature in the chapter
VP indicates visual problems
OWL interactive versions of these problems are assignable in OWL

Key Terms

acid (16.1)
base (16.1)
Arrhenius concept of acids and bases (16.1)
Brønsted–Lowry model (16.1)
conjugate acid (16.1)
conjugate base (16.1)
conjugate acid–base pair (16.1)
hydronium ion (16.1)
completely ionized (dissociated) (16.2)
strong acid (16.2)
weak acid (16.2)
diprotic acid (16.2)
oxyacid (16.2)
organic acid (16.2)
carboxyl group (16.2)
amphoteric substance (16.3)
ionization of water (16.3)
ion-product constant, K_w (16.3)
neutral solution (16.3)
acidic solution (16.3)
basic solution (16.3)
pH scale (16.4)
buffered solution (16.6)
buffered (16.6)

Summary

1. Acids or bases in water are commonly described by two different models. Arrhenius postulated that acids produce H^+ ions in aqueous solutions and that bases produce OH^- ions. The Brønsted–Lowry model is more general: an acid is a proton donor, and a base is a proton acceptor. Water acts as a Brønsted–Lowry base when it accepts a proton from an acid to form a hydronium ion:

   $$HA(aq) + H_2O(l) \rightleftharpoons H_3O^+(aq) + A^-(aq)$$
   Acid — Base — Conjugate acid — Conjugate base

   A conjugate base is everything that remains of the acid molecule after the proton is lost. A conjugate acid is formed when a proton is transferred to the base. Two substances related in this way are called a conjugate acid–base pair.
2. A strong acid or base is one that is completely ionized (dissociated). A weak acid is one that is ionized (dissociated) only to a slight extent. Strong acids have weak conjugate bases. Weak acids have relatively strong conjugate bases.
3. Water is an amphoteric substance—it can behave either as an acid or as a base. The ionization of water reveals this property; one water molecule transfers a

TEACHING TIP

Discuss the chemical properties that are necessary to produce a buffer. Why is it important to use a weak acid and its salt? Why can't we use a strong acid and its salt?

Lecture Demonstration: 16.3

ChemWork

Calculation of S Surroundings
Calculating Free Energy in a Chemical Reaction
Thermodynamic Properties of Vaporization
Calculating the Entropy of a Reaction from Entropy Data
Calculation of Entropy
Determining Entropy in Chemical Reactions
Determing Entropy in Chemical Reactions 2
Entropy Changes During Phase Transitions
Entropy of Vaporization
Calculating the Free Energy of a Reaction from Data
Calculation of Free Energy
Free Energy and Equilibrium
Free Energy for a Weak Acid
NO_2 Equilibrium
PCl_5 Equilibrium
Properties of Entropy
Relatioship of K and Enthalpy

proton to another water molecule to produce a hydronium ion and a hydroxide ion.

$$H_2O(l) + H_2O(l) \rightleftharpoons H_3O^+(aq) + OH^-(aq)$$

The expression

$$K_w = [H_3O^+][OH^-] = [H^+][OH^-]$$

is called the ion-product constant. It has been shown experimentally that at 25 °C,

$$[H^+] = [OH^-] = 1.0 \times 10^{-7}\ M$$

so $K_w = 1.0 \times 10^{-14}$.

4. In an acidic solution, $[H^+]$ is greater than $[OH^-]$. In a basic solution, $[OH^-]$ is greater than $[H^+]$. In a neutral solution, $[H^+] = [OH^-]$.

5. To describe $[H^+]$ in aqueous solutions, we use the pH scale.

$$pH = -\log[H^+]$$

Note that the pH decreases as $[H^+]$ (acidity) increases.

6. The pH of strong acid solutions can be calculated directly from the concentration of the acid, because 100% dissociation occurs in aqueous solution.

7. A buffered solution is one that resists a change in its pH even when a strong acid or base is added to it. A buffered solution contains a weak acid and its conjugate base.

Active Learning Questions

These questions are designed to be considered by groups of students in class. Often these questions work well for introducing a particular topic in class.

1. You are asked for the H^+ concentration in a solution of $NaOH(aq)$. Because sodium hydroxide is a strong base, can we say there is no H^+, since having H^+ would imply that the solution is acidic?

2. Explain why Cl^- does not affect the pH of an aqueous solution.

3. Write the general reaction for an acid acting in water. What is the base in this case? The conjugate acid? The conjugate base?

4. Differentiate among the terms *concentrated, dilute, weak,* and *strong* in describing acids. Use molecular-level pictures to support your answer.

5. What is meant by "pH"? True or false: A strong acid always has a lower pH than a weak acid does. Explain.

6. Consider two separate solutions: one containing a weak acid, HA, and one containing HCl. Assume that you start with 10 molecules of each.
   a. Draw a molecular-level picture of what each solution looks like.
   b. Arrange the following from strongest to weakest base: Cl^-, H_2O, A^-. Explain.

7. Why is the pH of water at 25 °C equal to 7.00?

8. Can the pH of a solution be negative? Explain.

9. Stanley's grade-point average (GPA) is 3.28. What is Stanley's p(GPA)?

10. A friend asks the following: "Consider a buffered solution made up of the weak acid HA and its salt NaA. If a strong base like NaOH is added, the HA reacts with the OH^- to make A^-. Thus, the amount of acid (HA) is decreased, and the amount of base (A^-) is increased. Analogously, adding HCl to the buffered solution forms more of the acid (HA) by reacting with the base (A^-). How can we claim that a buffered solution resists changes in the pH of the solution?" How would you explain buffering to your friend?

11. Mixing together aqueous solutions of acetic acid and sodium hydroxide can make a buffered solution. Explain.

12. Could a buffered solution be made by mixing aqueous solutions of HCl and NaOH? Explain.

13. Consider the equation: $HA(aq) + H_2O \rightleftharpoons H_3O^+(aq) + A^-(aq)$.
    a. If water is a better base than A^-, which way will equilibrium lie?
    b. If water is a better base than A^-, does this mean that HA is a strong or a weak acid?
    c. If water is a better base than A^-, is the value for K_a greater or less than 1?

14. Choose the answer that best completes the following statement and defend your answer. When 100.0 mL of water is added to 100.0 mL of 1.00 *M* HCl,
    a. the pH decreases because the solution is diluted.
    b. the pH does not change because water is neutral.
    c. the pH is doubled because the volume is now doubled.
    d. the pH increases because the concentration of H^+ decreases.
    e. the solution is completely neutralized.

15. You mix a solution of a strong acid with a pH of 4 and an equal volume of a strong acid solution with a pH of 6. Is the final pH less than 4, between 4 and 5, 5, between 5 and 6, or greater than 6? Explain.

VP 16. The following figures are molecular-level representations of acid solutions. Label each as a strong acid or a weak acid.

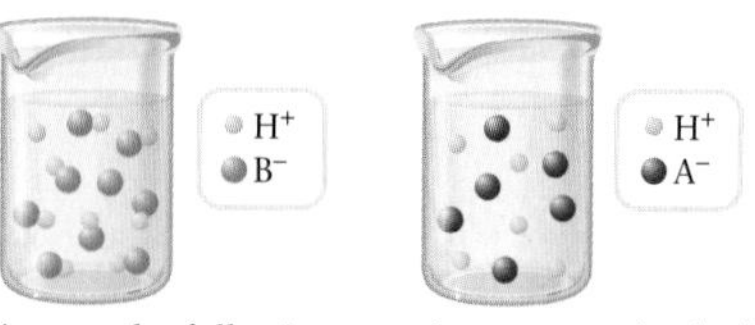

17. Answer the following questions concerning buffered solutions.
    a. Explain what a buffered solution does.
    b. Describe the substances that make up a buffered solution.
    c. Explain how a buffered solution works.

Answers to End-of-Chapter Exercises

1. Acids were recognized primarily from their sour taste; bases were recognized primarily from their bitter taste and their slippery feel on the skin.

2. $HCl(g) \xrightarrow{H_2O} H^+(aq) + Cl^-(aq)$; $NaOH(s) \xrightarrow{H_2O} Na^+(aq) + OH^-(aq)$

3. The Arrhenius definitions of acid and base are restricted to aqueous solutions in which a substance producing $H^+(aq)$ ions is considered an acid and a substance producing $OH^-(aq)$ ions is considered a base.

The Brønsted–Lowry definitions of acid and base are less restrictive and define an acid as a species capable of donating protons (regardless of the solvent) and a base as a species capable of receiving the protons being donated. In the equation $HA(aq) + H_2O(l) \rightarrow H_3O^+ + A^-$, HA is a Brønsted-Lowry acid because it donates a proton to water; water is a Brønsted-Lowry base because it receives the proton from HA.

4. A conjugate acid–base pair differs by one hydrogen ion, H^+. For example, $HC_2H_3O_2$ (acetic acid) differs from its conjugate base, $C_2H_3O_2^-$ (acetate ion), by a single H^+ ion.

$$HC_2H_3O_2(aq) \rightleftharpoons C_2H_3O_2^-(aq) + H^+(aq)$$

5. Water accepts a proton in going from H_2O to H_3O^+, which makes it a base in the Brønsted–Lowry model.

6. In addition to sodium bicarbonate, the gum also contains citric acid and malic acid. When the gum is exposed to moisture in the mouth, the bicarbonate ion behaves as a *base* and reacts with hydrogen ion from the acids: $H^+(aq) + HCO_3^-(aq) \rightarrow H_2O(l) + CO_2(g)$.

7. (a) conjugate pair; (b) not a conjugate pair; HClO, ClO^-; $HClO_2$, ClO_2^-; (c) not a conjugate pair; H_3PO_4, $H_2PO_4^-$; HPO_4^{2-}, PO_4^{3-}; (d) not a conjugate pair; H_2CO_3, HCO_3^-; HCO_3^-, CO_3^{2-}

8. (a) conjugate pair; (b) conjugate pair; (c) conjugate pair; (d) not a conjugate pair; H_2O, OH^-; OH^-, O^{2-}

9. (a) HF (acid), H_2O (base), F^- (base), H_3O^+ (acid); (b) CN^- (base), H_2O (acid), HCN (acid), OH^- (base); (c) HCO_3^- (base), H_2O (acid), H_2CO_3 (acid), OH^- (base)

10. (a) $NH_3(aq)$(base) + $H_2O(l)$(acid) $\rightleftharpoons$ $NH_4^+(aq)$ (acid) + $OH^-(aq)$(base); (b) $NH_4^+(aq)$(acid) + $H_2O(l)$ (base) $\rightleftharpoons$ $NH_3(aq)$(base) + $H_3O^+(aq)$(acid); (c) $NH_2^-(aq)$(base) + $H_2O(l)$ (acid) $\rightleftharpoons$ $NH_3(aq)$(acid) + $OH^-(aq)$(base)

11. (a) HPO_4^{2-}; (b) HIO_3; (c) HNO_3; (d) NH_3

12. (a) HClO; (b) HCl; (c) $HClO_3$; (d) $HClO_4$

13. (a) HS^-; (b) S^{2-}; (c) NH_2^-; (d) HSO_3^-

14. (a) BrO^-; (b) HSO_3^-; (c) SO_3^{2-}; (d) CH_3NH_2

Questions and Problems

16.1 Acids and Bases

QUESTIONS

1. What are some physical properties that historically led chemists to classify various substances as acids and bases?

2. Write an equation showing how HCl(*g*) behaves as an Arrhenius acid when dissolved in water. Write an equation showing how NaOH(*s*) behaves as an Arrhenius base when dissolved in water.

3. According to the Brønsted-Lowry model, an acid is a "proton donor" and a base is a "proton acceptor." Explain.

4. How do the components of a conjugate acid–base pair differ from one another? Give an example of a conjugate acid–base pair to illustrate your answer.

5. Given the general equation illustrating the reaction of the acid HA in water,

$$HA(aq) + H_2O(l) \rightarrow H_3O^+(aq) + A^-(aq)$$

explain why water is considered a *base* in the Brønsted-Lowry model.

6. The "Chemistry in Focus" segment *Gum That Foams* discusses Mad Dawg chewing gum. One of the ingredients in the gum is baking soda, sodium bicarbonate, $NaHCO_3$. Does baking soda behave as an acid or as a base in the gum?

PROBLEMS

7. Which of the following do *not* represent a conjugate acid–base pair? For those pairs that are not conjugate acid–base pairs, write the correct conjugate acid–base pair for each species in the pair.
   a. HI, I^-
   b. HClO, $HClO_2$
   c. H_3PO_4, PO_4^{3-}
   d. H_2CO_3, CO_3^{2-}

8. Which of the following do *not* represent a conjugate acid–base pair? For those pairs that are not conjugate acid–base pairs, write the correct conjugate acid–base pair for each species in the pair.
   a. $HClO_4$, ClO_4^-
   b. NH_4^+, NH_3
   c. NH_3, NH_2^-
   d. H_2O, O^{2-}

9. In each of the following chemical equations, identify the conjugate acid–base pairs.
   a. $HF(aq) + H_2O(l) \rightleftharpoons F^-(aq) + H_3O^+(aq)$
   b. $CN^-(aq) + H_2O(l) \rightleftharpoons HCN(aq) + OH^-(aq)$
   c. $HCO_3^-(aq) + H_2O(l) \rightleftharpoons H_2CO_3(aq) + OH^-(aq)$

10. In each of the following chemical reactions, identify the conjugate acid–base pairs.
   a. $NH_3(aq) + H_2O(l) \rightleftharpoons NH_4^+(aq) + OH^-(aq)$
   b. $NH_4^+(aq) + H_2O(l) \rightleftharpoons NH_3(aq) + H_3O^+(aq)$
   c. $NH_2^-(aq) + H_2O(l) \rightarrow NH_3(aq) + OH^-(aq)$

11. Write the conjugate *acid* for each of the following bases:
   a. PO_4^{3-}
   b. IO_3^-
   c. NO_3^-
   d. NH_2^-

12. Write the conjugate *acid* for each of the following bases.
   a. ClO^-
   b. Cl^-
   c. ClO_3^-
   d. ClO_4^-

13. Write the conjugate *base* for each of the following acids:
   a. H_2S
   b. HS^-
   c. NH_3
   d. H_2SO_3

14. Write the conjugate *base* for each of the following acids.
   a. HBrO
   b. HNO_2
   c. HSO_3^-
   d. $CH_3NH_3^+$

15. Write a chemical equation showing how each of the following species can behave as indicated when dissolved in water.
   a. HSO_3^- as an acid
   b. CO_3^{2-} as a base
   c. $H_2PO_4^-$ as an acid
   d. $C_2H_3O_2^-$ as a base

16. Write a chemical equation showing how each of the following species can behave as indicated when dissolved in water.
   a. O^{2-} as a base
   b. NH_3 as a base
   c. HSO_4^- as an acid
   d. HNO_2 as an acid

16.2 Acid Strength

QUESTIONS

17. What does it mean to say that an acid is *strong* in aqueous solution? What does this reveal about the ability of the acid's anion to attract protons?

18. What does it mean to say that an acid is *weak* in aqueous solution? What does this reveal about the ability of the acid's anion to attract protons?

19. How is the strength of an acid related to the fact that a competition for protons exists in aqueous solution between water molecules and the anion of the acid?

20. A strong acid has a weak conjugate base, whereas a weak acid has a relatively strong conjugate base. Explain.

All even-numbered Questions and Problems have answers in the back of this book and solutions in the Solutions Guide.

15. (a) $HSO_3^-(aq) + H_2O(l) \rightarrow SO_3^{2-}(aq) + H_3O^+(aq)$; (b) $CO_3^{2-}(aq) + H_2O(l) \rightarrow HCO_3^-(aq) + OH^-(aq)$; (c) $H_2PO_4^-(aq) + H_2O(l) \rightarrow HPO_4^{2-}(aq) + H_3O^+(aq)$; (d) $C_2H_3O_2^-(aq) + H_2O(l) \rightarrow HC_2H_3O_2(aq) + OH^-(aq)$

16. (a) $O^{2-}(aq) + H_2O(l) \rightarrow OH^-(aq) + OH^-(aq)$; (b) $NH_3(aq) + H_2O(l) \rightarrow NH_4^+(aq) + OH^-(aq)$; (c) $HSO_4(aq)^- + H_2O(l) \rightarrow SO_4^{2-}(aq) + H_3O^+(aq)$; (d) $HNO_2(aq) + H_2O(l) \rightarrow NO_2^-(aq) + H_3O^+(aq)$

17. A strong acid is one for which the equilibrium in water lies far to the right; a strong acid is almost completely converted to its conjugate base when dissolved in water, which means that the anion of a strong acid is very poor at attracting and holding onto protons.

18. If an acid is weak in aqueous solution, it does not easily transfer protons to water (and does not fully ionize). If an acid does not lose protons easily, then the acid's anion must strongly attract protons.

19. If water is a much stronger base than the anion of the acid, then protons will be attracted more strongly to water molecules than to the anion, and the acid will ionize well. If the anion of the acid is a much stronger base than water, then the anions will hold on to their protons and the acid will ionize poorly.

20. A strong acid loses its protons easily and fully ionizes in water; the acid's conjugate base is poor at attracting and holding protons and is a relatively weak base. A weak acid resists loss of its protons and does not ionize to a great extent in water; the acid's conjugate base attracts and holds protons tightly and is a relatively strong base.

21. Write the formula for the *hydronium* ion. Write an equation for the formation of the hydronium ion when an acid is dissolved in water.

22. Name four strong acids. For each of these, write the equation showing the acid dissociating in water.

23. Organic acids contain the carboxyl group

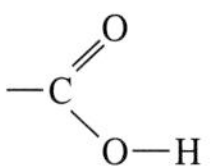

Using acetic acid, $CH_3—COOH$, and propionic acid, $CH_3CH_2—COOH$, write equations showing how the carboxyl group enables these substances to behave as weak acids when dissolved in water.

24. What is an *oxyacid?* Write the formulas of three acids that are oxyacids. Write the formulas of three acids that are *not* oxyacids.

25. Which of the following acids have relatively *strong* conjugate bases?

a. HCN
b. H_2S
c. $HBrO_4$
d. HNO_3

26. The "Chemistry in Focus" segment *Plants Fight Back* discusses how tobacco plants under attack by disease produce salicylic acid. Examine the structure of salicylic acid and predict whether it behaves as a monoprotic or a diprotic acid.

16.3 Water as an Acid and a Base

QUESTIONS

27. Water is the most common *amphoteric* substance, which means that, depending on the circumstances, water can behave either as an acid or as a base. Using HF as an example of an acid and NH_3 as an example of a base, write equations for these substances reacting with water, in which water behaves as a base and as an acid, respectively.

28. Anions containing hydrogen (for example, HCO_3^- and $H_2PO_4^{2-}$) show amphoteric behavior when reacting with other acids or bases. Write equations illustrating the amphoterism of these anions.

29. What is meant by the *ion-product constant* for water, K_w? What does this constant signify? Write an equation for the chemical reaction from which the constant is derived.

30. What happens to the hydroxide ion concentration in aqueous solutions when we increase the hydrogen ion concentration by adding an acid? What happens to the hydrogen ion concentration in aqueous solutions when we increase the hydroxide ion concentration by adding a base? Explain.

PROBLEMS

31. Calculate the $[H^+]$ in each of the following solutions, and indicate whether the solution is acidic or basic.

a. $[OH^-] = 2.32 \times 10^{-4}\ M$
b. $[OH^-] = 8.99 \times 10^{-10}\ M$
c. $[OH^-] = 4.34 \times 10^{-6}\ M$
d. $[OH^-] = 6.22 \times 10^{-12}\ M$

32. Calculate the $[H^+]$ in each of the following solutions, and indicate whether the solution is acidic or basic.

a. $[OH^-] = 3.44 \times 10^{-1}\ M$
b. $[OH^-] = 9.79 \times 10^{-11}\ M$
c. $[OH^-] = 4.89 \times 10^{-6}\ M$
d. $[OH^-] = 3.78 \times 10^{-7}\ M$

33. Calculate the $[OH^-]$ in each of the following solutions, and indicate whether the solution is acidic or basic.

a. $[H^+] = 4.01 \times 10^{-4}\ M$
b. $[H^+] = 7.22 \times 10^{-6}\ M$
c. $[H^+] = 8.05 \times 10^{-7}\ M$
d. $[H^+] = 5.43 \times 10^{-9}\ M$

34. Calculate the $[OH^-]$ in each of the following solutions, and indicate whether the solution is acidic or basic.

a. $[H^+] = 1.02 \times 10^{-7}\ M$
b. $[H^+] = 9.77 \times 10^{-8}\ M$
c. $[H^+] = 3.41 \times 10^{-3}\ M$
d. $[H^+] = 4.79 \times 10^{-11}\ M$

35. For each pair of concentrations, tell which represents the more acidic solution.

a. $[H^+] = 1.2 \times 10^{-3}\ M$ or $[H^+] = 4.5 \times 10^{-4}\ M$
b. $[H^+] = 2.6 \times 10^{-6}\ M$ or $[H^+] = 4.3 \times 10^{-8}\ M$
c. $[H^+] = 0.000010\ M$ or $[H^+] = 0.0000010\ M$

36. For each pair of concentrations, tell which represents the more *basic* solution.

a. $[H^+] = 3.99 \times 10^{-6}\ M$ or $[OH^-] = 6.03 \times 10^{-4}\ M$
b. $[H^+] = 1.79 \times 10^{-5}\ M$ or $[OH^-] = 4.21 \times 10^{-6}\ M$
c. $[H^+] = 7.81 \times 10^{-3}\ M$ or $[OH^-] = 8.04 \times 10^{-4}\ M$

16.4 The pH Scale

QUESTIONS

37. Why do scientists tend to express the acidity of a solution in terms of its pH, rather than in terms of the molarity of hydrogen ion present? How is pH defined mathematically?

38. Using Figure 16.3, list the approximate pH value of five "everyday" solutions. How do the familiar properties (such as the sour taste for acids) of these solutions correspond to their indicated pH?

39. For a hydrogen ion concentration of $2.33 \times 10^{-6}\ M$, how many *decimal places* should we give when expressing the pH of the solution?

All even-numbered Questions and Problems have answers in the back of this book and solutions in the Solutions Guide.

21. H_3O^+; for a general weak acid HA: $HA + H_2O \rightleftharpoons A^- + H_3O^+$

22. H_2SO_4 (sulfuric): $H_2SO_4 + H_2O \rightarrow HSO_4^- + H_3O^+$; HCl (hydrochloric): $HCl + H_2O \rightarrow Cl^- + H_3O^+$; HNO_3 (nitric): $HNO_3 + H_2O \rightarrow NO_3^- + H_3O^+$; $HClO_4$ (perchloric): $HClO_4 + H_2O \rightarrow ClO_4^- + H_3O^+$

23. $CH_3COOH + H_2O \rightleftharpoons CH_3COO^- + H_3O^+$; $CH_3CH_2COOH + H_2O \rightleftharpoons CH_3CH_2COO^- + H_3O^+$

24. An oxyacid is an acid containing a particular element that is bonded to one or more oxygen atoms. HNO_3, H_2SO_4, and $HClO_4$ are oxyacids. HCl, HF, and HBr are not oxyacids.

25. a and b

26. Salicylic acid is a monoprotic acid: only the hydrogen of the carboxyl group ionizes.

27. water as base: $HF + H_2O \rightleftharpoons F^- + H_3O^+$; water as acid: $NH_3 + H_2O \rightleftharpoons NH_4^+ + OH^-$

28. HCO_3^- can behave as an acid if it reacts with a substance that more strongly gains protons than does HCO_3^- itself. For example, HCO_3^- would behave as an acid when reacting with hydroxide ion (a much stronger base): $HCO_3^-(aq) + OH^-(aq) \rightarrow CO_3^{2-}(aq) + H_2O(l)$. Conversely, HCO_3^- would behave as a base when reacted with a substance that more readily loses protons than does HCO_3^- itself. For example, HCO_3^- would behave as a base when reacting with hydrochloric acid (a much stronger acid): $HCO_3^-(aq) + HCl(aq) \rightarrow H_2CO_3(aq) + Cl^-(aq)$. $H_2PO_4^- + OH^- \rightarrow HPO_4^{2-} + H_2O$ and $H_2PO_4^- + H_3O^+ \rightarrow H_3PO_4 + H_2O$.

29. The ion-product constant for water is the equilibrium constant for the reaction $H_2O + H_2O \rightleftharpoons H_3O^+ + OH^-$; the constant says that in water or an aqueous solution, there is an equilibrium between hydronium ion and hydroxide ion such that the product of their concentrations fulfills the value of the constant. $K_w = [H^+][OH^-] = 1.0 \times 10^{-14}$ at 25 °C.

30. The concentrations of H^+ and OH^- ions in water and in dilute aqueous solutions are *not* independent of one another. Rather, they are related by the ion product equilibrium constant, K_w. $K_w = [H^+(aq)][OH^-(aq)] = 1.00 \times 10^{-14}$ at 25 °C. If the concentration of one ion is *increased* by addition of a reagent producing H^+ or OH^-, then the concentration of the complementary ion will *decrease* so that the constant's value will hold true. If an acid is added to a solution, the concentration of hydroxide ion in the solution will decrease. Similarly, if a base is added to a solution, then the concentration of hydrogen ion will decrease.

31. (a) $[H^+] = 4.3 \times 10^{-11}\ M$; basic; (b) $[H^+] = 1.1 \times 10^{-5}\ M$; acidic; (c) $[H^+] = 2.3 \times 10^{-9}\ M$; basic; (d) $[H^+] = 1.6 \times 10^{-3}\ M$; acidic

40. The "Chemistry in Focus" segment *Garden-Variety Acid–Base Indicators* discusses acid–base indicators found in nature. What colors are exhibited by red cabbage juice under acid conditions? Under basic conditions?

PROBLEMS

41. Calculate the pH corresponding to each of the hydrogen ion concentrations given below, and indicate whether each solution is acidic or basic.

a. $[H^+] = 4.02 \times 10^{-3}\ M$
b. $[H^+] = 8.99 \times 10^{-7}\ M$
c. $[H^+] = 2.39 \times 10^{-6}\ M$
d. $[H^+] = 1.89 \times 10^{-10}\ M$

42. Calculate the pH corresponding to each of the hydrogen ion concentrations given below, and indicate whether each solution is acidic or basic.

a. $[H^+] = 9.35 \times 10^{-2}\ M$
b. $[H^+] = 3.75 \times 10^{-4}\ M$
c. $[H^+] = 8.36 \times 10^{-6}\ M$
d. $[H^+] = 5.42 \times 10^{-8}\ M$

43. Calculate the pH corresponding to each of the hydroxide ion concentrations given below, and indicate whether each solution is acidic or basic.

a. $[OH^-] = 4.73 \times 10^{-4}\ M$
b. $[OH^-] = 5.99 \times 10^{-1}\ M$
c. $[OH^-] = 2.87 \times 10^{-8}\ M$
d. $[OH^-] = 6.39 \times 10^{-3}\ M$

44. Calculate the pH corresponding to each of the hydroxide ion concentrations given below, and indicate whether each solution is acidic or basic.

a. $[OH^-] = 8.63 \times 10^{-3}\ M$
b. $[OH^-] = 7.44 \times 10^{-6}\ M$
c. $[OH^-] = 9.35 \times 10^{-9}\ M$
d. $[OH^-] = 1.21 \times 10^{-11}\ M$

45. Calculate the pH corresponding to each of the pOH values listed, and indicate whether each solution is acidic, basic, or neutral.

a. pOH = 4.32
b. pOH = 8.90
c. pOH = 1.81
d. pOH = 13.1

46. Calculate the pOH value corresponding to each of the pH values listed, and tell whether each solution is acidic or basic.

a. pH = 9.78
b. pH = 4.01
c. pH = 2.79
d. pH = 11.21

47. For each hydrogen ion concentration listed, calculate the pH of the solution as well as the concentration of hydroxide ion in the solution. Indicate whether each solution is acidic or basic.

a. $[H^+] = 4.76 \times 10^{-8}\ M$
b. $[H^+] = 8.92 \times 10^{-3}\ M$
c. $[H^+] = 7.00 \times 10^{-5}\ M$
d. $[H^+] = 1.25 \times 10^{-12}\ M$

48. For each hydrogen ion concentration listed, calculate the pH of the solution as well as the concentration of hydroxide ion in the solution. Indicate whether each solution is acidic or basic.

a. $[H^+] = 1.91 \times 10^{-2}\ M$
b. $[H^+] = 4.83 \times 10^{-7}\ M$
c. $[H^+] = 8.92 \times 10^{-11}\ M$
d. $[H^+] = 6.14 \times 10^{-5}\ M$

49. Calculate the hydrogen ion concentration, in moles per liter, for solutions with each of the following pH values.

a. pH = 9.01
b. pH = 6.89
c. pH = 1.02
d. pH = 7.00

50. Calculate the hydrogen ion concentration, in moles per liter, for solutions with each of the following pH values.

a. pH = 11.21
b. pH = 4.39
c. pH = 7.44
d. pH = 1.38

51. Calculate the hydrogen ion concentration, in moles per liter, for solutions with each of the following pOH values.

a. pOH = 4.95
b. pOH = 7.00
c. pOH = 12.94
d. pOH = 1.02

52. Calculate the hydrogen ion concentration, in moles per liter, for solutions with each of the following pH or pOH values.

a. pOH = 4.99
b. pH = 7.74
c. pOH = 10.74
d. pH = 2.25

53. Calculate the pH of each of the following solutions from the information given.

a. $[H^+] = 4.78 \times 10^{-2}\ M$
b. pOH = 4.56
c. $[OH^-] = 9.74 \times 10^{-3}\ M$
d. $[H^+] = 1.24 \times 10^{-8}\ M$

54. Calculate the pH of each of the following solutions from the information given.

a. $[H^+] = 4.39 \times 10^{-6}\ M$
b. pOH = 10.36
c. $[OH^-] = 9.37 \times 10^{-9}\ M$
d. $[H^+] = 3.31 \times 10^{-1}\ M$

16.5 Calculating the pH of Strong Acid Solutions

QUESTIONS

55. When 1 mole of gaseous hydrogen chloride is dissolved in enough water to make 1 L of solution, approximately how many HCl molecules remain in the solution? Explain.

All even-numbered Questions and Problems have answers in the back of this book and solutions in the Solutions Guide.

32. (a) $[H^+] = 2.9 \times 10^{-14}\ M$; basic; (b) $[H^+] = 1.0 \times 10^{-4}\ M$; acidic; (c) $[H^+] = 2.0 \times 10^{-9}\ M$; basic; (d) $[H^+] = 2.6 \times 10^{-8}$, basic

33. (a) $[OH^-] = 2.5 \times 10^{-11}\ M$; acidic; (b) $[OH^-] = 1.4 \times 10^{-9}\ M$; acidic; (c) $[OH^-] = 1.2 \times 10^{-8}\ M$; acidic; (d) $[OH^-] = 1.8 \times 10^{-6}\ M$; basic

34. (a) $[OH^-] = 9.8 \times 10^{-6}\ M$; acidic; (b) $[OH^-] = 1.02 \times 10^{-7}$ ($1.0 \times 10^{-7}\ M$); basic; (c) $[OH^-] = 2.9 \times 10^{-12}\ M$; acidic; (d) $[OH^-] = 2.1 \times 10^{-4}\ M$; basic

35. (a) $[H^+] = 1.2 \times 10^{-3}\ M$ is more acidic; (b) $[H^+] = 2.6 \times 10^{-6}\ M$ is more acidic; (c) $[H^+] = 0.000010\ M$ is more acidic

36. (a) $[OH^-] = 6.03 \times 10^{-4}\ M$; (b) $[OH^-] = 4.21 \times 10^{-6}\ M$; (c) $[OH^-] = 8.04 \times 10^{-4}\ M$

37. Scientific notation can be awkward when making comparisons of magnitude; $pH = -\log[H^+]$

38. Answers will depend on student choices.

39. three decimal places

40. pH 1-2, deep red; pH 4, purple; pH 8, blue; pH 11, green

41. (a) pH = 2.396; acidic; (b) pH = 6.046; acidic; (c) pH = 5.622; acidic; (d) 9.724; basic

42. (a) pH = 1.029; acidic; (b) pH = 3.426; acidic; (c) pH = 5.078; acidic; (d) pH = 7.266; basic

43. (a) pH = 10.68; basic; (b) pH = 13.78; basic; (c) pH = 6.46; acidic; (d) pH = 11.81; basic

44. (a) pH = 11.94; basic; (b) pH = 8.87; basic; (c) pH = 5.97; acidic; (d) pH = 3.08; acidic

45. (a) 9.68 (basic); (b) 5.10 (acidic); (c) 12.19 (basic); (d) 0.9 (acidic)

46. (a) pOH = 4.22; basic; (b) pOH = 9.99; acidic; (c) pOH = 11.21; acidic; (d) pOH = 2.79; basic

47. (a) pH = 7.322, $[OH^-] = 2.1 \times 10^{-7}\ M$, basic; (b) pH = 2.050, $[OH^-] = 1.1 \times 10^{-12}\ M$, acidic; (c) pH = 4.155, $[OH^-] = 1.4 \times 10^{-10}\ M$, acidic; (d) pH = 11.903, $[OH^-] = 8.0 \times 10^{-3}\ M$, basic

48. (a) pH = 1.719, $[OH^-] = 5.2 \times 10^{-13}\ M$; (b) pH = 6.316, $[OH^-] = 2.1 \times 10^{-8}\ M$; (c) pH = 10.050, $[OH^-] = 1.1 \times 10^{-4}\ M$; (d) pH = 4.212, $[OH^-] = 1.6 \times 10^{-10}\ M$

49. (a) $[H^+] = 9.8 \times 10^{-10}\ M$; (b) $[H^+] = 1.3 \times 10^{-7}\ M$; (c) $[H^+] = 9.5 \times 10^{-2}\ M$; (d) $[H^+] = 1.0 \times 10^{-7}\ M$

50. (a) $[H^+] = 6.2 \times 10^{-12}\ M$; (b) $[H^+] = 4.1 \times 10^{-5}\ M$; (c) $[H^+] = 3.6 \times 10^{-8}\ M$; (d) $[H^+] = 4.2 \times 10^{-2}\ M$

51. (a) $[H^+] = 8.9 \times 10^{-10}\ M$; (b) $[H^+] = 1.0 \times 10^{-7}\ M$; (c) $[H^+] = 8.7 \times 10^{-2}\ M$; (d) $[H^+] = 1.0 \times 10^{-13}\ M$

52. (a) $[H^+] = 9.8 \times 10^{-10}\ M$; (b) $[H^+] = 1.8 \times 10^{-8}\ M$; (c) $[H^+] = 5.5 \times 10^{-4}\ M$; (d) $[H^+] = 5.6 \times 10^{-3}\ M$

56. A bottle of acid solution is labeled "3 M HNO_3." What are the substances that are actually present in the solution? Are any HNO_3 molecules present? Why or why not?

PROBLEMS

57. Calculate the hydrogen ion concentration and the pH of each of the following solutions of strong acids.

a. 1.04×10^{-4} M HCl
b. 0.00301 M HNO_3
c. 5.41×10^{-4} M $HClO_4$
d. 6.42×10^{-2} M HNO_3

58. Calculate the pH of each of the following solutions of strong acids.

a. 1.21×10^{-3} M HNO_3
b. 0.000199 M $HClO_4$
c. 5.01×10^{-5} M HCl
d. 0.00104 M HBr

16.6 Buffered Solutions

QUESTIONS

59. What characteristic properties do buffered solutions possess?

60. What two components make up a buffered solution? Give an example of a combination that would serve as a buffered solution.

61. Which component of a buffered solution is capable of combining with an added strong acid? Using your example from Exercise 60, show how this component would react with added HCl.

62. Which component of a buffered solution consumes added strong base? Using your example from Exercise 60, show how this component would react with added NaOH.

PROBLEMS

63. Which of the following combinations would act as buffered solutions?

a. HCl and NaCl
b. CH_3COOH and KCH_3COO
c. H_2S and NaHS
d. H_2S and Na_2S

64. A buffered solution is prepared containing acetic acid, $HC_2H_3O_2$, and sodium acetate, $Na^+C_2H_3O_2^-$, both at 0.5 M. Write a chemical equation showing how this buffered solution would resist a decrease in its pH if a few drops of aqueous strong acid HCl solution were added to it. Write a chemical equation showing how this buffered solution would resist an increase in its pH if a few drops of aqueous strong base NaOH solution were added to it.

Additional Problems

65. The concepts of acid–base equilibria were developed in this chapter for aqueous solutions (in aqueous solutions, water is the solvent and is intimately involved in the equilibria). However, the Brønsted–Lowry acid–base theory can be extended easily to other solvents. One such solvent that has been investigated in depth is liquid ammonia, NH_3.

a. Write a chemical equation indicating how HCl behaves as an acid in liquid ammonia.
b. Write a chemical equation indicating how OH^- behaves as a base in liquid ammonia.

66. *Strong bases* are bases that completely ionize in water to produce hydroxide ion, OH^-. The strong bases include the hydroxides of the Group 1 elements. For example, if 1.0 mole of NaOH is dissolved per liter, the concentration of OH^- ion is 1.0 M. Calculate the $[OH^-]$, pOH, and pH for each of the following strong base solutions.

a. 0.10 M NaOH
b. 2.0×10^{-4} M KOH
c. 6.2×10^{-3} M CsOH
d. 0.0001 M NaOH

67. Which of the following conditions indicate an *acidic* solution?

a. pH = 3.04
b. $[H^+] > 1.0 \times 10^{-7}$ M
c. pOH = 4.51
d. $[OH^-] = 3.21 \times 10^{-12}$ M

68. Which of the following conditions indicate a *basic* solution?

a. pOH = 11.21
b. pH = 9.42
c. $[OH^-] > [H^+]$
d. $[OH^-] > 1.0 \times 10^{-7}$ M

69. Buffered solutions are mixtures of a weak acid and its conjugate base. Explain why a mixture of a *strong* acid and its conjugate base (such as HCl and Cl^-) is not buffered.

70. Which of the following acids are classified as *strong* acids?

a. HNO_3
b. CH_3COOH ($HC_2H_3O_2$)
c. HCl
d. HF
e. $HClO_4$

71. Is it possible for a solution to have $[H^+] = 0.002$ M and $[OH^-] = 5.2 \times 10^{-6}$ M at 25 °C? Explain.

72. Despite HCl's being a strong acid, the pH of 1.00×10^{-7} M HCl is *not* exactly 7.00. Can you suggest a reason why?

73. According to Arrhenius, bases are species that produce ________ ion in aqueous solution.

74. According to the Brønsted–Lowry model, a base is a species that ________ protons.

75. A conjugate acid–base pair consists of two substances related by the donating and accepting of a(n) ________.

All even-numbered Questions and Problems have answers in the back of this book and solutions in the Solutions Guide.

53. (a) 1.321; (b) 9.44; (c) 11.99; (d) 7.907

54. (a) 5.358; (b) 3.64; (c) 5.97; (d) 0.480

55. none; HCl ionizes completely

56. The solution contains water molecules, H_3O^+ ions (protons), and NO_3^- ions. Because HNO_3 is a strong acid that is completely ionized in water, no HNO_3 molecules are present.

57. (a) $[H^+] = 1.04 \times 10^{-4}$ M, pH = 3.983; (b) $[H^+] = 0.00301$ M, pH = 2.521; (c) $[H^+] = 5.41 \times 10^{-4}$ M, pH = 3.267; (d) $[H^+] = 6.42 \times 10^{-2}$ M, pH = 1.192

58. (a) pH = 2.917; (b) pH = 3.701; (c) pH = 4.300; (d) pH = 2.983

59. resists changes in pH

60. A buffered solution consists of a mixture of a weak acid and its conjugate base; one example of a buffered solution is a mixture of acetic acid ($HC_2H_3O_2$) and sodium acetate ($NaC_2H_3O_2$).

61. The conjugate base component combines with added strong acid.

62. The weak acid component of a buffered solution is capable of reacting with added strong base. For example, using the buffered solution given as an example in Exercise 60, acetic acid would consume added sodium hydroxide as follows: $HC_2H_3O_2(aq)$ + $NaOH(aq) \rightarrow NaC_2H_3O_2(aq)$ + $H_2O(l)$. Acetic acid *neutralizes* the added NaOH and prevents it from affecting the overall pH of the solution.

63. (a) not a buffer; (b) a buffer; (c) a buffer; (d) not a buffer

64. HCl: $H_3O^+ + C_2H_3O_2^- \rightarrow HC_2H_3O_2 + H_2O$; NaOH: $OH^- + HC_2H_3O_2 \rightarrow C_2H_3O_2^- + H_2O$

65. $HCl + NH_3 \rightarrow Cl^- + NH_4^+$; $OH^- + NH_3 \rightarrow H_2O + NH_2^-$

66. (a) $[OH^-(aq)] = 0.10$ M, pOH = 1.00, pH = 13.00; (b) $[OH^-(aq)] = 2.0 \times 10^{-4}$ M, pOH = 3.70, pH = 10.30; (c) $[OH^-(aq)] = 6.2 \times 10^{-3}$ M, pOH = 2.21, pH = 11.79; (d) $[OH^-(aq)] = 0.0001$ M, pOH = 4.0, pH = 10.0

67. a, b, d

68. b, c, d

69. A buffered solution must contain a species capable of strongly attracting protons, which the anion of a strong acid is unable to do very well.

70. a, c, e

71. No. For an aqueous solution, $[H^+][OH^-] = 1.0 \times 10^{-14}$ M at 25 °C.

72. Having a concentration as small as 10^{-7} M for HCl means that the contribution to the total hydrogen ion concentration from the dissociation of water must also be considered in determining the pH of the solution.

73. hydroxide

74. accepts

76. Acetate ion, $C_2H_3O_2^-$, has a stronger affinity for protons than does water. Therefore, when dissolved in water, acetate ion behaves as a(n) ______.

77. An acid such as HCl that strongly conducts an electric current when dissolved in water is said to be a(n) ______ acid.

78. Draw the structure of the carboxyl group, —COOH. Show how a molecule containing the carboxyl group behaves as an acid when dissolved in water.

79. Because of ______, even pure water contains measurable quantities of H^+ and OH^-.

80. The ion-product constant for water, K_w, has the value ______ at 25 °C.

81. The number of ______ in the logarithm of a number is equal to the number of significant figures in the number.

82. A solution with pH = 4 has a (higher/lower) hydrogen ion concentration than a solution with pOH = 4.

83. A 0.20 *M* HCl solution contains ______ *M* hydrogen ion and ______ *M* chloride ion concentrations.

84. A buffered solution is one that resists a change in ______ when either a strong acid or a strong base is added to it.

85. A(n) ______ solution contains a conjugate acid–base pair and through this is able to resist changes in its pH.

86. When sodium hydroxide, NaOH, is added dropwise to a buffered solution, the ______ component of the buffer consumes the added hydroxide ion.

87. When hydrochloric acid, HCl, is added dropwise to a buffered solution, the ______ component of the buffer consumes the added hydrogen ion.

88. Which of the following represent conjugate acid–base pairs? For those pairs that are not conjugates, write the correct conjugate acid or base for each species in the pair.

a. H_2O, OH^-
b. H_2SO_4, SO_4^{2-}
c. H_3PO_4, $H_2PO_4^-$
d. $HC_2H_3O_2$, $C_2H_3O_2^-$

89. In each of the following chemical equations, identify the conjugate acid–base pairs.

a. $CH_3NH_2 + H_2O \rightleftharpoons CH_3NH_3^+ + OH^-$
b. $CH_3COOH + NH_3 \rightleftharpoons CH_3COO^- + NH_4^+$
c. $HF + NH_3 \rightleftharpoons F^- + NH_4^+$

90. Write the conjugate *acid* for each of the following.

a. NH_3
b. NH_2^-
c. H_2O
d. OH^-

91. Write the conjugate *base* for each of the following.

a. H_3PO_4
b. HCO_3^-
c. HF
d. H_2SO_4

92. Write chemical equations showing the ionization (dissociation) in water for each of the following acids.

a. CH_3CH_2COOH (Only the last H is acidic.)
b. NH_4^+
c. H_2SO_4
d. H_3PO_4

93. Which of the following bases have relatively *strong* conjugate acids?

a. F^-
b. Cl^-
c. HSO_4^-
d. NO_3^-

94. Calculate $[H^+]$ in each of the following solutions, and indicate whether the solution is acidic, basic, or neutral.

a. $[OH^-] = 4.22 \times 10^{-3}\ M$
b. $[OH^-] = 1.01 \times 10^{-13}\ M$
c. $[OH^-] = 3.05 \times 10^{-7}\ M$
d. $[OH^-] = 6.02 \times 10^{-6}\ M$

95. Calculate $[OH^-]$ in each of the following solutions, and indicate whether the solution is acidic, basic, or neutral.

a. $[H^+] = 4.21 \times 10^{-7}\ M$
b. $[H^+] = 0.00035\ M$
c. $[H^+] = 0.00000010\ M$
d. $[H^+] = 9.9 \times 10^{-6}\ M$

96. For each pair of concentrations, tell which represents the more basic solution.

a. $[H^+] = 0.000013\ M$ or $[OH^-] = 0.0000032\ M$
b. $[H^+] = 1.03 \times 10^{-6}\ M$ or $[OH^-] = 1.54 \times 10^{-8}\ M$
c. $[OH^-] = 4.02 \times 10^{-7}\ M$ or $[OH^-] = 0.0000001\ M$

97. Calculate the pH of each of the solutions indicated below. Tell whether the solution is acidic, basic, or neutral.

a. $[H^+] = 1.49 \times 10^{-3}\ M$
b. $[OH^-] = 6.54 \times 10^{-4}\ M$
c. $[H^+] = 9.81 \times 10^{-9}\ M$
d. $[OH^-] = 7.45 \times 10^{-10}\ M$

98. Calculate the pH corresponding to each of the hydroxide ion concentrations given below. Tell whether each solution is acidic, basic, or neutral.

a. $[OH^-] = 1.4 \times 10^{-6}\ M$
b. $[OH^-] = 9.35 \times 10^{-9}\ M$
c. $[OH^-] = 2.21 \times 10^{-1}\ M$
d. $[OH^-] = 7.98 \times 10^{-12}\ M$

99. Calculate the pOH corresponding to each of the pH values listed, and indicate whether each solution is acidic, basic, or neutral.

a. pH = 1.02
b. pH = 13.4
c. pH = 9.03
d. pH = 7.20

All even-numbered Questions and Problems have answers in the back of this book and solutions in the Solutions Guide.

75. proton

76. base

77. strong

78. $-C(=O)OH$; $CH_3COOH + H_2O \rightleftharpoons C_2H_3O_2^- + H_3O^+$

79. autoionization

80. $1.0 \times 10^{-14}\ M$

81. decimal places

82. higher

83. 0.20, 0.20

84. pH

85. buffered

86. weak acid

87. conjugate base

88. (a) H_2O and OH^- are a conjugate acid–base pair (H_2O is the acid, having one more proton than the base, OH^-); (b) H_2SO_4 and SO_4^{2-} are *not* a conjugate acid–base pair (they differ by *two* protons). The conjugate base of H_2SO_4 is HSO_4^-; the conjugate acid of SO_4^{2-} is also HSO_4^-; (c) H_3PO_4 and $H_2PO_4^-$ are a conjugate acid–base pair (H_3PO_4 is the acid, having one more proton than the base, $H_2PO_4^-$); (d) $HC_2H_3O_2$ and $C_2H_3O_2^-$ are a conjugate acid–base pair ($HC_2H_3O_2$ is the acid, having one more proton than the base, $C_2H_3O_2^-$)

89. (a) CH_3NH_2 (base), $CN_3NH_3^+$ (acid), H_2O (acid), OH^- (base); (b) CH_3COOH (acid), CH_3COO^- (base), NH_3 (base), NH_4^+ (acid); (c) HF (acid), F^- (base), NH_3 (base), NH_4^+ (acid)

90. (a) NH_4^+; (b) NH_3; (c) H_3O^+; (d) H_2O

91. (a) $H_2PO_4^-$; (b) CO_3^{2-}; (c) F^-; (d) HSO_4^-

92. (a) $CH_3CH_2COOH + H_2O \rightleftharpoons CH_3CH_2COO^- + H_3O^+$; (b) $NH_4^+ + H_2O \rightleftharpoons NH_3 + H_3O^+$; (c) $H_2SO_4 + H_2O \rightarrow HSO_4^- + H_3O^+$; (d) $H_3PO_4 + H_2O \rightleftharpoons H_2PO_4^- + H_3O^+$

93. b, c, d

94. (a) $[H^+(aq)] = 2.4 \times 10^{-12}\ M$, solution is basic; (b) $[H^+(aq)] = 9.9 \times 10^{-2}\ M$, solution is acidic; (c) $[H^+(aq)] = 3.3 \times 10^{-8}\ M$, solution is basic; (d) $[H^+(aq)] = 1.7 \times 10^{-9}\ M$, solution is basic

95. (a) $[OH^-] = 2.4 \times 10^{-8}\ M$ (acidic); (b) $[OH^-] = 2.9 \times 10^{-11}\ M$ (acidic); (c) $[OH^-] = 1.0 \times 10^{-7}\ M$ (neutral); (d) $[OH^-] = 1.0 \times 10^{-9}\ M$ (acidic)

96. (a) $[OH^-(aq)] = 0.0000032\ M$; (b) $[OH^-(aq)] = 1.54 \times 10^{-8}\ M$; (c) $[OH^-(aq)] = 4.02 \times 10^{-7}\ M$

97. (a) pH = 2.827 (acidic); (b) pH = 10.82 (basic); (c) pH = 8.008 (basic); (d) pH = 4.87 (acidic)

100. For each hydrogen or hydroxide ion concentration listed, calculate the concentration of the complementary ion and the pH and pOH of the solution.

a. $[H^+] = 5.72 \times 10^{-4}\ M$
b. $[OH^-] = 8.91 \times 10^{-5}\ M$
c. $[H^+] = 2.87 \times 10^{-12}\ M$
d. $[OH^-] = 7.22 \times 10^{-8}\ M$

101. Calculate the hydrogen ion concentration, in moles per liter, for solutions with each of the following pH values.

a. pH = 8.34
b. pH = 5.90
c. pH = 2.65
d. pH = 12.6

102. Calculate the hydrogen ion concentration, in moles per liter, for solutions with each of the following pH or pOH values.

a. pH = 5.41
b. pOH = 12.04
c. pH = 11.91
d. pOH = 3.89

103. Calculate the hydrogen ion concentration, in moles per liter, for solutions with each of the following pH or pOH values.

a. pOH = 0.90
b. pH = 0.90
c. pOH = 10.3
d. pH = 5.33

104. Calculate the hydrogen ion concentration and the pH of each of the following solutions of strong acids.

a. $1.4 \times 10^{-3}\ M\ HClO_4$
b. $3.0 \times 10^{-5}\ M\ HCl$
c. $5.0 \times 10^{-2}\ M\ HNO_3$
d. $0.0010\ M\ HCl$

105. Write the formulas for *three* combinations of weak acid and salt that would act as buffered solutions. For each of your combinations, write chemical equations showing how the components of the buffered solution would consume added acid and base.

All even-numbered Questions and Problems have answers in the back of this book and solutions in the Solutions Guide.

98. (a) pH = 8.15, solution is basic; (b) pH = 5.97, solution is acidic; (c) pH = 13.34, solution is basic; (d) pH = 2.90, solution is acidic

99. (a) pOH = 12.98 (acidic); (b) pOH = 0.6 (basic); (c) pOH = 4.97 (basic); (d) pOH = 6.80 (acidic)

100. (a) $[OH^-(aq)] = 1.8 \times 10^{-11}\ M$, pH = 3.24, pOH = 10.76; (b) $[H^+(aq)] = 1.1 \times 10^{-10}\ M$, pH = 9.95, pOH = 4.05; (c) $[OH^-(aq)] = 3.5 \times 10^{-3}\ M$, pH = 11.54, pH = 2.46; (d) $[H^+(aq)] = 1.4 \times 10^{-7}\ M$, pH = 6.86, pOH = 7.14

101. (a) $[H^+] = 4.6 \times 10^{-9}\ M$; (b) $[H^+] = 1.3 \times 10^{-6}\ M$; (c) $[H^+] = 2.2 \times 10^{-3}\ M$; (d) $[H^+] = 3 \times 10^{-13}\ M$

102. (a) $[H^+] = 3.9 \times 10^{-6}\ M$; (b) $[H^+] = 1.1 \times 10^{-2}\ M$; (c) $[H^+] = 1.2 \times 10^{-12}\ M$; (d) $[H^+] = 7.8 \times 10^{-11}\ M$

103. (a) $[H^+] = 7.9 \times 10^{-14}\ M$; (b) $[H^+] = 0.13\ M$; (c) $[H^+] = 2 \times 10^{-4}\ M$; (d) $[H^+] = 4.7 \times 10^{-6}\ M$

104. (a) $[H^+(aq)] = 1.4 \times 10^{-3}\ M$, pH = 2.85; (b) $[H^+(aq)] = 3.0 \times 10^{-5}\ M$, pH = 4.52; (c) $[H^+(aq)] = 5.0 \times 10^{-2}\ M$, pH = 1.30; (d) $[H^+(aq)] = 0.0010\ M$, pH = 3.00

105. student selection of examples

Chapter 17

Objectives

In this chapter, our objectives are for the students to:

SECTION 17.1

- Understand the collision model of how chemical reactions occur.

SECTION 17.2

- Understand activation energy.
- Understand how a catalyst speeds up a reaction.

SECTION 17.3

- Learn how equilibrium is established.

SECTION 17.4

- Learn about the characteristics of chemical equilibrium.

SECTION 17.5

- Understand the law of chemical equilibrium and learn how to calculate values for the equilibrium constant.

SECTION 17.6

- Understand the role that liquids and solids play in constructing the equilibrium expression.

SECTION 17.7

- Learn to predict the changes that occur when a system at equilibrium is disturbed.

SECTION 17.8

- Learn to calculate equilibrium concentrations from equilibrium constants.

SECTION 17.9

- Learn to calculate the solubility product of a salt, given its solubility, and vice versa.

17 Equilibrium

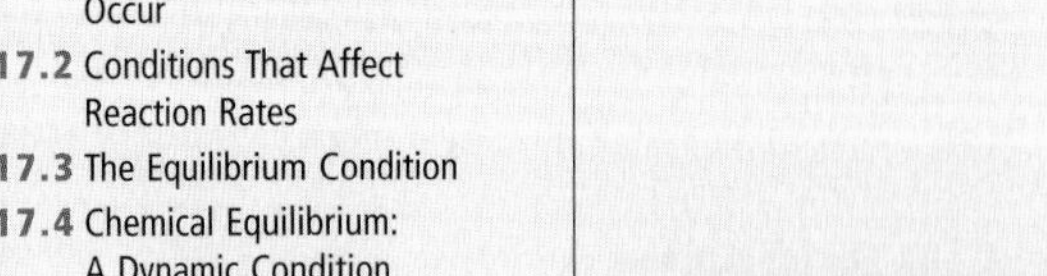

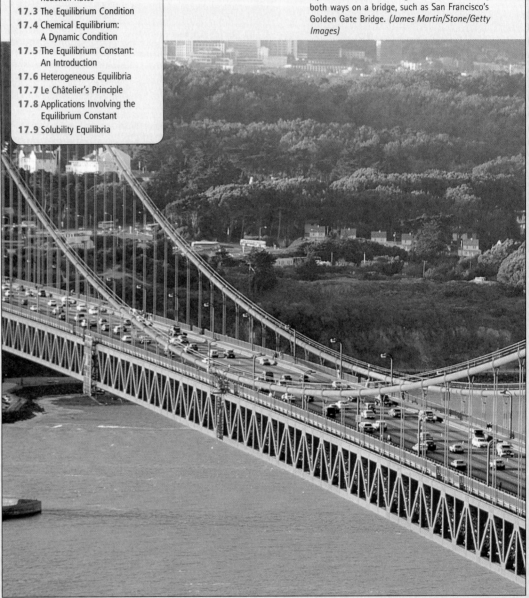

Equilibrium can be analogous to traffic flowing both ways on a bridge, such as San Francisco's Golden Gate Bridge. *(James Martin/Stone/Getty Images)*

ChemWork Refined over ten years of use by thousands of students, **ChemWork** builds and enhances students' problems-solving skills. Online assignments function as a "personal instructor" to help students learn how to solve challenging problems and learn how to think like chemists. Annotations for **ChemWork** assignments are included at the beginning of the end-of-chapter review.

PowerLecture This 2-DVD package includes the Chemistry Multimedia Library, which contains animations, simulations, and movies for all chemistry subjects, organized by topic for lecture presentations. Annotations for **PowerLecture** are referenced in the margins throughout the Annotated Instructor's Edition.

OWL Sign in to OWL at **www.cengage.com/owl** to view tutorials and simulations, develop problem-solving skills, and complete online homework assigned by your professor.

go Chemistry Download mini-lecture videos for key concept review and exam prep from OWL or purchase them from **www.ichapters.com**

Chemistry is mostly about reactions—processes in which groups of atoms are reorganized. So far we have learned to describe chemical reactions by using balanced equations and to calculate amounts of reactants and products. However, there are many important characteristics of reactions that we have not yet considered.

© Cengage Learning

Refrigeration prevents food spoilage.

For example, why do refrigerators prevent food from spoiling? That is, why do the chemical reactions that cause food to decompose occur more slowly at lower temperatures? On the other hand, how can a chemical manufacturer speed up a chemical reaction that runs too slowly to be economical?

Another question that arises is why chemical reactions carried out in a closed vessel appear to stop at a certain point. For example, when the reaction of reddish-brown nitrogen dioxide to form colorless dinitrogen tetroxide,

$$\underset{\text{Reddish-brown}}{2NO_2(g)} \rightarrow \underset{\text{Colorless}}{N_2O_4(g)}$$

is carried out in a closed container, the reddish-brown color at first fades but stops changing after a time and then stays the same color indefinitely if left undisturbed (see Figure 17.1). We will account for all of these important observations about reactions in this chapter.

Test Bank: 1

17.1 How Chemical Reactions Occur

Section 17.1

OBJECTIVE: To understand the collision model of how chemical reactions occur.

In writing the equation for a chemical reaction, we put the reactants on the left and the products on the right with an arrow between them. But how do the atoms in the reactants reorganize to form the products?

TEACHING TIP

Use the molecular-level view of molecules to show students what is happening during a molecular collision. Figure 17.2 shows how a collision results in a chemical reaction.

PowerLecture Animations:
Collision Theory: Effects of Molecular Energy
Collision Theory: Effects of Molecular Orientation
Collision Theory: A Successful Collision

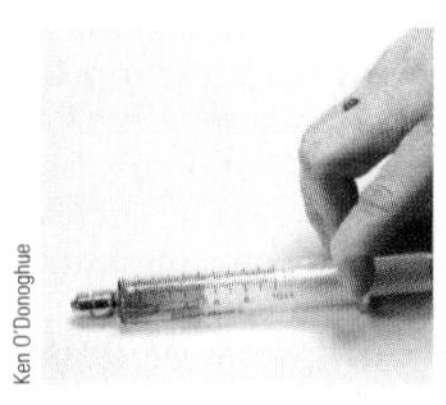

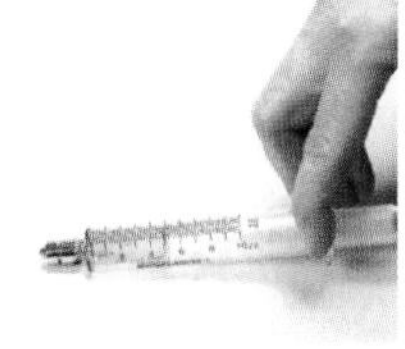

Ken O'Donoghue

Figure 17.1

a *A sample containing a large quantity of reddish-brown NO_2 gas.*

b *As the reaction to form colorless N_2O_4 occurs, the sample becomes lighter brown.*

c *After equilibrium is reached [$2NO_2(g) \rightleftharpoons N_2O_4(g)$], the color remains the same.*

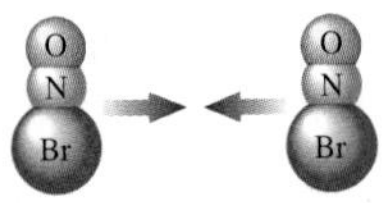

a — Two BrNO molecules approach each other at high speeds.

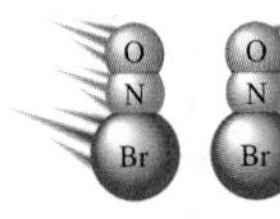

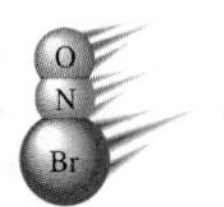

b — The collision occurs.

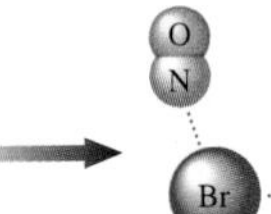

c — The energy of the collision causes the Br—N bonds to break and allows the Br—Br bond to form.

d — The products: one Br_2 and two NO molecules.

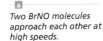

Figure 17.2 Visualizing the reaction $2BrNO(g) \rightarrow 2NO(g) + Br_2(g)$.

Chemists believe that molecules react by colliding with each other. Some collisions are violent enough to break bonds, allowing the reactants to rearrange to form the products. For example, consider the reaction

$$2BrNO(g) \rightleftharpoons 2NO(g) + Br_2(g)$$

which we picture to occur as shown in Figure 17.2. Notice that the Br—N bonds in the two BrNO molecules must be broken and a new Br—Br bond must be formed during a collision for the reactants to become products.

The idea that reactions occur during molecular collisions, which is called the **collision model,** explains many characteristics of chemical reactions. For example, it explains why a reaction proceeds faster if the concentrations of the reacting molecules are increased (higher concentrations lead to more collisions and therefore to more reaction events). The collision model also explains why reactions go faster at higher temperatures, as we will see in the next section.

17.2 Conditions That Affect Reaction Rates

OBJECTIVES: To understand activation energy. • To understand how a catalyst speeds up a reaction.

It is easy to see why reactions speed up when the *concentrations* of reacting molecules are increased: higher concentrations (more molecules per unit volume) lead to more collisions and so to more reaction events. But reactions also speed up when the *temperature* is increased. Why? The answer lies in the fact that not all collisions possess enough energy to break bonds. A minimum energy called the **activation energy (E_a)** is needed for a reaction to occur (see Figure 17.3). If a given collision possesses an energy greater than E_a, that collision can result in a reaction. If a collision has an energy less than E_a, the molecules will bounce apart unchanged.

Recall from Section 13.8 that the average kinetic energy of a collection of molecules is directly proportional to the temperature (K).

The reason that a reaction occurs faster as the temperature is increased is that the speeds of the molecules increase with temperature. So at higher temperatures, the average collision is more energetic. This makes it more likely that a given collision will possess enough energy to break bonds and to produce the molecular rearrangements needed for a reaction to occur.

Higher temperatures → Higher speeds → More high-energy collisions → More collisions that break bonds → Faster reaction

Test Bank: 2, 3

Section 17.2

TEACHING TIPS

- Use Figure 17.3 to illustrate the energy changes that occur when two BrNO molecules from Figure 17.2 interact.
- Compare the reaction curves from Figures 17.3 and 17.4. Emphasize the similarities between the two curves. Also point out that Figure 17.3 represents an exothermic reaction and Figure 17.4 represents an endothermic reaction. Discuss how we can tell from the graph whether the reaction is exothermic or endothermic.

Lecture Demonstration: 12.6, 12.7, 12.8, 12.9, 12.12, 12.20

DEMONSTRATION

Temperature and Reaction Rate

Materials 0.005 M $KMnO_4$, 0.75 M $H_2C_2O_4$ (saturated), 12 test tubes, 2 thermometers, water bath (at least a 600-mL beaker, one-third full of water), hot plate

Preparation Place 20 mL $KMnO_4$ in each of six test tubes. Place 20 mL $H_2C_2O_4$ in each of six additional test tubes. Set up the water bath. Place all test tubes in an empty large beaker.

Procedure Ask a student to determine room temperature. Record the temperature on the board. Place ten test tubes (five of each solution) in the water bath and begin heating the water. Assign one student to keep track of the temperature for the water bath. The student should tell you when the temperature of the water reaches 10 degrees higher than room temperature. While waiting for the water bath to heat, run the reactions at room temperature. Using the remaining tube of $KMnO_4$ and the remaining tube of $H_2C_2O_4$, explain that you will mix the solutions and students should time the reaction until the color has changed to pale yellow with no remaining purple. The timer should begin as soon as the solutions make contact. Pour the oxalic acid into the potassium permanganate solution. To mix them, pour the solutions back and forth twice. Be consistent in all trials. Record the time of reaction on the board. Place the reacted test tube back in the empty large beaker. Repeat this procedure with a second pair of test tubes when the temperature of the water bath is 10 degrees higher than room temperature. Record both the temperature and the time on the board. Continue to repeat the procedure at 10-degree intervals until all test tubes are reacted.

Teaching Notes It is possible to graph time versus temperature for this reaction on the board as you perform the demonstration. Ask students to determine what

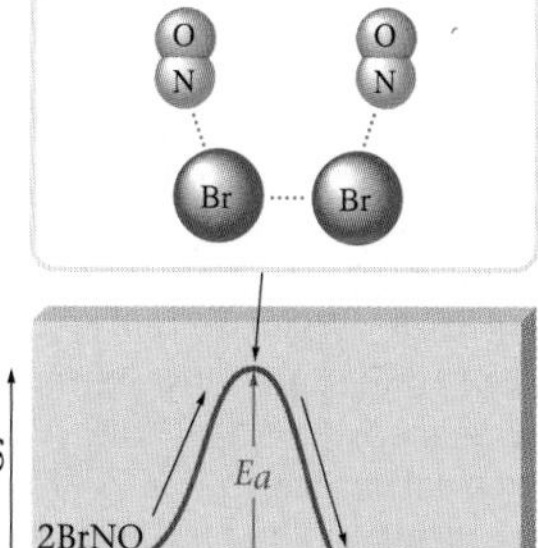

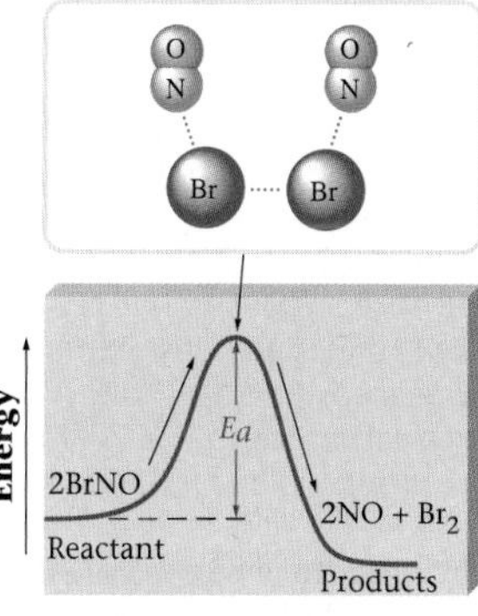

Figure 17.3 When molecules collide, a certain minimum energy called the activation energy (E_a) is needed for a reaction to occur. If the energy contained in a collision of two BrNO molecules is greater than E_a, the reaction can go "over the hump" to form products. If the collision energy is less than E_a, the colliding molecules bounce apart unchanged.

Is it possible to speed up a reaction without changing the temperature or the reactant concentrations? Yes, by using something called a **catalyst,** *a substance that speeds up a reaction without being consumed.* This may sound too good to be true, but it is a very common occurrence. In fact, you would not be alive now if your body did not contain thousands of catalysts called **enzymes.** Enzymes allow our bodies to speed up complicated reactions that would be too slow to sustain life at normal body temperatures. For example, the enzyme carbonic anhydrase speeds up the reaction between carbon dioxide and water

$$CO_2(g) + H_2O(l) \rightleftharpoons H^+(aq) + HCO_3^-(aq)$$

to help prevent an excess accumulation of carbon dioxide in our blood.

Although we cannot consider the details here, a catalyst works because it provides a new pathway for the reaction—a pathway that has a lower activation energy than the original pathway, as illustrated in Figure 17.4. Because of the lower activation energy, more collisions will have enough energy to allow a reaction. This in turn leads to a faster reaction.

A very important example of a reaction involving a catalyst occurs in our atmosphere; it is the breakdown of ozone, O_3, catalyzed by chlorine atoms. Ozone is one constituent of the earth's upper atmosphere that is especially crucial, because it absorbs harmful high-energy radiation from the sun. There are natural processes that result in both the formation and the destruction of ozone in the upper atmosphere. The natural balance of all these opposing processes has resulted in an amount of ozone that has been relatively constant over the years. However, the ozone level now seems to be decreasing, especially over Antarctica (Figure 17.5), apparently because chlorine atoms act as catalysts for the decomposition of ozone to oxygen by the following pair of reactions:

$$Cl + O_3 \rightarrow ClO + O_2$$
$$O + ClO \rightarrow Cl + O_2$$
$$\text{Sum: } Cl + O_3 + O + ClO \rightarrow ClO + O_2 + Cl + O_2$$

When species that appear on both sides of the equation are canceled, the end result is the reaction

$$O + O_3 \rightarrow 2O_2$$

Although O atoms are too reactive to exist near the earth's surface, they do exist in the upper atmosphere.

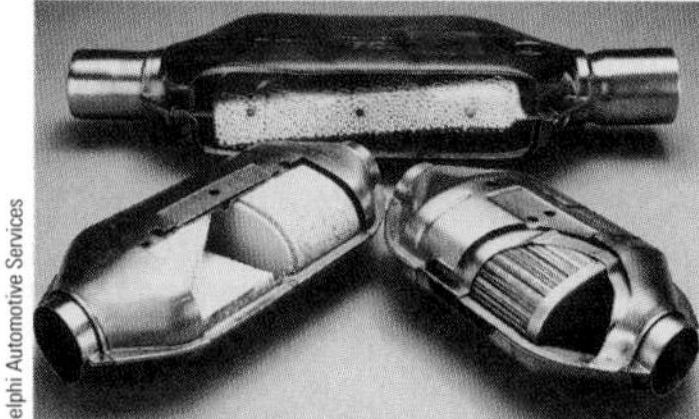

Cutaways of catalytic converters used in automobiles.

Uncatalyzed reaction pathway | Catalyzed reaction pathway

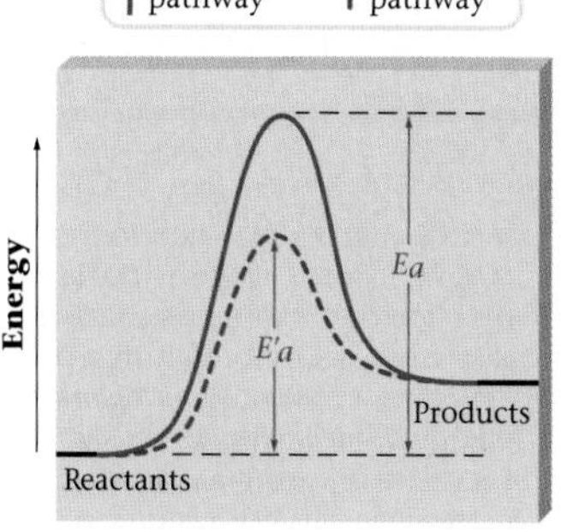

Figure 17.4 Comparison of the activation energies for an uncatalyzed reaction (E_a) and for the same reaction with a catalyst present (E_a'). Note that a catalyst works by lowering the activation energy for a reaction.

- Remind students that the kinetic energy of a collection of molecules is directly proportional to the temperature (K).

PowerLecture Animation: Transition States and Activation Energy

DEMONSTRATION

Sprinkling flour, lycopodium powder, or granular iron in a burner flame shows the dependence of combustion rate on particle size. Now is an excellent time to discuss events such as grain-dust explosions in storage silos or coal-dust explosions in mines.

PowerLecture Video: Reaction of Mg with Weak HCl and Strong HCl

DEMONSTRATION

You can illustrate the dependence of the speed of a reaction on surface area by using several different 2.0-g samples of zinc (use coarse grades through powdered zinc). Place the Zn samples in separate balloons. Place 30 mL of 1.0 M HCl in several 125-mL Erlenmeyer flasks. Next attach the balloons to cover the mouth of each flask, being careful not to spill any of the zinc into the flask or to tear the balloon. When you are ready to perform the demonstrations, have students carefully raise all the balloons to empty the zinc into the flasks at the same time. Observe the reaction as the assemblies stand on the table. The reaction rates should be apparent from the speeds at which the balloons fill.

is happening to the rate of the reaction as the temperature increases. This experiment produces reaction times that are halved for every 10-degree increase in temperature. This reaction is actually a study in complex kinetics, but it can be used to illustrate the effect of temperature on rate for beginning classes. The Mn^{2+} ion catalyzes the reaction, which contributes to the increase in rate. This point does not need to be discussed with students to effectively perform the demonstration. Times for the reaction vary from about 4 minutes at room temperature to about 5 seconds at the highest temperature.

TEACHING TIPS

- Most collisions do not result in a chemical reaction, as a consequence of energy requirements and positioning of the molecules. If all collisions resulted in a chemical reaction, life would be extremely unstable. Virtually everything would happen at a much higher speed (including our aging). Students should appreciate the vast number and types of chemical reactions that are occurring all around them (especially in an atmosphere rich in oxygen).

Lecture Demonstration: 12.22, 12.23, 12.25

PowerLecture Animation: Effect of Temperature on Reaction Rates

TEACHING TIP

Now is an excellent time to discuss the use of catalysts. Catalytic converters in automobiles use metals such as palladium and platinum to convert uncombusted hydrocarbons to carbon dioxide and water. The metals are used repeatedly in these processes. In the human body, enzymes act as catalysts, speeding up reactions that would take hours in the laboratory to fractions of a second in the body.

DEMONSTRATION

Reappearing Catalyst

Materials $KNaC_4H_4O_6$ crystals, $CoCl_2$ crystals, 400-mL beaker, 6% hydrogen peroxide, hot plate, teaspoon

Preparation Place 6 g of $KNaC_4H_4O_6$ crystals in the beaker. Add 100 mL distilled water and dissolve the crystals.

Procedure Warm the solution of $KNaC_4H_4O_6$ to about 60 °C. Add 40 mL of hydrogen peroxide. Add a few crystals (one-half teaspoon) of $CoCl_2$ crystals to the solution. A vigorous reaction occurs and the solution turns green with lots of bubbling. Eventually the solution will return to its original pink color.

Teaching Notes The green color is the color of the activated complex for the reaction. The tartaric acid is being oxidized by the hydrogen peroxide. The cobalt(II) ion is the catalyst for the reaction. The pink color at the beginning and end of the reaction indicates the presence of the catalyst, $Co^{2+}(aq)$.

CHEMISTRY *IN* FOCUS

Protecting the Ozone

Chlorofluorocarbons (CFCs) are ideal compounds for refrigerators and air conditioners because they are nontoxic and noncorrosive. However, the chemical inertness of these substances, once thought to be their major virtue, turns out to be their fatal flaw. When these compounds leak into the atmosphere, as they inevitably do, they are so unreactive they persist there for decades. Eventually these CFCs reach altitudes where ultraviolet light causes them to decompose, producing chlorine atoms that promote the destruction of the ozone in the stratosphere (see discussion in Section 17.2). Because of this problem, the world's industrialized nations have signed an agreement (called the Montreal Protocol) that banned CFCs in 1996 (with a 10-year grace period for developing nations).

Worldwide production of CFCs has already decreased to half of the 1986 level of 1.13 million metric tons. One strategy for replacing the CFCs has been to switch to similar compounds that contain carbon and hydrogen atoms substituted for chlorine atoms. For example, the U.S. appliance industry has switched from Freon-12 (CF_2Cl_2) to the compound CH_2FCH_3 (called HFC-134a) for home refrigerators, and most of the new cars and trucks sold in the United States have air conditioners that employ HFC-134a. Converting the 140 million autos currently on the road in the United States that use CF_2Cl_2 will pose a major headache, but experience suggests that replacement of Freon-12 with HFC-134a is less expensive than was originally feared. For example, Volvo Cars of North America estimates that a Volvo can be converted from Freon-12 to HFC-134a for around $300.

Courtesy, Amana

An Amana refrigerator, one of many appliances that now use HFC-134a. This compound is replacing CFCs, which lead to the destruction of atmospheric ozone.

A related environmental issue involves replacing the halons for firefighting applications. In particular, scientists are seeking an effective replacement for CF_3Br (halon-1301), the nontoxic "magic gas" used to flood enclosed spaces such as offices, aircraft, race cars, and military tanks in case of fire. The compound CF_3I, which appears to have a lifetime in the atmosphere of only a few days, looks like a promising candidate but much more research on the toxicology and ozone-depleting properties of CF_3I will be required before it receives government approval as a halon substitute.

The chemical industry has responded amazingly fast to the ozone depletion emergency. It is encouraging that we can act rapidly when an environmental crisis occurs. Now we need to get better at keeping the environment at a higher priority as we plan for the future.

Notice that a chlorine atom is used up in the first reaction but a chlorine atom is formed again by the second reaction. Therefore, the amount of chlorine does not change as the overall process occurs. This means that the chlorine atom is a true catalyst: it participates in the process but is not consumed. Estimates show that *one chlorine atom can catalyze the destruction of about one million ozone molecules per second.*

The chlorine atoms that promote this damage to the ozone layer are present because of pollution. Specifically, they come from the decomposition of compounds called Freons, such as CF_2Cl_2, which have been widely used in refrigerators and air conditioners. The Freons have leaked into the at-

PowerLecture Videos:
Catalysis: Decomposition of H_2O_2 Catalyzed by MnO_2
Homogeneous Catalysis

PowerLecture Animation:
Catalytic Converter on the Molecular Scale

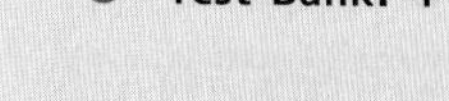
Test Bank: 4–5

Section 17.3

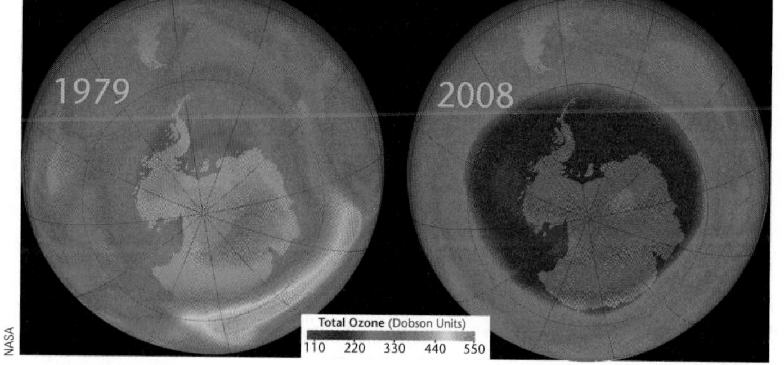

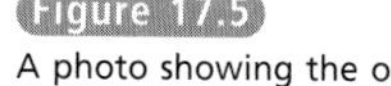
Figure 17.5
A photo showing the ozone "hole" over Antarctica.

Lecture Demonstration: 13.3

mosphere, where they are decomposed by light to produce chlorine atoms and other substances. As a result, the manufacture of Freons was banned by agreement among the nations of the world as of the end of 1996. Substitute compounds are now being used in newly manufactured refrigerators and air conditioners.

17.3 The Equilibrium Condition

OBJECTIVE: To learn how equilibrium is established.

Equilibrium is a word that implies balance or steadiness. When we say that someone is maintaining his or her equilibrium, we are describing a state of balance among various opposing forces. The term is used in a similar but more specific way in chemistry. Chemists define **equilibrium** as the *exact balancing of two processes, one of which is the opposite of the other.*

We first encountered the concept of equilibrium in Section 14.4, when we described the way vapor pressure develops over a liquid in a closed container (see Figure 14.9). This equilibrium process is summarized in Figure 17.6. The *equilibrium state* occurs when the rate of evaporation exactly equals the rate of condensation.

So far in this textbook we have usually assumed that reactions proceed to completion—that is, until one of the reactants "runs out." Indeed, many reactions *do* proceed essentially to completion. For such reactions we can assume that the reactants are converted to products until the limiting reactant is completely consumed. On the other hand, there are many chemical reactions that "stop" far short of completion when they are allowed to take place in a closed container. An example is the reaction of nitrogen dioxide to form dinitrogen tetroxide.

$$NO_2(g) + NO_2(g) \rightarrow N_2O_4(g)$$

The reactant NO_2 is a reddish-brown gas, and the product N_2O_4 is a colorless gas. Imagine an experiment where pure NO_2 is placed in an empty, sealed glass vessel at 25 °C. The initial dark brown color will decrease in intensity as the NO_2 is converted to colorless N_2O_4 (see Figure 17.1). However, even over a long period of time,

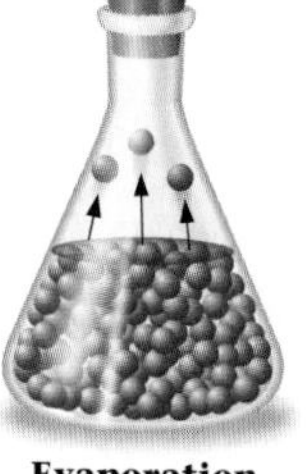
Evaporation

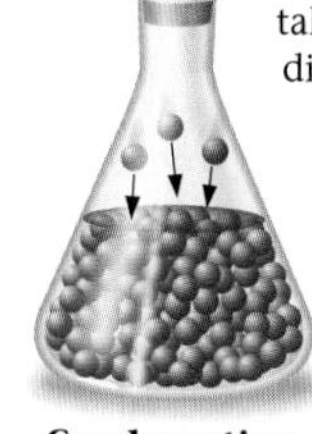
Condensation

TEACHING TIPS

- Point out that equilibrium can be reached only in closed systems, which include gases in closed containers and ions in solution (since the ions cannot escape). In industry, processes rarely reach equilibrium. Instead, processes are designed to maximize the amount of product formed (and avoid the limitation of equilibrium) by removing the product as it is formed.
- Emphasize that equilibrium is not a condition in which the reactants and the products are present in equal amounts. The balance is between the *rates* of the forward and reverse reactions.

PowerLecture Animation: $FeSCN^-$ Equilibrium

MISCONCEPTION

Students often think that equilibrium is a static condition. Emphasize that, although at the macroscopic level things appear to be constant at equilibrium, at the molecular level chemical reactions continue to take place. The rates of the forward and reverse reactions are equal.

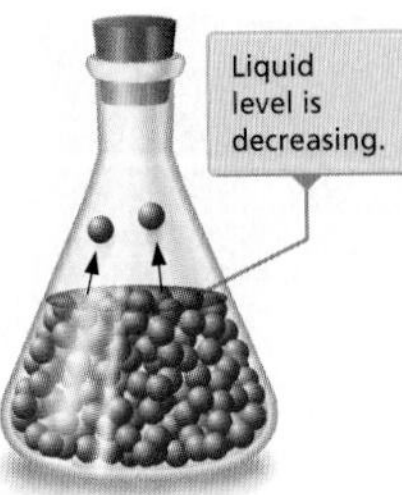

a At first there is a net transfer of molecules from the liquid state to the vapor state.

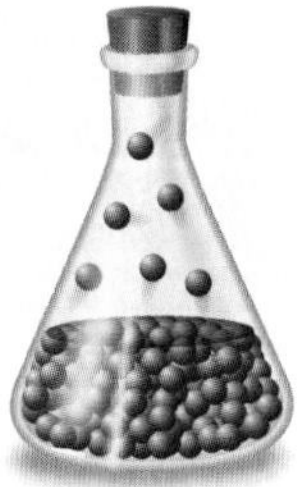

b After a while, the amount of the substance in the vapor state becomes constant—both the pressure of the vapor and the level of the liquid stay the same.

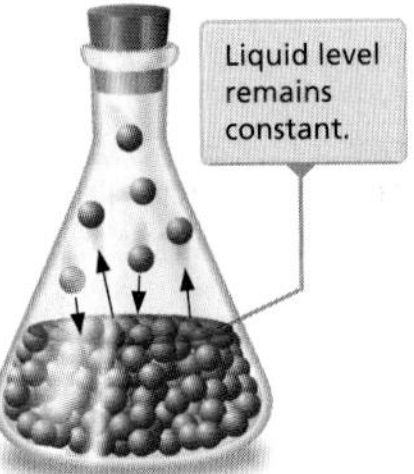

c The equilibrium state is very dynamic. The vapor pressure and liquid level remain constant because exactly the same number of molecules escape the liquid as return to it.

Figure 17.6

The establishment of the equilibrium vapor pressure over a liquid in a closed container.

the contents of the reaction vessel do not become colorless. Instead, the intensity of the brown color eventually becomes constant, which means that the concentration of NO_2 is no longer changing. This simple observation is a clear indication that the reaction has "stopped" short of completion. In fact, the reaction has not stopped. Rather, the system has reached **chemical equilibrium,** *a dynamic state where the concentrations of all reactants and products remain constant.*

This situation is similar to the one where a liquid in a closed container develops a constant vapor pressure, except that in this case two opposite chemical reactions are involved. When pure NO_2 is first placed in the closed flask, there is no N_2O_4 present. As collisions between NO_2 molecules occur, N_2O_4 is formed and the concentration of N_2O_4 in the container increases. However, the reverse reaction can also occur. A given N_2O_4 molecule can decompose into two NO_2 molecules.

$$N_2O_4(g) \rightarrow NO_2(g) + NO_2(g)$$

That is, chemical reactions are *reversible;* they can occur in either direction. We usually indicate this fact by using double arrows.

$$2NO_2(g) \underset{\text{Reverse}}{\overset{\text{Forward}}{\rightleftharpoons}} N_2O_4(g)$$

In this case the double arrows mean that either two NO_2 molecules can combine to form an N_2O_4 molecule (the *forward* reaction) or an N_2O_4 molecule can decompose to give two NO_2 molecules (the *reverse* reaction).

Equilibrium is reached whether pure NO_2, pure N_2O_4, or a mixture of NO_2 and N_2O_4 is initially placed in a closed container. In any of these cases, conditions will eventually be reached in the container such that N_2O_4 is being formed and is decomposing at exactly the same rate. This leads to chemical equilibrium, a dynamic situation where the concentrations of reactants and products remain the same indefinitely, as long as the conditions are not changed.

17.4 Chemical Equilibrium: A Dynamic Condition

OBJECTIVE: To learn about the characteristics of chemical equilibrium.

Equilibrium is a dynamic situation.

Because no changes occur in the concentrations of reactants or products in a reaction system at equilibrium, it may appear that everything has stopped. However, this is not the case. On the molecular level there is frantic activity. Equilibrium is not static but is a highly *dynamic* situation. Consider again the analogy between chemical equilibrium and two island cities connected by a single bridge. Suppose the traffic flow on the bridge is the same in both directions. It is obvious that there is motion (we can see the cars traveling across the bridge), but the number of cars in each city does not change because there is an equal flow of cars entering and leaving. The result is no *net* change in the number of cars in each of the two cities.

A double arrow ($\rightleftharpoons$) is used to show that a reaction is occurring in both directions.

To see how this concept applies to chemical reactions, let's consider the reaction between steam and carbon monoxide in a closed vessel at a high temperature where the reaction takes place rapidly.

$$H_2O(g) + CO(g) \rightleftharpoons H_2(g) + CO_2(g)$$

Assume that the same number of moles of gaseous CO and gaseous H_2O are placed in a closed vessel and allowed to react (Figure 17.7a).

When CO and H_2O, the reactants, are mixed, they immediately begin to react to form the products, H_2 and CO_2. This leads to a decrease in the concentrations of the reactants, but the concentrations of the products, which were initially at zero, are increasing (Figure 17.7b). After a certain

H_2O	7	5	2	2
CO	7	5	2	2
H_2	0	2	5	5
CO_2	0	2	5	5

Figure 17.7
The reaction of H_2O and CO to form CO_2 and H_2 as time passes. (a) Equal numbers of moles of H_2O and CO are mixed in a closed container. (b) The reaction begins to occur, and some products (H_2 and CO_2) are formed. (c) The reaction continues as time passes and more reactants are changed to products. (d) Although time continues to pass, the numbers of reactant and product molecules are the same as in (c). No further changes are seen as time continues to pass. The system has reached equilibrium.

Section 17.4

TEACHING TIP

The concept of equilibrium is one of the most difficult for students to understand. It is important to proceed slowly and use many examples in this chapter.

Lecture Demonstration: 13.1, 13.2

DEMONSTRATION
Reaching Equilibrium: Are We There Yet?

Materials Two large containers (plastic milk jugs cut in half work well), a large cup (15 oz), a small cup (5 oz), water, a marker, two volunteers

Preparation Add water to the two large containers and mark the level of water on each side of the container.

Presentation Each volunteer should fill the cup as much as possible by dipping it into his or her container and then pour the water into the other container. Repeat this process until the level of water in each container is no longer changing. It is important that the same number of transfers occur in each direction.

Discussion Students have difficulty with the idea that chemical equilibrium is a dynamic condition. This makes sense because we usually think of equilibrium as a balance, and something that is balanced—not moving. This is another example of the benefits of taking a microscopic approach to studying chemistry; that is, a system at equilibrium may appear to us to be unmoving, but at a molecular level it is dynamic. The balance is between the rates of forward and reverse reactions.

The number of transfers will vary, although equilibrium should be achieved within several minutes.

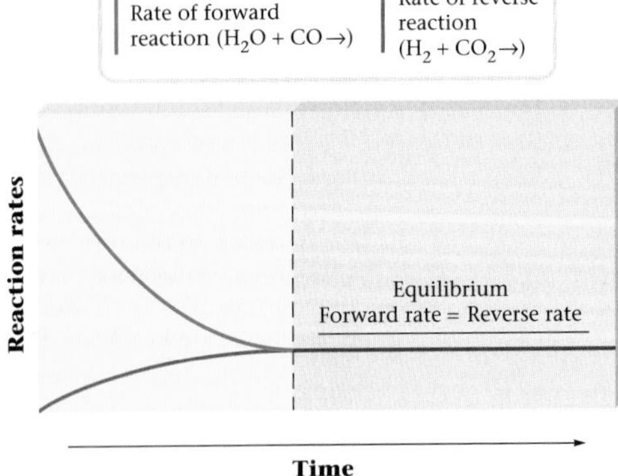

Figure 17.8
The changes with time in the rates of the forward and reverse reactions for $H_2O(g) + CO(g) \rightleftharpoons H_2(g) + CO_2(g)$ when equal numbers of moles of $H_2O(g)$ and $CO(g)$ are mixed. At first, the rate of the forward reaction decreases and the rate of the reverse reaction increases. Equilibrium is reached when the forward rate and the reverse rate become the same.

period of time, the concentrations of reactants and products no longer change at all—equilibrium has been reached (Figure 17.7c and d). Unless the system is somehow disturbed, no further changes in the concentrations will occur.

Why does equilibrium occur? We saw earlier in this chapter that molecules react by colliding with one another, and that the more collisions, the faster the reaction. This is why the speed of a reaction depends on concentrations. In this case the concentrations of H_2O and CO are lowered as the forward reaction occurs—that is, as products are formed.

$$H_2O + CO \rightarrow H_2 + CO_2$$

As the concentrations of the reactants decrease, the forward reaction slows down (Figure 17.8). But as in the traffic-on-the-bridge analogy, there is also movement in the reverse direction.

$$H_2 + CO_2 \rightarrow H_2O + CO$$

Initially in this experiment, no H_2 and CO_2 are present, so this reverse reaction cannot occur. However, as the forward reaction proceeds, the concentrations of H_2 and CO_2 build up and the speed (or rate) of the reverse reaction increases (Figure 17.8) as the forward reaction slows down. Eventually the concentrations reach levels at which *the rate of the forward reaction equals the rate of the reverse reaction*. The system has reached equilibrium.

Test Bank: 6–11, 40–42

17.5 The Equilibrium Constant: An Introduction

Section 17.5

OBJECTIVE: To understand the law of chemical equilibrium and to learn how to calculate values for the equilibrium constant.

Science is based on the results of experiments. The development of the equilibrium concept is typical. On the basis of their observations of many chemical reactions, two Norwegian chemists, Cato Maximilian Guldberg and Peter Waage, proposed in 1864 the **law of chemical equilibrium**

TEACHING TIPS

- Use balanced chemical equations including states for each chemical species in this section. The next section discusses heterogeneous equilibria, and students will need to distinguish among the states of the chemicals there.
- Once students understand how to set up the equilibrium expression for a reaction, you can talk about calculations involving the expression. It is important to distinguish between initial conditions and equilibrium conditions when students begin calculations.

PowerLecture Simulations:
The Meaning of the Equilibrium Constant
The Equilibrium State

Module 21: Chemical Equilibrium covers concepts in this section.

(originally called the *law of mass action*) as a general description of the equilibrium condition. Guldberg and Waage postulated that for a reaction of the type

$$aA + bB \rightleftharpoons cC + dD$$

where A, B, C, and D represent chemical species and *a*, *b*, *c*, and *d* are their coefficients in the balanced equation, the law of mass action is represented by the following **equilibrium expression:**

$$K = \frac{[C]^c[D]^d}{[A]^a[B]^b}$$

Square brackets, [ ], indicate concentration units of mol/L.

The square brackets indicate the concentrations of the chemical species *at equilibrium* (in units of mol/L), and *K* is a constant called the **equilibrium constant.** Note that the equilibrium expression is a special ratio of the concentrations of the products to the concentrations of the reactants. Each concentration is raised to a power corresponding to its coefficient in the balanced equation.

The law of chemical equilibrium as proposed by Guldberg and Waage is based on experimental observations. Experiments on many reactions showed that the equilibrium condition could always be described by this special ratio, called the equilibrium expression.

To see how to construct an equilibrium expression, consider the reaction where ozone changes to oxygen:

$$\underset{\text{Reactant}}{\overset{\text{Coefficient}}{2O_3(g)}} \rightleftharpoons \underset{\text{Product}}{\overset{\text{Coefficient}}{3O_2(g)}}$$

To obtain the equilibrium expression, we place the concentration of the product in the numerator and the concentration of the reactant in the denominator.

$$\frac{[O_2]}{[O_3]} \quad \begin{matrix}\leftarrow \text{Product} \\ \leftarrow \text{Reactant}\end{matrix}$$

Then we use the coefficients as powers.

$$K = \frac{[O_2]^3}{[O_3]^2} \quad \text{Coefficients become powers}$$

EXAMPLE 17.1 Writing Equilibrium Expressions

Write the equilibrium expression for the following reactions.

a. $H_2(g) + F_2(g) \rightleftharpoons 2HF(g)$ b. $N_2(g) + 3H_2(g) \rightleftharpoons 2NH_3(g)$

SOLUTION

Applying the law of chemical equilibrium, we place products over reactants (using square brackets to denote concentrations in units of moles per liter) and raise each concentration to the power that corresponds to the coefficient in the balanced chemical equation.

a. $$K = \frac{[HF]^2}{[H_2][F_2]} \quad \begin{matrix}\leftarrow \text{Product (coefficient of 2 becomes power of 2)} \\ \leftarrow \text{Reactants (coefficients of 1 become powers of 1)}\end{matrix}$$

Note that when a coefficient (power) of 1 occurs, it is not written but is understood.

b. $$K = \frac{[NH_3]^2}{[N_2][H_2]^3}$$

PowerLecture Simulation: Writing Equilibrium Expressions

Additional Examples

Example 17.1

Write the equilibrium expression for the following reactions.

1. $CH_3OH(g) \rightleftharpoons CH_2O(g) + H_2(g)$

$$K = \frac{[CH_2O(g)][H_2(g)]}{[CH_3OH(g)]}$$

2. $4NH_3(g) + 5O_2(g) \rightleftharpoons 4NO(g) + 6H_2O(g)$

$$K = \frac{[NO(g)]^4[H_2O(g)]^6}{[NH_3(g)]^4[O_2(g)]^5}$$

Self Check

Answer to Self-Check Exercise 17.1

$$K = \frac{[NO_2(g)]^4[H_2O(g)]^6}{[NH_3(g)]^4[O_2(g)]^7}$$

TEACHING TIPS

- Have students calculate the change in concentration for each of the species in Table 17.1. Make sure they understand that the ratio of concentration changes is the same ratio as the coefficients in the balanced equation.
- Use the results in Table 17.1 to emphasize the difference between "equilibrium position" and "equilibrium constant."
- When calculating K from concentrations of reactants and products, emphasize both initial and equilibrium concentrations so that students can distinguish between the two sets of data. This issue can be a major source of confusion for beginning students when working these problems.

Self-Check EXERCISE 17.1 Write the equilibrium expression for the following reaction.

$$4NH_3(g) + 7O_2(g) \rightleftharpoons 4NO_2(g) + 6H_2O(g)$$

See Problems 17.15 through 17.18. ■

What does the equilibrium expression mean? It means that, for a given reaction at a given temperature, the special ratio of the concentrations of the products to reactants defined by the equilibrium expression will always be equal to the same number—namely, the equilibrium constant K. For example, consider a series of experiments on the ammonia synthesis reaction

$$N_2(g) + 3H_2(g) \rightleftharpoons 2NH_3(g)$$

carried out at 500 °C to measure the concentrations of N_2, H_2, and NH_3 present at equilibrium. The results of these experiments are shown in Table 17.1. In this table, subscript zeros next to square brackets are used to indicate *initial concentrations:* the concentrations of reactants and products originally mixed together before any reaction has occurred.

Consider the results of experiment I. One mole each of N_2 and H_2 were sealed into a 1-L vessel at 500 °C and allowed to reach chemical equilibrium. At equilibrium the concentrations in the flask were found to be $[N_2] = 0.921\ M$, $[H_2] = 0.763\ M$, and $[NH_3] = 0.157\ M$. The equilibrium expression for the reaction

$$N_2(g) + 3H_2(g) \rightleftharpoons 2NH_3(g)$$

is

$$K = \frac{[NH_3]^2}{[N_2][H_2]^3} = \frac{(0.157)^2}{(0.921)(0.763)^3} = 0.0602 = 6.02 \times 10^{-2}$$

Similarly, as shown in Table 17.1, we can calculate for experiments II and III that K, the equilibrium constant, has the value 6.02×10^{-2}. In fact, whenever N_2, H_2, and NH_3 are mixed together at this temperature, the system *always* comes to an equilibrium position such that

$$K = 6.02 \times 10^{-2}$$

regardless of the amounts of the reactants and products that are mixed together initially.

Table 17.1 Results of Three Experiments for the Reaction $N_2(g) + 3H_2(g) \rightleftharpoons 2NH_3(g)$ at 500 °C

	Initial Concentrations			*Equilibrium Concentrations*			
Experiment	$[N_2]_0$	$[H_2]_0$	$[NH_3]_0$	$[N_2]$	$[H_2]$	$[NH_3]$	$\frac{[NH_3]^2}{[N_2][H_2]^3} = K^*$
I	1.000 M	1.000 M	0	0.921 M	0.763 M	0.157 M	$\frac{(0.157)^2}{(0.921)(0.763)^3} = 0.0602$
II	0	0	1.000 M	0.399 M	1.197 M	0.203 M	$\frac{(0.203)^2}{(0.399)(1.197)^3} = 0.0602$
III	2.00 M	1.00 M	3.00 M	2.59 M	2.77 M	1.82 M	$\frac{(1.82)^2}{(2.59)(2.77)^3} = 0.0602$

*The units for K are customarily omitted.

MATH MISCONCEPTION

Order of Operations and Calculators

When using calculators to determine equilibrium constants from equilibrium concentrations, students sometimes neglect the order of operations. For example, many students will take the expression

$$\frac{6}{4 \times 3}$$

and get 4.5 instead of 0.5. This is because they ente "6" "÷" "4" "×" "3" into the calculator. Thus they ge 6/4 = 1.5, and 1.5 × 3 = 4.5.

It is important to see from Table 17.1 that the *equilibrium concentrations are not always the same.* However, even though the individual sets of equilibrium concentrations are quite different for the different situations, the *equilibrium constant, which depends on the ratio of the concentrations, remains the same.*

For a reaction at a given temperature, there are many equilibrium positions but only one value for K.

Each *set of equilibrium concentrations* is called an **equilibrium position.** It is essential to distinguish between the equilibrium constant and the equilibrium positions for a given reaction system. There is only *one* equilibrium constant for a particular system at a particular temperature, but there are an *infinite* number of equilibrium positions. The specific equilibrium position adopted by a system depends on the initial concentrations; the equilibrium constant does not.

Note that in the above discussion, the equilibrium constant was given without units. In certain cases the units are included when the values of equilibrium constants are given, and in other cases they are omitted. We will not discuss the reasons for this. We will omit the units in this text.

EXAMPLE 17.2 Calculating Equilibrium Constants

The reaction of sulfur dioxide with oxygen in the atmosphere to form sulfur trioxide has important environmental implications because SO_3 combines with moisture to form sulfuric acid droplets, an important component of acid rain. The following results were collected for two experiments involving the reaction at 600 °C between gaseous sulfur dioxide and oxygen to form gaseous sulfur trioxide:

$$2SO_2(g) + O_2(g) \rightleftharpoons 2SO_3(g)$$

	Initial	Equilibrium
Experiment I	$[SO_2]_0 = 2.00\ M$	$[SO_2] = 1.50\ M$
	$[O_2]_0 = 1.50\ M$	$[O_2] = 1.25\ M$
	$[SO_3]_0 = 3.00\ M$	$[SO_3] = 3.50\ M$
Experiment II	$[SO_2]_0 = 0.500\ M$	$[SO_2] = 0.590\ M$
	$[O_2]_0 = 0$	$[O_2] = 0.045\ M$
	$[SO_3]_0 = 0.350\ M$	$[SO_3] = 0.260\ M$

The law of chemical equilibrium predicts that the value of K should be the same for both experiments. Verify this by calculating the equilibrium constant observed for each experiment.

Jenny Hager/The Image Works

Spruce needles turned brown by acid rain.

Additional Examples

Example 17.2

1. For the reaction

$$2NBr_3(g) \rightleftharpoons N_2(g) + 3Br_2(g)$$

the system at equilibrium at a particular temperature is analyzed and the following concentrations are found: $[NBr_3] = 2.07 \times 10^{-3}\ M$; $[N_2] = 4.11 \times 10^{-2}\ M$; $[Br_2] = 1.06 \times 10^{-3}\ M$. Calculate the value of K for the reaction at this temperature.

1.14×10^{-5}

2. At high temperatures, elemental bromine, Br_2, dissociates into individual bromine atoms:

$$Br_2(g) \rightleftharpoons 2Br(g)$$

This system at equilibrium at a particular temperature is analyzed and the following concentrations are found: $[Br_2] = 0.97\ M$; $[Br_2] = 3.4 \times 10^{-2}\ M$. Calculate the value of K for the reaction at this temperature.

1.2×10^{-3}

SOLUTION

The balanced equation for the reaction is

$$2SO_2(g) + O_2(g) \rightleftharpoons 2SO_3(g)$$

From the law of chemical equilibrium, we can write the equilibrium expression

$$K = \frac{[SO_3]^2}{[SO_2]^2[O_2]}$$

For experiment I we calculate the value of K by substituting the observed *equilibrium* concentrations,

$$[SO_3] = 3.50\ M$$
$$[SO_2] = 1.50\ M$$
$$[O_2] = 1.25\ M$$

into the equilibrium expression:

$$K_I = \frac{(3.50)^2}{(1.50)^2(1.25)} = 4.36$$

For experiment II at equilibrium

$$[SO_3] = 0.260\ M$$
$$[SO_2] = 0.590\ M$$
$$[O_2] = 0.045\ M$$

and

$$K_{II} = \frac{(0.260)^2}{(0.590)^2(0.045)} = 4.32$$

Notice that the values calculated for K_I and K_{II} are nearly the same, as we expected. That is, the value of K is constant, within differences due to rounding off and due to experimental error. These experiments show *two different equilibrium positions* for this system, but K, the equilibrium constant, is, indeed, constant. ■

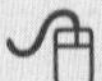 **Test Bank: 12–15, 34**

Section 17.6

TEACHING TIPS

- Students often forget the states of chemical species when writing equilibrium expressions. As a result, they may include pure liquids and solids in the equilibrium expression. It is important to remind them frequently of this point as they begin to write expressions for heterogeneous equilibria.
- Now is an excellent time to stress that the amounts represented in an equilibrium expression are concentrations. Solids and liquids have constant concentrations, so they are not included in the expression.

17.6 Heterogeneous Equilibria

OBJECTIVE: To understand the role that liquids and solids play in constructing the equilibrium expression.

So far we have discussed equilibria only for systems in the gaseous state, where all reactants and products are gases. These are examples of **homogeneous equilibria,** in which all substances are in the same state. However, many equilibria involve more than one state and are called **heterogeneous equilibria.** For example, the thermal decomposition of calcium carbonate in the commercial preparation of lime occurs by a reaction involving solids and gases.

In terms of amount produced, lime is among the top ten chemicals manufactured in the United States.

$$CaCO_3(s) \rightleftharpoons \underset{\text{Lime}}{CaO(s)} + CO_2(g)$$

Straightforward application of the law of equilibrium leads to the equilibrium expression

$$K = \frac{[CO_2][CaO]}{[CaCO_3]}$$

PowerLecture Animation: Ions of Lead Chloride in H_2O Attaining Dynamic Equilibrium

However, experimental results show that the *position of a heterogeneous equilibrium does not depend on the amounts of pure solids or liquids present.* The fundamental reason for this behavior is that the concentrations of pure solids and liquids cannot change. In other words, we might say that the concentrations of pure solids and liquids are constants. Therefore, we can write the equilibrium expression for the decomposition of solid calcium carbonate as

The concentrations of pure liquids and solids are constant.

$$K' = \frac{[CO_2]C_1}{C_2}$$

where C_1 and C_2 are constants representing the concentrations of the solids CaO and $CaCO_3$, respectively. This expression can be rearranged to give

$$\frac{C_2K'}{C_1} = K = [CO_2]$$

where the constants C_2, K', and C_1 are combined into a single constant K. This leads us to the following general statement: the concentrations of pure solids or pure liquids involved in a chemical reaction *are not included in the equilibrium expression* for the reaction. This applies *only* to pure solids or liquids. It does not apply to solutions or gases, because their concentrations can vary.

For example, consider the decomposition of liquid water to gaseous hydrogen and oxygen:

$$2H_2O(l) \rightleftharpoons 2H_2(g) + O_2(g)$$

where

$$K = [H_2]^2[O_2]$$

Water is not included in the equilibrium expression because it is a pure liquid. However, when the reaction is carried out under conditions where the water is a gas rather than a liquid,

$$2H_2O(g) \rightleftharpoons 2H_2(g) + O_2(g)$$

we have

$$K = \frac{[H_2]^2[O_2]}{[H_2O]^2}$$

because the concentration of water vapor can change.

EXAMPLE 17.3 Writing Equilibrium Expressions for Heterogeneous Equilibria

Write the expressions for K for the following processes.

a. Solid phosphorus pentachloride is decomposed to liquid phosphorus trichloride and chlorine gas.

b. Deep-blue solid copper(II) sulfate pentahydrate is heated to drive off water vapor and form white solid copper(II) sulfate.

SOLUTION

a. The reaction is

$$PCl_5(s) \rightleftharpoons PCl_3(l) + Cl_2(g)$$

In this case, neither the pure solid PCl_5 nor the pure liquid PCl_3 is included in the equilibrium expression. The equilibrium expression is

$$K = [Cl_2]$$

Additional Examples

Example 17.3

Write the expression for K for the following process.

$$ZrI_4(s) \rightleftharpoons Zr(s) + 2I_2(g)$$

$$K = [I_2(g)]^2$$

Answers to Self-Check Exercise 17.2

a. $K = [O_2]^3$

b. $K = [N_2O][H_2O]^2$

c. $K = \frac{1}{[CO_2]}$

d. $K = \frac{1}{[SO_3]}$

Test Bank: 16–39

Section 17.7

TEACHING TIP

Be sure to proceed slowly through this section, giving lots of examples. Students have a difficult time with these questions. Think through each example with students and be sure they understand how the concentrations change each time.

LABORATORY EXPERIMENT

A relevant laboratory experiment for this section is Experiment 25, Stresses Applied to Chemical Equilibrium, from *Introductory Chemistry in the Laboratory* by James Hall.

As solid copper(II) sulfate pentahydrate, $CuSO_4{\cdot}5H_2O$, is heated, it loses H_2O, eventually forming white $CuSO_4$.

b. The reaction is

$$CuSO_4 \cdot 5H_2O(s) \rightleftharpoons CuSO_4(s) + 5H_2O(g)$$

The two solids are not included. The equilibrium expression is

$$K = [H_2O]^5$$

Self-Check **EXERCISE 17.2** Write the equilibrium expression for each of the following reactions.

a. $2KClO_3(s) \rightleftharpoons 2KCl(s) + 3O_2(g)$

This reaction is often used to produce oxygen gas in the laboratory.

b. $NH_4NO_3(s) \rightleftharpoons N_2O(g) + 2H_2O(g)$

c. $CO_2(g) + MgO(s) \rightleftharpoons MgCO_3(s)$

d. $SO_3(g) + H_2O(l) \rightleftharpoons H_2SO_4(l)$

See Problems 17.25 through 17.28. ■

17.7 Le Châtelier's Principle

OBJECTIVE: To learn to predict the changes that occur when a system at equilibrium is disturbed.

It is important to understand the factors that control the *position* of a chemical equilibrium. For example, when a chemical is manufactured, the chemists and chemical engineers in charge of production want to choose conditions that favor the desired product as much as possible. That is, they want the equilibrium to lie far to the right (toward products). When the process for the synthesis of ammonia was being developed, extensive studies were carried out to determine how the equilibrium concentration of ammonia depended on the conditions of temperature and pressure.

In this section we will explore how various changes in conditions affect the equilibrium position of a reaction system. We can predict the effects of changes in concentration, pressure, and temperature on a system at equilibrium by using **Le Châtelier's principle,** which states that when *a change is imposed on a system at equilibrium, the position of the equilibrium shifts in a direction that tends to reduce the effect of that change.*

The Effect of a Change in Concentration

Let us consider the ammonia synthesis reaction. Suppose there is an equilibrium position described by these concentrations:

$$[N_2] = 0.399\ M \qquad [H_2] = 1.197\ M \qquad [NH_3] = 0.203\ M$$

What will happen if 1.000 mol/L of N_2 is suddenly injected into the system? We can begin to answer this question by remembering that for the system at equilibrium, the rates of the forward and reverse reactions exactly balance,

$$N_2(g) + 3H_2(g) \rightleftharpoons 2NH_3(g)$$

as indicated here by arrows of the same length. When N_2 is added, there are suddenly more collisions between N_2 and H_2 molecules. This increases the rate of the forward reaction (shown here by the greater length of the arrow pointing in that direction),

$$N_2(g) + 3H_2(g) \rightleftharpoons 2NH_3(g)$$

and the reaction produces more NH_3. As the concentration of NH_3 increases, the reverse reaction also speeds up (as more collisions between NH_3 molecules occur) and the system again comes to equilibrium. However, the new equilibrium position has more NH_3 than was present in the original position. We say that the equilibrium has shifted to the *right*—toward the products. The original and new equilibrium positions are shown below.

Equilibrium Position I		Equilibrium Position II
$[N_2] = 0.399\ M$	⇨	$[N_2] = 1.348\ M$
$[H_2] = 1.197\ M$	1.000 mol/L of N_2 added	$[H_2] = 1.044\ M$
$[NH_3] = 0.203\ M$		$[NH_3] = 0.304\ M$

Note that the equilibrium does, in fact, shift to the right; the concentration of H_2 decreases (from 1.197 *M* to 1.044 *M*), the concentration of NH_3 increases (from 0.203 *M* to 0.304 *M*), and, of course, because nitrogen was added, the concentration of N_2 shows an increase relative to the original amount present.

It is important to note at this point that, although the equilibrium shifted to a new position, the *value of K did not change.* We can demonstrate this by inserting the equilibrium concentrations from positions I and II into the equilibrium expression.

- Position I: $K = \dfrac{[NH_3]^2}{[N_2][H_2]^3} = \dfrac{(0.203)^2}{(0.399)(1.197)^3} = 0.0602$
- Position II: $K = \dfrac{[NH_3]^2}{[N_2][H_2]^3} = \dfrac{(0.304)^2}{(1.348)(1.044)^3} = 0.0602$

These values of *K* are the same. Therefore, although the equilibrium *position* shifted when we added more N_2, the *equilibrium constant K* remained the same.

Could we have predicted this shift by using Le Châtelier's principle? Because the change in this case was to add nitrogen, Le Châtelier's principle

which indicates that more $FeSCN^{2+}$ is forming. To the second Petri dish, add several drops of $Fe(NO_3)_3$ solution. Once again the solution color intensifies, which indicates further formation of $FeSCN^{2+}$. Both reactants are present in the original solution and neither reactant is limiting. To shift the equilibrium again, add a few crystals of solid Na_2HPO_4 to the first Petri dish. The HPO_4^{2-} reacts with the iron ions to form $FeHPO_4^{+}$. The red color disappears because the equilibrium of the initial reaction shifts to the left as iron ions are removed from the solution. To the second Petri dish, add a few drops of $AgNO_3$ solution. Once again the red color disappears. In this case the silver ions are reacting with the SCN^- ions to form AgSCN. Finally, add a few drops of HCl to the second Petri dish. The chloride ions react with the silver ions to form the white precipitate AgCl, but the red color of the solution returns because the SCN^- ions are released from the AgSCN and interact with the iron ions in solution once again to re-form $FeSCN^{2+}$.

Teaching Notes It is important during this demonstration to discuss each addition using the initial reaction to illustrate how the equilibrium is changing. Students need to be able to think about these changes as they occur.

DEMONSTRATION

$FeSCN^{2+}$ and Le Châtelier's Principle

Materials 0.20 *M* $Fe(NO_3)_2$, Na_2HPO_4 crystals, 0.2 *M* HCl, 0.002 *M* KSCN, solid KSCN, 0.20 *M* $AgNO_3$, 3 Petri dishes, eyedroppers, overhead projector

Procedure Cover the bottom of a Petri dish with the KSCN solution and place it on the overhead projector. Add several drops of $Fe(NO_3)_2$ to the Petri dish and swirl gently to mix well. The following reaction is occurring:

$$\underset{\text{Yellow}}{Fe^{3+}} + \underset{\text{Colorless}}{SCN^-} \rightleftharpoons \underset{\text{Red}}{FeSCN^{2+}}$$

Now divide the solution about equally among three Petri dishes. Place all three on the overhead projector. The third Petri dish will act as a standard for comparison. Add a small amount of solid KSCN to the first Petri dish. Notice that the solution becomes more strongly colored,

Lecture Demonstration: 13.3

PowerLecture Animations: Water Tank Equilibrium Demonstration (Parts 1–4)

DEMONSTRATION

Concentration Effects

To illustrate the effect of a change in concentration on equilibrium, you can use about 20 mL of 0.2 *M* $CoCl_2$ in a 250-mL flask. Observe the pink color of the solution. Add about 50 mL of concentrated HCl and show the students the color change from pink to blue. This change results from the formation of a cobalt complex:

$$\underset{\text{Pink}}{Co^{2+}(aq) + 4Cl^-(aq)} \rightleftharpoons \underset{\text{Blue}}{CoCl_4^{2-}(aq)}$$

Divide the solution into two equal parts in two 250-mL flasks. Add water to one of the flasks until the solution turns back to pink. This demonstration illustrates Le Châtelier's principle, as the water dilutes the chloride concentration and pulls the equilibrium to the left.

PowerLecture Animation: Binding of O_2 and CO to Hemoglobin Molecule

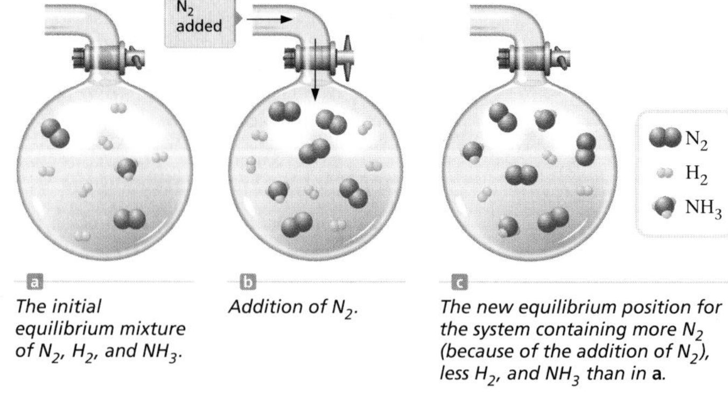

Figure 17.9

a The initial equilibrium mixture of N_2, H_2, and NH_3.

b Addition of N_2.

c The new equilibrium position for the system containing more N_2 (because of the addition of N_2), less H_2, and NH_3 than in **a**.

predicts that the system will shift in a direction that *consumes* nitrogen. This tends to offset the original change—the addition of N_2. Therefore, Le Châtelier's principle correctly predicts that adding nitrogen will cause the equilibrium to shift to the right (Figure 17.9) as some of the added nitrogen is consumed.

A system at equilibrium shifts in the direction that compensates for any imposed change.

If ammonia had been added instead of nitrogen, the system would have shifted to the left, consuming ammonia. Another way of stating Le Châtelier's principle, then, is to say that *when a reactant or product is added to a system at equilibrium, the system shifts away from the added component.* On the other hand, if *a reactant or product is removed, the system shifts toward the removed component.* For example, if we had removed nitrogen, the system would have shifted to the left and the amount of ammonia present would have been reduced.

A real-life example that shows the importance of Le Châtelier's principle is the effect of high elevations on the oxygen supply to the body. If you have ever traveled to the mountains on vacation, you may have noticed that you felt "light-headed" and especially tired during the first few days of your visit. These feelings resulted from a decreased supply of oxygen to your body because of the lower air pressure that exists at higher elevations. For example, the oxygen supply in Leadville, Colorado (elevation ~ 10,000 ft), is only about two-thirds that found at sea level. We can understand the effects of diminished oxygen supply in terms of the following equilibrium:

$$Hb(aq) + 4O_2(g) \rightleftharpoons Hb(O_2)_4(aq)$$

where Hb represents hemoglobin, the iron-containing protein that transports O_2 from your lungs to your tissues, where it is used to support metabolism. The coefficient 4 in the equation signifies that each hemoglobin molecule picks up four O_2 molecules in the lungs. Note by Le Châtelier's principle that a lower oxygen pressure will cause this equilibrium to shift to the left, away from oxygenated hemoglobin. This leads to an inadequate oxygen supply at the tissues, which in turn results in fatigue and a "woozy" feeling.

This problem can be solved in extreme cases, such as when climbing Mt. Everest or flying in a plane at high altitudes, by supplying extra oxygen from a tank. This extra oxygen pushes the equilibrium to its normal position. However, lugging around an oxygen tank would not be very practical for people who live in the mountains. In fact, nature solves this problem in a very interesting way. The body adapts to living at high elevations by producing additional hemoglobin—the other way to shift this equilibrium to the right. Thus, people who live at high elevations have significantly higher hemoglobin levels than those living at sea level. For example, the Sherpas who live in Nepal can function in the rarefied air at the top of Mt. Everest without an auxiliary oxygen supply.

EXAMPLE 17.4 Using Le Châtelier's Principle: Changes in Concentration

Arsenic, As_4, is obtained from nature by first reacting its ore with oxygen (called *roasting*) to form solid As_4O_6. (As_4O_6, a toxic compound fatal in doses of 0.1 g or more, is the "arsenic" made famous in detective stories.) The As_4O_6 is then reduced using carbon:

$$As_4O_6(s) + 6C(s) \rightleftharpoons As_4(g) + 6CO(g)$$

Predict the direction of the shift in the equilibrium position for this reaction that occurs in response to each of the following changes in conditions.

a. Addition of carbon monoxide

b. Addition or removal of $C(s)$ or $As_4O_6(s)$

c. Removal of $As_4(g)$

SOLUTION

a. Le Châtelier's principle predicts a shift away from the substance whose concentration is increased. The equilibrium position will shift to the left when carbon monoxide is added.

b. Because the amount of a pure solid has no effect on the equilibrium position, changing the amount of carbon or tetraarsenic hexoxide will have no effect.

c. When gaseous arsenic is removed, the equilibrium position will shift to the right to form more products. In industrial processes, the desired product is often continuously removed from the reaction system to increase the yield.

Self-Check EXERCISE 17.3

Novelty devices for predicting rain contain cobalt(II) chloride and are based on the following equilibrium:

$$\underset{\text{Blue}}{CoCl_2(s)} + 6H_2O(g) \rightleftharpoons \underset{\text{Pink}}{CoCl_2 \cdot 6H_2O(s)}$$

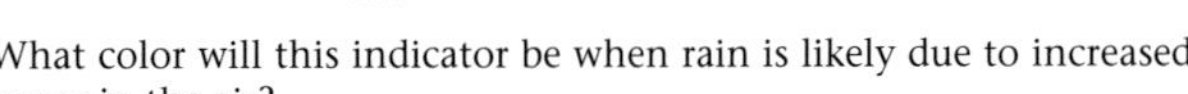

What color will this indicator be when rain is likely due to increased water vapor in the air?

See Problems 17.33 through 17.36. ■

When blue anhydrous $CoCl_2$ reacts with water, pink $CoCl_2 \cdot 6H_2O$ is formed.

The Effect of a Change in Volume

When the volume of a gas is decreased (when a gas is compressed), the pressure increases. This occurs because the molecules present are now contained in a smaller space and they hit the walls of their container more often, giving a greater pressure. Therefore, when the volume of a gaseous reaction system at equilibrium is suddenly reduced, leading to a sudden increase in pressure, by Le Châtelier's principle the system will shift in the direction that reduces the pressure.

Additional Examples

Example 17.4

Suppose the reaction system

$$2SO_2(g) + O_2(g) \rightleftharpoons 2SO_3(g)$$

has already reached equilibrium. Predict the effect of each of the following changes on the position of the equilibrium.

1. $SO_2(g)$ is added to the system.

   shifts to the right

2. The $SO_3(g)$ present is liquefied and removed from the system.

   shifts to the right

3. Some of the $O_2(g)$ is removed from the system.

   shifts to the left

Self Check

Answer to Self-Check Exercise 17.3

pink

DEMONSTRATION

Two everyday examples of Le Châtelier's principle are the novelty barometers often found in gift shops and commercial desiccants (containing Drierite with moisture indicator). In both cases $CoCl_2$ is used to indicate the level of moisture. The color change from blue to pink indicates an increase in the moisture content.

TEACHING TIPS

- Students have trouble understanding how a change in volume affects the system. The idea that decreasing the volume increases the pressure and therefore changes the concentration is difficult for many students to understand.
- When working with gases, students should remember that they must use a balanced equation to make their predictions.
- For students who would like a mathematical verification of the effect of a change in volume, discuss how the partial pressures of the gases change. For example, suppose that at some temperature the equilibrium concentrations of N_2, H_2, and NH_3 are all 1.0 *M* (thus at this temperature $K = 1.0$). If we suddenly double the volume, the concentration of each species initially decreases to 0.50 *M*. If we put these numbers into the equilibrium expression, we get a value of 4.0. This number is higher than *K* so the system must shift to the left to satisfy the equilibrium condition ($K = 1.0$). This is the direction predicted by Le Châtelier's principle.

For example, consider the reaction

$$CaCO_3(s) \rightleftharpoons CaO(s) + CO_2(g)$$

in a container with a movable piston (Figure 17.10). If the volume is suddenly decreased by pushing in the piston, the pressure of the CO_2 gas initially increases. How can the system offset this pressure increase? By shifting to the left—the direction that reduces the amount of gas present. That is, a shift to the left will use up CO_2 molecules, thus lowering the pressure. (There will then be fewer molecules present to hit the walls, because more of the CO_2 molecules have combined with CaO and thus have become part of the solid $CaCO_3$.)

Therefore, when the volume of a gaseous reaction system at equilibrium is decreased (thus increasing the pressure), *the system shifts in the direction that gives the smaller number of gas molecules.* So a decrease in the system volume leads to a shift that decreases the total number of gaseous molecules in the system.

Suppose we are running the reaction

$$N_2(g) + 3H_2(g) \rightleftharpoons 2NH_3(g)$$

and we have a mixture of the gases nitrogen, hydrogen, and ammonia at equilibrium (Figure 17.11a). If we suddenly reduce the volume, what will happen to the equilibrium position? Because the decrease in volume initially increases the pressure, the system moves in the direction that lowers its pressure. The reaction system can reduce its pressure by reducing the number of gas molecules present. This means that the reaction

$$\underset{\text{4 gaseous molecules}}{N_2(g) + 3H_2(g)} \rightleftharpoons \underset{\text{2 gaseous molecules}}{2NH_3(g)}$$

shifts to the right, because in this direction four molecules (one of nitrogen and three of hydrogen) react to produce two molecules (of ammonia), thus *reducing the total number of gaseous molecules present.* The equilibrium position shifts to the right—toward the side of the reaction that involves the smaller number of gaseous molecules in the balanced equation.

The opposite is also true. When the container volume is increased (which lowers the pressure of the system), the system shifts so as to increase its pressure. An increase in volume in the ammonia synthesis system produces a shift to the left to increase the total number of gaseous molecules present (to increase the pressure).

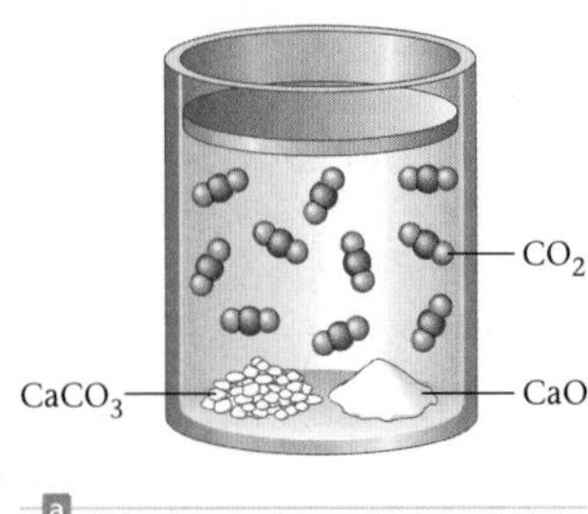

a The system is initially at equilibrium.

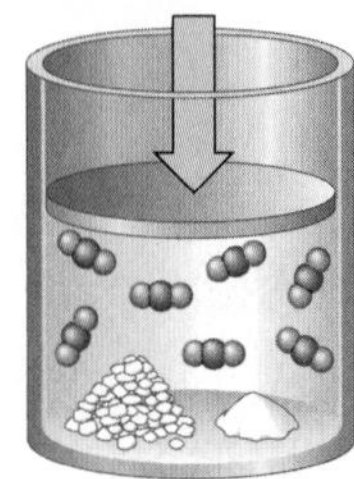

b Then the piston is pushed in, decreasing the volume and increasing the pressure. The system shifts in the direction that consumes CO_2 molecules, thus lowering the pressure again.

Figure 17.10 The reaction system $CaCO_3(s) \rightleftharpoons CaO(s) + CO_2(g)$.

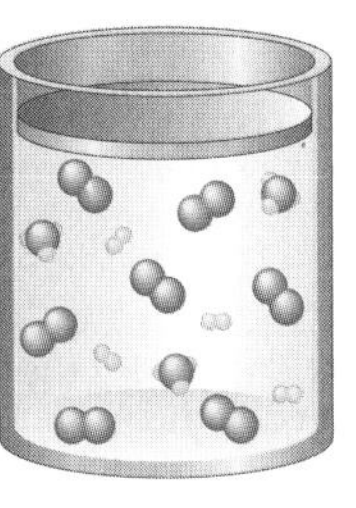

a A mixture of $NH_3(g)$, $N_2(g)$, and $H_2(g)$ at equilibrium.

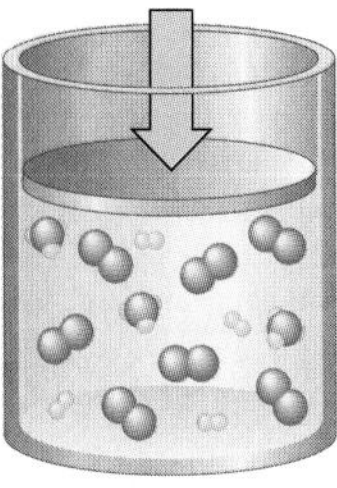

b The volume is suddenly decreased.

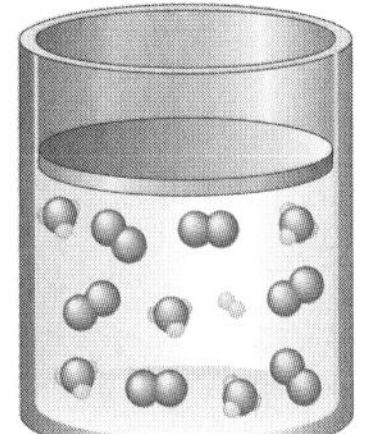

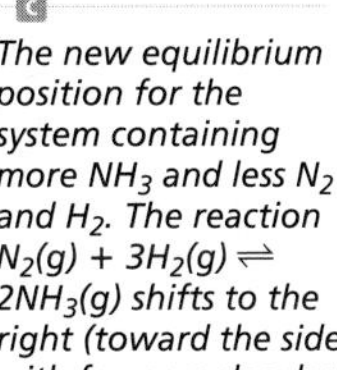

c The new equilibrium position for the system containing more NH_3 and less N_2 and H_2. The reaction $N_2(g) + 3H_2(g) \rightleftharpoons 2NH_3(g)$ shifts to the right (toward the side with fewer molecules) when the container volume is decreased.

Figure 17.11

EXAMPLE 17.5 **Using Le Châtelier's Principle: Changes in Volume**

Predict the shift in equilibrium position that will occur for each of the following processes when the volume is reduced.

a. The preparation of liquid phosphorus trichloride by the reaction

$$\underset{\text{6 gaseous molecules}}{P_4(s) + 6Cl_2(g)} \rightleftharpoons \underset{\text{0 gaseous molecules}}{4PCl_3(l)}$$

SOLUTION a

P_4 and PCl_3 are a pure solid and a pure liquid, respectively, so we need to consider only the effect on Cl_2. If the volume is decreased, the Cl_2 pressure will initially increase, so the position of the equilibrium will shift to the right, consuming gaseous Cl_2 and lowering the pressure (to counteract the original change).

b. The preparation of gaseous phosphorus pentachloride according to the equation

$$\underset{\text{2 gaseous molecules}}{PCl_3(g) + Cl_2(g)} \rightleftharpoons \underset{\text{1 gaseous molecule}}{PCl_5(g)}$$

SOLUTION b

Decreasing the volume (increasing the pressure) will shift this equilibrium to the right, because the product side contains only one gaseous molecule while the reactant side has two. That is, the system will respond to the decreased volume (increased pressure) by lowering the number of molecules present.

c. The reaction of phosphorus trichloride with ammonia:

$$PCl_3(g) + 3NH_3(g) \rightleftharpoons P(NH_2)_3(g) + 3HCl(g)$$

Additional Examples

Example 17.5

Predict the shift in equilibrium position that will occur for each of the following processes when the volume is increased.

1. $4NH_3(g) + 5O_2(g) \rightleftharpoons 2NO(g) + 6H_2O(g)$

   shift to the left

2. $NH_4NO_3(s) \rightleftharpoons N_2O(g) + 2H_2O(g)$

   shift to the right

Self Check

Answers to Self-Check Exercise 17.4

a. no change

b. shifts to left

c. shifts to right

PowerLecture Animation: N_2O_4/NO_2 Equilibrium: Temperature Dependence

DEMONSTRATION

Temperature Effect

To illustrate the effect of a change in temperature on equilibrium, you can use about 50 mL of 0.2 *M* $CoCl_2$ in a small beaker. Observe the pink color of the solution. Add concentrated HCl until the color of the solution changes from pink to blue. This change results from the formation of a cobalt complex:

$$\underset{\text{Pink}}{\text{Heat} + Co^{2+}(aq)} + 4Cl^-(aq) \rightleftharpoons \underset{\text{Blue}}{CoCl_4^{2-}(aq)}$$

To observe the effect of temperature on the reaction, place the solution in a large test tube and immerse the test tube about halfway into a beaker containing crushed ice and salt. The bottom part of the solution in the test tube will turn pink after several minutes because lowering the temperature pulls the endothermic reaction to the left.

Lecture Demonstration: 13.4

SOLUTION c

Both sides of the balanced reaction equation have four gaseous molecules. A change in volume will have no effect on the equilibrium position. There is no shift in this case, because the system cannot change the number of molecules present by shifting in either direction.

Self-Check EXERCISE 17.4 For each of the following reactions, predict the direction the equilibrium will shift when the volume of the container is increased.

a. $H_2(g) + F_2(g) \rightleftharpoons 2HF(g)$

b. $CO(g) + 2H_2(g) \rightleftharpoons CH_3OH(g)$

c. $2SO_3(g) \rightleftharpoons 2SO_2(g) + O_2(g)$

See Problems 17.33 through 17.36. ■

The Effect of a Change in Temperature

It is important to remember that although the changes we have just discussed may alter the equilibrium *position,* they do not alter the equilibrium *constant.* For example, the addition of a reactant shifts the equilibrium position to the right but has no effect on the value of the equilibrium constant; the new equilibrium concentrations satisfy the original equilibrium constant. This was demonstrated earlier in this section for the addition of N_2 to the ammonia synthesis reaction.

The effect of temperature on equilibrium is different, however, because *the value of K changes with temperature.* We can use Le Châtelier's principle to predict the direction of the change in *K*.

To do this we need to classify reactions according to whether they produce heat or absorb heat. A reaction that produces heat (heat is a "product") is said to be *exothermic.* A reaction that absorbs heat is called *endothermic.* Because heat is needed for an endothermic reaction, energy (heat) can be regarded as a "reactant" in this case.

In an exothermic reaction, heat is treated as a product. For example, the synthesis of ammonia from nitrogen and hydrogen is exothermic (produces heat). We can represent this by treating energy as a product:

$$N_2(g) + 3H_2(g) \rightleftharpoons 2NH_3(g) + \underset{\text{Energy released}}{92 \text{ kJ}}$$

Le Châtelier's principle predicts that when we add energy to this system at equilibrium by heating it, the shift will be in the direction that consumes energy—that is, to the left.

On the other hand, for an endothermic reaction (one that absorbs energy), such as the decomposition of calcium carbonate,

$$CaCO_3(s) + \underset{\text{Energy needed}}{556 \text{ kJ}} \rightleftharpoons CaO(s) + CO_2(g)$$

energy is treated as a reactant. In this case an increase in temperature causes the equilibrium to shift to the right.

In summary, to use Le Châtelier's principle to describe the effect of a temperature change on a system at equilibrium, *simply treat energy as a reactant (in an endothermic process) or as a product (in an exothermic process),* and *predict the direction of the shift* in the same way you would if an actual reactant or product were being added or removed.

EXAMPLE 17.6 Using Le Châtelier's Principle: Changes in Temperature

For each of the following reactions, predict how the equilibrium will shift as the temperature is increased.

a. $N_2(g) + O_2(g) \rightleftharpoons 2NO(g)$ (endothermic)

SOLUTION a

This is an endothermic reaction, so energy can be viewed as a reactant.

$$N_2(g) + O_2(g) + \text{energy} \rightleftharpoons 2NO(g)$$

Thus the equilibrium will shift to the right as the temperature is increased (energy added).

b. $2SO_2(g) + O_2(g) \rightleftharpoons 2SO_3(g)$ (exothermic)

SOLUTION b

This is an exothermic reaction, so energy can be regarded as a product.

$$2SO_2(g) + O_2(g) \rightleftharpoons 2SO_3(g) + \text{energy}$$

As the temperature is increased, the equilibrium will shift to the left.

Self-Check EXERCISE 17.5 For the exothermic reaction

$$2SO_2(g) + O_2(g) \rightleftharpoons 2SO_3(g)$$

predict the equilibrium shift caused by each of the following changes.

a. SO_2 is added.

b. SO_3 is removed.

c. The volume is decreased.

d. The temperature is decreased.

See Problems 17.33 through 17.42. ■

We have seen how Le Châtelier's principle can be used to predict the effects of several types of changes on a system at equilibrium. To summarize these ideas, Table 17.2 shows how various changes affect the equilibrium position of the endothermic reaction $N_2O_4(g) \rightleftharpoons 2NO_2(g)$. The effect of a temperature change on this system is depicted in Figure 17.12.

Table 17.2 Shifts in the Equilibrium Position for the Reaction $N_2O_4(g) + \text{Energy} \rightleftharpoons 2NO_2(g)$

Change	Shift
addition of $N_2O_4(g)$	right
addition of $NO_2(g)$	left
removal of $N_2O_4(g)$	left
removal of $NO_2(g)$	right
decrease in container volume	left
increase in container volume	right
increase in temperature	right
decrease in temperature	left

Additional Examples

Example 17.6

1. The reaction

$$C_2H_2(g) + 2Br_2(g) \rightleftharpoons C_2H_2Br_4(g)$$

is exothermic as written. Will an increase in temperature shift the position of equilibrium toward reactants or products?

reactants

2. The reaction

$$ZrI_4(s) \rightleftharpoons Zr(s) + 2I_2(g)$$

is endothermic as written. Will an increase in temperature shift the position of equilibrium toward reactants or products?

products

Self Check

Answers to Self-Check Exercise 17.5

a. shifts to the right

b. shifts to the right

c. shifts to the right

d. shifts to the right

Section 17.8

TEACHING TIP

Now is an excellent time to explain the relationship between the value of K and the extent of the reaction. Discuss the meaning of $K = 1$, $K < 1$, and $K > 1$.

Additional Examples

Example 17.7

1. The equilibrium constant for the reaction $H_2(g) + F_2(g) \rightleftharpoons 2HF(g)$ has the value 2.1×10^3 at a particular temperature. When the system is analyzed at equilibrium at this temperature, the concentrations of both $H_2(g)$ and $F_2(g)$ are found to be 0.0021 M. What is the concentration of $HF(g)$ in the equilibrium system under these conditions?

   $[HF(g)] = 9.6 \times 10^{-2}\ M$

2. The equilibrium constant for the reaction $2H_2O(g) \rightleftharpoons 2H_2(g) + O_2(g)$ has the value 2.4×10^{-3} at a particular temperature. When the system is analyzed at equilibrium at this temperature, it is found that $[H_2O(g)] = 1.1 \times 10^{-1}\ M$ and $[H_2(g)] = 1.9 \times 10^{-2}\ M$. What is the concentration of $O_2(g)$ in the equilibrium system under these conditions?

   $[O_2(g)] = 8.0 \times 10^{-2}\ M$

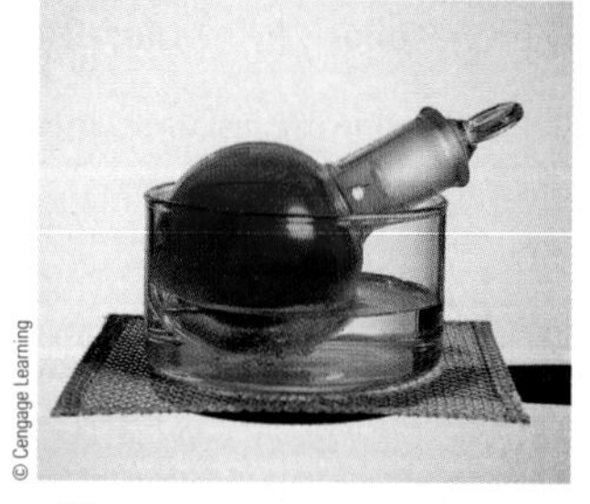

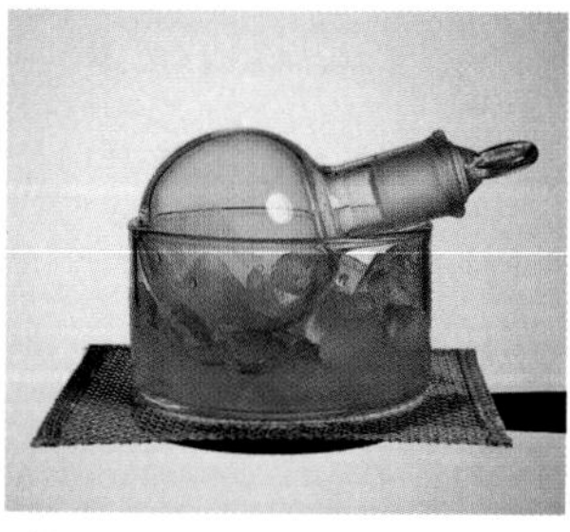

Figure 17.12 Shifting the $N_2O_4(g) \rightleftharpoons 2NO_2(g)$ equilibrium by changing the temperature.

a *At 100 °C the flask is definitely reddish-brown due to a large amount of NO_2 present.*

b *At 0 °C the equilibrium is shifted toward colorless $N_2O_4(g)$.*

17.8 Applications Involving the Equilibrium Constant

OBJECTIVE: To learn to calculate equilibrium concentrations from equilibrium constants.

Knowing the value of the equilibrium constant for a reaction allows us to do many things. For example, the size of K tells us the inherent tendency of the reaction to occur. A value of K much larger than 1 means that at equilibrium, the reaction system will consist of mostly products—the equilibrium lies to the right. For example, consider a general reaction of the type

$$A(g) \rightarrow B(g)$$

where

$$K = \frac{[B]}{[A]}$$

If K for this reaction is 10,000 (10^4), then at equilibrium,

$$\frac{[B]}{[A]} = 10{,}000 \quad \text{or} \quad \frac{[B]}{[A]} = \frac{10{,}000}{1}$$

That is, at equilibrium [B] is 10,000 times greater than [A]. This means that the reaction strongly favors the product B. Another way of saying this is that the reaction goes essentially to completion. That is, virtually all of A becomes B.

On the other hand, a small value of K means that the system at equilibrium consists largely of reactants—the equilibrium position is far to the left. The given reaction does not occur to any significant extent.

Another way we use the equilibrium constant is to calculate the equilibrium concentrations of reactants and products. For example, if we know the value of K and the concentrations of all the reactants and products except one, we can calculate the missing concentration. This is illustrated in Example 17.7.

EXAMPLE 17.7 Calculating Equilibrium Concentration Using Equilibrium Expressions

Gaseous phosphorus pentachloride decomposes to chlorine gas and gaseous phosphorus trichloride. In a certain experiment, at a temperature where

$K = 8.96 \times 10^{-2}$, the equilibrium concentrations of PCl_5 and PCl_3 were found to be $6.70 \times 10^{-3}\,M$ and $0.300\,M$, respectively. Calculate the concentration of Cl_2 present at equilibrium.

SOLUTION

Where Are We Going?

We want to determine $[Cl_2]$ present at equilibrium.

What Do We Know?

For this reaction, the balanced equation is

$$PCl_5(g) \rightleftharpoons PCl_3(g) + Cl_2(g)$$

and the equilibrium expression is

$$K = \frac{[PCl_3][Cl_2]}{[PCl_5]} = 8.96 \times 10^{-2}$$

We know that

$$[PCl_5] = 6.70 \times 10^{-3}\,M$$
$$[PCl_3] = 0.300\,M$$

How Do We Get There?

We want to calculate $[Cl_2]$. We will rearrange the equilibrium expression to solve for the concentration of Cl_2. First we divide both sides of the expression

$$K = \frac{[PCl_3][Cl_2]}{[PCl_5]}$$

by $[PCl_3]$ to give

$$\frac{K}{[PCl_3]} = \frac{\cancel{[PCl_3]}[Cl_2]}{\cancel{[PCl_3]}[PCl_5]} = \frac{[Cl_2]}{[PCl_5]}$$

Next we multiply both sides by $[PCl_5]$.

$$\frac{K[PCl_5]}{[PCl_3]} = \frac{[Cl_2]\cancel{[PCl_5]}}{\cancel{[PCl_5]}} = [Cl_2]$$

Then we can calculate $[Cl_2]$ by substituting the known information.

$$[Cl_2] = K \times \frac{[PCl_5]}{[PCl_3]} = (8.96 \times 10^{-2})\frac{(6.70 \times 10^{-3})}{(0.300)}$$
$$[Cl_2] = 2.00 \times 10^{-3}$$

The equilibrium concentration of Cl_2 is $2.00 \times 10^{-3}\,M$. ■

 Test Bank: 43–57

17.9 Solubility Equilibria

OBJECTIVE: To learn to calculate the solubility product of a salt, given its solubility, and vice versa.

Solubility is a very important phenomenon. Consider the following examples.

- Because sugar and table salt dissolve readily in water, we can flavor foods easily.

Section 17.9

TEACHING TIP

Now is an excellent time to review polyatomic ions and writing and balancing chemical equations. Students must be able to break compounds into their component ions and write equations for the dissociation to work with solubility equilibria.

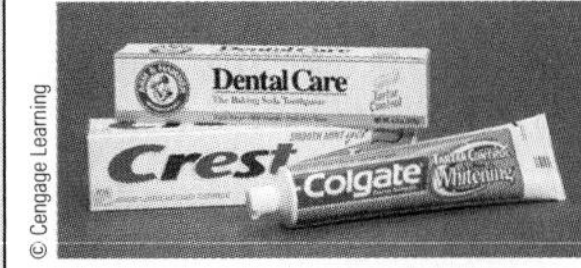

Toothpastes containing sodium fluoride, an additive that helps prevent tooth decay.

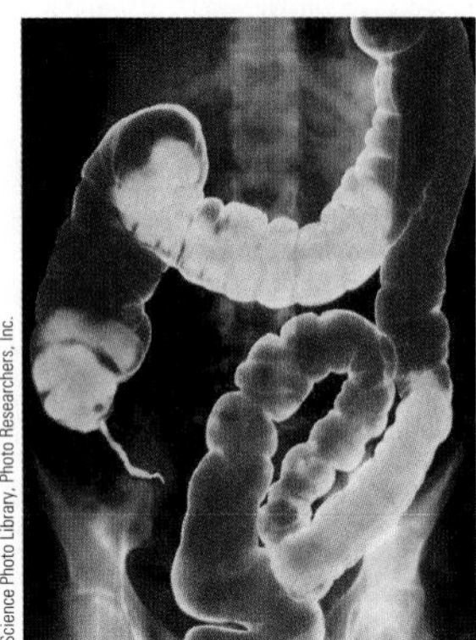

This X ray of the large intestine has been enhanced by the patient's consumption of barium sulfate.

- Because calcium sulfate is less soluble in hot water than in cold water, it coats tubes in boilers, reducing thermal efficiency.
- When food lodges between teeth, acids form that dissolve tooth enamel, which contains the mineral hydroxyapatite, $Ca_5(PO_4)_3OH$. Tooth decay can be reduced by adding fluoride to toothpaste. Fluoride replaces the hydroxide in hydroxyapatite to produce the corresponding fluorapatite, $Ca_5(PO_4)_3F$, and calcium fluoride, CaF_2, both of which are less soluble in acids than the original enamel.
- The use of a suspension of barium sulfate improves the clarity of X rays of the digestive tract. Barium sulfate contains the toxic ion Ba^{2+}, but its very low solubility makes ingestion of solid $BaSO_4$ safe.

In this section we will consider the equilibria associated with dissolving solids in water to form aqueous solutions. When a typical ionic solid dissolves in water, it dissociates completely into separate cations and anions. For example, calcium fluoride dissolves in water as follows:

$$CaF_2(s) \xrightarrow{H_2O(l)} Ca^{2+}(aq) + 2F^-(aq)$$

When the solid salt is first added to the water, no Ca^{2+} and F^- ions are present. However, as dissolving occurs, the concentrations of Ca^{2+} and F^- increase, and it becomes more and more likely that these ions will collide and re-form the solid. Thus two opposite (competing) processes are occurring—the dissolving reaction shown above and the reverse reaction to re-form the solid:

$$Ca^{2+}(aq) + 2F^-(aq) \rightarrow CaF_2(s)$$

Ultimately, equilibrium is reached. No more solid dissolves and the solution is said to be saturated.

We can write an equilibrium expression for this process according to the law of chemical equilibrium.

$$K_{sp} = [Ca^{2+}][F^-]^2$$

where $[Ca^{2+}]$ and $[F^-]$ are expressed in mol/L. The constant K_{sp} is called the **solubility product constant,** or simply the **solubility product.**

Pure liquids and pure solids are never included in an equilibrium expression.

Because CaF_2 is a pure solid, it is not included in the equilibrium expression. It may seem strange at first that the amount of excess solid present does not affect the position of the solubility equilibrium. Surely more solid means more surface area exposed to the solvent, which would seem to result in greater solubility. This is not the case, however, because both dissolving and re-forming of the solid occur at the surface of the excess solid. When a solid dissolves, it is the ions at the surface that go into solution. And when the ions in solution re-form the solid, they do so on the surface of the solid. So doubling the surface area of the solid doubles not only the rate of dissolving but also the rate of re-formation of the solid. The amount of excess solid present therefore has no effect on the equilibrium position. Similarly, although either increasing the surface area by grinding up the solid or stirring the solution speeds up the attainment of equilibrium, neither procedure changes the *amount* of solid dissolved at equilibrium.

Additional Examples

Example 17.8

Write the balanced equation for dissolving each of the following solids in water. Also write the K_{sp} expression for each solid.

1. $Cr(OH)_3(s)$

$Cr(OH)_3(s) \rightleftharpoons Cr^{3+}(aq) + 3OH^-(aq)$; $K_{sp} = [Cr^{3+}(aq)][OH^-(aq)]^3$

2. $Ca_3(PO_4)_2(s)$

$Ca_3(PO_4)_2(s) \rightleftharpoons 3Ca^{2+}(aq) + 2PO_4^{3-}(aq)$; $K_{sp} = [Ca^{2+}(aq)]^3 [PO_4^{3-}(aq)]^2$

EXAMPLE 17.8 Writing Solubility Product Expressions

Write the balanced equation describing the reaction for dissolving each of the following solids in water. Also write the K_{sp} expression for each solid.

a. $PbCl_2(s)$ b. $Ag_2CrO_4(s)$ c. $Bi_2S_3(s)$

SOLUTION

a. $PbCl_2(s) \rightleftharpoons Pb^{2+}(aq) + 2Cl^-(aq)$; $K_{sp} = [Pb^{2+}][Cl^-]^2$

b. $Ag_2CrO_4(s) \rightleftharpoons 2Ag^+(aq) + CrO_4^{2-}(aq)$; $K_{sp} = [Ag^+]^2[CrO_4^{2-}]$

c. $Bi_2S_3(s) \rightleftharpoons 2Bi^{3+}(aq) + 3S^{2-}(aq)$; $K_{sp} = [Bi^{3+}]^2[S^{2-}]^3$

Self-Check EXERCISE 17.6 Write the balanced equation for the reaction describing the dissolving of each of the following solids in water. Also write the K_{sp} expression for each solid.

a. $BaSO_4(s)$ b. $Fe(OH)_3(s)$ c. $Ag_3PO_4(s)$

See Problems 17.57 and 17.58. ■

EXAMPLE 17.9 Calculating Solubility Products

Copper(I) bromide, CuBr, has a measured solubility of 2.0×10^{-4} mol/L at 25 °C. That is, when excess CuBr(*s*) is placed in 1.0 L of water, we can determine that 2.0×10^{-4} mole of the solid dissolves to produce a saturated solution. Calculate the solid's K_{sp} value.

SOLUTION

Where Are We Going?

We want to determine the K_{sp} value for solid CuBr at 25 °C.

What Do We Know?

- The solubility of CuBr at 25 °C is 2.0×10^{-4} *M*.
- $CuBr(s) \rightleftharpoons Cu^+(aq) + Br^-(aq)$
- $K_{sp} = [Cu^+][Br^-]$

How Do We Get There?

We can calculate the value of K_{sp} if we know $[Cu^+]$ and $[Br^-]$, the equilibrium concentrations of the ions. We know that the measured solubility of CuBr is 2.0×10^{-4} mol/L. This means that 2.0×10^{-4} mole of solid CuBr dissolves per 1.0 L of solution to come to equilibrium. The reaction is

$$CuBr(s) \rightarrow Cu^+(aq) + Br^-(aq)$$

so

$$2.0 \times 10^{-4} \text{ mol/L } CuBr(s) \rightarrow 2.0 \times 10^{-4} \text{ mol/L } Cu^+(aq) + 2.0 \times 10^{-4} \text{ mol/L } Br^-(aq)$$

We can now write the equilibrium concentrations

$$[Cu^+] = 2.0 \times 10^{-4} \text{ mol/L}$$

and

$$[Br^-] = 2.0 \times 10^{-4} \text{ mol/L}$$

These equilibrium concentrations allow us to calculate the value of K_{sp} for CuBr.

$$K_{sp} = [Cu^+][Br^-] = (2.0 \times 10^{-4})(2.0 \times 10^{-4}) = 4.0 \times 10^{-8}$$

The units for K_{sp} values are omitted.

Self Check

Answers to Self-Check Exercise 17.6

a. $BaSO_4(s) \rightleftharpoons Ba^{2+}(aq) + SO_4^{2-}(aq)$;
$K_{sp} = [Ba^{2+}(aq)][SO_4^{2-}(aq)]$

b. $Fe(OH)_3(s) \rightleftharpoons Fe^{3+}(aq) + 3OH^-(aq)$;
$K_{sp} = [Fe^{3+}(aq)][OH^-(aq)]^3$

c. $Ag_3(PO_4)(s) \rightleftharpoons 3Ag^+(aq) + PO_4^{3-}(aq)$;
$K_{sp} = [Ag^+(aq)]^3[PO_4^{3-}(aq)]$

Additional Examples

Example 17.9

1. Zinc carbonate, $ZnCO_3(s)$, dissolves in water to give a solution that is 1.7×10^{-5} *M* at 22 °C. Calculate K_{sp} for $ZnCO_3(s)$ at this temperature.

   $K_{sp} = 2.9 \times 10^{-10}$

2. Copper(II) chromate, $CuCrO_4(s)$, dissolves in water to give a solution that is 1.1×10^{-5} g per liter at 23 °C. Calculate K_{sp} for $CuCrO_4(s)$ at this temperature.

   $K_{sp} = 3.8 \times 10^{-15}$

Self Check

Answer to Self-Check Exercise 17.7

$K_{sp} = 4.0 \times 10^{-32}$

Self-Check EXERCISE 17.7 Calculate the K_{sp} value for barium sulfate, $BaSO_4$, which has a solubility of 3.9×10^{-5} mol/L at 25 °C.

See Problems 17.59 through 17.62. ■

Solubilities must be expressed in mol/L in K_{sp} calculations.

We have seen that the known solubility of an ionic solid can be used to calculate its K_{sp} value. The reverse is also possible: the solubility of an ionic solid can be calculated if its K_{sp} value is known.

Additional Examples

Example 17.10

1. The K_{sp} value for $ZnCO_3(s)$ is 5.1×10^{-9}. Calculate the solubility of $ZnCO_3(s)$ in water in moles per liter.

   7.1×10^{-5} *M*

2. The K_{sp} value for $CoCO_3(s)$ is 1.5×10^{-13}. Calculate the solubility of $CoCO_3(s)$ in water in moles per liter.

   3.9×10^{-7} *M*

EXAMPLE 17.10 Calculating Solubility from K_{sp} Values

The K_{sp} value for solid AgI(*s*) is 1.5×10^{-16} at 25 °C. Calculate the solubility of AgI(*s*) in water at 25 °C.

SOLUTION

Where Are We Going?

We want to determine the solubility of AgI at 25 °C.

What Do We Know?

- $AgI(s) \rightleftharpoons Ag^+(aq) + I^-(aq)$
- At 25 °C, $K_{sp} = [Ag^+][I^-] = 1.5 \times 10^{-16}$

How Do We Get There?

Because we do not know the solubility of this solid, we will assume that x moles per liter dissolves to reach equilibrium. Therefore,

$$x\,\frac{\text{mol}}{\text{L}}\,AgI(s) \rightarrow x\,\frac{\text{mol}}{\text{L}}\,Ag^+(aq) + x\,\frac{\text{mol}}{\text{L}}\,I^-(aq)$$

and at equilibrium,

$$[Ag^+] = x\,\frac{\text{mol}}{\text{L}}$$

$$[I^-] = x\,\frac{\text{mol}}{\text{L}}$$

Substituting these concentrations into the equilibrium expression gives

$$K_{sp} = 1.5 \times 10^{-16} = [Ag^+][I^-] = (x)(x) = x^2$$

Thus

$$x^2 = 1.5 \times 10^{-16}$$

$$x = \sqrt{1.5 \times 10^{-16}} = 1.2 \times 10^{-8}\ \text{mol/L}$$

The solubility of AgI(*s*) is 1.2×10^{-8} mol/L.

Self Check

Answer to Self-Check Exercise 17.8

1.4×10^{-8} *M*

Self-Check EXERCISE 17.8 The K_{sp} value for lead chromate, $PbCrO_4$, is 2.0×10^{-16} at 25 °C. Calculate its solubility at 25 °C.

See Problems 17.69 and 17.70. ■

CHAPTER 17 REVIEW

Key Terms

collision model (17.1)
activation energy (E_a) (17.2)
catalyst (17.2)
enzyme (17.2)
equilibrium (17.3)
chemical equilibrium (17.3)
law of chemical equilibrium (17.5)
equilibrium expression (17.5)
equilibrium constant (17.5)
equilibrium position (17.5)
homogeneous equilibria (17.6)
heterogeneous equilibria (17.6)
Le Châtelier's principle (17.7)
solubility product (K_{sp}) (17.9)

 directs you to the *Chemistry in Focus* feature in the chapter
VP indicates visual problems
OWL interactive versions of these problems are assignable in OWL

Summary

1. Chemical reactions can be described by the collision model, which assumes that molecules must collide to react. In terms of this model, a certain threshold energy, called the activation energy (E_a), must be overcome for a collision to form products.
2. A catalyst is a substance that speeds up a reaction without being consumed. A catalyst operates by providing a lower-energy pathway for the reaction in question. Enzymes are biological catalysts.
3. When a chemical reaction is carried out in a closed vessel, the system achieves chemical equilibrium, the state where the concentrations of both reactants and products remain constant over time. Equilibrium is a highly dynamic state; reactants are converted continually into products, and vice versa, as molecules collide with each other. At equilibrium, the rates of the forward and reverse reactions are equal.
4. The law of chemical equilibrium is a general description of the equilibrium condition. It states that for a reaction of the type

$$aA + bB \rightleftharpoons cC + dD$$

the equilibrium expression is given by

$$K = \frac{[C]^c [D]^d}{[A]^a [B]^b}$$

where K is the equilibrium constant.

5. For each reaction system at a given temperature, there is only one value for the equilibrium constant, but there are an infinite number of possible equilibrium positions. An equilibrium position is defined as a particular set of equilibrium concentrations that satisfy the equilibrium expression. A specific equilibrium position depends on the initial concentrations. The amount of a pure liquid or a pure solid is never included in the equilibrium expression.
6. Le Châtelier's principle allows us to predict the effects of changes in concentration, volume, and temperature on a system at equilibrium. This principle states that when a change is imposed on a system at equilibrium, the equilibrium position will shift in a direction that tends to compensate for the imposed change.
7. The principle of equilibrium can also be applied when an excess of a solid is added to water to form a saturated solution. The solubility product (K_{sp}) is an equilibrium constant defined by the law of chemical equilibrium. Solubility is an equilibrium position, and the K_{sp} value of a solid can be determined by measuring its solubility. Conversely, the solubility of a solid can be determined if its K_{sp} value is known.

Active Learning Questions

These questions are designed to be considered by groups of students in class. Often these questions work well for introducing a particular topic in class.

1. Consider an equilibrium mixture of four chemicals (A, B, C, and D, all gases) reacting in a closed flask according to the following equation:

$$A + B \rightleftharpoons C + D$$

   a. You add more A to the flask. How does the concentration of each chemical compare to its original concentration after equilibrium is reestablished? Justify your answer.
   b. You have the original set-up at equilibrium, and add more D to the flask. How does the concentration of each chemical compare to its original concentration after equilibrium is reestablished? Justify your answer.

VP 2. The boxes shown on the following page represent a set of initial conditions for the reaction:

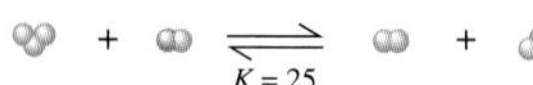

Draw a quantitative molecular picture that shows what this system looks like after the reactants are

ChemWork

Relative Oxidizing Abilities
Calculating Free Energy for an Electrochemical Cell
Cell Potential and Equilibrium
Copper Concentration Cell
K for Cell Reactions
Nernst Equation: Calculation of Concentration
Properties of Galvanic Cells
Electrolysis
Electrolysis of a Metal Ion in Solution
Properties of Electrochemical Cells

Chapter Review 571

mixed in one of the boxes and the system reaches equilibrium. Support your answer with calculations.

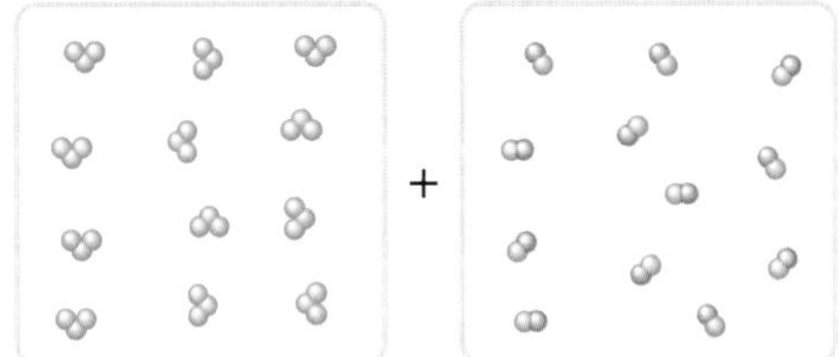

3. For the reaction $H_2 + I_2 \rightleftharpoons 2HI$, consider two possibilities: (a) you add 0.5 mole of each reactant, allow the system to come to equilibrium, and then add 1 mol H_2, and allow the system to reach equilibrium again, or (b) you add 1.5 mol H_2 and 0.5 mol I_2 and allow the system to come to equilibrium. Will the final equilibrium mixture be different for the two procedures? Explain.

4. Given the reaction $A + B \rightleftharpoons C + D$, consider the following situations:

   a. You have 1.3 *M* A and 0.8 *M* B initially.
   b. You have 1.3 *M* A, 0.8 *M* B, and 0.2 *M* C initially.
   c. You have 2.0 *M* A and 0.8 *M* B initially.

   Order the preceding situations in terms of increasing equilibrium concentration of D and explain your order. Give the order in terms of increasing equilibrium concentration of B and explain.

5. Consider the reaction $A + B \rightleftharpoons C + D$. A friend asks the following: "I know we have been told that if a mixture of A, B, C, and D is in equilibrium and more A is added, more C and D will form. But how can more C and D form if we do not add more B?" What do you tell your friend?

6. Consider the following statements: "Consider the reaction $A(g) + B(g) \rightleftharpoons C(g)$, for which at equilibrium [A] = 2 *M*, [B] = 1 *M*, and [C] = 4 *M*. To a 1-L container of the system at equilibrium you add 3 moles of B. A possible equilibrium condition is [A] = 1 *M*, [B] = 3 *M*, and [C] = 6 *M*, because in both cases, *K* = 2." Indicate everything you think is correct in these statements, and everything that is incorrect. Correct the incorrect statements, and explain.

7. The value of the equilibrium constant, *K*, is dependent on which of the following? (There may be more than one answer.)

   a. the initial concentrations of the reactants
   b. the initial concentrations of the products
   c. the temperature of the system
   d. the nature of the reactants and products

   Explain.

8. You are browsing through the *Handbook of Hypothetical Chemistry* when you come across a solid that is reported to have a K_{sp} value of zero in water at 25 °C. What does this mean?

9. What do you suppose happens to the K_{sp} value of a solid as the temperature of the solution changes? Consider both increasing and decreasing temperatures, and explain your answer.

10. Consider an equilibrium mixture consisting of $H_2O(g)$, $CO(g)$, $H_2(g)$, and $CO_2(g)$ reacting in a closed vessel according to the equation

$$H_2O(g) + CO(g) \rightleftharpoons H_2(g) + CO_2(g)$$

   a. You add more H_2O to the flask. How does the new equilibrium concentration of each chemical compare to its original equilibrium concentration after equilibrium is reestablished? Justify your answer.
   b. You add more H_2 to the flask. How does the concentration of each chemical compare to its original concentration after equilibrium is reestablished? Justify your answer.

11. Equilibrium is microscopically dynamic but macroscopically static. Explain what this means.

12. In Section 17.3 of your text, it is mentioned that equilibrium is reached in a "closed system." What is meant by the term "closed system," and why is it necessary for a system to reach equilibrium? Explain why equilibrium is not reached in an open system.

VP 13. Explain why the development of a vapor pressure above a liquid in a closed container represents an equilibrium. What are the opposing processes? How do we recognize when the system has reached a state of equilibrium.

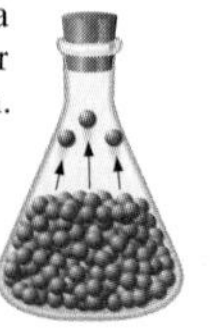

VP 14. Consider the figure below in answering the following questions.

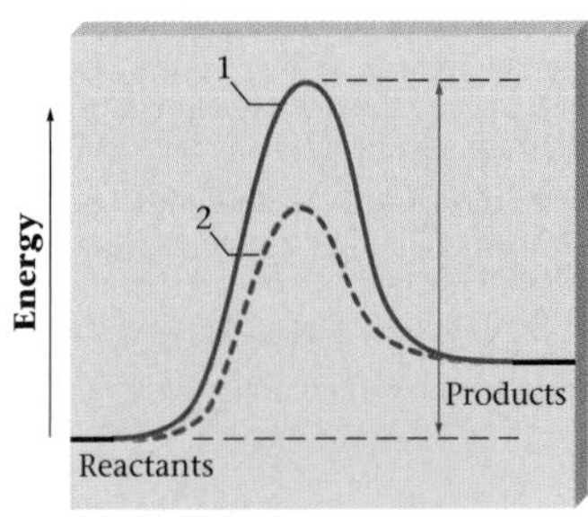

   a. What does a catalyst do to a chemical reaction?
   b. Which of the pathways in the figure is the catalyzed reaction pathway? How do you know?
   c. What is represented by the double-headed arrow?

Answers to End-of-Chapter Exercises

1. Answer depends on student choice of reaction.

2. Four C–H bonds and four Cl–Cl bonds must be broken; four C–Cl and four H–Cl bonds must form.

3. The collision model pictures chemical reactions taking place only when the reactant molecules physically collide with each other, with enough energy to break the bonds in the reactant molecules. The molecules must possess energy equivalent to the activation energy for reaction, or they just bounce off one another without reacting.

4. E_a represents the *activation energy* for the reaction, which is the minimum energy needed for the reaction to be able to occur.

5. A catalyst provides an alternative pathway, with a lower activation energy barrier, by which the reaction can take place.

6. Enzymes are biochemical catalysts that speed up the complicated reactions that would be too slow to sustain life at normal body temperatures.

7. An equilibrium represents two opposing processes going on at the same time at the same speed so that there is no net change in the system.

8. A state of equilibrium is attained when two opposing processes are exactly balanced. The development of a vapor pressure above a liquid in a closed container is an example of a physical equilibrium. Any chemical reaction that appears to "stop" before completion is an example of a chemical equilibrium.

9. We use a double-ended arrow (pointing both to the left and to the right): $\rightleftharpoons$

10. A system has reached equilibrium when no more product forms, even though significant amounts of all the needed reactants are present. This lack of further product creation indicates that the reverse process is now occurring at the same rate as the forward process—that is, every time a product molecule forms in the system, another product molecule reacts to give back the original reactants elsewhere in the system. Reactions that come to equilibrium are indicated by a double arrow.

11. The forward and reverse reactions are still going on, but at the same speed, so that there is no net change in the system.

12. The two curves come together when a state of chemical equilibrium has been reached, after which point the forward and reverse reactions are occurring at the same rate so that there is no further net change in concentration.

Questions and Problems

17.1 How Chemical Reactions Occur

QUESTIONS

1. For a chemical reaction to take place, some or all chemical bonds in the reactants must break, and new chemical bonds must form among the participating atoms to create the products. Write a simple chemical equation of your own choice, and list the bonds that must be broken and the bonds that must form for the reaction to take place.
2. For the simple reaction

$$CH_4(g) + 4Cl_2(g) \rightarrow CCl_4(l) + 4HCl(g)$$

list the types of bonds that must be broken and the types of bonds that must form for the chemical reaction to take place.

17.2 Conditions That Affect Reaction Rates

QUESTIONS

3. How do chemists envision reactions taking place in terms of the *collision model* for reactions? Give an example of a simple reaction and how you might envision the reaction's taking place by means of a collision between the molecules.
4. In Figure 17.3, the height of the reaction hill is indicated as E_a. What does the symbol E_a stand for, and what does it represent in terms of a chemical reaction?
5. How does a catalyst work to speed up a chemical reaction?
6. What are *enzymes* and why are they important?

17.3 The Equilibrium Condition

QUESTIONS

7. How does *equilibrium* represent the balancing of opposing processes? Give an example of an "equilibrium" encountered in everyday life, showing how the processes involved oppose each other.
8. How do chemists define a state of chemical equilibrium?
9. When writing a chemical equation for a reaction that comes to equilibrium, how do we indicate symbolically that the reaction is *reversible?*
10. How do chemists recognize a system that has reached a state of chemical equilibrium? When writing chemical equations, how do we indicate reactions that come to a state of chemical equilibrium?

17.4 Chemical Equilibrium: A Dynamic Condition

QUESTIONS

11. What does it mean to say that a state of chemical or physical equilibrium is *dynamic?*
12. Figure 17.8 shows a plot of the *rates* of the forward and reverse reactions versus the *time* for the reaction $H_2O(g) + CO(g) \rightleftharpoons H_2(g) + CO_2(g)$. What is the significance of the portion of the plot where the two curves join together to form a single curve as time increases?

17.5 The Equilibrium Constant: An Introduction

QUESTIONS

13. In general terms, what does the equilibrium constant for a reaction represent? What is the algebraic form of the equilibrium constant for a typical reaction? What do square brackets indicate when we write an equilibrium constant?
14. There is only one value of the equilibrium constant for a particular system at a particular temperature, but there are an infinite number of equilibrium positions. Explain.

PROBLEMS

15. Write the equilibrium expression for each of the following reactions.
    a. $C_2H_6(g) + Cl_2(g) \rightleftharpoons C_2H_5Cl(s) + HCl(g)$
    b. $4NH_3(g) + 5O_2(g) \rightleftharpoons 4NO(g) + 6H_2O(g)$
    c. $PCl_5(g) \rightleftharpoons PCl_3(g) + Cl_2(g)$
16. Write the equilibrium expression for each of the following reactions.
    a. $H_2(g) + CO_2(g) \rightleftharpoons H_2O(g) + CO(g)$
    b. $2N_2O(g) + O_2(g) \rightleftharpoons 4NO(g)$
    c. $CO(g) + 2H_2(g) \rightleftharpoons CH_3OH(g)$
17. Write the equilibrium expression for each of the following reactions.
    a. $NO_2(g) + ClNO(g) \rightleftharpoons ClNO_2(g) + NO(g)$
    b. $Br_2(g) + 5F_2(g) \rightleftharpoons 2BrF_5(g)$
    c. $4NH_3(g) + 6NO(g) \rightleftharpoons 5N_2(g) + 6H_2O(g)$
18. Write the equilibrium expression for each of the following reactions.
    a. $CO(g) + 2H_2(g) \rightleftharpoons CH_3OH(g)$
    b. $2NO_2(g) \rightleftharpoons 2NO(g) + O_2(g)$
    c. $P_4(g) + 6Br_2(g) \rightleftharpoons 4PBr_3(g)$
19. Suppose that for the reaction

$$PCl_5(g) \rightleftharpoons PCl_3(g) + Cl_2(g)$$

it is determined, at a particular temperature, that the equilibrium concentrations are $[PCl_5(g)] = 0.0711\ M$, $[PCl_3(g)] = 0.0302\ M$, and $[Cl_2(g)] = 0.0491\ M$. Calculate the value of K for the reaction at this temperature.

20. Suppose that for the reaction

$$COCl_2(g) \rightleftharpoons CO(g) + Cl_2(g)$$

it is determined, at a particular temperature, that the equilibrium concentrations are $[COCl_2(g)] = 0.00103\ M$, $[CO(g)] = 0.0345\ M$, and $[Cl_2(g)] = 0.0219\ M$. Calculate the value of K for the reaction at this temperature.

All even-numbered Questions and Problems have answers in the back of this book and solutions in the Solutions Guide.

15. (a) $K = \frac{[C_2H_5Cl][HCl]}{[C_2H_6][Cl_2]}$; (b) $K = \frac{[NO]^4[H_2O]^6}{[NH_3]^4[O_2]^5}$; (c) $K = \frac{[PCl_3][Cl_2]}{[PCl_5]}$

16. (a) $K = \frac{[H_2O][CO]}{[H_2][CO_2]}$; (b) $K = \frac{[NO]^4}{[N_2O]^2[O_2]}$; (c) $K = \frac{[CH_3OH]}{[CO][H_2]^2}$

17. (a) $K = \frac{[ClNO_2(g)][NO(g)]}{[NO_2(g)][ClNO(g)]}$; (b) $K = \frac{[BrF_5(g)]^2}{[Br_2(g)][F_2(g)]^5}$; (c) $K = \frac{[N_2(g)]^5[H_2O(g)]^6}{[NH_3(g)]^4[NO(g)]^6}$

18. (a) $K = \frac{[CH_3OH(g)]}{[CO(g)][H_2(g)]^2}$; (b) $K = \frac{[NO(g)]^2[O_2(g)]}{[NO_2(g)]^2}$; (c) $K = \frac{[PBr_3(g)]^4}{[P_4(g)][Br_2(g)]^6}$

19. $K = 2.09 \times 10^{-2}$

20. $K = 0.734$

13. In general terms, K is a ratio of the product concentrations to the reactant concentrations at equilibrium. For a reaction

$$aA + bB \rightleftharpoons cC + dD$$

the constant has the algebraic form $K = \frac{[C]^c[D]^d}{[A]^a[B]^b}$

14. The equilibrium constant is a *ratio* of the concentration of products to the concentration of reactants, all at equilibrium. Depending on the amount of reactant that was originally present, different amounts of reactants and products will be present at equilibrium, but their *ratio* will always be the same for a given reaction at a given temperature. For example, the ratios 4/2 and 6/3 involve different numbers, but each of these ratios has the value 2.

21. At high temperatures, elemental nitrogen and oxygen react with each other to form nitrogen monoxide.

$$N_2(g) + O_2(g) \rightleftharpoons 2NO(g)$$

Suppose the system is analyzed at a particular temperature, and the equilibrium concentrations are found to be $[N_2] = 0.041\ M$, $[O_2] = 0.0078\ M$, and $[NO] = 4.7 \times 10^{-4}\ M$. Calculate the value of K for the reaction.

22. Suppose that for the reaction

$$2N_2O(g) + O_2(g) \rightleftharpoons 4NO(g)$$

it is determined, at a particular temperature, that the equilibrium concentrations are $[NO(g)] = 0.00341\ M$, $[N_2O(g)] = 0.0293\ M$, and $[O_2(g)] = 0.0325\ M$. Calculate the value of K for the reaction at this temperature.

17.6 Heterogeneous Equilibria

QUESTIONS

23. What is a *homogeneous* equilibrium system? Give an example of a homogeneous equilibrium reaction. What is a *heterogeneous* equilibrium system? Write two chemical equations that represent heterogeneous equilibria.

24. Explain why the position of a heterogeneous equilibrium does not depend on the amounts of pure solid or pure liquid reactants or products present.

PROBLEMS

25. Write the equilibrium expression for each of the following heterogeneous equilibria.

a. $P_4(s) + 6F_2(g) \rightleftharpoons 4PF_3(g)$
b. $Xe(g) + 2F_2(g) \rightleftharpoons XeF_4(s)$
c. $2SiO(s) + 4Cl_2(g) \rightleftharpoons 2SiCl_4(l) + O_2(g)$

26. Write the equilibrium expression for each of the following heterogeneous equilibria.

a. $Fe(s) + H_2O(g) \rightleftharpoons FeO(s) + H_2(g)$
b. $4Al(s) + 3O_2(g) \rightleftharpoons 2Al_2O_3(s)$
c. $CH_4(g) + 4Cl_2(g) \rightleftharpoons CCl_4(l) + 4HCl(g)$

27. Write the equilibrium expression for each of the following heterogeneous equilibria.

a. $C(s) + H_2O(g) \rightleftharpoons H_2(g) + CO(g)$
b. $H_2O(l) \rightleftharpoons H_2O(g)$
c. $4B(s) + 3O_2(g) \rightleftharpoons 2B_2O_3(s)$

28. Write the equilibrium expression for each of the following heterogeneous equilibria.

a. $CS_2(g) + 3Cl_2(g) \rightleftharpoons CCl_4(l) + S_2Cl_2(g)$
b. $Xe(g) + 3F_2(g) \rightleftharpoons XeF_6(s)$
c. $4Fe(s) + 3O_2(g) \rightleftharpoons 2Fe_2O_3(s)$

17.7 Le Châtelier's Principle

QUESTIONS

29. In your own words, describe what Le Châtelier's principle tells us about how we can change the position of a reaction system at equilibrium.

30. Consider the reaction

$$2CO(g) + O_2(g) \rightleftharpoons 2CO_2(g)$$

Suppose the system is already at equilibrium, and then an additional mole of $CO(g)$ is injected into the system at constant temperature. Does the amount of $CO_2(g)$ in the system increase or decrease? Does the value of K for the reaction change?

31. For an equilibrium involving gaseous substances, what effect, in general terms, is realized when the volume of the system is decreased?

32. What is the effect on the equilibrium position if an endothermic reaction is carried out at a higher temperature? Does the net amount of product increase or decrease? Does the value of the equilibrium constant change if the temperature is increased?

PROBLEMS

33. For the reaction system

$$C(s) + H_2O(g) \rightleftharpoons H_2(g) + CO(g)$$

which has already reached a state of equilibrium, predict the effect that each of the following changes will have on the position of the equilibrium. Tell whether the equilibrium will shift to the right, will shift to the left, or will not be affected.

a. The pressure of hydrogen is increased by injecting an additional mole of hydrogen gas into the reaction vessel.
b. Carbon monoxide gas is removed as it forms by use of a chemical absorbent or "scrubber."
c. An additional amount of solid carbon is added to the reaction vessel.

34. For the reaction system

$$P_4(s) + 6F_2(g) \rightleftharpoons 4PF_3(g)$$

which has already reached a state of equilibrium, predict the effect that each of the following changes will have on the position of the equilibrium. Tell whether the equilibrium will shift to the right, will shift to the left, or will not be affected.

a. Additional fluorine gas is added to the system.
b. Additional phosphorus is added to the system.
c. Additional phosphorus trifluoride is added to the system.

35. Suppose the reaction system

$$CH_4(g) + 2O_2(g) \rightleftharpoons CO_2(g) + 2H_2O(l)$$

has already reached equilibrium. Predict the effect of each of the following changes on the position of the equilibrium. Tell whether the equilibrium will shift to the right, will shift to the left, or will not be affected.

a. Any liquid water present is removed from the system.
b. CO_2 is added to the system by dropping a chunk of dry ice into the reaction vessel.

All even-numbered Questions and Problems have answers in the back of this book and solutions in the Solutions Guide.

21. $K = 6.9 \times 10^{-4}$

22. $K = 4.85 \times 10^{-6}$

23. homogeneous: all substances in the same physical state; heterogeneous: substances in different physical states

24. Equilibrium constants represent ratios of the *concentrations* of products and reactants present at the point of equilibrium. The *concentration* of a pure solid or a pure liquid is constant and is determined by the density of the solid or liquid.

25. (a) $K = \dfrac{[PF_3]^4}{[F_2]^6}$; (b) $K = \dfrac{1}{[F_2]^2}$; (c) $K = \dfrac{[O_2]}{[Cl_2]^4}$

26. (a) $K = \dfrac{[H_2]}{[H_2O]}$; (b) $K = \dfrac{1}{[O_2]^3}$; (c) $K = \dfrac{[HCl]^4}{[CH_4][Cl_2]^4}$

27. (a) $K = \dfrac{[H_2][CO]}{[H_2O]}$; (b) $K = [H_2O(g)]$; (c) $K = \dfrac{1}{[O_2]^3}$

28. (a) $K = \dfrac{[S_2Cl_2(g)]}{[CS_2(g)][Cl_2(g)]^3}$; (b) $K = \dfrac{1}{[Xe(g)][F_2(g)]^3}$; (c) $K = \dfrac{1}{[O_2(g)]^3}$

29. When a change is made in a system at equilibrium, the position of the equilibrium shifts to reduce the effect of the change.

30. $[CO_2]$ increases; K does not change

31. When the volume is decreased, the pressure increases. This change shifts the equilibrium in the direction of the fewest number of moles of gas.

32. If heat is applied to an endothermic reaction (the temperature is raised), the equilibrium is shifted to the right. More product will be present at equilibrium than if the temperature had not been increased. The value of K increases.

33. (a) shifts left; (b) shifts right; (c) no change

34. (a) shifts right; (b) no change; (c) shifts left

c. The reaction is performed in a metal cylinder fitted with a piston, and the piston is compressed to decrease the total volume of the system.

d. Additional $O_2(g)$ is added to the system from a cylinder of pure O_2.

36. Consider the general reaction

$$2A(g) + B(s) \rightleftharpoons C(g) + 3D(g) \qquad \Delta H = +115 \text{ kJ/mol}$$

which has already come to equilibrium. Predict whether the equilibrium will shift to the left, will shift to the right, or will not be affected if the changes indicated below are made to the system.

a. Additional B(s) is added to the system.
b. C(g) is removed from the system as it forms.
c. The volume of the system is decreased by a factor of 2.
d. The temperature is increased.

37. Hydrogen gas and chlorine gas in the presence of light react explosively to form hydrogen chloride

$$H_2(g) + Cl_2(g) \rightleftharpoons 2HCl(g)$$

The reaction is strongly exothermic. Would an increase in temperature for the system tend to favor or disfavor the production of hydrogen chloride?

38. For the general reaction

$$A(g) + B(g) + \text{heat} \rightleftharpoons C(g)$$

would an increase in temperature tend to favor the forward or the reverse process? Why?

39. The reaction

$$C_2H_2(g) + 2Br_2(g) \rightleftharpoons C_2H_2Br_4(g)$$

is exothermic in the forward direction. Will an increase in temperature shift the position of the equilibrium toward reactants or products?

40. The reaction

$$4NO(g) + 6H_2O(g) \rightleftharpoons 4NH_3(g) + 5O_2(g)$$

is strongly endothermic. Will an increase in temperature shift the equilibrium position toward products or toward reactants?

41. Plants synthesize the sugar dextrose according to the following reaction by absorbing radiant energy from the sun (photosynthesis).

$$6CO_2(g) + 6H_2O(g) \rightleftharpoons C_6H_{12}O_6(s) + 6O_2(g)$$

Will an increase in temperature tend to favor or discourage the production of $C_6H_{12}O_6(s)$?

42. Consider the exothermic reaction

$$CO(g) + 2H_2(g) \rightleftharpoons CH_3OH(l)$$

Predict three changes that could be made to the system that would increase the yield of product over that produced by a system in which no change was made.

17.8 Applications Involving the Equilibrium Constant

QUESTIONS

43. Suppose a reaction has the equilibrium constant $K = 1.3 \times 10^8$. What does the magnitude of this constant tell you about the relative concentrations of products and reactants that will be present once equilibrium is reached? Is this reaction likely to be a good source of the products?

44. Suppose a reaction has the equilibrium constant $K = 1.7 \times 10^{-8}$ at a particular temperature. Will there be a large or small amount of unreacted starting material present when this reaction reaches equilibrium? Is this reaction likely to be a good source of products at this temperature?

PROBLEMS

45. For the reaction

$$Br_2(g) + 5F_2(g) \rightleftharpoons 2BrF_5(g)$$

the system at equilibrium at a particular temperature is analyzed, and the following concentrations are found: $[BrF_5(g)] = 1.01 \times 10^{-9}\ M$, $[Br_2(g)] = 2.41 \times 10^{-2}\ M$, and $[F_2(g)] = 8.15 \times 10^{-2}\ M$. Calculate the value of K for the reaction at this temperature.

46. Consider the reaction

$$SO_2(g) + NO_2(g) \rightleftharpoons SO_3(g) + NO(g)$$

Suppose it is found at a particular temperature that the concentrations in the system at equilibrium are as follows: $[SO_3(g)] = 4.99 \times 10^{-5}\ M$, $[NO(g)] = 6.31 \times 10^{-7}\ M$, $[SO_2(g)] = 2.11 \times 10^{-2}\ M$, and $[NO_2(g)] = 1.73 \times 10^{-3}\ M$. Calculate the value of K for the reaction at this temperature.

47. For the reaction

$$2CO(g) + O_2(g) \rightleftharpoons 2CO_2(g)$$

it is found at equilibrium at a certain temperature that the concentrations are $[CO(g)] = 2.7 \times 10^{-4}\ M$, $[O_2(g)] = 1.9 \times 10^{-3}\ M$, and $[CO_2(g)] = 1.1 \times 10^{-1}\ M$. Calculate K for the reaction at this temperature.

48. For the reaction

$$CO_2(g) + H_2(g) \rightleftharpoons CO(g) + H_2O(g)$$

the equilibrium constant, K, has the value 5.21×10^{-3} at a particular temperature. If the system is analyzed at equilibrium at this temperature, it is found that $[CO(g)] = 4.73 \times 10^{-3}\ M$, $[H_2O(g)] = 5.21 \times 10^{-3}\ M$, and $[CO_2(g)] = 3.99 \times 10^{-2}\ M$. What is the equilibrium concentration of $H_2(g)$ in the system?

49. The equilibrium constant for the reaction

$$H_2(g) + F_2(g) \rightleftharpoons 2HF(g)$$

has the value 2.1×10^3 at a particular temperature. When the system is analyzed at equilibrium at this

All even-numbered Questions and Problems have answers in the back of this book and solutions in the Solutions Guide.

44. A small equilibrium constant implies that not much product forms before equilibrium is reached. The reaction would not be a good source of the products unless Le Châtelier's principle can be used to force the reaction to the right.

45. $K = 1.18 \times 10^{-11}$

46. $K = 8.63 \times 10^{-7}$

47. $K = 8.7 \times 10^7$

48. $[H_2] = 0.119\ M$

35. (a) no change; (b) left (assuming the dry ice vaporizes); (c) right; (d) right

36. (a) no change (B is a solid); (b) shift right; (c) shift left; (d) shift right

37. disfavor

38. The forward reaction would be favored. The reaction is endothermic, and raising the temperature means heat is being added to the system.

39. shifts left

40. For an *endo*thermic reaction, an increase in temperature will shift the position of equilibrium to the right (toward products).

41. Production of dextrose will be favored.

42. add more $CO(g)$; add more $H_2(g)$; decrease the volume of the system

43. A large value for K means concentration of products will be large relative to remaining reactants.

temperature, the concentrations of both $H_2(g)$ and $F_2(g)$ are found to be 0.0021 *M*. What is the concentration of $HF(g)$ in the equilibrium system under these conditions?

50. For the reaction

$$2H_2O(g) \rightleftharpoons 2H_2(g) + O_2(g)$$

$K = 2.4 \times 10^{-3}$ at a given temperature. At equilibrium it is found that $[H_2O(g)] = 1.1 \times 10^{-1}\ M$ and $[H_2(g)] = 1.9 \times 10^{-2}\ M$. What is the concentration of $O_2(g)$ under these conditions?

51. For the reaction

$$3O_2(g) \rightleftharpoons 2O_3(g)$$

The equilibrium constant, *K*, has the value 1.12×10^{-54} at a particular temperature.

a. What does the very small equilibrium constant indicate about the extent to which oxygen gas, $O_2(g)$, is converted to ozone gas, $O_3(g)$, at this temperature?
b. If the equilibrium mixture is analyzed and $[O_2(g)]$ is found to be $3.04 \times 10^{-2}\ M$, what is the concentration of $O_3(g)$ in the mixture?

52. For the reaction

$$N_2O_4(g) \rightleftharpoons 2NO_2(g)$$

the equilibrium constant *K* has the value 8.1×10^{-3} at a particular temperature. If the concentration of $NO_2(g)$ is found to be 0.0021 *M* in the equilibrium system, what is the concentration of $N_2O_4(g)$ under these conditions?

17.9 Solubility Equilibria

QUESTIONS

53. Explain how the dissolving of an ionic solute in water represents an equilibrium process.

54. What is the special name given to the equilibrium constant for the dissolving of an ionic solute in water?

55. Why does the amount of excess solid solute present in a solution not affect the amount of solute that ultimately dissolves in a given amount of solvent?

56. Which of the following will affect the total amount of solute that can dissolve in a given amount of solvent?
a. The solution is stirred.
b. The solute is ground to fine particles before dissolving.
c. The temperature changes.

PROBLEMS

57. Write the balanced chemical equation describing the dissolving of each of the following sparingly soluble salts in water. Write the expression for K_{sp} for each process.
a. $AgIO_3(s)$
b. $Sn(OH)_2(s)$
c. $Zn_3(PO_4)_2(s)$
d. $BaF_2(s)$

58. Write the balanced chemical equation describing the dissolving of each of the following sparingly soluble salts in water. Write the expression for K_{sp} for each process.
a. $Bi_2S_3(s)$
b. $Ca(OH)_2(s)$
c. $Co(OH)_3(s)$
d. $Cu_2S(s)$

59. K_{sp} for copper(II) hydroxide, $Cu(OH)_2$, has a value 2.2×10^{-20} at 25 °C. Calculate the solubility of copper(II) hydroxide in mol/L and g/L at 25 °C.

60. K_{sp} for magnesium carbonate, $MgCO_3$, has a value 3.5×10^{-8} at 25 °C. Calculate the solubility of magnesium carbonate in mol/L and g/L at 25 °C.

61. A saturated solution of nickel(II) sulfide contains approximately 3.6×10^{-4} g of dissolved NiS per liter at 20 °C. Calculate the solubility product K_{sp} for NiS at 20 °C.

62. Most hydroxides are not very soluble in water. For example, K_{sp} for nickel(II) hydroxide, $Ni(OH)_2$, is 2.0×10^{-15} at 25 °C. How many grams of nickel(II) hydroxide dissolve per liter at 25 °C?

63. The solubility product constant, K_{sp}, for calcium carbonate at room temperature is approximately 3.0×10^{-9}. Calculate the solubility of $CaCO_3$ in grams per liter under these conditions.

64. Calcium sulfate, $CaSO_4$, is only soluble in water to the extent of approximately 2.05 g/L at 25 °C. Calculate K_{sp} for calcium sulfate at 25°C.

65. Approximately 1.5×10^{-3} g of iron(II) hydroxide, $Fe(OH)_2(s)$, dissolves per liter of water at 18 °C. Calculate K_{sp} for $Fe(OH)_2(s)$ at this temperature.

66. Chromium(III) hydroxide dissolves in water only to the extent of $8.21 \times 10^{-5}\ M$ at 25 °C. Calculate K_{sp} for $Cr(OH)_3$ at this temperature.

67. Magnesium fluoride dissolves in water to the extent of 8.0×10^{-2} g/L at 25 °C. Calculate the solubility of $MgF_2(s)$ in moles per liter, and calculate K_{sp} for MgF_2 at 25 °C.

68. Lead(II) chloride, $PbCl_2(s)$, dissolves in water to the extent of approximately $3.6 \times 10^{-2}\ M$ at 20 °C. Calculate K_{sp} for $PbCl_2(s)$, and calculate its solubility in grams per liter.

69. Mercury(I) chloride, Hg_2Cl_2, was formerly administered orally as a purgative. Although we usually think of mercury compounds as highly toxic, the K_{sp} of mercury(I) chloride is small enough (1.3×10^{-18}) that the amount of mercury that dissolves and enters the bloodstream is tiny. Calculate the concentration of mercury(I) ion present in a saturated solution of Hg_2Cl_2.

70. The solubility product of iron(III) hydroxide is very small: $K_{sp} = 4 \times 10^{-38}$ at 25 °C. A classical method of analysis for unknown samples containing iron is to add NaOH or NH_3. This precipitates $Fe(OH)_3$, which

All even-numbered Questions and Problems have answers in the back of this book and solutions in the Solutions Guide.

49. $[HF] = 9.6 \times 10^{-2}\ M$

50. $[O_2(g)] = 8.0 \times 10^{-2}\ M$

51. (a) The extent of conversion is very small; (b) $[O_3] = 5.61 \times 10^{-30}\ M$

52. $5.4 \times 10^{-4}\ M$

53. When a solute M^+X^- is placed in water, initially the solute dissolves, producing $M^+(aq)$ and $X^-(aq)$ ions. As the concentration of these ions increases, the likelihood of the ions reentering the solid increases. Eventually dissolving and undissolving reach the same speed, and the system is in equilibrium.

54. solubility product, K_{sp}

55. The solubility reflects the position of the equilibrium; using excess solid may allow the equilibrium to be reached more quickly, but will not affect the position of the equilibrium (how much solute dissolves).

56. only the temperature

57. (a) $AgIO_3(s) \rightleftharpoons Ag^+(aq) + IO_3^-(aq)$; $K_{sp} = [Ag^+(aq)][IO_3^-(aq)]$;
(b) $Sn(OH)_2(s) \rightleftharpoons Sn^{2+}(aq) + 2OH^-(aq)$; $K_{sp} = [Sn^{2+}(aq)][OH^-(aq)]^2$;
(c) $Zn_3(PO_4)_2(s) \rightleftharpoons 3Zn^{2+}(aq) + 2PO_4^{3-}(aq)$; $K_{sp} = [Zn^{2+}(aq)]^3[PO_4^{3-}(aq)]^2$;
(d) $BaF_2(s) \rightleftharpoons Ba^{2+}(aq) + 2F^-(aq)$; $K_{sp} = [Ba^{2+}(aq)][F^-(aq)]^2$

58. (a) $Bi_2S_3(s) \rightleftharpoons 2Bi^{3+}(aq) + 3S^{2-}(aq)$; $K_{sp} = [Bi^{3+}(aq)]^2[S^{2-}(aq)]^3$;
(b) $Ca(OH)_2(s) \rightleftharpoons Ca^{2+}(aq) + 2OH^-(aq)$; $K_{sp} = [Ca^{2+}(aq)][OH^-(aq)]^2$;
(c) $Co(OH)_3(s) \rightleftharpoons Co^{3+}(aq) + 3OH^-(aq)$; $K_{sp} = [Co^{3+}(aq)][OH^-(aq)]^3$;
(d) $Cu_2S(s) \rightleftharpoons 2Cu^+(aq) + S^{2-}(aq)$; $K_{sp} = [Cu^+(aq)]^2[S^{2-}(aq)]$

59. $1.8 \times 10^{-7}\ M$; 1.7×10^{-5} g/L

60. $1.9 \times 10^{-4}\ M$; 0.016 g/L

61. $K_{sp} = 1.6 \times 10^{-11}$

62. 7.4×10^{-4} g/L

63. 5.5×10^{-3} g/L

64. $K_{sp} = 2.27 \times 10^{-4}$

65. $K_{sp} = 1.9 \times 10^{-14}$

66. $K_{sp} = 1.23 \times 10^{-15}$

67. $K_{sp} = 8.4 \times 10^{-9}$

68. $K_{sp} = 1.9 \times 10^{-4}$; 10. g/L

can then be filtered and weighed. To demonstrate that the concentration of iron remaining in solution in such a sample is very small, calculate the solubility of $Fe(OH)_3$ in moles per liter and in grams per liter.

Additional Problems

71. Before two molecules can react, chemists envision that the molecules must first *collide* with one another. Is collision among molecules the only consideration for the molecules to react with one another?

72. Why does an increase in temperature favor an increase in the speed of a reaction?

73. The minimum energy required for molecules to react with each other is called the ______ energy.

74. A(n) ______ speeds up a reaction without being consumed.

75. Equilibrium may be defined as the ______ of two processes, one of which is the opposite of the other.

76. When a chemical system has reached equilibrium, the concentrations of all reactants and products remain ______ with time.

77. What does it mean to say that all chemical reactions are, to one extent or another, *reversible?*

78. What does it mean to say that chemical equilibrium is a *dynamic* process?

79. At the point of chemical equilibrium, the rate of the forward reaction ______ the rate of the reverse reaction.

80. Equilibria involving reactants or products in more than one state are said to be ______.

81. According to Le Châtelier's principle, when a large excess of a gaseous reactant is added to a reaction system at equilibrium, the amounts of products ______.

82. Addition of an inert substance (one that does not participate in the reaction) does not change the ______ of an equilibrium.

83. When the volume of a vessel containing a gaseous equilibrium system is decreased, the ______ of the gaseous substances present is initially increased.

84. Why does increasing the temperature for an exothermic process tend to favor the conversion of products back to reactants?

85. What is meant by the *solubility product* for a sparingly soluble salt? Choose a sparingly soluble salt and show how the salt ionizes when dissolved in water, and write the expression for its solubility product.

86. For a given reaction at a given temperature, the special ratio of products to reactants defined by the equilibrium constant is always equal to the same number. Explain why this is true, no matter what initial concentrations of reactants (or products) may have been taken in setting up an experiment.

87. Many sugars undergo a process called mutarotation, in which the sugar molecules interconvert between two isomeric forms, finally reaching an equilibrium between them. This is true for the simple sugar glucose, $C_6H_{12}O_6$, which exists in solution in isomeric forms called alpha-glucose and beta-glucose. If a solution of glucose at a certain temperature is analyzed, and it is found that the concentration of alpha-glucose is twice the concentration of beta-glucose, what is the value of K for the interconversion reaction?

88. Suppose $K = 4.5 \times 10^{-3}$ at a certain temperature for the reaction

$$PCl_5(g) \rightleftharpoons PCl_3(g) + Cl_2(g)$$

If it is found that the concentration of PCl_5 is twice the concentration of PCl_3, what must be the concentration of Cl_2 under these conditions?

89. For the reaction

$$CaCO_3(s) \rightleftharpoons CaO(s) + CO_2(g)$$

the equilibrium constant K has the form $K = [CO_2]$. Using a handbook to find density information about $CaCO_3(s)$ and $CaO(s)$, show that the *concentrations* of the two solids (the number of moles contained in 1 L of volume) are constant.

90. As you know from Chapter 7, most metal carbonate salts are sparingly soluble in water. Below are listed several metal carbonates along with their solubility products, K_{sp}. For each salt, write the equation showing the ionization of the salt in water, and calculate the solubility of the salt in mol/L.

Salt	K_{sp}
$BaCO_3$	5.1×10^{-9}
$CdCO_3$	5.2×10^{-12}
$CaCO_3$	2.8×10^{-9}
$CoCO_3$	1.5×10^{-13}

91. Teeth and bones are composed, to a first approximation, of calcium phosphate, $Ca_3(PO_4)_2(s)$. The K_{sp} for this salt is 1.3×10^{-32} at 25 °C. Calculate the concentration of calcium ion in a saturated solution of $Ca_3(PO_4)_2$.

92. Under what circumstances can we compare the solubilities of two salts by directly comparing the values of their solubility products?

93. How does the collision model account for the fact that a reaction proceeds faster when the concentrations of the reactants are increased?

94. How does an increase in temperature result in an increase in the number of successful collisions between reactant molecules? What does an increase in temperature mean on a molecular basis?

95. Explain why the development of a vapor pressure above a liquid in a closed container represents an equilibrium. What are the opposing processes? How do we recognize when the system has reached a state of equilibrium?

All even-numbered Questions and Problems have answers in the back of this book and solutions in the Solutions Guide.

84. In an exothermic process, heat is a product of the reaction. So adding heat (increasing the temperature) fights against the forward process.

85. K_{sp} is the equilibrium constant for the dynamic equilibrium between solution and undissolved solute.

86. An equilibrium reaction may come to many *positions* of equilibrium, but the numerical value of the equilibrium constant is fulfilled at each possible position. If different experiments vary the amounts of reactant, the *absolute amounts* of reactants and products present at the point of equilibrium will differ from one experiment to another, but the *ratio* that defines the equilibrium constant will remain the same.

87. $K = 0.5$

88. 9.0×10^{-3} M

89. From the densities, the "concentration" in the solids are $CaCO_3$, 29.3 M, and CaO, 58.8 M.

90. $BaCO_3(s) \rightleftharpoons Ba^{2+}(aq) + CO_3^{2-}(aq)$; 7.1×10^{-5} M
$CdCO_3(s) \rightleftharpoons Cd^{2+}(aq) + CO_3^{2-}(aq)$; 2.3×10^{-6} M
$CaCO_3(s) \rightleftharpoons Ca^{2+}(aq) + CO_3^{2-}(aq)$; 5.3×10^{-5} M
$CoCO_3(s) \rightleftharpoons Co^{2+}(aq) + CO_3^{2-}(aq)$; 3.9×10^{-7} M

91. $[Ca^{2+}] = 4.9 \times 10^{-7}$ M

69. $[Hg_2^{2+}] = 6.9 \times 10^{-7}$ M

70. 4×10^{-17} M; 4×10^{-15} g/L

71. The molecules must also have sufficient energy and the correct orientation for reaction.

72. increase in temperature increases the fraction of molecules with energy $> E_a$

73. activation

74. catalyst

75. balancing

76. constant

77. the reaction may occur in either direction

78. reaction is still taking place, but in opposing directions, at the same speeds

79. equals

80. heterogeneous

81. increase

82. position

83. pressure (and concentration)

92. Although a small solubility product generally implies a small solubility, comparisons of solubility based directly on K_{sp} values are valid only if the salts produce the same numbers of positive and negative ions per formula when they dissolve. For example, the solubilities of $AgCl(s)$ and $NiS(s)$ can be compared directly using K_{sp}, since each salt produces one positive and one negative ion per formula when dissolved. $AgCl(s)$ cannot be directly compared with a salt such as $Ca_3(PO_4)_2$, however.

93. higher concentration means more molecules, and therefore a greater frequency of collisions

94. At higher temperatures, the average kinetic energy of the reactant molecules is larger, as is the probability that a collision between molecules will be energetic enough for reaction to take place. On a molecular basis, a higher temperature means a given molecule will be moving faster.

95. When a liquid is confined to an empty closed container, evaporation takes place into the empty space. As the concentration increases in the vapor phase, condensation begins to occur. When evaporation and condensation are occurring at the same rate, the system has reached equilibrium. The pressure of vapor at this point is the equilibrium vapor pressure.

96. (a) $K = \dfrac{[HBr(g)]^2}{[H_2(g)][Br_2(g)]}$; (b) $K = \dfrac{[H_2S(g)]^2}{[H_2(g)]^2[S_2(g)]}$; (c) $K = \dfrac{[HCN(g)]^2}{[H_2(g)][C_2N_2(g)]}$

97. (a) $K = \dfrac{[O_2]^3}{[O_3]^2}$; (b) $K = \dfrac{[CO_2][H_2O]^2}{[CH_4][O_2]^2}$; (c) $K = \dfrac{[C_2H_4Cl_2]}{[C_2H_4][Cl_2]}$

96. Write the equilibrium expression for each of the following reactions.

a. $H_2(g) + Br_2(g) \rightleftharpoons 2HBr(g)$
b. $2H_2(g) + S_2(g) \rightleftharpoons 2H_2S(g)$
c. $H_2(g) + C_2N_2(g) \rightleftharpoons 2HCN(g)$

97. Write the equilibrium expression for each of the following reactions.

a. $2O_3(g) \rightleftharpoons 3O_2(g)$
b. $CH_4(g) + 2O_2(g) \rightleftharpoons CO_2(g) + 2H_2O(g)$
c. $C_2H_4(g) + Cl_2(g) \rightleftharpoons C_2H_4Cl_2(g)$

98. At high temperatures, elemental bromine, Br_2, dissociates into individual bromine atoms.

$$Br_2(g) \rightleftharpoons 2Br(g)$$

Suppose that in an experiment at 2000 °C, it is found that $[Br_2] = 0.97\ M$ and $[Br] = 0.034\ M$ at equilibrium. Calculate the value of K.

99. Gaseous phosphorus pentachloride decomposes according to the reaction

$$PCl_5(g) \rightleftharpoons PCl_3(g) + Cl_2(g)$$

The equilibrium system was analyzed at a particular temperature, and the concentrations of the substances present were determined to be $[PCl_5] = 1.1 \times 10^{-2}\ M$, $[PCl_3] = 0.325\ M$, and $[Cl_2] = 3.9 \times 10^{-3}\ M$. Calculate the value of K for the reaction.

100. Write the equilibrium expression for each of the following heterogeneous equilibria.

a. $4Al(s) + 3O_2(g) \rightleftharpoons 2Al_2O_3(s)$
b. $NH_3(g) + HCl(g) \rightleftharpoons NH_4Cl(s)$
c. $2Mg(s) + O_2(g) \rightleftharpoons 2MgO(s)$

101. Write the equilibrium expression for each of the following heterogeneous equilibria.

a. $P_4(s) + 5O_2(g) \rightleftharpoons P_4O_{10}(s)$
b. $CO_2(g) + 2NaOH(s) \rightleftharpoons Na_2CO_3(s) + H_2O(g)$
c. $NH_4NO_3(s) \rightleftharpoons N_2O(g) + 2H_2O(g)$

102. What is the effect on the position of a reaction system at equilibrium when an exothermic reaction is performed at a higher temperature? Does the value of the equilibrium constant change in this situation?

103. Suppose the reaction system

$$2NO(g) + O_2(g) \rightleftharpoons 2NO_2(g)$$

has already reached equilibrium. Predict the effect of each of the following changes on the position of the equilibrium. Tell whether the equilibrium will shift to the right, will shift to the left, or will not be affected.

a. Additional oxygen is injected into the system.
b. NO_2 is removed from the reaction vessel.
c. 1.0 mole of helium is injected into the system.

104. The reaction

$$PCl_3(l) + Cl_2(g) \rightleftharpoons PCl_5(s)$$

liberates 124 kJ of energy per mole of PCl_3 reacted. Will an increase in temperature shift the equilibrium position toward products or toward reactants?

105. For the process

$$CO(g) + H_2O(g) \rightleftharpoons CO_2(g) + H_2(g)$$

it is found that the equilibrium concentrations at a particular temperature are $[H_2] = 1.4\ M$, $[CO_2] = 1.3\ M$, $[CO] = 0.71\ M$, and $[H_2O] = 0.66\ M$. Calculate the equilibrium constant K for the reaction under these conditions.

106. For the reaction

$$N_2(g) + 3H_2(g) \rightleftharpoons 2NH_3(g)$$

$K = 1.3 \times 10^{-2}$ at a given temperature. If the system at equilibrium is analyzed and the concentrations of both N_2 and H_2 are found to be 0.10 M, what is the concentration of NH_3 in the system?

107. The equilibrium constant for the reaction

$$2NOCl(g) \rightleftharpoons 2NO(g) + Cl_2(g)$$

has the value 9.2×10^{-6} at a particular temperature. The system is analyzed at equilibrium, and it is found that the concentrations of $NOCl(g)$ and $NO(g)$ are 0.44 M and $1.5 \times 10^{-3}\ M$, respectively. What is the concentration of $Cl_2(g)$ in the equilibrium system under these conditions?

108. As you learned in Chapter 7, most metal hydroxides are sparingly soluble in water. Write balanced chemical equations describing the dissolving of the following metal hydroxides in water. Write the expression for K_{sp} for each process.

a. $Cu(OH)_2(s)$
b. $Cr(OH)_3(s)$
c. $Ba(OH)_2(s)$
d. $Sn(OH)_2(s)$

109. The three common silver halides (AgCl, AgBr, and AgI) are all sparingly soluble salts. Given the values for K_{sp} for these salts below, calculate the concentration of silver ion, in mol/L, in a saturated solution of each salt.

Silver Halide	K_{sp}
AgCl	1.8×10^{-10}
AgBr	5.0×10^{-13}
AgI	8.3×10^{-17}

110. Approximately 9.0×10^{-4} g of silver chloride, $AgCl(s)$, dissolves per liter of water at 10 °C. Calculate K_{sp} for $AgCl(s)$ at this temperature.

111. Mercuric sulfide, HgS, is one of the least soluble salts known, with $K_{sp} = 1.6 \times 10^{-54}$ at 25 °C. Calculate the solubility of HgS in moles per liter and in grams per liter.

112. Approximately 0.14 g of nickel(II) hydroxide, $Ni(OH)_2(s)$, dissolves per liter of water at 20 °C. Calculate K_{sp} for $Ni(OH)_2(s)$ at this temperature.

All even-numbered Questions and Problems have answers in the back of this book and solutions in the Solutions Guide.

98. $K = 1.2 \times 10^{-3}$

99. $K = 0.12$

100. (a) $K = \dfrac{1}{[O_2(g)]^3}$; (b) $K = \dfrac{1}{[NH_3(g)][HCl(g)]}$; (c) $K = \dfrac{1}{[O_2(g)]}$

101. (a) $K = \dfrac{1}{[O_2]^5}$; (b) $K = \dfrac{[H_2O]}{[CO_2]}$; (c) $K = [N_2O][H_2O]^2$

102. An *exo*thermic reaction liberates energy as heat. Increasing the temperature (adding heat) for such a reaction is fighting against the reaction's own tendency to liberate heat. The net effect of raising the temperature will be a shift to the left

113. For the reaction $N_2(g) + 3H_2(g) \rightarrow 2NH_3(g)$, list the types of bonds that must be broken and the type of bonds that must form for the chemical reaction to take place.

114. What does the *activation energy* for a reaction represent? How is the activation energy related to whether a collision between molecules is successful?

115. What are the catalysts in living cells called? Why are these biological catalysts necessary?

116. When a reaction system has reached chemical equilibrium, the concentrations of the reactants and products no longer change with time. Why does the amount of product no longer increase, even though large concentrations of the reactants may still be present?

117. Ammonia, a very important industrial chemical, is produced by the direct combination of the elements under carefully controlled conditions.

$$N_2(g) + 3H_2(g) \rightleftharpoons 2NH_3(g)$$

Suppose, in an experiment, that the reaction mixture is analyzed after equilibrium is reached and it is found, at a particular temperature, that $[NH_3(g)] = 0.34\ M$, $[H_2(g)] = 2.1 \times 10^{-3}\ M$, and $[N_2(g)] = 4.9 \times 10^{-4}\ M$. Calculate the value of K at this temperature.

118. Write the equilibrium expression for each of the following heterogeneous equilibria.

a. $2LiHCO_3(s) \rightleftharpoons Li_2CO_3(s) + H_2O(g) + CO_2(g)$
b. $PbCO_3(s) \rightleftharpoons PbO(s) + CO_2(g)$
c. $4Al(s) + 3O_2(g) \rightleftharpoons 2Al_2O_3(s)$

119. Suppose a reaction has the equilibrium constant $K = 4.5 \times 10^{-6}$ at a particular temperature. If an experiment is set up with this reaction, will there be large relative concentrations of products present at equilibrium? Is this reaction useful as a means of producing the products? How might the reaction be made more useful?

All even-numbered Questions and Problems have answers in the back of this book and solutions in the Solutions Guide.

109. AgCl: $1.3 \times 10^{-5}\ M$; AgBr: $7.1 \times 10^{-7}\ M$; AgI: $9.1 \times 10^{-9}\ M$

110. $K_{sp} = 3.9 \times 10^{-11}$

111. $[HgS] = 1.3 \times 10^{-27}\ M = 2.9 \times 10^{-25}$ g/L

112. $K_{sp} = 1.4 \times 10^{-8}$

113. The nitrogen–nitrogen triple bond in N_2 and the three hydrogen–hydrogen bonds must be broken; six nitrogen–hydrogen bonds must form.

114. The activation energy is the minimum energy that two colliding molecules must possess for the collision to result in a reaction.

115. enzymes; many of the biological reactions would not occur to any great extent at room temperature without the catalysts

116. Once a system has reached equilibrium, the net concentration of product no longer increases because molecules of product already present react to form the original reactants.

117. $K = 2.5 \times 10^{10}$

118. (a) $K = [H_2O][CO_2]$; (b) $K = [CO_2]$; (c) $K = \frac{1}{[O_2]^3}$

119. Reactions with small equilibrium constants are not very useful as a source of the products for the reaction, unless Le Châtelier's principle can be invoked to increase the amount of product produced.

and a decrease in the amount of product. To increase the amount of products in an exothermic reaction, heat must be *removed* from the system. Changing the temperature *does* change the numerical value of the equilibrium constant for a reaction.

103. (a) right; (b) right; (c) no effect

104. The reaction is *exo*thermic. An increase in temperature (addition of heat) will shift the reaction to the left (toward reactants).

105. $K = 3.9$

106. $[NH_3(g)] = 1.1 \times 10^{-3}\ M$

107. $[Cl_2] = 0.79\ M$

108. (a) $Cu(OH)_2(s) \rightleftharpoons Cu^{2+}(aq) + 2OH^-(aq)$; $K_{sp} = [Cu^{2+}(aq)][OH^-(aq)]^2$; (b) $Cr(OH)_3(s) \rightleftharpoons Cr^{3+}(aq) + 3OH^-(aq)$; $K_{sp} = [Cr^{3+}(aq)]\ [OH^-(aq)]^3$; (c) $Ba(OH)_2(s) \rightleftharpoons Ba^{2+}(aq) + 2OH^-(aq)$; $K_{sp} = [Ba^{2+}(aq)][OH^-(aq)]^2$; (d) $Sn(OH)_2(s) \rightleftharpoons Sn^{2+}(aq) + 2OH^-(aq)$; $K_{sp} = [Sn^{2+}(aq)][OH^-(aq)]^2$

Answers to Cumulative Review Exercises

Chapters 16–17

1. The Arrhenius and Brønsted–Lowry definitions both treat acids as a source of protons. The Arrhenius definition, however, is restricted to aqueous solutions, whereas the Brønsted–Lowry definition extends the idea of a "proton donor" to other situations. The two definitions differ in their treatment of bases. In the Arrhenius concept, the only real base is hydroxide ion because of the restriction to aqueous media. In the Brønsted–Lowry concept, a base is anything that receives a proton from an acid. Any Arrhenius acid will also be a Brønsted–Lowry acid. But because the Brønsted–Lowry definition applies in all media, some Brønsted–Lowry acids would not be acids in the Arrhenius sense.

2. A conjugate acid–base pair consists of two species related to one another by the donating or accepting of a single proton, H^+. An acid has one more H^+ than its conjugate base; a base has one less H^+ than its conjugate acid.

Brønsted–Lowry acids:

$$HCl(aq) + H_2O(l) \rightarrow Cl^-(aq) + H_3O^+(aq)$$

$$H_2SO_4(aq) + H_2O(l) \rightarrow HSO_4^-(aq) + H_3O^+(aq)$$

$$H_3PO_4(aq) + H_2O(l) \rightarrow H_2PO_4^-(aq) + H_3O^+(aq)$$

$$NH_4^+(aq) + H_2O(l) \rightarrow NH_3(aq) + H_3O^+(aq)$$

Brønsted–Lowry bases:

$$NH_3(aq) + H_2O(l) \rightarrow NH_4^+(aq) + OH^-(aq)$$

$$HCO_3^-(aq) + H_2O(l) \rightarrow H_2CO_3(aq) + OH^-(aq)$$

$$NH_2^-(aq) + H_2O(l) \rightarrow NH_3(aq) + OH^-(aq)$$

$$H_2PO_4^-(aq) + H_2O(l) \rightarrow H_3PO_4(aq) + OH^-(aq)$$

CUMULATIVE REVIEW for CHAPTERS 16-17

QUESTIONS

1. How are the Arrhenius and Brønsted–Lowry definitions of acids and bases similar, and how do these definitions differ? Could a substance be an Arrhenius acid but not a Brønsted–Lowry acid? Could a substance be a Brønsted–Lowry acid but not an Arrhenius acid? Explain.
2. Describe the relationship between a conjugate acid–base pair in the Brønsted–Lowry model. Write balanced chemical equations showing the following molecules/ions behaving as Brønsted–Lowry acids in water: HCl, H_2SO_4, H_3PO_4, NH_4^+. Write balanced chemical equations showing the following molecules/ions behaving as Brønsted–Lowry bases in water: NH_3, HCO_3^-, NH_2^-, $H_2PO_4^-$.
3. Acetic acid is a weak acid in water. What does this indicate about the affinity of the acetate ion for protons compared to the affinity of water molecules for protons? If a solution of sodium acetate is dissolved in water, the solution is basic. Explain. Write equilibrium reaction equations for the ionization of acetic acid in water and for the reaction of the acetate ion with water in a solution of sodium acetate.
4. How is the *strength* of an acid related to the *position* of its ionization equilibrium? Write the equations for the dissociation (ionization) of HCl, HNO_3, and $HClO_4$ in water. Since all these acids are strong acids, what does this indicate about the basicity of the Cl^-, NO_3^-, and ClO_4^- ions? Are aqueous solutions of NaCl, $NaNO_3$, or $NaClO_4$ basic?
5. Explain how water is an *amphoteric* substance. Write the chemical equation for the autoionization of water. Write the expression for the equilibrium constant, K_w, for this reaction. What values does K_w have at 25 °C? What are $[H^+]$ and $[OH^-]$ in pure water at 25 °C? How does $[H^+]$ compare to $[OH^-]$ in an acidic solution? How does $[H^+]$ compare to $[OH^-]$ in a basic solution?
6. How is the pH scale defined? What range of pH values corresponds to acidic solutions? What range corresponds to basic solutions? Why is pH = 7.00 considered *neutral?* When the pH of a solution changes by one unit, by what factor does the hydrogen ion concentration change in the solution? How is pOH defined? How are pH and pOH for a given solution related? Explain.
7. Describe a *buffered* solution. Give three examples of buffered solutions. For each of your examples, write equations and explain how the components of the buffered solution consume added strong acids or bases. Why is buffering of solutions in biological systems so important?
8. Explain the *collision model* for chemical reactions. What "collides"? Do all collisions result in the breaking of bonds and formation of products? Why? How does the collision model explain why higher concentrations and higher temperatures tend to make reactions occur faster?
9. Sketch a graph for the progress of a reaction illustrating the *activation energy* for the reaction. Define "activation energy." Explain how an increase in temperature for a reaction affects the number of collisions that possess an energy greater than E_a. Does an increase in temperature change E_a? How does a *catalyst* speed up a reaction? Does a catalyst change E_a for the reaction?
10. Explain what it means that a reaction "has reached a state of chemical equilibrium." Explain why equilibrium is a *dynamic* state: Does a reaction really "stop" when the system reaches a state of equilibrium? Explain why, once a chemical system has reached equilibrium, the concentrations of all reactants remain *constant* with time. Why does this *constancy* of concentration not contradict our picture of equilibrium as being *dynamic?* What happens to the *rates* of the forward and reverse reactions as a system proceeds to equilibrium from a starting point where only reactants are present?
11. Describe how we write the equilibrium expression for a reaction. Give three examples of balanced chemical equations and the corresponding expressions for their equilibrium constants.
12. Although the equilibrium constant for a given reaction always has the same value at the same temperature, the actual *concentrations* present at equilibrium may differ from one experiment to another. Explain. What do we mean by an *equilibrium position?* Is the equilibrium position always the same for a reaction, regardless of the amounts of reactants taken?
13. Compare *homogeneous* and *heterogeneous* equilibria. Give a balanced chemical equation and write the corresponding equilibrium constant expression as an example of each of these cases. How does the fact that an equilibrium is *heterogeneous* influence the expression we write for the equilibrium constant for the reaction?
14. In your own words, paraphrase Le Châtelier's principle. Give an example (including a balanced chemical equation) of how each of the following changes can affect the position of equilibrium in favor of additional products for a system: the concentration of one of the reactants is increased; one of the products is selectively removed from the system; the reaction system is compressed to a smaller volume; the temperature is increased for an endothermic reaction; the temperature is decreased for an exothermic process.
15. Explain how dissolving a slightly soluble salt to form a saturated solution is an *equilibrium* process. Give three balanced chemical equations for solubility processes and write the expressions for K_{sp} corresponding to the

580

3. When we say that acetic acid is a *weak* acid, we can take either of two points of view. Usually we say that acetic acid is a weak acid because it doesn't ionize very much when dissolved in water; not many acetic acid molecules dissociate. Alternatively, we could say that acetic acid doesn't dissociate much when we dissolve it in water because the acetate ion (the conjugate base of acetic acid) is extremely effective at holding on to protons; specifically, it is better at holding on to protons than water is at attracting them. Acetic acid doesn't dissociate much because the acetate ion won't let the proton go! What would happen if we had a source of free acetate ions (for example, sodium acetate) and placed them into water? Since acetate ion is better at attracting protons than water is, the acetate ions would pull protons out of water molecules, leaving hydroxide ions. An increase in hydroxide ion concentration would take place in the solution, so the solution would be basic. Although acetic acid is a weak acid, the acetate ion is a *base* in aqueous solution.

reactions you have chosen. When writing expressions for K_{sp}, why is the concentration of the sparingly soluble salt itself not included in the expression? Given the value for the solubility product for a sparingly soluble salt, explain how the molar solubility, and the solubility in g/L, may be calculated.

PROBLEMS

16. Choose 10 species that might be expected to behave as Brønsted–Lowry acids or bases in aqueous solution. For each of your choices, (a) write an equation demonstrating *how* the species behaves as an acid or base in water, and (b) write the formula of the conjugate base or acid for each of the species you have chosen.

17. a. Write the *conjugate base* for each of the following Brønsted–Lowry acids.

HNO_3, H_2SO_4, $HClO_4$, NH_4^+, H_2CO_3

b. Write the *conjugate acid* for each of the following Brønsted–Lowry bases.

Cl^-, HSO_4^-, NH_2^-, NH_3, CO_3^{2-}

18. Identify the Brønsted–Lowry conjugate acid–base pairs in each of the following.

a. $NH_3(aq) + H_2O(l) \rightleftharpoons NH_4^+(aq) + OH^-(aq)$
b. $H_2SO_4(aq) + H_2O(l) \rightleftharpoons HSO_4^-(aq) + H_3O^+(aq)$
c. $O^{2-}(s) + H_2O(l) \rightleftharpoons 2OH^-(aq)$
d. $NH_2^-(aq) + H_2O(l) \rightleftharpoons NH_3(aq) + OH^-(aq)$
e. $H_2PO_4^-(aq) + OH^-(aq) \rightleftharpoons HPO_4^{2-}(aq) + H_2O(l)$

19. For each of the following, calculate the indicated quantity.

a. $[OH^-] = 2.11 \times 10^{-4}\ M$, $[H^+] = ?$
b. $[OH^-] = 7.34 \times 10^{-6}\ M$, pH = ?
c. $[OH^-] = 9.81 \times 10^{-8}\ M$, pOH = ?
d. pH = 9.32, pOH = ?
e. $[H^+] = 5.87 \times 10^{-11}\ M$, pH = ?
f. pH = 5.83, $[H^+] = ?$

20. Calculate the pH and pOH values for each of the following solutions.

a. $0.00141\ M\ HNO_3$
b. $2.13 \times 10^{-3}\ M\ NaOH$
c. $0.00515\ M\ HCl$
d. $5.65 \times 10^{-5}\ M\ Ca(OH)_2$

21. Write the equilibrium constant expression for each of the following reactions.

a. $4NO(g) \rightleftharpoons 2N_2O(g) + O_2(g)$
b. $4PF_3(g) \rightleftharpoons P_4(s) + 6F_2(g)$
c. $CO(g) + 3H_2(g) \rightleftharpoons CH_4(g) + H_2O(g)$
d. $2BrF_5(g) \rightleftharpoons Br_2(g) + 5F_2(g)$
e. $S(s) + 2HCl(g) \rightleftharpoons H_2S(g) + Cl_2(g)$

22. Suppose that for the following reaction

$$Br_2(g) + Cl_2(g) \rightleftharpoons 2BrCl(g)$$

it is determined that, at a particular temperature, the equilibrium concentrations are as follows: $[Br_2(g)] = 7.2 \times 10^{-8}\ M$, $[Cl_2(g)] = 4.3 \times 10^{\times 6}\ M$, $[BrCl(g)] = 4.9 \times 10^{-4}\ M$. Calculate the value of K for the reaction at this temperature.

23. Write expressions for K_{sp} for each of the following sparingly soluble substances.

a. $Cu(OH)_2(s)$
b. $Co_2S_3(s)$
c. $Hg_2(OH)_2(s)$
d. $CaCO_3(s)$
e. $Ag_2CrO_4(s)$
f. $Hg(OH)_2(s)$

24. The solubility product of magnesium carbonate, $MgCO_3$, has the value $K_{sp} = 6.82 \times 10^{-6}$ at 25 °C. How many grams of $MgCO_3$ will dissolve in 1.00 L of water?

strong base is added to it. For example, water behaves as a base when HCl is dissolved in it.

$$HCl + H_2O \rightarrow Cl^- + H_3O^+$$

However, water would behave as an acid if the strong base $NaNH_2$ were added to it.

$$NH_2^- + H_2O \rightarrow NH_3 + OH^-$$

We can also demonstrate the amphoterism of water by the fact that water undergoes *autoionization,* in which some water molecules behave as an acid and some behave as a base.

$$H_2O + H_2O \rightarrow H_3O^+ + OH^-$$

Because this reaction is so important to our understanding of the relative acidity and basicity of aqueous solutions, the *equilibrium constant* for the autoionization of water is given a special symbol, K_w.

$$K_w = [H_3O^+][OH^-]$$

This equilibrium constant has the value 1.0×10^{-14} at 25 °C. Because hydronium ions and hydroxide ions are produced in equal numbers when water molecules undergo autoionization, and with the value for the equilibrium constant given, we know that in pure water

$$[H_3O^+] = [OH^-] = 1.0 \times 10^{-7}\ M$$

If a solution has a higher concentration of H_3O^+ ion than OH^- ion, we say the solution is *acidic.* If a solution has a lower concentration of H_3O^+ ion than OH^- ion, we say the solution is *basic.*

(Please refer to p. A32 in this book for answers to Exercises 6–24.)

4. The strength of an acid is a direct result of the position of the acid's dissociation (ionization) equilibrium. Acids whose dissociation equilibrium positions lie far to the right are called *strong* acids. Acids whose equilibrium positions lie only slightly to the right are called *weak* acids. For example, HCl, HNO_3, and $HClO_4$ are strong acids, which means that they are completely dissociated in aqueous solution (the position of equilibrium lies very far to the right):

$$HCl(aq) + H_2O(l) \rightarrow Cl^-(aq) + H_3O^+(aq)$$
$$HNO_3(aq) + H_2O(l) \rightarrow NO_3^-(aq) + H_3O^+(aq)$$
$$HClO_4(aq) + H_2O(l) \rightarrow ClO_4^-(aq) + H_3O^+(aq)$$

Since these are very strong acids, their anions (Cl^-, NO_3^-, ClO_4^-) must be very *weak* bases, and solutions of their sodium salts will *not* be basic.

5. When we say that water is an *amphoteric* substance, we are recognizing that water will behave as a *Brønsted–Lowry base* if a strong acid is added to it, but will behave as a *Brønsted–Lowry acid* if a

Chapter 18

Objectives

In this chapter our objectives are for the students to:

SECTION 18.1

- Learn about metal–nonmetal oxidation–reduction reactions.

SECTION 18.2

- Learn how to assign oxidation states.

SECTION 18.3

- Understand oxidation and reduction in terms of oxidation states.
- Learn to identify oxidizing and reducing agents.

SECTION 18.4

- Learn to balance oxidation–reduction equations by using half-reactions.

SECTION 18.5

- Understand the term *electrochemistry.*
- Learn to identify the components of an electrochemical (galvanic) cell.

SECTION 18.6

- Learn about the composition and operation of commonly used batteries.

SECTION 18.7

- Understand the electrochemical nature of corrosion and learn some ways of preventing it.

SECTION 18.8

- Understand the process of electrolysis and learn about the commercial preparation of aluminum.

18 Oxidation–Reduction Reactions and Electrochemistry

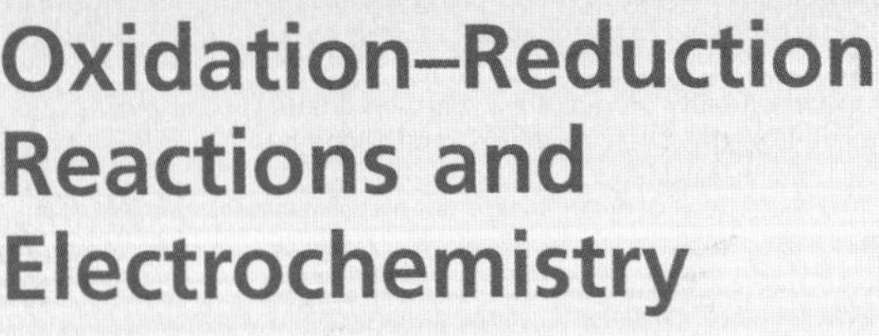

Workers in China apply paint to a wall to prevent rust. *(China Daily Information Corp/Reuters)*

ChemWork Refined over ten years of use by thousands of students, **ChemWork** builds and enhances students' problems-solving skills. Online assignments function as a "personal instructor" to help students learn how to solve challenging problems and learn how to think like chemists. Annotations for **ChemWork** assignments are included at the beginning of the end-of-chapter review.

PowerLecture This 2-DVD package includes the Chemistry Multimedia Library, which contains animations, simulations, and movies for all chemistry subjects, organized by topic for lecture presentations. Annotations for **PowerLecture** are referenced in the margins throughout the Annotated Instructor's Edition.

OWL Sign in to OWL at **www.cengage.com/owl** to view tutorials and simulations, develop problem-solving skills, and complete online homework assigned by your professor.

What do a forest fire, rusting steel, combustion in an automobile engine, and the metabolism of food in a human body have in common? All of these important processes involve oxidation–reduction reactions. In fact, virtually all of the processes that provide energy to heat buildings, power vehicles, and allow people to work and play depend on oxidation–reduction reactions. And every time you start your car, turn on your calculator, look at your digital watch, or listen to a radio at the beach, you are depending on an oxidation–reduction reaction to power the battery in each of these devices. In addition, battery-powered cars have become more common on U.S. roads. This will lead to increased reliance of our society on batteries and will spur the search for new, more efficient batteries.

In this chapter we will explore the properties of oxidation–reduction reactions, and we will see how these reactions are used to power batteries.

The power generated by an alkaline AA battery, a lithium battery, and a mercury battery results from oxidation–reduction reactions.

Test Bank: 1–4

18.1 Oxidation–Reduction Reactions

Section 18.1

OBJECTIVE: To learn about metal–nonmetal oxidation–reduction reactions.

TEACHING TIP

Some students wonder why the term *reduction* is used to describe a *gain* of electrons. When you discuss oxidation states in Section 18.2, emphasize that when an atom is reduced, its oxidation state is reduced.

Lecture Demonstration: 4.8, 4.9

In Section 7.5 we discussed the chemical reactions between metals and nonmetals. For example, sodium chloride is formed by the reaction of elemental sodium and chlorine.

$$2Na(s) + Cl_2(g) \rightarrow 2NaCl(s)$$

Because elemental sodium and chlorine contain uncharged atoms and because sodium chloride is known to contain Na^+ and Cl^- ions, this reaction must involve a transfer of electrons from sodium atoms to chlorine atoms.

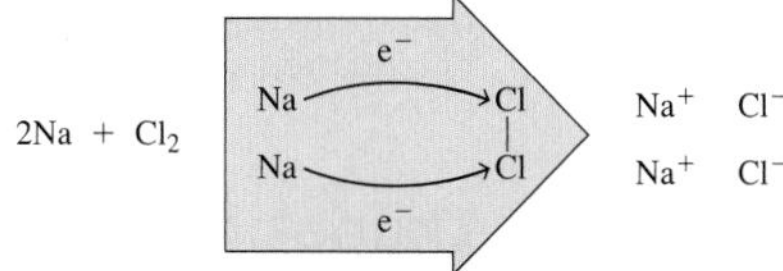

Some students use the mnemonic OIL RIG:

Oxidation Is Loss;
Reduction Is Gain.

Reactions like this one, in which one or more electrons are transferred, are called **oxidation–reduction reactions,** or **redox reactions. Oxidation** is defined as a *loss of electrons.* **Reduction** is defined as a *gain of electrons.* In the reaction of elemental sodium and chlorine, each sodium atom loses one electron, forming a 1+ ion. Therefore, sodium is oxidized. Each

TEACHING SUPPORT

HISTORICAL BACKGROUND

The discovery of oxygen by Joseph Priestley in 1774 was really the beginning of the use of the term *oxidation* for chemical reactions. When Lavoisier learned of Priestley's discovery of oxygen, he recognized that combustion is the reaction of substances with oxygen in the air. Combustion reactions were then known as oxidation reactions. When a substance lost oxygen, it was reduced in mass, so reactions involving the release of oxygen became known as reduction reactions. Not until the electron was discovered were oxidation–reduction reactions understood to involve the transfer of electrons.

chlorine atom gains one electron, forming a negative chloride ion, and is thus reduced. Whenever a metal reacts with a nonmetal to form an ionic compound, electrons are transferred from the metal to the nonmetal. So these reactions are always oxidation–reduction reactions where the metal is oxidized (loses electrons) and the nonmetal is reduced (gains electrons).

EXAMPLE 18.1 Identifying Oxidation and Reduction in a Reaction

In the following reactions, identify which element is oxidized and which element is reduced.

a. $2Mg(s) + O_2(g) \rightarrow 2MgO(s)$

b. $2Al(s) + 3I_2(s) \rightarrow 2AlI_3(s)$

Magnesium burns in air to give a bright, white flame.

SOLUTION

a. We have learned that Group 2 metals form 2+ cations and that Group 6 nonmetals form 2− anions, so we can predict that magnesium oxide contains Mg^{2+} and O^{2-} ions. This means that in the reaction given, each Mg loses two electrons to form Mg^{2+} and so is oxidized. Also each O gains two electrons to form O^{2-} and so is reduced.

b. Aluminum iodide contains the Al^{3+} and I^- ions. Thus aluminum atoms lose electrons (are oxidized). Iodine atoms gain electrons (are reduced).

Self-Check EXERCISE 18.1 For the following reactions, identify the element oxidized and the element reduced.

a. $2Cu(s) + O_2(g) \rightarrow 2CuO(s)$ b. $2Cs(s) + F_2(g) \rightarrow 2CsF(s)$

See Problems 18.3 through 18.6. ■

Although we can identify reactions between metals and nonmetals as redox reactions, it is more difficult to decide whether a given reaction between nonmetals is a redox reaction. In fact, many of the most significant redox reactions involve only nonmetals. For example, combustion reactions such as methane burning in oxygen,

$$CH_4(g) + 2O_2(g) \rightarrow CO_2(g) + 2H_2O(g) + \text{energy}$$

are oxidation–reduction reactions. Even though none of the reactants or products in this reaction is ionic, the reaction does involve a transfer of electrons from carbon to oxygen. To explain this, we must introduce the concept of oxidation states.

18.2 Oxidation States

OBJECTIVE: To learn how to assign oxidation states.

The concept of **oxidation states** (sometimes called *oxidation numbers*) lets us keep track of electrons in oxidation–reduction reactions by assigning charges to the various atoms in a compound. Sometimes these charges are

Additional Examples

Example 18.1

In the following reactions, identify which element is oxidized and which element is reduced.

1. $Cl_2(g) + Cu(s) \rightarrow CuCl_2(s)$

   copper is oxidized, chlorine is reduced

2. $O_2(g) + 2Ni(s) \rightarrow 2NiO(s)$

   nickel is oxidized, oxygen is reduced

3. $S(s) + 2Hg(l) \rightarrow Hg_2S(s)$

   mercury is oxidized, sulfur is reduced

Self Check

Answers to Self-Check Exercise 18.1

a. copper is oxidized, oxygen is reduced

b. cesium is oxidized, fluorine is reduced

 Test Bank: 5–33

Section 18.2

TEACHING TIP

It is easiest to introduce the oxidation states for ions before discussing covalent molecules. Since the charge on the ion is the same as the oxidation state, this idea makes sense to the students. Emphasize that the charge on an ion is acquired from a transfer of electrons. This point establishes the idea of assigning electrons to a particular atom. Then move to covalent molecules and begin assigning oxidation states to them.

DEMONSTRATION

A Silver Mirror

Materials 100-mL graduated cylinder, 250-mL Erlenmeyer flask, small flask and stopper to fit, 4 small beakers, sodium hydroxide, glucose, fructose, silver nitrate, ammonium nitrate, tartaric acid, ethanol, heating unit

Preparation Make the following solutions: (1) Dissolve 2.5 g glucose and 2.5 g fructose in 50 mL distilled water and add 0.6 g tartaric acid. Heat the solution to boiling; cool and then pour it into the 100-mL graduated cylinder. Add 10 mL of ethanol and dilute the solution to the 100-mL mark. Label it *A*. (2) Dissolve 4.0 g of silver nitrate in 50 mL water. Label it *B*. (3) Dissolve 6.0 g of ammonium nitrate in 50 mL water. Label it *C*. (4) Dissolve 10 g NaOH in 50 mL water. Label it *D*.

Clean the small flask thoroughly with concentrated nitric acid.

quite apparent. For example, in a binary ionic compound the ions have easily identified charges: in sodium chloride, sodium is +1 and chlorine is −1; in magnesium oxide, magnesium is +2 and oxygen is −2; and so on. In such binary ionic compounds the oxidation states are simply the charges of the ions.

Ion	Oxidation State
Na^+	+1
Cl^-	−1
Mg^{2+}	+2
O^{2-}	−2

In an uncombined element, all of the atoms are uncharged (neutral). For example, sodium metal contains neutral sodium atoms, and chlorine gas is made up of Cl_2 molecules, each of which contains two neutral chlorine atoms. Therefore, an atom in a pure element has no charge and is assigned an oxidation state of zero.

In a covalent compound such as water, although no ions are actually present, chemists find it useful to assign imaginary charges to the elements in the compound. The oxidation states of the elements in these compounds are equal to the imaginary charges we determine by assuming that the most electronegative atom (see Section 12.2) in a bond controls or possesses *both* of the shared electrons. For example, in the O—H bonds in water, it is assumed for purposes of assigning oxidation states that the much more electronegative oxygen atom controls both of the shared electrons in each bond. This gives the oxygen eight valence electrons.

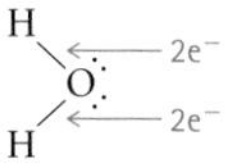

In effect, we say that each hydrogen has lost its single electron to the oxygen. This gives each hydrogen an oxidation state of +1 and the oxygen an oxidation state of −2 (the oxygen atom has formally gained two electrons). In virtually all covalent compounds, oxygen is assigned an oxidation state of −2 and hydrogen is assigned an oxidation state of +1.

Because fluorine is so electronegative, it is always assumed to control any shared electrons. So fluorine is always assumed to have a complete octet of electrons and is assigned an oxidation state of −1. That is, for purposes of assigning oxidation states, fluorine is always imagined to be F^- in its covalent compounds.

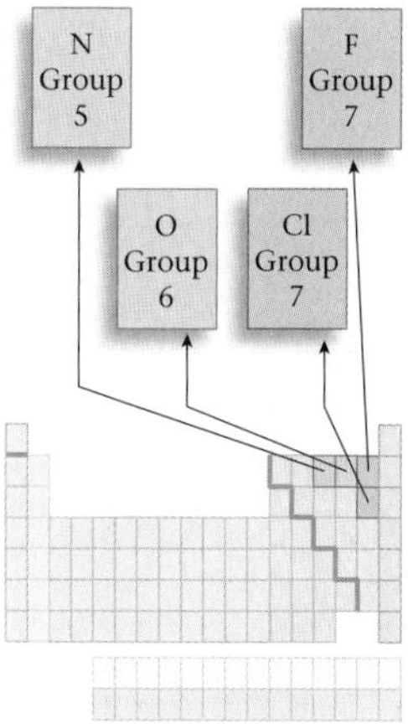

The most electronegative elements are F, O, N, and Cl. In general, we give each of these elements an oxidation state equal to its charge as an anion (fluorine is −1, chlorine is −1, oxygen is −2, and nitrogen is −3). When two of these elements are found in the same compound, we assign them in order of electronegativity, starting with the element that has the largest electronegativity.

$$F > O > N > Cl$$

Greatest electronegativity — Least electronegativity

For example, in the compound NO_2, because oxygen has a greater electronegativity than nitrogen, we assign each oxygen an oxidation state of −2. This gives a total "charge" of −4 (2 × −2) on the two oxygen atoms. Because the NO_2 molecule has zero overall charge, the N must be +4 to exactly balance the −4 on the oxygens. In NO_2, then, the oxidation state of *each* oxygen is −2 and the oxidation state of the nitrogen is +4.

DEMONSTRATION

Floating Pennies

Materials Post-1982 penny, file, 6 *M* HCl, large Erlenmeyer flask, parafilm or watch glass

Presentation Place about 100 mL of HCl in the large flask. Using the file, make four or five notches in the edge of the penny, being sure to break through the copper covering on the penny. Carefully drop the penny into the acid. Cover the flask and allow it to remain undisturbed for several days. Observe that the penny begins to float. Ask students to explain why.

Teaching Notes The penny floats because the zinc inside the copper plating reacts with the HCl to produce hydrogen gas that becomes trapped inside the penny. You can carefully pour out the HCl and retrieve the penny after washing it gently with water to remove the acid. If the penny is placed on a paper towel, it becomes evident that most of the penny has reacted, leaving only its "copper skin" behind. Have students write the oxidation–reduction reaction equation for the zinc and HCl.

resentation Place 30 mL of solution A into the clean ask. In a small beaker mix 15 mL of solution B with 5 mL of solution C. Add this mixture to the flask. Quickly dd 30 mL of solution D to the flask and mix the flask ith quick but gentle swirling motions. Be sure to cover e inside surface of the glass evenly while swirling. Coninue swirling until the silver mirror forms inside the ask. Immediately pour out the remaining solution and deactivate the solution by adding lots of water. Rinse the silvered flask with distilled water.

Teaching Notes Do not mix solutions B and C until the demonstration is performed; they are potentially unstable after mixing. Metallic silver forms on the surface of the glass when the silver ions oxidize the aldehyde on the sugar molecule. If the silver doesn't stick to the glass, it was not completely clean.

TEACHING TIPS

- Students need to learn the rules for assigning oxidation states. It is a good idea to give them a number of practice problems in assigning oxidation states to all of the elements in a compound.
- For beginning students, focus on compounds that obey the rules. If students ask about exceptions, use examples such as H_2O_2 and NaH.

PowerLecture Animations:
Hydrogen Fluoride Oxidation Numbers
Perchlorate Oxidation Numbers

The rules for assigning oxidation states are given below and are illustrated in Table 18.1. Application of these rules allows us to assign oxidation states in most compounds. The principles are illustrated by Example 18.2.

Rules for Assigning Oxidation States

1. The oxidation state of an atom in an uncombined element is 0.
2. The oxidation state of a monatomic ion is the same as its charge.
3. Oxygen is assigned an oxidation state of −2 in most of its covalent compounds. Important exception: peroxides (compounds containing the O_2^{2-} group), in which each oxygen is assigned an oxidation state of −1.
4. In its covalent compounds with nonmetals, hydrogen is assigned an oxidation state of +1.
5. In binary compounds, the element with the greater electronegativity is assigned a negative oxidation state equal to its charge as an anion in its ionic compounds.
6. For an electrically neutral compound, the sum of the oxidation states must be zero.
7. For an ionic species, the sum of the oxidation states must equal the overall charge.

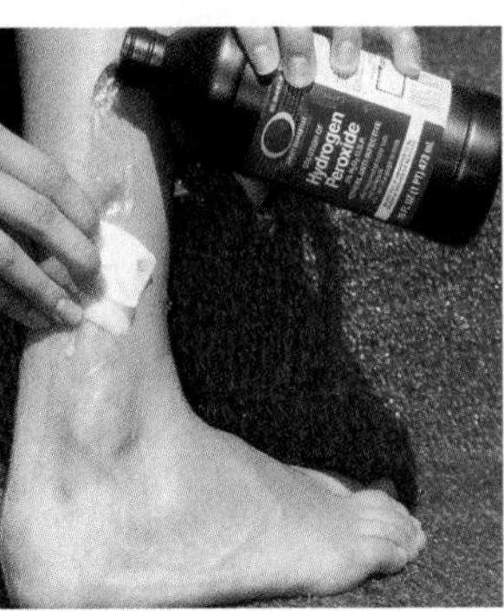

Hydrogen peroxide can be used to disinfect a wound.

Table 18.1 Examples of Oxidation States

Substance	Oxidation States	Comments
sodium metal, Na	Na, 0	rule 1
phosphorus, P	P, 0	rule 1
sodium fluoride, NaF	Na, +1 F, −1	rule 2 rule 2
magnesium sulfide, MgS	Mg, +2 S, −2	rule 2 rule 2
carbon monoxide, CO	C, +2 O, −2	 rule 3
sulfur dioxide, SO_2	S, +4 O, −2	 rule 3
hydrogen peroxide, H_2O_2	H, +1 O, −1	 rule 3 (exception)
ammonia, NH_3	H, +1 N, −3	rule 4 rule 5
hydrogen sulfide, H_2S	H, +1 S, −2	rule 4 rule 5
hydrogen iodide, HI	H, +1 I, −1	rule 4 rule 5
sodium carbonate, Na_2CO_3	Na, +1 O, −2 C, +4	rule 2 rule 3 For CO_3^{2-}, the sum of the oxidation states is $+4 + 3(-2) = -2$. rule 7
ammonium chloride, NH_4Cl	N, −3 H, +1 Cl, −1	rule 5 rule 4 For NH_4^+, the sum of the oxidation states is $-3 + 4(+1) = +1$. rule 7 rule 2

EXAMPLE 18.2 Assigning Oxidation States

Assign oxidation states to all atoms in the following molecules or ions.

a. CO_2

b. SF_6

c. NO_3^-

SOLUTION

a. Rule 3 takes precedence here: oxygen is assigned an oxidation state of −2. We determine the oxidation state for carbon by recognizing that because CO_2 has no charge, the sum of the oxidation states for oxygen and carbon must be 0 (rule 6). Each oxygen is −2 and there are two oxygen atoms, so the carbon atom must be assigned an oxidation state of +4.

CO_2: +4 (carbon); −2 for *each* oxygen

CHECK: $+4 + 2(-2) = 0$

b. Because fluorine has the greater electronegativity, we assign its oxidation state first. Its charge as an anion is always −1, so we assign −1 as the oxidation state of each fluorine atom (rule 5). The sulfur must then be assigned an oxidation state of +6 to balance the total of −6 from the six fluorine atoms (rule 7).

SF_6: +6 (sulfur); −1 for *each* fluorine

CHECK: $+6 + 6(-1) = 0$

c. Oxygen has a greater electronegativity than nitrogen, so we assign its oxidation state of −2 first (rule 5). Because the overall charge on NO_3^- is −1 and because the sum of the oxidation states of the three oxygens is −6, the nitrogen must have an oxidation state of +5.

NO_3^-: +5 (nitrogen); −2 for *each* oxygen gives −6 total

CHECK: $+5 + 3(-2) = -1$
This is correct; NO_3^- has a −1 charge.

Self-Check EXERCISE 18.2 Assign oxidation states to all atoms in the following molecules or ions.

a. SO_3

b. SO_4^{2-}

c. N_2O_5

d. PF_3

e. C_2H_6

See Problems 18.13 through 18.22. ■

Additional Examples

Example 18.2

Assign oxidation states to all atoms in the following molecules or ions.

1. NF_3

   nitrogen, +3; fluorine, −1

2. HOCl

   hydrogen, +1; oxygen, −2; chlorine, +1

3. CO_3^{2-}

   carbon, +4; oxygen, −2

Self Check

Answers to Self-Check Exercise 18.2

a. S, +6; O, −2

b. S, +6; O, −2

c. N, +5; O, −2

d. P, +3; F, −1

e. C, −3; H, +1

Test Bank: 39–49

Section 18.3

TEACHING TIPS

- You can use examples from earlier chapters, including single-displacement, synthesis, and decomposition reactions, to show students how many oxidation–reduction reactions they already know. You can assign oxidation states to all of the elements in the reactants and products of these reactions to illustrate that in an oxidation–reduction reaction something is oxidized at the same time that something is reduced.
- Students need to practice determining the number of electrons gained or lost in a reaction. This step is important to balance oxidation–reduction reactions correctly. Students sometimes have trouble applying the rules for oxidation states to compounds. For example, oxygen has a −2 oxidation state. In a compound such as SO_2, however, there are two oxygen atoms, which means that *four* electrons must have been transferred.

18.3 Oxidation–Reduction Reactions Between Nonmetals

OBJECTIVES: To understand oxidation and reduction in terms of oxidation states.
- To learn to identify oxidizing and reducing agents.

We have seen that oxidation–reduction reactions are characterized by a transfer of electrons. In some cases, the transfer literally occurs to form ions, such as in the reaction

$$2Na(s) + Cl_2(g) \rightarrow 2NaCl(s)$$

We can use oxidation states to verify that electron transfer has occurred.

$$2Na(s) + Cl_2(g) \rightarrow 2NaCl(s)$$

Oxidation state: 0 (element), 0 (element), +1 −1 $(Na^+)(Cl^-)$

Thus in this reaction, we represent the electron transfer as follows:

$$\text{Na} \xrightarrow{e^-} \text{Cl} \quad \Rightarrow \quad Na^+ \quad Cl^-$$

In other cases the electron transfer occurs in a different sense, such as in the combustion of methane (the oxidation state for each atom is given below each reactant and product).

$$CH_4(g) + 2O_2(g) \rightarrow CO_2(g) + 2H_2O(g)$$

Oxidation state: CH_4: −4, +1 (each H); O_2: 0; CO_2: +4, −2 (each O); H_2O: +1 (each H), −2

Note that the oxidation state of oxygen in O_2 is 0 because the oxygen is in elemental form. In this reaction there are no ionic compounds, but we can still describe the process in terms of the transfer of electrons. Note that carbon undergoes a change in oxidation state from −4 in CH_4 to +4 in CO_2. Such a change can be accounted for by a loss of eight electrons:

$$\underset{-4}{\text{C (in } CH_4)} \xrightarrow{\text{Loss of } 8e^-} \underset{+4}{\text{C (in } CO_2)}$$

or, in equation form,

$$\underset{-4}{CH_4} \rightarrow \underset{+4}{CO_2} + 8e^-$$

On the other hand, each oxygen changes from an oxidation state of 0 in O_2 to −2 in H_2O and CO_2, signifying a gain of two electrons per atom. Four oxygen atoms are involved, so this is a gain of eight electrons:

$$\text{4O atoms (in } 2O_2) \xrightarrow{\text{Gain of } 8e^-} 4O^{2-} \text{ (in } 2H_2O \text{ and } CO_2)$$

or, in equation form,

$$\underset{0}{2O_2} + 8e^- \rightarrow CO_2 + 2H_2O \quad 4(-2) = -8$$

Note that eight electrons are required because four oxygen atoms are going from an oxidation state of 0 to −2. So each oxygen requires two electrons.

Oxidation:
Loss of electrons
or
Increase in oxidation state

Reduction:
Gain of electrons
or
Decrease in oxidation state

Oxidizing agent:
Accepts electrons
Contains the element reduced

Reducing agent:
Furnishes electrons
Contains the element oxidized

No change occurs in the oxidation state of hydrogen, and it is not involved in the electron transfer process.

With this background, we can now define *oxidation* and *reduction* in terms of oxidation states. **Oxidation** is an *increase* in oxidation state (a loss of electrons). **Reduction** is a *decrease* in oxidation state (a gain of electrons). Thus in the reaction

$$2Na(s) + Cl_2(g) \rightarrow 2NaCl(s)$$

sodium is oxidized and chlorine is reduced. Cl_2 is called the **oxidizing agent (electron acceptor)** and Na is called the **reducing agent (electron donor).** We can also define the *oxidizing agent* as the reactant containing the element that is reduced (gains electrons). The *reducing agent* can be defined similarly as the reactant containing the element that is oxidized (loses electrons).

Concerning the reaction

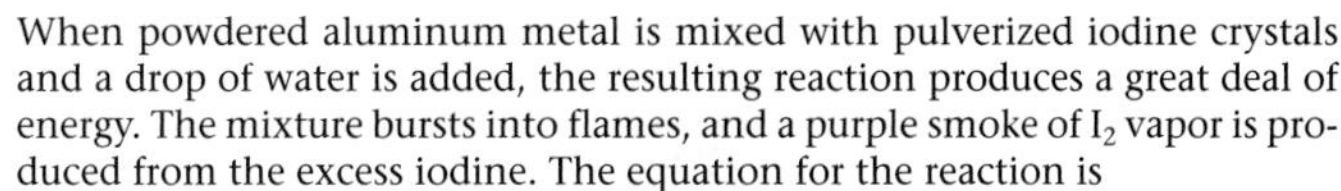

we can say the following:

1. Carbon is oxidized because there is an increase in its oxidation state (carbon has apparently lost electrons).
2. The reactant CH_4 contains the carbon that is oxidized, so CH_4 is the reducing agent. It is the reactant that furnishes the electrons (those lost by carbon).
3. Oxygen is reduced because there has been a decrease in its oxidation state (oxygen has apparently gained electrons).
4. The reactant that contains the oxygen atoms is O_2, so O_2 is the oxidizing agent. That is, O_2 accepts the electrons.

In a redox reaction, an oxidizing agent is reduced (gains electrons) and a reducing agent is oxidized (loses electrons).

Note that when the oxidizing or reducing agent is named, the *whole compound* is specified, not just the element that undergoes the change in oxidation state.

EXAMPLE 18.3

Identifying Oxidizing and Reducing Agents, I

When powdered aluminum metal is mixed with pulverized iodine crystals and a drop of water is added, the resulting reaction produces a great deal of energy. The mixture bursts into flames, and a purple smoke of I_2 vapor is produced from the excess iodine. The equation for the reaction is

$$2Al(s) + 3I_2(s) \rightarrow 2AlI_3(s)$$

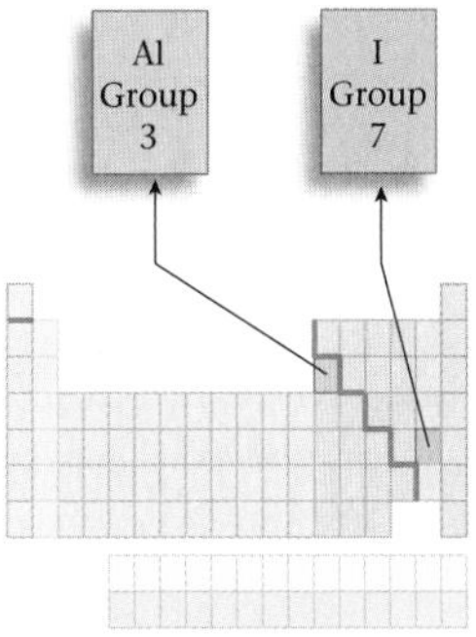

For this reaction, identify the atoms that are oxidized and those that are reduced, and specify the oxidizing and reducing agents.

SOLUTION

The first step is to assign oxidation states.

$$2Al(s) + 3I_2(s) \rightarrow 2AlI_3(s)$$

0 — 0 — Free elements

+3 −1 (each I) — $AlI_3(s)$ is a salt that contains Al^{3+} and I^- ions.

Additional Examples

Example 18.3

For the following reaction, identify the atoms that are oxidized and reduced, and specify the oxidizing and reducing agents.

$$Fe_2O_3(s) + 3CO(g) \rightarrow 2Fe(l) + 3CO_2(g)$$

Iron is reduced, carbon is oxidized; $Fe_2O_3(s)$ is the oxidizing agent, $CO(g)$ is the reducing agent

Because each aluminum atom changes its oxidation state from 0 to +3 (an increase in oxidation state), aluminum is *oxidized* (loses electrons). On the other hand, the oxidation state of each iodine atom decreases from 0 to −1, and iodine is *reduced* (gains electrons). Because Al furnishes electrons for the reduction of iodine, it is the *reducing agent.* I_2 is the *oxidizing agent* (the reactant that accepts the electrons).

Additional Examples

Example 18.4

For the following reaction, identify the atoms that are oxidized and reduced, and specify the oxidizing and reducing agents.

$$Cl_2O_3(g) + 2NaBr(aq) \rightarrow 2NaCl(aq) + Br_2(l)$$

Chlorine is reduced, bromine is oxidized; $Cl_2(g)$ is the oxidizing agent, NaBr(*aq*) is the reducing agent

EXAMPLE 18.4 Identifying Oxidizing and Reducing Agents, II

Metallurgy, the process of producing a metal from its ore, always involves oxidation–reduction reactions. In the metallurgy of galena (PbS), the principal lead-containing ore, the first step is the conversion of lead sulfide to its oxide (a process called *roasting*).

$$2PbS(s) + 3O_2(g) \rightarrow 2PbO(s) + 2SO_2(g)$$

The oxide is then treated with carbon monoxide to produce the free metal.

$$PbO(s) + CO(g) \rightarrow Pb(s) + CO_2(g)$$

For each reaction, identify the atoms that are oxidized and those that are reduced, and specify the oxidizing and reducing agents.

SOLUTION

For the first reaction, we can assign the following oxidation states:

$$\underset{+2\ \ -2}{PbS(s)} + \underset{0}{3O_2(g)} \rightarrow \underset{+2\ \ -2}{2PbO(s)} + \underset{+4\ \ -2\ \text{(each O)}}{2SO_2(g)}$$

The oxidation state for the sulfur atom increases from −2 to +4, so sulfur is oxidized (loses electrons). The oxidation state for each oxygen atom decreases from 0 to −2. Oxygen is reduced (gains electrons). The oxidizing agent (electron acceptor) is O_2, and the reducing agent (electron donor) is PbS.

For the second reaction, we have

$$\underset{+2\ \ -2}{PbO(s)} + \underset{+2\ \ -2}{CO(g)} \rightarrow \underset{0}{Pb(s)} + \underset{+4\ -2\ \text{(each O)}}{CO_2(g)}$$

Lead is reduced (gains electrons; its oxidation state decreases from +2 to 0), and carbon is oxidized (loses electrons; its oxidation state increases from +2 to +4). PbO is the oxidizing agent (electron acceptor), and CO is the reducing agent (electron donor).

Self Check

Answer to Self-Check Exercise 18.3

N_2 is the oxidizing agent, H_2 is the reducing agent

Self-Check EXERCISE 18.3 Ammonia, NH_3, which is widely used as a fertilizer, is prepared by the following reaction:

$$N_2(g) + 3H_2(g) \rightarrow 2NH_3(g)$$

Is this an oxidation–reduction reaction? If so, specify the oxidizing agent and the reducing agent.

See Problems 18.29 through 18.36. ■

CHEMISTRY *IN* FOCUS

Do We Age by Oxidation?

People (especially those over age 30) seem obsessed about staying young, but the fountain of youth sought since the days of Ponce de Leon has proved elusive. The body inevitably seems to wear out after 70 or 80 years. Is this our destiny or can we find ways to combat aging?

Why do we age? No one knows for certain, but many scientists think that oxidation plays a major role. Although oxygen is essential for life, it can also have a detrimental effect. The oxygen molecule and other oxidizing substances in the body can extract single electrons from the large molecules that make up cell membranes (walls), thus causing them to become very reactive. In fact, these activated molecules can react with each other to change the properties of the cell membranes. If enough of these changes accumulate, the body's immune system comes to view the changed cell as "foreign" and destroys it. This action is particularly harmful to the organism if the cells involved are irreplaceable, such as nerve cells.

Because the human body is so complex, it is very difficult to pinpoint the cause or causes of aging. Scientists are therefore studying simpler life forms. For example, Rajindar Sohal (currently at the University of California) and his coworkers at Southern Methodist University in Dallas are examining aging in common houseflies. Their work indicates that the accumulated damage from oxidation is linked to both the fly's vitality and its life expectancy. One study found that flies that were forced to be sedentary (couldn't fly around) showed much less damage from oxidation (because of their lower oxygen consumption) and lived twice as long as flies that had normal activities.

Accumulated knowledge from various studies indicates that oxidation is probably a major cause of aging. If this is true, how can we protect ourselves? The best way to approach the answer to this question is to study the body's natural defenses against oxidation. A study by Russel J. Reiter of the Texas Health Science Center at San Antonio has shown that melatonin—a chemical secreted by the pineal gland in the brain (but only at night)—protects against oxidation. In addition, it has long been known that vitamin E is an antioxidant. Studies have shown that red blood cells deficient in vitamin E age much faster than cells with normal vitamin E levels. On the basis of this type of evidence many people take daily doses of vitamin E to ward off the effects of aging.

Studies at the Center for Human Nutrition and Aging at Tufts University suggest that a diet rich in antioxidants can reduce the effects of brain aging. Rats that were fed a diet high in antioxidants appeared to have better memory and improved motor skills compared to rats that received a normal diet. Elderly rats fed blueberry diets even recovered some memory and motor skills lost as a result of normal brain aging.

Oxidation is only one possible cause of aging. Research continues on many fronts to find out why we get "older" as time passes.

Abiggerboat Inc/Iconica/Getty Images

Foods that contain natural antioxidants.

Test Bank: 50–66

Section 18.4

TEACHING TIPS

- Use the concept of half-reactions to emphasize that oxidation cannot occur without reduction, and vice versa.
- Students need help identifying the half-reactions. Writing half-reactions depends on correctly assigning oxidation states in compounds.
- Be sure that students balance both atoms and charges in the half-reactions. A common error is for students to place the electrons on the wrong side of the half-reaction.
- Remind students to equalize the number of electrons transferred. They often forget to do so when they begin to work with these equations. Explain that the electrons are transferred and so must be accounted for. This requirement means the number gained must equal the number lost.
- These reactions take time and practice to learn to balance. Students need to pay close attention to the details of the balancing process. Learning to use the half-reaction method on relatively simple equations makes it easier to balance more difficult equations later.

18.4 Balancing Oxidation–Reduction Reactions by the Half-Reaction Method

OBJECTIVE: To learn to balance oxidation–reduction equations by using half-reactions.

Many oxidation–reduction reactions can be balanced readily by trial and error. That is, we use the procedure described in Chapter 6 to find a set of coefficients that give the same number of each type of atom on both sides of the equation.

However, the oxidation–reduction reactions that occur in aqueous solution are often so complicated that it becomes very tedious to balance them by trial and error. In this section we will develop a systematic approach for balancing the equations for these reactions.

To balance the equations for oxidation–reduction reactions that occur in aqueous solution, we separate the reaction into two half-reactions. **Half-reactions** are equations that have electrons as reactants or products. One half-reaction represents a reduction process and the other half-reaction represents an oxidation process. In a reduction half-reaction, electrons are shown on the reactant side (electrons are gained by a reactant in the equation). In an oxidation half-reaction, the electrons are shown on the product side (electrons are lost by a reactant in the equation).

For example, consider the unbalanced equation for the oxidation–reduction reaction between the cerium(IV) ion and the tin(II) ion.

$$Ce^{4+}(aq) + Sn^{2+}(aq) \rightarrow Ce^{3+}(aq) + Sn^{4+}(aq)$$

This reaction can be separated into a half-reaction involving the substance being *reduced:*

Ce^{4+} gains $1e^-$ to form Ce^{3+} and is thus reduced.

$$e^- + Ce^{4+}(aq) \rightarrow Ce^{3+}(aq) \quad \text{reduction half-reaction}$$

and a half-reaction involving the substance being *oxidized:*

Sn^{2+} loses $2e^-$ to form Sn^{4+} and is thus oxidized.

$$Sn^{2+}(aq) \rightarrow Sn^{4+}(aq) + 2e^- \quad \text{oxidation half-reaction}$$

Notice that Ce^{4+} must gain one electron to become Ce^{3+}, so one electron is shown as a reactant along with Ce^{4+} in this half-reaction. On the other hand, for Sn^{2+} to become Sn^{4+}, it must lose two electrons. This means that two electrons must be shown as products in this half-reaction.

The key principle in balancing oxidation–reduction reactions is that the number of electrons lost (from the reactant that is oxidized) must equal the number of electrons gained (from the reactant that is reduced).

Number of electrons lost ← must be equal to → Number of electrons gained

In the half-reactions shown above, one electron is gained by each Ce^{4+} while two electrons are lost by each Sn^{2+}. We must equalize the number of electrons gained and lost. To do this, we first multiply the reduction half-reaction by 2.

$$2e^- + 2Ce^{4+} \rightarrow 2Ce^{3+}$$

Then we add this half-reaction to the oxidation half-reaction.

$$\begin{array}{r} 2e^- + 2Ce^{4+} \rightarrow 2Ce^{3+} \\ Sn^{2+} \rightarrow Sn^{4+} + 2e^- \\ \hline 2e^- + 2Ce^{4+} + Sn^{2+} \rightarrow 2Ce^{3+} + Sn^{4+} + 2e^- \end{array}$$

Finally, we cancel the $2e^-$ on each side to give the overall balanced equation

$$2e^- + 2Ce^{4+} + Sn^{2+} \rightarrow 2Ce^{3+} + Sn^{4+} + 2e^-$$
$$2Ce^{4+} + Sn^{2+} \rightarrow 2Ce^{3+} + Sn^{4+}$$

We can now summarize what we have said about the method for balancing oxidation–reduction reactions in aqueous solution:

1. Separate the reaction into an oxidation half-reaction and a reduction half-reaction.
2. Balance the half-reactions separately.
3. Equalize the number of electrons gained and lost.
4. Add the half-reactions together and cancel electrons to give the overall balanced equation.

It turns out that most oxidation–reduction reactions occur in solutions that are distinctly basic or distinctly acidic. We will cover only the acidic case in this text, because it is the most common. The detailed procedure for balancing the equations for oxidation–reduction reactions that occur in acidic solution is given below, and Example 18.5 illustrates the use of these steps.

The Half-Reaction Method for Balancing Equations for Oxidation–Reduction Reactions Occurring in Acidic Solution

Step 1 Identify and write the equations for the oxidation and reduction half-reactions.

Step 2 For each half-reaction:
a. Balance all of the elements except hydrogen and oxygen.
b. Balance oxygen using H_2O.
c. Balance hydrogen using H^+.
d. Balance the charge using electrons.

Step 3 If necessary, multiply one or both balanced half-reactions by an integer to equalize the number of electrons transferred in the two half-reactions.

Step 4 Add the half-reactions, and cancel identical species that appear on both sides.

Step 5 Check to be sure the elements and charges balance.

EXAMPLE 18.5

Balancing Oxidation–Reduction Reactions Using the Half-Reaction Method, I

H_2O and H^+ will be added to this equation as we balance it. We do not have to worry about them now.

Balance the equation for the reaction between permanganate and iron(II) ions in acidic solution. The net ionic equation for this reaction is

$$MnO_4^-(aq) + Fe^{2+}(aq) \xrightarrow{\text{Acid}} Fe^{3+}(aq) + Mn^{2+}(aq)$$

This reaction is used to analyze iron ore for its iron content.

Additional Examples

Example 18.5

Balance each of the following oxidation–reduction reactions using the half-reaction method.

1. $Ce^{4+}(aq) + H_3AsO_3(aq) \rightarrow Ce^{3+}(aq) + H_3AsO_4(aq)$

   $2Ce^{4+}(aq) + H_3AsO_3(aq) + H_2O(l) \rightarrow Ce^{3+}(aq) + H_3AsO_4(aq) + 2H^+(aq)$

2. $MnO_4^-(aq) + I^-(aq) \rightarrow Mn^{2+}(aq) + I_2(s)$

   $2MnO_4^-(aq) + 10I^-(aq) + 16H^+(aq) \rightarrow 2Mn^{2+}(aq) + 5I_2(s) + 8H_2O(l)$

PowerLecture Video: Reaction: $MnO_4^- + Fe^{2+}$

SOLUTION

Step 1 *Identify and write equations for the half-reactions.*
The oxidation states for the half-reaction involving the permanganate ion show that manganese is reduced.

Note that the left side contains oxygen but the right side does not. This will be taken care of later when we add water.

$$\underset{+7 \quad -2 \text{ (each O)}}{MnO_4^-} \rightarrow \underset{+2}{Mn^{2+}}$$

Because manganese changes from an oxidation state of +7 to +2, it is reduced. So this is the *reduction half-reaction*. It will have electrons as reactants, although we will not write them yet. The other half-reaction involves the oxidation of iron(II) to the iron(III) ion and is the *oxidation half-reaction.*

$$\underset{+2}{Fe^{2+}} \rightarrow \underset{+3}{Fe^{3+}}$$

This reaction will have electrons as products, although we will not write them yet.

Step 2 *Balance each half-reaction.*
For the reduction reaction, we have

$$MnO_4^- \rightarrow Mn^{2+}$$

a. The manganese is already balanced.

b. We balance oxygen by adding $4H_2O$ to the right side of the equation.

$$MnO_4^- \rightarrow Mn^{2+} + 4H_2O$$

The H^+ comes from the acidic solution in which the reaction is taking place.

c. Next we balance hydrogen by adding $8H^+$ to the left side.

$$8H^+ + MnO_4^- \rightarrow Mn^{2+} + 4H_2O$$

d. All of the elements have been balanced, but we need to balance the charge using electrons. At this point we have the following charges for reactants and products in the reduction half-reaction.

$$\underbrace{8H^+ + MnO_4^-}_{8+ \ + \ 1- \ = \ 7+} \rightarrow \underbrace{Mn^{2+} + 4H_2O}_{2+ \ + \ 0 \ = \ 2+}$$

A solution containing MnO_4^- ions (*left*) and a solution containing Fe^{2+} ions (*right*).

Ken O'Donoghue

594 Chapter 18 Oxidation–Reduction Reactions and Electrochemistry

Always add electrons to the side of the half-reaction with excess positive charge.

We can equalize the charges by adding five electrons to the left side.

$$\underbrace{5e^- + 8H^+ + MnO_4^-}_{2+} \rightarrow \underbrace{Mn^{2+} + 4H_2O}_{2+}$$

Both the *elements* and the *charges* are now balanced, so this represents the balanced reduction half-reaction. The fact that five electrons appear on the reactant side of the equation makes sense, because five electrons are required to reduce MnO_4^- (in which Mn has an oxidation state of +7) to Mn^{2+} (in which Mn has an oxidation state of +2).

For the oxidation reaction,

$$Fe^{2+} \rightarrow Fe^{3+}$$

the elements are balanced, so all we have to do is balance the charge.

$$\underbrace{Fe^{2+}}_{2+} \rightarrow \underbrace{Fe^{3+}}_{3+}$$

One electron is needed on the right side to give a net 2+ charge on both sides.

$$\underbrace{Fe^{2+}}_{2+} \rightarrow \underbrace{Fe^{3+} + e^-}_{2+}$$

The number of electrons gained in the reduction half-reaction must equal the number of electrons lost in the oxidation half-reaction.

Step 3 *Equalize the number of electrons transferred in the two half-reactions.* Because the reduction half-reaction involves a transfer of five electrons and the oxidation half-reaction involves a transfer of only one electron, the oxidation half-reaction must be multiplied by 5.

$$5Fe^{2+} \rightarrow 5Fe^{3+} + 5e^-$$

Step 4 *Add the half-reactions and cancel identical species.*

$$5e^- + 8H^+ + MnO_4^- \rightarrow Mn^{2+} + 4H_2O$$
$$5Fe^{2+} \rightarrow 5Fe^{3+} + 5e^-$$
$$\cancel{5e^-} + 8H^+ + MnO_4^- + 5Fe^{2+} \rightarrow Mn^{2+} + 5Fe^{3+} + 4H_2O + \cancel{5e^-}$$

Note that the electrons cancel (as they must) to give the final balanced equation

$$5Fe^{2+}(aq) + MnO_4^-(aq) + 8H^+(aq) \rightarrow 5Fe^{3+}(aq) + Mn^{2+}(aq) + 4H_2O(l)$$

Note that we show the physical states of the reactants and products—(*aq*) and (*l*) in this case—only in the final balanced equation.

Step 5 *Check to be sure that elements and charges balance.*

Elements 5Fe, 1Mn, 4O, 8H → 5Fe, 1Mn, 4O, 8H
Charges 17+ → 17+

The equation is balanced.

EXAMPLE 18.6

Balancing Oxidation–Reduction Reactions Using the Half-Reaction Method, II

When an automobile engine is started, it uses the energy supplied by a lead storage battery. This battery uses an oxidation–reduction reaction between elemental lead (lead metal) and lead(IV) oxide to provide the power to start

Additional Examples

Example 18.6

Balance each of the following oxidation–reduction reactions using the half-reaction method.

1. $MnO_4^-(aq) + C_2O_4^{2-}(aq) \rightarrow Mn^{2+}(aq) + CO_2(g)$

   $2MnO_4^-(aq) + 5C_2O_4^{2-}(aq) + 16H^+(aq) \rightarrow 2Mn^{2+}(aq) + 10CO_2(g) + 8H_2O(l)$

2. $BiO_3^-(aq) + Mn^{2+}(aq) \rightarrow Bi^{3+}(aq) + MnO_4^-(aq)$

   $5BiO_3^-(aq) + 2Mn^{2+}(aq) + 14H^+(aq) \rightarrow 5Bi^{3+}(aq) + 2MnO_4^-(aq) + 7H_2O(l)$

the engine. The unbalanced equation for a simplified version of the reaction is

$$Pb(s) + PbO_2(s) + H^+(aq) \rightarrow Pb^{2+}(aq) + H_2O(l)$$

Balance this equation using the half-reaction method.

SOLUTION

Step 1 First we identify and write the two half-reactions. One half-reaction must be

$$Pb \rightarrow Pb^{2+}$$

and the other is

$$PbO_2 \rightarrow Pb^{2+}$$

Because Pb^{2+} is the only lead-containing product, it must be the product in both half-reactions.

The first reaction involves the oxidation of Pb to Pb^{2+}. The second reaction involves the reduction of Pb^{4+} (in PbO_2) to Pb^{2+}.

Step 2 Now we will balance each half-reaction separately.

The oxidation half-reaction

$$Pb \rightarrow Pb^{2+}$$

a–c. All the elements are balanced.

d. The charge on the left is zero and that on the right is +2, so we must add $2e^-$ to the right to give zero overall charge.

$$Pb \rightarrow Pb^{2+} + 2e^-$$

This half-reaction is balanced.

The reduction half-reaction

$$PbO_2 \rightarrow Pb^{2+}$$

a. All elements are balanced except O.

b. The left side has two oxygen atoms and the right side has none, so we add $2H_2O$ to the right side.

$$PbO_2 \rightarrow Pb^{2+} + 2H_2O$$

c. Now we balance hydrogen by adding $4H^+$ to the left.

$$4H^+ + PbO_2 \rightarrow Pb^{2+} + 2H_2O$$

d. Because the left side has a +4 overall charge and the right side has a +2 charge, we must add $2e^-$ to the left side.

$$2e^- + 4H^+ + PbO_2 \rightarrow Pb^{2+} + 2H_2O$$

The half-reaction is balanced.

Step 3 Because each half-reaction involves $2e^-$, we can simply add the half-reactions as they are.

Step 4

$$\begin{array}{r} Pb \rightarrow Pb^{2+} + 2e^- \\ 2e^- + 4H^+ + PbO_2 \rightarrow Pb^{2+} + 2H_2O \\ \hline 2e^- + 4H^+ + Pb + PbO_2 \rightarrow 2Pb^{2+} + 2H_2O + 2e^- \end{array}$$

Canceling electrons gives the balanced overall equation

$$Pb(s) + PbO_2(s) + 4H^+(aq) \rightarrow 2Pb^{2+}(aq) + 2H_2O(l)$$

where the appropriate states are also indicated.

Copper metal reacting with nitric acid. The solution is colored by the presence of Cu^{2+} ions. The brown gas is NO_2, which is formed when NO reacts with O_2 in the air.

596 Chapter 18 Oxidation–Reduction Reactions and Electrochemistry

Step 5 Both the elements and the charges balance.

Elements $2Pb, 2O, 4H \rightarrow 2Pb, 2O, 4H$
Charges $4+ \rightarrow 4+$

The equation is correctly balanced.

Self-Check EXERCISE 18.4 Copper metal reacts with nitric acid, $HNO_3(aq)$, to give aqueous copper(II) nitrate, water, and nitrogen monoxide gas as products. Write and balance the equation for this reaction.

See Problems 18.45 through 18.48. ■

18.5 Electrochemistry: An Introduction

OBJECTIVES: To understand the term *electrochemistry.* • To learn to identify the components of an electrochemical (galvanic) cell.

Our lives would be very different without batteries. We would have to crank the engines in our cars by hand, wind our watches, and buy very long extension cords if we wanted to listen to a radio on a picnic. Indeed, our society sometimes seems to run on batteries. In this section and the next, we will find out how these important devices produce electrical energy.

A battery uses the energy from an oxidation–reduction reaction to produce an electric current. This is an important illustration of **electrochemistry,** *the study of the interchange of chemical and electrical energy.*

Electrochemistry involves two types of processes:

1. The production of an electric current from a chemical (oxidation–reduction) reaction
2. The use of an electric current to produce a chemical change

To understand how a redox reaction can be used to generate a current, let's reconsider the aqueous reaction between MnO_4^- and Fe^{2+} that we worked with in Example 18.5. We can break this redox reaction into the following half-reactions:

$$8H^+ + MnO_4^- + 5e^- \rightarrow Mn^{2+} + 4H_2O \quad \text{reduction}$$
$$Fe^{2+} \rightarrow Fe^{3+} + e^- \quad \text{oxidation}$$

When the reaction between MnO_4^- and Fe^{2+} occurs in solution, electrons are transferred directly as the reactants collide. No useful work is obtained from the chemical energy involved in the reaction. How can we harness this energy? The key is to *separate the oxidizing agent (electron acceptor) from the reducing agent (electron donor),* thus requiring the electron transfer to occur through a wire. That is, to get from the reducing agent to the oxidizing agent, the electrons must travel through a wire. The current produced in the wire by this electron flow can be directed through a device, such as an electric motor, to do useful work.

The energy involved in a chemical reaction is customarily not shown in the balanced equation. In the reaction of MnO_4^- with Fe^{2+}, energy is released that can be used to do useful work.

For example, consider the system illustrated in Figure 18.1. If our reasoning has been correct, electrons should flow through the wire from Fe^{2+} to MnO_4^-. However, when we construct the apparatus as shown, no flow of electrons occurs. Why? The problem is that if the electrons flowed from the right to the left compartment, the left compartment would become negatively charged and the right compartment would experience a build-up of

Self Check

Answer to Self-Check Exercise 18.4

$3Cu(s) + 8HNO_3(aq) \rightarrow 3Cu(NO_3)_2(aq) + 2NO(g) + 4H_2O(l)$

 **Test Bank: 67–73**

Section 18.5

DEMONSTRATION

Making a Galvanic Cell

Materials Two 250-mL beakers, strips of zinc and copper metal (approximately 4 in. × 1/2 in.), 1 *M* $CuSO_4$, 1 *M* $ZnSO_4$, 1 *M* KNO_3, large piece of filter paper, voltmeter (one that projects on an overhead projector is ideal), two wires with alligator clips at each end

Presentation Fill one beaker two-thirds full with $ZnSO_4$ solution and place the zinc electrode in it. Fill the second beaker two-thirds full of $CuSO_4$ and place the copper electrode in it. Connect a wire from each metal to the voltmeter. At this point the voltmeter should register 0 volts. Ask the students why this is true. No voltage registers because the circuit is incomplete (the two beakers are not connected by a "salt bridge"). Roll up the filter paper and dip it into the KNO_3 solution, wetting the entire filter paper. Then insert one end of the filter paper roll into each beaker, forming a "salt bridge." The voltmeter should register about 1 volt. Electrons can flow through the wire because ions can now flow through the "salt bridge."

Teaching Notes The solutions and electrodes can be safely stored and reused. If you don't have a voltmeter, you may be able to borrow one from the electronics classroom or purchase one at a local electronics store. Ask students to write the half-reaction equations and identify the cathode and the anode.

TEACHING TIP

Explain that electrochemical cells work differently from ordinary oxidation–reduction reactions because the half-reactions are separated from each other. The arrangement of the half-cells can be accomplished in several ways, as shown in Figure 18.4.

Lecture Demonstration: 18.1

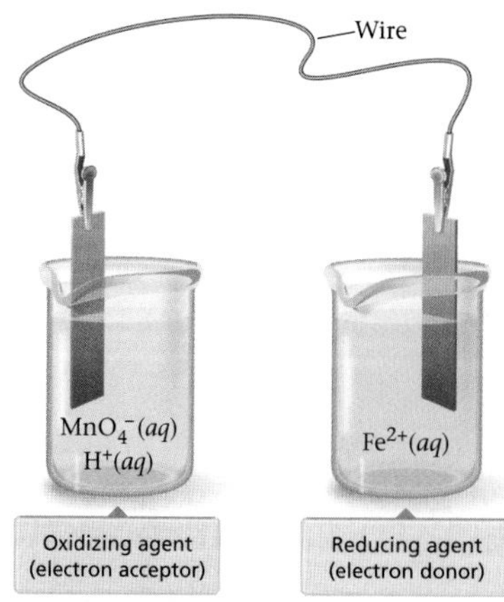

Figure 18.1
Schematic of a method for separating the oxidizing and reducing agents in a redox reaction. (The solutions also contain other ions to balance the charge.) This cell is incomplete at this point.

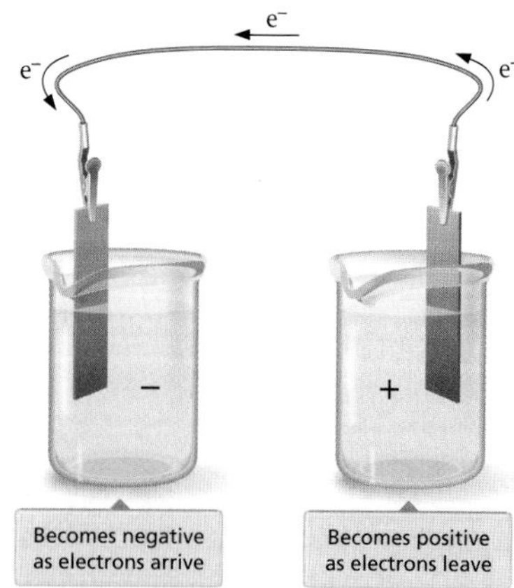

Figure 18.2
Electron flow under these conditions would lead to a build-up of negative charge on the left and positive charge on the right, which is not feasible without a huge input of energy.

PowerLecture Animation: Electron Travel in Voltaic Electrochemical Cell

positive charge (Figure 18.2). Creating a charge separation of this type would require large amounts of energy. Therefore, electron flow does not occur under these conditions.

We can, however, solve this problem very simply. The solutions must be connected (without allowing them to mix extensively) so that *ions* can also flow to keep the net charge in each compartment zero (Figure 18.3). This can be accomplished by using a salt bridge (a U-shaped tube filled with a strong electrolyte) or a porous disk in a tube connecting the two solutions (see Figure 18.4). Either of these devices allows ion flow but prevents extensive mixing of the solutions. When we make a provision for ion flow, the circuit is complete. Electrons flow through the wire from reducing agent to ox-

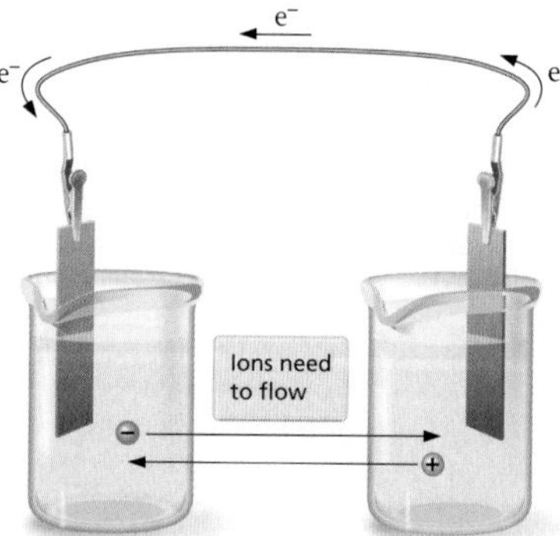

Figure 18.3
Here the ion flow between the two solutions keeps the charge neutral as electrons are transferred. This can be accomplished by having negative ions (anions) flow in the opposite direction to the electrons or by having positive ions (cations) flow in the same direction as the electrons. Both actually occur in a working battery.

Salt bridge

a The salt bridge contains a strong electrolyte either as a gel or as a solution; both ends are covered with a membrane that allows only ions to pass.

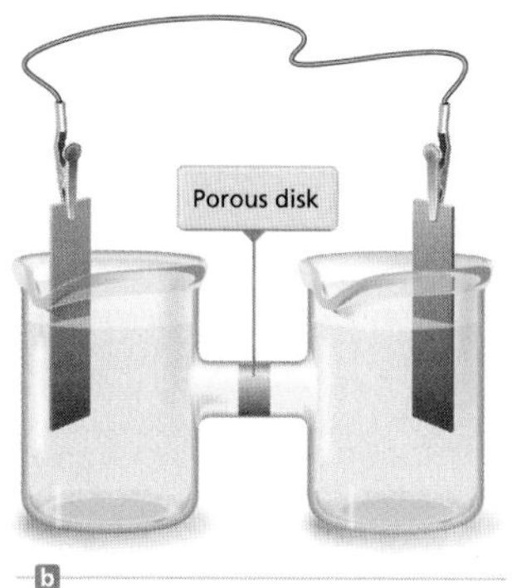

b The porous disk allows ion flow but does not permit overall mixing of the solutions in the two compartments.

Figure 18.4 A salt bridge or a porous-disk connection allows ions to flow, completing the electric circuit.

Lecture Demonstration: 17.2

PowerLecture Animation: Electrochemical Half-Reactions in a Galvanic Cell

PowerLecture Videos: Voltaic Cell: Anode Reaction
Voltaic Cell: Cathode Reaction

> The name *galvanic cell* honors Luigi Galvani (1737–1798), an Italian scientist generally credited with the discovery of electricity. These cells are sometimes called *voltaic cells* after Alessandro Volta (1745–1827), another Italian, who first constructed cells of this type around 1800.

> Anode: The electrode where oxidation occurs. Cathode: The electrode where reduction occurs.

idizing agent, and ions in the two aqueous solutions flow from one compartment to the other to keep the net charge zero.

Thus an **electrochemical battery,** also called a **galvanic cell,** is a device powered by an oxidation–reduction reaction where the oxidizing agent is separated from the reducing agent so that the electrons must travel through a wire from the reducing agent to the oxidizing agent (Figure 18.5).

Notice that in a battery, the reducing agent loses electrons (which flow through the wire toward the oxidizing agent) and so is oxidized. The electrode where oxidation occurs is called the **anode.** At the other electrode, the oxidizing agent gains electrons and is thus reduced. The electrode where reduction occurs is called the **cathode.**

We have seen that an oxidation–reduction reaction can be used to generate an electric current. In fact, this type of reaction is used to produce elec-

Alessandro Volta.

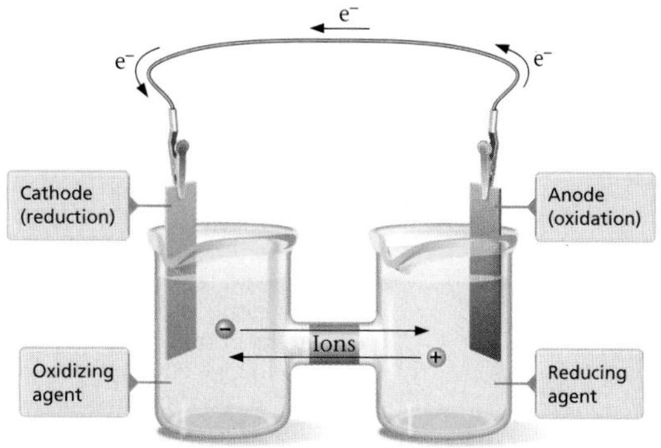

Figure 18.5 Schematic of a battery (galvanic cell).

18.5 Electrochemistry: An Introduction 599

tric currents in many space vehicles. An oxidation–reduction reaction that can be used for this purpose is hydrogen and oxygen reacting to form water.

$$2H_2(g) + O_2(g) \rightarrow 2H_2O(l)$$

Oxidation states: H_2: 0; O_2: 0; H_2O: +1 (each H), −2

Notice from the changes in oxidation states that in this reaction, hydrogen is oxidized and oxygen reduced. The opposite process can also occur. We can *force* a current through water to produce hydrogen and oxygen gas.

$$2H_2O(l) \xrightarrow[\text{energy}]{\text{Electrical}} 2H_2(g) + O_2(g)$$

This process, where *electrical energy is used to produce a chemical change,* is called **electrolysis.**

In the remainder of this chapter, we will discuss both types of electrochemical processes. In the next section we will concern ourselves with the practical galvanic cells we know as batteries.

Test Bank: 74–76

Section 18.6

TEACHING TIPS

- The remainder of this chapter explains practical applications of electrochemistry. Now is an excellent time for students to make connections between chemistry and their own lives.
- If you can obtain an old lead storage battery, drain it, and saw it in half, you can make a good model to use in class when explaining how lead storage batteries work. The model can be a permanent one for the classroom.

Lecture Demonstration: 17.7, 17.8

18.6 Batteries

OBJECTIVE: To learn about the composition and operation of commonly used batteries.

In the previous section we saw that a galvanic cell is a device that uses an oxidation–reduction reaction to generate an electric current by separating the oxidizing agent from the reducing agent. In this section we will consider several specific galvanic cells and their applications.

Lead Storage Battery

Since about 1915, when self-starters were first used in automobiles, the **lead storage battery** has been a major factor in making the automobile a practical means of transportation. This type of battery can function for several years under temperature extremes from −30 °F to 100 °F and under incessant punishment from rough roads. The fact that this same type of battery has been in use for so many years in the face of all of the changes in science and technology over that span of time attests to how well it does its job.

Remember: The oxidizing agent accepts electrons and the reducing agent furnishes electrons.

In the lead storage battery, the reducing agent is lead metal, Pb, and the oxidizing agent is lead(IV) oxide, PbO_2. We have already considered a simplified version of this reaction in Example 18.6. In an actual lead storage battery, sulfuric acid, H_2SO_4, furnishes the H^+ needed in the reaction; it also furnishes SO_4^{2-} ions that react with the Pb^{2+} ions to form solid $PbSO_4$. A schematic of one cell of the lead storage battery is shown in Figure 18.6.

In this cell the anode is constructed of lead metal, which is oxidized. In the cell reaction, lead atoms lose two electrons each to form Pb^{2+} ions, which combine with SO_4^{2-} ions present in the solution to give solid $PbSO_4$.

The cathode of this battery has lead(IV) oxide coated onto lead grids. Lead atoms in the +4 oxidation state in PbO_2 accept two electrons each (are reduced) to give Pb^{2+} ions that also form solid $PbSO_4$.

In the cell the anode and cathode are separated (so that the electrons must flow through an external wire) and bathed in sulfuric acid. The half-reactions that occur at the two electrodes and the overall cell reaction are shown on the following page.

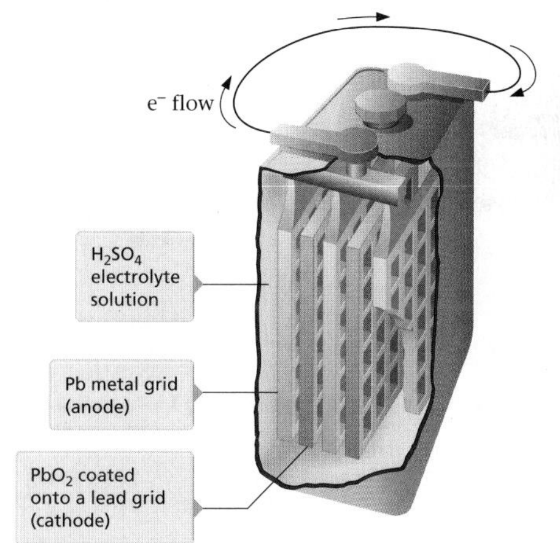

Figure 18.6
In a lead storage battery each cell consists of several lead grids that are connected by a metal bar. These lead grids furnish electrons (the lead atoms lose electrons to form Pb^{2+} ions, which combine with SO_4^{2-} ions to give solid $PbSO_4$). Because the lead is oxidized, it functions as the anode of the cell. The substance that gains electrons is PbO_2; it is coated onto lead grids, several of which are hooked together by a metal bar. The PbO_2 formally contains Pb^{4+}, which is reduced to Pb^{2+}, which in turn combines with SO_4^{2-} to form solid $PbSO_4$. The PbO_2 accepts electrons, so it functions as the cathode.

Anode reaction:

$$Pb + H_2SO_4 \rightarrow PbSO_4 + 2H^+ + 2e^- \quad \text{oxidation}$$

Cathode reaction:

$$PbO_2 + H_2SO_4 + 2e^- + 2H^+ \rightarrow PbSO_4 + 2H_2O \quad \text{reduction}$$

Overall reaction:

$$Pb(s) + PbO_2(s) + 2H_2SO_4(aq) \rightarrow 2PbSO_4(s) + 2H_2O(l)$$

The tendency for electrons to flow from the anode to the cathode in a battery depends on the ability of the reducing agent to release electrons and on the ability of the oxidizing agent to capture electrons. If a battery consists of a reducing agent that releases electrons readily and an oxidizing agent with a high affinity for electrons, the electrons are driven through the connecting wire with great force and can provide much electrical energy. It is useful to think of the analogy of water flowing through a pipe. The greater the pressure on the water, the more vigorously the water flows. The "pressure" on electrons to flow from one electrode to the other in a battery is called the **potential** of the battery and is measured in volts. For example, each cell in a lead storage battery produces about 2 volts of potential. In an actual automobile battery, six of these cells are connected to produce about 12 volts of potential.

Dry Cell Batteries

The calculators, electronic watches, CD players, and MP3 players that are so familiar to us are all powered by small, efficient **dry cell batteries.** They are called dry cells because they do not contain a liquid electrolyte. The common dry cell battery was invented more than 100 years ago by George Leclanché (1839–1882), a French chemist. In its *acid version,* the dry cell battery contains a zinc inner case that acts as the anode and a carbon (graphite) rod in contact with a moist paste of solid MnO_2, solid NH_4Cl, and carbon

DEMONSTRATION

Lemon Power

Materials Three lemons, 3 pennies, 3 galvanized nails, 4 pieces of wire, 6 alligator clips, access to a voltmeter; a small clock is optional

Preparation/Presentation Stick one nail and one penny into each lemon, making sure that they do not touch. Connect the penny from the first lemon to the nail of the second lemon using alligator clips and a piece of wire. Connect the second and third lemons the same way. Connect the nail of the first lemon to a terminal of a voltmeter using an alligator clip and a piece of wire. Connect the penny of the third lemon to the other terminal of the voltmeter in the same way.

Discussion The juice in the lemon is acidic and contains many ions (so it can carry a charge). In this battery, electrons flow from the iron nail to the copper penny.

The lemon battery should be able to supply 1.5 V, enough to power a small clock.

Lecture Demonstration: 17.9

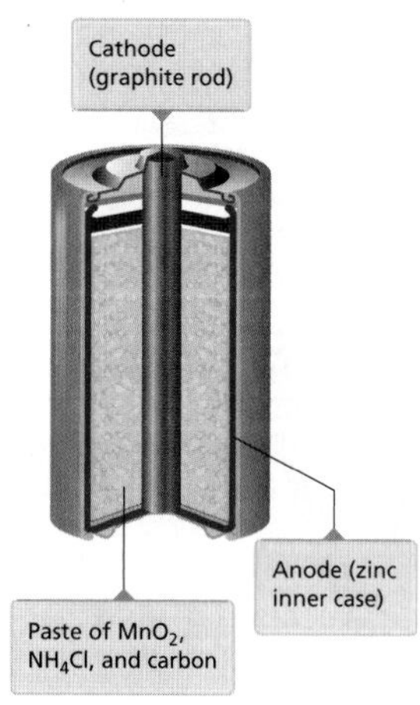

Figure 18.7
A common dry cell battery.

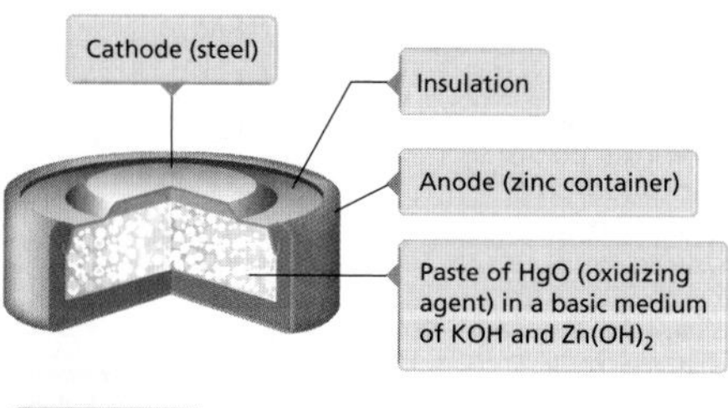

Figure 18.8
A mercury battery of the type used in small calculators.

that acts as the cathode (Figure 18.7). The half-cell reactions are complex but can be approximated as follows:

Anode reaction: $Zn \rightarrow Zn^{2+} + 2e^-$ oxidation

Cathode reaction:

$$2NH_4^+ + 2MnO_2 + 2e^- \rightarrow Mn_2O_3 + 2NH_3 + H_2O \quad \text{reduction}$$

This cell produces a potential of about 1.5 volts.

In the *alkaline version* of the dry cell battery, the NH_4Cl is replaced with KOH or NaOH. In this case the half-reactions can be approximated as follows:

Anode reaction: $Zn + 2OH^- \rightarrow ZnO(s) + H_2O + 2e^-$ oxidation

Cathode reaction: $2MnO_2 + H_2O + 2e^- \rightarrow Mn_2O_3 + 2OH^-$ reduction

The alkaline dry cell lasts longer, mainly because the zinc anode corrodes less rapidly under basic conditions than under acidic conditions.

Other types of dry cell batteries include the *silver cell,* which has a Zn anode and a cathode that employs Ag_2O as the oxidizing agent in a basic environment. *Mercury cells,* often used in calculators, have a Zn anode and a cathode involving HgO as the oxidizing agent in a basic medium (see Figure 18.8).

An especially important type of dry cell is the *nickel–cadmium battery,* in which the electrode reactions are

Anode reaction: $Cd + 2OH^- \rightarrow Cd(OH)_2 + 2e^-$ oxidation

Cathode reaction: $NiO_2 + 2H_2O + 2e^- \rightarrow Ni(OH)_2 + 2OH^-$ reduction

In this cell, as in the lead storage battery, the products adhere to the electrodes. Therefore, a nickel–cadmium battery can be recharged an indefinite number of times, because the products can be turned back into reactants by the use of an external source of current.

Lecture Demonstration: 17.10

 **Test Bank: 77–79**

Section 18.7

DEMONSTRATION

Dip a steel nail and a galvanized steel nail into two separate containers of diluted HCl for a few days. Students can compare the amount of rust formed on the two nails.

Lecture Demonstration: 17.12, 17.13

18.7 Corrosion

OBJECTIVE: To understand the electrochemical nature of corrosion and to learn some ways of preventing it.

Most metals are found in nature in compounds with nonmetals such as oxygen and sulfur. For example, iron exists as iron ore (which contains Fe_2O_3 and other oxides of iron).

PowerLecture Animations:
Diagram of Operation of Dry Cell Battery
Diagram of Operation of Alkaline Battery
Diagram of Operation of Mercury Battery
Diagram of Operation of Ni-Cad Battery
Diagram of Operation of 12-Volt Car Battery

CHEMISTRY IN FOCUS

Stainless Steel: It's the Pits

One of New York's giants, the Chrysler Building, boasts a much admired art-deco stainless steel pinnacle that has successfully resisted corrosion since it was built in 1929. Stainless steel is the nobility among steels. Consisting of iron, chromium (at least 13%), and nickel (with molybdenum and titanium added to more expensive types), stainless steel is highly resistant to the rusting that consumes regular steel. However, the cheaper grades of stainless steel have an Achilles heel—pit corrosion. In certain environments, pit corrosion can penetrate several millimeters in a matter of weeks.

Metallurgy, the science of producing useful metallic materials, almost always requires some kind of compromise. In the case of stainless steel, inclusions of MnS make the steel easier to machine into useful parts, but such inclusions are also the source of pit corrosion. Recently a group of British researchers analyzed stainless steel using a high-energy beam of ions that blasted atoms loose from the steel surface. Studies of the resultant atom vapor revealed the source of the problem. It turns out that when the stainless steel is cooling, the MnS inclusions "suck" chromium atoms from the surrounding area, leaving behind a chromium-deficient region. The corrosion occurs in this region, as illustrated in the accompanying diagram. The essential problem is that to resist corrosion steel must contain at least 13% Cr atoms. The low-chromium region around the inclusion is not stainless steel—so it corrodes just like regular steel. This corrosion leads to a pit that causes deterioration of the steel surface.

Now that the reason for the pit corrosion is understood, metallurgists should be able to develop methods of stainless steel formulation that avoid this problem. One British scientist, Mary P. Ryan, suggests that heat treatment of the stainless steel may solve the problem by allowing Cr atoms to diffuse from the inclusion back into the surrounding area. Because corrosion of regular steel is such an important issue, finding ways to make cheaper stainless steel will have a significant economic impact. We need stainless without the pits.

Built in New York in 1929, the Chrysler Building's stainless steel pinnacle has been cleaned only a few times. Despite the urban setting, the material shows few signs of corrosion.

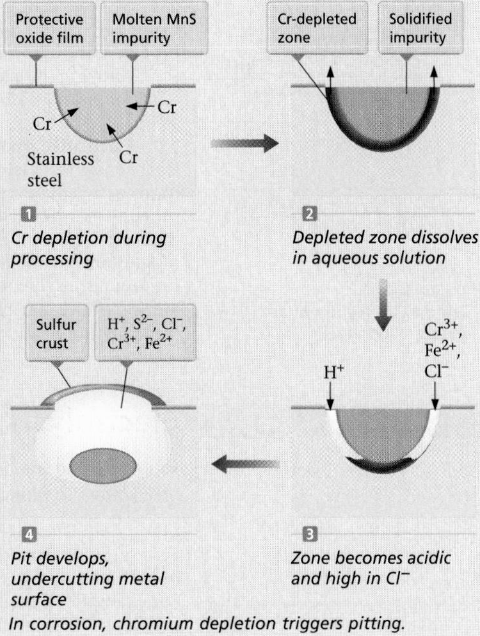

In corrosion, chromium depletion triggers pitting.

Corrosion can be viewed as the process of returning metals to their natural state—the ores from which they were originally obtained. Corrosion involves oxidation of the metal. Because corroded metal often loses its strength and attractiveness, this process causes great economic loss. For example, approximately one-fifth of the iron and steel produced annually is used to replace rusted metal.

Some metals, such as copper, gold, silver, and platinum, are relatively difficult to oxidize. They are often called noble metals.

Because most metals react with O_2, we might expect them to corrode so fast in air that they wouldn't be useful. It is surprising, therefore, that the problem of corrosion does not virtually prevent the use of metals in air. Part of the explanation is that most metals develop a thin oxide coating, which tends to protect their internal atoms against further oxidation. The best example of this is aluminum. Aluminum readily loses electrons, so it should be very easily oxidized by O_2. Given this fact, why is aluminum so useful for building airplanes, bicycle frames, and so on? Aluminum is such a valuable structural material because it forms a thin adherent layer of aluminum oxide, Al_2O_3, which greatly inhibits further corrosion. Thus aluminum protects itself with this tough oxide coat. Many other metals, such as chromium, nickel, and tin, do the same thing.

An alloy is a mixture of elements with metallic properties.

Iron can also form a protective oxide coating. However, this oxide is not a very effective shield against corrosion, because it scales off easily, exposing new metal surfaces to oxidation. Under normal atmospheric conditions, copper forms an external layer of greenish copper sulfate or carbonate called *patina*. *Silver tarnish* is silver sulfide, Ag_2S, which in thin layers gives the silver surface a richer appearance. Gold shows no appreciable corrosion in air.

Test Bank: 80

Preventing corrosion is an important way of conserving our natural supplies of metals and energy. The primary means of protection is the application of a coating—most often paint or metal plating—to protect the metal from oxygen and moisture. Chromium and tin are often used to plate steel because they oxidize to form a durable, effective oxide coating.

Alloying is also used to prevent corrosion. *Stainless steel* contains chromium and nickel, both of which form oxide coatings that protect the steel.

Cathodic protection is the method most often employed to protect steel in buried fuel tanks and pipelines. A metal that furnishes electrons more easily than iron, such as magnesium, is connected by a wire to the pipeline or tank that is to be protected (Figure 18.9). Because the magnesium is a better reducing agent than iron, electrons flow through the wire from the magnesium to the iron pipe. Thus the electrons are furnished by the magnesium rather than by the iron, keeping the iron from being oxidized. As oxidation of the magnesium occurs, the magnesium dissolves, so it must be replaced periodically.

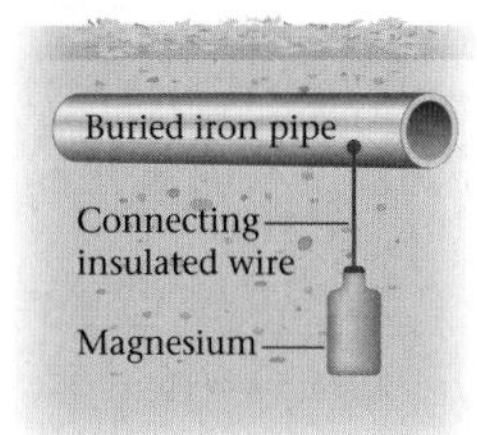

Figure 18.9
Cathodic protection of an underground pipe.

Section 18.8

TEACHING TIP

The lead storage battery is a practical example of electrolysis. Many students know that these batteries are "recharged" when the automobile engine runs. This is a good starting point for a discussion of electrolysis.

18.8 Electrolysis

OBJECTIVE: To understand the process of electrolysis and learn about the commercial preparation of aluminum.

Unless it is recharged, a battery "runs down" because the substances in it that furnish and accept electrons (to produce the electron flow) are consumed. For example, in the lead storage battery (see Section 18.6), PbO_2 and Pb are consumed to form $PbSO_4$ as the battery runs.

$$PbO_2(s) + Pb(s) + 2H_2SO_4(aq) \rightarrow 2PbSO_4(s) + 2H_2O(l)$$

PowerLecture Animations:
Redox Reaction of Iron Oxidation
Discharging and Recharging of Lead Storage Battery
Molecular Model of Protection of Aluminum from Oxidation by Oxygen

CHEMISTRY IN FOCUS

Water-Powered Fireplace

Hydrogen gas is being touted as an environmentally friendly fuel because, unlike fossil fuels, it does not produce the greenhouse gas carbon dioxide. The only product of combustion of H_2 is water. As a result, hydrogen is being investigated as a possible fuel for cars, trucks, and buses. Now comes a manufacturer, Heat & Glo, that is showcasing an in-home fireplace that uses water as the fuel. The Aqueon fireplace uses electrolysis to decompose the water to $H_2(g)$ and $O_2(g)$; the hydrogen is then burned to furnish heat for the home. The 31,000-Btu fireplace features copper and stainless steel and has a contemporary design (see accompanying photo). To operate, the fireplace is simply hooked up to the water and electrical supplies for the home.

Courtesy, Hearth & Home Technologies

However, one of the most useful characteristics of the lead storage battery is that it can be recharged. *Forcing* current through the battery in the direction opposite to the normal direction reverses the oxidation–reduction reaction. That is, $PbSO_4$ is consumed and PbO_2 and Pb are formed in the charging process. This recharging is done continuously by the automobile's alternator, which is powered by the engine.

An electrolytic cell uses electrical energy to produce a chemical change that would not otherwise occur.

The process of **electrolysis** involves *forcing a current through a cell to produce a chemical change that would not otherwise occur.*

One important example of this type of process is the electrolysis of water. Water is a very stable substance that can be broken down into its elements by using an electric current (Figure 18.10).

PowerLecture Video: Electrolysis of Water

$$2H_2O(l) \xrightarrow[\text{current}]{\text{Forced electric}} 2H_2(g) + O_2(g)$$

Charles D. Winters/Photo Researchers, Inc.

Figure 18.10
The electrolysis of water produces hydrogen gas at the cathode (on the left) and oxygen gas at the anode (on the right). A nonreacting strong electrolyte such as Na_2SO_4 is needed to furnish ions to allow the flow of current.

The electrolysis of water to produce hydrogen and oxygen occurs whenever a current is forced through an aqueous solution. Thus, when the lead storage battery is charged, or "jumped," potentially explosive mixtures of H_2 and O_2 are produced by the current flow through the solution in the battery. This is why it is very important not to produce a spark near the battery during these operations.

Another important use of electrolysis is in the production of metals from their ores. The metal produced in the greatest quantities by electrolysis is aluminum.

Aluminum is one of the most abundant elements on earth, ranking third behind oxygen and silicon. Because aluminum is a very reactive metal, it is found in nature as its oxide in an ore called *bauxite* (named after Les Baux, France, where it was discovered in 1821). Production of aluminum metal from its ore proved to be more difficult than the production of most other metals. In 1782, Lavoisier, the pioneering French chemist, recognized aluminum as a metal "whose affinity for oxygen is so strong that it cannot be overcome by any known reducing agent." As a result, pure aluminum

Figure 18.11 Charles Martin Hall (1863–1914) was a student at Oberlin College in Ohio when he first became interested in aluminum. One of his professors commented that anyone who could find a way to manufacture aluminum cheaply would make a fortune, and Hall decided to give it a try. The 21-year-old worked in a wooden shed near his house with an iron frying pan as a container, a blacksmith's forge as a heat source, and galvanic cells constructed from fruit jars. Using these crude galvanic cells, Hall found that he could produce aluminum by passing a current through a molten mixture of Al_2O_3 and Na_3AlF_6. By a strange coincidence, Paul Heroult, a French chemist who was born and died in the same years as Hall, made the same discovery at about the same time.

Lecture Demonstration: 17.15

ChemWork

Nuclear Particles

Nuclear Equations

Dating by Radioactive Decay

Decay of I-131

Radioactive Decay and Half-Life

Rate of Radioactive Decay

Calculating Nuclear Binding Energy

Properties of Nuclides

Table 18.2 The Price of Aluminum, 1855–1990

Date	Price of Aluminum ($/lb)*
1855	$100,000
1885	100
1890	2
1895	0.50
1970	0.30
1980	0.80
1990	0.74

*Note the precipitous drop in price after the discovery of the Hall-Heroult process in 1886.

metal remained unknown. Finally, in 1854, a process was found for producing metallic aluminum by using sodium, but aluminum remained a very expensive rarity. In fact, it is said that Napoleon III served his most honored guests with aluminum forks and spoons, while the others had to settle for gold and silver utensils!

The breakthrough came in 1886 when two men, Charles M. Hall in the United States (Figure 18.11) and Paul Heroult in France, almost simultaneously discovered a practical electrolytic process for producing aluminum, which greatly increased the availability of aluminum for many purposes. Table 18.2 shows how dramatically the price of aluminum dropped after this discovery. The effect of the electrolysis process is to reduce Al^{3+} ions to neutral Al atoms that form aluminum metal. The aluminum produced in this electrolytic process is 99.5% pure. To be useful as a structural material, aluminum is alloyed with metals such as zinc (for trailer and aircraft construction) and manganese (for cooking utensils, storage tanks, and highway signs). The production of aluminum consumes about 4.5% of all electricity used in the United States.

CHAPTER 18 REVIEW

Key Terms

oxidation–reduction (redox) reactions (18.1)
oxidation (18.1, 18.3)
reduction (18.1, 18.3)
oxidation states (18.2)
oxidizing agent (electron acceptor) (18.3)
reducing agent (electron donor) (18.3)
half-reactions (18.4)
electrochemistry (18.5)
electrochemical battery (galvanic cell) (18.5)
anode (18.5)
cathode (18.5)
electrolysis (18.5, 18.8)
lead storage battery (18.6)
potential (18.6)
dry cell battery (18.6)
corrosion (18.7)
cathodic protection (18.7)

Ⓕ directs you to the *Chemistry in Focus* feature in the chapter

VP indicates visual problems

OWL interactive versions of these problems are assignable in OWL

Summary

1. Oxidation–reduction reactions involve a transfer of electrons. Oxidation states provide a way to keep track of electrons in these reactions. A set of rules is used to assign oxidation states.
2. Oxidation is an increase in oxidation state (a loss of electrons); reduction is a decrease in oxidation state (a gain of electrons). An oxidizing agent accepts electrons, and a reducing agent donates electrons. Oxidation and reduction always occur together.
3. Oxidation–reduction equations can be balanced by inspection or by the half-reaction method. This method involves splitting a reaction into two parts (the oxidation half-reaction and the reduction half-reaction).
4. Electrochemistry is the study of the interchange of chemical and electrical energy that occurs through oxidation–reduction reactions.
5. When an oxidation–reduction reaction occurs with the reactants in the same solution, the electrons are transferred directly, and no useful work can be obtained. However, when the oxidizing agent is separated from the reducing agent, so that the electrons must flow through a wire from one to the other, chemical energy is transformed into electrical energy. The opposite process, in which electrical energy is used to produce chemical change, is called electrolysis.
6. A galvanic (electrochemical) cell is a device in which chemical energy is transformed into useful electrical energy. Oxidation occurs at the anode of a cell; reduction occurs at the cathode.
7. A battery is a galvanic cell, or group of cells, that serves as a source of electric current. The lead storage battery has a lead anode and a cathode of lead coated with PbO_2, both immersed in a solution of sulfuric acid. Dry cell batteries do not have liquid electrolytes but contain a moist paste instead.
8. Corrosion involves the oxidation of metals to form mainly oxides and sulfides. Some metals, such as aluminum, form a thin protective oxide coating that inhibits their further corrosion. Corrosion of iron can be prevented by a coating (such as paint), by alloying, and by cathodic protection.

Active Learning Questions

These questions are designed to be considered by groups of students in class. Often these questions work well for introducing a particular topic in class.

1. Sketch a galvanic cell, and explain how it works. Look at Figures 18.1 and 18.5. Explain what is occurring in each container and why the cell in Figure 18.5 "works," but the one in Figure 18.1 does not.
2. Make a list of nitrogen compounds with as many different oxidation states for nitrogen as you can.
3. Which of the following are oxidation–reduction reactions? Explain.
   a. $PCl_3 + Cl_2 \rightarrow PCl_5$
   b. $Cu + 2AgNO_3 \rightarrow Cu(NO_3)_2 + 2Ag$
   c. $CO_2 + 2LiOH \rightarrow Li_2CO_3 + H_2O$
   d. $FeCl_2 + 2NaOH \rightarrow Fe(OH)_2 + 2NaCl$
   e. $MnO_2 + 4HCl \rightarrow Cl_2 + 2H_2O + MnCl_2$
4. Which of the following statements is (are) true? Explain. (There may be more than one answer.)
   a. Oxidation and reduction cannot occur independently of each other.
   b. Oxidation and reduction accompany all chemical changes.
   c. Oxidation and reduction describe the loss and gain of electron(s), respectively.
5. Why do we say that when something gains electrons it is reduced? What is being reduced?
6. The equation $Ag^+ + Cu \rightarrow Cu^{2+} + Ag$ has equal numbers of each type of element on each side of the equation. This equation, however, is not balanced. Why is this equation not balanced? Balance the equation.
7. In balancing oxidation–reduction equations, why is it permissible to add water to either side of the equation?
8. What does it mean for a substance to be *oxidized*? The term "oxidation" originally came from substances reacting with oxygen gas. Explain why a substance that reacts with oxygen gas will always be oxidized.
9. VP Label the following parts of the galvanic cell.

   anode

   cathode

   reducing agent

   oxidizing agent

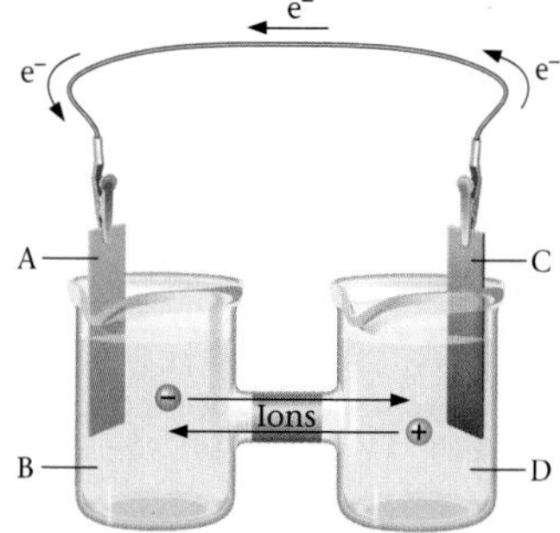

Answers to End-of-Chapter Exercises

1. batteries, corrosion and its prevention, combustion of fuels, metabolic processes, to name a few

2. Oxidation is a loss of one or more electrons by an atom or ion. Reduction is the gaining of one or more electrons by an atom or ion. Equations depend on student responses.

3. (a) chlorine is reduced; iodine is oxidized; (b) chlorine is reduced, lithium is oxidized; (c) sodium is oxidized; hydrogen is reduced; (d) bromine is oxidized; chlorine is reduced

4. (a) boron is oxidized; oxygen is reduced; (b) nitrogen is oxidized; oxygen is reduced; (c) carbon is oxidized; hydrogen is reduced; (d) magnesium is oxidized; copper is reduced

5. (a) calcium is oxidized; hydrogen is reduced; (b) hydrogen is oxidized; fluorine is reduced; (c) iron is oxidized; oxygen is reduced; (d) iron is oxidized; chlorine is reduced

6. (a) sulfur is oxidized, oxygen is reduced; (b) phosphorus is oxidized, oxygen is reduced; (c) hydrogen is oxidized, carbon is reduced; (d) boron is oxidized, hydrogen is reduced

7. The assignment of oxidation states allows us to keep track of electrons transferred between species in oxidation–reduction reactions.

8. Oxidation numbers represent a "relative charge" one atom has compared to another in a compound. In an element, all the atoms are equivalent.

9. For very electronegative elements like oxygen, we typically assign an oxidation state equal to the charge when the element forms an ion. Oxygen has an oxidation state of -1 in H_2O_2.

Questions and Problems

18.1 Oxidation–Reduction Reactions

QUESTIONS

1. Give some examples of how we make good use of oxidation–reduction reactions in everyday life.
2. How do chemists define the processes of *oxidation* and *reduction?* Write a simple equation illustrating each of your definitions.
3. For each of the following oxidation–reduction reactions, identify which element is being oxidized and which is being reduced.
   a. $Cl_2(g) + I_2(g) \rightarrow 2ICl(g)$
   b. $Cl_2(g) + 2Li(s) \rightarrow 2LiCl(s)$
   c. $2Na(s) + 2H_2O(l) \rightarrow 2NaOH(aq) + H_2(g)$
   d. $Cl_2(g) + 2NaBr(aq) \rightarrow 2NaCl(aq) + Br_2(l)$
4. For each of the following oxidation–reduction reactions, identify which element is being oxidized and which is being reduced.
   a. $4B(s) + 3O_2(g) \rightarrow 2B_2O_3(s)$
   b. $N_2(g) + 2O_2(g) \rightarrow 2NO_2(g)$
   c. $CaC_2(s) + H_2(g) \rightarrow CaH_2(g) + 2C(s)$
   d. $CuSO_4(aq) + Mg(s) \rightarrow MgSO_4(aq) + Cu(s)$
5. For each of the following oxidation–reduction reactions, identify which element is being oxidized and which is being reduced.
   a. $Ca(s) + 2H_2O(l) \rightarrow Ca(OH)_2(s, aq) + H_2(g)$
   b. $H_2(g) + F_2(g) \rightarrow 2HF(g)$
   c. $4Fe(s) + 3O_2(g) \rightarrow 2Fe_2O_3(s)$
   d. $2Fe(s) + 3Cl_2(g) \rightarrow 2FeCl_3(s)$
6. For each of the following oxidation–reduction reactions, identify which element is being oxidized and which is being reduced.
   a. $2Cr_2S_3(s) + 3O_2(g) \rightarrow 2Cr_2O_3(s) + 6S(s)$
   b. $P_4(s) + 5O_2(g) \rightarrow P_4O_{10}(s)$
   c. $CO_2(g) + H_2(g) \rightarrow CO(g) + H_2O(g)$
   d. $2B(s) + 3H_2(g) \rightarrow B_2H_6(g)$

18.2 Oxidation States

QUESTIONS

7. What is an oxidation state? Why do we define such a concept?
8. Why is the oxidation state of an element in the uncombined state equal to zero?
9. Explain why, although it is not an ionic compound, we still assign oxygen an oxidation state of −2 in water, H_2O. Give an example of a compound in which oxygen is *not* in the −2 oxidation state.
10. Why is fluorine always assigned an oxidation state of −1? What oxidation number is *usually* assigned to the other halogen elements when they occur in compounds? In an *interhalogen* compound involving fluorine (such as ClF), which atom has a negative oxidation state?
11. The sum of all the oxidation states of all the atoms in H_3PO_4 is ______.
12. The sum of all the oxidation states of all the atoms in PO_4^{3-} is ______.

PROBLEMS

13. Assign oxidation states to all of the atoms in each of the following.
    a. CBr_4 b. $HClO_4$ c. K_3PO_4 d. N_2O
14. Assign oxidation states to all of the atoms in each of the following.
    a. $CrCl_3$ b. $Ni(OH)_2$ c. H_2S d. CS_2
15. What is the oxidation state of *sulfur* in each of the following substances?
    a. S_8 b. H_2SO_4 c. $NaHSO_4$ d. Na_2S
16. What is the oxidation state of *nitrogen* in each of the following substances?
    a. N_2 b. NH_3 c. NO_2 d. $NaNO_3$
17. What is the oxidation state of *chlorine* in each of the following substances?
    a. ClF b. Cl_2 c. HCl d. HClO
18. What is the oxidation state of *manganese* in each of the following substances?
    a. $MnCl_2$ b. $KMnO_4$ c. MnO_2 d. $Mn(C_2H_3O_2)_3$
19. Assign oxidation states to all of the atoms in each of the following.
    a. $CuCl_2$ b. $KClO_3$ c. $KClO_4$ d. Na_2CO_3
20. Assign oxidation states to all of the atoms in each of the following.
    a. CaO b. Al_2O_3 c. PF_3 d. P_2O_5
21. Assign oxidation states to all of the atoms in each of the following ions:
    a. CO_3^{2-} b. NO_3^- c. PO_4^{3-} d. SO_4^{2-}

All even-numbered Questions and Problems have answers in the back of this book and solutions in the Solutions Guide.

10. Because fluorine is the most electronegative element, its oxidation state is always negative relative to other elements; because fluorine gains only one electron to complete its outermost shell, its oxidation number in compounds is always −1. The other halogen elements are almost always more electronegative than the atoms to which they bond, and almost always have −1 oxidation numbers. However, in an interhalogen compound involving fluorine and some other halogen, since fluorine is the most electronegative element of all, the other halogens in the compound will have positive oxidation states relative to fluorine.

11. zero

12. −3

13. (a) C, +4; Br, −1; (b) H, +1; Cl, +7; O, −2; (c) K, +1; P, +5; O, −2; (d) N, +1; O, −2

14. (a) Cr, +3; Cl, −1; (b) Ni, +2; O, −2; H, +1; (c) H, +1; S, −2; (d) C, +4; S, −2

15. (a) 0; (b) +6; (c) +6; (d) −2

16. (a) 0; (b) −3; (c) +4; (d) +5

17. (a) +1; (b) 0; (c) −1; (d) +1

18. (a) +2; (b) +7; (c) +4; (d) +3

19. (a) Cu, +2; Cl, −1; (b) K, +1; Cl, +5; O, −2; (c) K, +1; Cl, +7; O, −2; (d) Na, +1; C, +4; O, −2

20. (a) Ca, +2; O, −2; (b) Al, +3; O, −2; (c) P, +3; F, −1; (d) P, +5; O, −2

21. (a) C, +4; O, −2; (b) N, +5; O, −2; (c) P, +5; O, −2; (d) S, +6; O, −2

22. (a) H, +1; S, +6; O, −2; (b) Mn, +7; O, −2; (c) Cl, +5; O, −2; (d) Br, +7; O, −2

23. Losing an electron means losing negative charge; therefore, whatever is left after the electron is lost is more positive than it was before.

24. Electrons are negative; when an atom gains electrons, it gains one negative charge for each electron gained. For example, in the reduction reaction $Cl + e^- \rightarrow Cl^-$, the oxidation state of chlorine decreases from 0 to −1 as the electron is gained.

25. An oxidizing agent is a species that causes something else to be oxidized (while itself being reduced). A reducing agent is a species that causes something else to be reduced (while itself being oxidized).

26. Answer depends on student selection of example.

27. Oxidizing agents accept electrons; reducing agents donate them.

28. An antioxidant is a substance that prevents oxidation of some molecule in the body. It is not certain how all antioxidants work, but one example is

22. Assign oxidation states to all of the atoms in each of the following ions:

a. HSO_4^-　　c. ClO_3^-
b. MnO_4^-　　d. BrO_4^-

18.3 Oxidation–Reduction Reactions Between Nonmetals

QUESTIONS

23. Oxidation can be defined as a loss of electrons or as an increase in oxidation state. Explain why the two definitions mean the same thing, and give an example to support your explanation.

24. Reduction can be defined as a gain of electrons or as a decrease in oxidation state. Explain why the two definitions mean the same thing, and give an example to support your explanation.

25. What is an oxidizing agent? What is a reducing agent?

26. Give an example of a simple oxidation–reduction equation. Identify the species being oxidized and the species being reduced. Identify the oxidizing agent and the reducing agent in your example.

27. Does an oxidizing agent donate or accept electrons? Does a reducing agent donate or accept electrons?

F 28. The "Chemistry in Focus" segment *Do We Age by Oxidation?* discusses antioxidants. What does it mean for a chemical to be an antioxidant? How would it work chemically?

PROBLEMS

29. In each of the following reactions, identify which element is being oxidized and which is being reduced by assigning oxidation numbers.

a. $Fe(s) + CuSO_4(aq) \rightarrow FeSO_4(aq) + Cu(s)$
b. $Cl_2(g) + 2NaBr(aq) \rightarrow 2NaCl(aq) + Br_2(l)$
c. $3CuS(s) + 8HNO_3(aq) \rightarrow 3CuSO_4(aq) + 8NO(g) + 4H_2O(l)$
d. $2Zn(s) + O_2(g) \rightarrow 2ZnO(s)$

30. In each of the following reactions, identify which element is being oxidized and which is being reduced by assigning oxidation numbers.

a. $2Al(s) + 3S(s) \rightarrow Al_2S_3(s)$
b. $CH_4(g) + 2O_2(g) \rightarrow CO_2(g) + 2H_2O(g)$
c. $2Fe_2O_3(s) + 3C(s) \rightarrow 3CO_2(g) + 4Fe(s, l)$
d. $K_2Cr_2O_7(aq) + 14HCl(aq) \rightarrow 2KCl(aq) + 2CrCl_3(s) + 7H_2O(l) + 3Cl_2(g)$

31. In each of the following reactions, identify which element is being oxidized and which is being reduced by assigning oxidation states.

a. $2Cu(s) + S(s) \rightarrow Cu_2S(s)$
b. $2Cu_2O(s) + O_2(g) \rightarrow 4CuO(s)$
c. $4B(s) + 3O_2(g) \rightarrow 2B_2O_3(s)$
d. $6Na(s) + N_2(g) \rightarrow 2Na_3N(s)$

32. In each of the following reactions, identify which element is being oxidized and which is being reduced by assigning oxidation numbers.

a. $4KClO_3(s) + C_6H_{12}O_6(s) \rightarrow 4KCl(s) + 6H_2O(l) + 6CO_2(g)$
b. $2C_8H_{18}(l) + 25O_2(g) \rightarrow 16CO_2(g) + 18H_2O(l)$
c. $PCl_3(g) + Cl_2(g) \rightarrow PCl_5(g)$
d. $Ca(s) + H_2(g) \rightarrow CaH_2(g)$

33. Pennies in the United States consist of a zinc core that is electroplated with a thin coating of copper. Zinc dissolves in hydrochloric acid, but copper does not. If a small scratch is made on the surface of a penny, it is possible to dissolve away the zinc core, leaving only the thin shell of copper. Identify which element is oxidized and which is reduced in the reaction for the dissolving of the zinc by the acid.

$$Zn(s) + 2HCl(aq) \rightarrow ZnCl_2(aq) + H_2(g)$$

34. Iron ores, usually oxides of iron, are converted to the pure metal by reaction in a blast furnace with carbon (coke). The carbon is first reacted with air to form carbon monoxide, which in turn reacts with the iron oxides as follows:

$$F_2O_3(s) + 3CO(g) \rightarrow 2Fe(l) + 3CO_2(g)$$

Identify the atoms that are oxidized and reduced, and specify the oxidizing and reducing agents.

35. Although magnesium metal does not react with water at room temperature, it does react vigorously with steam at higher temperatures, releasing elemental hydrogen gas from the water.

$$Mg(s) + 2H_2O(g) \rightarrow Mg(OH)_2(s) + H_2(g)$$

Identify which element is being oxidized and which is being reduced.

36. Potassium iodide in solution reacts readily with many reagents. In the following reactions, identify the atoms that are being oxidized and reduced, and specify the oxidizing and reducing agents.

a. $Cl_2(g) + KI(aq) \rightarrow KCl(aq) + I_2(s)$
b. $2FeCl_3(aq) + 2KI(aq) \rightarrow 2FeCl_2(aq) + 2KCl(aq) + I_2(s)$
c. $2CuCl_2(aq) + 4KI(aq) \rightarrow 2CuI(s) + 4KCl(aq) + I_2(s)$

18.4 Balancing Oxidation–Reduction Reactions by the Half-Reaction Method

QUESTIONS

37. In what *two* respects must oxidation–reduction reactions be balanced?

38. Why is a systematic method for balancing oxidation–reduction reactions necessary? Why can't these equations be balanced readily by inspection?

All even-numbered Questions and Problems have answers in the back of this book and solutions in the Solutions Guide.

in preventing oxygen molecules and other substances from stripping electrons from cell membranes, leaving them vulnerable to destruction by the immune system.

29. (a) iron is oxidized; copper is reduced; (b) bromine is oxidized; chlorine is reduced; (c) sulfur is oxidized; nitrogen is reduced; (d) zinc is oxidized; oxygen is reduced

30. (a) aluminum is oxidized; sulfur is reduced; (b) carbon is oxidized; oxygen is reduced; (c) carbon is oxidized; iron is reduced; (d) chlorine is oxidized; chromium is reduced

31. (a) copper is oxidized, sulfur is reduced; (b) copper is oxidized, oxygen (of O_2) is reduced; (c) boron is oxidized, oxygen is reduced; (d) sodium is oxidized, nitrogen is reduced

32. (a) carbon is oxidized, chlorine is reduced; (b) carbon is oxidized, oxygen is reduced; (c) phosphorus is oxidized, chlorine is reduced; (d) calcium is oxidized, hydrogen is reduced

33. zinc is oxidized, hydrogen ion is reduced

34. Iron is reduced [+3 in $Fe_2O_3(s)$, 0 in $Fe(l)$]; carbon is oxidized [+2 in $CO(g)$, +4 in $CO_2(g)$]. $Fe_2O_3(s)$ is the oxidizing agent; $CO(g)$ is the reducing agent.

35. magnesium is oxidized, hydrogen is reduced

36. (a) chlorine is reduced, iodine is oxidized; chlorine is the oxidizing agent, iodide ion is the reducing agent; (b) iron is reduced, iodine is oxidized; iron(III) is the oxidizing agent, iodide ion is the reducing agent; (c) copper is reduced, iodine is oxidized; copper(II) is the oxidizing agent, iodide ion is the reducing agent

37. mass and charge

38. Oxidation–reduction reactions are often more complicated than "regular" reactions; the coefficients necessary to balance the number of electrons transferred are often large numbers.

39. When an overall equation is split into separate partial equations representing the oxidation and the reduction processes separately, the partial equations are called *half-reactions.*

40. Under ordinary conditions it is impossible to have "free" electrons that are not part of some atom, ion, or molecule. Thus, the total number of electrons lost by the species being oxidized must equal the total number of electrons gained by the species being reduced.

41. (a) $Cu \rightarrow Cu^{2+} + 2e^-$; (b) $Fe^{3+} + e^- \rightarrow Fe^{2+}$; (c) $2Br^- \rightarrow Br_2 + 2e^-$; (d) $Fe^{2+} + 2e^- \rightarrow Fe$

42. (a) $2Cl^-(aq) \rightarrow Cl_2(g) + 2e^-$; (b) $Fe^{2+}(aq) \rightarrow Fe^{3+}(aq) + e^-$; (c) $Fe(s) \rightarrow Fe^{3+}(aq) + 3e^-$; (d) $Cu^{2+}(aq) + e^- \rightarrow Cu^+(aq)$

39. What is a half-reaction? What does each of the two half-reactions that make up an overall process represent?

40. Why must the number of electrons lost in the oxidation equal the number of electrons gained in the reduction? Is it possible to have "leftover" electrons in a reaction?

PROBLEMS

41. Balance each of the following half-reactions.

a. $Cu(s) \rightarrow Cu^{2+}(aq)$
b. $Fe^{3+}(aq) \rightarrow Fe^{2+}(aq)$
c. $Br^-(aq) \rightarrow Br_2(l)$
d. $Fe^{2+}(aq) \rightarrow Fe(s)$

42. Balance each of the following half-reactions.

a. $Cl^-(aq) \rightarrow Cl_2(g)$
b. $Fe^{2+}(aq) \rightarrow Fe^{3+}(aq)$
c. $Fe(s) \rightarrow Fe^{3+}(aq)$
d. $Cu^{2+}(aq) \rightarrow Cu^+(aq)$

43. Balance each of the following half-reactions, which take place in acidic solution.

a. $HClO(aq) \rightarrow Cl^-(aq)$
b. $NO(aq) \rightarrow N_2O(g)$
c. $N_2O(aq) \rightarrow N_2(g)$
d. $ClO_3^-(aq) \rightarrow HClO_2(aq)$

44. Balance each of the following half-reactions, which take place in acidic solution.

a. $O_2(g) \rightarrow H_2O(l)$
b. $SO_4^{2-}(aq) \rightarrow H_2SO_3(aq)$
c. $H_2O_2(aq) \rightarrow H_2O(l)$
d. $NO_2^-(aq) \rightarrow NO_3^-(aq)$

45. Balance each of the following oxidation–reduction reactions, which take place in acidic solution, by using the "half-reaction" method.

a. $Mg(s) + Hg^{2+}(aq) \rightarrow Mg^{2+}(aq) + Hg_2^{2+}(aq)$
b. $NO_3^-(aq) + Br^-(aq) \rightarrow NO(g) + Br_2(l)$
c. $Ni(s) + NO_3^-(aq) \rightarrow Ni^{2+}(aq) + NO_2(g)$
d. $ClO_4^-(aq) + Cl^-(aq) \rightarrow ClO_3^-(aq) + Cl_2(g)$

46. Balance each of the following oxidation–reduction reactions, which take place in acidic solution, by using the "half-reaction" method.

a. $Al(s) + H^+(aq) \rightarrow Al^{3+}(aq) + H_2(g)$
b. $S^{2-}(aq) + NO_3^-(aq) \rightarrow S(s) + NO(g)$
c. $I_2(aq) + Cl_2(aq) \rightarrow IO_3^-(aq) + HCl(g)$
d. $AsO_4^-(aq) + S^{2-}(aq) \rightarrow AsO_3^-(aq) + S(s)$

47. Iodide ion, I^-, is one of the most easily oxidized species. Balance each of the following oxidation–reduction reactions, which take place in acidic solution, by using the "half-reaction" method.

a. $IO_3^-(aq) + I^-(aq) \rightarrow I_2(aq)$
b. $Cr_2O_7^{2-}(aq) + I^-(aq) \rightarrow Cr^{3+}(aq) + I_2(aq)$
c. $Cu^{2+}(aq) + I^-(aq) \rightarrow CuI(s) + I_2(aq)$

48. Nitric acid is a very strong acid, but is also a very strong oxidizing agent, and generally behaves as the latter. It will dissolve many metals. Balance the following oxidation–reduction reactions of nitric acid.

a. $Cu(s) + HNO_3(aq) \rightarrow Cu^{2+}(aq) + NO_2(g)$
b. $Mg(s) + HNO_3(aq) \rightarrow Mg^{2+}(aq) + H_2(g)$

18.5 Electrochemistry: An Introduction

QUESTIONS

49. Sketch a schematic representation of a typical galvanic cell, using a reaction of your choice. Indicate the direction of electron flow in your cell. How are the solutions placed in electrical contact to allow charge to balance between the chambers of the cell?

50. What is a salt bridge? Why is a salt bridge necessary in a galvanic cell? Can some other method be used in place of the salt bridge?

51. In which direction do electrons flow in a galvanic cell, from anode to cathode or vice versa?

52. What type of reaction takes place at the cathode in a galvanic cell? At the anode?

PROBLEMS

53. Consider the oxidation–reduction reaction

$$Al(s) + Ni^{2+}(aq) \rightarrow Al^{3+}(aq) + Ni(s)$$

Sketch a galvanic cell that makes use of this reaction. Which metal ion is reduced? Which metal is oxidized? What half-reaction takes place at the anode in the cell? What half-reaction takes place at the cathode?

54. Consider the oxidation–reduction reaction

$$Zn(s) + Pb^{2+}(aq) \rightarrow Zn^{2+}(aq) + Pb(s)$$

Sketch a galvanic cell that uses this reaction. Which metal ion is reduced? Which metal is oxidized? What half-reaction takes place at the anode in the cell? What half-reaction takes place at the cathode?

18.6 Batteries

QUESTIONS

55. Write the chemical equation for the overall cell reaction that occurs in a lead storage automobile battery. What species is oxidized in such a battery? What species is reduced? Why can such a battery be "recharged"?

56. Nickel–cadmium ("nicad") batteries are very common because, unlike ordinary dry cell batteries, they can be recharged an indefinite number of times. Write the half-reactions for the oxidation and reduction reactions that take place when a nicad battery operates.

All even-numbered Questions and Problems have answers in the back of this book and solutions in the Solutions Guide.

43. (a) $2e^- + H^+ + HClO \rightarrow Cl^- + H_2O$; (b) $2e^- + 2H^+ + 2NO \rightarrow N_2O + H_2O$; (c) $2e^- + 2H^+ + N_2O \rightarrow N_2 + H_2O$; (d) $3H^+ + 2e^- + ClO_3^- \rightarrow HClO_2 + H_2O$

44. (a) $4H^+ + 4e^- + O_2 \rightarrow 2H_2O$; (b) $4H^+ + 2e^- + SO_4^{2-} \rightarrow H_2SO_3 + H_2O$; (c) $2H^+ + 2e^- + H_2O_2 \rightarrow 2H_2O$; (d) $H_2O + NO_2^- \rightarrow NO_3^- + 2H^+ + 2e^-$

45. (a) $Mg + 2Hg^{2+} \rightarrow Mg^{2+} + Hg_2^{2+}$; (b) $8H^+ + 2NO_3^- + 6Br^- \rightarrow 3Br_2 + 2NO + 4H_2O$; (c) $2NO_3^- + 4H^+ + Ni \rightarrow 2NO_2 + 2H_2O + Ni^{2+}$; (d) $2H^+ + ClO_4^- + 2Cl^- \rightarrow ClO_3^- + H_2O + Cl_2$

46. (a) $2Al + 6H^+ \rightarrow 2Al^{3+} + 3H_2$; (b) $8H^+ + 2NO_3^- + 3S^{2-} \rightarrow 3S + 2NO + 4H_2O$; (c) $6H_2O + I_2 + 5Cl_2 \rightarrow 2IO_3^- + 2H^+ + 10HCl$; (d) $2H^+ + AsO_4^- + S^{2-} \rightarrow S + AsO_3^- + H_2O$

47. (a) $IO_3^- + 6H^+ + 5I^- \rightarrow 3I_2 + 3H_2O$; (b) $6I^- + Cr_2O_7^{2-} + 14H^+ \rightarrow 3I_2 + 2Cr^{3+} + 7H_2O$; (c) $2Cu^{2+} + 4I^- \rightarrow 2CuI + I_2$

48. $Cu(s) + 2HNO_3(aq) + 2H^+(aq) \rightarrow Cu^{2+}(aq) + 2NO_2(g) + 2H_2O(l)$; $Mg(s) + 2HNO_3(aq) \rightarrow Mg(NO_3)_2(aq) + H_2(g)$

49. Answer depends on student choice of reaction.

50. A salt bridge typically consists of a U-shaped tube filled with an inert electrolyte (one involving ions that are not part of the oxidation–reduction reaction). A salt bridge completes the electrical circuit in a cell. Any method that allows transfer of charge without allowing bulk mixing of the solutions may be used (another common method is to set up one half-cell in a porous cup, which is then placed in the beaker containing the second half-cell).

51. galvanic cell: electrons flow from anode (oxidation) to cathode (reduction)

52. Reduction takes place at the cathode and oxidation takes place at the anode.

53.

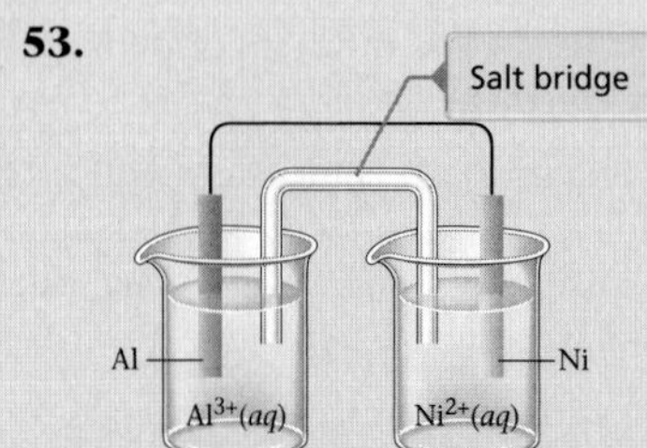

Ni^{2+} is reduced, Al(*s*) is oxidized.
Anode: $Al \rightarrow Al^{3+} + 3e^-$; cathode: $Ni^{2+} + 2e^- \rightarrow Ni$

54.

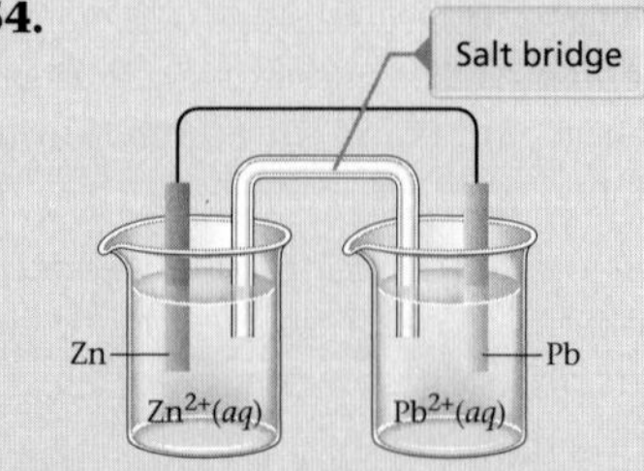

Pb^{2+} ion is reduced; Zn(*s*) is oxidized. The anode reaction is $Zn(s) \rightarrow Zn^{2+}(aq) + 2e^-$. The cathode reaction is $Pb^{2+}(aq) + 2e^- \rightarrow Pb(s)$.

18.7 Corrosion

QUESTIONS

57. What process is represented by the *corrosion* of a metal? Why is corrosion undesirable?

58. Explain how some metals, notably aluminum, naturally resist complete oxidation by the atmosphere.

59. Pure iron ordinarily rusts quickly, but steel does not corrode nearly as fast. How does steel resist corrosion?

60. The "Chemistry in Focus" segment *Stainless Steel: It's the Pits* discusses the fact that stainless steel can corrode if there is a deficit of chromium. How does chromium protect stainless steel?

18.8 Electrolysis

QUESTIONS

61. How does an *electrolysis* cell differ from a *galvanic* cell?

62. What reactions go on during the recharging of an automobile battery?

63. Although aluminum is one of the most abundant metals on earth, its price until the 1890s made it a "precious metal" like gold and platinum. Why?

64. The "Chemistry in Focus" segment *Water-Powered Fireplace* discusses a fireplace that uses the electrolysis of water to produce hydrogen gas. Write the balanced chemical equation for the electrolysis of water. Which element in water is oxidized? Which is reduced? Find the oxidation states to answer these questions. Also, how is heat generated by the fireplace?

Additional Problems

65. Reactions in which one or more ______ are transferred between species are called oxidation–reduction reactions.

66. Oxidation may be described as a(n) ______ of electrons or as an increase in ______.

67. Reduction may be described as a(n) ______ of electrons or as a decrease in ______.

68. In assigning oxidation states for a covalently bonded molecule, we assume that the more ______ element controls both electrons of the covalent bond.

69. The sum of the oxidation states of the atoms in a polyatomic ion is equal to the overall ______ of the ion.

70. What is an *oxidizing agent?* Is an oxidizing agent itself oxidized or reduced when it acts on another species?

71. An oxidizing agent causes the (oxidation/reduction) of another species, and the oxidizing agent itself is (oxidized/reduced).

72. To function as a good reducing agent, a species must ______ electrons easily.

73. When we balance an oxidation–reduction equation, the number of electrons lost by the reducing agent must ______ the number of electrons gained by the oxidizing agent.

74. To obtain useful electrical energy from an oxidation–reduction process, we must set up the reaction in such a way that the oxidation half-reaction and the reduction half-reaction are physically ______ one another.

75. An electrochemical cell that produces a current from an oxidation–reduction reaction is often called a(n) ______ cell.

76. Which process (oxidation/reduction) takes place at the anode of a galvanic cell?

77. At which electrode (anode/cathode) do species gain electrons in a galvanic cell?

78. What is an *electrolysis* reaction? Give an example of an electrolysis reaction.

79. The "pressure" on electrons to flow from one electrode to the other in a battery is called the ______ of the battery.

80. "Jump-starting" a dead automobile battery can be dangerous if precautions are not taken, because of the production of an explosive mixture of ______ and ______ gases in the battery.

81. The common acid dry cell battery typically contains an inner casing made of ______ metal, which functions as the anode.

82. Corrosion of a metal represents its ______ by species present in the atmosphere.

83. Although aluminum is a reactive metal, pure aluminum ordinarily does not corrode severely in air because a protective layer of ______ builds up on the metal's surface.

84. For each of the following unbalanced oxidation–reduction chemical equations, balance the equation by inspection, and identify which species is undergoing oxidation and which is undergoing reduction.

a. $Fe(s) + O_2(g) \rightarrow Fe_2O_3(s)$
b. $Al(s) + Cl_2(g) \rightarrow AlCl_3(s)$
c. $Mg(s) + P_4(s) \rightarrow Mg_3P_2(s)$

85. In each of the following reactions, identify which element is oxidized and which is reduced.

a. $Zn(s) + 2HCl(aq) \rightarrow ZnCl_2(aq) + H_2(g)$
b. $2CuI(s) \rightarrow CuI_2(s) + Cu(s)$
c. $6Fe^{2+}(aq) + Cr_2O_7^{2-}(aq) + 14H^+(aq) \rightarrow 6Fe^{3+}(aq) + 2Cr^{3+}(aq) + 7H_2O(l)$

All even-numbered Questions and Problems have answers in the back of this book and solutions in the Solutions Guide.

55. $Pb(s) + PbO_2(s) + 2H_2SO_4(aq) \rightarrow 2PbSO_4(s) + 2H_2O(l)$; Pb^0 is oxidized to Pb^{2+}, $Pb^{IV}O_2$ is reduced to Pb^{2+}; the battery can be recharged by passing an electric current from an outside source through the $PbSO_4$ solution.

56. $Cd + 2OH^- \rightarrow Cd(OH)_2 + 2e^-$ (oxidation); $NiO_2 + 2H_2O + 2e^- \rightarrow Ni(OH)_2 + 2OH^-$ (reduction)

57. Corrosion of a metal represents its oxidation; the metal oxide does not have the strength, flexibility, or other metallic properties of the metal itself.

58. Aluminum is a very reactive metal when freshly isolated in the pure state. Upon standing for even a relatively short period of time, aluminum metal forms a thin coating of Al_2O_3 on its surface from reaction with atmospheric oxygen. This Al_2O_3 coating is much less reactive than the metal and protects the metal's surface from further attack.

59. Chromium or nickel is added to steel; these metals form a protective oxide coating on the steel and prevent it from rusting as easily.

60. Chromium protects stainless steel by forming a thin coating of chromium oxide on the surface of the steel, which prevents oxidation of the iron in the steel.

61. In an electrolysis cell, an electric current from outside the cell is used to force an otherwise nonspontaneous oxidation–reduction reaction to occur. In a galvanic cell, a spontaneous oxidation–reduction reaction is used as a source of electric current.

62. The main recharging reaction for the lead storage battery is $2PbSO_4(s) + 2H_2O(l) \rightarrow Pb(s) + PbO_2(s) + 2H_2SO_4(aq)$. A major side reaction is the electrolysis of water, $2H_2O(l) \rightarrow 2H_2(g) + O_2(g)$, which produces an explosive mixture of hydrogen and oxygen that accounts for many accidents during the recharging of such batteries.

63. Aluminum is so reactive toward oxygen that no convenient chemical reducing agent could reduce aluminum ores to the metal. Widespread commercial preparation of aluminum became possible only when an electrolytic process was developed (see Figure 18.11).

64. The balanced equation is $2H_2O(l) \rightarrow 2H_2(g) + O_2(g)$. Oxygen is oxidized (going from −2 oxidation state in water to zero oxidation state in the free element). Hydrogen is reduced (going from +1 oxidation state in water to zero oxidation state in the free element). Heat is produced by burning the hydrogen gas produced by the electrolysis: since energy must be applied to water to electrolyze it, energy is released when hydrogen gas produced by the electrolysis and oxygen gas combine to form water in the fireplace.

65. electrons

66. loss; oxidation state

67. gain, oxidation number

68. electronegative

86. In each of the following reactions, identify which element is oxidized and which is reduced.

a. $2Al(s) + 6HCl(aq) \rightarrow 2AlCl_3(aq) + 3H_2(g)$
b. $2HI(g) \rightarrow H_2(g) + I_2(s)$
c. $Cu(s) + H_2SO_4(aq) \rightarrow CuSO_4(aq) + H_2(g)$

87. Carbon compounds containing double bonds (such compounds are called alkenes) react readily with many other reagents. In each of the following reactions, identify which atoms are oxidized and which are reduced, and specify the oxidizing and reducing agents.

a. $CH_2{=}CH_2(g) + Cl_2(g) \rightarrow ClCH_2{-}CH_2Cl(l)$
b. $CH_2{=}CH_2(g) + Br_2(g) \rightarrow BrCH_2{-}CH_2Br(l)$
c. $CH_2{=}CH_2(g) + HBr(g) \rightarrow CH_3{-}CH_2Br(l)$
d. $CH_2{=}CH_2(g) + H_2(g) \rightarrow CH_3{-}CH_3(g)$

88. Balance each of the following oxidation–reduction reactions by inspection.

a. $C_3H_8(g) + O_2(g) \rightarrow CO_2(g) + H_2O(g)$
b. $CO(g) + H_2(g) \rightarrow CH_3OH(l)$
c. $SnO_2(s) + C(s) \rightarrow Sn(s) + CO(g)$
d. $C_2H_5OH(l) + O_2(g) \rightarrow CO_2(g) + H_2O(g)$

89. Balance each of the following oxidation–reduction reactions, which take place in acidic solution.

a. $MnO_4^-(aq) + H_2O_2(aq) \rightarrow Mn^{2+}(aq) + O_2(g)$
b. $BrO_3^-(aq) + Cu^+(aq) \rightarrow Br^-(aq) + Cu^{2+}(aq)$
c. $HNO_2(aq) + I^-(aq) \rightarrow NO(g) + I_2(aq)$

90. For each of the following oxidation–reduction reactions of metals with nonmetals, identify which element is oxidized and which is reduced.

a. $4Na(s) + O_2(g) \rightarrow 2Na_2O(s)$
b. $Fe(s) + H_2SO_4(aq) \rightarrow FeSO_4(aq) + H_2(g)$
c. $2Al_2O_3(s) \rightarrow 4Al(s) + 3O_2(g)$
d. $3Mg(s) + N_2(g) \rightarrow Mg_3N_2(s)$

91. For each of the following oxidation–reduction reactions of metals with nonmetals, identify which element is oxidized and which is reduced.

a. $3Zn(s) + N_2(g) \rightarrow Zn_3N_2(s)$
b. $Co(s) + S(s) \rightarrow CoS(s)$
c. $4K(s) + O_2(g) \rightarrow 2K_2O(s)$
d. $4Ag(s) + O_2(g) \rightarrow 2Ag_2O(s)$

92. Assign oxidation states to all of the atoms in each of the following:

a. NH_3
b. CO
c. CO_2
d. NF_3

93. Assign oxidation states to all of the atoms in each of the following:

a. PBr_3
b. C_3H_8
c. $KMnO_4$
d. CH_3COOH

94. Assign oxidation states to all of the atoms in each of the following:

a. MnO_2
b. $BaCrO_4$
c. H_2SO_3
d. $Ca_3(PO_4)_2$

95. Assign oxidation states to all of the atoms in each of the following:

a. $CrCl_3$
b. K_2CrO_4
c. $K_2Cr_2O_7$
d. $Cr(C_2H_3O_2)_2$

96. Assign oxidation states to all of the atoms in each of the following:

a. BiO^+
b. PO_4^{3-}
c. NO_2^-
d. Hg_2^{2+}

97. In each of the following reactions, identify which element is oxidized and which is reduced by assigning oxidation states.

a. $C(s) + O_2(g) \rightarrow CO_2(g)$
b. $2CO(g) + O_2(g) \rightarrow 2CO_2(g)$
c. $CH_4(g) + 2O_2(g) \rightarrow CO_2(g) + 2H_2O(g)$
d. $C_2H_2(g) + 2H_2(g) \rightarrow C_2H_6(g)$

98. In each of the following reactions, identify which element is oxidized and which is reduced by assigning oxidation states.

a. $2B_2O_3(s) + 6Cl_2(g) \rightarrow 4BCl_3(l) + 3O_2(g)$
b. $GeH_4(g) + O_2(g) \rightarrow Ge(s) + 2H_2O(g)$
c. $C_2H_4(g) + Cl_2(g) \rightarrow C_2H_4Cl_2(l)$
d. $O_2(g) + 2F_2(g) \rightarrow 2OF_2(g)$

99. Balance each of the following half-reactions.

a. $I^-(aq) \rightarrow I_2(s)$
b. $O_2(g) \rightarrow O^{2-}(s)$
c. $P_4(s) \rightarrow P^{3-}(s)$
d. $Cl_2(g) \rightarrow Cl^-(aq)$

100. Balance each of the following half-reactions, which take place in acidic solution.

a. $SiO_2(s) \rightarrow Si(s)$
b. $S(s) \rightarrow H_2S(aq)$
c. $NO_3^-(aq) \rightarrow HNO_2(aq)$
d. $NO_3^-(aq) \rightarrow NO(g)$

101. Balance each of the following oxidation–reduction reactions, which take place in acidic solution, by using the "half-reaction" method.

a. $I^-(aq) + MnO_4^-(aq) \rightarrow I_2(aq) + Mn^{2+}(aq)$
b. $S_2O_8^{2-}(aq) + Cr^{3+}(aq) \rightarrow SO_4^{2-}(aq) + Cr_2O_7^{2-}(aq)$
c. $BiO_3^-(aq) + Mn^{2+}(aq) \rightarrow Bi^{3+}(aq) + MnO_4^-(aq)$

102. Potassium permanganate, $KMnO_4$, is one of the most widely used oxidizing agents. Balance each of the following oxidation–reduction reactions of the per-

All even-numbered Questions and Problems have answers in the back of this book and solutions in the Solutions Guide.

69. charge

70. An oxidizing agent is an atom, molecule, or ion that causes the oxidation of some other species, while itself being reduced.

71. oxidation, reduced

72. lose

73. equal

74. separate from

75. galvanic

76. oxidation

77. cathode

78. In an electrolysis reaction, an ordinarily nonspontaneous reaction is forced to occur by the application of an electric current of sufficient voltage. For example, water may be electrolyzed into its elements: $2H_2O(l) \rightarrow 2H_2(g) + O_2(g)$.

79. voltage or potential

80. hydrogen; oxygen

81. zinc

82. oxidation

83. aluminum oxide

84. (a) $4Fe(s) + 3O_2(g) \rightarrow 2Fe_2O_3(s)$; iron is oxidized, oxygen is reduced; (b) $2Al(s) + 3Cl_2(g) \rightarrow 2AlCl_3(s)$; aluminum is oxidized, chlorine is reduced; (c) $6Mg(s) + P_4(s) \rightarrow 2Mg_3P_2(s)$; magnesium is oxidized, phosphorus is reduced

85. (a) zinc is oxidized, hydrogen is reduced; (b) copper(I) is both oxidized to copper(II) and reduced to copper(0); (c) iron is oxidized, chromium is reduced

86. (a) Al is oxidized ($0 \rightarrow +3$); H is reduced ($+1 \rightarrow 0$); (b) H is reduced ($+1 \rightarrow 0$); I is oxidized ($-1 \rightarrow 0$); (c) Cu is oxidized ($0 \rightarrow +2$); H is reduced ($+1 \rightarrow 0$)

87. (a) carbon is oxidized, chlorine is reduced; Cl_2 is the oxidizing agent, ethylene is the reducing agent; (b) carbon is oxidized, bromine is reduced; Br_2 is the oxidizing agent, ethylene is the reducing agent; (c) the process does not involve electron transfer; (d) carbon is reduced, hydrogen is oxidized; H_2 is the reducing agent, ethylene is the oxidizing agent

88. (a) $C_3H_8(g) + 5O_2(g) \rightarrow 3CO_2(g) + 4H_2O(g)$; (b) $CO(g) + 2H_2(g) \rightarrow CH_3OH(l)$; (c) $SnO_2(s) + 2C(s) \rightarrow Sn(s) + 2CO(g)$; (d) $C_2H_5OH(l) + 3O_2(g) \rightarrow 2CO_2(g) + 3H_2O(g)$

89. (a) $2MnO_4^- + 6H^+ + 5H_2O_2 \rightarrow 2Mn^{2+} + 8H_2O + 5O_2$; (b) $6Cu^+ + 6H^+ + BrO_3^- \rightarrow 6Cu^{2+} + Br^- + 3H_2O$; (c) $2HNO_2 + 2H^+ + 2I^- \rightarrow 2NO + I_2 + 2H_2O$

90. (a) sodium is oxidized, oxygen is reduced; (b) iron is oxidized, hydrogen is reduced; (c) oxygen (O^{2-}) is oxidized, aluminum (Al^{3+}) is reduced; (d) magnesium is oxidized, nitrogen is reduced

91. (a) zinc is oxidized, nitrogen is reduced; (b) cobalt is oxidized, sulfur is reduced; (c) potassium is oxidized, oxygen is reduced; (d) silver is oxidized, oxygen is reduced

92. (a) H, +1; N, −3; (b) C, +2; O, −2; (c) C, +4; O, −2; (d) N, +3; F, −1

manganate ion in acidic solution by using the "half-reaction" method.

a. $MnO_4^-(aq) + C_2O_4^{2-}(aq) \rightarrow Mn^{2+}(aq) + CO_2(g)$
b. $MnO_4^-(aq) + Fe^{2+}(aq) \rightarrow Mn^{2+}(aq) + Fe^{3+}(aq)$
c. $MnO_4^-(aq) + Cl^-(aq) \rightarrow Mn^{2+}(aq) + Cl_2(g)$

103. Consider the oxidation–reduction reaction

$$Mg(s) + Cu^{2+}(aq) \rightarrow Mg^{2+}(aq) + Cu(s)$$

Sketch a galvanic cell that uses this reaction. Which metal ion is reduced? Which metal is oxidized? What half-reaction takes place at the anode in the cell? What half-reaction takes place at the cathode?

104. Explain to a friend who has not taken any chemistry courses what a *galvanic cell* consists of and how it may be used as a source of electricity.

All even-numbered Questions and Problems have answers in the back of this book and solutions in the Solutions Guide.

100. (a) $SiO_2(s) + 4H^+(aq) + 4e^- \rightarrow Si(s) + 2H_2O(l)$; (b) $S(s) + 2H^+(aq) + 2e^- \rightarrow H_2S(g)$; (c) $NO_3^-(aq) + 3H^+(aq) + 2e^- \rightarrow HNO_2(aq) + H_2O(l)$; (d) $NO_3^-(aq) + 4H^+(aq) + 3e^- \rightarrow NO(g) + 2H_2O(l)$

101. (a) $16H^+ + 10I^- + 2MnO_4^- \rightarrow 2Mn^{2+} + 8H_2O + 5I_2$; (b) $7H_2O + 2Cr^{3+} + 3S_2O_8^{2-} \rightarrow Cr_2O_7^{2-} + 14H^+ + 6SO_4^{2-}$; (c) $2Mn^{2+} + 14H^+ + 5BiO_3^- \rightarrow 2MnO_4^- + 5Bi^{3+} + 7H_2O$

102. (a) $16H^+(aq) + 2MnO_4^-(aq) + 5C_2O_4^{2-}(aq) \rightarrow 2Mn^{2+}(aq) + 8H_2O(l) + 10CO_2(g)$; (b) $8H^+(aq) + MnO_4^-(aq) + 5Fe^{2+}(aq) \rightarrow Mn^{2+}(aq) + 4H_2O(l) + 5Fe^{3+}(aq)$; (c) $16H^+(aq) + 2MnO_4^-(aq) + 10Cl^-(aq) \rightarrow 2Mn^{2+}(aq) + 8H_2O(l) + 5Cl_2(g)$

103.

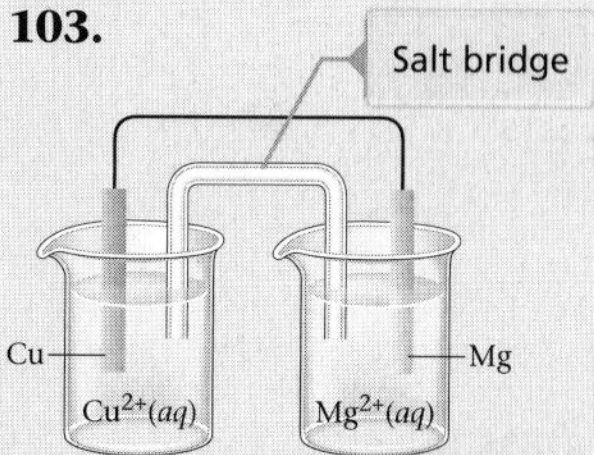

$Cu^{2+}(aq)$ is reduced; $Mg(s)$ is oxidized
Anode: $Mg(s) \rightarrow Mg^{2+}(aq) + 2e^-$; Cathode: $Cu^{2+}(aq) + 2e^- \rightarrow Cu(s)$

104. A galvanic cell is a battery. A spontaneous oxidation–reduction reaction is separated physically into the two half-reactions, and the electrons being transferred between the two half-cells are made available as an electric current.

93. (a) P, +3; Br, −1; (b) C, ; H, +1; (c) K, +1; Mn, +7; O, −2; (d) C, 0; H, +1; O, −2

94. (a) Mn, +4; O, −2; (b) Ba, +2; Cr, +6; O, −2; (c) H, +1; S, +4; O, −2; (d) Ca, +2; P, +5; O, −2

95. (a) Cr, +3; Cl, −1; (b) K, +1; Cr, +6; O, −2; (c) K, +1; Cr, +6; O, −2; (d) Cr, +2; C, 0; H, +1; O, −2

96. (a) Bi, +3; O, −2; (b) P, +5; O, −2; (c) N, +3; O, −2; (d) Hg, +1

97. (a) carbon is oxidized, oxygen is reduced; (b) carbon is oxidized, oxygen is reduced; (c) carbon is oxidized, oxygen is reduced; (d) hydrogen is oxidized, carbon is reduced

98. (a) oxygen is oxidized, chlorine is reduced; (b) germanium is oxidized, oxygen is reduced; (c) carbon is oxidized, chlorine is reduced; (d) oxygen is oxidized, fluorine is reduced

99. (a) $2I^- \rightarrow I_2 + 2e^-$; (b) $O_2 + 4e^- \rightarrow 2O^{2-}$; (c) $P_4 + 12e^- \rightarrow 4P^{3-}$; (d) $Cl_2 + 2e^- \rightarrow 2Cl^-$

Chapter 19

Objectives

In this chapter, our objectives are for the students to:

SECTION 19.1

- Learn the types of radioactive decay.
- Learn to write nuclear equations that describe radioactive decay.

SECTION 19.2

- Learn how one element may be changed into another by particle bombardment.

SECTION 19.3

- Learn about radiation detection instruments.
- Understand half-life.

SECTION 19.4

- Learn how objects can be dated by radioactivity.

SECTION 19.5

- Discuss the use of radiotracers in medicine.

SECTION 19.6

- Introduce fusion and fission as producers of nuclear energy.

SECTION 19.7

- Learn about nuclear fission.

SECTION 19.8

- Understand how a nuclear reactor works.

SECTION 19.9

- Learn about nuclear fusion.

SECTION 19.10

- See how radiation damages human tissue.

19 Radioactivity and Nuclear Energy

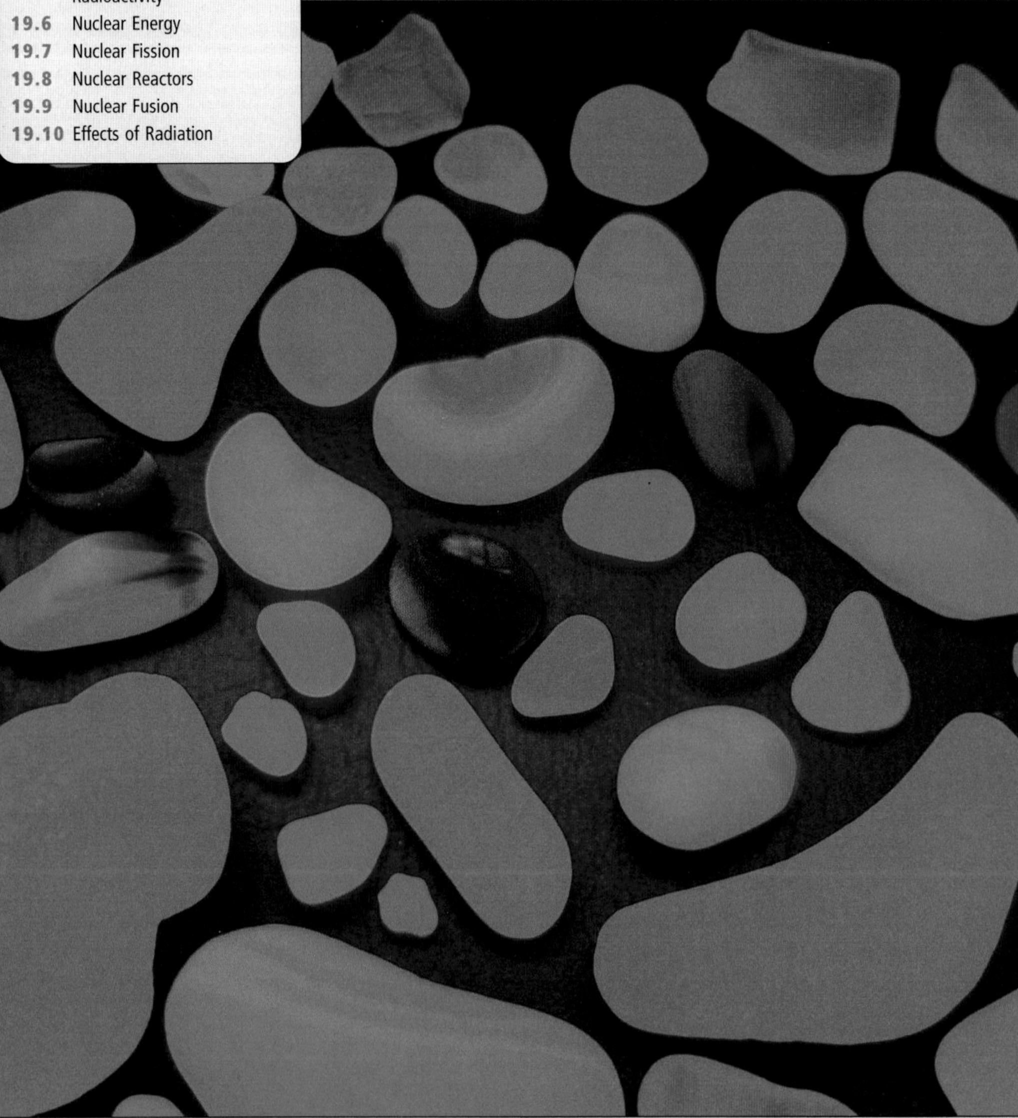

Radioactive sea glass. *(Courtesy, By the Bay Treasures, photo by Charles Peden)*

ChemWork Refined over ten years of use by thousands of students, **ChemWork** builds and enhances students' problems-solving skills. Online assignments function as a "personal instructor" to help students learn how to solve challenging problems and learn how to think like chemists. Annotations for **ChemWork** assignments are included at the beginning of the end-of-chapter review.

PowerLecture This 2-DVD package includes the Chemistry Multimedia Library, which contains animations, simulations, and movies for all chemistry subjects, organized by topic for lecture presentations. Annotations for **PowerLecture** are referenced in the margins throughout the Annotated Instructor's Edition.

OWL Sign in to OWL at **www.cengage.com/owl** to view tutorials and simulations, develop problem-solving skills, and complete online homework assigned by your professor.

Leslie Garland/Leslie Garland Picture Library/Alamy Images

Wooden artifacts such as this dragon figurehead from a Viking ship can be dated from their carbon-14 content.

Because the chemistry of an atom is determined by the number and arrangement of its electrons, the properties of the nucleus do not strongly affect the chemical behavior of an atom. Therefore, you might be wondering why there is a chapter on the nucleus in a chemistry textbook. The reason for this chapter is that the nucleus is very important to all of us—a quick reading of any daily newspaper will testify to that. Nuclear processes can be used to detect explosives in airline luggage (see "Chemistry in Focus: Measurement: Past, Present, and Future," page 22), to generate electric power, and to establish the ages of very old objects such as human artifacts, rocks, and diamonds (see "Chemistry in Focus: Dating Diamonds," page 624). This chapter considers aspects of the nucleus and its properties that you should know about.

Several facts about the nucleus are immediately impressive: its very small size, its very large density, and the energy that holds it together. The radius of a typical nucleus is about 10^{-13} cm, only a hundred-thousandth the radius of a typical atom. In fact, if the nucleus of the hydrogen atom were the size of a Ping-Pong ball, the electron in the 1*s* orbital would be, on the average, 0.5 km (0.3 mile) away. The density of the nucleus is equally impressive; it is approximately 1.6×10^{14} g/cm^3. A sphere of nuclear material the size of a Ping-Pong ball would have a mass of 2.5 *billion tons!* Finally, the energies involved in nuclear processes are typically millions of times larger than those associated with normal chemical reactions, a fact that makes nuclear processes potentially attractive for generating energy.

The nucleus is believed to be made of particles called **nucleons (neutrons and protons)**.

The atomic number (Z) represents the number of protons in a nucleus; the mass number (A) represents the sum of the numbers of protons and neutrons in a nucleus.

Recall from Chapter 4 that the number of protons in a nucleus is called the **atomic number (*Z*)** and that the sum of the numbers of neutrons and protons is the **mass number (*A*).** Atoms that have identical atomic numbers but different mass numbers are called **isotopes.** The general term **nuclide** is applied to each unique atom, and we represent it as follows:

Mass number
↓
$^{A}_{Z}\text{X}$ ← Element symbol
↑
Atomic number

where X represents the symbol for a particular element. For example, the following nuclides constitute the common isotopes of carbon: carbon-12, $^{12}_{6}\text{C}$; carbon-13, $^{13}_{6}\text{C}$; and carbon-14, $^{14}_{6}\text{C}$. Notice that all the carbon nuclides have six protons ($Z = 6$) and that they have six, seven, and eight neutrons, respectively.

Test Bank: 1, 2, 5–11

Section 19.1

TEACHING TIPS

- Balancing nuclear equations provides an excellent opportunity to review balancing by atoms and charge and the meanings of the mass number and atomic number in element notation.
- Students should be aware that in a nuclear decay the product is a different element. Therefore, we cannot balance the equation by balancing the atoms.
- Remind students that in forming ions, the number of electrons changes but the number of protons (and, therefore, the type of atom) remains the same. In nuclear equations, if the number of protons is changed, the atom's identity is also changed.
- Alchemists attempted to convert base metals (such as lead) into precious metals (such as gold) by chemical means. We now know that this transformation can be accomplished only by nuclear reactions, which is not practical.

LABORATORY EXPERIMENT

A relevant laboratory experiment for this section and Section 19.10 is Experiment 29, Radioactivity, from *Introductory Chemistry in the Laboratory* by James Hall.

19.1 Radioactive Decay

OBJECTIVES: To learn the types of radioactive decay. • To learn to write nuclear equations that describe radioactive decay.

Many nuclei are **radioactive;** that is, they spontaneously decompose, forming a different nucleus and producing one or more particles. An example is carbon-14, which decays as shown in the equation

$$^{14}_{6}C \rightarrow ^{14}_{7}N + ^{0}_{-1}e$$

where $^{0}_{-1}e$ represents an electron, which in nuclear terminology is called a **beta particle,** or **β particle.** This **nuclear equation,** which is typical of those representing radioactive decay, is quite different from the chemical equations we have written before. Recall that in a balanced chemical equation the atoms must be conserved. In a nuclear equation *both the atomic number (Z) and the mass number (A) must be conserved.* That is, the sums of the Z values on both sides of the arrow must be equal, and the same restriction applies to the A values. For example, in the above equation, the sum of the Z values is 6 on both sides of the arrow (6 and 7 − 1), and the sum of the A values is 14 on both sides of the arrow (14 and 14 + 0). Notice that the mass number for the β particle is zero; the mass of the electron is so small that it can be neglected here. Of the approximately 2000 known nuclides, only 279 do not undergo radioactive decay. Tin has the largest number of nonradioactive isotopes—ten.

Over 85% of all known nuclides are radioactive.

Types of Radioactive Decay

There are several different types of radioactive decay. One frequently observed decay process involves production of an **alpha (α) particle,** which is a helium nucleus ($^{4}_{2}He$). **Alpha-particle production** is a very common mode of decay for heavy radioactive nuclides. For example, $^{222}_{88}Ra$, radium-222, decays by α-particle production to give radon-218.

$$^{222}_{88}Ra \rightarrow ^{4}_{2}He + ^{218}_{86}Rn$$

Notice in this equation that the mass number is conserved (222 = 4 + 218) and the atomic number is conserved (88 = 2 + 86). Another α-particle producer is $^{230}_{90}Th$:

$$^{230}_{90}Th \rightarrow ^{4}_{2}He + ^{226}_{88}Ra$$

Notice that the production of an α particle results in a loss of 4 in mass number (A) and a loss of 2 in atomic number (Z).

β-particle production is another common decay process. For example, the thorium-234 nuclide produces a β particle as it changes to protactinium-234.

$$^{234}_{90}Th \rightarrow ^{234}_{91}Pa + ^{0}_{-1}e$$

Iodine-131 is also a β-particle producer:

$$^{131}_{53}I \rightarrow ^{0}_{-1}e + ^{131}_{54}Xe$$

Notice that both Z and A balance in each of these nuclear equations.

Recall that the β particle is assigned a mass number of 0 because its mass is tiny compared with that of a proton or neutron. The value of Z is −1 for the β particle, so the atomic number for the new nuclide is greater by 1 than the atomic number for the original nuclide. Therefore, *the net effect of β-particle production is to change a neutron to a proton.*

Production of a β particle results in no change in mass number (A) and an increase of 1 in atomic number (Z).

PowerLecture Animation: Nuclear Particles

PowerLecture Simulation: Stability of Isotopes

Table 19.1 Various Types of Radioactive Processes

Process	Example
β-particle (electron) production	$^{227}_{89}Ac \rightarrow ^{227}_{90}Th + ^{0}_{-1}e$
positron production	$^{13}_{7}N \rightarrow ^{13}_{6}C + ^{0}_{1}e$
electron capture	$^{73}_{33}As + ^{0}_{-1}e \rightarrow ^{73}_{32}Ge$
α-particle production	$^{210}_{84}Po \rightarrow ^{206}_{82}Pb + ^{4}_{2}He$
γ-ray production	excited nucleus $\rightarrow$ ground-state nucleus $+ ^{0}_{0}\gamma$ excess energy lower energy

A gamma ray is a high-energy photon produced in connection with nuclear decay.

The $^{0}_{0}\gamma$ notation indicates $Z = 0$ and $A = 0$ for a γ ray. A gamma ray is often simply indicated by γ.

A **gamma ray**, or **γ ray,** is a high-energy photon of light. A nuclide in an excited nuclear energy state can release excess energy by producing a gamma ray, and γ-ray production often accompanies nuclear decays of various types. For example, in the α-particle decay of $^{238}_{92}U$,

$$^{238}_{92}U \rightarrow ^{4}_{2}He + ^{234}_{90}Th + 2^{0}_{0}\gamma$$

two γ rays of different energies are produced in addition to the α particle ($^{4}_{2}He$). Gamma rays are photons of light and so have zero charge and zero mass number.

Production of a γ ray results in no change in mass number (A) and no change in atomic number (Z).

The **positron** is a particle with the same mass as the electron but opposite charge. An example of a nuclide that decays by **positron production** is sodium-22:

$$^{22}_{11}Na \rightarrow ^{0}_{1}e + ^{22}_{10}Ne$$

Note that the production of a positron appears to change a proton into a neutron.

Production of a positron results in no change in mass number (A) and a decrease of 1 in atomic number (Z).

Electron capture is a process in which one of the inner-orbital electrons is captured by the nucleus, as illustrated by the process

$$^{201}_{80}Hg + ^{0}_{-1}e \rightarrow ^{201}_{79}Au + ^{0}_{0}\gamma$$

Inner-orbital electron (↑ pointing to $^{0}_{-1}e$)

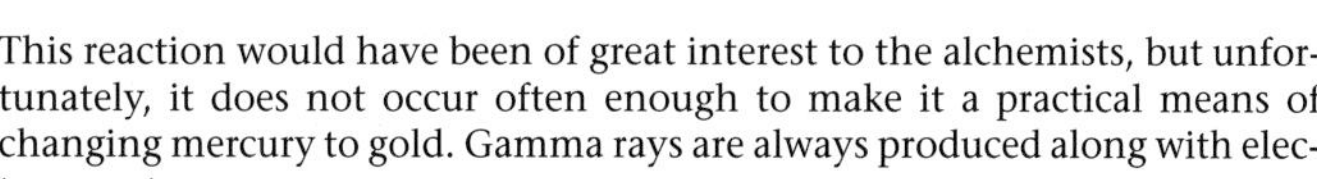

This reaction would have been of great interest to the alchemists, but unfortunately, it does not occur often enough to make it a practical means of changing mercury to gold. Gamma rays are always produced along with electron capture.

Table 19.1 lists the common types of radioactive decay, with examples.

Often a radioactive nucleus cannot achieve a stable (nonradioactive) state through a single decay process. In such a case, a **decay series** occurs until a stable nuclide is formed. A well-known example is the decay series that starts with $^{238}_{92}U$ and ends with $^{206}_{82}Pb$, as shown in Figure 19.1. Similar series exist for $^{235}_{92}U$:

$$^{235}_{92}U \xrightarrow[\text{decays}]{\text{Series of}} ^{207}_{82}Pb$$

and for $^{232}_{90}Th$:

$$^{232}_{90}Th \xrightarrow[\text{decays}]{\text{Series of}} ^{208}_{82}Pb$$

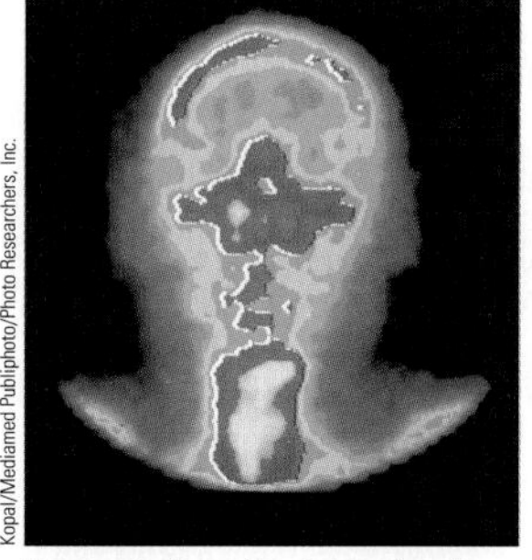

Kopal/Mediamed Publiphoto/Photo Researchers, Inc.

Bone scintigraph of a patient's cranium following administration of the radiopharmaceutical technetium-99.

19.1 Radioactive Decay 617

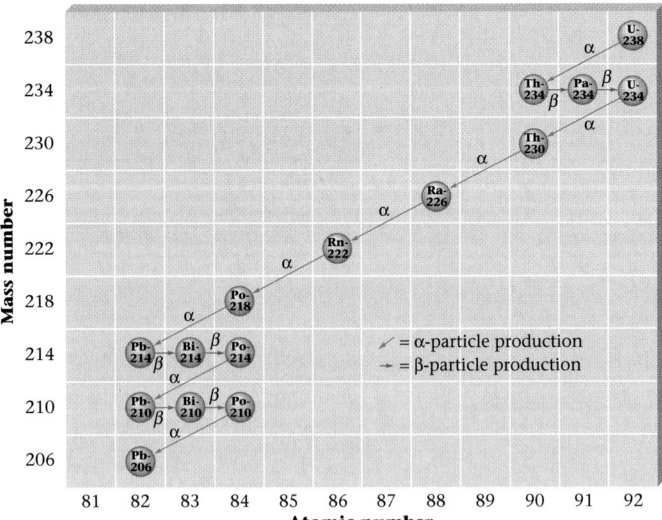

Figure 19.1
The decay series from $^{238}_{92}U$ to $^{206}_{82}Pb$. Each nuclide in the series except $^{206}_{82}Pb$ is radioactive, and the successive transformations (shown by the arrows) continue until $^{206}_{82}Pb$ is finally formed. The horizontal red arrows indicate β-particle production (Z increases by 1 and A is unchanged). The diagonal blue arrows signify α-particle production (both A and Z decrease).

Additional Examples

Example 19.1

Write balanced nuclear equations for each of the following processes.

1. $^{116}_{47}Ag$ produces a beta particle.

   $^{116}_{47}Ag \rightarrow {}^{0}_{-1}e + {}^{116}_{48}Cd$

2. $^{211}_{83}Bi$ produces an alpha particle.

   $^{211}_{83}Bi \rightarrow {}^{4}_{2}He + {}^{207}_{81}Tl$

EXAMPLE 19.1 Writing Nuclear Equations, I

Write balanced nuclear equations for each of the following processes.

a. $^{11}_{6}C$ produces a positron.

b. $^{214}_{83}Bi$ produces a β particle.

c. $^{237}_{93}Np$ produces an α particle.

SOLUTION

a. We must find the product nuclide represented by $^{A}_{Z}X$ in the following equation:

$$^{11}_{6}C \rightarrow {}^{0}_{1}e + {}^{A}_{Z}X$$

↑ Positron

The key to solving this problem is to recognize that both A and Z must be conserved. That is, we can find the identity of $^{A}_{Z}X$ by recognizing that the sums of the Z and A values must be the same on both sides of the equation. Thus, for X, Z must be 5 because $Z + 1 = 6$. A must be 11 because $11 + 0 = 11$. Therefore, $^{A}_{Z}X$ is $^{11}_{5}B$. (The fact that Z is 5 tells us that the nuclide is boron. See the periodic table on the inside front cover of the book.) So the balanced equation is $^{11}_{6}C \rightarrow {}^{0}_{1}e + {}^{11}_{5}B$.

CHECK:

Left Side		**Right Side**
$Z = 6$	→	$Z = 5 + 1 = 6$
$A = 11$		$A = 11 + 0 = 11$

b. Knowing that a β particle is represented by ${}_{-1}^{0}e$, we can write

$$ {}_{83}^{214}Bi \rightarrow {}_{-1}^{0}e + {}_{Z}^{A}X $$

where $Z - 1 = 83$ and $A + 0 = 214$. This means that $Z = 84$ and $A = 214$. We can now write

$$ {}_{83}^{214}Bi \rightarrow {}_{-1}^{0}e + {}_{84}^{214}X $$

Using the periodic table, we find that $Z = 84$ for the element polonium, so ${}_{84}^{214}X$ must be ${}_{84}^{214}Po$.

CHECK:	Left Side		Right Side
	$Z = 83$	$\rightarrow$	$Z = 84 - 1 = 83$
	$A = 214$		$A = 214 + 0 = 214$

c. Because an α particle is represented by ${}_{2}^{4}He$, we can write

$$ {}_{93}^{237}Np \rightarrow {}_{2}^{4}He + {}_{Z}^{A}X $$

where $A + 4 = 237$ or $A = 237 - 4 = 233$, and $Z + 2 = 93$ or $Z = 93 - 2 = 91$. Thus $A = 233$, $Z = 91$, and the balanced equation must be

$$ {}_{93}^{237}Np \rightarrow {}_{2}^{4}He + {}_{91}^{233}Pa $$

CHECK:	Left Side		Right Side
	$Z = 93$	$\rightarrow$	$Z = 91 + 2 = 93$
	$A = 237$		$A = 233 + 4 = 237$

Self-Check EXERCISE 19.1 The decay series for ${}_{92}^{238}U$ is represented in Figure 19.1. Write the balanced nuclear equation for each of the following radioactive decays.

a. Alpha-particle production by ${}_{88}^{226}Ra$

b. Beta-particle production by ${}_{82}^{214}Pb$

See Problems 19.25 through 19.28. ■

EXAMPLE 19.2 Writing Nuclear Equations, II

In each of the following nuclear reactions, supply the missing particle.

a. ${}_{79}^{195}Au + ? \rightarrow {}_{78}^{195}Pt$

b. ${}_{19}^{38}K \rightarrow {}_{18}^{38}Ar + ?$

SOLUTION

a. A does not change and Z for Pt is 1 lower than Z for Au, so the missing particle must be an electron.

$$ {}_{79}^{195}Au + {}_{-1}^{0}e \rightarrow {}_{78}^{195}Pt $$

CHECK:	Left Side		Right Side
	$Z = 79 - 1 = 78$	$\rightarrow$	$Z = 78$
	$A = 195 + 0 = 195$		$A = 195$

This is an example of electron capture.

b. For Z and A to be conserved, the missing particle must be a positron.

$$ {}_{19}^{38}K \rightarrow {}_{18}^{38}Ar + {}_{1}^{0}e $$

Self Check

Answers to Self-Check Exercise 19.1

a. ${}_{88}^{226}Ra \rightarrow {}_{2}^{4}He + {}_{86}^{222}Rn$

b. ${}_{82}^{214}Pb \rightarrow {}_{-1}^{0}e + {}_{83}^{214}Bi$

Additional Examples

Example 19.2

In each of the following nuclear reactions, supply the missing particle.

1. ${}_{89}^{210}Ac \rightarrow {}_{2}^{4}He + ?$

   ${}_{87}^{206}Fr$

2. ${}_{53}^{131}I \rightarrow {}_{54}^{131}Xe + ?$

   ${}_{-1}^{0}e$

3. ${}_{35}^{88}Br \rightarrow {}_{35}^{87}Br + ?$

   ${}_{0}^{1}n$

Self Check

Answers to Self-Check Exercise 19.2

a. $^{4}_{2}He$

b. $^{15}_{7}N$

Section 19.2

TEACHING TIPS

- Nuclear transformations are balanced in the same way as nuclear decay reactions.
- Radioisotopes are found in many household devices. Some examples are starters for fluorescent lamps and appliances (promethium-147, krypton-85, and thorium-232), antistatic devices (polonium-210), and smoke detectors (americium-241).

 **Test Bank: 12**

CHECK:	Left Side		Right Side
	$Z = 19$	$\rightarrow$	$Z = 18 + 1 = 19$
	$A = 38$		$A = 38 + 0 = 38$

Potassium-38 decays by positron production.

Self-Check EXERCISE 19.2 Supply the missing species in each of the following nuclear equations.

a. $^{222}_{86}Rn \rightarrow {}^{218}_{84}Po + ?$

b. $^{15}_{8}O \rightarrow ? + {}^{0}_{1}e$

See Problems 19.21 through 19.24. ■

19.2 Nuclear Transformations

OBJECTIVE: To learn how one element may be changed into another by particle bombardment.

Culver Pictures/The Granger Collection

Irene Curie and Frederick Joliot.

In 1919, Lord Rutherford observed the first **nuclear transformation,** *the change of one element into another.* He found that bombarding $^{14}_{7}N$ with α particles produced the nuclide $^{17}_{8}O$:

$$^{14}_{7}N + {}^{4}_{2}He \rightarrow {}^{17}_{8}O + {}^{1}_{1}H$$

with a proton ($^{1}_{1}H$) as another product. Fourteen years later, Irene Curie and her husband Frederick Joliot observed a similar transformation from aluminum to phosphorus:

$$^{27}_{13}Al + {}^{4}_{2}He \rightarrow {}^{30}_{15}P + {}^{1}_{0}n$$

where $^{1}_{0}n$ represents a neutron that is produced in the process.

Notice that in both these cases the bombarding particle is a helium nucleus (an α particle). Other small nuclei, such as $^{12}_{6}C$ and $^{15}_{7}N$, also can be used to bombard heavier nuclei and cause transformations. However, because these positive bombarding ions are repelled by the positive charge of the target nucleus, the bombarding particle must be moving at a very high speed to penetrate the target. These high speeds are achieved in various types of *particle accelerators.*

Neutrons are also employed as bombarding particles to effect nuclear transformations. However, because neutrons are uncharged (and thus not repelled by a target nucleus), they are readily absorbed by many nuclei, producing new nuclides. The most common source of neutrons for this purpose is a fission reactor (see Section 19.8).

By using neutron and positive-ion bombardment, scientists have been able to extend the periodic table—that is, to produce chemical elements that are not present naturally. Prior to 1940, the heaviest known element was uranium ($Z = 92$), but in 1940, neptunium ($Z = 93$) was produced by neutron bombardment of $^{238}_{92}U$. The process initially gives $^{239}_{92}U$, which decays to $^{239}_{93}Np$ by β-particle production:

$$^{238}_{92}U + {}^{1}_{0}n \rightarrow {}^{239}_{92}U \rightarrow {}^{239}_{93}Np + {}^{0}_{-1}e$$

Table 19.2 Syntheses of Some of the Transuranium Elements

Neutron Bombardment	neptunium ($Z = 93$)	$^{238}_{92}U + ^{1}_{0}n \rightarrow ^{239}_{92}U \rightarrow ^{239}_{93}Np + ^{0}_{-1}e$
	americium ($Z = 95$)	$^{239}_{94}Pu + 2\,^{1}_{0}n \rightarrow ^{241}_{94}Pu \rightarrow ^{241}_{95}Am + ^{0}_{-1}e$
Positive-Ion Bombardment	curium ($Z = 96$)	$^{239}_{94}Pu + ^{4}_{2}He \rightarrow ^{242}_{96}Cm + ^{1}_{0}n$
	californium ($Z = 98$)	$^{242}_{96}Cm + ^{4}_{2}He \rightarrow ^{245}_{98}Cf + ^{1}_{0}n$ or
		$^{238}_{92}U + ^{12}_{6}C \rightarrow ^{246}_{98}Cf + 4\,^{1}_{0}n$
	rutherfordium ($Z = 104$)	$^{249}_{98}Cf + ^{12}_{6}C \rightarrow ^{257}_{104}Rf + 4\,^{1}_{0}n$
	dubnium ($Z = 105$)	$^{249}_{98}Cf + ^{15}_{7}N \rightarrow ^{260}_{105}Db + 4\,^{1}_{0}n$
	seaborgium ($Z = 106$)	$^{249}_{98}Cf + ^{18}_{8}O \rightarrow ^{263}_{106}Sg + 4\,^{1}_{0}n$

In the years since 1940, the elements with atomic numbers 93 through 112, called the **transuranium elements,** have been synthesized. In addition, the production of element 114 (in 1999), elements 113 and 115 (in 2004), and element 118 (in 2006) have been reported. Table 19.2 gives some examples of these processes.

19.3 Detection of Radioactivity and the Concept of Half-life

OBJECTIVES: To learn about radiation detection instruments. • To understand half-life.

Geiger counters are commonly called *survey meters*.

The most familiar instrument for measuring radioactivity levels is the **Geiger–Müller counter,** or **Geiger counter** (Figure 19.2). High-energy particles from radioactive decay produce ions when they travel through matter. The probe of the Geiger counter contains argon gas. The argon atoms have no charge, but they can be ionized by a rapidly moving particle.

$$Ar(g) \xrightarrow[\text{particle}]{\text{High-energy}} Ar^{+}(g) + e^{-}$$

That is, the fast-moving particle "knocks" electrons off some of the argon atoms. Although a sample of uncharged argon atoms does not conduct a current, the ions and electrons formed by the high-energy particle allow a current to flow momentarily, so a "pulse" of current flows every time a particle enters the probe. The Geiger counter detects each pulse of current, and these events are counted.

A **scintillation counter** is another instrument often employed to detect radioactivity. This device uses a substance, such as sodium iodide, that

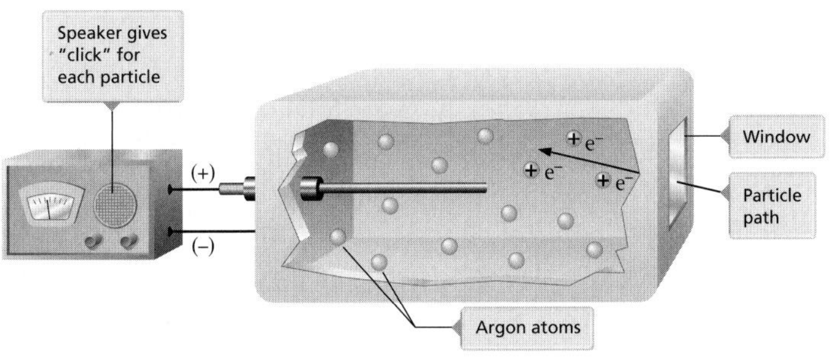

Figure 19.2 A schematic representation of a Geiger–Müller counter. The high-speed particle knocks electrons off argon atoms to form ions,

$$Ar \xrightarrow{\text{Particle}} Ar^{+} + e^{-}$$

and a pulse of current flows.

Test Bank: 13–19, 23

Section 19.3

DEMONSTRATION

If you have access to a Geiger counter, bring it to class for demonstration. A typical mantle from a gas camping lantern or a piece of orange Fiestaware pottery can be used as a source of radioactive material.

Lecture Demonstration: 21.1

MISCONCEPTION

Students have difficulty with the concept of half-life. They often believe that after two half-lives, all the material should be decayed.

TEACHING TIP

This is an excellent time to plot the amount of a radionuclide present versus time on the board to show the students the progression over time. You can use data from Table 19.3 to do this.

PowerLecture Animation: Geiger Counter

Additional Examples

Example 19.3

1. Gold-198 has a half-life of 2.7 days. It is used as an implant for cancer therapy. For an implant containing 50 μg of gold-198, approximately how much gold-198 remains after 1 week?

   Just over 6 μg (after 8.1 days, or four half-lives, 6.25 μg remains).

2. Krypton-76 has a half-life of 14.8 hours. About how long will it take to reach a point where a sample contains about 10% of its original krypton-76?

   About 2 days. After three half-lives (or around 44 hours), about 12.5% of the krypton-76 will remain.

PowerLecture Simulation: Rates of Radioactive Decay

gives off light when it is struck by a high-energy particle. A detector senses the flashes of light and thus counts the decay events.

One important characteristic of a given type of radioactive nuclide is its half-life. The **half-life** is the *time required for half the original sample of nuclei to decay*. For example, if a certain radioactive sample contains 1000 nuclei at a given time and 500 nuclei (half of the original number) 7.5 days later, this radioactive nuclide has a half-life of 7.5 days.

A given type of radioactive nuclide always has the same half-life. However, the various radioactive nuclides have half-lives that cover a tremendous range. For example, $^{234}_{91}Pa$, protactinium-234, has a half-life of 1.2 minutes, and $^{238}_{92}U$, uranium-238, has a half-life of 4.5×10^9 (4.5 *billion*) years. This means that a sample containing 100 million $^{234}_{91}Pa$ nuclei will have only 50 million $^{234}_{91}Pa$ nuclei in it (half of 100 million) after 1.2 minutes have passed. In another 1.2 minutes, the number of nuclei will decrease to half of 50 million, or 25 million nuclei.

$$100\text{ million } ^{234}_{91}Pa \xrightarrow[\text{minutes}]{1.2} 50\text{ million } ^{234}_{91}Pa \xrightarrow[\text{minutes}]{1.2} 25\text{ million } ^{234}_{91}Pa$$

(50 million decays) (25 million decays)

This means that a sample of $^{234}_{91}Pa$ with 100 million nuclei will show 50 million decay events (50 million $^{234}_{91}Pa$ nuclei will decay) over a time of 1.2 minutes. By contrast, a sample containing 100 million $^{238}_{92}U$ nuclei will undergo 50 million decay events over 4.5 billion years. Therefore, $^{234}_{91}Pa$ shows much greater activity than $^{238}_{92}U$. We sometimes say that $^{234}_{91}Pa$ is "hotter" than $^{238}_{92}U$.

Thus, at a given moment, a radioactive nucleus with a short half-life is much more likely to decay than one with a long half-life.

EXAMPLE 19.3 Understanding Half-life

Table 19.3 The Half-lives for Some of the Radioactive Nuclides of Radium

Nuclide	Half-life
$^{223}_{88}Ra$	12 days
$^{224}_{88}Ra$	3.6 days
$^{225}_{88}Ra$	15 days
$^{226}_{88}Ra$	1600 years
$^{228}_{88}Ra$	6.7 years

Table 19.3 lists various radioactive nuclides of radium.

a. Order these nuclides in terms of activity (from most decays per day to least).

b. How long will it take for a sample containing 1.00 mole of $^{223}_{88}Ra$ to reach a point where it contains only 0.25 mole of $^{223}_{88}Ra$?

SOLUTION

a. The shortest half-life indicates the greatest activity (the most decays over a given period of time). Therefore, the order is

Most activity (shortest half-life) → Least activity (longest half-life)

$$^{224}_{88}Ra > ^{223}_{88}Ra > ^{225}_{88}Ra > ^{228}_{88}Ra > ^{226}_{88}Ra$$

3.6 days 12 days 15 days 6.7 years 1600 years

b. In one half-life (12 days), the sample will decay from 1.00 mole of $^{223}_{88}Ra$ to 0.50 mole of $^{223}_{88}Ra$. In the next half-life (another 12 days), it will decay from 0.50 mole of $^{223}_{88}Ra$ to 0.25 mole of $^{223}_{88}Ra$.

$$1.00\text{ mol } ^{223}_{88}Ra \xrightarrow[\text{12 days}]{} 0.50\text{ mol } ^{223}_{88}Ra \xrightarrow[\text{12 days}]{} 0.25\text{ mol } ^{223}_{88}Ra$$

Therefore, it will take 24 days (two half-lives) for the sample to change from 1.00 mole of $^{223}_{88}Ra$ to 0.25 mole of $^{223}_{88}Ra$.

PowerLecture Animation: Half-Life of Nuclear Decay

Self-Check EXERCISE 19.3 Watches with numerals that "glow in the dark" formerly were made by including radioactive radium in the paint used to letter the watch faces. Assume that to make the numeral 3 on a given watch, a sample of paint containing 8.0×10^{-7} mole of $^{228}_{88}Ra$ was used. This watch was then put in a drawer and forgotten. Many years later someone finds the watch and wishes to know when it was made. Analyzing the paint, this person finds 1.0×10^{-7} moles of $^{228}_{88}Ra$ in the numeral 3. How much time elapsed between the making of the watch and the finding of the watch?

HINT: Use the half-life of $^{228}_{88}Ra$ from Table 19.3.

See Problems 19.37 through 19.42. ■

A watch dial with radium paint.

Self Check

Answer to Self-Check Exercise 19.3

20.1 years (2.0×10^1 with the correct number of significant figures).

19.4 Dating by Radioactivity

OBJECTIVE: To learn how objects can be dated by radioactivity.

Section 19.4

TEACHING TIPS

- Radiocarbon dating is a practical application of half-life.
- Carbon-14 is produced naturally in the environment. When it is incorporated into carbon dioxide, it can be fixed as a carbohydrate in plants. Carbon dioxide containing carbon-14 is an example of a natural source of radioactivity in the environment with which we come in contact.

Archaeologists, geologists, and others involved in reconstructing the ancient history of the earth rely heavily on the half-lives of radioactive nuclei to provide accurate dates for artifacts and rocks. A method for dating ancient articles made from wood or cloth is **radiocarbon dating,** or **carbon-14 dating,** a technique originated in the 1940s by Willard Libby, an American chemist who received the Nobel Prize for his efforts.

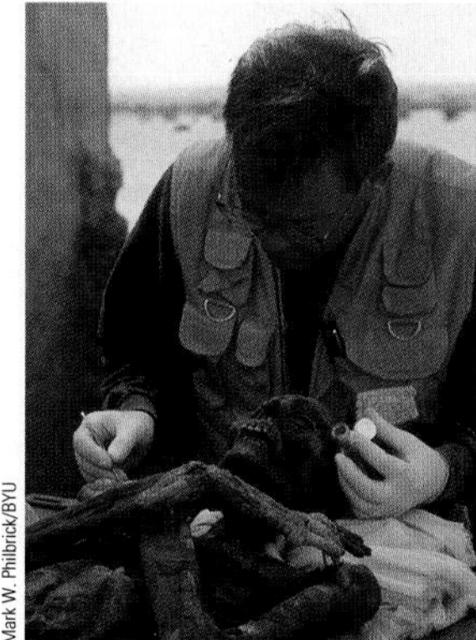

Brigham Young researcher Scott Woodward taking a bone sample for carbon-14 dating at an archaeological site in Egypt.

Radiocarbon dating is based on the radioactivity of $^{14}_{6}C$, which decays by β-particle production.

$$^{14}_{6}C \rightarrow {}^{0}_{-1}e + {}^{14}_{7}N$$

Carbon-14 is continuously produced in the atmosphere when high-energy neutrons from space collide with nitrogen-14.

$$^{14}_{7}N + {}^{1}_{0}n \rightarrow {}^{14}_{6}C + {}^{1}_{1}H$$

Just as carbon-14 is produced continuously by this process, it decomposes continuously through β-particle production. Over the years, these two opposing processes have come into balance, causing the amount of $^{14}_{6}C$ present in the atmosphere to remain approximately constant.

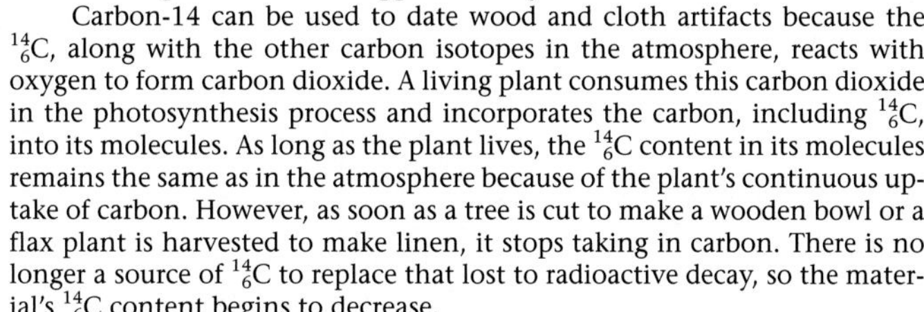

Carbon-14 can be used to date wood and cloth artifacts because the $^{14}_{6}C$, along with the other carbon isotopes in the atmosphere, reacts with oxygen to form carbon dioxide. A living plant consumes this carbon dioxide in the photosynthesis process and incorporates the carbon, including $^{14}_{6}C$, into its molecules. As long as the plant lives, the $^{14}_{6}C$ content in its molecules remains the same as in the atmosphere because of the plant's continuous uptake of carbon. However, as soon as a tree is cut to make a wooden bowl or a flax plant is harvested to make linen, it stops taking in carbon. There is no longer a source of $^{14}_{6}C$ to replace that lost to radioactive decay, so the material's $^{14}_{6}C$ content begins to decrease.

Because the half-life of $^{14}_{6}C$ is known to be 5730 years, a wooden bowl found in an archaeological dig that shows a $^{14}_{6}C$ content of half that found in currently living trees is approximately 5730 years old. That is, because half the $^{14}_{6}C$ present when the tree was cut has disappeared, the tree must have been cut one half-life of $^{14}_{6}C$ ago.

CHEMISTRY IN FOCUS

Dating Diamonds

While connoisseurs of gems value the clearest possible diamonds, geologists learn the most from impure diamonds. Diamonds are formed in the earth's crust at depths of about 200 kilometers, where the high pressures and temperatures favor the most dense form of carbon. As the diamond is formed, impurities are sometimes trapped, and these can be used to determine the diamond's date of "birth." One valuable dating impurity is $^{238}_{92}U$, which is radioactive and decays in a series of steps to $^{206}_{82}Pb$, which is stable (nonradioactive). Because the rate at which $^{238}_{92}U$ decays is known, determining how much $^{238}_{92}U$ has been converted to $^{206}_{82}Pb$ tells scientists the amount of time that has elapsed since the $^{238}_{92}U$ was trapped in the diamond as it was formed.

Using these dating techniques, Peter D. Kinney of Curtin University of Technology in Perth, Australia, and Henry O. A. Meyer of Purdue University in West Lafayette, Indiana, have identified the youngest diamond ever found. Discovered in Mbuji Mayi, Zaire, the diamond is 628 million years old, far younger than all previously dated diamonds, which range from 2.4 to 3.2 billion years old.

The great age of all previously dated diamonds had caused some geologists to speculate that all diamond formation occurred billions of years ago. However, this "youngster" suggests that diamonds have formed throughout geologic time and are probably being formed right now in the earth's crust. We won't see these diamonds for a long time, because diamonds typically remain deeply buried in the earth's crust for millions of years until they are brought to the surface by volcanic blasts called kimberlite eruptions.

It's good to know that eons from now there will be plenty of diamonds to mark the engagements of future couples.

Smithsonian Institution, Natural History Museum, Department of Mineral Sciences

The Hope diamond.

Section 19.5

TEACHING TIPS

- You could assign students to learn more about the applications in Table 19.4. Their summaries could be shared with the class as oral reports.
- The useful properties of radiotracers depend on their half-lives. Have your students compare the half-lives of radiotracers with the half-life of carbon-14.

19.5 Medical Applications of Radioactivity

OBJECTIVE: To discuss the use of radiotracers in medicine.

Nuclides used as radiotracers have short half-lives so that they disappear rapidly from the body.

Although we owe the rapid advances of the medical sciences in recent decades to many causes, one of the most important has been the discovery and use of **radiotracers**—radioactive nuclides that can be introduced into organisms in food or drugs and subsequently *traced* by monitoring their radioactivity. For example, the incorporation of nuclides such as $^{14}_{6}C$ and $^{32}_{15}P$ into nutrients has yielded important information about how these nutrients are used to provide energy for the body.

Iodine-131 has proved very useful in the diagnosis and treatment of illnesses of the thyroid gland. Patients drink a solution containing a small amount of NaI that includes ^{131}I, and the uptake of the iodine by the thyroid gland is monitored with a scanner (Figure 19.3).

Thallium-201 can be used to assess the damage to the heart muscle in a person who has suffered a heart attack because thallium becomes concentrated

PET, the Brain's Best Friend

One of the most valuable applications of radioactivity is in the use of radiotracers for medical diagnosis. Radiotracers are radioactive atoms that are attached to biologically active molecules. The resultant radioactivity is monitored to check on the functioning of organs such as the heart or to trace the path and final destination of a drug.

One particularly valuable radiotracer technique is called positron emission tomography (PET). As its name suggests, PET uses positron producers, such as ^{18}F and ^{11}C, as "labels" on biologic molecules. PET is especially useful for brain scans. For example, a modified form of glucose with ^{18}F attached is commonly used to map glucose metabolism. Areas of the brain where glucose is being rapidly consumed "light up" on the PET screen. The brain of a patient who has a tumor or who has Alzheimer's disease will show a much different picture than will a brain of a patient without Alzheimer's disease. Another application of PET is in seeing how much of a particular labeled drug reaches the intended target. This enables pharmaceutical companies to check the effectiveness of a drug and to set dosages.

One of the challenges of using PET is the speed required to synthesize the labeled molecule. For example, ^{18}F has a half-life of 110 minutes. Thus, in a little less than 2 hours after the ^{18}F has been produced in a particle accelerator, half of it has already decayed. Also, because of the dangers of handling radioactive ^{18}F, synthesis operations must be carried out by robotic manipulations inside a lead-lined box. The good news is that PET is incredibly sensitive—it can detect amounts of ^{18}F as small as 10^{-12} mol. The use of ^{11}C is even more challenging synthetically than the use of ^{18}F because ^{11}C has a half-life of only 20 minutes.

PET is a rapidly growing technology. In particular, more chemists are needed in this field to improve synthetic methods and to develop new radioactive tracers. If this is of interest to you, do some exploring to see how to prepare yourself for a job in this field.

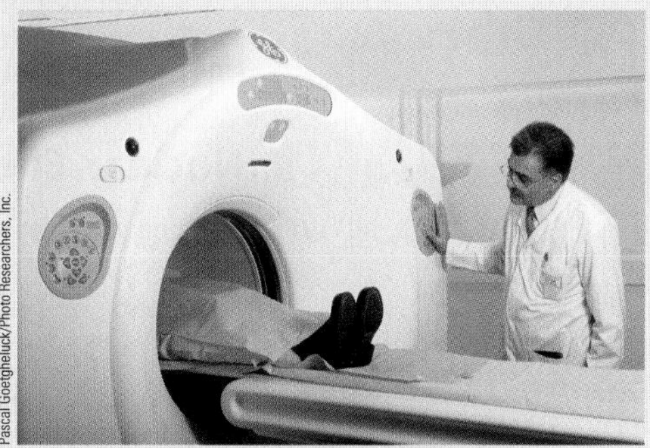
Pascal Goetgheluck/Photo Researchers, Inc.

A positron emission tomography (PET) scanner.

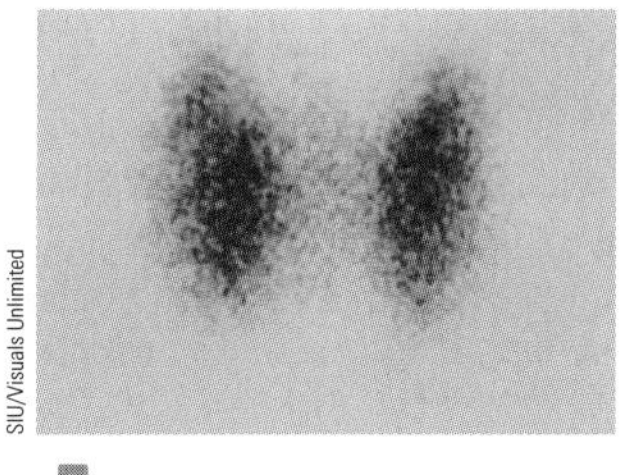
SIU/Visuals Unlimited

a *Scan of radioactive iodine in a normal thyroid.*

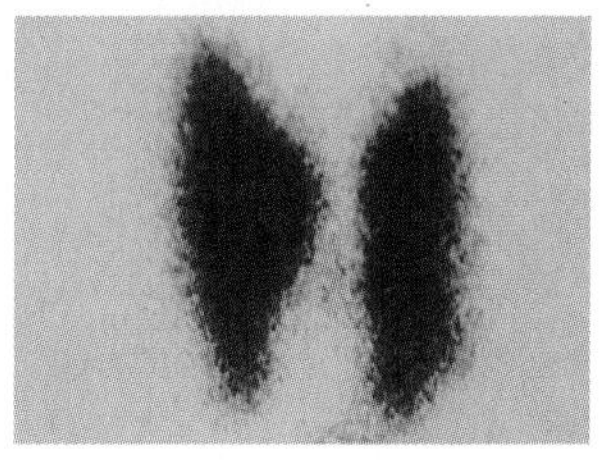
b *Scan of an enlarged thyroid.*

Figure 19.3
After consumption of $Na^{131}I$, the patient's thyroid is scanned for radioactivity levels to determine the efficiency of iodine absorption.

625

Table 19.4 Some Radioactive Nuclides, Their Half-lives, and Their Medical Applications as Radiotracers*

Nuclide	Half-life	Area of the Body Studied
^{131}I	8.1 days	thyroid
^{59}Fe	45.1 days	red blood cells
^{99}Mo	67 hours	metabolism
^{32}P	14.3 days	eyes, liver, tumors
^{51}Cr	27.8 days	red blood cells
^{87}Sr	2.8 hours	bones
^{99}Tc	6.0 hours	heart, bones, liver, lungs
^{133}Xe	5.3 days	lungs
^{24}Na	14.8 hours	circulatory system

*Z is sometimes not written when listing nuclides.

in healthy muscle tissue. Technetium-99, which is also taken up by normal heart tissue, is used for damage assessment in a similar way.

Radiotracers provide sensitive and nonsurgical methods for learning about biologic systems, for detecting disease, and for monitoring the action and effectiveness of drugs. Some useful radiotracers are listed in Table 19.4.

Section 19.6

19.6 Nuclear Energy

OBJECTIVE: To introduce fusion and fission as producers of nuclear energy.

The protons and the neutrons in atomic nuclei are bound together with forces that are much greater than the forces that bind atoms together to form molecules. In fact, the energies associated with nuclear processes are more than a million times those associated with chemical reactions. This potentially makes the nucleus a very attractive source of energy.

Because medium-sized nuclei contain the strongest binding forces ($^{56}_{26}Fe$ has the strongest binding forces of all), there are two types of nuclear processes that produce energy:

1. Combining two light nuclei to form a heavier nucleus. This process is called **fusion.**
2. Splitting a heavy nucleus into two nuclei with smaller mass numbers. This process is called **fission.**

Test Bank: 20–22

As we will see in the next several sections, these two processes can supply amazing quantities of energy with relatively small masses of materials consumed.

Section 19.7

19.7 Nuclear Fission

OBJECTIVE: To learn about nuclear fission.

TEACHING TIP

This is an excellent place for a student debate on the use of nuclear power.

Nuclear fission was discovered in the late 1930s when $^{235}_{92}U$ nuclides bombarded with neutrons were observed to split into two lighter elements.

$$^{1}_{0}n + ^{235}_{92}U \rightarrow ^{141}_{56}Ba + ^{92}_{36}Kr + 3\,^{1}_{0}n$$

PowerLecture Animation: Nuclear Fission

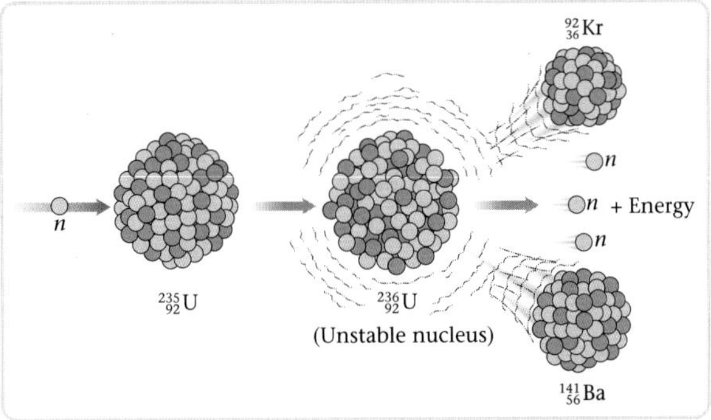

Figure 19.4 Upon capturing a neutron, the $^{235}_{92}U$ nucleus undergoes fission to produce two lighter nuclides, more neutrons (typically three), and a large amount of energy.

This process, shown schematically in Figure 19.4, releases 2.1×10^{13} joules of energy per mole of $^{235}_{92}U$. Compared with what we get from typical fuels, this is a huge amount of energy. For example, the fission of 1 mole of $^{235}_{92}U$ produces about *26 million times* as much energy as the combustion of 1 mole of methane.

The process shown in Figure 19.4 is only one of the many fission reactions that $^{235}_{92}U$ can undergo. In fact, over 200 different isotopes of 35 different elements have been observed among the fission products of $^{235}_{92}U$.

In addition to the product nuclides, neutrons are produced in the fission reactions of $^{235}_{92}U$. As these neutrons fly through the solid sample of uranium, they may collide with other $^{235}_{92}U$ nuclei, producing additional fission events. Each of these fission events produces more neutrons that can, in turn, produce the fission of more $^{235}_{92}U$ nuclei. Because each fission event produces neutrons, the process can be self-sustaining. We call it a **chain reaction** (Figure 19.5). For the fission process to be self-sustaining, at least one neutron from each fission event must go on to split another nucleus. If, on average, *less than one* neutron causes another fission event, the process dies out. If *exactly one* neutron from each fission event causes another fission event, the process sustains itself at the same level and is said to be *critical*. If *more than one* neutron from each fission event causes another fission event, the process rapidly escalates and the heat buildup causes a violent explosion.

To achieve the critical state, a certain mass of fissionable material, called the **critical mass,** is needed. If the sample is too small, too many

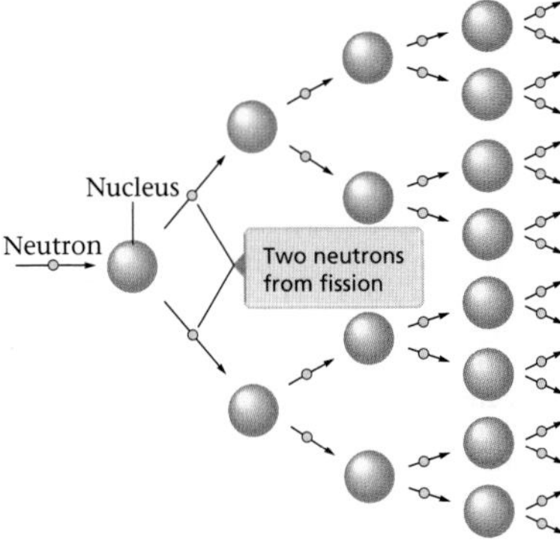

Figure 19.5 Representation of a fission process in which each event produces two neutrons that can go on to split other nuclei, leading to a self-sustaining chain reaction.

19.7 Nuclear Fission 627

neutrons escape before they have a chance to cause a fission event, and the process stops.

During World War II, the United States carried out an intense research effort called the Manhattan Project to build a bomb based on the principles of nuclear fission. This program produced the fission bomb, which was used with devastating effect on the cities of Hiroshima and Nagasaki in 1945. Basically, a fission bomb operates by suddenly combining two subcritical masses, which results in rapidly escalating fission events that produce an explosion of incredible intensity.

Section 19.8

Test Bank: 24

19.8 Nuclear Reactors

OBJECTIVE: To understand how a nuclear reactor works.

Natural uranium consists mostly of $^{238}_{92}U$.

Because of the tremendous energies involved, fission has been developed as an energy source to produce electricity in reactors where controlled fission can occur. The resulting energy is used to heat water to produce steam that runs turbine generators, in much the same way that a coal-burning power plant generates energy by heating water to produce steam. A schematic diagram of a nuclear power plant is shown in Figure 19.6.

In the reactor core (Figure 19.7), uranium that has been enriched to approximately 3% $^{235}_{92}U$ (natural uranium contains only 0.7% $^{235}_{92}U$) is housed in metal cylinders. A *moderator* surrounding the cylinders slows the neutrons down so that the uranium fuel can capture them more efficiently. *Control rods,* composed of substances (such as cadmium) that absorb neutrons, are used to regulate the power level of the reactor. The reactor is designed so that if a malfunction occurs, the control rods are automatically inserted into the core to absorb neutrons and stop the reaction. A liquid (usually water) is circulated through the core to extract the heat generated by the energy of fission. This heat energy is then used to change water to steam, which runs turbines that in turn run electrical generators.

The core of a nuclear power plant.

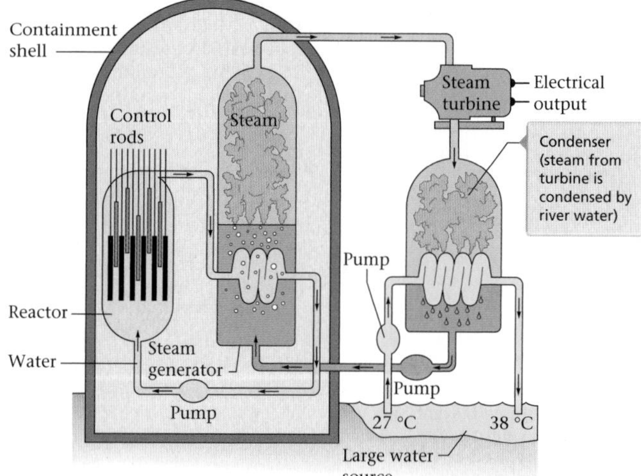

Figure 19.6
A schematic diagram of a nuclear power plant. The energy from the fission process is used to boil water, producing steam for use in a turbine-driven generator. Cooling water from a lake or river is used to condense the steam after it leaves the turbine.

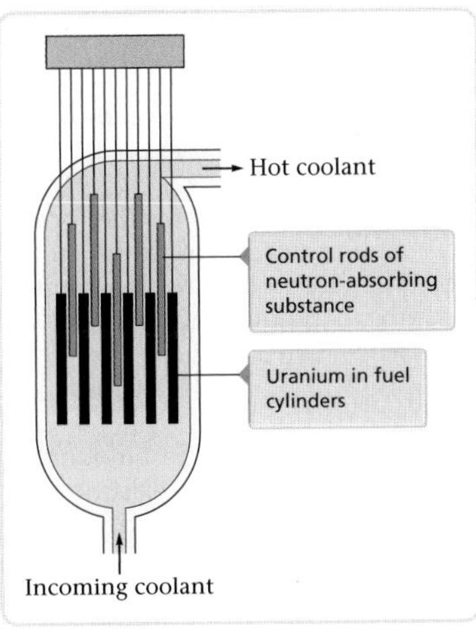

Figure 19.7
A schematic diagram of a reactor core.

Although the concentration of $^{235}_{92}U$ in the fuel elements is not great enough to allow an explosion such as that which occurs in a fission bomb, a failure of the cooling system can lead to temperatures high enough to melt the reactor core. This means that the building housing the core must be designed to contain the core even in the event of such a "meltdown." A great deal of controversy now exists about the efficiency of the safety systems in nuclear power plants. Accidents such as the one at the Three Mile Island facility in Pennsylvania in 1979 and the one at Chernobyl in the Soviet Union in 1986 have led many people to question the wisdom of continuing to build fission-based power plants.

Breeder Reactors

One potential problem facing the nuclear power industry is the limited supply of $^{235}_{92}U$. Some scientists believe that we have nearly depleted the uranium deposits that are rich enough in $^{235}_{92}U$ to make the production of fissionable fuel economically feasible. Because of this possibility, reactors have been developed in which fissionable fuel is actually produced while the reactor runs. In these **breeder reactors,** the major component of natural uranium, nonfissionable $^{238}_{92}U$, is changed to fissionable $^{239}_{94}Pu$. The reaction involves absorption of a neutron, followed by production of two β particles.

$$^{1}_{0}n + ^{238}_{92}U \rightarrow ^{239}_{92}U$$
$$^{239}_{92}U \rightarrow ^{239}_{93}Np + ^{0}_{-1}e$$
$$^{239}_{93}Np \rightarrow ^{239}_{94}Pu + ^{0}_{-1}e$$

As the reactor runs and $^{235}_{92}U$ is split, some of the excess neutrons are absorbed by $^{238}_{92}U$ to produce $^{239}_{94}Pu$. The $^{239}_{94}Pu$ is then separated out and used to fuel another reactor. Such a reactor thus "breeds" nuclear fuel as it operates.

Although breeder reactors are now used in Europe, the United States is proceeding slowly with their development because much controversy surrounds their use. One problem involves the hazards that arise in handling plutonium, which is very toxic and flames on contact with air.

19.9 Nuclear Fusion

Section 19.9

OBJECTIVE: To learn about nuclear fusion.

$^{2}_{1}H$ particles are called *deuterons.*

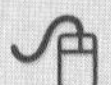
Test Bank: 25

PowerLecture Animation: Nuclear Fusion

The process of combining two light nuclei—called **nuclear fusion**—produces even more energy per mole than does nuclear fission. In fact, stars produce their energy through nuclear fusion. Our sun, which presently consists of 73% hydrogen, 26% helium, and 1% other elements, gives off vast quantities of energy from the fusion of protons to form helium. One possible scheme for this process is

$$^{1}_{1}H + ^{1}_{1}H \rightarrow ^{2}_{1}H + ^{0}_{1}e + \text{energy}$$
$$^{1}_{1}H + ^{2}_{1}H \rightarrow ^{3}_{2}He + \text{energy}$$
$$^{3}_{2}He + ^{3}_{2}He \rightarrow ^{4}_{2}He + 2\,^{1}_{1}H + \text{energy}$$
$$^{3}_{2}He + ^{1}_{1}H \rightarrow ^{4}_{2}He + ^{0}_{1}e + \text{energy}$$

Intense efforts are under way to develop a feasible fusion process because of the ready availability of many light nuclides (deuterium, $^{2}_{1}H$, in

CHEMISTRY IN FOCUS

Future Nuclear Power

Energy—a crucial commodity in today's world—will become even more important as the pace of world development increases. Because the energy content of the universe is constant, the challenge of energy is not its quantity but rather its quality. We must find economical and environmentally friendly ways to change the energy available in the universe to forms useful to humanity. This process always involves trade-offs. One of the most abundant sources of energy is the energy that binds the atomic nucleus together. We can derive useful energy by assembling small nuclei (fusion) or splitting large nuclei (fission). Although fusion reactors are being studied, a practical fusion reactor appears to be decades away. By contrast, fission reactors have been used since the 1950s. In fact, the production of electricity via fission reactors is widespread. At present, more than 430 nuclear reactors operate in 31 countries, producing over 370 billion watts of electrical power. More than 45 reactors are currently under construction. The 104 reactors currently operating in the United States produce over 100 billion watts of electricity—almost 20% of the country's electrical demands.

Forecasts indicate that the United States will need an additional 355 billion watts of generating capacity in the next 20 years. Where will this energy come from? A significant amount will be derived from coal-fired power plants. However, the major problems with these plants are air pollution and greenhouse gas (CO_2) production (see "Chemistry in Focus: Atmospheric Effects," on page 326).

Another potential source of power is solar energy. It should be an excellent pollution-free energy source, but significant technical problems remain to be solved before it sees widespread use.

Still another important potential power source is nuclear energy. To provide all of the needed 355 billion watts from nuclear energy would require hundreds of new nuclear reactors. However, nuclear power generation is very controversial because of safety, waste disposal, and cost issues.

To address these issues, huge amounts of money are being spent to improve existing reactor designs and to find new types of reactors that will be safer, be more efficient, and generate much less waste. An international consortium—the Generation IV International Forum (GIF)—was formed in 2000 and has decided to study six new reactor designs with the goal of development of one or more of these designs by 2030.

Nuclear power generation is too important to ignore. In the near future we must decide whether its use can be extended safely and economically.

A nuclear reactor.

seawater, for example) that can serve as fuel in fusion reactors. However, initiating the fusion process is much more difficult than initiating fission. The forces that bind nucleons together to form a nucleus become effective only at *very small* distances (approximately 10^{-13} cm), so for two protons to bind together and thereby release energy, they must get very close together. But protons, because they are identically charged, repel each other. This suggests that to get two protons (or two deuterons) close enough to bind together (the strong nuclear binding force is *not* related to charge), they must

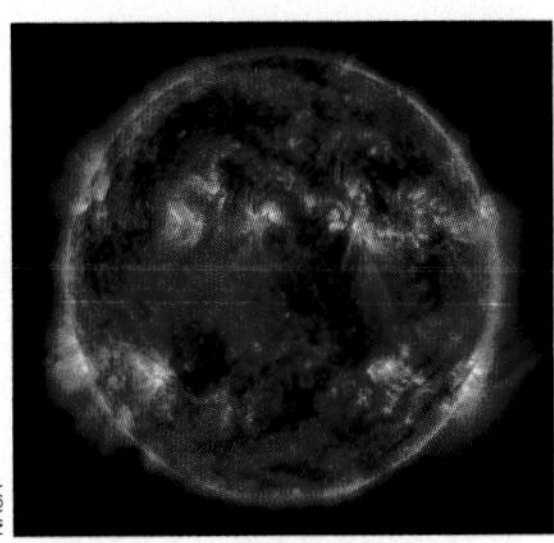

A solar flare erupts from the surface of the sun.

be "shot" at each other at speeds high enough to overcome their repulsion from each other. The repulsive forces between two $^{2}_{1}H$ nuclei are so great that temperatures of about 40 million K are thought to be necessary. Only at these temperatures are the nuclei moving fast enough to overcome the repulsions.

Currently, scientists are studying two types of systems to produce the extremely high temperatures required: high-powered lasers and heating by electric currents. At present, many technical problems remain to be solved, and it is not clear whether either method will prove useful.

Test Bank: 26

19.10 Effects of Radiation

OBJECTIVE: To see how radiation damages human tissue.

Everyone knows that being hit by a train is a catastrophic event. The energy transferred in such a collision is very large. In fact, any source of energy is potentially harmful to organisms. Energy transferred to cells can break chemical bonds and cause malfunctioning of the cell systems. This fact is behind our present concern about maintaining the ozone layer in the earth's upper atmosphere, which screens out high-energy ultraviolet radiation arriving from the sun. Radioactive elements, which are sources of high-energy particles, are also potentially hazardous. However, the effects are usually quite subtle, because even though high-energy particles are involved, the quantity of energy actually deposited in tissues *per decay event* is quite small. The resulting damage is no less real, but the effects may not be apparent for years.

Radiation damage to organisms can be classified as somatic or genetic damage. *Somatic damage* is damage to the organism itself, resulting in sickness or death. The effects may appear almost immediately if a massive dose of radiation is received; for smaller doses, damage may appear years later, usually in the form of cancer. *Genetic damage* is damage to the genetic machinery of reproductive cells, creating problems that often afflict the offspring of the organism.

The biologic effects of a particular source of radiation depend on several factors:

1. *The energy of the radiation.* The higher the energy content of the radiation, the more damage it can cause.
2. *The penetrating ability of the radiation.* The particles and rays produced in radioactive processes vary in their ability to penetrate human tissue: γ rays are highly penetrating, β particles can penetrate approximately 1 cm, and α particles are stopped by the skin (Figure 19.8).
3. *The ionizing ability of the radiation.* Because ions behave quite differently from neutral molecules, radiation that removes electrons from molecules in living tissues seriously disturbs their functions. The ionizing ability of radiation varies dramatically. For example, γ rays penetrate very deeply but cause only occasional ionization. On the other hand, α particles, although they are not very penetrating, are very effective at causing ionization and produce serious damage. Therefore, the ingestion of a producer of α particles, such as plutonium, is particularly damaging.

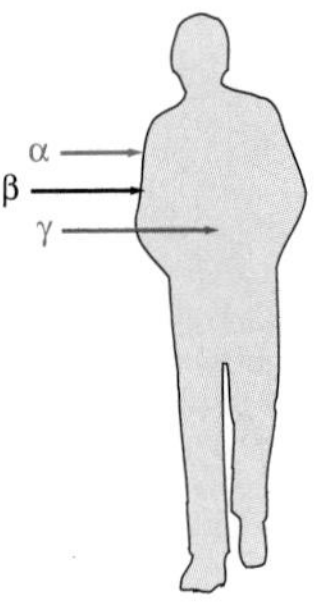

Figure 19.8
Radioactive particles and rays vary greatly in penetrating power. Gamma rays are by far the most penetrating.

Section 19.10

TEACHING TIPS

- This section is an opportunity to connect the study of chemistry to medicine and health. Many students do not understand the different effects of radiation on human tissue.
- The preservation of food by using gamma radiation was first approved by the Food and Drug Administration in 1963. The first foods approved for radiation preservation were wheat flour and potatoes. Not until 1986 could fruits and vegetables be preserved by radiation.

TEACHING SUPPORT

HISTORICAL BACKGROUND

During the early days of nuclear chemistry, scientists did not understand the hazards of radioactive substances. Many of the early scientists were exposed to harmful radiation. Marie Curie is a well-known example of radiation poisoning during her days of refining pitchblende. When doctors first began using X rays for diagnosis, patients were burned by the radiations. In 1896, Elihu Thompson (a physicist) deliberately exposed his hand to X rays in an effort to determine the effect of X-ray burns on the skin. One of Thomas Edison's assistants became fatally ill from X-ray exposure. Henri Becquerel also experienced radiation burns when he carried a radioactive sample with him in his pocket.

CHEMISTRY *IN* FOCUS

Nuclear Waste Disposal

Our society does not have a very impressive record for safe disposal of industrial wastes. We have polluted our water and air, and some land areas have become virtually uninhabitable because of the improper burial of chemical wastes. As a result, many people are wary about the radioactive wastes from nuclear reactors. The potential threats of cancer and genetic mutations make these materials especially frightening.

Because of its controversial nature, most of the nuclear waste generated over the past 50 years has been placed in temporary storage. However, in 1982 the U.S. Congress passed the Nuclear Waste Policy Act, which established a timetable for choosing and preparing sites for the deep underground disposal of radioactive materials.

The tentative disposal plan calls for incorporation of the spent nuclear fuel into blocks of glass that will be packed in corrosion-resistant metal containers and then buried in a deep, stable rock formation indicated by the rock layers in Figure 19.9.

There are indications that this method will isolate the waste until the radioactivity decays to safe levels. Some reassuring evidence comes from a natural fission "reactor" that has been discovered at Oklo in Gabon, Africa. Spawned about 2 billion years ago when uranium in ore deposits there formed a critical mass, this "reactor" produced fission and fusion products for several thousand years. Although some of these products have migrated away from the site in the intervening 2 billion years, most have stayed in place.

Finally, more than 25 years after the Nuclear Policy Act, we have begun to store nuclear waste. In 1998, the Waste Isolation Policy Plant (WIPP) in New Mexico was issued a license by the U.S. Environmental Protection Agency to begin receiving nuclear waste, and in March 1999, WIPP received its first waste. This facility employs tunnels carved into the salt beds of an ancient ocean. Once a repository room becomes full, the salt will collapse around the waste, encapsulating it forever.

Another waste depository, under Yucca Mountain in Nevada, may begin to store nuclear waste in the next several years. In June 2008, the Department of Energy submitted a license application to the Nuclear Regulatory Commission (NCR) to construct a repository. This process can take 3 to 4 years for approval and then more time to actually build the repository.

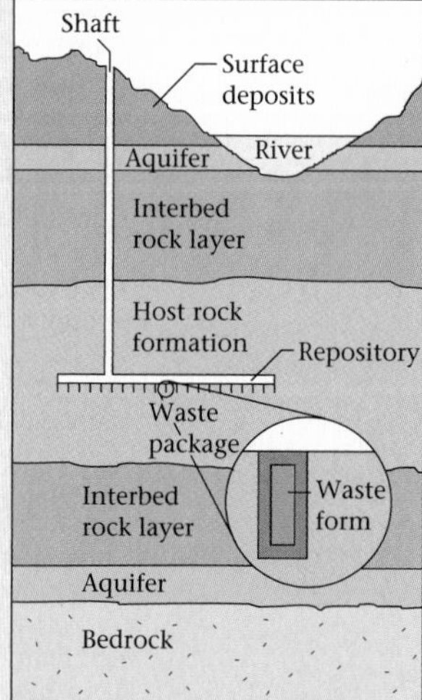

Figure 19.9
A schematic diagram for the tentative plan for deep underground isolation of nuclear waste. The disposal system would consist of a waste package buried in an underground repository. (Reprinted with permission from *Chemical & Engineering News,* July 18, 1983. Copyright © 1983 American Chemical Society.)

632

4. *The chemical properties of the radiation source.* When a radioactive nuclide is ingested, its capacity to cause damage depends on how long it remains in the body. For example, both $^{85}_{36}Kr$ and $^{90}_{38}Sr$ are β-particle producers. Because krypton, being a noble gas, is chemically inert, it passes through the body quickly and does not have much time to do damage. Strontium, on the other hand, is chemically similar to calcium. It can collect in bones, where it may cause leukemia and bone cancer.

Because of the differences in the behavior of the particles and rays produced by radioactive decay, we have invented a unit called the **rem** that indicates the danger the radiation poses to humans.

Table 19.5 shows the physical effects of short-term exposure to various doses of radiation, and Table 19.6 gives the sources and amounts of the radiation a typical person in the United States is exposed to each year. Note that natural sources contribute about twice as much as human activities do to the total exposure. However, although the nuclear industry contributes only a small percentage of the total exposure, controversy surrounds nuclear power plants because of their *potential* for creating radiation hazards. These hazards arise mainly from two sources: accidents allowing the release of radioactive materials, and improper disposal of the radioactive products in spent fuel elements.

Table 19.5 Effects of Short-Term Exposures to Radiation

Dose (rem)	Clinical Effect
0–25	nondetectable
25–50	temporary decrease in white blood cell counts
100–200	strong decrease in white blood cell counts
500	death of half the exposed population within 30 days after exposure

Table 19.6 Typical Radiation Exposures for a Person Living in the United States (1 millirem = 10^{-3} rem)

Source	Exposure (millirems/year)
cosmic	50
from the earth	47
from building materials	3
in human tissues	21
inhalation of air	5
Total from natural sources	126
X-ray diagnosis	50
radiotherapy X rays, radioisotopes	10
internal diagnosis and therapy	1
nuclear power industry	0.2
luminous watch dials, TV tubes,	
industrial wastes	2
radioactive fallout	4
Total from human activities	67
Total	193 = 0.193 rem

TEACHING TIPS

- Table 19.6 gives sources and amounts of radiation exposure for humans. This information can be used in a discussion of the natural sources and exposure to radioactivity expected in our lives.
- The use of nuclear imaging techniques is a good starting point for a discussion of the hazards and benefits of nuclear medicine.

CHAPTER 19 REVIEW

Key Terms

- nucleons (neutrons and protons) (p. 615)
- atomic number (Z) (p. 615)
- mass number (A) (p. 615)
- isotope (p. 615)
- nuclide (p. 615)
- radioactive (19.1)
- beta (β) particle (19.1)
- nuclear equation (19.1)
- alpha (α) particle (19.1)
- alpha (α)-particle production (19.1)
- beta (β)-particle production (19.1)
- gamma (γ) ray (19.1)
- positron (19.1)
- positron production (19.1)
- electron capture (19.1)
- decay series (19.1)
- nuclear transformation (19.2)
- transuranium elements (19.2)
- Geiger–Müller counter (Geiger counter) (19.3)
- scintillation counter (19.3)
- half-life (19.3)
- radiocarbon dating (carbon-14 dating) (19.4)
- radiotracers (19.5)
- fusion (19.6)
- fission (19.6)
- chain reaction (19.7)
- critical mass (19.7)
- breeder reactor (19.8)
- nuclear fusion (19.9)
- rem (19.10)

F directs you to the *Chemistry in Focus* feature in the chapter
VP indicates visual problems
OWL interactive versions of these problems are assignable in OWL

Summary

1. Radioactivity is the spontaneous decomposition of a nucleus to form another nucleus and produce one or more particles. We can write a nuclear equation to represent radioactive decay, in which both A (mass number) and Z (atomic number) must be conserved.
2. There are several types of radioactive decay: alpha-particle production, in which an alpha particle (helium nucleus) is produced; beta-particle (or electron) production; the production of gamma rays (high-energy photons of light); and electron capture, in which one of the inner-orbital electrons is captured by the nucleus. Often a series of decays occurs before a radioactive nucleus attains a stable state.
3. The production of new elements by nuclear transformation (the change of one element into another) is carried out by bombarding various nuclei with particles in accelerators. The transuranium elements have been synthesized in this way.
4. The half-life of a radioactive nuclide is the time required for one-half of the original sample to decay. Radiocarbon dating is based on the radioactivity of carbon-14.
5. Radiotracers—radioactive nuclides that can be introduced into organisms in food or drugs and whose pathways can be traced by monitoring their radioactivity—are used diagnostically in medicine.
6. Nuclear fusion is the process of combining two light nuclei to form a heavier, more stable nucleus. Nuclear fission involves the splitting of a heavy nucleus into two (more stable) lighter nuclei. Current nuclear reactors employ controlled fission.
7. Radiation can cause either direct damage to living tissues or damage to reproductive cells that manifests itself in the organism's offspring. The biological effects of radiation depend on the energy of the radiation, the radiation's penetrating ability and ionizing ability, and the chemical properties of the source of the radiation.

Active Learning Questions

These questions are designed to be considered by groups of students in class. Often these questions work well for introducing a particular topic in class.

1. It states in Section 19.1 of your text that approximately 2000 nuclides are known. How can this be possible if there are only about 100 elements?
2. By how many units does the mass number of a nucleus change when the nucleus produces an alpha particle? By how many units does the mass number of a nucleus change when the nucleus produces a beta particle? Is each change an increase or decrease in mass number?
3. Determine the number of half-lives that must pass for only 1% of a particular radioisotope to remain.
4. Hundreds of years ago, alchemists tried to turn lead into gold. Is this transformation possible? If not, why not? If yes, how would you do it?
5. Do radiotracers generally have long or short half-lives? Why?
6. Why is the nucleus of an atom a great source of energy?
7. Discuss what is meant by the term "critical mass" and explain why the ability to achieve a critical mass is essential to sustaining a nuclear reaction.

ChemWork

Thermodynamics of Hydrogen Production

Electrolysis of $CaCl_2$

Solubility of Magnesium Hydroxide

Formulas and Names

Properties of Groups 1–4

Structure and Hybridization of Group 4 Compounds

Answers to End-of-Chapter Exercises

1. The chemical properties of an atom are due almost exclusively to its electron structure; the nucleus has little or no effect.

2. The radius of a typical atomic nucleus is on the order of 10^{-13} cm, which is roughly 100,000 times smaller than the radius of an atom overall.

3. The atomic number represents the number of protons in the nucleus.

4. The mass number represents the total number of protons and neutrons in a nucleus.

5. Many elements consist of atoms that are not identical. These atoms contain the same number of protons and electrons, so they are *chemically* the same, but they contain different numbers of neutrons, which modifies some *physical* properties.

6. The atomic number (Z) is written as a left subscript, while the mass number (A) is written as a left superscript. That is, the general symbol for a nuclide is ${}^{A}_{Z}X$. As an example, consider the isotope of oxygen with 8 protons and 8 neutrons: its symbol is ${}^{16}_{8}O$.

7. ${}^{4}_{2}He$

8. electron

9. A beta particle is essentially an electron, ${}^{0}_{-1}e$. Emission of an electron increases the atomic number of the parent nucleus by one unit but does not change the mass number of the parent nucleus.

10. Emission of a neutron, ${}^{1}_{0}n$, does not change the atomic number of the parent nucleus but causes the mass number of the parent nucleus to decrease by one unit.

11. Some nuclei do not become stable on the emission of *one* particle. Such nuclei may decay through a *series of emissions* until they finally reach stability.

12. Gamma rays are high-energy photons of electromagnetic radiation; they are not normally considered to be particles. When a nucleus produces only gamma radiation, the atomic number and mass number of the nucleus do not change.

8. What makes fusion preferable over fission? What makes fusion more complicated?

9. Why is it difficult to determine the effects of radiation on humans?

VP 10. What type of radioactive decay must occur for each of the following transformations?

a. Transformation 1
b. Transformation 2
c. Transformation 3

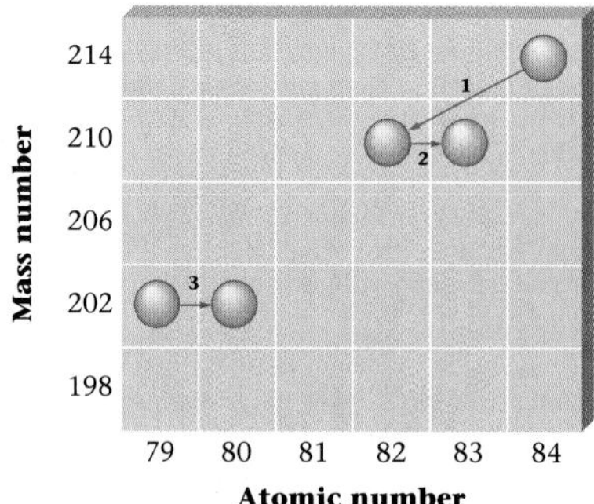

10. When a nucleus emits a neutron, does the atomic number of the nucleus change? Does the mass number of the nucleus change? Explain.

11. What is a *decay series?*

12. What changes, if any, take place to the atomic number and the mass number of an unstable nucleus when the nucleus emits a gamma ray?

13. What is a *positron?* What are the mass number and charge of a positron? How do the mass number and atomic number of a nucleus change when the nucleus produces a positron?

14. What do we mean when we say a nucleus has undergone an *electron capture* process? What type of electron is captured by the nucleus in this process?

PROBLEMS

15. Naturally occurring sulfur consists primarily (94.9%) of the isotope with mass number 32, but small amounts of the isotopes with mass numbers 33, 34, and 36 also are present. Write the nuclear symbol for each of the isotopes of sulfur. How many neutrons are present in each isotope? Is the average atomic mass of sulfur (32.07 g) consistent with the relative abundances of the isotopes?

16. Although naturally occurring potassium consists mostly of the isotope of mass number 39 (93.25%), isotopes of mass number 41 (6.73%) and 40 (0.01%) also are present. Write the nuclear symbol for each of the isotopes of potassium. How many neutrons are present in each isotope? Is the average atomic mass of potassium (39.10 g) consistent with the relative abundances of the isotopes?

17. Naturally occurring magnesium consists primarily of three isotopes, of mass numbers 24, 25, and 26. How many protons does each of these nuclides contain? How many neutrons does each of these nuclides contain? Write nuclear symbols for each of these isotopes.

18. Consider the three isotopes of magnesium discussed in Exercise 17. Given that the relative natural abundances of these isotopes are 79%, 10%, and 11%, respectively, without looking at the inside cover of this book, what is the *approximate* atomic molar mass of magnesium? Explain how you made your prediction.

19. Give the nuclear symbol for each of the following.

a. a beta particle
b. an alpha particle
c. a neutron
d. a proton

20. Name the particle that has the following nuclear symbol.

a. $^{0}_{-1}\text{e}$
b. $^{0}_{1}\text{e}$
c. $^{1}_{0}\text{n}$
d. $^{1}_{1}\text{H}$

Questions and Problems

19.1 Radioactive Decay

QUESTIONS

1. Does the nucleus of an atom strongly affect its chemical properties? Explain.

2. How large is a typical atomic nucleus, and how does the size of the nucleus of an atom compare with the overall size of the atom?

3. What does the *atomic number* of an atom represent?

4. What does the *mass number* of a nucleus represent?

5. What is meant by saying an element exists in several isotopic forms? Do isotopes of a given element have similar chemical properties? Explain.

6. Using *Z* to represent the atomic number and *A* to represent the mass number, give the general symbol for a nuclide of element X. Give also a specific example of the use of such symbolism.

7. Write the nuclear symbol for an *alpha* particle.

8. To which nuclear particle does the symbol $^{0}_{-1}\text{e}$ refer?

9. When a nucleus emits a *beta* particle, by how many atomic mass units does the mass of the nucleus change? By how many units does the atomic number of the nucleus change? Explain.

All even-numbered Questions and Problems have answers in the back of this book and solutions in the Solutions Guide.

13. A positron has the same mass (mass number 0) as an electron, but a positive charge (*atomic number* 1). When a nucleus emits a positron, the mass number of the nucleus does not change, but its atomic number decreases by 1 unit.

14. Electron capture occurs when one of the inner-orbital electrons is pulled into, and becomes part of, the nucleus.

15. The fact that the average atomic mass of sulfur is only slightly above 32 amu reflects the fact that the isotope of mass number 32 predominates.

Isotope	*Number of Neutrons*
$^{32}_{16}\text{S}$	16 neutrons
$^{33}_{16}\text{S}$	17 neutrons
$^{34}_{16}\text{S}$	18 neutrons
$^{36}_{16}\text{S}$	20 neutrons

16. The fact that the average atomic mass of potassium is only slightly above 39 amu reflects the fact that the isotope of mass number 39 predominates.

Isotope	*Number of Neutrons*
$^{39}_{19}\text{K}$	20 neutrons
$^{40}_{19}\text{K}$	21 neutrons
$^{41}_{19}\text{K}$	22 neutrons

17. $^{24}_{12}\text{Mg}$ (12 protons, 12 neutrons); $^{25}_{12}\text{Mg}$ (12 protons, 13 neutrons); $^{26}_{12}\text{Mg}$ (12 protons, 14 neutrons)

18. Based on the predominance of Mg-24, but with significant amounts of the other isotopes, one would expect the average atomic molar mass to be slightly higher than 24 (24.31 g).

19. (a) $^{0}_{-1}\text{e}$ or $^{0}_{-1}\beta$; (b) $^{4}_{2}\text{He}$ or $^{4}_{2}\alpha$; (c) $^{1}_{0}\text{n}$; (d) $^{1}_{1}\text{H}$

20. (a) electron; (b) positron; (c) neutron; (d) proton

21. (a) $^{4}_{2}\text{He}$; (b) $^{6}_{3}\text{Li}$; (c) $^{0}_{-1}\text{e}$

22. (a) $^{23}_{12}\text{Mg}$; (b) $^{5}_{3}\text{Li}$; (c) $^{4}_{2}\text{He}$

23. (a) $^{206}_{87}\text{Fr}$; (b) $^{0}_{-1}\text{e}$; (c) $^{1}_{0}\text{n}$

24. (a) $^{218}_{86}\text{Rn}$; (b) $^{0}_{+1}\text{e}$ (positron); (c) $^{137}_{56}\text{Ba}$

25. (a) $^{14}_{6}\text{C} \rightarrow {}^{0}_{-1}\text{e} + {}^{14}_{7}\text{N}$; (b) $^{140}_{55}\text{Cs} \rightarrow {}^{0}_{-1}\text{e} + {}^{140}_{56}\text{Ba}$; (c) $^{234}_{90}\text{Th} \rightarrow {}^{0}_{-1}\text{e} + {}^{234}_{91}\text{Pa}$

26. (a) $^{234}_{92}\text{U} \rightarrow {}^{4}_{2}\text{He} + {}^{230}_{90}\text{Th}$; (b) $^{222}_{86}\text{Rn} \rightarrow {}^{4}_{2}\text{He} + {}^{218}_{84}\text{Po}$; (c) $^{162}_{75}\text{Re} \rightarrow {}^{4}_{2}\text{He} + {}^{158}_{53}\text{Ta}$

27. (a) $^{188}_{74}\text{W} \rightarrow {}^{0}_{-1}\text{e} + {}^{188}_{75}\text{Re}$; (b) $^{40}_{19}\text{K} \rightarrow {}^{0}_{-1}\text{e} + {}^{40}_{20}\text{Ca}$; (c) $^{198}_{79}\text{Au} \rightarrow {}^{0}_{-1}\text{e} + {}^{198}_{80}\text{Hg}$

28. (a) $^{212}_{82}\text{Pb} \rightarrow {}^{0}_{-1}\text{e} + {}^{212}_{83}\text{Bi}$; (b) $^{212}_{81}\text{Tl} \rightarrow {}^{0}_{-1}\text{e} + {}^{212}_{82}\text{Pb}$; (c) $^{228}_{88}\text{Ra} \rightarrow {}^{0}_{-1}\text{e} + {}^{228}_{89}\text{Ac}$

29. transformation of one element into another, usually by bombardment of the nucleus

30. In a nuclear bombardment process, a target nucleus is bombarded with high-energy particles (typically subatomic particles or small atoms) from a particle accelerator. This may result in the transmutation of the target nucleus into some other element. For example, nitrogen-14 may be transmuted into oxygen-17 by bombardment with α-particles.

31. ${}^{9}_{4}Be + {}^{4}_{2}He \rightarrow {}^{12}_{6}C + {}^{1}_{0}n$

32. ${}^{24}_{12}Mg + {}^{2}_{1}H \rightarrow {}^{22}_{11}Na + {}^{4}_{2}He$

33. A Geiger counter probe contains argon gas, which is ionized by radioactive particles and which then conducts an electric current that can be detected and measured. A scintillation counter contains a light-emitting substance such as NaI, which flashes light when struck by radioactive particles, and the flashes of light are detected and counted.

34. The half-life of a nucleus is the time required for one-half of the original sample of nuclei to decay. A given isotope of an element always has the same half-life, although different isotopes of the same element may have greatly different half-lives. Nuclei of different elements have different half-lives.

35. One nucleus is "hotter" than another if it undergoes more decay events per time period. This is most commonly expressed in terms of half-life.

36. ${}^{226}_{88}Ra$ is the most stable (longest half-life); ${}^{224}_{88}Ra$ is the "hottest" (shortest half-life).

37. Highest Na > I > Co > H > C lowest

38. highest to lowest activity: ${}^{87}Sr > {}^{99}Tc > {}^{24}Na > {}^{99}Mo > {}^{133}Xe > {}^{131}I > {}^{32}P > {}^{51}Cr > {}^{59}Fe$

39. 25 μg

40. 4 half-lives, 1/16 (0.5^4) remains

41. Krypton-81 is the most stable; krypton-73 is the hottest; for krypton-73 and krypton-74, essentially none would remain after 24 hours; for krypton-76, 24 hours is approximately two half-lives, and ¼ would remain; for krypton-81, the half-life is much more than 24 hours, and essentially all would remain.

21. Complete each of the following nuclear equations by supplying the missing particle.
    a. ${}^{226}_{88}Ra \rightarrow ? + {}^{222}_{86}Rn$
    b. ${}^{9}_{4}Be + {}^{1}_{1}H \rightarrow ? + {}^{4}_{2}He$
    c. ${}^{17}_{8}O + ? \rightarrow {}^{14}_{6}C + {}^{3}_{1}H$

22. Complete each of the following nuclear equations by supplying the missing particle.
    a. ${}^{23}_{13}Al \rightarrow {}^{0}_{+1}\beta + ?$
    b. ${}^{1}_{1}H + {}^{4}_{2}He \rightarrow ?$
    c. ${}^{28}_{14}Si + {}^{1}_{0}n \rightarrow {}^{25}_{12}Mg + ?$

23. Complete each of the following nuclear equations by supplying the missing particle.
    a. ${}^{210}_{89}Ac \rightarrow {}^{4}_{2}He + ?$
    b. ${}^{131}_{53}I \rightarrow {}^{131}_{54}Xe + ?$
    c. ${}^{88}_{35}Br \rightarrow {}^{87}_{35}Br + ?$

24. Complete each of the following nuclear equations by supplying the missing particle.
    a. $? \rightarrow {}^{210}_{84}Po + {}^{4}_{2}He$
    b. ${}^{40}_{19}K \rightarrow {}^{40}_{18}Ar + ?$
    c. ${}^{137}_{57}La + {}^{0}_{-1}e \rightarrow ?$

25. Each of the following nuclides is known to undergo radioactive decay by production of a beta particle, ${}^{0}_{-1}e$. Write a balanced nuclear equation for each process.
    a. ${}^{14}_{6}C$ b. ${}^{140}_{55}Cs$ c. ${}^{234}_{90}Th$

26. Each of the following nuclides is known to undergo radioactive decay by production of an alpha particle, ${}^{4}_{2}He$. Write a balanced nuclear equation for each process.
    a. ${}^{234}_{92}U$ b. ${}^{222}_{86}Rn$ c. ${}^{162}_{75}Re$

27. Each of the following nuclides is known to undergo radioactive decay by production of a beta particle, ${}^{0}_{-1}e$. Write a balanced nuclear equation for each process.
    a. ${}^{188}_{74}W$ b. ${}^{40}_{19}K$ c. ${}^{198}_{79}Au$

28. Each of the following nuclides is known to undergo radioactive decay by production of a beta particle, ${}^{0}_{-1}e$. Write a balanced nuclear equation for each process.
    a. ${}^{212}_{82}Pb$ b. ${}^{212}_{81}Tl$ c. ${}^{228}_{88}Ra$

19.2 Nuclear Transformations

QUESTIONS

29. What does a *nuclear transformation* represent? How is a nuclear transformation performed?

30. What is meant by a *nuclear bombardment* process? Give an example of such a process, and describe what the net result of the process is.

31. Write a balanced nuclear equation showing the bombardment of ${}^{9}_{4}Be$ with alpha particles to produce ${}^{12}_{6}C$ and a neutron.

32. Write a balanced nuclear equation showing the bombardment of ${}^{24}_{12}Mg$ with deuterium atoms (the isotope of hydrogen with $A = 2$, ${}^{2}_{1}H$) to produce ${}^{22}_{11}Na$ and an alpha particle.

19.3 Detection of Radioactivity and the Concept of Half-life

QUESTIONS

33. Describe the operation of a Geiger counter. How does a Geiger counter detect radioactive particles? How does a scintillation counter differ from a Geiger counter?

34. What is the *half-life* of a radioactive nucleus? Does a given type of nucleus always have the same half-life? Do nuclei of different elements have the same half-life?

35. What do we mean when we say that one radioactive nucleus is "hotter" than another? Which element would have more decay events over a given period of time?

36. Consider the isotopes of radium listed in Table 19.3. Which isotope is most stable against decay? Which isotope is "hottest"?

PROBLEMS

37. The following isotopes (listed with their half-lives) have been used in the medical and biologic sciences. Arrange these isotopes in order of their relative decay activities: ${}^{3}H$ (12.2 years), ${}^{24}Na$ (15 hours), ${}^{131}I$ (8 days), ${}^{60}Co$ (5.3 years), ${}^{14}C$ (5730 years).

38. A list of several important radionuclides is given in Table 19.4. Which is the "hottest"? Which is the most stable to decay?

39. Nitrogen-13 (${}^{13}_{7}N$) is a radionuclide that decays by positron emission (${}^{0}_{+1}e$) to carbon-13 (${}^{13}_{6}C$) with a half-life very close to 10 minutes. If we begin with a sample containing 100 micrograms of nitrogen-13, how much N-13 will remain after a period of two half-lives?

40. Cobalt-62 (${}^{62}_{27}Co$) is a radionuclide with a half-life of 1.5 minutes. What fraction of an initial sample of Co-62 will remain after 6 min?

41. The element krypton has several radioactive isotopes. Below are listed several of these isotopes along with their half-lives. Which of the isotopes is most stable? Which of the isotopes is "hottest"? If we were to begin a half-life experiment with separate 125-μg samples of each isotope, *approximately* how much of each isotope would remain after 24 hours?

Isotope	Half-life
Kr-73	27 s
Kr-74	11.5 min
Kr-76	14.8 h
Kr-81	2.1×10^5 yr

All even-numbered Questions and Problems have answers in the back of this book and solutions in the Solutions Guide.

42. For an administered dose of 100 μg, 0.39 μg remains after 2 days. The fraction remaining is 0.39/100 = 0.0039; on a percentage basis, less than 0.4% of the original radioisotope remains.

43. We assume that an organism exchanges carbon-14 with the atmosphere while alive. When the organism dies, no further exchange takes place, so the amount of carbon-14 in the artifact is compared with the amount of carbon-14 in the atmosphere. Since the half-life of carbon-14 is known, the age of the artifact can be determined.

44. Carbon-14 is produced in the upper atmosphere by the bombardment of nitrogen with neutrons from space:

$${}^{14}_{7}N + {}^{1}_{0}n \rightarrow {}^{14}_{6}C + {}^{1}_{1}H$$

45. It is assumed that the concentration of carbon-14 in the atmosphere remains constant. When analyzing an artifact, we assume living cells

42. Technetium-99 has been used as a radiographic agent in bone scans ($^{99}_{43}Tc$ is absorbed by bones). If $^{99}_{43}Tc$ has a half-life of 6.0 hours, what fraction of an administered dose of 100 μg of $^{99}_{43}Tc$ remains in a patient's body after 2.0 days?

19.4 Dating by Radioactivity

QUESTIONS

43. Describe in general terms how an archaeological artifact is dated using carbon-14.

44. How is $^{14}_{6}C$ produced in the atmosphere? Write a balanced equation for this process.

45. In dating artifacts using carbon-14, an assumption is made about the amount of carbon-14 in the atmosphere. What is this assumption? Why is the assumption important?

46. Why does an ancient wood or cloth artifact contain less $^{14}_{6}C$ than contemporary or more recently fabricated articles made of similar materials?

19.5 Medical Applications of Radioactivity

QUESTIONS

47. The thyroid gland is interesting in that it is practically the only place in the body where the element iodine is used. How have radiotracers been used to study and treat illnesses of the thyroid gland?

48. The "Chemistry in Focus" segment *PET, The Brain's Best Friend* discusses the use of radiotracers to monitor the functioning of organs or to trace the path and final destination of a drug. The isotope ^{18}F is cited as a possible radiotracer and has a half-life of 110 minutes. From a sample of 1 mole of ^{18}F, about how many atoms are left after a day?

19.6 Nuclear Energy

QUESTIONS

49. How do the forces that hold an atomic nucleus together compare in strength with the forces between atoms in a molecule?

50. During nuclear ______, a large nucleus is transformed into lighter nuclei. During nuclear ______, small nuclei are combined to make a heavier nucleus. Both processes release energy, but nuclear ______ releases far more energy than does nuclear ______.

19.7 Nuclear Fission

QUESTIONS

51. How do the energies released by nuclear processes compare in magnitude with the energies of ordinary chemical processes?

52. Write an equation for the fission of $^{235}_{92}U$ by bombardment with neutrons.

53. What is a *chain reaction*? How does a chain reaction involving ^{235}U sustain itself?

54. What does it mean to say that fissionable material possesses a *critical mass?* Can a chain reaction occur when a sample has less than the critical mass?

19.8 Nuclear Reactors

QUESTIONS

55. Describe the purpose of each of the major components of a nuclear reactor (moderator, control rods, containment, cooling liquid, and so on).

56. Can a nuclear explosion take place in a reactor? Is the concentration of fissionable material used in reactors large enough for this?

57. What is a *meltdown,* and how can it occur? Most nuclear reactors use water as the cooling liquid. Is there any danger of a steam explosion if the reactor core becomes overheated?

58. The "Chemistry in Focus" segment *Future Nuclear Power* discusses nuclear power as an energy source. What are some advantages of nuclear power? What are some potential problems?

19.9 Nuclear Fusion

QUESTIONS

59. What is the nuclear *fusion* of small nuclei? How does the energy released by fusion compare in magnitude with that released by fission?

60. What are some reasons why no practical fusion reactor has yet been developed?

61. What type of "fuel" could be used in a nuclear fusion reactor, and why is this desirable?

62. The sun radiates vast quantities of energy as a consequence of the nuclear fusion reaction of ______ to form ______ nuclei.

19.10 Effects of Radiation

QUESTIONS

63. Although the energy transferred per event when a living creature is exposed to radiation is small, why is such exposure dangerous?

64. Explain the difference between *somatic* damage from radiation and *genetic* damage. Which type causes immediate damage to the exposed individual?

65. Describe the relative penetrating powers of alpha, beta, and gamma radiation.

66. Explain why, although gamma rays are far more penetrating than alpha particles, the latter are actually more likely to cause damage to an organism. Which radiation is more effective at causing ionization of biomolecules?

All even-numbered Questions and Problems have answers in the back of this book and solutions in the Solutions Guide.

in the artifact stopped exchanging carbon-14 with the atmosphere when they died, and we compare the amount of carbon-14 in the cells to the amount of carbon-14 in the atmosphere.

46. We assume that the concentration of C-14 in the atmosphere is effectively constant. A living organism is constantly replenishing C-14 through the processes of either metabolism (sugars ingested in foods contain C-14) or photosynthesis (carbon dioxide contains C-14). When a plant dies, it no longer replenishes itself with C-14 from the atmosphere. As the C-14 undergoes radioactive decay, its amount decreases with time.

47. Since iodine is used almost exclusively by the thyroid, a patient can be given a dose of a radioactive isotope of iodine in sodium iodide; the speed of the uptake of the iodine can be determined by measuring the radioactivity at the thyroid, and an effective picture of the thyroid can be taken using a detector (scanner). If a malignant tumor is found by the tracer, a larger dosage of another radioisotope of iodine can be applied to kill the tumor.

48. 1 day is about 13 half-lives for $^{18}_{9}F$. If we begin with 6.02×10^{23} atoms (1 mol), then after 13 half-lives, 7.4×10^{19} atoms of $^{18}_{9}F$ will remain.

49. Nuclear forces are *much* larger than chemical bonding forces.

50. fission, fusion, fusion, fission

51. Nuclear processes have energies on the order of 10^6 times the energies of ordinary chemical processes.

52. $^{1}_{0}n + ^{235}_{92}U \rightarrow ^{142}_{56}Ba + ^{91}_{36}Kr + 3^{1}_{0}n$

53. A chain reaction is a nuclear decay which, when initiated by an external particle, generates sufficient additional particles of the same type to continue the process on its own. In the fission of uranium-235, the chain reaction is initiated by bombarding uranium-235 with neutrons to start the reaction. However, the decay of the first bit of uranium-235 then produces additional neutrons, which continue the decay of the remaining uranium-235.

54. A critical mass of a fissionable material is the amount needed to provide a high enough internal neutron flux to sustain the chain reaction (production of enough neutrons to cause the continuous fission of further material). A sample with less than a critical mass is still radioactive, but cannot sustain a chain reaction.

55. The *moderator* surrounds the fuel rods and slows down the neutrons emitted so that they can be absorbed more easily by other nuclei; the *control rods* are made of a substance that absorbs neutrons and can be inserted into the reactor to control the power level; the *containment* is the special building where the

67. How do the *chemical properties* of radioactive nuclei (as opposed to the nuclear decay they undergo) influence the degree of damage they do to an organism?

68. Although nuclear processes offer the potential for an abundant source of energy, no nuclear power plants have been built in the United States for some time. In addition to the fear of a malfunction in such a plant (as happened at the Three Mile Island nuclear plant in Pennsylvania) or the threat of a terrorist attack against such a plant, there is the very practical problem of the regular disposal of the waste material from a nuclear power plant. Discuss some of the problems associated with nuclear waste and some of the proposals that have been put forth for its disposal.

Additional Problems

69. The number of protons contained in a given nucleus is called the ______.

70. A nucleus that spontaneously decomposes is said to be ______.

71. A(n) ______, when it is produced by a nucleus at high speed, is more commonly called a beta particle.

72. In a nuclear equation, both the atomic number and the ______ number must be conserved.

73. Production of a helium nucleus from a heavy atom is referred to as ______ decay.

74. The net effect of the production of a beta particle is to convert a ______ to a ______.

75. In addition to particles, many radioactive nuclei also produce high-energy ______ rays when they decay.

76. When a nuclide decomposes through a series of steps before reaching stability, the nuclide is said to have gone through a ______ series.

77. When a nuclide produces a beta particle, the atomic number of the resulting new nuclide is one unit ______ than that of the original nuclide.

78. When a nucleus undergoes alpha decay, the ______ of the nucleus decreases by four units.

79. Machines that increase the speed of species used for nuclear bombardment processes are called ______.

80. The elements with atomic numbers of 93 or greater are referred to as the ______ elements.

81. A ______ counter contains argon gas, which is ionized by radiation, making possible the measurement of radioactive decay rates.

82. The time required for half of an original sample of a radioactive nuclide to decay is referred to as the ______ of the nuclide.

83. The radioactive nuclide that has been used in determining the age of historical wooden artifacts is ______.

84. ______ are radioactive substances that physicians introduce into the body to enable them to study the absorption and metabolism of the substance or to analyze the functioning of an organ or gland that can make use of the substance.

85. Combining two small nuclei to form a larger nucleus is referred to as the process of nuclear ______.

86. A self-sustaining nuclear process, in which the bombarding particles needed to produce the fission of further material are themselves produced as the product of the initial fission, is called a ______ reaction.

87. The most common type of nuclear reactor uses the nuclide ______ as its fissionable material.

88. A nuclear reactor that generates additional fissionable fuel (in addition to producing heat for generating electricity) is referred to as a ______ reactor.

89. The decay series from uranium-238 to lead-206 is indicated in Figure 19.1. For each *step* of the process indicated in the figure, specify what type of particle is produced by the particular nucleus involved at that point in the series.

90. The U.S. Department of Energy sells an isotope of the transuranium element californium for approximately \$10 per microgram to qualified researchers. What would a pound of the Cf nuclide cost?

91. Each of the following isotopes has been used medically for the purpose indicated. Suggest reasons why the particular element might have been chosen for this purpose.
    a. cobalt-57, for study of the body's use of vitamin B_{12}
    b. calcium-47, for study of bone metabolism
    c. iron-59, for study of red blood cell function
    d. mercury-197, for brain scans before CAT scans became available

92. The fission of $^{235}_{92}U$ releases 2.1×10^{13} joules per mole of $^{235}_{92}U$. Calculate the energy released per atom and per gram of $^{235}_{92}U$.

93. During the research that led to production of the two atomic bombs used against Japan in World War II, different mechanisms for obtaining a supercritical mass of fissionable material were investigated. In one type of bomb, what is essentially a gun was used to shoot one piece of fissionable material into a cavity containing another piece of fissionable material. In the second type of bomb, the fissionable material was surrounded with a high explosive that, when detonated, compressed the fissionable material into a smaller volume. Discuss what is meant by critical mass, and explain why the ability to achieve a critical mass is essential to sustaining a nuclear reaction.

94. Zirconium consists of five primary isotopes, of mass numbers and abundances shown below:

Zr-90	51.5%
Zr-91	11.2%
Zr-92	17.1%
Zr-94	17.4%
Zr-96	2.8%

All even-numbered Questions and Problems have answers in the back of this book and solutions in the Solutions Guide.

core is located and which is designed to contain the fuel in the event of an accident; the *cooling liquid* is circulated through the reactor to draw off the heat produced by the reactor so that the heat can be converted to electrical energy in the turbines.

56. An actual nuclear explosion, of the type produced by a nuclear weapon, cannot occur in a nuclear reactor because the concentration of the fissionable materials is not sufficient to form a supercritical mass.

57. If the cooling system of the reactor fails, the reactor core might overheat and melt and might become hot enough to melt through the bottom of the reactor building and into the earth itself until the core reached cool groundwater and resolidified. If a water-cooled reactor were to have the cooling system blocked or breeched, then the reactor core would be hot enough to produce radioactive steam or to break down the water into hydrogen gas and oxygen gas, which could explode.

58. Some advantages: fuel available domestically, relative "clean," does not produce greenhouse gases fossil fuel plants produce. Some disadvantages: safety, waste disposal, cost.

59. Combining two light nuclei into one larger nucleus; energy release for fusion is much higher than for fission.

60. In one type of fusion reactor, two ^2_1H atoms fuse to produce ^4_2He. Because the hydrogen nuclei are positively charged, extremely high energies (temperatures of 40 million K) are needed to overcome the repulsion between the nuclei as they are shot into each other.

61. hydrogen; plentiful supply (from water)

62. protons (hydrogen), helium

63. The energy is sufficient to break chemical bonds, which may cause malfunctioning of a cellular system; this is especially problematic in a cell because so many biologic processes are chainlike, and the production of a single odd ion in the cell may have a cumulative effect. For example, ionization of a single bond in a sex cell may cause a drastic mutation in the resulting organism.

64. Somatic damage is damage directly to the organism itself, causing nearly immediate sickness or death to the organism. Genetic damage is damage to the genetic machinery of the organism, which will be manifested in future generations of

Write the nuclear symbol, $^{A}_{Z}X$, for each of these isotopes of zirconium.

95. The element zinc in nature consists of five isotopes with higher than 0.5% natural abundances, with mass numbers 64, 66, 67, 68, and 70. Write the nuclear symbol for each of these isotopes. How many protons does each contain? How many neutrons does each contain?

96. Aluminum exists in several isotopic forms, including $^{27}_{13}Al$, $^{28}_{13}Al$, and $^{29}_{13}Al$. Indicate the number of protons and the number of neutrons in each of these isotopes.

97. Complete each of the following nuclear equations by supplying the missing particle.

a. $^{226}_{88}Ra \rightarrow ^{222}_{86}Rn + ?$
b. $^{222}_{86}Rn \rightarrow ^{218}_{84}Po + ?$
c. $^{2}_{1}H + ^{3}_{1}H \rightarrow ^{4}_{2}He + ?$

98. Complete each of the following nuclear equations by supplying the missing particle.

a. $^{69}_{30}Zn \rightarrow ^{69}_{31}Ga + ?$
b. $^{74}_{35}Br \rightarrow ^{0}_{1}\beta + ?$
c. $^{244}_{94}Pu \rightarrow ^{4}_{2}He + ?$

99. Write a balanced nuclear equation for the bombardment of $^{14}_{7}N$ with alpha particles to produce $^{17}_{8}O$ and a proton.

100. Write a nuclear equation showing the bombardment of beryllium-9 with alpha particles, resulting in production of carbon-12 and a neutron.

101. How have $^{131}_{53}I$ and $^{201}_{81}Tl$ been used in medical diagnosis? Why are these particular nuclides especially well suited for this purpose?

102. The most common reaction used in breeder reactors involves the bombardment of uranium-238 with neutrons: ^{238}U is converted by this bombardment to ^{239}U. The uranium-239 then undergoes two beta decays, first to ^{239}Np, and then to ^{239}Pu, which is a fissionable material and the desired product. Write balanced nuclear equations for the bombardment reaction and the two beta-decay reactions.

103. Each of the following nuclides is known to undergo radioactive decay by production of an alpha particle, $^{4}_{2}He$. Write a balanced nuclear equation for each process.

a. $^{232}_{90}Th$ b. $^{220}_{86}Rn$ c. $^{216}_{84}Po$

All even-numbered Questions and Problems have answers in the back of this book and solutions in the Solutions Guide.

offspring.

65. Alpha particles are stopped by outer layers of skin; beta particles penetrate about 1 cm; gamma rays are deeply penetrating.

66. Gamma rays penetrate long distances, but seldom cause ionization of biological molecules. Because they are much heavier, although less penetrating, alpha particles ionize biological molecules very effectively and leave a dense trail of damage in the organism. Isotopes that decay by releasing alpha particles can be ingested or breathed into the body, where the damage from the alpha particles will be more acute.

67. Atoms that are chemically inert or that are not used by the body are excreted quickly. However, other nuclei, which form a part of the body's structure or metabolic processes, may be incorporated into the body and remain dangerous much longer.

68. Most reactor waste is still in "temporary" storage. Various suggestions have been made for a more permanent solution, such as casting the spent fuel into glass bricks to contain it and then storing the bricks in corrosion-proof metal containers deep underground.

(Please refer to page A27 in this book for answers to Exercises 69–103.)

Chapter 20

Objectives

In this chapter, our objectives are for the students to:

SECTION 20.1

- Understand the types of bonds formed by the carbon atom.

SECTION 20.2

- Learn about the alkanes—compounds that contain saturated carbon atoms.

SECTION 20.3

- Learn about structural isomers and how to draw their structural formulas.

SECTION 20.4

- Learn the system for naming alkanes and substituted alkanes.

SECTION 20.5

- Learn about the composition and uses of petroleum.

SECTION 20.6

- Learn various types of chemical reactions that alkanes undergo.

SECTION 20.7

- Learn to name hydrocarbons with double bonds (alkenes) and triple bonds (alkynes).
- Understand addition reactions.

SECTION 20.8

- Learn about the aromatic hydrocarbons.

SECTION 20.9

- Learn the system for naming aromatic compounds.

SECTION 20.10

- Learn the common functional groups in organic molecules.

SECTION 20.11

- Learn about simple alcohols and explain how to name them.

20 Organic Chemistry

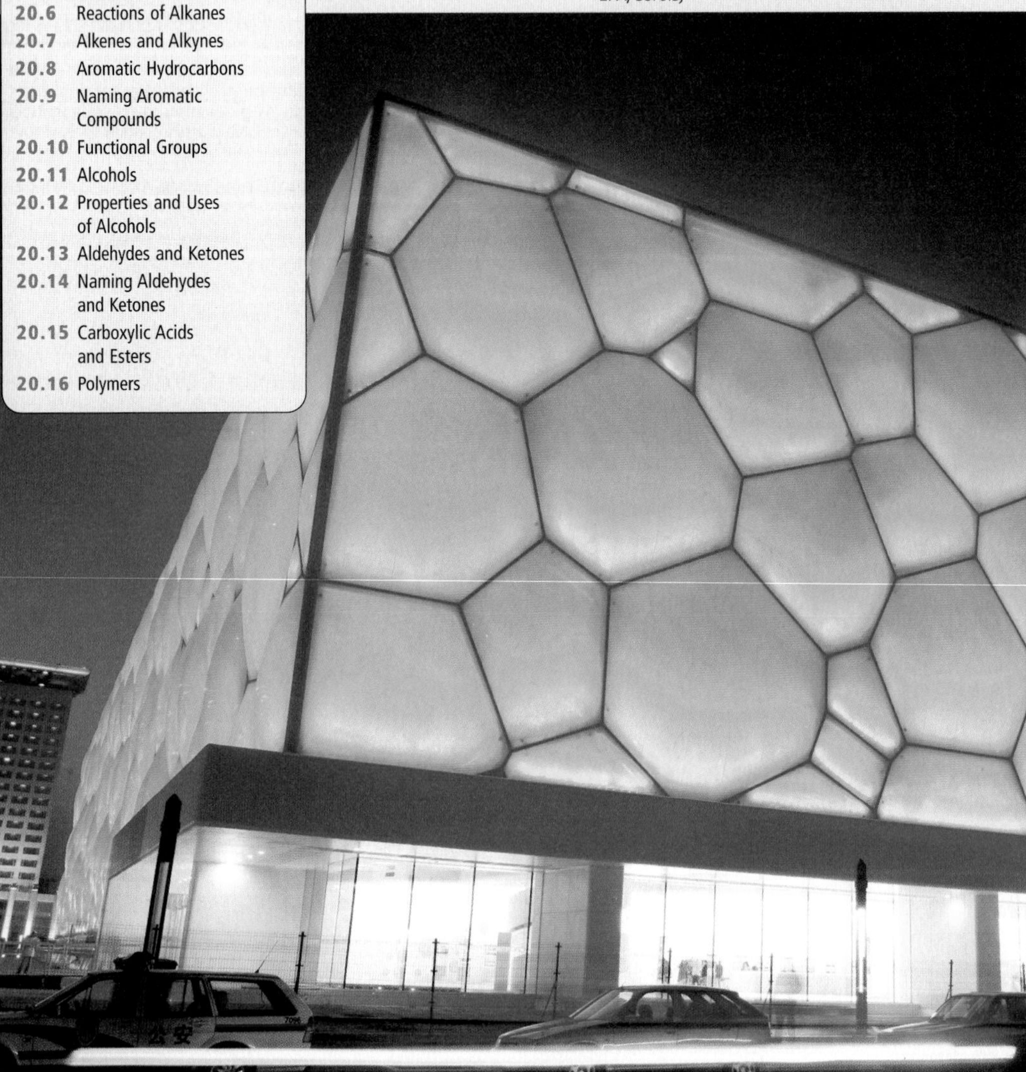

The National Aquatic Centre (also known as the "Water Cube") used in the 2008 Summer Olympics in Beijing, China. *(Michael Reynolds/EPA/Corbis)*

SECTION 20.12

- Learn about how some alcohols are made and used.

SECTION 20.13

- Learn the general formulas for aldehydes and ketones and some of their uses.

SECTION 20.14

- Learn the systems for naming aldehydes and ketones.

SECTION 20.15

- Learn the structures and names of the common carboxylic acids.

SECTION 20.16

- Learn about some common polymers.

OWL Sign in to OWL at **www.cengage.com/owl** to view tutorials and simulations, develop problem-solving skills, and complete online homework assigned by your professor.

go Chemistry Download mini-lecture videos for key concept review and exam prep from OWL or purchase them from **www.ichapters.com**

The study of carbon-containing compounds and their properties is called **organic chemistry.** The industries based on organic substances have truly revolutionized our lives. In particular, the development of polymers, such as nylon for fabrics; Velcro for fasteners; Kevlar for the composites used in exotic cars, airplanes, and bicycles; and polyvinyl chloride (PVC) for pipes, siding, and toys has produced a wondrous new world.

Two Group 4 elements, carbon and silicon, form the basis of most natural substances. Silicon, with its great affinity for oxygen, forms chains and rings containing Si—O—Si bonds to produce the silica and silicates that form the basic structures for most rocks, sands, and soils. Therefore, silicon compounds are the fundamental inorganic materials of the earth. What silicon is to the geologic world, carbon is to the organic or biologic world. Carbon has the unusual ability of bonding strongly to itself, forming long chains or rings of carbon atoms. In addition, carbon forms strong bonds to other nonmetals such as hydrogen, nitrogen, oxygen, sulfur, and the halogens. Because of these bonding properties, an extraordinary number of carbon compounds exists; several million are now known, and the number continues to grow rapidly. Among these many compounds are the **biomolecules,** molecules that make possible the maintenance and reproduction of life.

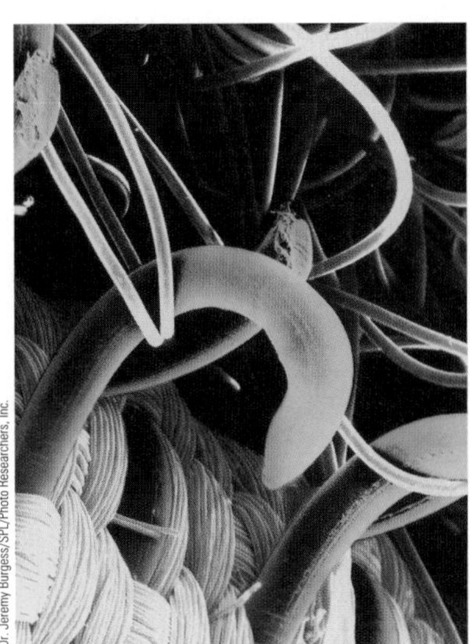

Dr. Jeremy Burgess/SPL/Photo Researchers, Inc.

A close-up photo of Velcro, a synthetic organic material used for fasteners.

Although a few compounds of carbon, such as the oxides of carbon and carbonates, are considered to be inorganic substances, the vast majority of carbon compounds are designated as organic compounds—compounds that typically contain chains or rings of carbon atoms. Originally, the distinction between inorganic and organic substances was based on whether they were produced by living systems. For example, until the early nineteenth century, it was believed that organic compounds had some kind of "life force" and could be synthesized only by living organisms. This misconception was dispelled in 1828 when the German chemist Friedrich Wöhler (1800–1882) prepared urea from the inorganic salt ammonium cyanate by simple heating.

$$\underset{\text{Ammonium cyanate}}{NH_4OCN} \xrightarrow{\text{Heat}} \underset{\text{Urea}}{H_2N-\underset{\underset{O}{\|}}{C}-NH_2}$$

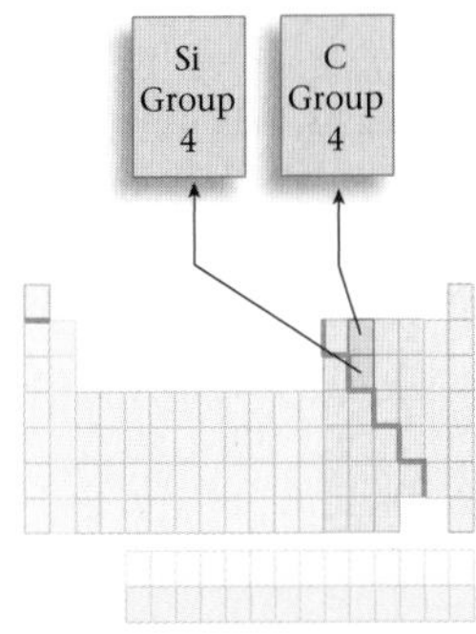

Urea is a component of urine, so it is clearly an organic material formed by living things, yet here was hard evidence that it could be produced in the laboratory as well.

Organic chemistry plays a vital role in our quest to understand living systems. Beyond that, the synthetic fibers, plastics, artificial sweeteners, and medicines that we take for granted are products of industrial organic chemistry. Finally, the energy on which we rely so heavily to power our civilization is based mostly on the combustion of organic materials found in coal and petroleum.

ChemWork Refined over ten years of use by thousands of students, **ChemWork** builds and enhances students' problems-solving skills. Online assignments function as a "personal instructor" to help students learn how to solve challenging problems and learn how to think like chemists. Annotations for **ChemWork** assignments are included at the beginning of the end-of-chapter review.

PowerLecture This 2-DVD package includes the Chemistry Multimedia Library, which contains animations, simulations, and movies for all chemistry subjects, organized by topic for lecture presentations. Annotations for **PowerLecture** are referenced in the margins throughout the Annotated Instructor's Edition.

Test Bank: 1, 2

Because organic chemistry is such a vast subject, we can introduce it only briefly in this text. We will begin with the simplest class of organic compounds, the hydrocarbons, and then show how most other organic compounds can be considered to be derived from hydrocarbons.

Section 20.1

TEACHING TIPS

- To introduce the topic of organic chemistry and its impact on our lives, ask the students what the classroom would look like without carbon-containing compounds. You will need to assist them in figuring out what things contain carbon, but it will not be long before they can appreciate how many of the objects surrounding us are organic compounds.
- You will find a good set of three-dimensional models very helpful in presenting this material. Use the models to illustrate the shapes of the molecules discussed in this section. The tetrahedral shape of methane is difficult to visualize without a model.
- Inexpensive classroom-sized models can be built from painted Styrofoam balls and wooden dowels.
- This section provides an excellent opportunity to review the concepts of covalent bonding.

20.1 Carbon Bonding

OBJECTIVE: To understand the types of bonds formed by the carbon atom.

So many carbon-containing compounds exist because carbon forms strong bonds to itself and to many other elements. A carbon atom can form bonds to a maximum of four other atoms; these can be either carbon atoms or atoms of other elements. One of the hardest, toughest materials known is diamond, a form of pure carbon in which each carbon atom is bound to four other carbon atoms (see Figure 4.18a).

One of the most familiar compounds of carbon is methane, CH_4, the main component of natural gas. The methane molecule consists of a carbon atom with four hydrogen atoms bound to it in a tetrahedral fashion. That is, as predicted by the VSEPR model (see Section 12.9), the four pairs of bonding electrons around the carbon have minimum repulsions when they are located at the corners of a tetrahedron.

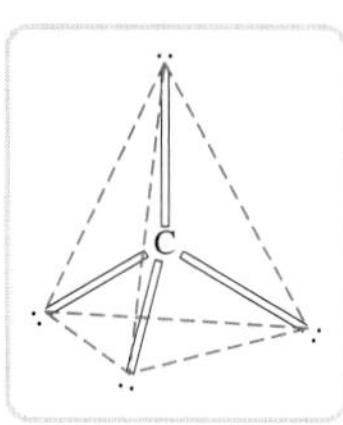

or

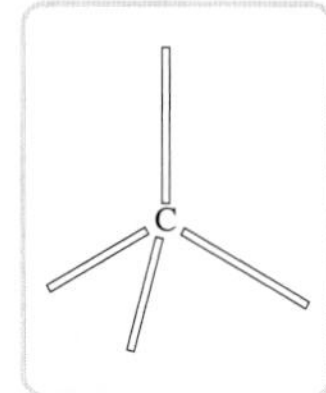

This leads to the structure for CH_4 shown in Figure 20.1. *When carbon has four atoms bound to it, these atoms will always have a tetrahedral arrangement about the carbon.*

Carbon can bond to fewer than four elements by forming one or more multiple bonds. Recall that a multiple bond involves the sharing of more than one pair of electrons. For example, a *double bond* involves sharing two pairs of electrons, as in carbon dioxide:

CO₂ and CO are classed as inorganic substances.

$$:\ddot{O}=C=\ddot{O}:$$

and a *triple bond* involves sharing three pairs of electrons, as in carbon monoxide:

$$:C\equiv O:$$

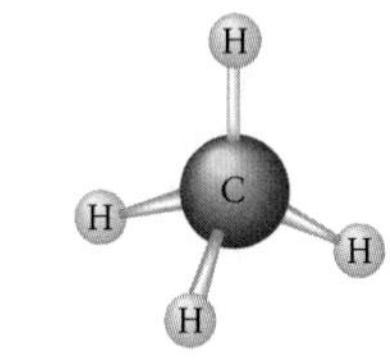

Figure 20.1
Methane is a tetrahedral molecule.

Note that carbon is bound to two other atoms in CO_2 and to only one other atom in CO.

Multiple bonding also occurs in organic molecules. Ethylene, C_2H_4, has a double bond:

```
H       H
 \     /
  C = C
 /     \
H       H
```

In this case, each carbon is bound to three other atoms (one C atom and two H atoms). A molecule with a triple bond is acetylene, C_2H_2:

$$H{-}C{\equiv}C{-}H$$

Here each carbon is bound to two other atoms (one carbon atom and one hydrogen atom).

More than any other element, carbon has the ability to form chains of atoms, as illustrated by the structures of propane and butane shown in Figure 20.3. In these compounds, each carbon atom is bound to four atoms in a tetrahedral fashion. We will discuss these molecules in detail in the next section.

PowerLecture Animation: Molecular Model: Acetylene

 **Test Bank: 3–8**

20.2 Alkanes

Section 20.2

OBJECTIVE: To learn about the alkanes—compounds that contain saturated carbon atoms.

Hydrocarbons, as the name indicates, are compounds composed of carbon and hydrogen. Those whose carbon–carbon bonds are all single bonds are said to be **saturated** because each carbon is bound to four atoms, the maximum number. Hydrocarbons containing carbon–carbon multiple bonds are described as being **unsaturated** because the carbon atoms involved in a multiple bond can bond to one or more additional atoms. This is shown by the *addition* of hydrogen to ethylene.

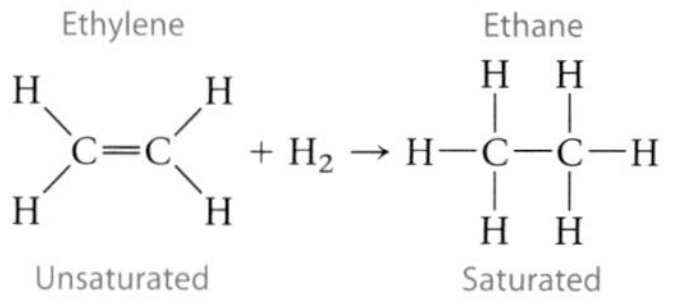

go Chemistry **Module 15: Naming Organic Compounds** covers concepts in this section.

Ethylene (Unsaturated) + H_2 → Ethane (Saturated)

$$H_2C{=}CH_2 + H_2 \rightarrow H_3C{-}CH_3$$

Note that each carbon in ethylene is bonded to three atoms (one carbon and two hydrogens) but can bond to one additional atom after one bond of the carbon–carbon double bond is broken. This leads to ethane, a saturated hydrocarbon (each carbon atom is bonded to four atoms).

Saturated hydrocarbons are called **alkanes.** The simplest alkane is *methane,* CH_4, which has a tetrahedral structure (see Figure 20.1). The next alkane, the one containing two carbon atoms, is *ethane,* C_2H_6, shown in Figure 20.2. Note that each carbon atom in ethane is bonded to four atoms.

The next two members of the series are *propane,* with three carbon atoms and the formula C_3H_8, and *butane,* with four carbon atoms and the

TEACHING TIPS

- Work slowly through this section with the students. Build the alkanes one at a time using the three-dimensional molecular models. Be sure that students see how the nomenclature and the structure are connected.
- By the time you get to a four-carbon molecule, the students should be able to see clearly that the carbon chain is not linear and that the hydrogen atoms can exist in many different orientations with respect to one another.

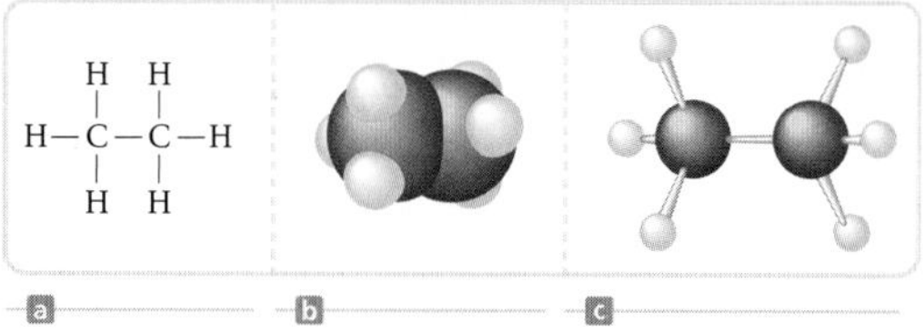

Figure 20.2 (a) The Lewis structure of ethane, C_2H_6. The molecular structure of ethane represented by (b) a space-filling model and (c) a ball-and-stick model.

PowerLecture Animation: Molecular Model: Ethene

PowerLecture Animation: Rotating Propane Molecule

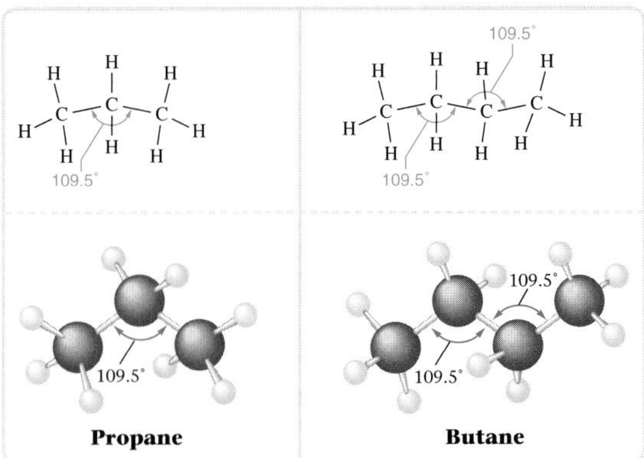

Figure 20.3 The structures of propane and butane.

Computer-generated model of ethane.

formula C_4H_{10}. These molecules are shown in Figure 20.3. Again, these are saturated hydrocarbons (alkanes); each carbon is bonded to four atoms.

Alkanes in which the carbon atoms form long "strings" or chains are called **normal, straight-chain,** or **unbranched hydrocarbons.** As Figure 20.3 illustrates, the chains in normal alkanes are not really straight but zigzag because the tetrahedral C—C—C angle is 109.5°. The normal alkanes can be represented by the structure

$$\mathrm{H{-}\overset{\displaystyle H}{\underset{\displaystyle H}{C}}{-}\left(\overset{\displaystyle H}{\underset{\displaystyle H}{C}}\right)_{m}{-}\overset{\displaystyle H}{\underset{\displaystyle H}{C}}{-}H}$$

where m is an integer. Note that each member is obtained from the previous one by insertion of a *methylene,* CH_2, group. We can condense the structural formulas by omitting some of the C—H bonds. For example, the general formula for normal alkanes shown above can be condensed to

$$CH_3{-}(CH_2)_m{-}CH_3$$

PowerLecture Animation: Rotating Hexane Molecule

EXAMPLE 20.1 **Writing Formulas for Alkanes**

Give the formulas for the normal (or straight-chain) alkanes with six and eight carbon atoms.

SOLUTION

The alkane with six carbon atoms can be written as

$$CH_3CH_2CH_2CH_2CH_2CH_3$$

which can be condensed to

$$CH_3{-}(CH_2)_4{-}CH_3$$

Notice that the molecule contains fourteen hydrogen atoms in addition to the six carbon atoms. Therefore, the formula is C_6H_{14}.

Additional Examples

Example 20.1

Give the formulas for the normal (or straight-chain) alkanes with five and twelve carbons.

C_5H_{12}: $CH_3CH_2CH_2CH_2CH_3$;
$C_{12}H_{26}$: $CH_3CH_2CH_2CH_2CH_2CH_2CH_2CH_2CH_2CH_2CH_2CH_3$

The alkane with eight carbons is

$$\underset{1}{CH_3}\underset{2}{CH_2}\underset{3}{CH_2}\underset{4}{CH_2}\underset{5}{CH_2}\underset{6}{CH_2}\underset{7}{CH_2}\underset{8}{CH_3}$$

which can be written in condensed form as

$$CH_3{-}(CH_2)_6{-}CH_3$$

This molecule has eighteen hydrogens. The formula is C_8H_{18}.

Self-Check **EXERCISE 20.1** Give the molecular formulas for the alkanes with ten and fifteen carbon atoms.

See Problems 20.11 through 20.14. ■

The first ten straight-chain alkanes are shown in Table 20.1. Note that all alkanes can be represented by the general formula C_nH_{2n+2}, where n represents the number of carbon atoms. For example, nonane, which has nine carbon atoms, is represented by $C_9H_{(2\times9)+2}$, or C_9H_{20}. The formula C_nH_{2n+2} reflects the fact that each carbon in the chain has two hydrogen atoms except the two end carbons, which have three each. Thus the number of hydrogen atoms present is twice the number of carbon atoms plus two (for the extra two hydrogen atoms on the ends).

EXAMPLE 20.2 Using the General Formula for Alkanes

Show that the alkane with fifteen carbon atoms can be represented in terms of the general formula C_nH_{2n+2}.

SOLUTION

In this case $n = 15$. The formula is $C_{15}H_{2(15)+2}$, or $C_{15}H_{32}$, as was found in Self-Check Exercise 20.1. ■

Table 20.1 Formulas of the First Ten Straight-Chain Alkanes

Name	Condensed Formula (C_nH_{2n+2})	Extended Formula
methane	CH_4	CH_4
ethane	C_2H_6	CH_3CH_3
propane	C_3H_8	$CH_3CH_2CH_3$
n-butane	C_4H_{10}	$CH_3CH_2CH_2CH_3$
n-pentane	C_5H_{12}	$CH_3CH_2CH_2CH_2CH_3$
n-hexane	C_6H_{14}	$CH_3CH_2CH_2CH_2CH_2CH_3$
n-heptane	C_7H_{16}	$CH_3CH_2CH_2CH_2CH_2CH_2CH_3$
n-octane	C_8H_{18}	$CH_3CH_2CH_2CH_2CH_2CH_2CH_2CH_3$
n-nonane	C_9H_{20}	$CH_3CH_2CH_2CH_2CH_2CH_2CH_2CH_2CH_3$
n-decane	$C_{10}H_{22}$	$CH_3CH_2CH_2CH_2CH_2CH_2CH_2CH_2CH_2CH_3$

Additional Examples

Example 20.2

Determine the number of hydrogens on an alkane with

1. eight carbons.

   eighteen

2. twenty-two carbons.

   forty-six

Self Check

Answers to Self-Check Exercise 20.1

$CH_3CH_2CH_2CH_2CH_2CH_2CH_2CH_2CH_2CH_3$;
$C_{10}H_{22}$
$CH_3CH_2CH_2CH_2CH_2CH_2CH_2CH_2CH_2CH_2CH_2CH_2CH_2CH_2CH_3$;
$C_{15}H_{32}$

Section 20.3

TEACHING TIPS

- Use the board to draw structural isomers with the students. Show them that structural isomers actually have a different order of atoms. Show them that rotating a carbon to point up or down on the end of a chain does not produce a new structure.
- Strings of children's pop beads can be used to illustrate that bending or twisting the string does not produce a change in the structure. To create a different order of beads, you must take apart the chain and put it together differently.

PowerLecture Animations:
Molecular Structure of Butane
Molecular Structure of Isobutane

20.3 Structural Formulas and Isomerism

OBJECTIVE: To learn about structural isomers and how to draw their structural formulas.

Butane and all succeeding alkanes exhibit structural isomerism. **Structural isomerism** occurs when two molecules have the same atoms but different bonds. That is, the molecules have the same formulas but different arrangements of the atoms. For example, butane can exist as a straight-chain molecule (normal butane, or *n*-butane) or as a branched-chain structure (called isobutane), as shown in Figure 20.4. Because of their different structures, these structural isomers have different properties.

EXAMPLE 20.3 Drawing Structural Isomers of Alkanes

Draw the structural isomers of pentane, C_5H_{12}.

SOLUTION

To find the isomeric structures for pentane, C_5H_{12}, we first write the straight carbon chain and then add the hydrogen atoms.

1. The straight-chain structure has the five carbon atoms in a row.

C—C—C—C—C

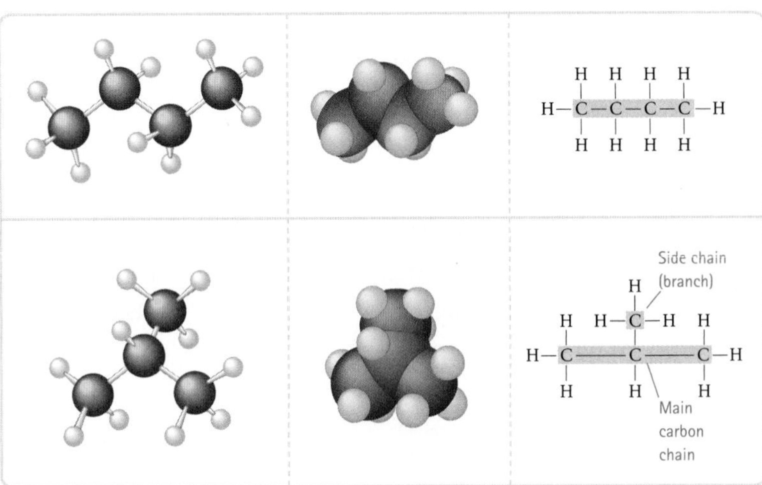

Figure 20.4
The structural isomers of C_4H_{10}. Each molecule is represented in three ways: a ball-and-stick structure, a space-filling structure, and a structure that shows the shared electrons as lines (a Lewis structure). (top) Normal butane (abbreviated *n*-butane). (bottom) The branched isomer of butane (called isobutane).

Additional Examples

Example 20.3

Draw three structural isomers of heptane, C_7H_{16}.

$CH_3CH_2CH_2CH_2CH_2CH_2CH_3$

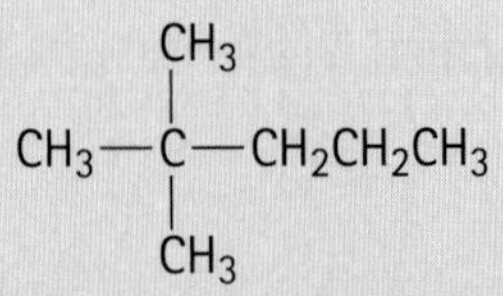

$CH_3—CH(CH_3)—CH_2CH_2CH_2CH_3$ (with CH_3 branch on the second carbon)

$CH_3—CH_2—CH(CH_3)—CH_2CH_2CH_3$ (with CH_3 branch on the third carbon)

$CH_3—CH(CH_3)—CH(CH_3)CH_2CH_3$

$CH_3—CH(CH_3)—CH_2—CH(CH_3)—CH_3$

$CH_3—C(CH_3)_2—CH(CH_3)—CH_3$

$CH_3—C(CH_3)_2—CH_2CH_2CH_3$

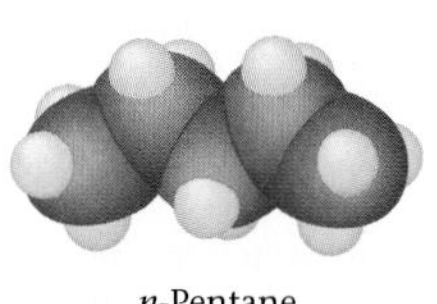

n-Pentane

We can now add the H atoms.

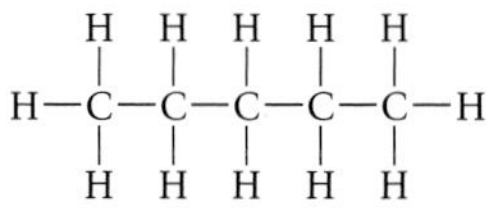

```
    H   H   H   H   H
    |   |   |   |   |
H—C—C—C—C—C—H
    |   |   |   |   |
    H   H   H   H   H
```

This can be written in shorthand form as

$$CH_3{-}CH_2{-}CH_2{-}CH_2{-}CH_3 \quad \text{or} \quad CH_3{-}(CH_2)_3{-}CH_3$$

and is called *n*-pentane.

2. Next we remove one C atom from the main chain and bond it to the second carbon in the chain.

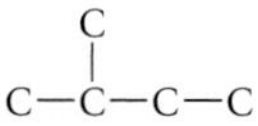

```
      C
      |
  C—C—C—C
```

Then we put on the H atoms so that each carbon has four bonds.

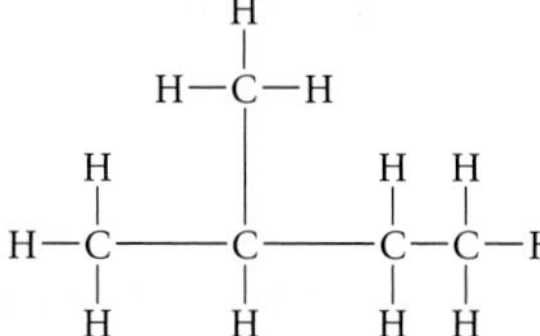

Isopentane

This structure can be represented as

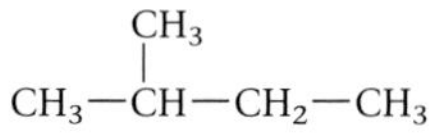

```
      CH3
      |
CH3—CH—CH2—CH3
```

and is called isopentane.

3. Finally, we take two carbons out of the chain to give the arrangement

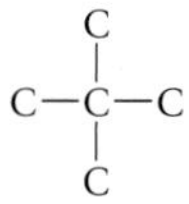

```
      C
      |
  C—C—C
      |
      C
```

Adding the H atoms gives

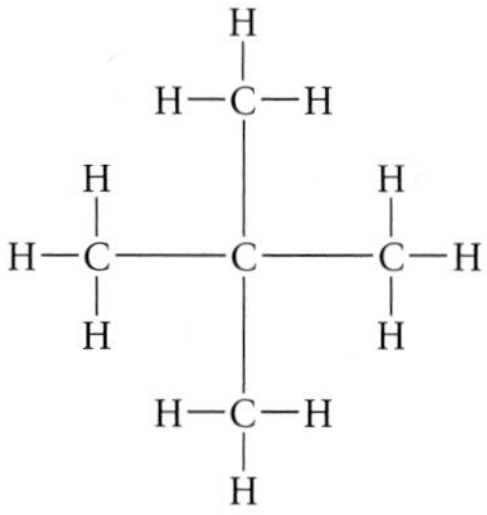

```
          H
          |
       H—C—H
          |
   H      |      H
   |      |      |
H—C——————C——————C—H
   |      |      |
   H      |      H
          |
       H—C—H
          |
          H
```

20.3 Structural Formulas and Isomerism 647

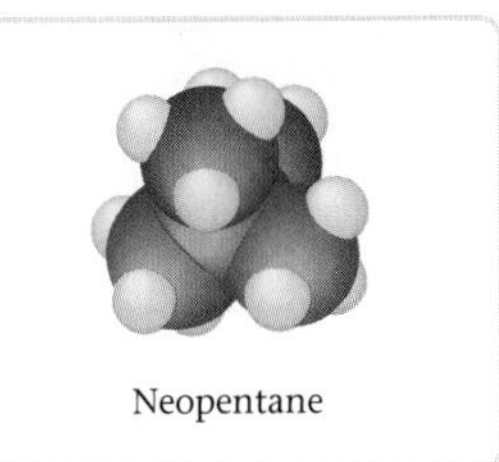
Neopentane

which can be written in shorthand form as

$$\begin{array}{c} CH_3 \\ | \\ CH_3-C-CH_3 \\ | \\ CH_3 \end{array}$$

This molecule is called neopentane.

The space-filling models for these molecules are shown in the margin. Note that all these molecules have the formula C_5H_{12}, as required. Also note that the structures

$$\begin{array}{c} \quad\quad\quad\quad CH_3 \\ \quad\quad\quad\quad | \\ CH_3-CH_2-CH-CH_3 \end{array} \quad \begin{array}{c} CH_3-CH-CH_2-CH_3 \\ | \quad\quad\quad\quad\quad \\ CH_3 \quad\quad\quad\quad \end{array} \quad \begin{array}{c} CH_3-CH_2-CH-CH_3 \\ \quad\quad\quad\quad | \\ \quad\quad\quad\quad CH_3 \end{array}$$

which might at first appear to be additional isomers, are actually identical to structure 2. All three of these structures have exactly the same skeleton of carbons as the structure shown in part 2. All these structures have four carbons in the chain with one carbon on the side:

$$\begin{array}{c} C-C-C-C \\ | \quad\quad \\ C \quad\quad \end{array}$$

■

Test Bank: 12–23

Section 20.4

20.4 Naming Alkanes

OBJECTIVE: To learn the system for naming alkanes and substituted alkanes.

Because there are literally millions of organic compounds, it would be impossible to remember common names for all of them. Just as we did in Chapter 5 for inorganic compounds, we must learn a systematic method for naming organic compounds. We will first consider the principles applied in naming alkanes and then summarize them as a set of rules.

1. The first four members of the alkane series are called methane, ethane, propane, and butane. The names of the alkanes beyond butane are obtained by adding the suffix *-ane* to the Greek root for the number of carbon atoms.

Number	Greek Root
5	*pent*
6	*hex*
7	*hept*
8	*oct*
9	*non*
10	*dec*

Therefore, the alkane

$$CH_3CH_2CH_2CH_2CH_2CH_2CH_2CH_3$$

which has eight carbons in the chain, is called octane.

(oct – ane)
Tells us there are eight carbons — Tells us it is an alkane

The complete name for this alkane is *n*-octane, the *n* indicating a straight-chain alkane.

TEACHING TIPS

- Organic nomenclature can seem overwhelming at first. It is not possible to memorize all the names and formulas for organic molecules. Students need to learn the names for the basic root and substituents. Once these are learned, naming organic compounds becomes a problem-solving activity.
- Be sure to include some examples where the longest carbon chain is not horizontal. Students find it difficult to understand that a carbon chain with several bends in it is not branched. It is helpful to tell the students that the longest chain is the one that they can follow without lifting their pencil along the carbons.
- Circling or highlighting the longest chain of carbons can help when you are teaching the students to identify the substituents.

PowerLecture Simulation: Naming Alkanes

2. For a branched hydrocarbon, the longest continuous chain of carbon atoms gives the root name for the hydrocarbon. For example, in the alkane

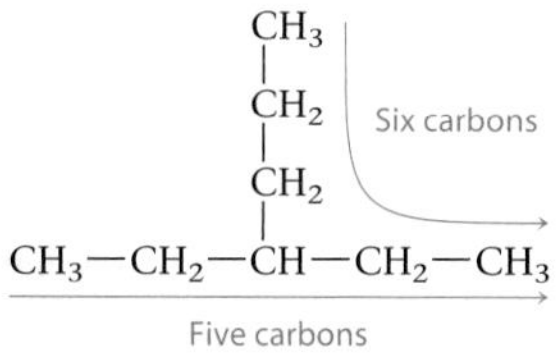

$$\begin{array}{c} CH_3 \\ | \\ CH_2 \\ | \\ CH_2 \\ | \\ CH_3-CH_2-CH-CH_2-CH_3 \end{array}$$

Six carbons

Five carbons

the longest continuous chain contains six carbon atoms. The specific name of this compound is not important at this point, but it will be named as a hexane (indicating a six-carbon chain).

3. Alkanes lacking one hydrogen atom can be attached to a hydrocarbon chain in place of one hydrogen atom. For example, the molecule

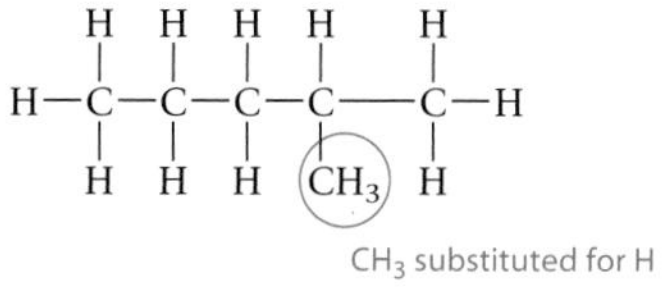

$$\begin{array}{ccccccccccc} & H & & H & & H & & H & & H & \\ & | & & | & & | & & | & & | & \\ H- & C & - & C & - & C & - & C & - & C & -H \\ & | & & | & & | & & | & & | & \\ & H & & H & & H & & CH_3 & & H & \end{array}$$

CH_3 substituted for H

can be viewed as a pentane (five-carbon chain) in which one hydrogen atom has been replaced by a $—CH_3$ group, which is a methane, CH_4, molecule with a hydrogen removed. When a group is substituted for a hydrogen on an alkane chain, we call this group a *substituent.* To name the $—CH_3$ substituent, we start with the name of its parent alkane, drop the *-ane,* and add *-yl.* Therefore, $—CH_3$ is called *methyl.* Likewise, when we remove one hydrogen from ethane, CH_3CH_3, we get $—CH_3CH_2$. Dropping the *-ane* ending and adding *-yl* gives this group the name *ethyl.* Removal of a hydrogen from the end carbon of propane, $CH_3CH_2CH_3$, yields $—CH_3CH_2CH_2$, which is called the *propyl* group.

There are two ways in which the propyl group can be attached as a substituent. A hydrogen can be removed from an end carbon to give the propyl group or from the middle carbon to give the isopropyl group.

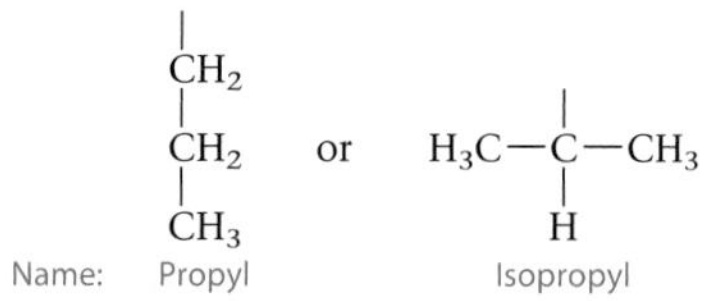

$$\begin{array}{c} | \\ CH_2 \\ | \\ CH_2 \\ | \\ CH_3 \end{array} \quad \text{or} \quad \begin{array}{c} | \\ H_3C-C-CH_3 \\ | \\ H \end{array}$$

Name: Propyl Isopropyl

When a hydrogen is removed from butane, $CH_3CH_2CH_2CH_3$, we get a butyl substituent. In the case of the butyl group, there are four ways in which the atoms can be arranged. These are shown, with their respective names, in Table 20.2.

The general name for an alkane when it functions as a substituent is *alkyl.* All the common alkyl groups are shown in Table 20.2.

4. We specify the positions of substituent groups by numbering sequentially the carbons in the longest chain of carbon atoms, starting at the

Table 20.2 The Most Common Alkyl Substituents and Their Names

Structure*	Name
$—CH_3$	methyl
$—CH_2CH_3$	ethyl
$—CH_2CH_2CH_3$	propyl
$CH_3\overset{\vert}{C}HCH_3$	isopropyl
$—CH_2CH_2CH_2CH_3$	butyl
$CH_3\overset{\vert}{C}HCH_2CH_3$	*sec*-butyl
$—CH_2—\overset{H}{\underset{CH_3}{C}}—CH_3$	isobutyl
$—\overset{CH_3}{\underset{CH_3}{C}}—CH_3$	*tert*-butyl

*The bond with one end open shows the point of attachment of the substituent.

20.4 Naming Alkanes 649

end closest to the branching (the place where the first substituent occurs). For example, the compound

Methyl substituent

$$\begin{array}{lcccccc} & & & CH_3 & & & \\ & & & | & & & \\ & CH_3- & CH_2- & CH- & CH_2- & CH_2- & CH_3 \\ \text{Correct numbering} & 1 & 2 & 3 & 4 & 5 & 6 \\ \text{Incorrect numbering} & 6 & 5 & 4 & 3 & 2 & 1 \end{array}$$

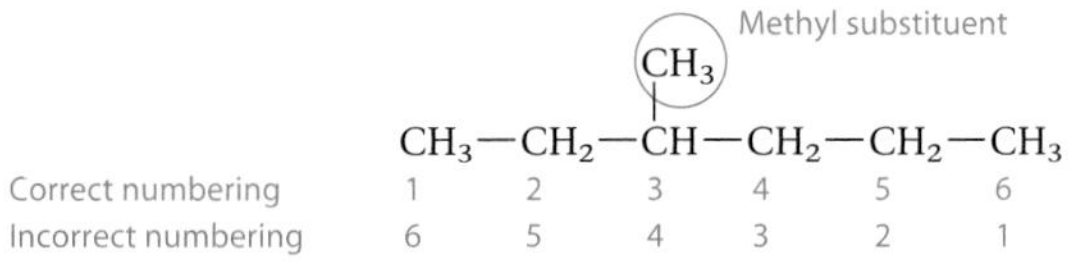

is called 3-methylhexane. Note that the top set of numbers is correct; the left end of the molecule is closest to the branching, and this gives the smallest number for the position of the substituent. Also note that a hyphen is written between the number and the name of the substituent.

5. When a given type of substituent occurs more than once, we indicate this by using a prefix. The prefix *di-* indicates two identical substituents, and *tri-* indicates three. For example, the compound

$$\begin{array}{ccccc} 1 & 2 & 3 & 4 & 5 \\ CH_3- & CH- & CH- & CH_2- & CH_3 \\ & | & | & & \\ & CH_3 & CH_3 & & \end{array}$$

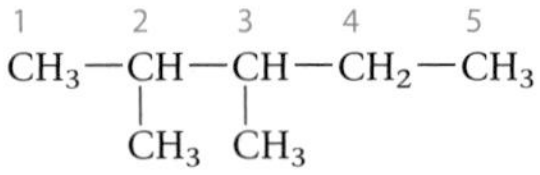

has the root name pentane (five carbons in the longest chain). We use *di-* to indicate the two methyl substituents and use numbers to locate them on the chain. The name is 2,3-dimethylpentane.

The following rules summarize the principles we have just developed.

Rules for Naming Alkanes

1. Find the longest continuous chain of carbon atoms. This chain (called the *parent chain*) determines the base alkane name.
2. Number the carbons in the parent chain, starting at the end closest to any branching (the first alkyl substituent). When a substituent occurs the same number of carbons from each end, use the next substituent (if any) to determine from which end to start numbering.
3. Using the appropriate name for each alkyl group, specify its position on the parent chain with a number.
4. When a given type of alkyl group occurs more than once, attach the appropriate prefix (*di-* for two, *tri-* for three, and so on) to the alkyl name.
5. The alkyl groups are listed in alphabetical order, *disregarding any prefix*.

Additional Examples

Example 20.4

Name three structural isomers of heptane, C_7H_{16}.

n-heptane

2-methylhexane

3-methylhexane

2,3-dimethylpentane

2,4-dimethylpentane

2,2,3-trimethylbutane

2,2-dimethylpentane

EXAMPLE 20.4 Naming Isomers of Alkanes

Draw the structural isomers for the alkane C_6H_{14}, and give the systematic name for each one.

SOLUTION

We proceed systematically, starting with the longest chain and then rearranging the carbons to form the shorter, branched chains.

1. $CH_3CH_2CH_2CH_2CH_2CH_3$
   1 2 3 4 5 6

This alkane has six carbons all in the same continuous chain, so we call it hexane or, more properly, *n*-hexane, indicating that all the carbon atoms are in the same chain.

2. We now take one carbon out of the main chain and make it a methyl substituent. This gives the molecule

$$\begin{array}{l} CH_3\underset{\displaystyle CH_3}{\underset{|}{C}}HCH_2CH_2CH_3 \end{array}$$

The carbon skeleton is as follows:

$$\begin{array}{ccccc} 1 & 2 & 3 & 4 & 5 \\ C- & C- & C- & C- & C \\ & | & & & \\ & C & & & \end{array}$$

Because the longest chain has five carbons, the base name is pentane. We have numbered the chain from the left, starting closest to the substituent, a methyl group. We indicate the position of the methyl group on the chain by the number 2, the number of the carbon to which it is attached. So the name is 2-methylpentane. Note that if we numbered the chain from the right end, the methyl group would be on carbon 4. We want the smallest possible number, so the numbering shown is correct.

Note that placing the $—CH_3$ group on carbon 4 gives the same molecule as placing it on carbon 2.

3. The methyl substituent also can be on the number 3 carbon:

$$\begin{array}{ccccc} 1 & 2 & 3 & 4 & 5 \\ CH_3 & CH_2 & CH & CH_2 & CH_3 \\ & & | & & \\ & & CH_3 & & \end{array}$$

The name is 3-methylpentane. We have now exhausted all possibilities for placing a single methyl group on pentane.

4. Next we take two carbons out of the original six-member chain.

$$\begin{array}{cccc} CH_3 & CH— & CH & CH_3 \\ & | & | & \\ & CH_3 & CH_3 & \end{array}$$

The carbon skeleton is

$$\begin{array}{cccc} 1 & 2 & 3 & 4 \\ C- & C- & C- & C \\ & | & | & \\ & C & C & \end{array}$$

The longest chain of this molecule has four carbons, so the root name is butane. Because there are two methyl groups (on carbons 2 and 3), we use the prefix *di-*. The name of the molecule is 2,3-dimethylbutane. Note that when two or more numbers are used, they are separated by a comma.

5. Two methyl groups also can be attached to the same carbon atom in the four-carbon chain to give the following molecule:

$$\begin{array}{ccc} & CH_3 & \\ & | & \\ CH_3— & C & —CH_2CH_3 \\ & | & \\ & CH_3 & \end{array}$$

TEACHING TIP

It is helpful to show students how to think about these isomer problems. An organized approach for drawing and naming isomers makes the process much simpler. Start with the longest carbon chain, remove one methyl group at a time, and try to place the methyl group on as many new carbons as possible without producing duplicates. Naming each molecule will help to eliminate duplicates. If the names are the same, then the molecules are the same, even if they look different in the drawing.

PowerLecture Animation: Rotating 2,2-Dimethylbutane

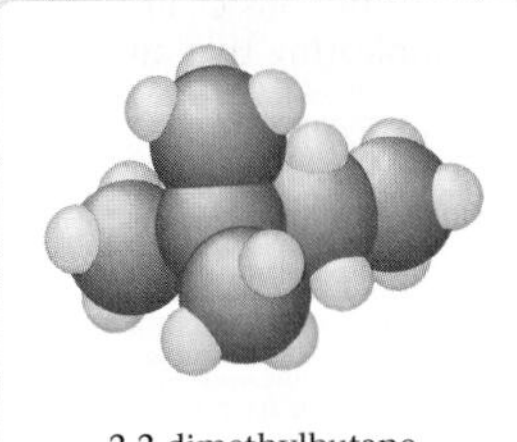

2,2-dimethylbutane

The carbon skeleton is

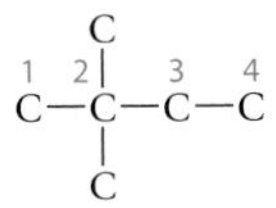

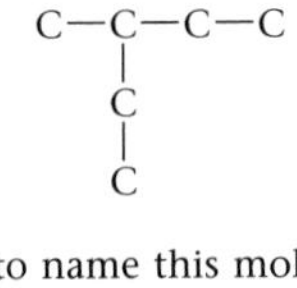

```
        C
  1  2  |  3  4
  C —— C —— C —— C
        |
        C
```

The root name is butane, and there are two methyl groups on the number 2 carbon. The name is 2,2-dimethylbutane.

6. As we search for more isomers, we might try to place an ethyl substituent on the four-carbon chain to give the molecule

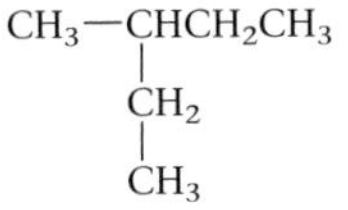

$$\begin{array}{l} CH_3{-}\underset{|}{C}HCH_2CH_3 \\ \quad\;\;\; \underset{|}{C}H_2 \\ \quad\;\;\; CH_3 \end{array}$$

The carbon skeleton is

```
C—C—C—C
  |
  C
  |
  C
```

We might be tempted to name this molecule 2-ethylbutane, but this is incorrect. Notice that there are five carbon atoms in the longest chain.

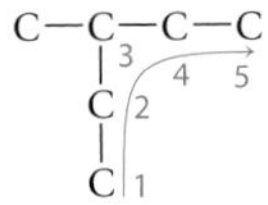

```
C—C—C—C
  | 3  4  5
  C  2
  |
  C  1
```

We can rearrange this carbon skeleton to give

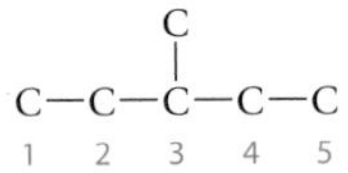

```
        C
        |
C—C—C—C—C
1  2  3  4  5
```

This molecule is, in fact, a pentane (3-methylpentane), because the longest chain has five carbon atoms, so it is not a new isomer.

In searching for more isomers, we might try a structure such as

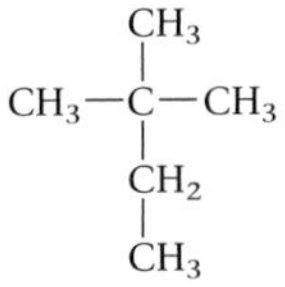

$$\begin{array}{c} CH_3 \\ | \\ CH_3{-}C{-}CH_3 \\ | \\ CH_2 \\ | \\ CH_3 \end{array}$$

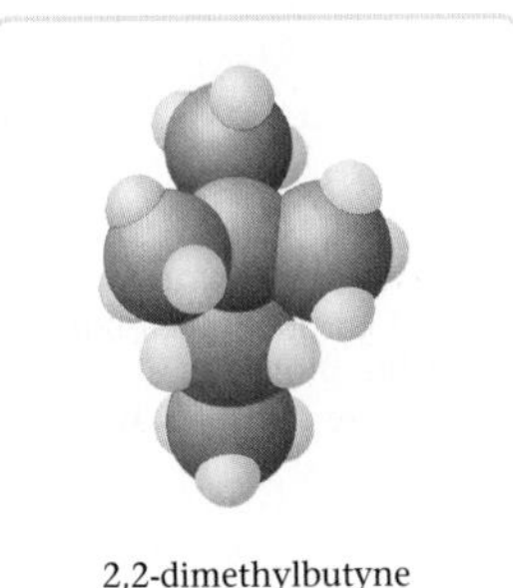

2,2-dimethylbutyne

As we have drawn it, this molecule might appear to be a propane. However, the molecule has a longest chain of four atoms (look vertically), so the correct name is 2,2-dimethylbutane.

Thus there are five distinct structural isomers of C_6H_{14}: *n*-hexane, 2-methylpentane, 3-methylpentane, 2,3-dimethylbutane, and 2,2-dimethylbutane.

Self-Check EXERCISE 20.2 Name the following molecules.

a. 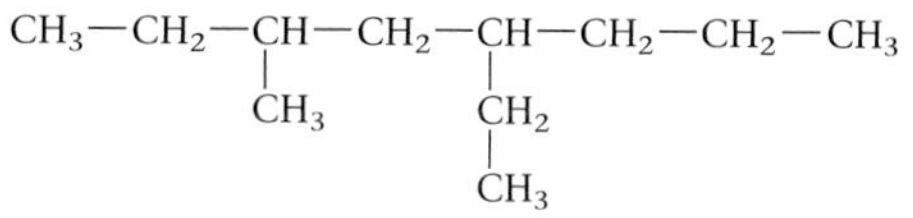
```
CH3—CH2—CH—CH2—CH—CH2—CH2—CH3
        |       |
        CH3     CH2
                |
                CH3
```

b. 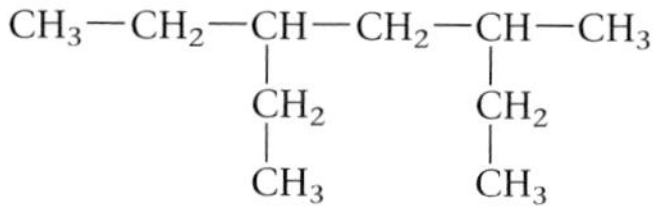
```
CH3—CH2—CH—CH2—CH—CH3
        |       |
        CH2     CH2
        |       |
        CH3     CH3
```

See Problems 20.25 and 20.26. ■

So far we have learned how to name a compound by examining its structural formula. We also must be able to do the reverse: write the structural formula from the name.

EXAMPLE 20.5 Writing Structural Isomers from Names

Write the structural formula for each of the following compounds.

a. 4-ethyl-3,5-dimethylnonane b. 4-*tert*-butylheptane

SOLUTION

a. The root name nonane signifies a nine-carbon chain. Therefore, we have the following main chain of carbons:

```
1   2   3   4   5   6   7   8   9
C—C—C—C—C—C—C—C—C
```

The name indicates an ethyl group attached to carbon 4 and two methyl groups, one on carbon 3 and one on carbon 5. This gives the following carbon skeleton:

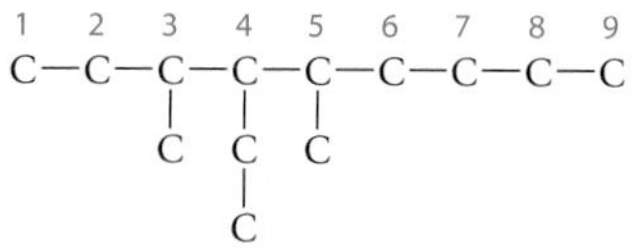

```
1   2   3   4   5   6   7   8   9
C—C—C—C—C—C—C—C—C
        |   |   |
        C   C   C
            |
            C
```

When we add the hydrogen atoms, we get the final structure

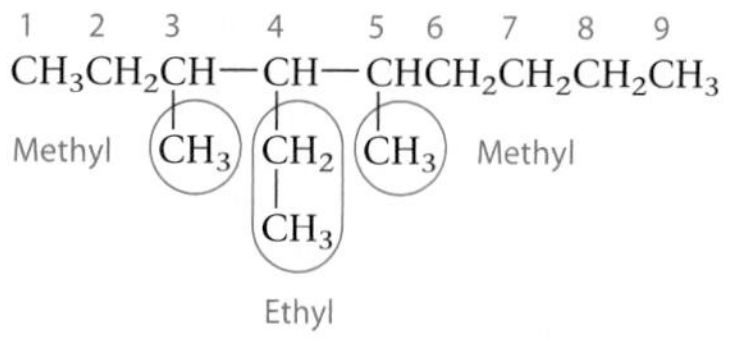

```
 1   2    3       4       5    6    7    8    9
CH3CH2CH—CH—CHCH2CH2CH2CH3
        |        |       |
Methyl (CH3) (CH2) (CH3) Methyl
                 |
               (CH3)
                Ethyl
```

b. Heptane signifies a seven-carbon chain, and the *tert*-butyl group (see Table 20.2) is

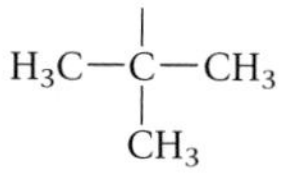

```
       |
H3C—C—CH3
       |
      CH3
```

Self Check

Answers to Self-Check Exercise 20.2

a. 5-ethyl-3-methyloctane

b. 5-ethyl-3-methylheptane

Additional Examples

Example 20.5

Draw the structural formula for each of the following compounds.

1. 3-methylheptane

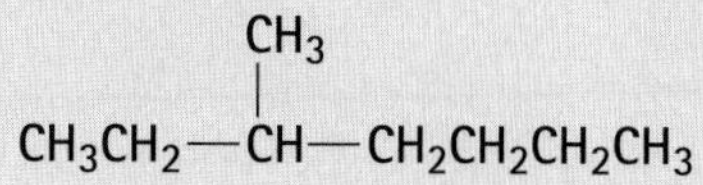

```
          CH3
          |
CH3CH2—CH—CH2CH2CH2CH3
```

2. 2,4-dimethylheptane

```
    CH3            CH3
    |              |
CH3CH—CH2—CHCH2CH2CH3
```

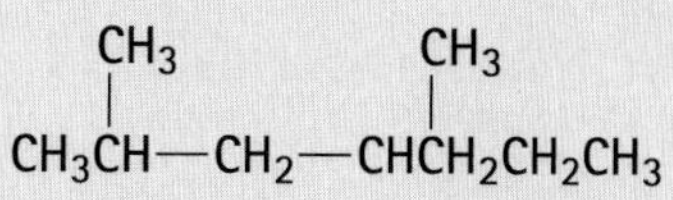

Thus we have the molecule

$$\begin{array}{c} \scriptstyle 1\ \ 2\ \ 3\ \ 4\ 5\ \ 6\ \ 7 \\ CH_3CH_2CH_2CHCH_2CH_2CH_3 \\ | \\ H_3C-C-CH_3 \\ | \\ CH_3 \end{array}$$

Self-Check **EXERCISE 20.3** Write the structural formula for 5-isopropyl-4-methyldecane.

See Problems 20.27 and 20.28. ■

Section 20.5

DEMONSTRATION

If you can obtain a sample of crude oil, bring it to class along with a sample of gasoline to show students the differences.

20.5 Petroleum

OBJECTIVE: To learn about the composition and uses of petroleum.

Woody plants, coal, petroleum, and natural gas provide a vast resource of energy that originally came from the sun. By the process of photosynthesis, plants store energy that we can claim by burning the plants themselves or, more commonly, burning the decay products that have been converted to fossil fuels. Although the United States currently depends heavily on petroleum for energy, this dependency is a relatively recent phenomenon (see Figure 10.7).

Petroleum and natural gas deposits probably formed from the remains of marine organisms that lived approximately 500 million years ago. **Petroleum** is a thick, dark liquid composed largely of hydrocarbons containing from 5 to more than 25 carbon atoms. **Natural gas,** which is usually associated with petroleum deposits, consists mostly of methane but also contains significant amounts of ethane, propane, and butane.

Distillation (separation by boiling) was discussed in Section 3.5.

To be used efficiently, petroleum must be separated by boiling into portions called *fractions*. The smaller hydrocarbons can be boiled off at relatively low temperatures; the larger molecules require successively higher temperatures. The major uses of various petroleum fractions are shown in Table 20.3.

The petroleum era began when the demand for lamp oil during the Industrial Revolution outstripped the traditional sources: animal fats and whale oil. In response to this increased demand, Edwin Drake drilled the first oil well in 1859 at Titusville, Pennsylvania. The petroleum from this well was refined to produce *kerosene* (fraction C_{10}–C_{18}), which served as an excellent lamp oil. *Gasoline* (fraction C_5–C_{12}) was of limited use and often was discarded. However, the importance of these fractions was reversed when the development of the electric light reduced the need for kerosene and the advent of the "horseless carriage" signaled the birth of the gasoline age.

As gasoline became more important, new ways were sought to increase the yield of gasoline obtained from each barrel of petroleum. William Burton invented a process called *pyrolytic cracking* at Standard Oil of Indiana. In this process, the heavier molecules of the kerosene fraction are heated to about 700 °C, which causes them to break (crack) into the smaller molecules characteristic of the gasoline fraction. As cars became larger, more efficient internal combustion engines were designed. Because of the uneven burning of the gasoline then available, these engines "knocked," producing unwanted noise and even engine damage. Intensive research to find additives that would promote smoother burning yielded tetraethyl lead, $(C_2H_5)_4Pb$, a very effective "antiknock" agent.

Table 20.3 Uses of the Various Petroleum Fractions

Petroleum Fraction*	Major Uses
C_5–C_{12}	gasoline
C_{10}–C_{18}	kerosene jet fuel
C_{15}–C_{25}	diesel fuel heating oil lubricating oil
$>C_{25}$	asphalt

*Shows the chain lengths present in each fraction.

Self Check

Answer to Self-Check Exercise 20.3

$$\begin{array}{c} CH_3 \\ | \\ CH_3CH_2CH_2CH-CH-CH_2CH_2CH_2CH_2CH_3 \\ | \\ CH_3-CH-CH_3 \end{array}$$

Adding tetraethyl lead to gasoline became a common practice, and by 1960, gasoline contained as much as 3 grams of lead per gallon. As we have discovered so often in recent years, technological advances can produce environmental problems. Lead in gasoline causes two important problems. First, it "poisons" the catalytic converters that have been added to exhaust systems to help prevent air pollution. Second, the use of leaded gasoline has greatly increased the amount of lead in the environment, where it can be ingested by animals and humans. For these reasons, the use of lead in gasoline has been largely discontinued. This has required extensive (and expensive) modifications of engines and of the gasoline-refining process.

20.6 Reactions of Alkanes

Section 20.6

OBJECTIVE: To learn various types of chemical reactions that alkanes undergo.

At low temperatures, alkanes are not very reactive because the C—C and C—H bonds in alkanes are relatively strong. For example, at 25 °C, alkanes do not react with acids, bases, or strong oxidizing agents. This chemical inertness makes alkanes valuable as lubricating materials and as the backbone for structural materials such as plastics.

At sufficiently high temperatures, however, alkanes *react vigorously with oxygen*. These **combustion reactions** are the basis for the alkanes' widespread use as fuels. For example, the combustion reaction of butane with oxygen is

$$2C_4H_{10}(g) + 13O_2(g) \rightarrow 8CO_2(g) + 10H_2O(g)$$

The alkanes also can undergo **substitution reactions**—reactions in which *one or more hydrogen atoms of the alkane are replaced* (substituted) *by different atoms*. We can represent the substitution reaction of an alkane with a halogen molecule as follows:

$$R—H + X_2 \rightarrow R—X + HX$$

where R represents an alkyl group and X represents a halogen atom. For example, methane can react successively with chlorine as follows:

The symbol *hv* signifies ultraviolet light used to furnish energy for the reaction.

$$CH_4 + Cl_2 \xrightarrow{hv} CH_3Cl + HCl$$

Chloromethane

$$CH_3Cl + Cl_2 \xrightarrow{hv} CH_2Cl_2 + HCl$$

Dichloromethane

$$CH_2Cl_2 + Cl_2 \xrightarrow{hv} CHCl_3 + HCl$$

Trichloromethane (chloroform)

$$CHCl_3 + Cl_2 \xrightarrow{hv} CCl_4 + HCl$$

Tetrachloromethane (carbon tetrachloride)

The *hv* above each arrow signifies that ultraviolet light is needed to furnish the energy to break the Cl—Cl bond to produce chlorine atoms:

$$Cl_2 \longrightarrow Cl\cdot + Cl\cdot$$

A chlorine atom has an unpaired electron, indicated by the dot, which makes it very reactive and able to disrupt the C—H bond.

TEACHING TIPS

- Classifying reactions is a new skill for students. It is important to help them practice classifying organic reactions. It is useful to explain to the students how you think about each reaction as you try to classify it.
- When discussing substitution reactions, remind students that any one of the hydrogens can be substituted. Not all substitutions will produce different products. This idea is often confusing to students. Use three-dimensional models to illustrate this concept one molecule at a time.
- For dehydrogenation reactions, point out that a hydrogen is removed from each of two adjacent carbons and that these two carbons form a double bond.

Lecture Demonstration: 22.1

Notice that each step in the process involves replacement of a C—H bond by a C—Cl bond. That is, a chlorine atom *substitutes* for a hydrogen atom. The names of the products of these reactions use the term *chloro* for the chlorine substituents with a prefix that gives the number of chlorine atoms present: *di-* for two, *tri-* for three, and *tetra-* for four. No number is used to describe the chlorine positions in this case because methane has only one carbon atom. Note that the products of the last two reactions have two names, the systematic name and the common name in parentheses.

Besides substitution reactions, alkanes also can undergo **dehydrogenation reactions** in which *hydrogen atoms are removed* and the product is an unsaturated hydrocarbon. For example, in the presence of a catalyst [chromium(III) oxide] at high temperatures, ethane can be dehydrogenated, yielding ethylene, C_2H_4.

Test Bank: 9, 10, 27–34

$$CH_3CH_3 \xrightarrow[500\ ^\circ C]{Cr_2O_3} \underset{\text{Ethylene}}{CH_2{=}CH_2} + H_2$$

Section 20.7

20.7 Alkenes and Alkynes

OBJECTIVES: To learn to name hydrocarbons with double bonds (alkenes) and triple bonds (alkynes). • To understand addition reactions.

TEACHING TIP

Use models to show the shapes of the alkene and alkyne molecules around the single and multiple bonds.

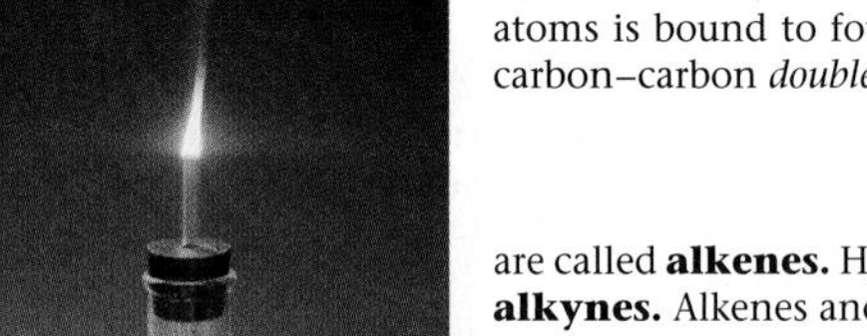

Acetylene gas burning. The acetylene is formed by the reaction of calcium carbide, CaC_2, with water in the flask.

We have seen that alkanes are saturated hydrocarbons—each of the carbon atoms is bound to four atoms by single bonds. Hydrocarbons that contain carbon–carbon *double bonds*

$$\gt C{=}C\lt$$

are called **alkenes.** Hydrocarbons with carbon–carbon *triple bonds* are called **alkynes.** Alkenes and alkynes are unsaturated hydrocarbons.

Multiple carbon–carbon bonds result when hydrogen atoms are removed from alkanes. Alkenes that contain a carbon–carbon double bond have the general formula C_nH_{2n}. The simplest alkene, C_2H_4, commonly known as *ethylene,* has the Lewis structure

$$\begin{matrix} H & & & & H \\ & \diagdown & & \diagup & \\ & & C{=}C & & \\ & \diagup & & \diagdown & \\ H & & & & H \end{matrix}$$

The ball-and-stick model of ethylene is shown in Figure 20.5.

The system for naming alkenes and alkynes is similar to the one we have used for alkanes. The following rules are useful.

PowerLecture Animations:
Rotating 2-Pentene Molecule
Rotating 2-Pentyne Molecule
Rotating 1-Propene Molecule

Figure 20.5 The ball-and-stick model of ethylene (ethene).

Rules for Naming Alkenes and Alkynes

1. Select the longest continuous chain of carbon atoms that contains the double or triple bond.
2. For an alkene, the root name of the carbon chain is the same as for the alkane, except that the *-ane* ending is replaced by *-ene*. For an alkyne, the *-ane* is replaced by *-yne*. For example, for a two-carbon chain we have

CH_3CH_3	$CH_2{=}CH_2$	$CH{\equiv}CH$
Ethane	Ethene	Ethyne

3. Number the parent chain, starting at the end closest to the double or triple bond. The location of the multiple bond is given by the lowest-numbered carbon involved in the bond. For example,

$$\underset{1}{CH_2}{=}\underset{2}{C}\underset{}{H}\underset{3}{CH_2}\underset{4}{CH_3}$$

is called 1-butene and

$$\underset{1}{CH_3}\underset{2}{CH}{=}\underset{3}{CH}\underset{4}{CH_3}$$

is called 2-butene.

4. Substituents on the parent chain are treated the same way as in naming alkanes. For example, the molecule $ClCH{=}CHCH_2CH_3$ is called 1-chloro-1-butene.

In writing shorthand formulas, the hydrogen atoms are often written just after the carbon to which they are attached. For example, the formula for $H{-}C{\equiv}C{-}H$ is often written as $CH{\equiv}CH$.

EXAMPLE 20.6 Naming Alkenes and Alkynes

Name each of the following molecules.

a. 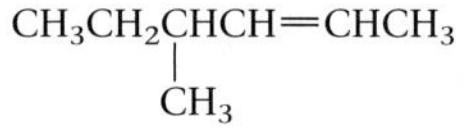 $CH_3CH_2\underset{\underset{CH_3}{|}}{C}HCH{=}CHCH_3$

b. 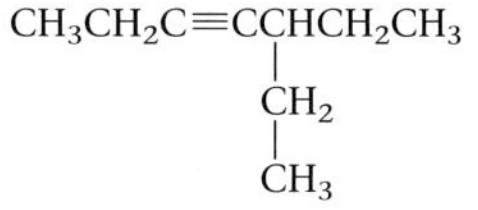 $CH_3CH_2C{\equiv}C\underset{\underset{\underset{CH_3}{|}}{CH_2}}{\underset{|}{C}}HCH_2CH_3$

SOLUTION

a. The longest chain contains six carbon atoms, and we number the carbons starting from the end closest to the double bond.

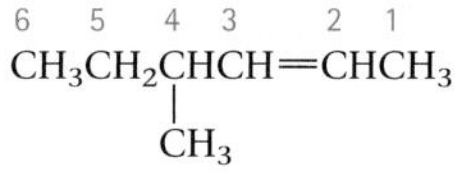

$$\overset{6}{C}H_3\overset{5}{C}H_2\underset{\underset{CH_3}{|}}{\overset{4}{C}}H\overset{3}{C}H{=}\overset{2}{C}H\overset{1}{C}H_3$$

Thus the root name for the hydrocarbon is 2-hexene. (Remember to use the lower number of the two carbon atoms involved in the double bond.) There is a methyl group attached to the number 4 carbon. Therefore, the name of the compound is 4-methyl-2-hexene.

b. The longest chain of carbon atoms is seven carbons long, and the chain is numbered as shown (starting from the end closest to the triple bond).

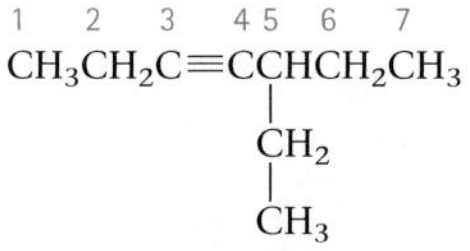

$$\overset{1}{C}H_3\overset{2}{C}H_2\overset{3}{C}{\equiv}\overset{4}{C}\underset{\underset{\underset{CH_3}{|}}{CH_2}}{\underset{|}{\overset{5}{C}}}H\overset{6}{C}H_2\overset{7}{C}H_3$$

The hydrocarbon is a 3-heptyne (we use the lowest-numbered carbon in the triple bond). Because there is an ethyl group on carbon number 5, the full name is 5-ethyl-3-heptyne.

Additional Examples

Example 20.6

Name each of the following molecules.

1. $CH_3CH{=}CHCH_2CH_2CH_2CH_2CH_2CH_2CH_3$

   2-decene

2. $CH_3CH_2C{\equiv}CCH_3$

   2-pentyne

Self Check

Answers to Self-Check Exercise 20.4

a. 2-methyl-3-octene

b. 1-pentyne

PowerLecture Animation: Addition Reaction: H_2 and Propene

TEACHING TIP

Molecules that have the same number of carbons and hydrogens but have double or triple bonds between different carbons are isomers. Students can identify which molecules are the same and which are structural isomers from the different locator numbers for the double and triple bonds in the names of the compounds.

DEMONSTRATION

You can show an addition reaction in class by adding a small amount of bromine dissolved in an inert solvent (such as trichloromethane) to some cyclohexene. The red color of the bromine disappears as the reaction occurs. Compare this result with the reaction after adding some of the bromine to a liquid alkane (such as hexane). The red color does not disappear.

Self-Check EXERCISE 20.4 Name the following molecules.

a. $CH_3CH_2CH_2CH_2CH{=}CHCHCH_3$ (with a CH_3 group attached to the second CH of CHCH)

$$\begin{array}{l} CH_3CH_2CH_2CH_2CH{=}CH\underset{\displaystyle |\atop \displaystyle CH_3}{C}HCH_3 \end{array}$$

b. $CH_3CH_2CH_2C{\equiv}CH$

See Problems 20.45 and 20.46. ■

Reactions of Alkenes

Because alkenes and alkynes are unsaturated, their most important reactions are **addition reactions,** in which *new atoms form single bonds to the carbons formerly involved in the double or triple bonds*. An addition reaction for an alkene changes the carbon–carbon double bond to a single bond, giving a saturated hydrocarbon (each carbon bonded to four atoms). For example, **hydrogenation reactions,** which use H_2 as a reactant, lead to the addition of a hydrogen atom to each carbon formerly involved in the double bond.

$$\underset{\text{1-Propene}}{CH_2{=}CHCH_3} + H_2 \xrightarrow{\text{Catalyst}} \underset{\text{Propane}}{CH_3CH_2CH_3}$$

Hydrogenation of molecules with double bonds is an important industrial process, particularly in the manufacture of solid shortenings. Unsaturated fats (fats containing double bonds) are generally liquids at room temperature, whereas saturated fats (those containing C—C single bonds) are solids. The liquid unsaturated fats are converted to solid saturated fats by hydrogenation.

Halogenation of unsaturated hydrocarbons involves the addition of halogen atoms. Here is an example:

$$\underset{\text{1-Pentene}}{CH_2{=}CHCH_2CH_2CH_3} + Br_2 \rightarrow \underset{\text{1,2-Dibromopentane}}{CH_2BrCHBrCH_2CH_2CH_3}$$

Another important reaction of certain unsaturated hydrocarbons is **polymerization,** a process in which many small molecules are joined together to form a large molecule. Polymerization will be discussed in Section 20.16.

20.8 Aromatic Hydrocarbons

OBJECTIVE: To learn about the aromatic hydrocarbons.

When mixtures of hydrocarbons from natural sources, such as petroleum or coal, are separated, certain of the compounds that emerge have pleasant odors and are thus known as **aromatic hydrocarbons.** When these substances, which include wintergreen, cinnamon, and vanillin, are examined, they are all found to contain a common feature: a six-membered ring of carbon atoms called the *benzene ring*. **Benzene** has the formula C_6H_6 and a planar (flat) structure in which all the bond angles are 120° (Figure 20.6).

Inga Spence/Visuals Unlimited

Cinnamon is an aromatic hydrocarbon.

When we examine the bonding in the benzene ring, we find that more than one Lewis structure can be drawn. That is, the double bonds can be located in different positions, as shown in Figure 20.7. Because the actual bonding is a combi-

Section 20.8

TEACHING TIPS

- A model that shows the difference between cyclohexane (a puckered ring) and benzene (a flat ring) would be useful in helping students understand aromatic hydrocarbons.
- You may wish to discuss the delocalization of the electrons in the benzene ring as an example of how our bonding model is limited. Drawing the benzene ring structure with the circle inside the hexagon reminds us that benzene behaves differently than a carbon molecule with a double bond.

 **Test Bank: 11**

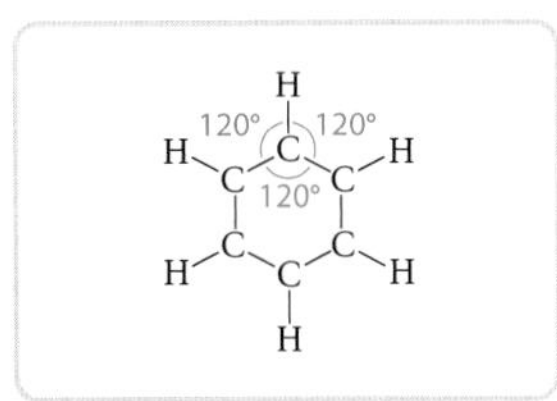

Figure 20.6 Benzene, C_6H_6, consists of six carbon atoms bonded together to form a ring. Each carbon has one hydrogen atom bonded to it. All the atoms in benzene lie in the same plane. This representation does not show all the bonds between the carbon atoms in the ring.

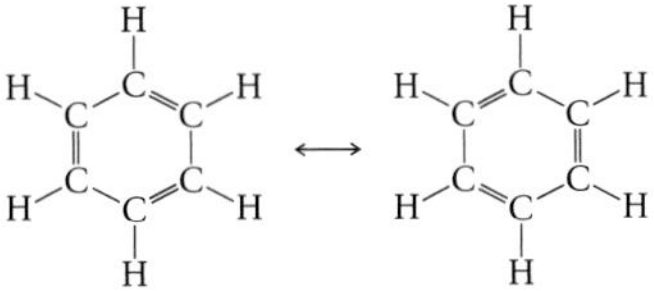

Figure 20.7 (Top) Two Lewis structures for the benzene ring. (Bottom) As a shorthand notation, the rings are usually represented without labeling the carbon and hydrogen atoms.

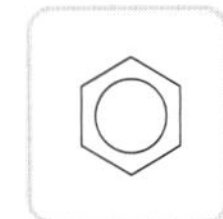

Figure 20.8 To show that the bonding in the benzene ring is a combination of different Lewis structures, the ring is drawn with a circle inside.

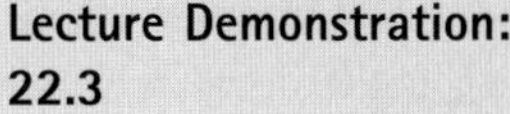

Lecture Demonstration: 22.3

PowerLecture Animation: Ring and Molecular Structure of Benzene

nation of the structures represented in Figure 20.7, the benzene ring is usually shown with a circle (Figure 20.8).

Test Bank: 35, 36

20.9 Naming Aromatic Compounds

OBJECTIVE: To learn the system for naming aromatic compounds.

Section 20.9

Substituted benzene molecules are formed by replacing one or more of the H atoms on the benzene ring with other atoms or groups of atoms. We will consider benzene rings with one substituent (called *monosubstituted benzenes*) first.

Monosubstituted Benzenes

The systematic method for naming monosubstituted benzenes uses the substituent name as a prefix of benzene. For example, the molecule

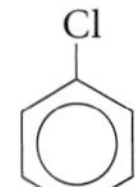

is called chlorobenzene, and the molecule

CH_2CH_3

is called ethylbenzene.

TEACHING TIPS

- Students need to learn the basic monosubstituted benzene molecule names because they are used repeatedly.
- Many students forget that when benzene is a substituent, the correct name for the group is *phenyl-*, not *benzyl-*.
- When naming disubstituted benzenes, give the names in both naming systems. Students find the system using numbers a little easier than the older (*ortho-*, *meta-*, *para-*) system.

TEACHING TIP

Naming disubstituted benzenes can be complicated. When both substituents are the same, two numbers are used as locators; when the substituents are different, only one number is used because we assume that the first substituent is on the number 1 carbon. You will need to help your students understand this distinction.

Sometimes, monosubstituted benzene compounds have special names. For example, the molecule

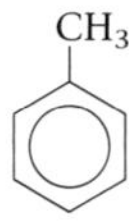

has the systematic name methylbenzene. However, for convenience, it is given the name toluene. Likewise, the molecule

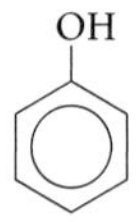

which might be called hydroxybenzene, has the special name phenol. Several examples of monosubstituted benzenes are shown in Figure 20.9.

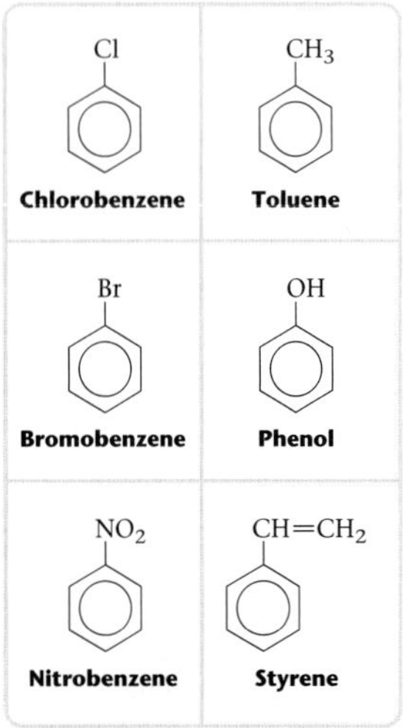
Cl
Chlorobenzene
CH3
Toluene
Br
Bromobenzene
OH
Phenol
NO2
Nitrobenzene
CH=CH2
Styrene

Figure 20.9 Names of some common monosubstituted benzenes.

Sometimes it is more convenient to name compounds if we view the benzene ring itself as a substituent. For example, the compound

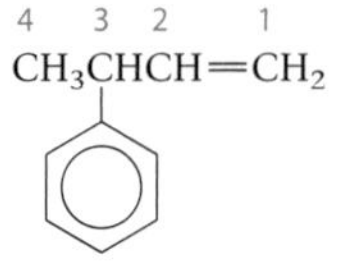

is most easily named as a 1-butene with a benzene ring as a substituent on the number 3 carbon. When the benzene ring is used as a substituent, it is called the **phenyl** (pronounced "fen′-ill") **group.** So the name of the preceding compound is 3-phenyl-1-butene. As another example, the compound

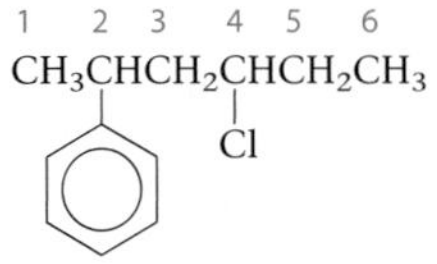

is named 4-chloro-2-phenylhexane. Remember, we start to number the chain from the end closest to the first substituent and name the substituents in alphabetical order (chloro before phenyl).

Disubstituted Benzenes

When there is more than one substituent on the benzene ring, numbers are used to indicate substituent position. For example, the compound

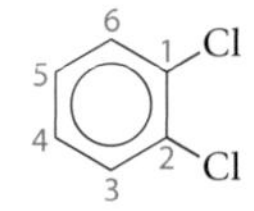

Ortho- (*o-*) means two adjacent substituents.

is named 1,2-dichlorobenzene. Another naming system uses the prefix *ortho-* (*o-*) for two adjacent substituents, *meta-* (*m-*) for two substituents with one carbon between them, and *para-* (*p-*) for two substituents opposite each

Para- (*p*-) means two substituents directly across the ring from each other.

Meta- (*m*-) means two substituents with one carbon between them.

other. This means that 1,2-dichlorobenzene also can be called *ortho*-dichlorobenzene or *o*-dichlorobenzene. Likewise, the compound

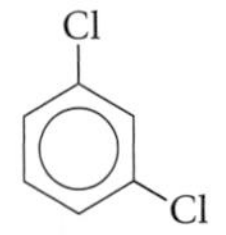

can be called 1,3-dichlorobenzene or *m*-dichlorobenzene. The compound

is named 1,4-dichlorobenzene or *p*-dichlorobenzene.

Benzenes that have two methyl substituents have the special name xylene. So the compound

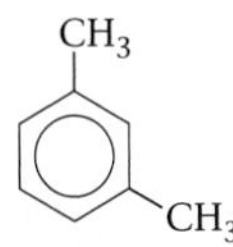

which might be called 1,3-dimethylbenzene, is instead called *m*-xylene (*meta*-xylene).

When two different substituents are present on the benzene ring, one is always assumed to be at carbon number 1, and this number is not specified in the name. For example, the compound

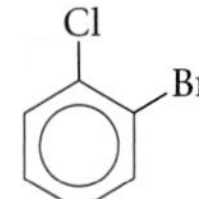

is named 2-bromochlorobenzene, not 2-bromo-1-chlorobenzene. Various examples of disubstituted benzenes are shown in Figure 20.10 on page 662.

Benzene is the simplest aromatic molecule. More complex aromatic systems can be viewed as consisting of a number of "fused" benzene rings. Some examples are given in Table 20.4.

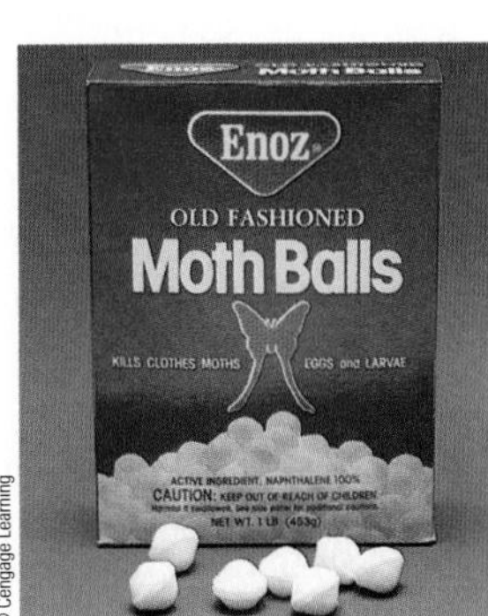

Mothballs used to contain naphthalene, composed of "fused" benzene rings, but now contain *p*-dichlorobenzene.

EXAMPLE 20.7 Naming Aromatic Compounds

Name the following compounds.

a. 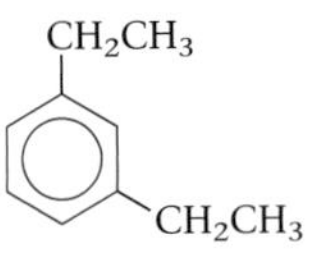 CH_2CH_3 / CH_2CH_3 (benzene ring, 1,3-substituted)

b.  CH_3 / Br (benzene ring, 1,4-substituted)

c. 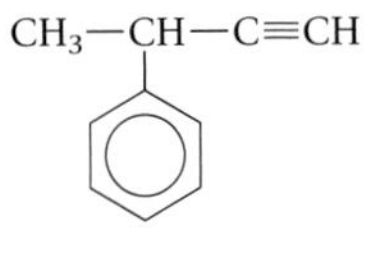 $CH_3—CH—C≡CH$ (phenyl on CH)

d. 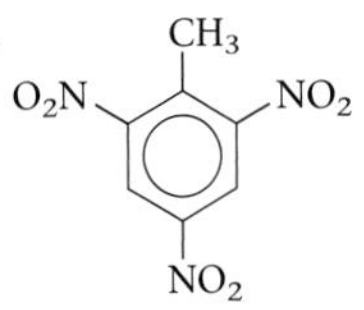 CH_3, O_2N, NO_2, NO_2 (benzene ring)

Additional Examples

Example 20.7

Name the following compounds.

1. 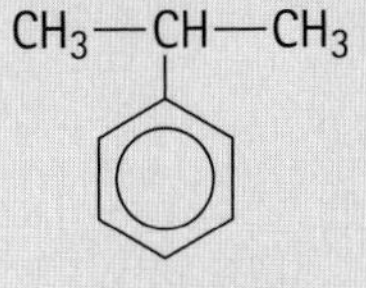 $CH_3—CH—CH_3$ (phenyl on CH)

   2-phenylpropane

2. 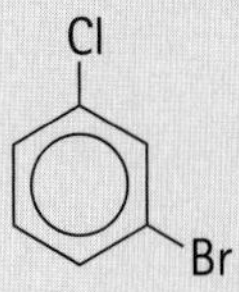 Cl / Br (benzene ring, 1,3-substituted)

   3-bromochlorobenzene

Pam Taylor/Bruce Coleman, Inc.

Dyed nylon rope.

1,2-Dibromobenzene (o-dibromobenzene)	1,3-Dibromobenzene (m-dibromobenzene)	1,4-Dibromobenzene (p-dibromobenzene)
1,4-Dimethylbenzene (p-xylene)	1,2-Dimethylbenzene (o-xylene)	1,3-Dimethylbenzene (m-xylene)
2-Nitrotoluene (o-nitrotoluene)	3-Bromonitrobenzene (m-bromonitrobenzene)	3-Chlorotoluene (m-chlorotoluene)

Figure 20.10 Some selected disubstituted benzenes and their names. Common names are given in parentheses.

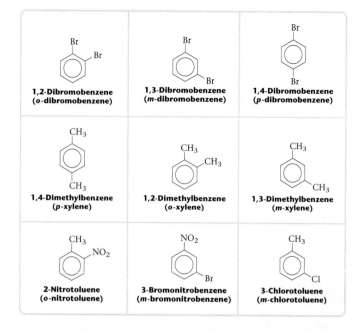

Table 20.4 More Complex Aromatic Molecules

Structural Formula	Name	Use
	naphthalene	Formerly used in mothballs
	anthracene	dyes
	phenanthrene	dyes, explosives, and synthesis of drugs

SOLUTION

a. There are ethyl groups in the 1 and 3 (or *meta-*) positions, so the name is 1,3-diethylbenzene or *m*-diethylbenzene.

b. The

CH_3 (benzene ring)

group is called toluene. The bromine is in the 4 (or *para-*) position. The name is 4-bromotoluene or *p*-bromotoluene.

CHEMISTRY IN FOCUS

Termite Mothballing

Termites typically do not get a lot of respect. They are regarded as lowly, destructive insects. However, termites are the first insects known to fumigate their nests with naphthalene, a chemical long used by humans to prevent moths from damaging wool garments. Although termites are not concerned about holes in their sweaters, they may use naphthalene to ward off microbes and predatory ants, among other pests.

Gregg Henderson and Jian Chen, of the Louisiana State University Agricultural Center in Baton Rouge, have observed that Formosan termites are unusually resistant to naphthalene. In fact, these insects build their underground galleries from chewed wood glued together with saliva and excrement. This "glue" (called *carton*) contains significant amounts of naphthalene, which evaporates and permeates the air in the underground tunnels. The source of the naphthalene is unknown—it might be a metabolite from a food source of the termites or it might be produced from the carton by organisms present in the nest. Whatever the source of the naphthalene, this interesting example shows how organisms use chemistry to protect themselves.

Naphthalene

Formosan subterranean termites.

PowerLecture Animation: Rotating Naphthalene Molecule

c. In this case, we name the compound as a butyne with a phenyl substituent. The name is 3-phenyl-1-butyne.

d. We name this compound as a substituted toluene (with the $—CH_3$ group assumed to be on carbon number 1). So the name is 2,4,6-trinitrotoluene. This compound is more commonly known as TNT, a component of high explosives.

Self Check

Answers to Self-Check Exercise 20.5

a. 2-chloronitrobenzene (or *o*-chloronitrobenzene)

b. 4-phenyl-2-hexene

Self-Check EXERCISE 20.5 Name the following compounds.

a.

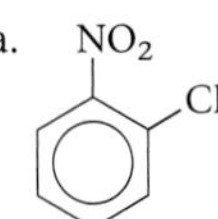

b. $CH_3CH_2CH—CH{=}CHCH_3$

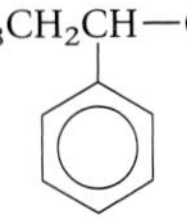

See Problems 20.55 and 20.56. ■

Test Bank: 24, 37–40

20.10 Functional Groups

Section 20.10

OBJECTIVE: To learn the common functional groups in organic molecules.

The vast majority of organic molecules contain elements in addition to carbon and hydrogen. However, most of these substances can be viewed as

663

DEMONSTRATION

If you have samples of molecules containing the functional groups you plan to discuss, bring them to class. These chemicals have interesting odors and physical properties.

TEACHING TIP

You may wish to spend some time drawing organic molecules on the board or overhead projector and having the students circle the functional groups. Learning to identify the functional group is the first step in being able to predict the organic reaction that occurs when chemicals are mixed.

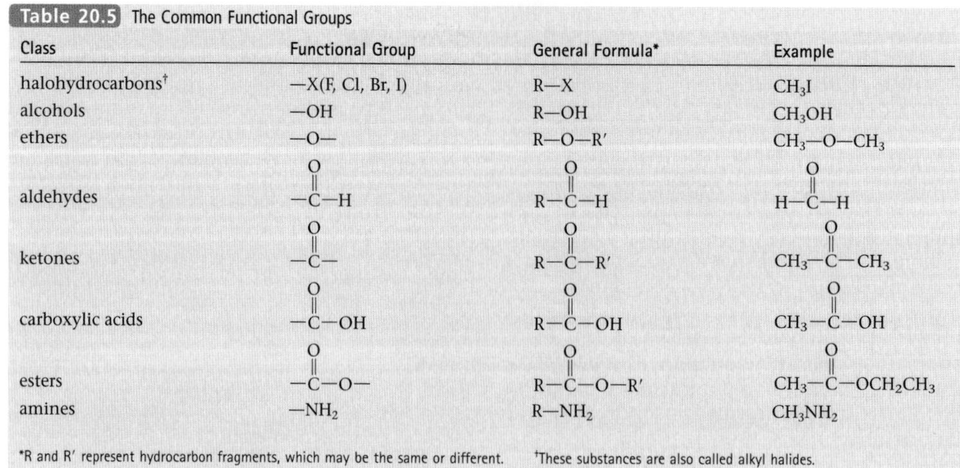

Table 20.5 The Common Functional Groups

Class	Functional Group	General Formula*	Example
halohydrocarbons†	—X(F, Cl, Br, I)	R—X	CH_3I
alcohols	—OH	R—OH	CH_3OH
ethers	—O—	R—O—R′	CH_3—O—CH_3
aldehydes	—C(=O)—H	R—C(=O)—H	H—C(=O)—H
ketones	—C(=O)—	R—C(=O)—R′	CH_3—C(=O)—CH_3
carboxylic acids	—C(=O)—OH	R—C(=O)—OH	CH_3—C(=O)—OH
esters	—C(=O)—O—	R—C(=O)—O—R′	CH_3—C(=O)—OCH_2CH_3
amines	—NH_2	R—NH_2	CH_3NH_2

*R and R′ represent hydrocarbon fragments, which may be the same or different. †These substances are also called alkyl halides.

hydrocarbon derivatives, molecules that are fundamentally hydrocarbons but that have additional atoms or groups of atoms called **functional groups.** The common functional groups are listed in Table 20.5; one example of a compound that contains that functional group is given for each. We will briefly describe some of these functional groups in the next few sections and learn to name the compounds that contain them.

Section 20.11

DEMONSTRATION

Bring samples of rubbing alcohol, methanol, and ethylene glycol (antifreeze) to class as examples of alcohols.

Test Bank: 42, 43

20.11 Alcohols

OBJECTIVE: To learn about simple alcohols and explain how to name them.

Alcohols are characterized by the presence of the —OH group. Some common alcohols are listed in Table 20.6. The systematic name for an alcohol is obtained by replacing the final *-e* of the parent hydrocarbon name with *-ol*. The position of the —OH group is specified by a number (where necessary) chosen such that it is the smallest of the substituent numbers.

The rules for naming alcohols follow.

Rules for Naming Alcohols

1. Select the longest chain of carbon atoms containing the —OH group.
2. Number the chain such that the carbon with the —OH group gets the lowest possible number.
3. Obtain the root name from the name of the parent hydrocarbon chain by replacing the final *-e* with *-ol*.
4. Name any other substituents as usual.

Table 20.6 Some Common Alcohols

Formula	Systematic Name	Common Name
CH_3OH	methanol	methyl alcohol
CH_3CH_2OH	ethanol	ethyl alcohol
$CH_3CH_2CH_2OH$	1-propanol	*n*-propyl alcohol
CH_3CHCH_3 (OH on C2)	2-propanol	isopropyl alcohol

PowerLecture Animation: Molecular Model: Methanol

For example, the compound

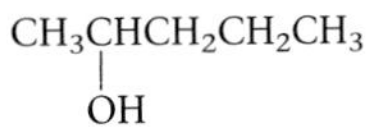

$$CH_3\underset{\displaystyle OH}{\underset{|}{C}}HCH_2CH_2CH_3$$

is called 2-pentanol because the parent carbon chain is pentane. The compound

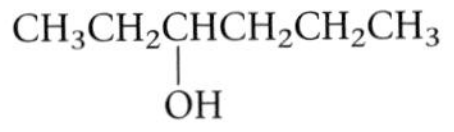

$$CH_3CH_2\underset{\displaystyle OH}{\underset{|}{C}}HCH_2CH_2CH_3$$

is called 3-hexanol.

Alcohols are classified according to the number of hydrocarbon fragments (alkyl groups) bonded to the carbon where the —OH group is attached. Thus we have

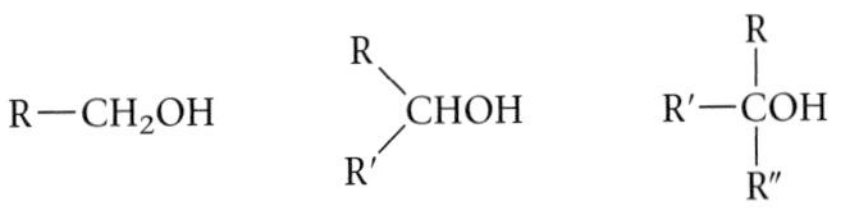

$R—CH_2OH$	$R(R')CHOH$	$R'—\overset{\displaystyle R}{\overset{|}{\underset{\displaystyle R''}{\underset{|}{C}}}}OH$
Primary alcohol (one R group)	*Secondary* alcohol (two R groups)	*Tertiary* alcohol (three R groups)

where R, R′, and R″ (which may be the same or different) represent hydrocarbon fragments (alkyl groups).

EXAMPLE 20.8 Naming Alcohols

Give the systematic name for each of the following alcohols, and specify whether the alcohol is primary, secondary, or tertiary.

a. 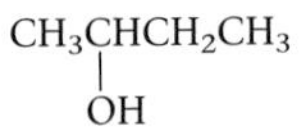 $CH_3\underset{\displaystyle OH}{\underset{|}{C}}HCH_2CH_3$

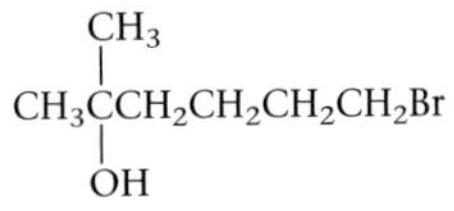

b. $ClCH_2CH_2CH_2OH$

c. $CH_3\overset{\displaystyle CH_3}{\overset{|}{\underset{\displaystyle OH}{\underset{|}{C}}}}CH_2CH_2CH_2CH_2Br$

SOLUTION

a. The chain is numbered as follows:

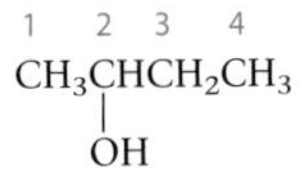

$$\overset{1}{CH_3}\underset{\displaystyle OH}{\underset{|}{\overset{2}{C}}}\overset{3}{H}\overset{}{CH_2}\overset{4}{CH_3}$$

Additional Examples

Example 20.8

Give the systematic names for each of the following alcohols, and specify whether the alcohol is primary, secondary, or tertiary.

1. 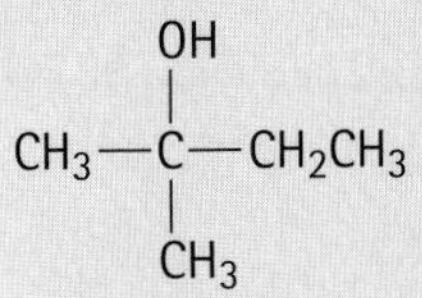 $CH_3—\overset{\displaystyle OH}{\overset{|}{\underset{\displaystyle CH_3}{\underset{|}{C}}}}—CH_2CH_3$

2-methyl-2-butanol; tertiary

2. 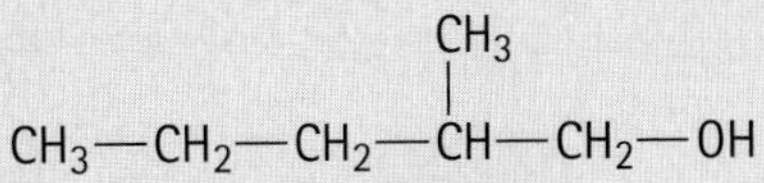 $CH_3—CH_2—CH_2—\overset{\displaystyle CH_3}{\overset{|}{C}}H—CH_2—OH$

2-methyl-1-pentanol; primary

TEACHING TIP

When determining whether an alcohol is primary, secondary, or tertiary, the focus should be on the carbon where the —OH is attached. Students often focus on the —OH group itself instead, but it does not tell anything about the classification.

The compound is called 2-butanol because the —OH group is located at the number 2 position of a four-carbon chain. Note that the carbon to which the —OH is attached also has two R groups (—CH_3 and —CH_2CH_3) attached. Therefore, this is a *secondary* alcohol.

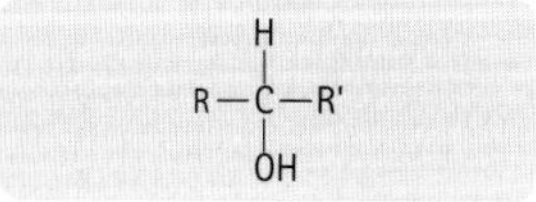

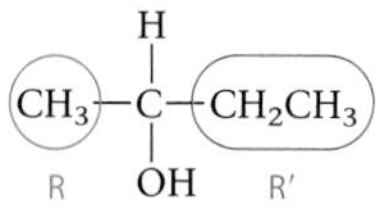

$$\text{R—C(H)(OH)—R'}$$

$$\underset{\text{R}}{CH_3}—\overset{H}{\underset{OH}{C}}—\underset{\text{R'}}{CH_2CH_3}$$

b. The chain is numbered as follows:

$$\overset{3}{Cl—CH_2}—\overset{2}{CH_2}—\overset{1}{CH_2}—OH$$

Remember that in naming an alcohol we give the carbon with the —OH attached the lowest possible number. The name is 3-chloro-1-propanol. This is a *primary* alcohol.

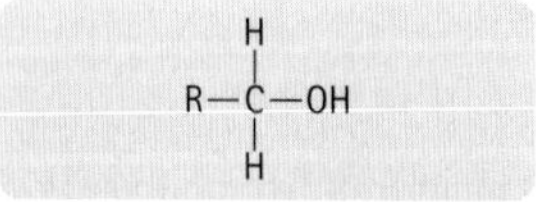

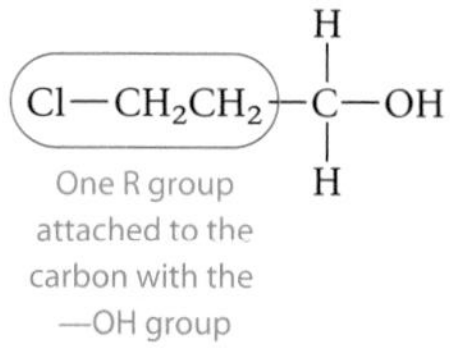

$$\text{R—C(H)(H)—OH}$$

$$Cl—CH_2CH_2—\overset{H}{\underset{H}{C}}—OH$$

One R group attached to the carbon with the —OH group

c. The chain is numbered as follows:

$$\overset{1}{CH_3}—\overset{2}{\overset{CH_3}{\underset{OH}{C}}}—\overset{3}{CH_2}—\overset{4}{CH_2}—\overset{5}{CH_2}—\overset{6}{CH_2Br}$$

$$\text{R—C(R')(OH)—R''}$$

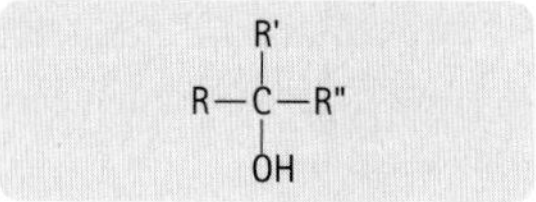

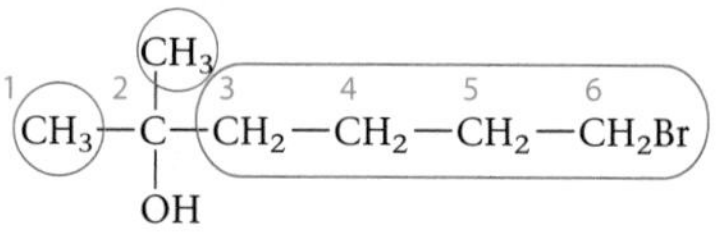

The name is 6-bromo-2-methyl-2-hexanol. This is a tertiary alcohol because the carbon where the —OH is attached also has three R groups attached.

Self Check

Answers to Self-Check Exercise 20.6

a. 1-pentanol; primary alcohol

b. 2-methyl-2-propanol (also known as *t*-butyl alcohol); tertiary alcohol

c. 5-bromo-2-hexanol; secondary alcohol

Self-Check EXERCISE 20.6 Name each of the following alcohols, and specify whether it is primary, secondary, or tertiary.

a. $CH_3CH_2CH_2CH_2CH_2OH$

b. 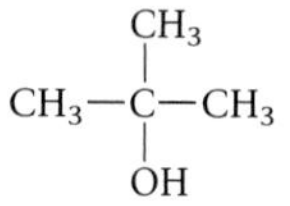 $CH_3—\overset{CH_3}{\underset{OH}{C}}—CH_3$

c. $CH_3—\underset{OH}{CH}—CH_2CH_2\overset{Br}{CH}CH_3$

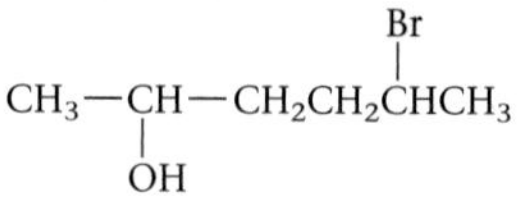

See Problems 20.61 and 20.62. ■

Test Bank: 46

Section 20.12

20.12 Properties and Uses of Alcohols

OBJECTIVE: To learn about how some alcohols are made and used.

TEACHING TIP

You may want to compare the toxicities of methanol, ethanol, and ethylene glycol.

Lecture Demonstration: 22.6

Although there are many important alcohols, the simplest ones, methanol and ethanol, have the greatest commercial value. Methanol, also known as *wood alcohol* because it was formerly obtained by heating wood in the absence of air, is prepared industrially (over 20 million tons per year in the United States) by the hydrogenation of carbon monoxide (catalyzed by a $ZnO–Cr_2O_3$ mixture).

$$CO + 2H_2 \xrightarrow[ZnO-Cr_2O_3]{400\ ^\circ C} CH_3OH$$

Methanol is used as a starting material for the synthesis of acetic acid and many types of adhesives, fibers, and plastics. It also can be used as a motor fuel. In fact, pure methanol has been used for many years in the engines of the cars that are driven in the Indianapolis 500 and similar races. Methanol is especially useful in racing engines because of its resistance to knock. It is advantageous for regular cars because it produces less carbon monoxide (a toxic gas) in the exhaust than does gasoline. Methanol is highly toxic to humans, and swallowing it can lead to blindness and death.

Ethanol is the alcohol found in beverages such as beer, wine, and whiskey; it is produced by the fermentation of the sugar glucose in corn, barley, grapes, and so on.

$$\underset{\text{Glucose}}{C_6H_{12}O_6} \xrightarrow{\text{Yeast}} \underset{\text{Ethanol}}{2CH_3CH_2OH} + 2CO_2$$

This reaction is catalyzed by the enzymes (biologic catalysts) found in yeast, and it can proceed only until the alcohol content reaches approximately 13% (that found in most wines), at which point the yeast can no longer survive. Beverages with higher alcohol content are made by distilling the fermentation mixture.

Ethanol, like methanol, can be burned in the internal combustion engines of automobiles and is now commonly added to gasoline to form *gasohol.* It is also used in industry as a solvent and for the preparation of acetic acid. The commercial production of ethanol (half a million tons per year in the United States) is carried out by reaction of water with ethylene.

PowerLecture Animation: Rotating Ethanol Molecule

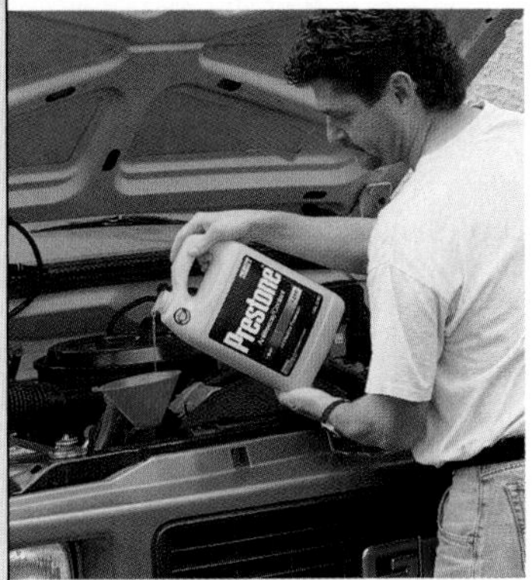

Ethylene glycol is a component of antifreeze, which is used to protect the cooling systems of automobiles.

$$CH_2{=}CH_2 + H_2O \xrightarrow[\text{Catalyst}]{\text{Acid}} CH_3CH_2OH$$

Many alcohols are known that contain more than one —OH group. The one that is the most important commercially is ethylene glycol,

$$\begin{array}{l} H_2C{-}OH \\ \ \ \ \ | \\ H_2C{-}OH \end{array}$$

a toxic substance that is the major constituent of most automobile antifreezes.

The simplest aromatic alcohol is

commonly called **phenol.** Most of the 1 million tons of phenol produced annually in the United States is used to produce polymers for adhesives and plastics.

20.12 Properties and Uses of Alcohols 667

Test Bank: 26, 47, 48

Section 20.13

DEMONSTRATION

Some interesting aldehydes and ketones to bring to class include cinnamaldehyde, citral (lemon), and vanillin. All of these compounds have a strong odor, so only a small amount of each is needed.

PowerLecture Animations: Rotating Diethylketone Molecule Rotating Propanal Molecule

20.13 Aldehydes and Ketones

OBJECTIVE: To learn the general formulas for aldehydes and ketones and some of their uses.

Aldehydes and ketones contain the **carbonyl group**

$$-\overset{\overset{\displaystyle O}{\|}}{C}-$$

In **ketones,** this group is bonded to two carbon atoms; an example is acetone:

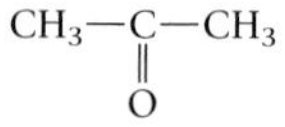

$$CH_3-\underset{\underset{\displaystyle O}{\|}}{C}-CH_3$$

The general formula for a ketone is

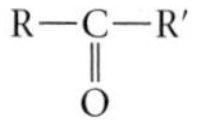

$$R-\underset{\underset{\displaystyle O}{\|}}{C}-R'$$

where R and R′ are alkyl groups that may or may not be the same. In a ketone, the carbonyl group is never at the end of the hydrocarbon chain. (If it were, it would be an aldehyde.)

In **aldehydes,** the carbonyl group always appears at the end of the hydrocarbon chain. There is always at least one hydrogen bonded to the carbonyl carbon atom. An example of an aldehyde is acetaldehyde:

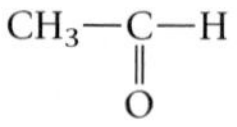

$$CH_3-\underset{\underset{\displaystyle O}{\|}}{C}-H$$

The general formula for an aldehyde is

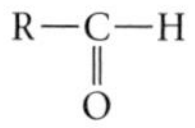

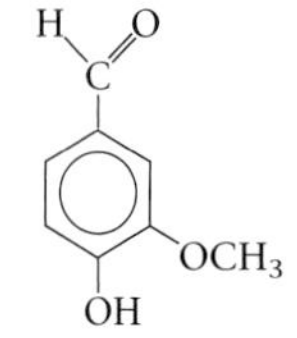

$$R-\underset{\underset{\displaystyle O}{\|}}{C}-H$$

Vanillin (benzene ring bearing CHO, OCH_3, OH)

Cinnamaldehyde ($C_6H_5-CH=CH-CHO$)

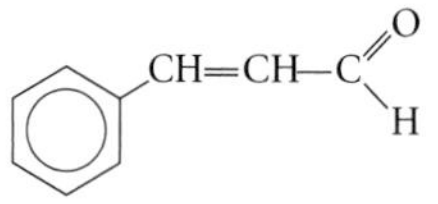

Butyraldehyde ($CH_3CH_2CH_2CHO$)

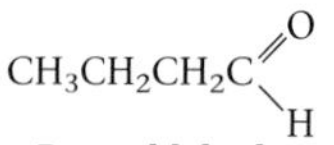

Figure 20.11 Some common aldehydes.

We often use compact formulas for aldehydes and ketones. For example, formaldehyde (where R = H) and acetaldehyde (where R = CH_3) are usually represented as HCHO and CH_3CHO, respectively. Acetone is often written as CH_3COCH_3 or $(CH_3)_2CO$.

Many ketones have useful solvent properties (acetone is often found in nail polish remover, for example) and are used frequently in industry for this purpose. Aldehydes typically have strong odors. Vanillin is responsible for the pleasant odor of vanilla beans; cinnamaldehyde produces the characteristic odor of cinnamon. On the other hand, the unpleasant odor of rancid butter arises from the presence of butyraldehyde (and butyric acid). (See Figure 20.11 for the structures of these compounds.)

Aldehydes and ketones are most often produced commercially by the oxidation of alcohols. Oxidation of a *primary* alcohol gives the corresponding aldehyde, for example,

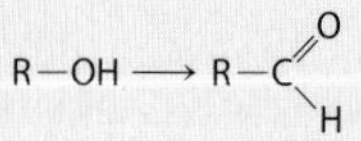

$$R-OH \longrightarrow R-CHO$$

$$CH_3CH_2OH \xrightarrow{\text{Oxidation}} CH_3CHO$$

Oxidation of a *secondary* alcohol results in a ketone:

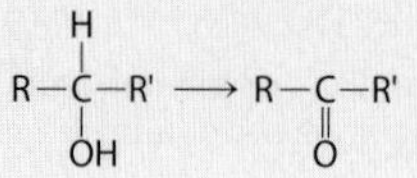

$$R-CH(OH)-R' \longrightarrow R-\underset{\underset{\displaystyle O}{\|}}{C}-R'$$

$$CH_3CH(OH)CH_3 \xrightarrow{\text{Oxidation}} CH_3\underset{\underset{\displaystyle O}{\|}}{C}CH_3$$

20.14 Naming Aldehydes and Ketones

OBJECTIVE: To learn the systems for naming aldehydes and ketones.

We obtain the systematic name for an aldehyde from the parent alkane by removing the final *-e* and adding *-al.* For ketones, the final *-e* is replaced by *-one,* and a number indicates the position of the carbonyl group where necessary. The carbon chain in ketones is numbered such that the

$$-\underset{\underset{\displaystyle O}{\|}}{C}-$$

carbon gets the lowest possible number. In aldehydes, the

$$-\underset{\underset{\displaystyle O}{\|}}{C}-H$$

is always at the end of the chain and is always assumed to be carbon number 1. The positions of other substituents are specified by numbers, as usual. The following examples illustrate these principles:

$H-\overset{\overset{\displaystyle O}{\|}}{C}-H$	$CH_3-\overset{\overset{\displaystyle O}{\|}}{C}-H$	$CH_3-\overset{\overset{\displaystyle O}{\|}}{C}-CH_3$	$CH_3-\overset{\overset{\displaystyle O}{\|}}{C}-CH_2CH_2CH_3$	$CH_3\underset{\underset{\displaystyle Cl}{\mid}}{C}HCH_2\overset{\overset{\displaystyle O}{\|}}{C}-H$
Methanal (formaldehyde)	Ethanal (acetaldehyde)	Propanone (acetone)	2-Pentanone	3-Chlorobutanal

The names in parentheses are common names that are used much more often than the systematic names.

Another common aldehyde is benzaldehyde (an aromatic aldehyde), which has the structure

$$C_6H_5-\overset{\overset{\displaystyle O}{\|}}{C}-H$$

Benzaldehyde

An alternative system for naming ketones specifies the substituents attached to the C=C group. For example, the compound

$$CH_3\underset{\underset{\displaystyle O}{\|}}{C}CH_2CH_3$$

is called 2-butanone when we use the system just described. However, this molecule also can be named methyl ethyl ketone and is commonly referred to in industry as MEK (*m*ethyl *e*thyl *k*etone):

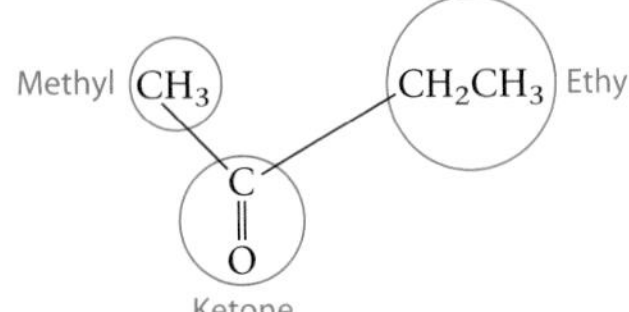

 **Test Bank: 49–55**

Section 20.14

TEACHING TIPS

- It is difficult to distinguish between *-ol* and *-al* in spoken language. Be sure to write the structure, say the name, and write the name when discussing these compounds in class so that students can distinguish clearly among the molecules.
- The aldehyde and ketone groups seem very similar to beginning students. Be sure to show them that in ketones the carbonyl group is located between two other carbons, whereas in aldehydes the carbonyl group is an end carbon.

Additional Examples

Example 20.9

Name the following molecules.

1.

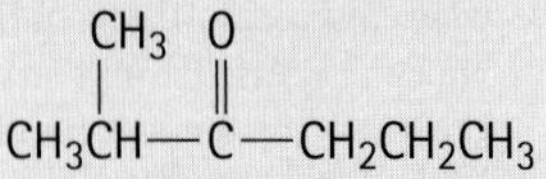

$$\mathrm{CH_3CH(CH_3)-C(=O)-CH_2CH_2CH_3}$$

2-methyl-3-hexanone

2.

$$\mathrm{CH_3CH_2CH(CH_3)-CH_2C(=O)-H}$$

3-methylpentanal

Another example is use of the name ketone for the compound

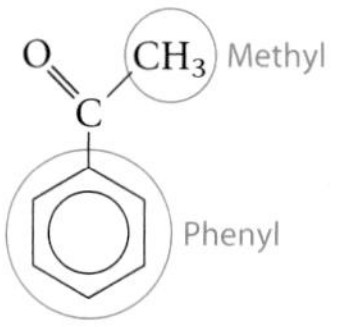

$$\mathrm{C_6H_5-C(=O)-CH_3}$$

(CH₃: Methyl; ring: Phenyl)

which is commonly called methyl phenyl ketone.

EXAMPLE 20.9 Naming Aldehydes and Ketones

Name the following molecules.

a. 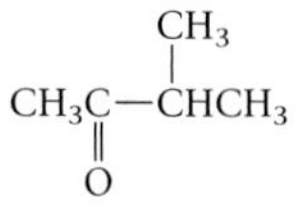 $\mathrm{CH_3C(=O)-CH(CH_3)CH_3}$ (Give two names.)

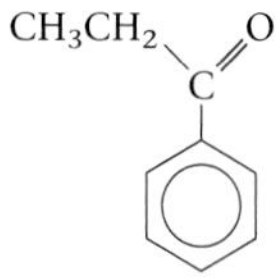

b. 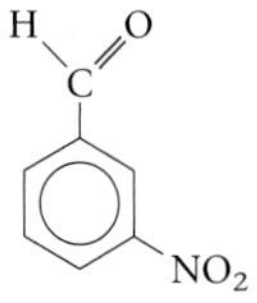 $\mathrm{H-C(=O)-C_6H_4-NO_2}$ (meta)

c. $\mathrm{CH_3CH_2-C(=O)-C_6H_5}$

d. 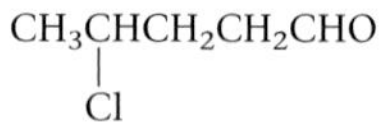 $\mathrm{CH_3CH(Cl)CH_2CH_2CHO}$

SOLUTION

a. We can name this molecule as a 2-butanone because the longest chain has four carbon atoms (butane root) with the

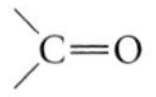

$$\mathrm{>C{=}O}$$

group in the number 2 position (the lowest possible number). Because the methyl group is in the number 3 position, the name is 3-methyl-2-butanone. We also can name this compound methyl isopropyl ketone.

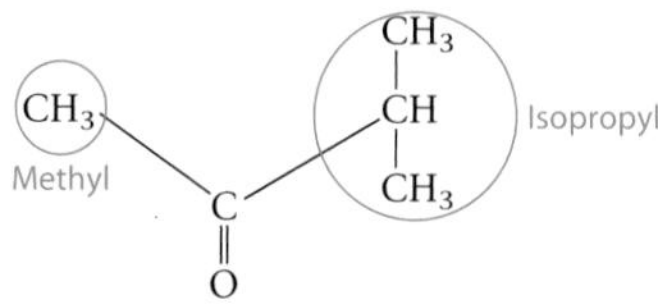

b. We name this molecule as a substituted benzaldehyde (the nitro group is in the number 3 position): 3-nitrobenzaldehyde. It also might be named *m*-nitrobenzaldehyde.

c. We name this molecule as a ketone: ethyl phenyl ketone.

d. The name is 4-chloropentanal. Note that an aldehyde group is always at the end of the chain and is automatically assigned as the number 1 carbon.

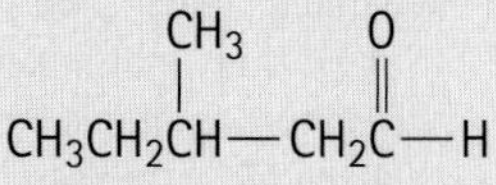

Self-Check **EXERCISE 20.7** Name the following molecules.

a.

$$CH_3CH_2\overset{\overset{O}{\|}}{C}\underset{\underset{CH_2CH_3}{|}}{C}HCH_2CH_3$$

b.

$$CH_3CH_2CH_2\underset{\underset{CH_3CHCH_3}{|}}{C}HCH_2CH_2CH_2CH_2CH_2CHO$$

See Problems 20.73 and 20.74. ■

20.15 Carboxylic Acids and Esters

OBJECTIVE: To learn the structures and names of the common carboxylic acids.

Carboxylic acids are characterized by the presence of the **carboxyl group,** —COOH, which has the structure

$$-C\begin{matrix}\nearrow O \\ \searrow O{-}H\end{matrix}$$

The general formula of a carboxylic acid is RCOOH, where R represents the hydrocarbon fragment. These molecules typically are weak acids in aqueous solution. That is, the dissociation (ionization) equilibrium

$$RCOOH(aq) + H_2O(l) \rightleftharpoons H_3O^+(aq) + RCOO^-(aq)$$

lies far to the left—only a small percentage of the RCOOH molecules are ionized.

We name carboxylic acids by dropping the final *-e* from the parent alkane (the longest chain containing the —COOH group) and adding *-oic*. Carboxylic acids are frequently known by their common names. For example, CH_3COOH, often written $HC_2H_3O_2$ and commonly called acetic acid, has the systematic name ethanoic acid because the parent alkane is ethane. Several carboxylic acids, their systematic names, and their common names are given in Table 20.7. Other examples of carboxylic acids are shown in Figure 20.12. Note that the —COOH group is always assigned the number 1 position in the chain.

Carboxylic acids can be produced by oxidizing primary alcohols with a strong oxidizing agent. For example, we can oxidize ethanol to acetic acid by using potassium permanganate.

$$CH_3CH_2OH \xrightarrow{KMnO_4(aq)} CH_3COOH$$

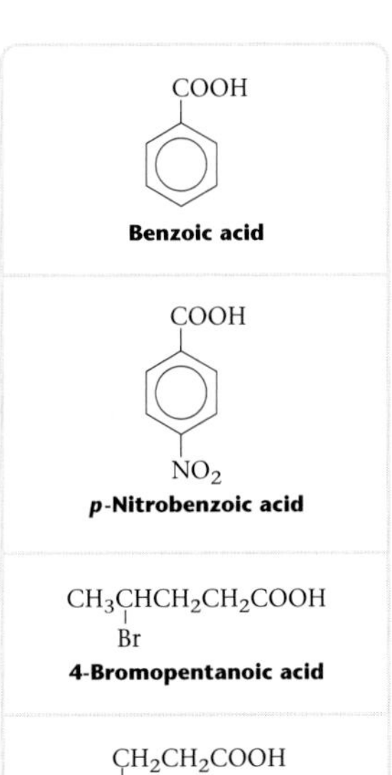

Figure 20.12 Some carboxylic acids.

Table 20.7 Several Carboxylic Acids, Their Systematic Names, and Their Common Names

Formula	Systematic Name	Common Name
$HCOOH$	methanoic acid	formic acid
CH_3COOH	ethanoic acid	acetic acid
CH_3CH_2COOH	propanoic acid	propionic acid
$CH_3CH_2CH_2COOH$	butanoic acid	butyric acid
$CH_3CH_2CH_2CH_2COOH$	pentanoic acid	valeric acid

Self Check

Answers to Self-Check Exercise 20.7

a. 4-ethyl-3-hexanone

b. 7-isopropyldecanal

Test Bank: 25, 44, 45, 56–58

Section 20.15

TEACHING TIPS

- When students look at the formula for an ester, it is difficult for them to tell which part of the molecule is derived from the acid and which from the alcohol. To help them figure this out, you can draw the formula so that the alcohol part of the molecule is below the main line for the formula.
- The aspirin molecule is the most complicated molecule the students have encountered. Now is an excellent time to point out that in this large molecule they can identify two functional groups on a benzene ring (an ester and a carboxylic acid).

PowerLecture Animations:
Rotating 1-Propanol Molecule
Rotating Molecular Structure of C_6H_5COOH
Rotating Propionic Acid Molecule
Rotating Ethyl Propionate Molecule

LABORATORY EXPERIMENT

Relevant laboratory experiments for this section are Experiment 30, Organic Chemical Compounds; Experiment 31, Ester Derivatives of Salicylic Acid; and Experiment 32, The Preparation of Fragrant Esters, from *Introductory Chemistry in the Laboratory* by James Hall.

DEMONSTRATION

If you have some available, bring samples of esters to class. Good examples include isobutyl formate (raspberries), octyl acetate (orange), and ethyl butyrate (pineapple). You may be able to obtain samples from an aromatherapy store in your neighborhood.

Lecture Demonstration: 22.8

A carboxylic acid reacts with an alcohol to form an ester and a water molecule. For example, the reaction of acetic acid and ethanol produces the ester ethyl acetate and water.

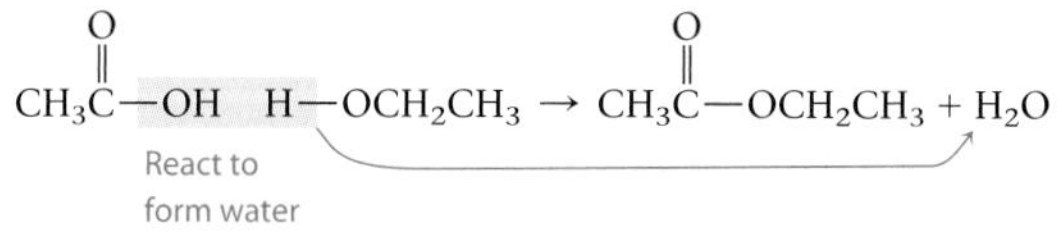

$$CH_3\overset{\overset{O}{\|}}{C}-OH \quad H-OCH_2CH_3 \rightarrow CH_3\overset{\overset{O}{\|}}{C}-OCH_2CH_3 + H_2O$$

React to form water

This reaction can be represented in general as follows:

$$\underset{\text{Acid}}{RCOOH} + \underset{\text{Alcohol}}{R'OH} \rightarrow \underset{\text{Ester}}{RCOOR'} + \underset{\text{Water}}{H_2O}$$

An **ester** has the following general formula:

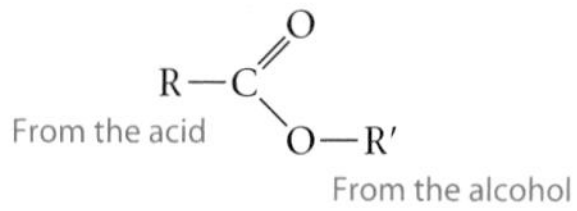

$$R-C(=O)-O-R'$$

From the acid — From the alcohol

Amyl is a common name for $CH_3CH_2CH_2CH_2CH_2-$.

Esters often have a sweet, fruity odor that contrasts markedly with the often-pungent odors of the parent carboxylic acids. For example, the odor of bananas derives from *n*-amyl acetate:

$$CH_3C(=O)OCH_2CH_2CH_2CH_2CH_3$$

and that of oranges from *n*-octyl acetate:

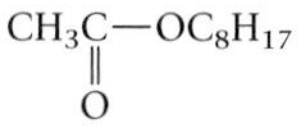

$$CH_3\underset{\underset{O}{\|}}{C}-OC_8H_{17}$$

Like carboxylic acids, esters are often referred to by their common names. The name consists of the alkyl name from the alcohol followed by the acid name, where the *-ic* ending is replaced by *-ate*. For example, the ester

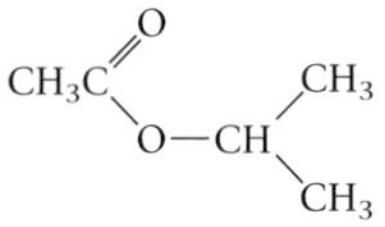

$$CH_3C(=O)-O-CH(CH_3)_2$$

is made from acetic acid, CH_3COOH, and isopropyl alcohol,

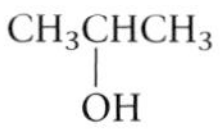

$$CH_3\underset{\underset{OH}{|}}{C}HCH_3$$

and is called isopropyl acetate. The systematic name for this ester is isopropylethanoate (from ethanoic acid, the systematic name for acetic acid).

Computer-generated space-filled model of acetylsalicylic acid (aspirin).

A very important ester is formed from the reaction of salicylic acid and acetic acid.

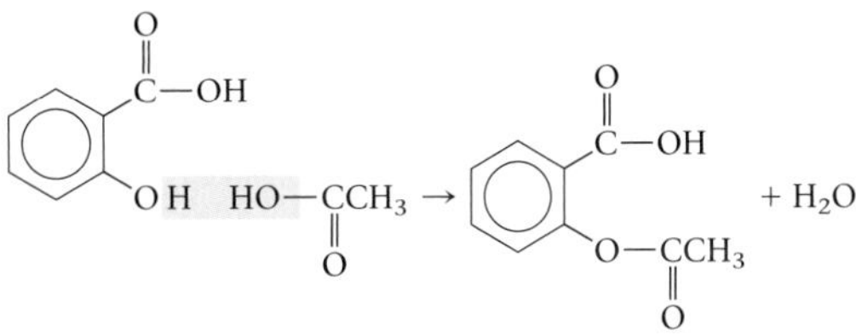

$$\text{C}_6\text{H}_4(\text{OH})\text{COOH} + \text{HO—C(=O)CH}_3 \rightarrow \text{C}_6\text{H}_4(\text{O—C(=O)CH}_3)\text{COOH} + H_2O$$

Salicylic acid Acetic acid Acetylsalicylic acid

The product is acetylsalicylic acid, commonly known as *aspirin,* which is manufactured in huge quantities and is widely used as an analgesic (painkiller).

 Test Bank: 59, 60

20.16 Polymers

OBJECTIVE: To learn about some common polymers.

Section 20.16

TEACHING TIPS

- Do not expect that students will be able to tell which functional groups should interact on monomers to form polymers.
- You can bring in common household items made from the polymers discussed in this section—for example, polyethylene bags and bottles, polystyrene toys, PVC pipe, Teflon-coated pans.

Polymers are large, usually chainlike molecules that are built from small molecules called *monomers.* Polymers form the basis for synthetic fibers, rubbers, and plastics and have played a leading role in the revolution brought about in our lives by chemistry during the past 50 years. (Many important biomolecules are also polymers.)

The simplest and one of the best-known synthetic polymers is *polyethylene,* which is constructed from ethylene monomers. Its structure is

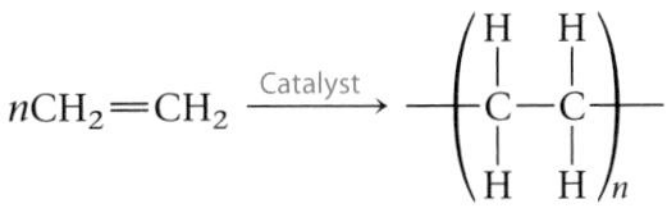

$$n\text{CH}_2\text{=CH}_2 \xrightarrow{\text{Catalyst}} \left(\text{—CH}_2\text{—CH}_2\text{—} \right)_n$$

Ethylene Polyethylene

where n represents a large number (usually several thousand). Polyethylene is a tough, flexible plastic used for piping, bottles, electrical insulation, film for packaging, garbage bags, and many other purposes. Its properties can be varied by using substituted ethylene monomers. For example, when tetrafluoroethylene is the monomer, the polymer Teflon is obtained.

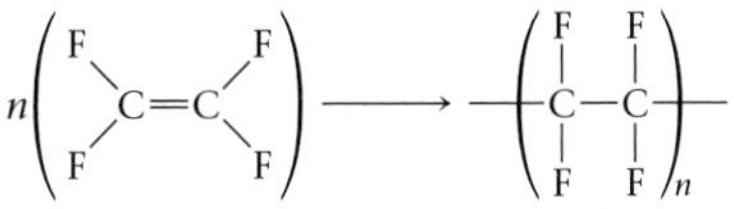

$$n\left(\text{F}_2\text{C=CF}_2 \right) \longrightarrow \left(\text{—CF}_2\text{—CF}_2\text{—} \right)_n$$

Tetrafluoroethylene Teflon

Because of the resistance of the strong C—F bonds to chemical attack, Teflon is an inert, tough, and nonflammable material that is widely used for electrical insulation, nonstick coatings for cooking utensils, and bearings for low-temperature applications.

Other similar polyethylene-type polymers are made from monomers containing chloro, methyl, cyano, and phenyl substituents (Table 20.8). In each case, the carbon–carbon double bond in the substituted ethylene monomer becomes a single bond in the polymer. The different substituents lead to a wide variety of properties.

Table 20.8 Some Common Synthetic Polymers, Their Monomers, and Applications

Monomer Name and Formula	Polymer Name and Formula	Applications
ethylene $H_2C{=}CH_2$	polyethylene $-(CH_2{-}CH_2)_n-$	plastic piping, bottles, electrical insulation, toys
propylene $H_2C{=}C(H)(CH_3)$	polypropylene $-(CH(CH_3){-}CH_2CH(CH_3){-}CH_2)_n-$	film for packaging, carpets, lab wares, toys
vinyl chloride $H_2C{=}C(H)(Cl)$	polyvinyl chloride (PVC) $-(CH_2{-}CH(Cl))_n-$	piping, siding, floor tile, clothing, toys
acrylonitrile $H_2C{=}C(H)(CN)$	polyacrylonitrile (PAN) $-(CH_2{-}CH(CN))_n-$	carpets, fabrics
tetrafluoroethylene $F_2C{=}CF_2$	Teflon $-(CF_2{-}CF_2)_n-$	coating for cooking utensils, electrical insulation, bearings
styrene $H_2C{=}C(H)(C_6H_5)$	polystyrene $-(CH_2CH(C_6H_5))_n-$	containers, thermal insulation, toys
butadiene $H_2C{=}C(H){-}C(H){=}CH_2$	polybutadiene $-(CH_2CH{=}CHCH_2)_n-$	tire tread, coating resin
butadiene and styrene (see above)	styrene-butadiene rubber $(CH(C_6H_5){-}CH_2{-}CH_2{-}CH{=}CH{-}CH_2)_n-$	synthetic rubber

PowerLecture Video: Girl Blowing Bubbles with Gum: Addition Polymer

PowerLecture Animations: Addition Polymerization Growth of Polymer Chain of Polyester

The polyethylene polymers illustrate one of the major types of polymerization reactions, called **addition polymerization,** in which the monomers simply "add together" to form the polymer and there are no other products.

Another common type of polymerization is **condensation polymerization,** in which a small molecule, such as water, is formed for each extension of the polymer chain. The most familiar polymer produced by condensation is *nylon*. Nylon is a **copolymer** because two different types of monomers combine to form the chain (a **homopolymer,** by contrast, results from the polymerizing of a single type of monomer). One common

The Chemistry of Music

Producing great instrumental music requires a combination of musical talent on the part of the performer and a high-quality instrument. The main component of stringed instruments such as acoustic guitars and violins is wood. Wood is a mixture of natural polymers including cellulose (a linear, high-molar-mass polysaccharide) and hemicellulose (a branched polysaccharide with lower molar mass). These components are held together by lignin, a complex branched polymer. In all wooden instruments, much of the sound comes from the body of the instrument. The specific wood used can have a profound effect on the sound by dampening certain frequencies and enhancing others.

One of the great mysteries relating to musical instruments is the legendary quality of the violins made in the seventeenth and early eighteenth centuries in Cremona, Italy, by Antonio Stradivari, Nicolo Amati, and Bartolomeo Giuseppe Guarneri. The instruments crafted by these masters have sounds unmatched by other violin makers before or since.

Joseph Nagyvary, a retired Texas A&M University biochemistry professor, has worked for the last 30 years to understand the unique properties of the Cremonian instruments. Using various scientific analyses, Nagyvary has decided that the secrets lie mainly in the treatment of the wood before the violins were constructed. First the wood was soaked as it floated downriver to Cremona. Then the wood was apparently treated with a chemical soak to prevent mold and to kill pests such as woodworms that might bore holes in the wood. Nagyvary's analyses indicate that this chemical soak was quite complex and was likely prepared by a local chemist for the violin makers. His studies also indicate that the wood may have been chemically treated by an alkaline solution, which reduced the hemicellulose content of the wood.

Nagyvary has used the knowledge he has gained from studying the Cremonian instruments to build more than 150 violins. He has achieved varying degrees of success in matching the sounds of the Cremonian instruments.

Chemistry is important in constructing modern instruments as well. In acoustic guitars, not only is the type of wood important but the coating used on the wood also influences the quality of the sound. A hard coating tends to emphasize high frequencies, whereas a softer coating resonates at lower frequencies.

Likewise, chemistry is important for the speakers of your audio system. To produce sounds, a speaker's components vibrate rapidly, generating a tremendous amount of heat. In fact, only 2% of the speaker's energy is converted to sound. The remaining 98% is heat. The louder the sound, the greater the heat. To withstand temperatures up to 150 °C, the polymers used in the speaker must be high-performance materials.

Great sounds require sound chemistry.

Joseph Nagyvary.

DEMONSTRATION

Making Nylon

Materials 250-mL beaker, copper wire, large test tube, 0.4 *M* NaOH, 1,6-hexanediamine, sebacoyl chloride, 1,1,1-trichloroethane

Preparations Dissolve 1.15 g of 1,6-hexanediamine in 25 mL of 0.4 *M* NaOH. Dissolve 2.3 g of sebacoyl chloride in 25 mL of 1,1,1-trichloroethane.

Presentation Pour the sebacoyl chloride solution into the 250-mL beaker. Carefully pour the 1,6-hexanediamine solution down the side of the beaker so that it floats on the sebacoyl chloride solution. Nylon forms at the interface of the two solutions. Bend the copper wire into a hook. Use the hook to grasp the nylon formed at the interface of the two solutions. Pull the nylon strand out of the solution, and wrap it around the outside of the large test tube. Rotate the test tube winding the nylon strand around it as you proceed. It is possible to obtain several feet of nylon from the interface of the solutions.

Teaching Notes Be careful when handling the nylon that is coated with HCl until it has been neutralized with $NaHCO_3(aq)$. Be sure to dispose of all excess chemicals as required.

Mother of Invention

Stephanie Kwolek is not very tall (4 feet 11 inches), but she has had a big impact on modern society. Ms. Kwolek is the scientist responsible for the discovery of Kevlar, a strong, light fiber used in "bulletproof" vests that are worn by many law enforcement officers. The DuPont company, which manufactures Kevlar, estimates that more than 3000 officers have survived life-threatening injuries because of the golden-colored fiber discovered by Stephanie Kwolek. In addition, countless soldiers have been saved. Nearly every U.S. service member has worn a helmet reinforced with Kevlar since 1991. Kevlar also has many other uses, including reinforcement for tires, special cables for suspension bridges, as a component of flame-resistant clothing, and in various types of sports equipment.

Ms. Kwolek was 42 years old in 1965 when she discovered the polymer (a long chain made up of many small units) that forms the basis of Kevlar. Tests showed that, pound for pound, Kevlar is five times stronger than steel. The unusual strength of Kevlar is principally due to the way the long chains "stick" to each other because of the strong attractions between atoms on adjacent strands. Also, instead of being random like a plate of spaghetti, the Kevlar chains tend to line up in parallel to maximize the interchain interactions.

Stephanie Kwolek attributes her scientific curiosity to her father, an amateur naturalist, who took her on many hikes to collect biologic samples in her native Pennsylvania. She was a chemistry major in college and initially wanted to become a doctor, but because she couldn't afford to go to medical school, she took a job in the chemical industry with DuPont, and the rest is history.

Ms. Kwolek has received many honors in her career, including induction into the National Inventors Hall of Fame in Akron, Ohio, in 1995.

The News Journal/Jennifer Corbett

Stephanie Kwolek wearing Kevlar gloves.

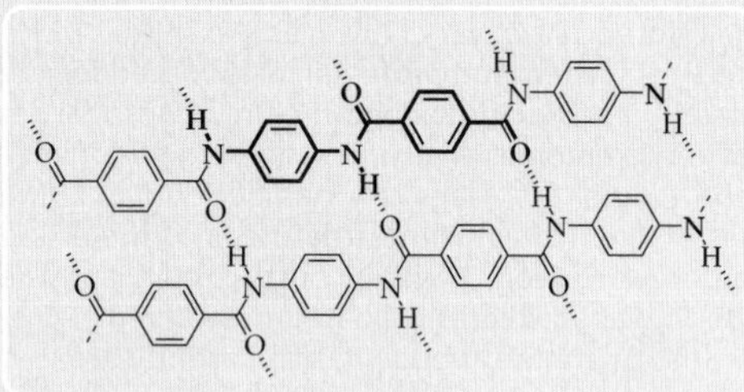

The structure of Kevlar

form of nylon is produced when hexamethylenediamine and adipic acid react by splitting out a water molecule to form a C—N bond:

$$\underset{\text{Hexamethylenediamine}}{H_2N\text{—}(CH_2)_6\text{—}N(H)\text{—}H} + \underset{\text{Adipic acid}}{H\text{—}O\text{—}\overset{O}{\overset{\|}{C}}\text{—}(CH_2)_4\text{—}\overset{O}{\overset{\|}{C}}\text{—}O\text{—}H} \rightarrow H_2N\text{—}(CH_2)_6\text{—}\overset{H}{\overset{|}{N}}\text{—}\overset{O}{\overset{\|}{C}}\text{—}(CH_2)_4\text{—}\overset{O}{\overset{\|}{C}}\text{—}O\text{—}H + H_2O$$

Figure 20.13
The reaction to form nylon can be carried out at the interface of two immiscible liquid layers in a beaker. The bottom layer contains adipyl chloride,

$$\mathrm{Cl-\overset{\displaystyle O}{\overset{\|}{C}}-(CH_2)_4-\overset{\displaystyle O}{\overset{\|}{C}}-Cl}$$

dissolved in CCl_4, and the top layer contains hexamethylenediamine,

$$\mathrm{H_2N-(CH_2)_6-NH_2}$$

dissolved in water. A molecule of HCl is formed as each C—N bond forms. This is a variation of the reaction to form nylon discussed in the text.

The molecule formed, which is called a **dimer** (two monomers joined), can undergo further condensation reactions because it has an amino group at one end and a carboxyl group at the other. Thus both ends are free to react with another monomer. Repetition of this process leads to a long chain of the type

$$\left(\mathrm{-\overset{\displaystyle H}{\overset{|}{N}}-(CH_2)_6-\overset{\displaystyle H}{\overset{|}{N}}-\overset{\displaystyle O}{\overset{\|}{C}}-(CH_2)_4-\overset{\displaystyle O}{\overset{\|}{C}}-}\right)_n$$

which is the general structure of nylon. The reaction to form nylon occurs quite readily and is often used as a lecture demonstration (Figure 20.13). The properties of nylon can be varied by changing the number of carbon atoms in the chain of the acid or amine monomers.

More than 1 million tons of nylon are produced annually in the United States for use in clothing, carpets, rope, and so on. Many other types of condensation polymers are also produced. For example, Dacron is a copolymer formed from the condensation reaction of ethylene glycol (a dialcohol) and *p*-terephthalic acid (a dicarboxylic acid).

$$\underset{\text{Ethylene glycol}}{\mathrm{HOCH_2CH_2O-H}}\ \ \underset{\text{p-Terephthalic acid}}{\mathrm{HO-\overset{\displaystyle O}{\overset{\|}{C}}-C_6H_4-\overset{\displaystyle O}{\overset{\|}{C}}-O-H}} \xrightarrow{} H_2O$$

The repeating unit of Dacron is

$$\left(\mathrm{-OCH_2CH_2-O-\overset{\displaystyle O}{\overset{\|}{C}}-C_6H_4-\overset{\displaystyle O}{\overset{\|}{C}}-}\right)_n$$

Note that this polymerization involves a carboxylic acid and an alcohol to form an ester group,

$$\mathrm{-O-\overset{\displaystyle O}{\overset{\|}{C}}-}$$

Thus Dacron is called a **polyester.** By itself or blended with cotton, Dacron is used widely in fibers for the manufacture of clothing.

PowerLecture Video: Synthesis of Nylon

CHAPTER 20 REVIEW

Key Terms

organic chemistry (p. 607)
biomolecules (p. 607)
hydrocarbon (20.2)
saturated (20.2)
unsaturated (20.2)
alkane (20.2)
normal (straight-chain or unbranched) hydrocarbon (20.2)
structural isomerism (20.3)
petroleum (20.5)
natural gas (20.5)
combustion reaction (20.6)
substitution reaction (20.6)
dehydrogenation reaction (20.6)
alkene (20.7)
alkyne (20.7)
addition reaction (20.7)
hydrogenation reaction (20.7)
halogenation (20.7)
polymerization (20.7)

ChemWork

Hybridization in Nitrogen Compounds
Production of N_2O
Structure of Nitrogen Compounds
Hybridization in Phosphorus Compounds
Geometric Structure of Phosphorus Compounds
Hybridization in Halogen Compounds
Geometric Structure of Halogen Compounds
Properties of Groups 5–8
Xenon in the Atmosphere

aromatic hydrocarbon (20.8)	functional group (20.10)	carboxylic acid (20.15)	condensation polymerization (20.16)
benzene (20.8)	alcohol (20.11)	carboxyl group (20.15)	copolymer (20.16)
phenyl group (20.9)	phenol (20.12)	ester (20.15)	homopolymer (20.16)
hydrocarbon derivative (20.10)	carbonyl group (20.13)	polymer (20.16)	dimer (20.16)
	ketone (20.13)	addition polymerization (20.16)	polyester (20.16)
	aldehyde (20.13)		

F directs you to the *Chemistry in Focus* feature in the chapter

VP indicates visual problems

OWL interactive versions of these problems are assignable in OWL

Summary

1. The study of carbon-containing compounds and their properties is called organic chemistry. Most organic compounds contain chains or rings of carbon atoms. The organic molecules responsible for maintaining and reproducing life are called biomolecules.
2. Hydrocarbons are organic compounds composed of carbon and hydrogen. Those that contain only C—C single bonds are saturated and are called alkanes, and those with carbon–carbon multiple bonds are unsaturated. Unsaturated hydrocarbons can become saturated by the addition of hydrogen, halogens, and/or other substituents.
3. All alkanes can be represented by the general formula C_nH_{2n+2}. Methane, CH_4, is the simplest alkane, and the next three in the series are ethane, C_2H_6; propane, C_3H_8; and butane, C_4H_{10}. In a saturated hydrocarbon, each carbon atom is bonded to four other atoms. Alkanes containing long chains of carbon atoms are called normal, or straight-chain, hydrocarbons.
4. Structural isomerism in alkanes involves the formation of branched structures. Specific rules for systematically naming alkanes indicate the point of attachment of any substituent group, the length of the root chain, and so on.
5. Alkanes can undergo combustion reactions to form carbon dioxide and water or substitution reactions in which hydrogen atoms are replaced by other atoms. Alkanes also can undergo dehydrogenation to form unsaturated hydrocarbons.
6. Hydrocarbons with carbon–carbon double bonds are called alkenes. The simplest alkene is ethylene, C_2H_4. Alkynes are unsaturated hydrocarbons with a carbon–carbon triple bond. The simplest in the series is acetylene, C_2H_2.
7. Unsaturated hydrocarbons undergo addition reactions such as hydrogenation (addition of hydrogen atoms) and halogenation (addition of halogen atoms). Ethylene and substituted ethylene molecules can undergo polymerization, a process by which many molecules (monomers) are joined together to form a large chain-like molecule.
8. Organic molecules that contain elements in addition to carbon and hydrogen can be viewed as hydrocarbon derivatives: hydrocarbons with functional groups. Each functional group exhibits characteristic chemical properties.
9. Alcohols contain the —OH functional group. Aldehydes and ketones contain the carbonyl functional group,

   $$\gt C{=}O$$

   In aldehydes, this group is bonded to at least one hydrogen atom. Carboxylic acids are characterized by the carboxyl functional group,

   $$-C(=O)-OH$$

   They can react with alcohols to form esters.
10. Polymers can be formed by addition polymerization, in which monomers add together, or by condensation polymerization, which involves the splitting out of small molecules (such as water) as the monomers react.

Active Learning Questions

These questions are designed to be considered by groups of students in class. Often these questions work well for introducing a particular topic in class.

1. What is meant by the term "unsaturated hydrocarbon"? What structural feature characterizes unsaturated hydrocarbons?
2. The following are named incorrectly, but a correct structure can be made from the name given. Draw the following incorrectly named compounds and name them correctly.
   a. 2-ethyl-3-methyl-5-isopropyl hexane
   b. 3-methyl-4-isopropylpentane
   c. 2-ethyl-3-butyne
3. When propane undergoes dehydrogenation, what is the product? Name it and draw a structural formula.

Answers to End-of-Chapter Exercises

1. Carbon has the unusual ability of bonding strongly to itself, forming long chains or rings of carbon atoms. Since there are many possible arrangements for a long chain, this results in many possible compounds.

2. Carbon has four valence electrons and can only make 4 bonds.

3. A double bond represents the sharing of two pairs of electrons between two bonded atoms.

4. A triple bond represents the sharing of three pairs of electrons between two bonded atoms. The sharing of three pairs imparts a linear geometry in the region of the triple bond.

5. tetrahedral arrangement; maximum separation of electron pairs

6. $\mathrm{\ddot{\underset{..}{O}}{=}C{=}\ddot{\underset{..}{O}}}$; $\mathrm{:C{\equiv}O:}$

7. b and c

8. a and c

9. In butane or propane, the four electron pairs around the carbon atoms have a basically tetrahedral orientation. This implies that the molecules cannot be linear.

10. In an alkane, carbons atoms make 4 separate bonds to adjacent atoms, with these bonds having the tetrahedral arrangement predicted by the VSEPR theory. With bond angles on the order of 109.5°, the molecule cannot be linear (180°).

11. C_nH_{2n+2}; for 20 carbon atoms, this would be $C_{20}H_{2\times20+2}$ = 42 hydrogen atoms ($C_{20}H_{42}$).

12. (a) 10; (b) 14; (c) 28; (d) 36

13. (a) octane; (b) decane; (c) hexane; (d) butane

14. (a) $CH_3—CH_2—CH_2—CH_2—CH_3$; (b) $CH_3—CH_2—CH_2—CH_2—CH_2—CH_2—CH_2—CH_2—CH_2—CH_2—CH_3$; (c) $CH_3—CH_2—CH_2—CH_2—CH_2—CH_2—CH_2—CH_2—CH_3$; (d) $CH_3—CH_2—CH_2—CH_2—CH_2—CH_2—CH_3$

15. Same atoms present, but atoms are arranged differently; the alkane butane is the first alkane to have an isomer.

$CH_3—CH_2—CH_2—CH_3$
Butane

$CH_3—CH(CH_3)—CH_3$
2-methylpropane

16. A branched alkane contains one or more shorter carbon-atom chains attached to the side of the main (longest) carbon-atom chain. The simplest branched alkane is 2-methylpropane,

$CH_3—CH(CH_3)—CH_3$

4. How many different possible "tetramethylbenzenes" exist? Provide structural formulas and names for each.

5. For the general formula $C_6H_{14}O$, draw the structures of three isomeric alcohols that illustrate primary, secondary, and tertiary structures.

6. Differentiate between an addition polymer and a condensation polymer and provide an example of each. Do the same for copolymer and homopolymer.

Questions and Problems

20.1 Carbon Bonding

QUESTIONS

1. What makes carbon able to form so many different compounds?

2. Your roommate, a chemistry major, claims to have synthesized the compound CH_5 in the lab. Why is that not possible?

3. What does a double bond represent? How many pairs of electrons are shared between the atoms in a double bond? Draw the Lewis structure of a simple molecule that contains a double bond.

4. How many electron pairs are shared when a triple bond exists between two carbon atoms? What must be the geometric arrangement around the carbon atoms in a triple bond? Draw the Lewis structure of a simple molecule that contains a triple bond.

5. When a carbon atom is bonded to four other atoms, what geometric arrangement occurs around the carbon atom? Why?

6. Draw the Lewis structures for carbon dioxide and carbon monoxide.

20.2 Alkanes

QUESTIONS

7. Which of the following molecules are *unsaturated*?

   a. $CH_3—CH_2—CH_2—CH_3$
   b. $CH_3—CH{=}CH—CH_3$
   c. $CH_3—C{\equiv}C—CH_3$
   d. $CH_3—CH_2—CH_3$

8. Which of the following molecules are *saturated*?

   a. $CH_3—CH_3$
   b. $CH_2{=}CH_2$
   c. $CH_3—CH_2—CH_2—CH_3$
   d. $CH_3—CH_2—CH{=}CH_2$

9. Figure 20.3 shows the structures of the hydrocarbons propane and butane. Discuss the arrangement of the electron pairs around each of the carbon atoms in these molecules. Are these molecules linear? Why or why not?

10. How do we know that the chain of carbon atoms in the "straight" chain alkanes actually must exist in a zig-zag arrangement? What are the bond angles around the carbon atoms in an alkane?

PROBLEMS

11. What is the "general" formula for an alkane? Show how this general formula can be used to determine the number of hydrogens that would be present for an alkane with twenty carbon atoms.

12. Without drawing a structural formula, tell how many hydrogen atoms would be present in the straight-chain alkanes with the following numbers of carbon atoms.

   a. four
   b. six
   c. thirteen
   d. seventeen

13. Give the name of each of the following straight-chain alkanes.

   a. $CH_3—CH_2—CH_2—CH_2—CH_2—CH_2—CH_2—CH_3$
   b. $CH_3—CH_2—CH_2—CH_2—CH_2—CH_2—CH_2—$ $CH_2—CH_2—CH_3$
   c. $CH_3—CH_2—CH_2—CH_2—CH_2—CH_3$
   d. $CH_3—CH_2—CH_2—CH_3$

14. Draw the structural formula for each of the following straight-chain alkanes.

   a. pentane
   b. undecane (eleven carbon atoms)
   c. nonane
   d. heptane

20.3 Structural Formulas and Isomerism

QUESTIONS

15. What are structural *isomers?* Which is the smallest alkane that has a structural isomer? Draw structures to illustrate the isomers.

16. What is a *branched* alkane? Draw the structure of a branched alkane and circle the branch.

PROBLEMS

17. Without looking back at the text, draw structural formulas and give the common names for the three isomers of pentane, C_5H_{12}.

18. Draw structural formulas for three isomeric alkanes having the formula C_6H_{14}.

All even-numbered Questions and Problems have answers in the back of this book and solutions in the Solutions Guide.

17.

```
    H  H  H  H  H
    |  |  |  |  |
 H—C—C—C—C—C—H
    |  |  |  |  |
    H  H  H  H  H

    H  H  H  H
    |  |  |  |
 H—C—C—C—C—H
    |  |  |  |
    H CH3 H  H

    H CH3 H
    |  |  |
 H—C—C—C—H
    |  |  |
    H CH3 H
```

18. carbon skeletons are shown:

```
   C
   |
C—C—C—C      C—C—C—C—C
   |                |
   C                C

C—C—C—C—C—C

C—C—C—C—C
    |
    C

  C  C
  |  |
C—C—C—C
```

19. propane (3), pentane (5), heptane (7), nonane (9)

20. The root name is derived from the number of carbon atoms in the *longest continuous chain* of carbon atoms.

21. An alkyl group is a hydrocarbon branch from the main chain; an alkyl group has one less hydrogen than its parent alkane.

22. The numbers indicate to which carbon atom of the longest continuous chain the substituents are attached. The longest continuous chain is numbered from the end closest to the first substituent so as to give the lowest possible numbers.

23. (a) *di-;* (b) *tetra-;* (c) *penta-;* (d) *tri-*

24. Multiple substituents are listed in alphabetical order, disregarding any prefix.

25. (a) 4,5-dimethylnonane; (b) 3,3,4,4-tetramethylheptane; (c) 3,4,5,5-tetramethyloctane; (d) 2,3,4-trimethylhexane

26. (a) 2,3,4-trimethylpentane; (b) 2,3-dimethylpentane; (c) 3,4-dimethylhexane; (d) 4,5-dimethyloctane

27.

```
(a) CH3—CH—CH—CH2—CH3;
        |    |
       CH3  CH3

(b) CH3—CH—CH2—CH—CH3;
        |        |
       CH3      CH3

(c)     CH3
        |
    CH3—C—CH2—CH2—CH3;
        |
        CH3

(d)             CH3
                |
    CH3—CH2—C—CH2—CH3
                |
                CH3
```

28. Answer appears at the bottom of the following page.

29. petroleum: hydrocarbons with five to more than 25 carbon atoms; natural gas: primarily methane; formed from decay of living organisms

30. *Number of*

C Atoms	*Use*
C_5-C_{12}	gasoline
$C_{10}-C_{18}$	kerosene, jet fuel
$C_{15}-C_{25}$	diesel fuel, heating oil
$>C_{25}$	asphalt

31. Pyrolytic cracking (using heat to break up petroleum fractions) of kerosene breaks it up into the smaller molecules characteristic of gasoline.

32. Tetraethyl lead was added to gasoline to prevent "knocking" of high-efficiency automobile engines. Its use is being discontinued because of the danger to the environment from the lead in this substance.

33. The C—C and C—H bonds are relatively strong and difficult to break.

34. Combustion reactions are used as a source of heat and light. $C_3H_8(g) + 5O_2(g) \rightarrow 3CO_2(g) + 4H_2O(g)$

35. CH_3Cl; (b) HCl; (c) $CHCl_3$; (d) Cl_2

36. A double bond is introduced; example depends on student choice.

37. (a) $2C_2H_6 + 7O_2 \rightarrow 4CO_2 + 6H_2O$; (b) $2C_4H_{10} + 13O_2 \rightarrow 8CO_2 + 10H_2O$; (c) $C_3H_8 + 5O_2 \rightarrow 3CO_2 + 4H_2O$

38.
(a) $2C_6H_{14}(l) + 19O_2(g) \rightarrow$

20.4 Naming Alkanes

QUESTIONS

19. Give the root names for the alkanes with three, five, seven, and nine carbon atoms.

20. To what does the root name for a *branched* hydrocarbon correspond?

21. What is an *alkyl* group? How is a given alkyl group related to its parent alkane?

22. In the systematic names of alkanes (such as 4-ethyl-3,5-dimethylnonane), what are *numbers* used to indicate? How are these numbers determined when naming an alkane?

23. What *prefixes* would be used in the systematic name of an alkane to indicate that the alkane contained the following numbers of methyl branches?

a. two
b. four
c. five
d. three

24. In giving the name of a hydrocarbon with several substituents, in what order do we list the substituents?

PROBLEMS

25. Give the systematic name for each of the following branched alkanes.

```
a. CH3—CH2—CH2—CH—CH—CH2—CH2—CH2
               |   |            |
              CH3 CH3          CH3

              CH3 CH3
               |   |
b. CH3—CH2—CH2—C———C—CH2—CH3
               |   |
              CH3 CH3

            CH3     CH3
             |       |
c. CH3—CH2—CH—CH——C—CH2—CH2
                |   |       |
               CH3 CH3     CH3

                CH3
                 |
d. CH3—CH2—CH—CH——CH—CH3
            |       |
           CH3     CH3
```

26. Give the systematic name for each of the following alkanes.

```
a. CH3—CH—CH—CH—CH3
        |   |   |
       CH3 CH3 CH3

b. CH3—CH—CH—CH2
        |   |   |
       CH3 CH3 CH3

c. CH2—CH—CH—CH2
   |    |   |   |
   CH3 CH3 CH3 CH3

d.        CH2—CH—CH—CH2
           |   |   |   |
   CH3—CH2 CH3 CH3 CH2—CH3
```

27. Draw a structural formula for each of the following branched alkanes.

a. 2,3-dimethylpentane
b. 2,4-dimethylpentane
c. 2,2-dimethylpentane
d. 3,3-dimethylpentane

28. Draw a structural formula for each of the following branched alkanes.

a. 2,2,4-trimethylheptane
b. 2,3,4-trimethylheptane
c. 3,3,4-trimethylheptane
d. 2,4,4-trimethylheptane

20.5 Petroleum

QUESTIONS

29. What are the major constituents of crude petroleum? What is the major constituent of natural gas? How were these mixtures formed?

30. List several petroleum fractions, and tell how each fraction is primarily used.

31. What is *pyrolytic cracking,* and why is the process applied to the kerosene fraction of petroleum?

32. Why was tetraethyl lead, $(C_2H_5)_4Pb$, added to gasoline in the past? Why is the use of this substance being phased out?

20.6 Reactions of Alkanes

QUESTIONS

33. Explain why alkanes are relatively unreactive.

34. Write an equation showing the *combustion* of propane, C_3H_8. How do we make use of combustion reactions?

35. Indicate the missing molecule in each of the following substitution reactions.

a. $CH_4 + Cl_2 \xrightarrow{hv} HCl + ?$
b. $CH_2Cl_2 + Cl_2 \xrightarrow{hv} CHCl_3 + ?$
c. $? + Cl_2 \xrightarrow{hv} CCl_4 + HCl$
d. $CH_3Cl + ? \xrightarrow{hv} CH_2Cl_2 + HCl$

36. When an alkane molecule is *dehydrogenated,* what sort of feature is introduced into the molecule? Give an example.

PROBLEMS

37. Complete and balance each of the following combustion reactions of alkanes.

a. $C_2H_6(g) + O_2(g) \rightarrow$
b. $C_4H_{10}(g) + O_2(g) \rightarrow$
c. $C_3H_8(g) + O_2(g) \rightarrow$

All even-numbered Questions and Problems have answers in the back of this book and solutions in the Solutions Guide.

28.

```
(a)     CH3
         |
   CH3—C—CH2—CH—CH2—CH2—CH3
         |        |
        CH3      CH3

(b)          CH3
              |
   CH3—CH—CH—CH—CH2—CH2—CH3
         |        |
        CH3      CH3

(c)               CH3
                   |
   CH3—CH2—C——CH—CH2—CH2—CH3
                   |   |
                  CH3 CH3

(d)      CH3          CH3
          |            |
   CH3—CH—CH2—C—CH2—CH2—CH3
                       |
                      CH3
```

680 Chapter 20 Organic Chemistry

38. Complete and balance each of the following chemical equations.

a. $C_6H_{14}(l) + O_2(g) \rightarrow$
b. $CH_4(g) + Cl_2(g) \rightarrow$
c. $CHCl_3(l) + Cl_2(g) \rightarrow$

20.7 Alkenes and Alkynes

QUESTIONS

39. What is an *alkene?* What structural feature characterizes alkenes? Give the general formula for alkenes.

40. What is an *alkyne?* What structural feature characterizes alkynes? Give the general formula for alkynes.

41. How is the *root name* of an alkane modified to indicate that a given hydrocarbon contains a double or triple bond in its longest continuous chain?

42. How is the *location* of a double or triple bond in the longest continuous chain of an unsaturated hydrocarbon indicated?

43. Indicate the missing molecule in each of the following reactions of alkenes.

a. $CH_2{=}CH{-}CH_3 + H_2 \xrightarrow{Pt} ?$
b. $? + Br_2 \rightarrow CH_2Br{-}CHBr{-}CH_3$
c. $2CH_2{=}CH{-}CH_3 + 9? \rightarrow 6CO_2 + 6H_2O$

44. How is *hydrogenation* used in the production of solid shortenings for cooking? Give an example of a hydrogenation reaction.

PROBLEMS

45. Give the systematic name for each of the following unsaturated hydrocarbons.

a. $CH_3{-}CH{=}CH{-}CH_2{-}CH_3$
b. $CH_3{-}CH_2{-}CH{=}CH{-}CH_3$
c. 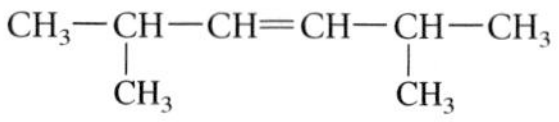 $CH_3{-}\underset{\displaystyle CH_3}{\underset{|}{CH}}{-}CH{=}CH{-}\underset{\displaystyle CH_3}{\underset{|}{CH}}{-}CH_3$
d. 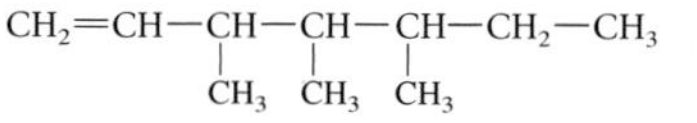 $CH_2{=}CH{-}\underset{\displaystyle CH_3}{\underset{|}{CH}}{-}\underset{\displaystyle CH_3}{\underset{|}{CH}}{-}\underset{\displaystyle CH_3}{\underset{|}{CH}}{-}CH_2{-}CH_3$

46. Give the systematic name for each of the following unsaturated hydrocarbons.

a. 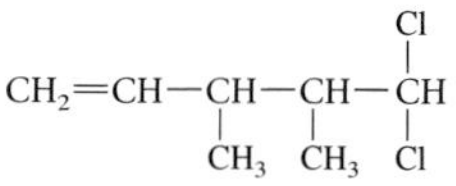 $CH_2{=}CH{-}\underset{\displaystyle CH_3}{\underset{|}{CH}}{-}\underset{\displaystyle CH_3}{\underset{|}{CH}}{-}\overset{\displaystyle Cl}{\overset{|}{\underset{\displaystyle Cl}{\underset{|}{CH}}}}$
b. 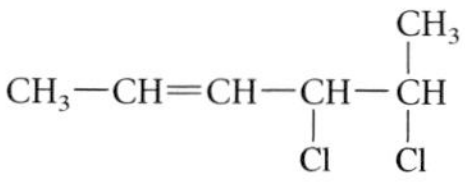 $CH_3{-}CH{=}CH{-}\underset{\displaystyle Cl}{\underset{|}{CH}}{-}\overset{\displaystyle CH_3}{\overset{|}{\underset{\displaystyle Cl}{\underset{|}{CH}}}}$
c. 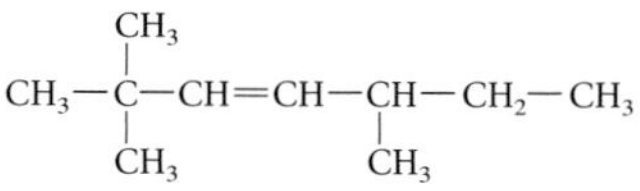 $CH_3{-}\overset{\displaystyle CH_3}{\overset{|}{\underset{\displaystyle CH_3}{\underset{|}{C}}}}{-}CH{=}CH{-}\underset{\displaystyle CH_3}{\underset{|}{CH}}{-}CH_2{-}CH_3$

d. 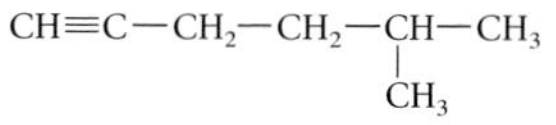 $CH{\equiv}C{-}CH_2{-}CH_2{-}\underset{\displaystyle CH_3}{\underset{|}{CH}}{-}CH_3$

47. Draw structural formulas and give the systematic names for at least *four* isomeric hydrocarbons containing seven carbon atoms and one double bond.

48. Draw structural formulas showing all possible molecules containing six carbon atoms and having one triple bond.

20.8 Aromatic Hydrocarbons

QUESTIONS

49. What structure do all aromatic hydrocarbons have in common?

50. Benzene exhibits resonance. Explain this statement in terms of the different Lewis structures that can be drawn for benzene.

20.9 Naming Aromatic Compounds

QUESTIONS

51. How is a monosubstituted benzene named? Give the structures and names of two examples. Also give two examples of monosubstituted benzenes that have special names.

52. How is the benzene ring named if it is considered a substituent in another molecule? Give the structures and names of two examples.

53. If a benzene ring contains several substituents, how are the relative locations of the substituents numbered in the systematic name given to the molecule?

54. What do the prefixes *ortho-*, *meta-*, and *para-* refer to in terms of the relative location of substituents in a disubstituted benzene?

PROBLEMS

55. Draw a structural formula for each of the following aromatic or substituted aromatic compounds.

a. naphthalene
b. 2-bromophenol
c. 3-methylstyrene
d. 4-nitrochlorobenzene
e. 1,3-dinitrobenzene

56. Name the following aromatic or substituted aromatic compounds.

a. 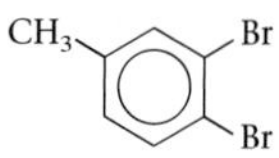 CH_3 (benzene ring with CH_3, Br, Br substituents)

b. 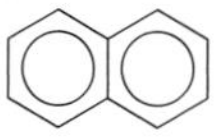 (fused two-ring structure)

All even-numbered Questions and Problems have answers in the back of this book and solutions in the Solutions Guide.

$12CO_2(g) + 14H_2O(g)$;
(b) $CH_4(g) + Cl_2(g) \rightarrow CH_3Cl(l) + HCl(g)$;
(c) $CHCl_3(l) + Cl_2(g) \rightarrow CCl_4(l) + HCl(g)$

39. Alkenes contain a carbon–carbon double bond. The general formula is C_nH_{2n}.

40. An alkyne is a hydrocarbon containing a carbon–carbon triple bond. The general formula is C_nH_{2n-2}.

41. Ending changed to *-ene* for alkenes and *-yne* for alkynes.

42. The location of a double or triple bond in the longest chain of an alkene or alkyne is indicated by giving the *number* of the lowest-number carbon atom involved in the bond.

43. (a) $CH_3{-}CH_2{-}CH_3$; (b) $CH_2{=}CH{-}CH_3$; (c) O_2

44. Hydrogenation converts unsaturated compounds to saturated (or less unsaturated) compounds. In the case of a liquid vegetable oil, this is likely to convert the oil to a solid:

$$C_2H_4(g) + H_2(g) \rightarrow C_2H_6(g)$$

45. (a) 2-pentene;
(b) 2-pentene;
(c) 2,5-dimethyl-3-hexene;
(d) 3,4,5-trimethyl-1-heptene

46. (a) 3,4-dimethyl-5,5-dichloro-1-pentene;
(b) 4,5-dichloro-2-hexene;
(c) 2,2,5-trimethyl-3-heptene;
(d) 5-methyl-1-hexyne

47. Obvious choices are 1-heptene, 2-heptene, and 3-heptene, followed by 2-methyl-1-hexene, 2-methyl-2-hexene, and so on

48. The carbon skeletons are

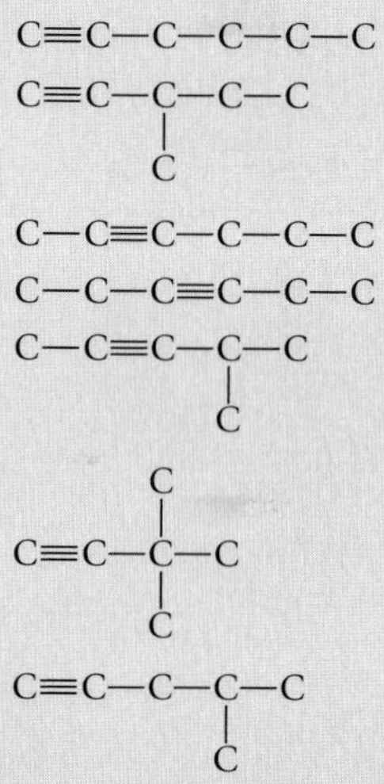

$C{\equiv}C{-}C{-}C{-}C{-}C$

$C{\equiv}C{-}\underset{\displaystyle C}{\underset{|}{C}}{-}C{-}C$

$C{-}C{\equiv}C{-}C{-}C{-}C$

$C{-}C{-}C{\equiv}C{-}C{-}C$

$C{-}C{\equiv}C{-}\underset{\displaystyle C}{\underset{|}{C}}{-}C$

$C{\equiv}C{-}\overset{\displaystyle C}{\overset{|}{\underset{\displaystyle C}{\underset{|}{C}}}}{-}C$

$C{\equiv}C{-}C{-}\underset{\displaystyle C}{\underset{|}{C}}{-}C$

49. the benzene ring (phenyl group)

50. For benzene, a set of equivalent Lewis structures can be drawn, with each structure differing only in the location of the three double bonds in the ring. Experimentally, benzene does not demonstrate the chemical properties expected for molecules having *any* double bonds.

51. The substituent is named as a prefix to the word *benzene.*

c. CH_3–C_6H_4–OH (para: CH_3 above ring, OH below)

d. NO_2–C_6H_4–NO_2 (para)

20.10 Functional Groups

PROBLEMS

57. Without looking back at the text, write the structural formula and the name for a representative compound from each of the following families (functional groups).
    a. amine
    b. alcohol
    c. carboxylic acid
    d. aldehyde
    e. ester
    f. ketone
    g. ether

58. Based on the functional group each molecule below contains, identify the family of organic compounds to which each belongs.
    a. $CH_3—CH_2—C(=O)OH$
    b. $CH_3—CH_2—CH_2—C(=O)H$
    c. $CH_3—CH_2—CH_2—C(=O)—CH_2—CH_3$
    d. $CH_3—CH_2—C(OH)(CH_2—CH_3)—CH_2—CH_3$

20.11 Alcohols

QUESTIONS

59. What functional group characterizes an alcohol? What ending is added to the name of the parent hydrocarbon to show that a molecule is an alcohol?

60. Distinguish among primary, secondary, and tertiary alcohols. Give a structural formula for an example of each type.

PROBLEMS

61. Give the systematic name for each of the following alcohols. Indicate whether the alcohol is primary, secondary, or tertiary.
    a. $CH_3—CH_2—C(OH)(CH_2—CH_3)—CH_2—CH_3$
    b. $CH_3—CH(CH_3)—CH(OH)—CH(CH_3)—CH_3$
    c. $CH_3—CH(OH)—CH_2—C(CH_3)_2—CH_3$
    d. $CH_3—CH(CH_3)—CH_2—C(CH_3)_2—CH_2—OH$

62. Without looking back at the text, draw the structures for examples of a primary, a secondary, and a tertiary alcohol, and name each of the compounds you choose.

20.12 Properties and Uses of Alcohols

QUESTIONS

63. Why is methanol sometimes called wood alcohol? Describe the modern synthesis of methanol. What are some uses of methanol?

64. Write the equation for the fermentation of glucose to form ethanol. Why can't ethanol solutions of greater than about 13% concentration be made directly by fermentation? How can the ethanol content be increased beyond this level in beverages?

65. Write the equation for the synthesis of ethanol from ethylene. What are some commercial uses of ethanol made by this process?

66. Give the names and structural formulas of two other commercially important alcohols. Cite the major use of each.

20.13 Aldehydes and Ketones

QUESTIONS

67. What functional group is *common* to both aldehydes and ketones?

68. What structural feature *distinguishes* aldehydes from ketones?

69. Mention some commercial uses of specific aldehydes and ketones.

All even-numbered Questions and Problems have answers in the back of this book and solutions in the Solutions Guide.

52. Answer appears at the bottom of the page.

53. With more than one substituent on a benzene ring, locator numbers are used with the substituent names to indicate their relative positions on the ring.

54. *ortho-*: adjacent substituents (1,2-); *meta-*: two substituents with one unsubstituted carbon atom between them (1,3-); *para-*: two substituents with two unsubstituted carbon atoms between them (1,4-)

55. (a)

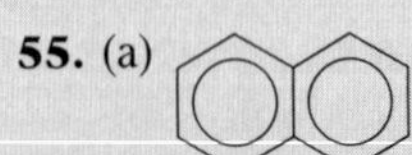

(b) C_6H_4 with OH and Br (ortho)

(c) C_6H_4 with $CH=CH_2$ and CH_3 (meta)

(d) $Cl—C_6H_4—NO_2$ (para)

(e) C_6H_4 with NO_2 and NO_2 (meta)

56. (a) 3,4-dibromo-1-methylbenzene, 3,4-dibromotoluene; (b) naphthalene; (c) 3-methylphenol; 3-hydroxytoluene; (d) 1,4-dinitrobenzene, *p*-dinitrobenzene

57. student examples

58. (a) carboxylic acid; (b) aldehyde; (c) ketone; (d) alcohol

59. hydroxyl group; ending *-ol* is added to root name

60. Answer appears at the bottom of the page.

52. When named as a substituent, the benzene ring is called the phenyl group. Two examples are

$CH_2=CH—CH(C_6H_5)—CH_3$

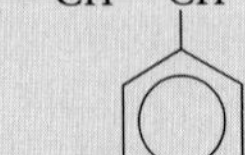

3-phenyl-1-butene

$CH_3—CH(C_6H_5)—CH_2—CH_2—CH_2—CH_3$

2-phenylhexane

60. Primary alcohols have one hydrocarbon fragment (alkyl group) bonded to the carbon atom where the —OH group is attached. Secondary alcohols have two alkyl groups attached, and tertiary alcohols contain three alkyl groups. Examples are

ethanol (primary) $CH_3—CH_2—OH$

2-propanol (secondary) $CH_3—CH(OH)—CH_3$

70. Write equations showing the oxidation of a primary alcohol and the oxidation of a secondary alcohol to produce an aldehyde and a ketone, respectively. Indicate the structure of each alcohol and of the principal organic products of the oxidations.

20.14 Naming Aldehydes and Ketones

QUESTIONS

71. Aldehydes and ketones both contain the carbonyl group, yet the properties of these two types of compounds are different enough that they are classified separately. Without looking back at the text, draw the structures of the ketone and the aldehyde that have three carbon atoms. Name each of these compounds.

72. Describe the alternative system for naming ketones. Give two examples of ketones, along with their names in both systems.

73. Give the systematic name for each of the following aldehydes or ketones.

a. $CH_3—CH(CH_3)—CH_2—C(CH_3)_2—C(=O)H$

b. $CH_3—CH(CH_3)—C(=O)—CH(CH_3)—CH_3$

c. $CH_3—C(=O)—C(CH_3)H—CH(Cl)—CH_2$

d. $CH_3—C(=O)H$

74. Draw structural formulas for each of the following aldehydes and ketones.

a. dimethyl ketone
b. 3-methyl-2-butanone
c. propanal
d. 2,2-dimethyl-3-pentanone

20.15 Carboxylic Acids and Esters

QUESTIONS

75. Draw the structure of the group that characterizes organic (carboxylic) acids. Give the general condensed formula for an organic acid.

76. Are carboxylic acids typically strong acids or weak acids? Write an equation showing the acid CH_3CH_2COOH ionizing in water.

77. What systematic ending is used to show that a molecule is a carboxylic acid? Give an example.

78. Complete the following equations with the structural formula of the principal organic product.

a. $CH_3—CH_2—CH_2—CH_2—OH \xrightarrow{\text{Mild oxidation}}$

b. $CH_3—CH_2—CH_2—OH \xrightarrow{\text{Strong oxidation}}$

c. $CH_3—CH_2—CH_2—C(=O)OH + HO—CH_2—CH_2—CH_3 \longrightarrow$

79. From what two families of organic compounds are esters synthesized? Give a specific example of a reaction in which an ester is formed, and indicate how the name of the ester in your example is derived from the compounds used to synthesize it.

80. Write an equation showing the synthesis of acetylsalicylic acid (aspirin).

PROBLEMS

81. Give the systematic name for each of the following organic acids:

a. $CH_3—CH_2—CH(CH_3)—C(=O)OH$

b. $C_6H_5—CH_2—C(=O)OH$

c. $CH_3—CH_2—C(CH_3)_2—CH_2—C(=O)OH$

d. $HO(O=)C—CH_2—C(CH_3)(CH_3)—CH_2Cl$

82. Draw a structural formula for each of the following:

a. methyl butanoate
b. ethyl acetate
c. *o*-chlorobenzoic acid
d. 2,2-dimethyl-3-chloro-butanoic acid

20.16 Polymers

QUESTIONS

83. What, in general terms, is a polymer? What is a monomer?

84. What is *addition polymerization?* Give an example of a common addition polymer.

All even-numbered Questions and Problems have answers in the back of this book and solutions in the Solutions Guide.

2-methyl-2-propanol (tertiary) $CH_3—C(CH_3)(OH)—CH_3$

61. (a) 3-ethyl-3-pentanol; tertiary; (b) 2,4-dimethyl-3-pentanol; secondary; (c) 4,4-dimethyl-2-pentanol; secondary; (d) 2,2,4-trimethyl-1-pentanol; primary

62. Structures depend on student choice. $CH_3—CH_2—CH_2OH$ (1°), $CH_3—CH(OH)—CH_3$ (2°), and $CH_3—C(CH_3)(OH)—CH_3$ (3°) are good examples.

63. "Wood" alcohol because it formerly was made by destructive distillation of wood; modern preparation is catalytic hydrogenation of CO; important industrial chemical (solvent, motor fuel, starting material for other organics)

64. $C_6H_{12}O_6 \xrightarrow{\text{yeast}} 2CH_3CH_2—OH + 2CO_2$

The yeast necessary for the fermentation process are killed if the concentration of ethanol is greater than 13%. More-concentrated ethanol solutions are most commonly made by distillation.

65. $CH_2{=}CH_2 + H_2O \rightarrow CH_3—CH_2OH$; solvent, fuel, starting material for synthesis of larger molecules

66. Methanol (CH_3OH): starting material for synthesis of acetic acid and many plastics; ethylene glycol ($CH_2OH—CH_2OH$): automobile antifreeze; isopropyl alcohol (2-propanol, $CH_3—CH(OH)—CH_3$): rubbing alcohol

67. carbonyl group

68. Both aldehydes and ketones contain the carbonyl group (C=O). Aldehydes and ketones differ in the *location* of the carbonyl function: aldehydes contain the carbonyl group at the end of a hydrocarbon chain (the carbon atom of the carbonyl group is bonded to a maximum of one other carbon atom); the carbonyl group of ketones represents one of the interior carbon atoms of a chain (the carbon atom of the carbonyl group is bonded to two other carbon atoms).

69. Methanal (tissue preservative); benzaldehyde, cinnamaldehyde, vanillin (flavorings/aromas); acetone, butanone (solvents)

70. Answer depends on student choice of alcohols

71. $H—CH_2—CH_2—CH{=}O$ (H—C(H)(H)—C(H)(H)—C(H)=O)

Propanal

$H—C(H)(H)—C(=O)—C(H)(H)—H$

Propanone

85. What is *condensation polymerization,* and how does it differ from addition polymerization? Give an example of a common condensation polymer.

86. The "Chemistry in Focus" segment *Mother of Invention* discusses Stephanie Kwolek and the invention of Kevlar. Is Kevlar a copolymer or a homopolymer?

PROBLEMS

87. List at least five common polymers discussed in this chapter, along with their common uses.

88. For the polymeric substances nylon and Dacron, sketch representations of the repeating unit in each.

Additional Problems

89. The first "organic" compound to be synthesized in the laboratory, rather than being isolated from nature, was ______, which was prepared from ______.

90. A carbon compound containing a carbon–carbon double or triple bond is said to be ______.

91. The general orientation of the four pairs of electrons around the carbon atoms in alkanes is ______.

92. Alkanes in which the carbon atoms form a single unbranched chain are said to be ______ alkanes.

93. Structural isomerism occurs when two molecules have the same number of each type of atom but exhibit different arrangements of the ______ between those atoms.

94. The systematic names of all saturated hydrocarbons have the ending ______ added to a root name that indicates the number of carbon atoms in the molecule.

95. For a branched hydrocarbon, the root name for the hydrocarbon comes from the number of carbon atoms in the ______ continuous chain in the molecule.

96. The positions of substituents along the hydrocarbon framework of a molecule are indicated by the ______ of the carbon atom to which the substituents are attached.

97. Kerosene may be converted to gasoline by ______, which means that the larger, heavier kerosene components are broken down by heat into smaller, lighter gasoline fragments.

98. Tetraethyl lead, $(C_2H_5)_4Pb$, was added to gasoline in the past as a(n) ______ agent.

99. The major use of alkanes has been in ______ reactions, as a source of heat and light.

100. With very reactive agents, such as the halogen elements, alkanes undergo ______ reactions, whereby a new atom replaces one or more hydrogen atoms of the alkane.

101. Alkenes and alkynes are characterized by their ability to undergo rapid, complete ______ reactions, by which other atoms attach themselves to the carbon atoms of the double or triple bond.

102. Unsaturated fats may be converted to saturated fats by the process of ______.

103. Benzene is the parent member of the group of hydrocarbons called ______ hydrocarbons.

104. An atom or group of atoms that imparts new and characteristic properties to an organic molecule is called a(n) ______ group.

105. A(n) ______ alcohol is one in which there is only one hydrocarbon group attached to the carbon atom holding the hydroxyl group.

106. The simplest alcohol, methanol, is prepared industrially by the hydrogenation of ______.

107. Ethanol is commonly prepared by the ______ of certain sugars by yeast.

108. Both aldehydes and ketones contain the ______ group, but they differ in where this group occurs along the hydrocarbon chain.

109. Aldehydes and ketones can be prepared by ______ of the corresponding alcohol.

110. Organic acids, which contain the ______ group, are typically weak acids.

111. The typically sweet-smelling compounds called ______ result from the condensation reaction of an organic acid with a(n) ______.

112. In ______ polymerization, the monomer units simply combine over and over again to form the polymer's long chain.

113. Show (by drawing structures) how the members of a series of alkanes differ from the previous or following member of the series by a $-CH_2-$ unit.

114. Draw at least three isomeric alkanes having the general formula C_7H_{16} and give the systematic name of each.

115. As the size of an organic molecule increases, the number of structural isomers that are possible increases dramatically. For the general alkane formula $C_{20}H_{42}$, draw structures showing the carbon framework of at least ten isomers. (You do not have to show all the hydrogen atoms.)

116. Give the systematic name of each of the following substituted alkanes.

a. $CH_3-CH(Cl)-CH_2-CH_3$

b. $CH_2(Br)-CH_2(Br)$

c. CHI_3

d. $CH_3-CH(Cl)-CH(Cl)-CH(Cl)-CH_3$

All even-numbered Questions and Problems have answers in the back of this book and solutions in the Solutions Guide.

72. Answer appears at the bottom of the page.

73. (a) 2,2,4-trimethylpentanal; (b) 2,4-dimethyl-3-pentanone; (c) 4-chloro-3-methyl-2-butanone; (d) ethanal (acetaldehyde)

74. (a) $CH_3-C(=O)-CH_3$

(b) $CH_3-C(=O)-CH(CH_3)-CH_3$

(c) $CH_3-CH_2-C(=O)H$

(d) $CH_3-C(CH_3)_2-C(=O)-CH_2-CH_3$

75. carboxyl group, $-C(=O)-OH$

The general formula for an acid is RCOOH.

76. Answer appears at the bottom of the page.

77. Ending is *-oic acid* added to the root hydrocarbon name; CH_3COOH, ethanoic acid.

78. Answer appears at the bottom of the page.

79. Esters are produced by the reaction of carboxylic acids with alcohols. Example depends on student choice of reactants.

80. (salicylic acid: benzene ring with COOH and OH) + $HO-C(=O)-CH_3$ → (benzene ring with COOH and $O-C(=O)-CH_3$) + H_2O

81. (a) 2-methylbutanoic acid;
(b) 2-phenylethanoic acid;
(c) 3,3-dimethylpentanoic acid;
(d) 4-chloro-3,3-dimethylbutanoic acid

82. Answer appears at the bottom of the following page.

72. In addition to their systematic names (based on the hydrocarbon root, with the ending *-one*), ketones can be named based on the groups attached to either side of the carbonyl carbon as alkyl groups, followed by the word *ketone.*

Methyl ethyl ketone (or 2-butanone) $CH_3-C(=O)-CH_2-CH_3$

Diethyl ketone (or 3-pentanone) $CH_3-CH_2-C(=O)-CH_2-CH_3$

76. Carboxylic acids are typically *weak* acids.

$CH_3-CH_2-COOH + H_2O \rightleftharpoons CH_3-CH_2-COO^- + H_3O^+$

78. (a) $CH_3-CH_2-CH_2-CHO$
(b) CH_3-CH_2-COOH
(c) $CH_3-CH_2-CH_2-C(=O)-O-CH_2-CH_2-CH_3$

e. 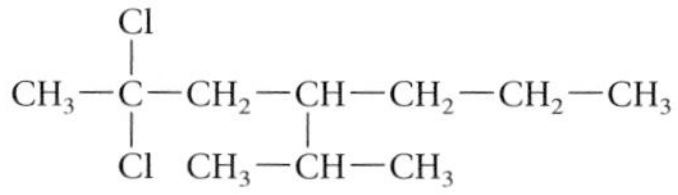
```
        Cl
        |
CH3—C—CH2—CH—CH2—CH2—CH3
        |         |
        Cl  CH3—CH—CH3
```

117. Give some examples of molecules containing "fused" benzene rings.

118. Write a structural formula for each of the following compounds.

a. 2,3-dimethylheptane
b. 2,2-dimethyl-3-chloro-1-octanol
c. 2-chloro-1-hexene
d. 1-chloro-2-hexene
e. 2-methylphenol

119. Draw the structural formula(s) for, and give the name(s) of, the organic product(s) of each of the following reactions. If a mixture of several, similar products is expected, indicate the type of product expected.

a. $CH_3—CH_3 + Cl_2 \xrightarrow{\text{Light}}$

b. $CH_3—CH{=}CH—CH_3 + H_2 \xrightarrow{\text{Pt}}$

c. 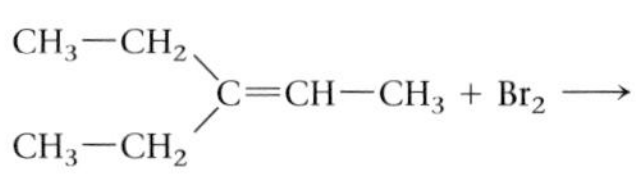 $(CH_3—CH_2)(CH_3—CH_2)C{=}CH—CH_3 + Br_2 \longrightarrow$

120. For the general formula $C_6H_{14}O$, draw the structures of three isomeric alcohols that illustrate *primary, secondary,* and *tertiary* alcohol structures.

121. The alcohol glycerol (glycerine), which is produced in the human body by the digestion of fats, has the following structure.

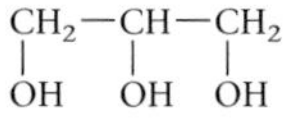

```
CH2—CH—CH2
|    |    |
OH   OH   OH
```

Give the systematic name of glycerol.

122. The sugar glucose could conceivably be given the name 2,3,4,5,6-pentahydroxyhexanal (though this name is never used because the actual sugar glucose has only one possible isomer having this name). Draw the structure implied by this name.

123. Draw a structure corresponding to each of the following names.

a. 2-methylpentanal
b. 3-hydroxybutanoic acid
c. 2-aminopropanal
d. 2,4-hexanedione
e. 3-methylbenzaldehyde

124. Write a structural formula for each of the following compounds.

a. methyl pentyl ketone
b. 3-methylpentanal
c. 2-methyl-1-pentanol
d. 1,2,3-propanetriol
e. 2-methyl-3-hexanone

125. Salicylic acid is an interesting molecule; it is both an acid and an alcohol, having a hydroxyl group attached to the aromatic ring (phenol). For this reason, salicylic acid can undergo two different esterification reactions depending on which functional group of salicylic acid reacts. For example, as discussed in this chapter, when treated with acetic acid—a stronger acid—salicylic acid behaves as an alcohol, and the ester produced is acetylsalicylic acid (aspirin). On the other hand, when reacted with methyl alcohol, salicylic acid behaves as an acid, and the ester methyl salicylate (oil of wintergreen) is produced. Methyl salicylate is also an analgesic and is part of the formulation of many liniments for sore muscles. Write an equation for the production of each of these esters of salicylic acid.

126. Alpha amino acids are organic acid molecules that also happen to contain an amino group ($—NH_2$) on the second carbon atom of the acid's chain. Proteins are condensation polymers of such alpha amino acids. The reaction by which the long chain of the protein forms is very similar to the reaction by which nylon forms, resulting in the formation of the linkage

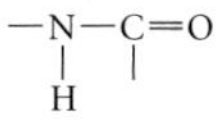

```
—N—C=O
 |  |
 H
```

which is called an "amide" (or "peptide") linkage. Show how the following two amino acids could react with each other to produce an amide linkage, resulting in the formation of a dimer (a "dipeptide").

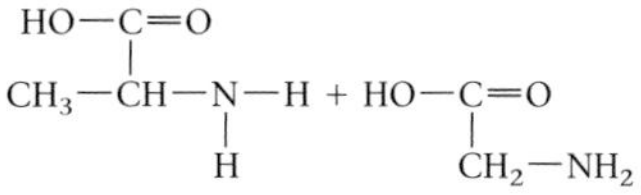

```
      HO—C=O
         |
CH3—CH—N—H + HO—C=O
         |         |
         H         CH2—NH2
```

How could this dipeptide then go on to react with additional amino acids to form a polypeptide?

127. Complete the following table with the name or structure as needed.

Name	Structure
pentane	________
________	$CH_3CH_2CH_2CH_2CH_2CH_2CH_2CH_3$
decane	________
________	$CH_3CH_2CH_2CH_2CH_3$
heptane	________

128. For each of the following numbers of carbon atoms, give the structure of the straight-chain alkane with that number of carbon atoms, and give its name.

a. eight carbon atoms
b. six carbon atoms
c. four carbon atoms
d. five carbon atoms

129. Draw structural formulas for all isomeric alkanes having the general formula C_7H_{16}.

All even-numbered Questions and Problems have answers in the back of this book and solutions in the Solutions Guide.

82. (a) 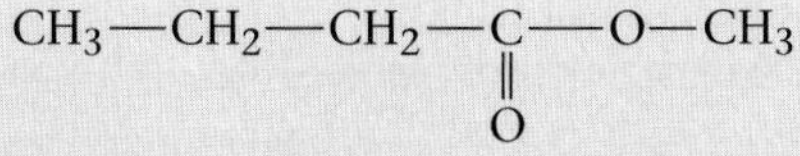 $CH_3—CH_2—CH_2—C({=}O)—O—CH_3$

(b) $CH_3—C({=}O)—O—CH_2—CH_3$

(c) COOH on benzene ring with Cl

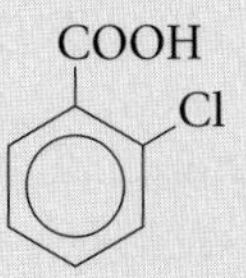

(d) 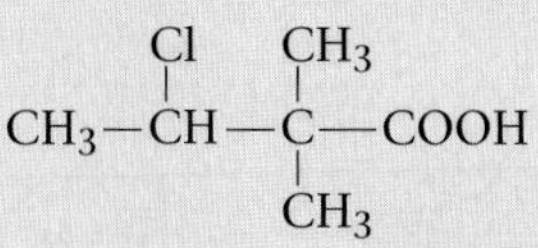
```
        Cl  CH3
        |   |
CH3—CH—C—COOH
            |
            CH3
```

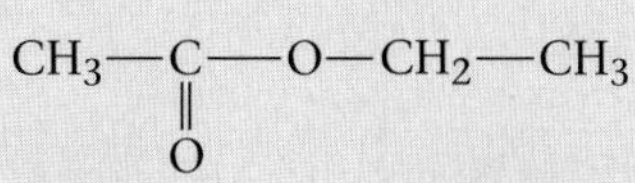

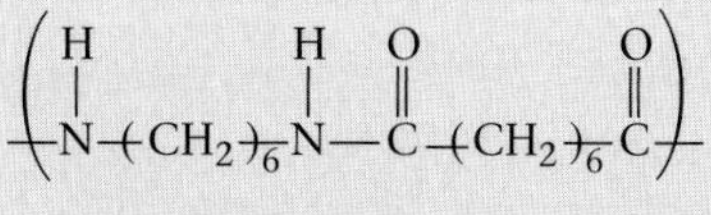

88. nylon $\left(\overset{H}{N} + CH_2 \right)_6 \overset{H}{N} — \overset{O}{\overset{\|}{C}} + CH_2)_6 \overset{O}{\overset{\|}{C}})$

Dacron $\left(O—CH_2—CH_2—O—\overset{O}{\overset{\|}{C}}—C_6H_4—\overset{O}{\overset{\|}{C}} \right)$

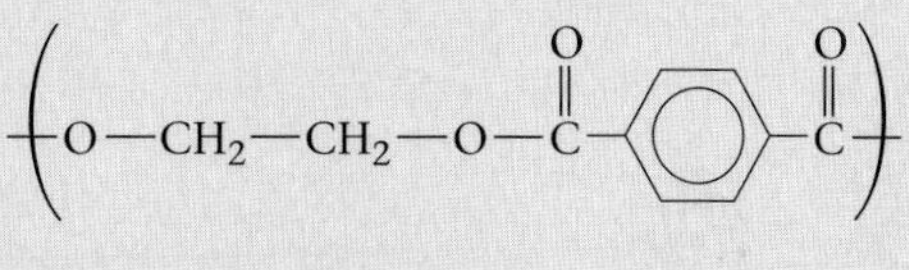

83. Polymers are large chainlike molecules that are built up from smaller molecules (monomers) that link together and repeat in the chain of the polymer hundreds or thousands of times.

84. In addition polymerization, the monomer units add together to form the polymer, with no other products. Polyethylene and polytetrafluoroethylene (Teflon) are examples.

85. In condensation polymerization, small molecules are formed and are split out as the monomer units combine to form the polymer chain; in addition polymerization, monomer units merely "add together" to form a longer chain. Nylon-66 is an example of a condensation polymer.

86. Kevlar is a co-polymer, since two different types of monomers combine to generate the polymer chain.

87. Answers depends on student choices.

88. Answer appears at the bottom of the page.

89. urea, ammonium cyanate

90. unsaturated

91. tetrahedral

92. straight-chain or normal

93. bonds

94. *-ane*

95. longest

96. number

97. pyrolytic cracking

98. antiknocking

99. combustion

100. substitution

101. addition

102. hydrogenation

103. aromatic

104. functional

105. primary

106. carbon monoxide

107. fermentation

130. Give the systematic name for each of the following alkanes.

a.
```
         CH3
         |
CH3—CH—CH—CH3
         |
         CH3
```

b.
```
CH3—CH2     CH2—CH3
        \  /
         C
        /  \
CH3—CH2     CH2—CH3
```

c.
```
CH3 CH3
|   |
CH—C—CH2—CH2—CH3
|   |
CH3 CH3
```

d.
```
CH3—CH—CH—CH—CH—CH—CH3
    |   |   |   |   |
    CH3 CH3 CH3 CH3 CH3
```

131. Draw a structural formula for each of the following compounds.

a. 2,2-dimethylhexane
b. 2,3-dimethylhexane
c. 3,3-dimethylhexane
d. 3,4-dimethylhexane
e. 2,4-dimethylhexane

132. Write the formula for the missing reactant or product in each of the following chemical equations.

a. $CH_4(g) + Cl_2(g) \rightarrow$ _____ $+ HCl(g)$
b. $CH_3CH_2CH_3(g) \rightarrow CH_3CH{=}CH_2(g) +$ _____
c. $CHCl_3(l) + Cl_2(g) \rightarrow CCl_4(l) +$ _____

133. Draw the structures for five different *unsaturated* hydrocarbons or substituted hydrocarbons and name your molecules.

134. Draw structural formulas showing all the isomers of the straight-chain alkyne with eight carbon atoms. Name each isomer.

135. Name each of the following aromatic or substituted aromatic compounds.

a. benzene ring with —CH3 and —CH3 on adjacent carbons

b. benzene ring with Br, Br, and Br (1,3,5 positions)

c. benzene ring with —NO2 and —Cl on adjacent carbons

d. two fused benzene rings

136. On the basis of the functional groups listed in Table 20.5, identify the family of organic compounds to which each of the following belongs.

a.
```
(C6H5)—CH2—CH2—C=O
                |
                OH
```

b.
```
CH3—CH2—CH2—C=O
             |
             (C6H5)
```

c.
```
CH3—CH2—C=O
        |
        O—CH2—CH2—(C6H5)
```

d. benzene ring with —OH and —CH2—CH3 on adjacent carbons

137. Draw a structural formula for each of the following alcohols. Indicate whether the alcohol is primary, secondary, or tertiary.

a. 2-propanol
b. 2-methyl-2-propanol
c. 4-isopropyl-2-heptanol
d. 2,3-dichloro-1-pentanol

138. Draw a structural formula for each of the following.

a. 3-methylpentanal
b. 3-methyl-2-pentanone
c. methyl phenyl ketone
d. 2-hydroxybutanal
e. propanal

139. How are carboxylic acids synthesized? Give an example of an organic acid and the molecule from which it is synthesized. What type of reaction is this?

140. Draw a structural formula for each of the following.

a. 3-methylbutanoic acid
b. 2-chlorobenzoic acid
c. hexanoic acid
d. acetic acid

141. Draw the structure of the monomer and the basic repeating unit for each of the following polymeric substances.

a. polyethylene
b. polyvinyl chloride
c. Teflon
d. polypropylene
e. polystyrene

All even-numbered Questions and Problems have answers in the back of this book and solutions in the Solutions Guide.

108. carbonyl

109. oxidation

110. carboxyl

111. esters, alcohol

112. addition

113. The general formula is C_nH_{2n+2}. Consider the following normal alkanes: each successive member differs from the previous by a —CH_2— unit:

CH_3—CH_3—CH_3—CH_2—CH_3
CH_3—CH_2—CH_2—CH_3
CH_3—CH_2—CH_2—CH_2—CH_3

114. Structures depend on student choices.

115. Structures depend on student choices.

116. (a) 2-chlorobutane; (b) 1,2-dibromoethane; (c) triiodomethane (common name: iodoform); (d) 2,3,4-trichloropentane; (e) 2,2-dichloro-4-isopropylheptane

117. Answer appears at the bottom of the page.

118. Answer appears at the bottom of the page.

119. (a) CH_3—CH_2Cl, CH_2Cl—CH_2Cl and various other chlorosubstituted compounds

(b) CH_3—CH_2—CH_2—CH_3

(c)
```
     CH3 H
     |   |
CH3—C—C—CH3
     |   |
     Br  Br
```

120. Answer appears at the bottom of the following page.

117.

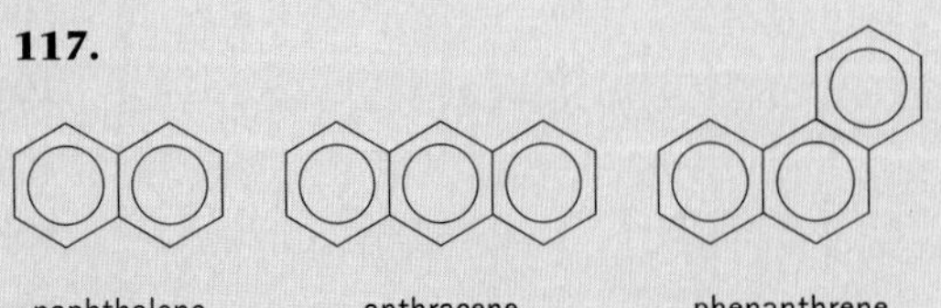

naphthalene anthracene phenanthrene

118.

(a)
```
CH3—CH—CH—CH2—CH2—CH2—CH3
    |   |
    CH3 CH3
```

(b)
```
                                 CH3
                                 |
CH3—CH2—CH2—CH2—CH2—CH—C—CH2—OH
                        |   |
                        Cl  CH3
```

(c)
```
CH3—CH2—CH2—CH2—C=CH2
                 |
                 Cl
```

(d) CH_3—CH_2—CH_2—$CH{=}CH$—CH_2—Cl

(e)

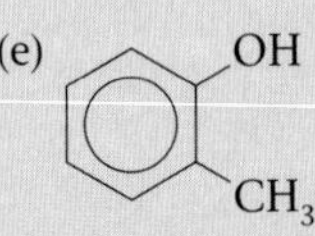

120.
primary $CH_3—CH_2—CH_2—CH_2—CH_2—CH_2—OH$;
secondary $CH_3—CH_2—CH_2—CH_2—\underset{\displaystyle OH}{\underset{|}{CH}}—CH_3$;
tertiary $CH_3—CH_2—\underset{\displaystyle OH}{\underset{|}{\overset{\displaystyle CH_3}{\overset{|}{C}}}}—CH_2—CH_3$
(there are other possibilities)

(Please refer to page A27 in this book for answers to Exercises 121–141.)

Chapter 21

Objectives

In this chapter, our objectives are for the students to:

SECTION 21.1

- Learn about proteins.

SECTION 21.2

- Understand the primary structure of proteins.

SECTION 21.3

- Understand the secondary structure of proteins.

SECTION 21.4

- Understand the tertiary structure of proteins.

SECTION 21.5

- Learn about various functions served by proteins.

SECTION 21.6

- Understand how enzymes work.

SECTION 21.7

- Understand the fundamental properties of carbohydrates.

SECTION 21.8

- Understand the fundamental nucleic acid structures.

SECTION 21.9

- Learn the four classes of lipids.

21 Biochemistry

The energy for exercise is furnished by chemical reactions in the body. *(John Blanding/The Boston Globe/Merlin-net.com)*

ChemWork Refined over ten years of use by thousands of students, **ChemWork** builds and enhances students' problems-solving skills. Online assignments function as a "personal instructor" to help students learn how to solve challenging problems and learn how to think like chemists. Annotations for **ChemWork** assignments are included at the beginning of the end-of-chapter review.

PowerLecture This 2-DVD package includes the Chemistry Multimedia Library, which contains animations, simulations, and movies for all chemistry subjects, organized by topic for lecture presentations. Annotations for **PowerLecture** are referenced in the margins throughout the Annotated Instructor's Edition.

OWL Sign in to OWL at **www.cengage.com/owl** to view tutorials and simulations, develop problem-solving skills, and complete online homework assigned by your professor.

Biochemistry, the study of the chemistry of living systems, is a vast and exciting field in which important discoveries about how life is maintained and how diseases occur are being made every day. In particular, there has been rapid growth in the understanding of how living cells manufacture and use the molecules necessary for life. This not only has been beneficial for detection and treatment of diseases but also has spawned a new field—**biotechnology,** which uses nature's "machinery" to synthesize desired substances. For example, insulin is a complex biomolecule that is used in the body to regulate the metabolism of sugars. People who have diabetes are deficient in natural insulin and must take insulin by injection or other means. In the past this insulin was obtained from animal tissues (particularly that of cows). However, our increased understanding of the biochemical processes of the cell has allowed us to "farm" insulin. We have learned to insert the "instructions" for making insulin into the cells of bacteria such as *Escherichia coli* so that as the bacteria grow they produce insulin that can then be harvested for use by diabetics. Many other products, including natural pesticides, are also being produced by the techniques of biotechnology.

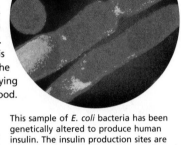

An understanding of biochemistry also allows our society to produce healthier processed foods. For example, the food industry is making great efforts to reduce the fat levels in food without destroying the good taste that fats bring to food.

Volker Steger/SPL/Photo Researchers, Inc.

This sample of *E. coli* bacteria has been genetically altered to produce human insulin. The insulin production sites are colored orange. The bacteria are cultured and pure human insulin is harvested from them.

We cannot hope to cover all the important aspects of this field in this chapter; we will concentrate here on the major types of biomolecules that support living organisms. First, however, we will survey the elements found in living systems and briefly describe the constitution of a cell.

At present, 30 elements are definitely known to be essential to human life. These **essential elements** are shown in color in Figure 21.1. The most abundant elements are hydrogen, carbon, nitrogen, and oxygen; sodium, magnesium, potassium, calcium, phosphorus, sulfur, and chlorine are also present in relatively large amounts. Although present only in trace amounts, the first-row transition metals are essential for the action of many enzymes (biologic catalysts). For example, zinc, one of the **trace elements,** is found in nearly 200 biologically important molecules. The functions of the essential elements are summarized in Table 21.1. In time, other elements probably will be found to be essential.

Life is organized around the functions of the **cell,** the smallest unit in living things that exhibits the properties normally associated with life, such as reproduction, metabolism, mutation, and sensitivity to external stimuli.

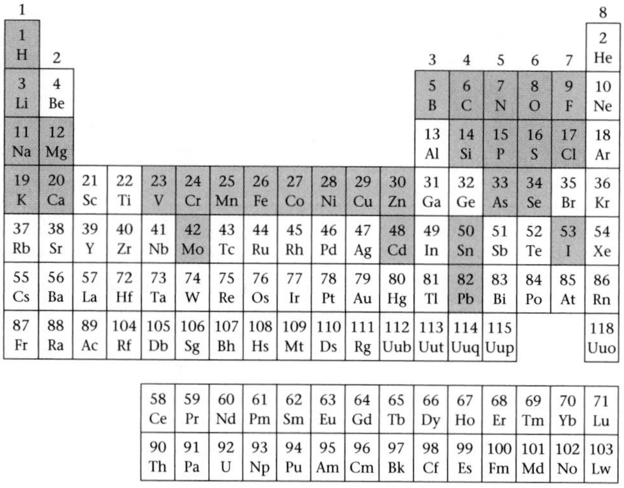

1	2											3	4	5	6	7	8
1 H																	2 He
3 Li	4 Be											5 B	6 C	7 N	8 O	9 F	10 Ne
11 Na	12 Mg											13 Al	14 Si	15 P	16 S	17 Cl	18 Ar
19 K	20 Ca	21 Sc	22 Ti	23 V	24 Cr	25 Mn	26 Fe	27 Co	28 Ni	29 Cu	30 Zn	31 Ga	32 Ge	33 As	34 Se	35 Br	36 Kr
37 Rb	38 Sr	39 Y	40 Zr	41 Nb	42 Mo	43 Tc	44 Ru	45 Rh	46 Pd	47 Ag	48 Cd	49 In	50 Sn	51 Sb	52 Te	53 I	54 Xe
55 Cs	56 Ba	57 La	72 Hf	73 Ta	74 W	75 Re	76 Os	77 Ir	78 Pt	79 Au	80 Hg	81 Tl	82 Pb	83 Bi	84 Po	85 At	86 Rn
87 Fr	88 Ra	89 Ac	104 Rf	105 Db	106 Sg	107 Bh	108 Hs	109 Mt	110 Ds	111 Rg	112 Uub	113 Uut	114 Uuq	115 Uup			118 Uuo

58 Ce	59 Pr	60 Nd	61 Pm	62 Sm	63 Eu	64 Gd	65 Tb	66 Dy	67 Ho	68 Er	69 Tm	70 Yb	71 Lu
90 Th	91 Pa	92 U	93 Np	94 Pu	95 Am	96 Cm	97 Bk	98 Cf	99 Es	100 Fm	101 Md	102 No	103 Lw

Figure 21.1 The chemical elements essential for life. Those most abundant in living systems are shown as purple. Nineteen elements, called the *trace elements,* are shown as green.

Table 21.1 Some Essential Elements and Their Major Functions

Element	Percent by Mass in the Human Body	Function
oxygen	65	in water and many organic compounds
carbon	18	in all organic compounds
hydrogen	10	in water and many inorganic and organic compounds
nitrogen	3	in both inorganic and organic compounds
calcium	1.5	in bone; essential to some enzymes and to muscle action
phosphorus	1.2	essential in cell membranes and to energy transfer in cells
potassium	0.2	cation in cell fluid
chlorine	0.2	anion inside and outside the cells
sulfur	0.2	in proteins
sodium	0.1	cation in cell fluid
magnesium	0.05	essential to some enzymes
iron	<0.05	in molecules that transport and store oxygen
zinc	<0.05	essential to many enzymes
cobalt	<0.05	found in vitamin B_{12}
iodine	<0.05	essential to thyroid hormones
fluorine	<0.01	in teeth and bones

As the fundamental building blocks of all living systems, aggregates of cells form tissues, which in turn are assembled into the organs that make up complex living systems. Therefore, to understand how life is maintained and reproduced, we must learn how cells operate on the molecular level. This is the main thrust of biochemistry.

690 Chapter 21 Biochemistry

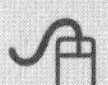

Test Bank: 1, 2

Section 21.1

TEACHING TIP

Table 21.1 gives mass percentages of elements and their functions. This is an excellent way to point out the importance of chemistry in everyday life.

21.1 Proteins

OBJECTIVE: To learn about proteins.

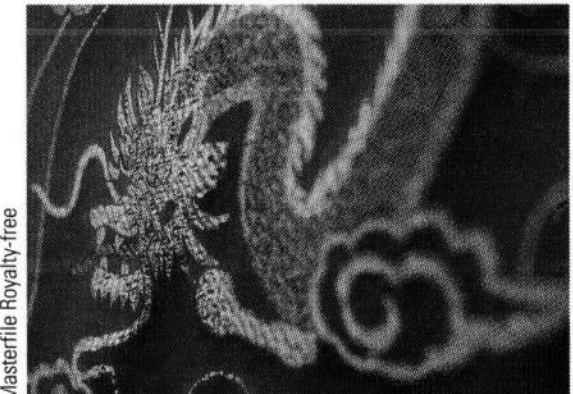

Masterfile Royalty-free

Silk is a naturally occurring polymer.

In Chapter 20 we saw that many useful synthetic materials are polymers. A great many natural materials are also polymers: starch, hair, silk and cotton fibers, and the cellulose in woody plants, to name only a few.

In this section we introduce a class of natural polymers, the **proteins,** which make up about 15% of our bodies and have molar masses that range from approximately 6000 to over 1,000,000 grams. Proteins have many functions in the human body. **Fibrous proteins** provide structural integrity and strength for many types of tissue and are the main components of muscle, hair, and cartilage. Other proteins, usually called **globular proteins** because of their roughly spherical shape, are the "worker" molecules of the body. These proteins transport and store oxygen and nutrients, act as catalysts for the thousands of reactions that make life possible, fight invasion of the body by foreign objects, participate in the body's many regulatory systems, and transport electrons in the complex process of metabolizing nutrients.

Test Bank: 3–5

Section 21.2

TEACHING TIPS

- This is an excellent place to review what causes a side group to be polar or nonpolar. Refer the students back to the ideas they learned in bonding, and work with them to determine why each of the side chains is classified as polar or nonpolar.
- The term *hydrophobic* is actually a misnomer. While the nonpolar side chains do not mix well with water, they do not repel the water. Water molecules are more attracted to other water molecules than to the nonpolar side chains.
- When students first begin to make peptide linkages, they often link the carboxyl group on one amino acid to the R group of the next. Be sure to work through several examples of the linkages with the students. It is helpful to mark the different parts of the amino acid (carboxyl, amine, R groups) with different colors so that students can more easily identify which groups should interact.

21.2 Primary Structure of Proteins

OBJECTIVE: To understand the primary structure of proteins.

The building blocks of all proteins are the **α-amino acids:**

α-Carbon

$$NH_2-\underset{\displaystyle R}{\overset{\displaystyle H}{C}}-C\begin{matrix}=O\\ -OH\end{matrix}$$

The R in this structure may represent H, CH_3, or more complex substituents. These molecules are called α-amino acids because the amino group ($-NH_2$) is always attached to the α-carbon, the one next to the carboxyl group ($-COOH$). The 20 amino acids most commonly found in proteins are shown in Figure 21.2.

At the pH in biologic fluids, the amino acids shown in Figure 21.2 exist in a different form, with the proton of the $-COOH$ group transferred to the $-NH_2$ group. For example, glycine would be in the form $H_3{}^+NCH_2COO^-$.

Note from Figure 21.2 that the amino acids are grouped into polar and nonpolar classes on the basis of the composition of the R groups, also called the **side chains.** Nonpolar side chains contain mostly carbon and hydrogen atoms; polar side chains contain nitrogen and oxygen atoms. This difference is important because polar side chains are *hydrophilic* (water-loving), but nonpolar side chains are *hydrophobic* (water-fearing). This greatly affects the three-dimensional structure of the resulting proteins, because they exist in aqueous media in living things.

The protein polymer is built by reactions between amino acids. For example, two amino acids can react as follows, forming a C—N bond with the elimination of water.

Peptide linkage

$$H_2N-\underset{\displaystyle R}{\overset{\displaystyle H}{C}}-C\begin{matrix}=O\\ -OH\end{matrix} + H-\underset{\displaystyle H}{N}-\underset{\displaystyle R'}{\overset{\displaystyle H}{C}}-C\begin{matrix}=O\\ -OH\end{matrix} \rightarrow H_2N-\underset{\displaystyle R}{\overset{\displaystyle H}{C}}-\overset{\displaystyle O}{\overset{\|}{C}}-\overset{\displaystyle H}{N}-\underset{\displaystyle R'}{\overset{\displaystyle H}{C}}-C\begin{matrix}=O\\ -OH\end{matrix} + H_2O$$

PowerLecture Animations:
Rotating Glycine and Leucine Molecules
Peptide Bonding between Glycine and Leucine Molecules

DEMONSTRATION

Use a set of children's pop beads to illustrate the primary structure of a protein. The different shapes of beads can be used to represent different amino acids. The pop connections can represent peptide linkages. You can have the students translate your primary structure into the three-letter-coded structure by assigning each bead a code sequence.

Nonpolar R Groups (hydrophobic)

Glycine (gly) **Alanine (ala)** **Proline (pro)** **Valine (val)**

Tryptophan (trp) **Isoleucine (ile)** **Methionine (met)** **Leucine (leu)** **Phenylalanine (phe)**

Polar R Groups (hydrophilic)

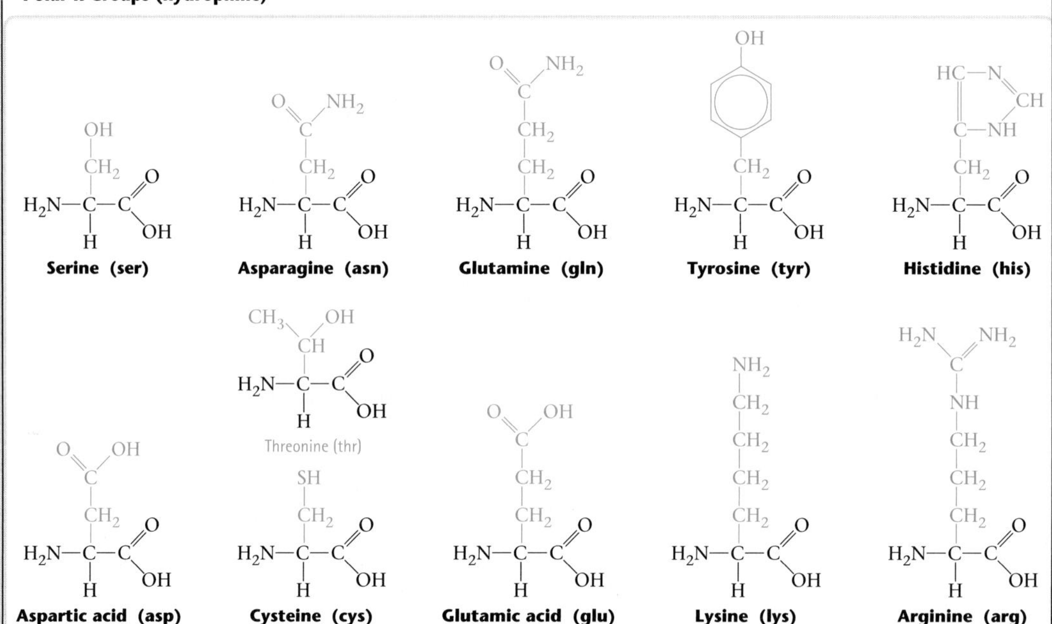

Figure 21.2
The 20 α-amino acids found in most proteins. The R group is shown in color.

The product shown on page 691 is called a **dipeptide.** The term *peptide* comes from the structure

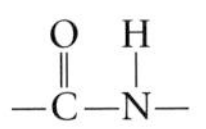

$$-\overset{\overset{\displaystyle O}{\|}}{C}-\overset{\overset{\displaystyle H}{|}}{N}-$$

which chemists call a **peptide linkage** or a peptide bond. The prefix *di-* indicates that two amino acids have been joined. Additional reactions lengthen the chain to produce a **polypeptide** and eventually a protein.

The 20 amino acids can be assembled in any order, which makes possible an enormous number of different proteins. This variety allows for the many types of proteins needed for the functions that organisms carry out.

The *order* or *sequence* of amino acids in the protein chain is called the **primary structure.** We indicate the primary structure by using three-letter codes for the amino acids (see Figure 21.2), where it is understood that the terminal carboxyl group is on the right and the terminal amino group is on the left. For example, one possible sequence for a tripeptide containing the amino acids lysine, alanine, and leucine is

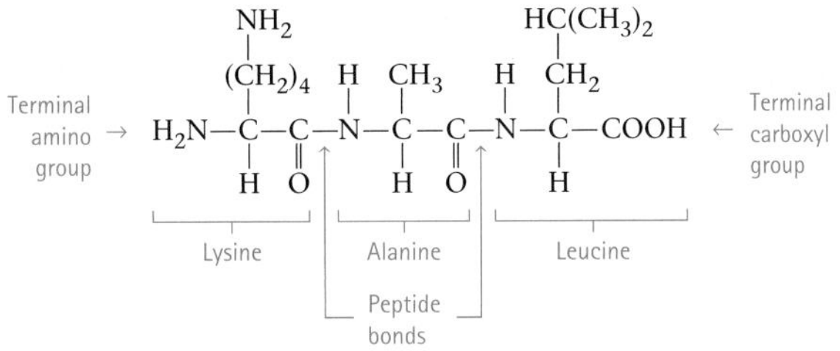

$$H_2N-\underset{\underset{\displaystyle H}{|}}{\overset{\overset{\displaystyle NH_2}{|}}{\overset{(CH_2)_4}{\overset{|}{C}}}}-\underset{\underset{\displaystyle O}{\|}}{C}-\overset{\overset{\displaystyle H}{|}}{N}-\underset{\underset{\displaystyle H}{|}}{\overset{\overset{\displaystyle CH_3}{|}}{C}}-\underset{\underset{\displaystyle O}{\|}}{C}-\overset{\overset{\displaystyle H}{|}}{N}-\underset{\underset{\displaystyle H}{|}}{\overset{\overset{\displaystyle HC(CH_3)_2}{|}}{\overset{CH_2}{\overset{|}{C}}}}-COOH$$

Terminal amino group → ; ← Terminal carboxyl group

Lysine | Alanine | Leucine

Peptide bonds

which is represented in the shorthand notation (three-letter codes) as

lys-ala-leu

EXAMPLE 21.1

Understanding Primary Structure

Write the sequences of all possible tripeptides composed of the amino acids tyrosine (tyr), histidine (his), and cysteine (cys).

SOLUTION

There are six possible sequences:

tyr-his-cys	his-tyr-cys	cys-tyr-his
tyr-cys-his	his-cys-tyr	cys-his-tyr ■

A striking example of the importance of the primary structure of polypeptides can be seen in the differences between *oxytocin* and *vasopressin.* Oxytocin is a hormone that triggers contraction of the uterus and milk secretion. Vasopressin raises blood pressure and regulates kidney function. Both these molecules are nine-unit polypeptides, and they differ by only two amino acids (Figure 21.3); yet they have completely different functions in the human body.

cys-tyr-ile-gin-asn-cys-pro-leu-gly

a

cys-tyr-phe-gin-asn-cys-pro-arg-gly

b

Figure 21.3

The amino acid sequences in a oxytocin and b vasopressin. The differing amino acids are enclosed in boxes.

Additional Examples

Example 21.1

Write the sequences of all possible tripeptides composed of the amino acids serine (ser), glutamic acid (glu), and arginine (arg).

ser-glu-arg	glu-arg-ser
ser-arg-glu	glu-ser-arg
arg-ser-glu	
arg-glu-ser	

Test Bank: 6, 7

Section 21.3

TEACHING TIP

An excellent model of secondary structure is the coiled cord from a telephone. Another possibility is to use children's pop beads and twist them into a helix to represent secondary structure while showing the primary structure by the order of the pop beads. A folded piece of paper can represent the pleated-sheet secondary structure.

PowerLecture Video: Interview: Linus Pauling

21.3 Secondary Structure of Proteins

OBJECTIVE: To understand the secondary structure of proteins.

So far we have considered the primary structure of proteins—the order of amino acids in the chain (Figure 21.4a). A second level of structure in proteins is the arrangement in space of the chain of the long molecule. This is called the **secondary structure** of the protein (Figure 21.4b).

One common type of secondary structure resembles a spiral staircase. This spiral structure is called an **α-helix** (Figure 21.5). A spiral-like secondary structure gives the protein elasticity (springiness) and is found in the fibrous proteins in wool, hair, and tendons. Another type of secondary structure involves joining several different protein chains in an arrangement called a **pleated sheet,** as shown in Figure 21.6. Silk has this arrangement of proteins, making its fibers flexible but very strong and resistant to stretching. The pleated sheet is also found in muscle fibers.

As you might imagine, a molecule as large as a protein has a great deal of flexibility and can assume a variety of overall shapes. The function the protein is to serve influences the specific shape that it will have. For long, thin structures such as hair, wool and silk fibers, and tendons, an elongated shape is required. This may involve an α-helical secondary structure, as found in the protein α-keratin in hair and wool or in the collagen that occurs in tendons (Figure 21.7a), or it may involve a pleated-sheet secondary

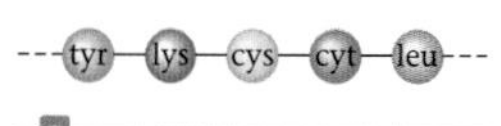

a

The primary structure of a protein describes the order of the amino acids in the chain. One example is shown.

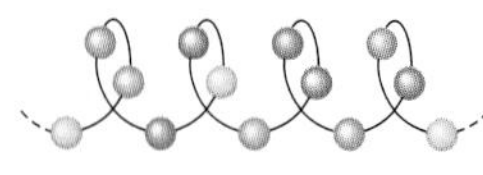

b

The secondary structure of a protein describes the arrangement of the chain in space. A spiral (helical) arrangement of the protein chain is shown.

Figure 21.4

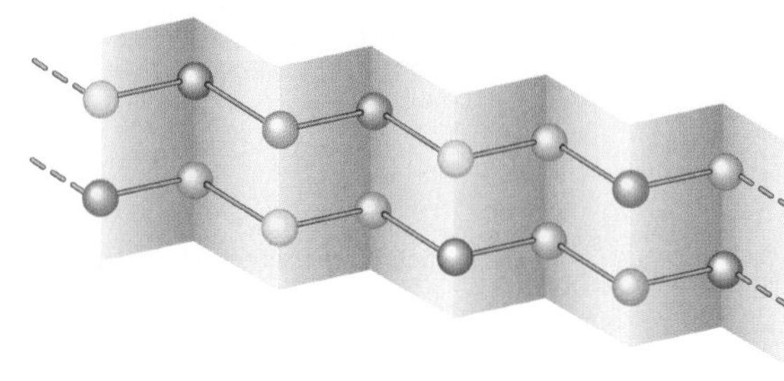

Figure 21.6

Two protein chains bound together in the pleated-sheet secondary structure. Each sphere represents an amino acid.

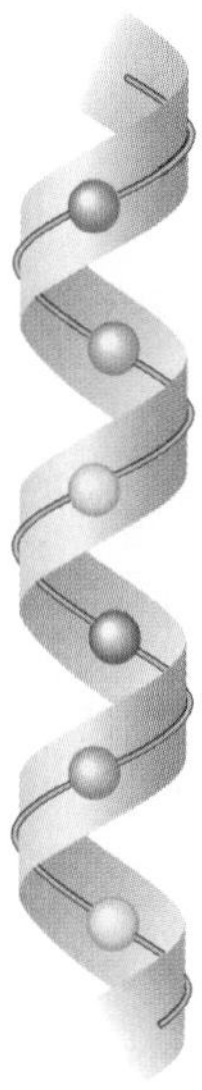

Figure 21.5

One type of secondary protein structure is like a spiral staircase and is called the α-helix. The circles represent individual amino acids.

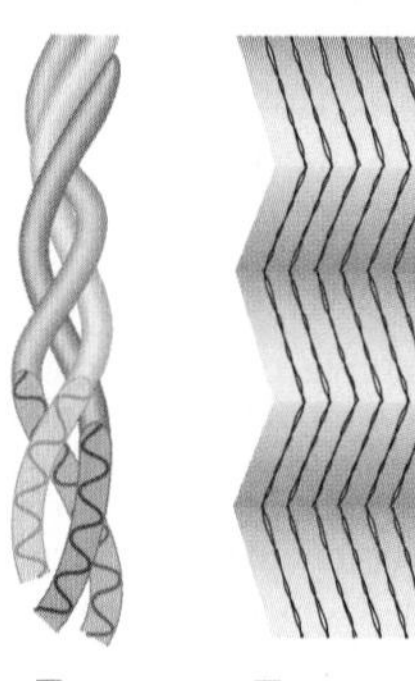

Figure 21.7

a Collagen, a protein found in tendons, consists of three protein chains (each with an α-helical structure) twisted together to form a superhelix. The result is a long, relatively narrow protein. b Many proteins are bound together in the pleated-sheet arrangement to form the elongated protein found in silk fibers.

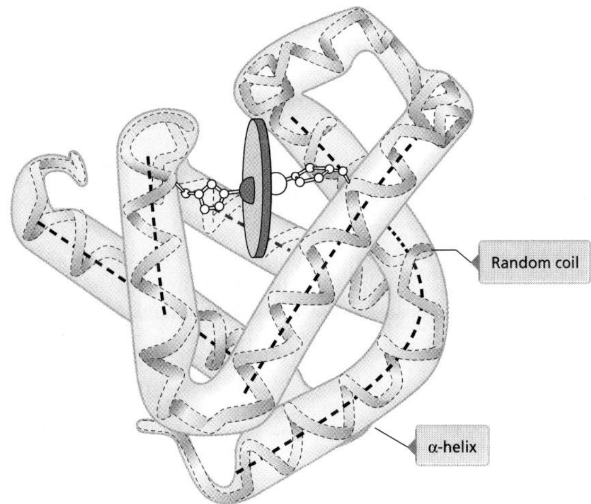

Figure 21.8
The protein myoglobin. Note that the secondary structure is basically α-helical except at the bends. The tertiary structure is globular.

structure, as found in silk (Figure 21.7b). Many of the proteins in the body that have nonstructural functions (such as serving as enzymes) are globular. One is myoglobin (Figure 21.8), which absorbs an O_2 molecule and stores it for use by the cells as it is needed. Note that the secondary structure of myoglobin is basically α-helical. However, in the areas where the chain bends to give the protein its compact globular structure, the α-helix breaks down so that the protein can "turn the corner."

21.4 Tertiary Structure of Proteins

Section 21.4

OBJECTIVE: To understand the tertiary structure of proteins.

The overall shape of the protein, long and narrow or globular, is called its **tertiary structure.** To make sure the difference between secondary and tertiary structure is clear, examine Figure 21.8 again. The secondary structure of the myoglobin protein is helical except in the regions where it bends back on itself to give the overall compact (globular) tertiary structure. If the bends did not occur, the tertiary structure would be like a long tube (tubular). In both tertiary arrangements (globular and tubular), the secondary structure of the protein is basically helical.

The amino acid *cysteine* (cys) plays a special role in stabilizing the tertiary structure of many proteins because the —SH groups on two cysteines can react to form an S—S bond called a **disulfide linkage.**

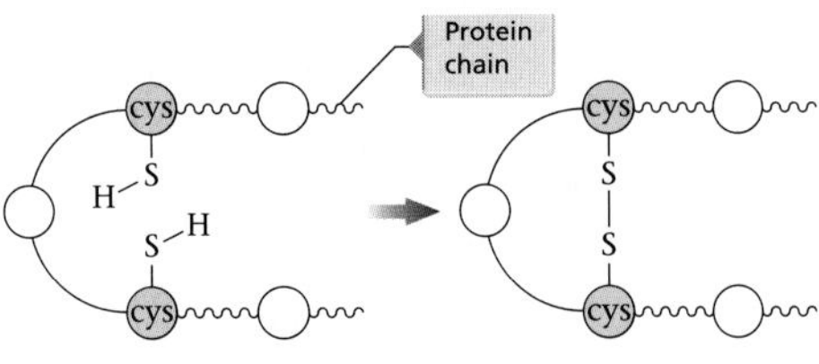

DEMONSTRATION

One way to illustrate tertiary structure is to use a coiled phone cord or a Slinky. The coils represent the secondary structure of the protein, which can be bent, folded, or coiled to illustrate the tertiary structure.

Figure 21.9 on page 696 shows how a permanent wave causes hair to curl. This is an interesting way to introduce denaturation of proteins and the disruption of protein function that can result. The formation of disulfide links demonstrates that the R groups can play an active role in protein structure (other than primary structure).

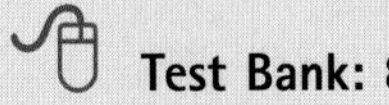
Test Bank: 8

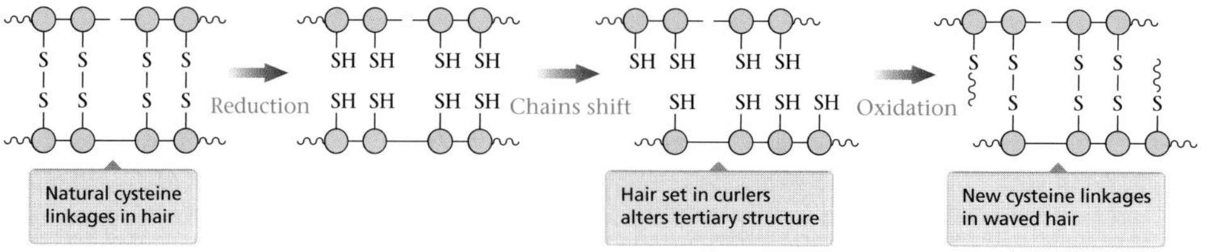

Reduction — Chains shift — Oxidation

Natural cysteine linkages in hair

Hair set in curlers alters tertiary structure

New cysteine linkages in waved hair

Figure 21.9
The permanent waving of hair.

The formation of a disulfide linkage can fasten together two parts of a protein chain to form and hold a bend in the chain, for example. A practical application of the chemistry of disulfide bonds is the permanent waving of hair (Figure 21.9). The S—S linkages in the protein of hair are broken by treatment with a reducing agent. Next the hair is set in curlers to change the tertiary protein structure to the desired shape. Then treatment with an oxidizing agent causes new S—S bonds to form, which make the hair protein retain the new structure.

Test Bank: 9–13

Section 21.5

21.5 Functions of Proteins

OBJECTIVE: To learn about various functions served by proteins.

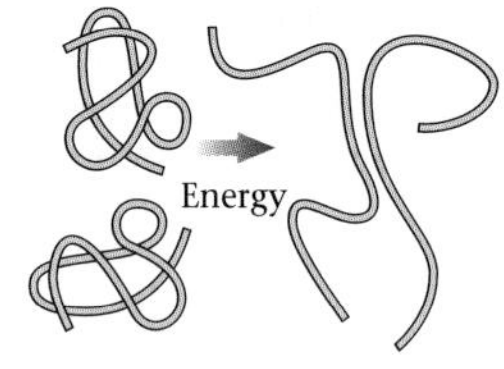

Figure 21.10
A schematic representation of the thermal denaturation of a protein.

The three-dimensional structure of a protein is crucial to its function. The process of breaking down this structure is called **denaturation** (Figure 21.10). For example, heat causes the denaturation of egg proteins when an egg is cooked. Any source of energy can cause denaturation of proteins and is thus potentially dangerous to living organisms. For example, ultraviolet radiation, X-ray radiation, or nuclear radioactivity can disrupt protein structure, which may lead to cancer or genetic damage. The metals lead and mercury, which have a very high affinity for sulfur, cause protein denaturation by disrupting disulfide bonds.

The tremendous variability in the several levels of protein structure allows proteins to be tailored specifically to serve a wide range of functions, some of which are given in Table 21.2.

DEMONSTRATION

You can easily demonstrate the denaturation of a protein by cooking an egg on a hotplate. The white is denatured as you cook it. You can produce the same result by adding sulfuric acid to the egg, but this renders it useless as food. You can denature milk protein by adding dilute acetic acid to nonfat dry milk dissolved in water. Students are familiar with the results of these reactions but usually do not associate them with chemistry.

Section 21.6

21.6 Enzymes

OBJECTIVE: To understand how enzymes work.

Enzymes are proteins that catalyze specific biologic reactions. Without the several hundred enzymes now known, life would be impossible. Almost all the critical biochemical reactions would occur far too slowly at the temperatures at which life exists. Enzymes are impressive for their tremendous efficiency (they are typically 1 to 10 million times as efficient as inorganic catalysts) and their incredible selectivity (an enzyme "ignores" the thousands of molecules in body fluids that are not involved in the reaction it catalyzes).

Although the mechanisms of enzyme activity are complex and not fully understood in most cases, a simple theory called the **lock-and-key model** (Figure 21.11) seems to fit many enzymes. This model postulates that the shapes of the reacting molecule (the **substrate**) and the enzyme are such that they fit together much as a key fits a specific lock. The substrate

An enzyme often changes shape slightly as the substrate is bound. This "clamps" the substrate into place.

TEACHING TIP

Use drawings to illustrate the lock-and-key model. Show that potential substrates will not react if they do not fit the active site.

Table 21.2 Common Functions of Proteins

Function	Comment/Example
Structure	Proteins provide the strength of tendons, bones, and skin. Cartilage, hair, wool, fingernails, and claws are mainly protein. Viruses have an outer layer of protein.
Movement	Proteins are the major components of muscles and are directly responsible for the ability of muscles to contract. The swimming of sperm results from the contraction of protein filaments in their tails.
Catalysis	Nearly all chemical reactions in living organisms are catalyzed by enzymes, which are almost always proteins.
Transport	Oxygen is carried from the lungs to tissues by the protein hemoglobin in red blood cells.
Storage	The protein *ferritin* stores iron in the liver, spleen, and bone marrow.
Energy transformation	Cytochromes are proteins found in all cells. They extract energy from food molecules by transferring electrons in a series of oxidation–reduction reactions.
Protection	*Antibodies* are special proteins that are synthesized in response to foreign substances and cells, such as bacterial cells. They then bind to those substances or cells and provide us with immunity to various diseases. Interferon, a small protein made and released by cells when they are exposed to a virus, protects other cells against viral infection. Blood-clotting proteins protect against bleeding (hemorrhage).
Control	Many *hormones* are proteins produced in the body that have specific effects on the activity of certain organs.
Buffering	Because proteins contain both acidic and basic groups on their side chains, they can neutralize both acids and bases and thus provide buffering for blood and tissues.

and enzyme attach to each other in such a way that the part of the substrate where the reaction is to occur occupies the **active site** of the enzyme. After the reaction occurs, the products are liberated, and the enzyme is ready for a new substrate. We can represent enzyme catalysis by the following steps:

Step 1 The enzyme E and the substrate S come together.

$$E + S \rightleftharpoons E \cdot S$$

Step 2 The reaction occurs to give the product P, which is released from the enzyme.

$$E \cdot S \rightarrow E + P$$

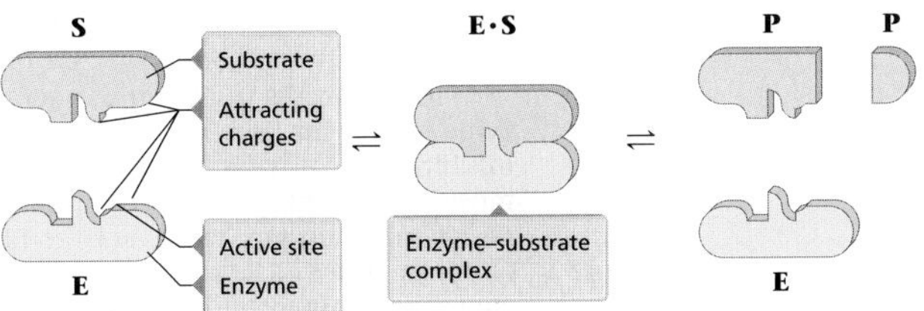

Figure 21.11 Schematic diagram of the lock-and-key model of the functioning of an enzyme.

21.6 Enzymes 697

CHEMISTRY *IN* FOCUS

Urine Farming

Nature is a very good chemist—organisms make hundreds of complex chemicals every second to survive. The rapidly expanding science of biotechnology is learning more every day about how to use natural chemical pathways to make valuable molecules. For example, insulin for diabetics is now made almost exclusively by "farming" genetically altered *Escherichia coli* or yeast.

Turning livestock into four-footed pharmaceutical factories has seemed an attractive option ever since we learned to carry out "genetic engineering." In fact, a great deal of effort has been expended on creating cows, sheep, and goats that are genetically modified to produce useful human proteins that are secreted into the animals' milk, from which they can then be harvested. None of these proteins has yet reached the market—tests are now under way to check their efficacy and safety—but a blood-clotting agent, antithrombin III, developed by Genzyme Transgenics Corporation of Framingham, Massachusetts, is close to commercial application. Creating a transgenic animal is expensive (costing approximately $60,000), but then standard breeding techniques can lead to an entire herd of animals programmed to produce commercially interesting molecules.

As a medium, milk has some disadvantages. It is produced only by mature females and contains a wide variety of proteins that complicate the purification process to obtain the desired product. Urine may be a better alternative. It contains fewer natural proteins and is produced at an early age by both male and female animals. Robert J. Wall and his colleagues at the U.S. Department of Agriculture in Beltsville, Maryland, have developed transgenic mice that produce human growth hormone in the walls of their bladders. For obvious reasons, mice are not ideal for large-scale production of chemicals, but Wall's experiments nevertheless show that the concept works. At present, it is too early to know whether urine farming will prove feasible. Yields from the bladder are about 10,000 times lower than those from the mammary glands. In addition, collecting urine from farm animals could prove to be a very tricky business.

Courtesy, Genzyme Transgenics Corporation

A New Zealand goat, one of the animals used for urine farming.

After the product is released, the enzyme is free to engage another substrate. Because this process occurs so rapidly, only a tiny amount of enzyme is required.

In some cases, a substance other than the substrate can bind to the enzyme's active site. When this occurs, the enzyme is said to be *inhibited*. If the inhibition is permanent, the enzyme is said to be inactivated. Some of the most powerful toxins act by inhibiting, or inactivating, key enzymes.

Because enzymes are crucial to life and because we hope to learn how to mimic their efficiency in our industrial catalysts, the study of enzymes occupies a prominent place in chemical research.

21.7 Carbohydrates

OBJECTIVE: To understand the fundamental properties of carbohydrates.

The **carbohydrates** are another class of biologically important molecules. Carbohydrates serve as food sources for most organisms and as structural materials for plants. Because many carbohydrates have the empirical formula CH_2O, it was believed originally that these substances were hydrates of carbon ($C{\cdot}H_2O$), which accounts for their name.

Like proteins, carbohydrates occur in almost bewildering varieties. Many of the most important carbohydrates are polymers—large molecules constructed by hooking together many smaller molecules. We have seen that proteins are polymers constructed from amino acids. The polymeric carbohydrates are constructed from molecules called **simple sugars** or, more precisely, **monosaccharides.** Monosaccharides are aldehydes or ketones that contain several hydroxyl (—OH) substituents. An example of a monosaccharide is fructose, with the structure

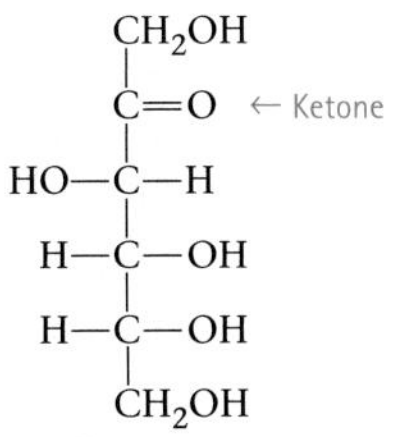

```
      CH2OH
       |
       C=O   ← Ketone
       |
  HO—C—H
       |
   H—C—OH
       |
   H—C—OH
       |
      CH2OH
```

Fructose

Fructose is a sugar found in honey and fruits. Monosaccharides can have various numbers of carbon atoms, and we name them according to the number of carbon atoms they contain by adding prefixes to the root *-ose*. The general names of monosaccharides are shown in Table 21.3. Notice that fructose is a ketone with six carbon atoms and five —OH substituents. Fructose is a member of the hexose family, where the prefix *hex-* means six.

The most important monosaccharides found in living organisms are pentoses and hexoses. The most common pentoses and hexoses are shown in Table 21.4.

USDA

Bread, a carbohydrate food source.

Mitch Hrdlicka/PhotoDisc/Getty Images

Fruit, a dietary source of fructose.

Test Bank: 14, 18, 20

Section 21.7

TEACHING TIPS

- Use glucose and fructose to compare the structures of common monosaccharides. Both have six carbons, but glucose has an aldehyde functional group on carbon 1, whereas fructose has a ketone on carbon 2. Both have —OH groups on the remaining carbons.
- It is helpful to illustrate how a sugar cyclizes by using a model. Build a model of glucose, and then carefully close the ring, showing the students what happens as you proceed.
- Be sure to point out to students that in glucose the aldehyde group reacts to form the ring, whereas in fructose the ketone groups react to form the ring. This changes the number of atoms in the ring for the two sugars.
- Students have difficulty seeing how starch and cellulose form from glucose. You will need to mark the molecules and number the carbons to show them that each time an —OH from carbon 1 links with an —OH from carbon 4.

Lecture Demonstration: 23.6

Table 21.3 The General Names of Monosaccharides

Number of Carbon Atoms	Prefix	General Name of Sugar
3	*tri-*	triose
4	*tetr-*	tetrose
5	*pent-*	pentose
6	*hex-*	hexose
7	*hept-*	heptose
8	*oct-*	octose
9	*non-*	nonose

Table 21.4 Some Important Monosaccharides

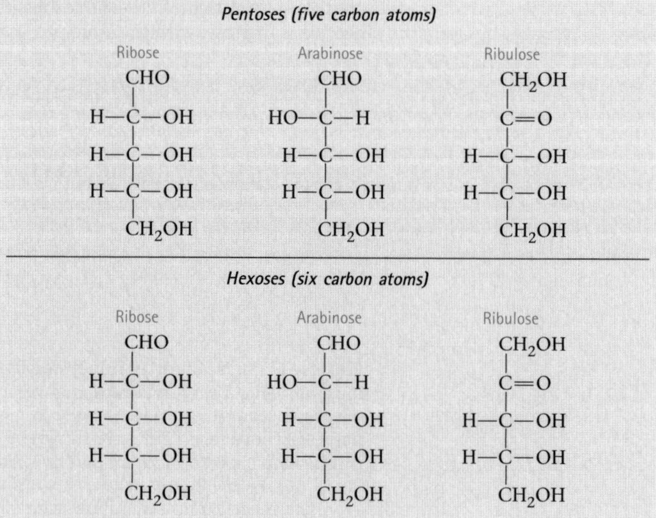

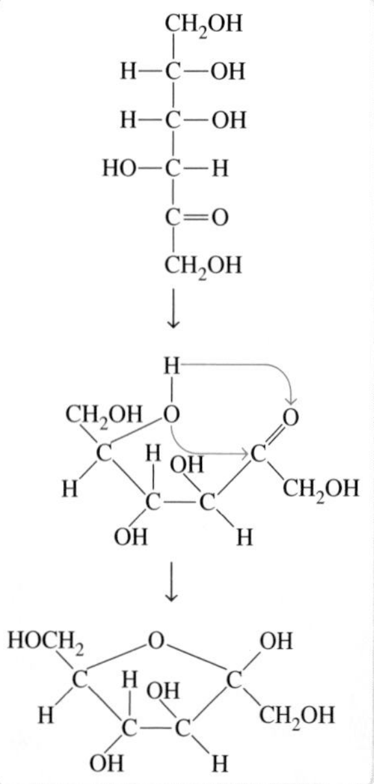

Pentoses (five carbon atoms)

Ribose	Arabinose	Ribulose
CHO	CHO	CH_2OH
H—C—OH	HO—C—H	C=O
H—C—OH	H—C—OH	H—C—OH
H—C—OH	H—C—OH	H—C—OH
CH_2OH	CH_2OH	CH_2OH

Hexoses (six carbon atoms)

Ribose	Arabinose	Ribulose
CHO	CHO	CH_2OH
H—C—OH	HO—C—H	C=O
H—C—OH	H—C—OH	H—C—OH
H—C—OH	H—C—OH	H—C—OH
CH_2OH	CH_2OH	CH_2OH

CH_2OH
H—C—OH
H—C—OH
HO—C—H
C=O
CH_2OH
↓
H, CH_2OH, O, O, C, H, OH, C, H, CH_2OH, C—C, OH, H
↓
$HOCH_2$, O, OH, C, H, OH, C, H, CH_2OH, C—C, OH, H

Figure 21.12
The formation of a ring structure for fructose.

Lecture Demonstration: 23.7

Although we have so far represented the monosaccharides as straight-chain molecules, they usually form ring structures in aqueous solution. Figure 21.12 shows how the ring forms for fructose. Note that a new bond is formed between the oxygen of a hydroxyl group and the carbon of the ketone group. In the cyclic form, fructose is a five-membered ring containing a C—O—C bond. Glucose, a hexose that is an aldehyde, forms a six-membered ring structure. The six-membered glucose ring is shown in Figure 21.13a. Note that the ring is nonplanar.

More complex carbohydrates are formed by the combining of monosaccharides. For example, two monosaccharides can combine to form a **disaccharide. Sucrose,** common table sugar, is a disaccharide formed from glucose and fructose by elimination of water to form a C—O—C bond between the rings that is called a **glycoside linkage** (Figure 21.13c). When sucrose is consumed in food, this reaction is reversed (the glycoside bond is broken). An enzyme in saliva catalyzes the breakdown of sucrose into its two monosaccharides.

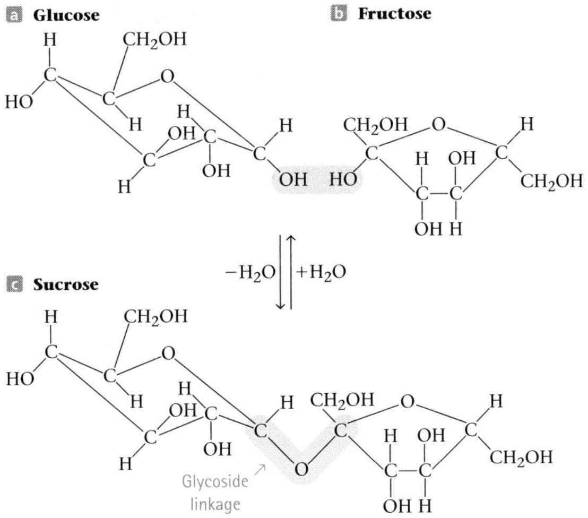

a Glucose

b Fructose

$-H_2O$ / $+H_2O$

c Sucrose

Glycoside linkage

Figure 21.13

Sucrose (c) is a disaccharide formed from glucose (a) and fructose (b).

Large polymers containing many monosaccharide units are called **polysaccharides** and can form when each ring forms two glycoside linkages, as shown in Figure 21.14. Three of the most important of these polymers are starch, cellulose, and glycogen. All these substances are polymers of glucose; they differ in the way the glucose rings are linked together.

Starch (Figure 21.14) is the carbohydrate reservoir in plants. It is the form in which glucose is stored by the plant for later use as cellular fuel—both by the plants themselves and by organisms that eat plants.

Cellulose, the major structural component of woody plants and natural fibers such as cotton, is also a polymer of glucose. However, in cellulose the way in which the glucose rings are linked is different from the way they are linked in starch. This difference in linkage has very important consequences. The human digestive system contains enzymes that can catalyze breakage of the glycoside bonds between the glucose molecules in starch. These enzymes are *not* effective on the glycoside bonds of cellulose, however, presumably because the different structure causes a poor fit between the enzyme's active site and the carbohydrate. Interestingly, the enzymes necessary to cleave the glycoside linkages in cellulose are found in bacteria that exist in the digestive tracts of termites, cows, deer, and many other animals. Therefore, unlike humans, these animals can derive nutrition from the cellulose in wood, hay, and other similar substances.

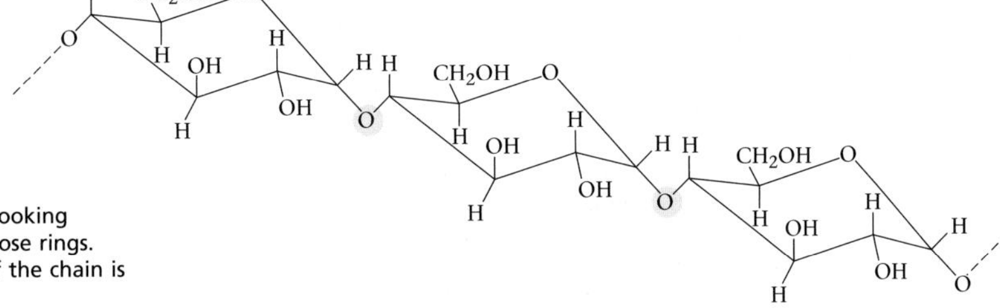

Figure 21.14

Starch is made by hooking together many glucose rings. Only a small part of the chain is shown here.

21.7 Carbohydrates 701

Test Bank: 15, 16, 21, 22

Section 21.8

TEACHING TIPS

- This is an excellent link to previous biology courses. The information presented here is much more detailed than students will have seen previously.
- Students should be able to determine that there are both differences and similarities between DNA and RNA. You may want to summarize these in a table for the students.

CHEMISTRY IN FOCUS

Great Expectations? The Chemistry of Placebos

Scientists have been intrigued by the "placebo effect" for more than 50 years. For example, a patient complaining of a pain is given a placebo (an inactive substance such as a sugar pill) but told it is really a drug to relieve the pain. In about one-third of the cases studied over many decades, the patient reports that the pain has gone away. But how does the placebo, which has no inherent medicinal value, relieve the pain? The first explanations had more to do with psychology than with chemistry. The most common explanation is that a patient feels better because the patient *expects* to feel better.

Recent studies, however, suggest there is chemistry involved in the placebo effect—specifically, the actions of endorphins. Endorphins, which were discovered in 1975, are neurotransmitters in the brain that are released when a person encounters stress. These endorphins have a pain-relieving quality much like codeine and morphine.

Researchers from the University of Michigan have found that the placebo effect correlates with an increase in endorphins being released from the brain. In their study, they injected highly concentrated saltwater solutions into the jaws of 14 healthy volunteers to produce pain. As this occurred, the brains of the subjects were scanned. During these scans the men rated their pain on a scale from 0 to 100, and were told when they would be given pain relief.

The brain scans revealed that the endorphin system was activated after the subjects were told that pain relief was coming and the placebo was given. The subjects responded to being told that pain relief was imminent by getting their bodies to release a natural pain reliever. Different studies have supported the link between the placebo effect and endorphin release by showing that when a patient who reports less pain due to a placebo is given naloxone (a drug that blocks endorphins), that person will report the reappearance of pain.

The next time someone tells you that pain is "all in your mind," you can counter by stating that chemistry has a lot to do with pain relief.

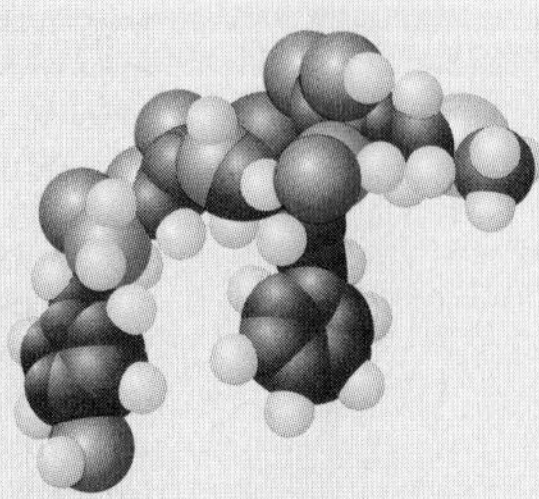

The structure of an endorphin molecule.

Glycogen is the main carbohydrate reservoir in animals. For example, it is found in muscles, where it can be broken down into glucose units when energy is required for physical activity.

21.8 Nucleic Acids

OBJECTIVE: To understand the fundamental nucleic acid structures.

Life is possible only because each cell, when it divides, can transmit the vital information about what it is to the next generation of cells. It has been known for a long time that this process involves the chromosomes in the nucleus of the cell. Only since 1953, however, have scientists understood the molecular basis of this intriguing cellular "talent."

Note that the prefix *de-* refers to the absence of the substance that follows. Thus deoxyribose means ribose with a missing oxygen (see Figure 21.15).

The substance that stores and transmits the genetic information is a polymer called **deoxyribonucleic acid (DNA),** a huge molecule with a molar mass as high as several billion grams. Together with other similar nucleic acids called the **ribonucleic acids (RNA),** DNA carries the information needed for the synthesis of the various proteins the cell requires to carry out its life functions. The RNA molecules, which are found in the cytoplasm outside the cell nucleus, are much smaller than DNA polymers, with molar mass values of only 20,000 to 40,000 grams.

Both DNA and RNA are polymers—they are constructed by the hooking together of many smaller units. The fundamental unit in these polymers is called a **nucleotide.** Each nucleotide in turn has three parts:

1. *A nitrogen-containing organic base*
2. *A five-carbon sugar*
3. *A phosphate group*

A nucleotide can be represented as follows:

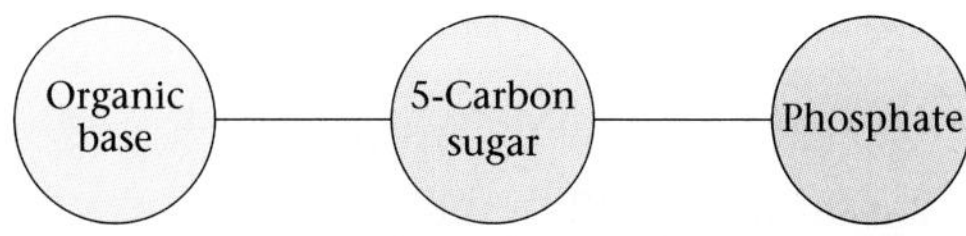

Figure 21.15
The structure of the pentoses (top) deoxyribose and (bottom) ribose. Deoxyribose is the sugar molecule present in DNA; ribose is found in RNA. The difference in these sugars is the substitution, in ribose, of an OH for one H in deoxyribose (shown in color).

In the DNA polymer, the five-carbon sugar is deoxyribose (Figure 21.15 top); in the RNA polymer, it is ribose (Figure 21.15 bottom). This difference in the sugar molecules present in the polymers is responsible for the names DNA (deoxyribonucleic acid) and RNA (ribonucleic acid).

The organic base molecules in the nucleotides of DNA and RNA are shown in Figure 21.16. Notice that some of these bases are found only in DNA, some are found only in RNA, and some are found in both. The formation of a specific nucleotide containing the base adenine and the sugar ribose is shown in Figure 21.17. To form the DNA and RNA polymers, the nucleotides are hooked together. DNA polymers can contain up to a *billion* nucleotide units. Figure 21.18 shows a small portion of a DNA chain.

The key to DNA's functioning is its *double-helical structure with complementary bases on the two strands.* Complementary bases form hydrogen bonds to each other, as shown in Figure 21.19. Note that the structures of cytosine and guanine make them perfect partners (complementary) for hydrogen bonding and that they are *always* found as pairs on the two strands of DNA. Thymine and adenine form similar hydrogen-bonding pairs.

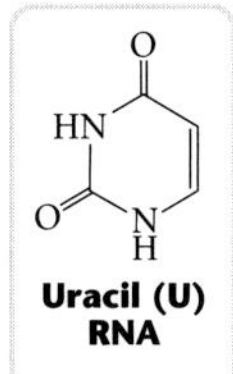

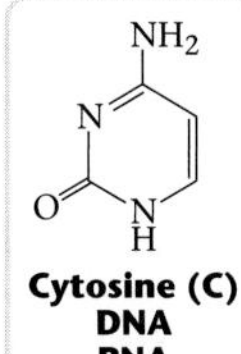

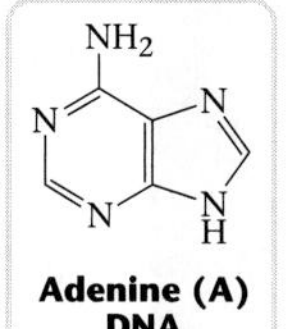

Guanine (G)
DNA
RNA

Figure 21.16
The organic bases found in DNA and RNA. Note that uracil is found only in RNA and that thymine is found only in DNA.

TEACHING TIP

You can use the analogy of a ladder to help students understand the structure of DNA. The sides of the ladder represent the alternating sugar and phosphate groups, and the rungs of the ladder represent the base pairs that are hydrogen-bonded together.

Adenine + Ribose → Adenosine + H_2O

Phosphoric acid + Adenosine → Adenosine 5-phosphoric acid + H_2O

Phosphate — Ribose — Base

Figure 21.17

(Top) Adenosine is formed by the reaction of adenine and ribose. (Bottom) The reaction of phosphoric acid with adenosine to form the ester adenosine 5-phosphoric acid, a nucleotide. (At biologic pH, the phosphoric acid would not be fully protonated as is shown here.)

A molecular model of part of the DNA structure.

There is much evidence to suggest that the two strands of DNA unwind during cell division and that new complementary strands are constructed on the unraveled strands (Figure 21.20). Because the bases on the strands always pair in the same way—cytosine with guanine and thymine with adenine—each unraveled strand serves as a template for attaching each complementary base (along with the rest of its nucleotide). This process results in two new double-helix DNA structures that are identical to the original one. Each new double strand contains one strand from the original DNA double helix and one newly synthesized strand. This replication of DNA makes possible the transmission of genetic information when cells divide.

DNA and Protein Synthesis

Besides replication, the other major function of DNA is **protein synthesis.** The proteins consumed by an organism in its food are typically not the specific proteins that organism needs to maintain its existence. The nutrient proteins are broken down into their constituent amino acids, which are then used to construct those proteins that the organism needs. The information for constructing each protein needed by a particular organism is stored in that organism's DNA. A given segment of the DNA, called a **gene,** contains the code for a specific protein. This code for the primary structure of

PowerLecture Animation: Rotating DNA Molecule

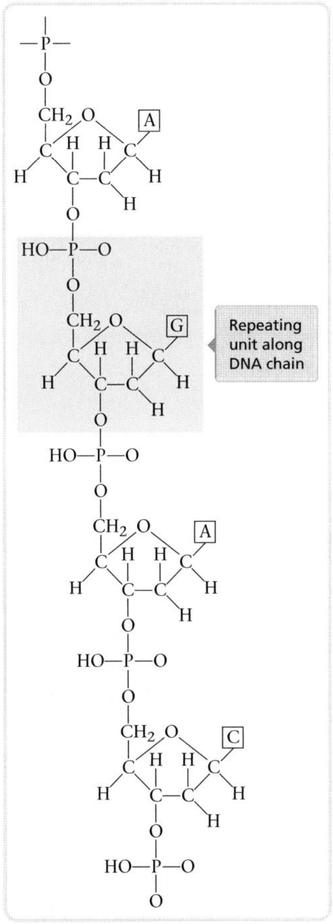

Repeating unit along DNA chain

Figure 21.18

A portion of a typical nucleic acid chain, half the DNA double helix shown in Figure 21.19.

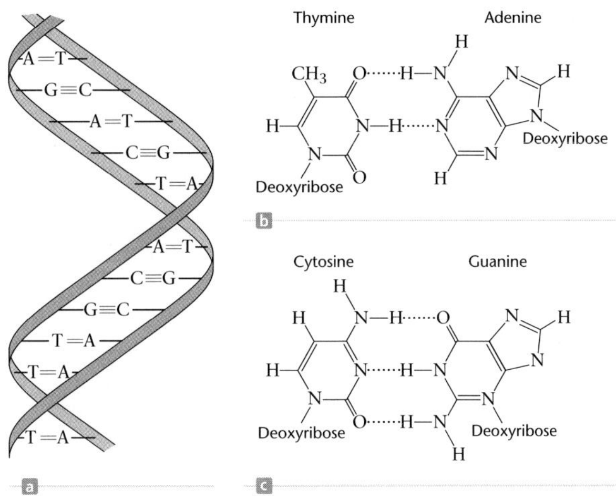

Figure 21.19

a The DNA double helix contains two sugar–phosphate backbones with the bases from the two strands hydrogen-bonded to each other. The b thymine–adenine and c cytosine–guanine pairs show complementarity. The hydrogen-bonding interactions are shown by dotted lines.

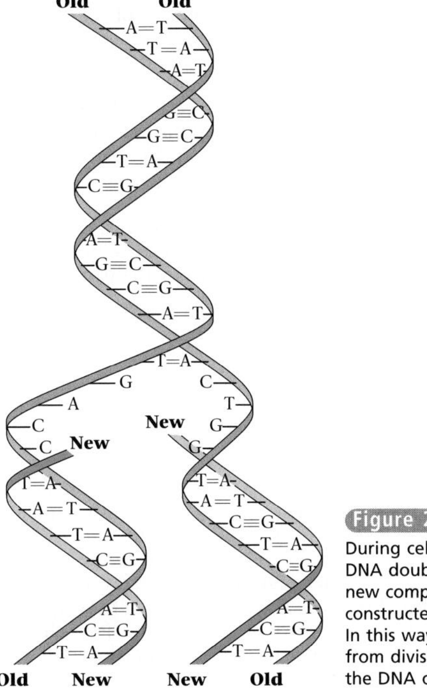

Figure 21.20

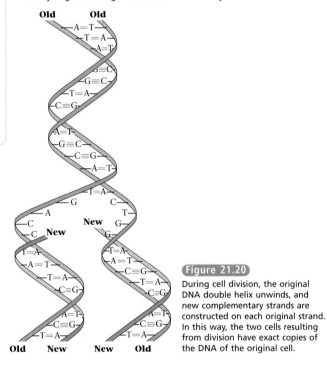

During cell division, the original DNA double helix unwinds, and new complementary strands are constructed on each original strand. In this way, the two cells resulting from division have exact copies of the DNA of the original cell.

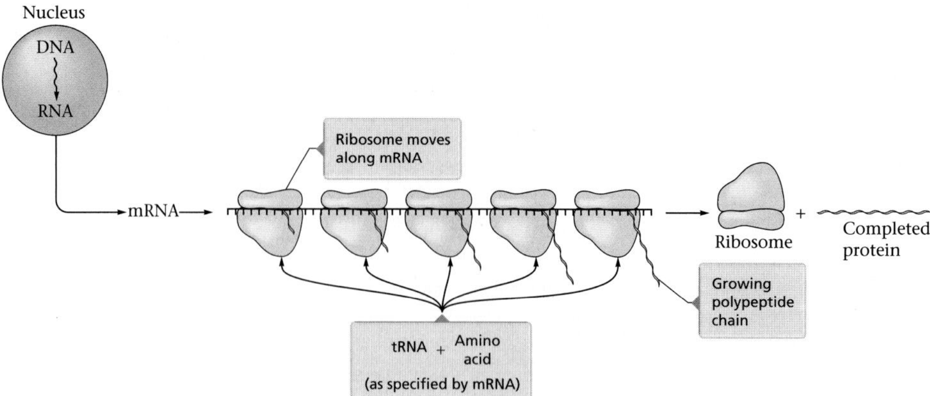

Figure 21.21
The mRNA molecule, constructed from a specific gene on the DNA, is used as the pattern for construction of a given protein with the assistance of ribosomes. The tRNA molecules attach to specific amino acids and put them in place, as dictated by the patterns on the mRNA. This sequence (left to right) shows the protein chain growing.

the protein (the sequence of amino acids) can be transmitted to the construction "machinery" of the cell.

DNA stores the genetic information, and RNA molecules are responsible for transmitting this information to cell components called *ribosomes,* where protein synthesis actually occurs. This process involves, first, the construction of a special RNA molecule called **messenger RNA (mRNA).** The mRNA is built in the cell nucleus, where a specific section of DNA (a gene) is used as the pattern. The mRNA then migrates from the nucleus into the cytoplasm of the cell, where, with the assistance of the ribosomes, the protein is synthesized.

Small RNA fragments, called **transfer RNA (tRNA)** molecules, attach themselves to specific amino acids and bring them to the growing protein chain as dictated by the pattern built into the mRNA. This process is summarized in Figure 21.21.

21.9 Lipids

OBJECTIVE: To learn the four classes of lipids.

The **lipids** are a group of substances defined in terms of their solubility characteristics. They are water-insoluble substances that can be extracted from cells by organic solvents such as benzene. The lipids found in the human body can be divided into four classes according to their molecular structure: fats, phospholipids, waxes, and steroids.

The most common **fats** are esters composed of the trihydroxy alcohol known as glycerol and long-chain carboxylic acids called **fatty acids** (Table 21.5). *Tristearin,* the most common animal fat, is typical of these substances.

Section 21.9

TEACHING TIPS

- This is a good time to discuss soaps and how they work. Figures 21.22 and 21.23 show how a micelle forms to break down globules of fats. Making soap in the laboratory is a good way for students to learn more about this process as well.
- Formation of lipids involves the same reaction as the formation of an ester, discussed in Chapter 20. The glycerol is a multihydroxyalcohol.
- Fats containing more unsaturated fatty acids are liquid at room temperature.
- Lipids are different from most other organic and biomolecules because they are distinguished not by a particular functional group but by their solubility in nonpolar solvents.

 Test Bank: 17, 19

Table 21.5 Some Common Fatty Acids and Their Major Sources

Name	Formula	Major Source
Saturated		
arachidic acid	$CH_3(CH_2)_{18}—COOH$	peanut oil
butyric acid	$CH_3(CH_2)_2—COOH$	butter
caproic acid	$CH_3(CH_2)_4—COOH$	butter
lauric acid	$CH_3(CH_2)_{10}—COOH$	coconut oil
stearic acid	$CH_3(CH_2)_{16}—COOH$	animal and vegetable fats
Unsaturated		
oleic acid	$CH_3(CH_2)_7CH{=}CH(CH_2)_7—COOH$	corn oil
linoleic acid	$CH_3(CH_2)_4CH{=}CH—CH_2—CH{=}CH(CH_2)_7—COOH$	linseed oil
linolenic acid	$CH_3CH_2CH{=}CH—CH_2CH{=}CH—CH_2—CH{=}CH—(CH_2)_7COOH$	linseed oil

$$
\begin{array}{l}
CH_2—O\boxed{H + H—O}—\overset{O}{\overset{\|}{C}}—(CH_2)_{16}—CH_3 \\
| \\
CH—O\boxed{H + H—O}—\overset{O}{\overset{\|}{C}}—(CH_2)_{16}—CH_3 \\
| \\
CH_2—O\boxed{H + H—O}—\overset{O}{\overset{\|}{C}}—(CH_2)_{16}—CH_3
\end{array}
\rightarrow
\begin{array}{l}
CH_2—O—\overset{O}{\overset{\|}{C}}—(CH_2)_{16}—CH_3 \\
| \\
CH—O—\overset{O}{\overset{\|}{C}}—(CH_2)_{16}—CH_3 + 3H_2O \\
| \\
CH_2—O—\overset{O}{\overset{\|}{C}}—(CH_2)_{16}—CH_3
\end{array}
$$

Glycerol — Three stearic acid molecules — Tristearin (fat)

Fats that are esters of glycerol are called **triglycerides** and have the general structure

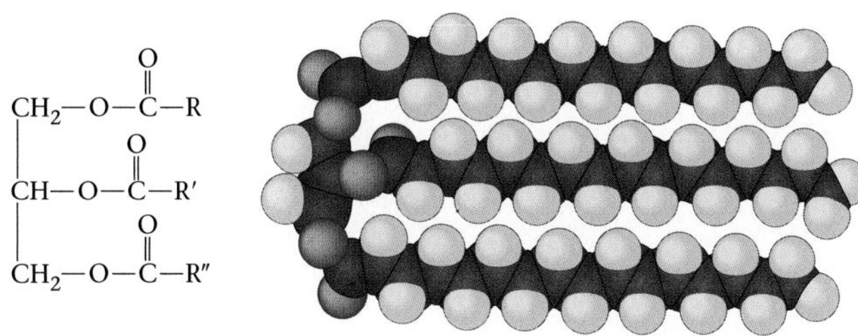

where the three R groups may be the same or different and may be saturated or unsaturated. Vegetable fats tend to be unsaturated and usually occur as oily liquids; most animal fats are saturated (contain only C—C single bonds) and occur as solids at room temperature.

Unsaturated fats contain one or more C=C bonds.

Triglycerides can be broken down by treatment with aqueous sodium hydroxide. The products are glycerol and the fatty acid salts; the latter are known as *soaps*. This process is called **saponification.**

21.9 Lipids 707

$$\begin{array}{l} CH_2{-}O{-}\overset{\displaystyle O}{\overset{\|}{C}}{-}R \\ | \\ CH{-}O{-}\overset{\displaystyle O}{\overset{\|}{C}}{-}R' \\ | \\ CH_2{-}O{-}\overset{\displaystyle O}{\overset{\|}{C}}{-}R'' \end{array} + 3NaOH \longrightarrow \begin{array}{l} CH_2OH + RCOONa \\ | \\ CHOH + R'COONa \\ | \\ CH_2OH + R''COONa \end{array}$$

Triglyceride — Sodium hydroxide — Glycerol — Soaps

Like dissolves like.

Much of what we call greasy dirt is nonpolar. Grease, for example, consists mostly of long-chain hydrocarbons. However, water, the solvent most commonly available to us, is very polar and does not dissolve "greasy dirt." We need to add something to the water that is somehow compatible with both the polar water and the nonpolar grease. Fatty-acid anions are perfect for this role because they have a long nonpolar tail and a polar head. For example, the stearate anion can be represented as

$$CH_3CH_2CH_2CH_2CH_2CH_2CH_2CH_2CH_2CH_2CH_2CH_2CH_2CH_2CH_2CH_2CH_2{-}\overset{\displaystyle O}{\overset{\|}{C}}{-}O^-$$

Nonpolar tail — Polar head

Such ions can be dispersed in water because they form **micelles** (Figure 21.22). These aggregates of fatty-acid anions have the water-incompatible tails in the interior; the anionic parts (the polar heads) point outward and

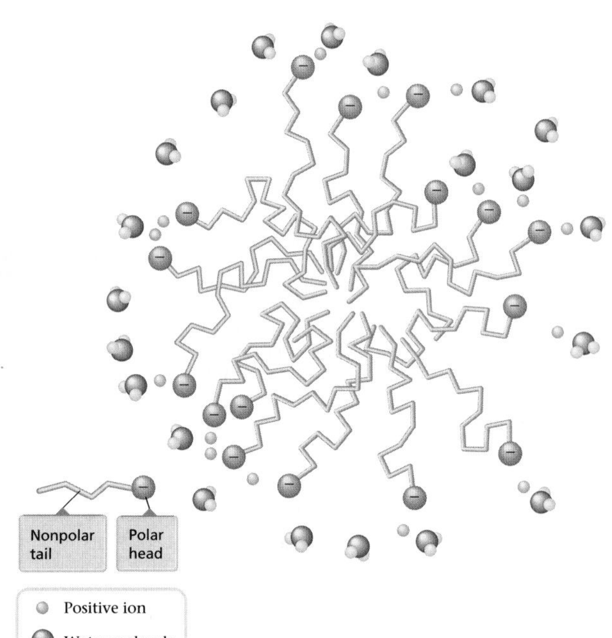

Figure 21.22 A two-dimensional "slice" of the structure of a micelle of fatty-acid anions.

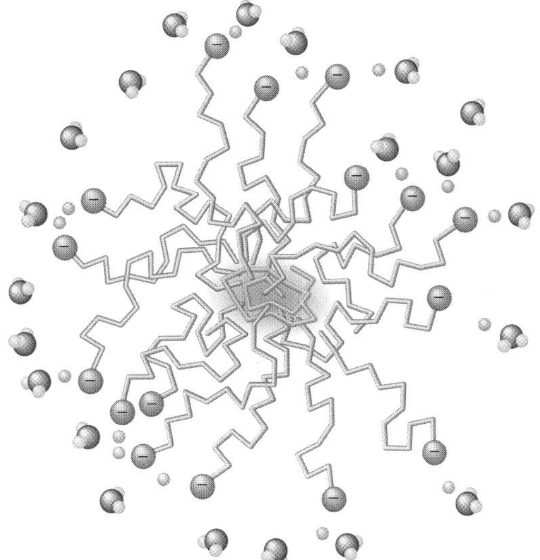

Figure 21.23
Soap micelles absorb grease molecules into their interiors so that the molecules are suspended in the water and can be washed away.

PowerLecture Animations: Surfactant–Oil Interaction
Micelle Formation: The Cleansing Action of Soap

interact with the polar water molecules. A soap solution does not contain *individual* fatty-acid anions dispersed in the water but rather groups of ions (micelles).

Soap dissolves grease by taking the grease molecules into the nonpolar interior of the micelle (Figure 21.23) so that they can be carried away by the water. Soap thus acts to suspend the normally incompatible grease in the water. Because of this ability to assist water in suspending nonpolar materials, soap is also called a *wetting agent,* or **surfactant.**

A major disadvantage is that soap anions form precipitates in hard water (water that contains large concentrations of ions such as Ca^{2+} and Mg^{2+}). These precipitates occur because the Ca^{2+} and Mg^{2+} ions form insoluble solids with soap anions. These precipitates ("soap scum") dull clothes and drastically reduce soap's cleaning efficiency. To help alleviate this problem, a huge industry has developed to produce artificial soaps, called *detergents.* Detergents are similar to natural soaps in that they have a long nonpolar tail and an ionic head. However, detergent anions have the advantage of not forming insoluble solids with Ca^{2+} and Mg^{2+} ions.

Phospholipids are similar in structure to fats in that they are esters of glycerol. Unlike fats, however, they contain only two fatty acids. The third group bound to glycerol is a phosphate group, which gives phospholipids two distinct parts: the long nonpolar "tail" and the polar substituted-phosphate "head" (Figure 21.24).

Waxes are another class of lipids. Like fats and phospholipids, waxes are esters, but unlike these other lipids, they involve monohydroxy alcohols instead of glycerol. For example, *beeswax,* a substance secreted by the wax glands of bees, is mainly myricyl palmitate,

$$CH_3(CH_2)_{14}-\overset{\overset{\displaystyle O}{\|}}{C}-O-(CH_2)_{29}-CH_3$$

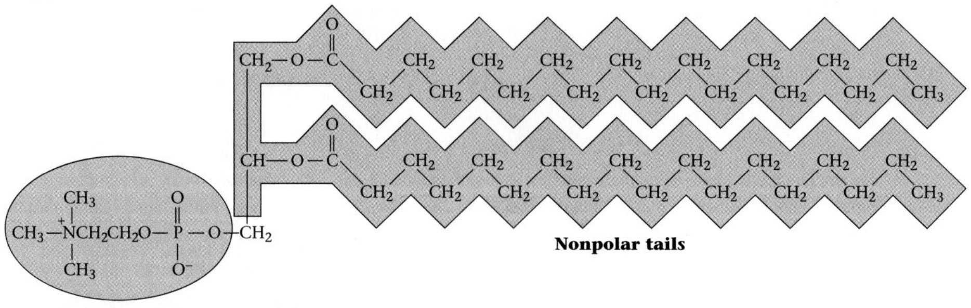

Figure 21.24
Lecithin, a phospholipid, with its long nonpolar tails and polar substituted-phosphate head.

formed from palmitic acid,

$$CH_3(CH_2)_{14}-C\begin{matrix}\diagup O \\ \diagdown OH\end{matrix}$$

and carnaubyl alcohol,

$$CH_3(CH_2)_{29}-OH$$

Waxes are solids that furnish waterproof coatings on leaves and fruit and on the skins and feathers of animals. Waxes are also important commercially. For example, whale oil is largely composed of the wax cetyl palmitate. It has been used in so many products, including cosmetics and candles, that the blue whale has been hunted almost to extinction.

Steroids are a class of lipids that have a characteristic carbon ring structure of the type

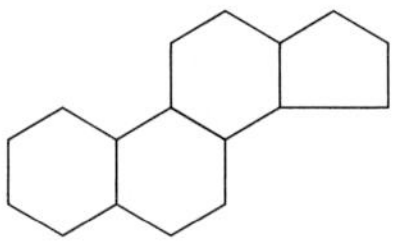

Steroids comprise four groups: cholesterol, adrenocorticoid hormones, sex hormones, and bile acids.

Cholesterol (Figure 21.25a) is found in virtually all organisms and is the starting material for the formation of the many other steroid-based molecules, such as vitamin D (Figure 21.25b). Although cholesterol is essential for human life, it has been implicated in the formation of plaque on the walls of arteries (a process called *atherosclerosis* or hardening of the arteries), which can lead eventually to clogging. This effect seems especially important in the arteries that supply blood to the heart. Blockage of these arteries leads to heart damage that often results in death from a heart attack.

The **adrenocorticoid hormones,** such as cortisol (Figure 21.25c), are synthesized in the adrenal glands (glands that lie next to each kidney) and are involved in various regulatory functions.

Of the **sex hormones,** the most important male hormone is *testosterone* (Figure 21.25d), a hormone that controls the growth of the reproductive organs and hair and the development of the muscle structure and deep voice that are characteristic of males. There are two types of female sex hormones of particular significance: *progesterone* (Figure 21.25e) and a group of

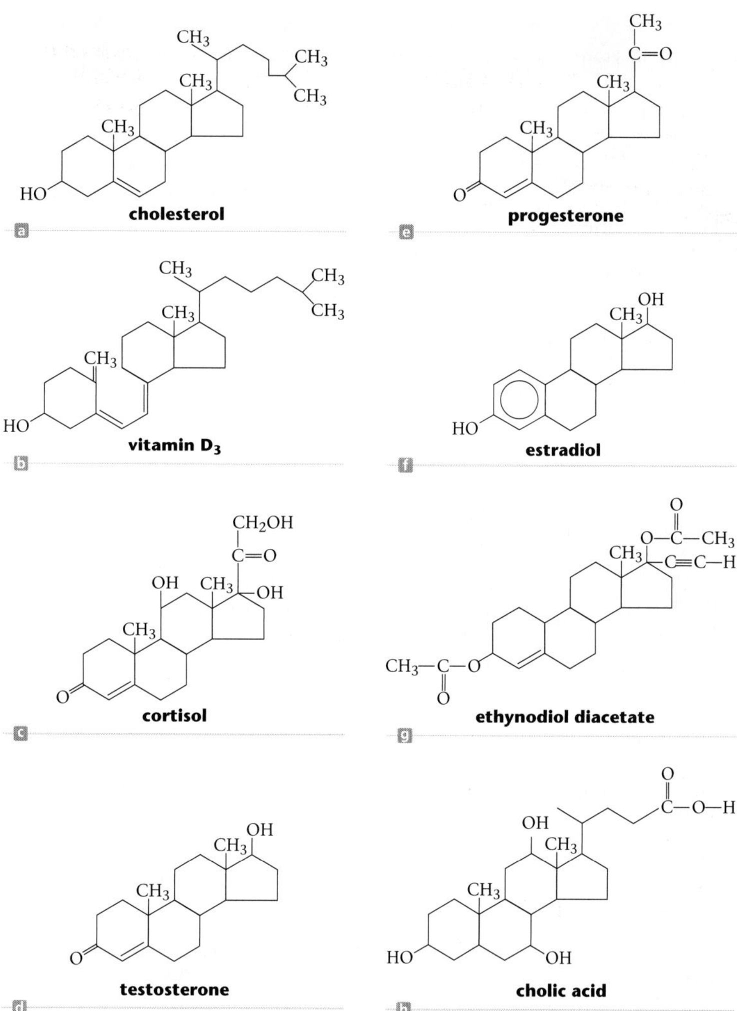

Figure 21.25 Several common steroids and steroid derivatives.

estrogens, one of which is *estradiol* (Figure 21.25f). Changes in the concentrations of these hormones cause the periodic changes in the ovaries and uterus that are responsible for the menstrual cycle. During pregnancy, a high level of progesterone is maintained, which prevents ovulation. This effect has led to the use of progesterone-type compounds as birth-control drugs. One of the most common of these is ethynodiol diacetate (Figure 21.25g).

The **bile acids** are produced from cholesterol in the liver and stored in the gallbladder. The primary human bile acid is *cholic acid* (Figure 21.25h), a substance that aids in the digestion of fats by emulsifying them in the intestine. Bile acids also can dissolve cholesterol ingested in food and are therefore important in controlling cholesterol in the body.

21.9 Lipids 711

ChemWork

- Alkane Nomenclature 1
- Alkane Nomenclature 2
- Cyclic Hydrocarbon Nomenclature
- Alkene Nomenclature 1
- Alkene Nomenclature 2
- Alkyne Nomenclature
- Aromatic Compounds Nomenclature
- Alcohol Nomenclature 1
- Alcohol Nomenclature 2
- Aldehyde Nomenclature
- Amine Nomenclature
- Carboxylic Acid Nomenclature
- Ester Formation
- Ester Nomenclature
- Ketone Nomenclature
- Reduction of Carbonyl Compounds
- Solubility of Organic Compounds

CHAPTER 21 REVIEW

F directs you to the *Chemistry in Focus* feature in the chapter
VP indicates visual problems
OWL interactive versions of these problems are assignable in OWL

Key Terms

biochemistry (p. 689)
biotechnology (p. 689)
essential elements (p. 689)
trace elements (p. 689)
cell (p. 689)
protein (21.1)
fibrous protein (21.1)
globular protein (21.1)
α-amino acid (21.2)
side chain (21.2)
dipeptide (21.2)
peptide linkage (21.2)
polypeptide (21.2)
primary structure (21.2)
secondary structure (21.3)
α-helix (21.3)
pleated sheet (21.3)
tertiary structure (21.4)
disulfide linkage (21.4)
denaturation (21.5)
enzyme (21.6)
lock-and-key model (21.6)
substrate (21.6)
active site (21.6)
carbohydrate (21.7)
monosaccharide (simple sugar) (21.7)
disaccharide (21.7)
sucrose (21.7)
glycoside linkage (21.7)
polysaccharide (21.7)
starch (21.7)
cellulose (21.7)
glycogen (21.7)
deoxyribonucleic acid (DNA) (21.8)
ribonucleic acid (RNA) (21.8)
nucleotide (21.8)
protein synthesis (21.8)
gene (21.8)
messenger RNA (mRNA) (21.8)
transfer RNA (tRNA) (21.8)
lipid (21.9)
fat (21.9)
fatty acid (21.9)
triglyceride (21.9)
saponification (21.9)
micelle (21.9)
surfactant (21.9)
phospholipid (21.9)
wax (21.9)
steroid (21.9)
cholesterol (21.9)
adrenocorticoid hormone (21.9)
sex hormone (21.9)
bile acid (21.9)

Summary

1. Thirty elements are currently known to be essential for life. The most abundant elements in the human body are hydrogen, carbon, nitrogen, and oxygen, but calcium, phosphorus, sodium, magnesium, potassium, sulfur, and chlorine are also present in large amounts. Other elements found only in trace amounts, such as zinc, are essential for the action of many enzymes.

2. Proteins are a class of natural polymers with molar masses ranging from 6000 to over 1,000,000 grams. Fibrous proteins are employed in the human body for structural purposes in muscle, hair, and cartilage. Globular proteins are molecules that transport and store oxygen and nutrients, act as catalysts, help regulate the body's systems, fight foreign objects, and so on.

3. The building blocks of proteins are the α-amino acids, which are classified as polar or nonpolar, depending on whether the side chain (R group) attached to the α-carbon is hydrophilic or hydrophobic. A protein polymer is built by successive condensation reactions that produce peptide linkages:

$$H_2N-CH(R)-C(=O)-OH + H-NH-CH(R')-C(=O)-OH \rightarrow H_2N-CH(R)-\underbrace{C(=O)-NH}_{\text{Peptide linkage}}-CH(R')-C(=O)-OH + H_2O$$

4. The order or sequence of amino acids in the protein chain is called the protein's primary structure. Differences in primary structure are what enable proteins to be tailored for different and very specific functions.

5. The secondary structure is the arrangement of the protein chain in space. The two most common secondary structures are the α-helix and the pleated sheet.

6. The overall shape of the protein is called its tertiary structure. Energy sources and a variety of chemicals can cause the breakdown of tertiary protein structure, which is called denaturation.

7. Enzymes are proteins that act as catalysts in biological reactions.

8. Carbohydrates serve as food sources for most organisms and as structural materials for plants. Simple carbohydrates, called monosaccharides, are most commonly five-carbon and six-carbon polyhydroxy ketones and aldehydes.

9. Monosaccharides combine to form more complex carbohydrates. For example, sucrose is a disaccharide, and starch and cellulose are polymers of glucose (polysaccharides).

Answers to End-of-Chapter Exercises

1. biochemistry

2. Trace elements are those elements present in the body in only very small amounts but which are essential to many biochemical processes in the body.

3. Proteins are large polymers of the α-amino acids, with molar masses in the range of 5000 to more than 1 million g/mol, which constitute approximately 15% of our bodies by mass.

4. Fibrous proteins provide structural integrity and strength for many types of tissue and are the main components of muscle, hair, and cartilage. Globular proteins are the "worker" molecules of the body, performing such functions as transporting oxygen throughout the body, catalyzing many of the reactions in the body, fighting infections, and transporting electrons during the metabolism of nutrients.

5. General amino acid formula:

$$H_2N-\underset{R}{\overset{H}{C}}-C(=O)-OH$$

6. All α-amino acids have the general structure

$$H_2N-\underset{R}{\overset{H}{C}}-COOH$$

The essential amino acids used by the body to construct proteins differ in the structure of the "R-group." Figure 21-2 shows the essential amino acids and their specific R-groups. Some amino acids con-

10. When a cell divides, the genetic information is transmitted via deoxyribonucleic acid (DNA), which has a double-helical structure. During cell division, the double helix unravels, and a new polymer forms along each strand of the original DNA, creating two double-helical DNA molecules. The DNA contains segments called genes, which store the primary structures of specific proteins. Various types of ribonucleic acid (RNA) molecules assist in protein synthesis.

11. Lipids are water-insoluble substances found in cells. They can be divided into four classes: fats, phospholipids, waxes, and steroids.

Active Learning Questions

These questions are designed to be considered by groups of students in class. Often these questions work well for introducing a particular topic in class.

1. Differentiate among primary, secondary, and tertiary structure in proteins.
2. Draw the structures of the simple dipeptides *gly-ala* and *ala-gly*.
3. How are proteins able to provide a buffering action?
4. What is meant by inhibition of an enzyme? What happens when an enzyme is irreversibly inhibited?
5. Differentiate between monosaccharide and disaccharide. Provide an example of each.
6. Sketch a representation of sucrose and clearly label the portion that originates from glucose, the portion that originates from fructose, and the glycoside linkage between the rings.
7. What is a polysaccharide? What monomer unit makes up starch and cellulose?
8. Describe the structure of a typical nucleotide.
9. Sketch the structures of the sugars ribose and deoxyribose. Which molecule, RNA or DNA, contains each sugar?
10. Sketch the general structure of a triglyceride. What are the components that go into making a typical triglyceride?
11. Describe the mechanism by which fatty acid salts are able to exert a cleaning action.

Questions and Problems

1. ________ is the study of the chemistry of living systems.
2. What are *trace elements,* and why are such elements important to the body's health?

21.1 Proteins

QUESTIONS

3. What are *proteins?* Are proteins *polymers?* Explain. What molar mass ranges are shown by proteins? What fraction of our bodies is made up of proteins?
4. What general functions do *fibrous* and *globular* proteins have in the body?

21.2 Primary Structure of Proteins

QUESTIONS

5. Consider the 20 most common amino acids shown in Figure 21.2. Although you may not be asked to *memorize* all these structures, it will help your study if you are *familiar* with them. Choose any five of the amino acids and sketch their structures. Also sketch the formula for a *general* amino acid. Circle the R group in each of your drawings.
6. What is meant by the *side chain* or "R group" of a protein? How does the internal structure of the side chain influence the relationship between the protein and water?
7. Nonpolar side chains in α-amino acids tend to be ________, whereas polar side chains are most often ________ in an aqueous medium.
8. Given the structures of the amino acids in Figure 21.2, choose two amino acids that you would expect to have hydrophobic side chains and two amino acids that you would expect to have hydrophilic side chains, and explain your choices in terms of the structure of the side chains involved.
9. Given the structures of the amino acids *alanine* and *serine* as shown in Figure 21.2, draw structures for each of the two dipeptides that these amino acids might form.
10. How many unique amino acid sequences are possible for a tripeptide containing only the amino acids *gly, ala,* and *cys,* with each amino acid occurring only once in each molecule?

PROBLEMS

11. What is a *peptide linkage?* Choose two amino acids from Figure 21.2 and draw structures for the two dipeptides those amino acids are capable of forming, circling the peptide linkage in each.
12. What does the *primary structure* of a protein represent? How are the individual units that make up the overall primary structure of a protein held together?

All even-numbered Questions and Problems have answers in the back of this book and solutions in the Solutions Guide.

tain R-groups that are nonpolar in nature, while other amino acids contain R-groups that are very polar and that may be capable of hydrogen bonding. Proteins with a preponderance of nonpolar R-groups tend to be insoluble in water, while proteins with a high content of polar R-groups tend to be soluble in water.

7. hydrophobic; hydrophilic

8. Answer depends on student choice of amino acids.

9.

```
       H   O   H   H
       |   ‖   |   |
  H2N—C—C—N—C—COOH
       |           |
      CH3         CH2OH

       H   O   H   H
       |   ‖   |   |
  H2N—C—C—N—C—COOH
       |           |
     CH2OH        CH3
```

10. six

11. The peptide linkage has the general structure

```
   O  H
   ‖  |
 —C—N—
```

Answer depends on student choice of amino acids.

12. The primary structure of a protein is the specific sequence of amino acids in the peptide chain. Adjacent amino acids are connected to each other by peptide (amide) linkages.

13. The secondary structure of a protein describes, in general, the arrangement in space of the protein's polypeptide chain. The most common secondary structures are the α-helix and the β-pleated sheet.

14. Long, thin, resilient proteins (such as hair) typically contain elongated, elastic α-helical protein molecules. Other proteins (such as silk) that form sheets or plates typically contain protein molecules having the β pleated-sheet secondary structure. Proteins that do not have a structural function in the body (such as hemoglobin) typically have a globular structure.

15. Collagen consists of three α-helical polypeptide chains twisted together to form a super helix.

16. Silk consists of a sheet structure in which the individual chains of amino acids are lined up lengthwise next to each other to form the sheet.

17. The tertiary structure of a protein represents its specific overall shape when it occurs in its natural environment and is influenced by that environment. To distinguish between the secondary and tertiary structures, consider this example: A given protein has an α-helical secondary structure (the protein's own amino acid chain coils in a helix); in the body, however, this helix itself is folded and twisted by interactions with the protein's environment until it

21.3 Secondary Structure of Proteins

QUESTIONS

13. In general terms, what does the secondary structure of a protein represent?

14. How is the secondary structure of a protein related to its function in the body? Give examples.

15. Describe the secondary structure of the protein collagen.

16. Describe the secondary structure of the protein found in silk.

21.4 Tertiary Structure of Proteins

QUESTIONS

17. In general terms, what does the tertiary structure of a protein describe? Clearly distinguish between the secondary and tertiary structures.

18. What is a *disulfide* linkage? Which of the amino acids commonly forms such linkages? Why is this linkage important?

21.5 Functions of Proteins

QUESTIONS

19. What is meant by *denaturation* of a protein? Give three examples of situations in which proteins are denatured.

20. What protein is responsible for the transport of oxygen through the bloodstream?

21. What name is given to proteins that catalyze biochemical reactions in the cell?

22. The protein *ferritin* is important because it helps store ______ in the liver, spleen, and bone marrow.

23. Give several examples of proteins that serve a protective function in the body.

24. How are proteins able to act as buffering agents in the blood and tissues?

21.6 Enzymes

QUESTIONS

25. How does the efficiency of an enzyme compare with that of inorganic catalysts? Are enzymes more or less efficient?

26. What does it mean to say that an enzyme is very *selective*?

27. What name is given to the specific portion of the enzyme molecule where catalysis actually occurs?

28. Describe the *lock-and-key model* for enzymes. Why are the *shapes* of the enzyme and its substrate important in this model? What does it mean to say that an enzyme is *inhibited* by a particular molecule? What happens if this inhibition is irreversible? Can you think of a situation in which it might be advantageous to be able to inhibit an enzyme?

21.7 Carbohydrates

QUESTIONS

29. Sketch the straight-chain representations of the aldehyde sugar glucose and of the ketone sugar fructose. Circle the aldehyde or ketone functional group in your structures.

30. Sugars can be referred to as *polyhydroxy carbonyl* compounds. Explain this terminology.

31. Sketch the ring structures of glucose and fructose. Based on the electron pairs surrounding the atoms of the rings, would you expect these rings to be planar (flat)?

32. What is a *pentose* sugar? Sketch the straight-chain representation of the pentose *ribose*.

33. What is a disaccharide? What monosaccharide units make up the disaccharide sucrose? What is the bond called that forms between the monosaccharide units?

34. Starch and cellulose both are polymers of glucose that are synthesized by plants. What do plants use starch for? What do they use cellulose for? Why is starch digestible by humans, but cellulose is not digestible?

PROBLEMS

35. Sketch a representation of the disaccharide sucrose (table sugar). Label clearly the portion of the disaccharide that originates from glucose, the portion that originates from fructose, and the glycoside linkage between the rings.

36. In addition to using *numerical* prefixes in the general names of sugars to indicate how many carbon atoms are present, we often use the prefixes *keto-* and *aldo-* to indicate whether the sugar is a ketone or an aldehyde. For example, the monosaccharide fructose is frequently called a ketohexose to emphasize that it contains the ketone functional group. For each of the monosaccharides shown in Table 21.4, classify the sugars as aldohexoses, aldopentoses, ketohexoses, or ketopentoses.

21.8 Nucleic Acids

QUESTIONS

37. ______ carries the information needed for the synthesis of the various proteins the cell requires to carry out its life functions.

38. A nucleotide consists of a nitrogen-containing organic base, a five-carbon sugar, and a ______ group bound together into a unit.

All even-numbered Questions and Problems have answers in the back of this book and solutions in the Solutions Guide.

forms a tight sphere. The fact that the helical protein is folded into a tight sphere indicates the tertiary structure of the protein.

18. A disulfide linkage represents an S—S bond between two sulfur-containing amino acids in a peptide chain. The amino acid cysteine forms such linkages. The presence of disulfide linkages produces bends and folds in the peptide chain and contributes greatly to the tertiary structure of a protein.

19. Denaturation of a protein represents the breaking down of the protein's tertiary structure. If the environment of a protein is changed from the normal environment of the protein, the specific folding and twisting of the protein's polypeptide chain will change to accommodate the new environment. If the protein's tertiary structure is changed, the protein most likely will no longer have whatever function in the body it ordinarily possesses. Cooking of an egg (adding heat to the environment of the protein) causes the protein albumin in the white of the egg to coagulate. Adding heavy metal ions (lead or mercury, for example) can disrupt the interchain linkages that contribute to the protein's tertiary structure. A permanent hair wave works by deliberately changing the hair protein's structure.

20. hemoglobin

21. Proteins that catalyze biochemical processes are called *enzymes*.

22. iron

23. Antibodies are special proteins that are synthesized in the body in response to foreign substances such as bacteria. Interferon is a protein that helps to protect cells against viral infection. The process of blood clotting involves several proteins.

24. Amino acids contain both a weak-acid and a weak-base group, and thus they can neutralize both bases and acids, respectively.

25. Enzymes are typically 1 to 10 million times more efficient than inorganic catalysts. Enzymes are much more efficient than any inorganic catalyst.

26. A given enzyme typically can react only with a specific molecule—the enzyme's substrate.

27. The action of an enzyme on its substrate takes place at a specific portion of the polypeptide chain called the *active site*.

28. The lock-and-key model for enzymes indicates that the structures of an enzyme and its substrate must be *complementary*, so that the substrate can approach and attach itself along the length of the enzyme at the enzyme's active sites. A given enzyme is intended to act upon a particular substrate: the substrate attaches itself to the enzyme, is acted upon, and then moves away from the enzyme. If a different molecule has a similar structure to the substrate, this other molecule may also be capable of attaching itself to the enzyme. Because this mole-

39. DNA nucleotides contain the pentose ______, whereas RNA nucleotides contain the pentose ______.

40. Name the five nitrogen bases found in DNA and RNA. Which base is found commonly in RNA but not in DNA? Which base is found commonly in DNA but not in RNA?

41. Describe the double-helical structure of DNA. What type of bonding occurs *within* the chain of each strand of the double helix? What type of bonding exists *between* strands to link them together?

42. The text states that the key to DNA's functioning is its *double-helical structure* with *complementary bases* on the two strands. Explain, with particular reference to how DNA is replicated.

43. What is a *gene?*

21.9 Lipids

QUESTIONS

44. Lipids are a group of substances defined in terms of their ______ characteristics.

45. What are the four *classes* of lipids? Give an example of a member of each class.

46. Sketch the general structure of a triglyceride. What are the components that go into making up a typical triglyceride?

47. Referring to Table 21.5, give an example of a *saturated* and an *unsaturated* fatty acid. Are triglycerides from animal sources generally saturated or unsaturated? Are triglycerides from plant sources generally saturated or unsaturated?

48. Using the general formula for a triglyceride, write an equation showing the process of *saponification.* What is a *soap?*

49. Describe the mechanism by which a soap is able to remove greasy dirt from clothing.

50. What is a *micelle?* How do the micelles formed by soap molecules suspend greasy dirt in a solution?

51. What is a *steroid?* What basic ring structure is common to all steroids? Sketch an example of a steroid found in the body, and highlight the basic ring structure that makes the molecule a steroid.

52. What steroid serves as the starting material in the body for the synthesis of other steroids? What dangers are involved in having too large a concentration of this substance in the body?

53. Give the names of several steroid sex hormones, and indicate their functions in the body.

54. What are *bile acids,* and from what are they synthesized by the body? What is the most common bile acid, and what function does it serve?

Additional Problems

MATCHING

For Exercises 55–76 choose one of the following terms to match the description given.

a. aldohexose	n. glycoside linkage
b. antibody	o. hormone
c. cellulose	p. hydrophobic
d. CH_2O	q. inhibition
e. cysteine	r. ketohexoses
f. denaturation	s. oxytocin
g. disaccharides	t. pleated sheet
h. disulfide	u. polypeptide
i. DNA	v. polysaccharides
j. enzymes	w. primary structure
k. fibrous	x. saliva
l. globular	y. substrate
m. glycogen	z. sucrose

55. polymer consisting of many amino acids
56. linkage that forms between two cysteine species
57. peptide hormone that triggers milk secretion
58. proteins with roughly spherical shape
59. sequence of amino acids in a protein
60. silk protein secondary structure
61. water-repelling amino acid side chain
62. amino acid responsible for permanent wave in hair
63. biological catalysts
64. breakdown of a protein's tertiary and/or secondary structure
65. molecule acted on by an enzyme
66. occurs when an enzyme's active site is blocked by a foreign molecule
67. special protein synthesized in response to foreign substance
68. substance that has a specific effect on a particular target organ
69. animal polymer of glucose
70. —C—O—C— bond between rings in disaccharide sugars
71. empirical formula leading to the name carbo*hydrate*

All even-numbered Questions and Problems have answers in the back of this book and solutions in the Solutions Guide.

cule is not the enzyme's proper substrate, however, the enzyme may not be able to act upon the molecule, and the molecule may remain attached to the enzyme, preventing proper substrate molecules from approaching the enzyme (irreversible inhibition). If the enzyme cannot act upon its proper substrate, then the enzyme is said to be inhibited. Irreversible inhibition might be a desirable feature in an antibiotic, which would bind to the enzymes of bacteria and prevent the bacteria from reproducing, thereby preventing or curing an infection.

29.

```
      CHO                 CH2OH
      |                   |
   H—C—OH                C=O
      |                   |
  HO—C—H              HO—C—H
      |                   |
   H—C—OH              H—C—OH
      |                   |
   H—C—OH              H—C—OH
      |                   |
     CH2OH               CH2OH

    glucose             fructose
```

30. Sugars contain an aldehyde or ketone functional group (carbonyl group), as well as several —OH groups (hydroxyl group).

31. These ring structures are shown in Figure 21.13. As indicated, the ring in glucose is not flat.

32. A pentose sugar is a carbohydrate containing 5 carbon atoms in the chain.

```
     CHO
     |
  H—C—OH
     |
  H—C—OH
     |
  H—C—OH
     |
    CH2OH

    ribose
```

33. A disaccharide consists of two monosaccharide units bonded together into a single molecule. Sucrose consists of a glucose molecule and a fructose molecule connected by an alpha-glycosidic linkage.

34. Starch is the form in which glucose is stored by plants for later use as cellular fuel. Cellulose is used by plants as their major structural component. Although starch and cellulose both are polymers of glucose, the linkage between adjacent glucose units differs in the two polysaccharides. Humans do not possess the enzyme needed to hydrolyze the linkage in cellulose.

35. Sucrose is a disaccharide formed from glucose and fructose by elimination of a water molecule to form a C—O—C linkage between the rings (called a *glycoside linkage*). The structure of sucrose is shown in Figure 21.13.

36. ribose (aldopentose); arabinose (aldopentose); ribulose (ketopentose); glucose (aldohexose); mannose (aldohexose); galactose (aldohexose); fructose (ketohexose)

37. DNA

38. phosphate

39. deoxyribose; ribose

40. uracil (RNA only); cytosine (DNA, RNA); thymine (DNA only); adenine (DNA, RNA); guanine (DNA, RNA)

41. In a strand of DNA, the phosphate group and the sugar molecule of adjacent nucleotides become bonded to each other. The chain portion of the DNA molecule, therefore, consists of alternating phosphate groups and sugar molecules. The nitrogen bases are found sticking out from the side of this phosphate–sugar chain, being bonded to the sugar molecules.

42. A DNA molecule consists of two chains of nucleotides, with the organic bases on the nucleotides arranged in complementary pairs (cytosine with guanine, adenine with thymine). The structures and properties of the organic bases are such that these pairs fit together well and allow the two chains of nucleotides to form the double-helix structure. When DNA replicates, the double helix unwinds, and then new molecules of the organic bases come in and pair up with their respective partner on the separated nucleotide chains, thereby replicating the original structure. See Figure 21.20.

43. A gene is a segment of the DNA molecule containing the code for synthesizing a particular protein.

44. solubility

45. The four types of lipids are fats (tristearin), phospholipids (lecithin), waxes (beeswax), and steroids (cholesterol).

(Please refer to page A27 in this book for answers to Exercises 46–106.)

72. where enzymes catalyzing the breakdown of glycoside links are found
73. six-carbon ketone sugars
74. structural component of plants, polymer of glucose
75. sugars consisting of two monomer units
76. six-carbon aldehyde sugars
77. The substance in the nucleus of the cell that stores and transmits genetic information is DNA, which stands for ______.
78. The basic repeating monomer units of DNA and RNA are called ______.
79. The pentose deoxyribose is found in DNA, whereas ______ is found in RNA.
80. The basic linkage in DNA or RNA between the sugar molecule and phosphoric acid is a phosphate ______ linkage.
81. The bases on opposite strands of DNA are said to be ______ to each other, which means the bases fit together specifically by hydrogen bonding to one another.
82. In a strand of normal DNA, the base ______ is always found paired with the base adenine, whereas ______ is always found paired with cytosine.
83. A given segment of the DNA molecule, which contains the molecular coding for a specific protein to be synthesized, is referred to as a ______.
84. During protein synthesis, ______ RNA molecules attach to and transport specific amino acids to the appropriate position on the pattern provided by ______ RNA molecules.
85. The codes specified by ______ are responsible for assembling the correct primary structure of proteins.
86. Substances in the cell are classified as ______ if they are insoluble in water but are soluble in nonpolar organic solvents.
87. ______ are esters of the polyhydroxyalcohol glycerol with long-chain carboxylic acids.
88. Vegetable oils tend to contain ______ fatty acids, whereas animal fats tend to be ______.
89. The process of ______ involves treating a fat with sodium hydroxide so that the fatty acids present are converted to their sodium salts.
90. Fatty acid anions make good soaps because they have both a ______ portion that is miscible with water and a ______ portion that is miscible with grease.
91. The aggregations of fatty acid anions that form when a soap is added to water are called ______.
92. Waxes are esters of ______ acids with monohydroxyl alcohols.
93. The starting material in the body for the synthesis of other steroids is ______.
94. During pregnancy, ovulation is prevented by secretion of the hormone ______.
95. Cholic acid and other bile acids act as ______ agents during digestion, helping to break fats up into smaller droplets that can then be acted on by enzymes.
96. What is meant by the *primary structure* of a protein?
97. How many possible primary structures exist for a small polypeptide containing four individual amino acids?
98. List three structural uses of proteins in the body.
99. What specific protein carries oxygen from the lungs to other body tissues?
100. How are proteins able to provide a buffering action?
101. What is meant by *inhibition* of an enzyme? What happens when an enzyme is irreversibly inhibited?
102. What general name is given to sugars containing five carbon atoms? six carbon atoms? three carbon atoms?
103. Although both starch and cellulose are polymers of glucose, starch is digestible by humans and cellulose is not. How do the structures of these polysaccharides differ, resulting in their different digestibility?
104. In the formation of a polynucleotide (a short portion of the DNA molecule), which components (sugar, base, or phosphate) on adjacent nucleotides bond to each other?
105. Describe the structure of a *wax*. Where do waxes occur naturally in living creatures, and what function do they serve?
106. What is a *phospholipid?* How does the structure of a phospholipid differ from that of a triglyceride? What is the function of the phospholipid lecithin?

All even-numbered Questions and Problems have answers in the back of this book and solutions in the Solutions Guide.

Using Your Calculator

In this section we will review how to use your calculator to perform common mathematical operations. This discussion assumes that your calculator uses the algebraic operating system, the system used by most brands.

One very important principle to keep in mind as you use your calculator is that it is not a substitute for your brain. Keep thinking as you do the calculations. Keep asking yourself, "Does the answer make sense?"

Addition, Subtraction, Multiplication, and Division

Performing these operations on a pair of numbers always involves the following steps:

1. Enter the first number, using the numbered keys and the decimal (.) key if needed.
2. Enter the operation to be performed.
3. Enter the second number.
4. Press the "equals" key to display the answer.

For example, the operation

$$15.1 + 0.32$$

is carried out as follows:

Press	Display
15.1	15.1
+	15.1
.32	0.32
=	15.42

The answer given by the display is 15.42. If this is the final result of a calculation, you should round it off to the correct number of significant figures (15.4), as discussed in Section 2.5. If this number is to be used in further calculations, use it exactly as it appears on the display. Round off only the final answer in the calculation.

Do the following operations for practice. The detailed procedures are given below.

a. $1.5 + 32.86$ c. 0.33×153

b. $23.5 - 0.41$ d. $\frac{9.3}{0.56}$ or $9.3 \div 0.56$

Procedures

a.

Press	Display
1.5	1.5
+	1.5
32.86	32.86
=	34.36
Rounded:	34.4

b.

Press	Display
23.5	23.5
−	23.5
.41	0.41
=	23.09
Rounded:	23.1

c.

Press	Display
.33	0.33
×	0.33
153	153
=	50.49
Rounded:	50.

d.

Press	Display
9.3	9.3
÷	9.3
.56	0.56
=	16.607143
Rounded:	17

Squares, Square Roots, Reciprocals, and Logs

Now we will consider four additional operations that we often need to solve chemistry problems.

The *squaring* of a number is done with a key labeled X^2. The *square root* key is usually labeled $\sqrt{X}$. To take the *reciprocal* of a number, you need the 1/X key. The *logarithm* of a number is determined by using a key labeled log or logX.

To perform these operations, take the following steps:

1. Enter the number.
2. Press the appropriate function key.
3. The answer is displayed automatically.

For example, let's calculate the square root of 235.

Press	Display
235	235
$\sqrt{X}$	15.32971
Rounded:	15.3

We can obtain the log of 23 as follows:

Press	Display
23	23
log	1.3617278
Rounded:	1.36

Often a key on a calculator serves two functions. In this case, the first function is listed on the key and the second is shown on the calculator just above the key. For example, on some calculators the top row of keys appears as follows:

	1/X	X^2		
2nd	R/S	$\sqrt{X}$	off	on/C

To make the calculator square a number, we must use 2nd and then $\sqrt{X}$; pressing 2nd tells the calculator we want the function that is listed *above* the key. Thus we can obtain the square of 11.56 on this calculator as follows:

Press	Display
11.56	11.56
2nd then $\sqrt{X}$	133.6336
Rounded:	133.6

We obtain the reciprocal of 384 (1/384) on this calculator as follows:

Press	Display
384	384
2nd then R/S	0.0026042
Rounded:	0.00260

Your calculator may be different. See the user's manual if you are having trouble with these operations.

Chain Calculations

In solving problems you often have to perform a series of calculations—a calculation chain. This is generally quite easy if you key in the chain as you read the numbers and operations in order. For example, to perform the calculation

$$\frac{14.68 + 1.58 - 0.87}{0.0850}$$

you should use the appropriate keys as you read it to yourself:

> 14.68 plus 1.58 equals; minus .87 equals; divided by 0.0850 equals

The details follow.

Press	Display
14.68	14.68
+	14.68
1.58	1.58
=	16.26
−	16.26
.87	0.87
=	15.39
÷	15.39
.0850	0.0850
=	181.05882
Rounded:	181

Note that you must press [=] after every operation to keep the calculation "up to date."

For more practice, consider the calculation

$$(0.360)(298) + \frac{(14.8)(16.0)}{1.50}$$

Here you are adding two numbers, but each must be obtained by the indicated calculations. One procedure is to calculate each number first and then add them. The first term is

$$(0.360)(298) = 107.28$$

The second term,

$$\frac{(14.8)(16.0)}{1.50}$$

can be computed easily by reading it to yourself. It "reads"

> 14.8 times 16.0 equals; divided by 1.50 equals

and is summarized as follows:

Press	Display
14.8	14.8
×	14.8
16.0	16.0
=	236.8
÷	236.8
1.50	1.50
=	157.86667

Now we can keep this last number on the calculator and add it to 107.28 from the first calculation.

Press	Display
+	157.86667
107.28	107.28
=	265.14667
Rounded:	265

To summarize,

$$(0.360)(298) + \frac{(14.8)(16.0)}{1.50}$$

becomes

$$107.28 + 157.86667$$

and the sum is 265.14667 or, rounded to the correct number of significant figures, 265. There are other ways to do this calculation, but this is the safest way (assuming you are careful).

A common type of chain calculation involves a number of terms multiplied together in the numerator and the denominator, as in

$$\frac{(323)(.0821)(1.46)}{(4.05)(76)}$$

There are many possible sequences by which this calculation can be carried out, but the following seems the most natural.

> 323 times .0821 equals; times 1.46 equals; divided by 4.05 equals; divided by 76 equals

This sequence is summarized as follows:

Press	Display
323	323
×	323
.0821	0.0821
=	26.5183
×	26.5183
1.46	1.46
=	38.716718
÷	38.716718
4.05	4.05
=	9.5596835
÷	9.5596835
76	76
=	0.1257853

The answer is 0.1257853, which, when rounded to the correct number of significant figures, is 0.13. Note that when two or more numbers are multiplied in the denominator, you must divide by *each* one.

Here are some additional chain calculations (with solutions) to give you more practice.

a. $15 - (0.750)(243)$

b. $\dfrac{(13.1)(43.5)}{(1.8)(63)}$

c. $\dfrac{(85.8)(0.142)}{(16.46)(18.0)} + \dfrac{(131)(0.0156)}{10.17}$

d. $(18.1)(0.051) - \dfrac{(325)(1.87)}{(14.0)(3.81)} + \dfrac{1.56 - 0.43}{1.33}$

Solutions

a. $15 - 182 = -167$

b. 5.0

c. $0.0411 + 0.201 = 0.242$

d. $0.92 - 11.4 + 0.850 = -9.6$

In performing chain calculations, take the following steps in the order listed.

1. Perform any additions and subtractions that appear inside parentheses.
2. Complete the multiplications and divisions of individual terms.
3. Add and subtract individual terms as required.

Basic Algebra

In solving chemistry problems you will use, over and over again, relatively few mathematical procedures. In this section we review the few algebraic manipulations that you will need.

Solving an Equation

In the course of solving a chemistry problem, we often construct an algebraic equation that includes the unknown quantity (the thing we want to calculate). An example is

$$(1.5)V = (0.23)(0.08206)(298)$$

We need to "solve this equation for V." That is, we need to isolate V on one side of the equals sign with all the numbers on the other side. How can we do this? The key idea in solving an algebraic equation is that *doing the same thing on both sides of the equals sign* does not change the equality. That is, it is always "legal" to do the same thing to both sides of the equation. Here we want to solve for V, so we must get the number 1.5 on the other side of the equals sign. We can do this by dividing *both sides* by 1.5.

$$\frac{(1.5)V}{1.5} = \frac{(0.23)(0.08206)(298)}{1.5}$$

Now the 1.5 in the denominator on the left cancels the 1.5 in the numerator:

$$\frac{(\cancel{1.5})V}{\cancel{1.5}} = \frac{(0.23)(0.08206)(298)}{1.5}$$

to give

$$V = \frac{(0.23)(0.08206)(298)}{1.5}$$

Using the procedures in "Using Your Calculator" for chain calculations, we can now obtain the value for V with a calculator.

$$V = 3.7$$

Sometimes it is necessary to solve an equation that consists of symbols. For example, consider the equation

$$\frac{P_1V_1}{T_1} = \frac{P_2V_2}{T_2}$$

Let's assume we want to solve for T_2. That is, we want to isolate T_2 on one side of the equation. There are several possible ways to proceed, keeping in mind that we always do the same thing on both sides of the equals sign. First we multiply both sides by T_2.

$$T_2 \times \frac{P_1V_1}{T_1} = \frac{P_2V_2}{\cancel{T_2}} \times \cancel{T_2}$$

This cancels T_2 on the right. Next we multiply both sides by T_1.

$$T_2 \times \frac{P_1V_1}{\cancel{T_1}} \times \cancel{T_1} = P_2V_2T_1$$

This cancels T_1 on the left. Now we divide both sides by P_1V_1.

$$T_2 \times \frac{\cancel{P_1V_1}}{\cancel{P_1V_1}} = \frac{P_2V_2T_1}{P_1V_1}$$

This yields the desired equation,

$$T_2 = \frac{P_2V_2T_1}{P_1V_1}$$

For practice, solve each of the following equations for the variable indicated.

a. $PV = k$; solve for P

b. $1.5x + 6 = 3$; solve for x

c. $PV = nRT$; solve for n

d. $\dfrac{P_1V_1}{T_1} = \dfrac{P_2V_2}{T_2}$; solve for V_2

e. $\dfrac{°F - 32}{°C} = \dfrac{9}{5}$; solve for °C

f. $\dfrac{°F - 32}{°C} = \dfrac{9}{5}$; solve for °F

Solutions

a. $\frac{PV\!\!\!/}{V\!\!\!/} = \frac{k}{V}$

$P = \frac{k}{V}$

b. $1.5x + 6 - 6 = 3 - 6$

$1.5x = -3$

$\frac{1.5x}{1.5} = \frac{-3}{1.5}$

$x = -\frac{3}{1.5} = -2$

c. $\frac{PV}{RT} = \frac{nRT}{RT}$

$\frac{PV}{RT} = n$

d. $\frac{P_1V_1}{T_1} \times T_2 = \frac{P_2V_2}{T_2} \times T_2$

$\frac{P_1V_1T_2}{T_1P_2} = \frac{P_2V_2}{P_2}$

$\frac{P_1V_1T_2}{T_1P_2} = V_2$

e. $\frac{°F - 32}{°C} \times °C = \frac{9}{5}°C$

$\frac{5}{9}(°F - 32) = \frac{5}{9} \times \frac{9}{5}°C$

$\frac{5}{9}(°F - 32) = °C$

f. $\frac{°F - 32}{°C} \times °C = \frac{9}{5}°C$

$°F - 32 + 32 = \frac{9}{5}°C + 32$

$°F = \frac{9}{5}°C + 32$

Scientific (Exponential) Notation

The numbers we must work with in scientific measurements are often very large or very small; thus it is convenient to express them using powers of 10. For example, the number 1,300,000 can be expressed as 1.3×10^6, which means multiply 1.3 by 10 six times, or

$$1.3 \times 10^6 = 1.3 \times \underbrace{10 \times 10 \times 10 \times 10 \times 10 \times 10}_{10^6 = 1 \text{ million}}$$

A number written in scientific notation always has the form:

> A number (between 1 and 10) times
> the appropriate power of 10

To represent a large number such as 20,500 in scientific notation, we must move the decimal point in such a way as to achieve a number between 1 and 10 and then multiply the result by a power of 10 to compensate for moving the decimal point. In this case, we must move the decimal point four places to the left.

2 0 5 0 0
4 3 2 1

to give a number between 1 and 10:

2.05

where we retain only the significant figures (the number 20,500 has three significant figures). To compensate for moving the decimal point four places to the left, we must multiply by 10^4. Thus

$$20{,}500 = 2.05 \times 10^4$$

As another example, the number 1985 can be expressed as 1.985×10^3. To end up with the number 1.985, which is between 1 and 10, we had to move the decimal point three places to the left. To compensate for that, we must multiply by 10^3. Some other examples are given in the accompanying list.

Number	Exponential Notation
5.6	5.6×10^0 or 5.6×1
39	3.9×10^1
943	9.43×10^2
1126	1.126×10^3

So far, we have considered numbers greater than 1. How do we represent a number such as 0.0034 in exponential notation? First, to achieve a number between 1 and 10, we start with 0.0034 and move the decimal point three places to the right.

0 . 0 0 3 4
1 2 3

This yields 3.4. Then, to compensate for moving the decimal point to the right, we must multiply by a power of 10 with a negative exponent—in this case, 10^{-3}. Thus

$$0.0034 = 3.4 \times 10^{-3}$$

In a similar way, the number 0.00000014 can be written as 1.4×10^{-7}, because going from 0.00000014 to 1.4 requires that we move the decimal point seven places to the right.

Mathematical Operations with Exponentials

We next consider how various mathematical operations are performed using exponential numbers. First we cover the various rules for these operations; then we consider how to perform them on your calculator.

Multiplication and Division

When two numbers expressed in exponential notation are multiplied, the initial numbers are multiplied and the exponents of 10 are *added.*

$$(M \times 10^m)(N \times 10^n) = (MN) \times 10^{m+n}$$

For example (to two significant figures, as required),

$$(3.2 \times 10^4)(2.8 \times 10^3) = 9.0 \times 10^7$$

When the numbers are multiplied, if a result greater than 10 is obtained for the initial number, the decimal point is moved one place to the left and the exponent of 10 is increased by 1.

$$\begin{aligned}(5.8 \times 10^2)(4.3 \times 10^8) &= 24.9 \times 10^{10}\\ &= 2.49 \times 10^{11}\\ &= 2.5 \times 10^{11} \text{ (two significant figures)}\end{aligned}$$

Division of two numbers expressed in exponential notation involves normal division of the initial numbers and *subtraction* of the exponent of the divisor from that of the dividend. For example,

$$\frac{4.8 \times 10^8}{\underbrace{2.1 \times 10^3}_{\text{Divisor}}} = \frac{4.8}{2.1} \times 10^{(8-3)} = 2.3 \times 10^5$$

If the initial number resulting from the division is less than 1, the decimal point is moved one place to the right and the exponent of 10 is decreased by 1. For example,

$$\begin{aligned}\frac{6.4 \times 10^3}{8.3 \times 10^5} = \frac{6.4}{8.3} \times 10^{(3-5)} &= 0.77 \times 10^{-2}\\ &= 7.7 \times 10^{-3}\end{aligned}$$

Addition and Subtraction

In order for us to add or subtract numbers expressed in exponential notation, *the exponents of the numbers must be the same.* For example, to add 1.31×10^5 and 4.2×10^4, we must rewrite one number so that the exponents of both are the same. The number 1.31×10^5 can be written 13.1×10^4: decreasing the exponent by 1 compensates for moving the decimal point one place to the right. Now we can add the numbers.

$$\begin{array}{r} 13.1 \times 10^4 \\ +\ 4.2 \times 10^4 \\ \hline 17.3 \times 10^4 \end{array}$$

In correct exponential notation, the result is expressed as 1.73×10^5.

To perform addition or subtraction with numbers expressed in exponential notation, we add or subtract only the initial numbers. The exponent of the result is the same as the exponents of the numbers being added or subtracted. To subtract 1.8×10^2 from 8.99×10^3, we first convert 1.8×10^2 to 0.18×10^3 so that both numbers have the same exponent. Then we subtract.

$$\begin{array}{r} 8.99 \times 10^3 \\ -0.18 \times 10^3 \\ \hline 8.81 \times 10^3 \end{array}$$

Powers and Roots

When a number expressed in exponential notation is taken to some power, the initial number is taken to the appropriate power and the exponent of 10 is *multiplied* by that power.

$$(N \times 10^n)^m = N^m \times 10^{m \times n}$$

For example,

$$\begin{aligned}(7.5 \times 10^2)^2 &= (7.5)^2 \times 10^{2\times 2}\\ &= 56. \times 10^4\\ &= 5.6 \times 10^5\end{aligned}$$

When a root is taken of a number expressed in exponential notation, the root of the initial number is taken and the exponent of 10 is divided by the number representing the root. For example, we take the square root of a number as follows:

$$\sqrt{N \times 10^n} = (N \times 10^n)^{1/2} = \sqrt{N} \times 10^{n/2}$$

For example,

$$\begin{aligned}(2.9 \times 10^6)^{1/2} &= \sqrt{2.9} \times 10^{6/2}\\ &= 1.7 \times 10^3\end{aligned}$$

Using a Calculator to Perform Mathematical Operations on Exponentials

In dealing with exponential numbers, you must first learn to enter them into your calculator. First the number is keyed in and then the exponent. There is a special key that must be pressed just before the exponent is entered. This key is often labeled (EE) or (exp). For example, the number 1.56×10^6 is entered as follows:

Press	Display
1.56	1.56
EE or exp	1.56 00
6	1.56 06

To enter a number with a negative exponent, use the change-of-sign key (+/−) after entering the exponent number. For example, the number 7.54×10^{-3} is entered as follows:

Press	Display
7.54	7.54
EE or exp	7.54 00
3	7.54 03
+/−	7.54 −03

Once a number with an exponent is entered into your calculator, the mathematical operations are performed exactly the same as with a "regular" number. For example, the numbers 1.0×10^3 and 1.0×10^2 are multiplied as follows:

Press	Display
1.0	1.0
EE or exp	1.0 00
3	1.0 03
×	1 03
1.0	1.0
EE or exp	1.0 00
2	1.0 02
=	1 05

The answer is correctly represented as 1.0×10^5.

The numbers 1.50×10^5 and 1.1×10^4 are added as follows:

Press	Display
1.5	1.50
EE or exp	1.50 00
5	1.50 05
+	1.5 05
1.1	1.1
EE or exp	1.1 00
4	1.1 04
=	1.61 05

The answer is correctly represented as 1.61×10^5. Note that when exponential numbers are added, the calculator automatically takes into account any difference in exponents.

To take the power, root, or reciprocal of an exponential number, enter the number first, then press the appropriate key or keys. For example, the square root of 5.6×10^3 is obtained as follows:

Press	Display
5.6	5.6
EE or exp	5.6 00
3	5.6 03
$\sqrt{X}$	7.4833148 01

The answer is correctly represented as 7.5×10^1.

Practice by performing the following operations that involve exponential numbers. The answers follow the exercises.

a. $7.9 \times 10^2 \times 4.3 \times 10^4$

b. $\dfrac{5.4 \times 10^3}{4.6 \times 10^5}$

c. $1.7 \times 10^2 + 1.63 \times 10^3$

d. $4.3 \times 10^{-3} + 1 \times 10^{-4}$

e. $(8.6 \times 10^{-6})^2$

f. $\dfrac{1}{8.3 \times 10^2}$

g. $\log(1.0 \times 10^{-7})$

h. $-\log(1.3 \times 10^{-5})$

i. $\sqrt{6.7 \times 10^9}$

Solutions

a. 3.4×10^7

b. 1.2×10^{-2}

c. 1.80×10^3

d. 4.4×10^{-3}

e. 7.4×10^{-11}

f. 1.2×10^{-3}

g. -7.00

h. 4.89

i. 8.2×10^4

Graphing Functions

In interpreting the results of a scientific experiment, it is often useful to make a graph. If possible, the function to be graphed should be in a form that gives a straight line. The equation for a straight line (a *linear equation*) can be represented in the general form

$$y = mx + b$$

where y is the *dependent variable*, x is the *independent variable*, m is the *slope*, and b is the *intercept* with the y axis.

To illustrate the characteristics of a linear equation, the function $y = 3x + 4$ is plotted in Figure A.1. For this equation $m = 3$ and $b = 4$. Note that the y intercept occurs when $x = 0$. In this case the y intercept is 4, as can be seen from the equation ($b = 4$).

The slope of a straight line is defined as the ratio of the rate of change in y to that in x:

$$m = \text{slope} = \frac{\Delta y}{\Delta x}$$

For the equation $y = 3x + 4$, y changes three times as fast as x (because x has a coefficient of 3). Thus the slope in

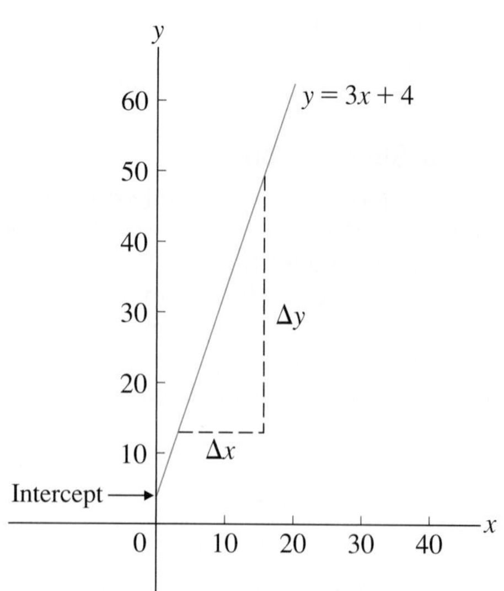

Figure A.1
Graph of the linear equation $y = 3x + 4$.

this case is 3. This can be verified from the graph. For the triangle shown in Figure A.1,

$$\Delta y = 15 - 16 = 36 \qquad \text{and} \qquad \Delta x = 15 - 3 = 12$$

Thus

$$\text{Slope} = \frac{\Delta y}{\Delta x} = \frac{36}{12} = 3$$

This example illustrates a general method for obtaining the slope of a line from the graph of that line. Simply draw a triangle with one side parallel to the y axis and the other side parallel to the x axis, as shown in Figure A.1. Then determine the lengths of the sides to get Δy and Δx, respectively, and compute the ratio $\Delta y/\Delta x$.

SI Units and Conversion Factors

These conversion factors are given with more significant figures than those typically used in the body of the text.

Length	SI Unit: Meter (m)
1 meter	= 1.0936 yards
1 centimeter	= 0.39370 inch
1 inch	= 2.54 centimeters (exactly)
1 kilometer	= 0.62137 mile
1 mile	= 5280. feet
	= 1.6093 kilometers

Mass	SI Unit: Kilogram (kg)
1 kilogram	= 1000 grams
	= 2.2046 pounds
1 pound	= 453.59 grams
	= 0.45359 kilogram
	= 16 ounces
1 atomic mass unit	= 1.66057×10^{-27} kilograms

Volume	SI Unit: Cubic Meter (m^3)
1 liter	= 10^{-3} m^3
	= 1 dm^3
	= 1.0567 quarts
1 gallon	= 4 quarts
	= 8 pints
	= 3.7854 liters
1 quart	= 32 fluid ounces
	= 0.94635 liter

Pressure	SI Unit: Pascal (Pa)
1 atmosphere	= 101.325 kilopascals
	= 760. torr (mm Hg)
	= 14.70 pounds per square inch

Energy	SI Unit: Joule (J)
1 joule	= 0.23901 calorie
1 calorie	= 4.184 joules

Chapter 2

Self-Check Exercise 2.1

$357 = 3.57 \times 10^2$
$0.0055 = 5.5 \times 10^{-3}$

Self-Check Exercise 2.2

a. Three significant figures. The leading zeros (to the left of the 1) do not count, but the trailing zeros do.
b. Five significant figures. The one captive zero and the two trailing zeros all count.
c. This is an exact number obtained by counting the cars. It has an unlimited number of significant figures.

Self-Check Exercise 2.3

a. $12.6 \times 0.53 = 6.678 = 6.7$ (Limiting)

b. $12.6 \times 0.53 = 6.7$; (Limiting)

$$\begin{array}{r} 6.7 \quad \text{Limiting} \\ -4.59 \\ \hline 2.11 = 2.1 \end{array}$$

c. $$\begin{array}{r} 25.36 \\ -4.15 \\ \hline 21.21 \end{array} \qquad \frac{21.21}{2.317} = 9.15408 = 9.154$$

Self-Check Exercise 2.4

$$0.750 \cancel{L} \times \frac{1.06 \text{ qt}}{1 \cancel{L}} = 0.795 \text{ qt}$$

Self-Check Exercise 2.5

$$225 \frac{\cancel{mi}}{h} \times \frac{1760 \cancel{yd}}{1 \cancel{mi}} \times \frac{1 \cancel{m}}{1.094 \cancel{yd}} \times \frac{1 \text{ km}}{1000 \cancel{m}} = 362 \frac{\text{km}}{\text{h}}$$

Self-Check Exercise 2.6

The best way to solve this problem is to convert 172 K to Celsius degrees. To do this we will use the formula $T_{°C} = T_K - 273$.

In this case

$$T_{°C} = T_K - 273 = 172 - 273 = -101$$

So 172 K = −101 °C, which is a lower temperature than −75 °C. Thus 172 K is colder than −75 °C.

Self-Check Exercise 2.7

The problem is 41 °C = ? °F.

Using the formula

$$T_{°F} = 1.80(T_{°C}) + 32$$

we have

$$T_{°F} = ?\ °F = 1.80(41) + 32 = 74 + 32 = 106$$

That is, 41 °C = 106 °F.

Self-Check Exercise 2.8

This problem can be stated as 239 °F = ? °C.

Using the formula

$$T_{°C} = \frac{T_{°F} - 32}{1.80}$$

we have in this case

$$T_{°C} = ?\ °C = \frac{239 - 32}{1.80} = \frac{207}{1.80} = 115$$

That is, 239 °F = 115 °C.

Self-Check Exercise 2.9

We obtain the density of the cleaner by dividing its mass by its volume.

$$\text{Density} = \frac{\text{mass}}{\text{volume}} = \frac{28.1 \text{ g}}{35.8 \text{ mL}} = 0.785 \text{ g/mL}$$

This density identifies the liquid as isopropyl alcohol.

Chapter 3

Self-Check Exercise 3.1

Items (a) and (c) are physical properties. When the solid gallium melts, it forms liquid gallium. There is no change in composition. Items (b) and (d) reflect the ability to change composition and are thus chemical properties. Statement (b) means that platinum does not react with oxygen to form some new substance. Statement (d) means that copper does react in the air to form a new substance, which is green.

Self-Check Exercise 3.2

a. Milk turns sour because new substances are formed. This is a chemical change.
b. Melting the wax is a physical change (a change of state). When the wax burns, new substances are formed. This is a chemical change.

Self-Check Exercise 3.3

a. Maple syrup is a homogeneous mixture of sugar and other substances dispersed uniformly in water.
b. Helium and oxygen form a homogeneous mixture.
c. Oil and vinegar salad dressing is a heterogeneous mixture. (Note the two distinct layers the next time you look at a bottle of dressing.)
d. Common salt is a pure substance (sodium chloride), so it always has the same composition. (Note that other substances such as iodine are often added to commercial preparations of table salt, which is mostly sodium chloride. Thus commercial table salt is a homogeneous mixture.)

Chapter 4

Self-Check Exercise 4.1

a. P_4O_{10} b. UF_6 c. $AlCl_3$

Self-Check Exercise 4.2

In the symbol $^{90}_{38}Sr$, the number 38 is the atomic number, which represents the number of protons in the nucleus of a strontium atom. Because the atom is neutral overall, it must also have 38 electrons. The number 90 (the mass number) represents the number of protons plus the number of neutrons. Thus the number of neutrons is $A - Z = 90 - 38 = 52$.

Self-Check Exercise 4.3

The atom $^{201}_{80}Hg$ has 80 protons, 80 electrons, and 201 − 80 = 121 neutrons.

Self-Check Exercise 4.4

The atomic number for phosphorus is 15 and the mass number is 15 + 17 = 32. Thus the symbol for the atom is $^{32}_{15}P$.

Self-Check Exercise 4.5

Element	Symbol	Atomic Number	Metal or Nonmetal	Family Name
a. argon	Ar	18	nonmetal	noble gas
b. chlorine	Cl	17	nonmetal	halogen
c. barium	Ba	56	metal	alkaline earth metal
d. cesium	Cs	55	metal	alkali metal

Self-Check Exercise 4.6

a. KI $(1+) + (1-) = 0$
b. Mg_3N_2 $3(2+) + 2(3-) = (6+) + (6-) = 0$
c. Al_2O_3 $2(3+) + 3(2-) = 0$

Chapter 5

Self-Check Exercise 5.1

a. rubidium oxide
b. strontium iodide
c. potassium sulfide

Self-Check Exercise 5.2

a. The compound $PbBr_2$ must contain Pb^{2+}—named lead(II)—to balance the charges of the two Br^- ions. Thus the name is lead(II) bromide. The compound $PbBr_4$ must contain Pb^{4+}—named lead(IV)—to balance the charges of the four Br^- ions. The name is therefore lead(IV) bromide.
b. The compound FeS contains the S^{2-} ion (sulfide) and thus the iron cation present must be Fe^{2+}, iron(II). The name is iron(II) sulfide. The compound Fe_2S_3 contains three S^{2-} ions and two iron cations of unknown charge. We can determine the iron charge from the following:

$$\underset{\text{Iron charge}}{2(?+)} + \underset{S^{2-}\text{ charge}}{3(2-)} = 0$$

In this case, ? must represent 3 because

$$2(3+) + 3(2-) = 0$$

Thus Fe_2S_3 contains Fe^{3+} and S^{2-}, and its name is iron(III) sulfide.
c. The compound $AlBr_3$ contains Al^{3+} and Br^-. Because aluminum forms only one ion (Al^{3+}), no Roman numeral is required. The name is aluminum bromide.
d. The compound Na_2S contains Na^+ and S^{2-} ions. The name is sodium sulfide. (Because sodium forms only Na^+, no Roman numeral is needed.)
e. The compound $CoCl_3$ contains three Cl^- ions. Thus the cobalt cation must be Co^{3+}, which is named cobalt(III) because cobalt is a transition metal and can form more than one type of cation. Thus the name of $CoCl_3$ is cobalt(III) chloride.

Self-Check Exercise 5.3

Compound	Individual Names	Prefixes	Name
a. CCl_4	carbon chloride	none *tetra-*	carbon tetrachloride
b. NO_2	nitrogen oxide	none *di-*	nitrogen dioxide
c. IF_5	iodine fluoride	none *penta-*	iodine pentafluoride

Self-Check Exercise 5.4

a. silicon dioxide
b. dioxygen difluoride
c. xenon hexafluoride

Self-Check Exercise 5.5

a. chlorine trifluoride
b. vanadium(V) fluoride
c. copper(I) chloride
d. manganese(IV) oxide
e. magnesium oxide
f. water

Self-Check Exercise 5.6

a. calcium hydroxide
b. sodium phosphate
c. potassium permanganate
d. ammonium dichromate
e. cobalt(II) perchlorate (Perchlorate has a 1− charge, so the cation must be Co^{2+} to balance the two ClO_4^- ions.)
f. potassium chlorate
g. copper(II) nitrite (This compound contains two NO_2^- (nitrite) ions and thus must contain a Cu^{2+} cation.)

Self-Check Exercise 5.7

	Compound	**Name**
a.	$NaHCO_3$	sodium hydrogen carbonate

Contains Na^+ and HCO_3^-; often called sodium bicarbonate (common name).

b.	$BaSO_4$	barium sulfate

Contains Ba^{2+} and SO_4^{2-}.

c.	$CsClO_4$	cesium perchlorate

Contains Cs^+ and ClO_4^-.

d.	BrF_5	bromine pentafluoride

Both nonmetals (Type III binary).

e.	NaBr	sodium bromide

Contains Na^+ and Br^- (Type I binary).

f.	KOCl	potassium hypochlorite

Contains K^+ and OCl^-.

g.	$Zn_3(PO_4)_2$	zinc(II) phosphate

Contains Zn^{2+} and PO_4^{3-}; Zn is a transition metal and officially requires a Roman numeral. However, because Zn forms only the Zn^{2+} cation, the II is usually left out. Thus the name of the compound is usually given as zinc phosphate.

Self-Check Exercise 5.8

	Name	**Chemical Formula**
a.	ammonium sulfate	$(NH_4)_2SO_4$

Two ammonium ions (NH_4^+) are required for each sulfate ion (SO_4^{2-}) to achieve charge balance.

b.	vanadium(V) fluoride	VF_5

The compound contains V^{5+} ions and requires five F^- ions for charge balance.

c.	disulfur dichloride	S_2Cl_2

The prefix *di-* indicates two of each atom.

d.	rubidium peroxide	Rb_2O_2

Because rubidium is in Group 1, it forms only 1+ ions. Thus two Rb^+ ions are needed to balance the 2− charge on the peroxide ion (O_2^{2-}).

e.	aluminum oxide	Al_2O_3

Aluminum forms only 3+ ions. Two Al^{3+} ions are required to balance the charge on three O^{2-} ions.

Chapter 6

Self-Check Exercise 6.1

a. $Mg(s) + H_2O(l) \rightarrow Mg(OH)_2(s) + H_2(g)$
Note that magnesium (which is in Group 2) always forms the Mg^{2+} cation and thus requires two OH^- anions for a zero net charge.

b. Ammonium dichromate contains the polyatomic ions NH_4^+ and $Cr_2O_7^{2-}$ (you should have these memorized). Because NH_4^+ has a 1+ charge, two NH_4^+ cations are required for each $Cr_2O_7^{2-}$, with it 2− charge, to give the formula $(NH_4)_2Cr_2O_7$. Chromium(III) oxide contains Cr^{3+} ions—signified by chromium(III)—and O^{2-} (the oxide ion). To achieve a net charge of zero, the solid must contain two Cr^{3+} ions for every three O^{2-} ions, so the formula is Cr_2O_3. Nitrogen gas contains diatomic molecules and is written $N_2(g)$, and gaseous water is written $H_2O(g)$. Thus the unbalanced equation for the decomposition of ammonium dichromate is

$$(NH_4)_2Cr_2O_7(s) \rightarrow Cr_2O_3(s) + N_2(g) + H_2O(g)$$

c. Gaseous ammonia, $NH_3(g)$, and gaseous oxygen, $O_2(g)$, react to form nitrogen monoxide gas, $NO(g)$, plus gaseous water, $H_2O(g)$. The unbalanced equation is

$$NH_3(g) + O_2(g) \rightarrow NO(g) + H_2O(g)$$

Self-Check Exercise 6.2

Step 1 The reactants are propane, $C_3H_8(g)$, and oxygen, $O_2(g)$; the products are carbon dioxide, $CO_2(g)$, and water, $H_2O(g)$. All are in the gaseous state.

Step 2 The unbalanced equation for the reaction is

$$C_3H_8(g) + O_2(g) \rightarrow CO_2(g) + H_2O(g)$$

Step 3 We start with C_3H_8 because it is the most complicated molecule. C_3H_8 contains three carbon atoms per molecule, so a coefficient of 3 is needed for CO_2.

$$C_3H_8(g) + O_2(g) \rightarrow 3CO_2(g) + H_2O(g)$$

Also, each C_3H_8 molecule contains eight hydrogen atoms, so a coefficient of 4 is required for H_2O.

$$C_3H_8(g) + O_2(g) \rightarrow 3CO_2(g) + 4H_2O(g)$$

The final element to be balanced is oxygen. Note that the left side of the equation now has two oxygen atoms, and the right side has ten. We can balance the oxygen by using a coefficient of 5 for O_2.

$$C_3H_8(g) + 5O_2(g) \rightarrow 3CO_2(g) + 4H_2O(g)$$

Step 4 ***Check:***

$$\underbrace{3\text{ C, 8 H, 10 O}}_{\text{Reactant atoms}} \rightarrow \underbrace{3\text{ C, 8 H, 10 O}}_{\text{Product atoms}}$$

We cannot divide all coefficients by a given integer to give smaller integer coefficients.

Self-Check Exercise 6.3

a. $NH_4NO_2(s) \rightarrow N_2(g) + H_2O(g)$ (unbalanced)
$NH_4NO_2(s) \rightarrow N_2(g) + 2H_2O(g)$ (balanced)

b. $NO(g) \rightarrow N_2O(g) + NO_2(g)$ (unbalanced)
$3NO(g) \rightarrow N_2O(g) + NO_2(g)$ (balanced)

c. $HNO_3(l) \rightarrow NO_2(g) + H_2O(l) + O_2(g)$ (unbalanced)
$4HNO_3(l) \rightarrow 4NO_2(g) + 2H_2O(l) + O_2(g)$ (balanced)

Chapter 7

Self-Check Exercise 7.1

a. The ions present are

$$\underbrace{Ba^{2+}(aq) + 2NO_3^-(aq)}_{\text{Ions in } Ba(NO_3)_2(aq)} + \underbrace{Na^+(aq) + Cl^-(aq)}_{\text{Ions in } NaCl(aq)} \rightarrow$$

Exchanging the anions gives the possible solid products $BaCl_2$ and $NaNO_3$. Using Table 7.1, we see that both substances are very soluble (rules 1, 2, and 3). Thus no solid forms.

b. The ions present in the mixed solution before any reaction occurs are

$$\underbrace{2Na^+(aq) + S^{2-}(aq)}_{\text{Ions in } Na_2S(aq)} + \underbrace{Cu^{2+}(aq) + 2NO_3^-(aq)}_{\text{Ions in } Cu(NO_3)_2(aq)} \rightarrow$$

Exchanging the anions gives the possible solid products CuS and $NaNO_3$. According to rules 1 and 2 in Table 7.1, $NaNO_3$ is soluble, and by rule 6, CuS should be insoluble. Thus CuS will precipitate. The balanced equation is

$$Na_2S(aq) + Cu(NO_3)_2(aq) \rightarrow CuS(s) + 2NaNO_3(aq)$$

c. The ions present are

$$\underbrace{NH_4^+(aq) + Cl^-(aq)}_{\text{Ions in } NH_4Cl(aq)} + \underbrace{Pb^{2+}(aq) + 2NO_3^-(aq)}_{\text{Ions in } Pb(NO_3)_2(aq)} \rightarrow$$

Exchanging the anions gives the possible solid products NH_4NO_3 and $PbCl_2$. NH_4NO_3 is soluble (rules 1 and 2) and $PbCl_2$ is insoluble (rule 3). Thus $PbCl_2$ will precipitate. The balanced equation is

$$2NH_4Cl(aq) + Pb(NO_3)_2(aq) \rightarrow PbCl_2(s) + 2NH_4NO_3(aq)$$

Self-Check Exercise 7.2

a. *Molecular equation:*
$Na_2S(aq) + Cu(NO_3)_2(aq) \rightarrow CuS(s) + 2NaNO_3(aq)$
Complete ionic equation:
$2Na^+(aq) + S^{2-}(aq) + Cu^{2+}(aq) + 2NO_3^-(aq) \rightarrow CuS(s) + 2Na^+(aq) + 2NO_3^-(aq)$
Net ionic equation:
$S^{2-}(aq) + Cu^{2+}(aq) \rightarrow CuS(s)$

b. *Molecular equation:*
$2NH_4Cl(aq) + Pb(NO_3)_2(aq) \rightarrow PbCl_2(s) + 2NH_4NO_3(aq)$
Complete ionic equation:
$2NH_4^+(aq) + 2Cl^-(aq) + Pb^{2+}(aq) + 2NO_3^-(aq) \rightarrow PbCl_2(s) + 2NH_4^+(aq) + 2NO_3^-(aq)$
Net ionic equation:
$2Cl^-(aq) + Pb^{2+}(aq) \rightarrow PbCl_2(s)$

Self-Check Exercise 7.3

a. The compound NaBr contains the ions Na^+ and Br^-. Thus each sodium atom loses one electron ($Na \rightarrow Na^+ + e^-$), and each bromine atom gains one electron ($Br + e^- \rightarrow Br^-$).

$$Na + Na + Br - Br \rightarrow (Na^+Br^-) + (Na^+Br^-)$$

(each Na transfers e^- to a Br atom)

b. The compound CaO contains the Ca^{2+} and O^{2-} ions. Thus each calcium atom loses two electrons ($Ca \rightarrow Ca^{2+} + 2e^-$), and each oxygen atom gains two electrons ($O + 2e^- \rightarrow O^{2-}$).

$$Ca + Ca + O - O \rightarrow (Ca^{2+}O^{2-}) + (Ca^{2+}O^{2-})$$

(each Ca transfers $2e^-$ to an O atom)

Self-Check Exercise 7.4

a. oxidation–reduction reaction; combustion reaction
b. synthesis reaction; oxidation–reduction reaction; combustion reaction
c. synthesis reaction; oxidation–reduction reaction
d. decomposition reaction; oxidation–reduction reaction
e. precipitation reaction (and double displacement)
f. synthesis reaction; oxidation–reduction reaction
g. acid–base reaction (and double displacement)
h. combustion reaction; oxidation–reduction reaction

Chapter 8

Self-Check Exercise 8.1

The average mass of nitrogen is 14.01 amu. The appropriate equivalence statement is 1 N atom = 14.01 amu, which yields the conversion factor we need:

$$23\ \cancel{\text{N atoms}} \times \frac{14.01\ \text{amu}}{\cancel{\text{N atom}}} = 322.2\ \text{amu}$$

(exact)

Self-Check Exercise 8.2

The average mass of oxygen is 16.00 amu, which gives the equivalence statement 1 O atom = 16.00 amu. The number of oxygen atoms present is

$$288\ \cancel{\text{amu}} \times \frac{1\ \text{O atom}}{16.00\ \cancel{\text{amu}}} = 18.0\ \text{O atoms}$$

Self-Check Exercise 8.3

Note that the sample of 5.00×10^{20} atoms of chromium is less than 1 mole (6.022×10^{23} atoms) of chromium. What fraction of a mole it represents can be determined as follows:

$$5.00 \times 10^{20}\ \cancel{\text{atoms Cr}} \times \frac{1\ \text{mol Cr}}{6.022 \times 10^{23}\ \cancel{\text{atoms Cr}}} = 8.30 \times 10^{-4}\ \text{mol Cr}$$

Because the mass of 1 mole of chromium atoms is 52.00 g, the mass of 5.00×10^{20} atoms can be determined as follows:

$$8.30 \times 10^{-4}\ \cancel{\text{mol Cr}} \times \frac{52.00\ \text{g Cr}}{1\ \cancel{\text{mol Cr}}} = 4.32 \times 10^{-2}\ \text{g Cr}$$

Self-Check Exercise 8.4

Each molecule of C_2H_3Cl contains two carbon atoms, three hydrogen atoms, and one chlorine atom, so 1 mole of C_2H_3Cl molecules contains 2 moles of C atoms, 3 moles of H atoms, and 1 mole of Cl atoms.

Mass of 2 mol C atoms:	$2 \times 12.01 =$	24.02 g
Mass of 3 mol H atoms:	$3 \times 1.008 =$	3.024 g
Mass of 1 mol Cl atoms:	$1 \times 35.45 =$	35.45 g
		62.494 g

The molar mass of C_2H_3Cl is 62.49 g (rounding to the correct number of significant figures).

Self-Check Exercise 8.5

The formula for sodium sulfate is Na_2SO_4. One mole of Na_2SO_4 contains 2 moles of sodium ions and 1 mole of sulfate ions.

1 mole of $Na_2SO_4 \rightarrow$ 1 mole of

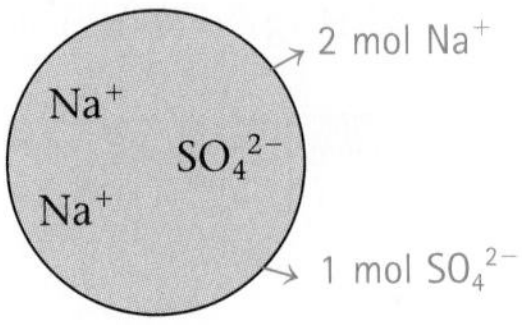

Mass of 2 mol Na^+	$= 2 \times 22.99$	$=$ 45.98 g
Mass of 1 mol SO_4^{2-}	$= 32.07 + 4(16.00)$	$=$ 96.07 g
Mass of 1 mol Na_2SO_4		$=$ 142.05 g

The molar mass for sodium sulfate is 142.05 g.

A sample of sodium sulfate with a mass of 300.0 g represents more than 1 mol. (Compare 300.0 g to the molar mass of Na_2SO_4.) We calculate the number of moles of Na_2SO_4 present in 300.0 g as follows:

$$300.0\ \cancel{\text{g } Na_2SO_4} \times \frac{1\ \text{mol } Na_2SO_4}{142.05\ \cancel{\text{g } Na_2SO_4}} = 2.112\ \text{mol } Na_2SO_4$$

Self-Check Exercise 8.6

First we must compute the mass of 1 mole of C_2F_4 molecules (the molar mass). Because 1 mole of C_2F_4 contains 2 moles of C atoms and 4 moles of F atoms, we have

$$2\ \cancel{\text{mol}}\ \text{C} \times \frac{12.01\ \text{g}}{\cancel{\text{mol}}} = 24.02\ \text{g C}$$

$$4\ \cancel{\text{mol}}\ \text{F} \times \frac{19.00\ \text{g}}{\cancel{\text{mol}}} = 76.00\ \text{g F}$$

Mass of 1 mole of C_2F_4: 100.02 g = molar mass

Using the equivalence statement 100.02 g C_2F_4 = 1 mole C_2F_4, we calculate the moles of C_2F_4 units in 135 g of Teflon.

$$135\ \cancel{\text{g } C_2F_4}\ \text{units} \times \frac{1\ \text{mol } C_2F_4}{100.02\ \cancel{\text{g } C_2F_4}} = 1.35\ \text{mol } C_2F_4\ \text{units}$$

Next, using the equivalence statement 1 mol = 6.022×10^{23} units, we calculate the number of C_2F_4 units in 135 mol of Teflon.

$$135\ \cancel{\text{mol}}\ C_2F_4 \times \frac{6.022 \times 10^{23}\ \text{units}}{1\ \cancel{\text{mol}}} = 8.13 \times 10^{23}\ C_2F_4\ \text{units}$$

Self-Check Exercise 8.7

The molar mass of penicillin F is computed as follows:

$$\text{C: } 14\ \cancel{\text{mol}} \times 12.01\ \frac{\text{g}}{\cancel{\text{mol}}} = 168.1\ \text{g}$$

$$\text{H: } 20\ \cancel{\text{mol}} \times 1.008\ \frac{\text{g}}{\cancel{\text{mol}}} = 20.16\ \text{g}$$

$$\text{N: } 2\ \cancel{\text{mol}} \times 14.01\ \frac{\text{g}}{\cancel{\text{mol}}} = 28.02\ \text{g}$$

$$\text{S: } 1\ \cancel{\text{mol}} \times 32.07\ \frac{\text{g}}{\cancel{\text{mol}}} = 32.07\ \text{g}$$

$$\text{O: } 4\ \cancel{\text{mol}} \times 16.00\ \frac{\text{g}}{\cancel{\text{mol}}} = 64.00\ \text{g}$$

Mass of 1 mole of $C_{14}H_{20}N_2SO_4$ = 312.39 g = 312.4 g

$$\text{Mass percent of C} = \frac{168.1\ \text{g C}}{312.4\ \text{g } C_{14}H_{20}N_2SO_4} \times 100\% = 53.81\%$$

$$\text{Mass percent of H} = \frac{20.16\ \text{g H}}{312.4\ \text{g } C_{14}H_{20}N_2SO_4} \times 100\% = 6.453\%$$

$$\text{Mass percent of N} = \frac{28.02\ \text{g N}}{312.4\ \text{g } C_{14}H_{20}N_2SO_4} \times 100\% = 8.969\%$$

$$\text{Mass percent of S} = \frac{32.07\ \text{g S}}{312.4\ \text{g } C_{14}H_{20}N_2SO_4} \times 100\% = 10.27\%$$

$$\text{Mass percent of O} = \frac{64.00\ \text{g O}}{312.4\ \text{g } C_{14}H_{20}N_2SO_4} \times 100\% = 20.49\%$$

Check: The percentages add up to 99.99%.

Self-Check Exercise 8.8

Step 1 0.6884 g lead and 0.2356 g chlorine

Step 2

$$0.6884\ \cancel{\text{g Pb}} \times \frac{1\ \text{mol Pb}}{207.2\ \cancel{\text{g Pb}}} = 0.003322\ \text{mol Pb}$$

$$0.2356\ \cancel{\text{g Cl}} \times \frac{1\ \text{mol Cl}}{35.45\ \cancel{\text{g Cl}}} = 0.006646\ \text{mol Cl}$$

Step 3 $\dfrac{0.003322 \text{ mol Pb}}{0.003322} = 1.000 \text{ mol Pb}$

$\dfrac{0.006646 \text{ mol Cl}}{0.003322} = 2.001 \text{ mol Cl}$

These numbers are very close to integers, so step 4 is unnecessary. The empirical formula is $PbCl_2$.

Self-Check Exercise 8.9

Step 1 0.8007 g C, 0.9333 g N, 0.2016 g H, and 2.133 g O

Step 2 $0.8007 \cancel{\text{g C}} \times \dfrac{1 \text{ mol C}}{12.01 \cancel{\text{g C}}} = 0.06667 \text{ mol C}$

$0.9333 \cancel{\text{g N}} \times \dfrac{1 \text{ mol N}}{14.01 \cancel{\text{g N}}} = 0.06662 \text{ mol N}$

$0.2016 \cancel{\text{g H}} \times \dfrac{1 \text{ mol H}}{1.008 \cancel{\text{g H}}} = 0.2000 \text{ mol H}$

$2.133 \cancel{\text{g O}} \times \dfrac{1 \text{ mol O}}{16.00 \cancel{\text{g O}}} = 0.1333 \text{ mol O}$

Step 3 $\dfrac{0.06667 \text{ mol C}}{0.06667} = 1.001 \text{ mol C}$

$\dfrac{0.06662 \text{ mol N}}{0.06667} = 1.000 \text{ mol N}$

$\dfrac{0.2000 \text{ mol H}}{0.06662} = 3.002 \text{ mol H}$

$\dfrac{0.1333 \text{ mol O}}{0.06662} = 2.001 \text{ mol O}$

The empirical formula is CNH_3O_2.

Self-Check Exercise 8.10

Step 1 In 100.00 g of Nylon-6 the masses of elements present are 63.68 g C, 12.38 g N, 9.80 g H, and 14.14 g O.

Step 2 $63.68 \cancel{\text{g C}} \times \dfrac{1 \text{ mol C}}{12.01 \cancel{\text{g C}}} = 5.302 \text{ mol C}$

$12.38 \cancel{\text{g N}} \times \dfrac{1 \text{ mol N}}{14.01 \cancel{\text{g N}}} = 0.8837 \text{ mol N}$

$9.80 \cancel{\text{g H}} \times \dfrac{1 \text{ mol H}}{1.008 \cancel{\text{g H}}} = 9.72 \text{ mol H}$

$14.14 \cancel{\text{g O}} \times \dfrac{1 \text{ mol O}}{16.00 \cancel{\text{g O}}} = 0.8838 \text{ mol O}$

Step 3 $\dfrac{5.302 \text{ mol C}}{0.8836} = 6.000 \text{ mol C}$

$\dfrac{0.8837 \text{ mol N}}{0.8837} = 1.000 \text{ mol N}$

$\dfrac{9.72 \text{ mol H}}{0.8837} = 11.0 \text{ mol H}$

$\dfrac{0.8838 \text{ mol O}}{0.8837} = 1.000 \text{ mol O}$

The empirical formula for Nylon-6 is $C_6NH_{11}O$.

Self-Check Exercise 8.11

Step 1 First we convert the mass percents to mass in grams. In 100.0 g of the compound, there are 71.65 g of chlorine, 24.27 g of carbon, and 4.07 g of hydrogen.

Step 2 We use these masses to compute the moles of atoms present.

$71.65 \cancel{\text{g Cl}} \times \dfrac{1 \text{ mol Cl}}{35.45 \cancel{\text{g Cl}}} = 2.021 \text{ mol Cl}$

$24.27 \cancel{\text{g C}} \times \dfrac{1 \text{ mol C}}{12.01 \cancel{\text{g C}}} = 2.021 \text{ mol C}$

$4.07 \cancel{\text{g H}} \times \dfrac{1 \text{ mol H}}{1.008 \cancel{\text{g H}}} = 4.04 \text{ mol H}$

Step 3 Dividing each mole value by 2.021 (the smallest number of moles present), we obtain the empirical formula $ClCH_2$.

To determine the molecular formula, we must compare the empirical formula mass to the molar mass. The empirical formula mass is 49.48.

Cl:	35.45
C:	12.01
2 H:	2 × (1.008)
$ClCH_2$:	49.48 = empirical formula mass

The molar mass is known to be 98.96. We know that

$$\text{Molar mass} = n \times (\text{empirical formula mass})$$

So we can obtain the value of n as follows:

$$\frac{\text{Molar mass}}{\text{Empirical formula mass}} = \frac{98.96}{49.48} = 2$$

$$\text{Molecular formula} = (ClCH_2)_2 = Cl_2C_2H_4$$

This substance is composed of molecules with the formula $Cl_2C_2H_4$.

Chapter 9

Self-Check Exercise 9.1

The problem can be stated as follows:

$$4.30 \text{ mol } C_3H_8 \underset{\text{yields}}{\rightarrow} ? \text{ mol } CO_2$$

From the balanced equation

$$C_3H_8(g) + 5O_2(g) \rightarrow 3CO_2(g) + 4H_2O(g)$$

we derive the equivalence statement

$$1 \text{ mol } C_3H_8 = 3 \text{ mol } CO_2$$

The appropriate conversion factor (moles of C_3H_8 must cancel) is 3 mol CO_2/1 mol C_3H_8, and the calculation is

$$4.30 \cancel{\text{mol } C_3H_8} \times \frac{3 \text{ mol } CO_2}{1 \cancel{\text{mol } C_3H_8}} = 12.9 \text{ mol } CO_2$$

Thus we can say

$$4.30 \text{ mol } C_3H_8 \text{ yields } 12.9 \text{ mol } CO_2$$

Self-Check Exercise 9.2

The problem can be sketched as follows:

$$C_3H_8(g) + 5O_2(g) \rightarrow 3CO_2(g) + 4H_2O(g)$$

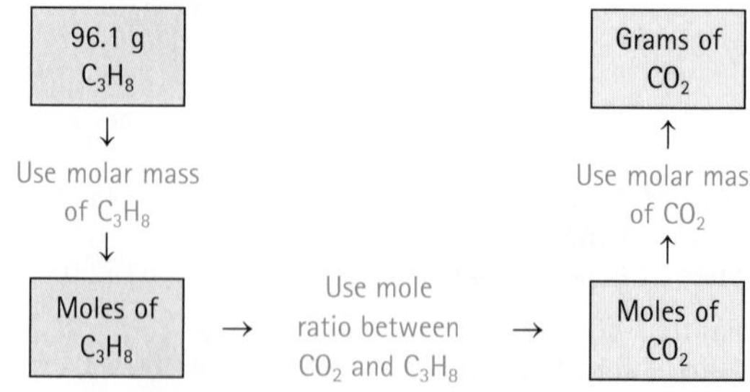

We have already done the first step in Example 9.4.

$$\boxed{96.1 \text{ g } C_3H_8} \rightarrow \frac{1 \text{ mol}}{44.09 \text{ g}} \rightarrow \boxed{2.18 \text{ mol } C_3H_8}$$

To find out how many moles of CO_2 can be produced from 2.18 moles of C_3H_8, we see from the balanced equation that 3 moles of CO_2 is produced for each mole of C_3H_8 reacted. The mole ratio we need is 3 mol CO_2/1 mol C_3H_8. The conversion is therefore

$$2.18\ \cancel{\text{mol } C_3H_8} \times \frac{3 \text{ mol } CO_2}{1\ \cancel{\text{mol } C_3H_8}} = 6.54 \text{ mol } CO_2$$

Next, using the molar mass of CO_2, which is 12.01 + 32.00 = 44.01 g, we calculate the mass of CO_2 produced.

$$6.54\ \cancel{\text{mol } CO_2} \times \frac{44.01 \text{ g } CO_2}{1\ \cancel{\text{mol } CO_2}} = 288 \text{ g } CO_2$$

The sequence of steps we took to find the mass of carbon dioxide produced from 96.1 g of propane is summarized in the following diagram.

96.1 g C_3H_8	→	$\frac{1 \text{ mol } C_3H_8}{44.09 \text{ g } C_3H_8}$	→	2.18 mol C_3H_8
2.18 mol C_3H_8	→	$\frac{3 \text{ mol } CO_2}{1 \text{ mol } C_3H_8}$	→	6.54 mol CO_2
6.54 mol CO_2	→	$\frac{44.01 \text{ g } CO_2}{1 \text{ mol } CO_2}$	→	288 g CO_2
Mass				Moles

Self-Check Exercise 9.3

We sketch the problem as follows:

$$C_3H_8(g) + 5O_2(g) \rightarrow 3CO_2(g) + 4H_2O(g)$$

96.1 g C_3H_8				Grams of H_2O
↓				↑
$\frac{1 \text{ mol } C_3H_8}{44.09 \text{ g}}$				$\frac{18.02 \text{ g}}{\text{mol } H_2O}$
↓				↑
Moles of C_3H_8	→	$\frac{4 \text{ mol } H_2O}{1 \text{ mol } C_3H_8}$	→	Moles of H_2O

Then we do the calculations.

96.1 g C_3H_8	→	$\frac{1 \text{ mol } C_3H_8}{44.09 \text{ g}}$	→	2.18 mol C_3H_8
2.18 mol C_3H_8	→	$\frac{4 \text{ mol } H_2O}{1 \text{ mol } C_3H_8}$	→	8.72 mol H_2O
8.72 mol H_2O	→	$\frac{18.02 \text{ g}}{\text{mol } H_2O}$	→	157 g H_2O

Therefore, 157 g of H_2O is produced from 96.1 g C_3H_8.

Self-Check Exercise 9.4

a. We first write the balanced equation.

$$SiO_2(s) + 4HF(aq) \rightarrow SiF_4(g) + 2H_2O(l)$$

The map of the steps required is

$$SiO_2(s) + 4HF(aq) \rightarrow SiF_4(g) + 2H_2O(l)$$

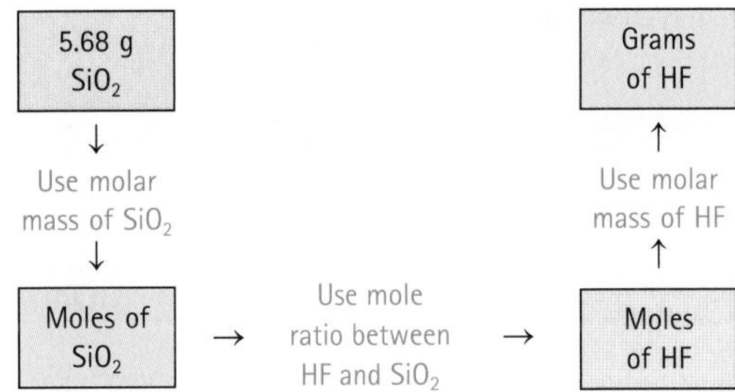

We convert 5.68 g of SiO_2 to moles as follows:

$$5.68\ \cancel{\text{g } SiO_2} \times \frac{1 \text{ mol } SiO_2}{60.09\ \cancel{\text{g } SiO_2}} = 9.45 \times 10^{-2} \text{ mol } SiO_2$$

Using the balanced equation, we obtain the appropriate mole ratio and convert to moles of HF.

$$9.45 \times 10^{-2}\ \cancel{\text{mol } SiO_2} \times \frac{4 \text{ mol HF}}{1\ \cancel{\text{mol } SiO_2}} = 3.78 \times 10^{-1} \text{ mol HF}$$

Finally, we calculate the mass of HF by using its molar mass.

$$3.78 \times 10^{-1}\ \cancel{\text{mol HF}} \times \frac{20.01 \text{ g HF}}{\cancel{\text{mol HF}}} = 7.56 \text{ g HF}$$

b. The map for this problem is

$$SiO_2(s) + 4HF(aq) \rightarrow SiF_4(g) + 2H_2O(l)$$

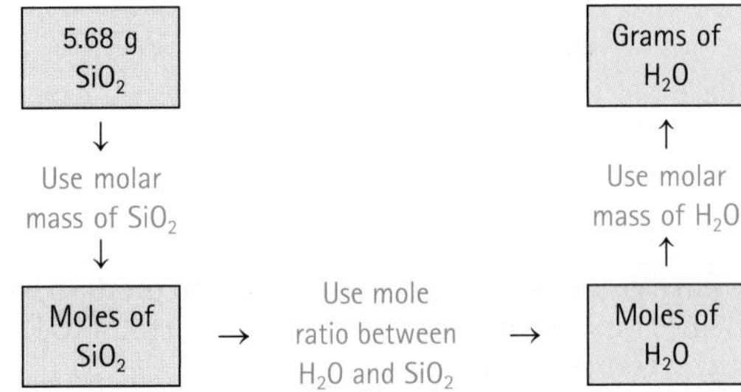

We have already accomplished the first conversion in part a. Using the balanced equation, we obtain moles of H_2O as follows:

$$9.45 \times 10^{-2}\ \cancel{\text{mol } SiO_2} \times \frac{2 \text{ mol } H_2O}{1\ \cancel{\text{mol } SiO_2}} = 1.89 \times 10^{-1} \text{ mol } H_2O$$

The mass of water formed is

$$1.89 \times 10^{-1}\ \cancel{\text{mol } H_2O} \times \frac{18.02 \text{ g } H_2O}{\cancel{\text{mol } H_2O}} = 3.41 \text{ g } H_2O$$

Self-Check Exercise 9.5

In this problem, we know the mass of the product to be formed by the reaction

$$CO(g) + 2H_2(g) \rightarrow CH_3OH(l)$$

and we want to find the masses of reactants needed. The procedure is the same one we have been following. We must first convert the mass of CH_3OH to moles, then use the balanced equation to obtain moles of H_2 and CO needed, and then convert these moles to masses. Using the molar mass of CH_3OH (32.04 g/mol), we convert to moles of CH_3OH.

First we convert kilograms to grams.

$$6.0\ \cancel{\text{kg}}\ CH_3OH \times \frac{1000 \text{ g}}{\cancel{\text{kg}}} = 6.0 \times 10^3 \text{ g } CH_3OH$$

Next we convert 6.0×10^3 g CH_3OH to moles of CH_3OH, using the conversion factor 1 mol CH_3OH/32.04 g CH_3OH.

$$6.0 \times 10^3\ \cancel{\text{g } CH_3OH} \times \frac{1 \text{ mol } CH_3OH}{32.04\ \cancel{\text{g } CH_3OH}} = 1.9 \times 10^2 \text{ mol } CH_3OH$$

Then we have two questions to answer:

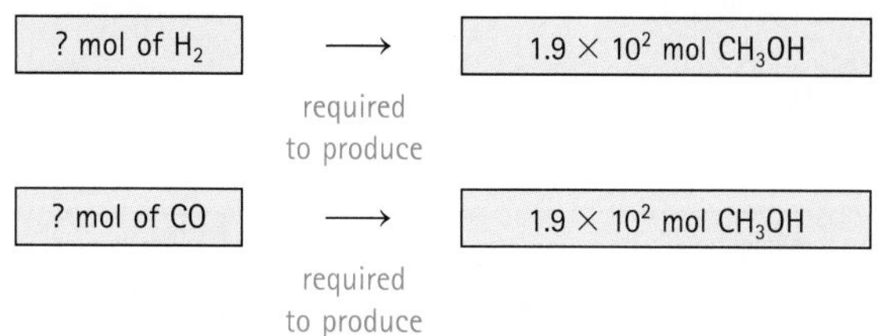

To answer these questions, we use the balanced equation

$$CO(g) + 2H_2(g) \rightarrow CH_3OH(l)$$

to obtain mole ratios between the reactants and the products. In the balanced equation the coefficients for both CO and CH_3OH are 1, so we can write the equivalence statement

$$1 \text{ mol CO} = 1 \text{ mol } CH_3OH$$

Using the mole ratio 1 mol CO/1 mol CH_3OH, we can now convert from moles of CH_3OH to moles of CO.

$$1.9 \times 10^2 \text{ mol } CH_3OH \times \frac{1 \text{ mol CO}}{1 \text{ mol } CH_3OH} = 1.9 \times 10^2 \text{ mol CO}$$

To calculate the moles of H_2 required, we construct the equivalence statement between CH_3OH and H_2, using the coefficients in the balanced equation.

$$2 \text{ mol } H_2 = 1 \text{ mol } CH_3OH$$

Using the mole ratio 2 mol H_2/1 mol CH_3OH, we can convert moles of CH_3OH to moles of H_2.

$$1.9 \times 10^2 \text{ mol } CH_3OH \times \frac{2 \text{ mol } H_2}{1 \text{ mol } CH_3OH} = 3.8 \times 10^2 \text{ mol } H_2$$

We now have the moles of reactants required to produce 6.0 kg of CH_3OH. Since we need the masses of reactants, we must use the molar masses to convert from moles to mass.

$$1.9 \times 10^2 \text{ mol CO} \times \frac{28.01 \text{ g CO}}{1 \text{ mol CO}} = 5.3 \times 10^3 \text{ g CO}$$

$$3.8 \times 10^2 \text{ mol } H_2 \times \frac{2.016 \text{ g } H_2}{1 \text{ mol } H_2} = 7.7 \times 10^2 \text{ } H_2$$

Therefore, we need 5.3×10^3 g CO to react with 7.7×10^2 g H_2 to form 6.0×10^3 g (6.0 kg) of CH_3OH. This whole process is mapped in the following diagram.

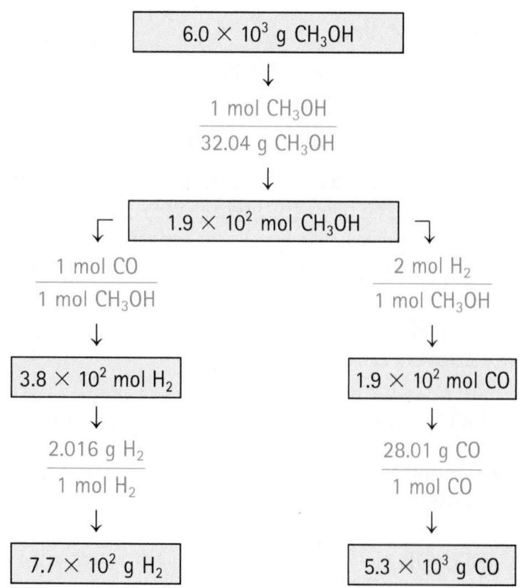

Self-Check Exercise 9.6

Step 1 The balanced equation for the reaction is

$$6Li(s) + N_2(g) \rightarrow 2Li_3N(s)$$

Step 2 To determine the limiting reactant, we must convert the masses of lithium (atomic mass = 6.941 g) and nitrogen (molar mass = 28.02 g) to moles.

$$56.0 \text{ g Li} \times \frac{1 \text{ mol Li}}{6.941 \text{ g Li}} = 8.07 \text{ mol Li}$$

$$56.0 \text{ g } N_2 \times \frac{1 \text{ mol } N_2}{28.02 \text{ g } N_2} = 2.00 \text{ mol } N_2$$

Step 3 Using the mole ratio from the balanced equation, we can calculate the moles of lithium required to react with 2.00 moles of nitrogen.

$$2.00 \text{ mol } N_2 \times \frac{6 \text{ mol Li}}{1 \text{ mol } N_2} = 12.0 \text{ mol Li}$$

Therefore, 12.0 moles of Li is required to react with 2.00 moles of N_2. However, we have only 8.07 mol of Li, so lithium is limiting. It will be consumed before the nitrogen runs out.

Step 4 Because lithium is the limiting reactant, we must use the 8.07 moles of Li to determine how many moles of Li_3N can be formed.

$$8.07 \text{ mol Li} \times \frac{2 \text{ mol } Li_3N}{6 \text{ mol Li}} = 2.69 \text{ mol } Li_3N$$

Step 5 We can now use the molar mass of Li_3N (34.83 g) to calculate the mass of Li_3N formed.

$$2.69 \text{ mol } Li_3N \times \frac{34.83 \text{ g } Li_3N}{1 \text{ mol } Li_3N} = 93.7 \text{ g } Li_3N$$

Self-Check Exercise 9.7

a. **Step 1** The balanced equation is

$$TiCl_4(g) + O_2(g) \rightarrow TiO_2(s) + 2Cl_2(g)$$

Step 2 The numbers of moles of reactants are

$$6.71 \times 10^3 \text{ g } TiCl_4 \times \frac{1 \text{ mol } TiCl_4}{189.68 \text{ g } TiCl_4} = 3.54 \times 10^1 \text{ mol } TiCl_4$$

$$2.45 \times 10^3 \text{ g } O_2 \times \frac{1 \text{ mol } O_2}{32.00 \text{ g } O_2} = 7.66 \times 10^1 \text{ mol } O_2$$

Step 3 In the balanced equation both $TiCl_4$ and O_2 have coefficients of 1, so

$$1 \text{ mol } TiCl_4 = 1 \text{ mol } O_2$$

and

$$3.54 \times 10^1 \text{ mol } TiCl_4 \times \frac{1 \text{ mol } O_2}{1 \text{ mol } TiCl_4} = 3.54 \times 10^1 \text{ mol } O_2 \text{ required}$$

We have 7.66×10^1 moles of O_2, so the O_2 is in excess and the $TiCl_4$ is limiting. This makes sense. $TiCl_4$ and O_2 react in a 1:1 mole ratio, so the $TiCl_4$ is limiting because fewer moles of $TiCl_4$ are present than moles of O_2.

Step 4 We will now use the moles of $TiCl_4$ (the limiting reactant) to determine the moles of TiO_2 that would form if the reaction produced 100% of the expected yield (the theoretical yield).

$$3.54 \times 10^1 \text{ mol } TiCl_4 \times \frac{1 \text{ mol } TiO_2}{1 \text{ mol } TiCl_4} = 3.54 \times 10^1 \text{ mol } TiO_2$$

The mass of TiO_2 expected for 100% yield is

$$3.54 \times 10^1 \text{ mol } TiO_2 \times \frac{79.88 \text{ g } TiO_2}{1 \text{ mol } TiO_2} = 2.83 \times 10^3 \text{ g } TiO_2$$

This amount represents the theoretical yield.

b. Because the reaction is said to give only a 75.0% yield of TiO_2, we use the definition of percent yield,

$$\frac{\text{Actual yield}}{\text{Theoretical yield}} \times 100\% = \%\ \text{yield}$$

to write the equation

$$\frac{\text{Actual yield}}{2.83 \times 10^3\ \text{g TiO}_2} \times 100\% = 75.0\%\ \text{yield}$$

We now want to solve for the actual yield. First we divide both sides by 100%.

$$\frac{\text{Actual yield}}{2.83 \times 10^3\ \text{g TiO}_2} \times \frac{100\%}{100\%} = \frac{75.0}{100} = 0.750$$

Then we multiply both sides by 2.83×10^3 g TiO_2.

$$2.83 \times 10^3\ \text{g TiO}_2 \times \frac{\text{Actual yield}}{2.83 \times 10^3\ \text{g TiO}_2} = 0.750 \times 2.83 \times 10^3\ \text{g TiO}_2$$

$$\text{Actual yield} = 0.750 \times 2.83 \times 10^3\ \text{g TiO}_2 = 2.12 \times 10^3\ \text{g TiO}_2$$

Thus 2.12×10^3 g of $TiO_2(s)$ is actually obtained in this reaction.

Chapter 10

Self-Check Exercise 10.1

The conversion factor needed is $\frac{1\ \text{cal}}{4.184\ \text{J}}$, and the conversion is

$$28.4\ \cancel{\text{J}} \times \frac{1\ \text{cal}}{4.184\ \cancel{\text{J}}} = 6.79\ \text{cal}$$

Self-Check Exercise 10.2

We know that it takes 4.184 J of energy to change the temperature of each gram of water by 1 °C, so we must multiply 4.184 by the mass of water (454 g) and the temperature change (98.6 °C − 5.4 °C = 93.2 °C).

$$4.184 \frac{\text{J}}{\cancel{\text{g}}\ \cancel{°\text{C}}} \times 454\ \cancel{\text{g}} \times 93.2\ \cancel{°\text{C}} = 1.77 \times 10^5\ \text{J}$$

Self-Check Exercise 10.3

From Table 10.1, the specific heat capacity for solid gold is 0.13 J/g °C. Because it takes 0.13 J to change the temperature of *one* gram of gold by *one* Celsius degree, we must multiply 0.13 by the sample size (5.63 g) and the change in temperature (32 °C − 21 °C = 11 °C).

$$0.13 \frac{\text{J}}{\text{g}\ °\text{C}} \times 5.63\ \text{g} \times 11\ °\text{C} = 8.1\ \text{J}$$

We can change this energy to units of calories as follows:

$$8.1\ \text{J} \times \frac{1\ \text{cal}}{4.184\ \text{J}} = 1.9\ \text{cal}$$

Self-Check Exercise 10.4

Table 10.1 lists the specific heat capacities of several metals. We want to calculate the specific heat capacity (s) for this metal and then use Table 10.1 to identify the metal. Using the equation

$$Q = s \times m \times \Delta T$$

we can solve for s by dividing both sides by m (the mass of the sample) and by ΔT:

$$\frac{Q}{m \times \Delta T} = s$$

In this case,

Q = energy (heat) required = 10.1 J
m = 2.8 g
ΔT = temperature change = 36 °C − 21 °C = 15 °C

so

$$s = \frac{Q}{m \times \Delta T} = \frac{10.1\ \text{J}}{(2.8\ \text{g})(15\ °\text{C})} = 0.24\ \text{J/g}\ °\text{C}$$

Table 10.1 shows that silver has a specific heat capacity of 0.24 J/g °C. The metal is silver.

Self-Check Exercise 10.5

We are told that 1652 kJ of energy is *released* when 4 moles of Fe reacts. We first need to determine what number of moles 1.00 g Fe represents.

$$1.00\ \text{g Fe} \times \frac{1\ \text{mol}}{55.85\ \text{g}} = 1.79 \times 10^{-2}\ \text{mol Fe}$$

$$1.79 \times 10^{-2}\ \text{mol Fe} \times \frac{1652\ \text{kJ}}{4\ \text{mol Fe}} = 7.39\ \text{kJ}$$

Thus 7.39 kJ of energy (as heat) is released when 1.00 g of iron reacts.

Self-Check Exercise 10.6

Noting the reactants and products in the desired reaction

$$S(s) + O_2(g) \rightarrow SO_2(g)$$

We need to reverse the second equation and multiply it by $\frac{1}{2}$. This reverses the sign and cuts the amount of energy by a factor of 2.

$$\tfrac{1}{2}[2SO_3(g) \rightarrow 2SO_2(g) + O_2(g)] \qquad \Delta H = \frac{198.2\ \text{kJ}}{2}$$

or

$$SO_3(g) \rightarrow SO_2(g) + \tfrac{1}{2}O_2(g) \qquad \Delta H = 99.1\ \text{kJ}$$

Now we add this reaction to the first reaction.

$$S(s) + \tfrac{3}{2}O_2(g) \rightarrow SO_3(g) \qquad \Delta H = -395.2\ \text{kJ}$$
$$SO_3(g) \rightarrow SO_2(g) + \tfrac{1}{2}O_2(g) \qquad \Delta H = 99.1\ \text{kJ}$$
$$S(s) + O_2(g) \rightarrow SO_2(g) \qquad \Delta H = -296.1\ \text{kJ}$$

Chapter 11

Self-Check Exercise 11.1

a. Circular pathways for electrons in the Bohr model.
b. Three-dimensional probability maps that represent the likelihood that the electron will occupy a given point in space.
c. The surface that contains 90% of the total electron probability.
d. A set of orbitals of a given type of orbital within a principal energy level. For example, there are three sublevels in principal energy level 3 (s, p, d).

Self-Check Exercise 11.2

Element	Electron Configuration	Orbital Diagram 1s	2s	2p	3s	3p
Al	$1s^22s^22p^63s^23p^1$ $[Ne]3s^23p^1$	↑↓	↑↓	↑↓ ↑↓ ↑↓	↑↓	↑ ☐ ☐
Si	$[Ne]3s^23p^2$	↑↓	↑↓	↑↓ ↑↓ ↑↓	↑↓	↑ ↑ ☐
P	$[Ne]3s^23p^3$	↑↓	↑↓	↑↓ ↑↓ ↑↓	↑↓	↑ ↑ ↑
S	$[Ne]3s^23p^4$	↑↓	↑↓	↑↓ ↑↓ ↑↓	↑↓	↑↓ ↑ ↑
Cl	$[Ne]3s^23p^5$	↑↓	↑↓	↑↓ ↑↓ ↑↓	↑↓	↑↓ ↑↓ ↑
Ar	$[Ne]3s^23p^6$	↑↓	↑↓	↑↓ ↑↓ ↑↓	↑↓	↑↓ ↑↓ ↑↓

Self-Check Exercise 11.3

F: $1s^22s^22p^5$ or $[He]2s^22p^5$
Si: $1s^22s^22p^63s^23p^2$ or $[Ne]3s^23p^2$
Cs: $1s^22s^22p^63s^23p^64s^23d^{10}4p^65s^24d^{10}5p^66s^1$ or $[Xe]6s^1$
Pb: $1s^22s^22p^63s^23p^64s^23d^{10}4p^65s^24d^{10}5p^66s^24f^{14}5d^{10}6p^2$ or $[Xe]6s^24f^{14}5d^{10}6p^2$
I: $1s^22s^22p^63s^23p^64s^23d^{10}4p^65s^24d^{10}5p^5$ or $[Kr]5s^24d^{10}5p^5$

Silicon (Si): In Group 4 and Period 3, it is the second of the "3*p* elements." The configuration is $1s^22s^22p^63s^23p^2$, or $[Ne]3s^23p^2$.
Cesium (Cs): In Group 1 and Period 6, it is the first of the "6*s* elements." The configuration is $1s^22s^22p^63s^23p^64s^23d^{10}4p^65s^24d^{10}5p^66s^1$, or $[Xe]6s^1$.
Lead (Pb): In Group 4 and Period 6, it is the second of the "6*p* elements." The configuration is $[Xe]6s^24f^{14}5d^{10}6p^2$.
Iodine (I): In Group 7 and Period 5, it is the fifth of the "5*p* elements." The configuration is $[Kr]5s^24d^{10}5p^5$.

Chapter 12

Self-Check Exercise 12.1

Using the electronegativity values given in Figure 12.3, we choose the bond in which the atoms exhibit the largest difference in electronegativity. (Electronegativity values are shown in parentheses.)

a. H—C (2.1)(2.5) > H—P (2.1)(2.1)
b. O—I (3.5)(2.5) > O—F (3.5)(4.0)
c. S—O (2.5)(3.5) > N—O (3.0)(3.5)
d. N—H (3.0)(2.1) > Si—H (1.8)(2.1)

Self-Check Exercise 12.2

H has one electron, and Cl has seven valence electrons. This gives a total of eight valence electrons. We first draw in the bonding pair:

H—Cl, which could be drawn as H:Cl

We have six electrons yet to place. The H already has two electrons, so we place three lone pairs around the chlorine to satisfy the octet rule.

H—C̈l: or H:C̈l: (with lone pairs above and below Cl)

Self-Check Exercise 12.3

Step 1 O_3: 3(6) = 18 valence electrons
Step 2 O—O—O
Step 3 O=O—O and O—O=O (with lone pairs completing each octet)

This molecule shows resonance (it has two valid Lewis structures).

Self-Check Exercise 12.4

See table on top of page A10.

Self-Check Exercise 12.5

a. NH_4^+

The Lewis structure is $\left[\begin{array}{c} H \\ | \\ H—N—H \\ | \\ H \end{array}\right]^+$

(See Self-Check Exercise 12.4.) There are four pairs of electrons around the nitrogen. This requires a tetrahedral arrangement of electron pairs. The NH_4^+ ion has a tetrahedral molecular structure (row 3 in Table 12.4), because all electron pairs are shared.

b. SO_4^{2-}

The Lewis structure is [:Ö—S—Ö: with :Ö: above and below S]$^{2-}$

(See Self-Check Exercise 12.4.) The four electron pairs around the sulfur require a tetrahedral arrangement. The SO_4^{2-} has a tetrahedral molecular structure (row 3 in Table 12.4).

c. NF_3

The Lewis structure is :F̈—N̈(—F̈:)—F̈: (N with one lone pair bonded to three F atoms)

(See Self-Check Exercise 12.4.) The four pairs of electrons on the nitrogen require a tetrahedral arrangement. In this case, only three of the pairs are shared with the fluorine atoms, leaving one lone pair. Thus the molecular structure is a trigonal pyramid (row 4 in Table 12.4).

d. H_2S

The Lewis structure is H—S̈—H

(See Self-Check Exercise 12.4.) The four pairs of electrons around the sulfur require a tetrahedral arrangement. In this case, two pairs are shared with hydrogen atoms, leaving two lone pairs. Thus the molecular structure is bent or V-shaped (row 5 in Table 12.4).

e. ClO_3^-

The Lewis structure is [:Ö—C̈l—Ö: with :Ö: below Cl]$^-$

(See Self-Check Exercise 12.4.) The four pairs of electrons require a tetrahedral arrangement. In this case, three pairs are shared with oxygen atoms, leaving one lone pair. Thus the molecular structure is a trigonal pyramid (row 4 in Table 12.4).

Molecule or Ion	Total Valence Electrons	Draw Single Bonds	Calculate Number of Electrons Remaining	Use Remaining Electrons to Achieve Noble Gas Configurations	*Check* Atoms	*Check* Electrons
a. NF_3	$5 + 3(7) = 26$	F—N(—F)—F	$26 - 6 = 20$	$:\ddot{F}—\ddot{N}—\ddot{F}:$ with $:\ddot{F}:$ below N	N F	8 8
b. O_2	$2(6) = 12$	O—O	$12 - 2 = 10$	$\ddot{O}=\ddot{O}$	O	8
c. CO	$4 + 6 = 10$	C—O	$10 - 2 = 8$	$:C\equiv O:$	C O	8 8
d. PH_3	$5 + 3(1) = 8$	H, H, H bonded to P	$8 - 6 = 2$	$H—\ddot{P}—H$ with H below P	P H	8 2
e. H_2S	$2(1) + 6 = 8$	H—S—H	$8 - 4 = 4$	$H—\ddot{S}—H$ (lone pairs above and below S)	S H	8 2
f. $SO_4{}^{2-}$	$6 + 4(6) + 2 = 32$	O—S—O with O above and below S	$32 - 8 = 24$	$[:\ddot{O}—S—\ddot{O}:]^{2-}$ with $:\ddot{O}:$ above and below S	S O	8 8
g. $NH_4{}^+$	$5 + 4(1) - 1 = 8$	H—N—H with H above and below N	$8 - 8 = 0$	$[H—N—H]^+$ with H above and below N	N H	8 2
h. $ClO_3{}^-$	$7 + 3(6) + 1 = 26$	O above Cl; O, O below Cl	$26 - 6 = 20$	$[:\ddot{O}—\ddot{Cl}—\ddot{O}:]^-$ with $:\ddot{O}:$ below Cl	Cl O	8 8
i. SO_2	$6 + 2(6) = 18$	O—S—O	$18 - 4 = 14$	$\ddot{O}=\ddot{S}—\ddot{O}:$ and $:\ddot{O}—\ddot{S}=\ddot{O}$	S O	8 8

Answer to Self-Check Exercise 12.4.

f. BeF_2

The Lewis structure is $:\ddot{F}—Be—\ddot{F}:$

The two electron pairs on beryllium require a linear arrangement. Because both pairs are shared by fluorine atoms, the molecular structure is also linear (row 1 in Table 12.4).

Chapter 13

Self-Check Exercise 13.1

We know that 1.000 atm = 760.0 mm Hg. So

$$525 \text{ mm Hg} \times \frac{1.000 \text{ atm}}{760.0 \text{ mm Hg}} = 0.691 \text{ atm}$$

Self-Check Exercise 13.2

Initial Conditions	**Final Conditions**
$P_1 = 635$ torr	$P_2 = 785$ torr
$V_1 = 1.51$ L	$V_2 = ?$

Solving Boyle's law ($P_1V_1 = P_2V_2$) for V_2 gives

$$V_2 = V_1 \times \frac{P_1}{P_2}$$

$$= 1.51 \text{ L} \times \frac{635 \text{ torr}}{785 \text{ torr}} = 1.22 \text{ L}$$

Note that the volume decreased, as the increase in pressure led us to expect.

Self-Check Exercise 13.3

Because the temperature of the gas inside the bubble decreases (at constant pressure), the bubble gets smaller. The conditions are

Initial Conditions

$T_1 = 28\ °C = 28 + 273 = 301$ K

$V_1 = 23\ cm^3$

Final Conditions

$T_2 = 18\ °C = 18 + 273 = 291$ K

$V_2 = ?$

Solving Charles's law,

$$\frac{V_1}{T_1} = \frac{V_2}{T_2}$$

for V_2 gives

$$V_2 = V_1 \times \frac{T_2}{T_1} = 23\ \text{cm}^3 \times \frac{291\ \cancel{\text{K}}}{301\ \cancel{\text{K}}} = 22\ \text{cm}^3$$

Self-Check Exercise 13.4

Because the temperature and pressure of the two samples are the same, we can use Avogadro's law in the form

$$\frac{V_1}{n_1} = \frac{V_2}{n_2}$$

The following information is given:

Sample 1	**Sample 2**
$V_1 = 36.7$ L	$V_2 = 16.5$ L
$n_1 = 1.5$ mol	$n_2 = ?$

We can now solve Avogadro's law for the value of n_2 (the moles of N_2 in sample 2):

$$n_2 = n_1 \times \frac{V_2}{V_1} = 1.5\ \text{mol} \times \frac{16.5\ \cancel{\text{L}}}{36.7\ \cancel{\text{L}}} = 0.67\ \text{mol}$$

Here n_2 is smaller than n_1, which makes sense in view of the fact that V_2 is smaller than V_1.

Note: We isolate n_2 from Avogadro's law as given above by multiplying both sides of the equation by n_2 and then by n_1/V_1,

$$\left(n_2 \times \frac{n_1}{V_1}\right)\frac{V_1}{n_1} = \left(n_2 \times \frac{n_1}{V_1}\right)\frac{V_2}{n_2}$$

to give $n_2 = n_1 \times V_2/V_1$.

Self-Check Exercise 13.5

We are given the following information:

$P = 1.00$ atm
$V = 2.70 \times 10^6$ L
$n = 1.10 \times 10^5$ mol

We solve for T by dividing both sides of the ideal gas law by nR:

$$\frac{PV}{nR} = \frac{\cancel{nR}T}{\cancel{nR}}$$

to give

$$T = \frac{PV}{nR} = \frac{(1.00\ \cancel{\text{atm}})(2.70 \times 10^6\ \cancel{\text{L}})}{(1.10 \times 10^5\ \cancel{\text{mol}})\left(0.08206\ \dfrac{\cancel{\text{L}}\ \cancel{\text{atm}}}{\text{K}\ \cancel{\text{mol}}}\right)}$$

$$= 299\ \text{K}$$

The temperature of the helium is 299 K, or 299 − 273 = 26 °C.

Self-Check Exercise 13.6

We are given the following information about the radon sample:

$n = 1.5$ mol
$V = 21.0$ L
$T = 33\ °\text{C} = 33 + 273 = 306$ K
$P = ?$

We solve the ideal gas law ($PV = nRT$) for P by dividing both sides of the equation by V:

$$P = \frac{nRT}{V} = \frac{(1.5\ \cancel{\text{mol}})\left(0.08206\ \dfrac{\cancel{\text{L}}\ \text{atm}}{\cancel{\text{K}}\ \cancel{\text{mol}}}\right)(306\ \cancel{\text{K}})}{21.0\ \cancel{\text{L}}}$$

$$= 1.8\ \text{atm}$$

Self-Check Exercise 13.7

To solve this problem, we take the ideal gas law and separate those quantities that change from those that remain constant (on opposite sides of the equation). In this case, volume and temperature change, and number of moles and pressure (and, of course, R) remain constant. So $PV = nRT$ becomes $V/T = nR/P$, which leads to

$$\frac{V_1}{T_1} = \frac{nR}{P} \quad \text{and} \quad \frac{V_2}{T_2} = \frac{nR}{P}$$

Combining these gives

$$\frac{V_1}{T_1} = \frac{nR}{P} = \frac{V_2}{T_2} \quad \text{or} \quad \frac{V_1}{T_1} = \frac{V_2}{T_2}$$

We are given

Initial Conditions

$T_1 = 5\ °\text{C} = 5 + 273 = 278$ K
$V_1 = 3.8$ L

Final Conditions

$T_2 = 86\ °\text{C} = 86 + 273 = 359$ K
$V_2 = ?$

Thus

$$V_2 = \frac{T_2V_1}{T_1} = \frac{(359\ \cancel{\text{K}})(3.8\ \text{L})}{278\ \cancel{\text{K}}} = 4.9\ \text{L}$$

Check: Is the answer sensible? In this case, the temperature was increased (at constant pressure), so the volume should increase. The answer makes sense.

Note that this problem could be described as a "Charles's law problem." The real advantage of using the ideal gas law is that you need to remember only *one* equation to do virtually any problem involving gases.

Self-Check Exercise 13.8

We are given the following information:

Initial Conditions

$P_1 = 0.747$ atm
$T_1 = 13\ °\text{C} = 13 + 273 = 286$ K
$V_1 = 11.0$ L

Final Conditions

$P_2 = 1.18$ atm
$T_2 = 56\ °\text{C} = 56 + 273 = 329$ K
$V_2 = ?$

In this case, the number of moles remains constant. Thus we can say

$$\frac{P_1V_1}{T_1} = nR \quad \text{and} \quad \frac{P_2V_2}{T_2} = nR$$

or

$$\frac{P_1V_1}{T_1} = \frac{P_2V_2}{T_2}$$

Solving for V_2 gives

$$V_2 = V_1 \times \frac{T_2}{T_1} \times \frac{P_1}{P_2} = (11.0\ \text{L})\left(\frac{329\ \cancel{\text{K}}}{286\ \cancel{\text{K}}}\right)\left(\frac{0.747\ \cancel{\text{atm}}}{1.18\ \cancel{\text{atm}}}\right)$$

$$= 8.01\ \text{L}$$

Self-Check Exercise 13.9

As usual when dealing with gases, we can use the ideal gas equation $PV = nRT$. First consider the information given:

$P = 0.91\ \text{atm} = P_{\text{total}}$
$V = 2.0$ L
$T = 25\ °\text{C} = 25 + 273 = 298$ K

Given this information, we can calculate the number of moles of gas in the mixture: $n_{total} = n_{N_2} + n_{O_2}$. Solving for n in the ideal gas equation gives

$$n_{total} = \frac{P_{total}V}{RT} = \frac{(0.91\ \text{atm})(2.0\ \text{L})}{\left(0.08206\ \frac{\text{L atm}}{\text{K mol}}\right)(298\ \text{K})} = 0.074\ \text{mol}$$

We also know that 0.050 mole of N_2 is present. Because

$$n_{total} = n_{N_2} + n_{O_2} = 0.074\ \text{mol}$$

↑ (0.050 mol)

we can calculate the moles of O_2 present.

$$0.050\ \text{mol} + n_{O_2} = 0.074\ \text{mol}$$

$$n_{O_2} = 0.074\ \text{mol} - 0.050\ \text{mol} = 0.024\ \text{mol}$$

Now that we know the moles of oxygen present, we can calculate the partial pressure of oxygen from the ideal gas equation.

$$P_{O_2} = \frac{n_{O_2}RT}{V} = \frac{(0.024\ \text{mol})\left(0.08206\ \frac{\text{L atm}}{\text{K mol}}\right)(298\ \text{K})}{2.0\ \text{L}} = 0.29\ \text{atm}$$

Although it is not requested, note that the partial pressure of the N_2 must be 0.62 atm, because

$$\underbrace{0.62\ \text{atm}}_{P_{N_2}} + \underbrace{0.29\ \text{atm}}_{P_{O_2}} = \underbrace{0.91\ \text{atm}}_{P_{total}}$$

Self-Check Exercise 13.10

The volume is 0.500 L, the temperature is 25 °C (or 25 + 273 = 298 K), and the total pressure is given as 0.950 atm. Of this total pressure, 24 torr is due to the water vapor. We can calculate the partial pressure of the H_2 because we know that

$$P_{total} = P_{H_2} + P_{H_2O} = 0.950\ \text{atm}$$

↑ 24 torr

Before we carry out the calculation, however, we must convert the pressures to the same units. Converting P_{H_2O} to atmospheres gives

$$24\ \text{torr} \times \frac{1.000\ \text{atm}}{760.0\ \text{torr}} = 0.032\ \text{atm}$$

Thus

$$P_{total} = P_{H_2} + P_{H_2O} = 0.950\ \text{atm} = P_{H_2} + 0.032\ \text{atm}$$

and

$$P_{H_2} = 0.950\ \text{atm} - 0.032\ \text{atm} = 0.918\ \text{atm}$$

Now that we know the partial pressure of the hydrogen gas, we can use the ideal gas equation to calculate the moles of H_2.

$$n_{H_2} = \frac{P_{H_2}V}{RT} = \frac{(0.918\ \text{atm})(0.500\ \text{L})}{\left(0.08206\ \frac{\text{L atm}}{\text{K mol}}\right)(298\ \text{K})} = 0.0188\ \text{mol} = 1.88 \times 10^{-2}\ \text{mol}$$

The sample of gas contains 1.88×10^{-2} mole of H_2, which exerts a partial pressure of 0.918 atm.

Self-Check Exercise 13.11

We will solve this problem by taking the following steps:

Grams of zinc ⇨ Moles of zinc ⇨ Moles of H_2 ⇨ Volume of H_2

Step 1 Using the atomic mass of zinc (65.38), we calculate the moles of zinc in 26.5 g.

$$26.5\ \text{g Zn} \times \frac{1\ \text{mol Zn}}{65.38\ \text{g Zn}} = 0.405\ \text{mol Zn}$$

Step 2 Using the balanced equation, we next calculate the moles of H_2 produced.

$$0.405\ \text{mol Zn} \times \frac{1\ \text{mol H}_2}{1\ \text{mol Zn}} = 0.405\ \text{mol H}_2$$

Step 3 Now that we know the moles of H_2, we can compute the volume of H_2 by using the ideal gas law, where

$P = 1.50$ atm
$V = ?$
$n = 0.405$ mol
$R = 0.08206$ L atm/K mol
$T = 19\ °C = 19 + 273 = 292$ K

$$V = \frac{nRT}{P} = \frac{(0.405\ \text{mol})\left(0.08206\ \frac{\text{L atm}}{\text{K mol}}\right)(292\ \text{K})}{1.50\ \text{atm}} = 6.47\ \text{L of H}_2$$

Self-Check Exercise 13.12

Although there are several possible ways to do this problem, the most convenient method involves using the molar volume at STP. First we use the ideal gas equation to calculate the moles of NH_3 present:

$$n = \frac{PV}{RT}$$

where $P = 15.0$ atm, $V = 5.00$ L, and $T = 25\ °C + 273 = 298$ K.

$$n = \frac{(15.0\ \text{atm})(5.00\ \text{L})}{\left(0.08206\ \frac{\text{L atm}}{\text{K mol}}\right)(298\ \text{K})} = 3.07\ \text{mol}$$

We know that at STP each mole of gas occupies 22.4 L. Therefore, 3.07 mol has the volume

$$3.07\ \text{mol} \times \frac{22.4\ \text{L}}{1\ \text{mol}} = 68.8\ \text{L}$$

The volume of the ammonia at STP is 68.8 L.

Chapter 14

Self-Check Exercise 14.1

Energy to melt the ice:

$$15\ \text{g H}_2\text{O} \times \frac{1\ \text{mol H}_2\text{O}}{18\ \text{g H}_2\text{O}} = 0.83\ \text{mol H}_2\text{O}$$

$$0.83\ \text{mol H}_2\text{O} \times 6.02\ \frac{\text{kJ}}{\text{mol H}_2\text{O}} = 5.0\ \text{kJ}$$

Energy to heat the water from 0 °C to 100 °C:

$$4.18\ \frac{\text{J}}{\text{g °C}} \times 15\ \text{g} \times 100\ \text{°C} = 6300\ \text{J}$$

$$6300\ \text{J} \times \frac{1\ \text{kJ}}{1000\ \text{J}} = 6.3\ \text{kJ}$$

Energy to vaporize the water at 100 °C:

$$0.83\ \text{mol H}_2\text{O} \times 40.6\ \frac{\text{kJ}}{\text{mol H}_2\text{O}} = 34\ \text{kJ}$$

Total energy required:

$$5.0\ \text{kJ} + 6.3\ \text{kJ} + 34\ \text{kJ} = 45\ \text{kJ}$$

Self-Check Exercise 14.2

a. Contains SO_3 molecules—a molecular solid.
b. Contains Ba^{2+} and O^{2-} ions—an ionic solid.
c. Contains Au atoms—an atomic solid.

Chapter 15

Self-Check Exercise 15.1

$$\text{Mass percent} = \frac{\text{mass of solute}}{\text{mass of solution}} \times 100\%$$

For this sample, the mass of solution is 135 g and the mass of the solute is 4.73 g, so

$$\text{Mass percent} = \frac{4.73 \text{ g solute}}{135 \text{ g solution}} \times 100\% = 3.50\%$$

Self-Check Exercise 15.2

Using the definition of mass percent, we have

$$\frac{\text{Mass of solute}}{\text{Mass of solution}} = \frac{\text{grams of solute}}{\text{grams of solute} + \text{grams of solvent}} \times 100\% = 40.0\%$$

There are 425 grams of solute (formaldehyde). Substituting, we have

$$\frac{425 \text{ g}}{425 \text{ g} + \text{grams of solvent}} \times 100\% = 40.0\%$$

We must now solve for grams of solvent (water). This will take some patience, but we can do it if we proceed step by step. First we divide both sides by 100%.

$$\frac{425 \text{ g}}{425 \text{ g} + \text{grams of solvent}} \times \frac{\cancel{100\%}}{\cancel{100\%}} = \frac{40.0\%}{100\%} = 0.400$$

Now we have

$$\frac{425 \text{ g}}{425 \text{ g} + \text{grams of solvent}} = 0.400$$

Next we multiply both sides by (425 g + grams of solvent).

$$\cancel{(425 \text{ g} + \text{grams of solvent})} \times \frac{425 \text{ g}}{\cancel{425 \text{ g} + \text{grams of solvent}}} = 0.400 \times (425 \text{ g} + \text{grams of solvent})$$

This gives

$$425 \text{ g} = 0.400 \times (425 \text{ g} + \text{grams of solvent})$$

Carrying out the multiplication gives

$$425 \text{ g} = 170. \text{ g} + 0.400 \text{ (grams of solvent)}$$

Now we subtract 170. g from both sides,

$$425 \text{ g} - 170. \text{ g} = \cancel{170. \text{ g}} - \cancel{170. \text{ g}} + 0.400 \text{ (grams of solvent)}$$

$$255 \text{ g} = 0.400 \text{ (grams of solvent)}$$

and divide both sides by 0.400.

$$\frac{255 \text{ g}}{0.400} = \frac{\cancel{0.400}}{\cancel{0.400}} \text{ (grams of solvent)}$$

We finally have the answer:

$$\frac{255 \text{ g}}{0.400} = 638 \text{ g} = \text{grams of solvent} = \text{mass of water needed}$$

Self-Check Exercise 15.3

The moles of ethanol can be obtained from its molar mass (46.1).

$$1.00 \text{ } \cancel{\text{g } C_2H_5OH} \times \frac{1 \text{ mol } C_2H_5OH}{46.1 \text{ } \cancel{\text{g } C_2H_5OH}} = 2.17 \times 10^{-2} \text{ mol } C_2H_5OH$$

$$\text{Volume in liters} = 101 \text{ } \cancel{\text{mL}} \times \frac{1 \text{ L}}{1000 \text{ } \cancel{\text{mL}}} = 0.101 \text{ L}$$

$$\text{Molarity of } C_2H_5OH = \frac{\text{moles of } C_2H_5OH}{\text{liters of solution}} = \frac{2.17 \times 10^{-2} \text{ mol}}{0.101 \text{ L}} = 0.215 \text{ } M$$

Self-Check Exercise 15.4

When Na_2CO_3 and $Al_2(SO_4)_3$ dissolve in water, they produce ions as follows:

$$Na_2CO_3(s) \xrightarrow{H_2O(l)} 2Na^+(aq) + CO_3^{2-}(aq)$$

$$Al_2(SO_4)_3(s) \xrightarrow{H_2O(l)} 2Al^{3+}(aq) + 3SO_4^{2-}(aq)$$

Therefore, in a 0.10 M Na_2CO_3 solution, the concentration of Na^+ ions is 2×0.10 M = 0.20 M and the concentration of CO_3^{2-} ions is 0.10 M. In a 0.010 M $Al_2(SO_4)_3$ solution, the concentration of Al^{3+} ions is 2×0.010 M = 0.020 M and the concentration of SO_4^{2-} ions is 3×0.010 M = 0.030 M.

Self-Check Exercise 15.5

When solid $AlCl_3$ dissolves, it produces ions as follows:

$$AlCl_3(s) \xrightarrow{H_2O(l)} Al^{3+}(aq) + 3Cl^-(aq)$$

so a 1.0×10^{-3} M $AlCl_3$ solution contains 1.0×10^{-3} M Al^{3+} ions and 3.0×10^{-3} M Cl^- ions.

To calculate the moles of Cl^- ions in 1.75 L of the 1.0×10^{-3} M $AlCl_3$ solution, we must multiply the volume by the molarity.

$$1.75 \text{ L solution} \times 3.0 \times 10^{-3} \text{ } M \text{ } Cl^-$$

$$= 1.75 \text{ } \cancel{\text{L solution}} \times \frac{3.0 \times 10^{-3} \text{ mol } Cl^-}{\cancel{\text{L solution}}}$$

$$= 5.25 \times 10^{-3} \text{ mol } Cl^- = 5.3 \times 10^{-3} \text{ mol } Cl^-$$

Self-Check Exercise 15.6

We must first determine the number of moles of formaldehyde in 2.5 L of 12.3 M formalin. Remember that volume of solution (in liters) times molarity gives moles of solute. In this case, the volume of solution is 2.5 L and the molarity is 12.3 moles of HCHO per liter of solution.

$$2.5 \text{ } \cancel{\text{L solution}} \times \frac{12.3 \text{ mol HCHO}}{\cancel{\text{L solution}}} = 31 \text{ mol HCHO}$$

Next, using the molar mass of HCHO (30.0 g), we convert 31 moles of HCHO to grams.

$$31 \text{ } \cancel{\text{mol HCHO}} \times \frac{30.0 \text{ g HCHO}}{1 \text{ } \cancel{\text{mol HCHO}}} = 9.3 \times 10^2 \text{ g HCHO}$$

Therefore, 2.5 L of 12.3 M formalin contains 9.3×10^2 g of formaldehyde. We must weigh out 930 g of formaldehyde and dissolve it in enough water to make 2.5 L of solution.

Self-Check Exercise 15.7

We are given the following information:

$M_1 = 12 \dfrac{\text{mol}}{\text{L}}$ $\qquad$ $M_2 = 0.25 \dfrac{\text{mol}}{\text{L}}$

V_1 = ? (what we need to find) $\qquad$ $V_2 = 0.75$ L

Using the fact that the moles of solute do not change upon dilution, we know that

$$M_1 \times V_1 = M_2 \times V_2$$

Solving for V_1 by dividing both sides by M_1 gives

$$V_1 = \frac{M_2 \times V_2}{M_1} = \frac{0.25 \frac{\cancel{\text{mol}}}{\cancel{\text{L}}} \times 0.75 \text{ L}}{12 \frac{\cancel{\text{mol}}}{\cancel{\text{L}}}}$$

and

$$V_1 = 0.016 \text{ L} = 16 \text{ mL}$$

Self-Check Exercise 15.8

Step 1 When the aqueous solutions of Na_2SO_4 (containing Na^+ and SO_4^{2-} ions) and $Pb(NO_3)_2$ (containing Pb^{2+} and NO_3^- ions) are mixed, solid $PbSO_4$ is formed.

$$Pb^{2+}(aq) + SO_4^{2-}(aq) \rightarrow PbSO_4(s)$$

Step 2 We must first determine whether Pb^{2+} or SO_4^{2-} is the limiting reactant by calculating the moles of Pb^{2+} and SO_4^{2-} ions present. Because 0.0500 *M* $Pb(NO_3)_2$ contains 0.0500 *M* Pb^{2+} ions, we can calculate the moles of Pb^{2+} ions in 1.25 L of this solution as follows:

$$1.25\ \cancel{L} \times \frac{0.0500\ \text{mol Pb}^{2+}}{\cancel{L}} = 0.0625\ \text{mol Pb}^{2+}$$

The 0.0250 *M* Na_2SO_4 solution contains 0.0250 *M* SO_4^{2-} ions, and the number of moles of SO_4^{2-} ions in 2.00 L of this solution is

$$2.00\ \cancel{L} \times \frac{0.0250\ \text{mol SO}_4^{2-}}{\cancel{L}} = 0.0500\ \text{mol SO}_4^{2-}$$

Step 3 Pb^{2+} and SO_4^{2-} react in a 1:1 ratio, so the amount of SO_4^{2-} ions is limiting because SO_4^{2-} is present in the smaller number of moles.

Step 4 The Pb^{2+} ions are present in excess, and only 0.0500 mole of solid $PbSO_4$ will be formed.

Step 5 We calculate the mass of $PbSO_4$ by using the molar mass of $PbSO_4$ (303.3 g).

$$0.0500\ \cancel{\text{mol PbSO}_4} \times \frac{303.3\ \text{g PbSO}_4}{1\ \cancel{\text{mol PbSO}_4}} = 15.2\ \text{g PbSO}_4$$

Self-Check Exercise 15.9

Step 1 Because nitric acid is a strong acid, the nitric acid solution contains H^+ and NO_3^- ions. The KOH solution contains K^+ and OH^- ions. When these solutions are mixed, the H^+ and OH^- react to form water.

$$H^+(aq) + OH^-(aq) \rightarrow H_2O(l)$$

Step 2 The number of moles of OH^- present in 125 mL of 0.050 *M* KOH is

$$125\ \cancel{\text{mL}} \times \frac{1\ \cancel{L}}{1000\ \cancel{\text{mL}}} \times \frac{0.050\ \text{mol OH}^-}{\cancel{L}} = 6.3 \times 10^{-3}\ \text{mol OH}^-$$

Step 3 H^+ and OH^- react in a 1:1 ratio, so we need 6.3×10^{-3} mole of H^+ from the 0.100 *M* HNO_3.

Step 4 6.3×10^{-3} mole of OH^- requires 6.3×10^{-3} mole of H^+ to form 6.3×10^{-3} mole of H_2O.

Therefore,

$$V \times \frac{0.100\ \text{mol H}^+}{\text{L}} = 6.3 \times 10^{-3}\ \text{mol H}^+$$

where *V* represents the volume in liters of 0.100 *M* HNO_3 required. Solving for *V*, we have

$$V = \frac{6.3 \times 10^{-3}\ \cancel{\text{mol H}^+}}{\dfrac{0.100\ \cancel{\text{mol H}^+}}{\text{L}}} = 6.3 \times 10^{-2}\ \text{L}$$

$$= 6.3 \times 10^{-2}\ \cancel{L} \times \frac{1000\ \text{mL}}{\cancel{L}} = 63\ \text{mL}$$

Self-Check Exercise 15.10

From the definition of normality, $N = \text{equiv/L}$, we need to calculate (1) the equivalents of KOH and (2) the volume of the solution in liters. To find the number of equivalents, we use the equivalent weight of KOH, which is 56.1 g (see Table 15.2).

$$23.6\ \cancel{\text{g KOH}} \times \frac{1\ \text{equiv KOH}}{56.1\ \cancel{\text{g KOH}}} = 0.421\ \text{equiv KOH}$$

Next we convert the volume to liters.

$$755\ \cancel{\text{mL}} \times \frac{1\ \text{L}}{1000\ \cancel{\text{mL}}} = 0.755\ \text{L}$$

Finally, we substitute these values into the equation that defines normality.

$$\text{Normality} = \frac{\text{equiv}}{\text{L}} = \frac{0.421\ \text{equiv}}{0.755\ \text{L}} = 0.558\ N$$

Self-Check Exercise 15.11

To solve this problem, we use the relationship

$$N_{acid} \times V_{acid} = N_{base} \times V_{base}$$

where

$$N_{acid} = 0.50\ \frac{\text{equiv}}{\text{L}}$$

$$V_{acid} = ?$$

$$N_{base} = 0.80\ \frac{\text{equiv}}{\text{L}}$$

$$V_{base} = 0.250\ \text{L}$$

We solve the equation

$$N_{acid} \times V_{acid} = N_{base} \times V_{base}$$

for V_{acid} by dividing both sides by N_{acid}.

$$\frac{N_{acid} \times V_{acid}}{N_{acid}} = \frac{N_{base} \times V_{base}}{N_{acid}}$$

$$V_{acid} = \frac{N_{base} \times V_{base}}{N_{acid}} = \frac{\left(0.80\ \cancel{\frac{\text{equiv}}{\text{L}}}\right) \times (0.250\ \text{L})}{0.50\ \cancel{\frac{\text{equiv}}{\text{L}}}}$$

$$V_{acid} = 0.40\ \text{L}$$

Therefore, 0.40 L of 0.50 *N* H_2SO_4 is required to neutralize 0.250 L of 0.80 *N* KOH.

Chapter 16

Self-Check Exercise 16.1

The conjugate acid–base pairs are

H_2O,	H_3O^+
Base	Conjugate acid

and

$HC_2H_3O_2$,	$C_2H_3O_2^-$
Acid	Conjugate base

The members of both pairs differ by one H^+.

Self-Check Exercise 16.2

Because $[H^+][OH^-] = 1.0 \times 10^{-14}$, we can solve for $[H^+]$.

$$[H^+] = \frac{1.0 \times 10^{-14}}{[OH^-]} = \frac{1.0 \times 10^{-14}}{2.0 \times 10^{-2}} = 5.0 \times 10^{-13}\ M$$

This solution is basic: $[OH^-] = 2.0 \times 10^{-2}\ M$ is greater than $[H^+] = 5.0 \times 10^{-13}\ M$.

Self-Check Exercise 16.3

a. Because $[H^+] = 1.0 \times 10^{-3}\ M$, we get pH = 3.00 because $\text{pH} = -\log[H^+] = -\log[1.0 \times 10^{-3}] = 3.00$.

b. Because $[OH^-] = 5.0 \times 10^{-5}\ M$, we can find $[H^+]$ from the K_w expression.

$$[H^+] = \frac{K_w}{[OH^-]} = \frac{1.0 \times 10^{-14}}{5.0 \times 10^{-5}} = 2.0 \times 10^{-10}\ M$$

$$\text{pH} = -\log[H^+] = -\log[2.0 \times 10^{-10}] = 9.70$$

Self-Check Exercise 16.4

$$\text{pOH} + \text{pH} = 14.00$$

$$\text{pOH} = 14.00 - \text{pH} = 14.00 - 3.5$$

$$\text{pOH} = 10.5$$

Self-Check Exercise 16.5

Step 1 pH = 3.50

Step 2 −pH = −3.50

Step 3 inv log $-3.50 = 3.2 \times 10^{-4}$

$[H^+] = 3.2 \times 10^{-4}\ M$

Self-Check Exercise 16.6

Step 1 $pOH = 10.50$

Step 2 $-pOH = -10.50$

Step 3 inv log $-10.50 = 3.2 \times 10^{-11}$

$[OH^-] = 3.2 \times 10^{-11}\ M$

Self-Check Exercise 16.7

Because HCl is a strong acid, it is completely dissociated:

$5.0 \times 10^{-3}\ M\ HCl \rightarrow 5.0 \times 10^{-3}\ M\ H^+$ and $5.0 \times 10^{-3}\ M\ Cl^-$

so $[H^+] = 5.0 \times 10^{-3}\ M$.

$pH = -\log(5.0 \times 10^{-3}) = 2.30$

Chapter 17

Self-Check Exercise 17.1

Applying the law of chemical equilibrium gives

$$K = \frac{[NO_2]^4[H_2O]^6}{[NH_3]^4[O_2]^7}$$

Coefficient of NO_2 (exponent 4 in numerator); Coefficient of H_2O (exponent 6); Coefficient of O_2 (exponent 7); Coefficient of NH_3 (exponent 4 in denominator)

Self-Check Exercise 17.2

a. $K = [O_2]^3$ The solids are not included.

b. $K = [N_2O][H_2O]^2$ The solid is not included. Water is gaseous in this reaction, so it is included.

c. $K = \dfrac{1}{[CO_2]}$ The solids are not included.

d. $K = \dfrac{1}{[SO_3]}$ Water and H_2SO_4 are pure liquids and so are not included.

Self-Check Exercise 17.3

When rain is imminent, the concentration of water vapor in the air increases. This shifts the equilibrium to the right, forming $CoCl_2 \cdot 6H_2O(s)$, which is pink.

Self-Check Exercise 17.4

a. No change. Both sides of the equation contain the same number of gaseous components. The system cannot change its pressure by shifting its equilibrium position.

b. Shifts to the left. The system can increase the number of gaseous components present, and so increase the pressure, by shifting to the left.

c. Shifts to the right to increase the number of gaseous components and thus its pressure.

Self-Check Exercise 17.5

a. Shifts to the right away from added SO_2.

b. Shifts to the right to replace removed SO_3.

c. Shifts to the right to decrease its pressure.

d. Shifts to the right. Energy is a product in this case, so a decrease in temperature favors the forward reaction (which produces energy).

Self-Check Exercise 17.6

a. $BaSO_4(s) \rightleftharpoons Ba^{2+}(aq) + SO_4^{2-}(aq)$; $K_{sp} = [Ba^{2+}][SO_4^{2-}]$

b. $Fe(OH)_3(s) \rightleftharpoons Fe^{3+}(aq) + 3OH^-(aq)$; $K_{sp} = [Fe^{3+}][OH^-]^3$

c. $Ag_3PO_4(s) \rightleftharpoons 3Ag^+(aq) + PO_4^{3-}(aq)$; $K_{sp} = [Ag^+]^3[PO_4^{3-}]$

Self-Check Exercise 17.7

$(3.9 \times 10^{-5})^2 = 1.5 \times 10^{-9} = K_{sp}$

Self-Check Exercise 17.8

$PbCrO_4(s) \rightleftharpoons Pb^{2+}(aq) + CrO_4^{2-}(aq)$

$K_{sp} = [Pb^{2+}][CrO_4^{2-}] = 2.0 \times 10^{-16}$

$[Pb^{2+}] = x$

$[CrO_4^{2-}] = x$

$K_{sp} = 2.0 \times 10^{-16} = x^2$

$x = [Pb^{2+}] = [CrO_4^{2-}] = 1.4 \times 10^{-8}$

Chapter 18

Self-Check Exercise 18.1

a. CuO contains Cu^{2+} and O^{2-} ions, so copper is oxidized ($Cu \rightarrow Cu^{2+} + 2e^-$) and oxygen is reduced ($O + 2e^- \rightarrow O^{2-}$).

b. CsF contains Cs^+ and F^- ions. Thus cesium is oxidized ($Cs \rightarrow Cs^+ + e^-$) and fluorine is reduced ($F + e^- \rightarrow F^-$).

Self-Check Exercise 18.2

a. SO_3

We assign oxygen first. Each O is assigned an oxidation state of −2, giving a total of −6 (3 × −2) for the three oxygen atoms. Because the molecule has zero charge overall, the sulfur must have an oxidation state of +6.

Check: $+6 + 3(-2) = 0$

b. SO_4^{2-}

As in part a, each oxygen is assigned an oxidation state of −2, giving a total of −8 (4 × −2) on the four oxygen atoms. The anion has a net charge of −2, so the sulfur must have an oxidation state of +6.

Check: $+6 + 4(-2) = -2$

SO_4^{2-} has a charge of −2, so this is correct.

c. N_2O_5

We assign oxygen before nitrogen because oxygen is more electronegative. Thus each O is assigned an oxidation state of −2, giving a total of −10 (5 × −2) on the five oxygen atoms. Therefore, the oxidation states of the *two* nitrogen atoms must total +10 because N_2O_5 has no overall charge. Each N is assigned an oxidation state of +5.

Check: $2(+5) + 5(-2) = 0$

d. PF_3

First we assign the fluorine an oxidation state of −1, giving a total of −3 (3 × −1) on the three fluorine atoms. Thus P must have an oxidation state of +3.

Check: $+3 + 3(-1) = 0$

e. C_2H_6

In this case, it is best to recognize that hydrogen is always +1 in compounds with nonmetals. Thus each H is assigned an oxidation state of +1, which means that the six H atoms account for a total of +6 (6 × +1). Therefore, the *two* carbon atoms must account for −6, and each carbon is assigned an oxidation state of −3.

Check: $2(-3) + 6(+1) = 0$

Self-Check Exercise 18.3

We can tell whether this is an oxidation–reduction reaction by comparing the oxidation states of the elements in the reactants and products:

$$N_2 + 3H_2 \rightarrow 2NH_3$$

Oxidation states: 0 (N in N_2), 0 (H in H_2), −3 (N in NH_3), +1 (each H)

Nitrogen goes from 0 to −3. Thus it gains three electrons and is reduced. Each hydrogen atom goes from 0 to +1 and is thus oxidized, so this is an oxidation–reduction reaction. The oxidizing agent is N_2 (it takes electrons from H_2). The reducing agent is H_2 (it gives electrons to N_2).

$$N_2 + 3H_2 \rightarrow 2NH_3$$

$6e^-$

Self-Check Exercise 18.4

The unbalanced equation for this reaction is

$$Cu(s) + HNO_3(aq) \rightarrow Cu(NO_3)_2(aq) + H_2O(l) + NO(g)$$

Copper metal | Nitric acid | Aqueous copper(II) nitrate (contains Cu^{2+}) | Water | Nitrogen monoxide

Step 1 The oxidation half-reaction is

$$Cu + HNO_3 \rightarrow Cu(NO_3)_2$$

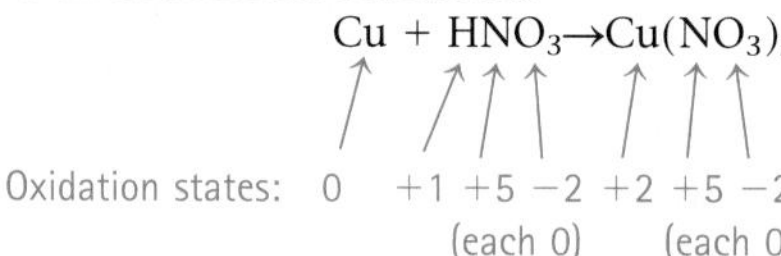

The copper goes from 0 to +2 and thus is oxidized. This reduction reaction is

$$HNO_3 \rightarrow NO$$

Oxidation states: +1 +5 −2 +2 −2 (each O)

In this case, nitrogen goes from +5 in HNO_3 to +2 in NO and so is reduced. Notice two things about these reactions:

1. The HNO_3 must be included in the oxidation half-reaction to supply NO_3^- in the product $Cu(NO_3)_2$.
2. Although water is a product in the overall reaction, it does not need to be included in either half-reaction at the beginning. It will appear later as we balance the equation.

Step 2 *Balance the oxidation half-reaction.*

$$Cu + HNO_3 \rightarrow Cu(NO_3)_2$$

a. Balance nitrogen first.

$$Cu + 2HNO_3 \rightarrow Cu(NO_3)_2$$

b. Balancing nitrogen also caused oxygen to balance.

c. Balance hydrogen using H^+.

$$Cu + 2HNO_3 \rightarrow Cu(NO_3)_2 + 2H^+$$

d. Balance the charge using e^-.

$$Cu + 2HNO_3 \rightarrow Cu(NO_3)_2 + 2H^+ + 2e^-$$

This is the balanced oxidation half-reaction.

Balance the reduction half-reaction.

$$HNO_3 \rightarrow NO$$

a. All elements are balanced except hydrogen and oxygen.

b. Balance oxygen using H_2O.

$$HNO_3 \rightarrow NO + 2H_2O$$

c. Balance hydrogen using H^+.

$$3H^+ + HNO_3 \rightarrow NO + 2H_2O$$

d. Balance the charge using e^-.

$$3e^- + 3H^+ + HNO_3 \rightarrow NO + 2H_2O$$

This is the balanced reduction half-reaction.

Step 3 We equalize electrons by multiplying the oxidation half-reaction by 3:

$$3 \times [Cu + 2HNO_3 \rightarrow Cu(NO_3)_2 + 2H^+ + 2e^-]$$

gives

$$3Cu + 6HNO_3 \rightarrow 3Cu(NO_3)_2 + 6H^+ + 6e^-$$

Multiplying the reduction half-reaction by 2:

$$2 \times [3e^- + 3H^+ + HNO_3 \rightarrow NO + 2H_2O]$$

gives

$$6e^- + 6H^+ + 2HNO_3 \rightarrow 2NO + 4H_2O$$

Step 4 We can now add the balanced half-reactions, which both involve a six-electron change.

$$3Cu + 6HNO_3 \rightarrow 3Cu(NO_3)_2 + 6H^+ + 6e^-$$
$$6e^- + 6H^+ + 2HNO_3 \rightarrow 2NO + 4H_2O$$
$$\cancel{6e^-} + \cancel{6H^+} + 3Cu + 8HNO_3 \rightarrow 3Cu(NO_3)_2 + 2NO + 4H_2O + \cancel{6H^+} + \cancel{6e^-}$$

Canceling species common to both sides gives the balanced overall equation:

$$3Cu(s) + 8HNO_3(aq) \rightarrow 3Cu(NO_3)_2(aq) + 2NO(g) + 4H_2O(l)$$

Step 5 Check the elements and charges.

Elements 3Cu, 8H, 8N, 24O → 3Cu, 8H, 8N, 24O
Charges 0 → 0

Chapter 19

Self-Check Exercise 19.1

a. An alpha particle is a helium nucleus, ^4_2He. We can initially represent the production of an α particle by $^{226}_{88}Ra$ as follows:

$$^{226}_{88}Ra \rightarrow ^4_2He + ^A_ZX$$

Because we know that both A and Z are conserved, we can write

$$A + 4 = 226 \quad \text{and} \quad Z + 2 = 88$$

Solving for A gives 222 and for Z gives 86, so ^A_ZX is $^{222}_{86}X$. Because Rn has $Z = 86$, ^A_ZX is $^{222}_{86}Rn$. The overall balanced equation is

$$^{226}_{88}Ra \rightarrow ^4_2He + ^{222}_{86}Rn$$

Check: $Z = 88 \rightarrow Z = 86 + 2 = 88$

$A = 226 \rightarrow A = 222 + 4 = 226$

b. Using a similar strategy, we have

$$^{214}_{82}Pb \rightarrow ^{0}_{-1}e + ^A_ZX$$

Because $Z - 1 = 82$, $Z = 83$, and because $A + 0 = 214$, $A = 214$. Therefore, $^A_ZX = ^{214}_{83}Bi$. The balanced equation is

$$^{214}_{82}Pb \rightarrow ^{0}_{-1}e + ^{214}_{83}Bi$$

Check: $Z = 82 \rightarrow Z = 83 - 1 = 82$

$A = 214 \rightarrow A = 214 + 0 = 214$

Self-Check Exercise 19.2

a. The missing particle must be ^4_2H (an α particle), because

$$^{222}_{86}Rn \rightarrow ^{218}_{84}Po + ^4_2He$$

is a balanced equation.

Check: $Z = 86 \rightarrow Z = 84 + 2 = 86$

$A = 222 \rightarrow A = 218 + 4 = 222$

b. The missing species must be $^{15}_{7}X$ or $^{15}_{7}N$, because the balanced equation is

$$^{15}_{8}O \rightarrow ^{15}_{7}N + ^{0}_{1}e$$

Check: $Z = 8 \rightarrow Z = 7 - 1 = 8$

$A = 15 \rightarrow A = 15 + 0 = 15$

Self-Check Exercise 19.3

Let's do this problem by thinking about the number of half-lives required to go from 8.0×10^{-7} mole to 1.0×10^{-7} mole of $^{228}_{88}Ra$.

$$8.0 \times 10^{-7} \text{ mol} \xrightarrow[\text{half-life}]{\text{First}} 4.0 \times 10^{-7} \text{ mol} \xrightarrow[\text{half-life}]{\text{Second}}$$
$$2.0 \times 10^{-7} \text{ mol} \xrightarrow[\text{half-life}]{\text{Third}} 1.0 \times 10^{-7} \text{ mol}$$

It takes three half-lives, then, for the sample to go from 8.0×10^{-7} mole of $^{228}_{88}Ra$ to 1.0×10^{-7} mole of $^{228}_{88}Ra$. From Table 19.3, we know that the half-life of $^{228}_{88}Ra$ is 6.7 years. Therefore, the elapsed time is 3(6.7 years) = 20.1 years, or 2.0×10^1 years when we use the correct number of significant figures.

Chapter 20

Self-Check Exercise 20.1

The alkane with ten carbon atoms can be represented as $CH_3—(CH_2)_8—CH_3$ and its formula is $C_{10}H_{22}$. The alkane with fifteen carbons,

$$CH_3—(CH_2)_{13}—CH_3$$

has the formula $C_{15}H_{32}$.

Self-Check Exercise 20.2

a. 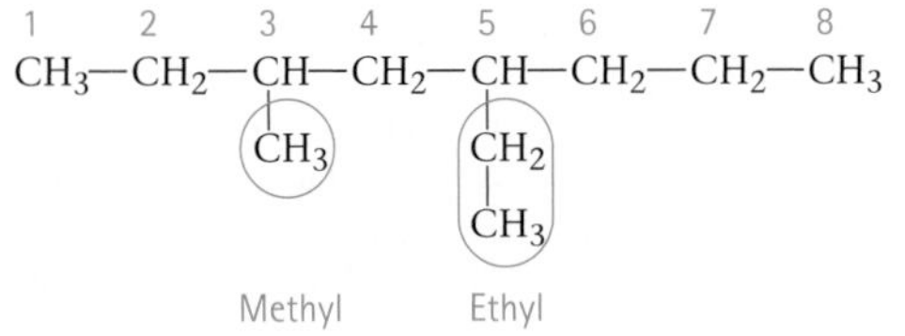
```
  1     2     3     4     5     6     7     8
CH3—CH2—CH—CH2—CH—CH2—CH2—CH3
              |           |
             (CH3)       (CH2)
                          |
                         (CH3)
           Methyl      Ethyl
```

This molecule is 5-ethyl-3-methyloctane.

b. 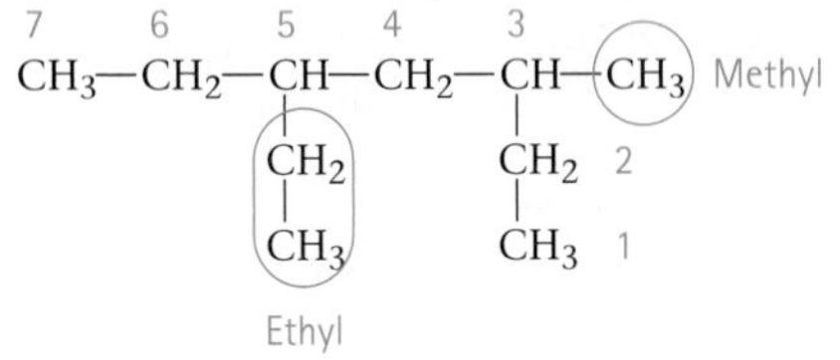
```
  7     6     5     4     3
CH3—CH2—CH—CH2—CH—(CH3) Methyl
              |           |
             (CH2)        CH2  2
              |           |
             (CH3)        CH3  1
           Ethyl
```

This molecule is 5-ethyl-3-methylheptane. Note that this chain could be numbered from the opposite direction to give the name 3-ethyl-5-methylheptane. These two names are equally correct.

Self-Check Exercise 20.3

The root name *decate* indicates a ten-carbon chain. There is a methyl group at the number 4 position and an isopropyl group at the number 5 position. The structural formula is

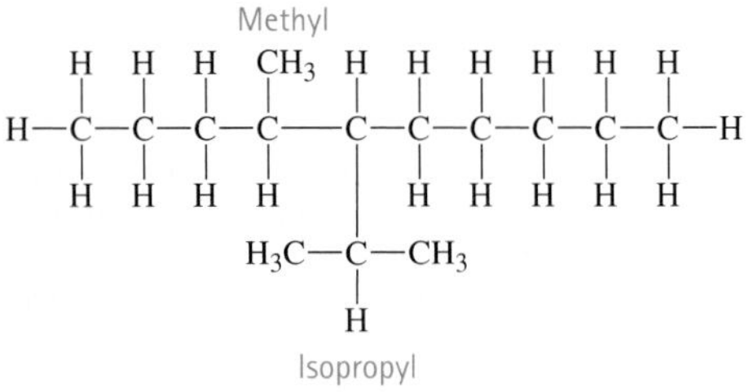

```
           Methyl
  H  H  H  CH3  H  H  H  H  H  H
  |  |  |  |    |  |  |  |  |  |
H—C—C—C—C————C—C—C—C—C—C—H
  |  |  |  |    |  |  |  |  |  |
  H  H  H  H    |  H  H  H  H  H
                |
           H3C—C—CH3
                |
                H
            Isopropyl
```

Self-Check Exercise 20.4

a. The longest chain has eight carbon atoms with a double bond, so the root name is octene. The double bond exists between carbons 3 and 4, so the name is 3-octene. There is a methyl group on the number-2 carbon. The name is 2-methyl-3-octene.

b. The carbon chain has five carbons with a triple bond between carbons 1 and 2. The name is 1-pentyne.

Self-Check Exercise 20.5

a. 2-chloronitrobenzene or *o*-chloronitrobenzene

b. 4-phenyl-2-hexene

Self-Check Exercise 20.6

a. 1-pentanol; primary alcohol

b. 2-methyl-2-propanol (but this alcohol is usually called tertiary butyl alcohol); tertiary alcohol

c. 5-bromo-2-hexanol; secondary alcohol

Self-Check Exercise 20.7

a. 4-ethyl-3-hexanone
   Because the compound is named as a hexanone, the carbonyl group is assigned the lowest possible number.

b. 7-isopropyldecanal

Chapter 11

97. (a) $1s^22s^22p^63s^23p^64s^23d^1$ or $[Ar]4s^23d^1$

1s [↑↓] 2s [↑↓] 2p [↑↓|↑↓|↑↓] 3s [↑↓] 3p [↑↓|↑↓|↑↓] 4s [↑↓]
3d [↑| | | |]

(b) $1s^22s^22p^63s^23p^3$ or $[Ne]3s^23p^3$

1s [↑↓] 2s [↑↓] 2p [↑↓|↑↓|↑↓] 3s [↑↓] 3p [↑|↑|↑]

(c) $1s^22s^22p^63s^23p^64s^23d^{10}4p^6$ or [Kr]

1s [↑↓] 2s [↑↓] 2p [↑↓|↑↓|↑↓] 3s [↑↓] 3p [↑↓|↑↓|↑↓] 4s [↑↓]
3d [↑↓|↑↓|↑↓|↑↓|↑↓] 4p [↑↓|↑↓|↑↓]

(d) $1s^22s^22p^63s^23p^64s^23d^{10}4p^65s^2$ or $[Kr]5s^2$

1s [↑↓] 2s [↑↓] 2p [↑↓|↑↓|↑↓] 3s [↑↓] 3p [↑↓|↑↓|↑↓] 4s [↑↓]
3d [↑↓|↑↓|↑↓|↑↓|↑↓] 4p [↑↓|↑↓|↑↓] 5s [↑↓]

(e) $1s^22s^22p^63s^23p^64s^23d^{10}$or $[Ar]4s^23d^{10}$

1s [↑↓] 2s [↑↓] 2p [↑↓|↑↓|↑↓] 3s [↑↓] 3p [↑↓|↑↓|↑↓] 4s [↑↓]
3d [↑↓|↑↓|↑↓|↑↓|↑↓]

98. (a) ns^2; (b) ns^2np^5; (c) ns^2np^4; (d) ns^1; (e) ns^2np^4

99. (a) four (or two if the *d* electrons are not counted); (b) seven; (c) two; (d) seven (or two if the *d* electrons are not counted)

100. (a) 2.7×10^{-12} m; (b) 4.4×10^{-34} m; (c) 2×10^{-35} m. The wavelengths for the ball and the person are infinitesimally small; the wavelength for the electron is nearly the same order of magnitude as the diameter of an atom.

101. 3.00×10^8 m/s

102. Light is emitted from the hydrogen atom only at certain fixed wavelengths. If the energy levels of hydrogen were continuous, a hydrogen atom would emit energy at all possible wavelengths.

103. As an electron moves to a higher principal energy level, its distance from the nucleus increases, and the attractive force from the nucleus becomes smaller.

104. The third principal energy level of hydrogen is divided into three sublevels (3*s*, 3*p*, and 3*d*); there is a single 3*s* orbital, a set of three 3*p* orbitals, and a set of five 3*d* orbitals. See Figures 11.25–11.28 for the shapes of these orbitals.

105. Orbitals in the 1*s* and 2*s* subshells can contain only two electrons.

106. a, c

107. Electrons are negatively charged particles that repel each other. By placing the three electrons in separate 2*p* orbitals (oriented at 90° to each other in space), the repulsion among the electrons is minimized. The electrons can also have the same spin if they are in separate orbitals but this is not discussed at length in the text.

108. (a) $1s^22s^22p^63s^23p^64s^23d^{10}4p^5$
(b) $1s^22s^22p^63s^23p^64s^23d^{10}4p^65s^24d^{10}5p^6$
(c) $1s^22s^22p^63s^23p^64s^23d^{10}4p^65s^24d^{10}5p^66s^2$
(d) $1s^22s^22p^63s^23p^64s^23d^{10}4p^4$

109. (a) 1s [↑↓] 2s [↑↓] 2p [↑↓|↑↓|↑↓] 3s [↑↓] 3p [↑↓|↑↓|↑↓] 4s [↑↓]
3d [↑| | | |]

(b) 1s [↑↓] 2s [↑↓] 2p [↑↓|↑↓|↑↓] 3s [↑↓] 3p [↑↓|↑|↑]

(c) 1s [↑↓] 2s [↑↓] 2p [↑↓|↑↓|↑↓] 3s [↑↓] 3p [↑↓|↑↓|↑↓] 4s [↑]

(d) 1s [↑↓] 2s [↑↓] 2p [↑|↑|↑]

110. (a) five (2*s*, 2*p*); (b) seven (3*s*, 3*p*); (c) one (3*s*); (d) three (3*s*, 3*p*)

111. transition metals

112. (a) $[Kr]5s^24d^2$; (b) $[Kr]5s^24d^{10}5p^5$; (c) $[Ar]4s^23d^{10}4p^2$; (d) $[Xe]6s^1$

113. (a) $[Ar]4s^23d^2$; (b) $[Ar]4s^23d^{10}4p^4$; (c) $[Kr]5s^24d^{10}5p^3$; (d) $[Kr]5s^2$

114. (a) Se; (b) Se; (c) Rb; (d) V

115. (a) $[Ar]4s^23d^8$; (b) $[Kr]5s^13d^4$; (c) $[Xe]6s^24f^{14}5d^2$; (d) $[Xe]6s^24f^{14}5d^{10}6p^5$

116. metals, low; nonmetals, high

117. (a) B and Al are very reactive; (b) Na; (c) F

118. (a) Ca; (b) P; (c) K

Chapter 14

75. lowest He(l) < CO(l) < H_2O(l) < NaCl(l) highest

76. London dispersion forces are relatively weak forces that arise among noble gas atoms and in nonpolar molecules. London forces arise from *instantaneous dipoles* that develop when one atom (or molecule) momentarily distorts the electron cloud of another atom (or molecule). London forces are typically weaker than either permanent dipole–dipole forces or covalent bonds.

77. (a) London dispersion forces; (b) hydrogen bonding, London dispersion forces; (c) London dispersion forces; (d) London dispersion forces

78. For each mole of liquid water that evaporates, several kilojoules of heat must be absorbed by the water from its surroundings to overcome attractive forces among the molecules.

79. Volatile liquids are liquids that evaporate relatively easily. Typically they have large vapor pressures, because the intermolecular forces in the liquid are relatively weak.

80. In NH_3, strong hydrogen bonding can exist. Because CH_4 molecules are nonpolar, only the relatively weak London dispersion forces exist.

81. Ionic solids typically have the highest melting points, because the ionic charges and close packing in the solids allow for very strong electrostatic forces among the ions.

82. Strong *hydrogen-bonding* forces are present in an ice crystal, while only the much weaker *London forces* exist in the crystal of a nonpolar substance like oxygen.

83. The electron sea model envisions a metal as a cluster of positive ions through which the valence electrons are able to move freely.

84. ice floats on liquid water; water expands when it is frozen

85. As a liquid is heated, the molecules of the liquid gain energy and begin to move faster and more randomly. At some point, some molecules of liquid will have sufficient kinetic energy and will be moving in the right direction so as to escape from the surface of the liquid. At the point where the pressure of vapor leaving the liquid is equal to the pressure above the liquid, the liquid is said to be boiling. Only intermolecular forces need to be overcome: no intramolecular bonds are broken.

86. Although they are at the same *temperature*, steam at 100 °C contains a larger amount of *energy* than hot water, equal to the heat of vaporization of water.

87. A dipole–dipole interaction exists when the positive end of one polar molecule is attracted to the negative end of another polar molecule. Examples depend on student choice.

88. Hydrogen bonding is a special case of dipole–dipole interactions that occur among molecules containing hydrogen atoms bonded to highly electronegative atoms such as fluorine, oxygen, or nitrogen. The bonds are very polar, and the small size of the hydrogen atom (compared to other atoms) allows the dipoles to approach each other very closely. Examples: H_2O, NH_3, HF.

89. Although the noble gas elements do not have *permanent* dipole moments, *instantaneous* dipole moments can arise in their atoms (London dispersion forces). For example, if two xenon atoms approach each other, the nuclear charge on the first atom could momentarily influence the electron cloud on the second atom. If the electron cloud on the second atom is affected so that the centers of negative and positive charge in the atom momentarily do not coincide, then the atom momentarily behaves as a weak dipole.

90. Evaporation and condensation are opposite processes. Evaporation is an endothermic process; condensation is an exothermic process. Evaporation requires an input of energy to provide the increased kinetic energy possessed by the molecules when they are in the gaseous state. It occurs when the molecules in a liquid are moving fast enough and randomly enough that molecules are able to escape from the surface of the liquid and enter the vapor phase.

Chapter 19

69. atomic number
70. radioactive
71. electron
72. mass
73. alpha
74. neutron; proton
75. gamma
76. radioactive decay
77. higher
78. mass number
79. particle accelerators
80. transuranium
81. Geiger
82. half-life
83. carbon-14
84. radiotracers
85. fusion
86. chain
87. $^{235}_{92}U$
88. breeder
89. The decay series, in order from the top right of the diagram, is alpha, beta, beta, alpha, alpha, alpha, alpha, alpha, beta, beta, alpha, beta, beta, alpha.
90. 4.5×10^9 dollars ($4.5 billion)

91. (a) Cobalt is a component of vitamin B_{12}; (b) bones consist partly of $Ca_3(PO_4)_2$; (c) red blood cells contain hemoglobin, an iron-protein compound; (d) mercury is absorbed by substances in the brain.

92. 3.5×10^{-11} J/atom; 8.9×10^{10} J/g

93. The material for the chain reaction must be dense enough that neutrons produced by the initial decay can go on and cause other nuclei to decay in turn; this is accomplished by having a large- and dense-enough sample.

94. $^{90}_{40}Zr$, $^{91}_{40}Zr$, $^{92}_{40}Zr$, $^{96}_{40}Zr$, $^{96}_{40}Zr$

95. $^{64}_{30}Zn$ (30 protons, 34 neutrons); $^{66}_{30}Zn$ (30 protons, 36 neutrons); $^{67}_{30}Zn$ (30 protons, 37 neutrons); $^{68}_{30}Zn$ (30 protons, 38 neutrons); $^{70}_{30}Zn$ (30 protons, 40 neutrons)

96. $^{27}_{13}Al$: 13 protons, 14 neutrons; $^{28}_{13}Al$: 13 protons, 15 neutrons; $^{29}_{13}Al$: 13 protons, 16 neutrons

97. (a) $^{4}_{2}He$; (b) $^{4}_{2}He$; (c) $^{1}_{0}n$

98. (a) $^{0}_{-1}e$; (b) $^{74}_{34}Se$; (c) $^{240}_{92}U$

99. $^{14}_{7}N + ^{4}_{2}He \rightarrow ^{17}_{8}O + ^{1}_{1}H$

100. $^{9}_{4}Be + ^{4}_{2}He \rightarrow ^{12}_{6}C + ^{1}_{0}n$

101. Iodine-131: diagnosis and treatment of thyroid problems, useful because only the thyroid uses iodine in the body; thallium-201: assessment of damage to heart muscle, useful because thallium-201 concentrates in healthy muscles, and a lack of uptake by heart muscles shows the damage.

102. $^{238}_{92}U + ^{1}_{0}n \rightarrow ^{239}_{92}U$;
$^{239}_{92}U \rightarrow ^{239}_{93}Np + ^{0}_{-1}e$;
$^{239}_{93}Np \rightarrow ^{239}_{94}Pu + ^{0}_{-1}e$

103. (a) $^{232}_{90}Th \rightarrow ^{4}_{2}He + ^{228}_{88}Ra$; (b) $^{220}_{86}Rn \rightarrow ^{4}_{2}He + ^{216}_{84}Po$; (c) $^{216}_{84}Po \rightarrow ^{4}_{2}He + ^{212}_{82}Pb$

Chapter 20

121. 1,2,3,-trihydroxypropane (1,2,3-propanetriol)

122.
```
CH2—CH—CH—CH—CH—C=O
|    |   |   |   |   |
OH   OH  OH  OH  OH  H
```

123. (a)
```
CH3—CH2—CH2—CH—CHO
             |
             CH3
```
(b) $CH_3—CH(OH)—CH_2—COOH$
(c) $CH_3—CH(NH_2)—CHO$
(d) $CH_3—C(=O)—CH_2—C(=O)—CH_2—CH_3$
(e)
```
              CH3
   O          |
    \\      /‾‾‾\
      C —  (  O  )
    /       \___/
   H
```

124. (a)
```
CH3—C—CH2—CH2—CH2—CH2—CH3
    ||
    O
```
(b)
```
CH3—CH2—CH—CH2—C=O
        |       |
        CH3     H
```
(c)
```
CH3—CH2—CH2—CH—CH2—OH
             |
             CH3
```
(d)
```
CH2—CH—CH2
|   |   |
OH  OH  OH
```
(e)
```
CH3—CH—C—CH2—CH2—CH3
    |   ||
    CH3 O
```

125.

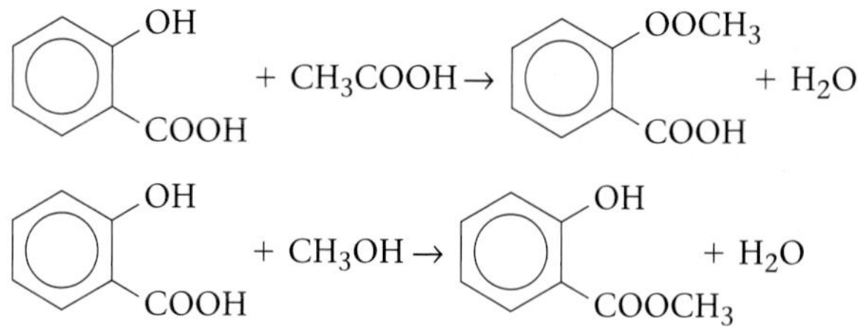

(benzene ring with OH, COOH) + CH_3COOH → (benzene ring with $OOCH_3$, COOH) + H_2O

(benzene ring with OH, COOH) + CH_3OH → (benzene ring with OH, $COOCH_3$) + H_2O

126.

```
        HO—C=O
           |
   CH3—CH—N—(H + HO)—C=O →
           |          |
           H          CH2—NH2

        HO—C=O
           |
   CH3—CH—N—C=O + H2O
           |  |
           H  CH2—NH2
```

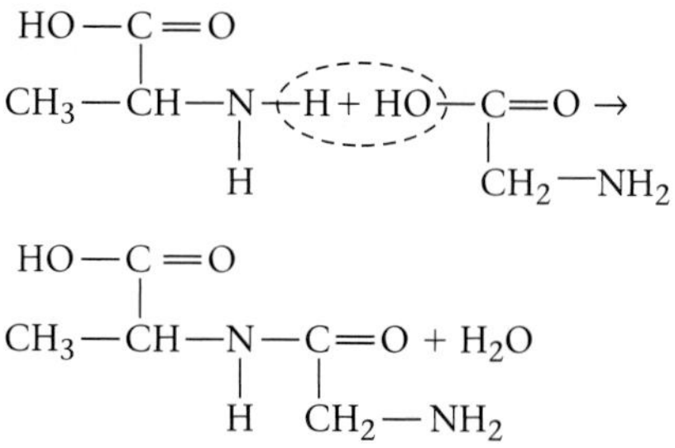

One end has —NH_2, which can react with the —COOH end of another of these dipeptides.

127.

Name	Structure
pentane	CH_3—CH_2—CH_2—CH_2—CH_3
octane	CH_3—CH_2—CH_2—CH_2—CH_2—CH_2—CH_2—CH_3
decane	CH_3—CH_2—CH_2—CH_2—CH_2—CH_2—CH_2—CH_2—CH_2—CH_3
pentane	CH_3—CH_2—CH_2—CH_2—CH_3
heptane	CH_3—CH_2—CH_2—CH_2—CH_2—CH_2—CH_3

128. (a)

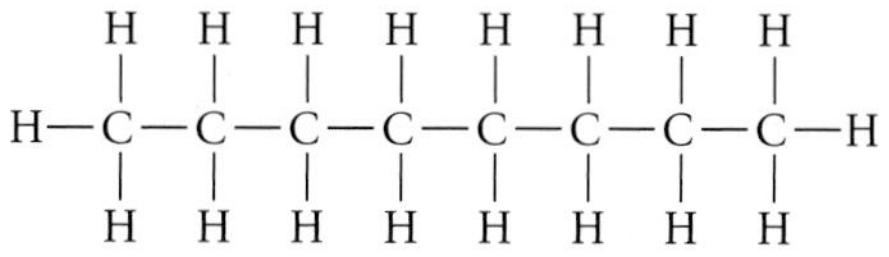

```
    H  H  H  H  H  H  H  H
    |  |  |  |  |  |  |  |
 H—C—C—C—C—C—C—C—C—H
    |  |  |  |  |  |  |  |
    H  H  H  H  H  H  H  H
```

octane, $CH_3CH_2CH_2CH_2CH_2CH_2CH_2CH_3$

(b)

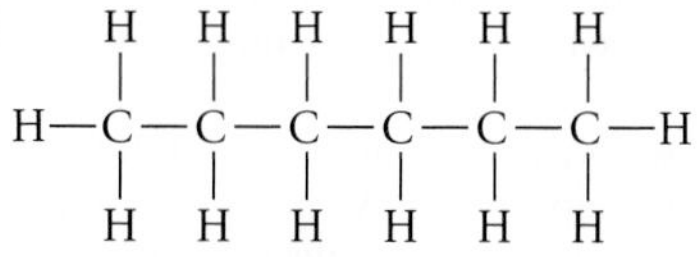

```
    H  H  H  H  H  H
    |  |  |  |  |  |
 H—C—C—C—C—C—C—H
    |  |  |  |  |  |
    H  H  H  H  H  H
```

hexane, $CH_3CH_2CH_2CH_2CH_2CH_3$

(c)

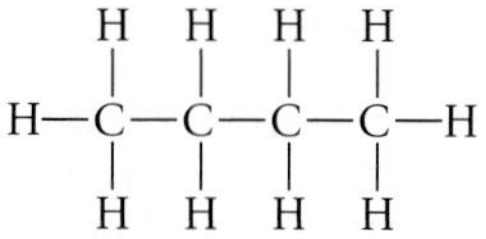

```
    H  H  H  H
    |  |  |  |
 H—C—C—C—C—H
    |  |  |  |
    H  H  H  H
```

butane, $CH_3CH_2CH_2CH_3$

(d)

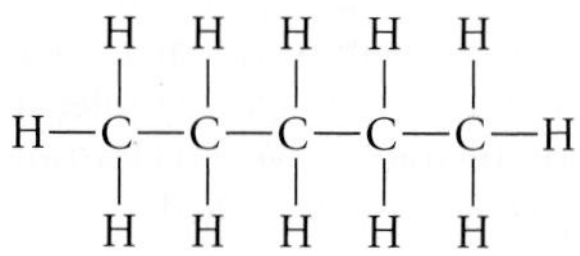

```
    H  H  H  H  H
    |  |  |  |  |
 H—C—C—C—C—C—H
    |  |  |  |  |
    H  H  H  H  H
```

pentane, $CH_3CH_2CH_2CH_2CH_3$

129. Some of the carbon skeletons are shown:

```
C—C—C—C—C—C—C

C—C—C—C—C—C
  |
  C

C—C—C—C—C—C
      |
      C

C—C—C—C—C
  |     |
  C     C

      C
      |
C—C—C—C—C
      |
      C

C—C—C—C—C
  |  |
  C  C

  C
  |
C—C—C—C—C
  |
  C
```

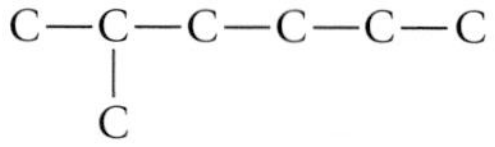

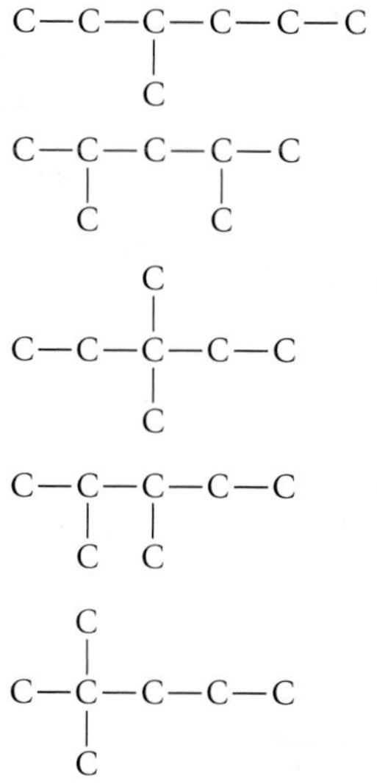

130. (a) 2,3-dimethylbutane; (b) 3,3-diethylpentane; (c) 2,3,3-trimethylhexane; (d) 2,3,4,5,6-pentamethylheptane

131.

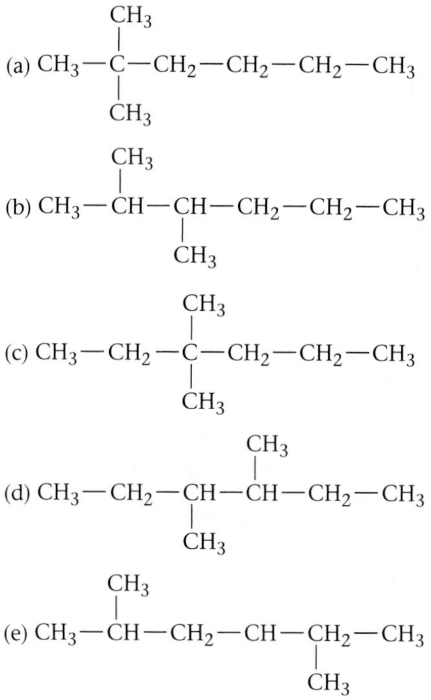

```
(a)        CH3
           |
     CH3—C—CH2—CH2—CH2—CH3
           |
           CH3

(b)        CH3
           |
     CH3—CH—CH—CH2—CH2—CH3
               |
               CH3

(c)               CH3
                  |
     CH3—CH2—C—CH2—CH2—CH3
                  |
                  CH3

(d)                     CH3
                        |
     CH3—CH2—CH—CH—CH2—CH3
                  |
                  CH3

(e)        CH3
           |
     CH3—CH—CH2—CH—CH2—CH3
                     |
                     CH3
```

132. (a) $CH_3Cl(g)$; (b) $H_2(g)$; (c) $HCl(g)$

133. Structures depend on student choices.

134.

$CH{\equiv}C$—CH_2—CH_2—CH_2—CH_2—CH_2—CH_3, 1-octyne;
CH_3—$C{\equiv}C$—CH_2—CH_2—CH_2—CH_2—CH_3, 2-octyne;
CH_3—CH_2—$C{\equiv}C$—CH_2—CH_2—CH_2—CH_3, 3-octyne;
CH_3—CH_2—CH_2—$C{\equiv}C$—CH_2—CH_2—CH_3, 4-octyne

135. (a) 1,2-dimethylbenzene; (b) 1,3,5-tribromobenzene; (c) 2-chloronitrobenzene; (d) naphthalene

136. (a) carboxylic acid; (b) ketone; (c) ester; (d) alcohol (phenol)

137. (a)

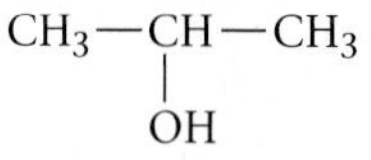

```
CH3—CH—CH3
     |
     OH
```

secondary

(b) $CH_3-\underset{\displaystyle OH}{\overset{\displaystyle CH_3}{\underset{|}{\overset{|}{C}}}}-CH_3$

tertiary

(c) $CH_3-\underset{\displaystyle OH}{\underset{|}{CH}}-CH_2-\overset{\displaystyle CH_3-CH-CH_3}{\overset{|}{CH}}-CH_2-CH_2-CH_3$

secondary

(d) $\underset{\displaystyle OH}{\underset{|}{CH_2}}-\underset{\displaystyle Cl}{\underset{|}{CH}}-\underset{\displaystyle Cl}{\underset{|}{CH}}-CH_2-CH_3$

primary

138. (a) 3-methylpentanal

$CH_3-CH_2-\underset{\displaystyle CH_3}{\underset{|}{CH}}-CH_2-\underset{\displaystyle H}{\underset{|}{C}}=O$

(b) 3-methyl-2-pentanone

$CH_3-CH_2-\underset{\displaystyle CH_3}{\underset{|}{CH}}-\underset{\displaystyle O}{\underset{\|}{C}}-CH_3$

(c) methyl phenyl ketone

$CH_3-\underset{\displaystyle O}{\underset{\|}{C}}-C_6H_5$

(d) 2-hydroxybutanal

$CH_3-CH_2-\underset{\displaystyle OH}{\underset{|}{CH}}-\underset{\displaystyle H}{\underset{|}{C}}=O$

(e) propanal

$CH_3-CH_2-\underset{\displaystyle H}{\underset{|}{C}}=O$

139. By strong oxidation of the corresponding primary alcohol; oxidation–reduction reaction:
$CH_3-CH_2-CH_2-OH \rightarrow CH_3-CH_2-COOH$

140. (a) $CH_3-\underset{\displaystyle CH_3}{\underset{|}{CH}}-CH_2-COOH$

(b) benzene ring bearing $-\overset{\displaystyle O}{\overset{\|}{C}}-OH$ and, on the adjacent carbon, $-Cl$

(c) $CH_3-CH_2-CH_2-CH_2-CH_2-COOH$
(d) CH_3-COOH

141. (a) $H_2C=CH_2 \quad \text{+}CH_2-CH_2\text{+}_n$

(b) $H_2C=\overset{\displaystyle H}{\overset{|}{\underset{\displaystyle Cl}{\underset{|}{C}}}} \quad \text{+}CH_2-\underset{\displaystyle Cl}{\underset{|}{CH}}\text{+}_n$

(c) $F_2C=CF_2 \quad \text{+}CF_2-CF_2\text{+}_n$

(d) $H_2C=\overset{\displaystyle H}{\overset{|}{\underset{\displaystyle CH_3}{\underset{|}{C}}}} \quad \text{+}\underset{\displaystyle CH_3}{\underset{|}{CH}}-CH_2-\underset{\displaystyle CH_3}{\underset{|}{CH}}-CH_2\text{+}_n$

(e) $H_2C=\overset{\displaystyle H}{\overset{|}{\underset{\displaystyle C_6H_5}{\underset{|}{C}}}} \quad \text{+}CH_2-\underset{\displaystyle C_6H_5}{\underset{|}{CH}}\text{+}_n$

Chapter 21

46. A triglyceride typically consists of a glycerol backbone, to which three separate fatty-acid molecules are attached by ester linkages.

$$\begin{array}{l} R-\overset{O}{\overset{\|}{C}}-O-CH_2 \\ \qquad\qquad\qquad | \\ \qquad\qquad\qquad CH-O-\overset{O}{\overset{\|}{C}}-R' \\ \qquad\qquad\qquad | \\ R''-\overset{O}{\overset{\|}{C}}-O-CH_2 \end{array}$$

47. Table 21.5 lists arachidic acid, butyric acid, caproic acid, lauric acid, and stearic acids as typical saturated fatty acids. Oleic acid, linoleic acid, and linolenic acid are given as examples of unsaturated fatty acids. Triglycerides from animals generally contain saturated fatty acids, whereas triglycerides from plant sources generally contain unsaturated fatty acids.

48. A soap is the salt of a long-chain organic (fatty) acid.

$$\begin{array}{lcl} CH_2-O-\overset{O}{\overset{\|}{C}}-R & & CH_2-OH \quad RCOONa \\ | & & | \\ CH-O-\overset{O}{\overset{\|}{C}}-R' \; + \; 3NaOH & \rightarrow & CH-OH \; + \; R'COONa \\ | & & | \\ CH_2-O-\overset{O}{\overset{\|}{C}}-R'' & & CH_2-OH \quad R''COONa \end{array}$$

49. Fatty-acid salts have a long hydrocarbon chain (that tends to be nonpolar in nature) but also are ionic (at the carboxylate end). Fatty acids are able to dissolve both in nonpolar substances (oils and grease) and in water. In water, a large number of fatty-acid molecules combine to form a spherical grouping called a *micelle,* in which the polar (ionic) ends of the fatty acids face out into the water and the nonpolar chains of the fatty acids are positioned into the interior of the micelle. Fatty-acid salts work as soaps to remove grease and oil from clothing by taking the grease or oil molecules into the interior of the micelles, allowing the grease or oil to be dispersed in the water in which the fatty-acid salts are themselves dispersed.

50. Soaps have both a nonpolar nature (from the long chain of the fatty acid) and an ionic nature (from the charge on the carboxyl group). In water, soap anions form aggregates called micelles, in which the water-repelling hydrocarbon chains are oriented toward the interior of the aggregate, with the ionic, water-attracting carboxyl groups oriented toward the outside. Most dirt has a greasy nature. A soap micelle interacts with a grease molecule, pulling the grease molecule into the hydrocarbon interior of the micelle. When clothing is rinsed, the micelle containing the grease is washed away (see Figures 21.22 and 21.23).

51. The group of lipids called *steroids* all contain the same basic cluster of four rings.

This common structure is sometimes referred to as the *steroid nucleus* or *kernel.*

52. Cholesterol is a naturally occurring steroid from which the body synthesizes other needed steroids. Because cholesterol is insoluble in water, having too large a concentration of this substance in the bloodstream may lead to its deposition and buildup on the walls of blood vessels, causing their eventual blockage.

53. Testosterone: male sex hormone that controls development of male reproductive organs and secondary sex characteristics

Estradiol: female sex hormone that controls development of female reproductive organs and secondary sex characteristics

Progesterone: female hormone secreted during pregnancy that prevents further ovulation during and immediately after the pregnancy.

54. The bile acids are synthesized from cholesterol in the liver and are stored in the gallbladder. Bile acids such as cholic acid act as emulsifying agents for lipids and aid in their digestion.

55. v 56. i 57. t
58. m 59. x 60. u
61. q 62. f 63. k
64. g 65. y 66. r
67. c 68. p 69. n
70. o 71. e 72. b
73. s 74. d 75. h
76. a

77. deoxyribonucleic acid
78. nucleotides
79. ribose
80. ester
81. complementary paired
82. thymine; guanine
83. gene
84. transfer, messenger
85. DNA
86. lipids
87. triglycerides
88. unsaturated, saturated
89. saponification
90. ionic, nonpolar
91. micelles
92. fatty
93. cholesterol
94. progesterone
95. emulsifying
96. The primary structure of a protein refers to the specific identity and ordering of amino acids in a protein's polypeptide chain. The primary structure is sometimes called the protein's amino acid *sequence*.
97. 24 (assuming no amino acid repeats)
98. tendons, bone (with mineral constituents), skin, cartilage, hair, fingernails
99. hemoglobin
100. Proteins contain both acidic (—COOH) and basic ($—NH_2$) groups in their side chains, which can neutralize both acids and bases.
101. An enzyme is inhibited if some other molecule, other than the enzyme's correct substrate, blocks the active sites of the enzyme. If the enzyme is inhibited irreversibly, the enzyme can no longer function and is said to have been *inactivated*.
102. pentoses (5 carbons); hexoses (6 carbons); trioses (3 carbons)
103. Although starch and cellulose are both polymers of glucose, the glucose rings in cellulose are connected in such a manner that the enzyme that ordinarily causes digestion of polysaccharides is not able to fit the shape of the substrate and is not able to act on it.
104. In a strand of DNA, the phosphate group and the sugar molecule of adjacent nucleotides become bound to each other. The chain portion of the DNA molecule, therefore, consists of alternating phosphate groups and sugar molecules. The nitrogen bases stick out from the side of this phosphate–sugar chain and are bonded to the sugar molecules.
105. A wax is an ester of a fatty acid with a long-chain monohydroxy alcohol. Waxes are solids that provide waterproof coatings on the fruits and leaves of plants and on the skins and feathers of animals.
106. Phospholipids are esters of glycerol. Two fatty acids are bonded to the —OH groups of the glycerol backbone, with the third —OH group of glycerol bonded to a phosphate group. The two fatty acids, but also the polar phosphate group, makes the phospholipid lecithin a good emulsifying agent.

Chapters 1–3

7. Scientists are careful about reporting their measurements to the appropriate number of significant figures so as to indicate to their colleagues the precision with which experiments were performed. That is, the number of significant figures reported indicates how "carefully" measurements were made. Suppose you were considering buying a new home, and the real estate agent told you that a prospective new house had "between 1000 and 2000 square feet of space," had "five or six rooms, more or less," and stood on "maybe an acre or two of land." Would you buy the house or would you look for another real estate agent? When a scientist says that a sample of material "has a mass of 3.126 grams," he or she is narrowing down the limits as to the actual, true mass of the sample: the mass is clearly slightly more than halfway between 3.12 and 3.13 grams.

   The rules for significant figures are covered in Section 2.5 of the text. These rules for experimentally measured numbers are as follows: (1) nonzero integers are always significant; (2) leading zeroes are never significant, captive zeroes are always significant, and trailing zeroes may be significant (if a decimal point is indicated); and (3) exact numbers (e.g., definitions) have an infinite number of significant figures.

   When we round off an answer to the correct number of significant figures (as limited by whatever measurement was least precise), we do so in a particular manner. If the digit to be removed is equal to or greater than 5, the preceding digit is increased by 1. If the digit to be removed is less than 5, the preceding digit is not changed. If you plan to perform a series of calculations involving a set of data, hold on to the digits in the intermediate calculations until you arrive at the final answer, and then round off the final answer to the appropriate number of significant figures.

   When doing arithmetic with experimentally determined numbers, the final answer is determined by the least precise measurement. In doing multiplication or division calculations, the number of significant figures in the result should be the same as that in the measurement with the fewest significant figures. In performing addition or subtraction, the number of significant figures in the result is limited by the number in the measurement with the fewest decimal places.

8. Dimensional analysis is a method of problem solving that pays particular attention to the units of measurements and uses these units as if they were algebraic symbols that multiply, divide, and cancel. Consider the following example: One dozen eggs costs \$1.25. Suppose we want to know how much one egg costs, and also how much three dozen eggs will cost. To solve these problems, we need two equivalence statements:

   1 dozen eggs = 12 eggs
   1 dozen eggs = \$1.25

   The calculations are:

   $$\frac{\$1.25}{12 \text{ eggs}} = \$0.104 = \$0.10$$

   as the cost of one egg and

   $$\frac{\$1.25}{1 \text{ dozen}} \times 3 \text{ dozen} = \$3.75$$

   as the cost of three dozen eggs. See Section 2.6 of the text for how we construct conversion factors from equivalence statements.

9. The Fahrenheit (°F) temperature scale is defined so that an ice/water bath has an equilibrium temperature of 32 °F, and a boiling water bath has a temperature of 212 °F, under normal atmospheric pressure. There are 180 degree divisions between these two reference points. The Celsius (°C) temperature scale is defined so that an ice/water bath has a temperature of 0 °C, whereas a boiling water bath has a temperature of 100 °C, with 100 degree divisions between these reference points. Both the Fahrenheit and Celsius temperature scales are human inventions that choose convenient, stable, reproducible reference points as their definitions.

   The Kelvin (K) or absolute temperature scale is based on a fundamental property of matter itself: the zero and lowest point (absolute zero) on the Kelvin temperature scale is the lowest possible temperature that can exist, and represents the temperature at which atoms and molecules are in their lowest possible energy states. All other temperatures on the Kelvin scale are positive relative to this point. As only one reference point is used to define the Kelvin scale, the size of the Kelvin degree was chosen to be the same size as the Celsius degree for convenience. The temperature of an ice/water bath is 273 K, and the temperature of a boiling water bath is 373 K.

10. Scientists say that matter is anything that "has mass and occupies space." Matter is the "stuff" of which everything is made. It can be classified and subdivided in many ways, depending on what we are trying to demonstrate. All the types of matter we have studied are made of atoms. They differ in whether these atoms are all of one element, or are of more than one element, and also in whether these atoms are in physical mixtures or chemical combinations.

    Matter can also be classified according to its physical state (solid, liquid, or gas). In addition, it can be classified as a pure substance (one type of molecule) or a mixture (more than one type of molecule).

11. Answer depends on student choice of substance.

12. An element is a fundamental substance that cannot be broken down into simpler substances by chemical methods. An element consists of atoms of only one type. Compounds, on the other hand, *can* be broken down into simpler substances. For example, both sulfur and oxygen are *elements*. When sulfur and oxygen are placed together and heated, the *compound* sulfur dioxide (SO_2) forms. Each molecule of sulfur dioxide contains one sulfur atom and two oxygen atoms. On a mass basis, SO_2 always consists of 50% each, by mass, sulfur and oxygen—that is, sulfur dioxide has a constant composition. Sulfur dioxide from any source would have the same composition (or it wouldn't be sulfur dioxide!).

13. A mixture is a combination of two or more substances that may be varied in its composition. Most commonly in chemistry, a mixture is a combination of two or more pure substances (either elements or compounds). A solution is a particular type of mixture that appears completely homogeneous throughout. Although a solution is homogeneous in appearance, realize, however, that it is still a mixture of two or more pure substances. If it were possible to see the individual particles of a solution, we would notice that different types of molecules were present.

In a sample of a pure substance, only one type of molecule is present. Two types of pure substances exist: elemental substances and compound substances. In an elemental substance, not only are all the molecules the same type, but all the atoms within those molecules are the same type. For example, the pure elemental substance oxygen consists of O_2 molecules (with no other type of molecule present). In addition, each O_2 molecule contains only one type of atom (O). In a sample of a compound substance, all the molecules are of the same type, but within each molecule are found atoms of different elements. For example, the pure compound substance water consists of H molecules (with no other type of molecule present). Within each H molecule, however, are found two different types of atoms (H and O). A compound is not a mixture, because the atoms of the different elements are chemically bonded (not just physically mixed), and the composition of the compound is not variable as to the relative amounts of each element present.

Two methods for separating mixtures are described in the text: filtration and distillation. Filtration can be used to separate a solid from a liquid. Distillation can be used to separate two liquids, or a dissolved solid from a liquid. Many other separation methods exist as well, but they are beyond the scope of this text.

14. (a) 8.917×10^{-4}; (b) 0.0002795; (c) 4913; (d) 8.51×10^{7}; (e) 1.219×10^{2}; (f) 3.396×10^{-9}
15. (a) 0.4932 kg; (b) 1.087 lb; (c) 14.99 km; (d) 4.917×10^{4} ft; (e) 13.84 ft; (f) 421.9 cm; (g) 0.4292 L; (h) 3.100 qt
16. (a) two; (b) two; (c) three; (d) three; (e) one; (f) two; (g) two; (h) three
17. (a) the sizes of the Kelvin and Celsius degree are the same; (b) the Celsius degree is larger than the Fahrenheit degree by a factor of 1.80; (c) 0 °C, 273 K, 32 °F; (d) 301 K, 81.5 °F; (e) 25 °C; 77 °F; (f) 37 °C; 310 K
18. (a) 0.785 g/mL; (b) 2.03 L; (c) 1.06 kg; (d) 9.33 cm^3; (e) 2.0×10^{2} g
19. (a) physical; (b) chemical; (c) physical; (d) physical; (e) chemical; (f) physical; (g) chemical; (h) chemical

Chapters 4–5

8. Isotopes represent atoms of the same element that have different atomic masses. Isotopes result from the different numbers of neutrons in the nuclei of atoms of a given element. They have the same atomic number (number of protons in the nucleus) but have different mass numbers (total number of protons and neutrons in the nucleus). The different isotopes of an atom are indicated by the form $^{A}_{Z}X$, in which Z represents the atomic number and A the mass number of element X. For example, $^{13}_{6}C$ represents a nuclide of carbon with atomic number 6 (6 protons in the nucleus) and mass number 13 (6 protons plus 7 neutrons in the nucleus). The various isotopes of an element have identical *chemical* properties. The *physical* properties of the isotopes of an element may differ slightly because of the small difference in mass.

9.

Symbol	Name	Atomic Number	Group Number
Ca	calcium	20	2
I	iodine	53	7
Cs	cesium	55	1
S	sulfur	16	6
As	arsenic	33	5
Sr	strontium	38	2
Si	silicon	14	4
Rn	radon	86	8
Ra	radium	88	2
Se	selenium	34	6

10. Most elements are too reactive to be found in nature in other than the combined form. Gold, silver, and platinum, and some of the gaseous elements (such as O_2, N_2, He, and Ar) are found in the elemental form.
11. Ions are electrically charged particles formed from atoms or molecules that have gained or lost one or more electrons. Isolated atoms typically do not form ions on their own, but are induced to gain or lose electrons by some other species (which loses or gains the electrons). Positively charged ions are called *cations*, while negative ions are called *anions*. A positive ion forms when an atom or molecule loses one or more of its electrons (negative charges). For example, sodium atoms and magnesium atoms form ions as follows:

$$\text{Na(atom)} \rightarrow \text{Na}^{+}\text{(ion)} + 1\text{e}^{-}$$
$$\text{Mg(atom)} \rightarrow \text{Mg}^{2+}\text{(ion)} + 2\text{e}^{-}$$

The resulting ions contain the same number of protons and neutrons in their nuclei as do the atoms from which they form, as the only change that has taken place involves the electrons (which are not in the nucleus). These ions obviously contain fewer electrons than the atoms from which they were formed, however. A negative ion forms when an atom or molecule gains one or more electrons from an outside source (another atom or molecule). For example, chlorine atoms and oxygen atoms form ions as follows:

$$\text{Cl(atom)} + \text{e}^{-} \rightarrow \text{Cl}^{-}\text{(ion)}$$
$$\text{O(atom)} + 2\text{e}^{-} \rightarrow \text{O}^{2-}\text{(ion)}$$

Because the periodic table is organized based on the electronic structure of the elements, in particular with the elements in the same vertical column having similar electronic structures, the mere location of an element in the periodic table indicates what simple ions the element forms. For example, the Group 1 elements all form 1+ ions (Li^+, Na^+, K^+, Rb^+, Cs^+) while the Group 7 elements all form 1− ions (F^-, Cl^-, Br^-, I^-). You will learn more about how the charge of an ion relates to an atom's electronic structure in a later chapter. For now, concentrate on learning the material shown in Figure 4.17.
12. Ionic compounds typically are hard, crystalline solids with high melting and boiling points. The ability of aqueous solutions of ionic substances to conduct electricity means that ionic substances consist of positively and negatively charged particles (ions). A sample of an ionic substance has no net electrical charge because the total number of positive charges is *balanced* by an equal number of negative charges. An ionic compound could not consist of only cations or only anions because a net charge of zero cannot be obtained when all ions have the same charge. Also, ions of like charge will repel each other.
13. The principle we use when writing the formula of an ionic compound is sometimes called the "principle of electroneutrality." That is, a chemical compound must have an overall net electrical charge of zero. For ionic compounds, the total number of positive charges on the positive ions present must equal the total number of negative charges on the negative ions present. For example, with sodium chloride, if we realize that an individual sodium ion has a 1+ charge, and that an individual chloride ion has a 1− charge, and if we combine one of each of these ions, the compound will have an overall net charge of zero: (1+) + (1−) = 0. On the other hand, with magnesium iodide, an individual magnesium ion has a 2+ charge, so clearly one iodide ion with its 1− charge will not lead to a compound with an overall charge of zero. We would need two iodide ions, each with a 1− charge, to bal-

ance the 2+ charge of the magnesium ion: (2+) + 2(1−) = 0. If we consider magnesium oxide, however, we would need only one oxide ion, with its 2− charge, to balance one magnesium with its 2+ charge [(2+) + (2−) = 0]. Thus the formula of magnesium oxide is just MgO.

14. When naming ionic compounds, the positive ion (cation) is named first. For simple binary Type I ionic compounds, the ending *-ide* is added to the root name of the negative ion (anion). For example, the name for K_2S would be "potassium sulf*ide*"—potassium is the cation, sulfide is the anion. Type II compounds, which involve elements that form more than one stable ion, are named by either of two systems: the "Roman numeral" system (which is preferred by most chemists) and the "*-ous/-ic*" system. For example, iron can react with oxygen to form either of two stable oxides, FeO or Fe_2O_3. Under the Roman numeral system, FeO would be named iron(II) oxide to show that it contains Fe^{2+} ions; Fe_2O_3 would be named iron(III) oxide to indicate that it contains Fe^{3+} ions. Under the "*-ous/-ic*" system, FeO is named ferr*ous* oxide and Fe_2O_3 is called ferr*ic* oxide. Type II compounds usually involve transition metals and nonmetals.

15. Type III binary compounds represent compounds involving only nonmetallic elements. In writing the name for such compounds, the element listed first in the formula is named first (using the full name of the element), and then the second element in the formula is named as though it were an anion (with the *-ide* ending). This is similar to the method used for naming ionic compounds (Type I). Often more than one compound is possible involving the same two nonmetallic elements, so the naming system for Type III compounds goes one step further than the system for ionic compounds by explicitly stating (by means of a numerical prefix) the number of atoms of each of the nonmetallic elements present in the molecules of the compound. For example, carbon and oxygen (both nonmetals) form two common compounds, CO and CO_2. To indicate clearly which compound is being discussed, the names of these compounds explicitly state the number of oxygen atoms present by using a numerical prefix.

CO, carbon monoxide (*mon-* or *mono-* is the prefix meaning "one")
CO_2, carbon dioxide (*di-* is the prefix meaning "two")

The prefix *mono-* is not normally used for the first element named in a compound if only one atom of the element is present, but numerical prefixes are used for the first element if more than one atom of that element is present. For example, nitrogen and oxygen form many binary compounds. Study closely how the examples following are named:

NO, nitrogen monoxide
NO_2, nitrogen dioxide
N_2O, dinitrogen monoxide
N_2O_4, dinitrogen tetroxide (*tetra-* or *tetr-* means "four")

16. A polyatomic ion is an ion containing more than one atom. Some common polyatomic ions are listed in Table 5.4. Parentheses are used in writing formulas containing polyatomic ions to indicate how many polyatomic ions are present. For example, the correct formula for calcium phosphate is $Ca_3(PO_4)_2$, which indicates that three calcium ions are combined for every two phosphate ions. If we did *not* write the parentheses around the formula for the phosphate ion (that is, if we wrote Ca_3PO_{42}), people might think that 42 oxygen atoms were present!

17. Several families of polyatomic anions contain an atom of a given element, combined with differing numbers of oxygen atoms. Such anions are called "oxyanions." For example, sulfur forms two common oxyanions, SO_3^{2-} and SO_4^{2-}. When there are two oxyanions in such a series (as for sulfur), the name of the anion with fewer oxygen atoms ends in *-ite* and the name of the anion with more oxygen atoms ends in *-ate*. Under this naming method, SO_3^{2-} is named *sulfite* and SO_4^{2-} is named *sulfate*. When there are more than two members of such a series, the prefixes *hypo-* and *per-* indicate the members of the series with the fewest and largest number of oxygen atoms. For example, bromine forms four common oxyanions. The formulas and names of these oxyanions are listed below.

Formula	Name
BrO^-	hypobromite (fewest number of oxygens)
BrO_2^-	bromite
BrO_3^-	bromate
BrO_4^-	perbromate (largest number of oxygens)

18. Acids are substances that produce protons (H^+ ions) when dissolved in water. For acids that do *not* contain oxygen, the prefix *hydro-* and the suffix *-ic* are used with the root name of the element present in the acid (for example: HCl, *hydro*chlor*ic* acid; H_2S, *hydro*sulfur*ic* acid; HF, *hydro*fluor*ic* acid). For acids whose anions contain oxygen, a series of prefixes and suffixes is used with the name of the central atom in the anion: these prefixes and suffixes indicate the relative (not actual) number of oxygen atoms present in the anion. Most elements that form oxyanions form *two* such anions—for example, sulfur forms sulf*ite* ion (SO_3^{2-}) and sulf*ate* ion (SO_4^{2-}). For an element that forms two oxyanions, the acid containing the anions will have the ending *-ous* if the *-ite* anion is involved and the ending *-ic* if the *-ate* anion is present. For example, H_2SO_3 is sulfur*ous* acid and H_2SO_4 is sulfur*ic* acid. The Group 7 elements each form *four* oxyanions/oxyacids. The prefix *hypo-* is used for the oxyacid that contains fewer oxygen atoms than the *-ite* anion, and the prefix *per-* is used for the oxyacid that contains more oxygen atoms than the *-ate* anion. For example,

Acid	Name	Anion	Name
HBrO	*hypo*brom*ous* acid	BrO^-	hypobromite
$HBrO_2$	brom*ous* acid	BrO_2^-	bromite
$HBrO_3$	brom*ic* acid	BrO_3^-	bromate
$HBrO_4$	*per*brom*ic* acid	BrO_4^-	perbromate

19.

Symbol	Name	Atomic Number	Group Number
Al	aluminum	13	3
Rn	radon	86	8
S	sulfur	16	6
Sr	strontium	38	2
Br	bromine	35	7
C	carbon	6	4
Ba	barium	56	2
Ra	radium	88	2
Na	sodium	11	1
K	potassium	19	1
Ge	germanium	32	4
Cl	chlorine	17	7

20. Elements in the same family have the same electron configuration and tend to undergo similar chemical reactions with other groups. For example, Li, Na, K, Rb, and Cs all react with elemental chlorine gas, Cl_2, to form an ionic compound of general formula M^+Cl^-.

21. (a) magnesium, 12; (b) gallium, 31; (c) tin, 50; (d) antimony, 51; (e) strontium, 38; (f) silicon, 14; (g) cesium, 55; (h) calcium, 20; (i) chromium, 24; (j) cobalt, 27; (k) copper, 29; (l) silver, 47; (m) uranium, 92; (n) arsenic, 33; (o) astatine, 85;

(p) argon, 18; (q) zinc, 30; (r) manganese, 25; (s) selenium, 34; (t) tungsten, 74; (u) radium, 88; (v) radon, 86; (w) cerium, 58; (x) zirconium, 40; (y) aluminum, 13; (z) palladium, 46

22. (a) 8, 8, 9; (b) 92, 92, 143; (c) 17, 17, 20; (d) 1, 1, 2; (e) 2, 2, 2; (f) 50, 50, 69; (g) 54, 54, 70; (h) 30, 30, 34
23. (a) Mg, Mg^{2+}; (b) F, F^-; (c) Ag, Ag^+; (d) Al, Al^{3+}; (e) O, O^{2-}; (f) Ba, Ba^{2+}; (g) Na, Na^+; (h) Br, Br^-; (i) K, K^+; (j) Ca, Ca^{2+}; (k) S, S^{2-}; (l) Li, Li^+; (m) Cl, Cl^-
24. (a) 12 protons, 10 electrons; (b) 26 protons, 24 electrons; (c) 26 protons, 23 electrons; (d) 9 protons, 10 electrons; (e) 28 protons, 26 electrons; (f) 30 protons, 28 electrons; (g) 27 protons, 24 electrons; (h) 7 protons, 10 electrons; (i) 16 protons, 18 electrons; (j) 37 protons, 36 electrons; (k) 34 protons, 36 electrons; (l) 19 protons, 18 electrons
25. K_3N, KBr, KCl, KH, K_2O, KI; Ca_3N_2, $CaBr_2$, $CaCl_2$, CaH_2, CaO, CaI_2; AlN, $AlBr_3$, $AlCl_3$, AlH_3, Al_2O_3, AlI_3; Ag_3N, AgBr, AgCl, AgH, Ag_2O, AgI

    Realize that most of the hydrogen compounds of the nonmetallic elements that are given as ions in this compound are, in fact, covalently bonded compounds (not ionic compounds): H_3N (NH_3, ammonia); HBr, HCl, H_2, H_2O, HI.

    Na_3N, NaBr, NaCl, NaH, Na_2O, NaI
26. (a) CuI; (b) $CoCl_2$; (c) Ag_2S; (d) Hg_2Br_2; (e) HgO; (f) Cr_2S_3; (g) PbO_2; (h) K_3N; (i) SnF_2; (j) Fe_2O_3
27. (a) incorrect; Ag forms 1+ ions; (b) incorrect; Fe forms only 2+ or 3+ ions; (c) incorrect; sodium *di*hydrogen phosphate; (d) incorrect; sulfur forms 2− ions; (e) correct; (f) correct; (g) correct; (h) incorrect; Ba forms 2+ ions; (i) correct; (j) incorrect; Ca forms 2+ ions
28. (a) NH_4^+, ammonium ion; (b) SO_3^{2-}, sulfite ion; (c) NO_3^-, nitrate ion; (d) SO_4^{2-}, sulfate ion; (e) NO_2^-, nitrite ion; (f) CN^-, cyanide ion; (g) OH^-, hydroxide ion; (h) ClO_4^-, perchlorate ion; (i) ClO^-, hypochlorite ion; (j) PO_4^{3-}, phosphate ion
29. Na^+: $NaNO_2$, $NaNO_3$, Na_2SO_3, Na_2SO_4, $NaHSO_4$, NaOH, NaCN, Na_3PO_4, Na_2HPO_4, NaH_2PO_4, Na_2CO_3, $NaHCO_3$, NaClO, $NaClO_2$, $NaClO_3$, $NaClO_4$, $NaC_2H_3O_2$, $NaMnO_4$, $Na_2Cr_2O_7$, Na_2CrO_4, Na_2O_2

    Ca^{2+}: $Ca(NO_2)_2$, $Ca(NO_3)_2$, $CaSO_3$, $CaSO_4$, $Ca(HSO_4)_2$, $Ca(OH)_2$, $Ca(CN)_2$, $Ca_3(PO_4)_2$, $CaHPO_4$, $Ca(H_2PO_4)_2$, $CaCO_3$, $Ca(HCO_3)_2$, $Ca(ClO)_2$, $Ca(ClO_2)_2$, $Ca(ClO_3)_2$, $Ca(ClO_4)_2$, $Ca(C_2H_3O_2)_2$, $Ca(MnO_4)_2$, $CaCr_2O_7$, $CaCrO_4$, CaO_2
30. (a) xenon dioxide; (b) iodine pentachloride; (c) phosphorus trichloride; (d) carbon monoxide; (e) oxygen difluoride; (f) diphosphorus pentoxide; (g) arsenic triiodide; (h) sulfur trioxide
31. (a) $HgCl_2$; (b) Fe_2O_3; (c) $H_2SO_3(aq)$; (d) CaH_2; (e) KNO_3; (f) AlF_3; (g) N_2O; (h) $H_2SO_4(aq)$; (i) K_3N; (j) NO_2; (k) $AgC_2H_3O_2$; (l) $HC_2H_3O_2(aq)$; (m) $PtCl_4$; (n) $(NH_4)_2S$; (o) $CoBr_3$; (p) $HF(aq)$

Chapters 6–7

9. The spectator ions in a precipitation reaction are, basically, the ions in the solution that do not precipitate. Since we take the actual chemical reaction in a precipitation process to be the formation of the solid, and since the spectator ions are not found in and do not participate in the formation of the solid, we leave them out of the net ionic equation for the reaction. Not including the spectator ions in the net ionic equation for a precipitation reaction also has another important implication: If we write the net ionic equation for the formation of silver chloride,

    $$Ag^+(aq) + Cl^-(aq) \rightarrow AgCl(s)$$

    we are indicating that it is these specific ions that will combine to form silver chloride, regardless of where they come from. If any soluble silver salt is combined with any soluble chloride, we should get a precipitate of silver chloride. For example, silver nitrate (a common soluble silver salt) reacts in exactly the same manner with NaCl, KCl, NH_4Cl, and HCl, which are all soluble compounds containing the chloride ion.

    Just because we leave the spectator ions out when writing a net ionic equation for a reaction does not mean that the spectator ions do not have to be present; the spectator ions are needed to provide a balance of charge in the reactant compounds for the ions that combine to form the precipitate. For the reaction above in which silver chloride is formed, it would not be possible to have a reagent bottle containing just silver ion (there would have to be some negative ion present) or just chloride ion (there would have to be some positive ion present).
10. Acids (such as the acetic acid found in vinegar) were first noted primarily because of their sour taste, whereas bases were first characterized by their bitter taste and slippery feel on the skin. Acids and bases neutralize each other, forming water: $H^+(aq) + OH^-(aq) \rightarrow H_2O(l)$. Strong acids and bases ionize *fully* when dissolved in water, which means they are also strong electrolytes.

    Strong acids: HCl, HNO_3, and H_2SO_4
    Strong bases: Group 1 hydroxides (for example, NaOH and KOH)
11. A salt is basically any ionic compound that contains any ions other than H^+ and OH^- (compounds containing these ions are called *acids* and *bases*, respectively). In particular, a salt is formed in the neutralization reaction between an acid and a base. Your textbook describes acid–base neutralization reactions as reactions that result in the formation of water; the water results from the combination of the $H^+(aq)$ ion from the acid with the $OH^-(aq)$ ion from the base:

    $$H^+(aq) + OH^-(aq) \rightarrow H_2O(l)$$

    However, the H^+ ion must have been paired with some negative ion in the original acid solution, and the OH^- ion must have been paired with some positive ion in the original base solution. These counterions to the acid–base ions are what constitute the salt that is formed during the neutralization.
12. Oxidation–reduction reactions; oxidation; reduction; No: if one species is going to lose electrons, there must be another species present capable of gaining them; Examples depend on student input.
13. Combustion reactions represent processes involving oxygen gas that release energy rapidly enough that a flame is produced. Combustion reactions are a special subclass of oxidation–reduction reactions (the fact that elemental oxygen gas is a reactant but combined oxygen is a product shows this). The most common combustion reactions are those we make use of through the burning of petroleum products as sources of heat, light, or other forms of energy. Combustion reactions of other types of substances are also possible, however. For example, magnesium metal burns in oxygen gas (with a very bright, intense flame) to produce magnesium oxide.
14. In a synthesis reaction, elements or simple compounds react to produce more complex substances. For example,

    $$N_2(g) + 3H_2(g) \rightarrow 2NH_3(g)$$
    $$NaOH(aq) + CO_2(g) \rightarrow NaHCO_3(s)$$

    Decomposition reactions represent the breakdown of complex substances into simpler substances. For example, $2H_2O_2(aq) \rightarrow 2H_2O(l) + O_2(g)$. Synthesis and decomposition reactions are often oxidation–reduction reactions, although not always. For example, the synthesis reaction between NaOH and CO_2 does *not* represent oxidation–reduction.

15. The different ways of classifying chemical reactions that have been discussed in the text are formation of a solid (precipitation), formation of water (acid–base), transfer of electrons (oxidation–reduction), combustion; synthesis (combination), decomposition, single displacement, double displacement.
16. (a) $C(s) + O_2(g) \rightarrow CO_2(g)$; (b) $2C(s) + O_2(g) \rightarrow 2CO(g)$; (c) $2Li(l) + 2C(s) \rightarrow Li_2C_2(s)$; (d) $FeO(s) + C(s) \rightarrow Fe(l) + CO(g)$; (e) $C(s) + 2F_2(g) \rightarrow CF_4(g)$
17. (a) $Na_2SO_4(aq) + BaCl_2(aq) \rightarrow BaSO_4(s) + 2NaCl(aq)$; (b) $Zn(s) + H_2O(g) \rightarrow ZnO(s) + H_2(g)$; (c) $3NaOH(aq) + H_3PO_4(aq) \rightarrow Na_3PO_4(aq) + 3H_2O(l)$; (d) $2Al(s) + Mn_2O_3(s) \rightarrow Al_2O_3(s) + 2Mn(s)$; (e) $2C_7H_6O_2(s) + 15O_2(g) \rightarrow 14CO_2(g) + 6H_2O(g)$; (f) $2C_6H_{14}(l) + 19O_2(g) \rightarrow 12CO_2(g) + 14H_2O(g)$; (g) $2C_3H_8O(l) + 9O_2(g) \rightarrow 6CO_2(g) + 8H_2O(g)$; (h) $Mg(s) + 2HClO_4(aq) \rightarrow Mg(ClO4)2(aq) + H_2(g)$
18. (a) $Ba(NO_3)_2(aq) + K_2CrO_4(aq) \rightarrow BaCrO_4(s) + 2KNO_3(aq)$; (b) $NaOH(aq) + HC_2H_3O_2(aq) \rightarrow H_2O(l) + NaC_2H_3O_2(aq)$ (then evaporate the water from the solution); (c) $AgNO_3(aq) + NaCl(aq) \rightarrow AgCl(s) + NaNO_3(aq)$; (d) $Pb(NO_3)_2(aq) + H_2SO_4(aq) \rightarrow PbSO_4(s) + 2HNO_3(aq)$; (e) $2NaOH(aq) + H_2SO_4(aq) \rightarrow Na_2SO_4(aq) + 2H_2O(l)$ (then evaporate the water from the solution); (f) $Ba(NO_3)_2(aq) + 2Na_2CO_3(aq) \rightarrow BaCO_3(s) + 2NaNO_3(aq)$
19. $HCl(aq) + NaOH(aq) \rightarrow NaCl(aq) + H_2O(l)$; $HNO_3(aq) + NaOH(aq) \rightarrow NaNO_3(aq) + N_2O(l)$; $H_2SO_4(aq) + 2NaOH(aq) \rightarrow Na_2SO_4(aq) + 2H_2O(l)$; $HCl(aq) + KOH(aq) \rightarrow KCl(aq) + H_2O(l)$; $HNO_3(aq) + KOH(aq) \rightarrow KNO_3(aq) + H_2O(l)$; $H_2SO_4(aq) + 2KOH(aq) \rightarrow K_2SO_4(aq) + 2H_2O(l)$
20. (a) $FeO(s) + 2HNO_3(aq) \rightarrow Fe(NO_3)_2(aq) + H_2O(l)$; acid–base; double-displacement; (b) $2Mg(s) + 2CO_2(g) + O_2(g) \rightarrow 2MgCO_3(s)$; synthesis; oxidation–reduction; (c) $2NaOH(s) + CuSO_4(aq) \rightarrow Cu(OH)_2(s) + Na_2SO_4(aq)$; precipitation; double-displacement; (d) $HI(aq) + KOH(aq) \rightarrow KI(aq) + H_2O(l)$; acid–base; double-displacement; (e) $C_3H_8(g) + 5O_2(g) \rightarrow 3CO_2(g) + 4H_2O(g)$; combustion; oxidation–reduction; (f) $Co(NH_3)_6Cl_2(s) \rightarrow CoCl_2(s) + 6NH_3(g)$; decomposition; (g) $2HCl(aq) + Pb(C_2H_3O_2)_2(aq) \rightarrow 2HC_2H_3O_2(aq) + PbCl_2(aq)$; precipitation; double-displacement; (h) $C_{12}H_{22}O_{11}(s) \rightarrow 12C(s) + 11H_2O(g)$; decomposition; oxidation–reduction; (i) $2Al(s) + 6HNO_3(aq) \rightarrow 2Al(NO_3)_3(aq) + 3H_2(g)$; oxidation–reduction; single-displacement; (j) $4B(s) + 3O_3(g) \rightarrow 2B_2O_3(s)$; synthesis; oxidation–reduction
21. For simplicity, the physical states are omitted.
$2Na + F_2 \rightarrow 2NaF$; $4Na + O_2 \rightarrow 2Na_2O$; $2Na + S \rightarrow Na_2S$; $2Na + Cl_2 \rightarrow 2NaCl$
$Ca + F_2 \rightarrow CaF_2$; $2Ca + O_2 \rightarrow 2CaO$; $Ca + S \rightarrow CaS$; $Ca + Cl_2 \rightarrow CaCl_2$
$2Al + 3F_2 \rightarrow 2AlF_3$; $4Al + 3O_2 \rightarrow 2Al_2O_3$; $2Al + 3S \rightarrow Al_2S_3$; $2Al + 3Cl_2 \rightarrow 2AlCl_3$
$Mg + F_2 \rightarrow MgF_2$; $2Mg + O_2 \rightarrow 2MgO$; $Mg + S \rightarrow MgS$; $Mg + Cl_2 \rightarrow MgCl_2$
22. Answer will depend on student examples.
23. Answer depends on student choice of examples.
24. (a) no reaction (all combinations are soluble); (b) $Ca^{2+}(aq) + SO_4^{2-}(aq) \rightarrow CaSO_4(s)$; (c) $Pb^{2+}(aq) + S^{2-}(aq) \rightarrow PbS(s)$; (d) $2Fe^{3+}(aq) + 3CO_3^{2-}(aq) \rightarrow Fe_2(CO_3)_3(s)$; (e) $Hg_2^{2+}(aq) + 2Cl^-(aq) \rightarrow Hg_2Cl_2(s)$; (f) $Ag^+(aq) + Cl^-(aq) \rightarrow AgCl(s)$; (g) $3Ca^{2+}(aq) + 2PO_4^{3-}(aq) \rightarrow Ca_3(PO_4)_2(s)$; (h) no reaction (all combinations are soluble)
25. (a) $Pb(NO_3)_2(aq) + Na_2S(aq) \rightarrow PbS(s) + 2NaNO_3(aq)$; (b) $AgNO_3(aq) + HCl(aq) \rightarrow AgCl(s) + HNO_3(aq)$; (c) $2Mg(s) + O_2(g) \rightarrow 2MgO(s)$; (d) $H_2SO_4(aq) + 2KOH(aq) \rightarrow K_2SO_4(aq) + 2H_2O(l)$; (e) $BaCl_2(aq) + H_2SO_4(aq) \rightarrow BaSO_4(s) + 2HCl(aq)$; (f) $Mg(s) + H_2SO_4(aq) \rightarrow MgSO_4(aq) + H_2(g)$; (g) $2Na_3PO_3(aq) + 3CaCl_2(aq) \rightarrow Ca_3(PO_3)_2(s) + 6NaCl(aq)$; (h) $2C_4H_{10}(l) + 13O_2(g) \rightarrow 8CO_2(g) + 10H_2O(g)$

Chapters 8–9

10. for O_2: $\frac{5 \text{ mol } O_2}{1 \text{ mol } C_3H_8}$; $0.55 \text{ mol } C_3H_8 \times \frac{5 \text{ mol } O_2}{1 \text{ mol } C_3H_8} = 2.8\ (2.75) \text{ mol } O_2$

for CO_2: $\frac{3 \text{ mol } CO_2}{1 \text{ mol } C_3H_8}$; $0.55 \text{ mol } C_3H_8 \times \frac{3 \text{ mol } CO_2}{1 \text{ mol } C_3H_8} = 1.7\ (1.65) \text{ mol } CO_2$

for H_2O: $\frac{4 \text{ mol } H_2O}{1 \text{ mol } C_3H_8}$; $0.55 \text{ mol } C_3H_8 \times \frac{4 \text{ mol } H_2O}{1 \text{ mol } C_3H_8} = 2.2 \text{ mol } H_2O$

11. Answer depends on student choice of example.
12. When arbitrary amounts of reactants are used, one reactant will be present, stoichiometrically, in the least amount: this substance is called the *limiting reactant*. It *limits* the amount of product that can form in the experiment, because once this substance has reacted completely, the reaction must *stop*. The other reactants in the experiment are present *in excess*, which means that a portion of these reactants will be present *unchanged* after the reaction ends.
13. Answer depends on student choice of example.
14. The *theoretical yield* for an experiment is the mass of product calculated assuming the limiting reactant for the experiment is completely consumed. The *actual yield* for an experiment is the mass of product actually collected by the experimenter. Any experiment is restricted by the skills of the experimenter and by the inherent limitations of the experimental method: for these reasons, the actual yield is often less than the theoretical yield. Although one would expect that the actual yield should never exceed the theoretical yield, in real experiments, sometimes this happens. However, an actual yield greater than a theoretical yield usually means that something is *wrong* in either the experiment (for example, impurities may be present) or the calculations.
15. (a) 0.0153 mol; (b) 0.0198 mol; (c) 0.0346 mol; (d) 0.00587 mol; (e) 0.0113 mol; (f) 0.0149 mol; (g) 0.0556 mol; (h) 0.00716 mol
16. (a) 92.25% C; (b) 32.37% Na; (c) 15.77% C; (d) 20.24% Al; (e) 88.82% Cu; (f) 79.89% Cu; (g) 71.06% Co; (h) 40.00% C
17. Na_2CO_3
18. (a) 53.0 g $SiCl_4$, 3.75 g C; (b) 20.0 g LiOH; (c) 12.8 g NaOH, 2.56 g O_2; (d) 9.84 g Sn, 2.99 g H_2O
19. (a) Cl_2; (b) H_2O; (c) Na_2O_2; (d) SnO_2
20. 11.7 g CO; 18.3 g CO_2
21. 0.3241 g theory; 92.41% of theory

Chapters 10–12

11. $Q = s \times m \times T$; so $T = Q/(m \times s)$. Because the specific heat capacity is found in the denominator of the fraction, the substance with the smallest heat capacity will demonstrate the largest temperature change. The sample of gold will undergo a temperature change of slightly over 38 °C.
12. (a) 464 kJ; (b) 69.3 kJ; (c) 1.40 mol (22.5 g)
14. An atom in its *ground state* is in its lowest possible energy state. When an atom possesses more energy than in its ground state,

the atom is in an *excited state.* An atom is promoted from its ground state to an excited state by absorbing energy; when the atom returns from an excited state to its ground state it emits the excess energy as electromagnetic radiation. Atoms do not gain or emit radiation randomly, but rather do so only in discrete bundles of radiation called *photons.* The photons of radiation emitted by atoms are characterized by the wavelength (color) of the radiation: longer-wavelength photons carry less energy than shorter-wavelength photons. The energy of a photon emitted by an atom corresponds *exactly* to the difference in energy between two allowed energy states in an atom.

15. Excited atoms definitely do not emit their excess energy in a random or continuous manner. Rather, an excited atom of a given element emits only discrete photons of characteristic wavelength and energy when going back to its ground state. Since an excited atom of a given element always emits photons of exactly the same energy, the internal structure of the atom must be such that there are only certain discrete allowed energy states for the electrons in atoms, and that the wavelengths of radiation emitted by an atom correspond to the exact energy differences between these allowed energy states. For example, excited hydrogen atoms always display the visible spectrum shown in Figure 11.11: we take this spectrum as evidence for the existence of only certain discrete energy levels within the hydrogen atom, and we describe it by saying that the energy levels of hydrogen are quantized. Previously, scientists had thought that atoms emitted energy continuously.

16. Bohr pictured the electron moving in certain circular orbits around the nucleus, with each orbit being associated with a specific energy (resulting from the attraction between the nucleus and the electron and from the kinetic energy of the electron). Bohr assumed that when an atom absorbs energy, the electron moves from its ground state ($n = 1$) to an orbit farther away from the nucleus ($n = 2, 3, 4, \ldots$). Bohr postulated that when an excited atom returns to its ground state, the atom emits the excess energy as radiation. Because the Bohr orbits are located at fixed distances from the nucleus and from each other, when an electron moves from one fixed orbit to another, the energy change is of a definite amount, which corresponds to the emission of a photon with a particular characteristic wavelength and energy. When the simple Bohr model for the atom was applied to the emission spectra of other elements, however, the theory could not predict or explain the observed emission spectra of these elements.

17. De Broglie and Schrödinger took the new idea that electromagnetic radiation behaved as if it were a steam of small particles (photons), as well as a traditional wave, and basically reversed the premise. That is, if something that had previously been considered to be entirely wave-like also has a particle-like nature, then perhaps small particles also have a wave-like nature under some circumstances. The wave mechanical theory for atomic structure developed by Schrödinger provided an exact model for the structure of the hydrogen atom that was consistent with all the observed properties of the hydrogen atom. Unlike Bohr's theory, which failed completely for atoms other than hydrogen, the wave mechanical model could be extended to describe other atoms with considerable success. Rather than the fixed "orbits" that Bohr had postulated, the wave mechanical model for the atom pictures the electrons of an atom as being distributed in regions of space called *orbitals.* The wave mechanical model for the atom does not describe in classical terms the exact motion or trajectory of an electron as it moves around the nucleus, but rather predicts the *probability* of finding the electron in a particular location within the atom. The orbitals that constitute the solutions to the mathematical formulation of the wave mechanical model for the atom represent probability contour maps for finding the electrons. When we draw a particular picture of a given orbital, we are saying that there is a 90% probability of finding the electron within the region indicated in the drawing.

18. The lowest-energy hydrogen atomic orbital is called the 1*s* orbital. The 1*s* orbital is spherical in shape (the electron density around the nucleus is uniform in all directions). The orbital does *not* have a sharp edge (it appears fuzzy) because the probability of finding the electron gradually decreases as distance from the nucleus increases. The orbital does *not* represent just a spherical surface on which the electron moves (this would be similar to Bohr's original theory)—instead, the 1*s* orbital represents a probability map of electron density around the nucleus for the first principal energy level.

19. When an atom (hydrogen, for example) absorbs energy, the electron moves to a higher energy state, which corresponds in the wave mechanical model to a different type of orbital. The orbitals are arranged in a hierarchy of *principal energy levels,* as well as sublevels of these principal levels. The principal energy levels (for hydrogen) correspond fairly well with the "orbits" of the Bohr theory, and are designated by an integer, *n,* called the *principal quantum number* ($n = 1, 2, 3, \ldots$). In the wave mechanical model, these principal energy levels are further subdivided into sets of equivalent orbitals called *subshells.* For example, the $n = 2$ principal energy level of hydrogen is further subdivided into an *s* and a *p* subshell (indicated as the 2*s* and 2*p* subshells, respectively). These subshells, in turn, consist of the individual orbitals in which the electrons reside. The 2*s* subshell consists of the single, spherically shaped 2*s* orbital, while the 2*p* subshell consists of a set of three equivalent, dumbbell-shaped 2*p* orbitals (which are often designated as $2p_x$, $2p_y$, and $2p_z$ to indicate their orientations in space). Similarly, the $n = 3$ principal energy level of hydrogen is subdivided into three subshells: the 3*s* subshell (one orbital), the 3*p* subshell (a set of three orbitals), and the 3*d* subshell (a set of five orbitals).

20. The third principal energy level of hydrogen is divided into three sublevels: the 3*s*, 3*p*, and 3*d* sublevels. The 3*s* subshell consists of the single 3*s* orbital, which is spherical in shape. The 3*p* subshell consists of a set of three equal-energy 3*p* orbitals: each of these 3*p* orbitals has the same shape ("dumbbell"), but each of the 3*p* orbitals is oriented in a different direction in space. The 3*d* subshell consists of a set of five 3*d* orbitals with shapes as indicated in Figure 11.28, which are oriented in different directions around the nucleus. The fourth principal energy level of hydrogen is divided into four sublevels: the 4*s*, 4*p*, 4*d*, and 4*f* orbitals. The 4*s* subshell consists of the single 4*s* orbital. The 4*p* subshell consists of a set of three 4*p* orbitals. The 4*d* subshell consists of a set of five 4*d* orbitals. The shapes of the 4*s*, 4*p*, and 4*d* orbitals are the *same* as the shapes of the orbitals of the third principal energy level—the orbitals of the fourth principal energy level are *larger* and *farther from the nucleus* than the orbitals of the third level, however. The fourth principal energy level also contains a 4*f* subshell consisting of seven 4*f* orbitals (the shapes of the 4*f* orbitals are beyond the scope of this text).

21. In simple terms, in addition to moving around the nucleus of the atom, an electron rotates (*spins*) on its own axis. A body spinning on its own axis can rotate in only two ways. In pre-digital watch days, these directions were often described as "clockwise" and "counterclockwise" motions, but basically this just means to the right or to the left (for example, the earth is rotating on its axis to the right). Since there are only two possible orientations for an electron's intrinsic spin, a given orbital can accommodate only two electrons (one spinning in each direction). The *Pauli exclusion principle* summarizes our theory about intrinsic electron spin: a given atomic orbital can hold a maximum of two electrons, and those two electrons must have opposite spins.

22. Atoms have a series of *principal energy levels* indexed by the letter n. The $n = 1$ level is closest to the nucleus, and the energies of the levels increase as the value of n (and distance from the nucleus) increases. Each principal energy level is divided into *sublevels* (sets of orbitals) of different characteristic shapes designated by the letters s, p, d, and f. Each s subshell consists of a single s orbital; each p subshell consists of a set of three p orbitals; each d subshell consists of a set of five d orbitals; and so on. An orbital can be empty or it can contain one or two electrons, but never more than two electrons (if an orbital contains two electrons, then the electrons must have opposite spins). The shape of an orbital represents a probability map for finding electrons—it does not represent a trajectory or pathway for electron movements.

23. The order in which the orbitals fill with electrons is indicated in Figure 11.32; this figure is especially useful since it also shows the specific number of orbitals of each type. Since the first principal level consists of only the 1s orbital, the $n = 1$ level can contain only two electrons. Since the second principal level consists of the 2s orbital and the set of three 2p orbitals, the $n = 2$ level can hold a maximum of $[2 + 3(2)] = 8$ electrons. Since any p subshell consists of three orbitals, a given p subshell can hold a maximum of six electrons. A particular p orbital (like any orbital) can hold only two electrons (of opposite spin). Since the three orbitals within a given p subshell are of exactly the same energy and differ only in their orientation in space, when we write the electron configuration of an element like N or O that has a partially filled p subshell, we place the electrons in separate p orbitals to minimize interelectronic repulsions. The configuration of nitrogen is written sometimes as $1s^2 2s^2 2p_x^{\,1} 2p_y^{\,1} 2p_z^{\,1}$ to emphasize this point.

24. The valence electrons are the electrons in an atom's outermost shell. The valence electrons are those most likely to be involved in chemical reactions because they are at the outside edge of the atom.

25. See the inside front cover of the text. An element is placed into a particular position in the periodic table because of its electron configuration—in particular, the number and arrangement of the valence electrons. Because all elements in a vertical group have similar valence electron configurations, they behave similarly in chemical reactions.

26. The general periodic table you drew for Exercise 25 should resemble that found in Figure 11.31. From the column and row location of an element, you should be able to determine its valence configuration. For example, the element in the third horizontal row of the second vertical column has $3s^2$ as its valence configuration. The element in the seventh vertical column of the second horizontal row has valence configuration $2s^2 2p^5$.

27. The *representative elements* are the elements in Groups 1–8 of the periodic table whose valence electrons are in s and p subshells. There are two groups of representative elements at the left side of the periodic table (corresponding to the s subshells) and six groups of representative elements at the right side of the periodic table (corresponding to the p subshells). Metallic character is largest at the left end of any horizontal row of the periodic table, and largest at the bottom of any vertical group. Overall, these two trends mean that the most metallic elements are at the lower-left corner of the periodic table, and the least metallic (the *nonmetals*) are at the upper-right corner of the periodic table. The *metalloids,* which have both metallic and nonmetallic properties, are found in the "stairstep" region indicated on most periodic tables.

28. The ionization energy of an atom represents the energy required to remove an electron from the atom in the gas phase. Moving from top to bottom in a vertical group on the periodic table, the ionization energies decrease. The ionization energies increase when going from left to right within a horizontal row within the periodic table. The relative sizes of atoms also vary systematically with the location of an element on the periodic table. Within a given vertical group, the atoms become progressively larger when going from the top of the group to the bottom. Moving from left to right within a horizontal row on the periodic table, the atoms become progressively smaller.

29. A *chemical bond* is a force that holds two or more atoms together and makes them function as a unit. The strength of a chemical bond is commonly described in terms of the *bond energy,* which is the quantity of energy required to break the bond. The principal types of chemical bonding are *ionic* bonding, *pure covalent* bonding, and *polar covalent* bonding.

30. To form an ionic compound, a metallic element reacts with a nonmetallic element, with the metallic element losing electrons to form a positive ion and the nonmetallic element gaining electrons to form a negative ion. The aggregate form of such a compound consists of a crystal lattice of alternating positively and negatively charged ions: a given positive ion is attracted by surrounding negatively charged ions, and a given negative ion is attracted by surrounding positively charged ions. Similar electrostatic attractions exist in three dimensions throughout the crystal of the ionic solid, leading to a very stable system (with very high melting and boiling points, for example). As evidence for the existence of ionic bonding, ionic solids do not conduct electricity (the ions are rigidly held), but melts or solutions of such substances do conduct electric current. For example, when sodium metal and chlorine gas react, a typical ionic substance (sodium chloride) results: $2Na(s) + Cl_2(g) \rightarrow 2Na^+Cl^-(s)$.

31. A *bond* between two atoms is, in general, *covalent* if the atoms share a pair of electrons in mutually completing their valence-electron shells. Covalent bonds can be classified according to whether they are pure (nonpolar) covalent or polar covalent. In a *nonpolar covalent* bond, two atoms of the same electronegativity (often this means the same type of atom) equally share a pair of electrons; the electron cloud of the bond is symmetrically distributed along the bond axis. In a *polar covalent* bond, one of the atoms of the bond has a higher electronegativity than the other atom and draws the shared pair of electrons more closely toward itself (pulling the electron cloud along the bond axis closer to the more electronegative atom). Because the more electronegative atom of a polar covalent bond ends up with a higher electron density than normal, a center of partial negative charge appears at this end of the bond. Conversely, because the less electronegative element of a polar covalent bond has one of its valence electrons pulled partly away from the atom, a center of positive charge develops at this end of the bond. A polar covalent bond, therefore, represents a partial transfer of an electron from one atom to another, but with the atoms still held together as a unit. This is in contrast with an *ionic* bond, in which one atom completely transfers an electron to a more electronegative atom, but with the resulting positive and negative ions able to separate and behave independently of one another (e.g., in solution).

32. Electronegativity represents the relative ability of an atom in a molecule to attract shared electrons to itself. The larger the difference in electronegativity between two atoms joined in a bond, the more polar is the bond. Examples depend on student choice of elements.

33. A molecule is said to possess an overall *dipole moment* if the centers of positive and negative charge in the molecule do not coincide. A distinction must be made as to whether individual bonds within a molecule are polar and whether the mole-

cule overall possesses a net dipole moment. Sometimes the geometric shape of a molecule is such that individual bond dipoles effectively cancel each other out, leaving the molecule nonpolar overall. For example, compare the two molecules H_2O and CO_2. From Chapter 12, you realize that the water molecule is nonlinear (bent or V-shaped), whereas the CO_2 molecule is linear because of the double bonds. Both the O—H and the C—O bonds are themselves polar (since the atoms involved do not have the same electronegativities). However, the CO_2 molecule is linear because the two individual bond dipoles lie in opposite directions on the same axis and cancel each other out, leaving CO_2 overall as a nonpolar molecule. In water, the two individual bond dipoles lie at an angle and combine to increase the negative charge on the oxygen atom, leading water to be a very polar molecule. Bond dipoles are in actuality vector quantities, and the overall dipole moment of the molecule represents the resultant of all the individual bond dipole vectors. The high polarity of the water molecule, combined with the existence of hydrogen bonding among water molecules, is responsible for the fact that water is a liquid at room temperature.

34. It has been observed over many, many experiments that when an active metal like sodium or magnesium reacts with a nonmetal, the sodium atoms always form Na^+ ions and the magnesium atoms always form Mg^{2+} ions. It has also been observed that when nonmetallic elements like nitrogen, oxygen, or fluorine form simple ions, the ions are always N^{3-}, O^{2-}, and F^-, respectively. Observing that these elements always form the same ions and those ions all contain eight electrons in the outermost shell, scientists speculated that a species that has an octet of electrons (like the noble gas neon) must be very fundamentally stable. The *repeated* observation that so many elements, when reacting, tend to attain an electron configuration that is isoelectronic with a noble gas led chemists to speculate that *all* elements try to attain such a configuration for their outermost shells. Covalently and polar covalently bonded molecules also strive to attain pseudo–noble gas electron configurations. For a covalently bonded molecule like F_2, each F atom provides one electron of the pair of electrons that constitutes the covalent bond. Each F atom feels also the influence of the other F atom's electron in the shared pair, and each F atom effectively fills its outermost shell.

35. The properties of typical ionic substances (hardness, rigidity, high melting and boiling points, and so on) suggest that the *ionic* bond is a very strong one. The formulas we write for ionic substances are really *empirical formulas,* showing the relative numbers of each type of atom present in the substance. For example, when we write $CaCl_2$ as the formula for calcium chloride, we are saying that there are two chloride ions for each calcium ion in the substance, not that there are distinct molecules of $CaCl_2$. Ionic substances in the bulk consist of crystals containing an extended lattice array of positive and negative ions, in a more or less alternating pattern (that is, a given positive ion typically has several negative ions as its nearest neighbors in the crystal). A typical ionic crystal lattice is shown in Figure 12.8. When an atom forms a *positive ion (cation),* it basically sheds its outermost electron shell (the valence electrons), leaving the resulting positive ion smaller than the atom from which it was formed. When an atom forms a *negative ion (anion),* the atom takes additional electrons into its outermost shell, which causes the outermost shell to increase in size because of the additional repulsive forces, leaving the negative ion larger than the atom from which it was formed. In the case of ionic compounds involving *polyatomic ions,* more than one type of bonding force is involved. First, ionic bonding exists between the positive and negative ions. Second, within the polyatomic ions themselves, the atoms that make up the polyatomic ion are held together by polar covalent bonds.

36. Bonding between atoms to form a molecule involves only the outermost electrons of the atoms, so only these *valence* electrons are shown in the Lewis structures of molecules. The most important requisite for the formation of a stable compound is that each atom of a molecule attain a noble gas electron configuration. In Lewis structures, arrange the bonding and nonbonding valence electrons to try to complete the octet (or duet) for as many atoms as possible.

37. Both the *duet* and *octet rules* are simplified statements of our basic guiding principle when discussing how atoms bond with one another to form molecules: when atoms of one element react with atoms of another element to form a compound, as many of the atoms as possible will end up with a noble gas–like electron configuration in the compound. The *duet rule* applies to only the element hydrogen: when a hydrogen atom forms a bond to another atom, the single electron of the hydrogen atom pairs up with an electron from the other atom to give the shared electron pair that constitutes the covalent bond. By sharing this additional electron, the hydrogen atom attains effectively the 1*s* configuration of the noble gas helium. The *octet rule* applies to the representative elements other than hydrogen: when one of these atoms forms bonds to other atoms, the atom shares enough electrons to end up with the *ns* (i.e., eight electrons—an *octet*) electron configuration of a noble gas. *Bonding electrons* are those electrons used in forming a covalent bond between atoms; in a molecule, they represent the electrons that are shared between atoms. *Nonbonding* (or *lone pair*) *electrons* are those valence electrons that are not used in covalent bonding, and that "belong" exclusively to one atom in a molecule. For example, in the molecule ammonia (NH_3), the Lewis structure shows that there are three pairs of bonding electrons (each pair constitutes a covalent bond between the nitrogen atom and one of the hydrogen atoms) as well as one nonbonding pair of electrons that belongs exclusively to the nitrogen atom. The presence of nonbonding pairs of electrons on an atom in a molecule can have a big effect on the geometric shape of the molecule and on the molecule's properties.

38. You could choose practically any molecules for your discussion. Let's illustrate the method for ammonia, NH_3. First, count the total number of valence electrons available in the molecule (without regard to their source). For NH_3, since nitrogen is in Group 5, one nitrogen atom would contribute five valence electrons. Since hydrogen atoms have only one electron each, the three hydrogen atoms provide an additional three valence electrons, for a total of eight valence electrons overall. Next, write down the symbols for the atoms in the molecule, and use one pair of electrons (represented by a line) to form a bond between each pair of bound atoms.

```
H—N—H
   |
   H
```

These three bonds use six of the eight valence electrons. Because each hydrogen already has its duet and the nitrogen atom has only six electrons around it so far, the final two valence electrons must represent a lone pair on the nitrogen.

```
   ..
H—N—H
   |
   H
```

39. A *double bond* between two atoms represents the atoms sharing two pairs of electrons (four electrons) between them. A *triple bond* represents two atoms sharing three pairs (six electrons) between them. When writing a *Lewis structure* for a molecule, if you discover (after writing down a pair of bonding electrons between each of the atoms to be connected) that there do not seem to be enough valence electrons remaining to complete independently the octet (or duet) for each atom, then it strongly suggests that multiple bonding must be present in the molecule. For example, if a molecule seems to be two electrons short of having enough to complete the octet independently, it suggests that there must be a second bond between two of the atoms (a double bond exists between those atoms). If a molecule seems to be four electrons short, it could mean either that a triple bond exists between two of the atoms or that two double bonds are present in the molecule. If it is possible to draw more than one valid Lewis structure for a molecule, differing only in the location of the double bonds, we say that the molecule exhibits *resonance*. The existence of resonance can markedly affect the geometry of the molecule and its resulting properties.

40. Boron and beryllium compounds sometimes do not fit the octet rule. For example, in BF_3, the boron atom has only six valence electrons in its outermost shell, whereas in BeF_2, the beryllium atom has only four electrons in its outermost shell. Other exceptions to the octet rule include any molecule with an odd number of valence electrons (such as NO or NO_2).

41. The general *geometric structure* of a molecule is determined by how many electron pairs surround the central atom in the molecule, and by which of those electron pairs are used for bonding to the other atoms of the molecule. Nonbonding electron pairs on the central atom do, however, cause minor changes in the bond angles, compared to the ideal regular geometric structure. In each of these structures, the central atom (C, N, or O) is surrounded by four pairs (an octet) of electrons. According to the *VSEPR theory,* the four pairs of electrons repel each other and orient themselves in space so as to be as far away from each other as possible. This leads to the electron pairs being oriented tetrahedrally, separated by angles of 109.5°. For CH_4, each of the four pairs of electrons around the C atom is a bonding pair. We therefore say that CH_4 itself has a *tetrahedral* geometry, with H—C—H bond angles of 109.5°. For NH_3, although there are four tetrahedrally arranged electron pairs around the nitrogen atom, only three of these pairs are bonding pairs; there is a lone pair on the nitrogen atom. We describe the geometry of NH_3 as a *trigonal pyramid;* the three hydrogen atoms lie below the nitrogen atom in space as a result of the presence of the lone pair on nitrogen. The H—N—H bond angles are slightly less than the tetrahedral angle of 109.5°. Finally, in H_2O, although we have four pairs of electrons around the oxygen atom, only two of these pairs are bonding pairs; there are two lone electron pairs on the oxygen atom. We describe the geometry of H_2O as *bent, V-shaped,* or *nonlinear;* the presence of the lone pairs makes the H—O—H bond angle not 180° (linear) but somewhat less than the tetrahedral angle of 109.5°.

42.

Number of Valence Pairs	Bond Angle	Examples
2	180°	BeF_2, BeH_2
3	120°	BCl_3
4	109.5°	CH_4, CCl_4, GeF_4

43. In predicting the geometric structure of a molecule, we treat a double (or triple) bond as a single entity (as if it were a single pair of electrons). This approach is reasonable, since all the electrons that bond together two particular atoms must be present in the same region of space between the atoms (whether there are one, two, or three electron pairs). For example, if we write the Lewis structure of acetylene, C_2H_2, we realize that each carbon atom in the molecule has effectively only two "things" attached to it: a bonding pair of electrons (which bonds the H atom) and a triple bond (which bonds the other C atom). As there are effectively only two things attached to each carbon atom, we would expect the bond angles for each carbon atom to be 180°, which makes the molecule *linear* overall.

44. (a) [Kr] $5s^2$; (b) [Ne] $3s^23p^1$; (c) [Ne] $3s^23p^5$; (d) [Ar] $4s^1$; (e) [Ne] $3s^23p^4$; (f) [Ar] $4s^23d^{10}4p^3$

45. (a) AlF_3; (b) Li_3N; (c) CaS; (d) Mg_3P_2; (e) Al_2O_3; (f) K_2S

46.

H—O—H — 4 electron pairs tetrahedrally oriented on O; nonlinear (bent, V-shaped) geometry; H—O—H bond angle slightly less than 109.5° because of lone pairs

H—P—H (with H below P) — 4 electron pairs tetrahedrally oriented on P; trigonal pyramidal geometry; H—P—H bond angles slightly less than 109.5° because of lone pair

:Br—C—Br: (with Br above and below C) — 4 electron pairs tetrahedrally oriented on C; overall tetrahedral geometry; Br—C—Br bond angles 109.5°

[:O—Cl—O: (with O above and below Cl)]⁻ — 4 electron pairs tetrahedrally-oriented on Cl; overall tetrahedral geometry; O—Cl—O bond angles 109.5°

F, F, F around B — 3 electron pairs trigonally oriented on B (exception to octet rule); overall trigonal geometry; F—B—F bond angles 120°

:F—Be—F: — 2 electron pairs linearly oriented on Be (exception to octet rule); overall linear geometry; F—Be—F bond angle 180°

Chapters 13–15

12. The main postulates of the kinetic molecular theory for gases are: (a) gases consist of tiny particles (atoms or molecules), and the size of these particles themselves is negligible compared with the bulk volume of a gas sample; (b) the particles in a gas are in constant random motion, colliding with each other and with the walls of the container; (c) the particles in a gas sample do not assert any attractive or repulsive forces on one another; and (d) the average kinetic energy of the gas particles is directly related to the absolute temperature of the gas sample. The pressure exerted by a gas results from the molecules colliding with (and pushing on) the walls of the container; the pressure increases with temperature because, at a higher temperature, the molecules move faster and hit the walls of the container with greater force. A gas fills the volume available to it because the molecules in a gas are in constant *random* motion: the randomness of the molecules' motion means that they eventually will move out into the available volume until the distribution of molecules is uniform; at constant pressure, the volume of a gas sample increases as the temperature is increased because with each collision having greater force, the container must expand so that the molecules are farther apart if the pressure is to remain constant.

13. The abbreviation *STP* stands for *standard temperature and pressure.* STP corresponds to a temperature of 0 °C and a pressure of 1 atm. These conditions were chosen as STP for comparisons of gas samples because they are easy to reproduce in any laboratory (an equilibrium mixture of ice and water has a temperature of 0 °C, and the pressure in most laboratories is very near to 1 atm). One mole of any ideal gas occupies a volume of 22.4 L at STP.

14. The molecules are much closer together in solids and liquids than in gaseous substances and interact with each other to a much greater extent. Solids and liquids have much greater densities than do gases, and are much less compressible, because so little room exists between the molecules in the solid and liquid states (the volume of a solid or liquid is not affected very much by temperature or pressure). We know that the solid and liquid states of a substance are similar to each other in structure, since it typically takes only a few kilojoules of energy to melt 1 mol of a solid, whereas it may take 10 times more energy to convert a liquid to the vapor state.

15. Water is a colorless, odorless, tasteless liquid that freezes at 0 °C and boils at 100 °C at 1 atm pressure. Water is one of the most important substances on earth. It acts as the solvent for most of the biochemical processes necessary for plant and animal life. Water in the oceans moderates the temperature of the earth. Because of its relatively large specific heat capacity and its great abundance, water is used as the primary coolant in industrial machinery. It provides a medium for transportation across vast distances on the earth. It provides a medium for the smallest plants and animals in many food chains.

16. The *normal* boiling point of water—that is, water's boiling point at a pressure of exactly 760 mm Hg—is 100 °C. Water remains at 100 °C while boiling, because the additional energy added to the sample is used to overcome attractive forces among the water molecules as they go from the condensed, liquid state to the gaseous state. The normal (760 mm Hg) freezing point of water is exactly 0 °C. A cooling curve for water is given in Figure 14.2.

17. Changes in state are simply physical changes: no chemical bonds are broken during the change and no new substances result (no changes in the intramolecular bonding forces take place). To melt a solid or to boil a liquid, the intermolecular forces that hold the molecules together in the solid or liquid must be overcome. The quantity of energy required to melt and to boil 1 mol of a substance are called the substance's *molar heat of fusion* and *molar heat of vaporization,* respectively. The molar heat of vaporization of water (or any substance) is much larger than the molar heat of fusion because to form a vapor, the molecules must move much farther apart, and virtually all the intermolecular forces must be overcome (when a solid melts, the intermolecular forces remaining in the liquid are still relatively strong). The boiling point of a liquid decreases with altitude because the atmospheric pressure (against which the vapor must be expanded during boiling) decreases with altitude (the atmosphere is thinner).

18. Dipole–dipole forces arise when molecules with permanent dipole moments try to orient themselves so that the positive end of one polar molecule can attract the negative end of another polar molecule. Dipole–dipole forces are not nearly as strong as ionic or covalent bonding forces (only about 1% as strong as covalent bonding forces) since electrostatic attraction is related to the *magnitude* of the charges of the attracting species and drops off rapidly with distance. Hydrogen bonding is an especially strong dipole–dipole attractive force that can exist when hydrogen atoms are directly bonded to the most electronegative atoms (N, O, and F). Because the hydrogen atom is so small, dipoles involving N—H, O—H, and F—H bonds can approach each other much more closely than can other dipoles; because the magnitude of dipole–dipole forces is related to distance, unusually strong attractive forces can exist. The much higher boiling point of water than that of the other covalent hydrogen compounds of the Group 6 elements is evidence for the special strength of hydrogen bonding.

19. *London dispersion forces* are the extremely weak forces that must exist to explain the fact that substances consisting of single atoms or nonpolar molecules can be liquefied and solidified. London forces are instantaneous dipole forces, which come about as the electrons of an atom move around the nucleus. Although we usually consider the electrons to be uniformly distributed in space around the nucleus, at any given instant there may be more electronic charge on one side of the nucleus than on the other, resulting in an instantaneous separation of charge and a small dipole moment. Such an *instantaneous dipole* may induce a similar instantaneous dipole in a neighboring atom, which produces an attractive force between the dipoles. Although an instantaneous dipole can arise in any molecule, in most cases other, much stronger intermolecular forces predominate. However, for substances that exist as single atoms (e.g., the noble gases) or nonpolar molecules (e.g., H_2, O_2), London forces are the only major intermolecular forces at work.

20. The vaporization of a liquid requires an input of energy to overcome the intermolecular forces that exist between the molecules in the liquid state. The large heat of vaporization of water is essential to life since much of the excess energy striking the earth from the sun is dissipated in vaporizing water. Condensation refers to the process by which molecules in the vapor state form a liquid. In a closed container containing a liquid with some empty space above the liquid, an equilibrium occurs between vaporization and condensation. When the liquid is first placed in the container, the liquid phase begins to evaporate into the empty space. As the number of molecules in the vapor phase increases, however, some of these molecules begin to reenter the liquid phase. Eventually, each time a molecule of liquid somewhere in the container enters the vapor phase, another molecule of vapor reenters the liquid phase. No further net change occurs in the amount of liquid phase. The pressure of the vapor in such an equilibrium situation is characteristic for the liquid at each temperature. A simple experiment to determine the vapor pressure of a liquid is shown in Figure 14.10. Typically, liquids with strong intermolecular forces have smaller vapor pressures (they have more difficulty in evaporating) than do liquids with very weak intermolecular forces.

21. *Crystalline solids* consist of a regular lattice array, which extends in three dimensions, of repeating component units (atoms, molecules, or ions); a small portion of a sodium chloride crystal lattice is shown in Figure 14.11. The three important types of crystalline solids are ionic solids, molecular solids, and atomic solids.

    Sodium chloride is a typical *ionic solid.* Its crystals consist of an alternating array of Na^+ ions and Cl^- ions. Each positive ion is surrounded by several negative ions, and each negative ion is surrounded by several positive ions. The electrostatic forces that develop in such an arrangement are very large, and the resulting substance is very stable and has very high melting and boiling points.

    Ice is a *molecular solid.* Its crystals consist of polar water molecules arranged in three dimensions so as to maximize dipole–dipole interactions (and hydrogen bonding). Figure 14.14(b) shows a representation of an ice crystal, indicating how the negative end of one water molecule is oriented toward the positive end of another water molecule and how this arrangement repeats. Because dipole–dipole forces are weaker than ionic bonding forces, molecular solids typically have much lower melting and boiling points.

    Atomic solids vary as to how the atoms are held together in the crystal. Substances such as the noble gases are held together in the solid only by very weak London dispersion forces. Such substances have extremely low melting and boiling points because these forces are so weak. In other atomic solids, such as the diamond form of carbon, adjacent atoms may actually form covalent bonds with each other, turning the entire crystal into one giant molecule. Such atomic solids have much higher boiling and melting points than those of substances held together by only London forces, as so much energy is held in the crystal's covalent bonds. Finally, the metallic substances are also atomic solids, in which strong, nondirectional bonding leads to the properties associated with metals. Metals are envisioned in terms of the *electron sea model*, in which a regular array of metal atoms are perfused with a sea of freely moving valence electrons.

22. The *electron sea model* explains many properties of metallic elements. This model pictures a regular array of metal atoms set in a "sea" of mobile valence electrons. The electrons can move easily throughout the metal to conduct heat or electricity, and the lattice of atoms and cations can be deformed with little effort, allowing the metal to be hammered into a sheet or stretched into wire. An alloy is a material that contains a mixture of elements that overall has metallic properties. *Substitutional* alloys consist of a host metal in which some of the atoms in the metal's crystalline structure are replaced by atoms of other metallic elements. For example, sterling silver is an alloy in which some silver atoms have been replaced by copper atoms. An *interstitial alloy* is formed when other, smaller atoms enter the interstices (holes) between atoms in the host metal's crystal structure. Steel is an interstitial alloy in which carbon atoms enter the interstices of a crystal of iron atoms.

23. A *solution* is a homogeneous mixture, in which the components are uniformly intermingled. When an ionic substance is dissolved in water to form a solution, the water plays an essential role in overcoming the strong interparticle forces in the ionic crystal (shown in Figure 15.2). Water is a highly polar substance: one end of the water molecule is strongly negative, and the other is strongly positive. In a crystal of sodium chloride, there is a negative chloride ion at one of the corners of the crystal. When this crystal is placed in water, water molecules surround the chloride ion, orienting themselves with the positive ends of their dipoles aimed at the negative chloride ion. When enough water molecules have arranged themselves in this manner, the resultant attraction of the several water molecules for the chloride ion becomes stronger than the attractive forces from the positive sodium ions in the crystal, and the chloride ion separates from the crystal and enters solution (still surrounded by the group of water molecules). Similarly, a positive sodium ion in a similar position would be attracted by a group of water molecules arranged with the negative ends of their dipoles oriented toward the positive ion. When enough water molecules had arranged themselves so as to overcome the attractive forces from negative ions in the crystal, the sodium ion would enter solution. Once the chloride ion and the sodium ion are in solution, they remain surrounded by a layer of water molecules (called a *hydration sphere*), which diminishes the effective charge each ion would feel from the other, which prevents the ions from easily recombining.

For a molecular solid (such as sugar) to dissolve in a solvent, there must be some portion or portions of the molecule that can be attracted by molecules of solvent. For example, common table sugar (sucrose) contains many hydroxyl groups, —OH. These hydroxyl groups are relatively polar and can be attracted by water molecule dipoles. When enough water molecules have attracted enough hydroxyl groups on a sugar molecule to overcome the attractive forces from other sugar molecules within the crystal, the molecule leaves the crystal and enters solution (naturally, the —OH groups can also hydrogen-bond with water molecules). For a substance to dissolve in water, not only must attractive forces be possible between water molecules and solute molecules, but these forces must also be strong enough to overcome the strong attractive forces that water molecules have for one another. For a substance to dissolve, the molecules of substance must also be capable of being dispersed among water molecules. If the water–solute interactions are not comparable to the water–water interactions, the substance will not dissolve.

24. A saturated solution contains as much solute as can dissolve at a particular temperature. Saying that a solution is *saturated* does not *necessarily* mean that the solute is present at a high concentration—for example, magnesium hydroxide dissolves only to a very small extent before the solution is saturated. A saturated solution is in equilibrium with undissolved solute: as molecules of solute dissolve from the solid in one place in the solution, dissolved molecules rejoin the solid phase in another part of the solution. Once the rates of dissolving and solid formation become equal, no further net change occurs in the concentration of the solution and the solution is saturated.

25. $$\text{mass percent} = \frac{\text{mass of solute}}{\text{total mass of solution}} \times 100 = \frac{5.00 \text{ g NaCl}}{(5.00 + 15.0) \text{ g total}} \times 100 = 25.0\%$$

$$5.00 \text{ g NaCl} = 5.00 \text{ g} \times \frac{1 \text{ mol}}{58.44 \text{ g}} = 0.0856 \text{ mol}$$

$$16.1 \text{ mL} = 0.0161 \text{ L}$$

$$\text{molarity} = \frac{0.0856 \text{ mol}}{0.0161 \text{ L}} = 5.32\ M$$

26. Adding more solvent to a solution to dilute the solution does *not* change the number of moles of solute present, but changes only the *volume* in which the solute is dispersed. If molarity is used to describe the solution's concentration, then the number of *liters* is changed when solvent is added and the number of *moles per liter* (the molarity) changes, but the actual number of *moles* of solute does *not* change. For example, 125 mL of 0.551 *M* NaCl contains 0.0689 mol of NaCl. The solution will *still* contain 0.0689 mol of NaCl after 250 mL of water is added to it. The volume and the concentration will change, but the number of moles of solute in the solution will *not* change. The 0.0689 mol of NaCl, divided by the total volume of the diluted solution in liters, gives the new molarity (0.184 *M*).

27. One *equivalent of an acid* is the amount of acid that can furnish one mole of H^+ ions; one *equivalent of a base* is the amount of base that can furnish one mole of OH^- ions. The *equivalent weight* of an acid or base is the mass of the substance representing one equivalent of the acid or base. The equivalent weight of a substance is determined from the molar mass of the substance, also taking into account how many H^+ or OH^- ions the substance furnishes per molecule. For example, HCl and NaOH have equivalent weights equal to their molar masses, since each furnishes one H^+ or OH^- ion per molecule, respectively. However, sulfuric acid (H_2SO_4) has an equivalent weight that is half its molar mass, since each H_2SO_4 molecule can produce two H^+ ions; therefore, only one-half mole of H_2SO_4 is needed to provide one mole of H^+ ion. Similarly, the equivalent weight of phosphoric acid (H_3PO_4) is one-third of its molar mass, since each H_3PO_4 molecule can provide three H^+ ions (and so only one-third mole of H_3PO_4 is needed to provide one mole of H^+ ions).

Similarly, bases such as $Ca(OH)_2$ and $Mg(OH)_2$ have equivalent weights that are half their molar masses, since each substance produces two moles of OH^- ion per mole of base (and so only one-half mole of base is needed to provide one mole of OH^-).

The *normality* of a solution is the number of equivalents of solute contained in one liter of the solution. A 1 *N* solution of an acid contains one mole of H^+ per liter; a 1 *N* solution of a base contains one mole of OH^- per liter. Since the equivalent weight and the molar mass of a substance are related by small whole numbers (representing the number of H^+ or OH^- ions that a molecule of the substance furnishes), the normality and molarity of a solution are also simply related by these same numbers. In fact, $N = n \times M$ for a solution.

28. (a) 105 mL; (b) 1.05×10^3 mm Hg
29. (a) 272 mL; (b) 84.0 mL
30. (a) 6.96 L; (b) $P_{hydrogen} = 5.05$ atm; $P_{helium} = 1.15$ atm; (c) 2.63 atm
31. 1.04 L
32. 0.550 g CO_2; 0.280 L CO_2 at STP
33. 0.259 L
34. (a) 9.65% NaCl; (b) 2.75 g $CaCl_2$; (c) 11.4 g NaCl
35. (a) 2.36 g NaOH; (b) 2.34 *M*; (c) 30.4 mol HCl
36. (a) 0.505 *M*; (b) 0.0840 *M*; (c) 0.130 *M*
37. (a) 34.6 mL; (b) 39.4 mL; (c) 18.3 mL
38. (a) 226 g; (b) 18.4 *M*; (c) 0.764 *M*; (d) 1.53 *N*; (e) 15.8 mL

Chapters 16–17

6. The pH of a solution is defined as $pH = -\log[H^+(aq)]$ for a solution. In pure water, the amount of $H^+(aq)$ ion present is *equal* to the amount of $OH^-(aq)$ ion—that is, pure water is *neutral*. Since $[H^+] = 1.0 \times 10^{-7}\,M$ in pure water, the pH of pure water is $-\log[1.0 \times 10^{-7}\,M] = 7.00$. Solutions in which $[H^+] > 1.0 \times 10^{-7}\,M$ (pH < 7.00) are acidic; solutions in which $[H^+] < 1.0 \times 10^{-7}\,M$ (pH > 7.00) are basic. The pH scale is logarithmic: a pH change of one unit corresponds to a change in the hydrogen ion concentration by a factor of *ten*. An analogous logarithmic expression is defined for the hydroxide ion concentration in a solution: $pOH = -\log[OH^-(aq)]$. The concentrations of hydrogen ion and hydroxide ion in water (and in aqueous solutions) are *not* independent of one another, but rather are related by the dissociation equilibrium constant for water, $K_w = [H^+][OH^-] = 1.0 \times 10^{-14}$ at 25 °C. From this expression it follows that pH + pOH = 14.00 for water (or an aqueous solution) at 25 °C.
7. A *buffered solution* is one that resists a change in its pH even when a strong acid or base is added to it. Buffered solutions consist of approximately equal amounts of two components: a weak acid (or base) and its conjugate base (or acid). The *weak acid* component of the buffered solution is capable of reacting with added *strong base*. The *conjugate base* component of the buffered solution is able to react with added *strong acid*. By reacting with (and effectively neutralizing) the added strong acid or strong base, the buffer is able to maintain its pH at a relatively constant level.

   Buffered solutions are crucial to the reactions in biological systems because many of these reactions are extremely pH-dependent: a change in pH of only one or two units can make some reactions impossible or extremely slow. Many biological molecules have three-dimensional structures that are extremely dependent on the pH of their surroundings. For example, protein molecules can lose part of their necessary structure and shape if the pH of their environment changes (if a protein's structure is changed it may not work correctly). For example, if a small amount of vinegar is added to whole milk, the milk instantly curdles: the solid that forms is the protein portion of the milk, which becomes less soluble at lower pH values.
8. Chemists envision that a reaction can take place between molecules only if the molecules physically *collide* with each other. Furthermore, when molecules collide, the molecules must collide with enough force for the reaction to be successful (there must be enough energy to break bonds in the reactants), and the colliding molecules must be positioned with the correct relative orientation for the products (or intermediates) to form. Reactions tend to be faster if higher concentrations are used for the reaction because if there are more molecules present per unit volume there will be more collisions between molecules in a given time period. Reactions are faster at higher temperatures because at higher temperatures the reactant molecules have a higher average kinetic energy, and the number of molecules that will collide with sufficient force to break bonds increases.
9. A graph illustrating the activation energy barrier for a reaction is given as Figure 17.4. The *activation energy* for a reaction represents the minimum energy the reactant molecules must possess for a reaction to occur when the molecules collide. Although an increase in temperature does not change the activation energy for a reaction itself, at higher temperatures the reactant molecules have a higher average kinetic energy, and a larger fraction of reaction molecules will possess enough energy for a collision to be effective. Recall from the kinetic-molecular theory that temperature is a direct measure of average kinetic energy. A *catalyst* speeds up a reaction by providing an alternative mechanism or pathway by which the reaction can occur, with such a mechanism or pathway having a lower activation energy than the original pathway.
10. Chemists define equilibrium as the exact balancing of two exactly opposing processes. When a chemical reaction is begun by combining pure reactants, the only process possible initially is

$$\text{reactants} \rightarrow \text{products}$$

   However, for many reactions, as the concentration of product molecules increases, it becomes more and more likely that product molecules will collide and react with each other,

$$\text{products} \rightarrow \text{reactants}$$

   giving back molecules of the original reactants. At some point in the process the rates of the forward and reverse reactions become equal, and the system attains chemical equilibrium. To an outside observer the system appears to have stopped reacting. On a microscopic basis, though, both the forward and reverse processes are still going on. Every time additional molecules of the product form, however, somewhere else in the system molecules of product react to give back molecules of reactant.

   Once the point is reached that product molecules are reacting at the same speed at which they are forming, there is no further net change in concentration. At the start of the reaction, the rate of the forward reaction is at its maximum, while the rate of the reverse reaction is zero. As the reaction proceeds, the rate of the forward reaction gradually decreases as the concentration of reactants decreases, whereas the rate of the reverse reaction increases as the concentration of products increases. Once the two rates have become equal, the reaction has reached a state of equilibrium.
11. The expression for the equilibrium constant for a reaction has as its numerator the *concentrations of the products* (raised to the powers of their stoichiometric coefficients in the balanced chemical equation for the reaction) and as its denominator the *concentrations of the reactants* (also raised to the powers of their stoichiometric coefficients). In general terms, for a reaction

$$aA + bB \rightleftharpoons cC + dD$$

the equilibrium constant expression has the form

$$K = \frac{[C]^c[D]^d}{[A]^a[B]^b}$$

in which square brackets [ ] indicate molar concentration.

12. The equilibrium constant for a reaction is a ratio of the concentration of products present at the point of equilibrium to the concentration of reactants still present. A *ratio* means that we have one number divided by another number (for example, the density of a substance is the ratio of a substance's mass to its volume). Since the equilibrium constant is a ratio, there are an infinite number of sets of data that can give the same ratio: for example, the ratios 8/4, 6/3, 100/50 all have the same value, 2. The actual concentrations of products and reactants will differ from one experiment to another involving a particular chemical reaction, but the ratio of the amount of product to reactant at equilibrium should be the same for each experiment.
13. In a *homogeneous equilibrium,* all reactants and products are in the same phase and have the same physical state (solid, liquid, or gas). In a *heterogeneous equilibrium,* one or more of the reactants or products exist in a phase or physical state different from the other substances. With a heterogeneous equilibrium, the concentrations of solids and pure liquids are left out of the expression for the equilibrium constant for the reaction: the concentration of a solid or pure liquid is a constant.
14. Your paraphrase of Le Châtelier's principle should go something like this: "When you make any change to a system in equilibrium, this throws the system temporarily out of equilibrium, and the system responds by reacting in whatever direction it will be able to reach a new position of equilibrium." There are various changes that can be made to a system in equilibrium. Here are examples of some of them.
    a. The concentration of one of the reactants is increased.
    $2SO_2(g) + O_2(g) \rightleftharpoons 2SO_3(g)$
    If additional SO_2 or O_2 is added to the system at equilibrium, then more SO_3 will result than if no change was made.
    b. The concentration of one of the products is decreased by selectively removing it from the system.
    $CH_3COOH + CH_3OH \rightleftharpoons H_2O + CH_3COOCH_3$
    If H_2O were to be removed from the system by, for example, use of a drying agent, then more CH_3COOCH_3 would result than if no change was made.
    c. The reaction system is compressed to a smaller volume.
    $3H_2(g) + N_2(g) \rightleftharpoons 2NH_3(g)$
    If this system is compressed to smaller volume, then more NH_3 would be produced than if no change was made.
    d. The temperature is increased for an endothermic reaction.
    $2NaHCO_3 + \text{heat} \rightleftharpoons Na_2CO_3 + H_2O + CO_2$
    If heat is added to this system, then more product would be produced than if no change was made.
    e. The temperature is decreased for an exothermic process.
    $PCl_3 + Cl_2 \rightleftharpoons PCl_5 + \text{heat}$
    If heat is removed from this system (by cooling), then more PCl_5 would be produced than if no change was made.
15. When a slightly soluble salt is placed in water, ions begin to leave the crystals of salt and enter the solvent to form a solution. As the concentration of ions in solution increases, ions from the solution are attracted to and rejoin the crystals of undissolved salt. Eventually every time ions leave the crystals to enter the solution in one place in the system, somewhere else ions leave the solution to rejoin the solid. At the point where dissolving and "undissolving" are going on at the same rate, we arrive at a state of *dynamic equilibrium.* We write the equilibrium constant (the *solubility product*), K_{sp}, for the dissolving of a slightly soluble salt in the usual manner. Since the concentration of the solid material is constant, we do not include it in the expression for K_{sp}.
16. Specific answer depends on student choices. In general, for a weak acid HA and a weak base B

    $HA + H_2O \rightleftharpoons A^- + H_3O^+$
    $B + H_2O \rightleftharpoons HB^+ + OH^-$
17. (a) NO_3^-, HSO_4^{2-}, ClO_4^-, NH_3, HCO_3^-;
    (b) HCl, H_2SO_4, NH_3, NH4$^+$, HCO_3^-
18. (a) $NH_3(aq)$(base) + $H_2O(l)$(acid) $\rightleftharpoons$ $NH_4^+(aq)$(acid) + $OH^-(aq)$(base);
    (b) $H_2SO_4(aq)$(acid) + $H_2O(l)$(base) $\rightleftharpoons$ $HSO_4^-(aq)$(base) + $H_3O^+(aq)$(acid);
    (c) $O^{2-}(s)$(base) + $H_2O(l)$(acid) $\rightleftharpoons$ $OH^-(aq)$(acid) + $OH^-(aq)$(base);
    (d) $NH_2^-(aq)$(base) + $H_2O(l)$(acid) $\rightleftharpoons$ $NH_3(aq)$(acid) + $OH^-(aq)$(base);
    (e) $H_2PO_4^-(aq)$(acid) + $OH^-(aq)$(base) $\rightleftharpoons$ $HPO_4^{2-}(aq)$(base) + $H_2O(l)$(acid)
19. (a) 4.7×10^{-11} *M;* (b) 8.87; (c) 7.01; (d) 4.68;
    (e) 10.23; (f) 1.5×10^{-6} *M*
20. (a) pH = 2.851; pOH = 11.149; (b) pOH = 2.672; pH = 11.328; (c) pH = 2.288; pOH = 11.712; (d) pOH = 3.947; pH = 10.053
21. (a) $\frac{[N_2O]^2[O_2]}{[NO]^4}$; (b) $\frac{[F_2]^6}{[PF_3]^4}$; (c) $\frac{[CH_4][H_2O]}{[CO][H_2]^3}$;
    (d) $\frac{[Br_2][F_2]^5}{[BrF_5]^2}$; (e) $\frac{[H_2S][Cl_2]}{[HCl]^2}$
22. 7.8×10^5
23. (a) $[Cu^{2+}][OH^-]^2$; (b) $[Co^{3+}]^2[S^{2-}]^3$; (c) $[Hg_2^{2+}][OH^-]^2$;
    (d) $[Ca^{2+}][CO_3^{2-}]$; (e) $[Ag^+]^2[CrO_4^{2-}]$; (f) $[Hg^{2+}][OH^-]^2$
24. 0.220 g/L

ANSWERS TO EVEN-NUMBERED END-OF-CHAPTER QUESTIONS AND EXERCISES

Chapter 1

2. The answer depends on the student's experiences.
4. Answers will depend on the student's responses.
6. Answers will depend on the student's choices.
8. Recognize the problem and state it clearly; propose possible solutions or explanations; decide which solution/explanation is best through experiments.
10. Answers will depend on student responses. A quantitative observation must include a number, such as "There are three windows in this room." A qualitative observation could include something like "The chair is blue."
12. The answer depends on the student's responses/examples.
14. Chemistry is not just a set of facts that have to be memorized. To be successful in chemistry, you have to be able to apply what you have learned to new situations, new phenomena, new experiments. Rather than just learning a list of facts or studying someone else's solution to a problem, your instructor hopes you will learn *how* to solve problems *yourself,* so that you will be able to apply what you have learned in future circumstances.
16. In real-life situations, the problems and applications likely to be encountered are not simple textbook examples. You must be able to observe an event, hypothesize a cause, and then test this hypothesis. You must be able to carry what has been learned in class forward to new, different situations.

Chapter 2

2. "Scientific notation" means we have to put the decimal point after the first significant figure, and then express the order of magnitude of the number as a power of 10. So we want to put the decimal point after the first 2:

$$2421 \rightarrow 2.421 \times 10^{\text{to some power}}$$

To be able to move the decimal point three places to the left in going from 2421 to 2.421 means you will need a power of 10^3 after the number, where the exponent 3 shows that you moved the decimal point three places to the left:

$$2421 \rightarrow 2.421 \times 10^{\text{to some power}} = 2.421 \times 10^3$$

4. (a) 10^4; (b) 10^{-3}; (c) 10^2; (d) 10^{-30}
6. (a) negative; (b) zero; (c) positive; (d) negative
8. (a) 2789; (b) 0.002789; (c) 93,000,000; (d) 42.89; (e) 99,990; (f) 0.00009999
10. (a) three places to the left; (b) one place to the left; (c) five places to the right; (d) one place to the left; (e) two places to the right; (f) two places to the left
12. (a) 6244; (b) 0.09117; (c) 82.99; (d) 0.0001771; (e) 545.1; (f) 0.00002934
14. (a) 3.1×10^3; (b) 1×10^6; (c) 1 or 1×10^0; (d) 1.8×10^{-5}; (e) 1×10^7; (f) 1.00×10^6; (g) 1.00×10^{-7}; (h) 1×10^1
16. Answer depends on the student's examples.
18. about ¼ pound **20.** about an inch **22.** 2-liter bottle
24. the woman **26.** (a) centimeter; (b) meter; (c) kilometer
28. d
30. Typically we read the scale on measuring devices to 0.1 unit of the smallest scale division on the device. We estimate this final significant figure, which makes the final significant figure in the measurement uncertain.
32. The scale of the ruler is marked to the nearest tenth of a centimeter. Writing 2.850 would imply that the scale was marked to the nearest hundredth of a centimeter (and that the zero in the thousandths place had been estimated).
34. (a) three: the relationship is exact; (b) two; (c) five; (d) probably two
36. It is better to round off only the final answer and to carry through extra digits in intermediate calculations. If there are enough steps to the calculation, rounding off in each step may lead to a cumulative error in the final answer.
38. (a) 4.18×10^{-6}; (b) 3.87×10^4; (c) 9.11×10^{-30}; (d) 5.46×10^6
40. (a) 8.8×10^{-4}; (b) 9.375×10^4; (c) 8.97×10^{-1}; (d) 1.00×10^3
42. The total mass would be determined by the number of decimal places available on the readout of the scale/balance. For example, if a balance whose readout is to the nearest 0.01 g were used, the total mass would be reported to the second decimal place. For example, 42.05 g + 29.15 g + 31.09 g would be reported as 102.29 to the second decimal place. Even though there are only four significant figures in each of the measurements, there are five significant figures in the answer because we look at the decimal place when adding (or subtracting) numbers.
44. Most calculators would say 0.66666666. If the 2 and 3 were experimentally determined numbers, this quotient would imply far too many significant figures.
46. none
48. (a) 2.3; (b) 9.1×10^2; (c) 1.323×10^3; (d) 6.63×10^{-13}
50. (a) one; (b) four; (c) two; (d) three
52. (a) 2.045; (b) 3.8×10^3; (c) 5.19×10^{-5}; (d) 3.8418×10^{-7}
54. an infinite number, a definition
56. $\frac{2.54 \text{ cm}}{1 \text{ in.}}$; $\frac{1 \text{ in.}}{2.54 \text{ cm}}$ **58.** $\frac{1 \text{ lb}}{\$0.79}$
60. (a) 50.5 in.; (b) 3.11 ft; (c) 452 mm; (d) 76.12 cm; (e) 1.32 qt; (f) 8.42 pt; (g) 13.7 lb; (h) 28.0 oz
62. (a) 1.03598 atm; (b) 3.13 qt; (c) 0.510 kg; (d) 1.007 cal; (e) 8617 ft; (f) 9.04 qt; (g) 262 g; (h) 1.76 qt
64. 4117 km **66.** 1×10^{-8} cm; 4×10^{-9} in.; 0.1 nm
68. freezing/melting **70.** 273
72. Fahrenheit (F)
74. (a) 195 K; (b) 502 °C; (c) 216 °C; (d) 297 K
76. (a) 173 °F; (b) 104 °F; (c) −459 °F; (d) 90. °F
78. (a) 2 °C; (b) 28 °C; (c) −5.8 °F (−6 °F); (d) −40 °C (−40 is where both temperature scales have the same value)
80. g/cm^3 (g/mL) **82.** 100 $in.^3$
84. Density is a characteristic property of a pure substance.
86. copper
88. (a) 22 g/cm^3; (b) 0.034 g/cm^3; (c) 0.962 g/cm^3; (d) 2.1×10^{-5} g/cm^3
90. 2.94×10^3 g; 159 mL **92.** float **94.** 11.7 mL
96. (a) 966 g; (b) 394 g; (c) 567 g; (d) 135 g
98. (a) 301,100,000,000,000,000,000,000; (b) 5,091,000,000; (c) 720; (d) 123,400; (e) 0.000432002; (f) 0.03001; (g) 0.00000029901; (h) 0.42
100. (a) cm; (b) m; (c) km; (d) cm; (e) mm

102. (a) 5.07×10^4 kryll; (b) 0.12 blim; (c) 3.70×10^{-5} blim^2
104. 20. in. **106.** \$1.33 **108.** °X = 1.26 °C + 14
110. 3.50 g/L (3.50×10^{-3} g/cm^3) **112.** 959 g
114. (a) negative; (b) negative; (c) positive; (d) zero; (e) negative
116. (a) 2, positive; (b) 11, negative; (c) 3, positive; (d) 5, negative; (e) 5, positive; (f) 0, zero; (g) 1, negative; (h) 7, negative
118. (a) 1, positive; (b) 3, negative; (c) 0, zero; (d) 3, positive; (e) 9, negative
120. (a) 0.0000298; (b) 4,358,000,000; (c) 0.0000019928; (d) 602,000,000,000,000,000,000,000; (e) 0.101; (f) 0.00787; (g) 98,700,000; (h) 378.99; (i) 0.1093; (j) 2.9004; (k) 0.00039; (l) 0.00000001904
122. (a) 1×10^{-2}; (b) 1×10^2; (c) 5.5×10^{-2}; (d) 3.1×10^9; (e) 1×10^3; (f) 1×10^8; (g) 2.9×10^2; (h) 3.453×10^4
124. kelvin, K **126.** centimeter **128.** 0.105 m
130. 1 kg **132.** 10
134. 2.8 (the hundredths place is estimated)
136. (a) 0.000426; (b) 4.02×10^{-5}; (c) 5.99×10^6; (d) 400.; (e) 0.00600
138. (a) 2149.6; (b) 5.37×10^3; (c) 3.83×10^{-2}; (d) -8.64×10^5
140. (a) 7.6166×10^6; (b) 7.24×10^3; (c) 1.92×10^{-5}; (d) 2.4482×10^{-3}
142. $\frac{1\text{ yr}}{12\text{ mo}}$; $\frac{12\text{ mo}}{1\text{ yr}}$
144. (a) 25.7 kg; (b) 3.38 gal; (c) 0.132 qt; (d) 1.09×10^4 mL; (e) 2.03×10^3 g; (f) 0.58 qt
146. for exactly 6 gross, 864 pencils
148. (a) 352 K; (b) −18 °C; (c) −43 °C; (d) 257 °F
150. 78.2 g **152.** 0.59 g/cm^3
154. (a) 23 °F; (b) 32 °F; (c) −321 °F; (d) −459 °F; (e) 187 °F; (f) −459 °F
156. (a) $100\text{ km} \times \frac{1\text{ mile}}{1.6093\text{ km}} = 62$ miles, or about 60 miles, taking significant figures into account.
(b) $22{,}300\text{ kg} \times \frac{2.2046\text{ lbs}}{1\text{ kg}} = 49{,}200$ lbs. of fuel was needed; 22,300 lbs. were added, so 26,900 additional pounds were needed.
158. $\frac{10^{-8}\text{ g}}{\text{L}} \times \frac{3.7854\text{ L}}{1\text{ gallon}} \times \frac{1\text{ lb.}}{453.59\text{ g}} \approx 10^{-11}$ lb/gal

Chapter 3

2. forces among the particles in the matter
4. liquids **6.** gaseous **8.** stronger
10. Because gases are mostly empty space, they can be *compressed* easily to smaller volumes. In solids and liquids, most of the sample's bulk volume is filled with the molecules, leaving little empty space.
12. chemical **14.** malleable; ductile **16.** c
18. (a) physical; (b) chemical; (c) chemical; (d) chemical; (e) physical; (f) physical; (g) chemical; (h) physical; (i) physical; (j) physical; (k) chemical
20. Compounds consist of two or more elements combined together chemically in a fixed composition, no matter what their source may be. For example, water on earth consists of molecules containing one oxygen atom and two hydrogen atoms. Water on Mars (or any other planet) has the same composition.
22. compounds
24. In general, the properties of a compound are very different from the properties of its constituent elements. For example, the properties of water are altogether different from the properties of the elements (hydrogen gas and oxygen gas) that make it up.
26. no; heating causes a reaction to form iron(II) sulfide, a pure substance
28. Heterogeneous mixtures: salad dressing, jelly beans, the change in my pocket; solutions: window cleaner, shampoo, rubbing alcohol
30. (a) primarily a pure compound, but fillers and anti–caking agents may have been added; (b) mixture; (c) mixture; (d) pure substance
32. Concrete is a mixture. It consists of sand, gravel, water, and cement (which consists of limestone, clay, shale, and gypsum). The composition of concrete can vary.
34. Consider a mixture of salt (sodium chloride) and sand. Salt is soluble in water; sand is not. The mixture is added to water and stirred to dissolve the salt, and is then filtered. The salt solution passes through the filter; the sand remains on the filter. The water can then be evaporated from the salt.
36. Each component of the mixture retains its own identity during the separation.
38. compound **40.** physical **42.** far apart
44. chemical **46.** physical **48.** electrolysis
50. (a) heterogeneous; (b) heterogeneous; (c) homogeneous (if no lumps!); (d) heterogeneous (although it may appear homogeneous); (e) heterogeneous
52. Answers depend on student responses.
54. physical; chemical
56. O_2 and P_4 are both still elements, even though the ordinary forms of these elements consist of molecules containing more than one atom (but all atoms in each respective molecule are the same). P_2O_5 is a compound, because it is made up of two or more different elements (not all the atoms in the P_2O_5 molecule are the same).
58. Assuming there is enough water present in the mixture to have dissolved all the salt, filter the mixture to separate out the sand from the mixture. Then distill the filtrate (consisting of salt and water), which will boil off the water, leaving the salt.
60. The most obvious difference is the physical states: water is a liquid under room conditions, hydrogen and oxygen are both gases. Hydrogen is flammable. Oxygen supports combustion. Water does neither.

Chapter 4

2. Robert Boyle
4. 116 elements are presently known; 88 occur naturally; the remainder are manmade. Table 4.1 lists the most common elements on the earth.
6. (a) Trace elements are elements that are present in tiny amounts. Trace elements in the body, while present in small amounts, are essential.
(b) Answers will vary. For example, chromium assists in the metabolism of sugars and cobalt is present in vitamin B_{12}.
8. Answer depends on student choices/examples.
10. (a) 9; (b) 6; (c) 8; (d) 12; (e) 11; (f) 13; (g) 3; (h) 5; (i) 4; (j) 2
12. zirconium; Cs; selenium; Au; cerium
14. B: barium, Ba; berkelium, Bk; beryllium, Be; bismuth, Bi; bohrium, Bh; boron, B; bromine, Br
N: neodymium, Nd; neon, Ne; neptunium, Np; nickel, Ni; niobium, Nb; nitrogen, N; nobelium, No
P: palladium, Pd; phosphorus, P; platinum, Pt; plutonium, Pu; polonium, Po; potassium, K; praseodymium, Pr; promethium, Pm; protactinium, Pa
S: samarium, Sm; scandium, Sc; seaborgium, Sg; selenium, Se; silicon, Si; silver, Ag; sodium, Na; strontium, Sr; sulfur, S
16. (a) Elements are made of tiny particles called atoms. (b) All atoms of a given element are identical; (c) The atoms of a

given element are different from those of any other element; (d) A given compound always has the same numbers and types of atoms; (e) Atoms are neither created nor destroyed in chemical processes. A chemical reaction simply changes the way the atoms are grouped together.

18. According to Dalton, all atoms of the same element are *identical;* in particular, every atom of a given element has the same *mass* as every other atom of that element. If a given compound always contains the *same relative numbers* of atoms of each kind, and those atoms always have the same *masses,* then the compound made from those elements always contains the same relative masses of its elements.

20. (a) CO_2; (b) CO; (c) $CaCO_3$; (d) H_2SO_4; (e) $BaCl_2$; (f) Al_2S_3

22. (a) False; Rutherford's bombardment experiments with metal foil suggested that the α particles were being deflected by coming near a *dense, positively charged* atomic nucleus; (b) False; the proton and the electron have opposite charges, but the mass of the electron is *much smaller* than the mass of the proton; (c) True

24. The protons and neutrons are found in the nucleus. The protons are positively charged; the neutrons have no charge. The protons and neutrons each weigh approximately the same.

26. neutron; electron **28.** The electrons; outside the nucleus

30. The atomic number represents the number of protons in the nucleus of the atom and makes the atom a particular element. The mass number represents the total number of protons and neutrons in the nucleus of an atom and distinguishes one isotope of an element from another.

32. Neutrons are uncharged and contribute only to the mass.

34. Atoms of the same element (atoms with the same number of protons in the nucleus) may have different numbers of neutrons, and so will have different masses.

36.

Z	Symbol	Name
14	Si	silicon
54	Xe	xenon
79	Au	gold
56	Ba	barium
53	I	iodine
50	Sn	tin
48	Cd	cadmium

38. (a) $^{54}_{26}Fe$; (b) $^{56}_{26}Fe$; (c) $^{57}_{26}Fe$; (d) $^{14}_{7}N$; (e) $^{15}_{7}N$; (f) $^{15}_{7}N$

40. Researchers have found that the concentrations of hydrogen-2 (deuterium) and oxygen-18 in drinking water vary significantly from region to region in the United States. By collecting hair samples around the country, they have also found that 86% of the variations in the hair samples' hydrogen and oxygen isotopes result from the isotopic composition of the local water.

42.

Name	Symbol	Atomic Number	Mass Number	Number of Neutrons
oxygen	$^{17}_{8}O$	8	17	9
oxygen	$^{17}_{8}O$	8	17	9
neon	$^{20}_{10}Ne$	10	20	10
iron	$^{56}_{26}Fe$	26	56	30
plutonium	$^{244}_{94}Pu$	94	244	150
mercury	$^{202}_{80}Hg$	80	202	122
cobalt	$^{59}_{27}Co$	27	59	32
nickel	$^{56}_{28}Ni$	28	56	28
fluorine	$^{19}_{9}F$	9	19	10
chromium	$^{50}_{24}Cr$	24	50	26

44. vertical; groups

46. Metallic elements are found toward the *left* and *bottom* of the periodic table; there are far more metallic elements than nonmetals.

48. nonmetallic gaseous elements: oxygen, nitrogen, fluorine, chlorine, hydrogen, and the noble gases; There are no metallic gaseous elements at room conditions

50. A metalloid is an element that has some properties common to both metallic and nonmetallic elements. The metalloids are found in the "stair-step" region marked on most periodic tables.

52. (a) fluorine, chlorine, bromine, iodine, astatine; (b) lithium, sodium, potassium, rubidium, cesium, francium; (c) beryllium, magnesium, calcium, strontium, barium, radium; (d) helium, neon, argon, krypton, xenon, radon

54. Arsenic is a metalloid. Other elements in the same group (5A) include nitrogen (N), phosphorus (P), antimony (Sb), and bismuth (Bi).

56. Most elements are too reactive to be found in the uncombined form in nature and are found only in compounds.

58. These elements are found uncombined in nature and do not readily react with other elements. Although these elements were once thought to form no compounds, this now has been shown to be untrue.

60. diatomic gases: H_2, N_2, O_2, F_2, Cl_2; monatomic gases: He, Ne, Kr, Xe, Rn, Ar

62. chlorine **64.** diamond **66.** electrons **68.** 3+

70. *-ide* **72.** nonmetallic

74. (a) 36; (b) 36; (c) 21; (d) 36; (e) 80; (f) 27

76. (a) two electrons gained; (b) three electrons gained; (c) three electrons lost; (d) two electrons lost; (e) one electron lost; (f) two electrons lost

78. (a) P^{3-}; (b) Ra^{2+}; (c) At^{-}; (d) no ion; (e) Cs^{+}; (f) Se^{2-}

80. Sodium chloride is an *ionic* compound, consisting of Na^{+} and Cl^{-} *ions*. When NaCl is dissolved in water, these ions are *set free* and can move independently to conduct the electric current. Sugar crystals, although they may *appear* similar visually, contain *no* ions. When sugar is dissolved in water, it dissolves as uncharged *molecules*. No electrically charged species are present in a sugar solution to carry the electric current.

82. The total number of positive charges must equal the total number of negative charges so that the crystals of an ionic compound have *no net charge*. A macroscopic sample of compound ordinarily has no net charge.

84. (a) CsI, BaI_2, AlI_3; (b) Cs_2O, BaO, Al_2O_3; (c) Cs_3P, Ba_3P_2, AlP; (d) Cs_2Se, BaSe, Al_2Se_3; (e) CsH, BaH_2, AlH_3

86. (a) 7, halogens; (b) 8, noble gases; (c) 2, alkaline earth elements; (d) 2, alkaline earth elements; (e) 4; (f) 6; (g) 8, noble gases; (h) 1, alkali metals

88.

	Element	Symbol	Atomic Number
Group 3	boron	B	5
	aluminum	Al	13
	gallium	Ga	31
	indium	In	49
Group 5	nitrogen	N	7
	phosphorus	P	15
	arsenic	As	33
	antimony	Sb	51
Group 6	oxygen	O	8
	sulfur	S	16
	selenium	Se	34
	tellurium	Te	52
Group 8	helium	He	2
	neon	Ne	10
	argon	Ar	18
	krypton	Kr	36

90. Most of an atom's mass is concentrated in the nucleus: the *protons* and *neutrons* that constitute the nucleus have similar masses and are each nearly 2000 times more massive than electrons. The chemical properties of an atom depend on the number and location of the *electrons* it possesses. Electrons are found in the outer regions of the atom and are involved in interactions between atoms.
92. $C_6H_{12}O_6$
94. (a) 29 electrons, 34 neutrons, 29 electrons; (b) 35 protons, 45 neutrons, 35 electrons; (c) 12 protons, 12 neutrons, 12 electrons
96. The chief use of gold in ancient times was as *ornamentation,* whether in statuary or in jewelry. Gold possesses an especially beautiful luster; since it is relatively soft and malleable, it can be worked finely by artisans. Among the metals, gold is inert to attack by most substances in the environment.
98. (a) I; (b) Si; (c) W; (d) Fe; (e) Cu; (f) Co
100. (a) Br; (b) Bi; (c) Hg; (d) V; (e) F; (f) Ca
102. (a) osmium; (b) zirconium; (c) rubidium; (d) radon; (e) uranium; (f) manganese; (g) nickel; (h) bromine
104. (a) CO_2; (b) $AlCl_3$; (c) $HClO_4$; (d) SCl_6
106. (a) ${}^{13}_{6}C$; (b) ${}^{13}_{6}C$; (c) ${}^{13}_{6}C$; (d) ${}^{44}_{19}K$; (e) ${}^{41}_{20}Ca$; (f) ${}^{35}_{19}K$

108.

Symbol	Number of Protons	Number of Neutrons	Mass Number
${}^{41}_{20}Ca$	20	21	41
${}^{55}_{25}Mn$	25	30	55
${}^{109}_{47}Ag$	47	62	109
${}^{45}_{21}Sc$	21	24	45

Chapter 5

2. A binary chemical compound contains only two elements; the major types are ionic (compounds of a metal and a nonmetal) and nonionic or molecular (compounds between two nonmetals). Answers depend on student responses.
4. cation (positive ion)
6. Some substances do not contain molecules; the formula we write reflects only the relative number of each type of atom present.
8. Roman numeral
10. (a) lithium chloride; (b) barium fluoride; (c) calcium oxide; (d) aluminum iodide; (e) magnesium sulfide; (f) rubidium oxide
12. (a) correct; (b) incorrect, copper(I) oxide; (c) incorrect; potassium oxide; (d) correct; (e) incorrect, rubidium sulfide
14. (a) copper(II) chloride; (b) chromium(III) oxide; (c) mercury(II) chloride; (d) mercury(I) oxide; (e) gold(III) bromide; (f) manganese(IV) oxide
16. (a) cobaltic chloride; (b) ferrous bromide; (c) plumbic oxide; (d) stannic chloride; (e) mercuric iodide; (f) ferrous sulfide
18. (a) chlorine pentafluoride; (b) xenon dichloride; (c) selenium dioxide; (d) dinitrogen trioxide; (e) diiodine hexachloride; (f) carbon disulfide
20. (a) lead(IV) sulfide, plumbic sulfide; (b) lead(II) sulfide, plumbous sulfide; (c) silicon dioxide; (d) tin(IV) fluoride, stannic fluoride; (e) dichlorine heptoxide; (f) cobalt(III) sulfide, cobaltic sulfide
22. (a) barium fluoride; (b) radium oxide; (c) dinitrogen oxide; (d) rubidium oxide; (e) diarsenic pent(a)oxide; (f) calcium nitride
24. An oxyanion is a polyatomic ion containing a given element and one or more oxygen atoms. The oxyanions of chlorine and bromine are given below:

Oxyanion	Name	Oxyanion	Name
ClO^-	hypochlorite	BrO^-	hypobromite
ClO_2^-	chlorite	BrO_2^-	bromite
ClO_3^-	chlorate	BrO_3^-	bromate
ClO_4^-	perchlorate	BrO_4^-	perbromate

26. *hypo-* (fewest); *per-* (most)
28. IO^-, hypoiodite; IO_2^-, iodite; IO_3^-, iodate; IO_4^-, periodate
30. (a) NO_3^-; (b) NO_2^-; (c) NH_4^+; (d) CN^-
32. CN^-, cyanide; CO_3^{2-}, carbonate; HCO_3^-, hydrogen carbonate; $C_2H_3O_2^-$, acetate
34. (a) ammonium ion; (b) dihydrogen phosphate ion; (c) sulfate ion; (d) hydrogen sulfite ion (bisulfite ion); (e) perchlorate ion; (f) iodate ion
36. (a) sodium permanganate; (b) aluminum phosphate; (c) chromium(II) carbonate, chromous carbonate; (d) calcium hypochlorite; (e) barium carbonate; (f) calcium chromate
38. oxygen
40. (a) hypochlorous acid; (b) sulfurous acid; (c) bromic acid; (d) hypoiodous acid; (e) perbromic acid; (f) hydrosulfuric acid; (g) hydroselenic acid; (h) phosphorous acid
42. (a) MgF_2; (b) FeI_2; (c) HgS; (d) Ba_3N_2; (e) $PbCl_2$; (f) SnF_4; (g) Ag_2O; (h) K_2Se
44. (a) N_2O; (b) NO_2; (c) N_2O_4; (d) SF_6; (e) PBr_3; (f) CI_4; (g) OCl_2
46. (a) $NH_4C_2H_3O_2$; (b) $Fe(OH)_2$; (c) $Co_2(CO_3)_3$; (d) $BaCr_2O_7$; (e) $PbSO_4$; (f) KH_2PO_4; (g) Li_2O_2; (h) $Zn(ClO_3)_2$
48. (a) HCN; (b) HNO_3; (c) H_2SO_4; (d) H_3PO_4; (e) HClO or HOCl; (f) HBr; (g) $HBrO_2$; (h) HF
50. (a) $Ca(HSO_4)_2$; (b) $Zn_3(PO_4)_2$; (c) $Fe(ClO_4)_3$; (d) $Co(OH)_3$; (e) K_2CrO_4; (f) $Al(H_2PO_4)_3$; (g) $LiHCO_3$; (h) $Mn(C_2H_3O_2)_2$; (i) $MgHPO_4$; (j) $CsClO_2$; (k) BaO_2; (l) $NiCO_3$
52. A moist paste of NaCl would contain Na^+ and Cl^- ions in solution and would serve as a *conductor* of electrical impulses.
54. $H \rightarrow H^+$ (hydrogen ion) + e^-; $H + e^- \rightarrow H^-$ (hydride ion)
56. ClO_4^-, $HClO_4$; IO_3^-, HIO_3; ClO^-, $HClO$; BrO_2^-, $HBrO_2$; ClO_2^-, $HClO_2$
58. (a) gold(III) bromide (auric bromide); (b) cobalt(III) cyanide (cobaltic cyanide); (c) magnesium hydrogen phosphate; (d) diboron hexahydride (common name diborane); (e) ammonia; (f) silver(I) sulfate (usually called silver sulfate); (g) beryllium hydroxide
60. (a) ammonium carbonate; (b) ammonium hydrogen carbonate, ammonium bicarbonate; (c) calcium phosphate; (d) sulfurous acid; (e) manganese(IV) oxide; (f) iodic acid; (g) potassium hydride
62. (a) $M(C_2H_3O_2)_4$; (b) $M(MnO_4)_4$; (c) MO_2; (d) $M(HPO_4)_2$; (e) $M(OH)_4$; (f) $M(NO_2)_4$
64. M^+ compounds: MD, M_2E, M_3F; M^{2+} compounds: MD_2, ME, M_3F_2; M^{3+} compounds: MD_3, M_2E_3, MF
66.

$Ca(NO_3)_2$	$CaSO_4$	$Ca(HSO_4)_2$	$Ca(H_2PO_4)_2$	CaO	$CaCl_2$
$Sr(NO_3)_2$	$SrSO_4$	$Sr(HSO_4)_2$	$Sr(H_2PO_4)_2$	SrO	$SrCl_2$
NH_4NO_3	$(NH_4)_2SO_4$	NH_4HSO_4	$NH_4H_2PO_4$	$(NH_4)_2O$	NH_4Cl
$Al(NO_3)_3$	$Al_2(SO_4)_3$	$Al(HSO_4)_3$	$Al(H_2PO_4)_3$	Al_2O_3	$AlCl_3$
$Fe(NO_3)_3$	$Fe_2(SO_4)_3$	$Fe(HSO_4)_3$	$Fe(H_2PO_4)_3$	Fe_2O_3	$FeCl_3$
$Ni(NO_3)_2$	$NiSO_4$	$Ni(HSO_4)_2$	$Ni(H_2PO_4)_2$	NiO	$NiCl_2$
$AgNO_3$	Ag_2SO_4	$AgHSO_4$	AgH_2PO_4	Ag_2O	AgCl
$Au(NO_3)_3$	$Au_2(SO_4)_3$	$Au(HSO_4)_3$	$Au(H_2PO_4)_3$	Au_2O_3	$AuCl_3$
KNO_3	K_2SO_4	$KHSO_4$	KH_2PO_4	K_2O	KCl
$Hg(NO_3)_2$	$HgSO_4$	$Hg(HSO_4)_2$	$Hg(H_2PO_4)_2$	HgO	$HgCl_2$
$Ba(NO_3)_2$	$BaSO_4$	$Ba(HSO_4)_2$	$Ba(H_2PO_4)_2$	BaO	$BaCl_2$

68. helium **70.** F_2, Cl_2 (gas); Br_2 (liquid); I_2, At_2 (solid)
72. 1− **74.** 1−
76. (a) $Al(13e) \rightarrow Al^{3+}(10e) + 3e^-$; (b) $S(16e) + 2e^- \rightarrow S^{2-}(18e)$; (c) $Cu(29e) \rightarrow Cu^{+}(28e) + e^-$; (d) $F(9e) + e^- \rightarrow F^-(10e)$; (e) $Zn(30e) \rightarrow Zn^{2+}(28e) + 2e^-$; (f) $P(15e) + 3e^- \rightarrow P^{3-}(18e)$
78. (a) Na_2S; (b) KCl; (c) BaO; (d) MgSe; (e) $CuBr_2$; (f) AlI_3; (g) Al_2O_3; (h) Ca_3N_2
80. (a) silver(I) oxide or just silver oxide; (b) correct; (c) iron(III) oxide; (d) plumbic oxide; (e) correct
82. (a) stannous chloride; (b) ferrous oxide; (c) stannic oxide; (d) plumbous sulfide; (e) cobaltic sulfide; (f) chromous chloride
84. (a) iron(III) acetate; (b) bromine monofluoride; (c) potassium peroxide; (d) silicon tetrabromide; (e) copper(II) permanganate; (f) calcium chromate
86. (a) CO_3^{2-}; (b) HCO_3^-; (c) $C_2H_3O_2^-$; (d) CN^-
88. (a) carbonate; (b) chlorate; (c) sulfate; (d) phosphate; (e) perchlorate; (f) permanganate
90. Answer depends on student choices.
92. (a) NaH_2PO_4; (b) $LiClO_4$; (c) $Cu(HCO_3)_2$; (d) $KC_2H_3O_2$; (e) BaO_2; (f) Cs_2SO_3

Chapter 6

2. Most of these products contain a peroxide, which decomposes and releases oxygen gas.
4. Bubbling takes place as the hydrogen peroxide chemically decomposes into water and oxygen gas.
6. The appearance of the black color actually signals the breakdown of starches and sugars in the bread to elemental carbon. You may also see steam coming from the bread (water produced by the breakdown of the carbohydrates).
8. atoms
10. Balancing an equation ensures that no atoms are created or destroyed during the reaction. The total mass after the reaction must be the same as the total mass before the reaction.
12. Solid, (*s*); liquid, (*l*); gas, (*g*)
14. $H_2O_2(aq) \rightarrow H_2(g) + O_2(g)$
16. $N_2H_4(l) \rightarrow N_2(g) + H_2(g)$
18. $C_3H_8(g) + O_2(g) \rightarrow CO_2(g) + H_2O(g)$; $C_3H_8(g) + O_2(g) \rightarrow CO(g) + H_2O(g)$
20. $CaCO_3(s) + HCl(aq) \rightarrow CaCl_2(aq) + H_2O(l) + CO_2(g)$
22. $SiO_2(s) + C(s) \rightarrow Si(s) + CO(g)$
24. $Fe(s) + H_2O(l) \rightarrow FeO(s) + H_2(g)$
26. $SO_2(g) + H_2O(l) \rightarrow H_2SO_3(aq)$; $SO_3(g) + H_2O(l) \rightarrow H_2SO_4(aq)$
28. $NO(g) + O_3(g) \rightarrow NO_2(g) + O_2(g)$
30. $P_4(s) + O_2(g) \rightarrow P_2O_5(s)$ **32.** $Xe(g) + F_2(g) \rightarrow XeF_4(s)$
34. $NH_3(g) + O_2(g) \rightarrow HNO_3(aq) + H_2O(l)$
36. To balance a chemical equation we must have the same number of each type of atom on both sides of the equation. In addition, we must balance the equation we are given, that is, we are not to change the nature of the substances.

For example, the equation $2H_2O_2(aq) \rightarrow 2H_2O(l) + O_2(g)$ can be represented as

The equation $H_2O_2(aq) \rightarrow H_2(g) + O_2(g)$ can be represented as

38. (a) $Zn(s) + CuO(s) \rightarrow ZnO(s) + Cu(l)$; (b) $P_4(s) + 6F_2(g) \rightarrow 4PF_3(g)$; (c) $Xe(g) + 2F_2(g) \rightarrow XeF_4(s)$; (d) $2NH_4Cl(g) + Mg(OH)_2(s) \rightarrow 2NH_3(g) + 2H_2O(g) + MgCl_2(s)$; (e) $2SiO(s) + 4Cl_2(g) \rightarrow 2SiCl_4(l) + O_2(g)$; (f) $Cs_2O(s) + H_2O(l) \rightarrow 2CsOH(aq)$; (g) $N_2O_3(g) + H_2O(l) \rightarrow 2HNO_2(aq)$; (h) $Fe_2O_3(s) + 3H_2SO_4(l) \rightarrow Fe_2(SO_4)_3(s) + 3H_2O(g)$
40. (a) $Na_2SO_4(aq) + CaCl_2(aq) \rightarrow CaSO_4(s) + 2NaCl(aq)$; (b) $3Fe(s) + 4H_2O(g) \rightarrow Fe_3O_4(s) + 4H_2(g)$; (c) $Ca(OH)_2(aq) + 2HCl(aq) \rightarrow CaCl_2(aq) + 2H_2O(l)$; (d) $Br_2(g) + 2H_2O(l) + SO_2(g) \rightarrow 2HBr(aq) + H_2SO_4(aq)$; (e) $3NaOH(s) + H_3PO_4(aq) \rightarrow Na_3PO_4(aq) + 3H_2O(l)$; (f) $2NaNO_3(s) \rightarrow 2NaNO_2(s) + O_2(g)$; (g) $2Na_2O_2(s) + 2H_2O(l) \rightarrow 4NaOH(aq) + O_2(g)$; (h) $4Si(s) + S_8(s) \rightarrow 2Si_2S_4(s)$
42. (a) $4NaCl(s) + 2SO_2(g) + 2H_2O(g) + O_2(g) \rightarrow 2Na_2SO_4(s) + 4HCl(g)$; (b) $3Br_2(l) + I_2(s) \rightarrow 2IBr_3(s)$; (c) $Ca(s) + 2H_2O(g) \rightarrow Ca(OH)_2(aq) + H_2(g)$; (d) $2BF_3(g) + 3H_2O(g) \rightarrow B_2O_3(s) + 6HF(g)$; (e) $SO_2(g) + 2Cl_2(g) \rightarrow SOCl_2(l) + Cl_2O(g)$; (f) $Li_2O(s) + H_2O(l) \rightarrow 2LiOH(aq)$; (g) $Mg(s) + CuO(s) \rightarrow MgO(s) + Cu(l)$; (h) $Fe_3O_4(s) + 4H_2(g) \rightarrow 3Fe(l) + 4H_2O(g)$
44. (a) $Ba(NO_3)_2(aq) + Na_2CrO_4(aq) \rightarrow BaCrO_4(s) + 2NaNO_3(aq)$; (b) $PbCl_2(aq) + K_2SO_4(aq) \rightarrow PbSO_4(s) + 2KCl(aq)$; (c) $C_2H_5OH(l) + 3O_2(g) \rightarrow 2CO_2(g) + 3H_2O(l)$; (d) $CaC_2(s) + 2H_2O(l) \rightarrow Ca(OH)_2(s) + C_2H_2(g)$; (e) $Sr(s) + 2HNO_3(aq) \rightarrow Sr(NO_3)_2(aq) + H_2(g)$; (f) $BaO_2(s) + H_2SO_4(aq) \rightarrow BaSO_4(s) + H_2O_2(aq)$; (g) $2AsI_3(s) \rightarrow 2As(s) + 3I_2(s)$; (h) $2CuSO_4(aq) + 4KI(s) \rightarrow 2CuI(s) + I_2(s) + 2K_2SO_4(aq)$
46. $Na(s) + O_2(g) \rightarrow Na_2O_2(s)$; $Na_2O_2(s) + H_2O(l) \rightarrow NaOH(aq) + O_2(g)$
48. $C_{12}H_{22}O_{11}(aq) + H_2O(l) \rightarrow 4C_2H_5OH(aq) + 4CO_2(g)$
50. $2Al_2O_3(s) + 3C(s) \rightarrow 4Al(s) + 3CO_2(g)$
52. $2Li(s) + S(s) \rightarrow Li_2S(s)$; $2Na(s) + S(s) \rightarrow Na_2S(s)$; $2K(s) + S(s) \rightarrow K_2S(s)$; $2Rb(s) + S(s) \rightarrow Rb_2S(s)$; $2Cs(s) + S(s) \rightarrow Cs_2S(s)$; $2Fr(s) + S(s) \rightarrow Fr_2S(s)$
54. $BaO_2(s) + H_2O(l) \rightarrow BaO(s) + H_2O_2(aq)$
56. $2KClO_3(s) \rightarrow 2KCl(s) + 3O_2(g)$
58. $NH_3(g) + HCl(g) \rightarrow NH_4Cl(s)$
60. The senses we call "odor" and "taste" are really chemical reactions of the receptors in our body with molecules in the food we are eating. The fact that the receptors no longer detect the "fishy" odor or taste suggests that adding the lemon juice or vinegar has changed the nature of the amines in the fish.
62. $Fe(s) + S(s) \rightarrow FeS(s)$
64. $K_2CrO_4(aq) + BaCl_2(aq) \rightarrow BaCrO_4(s) + 2KCl(aq)$
66. $2NaCl(aq) + 2H_2O(l) \rightarrow Cl_2(g) + H_2(g) + 2NaOH(aq, s)$; $2NaBr(aq) + 2H_2O(l) \rightarrow Br_2(l) + H_2(g) + 2NaOH(aq, s)$; $2NaI(aq) + 2H_2O(l) \rightarrow I_2(s) + H_2(g) + 2NaOH(aq, s)$
68. $CaC_2(s) + 2H_2O(l) \rightarrow Ca(OH)_2(s) + C_2H_2(g)$
70. $CuO(s) + H_2SO_4(aq) \rightarrow CuSO_4(aq) + H_2O(l)$
72. $Na_2SO_3(aq) + S(s) \rightarrow Na_2S_2O_3(aq)$
74. (a) $Cl_2(g) + 2KI(aq) \rightarrow 2KCl(aq) + I_2(s)$; (b) $CaC_2(s) + 2H_2O(l) \rightarrow Ca(OH)_2(s) + C_2H_2(g)$; (c) $2NaCl(s) + H_2SO_4(l) \rightarrow Na_2SO_4(s) + 2HCl(g)$; (d) $CaF_2(s) + H_2SO_4(l) \rightarrow CaSO_4(s) + 2HF(g)$; (e) $K_2CO_3(s) \rightarrow K_2O(s) + CO_2(g)$; (f) $3BaO(s) + 2Al(s) \rightarrow Al_2O_3(s) + 3Ba(s)$; (g) $2Al(s) + 3F_2(g) \rightarrow 2AlF_3(s)$; (h) $CS_2(g) + 3Cl_2(g) \rightarrow CCl_4(l) + S_2Cl_2(g)$
76. (a) $Pb(NO_3)_2(aq) + K_2CrO_4(aq) \rightarrow PbCrO_4(s) + 2KNO_3(aq)$; (b) $BaCl_2(aq) + Na_2SO_4(aq) \rightarrow BaSO_4(s) + 2NaCl(aq)$; (c) $2CH_3OH(l) + 3O_2(g) \rightarrow 2CO_2(g) + 4H_2O(g)$; (d) $Na_2CO_3(aq) + S(s) + SO_2(g) \rightarrow CO_2(g) + Na_2S_2O_3(aq)$; (e) $Cu(s) + 2H_2SO_4(aq) \rightarrow CuSO_4(aq) + SO_2(g) + 2H_2O(l)$; (f) $MnO_2(s) + 4HCl(aq) \rightarrow MnCl_2(aq) + Cl_2(g) + 2H_2O(l)$; (g) $As_2O_3(s) + 6KI(aq) + 6HCl(aq) \rightarrow 2AsI_3(s) + 6KCl(aq) + 3H_2O(l)$; (h) $2Na_2S_2O_3(aq) + I_2(aq) \rightarrow Na_2S_4O_6(aq) + 2NaI(aq)$

Chapter 7

2. Driving forces are types of *changes* in a system that pull a reaction in the *direction of product formation;* driving forces include formation of a *solid,* formation of *water,* formation of a *gas,* and transfer of electrons.

4. A reactant in aqueous solution is indicated with (*aq*); formation of a solid is indicated with (*s*).
6. There are twice as many chloride ions as magnesium ions.
8. The simplest evidence is that solutions of ionic substances conduct electricity.
10. Answer depends on student choices.
12. (a) soluble; Rule 3; (b) soluble; Rule 2; (c) soluble; Rule 2; (d) insoluble; Rule 5; (e) soluble; Rule 2; (f) soluble; Rule 1; (g) soluble; Rule 4; (h) insoluble; Rule 6
14. (a) Rule 6; (b) Rule 6; (c) Rule 6; (d) Rule 3; (e) Rule 4
16. (a) $MnCO_3$, Rule 6; (b) $CaSO_4$, Rule 4; (c) Hg_2Cl_2, Rule 3; (d) no precipitate, most sodium and nitrate salts are soluble; (e) $Ni(OH)_2$, Rule 5; (f) $BaSO_4$, Rule 4
18. (a) $Na_2CO_3(aq) + CuSO_4(aq) \rightarrow Na_2SO_4(aq) + \underline{CuCO_3(s)}$
(b) $HCl(aq) + AgC_2H_3O_2(aq) \rightarrow HC_2H_3O_2(aq) + \underline{AgCl(s)}$
(c) no precipitate
(d) $3(NH_4)_2S(aq) + 2FeCl_3(aq) \rightarrow 6NH_4Cl(aq) + Fe_2S_3(s)$
(e) $H_2SO_4(aq) + Pb(NO_3)_2(aq) \rightarrow 2HNO_3(aq) + \underline{PbSO_4(s)}$
(f) $2K_3PO_4(aq) + 3CaCl_2(aq) \rightarrow 6KCl(aq) + \underline{Ca_3(PO_4)_2(s)}$
20. (a) $CaCl_2(aq) + 2AgNO_3(aq) \rightarrow Ca(NO_3)_2(aq) + 2AgCl(s)$; (b) $2AgNO_3(aq) + K_2CrO_4(aq) \rightarrow Ag_2CrO_4(s) + 2KNO_3(aq)$; (c) $BaCl_2(aq) + K_2SO_4(aq) \rightarrow BaSO_4(s) + 2KCl(aq)$
22. (a) $Na_2CO_3(aq) + K_2SO_4(aq) \rightarrow$ no precipitate; all combinations are soluble (b) $CuCl_2(aq) + (NH_4)_2CO_3(aq) \rightarrow 2NH_4Cl(aq) + \underline{CuCO_3(s)}$ (c) $K_3PO_4(aq) + AlCl_3(aq) \rightarrow 3KCl(aq) + \underline{AlPO_4(s)}$
24. Spectator ions are ions that *remain in solution* during a precipitation/double-displacement reaction. For example, in the reaction $BaCl_2(aq) + K_2SO_4(aq) \rightarrow BaSO_4(s) + 2KCl(aq)$, the K^+ and Cl^- ions are spectator ions.
26. (a) $Ca^{2+}(aq) + SO_4^{2-}(aq) \rightarrow CaSO_4(s)$; (b) $Ni^{2+}(aq) + 2OH^-(aq) \rightarrow Ni(OH)_2(s)$; (c) $2Fe^{3+}(aq) + 3S^2(aq) \rightarrow Fe_2S_3(s)$
28. $Ag^+(aq) + Cl^-(aq) \rightarrow AgCl(s)$; $Pb^{2+}(aq) + 2Cl^-(aq) \rightarrow PbCl_2(s)$; $Hg_2^{2+}(aq) + 2Cl^-(aq) \rightarrow Hg_2Cl_2(s)$
30. $Co^{2+}(aq) + S^{2-}(aq) \rightarrow CoS(s)$; $2Co^{3+}(aq) + 3S^{2-}(aq) \rightarrow Co_2S_3(s)$; $Fe^{2+}(aq) + S^{2-}(aq) \rightarrow FeS(s)$; $2Fe^{3+}(aq) + 3S^{2-}(aq) \rightarrow Fe_2S_3(s)$
32. The strong bases are those hydroxide compounds that dissociate fully when dissolved in water. The strong bases that are highly soluble in water (NaOH, KOH) are also strong electrolytes.
34. acids: HCl (hydrochloric), HNO_3 (nitric), H_2SO_4 (sulfuric); bases: hydroxides of Group 1A elements: NaOH, KOH, RbOH, CsOH
36. A salt is the ionic product remaining in solution when an acid neutralizes a base. For example, in the reaction $HCl(aq) + NaOH(aq) \rightarrow NaCl(aq) + H_2O(l)$, sodium chloride is the salt produced by the neutralization reaction.
38. $RbOH(s) \rightarrow Rb^+(aq) + OH^-(aq)$; $CsOH(s) \rightarrow Cs^+(aq) + OH^-(aq)$
40. (a) $H_2SO_4(aq) + 2KOH(aq) \rightarrow K_2SO_4(aq) + 2H_2O(l)$
(b) $HNO_3(aq) + NaOH(aq) \rightarrow NaNO_3(aq) + H_2O(l)$
(c) $2HCl(aq) + Ca(OH)_2(aq) \rightarrow CaCl_2(aq) + 2H_2O(l)$
(d) $2HClO_4(aq) + Ba(OH)_2(aq) \rightarrow Ba(ClO_4)_2(aq) + 2H_2O(l)$
42. Answer depends on student choice of example: $Na(s) + Cl_2(g) \rightarrow 2NaCl(s)$ is an example.
44. The metal loses electrons, the nonmetal gains electrons.
46. Each magnesium atom would lose two electrons. Each oxygen atom would gain two electrons (so the O_2 molecule would gain four electrons). Two magnesium atoms would be required to react with each O_2 molecule. Magnesium ions are charged 2+, oxide ions are charged 2−.
48. Each potassium atom loses one electron. The sulfur atom gains two electrons. So two potassium atoms are required to react with one sulfur atom.

$2 \times (K \rightarrow K^+ + e^-)$
$S + 2e^- \rightarrow S^{2-}$

50. (a) $P_4(s) + 5O_2(g) \rightarrow P_4O_{10}(s)$; (b) $MgO(s) + C(s) \rightarrow Mg(s) + CO(g)$; (c) $Sr(s) + 2H_2O(l) \rightarrow Sr(OH)_2(aq) + H_2(g)$; (d) $Co(s) + 2HCl(aq) \rightarrow CoCl_2(aq) + H_2(g)$
52. The reaction includes aluminum metal as a reactant and products that contain aluminum ions. For this reaction, electrons must be transferred. That is, to make an aluminum cation, electrons must be removed from the metal. An oxidation reduction is one that involves transfers of electrons.
54. (a) oxidation–reduction; (b) oxidation–reduction; (c) acid–base; (d) acid–base, precipitation; (e) precipitation; (f) precipitation; (g) oxidation–reduction; (h) oxidation–reduction; (i) acid–base
56. oxidation–reduction
58. A decomposition reaction is one in which a given compound is broken down into simpler compounds or constituent elements. The reactions $CaCO_3(s) \rightarrow CaO(s) + CO_2(g)$ and $2HgO(s) \rightarrow 2Hg(l) + O_2(g)$ represent decomposition reactions. Such reactions often may be classified in other ways. For example, the reaction of HgO(*s*) is also an oxidation–-reduction reaction.
60. (a) $C_3H_8(g) + 5O_2(g) \rightarrow 3CO_2(g) + 4H_2O(g)$;
(b) $C_2H_4(g) + 3O_2(g) \rightarrow 2CO_2(g) + 2H_2O(g)$;
(c) $2C_8H_{18}(l) + 25O_2(g) \rightarrow 16CO_2(g) + 18H_2O(g)$
62. Answer depends on student selection.
64. (a) $8Fe(s) + S_8(s) \rightarrow 8FeS(s)$; (b) $4Co(s) + 3O_2(g) \rightarrow 2Co_2O_3(s)$; (c) $Cl_2O_7(g) + H_2O(l) \rightarrow 2HClO_4(aq)$
66. (a) $2Al(s) + 3Br_2(l) \rightarrow 2AlBr_3(s)$
(b) $Zn(s) + 2HClO_4(aq) \rightarrow Zn(ClO_4)_2(aq) + H_2(g)$
(c) $3Na(s) + P(s) \rightarrow Na_3P(s)$
(d) $CH_4(g) + 4Cl_2(g) \rightarrow CCl_4(l) + 4HCl(g)$
(e) $Cu(s) + 2AgNO_3(aq) \rightarrow Cu(NO_3)_2(aq) + 2Ag(s)$
68. (a) silver ion: $Ag^+(aq) + Cl^-(aq) \rightarrow AgCl(s)$; lead(II) ion: $Pb^{2+}(aq) + 2Cl^-(aq) \rightarrow PbCl_2(s)$; mercury(I) ion: $Hg_2^{2+}(aq) + 2Cl^-(aq) \rightarrow Hg_2Cl_2(s)$; (b) sulfate ion: $Ca^{2+}(aq) + SO_4^{2-}(aq) \rightarrow CaSO_4(s)$; carbonate ion: $Ca^{2+}(aq) + CO_3^{2-}(aq) \rightarrow CaCO_3(s)$; phosphate ion: $3Ca^{2+}(aq) + 2PO_4^{3-}(aq) \rightarrow Ca_3(PO_4)_2(s)$; (c) hydroxide ion: $Fe^{3+}(aq) + 3OH^-(aq) \rightarrow Fe(OH)_3(s)$; sulfide ion: $2Fe^{3+}(aq) + 3S^{2-}(aq) \rightarrow Fe_2S_3(s)$; phosphate ion: $Fe^{3+}(aq) + PO_4^{3-}(aq) \rightarrow FePO_4(s)$; (d) barium ion: $Ba^{2+}(aq) + SO_4^{2-}(aq) \rightarrow BaSO_4(s)$; calcium ion: $Ca^{2+}(aq) + SO_4^{2-}(aq) \rightarrow CaSO_4(s)$; lead(II) ion: $Pb^{2+}(aq) + SO_4^{2-}(aq) \rightarrow PbSO_4(s)$; (e) chloride ion: $Hg_2^{2+}(aq) + 2Cl^-(aq) \rightarrow Hg_2Cl_2(s)$; sulfide ion: $Hg_2^{2+}(aq) + S^{2-}(aq) \rightarrow Hg_2S(s)$; carbonate ion: $Hg_2^{2+}(aq) + CO_3^{2-}(aq) \rightarrow Hg_2CO_3(s)$; (f) chloride ion: $Ag^+(aq) + Cl^-(aq) \rightarrow AgCl(s)$; hydroxide ion: $Ag^+(aq) + OH^-(aq) \rightarrow AgOH(s)$; carbonate ion: $2Ag^+(aq) + CO_3^{2-}(aq) \rightarrow Ag_2CO_3(s)$
70. (a) $HNO_3(aq) + KOH(aq) \rightarrow H_2O(l) + \underline{KNO_3(aq)}$;
(b) $H_2SO_4(aq) + Ba(OH)_2(aq) \rightarrow \underline{BaSO_4(s)} + 2H_2O(l)$;
(c) $HClO_4(aq) + NaOH(aq) \rightarrow H_2O(l) + \underline{NaClO_4(aq)}$;
(d) $2HCl(aq) + Ca(OH)_2(aq) \rightarrow \underline{CaCl_2(aq)} + H_2O(l)$
72. (a) soluble (Rule 2: most potassium salts are soluble); (b) soluble (Rule 2: most ammonium salts are soluble); (c) insoluble (Rule 6: most carbonate salts are only slightly soluble); (d) insoluble (Rule 6: most phosphate salts are only slightly soluble); (e) soluble (Rule 2: most sodium salts are soluble); (f) insoluble (Rule 6: most carbonate salts are only slightly soluble); (g) soluble (Rule 3: most chloride salts are soluble)
74. (a) $AgNO_3(aq) + HCl(aq) \rightarrow \underline{AgCl(s)} + HNO_3(aq)$;
(b) $CuSO_4(aq) + (NH_4)_2CO_3(aq) \rightarrow \underline{CuCO_3(s)} + (NH_4)_2SO_4(aq)$;
(c) $FeSO_4(aq) + K_2CO_3(aq) \rightarrow \underline{FeCO_3(s)} + K_2SO_4(aq)$;
(d) no reaction; (e) $Pb(NO_3)_2(aq) + Li_2CO_3(aq) \rightarrow \underline{PbCO_3(s)} + 2LiNO_3(aq)$; (f) $SnCl_4(aq) + 4NaOH(aq) \rightarrow \underline{Sn(OH)_4(s)} + 4NaCl(aq)$

76. $Fe^{2+}(aq) + S^{2-}(aq) \rightarrow FeS(s)$; $2Cr^{3+}(aq) + 3S^{2-}(aq) \rightarrow Cr_2S_3(s)$; $Ni^{2+}(aq) + S^{2-}(aq) \rightarrow NiS(s)$
78. These anions tend to form insoluble precipitates with many metal ions. The following are illustrative for cobalt(II) chloride, tin(II) chloride, and copper(II) nitrate reacting with sodium salts of the given anions. (a) $CoCl_2(aq) + Na_2S(aq) \rightarrow CoS(s) + 2NaCl(aq)$; $SnCl_2(aq) + Na_2S(aq) \rightarrow SnS(s) + 2NaCl(aq)$; $Cu(NO_3)_2(aq) + Na_2S(aq) \rightarrow CuS(s) + 2NaNO_3(aq)$; (b) $CoCl_2(aq) + Na_2CO_3(aq) \rightarrow CoCO_3(s) + 2NaCl(aq)$; $SnCl_2(aq) + Na_2CO_3(aq) \rightarrow SnCO_3(s) + 2NaCl(aq)$; $Cu(NO_3)_2(aq) + Na_2CO_3(aq) \rightarrow CuCO_3(s) + 2NaNO_3(aq)$; (c) $CoCl_2(aq) + 2NaOH(aq) \rightarrow Co(OH)_2(s) + 2NaCl(aq)$; $SnCl_2(aq) + 2NaOH(aq) \rightarrow Sn(OH)_2(s) + 2NaCl(aq)$; $Cu(NO_3)_2(aq) + 2NaOH(aq) \rightarrow Cu(OH)_2(s) + 2NaNO_3(aq)$; (d) $3CoCl_2(aq) + 2Na_3PO_4(aq) \rightarrow Co_3(PO_4)_2(s) + 6NaCl(aq)$; $3SnCl_2(aq) + 2Na_3PO_4(aq) \rightarrow Sn_3(PO_4)_2(s) + 6NaCl(aq)$; $3Cu(NO_3)_2(aq) + 2Na_3PO_4(aq) \rightarrow Cu_3(PO_4)_2(s) + 6NaNO_3(aq)$
80. (a) $2Na(s) + O_2(g) \rightarrow Na_2O_2(s)$; (b) $Fe(s) + H_2SO_4(aq) \rightarrow FeSO_4(aq) + H_2(g)$; (c) $2Al_2O_3(s) \rightarrow 4Al(s) + 3O_2(g)$; (d) $2Fe(s) + 3Br_2(l) \rightarrow 2FeBr_3(s)$; (e) $Zn(s) + 2HNO_3(aq) \rightarrow Zn(NO_3)_2(aq) + H_2(g)$
82. (a) $2C_4H_{10}(l) + 13O_2(g) \rightarrow 8CO_2(g) + 10H_2O(g)$; (b) $C_4H_{10}O(l) + 6O_2(g) \rightarrow 4CO_2(g) + 5H_2O(g)$; (c) $2C_4H_{10}O_2(l) + 11O_2(g) \rightarrow 8CO_2(g) + 10H_2O(g)$
84. (a) $2NaHCO_3(s) \rightarrow Na_2CO_3(s) + H_2O(g) + CO_2(g)$; (b) $2NaClO_3(s) \rightarrow 2NaCl(s) + 3O_2(g)$; (c) $2HgO(s) \rightarrow 2Hg(l) + O_2(g)$; (d) $C_{12}H_{22}O_{11}(s) \rightarrow 12C(s) + 11H_2O(g)$; (e) $2H_2O_2(l) \rightarrow 2H_2O(l) + O_2(g)$
86. $Fe(s) + H_2SO_4(aq) \rightarrow FeSO_4(aq) + H_2(g)$; $Zn(s) + H_2SO_4(aq) \rightarrow ZnSO_4(aq) + H_2(g)$; $Mg(s) + H_2SO_4(aq) \rightarrow MgSO_4(aq) + H_2(g)$; $Co(s) + H_2SO_4(aq) \rightarrow CoSO_4(aq) + H_2(g)$; $Ni(s) + H_2SO_4(aq) \rightarrow NiSO_4(aq) + H_2(g)$
88. (a) one; (b) one; (c) two; (d) two; (e) three
90. The reaction $C(s) + O_2(g) \rightarrow CO_2(g)$ is such an example.
92. (a) $2C_3H_8O(l) + 9O_2(g) \rightarrow 6CO_2(g) + 8H_2O(g)$; oxidation–reduction, combustion; (b) $HCl(aq) + AgC_2H_3O_2(aq) \rightarrow AgCl(s) + HC_2H_3O_2(aq)$, precipitation, double-displacement; (c) $3HCl(aq) + Al(OH)_3(s) \rightarrow AlCl_3(aq) + 3H_2O(l)$, acid–base, double-displacement; (d) $2H_2O_2(aq) \rightarrow 2H_2O(l) + O_2(g)$, oxidation–reduction, decomposition; (e) $N_2H_4(l) + O_2(g) \rightarrow N_2(g) + 2H_2O(g)$, oxidation–reduction, combustion
94. $2Na(s) + Cl_2(g) \rightarrow 2NaCl(s)$; $2Al(s) + 3Cl_2(g) \rightarrow 2AlCl_3(s)$; $Zn(s) + Cl_2(g) \rightarrow ZnCl_2(s)$; $Ca(s) + Cl_2(g) \rightarrow CaCl_2(s)$; $2Fe(s) + 3Cl_2(g) \rightarrow 2FeCl_3(s)$

Chapter 8

2. The empirical formula is the lowest whole-number ratio of atoms in the compound. The graphic of PVDF shows four of each type of atom (carbon, hydrogen, and fluorine). So, the empirical formula is CHF.
4. The average atomic mass takes into account the various isotopes of an element and the relative abundances in which those isotopes are found.
6. (a) one; (b) five; (c) ten; (d) 50; (e) ten
8. A sample containing 35 tin atoms would weigh 4155 amu; 2967.5 amu of tin would represent 25 tin atoms.
10. 26.98 12. 3.011×10^{23} atoms Ne; 2.002 g He 14. 177 g
16. 1.99×10^{-23} g 18. 0.50 mol Ne atoms
20. (a) 3.500 moles of F atoms; (b) 2.000 mmol Hg; (c) 3.000 mol Si; (d) 0.2500 mol Pt; (e) 100.0 mol Mg; (f) 0.5000 mol Mo
22. (a) 0.221 g; (b) 0.0676 g; (c) 3.64×10^3 g; (d) 1.84×10^{-5} g; (e) 86.4 g; (f) 7.47×10^{-3} g
24. (a) 1.16×10^{-20} g; (b) 6.98×10^3 amu; (c) 2.24 mol; (d) 6.98×10^3 g; (e) 1.35×10^{24} atoms; (f) 7.53×10^{25} atoms
26. The molar mass is calculated by summing the individual atomic masses of the atoms in the formula.
28. (a) potassium hydrogen carbonate; 100.12 g; (b) mercury(I) chloride, mercurous chloride; 472.1 g; (c) hydrogen peroxide; 34.02 g; (d) beryllium chloride; 79.91 g; (e) aluminum sulfate; 342.2 g; (f) potassium chlorate; 122.55 g
30. (a) $LiClO_4$; 106.39 g; (b) $NaHSO_4$; 120.07 g; (c) $MgCO_3$; 84.32 g; (d) $AlBr_3$; 266.7 g; (e) Cr_2S_3; 200.2 g
32. (a) 0.463 mol; (b) 11.3 mol; (c) 7.18×10^{-3} mol; (d) 2.36×10^{-7} mol; (e) 0.362 mol; (f) 0.0129 mol
34. (a) 2.64×10^{-5} mol; (b) 38.1 mol; (c) 7.76×10^{-6} mol; (d) 3.49×10^{-2} mol; (e) 2.09×10^{-3} mol; (f) 2.69×10^{-2} mol
36. (a) 41.2 g; (b) 0.194 g; (c) 3.63×10^4 g; (d) 0.773 g; (e) 6.68×10^5 g; (f) 0.270 g
38. (a) 77.6 g; (b) 177 g; (c) 6.09×10^{-3} g; (d) 0.220 g; (e) 1.26×10^3 g; (f) 3.78×10^{-2} g
40. (a) 3.84×10^{24} molecules; (b) 1.37×10^{23} molecules; (c) 8.76×10^{16} molecules; (d) 1.58×10^{18} molecules; (e) 4.03×10^{22} molecules
42. (a) 0.0141 mol S; (b) 0.0159 mol S; (c) 0.0258 mol S; (d) 0.0127 mol S
44. less
46. (a) 80.34% Zn; 19.66% O; (b) 58.91% Na; 41.09% S; (c) 41.68% Mg; 54.86% O; 3.456% H; (d) 5.926% H; 94.06% O; (e) 95.20% Ca; 4.789% H; (f) 83.01% K; 16.99% O
48. (a) 81.10% Ba; (b) 89.56% Ba; (c) 26.94% Co; (d) 19.73% Co; (e) 62.61% Sn; (f) 45.57% Sn; (g) 87.32% Li; (h) 89.93% Al
50. (a) 78.16% I; (b) 63.65% N; (c) 46.68% N; (d) 73.89% Hg; (e) 84.98% Hg ; (f) 21.96% S; (g) 77.55% Xe; (h) 63.19% Mn
52. (a) 47.06% S^{2-}; (b) 63.89% Cl^-; (c) 10.44% O^{2-}; (d) 62.08% SO_4^{2-}
54. The empirical formula indicates the smallest whole-number ratio of the number and type of atoms present in a molecule. For example, NO_2 and N_2O_4 both have two oxygen atoms for every nitrogen atom and therefore have the same empirical formula.
56. a, c 58. NCl_3 60. BH_3 62. $SnCl_4$ 64. Co_2S_3
66. AlF_3 68. Li_2O 70. Li_3N
72. Co_2O_3 74. PCl_3, PCl_5
76. molar mass 78. C_6H_6 80. $C_4H_{10}O_2$
82. Both are 30.45% N, 69.55% O
84. 5.00 g Al, 0.185 mol, 1.12×10^{23} atoms; 0.140 g Fe, 0.00250 mole, 1.51×10^{21} atoms; 2.7×10^2 g Cu, 4.3 mol, 2.6×10^{24} atoms; 0.00250 g Mg, 1.03×10^{-4} mol, 6.19×10^{19} atoms; 0.062 g Na, 2.7×10^{-3} mol, 1.6×10^{21} atoms; 3.95×10^{-18} g U, 1.66×10^{-20} mol, 1.00×10^4 atoms
86. 24.8% X, 17.4% Y, 57.8% Z. If the molecular formula were actually $X_4Y_2Z_6$, the percent composition would be the same: the *relative* mass of each element present would not change. The molecular formula is always a whole-number multiple of the empirical formula.
88. Cu_2O, CuO
90. (a) 2.82×10^{23} H atoms, 1.41×10^{23} O atoms; (b) 9.32×10^{22} C atoms, 1.86×10^{23} O atoms; (c) 1.02×10^{19} C atoms and H atoms; (d) 1.63×10^{25} C atoms, 2.99×10^{25} H atoms, 1.50×10^{25} O atoms
92. (a) 4.141 g C, 52.96% C, 2.076×10^{23} C atoms; (b) 0.0305 g C, 42.88% C, 1.53×10^{21} C atoms; (c) 14.4 g C, 76.6% C, 7.23×10^{23} C atoms

94. 2.12 g Fe **96.** 7.86 g Hg **98.** 2.554×10^{-22} g

100. (a) 0.9331 g N; (b) 1.388 g N; (c) 0.8537 g N; (d) 1.522 g N

102. MgN_2O_6 [$Mg(NO_3)_2$]

104. The average mass takes into account not only the exact masses of the isotopes of an element, but also the relative abundance of the isotopes in nature.

106. 8.61×10^{11} sodium atoms; 6.92×10^{24} amu

108. (a) 2.0×10^2 g K; (b) 0.0612 g Hg; (c) 1.27×10^{-3} g Mn; (d) 325 g P; (e) 2.7×10^6 g Fe; (f) 868 g Li; (g) 0.2290 g F

110. (a) 151.9 g; (b) 454.4 g; (c) 150.7 g; (d) 129.8 g; (e) 187.6 g

112. (a) 0.311 mol; (b) 0.270 mol; (c) 0.0501 mol; (d) 2.8 mol; (e) 6.2 mol

114. (a) 4.2 g; (b) 3.05×10^5 g; (c) 0.533 g; (d) 1.99×10^3 g; (e) 4.18×10^3 g

116. (a) 1.15×10^{22} molecules; (b) 2.08×10^{24} molecules; (c) 4.95×10^{22} molecules; (d) 2.18×10^{22} molecules; (e) 6.32×10^{20} formula units (substance is ionic)

118. (a) 38.76% Ca, 19.97% P, 41.27% O; (b) 53.91% Cd, 15.38% S, 30.70% O; (c) 27.93% Fe, 24.06% S, 48.01% O; (d) 43.66% Mn, 56.34% Cl; (e) 29.16% N, 8.392% H, 12.50% C, 49.95% O; (f) 27.37% Na, 1.200% H, 14.30% C, 57.14% O; (g) 27.29% C, 72.71% O; (h) 63.51% Ag, 8.246% N, 28.25% O

120. (a) 36.76% Fe; (b) 93.10% Ag; (c) 55.28% Sr; (d) 55.80% C; (e) 37.48% C; (f) 52.92% Al; (g) 36.70% K; (h) 52.45% K

122. $C_3H_7NO_2$ **124.** HgO **126.** $BaCl_2$

Chapter 9

2. The coefficients of the balanced chemical equation indicate the *relative numbers of molecules* (or moles) of each reactant that combine, as well as the number of molecules (or moles) of each product formed.

4. Balanced chemical equations tell us in what molar ratios substances combine to form products, not in what mass proportions they combine.

6. (a) $(NH_4)_2CO_3(s) \rightarrow 2NH_3(g) + CO_2(g) + H_2O(g)$.
One formula unit of solid ammonium carbonate decomposes to produce two molecules of ammonia gas, one molecule of carbon dioxide gas, and one molecule of water vapor. One mole of solid ammonium carbonate decomposes into two moles of gaseous ammonia, one mole of carbon dioxide gas, and one mole of water vapor.
(b) $6Mg(s) + P_4(s) \rightarrow 2Mg_3P_2(s)$.
Six atoms of magnesium metal react with one molecule of solid phosphorus (P_4) to make two formula units of solid magnesium phosphide. Six moles of magnesium metal react with one mole of solid phosphorus (P_4) to produce two moles of solid magnesium phosphide.
(c) $4Si(s) + S_8(s) \rightarrow 2Si_2S_4(l)$.
Four atoms of solid silicon react with one molecule of solid sulfur (S_8) to form two molecules of liquid disilicon tetrasulfide. Four moles of solid silicon react with one mole of solid sulfur (S_8) to form two moles of liquid disilicon tetrasulfide.
(d) $C_2H_5OH(l) + 3O_2(g) \rightarrow 2CO_2(g) + 3H_2O(g)$.
One molecule of liquid ethanol burns with three molecules of oxygen gas to produce two molecules of carbon dioxide gas and three molecules of water vapor. One mole of liquid ethanol burns with three moles of oxygen gas to produce two moles of gaseous carbon dioxide and three moles of water vapor.

8. Balanced chemical equations tell us in what molar ratios substances combine to form products, not in what mass proportions they combine. How could 2 g of reactant produce a total of 3 g of products?

10. $\frac{3 \text{ mol } H_2SO_4}{1 \text{ mol } Fe_2O_3}$; $\frac{1 \text{ mol } Fe_2(SO_4)_3}{1 \text{ mol } Fe_2O_3}$; $\frac{3 \text{ mol } H_2O}{1 \text{ mol } Fe_2O_3}$

12. (a) 0.125 mol Bi_2O_3; (b) 0.250 mol Sn; 0.500 mol H_2O; (c) 0.250 mol SiO_2; 1.00 mol HCl; (d) 0.500 mol HNO_3

14. (a) 165 g CO_2; 81.1 g H_2O; (b) 27.0 g H_2O; 33.0 g CO_2; (c) 175 g $BaHPO_4$; 27.0 g H_2O; (d) 69.1 g C_2H_5OH; 66.0 g CO_2

16. (a) 0.469 mol O_2; (b) 0.938 mol Se; (c) 0.625 mol CH_3CHO; (d) 1.25 mol Fe

18. Stoichiometry is the process of using a chemical equation to calculate the relative masses of reactants and products involved in a reaction.

20. (a) 1.81×10^{-3} mol; (b) 0.692 mol; (c) 1.40×10^4 mol; (d) 9.37×10^{-6} mol; (e) 13.9 mol

22. (a) 98.3 g; (b) 0.361 g; (c) 3.55×10^8 g; (d) 0.0140 g; (e) 0.0103 g

24. (a) 0.0310 mol; (b) 0.00555 mol; (c) 0.00475 mol; (d) 0.139 mol

26. (a) 1.38 g B, 14.0 g HCl; (b) 13.5 g Cu_2O, 6.04 g SO_2; (c) 35.9 g Cu, 6.04 g SO_2; (d) 29.0 g $CaSiO_3$, 11.0 g CO_2

28. 1.52 g C_2H_2 **30.** 0.959 g Na_2CO_3

32. 2.68 g ethyl alcohol **34.** 0.443 g NH_3

36. 8.62 kg Hg **38.** 0.501 g C

40. Gas mileage is about 19 miles per gallon.
Balanced equation:
$2C_8H_{18} + 25O_2 \rightarrow 16CO_2 + 18H_2O$

$$1 \text{ gallon of gasoline} \times \frac{3.7854 \text{ L}}{1 \text{ gallon}} \times \frac{1000 \text{ mL}}{1 \text{ L}} \times \frac{0.75 \text{ g } C_8H_{18}}{1 \text{ mL}} \times \frac{1 \text{ mol } C_8H_{18}}{114.224 \text{ g } C_8H_{18}} \times \frac{16 \text{ mol } CO_2}{2 \text{ mol } C_8H_{18}} \times \frac{44.01 \text{ g } CO_2}{1 \text{ mol } CO_2} \times \frac{1 \text{ lb } CO_2}{453.59 \text{ g } CO_2} \times \frac{1 \text{ mile}}{1 \text{ lb } CO_2} = 19.29 \text{ miles traveled}$$

42. To determine the limiting reactant, first calculate the number of moles of each reactant present. Then determine how these numbers of moles correspond to the stoichiometric ratio indicated by the balanced chemical equation for the reaction. For each reactant, use the stoichiometric ratios from the balanced chemical equation to calculate how much of the *other* reactants would be required to react completely.

44. A reactant is present in excess if there is more of that reactant present than is required to react with the limiting reactant. The limiting reactant, by definition, cannot be present in excess. No.

46. (a) H_2SO_4 is limiting, 4.90 g SO_2, 0.918 g H_2O; (b) H_2SO_4 is limiting, 6.30 g $Mn(SO_4)_2$, 0.918 g H_2O; (c) O_2 is limiting, 6.67 g SO_2, 1.88 g H_2O; (d) $AgNO_3$ is limiting, 3.18 g Ag, 2.09 g $Al(NO_3)_3$

48. (a) O_2 is limiting, 0.458 g CO_2; (b) CO_2 is limiting, 0.409 g H_2O; (c) MnO_2 is limiting, 0.207 g H_2O; (d) I_2 is limiting, 1.28 g ICl

50. (a) CO is limiting reactant; 11.4 mg CH_3OH; (b) I_2 is limiting reactant; 10.7 mg AlI_3; (c) HBr is limiting reactant; 12.4 mg $CaBr_2$; 2.23 mg H_2O; (d) H_3PO_4 is limiting reactant; 15.0 mg $CrPO_4$; 0.309 mg H_2

52. CuO **54.** 1.79 g Fe_2O_3

56. Sodium sulfate is the limiting reactant; calcium chloride is present in excess.

58. 0.67 kg SiC

60. If the reaction occurs in a solvent, the product may have a substantial solubility in the solvent; the reaction may come to equilibrium before the full yield of product is achieved (see Chapter 17); loss of product may occur through operator error.

62. 1.86 g in theory; 81.3% yield

64. $2LiOH(s) + CO_2(g) \rightarrow Li_2CO_3(s) + H_2O(g)$. 142 g of CO_2 can be ultimately absorbed; 102 g is 71.8% of the canister's capacity.
66. theoretical, 2.72 g $BaSO_4$; percent, 74.3%
68. 28.6 g $NaHCO_3$
70. $C_6H_{12}O_6 + 6O_2 \rightarrow 6CO_2 + 6H_2O$; 1.47 g CO_2
72. at least 325 mg
74. (a) $UO_2(s) + 4HF(aq) \rightarrow UF_4(aq) + 2H_2O(l)$. One formula unit of uranium(IV) oxide combines with four molecules of hydrofluoric acid, producing one uranium(IV) fluoride molecule and two water molecules. One mole of uranium(IV) oxide combines with four moles of hydrofluoric acid to produce one mole of uranium(IV) fluoride and two moles of water; (b) $2NaC_2H_3O_2(aq) + H_2SO_4(aq) \rightarrow Na_2SO_4(aq) + 2HC_2H_3O_2(aq)$. Two molecules (formula units) of sodium acetate react exactly with one molecule of sulfuric acid, producing one molecule (formula unit) of sodium acetate and two molecules of acetic acid. Two moles of sodium acetate combine with one mole of sulfuric acid, producing one mole of sodium sulfate and two moles of acetic acid; (c) $Mg(s) + 2HCl(aq) \rightarrow MgCl_2(aq) + H_2(g)$. One magnesium atom reacts with two hydrochloric acid molecules (formula units) to produce one molecule (formula unit) of magnesium chloride and one molecule of hydrogen gas. One mole of magnesium combines with two moles of hydrochloric acid, producing one mole of magnesium chloride and one mole of gaseous hydrogen; (d) $B_2O_3(s) + 3H_2O(l) \rightarrow 2B(OH)_3(s)$. One molecule (formula unit) of diboron trioxide reacts exactly with three molecules of water, producing two molecules of boron trihydroxide (boric acid). One mole of diboron trioxide combines with three moles of water to produce two moles of boron trihydroxide (boric acid).
76. for O_2, 5 mol O_2/1 mol C_3H_8; for CO_2, 3 mol CO_2/1 mol C_3H_8; for H_2O, 4 mol H_2O/1 mol C_3H_8
78. (a) 0.0588 mol NH_4Cl; (b) 0.0178 mol $CaCO_3$; (c) 0.0217 mol Na_2O; (d) 0.0323 mol PCl_3
80. (a) 3.2×10^2 g HNO_3; (b) 0.0612 g Hg; (c) 4.49×10^{-3} g K_2CrO_4; (d) 1.40×10^3 g $AlCl_3$; (e) 7.2×10^6 g SF_6; (f) 2.13×10^3 g NH_3; (g) 0.9397 g Na_2O_2
82. 1.9×10^2 kg SO_3 84. 0.667 g O_2 86. 0.0771 g H_2
88. (a) Br_2 is limiting reactant, 6.4 g NaBr; (b) $CuSO_4$ is limiting reactant, 5.1 g $ZnSO_4$, 2.0 g Cu; (c) NH_4Cl is limiting reactant, 1.6 g NH_3, 1.7 g H_2O, 5.5 g NaCl; (d) Fe_2O_3 is limiting reactant, 3.5 g Fe, 4.1 g CO_2
90. 0.624 mol N_2, 17.5 g N_2; 1.25 mol H_2O, 22.5 g H_2O
92. 5.0 g

Chapter 10

2. Potential energy is energy due to position or composition. A stone at the top of a hill possesses potential energy because the stone may eventually roll down the hill. A gallon of gasoline possesses potential energy because heat will be released when the gasoline is burned.
4. The total energy of the universe is constant. Energy cannot be created or destroyed, but can only be converted from one form to another.
6. Ball A initially possesses potential energy by virtue of its position at the top of the hill. As ball A rolls down the hill, its potential energy is converted to kinetic energy and frictional (heat) energy. When ball A reaches the bottom of the hill and hits ball B, it transfers its kinetic energy to ball B. Ball A then has only the potential energy corresponding to its new position.
8. The hot tea is at a higher temperature, which means the particles in the hot tea have higher average kinetic energies. When the tea spills on the skin, energy flows from the hot tea to the skin, until the tea and skin are at the same temperature. This sudden inflow of energy causes the burn.
10. Temperature is the concept by which we express the thermal energy contained in a sample. We cannot measure the motions of the particles/kinetic energy in a sample of matter directly. We know, however, that if two objects are at different temperatures, the one with the higher temperature has molecules that have higher average kinetic energies than the molecules of the object at the lower temperature.
12. When the chemical system evolves energy, the energy evolved from the reacting chemicals is transferred to the surroundings.
14. exactly equal to 16. internal 18. losing
20. gaining
22. (a) $\frac{1\text{ J}}{4.184\text{ cal}}$; (b) $\frac{4.184\text{ cal}}{1\text{ J}}$; (c) $\frac{1\text{ kcal}}{1000\text{ cal}}$; (d) $\frac{1000\text{ J}}{1\text{ kJ}}$
24. 6540 J = 6.54 kJ
26. (a) 8.254 kcal; (b) 0.0415 kcal; (c) 8.231 kcal; (d) 752.9 kcal
28. (a) 243 kJ to three significant figures; (b) 0.004184 kJ; (c) 0.000251 kJ; (d) 0.4503 kJ
30. (a) 9.174×10^4 cal; (b) 425.7 cal; (c) 1.032 kcal; (d) 383.8 kJ
32. 5.8×10^2 J (two significant figures) 34. 29 °C
36. exothermic
38. 14.6 kJ (~15 kJ to one significant figure)
40. A calorimeter is an insulated device in which reactions are performed and temperature changes measured, enabling the calculation of heat flows. See Figure 10.6.
42. (a) −9.23 kJ; (b) −148 kJ; (c) +296 kJ/mol
44. (a) −29.5 kJ; (b) $\Delta H = -1360$ kJ; (c) 453 kJ/mol H_20
46. −220 kJ 48. −233 kJ
50. Once everything in the universe is at the same temperature, no further thermodynamic work can be done. Even though the total energy of the universe will be the same, the energy will have been dispersed evenly, making it effectively useless.
52. Concentrated sources of energy, such as petroleum, are being used so as to disperse the energy they contain, making that energy unavailable for further human use.
54. Petroleum consists mainly of hydrocarbons, which are molecules containing chains of carbon atoms with hydrogen atoms attached to the chains. The fractions are based on the number of carbon atoms in the chains: for example, gasoline is a mixture of hydrocarbons with 5–10 carbon atoms in the chains, whereas asphalt is a mixture of hydrocarbons with 25 or more carbon atoms in the chains. Different fractions have different physical properties and uses, but all can be combusted to produce energy. See Table 10.3.
56. Tetraethyl lead was used as an additive for gasoline to promote smoother running of engines. It is no longer widely used because of concerns about the lead being released into the environment as the leaded gasoline burns.
58. The greenhouse effect is a warming effect due to the presence of gases in the atmosphere that absorb infrared radiation that has reached the earth from the sun; the gases do not allow the energy to pass back into space. A limited greenhouse effect is desirable because it moderates the temperature changes in the atmosphere that would otherwise be more drastic between daytime when the sun is shining and nighttime. Having too high a concentration of greenhouse gases, however, will elevate the temperature of the earth too much, affecting climate, crops, the polar ice caps, the temperatures of the oceans, and so on. Carbon dioxide produced by combustion reactions is our greatest concern as a greenhouse gas.
60. If a proposed reaction involves either or both of those phenomena, the reaction will tend to be favorable.

62. Formation of a solid precipitate represents a concentration of matter.

64. The molecules in liquid water are moving around freely and are therefore more "disordered" than when the molecules are held rigidly in a solid lattice in ice. The entropy increases during melting.

66. (a) 110.5 kcal; (b) 4.369 kcal; (c) 0.2424 kcal; (d) 45.53 kcal

68. 7.65 kcal **70.** 2.0×10^2 J (two significant figures)

72. 3.8×10^5 J **74.** 62.5 °C = 63 °C **76.** 9.0 J

78.

Substance	Specific Heat Capacity	Temperature Change
water (*l*)	4.184 J/g °C	23.9 °C
water (*s*)	2.03 J/g °C	49.3 °C
water (*g*)	2.0 J/g °C	50. °C
aluminum	0.89 J/g °C	1.1×10^2 °C
iron	0.45 J/g °C	2.2×10^2 °C
mercury	0.14 J/g °C	7.1×10^2 °C
carbon	0.71 J/g °C	1.4×10^2 °C
silver	0.24 J/g °C	4.2×10^2 °C
gold	0.13 J/g °C	7.7×10^2 °C

80. (a) exothermic; (b) exothermic; (c) endothermic; (d) endothermic

82. $\frac{1}{2}\text{C} + \text{F} \rightarrow \text{A} + \text{B} + \text{D} \quad \Delta H = 47.0 \text{ kJ}$

84. Approximately 9 hr

Chapter 11

2. Rutherford's experiments determined that the atom had a nucleus containing positively charged particles called protons. He established that the nucleus was very small compared to the overall size of the atom. He was not able to determine where the electrons were in the atom or what they were doing.

4. The different forms of electromagnetic radiation all exhibit the same wavelike behavior and are propagated through space at the same speed (the "speed of light"). The types of electromagnetic radiation differ in their frequency (and wavelength) and in the resulting amount of energy carried per photon.

6. The frequency of electromagnetic radiation represents how many waves pass a given location per second. The speed of electromagnetic radiation represents how fast the waves propagate through space. The frequency and the speed are not the same.

8. The greenhouse gases do not absorb light in the visible wavelengths. Therefore, this light passes through the atmosphere and warms the earth, keeping the earth much warmer than it would be without these gases. As we are increasing our use of fossil fuels, the level of CO_2 in the atmosphere is increasing gradually but significantly. An increase in the level of CO_2 will warm the earth further, eventually changing the weather patterns on the earth's surface and melting the polar ice caps.

10. exactly equal to **12.** It is emitted as a photon.

14. absorbs

16. When excited hydrogen atoms emit their excess energy, the photons of radiation emitted always have exactly the same wavelength and energy. This means that the hydrogen atom possesses only certain allowed energy states, and that the photons emitted correspond to the electron changing from one of these allowed energy states to another allowed energy state. The energy of the photon emitted corresponds to the energy difference between the allowed states. If the hydrogen atom did *not* possess discrete energy levels, then the photons emitted would have random wavelengths and energies.

18. They are identical.

20. Energy is emitted at wavelengths corresponding to specific transitions for the electron among the energy levels of hydrogen.

22. The electron moves to an orbit farther from the nucleus of the atom.

24. Bohr's theory explained the experimentally observed line spectrum of hydrogen exactly. The theory was discarded because the calculated properties did not correspond closely to experimental measurements for atoms other than hydrogen.

26. An orbit refers to a definite, exact circular pathway around the nucleus, in which Bohr postulated that an electron would be found. An orbital represents a region of space in which there is a high probability of finding the electron.

28. The firefly analogy is intended to demonstrate the concept of a probability map for electron density. In the wave mechanical model of the atom, we cannot say specifically where the electron is in the atom; we can say only where there is a high probability of finding the electron. The analogy is to imagine a time-exposure photograph of a firefly in a closed room. Most of the time, the firefly will be found near the center of the room.

30. The drawing is a contour map, indicating a 90% probability that the electron is within the region of space bounded by that region. The electron may be anywhere within this region.

32. two-lobed ("dumbbell"-shaped); lower in energy and closer to the nucleus; similar shape

34. 1

36.

Value of *n*	Possible Subshells
1	1*s*
2	2*s*, 2*p*
3	3*s*, 3*p*, 3*d*
4	4*s*, 4*p*, 4*d*, 4*f*

38. Electrons have an intrinsic spin (they spin on their own axes). Geometrically, there are only two senses possible for spin (clockwise or counterclockwise). This means only two electrons can occupy an orbital, with the opposite sense or direction of spin. This idea is called the Pauli exclusion principle.

40. increases

42. paired (opposite spin)

44. (a) not possible; (b) possible; (c) possible; (d) not possible

46. For a hydrogen atom in its ground state, the electron is in the 1*s* orbital. The 1*s* orbital has the lowest energy of all hydrogen orbitals.

48. similar type of orbitals being filled in the same way; chemical properties of the members of the group are similar

50. (a) silicon; (b) beryllium; (c) neon; (d) argon

52. (a) selenium; (b) scandium; (c) sulfur; (d) iodine

54. (a) [↑↓] [↑↓] [↑↓|↑↓|↑↓] [↑↓]
1*s* 2*s* 2*p* 3*s*

(b) [↑↓] [↑↓] [↑↓|↑↓|↑↓] [↑↓] [↑↓|↑↓|↑↓]
1*s* 2*s* 2*p* 3*s* 3*p*

(c) [↑↓] [↑]
1*s* 2*s*

(d) [↑↓] [↑↓] [↑↓|↑↓|↑↓] [↑↓] [↑↓|↑↓|↑↓] [↑↓]
1*s* 2*s* 2*p* 3*s* 3*p* 4*s*
[↑↓|↑↓|↑↓|↑↓|↑↓] [↑|↑|↑]
3*d* 4*p*

56. Specific answers depend on student choice of elements. Any Group 1 element would have one valence electron. Any Group 3 element would have three valence electrons. Any Group 5 element would have five valence electrons. Any Group 7 element would have seven valence electrons.

58. The properties of Rb and Sr suggest that they are members of Groups 1 and 2, respectively, and so must be filling the 5*s* orbital. The 5*s* orbital is lower in energy than (and fills before) the 4*d* orbitals.
60. (a) aluminum; (b) potassium; (c) bromine; (d) tin
62. (a) [Ne]$3s^23p^3$; (b) [Ne]$3s^23p^5$; (c) [Ne]$3s^2$; (d) [Ar]$4s^23d^{10}$
64. (a) 1; (b) 2; (c) 0; (d) 10
66. (a) 5*f*; (b) 5*f*; (c) 4*f*; (d) 6*p* 68. [Rn]$7s^25f^{14}6d^5$
70. The metallic elements lose electrons and form positive ions (cations); the nonmetallic elements gain electrons and form negative ions (anions).
72. All exist as diatomic molecules (F_2, Cl_2, Br_2, I_2); are nonmetals; have relatively high electronegativities; and form 1− ions in reacting with metallic elements.
74. Elements at the left of a period (horizontal row) lose electrons most readily; at the left of a period (given principal energy level) the nuclear charge is the smallest and the electrons are least tightly held.
76. The elements of a given period (horizontal row) have valence electrons in the same subshells, but nuclear charge increases across a period going from left to right. Atoms at the left side have smaller nuclear charges and bind their valence electrons less tightly.
78. When substances absorb energy, the electrons become excited (move to higher energy levels). Upon returning to the ground state, energy is released, some of which is in the visible spectrum. Because we see colors, this tells us only certain wavelengths of light are released, which means that only certain transitions are allowed. This is what is meant by quantized energy levels. If all wavelengths of light were emitted, we would see white light.
80. (a) Li; (b) Ca; (c) Cl; (d) S
82. (a) Na; (b) S; (c) N; (d) F
84. speed of light 86. photons 88. quantized
90. orbital 92. transition metal 94. spins
96. (a) $1s^22s^22p^63s^23p^64s^1$; [Ar]$4s^1$;

[↑↓] [↑↓] [↑↓|↑↓|↑↓] [↑↓] [↑↓|↑↓|↑↓] [↑]
1*s* 2*s* 2*p* 3*s* 3*p* 4*s*

(b) $1s^22s^22p^63s^23p^64s^23d^2$; [Ar]$4s^23d^2$;

[↑↓] [↑↓] [↑↓|↑↓|↑↓] [↑↓] [↑↓|↑↓|↑↓] [↑↓]
1*s* 2*s* 2*p* 3*s* 3*p* 4*s*

[↑|↑| | |]
3*d*

(c) $1s^22s^22p^63s^23p^2$; [Ne]$3s^23p^2$;

[↑↓] [↑↓] [↑↓|↑↓|↑↓] [↑↓] [↑|↑|]
1*s* 2*s* 2*p* 3*s* 3*p*

(d) $1s^22s^22p^63s^23p^64s^23d^6$; [Ar]$4s^23d^6$;

[↑↓] [↑↓] [↑↓|↑↓|↑↓] [↑↓] [↑↓|↑↓|↑↓] [↑↓]
1*s* 2*s* 2*p* 3*s* 3*p* 4*s*

[↑↓|↑|↑|↑|↑]
3*d*

(e) $1s^22s^22p^63s^23p^64s^23d^{10}$; [Ar]$4s^23d^{10}$;

[↑↓] [↑↓] [↑↓|↑↓|↑↓] [↑↓] [↑↓|↑↓|↑↓] [↑↓]
1*s* 2*s* 2*p* 3*s* 3*p* 4*s*

[↑↓|↑↓|↑↓|↑↓|↑↓]
3*d*

98. (a) ns^2; (b) ns^2np^5; (c) ns^2np^4; (d) ns^1; (e) ns^2np^4
100. (a) 2.7×10^{-12} m; (b) 4.4×10^{-34} m; (c) 2×10^{-35} m; the wavelengths for the ball and the person are infinitesimally small, whereas the wavelength for the electron is nearly the same order of magnitude as the diameter of a typical atom.
102. Light is emitted from the hydrogen atom only at certain fixed wavelengths. If the energy levels of hydrogen were continuous, a hydrogen atom would emit energy at all possible wavelengths.
104. The third principal energy level of hydrogen is divided into three sublevels (3*s*, 3*p*, and 3*d*); there is a single 3*s* orbital, a set of three 3*p* orbitals, and a set of five 3*d* orbitals. See Figures 11.25 – 11.28 for the shapes of these orbitals.
106. Answer depends on student choice of examples.
108. (a) $1s^22s^22p^63s^23p^64s^23d^{10}4p^5$
(b) $1s^22s^22p^63s^23p^64s^23d^{10}4p^65s^24d^{10}5p^6$
(c) $1s^22s^22p^63s^23p^64s^23d^{10}4p^65s^24d^{10}5p^66s^2$
(d) $1s^22s^22p^63s^23p^64s^23d^{10}4p^4$
110. (a) five (2*s*, 2*p*); (b) seven (3*s*, 3*p*); (c) one (3*s*); (d) three (3*s*, 3*p*)
112. (a) [Kr]$5s^24d^2$; (b) [Kr]$5s^24d^{10}5p^5$; (c) [Ar]$4s^23d^{10}4p^2$; (d) [Xe]$6s^1$
114. (a) Se; (b) Se; (c) Rb; (d) V
116. metals, low; nonmetals, high
118. (a) Ca; (b) P; (c) K

Chapter 12

2. The *bond energy* represents the energy required to break a chemical bond.
4. A covalent bond represents the *sharing* of electrons by nuclei.
6. In H_2 and HF, the bonding is covalent in nature, with an electron pair being shared between the atoms. In H_2, the two atoms are identical and so the sharing is equal; in HF, the two atoms are different and so the bonding is polar covalent. Both of these are in marked contrast to the situation in NaF: NaF is an ionic compound, and an electron is completely transferred from sodium to fluorine, thereby producing the separate ions.
8. A bond is polar if the centers of positive and negative charge do not coincide at the same point. The bond has a negative end and a positive end. Any molecule in which the atoms in the bonds are not identical will have polar bonds (although the molecule as a whole may not be polar). Two simple examples are HCl and HF.
10. The difference in electronegativity between the atoms in the bond
12. (a) I is most electronegative, Rb is least electronegative; (b) Mg is most electronegative, Ca and Sr have similar electronegativities; (c) Br is most electronegative, K is least electronegative
14. (a) ionic; (b) polar covalent; (c) covalent
16. c and d
18. (a) O—Br; (b) N—F; (c) P—O; (d) H—O
20. (a) Ca–Cl; (b) Ba–Cl; (c) Fe–I; (d) Be–F
22. The presence of strong bond dipoles and a large overall dipole moment makes water a very polar substance. Properties of water that are dependent on its dipole moment involve its freezing point, melting point, vapor pressure, and ability to dissolve many substances.
24. (a) H; (b) Cl; (c) I
26. (a) $^{\delta+}S \rightarrow O^{\delta-}$; (b) $^{\delta+}S \rightarrow N^{\delta-}$; (c) $^{\delta+}S \rightarrow F^{\delta-}$; (d) $^{\delta+}S \rightarrow Cl^{\delta-}$
28. (a) $^{\delta+}H \rightarrow C^{\delta-}$; (b) $^{\delta+}N \rightarrow O^{\delta-}$; (c) $^{\delta+}S \rightarrow N^{\delta-}$; (d) $^{\delta+}C \rightarrow N^{\delta-}$;
30. preceding
32. Atoms in covalent molecules gain a configuration like that of a noble gas by sharing one or more pairs of electrons between atoms: such shared pairs of electrons "belong" to each of the bonding atoms at the same time. In ionic bonding, one atom completely donates one or more electrons to another atom, and then the resulting ions behave independently of one another (they are not "attached" to one another, although they are mutually attracted).
34. (a) Br^- [Kr]; (b) Cs^+ [Xe]; (c) P^{3-} [Ar]; (d) S^{2-} [Ar]

36. (a) F^-, O^{2-}, N^{3-}; (b) Cl^-, S^{2-}, P^{3-}; (c) F^-, O^{2-}, N^{3-}; (d) Br^-, Se^{2-}, As^{3-}

38. (a) $AlBr_3$; (b) Al_2O_3; (c) AlP; (d) AlH_3

40. Answers depend on student choice of examples.

42. An ionic solid such as NaCl consists of an array of alternating positively and negatively charged ions: that is, each positive ion has as its nearest neighbors a group of negative ions, and each negative ion has a group of positive ions surrounding it. In most ionic solids, the ions are packed as tightly as possible.

44. In forming an anion, an atom gains additional electrons in its outermost (valence) shell. Having additional electrons in the valence shell increases the repulsive forces between electrons, and the outermost shell becomes larger to accommodate this.

46. (a) F^- is larger than Li^+. The F^- ion has a filled $n = 2$ shell. A lithium atom has *lost* the electron from its $n = 2$ shell, leaving the $n = 1$ shell as its outermost. (b) Cl^- is larger than Na^+, since its valence electrons are in the $n = 3$ shell (Na^+ has lost its 3*s* electron). (c) Ca is larger than Ca^{2+}. Positive ions are always smaller than the atoms from which they are formed. (d) I^- is larger. Both Cs^+ and I^- have the same electron configuration (isoelectronic with Xe) and have their valence electrons in the same shell. However, Cs^+ has two more positive charges in its nucleus than does I^-; this charge causes the $n = 5$ shell of Cs^+ to be smaller than that of I^- (the electrons are pulled in closer to the nucleus by the positive charge).

48. (a) I; (b) F^-; (c) F^-

50. When atoms form covalent bonds, they try to attain a valence-electron configuration similar to that of the following noble gas element. When the elements in the first few horizontal rows of the periodic table form covalent bonds, they attempt to achieve the configurations of the noble gases helium (two valence electrons, duet rule) and neon and argon (eight valence electrons, octet rule).

52. These elements attain a total of eight valence electrons, giving the valence-electron configurations of the noble gases Ne and Ar.

54. Two atoms in a molecule are connected by a triple bond if the atoms share three pairs of electrons (six electrons) to complete their outermost shells. A simple molecule containing a triple bond is acetylene, C_2H_2 (H:C:::C:H).

56. (a) Mg: ; (b) :B̈r· ; (c) :S̈· ; (d) ·S̈i

58. (a) 24; (b) 16; (c) 20; (d) 17

60. (a) H—H (b) H—C̈l:

(c) CF_4: central C bonded to four :F̈: atoms (:F̈—C—F̈: with :F̈: above and below)

(d) C_2F_6: :F̈—C—C—F̈: with :F̈: above and below each C

62. (a) :C̈l—P̈—C̈l: with :C̈l: below P (b) $CHCl_3$: H above C, :C̈l—C—C̈l:, :C̈l: below C

(c) :C̈l—C—C—C̈l: with H above and below each C (d) H—N̈—N̈—H with H below each N

64. :O≡C—Ö: ⟷ Ö=C=Ö ⟷ :Ö—C≡O:

66. (a) ClO_3^- $\left(\text{:Ö—C̈l—Ö: with :Ö: below Cl}\right)^-$

(b) O_2^{2-} $(\text{:Ö—Ö:})^{2-}$

(c) $C_2H_3O_2^-$ (H—C—C—Ö: with H above and below the first C, :O: double-bonded above the second C)$^-$ ↔ (H—C—C=Ö with H above and below the first C, :Ö: single-bonded above the second C)$^-$

68. (a) $[CO_3]^{2-}$: three resonance structures, each with C bonded to three O atoms, one C=O double bond and two C—O single bonds, the double bond in a different position in each (↔ between structures), all in brackets with charge 2−

(b) $\left[\text{H—N—H with H above and below N}\right]^+$ (c) $\left[\text{:C̈l—Ö:}\right]^-$

70. The geometric structure of NH_3 is that of a trigonal pyramid. The nitrogen atom of NH_3 is surrounded by four electron pairs (three are bonding, one is a lone pair). The H—N—H bond angle is somewhat less than 109.5° (because of the presence of the lone pair).

72. SiF_4 has a tetrahedral geometric structure; eight pairs of electrons on Si; ~109.5°

74. The general molecular structure of a molecule is determined by how many electron pairs surround the central atom in the molecule, and by which of those pairs are used for bonding to the other atoms of the molecule.

76. Geometry shows that only two points in space are needed to indicate a straight line. A diatomic molecule represents two points in space.

78. In NF_3, the nitrogen atom has *four* pairs of valence electrons; in BF_3, only *three* pairs of valence electrons surround the boron atom. The nonbonding pair on nitrogen in NF_3 pushes the three F atoms out of the plane of the N atom.

80. (a) four pairs of electrons in a (distorted) tetrahedral arrangement; (b) four pairs of electrons in a (slightly distorted) tetrahedral arrangement; (c) four pairs of electrons in a tetrahedral arrangement

82. (a) trigonal pyramidal; (b) trigonal pyramidal; (c) nonlinear (bent, V-shaped)

84. (a) basically tetrahedral arrangement of the oxygens around the phosphorus; (b) tetrahedral; (c) trigonal pyramid

86. (a) approximately tetrahedral (a little less than 109.5°); (b) approximately tetrahedral (a little less than 109.5°); (c) tetrahedral (109.5°); (d) trigonal planar (120°) because of the double bond

88. 120° around the carbon atoms in the rings; 120° also for the C—N—N and N—N—C bond angles. The double bonds influence the bond angles greatly, with each atom having only three "effective pairs" of electrons around the atom.

90. double

92. (a) S—F; (b) P—O; (c) C—H

94. The bond energy is the energy required to break the bond.

96. (a) Be; (b) N; (c) F

98. a, c

100. (a) O; (b) Br; (c) I

102. (a) Al: $1s^22s^22p^63s^23p^1$; Al^{3+}: $1s^22s^22p^6$; Ne has the same configuration as Al^{3+}; (b) Br: $1s^22s^22p^63s^23p^64s^23d^{10}4p^5$; Br^-: $1s^22s^22p^63s^23p^64s^2\,3d^{10}4p^6$; Kr has the same configuration as Br^-; (c) Ca: $1s^22s^22p^63s^23p^64s^2$; Ca^{2+}: $1s^22s^22p^63s^23p^6$; Ar has the same configuration as Ca^{2+}; (d) Li: $1s^22s^1$; Li^+: $1s^2$; He has the same configuration as Li^+; (e) F: $1s^22s^22p^5$; F^-: $1s^22s^22p^6$; Ne has the same configuration as F^-.

104. (a) Na_2Se; (b) RbF; (c) K_2Te; (d) BaSe; (e) KAt; (f) FrCl

106. (a) Na^+; (b) Al^{3+}; (c) F^-; (d) Na^+

108. (a) 24; (b) 32; (c) 32; (d) 32

110. (a) N_2H_4
```
H—N̈—N̈—H
  |  |
  H  H
```
(b) C_2H_6
```
  H  H
  |  |
H—C—C—H
  |  |
  H  H
```
(c) NCl_3
```
:C̈l—N̈—C̈l:
     |
    :C̈l:
```
(d) $SiCl_4$
```
     :C̈l:
       |
:C̈l—Si—C̈l:
       |
     :C̈l:
```

112. (a) NO_3^-
```
[Ö=N—Ö:]⁻  ↔  [:Ö—N=Ö]⁻  ↔  [:Ö—N=Ö:]⁻
    |             |             ‖
   :Ö:           :Ö:           :Ö:
```
(b) CO_3^{2-}
```
[Ö=C—Ö:]²⁻  ↔  [:Ö—C=Ö]²⁻  ↔  [:Ö—C=Ö:]²⁻
    |              |              ‖
   :Ö:            :Ö:            :Ö:
```
(c) NH_4^+
```
[   H   ]⁺
    |
[ H—N—H ]
    |
[   H   ]
```

114. (a) four pairs arranged tetrahedrally; (b) four pairs arranged tetrahedrally; (c) three pairs arranged trigonally (planar)

116. (a) trigonal pyramid; (b) nonlinear (V-shaped); (c) tetrahedral

118. (a) nonlinear (V-shaped); (b) trigonal planar; (c) basically trigonal planar around C, distorted somewhat by H; (d) linear

120. Ionic compounds tend to be hard, crystalline substances with relatively high melting and boiling points. Covalently bonded substances tend to be gases, liquids, or relatively soft solids, with much lower melting and boiling points.

Chapter 13

2. Solids are rigid and incompressible and have definite shapes and volumes. Liquids are less rigid than solids; although they have definite volumes, liquids take the shape of their containers. Gases have no fixed volume or shape; they take the volume and shape of their container and are affected more by changes in their pressure and temperature than are solids or liquids.

4. A mercury barometer consists of a tube filled with mercury that is then inverted over a reservoir of mercury, the surface of which is open to the atmosphere. The pressure of the atmosphere is reflected in the height to which the column of mercury in the tube is supported.

6. Pressure units include mm Hg, torr, pascals, and psi. The unit "mm Hg" is derived from the barometer, because in a traditional mercury barometer, we measure the height of the mercury column (in millimeters) above the reservoir of mercury.

8. (a) 1.01 atm; (b) 1.05 atm; (c) 99.1 kPa; (d) 99.436 kPa

10. (a) 119 kPa; (b) 16.9 psi; (c) 3.23×10^3 mm Hg; (d) 15.2 atm

12. (a) 651 kPa; (b) 3.20×10^3 torr; (c) 1.04 atm; (d) 1.85 atm

14. Additional mercury increases the pressure on the gas sample, causing the volume of the gas upon which the pressure is exerted to decrease (Boyle's law).

16. $PV = k$; $P_1V_1 = P_2V_2$

18. (a) 423 mL; (b) 158 mL; (c) 8.67 L

20. (a) 689 mm Hg; (b) 1.20 atm; (c) 2.35 L

22. 0.520 L

24. 27.2 atm

26. Charles's law indicates that an ideal gas decreases by 1/273 of its volume for every Celsius degree its temperature is lowered. This means an ideal gas would approach a volume of zero at −273 °C.

28. $V = bT$; $V_1/T_1 = V_2/T_2$

30. 315 mL

32. (a) 80.2 mL; (b) −77 °C (196 K); (c) 208 mL (2.1×10^2 mL)

34. (a) 35.4 K = −238 °C; (b) 0 mL (absolute zero; a real gas would condense to a solid or liquid); (c) 40.5 mL

36. 69.4 mL (69 mL to two significant figures)

38. 90 °C, 124 mL; 80 °C, 121 mL; 70 °C, 117 mL; 60 °C, 113 mL; 50 °C, 110. mL; 40 °C, 107 mL; 30 °C, 103 mL; 20 °C, 99.8 mL

40. $V = an$; $V_1/n_1 = V_2/n_2$

42. 1744 mL (1.74×10^3 mL)

44. 80.1 L

46. Real gases behave most ideally at relatively high temperatures and relatively low pressures. We usually assume that a real gas's behavior approaches ideal behavior if the temperature is over 0 °C (273 K) and the pressure is 1 atm or lower.

48. For an ideal gas, $PV = nRT$ is true under any conditions. Consider a particular sample of gas (n remains constant) at a particular fixed pressure (P remains constant). Suppose that at temperature T_1 the volume of the gas sample is V_1. For this set of conditions, the ideal gas equation would be given by $PV_1 = nRT_1$. If the temperature of the gas sample changes to a new temperature, T_2, then the volume of the gas sample changes to a new volume, V_2. For this new set of conditions, the ideal gas equation would be given by $PV_2 = nRT_2$. If we make a *ratio* of these two expressions for the ideal gas equation for this gas sample, and cancel out terms that are constant for this situation (P, n, and R), we get

$$\frac{PV_1}{PV_2} = \frac{nRT_1}{nRT_2}, \text{ or } \frac{V_1}{V_2} = \frac{T_1}{T_2},$$

which can be rearranged to the familiar form of Charles's law,

$$\frac{V_1}{T_1} = \frac{V_2}{T_2}.$$

50. (a) 5.02 L; (b) 3.56 atm = 2.70×10^3 mm Hg; (c) 334 K
52. 0.747 atm
54. 304 K, 31 °C
56. 0.150 atm; 0.163 atm
58. 238 K/−35 °C
60. The helium (5.07 atm) is at a higher pressure than the argon (3.50 atm).
62. 0.332 atm; 0.346 atm
64. ~283 atm (2.8×10^2 atm)
66. As a gas is bubbled through water, the bubbles of gas become saturated with water vapor, thus forming a gaseous mixture. The total pressure for a sample of gas that has been collected by bubbling through water is made up of two components: the pressure of the sample gas and the pressure of water vapor. The partial pressure of the gas equals the total pressure of the sample minus the vapor pressure of water.
68. 0.314 atm
70. 3.00 g Ne; 5.94 g Ar
72. 3.07 atm
74. $P_{hydrogen}$ = 0.990 atm; 9.55×10^{-3} mol H_2; 0.625 g Zn
76. A theory is successful if it explains known experimental observations. Theories that have been successful in the past may not be successful in the future (for example, as technology evolves, more sophisticated experiments may be possible in the future).
78. pressure
80. no
82. If the temperature of a sample of gas is increased, the average kinetic energy of the particles of gas increases. This means that the speeds of the particles increase. If the particles have a higher speed, they hit the walls of the container more frequently and with greater force, thereby increasing the pressure.
84. STP = 0 °C, 1 atm pressure. These conditions were chosen because they are easy to attain and reproduce *experimentally*. The barometric pressure within a laboratory will usually be near 1 atm, and 0 °C can be attained with a simple ice bath.
86. 2.50 L O_2
88. 0.941 L
90. 0.941 L; 0.870 L
92. 5.03 L (dry volume)
94. 52.7 L
96. 28.1 L He; 23.6 L Ar
98. 40.5 L; P_{He} = 0.864 atm; P_{Ne} = 0.136 atm
100. 1.72 L
102. 0.365 g
104. twice
106. (a) $PV = k$; $P_1V_1 = P_2V_2$; (b) $V = bT$; $V_1/T_1 = V_2/T_2$; (c) $V = an$; $V_1/n_1 = V_2/n_2$; (d) $PV = nRT$; (e) $P_1V_1/T_1 = P_2V_2/T_2$
108. 125 balloons
110. 124 L
112. 0.0999 mol CO_2; 3.32 L wet; 2.68 L dry
114. 18.1 L O_2
116. (a) 1.00×10^5 Pa; (b) 4.52 atm; (c) 1087 (1.09×10^3) mm Hg; (d) 842 mm Hg
118. (a) 8.60×10^4 Pa; (b) 2.21×10^5 Pa; (c) 8.88×10^4 Pa; (d) 4.3×10^3 Pa
120. (a) 128 mL; (b) 1.3×10^{-2} L; (c) 9.8 L
122. 2.55×10^3 mm Hg
124. (a) 57.3 mL; (b) 448 K = 175 °C; (c) zero (absolute zero; a real gas would condense to a solid or liquid)
126. 123 mL
128. 2.59 g
130. (a) 61.8 K; (b) 0.993 atm; (c) 1.66×10^4 L
132. 487 mol gas needed; 7.79 kg CH_4; 13.6 kg N_2; 21.4 kg CO_2
134. 0.42 atm
136. 2.51×10^3 K
138. 32.4 L
140. 3.43 L N_2; 10.3 L H_2
142. 5.8 L O_2; 3.9 L SO_2
144. 7.8×10^2 L
146. 32 L; P_{He} = 0.86 atm; P_{Ar} = 0.017 atm; P_{Ne} = 0.12 atm
148. 22.4 L O_2

Chapter 14

2. less
4. Because it requires so much more energy to vaporize water than to melt ice, this suggests that the gaseous state is significantly different from the liquid state, but that the liquid and solid states are relatively similar.
6. See Figure 14.2.
8. When a solid is heated, the molecules begin to vibrate/move more quickly. When enough energy has been added to overcome the intermolecular forces that hold the molecules in a crystal lattice, the solid melts. As the liquid is heated, the molecules begin to move more quickly and more randomly. When enough energy has been added, molecules having sufficient kinetic energy will begin to escape from the surface of the liquid. Once the pressure of vapor coming from the liquid is equal to the pressure above the liquid, the liquid boils. Only intermolecular forces need to be overcome in this process: no chemical bonds are broken.
10. intramolecular; intermolecular
12. The quantity of energy that must be applied to melt 1 mole of the substance.
14. (a) In going from a liquid to a gas, a considerably larger amount of the heat being applied has to be converted to the kinetic energy of the atoms escaping from the liquid; (b) 10.9 kJ; (c) −2.00 kJ (heat is evolved); (d) 1.13 kJ
16. 2.44 kJ; −10.6 kJ (heat is evolved)
18. 2.60 kJ/mol
20. weaker
22. The hydrogen bonding that can exist when H is bonded to O (or N or F) is an additional intermolecular force, which means additional energy must be added to separate the molecules during boiling.
24. London dispersion forces are instantaneous dipole forces that arise when the electron cloud of an atom is momentarily distorted by a nearby dipole, temporarily separating the centers of positive and negative charge in the atom.
26. (a) London dispersion forces; (b) hydrogen bonding (H bonded to N); London dispersion forces; (c) London dispersion forces; (d) dipole–dipole forces (polar molecules); London dispersion forces
28. An increase in the heat of fusion is observed for an increase in the size of the halogen atom (the electron cloud of a larger atom is more easily polarized by a neighboring dipole, thus giving larger London dispersion forces).
30. For a homogeneous mixture to form, the forces between molecules of the two substances being mixed must be at least *comparable in magnitude* to the intermolecular forces within each separate substance. In the case of a water–ethanol mixture, the forces that exist when water and ethanol are mixed are stronger than water–water or ethanol–ethanol forces in the separate substances. Ethanol and water molecules can approach one another more closely in the mixture than either substance's molecules could approach a like molecule in the separate substances. Strong hydrogen bonding occurs in both ethanol and water.
32. When a liquid is placed into a closed container, a dynamic equilibrium is set up, in which vaporization of the liquid

and condensation of the vapor are occurring at the same rate. Once the equilibrium has been achieved, there is a net concentration of molecules in the vapor state, which gives rise to the observed vapor pressure.

34. A liquid is injected at the bottom of the column of mercury and rises to the surface of the mercury, where the liquid evaporates into the vacuum above the mercury column. As the liquid evaporates, the pressure of the vapor increases in the space above the mercury and presses down on the mercury. The level of mercury therefore drops, and the amount by which the mercury level drops (in mm Hg) is equivalent to the vapor pressure of the liquid.

36. (a) HF: Although both substances are capable of hydrogen bonding, water has two O—H bonds that can be involved in hydrogen bonding versus only one F—H bond in HF; (b) CH_3OCH_3: Because no H is attached to the O atom, no hydrogen bonding can exist. Thus, the molecule should be relatively more volatile than CH_3CH_2OH even though it contains the same number of atoms of each element; (c) CH_3SH: Hydrogen bonding is not as important for a S—H bond (because S has a lower electronegativity than O). Since there is relatively little hydrogen bonding, CH_3SH is more volatile than CH_3OH.

38. Both substances have the same molar mass. Ethyl alcohol contains a hydrogen atom directly bonded to an oxygen atom, however. Therefore, hydrogen bonding can exist in ethyl alcohol, whereas only weak dipole–dipole forces exist in dimethyl ether. Dimethyl ether is more volatile; ethyl alcohol has a higher boiling point.

40. *Ionic* solids have positive and negative ions as their fundamental particles; a simple example is sodium chloride, in which Na^+ and Cl^- ions are held together by strong electrostatic forces. *Molecular* solids have molecules as their fundamental particles, with the molecules being held together in the crystal by dipole–dipole forces, hydrogen-bonding forces, or London dispersion forces (depending on the identity of the substance); simple examples of molecular solids include ice (H_2O) and ordinary table sugar (sucrose). *Atomic* solids have simple atoms as their fundamental particles, with the atoms being held together in the crystal by either covalent bonding (as in graphite or diamond) or metallic bonding (as in copper or other metals).

42. sugar: molecular solid, relatively "soft," melts at a relatively low temperature, dissolves as molecules, does not conduct electricity when dissolved or melted; salt: ionic solid, relatively "hard," melts at a high temperature, dissolves as positively and negatively charged ions, conducts electricity when dissolved or melted.

44. Sodium chloride is an ionic substance in which a crystal lattice of alternating positive and negative ions holds the substance together with very strong forces that are difficult to overcome. Sucrose is a molecular substance in which the molecules are held together in the solid by dipole–dipole (and H-bonding) forces, which are weaker than the ionic forces.

46. In liquid hydrogen, the only intermolecular forces are weak London dispersion forces. In ethyl alcohol and water, hydrogen bonding is possible, but the hydrogen bonding forces are weaker in ethyl alcohol because of the influence of the remainder of the molecule. In sucrose, hydrogen bonding also is possible but now at several places in the molecule, leading to stronger forces. In calcium chloride, there exists an ionic crystal lattice with even stronger forces between the particles.

48. Although ions exist in both the solid and liquid states, in the solid state the ions are rigidly held in place in the crystal lattice and cannot move so as to conduct an electric current.

50. Nitinol is an alloy of nickel and titanium. When nickel and titanium are heated to a sufficiently high temperature during the production of Nitinol, the atoms arrange themselves in a compact and regular pattern of the atoms.

52. j

54. f

56. d

58. a

60. l

62. Diethyl ether has the larger vapor pressure. No hydrogen bonding is possible because the O atom does not have a hydrogen atom attached. Hydrogen bonding can occur *only* when a hydrogen atom is *directly* attached to a strongly electronegative atom (such as N, O, or F). Hydrogen bonding *is* possible in 1-butanol (1-butano contains an —OH group).

64. (a) H_2. London dispersion forces are the only intermolecular forces present in these nonpolar molecules; typically these forces become larger with increasing atomic size (as the atoms become bigger, the edge of the electron cloud lies farther from the nucleus and becomes more easily distorted); (b) Xe. Only the relatively weak London forces exist in a crystal of Xe atoms, whereas in NaCl strong ionic forces exist, and in diamond strong covalent bonding exists between carbon atoms; (c) Cl_2. Only London forces exist among such nonpolar molecules.

66. *Steel* is a general term applied to alloys consisting primarily of iron, but with small amounts of other substances added. Whereas pure iron itself is relatively soft, malleable, and ductile, steels are typically much stronger and harder and much less subject to damage.

68. Water is the solvent in which cellular processes take place in living creatures. Water in the oceans moderates the earth's temperature. Water is used in industry as a cooling agent, and it serves as a means of transportation. The liquid range is 0 °C to 100 °C at 1 atm pressure.

70. At higher altitudes, the boiling points of liquids are lower because there is a lower atmospheric pressure above the liquid. The temperature at which food cooks is determined by the temperature to which the water in the food can be heated before it escapes as steam. Thus, food cooks at a lower temperature at high elevations where the boiling point of water is lowered.

72. Heat of fusion (melt); heat of vaporization (boil). The heat of vaporization is always larger, because virtually all of the intermolecular forces must be overcome to form a gas. In a liquid, considerable intermolecular forces remain. Going from a solid to a liquid requires less energy than going from a liquid to a gas.

74. Dipole–dipole interactions are typically 1% as strong as a covalent bond. Dipole–dipole interactions represent electrostatic attractions between portions of molecules that carry only a *partial* positive or negative charge, and such forces require the molecules that are interacting to come *near* each other.

76. London dispersion forces are relatively weak forces that arise among noble gas atoms and in nonpolar molecules. London forces arise from *instantaneous dipoles* that develop when one atom (or molecule) momentarily distorts the electron cloud of another atom (or molecule). London forces are typically weaker than either permanent dipole–dipole forces or covalent bonds.

78. For each mole of liquid water that evaporates, several kilojoules of heat must be absorbed by the water from its surroundings to overcome attractive forces among the molecules.

80. In NH_3, strong hydrogen bonding can exist. Because CH_4 molecules are nonpolar, only the relatively weak London dispersion forces exist.

82. Strong *hydrogen-bonding* forces are present in an ice crystal, while only the much weaker *London forces* exist in the crystal of a nonpolar substance like oxygen.
84. Ice floats on liquid water; water expands when it is frozen.
86. Although they are at the same *temperature*, steam at 100 °C contains a larger amount of *energy* than hot water, equal to the heat of vaporization of water.
88. Hydrogen bonding is a special case of dipole–dipole interactions that occur among molecules containing hydrogen atoms bonded to highly electronegative atoms such as fluorine, oxygen, or nitrogen. The bonds are very polar, and the small size of the hydrogen atom (compared to other atoms) allows the dipoles to approach each other very closely. Examples: H_2O, NH_3, HF.
90. Evaporation and condensation are opposite processes. Evaporation is an endothermic process; condensation is an exothermic process. Evaporation requires an input of energy to provide the increased kinetic energy possessed by the molecules when they are in the gaseous state. It occurs when the molecules in a liquid are moving fast enough and randomly enough that molecules are able to escape from the surface of the liquid and enter the vapor phase.

Chapter 15

2. A *non*homogeneous mixture may differ in composition in various places in the mixture, whereas a solution (a homogeneous mixture) has the same composition throughout. Examples of nonhomogeneous mixtures include spaghetti sauce, a jar of jelly beans, and a mixture of salt and sugar.
4. solid
6. "Like dissolves like." The hydrocarbons in oil have intermolecular forces that are very different from those in water, so the oil spreads out rather than dissolving in the water.
8. Carbon dioxide is somewhat soluble in water, especially if pressurized (otherwise, the soda you may be drinking while studying chemistry would be "flat"). Carbon dioxide's solubility in water is approximately 1.5 g/L at 25 °C under a pressure of approximately 1 atm. The carbon dioxide molecule overall is nonpolar, because the two individual C—O bond dipoles cancel each other due to the linearity of the molecule. However, these bond dipoles are able to interact with water, making CO_2 more soluble in water than nonpolar molecules such as O_2 or N_2, which do not possess individual bond dipoles.
10. unsaturated
12. large
14. 100.
16. (a) 0.116%; (b) 0.0116%; (c) 10.4%; (d) 10.4%
18. (a) 20.5 g $FeCl_3$; 504.5 g (505 g) water; (b) 26.8 g sucrose; 198.2 g (198 g) water; (c) 181.3 g (181 g) NaCl; 1268.7 (1.27×10^3) g water; (d) 95.9 g KNO_3; 539.1 (539) g water
20. 957 g Fe; 26.9 g C; 16.5 g Cr
22. 19.6% $CaCl_2$
24. 7.81 g KBr
26. approximately 71 g
28. 9.5 g
30. 0.110 mol; 0.220 mol
32. b
34. (a) 3.35 *M*; (b) 1.03 *M*; (c) 0.630 *M*; (d) 4.99 *M*
36. (a) 0.403 *M*; (b) 0.169 *M*; (c) 0.629 *M*; (d) 0.829 *M*
38. 4.03 g KBr
40. 0.0902 *M*
42. 0.479 *M*
44. (a) 0.00130 mol; (b) 0.00609 mol; (c) 0.0184 mol; (d) 0.0356 mol
46. (a) 0.235 g; (b) 0.593 g; (c) 2.29 g; (d) 2.61 g
48. 9.51 g
50. (a) 4.60×10^{-3} mol Al^{3+}, 1.38×10^{-2} mol Cl^-; (b) 1.70 mol Na^+, 0.568 mol PO_4^{3-}; (c) 2.19×10^{-3} mol Cu^{2+}, 4.38×10^{-3} mol Cl^-; (d) 3.96×10^{-5} mol Ca^{2+}, 7.91×10^{-5} mol OH^-
52. 1.33 g
54. half
56. (a) 0.0717 *M*; (b) 1.69 *M*; (c) 0.0426 *M*; (d) 0.625 *M*
58. 0.541 L (541 mL)
60. Dilute 48.3 mL of the 1.01 *M* solution to a final volume of 325 mL.
62. 10.3 mL
64. 31.2 mL
66. 0.523 g
68. 0.300 g
70. 378 mL
72. 1.8×10^{-4} *M*
74. (a) 63.0 mL; (b) 2.42 mL; (c) 50.1 mL; (d) 1.22 L
76. 1 *N*
78. 1.53 equivalents OH^- ion. By definition, one equivalent of OH^- ion exactly neutralizes one equivalent of H^+ ion.
80. (a) 0.277 *N*; (b) 3.37×10^{-3} *N*; (c) 1.63 *N*
82. (a) 0.134 *N*; (b) 0.0104 *N*; (c) 13.3 *N*
84. 7.03×10^{-5} *M*, 1.41×10^{-4} *N*
86. 22.2 mL, 11.1 mL
88. 0.05583 *M*, 0.1117 *N*
90. Molarity is defined as the number of moles of solute contained in 1 liter of *total* solution volume (solute plus solvent after mixing). In the first example, the total volume after mixing is *not* known and the molarity cannot be calculated. In the second example, the final volume after mixing is known and the molarity can be calculated simply.
92. 3.3%
94. 12.7 g $NaHCO_3$
96. 56 mol
98. 1.12 L HCl at STP
100. 26.3 mL
102. 2.56 *M*
104. (a) 6.3% KNO_3; (b) 0.25% KNO_3; (c) 11% KNO_3; (d) 18% KNO_3
106. 4.7% C, 1.4% Ni, 93.9% Fe
108. 28 g Na_2CO_3
110. 9.4 g NaCl, 3.1 g KBr
112. (a) 4.0 *M*; (b) 1.0 *M*; (c) 0.73 *M*; (d) 3.6 *M*
114. 0.812 *M*
116. 0.026 *M*
118. (a) 0.446 mol, 33.3 g; (b) 0.00340 mol, 0.289 g; (c) 0.075 mol, 2.7 g; (d) 0.0505 mol, 4.95 g
120. (a) 0.938 mol Na^+, 0.313 mol PO_4^{3-}; (b) 0.042 mol H^+, 0.021 mol SO_4^{2-}; (c) 0.0038 mol Al^{3+}, 0.011 mol Cl^-; (d) 1.88 mol Ba^{2+}, 3.75 mol Cl^-
122. (a) 0.0909 *M*; (b) 0.127 *M*; (c) 0.192 *M*; (d) 1.6 *M*
124. 0.90 *M*
126. 50. mL
128. 35.0 mL
130. (a) 0.822 *N* HCl; (b) 4.00 *N* H_2SO_4; (c) 3.06 *N* H_3PO_4
132. 0.083 *M* NaH_2PO_4, 0.17 *N* NaH_2PO_4
134. 9.6×10^{-2} *N* HNO_3

Chapter 16

2. $HCl(g) \xrightarrow{H_2O} H^+(aq) + Cl^-(aq)$; $NaOH(s) \xrightarrow{H_2O} Na^+(aq) + OH^-(aq)$
4. A conjugate acid–base pair differs by one hydrogen ion, H^+. For example, $HC_2H_3O_2$ (acetic acid) differs from its conjugate base, $C_2H_3O_2^-$ (acetate ion), by a single H^+ ion.

$$HC_2H_3O_2(aq) \rightleftharpoons C_2H_3O_2^-(aq) + H^+(aq)$$

6. In addition to sodium bicarbonate, the gum also contains citric acid and malic acid. When the gum is exposed to moisture in the mouth, the bicarbonate ion behaves as a base and reacts with hydrogen ion from the acids: $H^+(aq) + HCO_3^-(aq) \rightarrow H_2O(l) + CO_2(g)$.
8. (a) conjugate pair; (b) conjugate pair; (c) conjugate pair; (d) not a conjugate pair; H_2O, OH^-; OH^-, O^{2-}
10. (a) $NH_3(aq)$(base) + $H_2O(l)$(acid) $\rightleftharpoons$ $NH_4^+(aq)$(acid) + $OH^-(aq)$(base);
(b) $NH_4^+(aq)$(acid) + $H_2O(l)$(base) $\rightleftharpoons$ $NH_3(aq)$(base) + $H_3O^+(aq)$(acid);
(c) $NH_2^-(aq)$(base) + $H_2O(l)$(acid) $\rightarrow$ $NH_3(aq)$(acid) + $OH^-(aq)$(base)
12. (a) $HClO$; (b) HCl; (c) $HClO_3$; (d) $HClO_4$
14. (a) BrO^-; (b) HSO_3^-; (c) SO_3^{2-}; (d) CH_3NH_2
16. (a) $O^{2-}(aq) + H_2O(l) \rightleftharpoons OH^-(aq) + OH^-(aq)$;
(b) $NH_3(aq) + H_2O(l) \rightleftharpoons NH_4^+(aq) + OH^-(aq)$;
(c) $HSO_4^-(aq) + H_2O(l) \rightleftharpoons SO_4^{2-}(aq) + H_3O^+(aq)$;
(d) $HNO_2(aq) + H_2O(l) \rightleftharpoons NO_2^-(aq) + H_3O^+(aq)$
18. If an acid is weak in aqueous solution, it does not easily transfer protons to water (and does not fully ionize). If an acid does not lose protons easily, then the acid's anion must strongly attract protons.
20. A strong acid loses its protons easily and fully ionizes in water; the acid's conjugate base is poor at attracting and holding protons and is a relatively weak base. A weak acid resists loss of its protons and does not ionize to a great extent in water; the acid's conjugate base attracts and holds protons tightly and is a relatively strong base.
22. H_2SO_4 (sulfuric): $H_2SO_4 + H_2O \rightarrow HSO_4^- + H_3O^+$;
HCl (hydrochloric): $HCl + H_2O \rightarrow Cl^- + H_3O^+$;
HNO_3 (nitric): $HNO_3 + H_2O \rightarrow NO_3^- + H_3O^+$;
$HClO_4$ (perchloric): $HClO_4 + H_2O \rightarrow ClO_4^- + H_3O^+$
24. An oxyacid is an acid containing a particular element that is bonded to one or more oxygen atoms. HNO_3, H_2SO_4, and $HClO_4$ are oxyacids. HCl, HF, and HBr are not oxyacids.
26. Salicylic acid is a monoprotic acid: only the hydrogen of the carboxyl group ionizes.
28. HCO_3^- can behave as an acid if it reacts with a substance that more strongly gains protons than does HCO_3^- itself. For example, HCO_3^- would behave as an acid when reacting with hydroxide ion (a much stronger base): $HCO_3^-(aq) + OH^-(aq) \rightarrow CO_3^{2-}(aq) + H_2O(l)$. On the other hand, HCO_3^- would behave as a base when reacted with a substance that more readily loses protons than does HCO_3^- itself. For example, HCO_3^- would behave as a base when reacting with hydrochloric acid (a much stronger acid): $HCO_3^-(aq) + HCl(aq) \rightarrow H_2CO_3(aq) + Cl^-(aq)$. $H_2PO_4^- + OH^- \rightarrow HPO_4^{2-} + H_2O$ and $H_2PO_4^- + H_3O^+ \rightarrow H_3PO_4 + H_2O$.
30. The concentrations of H^+ and OH^- ions in water and in dilute aqueous solutions are *not* independent of one another. Rather, they are related by the ion product equilibrium constant, K_w. $K_w = [H^+(aq)][OH^-(aq)] = 1.00 \times 10^{-14}$ at 25 °C. If the concentration of one ion is *increased* by addition of a reagent producing H^+ or OH^-, then the concentration of the complementary ion will *decrease* so that the constant's value will hold true. If an acid is added to a solution, the concentration of hydroxide ion in the solution will decrease. Similarly, if a base is added to a solution, then the concentration of hydrogen ion will decrease.
32. (a) $[H^+] = 2.9 \times 10^{-14}$ *M*; basic;
(b) $[H^+] = 1.0 \times 10^{-4}$ *M*; acidic;
(c) $[H^+] = 2.0 \times 10^{-9}$ *M*; basic;
(d) $[H^+] = 2.6 \times 10^{-8}$ *M*; basic
34. (a) $[OH^-] = 9.8 \times 10^{-8}$ *M*; acidic;
(b) $[OH^-] = 1.02 \times 10^{-7}$ *M* (1.0×10^{-7} *M*); basic;
(c) $[OH^-] = 2.9 \times 10^{-12}$ *M*; acidic;
(d) $[OH^-] = 2.1 \times 10^{-4}$ *M*; basic
36. (a) $[OH^-] = 6.03 \times 10^{-4}$ *M*; (b) $[OH^-] = 4.21 \times 10^{-6}$ *M*; (c) $[OH^-] = 8.04 \times 10^{-4}$ *M*
38. Answers will depend on student choices.
40. pH 1–2, deep red; pH 4, purple; pH 8, blue; pH 11, green
42. (a) pH = 1.029; acidic; (b) 3.426; acidic; (c) 5.078; acidic; (d) 7.266; basic
44. (a) pH = 11.94; basic; (b) pH = 8.87; basic; (c) pH = 5.97; acidic; (d) pH = 3.08; acidic
46. (a) 4.22, basic; (b) 9.99, acidic; (c) 11.21, acidic; (d) 2.79, basic
48. (a) pH = 1.719, $[OH^-] = 5.2 \times 10^{-13}$ *M*;
(b) pH = 6.316, $[OH^-] = 2.1 \times 10^{-8}$ *M*;
(c) pH = 10.050, $[OH^-] = 1.1 \times 10^{-4}$ *M*;
(d) pH = 4.212, $[OH^-] = 1.6 \times 10^{-10}$ *M*
50. (a) 6.2×10^{-12} *M*; (b) 4.1×10^{-5} *M*; (c) 3.6×10^{-8} *M*; (d) 4.2×10^{-2} *M*
52. (a) 9.8×10^{-10} *M*; (b) 1.8×10^{-8} *M*; (c) 5.5×10^{-4} *M*; (d) 5.6×10^{-3} *M*
54. (a) 5.358; (b) 3.64; (c) 5.97; (d) 0.480
56. The solution contains water molecules, H_3O^+ ions (protons), and NO_3^- ions. Because HNO_3 is a strong acid that is completely ionized in water, no HNO_3 molecules are present.
58. (a) pH = 2.917; (b) pH = 3.701; (c) pH = 4.300; (d) pH = 2.983
60. A buffered solution consists of a mixture of a weak acid and its conjugate base; one example of a buffered solution is a mixture of acetic acid ($HC_2H_3O_2$) and sodium acetate ($NaC_2H_3O_2$).
62. The weak acid component of a buffered solution is capable of reacting with added strong base. For example, using the buffered solution given as an example in Exercise 60, acetic acid would consume added sodium hydroxide as follows: $HC_2H_3O_2(aq) + NaOH(aq) \rightarrow NaC_2H_3O_2(aq) + H_2O(l)$. Acetic acid *neutralizes* the added NaOH and prevents it from affecting the overall pH of the solution.
64. $CH_3COO^- + HCl \rightarrow CH_3COOH + Cl^-$; $CH_3COOH + NaOH \rightarrow H_2O + NaCH_3COO$
66. (a) $[OH^-(aq)] = 0.10$ *M*, pOH = 1.00, pH = 13.00;
(b) $[OH^-(aq)] = 2.0 \times 10^{-4}$ *M*, pOH = 3.70, pH = 10.30;
(c) $[OH^-(aq)] = 6.2 \times 10^{-3}$ *M*, pOH = 2.21, pH = 11.79;
(d) $[OH^-(aq)] = 0.0001$ *M*, pOH = 4.0, pH = 10.0
68. b, c, d 70. a, c, e
72. Having a concentration as small as 10^{-7} *M* for HCl means that the contribution to the total hydrogen ion concentration from the dissociation of water must also be considered in determining the pH of the solution.
74. accepts
76. base
78. $-C(=O)OH$; $CH_3COOH + H_2O \rightleftharpoons C_2H_3O_2^- + H_3O^+$
80. 1.0×10^{-14}
82. higher

84. pH
86. weak acid
88. (a) H_2O and OH^- are a conjugate acid–base pair (H_2O is the acid, having one more proton than the base, OH^-); (b) H_2SO_4 and SO_4^{2-} are *not* a conjugate acid–base pair (they differ by *two* protons). The conjugate base of H_2SO_4 is HSO_4^-; the conjugate acid of SO_4^{2-} is also HSO_4^-; (c) H_3PO_4 and $H_2PO_4^-$ are a conjugate acid–base pair (H_3PO_4 is the acid, having one more proton than the base, $H_2PO_4^-$); (d) $HC_2H_3O_2$ and $C_2H_3O_2^-$ are a conjugate acid–base pair ($HC_2H_3O_2$ is the acid, having one more proton than the base, $C_2H_3O_2^-$)
90. (a) NH_4^+; (b) NH_3; (c) H_3O^+; (d) H_2O
92. (a) $CH_3CH_2COOH + H_2O \rightleftharpoons CH_3CH_2COO^- + H_3O^+$; (b) $NH_4^+ + H_2O \rightleftharpoons NH_3 + H_3O^+$; (c) $H_2SO_4 + H_2O \rightarrow HSO_4^- + H_3O^+$; (d) $H_3PO_4 + H_2O \rightleftharpoons H_2PO_4^- + H_3O^+$
94. (a) $[H^+(aq)] = 2.4 \times 10^{-12}$ *M*, solution is basic; (b) $[H^+(aq)] = 9.9 \times 10^{-2}$ *M*, solution is acidic; (c) $[H^+(aq)] = 3.3 \times 10^{-8}$ *M*, solution is basic; (d) $[H^+(aq)] = 1.7 \times 10^{-9}$ *M*, solution is basic
96. (a) $[OH^-(aq)] = 0.0000032$ *M*; (b) $[OH^-(aq)] = 1.54 \times 10^{-8}$ *M*; (c) $[OH^-(aq)] = 4.02 \times 10^{-7}$ *M*
98. (a) pH = 8.15; solution is basic; (b) pH = 5.97; solution is acidic; (c) pH = 13.34; solution is basic; (d) pH = 2.90; solution is acidic
100. (a) $[OH^-(aq)] = 1.8 \times 10^{-11}$ *M*, pH = 3.24, pOH = 10.76; (b) $[H^+(aq)] = 1.1 \times 10^{-10}$ *M*, pH = 9.95, pOH = 4.05; (c) $[OH^-(aq)] = 3.5 \times 10^{-3}$ *M*, pH = 11.54, pH = 2.46; (d) $[H^+(aq)] = 1.4 \times 10^{-7}$ *M*, pH = 6.86, pOH = 7.14
102. (a) $[H^+] = 3.9 \times 10^{-6}$ *M*; (b) $[H^+] = 1.1 \times 10^{-2}$ *M*; (c) $[H^+] = 1.2 \times 10^{-12}$ *M*; (d) $[H^+] = 7.8 \times 10^{-11}$ *M*
104. (a) $[H^+(aq)] = 1.4 \times 10^{-3}$ *M*, pH = 2.85; (b) $[H^+(aq)] = 3.0 \times 10^{-5}$ *M*, pH = 4.52; (c) $[H^+(aq)] = 5.0 \times 10^{-2}$ *M*, pH = 1.30; (d) $[H^+(aq)] = 0.0010$ *M*, pH = 3.00

Chapter 17

2. Four C—H bonds and four Cl—Cl bonds must be broken; four C—Cl and four H—Cl bonds must form.
4. E_a represents the *activation energy* for the reaction, which is the minimum energy needed for the reaction to be able to occur.
6. Enzymes are biochemical catalysts that speed up the complicated reactions that would be too slow to sustain life at normal body temperatures.
8. A state of equilibrium is attained when two opposing processes are exactly balanced. The development of a vapor pressure above a liquid in a closed container is an example of a physical equilibrium. Any chemical reaction that appears to "stop" before completion is an example of a chemical equilibrium.
10. A system has reached equilibrium when no more product forms, even though significant amounts of all the needed reactants are present. This lack of further product creation indicates that the reverse process is now occurring at the same rate as the forward process—that is, every time a product molecule forms in the system, another product molecule reacts to give back the original reactants elsewhere in the system. Reactions that come to equilibrium are indicated by a double arrow.
12. The two curves come together when a state of chemical equilibrium has been reached, after which point the forward and reverse reactions are occurring at the same rate so that there is no further net change in concentration.
14. The equilibrium constant is a *ratio* of the concentration of products to the concentration of reactants, all at equilibrium. Depending on the amount of reactant that was originally present, different amounts of reactants and products will be present at equilibrium, but their *ratio* will always be the same for a given reaction at a given temperature. For example, the ratios 4/2 and 6/3 involve different numbers, but each of these ratios has the value 2.
16. (a) $K = \dfrac{[H_2O][CO]}{[H_2][CO_2]}$; (b) $K = \dfrac{[NO]^4}{[N_2O]^2[O_2]}$; (c) $K = \dfrac{[CH_3OH]}{[CO][H_2]}$
18. (a) $K = \dfrac{[CH_3OH(g)]}{[CO(g)][H_2(g)]^2}$; (b) $K = \dfrac{[NO(g)]^2[O_2(g)]}{[NO_2(g)]^2}$; (c) $K = \dfrac{[PBr_3(g)]^4}{[P_4(g)][Br_2(g)]^6}$
20. $K = 0.734$
22. $K = 4.85 \times 10^{-6}$
24. Equilibrium constants represent ratios of the *concentrations* of products and reactants present at the point of equilibrium. The *concentration* of a pure solid or a pure liquid is constant and is determined by the density of the solid or liquid.
26. (a) $K = \dfrac{[H_2]}{[H_2O]}$; (b) $K = \dfrac{1}{[O_2]^3}$; (c) $K = \dfrac{[HCl]^4}{[CH_4][Cl_2]^4}$
28. (a) $K = \dfrac{[S_2Cl_2(g)]}{[CS_2(g)][Cl_2(g)]^3}$; (b) $K = \dfrac{1}{[Xe(g)][F_2(g)]^3}$; (c) $K = \dfrac{1}{[O_2(g)]^3}$
30. $[CO_2]$ increases; *K* does not change
32. If heat is applied to an endothermic reaction (the temperature is raised), the equilibrium is shifted to the right. More product will be present at equilibrium than if the temperature had not been increased. The value of *K* increases.
34. (a) shift right; (b) no change; (c) shift left
36. (a) no change (B is solid); (b) shift right; (c) shift left; (d) shift right
38. The forward reaction would be favored. The reaction is endothermic, and raising the temperature means heat is being added to the system.
40. For an *endo*thermic reaction, an increase in temperature will shift the position of equilibrium to the right (toward products).
42. Add more $CO(g)$; add more $H_2(g)$; decrease the volume of the system.
44. A small equilibrium constant implies that not much product forms before equilibrium is reached. The reaction would not be a good source of the products unless Le Châtelier's principle can be used to force the reaction to the right.
46. $K = 8.63 \times 10^{-7}$
48. $[H_2] = 0.119$ *M*
50. $[O_2(g)] = 8.0 \times 10^{-2}$ *M*
52. 5.4×10^{-4} *M*
54. solubility product, K_{sp}
56. only the temperature
58. (a) $Bi_2S_3(s) \rightleftharpoons 2Bi^{3+}(aq) + 3S^{2-}(aq)$; $K_{sp} = [Bi^{3+}(aq)]^2[S^{2-}(aq)]^3$; (b) $Ca(OH)_2(s) \rightleftharpoons Ca^{2+}(aq) + 2OH^-(aq)$; $K_{sp} = [Ca^{2+}(aq)][OH^-(aq)]^2$; (c) $Co(OH)_3(s) \rightleftharpoons Co^{3+}(aq) + 3OH^-(aq)$; $K_{sp} = [Co^{3+}(aq)][OH^-(aq)]^3$; (d) $Cu_2S(s) \rightleftharpoons 2Cu^+(aq) + S^{2-}(aq)$; $K_{sp} = [Cu^+(aq)]^2[S^{2-}(aq)]$

60. 1.9×10^{-4} *M*; 0.016 g/L
62. 7.4×10^{-4} g/L
64. $K_{sp} = 2.27 \times 10^{-4}$
66. $K_{sp} = 1.23 \times 10^{-15}$
68. $K_{sp} = 1.9 \times 10^{-4}$; 10. g/L
70. 4×10^{-17} *M*, 4×10^{-15} g/L
72. increase in temperature increases the fraction of molecules with energy $> E_a$
74. catalyst
76. constant
78. reaction is still taking place, but in opposing directions, at the same speeds
80. heterogeneous
82. position
84. In an exothermic process, heat is a product of the reaction. So adding heat (increasing the temperature) fights against the forward process.
86. An equilibrium reaction may come to many *positions* of equilibrium, but the numerical value of the equilibrium constant is fulfilled at each possible position. If different experiments vary the amounts of reactant, the *absolute amounts* of reactants and products present at the point of equilibrium will differ from one experiment to another, but the *ratio* that defines the equilibrium constant will remain the same.
88. 9.0×10^{-3} *M*
90. $BaCO_3(s) \rightleftharpoons Ba^{2+}(aq) + CO_3^{2-}(aq)$; 7.1×10^{-5} *M*
$CdCO_3(s) \rightleftharpoons Cd^{2+}(aq) + CO_3^{2-}(aq)$; 2.3×10^{-6} *M*
$CaCO_3(s) \rightleftharpoons Ca^{2+}(aq) + CO_3^{2-}(aq)$; 5.3×10^{-5} *M*
$CoCO_3(s) \rightleftharpoons Co^{2+}(aq) + CO_3^{2-}(aq)$; 3.9×10^{-7} *M*
92. Although a small solubility product generally implies a small solubility, comparisons of solubility based directly on K_{sp} values are valid only if the salts produce the same numbers of positive and negative ions per formula when they dissolve. For example, the solubilities of AgCl(*s*) and NiS(*s*) can be compared directly using K_{sp}, since each salt produces one positive and one negative ion per formula when dissolved. AgCl(*s*) cannot be directly compared with a salt such as $Ca_3(PO_4)_2$, however.
94. At higher temperatures, the average kinetic energy of the reactant molecules is larger, as is the probability that a collision between molecules will be energetic enough for reaction to take place. On a molecular basis, a higher temperature means a given molecule will be moving faster.
96. (a) $K = \dfrac{[HBr(g)]^2}{[H_2(g)][Br_2(g)]}$; (b) $K = \dfrac{[H_2S(g)]^2}{[H_2(g)]^2[S_2(g)]}$; (c) $K = \dfrac{[HCN(g)]^2}{[H_2(g)][C_2N_2(g)]}$
98. $K = 1.2 \times 10^{-3}$
100. (a) $K = \dfrac{1}{[O_2(g)]^3}$; (b) $K = \dfrac{1}{[NH_3(g)][HCl(g)]}$; (c) $K = \dfrac{1}{[O_2(g)]}$
102. An *exo*thermic reaction liberates energy as heat. Increasing the temperature (adding heat) for such a reaction is fighting against the reaction's own tendency to liberate heat. The net effect of raising the temperature will be a shift to the left and a decrease in the amount of product. To increase the amount of products in an exothermic reaction, heat must be *removed* from the system. Changing the temperature *does* change the numerical value of the equilibrium constant for a reaction.
104. The reaction is *exo*thermic. An increase in temperature (addition of heat) will shift the reaction to the left (toward reactants).
106. $[NH_3(g)] = 1.1 \times 10^{-3}$ *M*
108. (a) $Cu(OH)_2(s) \rightleftharpoons Cu^{2+}(aq) + 2OH^-(aq)$; $K_{sp} = [Cu^{2+}(aq)][OH^-(aq)]^2$; (b) $Cr(OH)_3(s) \rightleftharpoons Cr^{3+}(aq) + 3OH^-(aq)$; $K_{sp} = [Cr^{3+}(aq)][OH^-(aq)]^3$; (c) $Ba(OH)_2(s) \rightleftharpoons Ba^{2+}(aq) + 2OH^-(aq)$; $K_{sp} = [Ba^{2+}(aq)][OH^-(aq)]^2$; (d) $Sn(OH)_2(s) \rightleftharpoons Sn^{2+}(aq) + 2OH^-(aq)$; $K_{sp} = [Sn^{2+}(aq)][OH^-(aq)]^2$
110. $K_{sp} = 3.9 \times 10^{-11}$
112. $K_{sp} = 1.4 \times 10^{-8}$
114. The activation energy is the minimum energy that two colliding molecules must possess for the collision to result in a reaction.
116. Once a system has reached equilibrium, the net concentration of product no longer increases because molecules of product already present react to form the original reactants.
118. (a) $K = [H_2O][CO_2]$; (b) $K = [CO_2]$; (c) $K = \dfrac{1}{[O_2]^3}$

Chapter 18

2. Oxidation is a loss of one or more electrons by an atom or ion. Reduction is the gaining of one or more electrons by an atom or ion. Equations depend on student responses.
4. (a) boron is oxidized; oxygen is reduced; (b) nitrogen is oxidized; oxygen is reduced; (c) carbon is oxidized; hydrogen is reduced; (d) magnesium is oxidized; copper is reduced
6. (a) sulfur is oxidized, oxygen is reduced; (b) phosphorus is oxidized, oxygen is reduced; (c) hydrogen is oxidized, carbon is reduced; (d) boron is oxidized, hydrogen is reduced
8. Oxidation numbers represent a "relative charge" one atom has compared to another in a compound. In an element, all the atoms are equivalent.
10. Because fluorine is the most electronegative element, its oxidation state is always negative relative to other elements; because fluorine gains only one electron to complete its outermost shell, its oxidation number in compounds is always -1. The other halogen elements are almost always more electronegative than the atoms to which they bond, and almost always have -1 oxidation numbers. However, in an interhalogen compound involving fluorine and some other halogen, since fluorine is the most electronegative element of all, the other halogens in the compound will have positive oxidation states relative to fluorine.
12. -3
14. (a) Cr, +3; Cl, −1; (b) Ni, +2; O, −2; H, +1; (c) H, +1; S, −2; (d) C, +4; S, −2
16. (a) 0; (b) −3; (c) +4; (d) +5
18. (a) +2; (b) +7; (c) +4; (d) +3
20. (a) Ca, +2; O, −2; (b) Al, +3; O, −2; (c) P, +3; F, −1; (d) P, +5; O, −2
22. (a) H, +1; S, +6; O, −2; (b) Mn, +7; O, −2; (c) Cl, +5; O, −2; (d) Br, +7; O, −2
24. Electrons are negative; when an atom gains electrons, it gains one negative charge for each electron gained. For example, in the reduction reaction $Cl + e^- \rightarrow Cl^-$, the oxidation state of chlorine decreases from 0 to -1 as the electron is gained.
26. Answer depends on student selection of example.
28. An antioxidant is a substance that prevents oxidation of some molecule in the body. It is not certain how all antioxidants work, but one example is by preventing oxygen molecules and other substances from stripping electrons from

cell membranes, which leaves them vulnerable to destruction by the immune system.

30. (a) aluminum is oxidized; sulfur is reduced; (b) carbon is oxidized; oxygen is reduced; (c) carbon is oxidized; iron is reduced; (d) chlorine is oxidized; chromium is reduced

32. (a) carbon is oxidized, chlorine is reduced; (b) carbon is oxidized, oxygen is reduced; (c) phosphorus is oxidized, chlorine is reduced; (d) calcium is oxidized, hydrogen is reduced

34. Iron is reduced [+3 in $Fe_2O_3(s)$, 0 in $Fe(l)$]; carbon is oxidized [+2 in $CO(g)$, +4 in $CO_2(g)$]. $Fe_2O_3(s)$ is the oxidizing agent; $CO(g)$ is the reducing agent.

36. (a) chlorine is reduced, iodine is oxidized; chlorine is the oxidizing agent, iodide ion is the reducing agent; (b) iron is reduced, iodine is oxidized; iron(III) is the oxidizing agent, iodide ion is the reducing agent; (c) copper is reduced, iodine is oxidized; copper(II) is the oxidizing agent, iodide ion is the reducing agent

38. Oxidation–reduction reactions are often more complicated than "regular" reactions; the coefficients necessary to balance the number of electrons transferred are often large numbers.

40. Under ordinary conditions it is impossible to have "free" electrons that are not part of some atom, ion, or molecule. Thus, the total number of electrons lost by the species being oxidized must equal the total number of electrons gained by the species being reduced.

42. (a) $2Cl^-(aq) \rightarrow Cl_2(g) + 2e^-$; (b) $Fe^{2+}(aq) \rightarrow Fe^{3+}(aq) + e^-$; (c) $Fe(s) \rightarrow Fe^{3+}(aq) + 3e^-$; (d) $Cu^{2+}(aq) + e^- \rightarrow Cu^+(aq)$

44. (a) $4H^+ + 4e^- + O_2 \rightarrow 2H_2O$;
(b) $4H^+ + 2e^- + SO_4^{2-} \rightarrow H_2SO_3 + H_2O$;
(c) $2H^+ + 2e^- + H_2O_2 \rightarrow 2H_2O$;
(d) $H_2O + NO_2^- \rightarrow NO_3^- + 2H^+ + 2e^-$

46. (a) $2Al + 6H^+ \rightarrow 2Al^{3+} + 3H_2$;
(b) $8H^+ + 2NO_3^- + 3S^{2-} \rightarrow 3S + 2NO + 4H_2O$;
(c) $6H_2O + I_2 + 5Cl_2 \rightarrow 2IO_3^- + 2H^+ + 10HCl$;
(d) $2H^+ + AsO_4^- + S^{2-} \rightarrow S + AsO_3^- + H_2O$

48. $Cu(s) + 2HNO_3(aq) + 2H^+(aq) \rightarrow Cu^{2+}(aq) + 2NO_2(g) + 2H_2O(l)$; $Mg(s) + 2HNO_3(aq) \rightarrow Mg(NO_3)_2(aq) + H_2(g)$

50. A salt bridge typically consists of a U-shaped tube filled with an inert electrolyte (one involving ions that are not part of the oxidation–reduction reaction). A salt bridge completes the electrical circuit in a cell. Any method that allows transfer of charge without allowing bulk mixing of the solutions may be used (another common method is to set up one half-cell in a porous cup, which is then placed in the beaker containing the second half-cell).

52. Reduction takes place at the cathode and oxidation takes place at the anode.

54.

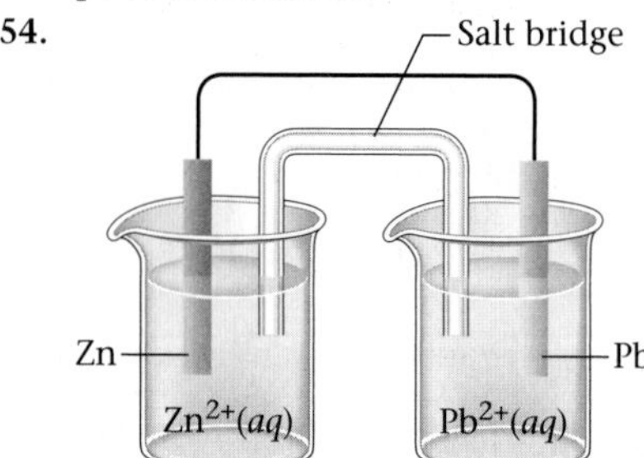

$Pb^{2+}(aq)$ ion is reduced; $Zn(s)$ is oxidized. The anode reaction is $Zn(s) \rightarrow Zn^{2+}(aq) + 2e^-$. The cathode reaction is $Pb^{2+}(aq) + 2e^- \rightarrow Pb(s)$.

56. $Cd + 2OH^- \rightarrow Cd(OH)_2 + 2e^-$ (oxidation);
$NiO_2 + 2H_2O + 2e^- \rightarrow Ni(OH)_2 + 2OH^-$ (reduction)

58. Aluminum is a very reactive metal when freshly isolated in the pure state. Upon standing for even a relatively short period of time, aluminum metal forms a thin coating of Al_2O_3 on its surface from reaction with atmospheric oxygen. This Al_2O_3 coating is much less reactive than the metal and protects the metal's surface from further attack.

60. Chromium protects stainless steel by forming a thin coating of chromium oxide on the surface of the steel, which prevents oxidation of the iron in the steel.

62. The main recharging reaction for the lead storage battery is $2PbSO_4(s) + 2H_2O(l) \rightarrow Pb(s) + PbO_2(s) + 2H_2SO_4(aq)$. A major side reaction is the electrolysis of water, $2H_2O(l) \rightarrow 2H_2(g) + O_2(g)$, which produces an explosive mixture of hydrogen and oxygen that accounts for many accidents during the recharging of such batteries.

64. The balanced equation is $2H_2O(l) \rightarrow 2H_2(g) + O_2(g)$. Oxygen is oxidized (going from −2 oxidation state in water to zero oxidation state in the free element). Hydrogen is reduced (going from +1 oxidation state in water to zero oxidation state in the free element). Heat is produced by burning the hydrogen gas produced by the electrolysis. Because energy must be applied to water to electrolyze it, energy is released when hydrogen gas produced by the electrolysis and oxygen gas combine to form water in the fireplace.

66. loss; oxidation state

68. electronegative

70. An oxidizing agent is an atom, molecule, or ion that causes the oxidation of some other species, while itself being reduced.

72. lose

74. separate from

76. oxidation

78. In an electrolysis reaction, an ordinarily nonspontaneous reaction is forced to occur by the application of an electric current of sufficient voltage. For example, water may be electrolyzed into its elements: $2H_2O(l) \rightarrow 2H_2(g) + O_2(g)$.

80. hydrogen; oxygen

82. oxidation

84. (a) $4Fe(s) + 3O_2(g) \rightarrow 2Fe_2O_3(s)$; iron is oxidized, oxygen is reduced; (b) $2Al(s) + 3Cl_2(g) \rightarrow 2AlCl_3(s)$; aluminum is oxidized, chlorine is reduced; (c) $6Mg(s) + P_4(s) \rightarrow 2Mg_3P_2(s)$; magnesium is oxidized, phosphorus is reduced

86. (a) Al is oxidized ($0 \rightarrow +3$); H is reduced ($+1 \rightarrow 0$);
(b) H is reduced ($+1 \rightarrow 0$); I is oxidized ($-1 \rightarrow 0$);
(c) Cu is oxidized ($0 \rightarrow +2$); H is reduced ($+1 \rightarrow 0$)

88. (a) $C_3H_8(g) + 5O_2(g) \rightarrow 3CO_2(g) + 4H_2O(g)$;
(b) $CO(g) + 2H_2(g) \rightarrow CH_3OH(l)$;
(c) $SnO_2(s) + 2C(s) \rightarrow Sn(s) + 2CO(g)$;
(d) $C_2H_5OH(l) + 3O_2(g) \rightarrow 2CO_2(g) + 3H_2O(g)$

90. (a) sodium is oxidized, oxygen is reduced; (b) iron is oxidized, hydrogen is reduced; (c) oxygen (O^{2-}) is oxidized, aluminum (Al^{3+}) is reduced; (d) magnesium is oxidized, nitrogen is reduced

92. (a) H, +1; N, −3; (b) C, +2; O, −2;
(c) C, +4; O, −2; (d) N, +3; F, −1

94. (a) Mn, +4; O, −2; (b) Ba, +2; Cr, +6; O, −2;
(c) H, +1; S, +4; O, −2; (d) Ca, +2; P, +5; O, −2

96. (a) Bi, +3; O, −2; (b) P, +5; O, −2;
(c) N, +3; O, −2; (d) Hg, +1

98. (a) oxygen is oxidized, chlorine is reduced; (b) germanium is oxidized, oxygen is reduced; (c) carbon is oxidized, chlorine is reduced; (d) oxygen is oxidized, fluorine is reduced

100. (a) $SiO_2(s) + 4H^+(aq) + 4e^- \rightarrow Si(s) + 2H_2O(l)$;
(b) $S(s) + 2H^+(aq) + 2e^- \rightarrow H_2S(g)$;
(c) $NO_3^-(aq) + 3H^+(aq) + 2e^- \rightarrow HNO_2(aq) + H_2O(l)$;
(d) $NO_3^-(aq) + 4H^+(aq) + 3e^- \rightarrow NO(g) + 2H_2O(l)$

102. (a) $16H^+(aq) + 2MnO_4^-(aq) + 5C_2O_4^{2-}(aq) \rightarrow 2Mn^{2+}(aq) + 8H_2O(l) + 10CO_2(g)$; (b) $8H^+(aq) + MnO_4^-(aq) + 5Fe^{2+}(aq) \rightarrow Mn^{2+}(aq) + 4H_2O(l) + 5Fe^{3+}(aq)$;
(c) $16H^+(aq) + 2MnO_4^-(aq) + 10Cl^-(aq) \rightarrow 2Mn^{2+}(aq) + 8H_2O(l) + 5Cl_2(g)$

104. A galvanic cell is a battery. A spontaneous oxidation–reduction reaction is separated physically into the two half-reactions, and the electrons being transferred between the two half-cells are made available as an electric current.

Chapter 19

2. The radius of a typical atomic nucleus is on the order of 10^{-13} cm, which is roughly 100,000 times smaller than the radius of an atom overall.
4. The mass number represents the total number of protons and neutrons in a nucleus.
6. The atomic number (Z) is written as a left subscript, while the mass number (A) is written as a left superscript. That is, the general symbol for a nuclide is ${}^{A}_{Z}X$. As an example, consider the isotope of oxygen with 8 protons and 8 neutrons: its symbol would be ${}^{16}_{8}O$.
8. electron
10. Emission of a neutron, ${}^{1}_{0}n$, does not change the atomic number of the parent nucleus, but it causes the mass number of the parent nucleus to decrease by one unit.
12. Gamma rays are high-energy photons of electromagnetic radiation; they are not normally considered to be particles. When a nucleus produces only gamma radiation, the atomic number and mass number of the nucleus do not change.
14. Electron capture occurs when one of the inner-orbital electrons is pulled into, and becomes part of, the nucleus.
16. The fact that the average atomic mass of potassium is only slightly above 39 amu reflects the fact that the isotope of mass number 39 predominates.

Isotope	Number of Neutrons
${}^{39}_{19}K$	20 neutrons
${}^{40}_{19}K$	21 neutrons
${}^{41}_{19}K$	22 neutrons

18. Based on the predominance of Mg-24, but with significant amounts of the other isotopes, one would expect the average atomic molar mass to be slightly higher than 24 (24.31 g).
20. (a) electron; (b) positron; (c) neutron; (d) proton
22. (a) ${}^{23}_{12}Mg$; (b) ${}^{5}_{3}Li$; (c) ${}^{4}_{2}He$
24. (a) ${}^{218}_{86}Rn$; (b) ${}^{0}_{1}e$ (positron); (c) ${}^{137}_{56}Ba$
26. (a) ${}^{234}_{92}U \rightarrow {}^{4}_{2}He + {}^{230}_{90}Th$; (b) ${}^{222}_{86}Rn \rightarrow {}^{4}_{2}He + {}^{218}_{84}Po$; (c) ${}^{162}_{75}Re \rightarrow {}^{4}_{2}He + {}^{158}_{73}Ta$
28. (a) ${}^{212}_{82}Pb \rightarrow {}^{0}_{-1}e + {}^{212}_{83}Bi$; (b) ${}^{212}_{81}Tl \rightarrow {}^{0}_{-1}e + {}^{212}_{82}Pb$; (c) ${}^{228}_{88}Ra \rightarrow {}^{0}_{-1}e + {}^{228}_{89}Ac$
30. In a nuclear bombardment process, a target nucleus is bombarded with high-energy particles (typically subatomic particles or small atoms) from a particle accelerator. This may result in the transmutation of the target nucleus into some other element. For example, nitrogen-14 may be transmuted into oxygen-17 by bombardment with α particles.
32. ${}^{24}_{12}Mg + {}^{2}_{1}H \rightarrow {}^{22}_{11}Na + {}^{4}_{2}He$
34. The half-life of a nucleus is the time required for one-half of the original sample of nuclei to decay. A given isotope of an element always has the same half-life, although different isotopes of the same element may have greatly different half-lives. Nuclei of different elements have different half-lives.
36. ${}^{226}_{88}Ra$ is the most stable (longest half-life); ${}^{224}_{88}Ra$ is the "hottest" (shortest half-life).
38. With a half-life of 2.6 hours, strontium-87 is the hottest; with a half-life of 45.1 days, iron-59 is the most stable to decay.
40. Four half-lives; 1/16 (0.5^4) remains
42. For an administered dose of 100 μg, 0.39 μg remains after 2 days. The fraction remaining is 0.39/100 = 0.0039; on a percentage basis, less than 0.4% of the original radioisotope remains.
44. Carbon-14 is produced in the upper atmosphere by the bombardment of nitrogen with neutrons from space:

$$ {}^{14}_{7}N + {}^{1}_{0}n \rightarrow {}^{14}_{6}C + {}^{1}_{1}H $$

46. We assume that the concentration of C-14 in the atmosphere is effectively constant. A living organism is constantly replenishing C-14 through the processes of either metabolism (sugars ingested in foods contain C-14) or photosynthesis (carbon dioxide contains C-14). When a plant dies, it no longer replenishes itself with C-14 from the atmosphere. As the C-14 undergoes radioactive decay, its amount decreases with time.
48. 1 day is about 13 half-lives for ${}^{18}_{9}F$. If we begin with 6.02×10^{23} atoms (1 mol), then after 13 half-lives, 7.4×10^{19} atoms of ${}^{18}_{9}F$ will remain.
50. fission, fusion, fusion, fission
52. ${}^{1}_{0}n + {}^{235}_{92}U \rightarrow {}^{142}_{56}Ba + {}^{91}_{36}Kr + 3{}^{1}_{0}n$
54. A critical mass of a fissionable material is the amount needed to provide a high enough internal neutron flux to sustain the chain reaction (production of enough neutrons to cause the continuous fission of further material). A sample with less than a critical mass is still radioactive, but cannot sustain a chain reaction.
56. An actual nuclear explosion, of the type produced by a nuclear weapon, cannot occur in a nuclear reactor because the concentration of the fissionable materials is not sufficient to form a supercritical mass.
58. Some advantages are that the fuel is available domestically, is relatively "clean," and does not produce the greenhouse gases that fossil fuel plants produce. Some disadvantages are safety, waste disposal, and cost.
60. In one type of fusion reactor, two ${}^{2}_{1}H$ atoms fuse to produce ${}^{4}_{2}He$. Because the hydrogen nuclei are positively charged, extremely high energies (temperatures of 40 million K) are needed to overcome the repulsion between the nuclei as they are shot into each other.
62. protons (hydrogen), helium
64. Somatic damage is damage directly to the organism itself, causing nearly immediate sickness or death to the organism. Genetic damage is damage to the genetic machinery of the organism, which will be manifested in future generations of offspring.
66. Gamma rays penetrate long distances, but seldom cause ionization of biological molecules. Because they are much heavier, although less penetrating, alpha particles ionize biological molecules very effectively and leave a dense trail of damage in the organism. Isotopes that decay by releasing alpha particles can be ingested or breathed into the body, where the damage from the alpha particles will be more acute.
68. Most reactor waste is still in "temporary" storage. Various suggestions have been made for a more permanent solution, such as casting the spent fuel into glass bricks to contain it and then storing the bricks in corrosion-proof metal containers deep underground.
70. radioactive
72. mass
74. neutron; proton
76. radioactive decay
78. mass number
80. transuranium
82. half-life

84. radiotracers
86. chain
88. breeder
90. 4.5×10^9 dollars (\$4.5 billion)
92. 3.5×10^{-11} J/atom; 8.9×10^{10} J/g
94. $^{90}_{40}Zr$, $^{91}_{40}Zr$, $^{92}_{40}Zr$, $^{94}_{40}Zr$, $^{96}_{40}Zr$
96. $^{27}_{13}Al$: 13 protons, 14 neutrons; $^{28}_{13}Al$: 13 protons, 15 neutrons; $^{29}_{13}Al$: 13 protons, 16 neutrons
98. (a) $^{0}_{-1}e$; (b) $^{74}_{34}Se$; (c) $^{240}_{92}U$
100. $^{9}_{4}Be + ^{4}_{2}He \rightarrow ^{12}_{6}C + ^{1}_{0}n$
102. $^{238}_{92}U + ^{1}_{0}n \rightarrow ^{239}_{92}U$;
$^{239}_{92}U \rightarrow ^{239}_{93}Np + ^{0}_{-1}e$;
$^{239}_{93}Np \rightarrow ^{239}_{94}Pu + ^{0}_{-1}e$

Chapter 20

2. Carbon has four valence electrons and can only make four bonds.
4. A triple bond represents the sharing of three pairs of electrons between two bonded atoms. The sharing of three pairs imparts a linear geometry in the region of the triple bond.
6. $\ddot{\underset{..}{O}}=C=\ddot{\underset{..}{O}}$; $:C\equiv O:$
8. a and c
10. In an alkane, carbons atoms make four separate bonds to adjacent atoms, with these bonds having the tetrahedral arrangement predicted by the VSEPR theory. With bond angles on the order of 109.5°, the molecule cannot be linear (180°).
12. (a) 10; (b) 14; (c) 28; (d) 36
14. (a) $CH_3—CH_2—CH_2—CH_2—CH_3$;
(b) $CH_3—CH_2—CH_2—CH_2—CH_2—CH_2—CH_2—CH_2—CH_2—CH_2—CH_3$;
(c) $CH_3—CH_2—CH_2—CH_2—CH_2—CH_2—CH_2—CH_2—CH_3$;
(d) $CH_3—CH_2—CH_2—CH_2—CH_2—CH_2—CH_3$
16. A branched alkane contains one or more shorter carbon-atom chains attached to the side of the main (longest) carbon-atom chain. The simplest branched alkane is 2-methylpropane,

```
CH3—CH—CH3
     |
    CH3
```

18. carbon skeletons are shown:

```
    C
    |
C—C—C—C        C—C—C—C—C      C—C—C—C—C
    |                |              |
    C                C              C

C—C—C—C—C—C         C  C
                    |  |
                  C—C—C—C
```

20. The root name is derived from the number of carbon atoms in the *longest continuous chain* of carbon atoms.
22. The numbers indicate to which carbon atom of the longest continuous chain the substituents are attached. The longest continuous chain is numbered from the end closest to the first substituent so as to give the lowest possible numbers.
24. Multiple substituents are listed in alphabetical order, disregarding any prefix.
26. (a) 2,3,4-trimethylpentane; (b) 2,3-dimethylpentane; (c) 3,4-dimethylhexane; (d) 4,5-dimethyloctane
28. (a)

```
      CH3
      |
CH3—C—CH2—CH—CH2—CH2—CH3;
      |         |
      CH3       CH3
```

(b)

```
              CH3
              |
CH3—CH—CH—CH—CH2—CH2—CH3;
      |       |
      CH3     CH3
```

(c)

```
              CH3
              |
CH3—CH2—C——CH—CH2—CH2—CH3;
              |     |
              CH3 CH3
```

(d)

```
       CH3          CH3
       |            |
CH3—CH—CH2—C—CH2—CH2—CH3;
                    |
                    CH3
```

30.

Number of C Atoms	Use
$C_5–C_{12}$	gasoline
$C_{10}–C_{18}$	kerosene, jet fuel
$C_{15}–C_{25}$	diesel fuel, heating oil
$>C_{25}$	asphalt

32. Tetraethyl lead was added to gasoline to prevent "knocking" of high-efficiency automobile engines. Its use is being discontinued because of the danger to the environment from the lead in this substance.
34. Combustion reactions are used as a source of heat and light: $C_3H_8(g) + 5O_2(g) \rightarrow 3CO_2(g) + 4H_2O(g)$
36. A double bond is introduced; example depends on student choice.
38. (a) $2C_6H_{14}(l) + 19O_2(g) \rightarrow 12CO_2(g) + 14H_2O(g)$;
(b) $CH_4(g) + Cl_2(g) \rightarrow CH_3Cl(l) + HCl(g)$;
(c) $CHCl_3(l) + Cl_2(g) \rightarrow CCl_4(l) + HCl(g)$
40. An alkyne is a hydrocarbon containing a carbon–carbon triple bond. The general formula is C_nH_{2n-2}.
42. The location of a double or triple bond in the longest chain of an alkene or alkyne is indicated by giving the *number* of the lowest-number carbon atom involved in the bond.
44. Hydrogenation converts unsaturated compounds to saturated (or less unsaturated) compounds. In the case of a liquid vegetable oil, this is likely to convert the oil to a solid. $C_2H_4(g) + H_2(g) \rightarrow C_2H_6(g)$
46. (a) 3,4-dimethyl-5,5-dichloro-1-pentene; (b) 4,5-dichloro-2-hexene; (c) 2,2,5-trimethyl-3-heptene; (d) 5-methyl-1-hexyne
48. The carbon skeletons are

```
C≡C—C—C—C—C

C≡C—C—C—C
      |
      C

C—C≡C—C—C—C

C—C—C≡C—C—C

C—C≡C—C—C
        |
        C

      C
      |
C≡C—C—C
      |
      C

C≡C—C—C—C
        |
        C
```

50. For benzene, a *set* of equivalent Lewis structures can be drawn, with each structure differing only in the location of the three double bonds in the ring. Experimentally, benzene does not demonstrate the chemical properties expected for molecules having *any* double bonds.

52. When named as a substituent, the benzene ring is called the phenyl group. Two examples are

$CH_2{=}CH{-}CH(C_6H_5){-}CH_3$

3-phenyl-1-butene

$CH_3{-}CH(C_6H_5){-}CH_2{-}CH_2{-}CH_2{-}CH_3$

2-phenylhexane

54. *ortho*-: adjacent substituents (1,2-); *meta*-: two substituents with one unsubstituted carbon atom between them (1,3-); *para*-: two substituents with two unsubstituted carbon atoms between them (1,4-)

56. (a) 3,4-dibromo-1-methylbenzene, 3,4-dibromotoluene; (b) naphthalene; (c) 3-methylphenol; 3-hydroxytoluene; (d) 1,4-dinitrobenzene, *p*-dinitrobenzene

58. (a) carboxylic acid; (b) aldehyde; (c) ketone; (d) alcohol

60. Primary alcohols have one hydrocarbon fragment (alkyl group) bonded to the carbon atom where the —OH group is attached. Secondary alcohols have two alkyl groups attached, and tertiary alcohols contain three alkyl groups. Examples are

ethanol (primary) $CH_3{-}CH_2{-}OH$

2-propanol (secondary) $CH_3{-}CH(OH){-}CH_3$

2-methyl-2-propanol (tertiary) $CH_3{-}C(CH_3)(OH){-}CH_3$

62. Structures depend on student choice. $CH_3{-}CH_2{-}CH_2OH$ (1°), $CH_3{-}CH(OH){-}CH_3$ (2°), and $CH_3{-}C(CH_3)(OH){-}CH_3$ (3°) are good examples.

64. $C_6H_{12}O_6 \xrightarrow{\text{yeast}} 2CH_3{-}CH_2{-}OH + 2CO_2$

The yeast necessary for the fermentation process are killed if the concentration of ethanol is greater than 13%. More concentrated ethanol solutions are most commonly made by distillation.

66. Methanol (CH_3OH): starting material for synthesis of acetic acid and many plastics; ethylene glycol ($CH_2OH{-}CH_2OH$): automobile antifreeze; isopropyl alcohol (2-propanol, $CH_3{-}CH(OH){-}CH_3$): rubbing alcohol

68. Both aldehydes and ketones contain the carbonyl group (C=O). Aldehydes and ketones differ in the *location* of the carbonyl function: aldehydes contain the carbonyl group at the end of a hydrocarbon chain (the carbon atom of the carbonyl group is bonded to a maximum of one other carbon atom); the carbonyl group of ketones represents one of the interior carbon atoms of a chain (the carbon atom of the carbonyl group is bonded to two other carbon atoms).

70. Answer depends on student choice of alcohols.

72. In addition to their systematic names (based on the hydrocarbon root, with the ending *-one*), ketones can be named based on the groups attached to either side of the carbonyl carbon as alkyl groups, followed by the word *ketone.*

methyl ethyl ketone (or 2-butanone) $CH_3{-}C({=}O){-}CH_2{-}CH_3$

diethyl ketone (or 3-pentanone) $CH_3{-}CH_2{-}C({=}O){-}CH_2{-}CH_3$

74. (a) $CH_3{-}C({=}O){-}CH_3$;
(b) $CH_3{-}C({=}O){-}CH(CH_3){-}CH_3$;
(c) $CH_3{-}CH_2{-}C({=}O){-}H$;
(d) $CH_3{-}C(CH_3)_2{-}C({=}O){-}CH_2{-}CH_3$;

76. Carboxylic acids are typically *weak* acids.
$CH_3{-}CH_2{-}COOH + H_2O \rightleftharpoons CH_3{-}CH_2{-}COO^- + H_3O^+$

78. (a) $CH_3{-}CH_2{-}CH_2{-}CHO$;
(b) $CH_3{-}CH_2{-}COOH$;
(c) $CH_3{-}CH_2{-}CH_2{-}C({=}O){-}O{-}CH_2{-}CH_2{-}CH_3$

80. $C_6H_4(COOH)(OH) + HO{-}C({=}O){-}CH_3 \longrightarrow C_6H_4(COOH)(O{-}C({=}O){-}CH_3) + H_2O$

82. (a) $CH_3{-}CH_2{-}CH_2{-}C({=}O){-}O{-}CH_3$;
(b) $CH_3{-}C({=}O){-}O{-}CH_2{-}CH_3$;
(c) $C_6H_4(COOH)(Cl)$ (ortho-chlorobenzoic acid, COOH and Cl adjacent)
(d) $CH_3{-}CH(Cl){-}C(CH_3)_2{-}COOH$

84. In addition polymerization, the monomer units add together to form the polymer, with no other products. Polyethylene and polytetrafluoroethylene (Teflon) are examples.

86. Kevlar is a copolymer, as two different types of monomers combine to generate the polymer chain.

88. nylon $\left({-}N(H){+}CH_2{+}_6N(H){-}C({=}O){+}CH_2{+}_6C({=}O){-}\right)$

Dacron $\left({-}O{-}CH_2{-}CH_2{-}O{-}C({=}O){-}C_6H_4{-}C({=}O){-}\right)$

90. unsaturated
92. straight-chain or normal
94. *-ane*
96. number
98. antiknocking
100. substitution
102. hydrogenation
104. functional
106. carbon monoxide
108. carbonyl

110. carboxyl

112. addition

114. Structures depend on student choices.

116. (a) 2-chlorobutane; (b) 1,2-dibromoethane; (c) triiodomethane (common name: iodoform); (d) 2,3,4-trichloropentane; (e) 2,2-dichloro-4-isopropylheptane

118.

```
(a) CH3—CH—CH—CH2—CH2—CH2—CH3
        |   |
       CH3 CH3

                                      CH3
                                       |
(b) CH3—CH2—CH2—CH2—CH2—CH—C—CH3—OH
                          |  |
                         Cl  CH3

(c) CH3—CH2—CH2—CH2—C=CH2
                    |
                    Cl

(d) CH3—CH2—CH2—CH=CH—CH2—Cl
```

(e) benzene ring bearing OH and CH_3 on adjacent carbons

120.

```
primary    CH3—CH2—CH2—CH2—CH2—CH2—OH;

secondary  CH3—CH2—CH2—CH2—CH—CH3;
                               |
                               OH

                    CH3
                     |
tertiary  CH3—CH2—C—CH2—CH3
                     |
                     OH
```

(there are other possibilities)

122.

```
CH2—CH—CH—CH—CH—C=O
|   |   |   |   |   |
OH  OH  OH  OH  OH  H
```

124.

```
(a) CH3—C—CH2—CH2—CH2—CH2—CH3
        ||
        O

(b) CH3—CH2—CH—CH2—C=O
             |       |
            CH3      H

(c) CH3—CH2—CH2—CH—CH2—OH
                 |
                CH3

(d) CH2—CH—CH2
    |   |   |
    OH  OH  OH

(e) CH3—CH—C—CH2—CH2—CH3
         |  ||
        CH3 O
```

126.

```
     HO—C=O
        |
CH3—CH—N—H + HO—C=O →
        |        |
        H        CH2—NH2

     HO—C=O
        |
CH3—CH—N—C=O + H2O
        |  |
        H  CH2—NH2
```

One end has —NH_2, which can react with the —COOH end of another of these dipeptides.

128.

```
(a)    H  H  H  H  H  H  H  H
       |  |  |  |  |  |  |  |
    H—C—C—C—C—C—C—C—C—H
       |  |  |  |  |  |  |  |
       H  H  H  H  H  H  H  H
```

octane, $CH_3CH_2CH_2CH_2CH_2CH_2CH_2CH_3$

```
(b)    H  H  H  H  H  H
       |  |  |  |  |  |
    H—C—C—C—C—C—C—H
       |  |  |  |  |  |
       H  H  H  H  H  H
```

hexane, $CH_3CH_2CH_2CH_2CH_2CH_3$

```
(c)    H  H  H  H
       |  |  |  |
    H—C—C—C—C—H
       |  |  |  |
       H  H  H  H
```

butane, $CH_3CH_2CH_2CH_3$

```
(d)    H  H  H  H  H
       |  |  |  |  |
    H—C—C—C—C—C—H
       |  |  |  |  |
       H  H  H  H  H
```

pentane, $CH_3CH_2CH_2CH_2CH_3$

130. (a) 2,3-dimethylbutane; (b) 3,3-diethylpentane; (c) 2,3,3-trimethylhexane; (d) 2,3,4,5,6-pentamethylheptane

132. (a) $CH_3Cl(g)$; (b) $H_2(g)$; (c) $HCl(g)$

134. CH≡C—CH_2—CH_2—CH_2—CH_2—CH_2—CH_3, 1-octyne; CH_3—C≡C—CH_2—CH_2—CH_2—CH_2—CH_3, 2-octyne; CH_3—CH_2—C≡C—CH_2—CH_2—CH_2—CH_3, 3-octyne; CH_3—CH_2—CH_2—C≡C—CH_2—CH_2—CH_3, 4-octyne

136. (a) carboxylic acid; (b) ketone; (c) ester; (d) alcohol (phenol)

138. (a) 3-methylpentanal

```
CH3—CH2—CH—CH2—C=O
         |       |
        CH3      H
```

(b) 3-methyl-2-pentanone

```
CH3—CH2—CH—C—CH3
         |  ||
        CH3 O
```

(c) methyl phenyl ketone

```
CH3—C—C6H5 (benzene ring)
    ||
    O
```

(d) 2-hydroxybutanal

```
CH3—CH2—CH—C=O
         |  |
         OH H
```

(e) propanal

```
CH3—CH2—C=O
         |
         H
```

140.

```
(a) CH3—CH—CH2—COOH
         |
        CH3
```

(b) benzene ring bearing —C(=O)—OH and —Cl on adjacent carbons

(c) CH_3—CH_2—CH_2—CH_2—CH_2—COOH

(d) CH_3—COOH

Chapter 21

2. Trace elements are those elements present in the body in only very small amounts but which are essential to many biochemical processes in the body.

4. Fibrous proteins provide structural integrity and strength for many types of tissue and are the main components of muscle, hair, and cartilage. Globular proteins are the "worker" molecules of the body, performing functions such as transporting oxygen throughout the body, catalyzing many of the reactions in the body, fighting infections, and transporting electrons during the metabolism of nutrients.

6. All α-amino acids have the general structure

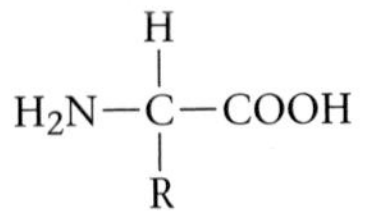

$$H_2N-\underset{R}{\overset{H}{\underset{|}{\overset{|}{C}}}}-COOH$$

The essential amino acids used by the body to construct proteins differ in the structure of the "R group." Figure 21-2 shows the essential amino acids and their specific R groups. Some amino acids contain R groups that are nonpolar in nature, while other amino acids contain R groups that are very polar and that may be capable of hydrogen bonding. Proteins with a preponderance of nonpolar R groups tend to be insoluble in water, while proteins with a high content of polar R groups tend to be soluble in water.

8. Answer depends on student choice of amino acids.
10. six
12. The primary structure of a protein is the specific sequence of amino acids in the peptide chain. Adjacent amino acids are connected to each other by peptide (amide) linkages.
14. Long, thin, resilient proteins (such as hair) typically contain elongated, elastic α-helical protein molecules. Other proteins (such as silk) that form sheets or plates typically contain protein molecules having the beta pleated-sheet secondary structure. Proteins that do not have a structural function in the body (such as hemoglobin) typically have a globular structure.
16. Silk consists of a sheet structure in which the individual chains of amino acids are lined up lengthwise next to each other to form the sheet.
18. A disulfide linkage represents a S—S bond between two sulfur-containing amino acids in a peptide chain. The amino acid cysteine forms such linkages. The presence of disulfide linkages produces bends and folds in the peptide chain and contributes greatly to the tertiary structure of a protein.
20. hemoglobin
22. iron
24. Amino acids contain both a weak-acid and weak-base group, and thus they can neutralize both bases and acids, respectively.
26. A given enzyme typically can react only with a specific molecule—the enzyme's substrate.
28. The lock-and-key model for enzymes indicates that the structures of an enzyme and its substrate must be *complementary*, so that the substrate can approach and attach itself along the length of the enzyme at the enzyme's active sites. A given enzyme is intended to act upon a particular substrate: the substrate attaches itself to the enzyme, is acted upon, and then moves away from the enzyme. If a different molecule has a similar structure to the substrate, this other molecule may also be capable of attaching itself to the enzyme. Because this molecule is not the enzyme's proper substrate, however, the enzyme may not be able to act upon the molecule, and the molecule may remain attached to the enzyme, preventing proper substrate molecules from approaching the enzyme (irreversible inhibition). If the enzyme cannot act upon its proper substrate, then the enzyme is said to be *inhibited*. Irreversible inhibition might be a desirable feature in an antibiotic, which would bind to the enzymes of bacteria and prevent the bacteria from reproducing, thereby preventing or curing an infection.
30. Sugars contain an aldehyde or ketone functional group (carbonyl group), as well as several —OH groups (hydroxyl group).
32. A pentose sugar is a carbohydrate containing five carbon atoms in the chain.

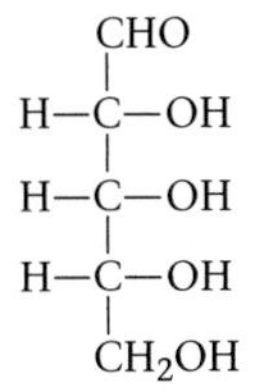

$$\begin{array}{c} CHO \\ | \\ H-C-OH \\ | \\ H-C-OH \\ | \\ H-C-OH \\ | \\ CH_2OH \end{array}$$

34. Starch is the form in which glucose is stored by plants for later use as cellular fuel. Cellulose is used by plants as their major structural component. Although starch and cellulose both are polymers of glucose, the linkage between adjacent glucose units differs in the two polysaccharides. Humans do not possess the enzyme needed to hydrolyze the linkage in cellulose.
36. ribose (aldopentose); arabinose (aldopentose); ribulose (ketopentose); glucose (aldohexose); mannose (aldohexose); galactose (aldohexose); fructose (ketohexose)
38. phosphate
40. uracil (RNA only); cytosine (DNA, RNA); thymine (DNA only); adenine (DNA, RNA); guanine (DNA, RNA)
42. A DNA molecule consists of two chains of nucleotides, with the organic bases on the nucleotides arranged in complementary pairs (cytosine with guanine, adenine with thymine). The structures and properties of the organic bases are such that these pairs fit together well and allow the two chains of nucleotides to form the double-helix structure. When DNA replicates, the double helix unwinds, and then new molecules of the organic bases come in and pair up with their respective partner on the separated nucleotide chains, thereby replicating the original structure. See Figure 21.20.
44. solubility
46. A triglyceride typically consists of a glycerol backbone, to which three separate fatty acid molecules are attached by ester linkages.

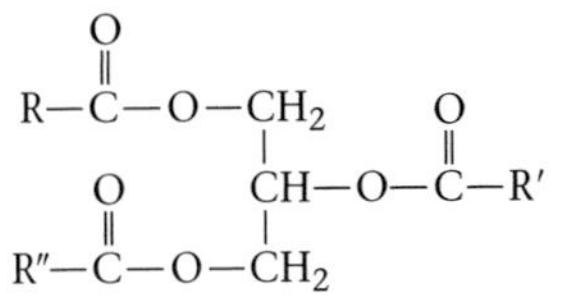

$$\begin{array}{l} R-\overset{O}{\overset{\|}{C}}-O-CH_2 \\ \qquad\qquad\quad | \\ \qquad\qquad\quad CH-O-\overset{O}{\overset{\|}{C}}-R' \\ \qquad\qquad\quad | \\ R''-\overset{O}{\overset{\|}{C}}-O-CH_2 \end{array}$$

48. A soap is the salt of a long-chain organic (fatty) acid.

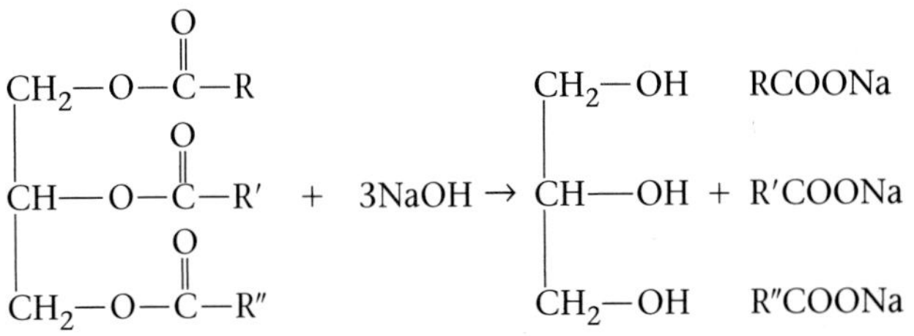

$$\begin{array}{l} CH_2-O-\overset{O}{\overset{\|}{C}}-R \\ | \\ CH-O-\overset{O}{\overset{\|}{C}}-R' \\ | \\ CH_2-O-\overset{O}{\overset{\|}{C}}-R'' \end{array} + 3NaOH \rightarrow \begin{array}{l} CH_2-OH \\ | \\ CH-OH \\ | \\ CH_2-OH \end{array} + \begin{array}{l} RCOONa \\ \\ R'COONa \\ \\ R''COONa \end{array}$$

50. Soaps have both a nonpolar nature (from the long chain of the fatty acid) and an ionic nature (from the charge on the carboxyl group). In water, soap anions form aggregates called micelles, in which the water-repelling hydrocarbon chains are oriented toward the interior of the aggregate, with the ionic, water-attracting carboxyl groups oriented toward the outside. Most dirt has a greasy nature. A soap micelle interacts with a grease molecule, pulling the grease molecule into the hydrocarbon interior of the micelle. When clothing is rinsed, the micelle containing the grease is washed away (see Figures 21.22 and 21.23).
52. Cholesterol is a naturally occurring steroid from which the body synthesizes other needed steroids. Because cholesterol is insoluble in water, having too large a concentration of this substance in the bloodstream may lead to its deposition

and buildup on the walls of blood vessels, causing their eventual blockage.

54. The bile acids are synthesized from cholesterol in the liver and are stored in the gallbladder. Bile acids such as cholic acid act as emulsifying agents for lipids and aid in their digestion.

56. i **58.** m **60.** u **62.** f **64.** g **66.** r

68. p **70.** o **72.** b **74.** d **76.** a

78. nucleotides **80.** ester

82. thymine; guanine **84.** transfer, messenger

86. lipids **88.** unsaturated, saturated

90. ionic, nonpolar

92. fatty

94. progesterone

96. The primary structure of a protein refers to the specific identity and ordering of amino acids in a protein's polypeptide chain. The primary structure is sometimes called the protein's amino acid *sequence*.

98. tendons, bone (with mineral constituents), skin, cartilage, hair, fingernails

100. Proteins contain both acidic (—COOH) and basic ($—NH_2$) groups in their side chains, which can neutralize both acids and bases.

102. pentoses (5 carbons); hexoses (6 carbons); trioses (3 carbons)

104. In a strand of DNA, the phosphate group and the sugar molecule of adjacent nucleotides become bound to each other. The chain portion of the DNA molecule, therefore, consists of alternating phosphate groups and sugar molecules. The nitrogen bases stick out from the side of this phosphate–sugar chain and are bonded to the sugar molecules.

106. Phopholipids are esters of glycerol. Two fatty acids are bonded to the —OH groups of the glycerol backbone, with the third —OH group of glycerol bonded to a phosphate group. Having the two fatty acids, but also the polar phosphate group, makes the phospholipid lecithin a good emulsifying agent.

ANSWERS TO EVEN-NUMBERED CUMULATIVE REVIEW EXERCISES

Chapters 1–3

2. After having covered three chapters in this book, you should have adopted an "active" approach to your study of chemistry. You can't just sit and take notes in class, or just review the solved examples in the textbook. You must learn to *interpret* problems and reduce them to simple mathematical relationships.
4. Some courses, particularly those in your major field, have obvious and immediate utility. Other courses—chemistry included—provide general *background* knowledge that will prove useful in understanding your own major, or other subjects related to your major.
6. Whenever a scientific measurement is made, we always employ the instrument or measuring device to the limits of its precision. This usually means that we *estimate* the last significant figure of the measurement. An example of the uncertainty in the last significant figure is given for measuring the length of a pin in the text in Figure 2.5. Scientists appreciate the limits of experimental techniques and instruments and always *assume* that the last digit in a number representing a measurement has been estimated. Because instruments or measuring devices always have a limit to their precision, uncertainty cannot be completely excluded from measurements.
8. Dimensional analysis is a method of problem solving that pays particular attention to the units of measurements and uses these units as if they were algebraic symbols that multiply, divide, and cancel. Consider the following example: One dozen eggs costs \$1.25. Suppose we want to know how much one egg costs, and also how much three dozen eggs will cost. To solve these problems, we need two equivalence statements:

   1 dozen eggs = 12 eggs

   1 dozen eggs = \$1.25

   The calculations are

   $$\frac{\$1.25}{12\text{ eggs}} = \$0.104 = \$0.10$$

   as the cost of one egg and

   $$\frac{\$1.25}{1\text{ dozen}} \times 3\text{ dozen} = \$3.75$$

   as the cost of three dozen eggs. See Section 2.6 of the text for how we construct conversion factors from equivalence statements.
10. Scientists say that matter is anything that "has mass and occupies space." Matter is the "stuff" of which everything is made. It can be classified and subdivided in many ways, depending on what we are trying to demonstrate. All the types of matter we have studied are made of atoms. They differ in whether these atoms are all of one element, or are of more than one element, and also in whether these atoms are in physical mixtures or chemical combinations.
    Matter can also be classified according to its physical state (solid, liquid, or gas). In addition, it can be classified as a pure substance (one type of molecule) or a mixture (more than one type of molecule).
12. An element is a fundamental substance that cannot be broken down into simpler substances by chemical methods. An element consists of atoms of only one type. Compounds, on the other hand, *can* be broken down into simpler substances. For example, both sulfur and oxygen are *elements*. When sulfur and oxygen are placed together and heated, the *compound* sulfur dioxide (SO_2) forms. Each molecule of sulfur dioxide contains one sulfur atom and two oxygen atoms. On a mass basis, SO_2 always consists of 50% each, by mass, sulfur and oxygen—that is, sulfur dioxide has a constant composition. Sulfur dioxide from any source would have the same composition (or it wouldn't be sulfur dioxide!).
14. (a) 8.917×10^{-4}; (b) 0.0002795; (c) 4913; (d) 8.51×10^{7}; (e) 1.219×10^{2}; (f) 3.396×10^{-9}
16. (a) two; (b) two; (c) three; (d) three; (e) one; (f) two; (g) two; (h) three
18. (a) 0.785 g/mL; (b) 2.03 L; (c) 1.06 kg; (d) 9.33 cm^3; (e) 2.0×10^2 g

Chapters 4–5

2. Although you don't have to memorize all the elements, you should at least be able to give the symbol or name for the most common elements (listed in Table 4.3).
4. The main postulates of Dalton's theory are: (1) elements are made up of tiny particles called atoms; (2) all atoms of a given element are identical; (3) although all atoms of a given element are identical, these atoms are different from the atoms of all other elements; (4) atoms of one element can combine with atoms of another element to form a compound that will always have the same relative numbers and types of atoms for its composition; and (5) atoms are merely rearranged into new groupings during an ordinary chemical reaction, and no atom is ever destroyed and no new atom is ever created during such a reaction.
6. The expression "nuclear atom" indicates that the atom has a dense center of positive charge (nucleus) around which the electrons move through primarily empty space. Rutherford's experiment involved shooting a beam of α particles at a thin sheet of metal foil. According to the "plum pudding" model of the atom, these positively charged α particles should have passed through the foil. Rutherford detected that a small number of α particles bounced backward to the source of α particles or were deflected from the foil at large angles. Rutherford realized that his observations could be explained if the atoms of the metal foil had a small, dense, positively charged nucleus, with a significant amount of empty space between nuclei. The empty space between nuclei would allow most of the α particles to pass through the foil. If an α particle were to hit a nucleus head-on, it would be deflected backward. If a positively charged α particle passed *near* a positively charged nucleus, then the α particle would be deflected by the repulsive forces. Rutherford's experiment disproved the "plum pudding" model, which envisioned the atom as a uniform sphere of positive charge, with enough negatively charged electrons scattered throughout to balance out the positive charge.
8. Isotopes represent atoms of the same element that have different atomic masses. Isotopes result from the different numbers of neutrons in the nuclei of atoms of a given element. They have the same atomic number (number of protons in the nucleus) but have different mass numbers (total number of protons and neutrons in the nucleus). The different isotopes of an atom are indicated by the form $^{A}_{Z}X$, in which Z

represents the atomic number and *A* the mass number of element X. For example, ${}^{13}_{6}C$ represents a nuclide of carbon with atomic number 6 (6 protons in the nucleus) and mass number 13 (6 protons plus 7 neutrons in the nucleus). The various isotopes of an element have identical *chemical* properties. The *physical* properties of the isotopes of an element may differ slightly because of the small difference in mass.

10. Most elements are too reactive to be found in nature in other than the combined form. Gold, silver, platinum, and some of the gaseous elements (such as O_2, N_2, He, and Ar) are found in the elemental form.

12. Ionic compounds typically are hard, crystalline solids with high melting and boiling points. The ability of aqueous solutions of ionic substances to conduct electricity means that ionic substances consist of positively and negatively charged particles (ions). A sample of an ionic substance has no net electrical charge because the total number of positive charges is *balanced* by an equal number of negative charges. An ionic compound could not consist of only cations or only anions because a net charge of zero cannot be obtained when all ions have the same charge. Also, ions of like charge will repel each other.

14. When naming ionic compounds, the positive ion (cation) is named first. For simple binary Type I ionic compounds, the ending *-ide* is added to the root name of the negative ion (anion). For example, the name for K_2S would be "potassium sulfide"—potassium is the cation, sulfide is the anion. Type II compounds, which involve elements that form more than one stable ion, are named by either of two systems: the Roman numeral system (which is preferred by most chemists) and the *-ous/-ic* system. For example, iron can react with oxygen to form either of two stable oxides, FeO or Fe_2O_3. Under the Roman numeral system, FeO would be named iron(II) oxide to show that it contains Fe^{2+} ions; Fe_2O_3 would be named iron(III) oxide to indicate that it contains Fe^{3+} ions. Under the *-ous/-ic* system, FeO is named ferr*ous* oxide and Fe_2O_3 is called ferr*ic* oxide. Type II compounds usually involve transition metals and nonmetals.

16. A polyatomic ion is an ion containing more than one atom. Some common polyatomic ions are listed in Table 5.4. Parentheses are used in writing formulas containing polyatomic ions to indicate how many polyatomic ions are present. For example, the correct formula for calcium phosphate is $Ca_3(PO_4)_2$, which indicates that three calcium ions are combined for every two phosphate ions. If we did *not* write the parentheses around the formula for the phosphate ion (that is, if we wrote Ca_3PO_{42}), people might think that 42 oxygen atoms were present!

18. Acids are substances that produce protons (H^+ ions) when dissolved in water. For acids that do *not* contain oxygen, the prefix *hydro-* and the suffix *-ic* are used with the root name of the element present in the acid (for example: HCl, *hydro*chloric acid; H_2S, *hydro*sulfuric acid; HF, *hydro*fluoric acid). For acids whose anions contain oxygen, a series of prefixes and suffixes is used with the name of the central atom in the anion: these prefixes and suffixes indicate the relative (not actual) number of oxygen atoms present in the anion. Most elements that form oxyanions form *two* such anions—for example, sulfur forms sulf*ite* ion (SO_3^{2-}) and sulf*ate* ion (SO_4^{2-}). For an element that forms two oxyanions, the acid containing the anions will have the ending *-ous* if the *-ite* anion is involved and the ending *-ic* if the *-ate* anion is present. For example, H_2SO_3 is sulfur*ous* acid and H_2SO_4 is sulfur*ic* acid. The Group 7 elements each form *four* oxyanions/oxyacids. The prefix *hypo-* is used for the oxyacid that contains fewer oxygen atoms than the *-ite* anion, and the prefix *per-* is used for the oxyacid that contains more oxygen atoms than the *-ate* anion. For example,

Acid	Name	Anion	Name
HBrO	*hypo*brom*ous* acid	BrO^-	hypobromite
$HBrO_2$	brom*ous* acid	BrO_2^-	bromite
$HBrO_3$	brom*ic* acid	BrO_3^-	bromate
$HBrO_4$	*per*brom*ic* acid	BrO_4^-	perbromate

20. Elements in the same family have the same electron configuration and tend to undergo similar chemical reactions with other groups. For example, Li, Na, K, Rb, and Cs all react with elemental chlorine gas, Cl_2, to form an ionic compound of general formula M^+Cl^-.

22. (a) 8, 8, 9; (b) 92, 92, 143; (c) 17, 17, 20; (d) 1, 1, 2; (e) 2, 2, 2; (f) 50, 50, 69; (g) 54, 54, 70; h) 30, 30, 34

24. (a) 12 protons, 10 electrons; (b) 26 protons, 24 electrons; (c) 26 protons, 23 electrons; (d) 9 protons, 10 electrons; (e) 28 protons, 26 electrons; (f) 30 protons; 28 electrons; (g) 27 protons, 24 electrons; (h) 7 protons, 10 electrons; (i) 16 protons, 18 electrons; (j) 37 protons, 36 electrons; (k) 34 protons, 36 electrons; (l) 19 protons, 18 electrons

26. (a) CuI; (b) $CoCl_2$; (c) Ag_2S; (d) Hg_2Br_2; (e) HgO; (f) Cr_2S_3; (g) PbO_2; (h) K_3N; (i) SnF_2; (j) Fe_2O_3

28. (a) NH_4^+, ammonium ion; (b) SO_3^{2-}, sulfite ion; (c) NO_3^-, nitrate ion; (d) SO_4^{2-}, sulfate ion; (e) NO_2^-, nitrite ion; (f) CN^-, cyanide ion; (g) OH^-, hydroxide ion; (h) ClO_4^-, perchlorate ion; (i) ClO^-, hypochlorite ion; (j) PO_4^{3-}, phosphate ion

30. (a) xenon dioxide; (b) iodine pentachloride; (c) phosphorus trichloride; (d) carbon monoxide; (e) oxygen diflouride; (f) diphosphorus pentoxide; (g) arsenic triiodide; (h) sulfur trioxide

Chapters 6–7

2. A chemical equation indicates the substances necessary for a given chemical reaction, and the substances produced by that chemical reaction. The substances to the left of the arrow are called the *reactants;* those to the right of the arrow are called the *products*. A *balanced* equation indicates the relative numbers of molecules in the reaction.

4. Never change the *subscripts* of a *formula:* changing the subscripts changes the *identity* of a substance and makes the equation invalid. When balancing a chemical equation, we adjust only the *coefficients* in front of a formula: changing a coefficient changes the *number* of molecules being used in the reaction, *without* changing the *identity* of the substance.

6. A precipitation reaction is one in which a solid is produced when two aqueous solutions are combined. The driving force in such a reaction is the formation of the solid, thus removing ions from the solution. Examples depend on student input.

8. Nearly all compounds containing the nitrate, sodium, potassium, and ammonium ions are soluble in water. Most salts containing the chloride and sulfate ions are soluble in water, with specific exceptions (see Table 7.1). Most compounds containing the hydroxide, sulfide, carbonate, and phosphate ions are *not* soluble in water (unless the compound also contains Na^+, K^+, or NH_4^+). For example, suppose we combine barium chloride and sulfuric acid solutions:

$$BaCl_2(aq) + H_2SO_4(aq) \rightarrow BaSO_4(s) + 2HCl(aq)$$
$$Ba^{2+}(aq) + SO_4^{2-}(aq) \rightarrow BaSO_4(s) \text{ [net ionic reaction]}$$

Because barium sulfate is not soluble in water, a precipitate of $BaSO_4(s)$ forms.

10. Acids (such as the acetic acid found in vinegar) were first noted primarily because of their sour taste, whereas bases were first characterized by their bitter taste and slippery feel on the skin.

Acids and bases neutralize each other, forming water: $H^+(aq) + OH^-(aq) \rightarrow H_2O(l)$. Strong acids and bases ionize *fully* when dissolved in water, which means they are also strong electrolytes.
Strong acids: HCl, HNO_3, and H_2SO_4
Strong bases: Group 1 hydroxides (for example, NaOH and KOH)

12. Oxidation–reduction reactions; oxidation; reduction; No: if one species is going to lose electrons, there must be another species present capable of gaining them; Examples depend on student input.
14. In a synthesis reaction, elements or simple compounds react to produce more complex substances. For example,

$$N_2(g) + 3H_2(g) \rightarrow 2NH_3(g)$$
$$NaOH(aq) + CO_2(g) \rightarrow NaHCO_3(s)$$

Decomposition reactions represent the breakdown of complex substances into simpler substances. For example, $2H_2O_2(aq) \rightarrow 2H_2O(l) + O_2(g)$. Synthesis and decomposition reactions are often oxidation–reduction reactions, although not always. For example, the synthesis reaction between NaOH and CO_2 does *not* represent oxidation–reduction.

16. (a) $C(s) + O_2(g) \rightarrow CO_2(g)$; (b) $2C(s) + O_2(g) \rightarrow 2CO(g)$; (c) $2Li(l) + 2C(s) \rightarrow Li_2C_2(s)$; (d) $FeO(s) + C(s) \rightarrow Fe(l) + CO(g)$; (e) $C(s) + 2F_2(g) \rightarrow CF_4(g)$
18. (a) $Ba(NO_3)_2(aq) + K_2CrO_4(aq) \rightarrow BaCrO_4(s) + 2KNO_3(aq)$; (b) $NaOH(aq) + HC_2H_3O_2(aq) \rightarrow H_2O(l) + NaC_2H_3O_2(aq)$ (then evaporate the water from the solution); (c) $AgNO_3(aq) + NaCl(aq) \rightarrow AgCl(s) + NaNO_3(aq)$; (d) $Pb(NO_3)_2(aq) + H_2SO_4(aq) \rightarrow PbSO_4(s) + 2HNO_3(aq)$; (e) $2NaOH(aq) + H_2SO_4(aq) \rightarrow Na_2SO_4(aq) + 2H_2O(l)$ (then evaporate the water from the solution); (f) $Ba(NO_3)_2(aq) + 2Na_2CO_3(aq) \rightarrow BaCO_3(s) + 2NaNO_3(aq)$
20. (a) $FeO(s) + 2HNO_3(aq) \rightarrow Fe(NO_3)_2(aq) + H_2O(l)$; acid–base; double-displacement; (b) $2Mg(s) + 2CO_2(g) + O_2(g) \rightarrow 2MgCO_3(s)$; synthesis; oxidation–reduction; (c) $2NaOH(s) + CuSO_4(aq) \rightarrow Cu(OH)_5(s) + Na_2SO_4(aq)$; precipitation; double-displacement; (d) $HI(aq) + KOH(aq) \rightarrow KI(aq) + H_2O(l)$; acid–base; double-displacement; (e) $C_3H_8(g) + 5O_2(g) \rightarrow 3CO_2(g) + 4H_2O(g)$; combustion; oxidation–reduction; (f) $Co(NH_3)_6Cl_2(s) \rightarrow CoCl_2(s) + 6NH_3(g)$; decomposition; (g) $2HCl(aq) + Pb(C_2H_3O_2)_2(aq) \rightarrow 2HC_2H_3O_2(aq) + PbCl_2(aq)$; precipitation; double-displacement; (h) $C_{12}H_{22}O_{11}(s) \rightarrow 12C(s) + 11H_2O(g)$; decomposition; oxidation–reduction; (i) $2Al(s) + 6HNO_3(aq) \rightarrow 2Al(NO_3)_3(aq) + 3H_2(g)$; oxidation–reduction; single-displacement; (j) $4B(s) + 3O_2(g) \rightarrow 2B_2O_3(s)$; synthesis; oxidation–reduction
22. Answer will depend on student examples.
24. (a) no reaction (all combinations are soluble)
(b) $Ca^{2+}(aq) + SO_4^{2-}(aq) \rightarrow CaSO_4(s)$
(c) $Pb^{2+}(aq) + S^{2-}(aq) \rightarrow PbS(s)$
(d) $2Fe^{3+}(aq) + 3CO_3^{2-}(aq) \rightarrow Fe_2(CO_3)_3(s)$
(e) $Hg_2^{2+}(aq) + 2Cl^-(aq) \rightarrow Hg_2Cl_2(s)$
(f) $Ag^+(aq) + Cl^-(aq) \rightarrow AgCl(s)$
(g) $3Ca^{2+}(aq) + 2PO_4^{3-}(aq) \rightarrow Ca_3(PO_4)_2(s)$
(h) no reaction (all combinations are soluble)

Chapters 8–9

2. On a microscopic basis, one mole of a substance represents Avogadro's number (6.022×10^{23}) of individual units (atoms or molecules) of the substance. On a macroscopic basis, one mole of a substance represents the amount of substance present when the molar mass of the substance in grams is taken. Chemists have chosen these definitions so that a simple relationship will exist between measurable amounts of substances (grams) and the actual number of atoms or molecules present, and so that the number of particles present in samples of *different* substances can easily be compared.
4. The molar mass of a compound is the mass in grams of one mole of the compound and is calculated by summing the average atomic masses of all the atoms present in a molecule of the compound. For example, for H_3PO_4: molar mass H_3PO_4 = 3(1.008 g) + 1(30.97 g) + 4(16.00 g) = 97.99 g.
6. The *empirical* formula of a compound represents the *relative* number of atoms of each type present in a molecule of the compound, whereas the *molecular* formula represents the *actual* number of atoms of each type present in a real molecule. For example, both acetylene (molecular formula C_2H_2) and benzene (molecular formula C_6H_6) have the same relative number of carbon and hydrogen atoms, and thus have the same empirical formula (CH). The molar mass of the compound must be determined before calculating the actual molecular formula. Since real molecules cannot contain fractional *parts* of atoms, the molecular formula is always a *whole-number multiple* of the empirical formula.
8. Answer depends on student examples chosen for Exercise 7.
10. for O_2: $\frac{5 \text{ mol } O_2}{1 \text{ mol } C_3H_8}$; $0.55 \text{ mol } C_3H_8 \times \frac{5 \text{ mol } O_2}{1 \text{ mol } C_3H_8} =$ 2.8 (2.75) mol O_2
for CO_2: $\frac{3 \text{ mol } CO_2}{1 \text{ mol } C_3H_8}$; $0.55 \text{ mol } C_3H_8 \times \frac{3 \text{ mol } CO_2}{1 \text{ mol } C_3H_8} =$ 1.7 (1.65) mol CO_2
for H_2O: $\frac{4 \text{ mol } H_2O}{1 \text{ mol } C_3H_8}$; $0.55 \text{ mol } C_3H_8 \times \frac{4 \text{ mol } H_2O}{1 \text{ mol } C_3H_8} =$ 2.2 mol H_2O
12. When arbitrary amounts of reactants are used, one reactant will be present, stoichiometrically, in the least amount: this substance is called the *limiting reactant*. It *limits* the amount of product that can form in the experiment, because once this substance has reacted completely, the reaction must *stop*. The other reactants in the experiment are present *in excess*, which means that a portion of these reactants will be present *unchanged* after the reaction ends.
14. The *theoretical yield* for an experiment is the mass of product calculated assuming the limiting reactant for the experiment is completely consumed. The *actual yield* for an experiment is the mass of product actually collected by the experimenter. Any experiment is restricted by the skills of the experimenter and by the inherent limitations of the experimental method: for these reasons, the actual yield is often less than the theoretical yield. Although one would expect that the actual yield should never exceed the theoretical yield, in real experiments, sometimes this happens. However, an actual yield greater than a theoretical yield usually means that something is *wrong* in either the experiment (for example, impurities may be present) or the calculations.
16. (a) 92.26% C; (b) 32.37% Na; (c) 15.77% C; (d) 20.24% Al; (e) 88.82% Cu; (f) 79.89% Cu; (g) 71.06% Co; (h) 40.00% C
18. (a) 53.0 g $SiCl_4$, 3.75 g C; (b) 20.0 g LiOH; (c) 12.8 g NaOH, 2.56 g O_2; (d) 9.84 g Sn, 2.99 g H_2O
20. 11.7 g CO; 18.3 g CO_2

Chapters 10–12

2. Temperature is a measure of the random motions of the components of a substance; in other words, temperature is a measure of the average kinetic energy of the particles in a sample. The molecules in warm water must be moving faster than the molecules in cold water (the molecules have the same

mass, so if the temperature is higher, the average velocity of the particles must be higher in the warm water). Heat is the energy that flows because of a difference in temperature.

4. Thermodynamics is the study of energy and energy changes. The first law of thermodynamics is the law of conservation of energy: the energy of the universe is constant. Energy cannot be created or destroyed, only transferred from one place to another or from one form to another. The internal energy of a system, *E*, represents the total of the kinetic and potential energies of all particles in a system. A flow of heat may be produced when there is a change in internal energy in the system, but it is not correct to say that the system "contains" the heat: part of the internal energy is *converted* to heat energy during the process (under other conditions, the change in internal energy might be expressed as work rather than a heat flow).
6. The enthalpy change represents the heat energy that flows (at constant pressure) on a molar basis when a reaction occurs. The enthalpy change is a state function (which we make great use of in Hess's law calculations). Enthalpy changes are typically measured in insulated reaction vessels called calorimeters (a simple calorimeter is shown in Figure 10.6).
8. Consider petroleum. A gallon of gasoline contains concentrated, stored energy. We can use that energy to make a car move, but when we do, the energy stored in the gasoline is dispersed throughout the environment. Although the energy is still there (it is conserved), it is no longer in a concentrated, useful form. Thus, although the energy content of the universe remains constant, the energy that is now stored in concentrated forms in oil, coal, wood, and other sources is gradually being dispersed to the universe, where it can do no work.
10. A driving force is an effect that tends to make a process occur. Two important driving forces are dispersion of energy during a process or dispersion of matter during a process (energy spread and matter spread). For example, a log burns in a fireplace because the energy contained in the log is dispersed to the universe when it burns. If we put a teaspoon of sugar into a glass of water, the dissolving of the sugar is a favorable process because the matter of the sugar is dispersed when it dissolves. Entropy is a measure of the randomness or disorder in a system. The entropy of the universe is constantly increasing because of matter spread and energy spread. A spontaneous process is one that occurs without outside intervention: the spontaneity of a reaction depends on the energy spread and matter spread if the reaction takes place. A reaction that disperses energy and also disperses matter will always be spontaneous. Reactions that require an input of energy may still be spontaneous if the matter spread is large enough.
12. (a) 464 kJ; (b) 69.3 kJ; (c) 1.40 mol (22.5 g)
14. An atom in its *ground state* is in its lowest possible energy state. When an atom possesses more energy than in its ground state, the atom is in an *excited state*. An atom is promoted from its ground state to an excited state by absorbing energy; when the atom returns from an excited state to its ground state it emits the excess energy as electromagnetic radiation. Atoms do not gain or emit radiation randomly, but rather do so only in discrete bundles of radiation called *photons*. The photons of radiation emitted by atoms are characterized by the wavelength (color) of the radiation: longer-wavelength photons carry less energy than shorter-wavelength photons. The energy of a photon emitted by an atom corresponds *exactly* to the difference in energy between two allowed energy states in an atom.
16. Bohr pictured the electron moving in certain circular orbits around the nucleus, with each orbit being associated with a specific energy (resulting from the attraction between the nucleus and the electron and from the kinetic energy of the electron). Bohr assumed that when an atom absorbs energy, the electron moves from its ground state ($n = 1$) to an orbit farther away from the nucleus ($n = 2, 3, 4, \ldots$). Bohr postulated that when an excited atom returns to its ground state, the atom emits the excess energy as radiation. Because the Bohr orbits are located at fixed distances from the nucleus and from each other, when an electron moves from one fixed orbit to another, the energy change is of a definite amount, which corresponds to the emission of a photon with a particular characteristic wavelength and energy. When the simple Bohr model for the atom was applied to the emission spectra of other elements, however, the theory could not predict or explain the observed emission spectra of these elements.
18. The lowest-energy hydrogen atomic orbital is called the 1*s* orbital. The 1*s* orbital is spherical in shape (the electron density around the nucleus is uniform in all directions). The orbital does *not* have a sharp edge (it appears fuzzy) because the probability of finding the electron gradually decreases as distance from the nucleus increases. The orbital does *not* represent just a spherical surface on which the electron moves (this would be similar to Bohr's original theory)—instead, the 1*s* orbital represents a probability map of electron density around the nucleus for the first principal energy level.
20. The third principal energy level of hydrogen is divided into three sublevels: the 3*s*, 3*p*, and 3*d* sublevels. The 3*s* subshell consists of the single 3*s* orbital, which is spherical in shape. The 3*p* subshell consists of a set of three equal-energy 3*p* orbitals: each of these 3*p* orbitals has the same shape ("dumbbell"), but each of the 3*p* orbitals is oriented in a different direction in space. The 3*d* subshell consists of a set of five 3*d* orbitals with shapes as indicated in Figure 11.28, which are oriented in different directions around the nucleus. The fourth principal energy level of hydrogen is divided into four sublevels: the 4*s*, 4*p*, 4*d*, and 4*f* orbitals. The 4*s* subshell consists of the single 4*s* orbital. The 4*p* subshell consists of a set of three 4*p* orbitals. The 4*d* subshell consists of a set of five 4*d* orbitals. The shapes of the 4*s*, 4*p*, and 4*d* orbitals are the *same* as the shapes of the orbitals of the third principal energy level—the orbitals of the fourth principal energy level are *larger* and *farther from the nucleus* than the orbitals of the third level, however. The fourth principal energy level also contains a 4*f* subshell consisting of seven 4*f* orbitals (the shapes of the 4*f* orbitals are beyond the scope of this text).
22. Atoms have a series of *principal energy levels* indexed by the letter *n*. The $n = 1$ level is closest to the nucleus, and the energies of the levels increase as the value of *n* (and distance from the nucleus) increases. Each principal energy level is divided into *sublevels* (sets of orbitals) of different characteristic shapes designated by the letters *s*, *p*, *d*, and *f*. Each *s* subshell consists of a single *s* orbital; each *p* subshell consists of a set of three *p* orbitals; each *d* subshell consists of a set of five *d* orbitals; and so on. An orbital can be empty or it can contain one or two electrons, but never more than two electrons (if an orbital contains two electrons, then the electrons must have opposite spins). The shape of an orbital represents a probability map for finding electrons—it does not represent a trajectory or pathway for electron movements.
24. The valence electrons are the electrons in an atom's outermost shell. The valence electrons are those most likely to be involved in chemical reactions because they are at the outside edge of the atom.
26. The general periodic table you drew for Question 25 should resemble that found in Figure 11.31. From the column and row location of an element, you should be able to determine its valence configuration. For example, the element in the third horizontal row of the second vertical column has $3s^2$ as its valence configuration. The element in the seventh vertical column of the second horizontal row has valence configuration $2s^22p^5$.

28. The ionization energy of an atom represents the energy required to remove an electron from the atom in the gas phase. Moving from top to bottom in a vertical group on the periodic table, the ionization energies decrease. The ionization energies increase when going from left to right within a horizontal row within the periodic table. The relative sizes of atoms also vary systematically with the location of an element on the periodic table. Within a given vertical group, the atoms become progressively larger when going from the top of the group to the bottom. Moving from left to right within a horizontal row on the periodic table, the atoms become progressively smaller.

30. To form an ionic compound, a metallic element reacts with a nonmetallic element, with the metallic element losing electrons to form a positive ion and the nonmetallic element gaining electrons to form a negative ion. The aggregate form of such a compound consists of a crystal lattice of alternating positively and negatively charged ions: a given positive ion is attracted by surrounding negatively charged ions, and a given negative ion is attracted by surrounding positively charged ions. Similar electrostatic attractions exist in three dimensions throughout the crystal of the ionic solid, leading to a very stable system (with very high melting and boiling points, for example). As evidence for the existence of ionic bonding, ionic solids do not conduct electricity (the ions are rigidly held), but melts or solutions of such substances do conduct electric current. For example, when sodium metal and chlorine gas react, a typical ionic substance (sodium chloride) results: $2Na(s) + Cl_2(g) \rightarrow 2Na^+Cl^-(s)$.

32. Electronegativity represents the relative ability of an atom in a molecule to attract shared electrons to itself. The larger the difference in electronegativity between two atoms joined in a bond, the more polar is the bond. Examples depend on student choice of elements.

34. It has been observed over many, many experiments that when an active metal like sodium or magnesium reacts with a nonmetal, the sodium atoms always form Na^+ ions and the magnesium atoms always form Mg^{2+} ions. It has also been observed that when nonmetallic elements like nitrogen, oxygen, or fluorine form simple ions, the ions are always N^{3-}, O^{2-}, and F^-, respectively. Observing that these elements always form the same ions and those ions all contain eight electrons in the outermost shell, scientists speculated that a species that has an octet of electrons (like the noble gas neon) must be very fundamentally stable. The *repeated* observation that so many elements, when reacting, tend to attain an electron configuration that is isoelectronic with a noble gas led chemists to speculate that *all* elements try to attain such a configuration for their outermost shells. Covalently and polar covalently bonded molecules also strive to attain pseudo–noble gas electron configurations. For a covalently bonded molecule like F_2, each F atom provides one electron of the pair of electrons that constitutes the covalent bond. Each F atom feels also the influence of the other F atom's electron in the shared pair, and each F atom effectively fills its outermost shell.

36. Bonding between atoms to form a molecule involves only the outermost electrons of the atoms, so only these *valence* electrons are shown in the Lewis structures of molecules. The most important requisite for the formation of a stable compound is that each atom of a molecule attain a noble gas electron configuration. In Lewis structures, arrange the bonding and nonbonding valence electrons to try to complete the octet (or duet) for as many atoms as possible.

38. You could choose practically any molecules for your discussion. Let's illustrate the method for ammonia, NH_3. First, count the total number of valence electrons available in the molecule (without regard to their source). For NH_3, since nitrogen is in Group 5, one nitrogen atom would contribute five valence electrons. Since hydrogen atoms have only one electron each, the three hydrogen atoms provide an additional three valence electrons, for a total of eight valence electrons overall. Next, write down the symbols for the atoms in the molecule, and use one pair of electrons (represented by a line) to form a bond between each pair of bound atoms.

```
H—N—H
  |
  H
```

These three bonds use six of the eight valence electrons. Because each hydrogen already has its duet and the nitrogen atom has only six electrons around it so far, the final two valence electrons must represent a lone pair on the nitrogen.

```
  ..
H—N—H
  |
  H
```

40. Boron and beryllium compounds sometimes do not fit the octet rule. For example, in BF_3, the boron atom has only six valence electrons in its outermost shell, whereas in BeF_2, the beryllium atom has only four electrons in its outermost shell. Other exceptions to the octet rule include any molecule with an odd number of valence electrons (such as NO or NO_2).

42.

Number of Valence Pairs	Bond Angle	Examples
2	180°	BeF_2, BeH_2
3	120°	BCl_3
4	109.5°	CH_4, CCl_4, GeF_4

44. (a) $[Kr]5s^2$; (b) $[Ne]3s^23p^1$; (c) $[Ne]3s^23p^5$; (d) $[Ar]4s^1$; (e) $[Ne]3s^23p^4$; (f) $[Ar]4s^23d^{10}4p^3$

46.

```
  ..
H—O—H
  ..
```

4 electron pairs tetrahedrally oriented on O; nonlinear (bent, V-shaped) geometry; H—O—H bond angle slightly less than 109.5° because of lone pairs

```
  ..
H—P—H
  |
  H
```

4 electron pairs tetrahedrally oriented on P; trigonal pyramidal geometry; H—P—H bond angles slightly less than 109.5° because of lone pair

```
      ..
     :Br:
  ..  |  ..
 :Br—C—Br:
  ..  |  ..
     :Br:
      ..
```

4 electron pairs tetrahedrally oriented on C; overall tetrahedral geometry; Br—C—Br bond angles 109.5°

```
      ..
  [  :O:   ]-
  ..  |  ..
  :O—Cl—O:
  ..  |  ..
     :O:
      ..
```

4 electron pairs tetrahedrally oriented on Cl; overall tetrahedral geometry; O—Cl—O bond angles 109.5°

```
 ..
:F
 ..\  ..
    B—F:
 ../  ..
:F
 ..
```

3 electron pairs trigonally oriented on B (exception to octet rule); overall trigonal geometry; F—B—F bond angles 120°

```
 ..     ..
:F—Be—F:
 ..     ..
```

2 electron pairs linearly oriented on Be (exception to octet rule); overall linear geometry; F—Be—F bond angle 180°

Chapters 13–15

2. The pressure of the atmosphere represents the mass of the gases in the atmosphere pressing down on the surface of the earth. The device most commonly used to measure the pres-

sure of the atmosphere is the mercury barometer, shown in Figure 13.2. A simple experiment to demonstrate the pressure of the atmosphere is shown in Figure 13.1.

4. Boyle's law says that the volume of a gas sample will decrease if you squeeze it harder (at constant temperature, for a fixed amount of gas). Two mathematical statements of Boyle's law are

$$P \times V = \text{constant}$$
$$P_1 \times V_1 = P_2 \times V_2$$

These two mathematical formulas say the same thing: if the pressure on a sample of gas is increased, the volume of the sample will decrease. A graph of Boyle's law data is given as Figure 13.5: this type of graph ($xy = k$) is known to mathematicians as a *hyperbola*.

6. Charles's law says that if you heat a sample of gas, the volume of the sample will increase (assuming the pressure and amount of gas remain the same). When the temperature is given in kelvins, Charles's law expresses a *direct* proportionality (if you *in*crease T, then V *in*creases), whereas Boyle's law expresses an *inverse* proportionality (if you *in*crease P, then V *de*creases). Two mathematical statements of Charles's law are $V = bT$ and $(V_1/T_1) = (V_2/T_2)$. With this second formulation, we can determine volume–temperature information for a given gas sample under two sets of conditions. Charles's law holds true only if the amount of gas remains the same (the volume of a gas sample would increase if more gas were present) and also if the pressure remains the same (a change in pressure also changes the volume of a gas sample). A graph of volume versus temperature (at constant pressure) for an ideal gas is a straight line with an intercept at –273 °C (see Figure 13.7).

8. Avogadro's law says that the volume of a sample of gas is directly proportional to the number of moles (or molecules) of gas present (at constant temperature and pressure). Avogadro's law holds true only for gas samples compared under the same conditions of temperature and pressure. Avogadro's law expresses a direct proportionality: the more gas in a sample, the larger the sample's volume.

10. The "partial" pressure of an individual gas in a mixture of gases represents the pressure the gas would exert in the same container at the same temperature if it were the *only* gas present. The *total* pressure in a mixture of gases is the sum of the individual partial pressures of the gases present in the mixture. The fact that the partial pressures of the gases in a mixture are additive suggests that the total pressure in a container is a function of the *number* of molecules present, and not of the identity of the molecules or of any other property (such as the molecules' inherent atomic size).

12. The main postulates of the kinetic molecular theory for gases are: (a) gases consist of tiny particles (atoms or molecules), and the size of these particles themselves is negligible compared with the bulk volume of a gas sample; (b) the particles in a gas are in constant random motion, colliding with each other and with the walls of the container; (c) the particles in a gas sample do not assert any attractive or repulsive forces on one another; and (d) the average kinetic energy of the gas particles is directly related to the absolute temperature of the gas sample. The pressure exerted by a gas results from the molecules colliding with (and pushing on) the walls of the container; the pressure increases with temperature because, at a higher temperature, the molecules move faster and hit the walls of the container with greater force. A gas fills the volume available to it because the molecules in a gas are in constant *random* motion: the randomness of the molecules' motion means that they eventually will move out into the available volume until the distribution of molecules is uniform; at constant pressure, the volume of a gas sample increases as the temperature is increased because with each collision having greater force, the container must expand so that the molecules are farther apart if the pressure is to remain constant.

14. The molecules are much closer together in solids and liquids than in gaseous substances and interact with each other to a much greater extent. Solids and liquids have much greater densities than do gases, and are much less compressible, because so little room exists between the molecules in the solid and liquid states (the volume of a solid or liquid is not affected very much by temperature or pressure). We know that the solid and liquid states of a substance are similar to each other in structure, since it typically takes only a few kilojoules of energy to melt 1 mole of a solid, whereas it may take 10 times more energy to convert a liquid to the vapor state.

16. The *normal* boiling point of water—that is, water's boiling point at a pressure of exactly 760 mm Hg—is 100 °C. Water remains at 100 °C while boiling, because the additional energy added to the sample is used to overcome attractive forces among the water molecules as they go from the condensed, liquid state to the gaseous state. The normal (760 mm Hg) freezing point of water is exactly 0 °C. A cooling curve for water is given in Figure 14.2.

18. Dipole–dipole forces arise when molecules with permanent dipole moments try to orient themselves so that the positive end of one polar molecule can attract the negative end of another polar molecule. Dipole–dipole forces are not nearly as strong as ionic or covalent bonding forces (only about 1% as strong as covalent bonding forces) since electrostatic attraction is related to the *magnitude* of the charges of the attracting species and drops off rapidly with distance. Hydrogen bonding is an especially strong dipole–dipole attractive force that can exist when hydrogen atoms are directly bonded to the most electronegative atoms (N, O, and F). Because the hydrogen atom is so small, dipoles involving N—H, O—H, and F—H bonds can approach each other much more closely than can other dipoles; because the magnitude of dipole–dipole forces is related to distance, unusually strong attractive forces can exist. The much higher boiling point of water than that of the other covalent hydrogen compounds of the Group 6 elements is evidence for the special strength of hydrogen bonding.

20. The vaporization of a liquid requires an input of energy to overcome the intermolecular forces that exist between the molecules in the liquid state. The large heat of vaporization of water is essential to life since much of the excess energy striking the earth from the sun is dissipated in vaporizing water. Condensation refers to the process by which molecules in the vapor state form a liquid. In a closed container containing a liquid with some empty space above the liquid, an equilibrium occurs between vaporization and condensation. When the liquid is first placed in the container, the liquid phase begins to evaporate into the empty space. As the number of molecules in the vapor phase increases, however, some of these molecules begin to reenter the liquid phase. Eventually, each time a molecule of liquid somewhere in the container enters the vapor phase, another molecule of vapor reenters the liquid phase. No further net change occurs in the amount of liquid phase. The pressure of the vapor in such an equilibrium situation is characteristic for the liquid at each temperature. A simple experiment to determine the vapor pressure of a liquid is shown in Figure 14.10. Typically, liquids with strong intermolecular forces have smaller vapor pressures (they have more difficulty in evaporating) than do liquids with very weak intermolecular forces.

22. The *electron sea model* explains many properties of metallic elements. This model pictures a regular array of metal atoms set in a "sea" of mobile valence electrons. The electrons can

move easily throughout the metal to conduct heat or electricity, and the lattice of atoms and cations can be deformed with little effort, allowing the metal to be hammered into a sheet or stretched into wire. An alloy is a material that contains a mixture of elements that overall has metallic properties. *Substitutional* alloys consist of a host metal in which some of the atoms in the metal's crystalline structure are replaced by atoms of other metallic elements. For example, sterling silver is an alloy in which some silver atoms have been replaced by copper atoms. An *interstitial alloy* is formed when other, smaller atoms enter the interstices (holes) between atoms in the host metal's crystal structure. Steel is an interstitial alloy in which carbon atoms enter the interstices of a crystal of iron atoms.

24. A saturated solution contains as much solute as can dissolve at a particular temperature. Saying that a solution is *saturated* does not *necessarily* mean that the solute is present at a high concentration—for example, magnesium hydroxide dissolves only to a very small extent before the solution is saturated. A saturated solution is in equilibrium with undissolved solute: as molecules of solute dissolve from the solid in one place in the solution, dissolved molecules rejoin the solid phase in another part of the solution. Once the rates of dissolving and solid formation become equal, no further net change occurs in the concentration of the solution and the solution is saturated.
26. Adding more solvent to a solution to dilute the solution does *not* change the number of moles of solute present, but changes only the *volume* in which the solute is dispersed. If molarity is used to describe the solution's concentration, then the number of *liters* is changed when solvent is added and the number of *moles per liter* (the molarity) changes, but the actual number of *moles* of solute does *not* change. For example, 125 mL of 0.551 *M* NaCl contains 0.0689 mole of NaCl. The solution will *still* contain 0.0689 mole of NaCl after 250 mL of water is added to it. The volume and the concentration will change, but the number of moles of solute in the solution will *not* change. The 0.0689 mole of NaCl, divided by the total volume of the diluted solution in liters, gives the new molarity (0.184 *M*).
28. (a) 105 mL; (b) 1.05×10^3 mm Hg
30. (a) 6.96 L; (b) $P_{hydrogen} = 5.05$ atm; $P_{helium} = 1.15$ atm; (c) 2.63 atm
32. 0.550 g CO_2; 0.280 L CO_2 at STP
34. (a) 9.65% NaCl; (b) 2.75 g $CaCl_2$; (c) 11.4 g NaCl
36. (a) 0.505 *M*; (b) 0.0840 *M*; (c) 0.130 *M*
38. (a) 226 g; (b) 18.4 *M*; (c) 0.764 *M*; (d) 1.53 *N*; (e) 15.8 mL

Chapters 16–17

2. A conjugate acid–base pair consists of two species related to one another by the donating or accepting of a single proton, H^+. An acid has one more H^+ than its conjugate base; a base has one less H^+ than its conjugate acid.

   Brønsted–Lowry acids:

   $HCl(aq) + H_2O(l) \rightarrow Cl^-(aq) + H_3O^+(aq)$
   $H_2SO_4(aq) + H_2O(l) \rightarrow HSO_4^-(aq) + H_3O^+(aq)$
   $H_3PO_4(aq) + H_2O(l) \rightarrow H_2PO_4^-(aq) + H_3O^+(aq)$
   $NH_4^+(aq) + H_2O(l) \rightarrow NH_3(aq) + H_3O^+(aq)$

   Brønsted–Lowry bases:

   $NH_3(aq) + H_2O(l) \rightarrow NH_4^+(aq) + OH^-(aq)$
   $HCO_3^-(aq) + H_2O(l) \rightarrow H_2CO_3(aq) + OH^-(aq)$
   $NH_2^-(aq) + H_2O(l) \rightarrow NH_3(aq) + OH^-(aq)$
   $H_2PO_4^-(aq) + H_2O(l) \rightarrow H_3PO_4(aq) + OH^-(aq)$
4. The strength of an acid is a direct result of the position of the acid's dissociation (ionization) equilibrium. Acids whose dissociation equilibrium positions lie far to the right are called *strong* acids. Acids whose equilibrium positions lie only slightly to the right are called *weak* acids. For example, HCl, HNO_3, and $HClO_4$ are strong acids, which means that they are completely dissociated in aqueous solution (the position of equilibrium is very far to the right):

   $$HCl(aq) + H_2O(l) \rightarrow Cl^-(aq) + H_3O^+(aq)$$
   $$HNO_3(aq) + H_2O(l) \rightarrow NO_3^-(aq) + H_3O^+(aq)$$
   $$HClO_4(aq) + H_2O(l) \rightarrow ClO_4^-(aq) + H_3O^+(aq)$$

   Since these are very strong acids, their anions (Cl^-, NO_3^-, ClO_4^-) must be very *weak* bases, and solutions of their sodium salts will *not* be basic.
6. The pH of a solution is defined as $pH = -\log[H^+(aq)]$ for a solution. In pure water, the amount of $H^+(aq)$ ion present is *equal* to the amount of $OH^-(aq)$ ion—that is, pure water is *neutral*. Since $[H^+] = 1.0 \times 10^{-7}$ *M* in pure water, the pH of pure water is $-\log[1.0 \times 10^{-7}\ M] = 7.00$. Solutions in which $[H^+] > 1.0 \times 10^{-7}$ *M* (pH < 7.00) are acidic; solutions in which $[H^+] < 1.0 \times 10^{-7}$ *M* (pH > 7.00) are basic. The pH scale is logarithmic: a pH change of one unit corresponds to a change in the hydrogen ion concentration by a factor of *ten*. An analogous logarithmic expression is defined for the hydroxide ion concentration in a solution: $pOH = -\log[OH^-(aq)]$. The concentrations of hydrogen ion and hydroxide ion in water (and in aqueous solutions) are *not* independent of one another, but rather are related by the dissociation equilibrium constant for water, $K_w = [H^+][OH^-] = 1.0 \times 10^{-14}$ at 25 °C. From this expression it follows that pH + pOH = 14.00 for water (or an aqueous solution) at 25 °C.
8. Chemists envision that a reaction can take place between molecules only if the molecules physically *collide* with each other. Furthermore, when molecules collide, the molecules must collide with enough force for the reaction to be successful (there must be enough energy to break bonds in the reactants), and the colliding molecules must be positioned with the correct relative orientation for the products (or intermediates) to form. Reactions tend to be faster if higher concentrations are used for the reaction because if there are more molecules present per unit volume there will be more collisions between molecules in a given time period. Reactions are faster at higher temperatures because at higher temperatures the reactant molecules have a higher average kinetic energy, and the number of molecules that will collide with sufficient force to break bonds increases.
10. Chemists define equilibrium as the exact balancing of two exactly opposing processes. When a chemical reaction is begun by combining pure reactants, the only process possible initially is

    $$\text{reactants} \rightarrow \text{products}$$

    However, for many reactions, as the concentration of product molecules increases, it becomes more and more likely that product molecules will collide and react with each other,

    $$\text{products} \rightarrow \text{reactants}$$

    giving back molecules of the original reactants. At some point in the process the rates of the forward and reverse reactions become equal, and the system attains chemical equilibrium. To an outside observer the system appears to have stopped reacting. On a microscopic basis, though, both the forward and reverse processes are still going on. Every time additional molecules of the product form, however, somewhere else in the system molecules of product react to give back molecules of reactant.

    Once the point is reached that product molecules are reacting at the same speed at which they are forming, there is no further net change in concentration. At the start of the reaction, the rate of the forward reaction is at its maximum, while the rate of the reverse reaction is zero. As the reaction proceeds, the rate of the forward reaction gradually decreases as the concentration of reactants decreases, whereas the rate of the reverse reaction increases as the concentration of products increases. Once the two rates have become equal, the reaction has reached a state of equilibrium.

12. The equilibrium constant for a reaction is a ratio of the concentration of products present at the point of equilibrium to the concentration of reactants still present. A *ratio* means that we have one number divided by another number (for example, the density of a substance is the ratio of a substance's mass to its volume). Since the equilibrium constant is a ratio, there are an infinite number of sets of data that can give the same ratio: for example, the ratios 8/4, 6/3, 100/50 all have the same value, 2. The actual concentrations of products and reactants will differ from one experiment to another involving a particular chemical reaction, but the ratio of the amount of product to reactant at equilibrium should be the same for each experiment.

14. Your paraphrase of Le Châtelier's principle should go something like this: "When you make any change to a system in equilibrium, this throws the system temporarily out of equilibrium, and the system responds by reacting in whatever direction it will be able to reach a new position of equilibrium." There are various changes that can be made to a system in equilibrium. Here are examples of some of them.
    a. The concentration of one of the reactants is increased.
    $2SO_2(g) + O_2(g) \rightleftharpoons 2SO_3(g)$
    If additional SO_2 or O_2 is added to the system at equilibrium, then more SO_3 will result than if no change was made.
    b. The concentration of one of the products is decreased by selectively removing it from the system.
    $CH_3COOH + CH_3OH \rightleftharpoons H_2O + CH_3COOCH_3$
    If H_2O were to be removed from the system by, for example, use of a drying agent, then more CH_3COOCH_3 would result than if no change was made.
    c. The reaction system is compressed to a smaller volume.
    $3H_2(g) + N_2(g) \rightleftharpoons 2NH_3(g)$
    If this system is compressed to smaller volume, then more NH_3 would be produced than if no change was made.
    d. The temperature is increased for an endothermic reaction.
    $2NaHCO_3 + \text{heat} \rightleftharpoons Na_2CO_3 + H_2O + CO_2$
    If heat is added to this system, then more product would be produced than if no change was made.
    e. The temperature is decreased for an exothermic process.
    $PCl_3 + Cl_2 \rightleftharpoons PCl_5 + \text{heat}$
    If heat is removed from this system (by cooling), then more PCl_5 would be produced than if no change was made.

16. Specific answer depends on student choices. In general, for a weak acid HA and a weak base B,
    $HA + H_2O \rightleftharpoons A^- + H_3O^+$
    $B + H_2O \rightleftharpoons HB^+ + OH^-$

18. (a) $NH_3(aq)$(base) + $H_2O(l)$(acid) $\rightleftharpoons$ $NH_4^+(aq)$(acid) + OH^- (aq)(base); (b) $H_2SO_4\,(aq)$(acid) + $H_2O(l)$(base) $\rightleftharpoons$ $HSO_4^-\,(aq)$(base) + H_3O^+ (aq)(acid); (c) $O^{2-}(s)$(base) + $H_2O(l)$(acid) $\rightleftharpoons$ $OH^-(aq)$(acid) + OH^- (aq)(base); (d) $NH_2^-\,(aq)$(base) + $H_2O(l)$(acid) $\rightleftharpoons$ $NH_3(aq)$(acid) + OH^- (aq)(base); (e) $H_2PO_4^-\,(aq)$(acid) + $OH^-(aq)$(base) $\rightleftharpoons$ $HPO_4^{2-}(aq)$(base) + $H_2O(l)$(acid)

20. (a) pH = 2.851; pOH = 11.149; (b) pOH = 2.672; pH = 11.328; (c) pH = 2.288; pOH = 11.712; (d) pOH = 3.947; pH = 10.053

22. 7.8×10^5

24. 0.220 g/L

INDEX AND GLOSSARY

Page numbers followed by *n* refer to margin notes. Page numbers followed by *f* refer to figures. Page numbers followed by *t* refer to tables.

Table 5.1 Common Simple Cations and Anions

Cation	Name	Anion	Name*
H^+	hydrogen	H^-	hydride
Li^+	lithium	F^-	fluoride
Na^+	sodium	Cl^-	chloride
K^+	potassium	Br^-	bromide
Cs^+	cesium	I^-	iodide
Be^{2+}	beryllium	O^{2-}	oxide
Mg^{2+}	magnesium	S^{2-}	sulfide
Ca^{2+}	calcium		
Ba^{2+}	barium		
Al^{3+}	aluminum		
Ag^+	silver		
Zn^{2+}	zinc		

*The root is given in color.

Table 5.2 Common Type II Cations

Ion	Systematic Name	Older Name
Fe^{3+}	iron(III)	ferric
Fe^{2+}	iron(II)	ferrous
Cu^{2+}	copper(II)	cupric
Cu^+	copper(I)	cuprous
Co^{3+}	cobalt(III)	cobaltic
Co^{2+}	cobalt(II)	cobaltous
Sn^{4+}	tin(IV)	stannic
Sn^{2+}	tin(II)	stannous
Pb^{4+}	lead(IV)	plumbic
Pb^{2+}	lead(II)	plumbous
Hg^{2+}	mercury(II)	mercuric
Hg_2^{2+}*	mercury(I)	mercurous

*Mercury(I) ions always occur bound together in pairs to form Hg_2^{2+}.

Table 5.4 Names of Common Polyatomic Ions

Ion	Name	Ion	Name
NH_4^+	ammonium	CO_3^{2-}	carbonate
NO_2^-	nitrite	HCO_3^-	hydrogen carbonate (bicarbonate is a widely used common name)
NO_3^-	nitrate		
SO_3^{2-}	sulfite		
SO_4^{2-}	sulfate	ClO^-	hypochlorite
HSO_4^-	hydrogen sulfate (bisulfate is a widely used common name)	ClO_2^-	chlorite
		ClO_3^-	chlorate
		ClO_4^-	perchlorate
OH^-	hydroxide	$C_2H_3O_2^-$	acetate
CN^-	cyanide	MnO_4^-	permanganate
PO_4^{3-}	phosphate	$Cr_2O_7^{2-}$	dichromate
HPO_4^{2-}	hydrogen phosphate	CrO_4^{2-}	chromate
$H_2PO_4^-$	dihydrogen phosphate	O_2^{2-}	peroxide